THE
ALL ENGLAND
LAW REPORTS

1980

Volume 1

Editor
PETER HUTCHESSON LL M
Barrister, New Zealand

Assistant Editor
BROOK WATSON
of Lincoln's Inn, Barrister
and of the New South Wales Bar

Consulting Editor
WENDY SHOCKETT
of Gray's Inn, Barrister

London
BUTTERWORTHS

ENGLAND:	Butterworth & Co (Publishers) Ltd London: 88 Kingsway, WC2B 6AB
AUSTRALIA:	Butterworths Pty Ltd Sydney: 586 Pacific Highway, Chatswood, NSW 2067 Also at Melbourne, Brisbane, Adelaide and Perth
CANADA:	Butterworth & Co (Canada) Ltd Toronto: 2265 Midland Avenue, Scarborough, M1P 4S1
NEW ZEALAND:	Butterworths of New Zealand Ltd Wellington: T & W Young Building, 77–85 Customhouse Quay
SOUTH AFRICA:	Butterworth & Co (South Africa) (Pty) Ltd Durban: 152–154 Gale Street
USA:	Butterworth & Co (Publishers) Inc Boston: 10 Tower Office Park, Woburn, Mass 01801

©

Butterworth & Co (Publishers) Ltd

1980

ISBN 0 406 85136 0

Typeset by CCC, printed and bound in Great Britain by William Clowes (Beccles) Limited, Beccles and London

House of Lords

The Lord High Chancellor: Lord Hailsham of St Marylebone

Lords of Appeal in Ordinary

Lord Wilberforce
Lord Diplock
Viscount Dilhorne
Lord Salmon
Lord Edmund-Davies
Lord Fraser of Tullybelton
Lord Russell of Killowen

Lord Keith of Kinkel
Lord Scarman
Lord Lane
(appointed Lord Chief Justice of England,
15th April 1980)
Lord Roskill
(appointed 15th April 1980)

Court of Appeal

The Lord High Chancellor

The Lord Chief Justice of England
Lord Widgery (resigned 14th April 1980)
Lord Lane (appointed 15th April 1980)

The Master of the Rolls: Lord Denning

The President of the Family Division: Sir John Lewis Arnold

Lords Justices of Appeal

Sir John Megaw
Sir Denys Burton Buckley
Sir John Frederick Eustace Stephenson
Sir Alan Stewart Orr
(retired 1st February 1980)
Sir Eustace Wentworth Roskill
(appointed Lord of Appeal in Ordinary,
15th April 1980)
Sir Frederick Horace Lawton
Sir Roger Fray Greenwood Ormrod
Sir Patrick Reginald Evelyn Browne
(retired 10th January 1980)
Sir Reginald William Goff
(died 17th January 1980)
Sir Nigel Cyprian Bridge
Sir Sebag Shaw

Sir George Stanley Waller
Sir James Roualeyn Hovell-Thurlow
Cumming-Bruce
Sir Edward Walter Eveleigh
Sir Henry Vivian Brandon
Sir Sydney William Templeman
Sir John Francis Donaldson
Sir John Anson Brightman
Sir Desmond James Conrad Ackner
(appointed 11th January 1980)
Sir Robin Horace Walford Dunn
(appointed 29th February 1980)
Sir Peter Raymond Oliver
(appointed 29th February 1980)
Sir Tasker Watkins VC
(appointed 15th April 1980)

Chancery Division

The Lord High Chancellor

The Vice-Chancellor: Sir Robert Edgar Megarry

Sir John Patrick Graham
Sir Peter Harry Batson Woodroffe Foster
Sir John Norman Keates Whitford
Sir Ernest Irvine Goulding
Sir Raymond Henry Walton
Sir Peter Raymond Oliver
  (appointed Lord Justice of Appeal,
  29th February 1980)

Sir Michael John Fox
Sir Christopher John Slade
Sir Nicolas Christopher Henry Browne-
  Wilkinson
Sir John Evelyn Vinelott
Sir George Brian Hugh Dillon
Sir Martin Charles Nourse
  (appointed 14th April 1980)

Queen's Bench Division

The Lord Chief Justice of England

Sir Alan Abraham Mocatta
Sir John Thompson
Sir Helenus Patrick Joseph Milmo
Sir Joseph Donaldson Cantley
Sir Hugh Eames Park
Sir Stephen Chapman
Sir John Ramsay Willis
Sir Graham Russell Swanwick
  (retired 9th January 1980)
Sir Patrick McCarthy O'Connor
Sir Bernard Caulfield
Sir Hilary Gwynne Talbot
Sir William Lloyd Mars-Jones
Sir Ralph Kilner Brown
Sir Phillip Wien
Sir Peter Henry Rowley Bristow
Sir Hugh Harry Valentine Forbes
Sir Desmond James Conrad Ackner
  (appointed Lord Justice of Appeal,
  11th January 1980)
Sir William Hugh Griffiths
Sir Robert Hugh Mais
Sir Neil Lawson
Sir David Powell Croom-Johnson
Sir Tasker Watkins VC
  (appointed Lord Justice of Appeal,
  15th April 1980)
Sir John Raymond Phillips
Sir Leslie Kenneth Edward Boreham

Sir John Douglas May
Sir Michael Robert Emanuel Kerr
Sir Alfred William Michael Davies
Sir John Dexter Stocker
Sir Kenneth George Illtyd Jones
Sir Haydn Tudor Evans
Sir Peter Richard Pain
Sir Kenneth Graham Jupp
Sir Robert Lionel Archibald Goff
Sir Stephen Brown
Sir Gordon Slynn
Sir Roger Jocelyn Parker
Sir Ralph Brian Gibson
Sir Walter Derek Thornley Hodgson
Sir James Peter Comyn
Sir Anthony John Leslie Lloyd
Sir Frederick Maurice Drake
Sir Brian Thomas Neill
Sir Roderick Philip Smith
Sir Michael John Mustill
Sir Barry Cross Sheen
Sir David Bruce McNeill
Sir Harry Kenneth Woolf
Sir Thomas Patrick Russell
  (appointed 10th January 1980)
Sir Peter Edlin Webster
  (appointed 14th April 1980)
Sir Thomas Henry Bingham
  (appointed 14th April 1980)

Family Division

The President of the Family Division

Sir John Brinsmead Latey
Sir Robin Horace Walford Dunn
  (appointed Lord Justice of Appeal,
  29th February 1980)
Sir Alfred Kenneth Hollings
Sir Charles Trevor Reeve
Sir Francis Brooks Purchas
Dame Rose Heilbron
Sir Brian Drex Bush
Sir Alfred John Balcombe

Sir John Kember Wood
Sir Ronald Gough Waterhouse
Sir John Gervase Kensington Sheldon
Sir Thomas Michael Eastham
Dame Margaret Myfanwy Wood Booth
Sir Christopher James Saunders French
Sir Anthony Leslie Julian Lincoln
Dame Ann Elizabeth Oldfield Butler-Sloss
Sir Anthony Bruce Ewbank
  (appointed 7th March 1980)

CITATION

These reports are cited thus:

[1980] 1 All ER

REFERENCES

These reports contain references, which follow the headnotes, to the following major works of legal reference described in the manner indicated below.

Halsbury's Laws of England

The reference 35 Halsbury's Laws (3rd Edn) 366, para 524, refers to paragraph 524 on page 366 of volume 35 of the third edition, and the reference 26 Halsbury's Laws (4th Edn) para 577 refers to paragraph 577 on page 296 of volume 26 of the fourth edition of Halsbury's Laws of England.

Halsbury's Statutes of England

The reference 5 Halsbury's Statutes (3rd Edn) 302 refers to page 302 of volume 5 of the third edition of Halsbury's Statutes of England.

English and Empire Digest

References are to the replacement volumes (including reissue volumes) of the Digest, and to the continuation volumes of the replacement volumes.

The reference 44 Digest (Repl) 144, 1240, refers to case number 1240 on page 144 of Digest Replacement Volume 44.

The reference 28(1) Digest (Reissue) 167, 507, refers to case number 507 on page 167 of Digest Replacement Volume 28(1) Reissue.

The reference Digest (Cont Vol D) 571, 678b, refers to case number 678b on page 571 of Digest Continuation Volume D.

Halsbury's Statutory Instruments

The reference 12 Halsbury's Statutory Instruments (Third Reissue) 125 refers to page 125 of the third reissue of volume 12 of Halsbury's Statutory Instruments; references to subsequent reissues are similar.

CORRIGENDA

[1979] 3 All ER
p 92. **B v W (wardship: appeal).** Line *e* 5: for 'But for the purposes' read 'But for present purposes'.
p 119. **Cedar Holdings Ltd v Green.** Counsel for the wife: for *'Alastair Norris'* read *'Paul Norris'*.
p 992. **Vestey v Inland Revenue Comrs (Nos 1 and 2).** Line *c* 2: for 'taxpayers' read 'Crown'.

[1980] 1 All ER
p 67. **Express Newspapers Ltd v MacShane.** Counsel for the appellants: for *'John Heady'* read *'John Hendy'*.
p 165. **J(HD) v J(AM).** Line *c* 6: the following line was inadvertently omitted, 'In conclusion, dealing with both applications together, there will be no order on either'. The missing line should follow immediately after line *c* 5 which ends with the word 'it'.
p 168. **Farrell v Secretary of State.** Counsel for the Ministry: add *'John Laws* and *John A H Martin'*.
p 373. **Federated Homes Ltd v Mill Lodge Properties Ltd.** Counsel for the plaintiffs: for *R G B McComber* read *R G B McCombe*.
p 449. **Co-operative Retail Services Ltd v Secretary of State for the Environment.** Line *h* 1: for 'the cause of an appeal' read 'the course of an appeal'.
p 622. **United Kingdom Association of Professional Engineers v Advisory, Conciliation and Arbitration Service.** Solicitors for the plaintiffs: read *'Gregory, Rowcliffe & Co,* agents for *Jonathan S Lawton & Co,* Chorley' instead of as printed.
p 644. **Liff v Peasley.** Line *a* 4: Solicitors: *Greenwoods* (for the second defendant); *Outred & Co,* Weybridge (for the plaintiff); *Stevensons* (for the first defendant) instead of as printed.
p 886. **Inland Revenue Comrs v McMullen.** Line *d* 3: for 'Anthony Derek McMullen' read 'Arthur Derek McMullen'. Line *h* 5: Solicitors for the trustees: read *'Chethams'* instead of as printed.

Cases reported in volume 1

Levermore v Levermore

b
FAMILY DIVISION
BALCOMBE J
2nd MAY 1979

Execution – Equitable execution – Appointment of receiver – Appointment of receiver over
debtor's interest under trust for sale of property – Purpose of appointment to effect sale of
property and discharge debt out of proceeds of sale – Court order for payment of lump sum by
c *husband to wife – Husband not making payment – Husband's sole asset beneficial interest in*
proceeds of sale of house held by him and another as tenants in common – Wife applying for
appointment of receiver of husband's interest for purpose of procuring sale of house and payment
of lump sum out of proceeds – Whether court entitled to appoint receiver with power to bring
proceedings for sale in husband's name.

d Following dissolution of the marriage of the husband and wife (who had children in
respect of whom a custody application was pending), a consent order was made on 15th
May 1978 ordering the husband to pay the wife a lump sum of £2,000 on or before 31st
July 1978. The husband never paid that sum. His only asset was an interest under a trust
for sale of the matrimonial home, which he and his brother owned as tenants in
common. The brother lived abroad and would not consent to a sale of the house. The
e husband was living in the house. Because his interest was not one in land, but merely an
interest in the proceeds of sale of the house, legal execution of the order of 15th May 1978
(by a charging order charging the husband's interest) was impossible. To enforce the
consent order the wife therefore applied for the appointment of a receiver of the
husband's interest by way of equitable execution and also sought an order authorising the
receiver to bring proceedings in the husband's name, under s 30 of the Law of Property
f Act 1925 or otherwise, to procure a sale of the house and payment of the lump sum out
of the husband's interest in the proceeds. The husband conceded there was jurisdiction
to appoint a receiver by way of equitable execution but contended that to appoint a
receiver for the purpose of procuring a sale of the house was beyond the permissible
limits of such an appointment.

Held – The court was entitled, in an appropriate case, to authorise a receiver appointed
g by way of equitable execution to bring any necessary proceedings in the name of the
estate owner of the property of which he had been appointed receiver. In the instant case
the interests of justice would be served by appointing a receiver by way of equitable
execution over the husband's interest in the house coupled with liberty to the receiver to
take such proceedings in the husband's name as might be necessary to enforce a sale of
the house, and the court would make an order accordingly (see p 5 g h and p 6 c d, post).
h
Re Shephard (1889) 43 Ch D 131 applied.
Ideal Bedding Co Ltd v Holland [1907] 2 Ch 157 and *Re No 39 Carr Lane, Acomb, Stevens*
v Hutchinson [1953] 1 All ER 699 considered.
Per Curiam. Where parties no longer married are the parents of children in relation
to whom custody proceedings are pending, the court will seek methods of enforcing its
orders which will avoid, where possible, the necessity of committing a party to prison
j (see p 2 g h, post).

Notes
For equitable execution against property other than land and interests in land, see 17
Halsbury's Laws (4th Edn) paras 576–578, and for cases on the subject, see 21 Digest
(Repl) 772–777, 2580–2629.

Cases referred to in judgment

Bailey, Re (bankrupt), ex parte trustee of bankrupt v Bailey [1977] 2 All ER 26, [1977] 1 WLR a
278, DC.

Carr Lane (No 39), Acomb, Re, Stevens v Hutchinson [1953] 1 All ER 699, [1953] Ch 299,
[1953] 2 WLR 545, 21 Digest (Repl) 781, 2652.

Debtor, Re a, ex parte Trustee v Solomon [1966] 3 All ER 255, [1967] Ch 573, [1967] 2 WLR
172, 5 Digest (Reissue) 725, 6237.

Ideal Bedding Co Ltd v Holland [1907] 2 Ch 157, 76 LJ Ch 411, 96 LT 774, 14 Mans 113, b
21 Digest (Repl) 759, 2436.

Irani Finance Ltd v Singh [1970] 3 All ER 199, [1971] Ch 59, [1970] 3 WLR 330, 21 P &
CR 843, CA, Digest (Cont Vol C) 342, 1628 Aa.

Shephard, Re, Atkins v Shephard (1889) 43 Ch D 131, 59 LJ Ch 83, 62 LT 337, CA, 21 Digest
(Repl) 772, 2580.

c

Cases also cited

Vine v Raleigh (1883) 24 Ch D 238.
Wills v Luff (1888) 38 Ch D 197.

Application

By a notice of application dated 29th January 1979 the wife applied for an order that a d
receiver be appointed by way of equitable execution, under RSC Ord 51, r 1, to enforce
a consent order made on 15th May 1978 whereby the husband was ordered to pay the
wife a lump sum of £2,000. The application came before Mr Registrar Bayne-Powell on
27th February 1979. He adjourned it to a judge of the Family Division. The application
was heard and judgment given in open court. The facts are set out in the judgment.

e

Jeffrey Littman for the wife.
Jonathan Cohen for the husband.

BALCOMBE J. This is an application which raises a short but interesting point of law.
I have been very much assisted by counsel who have prepared and put before me an f
agreed memorandum of facts so that the question is purely one of law.

It arises in this way. The parties were husband and wife, and I propose to call them
that. The facts agreed are these: the marriage between the husband and the wife
celebrated on 29th June 1968 was dissolved by decree nisi on 9th April 1975 made
absolute on 25th May 1975. Then there are references to various maintenance orders
and also to the children of the family, and to a custody application which is pending, and g
the only relevance of the custody application appears to me to be this. Where one has
parties such as these who, although no longer married, are the parents of children in
relation to whom custody proceedings are pending, the court will undoubtedly seek for
methods of enforcing its orders which will avoid, where possible, the necessity of having
to commit a party to prison. It cannot do any good to commit to prison a party who does
not obey the order of the court, particularly where there are children, unless there is no h
other effective method available.

On 29th January 1976 the wife gave notice of her intention to proceed with an
application for ancillary relief. That application was heard by Mr Registrar Bayne-Powell
on 15th May 1978 when a consent order was made. That consent order provided that the
husband should pay to the wife by way of lump sum payment the sum of £2,000, the
said sum to be paid on or before 31st July 1978 to the wife's solicitor. In the event that j
the said sum of £2,000 or any part thereof remained unpaid after 31st July 1978 interest
should accrue on the sum outstanding at the rate of 10% per annum. If base rate
exceeded 10% there should be liberty to the wife to apply as to the rate of interest. The
agreed memorandum of facts continues: no part of the lump sum has been paid.

The husband and his brother Egbert own the former matrimonial home at 116

Hubert Grove, London SW9, where the husband continues to live. There are no assets
a or resources of the husband, other than his interest in that property, out of which it is
practicable for the husband to raise the money with which to pay his judgment debt.
But if the property were sold the net proceeds after discharging a mortgage debt would
be in excess of £9,000.

Egbert, to whom notice of these proceedings was sent, lives in New York and regards
himself as entitled to a half beneficial interest in the property and, in his own words,
b vehemently opposes any sale of it and may wish to return to live in it.

The husband alleges, and the wife accepts for the purposes of this hearing and as
against the husband only, that the property was acquired and treated as follows. In 1963
the husband and Egbert borrowed £2,250 from the Greater London Council, or its
predecessor, which has been duly served herein, which sum was charged on the
property. They utilised cash from their own resources in order to buy the freehold for
c £3,225. Then the husband and Egbert registered title absolute to the property in their
names together with a restriction in the common form in the case of registered land
where the beneficial interests are held under a tenancy in common. Then for some years
until Egbert left in 1971 or 1973 the husband and his family lived in one part of the
house and Egbert and his family lived in another part of it. There is no evidence that any
part of the house, even that part previously occupied by Egbert and his family, is at the
d moment let so as to bring in an income and counsel for the husband has told me on
instructions that the husband now lives in the whole house.

On 17th November 1978 Mrs Registrar Butler-Sloss made an order for transfer to the
High Court and a charging order nisi charging the husband's interest in the house with
the sum of £2,000 and interest. But on the 15th December 1978 the same registrar by
consent made an order discharging the charging order nisi. The reason why the charging
e order nisi was discharged was because it was appreciated, which it had not been at the
time when the order was applied for, that the effect of the Court of Appeal decision in
Irani Finance Ltd v Singh[1] was that the husband's interest in the house was not an interest
in land and therefore no charging order could properly be made. It was appreciated that
the husband has an interest under a trust for sale and that is his only interest (other than
as a trustee) and therefore the charging order should not have been made. In those
f circumstances the wife issued an application for the appointment of a receiver by way of
equitable execution over the husband's interest in this house which interest, as I have
said, is an interest under a trust for sale. I am not told whether the trust for sale is one
which arises by express creation or by operation of law, but it matters not for this
purpose. That application by the wife for the appointment of a receiver came before Mr
Registrar Bayne-Powell on 27th February 1979, when the husband's counsel submitted
g before the registrar that the effect of the case (to which I shall be referring in a moment)
of *Re No 39 Carr Lane, Acomb, Stevens v Hutchinson*[2] was to render the appointment of a
receiver futile, and the application was therefore adjourned into court and it has come
before me. Since it seems to me to raise a pure question of law I thought it right to
adjourn the application, both for argument and for judgment, into open court.

Before I turn to consider *Re No 39 Carr Lane, Acomb, Stevens v Hutchinson*[2] and the other
h cases to which I have referred, it would be, I think, convenient to refer to what the
appointment of a receiver by way of equitable execution is intended to do. I derive
assistance from a note in the Supreme Court Practice 1979[3] where in referring to
equitable execution it says:

> 'There are various interests in property to which a judgment debtor may be
> entitled, yet which cannot be taken in execution under any of the processes specified
j > in these Rules. Such interest may generally be reached by the appointment of a

---

1   [1970] 3 All ER 199, [1971] Ch 59
2   [1953] 1 All ER 699, [1953] Ch 299
3   Vol 1, para 51/1–3/2, p 799

receiver, supplemented if necessary by an injunction restraining the judgment debtor from dealing with the property.'

a

As I have said, the effect of *Irani Finance Ltd v Singh*[1] is undoubtedly to stop execution, in this case to enforce payment of the lump sum of £2,000 and interest, by way of a charging order. It is accepted that it would be open to the court, if a judgment summons were taken out against the husband, to make an order committing him to prison for his failure to observe the court order. That would seem to be a somewhat pointless exercise because the husband has no assets out of which to satisfy this judgment except his *b* interest in the house. But he cannot enforce that interest without the concurrence of his brother Egbert. It is true that this procedure might have the effect of persuading the husband to bring proceedings against his brother Egbert, but that does seem to be a very roundabout way of having to go about it. Equally, it is said that it would be possible for the wife to apply to have the husband made bankrupt and if, in due course, a trustee in bankruptcy were appointed, the trustee in bankruptcy would be able to bring proceedings *c* to enforce a sale of this house, as would appear from *Re a Debtor, ex parte Trustee v Solomon*[2] and *Re Bailey*[3]. I ask myself the question: why should the court have to go this roundabout way of enforcing the wife's judgment if there is a more direct way available?

Counsel for the husband fairly concedes that there is jurisdiction here to appoint a receiver by way of equitable execution, but he submits that I should not exercise that jurisdiction because to do so would be pointless. He relied on *Re No 39 Carr Lane, Acomb, d Stevens v Hutchinson*[4], a decision of Upjohn J at first instance. The headnote says this[5]:

'A judgment creditor was appointed as receiver by way of equitable execution of the debtor's interest in a house, which was held by the debtor and his wife on trust for sale as tenants in common. The creditor asked the court for an order for sale under section 30 of the Law of Property Act, 1925, as being a "person interested" *e* within the meaning of that section, either as being an equitable chargee under section 195 of that Act, or alternatively by virtue of his position as receiver. The evidence was that this was the matrimonial home, and that the debtor was a spendthrift who had been repeatedly lent money by his wife:— *Held,* (1) that the judgment creditor was not, by virtue simply of his position as receiver, a "person interested" within the meaning of section 30, which meant a person interested in *f* some proprietary right under the trust.'

It is to be noted that in that case the judgment creditor, who had had himself appointed receiver by way of equitable execution, was himself the plaintiff in the application for the sale of the property under s 30 of the Law of Property Act 1925. And that section provides that if trustees for sale refuse to sell, any person interested may *g* apply to the court for an order directing the trustees for sale to sell. That is the general effect of the section. The question there was: was the receiver appointed in that case by way of equitable execution a person interested who had a locus standi under s 30? Upjohn J held after argument that he was not such a person. I do not think it either necessary or desirable that I should express any view as to the correctness of that decision. What I do say is this: it was certainly contrary to what I would have expected *h* to be the usual practice for the receiver to bring the action, as he did in that case, in his own name. The invariable practice, as is made clear in the standard textbook on receivers[6], is for the receiver, if he needs for the purpose of his appointment to bring proceedings, to seek the authority of the court to bring such proceedings in the name of

j

1　[1970] 3 All ER 199, [1971] Ch 59
2　[1966] 3 All ER 255, [1967] Ch 573
3　[1977] 2 All ER 26, [1977] 1 WLR 278
4　[1953] 1 All ER 699, [1953] Ch 299
5　[1953] Ch 299 at 299–300
6　Kerr on Receivers (15th Edn, 1978), p 181

the estate owner of the property over which he has been appointed receiver. By the time

a that *Re No 39 Carr Lane, Acomb, Stevens v Hutchinson*[1] was before Upjohn J that point had passed; the receiver was already the plaintiff and on the ground that the receiver, the plaintiff in that action, was not a person interested Upjohn J dismissed the action. I do not find it very persuasive that nobody in that case, either in the course of argument or, indeed in the judgment, referred to the possibility of the receiver bringing the action in the name of the judgment creditor, and I can see no reason why he should not have done

b so.

I mentioned this possibility to counsel for the wife in the course of his opening the case and he now invites me to make an order both appointing a receiver by way of equitable execution and authorising such receiver to bring proceedings, whether under s 30 of the 1925 Act or otherwise as may be appropriate, in the name of the husband, so as to procure a sale of this property and thereby get into his hands the moneys representing

c the husband's interest out of which the order in favour of the wife can be paid.

Counsel for the husband resists that application. He does so on the ground that this would be stretching beyond permissible limits the appointment of a receiver by way of equitable execution. I do not accept that submission. I find of assistance the explanation of the effect of the appointment of a receiver by way of equitable execution which is to be found in the decision of the Court of Appeal in *Re Shephard*[2] where Cotton LJ says:

d
> 'Confusion of ideas has arisen from the use of the term "equitable execution". The expression tends to error. It has often been used by judges and occurs in some orders, as a short expression indicating that the person who obtains the order gets the same benefit as he would have got from legal execution. But what he gets by the appointment of a receiver is not execution, but equitable relief, which is granted on the ground that there is no remedy by execution at law; it is a taking out of the

e way a hindrance which prevents execution at common law.'

Bowen LJ[3] is to the like effect. 'Equitable execution', he says, 'is not like legal execution; it is equitable relief, which the Court gives because execution at law cannot be had. It is not execution, but a substitute for execution.'

Here execution at law is impossible because of the effect of the decision in *Irani Finance*

f *Ltd v Singh*[4]. It would be, in my judgment, a blot on our jurisprudence if the wife in this case had to take a sledgehammer to crack a nut, an expression which was used in the course of argument, either by making the husband bankrupt or by seeking to commit him to prison as an indirect way of making him bring proceedings against his brother, when there is a form of machinery which ought to be ready and available to her and, in my judgment, is so available. As I have said it is not uncommon as a matter of practice

g when a receiver is appointed, whether by way of equitable execution or for the interim preservation of property, to authorise the receiver in an appropriate case to bring any necessary proceedings in the name of the estate owner of the property of which he has been appointed receiver. That, in my judgment, can and should be done in the present case.

Counsel for the husband further relied on *Ideal Bedding Co Ltd v Holland*[5] where

h Kekewich J says something about the effects of equitable execution. He says that the appointment of a receiver by way of equitable execution has certain limiting effects, namely that it prevents the debtor from dealing with the property over which he has been appointed to the prejudice of the judgment creditors. It also prevents any subsequent judgment creditor from gaining priority over the creditor obtaining the order. The judgment of Kekewich J in *Ideal Bedding Co Ltd v Holland*[5] was cited by

j
1 [1953] 1 All ER 699, [1953] Ch 299
2 (1889) 43 Ch D 131 at 135
3 43 Ch D 131 at 137
4 [1970] 3 All ER 119, [1971] Ch 59
5 [1907] 2 Ch 157

Upjohn J in *Re No 39 Carr Lane, Acomb, Stevens v Hutchinson*[1] as if it were an exhaustive definition of the effect of an appointment of a receiver by way of equitable execution. But it is worthy of note that Kekewich J himself considered it nothing of the sort. He says quite clearly that[2]:

> 'After consulting many authorities and pondering over the matter, I have come to the conclusion that full treatment of this question would require something in the nature of a lecture or treatise, which it is better to avoid unless absolutely necessary. My observations, therefore, do not pretend to be exhaustive.'

Regrettably, Upjohn J did not cite that earlier part of Kekewich J's judgment, but I do not interpret the judgment in *Re No 39 Carr Lane, Acomb, Stevens v Hutchinson*[1] as intending to accept the definition in *Ideal Bedding Co Ltd v Holland*[3] as an exhaustive definition, and if it were so intended it would be inconsistent with other authorities which are binding on me, and I would not therefore be minded to follow it.

It seems to me therefore that the interests of justice can be served in this case by appointing a receiver by way of equitable execution over the husband's interest in the property known as 116 Hubert Grove, London SW9, and coupling with that appointment liberty to the receiver in the name of the husband to take any such proceedings as may be necessary to enforce a sale of the property and I propose so to order.

Order accordingly.

Solicitors: *Judith Walker, Tayar & Co* (for the wife); *Baldwin, Mellor & Co* (for the husband).

Georgina Chambers   Barrister.

---

1   [1953] 1 All ER 699, [1953] Ch 299
2   [1907] 2 Ch 157 at 168
3   [1907] 2 Ch 157

Roberts and others v Ramsbottom

QUEEN'S BENCH DIVISION AT MANCHESTER

NEILL J

31st JANUARY, 7th FEBRUARY 1979

*Negligence – Defence – Sudden event or affliction – Malfunction of mind – Road accident –
Driver suffering stroke shortly before accident – Stroke causing impairment of driver's
consciousness – Driver's control of vehicle impaired – Driver not aware of stroke – Driver aware
of feeling queer at time of accident – Whether impairment of consciousness a defence – Whether
driver liable for damage caused by accident.*

On 4th June 1976 at about 10.20 am Mrs R, the second plaintiff, parked a car belonging
to her husband, the first plaintiff, outside a launderette.   As she alighted from the car a
car driven by the defendant, who was aged 73, collided head on with it damaging it
beyond repair and she and her daughter, the third plaintiff, who was with her in the car,
were injured.   Mrs R's husband brought an action against the defendant in respect of the
damage to his car and certain other loss resulting from the collision, and Mrs R and her
daughter claimed damages against the defendant in respect of the injuries they had
suffered.   No criticism was made of Mrs R's driving and it was not in dispute that the
circumstances of the collision established a prima facie case of negligence against the
defendant entitling the plaintiffs to damages.   The defendant contended however that he
was not liable to the plaintiffs because 20 minutes before the accident he had suffered a
stroke which so clouded his consciousness that from that moment he had been, through
no fault of his own, unable properly to control his car or to appreciate that he was no
longer fit to drive.   The evidence showed that on the day of the accident the defendant
had left his home at about 10 am to go to his office some 2½ miles away.   He had left
without taking his wife with him contrary to arrangement.   His journey involved him
in travelling through a busy part of the town and going round a number of corners.
Shortly before colliding with the first plaintiff's car the defendant had struck a parked
van, insisting when asked by its occupants that he was all right, and had knocked a boy
off his bicycle although there had been plenty of room for him to pass.   The defendant
told a police constable at the hospital where he was taken after the collision with the first
plaintiff's car that after each collision he had felt queer but had felt all right afterwards.
The next day the defendant could remember nothing of the journey.   The judge found
that the defendant had suffered a stroke shortly before leaving his home on the day of the
accident, that before he suffered the stroke he had had no previous symptoms or warning
signs, that following the onset of the stroke his consciousness had been impaired and that
state of impaired or clouded consciousness had continued throughout the journey from
his home to the point of impact with the first plaintiff's car, that he had experienced the
feelings of queerness which he had described to the constable and did know at the time
it had happened that he had hit the parked van, that throughout the journey and up to
the moment of impact with the first plaintiff's car he had been sufficiently in possession
of his faculties to have some, though an impaired, awareness of his surroundings and the
traffic conditions and to make a series of deliberate and voluntary though insufficient
movements of his hands and legs to manipulate the controls of his car, and that he had
at no time been aware of the fact that he had been unfit to drive.   On the question
whether the defendant's physical condition absolved him from liability for negligence.

Held – In an action for negligence arising out of a motor vehicle accident where shortly
before the accident the defendant suffered a malfunction of the mind which so clouded
his consciousness that from that moment he was, through no fault of his own, unable
properly to control his vehicle or to appreciate that he was no longer fit to drive, the
defendant was not able to escape liability unless his actions had been wholly beyond his
control, as in cases of sudden unconsciousness, ie he could only avoid liability where the

facts established what the law recognised as automatism. But, if he retained some
control, albeit imperfect, and his driving, judged objectively, was below the required *a*
standard, he remained liable, in the same way as a driver who was old or infirm. It was
clear from the medical evidence that the defendant's condition did not amount in law to
automatism, and he was accordingly liable to the plaintiffs. Alternatively he was liable
on the ground that he had continued to drive when he was unfit to do so and should have
been aware of his unfitness. Although he was, owing to his mental state, unable to
appreciate that he should have stopped and although he was in no way morally to blame, *b*
that was irrelevant to the question of legal liability, since impairment of judgment was
not a defence. There would accordingly be judgment for the plaintiffs (see p 15 *f* to p 16
b, post).

 Hill v Baxter [1958] 1 All ER 193 and *Watmore v Jenkins* [1962] 2 All ER 868 applied.

Notes   *c*
For the standard of care required of a person generally, see 28 Halsbury's Laws (3rd Edn)
10, para 8, and for negligence of drivers of motor vehicles, see 33 ibid 373, para 631.

Cases referred to in judgment
Glasgow Corpn v Muir [1943] 2 All ER 44, [1943] AC 448, 112 LJPC 1, 169 LT 53, 107 JP
 140, 41 LGR 173, HL, 36(1) Digest (Reissue) 86, *337*.
Gordon v Wallace (1973) 42 DLR (3d) 342, 2 OR (2d) 202, 36(1) Digest (Reissue) 169,   *d*
 *1057.
Hill v Baxter [1958] 1 All ER 193, [1958] 1 QB 277, [1958] 2 WLR 76, 122 JP 134, 56 LGR
 117, 42 Cr App 51, DC, 45 Digest (Repl) 35, *119*.
Jones v Dennison [1971] RTR 174, CA, 36(1) Digest (Reissue) 233, *923*.
Nettleship v Weston [1971] 3 All ER 581, [1971] 2 QB 691, [1971] 3 WLR 370, [1971] RTR
 425, CA, 36(1) Digest (Reissue) 245, *952*.   *e*
R v Gosney [1971] 3 All ER 220, [1971] 2 QB 674, [1971] 3 WLR 343, 135 JP 529, 55 Cr
 App R 502, [1971] RTR 321, CA, Digest (Cont Vol D) 875, *291c*.
R v Isitt [1978] RTR 211, CA.
R v Spurge [1961] 2 All ER 688, [1961] 2 QB 205, [1961] 3 WLR 23, 125 JP 502, 59 LGR
 323, 45 Cr App 191, CCA, 45 Digest (Repl) 87, *291*.
Watmore v Jenkins [1962] 2 All ER 868, [1962] 2 QB 572, [1962] 3 WLR 463, 126 JP 432,   *f*
 60 LGR 325, DC, 45 Digest (Repl) 95, *329*.
Waugh v James K Allan Ltd 1964 SC (HL) 102, 1964 SLT 269, [1964] 2 Lloyd's Rep 1, HL,
 36(1) Digest (Reissue) 169, **1059*.

Action
By a writ dated 30th June 1976 the plaintiffs, Jack Roberts, Jean Roberts (his wife) and *g*
Karen Jane Roberts (their daughter, an infant suing by Jack Roberts her father and next
friend), brought an action against the defendant, Arthur Ramsbottom, claiming damages
for personal injuries and loss caused by negligent driving by the defendant of a Volvo
motor car on 4th June 1976 in Bolton Road, Bury, when it collided head on with a
Triumph motor car owned by the first named plaintiff and injured the second and third
named plaintiffs. The first named plaintiff claimed damages of £968·87 in respect of the *h*
damage to his car and certain other loss resulting from the collision, and the second and
third named plaintiffs claimed damages for personal injuries. The facts are set out in the
judgment.

John Stannard for the plaintiffs.
H K Goddard and *R D Machell* for the defendant.

            Cur adv vult   *j*

7th February. **NEILL J** read the following judgment: Mr and Mrs Roberts live at 171
Ainsworth Road, Bury. On 4th June 1976 Mrs Roberts drove in her husband's Triumph
car to a launderette in Bolton Road, Bury. Her daughter Karen, who was born on 1st

a February 1964, was with her sitting in the front passenger seat. The launderette was called Laundercentre. It was on the south side of Bolton Road between Buxton Street and Fountain Street. Mrs Roberts approached the shop from the south-west, that is from the direction of Bolton. She waited for a gap in the traffic and then drove across to the offside of the road and parked outside Laundercentre facing toward Bury. Mrs Roberts opened the door and prepared to get out on the pavement. She turned to pick up her handbag. A moment later she was thrown out onto the pavement. A Volvo car driven

b by the defendant had come up the road from the direction of Bury and had collided head-on with the Triumph car driven by Mrs Roberts. Karen had seen the car approaching and had ducked beneath the dash board but the windscreen of the Triumph car was shattered and Karen was seriously injured by broken glass. Mrs Roberts also was injured but less seriously. The Triumph car was damaged beyond repair. The collision took place at about 10.20 am.

c   No criticism whatever is made of Mrs Roberts's driving. It is accepted on behalf of the defendant that the facts which I have outlined and which are not in dispute would, if unexplained, entitle the plaintiffs to damages caused by negligent driving by the defendant. The first plaintiff, Mr Jack Roberts, sues in respect of the damage to his car and in respect of certain other loss resulting from the collision. His claim is agreed subject to liability at £968·87. The second plaintiff is Mrs Jean Roberts. She was the

d driver. She sues in respect of the injuries she suffered. The third plaintiff is Miss Karen Roberts, the daughter. She also sues for damages for personal injuries.

   The defendant is Mr Arthur Ramsbottom. He lives at 396 Brandlesholme Road, Bury. He was born on 2nd December 1902. He was therefore 73 at the date of the collision. His defence is that approximately 20 minutes before the collision he suffered a stroke, that is a cerebral haemorrhage, which so clouded his consciousness that from

e that moment he was, through no fault of his own, unable properly to control his car or to appreciate that he was no longer fit to drive. Accordingly, argued counsel on behalf of the defendant, the defendant was not negligent.

   It is therefore necessary for me to consider the evidence as to the defendant's driving before the collision and the medical evidence as to the effect of his stroke. It is also necessary for me to consider the relevant principles of law.

f

The defendant's journey to Bolton Road

   By profession Mr Ramsbottom was an accountant. When he was 65 he retired from full-time work but he continued to go to work for part of the day. He used to drive every day from his home at 396 Brandlesholme Road to his office in East Street in Bury. It was

g a journey of about two miles or a little more. Sometimes his wife went with him in order to go shopping. On 4th June 1976 he got ready to leave about 10 o'clock. It was a day his wife was going to go with him. Mrs Ramsbottom went upstairs to get her coat. She came down. She found that her husband had gone without her. She was astonished because he had never gone off like this before, leaving her behind when he had arranged to take her. It was so unusual an event that after a time she telephoned the

h police.

   Meanwhile, Mr Ramsbottom had set off towards the centre of Bury in his blue Volvo car. There was no evidence before me relating to the earlier part of his journey. Mr Ramsbottom himself cannot now remember any part of his journey or any of the events of that morning and no other witness threw light on Mr Ramsbottom's movements before he reached Irwell Street. I am entitled to infer, however, and I do infer, that Mr

j Ramsbottom drove down Brandlesholme Road from his home at no 396 and then along Crostons Road into Bolton Street and round the roundabout into the continuation of Bolton Street on the east side of the roundabout. If he had followed his usual route Mr Ramsbottom would have then continued eastwards to the Market Place, turned right into Market Street and then driven into Angouleme Way and Spring Street to his office in East Street. On that morning, however, instead of following his usual route, Mr

Ramsbottom turned south just beyond the roundabout in Bolton Street and went down Irwell Street.

About half-way along Irwell Street on the east side there is a police station. About 10.15 am on 4th June there was a van parked outside the police station. Sitting in the van were Mr Kay and Mr Banks. They were waiting for a colleague. Both Mr Kay and Mr Banks gave evidence and there was some conflict of recollection between them about what they saw. I prefer the evidence of Mr Banks and I accept his account of what happened. This is what he said. He was sitting in the van when he felt a bang at the rear of the van. He got out and saw that the offside corner at the back of the van had been hit by a blue Volvo. It was the defendant's car. The Volvo was at an angle as though it had been trying to overtake too late. The defendant tried to reverse. He had difficulty in getting into gear and when he reversed he moved the car in a jerky manner. Mr Banks walked back to where the car was. By then the defendant had got out and was walking across the road to the path on the other side. As he crossed the road the defendant was narrowly missed by a gas board van. Mr Banks asked him if he was all right. He said, 'Yes, yes, yes.' Mr Banks asked him if he was sure. 'Yes, yes,' he said. The defendant gave Mr Banks the impression that he was slightly dazed and his speech seemed slightly slurred. Mr Banks noticed when he crossed the road, that he had an uneven gait. The defendant got back in his car and moved forward. He pulled up just behind the van, only a foot away. Once more he had to reverse. Mr Banks again asked him if he was all right and he said he was. 'Are you sure now?' said Mr Banks. 'Yes,' said the defendant. After he had reversed the second time the defendant drove forward. On this occasion he avoided the van by a good margin and drove off down Irwell Street. As the defendant went down the road, however, Mr Banks saw that he narrowly missed two men working in the road who waved and shouted. The defendant passed from view. A few minutes later Mr Banks was joined by the third man in the van and he drove off. By chance his route took him to Bolton Road. There he saw the blue Volvo again. It was outside the Laundercentre. It had collided with the Triumph. The defendant was walking about in the road in a dazed condition.

It is clear that from Irwell Street the defendant had driven across into Tenterden Street and had then turned right into Millett Street. At the end of Millett Street he turned left into Bolton Street and then along Bolton Road. In Bolton Road, about 100 yards or so before he collided with the Triumph, the defendant's car brushed past a boy on a bicycle. The boy, young Mr Hardman, was just by the Manchester Motor Mart in Bolton Road. He was riding a few inches from the kerb. He was knocked off his bicycle and fell on the pavement. There was plenty of room in the road for the defendant to have passed him normally. A few moments later Mr Hardman saw the defendant's car crash into the Triumph.

The distance travelled by the defendant from his home to where he collided with the Triumph car was about $2\frac{1}{2}$ miles and involved travelling round a busy part of Bury and going round a number of corners.

The events following the collision

After the collision Mrs Roberts, Karen and the defendant were taken together by ambulance to hospital. At the hospital it was not appreciated at once that the defendant had had a stroke.

At 11.30 am he was seen at the hospital by a police officer, Pc Flanagan. No criticism whatever can be made of the officer for interviewing the defendant. He asked a nurse if he could see the defendant and had been told that he could. He described the defendant as appearing to be dazed. Pc Flanagan told the defendant that he was making enquiries about the collision. He cautioned the defendant. This is what the defendant told him: 'I suddenly felt queer and I ran into the van. I felt all right after that and I carried on. I felt queer again later and I hit the car.' A little later he said: 'I felt a bit queer before I ran into the van. I went away and felt all right. After that I felt a bit queer again and I hit the other car.'

The defendant that morning was also questioned by the medical staff at the hospital.
a I have not seen the hospital notes but it is common ground that the relevant parts of the hospital notes were reproduced by Dr Riley in a letter which he wrote to the defendant's insurers dated 24th August 1976. The second paragraph of that letter contains these sentences:

> 'He was then driving his car at about 10.0 a.m. when he felt rather dizzy for about
> 15 minutes and then nauseated. He kept on driving and then he remembers
b crashing his car before losing consciousness and he was apparently unconscious for
> about two minutes. He was admitted to Bury General Hospital.'

I am satisfied that the information in that paragraph and in the hospital notes must have come originally from the defendant. I consider, however, that there is force in counsel's argument for the defendant, which was supported by the medical evidence,
c that the information may well have been based on questions and answers and the defendant may have done no more than say yes to various questions which were put to him. I do not therefore attach great importance to what the defendant appears to have told the doctors. But I do attach considerable significance to the defendant's interview with Pc Flanagan. There is no suggestion that the police officer put any words into the defendant's mouth.

d *The medical evidence*

On the day after the collision the defendant was seen by Dr M E Benaim, a consultant physician at Bury General Hospital, where the defendant had been detained. By this stage the defendant was unable to remember anything about his journey to Bolton Road. I understand it is typical for a stroke to be followed by progressive amnesia. He told Dr Benaim he had blacked out and could not remember any more. The defendant
e was under Dr Benaim's care at the hospital. He was very confused for several days and was discharged after about a fortnight. Dr Benaim was satisfied that the defendant had had a stroke and also thought at one time that he might have had an epileptic attack as well. He agreed with Dr Evans (to whose evidence I shall have to refer later) that the stroke probably started just before the defendant left home. He expressed the following opinions. First, that once the stroke had started the defendant would not have been
f completely normal and he would not have been able to judge the quality of his own driving. Secondly, that the defendant's mental condition following the onset of the stroke could be correctly termed a clouding of consciousness. Thirdly, in order to drive in traffic it is necessary for a driver to exercise his will and his capacity to think, and that when stopping and giving way to approaching traffic a deliberate decision has to be made. Fourthly, on the subject of what the defendant said to the police officer and may
g have told the medical staff on 4th June, Dr Benaim said that he was not certain that the defendant would in fact have felt dizzy and that when he saw the defendant the next day, he himself would not have placed any reliance on what the defendant said. In cross-examination, however, he agreed that the case notes might be an accurate account of what the defendant actually experienced and, further, that he had no reason to doubt that what the defendant said to the police officer was accurate.
h The main medical evidence called on behalf of the defendant was the evidence of Dr John Evans, who is a consultant neurologist of the Salford group of hospitals and a lecturer in medicine at the University of Manchester. In addition to giving oral evidence he produced a medical report dated 11th July 1977. In the witness box Dr Evans told me that he remained of the opinion expressed in that report under the heading 'Conclusion'. Dr Evans wrote:
j

> 'At my examination today [that is 11th July 1977] Mr. Ramsbottom shows
> evidence of a moderately severe left hemiparesis with sensory loss down the left side
> of the body and sensory inattention to visual stimuli in the left half of his visual
> field. In addition he shows an impairment of intellect characterised by a marked
> impairment of short term memory. These neurological signs have been present

since the episode on 4th June 1976. I am of the opinion that while his wife was
upstairs changing preparatory to going out Mr. Ramsbottom sustained a stroke *a*
causing severe disorientation of thought and impairment of memory, weakness of
the left side of the body and inattention of his left visual field. It was in this
disorientated condition that he went off in his car, forgetting to take his wife with
him, and it was in the same disorientated state that he collided with the bicycle and
the van and the car. It is clear that Mr. Ramsbottom was ill at the time of this
incident, he did not fully appreciate what he was doing and he had no full control *b*
over his movements. He was, in effect, acting in a state of automatism and he was
not responsible for his actions. At the same time Mr. Ramsbottom was not aware
of the severity of his incapacity and he was not in a position to judge whether or not
he was fit enough to take the wheel of his car. He has made a partial recovery from
his stroke but still remains severely incapacitated. He is not fit to drive a car. He
will continue to need help and care and attention from his wife.'   *c*

Then Dr Evans dealt with the suggestion that the defendant might have suffered an
epileptic fit and expressed the view that in his opinion he had not.
   In his evidence-in-chief Dr Evans repeated what he had said in his report about
automatism. He said that in his view there was no evidence in favour of an epileptic fit
having occurred and that he was certain when the defendant had been driving along he *d*
was not capable of forming any rational opinion whether he was able to drive. And later
he said that the clouding of consciousness resulted in the defendant being unable to
appreciate fully what had happened or to appreciate that he was incapable of driving
the car properly. He described, as I have said, the defendant's condition as a clouding of
consciousness. He also expressed the opinion that a person in the defendant's condition
on 4th June following his stroke would have given a most misleading account to a police *e*
officer or anyone else as to what had happened. In cross-examination, however, Dr
Evans accepted that a person in the defendant's condition might have felt queer and
rather dizzy and might have experienced a feeling of nausea. He also agreed that the
defendant could have experienced what he described to the police officer.
   He was also questioned about the extent of the defendant's consciousness. He agreed
that the defendant was not unconscious but that his consciousness was impaired or *f*
clouded from the time he set out. He accepted that the defendant's movements in
driving were deliberate movements and that to drive along the route which the
defendant followed involved purposeful acts. He described the defendant's state at the
time of collision with the Triumph as a state of impaired consciousness. Nevertheless, Dr
Evans remained unshaken in his evidence that the defendant did not know that he was
driving badly or that he was unfit to drive. He told me that after the initial onset of the *g*
stroke further damage to the brain would have occurred all the time during the next
hour or so. During that period the defendant's capacity to drive might have fluctuated
somewhat but his physical condition must have got worse.
   I have summarised the main points of the evidence and I must now state my findings
of fact in relation to the defendant's driving and his condition when driving.
   It is not in dispute that the circumstances of the collision establish a prima facie case *h*
of negligence. I can set out my findings shortly as follows. First, I find that the
defendant suffered a stroke on 4th June 1976 and that the onset of the stroke began
shortly before he left home at about 10.00 am. Second, that before he suffered that
stroke the defendant had no previous symptoms or warning signs. Third, that following
the onset of the stroke the defendant's consciousness was impaired. Fourth, that this
state of impaired or clouded consciousness continued throughout the defendant's journey *j*
from his home to the point of impact in Bolton Road. Fifth, that the defendant did
experience the feelings of queerness which he described to the police officer and did
know at the time it happened that he had hit the van. Sixth, that throughout the
journey to Bolton Road and up to the moment of impact with the Triumph car the
defendant was sufficiently in possession of his faculties (i) to have some, though an

impaired, awareness of his surroundings and the traffic conditions and (ii) to make a
a series of deliberate and voluntary though inefficient movements of his hands and legs to
manipulate the controls of his car. Seventh, that the defendant was at no time aware of
the fact that he was unfit to drive; accordingly no moral blame can be attached to him
for continuing to do so.

I must turn therefore to consider the law applicable to these facts. The standard of care
by which a driver's actions are to be judged in an action based on negligence is an
b objective standard. Every driver, including a learner-driver—

> 'must drive in as good a manner as a driver of skill, experience and care, who is
> sound in wind and limb, who makes no errors of judgment, has good eyesight and
> hearing, and is free from any infirmity'

(per Lord Denning MR in *Nettleship v Weston*[1]). It is the same standard as that which is
c applied in the criminal law in relation to offences of dangerous driving and driving
without due care and attention. The standard 'eliminates the personal equation and is
independent of the idiosyncrasies of the particular person whose conduct is in question'
(see per Lord Macmillan in *Glasgow Corpn v Muir*[2]). As Salmon LJ said in *Nettleship v
Weston*[3]: 'On grounds of public policy, neither this criminal nor civil responsibility is
affected by the fact that the driver in question may be a learner, infirm or drunk.'
d The liability of a driver in tort is not, however, a strict liability. Nor is the offence of
dangerous driving an absolute offence. In *R v Gosney*[4] Megaw LJ said in relation to a
charge of dangerous driving:

> 'It is not an absolute offence. In order to justify a conviction there must be, not
> only a situation which, viewed objectively, was dangerous, but there must also have
e > been some fault on the part of the driver, causing that situation. "Fault" certainly
> does not necessarily involve deliberate misconduct or recklessness or intention to
> drive in a manner inconsistent with proper standards of driving. Nor does fault
> necessarily involve moral blame. Thus there is fault if an inexperienced or a
> naturally poor driver, while straining every nerve to do the right thing, falls below
> the standard of a competent and careful driver. Fault indicates a failure; a falling
f > below the care or skill of a competent and experienced driver, in relation to the
> manner of the driving and to the relevant circumstances of the case. A fault in that
> sense, even though it be slight, even though it be a momentary lapse, even though
> normally no danger would have arisen from it, is sufficient.'

As Megaw LJ said a little later in his judgment in *R v Gosney*[4]: 'Such a fault will often be
g sufficiently proved as an inference from the very facts of the situation.' But there may
be cases where the driver will be able to raise some matter sufficient to avoid the
inference of fault.

In the criminal cases concerned with dangerous driving guidance is given as to the
circumstances in which some sudden event will provide a defence. In *R v Spurge*[5]
Salmon J, in delivering the judgment of the Court of Criminal Appeal, said:

h
> 'If, however, a motor car endangers the public solely by reason of some sudden
> overwhelming misfortune suffered by the man at the wheel for which he is in no
> way to blame – if, for example, he suddenly has an epileptic fit or passes into a coma,
> or is attacked by a swarm of bees or stunned by a blow on the head from a stone,
> then he is not guilty of driving in a manner dangerous to the public (*Hill* v.

j

---

1   [1971] 3 All ER 581 at 586, [1971] 2 QB 691 at 699
2   [1943] 2 All ER 44 at 48, [1943] AC 448 at 457
3   [1971] 3 All ER 581 at 589, [1971] 2 QB 691 at 703
4   [1971] 3 All ER 220 at 224, [1971] 2 QB 674 at 680
5   [1961] 2 All ER 688 at 690, [1961] 2 QB 205 at 210

Baxter[1]). It would be otherwise if he had felt an illness coming on but still continued to drive, for that would have been a manifestly dangerous thing to do.'

A little later, in relation to a defect in the vehicle, he went on[2]:

> 'There does not seem to this court to be any real distinction between a man being suddenly deprived of control of a motor car by some sudden affliction of his person and being so deprived by some defect suddenly manifesting itself in the motor car. In both cases the motor car is suddenly out of control of its driver through no fault of his.'

In the course of his judgment Salmon J[3] also explained that the defendant in what may be called the 'sudden affliction' cases may be able to escape liability on the additional ground that he was not driving at all. It was this ground which was considered by the Divisional Court in *Hill v Baxter*[1]. Lord Goddard CJ said[4]: '. . . there may be cases where the circumstances are such that the accused could not really be said to be driving at all.' And Pearson J put the matter in these terms[5]:

> 'In any ordinary case when once it has been proved that the accused was in the driving seat of a moving car, there is prima facie an obvious and irresistible inference that he was driving it. No dispute or doubt will arise on that point unless and until there is evidence tending to show that by some extraordinary mischance he was rendered unconscious or otherwise incapacitated from controlling the car.'

In civil cases too a defendant may be able to rebut a prima facie case of negligence by showing that a sudden affliction has rendered him unconscious or otherwise wholly incapable of controlling the vehicle. In *Waugh v James K Allan Ltd*[6] it was contended in the Inner House of the Court of Session that the driver had been driving negligently. But Lord Clyde said[7]:

> 'In the first place it was contended that Gemmell was driving his lorry in a negligent and dangerous manner and was therefore guilty of negligence. But it seems to me clear on the evidence that the driver was at the time of the accident to the pursuer so completely disabled by the sudden onset of the coronary thrombosis as to have ceased to be responsible for the alarming manoeuvres of his lorry, and the Lord Ordinary had ample evidence upon which he was entitled to negative this ground of fault.'

This ground of negligence was not pursued in the House of Lords, where the only question which was debated was whether the driver should have realised that he was unfit to drive. *Jones v Dennison*[8] is a similar case. The driver, who was an epileptic, had a sudden blackout but the argument in the Court of Appeal was concerned wholly with the question whether he was or ought reasonably to have been aware of a tendency on his part to suffer a blackout. See also the Canadian case of *Gordon v Wallace*[9] and the cases there referred to.

In the present case, however, I am not concerned with a total loss of consciousness but with a clouding or impairment of consciousness. I must turn again for assistance to the criminal cases where specific consideration has been given to what is called the defence of automatism.

1   [1958] 1 All ER 193, [1958] 1 QB 277
2   [1961] 2 All ER 688 at 690, [1961] 2 QB 205 at 210–211
3   [1961] 2 All ER 688 at 690, [1961] 2 QB 205 at 210
4   [1958] 1 All ER 193 at 195, [1958] 1 QB 277 at 283
5   [1958] 1 All ER 193 at 197, [1958] 1 QB 277 at 286
6   [1964] 2 Lloyd's Rep 1
7   [1964] 2 Lloyd's Rep 1 at 2
8   [1971] RTR 174
9   (1973) 42 DLR (3d) 342

In *Watmore v Jenkins*[1] the defendant was charged with three offences including
a dangerous driving and driving without due care and attention. The defendant was a
diabetic who had had an attack of infective hepatitis. In the course of driving home from
his office he suffered a hypoglycaemic episode and in a gradually worsening state of
concussion he drove from Mitcham to a point about five miles away in Coulsdon where
he crashed into the back of a car. The defendant had no recollection of this part of his
journey and had had no warning of the onset of the episode. The justices acquitted the
b defendant on the grounds that at all material times he was in a state of automatism. The
Divisional Court, consisting of five judges presided over by Lord Parker CJ, remitted the
case to the justices with a direction to convict. Winn J, who delivered the judgment of
the court, said[2]:

c 'It is ... a question of law what constitutes a state of automatism ... this
expression is no more than a modern catchphrase which the courts have not
accepted as connoting any wider or looser concept than involuntary movement of
the body or limbs of a person.'

And later he referred[3] to 'such a complete destruction of voluntary control as could
constitute in law automatism'.
To the same effect was the judgment of the Court of Appeal in *R v Isitt*[4], where Lawton
d LJ referred to acts done during an epileptic attack, and continued: 'What the accused does
in those circumstances is involuntary. Acts performed involuntarily have come to be
known as automatism.' But he added[4]:

'It is a matter of human experience that the mind does not always operate in top
gear. There may be some difficulty in functioning. If the difficulty does not
e amount in law to either insanity or automatism, is the accused to be entitled to say
"I am not guilty because my mind was not working in top gear"? In my judgment
he is not.'

In *R v Isitt*[5] there was medical evidence that at the material time the defendant was
suffering from some malfunction of the mind. But the facts showed that he had driven
f in that state for a considerable distance and his driving was described by Lawton LJ[4] as
'purposeful driving'.
Finally, the decision of the Divisional Court in *Hill v Baxter*[6], to which I have already
referred, provides additional support for the proposition that in law a state of automatism
involves a complete loss of consciousness. I am satisfied that in a civil action a similar
approach should be adopted. The driver will be able to escape liability if his actions at the
g relevant time were wholly beyond his control. The most obvious case is sudden
unconsciousness. But if he retained some control, albeit imperfect control, and his
driving, judged objectively, was below the required standard, he remains liable. His
position is the same as a driver who is old or infirm. In my judgment unless the facts
establish what the law recognises as automatism the driver cannot avoid liability on the
basis that owing to some malfunction of the brain his consciousness was impaired.
h Counsel for the plaintiff put the matter accurately, as I see it, when he said 'One cannot
accept as exculpation anything less than total loss of consciousness'.
It is true that in the present case Dr Evans described the defendant's condition as one
of automatism. I am satisfied, however, that his condition did not amount to automatism
as that word has been used in the decided cases.

j 1   [1962] 2 All ER 868, [1962] 2 QB 572
2   [1962] 2 All ER 868 at 874, [1962] 2 QB 572 at 586
3   [1972] 2 All ER 868 at 874, [1962] 2 QB 572 at 587
4   [1978] RTR 211 at 216
5   [1978] RTR 211
6   [1958] 1 All ER 193, [1958] 1 QB 277

I therefore consider that the defendant is liable in law for his driving when he collided with the Triumph car in Bolton Road. I also consider that the plaintiffs would be entitled *a* to succeed, if necessary, on the alternative ground put forward, that is, that the defendant continued to drive when he was unfit to do so and when he should have been aware of his unfitness. He was aware that he had been feeling queer and had hit the van. Owing to his mental state he was unable to appreciate that he should have stopped. As I have said, and I repeat, the defendant was in no way morally to blame, but that is irrelevant to the question of legal liability in this case. An impairment of judgment does not *b* provide a defence. I consider that the defendant was in law guilty of negligence in continuing to drive because he was aware of his disabling symptoms and of his first collision even though he was not able to appreciate their proper significance.

I turn therefore to the question of damages. [His Lordship awarded the first plaintiff damages of £968·87, the second plaintiff damages of £700, and the third plaintiff damages of £2,500, all the awards being subject to the addition of interest.] *c*

Judgment for plaintiffs accordingly.

Solicitors: *Frederick Howarth Son & Maitland,* Bury, (for the plaintiffs); *A W Mawer & Co,* Manchester (for the defendant).

d

M Denise Chorlton Barrister.

a Leakey and others v National Trust for Places of Historic Interest or Natural Beauty

COURT OF APPEAL, CIVIL DIVISION

MEGAW, SHAW AND CUMMING-BRUCE LJJ

b 11th, 12th, 13th, 14th, 15th JUNE, 31st JULY 1979

Nuisance – Natural processes – Change in nature of land itself – Change giving rise to state of affairs constituting hazard to neighbouring properties – Occupier aware of hazard – Duty of occupier to abate hazard – Plaintiff's house adjacent to steep mound owned and occupied by defendant – Earth movements taking place in mound as a result of natural causes – Movements giving rise to danger of bank collapsing onto houses – Whether defendant under a duty to take c *reasonable steps to abate danger.*

The defendants owned and occupied a parcel of land consisting of a conical shaped hill composed of soil which made it peculiarly liable to cracking and slipping as a result of weathering. The plaintiffs were the owners of two houses at the base of the hill, the hill rising in a steep bank from a narrow strip of land lying at the back of the houses. The d boundary between the defendants' land and the houses ran along the bottom of the bank, so that the bank formed part of the defendants' property. For many years there had from time to time been slides of soil, rocks, tree-roots and other debris from the bank onto the plaintiffs' land caused by the effect of natural weathering on the land. In 1976 a prolonged summer drought followed by an unusually wet autumn aggravated the process of natural weathering and in September 1976 one of the plaintiffs pointed out to e the defendants that a large crack had opened up in the bank above her house and that there was a grave danger of a major collapse of the bank onto her house. The defendants replied that they were not obliged to do anything about it because it was caused by the natural movement of the earth. Some weeks later there was a large fall of the bank onto the land of the plaintiff who had complained, extending up against the house and, it was alleged, putting it at risk if there were further falls. The defendants were asked to clear f the fallen earth and debris but they refused saying they were not responsible for what had occurred. The cost of clearing the material and subsequent protective works amounted to some £6,000. In January 1977 the plaintiffs joined in issuing a writ against the defendants seeking injunctions requiring them to remove the fallen soil and debris and to prevent future falls of earth, soil and tree-stumps onto the plaintiffs' land, and damages for nuisance. There was no express pleading of negligence. The judge[a] held g that the defendants were liable in nuisance. The defendants appealed, contending that in English law there was no liability owed to an adjoining owner where natural mineral material encroached or threatened to encroach onto adjoining land causing damage. They further contended that if there was any liability it was a liability in negligence and not in nuisance and that therefore the plaintiffs' claim having been pleaded only in nuisance it necessarily failed.
h

Held – The appeal would be dismissed for the following reasons—

(i) (Shaw LJ dubitante) Under English law there was both in principle and on authority a general duty imposed on occupiers in relation to hazards occurring on their land, whether the hazards were natural or man-made. A person on whose land a hazard naturally occurred, whether in the soil itself or in something on or growing on the land, j and which encroached or threatened to encroach onto another's land thereby causing or threatening to cause damage, was under a duty, if he knew or ought to have known of the risk of encroachment, to do what was reasonable in all the circumstances to prevent

---

a [1978] 3 All ER 234

or minimise the risk of the known or foreseeable damage or injury to the other person
or his property, and was liable in nuisance if he did not. Where a substantial expenditure *a*
was required to prevent or minimise the risk of damage the occupier's financial resources,
assessed on a broad basis, were a relevant factor in deciding what was reasonably required
of him to discharge the duty, and the neighbour's ability, similarly assessed on a broad
basis, to protect himself from damage might also be a relevant factor to be taken into
account, depending on the circumstances. Because the duty was part of English law and
because the defendants knew that the instability of their land was a hazard which *b*
threatened the plaintiffs' property, that duty applied to them (see p 25 *d* to *g*, p 26 *f*, p 27
a b f g, p 28 *c* to *e*, p 35 *c* to *e*, p 37 *b* to *d* and *f* to p 38 *c*, p 39 *g h* and p 40 *a*, post); dicta
of Scrutton LJ in *Job Edwards Ltd v Birmingham Navigations* [1924] 1 KB at 360, of Rowlatt
J and of Wright J in *Noble v Harrison* [1926] All ER Rep at 287, 288, *Sedleigh-Denfield v
O'Callagan* [1940] 3 All ER 349 and *Goldman v Hargrave* [1966] 2 All ER 989 applied;
Davey v Harrow Corpn [1957] 2 All ER 305 approved; *Rylands v Fletcher* [1861–73] All ER *c*
Rep 1 distinguished; dictum of Lord Cairns LC in *Rylands v Fletcher* [1861–73] All ER
Rep at 12–13 explained; *Rouse v Gravelworks Ltd* [1940] 1 All ER 26 criticised; *Giles v
Walker* [1886–90] All ER Rep 501 and *Pontardawe Rural District Council v Moore-Gwyn*
[1929] 1 Ch 656 overruled.

(ii) (Per Megaw and Cumming-Bruce LJJ) The plaintiffs' claim, in alleging breach of
a duty to take reasonable care to prevent part of the defendants' land from falling onto *d*
the plaintiffs' property, was properly described as a claim in nuisance, but in any event
the defendants had not been prejudiced by any failure expressly to plead negligence (see
p 26 *a b* and p 40 *a*, post).

Decision of O'Connor J [1978] 3 All ER 234 affirmed.

Notes   *e*

For ordinary and reasonable user of land, see 28 Halsbury's Laws (3rd Edn) 133–135,
paras 169–172, and for cases on the subject, see 36(1) Digest (Reissue) 460–463, 412–429.

Cases referred to in judgments

Attorney-General v Tod Heatley [1897] 1 Ch 560, [1895–9] All ER Rep 636, 66 LJ Ch 275, *f*
    76 LT 174, 61 JP 164, 36(1) Digest (Reissue) 432, 253.
Barker v Herbert [1911] 2 KB 633, [1911–13] All ER Rep 509, 80 LJKB 1329, 105 LT 349,
    75 JP 481, 9 LGR 1083, CA, 36(1) Digest (Reissue) 465, 441.
British Railways Board v Herrington [1972] 1 All ER 749, [1972] AC 877, [1972] 2 WLR
    537, HL, 36(1) Digest (Reissue) 121, 466.
Davey v Harrow Corpn [1957] 2 All ER 305, [1958] 1 QB 60, [1957] 2 WLR 941, CA, 1
    Digest (Repl) 38, 281.   *g*
Donoghue v Stevenson [1932] AC 562, [1932] All ER Rep 1, 101 LJPC 119, 147 LT 281, 37
    Com Cas 350, 1932 SC (HL) 31, 1932 SLT 317, HL, 36(1) Digest (Reissue) 144, 562.
French v Auckland City Corpn [1974] 1 NZLR 340, 36(1) Digest (Reissue) 454, *160.
Giles v Walker (1890) 24 QBD 656, [1886–90] All ER Rep 501, 59 LJQB 416, 62 LT 933,
    54 JP 599, DC, 36(1) Digest (Reissue) 462, 423.   *h*
Goldman v Hargrave [1966] 2 All ER 989, [1967] 1 AC 645, [1966] 3 WLR 513, [1966] 2
    Lloyd's Rep 65, 115 CLR 458, [1967] ALR 113, PC; *rvsg* sub nom *Hargrave v Goldman*
    (1963) 110 CLR 40, [1964] ALR 377, HC of Aust, 36(1) Digest Reissue 123, 469.
Job Edwards Ltd v Birmingham Navigations [1924] 1 KB 341, 93 LJKB 261, 130 LT 522,
    36(1) Digest (Reissue) 485, 632.
Margate Pier and Harbour (Co of Proprietors) v Margate Town Council (1869) 20 LT 564, 33 *j*
    JP 437, 36(1) Digest (Reissue) 437, 282.
Noble v Harrison [1926] 2 KB 332, [1926] All ER Rep 284, 95 LJKB 813, 135 LT 325, 90
    JP 188, DC, 36(1) Digest (Reissue) 449, 355.
Pontardawe Rural District Council v Moore-Gwyn [1929] 1 Ch 656, 98 LJ Ch 242, 141 LT
    23, 93 JP 141, 27 LGR 493, 36(1) Digest (Reissue) 463, 429.

Read v J Lyons & Co Ltd [1946] 2 All ER 471, [1947] AC 156, [1947] LJR 39, 175 LT 413,
a   HL, 36(1) Digest (Reissue) 459, 400.
Rickards v Lothian [1913] AC 263, [1911-13] All ER Rep 71, 82 LJPC 42, 108 LT 225, PC,
      36(1) Digest (Reissue) 461, 417.
Rouse v Gravelworks Ltd [1940] 1 All ER 26, [1940] 1 KB 489, 109 LJKB 408, 162 LT 230,
      CA, 19 Digest (Repl) 189, *1294.*
Rylands v Fletcher (1868) LR 3 HL 330, [1861–73] All ER Rep 1, 37 LJ Ex 161, 19 LT 220,
b   33 JP 70, HL; *affg* (1866) LR 1 Exch 265, 4 H & C 263, 35 LJ Ex 154, 14 LT 523, 30
      JP 436, 12 Jur NS 603, Ex Ch 36(1) Digest (Reissue) 446, *349.*
St Anne's Well Brewery Co v Roberts 140 LT 1, [1928] All ER Rep 28, 92 JP 180, 26 LGR
      638, CA, 36(1) Digest (Reissue) 460, *412.*
Sedleigh-Denfield v O'Callaghan [1940] 3 All ER 349, [1940] AC 880, 109 LJKB 893, 164 LT
      72, HL, 36(1) Digest (Reissue) 486, *633.*
c *Smith v Kenrick* (1849) 7 CB 515, [1843–60] All ER Rep 273, 18 LJCP 172, 12 LTOS 556,
      13 Jur 362, 137 ER 205, 36(1) Digest (Reissue) 403, *8.*
Thomas and Evans Ltd v Mid-Rhondda Co-operative Society Ltd [1940] 4 All ER 357, [1941]
      1 KB 381, 110 LJKB 699, 164 LT 303, CA, 47 Digest (Repl) 696, *453.*
Wilkins v Leighton [1932] 2 Ch 106, [1932] All ER Rep 55, 101 LJ Ch 385, 147 LT 495,
      36(1) Digest (Reissue) 460, *413.*
d

Cases also cited
Attorney-General v Cory Bros & Co Ltd, Kennard v Cory Bros & Co Ltd [1921] 1 AC 521, HL.
Bamford v Turnley (1862) 3 B & S 62, 122 ER 25; *rvsd* 3 B & S 66, [1861–73] All ER Rep
      706, Ex Ch.
e *British Road Services Ltd v Slater* [1964] 1 All ER 816, [1964] 1 WLR 498.
Broder v Saillard (1876) 2 Ch D 692.
Home Office v Dorset Yacht Co Ltd [1970] 2 All ER 294, [1970] AC 1004, HL.
Hurdman v North Eastern Railway Co (1878) 3 CPD 168, [1874–80] All ER Rep 735, CA.
Laugher v Pointer (1826) 5 B & C 546, [1824–34] All ER Rep 388.
Lemmon v Webb [1893] 3 Ch 1, CA; *affd* [1895] AC 1, [1891–4] All ER Rep 749, HL.
f *Morgan v Khyatt* [1964] 1 WLR 475, PC.
Neath Rural District Council v Williams [1950] 2 All ER 625, [1951] 1 KB 115, DC.
Slater v Worthington's Cash Stores (1930) Ltd [1941] 3 All ER 28, [1941] KB 488, CA.
Smith v Giddy [1904] 2 KB 448, [1904–7] All ER Rep 289, DC.
Trevett v Lee [1955] 1 All ER 406, [1955] 1 WLR 113, CA.
Wagon Mound, The, Overseas Tankship (UK) Ltd v Miller Steamship Co Pty Ltd (No 2) [1966]
g   2 All ER 709, [1967] 1 AC 617, PC.
Whalley v Lancashire and Yorkshire Railway Co (1884) 13 QBD 131, CA.
Wooldridge v Sumner [1962] 2 All ER 878, [1963] 2 QB 43, CA.
Wringe v Cohen [1939] 4 All ER 241, [1940] 1 KB 229, CA.

h **Appeal**
By a writ issued on 31st January 1977 the plaintiffs, Leslie McDonald Leakey, Doris Irene
Leakey (his wife) and Edward Charles Storey, brought an action against the defendants,
the National Trust for Places of Historic Interest or Natural Beauty, seeking (i) an
injunction restraining them from permitting soil, earth and tree stumps to move from
the defendants' land known as Burrow Mump, Burrowbridge, in Somerset, onto land
j adjoining thereon owned by the plaintiffs, (ii) an order that the defendants take all
necessary steps to remove and stop and prevent soil, earth and tree stumps moving from
their land onto the plaintiffs' land, and (iii) damages for nuisance. On 1st March 1977
Bristow J granted an interlocutory injunction against the defendants ordering them
forthwith to take all necessary steps to stop and prevent soil, earth and tree stumps
moving from the defendants' land onto the plaintiffs' land and ordered an early trial of

the action. In April 1977 the defendants carried out the work required to abate the
nuisance at a cost of £2,175. On 20th January 1978 at the trial of the action O'Connor **a**
J¹ held that the defendants were liable in nuisance and awarded damages of £50 to Mr
and Mrs Leakey and nominal damages of £2 to Mr Storey. The judge refused to grant
the injunctions because he was satisfied that the work carried out by the defendants had
successfully averted any serious risk to the plaintiffs' properties. The defendants
appealed. The plaintiffs by a respondent's notice claimed that the judge should have
granted the injunctions but the cross-notice was abandoned on appeal. After the trial **b**
and before the appeal the defendants carried out further protective work costing a
further £4,000. The facts are set out in the judgment of Megaw LJ.

Iain Glidewell QC and *Joseph Harper* for the defendants.
Hubert Dunn for the plaintiffs.

c

Cur adv vult

31st July. The following judgments were read.

MEGAW LJ. This appeal from the judgment of O'Connor J¹ raises questions which are **d**
of importance in the development of English law. The learned judge held that the
defendants are liable to the plaintiffs in damages, on a claim framed in nuisance, based
on the fact that soil and other detritus had fallen from property owned and occupied by
the defendants onto the plaintiffs' properties. It was accepted by the parties that the
instability of the defendants' land which made it labile, and which had caused, and was
likely to continue to cause, falls of detritus on the plaintiffs' land, was not caused by, nor **e**
was it aggravated by, any human activities on the defendants' land. It was caused by
nature: the geological structure, content and contours of the land, and the effect thereon
of sun, rain, wind and frost and suchlike natural phenomena. It was held by the learned
judge, and is not now in dispute, that, at least since 1968, the defendants knew that the
instability of their land was a threat to the plaintiffs' property because of the possibility
of falls of soil and other material. Although requested by the plaintiffs to take steps to **f**
prevent such falls, the defendants had not taken any action, because they held the view,
no doubt on legal advice, that in law they were under no liability in respect of any
damage which might be caused to neighbouring property in consequence of the natural
condition of their own property and the operation of natural forces thereon.

O'Connor J has held that that view of the law is wrong. He based his decision on the
judgment of the Judicial Committee of the Privy Council in *Goldman v Hargrave*². The
main issue in this appeal is whether *Goldman v Hargrave*² accurately states the law of **g**
England. If it does, the appeal fails, and the defendants are liable.

The opinion of the Judicial Committee in *Goldman v Hargrave*², an appeal from the
High Court of Australia, emanating originally from the Supreme Court of Western
Australia, was delivered by Lord Wilberforce, the Board consisting of Lord Reid, Lord
Morris of Borth-y-Gest, Lord Pearce, Lord Wilberforce and Lord Pearson. We in this **h**
court are not bound by that decision, as we should have been bound if their Lordships
had been sitting as an Appellate Committee of the House of Lords. But there can be no
suggestion that the Board regarded the law of Western Australia, on the issues which
they decided, as differing in any way from the law of England. I need scarcely say that
in those circumstances it would be only after the most mature consideration that this
court could regard it as right to conclude that the unanimous view of the Board did not **j**
accurately represent the law of England. Nevertheless, as the defendants in this appeal,

1   [1978] 3 All ER 234, [1978] QB 849
2   [1966] 2 All ER 989, [1967] 1 AC 645

a perfectly properly and with powerful and carefully marshalled arguments, ask us to say that *Goldman v Hargrave*[1] is not the law of England, we must, equally, give these submissions the mature consideration to which they are entitled.

I shall, of course, have to return to these submissions in more detail later. But it may be helpful if at this stage I indicate briefly that the criticism offered of the decision in *Goldman v Hargrave*[1] is, in essence, that that decision involves the disregard, perhaps by inadvertence, of a principle of law laid down by the House of Lords in *Rylands v Fletcher*[2],

b which has, it is said, ever since been accepted and followed. If the Judicial Committee's decision assumes, or involves the proposition, that the House of Lords in *Sedleigh-Denfield v O'Callagan*[3] had departed from that principle, then that was a decision which the House of Lords themselves had not been entitled to reach in 1940, in the light of the then prevailing doctrine of precedent in the House of Lords; and it should not be assumed that the House of Lords had so decided, contrary to that doctrine. Alternatively, the

c defendants submit that, at most, the ratio decidendi of *Sedleigh-Denfield v O'Callagan*[3] leaves it open for, but not obligatory on, lower courts thereafter to decide that a landowner could be liable for damage to his neighbour's property although there was no unnatural use of the land and the nuisance resulted solely from the operation of the forces of nature. If that be the position as regards authority, then, the defendants submit, despite the great weight which ought to be given to the view of the Privy Council, this

d court ought, with the greatest respect to that view, to reject it and to decide the question in the opposite way. It is free to do so. It should, it was submitted, hold that there is no such liability.

Having thus stated, as I thought to be desirable at an early stage of this judgment, the broad nature of the important issue which arises on this appeal, I shall now return to a more detailed statement of the facts and events which led up to this appeal. But I do not

e propose to go into great detail, for the issues to be decided do not depend on detail. I shall try to say no more than is desirable as giving the background to the appeal.

Near Bridgwater, in Somerset, there is a hill rejoicing in the name of Burrow Mump. It has since 1946 been owned by the defendants, the National Trust. It is a conical hill which rises steeply, on all its sides, from the Somerset plain. Geologically, it is composed of Keuper marl, which, as I understand it, makes it peculiarly liable to cracking and

f slipping as a result of weathering. At the base of its western side lie two adjacent houses, which belong to the plaintiffs. Elm Glen belongs to Mr and Mrs Leakey, the first and second plaintiffs. Hillside, which is immediately to the north of Elm Glen, belongs to Mr Storey, the third plaintiff. The latter house had been constructed by the amalgamation of two cottages which had stood on the site for, perhaps, 200 or 300 years. Elm Glen was built in 1915, but there had been an earlier house or houses on the same site, going back

g to a time, to use the picturesque phrase, 'whereof the memory of man runneth not to the contrary'.

The lower part of the western hillside of the Mump, which looms over these two houses, is particularly steep. At that place it takes the form of a bank. At some unknown time in the past, it is thought, there was some cutting, by human hands and implements, for some unknown reason, of the hillside at this point. The consequence may have been

h to make what I have called 'the bank' steeper than it would have been if nature had been left to its own workings. But, though issues were raised about this in the pleadings in the action, nothing now turns on the fact, or the possibility, that there had been this remotely distant human intervention. It is accepted by all parties that the legal rights and liabilities are to be ascertained on the assumption that the contours of the defendants' property are as nature made or developed them.

j

---

1   [1966] 2 All ER 989, [1967] 1 AC 645
2   (1868) LR 3 HL 330, [1861–73] All ER Rep 1
3   [1940] 3 All ER 349, [1940] AC 880

It is also to be assumed that, as admitted by the defendants in their pleading, they were not only the owners, but also the occupiers, of Burrow Mump at all relevant times. We were told by the defendants' counsel that in fact the Mump, or part of it, had been occupied on lease or licence by someone to whom the defendants had given grazing rights. But, for the purpose of this appeal, the defendants, fairly and properly, do not seek to go back on their admission that they are the occupiers. It is not, therefore, a question for consideration in this appeal whether it would have affected the issue of the defendants' liability if someone else had been the occupier.

Another fact which I have already mentioned as not being in dispute, but which it is right should be emphasised, is that there has been no human activity, whether the possible long-distant cutting of the hillside already mentioned, or any bringing of anything on to the defendants' land, or the carrying out of any work or operations of any sort on the land, which has in any way affected or increased the labile condition of the land. Its instability, its propensity to slip, which admittedly exists, is caused by nature: the contours, the geological structure and material, and the effect thereon of sun, rain, wind, frost and other natural agencies.

As a result of the operation of natural agencies on the steep contours of Burrow Mump, where its western slope rises in a bank at the back of the plaintiffs' houses, there have from time to time over the years, for many years past, been slides, often quite minor, sometimes more substantial, of soil, rocks, tree-roots and such-like detritus, from the bank, which belongs to the defendants, onto land belonging to each of the plaintiffs, onto a strip of land lying at the backs of the houses, between them and the bank, and also, on occasion, onto a piece of the Leakeys' land to the south of their house, where there was an outhouse belonging to them. There were earlier complaints and discussions, into which I need not go. But, as I have already said, there is now no dispute but that, since 1968 at least, the defendants appreciated that the bank was a part of their property and that it was a threat to the houses below because of the real possibility of falls of material from it.

The present action has its origin in developments following the exceptionally hot, dry summer of 1976 and the unusually heavy rainfall of the ensuing autumn. Mrs Leakey, in September of that year, noticed that a big crack had opened up in the bank above her property. She drew the attention of the defendants to it, pointing out that there was a grave danger of a major collapse of the bank onto her house. The defendants told her that this was a natural movement and that they were not obliged to do anything about it. She offered to pay half the cost of reducing the bank. At that time she thought that the cost would be about £1,000. That offer was rejected.

A few weeks later there was a large fall of the bank. Part of the intrusion into the plaintiffs' properties involved the piling up of detritus against the outside wall of the Leakeys' kitchen. A letter was sent by solicitors acting for the Leakeys to the defendants saying that the house was at risk of further falls and that there were large tree-stumps in the material which had already fallen. They asked the defendants to remove the fallen debris. The defendants refused, denying responsibility; but they said that they would be glad to give the Leakeys a licence to go onto the defendants' land to abate the nuisance to their property. The Leakeys and Mr Storey then joined forces in launching the action out of which this appeal arises. I mention at this stage, simply to show the seriousness of the case, that the cost of clearance and of protective works hitherto undertaken is about £6,000.

The writ was issued on 31st January 1977 claiming, first, a mandatory injunction, restraining the defendants from permitting soil, earth and tree-stumps to move onto the plaintiffs' properties, secondly, an order to remove the soil etc which had already fallen, and, thirdly, damages for nuisance. The defendants stress that there was no express pleading of negligence, nor any formulation of the claim other than in nuisance. The defendants by their defence denied any liability. I need not consider the pleadings more deeply.

The plaintiffs sought an interlocutory injunction. The defendants sought, courageously
a in the light of *Goldman v Hargrave*[1], to strike out the statement of claim as disclosing no
reasonable cause of action. The two interlocutory applications were heard by Bristow J
on 1st March 1977. He dismissed the defendants' application. He granted the plaintiffs
an interlocutory injunction, on the plaintiffs' undertaking as to damages. The judge
ordered the defendants to take steps to prevent soil etc moving from Burrow Mump onto
the plaintiffs' properties. The defendants carried out work on the land. That work was
b completed in April 1977 at a cost to the defendants of £2,175. No further falls occurred
before the hearing of the action.

The action was thereafter tried before O'Connor J. On 20th January 1978 he delivered
judgment[2]. He held that the defendants were liable in nuisance. He awarded damages
of £50 to Mr and Mrs Leakey and nominal damages of £2 to Mr Storey. The damages
were relatively small because, first, the defendants had undertaken and paid for the
c protective work under the interlocutory injunction, which included the removal of the
fallen soil from the Leakeys' property, and, secondly, because, while refusing to grant an
injunction, the judge made it clear that if there should, unfortunately, be further
encroachments, the plaintiffs, or either of them, would be free to present a fresh claim
for damages. In fact, since O'Connor J's judgment, the defendants, no doubt wisely and
properly, have caused further protective works to be carried out, which have cost, we
d have been told, a further sum of approximately £4,000. Hence the £6,000 to which I
have referred earlier as having been the cost of clearing and protective works hitherto.

At the trial, an undertaking was given on behalf of the defendants that, if the defence
were to succeed, the defendants would not seek to enforce the undertaking given by the
plaintiffs on the granting of the interlocutory injunction. That undertaking would have
involved a payment to the defendants of a sum of £2,175, as the amount then was.
e Before us, counsel for the defendants renewed that undertaking and further undertook
that, if the appeal were to succeed, the defendants would not seek to recover from the
plaintiffs any part of the further £4,000 or so which has since been expended by the
defendants on protective work. While it is right to record this generous offer by the
defendants, it cannot, of course, and was not intended to, influence the decision in any
way. It was made clear, further, that the undertaking did not relate to the cost of any
f further protective works.

From O'Connor J's judgment the defendants appeal. They submit that the question
is not only one of great moment as affecting themselves, the National Trust, by reason of
potential liabilities, if the decision is upheld, in respect of many properties which they
own for the benefit of the public in many parts of the United Kingdom, but also, they
submit, it is a question of general importance in the law. If *Goldman v Hargrave*[1] were
g to be treated as a part of the law of England, that, the defendants say, would be a
development of the law which would not only be inconsistent with long-standing
authority binding on this court, but also be undesirable from the point of view of the
general public interest and of fairness to persons, wealthy or poor, who own or occupy
land, large or small, in extent.

There was a cross-notice by the plaintiffs (strictly, it should have been a cross-appeal)
h asking that injunctions should be granted. However, it was abandoned.

For the defendants in this appeal, the fundamental proposition was formulated by
counsel as follows: in English law, neither the owner nor the occupier of land from
which, solely as the result of natural causes, natural mineral material encroaches onto, or
threatens to encroach onto, adjoining land, causing damage, is under any liability to the
adjoining land owner.
j Certain points should be made at once as to that proposition. First, the opening words,

---

1   [1966] 2 All ER 989, [1967] 1 AC 645
2   [1978] 3 All ER 234, [1978] QB 849

'In English law', are properly and deliberately included so as to emphasise that, even if the proposition has to be treated as being inconsistent with the ratio decidendi of *a* *Goldman v Hargrave*[1], that case, however persuasive, does not have the status of a binding authority as to English law. Secondly, the phrase 'solely as the result of natural causes' is intended to connote, if the negative form of words were to be used, 'not being the result of any human action, activity or use of land'. Thirdly, the proposition applies irrespective of whether or not the owner or occupier of the potentially encroaching land has knowledge of the risk that the encroachment will or may take place. Fourthly, the *b* proposition applies both to natural material making up the solid ground and to water naturally on or under land. In relation to this 'fourthly', I believe that the adjective which was included in the proposition as formulated by counsel, 'mineral' in 'natural mineral material', was included as providing a possible basis of distinction according as the substance of the encroaching material is, on the one hand, mineral, such as rocks or soil (if soil is mineral), and, on the other hand, vegetable, such as a tree trunk or the roots *c* or the branch of a tree. This, at first sight, unattractive distinction of 'animal, mineral or vegetable?' is, I believe, introduced into the proposition in order to prevent the proposition from coming into obvious conflict with authorities, such as *Davey v Harrow Corpn*[2], binding on this court, as to damage caused by trees.

The defendants' second proposition, which I propose to consider in the course of considering the first proposition, is that, if the first proposition be wrong, so that *Goldman* *d* *v Hargrave*[1] does represent the law of England, nevertheless the liability which is imposed under the *Goldman v Hargrave*[1] principle is a liability in negligence and not in nuisance. The present claim was pleaded, and pleaded only, in nuisance. Hence, it is said, it must fail.

There is a third proposition of the defendants as to the scope of the duty, if duty there be, affecting the defendants. I shall leave the consideration of that proposition until I *e* have dealt with the earlier two propositions affecting the existence of the duty.

Counsel for the plaintiffs formulated, and at our request put before us in a document, a series of 12 propositions. It involves no disrespect to that clear and very helpful formulation of the arguments for the plaintiffs that I do not find it necessary to set them out and consider them specifically as they were framed. So far as I find it necessary to reach conclusions on those propositions, I shall do so in the course of my discussion of the *f* defendants' propositions.

Because of the conclusion which I have reached on this main issue, and my reasons for that conclusion, which I do not think differ for the most part in any substantial respect from the reasons expressed in the judgment of O'Connor J, I think that the simplest and most satisfactory method of dealing with the main issue is to start by a brief summary of the facts of, and the decision in, *Goldman v Hargrave*[1]. *g*

The relevant facts of *Goldman v Hargrave*[1] were simple. A redgum tree, 100 feet high, on the defendant's land was struck by lightning and caught fire. The defendant caused the land around the burning tree to be cleared and the tree was then cut down and sawn into sections. So far there could be no complaint that the defendant had done anything which he ought not to have done or left undone anything which he ought to have done, so as in any way to increase the risk which had been caused by this act of natural forces *h* setting fire to the tree. Thereafter the defendant (this was the state of the facts on which the Judicial Committee based their decision) did not do anything which he ought not to have done. He took no positive action which increased the risk of the fire spreading. But he failed to do something which he could have done without any substantial trouble or expense, which would, if done, have eliminated or rendered unlikely the spreading of the fire, that is, to have doused with water the burning or smouldering sections of the *j*

---

1   [1966] 2 All ER 989, [1967] 1 AC 645
2   [1957] 2 All ER 305, [1958] 1 QB 60

tree as they lay on the ground. Instead, the defendant chose to allow or encourage the
a fire to burn itself out. Foreseeably (again it was the forces of nature and not human
action), the weather became even hotter and a strong wind sprang up. The flames from
the tree spread rapidly through the defendant's land to the land of neighbours where it
did extensive damage to their properties.

The judgment of the Board was delivered by Lord Wilberforce. It was held that the
risk of the consequence which in fact happened was foreseeable. This, it is said, 'was not
b really disputed'. The legal issue was then defined[1]:

> '. . . the case is not one where a person has brought a source of danger on to his
> land, nor one where an occupier has so used his property as to cause a danger to his
> neighbour. It is one where an occupier, faced with a hazard accidentally arising on
> his land, fails to act with reasonable prudence so as to remove the hazard. The issue
> is therefore whether in such a case the occupier is guilty of legal negligence, which
> *c* involves the issue whether he is under a duty of care, and, if so, what is the scope of
> that duty.'

It is to my mind clear, from this passage and other passages in the judgment, that the
duty which is being considered, and which later in the judgment is held to exist, does not
involve any distinction of principle between what, in another sphere of the law, used to
d be known as misfeasance and non-feasance. A failure to act may involve a breach of the
duty, though, since the duty which emerges is a duty of reasonable care, the question of
misfeasance or non-feasance may have a bearing on the question whether the duty has
been broken. It is to my mind clear, also, that no distinction is suggested in, or can
properly be inferred from, the judgment as between a hazard accidentally arising on the
defendant's land which, on the one hand, gives rise to a risk of damage to a neighbour's
e property by the encroachment of fire and, on the other hand, gives rise to such a risk by
the encroachment of the soil itself, falling from the bank onto the neighbour's land.
There is no valid distinction, to my mind, between an encroachment which consists, on
the one hand, of the spread of fire from a tree on fire on the land, and, on the other hand,
of a slip of soil or rock resulting from the instability of the land itself, in each case, the
danger of encroachment, and the actual encroachment, being brought about by the
f forces of nature.

If any such distinctions as I have referred to in the previous paragraph were sought to
be made, I should have thought that their acceptance as being material, as leading to
different conclusions of principle in law, would make the law on this topic incoherent,
artificial, uncertain and unpredictable. In other words, they would lead to bad law.

At the point in the Board's judgment immediately following the passage which I have
g quoted above, the judgment goes on to deal briefly with the question of the appropriate
description of the cause of action. Their Lordships in that case found it unnecessary to
decide[2]—

> 'whether if responsibility is established it should be brought under the heading
> of nuisance or placed in a separate category . . . The present case is one where
> liability, if it exists, rests on negligence and nothing else; whether it falls within or
> *h* overlaps the boundaries of nuisance is a question of classification which need not
> here be resolved.'

It is convenient at this stage to deal with the second proposition put forward by the
defendants in the present appeal. The plaintiffs' claim is expressed in the pleadings to be
founded in nuisance. There is no express reference to negligence in the statement of
j claim. But there is an allegation of a breach of duty, and the duty asserted is, in effect, a
duty to take reasonable care to prevent part of the defendants' land from falling onto the

---

1   [1966] 2 All ER 989 at 991, [1967] 1 AC 645 at 656
2   [1966] 2 All ER 989 at 992, [1967] 1 AC 645 at 656

plaintiffs' property. I should, for myself, regard that as being properly described as a claim in nuisance. But even if that were, technically, wrong, I do not think that the point could or should avail the defendants in this case. If it were to do so, it would be a regrettable modern instance of the forms of action successfully clanking their spectral chains; for there would be no conceivable prejudice to the defendants in this case that the word 'negligence' had not been expressly set out in the statement of claim. The suggestion that if it had been so pleaded the defendants could have raised a defence of volenti non fit injuria, which they could not raise as against a claim pleaded in nuisance, is, in my judgment, misconceived. As counsel for the plaintiffs submitted, while it is no defence to a claim in nuisance that the plaintiff has 'come to the nuisance', it would have been a properly pleadable defence to this statement of claim that the plaintiffs, knowing of the danger to their property, by word or deed, had shown their willingness to accept that danger. Moreover, I find it hard to imagine circumstances in which the facts which would provide a defence of volenti non fit injuria would not also provide a defence in a case such as the present in the light of the scope of the duty which falls to be considered hereafter.

If the defendants' first and main proposition is wrong, I do not see that they can succeed on their second proposition.

I return to the judgment in *Goldman v Hargrave*[1]. The law of England as it used to be is set out in the following passage:

'. . . it is only in comparatively recent times that the law has recognised an occupier's duty as one of a more positive character than merely to abstain from creating, or adding to, a source of danger or annoyance. It was for long satisfied with the conception of separate or autonomous proprietors, each of which was entitled to exploit his territory in a "natural" manner and none of whom was obliged to restrain or direct the operations of nature in the interest of avoiding harm to his neighbours.'

The judgment of the Board then goes on to review the development of the law which, as the Board held[2], had changed the law so that there now exists 'a general duty on occupiers in relation to hazards occurring on their land, whether natural or man-made'. That change in the law, in its essence and in its timing, corresponds with, and may be viewed as being a part of, the change in the law of tort which achieved its decisive victory in *Donoghue v Stevenson*[3], though it was not until eight years later, in the House of Lords decision in *Sedleigh-Denfield v O'Callagan*[4], that the change as affecting the area with which we are concerned was expressed or recognised in a decision binding on all English courts, and, even then, the full, logical effect of the decision in altering what had hitherto been thought to be the law was not immediately recognised. But *Goldman v Hargrave*[5] has now demonstrated what that effect was in English law.

The *Sedleigh-Denfield* case[4] approved the dissenting judgment of Scrutton LJ in *Job Edwards Ltd v Birmingham Navigations*[6]. Thus, as the Judicial Committee recognised in

---

1   [1966] 2 All ER 989 at 992, [1967] 1 AC 645 at 657
2   [1966] 2 All ER 989 at 995, [1967] 1 AC 645 at 661–662
3   [1932] AC 562, [1932] All ER Rep 1
4   [1940] 3 All ER 349, [1940] AC 880
5   [1966] 2 All ER 989, [1967] 1 AC 645
6   [1924] 1 KB 341

Goldman v Hargrave[1], it was that great judge whose judgment in the *Job Edwards* case[2]
'marked a turning point in the law', eight years before *Donoghue v Stevenson*[3]. In the *Job
Edwards* case[2], Scrutton LJ took the view that the case required to be sent back for a new
trial because insufficient facts had been found. But the principle which, differing from
Bankes LJ and Astbury J, Scrutton LJ stated was[4]:

> '. . . the landowner in possession is liable for a nuisance created by a trespasser,
> which causes damage to others, if he could, after he knows or ought to have known
> of it, prevent by reasonable care its spreading.'

Earlier Scrutton LJ[5] had used words which are quoted in the judgment in *Goldman v
Hargrave*[1], which I need not here repeat. I should merely mention that, for the
defendants in this case, much stress is laid on the fact that Scrutton LJ in that passage used
the phrase '. . . if a man finds a dangerous *and artificial* thing on his land' (emphasis
mine). The defendants submit that the inclusion of the words 'and artificial' makes all
the difference in the subsequent development of the law. For reasons which I shall give,
I think not.

Again, in his judgment in the *Job Edwards* case[6], Scrutton LJ referred with approval to
what was said in Salmond on the Law of Torts[7], in a passage which was later given express
approval by Viscount Maugham and by Lord Wright in the *Sedleigh-Denfield* case[8]. Sir
John Salmond wrote:

> 'When a nuisance has been created by the act of a trespasser or otherwise without
> the act, authority or permission of the occupier, the occupier is not responsible for
> that nuisance unless, with knowledge or means of knowledge of its existence, he
> suffers it to continue without taking reasonably prompt and efficient means for its
> abatement.'

After the *Job Edwards* case[2] and before the *Sedleigh-Denfield* case[9] came the judgment of
Rowlatt J in the Queen's Bench Divisional Court in *Noble v Harrison*[10], in which he said:

> '. . . a person is liable for a nuisance constituted by the state of his property: (1.) if
> he causes it; (2.) if by neglect of some duty he allowed it to arise; and (3.) if, when
> it has arisen without his own act or default, he omits to remedy it within a
> reasonable time after he did or ought to have become aware of it.'

It is head (3) which is relevant for present purposes. If this is the law of England, then
Goldman v Hargrave[11] correctly represents the law of England in its assertion of 'a general
duty on occupiers in relation to hazards occurring on their land, whether natural or man-
made'. I shall refer later to a passage in the judgment of Wright J the other member of
the court in *Noble v Harrison*[12].

---

1   [1966] 2 All ER 989 at 993, [1967] 1 AC 645 at 659
2   [1924] 1 KB 341
3   [1932] AC 562, [1932] All ER Rep 1
4   [1924] 1 KB 341 at 360
5   [1924] 1 KB 341 at 357–358
6   [1924] 1 KB 341 at 359–360
7   5th Edn (1920) pp 258–265; see now 17th Edn (1977) pp 64–68
8   [1940] 3 All ER 349 at 357, 369, [1940] AC 880 at 893, 910
9   [1940] 3 All ER 349, [1940] AC 880
10 [1926] 2 KB 332 at 338, [1926] All ER Rep 284 at 287
11 [1966] 2 All ER 989 at 995, [1967] 1 AC 645 at 661–662
12 [1926] 2 KB 332, [1926] All ER Rep 284

In the *Sedleigh-Denfield* case[1], a local authority had trespassed on the defendant's land, without the defendant's knowledge or consent, and had placed a culvert in a ditch on that *a* land. By the improper placing of a grid at the mouth of the culvert, instead of further back, those who did the work created a danger of flooding which would be likely to spread to the plaintiff's land. The defendant, through his servants, came to know what had been done. He should have realised that it created a real risk of flooding of his neighbour's land. He did nothing. A heavy rainstorm caused the ditch to flood, because of the trespassers' work. The plaintiff's land was damaged. The House of Lords held that *b* the defendant was liable. The defendant himself had not done anything which was an 'unnatural user' of his land. He had not himself brought anything 'unnatural' onto his land. But when he knew or ought to have known of the risk of flood water from his land encroaching on his neighbour's land he had done nothing towards preventing it. Prevention could have been achieved without any great trouble or expense.

The approval by the House of Lords in the *Sedleigh-Denfield* case[1] of Scrutton LJ's *c* judgment in the *Job Edwards* case[2] meant, at any rate unless it could properly be said that it was a decision inconsistent with an earlier decision of the House of Lords, that it was thereafter the law of England that a duty existed under which the occupier of land might be liable to his neighbour for damage to his neighbour's property as a result of a nuisance spreading from his land to his neighbour's land, even though the existence and the operative effect of the nuisance were not caused by any 'non-natural' use by the defendant *d* of his own land. But the liability was not a strict liability such as that which was postulated by the House of Lords in *Rylands v Fletcher*[3] as arising where damage was caused to another by an 'unnatural' user of land. The obligation postulated in the *Sedleigh-Denfield* case[1], in conformity with the development of the law in *Donoghue v Stevenson*[4], was an obligation to use reasonable care. A defendant was not to be liable as a result of a risk of which he neither was aware nor ought, as a reasonable careful *e* landowner, to have been aware.

The decision in the *Sedleigh-Denfield* case[1] was in a case where, on the facts, something which might be described as 'not natural' had been introduced onto the defendant's land in the building of the culvert, but not by the defendant. It had been done by a trespasser without the defendant's knowledge or consent. It was not a case in which the potential damage to the neighbour's land had been brought about by natural causes. Therefore it *f* may be said that the *Sedleigh-Denfield* case[1] did not decide, so as to bind lower courts in England, that an owner or occupier of land was under a duty to exercise reasonable care where natural causes, as distinct from the act of a trespasser, brought about the dangerous condition of the land, of which he, the owner or occupier, knew or which he should have realised. If I had taken the view that the *Sedleigh-Denfield* case[1] does not bear on the question raised by the present appeal (and therefore also ought not to have influenced the *g* decision in *Goldman v Hargrave*[5]), I should have reached a different conclusion on this appeal. I do not, however, accept the suggested distinction.

My first comment is that the whole tenor of the speeches in the *Sedleigh-Denfield* case[1] suggests that the view of their Lordships, if not their decision, was that the same duty

h

1   [1940] 3 All ER 349, [1940] AC 880   *j*
2   [1924] 1 KB 341
3   (1868) LR 3 HL 330 [1861–73] All ER Rep 1
4   [1932] AC 562, [1932] All ER Rep 1
5   [1966] 2 All ER 989, [1967] 1 AC 645

arose. The approval of the passage in Salmond on the Law of Torts[1], to which I have
a previously referred, so suggests. A passage in Lord Wright's speech[2] gives, I believe, a fair
reflection of the attitude of their Lordships:

> 'The liability for a nuisance is not, at least in modern law, a strict or absolute
> liability. If the defendant, by himself or those for whom he is responsible, has
> created what constitutes a nuisance, and if it causes damage, the difficulty now
> being considered does not arise; but he may have taken over the nuisance, ready
> *b* made as it were, when he acquired the property, or the nuisance may be due to a
> latent defect or to the act of a trespasser or stranger. Then he is not liable unless he
> continued or adopted the nuisance, or, more accurately, did not without undue
> delay remedy it when he became aware of it, or with ordinary and reasonable care
> should have become aware of it. This rule seems to be in accord with good sense
> and convenience.'

c
I am confident that Lord Wright's words 'latent defect' were intended to include a
defect in the land itself. Lord Wright was making the same point, the lack of any valid
distinction, in this context, between a trespasser's act and an act of nature, as he had made
when he was Wright J, in *Noble v Harrison*[3]. There, after referring to *Barker v Herbert*[4],
he said:

d
> 'The nuisance in that case was caused by the act of a trespasser, but I think the
> same principle applies to a nuisance (in this case the latent crack in the branch with
> the resulting risk that some day it would fall) caused by a secret and unobservable
> operation of nature.'

So long as the defect remains 'latent' there is no duty on the occupier, whether the defect
e has been caused by a trespasser or by nature. Equally, once the latent becomes patent, a
duty will arise, whether the causative agent of the defect is man or nature. But the mere
fact that there is a duty does not necessarily mean that inaction constitutes a breach of the
duty.

My second comment on the suggested distinction is that it involves a fallacy. I cite a
passage from the judgment in *Goldman v Hargrave*[5] which, I respectfully suggest, makes
f this clear beyond dispute:

> 'It was suggested as a logical basis for the distinction that in the case of a hazard
> originating in an act of man, an occupier who fails to deal with it can be said to be
> using his land in a manner detrimental to his neighbour and so to be within the
> classical field of responsibility in nuisance, whereas this cannot be said when the
> hazard originates without human action so long at least as the occupier merely
> *g* abstains. The fallacy of this argument is that, as already explained, the basis of the
> occupier's liability lies not in the use of his land: in the absence of "adoption" there
> is no such use; but in the neglect of action in the face of something which may
> damage his neighbour. To this, the suggested distinction is irrelevant.'

The late Professor Goodhart, in an article published in 1932[6], made trenchant criticism
h of the suggested distinction. He said:

> 'In brief, an occupier must use reasonable care to see that his land does not cause
> harm to others outside the land. Is there an exception to this rule when the harm

---

j 1   5th Edn (1920) pp 258–265
2   [1940] 3 All ER 349 at 365, [1940] AC 880 at 904
3   [1926] 2 KB 332 at 341, [1926] All ER Rep 284 at 288
4   [1911] 2 KB 633, [1911–13] All ER Rep 509
5   [1966] 2 All ER 989 at 995, [1967] 1 AC 645 at 661
6   Liability for Things Naturally on Land (1932) 4 CLJ 13 at 26

is caused by a natural condition? An artificial pond in my land becomes stagnant
and infects the neighbourhood. I am liable. A natural pond becomes stagnant. *a*
May I sit by and do nothing? Refuse is thrown on my land by strangers. It is my
duty to use reasonable care to abate the nuisance. Refuse is blown on my land by
the wind. May I permit it to remain? A trespasser injures one of my planted trees
so that it is about to fall into the highway. It is my duty to cut down the tree. A
storm half uproots one of my self-grown trees. May I allow it to crash into the
highway? Such an astonishing exception to the general rule that an occupier must *b*
take reasonable care of his property ought to be established by clear authority before
it is recognised.'

Is there, then, anything in the ratio decidendi of *Rylands v Fletcher*[1], or in any
subsequent authority binding on this court, which requires or entitles us to disregard the
decision in the *Sedleigh-Denfield* case[2] or to prevent us from accepting the logical extension *c*
of it (so far as it is an extension) which was regarded as proper in *Goldman v Hargrave*[3]?
    The application of the decision and of the dicta in *Rylands v Fletcher*[1] has given rise to
continual trouble thereafter in the law of England. But, as I see it, the true ratio
decidendi of *Rylands v Fletcher*[1] is not relevant to the issue with which we are concerned.
In *Rylands v Fletcher*[1] the defendant was held to be liable because he had erected or
brought on his land something of an unusual nature, which was essentially dangerous in *d*
itself. That, said Wright J in *Noble v Harrison*[4], 'expresses the true principle of *Rylands v.
Fletcher*'. The decision was that, on such facts, there was strict liability. It would be no
answer for the defendant to say 'I did not know of the danger and had no reason to know
of it'. It was no part of the decision, as distinct from dicta, in *Rylands v Fletcher*[1] that one
who has not himself brought something of an unusual nature on his land, or used his
land in an unnatural way (whatever that may mean or include), is in no circumstances *e*
liable if something from his land encroaches on his neighbour's land. That was why
Viscount Maugham in the *Sedleigh-Denfield* case[5] said:

'My Lords, I will begin by saying that, in my opinion, the principle laid down in
Rylands v. Fletcher[1] does not apply to the present case. That principle applies only to *f*
cases where there has been some special use of property bringing with it increased
danger to others, and does not extend to damages caused to adjoining owners as the
result of the ordinary use of the land: see *Rickards v. Lothian*[6].'

If *Rylands v Fletcher*[1] was thus irrelevant in the *Sedleigh-Denfield* case[2], it is not relevant in
this case. *g*
    Rylands v Fletcher[1] does not impose strict liability except where there has been some
non-natural use of the land. But it does not hold, by way of binding authority, that there
can be no duty where there has not been a 'non-natural' use of the land. The well-known
passage, cited with approval by Lord Cairns LC[7], from the judgment of Blackburn J

h

1   (1868) LR 3 HL 330, [1861–73] All ER Rep 1
2   [1940] 3 All ER 349, [1940] AC 880
3   [1966] 2 All ER 989, [1967] 1 AC 645
4   [1926] 2 KB 332 at 342, [1926] All ER Rep 284 at 289
5   [1940] 3 All ER 349 at 354, [1940] AC 880 at 888
6   [1913] AC 263 at 280, [1911–13] All ER Rep 71 at 80
7   LR 3 HL 330 at 339, [1861–73] All ER Rep 1 at 13

j

when *Rylands v Fletcher*[1] was decided in the Court of Exchequer Chamber, which does
a provide the ratio decidendi of *Rylands v Fletcher*[2], is concerned only with strict liability
where a man 'for his own purpose brings on his land and collects and keeps there
something likely to do mischief if it escapes'. He must, it is said, 'keep it in at his
peril'. But it is obiter dictum when Lord Cairns LC says[3]:

> *b*   'The Defendants . . . might lawfully have used that close for any purpose for
> which it might in the ordinary course of the enjoyment of land be used; and if, in
> what I may term the natural user of that land, there had been any accumulation of
> water either on the surface or underground, and if, by the operation of the laws of
> nature, the accumulation of water had passed off into the close occupied by the
> Plaintiff, the Plaintiff could not have complained that that result had taken place.
> If he had desired to guard against it, it would have lain upon him to have done so,
> *c*   by leaving, or by interposing, some barrier between his close and the close of the
> Defendants in order to have prevented the operation of the laws of nature.'

I do not believe that in that dictum Lord Cairns LC had in mind, or was purporting
to express any view on, the question with which we are here concerned. I believe he was
merely intending to stress that the strict duty, in no way dependent on the existence of
d negligence, which he was holding to exist in respect of 'unnatural user of land', did not
apply where the user was not 'unnatural'. Certainly, the authority which he cited for
absence of liability for damage where the defendant's user was 'natural', *Smith v Kenrick*[4],
was a very special and peculiar case on its facts. A trespasser, for whose acts the defendant
was in no way responsible, had bored holes through the coal-face which belonged to the
plaintiff, on the plaintiff's land, with the result that water from the defendant's coal-
workings could and did run through those holes. Presumably the plaintiff knew that
e these holes existed in his own coal-face and that his own natural defences on his own land
had been rendered ineffective, and yet he took no steps to repair his own defences. I find
nothing in the elaborate pleadings for the plaintiff in that case to suggest the contrary.
This explains the reference by Lord Cairns LC to 'interposing some barrier between his
close and the close of the defendants'. It is to be noted, also, that in the judgment of the
f Court of Common Pleas in *Smith v Kenrick*[5] Cresswell J, delivering the judgment of the
court, said:

> '. . . it would seem to be the natural right of each of the owners of two adjoining
> coal-mines . . . to work his own in the manner most convenient and beneficial to
> himself, although the natural consequence may be that some prejudice will accrue
> to the owner of the adjoining mine, *so long as that does not arise from the negligent or*
> *g*   *malicious conduct of the party.*'

It is, I think, that passage from the judgment in *Smith v Kenrick*[5], and not anything
which was said in the speeches of Lord Cairns LC or Lord Cranworth in *Rylands v
Fletcher*[2], which led the reporter of the House of Lords decision in *Rylands v Fletcher*[6] to
begin the headnote with the words 'Where the owner of land, *without wilfulness or*
h *negligence*, uses his land in the ordinary manner of its use . . .'
So I find nothing in *Rylands v Fletcher*[2], or at least in its ratio decidendi, which could

---

j
1   (1866) LR 1 Exch 265 at 279–280, [1861–73] All ER Rep 1 at 7
2   (1868) LR 3 HL 330, [1861–73] All ER Rep 1
3   LR 3 HL 330 at 338–339, [1861–73] All ER Rep 1 at 12–13
4   (1849) 7 CB 515, [1843–60] All ER Rep 273
5   7 CB 515 at 564, [1843–60] All ER Rep 273 at 278
6   LR 3 HL 330

properly be used to justify the suggestion that the House of Lords in 1940 in the *Sedleigh-Denfield* case[1] departed, consciously or unconsciously, from the law as laid down in *Rylands v Fletcher*[2], or which was inconsistent with the extension, if it be an extension, of the *Sedleigh-Denfield*[1] decision to defects naturally arising on land which constitute nuisances and give rise to damage to the land of neighbours. The House of Lords was not in 1940 precluded by earlier decisions of the House from following the *Donoghue v Stevenson*[3] approach or from holding that the neighbour in Lord Atkin's speech in *Donoghue v Stevenson*[4] included one who was a neighbour in the literal sense as being the owner of adjoining land.

    Is there, then, any subsequent authority binding on this court which prevents it, by the doctrine of precedent, from holding that the law of England, as laid down in the *Sedleigh-Denfield* case[1], is extended by what the Judicial Committee of the Privy Council regarded as inevitable logic?

    I do not find it necessary to consider all the numerous cases (only a fraction, be it said, of the total number of such reported cases) to which we were referred in argument, in which *Rylands v Fletcher*[2] has been discussed in relation to 'natural user' of land: what is and what is not natural user, and what are and what are not 'things naturally on land'. It is notorious that those cases involve apparent anomalies and grave difficulties of reconciliation one with another. As Viscount Simon, with no doubt studied moderation, said in *Read v J Lyons & Co Ltd*[5]: 'I confess to finding this test of "non-natural" user (or of bringing on the land what was not "naturally there", which is not the same test) difficult to apply.' Viscount Simon went on to give as an example of his difficulty the fact that in the oft-quoted passage in Blackburn J's judgment in the Court of Exchequer Chamber in *Rylands v Fletcher*[6], to which I have previously referred, that learned judge 'treats cattle-trespass as an example of his generalization'. Yet, says Viscount Simon, 'The pasturing of cattle must be one of the most ordinary uses of land . . .' So the pasturing of cattle is said by implication not to be a natural user of land. Yet in *Wilkins v Leighton*[7], Luxmoore J held, citing as authority Scrutton LJ in *St Anne's Well Brewery Co Ltd v Roberts*[8], that 'one of the most normal uses of land' (for the purposes of the *Rylands v Fletcher*[2] doctrine) '. . . is to put buildings on it'. The pasturing of cattle on land is not a normal user. The building of houses on land is one of the most normal uses. So it is said. The anomalies, if not the absurdities, of the development of this supposed doctrine are fully discussed in the late Professor Goodhart's article 'Liability for Things Naturally on Land' in the Cambridge Law Journal[9], a passage from which I have already cited. That article clearly was a powerful influence on the decision of this court in *Davey v Harrow Corpn*[10], as was mentioned by Lord Goddard, CJ[11], who delivered the judgment of the court, consisting of himself, Jenkins and Morris LJJ. The same article is referred to as 'a formative article' in the judgment in *Goldman v Hargrave*[12].

---

1   [1940] 3 All ER 349, [1940] AC 880
2   (1868) LR 3 HL 330, [1861–73] All ER Rep 1
3   [1932] AC 562, [1932] All ER Rep 1
4   [1932] AC 562 at 580, [1932] All ER Rep 1 at 11
5   [1946] 2 All ER 471 at 474, [1947] AC 156 at 166
6   (1866) LR 1 Exch 265 at 279–280, [1861–73] All ER Rep 1 at 7
7   [1932] 2 Ch 106 at 113, [1932] All ER Rep 55 at 58
8   (1928) 140 LT 1, [1928] All ER Rep 28
9   (1932) 4 CLJ 13
10   [1957] 2 All ER 305, [1958] 1 QB 60
11   [1957] 2 All ER 305 at 311, [1958] 1 QB 60 at 73
12   [1966] 2 All ER 989 at 995, [1967] 1 AC 645 at 662

In *Davey v Harrow Corpn*[1] it was held that the encroachment onto a neighbour's land

a of roots or branches of trees, causing damage, gives the neighbour an action in nuisance; and that no distinction is to be drawn between trees which may have been self-sown and trees which were deliberately planted on the land. Contrast the decision with *Rouse v Gravelworks Ltd*[2]. There the defendants had dug out gravel from their land, leaving a large hole adjacent to the boundary with the plaintiff's land. It was held by this court, a two judge court consisting of Slesser and Goddard LJJ, that the plaintiff's claim failed

b because the damage to his land was caused by 'natural agencies'. It would seem that the decision would have been different if the water which filled the hole left by the excavation of the gravel had been brought in by pumping or perhaps even by percolation emanating from outside the defendants' land and induced by the excavation to flow into that land. If so, I should have thought that few people would regard this as a satisfactory state of the law. It may, perhaps, be arguable that, following *Rylands v Fletcher*[3], there is

c some special doctrine relating to the rights of landowners to dig out coal or gravel from their land as being a 'natural user'. If there is no such valid distinction, then, in my judgment, the decision in *Rouse v Gravelworks Ltd*[2] cannot stand with the decision in *Davey v Harrow Corpn*[1]. In that event I have no hesitation in preferring the later decision as stating the law as it now is, subject to the proviso that the duty arising from a nuisance which is not brought about by human agency does not arise unless and until the

d defendant has, or ought to have had, knowledge of the existence of the defect and the danger thereby created.

The decision of this court in *Thomas and Evans Ltd v Mid-Rhondda Co-operative Society Ltd*[4] is not to be explained on the basis of some special principle of 'naturalness' applicable to the digging of minerals on one's land. That was a case of flooding from a river. But the decision itself, it appears to me, can be justified without any inconsistency with the

e *Goldman v Hargrave*[5] development of the law. There was nothing whatever which could be described as unreasonable, bearing in mind that an occasional flood in the river was foreseeable, in the defendants taking down an old protective wall on their own land in order to rebuild it. The fact that a flood happened to come before the wall was completely rebuilt could not, on any view, of itself give rise to liability on the defendants. But the potential liability of an owner or occupier to his neighbours for the overflow of a stream

f from his land onto their land does, indeed, give rise to consideration as to possible injustice. To this I shall return later.

It is not without significance that in at least two of the cases in which it has been held that there was no liability for nuisance because of the 'natural user' doctrine it was suggested that the position at least might have been different if the owner or occupier had had knowledge of the existence of the danger: see the decision of the Privy Council

g in *Rickards v Lothian*[6], and *Wilkins v Leighton*[7], where Luxmoore J said: 'To make the occupier liable the plaintiff must prove that he had knowledge of the existence of the nuisance.'

Lord Wright in the *Sedleigh-Denfield* case[8] referred to that judgment in *Wilkins v Leighton*[9] with approval, on the basis, as I think is clear from the context, that the

h

---

1 [1957] 2 All ER 305, [1958] 1 QB 60
2 [1940] 1 All ER 26, [1940] 1 KB 489
3 (1868) LR 3 HL 330, [1861–73] All ER Rep 1
4 [1940] 4 All ER 357, [1941] 1 KB 381
j 5 [1966] 2 All ER 989, [1967] 1 AC 645
6 [1913] AC 263 at 281–282, [1911–13] All ER Rep 71 at 81–82
7 [1932] 2 Ch 106 at 114, [1932] All ER Rep 55 at 58
8 [1940] 3 All ER 349 at 367, [1940] AC 880 at 907
9 [1932] 2 Ch 106, [1932] All ER Rep 55

defendant in that case did not know of the defect. In other words, it would not have
been enough to provide a defence that the user was 'natural' if the defendant had had   *a*
knowledge of the danger.

I should refer briefly to two other cases on which much reliance was placed by the
defendants. The first is *Giles v Walker*[1]. That was not, as O'Connor J thought[2], a decision of this
court. Despite the fact that one of the two members of the court was Lord Esher MR, it
was a decision of the Queen's Bench Divisional Court. It is thus not binding on us. *Giles*   *b*
v Walker[1], the thistledown case, is discussed at length in Professor Goodhart's article[3]. In
Davey v Harrow Corpn[4] it was said in the judgment of the court: 'We think such an action
[that is, *Giles v Walker*[1]] today . . . might well be decided differently.' We were referred
to a very careful and helpful review of the authorities in the judgment of McMullin J in
the New Zealand Supreme Court in *French v Auckland City Corpn*[5]. McMullin J declined
to follow *Giles v Walker*[1]. I think he was right. I think this court should overrule *Giles*   *c*
v Walker[1].

The second case is *Pontardawe Rural District Council v Moore-Gwynn*[6]. Again, though
the actual decision may be supported on the basis suggested as a possibility in the
judgment in *Goldman v Hargrave*[7], I would hold that the reasoning in support of the
decision is not now good law.

Suppose that we are not bound by *Rylands v Fletcher*[8] or any other authority to hold in   *d*
favour of the defendants where the nuisance arises solely from natural forces; but
suppose also that we are not bound by the decision in *Sedleigh-Denfield*[9] or other binding
authority to hold that there is a duty on the defendants in a case such as the present.
Ought we as a matter of policy to develop the law by holding that there is a duty in a case
such as the present?

If, as a result of the working of the forces of nature, there is, poised above my land, or   *e*
above my house, a boulder or a rotten tree, which is liable to fall at any moment of the
day or night, perhaps destroying my house, and perhaps killing or injuring me or
members of my family, am I without remedy? (Of course the standard of care required
may be much higher where there is risk to life or limb as contrasted with mere risk to
property, but can it be said that the duty exists in the one case and not in the other?)
Must I, in such a case, if my protests to my neighbour go unheeded, sit and wait and hope   *f*
that the worst will not befall? If it is said that I have in such circumstances a remedy of
going on my neighbour's land to abate the nuisance, that would, or might, be an
unsatisfactory remedy. But in any event, if there were such a right of abatement, it
would, as counsel for the plaintiffs rightly contended, be because my neighbour owed me
a duty. There is, I think, ample authority that, if I have a right to abatement, I have also
a remedy in damages if the nuisance remains unabated and causes me damage or   *g*
personal injury. That is what Scrutton LJ said in the *Job Edwards* case[10] with particular

h

1   (1890) 24 QBD 656, [1886–90] All ER Rep 501
2   [1978] 2 WLR 774 at 783; but cf [1978] 3 All ER 234 at 242, [1978] QB 849 at 858
3   (1932) 4 CLJ 13
4   [1957] 2 All ER 305 at 310, [1958] 1 QB 60 at 72
5   [1974] 1 NZLR 340
6   [1929] 1 Ch 656
7   [1966] 2 All ER 989 at 996, [1967] 1 AC 645 at 663
8   (1868) LR 3 HL 330, [1861–73] All ER Rep 1
9   [1940] 3 All ER 349, [1940] AC 880
10 [1924] 1 KB 341 at 359

j

a reference to *Attorney-General v Tod Heatley*[1]. It is dealt with also in the speech of Viscount
Maugham in the *Sedleigh-Denfield* case[2], and in the speech of Lord Atkin[3].

In the example which I have given above, I believe that few people would regard it as
anything other than a grievous blot on the law if the law recognises the existence of no
duty on the part of the owner or occupier. But take another example, at the other end
of the scale, where it might be thought that there is, potentially, an equally serious
injustice the other way. If a stream flows through A's land, A being a small farmer, and
b there is a known danger that in times of heavy rainfall, because of the configuration of
A's land and the nature of the stream's course and flow, there may be an overflow, which
will pass beyond A's land and damage the property of A's neighbours: perhaps much
wealthier neighbours. It may require expensive works, far beyond A's means, to prevent
or even diminish the risk of such flooding. Is A to be liable for all the loss that occurs
when the flood comes, if he has not done the impossible and carried out these works at
c his own expense?

In my judgment, there is, in the scope of the duty as explained in *Goldman v Hargrave*[4],
a removal, or at least a powerful amelioration, of the injustice which might otherwise be
caused in such a case by the recognition of the duty of care. Because of that limitation on
the scope of the duty, I would say that, as a matter of policy, the law ought to recognise
such a duty of care.

d This leads to the question of the scope of the duty. This is discussed, and the nature
and extent of the duty is explained, in the judgment in *Goldman v Hargrave*[5]. The duty
is a duty to do that which is reasonable in all the circumstances, and no more than what,
if anything, is reasonable, to prevent or minimise the known risk of damage or injury to
one's neighbour or to his property. The considerations with which the law is familiar are
all to be taken into account in deciding whether there has been a breach of duty, and, if
e so, what that breach is, and whether it is causative of the damage in respect of which the
claim is made. Thus, there will fall to be considered the extent of the risk. What, so far
as reasonably can be foreseen, are the chances that anything untoward will happen or that
any damage will be caused? What is to be foreseen as to the possible extent of the
damage if the risk becomes a reality? Is it practicable to prevent, or to minimise, the
happening of any damage? If it is practicable, how simple or how difficult are the
f measures which could be taken, how much and how lengthy work do they involve, and
what is the probable cost of such works? Was there sufficient time for preventive action
to have been taken, by persons acting reasonably in relation to the known risk, between
the time when it became known to, or should have been realised by, the defendant, and
the time when the damage occurred? Factors such as these, so far as they apply in a
particular case, fall to be weighed in deciding whether the defendant's duty of care
g requires, or required, him to do anything, and, if so, what.

There is a passage in this part of the judgment in *Goldman v Hargrave*[6] defining the
scope of the duty, which, on the one hand, is said to be likely, if accepted, to give rise to
insuperable difficulties in its practical working, and, on the other hand, is said to provide
a sensible and just limitation on the scope of the duty, avoiding the danger of substantial
injustice being caused, even in exceptional cases, by the existence of the duty. The
h passage in question reads as follows:

'... the owner of a small property where a hazard arises which threatens a
neighbour with substantial interests should not have to do so much as one with

i   1   [1897] 1 Ch 560, [1895–9] All ER Rep 636
j   2   [1940] 3 All ER 349 at 357–358, [1940] AC 880 at 893–894
    3   [1940] 3 All ER 349 at 361–362, [1940] AC 880 at 899–900
    4   [1966] 2 All ER 989, [1967] 1 AC 645
    5   [1966] 2 All ER 989 at 996, [1967] 1 AC 645 at 663–664
    6   [1966] 2 All ER 989 at 996, [1967] 1 AC 645 at 663

larger interests of his own at stake and greater resources to protect them: if the small
owner does what he can and promptly calls on his neighbour to provide additional *a*
resources, he may be held to have done his duty: he should not be liable unless it is
clearly proved that he could, and reasonably in his individual circumstances should,
have done more.'

It is then suggested in the judgment that the anticipated cost of the remedies in those
cases may have justified the actual decisions against liability in the *Job Edwards* case[1] and
in the *Pontardawe* case[2].   *b*

What are the submissions of the parties in this case as to the exposition in the
judgment in *Goldman v Hargrave*[3] of the scope of the duty? The plaintiffs accept, and
invite us to adopt as being the law of England, the exposition, including the passage
above cited. The submissions of the defendants on this aspect of the case are more
complex. I said early in this judgment that there was a third proposition of the
defendants which I would consider later. That third proposition, as it was originally *c*
presented to us, was that, if the defendants were wrong on their first two propositions,
as to the existence of the duty, then, applying the principles of *Goldman v Hargrave*[4] as to
the scope of the duty, O'Connor J ought to have held that the quantity and cost of the
work required in this case, while not going beyond the financial or other capacities of the
defendants, were greater than necessary to deal with the actual damage caused to the
plaintiffs. But in his speech in reply counsel for the defendants on instructions withdrew *d*
that submission. So, as I understand it, if there be a duty and if its scope is as expounded
in *Goldman v Hargrave*[3], the defendants do not now challenge the judgment against
them. They say, however, that there is no duty; and one of their arguments for saying
that this court, if free to do so, should refrain from holding that such a duty exists is that
an essential element of such a duty, if it is to conform with the dictates of justice, is the
factor of relative financial resources; but, they say, the introduction of that factor would *e*
make the law unworkable. However, if that submission is wrong, and if there is a duty,
then the defendants accept that the scope of the duty should be as expounded in *Goldman
v Hargrave*[3]. I hope that I have correctly expressed the substance of the defendants'
submission.

The difficulties which are foreseen, arising out of the passage which I have quoted,
include unpredictability of the outcome of litigation, delay in reaching decisions (which *f*
in everyone's interests ought to be made promptly) as to protective measures to prevent
damage, and the increased complexity, length and expense of litigation, if litigation is
necessary. All this, and other disadvantages, would arise, it is suggested, because the
parties and their advisers, before they could form a fair and confident view of their
respective rights and liabilities, and before they could safely ask the court to decide these
matters, whether finally or at an interlocutory hearing, would find it necessary, or at least *g*
desirable, to put themselves in a position to ascertain and compare the respective financial
resources of the parties. This might involve detailed, embarrassing and prolonged
investigation, even before the stage of discovery in an action.

If I thought that that sort of result would be likely to follow, or to follow in a
substantial number or proportion of cases where this duty comes in question, I should,
at least, hesitate long before accepting that this factor could be regarded as a proper factor *h*
in deciding whether the duty had or had not been broken in a particular case. But I do
not think that anything of that sort is contemplated by *Goldman v Hargrave*[4], any more

j

1   [1924] 1 KB 341
2   [1929] 1 Ch 656
3   [1966] 2 All ER 989 at 996, [1967] 1 AC 645 at 663
4   [1966] 2 All ER 989, [1967] 1 AC 645

a than the decision of the House of Lords in *British Railways Board v Herrington*[1] contemplated, or leads to the possibility of, a detailed examination of the financial position of the defendant landowner or occupier who is sued for damages by a trespasser who has been injured while on the defendant's land. The extent of the defendant's duty, and the question whether he has or has not fulfilled that duty, may, it is clear as a matter of English law, depend on the defendant's financial resources: see the speech of Lord Reid in *British Railways Board v Herrington*[2]. I do not believe that there was any contemplation

b that in such a case there would be discovery of the defendant's bank account or any detailed examination of his financial resources.

So here. The defendant's duty is to do that which it is reasonable for him to do. The criteria of reasonableness include, in respect of a duty of this nature, the factor of what the particular man, not the average man, can be expected to do, having regard, amongst other things, where a serious expenditure of money is required to eliminate or reduce the danger, to his means. Just as, where physical effort is required to avert an immediate

c danger, the defendant's age and physical condition may be relevant in deciding what is reasonable, so also logic and good sense require that, where the expenditure of money is required, the defendant's capacity to find the money is relevant. But this can only be in the way of a broad, and not a detailed, assessment; and, in arriving at a judgment on reasonableness, a similar broad assessment may be relevant in some cases as to the

d neighbour's capacity to protect himself from damage, whether by way of some form of barrier on his own land or by way of providing funds for expenditure on agreed works on the land of the defendant.

Take, by way of example, the hypothetical instance which I gave earlier: the landowner through whose land a stream flows. In rainy weather, it is known, the stream may flood and the flood may spread to the land of neighbours. If the risk is one which can readily

e be overcome or lessened, for example by reasonable steps on the part of the landowner to keep the stream free from blockage by flotsam or silt carried down, he will be in breach of duty if he does nothing or does too little. But if the only remedy is substantial and expensive works, then it might well be that the landowner would have discharged his duty by saying to his neighbours, who also know of the risk and who have asked him to do something about it, 'You have my permission to come onto my land and to do

f agreed works at your expense', or, it may be, 'on the basis of a fair sharing of expense'. In deciding whether the landowner had discharged his duty of care, if the question were thereafter to come before the courts, I do not think that, except perhaps in a most unusual case, there would be any question of discovery as to the means of the plaintiff or the defendant, or evidence as to their respective resources. The question of reasonableness of what had been done or offered would fall to be decided on a broad basis, in which, on

g some occasions, there might be included an element of obvious discrepancy of financial resources. It may be that in some cases the introduction of this factor may give rise to difficulties to litigants and to their advisers and to the courts. But I believe that the difficulties are likely to turn out to be more theoretical than practical. I have not heard or seen anything to suggest that the principle laid down in *British Railways Board v Herrington*[1] has given rise to difficulties in trespasser cases. If and when problems do

h arise, they will have to be solved. I do not think that the existence of such potential difficulties justifies a refusal to accept as a part of the law of England the duty as laid down in *Goldman v Hargrave*[3], including the whole of the exposition as to the scope of the duty. As I have said, no difficulty now arises in this present appeal as regards the

j

1   [1972] 1 All ER 749, [1972] AC 877
2   [1972] 1 All ER 749 at 758, [1972] AC 877 at 898
3   [1966] 2 All ER 989, [1967] 1 AC 645

application of the *Goldman v Hargrave*[1] scope of the duty, once it is held that the duty exists.   *a*
I would dismiss the appeal.

SHAW LJ (read by Cumming-Bruce LJ). I must confess to substantial misgivings as to what is the course which the law of England has taken in regard to the liability of a landowner for a nuisance arising on his land independently of the intervention of any *b* human agency. In the end, having had the advantage of reading the judgment which has just been delivered I have come to the view that, if I may respectfully say so, the weight and direction of authority support the conclusions of Megaw LJ as to the incidence of liability.

One begins by recognising that the negative proposition for which *Rylands v Fletcher*[2] is generally cited as authority was not a necessary part of the decision of that appeal. On *c* the facts which were there admitted by the defendant landowner he had used his land for what was described by Lord Cairns LC as 'a non-natural use'. It was not, therefore, necessary to decide what the landowner's legal position would have been if the same injury had been occasioned to the plaintiff by a natural use of the land. Accordingly, as Megaw LJ has pointed out, the opinion expressed by their Lordships that a landowner would not be liable for damage resulting from a natural use of the land was obiter and *d* does not constitute a binding authority of the House of Lords for that proposition. None the less it has long been accepted as stating the law and, having regard to its source, must be treated with respect. It does not appear to me to be necessarily weakened by the anomalous exception as to encroachment by trees. This may be a consequence of the obvious fact that trees though naturally on land are living things which grow and extend root and branch and are a readily recognisable and remediable source of damage by *e* encroachment.

However, as is clear from the citation in the judgment of Megaw LJ of the passage in Professor Goodhart's article in the Cambridge Law Journal[3], the view that liability for nuisance does not extend to nuisances which arise solely from a natural use of land has been subjected to formidable criticism. Elsewhere in that article the learned author referred to the decision of a Divisional Court in *Margate Pier and Harbour (Co of* *f* *Proprietors) v Margate Town Council*[4] as supporting the view that an owner could be liable for nuisances arising naturally on his property. In a special and limited sense this was so, but the decision was based on a special duty created by a local Act of Parliament; It does nothing to fortify the general principle for which Professor Goodhart contended. The logical argument developed in his article is none the less an impressive one without the assistance of any judicial decision.

The underlying theory of this approach is the correlation of control and *g* responsibility. As the owner of land is normally in the best position to obviate or to contain or to reduce the effect of nuisances arising naturally on his land, he should be primarily responsible for avoiding the consequences of such nuisances or for compensating those who suffer by their occurring. This principle is reflected in the judgment of McMullin J in the New Zealand case of *French v Auckland City Corpn*[5]. *h* There are, however, so it seems to me, powerful arguments the other way. Why should a nuisance which has its origin in some natural phenomenon and which manifests itself without any human intervention cast a liability on a person who has no other

---

1   [1966] 2 All ER 989, [1967] 1 AC 645   *j*
2   (1868) LR 3 HL 330, [1861–73] All ER Rep 1
3   (1932) 4 CLJ 13 at 26
4   (1869) 20 LT 564
5   [1974] 1 NZLR 340

connection with that nuisance than the title to the land on which it chances to
a originate? This view is fortified inasmuch as a title to land cannot be discarded or
abandoned. Why should the owner of land in such a case be bound to protect his
neighbour's property and person rather than that the neighbour should protect his
interests against the potential danger?

The old common law duty of a landowner on whose land there arose a nuisance from
natural causes only, without any human intervention, was to afford a neighbour whose
b property or person was threatened by the nuisance a reasonable opportunity to abate that
nuisance. This entailed (1) that the landowner should on becoming aware of the nuisance
give reasonable warning of it to his neighbour, (2) that the landowner should give to the
neighbour such access to the land as was reasonably requisite to enable him to abate the
nuisance.

The principle was relatively clear in its application and served in broad terms to do
c justice between the parties concerned. The development of 'the good neighbour' concept
has however blurred the definition of rights and liabilities between persons who stand in
such a relationship as may involve them in reciprocal rights and liabilities.

It has culminated in the judgment of the Privy Council in *Goldman v Hargrave*[1].
Though not binding on this court, it is of great persuasive authority. It might have been
possible to explain the result of that case in the context of its special facts, for the
d defendant had added his own ill-directed exertions to what the forces of nature had
initiated. However, the judgment of the Board is in general terms and expounds a
universal principle. It is for this reason that it has to be seen as powerful support for a
development in the law relating to the liability of a landowner for nuisance. It is to be
observed that the judgment was expressly stated to be founded on negligence[2] and it
repudiated any necessity to resolve jurisprudential distinctions between a liability arising
e from a duty to take care on the one hand and on the other a liability not directly related
to any duty of care but absolute in its character as in the case of what is understood as
nuisance in the English common law. It is readily understandable that the scope of
absolute liability must be bounded by relatively narrow limits, and that it is right to
hesitate before adopting a principle which will have the effect of extending those limits
in the law of nuisance. I do not for myself, if I may respectfully venture to say so, see
f how the difficulty is disposed of by transmuting a liability in nuisance (howsoever
occasioned) into a duty to do what can reasonably be done in the circumstances of a
particular case to prevent or to diminish the consequences of a nuisance. This formulation
may, so it seems to me, create fresh problems, and the derivative problems may defy
resolution.

However, a judgment based on general principle and given by a tribunal so
g commanding of attention and esteem must, even though not authoritative in the courts
of England, be regarded as relating to the law of England and as being an induction of
that law.

Seen in the light of Megaw LJ's analysis and exposition of the long line of cases, the
judgment in *Goldman v Hargrave*[1] may represent the climax of a movement in the law
of England expanding that part of the law which relates to liability for nuisance.

h It is in this attitude of mind that I find myself in agreement with the conclusions
which Megaw LJ has stated.

Accordingly, albeit with diffident reluctance, I would dismiss the appeal.

j

---

1   [1966] 2 All ER 989, [1967] 1 AC 645
2   [1966] 2 All ER 989 at 992, [1967] 1 AC 645 at 657

CUMMING-BRUCE LJ. I agree with the order proposed by Megaw LJ, for the reasons stated in his judgment.

a

Appeal dismissed. Leave to appeal granted, the defendants through counsel undertaking not to ask in the House of Lords for an order that their costs be paid by any other party at any stage of the proceedings.

Solicitors: *Dawson & Co* (for the defendants); *Gamlens*, agents for *Pardoe, David & Shaw*, Bridgwater (for the plaintiffs).

b

Mary Rose Plummer   Barrister.

Re Moorgate Mercantile Holdings Ltd

c

CHANCERY DIVISION

SLADE J

18th, 19th, 20th, 26th JUNE 1979

Company – Resolution – Special resolution – Validity – Special resolution proposing that share   *d*
premium account of £1,356,900 be cancelled entirely – Resolution passed stating that account be reduced to £321 – Application to court to confirm reduction of account – Whether resolution as passed substantially the same as that proposed – Whether court having jurisdiction to confirm reduction – Companies Act 1948, s 141(2).

A company's articles of association empowered it by special resolution to reduce its share   *e*
premium account. On 2nd April 1979 the secretary sent a notice to each of the company's members informing them that an extraordinary general meeting of the company would be held on 26th April 1979 at which a special resolution would be proposed to the effect that 'the share premium account of the Company amounting to £1,356,900·48p be cancelled'. That figure included the sum of £321·17 which had been credited to the share premium account on 12th March 1979 by virtue of an issue of   *f*
shares made on that day and which could not be regarded as lost when, as it was proposed to do, the court was asked to approve the proposed cancellation of the share account on the basis that the amount credited to the account had all been lost. Before the meeting on 26th April the company was advised of the consequent legal difficulty that there was no other basis on which the cancellation of the £321·17 could be justified. Therefore, at the extraordinary general meeting on 26th April the chairman, acting on legal advice,   *g*
proposed that the special resolution should be passed in the form: 'That the share premium account of the Company amounting to £1,356,900·48p be reduced to £321·17p.' Not all the members of the company entitled to vote at the meeting were present but the amended version of the resolution was passed unanimously on a show of hands by those who were there and a poll was not demanded. By a petition the company   *h*
asked the court to confirm the reduction of the company's share premium account. The petition alleged that before the passing of the special resolution on 26th April the entire share premium account had been lost with the exception of the £321·17 credited to it in March 1979. No member or creditor of the company appeared before the court to oppose the petition. At the hearing of the petition the question arose whether the resolution of 26th April had been validly passed, ie whether one of the conditions   *j*
precedent to the validity of a special resolution imposed by s 141(2)[a] of the Companies Act 1948 had been complied with, namely whether the resolution had been passed at a general meeting of which requisite notice 'specifying the intention to propose the resolution as a special resolution [had] been duly given'. The company contended that

---

a   Section 141(2), so far as material, is set out at p 44c, post

a it had, despite the difference in wording between the resolution as set out in the notice and the resolution as passed, because (i) no member who had formed a view or intention on the resolution as circulated in the notice could reasonably have adopted a different view on the amended version of the resolution or alternatively, (ii) the effect of the amendment was merely to whittle down the effect of the special resolution as set out in the notice.

b **Held** – (i) A notice of intention to propose a special resolution was valid for the purpose of s 141(2) of the 1948 Act only if it identified the intended resolution by specifying either the text or the entire substance of the resolution which it was intended to propose, and a special resolution was validly passed in accordance with s 141(2) only if it was the same resolution as that identified in the preceding notice. In deciding whether there was complete identity between the substance of the resolution as passed and the substance of the intended resolution as notified there was no room for the application of the de

c minimis principle. If, however, the resolution as passed either departed in some respects from the text of the resolution set out in the preceding notice (eg on account of the correction of grammatical or clerical errors or the use of more formal language) or was reduced into the form of a new text which was not included in the notice, it could properly be regarded as 'the resolution' identified in the notice provided there had been no departure from the substance of the circulated text. Otherwise only where all the

d members, or a class of members, of a company unanimously agreed to waive their rights to notice under s 141(2) could a special resolution be validly passed (see p 44h to p 45a, p 52g to p 53c, p 54a to g and p 55f, post); MacConnell v E Prill & Co Ltd [1916] 2 Ch 57, Re Pearce, Duff & Co Ltd [1960] 3 All ER 222 and Re Duomatic Ltd [1969] 1 All ER 161 applied; Re Bridport Old Brewery Co (1867) LR 2 Ch App 191, Henderson v Bank of Australasia (1890) 45 Ch D 330, Re Teede & Bishop Ltd (1901) 70 LJ Ch 409 and Torbock v

e Lord Westbury [1902] 2 Ch 871 considered.

(ii) In the instant case the resolution had not been validly passed in accordance with s 141(2) because it differed not only in form but also in substance from the one set out in the notice of 2nd April and the members of the company had not unanimously agreed to waive their rights to notice under s 141(2). Accordingly the court had no jurisdiction to confirm the reduction of the share premium account and the petition would be

f dismissed (see p 44gh and p 55g to p 56a, post).

Per Curiam. In the case of notice of intention to propose a special resolution nothing is achieved by the addition of such words as 'with such amendments and alterations as shall be determined on at the general meeting' (see p 54c, post).

Notes

g For amendments to company resolutions, see 7 Halsbury's Laws (4th Edn) para 589, and for cases on resolutions, see 9 Digest (Reissue) 637–640, 3811–3840, and 10 Digest (Reissue) 1130–1132, 7017–7024.

For the Companies Act 1948, s 141, see 5 Halsbury's Statutes (3rd Edn) 223.

Cases referred to in judgment

Betts & Co Ltd v Macnaghten [1910] 1 Ch 430, 79 LJ Ch 207, 100 LT 922, 17 Mans 71, 9

h Digest (Reissue) 621, 3703.

Bridport Old Brewery Co, Re (1867) LR 2 Ch App 191, 15 LT 643, 10 Digest (Reissue) 1130, 7017.

Caldwell v Caldwell & Co (Papermakers) Ltd [1916] WN 70, HL, 9 Digest (Reissue) 169, 977.

j Duomatic Ltd, Re [1969] 1 All ER 161, [1969] 2 Ch 365, [1969] 2 WLR 114, 9 Digest (Reissue) 483, 2879.

Henderson v Bank of Australasia (1890) 45 Ch D 330, 59 LJ Ch 794, 63 LT 597, CA, 9 Digest (Reissue) 627, 3737.

Hoare & Co Ltd, Re [1904] 2 Ch 208, [1904–7] All ER Rep 635, 73 LJ Ch 601, 91 LT 115, 11 Mans 307, 9 Digest (Reissue) 153, 850.

MacConnell v E Prill & Co Ltd [1916] 2 Ch 57, 85 LJ Ch 674, 9 Digest (Reissue) 620, 3700.

Pearce, Duff & Co Ltd, Re [1960] 3 All ER 222, [1960] 1 WLR 1014, 9 Digest (Reissue) 639, 3830.

Picturesque Atlas and Publishing Co Ltd, Re (1892) 13 LR(NSW) Eq 44, 9 Digest (Reissue) 162, *285.

Teede & Bishop Ltd, Re (1901) 70 LJ Ch 409, 84 LT 561, 2 Mans 217, 9 Digest (Reissue) 625, 3723.

Tiessen v Henderson [1899] 1 Ch 861, 68 LJ Ch 353, 80 LT 483, 6 Mans 340, 9 Digest (Reissue) 620, 3698.

Torbock v Lord Westbury [1902] 2 Ch 871, 71 LJ Ch 845, 87 LT 165, 9 Digest (Reissue) 625, 3725,

Cases also cited

Boschoek Proprietary Co Ltd v Fuke [1906] 1 Ch 148.

Cheshire v Gordon Hotels [1953] The Times, 14th February.

Clinch v Financial Corpn (1868) LR 5 Eq 450.

Floating Dock Co of St Thomas Ltd, Re [1895] 1 Ch 691.

Foster v New Trinidad Lake Asphalt Co Ltd [1901] 1 Ch 208.

Welsbach Incandescent Gas Light Co Ltd, Re [1904] 1 Ch 87, CA.

Wright's case, Re London and Mediterranean Bank (1871) LR 12 Eq 331.

Petition

This was a petition by Moorgate Mercantile Holdings Ltd ('the company') asking the court to confirm the reduction of the share premium account of the company from £1,356,900·48 to £321·17 expressed to be effected by a special resolution passed on 26th April 1979. The facts are set out in the judgment.

Ralph Instone for the company.
Mary Arden as amicus curiae.

Cur adv vult

26th June. **SLADE J** read the following judgment: This is a petition of Moorgate Mercantile Holdings Ltd ('the company') asking for the confirmation of the reduction of its share premium account. The company was incorporated in September 1969 under the Companies Acts, its objects being to acquire and hold shares and other investments, and other objects specified in its memorandum of association.

The share capital of the company was originally 14s divided into seven shares of 2s each. By virtue of subsequent increases, it is now £3,500,000, divided into 35 million ordinary shares of 10p each, of which 15,294,293 shares have been issued and are fully paid up. The remainder are unissued.

There is standing to the credit of the share premium account of the company the sum of £1,356,900·48, which represents the aggregate amount of premiums received in cash or otherwise by the company on the issue of shares at a premium, less the aggregate amount applied thereout in accordance with the provisions of s 56(2) of the Companies Act 1948.

Article 9 of the company's articles of association empowers it, inter alia, by special resolution to reduce its share premium account. The share premium account of the company, which reflected premiums received on the issue of shares as consideration for the acquisition of subsidiaries prior to 1973, less a scrip issue in 1973 and certain issue expenses, stood from then onwards until 12th March 1979 at £1,356,579·31. On 12th March 1979 a small issue of shares was made on the acquisition of the outstanding minority interests in a subsidiary. This resulted in the increase in the share premium account by £321·17, so that it has since then stood at £1,356,900·48.

On 2nd April 1979 the secretary of the company sent a notice to the company's members, which was signed by him and accompanied by an explanatory circular letter

from the company's chairman convening an extraordinary general meeting of the
a company. The notice was in the following terms:

'NOTICE IS HEREBY GIVEN that an extraordinary general meeting of the Company
will be held at Moorgate House, 312 High Road, Tottenham, London, N.15, on
Thursday the 26th April 1979, at 11 a.m., when the following resolution will be
proposed as a special resolution: "That the share premium account of the Company
amounting to £1,356,900·48p be cancelled."'

b
There was added to the notice the usual note stating that a member entitled to attend and
vote at the meeting was entitled to appoint a proxy or proxies, who need not be
members, to attend and, on a poll, to vote on his behalf.

Before the holding of the meeting, valid instruments of proxy had been received,
under which a total of 7,278,460 shares were voted in favour of the resolution as
c circulated and 7,212 shares against it. The figure specified as the amount of the share
premium account, in the form of the special resolution printed and circulated in the
notice of the meeting, was accurately stated as being £1,356,900·48. This figure,
however, included the sum of £321·17 credited to the share premium account on 12th
March 1979 by virtue of the issue of shares made on that day. The draftsman of the
notice was unaware that this issue either had taken place or was about to take place.

d Before the members' meeting was held on 26th April 1979, the company was advised
of a consequent legal difficulty. The court was to be asked to approve the proposed
cancellation of the company's entire share premium account on the basis that the
amount credited to the share premium account had all been lost. The amount of
£321·17, however, resulting from the recent issue of shares, could not on any footing be
regarded as having been lost. Accordingly, the company was advised there was no basis
e on which the cancellation of this sum could be justified.

In these circumstances, when the extraordinary general meeting of the company came
to be held on 26th April 1979, the chairman of the company, Mr Julius Silman, in
accordance with legal advice received by him, proposed that the special resolution be
passed in an amended form as follows: 'That the share premium account of the Company
amounting to £1,356,900·48p be reduced to £321·17p.' The chairman had been advised
f that the amendment could not affect the validity of the resolution, on the grounds that
no shareholder, who had made up his mind how to vote on the resolution in its original
form, could reasonably adopt a different attitude to the amended form. He explained
the reason for the amendment to the meeting, which was attended by seven members in
person (a sufficient quorum under the company's articles). The amended version of the
resolution was passed unanimously on a show of hands and a poll was not demanded.

g The company, by this petition, asks that the reduction of the share premium account
of the company from £1,356,900·48 to £321·17, expressed to be effected by the special
resolution passed on 26th April 1979, may be confirmed by the court. The petition
alleges that, before the passing of this resolution, the entire share premium account had
been lost, with the exception of £321·17 credited thereto in March 1979. The registrar
has dispensed with an enquiry as to creditors.

h No member or creditor has appeared before me to oppose the petition. Since, however,
the case seemed to me to raise an important question of principle, namely as to the
extent, if any, to which the form of a special resolution may be validly amended, I asked
for the assistance of an amicus curiae. Counsel, instructed by the Treasury Solicitor, has
appeared in this capacity. She and counsel for the company have both given me valuable
assistance, for which I am grateful. Since there seemed to be possible doubts as to the
j sufficiency of the evidence of loss of the share premium account, I requested counsel as
amicus curiae to address submissions to me on this point also.

In the event, therefore, two quite separate questions have fallen to be argued: first, was
the special resolution of 26th April 1979 validly passed? Secondly, if the answer to the
first question is Yes, has the alleged loss been sufficiently proved and how should the
court's discretion be exercised? I will begin by dealing with the first question.

Was the resolution of 26th April 1979 validly passed?

Section 141(1) of the Companies Act 1948 defines an extraordinary resolution as follows:

'A resolution shall be an extraordinary resolution when it has been passed by a majority of not less than three fourths of such members as, being entitled so to do, vote in person or, where proxies are allowed, by proxy, at a general meeting of which notice specifying the intention to propose the resolution as an extraordinary resolution has been duly given.'

Section 141(2) of that Act, omitting an immaterial proviso, defines a 'special resolution' as follows:

'A resolution shall be a special resolution when it has been passed by such a majority as is required for the passing of an extraordinary resolution and at a general meeting of which not less than twenty-one days' notice, specifying the intention to propose the resolution as a special resolution, has been duly given . . .'

Section 141(5) provides that for the purposes of the section—

'. . . notice of a meeting shall be deemed to be duly given and the meeting to be duly held when the notice is given and the meeting held in manner provided by this Act or the articles.'

The company's articles, so far as I am aware, contain no provisions which are relevant to the question which I have to decide. The doubts as to the validity of the special resolution of 26th April 1979 arise solely from the provisions of s 141(2).

It will be seen that, under the terms of s 141(2), one of the conditions precedent to the validity of any special resolution is that '. . . not less than 21 days' notice, specifying the intention to propose the resolution as a special resolution, has been duly given'. As counsel as amicus curiae has submitted, the phrase 'the resolution' in this context in my judgment manifestly means 'the aforesaid resolution', that is to say, the resolution which has been actually passed. This is a point of crucial importance in the present case.

The problem which now arises may be briefly summarised as follows. The notices dated 2nd April 1979 specified the intention to propose as a special resolution the resolution that 'the share premium account of the Company amounting to £1,356,900·48p be cancelled'. However, the resolution which was actually passed at the meeting of 26th April 1979 was a resolution that 'the share premium account of the Company amounting to £1,356,900·48p be reduced to £321·17p'. In these circumstances, did the notices of 2nd April 1979 give notice within the meaning of s 141(2), specifying the intention to propose the resolution which was in the event actually passed?

In the absence of authority, I would have thought that the answer to this short question of statutory construction was manifestly No. The notices of 2nd April 1979 specified the intention to propose one resolution; the resolution actually passed at the meeting of 26th April 1979 was another, different resolution. Furthermore, the difference was not one merely of form but also of substance, albeit of slight substance, inasmuch as one resolution provided for the entire cancellation of the company's share premium account, while the other provided merely for its reduction, albeit by almost the entirety thereof.

The terms of s 141(2), at least if read in isolation and in the absence of authority, would seem to me to require that, if a special resolution passed at a meeting of members is to be valid, it must be the same resolution as that which the requisite notice has specified the intention to propose. As I have already indicated, the phrase 'the resolution' appearing in the later words of the subsection clearly refers back to and echoes the phrase 'a resolution' appearing at the beginning of the subsection. I can see strong arguments for contending that a resolution passed at a meeting of members may properly be regarded as *the* resolution (that is, the same resolution as that) referred to in the preceding notice, if the only differences between the two are merely clerical or grammatical; I will revert

a
to this point later. If, however, there is any difference whatsoever of substance between the two I would not, in the absence of authority, have regarded the later resolution, which was actually passed, as having been preceded by proper notice for the purpose of s 141(2).

Do the authorities lead me to a different conclusion? Counsel for the company submitted that they imperatively should. He referred me in this context to a number of authorities in relation to statutes preceding the Companies Act 1929 and the Companies

b
Act 1948, though neither he nor counsel as amicus curiae were able to produce any later authority directly relevant to the present question. I shall now refer chronologically to the relevant earlier statutory provisions mentioned by counsel for the company and the authorities relied on by him in the present context.

Section 51 of the Companies Act 1862 contained a definition of a special resolution which, so far as material for present purposes, read as follows:

c
'A Resolution passed by a Company under this Act shall be deemed to be special whenever a Resolution has been passed by a Majority of not less than Three Fourths of such Members of the Company for the Time being entitled, according to the Regulations of the Company, to vote as may be present, in Person or by Proxy (in Cases where by the Regulations of the Company Proxies are allowed), at any General Meeting of which Notice specifying the Intention to propose such Resolution has

d
been duly given, and such Resolution has been confirmed by a Majority of such Members for the Time being entitled, according to the Regulations of the Company, to vote as may be present, in Person or by Proxy, at a subsequent General Meeting, of which Notice has been duly given, and held at an Interval of not less than Fourteen Days, nor more than One Month from the Date of the Meeting at which such Resolution was first passed . . .'

e
The procedure for the passing of special resolutions embodied in the 1862 Act, unlike that of the 1948 Act, thus contemplated that, if a resolution was to be validly passed as a special resolution, it not only had to be passed by the requisite majority at a meeting of members of the company, but also had to be confirmed at a subsequent general meeting of which proper notice had been given.

f
Section 129(3) of the Companies Act 1862 introduced the concept of an 'extraordinary resolution'. That section, so far as material for present purposes, read as follows:

'A Company under this Act may be wound up voluntarily . . . (2.) Whenever the Company has passed a Special Resolution requiring the Company to be wound up voluntarily: (3.) Whenever the Company has passed an Extraordinary Resolution to the Effect that it has been proved to their Satisfaction that the Company cannot by

g
reason of its Liabilities continue its Business, and that it is advisable to wind up the same: For the Purposes of this Act any Resolution shall be deemed to be extraordinary which is passed in such Manner as would, if it had been confirmed by a subsequent Meeting, have constituted a Special Resolution, as herein-before defined.'

h
In Re Bridport Old Brewery Co[1] notice had been given to shareholders of a company that an extraordinary meeting of the shareholders would be held at a stated place, date and time '. . . for the purpose of considering and, if so determined on, of passing, a resolution to wind up the company voluntarily . . .'. The meeting passed (inter alia) a resolution that it had been proved to the satisfaction of the company that it could not, by reason of its liabilities, continue its business and it was advisable to wind it up. No meeting was

j
ever called to confirm this resolution, so that it could not be treated as a special resolution; it could only have been valid (if at all) as an extraordinary resolution. The Court of Appeal held that it was not valid as such. Turner LJ said[2]:

---

1   (1867) LR 2 Ch App 191
2   LR 2 Ch App 191 at 194

'The first part of this resolution is, that it had been proved to the satisfaction of the company, that the company could not, by reason of its liabilities, continue its *a* business. But the notice did not state that an extraordinary resolution to wind up the company would be proposed; nor did it give any intimation that it was proposed to consider at the meeting the question whether the company was able to continue its business. Now it is evidently of great importance to shareholders that they should have proper notice what subjects are proposed to be considered at a meeting, and I do not think that in the present case they had such notice. I do not say that it *b* was necessary to follow in the notice the precise terms of the *Companies Act*, sect. 129, clause 2 [sic]; but it appears to me that the shareholders were entitled to have a notice which would give them to understand that it was proposed to pass an extraordinary resolution to wind up the company. It is of great importance that the steps taken in a matter of such consequence as the resolving to wind up a company should be perfectly regular, and in the present case I think that there was no *c* sufficient notice . . .'

Cairns LJ said[1]:

'I am of the same opinion, and on the same grounds . . . In the present case, it appears to me that the provisions of the Act have not been complied with; the notice which was given, though sufficient for the purpose of passing a resolution requiring *d* confirmation, being insufficient for the purpose of passing a resolution requiring no confirmation.'

In its context, the reference by Turner LJ to s 129(2), as reported, must, in my opinion, have been intended as a reference to s 129(3) of the 1862 Act. I do not think that his judgment is of any assistance or relevance in relation to the question whether the notice given would have been sufficient for the purpose of passing a special resolution. The *e* only point to be derived from his judgment which is marginally relevant for present purposes is that by implication it indicates his view that a notice could be sufficient for the purpose of passing an extraordinary resolution, within the meaning of s 129 of the 1862 Act, even if it did not specify the precise words of the resolution intended to be passed. The difficulty in that case, as the court thought, was that the members did not have sufficient warning of the subjects proposed to be considered at the relevant meeting. *f*

Counsel for the company further relied on the passage in the judgment of Cairns LJ[1] in which he expressed the view that the notice was '. . . sufficient for the purpose of passing a resolution requiring confirmation', in other words, for the purpose of passing a special resolution. Since, however, this view was expressed by Cairns LJ (obiter) in the context of an act which made a subsequent, confirmatory meeting obligatory if a special resolution was to be valid and effective, I do not think that it is of any assistance in the *g* interpretation of s 141 of the Companies Act 1948, by which the legislature has required no such confirmatory meeting and therefore might well see fit to require preceding notices to be in more specific terms.

The next case in order of date relied on by counsel for the company was *Henderson v Bank of Australasia*[2]. That case concerned a bank which was a deed of settlement company. A proprietor brought an action to test the validity of certain resolutions *h* altering the deed of settlement. The advertisement of the proposed meeting had described[3] the proposed resolutions as 'special resolutions' and stated that, if they should be duly passed, they would be submitted for confirmation to a second extraordinary meeting of the proprietors, which would be subsequently convened. It also appears[4] that

j

---

1 (1867) LR 2 Ch App 191 at 195
2 (1890) 45 Ch D 330
3 45 Ch D 330 at 332–333
4 45 Ch D 330 at 333

the full text of the proposed resolutions had been circulated before the meeting was
a held. The plaintiff contended that the resolutions were invalid, substantially, first, on
the grounds that no proper notice of the meeting was given and, secondly, that even
supposing the meeting was duly summoned the resolutions passed at it were invalid,
because the chairman declined to put an amendment which the plaintiff wished to put.
The Court of Appeal, in allowing the plaintiff's appeal from Chitty J, was unanimous in
the view that the chairman was wrong in refusing to put the amendment. While Lopes
b LJ[1] expressed doubts whether the notice was sufficient, Cotton LJ[2], without deciding the
point, expressed the view obiter that the notice was adequate on the grounds that it '. . .
fairly and reasonably expressed to the shareholders what matters were going to be
discussed at the meeting', and Fry LJ[3] expressed entire agreement with the judgment of
Cotton LJ.
    Counsel for the company, in effect, relied on this case as authority for two general
c propositions: first, that if an amended form of a resolution is proposed to a meeting and
is passed thereat, it may be validly passed, provided that the amended version does not
stray too far from the version contained in the notice of the meeting; secondly, that this
result may ensue, even though the actual text of the resolution in its unamended form
had been circulated to shareholders before the meeting. I accept that these particular
propositions were, by necessary implication, accepted by the Court of Appeal on the
d particular facts of *Henderson v Bank of Australasia*[4]. I am, however, unable to accept that
this decision affords any assistance at all in the construction of s 141(2) of the Companies
Act 1948, if only for two reasons. First, no statutory provisions were under consideration
by the Court of Appeal in that case, and none were referred to in the judgments.
Everything turned on the provisions of the relevant deed of settlement, the form of the
relevant notices and the course of the relevant meeting; in other words, it was a decision
e entirely on its special facts. Secondly, in my judgment, as I have already indicated,
considerations quite different from those applicable to the present case may apply in
considering the sufficiency of a notice convening a meeting at which there is to be
considered a resolution which, if passed, has to be submitted for confirmation to a second
meeting. Correspondingly, in my judgment, considerations quite different from those
applicable to the *Henderson* case[4] may apply in considering whether an amendment of a
f special resolution, intended to be passed under Section 141 of the Companies Act, 1948,
may properly be put to a meeting.
    Counsel for the company next referred to *Re Teede & Bishop Ltd*[5]. In that case notices
were sent to the shareholders of a company stating that an extraordinary general meeting
would be held on a stated date for the purpose of considering and, if thought fit, passing
three resolutions, the text of which was stated in the notices. These resolutions were to
g the following effect, namely (1) that a reconstruction of the company was desirable and
that the company therefore be wound up voluntarily and that a named person be
appointed its liquidator, (2) that the liquidator should be authorised to consent to the
registration of a new company, and (3) that the liquidator should be authorised, pursuant
to s 161 of the Companies Act 1862, to enter into an agreement with the new company,
when incorporated, in the terms of a draft agreement submitted to the meeting. At the
h subsequent meeting, only one resolution was put to the meeting and purportedly passed
as a special resolution under s 51 of the Companies Act 1862. This was a resolution for
the voluntary winding up of the company and the appointment of a liquidator. This
resolution was subsequently confirmed as a special resolution at another meeting.
Certain creditors of the company subsequently claimed that the resolution for the

j

1   (1890) 45 Ch D 330 at 349
2   45 Ch D 330 at 343
3   45 Ch D 330 at 346
4   45 Ch D 330
5   (1901) 70 LJ Ch 409

voluntary winding up was invalid, on the grounds that the single resolution passed did
not accord with the three contemplated resolutions of which notice had been given. *a*
Cozens-Hardy J upheld this claim. Having referred to the three resolutions which had
been set out in the notices, and the single resolution which was actually put to and passed
at the meeting, he said[1]:

> 'That is altogether different in its results and objects from what was contemplated
> in the notice, and not such a resolution as an absent shareholder was entitled to
> suppose would be brought before the meeting, under which he could claim *b*
> compensation under sect. 161. It would not bring sect. 161 into operation, and it
> would not limit the amount of the expenses; and, in fact, it was not the resolution
> of which notice had been given. A shareholder receiving the notice might very well
> say that he would not trouble to attend an ordinary reconstruction meeting, and at
> the same time might have the strongest objection to an ordinary voluntary winding-
> up, which is something more than a winding-up for the limited purpose of *c*
> reconstructing the company.'

The decision in *Re Teede & Bishop Ltd*[2] is of some interest for present purposes, since it
does concern a case where a meeting of members of a company purported to pass a
special resolution, but the resolution took a different form from the contemplated
resolution or resolutions of which the text had previously been circulated to members in *d*
the preceding notices. Furthermore, in the event the resolution was held to be invalid.
Nevertheless, counsel for the company sought to derive some assistance from the passage
in the judgment of Cozens-Hardy J which I have already read. If I understood him
correctly, he suggested that the corollary of the reasoning of that passage was that if a
special resolution was *not* altogether different in its result and object from what was
contemplated in the notice, it could be valid, even if it represented an amended version *e*
of the text set out in the notices preceding the meeting. He suggested that the decision
was at least by inference authority for the proposition that, if the text of a special
resolution has been circulated, an amendment thereof at the meeting is permissible, if it
satisfies the criterion that a shareholder, who had formed a view of intention on the
resolution as circulated, could not reasonably adopt a different view on the amended
version. *f*

Possibly this would have been Cozens-Hardy J's opinion, but I am unable to draw this
inference from the brief report of his judgment. A little later in the same passage he
stated[3]: '. . . in fact, it was not the resolution of which notice had been given.' These
words, at least if read in isolation, suggest rather the contrary, namely that no amendment
is permissible.

On any footing, therefore, this case is, in my judgment, of little assistance to the *g*
company in the present case; first, because the amendment of the special resolution was
in the event there held impermissible; secondly, because Cozens-Hardy J did not clearly
specify the circumstances, if any, in which he would have held an amendment
permissible; and, thirdly, because the decision was based on the construction of the 1862
Act, s 51 of which differed materially from s 141(2) of the 1948 Act.

This third comment also applies in relation to the next decision relied on by counsel *h*
for the company, namely *Torbock v Lord Westbury*[4]. Subject to this comment, however,
this decision provides him with rather more substantial ammunition. In that case the
board of a company had given its members notice that an extraordinary general meeting
would be held for the purpose of considering and, if thought fit, passing a resolution, the
text of which was circulated. This resolution would have provided for the company's
articles of association to be altered by allocating 40% of the profits of the company, after *j*

---

1   (1901) 84 LT 561 at 562; cf 70 LJ Ch 409 at 411
2   70 LJ Ch 409
3   70 LJ Ch 409 at 411
4   [1902] 2 Ch 871

payment of certain dividends, by way of remuneration to the directors of the company,
a in the proportions of 20% to the managing director and the balance between the
remaining directors in such proportions as they might decide. The first meeting was
held and the proposed resolution was amended by altering the 40% to 30% and reducing
the proportions to be received by the individual directors pro tanto. The amended
resolution was passed at the meeting and was confirmed at a subsequent meeting. The
plaintiff claimed that, owing to the amendment, no notice had been given of the
b resolution actually passed and that it was therefore invalid as a special resolution. Eve KC,
arguing against this claim, submitted[1]:

> 'There is no doubt that an entirely new resolution cannot be proposed under the
> guise of an amendment, but though the point must often have arisen in similar
> cases, it has never been contended that an amendment in pari materiâ with the
> resolution specified in the notice contravenes the statute and thereby necessitates a
c fresh notice.'

Swinfen Eady J in effect accepted this submission and rejected the plaintiff's
contention. He said[2]:

> 'This contention is not well founded. The resolution confirmed at the second
> meeting must no doubt be in the same form as that passed at the first meeting. In
d other words, the second meeting can only say Aye or No to the resolution passed at
> the first meeting. But it is not necessary that the resolution passed at the first
> meeting should be in the identical terms of the resolution specified in the notice.
> Sect. 51 requires a resolution to be passed "at any general meeting of which notice
> specifying the intention to propose such resolution has been duly given." If,
> therefore, proper and sufficient notice of the intention to propose the resolution is
e given, nothing more is required, and the resolution is not invalidated if, owing to
> an amendment at the first meeting, the resolution passed is not identical with that
> of the notice. In the present case full notice was given of the intention to fix the
> directors' remuneration, and the only difference between the proposed resolution,
> as set forth in the notice of the first meeting, and the resolution actually passed was
> the reduction of the proposed remuneration from 40 to 30 per cent., the proportion
f allocated to the general manager being unaltered. I hold that this alteration did not
> invalidate the resolution . . .'

This case is thus, in my judgment, clear authority for the following propositions. (i) If
the members of a company passed a special resolution it could, in appropriate
circumstances, be legitimately claimed that 'notice specifying the intention to propose
such a resolution has been duly given', within the meaning of s 51 of the 1862 Act, even
g though, owing to an amendment at the first meeting, the resolution passed was not in
the identical terms of the resolution referred to in the notice. (ii) All that was necessary
was that 'proper and sufficient notice' of the intention to propose the resolution had been
given. (iii) The special resolution confirmed at the second meeting had, nevertheless, to
be in the identical terms of that passed at the first meeting.
h Swinfen Eady J did not elaborate as to the test which should be applied in deciding
whether 'proper and sufficient notice' had been given. But it seems plain from his
judgment that he regarded it as having been given on the facts of that case, on the
grounds that members had been given notice of the intention to fix the directors'
remuneration, and the only difference in the resolution passed from that of which notice
had been given was a reduction in the amount of the remuneration. I will revert to his
j judgment hereafter.
Sections 51 and 129 of the Companies Act 1862 were partially repealed by the
Companies Act 1907, Sch 4, but the Companies Act 1907 was itself repealed by the

---

1 [1902] 2 Ch 871 at 873
2 [1902] 2 Ch 871 at 873–874

Companies (Consolidation) Act 1908 which introduced entirely new definitions of an
'extraordinary resolution' and a 'special resolution'. Section 69(1) provided: *a*

'A resolution shall be an extraordinary resolution when it has been passed by a
majority of not less than three fourths of such members entitled to vote as are
present in person or by proxy (where proxies are allowed) at a general meeting of
which notice specifying the intention to propose the resolution as an extraordinary
resolution has been duly given.'

b

Section 69(2) provided:

'A resolution shall be a special resolution when it has been—(a) passed in manner
required for the passing of an extraordinary resolution; and (b) confirmed by a
majority of such members entitled to vote as are present in person or by proxy
(where proxies are allowed) at a subsequent general meeting, of which notice has
been duly given, and held after an interval of not less than fourteen days, nor more   *c*
than one month, from the date of the first meeting.'

The form of s 69(2) of the 1908 Act relating to special resolutions thus bears little
similarity to s 141(2) of the Act of 1948. For present purposes, the significance of the
1908 Act lies rather in the definition of an 'extraordinary resolution' in s 69(1) for two
reasons, First, the language of sub-ss (1) and (2) of s 141 of the 1948 Act clearly derives   *d*
its descent from this definition. Secondly, this definition itself clearly derives its own
descent from the opening limb of s 51 of the 1862 Act (defining a special resolution),
which it quite closely resembles but with certain apparently deliberate departures from
its wording. The departure from that wording most significant for present purposes is
the substitution of the phrase 'notice specifying the intention to propose *the* resolution'
for the phrase 'notice specifying the intention to propose *such* resolution' (emphasis   *e*
mine).
Counsel for the company submits that this is a distinction without a difference, but I
cannot accept this submission. As counsel appearing as amicus curiae pointed out, the
primary definition of the word 'such' to be found in the Shorter Oxford English
Dictionary[1] is 'Of the character, degree, or extent described, referred to, or implied in
what has been said'. As the dictionary shows, in appropriate contexts the word can also   *f*
bear the meaning 'the previously described or specified' but this is not the primary
meaning of the word. It must have been at least strongly arguable that, in the context
of s 51 of the 1862 Act, the word 'such' bore its primary meaning, with the result that it
would have sufficed for a notice to specify the intention to propose a special resolution of
the character which was in fact passed, in other words a resolution in pari materia (see, for
example, the argument of Eve KC in the *Torbock* case[2] already quoted). It seems to me   *g*
highly probable that in the drafting of s 69(1) of the 1908 Act the legislature deliberately
abandoned the word 'such' and adopted the word 'the' (meaning 'the aforesaid') so as to
make it plain that prior notice of the actual resolution, not merely of the character of the
resolution, had to be given if an extraordinary resolution was to be valid. One obvious
reason for so providing was that an extraordinary resolution did not require the
confirmation by a subsequent meeting, which a special resolution at that time did   *h*
require.
This conclusion as to the intention of the legislature in 1908, in my judgment derives
a measure of support from a comparison of the wording of s 69(1) with that of art 49 in
Table A in Sch 1 to that Act. That article so far as material provides:

'Seven days notice at the least . . . specifying the place, the day, and the hour of   .
meeting and, in case of special business, the general nature of that business shall be   *j*
given in manner hereinafter mentioned . . .'

1   3rd Edn (1944)
2   [1902] 2 Ch 871 at 873

In the case of a special resolution, it was clearly not intended to suffice to specify the 'general nature' of the proposed resolution.

a   The next case referred to by counsel for the company is a significant one, because it concerned the construction of s 69(1) of the 1908 Act, the wording of which closely resembles that of s 141(2) of the 1948 Act in all respects material for present purposes. In *MacConnell v E Prill & Co Ltd*[1] the articles of the company in question incorporated the last mentioned art 49. The company, which had a nominal share capital of £2,000, sent a notice to shareholders convening an extraordinary general meeting, of which the

b   agenda was stated to be 'to pass resolution to increase capital of the company'. The company subsequently passed an extraordinary resolution that the capital of the company be increased to £3,500 by the creation and issue of 1,500 shares of £1 each. The plaintiff claimed that the notice was insufficient on two grounds, both depending on the language of s 69 of the 1908 Act. Sargant J summarised the grounds of objection as follows[2]:

c

'In the first place it is said that the notice convening the meeting did not specify *the* resolution, and in the next place it is said that the notice did not specify the intention to pass the resolution as an extraordinary resolution.'

d   Sargant J held that both objections were well founded. In relation to the first objection, the material one for present purposes, he said[2]:

'As regards the first objection, it is obvious that the notice signifies merely an intention to propose some increase or other in the capital of the company, and not an intention to make the specific increase embodied in the resolution that was actually passed. It seems to me of great importance that shareholders should be

e   protected in matters of this kind by specific notice of what is intended to be done. And there is a marked difference between the very definite language in this respect of s. 69 of the Act of 1908 and the much looser and general language of art. 49 in the Table A of that Act with regard to notice of any special business that is proposed to be transacted at a meeting of the company. In the latter case notice is required only of the general nature of any special business to be transacted, while in the case of an

f   extraordinary resolution the notice has to specify the resolution.'

Counsel for the company, as I understood him, accepted that the decision of Sargant J was correct on its particular facts. He submitted, however, that he was wrong in saying 'in the case of an extraordinary resolution the notice has to specify the resolution'. He submitted that this dictum was obiter and ought to be disregarded as being inconsistent

g   with the *Bridport*[3], *Henderson*[4] and *Torbock*[5] decisions, the last two of which were not apparently cited to Sargant J. Counsel for the company submitted that all three decisions show that a resolution can be validly passed, even if not identical to the notified form. He reminded me that what had to be notified under the terms of s 69(1) of the 1908 Act (as under s 141(2) of the 1948 Act) was simply the *intention* to propose the relevant resolution. He submitted that there was no reason why the freedom of the members at

h   the meeting to translate the intention into action should be fettered by the form of wording chosen by the conveners.

No authorities subsequent to that of *MacConnell's* case[1] directly relevant to the present point were cited to me. After amendment by the Companies Act 1928, s 69 of the 1908 Act was wholly repealed by the Companies Act 1929, of which s 117 is the forerunner of

j

1   [1916] 2 Ch 57
2   [1916] 2 Ch 57 at 61
3   (1867) LR 2 Ch App 191
4   (1890) 45 Ch D 330
5   [1902] 2 Ch 871

of s 141 of the 1948 Act. In relation to special resolutions, however, s 117 of the 1929 Act
embodied at least one important alteration in the 1908 law. Under the 1929 Act (as *a*
under the 1948 Act) a second confirmatory meeting was not made requisite in relation
to a special resolution, so that in this respect special resolutions were equated with
extraordinary resolutions.

As I have indicated, the source of the wording of s 141(2) of the 1948 Act relating to
special resolutions can be traced back to the wording of s 69(1) of the 1908 Act, relating
to extraordinary resolutions. In all the circumstances it was, I think, common ground *b*
between counsel that the decision of Sargant J in *MacConnell's* case[1] in relation to the
construction of s 69(1) of the 1908 Act must, so far as this decision is correct, be applicable
to the interpretation of s 141(2) of the 1948 Act. This, I conceive, is why counsel for the
company took such pains to satisfy me that Sargant J was wrong in stating that, in the
case of an extraordinary resolution, the notice had to 'specify the resolution'. In the case
of an extraordinary resolution under the 1908 Act, and in the case of a special resolution *c*
under the 1948 Act, he submitted in effect that all that is necessary is to give notice of the
nature of what the resolution is to do. It is not the law, he submitted, that the actual
wording of the proposed resolution must be notified or that, if it is notified, no
amendment is permissible. Following the service of a notice in sufficient form, an
amendment of the proposed resolution at the meeting will be permissible, he submitted,
provided only that any shareholder who had formed a view or intention on the resolution *d*
as circulated could not reasonably have adopted a different view on the amended
version. This latter criterion he conveniently termed the 'limits of tolerance'. In reply,
he submitted in the alternative, in reliance on the *Torbock* case[2], that if the effect of an
amendment is merely to 'whittle down' the effect of the form of a special resolution as
set out in a notice of a meeting, such an amendment must prima facie be permissible
unless it is so substantial as significantly to change the nature of the transaction. *e*

Counsel appearing as amicus curiae drew my attention to an Australian case, *Re
Picturesque Atlas and Publishing Ltd*[3], on the particular facts of which the amendment of a
special resolution was held not to affect its validity. While I found this decision
interesting, I did not find it of any real assistance in the present case, since it apparently
centred on the construction of a section (s 83) of an Australian statute (the Companies Act
1874 (NSW)) in materially different terms from s 141(2) of the 1948 Act, in particular *f*
because it embodied the phrase 'such resolution', not 'the resolution'. Neither did I
derive much help from the conflicting views of textbook writers.

Having referred to all the authorities cited to me which I consider directly relevant for
present purposes, I shall now attempt to express my own views on the decision in
MacConnell's case[1] and to formulate the principles applicable to the case before me.

If (which I doubt) Sargant J, in stating that 'in the case of an extraordinary resolution *g*
the notice has to specify the resolution', intended to say that the notice must set out the
precise text of the proposed resolution, I would agree with counsel for the company that
he went a little too far. The relevant condition precedent to the validity of an
extraordinary resolution, as set out in s 69(1) of the 1908 Act, is that 'notice specifying the
intention to propose the resolution as an extraordinary resolution has been duly given'.
Strictly, therefore, it is the relevant *intention* of which notice must be given. I do not *h*
think it can be possible to give notice specifying the relevant intention without also
specifying the entire substance of the actual resolution which it is intended to propose.
Nevertheless, as counsel as amicus curiae pointed out, it is well established that notices
are not to be construed with excessive strictness, if they give reasonable notice of that of

_____ *j*

1   [1916] 2 Ch 57
2   [1902] 2 Ch 871
3   (1892) 13 LR (NSW) Eq 44

which they are supposed to give notice: see Buckley on the Companies Act[1] and the cases
a there cited. In my judgment, it is perfectly possible to conceive a form of notice which
may properly be said to give notice specifying the intention to propose a particular
resolution, even though it does not set out in terms the text of the proposed resolution.
Provided that the notice specifies both *the entire substance* of the intended resolution (that
is the entire substance of what is to be decided) and the intention to propose it, it can, in
my judgment, be properly claimed that notice has been given 'specifying the intention
b to propose the resolution' within the meaning of s 69(1) of the 1908 Act or s 141(1) or
(2) of the 1948 Act. In such circumstances it can also properly be said that the resolution
subsequently passed is 'the resolution' referred to in the notice.

The fact remains, however, that under the terms of each of these three last-mentioned
subsections, if a resolution is to be validly passed, it must be *the* resolution (ie the same
resolution) as that identified in the preceding notice. This, as I read it, was the crucial
c point on which the whole of Sargant J's reasoning in the *MacConnell* case[2] was based in the
present context and I respectfully agree with it. The difficulty in that case was, as he said,
that the notice in question signified 'merely an intention to propose some increase or
other in the capital of the company and not an intention to make the specific increase
embodied in the resolution that was actually passed'. Neither the precise form nor the
substance of the intended resolution was communicated to the shareholders, and this
d necessarily rendered the notice invalid.

With the one possible qualification to which I have referred, I therefore respectfully
agree with and adopt the reasoning of Sargant J's judgment in the *MacConnell* case[2]. I feel
unable to accept counsel's submission for the company that it was inconsistent with the
Bridport[3], *Henderson*[4] and *Torbock*[5] decisions. Sargant J[6] himself referred to the *Bridport*[3]
decision as being a case which turned merely on—
e

'. . . the question whether the notice which had been sent gave shareholders
sufficient warning that it was intended to put the company into liquidation by a
single extraordinary resolution under s. 129, sub-s. 3, of the [1862] Act rather than
by the more normal process of a special resolution.'

f
This entirely accords with my own earlier analysis of this decision. The *Henderson*
decision[4], as I have indicated, was a decision on its own, entirely special, facts. Though it
is perhaps regrettable that the *Torbock* decision[5] was apparently not cited to Sargant J, I
cannot think that it would have made any difference to his own decision, bearing in
mind that the *Torbock* decision[5] (i) related to s 51 of the Companies Act 1862, which used
g the phrase 'such resolution', as opposed to the words 'the resolution', to which Sargant J
in my judgment rightly attached such significance, and (ii) concerned a special resolution
which, at the time when the *Torbock* case[5] was decided, required a second meeting for its
confirmation, so that the need for exact precision in the notice calling the first meeting
was clearly less acute.

I therefore find nothing in the authorities which precludes me from reaching the
h conclusion as to the construction of s 141(2) of the 1948 Act which I would have reached

j 1   13th Edn (1957) p 331, note (k)
    2   [1916] 2 Ch 57
    3   (1867) LR 2 Ch App 191
    4   (1890) 45 Ch D 330
    5   [1902] 2 Ch 871
    6   [1916] 2 Ch 57 at 62

in the absence of authority and indeed I think this conclusion derives strong support
from the *MacConnell* decision[1]. In the light of this analysis of the authorities and of the *a*
wording of s 141(2), I shall now attempt to summarise what are in my judgment the
relevant principles relating to notices of, and the subsequent amendment of, special
resolutions:

(1) If a notice of the intention to propose a special resolution is to be a valid notice for
the purpose of s 141(2), it must identify the intended resolution by specifying either the
text or the entire substance of the resolution which it is intended to propose. In the case *b*
of a notice of intention to propose a special resolution, nothing is achieved by the
addition of such words as 'with such amendments and alterations as shall be determined
on at such meeting'.

(2) If a special resolution is to be validly passed in accordance with s 141(2), the
resolution as passed must be the same resolution as that identified in the preceding
notice; the phrase 'the resolution' in s 141(2) means 'the aforesaid resolution'. *c*

(3) A resolution as passed can properly be regarded as 'the resolution' identified in a
preceding notice, even though (i) it departs in some respects from the text of a resolution
set out in such notice (for example by correcting those grammatical or clerical errors
which can be corrected as a matter of construction, or by reducing the words to more
formal language) or (ii) it is reduced into the form of a new text, which was not included
in the notice, provided only that in either case there is no departure whatever from the *d*
substance.

(4) However, in deciding whether there is complete identity between the substance of
a resolution as passed and the substance of an intended resolution as notified, there is no
room for the court to apply the de minimis principle or a 'limit of tolerance'. The
substance must be identical. Otherwise the condition precedent to the validity of a
special resolution as passed, which is imposed by s 141(2), namely that notice has been *e*
given 'specifying the intention to propose the resolution as a special resolution' is not
satisfied.

(5) It necessarily follows from the above propositions that an amendment to the
previously circulated text of a special resolution can properly be put to and voted on at
a meeting if, but only if, the amendment involves no departure from the substance of the
circulated text, in the sense indicated in propositions (3) and (4) above. *f*

(6) References to notices in the above propositions are intended to include references
to circulars accompanying notices. In those cases where notices are so accompanied, the
notices and circulars can and should, in my judgment, ordinarily be treated as one
document.

(7) All the above propositions may be subject to modification where all the members,
or a class of members, of a company unanimously agree to waive their rights to notice *g*
under s 141(2): see s 143(4)(*d*) of the 1948 Act, *Re Pearce, Duff & Co Ltd*[2] and *Re Duomatic
Ltd*[3].

I would emphasise that these propositions are directed solely to special resolutions.
Very different considerations may apply in the case of ordinary resolutions, in relation to
which the criteria of permissible amendments suggested by counsel for the company
could well be very relevant: see, for example, *Betts & Co Ltd v Macnaghten*[4]. In relation *h*
to special resolutions, however, I think that my conclusions of principle accord not only
with the wording of the 1948 Act and with the authorities, but also with the following
considerations of public policy. The 1948 Act requires a special resolution only in about
ten circumstances. Thus, for example, such a resolution is required by s 5 for the
alteration of a company's memorandum, by s 10 for the alteration of its articles, by

j

1   [1916] 2 Ch 57
2   [1960] 3 All ER 222, [1960] 1 WLR 1014
3   [1969] 1 All ER 161, [1969] 2 Ch 365
4   [1910] 1 Ch 430

s 18(1) for the change of its name, by s 66 for the reduction of its capital, by s 222(a) for
a a resolution that the company may be wound up by the court, and is also required for a
resolution for voluntary winding-up passed under s 278(1)(b). It may, I think, fairly be
said that all the situations in which special resolutions are required are special situations,
where the resolutions in question are by their nature likely either to affect the company's
constitution or to have an important effect on its future. Since the passing of the 1929
legislation, the shareholders of a company, when faced with the intention to propose a
b special resolution, no longer have the protection of a locus poenitentiae in the shape of
a second confirmatory meeting, at which they can accept or reject a special resolution
passed at the first meeting It is therefore all the more important that each shareholder
should now have clear and precise advance notice of the substance of any special
resolution which it is intended to propose, so that he may decide whether he should
attend the meeting or is content to absent himself and leave the decision to those who do;
c the provisions imposed by s 141(2) of the 1948 Act must be intended as much for the
protection of the members who in the event decide to absent themselves as for those who
decide to attend: see for example *Tiessen v Henderson*[1] per Kekewich J. If it were open to
the members who did attend to propose and vote on a special resolution differing in
substance (albeit slightly) from the resolution of which notice had been given, there
would be a risk of unfair prejudice to those members who, after due consideration, had
d deliberately absented themselves. I do not think that their interests would be sufficiently
protected by the safeguard suggested by counsel for the company, namely that an
amendment could properly be put to and voted on by the meeting only if a member,
who had formed a view or intention with regard to a resolution as circulated, could not
reasonably adopt a different view on the amended version. Nor do I think that the
alternative 'whittling down' criterion suggested by him would offer them adequate
e protection. In many circumstances, albeit not on the facts of the particular case, either
test when applied in practice could involve serious uncertainties and difficult questions
of degree. Furthermore, in many cases it would present substantial embarrassment both
to the chairman of the meeting who had to apply it and to any persons holding 'two-way'
proxies on behalf of absent members. The absent members would be correspondingly
faced with unpredictable risks.
f   These considerations strengthen my conclusion that the strict interpretation which I
have placed on s 141(2) is likely to represent the true intention of the legislature, as well
as the grammatical meaning of the words used. There must be absolute identity, at least
in substance, between the intended resolution referred to in the notice and the resolution
actually passed.
      I now turn to apply the seven propositions set out above to the facts of the present case.
g The qualifications referred to in the last of them are not revelant here, since not all
members of the company entitled to vote thereat were present at the meeting of 26th
April 1979. While I have no reason to doubt that the amendment to the resolution was
put to the meeting in good faith and on legal advice, it was in my judgment improperly
put and voted on. Counsel as amicus curiae accepted, and I accept, the correctness of the
advice given to Mr Silman, on the facts, that no shareholder who had made up his mind
h how to vote on the resolution in its original form could reasonably have adopted a
different view in regard to the amended form. For this reason I have a measure of
sympathy with this petition. This point, however, in my judgment is irrelevant in
law. In my judgment, the crucial point is that the resolution which the meeting of 26th
April 1979 approved was not the same resolution, either in form or in substance, as that
of which the text had been circulated to shareholders in the notices of 2nd April 1979.
j There is no room for the application of any 'de minimis' principle; a resolution to reduce
the share premium account of a company to £321 could not even be deemed to be the
same as a resolution to reduce it to £320.

---

1   [1899] 1 Ch 861 at 866–867, 870–871

In the circumstances the resolution was not in my judgment validly passed in accordance with s 141(2) of the 1948 Act. The court, therefore, has no jurisdiction to *a* confirm the reduction of the share premium account as asked for by this petition.

The exercise of the court's discretion
The second principal point which has been argued before me relates to the exercise of the court's discretion and arises in the following circumstances. The petition invokes this discretion to approve the reduction of the share premium account on the grounds *b* that, as alleged in the petition, 'previously to the passing of the said resolution the entire share premium account of £1,356,900·48p had been lost with the exception of £321·17p credited thereto in March 1979'. The petition is thus founded on loss and echoes the wording of s 66(1)(b) of the 1948 Act. This section provides:

'Subject to confirmation by the court, a company limited by shares or a company limited by guarantee and having a share capital may, if so authorised by its articles, *c* by special resolution reduce its share capital in any way, and in particular, without prejudice to the generality of the foregoing power, may—(a) extinguish or reduce the liability on any of its shares in respect of share capital not paid up; or (b) either with or without extinguishing or reducing liability on any of its shares, cancel any paid-up share capital which is lost or unrepresented by available assets; or (c) either with or without extinguishing or reducing liability on any of its shares, pay off any *d* paid-up share capital which is in excess of the wants of the company; and may, if and so far as is necessary, alter its memorandum by reducing the amount of its share capital and of its shares accordingly.'

Section 56(1) renders the provisions of s 66 relating to the reduction of the share capital of a company applicable (mutatis mutandis) to an application for the reduction of a *e* company's share premium account.

The decision of the Court of Appeal in *Re Hoare & Co*[1], to which counsel for the company referred me, indicates that the references in s 66(1) to capital being 'lost' and capital 'unrepresented by available assets' are alternatives. Furthermore, in view of the words 'without prejudice to the generality of the foregoing power' to be found in s 66(1), the court would have jurisdiction to approve a reduction expressed to be founded on loss, *f* even if it were not satisfied that the loss was wholly proved.

Nevertheless, for reasons appearing from the decision of the House of Lords in *Caldwell v Caldwell & Co Ltd*[2] it is the practice of the court to require evidence of loss where a reduction petition is founded on loss of capital and, as the price for approving a reduction, to require provisions for the safeguarding of the creditors, in so far as the proven loss is less than the amount of capital proposed to be reduced.

g

The evidence of loss in the present case is to be found in an affidavit sworn by Mr Silman on 26th April 1979, to which were exhibited the company's accounts for the year ended 31st March 1978. Very briefly, the greatest part of this loss is said to have been incurred by the company because of a severe decline in the value of the company's shareholdings in certain subsidiaries in 1973 and 1974. These decreases in value were reflected in the writing down of the relevant assets in the company's subsequent balance *h* sheets. There is, however, no direct evidence as to the *present* value of the relevant shareholdings in subsidiaries which are still retained by the company. Counsel as amicus curiae submitted that there is thus no evidence of a permanent deficiency, that there must be such a deficiency to establish a reduction on the basis of loss and that the court should, in the exercise of its discretion, decline to confirm the reduction unless appropriate steps are first taken to ensure that creditors cannot be adversely affected. *j*

Counsel, while offering on behalf of the company certain undertakings for the

1   [1904] 2 Ch 208, [1904–7] All ER Rep 635
2   [1916] WN 70

protection of creditors if the court should think fit to exact them, strenuously submitted
a that the court should not exact them. He further submitted in effect that the principles
suggested by counsel as amicus curiae as the relevant principles were not wholly the
correct ones and that the evidence before the court would be amply sufficient to justify
it in approving the reduction without taking any further steps for the protection of
creditors.

In this context, both counsel made reference to a number of authorities, indicating the
b court's approach to the exercise of its discretion in this kind of case, and have taken me
through the evidence in some detail. The question clearly involves a point of principle
of some general importance, namely whether, as counsel as amicus curiae in effect
submitted, the court should in practice always insist on evidence as to the *current* net
value of a company's assets in the case of a petition for reduction expressed to be founded
on alleged loss, where creditors are not provided for.

c I hope that counsel will not think I am failing to do justice to their arguments in this
context if I decline to express any view on this question of principle. The expression of
any such view would in any event be obiter. To express it without reasons would be of
no assistance to any subsequent court. To express it with reasons and to analyse the
evidence as to loss in this case would, I think, involve an unjustified prolongation of this
already lengthy judgment.

d
Conclusion
I therefore do not propose to state how I would have been minded to exercise my
discretion if I had had jurisdiction to approve the proposed reduction. As things are, I
find that the requirements of s 141(2) not having been complied with, I have no
jurisdiction to approve it and must decline to make the order sought.

e
Petition dismissed.

Solicitors: *Nicholson, Graham & Jones* (for the company); *Treasury Solicitor.*

Jacqueline Metcalfe   Barrister.

Department of the Environment v Fox and another

a

EMPLOYMENT APPEAL TRIBUNAL

SLYNN J, MRS D EWING AND MR J JACK

17th MAY 1979

b

Employment – Discrimination against a woman – Crown service – Service on behalf of the Crown as statutory officer holder or as member of statutory body – Refusal to put woman's name on list of candidates for position of rent officer – Whether sex discrimination legislation applicable to service as rent officer – Whether public service which is not service on behalf of a Minister or government department is service on behalf of Crown – Whether service 'for purposes of' a person holding a statutory office includes service of statutory office holder himself – Whether service of *c* *rent officer service for purposes of a statutory body, namely a rent assessment committee – Whether service as rent officer service 'on behalf of the Crown' – Sex Discrimination Act 1975, s 85(2)(b).*

The claimant, a woman, complained to an industrial tribunal alleging that either a local authority or the Department of the Environment had discriminated against her on the *d* ground of her sex, contrary to s 6(1) of the Sex Discrimination Act 1975, by the refusal to include, or the deliberate omission of, her name from the list of candidates for the post of rent officer advertised by the local authority. The department took the preliminary point that the tribunal had no jurisdiction to entertain the claim because s 6 did not apply to service as a rent officer since it was not Crown service to which the 1975 Act applied. The industrial tribunal decided, in accordance with the claimant's contentions, *e* that service as a rent officer was 'service on behalf of the Crown for purposes of a person holding a statutory office', within s 85(2)(b)ᵃ of the 1975 Act, and was therefore Crown service to which the Act applied, because (i) being public service under a statute it was service 'on behalf of the Crown', in the Crown's general manifestation as the embodiment of authority in the state, and (ii) it was service for the purposes of a person holding a statutory office, ie a rent officer, since service 'for purposes of' included the activities of *f* the statutory office holder himself and was not confined to service by others on his behalf. The tribunal accordingly decided that it had jurisdiction to entertain the claim. The department appealed to the Employment Appeal Tribunal, contending (i) that for the purpose of s 85(2)(b) a distinction was to be drawn between service on behalf of the Crown in the limited sense of service on behalf of a specified Minister or government department and public service in the broader sense, e g under a statute, and that the latter *g* was not service 'on behalf of the Crown', and (ii) that service by the statutory office holder himself was not service 'for purposes of' a statutory office holder within s 85(2)(b). On the appeal the claimant further contended that the work done by a rent officer was service 'for purposes of a statutory body', within s 85(2)(b), because the work was done for the purposes of a rent assessment committee as part of the process of the fixing of fair rents by such a committee under the Rent Act 1977. *h*

Held – (i) On the true construction of s 85(2)(b) of the 1975 Act there was no distinction between 'service on behalf of the Crown' in the limited sense of service on behalf of a Minister or department and public service generally unless the statute setting up the particular statutory office or body made it plain that the service to be performed was *j* independent of the Crown. It followed that the carrying out of a function of the kind imposed on a rent officer under the 1977 Act was service 'on behalf of the Crown' within

---

a   Section 85, so far as material, is set out at p 61 *a* to *c*, post

s 85(2)(b) (see p 62 d to f, post); Tamlin v Hannaford [1949] 2 All ER 327, Attorney-General
a for New South Wales v Perpetual Trustee Co [1955] 1 All ER 846 and R v Metropolitan Police
Comr, ex parte Blackburn [1968] 1 All ER 763 considered.

(ii) However the activities of a rent officer were not service on behalf of the Crown 'for
purposes of a person holding a statutory office' within s 85(2)(b) because that only
referred to the service of persons other than the statutory office holder himself performed
for the purposes of the statutory office holder, and a rent officer was himself the statutory
b office holder. In any event, under the 1977 Act a rent officer had his own functions and
what he did, therefore, was done for the purposes of his own office, and not for the
purposes of a rent assessment committee. It followed that service of a rent officer was not
'service for purposes of a statutory body' within s 85(2)(b) and accordingly the appeal
would be allowed (see p 62 j to p 63 d and p 64 b to d, post).

Notes
c For the employment of women under or for the purposes of a Minister of the Crown or
government department, see 8 Halsbury's Laws (4th Edn) para 1105, and for the
application of employment protection legislation to the Crown generally, see 16 ibid
para 786:46.

For the Sex Discrimination Act 1975, s 85, see 45 Halsbury's Statutes (3rd Edn) 286.

d **Cases referred to in judgment**
Attorney-General for New South Wales v Perpetual Trustee Co (Ltd) [1955] 1 All ER 846,
[1955] AC 457, [1955] 2 WLR 707, 119 JP 312, PC, 34 Digest (Repl) 224, 1631.
Knight v Attorney-General [1979] ICR 194.
London Housing and Commercial Properties Ltd v Cowan [1976] 2 All ER 385, [1977] 1 QB
148, [1976] 3 WLR 115, 31 P & CR 387, DC.
e Metropolitan Properties Co (FGC) Ltd v Lannon [1968] 3 All ER 304, [1969] 1 QB 577,
[1968] 3 WLR 694, 19 P & CR 856, sub nom R v London Rent Assessment Panel
Committee, ex parte Metropolitan Properties Co (FGC) Ltd [1968] RVR 490, CA, 31(2)
Digest (Reissue) 1071, 8400.
R v Metropolitan Police Comr, ex parte Blackburn [1968] 1 All ER 763, [1968] 2 QB 118,
[1968] 2 WLR 893, CA, Digest (Cont Vol C) 279, 1113a.
f Tamlin v Hannaford [1949] 2 All ER 327, [1950] 1 KB 18, CA, 11 Digest (Reissue) 682,
160.

Appeal
The applicant, Mrs L Fox, applied to an industrial tribunal complaining that the first
respondent, Mr R G Brooke, the director of administration for West Yorkshire
Metropolitan County Council, discriminated against her, contrary to the Sex Discrimi-
g nation Act 1975, by refusing to include, or deliberately omitting, her name from a list
of applicants to be interviewed for the post of rent officer in Leeds. The applicant was
given leave to add the Department of the Environment ('the department') as second
respondent to the application. The department resisted the claim on the ground (inter
alia) that Part II of the 1975 Act did not apply to the application because appointment to
the office of rent officer did not come within s 85(2) of the 1975 Act and therefore the
h tribunal had no jurisdiction to adjudicate on the claim. Mrs Fox abandoned her claim
against the first respondent because he was not the employer of rent officers in the area
in question. By a decision dated 20th November 1978 an industrial tribunal (chairman
J H Morrish Esq) sitting at Leeds decided that the office of rent officer came within the
scope of s 85(2)(b) of the 1975 Act and that accordingly the tribunal had jurisdiction to
hear Mrs Fox's claim against the department. The department appealed to the
j Employment Appeal Tribunal. The facts are set out in the judgment of the appeal
tribunal.

S Lawson Rogers for the department.
Stephen Sedley (who did not appear below) for Mrs Fox.
Mr S Walker, solicitor, for the first respondent.

SLYNN J delivered the following judgment of the appeal tribunal: Mrs Fox was employed by the West Yorkshire Metropolitan County Council as a referencer. The local *a* authority advertised a vacancy as a 'rent officer' for the purposes of the Rent Act 1977. Mrs Fox applied, amongst other people, for that job. She did not get it. She then brought a claim before an industrial tribunal that the county rent officer had refused to include or had deliberately omitted her name from the list of candidates who were to be interviewed for the appointment which was to be apparently carried out in Leeds. She said there was discrimination contrary to s 6(1) of the Sex Discrimination Act 1975 in the *b* arrangements that had been made for the purpose of determining who should be offered employment, or by a refusal or a deliberate omission to offer her that employment.

Mrs Fox began her case against Mr Brooke, who was the director of administration of the local authority and who is the proper officer under the Rent Act 1977 as defined in the local government legislation. Subsequently, the Department of the Environment ('the department') were joined as a second respondent to the application on the basis that *c* if Mrs Fox was not employed by Mr Brooke as the proper officer then Mrs Fox was employed by the department.

The industrial tribunal had to consider a preliminary point which was taken as to their jurisdiction. It was contended that Part II of the 1975 Act which is dealing with discrimination in the employment field, and in which s 6 falls, was not applicable to the particular service which Mrs Fox desired to undertake and, accordingly, it was said that *d* she could not bring a claim under s 6 of the Act. The industrial tribunal considered solely that question of jurisdiction and at the end of the day they concluded that by virtue of s 85(2)(*b*) of the 1975 Act they had jurisdiction to hear the claim. They did not proceed further since that was the only matter before them on this occasion.

It is important to stress that this is the only matter which arose for decision, and this case proceeded on the basis that Mr Brooke had not been properly joined in the first place, *e* that he was not the employer so that, accordingly, he was dismissed from the proceedings and in fact costs were awarded in his favour. So in this case, no question arose whether under s 41 of the 1975 Act it could be said that the department were vicariously responsible for the acts of Mr Brooke if he had in fact discriminated contrary to the terms of s 6. Moreover, there was no question raised here, because of the preliminary concessions which were made, whether a rent officer would be a person in the *f* employment of the local authority, or its proper officer, so that a claim could be made direct under Part II of the 1975 Act without any complications as to the position of the Crown being raised.

It is also important to state that here no claim was pursued before the industrial tribunal, or is raised before us, whether Mrs Fox could contend that there had been discrimination against her, as a person for the time being employed by the local *g* authority, in the way in which access had been afforded to her for promotion, transfer, training or other benefits or facilities. That is a claim which of course could only be pursued, as we see it on the facts of the present case, against the local authority as her employers for the time being. That matter, we repeat, does not arise in the present case.

The sole question which we have to decide is whether the tribunal reached a correct conclusion when they decided that s 85(2)(*b*) entitled Mrs Fox to maintain her claim *h* under s 6(1) of the 1975 Act against the department.

The industrial tribunal considered the terms of the appropriate legislation. It is important to refer to the provisions of s 85. Subsection (1) provides that the Act applies to an act done by, or for the purposes of, a Minister of the Crown or government department, or to an act done on behalf of the Crown by a statutory body or a person holding a statutory office as it applies to an act done by a private person. We interpose *j* that no point has been argued before us under this particular subsection nor, as we understand it, was any such point taken before the industrial tribunal. It may be if this case goes further that counsel for Mrs Fox might wish to address arguments on the proper construction of that subsection. Subsection (2) reads as follows:

'Parts II and IV apply to—(a) service for purposes of a Minister of the Crown or
government department, other than service of a person holding a statutory office,
or (b) service on behalf of the Crown for purposes of a person holding a statutory
office or purposes of a statutory body, as they apply to employment by a private
person, and shall so apply as if references to a contract of employment included
references to the terms of service.'

By s 85(10):

'In this section "statutory body" means a body set up by or in pursuance of an
enactment, and "statutory office" means an office so set up . . .'

It is unnecessary to read the rest of s 85(10).

The tribunal referred to the scheme which is set up under the Rent Act 1977. It is
unnecessary for us to refer to many of the provisions of that Act, but it is important for
us to remind ourselves that Part III of the 1977 Act makes provision for rents under
regulated tenancies. It provides that where rents are registered under Part IV of the Act,
then the rent recoverable for any contractual period shall be limited to the registered
rent. The scheme for the registration of rents under regulated tenancies is dealt with in
Part IV of the Act. That provides that registration areas shall be constituted for the
purposes of the Act. Under s 63, the Secretary of State is to draw up for each registration
area a scheme providing for the appointment by the proper officer of the local authority
of such number of rent officers as may be determined and of deputies, and the scheme
is to provide for the payment of remuneration in accordance with scales approved by the
Secretary of State and to deal with matters such as the dismissal, or the prohibition of
dismissal, of a rent officer without the authority of the Secretary of State. The scheme is
also to provide for certain other administrative arrangements which necessarily fall to be
made. By sub-s (3) a rent officer is to be deemed to be an officer in the employment of
the local authority for whose area the scheme is made for the purposes of the
Superannuation Act 1972 and any other local Act scheme, and for certain purposes under
the Social Security Pensions Act 1975 and the Social Security Act 1975. The duties of a
rent officer as to the maintenance of a register of rents and as to the way in which
applications for the registration of a rent are to be made are laid down by subsequent
provisions of the 1977 Act, and it is unnecessary for us to refer to those in detail. The
principal provisions are ss 66 and 67 and Sch 11 to the 1977 Act.

It is conceded before us that a rent officer is a person holding a statutory office within
the meaning of s 85(2)(b). Accordingly, the questions which arose before the industrial
tribunal were whether a rent officer is a person carrying out service on behalf of the
Crown, and, secondly, whether he was a person who was carrying out such services for
the person holding a statutory office. Before us, counsel for Mrs Fox, without opposition
from counsel for the department, has argued in the alternative, that this is service for the
purposes of a statutory body, it being conceded that a rent assessment committee, to
which we shall in due course refer, is such a statutory body.

Now on the first point, the industrial tribunal took the view that what was being done
by a rent officer was service on behalf of the Crown. They said:

'. . . service on behalf of the Crown, however, would seem to be service by those who
are working, not for the purposes of a specific Minister or a government department,
but for the Crown in its more general manifestation as the embodiment of authority
in the state.'

Counsel for the department submits that they have erred in this part of their
decision. He says that a rent officer is not a person carrying out service on behalf of the
Crown; he is a creature of statute; he is carrying out independent functions given to him
by the legislation; he has duties which he must perform, and it is said those duties given
to him by the Act of Parliament are duties to the public or to the state. He asks us to
draw a distinction between the service on behalf of the Crown (properly understood) and

public service in a broader sense. For that proposition he relies in part on the decision of
the Court of Appeal in *Tamlin v Hannaford*[1]. That was a case which raised the question   *a*
whether the British Transport Commission was a servant or agent for the Crown entitled
to claim Crown privilege. The Court of Appeal held that it was not. They found that on
the particular statute which set up the British Transport Commission, namely the
Transport Act 1947, the British Transport Commission was a public authority with
public purposes but it was not a government department, nor did its powers fall within
the province of government. They felt there was there set up a separate entity which was   *b*
not as it were an emanation of the Crown.

In addition, counsel for the department has referred us to another decision of the
Court of Appeal in *R v Metropolitan Police Comr, ex parte Blackburn*[2]. There, Lord
Denning MR[3] referred to the duty of the Commissioner of Police. He found that the
commissioner, like every other constable, was independent of the executive; he was not
subject to the orders of the Secretary of State. No Minister of the Crown could tell him   *c*
what he should do. He was answerable to the law and to the law alone.

Those two cases, says counsel for the department, show that a distinction is to be drawn
between service for the Crown and public service which is not due under a duty to the
Crown.

On the other hand, counsel for Mrs Fox has referred us to what has been said in
Attorney-General for New South Wales v Perpetual Trustee Co (Ltd)[4]. There, the Privy   *d*
Council considered the position of a police officer and they were prepared to accept that
he might be called a servant in the sense in which any holder of a public office may be
called a servant of the Crown or of the state.

It seems to us that on a proper construction of s 85(2)(*b*), it would be wrong to draw a
distinction between service on behalf of the Crown and other public service, unless the
Act of Parliament setting up the particular statutory office or statutory body made it   *e*
plain that what was to be done was independent of or cut off from the Crown. It seems
to us that here Crown service does involve the carrying out of a function of the kind
which is imposed on rent officers under the 1977 Act, and we decline to draw the
distinction which has been put forward by counsel on behalf of the department. It seems
to us that on this first point, the conclusion which was reached by the industrial tribunal
was a correct one.   *f*

The second point which is taken involves the correct meaning of the phrase, 'service
for the purposes of a person holding a statutory office'. The industrial tribunal's
conclusions on this have been adopted by counsel for Mrs Fox in argument, really
without elaboration because he says they are aptly set out. The industrial tribunal say
that they consider that a holder of a statutory office can be working for his own purposes
just in the same way as one who sets up a business on his own and is working for his own   *g*
purposes:

> 'The wording is not "for the person . . ." nor are there words of exclusion of that
> person himself. We consider the words "for the purposes of" refer to the general
> objects of the statutory function of a rent officer, objects which delineate the work
> which the rent officer will do either in person or through others on his staff.'   *h*

The tribunal go on to say that they would be very surprised if rent officers were left
outside the jurisdiction of the 1975 Act because they find that they are carrying out a
function which is similar to that carried on by others in the process of the valuation of
property. That to us does not seem to be a matter which we should take into account.
It may be that a rent officer, as has been argued, does not have all the trappings of some   *j*

1   [1949] 2 All ER 327, [1950] 1 KB 18
2   [1968] 1 All ER 763, [1968] 2 QB 118
3   [1968] 1 All ER 763 at 769, [1968] 2 QB 118 at 135
4   [1955] 1 All ER 846, [1955] AC 457

of the other offices under the Crown, but once it is accepted that he is a person holding
a a statutory office, the sole question is one of the construction of these few words. It seems
to us here that these words are directed to cover the service of persons who are acting for
the purposes of the person holding the statutory office but not the service of the person
himself. It is clear that where a service is done for the purpose of a Minister of the Crown
or a government department, service of a person holding statutory office is excluded.
Counsel for Mrs Fox argues that, because that exclusion is not repeated in 85(2)(*b*), we
b should lean in favour of a construction which includes the activities of the person
himself. He says that what is done by a person holding a statutory office is done for the
purposes of the person holding that office. We do not accept that argument. It seems to
us that the service which is referred to is the service of other persons on behalf of the
Crown for the purposes of the person who is the statutory office holder.

This matter was considered by this tribunal in the case of *Knight v Attorney-General*[1].
c In that case a similar argument was put forward on behalf of the appellant. Counsel
there conceded that in order to make his point, he had to substitute the word 'by' for the
words 'for the purposes of'. We rejected that argument. Counsel for Mrs Fox of course
does not rely entirely on that argument. He would say that the words, 'for the purposes
of' are wide enough to include the service both of people working with or for the person
holding the statutory office and of that person himself. For reasons which we have
d given, we do not consider that, properly construed, the acts of the person holding the
statutory office are acts done for his purposes; they are done either for the purposes of the
office or for the purposes of the legislation; they are not done for his purposes.
Accordingly, we would here differ from the view which was taken by the industrial
tribunal.

The third point which arises before us is the contention that what a rent officer does
e is done for the purposes of a statutory body, namely a rent assessment committee. This
point really involves consideration, albeit not in detail, of the function of the rent
officer. It is clear that when an application is made for the registration of a rent, then the
rent officer has to enquire into the matter. He will generally call the parties together
under his powers under para 4(2) of Sch 11 to the 1977 Act for the purposes of a
consultation, and if such a consultation is held or even if such a consultation is not held,
f he must then determine a fair rent and register it. If the parties are not satisfied with
what he has done, then there is power for the matter to be referred to a rent assessment
committee and then it is for them, under the provisions of the 1977 Act (s 65 in
particular and the other provisions dealing with rent assessment committees in para 7
and following in Sch 11 to the Act), to determine a fair rent. And it is for them, if they
so decide, to call for such information as is necessary for them to make their decision.

g Counsel for Mrs Fox says that a rent officer is in a very different category from a rent
assessment committee or a rent tribunal. He has put forward a number of detailed
differences between them. He says that a rent officer is appointed under a scheme made
by the Secretary of State and under the terms of the scheme applicable in the particular
area to which we have been referred, there is provision for a considerable element of
control as to certain aspects of the work of the rent officer. Moreover, he says that the
h rent officer is not a body who is required to give reasons; he is not an officer who is
scheduled to the Tribunals and Inquiries Act 1958 who is required to give reasons, and
he is not a person who should be regarded as in any sense a judicial tribunal; he is not a
body from whom there is an appeal. He says that when the Court of Appeal in
Metropolitan Properties Co (FGC) Ltd v Lannon[2] talked about an appeal to a rent assessment
committee, they were not strictly accurate. He says the real position is that which is
j referred to as having been submitted by counsel for the Crown in the case of *London
Housing and Commercial Properties Ltd v Cowan*[3], namely that a rent officer and a rent

1　[1979] ICR 194
2　[1968] 3 All ER 304, [1969] 1 QB 577
3　[1976] 2 All ER 385, [1977] 1 QB 148

assessment committee are really part of a unified whole created for the purpose of fixing fair rents. Accordingly, counsel for Mrs Fox says here that what a rent officer is really *a* doing is work which is for the purposes of the rent assessment committee; he is a small cog in a larger machine; he is simply one stage in the process and what he is doing is not for the purposes of his office, but is merely a stage in the process of fixing fair rents by the rent assessment committee.

We do not accept this argument. It seems to us that a rent officer under the Rent Act 1977 has his own functions. He may be carrying out a process which is merely one stage, *b* but it is a separate process and he is required to exercise the functions and carry out the duties in regard to the fixing of rents and to the maintenance of the register which Parliament has laid on him. Moreover, it is accepted that the majority of cases of an application for the registration of a fair rent do not go beyond the rent officer himself. They are dealt with by him either after agreement between the parties at the consultation or by the parties' acceptance of his decision. That being the case and having looked at the *c* many sections of the 1977 Act to which we have been referred, we are quite satisfied that what the rent officer does is for the purposes of his office and for the purpose of carrying out his duties. It is not done for the purposes of the rent assessment committee.

Accordingly, we would reject this argument put forward by counsel for Mrs Fox despite the fact that it was put forward with his usual skill and ability. In the result, we hold that what is done by a rent officer is not service on behalf of the Crown for the *d* purpose of a person holding a statutory office, or for the purposes of a statutory body. The appeal is accordingly allowed.

Appeal allowed. Leave to appeal to the Court of Appeal.

Solicitors: *Treasury Solicitor; P Grant* (for Mrs Fox); *S Walker*.   *e*

Salim H J Merali Esq   Barrister.

a # Express Newspapers Ltd v MacShane and another

HOUSE OF LORDS

LORD WILBERFORCE, LORD DIPLOCK, LORD SALMON, LORD KEITH OF KINKEL AND LORD SCARMAN

5th, 6th NOVEMBER, 13th DECEMBER 1979

b

Trade dispute – Acts done in contemplation or furtherance of trade dispute – In contemplation or furtherance of – Claim by party that he had acted in furtherance of trade dispute – Employees of national newspaper company instructed by their union to black copy from Press Association – Union genuinely believing that blacking of copy would advance cause of provincial members involved in pay dispute with provincial newspaper proprietors – Whether union officers acting
c *'in . . . furtherance of' trade dispute – Trade Union and Labour Relations Act 1974, s 13(1) (as substituted by the Trade Union and Labour Relations (Amendment) Act 1976, s 3(2)).*

In 1978 there was a dispute over pay between the proprietors of provincial newspapers and those of their employees who were members of the National Union of Journalists ('the union'). In an attempt to bring pressure to bear on the proprietors, the union's
d national executive council called the union's journalists on provincial newspapers out on strike. That action did not completely immobilise the provincial newspapers because as well as copy from their own journalists they also used news copy supplied by the Press Association, and were thus able to continue publication using that copy, albeit with a reduced coverage. To make the primary strike more effective the union's national executive council called on journalists employed by the Press Association (many of
e whom were union members) to come out on strike. About half the union's journalists at the Press Association obeyed the national executive council's strike call, so that the Press Association was still able to supply copy to the provincial newspapers. The national executive council thereupon instructed union members working on national newspapers, including that owned by the plaintiffs, to 'black' (ie refuse to use) news copy sent out by the Press Association. This secondary action affected both the Press Association and the
f national newspapers neither of whom were involved in the provincial newspapers' pay dispute. The plaintiffs brought an action against the defendants, who were members of the union's national executive council, seeking (i) an injunction restraining the defendants from inducing or procuring those of the plaintiffs' employees who were members of the union to break or not to perform their contracts of employment by refusing to use material provided to the plaintiffs by the Press Association, and (ii) damages for inducing
g or procuring such breaches of contract. The plaintiffs also applied for an interlocutory injunction pending the trial of the action, in the same terms as the injunction sought in the writ, and a mandatory injunction ordering the defendants to withdraw instructions given to the plaintiffs' employees to break or not to perform their contracts of employment. The defendants claimed that their action in calling on the union members of national newspapers to black copy from the Press Association was done 'in . . .
h furtherance of a trade dispute' and was accordingly protected by s 13(1)[a] of the Trade Union and Labour Relations Act 1974. The judge held that their action did not come within s 13(1) because it did not advance the interest of the provincial journalists in a concrete way and that the injunctions should be granted. This decision was upheld by the Court of Appeal[b]. The defendants appealed to the House of Lords.

j **Held** (Lord Wilberforce dissenting) – On the ordinary and natural meaning of s 13(1) of the 1974 Act, an act was done 'in . . . furtherance of a trade dispute', and the person doing

---

a   Section 13(1), so far as material, is set out at p 75 j, post
b   [1979] 2 All ER 360

the act was accordingly protected by s 13 against an action for tort, if he honestly believed
that the act might further the cause of those taking part in the dispute. Although the *a*
genuineness of the person's belief could be tested by the courts by applying the usual tests
of credibility (ie by asking itself whether a reasonable man could have thought that his
action would support his side of the dispute, or whether the link between his actions and
purpose was so tenuous that his evidence could not be believed), the test of whether the
act was done in furtherance of a trade dispute was a subjective one, and it was not
necessary for the person doing the act to prove that it was reasonably capable of achieving *b*
his object. Since the evidence clearly established that the defendants honestly and
reasonably believed that the action taken was fairly 'in . . . furtherance of a trade dispute',
it followed (Lord Wilberforce, applying an objective test, concurring) that the appeal
would be allowed and the injunctions discharged (see p 71 *f* to *h*, p 72 *a* and *g* to *j*, p 73
f and *h* to p 74 *b*, p 75 *b* to *d* and *g*, p 76 *e* to *h*, p 77 *a* to *h*, p 78 *c* to *g* and p 79 *e*, post).
    Conway v Wade [1908–10] All ER Rep 344 applied. *c*
    British Broadcasting Corpn v Hearn [1978] 1 All ER 111 approved.
    Per Lord Diplock. The belief of the doer of the act need not be wise and it need not
take account of the damage it will cause to innocent and disinterested third parties. Nor
need the benefit deriving from the act be proportional to the damage it causes (see p 72
j to p 73 *b* and *f*, post).
    Per Lord Scarman. Where action alleged to be in contemplation or furtherance of a *d*
trade dispute endangers the nation or puts at risk such fundamental rights as the right of
the public to be informed and the freedom of the Press, the law does not preclude the
possibility of the court in a proper case exercising its discretion to restrain the industrial
action pending trial (see p 79 *d e*, post).
    Decision of the Court of Appeal [1979] 2 All ER 360 reversed.

    e

Notes
For the legal liability of trade unions, see Supplement to 38 Halsbury's Laws (3rd Edn)
para 677B.3.
    For the Trade Union and Labour Relations Act 1974, s 13(1), as substituted by the
Trade Union and Labour Relations (Amendment) Act 1976, s 3(2), see 46 Halsbury's
Statutes (3rd Edn) 1941. *f*

Cases referred to in opinions
Associated Newspapers Group Ltd v Wade [1979] 1 WLR 697, [1979] ICR 664, [1979] IRLR
    201, CA.
Beaverbrook Newspapers Ltd v Keys [1978] ICR 582, [1978] IRLR 34, CA.
British Broadcasting Corpn v Hearn [1978] 1 All ER 111, [1977] 1 WLR 1004, [1977] ICR *g*
    685, [1977] IRLR 273, CA.
Conway v Wade [1909] AC 506, [1908–10] All ER Rep 344, 78 LJKB 1025, 101 LT 248,
    HL, 45 Digest (Repl) 572, *1436.*
NWL Ltd v Woods, NWL Ltd v Nelson [1979] 3 All ER 614, [1979] 1 WLR 1294, HL.
United Biscuits (UK) Ltd v Fall [1979] IRLR 110.

    h

Appeal
By a writ issued on 11th December 1978 the respondents, Express Newspapers Ltd,
brought an action against the appellants, Denis MacShane and Kenneth Ashton (sued
personally and as representing the members of the National Executive Council of the
National Union of Journalists resident in England and Wales who were present at the
meeting of the council on 1st December 1978), claiming (i) an injunction restraining the *j*
appellants and each of them, whether by themselves, their servants or agents or otherwise
howsoever from inducing or procuring those of the respondents' employees who were
members of the National Union of Journalists, or any of them, to break or not to perform
their contracts of employment by refusing to handle or use material provided to the
respondents by the Press Association, and (ii) damages for inducing or procuring breaches

of contract. Pending the trial of the action the respondents applied by summons on 12th
a December for (i) an injunction in the same terms as that sought in the writ, and (ii) a
mandatory injunction ordering the appellants to withdraw any instructions, directions
or recommendations given by themselves, or their servants or agents to the employees
to break or not perform their contracts of employment. On 14th December Lawson J
granted the relief sought in the summons. On 21st December the Court of Appeal[1]
(Lord Denning MR, Lawton and Brandon LJJ) dismissed an appeal by the appellants who
b appealed to the House of Lords pursuant to leave of the House granted on 1st February
1979. The facts are set out in the opinion of Lord Wilberforce.

J Melville Williams QC and *John Heady* for the appellants.
Denis R M Henry QC and *Thomas Morison* QC for the respondents.

c Their Lordships took time for consideration.

13th December. The following opinions were delivered.

LORD WILBERFORCE. My Lords, this appeal is concerned with the immunity
from suit granted to trade unions and others in respect of acts done 'in . . . furtherance of
d a trade dispute'. These words have appeared in legislation since 1875 and are now
contained in s 13(1) of the Trade Union and Labour Relations Act 1974, as amended.
How far does this immunity extend? Is it sufficient for those claiming the immunity to
have a genuine intention to further an existing trade dispute? Or is it necessary to show,
in addition, that the act done is in fact reasonably capable of furthering the trade dispute
or gives practical support to the trade dispute? These are broadly the questions raised.
e They have not, so far, arisen for decision in this form in this House.

The trade dispute, a normal one between employers and employees, arose between the
National Union of Journalists ('the NUJ'), a trade union with about 30,000 members, and
a body called the Newspaper Society which represents the proprietors of provincial
newspapers. This started towards the end of 1978. On 1st December of that year the
National Executive Council ('the NEC') of the NUJ voted in favour of a recommendation
f for an all-out provincial newspaper strike from 12 noon on 4th December.

Provincial newspapers, as do national newspapers, derive much of their supply of news
from the Press Association ('the PA'). This is a company owned by provincial daily and
Sunday newspapers. It provides a news agency service to its shareholders and also to
subscribers who include national newspapers, some radio and television networks, and
overseas agencies. The PA employs about 250 journalists, not all members of the NUJ.
g The NEC at the same meeting of 1st December decided to call a strike of NUJ members
employed by the PA so as to stop it from supplying copy to provincial newspapers. This
strike was also to take effect from noon on 4th December. Its purpose was, by pressure
on the PA, with which, as such, the NUJ had no dispute, to reduce or cut off supplies of
news to the provincial newspapers. This type of action, against a supplier of a party to a
trade dispute, is sometimes called 'secondary' action.
h Further action was taken by the NEC. On 3rd December the NEC by letter instructed
NUJ members employed on *national* newspapers, including the Daily Express, to 'black'
(ie not to handle) all copy emanating from the PA after noon on 4th December. The
NUJ had at this time no dispute with the national newspapers. There is no doubt that
this instruction constituted what, apart from any immunity conferred by statute, would
be an actionable wrong, viz wrongfully procuring the journalists employed by national
j newspapers to break their contracts of employment.

After this instruction had been sent out, namely on 4th December, there was a
meeting of the NUJ chapel at the PA. At that meeting the members voted by 86 to 76

---

1   [1979] 2 All ER 360, [1979] 1 WLR 390

not to obey the strike instruction. After this vote the chairman told the meeting that they were instructed to strike and that any copy produced by them would be regarded *a* as 'black'. The 76 members went on strike and were 'soon afterwards' joined by 26 others and later by a further six journalists. The result of this was to cut down the PA service to its subscribers, including the national newspapers, by about half.

There was a good deal of evidence given on affidavit as to the instructions given to the NUJ members employed by national newspapers. Mr MacShane, the president of the NUJ, said that the sole reason for the instructions was to make the strike (ie with the *b* provincial newspapers) more effective. He believed that the NUJ members employed by the PA would be discouraged from joining or continuing the strike if they knew that the copy sent out by those who were 'strike breakers' was being handled and used by other NUJ members. The factor of morale is very important in a strike. Similar evidence was given by Mr Ashton, the general secretary of the NUJ. Mr Dennis, acting father of the NUJ chapel at the PA, said that it would be a serious blow to the morale of those PA *c* members who were on strike if fellow NUJ members in national newspapers and broadcasting were to handle PA copy. It might so discourage those who were on strike that some would go back to work and it certainly would not help him to persuade those at work to join the strike. This evidence was given on 13th December, after the split vote at the PA had occurred, but it is likely that the possibility of a split was foreseen when the strike action at the PA was called. *d*

On 11th December Express Newspapers Ltd issued a writ against the appellants, who were president and general secretary of the NUJ, sued as representing the members of the NEC, claiming an injunction. On the same day, after a notification pursuant to s 17(1) of the 1974 Act, as amended, they applied to a judge for an interlocutory injunction. This was heard on 14th December when Lawson J granted injunctions against the appellants ordering them to withdraw the instructions given to black PA *e* copy and restraining them from giving any such instructions. The judge held, pursuant to s 17(2), that the appellants' claim that they had a defence under s 13 was unlikely to succeed. On appeal, the judge's order was upheld by the Court of Appeal[1].

Although the injunctions have ceased to be operative, since the provincial journalists' claims have been settled, an Appeal Committee of this House gave leave to appeal on the ground that an important point of principle arose, namely as to the scope of s 13, and in *f* particular as to the meaning of 'act done . . . in . . . furtherance of a trade dispute', which might well affect other cases. In fact the decision given by the Court of Appeal has already been followed at first instance.

My Lords, the issue which has to be resolved in the present case arises out of the very great extension of industrial action which has occurred in recent years. When trade disputes were confined to disputes between employees in an undertaking and their *g* employers or between employees in an undertaking, it was not difficult to decide whether industrial action was in contemplation or furtherance of a trade dispute. The argument normally centred on the issue whether the dispute was a trade dispute. This was the case in *Conway v Wade*[2], a decision to which I shall return. The definition of 'trade dispute' has been extended; it was further enlarged by the 1974 Act and by the Trade Union and Labour Relations (Amendment) Act 1976. There is now a very wide *h* definition which includes a dispute between employers and workers or between workers and workers, which 'is connected with' one or more of a list of seven matters (s 29(1) as amended). Correspondingly, industrial action has been greatly widened. It may extend to customers or suppliers of a party to the dispute, on the basis that through them pressure on the party is intensified. In still other cases, of which *Associated Newspapers Group Ltd v Wade*[3] is one and this is another, it may extend to customers or suppliers of *j*

---

1   [1979] 2 All ER 360, [1979] 1 WLR 390
2   [1909] AC 506, [1908–10] All ER Rep 344
3   [1979] 1 WLR 697

such suppliers or customers. Such second stage customers or suppliers may, and probably will, have no dispute with those calling for the industrial action, and no interest in the first stage dispute though some of their workers may have sympathy with it. Moreover they may, as here, have no means of influencing that dispute or of making concessions which might bring that dispute to an end. The question therefore whether action against such innocent and powerless third parties or parties even more remote from the original trade dispute is in 'furtherance' of that dispute becomes one that is difficult to answer. The answer must depend on some test other than the possibility of pressure being exercised on the original party, because none can be so exercised.

The answer given to this question by the appellants is that it is enough if there is a genuine belief that action against the innocent and powerless third party will further the cause of those taking the action. By 'to further' they mean, and this fits the dictionary definition, to help or encourage. So what is asserted is a purely subjective test, such as might be satisfied by Mr Ashton's words: 'I believe that this trend [viz of PA journalists to join the PA strike] may be damaged or reversed if copy produced by those breaking the strike . . . is handled by our Members elsewhere.' My Lords, with all deference to those of your Lordships who are of this opinion, I am unable to accept this. I recognise, of course, that the trend of recent legislation has been to widen, and to widen greatly, the extent of immunity from civil action of trade unions and officials and members of trade unions. The policy no doubt is to substitute for judicial control or review over trade disputes and their consequences other machinery including conciliation procedures. But it would be wrong, in my opinion, to suppose that judicial review has been excluded altogether. The observations in this House in *NWL Ltd v Woods*[1], directed as they were to the facts of that case, do not so suggest, nor do the recent statutes lead to that conclusion. I take one example. Wide though the definition of 'trade dispute' in s 29 of the 1974 Act may be, it cannot be suggested that the courts are precluded from considering whether a particular dispute 'is connected' with any one or more of the matters listed in that section. The very fact that a list of such a detailed character is provided suggests otherwise: it would serve no purpose if it were excluded from judicial consideration. The court in fact examined 'connection' in *British Broadcasting Corpn v Hearn*[2], in a decision which I regard as correct. So I see no reason why the courts should not examine the words which are critical here, 'An act done . . . in contemplation or furtherance of a trade dispute'. Indeed that they may do so is clearly shown by s 17 of the 1974 Act which certainly does not make a 'claim' that these words apply conclusively. So I have no doubt that the courts may at least ask the questions whether the test, in relation to both or either of these words, is purely subjective or not.

As a first approach, to argue for a subjective test appears unattractive. To accept it would mean that immunity from civil suit, as regards all those persons who may now be affected by industrial action, would depend on an assertion by the person or persons taking the action as to his or their state of mind, subject only to some qualification as to bona fides or genuine belief, a safeguard of obvious weakness. Given the strong feelings which usually accompany the taking of industrial action, this would give no protection to such persons against action by enthusiasts, extremists and fanatics, so long as the action was accompanied by a statement that those taking it had the necessary belief. I do not find the courts' reluctance to accept this at all unreasonable, or as reflecting outdated prejudices. To confer very wide immunity from civil suit by an innocent and powerless third party is one thing; to make such immunity depend on the state of mind of the other party, to which only he can testify, is another which does not necessarily follow from the policy giving rise to the former.

The appellants indeed in their printed case, and at the hearing, modified this position. They seemed prepared to agree that some examination may be made of the

---

1   [1979] 3 All ER 614, [1979] 1 WLR 1294
2   [1978] 1 All ER 111, [1977] 1 WLR 1004

factual capability of the action taken to further the trade dispute. But this is to be only by way of a check, or verification, on the genuineness of the belief held by those directing *a* the action. If, they say, an examination of the nature of the act proposed to be done shows that no responsible person in the position of those directing the action could think that the action would further the dispute, then, notwithstanding their expressed belief, the court may decide that the action could not be in furtherance of the dispute.

My Lords, this presentation has some attraction since it appears to avoid a judicial interference in trade disputes decided on and managed by unions or their officers or *b* members. But I regret that I cannot agree with it. I think indeed that this formula has the worst of both worlds. It destroys or emasculates the subjective test, because a man may perfectly well have a genuine belief that something is practicable which is in fact not practicable, or more exactly which a judge thinks is not practicable. It does not substitute an objective test, for what is enquired into is not what the action is capable of achieving but what a person in the position of the initiator of the action might reasonably think it *c* capable of achieving. Moreover it is likely to be just as unacceptable to the initiator of the action to have the bona fides or reasonableness of his expressed belief enquired into by a judge as it is to have an enquiry into what good the action may in fact do. The choice is, to my mind, a bleak choice between a purely subjective test, in which all that matters is the belief of the initiator, which is what the appellants really claim, and some objective test, based on an impartial assessment by the court. This cannot be burked by *d* acceptance of a hybrid.

So I must now examine the arguments for an objective test.

In the first place I do not find it to be excluded by the words of the section. It is clear enough that 'in contemplation . . . of' are not words exclusively subjective. It cannot be enough for someone to depose, in general terms, which cannot be probed, that he had a trade dispute in mind. The words, to me, presuppose an actual or emerging trade *e* dispute as well as the mental contemplation of it. Similarly, 'in . . . furtherance' may quite well include, as well as an intention to further, an actual furtherance (help or encouragement) or the capability of furtherance. Secondly, so to construe the phase is not to impose on it a limitation. There is much in the cases to the effect that 'the words must be given some limitation' and to this the appellants object. The words, they say, and I agree, must be given their natural meaning and the courts must not approach them *f* with a disposition to cut them down. But it is always open to the courts, indeed their duty, with open-ended expressions such as those involving cause, or effect, or remoteness, or in the context of this very Act, connection with (cf *British Broadcasting Corpn v Hearn*[1]), to draw a line beyond which the expression ceases to operate. This is simply the common law in action. It does not involve the judges in cutting down what Parliament has given; it does involve them in interpretation in order to ascertain how far Parliament *g* intended to go.

If there is to be an objective test what should it be? The Court of Appeal found difficulty in this. Lord Denning MR, through various revisions, finally settled I think on practical effect. This I think with respect goes too far: it involves judging the matter by results (at what time?), a very uncertain process in the complex, and sometimes irrational world of industrial relations. He did, as I read his judgment, take into account the actual *h* effect of the action as he saw it. But one cannot use hindsight to interpret or apply the expression: the act must be appraised when it is done. Lawton LJ, and Brandon LJ agreed, did not go so far. The acts done, pursuant to the genuine intention, must in his view be reasonably capable of achieving the objective; it is not necessary to prove that what is done *will* achieve the objective. The test involves, necessarily, finding some connection between the action taken, or proposed, and the result, and to that extent is a *j* test based on remoteness. In my opinion, this test is in line with sound accepted principle and I find myself able to accept it. In applying it the court must take into

---

1   [1978] 1 All ER 111, [1977] 1 WLR 1004

account the belief of the initiators of the action as to the capability of that action to
a achieve the objective. If these are, as in most but not all cases they will be, experienced
trade union officials, if they express a clear opinion as to the 'capability' of the action, and
if there is no evidence the other way, the court will or should be very reluctant to
substitute its own judgment for theirs. The court may have to form its own judgment,
either if there is no such clear expression of opinion (cf *United Biscuits (UK) Ltd v Fall*[1]) or
it comes from a source less fitted to form a judgment, or, rarely, if the conclusion
b suggested is so implausible or the connection between the action called for and the
objective so remote and tenuous that the court feels justified in disregarding it. This it
should do directly rather than by the indirect device of questioning the initiator's belief.

My Lords, most of the cases which have preceded the present proceed on the basis of
an objective test, though the nature of this test is expressed without complete
consistency. Ackner J in the *United Biscuits* case[2] neatly stated the alternatives available.
c I do not go through these cases because though contributing to a solution of the present
difficulty they provide no certain guide and because your Lordships are not bound by
them. *Conway v Wade*[3] as a decision of this House would be entitled to great respect, in
spite of its age, if it bore on the point. But it does not. The question the House was
considering was whether there was a trade dispute between the employer and Wade;
they held him to be an intermeddler and a mischief maker. It was to this issue that both
d Lord Loreburn LC and Lord Shaw of Dunfermline addressed their remarks. They were
not concerned to analyse, or to discuss the nature of, the acts 'in contemplation or
furtherance', and they certainly had no such problem as the present in mind. Here there
is no argument as to the existence of the dispute; everything turns on the nature of the
acts.

The clearest statement now prevailing is that by Lawton and Brandon LJJ in the Court
e of Appeal. If I apply this test here, I find no difficulty in reaching a conclusion, but it is
not that of the Court of Appeal. I have summarised the relevant evidence above. We
find Mr MacShane, Mr Ashton and Mr Dennis all expressing the view that, on the one
hand, if NUJ members elsewhere were to handle PA material it would weaken the strike
at the PA, and that, on the other hand, if these members were not to handle the PA
material it would encourage NUJ members at the PA to join the strike. The Court of
f Appeal discounted this evidence on the ground that it only bore on the morale of the NUJ
members at the PA and so was insufficiently concrete, but I disagree on both points.
Morale is a vital factor in all confrontations, whether at Alamein or in Fleet Street, not the
only factor, and bare assertions regarding it must be critically viewed. But here the
evidence goes beyond morale well into the capability of practical effect; it shows that to
persuade the PA journalists to join the PA strike could well further both that strike and
g the initial strike against the Newspaper Society; to discourage such journalists from
doing so could effect the opposite. The evidence here as to reasonable capability is all one
way, and is persuasive. It is not possible for the courts to reject it on a view of their
own. Quite apart from s 17(2) of the 1974 Act, as amended, the injunctions should not
have been granted.

To sum up: in my opinion there is an objective element in 'furtherance' which the
h court must appraise. It should do so in the light of the evidence, giving due weight but
not conclusive force to the genuine belief of those who initiate the action in question.
On the facts of this case and on the evidence available, the action taken (viz of blacking
the PA copy) was reasonably capable of furthering the trade dispute. I would only add
that I must reserve my opinion on the 'second point' raised in the opinion of my noble
and learned friend, Lord Scarman. This was not an issue in the appeal. It raises what
j may be interesting questions, but I am left with more than a little doubt whether the
stark effect of the 'subjective' interpretation can be mitigated by the use, in certain cases

---

1 [1979] IRLR 110
2 [1979] IRLR 110 at 113
3 [1909] AC 506, [1908–10] All ER Rep 344

only, of a residual discretion to grant an injunction. I must not be taken to agree that such a discretion is capable of being exercised in cases such as the present. I would allow *a* the appeal and discharge the injunctions.

LORD DIPLOCK. My Lords, during the past two years there has been a series of judgments in the Court of Appeal given on applications for interlocutory injunctions against trade union officials. These have the effect of imposing on the expression 'An act done by a person in contemplation or furtherance of a trade dispute', for which immunity *b* from civil actions for specified kinds of torts is conferred by s 13(1) of the Trade Union and Labour Relations Act 1974 (as now amended), an interpretation restrictive of what, in common with the majority of your Lordships, I believe to be its plain and unambiguous meaning. The terms in which the limitations on the ambit of the expression have been stated are not identical in the various judgments, but at the root of all of them there appears to lie an assumption that Parliament cannot really have *c* intended to give so wide an immunity from the common law of tort as the words of ss 13 and 29 would, on the face of them, appear to grant to everyone who engages in any form of what is popularly known as industrial action.

My Lords, I do not think that this is a legitimate assumption on which to approach the construction of the 1974 Act, notwithstanding that the training and traditions of anyone whose life has been spent in the practice of the law and the administration of justice in *d* the courts must make such an assumption instinctively attractive to him. But the manifest policy of the Act was to strengthen the role of recognised trade unions in collective bargaining, so far as possible to confine the bargaining function to them, and, as my noble and learned friend Lord Scarman recently pointed out in *NWL Ltd v Woods*[1], to exclude trade disputes from judicial review by the courts. Parliament, as it was constituted when the Act and the subsequent amendments to it were passed, may well *e* have felt so confident that trade unions could be relied on always to act 'responsibly' in trade disputes that any need for legal sanctions against their failure to do so could be obviated.

This being so, it does not seem to me that it is a legitimate approach to the construction of the sections that deal with trade disputes, to assume that Parliament did *not* intend to give to trade unions and their officers a wide discretion to exercise their own judgment *f* as to the steps which should be taken in an endeavour to help the workers' side in any trade dispute to achieve its objectives. And, if their plain and ordinary meaning is given to the words 'An act done by a person in contemplation or furtherance of a trade dispute', this, as it seems to me, is what s 13 does. In the light of the express reference to the 'person' by whom the act is done and the association of 'furtherance' with 'contemplation' (which cannot refer to anything but the state of mind of the doer of the act) it is, in my *g* view, clear that 'in furtherance' too can only refer to the state of mind of the person who does the act, and means 'with the purpose of helping one of the parties to a trade dispute to achieve their objectives in it'.

Given the existence of a trade dispute (the test of which, though broad, is nevertheless objective: see *NWL Ltd v Woods*[2]), this makes the test of whether an act was done 'in . . . furtherance of' it a purely subjective one. If the party who does the act honestly thinks *h* at the time he does it that it may help one of the parties to the trade dispute to achieve their objectives and does it for that reason, he is protected by the section. I say 'may' rather than 'will' help, for it is the nature of industrial action that success in achieving its objectives cannot be confidently predicted. Also there is nothing in the section that requires that there should be any proportionality between on the one hand the extent to which the act is likely to, or be capable of, increasing the 'industrial muscle' of one side *j* to the dispute and on the other hand the damage caused to the victim of the act which,

1 [1979] 3 All ER 614 at 630, [1979] 1 WLR 1294 at 1312
2 [1979] 3 All ER 614, [1979] 1 WLR 1294

but for the section, would have been tortious. The doer of the act may know full well
a that it cannot have more than a minor effect in bringing the trade dispute to the
successful outcome that he favours, but nevertheless is bound to cause disastrous loss to
the victim, who may be a stranger to the dispute and with no interest in its outcome.
The act is none the less entitled to immunity under the section.

It is, I think, these consequences of applying the subjective test that, not surprisingly,
have tended to stick in judicial gorges: that so great damage may be caused to innocent
b and disinterested third parties in order to obtain for one of the parties to a trade dispute
tactical advantages which in the court's own view are highly speculative and, if obtained,
could be no more than minor. This has led the Court of Appeal to seek to add some
objective element to the subjective test of the bona fide purpose of the person who did
the act.

In the reported cases, which have already been cited by my noble and learned friend,
c Lord Wilberforce, three somewhat different tests have been suggested. They are
conveniently stated in summary form by Ackner J in *United Biscuits (UK) Ltd v Fall*[1]. First
there is a test based on remoteness. The help given to the party to the trade dispute must
be direct. 'You cannot', said Lord Denning MR in *Beaverbrook Newspapers v Keys*[2], 'chase
consequence after consequence after consequence in a long chain and say everything that
follows a trade dispute is in "furtherance" of it'. The second test, suggested by Lord
d Denning MR in the instant case, is that the act done must have some 'practical' effect in
bringing pressure to bear on the opposite side to the dispute; acts done to assist the
morale of the party to the dispute whose cause is favoured are not protected. Thirdly
there is the test favoured by Lawton and Brandon LJJ in the instant case: the act done
must, in the view of the court, be reasonably capable of achieving the objective of the
trade dispute.

e My Lords, these tests though differently expressed, have the effect of enabling the
court to substitute its own opinion for the bona fide opinion held by the trade union or
its officers whether action proposed to be taken or continued for the purpose of helping
one side or bringing pressure to bear on the other side to a trade dispute is likely to have
the desired effect. Granted bona fides on the part of the trade union or its officer this is
to convert the test from a purely subjective to a purely objective test and for the reasons
f I have given I do not think the wording of the section permits of this. The belief of the
doer of the act that it will help the side he favours in the dispute must be honest; it need
not be wise, nor need it take account of the damage it will cause to innocent and
disinterested third parties. On an application for an interlocutory injunction the
evidence may show positively by admission or by inference from the facts before the
court that the act was not done to further an existing trade dispute but for some ulterior
g purpose such as revenge for previous conduct. Again, the facts in evidence before the
court may be such as will justify the conclusion that no reasonable person versed in
industrial relations could possibly have thought that the act was capable of helping one
side in a trade dispute to achieve its objectives. But this too goes to honesty of purpose
alone and not to the reasonableness of the act, or its expediency.

My Lords, on what I have held to be the true construction of the Act, I agree with your
h Lordships that this appeal must be allowed. There was unquestionably a trade dispute
between provincial journalists and their employers. There was, I think, what could
properly be described as a continuing dispute between the PA and the NUJ as to the
blacking of PA copy to provincial newspapers whose journalists were on strike, which
flared up whenever such a strike occurred but in the meantime remained quiescent.
This dispute, however, did not qualify as a trade dispute under s 29. The withdrawal of
j PA copy from the provincial newspapers would be a crucial factor in strengthening the
bargaining position of the striking journalists, but in view of the PA's attitude this could

1 [1979] IRLR 110 at 113
2 [1978] ICR 582 at 586

only be achieved by forcing it to close down or at any rate to reduce its services
drastically, by withdrawing journalistic labour from it. The PA was not an NUJ closed *a*
shop and for economic reasons even the NUJ members on its staff were not likely to be
enthusiastic at the prospect of being called out on strike. For my part I see no reason for
doubting the honesty of the belief held by Mr MacShane and Mr Dennis that the
response of their members to the strike call at the PA might well be less numerous and
less enduring if they knew that fellow members of their union on the national
newspapers were continuing to make use of copy produced by those whom they would *b*
regard as 'blacklegs' at the PA.
    I would allow this appeal.

LORD SALMON. My Lords, towards the end of 1978 a trade dispute arose between
a trade union, the National Union of Journalists ('the NUJ'), and most of the provincial
newspapers which are represented by the Newspaper Society. The NUJ asserted that the *c*
journalists employed by the provincial newspapers were being underpaid and demanded
an increase in the journalists' wages. The Newspaper Society refused to agree to any such
increase in wages. As a result the provincial journalists came out on strike on 4th
December 1978. The provincial newspapers normally obtain most of their news from
the journalists in their employment. They also obtain much of their news from the Press
Association ('the PA') as do the national newspapers and some radio and television *d*
networks. The PA employ about 250 journalists, some of whom are members of the
NUJ. As long as the PA was able to supply the provincial newspapers with its usual
service, they could carry on business, maybe with some difficulty, in spite of the fact that
the journalists whom it normally employed were out on strike. Accordingly, on 4th
December, the NUJ, which had no dispute with the PA, called out on strike all its
members who were employed by the PA. The NUJ's object in calling this strike was to *e*
reduce the provincial newspapers' supply of news from the PA to such an extent that the
provincial newspapers would be obliged to cease publishing their newspapers unless they
agreed to increase the wages of their journalist employees, and so brought them back
into the fold.
    At the meeting on 4th December, 86 of the members of the NUJ who were employed
by the PA voted against the strike and 76 for it. The chairman told the meeting that any *f*
copy produced for the PA by those who had been instructed to strike but had disobeyed
the instruction would be 'blacked'. The 76 members who had voted for the strike went
out on strike and were shortly joined by 32 others. This meant that the PA was able to
render a little less than half its normal services to its usual customers.
    On 3rd December, no doubt because it foresaw the difficulties which did arise in
persuading its members in the PA to come out on strike, the NUJ wrote to its members *g*
employed by the national Press, including the Daily Express, instructing them to black,
i e not to make use of, any copy coming from the PA after noon on 4th December. The
NUJ had at that time no dispute with any of the owners of the national Press. Its
instructions to black amounted to the commission by the NUJ of the tort of procuring
its members to commit a breach of their contracts of employment with the national
Press. The NUJ would be liable in damages for this tort unless s 13(1) of the Trade *h*
Unions and Labour Relations Act 1974 (as amended) entitles the NUJ to immunity for
committing this tort. This would depend on whether the giving of instructions by the
NUJ to its members employed by the national Press to black all news obtained from the
PA amounted to 'An act done . . . in . . . furtherance of a trade dispute'.
    The evidence seems to me to prove clearly that the NUJ gave its instructions in relation
to blacking for the purpose of furthering on behalf of its provincial members the trade *j*
dispute between them and their employers, the provincial newspapers. If the NUJ
members employed by the national Press consented to handle the newscopy compiled by
the PA's NUJ strike-breakers this might well undermine the morale of the PA's NUJ
strikers and induce them to abandon the strike; it certainly would not encourage any of
the PA's NUJ non-strikers to join in the strike. Accordingly, there would then be a real

danger that the strike of the PA's NUJ members would collapse and thus enable the PA
a to resume its normal services to the provincial Press, which would help to break the
strike of its NUJ employees. Morale, and lack of it, are, in certain circumstances, just as
likely to win or lose a trade dispute as a battle.

I recognise and regret how much the national Press must have been incommoded and
put to serious expense by the strike at the PA and the blacking of the PA's newscopy. In
my opinion, however, the strike at the PA and the blacking may well have helped the
b NUJ members to succeed in their trade dispute with the provincial newspapers. It
appears the strike ended quite quickly by the provincial newspapers' journalists having
their pay substantially increased. In any event, I do not think that the evidence before
the court could justify a finding that no sensible officers of the NUJ could reasonably have
believed that the strike at the PA and the blacking would further the trade dispute to
which I have referred.

c   The words 'An act done by a person in . . . furtherance of a trade dispute' must be given
their ordinary and natural meaning in their context. That meaning, in my view, is that
the person doing the act must honestly and reasonably believe that it may further the
trade dispute. If he does not honestly and reasonably believe that, but does the act out of
spite or in order to show his 'muscle' or is an embittered fanatic who believes, wholly
unreasonably, that the act he does is in furtherance of a trade dispute, I do not think that
d s 13(1) was intended by Parliament to afford protection to him or persons such as him.

I entirely agree that the courts are not the appropriate places in which trade disputes
should be decided. Section 13(1) however deals with the commission of a tort, ie a
breach of the law, and the circumstances in which the tortfeasor may be entitled to
immunity when those against whom the tort is committed may suffer seriously. This,
in my opinion, is a matter to be decided in the courts; and I have no doubt that the courts
e will be very slow to hold that an act is wholly unreasonable if those of great experience
in the trade give evidence that the act had a reasonable prospect of furthering the trade
dispute in question.

On the other hand, there have been cases in which tortious acts have been done which
constituted inhuman conduct causing the most grievous harm. For example, quite
recently patients in the Charing Cross Hospital being treated for cancer were brought
f near to death because industrial action had been taken to prevent fuel oil from being
brought into the hospital. This made the hospital intolerably cold when warmth was
necessary in order to provide any chance of keeping the patients alive. No doubt some
of those who were responsible for preventing the fuel from entering the hospital firmly,
but certainly not reasonably, believed that they were doing an act ' in . . . furtherance of
a trade dispute', within the meaning of those words in s 13(1), and were therefore
g immune. They may have been; but if this is the law, surely the time has come for it to
be altered.

My Lords, I am satisfied that in the present case the evidence established that the
officers of the NUJ honestly and reasonably believed that the action which they took was
fairly 'in . . . furtherance of a trade dispute', and for these reasons I would allow the
appeal.

h

LORD KEITH OF KINKEL. My Lords, this appeal is concerned with s 13(1)(*a*) of
the Trade Union and Labour Relations Act 1974, as amended in 1976, which provides:

> 'An act done by a person in contemplation or furtherance of a trade dispute shall
> not be actionable in tort on the ground only—(*a*) that it induces another person to
j break a contract or interferes or induces any other person to interfere with its
> performance . . .'

The material facts may be briefly stated. Late in 1978 a trade dispute arose between
the National Union of Journalists ('the NUJ') and the Newspaper Society representing the
proprietors of provincial newspapers. The dispute was about the pay of journalists

employed by the latter. A strike of these journalists was called. At the same time a strike was called of journalists employed by the Press Association ('the PA'), a company *a* providing a news agency service to newspapers and others. The only purpose of this was to render more effective the strike by journalists employed by the provincial newspapers, by depriving these newspapers of copy which might otherwise enable them to carry on limited production. There was some reason to doubt the likely measure of response to the PA strike call, so before it was due to take effect the NUJ issued instructions to members employed by national newspapers, including the Daily Express, to refuse to *b* handle, i e to black, all copy sent out by the PA after the time at which the strike there was due to begin. In the result, about half the NUJ members at the PA obeyed the strike call and the remainder did not. The service provided by the PA was proportionately reduced.

The respondents in this appeal, the proprietors of the Daily Express, commenced proceedings against the appellants, the President and General Secretary of the NUJ as representing the members of its National Executive Council, claiming an injunction *c* against their inducing members working for the Daily Express to break their contracts of employment by refusing to handle PA copy. An interlocutory injunction was granted by Lawson J on 14th December 1978, and his decision was, on appeal, affirmed by the Court of Appeal. It was held that the defence which the appellants claimed to be available to them under s 13(1) of the 1974 Act was not likely to succeed, because the act of instructing NUJ members employed by national newspapers to black PA copy was not, *d* according to the true construction of the words, 'in . . . furtherance of' the trade dispute between the NUJ and the Newspaper Society. Lord Denning MR said[1]: 'To be "in furtherance of" a [trade] dispute, an act must give practical support to one side or the other and not merely moral support.' He took the view that the instructions to black PA copy had had, on the evidence, no practical effect at all on the dispute between provincial newspapers and their journalists. Lawton and Brandon LJJ both expressed the opinion *e* that the act must be reasonably capable or have a reasonable prospect of achieving furtherance of the dispute, and they did not consider that this was so in the present case.

In my opinion there is no room for serious doubt about the natural and ordinary meaning of the words 'in . . . furtherance of' in section 13(1). In *Conway v Wade*[2] Lord Shaw of Dunfermline, speaking of the similar wording in s 3 of the Trade Disputes Act 1906, put the matter thus: *f*

'With regard to the term "furtherance" of a trade dispute, I think that must apply to a trade dispute in existence, and that the act done must be in the course of it and for the purpose of promoting the interests of either party or both parties to it.'

I consider this to be correct. The only alternative would be to hold that the act must be one which actually does further the dispute, but as the quality of the act falls to be judged *g* as at the time when it is done, that reading does not seem to me to be open.

The task of ascertaining the purpose for which a particular act was done is one familiar to courts of law in a variety of statutory contexts. It involves looking into the state of mind of the person doing the act at the time when he did it. The common situation is where the person doing the act is concerned to deny the particular purpose alleged, and his opponent in the litigation is concerned to assert it. In that situation the court is *h* naturally inclined to place more reliance on facts and circumstances from which the purpose may be inferred than on the statement of the person who has done the act. In cases where a defence under s 13(1) is put forward, the defendant's interest lies in establishing the requisite purpose, and although no doubt he knows best what was the state of his mind at the relevant time, a court may well be reluctant to accept his evidence unless it is supported by facts and circumstances objectively ascertained. This reluctance *j* no doubt stems from the far-reaching nature of the indemnity given by the enactment

1   [1979] 2 All ER 360 at 365, [1979] 1 WLR 390 at 396
2   [1909] AC 506 at 522, [1908–10] All ER Rep 344 at 351–352

and the consideration that extremely serious damage may have been sustained by the
a plaintiff as a result of the act complained of. But the burden of proof resting on the
defendant is the normal one in civil cases, and the court must deal with the issue as to his
purpose in the ordinary way with that in mind. This will no doubt involve the
consideration of all relevant facts and circumstances which may throw light on the
genuineness of the defendant's statement as to his purpose. If it should appear that no
reasonable person versed in industrial relations could take the view that the act called in
b question was capable of furthering the dispute, that might lead to rejection of the
defendant's evidence, particularly if some other purpose were alleged by the
plaintiff. But in my opinion considerations of that sort, which may be appropriate for
the purpose of reaching a conclusion on the weight of the evidence in particular cases, are
not properly to be imported into the construction of s 13(1) itself. One can understand,
without necessarily agreeing with, the inclination to set some limits to the width of the
c immunity thereby conferred, and to avoid allowing it to depend entirely on the evidence
about his own state of mind given by the person claiming it. But in my opinion the
proper construction of the enactment does not permit of the glosses which the Court of
Appeal placed on it in order to introduce a more objective element. On that construction
the function of the court is simply to ascertain and pronounce on the purpose with which
the act was done.
d   On the evidence in the present case, I am of opinion that the appellants have presented
a good prima facie case that the instructions to NUJ members working with national
newspapers to black PA copy were given with the purpose of promoting the interests of
the journalists' side in the dispute with the provincial newspaper proprietors. It is not in
dispute that the appellants genuinely hoped and believed that their action would help to
achieve that result, and no other purpose is suggested by the respondents. It cannot be
e said at this stage that there were no reasonable grounds for this hope and belief. The
blacking of PA copy by journalists on national newspapers might not unreasonably be
thought to have some prospect of increasing participation in the strike of PA journalists,
or at least of reducing the chances of it withering away completely. That in turn would
assist in increasing or at least maintaining the pressure exerted on the provincial
newspapers by the strike of their own journalists.
f   My Lords, for these reasons I would allow the appeal.

LORD SCARMAN. My Lords, this appeal raises directly one question and less
directly a second. The direct question, which was fully argued at the bar, may be put as
follows: was the National Union of Journalists' instruction to those of its members in the
g employ of Express Newspapers to 'black' Press Association copy 'An act done by a person
in . . . furtherance of a trade dispute'? Undoubtedly the NUJ and its officers honestly
believed that it was; and, if it was, it was not actionable in tort; for such is the effect of
s 13(1) of the Trade Union and Labour Relations Act 1974, as amended by s 3(2) of the
Trade Union and Labour Relations (Amendment) Act 1976. And it would follow that
Express Newspapers Ltd, who are the respondents in your Lordships' House and the
h plaintiffs in the action, were not entitled to any relief or remedy in our courts. The
question is one of interpretation of the subsection.
    There was certainly a trade dispute. It was between the NUJ and those provincial
newspapers (virtually every local provincial newspaper published in England and Wales)
who are represented by the Newspaper Society, and it concerned the rates of pay of
journalists employed by provincial newspapers. It resulted in the NUJ calling its
j members in their employ out on strike on 4th December 1978. It was in support of this
strike, to which the Daily Express was not a party, and over the conduct of which it had
no control, that the NUJ issued its instruction to its members in the employ of the
newspaper. Put in the jargon of industrial relations, the problem in the case is 'secondary
blacking'. If an employer, as in this case the Daily Express has done, issues a writ seeking
to prevent or stop the blacking, the court does have power, at its discretion, to grant an

injunction prohibiting it pending hearing of the case and before a final decision whether the blacking was in contemplation or furtherance of a trade dispute has been reached. *a* Section 17(2) of the 1974 Act, as amended, which regulates the exercise of this discretion, requires the court to have regard to the likelihood of a defence under s 13 succeeding. The existence of this discretionary power, notwithstanding the likelihood of the defence succeeding, gives rise to the second question, which some of your Lordships (including myself) raised in argument, but which was not taken up by counsel. Nevertheless its importance is great. The question is: if industrial action poses a substantial threat to a *b* defined public interest, eg the freedom of the Press and the right of the public to be informed, is the threat a factor which the court should properly put into the balance together with the other relevant factors when asked to grant an interlocutory injunction restraining the industrial action? The facts of the present case are sufficiently close to that situation to require a consideration of, if not a final answer to, the question.

On the first question, ie the interpretation of s 13(1), I find myself in agreement with *c* my noble and learned friend, Lord Diplock. The words 'An act done by a person in contemplation or furtherance of a trade dispute' seem to me, in their natural and ordinary meaning, to refer to the person's purpose, his state of mind. The court must satisfy itself that it was his purpose, and, before reaching its decision, will test his evidence by investigating all the circumstances and applying the usual tests of credibility: that is to say, it will ask itself whether a reasonable man could have thought that what he *d* was doing would support his side of the dispute, or whether the link between his actions and his purpose was so tenuous that his evidence is not to be believed. But, at the end of the day, the question for the court is simply: is the defendant to be believed when he says that he acted in contemplation or in furtherance of a trade dispute?

I accept that this construction limits the extent of judicial review. But it does not exclude it. An effective judicial review remains. 'To "contemplate a trade dispute" is to *e* have before the mind some objective event or situation ... but does not mean ... something as yet wholly within the mind and of a subjective character': per Lord Shaw of Dunfermline in *Conway v Wade*[1]. Likewise, to further a trade dispute presupposes that a dispute exists. In either case, the court must ask itself whether a trade dispute as defined in s 29 of the 1974 Act is either imminent or actual; and, unless it is, it cannot be said that the defendant acted in contemplation or furtherance of it. A fanciful *f* suggestion of a dispute will not do: the defendant must have in mind 'an objective event or situation'. The effectiveness of this objective factor in the exercise of judicial review is well shown by *British Broadcasting Corpn v Hearn*[2], a decision of the Court of Appeal to which I was a party and which I continue to think was correctly decided.

It follows therefore that, once it is shown that a trade dispute exists, the person who acts, but not the court, is the judge of whether his acts will further the dispute. If he is *g* acting honestly, Parliament leaves to him the choice of what to do. I confess that I am relieved to find that this is the law. It would be a strange and embarrassing task for a judge to be called on to review the tactics of a party to a trade dispute and to determine whether in the view of the court the tactic employed was likely to further, or advance, that party's side of the dispute. And the difficulties which have beset the Court of Appeal in their attempts to formulate a test are a persuasive argument for keeping this act of *h* judgment in the industrial arena and out of the judicial forum. Without going further afield than the present case, Lord Denning MR has made two attempts to formulate a test: 'remoteness' and 'practical effect'. Lawton and Brandon LJJ have favoured one of seeing whether the act done is reasonably capable of achieving the party's objective in the dispute. It is, not surprisingly, a case of quot praetores, tot sententiae. It would need very clear statutory language to persuade me that Parliament intended to allow the *j* courts to act as some sort of a backseat driver in trade disputes.

---

1   [1909] AC 506 at 522, [1908–10] All ER Rep 344 at 351
2   [1978] 1 All ER 111, [1977] 1 WLR 1004

I turn now to the second question. On the facts of the present case there was no threat
a to the freedom of the Press. But, if a union of print workers or journalists should seek
to further its side of a trade dispute with one or more newspapers by calling on its
members to withdraw their labour from all newspapers including the nationals, the
threat to the public interest could be very serious. Our law, as it stands, would confer on
the union and its members the immunity contained in s 13 of the 1974 Act. If a
newspaper, which was not a party to the dispute, found itself threatened and sought an
b interim injunction, would the court be able to grant it, notwithstanding it was more
likely than not that at trial the defendants would succeed in showing that they had acted
in furtherance of a trade dispute? In *NWL Ltd v Woods*[1] your Lordships' House recognised
that s 17(2) of the 1974 Act, as amended, left with the court a residual discretion, even in
such circumstances, to grant an interim injunction. In that case, my noble and learned
friend Lord Diplock, after commenting that ordinarily judges would refuse an injunction
c when it was more likely than not that the defendant would succeed in his defence of
statutory immunity, added[2]:

'. . . but this does not mean that there may not be cases where the consequences
to the employer or to third parties or the public and perhaps the nation itself, may
be so disastrous that the injunction ought to be refused, unless there is a high degree
of probability that the defence will succeed.'

d
My Lords, in a case where action alleged to be in contemplation or furtherance of a trade
dispute endangers the nation or puts at risk such fundamental rights as the right of the
public to be informed and the freedom of the Press, it could well be a proper exercise of
the court's discretion to restrain the industrial action pending trial of the action. It
would, of course, depend on the circumstances of the case; but the law does not preclude
e the possibility of the court exercising its discretion in that way. I would, therefore, give
an affirmative answer to the second question.

Nevertheless for the reasons previously given I consider that the judge and the Court
of Appeal fell into an error of law. I would, therefore, allow the appeal.

Appeal allowed. Injunctions discharged.

f
Solicitors: *Vizards* (for the appellants); *Lovell, White & King* (for the respondents).

Mary Rose Plummer   Barrister.

---

1   [1979] 3 All ER 614, [1979] 1 WLR 1294
2   [1979] 3 All ER 614 at 626, [1979] 1 WLR 1294 at 1307

Inland Revenue Commissioners and another *a*
v Rossminster Ltd
and related appeals

HOUSE OF LORDS

LORD WILBERFORCE, VISCOUNT DILHORNE, LORD DIPLOCK, LORD SALMON AND LORD SCARMAN   *b*

29th, 30th, 31st OCTOBER, 13th DECEMBER 1979

Income tax – Offence – Fraud – Suspected offence – Warrant to enter and seize documents – Validity – Warrant not specifying offence suspected but drawn in general terms of provision empowering issue of warrant – Proceedings for judicial review of warrant and seizure – Whether warrant ought to specify nature of suspected offence – Whether Revenue sole arbiter that *c* *reasonable belief documents required as evidence of an offence existed – Whether Revenue entitled to withhold grounds for seizure – Whether in proceedings for judicial review court entitled to make final declaration that seizure unlawful where action claiming damages for unlawful seizure pending – Taxes Management Act 1970, s 20c(1)(3) (as inserted by the Finance Act 1976, s 57(1), Sch 6) – RSC Ord 53.*

An officer of the Board of Inland Revenue, acting under the provisions of s 20c[a] of the   *d* Taxes Management Act 1970, laid an information on oath before a circuit judge alleging that there was reasonable ground for suspecting that an offence involving a tax fraud had been committed and that incriminating documents would be found on the premises, both private and business, belonging to the respondents and specified in the information. The judge issued search warrants under s 20c(1). The warrants did not   *e* specify that any particular offence was suspected but simply stated, in the words of s 20c(1) and (3), that there was 'reasonable ground for suspecting that an offence involving fraud in connection with or in relation to tax has been committed and that evidence of it is to be found on the premises described [therein]', and authorised officers of the Revenue to enter those premises, search them and seize and remove 'any things whatsoever found there which [they had] reasonable cause to believe may be required as   *f* evidence for the purposes of proceedings in respect of such an offence'. In executing the warrants the officers entered the specified premises and seized and removed numerous files, papers and documents of all kinds. The respondents contended that the officers did not examine the bulk of the articles before seizing them, or did not examine them in enough detail to form an opinion on their evidential value, although the Revenue asserted that the officers had detailed instructions what to look for. The respondents   *g* commenced an action in the Chancery Division against the Revenue claiming, inter alia, damages for wrongful interference with goods. Subsequently, in the Divisional Court of the Queen's Bench Division, the applicants applied for judicial review of the seizure, under RSC Ord 53, and in those proceedings sought an order of certiorari to quash the warrants and a declaration that the seizure was unlawful and that the Revenue ought to return to the applicants all the articles seized, and all copies and notes taken of them. The   *h* Divisional Court[b] dismissed the application for judicial review. The applicants appealed contending (1) that the warrants were invalid under s 20c(1) because they did not specify the particular offence involving fraud which was suspected and (2) that the seizure was unlawful because the articles taken were so numerous and inspection of the bulk of them so cursory that the officers could not at the time of the seizure have had reasonable grounds for believing they might be required as evidence of an offence, within   *i* s 20c(3). The Court of Appeal[b] upheld those contentions, allowed the appeal and, because   *j* an interim injunction or declaration could not be made against the Crown, made a final declaration that the seizure was unlawful. The Crown appealed.

---

a Section 20c, so far as material, is set out at p 97 *g* to *j*, post

b [1979] 3 All ER 385

Held (Lord Salmon dissenting) – The appeal would be allowed for the following
a reasons—
(i) On the true construction of s 20c(1) of the 1970 Act all that was required to be
specified in a warrant to search issued under s 20c was the address of the premises to be
searched and the name of the officer authorised to carry out the search, and although the
circuit judge issuing the warrant was himself required to be satisfied that there was
reasonable ground for suspecting that a tax fraud had been committed and that evidence
b of it was to be found on the premises to be searched, the fact that the judge was so
satisfied was not required to be stated in the warrant. Since the warrants in the instant
case were within the terms of s 20c(1) they were not invalid (see p 83 f g and j to p 84 e,
p 85 d, p 87 b c and j to p 88 a d f and h, p 90 a, p 91 e, p 92 b and g, p 101 f g, p 102 b and
d to p 103 e and g, p 104 j to p 105 b and 106 a b, post).
(ii) Although a revenue officer was required, under s 20c(3), to have 'reasonable cause
c to believe' that what was seized under a warrant might be required as evidence of a tax
fraud, on an application for judicial review made prior to the criminal prosecution public
interest immunity entitled the officer to refuse to give any reason for his decision to seize
particular documents and his decision could only be attacked if it was shown to be ultra
vires because he had no reasonable cause to believe or did not believe that what was seized
might be required as evidence, and the respondents' case fell short of doing that.
d Therefore, although in the respondents' action for wrongful interference with goods the
Revenue officers would have to disclose and substantiate the grounds of their belief, the
respondents' applications for judicial review failed (see p 84 j to p 85 a and d, p 89 e f, p 90
a, p 93 b to d, p 94 f to p 95 c, p 101 f g, p 103 h j, p 105 e to g and p 106 a b, post).
(iii) In any event because there was a substantial conflict of evidence as to the manner
in which the searches were carried out, the Court of Appeal had been wrong to make a
e final declaration, since such a declaration should not be made unless there was no dispute
as to the material facts or the dispute as to those facts had been determined after an
enquiry in the nature of a trial (see p 84 g h, p 85 d, p 89 h, p 90 a, p 95 h, p 101 f g, p 104
h and p 106 a b, post).
Decision of the Court of Appeal sub nom *R v Inland Revenue Comrs, ex parte Rossminster
Ltd* [1979] 3 All ER 385 reversed.

f **Notes**
For the powers of an officer of the Commissioners of Inland Revenue to enter and search
premises in a case in which there are reasonable grounds for suspecting that a tax fraud
has been committed, see 23 Halsbury's Laws (4th Edn) para 1563.
For s 20c of the Taxes Management Act 1970 (as inserted by the Finance Act 1976,
g s 57(1), Sch 6), see 46 Halsbury's Statutes (3rd Edn) 1790.

Cases referred to in opinions
Cassell & Co Ltd v Broome [1972] 1 All ER 801, [1972] AC 1027, [1972] 2 WLR 645, HL,
17 Digest (Reissue) 82, 17.
Chic Fashions (West Wales) Ltd v Jones [1968] 1 All ER 229, [1968] 2 QB 299, [1968] 2 WLR
h 201, 132 JP 175, CA, 14(1) Digest (Reissue) 215, 1573.
Conway v Rimmer [1968] 1 All ER 874, [1968] AC 910, [1968] 2 WLR 998, HL, 18 Digest
(Reissue) 155, 1273.
D v National Society for the Prevention of Cruelty to Children [1977] 1 All ER 589, [1978] AC
171, [1977] 2 WLR 201, HL.
Entick v Carrington (1765) 2 Wils 275, 19 State Tr 1029, 95 ER 807, 14(1) Digest (Reissue)
215, 1566.
j *Home v Bentinck* (1820) 2 Brod & Bing 130, 8 Price 225, 1 State Tr NS App 1348, 4 Moore
CP 563, 129 ER 907, Ex Ch, 22 Digest (Reissue) 429, 4285.
Huckle v Money (1763) 2 Wils 205, 95 ER 768, 17 Digest (Reissue) 219, 903.
International General Electric Co of New York Ltd v Customs and Excise Comrs [1962] 2 All ER
398, [1962] Ch 784, [1962] 3 WLR 20, [1962] RPC 235, CA, Digest (Cont Vol A) 457,
483a.

Liversidge v Anderson [1941] 3 All ER 338, [1942] AC 206, 110 LJKB 724, 166 LT 1, HL, 17 Digest (Reissue) 467, *28.*

Nakkuda Ali v M F de S Jayaratne [1951] AC 66, PC, 8(2) Digest (Reissue) 811, *621.*

R v Wilkes (1763) 2 Wils 151, 19 State Tr 982, 95 ER 737, 32 Digest (Reissue) 337, *2811.*

Rookes v Barnard [1964] 1 All ER 367, [1964] AC 1129, [1964] 2 WLR 269, [1964] Lloyd's Rep 28, HL, 17 Digest (Reissue) 81, *14.*

Appeals

The Inland Revenue Commissioners and Raymond Quinlan, one of Her Majesty's Inspector of Taxes, appealed against the decision of the Court of Appeal[1] (Lord Denning MR, Browne and Goff LJJ) given on 16th August 1979 allowing the appeal of the respondents, Rossminster Ltd, A J R Financial Services Ltd, Ronald Anthony Plummer and Ray Clifford Tucker, against the decision of the Divisional Court[1] (Eveleigh LJ, Park and Woolf JJ) given on 1st August 1979 refusing the respondents' application by motion pursuant to RSC Ord 53 for judicial review. The facts are set out in the opinion of Viscount Dilhorne.

Robert Gatehouse QC, Brian Davenport and *Michael Neligan* for the Crown.

Andrew J Bateson QC, Michael Tugendhat and *Michael Oliver* for the respondents.

Their Lordships took time for consideration.

13th December. The following opinions were delivered.

LORD WILBERFORCE. My Lords, the organised searches by officers of the Inland Revenue on Friday, 13th July 1979, on the respondents' office and private premises were carried out under powers claimed to be conferred by Act of Parliament: the Finance Act 1976, s 57, and Sch 6, inserting s 20c in the Taxes Management Act 1970.

The integrity and privacy of a man's home, and of his place of business, an important human rights has, since the Second World War, been eroded by a number of statutes passed by Parliament in the belief, presumably, that this right of privacy ought in some cases to be overridden by the interest which the public has in preventing evasions of the law. Some of these powers of search are reflections of dirigisme and of heavy taxation, others of changes in mores. Examples of them are to be found in the Exchange Control Act 1947, the Finance Act 1972 (in relation to value added tax) and in statutes about gaming or the use of drugs. A formidable number of officials now have powers to enter people's premises, and to take property away, and these powers are frequently exercised, sometimes on a large scale. Many people, as well as the respondents, think that this process has gone too far; that is an issue to be debated in Parliament and in the Press.

The courts have the duty to supervise, I would say critically, even jealously, the legality of any purported exercise of these powers. They are the guardians of the citizens' right to privacy. But they must do this in the context of the times, ie of increasing Parliamentary intervention, and of the modern power of judicial review. In my respectful opinion appeals to 18th century precedents of arbitrary action by Secretaries of State and references to general warrants do nothing to throw light on the issue. Furthermore, while the courts may look critically at legislation which impairs the rights of citizens and should resolve any doubt in interpretation in their favour, it is no part of their duty, or power, to restrict or impede the working of legislation, even of unpopular legislation; to do so would be to weaken rather than to advance the democratic process.

It is necessary to be clear at once that Parliament, in conferring these wide powers, has introduced substantial safeguards. Those relevant to this case are three:

(1) No action can be taken under s 20c without the approval of the Board of Inland Revenue, viz two members, at least, acting personally. This Board consists of senior and responsible officials expert in the subject-matter, who must be expected to weigh carefully the issues of public interest involved.

---

1   [1979] 3 All ER 385

(2) No warrant to enter can be issued except by a circuit judge, not, as is usually the
a case, by a magistrate. There has to be laid before him information on oath, and on this
he must be satisfied that there is reasonable ground for suspecting the commission of a
'tax fraud' and that evidence of it is to be found in the premises sought to be searched.
If the judge does his duty (and we must assume that the learned Common Serjeant did
in the present case) he must carefully consider for himself the grounds put forward by
the Revenue officer and judicially satisfy himself, in relation to each of the premises
b concerned, that these amount to reasonable grounds for suspecting etc. It would be quite
wrong to suppose that he acts simply as a rubber stamp on the Revenue's application.
(3) The courts retain their full powers of supervision of judicial and executive
action. There is nothing in s 20c which cuts these down; on the contrary, Parliament, by
using such phrases as 'is satisfied' and 'has reasonable cause to believe', must be taken to
accept the restraints which courts in many cases have held to be inherent in them.
c   The courts are concerned, in this case, only with two matters bearing on legality. First,
were the warrants valid? Secondly, can the actual action taken under s 20c(3) be
challenged on the ground that the officers did not have, or could not have had, reasonable
cause to believe that the documents they seized might be required as evidence for the
purposes of proceedings in respect of a 'tax fraud'? A third possible issue, namely that
there was not before the judge sufficient material on which to be satisfied as the section
d requires was not pursued, nor thought sustainable by the Court of Appeal. It is not an
issue now.
The two first mentioned are the only issues in the case. Three judges have decided
them in favour of each side. For myself I have no doubt that the view taken by the
Divisional Court on each was correct and I am willing to adopt their judgment. I add a
few observations of my own.
e   1. I can understand very well the perplexity, and indeed indignation, of those present
on the premises, when they were searched. Beyond knowing, as appears in the warrant,
that the search was in connection with a 'tax fraud', they were not told what the precise
nature of the fraud was, when it was committed, or by whom it was committed. In the
case of a concern with numerous clients, e g a bank, without this knowledge the occupier
of the premises is totally unable to protect his customers' confidential information from
f investigation and seizure. I cannot believe that this does not call for a fresh look by
Parliament. But, on the plain words of the enactment, the officers are entitled, if they
can persuade the Board and the judge, to enter and search *premises* regardless of whom
they belong to: a warrant which confers this power is strictly and exactly within the
Parliamentary authority, and the occupier has no answer to it. I accept that some
information as regards the person(s) alleged to have committed an offence and possibly
g as to the approximate dates of the offences must almost certainly have been laid before
the Board and the judge. But the occupier has no right to be told of this at this stage, nor
has he the right to be informed of the 'reasonable grounds' of which the judge was
satisfied. Both courts agree as to this: all this information is clearly protected by the
public interest immunity which covers investigations into possible criminal offences.
With reference to the police, Lord Reid stated this in *Conway v Rimmer*[1] in these words:

h   'The police are carrying on an unending war with criminals many of whom are
today highly intelligent. So it is essential that there should be no disclosure of
anything which might give any useful information to those who organise criminal
activities; and it would generally be wrong to require disclosure in a civil case of
anything which might be material in a pending prosecution, but after a verdict has
been given, or it has been decided to take no proceedings, there is not the same need
j   for secrecy.'

The Court of Appeal took the view that the warrants were invalid because they did not
sufficiently particularise the alleged offence(s). The court did not make clear exactly
what particulars should have been given, and indeed I think that this cannot be done.

1   [1968] 1 All ER 874 at 889, [1968] AC 910 at 953–954

The warrant followed the wording of the statute, 'fraud in connection with or in relation to tax', a portmanteau description which covers a number of common law offences *a* (cheating) and statutory offences (under the Theft Act 1968 et al). To require specification at this investigatory stage would be impracticable given the complexity of 'tax frauds' and the different persons who may be involved (companies, officers of companies, accountants, tax consultants, taxpayers, wives of taxpayers etc). Moreover, particularisation, if required, would no doubt take the form of a listing of one offence and/or another or others and so would be of little help to those concerned. Finally, there would clearly *b* be power, on principles well accepted in the common law, after entry had been made in connection with one particular offence, to seize material bearing on other offences within the portmanteau. So, particularisation, even if practicable, would not help the occupier.

I am unable, therefore, to escape the conclusion, that adherence to the statutory formula is sufficient.

The warrants, being valid, confer an authority to enter and search: see s 20c(1). This *c* being in terms stated in the Act, I do not appreciate the relevance of an enquiry into the form of search warrants at common law (which in any case admitted of some flexibility in operation) and still less into that of warrants of arrest. There is no mystery about the word 'warrant': it simply means a document issued by a person in authority under power conferred in that behalf authorising the doing of an act which would otherwise be illegal. The person affected, of course, has the right to be satisfied that the power to issue *d* it exists: therefore the warrant should (and did) contain a reference to that power. It would be wise to add to it a statement of satisfaction on the part of the judicial authority as to the matters on which he must be satisfied, but this is not a requirement and its absence does not go to validity. To complain of its absence in the present case when, as is admitted, no challenge can be made as to the satisfaction, in fact, of the judge, would be technical and indeed irrational. I can find no ground for holding these warrants *e* invalid.

2. The second matter, on which the intervention of the court may be called for, arises under s 20c(3). This confers a statutory power independent of any authority in the warrant to seize and remove. Like all statutory powers conferred on executive officers it is subject to supervision by the courts exercising their classic and traditional powers of judicial review. It is undisputed that the words 'has reasonable cause to believe' are open *f* to examination in spite of their subjective form: see *Nakkuda Ali v M F de S Jayaratne*[1]. The existence of this reasonable cause, and of the belief founded on it, is ultimately a question of fact to be tried on evidence.

So far as regards these appeals this issue is complicated in three ways. First, it has been raised at an interlocutory stage, and at the very beginning of the investigation, on affidavit evidence. Secondly, the Revenue have refused, so far, to disclose their reasonable *g* grounds, claiming immunity from so doing, on the grounds stated above. Thirdly, the defendants being, in effect, the Crown or Crown servants, an interlocutory injunction cannot be granted (see s 21 of the Crown Proceedings Act 1947).

The Court of Appeal sought to meet this situation by granting a declaration; and recognising, rightly in my opinion, that an interim declaration could not be granted, gave a final declaration in effect that the Revenue had exceeded their powers. I regret *h* that I cannot agree that this was correct. It is to me apparent that there was a substantial conflict of evidence as to the manner in which the searches were carried out, the respondents broadly contending that the officers gave no real consideration to the question whether individual documents might be required as evidence, the Revenue asserting that they had detailed instructions what to look for and seize and that these were complied with. I shall not further analyse this issue which was fully and *j* satisfactorily treated by the Divisional Court, for I am satisfied that, even if, which I doubt, there might have been enough evidence to justify the granting of interlocutory relief, this fell very far short of supporting a final declaration. I believe that the Court of

---

1   [1951] AC 66

Appeal was itself really of this opinion. The final declaration granted must clearly be set
a aside.
Two remarks in conclusion. First, I would wish to make it clear that the failure of the
respondents at this stage is not necessarily the end of the matter. They can proceed with
an action against the Revenue for, in effect, excess of power and for trespass and any
aggravation can be taken into account. At some stage, which cannot be particularised
now with precision but which broadly would be when criminal proceedings are over, or,
b within a reasonable time, are not taken, the immunity which exists at the stage of initial
investigation will lapse. Then the Revenue will have to make good and specify the
existence and cause of their belief that things removed might be required as evidence for
the purpose of 'tax fraud' proceedings and the issue will be tried in a normal manner.
Secondly, I must express reservations as to the suggestion that the law ought to be
changed so as to allow interim declarations to be granted. As regards persons other than
c the Crown, I see no need for this head of relief, given the power to grant interim
injunctions. As regards the Crown I can see that there may be formidable objections
against allowing, on incomplete evidence, a form of relief which, in effect, may have
much the same effect as an injunction. As I have already commented in another context,
sensible limits have to be set on the courts' powers of judicial review of administrative
action; these I think, as at present advised, are satisfactorily set by the law as it stands.
d The appeals must be allowed and the judgment and orders of the Court of Appeal set
aside.

VISCOUNT DILHORNE. My Lords, on 12th July 1979 the Common Serjeant at the
instance of the Crown issued four warrants under s 20c of the Taxes Management Act
1970, as amended, authorising the search of four premises named in the warrants by the
e appellant Mr Raymond Quinlan, a senior inspector of taxes, and other persons named in
each warrant. The four premises were the homes of Mr Ronald Arthur Plummer,
managing director of Rossminster Ltd, and of Mr Roy Clifford Turner, and the offices of
Rossminster Ltd at 1 Hanover Square, London W1 and the adjoining offices of AJR
Financial Services Ltd at 19–24 St George Street. Each warrant was in similar form.
That in relation to Rossminster's offices authorised their search by Mr Quinlan and 63
f other officers of the Inland Revenue.
The next day, 13th July at 7 am, named officers of the Inland Revenue accompanied
by police officers came to Mr Plummer's and Mr Tucker's homes to execute the search
warrants relating to those premises. At the same time other officers of the Inland
Revenue accompanied by police officers went to Rossminster's offices and those of AJR
Financial Services. There they waited until an employee arrived to let them in, but at Mr
g Plummer's and Mr Tucker's homes they demanded admittance at 7 am.
The Revenue sought to justify this early visit on the ground that they wanted to get
to these homes while someone was at home so as to avoid having to force an entry. This
does not appear to me to be a good ground for arriving at that time. If they had come
a little later, they might have caused less disturbance and distress and still have found
someone at home. It cannot, however, be said that they acted illegally by demanding
h entry at that time for a warrant issued under s 20c authorises entry 'at any time', even in
the middle of the night. If this section is revised, consideration might be given to
restricting the time within which such a search warrant can be executed, as is done by
some other Acts.
The search and seizure of documents and things in the offices of Rossminster and AJR
Financial Services continued throughout the day but came to an end that evening on it
j being learnt that at the instance of Mr Plummer, Mr Tucker, Rossminster and AJR
Financial Services, Walton J had granted an injunction against the appellants. In view of
the terms of s 21 of the Crown Proceedings Act 1947, this injunction should not have
been granted.
On 16th July the respondents issued a writ in the Chancery Division against the
appellants claiming damages for wrongful interference with their goods, an injunction

and delivery up of anything removed by an officer of the Inland Revenue in respect of
which that officer had not reasonable cause for belief that it might be required as *a*
evidence for the purpose of proceedings in respect of an offence involving fraud in
connection with or in relation to tax.

On 17th July the respondents obtained the leave of the Divisional Court to move that
court for an order of mandamus, an injunction and a declaration that the appellants were
not entitled to remove and were bound to deliver up all documents and other things in
respect of which there was no reasonable cause for belief that they might be required as *b*
evidence in such proceedings.

That motion was heard by the Divisional Court (Eveleigh LJ, Park and Woolf JJ) on 1st
August and dismissed. The respondents' appeal from that decision was allowed by the
Court of Appeal (Lord Denning MR, Browne and Goff LJJ) on 16th August. That court
made orders of certiorari quashing the search warrants and granted a declaration, not to
take effect until the appeal to this House had been heard or abandoned, that Mr Quinlan *c*
and the other officers of the Inland Revenue were not entitled to remove the documents
and other things taken from the premises searched and ought to deliver them up and to
destroy all copies, all extracts and notes etc they had made.

The warrant authorising the search of Rossminster's offices was in the following
terms:

'IN THE CENTRAL CRIMINAL COURT. SEARCH WARRANT. TO: RAYMOND QUINLAN *d*
AND TO THE PERSONS NAMED IN THE FIRST SCHEDULE ANNEXED TO THIS WARRANT Officers
of the Board of Inland Revenue

'INFORMATION on oath having been laid this day by Raymond Quinlan in
accordance with the provisions of Section 20C of the Taxes Management Act 1970
stating that there is reasonable ground for suspecting that an offence involving
fraud in connection with or in relation to tax has been committed and that evidence *e*
of it is to be found on the premises described in the second schedule annexed hereto.

'YOU ARE HEREBY AUTHORISED to enter those premises, together with all or any of
the officers of the Board of Inland Revenue named in the first schedule hereto and
together with such constables as you may require, if necessary by force, at any time
within 14 days from the time of issue of this Warrant, and search them; and on
entering those premises with this Warrant you may seize and remove any things *f*
whatsoever found there which you have reasonable cause to believe may be required
as evidence for the purposes of proceedings in respect of such an offence.

'DATED THIS 12th DAY OF JULY 1979 [signed by the circuit judge].

'THE FIRST SCHEDULE [63 names]

'THE SECOND SCHEDULE 1 Hanover Square London W1R 9RD

'DATED 12th July 1979 [signed by the circuit judge].' *g*

Section 20C(1) and (2) reads as follows:

'(1) If the appropriate judicial authority is satisfied on information on oath given
by an officer of the Board that—(a) there is reasonable ground for suspecting that an
offence involving any form of fraud in connection with, or in relation to, tax has
been committed and that evidence of it is to be found on premises specified in the
information; and (b) in applying under this section, the officer acts with the approval *h*
of the Board given in relation to the particular case, the authority may issue a
warrant in writing authorising an officer of the Board to enter the premises, if
necessary by force, at any time within 14 days from the time of issue of the warrant,
and search them.

'(2) Section 4A of the Inland Revenue Regulation Act 1890 (Board's functions to *i*
be exercisable by an officer acting under their authority) does not apply to the
giving of Board approval under this section.'

Section 20D provides that a circuit judge is the appropriate judicial authority in
England and Wales for the purposes of s 20C, a section which is free from any kind of
ambiguity and in my opinion a model of clarity.

If the terms of this section are reconsidered by Parliament, it might be thought
_a_ desirable to replace a circuit judge by a High Court judge as the appropriate judicial
authority. The power given by s 20C to seize and remove other person's property and the
fact that tax frauds more often than not are of great complexity suggest that it should be
the responsibility of a High Court judge to satisfy himself of the matters specified in sub-
s (1)(a) and (b). In saying that I do not wish to cast any reflection on the Common
Serjeant. As the requirement that a judge should be so satisfied is the final safeguard
_b_ against abuse of the powers given by the section, it might be preferable to place the
responsibility for their exercise on a more senior judge.

The Act does not prescribe that such a warrant must be in any particular form. It does
not say that it must state that requirements for its issue have been complied with. If the
warrants in this case had omitted their first paragraphs and, after stating to whom the
warrants were addressed, had just stated that the persons named in it were authorised to
_c_ enter and to search the premises named, I can see no ground on which their validity
could have been successfully challenged.

These warrants, however, no doubt with the intention of showing that the
requirements for their issue had been complied with, said that information on oath had
been laid in accordance with the provisions of s 20C 'stating that there is reasonable
ground for suspecting that an offence involving fraud' had been committed and that
_d_ evidence of it was to be found on the premises named.

It cannot in my view be emphasised too strongly that the section requires that the
appropriate judicial authority should himself be satisfied of these matters and that it does
not suffice for the person laying the information to say that he is.

Does the fact that the warrants did not state that the Common Serjeant had satisfied
himself of these matters lead to the conclusion that the warrants were in law invalid?
_e_ That in my opinion would be so if the omission meant that he had not done so.
Applications for the issue of warrants under this section cannot, I think, be so very
frequent that circuit judges are familiar with the terms of the section. I do not doubt
that before issuing these warrants authorising such extensive searches the Common
Serjeant would have looked at the section. If he did, he must have realised that he had
to be satisfied and that he was not empowered to act on another person being satisfied.
_f_ The warrants were not, I expect, drawn up by him and when he signed them, it is much
more likely that he failed to notice the omission than that he failed to discharge the duty
laid on him. I see no grounds whatsoever for assuming or inferring that the Common
Serjeant misconstrued the section. If he thought, and there is no ground for thinking
that he did, that he was entitled to authorise the issue of the warrants merely in reliance
on Mr Quinlan stating on oath that there was reasonable ground for the Board's
_g_ suspicions, then indeed he would be blameworthy having regard to the clear language of
the section.

Although it is not made necessary by the section, I think that it is most desirable that
a warrant issued under this section should make it clear that the statutory conditions
precedent to the issue of a valid warrant have been complied with, and also that the
warrant should state accurately what it authorises to be done.

_h_ The issue of a warrant only authorises entry and search. It does not authorise seizure
and removal of anything. The power to seize and remove is given by s 20C(3) which is
in the following terms:

> 'On entering the premises with a warrant under this section, the officer may seize
> and remove any things whatsoever found there which he has reasonable cause to
> believe may be required as evidence for the purposes of proceedings in respect of
_j_ > such an offence as is mentioned in subsection (1) above . . .'

Anyone reading the warrants issued in this case might reasonably conclude that the
warrants themselves authorised seizure and removal. If that were the case, then it might
lend some force to the contention that the warrants should give some indication of the
nature of the things which might be seized and removed. Strictly I see no need for the

warrant to refer at all to the power to seize and remove but if it is thought desirable to do so, then it should be stated that the power of seizure and removal is exercisable by *a* virtue of this subsection.

The respondents contend that the warrants should have given some indication of what was being searched for. To be valid, they say, the warrants should have specified or sufficiently identified the nature of the offence or offences suspected. They say that the information contained in the warrants was not specific enough to enable the officers of the Board, the owners of the documents and the respondents to know what the officers *b* were authorised to search for, seize and remove or to enable a court to determine whether the officers had had belief and reasonable cause to believe that a document might be required as evidence.

These contentions found favour in the Court of Appeal, Lord Denning MR[1] saying that to be valid, a warrant must specify the offence suspected and that 'the seizure is limited to those things authorised by the warrant'. Browne LJ[2] held that a warrant must *c* specify at least the general nature of the offence or offences suspected and Goff LJ[3] that to be valid it must state on its face 'that it relates to all or to some one or more' of the criminal offences to which a tax fraud could give rise.

My Lords, I do not find myself able to agree. The section does not require the warrant to state what criminal offence or offences are suspected. Officers of the Board when making their searches and deciding what to seize, act in accordance with the instructions *d* they have received and do not rely on the terms of the warrant for guidance. The warrant does not authorise seizure or say what may be seized. It is sub-s (3) that does that. Tax frauds may take many forms and lead to a variety of criminal charges. If the Court of Appeal is right, it means that, before any evidence secured by the search has been considered and when the circuit judge has only to be satisfied that there is reasonable ground for suspecting the commission of 'an' offence involving a tax fraud, for the *e* warrant the section then authorises him to issue to be valid, it must specify the offence or offences suspected.

My Lords, I do not think that these contentions of the respondents and the conclusions of the Court of Appeal on this are right. A warrant issued under the section will be invalid if the provisions of the section are not complied with or if there is some rule of law independent of the section that requires the particular offence or offences to be *f* stated. These warrants did comply with the section, and I know of no rule of law that requires that. In the course of the argument reference was made to general warrants. Lord Denning MR also referred to them. In my view the old well-known cases on general warrants really have no reference to this case. Here the warrants were not general. They authorised named persons to enter named premises and to search them. On entry with such a warrant, their power of seizure and removal was limited by, *g* controlled by and authorised by sub-s (3). It may be that there are many persons who think that in 1976 too wide a power was given to the Revenue. If it was, and I express no opinion on that, it must be left to Parliament to narrow the power it gave. That, in my view, cannot be done by judicial interpretation when the language of the enactment is clear and does not warrant it and when that cannot be done in accordance with any rule of law. *h*

For these reasons in my opinion the warrants were not invalid and should not have been held to be.

The respondents also contended that the way in which the search was conducted showed that the officers searching could not reasonably have formed the belief in respect of many of the document seized that they might be required as evidence in criminal proceedings. Affidavits were sworn by Mr Plummer, Mr Tucker and others to establish *j*

---

1   [1979] 3 All ER 385 at 403
2   [1979] 3 All ER 385 at 405
3   [1979] 3 All ER 385 at 408

this and affidavits were filed in reply by a number of officers of the Inland Revenue. It
a would not serve any useful purpose to summarise the contents of these affidavits. It
suffices to say that there was a conflict of evidence on a number of matters and that the
main contention of the respondents was that the times of seizure of the various
documents and files shown on lists prepared by the Revenue's officers showed that a great
many of them could not possibly have been examined before seizure, and in the absence
of examination there could not have been any reasonable belief that they might be
b required as evidence.

A great many documents were seized and removed. Many officers were employed in
the operation. Lists were made up of what was seized and the time of seizure recorded.
A short interval of time between two entries on a list would be a strong indication that
there could not have been a proper examination, if one officer dealt with the documents
referred to in those two entries, but with a number of officers searching and examining
c documents, the times of seizure do not in my opinion provide the slightest indication of
whether or not before seizure there was examination. The time necessary to form a view
whether a file or a document might be required as evidence would vary. If the fraud
suspected involved inter-company transactions between a large number of companies, it
would not take up much time to decide that a file relating to one of the companies might
reasonably be believed as likely to contain material which might be required as evidence;
d and such a conclusion might properly be reached without looking at every document in
the file.

The respondents satisfied the Court of Appeal that the seizure and removal were
unlawful. When taking so many documents as were taken in this case, mistakes may
occur and some documents may be taken that should not have been. But the fact that
they should not have been does not, in my opinion, justify the conclusion that the other
e documents taken were not taken after adequate examination and in the belief that they
might be required in evidence. Omnia praesumuntur rite esse acta. If the respondents
claimed the entry into their premises was a trespass, they would be met with the answer
that the warrants made the entry legal. If they assert that, following a lawful entry,
documents and things were seized and removed when there was no right to take them,
the onus, in my opinion, lies on them to establish a prima facie case of that and that, in
f my opinion, they have not done.

In these proceedings for a judicial review the Court of Appeal made a final declaration
that the appellants should deliver up all they had taken. No injunction can be granted
against the Crown but one would expect the Crown to comply with any declaration
made. No interim declaration can be made and, while I do not wish to express an
opinion on the point, I doubt very much whether it would be advisable that the courts
g should have power to grant one affecting the Crown which would have much the same
effect as an interim injunction.

The Court of Appeal, not having power to make an interim declaration, made a final
one. While I would not go so far as to say that there can never be a case where on a
judicial review a final declaration against the Crown can properly be made, such a case
should, I think, be very exceptional. Such a declaration should not be made unless there
h is no dispute as to the material facts, which is not the case here, or unless the dispute as
to the facts has been determined after something in the nature of a trial, which again did
not happen here.

In my opinion no final declaration should have been made.

One does not know the nature of the tax fraud, the commission of which the Common
Serjeant was satisfied there were reasonable grounds to suspect. It may have been, one
j does not know, a tax fraud of great magnitude, involving a number of persons and a lot
of money. The purpose of the warrants was to enable entry to be made onto premises
where it was thought evidence of the fraud might be found.

The effect of the Court of Appeal's order was to prevent evidence which might be
required for a criminal prosecution being secured.

If this appeal is allowed, it will not prevent the respondents continuing their action for

damages for the wrongful seizure of documents, though if there is a prosecution, it may
well be desirable that that action should not be tried until after the conclusion of the   *a*
criminal case.

In my opinion, for the reasons I have stated, this appeal should be allowed.

LORD DIPLOCK. My Lords, all the events with which this appeal is concerned took
place in the course of an investigation by officers of the Board of Inland Revenue into
suspected criminal offences. Two competing public interests are involved: that offences   *b*
involving tax frauds should be detected and punished, and that the right of the individual
to the protection of the law from unjustified interference with his use and enjoyment of
his private property should be upheld. What underlies the questions of law which this
House must now determine is how those two competing, and at times conflicting, public
interests can be reconciled under the new procedure for judicial review for which RSC
Ord 53 now provides.   *c*

Three questions of law are raised in this appeal. The first is how much information
must be disclosed on the face of a search warrant issued by a circuit judge under s 20C(1)
of the Taxes Management Act 1970; the second is whether on an application for judicial
review of acts of an officer of the Board of Inland Revenue in seizing and removing
documents under s 20C(3) any onus lies on the applicant to show that the officer did not
have reasonable grounds for believing that the documents seized might be required as   *d*
evidence for the purpose of such proceedings as are referred to in that subsection; and the
third is whether if there is an unresolved conflict of affidavit evidence of relevant fact it
is nevertheless a proper exercise of judicial discretion to make a final declaration in
favour of the applicant.

                                                                                             e
The validity of the warrant

What has to be disclosed on the face of the search warrant depends on the true
construction of the statute. The construing court ought, no doubt, to remind itself, if
reminder should be necessary, that entering a man's house or office, searching it and
seizing his goods against his will are tortious acts against which he is entitled to the
protection of the court unless the acts can be justified either at common law or under   *f*
some statutory authority. So, if the statutory words relied on as authorising the acts are
ambiguous or obscure, a construction should be placed on them that is least restrictive of
individual rights which would otherwise enjoy the protection of the common law. But
judges, in performing their constitutional function of expounding what words used by
parliament in legislation mean, must not be over-zealous to search for ambiguities or
obscurities in words which on the face of them are plain, simply because the members   *g*
of the court are out of sympathy with the policy to which the Act appears to give effect.

My Lords, it does not seem to me that in construing s 20C of the Taxes Management
Act 1970 any assistance is to be gained from a consideration of those mid-18th century
cases centring on John Wilkes and culminating in *Entick v Carrington*[1], which established
the illegality of 'general warrants' and were cited by Lord Denning MR in his judgment
in the instant case. *R v Wilkes*[2] was not concerned with a warrant for arrest and seizure   *h*
of documents but with a warrant of commitment to the Tower of London of John
Wilkes by name and was decided on a point of parliamentary privilege from arrest
alone. *Huckle v Money*[3] was a case reported on the question of the right of the Court of
Common Pleas to order a new trial on the ground that excessive damages had been
awarded by a jury. It was an action for false imprisonment brought by a journeyman
printer who apparently had played no part in printing the famous issue No 45 of 'The   *j*

---

1 (1765) 2 Wils 275, 95 ER 807
2 (1763) 2 Wils 151, 95 ER 737
3 (1763) 2 Wils 205, 95 ER 768

North Briton' but had been arrested under a warrant issued by a Secretary of State
a authorising a King's messenger to arrest the authors, printers and publishers of that issue
(without naming or identifying any of them), to seize all their papers and to bring them
before the Secretary of State to be examined by him. Pratt CJ referred to the fact that in
this particular case the warrant did not name the persons to be arrested under it as a
matter which might be taken into account in aggravation of damages; but as was
ultimately held in *Entick v Carrington*[1] the invalidity of warrants of this kind did not
b depend on the absence of the name of the person to be arrested, for Entick was so
named. Their invalidity was more fundamental: a Secretary of State, it was held, did not
have any power at common law or under the prerogative to order the arrest of any
citizen or the seizure of any of his property for the purpose of discovering whether he
was guilty of publishing a seditious libel.

In the instant case the search warrant did not purport to be issued by the circuit judge
c under any common law or prerogative power but pursuant to s 20c(1) of the Taxes
Management Act 1970 alone. That subsection makes it a condition precedent to the
issue of the warrant that the circuit judge should himself be satisfied by information on
oath that facts exist which constitute reasonable ground for suspecting that an offence
involving some form of fraud in connection with or in relation to tax has been
committed, and also for suspecting that evidence of the offence is to be found on the
d premises in respect of which the warrant to search is sought. It is not, in my view, open
to your Lordships to approach the instant case on the assumption that the Common
Serjeant did not satisfy himself on both these matters, or to imagine circumstances which
might have led him to commit so grave a dereliction of his judicial duties. The
presumption is that he acted lawfully and properly; and it is only fair to him to say that,
in my view, there is nothing in the evidence before your Lordships to suggest the
e contrary; nor, indeed, have the respondents themselves so contended.

All that the subsection expressly requires shall be specified in the warrant are the
address of the premises to be searched and the name of the officer or officers of the Board
who are authorised to search them. The premises need not be in the occupation of the
person suspected of the offence; they may be premises of some wholly innocent custodian
or third party. The matter is still at the investigatory stage; good grounds must exist for
f suspecting that a tax fraud has been committed, but as yet there is not sufficient evidence
in a form admissible at a criminal trial to prove it. The sole purpose of the search is to
obtain such evidence.

Even though the statute may not strictly so require (a matter on which I express no
concluded opinion) the warrant in my view ought to state on its face the statutory
authority under which it has been issued. This the form of warrant issued in the instant
g case does, though I agree with my noble and learned friend, Viscount Dilhorne, that the
wording of the recital of the fulfilment of the two statutory conditions precedent to its
issue might be improved. But for the reference to s 20c in accordance with whose
provisions the information is stated to have been laid, the wording of the warrant would
be consistent with its meaning that the information had not specified for consideration
by the judge the grounds of suspicion on which the informant relied; but the express
h reference to the section, in my view, resolves any ambiguity and makes untenable the
suggestion that the preamble to the warrant constitutes an admission by the judge that
he had adopted blindly a statement of the informant that there existed some reasonable
grounds for suspicion the nature of which, however, was not disclosed. This was not a
contention that the respondents were willing to advance. The warrant, in my view,
ought also to state what are the things found on the premises that the searching officers
j are entitled to seize and to remove, ie potential evidence of a particular category of
offences. This the form of warrant in the instant case also does by reproducing the terms
of s 20c(3).

---

1   (1765) 2 Wils 275, 95 ER 807

Ought it to disclose more in order to be a valid warrant under the section? It was submitted on behalf of the respondents that it was defective in three respects. First, it *a* was said, it ought to identify the suspected offender, secondly, it ought to specify which one or more of the six or more species of offences which fall within the genus 'an offence involving any form of fraud in connection with, or in relation to, tax' the suspect is suspected of having committed, and, thirdly, it ought to state the date of any offences of which he is suspected.

My Lords, if the subsection does indeed require that any of this additional information *b* should be disclosed on the face of the warrant, this must be by necessary implication only. There is no express requirement; and for my part I cannot see that any such implication is justified. The information would not protect the innocent; it might well assist the guilty to destroy or to remove beyond the jurisdiction of the court of trial the documentary evidence of their tax frauds. Tax frauds generally involve the use of confederates, whether ignorant of or parties to the fraud. To identify a suspect where the *c* search extends to premises that are not in his personal occupation is to alert him to the suspicions of the Revenue, and if they are well founded it may be give him an opportunity of covering his tracks; while if the suspicions ultimately turn out to be groundless his reputation with those whose premises have been searched will be unnecessarily besmirched. It is to be observed that the form of warrant at common law to search premises for stolen goods does not state who is alleged to have been the thief. *d* As regards more detailed specification in the warrant of the offence of which the circuit judge was satisfied that there were reasonable grounds for suspecting had been committed this would not help the person whose premises were searched to know what documents were liable to be seized, since the right of seizure under sub-s (3) is not limited to documents that may be required as evidence in proceedings for that offence alone but, on the true construction of the subsection, extends to documents that may be required as *e* evidence in proceedings for any other offence that falls within the genus of offences 'involving any kind of fraud in connection with, or in relation to, tax'. This, as it seems to me, is the plain meaning of the words 'such an offence as is mentioned in subsection (1) above'. Nor do I find it surprising that Parliament should grant a power of search under the warrant wider in its scope than those things which it was already suspected would be found on the premises when the warrant was issued. Even at common law as *f* it had developed by the time the Act was passed a warrant to search premises for stolen goods particularised in the warrant justified seizure of other goods found on the premises at the time the warrant was executed if there were reasonable grounds for believing that those other goods were stolen (*Chic Fashions (West Wales) Ltd v Jones*[1]).

In agreement with the Divisional Court I would accordingly uphold the sufficiency and validity of the search warrant. *g*

The onus of proof on an application for judicial review

With the issue of the warrant the functions and responsibilities of the circuit judge come to an end. The power of the officer of the Board to seize and remove things that he finds on the premises which the warrant authorises him to enter and search is *h* conferred directly on him by sub-s (3) which limits his powers of seizure and removal to things 'which he has reasonable cause to believe may be required as evidence for the purposes of proceedings' for an offence involving a tax fraud. These words appearing in a statute do not make conclusive the officer's own honest opinion that he has reasonable cause for the prescribed belief. The grounds on which the officer acted must be sufficient to induce in a reasonable person the required belief before he can validly seize and *j* remove anything under the subsection. This was affirmed in *Nakkuda Ali v M F de S*

---

1   [1968] 1 All ER 229, [1968] 2 QB 299

Jayaratne[1], a decision of the Privy Council in which Lord Radcliffe writing for the Board
a expressed the view that the majority speeches in *Liversidge v Anderson*[2], in which a
contrary construction had been placed on similar words in the wartime emergency
regulations, the Defence (General) Regulations 1939, reg 18B, should be regarded as an
authority for the meaning of that phrase in that particular regulation alone. For my part
I think the time has come to acknowledge openly that the majority of this House in
Liversidge v Anderson[2] were expediently and, at that time, perhaps, excusably, wrong and
b the dissenting speech of Lord Atkin was right.

I would also accept that, since the act of handling a man's goods without his permission
is prima facie tortious, at the trial of a civil action for trespass to goods based on the
seizure and removal of things by an officer of the Board in purported exercise of his
powers under the subsection the onus would be on the officer to satisfy the court that
there did in fact exist reasonable grounds that were known to him for believing that the
c documents he removed might be required as evidence in proceedings for some offence
involving a tax fraud, not that they *would* be so required, for that the seizing officer could
not know, but that they *might* be required if sufficient admissible evidence were
ultimately forthcoming to support a prosecution for the offence and it were decided to
prosecute. But although this onus would lie on the officer at the trial there remains the
question: at what stage in the civil action is the officer bound to disclose the grounds of
d his belief? It is at this point that the problem is reached of reconciling the two competing
and conflicting public interests which I mentioned at the outset that offences involving
tax frauds should be detected and punished, and that the right of the individual to the
protection of the law from unjustified interference with his private property should be
upheld.

What is required for the protection of the former public interest was stated by Lord
e Reid in that part of his speech in *Conway v Rimmer*[3] which dealt with public interest
immunity from discovery in civil actions of documents and information in the hands of
the police. What he said appears to me to apply with equal force to the Board of Inland
Revenue as to the police and to those who perpetrate tax frauds as it does to those who
organise other criminal activities:

f   'The police are carrying on an unending war with criminals many of whom are
today highly intelligent. So it is essential that there should be no disclosure of
anything which might give any useful information to those who organise criminal
activities; and it would generally be wrong to require disclosure in a civil case of
anything which might be material in a pending prosecution, but after a verdict has
been given, or it has been decided to take no proceedings, there is not the same need
g   for secrecy.'

The public interest in immunity from disclosure of the grounds of the officer's belief
that a document that he seized may be required as evidence in a future prosecution for
an offence involving a tax fraud is thus, in general, temporary in its nature, except as
regards identity of informants (cf *D v National Society for the Prevention of Cruelty to
h Children*[4]) and possibly new and unusual methods of investigation used by the Inland
Revenue. This, as it seems to me, provides an obvious method of reconciling the two
conflicting public interests where an ordinary civil action is involved. If there is to be a
criminal prosecution it is, in my view, clearly in the public interest in the proper
administration of justice, both criminal and civil, that the civil action should not proceed
to trial until the criminal trial is over; so discovery, whether of documents or by

j

1   [1951] AC 66
2   [1941] 3 All ER 338, [1942] AC 206
3   [1968] 1 All ER 874 at 889, [1968] AC 910 at 953–954
4   [1977] 1 All ER 589, [1978] AC 171

interrogatories, directed to eliciting the factual grounds for the officer's belief can be deferred at least until the Inland Revenue have had a reasonable time to complete their *a* investigations into suspected tax frauds and to decide whether to bring criminal proceedings at all and, if so, for what offences. If they decide to bring proceedings the public interest immunity would continue to apply until the conclusion of the criminal trial; if they decide not to bring any criminal proceedings the public interest immunity would come to an end with that decision. The court in the civil action could and should be vigilant to see that the Inland Revenue proceeded with their investigations with *b* reasonable dispatch and reached their decision whether to prosecute or not without unreasonable delay. If this were not done the court could properly hold continuation of the immunity to be no longer justified in the public interest, and allow discovery to go ahead.

In cases where those claiming a public interest immunity against premature disclosure of information relating to criminal investigations or pending prosecutions are not (unlike *c* the appellants in the instant case) protected against injunctive relief by s 21 of the Crown Proceedings Act 1947, the immunity would, in my view, extend to applications for an interlocutory mandatory order for return of the documents seized. Despite the fact that when the action came to be tried the onus would lie on the defendant to show that there existed reasonable grounds for his belief that they might be required as evidence in criminal proceedings, the court should not require him to disclose the grounds of his *d* belief in opposition to the claim for interlocutory relief, but should be satisfied with his statement on affidavit that he had reasonable grounds for his belief, unless the other evidence on the application was strong enough to justify the inference that no reasonable person could have thought so. It is to be borne in mind that if at the trial it should turn out that the defendant was unable to satisfy the onus of proving that reasonable grounds did in fact exist the plaintiff has the advantage that the action falls into one of those *e* exceptional categories in which punitive damages may still be awarded (*Rookes v Barnard*[1] and *Cassell & Co Ltd v Broome*[2]).

In the same way, it would not in my view be open to a person claiming to have been injured by the purported but unlawful exercise by a public officer of statutory powers to circumvent the public interest immunity against premature disclosure of the grounds on which the officer's exercise of the power was based by applying under RSC Ord 53 for *f* judicial review instead of bringing a civil action. RSC Ord 53 amends and simplifies the procedure for obtaining on a single application the kind of relief that was formerly obtainable only in an ordinary civil action against a public officer or authority and the kind of relief that was formerly obtainable only on an application for a prerogative order of mandamus, prohibition or certiorari; but it does not alter the differing roles played by the court in applications for these two categories of relief. *g*

Seizure of documents by an officer of the Board under s 20c(3) involves a decision by the officer as to what documents he may seize. The subsection prescribes what the state of mind of the officer must be in order to make it lawful for him to decide to seize a document: he must believe that the document may be required as evidence in criminal proceedings for some form of tax fraud and that belief must be based on reasonable grounds. The decision-making power is conferred by the statute on the officer of the *h* Board. He is not required to give any reasons for his decision and the public interest immunity provides justification for any refusal to do so. Since he does not disclose his reasons there can be no question of setting aside his decision for error of law on the face of the record and the only ground on which it can be attacked on judicial review is that it was ultra vires because a condition precedent to his forming the belief which the statute prescribes, viz that it should be based on reasonable grounds, was not satisfied. *j*

Where Parliament has designated a public officer as decision-maker for a particular class

1   [1964] 1 All ER 367, [1964] AC 1129
2   [1972] 1 All ER 801, [1972] AC 1027

of decisions the High Court, acting as a reviewing court under RSC Ord 53, is not a court
a of appeal. It must proceed on the presumption omnia praesumuntur rite esse acta until
that presumption can be displaced by the applicant for review, on whom the onus lies of
doing so. Since no reasons have been given by the decision-maker and no unfavourable
inference can be drawn for this fact because there is obvious justification for his failure
to do so, the presumption that he acted intra vires can only be displaced by evidence of
facts which cannot be reconciled with there having been reasonable cause for his belief
b that the documents might be required as evidence or alternatively which cannot be
reconciled with his having held such belief at all.

I agree with my noble and learned friend, Viscount Dilhorne, that the evidence filed
on behalf of the applicants in the instant case, the respondents in this House, would have
fallen short of that even if there had been no affidavits in answer filed on behalf of the
Board to throw a different light on the matter. So I would hold, as the Divisional Court
c did, that the respondents have failed to establish on their application for judicial review
that the officers of the Board acted ultra vires or otherwise unlawfully in seizing any of
the documents that they seized.

The final declaration
There was a clear conflict of affidavit evidence of relevant facts before the Court of
d Appeal as to the time spent by officers in examining individual documents and files
before deciding to seize them. The respondents contend the time spent on examining
at any rate some of the documents seized was too short to enable the officer concerned to
consider whether or not there was reasonable cause to believe that the document might
be required as evidence in criminal proceedings; the appellants deny this. Clearly there
are issues of fact to be resolved which cannot with justice be disposed of on the existing
e affidavit evidence.

The Court of Appeal were of opinion, which I do not share, that on the affidavit
evidence before them the respondents had made out a prima facie case that all the
documents had been seized unlawfully, and ought to be delivered up to the
respondents. But for the fact that the appellants were officers of the Crown against
whom there was no jurisdiction to grant injunctive relief, it would appear that the Court
f of Appeal would have thought it appropriate to grant an interlocutory injunction only,
leaving the question of whether the respondents were entitled to a final injunction to be
decided on full oral evidence at the trial. However, s 21 of the Crown Proceedings Act
1947 permits only a declaration of the rights of the parties in lieu of an injunction against
officers of the Crown and it has been held, in my continued view correctly, that this does
not empower the court to grant interlocutory declarations which would be a contradiction
g in terms (*International General Electric Co of New York Ltd v Customs and Excise Comrs*[1]).
Faced with this dilemma the Court of Appeal made a final declaration instead.

In so far as this declaration was based on the quashing of the search warrant only it may
be that a final declaration was appropriate, though I express no concluded view on that;
but, in so far as it was based in the alternative on the court's prima facie view only,
formed on conflicting affidavit evidence, that even if the warrant were valid the actual
h seizure of documents by the officers of the Board was unlawful, it was, in my view,
clearly wrong to make a final declaration which would have the effect of making this
hotly disputed issue res judicata between the parties without any proper trial.

My Lords, this serves once again to draw attention to what, for my part, I regard as a
serious procedural defect in the English system of administrative law: it provides no
means of obtaining interlocutory relief against the Crown and its officers. The useful
j reforms effected by the amendment to the rules of court by substituting the new Ord 53
for the old system of prerogative orders, could not overcome this procedural defect,
which would require primary legislation. Such legislation has been recommended in

---

1   [1962] 2 All ER 398, [1962] Ch 784

the Report of the Law Commission[1] on which the revision of RSC Ord 53 was based. It is greatly to be hoped that the recommendation will not continue to fall on deaf parliamentary ears.

LORD SALMON. My Lords, it is very much in the public interest that anyone who commits an offence involving any form of fraud in relation to tax a very grave offence should be brought to justice. It is at least equally in the public interest that individual liberty should be protected by the judges who have the traditional right and duty to protect individuals from an abuse of power by the executive. Accordingly, at common law, it would be unlawful for any officer of the Inland Revenue or any member of the police to force his way into the home or business premises of any person and search for and seize any documents he might find there, even if he believed that there was reasonable ground for suspecting that an offence involving any form of fraud in relation to tax had been committed and that the documents seized might be required as evidence for the purpose of proceedings in respect of the offence which he suspected.

The uncontradicted evidence shows that in the early morning of Friday, 13th July 1979, (i) several officers of the Inland Revenue and a detective inspector entered 27 Radnor Place, London W2, the home of Mr R A Plummer, on a warrant (to which I shall refer later). Mr Plummer is a chartered accountant, a Fellow of the Institute of Taxation and the managing director of Rossminster Ltd. This company carries on business as a bank and is a member of the Rossminster group of companies. Virtually all the papers and documents which Mr Plummer's house contained were seized and removed. (ii) A large number of officers of the Inland Revenue and of the police entered the Rossminster bank on a warrant and took away van loads of documents leaving very few behind them. They remained in the premises all day and left them shortly after 6 pm. The banking business of Rossminster Ltd was carried on in a separate part of the premises at 1 Hanover Square, London W1. Other parts of those premises were occupied by other companies of the Rossminster group whose business it was to devise lawful schemes to enable clients lawfully to avoid tax. (iii) Much the same as occurred at 1 Hanover Square occurred at the premises of AJR Financial Services Ltd at 19–24, St George Street, London W1. AJR carries on the business of providing secretarial and accounting services to several hundred clients. The Rossminster group of companies is one of its best clients but otherwise has no connection with it. (iv) Much the same occurred at Mr R C Tucker's house as occurred at Mr Plummer's. Mr Tucker, who is a chartered accountant, has had a close business relationship with the Rossminster group of companies for some time. Recently, before 13th July, he left his own offices which he had occupied for seven years and moved into 1 Hanover Square for the time being.

The Inland Revenue was asked by or on behalf of everyone whose home or offices were searched and whose papers and documents were seized what offence was alleged to have been committed and by whom. The Inland Revenue refused to give any answer to either part of that question.

It seems to me to be obvious that the news of the events I have described must have spread like wildfire and been a calamity for those who experienced them. Their names must have been seriously tarnished and they have no doubt suffered serious financial loss. This must apply also to the Rossminster group of companies, in particular those companies in the group whose business was to devise lawful schemes for avoiding tax which would otherwise have been exigible from their clients. No sensible client would be likely to continue to employ anyone to draw up such a scheme for him if he contemplated that the scheme might land him in prison.

On Friday 13th July the bank had an issued share capital of £1,250,000, about one thousand customers with current accounts and more than £6,000,000 held for customers

---

1   Remedies in Administrative Law (1976) Law Com 73, Cmnd 6407

on deposit. On Monday 16th July there was a run on the bank; on that day, £1,956,695
a was withdrawn by customers and instructions given for the withdrawal of over £400,000
on the following day; these instructions were obeyed.

The bank had intended to apply to the Bank of England for an important licence
under the Banking Act 1979 and had been reporting quarterly to the Bank of England
on its financial position since its inception.

On the afternoon of Monday 16th July Mr Roper of the Bank of England telephoned
b a director of the bank enquiring about the circumstances surrounding the Inland
Revenue's seizure of the bank's documents on the previous Friday. The director
explained what had happened and Mr Roper informed him that it was unlikely that the
Bank of England would entertain any application for a licence until the situation with
the Inland Revenue had been clarified.

It is impossible at this stage to know when the prosecution (if there is to be a
c prosecution) will take place or, if there is to be no prosecution, when the Inland Revenue
will announce its decision. More than four months have already gone by and no decision
has been made, and none may be made for years. In the meantime, vast sums of money
may be lost as a result of the acts done by the Inland Revenue on 13th July; and the
persons concerned may be ruined. Moreover, I doubt whether these persons will ever be
able to recover the loss they will have suffered even if the search warrants are invalid.
d The Inland Revenue would no doubt put forward the defence to any proceedings
brought against them for damages for entering the premises concerned that they had
entered on the authority of a warrant permitting them to enter and issued on 12th July
by a circuit judge.

I express no concluded view whether the plaintiffs would be able to discharge the onus
of proof (which would undoubtedly be on them) of showing, maybe many years after
e 12th July 1979, (a) that on that date, there had been no reasonable ground for suspecting
that an offence involving any form of fraud in relation to tax had been committed and
(b) that the Inland Revenue had no reasonable cause to believe that the documents which
they seized and removed might be required in respect of an offence of the kind I have
mentioned.

Prior to 1976 I should have thought that the law afforded the Inland Revenue ample
f power to detect offences involving any form of fraud in relation to tax. Nevertheless
s 20C inserted into the Taxes Management Act 1970 by s 57 of the Finance Act 1976
greatly increased the Inland Revenue's pre-1976 powers by introducing what I regard as
an altogether unnecessary power which, in my view, dangerously encroaches on
individual liberty.

Section 20C, so far as relevant, reads as follows:

g
'(1) If the appropriate judicial authority is satisfied on information on oath given
by an officer of the Board that—(a) there is reasonable ground for suspecting that an
offence involving any form of fraud in connection with, or in relation to, tax has
been committed and that evidence of it is to be found on premises specified in the
information; and (b) in applying under this section, the officer acts with the approval
h of the Board given in relation to the particular case, the authority may issue a
warrant in writing authorising an officer of the Board to enter the premises, if
necessary by force, at any time within 14 days from the time of issue of the warrant,
and search them . . .

'(3) On entering the premises with a warrant under this section, the officer may
seize and remove any things whatsoever found there which he has reasonable cause
j to believe may be required as evidence for the purposes of proceedings in respect of
such an offence as is mentioned in subsection (1) above . . .'

However much the courts may deprecate an Act they must apply it. It is not possible
by torturing its language or by any other means to construe it so as to give it a meaning

which Parliament clearly did not intend it to bear. I am certain my noble and learned friend, Lord Denning MR, was not departing from that principle when he said[1]:   *a*

'Once great power is granted, there is a danger of it being abused. Rather than risk such abuse, it is . . . the duty of the courts so to construe the statute as to see that it encroaches as little as possible on the liberties of the people of England.'

I respectfully agree with this passage which I think is consistent with the view that the   *b*
courts should construe a statute which encroaches on liberty so that it encroaches on it no more than the statute allows, expressly or by necessary implication.

Section 20C says nothing more in express terms about the contents of a warrant than that the appropriate judicial authority 'may issue a warrant in writing authorising an officer of the Board to enter the premises, if necessary by force, at any time within 14 days from the time of issue of the warrant, and search them'.

It may be that a warrant is valid which says nothing more than that it authorises   *c*
officers of the Inland Revenue Board to enter the premises and search them. Such a warrant may be sufficient to state by implication that the important conditions in s 20C(1)(a) and (b) have been complied with. I express no concluded view on this topic because the warrants in the present case are very different in form from those that I have postulated. In my view, they show that s 20C(1)(a) was not complied with for reasons   *d*
which I shall presently explain.

To issue search warrants which are based on no more than suspicion can lead to disastrous results for persons who may be innocent of fraud. Suspicion can easily be aroused, and honestly aroused in some more easily than in others, without any reasonable ground to support it. Officers of the Inland Revenue Board are not immune from having such suspicions any more than many other highly respectable bodies of people.   *e*
That, I think, is why Parliament, certainly not as clearly as it should have done, laid down in 20C(1)(a) that if officers of the Board require search warrants, they must give evidence on oath, laying before a circuit judge the grounds for their suspicion, and that the duty of the judge must then be to consider the evidence and decide whether he (the judge) is satisfied that it establishes reasonable ground for the Board's suspicion. In a complicated case such as the present, it would probably take a long time for the judge, before reaching   *f*
his decison, to sift and weigh the evidence laid before him on oath.

In the present case the judge to whom the application for the warrants was made held the distinguished office of Common Serjeant at the Central Criminal Court. He, like all other circuit judges trying crime, particularly at the Old Bailey, is kept extremely busy. Issuing ordinary search warrants is not regarded as being a matter which takes up more than a few minutes. They are normally issued by justices of the peace.

We do not know whether the Common Serjeant was told anything in advance to   *g*
suggest that the application for the search warrants in the present case was likely to take a long time. It may well be that no papers had been submitted before the application and that all the Common Serjeant had been told was that the Board were going to apply to him for some search warrants under the Taxes Management Act 1970. I should be surprised if any copy of that Act is to be found in the Old Bailey's library.

Mr Raymond Quinlan, one of the Board's inspectors, represented the Board on the   *h*
application for the warrants. He probably handed the judge a copy of the Act. His affidavit, sworn in the present proceedings, shows that he had made a thorough investigation of the activities of the Rossminster group of companies and other persons and bodies with whom the group had special relationships. He informed the Common Serjeant on oath (as the warrant signed by the Common Serjeant shows) that he had   *j*
reasonable ground for suspecting that an offence involving fraud in relation to tax had been committed and that evidence establishing fraud might be found on the premises described later in Sch 2 annexed to the warrants. No one could blame the Common

---

1   [1979] 3 All ER 385 at 399

a Serjeant for thinking that Mr Quinlan's oath stating that there was reasonable ground for
the Board's suspicion was something on which he could and indeed should rely; and he
accordingly signed the search warrants. I would like to make it plain that, in my
respectful view, no blame of any kind can be attributed to the learned judge. Section 20c
is by no means as clear as it should be, and there is no reason to suppose that the judge had
had sufficient opportunity to study it at length before the application in the present case
was made.

b The section is, in my view, so drafted that if an officer of the Inland Revenue who had
made a long and careful investigation of the respondents' affairs, informed the judge on
oath that there was reasonable ground for suspecting that an offence or offences involving
fraud in relation to tax had been committed etc the judge might well make the mistake
of misconstruing the section as meaning that the information given on oath was
sufficient to satisfy him that there was reasonable ground for suspicion and to empower
c him to issue the warrants.

Each of the warrants read as follows:

'SEARCH WARRANT. TO: RAYMOND QUINLAN AND TO THE PERSONS NAMED IN THE
FIRST SCHEDULE ANNEXED TO THIS WARRANT Officers of the Board of Inland Revenue
'INFORMATION on oath having been laid this day by Raymond Quinlan in
d accordance with the provisions of Section 20c of the Taxes Management Act 1970
stating [emphasis mine] that there is reasonable ground for suspecting that an
offence involving fraud in connection with or in relation to tax has been committed
and that evidence of it is to be found on the premises described in the second
schedule annexed hereto.
'YOU ARE HEREBY AUTHORISED to enter those premises, together with all or any of
e the officers of the Board of Inland Revenue named in the first schedule hereto and
together with such constables as you may require, if necessary by force, at any time
within 14 days from the time of issue of this Warrant, and search them; and on
entering those premises with this Warrant you may seize and remove any things
whatsoever found there which you have reasonable cause to believe may be required
as evidence for the purposes of proceedings in respect of such an offence.
f 'DATED THIS 12th DAY OF JULY 1979 [signed by the circuit judge] . . . '

The first part of the warrant explains the grounds on which the warrant is issued. In
my view, this part of the warrant makes it plain that the warrant was issued on the faith
of the information on oath by Raymond Quinlan stating that there was reasonable
ground for suspecting etc. It follows therefore that s 20c(1)(a) was not complied with.
g If it had been, the first part of the warrant would have read quite differently, perhaps
somewhat as follows: 'Evidence on oath which establishes that there is reasonable ground
for suspecting etc having been laid before me this day by Raymond Quinlan, I am
satisfied in accordance with the provisions of s 20c of the Taxes Management Act 1970
that there is reasonable ground for suspecting etc . . . '

Section 20c makes a wide inroad into the citizen's basic human rights, the right to
h privacy in his own home and business premises and the right to keep what belongs to
him. It allows the Inland Revenue the power to force its way into a man's home or
offices and deprive him of his private papers and books. In my view, it provides only one
real safeguard against an abuse of power. That safeguard is not that the Inland Revenue
is satisfied that there is reasonable ground for suspecting that an offence involving fraud
in relation to tax has been committed, but that the judge who issues the search warrant
j is so satisfied after he has been told on oath by the Inland Revenue full details of the facts
which it has discovered. That is why I am inclined to the view that it is implicit in s 20c
that a search warrant signed by the judge should state that he is so satisfied, ie that the
warrant should always give the reason for its issue. In any event, I hope that in the future
the practice will always be that such warrants state plainly that the judge who signed
them is so satisfied.

I am, however, convinced that search warrants like the present are invalid because they recite as the reason for their issue only that an officer of the Inland Revenue has stated on *a* oath that there is reasonable ground for suspecting that an offence involving fraud in relation to tax has been committed. If the judge gives that as his reason for issuing a warrant, it seems to me to follow that his reason for issuing it cannot be that he is so satisfied by the information given to him on oath by an officer of the Inland Revenue of the detailed facts which the officer has ascertained, but that the judge's reason for issuing the warrant was because the officer had stated on oath that there is reasonable ground to *b* suspect etc. I am afraid that I do not agree that the warrants in the present case make it clear that they were issued by the judge pursuant to the powers conferred on him by s 20C. Indeed, for the reasons I have given, I consider that the exact contrary is made clear by these warrants.

It had never occurred to me before reading some of your Lordships' speeches that anyone could imagine that I was suggesting that this highly respected judge had acted *c* improperly and unfairly. I had hoped that I had made it crystal clear that I was suggesting no more than that, in my opinion, the judge had misconstrued a statutory provision (s 20C) whose meaning was not very clear, the sort of mistake which every judge, except perhaps the infallible, would agree that he has made at some time during his career. To make such a mistake surely cannot be regarded as improper or unfair, still less as a dereliction by the judge of his judicial duties. *d*

I think that the point that I have been making is covered by the following words in the notice pursuant to RSC Ord 53, r 6(3), dated 23rd July 1979:

'That the learned Judge erred in law . . . in issuing the said warrants in that he was not satisfied . . . that there was reasonable grounds for suspecting that any . . . person had at any . . . time done any . . . act such as to constitute an act involving fraud . . . in relation to tax.' *e*

This point, however, was not argued in the Divisional Court or in the Court of Appeal or in your Lordships' House, nor did it appear in the respondents' case. I did, however, put it to counsel for the appellants in the course of his argument.

I recognise, of course, that in any ordinary case between litigant and litigant the point could not be allowed to be relied on now. This, however, is by no means any ordinary *f* case. It is a case of great constitutional importance which can seriously affect individual liberty. The point which I have ventured to make, as I have already said, in my opinion affords the only real safeguard against an abuse of power by the Inland Revenue. I recognise that s 20C, not very clearly, indicates that a warrant is invalid if it shows on its face (as, in my opinion, each of the four relevant warrants does) that it was issued by the judge not because he was satisfied by any evidence of facts discovered by the Inland *g* Revenue and put before him on oath that there was reasonable ground for suspecting that an offence involving fraud relating to tax had been committed etc but because he was told on oath by an officer of the Inland Revenue that there was reasonable ground for suspecting that such an offence had been committed. In my view, the judge misconstrued s 20C by thinking that it laid down that what he had been told on oath by the officer of the Inland Revenue was sufficient to allow the warrants to be issued. *h*

I entirely agree with your Lordships for the reasons which you have given that the warrants cannot be successfully attacked on the ground that they do not sufficiently particularise the offences to which they refer; and that the well-known mid-18th century authorities on which the Court of Appeal relied lend no real support to the contrary view.

The genus of the offences specified in s 20C is specified in the warrants. There are six or more species of that genus. If the warrants were to set out these species in the *j* alternative to each other, as they might do, they could not help the persons whose homes or offices were entered and searched.

I agree for the reasons stated by my noble and learned friend, Viscount Dilhorne, that so long as s 20C remains on the statute book it is highly desirable that it should be amended so that the application for a warrant should be made to a High Court judge.

This is certainly not out of any disrespect for the circuit judges but because of the
a enormous powers conferred on the Inland Revenue under s 20c, the great harm it may
do to individual liberty and the ruin it may inflict on those on whom it is exercised,
however innocent they may be.

I also agree that having regard to the conflicting affidavit evidence, it was wrong to
hold that, even if the warrants were valid, the seizure of documents by the officers of the
Board was unlawful because their failure properly to examine the documents which they
b seized made it impossible for them to have reasonable cause to believe that the documents
might be required as evidence. Such an issue could only be properly decided by a judge
at an ordinary trial after he had seen the witnesses on each side examined and cross-
examined. This however is of no great importance since s 20c(3) empowers an officer
'on entering the premises with a warrant under this section' to seize and remove
documents which he has reasonable cause to believe might be required as evidence. The
c warrant referred to in sub-s (3) must, in my view, be a valid warrant. And accordingly
the powers conferred by the subsection cannot operate if the warrants were invalid as, in
my opinion, they were.

My Lords, for the reasons I have stated I would dismiss the appeal.

d **LORD SCARMAN.** My Lords, these appeals raise two questions: the validity of the
search warrants issued by the Common Serjeant, and the legality of the seizure and
removal by officers of the Inland Revenue of the documents found on the premises
searched. The respondents are applicants for judicial review of the validity of the
warrants and of the legality of the seizure. They attack the warrants by seeking an order
of certiorari to remove them into the Queen's Bench Division so that they may be
e quashed: and they seek a declaration that the seizure and removal of the documents were
unlawful. If they fail in their case against the warrants, they may yet succeed in their
case against the seizure and removal of the documents. But, if they succeed against the
warrants, it does not necessarily follow that they must succeed in their attack on the
seizure and removal of the documents. Both forms of relief were sought, as is now
possible, by applying for judicial review. The Divisional Court refused the applicants
f any relief. The Court of Appeal upheld the applicants' appeal, quashing the warrants and
declaring that the officers of the Inland Revenue 'were at no material time entitled to
remove' the documents and things taken from the premises searched.

My Lords, I agree that these appeals should be allowed and add some observations only
because of the importance of the issues raised, and because I share the anxieties felt by the
Court of Appeal. If power exists for officers of the Board of Inland Revenue to enter
g premises, if necessary by force, at any time of the day or night and then seize and remove
any things whatsoever found there which they have reasonable cause to believe may be
required as evidence for the purposes of proceedings in respect of any offence or offences
involving any form of fraud in connection with, or in relation to, tax, it is the duty of the
courts to see that it is not abused: for it is a breath-taking inroad on the individual's right
of privacy and right of property. Important as is the public interest in the detection and
h punishment of tax frauds, it is not to be compared with the public interest in the right
of men and women to be secure in the privacy of their homes, their offices and their
papers. Yet if the law is that no particulars of the offence or offences suspected, other that
that they are offences of tax fraud, need be given, how can the householder, or occupier
of premises, hope to obtain an effective judicial review of the entry, search and seizure at
the time of the events or shortly thereafter? And telling the victim that long after the
j event he may go to law and recover damages if he can prove the Revenue acted
unlawfully is cold comfort, even if he can afford it.

It is therefore with regret that I have to accept that, if the requirements of s 20c of the
Taxes Management Act 1970, a section which entered the law as an amendment
introduced by s 57 of the Finance Act 1976, are met, the power exists to enter and search
premises, and seize and remove things there found and that the prospect of an immediate

judicial review of the exercise of the power is dim. Nevertheless, what Lord Camden CJ
said in *Entick v Carrington*[1] in 1765 remains good law today: *a*

> 'No man can set his foot upon my ground without my licence, but he is liable to
> an action, though the damage be nothing . . . If he admits the fact, he is bound to
> shew by way of justification, that some positive law has empowered or excused
> him.'

The positive law relied on in this case is the statute. If the requirements of the statute   *b*
have been met, there is justification, but, if they have not, there is none.

The essential requirement of the statute is the issue under sub-s (1) of the section by a
judicial authority of a warrant in writing authorising an officer of the Board to enter the
premises, if necessary by force, at any time within 14 days from the time of issue of the
warrant and search them. The subsection provides that the appropriate judicial authority   *c*
(in England and Wales, a circuit judge) may issue a warrant only if satisfied on
information on oath given by an officer of the Board of two matters: first, that there is
reasonable ground for suspecting that an offence involving a tax fraud has been
committed and that evidence of it is to be found on premises specified in the information,
and, secondly, that in making his application the officer has the approval of the Board
given (by at least two members) in relation to the particular case.

The judge must himself be satisfied. It is not enough that the officer should state on   *d*
oath that he is satisfied, which is all that the warrants say in the present case. The issue
of the warrant is a judicial act, and must be preceded by a judicial enquiry which satisfies
the judge that the requirements for its issue have been met.

There is no reason to believe, nor is it possible, as counsel for the respondents properly
conceded, to suggest, that in this case the Common Serjeant failed in his judicial duty.   *e*
I cannot agree with my noble and learned friend, Lord Salmon, that the words of the
warrant make clear that the Common Serjeant was content to rely solely on Mr Quinlan's
oath, and so neglected to satisfy himself. They do not even, in my view raise a doubt.
It is not to be supposed, in the absence of evidence, that a circuit judge will have been so
careless of the rights of citizens as to fail to carry out his duty, when a statute plainly
requires him to act as the protector of those rights. Neither in the Divisional Court   *f*
where the respondents lost nor in the Court of Appeal where they succeeded was any
such suggestion made, though it had found a place in the amended statement filed by the
respondents in support of their application for judicial review. The point which the
respondents have taken on the four warrants is a different one, namely that the warrants
did not state by whom and when there are reasonable grounds for suspecting an offence
has been committed or the precise nature or the particular acts constituting the suspected
offence.   *g*

It is, therefore, necessary to approach the case on the basis that the judge did satisfy
himself on the matters on which he was required to be satisfied before issuing the
warrants.

The only warrant required by the statute is one authorising entry and search. Clearly
it must specify the premises to be entered and searched. But that is the limit of the
authority given by the warrant. The judge's warrant is not the authority for seizing and   *h*
removing things found on the premises. That power is conferred by the statute, i e sub-s
(3). As the Divisional Court well said, the warrant is only the key of the door, it does not
confer the power to seize and remove, although, until and unless it opens the door, the
power to seize and remove does not arise.

Each of the four warrants which the judge issued did in terms authorise the officers it
named to enter and search the premises which it identified. Each warrant also made   *j*
clear that it was issued by the judge pursuant to s 20c of the Taxes Management Act
1970. The warrants therefore contained sufficient information to enable an occupier of

---

1   (1765) 19 State Tr 1029 at 1066

premises to know that they were issued under s 20c(1) and to identify the premises to be
a searched.

If the warrant to be valid must also contain particulars of the offences suspected, I
would have expected to find this requirement expressly stated in, or necessarily to be
implied from the language of, sub-s (3) which confers the power to seize and remove
things of possible evidential value. But, in my judgment, sub-s (3) says nothing of the
sort. An officer can enter only if armed with a warrant issued under sub-s (1), ie a
b warrant authorising entry and search. Having entered, he may seize and remove
anything which he has reasonable cause to believe may be required as evidence '. . . in
respect of such an offence as is mentioned in subsection (1) above'. I construe these words
as a reference to the kind of offence there mentioned and not limited to the particular
offences suspected, ie to any offence involving any form of fraud in connection with or
in relation to tax. Such a construction is, as my noble and learned friend, Lord Diplock,
c points out, consistent with the power of seizure of goods other than those mentioned in
the warrant conferred by a common law warrant to search premises for stolen goods (*Chic
Fashions (West Wales) Ltd v Jones*[1]). There being nothing in the section to require the
warrant to give particulars of the offences suspected, does the general law import the
requirement? For the reasons given by my noble and learned friends I think not.
Indeed, I would think it a wrong approach to modern legislation to reason by analogy
d from common law powers. The relevance of *Entick v Carrington*[2] is that it recognises
that, where the justification for what would otherwise be a trespass is a statute, the judge
must look to the statute. Today that means looking to the legislative purpose of the
enactment as well as the words and context of the specific provision. If that approach be
adopted, there are strong grounds for holding that the statute does not require the
Revenue, before it has decided to take proceedings and when it is still at the investigatory
e stage of a case, to reveal to a possible wrongdoer its suspicions or the extent of its
knowledge.

I therefore reject the submission of counsel for the respondents that the warrants
should have given particulars of the offences suspected. One criticism may, however,
fairly be made, but was not made by counsel for the respondents, of the warrants in this
case. It is that they fail to recite that the judge was himself satisfied as to the matters on
f which he has to be satisfied. No doubt, and absolutely correctly, counsel took the view
that the omission was not fatal to the validity of the warrants. Nevertheless the recital in
the warrants is incomplete. If anything was going to be recited as to the proceedings
before the judge, the fact that the judge was satisfied should have been. In a matter of
such importance as the issue of these warrants it is, I think, desirable to include a recital
of the essential fact that the judge was satisfied that there were reasonable grounds for
g suspicion and that the Board itself had authorised the application.

For these reasons I conclude that the warrants, which are the only record of the judge's
decision to issue them, disclose on their face no error of law. Certiorari, therefore, does
not lie. But, even if there was error of law in their issue, it would not necessarily follow
that the actions of the officers of the Inland Revenue in entering the premises and
exercising their statutory powers of seizure were unlawful. Like my noble and learned
h friend, Lord Diplock, I would not wish to prejudge a question not raised in this appeal,
namely whether an entry and seizure made in the bona fide belief that the warrant was
properly issued would be illegal, provided always the appropriate judicial authority had
issued the warrant and the officer, who had entered relying on it, had reasonable cause
to believe that what he seized might be required as evidence.

The main thrust of the respondents' submissions in your Lordships' House was directed
j against the lawfulness of the seizure and removal of the respondents' papers. Subsection
(3) provides that an officer may seize and remove anything which he has reasonable cause

---

1   [1968] 1 All ER 229 at 237, [1968] 2 QB at 314
2   (1765) 2 Wils 275, 95 ER 807

to believe may be required as evidence. The Revenue conceded that the officer must in fact have had reasonable cause for this belief and that it is not enough merely to show *a* that he honestly believed he had such cause. The ghost of *Liversidge v Anderson*[1] therefore casts no shadow on this statute. And I would think it need no longer haunt the law. It was laid to rest by Lord Radcliffe in *Nakkuda Ali v M F de S Jayaratne*[2], and no one in this case has sought to revive it. It is now beyond recall.

There being, therefore, no challenge to the requirement of an objective test of reasonable cause, the respondents seek a judicial review of the exercise of the power of *b* seizure. They say there was an abuse of power and that the evidence does not support the Revenue's assertion that the officers who conducted the search had reasonable cause for their belief. They have endeavoured to support the submission by an analysis of the available evidence to show that the officers seized a great quantity of documents without reading them, or even looking at some of them.

The Divisional Court held that the question of reasonable cause could not be decided *c* on the basis of contested affidavits and, in effect, dismissed as premature the application for judicial review. The Court of Appeal, noting that the Revenue refused to disclose the grounds for believing that the documents seized may be required as evidence, concluded that, since in many instances the officers seized documents without reading them, the existence of reasonable cause for their belief could not be proved, and that the quantity of such unexamined material was such that the whole exercise of seizure and removal *d* must be held illegal: the 'all or nothing' argument, as it was described.

The application for judicial review is a recent procedural innovation in our law. It is governed by RSC Ord 53, r 2, which was introduced in 1977. The rule made no alteration to the substantive law; nor did it introduce any new remedy. But the procedural reforms introduced are significant and valuable. Judicial review is now the procedure for obtaining relief by way of prerogative order, i e mandamus, prohibition or *e* certiorari. But it is not confined to such relief: an applicant may now obtain a declaration or injunction in any case where in the opinion of the court 'it would be just and convenient for the declaration or injunction to be granted on an application for judicial review'. Further, on an application, the court may award damages, provided that the court is satisfied that damages could have been awarded, had the applicant proceeded by action. The rule also makes available at the court's discretion discovery, interrogatories *f* and cross-examination of deponents. And, where the relief sought is a declaration, an injunction or damages but the court considers it should not be granted on an application for judicial review, the court may order the proceedings to continue as if they had been begun by writ.

Thus the application for judicial review, where a declaration, an injunction or damages are sought, is a summary way of obtaining a remedy which could be obtained at trial in *g* an action begun by writ; and it is available only where in all the circumstances it is just and convenient. If issues of fact, or law and fact, are raised which it is neither just nor convenient to decide without the full trial process, the court may dismiss the application or order, in effect, a trial. In the present case there are, in my judgment, insuperable objections to the granting of a declaration in proceedings for judicial review. With all respect to the Court of Appeal, the evidence is not such that a court could safely say at this *h* stage that the officers had no reasonable cause to believe that what they seized might be required as evidence. A trial is necessary if justice is to be done. The applicants could have asked for the proceedings to be continued as if begun by writ, but did not, no doubt because they have already begun proceedings by writ issued in the Chancery Division. I agree with the views expressed by the Divisional Court on this point as well as on the point relating to the validity of the warrants. *j*

At the end of the day one fundamental issue divides the parties and calls for the

---

1 [1941] 3 All ER 338, [1942] AC 206
2 [1951] AC 66 at 75

decision of the House. Is it a requirement of the law that particulars of the offences
a suspected to have been committed be shown either on the face of the warrant or by the
Revenue, if challenged, in proceedings for judicial review? The statute contains no
express provision spelling out such a requirement. Is the requirement to be implied? I
know of no common law rule which compels the implication. Indeed, the common law
supports the converse, for the nearest common law analogy is the rule, based on public
policy, which protects from disclosure police sources of information: *Home v Bentinck*[1].
b Talk of general warrants is beside the point: these warrants make clear that they are
issued by judicial authority in the exercise of the power conferred in the statute. When
one turns from the common law to consider the legislative purpose of the section, it is
plain that the purpose could be defeated if a warrant must particularise the offences
suspected: for warrants are issued at the stage of investigation when secrecy may be vital
to the success of detection. But can the Revenue, if their seizure be challenged in
c proceedings for judicial review, refuse at that stage to disclose particulars of the offences
suspected? That is a matter for their decision. If the Revenue chooses, as in this case, not
to disclose them, it runs the risk of failing to show that there is a triable issue as to
'reasonable cause'. But if, as in the present case, the affidavits disclose evidence sufficient
to show a triable issue, it is 'just and convenient' to leave the issue to trial. And, as my
noble and learned friends, Lord Wilberforce and Lord Diplock, have emphasised, trial
d (or an investigation in substitute for trial, if undertaken in the proceedings for judicial
review) should ordinarily be delayed until after criminal proceedings have been
completed or abandoned or, if none are begun, after a reasonable period, in which to take
a decision whether or not to institute such proceedings, has elapsed.

Two questions were canvassed in the course of argument on which I wish to
comment. The first was the suggestion that the burden of proving the legality of the
e seizure was on the Revenue. The suggestion rests on a misunderstanding. An applicant
for judicial review has to satisfy the court that he has a case. If he proves that his house
has been entered or his documents seized without his consent, he establishes a prima
facie case. But as soon as the respondent pleads justification, eg in this case the statute,
and leads evidence to show that he has acted within the power conferred on him by law,
issue is joined and the prima facie case has to be judged against the strength of the
f matters urged in defence. Unless the court on judicial review can safely say that the
defence will surely fail, it cannot be just to grant final relief, and it must be convenient
to allow the issue to go to trial. The summary proceedings are a substitute for trial only
if the court can be confident that the trial is unneccessary. The only rider I would add is
that the court can, if it thinks fit, grant an interlocutory injunction (save against the
Crown) or test evidence by allowing discovery, interrogatories or cross-examination, in
g which case it may be able to reach a decision without the need of sending the case to trial
by a single judge. But these are powers to be sparingly used, if the new procedure is to
be a success.

The second point on which I desire to comment is as to the possibility of an 'interim
declaration'. Under existing law only a final and conclusive declaration may be granted
by a court. This means that, where the Crown is defendant or respondent, relief
h analogous to an interim injunction is not available. Many commentators, including the
Law Commission[2], recommend that interim relief should be available against the Crown
and that an 'interim declaration' would be the appropriate way of providing it. I gravely
doubt the wisdom of interim relief against the Crown. The state's decisions must be
respected unless and until they are shown to be wrong. Judges neither govern nor
administer the state: they adjudicate when required to do so. The value of judicial
j review, which is high, should not be allowed to obscure the fundamental limits of
the judicial function. And, if interim relief against the Crown be acceptable, the

---

1   (1820) 2 Brod & Bing 130
2   Remedies in Administrative Law (1976) Law Com 73, Cmnd 6407

interlocutory declaration is not the way to provide it. For myself, I find absurd the posture of a court declaring one day in interlocutory proceedings that an applicant has *a* certain rights and on a later day that he has not. Something less risible must be devised. For these reasons I would allow the appeals.

Appeals allowed.

Solicitors: *Solicitor of Inland Revenue*; *Roney, Vincent & Co* (for the respondents).   *b*

Mary Rose Plummer   Barrister.

Earl of Normanton v Giles and another   *c*

HOUSE OF LORDS

LORD WILBERFORCE, VISCOUNT DILHORNE, LORD DIPLOCK, LORD SALMON AND LORD RUSSELL OF KILLOWEN

1St NOVEMBER, 13th DECEMBER 1979   *d*

Rent restriction – Agricultural worker – Agriculture – Livestock keeping – Animals kept for production of food – Keeping and rearing of pheasants for sport – Gamekeeper occupying cottage on agricultural holding – Gamekeeper employed to keep and rear pheasants for sport – Majority of birds killed sold to butchers and game dealers – Whether pheasants 'livestock' – Whether gamekeeper keeping and breeding livestock – Whether gamekeeper employed in 'agriculture' –   *e* *Rent (Agriculture) Act 1976, s 1.*

The first appellant was employed by the respondent as head gamekeeper on his estate and as such he occupied with his wife, the second appellant, a cottage on the estate. His duties included providing a sufficient number of pheasants for the respondent's shoot *f* and he was also responsible for rearing pheasants. After the shooting season was over he would catch birds, clip their wings and put them in pens in a walled garden adjacent to his cottage for the purpose of their breeding. After laying and incubation of the eggs, the poults were put into release pens in the woods and when sufficiently grown were free to escape and in due course would, it was hoped, become wild and available for shooting. The primary object of breeding, rearing and keeping the pheasants was for the sport of *g* shooting. They were not reared and kept for food although the great majority of the pheasants which were shot were sold to butchers and game dealers and were ultimately consumed as food. The proceeds of sale went to maintain the shoot. The first appellant continued to occupy the cottage after he had ceased to be employed as gamekeeper and the respondent brought proceedings against him to recover possession. The first appellant contended that since the pheasants were animals kept for the production of *h* food they were 'livestock' within s 1(2)*ᵈ* of the Rent (Agriculture) Act 1976, and that accordingly he was employed in 'agriculture' within s 1(1)(*a*)(i) of that Act and entitled to security of tenure thereunder. The county court judge held that the first appellant's job was to keep and rear pheasants for sport. It was no part of food production or the keeping of livestock, and therefore his employment did not fall within the definition of 'agriculture' in s 1 of the 1976 Act and accordingly he was not entitled to security of *j* tenure under the Act. The judge granted the plaintiff an order for possession, and his decision was upheld by the Court of Appeal. The appellants appealed to the House of Lords.

---

a   Section 1, so far as material, is set out at p 115 *h* to p 116*a*, post

Held – The pheasants were not 'livestock' within s 1(2) of the 1976 Act since they were
a not kept and bred for the production of food but were kept for sport which was not an
agricultural activity. It followed that the keeping and breeding of the pheasants did not
come within 'agriculture' in s 1(1) and the first appellant was not therefore entitled to
security of tenure under the 1976 Act. The appeal would accordingly be dismissed (see
p 108 *g* to *j*, p 109 *a b*, p 111 *b* to *f*, p 113 *e f* and *j* to p 114 *b* and *h* to p 115 *e* and p 116 *c*
to *f*, post).
b   *Lord Glendyne v Rapley* [1978] 2 All ER 110 applied.

Notes
For the meaning of agriculture, see 1 Halsbury's Laws (4th Edn) para 1002, and for the
protection of agricultural workers from eviction, see ibid para 1624.
     For the Rent (Agriculture) Act 1976, s 1, see 46 Halsbury's Statutes (3rd Edn) 53.

c **Cases referred to in opinions**
Glendyne (Lord) v Rapley [1978] 2 All ER 110, [1978] 1 WLR 601, CA.
Kendall (Henry) & Sons (a firm) v William Lillico & Sons Ltd [1968] 2 All ER 444, [1969] 2
     AC 31, [1968] 3 WLR 110, sub nom *Hardwick Game Farm v Suffolk Agricultural and
     Poultry Producers' Association Ltd* [1969] 1 Lloyd's Rep 547, HL, Digest (Cont Vol C) 15,
     1166b.
d *Minister of Agriculture, Fisheries and Food v Appleton* [1969] 3 All ER 1051, [1970] 1 QB
     221, [1969] 3 WLR 755, 48 ATC 243, DC, Digest (Cont Vol C) 848, 841 *Anb*.
Peterborough Royal Foxhound Show Society v Inland Revenue Comrs [1936] 1 All ER 813,
     [1936] 2 KB 497, 105 LJKB 427, 155 LT 134, 20 Tax Cas 249, 28(1) Digest (Reissue)
     475, 1706.
Smith v Coles [1905] 2 KB 827, 75 LJKB 16, 93 LT 754, 8 WCC 116, CA, 34 Digest (Repl)
e   337, 2597.
Stephens and Branthwaite (trading as Meresdale Fur Farm) and Otway, Re, Re Hume and Croft
     [1938] 3 All ER 311, sub nom *Re Stephens' Application* [1938] 2 KB 675, sub nom
     Minister of Labour v Stephens, 107 LJKB 614, 159 LT 120, 35 Digest (Repl) 804, 18.
Vellacott, Re [1922] 1 KB 466, 126 LT 412, 35 Digest (Repl) 805, 32.
Walters v Wright [1938] 4 All ER 116, 159 LT 555, 102 JP 487, 36 LGR 666, DC, 2 Digest
f   (Repl) 161, 1175.

Appeal
The defendants, Stanley Giles and Diana Mary Giles, his wife, appealed by leave of the
House of Lords against an order of the Court of Appeal (Stephenson and Lawton LJJ)
dated 25th July 1978 dismissing their appeal from an order made by his Honour Judge
g Lee QC on 18th February 1977 in the Salisbury County Court whereby the plaintiff,
Shaun James Christian Welbore Ellis Agar, sixth Earl of Normanton, was granted
possession against the defendants of a cottage known as Old Somerley, Somerley Park,
Ringwood, Hampshire. The plaintiff was the life tenant of Somerley Park, an estate
which consisted of approximately 3,500 acres of woodland and farmland let to four
tenant farmers. The plaintiff retained the shooting rights over the estate and organised
h a syndicate of other persons ('guns') who contributed to the expenses of operating the
shoot in return for shooting rights over the estate at certain times. The first defendant
was employed by the plaintiff from 7th March 1973 until 27th March 1976 as head
gamekeeper on the estate and as such he occupied the cottage. The facts are set out in the
opinion of Lord Wilberforce.

j   The first appellant appeared in person on his own behalf and that of his wife.
     Robert Johnson QC and *Hugh Bennett* for the respondent.

Their Lordships took time for consideration.

13th December. The following opinions were delivered.

LORD WILBERFORCE. My Lords, is a gamekeeper a person working wholetime in agriculture? If so, he is, as a qualifying worker, entitled to the protection conferred by *a* the Rent (Agriculture) Act 1976 as regards occupation of his cottage.

This is partly a question of impression, partly a question of statutory interpretation. It is no easier to discard deep-seated preconceptions as to the former than it is to unravel the confusions of the latter. There is no doubt that the apparent simplicity of the case is deceptive.

Mr Giles was gamekeeper to the Earl of Normanton, and as such, until he was given *b* notice to quit, he occupied Old Somerley, a cottage on the estate. There was detailed evidence as to his duties and the case must be decided on it, but it is probably true to say that they were fairly typical. He had the normal task of producing pheasants during shoots and of preventing poaching: he cleared vermin and controlled deer. Also (and this was what he relied on) he was responsible for rearing pheasants. In the spring he would catch birds for laying, clip their wings and put them in pens. These were in a *c* walled garden adjoining his cottage. After laying and incubation of the eggs, the poults were put into release pens and as they grew they walked out and in due course, it was hoped, became wild and available for shooting. Some figures were provided as to the number of birds reared and shot in several seasons, interesting to the sportsman but not legally significant. The one relevant point was that the great majority of the birds shot were sold to butchers and game dealers, and no doubt ultimately to individuals by whom *d* they were consumed as food. The proceeds went to maintain the shoot.

I must now refer to the relevant provisions in the 1976 Act. These are the following:

'1.—(1) In this Act—(a) "agriculture" includes—(i) dairy-farming and livestock keeping and breeding (whether those activities involve the use of land or not) . . .

'(2) For the purposes of the definition in subsection (1)(a) above—"consumable produce" means produce grown for consumption or other use after severance or *e* separation from the land or other growing medium on or in which it is grown; "livestock" includes any animal which is kept for the production of food, wool, skins or fur, or for the purpose of its use in the carrying on of any agricultural activity, and for the purposes of this definition "animal" includes bird but does not include fish. . .'

On these facts and this law the case was tried in Salisbury County Court by his Honour Judge Lee QC who, it can safely be assumed, was not blind or oblivious to the realities of country life. Before him, and subsequently, the main reliance was placed on sub-s (2) above. Mr Giles contended that pheasants, or at any rate his pheasants, were animals kept for the production of food; therefore they were 'livestock'. This made them livestock kept and bred within s 1(1)(a)(i); therefore keeping and breeding of them was *g* 'agriculture'.

My Lords, I think that there are two good reasons why this argument does not succeed. First, it was found by the judge that—

'The production of food is not the purpose for which birds are reared or for which [Mr Giles] was employed. The job of the gamekeeper is to get as many pheasants into the woods [sic] so that they become wild . . . A gamekeeper is there to keep *h* game, for the purpose of shooting and enjoyment. The purpose of shooting pheasants is sport. It is no part of food production or the keeping of livestock.'

There was clearly evidence to support these findings and they are fatal to the argument. It may be the case that unless people in general were willing to eat pheasants and to pay for that pleasure, shooting would become uneconomic, but it does not follow *j* from this that pheasants are produced for food. If they were to be so produced many easier ways of rearing and killing them could be found.

But secondly, the argument fails, in my opinion, on another ground. The section does not say 'produced for food' but 'kept for the production of food'. This seems to me to be a different thing altogether and to be directed toward animals such as bees, or (as to skins

or fur) mink or silver foxes. Animals kept and bred for food, ie to be eaten, such as cattle
a or chickens, come under s 1. The presence of 'wool' in sub-s (2) is puzzling, but I cannot
believe that sheep, kept as prospective mutton or lamb, do not come under sub-s (1);
there could scarcely be anything which more obviously does. Sub-section (2) is not
needed to bring them in under 'agriculture'. If this is right, it is clear that pheasants do
not come within sub-s (2) at all. Whatever they do, they do not produce food: on the
contrary they consume it.

b   This conclusion however does not, as seems to have been thought, conclude the
matter. It only leads to the real point as I see it: ie whether pheasants are livestock and
whether Mr Giles kept and bred livestock. Section 1(1)(a) is quite independent of s 1(2):
the latter says what is *included* in livestock, not what 'livestock' *means*. That 'includes'
here signifies 'includes' is shown by the preceding definition of 'consumable produce'
which takes the form 'means . . .' So we still have to consider whether, apart from the
c special inclusions, pheasants can be described as 'livestock'. Though many people would
instinctively deny this, it does, on the authorities, seem to be a puzzling question.

We were shown a number of other definitions in other Acts which are remarkable for
their variety. In the Animals Act 1971 (s 11) 'livestock' is said to mean cattle etc, and, in
certain sections 'while in captivity, pheasants, partridges and grouse'. But I think this is
a special provision designed to give their keepers protection from dogs. In the Diseases
d of Animals Act 1950 (s 84) pheasants and partridges are classified as poultry, but this does
not necessarily mean they are livestock: they are not, in that Act, regarded as 'animals'.
For value added tax purposes 'game birds' are zero-rated together with other edible
animals which undoubtedly are 'livestock' as contrasted with horses and racing pigeons,
on the basis that they are held to be food for human consumption. But this does not
mean that before the stage of consumption they are necessarily 'livestock'. So these
e statutes in the end are inconclusive.

Mr Giles, with exemplary relevance and economy, referred us to a number of cases.
In *Smith v Coles*[1] it was held that a man employed three months in the year as a
gamekeeper and who assisted at hay and corn harvests, rick-making, and mangel-carting,
and who also acted as farm carpenter, was employed in agriculture for the purpose of
workmen's compensation, but the question was whether the county court judge could
f so find in spite of his work as farm carpenter. It was not necessary to decide, and the
court did not decide, whether as gamekeeper he was employed in agriculture. Indeed,
Romer LJ[2] was careful to leave this question open: 'Sometimes he was engaged in what
are admittedly agricultural pursuits, at other times he did work essential to the proper
conduct of the farm such as the repair of fences, and for part of his time he acted as
gamekeeper'. On this total picture he could be said to be employed in agriculture.

g   In *Walters v Wright*[3] Lord Hewart CJ said that there was much to be said for a
definition of 'agriculture' as including 'any use of land in connection with breeding or
keeping any animal 'ordinarily found on a farm'. The animals there in question were
poultry, and two Scottish cases[4] had decided that poultry farms could be husbandry or
agriculture: it seems that rent was sometimes paid by farmers in 'kain hens'. But even
if 'pheasants' are for some purposes 'poultry' that does not mean that the keeping of them
h is agriculture: the question remains whether they are animals 'ordinarily kept on a farm',
a question to which I shall have to return. In *Peterborough Royal Foxhound Show Society v
Inland Revenue Comrs*[5], a case concerned with foxhound breeding, Lawrence J said: 'the
words "live stock" are ordinarily and properly used in contrast with dead stock and
include all live animals and birds the breeding of which is regulated by man'. This is

j

1   [1905] 2 KB 827
2   [1905] 2 KB 827 at 831
3   [1938] 4 All ER 116 at 118
4   *Lean v Ball (Inspector of Taxes)* 1926 SC 15; *Lanarkshire Assessor v Smith* 1933 SC 366
5   [1936] 1 All ER 813 at 814–815, [1936] 2 KB 497 at 500

helpful to Mr Giles but later the judge made it clear that he had in mind animals bred in
the ordinary course of agriculture and shown throughout the country, for example, *a*
hackneys, hunters, racehorses, dogs and fur-bearing animals. The question still remains
whether pheasants bred for shooting would come within this conception. In *Re Stephens*[1],
it was held that a man employed on a farm for breeding silver foxes, nutria, etc, for their
pelts, and having general duties on the farm, was 'employed in agriculture'. Branson J
took the view, as a matter of impression, that since breeding sheep for wool rather than
for food must clearly be an agricultural pursuit, so must breeding animals for pelts, *b*
particularly when the breeding and feeding of them was integrated with the farm as a
whole. This view of the matter (on which there was contrary opinion in Scotland) was
evidently endorsed by Parliament in various Acts preceding and in s 1(2) of the 1976 Act,
and may explain the appearance of 'wool' in sub-s (2).

Counsel for Lord Normanton contributed his share to the learning on this subject. In
Re Vellacott[2] questions arose whether a list of persons of various occupations were (a) *c*
employed in agriculture or (b) employed in domestic service; in either of which cases
they were exempt from insurance against unemployment. A gamekeeper was held to be
exempt but on the, some may think curious, ground that he was employed in domestic
service, as were a huntsman of a pack of foxhounds and the whippers-in. A river keeper
was similarly treated and Roche J[3] said of him:

> 'He is engaged by a private employer for the purpose of looking after the fishing, *d*
> which is one of the interests and amusements in life of his employer. Sport has
> universally been held to be one of the wants and needs of the average ordinary
> Englishman.'

This is not conclusive that the gamekeeper was not, also, employed in agriculture but
certainly does not support the contention that he is.   *e*

An interesting citation was produced from the unlikely source of *Henry Kendall & Sons
(a firm) v William Lillico & Sons Ltd*[4]. Lord Reid said:

> 'I do not think that these pheasants were poultry. They were reared for the
> purpose of being released to serve as targets for sportsmen, and pheasants which
> have never been in captivity are clearly not poultry. It may well be that, if it should
> prove profitable to rear and keep pheasants in captivity until killed for human *f*
> consumption, such pheasants should be regarded as poultry. But the mere fact that
> these pheasants like other game will come to the table after they have been shot
> seems to me to be immaterial. It would not in my view be in accordance with the
> ordinary use of language to say that they were poultry until released and then
> became game. They were game throughout and the farm where they were reared
> was properly called a game farm.'   *g*

Some similar observations appear in the speeches of Lord Guest[5] and myself[6]. I think
that these reinforce the common impression that the rearing of pheasants for sport is sui
generis and is not to be equated with the rearing of other livestock.

In *Minister of Agriculture, Fisheries and Food v Appleton*[7], the court had to decide whether
the breeding of cats and dogs was livestock breeding and keeping. The relevant Act (the *h*
Selective Employment Payments Act 1966) contained definitions of 'agriculture' and of
'livestock' very similar to those in s 1(1) and (2) of the 1976 Act. It was held that it was
not. The definition of 'livestock' showed that the word was not intended to refer to the

---

1   [1938] 3 All ER 311, [1938] 2 KB 675
2   [1922] 1 KB 466
3a   [1922] 1 KB 466 at 473
4   [1968] 2 All ER 444 at 458, [1969] 2 AC 31 at 85
5   [1968] 2 All ER 444 at 480, [1969] 2 AC 31 at 111
6   [1968] 2 All ER 444 at 493, [1969] 2 AC 31 at 126
7   [1969] 3 All ER 1051, [1970] 1 QB 221

j

breeding and keeping of animals of any sort, but only to those either within the separate

a definition (as in our sub-s (2)) or in the course of an activity which could properly be brought within the meaning of agriculture. In his judgment Lord Parker CJ quoted from an earlier decision of his[1] in which, referring to the definition of livestock (as in our sub-s (2)) he had said: ' . . . that is clearly an extension to cover, no doubt, an argument that, for instance, bees, *possibly pheasants* and fish are not livestock' (emphasis mine).

I do not think that this helps Mr Giles, if I am right in thinking that pheasants are not

b within the extension. On the definition of 'agriculture' which we are now considering this case decidedly favours Lord Normanton.

Finally, I come to the recent decision of the Court of Appeal in *Lord Glendyne v Rapley*[2] which raised exactly the same question as that now before us and which was followed by the Court of Appeal in the present case. Lord Scarman gave a short judgment in which he held as follows[3]:

c

> ' . . . not every rural or country activity is intended to be included in the definition of agriculture. Fishing, for example, is clearly excluded. The definition is really directed towards including all operations involved in farming land for commercial purposes of which the one relevant to this appeal is the production of food. The finding that these pheasants were kept for sport, although 80 per cent of those killed
> *d* and retrieved were in fact sold, is, in our judgment, conclusive. The defendant's employment was to promote not agriculture but a field sport. This is a country activity but not an agricultural one.'

Apart from the reference to the 'production of food', which to my mind is not the critical issue in this case, I agree with this passage. I think that it is in line with the tenor of the

e cases I have referred to, and in particular with the judgment of Lord Parker CJ just mentioned. Agriculture, however wide that activity has become, does not include everything that goes on in the country. Rearing and keeping pheasants for sport is not thought of as, and there is no statutory or case authority for holding it to be, an agricultural occupation: pheasants so kept and reared are not 'livestock' in an agricultural context: only such 'livestock' is designated in s 1 of the 1976 Act.

f I cannot therefore, in the end, accept Mr Giles's argument and his appeal must be dismissed.

VISCOUNT DILHORNE. My Lords, the first appellant, Mr Giles, who appeared in person, was employed by the respondent as head gamekeeper on his estate, Somerley Park, Ringwood, Hampshire. His employment began on 7th March 1973, and throughout it he and his wife, the second appellant, lived in a cottage on the estate called 'Old

g Somerley'. The respondent gave him notice terminating his employment on 27th March 1976, and sought to recover possession of the cottage through the county court. On 16th July his Honour Judge Lee QC held that it was a term of the first appellant's employment that it was only terminable by notice given on or before 1st December in any year to expire on 1st February following. So on 27th July 1976 the respondent gave the first appellant a fresh notice terminating his employment with effect from 1st

h February 1977 and requiring him to give up possession of the cottage. The first appellant did not do so and so a summons for possession was issued and on 18th February 1977 Judge Lee made an order for possession.

The Rent (Agriculture) Act 1976 came into force on 1st January 1977 and it was contended on behalf of Mr Giles in the county court and in the Court of Appeal, and by him in this House, that by virtue of that Act, he was a protected occupier and entitled to

j continue to occupy the cottage.

Section 2(1) of the Act provides:

---

1   *Belmont Farm Ltd v Minister of Housing and Local Government* (1962) 60 LGR 319 at 322
2   [1978] 2 All ER 110, [1978] 1 WLR 601
3   [1978] 2 All ER 110 at 112, [1978] 1 WLR 601 at 603–604

'Where a person has, in relation to a dwelling-house, a relevant licence or tenancy and the dwelling-house is in qualifying ownership . . . at any time during the *a* subsistence of the licence or tenancy . . . he shall be a protected occupier of the dwelling-house if (*a*) he is a qualifying worker, or (*b*) he has been a qualifying worker at any time during the subsistence of the licence or tenancy . . .'

So to establish that he was a protected occupier, Mr Giles had to show that the cottage was in qualifying ownership and that he was or had been a qualifying worker.

Schedule 3, para 3, of the Act states that a dwelling-house is in qualifying ownership *b* at any time if, at that time, the occupier is employed in agriculture and the occupier's employer is the owner of the dwelling-house; and para 1 of the schedule provides that a person is a qualifying worker at any time if, at that time, he has worked whole-time in agriculture. There was no dispute that if Mr Giles had been employed in agriculture and had worked in agriculture, the cottage was in qualifying ownership and he was or had been a qualifying worker. The only question for decision in this litigation is whether he *c* had been employed and had worked in agriculture.

The Act does not attempt to define 'agriculture' but by s 1(1)(*a*) it states that 'agriculture' includes: '(i) dairy-farming and livestock keeping and breeding (whether those activities involve the use of land or not)', and s 1(2) states that 'livestock' includes—

'any animal which is kept for the production of food, wool, skins or fur, or for the *d* purpose of its use in the carrying on of any agricultural activity, and for the purposes of this definition "animal" includes bird but does not include fish.'

So as these definitions are not exhaustive, one must first consider whether if they were not in the Act, Mr Giles should be held to have been engaged in agriculture; and secondly, taking these definitions into account, he should be held to have been so employed. *e*

'Agriculture' is defined in the Oxford English Dictionary as 'The science and art of cultivating the soil; including the allied pursuits of gathering in the crops and rearing livestock'; and 'livestock' is defined in the dictionary as 'Domestic animals generally; animals of any kind kept or dealt in for use or profit'.

Mr Giles, who had two keepers under him, was employed in looking after the respondent's pheasant shoot and he did the usual work of a gamekeeper so employed, *f* catching up cocks and hens after the shooting season was over, putting them in a walled-in garden by his cottage, collecting the eggs, putting them in incubators, looking after the incubators and the hatched out chicks, and then when the time was right, putting the pheasant poults in release pens in the woods. No doubt on shooting days he supervised the beaters and saw that the drives were properly conducted.

The pheasants which were shot, a number far less than the number reared, were for *g* the most part sold to dealers. Some were given to the guns and some to the beaters at Christmas. However disposed of, there is no doubt that they were consumed as food. The receipts from the sale of the dead pheasants went to meet some of the expense of the shoot.

Mr Giles stated that the pheasants were reared and kept for shooting. They were not reared and kept for eating. This use for food was consequently a by-product of the *h* shooting.

I do not think that pheasants kept and reared for shooting, and which when sufficiently grown are released from captivity, can properly be regarded as 'domestic animals' or as being kept for use or profit. They cease to be kept when they are let go free. I do not therefore consider that the pheasants looked after by Mr Giles were within the definition of livestock in the dictionary and consequently the rearing and keeping of them does not *j* come within the definition in the dictionary of agriculture.

I do not think that the decision of Lawrence J in *Peterborough Royal Foxhound Show Society v Inland Revenue Comrs*[1] that foxhound breeding was livestock breeding, is of any

---

1   [1936] 1 All ER 813, [1936] 2 KB 497

assistance to Mr Giles, for I do not think it follows from that decision that the rearing of
a pheasants which are to be freed and which is for shooting is to be similarly regarded.
'Livestock' was contrasted by Lawrence J with 'dead stock' and he did not have to deal
with a definition of agriculture which included livestock (see *Minister of Agriculture,
Fisheries and Food v Appleton*[1] per Lord Parker CJ). In my view the word 'livestock' is
usually used to cover all forms of stock found on farms in the course of farming.

In *Re Vellacott*[2] Roche J had to decide whether a variety of persons were excepted from
b the provisions of the Unemployment Insurance Act 1920 as to insurance against
unemployment. They were excepted if employed in agriculture or in domestic
services. He held that a gamekeeper was exempt not because he was employed in
agriculture but because he was a domestic servant. He also held that a river keeper was
a domestic servant, saying[3]:

c   'He is engaged by a private employer for the purpose of looking after the fishing,
         which is one of the interests and amusements in life of his employer. Sport has
         universally been held to be one of the wants and needs of the average ordinary
         Englishman.'

If one replaces the word 'fishing' by the word 'shooting' this passage would be apt in its
d application to Mr Giles. I cannot regard any of his activities which I have described as
agricultural activities. They were all directed to one end, to provide good sport for the
respondent and those who came to shoot with him. In my opinion, ignoring the
definitions in the Act, it is not right to say that Mr Giles when working for the
respondent was employed in or worked in agriculture.

I now turn to the second question. Is he to be regarded as having been engaged in
e agriculture by virtue of the definitions in the Act? This appears to me to depend on
whether the pheasants were livestock as defined. If they were kept for the production of
food they were, but not otherwise.

As I have said, Mr Giles said they were kept and reared for shooting, and Judge Lee
held, in my opinion rightly, that 'The production of food is not the purpose for which
the birds are reared or for which [Mr Giles] was employed.' To say that the pheasants
f were kept for the production of food when they were reared for shooting because the
shot pheasants were eaten is in my opinion to confuse an incidental result of the shooting
with the purpose for which the pheasants were reared.

In *Henry Kendell & Sons (a firm) v William Lillico & Sons Ltd*[4] Lord Reid had to consider
whether pheasants were poultry and he said:

g   'I do not think that these pheasants were poultry. They were reared for the
         purpose of being released to serve as targets for sportsmen, and pheasants which
         have never been in captivity are clearly not poultry. It may well be that, if it should
         prove profitable to rear and keep pheasants in captivity until killed for human
         consumption, such pheasants should be regarded as poultry. But the mere fact,
         however, that these pheasants like other game will come to the table after they have
h   been shot seems to me to be immaterial. It would not in my view be in accordance
         with the ordinary use of language to say that they were poultry until released and
         then became game. They were game throughout . . .'

In my opinion the definitions in the Act do not help Mr Giles and I am fortified in this
conclusion by the decision of the Court of Appeal on the same question in *Lord Glendyne*
j

1 [1969] 3 All ER 1051 at 1053, [1970] 1 QB 221 at 225
2 [1922] 1 KB 466
3 [1922] 1 KB 466 at 473
4 [1968] 2 All ER 444 at 458, [1969] 2 AC 31 at 85

v Rapley[1] when the judgment of the court was given by my noble and learned friend, Lord Scarman.

In my opinion definitions in other Acts are of no assistance in construing this Act and I do not therefore refer to them.

In my opinion the Court of Appeal in the present case and Judge Lee came to the right conclusion and for the reasons stated, I would dismiss this appeal with costs.

LORD DIPLOCK. My Lords. I have had the advantage of reading in draft the opinion of my noble and learned friend, Viscount Dilhorne, with which I agree, and I would therefore dismiss the appeal.

LORD SALMON. My Lords, this appeal turns on a short but, in my view, not very easy point of construction of the Rent (Agriculture) Act 1976. The question to be decided is whether Mr Giles, who was the Earl of Normanton's head gamekeeper and occupied one of his cottages, was entitled to security of tenure.

The relevant facts are all set out in the speech of my noble and learned friend, Lord Wilberforce, which I gratefully adopt. The dictionary definition of agriculture and many interesting authorities (none of which related to the Act with which this appeal is concerned) and a number of other Acts dealing with agriculture were cited both by Mr Giles (who conducted his case extremely well) and by counsel for Lord Normanton. No doubt that to describe a gamekeeper as an agricultural worker sounds somewhat incongruous, but no more so than to describe him as a domestic servant. All the learning relied on by both parties was of considerable interest but in my view shed little light on the point which this House has to decide.

I will now set out the relevant parts of the 1976 Act. Section 2(1) provides:

'Where a person has, in relation to a dwelling-house, a relevant licence or tenancy . . . he shall be a protected occupier . . . if—(a) he is a qualifying worker . . .'

And Sch 3 provides:

'1. A person is a qualifying worker for the purpose of this Act at any time if, at that time, he has worked whole-time in agriculture . . .
'3.—(1) A dwelling-house in relation to which a person ("the occupier") has a licence or tenancy is in qualifying ownership for the purposes of this Act at any time if, at that time, the occupier is employed in agriculture and the occupier's employer . . . (a) is the owner of the dwelling-house . . .'

I now come to s 1, the interpretation section of the Act, parts of which are of great importance.

'(1) In this Act—(a) "agriculture" includes—(i) dairy-farming and livestock keeping and breeding . . .
'(2) For the purposes of the definition in subsection (1)(a) above—. . . "livestock" includes any animal which is kept for the production of food, wool, skins or fur, or for the purpose of its use in the carrying on of any agricultural activity, and for the purposes of this definition "animal" includes bird but does not include fish.'

This appeal, in my opinion, turns entirely on whether the pheasants kept by Lord Normanton were kept by him for the production of food.

The dictionary's definition of 'livestock' is 'Domestic animals generally; animals of any kind kept or dealt in for use or profit'. That definition covers a wide range of animals including dogs and horses. This may be why the Act set out in s 1(2) the meaning of 'livestock' in the sense in which it is used in s 1(1). I cannot accept that the word 'food' in the phrase 'any animal which is kept for the production of food' is confined to milk

_____

1   [1978] 2 All ER 110, [1978] 1 WLR 601

and honey. Nor do I think that the phrase is in any way inept when applied to beef cattle,
a sheep or poultry, for, in my view, all these are kept for the production of food. The only
question is, does the phrase apply to Lord Normanton's pheasants? None of these birds
were wild birds but they were bred and reared by the head gamekeeper in a walled
garden behind the cottage in which he lived. Well before the shooting season began, the
keeper put the birds out into his employer's woods and with the help of the two junior
gamekeepers protected them by keeping down vermin and poachers.

b There is no doubt that the primary object of breeding, rearing and keeping the
pheasants was for the sport of shooting: indeed it is obvious that no gamekeepers would
have been employed nor any pheasants bred and reared but for the shooting. There is,
however, no doubt that all the pheasants which are shot down and retrieved, whether
given to the guns and, as they sometimes were, to the gamekeepers and to some of the
beaters, or sold, as the bulk of them were, to butchers and merchants, every bird brought
c down and retrieved at a shoot would eventually become food on someone's table. If
pheasants were not edible but only decorative and rare, I wonder if pheasant shooting
would continue to be in vogue. I think not: indeed it would probably be illegal. It is
perhaps obvious that everyone who keeps pheasants must know that those which are
shot and retrieved will become food which will be eaten. Accordingly, there is, in my
view, a good deal to be said for the proposition that if you keep pheasants for shooting,
d it necessarily follows that you must also keep them for the production of food. I have no
doubt, however (as I have already indicated), that the main purpose for which pheasants
are kept is shooting and, indeed, that, but for the shooting, they would not be kept at all.

My Lords, although I have considerable doubt about the point at issue, I am not
prepared to dissent from the view that since the principal reason for keeping the
pheasants was the sport of shooting them, the appeal should be dismissed.

e
LORD RUSSELL OF KILLOWEN. My Lords, the question in this appeal is a short
one. The first appellant was employed by the respondent on his estate as head
gamekeeper. As such he was provided with a cottage on the respondent's estate. The
respondent, having by notice determined that employment, obtained from the county
court judge an order for possession, which was upheld in the Court of Appeal. Whether
f that order was correctly made depends on whether the appellant was entitled to the
protection of the Rent (Agriculture) Act 1976. In order to assert that protection the
appellant must show that he was 'employed to work in agriculture'. The short question
is, was he?

I pause to say that in fact during the litigation the first appellant vacated the cottage
and his successor in his employment has been installed in the cottage. If the first
g appellant is correct in his contentions, presumably his successor would be entitled to the
same protection, and the outcome of success in this appeal would be, to say the least,
obscure.

Returning to the short question, the 1976 Act provides in s 1:

'(1) In this Act—(*a*) "agriculture" includes—(i) dairy-farming and livestock
h keeping and breeding (whether those activities involve the use of land or not); (ii)
the production of any consumable produce which is grown for sale or for
consumption or other use for the purposes of a trade or business or of any other
undertaking (whether carried on for profit or not); (iii) the use of land as grazing,
meadow or pasture land or orchard or osier land; (iv) the use of land for market
gardens or nursery grounds; and (v) forestry; (*b*) "forestry" includes—(i) the use of
j land for nursery grounds for trees, and (ii) the use of land for woodlands where that
use is ancillary to the use of land for other agricultural purposes.

'(2) For the purposes of the definition in subsection (1)(*a*) above—"consumable
produce" means produce grown for consumption or other use after severance or
separation from the land or other growing medium on or in which it is grown;
"livestock" includes any animal which is kept for the production of food, wool, skins

or fur, or for the purpose of its use in the carrying on of any agricultural activity, and for the purposes of this definition "animal" includes bird but does not include *a* fish . . .'

I observe that sub-s (2) refers to sub-s (1)(*a*) as a 'definition': and s 1(3) says that the expressions listed in column 1 of Sch 1 to the Act have for the purposes of the Act 'the meanings' given by the provisions shown in column 2 of that schedule. 'Agriculture' is one such expression, and against it is a reference to s 1(1). Schedule 1 is headed 'Index of General Definitions'. Nevertheless it cannot be ignored that 'includes' is not ordinarily *b* to be regarded as the same as 'means'.

The respondent preserves and breeds pheasants on his estate for the sport of shooting. Others of your Lordships have described the activities involved, and the part played in those activities by the appellant in the course of his employment as head gamekeeper, which were those to be expected from that designation. I need not enlarge *c* further on them.

In my opinion 'agriculture' per se is not a word appropriate to the preservation and breeding of pheasants for sporting purposes. Further, the fact that in the Act 'agriculture' includes 'livestock keeping and breeding' cannot in my opinion per se be regarded in the context as embracing within the word 'livestock' pheasants bred and kept for that purpose. I consider that the provisions of s 1(2) reinforce that last conclusion. These *d* pheasants are in no sense birds 'kept for the production of food'. In so far as both home-bred pheasants and others are 'preserved' in the woods on the estate this is done so that they may by way of sport be in due season shot at. The fact that those which are successfully shot at are for the most part sold and eaten is not the reason for their keeping, they are not 'kept for' that. Accordingly in my opinion the provisions of sub-s (2) do not extend 'livestock keeping and breeding' in sub-s (1)(*a*) to cover this case. If anything the stress in sub-s (2) of 'kept for the production of food' tends to confirm the view that the *e* language of sub-s (1)(*a*) does not embrace a case such as the present.

In my opinion the decision of the Court of Appeal, and the earlier decision of the Court of Appeal which it followed, that of *Lord Glendyne v Rapley*[1], were correct, and this appeal should be dismissed.

Mr Giles, the appellant, concluded his case with relevance and courtesy. I wish only *f* to add that he raised a point of complaint in that the county court judge, in consultation with both counsel approved several alterations to counsel's original draft of his reasons for judgment. He is to be assured that there was nothing unusual (let alone improper) in this, and that there is no cause for suspicion in the fact that the alterations in the copy signed as approved by the judge were in the handwriting of his opponent's counsel.

Appeal dismissed.   *g*

Solicitors: *Payne Hicks Beach & Co* (for the respondent).

Mary Rose Plummer   Barrister.

_____ *h*

1 [1978] 2 All ER 110, [1978] 1 WLR 601

a

Re Mesco Properties Ltd

COURT OF APPEAL, CIVIL DIVISION

BUCKLEY, BRIDGE AND TEMPLEMAN LJJ

12th JULY 1979

b   *Company – Compulsory winding-up – Corporation tax on chargeable gains – Priority of liquidator's fees over tax – Company compulsorily wound up – Assets sold following winding-up order – Resulting liability to corporation tax on chargeable gains – Liquidator's balance less than amount liable to corporation tax – Whether corporation tax an expense incurred in realising assets – Whether corporation tax a necessary disbursement by the liquidator – Whether corporation tax a charge or expense incurred in the winding-up – Companies Act 1948, s 267*

c   *– Companies (Winding-up) Rules 1949 (SI 1949 No 330), r 195(1).*

A company in respect of which a compulsory winding-up order had been made sold several properties at a profit. In consequence it became liable to corporation tax on chargeable gains arising on the disposal in the sum of £634,440. The liquidator, who held a balance of not more than £520,000, sought the determination of the court whether the company's liability to account to the Crown in respect of corporation tax was

d   (i) part of 'the fees or expenses properly incurred in preserving, realising or getting in the assets' of the company or part of the 'necessary disbursements of [the] liquidator' within r 195(1)*a* of the Companies (Winding-up) Rules 1949 or (ii) part of the 'costs, charges and expenses incurred in the winding up' within s 267*b* of the Companies Act 1948. The judge*c* held that the corporation tax was not an expense incurred in realising the assets

e   but was a necessary disbursement within the meaning of r 195(1) and, further, that it was a charge or expense incurred in the winding-up within s 267 of the 1948 Act. The liquidator appealed.

Held – Where a company had incurred a liability to tax in consequence of the realisation of its assets after the commencement of its winding-up, the discharge of such liability constituted a 'charge or expense incurred in the winding-up' within s 267 of the 1948

f   Act; and further, taking into account the fact that the company was bound to pay the tax and that the liquidator was the proper officer to pay it, the liability to tax was a 'necessary disbursement' of the liquidator within r 195(1) of the 1949 rules. The liability to tax was not, however, an 'expense properly incurred in . . . realising . . . the asset' within r 195(1) since it was not a direct, but only a possible, consequence of the realisation of the assets of the company. It followed, therefore, that the company's liability to corporation tax in

g   the sum of £634,440 was a 'necessary disbursement' of the company's liquidator within r 195(1) of the 1949 rules and was a 'charge or expense incurred in the winding up' of the company within s 267 of the 1948 Act. The appeal would accordingly be dismissed (see p 120 *g* to *j* and p 121 *b* to *e*, post).

Decision of Brightman J [1979] 1 All ER 302 affirmed.

h   *a*   Rule 195(1), so far as material, provides: 'The assets of a Company in a winding-up by the Court remaining after payment of the fees and expenses properly incurred in preserving, realising or getting in the assets . . . shall . . . be liable to . . . payments, which shall be made in the following order . . . First.—The taxed costs of the petition . . . Next.—The remuneration of the special manager (if any). Next.—The costs and expenses of any person who makes or concurs in making, the Company's statement of affairs. Next.—The taxed charges of any shorthand writer . . . Next.—

j   The necessary disbursements of any Liquidator . . . other than expenses properly incurred in preserving, realising or getting in the assets . . . Next.—The costs of any person properly employed by such Liquidator. Next.—The remuneration of any such Liquidator . . .'

    b   Section 267 provides: 'The court may, in the event of the assets being insufficient to satisfy the liabilities, make an order as to the payment out of the assets of the costs, charges and expenses incurred in the winding up in such order of priority as the court thinks just.'

    c   [1979] 1 All ER 302, [1979] STC 11

Notes
For priority for payment of tax in a winding-up, see 7 Halsbury's Laws (4th Edn) paras **a**
1285, 1316, for the application of assets in a winding-up, see ibid paras 1310, 1497, and
for cases on the subject, see 10 Digest (Reissue) 1075–1076, 1148, 6596–6600, 7146–
7149.
   For the Companies Act 1948, s 267, see 5 Halsbury's Statutes (3rd Edn) 319.
   For the Companies (Winding-up) Rules 1949, r 195, see 4 Halsbury's Statutory
Instruments (Third Reissue) 186. **b**

Cases referred to in judgments
Beni-Felkai Mining Co Ltd, Re [1934] Ch 406, [1933] All ER Rep 693, 18 Tax Cas 632, 103
   LJ Ch 187, 150 LT 370, [1934] B & CR 14, 10 Digest (Reissue) 1152, 7170.
Sadd v Griffin [1908] 2 KB 510, 77 LJKB 775, 99 LT 502, CA, 43 Digest (Repl) 173, 1605. **c**

Appeals
By two summonses dated 28th April 1978 Gerhard Adolf Weiss, who was appointed the
liquidator of Mesco Properties Ltd and Mesco Laboratories Ltd ('the companies') on 4th
February 1971 following the compulsory winding-up of the companies on 21st
December 1970, sought the determination of the following questions and the following **d**
relief: (1) whether the liability of the companies to account to the respondents to the
summonses, the Inland Revenue Commissioners, in respect of chargeable gains on
disposals by (i) the Co-operative Bank Ltd ('the bank') in exercise of its powers as
mortgagee of certain of the companies' properties which had been charged in its favour,
(ii) the receiver appointed by the bank in exercise of its powers as mortgagee of certain
other of the companies' properties which had been charged in favour of the bank and (iii) **e**
the liquidator of the companies during winding-up by the court of assets vested in the
companies arose (a) as a fee or expense properly incurred in preserving, realising or
getting in the companies' assets within the meaning of r 195(1) of the Companies
(Winding-up) Rules 1949[1] or (b) as a necessary disbursement of the liquidator within the
meaning of r 195(1) or (c) as a debt or some other liability ranking pari passu with the
claims of the ordinary unsecured creditors of the companies or (d) as some other liability; **f**
(2) whether in any event the liability was a cost, charge or expense of the winding-up
within the meaning of s 267 of the Companies Act 1948; and (3) in the event that the
liability ranked in order of priority ahead of the remuneration of the liquidator within
r 195(1) an order under s 267 of the 1948 Act that the remuneration of the liquidator
down to his release be allowed in full in priority to the liability. On 7th November 1978
Brightman J[2] declared that the liability of the companies to account to the Inland **g**
Revenue Commissioners in respect of corporation tax on the chargeable gains arising on
disposal of the companies' assets during the compulsory winding-up was a necessary
disbursement of the liquidator within r 195(1) of the 1949 rules. The Crown gave notice
that it would on the appeal contend that the decision of the judge should be varied in the
event of the appeal being allowed to the extent of the discharge of the declaration made
by the judge that the liability of the companies to account to the Crown in respect of the **h**
corporation tax arose as an expense properly incurred in realising or getting in the assets
of the companies within r 195(1) or, alternatively, that the liability in respect of tax
ranked after the matters provided for in r 195(1) but before the claim of creditors with
provable debts.

G B H Dillon QC and *James Munby* for the liquidator. **j**
Peter Gibson for the Crown.

---

1 SI 1949 No 330
2 [1979] 1 All ER 302, [1979] 1 WLR 558, [1979] STC 11

BUCKLEY LJ. We have before us two appeals from decisions of Brightman J[1], one in
a the matter of Mesco Properties Ltd, and the other, notwithstanding the way in which the
case is listed, in the matter of Mesco Laboratories Ltd. The appeals arise on decisions of
the learned judge on two summonses, each issued in the compulsory liquidation of the
company in question. The facts of the two cases are in all significant respects the same,
so that the fate of one appeal must dictate the fate of the other; I can confine myself to the
appeal in the matter of Mesco Properties Ltd.

b   The facts are set out in the report of the learned judge's decision[1]; I need not repeat
them at any length.

After the commencement of the winding-up of the company, certain immovable
properties of the company were sold, some of them by receivers appointed by mortgagees,
some by mortgagees and some by the liquidator, at prices which realised profits over the
cost of those properties to the company. Consequently the company became liable to
c corporation tax in the considerable sum of £634,440, in respect of chargeable gains so
realised. The liquidator has a balance in hand in the winding-up of no more than about
£520,000.

In these circumstances the liquidator, by the summons, asks (1) whether the
corporation tax is (a) a fee or other expense properly incurred in preserving, realising or
getting in the assets of the company within the meaning of r 195(1) of the Companies
d (Winding-up) Rules 1949 or (b) a necessary disbursement of the liquidator within the
meaning of that rule. I need not read paras (c) and (d) of para (1) of the summons: (c) has
been abandoned and (d) does not in fact arise.

The liquidator also asks, by para (2) of the summons, whether in any event the liability
for the tax is a cost, charge or expense of the winding-up within the meaning of s 267 of
the Companies Act 1948. The summons also raised a further question about how the
e liquidator's own remuneration should rank, but we are not now concerned with that.

Brightman J answered para (1)(a) of the summons in the negative, para (1)(b) in the
affirmative and para (2) in the affirmative. The liquidator appeals against that decision.

It is common ground that the Crown cannot prove in the winding-up for tax the
liability for which arose after the commencement of the winding-up. It is also common
ground that neither the liquidator, nor any mortgagee or receiver is liable for any of the
f tax: the company alone is liable.

In the events which have happened the liquidator is the proper officer of the company
to pay the tax (see the Taxes Management Act 1970, s 108(1) and (3)(a)). Under the
Income and Corporation Taxes Act 1970, s 238(1), corporation tax is charged on a
company's profits which, by virtue of sub-s (4) means income and chargeable gains.
Chargeable gains for this purpose are to be computed in accordance with capital gains tax
g principles (see s 265(2) of that Act) and the amount to be included in respect of chargeable
gains in a company's total profits for any accounting period are the total amount of
chargeable gains accruing to the company in that period after deducting allowable
losses. Corporation tax assessed for an accounting period is in general payable within
nine months from the end of that period or, if later, within one month from assessment
(see s 243(4)).

h   Counsel for the liquidator, submits that the learned judge was wrong to hold that the
tax is a disbursement within r 195 of the 1949 rules, because the liquidator has not paid
the tax and does not wish to pay it unless, in accordance with the proper priority in which
the company's liabilities should be discharged, he is bound to do so; and because the
payment of the tax will not advance the liquidation in the sense of making the liquidator
more able to distribute the company's assets among its creditors.

j   Counsel for the Crown submits that the judge was right in holding that the tax
constitutes a disbursement within the meaning of r 195. He says that all liabilities which
properly fall within the description of costs, charges and expenses of a winding-up rank

---

1   [1979] 1 All ER 302, [1979] 1 WLR 558, [1979] STC 11

in front of the general body of creditors at the commencement of the winding-up having
provable debts, and that they are, inter se, to be satisfied in the order of priority laid down   *a*
in r 195, subject to any order of the court under s 267 of the Companies Act 1948, and
he submits that the tax ranks as a necessary disbursement of the liquidator and so falls
within the fifth of the paragraphs set out in para (1) of r 195.

The Crown has by a respondent's notice asserted that in the event of the liquidator's
appeal being allowed, the learned judge's order should be varied so as to declare that the
liability for the tax is an expense properly incurred in realising or getting in the assets of   *b*
the company within the opening words of r 195.

The first question for consideration is, I think, whether Brightman J was right in
holding that the tax constitutes a necessary disbursement within the meaning of the
rule. It would, in my view, be a very remarkable thing if the proper priority of a liability
under r 195 were to depend on whether the liquidator decided to pay it or not, which
seems to be the effect of the argument of counsel for the liquidator, for he says that if the   *c*
liquidator had paid the tax it could properly be described as a disbursement, but that
until he pays it, it cannot be so described.

He referred us in this connection to *Sadd v Griffin*[1] where it was held that a solicitor
could not charge his client, as disbursements, for counsel's fees which had not yet been
paid. That case is so far from the present case on the facts and the considerations
involved, that I do not think it of any assistance in construing r 195. It must, in my view,   *d*
be open to a liquidator to apply to the court for guidance on the question whether, if he
discharges a certain liability of the company in liquidation, the payment will be a
necessary disbursement within the meaning of r 195. That is what the liquidator is
doing in this case. The company is liable for the tax which is due. The tax ought to be
paid. The liquidator is the proper officer to pay it. When he pays it, he will clearly make
a disbursement. In my judgment it will be a necessary disbursement within the meaning   *e*
of the rule. Moreover, common sense and justice seem to me to require that it should be
discharged in full in priority to the unsecured creditors, and to any expenses which rank
lower in priority under r 195. The tax is a consequence of the realisation of the assets in
the course of the winding-up of the company. That realisation was a necessary step in the
liquidation; that is to say, in the administration of the insolvent estate. The fact that in
the event there may be nothing available for the unsecured creditors does not, in my   *f*
view, mean that the realisation was not a step taken in the interests of all who have claims
against the company. Those claims must necessarily be met out of the available assets in
due order of priority. Superior claims may baulk inferior ones, but the liquidator's duty
is to realise the assets for the benefit of all in accordance with their rights. If in
consequence of the realisation, the company incurs a liability, the discharge of such
liability must, in my judgment, constitute a charge or expense incurred in the winding-   *g*
up within the Companies Act 1948, s 267 and must also, in my view, fall within r 195.

The learned judge pointed out that under the Income and Corporation Taxes Act
1970, s 243(2), a company is expressly made chargeable to corporation tax on a capital
gain arising in a winding-up. He said[2]:

> 'It follows that the tax is a charge which the liquidator is bound to discharge by   *h*
> payment, to the extent that assets are available. It is, therefore, to my mind, beyond
> argument that the payment of the tax is a "necessary disbursement" of the liquidator
> and must come within the fifth paragraph of r 195(1) of the 1949 rules unless it is
> an expense "properly incurred in preserving, realising or getting in the assets", in
> which case it is excepted from the fifth paragraph because it falls within the opening
> words of the sub-r (1).'

j

I agree.

---

1   [1908] 2 KB 510
2   [1979] 1 All ER 302 at 304–305, [1979] 1 WLR 558 at 561, [1979] STC 11 at 13–14

He went on to refer to certain dicta of Maugham J in *Re Beni-Felkai Mining Co Ltd*[1].

a That case was concerned with a voluntary winding-up and with income tax which had become due in respect of profits earned after the commencement of the winding-up. Maugham J expressed the view[2] that the tax could not be properly described as 'fees or actual expenses incurred in realising or getting in the assets', but said that he was more doubtful whether it might come within 'the liquidator's necessary disbursements'.

Brightman J expressed the opinion[3] that corporation tax on a capital gain, made when

b a liquidator sells an asset, is not 'an expense incurred in realising' that asset. I agree with this. The liability to tax is a consequence of, amongst other things, the realisation, but it is not a direct consequence of the realisation. It depends on the amount of the company's 'profits' as defined in s 238 of the Income and Corporation Taxes Act 1970 (if any) for the entire relevant accounting period. It is, as the learned judge said[3], 'merely a possible consequence' of a sale at a profit. He consequently reached the conclusion that

c the tax did not fall within the expression 'fees and expenses incurred in realising the assets' in the opening words of r 195, but did not fall within the words 'the necessary disbursements of any liquidator appointed in the winding up by the court' in the fifth sub-paragraph of para (1) of the rule.

On the question raised by para (2) of the summons, he held that the corporation tax was a charge or expense incurred in the winding-up, within s 267.

d In my judgment the learned judge's conclusions were correct and I would dismiss both appeals.

BRIDGE LJ. I agree, both with the judgment just delivered by Buckley LJ and with that of Brightman J which is under appeal.

There is nothing of my own that I can usefully add. I too would dismiss the appeals.

e

TEMPLEMAN LJ. I agree.

Appeals dismissed. Liquidator to be at liberty to retain his costs (to be taxed on trustee basis) out of assets. Leave to appeal to House of Lords refused.

f Solicitors: *Herbert Smith & Co* (for the liquidator); *Solicitor of Inland Revenue*.

J H Fazan Esq   Barrister.

---

1   [1934] Ch 406, [1933] All ER Rep 693, 18 Tax Cas 632
2   [1934] Ch 406 at 417, [1933] All ER Rep 693 at 696–697, 18 Tax Cas 632 at 634–635
3   [1979] 1 All ER 302 at 306, [1979] 1 WLR 558 att 563, [1979] STC 11 at 15

Dunford v Dunford   *a*

COURT OF APPEAL, CIVIL DIVISION
LORD DENNING MR AND EVELEIGH LJ
28th JUNE 1979

Divorce – Financial provision – Matters to be considered by court when making order – Financial *b*
needs, obligations and responsibilities of parties – Principle of 'clean break' – Matrimonial home
purchased in joint names – Wife living in matrimonial home with children after dissolution of
marriage – Children aged between 15 and 11 – Husband living in lodgings – Husband having
better financial position and prospects than wife – Husband ordered to transfer his interest in
matrimonial home to wife – In the event of the wife selling the matrimonial home or dying, husband
to have 25% of the net proceeds – Husband also ordered to pay wife 5p per annum and each child *c*
£7.50 a week until child 17 – Whether order consistent with principle of 'clean break' – Whether
order proper in circumstances.

The husband and wife married in 1962 and had three children. In 1971 they bought a
house for £3,950 in their joint names on a 100% mortgage. In 1978 the wife petitioned *d*
for a divorce and applied for financial provision for herself and the children and a
property adjustment order. The husband did not oppose the petition and the wife was
granted a decree nisi in the county court. By then the husband had moved into lodgings
but the wife was still living in the matrimonial home with the three children, who were
aged 15, 13 and 11 respectively. Only £350 of the mortgage had been paid off. The
husband was earning £93 a week gross. The wife was earning £37 a week gross, *e*
working part-time in a school, and in addition was receiving a family allowance and
various other social security benefits. She wished to bring up the children in the
matrimonial home, which was by then worth between £14,000 and £15,000. The
judge ordered (i) that the husband's interest in the matrimonial home should be
transferred to the wife within three months and that she should be responsible for all the
outgoings in respect of the house including the mortgage repayments, (ii) that the house *f*
should be charged with payment to the husband of 25% of the net proceeds of sale should
the wife sell the home or die, (iii) that the husband should continue to pay £7.50 a week
for each child until the child attained the age of 17, and (iv) that the maintenance
payments for the wife should be reduced to the nominal sum of 5p per annum. The
husband appealed contending that the matrimonial home should be sold on the youngest
child completing her full-time education or on the wife's remarriage, whichever was the *g*
earlier, and that he should be required to transfer to the wife only such of his interest in
the matrimonial home as was necessary for her future needs. The wife cross-appealed,
contending that the provision in the judge's order for a charge on the matrimonial home
should be struck out.

h

Held – The judge's order produced certainty in that both parties knew exactly where
they stood and furthermore was generally consistent with the modern principle that
after the breakdown of a marriage the financial and property issues should be settled once
and for all so as to enable the parties to make a clean break with the past and begin a new
life. The order departed from that principle only in so far as it required the husband to
pay the wife maintenance of 5p per annum. The order was the appropriate one in the *j*
circumstances and would be varied only to the extent of striking out the requirement as
to maintenance payments for the wife. It followed that both the appeal and cross-appeal
would be dismissed (see p 124 *j*, p 125 *c* to *h* and p 126 *a*, post).

Hanlon v Hanlon [1978] 2 All ER 889, *Minton v Minton* [1979] 1 All ER 79 and *Jessel v*
Jessel [1979] 3 All ER 645 applied.

Notes

a For financial provision and property adjustment orders on divorce and the matters to which the court must have regard, see 13 Halsbury's Laws (4th Edn) paras 1052–1053, 1060.

Cases referred to in judgments

Hanlon v Hanlon [1978] 2 All ER 889, [1978] 1 WLR 592, CA.

b *Jessel v Jessel* [1979] 3 All ER 645, [1979] 1 WLR 1148, CA.

Mesher v Mesher and Hall p 126, post, CA.

Minton v Minton [1979] 1 All ER 79, [1979] AC 593, [1979] 2 WLR 31, HL.

Interlocutory appeal

In September 1978 the wife filed a petition for divorce. Her petition included a prayer c for financial provision for herself and the three children of the marriage and a property adjustment order. In December 1978 she was granted a decree nisi in the Portsmouth County Court. By an order dated 22nd March 1979 the registrar in the Portsmouth County Court, Mr Registrar J H Wroath, ordered (i) that the matrimonial home in Portsmouth should not be sold until the youngest child completed her full-time education, (ii) that the husband should pay the the wife maintenance pending suit at the d rate of £5 a week and that such payment should rank as periodical payments from the date that the decree nisi was made absolute, (iii) that the husband should pay from 22nd March 1979 periodical payments to each child of the marriage until the child attained 17 years of age, or further order, at the rate of £7·50 per week. The wife appealed against the order. On 21st May 1979 in the Portsmouth County Court his Honour Judge Galpin allowed the appeal and ordered (i) that the husband should transfer his interest in the e matrimonial home to the wife within three months of the order, (ii) that the wife should be responsible for all future outgoings including mortgage repayments on the property and indemnify the husband against any future payments; (iii) that the matrimonial home should be charged with payment to the husband of 25% of the net proceeds of sale when sold or on the death of the wife, such sum to be calculated without regard to any future mortgage taken out by the wife, (iv) that the order for periodical payments for the f wife should be varied to 5p per annum, and (v) that the order for periodical payments in respect of the children should remain the same. The husband appealed against the order, contending that the matrimonial home should be sold on the youngest child completing her full-time education or the wife's earlier remarriage and that he should be required to transfer to the wife only such of his interest in the matrimonial home as would be necessary for the wife's future needs. The wife cross-appealed, contending that the g provision in the judge's order for a charge on the matrimonial home should be struck out. The facts are set out in the judgment of Lord Denning MR.

Keith Cutler for the husband.
F R N K Massey for the wife.

h

LORD DENNING MR. This is an interesting case about a matrimonial home. The husband and wife were married on 14th July 1962, when he was 21 and she was 19. They have three children: boys of 15 and 13 and a girl of 11. They separated after 16 years of marriage in August 1978. Divorce proceedings have gone through very expeditiously. The wife took out a petition for divorce in September 1978 on the ground j that the husband had behaved in such a way that she could not be expected to live with him any more and that the marriage had broken down irretrievably. The husband did not dispute it. He submitted to an order by consent. That can often be done nowadays just on an affidavit without going to court at all. The wife alleged that from 1974 onwards the husband drank to excess despite her repeated pleadings and became an alcoholic. She gave details of events in the August before the final breakdown of the

marriage; how he went out drinking and when he returned home he behaved
abominably to her. So much so that he struck her and the like. At all events, she said *a*
that owing to his conduct the marriage had broken down. The husband did not oppose
it. The decree nisi was made in December 1978.

There arose the question of the arrangements for the children. The wife stayed with
the children in the matrimonial home at 2 Minstead Road, Milton, Portsmouth. She
looked after them there, seeing them off to school, and working part-time while they
were at school. The question then arose as to what should be done with the matrimonial *b*
home. Under the new legislation the court has a very wide power to transfer the interest
in the home from one spouse to the other.

In this case the matrimonial home had been a council house. The husband and wife
had bought it in 1971. They did not have to put down a deposit. They obtained a 100%
mortgage from the Portsmouth Council. The total price for that three-bedroomed house
in 1971 was £3,950. But during the last eight years the value of the house has gone up *c*
to £14,000 or £15,000. The question is: what is to be done about the house? The wife
wants to stay there, and ought to be able to stay there, to bring up the family. The house
is still on mortgage; and over the years, when the husband and wife were both living
there, they paid off the interest and a little off the capital. At present time there is on the
mortgage a sum of about £3,600 outstanding.

The position of the parties is this. The husband is a press room assistant. That is a *d*
good position. His gross income is £93 a week. The wife now has part-time work
concerned with school meals. She earns £37 a week gross. He has to pay maintenance
of £7·50 a week for each of the three children, which totals £22·50. She receives family
allowance, one-parent benefit, and so forth. The husband, of course, has had to move
into lodgings elsewhere.

The matter first came before the registrar of the Portsmouth County Court. He went *e*
by a decision which was made some years ago. It is *Mesher v Mesher*[1]. In our present case
the house was in joint names and belonged to the husband and wife in equal
proportions. The registrar ordered that the house was not to be sold until the youngest
child had finished her schooling, which would be when she is 17 or 18 years of age.
Presumably, after that time, it could be sold and the proceeds divided equally between
the parties. Meanwhile the registrar ordered the husband to pay maintenance of £5 a *f*
week for the wife together with the sums of £7·50 a week for each of the children.

That order left the parties in complete uncertainty as to the future. After six or seven
years the house would have to be sold and the husband would take a half-share of the
proceeds, and the wife would be left with insufficient money to buy another house. The
wife's solicitors appealed. The judge made a different order. He ordered that the whole
of the interest in the house should be transferred to the wife within three months. He *g*
realised that if it were transferred, the wife would have to pay the mortgage instalments,
the rates, and all the other outgoings on the house. But the judge realised that the wife
might die or might sell the house some time in the future. If that should happen, the
judge ordered that the husband should then have 25% of the equity. His actual order
was:

h

'The matrimonial home to be charged with payment to the husband of 25% of
the net proceeds of sale when sold or on the death of the wife such sum to be
calculated without regard to any future mortgage taken out by the wife.'

By making that order, the parties would know exactly where they stood with
regard to the future. In so ordering, the judge applied the principle which is now *i*
flowing through these cases. It was indicated in the recent case of *Hanlon v Hanlon*[2] by

---

1 Page 126, post
2 [1978] 2 All ER 889 at 895, [1978] 1 WLR 592 at 599

Ormrod LJ. When it was suggested that there should be a postponement of the sale and
a then a distribution on a fifty-fifty basis, he said:

'. . . I do not think that that, in this case, would be in the least satisfactory; it
would leave the wife in a state of perpetual uncertainty and neither party would
know where ultimately they were going to be. It seems to me far better that the
parties' interests should be crystallised now, once and for all, so that the wife can
know what she is going to do about the property and the husband can make up his
b mind about what he is going to do about rehousing.'

That principle was expressed again in the recent case of *Minton v Minton*[1] by Lord
Scarman. He drew attention to the principle of the clean break. He said:

'The law now encourages spouses to avoid bitterness after family break down and
to settle their money and property problems. An object of the modern law is to
c encourage the parties to put the past behind them and to begin a new life which is
not overshadowed by the relationship which has broken down.'

There is only one variation which I think should be made to the order of the judge.
He ordered that the order for periodical payments for the wife should be 5p per annum,
a nominal sum. That should not be included in an order when you want a clean break.
d We recently had the case of *Jessel v Jessel*[2] in this court. We said that if an order for
periodical payments were included, it kept the position fluid and the wife could come
back later on for more and more maintenance. In order to avoid any such renewal of the
past, the right thing is to have no order for periodical payments inserted at all, as in
Minton v Minton[3]. So I think in this case the order of the judge should be varied by
striking out the order for periodical payments of 5p a year. In that way we have the
e 'clean break'. The wife knows exactly where she stands. The house is vested in her. She
has the property in it, and she can keep the family together. She can keep it as a home
for the family as they grow up. She can keep it going indefinitely, knowing exactly
where she stands. But if it should happen that she should sell the house (or should die)
then the husband is to have one-quarter of the net proceeds.

It has to be remembered that she has to bear the expense of the outstanding mortgage
f of nearly £4,000. This is a legal aid case, so there will probably be a charge on the house
to cover the costs of both parties. But, subject to those charges, if the house is sold, the
husband will receive 25% and the wife will receive 75% of the net proceeds.

It seems to me that the judge made his order in accordance with the modern principle
of the 'clean break' so that both parties will know hereafter exactly where they stand. At
all events, subject to the variation which I have indicated, it seems to me that the order
g of the judge was right, and I would dismiss the appeal and, incidentally, the cross-appeal.
I do not think the wife should have this house vested in her completely as she wanted.

So I would dismiss the appeal and the cross-appeal subject to the variation that the
order for periodical payments should be struck out.

h

EVELEIGH LJ. I agree. It is true that the husband is losing his share in the equity of
the house, but it is a house where the mortgage is still at the original figure and the wife
has the obligation of paying that off. The husband's capital prospects are very much
greater than those of the wife. He has a superior earning capacity; and, in the not too
distant future when the children's payments come to an end, the difference between
j their earning capacity or their income will be even more pronounced.

---

1   [1979] 1 All ER 79 at 87–88, [1979] AC 593 at 608
2   [1979] 3 All ER 645, [1979] 1 WLR 1148
3   [1979] 1 All ER 79, [1979] AC 593

In those circumstances, I think that his prospects, as I say, of acquiring a house in due
course are really quite good.   *a*
I agree with the order proposed by Lord Denning MR.

Appeal and cross-appeal dismissed. Order accordingly.

Solicitors: *Warner, Goodman & Co* (for the husband); *Innes, Pitassi & Co* (for the wife).
                                                                                                                      b
Sumra Green   Barrister.

Note
Mesher v Mesher and Hall   *c*

COURT OF APPEAL, CIVIL DIVISION
DAVIES, CAIRNS AND STAMP LJJ
12th FEBRUARY 1973

Divorce – Property – Adjustment order – Transfer of property – Matrimonial home – Matters   *d*
to be considered by court when making order – Financial needs, obligations and responsibilities of
parties.

Case referred to in judgments
Wachtel v Wachtel [1973] 1 All ER 829, [1973] Fam 72, [1973] 2 WLR 366, CA, Digest
(Cont Vol D) 425, 6962Aa.   *e*

Appeal
This was an appeal by the respondent husband from an order made by Latey J at
Winchester on 4th October 1972 on the wife's application for ancillary relief. The judge
ordered, on an undertaking by the wife not to take any action to recover any arrears due
to her on any existing order, that the former matrimonial home be transferred to the   *f*
wife and that the husband pay £4 per week for the benefit of the child of the marriage.
He adjourned the question of periodical payments for the wife. Both husband and wife
planned to remarry partners with children by previous marriages resulting in two family
units with similar resources. The husband complained that in the circumstances it
would be unfair and unreasonable to deprive him of the whole of his interest in the
former matrimonial home. The facts are set out in the judgment of Davies LJ.   *g*

B R O Carter for the husband.
Susan Trevethan for the wife.

DAVIES LJ. This is the respondent husband's appeal, by leave, from an order made by
Latey J at Winchester on 4th October 1972, on the wife's application for a periodical   *h*
payments order for herself and the child of the marriage, a lump sum order, and a
transfer of property order in respect of the former matrimonial home, 11 Burnbrae
Road, Ferndown, Dorset, which had at all material times been in the joint names of the
parties. So far as periodical payments are concerned, there had been in force an interim
order for the wife of £4 per week and for the child of £3 per week. At the date of the   *j*
hearing before the judge the payments due to the wife were in arrear.
    The order which the judge made was as follows:

    'Upon the Judge making no order for lump sum And Upon [the wife] undertaking
    by her Counsel not to take any action to recover any arrears due to her on any
    existing order It is Ordered that the property known as 11 Burnbrae Road, West

Parley, Ferndown in the County of Dorset be transferred to [the wife] And it is
Ordered that [the husband] do pay to [the wife] for the benefit of the child of the
marriage Gillian Nicola the sum of £4 per week, payable weekly, the first such
payment to be made on the 4th October, 1972 It is Further Ordered that [the wife]
do apply forthwith to have the decree nisi pronounced on the 4th August, 1971,
made absolute And it is Further Ordered that the question of periodical payments
[that is periodical payments for the wife, of course] do stand adjourned generally.'

The husband complains that in the circumstances it is unfair and unreasonable that he
should be deprived of the whole of his interest in the former matrimonial home and
submits that the proper order is that he and the wife should share it equally. There is, as
will appear, a dispute between the parties as to its probable present-day value.

The marriage took place on 12th May 1956 and there has been one child, a girl, now
approaching nine years of age, who lives with her mother. The house at Burnbrae Road,
which was the third matrimonial home, each of which had been in joint names, was
bought in 1966. I shall return to figures later. Apparently the husband commenced to
commit adultery with Mrs Hall, the second respondent, in 1968; and in June 1970 he left
to go to take up residence with her. Since April 1971 they have lived at 12 Chichester
Walk, Canford Magna, as to which more later. On 11th May 1971 the wife petitioned
for dissolution, and on 4th August of that year a decree nisi was pronounced. It has not
yet been made absolute, and an application made by the husband on 17th February 1972
for the decree to be made absolute was on 6th March adjourned pending the decision on
the wife's application for ancillary relief. If and when the decree is made absolute, the
husband and Mrs Hall, who is free to marry, intend to marry; and similarly the wife
intends to marry a Mr Jones, who is also free to marry. He was previously married and
has to support his former wife and two children.

I turn now to consider the financial aspect of the case, and deal first with the two
houses. The former matrimonial home at Burnbrae Road was bought in 1966, as I have
said, in joint names, for £6,750, and on it there is an outstanding mortgage of £3,500.
Various estimates as to its present-day value were before the judge. In broad outline, the
husband's case is that it is worth something in the neighbourhood of £22,000; the figure
which the wife puts on it is some £16,000 to £16,500. On any view it is a substantial
capital asset. The house where the husband is now living with Mrs Hall in Chichester
Walk was bought in April 1971 for £6,200, in the joint names of the husband and Mrs
Hall. Of this sum Mrs Hall provided £3,000 and the balance was covered by a
mortgage. Here again there is a dispute about the present value, the husband putting it
at about £12,000 and the wife at about £14,000. So far as concerns Mr Jones, he has no
house, having transferred his former matrimonial home to his former wife.

The income positions of the two families, treating the husband and Mrs Hall as one
family and the wife and Mr Jones as another, which it is convenient to do in view of the
impending marriages, are remarkably similar the one to the other. The latest
information about the husband's income position is that he has a gross annual earned
income, that is to say before tax, of £1,945, and Mrs Hall earns £624, a total of, say,
£2,500. In addition, Mrs Hall receives maintenance of £3·50 per week, or £182 a year,
from her former husband for the maintenance of her one child. The husband estimates
the outgoings in respect of Chichester Walk at £579. He has debts of just over £1,000
and, of course, he has to pay £4 a week, or £208 a year, for the maintenance of the child
of the marriage. The two orders for maintenance nearly cancel each other out. Mr
Jones's earnings are higher, namely £3,250 before tax. But he has to pay his former wife
and children £15 per week, or £780 a year. Thus both families are in the £2,500
bracket. The outgoings on Burnbrae Road as estimated by the husband were £543 per
annum. Mr Jones has debts of approximately £1,300. The maintenance of £4 per week
which the wife receives in respect of the child I have already dealt with.

So it is to be seen that matters are very evenly balanced; and in these circumstances
counsel for the husband submits that it would be quite wrong to deprive the husband of

the substantial asset which his half-interest in the house represents. Indeed he referred us to the very recent decision of this court in *Wachtel v Wachtel*[1] and suggested that as a *a* result of the observations of Lord Denning MR in that case there would be something to be said for cutting down the wife's share to one-third. But he did not ask for such an order. He was content that this valuable asset should be divided equally.

Counsel for the wife, however, strongly supported the order. She pointed out that, after 14 years of marriage, it was the husband who broke it up, as the judge rightly said, and that, despite what this court said in *Wachtel v Wachtel*[1], under the express words of *b* s 5(1) of the Matrimonial Proceedings and Property Act 1970, conduct is a matter to put into the scales. She points out that owing to the forthcoming marriage between the wife and Mr Jones, the husband will be absolved from the liability to maintain the wife and that the order of £4 per week in respect of the daughter is on the low side.

So far as that last point is concerned, it is obviously open to the wife to apply for an increase if the circumstances justify it. But as far as the main problem is concerned, one *c* has to take a broad approach to the whole case. What is wanted here is to see that the wife and daughter, together no doubt in the near future with Mr Jones, should have a home in which to live rather than that she should have a large sum of available capital. With that end in view, I have come to the conclusion that counsel's submission for the husband is right. It would, in my judgment, be wrong to strip the husband entirely of any interest in the house. I would set aside the judge's order so far as concerns the house and *d* substitute instead an order that the house is held by the parties in equal shares on trust for sale but that it is not to be sold until the child of the marriage reaches a specified age or with the leave of the court.

That, I think, in all the circumstances, would be the fairest disposal of this matter. I would allow the appeal accordingly. The precise terms of the order can no doubt be discussed with counsel after Cairns and Stamp LJJ have given judgment.   *e*

CAIRNS LJ. I agree, and have nothing to add.

STAMP LJ. I agree, and have nothing to add.

Appeal allowed. Transfer order set aside. Order that the matrimonial home to be held on trust *f* *for sale to hold the net proceeds of sale and rents and profits until sale in equal shares, provided that as long as the child of the marriage be under the age of 17 or until further order the house not be sold; the wife to be at liberty to live there rent-free, paying and discharging all rates, taxes and outgoings, including mortgage interest, and indemnifying the husband therefor; any repayments of capital to be borne in equal shares; undertaking by wife to stand. Leave to appeal to the House of Lords refused.*   *g*

Solicitors: *Ward Bowie & Co*, agents for *Trevanion, Walker & Coombs*, Bournemouth (for the husband); *Peacock & Goddard*, agents for *Lester & Russell*, Bournemouth (for the wife).

Avtar S Virdi Esq   Barrister. *h*

---

1   [1973] 1 All ER 829, [1973] Fam 72

Re a debtor (No 37 of 1976, Liverpool), ex parte Taylor v The debtor and another

CHANCERY DIVISION

FOX AND BROWNE-WILKINSON JJ

14th, 15th, 16th, 17th, 18th, 21st MAY, 13th JULY 1979

Bankruptcy – Annulment – Application to annul adjudication – Cross-examination of bankrupt – Affidavit of bankrupt used in court – Cross-examination on affidavit – Discretion of court to refuse to allow cross-examination.

Bankruptcy – Annulment – Application to annul adjudication – No public examination of bankrupt held – Whether public examination a condition precedent to annulment – Bankruptcy Act 1914, ss 15(1), 29(1).

In 1970 the debtor and the petitioning creditor began trading as land developers under the name of M Ltd. In 1972 the debtor instituted a succession of legal proceedings, in the name of M Ltd, against the petitioning creditor and a number of companies, in which he contested the disposal of a piece of land known as the Forum site. In order to finance the legal proceedings he borrowed large sums of money. In March 1976 the petitioning creditor filed a bankruptcy petition against the debtor on a debt due to the petitioning creditor under a High Court order. A receiving order was made on the petition on 11th May 1976. The debtor's public examination was fixed for 29th June 1976 but on that date the examination was adjourned to 6th July. The debtor failed to attend on 6th July. An adjudication order was made and the public examination adjourned sine die. The date for the public examination was subsequently fixed for 14th September but on that date it had to be adjourned sine die because the debtor again failed to attend. As a result he was committed to prison for contempt of court but was released on giving an undertaking to attend the public examination. In November 1977 he brought an action in the name of M Ltd against the petitioning creditor and various companies to recover the Forum site. On 20th February 1978 the court made an order for the speedy trial of the action. A fortnight later, on the application of the Official Receiver, the public examination of the debtor was reinstated for hearing on 11th April. On 4th April the debtor applied for, and was granted, an adjournment of the public examination to 19th September on the grounds that his main asset in his bankruptcy was his shares in M Ltd and that he might be asked questions which might be prejudicial to the outcome of the action and consequently to M Ltd and to the creditors in the bankruptcy. The action was dismissed by consent on 20th June 1978, after the debtor had been legally advised that although he himself might have a cause of action M Ltd did not. On 6th September 1978 the debtor applied for the annulment of the adjudication order under s 29(1)[a] of the Bankruptcy Act 1914 on the ground that all the debts had been paid in full. He filed an affidavit in support of his application. On 14th September the public examination was ordered to be adjourned to 31st October and the application for annulment was ordered to be heard on 4th October. The petitioning creditor was the only one of the debtor's creditors to oppose the application. He applied for, and was granted, leave to appear on the application for annulment. The Official Receiver submitted a report to the registrar in which he stated, inter alia, (i) that the debts had been paid in full from third party funds, (ii) that had he been required to report on an application to discharge under s 26 of the 1914 Act he would have had to state that the debtor's assets were not equal to 50p

---

a Section 29(1), so far as material, provides: 'Where . . . it is proved to the satisfaction of the court that the debts of the bankrupt are paid in full, the court may, on the application of any person interested, by order annul the adjudication.'

in the pound on the amount of his unsecured liabilities, but that he did not think that
would, by itself, have been sufficient reason for refusing a discharge under s 26, and (iii) *a*
that in the circumstances he did not think there was any need for a public examination
of the debtor. The debtor's affidavit was used at the hearing. The petitioning creditor
filed no evidence but applied at the hearing for leave to cross-examine the debtor. He did
not formulate any specific issue on which he wished to cross-examine the debtor. The
debtor contended that the cross-examination should not be allowed because in the
circumstances it would be oppressive. The registrar refused to grant the petitioning *b*
creditor leave to cross-examine and then made an order annulling the adjudication order
on the ground that the debts had been paid in full. Five days later the debtor instituted
legal proceedings against the petitioning creditor and three companies in relation to the
Forum site. The petitioning creditor appealed against the registrar's order, contending
that it should be set aside because (i) the proceedings before the registrar were
fundamentally defective in that he had refused to allow the petitioning creditor to cross- *c*
examine the debtor and (ii) the registrar should not, in any event, have granted an
annulment of the adjudication order, especially as the debtor had not been publicly
examined as to his conduct, dealings and property in accordance with s 15(1)[b] of the 1914
Act.

Held – The appeal would be dismissed for the following reasons—
(i) The registrar had a discretion whether to allow or refuse cross-examination, and, *d*
since the petitioning creditor had filed no evidence, had asserted no new facts and had
not controverted any specific statements in the debtor's affidavit, cross-examination of
the debtor could well have been oppressive and the case was one of those exceptional
cases where a refusal to allow it was justified (see p 133 *g* and *j* to p 134 *c* and p 138 *d*,
post); *Comet Products UK Ltd v Hawkex Plastics Ltd* [1971] 1 All ER 1141 applied.
(ii) There were no grounds for interfering with the registrar's decision to annul the *e*
adjudication order because (a) the discretion which the court was given by s 29 of the
1914 Act to annul an adjudication order on the ground that the bankrupt's debts had
been paid in full was not restricted by the requirements of s 15(1) of that Act to cases
where the public examination had already been held, but was unfettered and could be
exercised in a case where a bankrupt had not been publicly examined if the court was
satisfied, in the light of all the circumstances, that the examination would not serve any *f*
useful purpose, (b) even if it was the law that, in the absence of special circumstances, the
court should not exercise its discretion under s 29 in a case where the bankrupt would not
have been granted an order of discharge on an application under s 26 of the Act, there
was no reason to think that the court would have refused to grant the debtor an order of
discharge if he had applied for one, and (c) in all the circumstances it could not be said
that the way in which the registrar had exercised his discretion was manifestly wrong or *g*
unjust (see p 134 *h* to p 135 *a* and *c g*, p 137 *b* and *e* to p 138 *d*, post); *Beck v Value Capital
Ltd (No 2)* [1976] 2 All ER 102 applied; dictum of Stirling LJ in *Re Keet* [1904–7] All ER
Rep at 840 considered.
Per Browne-Wilkinson J. In weighing the facts relevant to the exercise of the
discretionary powers to order cross-examination or to grant an annulment, it is proper to
take into account the petitioning creditor's motive for asking for the cross-examination *h*
and opposing the annulment (see p 138 *f g*, post).

Notes
For public examination of debtor, see 3 Halsbury's Laws (4th Edn) paras 399–407, and
for cases on the subject, see 5 Digest (Reissue) 653–656, 5697–5743.
For the Bankruptcy Act 1914, ss 15, 26, 29, see 3 Halsbury's Statutes (3rd Edn) 53, 69, *j*
77.

Cases referred to in judgments
Beck v Value Capital Ltd (No 2) [1976] 2 All ER 102, [1976] 1 WLR 572, CA.

---

b   Section 15(1) is set out at p 134 *g h*, post

Comet Products UK Ltd v Hawkex Plastics Ltd [1971] 1 All ER 1141, [1971] 2 QB 67, [1971]
a   2 WLR 361, [1972] RPC 691, CA, 22 Digest (Reissue) 511, 5185.

Debtor (No 446 of 1918), Re a, [1920] 1 KB 461, [1918–19] All ER Rep 397, 89 LJKB 113,
    122 LT 354, [1920] B & CR 31, CA, 4 Digest (Reissue) 184, *1636*.

Keet, Re [1905] 2 KB 666, [1904–7] All ER Rep 836, 74 LJKB 694, 93 LT 259, 12 Mans
    235, CA, 4 Digest (Reissue) 213, *1887*.

Paget, Re, ex parte Official Receiver [1927] 2 Ch 85, [1927] All ER Rep 465, 96 LJ Ch 377,
b   137 LT 369, [1927] B & CR 118, CA, 5 Digest (Reissue) 654, *5720*.

Cases also cited

Baden's Deed Trusts, Re, Baden v Smith [1967] 3 All ER 159, [1967] 1 WLR 1457.
Baron, Re, ex parte the debtor v Official Receiver [1943] 2 All ER 662, [1943] Ch 177, DC.
Beer, Re, ex parte Beer [1903] 1 KB 628, CA.
c *Burn, Re, Dawson v McClellan* (1931) 101 LJ Ch 113.
Burr, Re, ex parte Board of Trade [1892] 2 QB 467, CA.
Debtor (No 12 of 1970), Re a, ex parte Official Receiver v The debtor [1971] 2 All ER 1494,
    [1971] 1 WLR 1212, CA.
Debtor (No 2283 of 1976), Re a, ex parte the debtor v Hill Samuel & Co Ltd [1979] 1 All ER
    434, [1978] 1 WLR 1512, CA.
d *Gawthrop v Boulton* [1978] 3 All ER 615, [1979] 1 WLR 268.
Izod, Re, ex parte Official Receiver [1898] 1 QB 241, [1895–9] All ER Rep 1259, CA.
Lindwall v Lindwall [1967] 1 All ER 470, [1967] 1 WLR 143, CA.
London Fish Market and National Fishing Co, Re (1883) 27 Sol Jo 600.
Mundell, Re, Fenton v Cumberlege (1883) 48 LT 776.
Reed, Bowen & Co, Re, ex parte Official Receiver (1887) 19 QBD 174, CA.
e *Strauss v Goldschmidt* (1892) 8 TLR 239, DC.
Sultzberger, Re, ex parte Sultzberger (1887) 4 Morr 82, DC.
Taylor, Re, ex parte Taylor [1901] 1 KB 744, DC.
Van Laun, Re, ex parte International Assets Co Ltd (1907) 14 Mans 281, CA.
Ward v James [1965] 1 All ER 563, [1966] 1 QB 273, CA.
Ward, Re, ex parte Ward (1880) 15 Ch D 292, CA.

f

Appeal

This was an appeal by the petitioning creditor against an order of Mr Registrar Metcalfe,
made at Liverpool County Court on 4th October 1978, annulling an adjudication order
made against the debtor on 6th July 1976. The facts are set out in the judgment of Fox J.

g

Muir Hunter QC and *T M Ashe* for the petitioning creditor.
David Graham QC and *Charles Purle* for the debtor.
Roger Kaye for the Official Receiver.

                                                  Cur adv vult

h 13th July. The following judgments were read.

FOX J. This is an appeal by the petitioning creditor against an order of Mr Registrar
Metcalfe at the Liverpool County Court annulling an adjudication order made against
the debtor in July 1976. The petition was filed on 29th March 1976 on a debt of £3,740
due to the petitioning creditor from the debtor in respect of taxed costs under an order
j of the High Court. On 11th May a receiving order was made on that petition. The
public examination was fixed for 29th June but on that date the examination was
adjourned to 6th July. On 6th July the public examination was adjourned sine die,
under the provisions of r 192(*b*) of the Bankruptcy Rules 1952[1], because the debtor had

---

1 SI 1952 No 2113

failed to attend, and it was on 6th July that the adjudication order was made. On 24th
August an order was made that the public examination be held on 14th September but *a*
on the latter date the examination was adjourned sine die because the debtor had failed
to attend. On 15th October a warrant was issued for the arrest of the debtor in
consequence of his failure to attend the public examination. On 18th January 1977 the
debtor applied to this court for leave to appeal out of time against the receiving order and
the adjudication order. That application was dismissed on 8th February. On 29th
March the debtor was committed to prison for contempt of court in failing to attend his *b*
public examination. On 1st April the debtor was released from prison on certain
undertakings, including an undertaking to attend his public examination. On 6th
March 1978, on the application of the Official Receiver, the public examination which
had been adjourned sine die on 14th September 1976 was reinstated for hearing on 11th
April 1978. On 4th April 1978, on the application of the debtor, it was ordered that the
public examination be adjourned to 19th September 1978. *c*
    The grounds of the debtor's application were set out in his affidavit of 31st March
1978, paras 4, 5 and 6 of which read as follows:

> '4. I wish to draw to the attention of this Honourable Court the fact that the main
> asset in my Bankruptcy is my shares in Messina Securities Limited (hereinafter
> called the Company). The Company has been involved since 1971 in litigation with
> a number of parties. The said litigation arose out of the disposal of a piece of land *d*
> known as the Forum Site at Southport. [The petitioning creditor] is intimately
> concerned with the outcome of the said proceedings.
>   '5. The Company commenced an action to recover the Forum Site in November
> 1977. On the 20th day of February 1978 an Order was made by His Honour Judge
> FitzHugh Q.C. for a speedy Trial on a date to be fixed not before the 1st day of July
> 1978. Within two weeks of the said Order for a speedy Trial being made my said *e*
> Public Examination had been reinstated.
>   '6. I have no wish to avoid my Public Examination but I would respectfully draw
> to the attention of this Honourable Court that if the Public Examination were to
> proceed and if I were to be examined with regard to the said proceedings concerning
> the Company I respectfully submit that these questions might well be asked which
> will be prejudicial to the outcome of the said proceedings. They could I submit *f*
> with respect be prejudicial to the Company and consequently to the Creditors in the
> Bankruptcy.'

On 20th June 1978 the action by Messina Securities Ltd was dismissed by consent. On
6th September 1978 the debtor applied for the annulment of the adjudication on the
ground that all the debts had been paid in full. On 14th September it was ordered that *g*
the public examination be adjourned to 31st October and that the application for
annulment be heard on 4th October. On 18th September the petitioning creditor
applied to the court under r 184(3) for leave to appear on the application for
annulment. On 26th September the petitioning creditor was given leave to appear. On
4th October Mr Registrar Metcalfe made an order annulling the adjudication on the
ground that all the proved debts had been paid in full. *h*
    The Official Receiver's report is dated 27th September 1978 and contains, inter alia,
the following statements. (1) The proved debts had been paid in full from third party
funds. We were informed by counsel for the debtor that this payment was made by his
wife. (2) The debtor, who was aged about 48, was, up to 1971, variously employed as a
land consultant, earning between £6,000 and £8,000 a year. (3) In April 1970 the debtor
began to trade with the petitioning creditor as land developers under the style of Messina *j*
Securities Ltd on terms that he received 55% of the profits. (4) Since 1972 the debtor has
conducted some 36 legal actions in the name of Messina Securities Ltd against the
petitioning creditor and certain companies contesting the ownership of land. (5) In
about November 1971 the debtor mortgaged his house, 30 Liverpool Road, in order to
finance the legal proceedings. From 1971 onwards he borrowed money from four banks

for the same purpose and for living expenses. During this period he also received gifts
a from relatives totalling £6,000 which he used partly for living expenses and partly for
litigation. (6) The debtor had produced no books of account and alleged that he had not
traded personally since October 1971. (7) The deficiency in the debtor's assets as disclosed
by his statement of affairs was £46,682. (8) Had the Official Receiver been required to
report, on an application to discharge, any facts on proof of which the court would, under
s 26(3) of the Bankruptcy Act 1914, be bound to refuse, suspend or qualify an order to
b discharge, he would have reported that the debtor's assets were not equal to 50p in the
pound on the amount of his unsecured liabilities.

I have already mentioned that on 20th June 1978 the action by Messina Securities Ltd
was dismissed by consent. The action appears to have been misconceived. The debtor
has been so advised when abandoning the proceedings. There was no cause of action in
Messina Securities Ltd.

c On 9th October 1978 the debtor himself instituted proceedings in the Chancery
Division against the petitioning creditor and three companies in relation to the land
known as the Forum site and claiming to be entitled thereto. These proceedings were
commenced on the advice of leading counsel.

In the present appeal counsel for the petitioning creditor asks that the order of 4th
October 1978 annulling the adjudication be set aside. Two reasons are advanced in
d support of that. First, it is said that the proceedings before the registrar were
fundamentally defective because the registrar refused to allow counsel on behalf of the
petitioning creditor to cross-examine the debtor. Secondly, it is said that in any event the
registrar erred in principle and was manifestly wrong in exercising his discretion to
annul, having regard in particular to the fact that the debtor had not been publicly
examined. I take these submissions in turn.

e First, as to cross-examination. The debtor had filed an affidavit in support of the
application for annulment. It was largely formal. It merely recorded the amount of the
debts, that the Official Receiver had been kept informed of the proposed arrangements
to discharge them, and that although he, the debtor, had never accepted that he was
indebted to the petitioning creditor he was content that the indebtedness claimed by the
petitioning creditor should be discharged. No evidence was filed by the petitioning
f creditor.

At the hearing on 4th October 1978 counsel for the petitioning creditor asked for leave
to cross-examine the debtor. This was opposed by counsel on behalf of the debtor on the
ground that such cross-examination would be oppressive. Having heard counsel on both
sides, the registrar rejected the application for cross-examination.

The first question is whether the registrar had a discretion whether to allow or refuse
g cross-examination. I think that he had. It is true, of course, that the debtor's affidavit
had not merely been filed but used in the proceedings. But I do not think that that is
conclusive. In *Comet Products UK Ltd v Hawkex Plastics Ltd*[1], where the deponent's
affidavit had been read, Lord Denning MR said:

'If he has filed an affidavit, and in addition, if he has gone on to use it in the court,
then he is liable to be cross-examined on it if the court thinks it right so to order.
h I would not say that the mere filing is sufficient, but I do say that when it is not only
filed but used, the defendant does expose himself to a liability to be cross-examined
if the judge so rules. So that brings me to the final question: ought a judge to rule
that the second defendant should be cross-examined on his affidavit? It is to be
remembered that this power to cross-examine is a matter for the discretion of the
judge who is trying the case.'

j Cross LJ said[2]: '. . . I have no doubt that the judge had jurisdiction to order cross-

---

1   [1971] 1 All ER 1141 at 1144–1145, [1971] 2 QB 67 at 74
2   [1971] 1 All ER 1141 at 1147, [1971] 2 QB 67 at 77

examination and that the only question for determination on this appeal is whether he
was right to order it.'   *a*

In my view, therefore, the registrar had a discretion. Did he exercise it wrongly? As
Cross LJ observed in a further passage in the *Comet Products* case[1]: 'It is, I think, only in
a very exceptional case that a judge ought to refuse an application to cross-examine a
deponent on his affidavit'. But in my view the circumstances in the present case justify
the registrar's decision. The petitioning creditor had filed no evidence. He was asserting
no new facts and does not appear to have been controverting any specific statements in   *b*
the debtor's affidavit. No specific issue was formulated by the petitioning creditor in
respect of which it was suggested that cross-examination would be material. The fact is
that what the petitioning creditor wanted was a roving commission to cross-examine the
debtor generally in the hope that something might emerge to the discredit of the debtor
which might justify a submission that it was not a proper case to grant an annulment.
It seems to me that such cross-examination could well be oppressive and that, in the   *c*
absence of any attempt on behalf of the petitioning creditor to define clear issues of fact
to which cross-examination could be directed, the registrar was quite justified in his
decision.

It was suggested before us that there was an issue as to statutory interest on which
cross-examination would or might have been relevant, and the matter arises in this
way. Statutory interest is payable only out of the assets of the bankrupt. It is said that   *d*
the fact that the debts were being paid by the debtor's wife is a circumstance of some
suspicion and that it is possible that the debts are in fact being paid out of undisclosed
assets of the debtor; and that accordingly the debtor may have assets out of which
statutory interest could be paid. Accordingly it is said that cross-examination could
properly have been directed to this issue. I do not think that this contention is well
founded. It appears from the agreed note of the proceedings which is before us that the   *e*
matter of statutory interest was not raised on the question of cross-examination at all. It
was mentioned at a later stage in the proceedings after the registrar had refused leave to
cross-examine.

I may add that counsel for the petitioning creditor in his argument before us quite
frankly accepted that the question of statutory interest was of no real consequence in his
client's attitude to the case at all, and the amount involved, about £150, is small. What   *f*
the petitioning creditor wants is not statutory interest but the continuation of the
debtor's status of bankruptcy.

I turn to the second of counsel's principal submissions for the petitioning creditor:
that, there having been no public examination of the debtor, the registrar should not
have granted an annulment. Counsel submitted first that s 15 of the Bankruptcy Act
1914 contains a mandatory requirement for a public examination in every case. Section   *g*
15(1) provides:

> 'Where the court makes a receiving order, it shall, save as in this Act provided,
> hold a public sitting, on a day to be appointed by the court, for the examination of
> the debtor, and the debtor shall attend thereat, and shall be examined as to his
> conduct, dealings, and property.'
>   *h*

It will be observed that this provision is expressed to be 'save as in this Act provided'.
The specific provisions of the Act which limit the requirement of public examination are
to be found in ss 15(10) and 16(7). But in my view those provisions do not exhaust the
operation of the saving provision. Section 29 confers on the court a power to annul the
adjudication altogether. In cases to which the section applies, that discretion is
unfettered, and I see no reason why it should be treated as subject to a limitation that a   *j*
public examination must be held before annulment can be granted. The public
examination is, no doubt, a necessary step in the ordinary process of a bankruptcy. But

---

1   [1971] 1 All ER 1141 at 1147, [1971] 2 QB 67 at 77

by s 29 the court is authorised to bring to a halt the ordinary process of a bankruptcy by
a annulling the adjudication. Accordingly, it seems to me that in a case where the court
sees fit to exercise its discretion under s 29, the provisions of s 15(1) are, by implication,
displaced. It is to be observed that one of the circumstances in which the power
conferred by s 29 operates is where the debtor ought not to have been adjudged
bankrupt. If the court is satisfied of that fact, for example in the case of fraud, I find it
difficult to suppose that Parliament can have intended that nevertheless a public
b examination must, in every case, be insisted on.

Section 29 contains no reference to a public examination. It is, I think, significant
that s 16, dealing with compositions and schemes of arrangement, provides that the
application to approve the composition or scheme shall not be made until after the
conclusion of the public examination.

Again, s 26, dealing with discharge, provides that no application for discharge shall be
c made until the public examination has been completed. The result, in my view, is that
the provisions of s 29 displace those of s 15(1), and accordingly are within the saving
provision of s 15(1). Accordingly I think that the court has jurisdiction to grant an
annulment even though the public examination has not taken place.

Counsel for the petitioning creditor, however, makes a second submission on wider
grounds. He says, in effect, that, in the public interest, for the proper administration of
d the bankruptcy laws it is wrong in principle that a bankruptcy should be annulled if the
debtor has not been subjected to a public examination. We were referred to the
observations of Lord Hanworth MR in *Re Paget*[1]. He said:

> '. . . the object of the examination [is] not merely for the purpose of collecting the
> debts on behalf of the creditors or of ascertaining simply what sum can be made
> available for the creditors who are entitled to it, but also for the purpose of the
e > protection of the public in the cases in which the bankruptcy proceedings apply, and
> that there shall be a full and searching examination as to what has been the conduct
> of the debtor in order that a full report may be made to the Court by those who are
> charged to carry out the examination of the debtor.'

Further, we have been provided by the Chief Registrar with a statement as to the
f practice of the High Court registrars on applications for annulment. He states:

> 'Unless the public examination has been dispensed with under s 15(10) of the
> Bankruptcy Act 1914 (or, since the coming into force of the Insolvency Act 1976,
> under s 6 of that Act) it is the practice of the High Court not to entertain, except in
> exceptional circumstances, an application for annulment under s 29 of the Act, on
> the ground of payment in full, until the bankrupt has undergone a public
g > examination and that examination has been concluded.'

In general, that seems to me to be a salutary rule. It must, however, be borne in mind
that under s 29 the registrar has a complete discretion in the matter. He must exercise
that discretion in the light of all the circumstances of the case, and if he concludes that
a public examination would serve no sufficiently useful purpose he is, in the exercise of
h this discretion, entitled to give effect to that.

I come now to a number of matters relied on by counsel for the petitioning creditor
as indicating that this was a case in which a public examination was necessary, or as
indicating that the registrar had manifestly erred in his decision.

(1) There was a history of misconduct by the debtor. His conduct was, indeed, highly
unsatisfactory in that he disobeyed orders of the court. For that he was quite rightly sent
j to prison for contempt. However, he apologised for that contempt and was released.
There were no subsequent instances of misconduct. We are informed by counsel for
the Official Receiver that after the debtor was released from prison he was helpful and

---

1   [1927] 2 Ch 85 at 87, [1927] All ER Rep 465 at 466

co-operative. It seems to me that the debtor has purged his contempt, that there was no
subsequent misconduct, and that accordingly any further enquiry as to misconduct *a*
would not be useful.

(2) It is said that the debtor failed to keep books of account. The Official Receiver's
report merely records that the bankrupt has not produced any books of account and
alleges that he has not traded since 1971. We understand that the Official Receiver has
no reason to suppose that the debtor did trade after 1971. In 1970 he entered into
partnership with the petitioning creditor. Any accounts of that business would be *b*
available to the petitioning creditor. Prior to 1971 the debtor was employed as a land
consultant. There was no positive evidence of failure to keep books of account in any
business carried on by the debtor.

(3) The debtor's assets were not of a value equal to 50p in the pound on the amount of
his unsecured liabilities. That is true but is not, I think, a matter of great significance,
bearing in mind that the creditors were paid in full. At the hearing, the Official Receiver *c*
said that the fact would not generally be regarded as sufficient reason to refuse a
discharge under s 26. That, I think, is correct.

(4) It is said that the debtor contracted debts without any reasonable or probable
grounds of expectation of being able to repay. In 1971 he borrowed money on mortgage
to finance legal actions. From 1971 onwards he borrowed money from four banks for
the same purpose and for living expenses. He also borrowed £8,000 from a business *d*
acquaintance and guaranteed an overdraft of Messina Securities Ltd with Lloyds Bank for
£7,000. Essentially the motive for these borrowings was the debtor's determination that
Messina Securities Ltd should pursue claims in respect of the Forum site. We were
informed by counsel for the Official Receiver that, from the Official Receiver's enquiries
and discussions with the debtor, it appeared to the Official Receiver that, at the time of
the borrowings, the debtor did believe that the actions would produce large gains for *e*
Messina Securities Ltd in which he was a substantial shareholder.

(5) It is said that the debtor brought frivolous or vexatious proceedings. As I have
mentioned, since 1972 the debtor has brought some 36 legal proceedings in the name of
Messina Securities Ltd against the petitioning creditor and others, contesting the
ownership of land. We know nothing of the details of those proceedings and can reach
no conclusion as to their merits. The petitioning creditor put in no evidence relating to *f*
this. We were told that there were not 36 separate actions but 36 applications to the
court in a number of different actions. We understand from the Official Receiver that
it appears to him that the debtor had professional representation in those cases. The
main dispute appears to be in relation to the Forum site, as to which the debtor is now
advised by leading counsel that the cause of action is in the debtor and not in Messina
Securities Ltd, and that new proceedings have been started accordingly, as I have already *g*
mentioned.

(6) It is said that the debtor failed to account satisfactorily for losses of assets or
deficiencies of assets. We were informed that the Official Receiver knows of no instance
of failure to account for loss of assets and the documents before us do not indicate such
an instance. As regards deficiencies of assets, the extent of the deficiency is £46,000 odd,
and is particularised in the Official Receiver's report. The Official Receiver does not *h*
suggest that there has been any failure to account for the deficiency.

On the conclusion of the arguments the registrar said: 'I have listened carefully to the
arguments put by counsel. I feel I should exercise my discretion in favour of the
bankrupt.' He did not give reasons. The registrar plainly had a discretion to grant an
annulment. In what circumstances can we interfere with the exercise of his discretion?
I take the law stated by Buckley LJ in *Beck v Value Capital Ltd (No 2)*[1] as follows: *j*

'Where a trial judge is not shown to have erred in principle, his exercise of a
discretionary power should not be interfered with unless the appellate court is of

---

1   [1976] 2 All ER 102 at 109, [1976] 1 WLR 572 at 574

opinion that his conclusion is one that involves injustice, or, to use the language of
a Lord Wright[1], the appellate court is clearly satisfied that the judge of first instance
was wrong.'

Did the registrar err in principle? There are two matters to which I shall refer. The
first is the absence of a public examination. In essence, the case of counsel for the
petitioning creditor is that it was wrong in principle to grant an annulment in those
circumstances. As I have indicated, it seems to me that the registrar was not compelled
b to refuse an annulment in the absence of a public examination. He had a discretion to
be exercised in the light of all the circumstances of the case.

I think the most serious complaint against the debtor is that he engaged in irresponsible
litigation and financed it by borrowing which he could not reasonably expect to repay.
Let it be assumed that this complaint is established. The facts remain that the proved
debts have been repaid, that no creditor except the petitioning creditor objects to the
c annulment, and that the litigation is now being conducted on the advice of leading
counsel. Further, the Official Receiver expressed to the registrar the opinion that a
public examination would not be of assistance. That, in my view, is a circumstance of
considerable importance. Under s 73, the Official Receiver is charged with the duty of
investigating the conduct of the debtor. If he considers that a public examination would
not be of assistance, I think that is a fact to which the registrar is entitled to give
d weight. The Official Receiver's opinion is not binding on the registrar, who must
exercise his own discretion: see *Re a Debtor (No 446 of 1918)*[2]. But the registrar can and
should give proper weight to it. It is a special circumstance in the present case, since it
is, I think, common ground that it is not usual for the Official Receiver so to advise. It
was suggested that the Official Receiver had been unduly swayed by the debtor's
persuasiveness. I see no justification for that contention.
e Bearing in mind that the registrar had a full discretion, that the proved debts were
being paid and that the Official Receiver saw no need for a public examination, I find it
impossible to say that the registrar could not reasonably conclude that he should grant an
annulment without a public examination, though I give full weight to the general
desirability of holding a public examination. In my view the registrar did not err in
f principle so far as the absence of a public examination is concerned.
The second matter of principle is this. We were referred to the observations of Stirling
LJ in *Re Keet*[3] that—

'. . . in the absence of special circumstances, it would not be a good exercise of
discretion to make an order of annulment where, if the bankrupt were applying for
his order of discharge, an order of discharge would not be granted.'

g That dictum is not repeated in the other judgments but, if it be the law, I do not think
that it compels the conclusion that an annulment must be refused in the present case.
Section 26(3) refers to 12 facts, any of which, if proved, limits the powers of the court
to grant a discharge. Of those 12 grounds, there are seven which it is not suggested are
applicable here, that is to say those in paras (*c*), (*f*), (*g*), (*i*), (*j*), (*k*) and (*l*). Of the
h remaining five, one is clearly established. That is the fact set out in para (*a*) that the
bankrupt's assets are not of a value equal to 50p in the pound on the amount of his
liabilities. But, as I have said, I think that the Official Receiver is correct in his view that
that circumstance would not itself be regarded as sufficient reason for refusing a
discharge.
Three of the remaining grounds, those in paras (*b*), (*e*) and (*h*), do not appear to me to
j be proved. That leaves para (*d*), contracting debts without a reasonable expectation of

---

1   In *Evans v Bartlam* [1937] 2 All ER 646 at 654, [1937] AC 473 at 486
2   [1920] 1 KB 461, [1918–19] All ER Rep 397
3   [1905] 2 KB 666 at 677, [1904–7] All ER Rep 836 at 840

being able to pay. Since the burden of proof is on the bankrupt as regards para (d), I will assume this fact is established. But I do not think the consequence is that the court must necessarily refuse a discharge in a case where the proved debts have been paid in full. Under s 26(2) the court is entitled, even though any of the facts in s 26(3) are proved, to grant a discharge suspended until a dividend of not less than 50p in the pound has been paid, or to require the bankrupt, as a condition of the discharge, to consent to a judgment for the unpaid balance of provable debts. If the debts have been paid in full, it is difficult to see why anything more than a purely nominal suspension of discharge should be necessary to satisfy the language of s 26. I see no reason in principle why, on a comparison with the position on an application under s 26, an annulment should not have been granted in the present case.

Can it be said that the registrar's decision was manifestly wrong or unjust? I do not think so. Where the debts have been paid in full and where the majority of creditors and the Official Receiver do not oppose the application, and the Official Receiver sees no need for a public examination, I do not think that it can be said that a tribunal properly instructed as to the law could not reasonably have come to the conclusion that an annulment should be granted. I would dismiss the appeal.

For completeness, I should mention that it was conceded that the petitioning creditor was a person aggrieved for the purposes of appealing from the registrar's order, and that the debtor's cross-notice, raising the objection that the petitioning creditor had taken a benefit under the registrar's order, was abandoned.

BROWNE-WILKINSON J. I agree. I have only a few words to add. For myself, I think it is material to take into account the position of the petitioning creditor. Apart from the very remote possibility of obtaining statutory interest if both the annulment were set aside and assets were discovered sufficient to pay the debts in full plus statutory interest, the petitioning creditor has no direct financial interest in keeping this bankruptcy on foot. His real concern is to ensure that the debtor remains bankrupt and therefore incompetent to conduct the litigation relating to the Forum site. I do not suggest that the petitioning creditor had no locus standi to be heard on the application. But it seems to me relevant to take into account the fact that he is motivated not by any legitimate financial interest likely to be satisfied in the distribution of the debtor's estate in bankruptcy, but by extraneous advantages that he would achieve by ensuring that the disability of bankruptcy continued to affect the debtor. I do not think the bankruptcy court should be used as a means of stopping litigation alleged to be vexatious. There are other and better ways of stopping vexatious litigants.

I therefore consider that, in weighing the facts relevant to the exercise of the discretionary powers to order cross-examination or to grant an annulment, it is proper to take into account the fact that the person asking for cross-examination and opposing the annulment desires to achieve from the bankruptcy personal advantages which the law of bankruptcy was not designed to provide for him. I should add that I am expressing no view, one way or the other, as to the merits of the debtor's claim relating to the Forum site, of which we know nothing.

Appeal dismissed.

Solicitors: *Brett Ackerley & Cooke,* Manchester (for the petitioning creditor); *Hodge & Halsall,* Southport (for the debtor); *Treasury Solicitor.*

Jacqueline Metcalfe   Barrister.

Bartlett and others v Barclays Bank Trust Co Ltd

CHANCERY DIVISION

BRIGHTMAN J

2nd, 3rd, 4th, 8th, 9th, 10th, 11th, 14th, 15th, 16th, 17th, 18th, 21st, 22nd, 23rd, 24th, 25th MAY, 6th, 7th, 8th, 11th, 12th, 13th, 14th, 15th, 19th, 20th, 21st, 22nd, 25th, 26th, 27th, 28th, 29th JUNE, 2nd, 3rd, 4th, 5th, 6th, 9th, 10th, 11th, 12th, 31st JULY 1979

Trust and trustee – Breach of trust – Investments – Trust being major shareholder in private company – Duty of trustee in regard to management of company – Trust corporation – Bank trustee of settlement – Trust fund consisting of majority of shares in private property company – Bank not represented at board meetings and not insisting on regular flow of information from board – Bank content to receive information dispensed at annual general meetings – Company suffering substantial loss through hazardous investment in property development – Bank unaware of nature of investment – Whether bank in breach of trust – Whether bank under duty to obtain regular flow of information from board – Whether bank entitled to set off profit from one speculative investment against loss in another – Trustee Act 1925, s 61.

Limitation of action – Concealment of right of action by fraud – Fraud – Action against trustee for breach of trust – Bank trustee of a fund consisting of controlling interest in a company – Bank failing to secure adequate information from board on company's activities – Company sustaining loss through speculative investment – Loss to trust fund – Action by beneficiaries against trustee – Whether bank's omission to secure information unconscionable conduct amounting to fraud – Limitation Act 1939, s 26(b).

In 1920 the settlor made a settlement of property consisting of debenture stock and 99·8% of the shares in a private company ('BTL') for the benefit of his wife and issue. BTL had been incorporated earlier in 1920 to manage the settlor's properties. The trustee of the settlement was a bank and subsequently a trust corporation controlled by the bank ('the bank'). The bank as trustee therefore had a controlling interest in BTL's shares. By 1960, the settlor and his wife were dead, there were seven settled shares in the trust fund and the trust was in the closing stages of its life. Down to 1960 BTL's board had included members of the settlor's family but in 1960 the composition of the board was changed due to illness, and thereafter no beneficiary or member of the family was on the board, and there was no director who regarded himself as the bank's representative or nominee. From 1960 the board consisted of two surveyors, an accountant and a solicitor, the chairman of the board being one of the surveyors. During 1960 the bank needed to raise moneys for death duties on the cesser of certain life interests in the trust fund and asked the board to examine the possibility of a public quotation of BTL's shares. At the same time the chairman wished to extend BTL's role in the property world. At a meeting in February 1961 the board told the bank that brokers had advised that a public quotation would go better if BTL had investments in property development. The bank indicated that it would give favourable consideration to the policy of investing in property development provided that the policy was required for a successful public quotation, that the life tenants would not be left short of income during the development period and that the investment would be limited to the proceeds of sale of the BTL property. At the 1961 annual general meeting the chairman stated that the board intended to invest available moneys in development projects but did not link such investment to the proposed public quotation. This represented a major change of direction for BTL, but the bank's representative at the meeting raised no objections, did not indicate that the bank had not yet given its approval to the change of investment policy and merely recorded in his attendance note that he was satisfied everything was under control. Thereafter at the board's monthly meetings (at which the bank was not represented) the chairman put forward various development projects for the board's *a* consideration, and, without consulting the bank, the board embarked on two projects, at sites at Guildford and the Old Bailey, London. The board invested substantial sums in those projects. Both projects were hazardous speculations, but whereas the Guildford project ultimately produced, by sheer luck, a substantial capital profit (which was used to finance the Old Bailey project) the Old Bailey project involved buying into the site at prices exceeding the investment value of the properties, on the chance that planning *b* permission for development would be granted, and was unsuccessful, with the result that BTL sustained a large loss. Because the board did not provide the bank with, and the bank did not insist on receiving, a regular flow of information on BTL's activities, and the bank was content to receive only such information on the projects as was dispensed at the annual general meetings, it was unaware of the hazardous nature of the projects and did not intervene to stop BTL from embarking on them or require the board to *c* accept an offer made half way through the project to buy out its share at little or no loss. The loss sustained by BTL from its investment in the Old Bailey project reduced the market value of its shares and thereby caused a substantial loss to the trust fund. The plaintiffs, the beneficiaries under the settlement, brought an action against the bank claiming that it was liable as trustee to make good the loss suffered by the trust because it was caused by the bank's default in permitting BTL to engage in the Old Bailey *d* project. The bank contended that the high calibre of the BTL board entitled it to rely on the information dispensed at the annual general meetings and that therefore, under s 61[a] of the Trustee Act 1925, it ought fairly to be excused for any breach of trust. The bank further contended that in any event, by virtue of s 19 of the Limitation Act 1939 the action had been brought after the expiration of the limitation period in relation to any loss occurring before 19th August 1971, ie six years before the date of the writ. In the *e* event that the bank was held to be in breach of trust, it sought to set off the profit resulting from the Guildford project against the loss resulting from the Old Bailey project.

Held – (i) It was a trustee's duty to conduct trust business with the care that a reasonably prudent businessman would extend to his own affairs, and, in the case of a private *f* company in which he was a majority shareholder, a prudent businessman would not be content to receive only such information on that company's activities as was dispensed at annual general meetings. Moreover, a professional corporate trustee, such as the bank, owed a higher duty of care and was liable for loss caused to a trust by neglect to exercise the special care and skill which it professed to have. It followed that, notwithstanding the calibre of the board, the bank, as the controlling shareholder under the settlement, *g* was under a duty as trustee of the settlement to ensure that it received an adequate flow of information from the board on BTL's activities in time to enable it to make use of the information to protect the beneficiaries' interests by preventing the Old Bailey project from being commenced and later from becoming the financial disaster it did. The bank was therefore in breach of trust in neglecting to ensure that it received such information and in confining itself to the receipt of the information dispensed at the annual general *h* meetings. Even without such information, however, the bank had known enough to put it on enquiry about the projects. Since the loss to the trust fund would not have occurred if the bank had intervened to prevent BTL's participation in the Old Bailey project, as it ought to have done, it followed that the bank's breach of trust had caused the loss and that it was liable for that loss (see p 149 *f*, p 150 *h* to p 151 *b* and *j* to p 152 *a* and

j

---

a   Section 61, so far as material, provides, 'If it appears to the court that a trustee . . . is or may be personally liable for any breach of trust . . . but has acted honestly and reasonably, and ought fairly to be excused for the breach of trust . . . then the court may relieve him either wholly or partly from personal liability for the same.'

c to p 153 *b* and *j* and p 154 *a*, post); *Speight v Gaunt* (1883) 9 App Cas 1 and *Re Lucking's*
a *Will Trusts, Renwick v Lucking* [1967] 3 All ER 726 applied.

(ii) The bank was entitled to rely on s 19 of the 1939 Act as a defence to the claim in
respect of income lost on money spent by BTL prior to 19th August 1971, ie six years
before the writ in the action was issued, because it could not be said that the right of
action in relation to that income had been concealed by the bank's 'fraud', within s 26(*b*)[b]
of the 1939 Act. 'Fraud' in that context envisaged unconscionable conduct in regard to
b the parties' relationship, whereas the bank's conduct had not been unconscionable since
it did not know that it was acting in breach of trust and there had not been, therefore, any
concealment by it (see p 154 *e* to p 155 *b*, post); *Kitchen v Royal Air Forces Association*
[1958] 2 All ER 241 and dictum of Lord Denning MR in *King v Victor Parsons & Co*
[1973] 1 All ER at 209 applied.

(iii) The bank was not, however, entitled to rely on s 61 of the 1925 Act as a defence
c for, although it had acted 'honestly', it had not acted 'reasonably' within s 61, and,
moreover, it would be unfair to excuse the bank at the expense of the beneficiaries (see
p 155 *b c*, post).

(iv) Although the Guildford project and the Old Bailey project were different
transactions, they stemmed from the same policy of BTL to make speculative investments
in property development, and it would be unjust to deprive the bank of a right to set off
d the profit resulting from the Guildford project against the loss resulting from the Old
Bailey project (see p 155 *e f*, post).

Notes

For a trustee's duty to use diligence and prudence, see 38 Halsbury's Laws (3rd Edn) 969,
para 1679, and for cases on the subject, see 47 Digest (Repl) 355–357, 3202–3220.

For relief for breach of trust where a trustee has acted honestly and reasonably, see 38
e Halsbury's Laws (3rd Edn) 1056, para 1828.

For the nature of fraud for the purpose of postponing the limitation period, see 24 ibid
316–317, paras 628–629, and for cases on the subject, see 32 Digest (Repl) 605–607,
1891–1900.

For the Trustee Act 1925, s 61, see 38 Halsbury's Statutes (3rd Edn) 184.

For the Limitation Act 1939, ss 19, 26, see 19 ibid 79, 86.
f

Cases referred to in judgment

Archer v Moss, Applegate v Moss [1971] 1 All ER 747, [1971] 1 QB 406, [1971] 2 WLR 541,
CA, Digest (Cont Vol D) 616, 1900b.
Chapman, Re, Cocks v Chapman [1896] 2 Ch 763, [1895–9] All ER 1104, 65 LJ Ch 892, 75
LT 196, CA, 47 Digest (Repl) 458, 4093.
g *Godfrey, Re, Godfrey v Faulkner* (1883) 23 Ch D 483, 52 LJ Ch 821, 48 LT 853, 47 Digest
(Repl) 355, 8208.
King v Victor Parsons & Co [1972] 2 All ER 625, [1972] 1 WLR 801, [1972] 1 Lloyds Rep
213; *affd* [1973] 1 All ER 206, [1973] 1 WLR 29, [1973] 1 Lloyds Rep 189, CA, Digest
(Cont Vol D) 617, 1900c.
Kitchen v Royal Air Forces Association [1958] 2 All ER 241, [1958] 1 WLR 563, CA, 32
h Digest (Repl) 713, 5196.
Lucking's Will Trusts, Re, Renwick v Lucking [1967] 3 All ER 726, [1968] 1 WLR 866,
Digest (Cont Vol C) 1049, 4219a.
Miller's Deed Trusts, Re, Miller v Littner (21st March 1978) unreported, [1978] LS Gaz 454.
Speight v Gaunt (1883) 9 App Cas 1, 53 LJ Ch 419, 50 LT 330, 48 JP 84, HL; *affg* sub nom
Re Speight, Speight v Gaunt 22 Ch D 727, CA, 47 Digest (Repl) 387, 3462.

j

---

b Section 26, so far as material, provides: 'Where, in the case of any action for which a period of
limitation is prescribed by this Act ... (*b*) the right of action is concealed by the fraud of [the
defendant or his agent or of any person through whom he claims or his agent] ... the period of
limitation shall not begin to run until the plaintiff has discovered the fraud ... or could with
reasonable diligence have discovered it.'

Waterman's Will Trusts, Re, Lloyds Bank Ltd v Sutton [1952] 2 All ER 1054, 24 Digest (Repl)
    666, 6546.   *a*
Whiteley, Re, Whiteley v Learoyd (1886) 33 Ch D 347, 55 LJ Ch 864, 55 LT 564, 51 JP 100,
    CA; *affd* sub nom *Learoyd v Whiteley* (1887) 12 App Cas 727, HL, 47 Digest (Repl) 464,
    4149.
Wynn's Will Trusts, Re, Public Trustee v Newborough [1952] 1 All ER 341, [1952] Ch 271,
    48 Digest (Repl) 390, 3388.

Cases also cited   *b*
Abbey, Malvern Wells Ltd v Ministry of Local Government and Planning [1951] 2 All ER 154,
    [1951] Ch 728.
Bell Houses Ltd v City Wall Properties Ltd [1966] 2 All ER 674, [1966] 2 QB 656, CA.
Cable (Lord) (deceased), Re, Garratt v Waters [1976] 3 All ER 417, [1977] 1 WLR 7.
Charterbridge Corpn Ltd v Lloyds Bank Ltd [1969] 2 All ER 1185, [1970] Ch 62.
City Equitable Fire Insurance Co Ltd, Re [1925] Ch 407, CA.   *c*
Dimes v Scott (1827) 4 Russ 195, [1824–34] All ER Rep 653, LC.
Elliott v Turner (1843) 13 Sim 477.
Fletcher v Green (1864) 33 Beav 426, 55 ER 433.
French Protestant Hospital, Re [1951] 1 All ER 938, [1951] Ch 567.
Garrett v Noble (1834) 6 Sim 504.
German Date Coffee Co, Re (1882) 20 Ch D 169, [1881–5] All ER Rep 372, CA.   *d*
Jobson v Palmer [1893] 1 Ch 71.
National Trustees Co of Australasia Ltd v General Finance Co of Australasia Ltd [1905] AC
    373, PC.
Pauling's Settlement Trusts, Re, Younghusband v Coutts & Co [1963] 3 All ER 1, [1964] Ch
    303, CA.
Pecz̧enik's Settlement, Re, Cole v Ingram [1964] 2 All ER 339, [1964] 1 WLR 720.   *e*
Rae v Meek (1889) 14 App Cas 558, HL.
Wiles v Gresham (1854) 2 Drew 258; *on appeal* 5 De GM & G 770, LJJ.

Action
By a writ dated 19th August 1977 and a subsequent statement of claim the plaintiffs, Sir
Basil Bartlett Bt, Irene Theodora Bartlett, Henry David Hardington Bartlett, Sheila   *f*
Bartlett, Norman Alaric Bartlett, Hazel Leslie Ellwood, Derek Bartlett and Edwina
Boldero, beneficiaries under a settlement dated 23rd July 1920, claimed against the
defendant, Barclays Bank Trust Co Ltd ('the bank'), the trustee of the settlement,
declarations that the bank was liable to reconstitute the trust fund subject to the
settlement by making good to the fund all loss which had accrued or might accrue to the
fund by reason of certain alleged breaches of trust, and an enquiry as to the loss which   *g*
had already accrued or might accrue to the fund by reason of the breaches of trust. The
facts are set out in the judgment.

Edward Nugee QC and *Jules Sher* for the plaintiffs.
Paul V Baker QC and *Alan Sebestyen* for the bank.

                                                                          Cur adv vult *h*

31st July. **BRIGHTMAN J** read the following judgment: This is an action against a
trust corporation for breach of trust. It is claimed that the trust corporation, and its
banking predecessor ('the bank'), failed to exercise proper supervision over the
management of a family company which they controlled. As a result, it is said, the trust
suffered an avoidable loss in excess of £½ million due to a disastrous property speculation
by the company.   *j*
   On 23rd July 1920 Sir Herbert Bartlett Bt made a settlement for the benefit of his wife
and issue. The trustee was Barclays Bank Ltd. The settled property consisted of
debenture stock and 498 (later 499) out of 500 shares in Bartletts Trust Ltd ('BTL'). This
company had been incorporated in the previous May to take over and manage properties

belonging to Sir Herbert and his wife. By 1960, after both had died, there were seven
a settled shares in the trust fund. Five of the settled shares were held on trusts for the
benefit of the settlor's five surviving children. Each child had a life interest and a power
to appoint income to a surviving spouse. Subject thereto the capital was divisible
between the issue of the life tenant living at the life tenant's death; failing issue, there
was an accruer to the other shares.

The five surviving children were: (1) Mrs Graham, born 1876; she had a husband but
b no issue; (2) Robert, born 1880; he had a wife, born 1899, but no issue; (3) Eric, born
1882; he had a wife and two children; (4) Ruby, born 1886, who was a spinster; and (5)
Norman, born 1888; he had a wife and two children. A further share was held in trust
for Irene, the widow of the settlor's eldest son. She was born in 1874. After her death
the capital of her settled share was divisible between her issue then living per stirpes. She
had three children who are the first three plaintiffs: Sir Basil Bartlett Bt, born 1905, Miss
c Irene Bartlett, born 1908, and Mr David Bartlett, born 1912. The remaining share was
held in trust for Sir Basil for life with remainder to the successor to the baronetcy, The
presumptive successor is his brother, Mr David Bartlett.

The directors of BTL at the beginning of 1960 were: Mr Graham, a solicitor, who was
the husband of the Mrs Graham I have mentioned; he had been chairman and managing
director since 1936; Mr David Bartlett; Mr Clee, who had been the surveyor of BTL since
d 1946 and dealt with the day-to-day affairs of the company; Mr Fereday, a partner in the
firm of accountants responsible for the company's audit; and Mr Roberts, a partner in a
well-known firm of surveyors and estate agents who acted professionally for BTL. Mr
Roberts and Mr Fereday were part-time directors.

The property of BTL consisted at this time mainly of some 21 freehold properties with
a book value of about £300,000 and ten leasehold properties with a book value of about
e £250,000. The leases had about 24 to 45 years to run. There were also a number of
freehold properties, including reversions to two of the leaseholds, held in a sinking fund
for amortising leaseholds, and some investments and a few other assets. The properties
were mainly office blocks, shop properties and residential properties, with a rent roll of
about £93,000. The company had an office in Victoria Street, London, and at one time
a work force for maintenance of buildings.

f In 1960 the BTL board underwent a significant change in its composition. Mr
Graham became ill and could not attend board meetings after the beginning of that
year. Mr Roberts acted as chairman from March onwards, and was formally so appointed
in November on the resignation of Mr Graham. Mr David Bartlett also became ill and
he left the board in December. Mr Albert, a solicitor, joined the board in the following
year. Thereafter until 1976 the board consisted only of Mr Roberts, Mr Fereday, Mr Clee
g (who became managing director at the end of 1960 in place of Mr Graham) and Mr
Albert. Down to 1960 the interests of the beneficiaries were to some extent represented
by the presence on the board of Mr Graham, the husband of a beneficiary, and Mr David
Bartlett, a reversionary beneficiary. Thereafter the position radically changed. There
was no beneficiary or member of the family on the board and no director who regarded
himself as the particular representative or nominee of the trustee.

h Mr Roberts had joined the board of BTL in 1951 as a non-executive director, when he
was about 40 years of age. He was known to Mr David Bartlett from pre-war days. Mr
Bartlett had a high regard for him as a surveyor and it was at Mr Bartlett's suggestion that
he became a director. He had undergone training with a firm of surveyors for four years
after he left school in 1933, and he was offered a partnership in the firm when he came
back from the war in 1945. At that time the firm had only one office and about five
j partners. By 1974 it was a large and well-known concern with 16 partners and 16
associates, and 3 architects on the staff.

The affairs of the trust were conducted at the City office of the bank's trustee
department. In earlier days the manager of the City office was Mr M W Lockyer. He left
the City office in 1959 and became trustee manager of the bank's chief office. His

successor as manager of the City office was Mr C Mahony. Mr Mahony remained there until 1965, when he succeeded Mr Lockyer as trustee manager of the chief office. A Mr Dale then became manager of the City office, but he remained for only about a year. He was appointed to undertake a special job elsewhere, seemingly at short notice because there was no hand-over when he was succeeded by Mr P L Daly. Mr Daly was manager of the City office until 1975; to be accurate from 1970 he filled an equivalent position as manager of the City trustee office of the newly formed Barclays Bank Trust Co Ltd. Mr Dale plays no significant part in the story, and he was not called as a witness. The representatives of the bank who gave evidence were Mr Mahony and Mr Daly, and they effectively cover the period 1960 to 1975.

The manager of the City office of the bank's trustee department had a staff to assist him which included an assistant manager, trust officers and trust administrators. The trust officer or administrator allocated to a trust would deal with routine matters; important things were done by the manager, who in any event had overall responsibility for the trust. The manager could, however, refer difficult problems to his superior, the trustee manager at the chief office, or the assistant general manager of the bank responsible for trust matters, but such references were rare.

It was the custom of the BTL board to hold regular monthly meetings, usually on the last Tuesday of each month. The proceedings at board meetings appear to have been meticulously minuted. I have nearly 800 pages of minutes before me, and they are the foundation of the almost perfect contemporary documentary notation which is a feature of this case. Mr Roberts also held fortnightly management meetings with Mr Clee and the secretary of BTL.

During the year 1960 there were two particular matters which came under consideration by the board. First, the bank was faced with the prospect of raising money for death duties on the cesser of the life interests of six very elderly beneficiaries. With this in mind, in January 1960 the bank and Mr David Bartlett asked Mr Fereday to examine with his co-directors the possibility of the introduction of BTL's shares and debentures to the Stock Exchange. Secondly, Mr Roberts, who was about to become the real power on the board, had a poor opinion of the rôle of BTL in the property world. He did not think it right that BTL should exist merely as a rent collecting agency, as he described it. In fact, BTL had a more important function than that. Mr Roberts, nevertheless, envisaged an undertaking of greater stature. In the course of the October 1960 meeting, at which he presided, he pointed out to his colleagues that BTL had very little of what he described as 'risk' property. He said that it might be advisable to consider factory and commercial investments as future funds became available, yielding 10% instead of the 6% obtainable on the steadier type of property investment. (The plaintiffs have no criticism of this advice.) This led Mr Fereday to observe that a re-statement of the investment policy of the company was desirable. This was a matter of immediate relevance because purchasers were known to be in the field for BTL's leasehold property, Albany Buildings, at a price likely to be in excess of half a million pounds, and there would therefore be money to re-invest.

[His Lordship, having reviewed the relevant evidence, found the following facts. At a meeting with the BTL board, in February 1961, Mr Mahony was told that brokers had advised the board, in connection with the proposed public issue of BTL shares, that it would be better if BTL had investments in property development. Mr Mahony promised to give favourable consideration to such investment by BTL on the footing that any investment was limited to the net proceeds from the sale of the Albany Buildings, ie to some £500,000 to £600,000. At BTL's 1961 annual general meeting the speech of Mr Roberts, the chairman, included a statement that the BTL board intended to invest available moneys in property development and did not link such investment with the proposed public quotation of BTL shares. The statement disclosed a major change of direction for BTL (into property development) to be taken in the closing stages of the life of the trust. However, Mr Mahony, though present at the meeting, did not remind Mr

Roberts that the bank had not yet taken advice on, or given further consideration to the
a policy of investment in property development, and his attendance note merely recorded
that everything was under control. Moreover he gave evidence that he regarded the BTL
board as a team of well-equipped professionals and was content to leave things to them.
From 1961 onwards Mr Roberts, at BTL's monthly board meetings, introduced various
development schemes for consideration by the board but merely disclosed to the bank,
at BTL's annual general meetings, such information relating to the schemes as it was
b considered appropriate to disclose. The board adopted a system of not consulting the
bank, unless it was directly involved as a shareholder, and not providing it with a regular
flow of information, and merely gave it information in advance of and at BTL's annual
general meetings. The transition of BTL to a policy of speculative development did not
provoke the bank to make any particular enquiries or alert it to the need for special
vigilance. Two of the development projects put forward by Mr Roberts were at
c Guildford, a scheme which was likely to cost some £1,250,000, and the redevelopment
of a site at the Old Bailey in the City of London. The board embarked on those schemes
without consulting the bank. However, throughout Mr Roberts had acted in a way he
thought was justified and calculated to bring benefit to the trust estate. At the November
1962 board meeting Mr Roberts reported that details of the Old Bailey scheme were
being prepared, that planning consent would 'probably' be available for office user on
d redevelopment of the area and that a company called Far Investments Ltd ('Far') was to
be incorporated to make purchases on the site. Mr Mahony first learned of the Old
Bailey scheme at a meeting with Mr Roberts in January 1963 and despite Mr Roberts'
promise to give the bank written details of the scheme, he never did so and Mr Mahony
did not remind him to do so. Consequently the bank did not see any report or appraisal
of the scheme, did not know which properties were involved, or the expected cost and
e benefit of the scheme, did not know how the scheme was to be financed or whether
planning consent would be forthcoming for office development. Nor did the bank learn
of a joint development scheme for the site which BTL entered into in March 1963 with
Stock Conversion and Investment Trust Ltd ('Stock Conversion'), until the 1973 annual
general meeting held in June 1973 and even then the bank did not ask for and never saw
a copy of the agreement between BTL and Stock Conversion and did not, therefore,
f know the extent of BTL's commitment to the scheme or the terms on which it could
withdraw from it. At the 1963 annual general meeting it was not disclosed that the
application for planning permission to develop the Old Bailey site had been withdrawn,
because of adverse government policy. An application for permission to develop the site
was refused in March 1964 but the refusal was not disclosed to the bank at the 1964
annual general meeting. The disclosure by Mr Roberts to Mr Mahony, in January 1965,
g that planning consent for the site had not been obtained and that it could be ten years
before development of the site could be undertaken elicited no reaction from Mr
Mahony. At the 1965 annual general meeting, at which Mr Mahony's successor was
present, it was reported that negotiations with the City of London Corporation on the
Old Bailey scheme had been suspended but that the board were satisfied the scheme
would eventually be carried out and would produce an adequate return. In fact prospects
h for the scheme were poor. No report on the scheme appeared in the bank's files in
consequence of the report made at the 1965 annual general meeting. The Guildford
development scheme, due to the intervention of another development company, resulted
in a capital profit of £271,000. At the 1966 annual general meeting the board reported
that the Old Bailey scheme had been halted because of planning and licensing difficulties
but that interim arrangements were being made to increase the present income from the
j scheme until it could be revived. In fact Far had decided not to buy any further
properties on the site unless they would show an adequate return. At the end of 1967
BTL became a wholly owned subsidiary of Bartlett Trust Holdings Ltd ('BTH'). By the
end of 1967 the Old Bailey scheme was a white elephant and the BTH board authorised
Mr Roberts to approach the City of London Corporation with a view to selling the site to

the corporation. As at 31st March 1968 BTL's loan to Far amounted to the principal sum
of £245,650, and arrears of interest from Far amounted to over £49,000. No mention **a**
was made at the 1967 annual general meeting that the site was up for sale. At the 1969
annual general meeting (at which the bank was not represented) the loan to Far was
written down in the accounts by £40,000 on the ground that there was a contingent
deficiency of that sum on the loan account to Far if the properties purchased by Far were
considered purely as investments. The bank made no enquiries consequent on that
observation in the accounts. At the 1970 annual general meeting Mr Roberts stated that **b**
a considerable time would elapse before anything could be done in connection with the
Old Bailey scheme but that statement did not cause the bank to re-examine the scheme
and its impact on the trust. In 1970 the bank's trustee business was transferred to the
defendants, Barclays Bank Trust Co Ltd. At the 1971 annual general meeting Mr
Roberts stated that although little progress had been made with the scheme further
property within the development area was purchased and a further advance of £84,000 **c**
was to be made to Far. The bank's representative at the meeting asked no questions
about that. Unknown to the bank, BTH could have, in 1972, negotiated the disposal of
its interest in Far to Stock Conversion at little or no loss, but at the April 1972 board
meeting BTL chose to continue its participation in the Old Bailey scheme. At the 1972
annual general meeting Mr Roberts reported that BTH had advanced further capital of
£122,500, to Far in connection with the scheme but that further capital commitment on **d**
the scheme would not be made. However at the 1973 annual general meeting it was
reported that further property purchases on the site were being negotiated by Far to give
BTH more than 50% of the proposed development site and that BTH might put up
further cash of £550,000 for the purchase of the properties. Further properties on the
site were bought in 1973 as a result of which the loan account to Far, as shown in the
1973 accounts, increased to £1,035,750, compared with the figure of £376,000 shown **e**
in the accounts for the previous year. The end of the property boom put an end to the
Old Bailey scheme, and BTH incurred substantial losses on its investment in the scheme
with Far, which was probably insolvent. His Lordship continued:] The venture, begun
15 years earlier, without prior consultation with the bank, and continued without any
such consultation, had turned out to be an unqualified disaster.

The shares in BTH were sold in September 1978 for £4,490,000. The market value of **f**
the shares in BTH would have been greater if BTH had not lost a large sum of money on
its investment in Far. By how much the value would have been increased has not yet
been argued.

In August 1977 a writ was issued against Barclays Bank Trust Co. The plaintiffs are Sir
Basil Bartlett, life tenant of a quarter settled share of the trust fund, and also entitled to
one-third of the capital of Mrs Irene Bartlett's settled share since the latter's death in 1974; **g**
Miss Irene Bartlett and Mr David Bartlett, who have been similarly entitled to shares of
capital since 1974; Mrs Sheila Bartlett, who has been entitled to part or all of the income
of Norman's settled share since his death in 1972; and Mr Norman Bartlett (junior), Mrs
Ellwood, Mr Derek Bartlett and Mrs Boldero, the children of Mr Norman Bartlett
(senior), who are entitled to the capital of his settled share. This leaves out only Mrs
Hedley and Mrs Bruce, the children of Mr Eric Bartlett, who or whose trustees have **h**
been interested in his settled share since his death in 1968. The plaintiffs claim that the
bank is liable to make good to the trust fund all loss accruing by reason of the various
defaults specified in paras 24 to 35 of the statement of claim, broadly speaking the default of the bank in permitting BTL and BTH to engage in property development of the
sort which I have indicated. They seek appropriate enquiries in order to establish their
loss. **j**

Before I turn to the argument, I wish to make some observations on the evidence. The
development of a defined area of land may be simple or complex. It may or may not be
attended by financial risk. If the developer is the owner of the entire site, and has
planning permission, the requisite finance, and a prospective tenant or tenants, the
development is a simple project, the financial involvement can be calculated with some

precision and the risk is small. On the other hand, if the development site is in multiple
a ownership, and planning permission for a viable development does not exist and may
not be obtainable, and the developer does not own and has not arranged the requisite
finance, the development is a complex one; considerable risk will be incurred by a
developer who enters on the process of buying into the site with his problems of
planning and finance unresolved. In such a case there are the following risks: (1) the
developer may be unable to purchase all the interests, so that the development is
b frustrated; (2) the price will tend to rise as assembly of the site proceeds, and the
developer may be held to ransom before assembly is complete. Mr Roberts admitted in
evidence that it is impossible to keep the assembling of a large development site secret.
Word gets around and everyone knows about it. If a planning application is made,
notices have to be served. A person buying for investment is in the position of a willing
purchaser bargaining with a willing vendor who has voluntarily placed his property on
c the market. A developer, on the other hand, is a willing purchaser who has to seek out
a vendor who may have had no intention of selling, and this alone is likely to lead to high
prices; (3) planning permission for a viable development may prove to be unobtainable.
In that case the developer is left with properties bought at prices in excess of existing use
values, which will probably have to be sold at a loss or retained as low-yielding
investments; (4) the completion of the assembly of the site or the obtaining of planning
d permission may be delayed longer than expected, with resultant loss of income (if the
developer is using his own money) or larger interest charges than anticipated (if the
developer is using borrowed money); (5) the completion of the assembly and development
of a site can easily take seven to ten years. During this period market conditions may
change and letting conditions may deteriorate; (6) there is in any event no certainty in
times of inflation that rents will increase in line with inflation; building costs may
e escalate more steeply than rents or vice versa.

For these reasons the development of a site in multiple ownership without prior
planning permission will usually offer the developer a big profit if successful, in order to
offset the risk of heavy loss if the scheme fails. Mr Roberts told me that one would look
for a profit margin of 30% to 50%. The Old Bailey project was a complex development
of this type, although it was by no means satisfactorily proved in evidence that it ever
f offered a rich reward. The risks were well explained in the evidence of the plaintiffs'
expert, Mr Murray. I accept his evidence. On the few occasions when his evidence
significantly differs from that of the defendants' expert, Mr Spooner, I prefer the evidence
of Mr Murray. To put the matter briefly, the Old Bailey project was a gamble, and not,
on the evidence I have heard, a very good gamble.

Mr Roberts made it perfectly clear what his attitude was to his principal shareholder.
g Whereas Mr Graham, when chairman of the board, frequently referred matters to the
bank before acting, Mr Roberts did not think that the board was under any obligation to
discuss things with the bank. 'We told them', he said, 'what information we thought
necessary'. If the board were effecting a large purchase or sale, the bank would be advised
after the transaction had been done. He added that if the board were effecting any great
change of policy, the board would tell the bank what was proposed to be done, and
h discuss it. There does not seem, however, to have been any discussion with the bank
before the board embarked on the Guildford and Old Bailey development schemes,
which represented a pretty big change of policy. Mr Roberts regarded the board as
having a mandate to run the company efficiently without bothering the bank over
details. It was not the board's policy to send the bank any reports or documents dealing
with development projects, although information would have been given if asked for.
j The board considered that development projects would redress the balance between life
tenants and remaindermen. The remaindermen were prejudiced by the short leaseholds
in BTL's portfolio. Successful developments would improve their position, without
significantly affecting the spendable income of the life tenants. Mr Roberts told me that
he saw little risk in the Old Bailey development when BTL embarked on it. On the
evidence which I have heard I find that his confidence was wholly misplaced.

Mr Roberts was asked whether, at the inception of the Guildford and Old Bailey schemes, the board intended to assemble and develop the site in order to sell at a profit, *a* or in order to retain and enjoy the income. He replied:

> 'We had a fairly open mind on it . . . but from a property point of view, my own view (and I cannot say that definitely we formulated a view on the board) was to create an income position, having got our money back from an association with a fund, whereby they would virtually take over as partners. They would finance the *b* scheme, come in on the scheme as partners and Bartlett Trust would be left with whatever the due percentage was due to the financial arrangements—a cut of the equity virtually: obviously very much smaller than the total revenue received from the building, from the development, and that interest, if required, was saleable. I mean one did not know what the future was going to hold.'

And later— *c*

> 'We talked all around various ways of finance, and we discussed it pretty extensively . . . we thought that all options could be open to us. By that I mean we could . . . sell out complete our share in the completed development.'

I think it appears from this answer, despite some obscurity of expression, that the board had no fixed idea how the development would proceed in its later stages, but probably *d* the board would sell a share of the development to some financial source in return for the provision of the money needed to complete the development, BTL's share in which would then be retained as an investment or sold in order to realise a capital profit.

When Mr Mahony came on the scene in 1959 as manager of the City office branch, his predecessor impressed on him, when handing over, the need for liquidity because of the ages of the life tenants, the heavy estate duty liabilities that would arise when they died, *e* and the fact that most of the reversioners would be more interested in cash than shares in a private property company. Mr Mahony did not know Mr Roberts personally before 1960. He achieved a fairly close relationship with him on an informal basis, and Mr Roberts would always find time to see him at short notice. He accepted that Mr Roberts was not going to refer matters to the bank in the same way as Mr Graham had done when he was chairman. Mr Mahony viewed the board as a well-equipped team of professionals *f* who knew their job, and nothing occurred to change his opinion. He was never given any details at all about any development project but was quite satisfied that that should be so. His attitude was that he had agreed in principle to a measure of development (as he put it) and that the board should be left to carry out that policy. He placed complete confidence in the board and assumed they knew what they were doing and would do nothing stupid. He did not direct his mind to the problem how development projects *g* would be financed. With hindsight, he was disposed to agree that he might have asked more questions. At the time he was content that all decisions in relation to the management of BTL and the conduct of its affairs should be left to the board.

When Mr Daly took over in 1966, he regarded the Old Bailey project as a dormant matter. He learned that there was a site opposite the Old Bailey where certain properties had been acquired in conjunction with Stock Conversion, and that it was the intention *h* to assemble the site when conditions were favourable, and ultimately to demolish the existing buildings and erect a new one. He did not have a plan of the site, and knew nothing of the planning difficulties. He was not worried because he was aware that Mr Mahony was content with the position and had reposed complete confidence in the board. Mr Daly himself considered the directors to be highly competent and professional. Mr Roberts always expressed himself to Mr Daly as extremely confident *j* that the Old Bailey development would be successfully completed within a reasonable period. Mr Daly was under the impression that Mr Roberts was enthusiastic about it, and he knew nothing of the proposal in 1972 to sell out to Stock Conversion. The decision to buy into the site had been made at an earlier time. He was sure that it had

been considered in depth both by Mr Mahony and the board, and he did not think that
a it was for him to reconsider it. Furthermore, a well-known and prosperous development
company was backing the scheme with an equal participation. He saw no cause for
alarm. He believed that the Old Bailey project would turn out to be a very valuable
asset. As regards finance, he understood that there would be no question of committing
the assets of BTL in any way, and that the money would be put up on some participation
basis by an insurance company.

b   The situation may be summed up as follows. BTH made a large loss as a result of the
involvement of itself and BTL in the Old Bailey project. This loss reduced the value of
the BTH shares and thereby caused a loss to the trust fund of the 1920 settlement. The
bank, had it acted in time, could by reason of its shareholding have stopped the board of
BTL embarking on the Old Bailey project; and, had it acted in time, could have stopped
the board of BTL and later the board of BTH (it is unnecessary to differentiate) from
c continuing with the project; and could, had it acted in time, have required BTH to sell
its interest in Far to Stock Conversion on the no-loss or small-loss terms which (as I find)
were available for the asking. This would not have necessitated the draconian course of
threatening to remove, or actually removing, the board in favour of compliant
directors. The members of the board were reasonable persons, and would (as I find) have
followed any reasonable policy desired by the bank had the bank's wishes been indicated
d to the board. The loss to the trust fund could have been avoided (as I find) without
difficulty or disruption had the bank been prepared to lead, in a broad sense, rather than
to follow.

What, then, was the duty of the bank and did the bank fail in its duty? It does not
follow that because a trustee could have prevented a loss it is therefore liable for the
loss. The questions which I must ask myself are: (1) what was the duty of the bank as the
e holder of 99·8% of the shares in BTL and BTH? (2) was the bank in breach of duty in any
and if so what respect? (3) if so, did that breach of duty cause the loss which was suffered
by the trust estate? (4) if so, to what extent is the bank liable to make good that loss? In
approaching these questions, I bear in mind that the attack on the bank is based, not on
wrongful acts, but on wrongful omissions, that is to say, non-feasance not misfeasance.

The cases establish that it is the duty of a trustee to conduct the business of the trust
f with the same care as an ordinary prudent man of business would extend towards his
own affairs: see *Re Speight, Speight v Gaunt*[1] per Jessel MR and Bowen LJ (affirmed on
appeal[2] and see Lord Blackburn[3]). In applying this principle, Lindley LJ (who was the
third member of the court in *Re Speight*[4]) added in *Re Whiteley*[5]:

g   '. . . care must be taken not to lose sight of the fact that the business of the trustee,
and the business which the ordinary prudent man is supposed to be conducting for
himself, is the business of investing money for the benefit of persons who are to
enjoy it at some future time, and not for the sole benefit of the person entitled to the
present income. The duty of a trustee is not to take such care only as a prudent man
h   would take if he had only himself to consider; the duty rather is to take such care as
an ordinary prudent man would take if he were minded to make an investment for
the benefit of other people for whom he felt morally bound to provide. That is the
kind of business the ordinary prudent man is supposed to be engaged in; and unless
this is borne in mind the standard of a trustee's duty will be fixed too low; lower

j   1   (1883) 22 Ch D 727 at 739, 762
     2   (1883) 9 App Cas 1
     3   9 App Cas 1 at 19
     4   22 Ch D 727
     5   (1886) 33 Ch D 347 at 355

than it has ever yet been fixed, and lower certainly than the House of Lords or this Court endeavoured to fix it in *Speight* v. *Gaunt*[1].'

On appeal Lord Watson added[2]:

'Business men of ordinary prudence may, and frequently do, select investments which are more or less of a speculative character; but it is the duty of a trustee to confine himself to the class of investments which are permitted by the trust, and likewise to avoid all investments of that class which are attended with hazard.'

That does not mean that the trustee is bound to avoid all risk and in effect act as an insurer of the trust fund: in *Re Godfrey*[3] Bacon V-C said:

'No doubt it is the duty of a trustee, in administering the trusts of a will, to deal with property intrusted into his care exactly as any prudent man would deal with his own property. But the words in which the rule is expressed must not be strained beyond their meaning. Prudent businessmen in their dealings incur risk. That may and must happen in almost all human affairs.'

The distinction is between a prudent degree of risk on the one hand, and hazard on the other. Nor must the court be astute to fix liability on a trustee who has committed no more than an error of judgment, from which no business man, however prudent, can expect to be immune: in *Re Chapman*[4] Lopes LJ said:

'A trustee who is honest and reasonably competent is not to be held responsible for a mere error in judgment when the question which he has to consider is whether a security of a class authorized, but depreciated in value, should be retained or realized, provided he acts with reasonable care, prudence, and circumspection.'

If the trust had existed without the incorporation of BTL, so that the bank held the freehold and leasehold properties and other assets of BTL directly on the trusts of the settlement, it would in my opinion have been a clear breach of trust for the bank to have hazarded trust money in the Old Bailey development project in partnership with Stock Conversion. The Old Bailey project was a gamble, because it involved buying into the site at prices in excess of the investment values of the properties, with no certainty or probability, with no more than a chance, that planning permission could be obtained for a financially viable redevelopment, that the numerous proprietors would agree to sell out or join in the scheme, that finance would be available on acceptable terms, and that the development would be completed, or at least become a marketable asset, before the time came to start winding up the trust. However one looks at it, the project was a hazardous speculation on which no trustee could properly have ventured without explicit authority in the trust instrument. I therefore hold that the entire expenditure in the Old Bailey project would have been incurred in breach of trust, had the money been spent by the bank itself. The fact that it was a risk acceptable to the board of a wealthy company like Stock Conversion has little relevance.

I turn to the question, what was the duty of the bank as the holder of shares in BTL and BTH? I will first answer this question without regard to the position of the bank as a specialist trustee, to which I will advert later. The bank, as trustee, was bound to act in relation to the shares and to the controlling position which they conferred, in the same manner as a prudent man of business. The prudent man of business will act in such manner as is necessary to safeguard his investment. He will do this in two ways. If facts come to his knowledge which tell him that the company's affairs are not being conducted as they should be, or which put him on enquiry, he will take appropriate action.

1 (1883) 22 Ch D 727, 9 App Cas 1
2 (1887) 12 App Cas 727 at 733
3 (1883) 23 Ch D 483 at 493
4 [1896] 2 Ch 763 at 778, [1895–9] All ER Rep 1104 at 1110

a Appropriate action will no doubt consist in the first instance of enquiry of and consultation with the directors, and in the last but most unlikely resort, the convening of a general meeting to replace one or more directors. What the prudent man of business will *not* do is to content himself with the receipt of such information on the affairs of the company as a shareholder ordinarily receives at annual general meetings. Since he has the power to do so, he will go further and see that he has sufficient information to enable him to make a responsible decision from time to time either to let matters proceed as

b they are proceeding, or to intervene if he is dissatisfied. This topic was considered by Cross J in *Re Lucking's Will Trusts*[1]. In that case nearly 70% of the shares in the company were held by two trustees, L and B, as part of the estate of the deceased; about 29% belonged to L in his own right, and 1% belonged to L's wife. The directors in 1954 were Mr and Mrs L and D, who was the manager of the business. In 1956 B was appointed trustee to act jointly with L. The company was engaged in the manufacture and sale of

c shoe accessories. It had a small factory employing about 20 people, and one or two travellers. It also had an agency in France. D wrongfully drew some £15,000 from the company's bank account in excess of his remuneration, and later became bankrupt. The money was lost. Cross J[2] said this:

d 'The conduct of the defendant trustees is, I think, to be judged by the standard applied in *Re Speight, Speight* v. *Gaunt*[3], namely, that a trustee is only bound to conduct the business of the trust in such a way as an ordinary prudent man would conduct a business of his own. Now, what steps, if any, does a reasonably prudent man who finds himself a majority shareholder in a private company take with regard to the management of the company's affairs? He does not, I think, content himself with such information as to the management of the company's affairs as he

e is entitled to as shareholder, but ensures that he is represented on the board. He may be prepared to run the business himself as managing director or, at least, to become a non-executive director while having the business managed by someone else. Alternatively, he may find someone who will act as his nominee on the board and report to him from time to time as to the company's affairs. In the same way, as it seems to me, trustees holding a controlling interest ought to ensure so far as

f they can that they have such information as to the progress of the company's affairs as directors would have. If they sit back and allow the company to be run by the minority shareholder and receive no more information than shareholders are entitled to, they do so at their risk if things go wrong.'

g I do not understand Cross J to have been saying that in every case where trustees have a controlling interest in a company it is their duty to ensure that one of their number is a director or that they have a nominee on the board who will report from time to time on the affairs of the company. He was merely outlining convenient methods by which a prudent man of business (as also a trustee) with a controlling interest in a private company, can place himself in a position to make an informed decision whether any action is appropriate to be taken for the protection of his asset. Other methods may be

h equally satisfactory and convenient, depending on the circumstances of the individual case. Alternatives which spring to mind are the receipt of the copies of the agenda and minutes of board meetings if regularly held, the receipt of monthly management accounts in the case of a trading concern, or quarterly reports. Every case will depend on its own facts. The possibilities are endless. It would be useless, indeed misleading, to seek to lay down a general rule. The purpose to be achieved is not that of monitoring every

j move of the directors, but of making it reasonably probable, so far as circumstances

---

1 [1967] 3 All ER 726, [1968] 1 WLR 866
2 [1967] 3 All ER 726 at 732–733, [1968] 1 WLR 866 at 874–875
3 (1883) 22 Ch D 727

permit, that the trustee or (as in *Re Lucking's Will Trusts*[1]) one of them will receive an adequate flow of information in time to enable the trustees to make use of their *a* controlling interest should this be necessary for the protection of their trust asset, namely the shareholding. The obtaining of information is not an end in itself, but merely a means of enabling the trustees to safeguard the interests of their beneficiaries.

The principle enunciated in *Re Lucking's Will Trusts*[1] appears to have been applied in *Re Miller's Deed Trusts* decided by Oliver J. No transcript of the judgment is available but the case is briefly noted in a journal of the Law Society[2]. There are also a number of *b* American decisions proceeding on the same lines, to which counsel has helpfully referred me.

So far, I have applied the test of the ordinary prudent man of business. Although I am not aware that the point has previously been considered, except briefly in *Re Waterman's Will Trusts*[3], I am of opinion that a higher duty of care is plainly due from someone like a trust corporation which carries on a specialised business of trust management. A trust *c* corporation holds itself out in its advertising literature as being above ordinary mortals. With a specialist staff of trained trust officers and managers, with ready access to financial information and professional advice, dealing with and solving trust problems day after day, the trust corporation holds itself out, and rightly, as capable of providing an expertise which it would be unrealistic to expect and unjust to demand from the ordinary prudent man or woman who accepts, probably unpaid and sometimes *d* reluctantly from a sense of family duty, the burdens of a trusteeship. Just as, under the law of contract, a professional person possessed of a particular skill is liable for breach of contract if he neglects to use the skill and experience which he professes, so I think that a professional corporate trustee is liable for breach of trust if loss is caused to the trust fund because it neglects to exercise the special care and skill which it professes to have. The advertising literature of the bank was not in evidence (other than the scale of fees) *e* but counsel for the bank did not dispute that trust corporations, including the bank, hold themselves out as possessing a superior ability for the conduct of trust business, and in any event I would take judicial notice of that fact. Having expressed my view of the higher duty required from a trust corporation, I should add that the bank's counsel did not dispute the proposition.

In my judgment the bank wrongfully and in breach of trust neglected to ensure that *f* it received an adequate flow of information concerning the intentions and activities of the boards of BTL and BTH. It was not proper for the bank to confine itself to the receipt of the annual balance sheet and profit and loss account, detailed annual financial statements and the chairman's report and statement, and to attendance at the annual general meetings and the luncheons that followed, which were the limits of the bank's regular sources of information. Had the bank been in receipt of more frequent *g* information it would have been able to step in and stop, and ought to have stopped, Mr Roberts and the board embarking on the Old Bailey project. That project was imprudent and hazardous and wholly unsuitable for a trust whether undertaken by the bank direct or through the medium of its wholly owned company. Even without the regular flow of information which the bank ought to have had, it knew enough to put it on enquiry. There were enough obvious points at which the bank should have intervened *h* and asked questions. Assuming, as I do, that the questions would have been answered truthfully, the bank would have discovered the gamble on which Mr Roberts and his board were about to embark in relation to the Old Bailey site, and it could have, and should have, stopped the initial move towards disaster, and later on arrested further

j

1 [1967] 3 All ER 726, [1968] 1 WLR 866
2 [1978] LS Gaz 454
3 [1952] 2 All ER 1054

progress towards disaster. I have indicated in the course of this judgment a number of obvious points at which the bank should have intervened, and it would be repetitive to summarise them.

I hold that the bank failed in its duty whether it is judged by the standard of the prudent man of business or of the skilled trust corporation. The bank's breach of duty caused the loss which was suffered by the trust estate. If the bank had intervened as it could and should have, that loss would not have been incurred. By 'loss', I mean the depreciation which took place in the market value of the BTL and BTH shares, by comparison with the value which the shares would have commanded if the loss on the Old Bailey project had not been incurred, and reduction of dividends through loss of income. The bank is liable for the loss so suffered by the trust estate, except to the extent that I shall hereafter indicate.

The bank's defences to the main charge simply do not stand up to examination. For instance: (1) para 15 of the defence: '. . . the Trustees maintained close and regular contact with the Board of the Company, and in particular with Mr Roberts.' This is untrue in any meaningful sense; (2) para 19: '. . . the Bank acting by Mr Mahoney . . . reached the conclusion that the best prospects for the Old Company lay in the field of property development.' In fact, the bank, through its officers, merely accepted, without proper examination, a series of faits accomplis; (3) para 25: the participation of Stock Conversion 'was considered by the Bank . . . to be of great benefit to the eventual success' of the development. Mr Mahoney knew nothing whatever about Stock Conversion's participation until months after the event, and even then the name meant nothing to him at the time; (4) para 34(1): 'Mr Roberts . . . fulfilled the role of a nominee of the Trustees . . .' He did not; (5) para 34(2): the bank gave 'full and anxious consideration to the future direction of the Company's efforts'. The bank gave neither full nor anxious consideration to those efforts in so far as they were directed towards the Old Bailey development; (6) para 34(4): 'The trustees discussed with Mr Roberts on several occasions what steps, if any, were necessary or desirable in connection with the Old Bailey Site.' No significant discussions ever took place on this topic; (7) para 36: 'The Old Bailey project was not a speculative adventure.' It not only was but could always be seen to be; (8) para 46: '. . . given the primary duty of the Trustees under Clause 1 of the Settlement [ie to retain the shares in their present state unless for the purposes of division or for some other good and sufficient cause a sale is necessary or desirable] the economic position in the early 1960s and the then portfolio of the Old Company, it was the act of a reasonably prudent man to allow the Old Company to engage in property development.' None of these three factors would have persuaded a prudent trustee to allow BTL to accept the hazards of the Old Bailey project; (9) para 46(2): '. . . the Trustees at all times received full information as to the developments which occurred in relation to the Old Bailey Site project.' I would substitute the word 'inadequate' for the word 'full'.

Counsel in his able submissions on behalf of the bank put the defence on a broader basis, in the light of the documentary and oral evidence. The real issue, he said, was whether it was the duty of the bank (a) to ensure that it received regular reports from the board, either by its nominee or otherwise, or (b) to probe only if and when alerted. He submitted that in the context of this type of company and calibre of board, trustees are entitled to rely on the information dispensed annually until something occurs to warn them that, as prudent men of business, they should exercise greater vigilance. He submitted that the board of this company was of high calibre, and was rightly trusted. If one accepts, as I accept, what was said by Cross J in Re Lucking's Will Trusts[1], this argument breaks down at the outset. The judge said, and I agree, that a reasonably prudent man who finds himself a majority shareholder in a private company does not content himself with such information as to the management of the company's affairs as he is entitled to as a shareholder. Still less does he do so if his shareholding in the

---

1 [1967] 3 All ER 726 at 732–733, [1968] 1 WLR 866 at 874–875

company represents his entire fortune; so far as I am aware, there were never any assets of significance in the settlement at the relevant time except the debentures and shares in *a* BTL and BTH. I do not think that the calibre of the board is relevant, save that the extent and regularity of the information that a trustee should be content to receive must be much greater in the case of an inexperienced board. Everyone without exception spoke highly of the calibre of the BTL board when it confined itself to estate management. But as an expert on development Mr Roberts and his colleagues had no claim to exceptional ability. His initial costings of the Old Bailey project were easily faulted in cross- *b* examination, his forecasts were continually falsified by events and he claimed and displayed no expertise in matters of finance or planning.

The bank also relies on cll 18 and 26 of the settlement. Clause 18 entitled the bank to—

> 'act in relation to [BTL] or any other company and the shares securities and properties thereof in such way as it shall think best calculated to benefit the trust *c* premises and as if it was the absolute owner of such shares securities and property.'

In my judgment this is a clause which confers on the bank power to engage in a transaction which might otherwise be outside the scope of its authority; it is not an indemnity protecting the bank against liability for a transaction which is a breach of trust because it is one that a prudent man of business would have eschewed. Clause 26 will be *d* recognised by conveyancers of an earlier generation as a not unusual 'apportionment clause' at the end of which the draftsman tagged on a purported power to determine all questions of doubt. It has no conceivable relevance. For the clause, and its undoing, see *Re Wynn's Will Trusts*[1].

Two particular defences remain. The Limitation Act 1939 is pleaded. It is relied on in relation to any income lost by Sir Basil on money spent in breach of trust prior to 19th *e* August 1971, six years before the writ was issued. The defence is sound unless it can be said that the right of action in relation to the lost income was 'concealed by the fraud' of the bank within the meaning of s 26(b) of the 1939 Act. The purpose of the 1939 Act is to protect a defendant against stale claims, particularly where evidence for the defence may have been obscured or lost by the passage of time. Nothing like that has happened here. The beneficiaries never received the annual accounts or reports of BTL and BTH, *f* or copies of board minutes or the chairman's statements. Sir Basil could not be expected by the bank to know of the various wrongful purchases into the Old Bailey site at inflated prices, or the diminished income resulting therefrom. Nor is it usual, in my experience, for life tenants to be sent annual trust accounts. 'Fraud', in the context of s 26(b), does not mean common law fraud or deceit. But it does seem to envisage conduct which, if not fraudulent in the more usual sense, is unconscionable having regard to the relationship *g* between the parties: see *Kitchen v Royal Air Forces Association*[2]. 'Fraud' is used in the equitable sense to denote conduct by the defendant or his agent such that it would be against conscience for him to avail himself of the lapse of time. As Lord Denning MR said in *Applegate v Moss*[3]:

> 'The section applies whenever the conduct of the defendant or his agent has been such as to hide from the plaintiff the existence of his right of action, in such *h* circumstances that it would be inequitable to allow the defendant to rely on the lapse of time as a bar to the claim.'

and in *King v Victor Parsons & Co*[4]:

j

---

1 [1952] 1 All ER 341, [1952] Ch 271
2 [1958] 2 All ER 241, [1958] 1 WLR 536
3 [1971] 1 All ER 747 at 750, [1971] 1 QB 406 at 413
4 [1973] 1 All ER 206 at 209, [1973] 1 WLR 29 at 34

> 'If the defendant was, however, quite unaware that he was committing a wrong
> or a breach of contract, it would be different'.

In the instant case there was no cover-up by the bank. The bank had no inkling that it was acting in breach of trust. The defence is, in my judgment, available to the bank if its conscience permits it to rely on it having regard to the fact that the passage of time caused no prejudice whatever to the bank.

It follows that Sir Basil is not entitled to claim against the bank a share in any increased dividends which ought to have been declared by BTL over the six years prior to the issue of the writ.

Section 61 of the Trustee Act 1925 is pleaded. There is no doubt that the bank acted honestly. I do not think it acted reasonably. Nor do I think it would be fair to excuse the bank at the expense of the beneficiaries.

There remains this defence, which I take from para 26 of the amended pleading:

> 'In about 1963 the Old Company purchased a site at Woodbridge Road, Guildford,
> pursuant to the policy pleaded in paragraph 19 hereof, for the sum of £79,000, and
> re-sold the same for £350,000 to MEPC Ltd. in 1973. The net profit resulting from
> such sale was £271,000. If, which is denied, the Defendant is liable for breach of
> trust, whether as alleged in the amended Statement of Claim or otherwise, the
> Defendant claims credit for such sum of £271,000 or other sum found to be gained
> in taking any accounts or inquiries.'

The general rule as stated in all the textbooks, with some reservations, is that where a trustee is liable in respect of distinct breaches of trust, one of which has resulted in a loss and the other in a gain, he is not entitled to set off the gain against the loss, unless they arise in the same transaction: see Halsbury's Laws of England[1], Snell's Equity[2], Lewin on Trusts[3], Underhill's Law of Trusts and Trustees[4]. The relevant cases are, however, not altogether easy to reconcile. All are centenarians and none is quite like the present. The Guildford development stemmed from exactly the same policy and (to a lesser degree because it proceeded less far) exemplified the same folly as the Old Bailey project. Part of the profit was in fact used to finance the Old Bailey disaster. By sheer luck the gamble paid off handsomely, on capital account. I think it would be unjust to deprive the bank of this element of salvage in the course of assessing the cost of the shipwreck. My order will therefore reflect the bank's right to an appropriate set-off.

There is one final point. BTL and BTH by the terms of their respective memoranda of association existed for the purpose only of investment. It is pleaded by the plaintiffs that participation in the Old Bailey project was ultra vires. I think that may well be correct. If so, it would have been a breach of trust for the bank to have permitted the board to pursue activities ultra vires the company. It is not, however, necessary that I should reach a concluded view on this point, and I content myself with recording a doubt.

This action has lasted well over 40 days. It was obvious from the time when the documentation was complete that most of the matters alleged in the defence were unsustainable. It was equally obvious that the defence could not succeed in this court unless I were persuaded to depart from the law as stated by Cross J in *Re Lucking's Will Trusts*[5]. Furthermore, the defence could not succeed if the advice given to trust managers and officers in the bank's current rule book was correct. The plaintiffs' counsel made it

---

1 38 Halsbury's Laws (3rd Edn) 1046, para 1804
2 27th Edn (1973) p 276
3 16th Edn (1964) p 670
4 12th Edn (1970) p 634
5 [1967] 3 All ER 726 at 732–733, [1968] 1 WLR 866 at 874–875

clear in opening his case, and at a later stage, that his clients had no desire to squeeze the
last penny from the bank, and that they were open to reasonable suggestions for resolving   *a*
the dispute. This offer was not taken up. In the circumstances I think it is a pity that a
large and responsible trust corporation should have put the Bartlett family to the expense
and anxiety of a marathon court proceeding.

Order accordingly

b

Solicitors: *Frere Cholmeley & Co* (for the plaintiffs): *Simmons & Simmons* (for the bank).

Evelyn M C Budd   Barrister.

J (HD) v J (AM)

c

FAMILY DIVISION
SHELDON J
5th, 6th, 9th, 30th JULY 1979

*Divorce – Financial provision – Conduct of parties – Duty of court to have regard to conduct –
Circumstances in which regard to be had to conduct – Conduct after dissolution of marriage –*   *d*
*Conduct between order for financial provision and application to vary order – Wife conducting
sustained campaign of malice and persecution against husband and his new wife – Whether wife's
conduct subsequent to order for periodical payments relevant on application by husband to vary
order – Whether wife's conduct of such gravity as to effect financial provision for her –
Matrimonial Causes Act 1973, s 31(7).*

e

The marriage between the husband and wife was dissolved by decree nisi of 5th March
1969 which was made absolute on 13th March 1970. There were two children of the
marriage, a son and daughter. On the wife's application for ancillary relief, consent
orders were made on 18th December 1972 whereby, inter alia, the husband was ordered
to make periodical payments for the wife of £1,000 per annum less tax. On the same   *f*
date the husband remarried. From the date of his remarriage the wife conducted a
sustained campaign of malice and persecution against the husband and his new wife,
subjecting them to a stream of letters and telephone calls, some of which were violently
abusive. The wife also called at their home, and on one such visit violently attacked the
husband's new wife, as a result of which she was convicted of assault. On numerous
occasions the wife also breached an injunction issued against her restraining her from
molesting the husband and his new wife. Although the wife's conduct was partly due to   *g*
psychiatric illness, it also contained a significant element of intentional harassment of the
husband and his new wife. Moreover, her conduct exacerbated a psychiatric illness from
which the husband suffered. On 28th February 1978 the husband applied to the court
under s 31(1) of the Matrimonial Causes Act 1973 for a variation of the order for
periodical payments made on 18th December 1972 seeking in effect to have the payments
reduced to a nominal amount because of the wife's conduct. The husband contended   *h*
that the wife's conduct was a matter to which the court, in exercising its power to vary
the order of 18th December 1972, was required, by s 31(7)[a], to have regard as part of 'all
the circumstances of the case'. The wife contended, inter alia, that conduct of a party
after dissolution of the marriage, or alternatively after a party's right to financial relief
had been established by a court order, could not be taken into account and that, in any
event, her conduct was not sufficiently gross and obvious to warrant her being deprived   *j*
completely of the periodical payments under the order. On the hearing of the application
the wife cross-applied for an increase of the periodical payments.

---

a   Section 31(7), so far as material, is set out at p 160 *e f*, post

Held – (i) On an application to vary an order for periodical payments the court could
a take into account not only a party's conduct between the dissolution of the marriage and
the original order for financial relief but also his or her conduct between the making of
the original order and the hearing of the application to vary it, for conduct during the
latter period was part of 'all the circumstances of the case' for the purposes of s 31(7) of
the 1973 Act and as such was material to the court's consideration of the application to
vary the order.   Furthermore, any conduct during those periods which interfered with
b the other party's life or standard of living (whether or not it affected the other party's
finances) and which was so gross and obvious that to order the other party to support the
party whose conduct was in question would be repugnant to justice was relevant in
considering the application to vary an order (see p 162 *a b d* and *g h* and p 163 *a* to *c*, post);
Wachtel v Wachtel [1973] 1 All ER 829, *Jones v Jones* [1975] 2 All ER 12 and dictum of Sir
George Baker P in *W v W* [1975] 3 All ER at 972 applied.
c   (ii) In assessing the effect of a party's conduct on the question of financial provision, the
test to be applied was whether, after making all allowances for his or her disabilities and
for the temperaments of both parties, the character and gravity of the conduct was such
that it would be repugnant to justice to ignore it in deciding the provision that was to be
made by the other party (see p 164 *c d*, post); *Williams v Williams* [1963] 2 All ER 994 and
Katz v Katz [1972] 3 All ER 219 applied.
d   (iii) In all the circumstances, the wife's conduct since 18th December 1972 was of such
a character that it could not be ignored in deciding the provision that should be made by
the husband, but, taking a broad view of the matter and bearing in mind that the wife
still had a contribution to make by bringing up the daughter of the marriage until her
education was completed, that the husband was in arrears with payments due under the
order of 18th December 1972 and that the wife was unlikely to recover those arrears, it
e would be fair to dismiss both the application and the cross-application and leave the
periodical payments at the rate of £1,000 per annum, payable without deduction of tax,
since an order for the payment of maintenance of £1,000 was now a small maintenance
order (see p 164 *e* to *h* and p 165 *d e* post).

f **Notes**
For financial provision after a decree of divorce and the extent to which the court must
have regard to the conduct of the parties, see 13 Halsbury' Laws (4th Edn) paras 1060,
1062.
     For the Matrimonial Causes Act 1973, s 31, see 43 Halsbury's Statutes (3rd Edn) 576.

g
Cases referred to in judgment
Hadkinson v Hadkinson [1952] 2 All ER 567, [1952] P 285, CA, 16 Digest (Repl) 104, 1188.
Jones v Jones [1975] 2 All ER 12, [1976] Fam 8, [1975] 2 WLR 606, CA, Digest (Cont Vol
     D) 426, 6962 Abc.
Katz v Katz [1972] 3 All ER 219, [1972] 1 WLR 955, Digest (Cont Vol D) 403, 2631a.
h *W v W* [1975] 3 All ER 970, [1976] Fam 107, [1975] 3 WLR 752, Digest (Cont Vol D)
     428, 6962Ae.
Wachtel v Wachtel [1973] 1 All ER 829, [1973] Fam 72, [1973] 2 WLR 366, CA, Digest
     (Cont Vol D) 425, 6962Aa.
West v West [1977] 2 All ER 705, [1978] Fam 1, [1977] 2 WLR 933, CA.
Williams v Williams [1963] 2 All ER 994, [1964] AC 698, [1963] 3 WLR 215, HL, 27(1)
j   Digest (Reissue) 387, 2833.

Case also cited
Bateman v Bateman [1979] Fam 25.

Summons

By a summons dated 28th February 1978 the respondent, the husband, applied to the   *a*
court for variation of an order dated 18th December 1972 for periodical payments to the
petitioner, the wife, by reduction of the order to a nominal amount because of the wife's
conduct since the date of the order. The facts are set out in the judgment.

Michael Connell for the respondent.
Quintin Iwi for the petitioner.   *b*

                                                     Cur adv vult

30th July. **SHELDON J** read the following judgment: The parties to these proceedings
were married on 25th June 1960, when the petitioner was 32 and the husband was 27   *c*
years of age.

They have two children, a son born on 5th February 1961 and a daughter born on 18th
August 1963.

In general terms, however, the marriage was never happy, and in 1967 the husband
left home, the children (who were then only six and four) remaining with the wife.

In the same year he commenced his association with his present wife, and on 17th   *d*
November 1967, relying on their adultery, the wife presented her petition for divorce.
The petition was not defended; and in due course their marriage was dissolved by a
decree nisi of 5th March 1969, which was made absolute on 13th March 1970.

On 18th December 1972, on the wife's application for ancillary relief, including
variation of settlement and periodical payments, orders were made, by consent, first that
the husband would make periodical payments to the wife of £1,000 per annum less tax   *e*
for herself and of £480 per annum for each child, and second that, on or before 31st
December 1973, he would transfer to her the whole of his beneficial interest in the
matrimonial home and in the assurance policy with the mortgagees, the Equitable Life
Assurance Society, on the petitioner's undertaking, with effect from 1st June 1973, to
assume responsibility for all further mortgage repayments and premiums.

In fact, although all further payments after that date in connection with the mortgage   *f*
and assurance policy have been paid by the petitioner, the property itself has not yet been
transferred to her, a delay which has been due in part to the unwillingness of the
mortgagees to concur in the transaction and partly to other factors for none of which, as
I am satisfied, was the respondent in any way to blame. Nor, indeed, in my opinion, has
the delay had any effect whatever on the events which have led to the application now
before me. I also accept that the respondent is prepared to take whatever steps may be   *g*
required of him to give effect to the order.

On the same day as that on which the order was made the respondent and his present
wife were married, and on 20th November 1974 their child, C, was born.

Regrettably, however, from the date of their marriage the petitioner has conducted
against them what the respondent, with some justification, has described in an affidavit
of 7th September 1977 as 'a sustained campaign of malice and persecution', subjecting   *h*
them to relentless and unwelcome streams of letters and telephone calls, ranging 'from
the irrational to the violently abusive' and in some instances containing false reports of
some serious accident to their (the petitioner's and the respondent's) daughter. In
addition she has repeatedly made attempts to see him or to speak to him at his place of
work.

The telephone calls to his home, indeed, became so disturbing, (on one occasion in July   *j*
1974 amounting to some twenty or more in the course of the evening) that in 1975 the
respondent was obliged to go 'ex-directory' and to have his telephone number changed.

The petitioner also became an unwelcome caller at the respondent's home, and, on one
such visit, on 28th August 1976, gained admittance and violently attacked the
respondent's present wife, punching her in the face and stamping on her foot. Her

violence, indeed, was so extreme that it was only with difficulty that she was prevented
a from going upstairs to the child C and was evicted. It was an incident which led, after
a contested hearing, to her conviction on 8th February 1977 at Horseferry Road
Magistrates' Court of assault and to her then being given a three-year conditional
discharge and being ordered to pay £25 towards the complainant's costs. It is difficult,
moreover, not to believe the justices were not aware that the incident had so incensed the
respondent that from its date and until the date of the hearing he had paid little or
b nothing under the periodical payments order of 18th December 1972, an accumulation
of arrears, still outstanding, of some £814·98. Nor, to date, has the petitioner taken any
steps to enforce those arrears or to apply for the leave to do so which, by reason of the
lapse of time, has now become necessary by virtue of the Matrimonial Causes Act 1973,
s 32(1); nor, somewhat surprisingly, did counsel on her behalf accede to the invitation to
make such an application at this hearing before me.

c   Unfortunately that conviction seems to have had little effect in stemming the
petitioner's harassment of the respondent and his wife. The flow of letters still continued,
she continued to call at or to telephone his place of work and she was unable to keep away
from his home. On one such occasion, 18th June 1977, indeed, as I accept, she seriously
alarmed the respondent's wife (who, for protection, had put the door on a chain) by
hammering at it for an appreciable time after she had been refused admittance.

d   In these circumstances, on 28th February 1978, the respondent issued his present
summons for variation of the maintenance order of 18th December 1972, asking in
effect that, because of her conduct, the periodical payments for the petitioner herself
should be reduced to a nominal amount.

Even that, however, failed to curb her activities, with the result that on 11th May 1978
application was made by the respondent for an injunction to restrain her from molesting
e him or his wife, from communicating with them save through solicitors and from
calling at or loitering in the vicinity of their home. At three successive hearings,
moreover, on 23rd May, 20th June and 4th July 1978, orders were made to such effect.

Even so, the petitioner would not leave them alone. As soon as 18th August 1978 she
was back at their house, pounding on the door to gain admittance. She was again at the
house at 9.40 in the evening on 2nd September 1978, again during the evening of 5th
f December 1978, and again during the early evening of 10th March 1979, when by
ringing the bell and by hammering on the door she made repeated efforts to gain
admission. In the meanwhile, on several occasions, she has attempted to communicate
with the respondent through his office.

In the event and perhaps not surprisingly, application was made for the petitioner's
committal for breaches of the injunction. It was heard on 25th May 1979 before his
g Honour Judge Callman when the judge, although adjourning the application generally
with liberty to restore, made it plain that, if the matter were restored before him, any
further breach would result in an immediate custodial sentence.

Fortunately, perhaps, for all concerned, for the greater part of the time since then the
respondent and his wife have been on holiday, though it is some reflection on the state
of affairs that they have gone out of their way to keep the petitioner in ignorance of their
h movements.

Thus it is that I now have to adjudicate on the respondent's application for variation of
the order of 18th December 1972 by the reduction to no more than a nominal amount
of the order for periodical payments to be made for the petitioner.

Before doing so, however, I should give brief details of their present incomes and of
the situations of their two children.

j   As to their incomes it is sufficient to say that the respondent, after some 20 years with
the same employers, is currently in receipt of a gross salary of £9,941 per annum, which
is his only source of income and one that is precarious to this extent that he is on sick
leave and not expected back to work until September next after an orchidectomy
(involving the removal of a malignant tumour) on 25th October 1978. Happily the
prognosis is good, although he is still suffering from the after-effects of the operation and

of the radiotherapy which followed it, and still has to undergo regular checks to ensure
that there is no sign of any recurrent disease.   *a*

The petitioner, however, is not employed, so that her only present income is whatever
may be provided by the respondent, together with a disability allowance from the
Department of Health and Social Security currently amounting to some £25·45 per
week, and a further £5 per week by way of child benefit.

In general terms, their only significant assets are the homes in which they live (the
petitioner's home (hers or to be hers by virtue of the order of 18th December 1972) *b*
representing (apart from its contents, most of which she appears to enjoy) the sole assset
of the parties at the end of their marriage, of a present value of some £30,000, subject to
a mortgage of £4,000 on which she has to pay by way of premiums and mortgage
repayments some £32 per month) and the respondent's house, which he bought in 1975
for about £19,000, on which there is outstanding a mortgage of £15,460 repayable at the
monthly rate of £181·77.   *c*

As regards the children, for some years after the respondent left home both children
lived with the petitioner. In about 1974, however, the boy (then 13) left home to live
first with an aunt and then with his maternal grandmother in Surrey, where he also went
to school. It also appears likely that, as he is now 18 and has been offered work in that
neighbourhood, this summer term at school has been his last. The girl, however, still
lives with the petitioner and, at the age of almost 16, still has at least two more years of *d*
education before her. It has also been agreed between the parties that the order of 18th
December 1972 should be varied by increasing the periodical payments for her to the
rate of £624 per annum.

As to the relationship between the respondent and these children, as it has not been the
subject of any detailed investigation, I will say no more than that it has clearly been
subjected to great strain by the bitterness of feeling between their parents.   *e*

Section 31(7) of the Matrimonial Causes Act 1973 provides that in exercising its power
to vary an order (in this instance for periodical payments) previously made—

'... the court shall have regard to all the circumstances of the case, including any
change in any of the matters to which the court was required to have regard when
making the order to which the application [to vary] relates ...'   *f*

Some of the particular matters to which the court was required to have regard when
making the original order are specified in s 25(1) of the 1973 Act which concludes by
enjoining the court—

'... to place the parties, so far as it is practicable and, having regard to their
conduct, just to do so, in the financial position in which they would have been if the *g*
marriage had not broken down ...'

In these circumstances, in general terms, the respondent's contention is that,
notwithstanding that the original order was an order made by consent, the conduct of
the petitioner since the dissolution of their marriage is a matter to which the court
should now have regard in deciding whether or to what extent it is just that the
periodical payments should continue.   *h*

It is a contention which has been opposed by counsel on behalf of the petitioner on
several grounds which may be tabulated as follows: (i) that as the respondent is himself
in contempt of the order in question (in having failed to pay arrears of £814·98 or to
transfer to the petitioner his share in their previous matrimonial home) it is not open to
him, or the court should not permit him, to seek to have it amended; (ii) that the conduct
of a party, after dissolution of their marriage, as it could no longer be described as *j*
'matrimonial conduct', cannot be taken into account; (iii) that, in any event, such
conduct could be considered only if it was 'both gross and obvious' in the sense in which
that expression is used in *Wachtel v Wachtel*[1], and that, on the facts, the petitioner's

1   [1973] 1 All ER 829, [1973] Fam 72

behaviour falls well below that standard; (iv) that even if conduct after divorce can be
a considered at all it cannot be brought into account after the party's right to financial relief
(whether by way of lump sum, variation of settlement or periodical payments) has
finally been established, as in this case they were by the order of 18th December 1972;
(v) that, having regard to the parallel proceedings taken by the respondent for an
injunction and for the petitioner's committal, now also to reduce her entitlement to
periodical payments would be to impose a double penalty on her for the same behaviour;
b (vi) that, in all the circumstances, the petitioner's conduct was not such as warranted her
being deprived of more than a relatively small proportion of the periodical payments to
which she would otherwise have been entitled.

In conclusion, turning defence into attack, counsel for the petitioner at the outset of
the hearing asked for (and was given by me) leave to the petitioner herself to apply for
an increase in the periodical payments ordered on 18th December 1972. As to that, he
c submitted (and I did not understand this seriously to be challenged by counsel for the
respondent) that, on financial considerations alone, a proper rate would be that of £2,500
per annum.

It will be convenient to deal with these propositions seriatim.

In my opinion, it is clear from the authorities, as in the event counsel for the petitioner
conceded, that the court always has a discretion whether or not to permit a party in
d contempt to be heard on some further application by him in the same suit, balancing 'the
plain and unqualified obligation of every person against, or in respect of, whom an order
is made by a court of competent jurisdiction to obey it unless and until that order is
discharged' against the need to do justice between the parties in the particular
circumstances of the case: see *Hadkinson v Hadkinson*[1], in which Romer LJ gives examples
of what he describes as exceptions from the general rule which would debar a party in
e contempt from being heard by the courts whose order he has disobeyed. In my view, the
court's discretion in such a case is unfettered; but if guidelines are required, they are to
be found in the judgment in the same case of Denning LJ which, after a review of the
history of the general rule, contains the following passage[2]:

f 'It is a strong thing for a court to refuse to hear a party to a cause and it is only to
be justified by grave considerations of public policy. It is a step which a court will
only take when the contempt itself impedes the course of justice and there is no
other effective means of securing his compliance . . . Appling this principle I am of
the opinion that the fact that a party to a cause has disobeyed an order of the court
is not in itself a bar to his being heard, but, if his disobedience is such that, so long
as it continues, it impedes the course of justice in the cause, by making it more
difficult for the court to ascertain the truth or to enforce the orders which it may
g make, then the court may in its discretion refuse to hear him until the impediment
is removed or good reason is shown why it should not be removed.'

I have stated already that I do not regard the respondent as having been in contempt
in one of the respects suggested by counsel for the petitioner, in that he was not in any
way to blame for the failure to date to transfer to the petitioner his interest in their
h previous matrimonial home. On the other hand he was clearly in contempt of the order
of 18th December 1972 in discontinuing for a time after the incident of 26th August
1976 the periodical payments to which she was prima facie entitled, although the reason
for his action is not difficult to understand.

However that may be, in the exercise of my discretion in accordance with the
principles to which I have referred, I have no doubt that I should not, because of that
j contempt, now refuse to hear the respondent's application for the variation of the order
in question.

1   [1952] 2 All ER 567 at 569, [1952] P 285 at 288
2   [1952] 2 All ER 567 at 574–575, [1952] P 285 at 298

I would add that, for similar reasons, I am satisfied that I should not refuse to hear the petitioner's cross-application for an increase in the periodical payments, notwithstanding *a* that, on her own admission, she had committed several 'serious breaches' of the injunction made on 4th July 1978.

I also reject counsel's second submission for the petitioner that, on an application to vary an order for periodical payments, the court cannot take into account a party's conduct after the dissolution of the marriage. In my judgment, indeed, not only is *Jones v Jones*[1] clear authority to the contrary, but to accede to such a proposition would be to *b* ignore the provisions of s 31(7) of the 1973 Act and to act contrary to plain justice and common sense. Counsel for the petitioner has argued that that decision is obiter because, although the point was raised in argument, as stated by Orr LJ[2], it was 'certainly not pressed' (possibly because its lack of merit had soon become apparent). I am not prepared so to treat the judgment. In that case the conduct in question was that of a husband who, two months after the decree absolute, had violently attacked the wife with a razor. It was *c* conduct which it was held could be applied to increase the wife's claim for financial relief; in the judgment of Orr LJ[3] it was '. . . a case in which the conduct of the husband had been of such a gross kind that it would be offensive to a sense of justice that it should not be taken into account'. As was stressed by Megaw LJ[4], moreover, the word 'conduct' in the context of s 25(1) of the 1973 Act (and so, in my view, in the context of a review within s 37(7)) 'is not to be treated as being confined to matrimonial misconduct.' *d*

I also reject counsel's further submission for the petitioner that if a party's conduct after divorce is relevant at all to a claim for financial relief it is to be limited to conduct between the divorce and the date on which that claim is finally adjudicated. Certainly that was not a question which arose for decision in *Jones v Jones*[1], as the husband's conduct in that case occurred during that interval and the court was concerned merely to decide whether it could be taken into account in determining the parties' appropriate shares in *e* the family assets. Clearly also, in the present context, a party's conduct after the making of a financial provision or property adjustment order is relevant only to those cases in which the court has power to vary or even to discharge the original order. It cannot, therefore, affect orders already made for a lump sum or for the adjustment or settlement of property save in the limited respects provided by s 31(2)(d), (e) and (4). Thus, in general terms, in regard to orders made in divorce proceedings or on or after the grant *f* of a decree of divorce, the only cases to which s 31 applies, and accordingly to which conduct after the making of the order could be relevant, are those which provide for periodical payments or payments of maintenance or of lump sum instalments. In my judgment, however, a party's conduct between the making of the original order and the hearing of the application for its discharge or variation may be as much a part of 'all the circumstances of the case' and as material to the court's consideration as the husband's *g* conduct (between the decree absolute and the making of the orders for financial provision) was held to be in *Jones v Jones*[1].

Clearly, in this context, any conduct might be relevant to the extent that it effectively reduced the other party's means, income or ability to earn his living, where, to adopt the words of Sir George Baker P in *W v W*[5], 'it directly affects the [other party's] finances'. In that case, however, the learned President was concerned to exclude from consideration *h* behaviour on the part of the wife which, after the dissolution of their marriage, was of

j

1   [1975] 2 All ER 12, [1976] Fam 8
2   [1975] 2 All ER 12 at 16, [1976] Fam 8 at 15
3   [1975] 2 All ER 12 at 17, [1976] Fam 8 at 15
4   [1975] 2 All ER 12 at 17, [1976] Fam 8 at 16
5   [1975] 3 All ER 970 at 972, [1976] Fam 107 at 110

'no concern to her ex-husband'. I do not understand him as having intended to deal with
a the wider question now before me.

In my judgment, indeed, any conduct by a party may be relevant in the present
context which, whether or not it directly affects the other's finances, is such as to interfere
with his or her life and standard of living and which is covered by the well-known
passage in the judgment of Lord Denning MR in *Wachtel v Wachtel*[1], that is conduct
which is '"both gross and obvious", so much so that to order one party to support another
b whose conduct falls into this category is repugnant to anyone's sense of justice'. Or to put
the question into other words, as used by Sir George Baker P in *W v W*[2], is conduct 'of the
kind that would cause the ordinary mortal to throw up his hands and say, "Surely that
woman is not going to be given any money", or "is not going to get a full award"'.

In counsel's submission for the petitioner, however, the petitioner's conduct since the
order of 18th December 1972, however reprehensible, falls far short of any such
c standard. I disagree.

Two important features in this case are the medical histories of the two parties.
According to the medical reports placed before me the petitioner suffers from chronic
schizophrenia in respect of which she has been 'a very long-standing' hospital patient,
both as an in-patient and out-patient, 'almost continuously since her first admission in
1950'. It is an illness in which rational intervals have been punctuated by bouts of
d depression, outbursts of physical violence, threats of suicide and other irrational
manifestations. Unfortunately, moreover, she has only allowed herself to be treated
sporadically with medication, so that, although she has shown some signs of improvement
over the years, this has not been as great as might otherwise have been achieved. Thus
on 28th August 1978 the consultant psychiatrist whose patient she is was able to say only
that there was a 'reasonable chance' that she would obey the injunction that was then in
e force and that was renewed on 4th July 1978. In fact, she did not obey its terms and in
a later report of 18th May 1979 he recorded that 'her willingness or ability to co-operate
with treatment had been just as sporadic' and that, in the interval, there had been several
occasions on which she had behaved 'very aggressively', conduct which was manifested
usually by 'hair-pulling or smashing furniture'.

The respondent, too, has a psychiatric history and, indeed, it was in consequence of
f that that on an admission to hospital for treatment he first met the petitioner. His
condition, from which he had suffered for several years, is described as one of 'nervous
depression', as to which, in a report of May 1978, the consultant psychiatrist who had
been treating him wrote as follows:

> 'Although he has, with the aid of treatment, been enabled to remain at work
g during most of this time, his capacity is seriously impaired by exacerbations of the
> symptoms of his illness, particularly by inability to concentrate, headaches,
> insomnia, morbid anxiety and feelings of depression ... An important factor in
> bringing about these exacerbations and, indeed, in perpetuating the illness, has been
> the anxiety induced by the vagaries of [the petitioner's] behaviour [and that]
> continuation of this strain entails a real risk ... of further breakdown and loss of
> earning capacity.'
h

So also, in a further report of 28th March 1979 he wrote that the petitioner's behaviour
was continuing to adversely affect his health and added:

> 'The continued apprehension about the possibility of a recurrence of an assault
> on, or other harm to his [present] wife, as well as her own anxiety in this connection,
> contributes significantly to his state of anxiety and to the subsequent morbid
j depression.'

---

1   [1973] 1 All ER 829 at 835–836, [1973] Fam 72 at 90
2   [1975] 3 All ER 970 at 972, [1976] Fam 107 at 110

I would add also that, having seen both the respondent and his present wife (in addition to the petitioner), I have no doubt as to the genuineness of their fears, nor am I prepared to say they are without justification. Clearly also these fears have significantly affected their way and enjoyment of life, even to the extent of having made them consider leaving England (and the respondent's employment) for permanent residence abroad.

In my judgment, indeed, as I have already stated, the respondent has cause for saying, as in his affidavit of 7th September 1977, that the petitioner has been making his life and that of his present wife 'a burden and a misery' and for describing her conduct as 'a sustained campaign of malice and persecution'.

I accept, of course, that the petitioner's behaviour is due to some, maybe to a considerable, extent to her illness, although I cannot escape the conclusion that it has also contained a significant intentional element in the sense that she has deliberately set out to harass the respondent and his present wife. I am also of the opinion that, in assessing the gravity of a party's conduct in the context of financial provision, the test to be applied is similar to that propounded by Lord Reid in *Williams v Williams*[1] in regard to 'cruelty', as applied by Sir George Baker P in *Katz v Katz*[2] in connection with 'behaviour' in the context of s 2(1) (b) of the Divorce Reform Act 1969, that is to say that a party's conduct would be of sufficient gravity to affect the issue if the facts are such that, after making all allowances for his disabilities and for the temperaments of both parties, the character and gravity of his behaviour was of such a nature that it would be repugnant to anyone's sense of justice to ignore it in deciding the provision to be made by one for the other or what should be their appropriate shares in the family assets. In *West v West*[3], indeed, it was emphasised that no moral judgment is necessarily to be inferred from a finding that a party's conduct was of such a nature. In all the circumstances, moreover, as I have already indicated, I am satisfied that the petitioner's conduct since 18th December 1972 has fallen within that category.

In deciding how that finding is to be reflected in financial terms, it will be convenient to consider together the cross-applications of both parties. In all the circumstances, moreover, bearing in mind particularly that the wife still has a contribution to make by bringing up their daughter until her education is completed, I am of the opinion that, although it would not be doing justice between the parties to give her what might be described as a full award of periodical payments, she should by no means be deprived of all financial provision in that respect. I bear in mind also (a) that the respondent has abandoned all claim to a share in their previous matrimonial home, substantially their only family asset, and (b) that, in the circumstances I have described, the periodical payments due under the order of 18th December 1972 are £814·98 in arrear, arrears which, as it seems to me, she is unlikely ever to be able to recover. Indeed, as she ignored the opportunity offered to her to apply in these proceedings for leave to enforce them, I consider it unlikely that some later application under s 32(1) of the Matrimonial Causes Act 1973 would be regarded with favour. I have regard also to the figures suggested by counsel for the petitioner as appropriate to a full order, although I am not persuaded that, if she were to make a real effort, the petitioner could not obtain at least some part-time employment to supplement her income. In the event, taking a broad view of the matter, I have come to the conclusion that a fair result would be, in this context, to dismiss both applications and to leave the periodical payments to the petitioner at the present rate of £1,000 per annum, although in such an event, as that is now a small maintenance order, the payments would be made without deduction of tax.

Nor do I accept counsel's final submission for the petitioner that, having regard to the previous proceedings initiated by the respondent for an injunction and for the committal of the petitioner, to deprive her now of a right to a full award would be to penalise her

---

1   [1963] 2 All ER 994, [1964] AC 698
2   [1972] 3 All ER 219, [1972] 1 WLR 955
3   [1977] 2 All ER 705, [1978] Fam 1

twice. Apart from the fact that no order was made and no penalty was imposed on the
a committal application, a restraint on future behaviour does not amount automatically to
forgiveness for the past and for a court to punish a party for contempt of its order cannot
preclude the victim from claiming any other relief to which he may be entitled.

I would add also this by way of warning to the petitioner, that, in my opinion, if she
were to persist in unjustified harassment of the respondent or his present family, the
stage might well be reached at which a court would say that it would be repugnant to
b anyone's sense of justice that the respondent should continue to maintain her at all.

There is one further matter I would mention. In the course of the hearing the
respondent, by counsel, made an open offer to the petitioner to compound her
entitlement to periodical payments for herself by the immmediate payment to her of
£6,000, the most that he said he could obtain on a further mortgage of his house, the
only condition being that £4,000 of that sum should be used to discharge the mortgage
c on their previous matrimonial home. It was an offer which the petitioner rejected. It
would, however, have been one further step to the clean break which, in my view, would
be likely to benefit both parties; nor, having regard to all the circumstances and to their
respective states of health, is it, in my view, without merit. As it was not a solution,
however, which I had any jurisdiction to impose, I will say no more about it.

In conclusion, dealing with both applications together, there will be no order on either
d application save that (1) the order of 18th December 1972 of Mr Registrar Stranger-Jones
will be varied to provide (a) that, with effect from 9th July 1979, the periodical payments
to be made by the respondent to the petitioner for herself shall be at the rate of £1,000
per annum, payable monthly without deduction of tax, and (b) that, with effect from 9th
July 1979, the periodical payments to be made to the daughter shall be at the rate of £624
per annum payable monthly, and (2) that there be no order as to costs, save legal aid
e taxation of the petitioner's costs.

Order accordingly.

Solicitors: *Lambert, Hale & Proctor* (for the petitioner); *Charles Russell & Co* (for the
f respondent).

Georgina Chambers   Barrister.

Farrell v Secretary of State for Defence   *a*

HOUSE OF LORDS

VISCOUNT DILHORNE, LORD EDMUND-DAVIES, LORD FRASER OF TULLYBELTON, LORD RUSSELL OF
KILLOWEN AND LORD LANE

5th, 6th NOVEMBER, 19th DECEMBER 1979

b

Negligence – Withdrawal of issue from jury – Suspected terrorists shot dead in Northern Ireland by army patrol of four soldiers protecting bank – Action by widow against Ministry of Defence claiming damages – Allegation in statement of claim that soldiers negligent – No allegation of negligence made against anyone else in planning operation to protect bank – Trial judge withdrawing issue of negligence from jury – Whether issue of negligence should have been withdrawn from jury.

c

Trespass to the person – Assault – Defence – Use of force in prevention of crime – Suspected terrorists shot dead in Northern Ireland by army patrol protecting bank – Whether circumstances in which operation to protect bank planned relevant in determining whether use of force by soldiers reasonable 'in the circumstances' to prevent crime – Criminal Law Act (Northern Ireland) 1967, s 3(1).

d

On 23rd October 1971 the officer in command of a detachment of troops in Newry, Northern Ireland ('soldier X') received information that a bomb attack by three men was likely to take place that night on a bank in the town. He informed soldier A and instructed him to go with three other soldiers, B, C and D, and take up a position on the *e* roof of a building opposite the bank. The four soldiers took up their position at about 10.30 pm. While soldier B was alone on the front of the roof he saw two men walking towards the bank and go to the night safe which they appeared to be trying to open. He then saw three other men cross the road to the night safe. There was a scuffle with the two already there. Soldier B called soldier A who saw the three men close to the night safe with their backs towards him. Soldier A ordered them to halt. The men stopped *f* what they were doing and looked up and down the street. One shouted to the others to run and all three ran off. Soldier A cocked his rifle and again ordered them to halt stating that he was ready to fire. The men did not stop. He and the other three soldiers then fired killing all three men. It turned out that none of the men was armed or carrying a bomb. They had been attempting to rob one of the other two men who was putting money in the night safe. That autumn there had been 35 bomb explosions in Newry and *g* two days before the incident a bomb had been placed outside a bank. The respondent, who was the widow and administratrix of one of the three men killed, brought an action against the Ministry of Defence claiming damages on the ground that his death was caused by the negligence of the Ministry, its servants and agents and by assaults and batteries committed by them. The negligence pleaded related solely to alleged acts and omissions by the four soldiers and there was no allegation in the statement of claim that *h* there had been any negligence on the part of anyone else in the planning of the operation to protect the bank. At the trial, however, in the course of cross-examination of the soldiers, it was elicited that soldier X had only selected and instructed one soldier, that he had given no instructions about summoning help, that there was no agreed procedure for the four soldiers reporting back to their base, that only four soldiers out of 80 under soldier X's command had been selected for the operation and that they did not have a *j* loud-hailer with them and could only stop or apprehend a terrorist or suspected terrorist who refused to stop by firing at him. After the evidence was heard the judge withdrew the issue of negligence from the jury but left to them a series of questions directed to the assaults and battery and possible defences to that claim, which the jury answered in favour of the soldiers. Judgment was given for the Ministry. The respondent appealed *a*   to the Court of Appeal in Northern Ireland contending, inter alia, that the judge should have left to the jury the question whether there had been negligence on the part of persons other than the four soldiers. The Court of Appeal allowed the appeal and ordered a new trial on the ground that, in considering whether the use of force by the four soldiers was, in the circumstances, reasonable for the prevention of crime, within s 3(1)*ᵃ* of the Criminal Law Act (Northern Ireland) 1967, the jury should have been directed to take into account not only the immediate conduct of the four soldiers but also

b   the circumstances in which the operation was planned and conceived, or, alternatively, that the question of negligence should have been left to the jury in order to ensure that the reasonableness of the planning and preparatory actions was considered by them. The Ministry appealed to the House of Lords contending that the phrase 'in the circumstances' in s 3(1) related solely to the immediate circumstances in which the force was used. At the hearing before the House the plaintiff did not contend that there should be a new

c   trial on account of the issue of negligence not being left to the jury.

Held – Section 3 of the 1967 Act provided a defence only for a person accused of a crime, or a person sued in tort, who had used force. In each case when such a defence was put forward the question to be determined was whether the person who was accused or sued

d   had used such force as was reasonable in the circumstances in which he was placed in the prevention of crime or in bringing about a lawful arrest of an offender or suspected offender. It followed therefore that the only circumstances which were relevant for the purposes of s 3(1) were the immediate circumstances in which the force was used and the phrase 'in the circumstances' in the subsection was to be construed accordingly. Therefore, since the only persons who had used force within the meaning of the subsection were the four soldiers in the patrol, s 3(1) would provide no defence to soldier

e   X in respect of a claim for negligence in the planning of the operation, and the jury had not been entitled to have regard to the circumstances in which the operation had been planned in determining whether the defence under s 3(1) had been established. The trial judge had therefore been right to withdraw the issue of negligence from the jury and in omitting from his direction to them any suggestion that they were entitled to have regard to soldier X's conduct in planning the operation. In the circumstances the

f   respondent had not been deprived of a fair trial and a new trial should not have been ordered. The appeal would therefore be allowed (see p 170 *b*, p 172 *f* to *h*, p 173 *a c d* and p 174 *j* to p 175 *d*, post).

     Per Lord Edmund-Davies, Lord Fraser of Tullybelton, Lord Russell of Killowen and Lord Lane. (i) Pleadings continue to play an essential part in civil actions, and although there has been a wide power to permit amendments since the enactment of the Civil

g   Procedure Act 1833 circumstances may arise when the grant of permission could work injustice or necessitate an adjournment which may prove particularly unfortunate in trials with a jury. Because the primary purpose of pleadings is to define the issues and thereby inform the parties in advance of the case they have to meet and so enable them to take steps to deal with it, it is bad law and bad practice to shrug off a criticism as 'a mere pleading point' (see p 173 *e* to *g* and p 175 *b* to *d*, post).

h   (ii) Latitude extended by a trial judge in relation to cross-examination does not per se broaden the pleaded issues, but it may give rise to a successful application for leave to amend if such cross-examination proves fruitful (see p 173 *j* to p 174 *a* and p 175 *b* to *d*, post).

Notes

j   For the use of force in making an arrest, see 11 Halsbury's Laws (4th Edn) para 103.

---

   a   Section 3(1) provides: 'A person may use such force as is reasonable in the circumstances in the prevention of crime, or in effecting or assisting in the lawful arrest of offenders or suspected offenders or of persons unlawfully at large.'

Section 3(1) of the Criminal Law Act (Northern Ireland) 1967 corresponds to s 3(1) of the Criminal Law Act 1967. For s 3 of the latter Act, see 8 Halsbury's Statutes (3rd Edn) 554.

Appeal

By a writ issued on 19th April 1973 the respondent, Olive Farrell (formerly Olive McLaughlin), brought an action on behalf of herself and on behalf of the estate of James Thomas McLaughlin deceased against the Ministry of Defence, claiming as widow and administratrix damages under and by virtue of the Law Reform (Miscellaneous Provisions) Act (Northern Ireland) 1937 and the Fatal Accidents Acts (Northern Ireland) 1846 to 1959 for loss and damage sustained by her and by other dependants of the deceased and by his estate by reason of his death which she alleged had been caused by the negligence of, and further or alternatively by assaults on and batteries to the deceased by, the Ministry, its servants and agents, in and about Marcus Square, Hill Street, Newry, County Down, Northern Ireland, on 23rd October 1971, when he was shot and killed. The Ministry denied liability. On 25th February 1977 the High Court in Northern Ireland (Gibson LJ sitting with a jury) gave judgment for the Ministry. The respondent appealed to the Court of Appeal in Northern Ireland and on 20th December 1978 that court (Lowry LCJ, Jones and McGonigal LJJ) allowed the appeal, set aside the judgment and verdict, and ordered a new trial. The Ministry appealed to the House of Lords. The facts are set out in the opinion of Viscount Dilhorne.

The Attorney-General (Sir Michael Havers QC) and *Simon Brown* for the Ministry.
Richard Ferguson QC and *D Morgan* (both of the Northern Ireland Bar) for the respondent.

Their Lordships took time for consideration.

19th December. The following opinions were delivered.

VISCOUNT DILHORNE. My Lords, the respondent was the widow of one of three men shot and killed in Newry in Northern Ireland during the night of 23rd October 1971. During that day soldier X, the officer in command of a detachment of troops in the town, received information that it was highly likely that a bomb attack would be made that night by three men on the National Provincial Bank in Hill Street in that town.

Soldier X told soldier A this and told him to go with three other soldiers B, C and D, and take up a position on the roof of a building in Hill Street opposite the National Provincial Bank. The four soldiers did so at about 10.30 pm. Soldier A told the soldiers with him that on no account were they to open fire until he did. The street was well lit and the soldiers on the roof were above the street lights and so difficult, if not impossible, to see from the ground.

At a moment when soldier B was alone on the front of the roof, he saw two men walking up Hill Street towards the National Provincial Bank. He saw them cross the road and go to the night safe of the bank. They appeared to be trying to open it. He then saw three men cross the road to the night safe and then there was a scuffle with the two already there. Soldier B called soldier A who saw the three men close to the night safe, with their backs towards him. He did not see the two who had got there first. After about 10 to 15 seconds soldier A shouted 'Halt'. He saw the three men stop what they were doing and look up and down the street. One of them shouted 'Run' and the three of them took to their heels. Soldier A cocked his rifle and shouted 'Halt, I am ready to fire'. The men did not stop. He fired and the three soldiers with him also fired, with the result that the three men were killed. It turned out that none of them was armed or carrying a bomb. One was found to be carrying a bag which had been in the possession

of one of the two men who went first to the night safe. That bag contained a coat. The
a other of the two men had a bag containing cash which presumably he had intended to
put in the night safe. That autumn there had been about 35 bomb explosions in Newry
and two days before a bomb had been put outside the local savings bank.

On 19th April 1973, about 18 months later, the respondent issued a writ claiming as
widow and administratrix of McLaughlin, one of the three men killed, damages from
the Ministry of Defence on the ground that his death was caused by the negligence of the
b Ministry, its servants and agents, and by assault and batteries committed by them. It was
not until 23rd January 1974 that the statement of claim was delivered. Paragraph 2
thereof, so far as material, reads as follows:

'2 ... by reason of the negligence of the servants and agents of the Defendants,
and further and in the alternative by reason of the assaults on and batteries to the
deceased by the said servants and agents of the Defendants, the deceased was struck
c by a bullet or bullets which had been discharged from a firearm by one or more of
the said servants or agents, whereby the deceased sustained such severe personal
injuries that he died as a result thereof on the 23rd day of October 1971.

'PARTICULARS OF NEGLIGENCE

'(i) Failing and omitting to give any or adequate warning to the plaintiff. (ii)
d Causing and permitting a firearm to be discharged at the deceased in the
circumstances. (iii) Discharging a firearm at the deceased with intent to kill him or
cause him grievous bodily harm. (iv) Failing and omitting to fire a warning shot.
(v) Failing and omitting to fire at the deceased in a fashion which would have
minimised the risk of causing him serious injury or death. (vi) Striking a blow
which was out of proportion to the occasion. (vii) Using excessive force to effect an
e arrest. (viii) Causing and permitting a firearm to be discharged at the deceased at
all.

'PARTICULARS OF ASSAULTS AND BATTERIES

'The Plaintiff repeats the above particulars of negligence and says that the
circumstances in which the deceased was killed by the servants or agents of the
Defendants were such that they constituted in law an assault and battery upon his
f person. In particular the Plaintiff complains that the force used in executing an
arrest of the deceased was excessive and unnecessary and unreasonable in the
circumstances and was, therefore, out of proportion to the occasion.'

It is apparent from this paragraph that the case the respondent sought to establish and
the case that the Ministry had to meet was that it was negligence on the part of the four
g soldiers who fired the shots and, alternatively, assaults and batteries committed by them
that brought about the death of McLaughlin.

There was no allegation in the statement of claim that there had been any negligence
on the part of anyone else or in the planning of the operation to protect the bank.

In their amended defence, the Ministry, inter alia, pleaded:

'If any servant or agents of the defendants discharged any bullet from any firearm
h and the deceased was struck thereby, which is denied, such person in doing so was
using such force as was reasonable in the circumstances in the prevention of crime
and/or the effecting or assisting in the lawful arrest of the deceased, who (a) was
attempting to escape after the commission or attempted commission of offences of
robbery, assault and battery, and was unlawfully at large; (b) was reasonably thought
by such person to have been attempting to destroy or damage bank premises in the
j town of Newry by the use of a bomb or incendiary device at a time when in the
recent past there had been many attacks by bombs and incendiary devices upon
premises in Newry.'

The trial of this action took place before Gibson LJ and a Belfast jury. After the
evidence was heard, counsel made a number of submissions to Gibson LJ. In the course

of the discussion, counsel for the respondent suggested that a question should be left to
the jury along the lines 'Did the soldiers shoot the deceased without lawful cause or *a*
excuse?' and that the second question left to them should be 'Were the soldiers guilty of
negligence causing the death of the deceased?' It is clear that both these questions were
directed to the conduct of the soldiers who had been on the roof in Hill Street and who
had fired and were not directed to any question of anyone else being guilty of
negligence. After the discussion, Gibson LJ decided not to leave the question of
negligence to the jury. In my opinion he was right not to do so, for if the soldiers had *b*
an answer to the claim based on assault and battery, that would also be an answer to the
claim against them based on negligence and to leave both questions to the jury would
only confuse. In this House counsel for the respondent did not contend that there should
be a new trial on account of negligence not being left to the jury.

Gibson LJ invited the jury to answer the following eight questions and I append to
them the answers that they gave: *c*

'1. Did the soldiers fire because soldier A suspected with reasonable cause—(a)
that the husband of the plaintiff and two other men had attempted to place an
explosive bomb or an incendiary device in or at the Provincial Bank and (b) that such
explosive bomb or incendiary device would endanger life? [*Answer*: (a) Yes (b) Yes]

'2. If the answers to questions 1(a) and 1(b) or to question 1(a) is Yes, was it *d*
reasonable in the circumstances (including the reasonable suspicion of soldier A) in
the prevention of crime for the soldiers to fire to kill? [*Answer*: Yes]

'3. If the answers to questions 1(a) and 1(b) or to question 1(a) is Yes, was it
reasonable in the circumstances (including the reasonable suspicion of soldier A) in
effecting the lawful arrest of the three men for the soldiers to fire to kill? [*Answer*:
Yes]

'4. Did the soldiers fire after soldier A had twice shouted at the three men to *e*
halt? [*Answer*: Yes]

'5 When the barman Mr O'Neill was at the night safe in the front wall of the
Provincial Bank did the husband of the plaintiff and two other men attempt to rob
him of the money he was going to place in the night safe? [*Answer*: Yes]

'6. Was the shooting entirely out of proportion to the occasion? [*Answer*: No]

'7. Was there fault on the part of the husband of the plaintiff which contributed *f*
to his death? [*Answer*: Yes]

'8. If answers to questions 2 and 3 are No and answer to question 7 is Yes what
percentage reduction should be made in the damages having regard to the
responsibility of the plaintiff's husband for his own death? [*Not Answered*]'

Gibson LJ accordingly gave judgment for the Ministry. The respondent appealed to *g*
the Court of Appeal on the following grounds:

'1. That the learned trial judge was wrong in law in withdrawing the issue of
negligence from the jury. 2. That the learned trial judge was wrong in law in
directing the jury that the test to be applied to the conduct of the soldiers was a
subjective test. 3. That the learned trial judge was wrong in law in failing to direct *h*
the jury that the test to be applied to the conduct of the soldiers was an objective
test. 4. That the learned trial judge wrongly admitted evidence of acts of terrorism
in Newry and the surrounding district. 5. That the questions put to the jury were
of such a nature and couched in such a form as to deprive the appellant of a fair
trial. 6. That the learned trial judge failed to put the case for the appellant
adequately to the jury. 7. That the finding that the appellant was not entitled to *j*
damages was perverse and unreasonable.'

It was not suggested in the course of the trial that there had been negligence on the
part of anyone other than the four soldiers and failure to leave to the jury the question
of negligence on the part of anyone else was not a ground of appeal. Counsel for the

respondent nevertheless, in the Court of Appeal, contended that Gibson LJ should have
a left to the jury the question whether there had been negligence on the part of any other
servant or agent of the Ministry. In the course of the cross-examination of the soldiers
who gave evidence, it was elicited that soldier X had only selected and instructed one
soldier; that he had given no instructions about summoning help; that there was no
agreed procedure for the four soldiers reporting back to their base; that only four soldiers
out of 80 under soldier X's command were selected for this operation; that all four were
b ordered to go on the roof; that they did not have with them a loud-hailer; and that they
were left in a situation in which the only way they could stop or apprehend a terrorist or
suspected terrorist if he refused to stop was by firing at him.

In this House counsel for the respondent contended that these matters were
circumstances which the jury should have been directed to take into account in relation
to the use of force by the four soldiers.

c   Section 3 of the Criminal Law Act (Northern Ireland) 1967 reads as follows:

'(1) A person may use such force as is reasonable in the circumstances in the
prevention of crime or in effecting or assisting in the lawful arrest of offenders or
suspected offenders or of persons unlawfully at large.

'(2) Subsection (1) shall replace the rules of the common law as to the matters
dealt with by that subsection.'

d
In the Court of Appeal Lowry LCJ said:

'When the cause of action is framed in trespass and the assault *in fact* is proved, the
defendants must then prove the defence of justification and, when debating that
issue, it is not only the conduct of the soldiers on the ground which must be looked
at but all the circumstances which led to the commission of the act complained of.'

e
He thought that it was in order to leave only the issues of assault and battery and the
alleged justification thereof to the jury where there was no separate issue of negligence.
But in his opinion that depended on the proper direction being given as to the phrase 'in
the circumstances' in s 3(1). This meant, he said—

f   'the circumstances in which an operation is conceived and planned and in which
the preparatory steps are taken as well as those in which the final decisive act is
performed.'

If he was wrong as to this, then in his opinion the question of negligence should have
been left to the jury '. . . in order to ensure that the reasonableness of the planning and
g preparatory actions is considered by the jury.'

He considered that Gibson LJ had erred because he omitted a question on negligence
and—

'charged the jury in a manner which invited their attention only to the immediate
conduct of soldier A and his detachment at the precise time and place of the
h   shooting. Liability was made to depend solely on the liability of the men on the
spot viewed at the time of the shooting.'

Jones LJ said:

'. . . there was more to the case, as it seems to me, than merely the shooting by the
j   soldiers. That was the central incident and the one which led directly to the
bringing of this action. Indeed that was what the action was about. But it by no
means exhausted the relevant matters because the scene was set by the Ministry or
at any rate by its officers. They laid on the operation, chose the location of the post
and positioned the soldiers. They made the plan and provided the men and the
equipment with which to carry out the plan.'

McGonigal LJ said that the claim in negligence was based on—

'a failure to take reasonable care for the safety of the men engaged in that robbery
in that (1) the scene for the counter-action was set by soldier X regardless of the fact
that the likely result would be what did occur and (2) no regard was had to any
attempt to reduce the risk of serious injury to the robbers by, for example,
establishing fixed ground positions or back-up ground patrols which might have
enabled an arrest rather than a killing to result, or by the use of a loud-hailer coupled
with a clearer indication of who was challenging and where the challenge came
from to enhance the possibility that the men challenged would stop instead of
trying to escape by running away.'

My Lords, I have already made it clear that no such allegations of negligence were
contained in the statement of claim and that at the trial no such allegations of negligence
were advanced. If in the statement of claim any such allegations had been put forward,
the defence would have been notified of the fact that evidence might be required to meet
them and the trial would have then taken a very different course.

Soldier X envisaged that persons challenged would stop, not that the likely result
would be that they would be shot. He considered that a soldier at ground level at a static
position would have been at considerable risk from a terrorist gunman. There were
mobile patrols in Newry. They were diverted to the area after the shooting. One arrived
in about five minutes. If the four soldiers had waited for their arrival, there can be no
doubt that the three men would have made good their escape. As there was no doubt
that the three men heard the challenges, the provision of a loud-hailer would have made
no difference. The use of a loud-hailer would not have indicated who was challenging or
where the challenge came from, nor can I see any reason for thinking that the use of one
would have enhanced the possibility that the men challenged would stop.

My Lords, I do not consider that the information elicited in the course of cross-
examination, to which I have referred, amounted to prima facie evidence of negligence
on the part of anyone in the planning of this operation. Indeed, if on this evidence
Gibson LJ had been invited to hold that there was a prima facie case of such negligence,
he would, in my opinion, have been right, indeed obliged, to rule that there was not.

Further, my Lords, I am unable to agree that the phrase 'in the circumstances' in s 3(1)
should be given the wide interpretation given to it in the Court of Appeal. That section
is contained in a statute dealing with the criminal law. It may provide a defence for a
person sued. In each case when such a defence is put forward the question to be
determined is whether the person who is accused or sued used such force as was
reasonable in the circumstances in which he was placed in the prevention of crime or in
bringing about a lawful arrest of an offender or suspected offender.

Section 3(1) would provide no defence to soldier X in respect of a claim for negligence
in the planning of the operation. It can only provide a defence for those who used force
and if the force the four soldiers used was reasonable in the circumstances in which they
used it, the defects, if there were any, in the planning of the operation would not deprive
them of that defence and render the force used unreasonable.

Further, I am unable to agree with Lowry LCJ that the questions put to the jury were
of such a nature and couched in such a form as to deprive the respondent of a fair trial.
The questions must not be considered in isolation, but with the charge of Gibson LJ in
regard to them. And reading them with the charge to the jury, I do not consider them
to have deprived the respondent of a fair trial. It is true Gibson LJ did say that he thought
one would still be preventing a crime if one saw a man trying to commit a crime and
chased after him and shot him while trying to catch him. Soldier A said that he
suspected that the three men were trying to put a bomb or incendiary in the night
safe. His challenge stopped their actions. If they had gone to the bank with a bomb or
incendiary device, he could not say whether they had succeeded in placing it in the night
safe. If they had not, then it might be said that the force used was used in the prevention

of crime, for it could not be assumed that the bomb or device would not be used
a elsewhere. However this may be, this observation in the course of a long charge to the
jury did not, in my opinion, suffice to render the trial unfair.

The Court of Appeal ordered a new trial. In my opinion they should not have done
so. If, following on their order, there was a trial conducted on the lines they suggest the
original trial should have been, it would have been a trial of a very different case from
that pleaded and presented to the jury in the trial before Gibson LJ.

b It could have been pleaded that there was negligence on the part of persons other than
the four soldiers. Any such allegations would have to have been properly formulated,
and if such a case had been pleaded and presented, then the question whether any and if
so what duty of care was owed to persons reasonably suspected of attempting to commit
or of committing a serious crime would have arisen for consideration. Although debated
in the Court of Appeal, no useful purpose would, in my opinion, be served by considering
c that question in this appeal, for determination of it would in no way affect the question
whether or not the order of the Court of Appeal that there should be a new trial was
correct. I do not propose to comment on the views expressed on this question by the
Court of Appeal, but it is not to be assumed that I agree with them.

In my opinion, for the reasons stated, this appeal should be allowed.

d
LORD EDMUND-DAVIES. My Lords, I am in respectful agreement with the speech
prepared by my noble and learned friend Viscount Dilhorne, which I have had the
advantage of seeing in draft, and I desire to add no more than a few observations.

It has become fashionable in these days to attach decreasing importance to pleadings,
and it is beyond doubt that there have been times when an insistence on complete
e compliance with their technicalities put justice at risk, and, indeed, may on occasion have
led to its being defeated. But pleadings continue to play an essential part in civil actions,
and although there has been since the Civil Procedure Act 1833 a wide power to permit
amendments, circumstances may arise when the grant of permission would work
injustice or, at least, necessitate an adjournment which may prove particularly
unfortunate in trials with a jury. To shrug off a criticism as 'a mere pleading point' is
f therefore bad law and bad practice. For the primary purpose of pleadings remains, and
it can still prove of vital importance. That purpose is to define the issues and thereby to
inform the parties in advance of the case they have to meet and so enable them to take
steps to deal with it.

I have regretfully to say that in my judgment this basic requirement received
insufficient consideration by the Court of Appeal in Northern Ireland. The relevant
g parts of the statement of claim have already been set out in the speech of my noble and
learned friend Viscount Dilhorne, and I need only point out that, in support of the
allegation in para 2 thereof of 'the negligence of the servants and agents of the
Defendants', the only particulars pleaded related solely to alleged acts or omissions by the
soldiers stationed on the roof-top opposite the National Provincial Bank premises.
Indeed, after observing critically that, in the trial judge's direction to the jury, 'Liability
h was made to depend solely on the liability of the men on the spot . . . at the time of the
shooting', Lowry LCJ correctly commented: 'It must, in fairness, be said that the
particulars of negligence in the Statement of Claim appear to look solely to the alleged
acts and omissions of the men on the spot . . .' He continued: '. . . but Mr Ferguson, for
the plaintiff, briefly cross-examined soldiers X and A on broader grounds without
objection'.

j My Lords, I have studied with care the short cross-examination of soldier X and I have
been unable to find in it any accusation levelled against him that he failed in his duty in
any respect, and certainly no admission by him of any neglect. Nor was the cross-
examination of soldier A directed to establish negligence by soldier X or any other officer
or NCO. It is therefore unnecessary to consider what should have been done had useful
admissions been elicited, save to say that latitude extended by a trial judge in relation to

cross-examination does not per se broaden the pleaded issues, though it may give rise to a successful application for leave to amend if such cross-examination proves fruitful. In *a* the present case no such application was made, and that for the good reason that nothing useful to the plaintiff's case emerged.

So the case in negligence remained at all times restricted to the conduct of the soldiers on the roof-top. Yet Jones LJ stressed that—

> '... the Ministry of Defence ... was, of course, the defendant and ultimately *b* responsible not only for the acts and omissions of the soldiers on the ground but also for the layout of the operation, the setting in which the soldiers found themselves.'

McGonigal LJ said:

> 'The claim in negligence is based on a failure to take reasonable care for the safety *c* of the men engaged in that robbery in that (1) the scene for the counter-action was set by soldier X regardless of the fact that the likely result would be what did occur, and (2) no regard was had to any attempt to reduce the risk of serious injury to the robbers by, for example, establishing fixed ground positions or back-up ground patrols which might have enabled an arrest rather than a killing to result, or by the use of a loud hailer coupled with a clearer indication of who was challenging and *d* where the challenge came from to enhance the possibility that the men challenged would stop instead of trying to escape by running away.'

Now, not only were these matters never pleaded, but, as I have already pointed out, no opportunity appears to have been given to soldier X to deal with them. Had they been, the proper course would have been to insist on the statement of claim being amended to *e* meet with the entirely new case which for the first time was being developed. For my part I cannot accept that the failure in this respect was attributable solely to the trial judge's ruling that the issue of negligence was not to go to the jury, as to the rightness of which I need only recall that learned counsel for the respondent told your Lordships, 'If the soldiers alone had been sued, I agree that they could not have been found liable'. Despite that ruling, the view of McGonigal LJ was that—   *f*

> '... the learned trial judge should have so worded the questions or so directed the jury as to lead them to consider the reasonableness of the force in relation not only to the immmediate circumstances but to events prior to the patrol getting into position and, in particular, to Soldier X's actions and preparations which set the scene in which the actual force used ... was made necessary ... the jury should have *g* had an opportunity when dealing with questions 2 and 3 to consider all the relevant circumstances, not only those at the time the urgency of the incident took over control, but those prevailing at the earlier stage when there was time for planning and consideration that could have dictated the amount of force which might be required to be used later.'

h

My Lords, such allegations of negligence in preparation as were thus canvassed by the Court of Appeal were of gravity and importance. Had they been made timeously, that is to say, in the statement of claim, they would have demanded careful consideration by the defendant Ministry before the case came to trial. But they had found no place there, and the most that can be said of the trial is that, during the cross-examination of soldiers X and A, there was slight skirmishing which led nowhere.   *j*

In the result, not only was the trial judge right in withdrawing negligence from the jury but he was both correct and fair in omitting from his direction to them any suggestion that they were entitled to have regard to the adequacy or otherwise of the preparation for which soldier X appears to have been responsible. Indeed, I consider that a justice would have been denied to the defendant Ministry had he followed a different course.

I therefore concur in holding that no new trial should have been ordered and that the appeal should be allowed.

LORD FRASER OF TULLYBELTON. My Lords, I have had the advantage of
b reading in draft the speeches prepared by my noble and learned friends Viscount Dilhorne and Lord Edmund-Davies. I agree with both of them, and I would particularly associate myself with Lord Edmund-Davies' emphatic reminder of the importance of pleadings in defining the issue before the court in actions of this sort.

I would allow the appeal.

c
LORD RUSSELL OF KILLOWEN. My Lords, I have had the advantage of reading the speeches prepared by my noble and learned friends Viscount Dilhorne and Lord Edmund-Davies. I agree with them and I also would allow this appeal.

d **LORD LANE.** My Lords, for the reasons expressed in the speeches of my noble and learned friends Viscount Dilhorne and Lord Edmund-Davies, I would allow this appeal.

Appeal allowed.

Solicitors: *Treasury Solicitor ; Ingledew Brown Bennison & Garrett* (for the respondent).

e
                                    Mary Rose Plummer   Barrister.

Note

Ward v Ward and Greene

COURT OF APPEAL, CIVIL DIVISION
ORMROD LJ AND SIR DAVID CAIRNS
1st MAY 1979

Husband and wife – Matrimonial home – Sale under trust for sale – Divorce – Power of judge or registrar to order sale of matrimonial home – Pro forma summons not required to be issued before judge or registrar can order sale – Married Women's Property Act 1882, s 17 – Law of Property Act 1925, s 30 – Matrimonial Causes Act 1973, ss 23, 24.

ORMROD LJ (with whom Sir David Cairns agreed), after dismissing the husband's appeal against an order for periodical payments, said: Before leaving the appeal finally, however, there is one point with which I want to deal. At the outset of his judgment the learned judge referred to the fact that he had suggested that the husband should issue a pro forma summons under s 17 of the Married Women's Property Act 1882 asking for the sale of the former matrimonial home. This is a point which has been raised from time to time, which I know is concerning the Law Commission at the moment. I have heard it suggested on a number of occasions that in order for the court to make an order for a sale under the Matrimonial Causes Act 1973, ss 23 and 24, it is necessary to issue proceedings either under s 17 of the 1882 Act or, in appropriate cases, under s 30 of the Law of Property Act 1925.

For my part, I have never understood the advantages of multiplying pieces of paper intituled in particular statutes named at the head of the summons. It seems to me to be quite clear that s 17 of the 1882 Act gives the court power to order a sale (certainly as clarified by the Matrimonial Causes (Property and Maintenance) Act 1958) in proceedings between husband and wife in connection with property. Section 30 of the Law of Property Act 1925 gives the court power to order a sale where there is a trust for sale, and to my mind it cannot matter what the nature of the proceedings are; what matters is whether the circumstances are such as to bring the case within one or other of those Acts which give the necessary power to the court to order the sale. So I think it may be helpful if we were to say that it is not necessary to intitule proceedings as being under the Married Women's Property Act 1882 or the Law of Property Act 1925, or to issue pro forma summonses to enable the court to exercise its powers to order a sale where the circumstances justify it under one or other of those Acts. I hope that may be a helpful observation.

Mary Rose Plummer   Barrister.

Jackson v Hall and another
Williamson v Thompson and another

HOUSE OF LORDS

VISCOUNT DILHORNE, LORD EDMUND-DAVIES, LORD FRASER OF TULLYBELTON, LORD RUSSELL OF KILLOWEN AND LORD LANE

12th, 13th, 14th NOVEMBER, 19th DECEMBER 1979

Agricultural holding – Tenancy – Death of tenant – Eligibility of survivor of tenant for grant of new tenancy – Date at which eligibility to be determined – Tenant of agricultural holding dying – Whether survivor of tenant required to be eligible at date of tenant's death – Whether survivor who later acquires eligibility entitled to apply for a new tenancy – Whether joint occupier eligible – Agriculture (Miscellaneous Provisions) Act 1976, s 18(2).

Statute – Construction – Statutory instrument – Use of rules made by Lord Chancellor for interpretation of section of statute.

In two separate appeals relating to the grant of a new tenancy to the survivor of an agricultural tenant who had died, the questions arose (i) whether a survivor who was not eligible for the grant of a new tenancy at the date of the tenant's death could later satisfy the conditions of eligibility and so become entitled to be granted a new tenancy, and (ii) whether a survivor who was a joint tenant of other land was thereby prevented from being eligible for the grant of a new tenancy.

In the first case, a father and his two sons farmed in partnership two adjacent farms, a freehold property and a leasehold property. The freehold farm, which was a commercial unit within the meaning of Part II of the Agriculture Act 1967, was owned by the father but leased to the partnership. When the father died the sons continued to farm both farms as partners, but the lessors of the leasehold farm gave the father's executors notice to quit. Very shortly after, one of the sons (the applicant) assigned to his brother all his estate and interest in the freehold farm and then applied to an agricultural land tribunal for a direction entitling him to a tenancy of the leasehold farm under s 20[a] of the Agriculture (Miscellaneous Provisions) Act 1976 claiming to be eligible for the grant of a tenancy by virtue, inter alia, of being a 'survivor of the deceased' and 'not [being] the occupier of a commercial unit of agricultural land' for the purposes of s 18(2)[b] of that Act. The lessors contended that the preconditions of eligibility laid down by s 18(2) had to be fulfilled by an applicant at the date of the deceased tenant's death and that at the date of his father's death the applicant was, together with his brother, the occupier of a commercial unit and therefore not eligible for the grant of a tenancy. The tribunal decided that the appropriate date for determining the preconditions of eligibility was the date of the father's death and dismissed the application. On a case stated to the High Court the judge upheld the tribunal's decision. The applicant appealed to the Court of Appeal[c] which allowed his appeal holding that it was sufficient for the applicant to be eligible at the date of the application and hearing and that accordingly he was entitled to have his application considered on its merits by the tribunal. On appeal by the lessors to the House of Lords the applicant was granted leave to take the further point that he was not barred by his joint occupation of the commercial unit from applying for a direction.

In the second case, agricultural land of which a father was the tenant ('the riverside land') had been farmed by his two sons in partnership since 1971 as part of an agricultural

---

a Section 20, so far as material, is set out at p 180 *e*, post
b Section 18(2), so far as material, is set out at p 180 *f g*, post
c [1979] 1 All ER 449

unit which comprised other land. The sons were joint occupiers of the other land which was a commercial unit within the meaning of Part II of the 1967 Act. Following the *a* father's death one of the sons applied to an agricultural land tribunal pursuant to s 20(1) of the 1976 Act claiming to be eligible for the grant of a new tenancy of the riverside land by virtue, inter alia, of 'not [being] the occupier of a commercial unit of agricultural land' for the purposes of s 18(2) of the 1976 Act. The lessors opposed the application on the ground that the applicant was the occupier of a commercial unit and was therefore disqualified from being eligible for the grant of a new tenancy. The applicant contended *b* that, since his occupation of the commercial unit in question was joint or shared and not sole, he was not, within para (c) of the definition of 'eligible person' in s 18(2) of the 1976 Act, 'the occupier' of it for the purposes of the Act. The tribunal upheld his contention and made a direction entitling him to a tenancy of the holding. On a case stated to the High Court the judge overruled the opinion of the tribunal and held that s 18(2) disqualified joint occupiers as well as sole occupiers of commercial units from claiming *c* the benefits of the 1976 Act. The applicant appealed directly to the House of Lords.

Held – (i) The material date for determining for the purposes of s 18(2) of the 1976 Act whether a survivor of a deceased tenant was eligible to apply for a direction entitling him to a tenancy was the date of death of the tenant. Moreover eligibility had to continue to *d* exist until the dates of the application and the hearing. Accordingly, a person who was, at the date of the tenant's death, ineligible because he was the occupier of a commercial unit could not bring himself within the class of eligible persons by divesting himself of that occupation (see p 182 *b* to *f*, p 183 *j*, p 187 *g* to p 188 *d*, p 189 *h j* and p 191 *f*, post).

(ii) (Lord Russell of Killowen dissenting) The expression 'the occupier' in para (c) of the definition of 'eligible person' in s 18(2) of the 1976 Act was to be construed in its *e* ordinary and natural sense rather than in its strict literal sense to include not only a sole occupier but also a joint occupier, having regard to the fact that the Act represented an encroachment on the landlord's right to control his own property. Accordingly joint occupation of a commercial unit deprived an applicant of eligibility to apply for a new tenancy of the holding (see p 183 *c* to *j*, p 185 *a* to *g*, p 187 *b e* and p 191 *f*, post).

(iii) It followed therefore that the appeal in the first case would be allowed and (Lord *f* Russell of Killowen dissenting) that the appeal in the second case would be dismissed (see p 183 *h j*, p 187 *b*, p 188 *d*, p 190 *a b* and p 191 *f*, post).

Per Viscount Dilhorne, Lord Edmund-Davies, Lord Fraser of Tullybelton and Lord Lane. Rules made by the Lord Chancellor in the exercise of a statutory power which do not have the express approval of Parliament cannot be relied on as an aid to the construction of the statute itself (see p 183 *a j*, p 186 *f* to p 187 *c* and p 191 *f*, post); dictum *g* of Mellish LJ in *Re Wier, ex parte Wier* (1871) LR 6 Ch App at 879 disapproved.

Decision of the Court of Appeal in *Jackson v Hall* [1979] 1 All ER 449 reversed.

Notes

For succession on death of a tenant of an agricultural holding, see Supplement to 1 Halsbury's Laws (4th Edn) para 101A.1–3. *h*

For the Agriculture (Miscellaneous Provisions) Act 1976, ss 18, 20, see 46 Halsbury's Statutes (3rd Edn) 31, 36.

Cases referred to in opinions

Hales v Bolton Leathers Ltd [1951] 1 All ER 643, [1951] AC 531, HL, 34 Digest (Repl) 338, *j* 2607.

Jacobs v Chaudhuri [1968] 2 All ER 124, [1968] 2 QB 470, [1968] 2 WLR 1098, 19 P & CR 286, CA, 31(2) Digest (Reissue) 955, 7761.

Wier, Re, ex parte Wier (1871) LR 6 Ch App 875, 41 LJ Bcy 14, 25 LT 369, 44 Digest (Repl) 248, 724.

Appeals

a

Jackson v Hall and another

On 23rd June 1977 the respondent, Graham Christopher Jackson, applied to the agricultural land tribunal for the Yorkshire/Lancashire area (chairman Mr F Stephenson) pursuant to s 20(1) of the Agriculture (Miscellaneous Provisions) Act 1976 seeking a direction that he was entitled to a tenancy of the holding known as Grange Farm,

b Keyingham, owned by the appellants, William Horner Hall and Geoffrey Alan Marr, trustees of the estate of Geoffrey Edwards Marr, deceased. On 9th September 1977 the appellants applied under s 22 of the Act for the consent of the tribunal to the operation of a notice to quit dated 4th April 1977. Both applications came before the tribunal on 9th November 1977 when the tribunal first dealt with the preliminary point whether the respondent was a person eligible to apply for a direction under s 20 of the Act. The

c tribunal held that the respondent was not eligible and refused to grant the direction sought. On 11th April 1978 at the respondent's request the tribunal stated a case for the determination of the High Court, the question being whether the tribunal came to the correct conclusion in law in holding that the respondent did not qualify as an 'eligible person' within s 18(2) of the 1976 Act and thereby refusing a direction under that Act entitling the applicant to a tenancy of the holding. On 5th July 1978 Sir Douglas Frank

d QC, sitting as a deputy judge of the High Court, affirmed the tribunal's conclusion and refused the respondent leave to appeal. The respondent appealed with leave of the Court of Appeal granted on 17th July 1978. On 21st December 1978 the Court of Appeal[1] (Lord Denning MR and Lawton LJ, Brandon LJ dissenting) allowed the respondent's appeal. The appellants appealed to the House of Lords with leave of the Court of Appeal. The facts are set out in the opinion of Viscount Dilhorne.

e

Williamson v Thompson and another

On 29th March 1978 the appellant, Lewis Williamson, applied to the agricultural land tribunal for the West Midlands area (chairman Mr John Wilson) under s 20(1) of the Agriculture (Miscellaneous Provisions) Act 1976 for a direction entitling him to a new tenancy of a holding of 22.439 hectares of riverside land forming part of the Eardington

f Estate at Bridgnorth, Salop, of which he was the joint occupier. The land was owned by the respondents, Peter Howard Thompson and James Montagu Carpenter, who opposed the application. On 15th August 1978 the tribunal held the appellant to be both eligible and suitable and, the respondents having withdrawn a cross application for the tribunal's consent to the operation of a notice to quit, made a direction entitling him to a tenancy of the holding. On 9th November 1978 at the request of the respondents the tribunal

g stated a special case for the opinion of the High Court, the question being whether a person who was the joint owner of certain land and a joint occupier of other land and in joint occupation of all such land in partnership, such land being certified by the Minister in accordance with s 18(6) of the 1976 Act as a commercial unit within the meaning of Part II of the Agriculture Act 1967, was the occupier of a commercial unit of agricultural land within the meaning of Part II of the 1967 Act for the purposes of para (c) of the

h definition of 'eligible person' in s 18(2) of the 1976 Act. On 15th June 1979 Mr Michael Kempster QC, sitting as a deputy judge of the High Court, overruled the opinion of the tribunal and answered the question in the affirmative. The appellant appealed directly to the House of Lords pursuant to s 12 of the Administration of Justice Act 1969 and by leave granted by the House of Lords on 4th October 1979. The facts are set out in the

j opinion of Viscount Dilhorne.

Leolin Price QC and *Alan Sebestyen* for the appellants Hall and Marr.
E C Evans-Lombe QC and *Clifford Joseph* for the respondent Jackson.

---

1 [1979] 1 All ER 449, [1979] 2 WLR 505

Derek Wood QC and *Joanne Moss* for the appellant Williamson.
Gavin Lightman for the respondents Thompson and Carpenter.   *a*

Their Lordships took time for consideration.

19th December. The following opinions were delivered.

VISCOUNT DILHORNE. My Lords, s 24(2)(*g*) of the Agricultural Holdings Act   *b*
1948 enabled a landlord of an agricultural holding to give notice to quit that holding if
the tenant had died within three months before the date of the giving of the notice, and
it was stated that the notice was given for that reason. This provision was replaced by a
provision that such a notice could only be given where a person was the sole or sole
surviving tenant under a contract of tenancy immediately before his death (Agriculture
(Miscellaneous Provisions) Act 1976, s 16(1)). Part II of the 1976 Act made provision for   *c*
succession on the death of the tenant of such a holding. Section 18(1) provides that
where the sole or sole surviving tenant dies and is survived by any of the following
persons—

> '(*a*) the wife or husband of the deceased; (*b*) a brother or sister of the deceased; (*c*)
> a child of the deceased; (*d*) any person (not within (*b*) or (*c*) above) who, in the case
> of any marriage to which the deceased was at any time a party, was treated by the   *d*
> deceased as a child of the family in relation to that marriage,'

the following provisions of that Part of the Act are to apply.
Section 20(1) reads as follows:

> 'Any eligible person may within the relevant period apply to the Tribunal for a
> direction entitling him to a tenancy of the holding.'   *e*

'Eligible person' is defined by s 18(2) as meaning, subject to sub-s (3) of that section
(which does not apply in these cases) and without prejudice to s 21—

> 'a survivor of the deceased in whose case the following conditions are satisfied—
> (*a*) he falls within paragraphs (*a*) to (*d*) of subsection (1) above; (*b*) in the seven years   *f*
> ending with the date of death his only or principal source of livelihood throughout
> a continuous period of not less than five years, or two or more discontinuous periods
> together amounting to not less than five years, derived from his agricultural work
> on the holding or on an agricultural unit of which the holding forms part; and (*c*)
> he is not the occupier of a commercial unit of agricultural land within the meaning
> of Part II of the Agriculture Act 1967 or, if he is, occupies it as a licensee only.'
>   *g*

Section 21 gave the tribunal discretion to treat a survivor as an eligible person even
though he was unable to show that condition (*b*) above was fully satisfied. If he was able
to show that it was satisfied to a material extent, and in all the circumstances it appeared
fair and reasonable for the applicant to be able to apply for a direction entitling him to
a tenancy of the holding, the tribunal could allow him to apply. No such discretion is
given to the tribunal in relation to condition (*c*). If the applicant is the occupier of a   *h*
commercial unit as defined, he is not an eligible person and so is not qualified to apply
to the tribunal for such a direction.

On 28th March 1977 Mr James William Jackson died. He was the tenant of Grange
Farm, Keyingham which he farmed with his two sons. Following on his death notice to
quit was given and then his two sons, Mr Graham Christopher Jackson and Mr Martin
James Jackson, lodged an application for a direction entitling them to a tenancy of that   *j*
holding. At the opening of the hearing before the tribunal, Mr Martin James Jackson
withdrew his application.

Adjoining Grange Farm lies White House Farm which had been farmed by the
deceased and his two sons in partnership. On 19th September 1967 he had entered into
a tenancy agreement letting it to himself and his two sons on a yearly tenancy. White

a   House Farm was certified on 19th August 1977 to be a commercial unit within the meaning of Part II of the Agriculture Act 1967.

'Commercial unit' is defined by s 40 of that Act as meaning—

'An agricultural unit which in the opinion of the appropriate Minister is capable, when farmed under reasonably skilled management, of providing full-time employment for an individual occupying it and for at least one other man (or full-

b   time employment for an individual occupying it and employment for members of his family or other persons equivalent to full-time employment for one man).'

This part of the 1967 Act makes provision for, inter alia, grants towards expenditure incurred in securing amalgamations of farm land so as to form 'an intermediate unit' (also defined in s 40) or a commercial unit. Such a unit may of course provide full-time employment for a large number of people. The definition states the minimum number
c   for whom employment is to be provided for that unit to be treated as commercial.

At the time of Mr Jackson's death Graham Christopher Jackson and his brother were in joint occupation of White House Farm and it appears then to have been thought that he was consequently ineligible, if he remained a joint occupier, for applying for a direction entitling him to a tenancy of Grange Farm.

d   On 22nd June 1977 he assigned all his interest in White House Farm to his brother, and it was his contention that, as he had ceased to be in occupation at the date of the application, condition (c) did not render him ineligible to make the application. The tribunal thought that the meaning of ss 18 and 20 was plain and that the date that mattered in deciding whether an applicant was the occupier of a commercial unit was the date of the death of the tenant of the holding in respect of which the application was made.

e   Mr Jackson appealed to the High Court and Sir Douglas Frank QC, sitting as a deputy High Court judge, dismissed his appeal on the ground that he had to be eligible at the date of his father's death. The Court of Appeal[1], however, held by a majority (Lord Denning MR and Lawton LJ, Brandon LJ dissenting) that it sufficed that the applicant should be eligible at the date of the application and at that of the hearing. Throughout
f   this litigation until this case came to this House it appears to have been assumed that joint occupation of a commercial unit was a bar to eligibility.

I now turn to the facts of the other appeal. Mr George Williamson died on 17th January 1968. He was the tenant of land known as riverside land which formed part of the Eardington estate. This land was part of an agricultural unit farmed by the two sons of Mr Williamson. That agricultural unit, excluding the riverside land, was a commercial unit within the meaning of Part II of the 1967 Act. Mr Lewis Williamson, one of the
g   sons, applied for a direction entitling him to a tenancy of the riverside land.

The agricultural land tribunal which heard his application held that he was eligible to do so. On appeal Mr Kempster, sitting as a deputy High Court judge, allowed the appeal, holding that a joint occupier of a commercial unit is the occupier for the purposes of condition (c). He was given leave to appeal directly to this House in the belief that
h   now appears was erroneous, that in Jackson v Hall[1] it had been decided, when it was merely assumed, that joint occupation of a commercial unit was a bar to eligibility. At the commencement of the hearing of these appeals, application was made on behalf of Mr Jackson to take the point that he was not debarred by joint occupation of the commercial unit from applying to the tribunal for a direction. Leave to do so was granted.

j   So there are two questions to be decided in these appeals. The first, common to both, may be expressed thus: does condition (c) render only a sole occupier of a commercial unit ineligible? and the second thus: if a joint occupier of such a unit at the time of the death of the tenant of the holding in respect of which a direction is sought is ineligible,

---

1   [1979] 1 All ER 449, [1979] 2 WLR 505

can he make himself eligible by divesting himself of that occupation before he applies for
a direction?   *a*

I propose to consider the second question first. Lord Denning MR based his
conclusion, that a person was eligible provided conditions (*a*) and (*b*) were satisfied, if he
was not the occupier of a commercial unit at the date of his application and at the date
of the hearing, primarily on the use of the present tense in s 20. Lawton LJ based his
conclusion to the like effect on the ground that being a survivor was a continuing state,
and on the absence in condition (*c*) of any reference to the date of death. Brandon LJ, as   *b*
I have said, dissented.

In my opinion Brandon LJ came to the right conclusion. Section 20, which provides
that any eligible person may apply within the relevant period (in the majority of cases
within three months beginning with the day after the date of death), to my mind gives
no indication of when eligibility must arise, though I agree with Lord Denning MR that
the applicant must be eligible both at the date of the application and at the date of the   *c*
hearing.

Section 18(1) defines the persons who may satisfy condition (*a*). It provides that
'Where . . . the . . . tenant of an agricultural holding dies and is survived by any of the
following persons . . .' This to my mind signifies that one has to determine who were
the survivors at the date of the death. True it is that those who fell within paras (*a*) to
(*d*) of s 18(1) then will remain within that class as survivors of the deceased for the rest of   *d*
their lives, but the conjunction of the words 'dies and is survived by' seems to me a clear
indication that the point of time that has to be considered is the time of death. Condition
(*b*) states that the period to be considered in relation to that condition ends at the date of
the death, and it would I think be very odd if condition (*c*) could be satisfied at a different
time.

I entirely agree with the conclusion reached by Brandon LJ and with his reasons. In   *e*
my view eligibility has to arise at the date of the death. The persons who are then eligible
can apply, though eligibility must continue to exist at the date of the hearing and at the
date of the application. I do not think that Parliament can ever have intended that a
person who was at the date of death ineligible as the sole occupier of a commercial unit
could bring himself later within the class of eligible persons by divesting himself of that
occupation. So my answer to the second question I have posed is in the negative.   *f*

I now turn to the first question, which is one of more difficulty. The answer to it
depends on the meaning to be given to the words 'he is not the occupier'. Do they mean
the sole occupier? If that had been the intention of Parliament it could easily have been
expressed. On this construction great weight has to be placed on the article 'the'. Or
should they be read as if instead of 'the' the word 'an' was there? So read a joint occupier
would be ineligible. If it was Parliament's intention that he should be, why was 'an' not   *g*
the word used?

The argument was advanced that the rules made by the Agricultural Land Tribunals
(Succession to Agricultural Tenancies) Order 1976[1] might be relied on as an aid to the
construction of the statute. Those rules provide that the applicant for a direction must
complete a form which requires him to give particulars of the holding in respect of
which the application is made, and para 11 of the form reads as follows: *h*

'(*a*) I occupy as owner-occupier/tenant/licensee the following agricultural land
[*give particulars of land occupied, including area*]:—

'(*b*) I do not occupy any other agricultural land.'

The applicant is told to strike out whichever of these two statements is inapplicable.   *j*
The 'any other agricultural land' in (*b*) must I think mean land other than the holding in
respect of which the application is made.

---

1   SI 1976 No 2183

My Lords, I have no hesitation in rejecting the contention that rules made in the *a* exercise of a statutory power can be relied on as an aid to the construction of a statute. As Lawton LJ[1] said in the Court of Appeal: 'The form cannot, of course, be a guide to the construction of s 18(2). Such value as it has lies only in showing what a draftsman, used to looking closely at words, thought the ones used in s 18(2) meant.'

Our task is to give effect to the intention of Parliament as revealed by the words of the enactment. The difficulty is that the Act gives no clear indication whether the intention *b* was to exclude only sole occupiers, or to exclude both sole and joint occupiers, ie to exclude anyone in occupation of a commercial unit. The Act shows that Parliament recognised that there might be a number of persons who fell within paras (*a*) to (*d*) of s 18(1) and the Act makes provision for dealing with claims by individuals who are eligible applicants, but no provision was made for a direction entitling two applicants to a joint tenancy of a holding. It may be, one does not know, that Parliament just *c* overlooked the possibility that there might be joint ownership of a commercial unit and so made no provision for that.

It is clear from the terms of the Act that it made, and was intended to make, a further encroachment on the rights of landlords of agricultural holdings. It gave a person who came within s 18(1) (*a*) to (*d*) and who could show that he had derived his livelihood either entirely or principally from work on the holding for the requisite period the right *d* to apply for a direction provided that he was not the occupier of a commercial unit. Whether the land was a commercial unit does not depend on the number of persons who can gain their livelihood from it. However many or few they may be, the test of whether it is a commercial unit depends on the number of persons employed thereon.

What in my view Parliament has in effect enacted is that a survivor may apply if he comes within s 18(2) and can satisfy condition (*b*), but that he cannot do so if he already *e* occupies a commercial unit, which must I think be taken to be a viable farm. If he does occupy such a unit, then Parliament has not thought it right that a landlord should be deprived by the grant of a direction of the advantages which may enure to him from vacant possession.

That is a short and I hope not inaccurate summary of the Act, and in the light of it I cannot think that Parliament intended to give each of two joint occupiers of a commercial *f* unit, which it may be is of such a size and character as to provide them with a good living, the right to apply for a direction entitling them to a tenancy of the holding. To hold that only a sole occupier is barred is I think putting weight on the word 'the' which it does not bear.

A person in joint occupation of a farm if asked 'Do you occupy that farm?' could not truthfully answer 'No'. A truthful answer would be 'Yes, I occupy it and I occupy it with *g* someone else'.

My Lords, it is to be regretted that this lengthy and no doubt expensive litigation has been brought about by the inadequacy of the drafting of this Act.

I do not find the answer to the first question easy. My conclusion is that the words 'he is not the occupier' are just another way of saying 'he does not occupy,' and so read the result is that the applicant in each of these cases was ineligible to apply for a direction.

h   For the reasons I have stated, in my opinion the appeal in *Jackson v Hall* should be allowed with costs here and below and in *Williamson v Thompson* the appeal should be dismissed with costs.

LORD EDMUND-DAVIES. My Lords, for the reasons set out in the speeches of my *j* noble and learned friends Viscount Dilhorne and Lord Fraser of Tullybelton, I would allow the appeal in *Jackson v Hall* and dismiss the appeal in *Williamson v Thompson*. I also agree with their opinions regarding the orders as to costs.

---

1   [1979] 1 All ER 449 at 453–454, [1979] 2 WLR 505 at 510

LORD FRASER OF TULLYBELTON. My Lords, these two appeals were heard together. In the *Williamson* appeal, the only question is whether the words 'the occupier' *a* in para (*c*) of the definition of 'eligible person' in s 18(2) of the Agriculture (Miscellaneous Provisions) Act 1976 include a joint occupier. I shall refer to that as 'the *Williamson* question'. In the *Jackson* appeal that question was not raised in the courts below and in view of the decision of the majority in the Court of Appeal it would have made no difference to the result if it had been raised there. All the courts proceeded on the assumption that the *Williamson* question, if it had been raised, would have been answered *b* in favour of the landlord. But the Court of Appeal decided (by a majority) in favour of the applicant on another ground. At the beginning of the hearing in this House, counsel for the respondent in the *Jackson* appeal asked to be allowed to raise the *Williamson* point and, after hearing counsel for the appellants (the landlords) who opposed that course, the respondent's application was granted. Accordingly the *Williamson* question now arises in both appeals. I shall deal with that question first.   *c*

In the *Williamson* appeal the appellant's father was the tenant of an agricultural holding ('the holding') at the date of his death on 17th January 1978. He was survived by two sons, the appellant and his brother, who had farmed the holding in partnership since 1971 as part of an agricultural unit which also included other land. The appellant and his brother were joint occupiers of the land, being joint owners of part of it and joint tenants of the rest of it. The other land, that is the land excluding the holding, was a 'commercial *d* unit of agricultural land' within the meaning of Part II of the Agriculture Act 1967.

If the appellant was 'the occupier' of that commercial unit within the meaning of s 18(2)(*c*) of the 1976 Act, he is disqualified from being an 'eligible person' entitled to apply under s 20 of the Act for a direction entitling him to succeed his father as tenant of the holding. If he was not the occupier of a commercial unit, it is conceded that he fulfils the other qualifications for being an 'eligible person'.   *e*

The agricultural land tribunal for the West Midlands Area held that the appellant was not the occupier of a commercial unit, and found that he was an eligible person and a suitable person to become the tenant and made a direction in his favour. The tribunal stated a case for the opinion of the High Court on a question of law and the question was answered by the deputy judge, Mr Michael Kempster QC, in the sense opposite to the decision of the tribunal. As there are conflicting decisions in the High Court on this *f* question, the appeal has been made directly to this House under s 12 of the Administration of Justice Act 1969.

In the *Jackson* appeal the facts, so far as this question is concerned, were very similar to those in the *Williamson* appeal. The respondent's father, the tenant of the holding, died on 28th March 1977 and was survived by two sons, the respondent and his brother Martin. The father also owned most of the land forming an adjacent farm and he let this *g* land to a partnership consisting of himself, the respondent and Martin. A small part of the adjacent farm belonged to the respondent and Martin jointly and was occupied by them. Both farms were being farmed as one unit by the partnership. The adjacent farm was a commercial unit of agricultural land. Within three months after his father's death the respondent divested himself of his interest in the tenancy of the adjacent farm and ceased to be a joint occupier of it. The only question raised before the tribunal and the *h* Court of Appeal was whether the material date for considering whether he was a joint occupier was the date of his father's death or some later date. I shall refer to that question later on.

The provisions of the Agriculture (Miscellaneous Provision) Act 1976 which are directly relevant here have been quoted by my noble and learned friend Viscount Dilhorne and I need not repeat them.   *j*

The appellant in the *Williamson* appeal duly applied within the relevant period of three months after his father's death for a direction entitling him to a new tenancy of the holding. It is conceded by the respondents that he satisfies the conditions of paras (*a*) and (*b*) of the definition of 'eligible person' in s 18(2) in that he is a child of the deceased and that during the seven years ending with the date of death of the deceased his only or a principal source of livelihood was from agricultural work on the holding. The only question in dispute is whether he also satisfies the condition in para (c).

The foundation of the argument for the appellant is that the only person who is disqualified by para (c) of the definition of 'eligible person' in s 18(2) is 'the occupier' of a commercial unit and that those words can only apply to a sole occupier. On a strictly literal reading of the section I recognise that that is undoubtedly correct, but in my opinion the words ought to be read in their ordinary and natural sense, which in this case

b appears to me to be different from the literal sense. In its ordinary and natural sense the expression 'the occupier' seems to me to include not only the sole occupier but also each of several joint occupiers. The argument for the appellant depends on emphasising the definite article 'the' in a way that impresses me as unnatural and somewhat forced. The emphasis should, I think, be on the word 'occupier' which is the significant word. I find another example of the same sort of usage in the appellant's printed case in the appeal

c where he says that he is 'the son' of the deceased, although he is not the only son; that of course cannot be in any way conclusive of the question in the appeal. If the intention of Parliament had been that para (c) was to apply only to a sole occupier that could easily have been stated expressly, as we see in slightly different contexts in sub-ss (1) and (4)(e) of s 18 of the Act. Moreover, it is of some importance that para (c) of the definition of 'eligible person' in s 18(2) is expressed in the negative. The applicant must therefore

d show that he is *not* the occupier of a commercial unit, and I do not think that he can do that. If he were asked a direct question 'Are you the occupier?' he could not truthfully answer with an unqualified 'No'. He would have to answer either, 'No, but I am one of two joint occupants,' or possibly 'Yes, but I am only one of two joint occupants'. Either of these answers would, I think, be true but it seems clear that he cannot give a straight denial.

e The view that I have formed on the natural reading of the words seems to receive support from a consideration of the policy of the Act. In a general sense the object of Part II of the Act clearly is to give some security of tenure to the family of a deceased tenant. In pursuit of that object the policy is to hold a fair balance between the landlord on one side and the tenant's family on the other, as is shown by the conditions which a member of the family must satisfy if he is to be qualified as an eligible person. As well as being

f a member of the deceased's family an applicant must fulfil two conditions, one positive and the other negative, both of an economic character. The positive condition laid down in para (b) is that his only or principal source of livelihood must have been derived from the holding for five out of the last seven years, though that condition may be relaxed by the tribunal under s 21(1)(b) if it has been not fully satisfied but satisfied to a material extent. The negative condition with which this appeal is concerned is laid down in para

g (c) under which he must not be the occupier of land sufficiently large or of sufficient quality to be a 'commercial unit'. That expression is taken from the Agriculture Act 1967, s 40(2), where it is defined as meaning—

h 'an agricultural unit which in the opinion of the appropriate Minister is capable when farmed under reasonably skilled management, of providing full-time employment for an individual occupying it and for at least one other man (or full-time employment for an individual occupying it and employment for members of his family or other persons equivalent to full-time employment for one man).'

j In the 1967 Act a commercial unit was defined for quite a different purpose, connected with government grants, but it has evidently been adopted in para (c) of the definition of 'eligible person' in s 18(2) of the 1976 Act as an objective measure of a substantial agricultural unit. It was submitted on behalf of the appellant that if para (c) included the joint occupier hardship might result in a case where three or more children, or other close relatives of the deceased, were joint occupiers of a commercial unit as none of them could then qualify as an eligible person for a new tenancy of the holding, although the

commercial unit might be only just large enough to provide employment for two
persons. No doubt that may be so, but it has to be remembered that a commercial unit   *a*
is defined by reference only to the minimum standard (capable of providing employment
for an individual and 'at least' one other man). It may in fact be capable of providing
employment for several other men. If the appellant's construction were correct, it might
be thought to lead to hardship on the landlord because a joint tenant of a commercial
unit, however large or productive it might be, would not be disqualified so long as his
principal source of livelihood was the holding; so the larger the holding, the larger could   *b*
be the commercial unit without its leading to disqualification. Considerations of possible
hardship seem to me to be out of place here. The minimum standard for a commercial
unit is enough to ensure that it must be of substantial size or productiveness, but bearing
in mind that the security given to the deceased tenant's family is at the cost of encroaching
on the landlord's right to control his own property I see no reason to imply that the unit
should be capable of supporting a large family.   *c*

We were referred to some decisions under other Acts, none of which is in my opinion
of assistance in construing the words of this particular Act. The case which is perhaps
closest to the present is *Jacobs v Chaudhuri*[1], which held that one of two joint tenants was
not 'the tenant' within the meaning of s 24(1) of the Landlord and Tenant Act 1954. But
the context there was quite different, particularly in respect that if 'the tenant' had
included a joint tenant then each joint tenant would have been entitled to apply for a   *d*
new tenancy and there was no machinery for deciding between competing applicants.
In the 1976 Act, on the other hand, such machinery is provided by s 20(6), which directs
the tribunal to select the most suitable applicant.

An argument was advanced in support of the landlord's construction of para (c) based
on the terms of a form contained in the Agricultural Land Tribunals (Succession to
Agricultural Tenancies) Order 1976; it was said that the order could be used as an aid to   *e*
construction of the Act itself, and that submission was accepted by Mr Kempster QC, the
deputy judge. If it were permissible to use the order, and the form contained in it, for
that purpose, I would agree with the learned deputy judge that the terms of para 11(a)
and (b) of the form do support the contention of the landlord. But in my opinion it is not
legitimate to use the order as an aid to construing the Act. This question was considered
by your Lordships' House in *Hales v Bolton Leathers Ltd*[2] in relation to regulations made   *f*
under the National Insurance (Industrial Injuries) Act 1946, which were subject to a
negative resolution of either House: see s 87(2) of that Act. In that case Lord Simonds[3]
said that he 'much doubted' whether he was entitled to look to regulations for guidance
on the meaning of words in the Act under which they were made, and Lord Normand[4]
and Lord Oaksey[5] said that the words of the regulations could not control or alter the
construction of the Act, although Lord Oaksey added that they might be looked at as   *g*
being an interpretation placed by the appropriate government department on the words
of the statute. I would respectfully agree with the views of Lord Normand and Lord
Oaksey and would apply them to the 1976 order.

It was made by the Lord Chancellor under s 73(3) of the Agriculture Act 1947, as
amended, and was also subject to a negative resolution by either House: see s 108(1). It
does not, therefore, have the express approval of Parliament. The fact that it was made   *h*
by the Lord Chancellor does not invest it with the authority that it would have if it had
been approved by the holder of that office in his judicial capacity. The order has, in my
opinion, no greater weight than if it had been made by any other Minister acting under
statutory authority and it merely gives effect to the views of the Minister, or of his
department, as to the effect of the Act. It ought not, in my opinion, to be treated by the

j

1   [1968] 2 All ER 124, [1968] 2 QB 470
2   [1951] 1 All ER 643, [1951] AC 531
3   [1951] 1 All ER 643 at 646, [1951] AC 531 at 539
4   [1951] 1 All ER 643 at 649, [1951] AC 531 at 544
5   [1951] 1 All ER 643 at 651, [1951] AC 531 at 548

courts as an aid to construction of the Act. A view to the opposite effect was expressed
in *Re Wier, ex parte Wier*[1] by Mellish LJ who said:

> '... where the construction of the Act is ambiguous and doubtful on any point,
> recourse may be had to the rules which have been made by the Lord Chancellor
> under the authority of the Act, and if we find that in the rules any particular
> construction has been put on the Act ... it is our duty to adopt and follow that
> construction.'

In my opinion that statement is erroneous, at least in relation to rules like the 1976
rules, which have not been affirmatively approved by Parliament, and it should not be
treated as authoritative in relation to such rules.

For these reasons I would dismiss the appeal in *Williamson v Thompson* and I would
answer the *Williamson* question in the *Jackson* appeal in favour of the appellants, the
trustees.

I turn now to consider the original question in the *Jackson* appeal. The respondent in
that appeal was at the date of his father's death, which occurred on 28th March 1977, a
joint occupier with his brother of an agricultural unit called White House Farm. His
father had been the tenant of Grange Farm ('the holding') and on 4th April the appellants
served notice to quit the holding on the father's personal representatives. On 22nd June,
just within the period of three months after his father's death, the respondent assigned
all his interest in White House Farm to his brother Martin, but he continued to work the
farm jointly with Martin as his partner. On 23rd June the respondent applied to the
agricultural land tribunal for a direction entitling him to a new tenancy of the holding.
On 19th August the Minister of Agriculture certified that White House Farm was a
commercial unit of agricultural land. In these circumstances the question is whether the
respondent is disqualified from being an eligible person because he was a joint occupier
(and therefore, as all parties assumed, and as I would now hold, 'the occupier') of a
commercial unit at the date of his father's death, or whether the material date is the date
of his application to the tribunal. Whichever of those dates is the material one, he will
of course be disqualified if he is the occupier at the date of the decision by the tribunal.
The agricultural land tribunal for Yorkshire and Lancashire held that the material date
was the date of his father's death and that he was therefore disqualified. The tribunal
stated a case in which the question of law was whether it had come to a correct conclusion
of law in so holding. The case came before Sir Douglas Frank QC sitting as a deputy
judge of the High Court, who affirmed the decision of the tribunal. The respondent
appealed, by leave of the Court of Appeal, to the Court of Appeal, which by a majority
(Lord Denning MR and Lawton LJ, Brandon LJ dissenting) answered the question of law
in the negative. From that decision the appellants, the landlords, have appealed to this
House.

I should say that I regard the respondent's act in assigning his interest in White House
Farm to his brother as perfectly genuine and legitimate. Sir Douglas Frank regarded it
as subterfuge, but with respect I do not agree with that view. Nevertheless, I am of
opinion that it cannot avail the respondent for the purpose of this application. If a person
in the position of the respondent is not eligible at the date of his parent's death, he cannot
in my opinion acquire eligibility thereafter. The whole of s 18 seems to be defining and
referring to a state of affairs existing at or before the parent's date of death. The scene is
set by the opening words of s 18(1) which are 'Where ... the sole ... tenant ... dies and
is survived by any of the following persons'. Plainly that is looking at the date of death.
It then defines 'the following persons' by their relationship to the deceased, which
obviously cannot change after his death. Then in subs (2) the definition of 'eligible
person', after referring back to the family relationship, sets out the two economic
qualifications that I have already mentioned in relation to the *Williamson* question. The
qualification set out in para (*b*) is necessarily dependent on events that have occurred 'in

---

1   (1871) LR 6 Ch App 875 at 879

the seven years ending with the date of death'. Nothing occurring after the date of death can affect that qualification. The qualification in para (c) is that the person 'is not' the occupier of a commercial unit, and the present tense must, I think, mean 'is not at the date of death'. Any other meaning seems to me hardly possible. Similarly the use of the present tense in s 20(2) in the phrase 'the Tribunal, if sa.:sfied that the applicant *is* an eligible person, shall determine whether he *is* in their opinion a suitable person' (emphasis mine) must mean that the applicant must be eligible and suitable also at the date of the tribunal's decision. Accordingly he may lose eligibility before that date. But it is accepted that the applicant must have been eligible for at least some period before the date of the decision. The respondent says that the period begins with the date of his application to the tribunal, but for the reason I have stated, I consider that it begins with the date of death.

A separate and powerful reason why eligibility cannot be acquired after the date of death is that otherwise it would be easy for a child of a deceased tenant to divest himself of an interest in a commercial unit immediately after the parent's death and the condition in para (c) would for practical purposes be almost ineffective. He would have three months in which to acquire eligibility and he might do so by divesting himself of the disqualifying interest. I do not consider that Parliament can have intended to leave open such an obvious and comparatively easy method of circumventing the requirement of para (c).

Accordingly I would answer the original question in the *Jackson* appeal in the affirmative. I would allow the appeal in that case with costs in this House and below to the appellants.

LORD RUSSELL OF KILLOWEN.
Jackson v Hall

My Lords, in this case the applicant under Part II of the Agriculture (Miscellaneous Provisions) Act 1976 was at the death of his father (the tenant of the holding) joint occupier of an agricultural unit within the definition of a 'commercial unit' with his partner brother. They were the joint lessees of that unit under a lease to the partnership granted by the deceased father (who had himself been a partner). Before the application for a grant of a tenancy of the holding the applicant and his brother executed a document by which the applicant assigned to his brother all his beneficial interest as joint tenant in the leasehold of the unit and the brothers as trustees assigned the leasehold to the non-applicant brother, who thereby covenanted with the applicant to pay the rent and perform the covenants under the lease and indemnify the applicant against liability therefor. The applicant asserts that since that assignment his occupation of the unit has been as licensee only, I suppose as licensee of his brother. I do not find it obvious that this is so. The brothers farmed the unit in partnership, with the tenancy relevantly the sole partnership asset; the partnership presumably continued unaffected by the assignment with, for example, any growing crops or dairy herd or dead stock thereon as assets of the partnership and the applicant would supposedly have some rights as co-partner in respect of entry on the land. The respondent applicant in his case to this House states that after the assignment he continued to occupy the unit jointly with his brother as his partner. However no point was suggested on those lines, and I say no more about it. The situation is to be accepted that the applicant from the date of the assignment occupied the unit as licensee only.

The applicant was obviously advised to enter into this deed of assignment by someone shrewd enough, or prophetic enough, to recognise that the applicant's occupation as joint tenant would suffice (as the majority of your Lordships have just held in the *Williamson* case) to deny eligibility to the applicant, if continued; and this was assumed below. Leave was given to dispute that in this House for the first time in this case. Confessing the error of my ways in my dissent on the point in the *Williamson* case[1], I now loyally

---

1   See pp 190–191, post

concur in holding in the instant case that occupation as a joint tenant is within para (c)
a of the definition of 'eligible person' in s 18(2) of the 1976 Act, contenting myself with the
observation that had my dissenting opinion found favour in the *Williamson* case the point
in the instant appeal which must now be dealt with would not have arisen for decision
by your Lordships.

The point now for decision is whether, when a situation under para (c) of the definition
of 'eligible person' in s 18(2) prohibiting eligibility exists at the death of the tenant of the
b holding, an alteration to that situation can be achieved, so as to cure the lack of
eligibility. Put shortly, must the applicant for the purposes of para (c) of the definition
of 'eligible person' in s 18(2) be eligible at that death? The area agricultural land tribunal,
the deputy judge before whom the question came on a case stated, and Brandon LJ
answered that question in the affirmative. The majority of the Court of Appeal took the
other view, and held that the ban on eligibility imposed by para (c) of the definition of
c 'eligible person' in s 18(2) was to be examined in the light of circumstances as existing at
the date of application for a tenancy, and not at the death.

Section 18(1) of the Act raises the curtain on the whole of that group of sections dealing
with 'Provision for succession on death of tenant'; it applies the sections that follow
'Where . . . the . . . tenant . . . dies and is survived by . . .' members of his family as
listed. That clearly speaks of survival at the moment of death; but then it could not
d speak otherwise. Section 18(2) provides that '"eligible persons" means . . . a survivor of
the deceased . . .' fulfilling the stated qualifications. The first is that of relationship, and
I would only note that I would not suppose that a precipitately remarrying wife would
thereby lose eligibility. The second requirement for eligibility is related to an applicant's
activities during a period expressed to end with the tenant's death; under this head
nothing after the death can contribute to eligibility or qualification. The third
e requirement for qualification is that now directly relevant, relating to occupation; that
'he is not the occupier of a commercial unit . . .' except as a licensee only.

Section 20(1) provides for application for a direction by the tribunal entitling the
applicant to a tenancy of the holding: 'Any eligible person may . . . apply . . .' Application
must be made within three months beginning with the day after the date of the death
of the tenant. Section 20(2) deals with the case of only one applicant: 'the Tribunal, if
f satisfied that the applicant *is* an eligible person, shall determine whether he *is* in their
opinion a suitable person to become the tenant of the holding' (emphasis mine). Other
provisions of s 20 cover cases where more than one eligible person applies, it falling to the
tribunal to decide which is the more suitable. The question of suitability falls to be
determined by the tribunal having regard, inter alia, to agricultural experience, age,
health, financial standing, and the views expressed by the landlord on suitability, of the
g applicant.

Section 21 in effect enables the tribunal to treat as an eligible person 'Any survivor of
the deceased' who does not quite fulfil the earlier requirements for eligibility related to
activities of the applicant during the seven years preceding the death of the tenant.

So, after this summary of the statutory provisions, the question remains whether the
applicant, not being qualified (eligible) at the death of his father, can attain eligibility
h thereafter by rearranging his occupational rights in respect of the relevant commercial
unit.

Having considered the views expressed below I am, my Lords, persuaded that the
correct conclusion is that expressed by the tribunal, the judge and Brandon LJ. It appears
to me most unlikely that Parliament should have intended that qualification might be
achieved after the death of the tenant. The landlord should, it would be expected, be able
j on advice to know where at that moment he would stand in relation to the holding. I do
not think that, in relation to qualification, the tribunal on hearing an application is
entitled to consider whether an applicant, previously not qualified, is then qualified.

It is of course true to say that the applicant might by a similar transaction before the
death of the tenant have denuded himself of a right to occupy the unit, and this ability
did much to influence Lord Denning MR in his conclusion that he could equally

effectively take the same action to avoid the impact of para (c) of the definition of 'eligible person' in s 18(2) after the death. I am not persuaded by this possibility to the same view; arrangements in a farming family based on an assumption of the father's death seem highly improbable.

I find myself, my Lords, persuaded by the cogent judgment of Brandon LJ on this question, and for the reasons which he gives I would allow this appeal.

Williamson v Thompson

In this appeal the appellant at all material times occupied and farmed in partnership with his brother land totalling nearly 400 acres, the brothers being joint owners of part and joint tenants under two tenancies of other parts. The whole was a 'commercial unit'. The question for decision is whether, as was held by the learned deputy judge, that joint occupation disqualified the appellant from ability to apply for a tenancy of the holding of which the appellant's father was the tenant at his death. This question depends on the true construction of the Agriculture (Miscellaneous Provisions) Act 1976, and in particular of para (c) of the definition of 'eligible person' in s 18(2). By that last provision, in order to qualify as an applicant for a tenancy of his late father's holding as an 'eligible person', it is necessary that he should show that 'he is not the occupier of a commercial unit of agricultural land within the meaning of Part II of the Agriculture Act 1967 or, if he is, occupies it as a licensee only'. Does this cover the case where his occupation is that of a joint owner or joint tenant, or does it cover only the case of a sole occupier or tenant? The learned deputy judge, from whom this is a 'leapfrog' appeal, held that joint occupation of a commercial unit sufficed to exclude the relation from eligibility to apply for a grant of a tenancy of the deceased's holding.

The policy of this part of the 1976 statute is to meet (for the first time) in a particular way the event of death of a tenant farmer, which death would otherwise give to the landowner an unrestricted right to determine the tenancy. The particular way adopted was in that event to give to a member of the deceased's family a chance of obtaining a tenancy of the holding against the will of the landowner, when that member had derived his principal source of livelihood from his agricultural work on the holding or on any agricultural unit including the holding. In general this was a recognition of a family's interest in a family worked farm, and no doubt it was thought to encourage good farming by the prospect of succession on the death of the tenant.

Paragraph (c) of the definition of 'eligible person' in s 18(2) states a situation in which it was thought proper to negative a right to apply for a new tenancy; and that situation was related to an applicant's ability to continue with security of tenure to farm elsewhere, notwithstanding the loss of his principal livelihood in farming the holding. To be eligible to apply he must (inter alia) show that he satisfies the condition that 'he is not the occupier of a commercial unit of agricultural land within the meaning of Part II of the Agriculture Act 1967 or, if he is, occupies it as a licensee only'.

It would obviously have been too stringent an exclusion to relate the occupation to too small or otherwise unviable an area of farming land. So the device was chosen of relating it to a commercial unit, which is defined in the 1967 Act for a quite different purpose, in connection with rationalisation of the farming industry by encouraging the formation of sufficiently viable farm holdings. In the 1967 Act—

> '"commercial unit" means an agricultural unit which in the opinion of the appropriate Minister is capable, when farmed under reasonably skilled management, of providing full-time employment for an individual occupying it and for at least one other man (or full-time employment for an individual occupying it and employment for members of his family or other persons equivalent to full-time employment for one man).'

Now this definition was, as I have said, originally for a wholly different purpose, and constitutes a minimum objective yardstick for that purpose. But its form is to be expected to have been in the mind of the draftsman of para (c) of the definition of

'eligible person' in s 18(2), and in construing that latter provision and determining
a whether 'the occupier' is to be taken to indicate 'an occupier' or 'the sole occupier' it is not
I think without some significance that the definition of commercial unit speaks of one
individual occupier of the agricultural unit.

In the present case, no doubt the appellant in joint occupation of the particular land
with his brother has ample opportunity for earning a good living in farming it without
any necessity to extend (or continue) his farming activities to or on the holding of the
b deceased tenant. But this particularity of the case should not lead your Lordships to lean
in favour of exclusion from eligibility of a joint occupier. In another case the applicant
may be in joint occupation of an agricultural unit only just within the definition of
commercial unit, and with more than one other.

Of course there are many contexts in which the definite article is not used as an
indication of uniqueness: to say for example of X that he is the son of Y is not to be taken
c as indicating that Y had no other son. Many examples may be given in which the
definite article means no more than would the indefinite article: some of them in cases
cited in this appeal. The arguments in this appeal really rest on what is *not* said. On the
one hand it is pointed out that if the draftsman meant sole occupier he could have said
it; and other provisions of this part of the statute show that (in a different context) the
draftsman was aware of and used the word 'sole'. On the other hand if joint occupation
d were in mind in para (c) of the definition of 'eligible person' in s 18(2) the question is why
the draftsman selected the definite article, which I take to point prima facie to
singularity. He might have said 'he is not an occupier'; or 'he is not in occupation of', or
'he does not occupy . . . or, if he does, occupies it as licensee'. Three choices of language
were readily available to make it plain that a joint occupation was intended, and none
were chosen.

e This, as is sometimes said, is a matter of impression; I conclude that the joint
occupation of the appellant does not deprive him of the eligibility to apply for a tenancy
of his deceased father's holding and I would allow this appeal.

LORD LANE. My Lords, I have had the advantage of reading the speeches of my noble
and learned friends Viscount Dilhorne and Lord Fraser of Tullybelton. For the reasons
f expressed in those speeches I would allow the appeal in the case of *Jackson v Hall* and
dismiss the appeal in *Williamson v Thompson*.

Appeal in Jackson v Hall allowed; appeal in Williamson v Thompson dismissed.

Solicitors: *Collyer-Bristow,* agents for *Chambers Thomas & Williamson,* Hull (for the
g appellants Hall and Marr); *Warren Murton & Co,* agents for *Stamp, Jackson & Procter,* Hull
(for the respondent Jackson); *Ellis & Fairbairn,* agents for *Burgess, Salmon & Co,* Bristol (for
the appellant Williamson); *Wedlake Bell,* agents for *Ivens & Morton,* Kidderminster (for
the respondents Thompson and Carpenter).

Mary Rose Plummer   Barrister.

Air-India v Wiggins   *a*

QUEEN'S BENCH DIVISION
LORD WIDGERY CJ, EVELEIGH LJ AND KILNER BROWN J
15th OCTOBER 1979

Carriage by air – Carriage of animals – Carriage of animal by air in way which is likely to cause *b*
it injury or unnecessary suffering forbidden by regulation – Carriage of birds from Bombay to
London via Kuwait by foreign national corporation – Delay in Kuwait – Birds suffering privation
in Kuwait and dying before aircraft entering English air space – Whether regulation having
extra-territorial effect – Whether proceedings could be brought against foreign corporation in
England – Diseases of Animals Act 1950, s 23 (as applied by s 11(1) of the Agriculture
(Miscellaneous Provisions) Act 1954) – Transit of Animals (General) Order 1973 (SI 1973 *c*
No 1377), arts 3(3), 5(2).

A foreign airline loaded 2,120 birds in Bombay for carriage to London via Kuwait. The
aircraft developed engine trouble in Kuwait and had to remain there longer than was
intended. During that period the birds suffered great privation and only 89 of them
were alive when the aircraft landed at London airport. The airline was charged with, and *d*
convicted by justices of, an offence under the Diseases of Animals Act 1950 in that they
had carried the birds by air in a way which was likely to cause them injury or unnecessary
suffering, contrary to art 5(2)[a] of the Transit of Animals (General) Order 1973, made
under s 23[b] of the Act as applied by s 11(1)[c] of the Agriculture (Miscellaneous Provisions)
Act 1954. On appeal the Crown Court found, inter alia, (i) that the birds which had died
had almost certainly done so as a result of the heat and lack of ventilation during the
period spent in Kuwait, and (ii) that they were almost certainly dead before the aircraft *e*
entered English air space. The Crown Court held that art 5(2) of the 1973 order had
extra-territorial effect by virtue of art 3(3)[d] of the order, which provided that, in relation
to carriage by air, the provisions of the order were to 'apply to animals carried on any
... aircraft to or from an ... airport in Great Britain, whether or not such animals are
loaded or unloaded at such ... airport'. The airline was convicted and appealed, *f*
contending that proceedings could not be brought against it in England because (i) it was
a foreign national, (ii) any offence which might have been committed had been
committed outside English air space, and (iii) art 3(3) of the order did not extend the
provisions of the 1973 order to flights outside British territorial limits.

Held – On the true construction of art 3(3) of the 1973 order the provisions of the order
applied to acts committed by a foreign national in foreign territory if the aircraft in *g*
which such acts were committed landed in Great Britain during or at the conclusion of
the same flight. It followed that the case was not outside the jurisdiction of the English
courts and the appeal would be dismissed (see p 196 c d and p 197 a b, post).

h

---

a   Article 5(2), so far as material, provides: 'No person shall carry any animal by ... air ... or cause
     or permit any animal to be so carried, in a way which is likely to cause ... unnecessary suffering
     to the said animal.'
b   Section 23, so far as material, is set out at p 195 j, post
c   Section 11 (1) provides: 'The Diseases of Animals Act, 1950 (which includes provision for regulating
     the import, export and movement of animals by sea or by inland waters, and similar matters), shall
     apply in relation to aircraft and aerodromes, and to shipment in or landing from aircraft, as it *j*
     applies in relation to vessels and ports, and to shipment in and landing or disembarking from
     vessels, but with the adaptations provided for by the Second Schedule to this Act.' By s 45 of the
     1950 Act and r 2(b) of the 1973 order the Act has the same effect in relation to birds of any species
     as it has to animals.
d   Article 3(3), is set out at p 196 c, post

Notes

a For offences relating to carriage of animals, see 2 Halsbury's Laws (4th Edn) para 391, and
for cases on the subject, see 2 Digest (Reissue) 399–401, 2216–2228.

    For the Diseases of Animals Act 1950, s 23, see 2 Halsbury's Statutes (3rd Edn) 327.

    For the Agriculture (Miscellaneous Provisions) Act 1954, s 11, see ibid 376.

    For the Transit of Animals (General) Order 1973, art 3, see 2 Halsbury's Statutory
Instruments (4th Reissue) 278.

b

Cases cited

Cox v Army Council [1962] 1 All ER 880, [1963] AC 48, HL.
Philipson-Stow v Inland Revenue Comrs [1960] 3 All ER 814, [1961] AC 727, HL.
R v Jameson [1896] 2 QB 425.
R v Martin [1956] 2 All ER 86, [1956] 2 QB 272.

c *Theophile v Solicitor-General* [1950] 1 All ER 405, [1950] AC 186, HL.

Case stated

This was an appeal by Air-India by way of a case stated by his Honour Judge Oliver
Martin QC and the justices for the Middlesex Commission Area in respect of their
adjudication at the Crown Court at Middlesex Guildhall on appeal from the Uxbridge

d Magistrates' Court.

    On 17th June 1976 the justices for the Metropolitan Commission Area of Greater
London, Petty Sessional Division of Uxbridge, heard 36 summonses preferred by the
respondent, Geoffrey Stuart Wiggins, against the appellant under the Transit of Animals
(General) Order 1973[1] and the Diseases of Animals Act 1950. The offences alleged
against the appellant were as follows: under art 5(2) of the order that it had carried a

e consignment of birds from Bombay to London in such a way as was likely to cause them
injury or unnecessary suffering; under art 6(1)(a) that it had failed to ensure that the birds
were adequately fed and watered at suitable intervals during carriage; under art 6(1)(b)
that it had failed to ensure that adequate supplies of food and water appropriate to the
species of birds were available in the aircraft in which the birds were carried. The justices
convicted on all 36 summonses, and fined the appellant.

f   The appellant appealed to the Crown Court, Westminster, by notice dated 23rd June
1976 and amended on 2nd July 1976, on the following grounds: (i) against conviction in
respect of all summonses, as the convictions were unsound in law and on the facts and
(ii) against sentence in respect of all summonses, as the sentences were harsh and
excessive in all the circumstances.

    The Crown Court heard the appeal and found the following facts: (i) on 30th

g September 1975, 2,120 birds were consigned from Bombay to London, Heathrow
Airport, via Kuwait, aboard one of the appellant's flights; (ii) the aircraft carrying the
birds developed a technical fault at Kuwait and remained on the tarmac at Kuwait for 31
hours; (iii) during the delay at Kuwait the birds remained in the hold of the aircraft
without the hold being opened or otherwise ventilated; (iv) on arrival at the RSPCA
hostel at Heathrow Airport on 1st October 1975, 89 of the birds were alive and 2,031

h were dead; (v) the overwhelming probability was that the birds which had died did so as
a result of the heat and lack of ventilation during the period that they spent in Kuwait,
and in consequence it was highly probable that the great majority of the birds were dead
before the aircraft entered British air space; (vi) by reason of the lack of ventilation at
Kuwait all the birds had been carried in a way which was likely to cause them injury or
unnecessary suffering. The Crown Court did not find that the boxes in which the birds

j had travelled had been overcrowded; (vii) the appellant was at all material times a foreign
national corporation.

    At the close of the case for the respondent it was contended by the appellant that: (i)
the 1950 Act and the 1973 order applied only to live animals because dead animals were

---

1   SI 1973 No 1377

incapable of suffering; (ii) accordingly an offence under s 78 of the Act and the order
could only be committed in relation to live animals; (iii) since only 89 birds were alive   *a*
at Heathrow Airport, and there was no way in which it could be established that more
than 89 birds were alive during the time that the aircraft had been in British airspace, it
followed that except in relation to 89 birds any offence which may have been committed
against British law had been committed (a) by a foreign national and (b) outside British
territory; (iv) that such offences as might have been committed were accordingly outside
the jurisdiction of the British courts unless it was established as a matter of law that the   *b*
Act and the order which together created the offences had extra-territorial effect. The
Crown Court agreed with contentions (i) and (ii).

Since the appellant admitted that it was by its agents responsible for the failure to
ventilate the birds at Kuwait and likewise admitted that such a failure would be caught
by the words of art 5(2) of the order if the Act and order had extra-territorial effect, the
question on which the appeal before the Crown Court largely turned was whether the   *c*
Act and the order did have extra-territorial effect.

It was contended by the respondent: (i) that the Diseases of Animals Act 1950, having
particular regard to ss 20, 23 and 83 of the Act, had extra-territorial effect; (ii) that by art
3(3) of the 1973 order the provisions of the order were applied with extra-territorial
effect. For the respondent, who contended that the Act and the order did have extra-
territorial effect, it was submitted: (i) that by art 3(3) of the 1973 order the provisions of   *d*
the order applied to 'animals carried on any vessel or aircraft to or from a port or airport
in Great Britain whether or not such animals [were] loaded or unloaded at such port or
airport'; (ii) that by s 83(3) of the 1950 Act, which provided that: 'Every offence against
this Act shall be deemed to have been committed, and every cause of complaint or matter
for summary proceeding under this Act or an order of the Minister or regulation of a
local authority shall be deemed to have arisen, either in any place where the same was   *e*
actually committed or arose, or in any place where the person charged or complained of
or proceeded against happens to be at the time of the institution or commencement of
the charge, complaint, or proceedings', such words gave to the Act extra-territorial effect.

For the appellant, who contended that the Act and order did not have extra-territorial
effect, it was submitted: (i) that by reason of the comity of nations and by analogy with
other Acts of Parliament, no statute of the British Parliament could have extra-territorial   *f*
effect unless it said as much in the clearest terms (the Crown Court was referred, inter
alia, to the following Acts which did in terms assume extra territorial application: the
Geneva Conventions Act 1957, s 1(1); the Hijacking Act 1971, s 1; the Protection of
Aircraft Act 1973, s 1; the court was also referred to the Civil Aviation Act 1949, s 59(1),
and to the Tokyo Convention Act 1967); (ii) that s 83(3) of the 1950 Act was procedural
only and provided for venue rather than extending the provisions of the Act to world-   *g*
wide application; and (iii) that art 3(3) of the 1973 order could not assume greater
powers than were originally provided for in the Act by the authority of which the order
was made.

The Crown Court concluded that the 1950 Act and the 1973 order had extra-territorial
effect and were to be applied throughout the carriage from the point of loading whether
or not that was within the jurisdiction, where the animals were carried to or from a port   *h*
or airport in Great Britain, applying art 3(3) of the order.

After the Crown Court's ruling on the appellants' submission, the appellants called no
evidence.

The Crown Court was of the opinion that in the light of the facts which it found and
its ruling on the law the justices had been correct in finding the 12 summonses under art
5(2) proved but that there was insufficient evidence to support convictions on the 24   *j*
summonses under art 6(1)(a) and (b). Accordingly, it dismissed the appeals against
conviction in respect of the 12 summonses under art 5(2) and allowed the appeals against
conviction in respect of the 24 summonses under art 6(1)(a) and (b).

The question for the opinion of the High Court was whether the Crown Court was
correct in holding that the provisions of the 1973 order applied to acts done by foreign

a nationals in foreign territory provided that the vessel or aircraft in which such acts were done landed or docked in Great Britain during or at the conclusion of the voyage.

Keith Evans and *Frank Panford* for Air-India.
Roger Cox for the respondent.

b **LORD WIDGERY CJ.** This is a case stated by the Crown Court at Middlesex Guildhall on appeal from the Uxbridge Magistrates' Court.

On 17th June 1976, which was the day the summonses were presented, there were a total of 36 summonses issued against the appellant, Air-India, alleging in broad terms cruel treatment or insufficient attention paid to a cargo of birds which Air-India was at that time transporting.

c What had happened was that about 2,100 birds left Bombay destined to go to London. The aircraft was due to touch down at Kuwait en route. It did touch down at Kuwait. Some fault developed in the engine and it had to remain there for very much longer than was intended, and during that period the birds obviously suffered great privation, and of the 2,120 consigned from Bombay only 89 were alive when the aeroplane reached Heathrow Airport, London. The consequence of that was that it was *d* almost clear beyond doubt that the death of the birds in question had occurred before the aeroplane entered English air space.

At a very early stage in the proceedings the point was taken that, given the background facts which I have described, no proceedings could be brought in this country against Air-India because Air-India was a foreign national and the offence had been committed outside English air space somewhere in the Gulf of Kuwait.

e This case raises a very short and very interesting, and no doubt very important, point as to how far these days, when animals are carried by air in such large quantities, the carrier is responsible for looking after them and how far that obligation falls on the consignor.

The view taken by the Crown Court was that the answer to this problem had to be found in the relevant regulations which presently apply to the carriage of animals by *f* air. The court seems to have been properly advised at all times that as a general principle the law of England is a domestic law in so far as the criminal law is concerned, and consequently there are very powerful authorities that require the justices in the first instance, and us later on, to recognise that fact and not to create or be party to the creation of criminal offences which are extra-territorial in the sense that they can be committed outside the country.

g Coming immediately to the situation affecting animals carried by air, one has to look under the relevant authorities first of all at the Diseases of Animals Act 1950. Section 20 of that Act is headed 'Regulation of movement of animals etc'. It provides: 'The Minister may make such orders as he thinks fit, subject and according to the provisions of this Act, for all or any of the following purposes . . .' If one goes down to para (x), we find that the tenth purpose for which regulations can be made is 'for protecting animals from *h* unnecessary suffering during inland transit or while exposed for sale or awaiting removal after being exposed for sale . . .' That is a clear power to the Minister to make regulations to protect the birds against unnecessary suffering, but it is confined, and was confined at that stage, to inland transit.

The matter has been supplemented since, as development occurred in air transport. Regulations have been made, as we shall shortly see, under s 23 of the 1950 Act, which *j* is in these terms:

> 'The Minister may make such orders as he thinks fit . . . (*b*) for ensuring for animals carried by sea a proper supply of food and water and proper ventilation during the passage and on landing; (*c*) for protecting them from unnecessary suffering during the passage and on landing.'

There again one has comprehensive power in the Minister to make regulations for the welfare of animals in the circumstances, but it will be observed that s 23 as originally *a* enacted was confined to passage by land.

The final reference is made now to the Agriculture (Miscellaneous Provisions) Act 1954, s 11 of which applies the provisions of s 23 of the 1950 Act to travel by air as it had formerly applied to travel by land.

The stage is set for the making of regulations on which the protection of animals is to depend, and for this we go to the Transit of Animals (General) Order 1973[1]. Article 1 *b* applies the order to Great Britain, and art 3 contains extensive definitive provisions about the words used in the regulations. I do not find it necessary to refer to art 3(1) and (2), but art 3(3) is, in my judgment, the core and heart of this case. Under that paragraph it is provided:

> 'In relation to carriage by sea or air, the provisions of this order shall apply to animals carried on any vessel or aircraft to or from a port or airport in Great Britain, *c* whether or not such animals are loaded or unloaded at such port or airport.'

It seems to me (and I do not think it will be disputed) that that paragraph, if the words it contains are given their ordinary meaning in the English language, will be wide enough to enable the Secretary of State to make orders extending beyond the territorial limits of this country and including such animal-carrying flights as the one with which *d* we are concerned here.

On the appeal the Crown Court took the view that the power was thus extensive and had thus been exercised, and therefore in the cases where there was no other defence it convicted on the summonses.

It is said today, and there is just the one point, that the Crown Court was wrong because it failed to construe art 3(3) correctly and it was wrong in allowing it to extend *e* to flights outside the territorial limits of this country.

One can say at once that it is a very short point, and so far as I can judge the only point for consideration is whether the Crown Court erred in the construction which it was minded to give to art 3(3).

It seems to me, and has seemed to me throughout the case, that, if one excluded extra-territorial activities because they should be excluded from the regulation, there was *f* nothing left in the regulations at all. I took the liberty of pressing counsel for Air-India at one stage to show us what the effect of the regulations would be under any other approach to the construction of the regulations. It seems to me, with respect to him, that he did not ever answer my question, and it certainly seems to me now that the only alternatives in regard to construction is that the regulation operates fully in giving the words their natural meaning, or for all practical purposes it is a dead provision with no *g* life left in it at all. Those are the alternatives before us, and I have no hesitation, speaking for myself, in saying that we should give this regulation its full meaning.

There are many pointers in it which indicate that the draftsmen and the Secretary of State had that in mind. Indeed one must remember that we are now in the jet age and all sorts of regulations about transit and transit of animals have to be revised in the modern setting. As was pointed out in argument, another pointer to the construction of *h* the regulations being the one which I have favoured is that in art 3(3) of the 1973 order there is a reference to animals being carried on a vessel or aircraft to or from a port in the United Kingdom. That seems to me to be an expression properly related to international transport, and, as I say, it seems to me that in the year 1979 one has to have considerable international agreement on matters which are strictly of a criminal nature because it is nowadays with the shortening of length of journeys, impossible to say which country's *j* domestic law should remain entirely domestic.

I think that the Crown Court reached a proper conclusion, and I turn to the question which it has asked us in the case. It is this:

---

1   SI 1973 No 1377

'Were we correct in holding that the provisions of the Transit of Animals (General) Order 1973 apply to acts done by foreign nationals in foreign territory provided that the vessel or aircraft in which such acts are done lands or docks in Great Britain during or at the conclusion of the same voyage.'

The Crown Court thought the answer to that question would be Yes. I think so too, and I would dismiss the appeal.

b EVELEIGH LJ. I agree.

KILNER BROWN J. I also agree.

Appeal dismissed.

c 2nd November. The court refused leave to appeal to the House of Lords but certified, under s 1(2) of the Administration of Justice Act 1960, that the following point of law of general public importance was involved in the decision: was there an offence punishable in England under the Diseases of Animals Act 1950, and regulations made thereunder, if an airline carried animals from India to London Airport in conditions which constituted a breach of such regulations, but the animals were dead before the aircraft entered English airspace.

d

Solicitors: *Bulcraig & Davis* (for Air-India); *Stanley F Heather*, Comptroller and City Solicitor (for the respondent).

N P Metcalfe Esq   Barrister.

Re Sharpe (a bankrupt), ex parte the trustee of the bankrupt v Sharpe and another

CHANCERY DIVISION
BROWNE-WILKINSON J
23rd, 24th, 30th JULY 1979

Bankruptcy – Trustee in bankruptcy – Title of trustee – Property – Trustee contracting to sell property – Irrevocable licence to occupy property conferred prior to bankruptcy – Aunt lending money to debtor to purchase property in return for right to live in property with debtor and his family and be cared for by them – Whether loan conferring interest in property under a resulting trust or an irrevocable licence to remain in property until loan repaid – Whether aunt having an interest in the property as against the trustee.

In January 1975 the debtor purchased a property for £17,000 with the help of £12,000 lent to him by his aunt as part of an arrangement whereby the aunt was to live with the debtor and his wife in the property and they were to look after her. On 27th April 1978 a receiving order was made against the debtor. On 30th April his trustee in bankruptcy contracted to sell the property with vacant possession to a purchaser for £17,000. Prior to the contract the trustee twice wrote to the aunt asking whether the £12,000 was a gift or a loan and if it was a loan whether any consideration or security had been given for it, but she did not reply to the letters, probably because of her old age and bad health. After the date of the contract, however, she made a claim to the property, claiming either a beneficial interest under a resulting trust by virtue of the loan or alternatively a right under an irrevocable licence to occupy the property until repayment of the loan. The trustee in bankruptcy claimed possession of the property against the debtor and his aunt. The questions arose (i) whether the aunt had any interest in the property and (ii) if so whether it was binding on the trustee in bankruptcy.

Held – (i) Where moneys were advanced by way of loan to purchase a property the lender was not entitled to an interest in the property under a resulting trust because if he were to have such an interest he would get his money back twice, ie on repayment of the loan and on taking his share of the proceeds of sale. It followed that the aunt did not have an equitable interest in the property under a resulting trust (see p 200 *j* and p 201 *d e*, post); *Hussey v Palmer* [1972] 3 All ER 744 explained.

(ii) Where, however, parties proceeded on a common assumption that one of them was to enjoy a right to occupy the property and in reliance on that assumption he expended money or otherwise acted to his detriment, the other party would not be allowed to go back on that assumption, and the court would imply an irrevocable licence or constructive trust giving effect to the arrangement. As against the debtor, the circumstances in which the aunt had provided the loan for the debtor to purchase the property meant that the aunt had an irrevocable licence to occupy the house until the loan was repaid. Furthermore, the aunt's irrevocable licence was not merely a contractual licence but arose under a constructive trust and as such conferred on her an interest in the property binding on the trustee in bankruptcy (see p 201 *g h*, p 202 *a* to *d g*, p 203 *d* and p 204 *a b*, post); *Errington v Errington* [1952] 1 All ER 149, *Tanner v Tanner* [1975] 3 All ER 776, *DHN Food Distributors Ltd v London Borough of Tower Hamlets* [1976] 3 All ER 462 and *Hardwick v Johnson* [1978] 2 All ER 935 applied.

(iii) The aunt's conduct in failing to reply to the trustee in bankruptcy's enquiries prior to the contract for the sale of the house was not such as to preclude her from enforcing her interest. Accordingly the trustee took the property subject to the aunt's interest, and as against the trustee (but not necessarily the purchaser from the trustee) the aunt was entitled to remain in the property until the loan was repaid (see p 204 *c* to *g*, post).

Notes

a For the estate or right taken by a trustee in bankruptcy, see 3 Halsbury's Laws (4th Edition) para 594, and for cases on the subject see 5 Digest (Reissue) 675–682, 5905–5968.

Cases referred to in judgment

Banister v Banister [1948] 2 All ER 133, CA, 47 Digest (Reissue) 101, 733.

b Binions v Evans [1972] 2 All ER 70, [1972] Ch 359, [1972] 2 WLR 729, 23 P & CR 192, CA, Digest (Cont Vol D) 814, 2771a.

DHN Food Distributors Ltd v London Borough of Tower Hamlets [1976] 3 All ER 462, [1976] 1 WLR 852, 74 LGR 506, 32 P & CR 240, [1976] RVR 269, CA.

Dodsworth v Dodsworth (1973) 228 Estates Gazette 1115.

Errington v Errington and Woods [1952] 1 All ER 149, [1952] 1 KB 290, CA, 31(1) Digest

c (Reissue) 208, 1734.

Hardwick v Johnson [1978] 2 All ER 935, [1978] 1 WLR 683, CA.

Hussey v Palmer [1972] 3 All ER 744, [1972] 1 WLR 1286, CA, Digest (Cont Vol D) 1007, 814b.

Ramsden v Dyson (1866) LR 1 HL 129, 21 Digest (Repl) 453, 1551.

Siew Soon Wah v Yong Tong Hong [1973] AC 836, [1973] 2 WLR 713, PC, Digest (Cont Vol

d D) 579, *739a.

Tanner v Tanner [1975] 3 All ER 776, [1975] 1 WLR 1346, CA, Digest (Cont Vol D) 578, 1732a.

Summons

By a notice of motion dated 17th May 1979 the trustee of the property of the first

e respondent, Thomas Anthony Sharpe, a bankrupt, applied against the first respondent and against the second respondent, Dorothy Annie Johnson, for an order for vacant possession of leasehold property known as 30 Englands Lane, London (save for such parts of the property as had been let to the trustee) and for such further or other relief as the court might think fit. The facts are set out in the judgment.

f Gabriel Moss for the trustee.
John Vallat for Mrs Johnson.

Cur adv vult

30th July. **BROWNE-WILKINSON J** read the following judgment: This case arises

g out of the bankruptcy of Thomas Anthony Sharpe, against whom a receiving order was made on 27th April 1978. The applicant, who is his trustee in bankruptcy, claims against the debtor and his aunt, Dorothy Annie Johnson, possession of certain premises, 30 Englands Lane, London NW3. That is a leasehold property which was purchased by the debtor for £17,000 in January 1975. It consists of a shop with a maisonette above, which is at present occupied by the debtor, his wife and Mrs Johnson. There are also two

h other tenants on the premises.

On 30th April 1979 the trustee contracted to sell the premises to a Mr Promitzer for £17,000 with vacant possession of the shop and maisonette. Completion was to be on 29th May 1979. After the date of that contract, Mrs Johnson for the first time put forward a claim to an interest in the premises. I have to decide whether she has such an interest and, if so, whether it is binding on the trustee in bankruptcy. The purchaser

j from the trustee in bankruptcy is not a party to this application and I cannot decide any question of priorities as between him and Mrs Johnson.

Mrs Johnson is a widow and is now 82 years old. She suffers from Parkinson's disease and senile arteriosclerosis. She is being looked after by the debtor and his wife.

When her husband died in 1960 she inherited a property, 11 Chalcot Gardens, parts of which were let out as flatlets. The debtor is a nephew of Mrs Johnson and he and his wife

occupied one of those flatlets. In 1972 Mrs Johnson's health declined. She decided to sell
11 Chalcot Gardens and agreed with the debtor and his wife that they would live *a*
together and look for somewhere else permanent to live. She sold 11 Chalcot Gardens in
March 1972 for about £38,000 and they all went to live in a rented flat at 92 Fellowes
Road. Mrs Johnson lived there with the debtor and his wife, the rent, rates and telephone
bills being shared.

Eventually, the debtor, who had apparently been carrying on a newsagent business at
another shop in Englands Lane, found the shop and maisonette at 30 Englands Lane. He *b*
told Mrs Johnson that it would cost some £17,000 and she agreed to provide £12,000,
the rest being raised on mortgage. She made three payments totalling £12,000 in
November and December 1974. In her affidavit she says this:

> 'I made these payments to the Bankrupt in order that he could buy the said
> premises. I cannot remember much about the circumstances now. However, I
> knew that I would be able to stay at the said premises as long as I wanted and that *c*
> I would be looked after by the Bankrupt and his wife. I am told that at his public
> examination the Bankrupt stated that the £12,000 was a gift. This is not right. It
> represented a very substantial part of my wealth and I hoped that if the Bankrupt's
> business prospered he might be able to repay me. I do not think that anything was
> said about the terms of repayment, but I knew that he could not hope to pay me *d*
> back so long as we lived at the said premises.'

Mrs Johnson, the debtor and his wife moved into the maisonette in the autumn of
1975 and she made certain further payments in 1975 for decorations and fittings to the
property, the cost of which to her totalled some £2,271·16.

Before the trustee in bankruptcy offered the property for sale steps were taken to find
out from Mrs Johnson what rights, if any, she claimed arising out of the provision of the *e*
£12,000. On 1st June 1978 the Official Receiver wrote to Mrs Johnson a letter addressed
to her at 30 Englands Lane. The letter is headed, 'Re: Thomas Anthony Sharpe' and
continues:

> 'The debtor has informed me that you gave him a sum of money in order that he
> could purchase the property 30 Englands Lane, London NW3. I would be assisted *f*
> therefore if you will let me know: 1 whether the sum involved was a gift or a loan;
> 2 the amount and the date given; 3 whether any security or consideration was given
> if the sum involved was a loan. A franked addressed label is enclosed for your reply.'

It is to be noted that that letter does not in terms refer to her claiming any equitable or
other interest in the property, otherwise than by way of secured loan.

No reply was received to that letter and on 1st August 1978 the trustee in bankruptcy *g*
again wrote to Mrs Johnson, referring back to the Official Receiver's letter and asking for
any comment. There was again no reply to that letter. Mrs Johnson in her affidavit
states that she never received those letters. That seems to me improbable. I think she
probably received them, but, in view of her age, took no steps about them and has since
forgotten their receipt.

On these facts Mrs Johnson claims to have either a beneficial interest in the property *h*
and its proceeds of sale or alternatively a right to stay in the property by virtue of an
irrevocable licence or equitable right. I should mention that in addition to the substantial
sums she provided to acquire and decorate the property, she paid debts of the debtor
amounting to more than £9,000 in order to try to stave off his bankruptcy.

I will first consider whether she has established an equitable interest in the property *j*
and its proceeds of sale by virtue of having provided the bulk of the purchase money, that
is to say, has she an interest under a resulting trust? I have no doubt that she has not
established any such interest. It is clear that the parties never worked out in any detail
what was the legal relationship between them, but no one has suggested that Mrs
Johnson advanced the money to the debtor otherwise than by way of gift or loan. In his

public examination the debtor suggested that the moneys were a gift, but I find as a fact
a that the moneys were advanced by way of loan.

In September 1975, on the advice of her solicitor, Mrs Johnson got the debtor to sign
a promissory note for £15,700. The reason for the promissory note was that by her will
Mrs Johnson had left her estate to her three nephews equally and she felt it would be
unfair if the debtor were to take one third of what remained without bringing into
account what he had received already. The parties having, by the promissory note,
b expressed the moneys to be repayable, the result must, in my judgment, be that the
moneys were paid by way of loan, not gift. I do not think it matters which for the
purposes of this aspect of the argument. In either case it is clear that Mrs Johnson and her
estate were not to have a beneficial share in the value of the property, which was to
belong solely to the debtor. Counsel for Mrs Johnson on this aspect of the case relied on
Hussey v Palmer[1] where the Court of Appeal by a majority held that, even though the
c plaintiff in that case described moneys used to improve a property as having been paid
by way of loan to the owner of the property, she was entitled to an equitable interest in
the property. However, her equitable interest was not apparently a share of the proceeds
of sale, but something akin to a lien for the moneys advanced. The facts in that case were
very special and I think the clue to the decision may be that the court reached the view
that, although described in evidence as a loan, the parties did not in fact intend a loan
d since there was never any discussion of repayment (see per Lord Denning MR[2]).

In my judgment, if, as in this case, moneys are advanced by way of loan there can be
no question of the lender being entitled to an interest in the property under a resulting
trust. If he were to take such an interest, he would get his money twice: once on
repayment of the loan and once on taking his share of the proceeds of sale of the property.

I turn then to the alternative claim that Mrs Johnson is entitled to something less than
e an aliquot share of the equity in the premises, namely the right to stay on the premises
until the money she provided indirectly to acquire them has been repaid. This right is
based on the line of recent Court of Appeal decisions which has spelt out irrevocable
licences from informal family arrangements, and in some cases characterised such
licences as conferring some equity or equitable interest under a constructive trust. I do
not think that the principles lying behind these decisions have yet been fully explored
f and on occasion it seems that such rights are found to exist simply on the ground that to
hold otherwise would be a hardship to the plaintiff. It appears that the principle is one
akin to, or an extension of, a proprietary estoppel stemming from Lord Kingsdown's
well-known statement of the law in *Ramsden v Dyson*[3]. In a strict case of proprietary
estoppel the plaintiff has expended his own money on the defendant's property in an
expectation encouraged by, or known to, the defendant that the plaintiff either owns the
g property or is to have some interest conferred on him. Recent authorities have extended
this doctrine and, in my judgment, it is now established that, if the parties have
proceeded on a common assumption that the plaintiff is to enjoy a right to reside in a
particular property and in reliance on that assumption the plaintiff has expended money
or otherwise acted to his detriment, the defendant will not be allowed to go back on that
common assumption and the court will imply an irrevocable licence or trust which will
h give effect to that common assumption. Thus in *Errington v Errington and Woods*[4]
Denning LJ held that the son, who had paid the instalments under the mortgage in the
expectation that the property would eventually become his, had an equitable right to
stay in occupation until the mortgage was paid off. In *Tanner v Tanner*[5] the plaintiff was
held entitled to a licence to occupy a house bought in contemplation of it being a home

j

1   [1972] 3 All ER 744, [1972] 1 WLR 1286
2   [1972] 3 All ER 744 at 745, [1972] 1 WLR 1286 at 1288
3   (1866) LR 1 HL 129 at 170
4   [1952] 1 All ER 149, [1952] 1 KB 290
5   [1975] 3 All ER 776, [1975] 1 WLR 1346

for herself and her children, there being no express contract to that effect. In *Hardwick v Johnson*[1], where the plaintiff's house had been occupied by the plaintiff's son and his   **a** first wife under an informal family arrangement, the Court of Appeal imputed an intention to grant an irrevocable licence to the wife on payment by her of a weekly sum.

Applying those principles to the present case, I have little doubt that as between the debtor on the one hand and Mrs Johnson on the other, the circumstances in which she provided the money by way of loan in order to enable the premises to be bought do give rise to some right in Mrs Johnson. It is clear that she only lent the money as part of a   **b** wider scheme, an essential feature of which was that she was to make her home in the property to be acquired with the money lent. Suppose that, immediately after the property had been bought, the debtor had tried to evict Mrs Johnson without repaying the loan; can it be supposed that the court would have made an order for possession against her? In my judgment, whether it be called a contractual licence or an equitable licence or an interest under a constructive trust, Mrs Johnson would be entitled as against   **c** the debtor to stay in the house. *Dodsworth v Dodsworth*[2] shows that there are great practical difficulties in finding that she is entitled to a full life interest: but there is no reason why one should not imply an intention that she should have the right to live there until her loan is repaid, which was the result reached in *Dodsworth v Dodsworth*[2].

Unfortunately, this case does not arise for decision simply between Mrs Johnson on the one hand and the debtor on the other. She has to show some right good against the   **d** trustee in bankruptcy and the purchaser from the trustee in bankruptcy. Due to an unfortunate procedural position, the purchaser is not a party to this application and nothing I can say can or is intended to bind him. As an antidote to the over-indulgence of sympathy which everyone must feel for Mrs Johnson, I put on record that the purchaser's plight is little better. He apparently had no reason to suspect that there was any flaw in the trustee's right to sell with vacant possession. As a result of the trustee's   **e** inability to complete the sale he cannot open the business he intended and he and his wife and two children are being forced to live in a small motorised caravan parked in various places on or near Hampstead Heath.

Is then Mrs Johnson's right against the debtor binding on the trustee in bankruptcy? This is an important and difficult point and, were it not for the urgency of the matter and the late stage of the term, I would like to have given it longer consideration. In general   **f** the trustee in bankruptcy steps into the shoes of the debtor and takes the debtor's property subject to all rights and equities affecting it (see Halsbury's Laws of England[3]). However, the trustee in bankruptcy is free to break any merely contractual obligation of the debtor, leaving the other party to his remedy in damages, which damages will only give rise to a right to prove in the bankruptcy.

Are rights of the kind spelt out in the cases I have referred to merely contractual   **g** licences or do they fetter the property and create some right over it? On the authorities as they stand, I think I am bound to hold that the rights under such an irrevocable licence bind the property itself in the hands of the trustee in bankruptcy. Lord Denning MR has, on a number of occasions, said that these licences arise under a constructive trust and are binding on the third party's acquiring with notice. These statements are for the most part obiter dicta with which other members of the court have not associated themselves,   **h** preferring to rest their decision on there being a contractual licence. But in *Binions v Evans*[4] a third party taking with notice of, and expressly subject to, such a licence was held bound by it. In that case the liability could not have depended merely on contract. Closer to the present case is a decision which was not referred to in argument and therefore my comments on it must be treated with some reserve. In *DHN Food*

j

---

1   [1978] 2 All ER 935, [1978] 1 WLR 683
2   (1973) 228 Estates Gazette 115
3   3 Halsbury's Laws (4th Edn) para 594
4   [1972] 2 All ER 70, [1972] Ch 359

Distributors Ltd v London Borough of Tower Hamlets[1] certain premises were legally owned
a by one company (Bronze) but occupied by an associated company (DHN) under an
informal arrangement between them. The premises were compulsorily acquired and
the question was whether any compensation for disturbance was payable, it being said
that Bronze had not been disturbed. The Court of Appeal held that DHN had an
irrevocable licence to remain in the premises indefinitely and this gave DHN a
compensatable interest in the land. Lord Denning MR said this[2]:

b
 'It was equivalent to a contract between the two companies whereby Bronze
 granted an irrevocable licence to DHN to carry on their business on the premises.
 In this situation counsel for the claimants cited to us *Binions v Evans*[3] to which I
 would add *Bannister v Bannister*[4] and *Siew Soon Wah alias Siew Pooi Tong v Yong Tong
 Hong*[5]. Those cases show that a contractual licence (under which a person has the
 right to occupy premises indefinitely) gives rise to a constructive trust, under which
c
 the legal owner is not allowed to turn out the licensee. So here. This irrevocable
 licence gave to DHN a sufficient interest in the land to qualify them for
 compensation for disturbance.'

Goff LJ[6] also made this a ground of his decision.
 It seems to me that this is a decision that such contractual or equitable licence does
d confer some interest in the property under a constructive trust. Accordingly, in my
judgment, it follows that the trustee in bankruptcy takes the property subject to Mrs
Johnson's right to live there until she is repaid the moneys she provided to acquire it.
 Counsel for the trustee in bankruptcy argued that this was the wrong approach. He
said that the species of constructive trust which Lord Denning MR was considering in
the cases was different from the traditional constructive trust known to equity lawyers.
e It is not, counsel says, a substantive right but an equitable remedy (see per Lord Denning
MR in *Hussey v Palmer*[7] and in *Binions v Evans*[8]). Then, says counsel, the time to decide
whether to grant such a remedy is when the matter comes before the court in the light
of the then known circumstances. In the present case those circumstances are that the
debtor is a bankrupt and Mrs Johnson has failed to put forward her claim until after the
trustee has contracted to sell the property to an innocent third party, notwithstanding
f two enquiries as to whether she had a claim. Accordingly, he says, it would not be
equitable to grant her an interest under a constructive trust at this time.
 I cannot accept that argument in that form. Even if it be right to say that the courts
can impose a constructive trust as a remedy in certain cases (which to my mind is a novel
concept in English law), in order to provide a remedy the court must first find a right
which has been infringed. So far as land is concerned an oral agreement to create any
g interest in it must be evidenced in writing: see the Law of Property Act 1925, s 40.
Therefore if these irrevocable licences create an interest in land, the rights cannot rest
simply on an oral contract. The introduction of an interest under a constructive trust is
an essential ingredient if the plaintiff has any right at all. Therefore in cases such as this,
it cannot be that the interest in property arises for the first time when the court declares
it to exist. The right must have arisen at the time of the transaction in order for the
h plaintiff to have any right the breach of which can be remedied. Again, I think the *DHN
Food* case[1] shows that the equity predates any order of the court. The right to

---

 1 [1976] 3 All ER 462, [1976] 1 WLR 852
j 2 [1976] 3 All ER 462 at 466–467, [1976] 1 WLR 852 at 859
 3 [1972] 2 All ER 70, [1972] Ch 359
 4 [1948] 2 All ER 133
 5 [1973] AC 836
 6 [1976] 3 All ER 462 at 467–468, [1976] 1 WLR 852 at 860–861
 7 [1972] 3 All ER 744 at 747 [1972] 1 WLR 1286 at 1289–1290
 8 [1972] 2 All ER 70 at 76, [1972] Ch 359 at 368

compensation in that case depended on substantive rights at the date of compulsory
acquisition, not on what remedy the court subsequently chose to grant in the subsequent   *a*
litigation.

Accordingly, if I am right in holding that as between the debtor and Mrs Johnson she
had an irrevocable licence to remain in the property, authority compels me to hold that
that gave her an interest in the property before the bankruptcy and the trustee takes the
property subject to that interest. In my judgment the mere intervention of the
bankruptcy by itself cannot alter Mrs Johnson's property interest. If she is to be deprived   *b*
of her interest as against the trustee in bankruptcy, it must be because of some conduct
of hers which precludes her from enforcing her rights, that is to say, the ordinary
principles of acquiescence and laches which apply to all beneficiaries seeking to enforce
their rights apply to this case.

I am in no way criticising the trustee in bankruptcy's conduct; he tried to find out if
she made any claim relating to the £12,000 before he contracted to sell the property.   *c*
But I do not think that on ordinary equitable principles Mrs Johnson should be prevented
from asserting her rights even at this late stage. She is very old and in bad health. No
one had ever advised her that she might have rights to live in the property. As soon as
she appreciated that she was to be evicted she at once took legal advice and asserted her
claim. This, in my judgment, is far removed from conduct which precludes enforcement
by a beneficiary of his rights due to his acquiescence, the first requirement of acquiescence   *d*
being that the beneficiary knows his or her rights and does not assert them.

Accordingly, I hold that Mrs Johnson is entitled as against the trustee in bankruptcy
to remain in the property until she is repaid the sums she advanced. I reach this
conclusion with some hesitation since I find the present state of the law very confused
and difficult to fit in with established equitable principles. I express the hope that in the
near future the whole question can receive full consideration in the Court of Appeal, so   *e*
that, in order to do justice to the many thousands of people who never come into court
at all but who wish to know with certainty what their proprietary rights are, the extent
to which these irrevocable licences bind third parties may be defined with certainty.
Doing justice to the litigant who actually appears in the court by the invention of new
principles of law ought not to involve injustice to the other persons who are not litigants
before the court but whose rights are fundamentally affected by the new principles.   *f*

Finally, I must reiterate that I am in no way deciding what are the rights of the
purchaser from the trustee as against Mrs Johnson. It may be that as a purchaser without
express notice in an action for specific performance of the contract his rights will prevail
over Mrs Johnson's. As to that, I have heard no argument and express no view. I do,
however, express my sympathy for him in the predicament in which he finds himself.

I therefore dismiss the trustee's application for possession against Mrs Johnson.   *g*

Motion dismissed.

Solicitors: *Peard Son & Webster* (for the trustee); *Edwin Coe & Calder Woods* (for Mrs
Johnson).

h

Azza M Abdallah Barrister.

Chartered Bank v Daklouche and another

COURT OF APPEAL, CIVIL DIVISION

LORD DENNING MR, EVELEIGH LJ AND SIR STANLEY REES

15th, 16th MARCH 1979

Injunction – Interlocutory – Danger that defendant may transfer assets out of jurisdiction – Injunction restraining removal of assets out of the jurisdiction – Injunction in advance of plaintiff's claim – Action alleging Lebanese husband and wife defrauding husband's creditors in Abu Dhabi – Husband transferring money to wife in Abu Dhabi instead of paying creditors – Wife transferring money from Abu Dhabi to her bank account in England – Wife present and owning house in England – Whether jurisdiction to grant Mareva injunction where defendant is temporarily within the jurisdiction and can be served here – Whether cause of action against husband in respect of which he could be served out of jurisdiction – Whether jurisdiction to grant injunction against him.

The husband and the wife were Lebanese citizens who carried on business in Abu Dhabi. The business was very successful and the wife purchased a house in England in her name to provide a base for herself and her husband during their periodic visits to England where their daughters were being educated. In January 1979 the husband ran into financial difficulties and his firm's account with the branch of the plaintiff bank in Abu Dhabi became heavily overdrawn. He told the branch manager that he would pay off the overdraft with the proceeds of trade debts owing to him. However, in the same month the husband paid into his personal account at another bank in Abu Dhabi cheques amounting to £70,000 received by his firm in respect of trade debts. Soon after, he drew out the £70,000 in cash and closed the account. He apparently handed the £70,000 to his wife in Abu Dhabi, and she paid the money into banks in Abu Dhabi to be transferred to accounts in her name at a London bank. A short time later the husband disappeared and the wife came to England The plaintiff bank commenced an action in England against the husband and the wife claiming, inter alia, damages for fraud and/or conspiracy, and applied for a Mareva[1] injunction restraining the husband and wife from disposing of the £70,000 standing in the wife's name at the London bank. Mocatta J in the Commercial Court granted the injunction and gave leave to serve it on the husband out of the jurisdiction. The wife was served with notice of the injunction in England. The wife applied to the Commercial Court to discharge the injunction and Donaldson J held that it should be discharged, on the ground that the court had no jurisdiction to grant it because the transactions in question took place in Abu Dhabi. However, the injunction was continued pending appeal. The plaintiff bank appealed, seeking reinstatement of the injunction until further order or trial of the action. On the appeal the wife contended that where a defendant to an action was within the jurisdiction of the English court and had assets within the jurisdiction the court could not grant a Mareva injunction in advance of trial of the action.

Held – An English court had jurisdiction to grant a Mareva injunction against both the husband and the wife, and such an injunction should be granted, for the following reasons—

(i) Even though a defendant was present in England and could be served there the court had jurisdiction to grant a Mareva injunction if his presence in England was only fleeting and he was likely to leave at short notice, or if there was a danger that he might abscond out of the jurisdiction with assets. Because the wife was not based in England and was likely to leave the country at short notice, there was jurisdiction to grant a Mareva injunction against her even though she was present and could be served in

---

1 See *Mareva Compania Naviera v International Bulkcarriers SA*, p 213, post

England (see p 209 *j*, p 210 *d* to *f*, p 211 *f* and p 212 *e f*, post); dicta of Lord Denning MR
in *Rasu Maritima SA v Perusahaan Pertambangan Minyak Dan Gas Bumi Negara (Pertamina)* *a*
[1977] 3 All ER at 332 and of Lord Hailsham of St Marylebone in *Siskina (Owners) v Distos
Compania Naviera SA, The Siskina* [1977] 3 All ER at 829 explained.

(ii) Since fraud had been pleaded against the husband there was a cause of action
against him which was justiciable in England. Furthermore, because he was a person out
of the jurisdiction who was a proper party to the action, the writ could be served on him
out of the jurisdiction under RSC Ord 11, r 1(1)(*j*)ᵃ, and that being so, he came within the *b*
ambit of a Mareva injunction as a person who was out of the jurisdiction, who could be
served out of the jurisdiction and who had assets within the jurisdiction (ie the £70,000
standing in the wife's accounts) which might disappear unless the injunction were
granted (see p 210 *a* to *d*, p 211 *g* and p 212 *b* to *f*, post); *Siskina (Owners) v Distos Compania
Naviera SA, The Siskina* [1977] 3 All ER 803 distinguished.

(iii) In all the circumstances the proper course was to continue the injunction, and the *c*
appeal would be allowed accordingly (see p 210 *f g* and p 212 *e f*, post).

Notes
For an injunction restraining disposition of property, see 24 Halsbury's Laws (4th Edn)
para 1018.

For service of the writ or notice thereof out of the jurisdiction where an injunction is *d*
sought, see ibid para 1047 and 30 Halsbury's Laws (3rd Edn) 323–328, paras 588–594,
and for cases on the subject, see 50 Digest (Repl) 353–355, 773–789.

Cases referred to in judgments
Cadogan v Cadogan [1977] 3 All ER 831, [1977] 1 WLR 1041, 35 P & CR 92, CA.
Mareva Compania Naviera SA v International Bulkcarriers SA, The Mareva, p 213, post, *e*
[1975] 2 Lloyd's Rep 509, CA.
Midland Bank Trust Co Ltd v Green (No 3) [1979] 2 All ER 193, [1979] 2 WLR 594.
*Rasu Maritima SA v Perusahaan Pertambangan Minyak Dan Gas Bumi Negara (Pertamina)
and Government of Indonesia (as interveners)* [1977] 3 All ER 324, [1978] QB 644, [1977]
3 WLR 518, [1977] 2 Lloyd's Rep 397, CA.
Siskina (Owners) v Distos Compania Naviera SA, The Siskina [1977] 3 All ER 803, [1979] AC *f*
210, [1977] 3 WLR 818, [1978] 1 Lloyd's Rep 1, HL.

Cases also cited
Director of Public Prosecutions v Doot [1973] 1 All ER 940, [1973] AC 807, HL.
Mawji v R [1957] 1 All ER 385, [1957] AC 126, PC.
Lister & Co v Stubbs (1890) 45 Ch D 1, [1886–90] All ER Rep 797, CA. *g*
Rye v Rye [1962] 1 All ER 146, [1962] AC 496, HL.

Interlocutory appeal
By a writ and statement of claim dated 8th February 1979 the plaintiff, the Chartered
Bank (a body incorporated by royal charter) which had a branch in Abu Dhabi, brought
an action against the defendants, Suhail Daklouche ('the husband') and his wife, Salwa *h*
Daklouche ('the wife') claiming against the husband (a) 193,974·08 Dirhams, or the
sterling equivalent, as moneys lent, (b) 138,786·40 Dirhams, or the sterling equivalent,
as moneys lent, (c) interest thereon, and (d) damages for fraud; and against both the
husband and the wife (a) a declaration that dispositions by the husband of moneys from
his account at the First National Bank of Chicago in Abu Dhabi made in January 1979
were voidable under s 172 of the Law of Property Act 1972, (b) an order that the *j*
dispositions be set aside and (c) an injunction restraining the husband and wife and each
of them whether by themselves, their servants or agents or otherwise howsoever, from

---

a Rule 1(1), so far as material, is set out at p 210 *c*, post

removing or taking any steps to remove any of their assets from within the jurisdiction
a of the court or otherwise disposing of them and in particular, restraining them from so
removing or disposing of the moneys presently standing to the wife's credit in any bank
within the court's jurisdiction. Subsequently the writ and statement of claim were
amended to claim a declaration that moneys standing in bank accounts in the wife's
name in London were the husband's moneys, and to claim against both the husband and
the wife damages for conspiracy and/or breach of trust and/or fraud. The Chartered
b Bank applied ex parte for an interim injunction against the husband and wife to restrain
them from disposing of moneys standing to the wife's credit in accounts with the First
National Bank of Chicago in London. On 7th February 1979 Mocatta J in the
Commercial Court granted an injunction restraining the husband and wife and each of
them from removing or taking any steps to remove or dispose of any moneys presently
standing to the wife's credit in any bank account within the jurisdiction of the court until
c trial of the action or further order. The wife applied to have that injunction set aside and
on 6th March Donaldson J in the Commercial Court held that the injunction should be
discharged, on the ground that the English courts had no jurisdiction to grant it because
the transactions in question took place in Abu Dhabi. However, the judge continued the
injunction pending an appeal. The Chartered Bank appealed, seeking an injunction to
restrain the wife from dealing with the moneys standing to the credit of accounts in her
d name with the First National Bank of Chicago in London. The grounds of the appeal
were that Donaldson J ought to have held that he had jurisdiction to grant the interim
injunction sought by virtue of the fact that the moneys in the wife's account in London
were transferred there pursuant to a conspiracy between the husband and the wife to
defraud the husband's creditors such as the Chartered Bank and/or that the moneys in the
acccounts were impressed with a trust for the benefit of the Chartered Bank as a creditor
e of the husband; and that the judge ought to have granted an injunction in the terms
sought until trial or further order. The facts are set out in the judgment of Lord
Denning MR.

Roger Buckley for the Chartered Bank.
Anthony Boswood for the wife.

f

LORD DENNING MR. The Lebanese are born traders. They set up businesses far
and wide. Two of them are husband and wife, Suhail and Salwa Daklouche. They did
g well in Abu Dhabi in the Persian Gulf. That is a place grown rich on oil. The husband
traded there under the business name of Gulf Trading and Cold Storage. He supplied
food and drink wholesale to caterers at the airport and at clubs. Some of his business was
retail. He set up a supermarket and supplied goods retail to the public. His wife helped
him a good deal in both businesses. At all events, on her own admission, she helped him
quite a lot in managing the supermarket.
h   The business was very successful. So much so that they were attracted to England.
They, or at least the wife, purchased a large house at Beech, which is near Alton in
Hampshire. It was conveyed into the wife's name. In 1977 it cost £50,000. The money
seems to have been available without any need to raise anything on mortgage. It is now
worth £80,000. The wife is having building work done on it to a value, she says, of more
than £34,000. Mr and Mrs Daklouche have two daughters aged 15 and 13 who are at
j boarding school in England. They hope to go on to a university here.
      Meanwhile the husband has been carrying on the business in Abu Dhabi. From
January 1976 he has had an account with the branch of the Chartered Bank there. That
account is in the firm's name of Gulf Trading and Cold Storage. But both husband and
wife have power to operate it individually on their sole signature. Each gave specimen
signatures to the bank in regard to the operation of that account.

All seems to have gone reasonably well until January of this year. Then the husband ran into financial difficulties. The account of the firm with the Chartered Bank became *a* very much overdrawn. He told the manager of the branch at Abu Dhabi that he had many trade debts owing to him and that he would pay off the overdraft with the proceeds of these trade debts which he would get in by 20th January 1979. Other creditors were also pressing for payment of unpaid bills. We are told that one of them called in the local police to help recover his debt.

During January 1979 three cheques were received by the Gulf Trading and Cold *b* Storage company. Two of them were from the Abu Dhabi International Airport Caterers and one was from the Abu Dhabi Club. They were all marked 'Account payee'. They were given in local currency, but in sterling they came to about £70,000. The husband, however, did not pay these cheques into the Chartered Bank to clear the overdraft. He paid them into his own account which he had in Abu Dhabi with the First National Bank of Chicago there. Soon afterwards he drew out the amount in cash and closed his account *c* with the First National Bank in Abu Dhabi. Although there is some conflict, it appears very likely from the evidence that on the very next day, having drawn out the cash from the First National Bank, he handed it to his wife. Then she paid it into two banks in Abu Dhabi, Citibank and Barclays Bank International. She then asked those two banks to transfer the money by telegraph to her personal account in London with the First National Bank of Chicago. This was done. So the £70,000 stood in her name in the bank *d* in London.

Soon afterwards she came back to England. But we do not know what happened to the husband. He seems to have disappeared without trace. The court officials in Abu Dhabi have taken possession of his premises. They have sealed them up, and have put up a notice calling on creditors to put in their claim.

The Chartered Bank seems to have got wind of some of these happenings. At first they *e* had very little knowledge about it. They found out that there was quite a large sum of money to the credit of the wife in the First National Bank of Chicago in London. So they issued a writ trying to stop it being dealt with. They issued a writ against both husband and wife here. They moved the court for a Mareva[1] injunction so as to stop any disposal of that £70,000 in the First National Bank which stood in the wife's name. Mocatta J granted the injunction to stop the money being dealt with; and he further gave leave to *f* serve the husband out of the jurisdiction. As for the wife, she was here in England. So she was duly served, I suppose at her house at Alton. At all events, the judge granted a Mareva injunction to stop any dealings with the money. First National Bank was told. Everything was held up.

Thereupon the wife moved the court to discharge the injunction. The matter came before Donaldson J. He did discharge the injunction. He gave his reasons quite *g* shortly. He said:

'This matter should be dealt with by order of the court in whose jurisdiction the transaction took effect and in my view this is Abu Dhabi since orders of English courts do not have extra-territorial effect.'

h

So Donaldson J refused the injunction because he said this matter could not be dealt with in England. He would not even restrain the moneys from going out of England. The only course open to the Chartered Bank was to go to Abu Dhabi, sue the husband there, get judgment there and put the husband in bankruptcy there. It was only after all that was done that the Chartered Bank might stop any dealings with the money in London.

By that time I doubt whether there would be any money in the London bank. It is *j* very easy to transfer money from one bank to another bank at a moment's notice. It could be transferred to Switzerland or Chicago, or wherever it may be.

---

1   See *Mareva Compania Naviera SA v International Bulkcarriers SA* p 213, post

Donaldson J, realising it is a difficult point, extended the injunction pending the
a appeal to this court until today. So we have heard it, and now have to give our decision.
There has been additional evidence filed on both sides. So we know a good deal more
about the case. Earlier on the wife had said that this money was not given to her by her
husband. She said it was never her husband's money at all. She said she was an
entrepreneur on her own account. She said in her affidavit: 'I am a Lebanese citizen and
I am not a resident of the United Kingdom.' She explained that she purchased the house
b in order to provide a base for herself and her husband because her two daughters were
being educated at school here. She said:

> 'Since I purchased the house here and before that date, I have transferred sums of
> money to my account with the First National Bank of Chicago in London. The
> money transferred has always been my own money, owned by me in my own
> right. I own money which has come to me through my own family, from
c > transactions entered into by me in Abu Dhabi on the gold market there, from land
> transactions entered into by me in Sharjah and from other business interests.
> Furthermore, my relatives often give me money to transfer for them to London.
> During the year 1978 I remitted over £60,000 to London.'

Then she deals with these specific items: the cheques which I have mentioned, which
d were in favour of the Gulf Trading and Cold Storage Co and which were traced here. As
to those, she said they were not her husband's at all. She said that they were sent to her
by a family friend in Jordan and also from an uncle in Beirut, and she remitted those
moneys to London.

That is what she said at first. But later the bank were able to get further evidence.
They got the cheques and traced them all through. As a result it appears that her story
e was altogether wrong. She had previously said that they were her moneys, given to her
by her uncle and other friends and relatives. Now the evidence goes to show that they
were the firm's moneys, drawn out by the husband in Abu Dhabi, handed to her, and she
then put them in her name into the London bank. The reason is pretty plain. He
wanted to get the moneys out of the reach of his creditors. So, as often happens, the
moneys were put into the wife's name. It appears on the evidence that she was the agent
f or nominee of the husband, whatever you like to call it, and they were his moneys still,
or the firm's moneys.

That being the case, the question became one of law. Has this court any jurisdiction
to grant an injunction restraining the defendants from removing these moneys out of
the jurisdiction? In this regard, it is as well to take the wife and husband separately,
because she is in this country, and he is not.
g Counsel for the wife said: 'She has these large assets here. You cannot get an injunction
against her in regard to these moneys.' He referred to what I myself said in *Rasu
Maritima SA v Perusahaan Pertambangan Minyak Dan Gas Bumi Negara (Pertamina) and
Government of Indonesia (as interveners)*[1]:

> 'So far as concerns defendants who are within the jurisdiction of the court and
h > have assets here, it is well established that the court should not, in advance of any
> order or judgment, allow the creditor to seize any of the money or goods of the
> debtor or to use any legal process to do so.'

In making that statement I only had in mind the cases where defendants were
permanently settled here and had their assets here. I would not extend that statement so
as to cover a case such as this. The wife declared at the beginning that she was a Lebanese
j citizen. Next, at a very late stage, she altered it and said she intended to live here
permanently. If a defendant is likely to leave England at short notice, a Mareva
injunction may well be granted.

---

1   [1977] 3 All ER 324 at 332, [1978] QB 644 at 659

Then, as regards the husband, counsel suggested that *Siskina (Owners) v Distas Compania Naviera SA*[1] in the House of Lords precluded a Mareva injunction being granted against **a** him. But that was a case where there was no ground for serving the writ out of the jurisdiction. Here there is a cause of action on which the husband could be served out. An amended writ has been issued with amended pleadings. There is a claim for a declaration that the moneys, although standing in the wife's name, are the husband's moneys, and there is a claim for an injunction. There is also a claim for damages for conspiracy and/or breach of trust and/or fraud. That is a claim against both the husband **b** and wife. It has recently been held by Oliver J that a husband and wife can be liable in a civil action against them for conspiracy: see *Midland Bank v Green (No 3)*[2]. The husband is a proper party to those causes of action. The case comes within the provisions of RSC Ord 11, r 1(1)(*j*):

> 'if the action begun by the writ being properly brought against a person duly **c** served within the jurisdiction, a person out of the jurisdiction is a necessary or proper party thereto . . .'

So it seems to me that the husband is brought within the Mareva principle of a person who is out of the jurisdiction, and can be served out of the jurisdiction, and has assets here which may disappear unless the injunction is ordered.

But I would not limit the Mareva principle. It seems to me, as Lord Hailsham of St **d** Marylebone indicated in the *Siskina* case[3], that the law is developing in this field. Even when a defendant may be present in this country and is served here, it is quite possible that a Mareva injunction can be granted. Counsel for the Chartered Bank told us that it has already been done from time to time in the Commercial Court. Eveleigh LJ made this suggestion: suppose a person was able to be served here because he was on a short visit for a weekend, or had dropped in for an hour or two, and was served, would that **e** make all the difference as to whether a Mareva injunction could be granted or not? That cannot be. The law should be that there is jurisdiction to grant a Mareva injunction, even though the defendant may be served here. If he makes a fleeting visit, or if there is a danger that he may abscond or that the assets or moneys may disappear and be taken out of the reach of the creditors, a Mareva injunction can be granted. That seems to me to be this very case. Here is this £70,000 lying in a bank in England which can be **f** removed at the stroke of a pen from England outside the reach of the creditors.

For this reason it seems to me that the right thing would be to continue the injunction granted by Mocatta J, and to grant an injunction preventing the disposition of these moneys until further order of the court. Notice will be given to the First National Bank accordingly.

I would allow the appeal accordingly. **g**

EVELEIGH LJ. The Mareva injunction is now established in my opinion so far as this court is concerned. I take that also to be the view of Lord Diplock in *Siskina v Distos Compania Naviera SA*[4]. He said:

> 'In the view that I take of the instant appeal, however, it can be disposed of on the **h** grounds adopted by Kerr J and Bridge LJ. They distinguished it from the *Mareva*[5] and *Pertamina*[6] cases by which decisions they were bound.'

What is required for such an injunction? First, that there should be assets here, and, secondly, that there should be a substantial cause of action to which the injunction will

1   [1977] 3 All ER 803, [1979] AC 210
2   [1979] 2 All ER 193, [1979] 2 WLR 594
3   [1977] 3 All ER 803 at 829, [1979] AC 210 at 261–262
4   [1977] 3 All ER 803 at 822, [1979] AC 210 at 254
5   Page 213, post
6   [1977] 3 All ER 324, [1978] QB 644

j

a be ancillary. So far as assets here are concerned, the affidavits, in my view, establish this. It may be argued that one cannot ascertain whether they are the husband's or the wife's or whether they belong to both. In a situation like this, I do not think that is a difficulty which should stand in the way of the court. They were assets of the husband. They were transferred fraudulently, as is claimed, to avoid the husband's liability to the bank. I therefore regard them from the point of view of the husband and the point of view of the wife as assets which could be made the subject of an injunction.

b   Furthermore, as this case was presented to the court, the money is the subject-matter of the action. I am aware of the difficulties of tracing money, but it seems to me in the present case that the moneys which the husband diverted in order to defraud the bank are moneys which rest in the account which is in the name of the wife in London. That being so, what are the objections to this injunction? It is said that the wife has been served here, and reliance has been placed on the words of Lord Hailsham of St Marylebone

c in the *Siskina* case[1]; and counsel has argued that in the case of a person who is served here this injunction is not appropriate. But Lord Hailsham did not use the word 'served'. He said:

> 'Either the position of a plaintiff making a claim against an English based defendant will have to be altered or the principle of the Mareva cases will have to be modified.'

d
In her first affidavit before this court the wife said:

> 'I am a Lebanese citizen and I am not a resident of the United Kingdom. However, in September 1977 I purchased the house at the aforesaid address in Alton, Hampshire so as to provide a base for myself and my husband when we periodically came to England to visit our two children, who are being educated at schools here.'

e
That is not the kind of base that I regard Lord Hailsham as referring to in his speech in the *Siskina* case[2]. According to that affidavit, the wife is certainly not based in this country. It is true that a subsequent affidavit sought to claim that she was resident here, but I would not place any reliance on that. That being so, I take the view that a Mareva injunction is possible in the case of a person such as the wife who was served in this

f country. Were it otherwise the situation would be ridiculous for, as counsel has pointed out, a person who anticipates that he is going to be served with notice of a writ will come to this country and accept actual service and thus defeat a Mareva injunction. I do not believe that the law could be so futile.

So one is then concerned to see what causes of action there are. Fraud is alleged in this case; and, if the money is to be regarded as strictly speaking the money of the husband,

g it is pertinent to consider what part in the fraud he has played which is justiciable in this country. In *Cadogan v Cadogan*[3] Buckley LJ said:

> 'If the voluntary conveyance was tainted with a fraudulent intention on the part of the husband to defeat a legitimate claim on him by the plaintiff, can the plaintiff seek to have it set aside to such extent as may be necessary to recompense her for any damage she may have suffered in consequence of the conveyance, notwithstanding
h that that damage has not taken the form of her being deprived of a particular claim which the conveyance was actually directed to defeating? The position can perhaps be made clearer in this way. There were two possibilities at the time of the voluntary conveyance: either the husband would succeed in obtaining a decree absolute or he would not. If he had survived and had obtained a decree absolute, the plaintiff would have been entitled to pursue her claim against him under the
j Matrimonial Causes Act 1973 for financial provisions.'

---

1 [1977] 3 All ER 803 at 829, [1979] AC 210 at 261
2 [1977] 3 All ER 803, [1979] AC 210
3 [1977] 3 All ER 831 at 837, [1977] 1 WLR 1041 at 1057

Buckley LJ went on to say that the wife's claim as pleaded disclosed a cause of action known to law. Goff LJ[1] concurring referred to a passage from Kerr on Fraud and *a*
Mistake[2]:

> 'Civil Courts have an original independent and inherent jurisdiction to relieve against every species of fraud not being relief of a penal nature. Every transfer or conveyance of property, by whatever means it be done, is vitiated by fraud. Deeds, obligations, contracts, awards, judgments, or decrees may be the instruments to *b*
> which parties may resort to cover fraud, and through which they may obtain the most unrighteous advantages, but none of such devices or instruments will be permitted by a Court of Equity to obstruct the requirements of justice.'

Those words are apt to cover the facts alleged in the present case.

It is also alleged that there was a conspiracy by the husband and the wife. I do not regard it as necessary to determine the question whether a husband and wife can conspire *c*
together. The fact is that they were acting jointly and acting wrongly in committing a fraud: whether one calls it 'conspiracy' or not is not to my mind important.

It was also urged in argument that the husband could not be served with notice under RSC Ord 11 in this case. For the reasons stated by Lord Denning MR, I am of the opinion that he can. I think that he is a proper party whether or not he is said to be a necessary party as well. *d*

I further take the view that on the facts alleged in this case both the husband and wife are perpetuating their fraud here in this country by secreting the money in the London bank out of the reach of the bank in Abu Dhabi. By their fraud they are depriving the plaintiffs of their full lawful right to bring an action. That right which they undoubtedly have, be it in Abu Dhabi or be it here, has in effect, if the fraud is successful, been rendered worthless. *e*

For these reasons I agree that this appeal should be allowed.

SIR STANLEY REES. I agree that this appeal should be allowed and I agree with both judgments which have been delivered.

Appeal allowed.   *f*

Solicitors: *Coward Chance* (for the Chartered Bank); *Pothecary & Barratt* (for the wife).

Frances Rustin   Barrister.

---

1   [1977] 3 All ER 831 at 841, [1977] 1 WLR 1041 at 1061
2   7th Edn (1952) p 6

Note
Mareva Compania Naviera SA v
International Bulkcarriers SA
The Mareva

COURT OF APPEAL, CIVIL DIVISION
LORD DENNING MR, ROSKILL AND ORMROD LJJ
23rd JUNE 1975

Injunction – Interlocutory – Danger that defendant may transfer assets out of jurisdiction – Injunction restraining disposition of defendant's assets within jurisdiction – Whether court having jurisdiction to grant injunction in advance of judgment – Supreme Court of Judicature (Consolidation) Act 1925, s 45(1).

Cases referred to in judgments

Beddow v Beddow (1878) 9 Ch D 89, 47 LJ Ch 588, 28(2) Digest (Reissue) 959, 22.
Lister & Co v Stubbs (1890) 45 Ch D 1, [1886-90] All ER Rep 797, 59 LJ Ch 570, 63 LT 75, CA, 1 Digest (Repl) 549, 1715.
Nippon Yusen Kaisha v Karageorgis [1975] 3 All ER 282, [1975] 1 WLR 1093, [1975] 2 Lloyd's Rep 137, CA, Digest (Cont Vol D) 534, 79a.
North London Railway Co v Great Northern Railway Co (1883) 11 QBD 30, 52 LJQB 380, 48 LT 695, CA, 28(2) Digest (Reissue) 959, 24.

Appeal

The plaintiffs, Mareva Compania Naviera SA ('the shipowners'), issued a writ on 25th June 1975 claiming against the defendants, International Bulkcarriers SA ('the charterers'), unpaid hire and damages for repudiation of a charterparty. On an ex parte application Donaldson J granted an injunction until 17.00 hours on 23rd June restraining the charterers from removing or disposing out of the jurisdiction moneys standing to the credit of the charterers' account at a London bank. The shipowners appealed against Donaldson J's refusal to extend the injunction beyond 17.00 hours on 23rd June. The facts are set out in the judgment of Lord Denning MR.

Bernard Rix for the shipowners.
The charterers were not represented.

LORD DENNING MR. This raises a very important point of practice. It follows a recent case, *Nippon Yusen Kaisha v Karageorgis*[1]. The plaintiffs are shipowners who owned the vessel Mareva. They let it to the defendants ('the charterers') on a time charter for a trip out to the Far East and back. The vessel was to be put at the disposal of the charterers at Rotterdam. Hire was payable half monthly in advance and the rate was $US3,850 a day from the time of delivery. The vessel was duly delivered to the charterers on 12th May 1975. The charterers sub-chartered it. They let it on a voyage charter to the President of India. Freight was payable under that voyage charter: 90% was to be paid against the documents and the 10% later.

Under that voyage charter the vessel was loaded at Bordeaux on 29th May 1975 with a cargo of fertiliser consigned to India. The Indian High Commission, in accordance with the obligations under the voyage charter, paid 90% of the freight. But paid it to a bank in London. It was paid out to the Bank of Bilbao in London to the credit of the

1   [1975] 3 All ER 282, [1975] 1 WLR 1093

charterers. The total sum which the Indian High Commission paid into the bank was
£174,000. Out of that the charterers paid to the shipowners, the plaintiffs, the first two *a*
instalments of the half monthly hire. They paid those instalments by credit transferred
to the shipowners. The third was due on 12th June 1975, but the charterers failed to pay
it. They could easily have done it, of course, by making a credit transfer in favour of the
shipowners. But they did not do it. Telexes passed which make it quite plain that the
charterers were unable to pay. They said they were not able to fulfil any part of their
obligations under the charter, and they had no alternative but to stop trading. Their *b*
efforts to obtain further financial support had been fruitless.

Whereupon the shipowners treated the charterers' conduct as a repudiation of the
charter. They issued a writ on 20th June. They claimed the unpaid hire, which comes
to $US30,800, and damages for the repudiation. The total will be very large. They have
served the writ on agents here, and they have applied also for service out of the
jurisdiction. But meanwhile they believe that there is a grave danger that these moneys *c*
in the bank in London will disappear. So they have applied for an injunction to restrain
the disposal of those moneys which are now in the bank. They rely on the recent case of
Nippon Yusen Kaisha v Karageorgis[1]. Donaldson J felt some doubt about that decision
because we were not referred to *Lister & Co v Stubbs*[2]. There are observations in that case
to the effect that the court has no jurisdiction to protect a creditor before he gets
judgment. Cotton LJ said[3]: *d*

> 'I know of no case where, because it was highly probable that if the action were
> brought to a hearing the plaintiff could establish that a debt was due to him from
> the defendant, the defendant has been ordered to give security until that has been
> established by the judgment or decree.'

And Lindley LJ said[4]: '. . . we should be doing what I conceive to be very great mischief *e*
if we were to stretch a sound principle to the extent to which the Appellants ask us to
stretch it . . .'

Donaldson J felt that he was bound by *Lister & Co v Stubbs*[2] and that he had no power
to grant an injunction. But, in deference to the recent case, he did grant an injunction,
but only until 17.00 hours today (23rd June 1975), on the understanding that by that
time this court would be able to reconsider the position. *f*

Now counsel for the charterers has been very helpful. He has drawn our attention not
only to *Lister & Co v Stubbs* but also to s 45 of the Supreme Court of Judicature
(Consolidation) Act 1925, which repeats s 25(8) of the Judicature Act 1873. It says:

> 'A mandamus or an injunction may be granted or a receiver appointed by an
> interlocutory Order of the Court in all cases in which it shall appear to the Court to
> be just or convenient . . .' *g*

In *Beddow v Beddow*[5] Jessel MR gave a very wide interpretation to that section. He said:
'I have unlimited power to grant an injunction in any case where it would be right or just
to do so . . .'

There is only one qualification to be made. The court will not grant an injunction to
protect a person who has no legal or equitable right whatever. That appears from *North* *h*
London Railway Co v Great Northern Railway Co[6]. But, subject to that qualification, the
statute gives a wide general power to the courts. It is well summarised in Halsbury's
Laws of England[7]:

---

1   [1975] 3 All ER 282, [1975] 1 WLR 1093
2   (1890) 45 Ch D 1, [1886–90] All ER Rep 797   *j*
3   45 Ch D 1 at 13, [1886–90] All ER Rep 797 at 799
4   45 Ch D 1 at 15, [1886–90] All ER Rep 797 at 800
5   (1878) 9 Ch D 89 at 93
6   (1883) 11 QBD 30
7   21 Halsbury's Laws (3rd Edn) 348, para 729; see now 24 Halsbury's Laws (4th Edn) para 918

a   '. . . now, therefore, whenever a right, which can be asserted either at law or in equity, does exist, then, whatever the previous practice may have been, the Court is enabled by virtue of this provision, in a proper case, to grant an injunction to protect that right.'

In my opinion that principle applies to a creditor who has a right to be paid the debt owing to him, even before he has established his right by getting judgment for it. If it appears that the debt is due and owing, and there is a danger that the debtor may dispose
b   of his assets so as to defeat it before judgment, the court has jurisdiction in a proper case to grant an interlocutory judgment so as to prevent him disposing of those assets. It seems to me that this is a proper case for the exercise of this jurisdiction. There is money in a bank in London which stands in the name of these charterers. The charterers have control of it. They may at any time dispose of it or remove it out of this country. If they do so, the shipowners may never get their charter hire. The ship is now on the high
c   seas. It has passed Cape Town on its way to India. It will complete the voyage and the cargo will be discharged. And the shipowners may not get their charter hire at all. In face of this danger, I think this court ought to grant an injunction to restrain the charterers from disposing of these moneys now in the bank in London until the trial or judgment in this action. If the charterers have any grievance about it when they hear of it, they can apply to discharge it. But meanwhile the shipowners should be protected.
d   It is only just and right that this court should grant an injunction. I would therefore continue the injunction.

ROSKILL LJ. I agree that this injunction should be extended until judgment in the action or until further order. The application to this court is made ex parte, and is necessitated by the fact that the learned judge, Donaldson J, understandingly in the
e   circumstances, refused to extend the jurisdiction beyond 17.00 hours this afternoon (23rd June 1975). Though the admirable argument to which we have listened puts the case very fairly both for and against continuing the injunction, the fact remains that, we have only heard argument from one side and I do not think it would be right to express any opinion as to what the result would be were this matter hereafter to be argued fully. But, as at present advised, it seems reasonably clear, first, that this court has
f   jurisdiction to continue this injunction, and, secondly, that the difficult question is whether on the present facts this court ought at this stage to continue it until judgment or further order. Donaldson J, in his judgment of which we have a full note, has asked a number of other questions of this court which at present it would be wrong for us to seek to answer. If the charterers were represented, it would no doubt be said on their behalf that the decision of this court in *Lister & Co v Stubbs*[1] precludes this court, not as
g   a matter of jurisdiction but as a matter of practice, from granting this injunction.

Indeed it is right to say that, as far as my own experience in the Commercial Court is concerned, an injunction in this form has in the past from time to time been applied for but has been consistently refused. This court should not, therefore, on an ex parte interlocutory application be too ready to disturb the practice of the past save for good reasons. But on the facts of this case, there are three good reasons for granting this
h   injunction. First, this ship was on time charter from the plaintiffs to the defendants on the New York Produce form, which provided, a little unusually, for a daily rate of hire payable half-monthly in advance and only the first two half-monthly instalments have been paid; secondly, there has been what would seem to be a plain and unexcused default in the payment of the third half-monthly instalment, and indeed a repudiation of the time charter by the charterers; thirdly, that third instalment fell due when the ship was
j   under voyage charter from the time charterers to the President of India as voyage charterers.

On the evidence the charterers have already received £174,000 from the voyage charterers. Yet they have sent a telex to the shipowners in London on 17th June stating

1   (1890) 45 Ch D 1, [1886–90] All ER Rep 797

that their efforts to raise further financial support have been fruitless and that they have no alternative but to stop trading. If therefore this court does not interfere by injunction, it is apparent that the shipowners will suffer a grave injustice which this court has the power to help avoid; the injustice being that the ship will have to continue on her voyage to India and perhaps, as is not unknown in Indian ports, wait a long time there for discharge without remuneration while the charterers will be able to dissipate that £174,000.

In my judgment it would be wrong to tolerate this if it can be avoided. If it is necessary to find a reason for distinguishing this case from *Lister & Co v Stubbs*[1], I would venture to suggest that it is at least arguable that the court should interfere to protect the shipowners' rights which arise under cl 18 of the time charter. The relevant part reads: 'That the Owners shall have a lien upon all cargoes, and all sub-freights for any amounts due under this Charter, including General Average contributions.'

There is or may be a legal or perhaps equitable right which the shipowners may be entitled to have protected by the court. The full extent and nature of that right has long been a controversial matter which may have to be resolved hereafter and I therefore say no more about it.

For those rather narrow reasons I should continue this injunction until judgment or further order. It is open to the charterers to apply to discharge the injunction or to apply for a stay under the arbitration clause at any time if they are so advised. I agree with the order proposed by Lord Denning MR.

ORMROD LJ. I agree. In my judgment the charterers here have a very strong case on the merits. We have not heard any argument from the other side because it is an ex parte application. In these circumstances I would reserve my own views until I have heard argument from the other side if any such argument is put forward. But, in the absence of any such argument, in my view this injunction should be continued.

Appeal allowed. Injunction continued.

Solicitors: *Holman, Fenwick & Willan* (for the shipowners).

Edwina Epstein   Barrister.

---

1 (1890) 45 Ch D 1, [1886–90] All ER Rep 797

R v Folan

a

COURT OF APPEAL, CRIMINAL DIVISION
WALLER LJ, LAWSON AND JUPP JJ
13th FEBRUARY 1979

b *Sentence – Suspended sentence – Fresh offence committed during period of suspension – Court dealing with fresh offence making no order regarding suspended sentence – Whether subsequent court has power to activate suspended sentence for same breach – Powers of Criminal Courts Act 1973, s 23(1)(d).*

Where, during the operational period of a suspended sentence, an offender before a court admits that on an earlier occasion a suspended sentence was passed on him and the court
c takes no action in respect of that suspended sentence, that court in so taking no action has made a decision under s 23(1)(d)[a] of the Powers of Criminal Courts Act 1973 to 'make no order with respect to the suspended sentence', and there is no power in any subsequent court to deal again with the same breach of the suspended sentence (see p 218 *f g*, post).

Notes
d For the power of the court on the conviction of an offender during the operational period of a suspended sentence, see 11 Halsbury's Laws (4th Edn) para 504.
     For the Powers of Criminal Courts Act 1973, s 23, see 43 Halsbury's Statutes (3rd Edn) 317.

Application
Peter Paul Folan applied for leave to appeal against an order made on 2nd July 1978 by
e his Honour Judge Randolph in the Crown Court at Huddersfield activating a suspended sentence of two years' imprisonment imposed on the applicant previously and requiring him to serve six months of the sentence consecutively with a sentence of 12 months' imprisonment imposed by the judge for failure to comply with a community service order. The facts are set out in the judgment of the court.

f *Gordon Lakin* for the applicant.
The Crown was not represented.

JUPP J delivered the following judgment of the court: This is an application for leave to appeal against an order made on 20th July 1978 in the Huddersfield Crown Court. The applicant had been brought there, committed by the magistrates, for failing to
g comply with a community service order made on an earlier occasion. Little need be said about the offence in respect of which the community service order was passed. It had taken place on 12th September 1977. A drinking club had been broken into and the defendant was charged with burglary. He was with another man. Together they took a total of £260 from the cash box and the till. There was something of a scene when policemen with a police dog went into the club to arrest them.
h   The learned judge dealt with the matter under s 16 of the Powers of Criminal Courts Act 1973. He revoked the community service order, and sentenced the applicant to 12 months' imprisonment for that offence.
     It has not been suggested before this court that there is anything wrong with that sentence; nor could it be, considering the applicant's record. He had been before a court no less than nine times as a juvenile for various offences of dishonesty. Following that he
j went to Borstal training for burglary in 1973, and he was sentenced to three months' imprisonment for burglary and wounding in 1974. There were fines for further burglary offences after that, and he was also in trouble for drug offences and a small matter of disorderly conduct before the community service order was made against him.

---

a   Section 23(1), so far as material, is set out at p 218 *c d*, post

The matter for appeal arises out of a further order made on 20th July 1978 at Huddersfield. It was made to appear to the learned judge that on 23rd January 1976, also *a* for burglary and with six other offences taken into consideration, the applicant had been sentenced to 18 months' imprisonment suspended for two years. It followed that the commission of the burglary at the club in September 1977 was committed during the currency of the suspended sentence, some 17 months after it was passed. The judge ordered six months of the suspended sentence to come into effect to be served consecutively to the 12 months he had already passed. The question is whether the *b* learned judge had jurisdiction to deal with the suspended sentence when dealing with the offence in respect of which the community service order had been made. The answer depends on whether or not the court which made the community service order dealt at the same time with the breach of the suspended sentence. It is clear from the 1973 Act that the matter might fall within one of two categories. Under s 23 of the Act the court before whom an offender is convicted of an offence punishable with *c* imprisonment committed during the operation period of a suspended sentence 'shall consider his case and deal with him by one of the following methods . . .' The four methods are set out in paras (*a*) to (*d*). Paragraph (*d*) reads: 'it may make no order with respect to the suspended sentence.' On the other hand it is clear that the 1973 Act does contemplate circumstances, under s 25, where the court just does not deal with a suspended sentence at all. The heading to that section is: 'Procedure where court *d* convicting of further offence does not deal with suspended sentence.' In this case it is unfortunate that counsel for the prosecution informed the learned judge that no action had been taken in respect of the suspended sentence by the court which made the community service order. It is true that later the matter is referred to by saying no order was made and it is also true that in a copy of the antecedents which counsel has shown this court the matter is entered as 'no action re breach'. This must have been misleading *e* for it uses words which are quite unsuited to what in fact happened.

Counsel who appears before us was present in court on the earlier occasion when the community service order was made, and he tells us that on that occasion his client was asked whether he admitted that a suspended sentence had been passed on him earlier. He did so. The court therefore had before it the question of the suspended sentence and was, under s 23, bound to deal with the matter. Accordingly it must follow that, when *f* the court made no order, it was making a decision under s 23(1)(*d*) to make no order, which is one of the methods by which the court may deal with the offender. That being so, undoubtedly there was no power in any subsequent court to deal again with the same breach of suspended sentence. The suspended sentence of course continued and if there was a further breach it may well have been dealt with, but that breach had been considered and dealt with under s 23 of the 1973 Act by the court deciding that no *g* further action should be taken. Accordingly the judge at the Huddersfield Crown Court on 20th July 1978 had no power to order the suspended sentence to come into operation.

In effect this is a point of law and no leave is, in the event, required for the submission that has been made to us. The appeal will be allowed by quashing the sentence of six months' imprisonment consecutive. The sentence of 12 months' imprisonment stands.

h

Appeal allowed.

Solicitors: *Registrar of Criminal Appeals.*

Sepala Munasinghe Esq   Barrister.

a

Re Bourke's Will Trusts
Barclays Bank Trust Co Ltd v Canada
Permanent Trust Co and others

CHANCERY DIVISION

b SLADE J

28th, 29th JUNE, 3rd JULY 1979

Will – Gift – Specific donees – Heirs and surviving issue – Ascertainment of class comprising heirs and surviving issue – 'Heirs' of deceased person – Law of Property Act 1925, s 132.

c The testator had a wife, a brother (John), a half brother (Rowland) and two half sisters (Winifred and Eva). In 1938 he wrote out his own will, in cl 9 of which he bequeathed the residue of his estate to his trustees on trust to pay half the income to his wife and half to his brother John for life, the survivor to receive the whole of the income. If there was no issue of the marriage, the capital was to be divided equally between Rowland, Winifred and Eva 'or their heirs & surviving issue on the death of my wife & Brother'.

d There was no issue of the marriage and the testator died in 1943 survived by his wife, John, Rowland, Winifred and Eva. John died in 1953 and Rowland died in 1958 without issue. Rowland's wife survived him and was his sole beneficiary. Eva died in 1969 leaving three children, 13 grandchildren and two great grandchildren. Rowland's widow died on 27th January 1971 and the testator's wife died on 18th April 1971. Winifred and Eva's children, grandchildren and great grandchildren were then still living. The testator's trustee applied by summons for the determination of the questions

e (1) whether Rowland's share of the residue was to be held on trust (a) for Rowland's personal representatives as part of Rowland's estate or (b) for Winifred or (c) for some other person or persons and, if so, in what shares and proportions, and (2) whether Eva's share of the residue was to be held on trust (a) for Eva's personal representatives as part of her estate or (b) for her three children and, if so, whether as joint tenants or as tenants

f in common in equal shares or (c) for all of Eva's children and remoter issue living at the date of her death and, if so, whether as joint tenants or as tenants in common in equal shares or (d) for some other person or persons and, if so, in what shares and proportions.

Held – (i) On the true construction of the will, on the death of the testator's wife and brother the residue was to be divided equally between Rowland, Winifred and Eva, and

g if any of them was not alive at that time, then, because the gift over was substitutional in nature, his or her share was to be divided among his or her respective heirs and surviving issue. Furthermore the gift over was a gift to two separate categories of beneficiary, namely (a) heirs and (b) surviving issue, and was not a gift to a composite class of those who were both heirs and surviving issue (see p 223 *j* to p 224 *c*, p 226 *h* and p 227 *a b*, post); *Re Kilvert (deceased)* [1957] 2 All ER 196 distinguished.

h (ii) The word 'heirs' in the phrase 'heirs & surviving issue' meant heirs in the strict pre-1926 sense and, since the limitation of real and personal property of the testator in favour of the heir of the deceased person (ie Rowland, Winifred and Eva as the case might be) would, if it had been limited in respect of freehold land immediately before 1st January 1926, have conferred on the heir an estate in land by purchase, it followed that the substitutional gift operated, by virtue of s 132[a] of the Law of Property Act 1925, to confer

j a corresponding equitable interest in the property on the person or persons who, if the general law immediately before 1st January 1926 had remained unaffected, would have answered the description of heir of the deceased in respect of his freehold land either at the date of death of the deceased or at the time named in the limitation as the case might

---

a Section 132, so far as material, is set out at p 227 *c d*, post

be. Furthermore the words 'surviving issue' meant surviving children and not surviving issue of all degrees, while the word 'surviving' meant surviving the praepositus. The *a* category of heirs and the category of surviving issue had each to be ascertained at the same date, and therefore the date for ascertaining the category of heirs and of surviving issue was the date of death of the relevant praepositus and not the date of ultimate distribution (ie the date of death of the last surviving tenant for life, viz the testator's wife); and since there was nothing in the will to indicate severance the heirs and surviving issue of each praepositus took as joint tenants and not as tenants in common *b* (see p 224 *c* to *h*, p 225 *d*, p 228 *c d*, p 229 *g* and p 230 *c* to *e*, post); *Re Noad (deceased)* [1951] 1 All ER 467 applied; *Re Kilvert (deceased)* [1957] 2 All ER 196 distinguished.

(iii) It followed that on the death of Rowland without issue, Winifred and Eva became his 'heirs' in the strict sense and were absolutely entitled in reversion as beneficial joint tenants to the share of the testator's residuary estate bequeathed to Rowland, subject only to the life interest therein of the testator's wife. Prima facie, therefore, Winifred, as the *c* survivor of herself and Eva, would have become entitled to Rowland's share on the death of the testator's wife, but as it was possible that Eva might have severed the joint tenancy before she died, her personal representatives would be given liberty to apply within six months for an enquiry whether there had been any such severance, and if no such application were made within six months the testator's trustee was to be at liberty to distribute Rowland's share of the residuary estate on the footing that there had been no *d* severance (see p 227 *e* and p 230 *e* to p 231 *b*, post); *Re Osoba (deceased)* [1979] 2 All ER 393 considered.

(iv) It also followed that on the death of Eva her three children became absolutely entitled in reversion as beneficial joint tenants to the share of the testator's residuary estate bequeathed to her, subject only to the life interest of the testator's wife (see p 231 *b c*, post). *e*

Notes

For a gift to a person 'or his heirs', for survivorship and for ascertainment of class of beneficiaries, see 39 Halsbury's Laws (3rd Edn) 1065, 1044–1048, 1053, paras 1591, 1566–1570, 1577, and for cases on the subjects, see 49 Digest (Repl) 781–782, 1124– *f* 1143, 708–709, 7331–7350, 10427–10600, 6644–6554, respectively.

For the Law of Property Act 1925, s 132, see 27 Halsbury's Statutes (3rd Edn) 544.

Cases referred to in judgment

Gansloser's Will Trusts, Re, Chartered Bank of India, Australia and China v Chillingworth [1951] 2 All ER 936, [1952] Ch 30, CA, 49 Digest (Repl) 797, 7492.

Jones' Estate, Re, Hume v Lloyd (1878) 47 LJ Ch 775, 26 WR 828, 49 Digest (Repl) 709, *g* 6653.

Keay v Boulton (1883) 25 Ch D 212, 54 LJ Ch 48, 49 LT 631, 49 Digest (Repl) 778, 7303.

Kilvert (deceased), Re, Midland Bank Executor and Trustee Co Ltd v Kilvert [1957] 2 All ER 196, [1957] Ch 388, [1957] 2 WLR 854, 49 Digest (Repl) 822, 7772.

Noad (deceased), Re, Noad v Noad [1951] 1 All ER 467, [1951] Ch 553, 49 Digest (Repl) 770, 7226. *h*

Osoba (deceased), Re, Osoba v Osoba [1979] 2 All ER 393, [1979] 1 WLR 247, CA.

Reed v Braithwaite (1871) LR 11 Eq 514, 40 LJ Ch 355, 24 LT 351, 49 Digest (Repl) 1092, 10162.

Smith v Butcher (1878) 10 Ch D 113, 48 LJ Ch 136, 49 Digest (Repl) 778, 7294.

Whitehead, Re, Whitehead v Hemsley [1920] 1 Ch 298, 89 LJ Ch 155, 122 LT 767, 49 Digest (Repl) 782, 7342. *j*

Wingfield v Wingfield (1878) 9 Ch D 658, 47 LJ Ch 768, 39 LT 227, 49 Digest (Repl) 708, 6649.

Cases also cited

Brown v Gould [1971] 2 All ER 1505, [1972] Ch 53.

Browne v Moody [1936] 2 All ER 1695, [1936] AC 635, PC.

a *Manly's Will Trusts, Re* [1969] 3 All ER 1011, [1969] 1 WLR 1818.

Powell v Boggis (1866) 35 Beav 535, 55 ER 1004.

Ralph v Carrick (1879) 11 Ch D 873, [1874–80] All ER Rep 1054, CA.

Sibley's Trusts, Re (1877) 5 Ch D 494, [1874–80] All ER Rep 250.

Adjourned summons

b The plaintiffs, Barclays Bank Trust Co Ltd, as the trustees of the will dated 11th June 1938 of the testator, Isidore McWilliam Bourke deceased, applied by summons to the court for the determination of the following questions and for the following relief: by para 1, whether on the true construction of the will and in the events which had happened (1) the share of the testator's residuary estate bequeathed to his half brother Rowland Richard Bourke was held on trust (a) for the personal representatives of the half c brother as part of his estate or (b) for the testator's half sister Winifred Louis or (c) for some other person or persons and, if so, in what shares and proportions, (2) the share of the testator's residuary estate bequeathed to his half sister Eva Venables was held on trust (a) for her personal representatives as part of her estate or (b) for her three children, Albert John Venables, Mary Frances Vernon Reaney and John Michael Venables, and, if so, whether as joint tenants or as tenants in common in equal shares or (c) for all the children d and remoter issue of Eva Venables living at her death and, if so, whether as joint tenants or as tenants in common in equal shares or (d) for some other person or persons and, if so, in what shares and proportions; by para 2, that for the purpose of the proceedings (1) Canada Permanent Trust Co might be appointed to represent the estates of the half brother and his widow (2) Jocelyn Comyn Reaney might be appointed to represent all the grandchildren and remoter issues of Eva Venables deceased. The defendants were (1) e Canada Permanent Trust Co (as the executor in Canada of Rosalind Thelma Bourke the widow and sole executrix in Canada and beneficiary under the will of the half brother), (2) Winifred Louis, (3) Albert John Venables (4) Mary Frances Vernon Reaney, (5) John Michael Venables, (6) Jocelyn Comyn Reaney. The second defendant died after the issue of the summons. By an order of Master Gowers dated 22nd March 1979 Judith Valentine Winifred Jones was appointed to represent for the purposes of the proceedings the estate f of the second defendant and it was ordered that the proceedings be carried on with her as seventh defendant. The summons was amended to include in para 2 a claim that she might be appointed to represent the estate of the second defendant. The facts are set out in the judgment.

John Monckton for the plaintiffs.
g *Richard Fawls* for the first defendant.
James Munby for the second and seventh defendants.
Christopher Semken for the third, fourth and fifth defendants.
Richard de Lacy for the sixth defendant.

h   *Cur adv vult*

3rd July. **SLADE J** read the following judgment: This originating summons raises certain questions of construction on the will of the late Isidore McWilliam Bourke. The will was dated 11th June 1938. The testator died on 2nd February 1943, domiciled in England, and probate of his will was granted to Barclays Bank Ltd, as the sole surviving j executor named in the will, out of the Principal Probate Registry on 30th October 1943. On 1st October 1970 the plaintiff, Barclays Bank Trust Co Ltd, became sole trustee of the will in the place of Barclays Bank Ltd.

The will was a holograph document made by a testator who described himself therein as having the qualifications 'FRCS. MRCS. DPh.' Though it was apparently a home-made one, it was made by a man who seems to have had considerable knowledge of legal

phraseology. It is a concisely drawn will, and, with the exception of one short phrase,
which has given rise to all the difficulties in the present case, a well drawn one.   *a*

By the will the testator, having appointed as his executors Barclays Bank Ltd and one
Edward Orford Capon, who predeceased him, by cll 1 to 8 gave a number of pecuniary
and specific legacies. Of these clauses I need only read cll 1 and 5:

> '1. To my wife Dorothy Gladys £300 & £500 for each surviving issue of our
> marriage . . .
> '5. To my aforesaid Brother John my A.C.A. Championship Silver Bowl as an   *b*
> heirloom & thence to my ½ brother R. R. Bourke V.C. D.S.O. [and an address is
> given] and thence to Reg Louis & Bert Venables in that order nephews of R. R.
> Bourke V.C. D.S.O.'

The will then proceeded as follows: *c*

> 'I bequeath all my real & the residue of my personal estate & effects unto my
> trustees upon trust to sell call in & convert the same into money (with power in
> their discretion to postpone such sale calling in and conversion) & after paying all
> debts, funeral, and testamentary expenses to stand possessed of the proceeds of sale
> of such investments & of all parts of my estate for the time being unsold (Residuary
> Estate) upon trust as to the income of one half to my wife Dorothy Gladys for life   *d*
> & remaining half to my aforesaid brother John Joseph Fitz Adlem Bourke of Eagle,
> Alaska U.S.A. & on death of either survivor to receive income of whole. Provided
> Always that if there be issue of my marriage with Dorothy Gladys McW Bourke
> such issue shall receive the benefit on her death if previous to my Brother of her
> income & on my brother's death of his income also & aforesaid issue shall on
> reaching the age of 21 succeed to the capital. If no issue or none reach the age of 21   *e*
> the capital shall be divided equally between the aforesaid R. R. Bourke; Winifred
> Louis; & Eva Venables or their heirs & surviving issue on the death of my wife &
> Brother.'

In conclusion the will contained two brief administrative provisions which I need not
read.   *f*

The testator's widow, Dorothy Gladys Bourke, survived him and died on 18th April
1971. His brother, John Joseph Fitz Adlem Bourke, also survived him but died long
before the testator's widow, namely on 14th December 1953. Accordingly, at the date
of her death she was, in accordance with the terms of the will, entitled to receive the
whole income of the testator's residuary estate. There were no children of the testator's
marriage to her. Accordingly, on her death, the residuary estate fell to be disposed of in   *g*
accordance with the last sentence of the residuary gift contained in the will, which I read
again: 'If no issue or none reach the age of 21 the capital shall be divided equally between
the aforesaid R. R. Bourke; Winifred Louis; & Eva Venables or their heirs & surviving
issue on the death of my wife & Brother.'

It is now necessary to explain who these three named persons were. The testator's
father, who had predeceased the testator, had been married twice. The testator and his   *h*
brother John Joseph Fitz Adlem Bourke, one of the life tenants of residue named in the
will, had been the only two children of the first marriage. Of the second marriage of the
testator's father there had been three children, namely the testator's half brother,
Rowland Richard Bourke, and the testator's half sisters, Winifred Louis and Eva Venables.

Rowland Richard Bourke died on 29th August 1958 without having had any issue.
His will dated 19th April 1952 was proved by his widow, Rosalind Thelma Bourke, the   *j*
sole executrix named in it and the sole beneficiary thereunder. She herself died on 27th
January 1971 and her will dated 7th October 1969 was proved by Canada Permanent
Trust Co, the sole executor named in it. Canada Permanent Trust Co is the first
defendant in these proceedings and is there to represent both the estates of Rowland
Richard Bourke and Rosalind Thelma Bourke.

a Winifred Louis was still alive when this originating summons was issued on 31st July 1975 and was joined as second defendant to the proceedings. Since she survived the period of distribution, no questions arise concerning the one-third share of residue bequeathed to her. She died, however, on 27th June 1976. Letters of administration with the will annexed of her estate were granted on 10th March 1978 out of the Supreme Court of British Columbia to Judith Valentine Winifred Jones. Winifred Louis has no personal representative constituted within the jurisdiction of this court. Accordingly, by *b* order of 22nd March 1979 Master Gowers appointed Judith Valentine Winifred Jones to represent for the purpose of these proceedings the estate of Winifred Louis and ordered that proceedings be carried on with her as an added defendant. The originating summons has been amended to add her as the seventh defendant.

Eva Venables died on 31st July 1969, a widow and intestate, having had three children only, all of whom survived her, namely the third defendant, Albert John Venables, the *c* fourth defendant, Mary Frances Vernon Reaney, and the fifth defendant, John Michael Venables. At her death she had 13 grandchildren and two great grandchildren, all of whom survived the testator's widow and are still living. No grant of administration to the estate of Eva Venables has been obtained, but the evidence is that her three children are entitled to any such estate in equal shares. One of the adult grandchildren of Eva Venables is Jocelyn Comyn Reaney, who has been joined as the sixth defendant to these *d* proceedings for the purpose of representing all other grandchildren and remoter issue of Eva Venables.

The two questions asked by para 1 of the amended originating summons are as follows:

e 'Whether upon the true construction of the said will and in the events which have happened (1) the share of his residuary estate bequeathed by the above-named Testator to his half brother Rowland Richard Bourke is held upon trust (a) for the personal representatives of the said Rowland Richard Bourke as part of his estate, or (b) for the Testator's half-sister the Defendant Winifred Louis or (c) for some other person or persons and if so in what shares and proportions (2) the share of his residuary estate bequeathed by the above-named Testator to his half sister Eva *f* Venables is held upon trust (a) for the personal representatives of the said Eva Venables as part of her estate, or (b) for the three children of the said Eva Venables and if so whether as joint tenants or as tenants in common in equal shares, or (c) for all the children and remoter issue of the said Eva Venables living at her death and if so whether as joint tenants or as tenants in common in equal shares or (d) for some other person or persons and if so in what shares and proportions.'

g Paragraph 2(1) of the amended originating summons seeks an order that Canada Permanent Trust Co may be appointed to represent the estates of Rowland Richard Bourke and Rosalind Thelma Bourke. Paragraph 2(2) seeks an order that Jocelyn Comyn Reaney may be appointed to represent all other grandchildren and remoter issue of Eva Venables. Paragraph 2(3) seeks an order that Judith Valentine Winifred Jones may be appointed to represent the estate of Winifred Louis.

h The two problems reflected in para 1 of the originating summons centre round the use by the testator of the phrase 'If no issue or none reach the age of 21 the capital shall be divided equally between the aforesaid R. R. Bourke; Winifred Louis; & Eva Venables or their heirs & surviving issue on the death of my wife & Brother'. More particularly the problems centre round the phrase 'or their heirs & surviving issue'. While this latter phrase gives rise to a number of doubts and uncertainties, four points are in my *j* judgment reasonably clear, and it will be convenient to state them at once, as a starting point.

First, in view of the use of the word of division, 'equally', in this phrase, it is obvious that if all of R R Bourke, Winifred Louis and Eva Venables had been alive at the date of ultimate distribution, there would have been a division of the residuary estate into equal third shares. Correspondingly, there is in my judgment no doubt that the words or their heirs and surviving issue' mean 'or the respective heirs and surviving issue of each of them': compare *Re Kilvert (deceased)*[1] per Roxburgh J.

Secondly, the words 'or their heirs and surviving issue' constitute *substitutional* gifts to the respective 'heirs and surviving issue' (whatever that may mean) of the one-third shares of the residuary estate given to R R Bourke, Winifred Louis and Eva Venables, intended to take effect if he or she is not still alive to take at the relevant time (whatever that may be). That the gift is substitutional in nature is, I think, made clear not only by the use of the introductory word 'or', but also by the nature of the succeeding description of the class that is to take. The relevant principles are to be found set out in Jarman on Wills[2].

Thirdly, the words 'on the death of my wife and brother' in my judgment relate back to the phrase 'shall be divided equally'. As a matter of ordinary grammar, I think that they designate the time of such division. I cannot accept a submission that they fall to be read merely with the phrase 'their heirs and surviving issue' or, alternatively, with the phrase 'surviving issue'; such a construction would seem to me to involve an unnatural distortion of language.

Fourthly, the reference to 'surviving issue' must in my judgment be construed in its context as a reference to surviving children rather than surviving issue of all degrees. I accept counsel's submission to this effect on behalf of the third, fourth and fifth defendants. It is true that, as counsel has pointed out on behalf of the sixth defendant, in the absence of any future assisting context, the court will generally construe the word 'issue', when used in a will, as meaning issue of all degrees. In my judgment, however, there is an overwhelming context here showing that this testator intended the phrase 'surviving issue' to be restricted to his children. He had used the word 'issue' on five previous occasions in this will, and on every single occasion he had in my judgment used it in the sense of 'children'.

By cl 1 he had bequeathed '£500 to each surviving issue of our marriage'. I respectfully agree with what Roxburgh J said in *Re Noad (deceased)*[3] that—

> '"Issue of our marriage" ought to mean to the court, as it undoubtedly would mean to any layman, the children of the person using the words and of the other person to whom he was referring, i.e., of himself and his wife . . .'

In this case Roxburgh J himself followed the decision of Malins V-C in *Reed v Braithwaite*[4] and held that, in a gift by a testator to his named wife for life 'and upon her death to be equally divided between the issue of our marriage', the phrase 'issue of our marriage' meant children. Following the decision in *Re Noad*[5], I therefore think that the word 'issue' in cl 1 of this will means 'children'; and indeed the contrary has not been contended in relation to cl 1. The same interpretation must be given to the word 'issue', when it appears in the phrase 'issue of my marriage', which is contained in the bequest of the testator's residuary estate. The same interpretation too must be given to the phrases 'such issue', 'aforesaid issue' and 'if no issue', which appear in this bequest of residue.

I accept that, where the context furnishes a clear guide to a testator's meaning, the word 'issue' may bear the narrower meaning of 'children' in the earlier part of a will and the wider meaning of 'issue of all degrees' in a later part. Although, in the absence of further guidance, the court will tend to put the same construction on the same word when it occurs twice or more in the same will, this canon of construction will always yield to a contrary context: see Jarman on Wills[6]. Nevertheless in the will now before me

1   [1957] 2 All ER 196 at 198, [1957] Ch 388 at 391
2   8th Edn (1951) vol 2, pp 1304–1305
3   [1951] Ch 553 at 557, cf [1951] 1 All ER 467 at 469
4   (1871) LR 11 Eq 514
5   [1951] 1 All ER 467, [1951] Ch 553
6   8th Edn (1951) vol 3, p 1594

I can see no sufficient contrary context. The very sentence, in which the crucial phrase
a 'their heirs and surviving issue' appears, is introduced by the phrase 'If no issue . . .' As
I have indicated, the word 'issue' in the latter phrase plainly means 'children'. As counsel
has pointed out on behalf of the sixth defendant, the word 'issue' in this phrase clearly
refers back to 'issue of my marriage', while the word 'issue', when appearing for the
second time in this sentence of the will, does not so refer. Nevertheless in my judgment
it is more or less inconceivable that this obviously literate testator would have chosen to
b use the very same word in the very same sentence in two quite different senses.

Counsel for the sixth defendant also pointed out that the testator might have foreseen
that the ultimate distribution of his residuary estate would not take place until a distant
date and that this is one reason for concluding that he might well have intended issue of
his half-brother and half-sisters, more remote than children, to be qualified to participate.
I think, however, that this point is more than outweighed by two others. First, the
c testator plainly did not intend that his own issue more remote than children should
participate in the ultimate distribution of residue. Secondly, he did not direct the
distribution among heirs and issue to be per stirpes. I would regard it as inherently
improbable that he would have contemplated a distribution among heirs and issue of all
degrees per capita, in which parents and children would have competed with one
another.

d These are the main reasons which have led me to the fourth conclusion, which I have
already described as reasonably clear, namely that the reference to 'surviving issue' in the
phrase 'their heirs and surviving issue' must be construed as a reference to 'surviving
children'.

I now approach territory which is a little less easy to traverse. The next problem, I
think, is whether, on the basis of the conclusions already reached, the substitutional gift
e to 'their heirs and surviving issue' should be construed as a gift to the members of a class
comprising one composite category or to the members of a class comprising two
categories. Putting the point another way, should it be construed as a gift both to the
heirs of the relevant person and also to his or her surviving children? Or should it be
construed as a gift to one class only, namely to that class of persons who qualify both as
heirs and surviving children of such person?

f In *Re Kilvert (deceased)*[1], Roxburgh J had to consider a will of which the phraseology
bore strong superficial resemblances to the present case. In that case[2] (I read from the
headnote to the report)—

> 'A testator, by his will, dated June 4, 1948, gave his wife the use of certain chattels
> for her life, and then provided that they should be "returned to my brothers and
> sister or their heirs and successors at her death." He gave his residuary estate "to be
g > equally divided between my brothers E. and W. and my sister S. or their heirs and
> successors. . . ." The testator died in 1954. One brother was alive at the date of the
> summons, one brother had predeceased the testator leaving a wife and son and
> daughter, and the sister had survived the testator and his widow, but was now dead.'

There then followed a summons to determine who was entitled to take under the
h words 'heirs and successors' and in what shares or proportions so the persons entitled
took. Roxburgh J held[3]:

> '(1) that no distinction should be drawn between the gifts of the personalty and
> realty, and that those entitled were the persons entitled to the real and personal
> estate under the law of intestate succession as it had stood since January 1, 1926 . . .
j > (2) that the words "heirs and successors" did not constitute such a reference to the
> Statutes of Distribution as to oust the general rule that members of a class took as
> joint tenants.'

---

1   [1957] 2 All ER 196, [1957] Ch 388
2   [1957] Ch 388 at 388–389
3   [1957] Ch 388 at 389

The property in question in that case consisted partly of real estate and partly of personal estate and there was nothing to convert the real estate into personal estate for the *a* purpose of distribution. Roxburgh J[1] summarised the three lines of argument that had been put before him as follows:

'One is that the person entitled is the person who would have been the heir on an intestacy before January 1, 1926. Another view is that there is no differentiation to be made since 1925 between real and personal estate, and that the persons entitled *b* are those who are entitled to property undisposed of under the existing law in intestate succession. The third view has been that the words "and successors" introduce such a degree of uncertainty as to vitiate not only themselves but their co-partner, the word "heirs," and thus produce an intestacy, on the ground of uncertainty.'

He held[2]:   *c*

'It seems to me most probable that, at the present time, in the case of a gift to a class of persons or their heirs, both realty and personalty would be distributed in accordance with the present law of intestate succession, making no distinction between realty and personalty. That, I think, is most probable, but I must not put it higher, because that is not the position here. I have the words "and successors"; and, in my view, the words "and successors" are words of a much wider and more *d* general application than the words "heirs." There is about them no flavour or savour of realty at all. The word "heirs," of course, historically and in a legal vocabulary has a very strong flavour of realty, though no doubt lay people often use it and have used it in connexion with personalty; but the word "successors" has no such savour. It is no more akin to realty than to personalty; and the phrase is "heirs and successors." In my judgment, that does not mean the same as "heirs or *e* successors," which might have suggested a different construction. I think that where one has the presence of the word "successors" as well as the word "heirs"— and that is what I have to decide—the court will construe those words as referring to the persons entitled to the real and personal estate under the law of intestate succession applicable at the date when the testator died.'
f

In *Re Kilvert*[3] it seems to have been the implicit assumption of the court and all counsel that, if the gift to 'their heirs and successors' took effect at all, it took effect in favour of a class comprising one category only, namely those persons who qualified as 'heirs and successors' of the relevant deceased person. The contrary does not appear to have been argued. That, however, was a case where the phrase in question was such as to be readily capable of interpretation as referring to a class comprising one category, namely the *g* persons entitled to the real and personal estate of the relevant deceased person under the law of intestate succession applicable at the date when the testator died. This was the construction which Roxburgh J ultimately attributed to the phrase.

In contrast, in the present case, the relevant phrase 'their heirs and surviving issue' is not in my judgment capable of interpretation as referring to a class comprising one single category. In my judgment there is no such single category to which the words are *h* apt to refer. For this reason, among others, counsel on behalf of the first defendant submitted that the whole of the substitutional gift over is void for uncertainty. Accordingly, he submitted that, in the events which have happened, the share of the residue bequeathed to Rowland Richard Bourke is held on trust for the estate of Rowland, which has a vested interest in his share that cannot now be divested. The very fact, however, that a reference to 'heirs and surviving issue', as a class comprising one single *j* category, would have produced potential uncertainty so obvious to any intelligent

1   [1957] Ch 388 at 392, cf [1957] 2 All ER 196 at 198
2   [1957] Ch 388 at 393–394, cf [1957] 2 All ER 196 at 199
3   [1957] 2 All ER 196, [1957] Ch 388

a testator is in my judgment a good reason for concluding that he regarded the gift to 'their heirs and surviving issue' as a gift to the members of a class comprising two separate categories, namely, first, 'heirs' and, secondly, 'surviving issue'. In my judgment this is a perfectly reasonable meaning to attribute to the words and is the proper construction of the phrase.

As any informed layman such as this testator would have realised, the word 'heirs' in any legal document would ordinarily fall to be construed in a very different sense from
b the word 'issue'. Thus in my judgment this testator must be deemed to have intended, by the substitutional gift in question, to benefit two separate, albeit perhaps overlapping categories, namely 'heirs' and 'issue'.

In the light of my conclusions so far, I now turn to consider the meaning of the word 'heirs' in the context of this will. Section 132(1) of the Law of Property Act 1925 provides as follows:

c
> 'A limitation of real or personal property in favour of the heir, either general or special, of a deceased person which, if limited in respect of freehold land before the commencement of this Act, would have conferred on the heir an estate in the land by purchase, shall operate to confer a corresponding equitable interest in the property on the person who would, if the general law in force immediately before
d > such commencement had remained unaffected, have answered the description of the heir, either general or special, of the deceased in respect of his freehold land, either at the death of the deceased or at the time named in the limitation, as the case may require.'

In the relevant clause of this will, one finds a limitation of the real and the personal property of the testator 'in favour of the heir of a deceased person', namely R R Bourke,
e Winifred Louis and Eva Venables, as the case may be. Applying the wording of s 132 therefore, the question then arises: if such limitation had been limited in respect of *freehold land* before 1st January 1926 (this being the hypothesis which the section poses), would it have conferred on the heir an estate in the land by purchase? The general rule appertaining before 1926 was as stated in Jarman on Wills[1] as follows:

f
> 'Like all other legal terms, the word *heir*, when unexplained and uncontrolled by the context, must be interpreted according to its strict and technical import; in which sense it obviously designates the person or persons appointed by law to succeed to the real estate in question in case of intestacy . . . And in the circumstance that the expression is *heir* (in the singular) and that the heirship resides in, and is divided among, several individuals as co-heirs or co-heiresses, would create no difficulty in the application of this rule of construction; the word "heir" being in
g > such cases used in a collective sense, as comprehending any number of persons who may happen to answer the description; and which persons, if more than one, would, if there were no words to sever the tenancy, be entitled as joint tenants.'

Before 1926, in the absence of the contrary context, the word 'heir' was taken to be used in its strict sense, even where the entire subject of the bequest was personal
h property: see Jarman on Wills[2]. I have, however, been referred to a number of pre-1926 cases where, on the provisions of particular wills, it was held that this strict interpretation of the word 'heir' yielded to a contrary context in regard to personal estate: see *Wingfield v Wingfield*[3], *Keay v Boulton*[4], *Re Whitehead*[5], though compare *Smith v Butcher*[6]. In my

---

j 1 8th Edn (1951) vol 3, p 1544
2 Ibid p 1565
3 (1878) 9 Ch D 658
4 (1883) 25 Ch D 212
5 [1920] 1 Ch D 298
6 (1878) 10 Ch D 113

judgment, however, these cases are of little or no assistance in the present context since they related to mixed gifts of realty and personalty, or personalty alone.   *a*

For the purpose of testing the applicability of s 132 of the Law of Property Act 1925 to the substitutional gift contained in this testator's will, I have first to assume that it was a gift limited solely in respect of freehold land, taking effect before 1st January 1926. On this hypothetical assumption, I can see no sufficient context that would have entitled the court to give the word 'heirs' anything other than its strict and technical import, as referred to in Jarman[1].   *b*

The testator having provided for conversion of all his real estate into personalty could easily have used the phrase 'next of kin', but deliberately chose to use the technical word 'heirs'. Further, the provisions of cl 5 of his will give some indication, albeit slight, that he was well familiar with the concept of heirship, usually connected with realty, being made applicable in the context of personalty.

On the hypothetical assumption mentioned above, the gift in this will would have   *c* conferred on the heir an estate in land by purchase. It follows in my judgment that, by virtue of s 132 of the Law of Property Act 1925, the substitutional gift operates to confer a corresponding equitable interest in the property on the person or persons who, if the general law immediately before 1st January 1926 had remained unaffected, would have answered the description of the heir of the deceased in respect of his freehold land 'either at the death of the deceased or at the time named in the limitation as the case may   *d* require'.

I will consider the relevant date in one moment. Beyond attempting to ascertain them from the language which he has used, I do not attempt to guess at the testator's true intentions in this context or in any other passage of his will. I see no sufficient reason, however, why the use by him of the word 'heirs' should not have operated as an effectual invocation of s 132 of the Law of Property Act 1925.   *e*

For the sake of clarity, however, I should perhaps add this. In *Re Kilvert*[2] Roxburgh J referred to *Re Whitehead*[3], the effect of which decision he summarised as follows[4]:

'Sargant, J., held that where, as in that case, the words "or their heirs" were referable to a mixed fund, they were words of substitution and not words of limitation, both in regard to realty and in regard to personalty, and accordingly that personalty went to the statutory next of kin and (as far as I can make out) that realty   *f* went to the heir at law, though that is not, I think, expressly stated.'

Roxburgh J then proceeded to make the following observations[5]:

'That would, at any rate, be the position as it was in 1920; but what I have to consider is first of all whether that would be true now and, secondly, even if it would be true of a gift to a class or their heirs, it would be equally true of a gift to   *g* a class or their heirs and successors. Of course, the important thing that has happened since 1920 is the assimilation of the devolution of real and personal property on an intestacy. No doubt there are certain saving provisions, but I do not think that they have any application to the present case. It seems to me most probable that, at the present time, in the case of a gift to a class of persons or their heirs, both realty and personalty would be distributed in accordance with the   *h* present law of intestate succession, making no distinction between realty and personalty. That, I think, is most probable, but I must not put it higher, because that is not the position here.'

The important penultimate sentence of this passage, which I have already read, clearly

     j

1 8th Edn (1951) vol 3, p 1544
2 [1957] 2 All ER 196, [1957] Ch 388
3 [1920] 1 Ch 298
4 [1957] 2 All ER 196 at 199, [1957] Ch 388 at 393
5 [1957] Ch 388 at 393–394, cf [1957] 2 All ER 196 at 199

represented an obiter observation. With great respect to Roxburgh J, I think it should be
a approached with considerable caution, since it appears to me to attach inadequate weight
to the possible relevance of s 132 of the Law of Property Act 1925, to which he did not
refer in his judgment, though it was referred to in argument. I do not suggest that the
actual decision in *Re Kilvert*[1] was incorrect, since it might well have been supported on
the footing that a substitutional gift of property in favour of the 'heirs and successors' of
a named praepositus, even if limited in respect of freehold land before 1926, would not
b have conferred on the heir an estate in the land by purchase, and that therefore s 132 had
no application. This presumably was in fact Roxburgh J's implicit reasoning. I seek,
however, to make it plain that I do not regard the present case as being on all fours with
Re Kilvert[1].

Having concluded, as I have concluded, that in the relevant phrase the word 'heirs'
means heirs in the strict pre-1926 sense and that the word 'issue' means children, I now
c have to consider at what time the relevant classes should be ascertained. The general
prima facie rule is that—

'. . . inasmuch as the proper time for the operation of the Statutes of Distribution
in relation to the estate of any person is the death of that person, therefore, *prima
facie*, the reference to next of kin according to the statutes involves by implication
the ascertainment of those persons at the proper time, namely, the death of the
d person whose next of kin according to the statutes are referred to'.

(*Re Gansloser's Will Trusts*[2] per Jenkins LJ; see also per Evershed MR[3]). On the particular
facts of that case, the Court of Appeal held that there was something in the terms of the
particular will under consideration which, despite the prima facie rule, showed that it
was not intended that the ascertainment of the next of kin of the relevant person
e according to the statutes should take place at the death of such person. In my judgment,
however, the prima facie rule still applies and must, by parity of reasoning, in the
absence of a contrary context be applicable to a gift to the 'heirs' of a named person: see
Wingfield v Wingfield[4] and *Re Whitehead*[5].

In contrast the general rule as stated in Jarman[6] in relation to substitutional gifts to
issue, is, as counsel pointed out on behalf of the second defendant, as follows:

f
'The question frequently arises where there is a prior life estate, as in the case of
a gift to A for life and after his death to B or his issue; if B dies in the testator's
lifetime, the class is ascertained at the testator's death, while if he survives the
testator and dies in A's lifetime, the class consists of all issue coming into existence
before the death of the tenant for life'

g (see, for example, *Re Jones's Estate*[7]).

I feel no doubt that the category of 'heirs' and the category of 'surviving issue' in the
present case must each fall to be ascertained at the same date; for this purpose no
differentiation can be made between the two categories. The choice is thus between (a)
the death of the relevant praepositus and (b) the date of ultimate distribution, being the
date of death of the last surviving tenant for life, 18th April 1971.
h   An attempt was made to bolster up the argument in favour of construction (b) by
inviting me to read the words 'on the death of my wife and brother' along with the

---

j
1 [1957] 2 All ER 196, [1957] Ch 388
2 [1951] 2 All ER 936 at 945, [1952] Ch 30 at 44
3 [1951] 2 All ER 936 at 940, [1952] Ch 30 at 37
4 (1878) 9 Ch D 658 at 666
5 [1920] 1 Ch 298 at 304
6 8th Edn (1951) vol 2, p 1304
7 (1878) 47 LJ Ch 775

phrase 'or their heirs and surviving issue'; but I have already indicated that I reject this point. The phrase 'on the death of my wife and brother' in my judgment falls to be read *a* with the phrase 'shall be divided equally', and accordingly affords no direct assistance to the argument in favour of construction (b).

In deciding which of the two constructions is correct, the most important point, it seems to me, is that construction (b) would or could involve the treatment of a person for the purpose of this will as being the heir of a praepositus, when he was in no sense his true heir. If, for example, one of R R Bourke, Winifred Louis or Eva Venables were to *b* die during the lifetime of the survivor of the testator's widow and his brother John, leaving X as his or her heir in the strict sense, X might predecease such survivor, in which case, for the purpose of applying construction (b), the heir of the praepositus would have to be ascertained on an entirely artificial hypothesis, namely that the praepositus had died at a date when he or she did not die.

Construction (a) in contrast involves no artificiality of this kind. Furthermore, it gives *c* rise to no difficulties in construing the phrase 'surviving issue', if the word 'surviving' is construed (as I think it readily can and should be construed) as meaning 'surviving the praepositus'. I do not therefore accept the submission that the word 'surviving' necessarily means surviving the date of distribution. Accordingly, I hold that construction (a) above is the correct one and that the date of ascertainment is the death of the relevant praepositus.   *d*

It is in my judgment clear that, under the terms of the will, the members of the class of heirs and surviving issue of each praepositus take as joint tenants rather than as tenants in common. The will contains no express words of severance and nothing which indicates that the testator intended severance: compare *Re Osoba (deceased)*[1] per Goff LJ.

I will now attempt to apply these conclusions as to the interpretation of the wording of the will to the actual facts of this case. As to the share of Rowland Richard Bourke, this *e* half brother of the testator had died on 29th August 1958, before the testator's widow, leaving no issue but leaving his two sisters, Winifred Louis and Eva Venables as his 'heirs' in the strict sense. It follows from my earlier conclusions that on Rowland's death, Winifred Louis and Eva Venables became entitled to a vested interest in the reversion of Rowland's share as joint tenants, expectant only on the death of the testator's widow. Prima facie therefore Winifred Louis, as the survivor of herself and Eva Venables, would *f* have become entitled to Rowland's share on the death of the testator's widow. It is, however, possible that Eva Venables may have severed this joint tenancy before she died. The available evidence gives no indication as to the facts on this point, one way or the other. The situation in this respect is thus substantially the same as that which faced the Court of Appeal in *Re Osoba*[2]. In that case the court ordered an enquiry whether or not there had, since the death of the testator, been any severance of the relevant joint *g* tenancy; this appears from the report[3] and a transcript of the colloquy following the judgments, which I have seen.

I have not been invited in the present case to make an immediate order for a similar enquiry, but have been invited to give the persons interested in the estate of Eva Venables liberty to apply for one. I think that some time limit should be imposed on the period within which this application is to be made, if at all, and that, if the application *h* is to be made, it should be made by Eva Venables's personal representatives, if and when duly constituted.

Subject therefore to the submissions of counsel, I propose to declare, in answer to question (1) in para 1 of the amended originating summons, that on the true construction of the will, on the death of Rowland Richard Bourke and in the events which had happened, Winifred Louis and Eva Venables became absolutely entitled in reversion, as *j* beneficial joint tenants, to the share of his residuary estate bequeathed by the testator to

---

1   [1979] 2 All ER 393 at 406, [1979] 1 WLR 247 at 261
2   [1979] 2 All ER 393, [1979] 1 WLR 247
3   [1979] 2 All ER 393 at 403, [1979] 1 WLR 247 at 259

Rowland, subject only to the life interest therein of Dorothy Gladys Bourke. Subject
a likewise to the submissions of counsel, I propose further to give the personal
representatives of Eva Venables, if and when duly constituted, liberty to apply within six
months of today's date for an enquiry whether or not there has, since the death of the
testator, been any severance of the said joint tenancy. I propose so far as necessary to
reserve the costs of any such application and any subsequent enquiry.

In default of any such application being made within the said six months' period, I
b propose to give the plaintiffs liberty to distribute this share of the residuary estate on the
footing that there has been no such severance.

In answer to question (2) in para 1 of the amended originating summons, I propose to
declare that on the true construction of the will and in the events which had happened,
on the death of Eva Venables the third, fourth and fifth defendants became absolutely
entitled in reversion as beneficial joint tenants to the share of the testator's residuary
c estate bequeathed to Eva Venables, subject only to the life interest therein of Dorothy
Gladys Bourke.

I propose to make the representation orders sought by para 2(1), (2) and (3) of the
amended originating summons. Subject to the submissions of counsel, I propose also to
make a further representation order to the effect that, for the purpose of the proceedings,
the third, fourth and fifth defendants be appointed to represent the estate of Eva
d Venables.

Declarations and order accordingly.

Solicitors: *Sharpe Pritchard & Co,* agents for *Whitehead Monckton & Co,* Maidstone (for all
e parties).

Jacqueline Metcalfe   Barrister.

f

Spillers-French (Holdings) Ltd v Union of Shop, Distributive and Allied Workers

EMPLOYMENT APPEAL TRIBUNAL
g SLYNN J, MR E ALDERTON AND MRS D EWING
28th JUNE 1979

Redundancy – Employer's duty to consult appropriate trade union – Failure to consult union –
Protective award against employer – Jurisdiction – Purpose of award – Factors to be considered
in deciding to make award – Employees continuing in employment with purchasers of business –
h *No hardship or loss of remuneration – Whether jurisdiction to make protective award – Whether*
purpose of award to compensate for lost renumeration or to punish employer for failing to consult
union – Whether payments under contract of employment made by another employer during
protected period discharging defaulting employer's liability under protective award –
Employment Protection Act 1975, ss 101(3)(4), 102(3).

j The employers owned 36 bakeries. On 7th April 1978 they announced that the bakeries
were to close. The closure took effect on 26th April but in the meantime 13 of the
bakeries were sold to other companies as going concerns and most of the employees in
those bakeries were taken on by the new owners without any break in their
employment. Because of the short time between the announcement and the closure the
employers did not consult the employees' union at least 90 days before the proposed

closure, as required by s 99[a] of the Employment Protection Act 1975, but when the union made a complaint to an industrial tribunal asking for a protective award under s 101(3) and (4)[b], the employers denied that those employees had any right to a protective award. The industrial tribunal decided, as a preliminary issue, that it had jurisdiction under s 101 to make a protective award even though the employees had not suffered any loss and the award would, therefore, be punitive in nature, because the object of such an award was both compensatory and penal. The employers appealed, contending (i) that a protective award could only be made to compensate for loss of remuneration, and (ii) that if they were under any liability under a protective award that liability had been discharged under s 102(3)[c] of the Act by the wages paid by the new employers, since those wages were a 'payment made to an employee by an employer under his contract of employment during the [protected] period' which went towards discharging the original employers' liability to pay remuneration during that period.

Held – (i) The purpose of a protective award was to compensate for an employer's failure to consult the appropriate union within the required time in respect of proposed dismissals for redundancy, and not merely to compensate for loss or potential loss of the employees' remuneration. The relevant factors, therefore, in deciding whether to make a protective award were the number of days of consultation lost by the employer's breach of s 99 of the 1975 Act and the seriousness of the breach. Moreover, on the true construction of s 102(3) of that Act, only payments by the defaulting employer could go to reduce that employer's liability under a protective award, and remuneration paid by another employer during the protected period was irrelevant (see p 239 c to e and p 240 a to e, post); dicta of Lord McDonald in *Association of Patternmakers & Allied Craftsmen v Kirvin Ltd* [1978] IRLR at 319 and of Geoffrey Lane LJ in *Clarks of Hove Ltd v Bakers' Union* [1979] 1 All ER at 154 applied.

(ii) Thus, even assuming that the employees transferred to new employment had not suffered any financial loss or hardship, the industrial tribunal still had jurisdiction to enquire into the merits of making a protective award in respect of them. Accordingly, the appeal would be dismissed and the case would be remitted to the tribunal to consider whether such an award should be made and, if so, the period of the award (see p 240 e to g, post).

Notes

For the duty of an employer who proposes to dismiss employees as redundant to consult a trade union and for the jurisdiction of an industrial tribunal to make a protective award, see 16 Halsbury's Laws (4th Edn) paras 654:1–654:2.

For the Employment Protection Act 1975, ss 99, 101, 102, see 45 Halsbury's Statutes (3rd Edn) 2412, 2415, 2416.

Cases referred to in judgment

Association of Patternmakers & Allied Craftsmen v Kirvin Ltd [1978] IRLR 318, EAT.
Barratt Developments (Bradford) Ltd v UCATT [1977] IRLR 403, EAT.
Brassington v Cauldon Wholesale Ltd [1978] ICR 405, EAT.
Clarks of Hove Ltd v Bakers' Union [1979] 1 All ER 152, [1978] 1 WLR 1207, CA.
Clarkson International Tools Ltd v Short [1973] ICR 191, NIRC.

---

a   Section 99, so far as material, provides:
     '(1) An employer proposing to dismiss as redundant an employee of a description in respect of which an independent trade union is recognised by him shall consult representatives of that trade union about the dismissal in accordance with the following provisions of this section . . .
     '(3) The consultation required by this section shall begin at the earliest opportunity, and shall in any event begin—(a) where the employer is proposing to dismiss as redundant 100 or more employees at one establishment within a period of 90 days or less, at least 90 days before the first of those dismissals takes effect . . .'
b   Section 101, so far as material, is set out at p 234 h, post.
c   Section 102(3) is set out at p 235 d, post.

National Union of Teachers v Avon County Council [1978] ICR 626, 76 LGR 403, EAT

a   *TGWU v Gainsborough Distributors (UK) Ltd* [1978] IRLR 460

Talke Fashions Ltd v Amalgamated Society of Textile Workers and Kindred Trades [1978] 2 All
   ER 649, [1978] 1 WLR 558, [1977] ICR 833, EAT.

Union of Construction, Allied Trades and Technicians v H Rooke & Son (Cambridge) Ltd [1978]
   ICR 818, EAT.

Wilson (Joshua) & Brothers Ltd v Union of Shop, Distributive and Allied Workers [1978] 3 All
b   ER 4, [1978] ICR 614, EAT.

Appeal

By an originating application to an industrial tribunal made on 6th July 1978 the Union
of Shop, Distributive and Allied Workers ('the union') claimed that a protective award
should be made against the employers, Spillers-French (Holdings) Ltd ('the company'),
c   who carried on business at a number of bakeries, in respect of all employees who were
members of the union and who were dismissed by the company as redundant. The
company denied that in respect of employees transferred to the employment of the
purchasers of 13 of the bakeries there was any right to a protective award. By a decision
sent to the parties on 16th February 1979 an industrial tribunal sitting in South London
(chairman D J Walker Esq) decided that it had power under s 101(3)(4) of the
d   Employment Protection Act 1975 to make a protective award in circumstances where
there was no loss to any employee who came within s 99(1) of the 1975 Act because they
had been transferred to other employment with the new owners of the bakeries. The
company appealed to the Employment Appeal Tribunal. The facts are set out in the
judgment of the appeal tribunal.

e   *Alexander Irvine QC* and *Mark Cran* for the company.
J Hand for the union.

SLYNN J delivered the following judgment of the appeal tribunal: For the purposes of
this case the facts are largely agreed and can be shortly stated. Spillers-French (Holdings)
Ltd carried on business at some 36 bakeries in Great Britain. On 7th April 1978, without
f   having consulted with the unions representing the workers at the bakeries, they
announced that the 36 bakeries were to close. The closure in effect took place on 26th
April and most of the persons who had previously been employed by the company ceased
to work for them. The company sold 13 of the bakeries to other companies as going
concerns, and apart from a very small number all the employees continued to be
employed by the new owners without any break in their employment. This only gave
g   some 15 days in which the company could discuss with the unions the position that
arose. Some of the employees at bakeries which were closed were not transferred to the
new employers.

As a result the union claimed that the company had not complied with the provisions
of s 99 of the Employment Protection Act 1975. They said that a protective award
should be made in respect of all employees who were members of the union and who
h   were dismissed as redundant.

The union (Union of Shop, Distributive and Allied Workers) made an originating
application to an industrial tribunal on 6th July 1978. The company, as we understand
it, consented to a protective award for a period of 90 days in respect of employees of
agreed description in the bakeries which had been closed. However, they denied that
there was any right to a protective award in respect of the employees at the bakeries
j   which were transferred to the new purchaser.

It was agreed that the industrial tribunal should deal with one matter as a preliminary
issue. That preliminary issue was stated to be whether the tribunal was empowered to
make a protective award which, by reason of the fact that none of the employees of the
transferred bakeries had suffered any loss and there were no concomitant sad features
from their transfer, would be punitive in nature.

The issue which arises before us has been summarised in this form: can an industrial tribunal make a protective award under s 101 of the 1975 Act arising out of a complaint *a* by a union that the employers have not consulted the representatives of the union about the proposed redundancies in a case where the employees have suffered no loss by reason of the lack of consultation?

The industrial tribunal heard the matter and, after analysing the sections and a substantial body of law cited to them, came to the conclusion that a protective award in effect might be made where there was no loss. They found that the object of a protective *b* award was both compensatory and penal. They recognised that it was not necessary in every case to include a penal element in the award. Dealing with the matter solely as one of jurisdiction, as in effect the preliminary issue was, they were satisfied that they could enquire into the matter. However, they made it plain that they were giving no indication of what would happen when the matter came for substantive hearing. They recognised that it was a question of discretion and that they would have to look into the *c* detail and consider whether or not any, and if so what, award should be made. The company has appealed against that decision.

The Employment Protection Act 1975 contains important provisions in Part IV laying down a procedure for handling redundancies. By s 99 it is provided that an employer, proposing to dismiss as redundant an employee of a description in respect of which an independent trade union is recognised by him, shall consult representatives of that trade *d* union about the dismissal in accordance with the provisions of the section. One of those provisions is that the consultation is to begin at the earliest opportunity, and where it is proposed to dismiss more than 100 employees at one establishment within a period of 90 days or less, consultation shall begin at least 90 days before the first of the dismissals takes place. There are other provisions relating to a smaller number of employees where consultation shall take place at least 60 days before the dismissals take place. The *e* employers are required by the Act to produce certain information in writing. One of the matters which have to be disclosed to the trade union representatives is the number and description of employees whom it is proposed to dismiss as redundant. It is necessary to indicate the total number of employees of such description and the proposed method of selecting those employees. By s 100 of the Act, in certain circumstances the employer is required to notify the Secretary of State for Employment of his proposals. A copy of that *f* notice must be handed to a representative of the appropriate trade union. The details of the notice which must be given are not relevant for present purposes.

By s 101 of the Act, an appropriate trade union (which is an independent trade union recognised by the employer in respect of the particular description of employee which is relevant) may present a complaint to an industrial tribunal that an employer has dismissed as redundant, or is proposing to dismiss as redundant, one or more employees, *g* not having complied with any of the requirements of s 99 of the Act. If a tribunal finds that such a complaint is well founded it is required under the Act to make a declaration to that effect (see s 101(3)). It may also make a protective award in accordance with s 101(4). A protective award is defined in sub-s (4) as—

'. . . an award that in respect of such descriptions of employees as may be specified *h* in the award, being employees who have been dismissed, or whom it is proposed to dismiss, as redundant, and in respect of whose dismissal or proposed dismissal the employer has failed to comply with any requirement of section 99 above, the employer shall pay remuneration for a protected period.'

By sub-s (5) a protected period is—

'. . . a period beginning with the date on which the first of the dismissals to which *j* the complaint relates takes effect, or the date of the award, whichever is the earlier, of such length as the tribunal shall determine to be just and equitable in all the circumstances having regard to the seriousness of the employer's default in complying with any requirement of section 99 [of the Act] . . .'

not exceeding, in the case of a proposal to dismiss 100 or more employees within a period
of 90 days, 90 days. In a case where more than ten employees are to be dismissed at one
establishment within a period of 30 days or less, the period is 60 days, and in any other
case it is 28 days.

There are provisions in the Act that entitle the employer to show special circumstances
which rendered it not reasonably practicable for the employer to comply with the
requirements of the section and that he took all steps which were in the circumstances
reasonably practicable to comply with the requirements of s 99.

By s 102, where an industrial tribunal has made a protective award under s 101, every
employee of the description to which the award relates shall be entitled (subject to the
following provisions of the section) to be paid remuneration by his employer for the
protected period specified in the award. The rate of remuneration payable under the
award is to be a week's pay for each week of the protected period or, if a part of a week,
a proportionate reduction.

Section 102(3) is important. It provides as follows:

> 'Any payment made to an employee by an employer under his contract of
> employment, or by way of damages for breach of that contract, in respect of a period
> falling within a protected period, shall go towards discharging the employer's
> liability to pay remuneration under the protective award in respect of that first
> mentioned period, and conversely any payment of remuneration under a protective
> award in respect of any period shall go towards discharging any liability of the
> employer under, or in respect of breach of, the contract of employment in respect
> of that period.'

Subsection (4) provides that if an employee would not have been entitled to be paid by
his employer in respect of the relevant period, either under his contract or by virtue of
the provisions of the Contracts of Employment Act 1972 relating to notice, he shall not
be entitled to remuneration under a protective award in respect of that period.

There are other provisions in the section which disentitle an employee to the amount
of remuneration or an award if, for example, an offer of re-employment is made and is
unreasonably refused.

The provisions of s 103 relate to the ability of an employee himself to go to an
industrial tribunal. By sub-s (1) it is provided that:

> 'An employee may present a complaint to an industrial tribunal on the ground
> that he is an employee of a description to which a protective award relates and that
> his employer has failed, wholly or in part, to pay him remuneration under that
> award.'

In this case counsel for the company has submitted that the object of this section is to
provide compensation for loss of remuneration resulting from failure to consult. He
does not accept that there is any power in a tribunal to make an award at all, if it is shown
that there was no loss of remuneration. He specifically challenges the assumption in one
of the cases that what had been called 'concomitant sad features' justify the making of an
award by way of solatium. Accordingly he would say the fact that there is some form of
hardship or disruption in the life of the employees, when they seek to obtain other work
or find their domestic arrangements disturbed, is wholly irrelevant. His contention is
that this legislation, properly construed, relates only to the payment of compensation for
wages which have been lost and nothing else. In support of that contention he has
referred us to a number of authorities. For example, he has referred to *Clarkson
International Tools Ltd v Short*[1]. That was a case in which the court said that the assessment
of compensation was not to express disapproval of industrial relations policies; it was to

---

1   [1973] ICR 191

compensate for financial loss. It is however right to bear in mind that that was a claim in respect of unfair dismissal; a situation where an industrial tribunal has to decide whether in all the circumstances an employer has behaved reasonably in determining employment. There the court was satisfied that the object of compensation provided by s 161 of the Industrial Relations Act 1971 was limited to the assessment of financial loss; but there one must bear in mind that the section provided that compensation was to be such amount as the tribunal considered just and equitable in all the circumstances having regard to the loss sustained by the aggrieved party as a consequence of the matters to which the complaint related. We do not think that we get direct assistance from the provisions of that particular Act, in the context of the present inquiry where the wording is very different.

Then counsel for the company has referred us to ss 53 to 56 of the 1975 Act. There, where a complaint is made to an industrial tribunal, under s 54, that action has been taken against an employee in relation to union or proposed union activities, the tribunal may assess compensation. The compensation is specifically said to be such amount as is considered just and equitable in all the circumstances having regard to the infringement of the complainant's right under s 53 by his employer's action complained of and to any loss sustained by the complainant which is attributable to the action. Once again there is a specific reference to the loss suffered by the complainant in the case. Therefore, it is perhaps not surprising that in *Brassington v Cauldon Wholesale Ltd*[1] this tribunal should have come to the conclusion that what had to be assessed was the compensation for loss, and that Parliament was not in this section laying down simply a penalty. Again, we do not think that the words of those sections or that case really assist us in the present dispute.

It is quite right, as counsel for the company has said, that even before the 1975 Act, Parliament sought to encourage consultation before redundancies took place, as did the National Industrial Relations Court, in order to avoid dismissals being unfair. But it is equally the case that in this body of legislation there are provisions where sums are to be paid without any assessment of actual loss being made. Thus, for example, in s 70 of the 1975 Act it is provided that an employee is entitled to be given a statement, on the termination of his employment, which contains particulars of the reason for his dismissal. If complaint is made that that has been unreasonably refused, a tribunal may make a declaration as to the reasons and, more important for our purposes, shall make an award that the employer pay to the employee an amount equal to two weeks' pay. Also it is clear that there is, in s 100 of the Act, in the group of sections with which we are concerned, a specific financial penalty provided if a notice is not given to the Secretary of State.

So it seems to us that despite this background of the desire to encourage consultation in order to avoid liability for unfair dismissal, and also despite the fact that in some areas the object of Parliament is clearly seen to be purely one of compensation, we have to look at the particular sections with which we are concerned and decide what precisely they lay down.

It seems to us that here it is important to bear in mind that the obligation which is imposed on an employer is one in respect of descriptions of employees. As we read it, there is no necessary obligation on an employer, when launching the necessary consultation, to identify the particular employees concerned. He may be able to do so; he may not. Indeed the object of this legislation quite clearly is to give an opportunity for consultation between the employer, trade unions and the Secretary of State. The consultation may result in new ideas being ventilated which avoid the redundancy situation altogether. Equally it may lead to a lesser number of persons being made redundant than was originally thought necessary. Or it may be that alternative work can be found during the period of consultation. So one has to bear in mind that at this first stage the duty is to give the 'numbers and descriptions' of employees concerned. When

---

1   [1978] ICR 405

the award is made, it is an award in respect of descriptions of employees who are specified
a in the award, being employees who have been dismissed or whom it is proposed to
dismiss as redundant. There it may be that the terms of the award can be general. When
a particular individual seeks to bring a claim, if the remuneration has not been paid to
him, he is not required under s 103 of the Act to show that he was a person named in the
protective award. What he has to show is that he is an employee of a description to
which the protective award relates. Those matters, it seems to us, are of relevance when
b one comes to consider the kinds of matter with which the protective award is concerned.
Section 101(5) does not provide that the protected period is to be in respect of the date
when each particular employee is dismissed; it is to be when the first of the dismissals to
which the complaint relates take effect, or, in a case where it is still proposed to dismiss
employees, the date of the award (whichever is the earlier). So, clearly there is power in
an industrial tribunal to make a protective award which may take effect earlier than the
c date when particular employees are in fact dismissed. When the tribunal comes to
exercise its power, it is required to consider the relevant period. The relevant period is
such period beginning with the appropriate date as the tribunal shall determine to be just
and equitable in all the circumstances having regard to the seriousness of the employer's
default in complying with any requirement of s 99 of the Act. It is striking that that
provision does not refer, as did the definition of compensation under the Industrial
d Relations Act 1971, or the definition in relation to trade union activities in s 56 of the
1975 Act, to the loss suffered by the employee.

So it would seem that basically the question is, how serious was the employer's default
in complying with the requirements of s 99? Obviously there can be defaults of
different gravity. For example, one requirement of the Act is that necessary information
shall be disclosed in writing. It might be that if all the information had been given orally
e to a trade union representative, a tribunal would not take a very serious view of that as
a failure to comply with a requirement. On the other hand, failure to give reasons at all,
or failure to include one of the matters specified in s 99(5), might be more serious. A
failure to consult at all, or consultation only at the last minute, might be taken to be even
more serious.

One of the main questions which arises in this case is whether the words 'just and
f equitable in all the circumstances' require or entitle the tribunal to go further. Counsel
for the company submits that what they are required to do is to look at the effect on the
employee of the particular breach. He says in effect that the real question is: what are the
consequences that flow from the breach, consequences which really only are to be seen
in terms of loss of wages? He says that that is to some extent supported by previous
decisions of this tribunal. He has referred us to a number of those decisions. Most
g important, we think it is agreed by both sides, is *Talke Fashions Ltd v Amalgamated Society
of Textile Workers and Kindred Trades*[1]. There, in giving the decision of the tribunal,
Kilner Brown J considered the meaning and effect of some of these provisions. In that
case the tribunal said that they considered that in the linking of the period of an award
with a period of notice to a trade union for purposes of consultation the primary
consideration is to assess the consequences to the employees. They added[2]:

h   'Plainly the seriousness of the employer's default has also to be considered.
    However, neither should be considered in isolation. Whether or not the employer's
    conduct should be penalised seems to us to beg the question. In other words the
    seriousness of the default ought to be considered in its relationship to the employees
    and not in its relationship to the trade union representative who has not been
    consulted.'

j The majority of the tribunal took the view that the degree of the employer's default was
a factor for increasing the period from short to long. That is some support for counsel's
submission for the company here that it is the consequences to the employees which are

1   [1978] 2 All ER 649, [1978] 1 WLR 558
2   [1978] 2 All ER 649 at 652, [1978] 1 WLR 558 at 561

to be taken into account. It is however to be noticed, as we see it, that in that case the
tribunal was concerned in assessing the consequences by the number of days of *a*
consultation denied to the employees through their union representative. We do not see
that in that case this tribunal was concerned with the extent to which, if any, the
employees had obtained alternative remuneration. We do not see that that case is really
decisive of the issue which we have to consider.

Another case which has involved this group of sections is *National Union of Teachers v
Avon County Council*[1]. That was a case in which Phillips J, in dealing with the *Talke* *b*
Fashions case[2], referred to it without disapproval so far as this particular point is
concerned; but it adds nothing for the present decision as it is really concerned with the
question of the relevant period.

There are a number of other authorities to which counsel for the company has referred
us, which he says go to support his contention that this is really compensatory *Joshua
Wilson & Brothers Ltd v Union of Shop, Distributive and Allied Workers*[3]. In that case Kilner *c*
Brown J, giving the decision of the tribunal, again stressed that though consideration had
to be given to the employer's default, the concept of the protective award was not
punitive but was basically compensatory. So there is a case where clearly the tribunal
was once again saying that it was compensatory.

In *Barratt Developments (Bradford) Ltd v UCATT*[4] the point arose once again. This
tribunal said that the industrial tribunal had approached the matter correctly when it *d*
had considered that the problem was one of compensation. There it is to be observed
that what the tribunal said was this[5]:

'What the protective award ought to be is the amount of money, either by way
of wages or in lieu of notice, that the employee would have got if the proper
consultation procedures required by the Act had been applied.'
  e

They began with the maximum period, knocked off several days when they had time to
consult, and they also took off some days in respect of which holiday money had been
paid. That method has been attacked by counsel for the union in its detail; but clearly
the general approach there was to look at the number of days when consultation ought
to have but had not taken place. The tribunal was not there investigating, as we see it,
the question whether there had been any financial loss or whether it had been made up *f*
by earnings from other sources.

On the other side of the coin there are cases which indicate that the object of this
legislation is not merely to compensate for loss of money but has a penal or punitive or
deterrent effect. These we can refer to shortly. In *Clarks of Hove Ltd v Bakers' Union*[6] the
Court of Appeal makes reference to this legislation. Geoffrey Lane LJ, in the first
judgment of the court, sets out the statutory provisions and refers to the penalty which *g*
may be imposed if no notice is given to the Secretary of State. He adds[7]:

'So that there are two forms of what may loosely be described as "penalty". If the
employer fails to comply with his duties to notify the union he may find himself
faced with the necessity of paying a protective award; if he fails to comply with his
duty to notify the Secretary of State he may, on summary conviction, be fined up to
a sum of £400.'
  h

Then we should mention *Association of Patternmakers & Allied Craftsmen v Kirvin Ltd*[8].
There, Lord McDonald, giving the decision of this tribunal, set out the legislative
provisions in summary form and, having referred to the need for the tribunal to

---

1   [1978] ICR 626
2   [1978] 2 All ER 649, [1978] 1 WLR 558   *j*
3   [1978] 3 All ER 4
4   [1977] IRLR 403
5   [1977] IRLR 403 at 404
6   [1979] 1 All ER 152, [1978] 1 WLR 1207
7   [1979] 1 All ER 152 at 154, [1978] 1 WLR 1207 at 1209
8   [1978] IRLR 318

determine the period and amount of the award by paying regard to the seriousness of the
a employer's default, added[1]:

> 'This introduces a punitive element into the jurisdiction of an Industrial Tribunal
> and is in contrast with e g, the calculations of a compensatory award which is based
> upon what is just and equitable having regard to the loss sustained.'

Finally we observe, from the authorities cited to us, that in *Union of Construction, Allied*
b *Trades and Technicians v H Rooke & Son (Cambridge) Ltd*[2] this tribunal considered in detail
a submission made on behalf of the employers that they had been misled into the steps
that they had taken. That was one of the factors which it was thought to be proper to
take into account when considering whether a protective award should be made and for
what period.

So it can be said here that there is, particularly in the *Talke Fashions* case[3] and in *TGWU*
c *v Gainsborough Distributors (UK) Ltd*[4] (which followed the *Talke*[3] decision) support for the
view that what is to be done is to compensate.

But that does not seem to us to be the end of the question. The question is: to
compensate for what? It seems to us that it is to compensate for the failure to consult.
It seems to us that here Parliament is providing that employers should, in this kind of
potential or actual redundancy situation, discuss the matter with the union and the
d Secretary of State in the hope of achieving one or other of the alternative courses to which
we have referred. True it is that the tribunal has power to make a declaration. It seems
to us that there is a duty, in the appropriate case, to make a declaration. In addition it
seems to us that Parliament has given to the industrial tribunals the power, if they so
decide, also to make a protective award which involves the payment of money. It seems
to us that when that decision is taken, the question that has to be looked at is not the loss
e or potential loss of actual remuneration during the relevant period by the particular
employee. It is to consider the loss of days of consultation which have occurred. The
tribunal will have to consider, how serious the breach on the part of the employer was.
It may be that the employer has done everything that he can possibly do to ensure that
his employees are found other employment. If that happens, a tribunal may well take
the view that either there should be no award or, if there is an award, it should be
f nominal. It does not seem to us that the tribunal has to be satisfied, before it can make
an award, that the employees have not been paid during the relevant period. Indeed, if
the application is made before the dismissals take place, these facts may not be known.
It might be quite impossible to know, until the end of the period, what is the position so
far as earnings from the same employer or from other sources are concerned.

Counsel for the company (to whom we are indebted for a very careful and, if we may
g say so, able argument in this case which has put all possible points and authorities before
us) has relied on s 102(3) of the 1975 Act. That is clearly an important section in
considering what is the entitlement of an employee. It does not go so much to the
making of the award itself as to the entitlement of an employee to an award. It provides
that any payment made to an employee by an employer under his contract of
employment, or by way of damages for breach of contract in respect of a period falling
h within a protected period, shall go towards discharging the employer's liability to pay
remuneration under the protective award in respect of that first-mentioned period.
What is said here by counsel for the company, and said with force, is that the reference
to 'any payment made to an employee by an employer under his contract of employment
during the relevant period' is to any payment made to the employee by any employer
under any contract of employment which exists during the relevant period. So counsel
j for the company would say that if, after dismissal, an employee finds another job and is
paid a wage during the protected period, then that amount is to be taken as discharging

---

1   [1978] IRLR 318 at 319
2   [1978] ICR 818
3   [1978] 2 All ER 649
4   [1978] IRLR 460

the employer's liability to pay remuneration under the protective award. He contends that 'an employer', when first used in the subsection, would otherwise have been 'the employer'. 'An employer' he says in effect must be interpreted as any employer. We do not find it possible to accept that submission. It seems to us that this section is dealing with the position of the employer who has actually failed in his obligations and who has been made liable to pay remuneration under the protective award. In other words, where the words 'the employer' occur the second time, it is really that defaulting employer's liability which is referred to. It seems to us that it is quite clearly only payments which are made under the contract of employment, or by way of damages for breach, by the particular employer who dismisses without consultation, which can go to satisfy that employer's obligation to pay money under the protective award. In the same way it seems to us plain that the second part of the subsection, which is providing for the discharge of a liability under the contract, or in respect of breach of contract, to be discharged pro tanto by any payment made under the protective award, is talking in both places of the same employer. It is payments under the protective award which go only to discharge the obligations of the particular employer who is concerned.

Accordingly it seems to us here that Parliament has declared that the payments by way of wages, or for damages for breach of contract, which are relevant to reduce the amount of the protective award are only those made by the employer in default. Parliament has so provided, but has left out of the statutory provision reference to any other payments by any other employers. It seems to us clear that those other payments are not to be taken into account so as to eliminate the possibility of a protective award being made at all, if it can be shown that during the relevant period there is no loss of wages, or, as was conceded here, any other kind of hardship suffered.

Accordingly it seems to us that (though perhaps for reasons which are not entirely the same as those referred to by the industrial tribunal) the tribunal came to the correct conclusion in deciding on the facts agreed for the purposes of this preliminary issue (but only for that) that assuming that there was no loss, no hardship, they had jurisdiction to go further and deal with the application on its merits. Therefore this case will now go back to the industrial tribunal for them to decide, on the material before them, whether there should be a protective award and, if so, what should be the length of the period which they find to be just and equitable in all the circumstances having regard to the seriousness of the employer's default in complying with the requirements of the section. That, as the cases to which we have referred show quite clearly, will involve a consideration of the length of period, the nature of the default, and the 'just and equitable' provision. It will also involve a consideration of the steps which were taken by the employer to deal with the situation which arose and to obtain other employment for their employees, even though they were in breach of the obligation to consult.

Accordingly, despite the arguments put forward powerfully by counsel for the company, this appeal is dismissed.

Appeal dismissed. Leave to appeal to Court of Appeal.

Solicitors: *Linklaters & Paines* (for the company); *Rowleys & Blewitts*, Manchester (for the union).

Salim H J Merali Esq   Barrister.

Stonegate Securities Ltd v Gregory

COURT OF APPEAL, CIVIL DIVISION

BUCKLEY, GOFF LJJ AND SIR DAVID CAIRNS

4th, 5th OCTOBER 1979

b   *Company – Compulsory winding-up – Petition by creditor – Disputed debt – Demand for payment of £33,000 served on company – Company denying that any part of sum due – Company admitting that creditor a contingent creditor – Whether company entitled as of right to injunction restraining presentation of petition – Whether court may impose condition requiring directors to file declaration of solvency – Companies Act 1948, s 223(a).*

c   On 25th January 1979 the defendant served on the plaintiff company a notice under s 223(a)[a] of the Companies Act 1948 requiring it to pay within 21 days £33,000 which he alleged was due to him from the company. The company denied that it presently owed him £33,000 or any part of that sum, and claimed that he was merely a contingent creditor of the company for £33,000. On 5th February it issued a writ seeking an injunction restraining him from presenting a petition to wind up the company based on the alleged debt of £33,000 and, by notice of motion, sought an injunction to restrain *d*   him from doing so until the trial of the action or further order. On 20th March, at the hearing of the motion, the judge held (i) that it had not been established that any part of the debt of £33,000 was presently due to the defendant from the company, (ii) that in the circumstances the defendant would not be allowed to base a petition on the notice of 25th January and (iii) that the defendant was nonetheless entitled to know whether the company had any assets. He made an order restraining the defendant 'for a period of *e*   three weeks from the 20th March 1979 (if during the said period of three weeks, all the Directors of the Plaintiff Company make a Declaration of Solvency of the Plaintiff Company as at the 21st March 1979) and thereafter until the trial of [the] Action or further Order from presenting . . . any petition under The Companies Act 1948 for the winding up of the [company] in respect of an alleged debt of £33,000·00 referred to in *f*   [the] notice dated 25th January 1979 and purported to be served upon the Plaintiff Company under Section 223(a) of The Companies Act 1948'. The company appealed against the order in so far as it was conditional on the directors filing a declaration of solvency. At the hearing of the appeal the defendant conceded (i) that there was a bona fide dispute whether any part of the £33,000 was presently due and (ii) that, if the order merely restrained him from presenting a petition based on the statutory notice or one based on an averment that £33,000 was presently due to him from the company, the *g*   condition as to the declaration of solvency could not be justified. He submitted however that the order in fact restrained not only the presentation of a petition founded on an immediate debt but also one founded on a contingent debt and that in the circumstances it was open to the judge to append the condition.

h   **Held** – On its true construction the order merely restrained the presentation of a petition founded on the statutory notice, or possibly one founded on an averment that £33,000 was presently due to the defendant, and there was no justification for the imposition of the condition contained in it. Since there was a bona fide dispute whether the money was presently due from the company to the defendant and there was evidence that the defendant was nonetheless threatening to present a petition on the basis that it was so

j

---

     a   Section 223, so far as material, provides: 'A company shall be deemed to be unable to pay its debts— (a) if a creditor . . . to whom the company is indebted in a sum exceeding fifty pounds then due has served on the company . . . a demand under his hand requiring the company to pay the sum so due and the company has for three weeks thereafter neglected to pay the sum or to secure or compound for it to the reasonable satisfaction of the creditor . . .'

due, the company was entitled as of right to an injunction restraining the defendant
from presenting a petition for the winding-up of the company on that basis or any basis *a*
other than being treated for the purposes of the petition as a contingent creditor of the
company for £33,000. The appeal would therefore be allowed and an injunction in
those terms would be substituted for the injunction granted by the judge (see p 245 *g h*,
p 247 *e* to *j*, p 249 *h j* and p 251 *c* to *g*, post).

Per Curiam. Winding-up proceedings are not suitable proceedings in which to
determine a genuine dispute whether the company owes the sum in question. Neither *b*
are such proceedings suitable for determining whether that liability is an immediate
liability or only a prospective or contingent one. It may be that in some cases the point
is so simple and straightforward that the Companies Court may be able to deal with it,
but it is not right to say that, in a case where there is a dispute of that nature, the only
course which the court to which the application is made to restrain presentation of the
petition can follow is to leave it to the Companies Court to resolve all the issues between *c*
the parties (see p 243 *g* to p 244 *a*, p 249 *c* to *e*, p 250 *h* and p 251 *a* to *c* and *g*, post).

Dictum of Ungoed-Thomas J in *Mann v Goldstein* [1968] 2 All ER at 775 approved.

Dictum of Goulding J in *Holt Southey Ltd v Catnic Components Ltd* [1978] 2 All ER at 280
disapproved.

Notes

For injunctions to restrain a winding-up petition generally, see 7 Halsbury's Laws (4th *d*
Edn) para 1004, and for cases on the subject, see 10 Digest (Reissue) 934-935, 5457-5463.

For the Companies Act 1948, s 223, see 5 Halsbury's Statutes (3rd Edn) 292.

Cases referred to in judgment

Bryanston Finance Ltd v de Vries (No 2) [1976] 1 All ER 25, [1976] Ch 63, [1976] 2 WLR
41, CA.   *e*

Holt Southey Ltd v Catnic Components Ltd [1978] 2 All ER 276, [1978] 1 WLR 630.

Imperial Guardian Life Assurance Society, Re (1869) LR 9 Eq 447, 39 LJ Ch 147, 10 Digest
(Reissue) 934, 5455.

Mann v Goldstein [1968] 2 All ER 769, [1968] 1 WLR 1091, 10 Digest (Reissue) 935, 5463.

Cases also cited

Atlantic Star, The [1973] 2 All ER 175, [1974] AC 436, HL; *rvsg* [1972] 3 All ER 705, *f*
[1973] QB 364, CA.

JN2 Ltd, Re [1977] 3 All ER 1104, [1978] 1 WLR 183.

Appeal

The plaintiff company, Stonegate Securities Ltd, appealed against an order of Blackett-
Ord V-C, sitting as a judge of the High Court in Leeds on 20th March 1979, whereby he *g*
granted it an injunction restraining the defendant, Philip Howard Gregory, for a period
of three weeks from 20th March 1979 (if during that period of three weeks all the
directors of the company made a declaration of solvency of the company as at 21st March
1979) and thereafter until the trial of the company's action against the defendant or
further order, from presenting a petition under the Companies Act 1948 for the winding
up of the company in respect of an alleged debt of £33,000 referred to in a notice dated *h*
25th January 1979 and purported to be served on the company under s 223(*a*) of the 1948
Act, and sought in lieu thereof an injunction restraining the defendant until judgment
in the company's action or further order from presenting a petition under the 1948 Act
for the winding up of the company (a) on the basis that a sum of £33,000 was allegedly
due from and/or immediately payable by the company to the defendant or (b) on any
basis other than that the defendant be treated for the purposes of the petition as a *j*
contingent creditor of the company in a sum of £33,000. The facts are set out in the
judgment of Buckley LJ.

W F Stubbs QC and *Leonard Porter* for the company.
Jonathan Parker QC and *J H Allen* for the defendant.

BUCKLEY LJ. This is an appeal from an order of Blackett-Ord V-C, sitting as an
a additional judge of the Chancery Division in Leeds on 20th March 1979, whereby he
granted an injunction in terms which I shall have to explain later, restraining the
defendant from presenting a petition for the winding up of the plaintiff company; he
made his injunction subject to a condition which also I shall have to explain in due
course.

The relevant statutory provisions are contained in ss 222, 223 and 224 of the
b Companies Act 1948. Section 222, as is very familiar, provides that a company may be
wound up by the court if '. . . (*e*) the company is unable to pay its debts'. Section 223
provides that a company shall be deemed to be unable to pay its debts if, among other
things, a creditor to whom the company is indebted in a sum exceeding £50 then due,
and I emphasise those last two words, has served a statutory demand on the company and
the company has failed for three weeks to comply with it. That provision has no
c application to a case in which the creditor is a creditor in respect of a sum which is not
presently due. Section 224 indicates who may present a winding-up petition, and it
provides that an application for the winding up of a company shall be by petition
presented either by the company or by any creditor or contributory of the company.
Then there are provisos, and proviso (*c*) is in the following terms:

> *d*   '. . . the court shall not give a hearing to a winding-up petition presented by a
> contingent or prospective creditor until such security for costs has been given as the
> court thinks reasonable and until a prima facie case for winding up has been
> established to the satisfaction of the court . . .'

In that context, in my opinion, the expression 'contingent creditor' means a creditor in
respect of a debt which will only become due in an event which may or may not occur;
e and a prospective creditor is a creditor in respect of a debt which will certainly become
due in the future, either on some date which has been already determined or on some
date determinable by reference to future events.

Where a creditor petitions for the winding up of a company, the proceedings will take
one of two courses, depending on whether the petitioner is a creditor whose debt is
presently due, or one whose debt is contingent or prospective by reason of the proviso in
f s 224(1), proviso (c). If the creditor petitions in respect of a debt which he claims to be
presently due, and that claim is undisputed, the petition proceeds to hearing and
adjudication in the normal way. But if the company in good faith and on substantial
grounds disputes any liability in respect of the alleged debt, the petition will be dismissed
or, if the matter is brought before a court before the petition is issued, its presentation
will in normal circumstances be restrained. That is because a winding-up petition is not
g a legitimate means of seeking to enforce payment of a debt which is bona fide disputed.
Ungoed-Thomas J put the matter thus in *Mann v Goldstein*[1]:

> 'For my part, I would prefer to rest the jurisdiction directly on the comparatively
> simple propositions that a creditor's petition can only be presented by a creditor,
> that the winding-up jurisdiction is not for the purpose of deciding a disputed debt
> (that is, disputed on substantial and not insubstantial grounds) since, until a creditor
> *h*   is established as a creditor he is not entitled to present the petition and has no locus
> standi in the companies court; and that, therefore, to invoke the winding-up
> jurisdiction when the debt is disputed (that is, on substantial grounds) or after it has
> become clear that it is so disputed is an abuse of the process of the court.'

I gratefully adopt the whole of that statement, although I think it could equally well have
j ended at the reference to want of locus standi. In my opinion a petition founded on a
debt which is disputed in good faith and on substantial grounds is demurrable for the
reason that the petitioner is not a creditor of the company within the meaning of

---

1   [1968] 2 All ER 769 at 775, [1968] 1 WLR 1091 at 1098–1099

s 224(1) at all, and the question whether he is or is not a creditor of the company is not appropriate for adjudication in winding-up proceedings.

The circumstances may, however, be such that the company adopts an intermediate position, denying that the debt is presently due but not denying that it will or may become due in the future, in other words, accepting it as a contingent or prospective debt. The present case is of the last-mentioned kind and the present appeal involves consideration of what is proper in such a case.

On 25th January 1979 the defendant served on the company a notice in the following terms:

'TAKE NOTICE that you are required to pay [the defendant, and an address is given] within 21 days from the date of this Notice the sum of £33,000 . . . which sum is due and owing by you to [the defendant]. This Notice is served in accordance with the provisions of Section 223(a) of the Companies Act 1948.'

That is clearly a notice which affirms that the whole of the sum of £33,000 was presently due and owing from the company to the defendant; indeed, it was only on that basis that such a statutory demand could have been served.

The debt of £33,000 relied on is said to have arisen out of a transaction relating to certain shares in a company called Trinette Ltd, which were sold by the defendant to the company. In February 1972 it appears that the defendant was the holder of 24 shares out of the total issued share capital of 100 shares of Trinette Ltd, and he agreed to sell those 24 shares to the company for £80,000. That agreement was later modified by mutual agreement between the parties so that the sale was restricted to 14 only of the shares and the purchase price was reduced from £80,000 to £67,000. Trinette Ltd was a company engaged in a speculative development of certain land and had the benefit of a contract connected with that project, but no planning permission had at that time been obtained. By the agreement that was entered into in July 1972 modifying the original sale agreement, it was provided that completion of the transfer of the 14 shares which were then to be sold should take place following the grant of outline planning permission in respect of the development; and it was further provided that £35,000, part of the £67,000 purchase price, would be payable on completion and that the balance of the consideration, £32,000, would become payable on the acquisition by Trinette Ltd of the whole of the proposed site or such part of it as would enable Trinette Ltd to proceed with, and complete, the redevelopment in accordance with the outline planning consent.

In 1973 the company paid the defendant £17,500, part of the purchase price payable under the agreement, that is to say half of the £35,000, and in May of that year the 14 shares were transferred to the company. It was then agreed that the balance of £17,500, the other half of the £35,000, should be paid only on obtaining detailed planning consent for the development, so that was a further modification of the sale agreement and, as the learned judge pointed out in his judgment, nobody could foresee whether the £17,500 which was to be paid on detailed planning permission being obtained would become payable before the £32,000, or whether the £32,000 would become payable before the £17,500. There were various payments made to the defendant on account during 1974 and 1975, and in 1976 there was a further agreement between the parties that the purchase price should be reduced by the sum of £5,500. Allowing for that, the learned judge said that there was left outstanding under the sale agreement a sum of £33,000, of which it was suggested that at least £1,000 must be payable forthwith. The company now admits that the defendant is a contingent creditor at any rate in a sum of £33,000, but not that any part of that sum is immediately due. The defendant alleges that at least some part of the £33,000 is immediately due, but Blackett-Ord V-C held that this was not established on the evidence, and the defendant now accepts that there is a bona fide dispute whether any part of the £33,000 is now due, and he further admits that in so far as the debt is contingent, the relevant contingency may never happen. So the situation is such that the defendant cannot petition to wind the company up on the basis that he is a debtor for a sum which is presently due, because that position is disputed in

good faith and on substantial grounds; but he is competent to petition as a contingent
a creditor. As a petitioner in that capacity, however, he would have to comply with the
requirements of s 224(1) proviso (*c*), under which the burden rests on him of establishing
a prima facie case for winding-up the company.

Consequent on the service of the statutory demand, the company issued its writ in the
action in which the present appeal arises on 5th February 1979. On the same day it
served notice of motion for interlocutory relief in the following terms: the notice of
b motion asks for an order—

'restraining the Defendant whether by himself or by his servants or agents or any
of them or otherwise howsoever until the trial of this action or further or other
Order from presenting a Petition for the Winding Up of the Plaintiff Company
based upon an alleged debt of £33,000 referred to in a Notice dated the 25th day of
January 1979 purported to be served upon the Plaintiff Company under Section
c 223(*a*) of the Companies Act 1948,'

and then it asks in the alternative for an injunction restraining advertisement of any such
petition.

Blackett-Ord V-C in effect granted relief in accordance with para 1 of the notice of
motion, but he made such relief conditional; I will read the form of his order. After the
d formal parts it provides as follows:

'THIS COURT DOTH ORDER that the Defendant be restrained for a period of three
weeks from the 20th March 1979 (if during the said period of three weeks, all the
Directors of the Plaintiff Company make a Declaration of Solvency of the Plaintiff
Company as at the 21st March 1979) and thereafter until the trial of this Action or
further Order from presenting whether by himself or by his agents or servants or
e otherwise howsoever any petition under The Companies Act 1948 for the winding
up of [the company] in respect of an alleged debt of £33,000·00 referred to in a
notice dated 25th January 1979 and purported to be served upon the Plaintiff
Company under Section 223(*a*) of The Companies Act 1948.'

Then provision was made for the order to be suspended in the event of any appeal being
made against the order, such appeal being prosecuted with due diligence.
f That order is certainly ineptly drafted in one respect; the words in parenthesis, 'if
during the said period of 3 weeks, all the Directors of the Plaintiff Company make a
Declaration of Solvency of the plaintiff company as at the 21st March 1979', have, I think,
quite clearly got in in the wrong place; they should follow the words 'and thereafter'. It
is also, I think, not crystal clear whether the injunction was one intended to restrain the
presentation of any petition founded on a debt of £33,000, or whether it was only
g intended to restrain the presentation of a petition founded on an allegation that that sum
was presently due to the petitioner. We are however told by counsel that it was made
clear in the court below that the company was not seeking an injunction which would
restrain a petition based on the debt of £33,000 as a contingent debt, and from the terms
of Blackett-Ord V-C's judgment I think it was certainly his intention that the injunction
should restrain, and restrain only, the presentation of a petition founded on the statutory
h demand, or possibly founded on an averment that the £33,000 was presently due to the
plaintiff.

The company appeals, in effect, against so much of the order as makes the injunction
conditional. By its notice of motion the company seeks to have Blackett-Ord V-C's order
discharged in whole, and in lieu thereof an order in the following form, which I read
from the notice of motion, interpolating certain additional words which it seems to me
j are necessary to give it satisfactory form. The notice asks for—

'An Order that (upon the Plaintiff by its Counsel giving the normal cross-
undertaking as to damages) the Defendant be restrained until judgment in this
action or further Order from presenting (whether by himself or by his servants or
agents or otherwise howsoever) any petition [for the winding up of the company]

under the Companies Act, 1948, (a) on the basis that a sum of £33,000 is allegedly due from and/or immediately payable by the Plaintiff to the Defendant; or (b) on any basis other than that the Defendant [must be treated for the purposes of the petition] as a contingent creditor of the Plaintiff in a sum of £33,000.'

There is no cross-appeal. Counsel for the defendant contends that Blackett-Ord V-C was entitled in his discretion to grant the injunction which he did grant in its conditional form.

The legal position appears to me to be this. (1) The defendant could not properly petition as a creditor who had an established or undisputed debt immediately due. (2) The defendant was, and is, entitled to petition as a contingent creditor. (3) When the injunction was granted the company had sound reasons for supposing that the defendant proposed to present a petition based on his statutory demand; that is, on the basis of a debt of £33,000 immediately due. Such a petition would not on its face have fallen within the terms of s 224(1) proviso (c): it would have been a petition on which the defendant could not have proceeded, at any rate without amendment, on account of the fact that immediate liability to pay was bona fide disputed; it would in effect have been demurrable and, unless amended to recognise the debt as being for the purposes of the petition (although not for any other purposes) a contingent one, it would have been bound to be dismissed. (4) In these circumstances in my judgment the company was entitled to an injunction restraining the presentation of a petition which did not restrict the alleged indebtedness in that way, that is to say, which did not proceed on the footing that for the purposes of the petition the petitioner was content to be treated merely as a contingent creditor.

There remains the question whether Blackett-Ord V-C was justified in making the injunction conditional in the way he did. He stated his reasons for doing so as follows:

'I think therefore that the defendant should not be allowed to base a petition on the notice of 25th January 1979 . . . [I pause there to say that from that I think it is reasonably clear that Blackett-Ord V-C did not think that he was restraining the presentation of any petition except one that was based on the statutory notice or, possibly, one which in terms alleged that the £33,000 was presently due and owing to the petitioner] . . . but I also consider that he is entitled to know if the company has any assets. It apparently has not filed an annual return since 1976 . . . [Again I pause to interpolate that that position has now been rectified; an annual return has been filed down to 30th September 1977] . . . and such assets as it is said to have consist, or consisted at that date, of inter-group credits, nothing, if I may say so, that one could really get one's teeth into. I propose, therefore, to grant an injunction in accordance with para 1 of the notice of motion, and the injunction will take effect forthwith, but it will be subject to the company, all the directors of the company joining in making a statutory declaration of the solvency of that company in the form which would be applicable in the case of a members' voluntary winding up except that instead of a reference to the date of the commencement of the winding up the reference should be today's date. It will, of course, schedule the assets and liabilities in the usual way, and that must be supplied to the defendant within 21 days. If it is not, the injunction will cease. If this term is complied with the defendant must pay the costs of the motion, and if not, the plaintiff will pay the costs.'

As counsel for the company has pointed out, the preparation of a declaration of solvency is an onerous business, and may be a very difficult one. It involves, or may involve, making estimates of the value of assets (such, for instance, as contracts and book debts) which may be speculative and very difficult to value. It also involves putting a value on future or contingent liabilities, which also may be very difficult to assess. It is not a declaration as to the commercial solvency of the company, that is to say, as to its ability to pay its debts as they fall due, but of its ability to discharge all its debts, whatever their character, within 12 months. Realisation of the company's assets within that

period might well be an improvident act; directors might well feel difficulty about
a making such a declaration under the sanctions of the Perjury Act 1911, notwithstanding
that the company might be fully commercially solvent. If the only established footing
on which the defendant can petition to wind up the company is as a contingent or
prospective creditor, the burden rests on him to show prima facie that there is a case for
winding up the company. If the ground for seeking a winding-up order is that the
company is unable to pay its debts, and no other ground is suggested here, it would be
b incumbent on the defendant to establish a prima facie case that this was so. The
condition of Blackett-Ord V-C's order seems to me to reverse this burden of proof, for if
the condition is not complied with it would be open to the petitioner to rely on that fact
as some evidence of the company's inability to pay its debts; and moreover, having
regard to the nature of the declaration of solvency which I have mentioned, the condition
imposes on the company, through its directors, a heavier burden of proof than the
c burden of establishing merely that the company is commercially solvent: it imposes the
burden of proof of establishing that the company will ultimately be solvent on the basis
of a prospective liquidation within 12 months. It seems to me that such a condition
cannot be supported in principle.

In the first place, Blackett-Ord V-C was, I think, with deference to him, mistaken in
saying that the defendant, that is the prospective petitioner in the present case, was
d entitled to know if the company had any assets. Of course, a creditor is entitled to have
access to the published public documents of the company; he is entitled to see the annual
returns which are filed in the registry. But he is not entitled to have access to the
company's books and he is not entitled to demand to have any information with regard
to the company's financial position. In any event, for the reasons which I have
adumbrated, it seems to me that this is placing on the company a quite unreasonable
e burden and one which cannot be justified in principle.

Counsel for the defendant concedes that, if on its true construction and effect the
injunction should be treated as restricted to restraining the presentation of a petition
either founded on the statutory declaration or founded on an averment that the £33,000
is presently due to the defendant, he could not justify any effort to uphold the correctness
of the condition; but he has contended that on its true interpretation Blackett-Ord V-C's
f order is appropriate to restrain the presentation of a petition founded on the debt of
£33,000, whether immediately due or contingent, and he says that in those circumstances
it was open to Blackett-Ord V-C in his discretion to append the condition to the
injunction. In my judgment that is not a proposition which can stand up to
investigation. If the injunction, on its true construction, forbids the presentation of a
petition based on the debt of £33,000, whether immediately due or only contingently
g due, then in my judgment it was the wrong injunction to grant and the appeal should
succeed on the ground that the injunction was too wide and not justified by the
circumstances of the case.

If, on the other hand, on its true construction it does no more than restrain the
presentation of a petition founded on an assertion that the £33,000 was immediately
due, or based on a statutory declaration which embraces the same assertion, then there
h is no justification for adding any condition to the injunction, for that is an injunction to
which in my judgment the company was clearly entitled. So it seems to me that for
those reasons this appeal must succeed, on the basis that the conditional character of the
injunction is not one which can be upheld on principle.

The way in which the order is framed does not, in my opinion, express with happy
clarity what I think was the true intention of Blackett-Ord V-C. I would allow the appeal
j and substitute for the injunction as framed in the order an injunction in the terms which
I have read out, taken from the notice of appeal with the minor amendments which I
incorporated in my reading of the notice of appeal.

In the course of the argument we were referred to the decision of Goulding J in *Holt
Southey Ltd v Catnic Components Ltd*[1]; indeed, that was a case which was referred to by

1   [1978] 2 All ER 276, [1978] 1 WLR 630

Blackett-Ord V-C in his judgment under appeal. In that case a statutory demand had been served in respect of an alleged debt of £39,000-odd said to be due from the *a* company, Holt Southey Ltd to the proposed petitioner. That debt appears to have been disputed, though exactly what the full nature of the dispute was does not clearly emerge from the report. As regards £20,000, part of the £39,000, the dispute was whether that part of the debt was immediately payable or whether it was only payable in the future; there seems to have been no dispute about the fact that it was at any rate payable at some time. What the position was with regard to the balance of the £39,000 does not clearly *b* appear, but I think it must have been the case that there was a bona fide dispute with regard to that part of the liability.

Goulding J held that, although the circumstances and the evidence showed that there was a substantial dispute, the presentation of the petition could not be restrained, since the prospective petitioner was at any rate a prospective creditor in respect of the £20,000, and as a prospective creditor the proposed petitioner was qualified to petition to wind up *c* the company. Goulding J considered that in these circumstances he should leave it to the Companies Court to weigh up and decide by its own process the allegations which might be made in the petition, and accordingly he declined to restrain the presentation of the petition.

In the course of his judgment he referred to Ungoed-Thomas J's decision in *Mann v Goldstein*[1], and to the decision of this court in *Bryanston Finance Ltd v de Vries (No 2)*[2] and *d* towards the end of his judgment Goulding J said this[3]:

> 'Then counsel for the plaintiff makes an alternative submission, assuming I get to the point (at which I have in fact arrived) of holding that there is a substantial dispute regarding the debt alleged in the statutory demand, but at the same time thinking that I ought not to ignore the defendant's locus standi as a prospective *e* creditor for a sum admitted in that respect. Counsel for the plaintiff suggests that I ought, nonetheless, to restrain the defendant until further order from presenting a winding-up petition otherwise than as a prospective creditor. He asks me also to restrain the advertisement of a petition presented on that footing until prior notice has been given to the plaintiff. I have hesitated over that application, but it seems to me that I ought not to accede to it. As I have said, I am very loath to extend this *f* type of proceeding. As I have also said more than once, I think the basis of *Mann v Goldstein*[1] is that it is an abuse for a person who is not qualified as a petitioner under the terms of the 1948 Act to present a petition. If he is qualified, it seems to me that the only satisfactory course is to leave the Companies Court itself to weigh up and decide by its own process all the allegations that may be made in the petition. It was said by James V-C in *Re Imperial Guardian Life Assurance Society*[4] quoted in *Mann v* *g* *Goldstein*[5] that "A winding-up petition is not to be used as machinery for trying a common law action", and that of course is the whole basis of the application before me. But that does not mean that the Companies Court may not have to decide on the validity or terms of an alleged liability once the petitioner has established his locus standi to petition before that court.'

h

If when a matter is brought before a court a prospective petitioner has not yet made clear in what form, or on what basis, he proposes to petition, whether as a creditor in respect of a debt presently due or in respect of a contingent or prospective debt, an application to restrain presentation of the petition might well be premature if the only

j

---

1 [1968] 2 All ER 769, [1968] 1 WLR 1091
2 [1976] 1 All ER 25, [1976] Ch 63
3 [1978] 2 All ER 276 at 280, [1978] 1 WLR 630 at 634
4 (1869) LR 9 Eq 447 at 450
5 [1968] 2 All ER 769 at 773, [1968] 1 WLR 1091 at 1097

dispute as to liability was whether it was immediate or prospective. But if the prospective

a petitioner has made it clear that he proposes to petition on the footing of a debt alleged to be presently due, and there is a bona fide dispute on substantial grounds as to its being presently due, it seems to me that on principle, and in accordance with the principles that I have been discussing earlier in this judgment the court ought to restrain the presentation of a petition otherwise than in terms which make it plain that for the purposes of the petition the petitioner is content to be treated as being no more than a

b prospective or contingent creditor. If Goulding J, in the passage which I have read, meant that in the case in which there was such a dispute it would be right to allow the petition to be presented in a way which claimed the debt to be presently due, and sought to obtain winding up on that basis, and if he intended to say that in such circumstances the Companies Court should decide whether or not, on the true view of the facts, the debt was in fact presently due then, with all deference to Goulding J, I think the learned

c judge went too far. The whole of the doctrine of this part of the law is based on the view that winding-up proceedings are not suitable proceedings in which to determine a genuine dispute about whether the company does or does not owe the sum in question; and equally I think it must be true that winding-up proceedings are not suitable proceedings in which to determine whether that liability is an immediate liability or only a prospective or contingent liability. It might be that in some case the point was so

d simple and straightforward that the winding-up court might be able to deal with it, but I feel certain that it cannot be right to say that, in a case where there is a dispute of that nature, the only course which the court to which application is made to restrain presentation of the petition can follow is to leave it to the Companies Court to resolve all the issues between the parties. Accordingly, I do not think that the observations of Goulding J in the paragraph that I have read can be regarded as satisfactory.

e

GOFF LJ. Some confusion has been imported into this case by reason of the fact that the defendant and his advisers took the view that the injunction would restrain the defendant from presenting a petition to the court even on the footing that the defendant conceded, for the purposes of the petition but for such purposes only, that he was no more than he

f is admitted to be, namely a contingent creditor. If that were the true construction of the order, then in my judgment it was plainly too wide and such an injunction ought not to have been granted. Moreover, I cannot see that the vice of ordering too wide an injunction could be cured by making it subject to a condition which, with all respect to Blackett-Ord V-C, was too onerous and also calculated to place the defendant in a better position vis-à-vis the debtor than that in which under s 224(1) proviso (c) of the

g Companies Act 1948 he ought to stand.

However, it is clear that the company never asked for so wide an injunction; all it sought was an injunction to restrain the defendant from presenting a petition on any other basis than as a contingent creditor. Moreover, I think it is clear that Blackett-Ord V-C did not intend to do more than that, and, although I agree that the wording of the order (which is in fact taken from the notice of motion) is not happily phrased, in my

h judgment that is its true construction.

Once one reaches that conclusion, it seems beyond doubt that the injunction ought to stand, but to be discharged as to the condition, and I would agree, as Buckley LJ has proposed, that it should be worded in the form of the notice of appeal, with certain minor amendments which have been indicated.

The defendant, by serving a statutory notice under s 223, threatened and intended to

j present a petition based on the contention that the debt was immediately payable and based on default in compliance with the notice as evidence of inability on the part of the company to pay its debts. It has never effectively resiled from that position, at all events until the appeal came to be heard.

I agree, therefore, that the appeal should be allowed, and that the order should be in the form proposed by Buckley LJ.

I would, however, wish to add some observations on the decision of Goulding J in *Holt Southey Ltd v Catnic Components Ltd*[1]. His Lordship said: 'Thus it seems to me that the point taken by counsel for the defendant is a good one and that at least I ought not to prevent the presentation of a petition based on a prospective debt.' So far I find nothing to quarrel with in that conclusion. But Goulding J then went on to say[1]:

'Then counsel for the plaintiff makes an alternative submission, assuming I get to the point (at which I have in fact arrived) of holding that there is a substantial dispute regarding the debt alleged in the statutory demand, but at the same time thinking that I ought not to ignore the defendant's locus standi as a prospective creditor for a sum admitted in that respect. Counsel for the plaintiff suggests that I ought, nonetheless, to restrain the defendant until further order from presenting a winding-up petition otherwise than as a prospective creditor. He asks me also to restrain the advertisement of a petition presented on that footing until prior notice has been given to the plaintiff. I have hesitated over that application, but it seems to me that I ought not to accede to it. As I have said, I am very loath to extend this type of proceeding. As I have also said more than once, I think the basis of *Mann v Goldstein*[2] is that it is an abuse for a person who is not qualified as a petitioner under the terms of the 1948 Act to present a petition. If he is qualified, it seems to me that the only satisfactory course is to leave the Companies Court itself to weigh up and decide by its own process all the allegations that may be made in the petition. It was said by James V-C in *Re Imperial Guardian Life Assurance Society*[3] quoted in *Mann v Goldstein*[4] that "A winding-up petition is not to be used as machinery for trying a common law action", and that of course is the whole basis of the application before me. But that does not mean that the Companies Court may not have to decide on the validity or terms of an alleged liability once the petitioner has established his locus standi to petition before that court.'

The learned judge there appears to me to be saying that even where the court is satisfied that there is a bona fide dispute whether the debt is presently payable, but it is established or conceded that the would-be petitioner is at least a contingent or prospective creditor, then he should be allowed to present a petition based on his claim that he is a creditor presently entitled, with or without an alternative claim as a contingent or prospective creditor, leaving the Companies Court to resolve the dispute, that is to determine the rights of the parties, not merely the issue whether there is a bona fide dispute.

I say that because, in the opening part of the passage I have cited Goulding J said[1]:

'. . . assuming I get to the point (at which I have in fact arrived) of holding that there is a substantial dispute regarding the debt alleged in the statutory demand, but at the same time thinking that I ought not to ignore the defendant's locus standi as a prospective creditor for a sum admitted in that respect,'

and because he then went on at the end of the passage to say that the quotation from *Mann v Goldstein*[2] did not mean that the Companies Court might not have to decide on the validity or terms of an alleged liability once the petitioner has established his locus standi to petition. So he was proceeding on the basis that he had already satisfied himself that there was a bona fide dispute, and therefore all that could be left to the Companies Court, if anything was to be left to it at all, would be to resolve that dispute. If that be what the learned judge meant, then in my judgment, with all respect to him, that is wrong.

1 [1978] 2 All ER 276 at 280, [1978] 1 WLR 630 at 634
2 [1968] 2 All ER 769, [1968] 1 WLR 1091
3 (1869) LR 9 Eq 447 at 450
4 [1968] 2 All ER 769 at 773, [1968] 1 WLR 1091 at 1097

Once the court is satisfied that there is a bona fide dispute as to the right of an alleged
a creditor to claim as one to whom a debt is presently due then, unless he elects for the
purposes of the petition, to proceed on the basis, if that be not also disputed, that he is
only a contingent or prospective creditor, then he ought to be restrained. If, however,
the learned judge meant no more than that it should be left to the Companies Court to
decide whether or not there was a bona fide dispute, then, with all respect, I find that
rather surprising in view of his own conclusion that there was. It may well be right, if
b the court which is asked to grant an injunction is not satisfied on the question whether
there is a bona fide dispute or whether it is insubstantial or trumped up, to leave the
creditor to present his petition on his own claim, with or without an alternative claim as
a contingent or prospective creditor, and to leave the Companies Court to decide for itself
whether there is a bona fide dispute or not; but, given the premise that there is a bona
fide dispute, it seems to me that the company is entitled as of right to an injunction to
c restrain a petition which it is threatened shall be brought on the basis, in effect, that there
is no such dispute.

Accordingly, I agree with the order proposed.

SIR DAVID CAIRNS. I agree that this appeal should be allowed.

At the time of the hearing before Blackett-Ord V-C it was clear that there was a bona
d fide dispute whether any debt was presently due from the company to the defendant.
The defendant was nevertheless threatening to present a petition on the basis that there
was a debt of £33,000 presently due. The company was therefore entitled, as of right, to
an injunction to restrain the presentation of such a petition.

In my opinion, the language used by Blackett-Ord V-C in his judgment shows that it
was only an injunction to that effect that he intended to grant. If that is so, I do not
e consider that it was open to him to impose any such condition as he did impose on the
grant or continuance of the injunction.

It was contended by counsel for the defendant that the order as drawn up restrained
the defendant from presenting any petition in his capacity as a creditor for £33,000, even
on the basis of its being a contingent debt. I would not so construe the order as drawn
up, although I agree that it would be desirable to amend the language as proposed in his
f notice of appeal with the further slight amendments mentioned by Buckley LJ to make
it clearer.

If, however, the defendant had been enjoined from petitioning even as a contingent
creditor, I consider that such an injunction would not have been one which could, as a
matter of discretion, have been granted conditionally, but one which ought not to have
been granted at all.

g However, for the reasons I have already given, and for those which have been given
more fully by Buckley and Goff LJJ, I agree that the right course for this court to take is
to delete the condition and to make the amendments necessary to make quite plain what
the defendant is restrained from doing.

Appeal allowed. Order accordingly.

h
Solicitors: *Halliwell Landau & Co,* Manchester (for the company); *Willey, Hargrave & Co*
(for the defendant).

J H Fazan Esq Barrister.

Carter v Credit Change Ltd

a

COURT OF APPEAL, CIVIL DIVISION
STEPHENSON, BRIDGE AND CUMMING-BRUCE LJJ
27th, 30th JULY 1979

Industrial tribunal – Procedure – Decision – Postponement of hearing of proceedings – Discretion – Proceedings for unfair dismissal – Industrial tribunal postponing hearing pending outcome of b *High Court proceedings between employer and employee – Principles on which Employment Appeal Tribunal entitled to interfere with exercise of discretion to postpone – Whether unfair dismissal claim required to be heard before High Court proceedings unless special circumstances justifying postponement of claim – Industrial Tribunals (Labour Relations) Regulations 1974 (SI 1974 No 1386), Sch, r 11(2)(b).*

c

The employers employed the employee as their general manager, his main task being to acquire new sites for shops. On 18th December 1978 the employers commenced proceedings in the High Court against the employee in respect of the acquisition of three sites, alleging fraud and forgery against him, and on 20th December they dismissed him from his employment. On 7th January 1979 the employee commenced proceedings before an industrial tribunal for compensation for unfair dismissal. On 16th March the d chairman of the industrial tribunal, in the exercise of his discretion under r 11(2)(b)[a] of the schedule to the Industrial Tribunals (Labour Relations) Regulations 1974, ordered that the unfair dismissal proceedings should be postponed pending the outcome of the High Court proceedings, on the ground, inter alia, that there were complex issues common to both proceedings involving serious allegations by both sides and it was in the interests of justice that those issues should be dealt with first in the High Court where e stricter rules of evidence applied, and that, as the employee was not seeking reinstatement, delay in hearing the unfair dismissal proceedings was acceptable and was in any event outweighed by the need in the interests of justice for an orderly sequence in the two sets of proceedings. An appeal by the employee was allowed by the Employment Appeal Tribunal, which ordered that the unfair dismissal claim should proceed, on the grounds that, in principle, unfair dismissal claims should be dealt with speedily and therefore f where a party to such a claim wished it to be heard an industrial tribunal should proceed to hear it even though High Court proceedings raising similar issues were pending, unless there were special circumstances justifying a postponement of the hearing, and that in the particular case there were no special circumstances justifying postponement. The employers appealed to the Court of Appeal contending that that principle was erroneous. g

Held – Rule 11(2)(b) of the schedule to 1974 regulations conferred a complete discretion on an industrial tribunal to postpone proceedings before it if that was in the best interests of justice. Accordingly the Employment Appeal Tribunal could only interfere with an exercise of that discretion if there had been error of law in the exercise of it by the industrial tribunal's failing to take into account any relevant factor or by its taking into h account an irrelevant factor, or where the decision to postpone was one which no reasonable tribunal could have reached; it was not the appeal tribunal's function to approve the exercise of the discretion. It followed that the principle applied by the appeal tribunal was erroneous and that, as it had not been shown that the industrial tribunal had fallen into any error of law but that, on the contrary, the postponement had been ordered for good reasons, the appeal would be allowed and the postponement order j restored (see p 257 b to h and p 258 a to h, post).
    Dictum of Arnold J in *Bastick v James Lane (Turf Accountants) Ltd* [1979] ICR at 782 applied.

---

a   Rule 11(2), so far as material, is set out at p 254 d, post

Notes

a For the power of an industrial tribunal to postpone or adjourn a hearing, see 16 Halsbury's Laws (4th Edn) para 1019.

Cases referred to in judgments

Bastick v James Lane (Turf Accountants) Ltd [1979] ICR 778, EAT.
Cahm v Ward & Goldstone Ltd (6th April 1979) unreported, EAT.
b Griffiths (James) Ltd v James (15th February 1978) unreported, EAT.
Jacobs v Norsalta Ltd [1977] ICR 189, EAT.

Appeal

By a decision dated 16th March 1979 an industrial tribunal sitting at London (chairman Mr G H Brown) ordered that proceedings in which the applicant, Edward Carter, claimed
c that he was unfairly dismissed by his former employers, Credit Change Ltd ('the employers'), were to be postponed pending the outcome of proceedings in the Queen's Bench Division of the High Court of Justice between the employers and Mr Carter, entitled Credit Change Ltd v Carter and others. Mr Carter appealed to the Employment Appeal Tribunal. On 27th June 1979 the appeal tribunal (Slynn J, Mr E Alderton JP and Mrs D Ewing) allowed the appeal, set aside the decision to postpone the industrial
d tribunal proceedings and ordered that they should proceed. The appeal tribunal refused leave to appeal. On 1st July the Court of Appeal granted the employers leave to appeal from the appeal tribunal's decision. The facts are set out in the judgment of Stephenson LJ.

Peter Cresswell for the employers.
e Mr Carter appeared in person.

STEPHENSON LJ. This is an appeal by the employers, Credit Change Ltd, from a decision of the Employment Appeal Tribunal given by Slynn J on 27th June 1979. By that decision the Employment Appeal Tribunal reversed a decision of the chairman of an industrial tribunal, who had postponed proceedings by Mr Carter, the respondent to this
f appeal, for compensation for unfair dismissal, until after the hearing of High Court proceedings which had been brought against him, as it happens, though this is, in my view, immaterial, just before he brought his claim against his employers for compensation. The Employment Appeal Tribunal refused leave to appeal, but this court granted the employers that leave on 1st July, and we have to consider whether the Employment Appeal Tribunal was justified in reversing an exercise of discretion to
g postpone by the chairman of the industrial tribunal.

Not much, I think, need be said about the facts. The employers operate bureaux de change and in August 1976 they employed Mr Carter as their general manager. His main task was to acquire for them new sites for their bureaux. He procured altogether three sites and they believed that he was procuring them by arm's length transactions from a company called Luxane Ltd. It is their case that Luxane Ltd was operated by a Mr
h Bartram. Mr Bartram, a retired civil servant, was merely a nominee of Mr Carter, was in fact his father-in-law, and Mr Carter was the majority shareholder in Luxane Ltd, his wife and his father-in-law, Mr Bartram, and his mother-in-law, Mrs Bartram, holding all the other shares. Furthermore, it is their case, and their case in the High Court proceedings which they brought against Mr Carter, that he drafted and signed letters from Luxane Ltd, or purporting to be from that company, in the name of Mr Bartram
j and forged, in effect, Mr Bartram's signature.

Of course, it is not for this court to pronounce on the correctness of these allegations, but when these matters came to the notice of the employers they dismissed Mr Carter from his employment on 20th December 1978, having issued two days before that the writ which initiated the High Court proceedings giving rise to the postponement of the unfair dismissal claim.

On 21st December Forbes J granted ex parte injunctions in respect of these sites against Mr Carter. On 4th January 1979 Waterhouse J continued those injunctions and *a* directed a speedy trial of the employers' action against Mr Carter. On 11th May, there having been a delay in discovery, an 'unless' order was made against Mr Carter, against Luxane Ltd and against Mr Bartram, all three of whom, I should have said, were parties to the High Court proceedings; the 'unless' order being a dismissal of their defences unless they complied with orders already made for discovery. On 18th June Swanwick J dismissed an application made by Mr Carter, through counsel, to discharge the *b* injunctions, and he continued them. The date fixed for trial of the High Court action against Mr Carter, Luxane Ltd and Mr Bartram, an action which it is estimated will take three days, is now 5th November.

The application to the industrial tribunal was made by Mr Carter on 7th January, and it was on 16th March that the industrial tribunal chairman stayed those proceedings until after the High Court proceedings. Mr Carter appealed against that on 4th May to *c* the Employment Appeal Tribunal who allowed his appeal, as I stated, on 27th June.

The industrial tribunal chairman gave a carefully reasoned decision for postponing the proceedings before the industrial tribunal. Before I go any further, the rule which gives him jurisdiction to postpone or not is r 11(2)(b) of the schedule to the Industrial Tribunals (Labour Relations) Regulations 1974[1], which provides: 'A tribunal may, if it thinks fit . . . (b) postpone the day or time fixed for, or adjourned for any hearing . . .', a rule which *d* appears to confer a complete judicial discretion on the chairman of an industrial tribunal.

In a decision running to nearly three pages the chairman expressed his reasons for granting the postponement. He referred to the arguments on both sides of counsel for the employers and of Mr Carter appearing in person. He said in para 11:

> 'I am satisfied that a number of the important issues which are of some complexity in both sets of proceedings are the same: that as serious allegations are made by both *e* sides it is in the interest of justice that they should be dealt with first in the High Court, where both sides will be represented by counsel and solicitors and where the rules of evidence are applied more strictly than in tribunal proceedings; that especially as Mr Carter is not seeking reinstatement the delay factor in postponing the tribunal proceedings ought to be accepted; that the delay factor is outweighed by the need in the interest of justice to have an orderly sequence in the two sets of *f* proceedings; that the possibility of an appeal (with or without a review) from an industrial tribunal decision could lead to additional expense and delay in the High Court proceedings militating against the speedy trial ordered; that although the parties are not identical the second and third defendants [that is Luxane Ltd and Mr Bartram] are mentioned in Mr Carter's said statement and the events surrounding them will almost certainly form part of the tribunal proceedings; that there is an *g* advantage in this litigation in having the High Court proceedings heard first which have pleadings on affidavit.'

He then referrred to two cases, *Jacobs v Norsalta Ltd*[2] and a further unreported case of *James Griffiths Ltd v D A James*[3]. 'In the result', he concluded, 'in the exercise of my discretion under the rules of procedure . . . I order that the industrial tribunal proceedings *h* be postponed pending the outcome of the High Court proceedings.'

I should have said that the industrial tribunal can hear, over a period of four days from 13th to 16th August and I assume could complete a hearing if it did not finish in those four days, Mr Carter's application for compensation for unfair dismissal.

The Employment Appeal Tribunal in an equally careful judgment reversed that *j*

---

1   SI 1974 No 1386
2   [1977] ICR 189
3   (15th February 1978) unreported

decision. Slynn J said that he understood the factors which had influenced the chairman
a to postpone and he also stated that it was not the practice of the Employment Appeal
Tribunal, as he put it, to interfere with the exercise of the discretion of a tribunal on an
order of this kind, 'unless we consider that it is wrong in principle or is in some way
unsupported by the material which has been placed before the tribunal'. Slynn J went
on to consider the different issues which were raised by the claim before the tribunal and
the proceedings in the High Court, and he stated the issues before the tribunal perfectly
b correctly. He then said:

> '. . . as we have said on many occasions, the issue [that is before the tribunal] is not
> in fact whether there was fraud, forgery or some other act which was an offence.
> The question is whether, on the material which they had or ought to have had at the
> time, the employers had reasonable grounds for dismissing [Mr Carter] and whether
c > they behaved fairly in so doing. It seems to us that Parliament intended that these
> claims of unfair dismissal should be dealt with as quickly and simply as the issues in
> the case allowed. We think that in principle it is right that claims of this kind, of
> unfair dismissal, should go ahead regardless of the existence of High Court
> proceedings if one of the parties wishes it as the applicant does here. That is so even
> if those High Court proceedings may have been started first and even if there is to
d > some extent an overlap of the issues. That in our view is the starting point. A
> claimant, and indeed a respondent, is entitled to have those matters dealt with
> speedily. We think that the starting point is that they should be allowed to proceed,
> unless there are special reasons why the matter should be delayed.'

That was the principle and Slynn J described it as the 'general principle', which the
Employment Appeal Tribunal applied and which they decided the industrial tribunal
e chairman had disregarded. The main thrust of counsel's submission on behalf of the
employers in this court was that that statement of principle was an error. It does not state
the correct principle, correct on the wording of the rule giving the industrial tribunal
power to postpone or on the authorities in which the Employment Appeal Tribunal has
considered the exercise of that discretion.

Before I refer further to that main submission I should say that the Employment
f Appeal Tribunal went on to consider and to state reasons in this particular case for
following what they declared to be the general principle: mainly, I think, the
complication of the High Court case; the possibility of an appeal to the Court of Appeal
from the High Court causing further delay; and the consideration that, though there was
some overlap on issues of fact, the central issues, 'had the employers reasonable grounds
for dismissal? had they behaved fairly in dismissing Mr Carter?', were not essentially the
g same as the issues raised by the accusations of fraud and forgery, and so on, in the High
Court proceedings, a consideration so stated as to underestimate the extent and
importance of the ground common to both proceedings. We have been referred to four
cases in which the Employment Appeal Tribunal has considered the exercise of this
discretion by chairmen of industrial tribunals, and it is not without interest that in every
case, whether the industrial tribunal chairman had refused a stay or granted a stay, the
h Employment Appeal Tribunal upheld the industrial tribunal chairman. This is the first
case, as far as counsel for the employers is able to inform us, in which the Employment
Appeal Tribunal has reversed the decision of the industrial tribunal chairman. That is
less surprising when one remembers that an appeal lies from an industrial tribunal to the
Employment Appeal Tribunal on a point of law only, as it does from an Employment
Appeal Tribunal to this court on a point of law only.
j The first of the authorities to which we were referred is the first of the two cases cited
to and by the chairman of the industrial tribunal, *Jacobs v Norsalta Ltd*[1]. In that case

---

1   [1977] ICR 189

Phillips J, presiding over the Employment Appeal Tribunal, referred to the rule which
I have read, and said this[1]:   **a**

> 'We accept, of course, that the power under rule 11(2)(b) must not be used
> arbitrarily or capriciously. It must certainly not be used in order to defeat the
> general object of the legislation. But subject to that, it seems to us that the industrial
> tribunal has a complete discretion, so long as it exercises it judicially, to postpone or
> adjourn any case provided there is a good, reasonable ground for so doing.'   **b**

The learned judge also made the statement which is cited in Mr Carter's notice of appeal
to the Employment Appeal Tribunal[2]:

> 'We are also impressed [said Phillips J] by the point that, ordinarily speaking, a
> claimant before an industrial tribunal is entitled to have his claim quickly disposed
> of in what is intended to be a simple, readily available form of proceedings; and it
> is not desirable, except in unusual cases, to have to delay or postpone the hearing in **c**
> order to await the outcome of other proceedings.'

Finally, dealing with the merits of the matter, because he said it is always more
satisfactory for an appellate tribunal to say not merely that it did not feel it ought to
interfere with the decision of the tribunal below but that it agreed with it, he referred[3]
to the fact that the delay in that case was an acceptable one 'because on the whole we **d**
think that greater simplicity will result in the end', that is, from the postponement of the
tribunal proceedings until the hearing of the High Court proceedings.

That was a decision in July 1976. The next decision cited to and by the chairman of
the industrial tribunal was *Griffiths v James*[4], a decision again of Phillips J presiding over
the Employment Appeal Tribunal nearly two years later in February 1978. There the
learned judge made a statement, relied on by counsel for the employers in his notice of **e**
appeal and in his submissions to us, in these terms:

> 'The decision which the industrial tribunal chairman had to make was one, of
> course, which lay within her discretion, and before we can interfere with it, it has
> to be shown that in some way or another the discretion was not properly exercised
> or that the decision was so surprising that we can conclude that it must be wrong,
> or perhaps we should say, so wrong that it must have been given for some wrong **f**
> reason.'

There the tribunal decided that 'the decision was a reasonable and sensible decision and,
we think, the one which we would have reached'.

There were two later cases. One was in April 1979, in which the judgment for the
Employment Appeal Tribunal was given by Bristow J, a decision in *Cahm v Ward &* **g**
Goldstone Ltd[5]. That decision is interesting because there is no reference there to the need
to find an error in law on the part of the industrial tribunal chairman, yet there is clear
approval, in a case closer on its facts to this than any of the others which have been cited,
of a decision to postpone a tribunal claim until after the hearing of other proceedings; in
that case proceedings which had been originally brought in the county court and then
transferred to the High Court, and criminal proceedings which had ended in an **h**
acquittal. It is true that there are references in that case to public interest and to the
importance of a hearing in public, and perhaps more suitably in public in the High
Court, on which Mr Carter relies. But it is an instance of a case in which it was thought
right by two tribunals to postpone a claim until after certain serious allegations, there of
breach of confidence, and so on, had been ventilated in an action brought by employers
against the applicant employee in the High Court.   **j**

1   [1977] ICR 189 at 191
2   [1977] ICR 189 at 192
3   [1977] ICR 189 at 193
4   (15th February 1978) unreported
5   (6th April 1979) unreported

The last case is *Bastick v James Lane (Turf Accountants) Ltd*[1] in which Arnold J gave the
a judgment of the Employment Appeal Tribunal in May 1979, in which it is to be noted
that the Employment Appeal Tribunal refused to upset a decision of an industrial
tribunal chairman *refusing* to postpone an employee's claim to compensation for unfair
dismissal until after a criminal trial. Arnold J[2] recognised that the discretion was the
industrial tribunal chairman's and not the discretion of the Employment Appeal
Tribunal, and to reverse that decision—

b
> 'Either we must find, in order so to do, that the tribunal, or its chairman, has
> taken into account some matter which it was improper to take into account or has
> failed to take into account some matter which it was necessary to take into account
> in order that the discretion might be properly exercised; or, alternatively if we do
> not find that, that the decision which was made by the tribunal, or its chairman, in
> the exercise of its discretion was so far beyond what any reasonable tribunal or
> *c* chairman could have decided that we are entitled to reject it as perverse.'

And he concluded[3] that—

> '. . . having weighed the matter up as best we can, we are bound to conclude that
> although it would have been perfectly reasonable [and I stress these words] to come
> *d* to an opposite conclusion, nevertheless the conclusion which this chairman reached
> is not so unreasonable a conclusion as to lead us to a finding of perversity. In those
> circumstances we are obliged to dismiss the appeal.'

For my part I regard the statements of the principle on which the Employment Appeal
Tribunal acts by Phillips J in the *Jacobs* case[4] and the *Griffiths* case[5] and by Arnold J in the
Bastick case[1] as correct statements of the law, correctly interpreting the law as giving to
e the chairmen of industrial tribunals a complete and wide discretion to postpone or not
as they think best in the interest of justice. As it seems to me, the error, what I find to
be an error, with all respect to the Employment Appeal Tribunal in this case, of their
decision is that they elevate into a general principle what Phillips J in the *Jacobs* case[4]
considered, and rightly considered, a factor, and an important factor, in arriving at a just
decision and a decision which would simplify matters without doing injustice to the
f parties. The Employment Appeal Tribunal seems to me in this case to have stepped out
of line in seeking to lay down a general principle that an industrial tribunal must hear a
claim before High Court proceedings are heard unless there are special reasons or unusual
circumstances. I would not wish to underrate the importance of a quick and expeditious
settlement of straightforward claims for unfair dismissal; but I would deplore any
attempt to take from the chairmen of industrial tribunals the discretion which the rule
g gives them to decide what is best to do in each individual case in all the circumstances
when faced with an application to postpone. Naturally it is the employee who usually
wishes to press on with his claim for unfair dismissal and I appreciate and give full
weight to Mr Carter's point that it would be disastrous if our decision could be interpreted
as a precedent for encouraging employers to use the device of a stopping writ, as it were,
a writ issued simply in order to stop and delay claims for unfair dismissal. But, in my
h judgment, it is for the tribunal chairman in every case to consider the nature and the
object of the High Court or other proceedings for which he is asked to postpone the
hearing of an application to his or her tribunal, and any abuse of postponement
proceedings is something which, in my judgment, industrial tribunal chairmen can be
trusted to deal with robustly and clear-sightedly.

j
_____

1   [1979] ICR 778
2   [1979] ICR 778 at 782
3   [1979] ICR 778 at 784
4   [1977] ICR 189
5   (15th February 1978) unreported

I accept counsel's submission for the employers that the Employment Appeal Tribunal erred in law in the principle which they sought to lay down. I would lay down no *a* principle except the principle (if it can be called a principle) that the industrial tribunal chairman should attempt to do justice as best he or she can in each individual case. I think it unnecessary and undesirable to go on to examine the reasons for the decision of the chairman in this case or the correctness of those reasons; but I think I have read enough of them to show how difficult it is to mount any argument that his decision was not a reasonable and sensible decision, and how impossible, in my judgment, it would be *b* to argue that he had failed to take into account any relevant factors or taken into account any irrelevant factors in reaching the conclusion to which he came. All the reasons which he gave seem to me to be good reasons for the decision to which he came; many important issues are indeed the same in both proceedings; and if it were necessary for me to express my agreement with his exercise of discretion I do not think I would find any difficulty in doing it: but I do not regard it as a function of this court, or the function of *c* the Employment Appeal Tribunal, to approve the exercise of the industrial tribunal's discretion to postpone. All the Employment Appeal Tribunal has to do is to see whether there is an error in law, and they can only do that, it seems to me, in accordance with the guidance given by the precedents of the Employment Appeal Tribunal in other cases: they must look to see whether there is anything wrong in law with the decision, and whether it is so surprising that something must have gone wrong with it and that it *d* could be characterised as perverse or a decision which no reasonable tribunal could have come to.

In this case, as it seems to me, after hearing Mr Carter's very clear submissions and studying the grounds he gave in his notice of appeal, they do not come near to showing that there is any error of the kind which is necessary for interfering with the chairman's decision. Mr Carter points out, quite rightly, that some delay will be occasioned, it may *e* not be very much as it turns out, by the postponement of his application, and it may be that any delay is going to prolong the period of his unemployment. He has apparently made 23 applications for posts and until his reputation is cleared, and I would have thought it would be better and more demonstrably cleared in the High Court than before the industrial tribunal, he may be suffering from unemployment, and if in the long run it turns out he is entitled to compensation it is unfortunate that there will have *f* been delay in paying it. But I do not think it necessary to go into other suggested advantages of his claim being heard first, or the reasons why it is suggested that one party or the other may have found it necessary to ask for one set of proceedings to be heard before the other. I content myself with saying that I can see nothing wrong in law, and indeed nothing wrong at all, in the decision of the chairman of the industrial tribunal in this case, and for these reasons I think that the Employment Appeal Tribunal were *g* wrong to upset it; the appeal from their decision should be allowed, and the decision of the chairman of the industrial tribunal postponing Mr Carter's application until after the hearing of the High Court proceedings restored.

BRIDGE LJ. I so fully agree with the judgment delivered by Stephenson LJ that I do not think I can usefully add anything.   *h*

CUMMING-BRUCE LJ. I agree.

Appeal allowed. Order of Employment Appeal Tribunal set aside. Order of industrial tribunal restored.

j

Solicitors: *Fremont & Co* (for the employers).

K Mydeen Esq   Barrister.

a
Re Stott (deceased)
Klouda v Lloyds Bank Ltd and others

CHANCERY DIVISION
SLADE J
b 3rd, 11th MAY 1979

Probate – Pleading – Contents of pleading – Nature of case relied on required to be specified –
Allegation which would be relevant in support of plea of undue influence – Party pleading that
testator did not know and approve of contents of will when executing it – Party alleging in
support of that plea matters which would also support plea of undue influence – Party precluded
c *from doing so unless undue influence also pleaded – Whether party's allegations in support of plea*
of want of knowledge and approval an allegation which would be 'relevant in support of ' plea of
undue influence – RSC Ord 76, r 9(3).

From November 1975 until her death in 1977 the deceased resided in a nursing home
managed by the plaintiff. After the deceased's death the plaintiff sought to propound a
d will signed by the deceased in 1976 and naming the plaintiff as sole residuary
beneficiary. The defendant, who was the residuary beneficiary under a will executed by
the deceased in 1972, asked the court to pronounce against the 1976 will and for the 1972
will on the ground that at the time when the 1976 will was executed the deceased did not
know and approve of its contents, or alternatively was not of sound mind, memory and
understanding. The defendant set out in his defence particulars in support of his plea of
e the deceased's want of knowledge and approval of the 1976 will and of her lack of
testamentary capacity. In relation to the former he alleged, inter alia, in para 1 of his
defence (i) that in December 1975, when she was residing in the plaintiff's nursing
home, the deceased had written, with the assistance of one of the plaintiff's employees or
associates, to a firm of solicitors, with whom she had not previously dealt, asking them
to prepare a will under which the plaintiff was to be the sole residuary beneficiary (the
f 1976 will), (ii) that the deceased was then in a confused and disturbed mental state and
unaware of the extent of her estate, (iii) that there was no good reason why the deceased
should have wished to give her residuary estate to the plaintiff and that in her three
previous wills the deceased had shown a consistent desire to benefit the defendant, (iv)
that the deceased had not at any time spoken to a representative of the firm of solicitors
and had received no independent legal advice in connection with the 1976 will, (v) that
g at the date of the letter to the solicitors the deceased was under the plaintiff's control and
on the plaintiff's instructions confined to the nursing home, and (vi) that the plaintiff had
arranged for the deceased to be accompanied either by the plaintiff or by a member of
her family or by a member of the plaintiff's staff on all occasions when the deceased was
visited by friends or relations. The defendant made no express plea of undue influence
or fraud. The plaintiff applied by summons to have many of the allegations in para 1 of
h the defence struck out as contravening RSC Ord 76, r 9(3)[a], in that, although all the
allegations made in para 1 were material for the purposes of a plea of want of knowledge
and approval, the defendant should not be permitted to include many of them in his
defence because they would also be relevant in support of a plea of undue influence
which the defendant had not pleaded, since under r 9(3) 'no allegation in support of [a
plea of want of knowledge and approval] which would be relevant in support of a plea of'
j undue influence or fraud was to be made unless undue influence or fraud was also
pleaded.

Held – On its true construction RSC Ord 76, r 9(3) applied only to cases where, under

a Rule 9(3) is set out at p 262 *h* to p 263 *a*, post

cover of a plea of want of knowledge and approval, a pleader was in substance
affirmatively alleging undue influence or fraud without specifically introducing it as an *a*
alternative plea. An allegation was not 'relevant' within r 9(3) unless it would, if
established, either alone or in conjunction with other facts also pleaded, affirmatively
prove the relevant alternative plea, and the mere fact that an allegation, if proved, might
constitute evidence that could incidentally assist proof of the relevant alternative plea, if
raised, did not bring it within r 9(3). On that construction, the allegations to which the
plaintiff objected were not allegations which would be relevant in support of a plea of *b*
undue influence within r 9(3) and therefore they should not be struck out. The
summons would accordingly be dismissed (see p 264 *g h*, p 265 *a b d* to *g* and p 266 *b*,
post).

   Wintle v Nye [1959] 1 All ER 552 applied.
   Re R (deceased) [1950] 2 All ER 117 distinguished.

                                                                                    c
Notes
For contents of pleadings in probate actions, see 17 Halsbury's Laws (4th Edn) para 874.
   For opposition to the grant of probate on the ground of want of knowledge and
approval, see ibid paras 905–910, and for cases on the subject, see 23 Digest (Repl) 130–
134, 1354–1389.
   For jurisdiction to strike out proceedings, see 30 Halsbury's Laws (3rd Edn) 407, para *d*
767, and for cases on the subject, see 50 Digest (Repl) 60–72, 491–563.

Cases referred to in judgment
Barry v Butlin (1838) 2 Moo PCC 480, 1 Curt 637, 12 ER 1089, 23 Digest (Repl) 131, 1357.
Fuld (deceased), In the estate of, (No 3), Hartley v Fuld [1965] 3 All ER 776, [1968] P 675,
   [1966] 2 WLR 717, Digest (Cont Vol B) 126, 666a.   *e*
R (deceased), Re [1950] 2 All ER 117, [1951] P 10, 23 Digest (Repl) 134, 1389.
Wintle v Nye [1959] 1 All ER 552, [1959] 1 WLR 284, Digest (Cont Vol A) 555, 3169a.

Procedure summons
By a summons dated 24th November 1978 Alice Klouda, the plaintiff in a probate action
against the first defendant, Lloyds Bank Ltd, the second defendant, Norman Jones, and *f*
the third defendant, Herbert Gardner, applied to have parts of the defence of the third
defendant struck out as contravening RSC Ord 76, r 9(3). The facts are set out in the
judgment.

John H Weeks for the plaintiff.
Peter Rawson for the third defendant.   *g*
The first defendant was not represented.
The second defendant did not appear.

                                                                      Cur adv vult

11th May. **SLADE J** read the following judgment: By this summons application is *h*
made by the plaintiff to strike out parts of the defence of the third defendant in an
action. It raises a pleading point which is not easy and is of some general importance in
the context of probate actions. I am surprised that, apparently, it has not been decided
in any earlier reported case.
   The action concerns the estate of the late May, Lady Stott ('the deceased') who died on
2nd January 1977. The plaintiff, Mrs Alice Klouda, is named as the residuary beneficiary *j*
in what purports to be a will executed by the deceased on 17th February 1976, under
which she appointed the first defendant, Lloyds Bank Ltd, executor and trustee.
   The third defendant, Mr Herbert Gardner, is named as the residuary beneficiary in
what purports to be a will executed by the deceased on 25th May 1972, by which she
appointed the second defendant, Mr Norman Jones, executor and trustee.

By her writ, endorsed with a statement of claim in the abbreviated form commonly
a used in such cases, the plaintiff propounds the will of 1976. By counterclaim the third
defendant asks, inter alia, that the court pronounce against the will of 1976, and for the
will of 1972.

The first and second defendants have filed defences which show that, effectively, they
are both adopting a neutral stance in the proceedings. They have not appeared before me
on this application. The contest is effectively between the plaintiff and the third
b defendant, who opposes probate of the will of 1976, first, on the grounds of want of
knowledge and approval of its contents, and secondly, on the grounds of testamentary
incapacity. There is no express plea by the third defendant of undue influence or fraud.

Paragraph 1 of the third defendant's defence, which contains the plea of want of
knowledge and approval, reads as follows:

c
'At the time of execution of the alleged will dated the 17th February 1976 May
Lady Stott (hereinafter called "the deceased") did not know and approve of the gift
of residue in favour of the Plaintiff contained in Clause 4 thereof.

'PARTICULARS

'(a) The Plaintiff is and has at all material times been the proprietress or
d manageress of a nursing home at 20 Fitz-James Avenue, London W.14. (b) The
deceased took up residence at the said nursing home on or about the 14th November
1975. (c) At the date of taking up residence the deceased was 91 years old and
suffering from senile dementia, so that she was incapable of living by herself. (d)
The deceased gave instructions for the said alleged will by a letter dated the 5th
December 1975 to Messrs. Freeborough Slack & Co. At the date of said letter the
e deceased was in a confused and disturbed mental state and was unaware of the
extent of her free estate. (e) The said letter was written with the assistance of one
Davey, an employee or associate of the Plaintiff. (f) By the said letter the deceased
purported to instruct Messrs. Freeborough Slack & Co., to prepare a Will under
which the Plaintiff was the sole residuary beneficiary. There was no good reason
why the deceased should have wished to give her entire residuary estate to the
f Plaintiff. In three previous Wills dated respectively the 2nd March 1957, the 4th
October 1968 and the 25th May 1972 the deceased had shown a consistent desire to
benefit the Third Defendant. (g) The deceased did not at any time see or speak to
any partner or other representative of Messrs. Freeborough Slack & Co., in relation
to her said alleged Will and received no independent legal advice from any other
source in connection therewith. The deceased had never previously consulted the
g said firm. (h) At the date of the said letter the deceased was under the control of the
Plaintiff and was on the instructions of the Plaintiff confined to the said nursing
home. The Plaintiff kept the doors of the same locked at all times and did not
permit the deceased to use the key for the same or to leave the said nursing home
unattended. The Plaintiff further arranged for the deceased to be accompanied
either by herself or by a member of her family or by the said Davey on all occasions
h when she was visited by friends or relations. (i) The Third Defendant accordingly
puts the Plaintiff to proof that the said alleged Will was, in respect of the gift of
residue contained in Clause 4 thereof, the Will of a free and capable testatrix who
knew and understood the effect thereof.'

Paragraph 2 of this defence, containing the plea of testamentary incapacity, begins
with the following words: 'Further or in the alternative the deceased at the time when
j the said alleged Will purports to have been executed was not of sound mind, memory or
understanding.' There then follow, in para 2, lengthy particulars of the alleged lack of
testamentary capacity, such particulars, in certain respects, overlapping with those
contained in para 1. Paragraph 3 of this defence reads as follows:

'In the premises the Third Defendant puts the Plaintiff to proof that the deceased knew and approved the contents of Clause 4 of the said alleged Will or alternatively that the deceased was of sound mind, memory and understanding when she *a* purported to execute the same.'

The pleading then contains a counterclaim by the third defendant, which I need not read for present purposes.

By paras 1 and 3 of the defence, the pleader clearly intends to rely on the general principle of law that, where a will is prepared and executed in circumstances which *b* excite the vigilance and suspicion of the court, the burden is placed on the person propounding it to remove the suspicion and prove that the testator knew and approved of its contents. In particular this principle is likely to be applied where the court is satisfied on the evidence that a person has, by himself or his agents, been instrumental in preparing a will under which he himself takes a benefit: see for example *Wintle v Nye*[1].

In the light of these principles counsel for the plaintiff does not dispute that each and every one of the allegations contained in para 1 of the third defendant's defence is *c* relevant to the plea of want of knowledge and approval. In this important respect, at least, the present case is distinguishable from *Re R (deceased)*[2] to which he referred me. In that case the defendants in a probate action alleged, inter alia, that, at the apparent time of execution of the relevant will, the deceased did not know or approve of its contents. Under that heading, in their pleadings, they made derogatory allegations *d* concerning the relationship between the beneficiary and the testator. Willmer J struck out these allegations, primarily on the grounds that they were 'scandalous' and might 'tend to embarrass or delay the fair trial of the action', within what was then RSC Ord 19, r 27. The grounds of Willmer J's decision[3] were that, where a question is raised concerning knowledge and approval of the contents of a will, 'the circumstances which are held to excite the suspicions of the court must be circumstances attending, or at least relevant to, the preparation and execution of the will itself'. He accepted[4] that the *e* allegations could be relevant to the testamentary capacity of the deceased or to a plea of undue influence. Since, however, the allegations could not be relevant to the issue of want of knowledge and approval, within the test which he had formulated, he struck them out.

In the present case, counsel for the plaintiff does not dispute that each and every one *f* of the allegations made in para 1 of the third defendant's defence is a circumstance attending, or relevant to, the preparation and execution of the will of 1976 and is thus a material fact in respect of which the third defendant will, understandably, wish to rely in support of his plea of want of knowledge and approval, to the extent that such fact is provable by evidence and that the rules permit it.

He submits, however, that the allegations pleaded in sub-paras (a), (b), (e), the second sentence of sub-para (f) and sub-paras (g) and (h) of para (1), though allegations of facts *g* material for purposes of the plea, are not allegations which it is permissible for the third defendant to insert in his defence, in its present form, having regard to RSC Ord 76, r 9(3). For this reason he seeks to have them struck out. Order 76, r 9(3) provides as follows:

'Without prejudice to Order 18, rule 7, any party who pleads that at the time *h* when a will, the subject of the action, was alleged to have been executed the testator did not know and approve of its contents must specify the nature of the case on which he intends to rely, and no allegation in support of that plea which would be relevant in support of any of the following other pleas, that is to say:—(a) that the will was not duly executed, (b) that at the time of the execution of the will the testator was not of sound mind, memory and understanding, and (c) that the *j*

---

1   [1959] 1 All ER 552, [1959] 1 WLR 284
2   [1950] 2 All ER 117, [1951] P 10
3   [1950] 2 All ER 117 at 121, [1951] P 10 at 17
4   [1950] 2 All ER 117 at 123, [1951] P 10 at 20

execution of the will was obtained by undue influence or fraud, shall be made by
that party unless that other plea is also pleaded.'

Counsel for the plaintiff submits that each of the allegations under attack would also
be relevant in support of a plea that the execution of the will of 1976 was obtained by
undue influence on the part of the plaintiff. Accordingly, he submits, para (3)(c) of Ord
76, r 9 must render such allegations impermissible in a pleading, such as this, where
undue influence is not specifically pleaded. He submits that it would be wrong for the
court to allow the third defendant to insinuate what is effectively a plea of undue
influence under cover of a plea of want of knowledge and approval. If the third
defendant wants to plead undue influence, counsel for the plaintiff suggests, he should
do so expressly with all the potential consequences as to costs that such a pleading may
entail. He submits that further support for his general argument is to be found in a
passage from the judgment in *Re R (deceased)*[1] in which Willmer J, having decided that
the allegations there sought to be struck out should be struck out under the then RSC
Ord 19, r 27, proceeded further to decide that they should also be struck out as being in
direct contravention of the last sentence of r 40A of the Contentious Probate Rules 1862.

At the time Willmer J made this decision, r 40A was still in force; he rejected[2] an
argument that it had been entirely superseded by what was then RSC Ord 19, r 25(a).
However, the Contentious Probate Rules 1862 were wholly revoked by the Rules of the
Supreme Court (Revision) Order 1962, which introduced a new special Ord 76, dealing
with probate proceedings. This revision was effected only two or three years after the
House of Lords had given its decision, concerning the plea of want of knowledge and
approval, in *Wintle v Nye*[3]. It seems to me readily conceivable in principle that the
revision was intended substantially to alter the rules of practice and procedure relating to
this plea. I therefore think that any reference to r 40A of the old Contentious Probate
Rules 1862 or to that part of the judgment of Willmer J in *Re R (deceased)*[4] dealing with
that rule is of little assistance in the present case. The attack of the plaintiff on the third
defendant's pleading must stand or fall on the wording of the present RSC Ord 76, r 9(3).

On a first literal reading of the wording of this rule, I think there is considerable force
in the basic submission of counsel for the plaintiff, that a party in a probate action may
never plead an allegation in support of a plea of want of knowledge and approval, if such
allegation would in any sense at all be relevant in support of a plea of undue influence,
but a plea of undue influence is not itself made in the action. This submission however,
if correct, would have such surprising results as to make me doubt whether this can have
been the intention of those responsible for introducing Ord 76, r 9(3).

For the purpose of testing the correctness of the submission as a matter of principle, I
have to assume that the third defendant would be in a position to prove at the trial all the
allegations of fact which are now under attack. As I have said, it is not disputed that they
are all material to a plea of want of knowledge and approval (though I would myself raise
a small query, not raised in argument, in relation to the materiality in this context of the
second and third sentences of para 1(f)). With this one possible exception, it seems to me
that all the relevant allegations are matters of fact which, if proved, in conjunction with
the other facts pleaded in para 1 of the third defendant's defence, the trial judge would
be likely to regard as creating a suspicion that fell to be removed by the person
propounding the will, within the principle of such cases as *Wintle v Nye*[3] and the much
earlier decision in *Barry v Butlin*[5] per Parke B.

1   [1950] 2 All ER 117 at 123–124, [1951] P 10 at 20–21
2   [1950] 2 All ER 117 at 123, [1951] P 10 at 20
3   [1959] 1 All ER 552, [1959] 1 WLR 284
4   [1950] 2 All ER 117, [1951] P 10
5   (1838) 2 Moo PC 480 at 482, 12 ER 1089 at 1090

Accordingly, apart from Ord 76, r 9(3), the relevant allegations are eminently suitable matters for a pleader to allege, on instructions, in support of a plea of want of knowledge *a* and approval; if true, they would give rise to reasonable suspicion. Furthermore, Ord 18, r 7, to which Ord 76, r 9(3) is expressly stated to be 'without prejudice', expressly provides that every pleading must contain a statement in summary form of the facts on which the party pleading relies for his claim, or defence, as the case may be, though 'not the evidence by which those facts are to be proved'.

In contrast, however, an affirmative plea of undue influence ought never to be put *b* forward unless the person who pleads it has reasonable grounds to support it. In the present case the third defendant does not wish to put forward an affirmative plea of undue influence. It seems a fair assumption, though I do not actually know, that the reason for this reluctance is that he and his legal advisers consider that, on the information available to them, there are no sufficient grounds to support such a plea. The third defendant, after all, presumably has little or no personal knowledge of the circumstances *c* in which the will of 1976 came to be made, but must rely on what he has been told by others. Yet, if the submissions of the plaintiff on the interpretation and effect of Ord 76, r 9(3) are correct, the third defendant, and defendants in a similar position in other probate actions, will find themselves obliged for practical purposes either (a) wholly to abandon a number of material allegations of fact, which are of crucial importance to their plea of want of knowledge and approval, or (b) to raise an affirmative plea of undue *d* influence, which they have no reasonable grounds to support.

The resulting anomalies become even more apparent from references made by counsel for the third defendant to cases. First, as appears from the speech of Lord Simonds in *Wintle v Nye*[1], it is open to a party alleging want of knowledge and approval to cross-examine the person propounding the will on matters which may result in establishing fraud on the part of such person, even though fraud has not been pleaded. The same *e* must, I think, apply to undue influence.

Further, Scarman J in *In the estate of Fuld (deceased) (No 3)*[2] made it clear that he did not regard the failure or deliberate omission of a party, who had raised a plea of want of knowledge and approval in a probate action, also to plead undue influence, as precluding such party from introducing, in support of his plea, matters of fact which would also, at least in a broad sense, be relevant in support of a plea of undue influence. *f*

These various points guide me towards the conclusion that the basic submission made by counsel for the plaintiff cannot be right. In my judgment the answer to it is, in the end, a short and simple one.

In my judgment, the second limb of Ord 76, r 9(3), beginning with the words 'and no allegation . . .', though not perhaps very happily drafted, must be read in a somewhat restricted sense, as being intended to apply merely to the case where, under cover of a *g* plea of want of knowledge and approval, a pleader is in substance making affirmative allegations of lack of proper execution, or lack of testamentary capacity, or undue influence, or fraud, as the case may be, without specifically introducing the appropriate alternative plea. In other words, so far as it relates to fraud and undue influence, it is intended to cover the case where the pleader is willing to wound, but afraid to strike.

Willmer J in *Re R (deceased)*[3] himself referred to the principle that the defence of want *h* of knowledge and approval is not to be 'used as a screen behind which one man is to be at liberty to charge another with fraud or dishonesty without assuming the responsibility of making that charge in plain terms'. Paragraph (c) of the second limb of Ord 76, r 9(3), in my judgment, reflects this principle.

A little later in the same judgment, however, Willmer J observed[3]: 'It is obvious that

j

1   [1959] 1 All ER 552 at 560, [1959] 1 WLR 284 at 294
2   [1965] 3 All ER 776 at 783, [1968] P 675 at 722
3   [1950] 2 All ER 117 at 123, [1951] P 10 at 19

in the nature of things a fair measure of latitude must be allowed to the pleader in
a alleging facts in support of a plea of want of knowledge and approval.'

By the like token, in construing Ord 76, r 9(3) a reasonably narrow meaning should,
I think, be attributed to the phrase 'which would be relevant in support of any of the
following other pleas'. An allegation should not, in my judgment, be treated as being
'relevant' within this meaning, unless it would, if established either alone or in
conjunction with other facts also pleaded, *affirmatively prove* the relevant alternative
b plea. The mere fact that the allegation, if proved, might constitute evidence that could
incidentally assist the proof of the relevant alternative plea, if raised, does not seem to me
to bring it within this second limb of Ord 76, r 9(3).

If the position were otherwise it is hard to see where the line could be drawn. For in
any case there are likely to be numerous facts which, in a broad sense, could be said to be
relevant in support of a plea of undue influence, as well as a plea of want of knowledge
c and approval. Simply for example, on facts similar to those in *Wintle v Nye*[1], it would
not, if the plaintiff's present contentions are correct, even be open to a party, who seeks
to assert a plea of want of knowledge and approval without affirmatively alleging fraud
or undue influence, to allege that the person who prepared the relevant will, and was the
residuary legatee thereunder, was the testator's solicitor. In one sense such an allegation
might be said to be 'relevant in support of' a plea that the execution of the will was
d obtained by undue influence or fraud, because the fact alleged would, or might,
constitute important evidence of the circumstances and background against which undue
influence or fraud was affirmatively alleged. In my judgment, however, it would not be
'relevant in support of' such a plea, within the meaning of Ord 76, r 9(3), unless it formed
one of a number of allegations which, taken together, would, if established, affirmatively
prove undue influence or fraud.

e Order 76, r 9(3) is expressed to operate subject to Ord 18, r 7. As Ord 18, r 7 itself
shows, a crucial distinction is to be drawn between facts on which a party relies to
support a plea and the evidence on which he relies to prove such facts.

In the present case, I can well see that some or all of the allegations made in para 1 of
the third defendant's defence would incidentally go some way towards assisting him to
make out a case of undue influence if he were minded to put forward such a plea.
f However they do not, in my judgment, constitute a screen behind which the third
defendant is implicitly charging the plaintiff with undue influence without expressly
alleging it. Even if they were all established they would not serve affirmatively to prove
undue influence, since, even then, they would not necessarily be inconsistent with
complete innocence of such a charge on the part of the plaintiff. In these circumstances
the relevant allegations are not, in my judgment, allegations which would be 'relevant in
g support of' a plea of undue influence, within the true meaning of Ord 76, r 9(3).

The assertion of a plea of want of knowledge and approval is not by itself treated by the
court as an example of an attempt to wound made by someone who is yet afraid to
strike. Its very nature is such that it will often be put forward by persons who, through
no fault of their own, have very limited information as to the precise circumstances in
which the relevant will was made, but who are entitled to submit that the circumstances
h which *are* known to them should excite the vigilance of the court and place on the person
propounding the will the onus of proving that the testator knew and approved of its
contents. The very nature of the plea is also such that the facts on which the pleader may
rely in support of it will often overlap with the evidence which he might wish to adduce
in support of an affirmative plea of fraud or undue influence. An analogy is to be found
in the case where a person seeks to set aside a transaction in equity on the alternative
j grounds of presumed undue influence and of actual undue influence; the facts on which
he will rely to support the presumption must often overlap with the evidence with
which he will adduce in support of the plea of actual undue influence.

If, however, RSC Ord 76, r 9(3) were to be construed as having the far-reaching effect

---

1   [1959] 1 All ER 552, [1959] 1 WLR 284

contended for by the plaintiff in the present case, this would, I think, have one or both
of two most undesirable results. Either it would have the effect of emasculating the *a*
scope of the plea of want of knowledge and approval, in a manner quite inconsistent with
the House of Lords decision in *Wintle v Nye*[1] and contrary to the public interest, or
alternatively it would encourage parties and their counsel to put forward specific pleas of
fraud or undue influence merely as a precautionary measure and without sufficient
grounds. For the reasons which I have tried to indicate I do not think that the
construction of the rule suggested on behalf of the plaintiff is either the necessary or the *b*
correct one.

I must, accordingly, dismiss this application.

Application dismissed.

Solicitors: *Farrer & Co* (for the plaintiff); *Speechly, Bircham & Co* (for the third defendant). *c*

Jacqueline Metcalfe   Barrister.

Re Beaumont (deceased),
Martin v Midland Bank Trust Co Ltd   *d*

CHANCERY DIVISION
SIR ROBERT MEGARRY V-C
17th, 18th, 21st, 25th MAY 1979

Family provision – Person who immediately before deceased's death was being maintained by *e*
deceased – Dependant – Substantial contribution by deceased towards applicant's needs otherwise
than for full valuable consideration – Full valuable consideration – Maintenance of applicant
immediately before death of deceased – Assumption of responsibility for maintenance – Couple
living together as man and wife – Woman owning bungalow – Each earning and contributing
towards household expenses – Joint establishment – On death woman leaving estate of £17,000
to sisters but nothing to man – Whether man being 'maintained' by deceased 'immediately' before *f*
deceased's death – Whether deceased had 'assumed responsibility for' applicant's maintenance –
Whether man qualifying to apply for provision out of estate – Inheritance (Provision for Family
and Dependants) Act 1975, ss 1(1)(c)(3), 3(4).

Practice – Chambers proceedings – Adjournment to judge – Originating summons – Discretion
of master to adjourn summons unheard or to hear it first – Parties informing master that *g*
whatever his decision adjournment to judge would be sought – Summons raising difficult point of
law – Whether master should hear summons before adjourning it to judge – RSC Ord 32,
r 14(1)(4).

From 1940 until her death in December 1976 the deceased and the plaintiff lived
together as man and wife in the deceased's bungalow. After the retirement of the *h*
deceased in 1964 and the plaintiff in 1966, they each received a state pension. The
deceased also received a civil service pension. The plaintiff continued in part-time
employment until 1976 earning £20 per week or less. From 1945 onwards the plaintiff
paid the deceased £2 or £3 a week increasing to £5 a week by 1966 for his
accommodation. The plaintiff also contributed to the weekly shopping bill. The
deceased paid the outgoings on the bungalow and did the cooking and housework. The *i*
plaintiff did various household and gardening jobs, and decorated the bungalow for
which he was paid by the deceased. He bought a car for their joint use; the deceased paid

---

1   [1959] 1 All ER 552, [1959] 1 WLR 284

a the insurance and the plaintiff paid the other running costs. Each nursed the other in sickness. In the last year of her life the deceased was in hospital for three months; the plaintiff then nursed her at home for five weeks, and she returned to hospital for the last ten days of her life. The deceased left a net estate of £17,000. By her will made in 1974 the deceased left her estate to her three sisters and nothing to the plaintiff. However, about a year after making her will the deceased nominated savings certificates to the value of £550 in favour of the plaintiff. After the deceased died the plaintiff issued an

b originating summons under the Inheritance (Provision for Family and Dependants) Act 1975 seeking an order for reasonable financial provision out of the deceased's estate, on the ground that he qualified for such provision as a person who 'immediately before the death of the deceased was being maintained, either wholly or partly, by the deceased' within s 1(1)(e)[a] of the 1975 Act. The executors and beneficiaries of the will applied by summons to strike out the proceedings as disclosing no reasonable cause of action because

c the plaintiff did not qualify under s 1(1)(e) for financial provision out of the estate. When the summons to strike out came on before the master both sides informed him that whatever his decision on the summons was they would ask for the matter to be adjourned to a judge. The master held that the plaintiff was entitled to apply for provision out of the estate and dismissed the summons. The summons was then adjourned to the judge.

d **Held** – (i) On the true construction of the 1975 Act, s 1(1)(e) was qualified by both ss 1(3)[b] and 3(4)[c] so that a person could claim financial provision from a deceased's estate under s 1(1)(e), by virtue of being maintained by the deceased, only if he satisfied the preconditions of showing—

(a) that he was being maintained 'immediately before' the death of the deceased, which, on the true construction of s 1(1)(e) required the court to look, not at the de facto

e state of maintenance existing at the moment of death, but at the settled and enduring basis or arrangement then generally existing between the parties, using the date of death as the day on which that arrangement was to be considered. The degree of maintenance to be considered therefore was not the maintenance existing at the moment of death but the degree of maintenance normally and habitually existing under the arrangement (see p 271 j, p 272 a to d and p 275 a to c and g h, post).

f (b) that for the purposes of s 1(3) the deceased had 'made a substantial contribution in money or money's worth towards the reasonable needs' of the applicant 'otherwise than for full valuable consideration'. The exclusion of claims where the contribution towards the applicant's needs had been provided in return for full valuable consideration was not restricted to contributions supplied under a contract but extended to any contribution provided for full consideration. Thus, if a couple living together made equal

g contributions towards the maintenance of each other by way of bearing half the cost of a joint establishment, then although both would be making a substantial contribution in money or money's worth towards the reasonable needs of the other they would be doing so for full valuable consideration and would therefore be barred from claiming against each other's estate (see p 272 h to p 273 a, post); *Re Wilkinson (deceased)* [1978] 1 All ER 221 applied.

h (c) that the deceased had 'assumed responsibility' for the applicant for the purposes of s 3(4). That was a matter which could not be established by the mere fact of maintaining someone but which required an act demonstrating an undertaking or assumption of responsibility (see p 274 c d, p 275 h and p 276 e f, post).

(ii) The plaintiff had not proved that the deceased had assumed responsibility for his maintenance but, on the contrary, had shown himself to be one of two people with

j independent means who had chosen to pool their individual resources to enable them to live together without either undertaking any responsibility for maintaining the other.

---

a   Section 1(1), so far as material, is set out at p 270 e, post
b   Section 1(3) is set out a p 270 f, post
c   Section 3(4), so far as material, is set out at p 273 h, post

It followed that the plaintiff was not qualified under s 1(1)(e) to apply for financial provision out of the deceased's estate and that his claim was bound to fail. Accordingly, *a* the defendant's summons to strike out the proceedings succeeded (see p 276 *a* to *e g j* and p 278 *f*, post).

Per Curiam. (i) It may be that in some cases where there is neither a negation of responsibility nor a positive undertaking of it, it is possible to infer from the circumstances attending the fact of maintenance that there has been an undertaking of responsibility. It may also be that would-be benefactors who wish to protect their *b* families ought to obtain from anyone to whose maintenance they propose to contribute an acknowledgment that they are undertaking no responsibility for his maintenance (see p 276 *f h j*, post).

(ii) Where the parties to a procedure summons initially assert before the master that in any event they will require an adjournment of the summons to the judge, the master in exercising his discretion whether to adjourn the case to the judge unheard or to hear *c* it first should bear in mind, where there is plainly a difficult point of law on the summons, that by virtue of RSC Ord 32, r 14(4)^*d* nothing in Ord 32, r 14(1) authorises him to determine a question of law raised by an originating summons for the determination of the court. In any event, in deciding whether to hear a summons which is to be adjourned to the judge, a master should bear in mind the burden of costs, especially where modest sums are at stake (see p 278 *e f*, post). *d*

Notes

For persons for whom provision may be made out of the deceased's estate, and for matters to which the court is to have regard, see 17 Halsbury's Laws (4th Edn) paras 1321, 1337.

For the Inheritance (Provision for Family and Dependants) Act 1975, ss 1, 3, see 45 *e* Halsbury's Statutes (3rd Edn) 496, 501.

Case referred to in judgment

Wilkinson (deceased), Re, Neale v Newell [1978] 1 All ER 221, [1978] Fam 22, [1977] 3 WLR 514.

Cases also cited

Bowlas v Bowlas [1965] 3 All ER 40, [1965] P 450, CA. *f*
Snow v Snow [1971] 3 All ER 833, [1972] Fam 74, CA.

Adjourned summonses

By an originating summons dated 20th December 1977 issued by the plaintiff, Albert Martin, against the defendants, Midland Bank Trust Co Ltd, the executors of the will dated 18th February 1974 of Ethel Maud Beaumont ('the deceased'), and Elsie Clutterbuck, Mabel Plumb and Ivy Egleton, the deceased's sisters who were beneficially *g* entitled in equal shares to the residue of the deceased's estate, the plaintiff applied for an order under s 2 of the Inheritance (Provision for Family and Dependants) Act 1975 for reasonable financial provision out of the deceased's estate and such further or other relief as to the court might seem proper. By a summons dated 8th September 1978 the defendants applied to strike out the originating summons on the ground that it disclosed no reasonable cause of action in that the plaintiff was not a person qualified within s 1(1) *h*

---

d Rule 14, so far as material, provides:

'(1) The masters of the Chancery Division shall, subject to the right of any party, as provided by paragraph (3), to have an adjournment to the judge in person without any fresh summons for the purpose, have power to transact all such business and exercise all such authority and jurisdiction as may be transacted and exercised by a judge in chambers, except such business, authority and jurisdiction as the judges of that Division may from time to time direct to be transacted or *j* exercised by a judge in person or as may by any of these rules be expressly directed to be transacted or exercised by a judge in person . . .

'(4) Where an originating summons raises for the determination of the Court a question as to the construction of a document or a question of law, nothing in paragraph (1) shall authorise a master to determine that question.'

of the 1975 Act to make a claim for provision under that Act. The summons to strike
a   out came on before Master Gowers on 9th October 1978. Both sides informed the master
that whatever his decision they would ask for the case to be adjourned to a judge. The
plaintiff applied to the master for interim maintenance under the 1975 Act and the
master directed him to issue a pro forma summons applying for interim maintenance.
The master then proceeded to hear the summons to strike out, but not the summons for
interim maintenance, and on 9th October decided that the plaintiff was qualified under
b   s 1(1)(e) of the 1975 Act to apply for reasonable provision out of the deceased's estate and
dismissed the summons. The summons to strike out and the summons for interim
maintenance were then adjourned into court. The facts are set out in the judgment.

J G Ross Martyn for the plaintiff.
P M Mottershead QC for the defendants.

c   *Cur adv vult*

25th May. **SIR ROBERT MEGARRY V-C** read the following judgment: In this case
the plaintiff, Albert Martin, has issued an originating summons which seeks an order in
his favour under the Inheritance (Provision for Family and Dependants) Act 1975. What
is before me is a summons taken out by the defendants in those proceedings, seeking to
d   have them struck out or dismissed as disclosing no reasonable cause of action, in that the
plaintiff is not a person who under s 1(1) of the Act is qualified to make a claim under the
Act. The summons is in terms which indicate that it was taken out under RSC Ord 18,
r 19(1)(a); but after reference had been made to affidavit and oral evidence, it was pointed
out to counsel for the defendants that r 19(2) excluded any evidence on such an
application. He thereupon sought leave to amend his summons by alternatively relying
e   on the inherent jurisdiction, under which there is nothing to exclude evidence; and in
view of the course that the summons had taken, counsel for the plaintiff did not oppose
the amendment. I therefore allowed it.

The summons raises points of some importance on the law; and there is a question of
procedure. Before I turn to these, I should set out the basic facts. These lie within a
relatively narrow compass. The plaintiff is between 77 and 78 years of age; and he is
f   seeking an order under the 1975 Act for payments to be made to him on the ground that
Mrs Beaumont, the deceased, had failed to make reasonable financial provision for him.
She died on 13th December 1976, leaving a net estate for the purposes of the Act of some
£17,000. By her will dated 18th February 1974 she gave a legacy of £100 to one of her
executors if he proved the will, and then gave the whole of her residue equally among
her three sisters. The will gave nothing to the plaintiff; but by a nomination made
g   rather over a year after the date of the will the deceased made a nomination in his favour
of 425 units of her savings certificates, worth over £550, as well as nominating other
units to other persons. The defendants to the summons are the two executors and the
three sisters of the deceased. Neither the plaintiff nor the three sisters could be described
as being affluent.

The plaintiff and the deceased were never married to each other. They began living
h   together in 1940, some two years after the deceased had become a widow; and apart from
separations during the war years, and shortly afterwards, they lived together as man and
wife until the death of the deceased at the end of 1976. The deceased, who was nearly 79
at her death, had been a civil servant; but she retired in 1964. She had a civil service
pension as well as a state pension. The plaintiff, who held a variety of jobs, for the most
part worked as a driver with various employers. He retired from full-time employment
j   in 1966, though for another ten years he had some part-time employment which
brought him in somewhere about £20 a week net, subject, towards the end, to reductions
for periods of sickness. According to the plaintiff's evidence, the general pattern of his
life with the deceased was that they lived together in a bungalow in Potters Bar,
Hertfordshire, which belonged to her. From 1945 onwards he paid her a weekly sum of
a fixed amount in return for the accommodation that she provided, and in addition he

contributed something to the weekly shopping bill. At first, the weekly sum was £2 or
£3. By 1964 it was £4, and by 1966 it had become £5, at which figure it remained. The
contributions to the weekly shopping bill, which at first were occasional, had become
regular by 1953: and at any rate latterly the contributions were of the order of £3, £4 or
£5 a week, depending on what was spent. In addition, the plaintiff drove the deceased
about in a car which he owned. He bought the car out of his own money, and paid all
the expenses of running it, apart from insurance, for which the deceased paid. The
plaintiff and the deceased each nursed the other in sickness, the deceased paid the
outgoings on the bungalow and did the cooking and housework and other household
chores, and the plaintiff did various household and gardening jobs. During the last year
before the deceased died, when the plaintiff's part-time work had come to an end, his
only income seems to have been a state pension of £13·40 a week, which rose to £15·40
a week a month before the deceased died. This sum provided the regular £5 a week that
the plaintiff paid to the deceased (even while she was in hospital), and also his contribution
to food and general expenses, as well as his personal expenses. During the last year of her
life the deceased was in hospital for August, September and October 1976, and also for
the last ten days before her death on 13th December 1976. For some five weeks in
November and the first few days of December the plaintiff nursed the deceased at home.

With that, I turn to the 1975 Act. Section 1(1) sets out the persons who may apply for
financial provision under the Act. Put shortly, paras (a) to (d) include the spouse of the
deceased; a former spouse who has not remarried; a child of the deceased; and a person
treated by the deceased as a child of a marriage to which the deceased was a party. There
is then para (e). This runs:

'any person (not being a person included in the foregoing paragraphs of this
subsection) who immediately before the death of the deceased was being maintained,
either wholly or partly, by the deceased.'

One has only to read this to see the problems that are likely to arise in applying the
expression 'immediately before the death of the deceased'. To these and other problems
I shall come in due course. I must also read s 1(3):

'For the purposes of subsection (1)(e) above, a person shall be treated as being
maintained by the deceased, either wholly or partly, as the case may be, if the
deceased, otherwise than for full valuable consideration, was making a substantial
contribution in money or money's worth towards the reasonable needs of that
person.'

These two provisions are newcomers to this legislation. One question is that of their
relationship to each other. Does s 1(3) provide an alternative to s 1(1)(e), or does it narrow
or qualify s 1(1)(e)? Grammatically it appears to provide an alternative. A person may
apply under the Act if immediately before the death of the deceased he was either 'being
maintained' by him within s 1(1)(e), or else he was to be 'treated as being maintained' by
him within s 1(3). On this reading, s 1(3) provides something of a deeming: someone
who is not in fact being maintained may nevertheless be treated as being maintained,
thus extending the ambit of s 1(1) (e). There is nothing in s 1(3) to state that someone
who falls within s 1(1)(e) is to be driven out of it unless he also satisfies s 1(3).

Grammatically that seems clear enough. The only difficulty about it is that it produces
an absurd result that I would not attribute to Parliament. Suppose the proprietor of an
old persons' home, a boarding house or a hotel were to die. Many of the residents who
were paying for full board could say that they were being at least partly maintained by
the proprietor immediately before his death, and so they satisfy s 1(1)(e): but plainly they
do not satisfy s 1(3), for the proprietor was partly maintaining them for full valuable
consideration. I can see no sensible grounds on which it could be said that Parliament
intended such persons to be able to make a claim under the Act. To avoid producing an
absurd result it therefore seems necessary to construe s 1(3) as if it contained a word or
words that in fact it does not, converting it from a positive or alternative provision into

a negative or restrictive provision. The clearest way, I think, is to construe it as if 'shall
a be treated' read 'shall not be treated', and as if the word 'if' were 'unless': a person 'shall
not be treated' as being maintained by the deceased 'unless' the deceased, otherwise than
for full valuable consideration, was making a substantial contribution, and so on. A
simpler alternative would be to read the subsection as if the word 'only' had been inserted
between 'be' and 'if': a person shall be treated as being maintained by the deceased 'only
if' the deceased, and so on.

b   Whatever the means, I think that it is necessary to read the section in such a way as to
prevent a claim being made under s 1(1)(e) unless the requirements of s 1(3) are satisfied.
I appreciate, of course, that if this is wrong, and a claimant can satisfy s 1 simply by
complying with s 1(1)(e), his failure to satisfy s 1(3) will mean that his claim, when heard,
will have scant prospects of success. But it is to the advantage of all concerned that
hopeless claims should be excluded in limine and not be left to a later stage when the
c costs and the lapse of time have become more burdensome.

   I turn to the phrase 'immediately before the death of the deceased was being
maintained', in s 1(1)(e), and particularly the word 'immediately'. Does this require
consideration to be given only to the state of affairs existing at the instant before the
death of the deceased, or does it allow a wider approach? In particular, what if the state
of affairs at that instant differs from the normal state of affairs? Suppose that C is being
d maintained by D, living in D's house, eating D's food and having clothes bought for him
by D. C falls ill and goes to a national health service hospital. A day, a week, a month
or a year later D dies. At the instant before D's death, D had not been providing anything
for C, whether food, lodging, clothing or anything else, and had not been making any
'substantial contribution in money or money's worth towards the reasonable needs' of
C. If only the instant before death is to be considered, C appears to have no claim. Yet
e if C had been discharged from hospital and had returned to D's home, however shortly
before D's death, presumably C can claim against D's estate.

   Again, suppose B has maintained C for years. B falls ill, and her sister, D, fetches both
B and C to live with her until B is better. If B dies the next day, must C's claim against
her estate fail? If instead D dies the next day, can C claim against her estate? Other
examples abound. Let me assume that the effect of s 1(3) is that where two people share
f the expenses of a common home, the one whose contribution is substantially more
valuable than the other's will be taken to be partly maintaining that other. That is a
point that I shall have to discuss in due course; but for the moment I shall make an
assumption broadly to that effect. Clearly the balance between the relative contributions
made by the two is liable to be changed at any moment, sometimes suddenly. Suppose
that C is contributing substantially less than D, in whose house they both live, and D is
g then taken ill. If C thereupon nurses D devotedly until D dies, the value of C's
contribution to D's maintenance may then greatly outstrip that of D's contribution to C's
maintenance, so that if matters are tested as at the moment before D's death, C's devotion
may have destroyed any claim under the Act. But if the day before dying D had been
removed to hospital, this would make it possible to contend that the former position of
D partly maintaining C had been restored, so that C could make a claim. Furthermore,
h if C and D have for years lived together on a basis of equality of contribution, both
financially and in domestic work, C will have no claim. Yet if through illness or laziness
or obstinacy C's contribution is reduced sufficiently, it may then be possible to say that
D is maintaining C: and so long as this occurs before D's death, however short the period,
C can claim under the Act. One may also take the case of two students who share
accommodation, one poor and the other wealthy. If from generosity Dives is
j contributing substantially more than his fair share of the expenses just before his death,
Lazarus may then be said to be entitled to claim against his estate.

   The contemplation of possible examples such as these suggests certain consequences.
First, it seems to me improbable that the word 'immediately' in s 1(1)(e) was intended to
confine the gaze of the court to whatever was the state of maintenance existing at that
precise moment. I very much doubt whether Parliament can have intended people to

shuffle in and out of s 1(1)(e) and 1(3) with every variation in the state of maintenance between them, so that last week C was partly maintaining D with substantial contributions, this week neither is maintaining the other, and next week D will be maintaining C with substantial contributions. Given that the moment at which the examination must be made is the moment before the death of the deceased, what has to be examined ought not, I think, to be the de facto state or balance of maintenance at that moment, but something more substantial and enduring.

The question is what that something is. If at the moment before the death of the deceased there is some settled basis or arrangement between the parties as regards maintenance, then I think that s 1 should be applied to this rather than to any de facto variation in the actual maintenance that may happen to exist at that moment. If the general arrangement between the parties is that D is substantially maintaining C, then matters ought to be decided on that basis. This should be so even if, at the moment before D dies, C is in fact making such contributions, whether in personal services such as nursing or in the provision of money or goods, that on balance C is substantially maintaining D. The word 'immediately' plainly confines the court to the basis or arrangement subsisting at the moment before death, and excludes whatever previously subsisted but has ended, and the state of affairs under it. The nature or the quality of the basis or arrangement in question is a matter that I shall consider in due course. At this stage I shall only add that under all the other heads of s 1(1) the qualification is of an enduring nature. There must be a past or present marriage, paternity or maternity, or the treatment of the claimant as a child of the marriage of the deceased. If para (e) made no more than a transient and fluctuating requirement, it would be strikingly out of line with the other paragraphs.

Second, there is the assumption that I made a short while ago in relation to s 1(3). What is the meaning of the parenthetic phrase 'otherwise than for full valuable consideration' in the subsection? Does it merely mean, as I assumed, that you weigh up the value of the respective contributions in money or money's worth made by C and D towards the reasonable needs of the other, strike a balance, and then say whether the balance of contributions (if any) is substantial? One of counsel's contentions for the plaintiff was that this was wrong. Anything provided for full valuable consideration should be disregarded, he said, if it was provided under a contract: this was necessary in order to protect the proprietor of an old persons' home, for example, from being treated as maintaining all those in his home despite their paying in full for their board and lodging. But unless there was a contract, the parenthetic phrase did not apply.

I can see no justification for reading into the subsection a reference to a contract that does not appear in it. The reference to 'valuable consideration' suggests that thoughts of contract were not likely to have been far from the draftsman's mind; and yet there is no mention of any contract in the subsection. Furthermore, if D is providing full board and lodging for C, but C, without being contractually bound to do so, regularly gives D, in money or money's worth, more than the value of the board and lodging, I find it difficult to see how, in any real sense of the words, it could be said that C 'was being maintained' by D, or that D, by providing C with board and lodging worth less than C gives for it, was making 'a substantial contribution in money or money's worth' towards C's reasonable needs. Quite apart from language, it would be quite contrary to the whole tenor of the Act to allow C to make a claim under it in such a case.

One other consideration is that of the position of C and D if, without any contract, each makes contributions of equal value towards the maintenance of the other, one providing the home and the other the food and drink. Neither in any real sense of the word is maintaining the other: each is bearing a half share of the cost of the joint establishment. Yet if contributions are to be ignored only if made under contract, plainly each is making a substantial contribution in money or money's worth towards the reasonable needs of the other, and so whichever dies first, the other could claim under the Act against the estate of the deceased. Yet if a contract could be spelled out of the arrangements which they made, neither could make such a claim. I cannot see why so much should turn on the presence or absence of a contract.

For these reasons I reject the contention that the parenthetic words in s 1(3) apply only
to full valuable consideration under a contract. Instead, I think that they apply whenever
full valuable consideration is given, whether under a contract or otherwise. This view
accords, I think, with the view taken by Arnold J in *Re Wilkinson*[1]. In that case, I may say,
the judge weighed up the value of the services rendered by the applicant to the deceased,
her sister, with whom she lived, and with some hesitation reached the conclusion that
those services did not amount to full valuable consideration for the maintenance of the
claimant that the deceased had provided. The claimant was accordingly entitled to
proceed with her claim. (I may say that the obscure sentence in the Law Reports[2] which
begins 'According to the question' makes sense if 'Accordingly, the question'[3] is
substituted.)

With that, I can return to the question of the nature or quality of the basis or
arrangement existing immediately before the death that has to be examined. Counsel's
contention for the defendants was that what was required was an assumption of
responsibility by the deceased for the maintenance of the applicant. That might be
contractual, or it might be informal; it might be express or it might be implied; but not
unless it could be said that immediately before the death of the deceased there existed
such an assumption of responsibility could an applicant claim against the estate of the
deceased. Counsel for the defendants accepted, of course, that there was not a word
about this assumption of responsibility in s 1, which prescribes the persons who can
make a claim; but he said that s 3, which deals with matters to which the court must have
regard in considering a claim under the Act, must be treated as qualifying s 1 in this
respect. Alternatively, even if s 3 had no effect on s 1, and a claimant satisfied s 1, his
claim should be struck out if s 3 showed that when his claim came to be considered it was
bound to fail. I must therefore turn to s 3.

In s 3, sub-ss (1) and (2) set out a long list of matters to which the court must have
regard in any application for an order under s 2. These include the financial resources
and financial needs of the applicant, of other possible applicants, and of the beneficiaries,
any obligations and responsibilities which the deceased had towards the applicant, and so
on. Then sub-s (3) deals with applicants under paras (c) and (d) of s 1(1), being respectively
children of the deceased and those who were treated by him as children of the family.
In the latter case (that is, under para (d)), one of the matters to which the court must have
regard is—

'whether the deceased had assumed any responsibility for the applicant's
maintenance and, if so, the extent to which and the basis upon which the deceased
assumed that responsibility and to the length of time for which the deceased
discharged that responsibility.'

On the other hand, sub-s (4) deals with para (e) of s 1(1), the paragraph with which I am
concerned, relating to a person who immediately before the death of the deceased 'was
being maintained, either wholly or partly, by the deceased'. Here, said counsel for the
defendants, there is a striking contrast in the wording. There is no reference to 'whether'
the deceased had assumed any responsibility for the applicant's maintenance, and no
'and, if so': instead, there is an implicit assumption that the deceased has assumed this
responsibility. In a para (e) case, sub-s (4) requires the court to 'have regard to the extent
to which and the basis on which the deceased assumed responsibility for the maintenance
of the applicant, and to the length of time for which the deceased discharged that
responsibility'. With sub-ss (3) and (4) cheek by jowl, and with the close similarity in the
portions of the wording that I have quoted, the difference as to the presence or absence
of the 'whether', and the 'and, if so', points strongly to a difference in meaning. In para
(d) cases, the assumption of responsibility is not essential to success: in para (e) cases it is.
If in drafting the Act it had, for some reason not at present apparent, been thought

1   [1978] 1 All ER 221, [1978] Fam 22
2   [1978] Fam 22 at 23 F
3   [1978] 1 All ER 221 at 223 a

desirable to use different language without conveying any difference of meaning, it would have been easy enough to insert in sub-s (4), in one or more suitable places, the *a* words 'if any' in brackets: but this has not been done. Accordingly, sub-s (4) makes it plain that an essential of a claim under s 1(1)(e) is that the deceased should have assumed responsibility for the maintenance of the applicant; and if the applicant could not establish this, his claim was bound to fail. Thus ran the argument.

To this contention counsel for the plaintiff had no answer that seemed to me to be of any degree of cogency. He stressed, of course, that s 3 appeared to be speaking only as to *b* the hearing of the claim and not as to whether a person was entitled to make a claim, a matter dealt with by s 1. Accordingly it was said that s 3 could not be used to support any contention that a would-be applicant was not entitled to make a claim, and so any claim that he made should be struck out. I do not, however, think that there is any reality in this. If an applicant faces an insurmountable barrier, I do not think that it matters much whether it stands in his path at the door of the court or at the seat of judgment. Of course *c* s 3 is dealing only with the matters to which the court must have regard, and it does not per se exclude any claim which lacks one or more of these matters. But s 3(4) assumes that in any case within para (e) which reaches that stage there has in fact been an assumption of responsibility, and so I think it excludes from the Act any such case where there has been no such assumption of responsibility.

In this connection I should mention something that occurred during the argument. *d* The Act, as is well-known, was engendered by the Law Commission. In its second report on family property, Family Provision on Death[1], the Law Commission recommended legislation on the lines of the Act, and appended a draft bill. In all material respects the relevant provisions of the draft bill (and especially cll 1(1)(e) and 3(3) and (4)) appear to be identical with the corresponding sections of the Act. In particular, there is the same structure whereby s 1 states who can claim and ss 2 and 3 provide what orders the court *e* can make, and what matters must be considered by the court. Counsel for the plaintiff referred me to the report, and without objection by counsel for the defendants (not surprisingly, in the event) adopted certain passages as part of his argument, including para 91[2]. This is dealing with the new category of those being maintained by the deceased, that is, category (e) cases. In that paragraph there is a sentence which states that— *f*

> 'it could (and should) be made clear that, if those who were dependent on the deceased at the time of his death are to be entitled to apply for family provision, the court should give special consideration to the basis upon which the deceased undertook responsibility for that person's maintenance.'

This plainly appears to envisage that only dependants for whose maintenance the *g* deceased had undertaken responsibility were to be 'entitled to apply' for an order; and this is in accordance with counsel's submission for the defendants. The fact that the Law Commission's draft bill does not make the undertaking of responsibility a requirement for the right to apply under s 1, but instead includes it as part of what has to be considered under s 3 when the application has been made, is, of course, curious: but I cannot see that it vitiates counsel's argument for the defendants in any way. When s 3(4) provides that *h* where a claim is made under para (e) the court 'shall have regard' to the assumption of responsibility by the deceased, and in fact there has been no such assumption of responsibility, the choice is between holding that the claim must fail because of the absence of an element which the court is required to have regard to, and holding that the court must disobey the statute because it is impossible to obey it. No doubt the disobedience could be softened or conjured away by implying into the subsection the *j*

1 Law Com 61 (1974)
2 Ibid p 24

a words 'if any' in appropriate places; but as I have indicated the contrast with the language of s 3(3) discourages such an approach.

I do not pretend that the question is easy. Nevertheless, it seems to me that what I have said in relation to the word 'immediately' strongly indicates that the first of the alternatives ought to be adopted. If one is to reject a mere examination of the de facto state of affairs existing at the instant before the death, and seek to discover something more substantial and enduring than that, then an assumption by the deceased of *b* responsibility for the maintenance of the applicant seems to me to be the relationship which has to be considered. If immediately before the death of the deceased such an assumption of responsibility by the deceased for the applicant was in existence, and under it the applicant was being maintained, wholly or partly, by the deceased, then the applicant may claim under the Act. In such a case, the degree of maintenance would not be whatever degree existed at the instant before death, but whatever degree normally *c* and habitually existed under the assumption of responsibility which was then in existence. In general, the requirement of an assumption of responsibility seems to me to be suitable for excluding most cases which appear to be outside the general purport and intent of this part of the Act without excluding those cases which ought to fall within it. No doubt there may be debatable cases: but I have to do the best I can on the material that is before me.

d   While I do not, of course, rely on the report of the Law Commission[1] as an authority, I cannot think that my conclusion is any the worse for appearing to be in accordance with the report on this point. I may perhaps also observe that a process of balancing contributions to a common home and considering what is provided otherwise than for full valuable consideration, irrespective of any contract, seems to me to be consonant with para 98[2] of the report; and it seems clear[3] that s 1(3) was indeed intended merely to *e* explain s 1(1)(e). I may add that although of course much must have been debated by the Law Commission before making the report, neither in para 98 of the report nor elsewhere is there any discussion of most of the examples mentioned in this judgment. Indeed, I remain uncertain how far the concept that lies behind s 1(1)(e) has been fully worked out. Let me take one more example, by no means uncommon. The members of a family take it in turns to provide a home for C, an old and poor relation of theirs. *f* C lives with each in turn for some two or three months, and then moves on. If a member of the family dies, does C's right to claim against the deceased depend on whether or not at the death C was living with the deceased?

I return at last to the facts of this case. If I am right in the views that I have expressed, then I have to examine the state of affairs existing immediately before the death of the deceased to discover if at that moment there existed an assumption of responsibility by *g* the deceased for the maintenance of the plaintiff, and the extent to which, in the normal state of affairs under that assumption of responsibility, the plaintiff was being maintained by the deceased. In doing that I have to consider whether the deceased, otherwise than for full valuable consideration (and irrespective of the existence of any contract), was making a substantial contribution in money or money's worth towards the reasonable needs of the plaintiff. As this is an application by the defendants to strike out the claim *h* of the plaintiff, in the nature of a demurrer (as was the case in *Re Wilkinson*[4]), I have to do this on the basis that for this purpose the plaintiff's evidence is accepted.

The central question is whether the deceased assumed responsibility for the maintenance of the plaintiff. On this, the onus, I think, must lie on the plaintiff, both on general principles and on the decision in *Re Wilkinson*[4]. There, it was held that the onus of bringing the claimant within the definition of a person within s 1(1)(e) 'rests squarely

j

---

1   Law Com 61 (1974)
2   Ibid p 26
3   See ibid p 85
4   [1978] 1 All ER 221, [1978] Fam 22

throughout on the applicant'[1]. The plaintiff and the deceased in the present case, of
course, lived together as man and wife for some 30 years or more; but the whole picture *a*
presented by the plaintiff is one of two people, each with their own earnings and, latterly,
their own pensions, who chose to pool such of their individual resources as were needed
for them to be able to live with each other without either undertaking any responsibility
for maintaining the other. Each paid his or her own way, and there is nothing to suggest
that any change in this state of affairs was even contemplated. The deceased seems to
have been a woman of some independence of character, concerned to make it clear that *b*
her bungalow and all improvements to it were hers alone. She kept accounts of all that
she spent, and from time to time paid sums of money to the plaintiff in respect of
decorating work that he did to the bungalow, recording these payments on slips of paper,
some of which have survived. The plaintiff says that these payments were not for the
work that he did, but were in the nature of cash for him to buy a drink after a hard day's
decorating, a distinction that is not very easy to comprehend. I do not think that the fact *c*
that in sickness each nursed the other in any way affects the picture of two people with
means that are independent of each other sharing their lives without either of them
doing anything which showed any intention to assume any responsibility for the
maintenance of the other. Indeed, when cross-examined on his affidavits before the
master, the plaintiff accepted that the deceased had never agreed in any way to be
responsible for his maintenance.   *d*
    Counsel for the plaintiff argued in the alternative that if the deceased was in fact
maintaining the plaintiff (as he said that she was), that of itself showed that the deceased
had assumed responsibility for his maintenance: the fact of maintaining sufficed to
establish an assumption of responsibility. I do not think that this can be right. The Act
is drafted in language which treats 'being maintained' and the assumption of
'responsibility for the maintenance' as being distinct. Furthermore, I can see no reason *e*
why the provision of maintenance should not be accompanied by an express or tacit
negation of any responsibility for maintenance. In such a case it would be impossible to
treat the fact of maintenance as proving an assumption of that responsibility which has
been denied. The word 'assumes', too, seems to me to indicate that there must be some
act or acts which demonstrate an undertaking of responsibility, or the taking of the
responsibility on oneself.   *f*
    It may be that in some cases where there is neither a negation of responsibility nor a
positive undertaking of it, it will be possible to infer from the circumstances attending
the fact of maintenance that there has indeed been an undertaking of responsibility. But
it is for the plaintiff to establish that there has been an assumption of responsibility, and
not for the defendants to have to rebut any presumption of an assumption of
responsibility which is to be drawn from the bare fact of maintenance. In this case I can *g*
see nothing to indicate that the deceased assumed any responsibility for the maintenance
of the plaintiff. I may add that if from kindness D, out of his substantial earned income,
has been partly maintaining C, an aged and indigent friend or relation or former servant,
in circumstances which make it clear that D was undertaking no responsibility for C's
maintenance, I think it would be remarkable if it were to be held that s 1(1)(*e*) permitted
C to make a claim against D's estate. To say that the claim, when heard, is likely to fail *h*
would be small comfort to D's widow and family when confronted by the nuisance value
of C's claim. It may be that would-be benefactors who wish to protect their families
ought to obtain from anyone to whose maintenance they propose to contribute an
acknowledgment that they are undertaking no responsibility for his or her maintenance. Unless this suffices, the path of safety seems, rather sadly, to be simply to abstain
from any such generosity.   *i*
    For the reasons that I have given, I think that the plaintiff's claim is bound to fail, so
that the defendants' summons to strike out or dismiss the plaintiff's proceedings under
the originating summons should succeed. There is another summons before me, a pro

---

1   [1978] 1 All ER 221 at 222, [1978] Fam 22 at 23

a forma summons by the plaintiff for an interim order under the Act, issued on the directions of the master. As the originating summons will be struck out or dismissed, the plaintiff's summons necessarily falls to the ground, and will be dismissed. That brings me to the matter of procedure that I mentioned at the outset of this judgment.

Both summonses come before me on adjournment from the master. The course that the case followed before the master was, I hope, unusual. I set it out on what both counsel told me and on the master's notes and his judgment. Before the defendants'
b summons to strike out the application came to be heard, the master had directed that all witnesses should attend for cross-examination before him. The case came on for hearing before the master on 9th October. Both counsel informed the master that whatever his decision they would ask for the case to be adjourned to the judge; and this attitude, said the master, he considered to be entirely reasonable. Counsel for the plaintiff told the master that he sought interim maintenance, and so the master directed the plaintiff to
c issue a pro forma summons for this purpose, returnable that day; and he said that he would deal with both summonses at the same time. He then said that under the defendants' summons to strike out the proceedings, the first point was whether the plaintiff was qualified under s 1(1)(e); and he ruled that this should be dealt with after cross-examination as it so much depended on fact, and it gave the plaintiff an opportunity to explain.

d I pause at that point. As the defendants' summons stood at that time it was worded substantially in terms of RSC Ord 18, r 19(1)(a); and, as I have mentioned, in such cases, by r 2, no evidence is admissible. It was for that reason that when the summons came before me it was amended so as to rely also on the inherent jurisdiction, where there is no such limitation. Nevertheless, although before the master counsel argued that the proceedings were in the nature of a demurrer, as in *Re Wilkinson*[1], the master insisted on
e all the affidavits save one being read, and there were about eight pages of cross-examination (with a gap in the middle when the tape recorder was switched off), over half a page of re-examination, and then less than half a page of cross-examination of one of the defendants. This latter was not very illuminating: the transcript reveals one question to the witness, asking her if she had her affidavit, and then three more questions to which the answers were inaudible. After this, counsel argued the case, particularly on
f the point as to the assumption of responsibility for maintenance; and I think that the case as a whole took a day to hear, solely on the defendant's summons to strike out. The summons for an interim order was not dealt with. The next morning the master read a ten-page judgment, dated the previous day. In this, he dismissed the defendants' summons to strike out the proceedings, rejecting the defendants' contention that an assumption of responsibility by the deceased for the maintenance of the plaintiff was
g requisite. He then adjourned to the judge both the defendants' summons to strike out the proceedings and the plaintiff's summons for an interim order, which, of course had not been heard.

The reasons stated by the master for taking the course that he did were that in view of the plaintiff's straitened circumstances the substance of his application should be dealt with at an early date 'by opening a way to avoid the proceedings going through three
h stages, viz jurisdiction, interim application, final application'. He also said that to save the time and expense of all concerned (bearing in mind the inevitable adjournment to the judge) he would deal first with the question whether the plaintiff was entitled to apply under the Act. This point, of course, arose both under the defendants' summons and under the plaintiff's summons for an interim order: see ss 1(1)(e), 2 and 5.

It is plain that the master was concerned to do the best that he could to assist the
j parties. Nevertheless, I think that the course that the case took was in some respects unfortunate. I cannot see why all the witnesses should have been required to attend for cross-examination. Their evidence was not admissible on the summons to strike out which the master heard, and the master never heard the summons for an interim order,

---

1   [1978] 1 All ER 221, [1978] Fam 22

on which their oral evidence might have been of some value. It took some time to get
a transcript of the cross-examination, and it cost some £30, I was told. Furthermore, the *a*
master's decision on the defendants' summons to strike out meant that the plaintiff had
been held eligible to apply for an interim order, which can be made if it appears to the
court that the applicant 'is in immediate need of financial assistance' (s 5(1)(a)): yet that
was the application that was left undecided.

A Chancery master's discretion whether to adjourn a matter to the judge unheard or
whether to hear it first before adjourning it must sometimes be difficult to exercise. *b*
However strongly counsel may initially assert before the master that in any event they
will require an adjournment to the judge, there are some cases where, once the master's
decision has been announced, no adjournment will in fact be sought, and the parties will
be saved the costs and delay that are inevitable in any such adjournment. The master's
decision may convince the loser that to take the case to the judge will merely be to throw
good money after bad. But where, as in this case, there is plainly a difficult point of law *c*
on one summons, and the decision on that summons shows that the plaintiff is entitled
to proceed on the other summons, I find it very difficult to see what advantage there is
to anyone in deciding the first summons and then adjourning the other summons
without judgment. Such a course makes even more inevitable the adjournment to the
judge which in any case the master recognises as being inevitable, and seems to do little
save to increase costs. *d*

Such a course also seems to ensure that the case will go through the three stages that
the master very properly sought to avoid, namely jurisdiction, interim application and
final application, instead of making it at least possible that the first two would go no
further than the master, having both been decided by him. It will be remembered that
by RSC Ord 32, r 14(4), nothing in r 14(1), which provides for the exercise of jurisdiction
by Chancery masters, is to authorise a master to determine a question of law raised by an *e*
originating summons for the determination of the court. I think that masters should
bear this in mind in cases where the heart and core of a procedure summons consists of
a difficult point of law and all the parties state that in any case they will require the case
to be adjourned to the judge; and of course in deciding what course to follow one factor
that must never be lost sight of is which course will be likely to increase the burden of
costs the least, especially where modest sums are at stake. *f*

I do not think that I need to say any more about the procedure. It only remains for me
to say that the originating summons will be struck out or dismissed (whichever is the
appropriate term), and the plaintiff's summons for an interim order will be dismissed.

Order accordingly.

g
Solicitors: *Stanley de Leon & Co*, Potters Bar (for the plaintiff); *Reading & Co*, Potters Bar
(for the defendants).

Azza M Abdallah   Barrister.

a
Re St Mary Magdalene, Paddington

LONDON CONSISTORY COURT
CHANCELLOR G H NEWSOM QC
2nd MAY, 5th NOVEMBER 1979

Ecclesiastical law − Incumbent − Freehold − Unconsecrated churchyard − Power to convey −
b *Whether power at common law as well as under statute − Whether consistory court can authorise*
sale at common law and direct application of proceeds − Whether court restricted to authorising
sale under statute with consequent restrictions on sale and on application of proceeds − New
Parishes Measure 1943, s 17.

Ecclesiastical law − Unconsecrated curtilage of church − Curtilage − Churchyard − Churchyard
greater than curtilage − Whether churchyard within jurisdiction of consistory court − Faculty
c *Jurisdiction Measure 1964, s 7(1).*

An incumbent in whom the freehold of the churchyard is vested has power, either at
common law or under s 17[a] of the New Parishes Measure 1943, to sell, with the authority
of a consistory court, unwanted unconsecrated churchyard. Accordingly, a consistory
court is not restricted to authorising the sale of such land under the s 17 procedure
d (which requires certain consents to be obtained and the proceeds of the sale to be applied
in accordance with s 17(4)) but can adopt the simpler procedure of authorising a sale at
common law involving only the parties to the sale and the court, and under such
procedure the court itself can direct the application of the proceeds of sale (see p 280 *f* to
h, p 282 *f* to *h* and p 283 *a b*, post).

Re St George's Church, Oakdale [1975] 2 All ER 870 not followed.

e Unconsecrated churchyard has always been within the jurisdiction of the consistory
court. Section 7(1)[b] of the Faculty Jurisdiction Measure 1964, which provides that the
court has jurisdiction over unconsecrated land forming part of the 'curtilage' of a church,
is declaratory, and where the churchyard is greater than the 'curtilage' the court has
jurisdiction over the whole churchyard (see p 280 *f*, post).

f **Petition for faculty**
This was a petition by the Reverend Michael James Stephenson, vicar of St Mary
Magdalene, Paddington, and Mr Frederick George Wright and Mrs Elsie Muriel Hyett,
churchwardens, for the grant of a faculty authorising the sale of a strip of land comprising
unconsecrated churchyard immediately adjacent to the church to the Westminster City
Council for the sum of £750 plus legal costs and a contribution to the surveyors' fees.
The Church Commissioners for England were represented at the hearing since their
g consent would be required in the event of the sale of the land under s 17 of the New
Parishes Measures 1943. The facts are set out in the judgment.

Mr Ian Gower Williams, solicitor, for the petitioners.
Mr George Atkinson, solicitor, for the council.
h Mr Barry G Hall, solicitor, for the commissioners.

Notes
For faculties relating to churchyards, see 14 Halsbury's Laws (4th Edn) para 1315, and for
cases on the grant of faculties, see 19 Digest (Repl) 377−378, 1752-1766.
For the New Parishes Measure 1943, s 17, see 10 Halsbury's Statutes (3rd Edn) 654.
For the Faculty Jurisdiction Measure 1964, s 7, see ibid 309.
j

---

a   Section 17, so far as material, is set out at p 280 *g h*, post
b   Section 7(1) provides: 'For the avoidance of doubt it is hereby declared that where unconsecrated
land forms, or is part of, the curtilage of a church within the jurisdiction of a court that court has
the same jurisdiction over such land as over the church.'

Cases referred to in judgment

Christ Church, Chislehurst, Re [1974] 1 All ER 146, [1973] 1 WLR 1317, Digest (Cont **a**
    Vol D) 284, *1763a*.
St George's Church, Oakdale, Re [1975] 2 All ER 870, [1976] Fam 210, [1975] 3 WLR 804,
    Digest (Cont Vol D) 285, *1799aa*.
St John's Church, Bishop's Hatfield, Re [1966] 2 All ER 403, [1967] P 113, [1966] 2 WLR
    705, Digest (Cont Vol B) 233, *1799a*.
St Peter's, Burley Heath [1971] 2 All ER 704, [1971] 1 WLR 357, 30 Digest (Reissue) 284, **b**
    928.

Cur adv vult

5th November. **THE CHANCELLOR** read the following judgment: This case
concerns a strip of land immediately adjacent to the church on its north side, which was
conveyed in 1868 to the then Ecclesiastical Commission along with the land which **c**
became the site of the church itself. The church was consecrated; the strip was not. On
the consecration of the church both church site and strip became vested in the incumbent
as a corporation sole under the legislation then in force. The strip was thus unconsecrated
churchyard. Moreover, it was so close to the church as necessarily to be curtilage of the
church within s 7 of the Faculty Jurisdiction Measure 1964, however the word curtilage
is to be construed. The strip is now wanted by the Westminster City Council to become **d**
part of their canalside walk and to be held by them as a public open space under the Open
Spaces Act 1906. The purpose is laudable, the terms are in my opinion satisfactory, and
I propose to authorise the strip to be conveyed to the council.

However, questions arise as to the form of, and the parties to, the proposed conveyance,
and as to the disposition of the proceeds of sale. There is some apparent conflict between
the recent reported authorities, and I therefore said at the hearing in chambers that I **e**
should put my judgment on these points into writing for the guidance of those who are
concerned in the Diocese of London with cases of this sort, which are not by any means
infrequent.

There is, in my opinion, no doubt that unconsecrated churchyard has always been
within the jurisdiction of the Consistory Court. Section 7 of the 1964 Measure uses the
word 'curtilage' and is declaratory. But 'curtilage' may well be smaller than 'churchyard' **f**
and the greater includes the less. When it comes to making a conveyance of the strip,
whether it be designated as curtilage or as unconsecrated churchyard, the first possibility,
and much the simplest, is that the incumbent, who has the freehold, should convey it to
the council under the authority of a faculty. The other, and more complicated, possibility
is that a faculty should authorise title to be made under s 17 of the New Parishes Measure
1943, as substituted by s 6 of the Church Property (Miscellaneous Provisions) Measure **g**
1960. Under this latter provision the incumbent (with the authority of a faculty, since
sub-s (5) says that 'Nothing in this section shall . . . affect the jurisdiction of the Consistory
Court', which undoubtedly has jurisdiction over the strip) can sell it, but only with the
consent of the Church Commissioners and of the bishop (see the proviso to sub-s (1)).
The proceeds of sale have to be 'paid to the Commissioners and . . . applied by them . . .
for the benefit of the benefice . . . or charitable purposes relating to [the] district, as may **h**
be agreed between the Commissioners and the bishop after consultation with [the
incumbent]': see sub-s (4). The commissioners were represented before me and I was
informed that they do not particularly welcome being invited to act in such a case as this,
which makes work for them which would not otherwise come their way and takes up
their time. Nor, so far as I can see, would there be any advantage to the bishop in being
brought in if the work can be done by his court. **j**

In *Re St George's Church, Oakdale*[1], a case in the Diocese of Salisbury, Chancellor Ellison
held that the procedure under the New Parishes Measure 1943 was the only possible

_____

1   [1975] 2 All ER 870, [1976] Fam 210

one. The basis of his decision was that at common law an incumbent had no power to
a convey away unconsecrated churchyard which was not needed as such. Admittedly,
various Union of Beneficies Acts and Measures conferred specific powers of disposition;
but the provisions of the New Parishes Measure 1943, which correspond to the present
s 17, was, he said, the first general power for an incumbent to convey such land. Hence,
said Chancellor Ellison, the court could confer no other power on him. Further, he held
that the provision of the present s 17(5), which apparently saves the existing jurisdiction
b of the Consistory Court, amounts only to a recognition that the court has jurisdiction
over the *user* of unconsecrated churchyard, and it does not mean that the court can
authorise the ultimate disposal of such land[1]. He also observed that he had heard no less
an authority than my predecessor, the late Dr W S Wigglesworth QC, voice anxiety about
the uncertain meaning of s 17(5). This last statement is a little surprising in view of the
part played by Dr Wigglesworth in *Re St John's Church, Bishop's Hatfield*[2], to which I refer
c later.

    The major premise on which the reasoning of Chancellor Ellison rests is that at
common law the incumbent had no power, even under a faculty, to dispose of pieces of
unconsecrated and unwanted churchyard or curtilage[3]. But my attention has been
drawn to a decision of Chancellor Tristram, sitting as the Commissary-General of the
City and Diocese of Canterbury in 1897, where he authorised precisely that thing to be
d done. The case is referred to briefly in the judgment of Chancellor Goodman in *Re Christ
Church, Chislehurst*[4], a later case about the same churchyard, but in the Consistory Court
of the Diocese of Rochester, the parish having in the meantime been transferred from,
the Diocese of Canterbury to that of Rochester. The decision of Chancellor Tristram
authorised an unwanted part of the unconsecrated churchyard of Christ Church to be
conveyed by the incumbent to a Miss Quincey, subject to certain restrictive covenants,
e for the sum of £150 and he directed that the purchase money should be applied first in
payment of the costs of the proceedings and then in reduction of a debt to Martins Bank
for money which the bank had lent towards the purchase of the parsonage house. Here,
then, we find, in 1897, long before the New Parishes Measure 1943, that the Consistory
Court was treating itself as entitled to authorise the incumbent to make a conveyance of
the kind in question and to direct what was to be done with the proceeds of sale.
f Chancellor Goodman has supplied me with a photostat copy of what appears to be the
actual order of Chancellor Tristram, or perhaps a final draft of it, which he has obtained
from the Canterbury Registry. It is added to this present judgment by way of appendix[5].
I cannot think that the existence of this order was known to Chancellor Ellison; for it is
not mentioned in his judgment in the *Oakdale* case[6] and it is fundamentally inconsistent
with his decision there. I should mention that nothing on the face of the order indicates
g that the case was contested or argued. But, if there had been any doubt about the
jurisdiction (and at this date if there was no power of sale at common law the sale could
not be made at all), Chancellor Tristram would surely have set the case down for
hearing. It is, in my judgment, much more likely that he was exercising an accepted and
familiar jurisdiction.

    Chancellor Tristram was chancellor of several dioceses and by 1897 had already been
h chancellor of the Diocese of London for well over 20 years. I should be slow indeed to
say that he acted without jurisdiction. Of course, a decision of his in the Canterbury
Diocese is not strictly binding on me in London. But it is a great persuasive authority
and I propose respectfully to follow it in the present case. I shall therefore authorise the

---

j
1   [1975] 2 All ER 870 at 877–878, [1976] Fam 210 at 218
2   [1966] 2 All ER 403, [1967] P 113
3   [1975] 2 All ER 870 at 875, [1976] Fam 210 at 215
4   [1974] 1 All ER 146 at 148, 151, [1973] 1 WLR 1317 at 1319, 1321
5   See p 283, post
6   [1975] 2 All ER 870, [1976] Fam 210

incumbent to convey the land to the council and at the request of the incumbent I shall direct that the purchase money and interest (for this completion has been long delayed) *a* shall be paid to the parochial church council to be held as part of the fabric fund for the charitable purpose of the upkeep of the church building itself.

Though that disposes of this case, it may be as well that I should put on record certain matters relating to two decisions of my own as Chancellor of the Diocese of St Albans and one decision of Chancellor Goodman in the recent case of *Re Christ Church, Chislehurst*[1], since they are criticised in the *Oakdale*[2] judgment. The first of my decisions, *Re St John's* *b* *Church, Bishop's Hatfield*[3], was a case where a piece of unconsecrated churchyard or curtilage, belonging to a very new church, was needed for a secular building. The problem was to get rid of the jurisdiction of the court. Dr Wigglesworth appeared before me as counsel for the petitioners and he did not suggest that I had no jurisdiction. On the contrary, at his express instance, I destroyed my jurisdiction by granting a faculty authorising the secular building to be put up, that being a building *c* whose existence was wholly inconsistent with the concept that its site would continue to be church curtilage or indeed churchyard. Having destroyed the jurisdiction, there was no room for the application of the power exercised by Chancellor Tristram in 1897, and the conveyancing was dealt with, out of court, under the supervision of Dr Wigglesworth himself, by means of the New Parishes Measure 1943 as altered in 1960. The only present relevance of that case is that the proceedings were founded on the proposition *d* that the court had jurisdiction and that it was Dr Wigglesworth who proceeded on that footing, notwithstanding what was later said about him in the *Oakdale* case[2].

The next case was *Re St Peter's, Bushey Heath*[4]; but in that case I merely authorised the grant of a right of way over a piece of unconsecrated churchyard or curtilage; thus there was no question of my allowing a conveyance which would terminate the jurisdiction of the court over the area in question. So this case too does not bear on the present problem. *e* In recent *Chislehurst case*[5], the court, having adopted my reasoning about 'curtilage', and distinguishing the *Bushey Heath* case[4] on the facts, authorised the sale of the land and referred the actual conveyancing to be considered in chambers. It appears however from the remarks of Chancellor Goodman[6] that he considered that the conveyance would be made under the New Parishes Measure 1943 and that he would therefore have no control over the proceeds of sale. He has informed me that the documents had already been *f* prepared on that basis and that the faculty transfer authorised the sale to proceed in that manner.

There are two possible procedures and in my judgment they are alternatives, since there was a power at common law and the 1943 Measure gives an extra power; it is not designed to abridge existing powers. Subject always to the jurisdiction of the Consistory Court, each power exists side by side with the other. If, as in the recent *Chislehurst* case[1], *g* the court chooses to authorise the incumbent to use the power given by the 1943 Measure, it follows that the consents required by that Measure are necessary as well as a faculty and that the proceeds of sale must be dealt with as the Measure provides. But if, as in the present case, the court chooses to use the method employed by Chancellor Tristram, then, like him, the court can direct the application of the proceeds of sale. The powers are alternative, and each is independent of the other. The court must not blur *h* the distinction. But the authority of the court is necessary whichever way the conveyancing is to be done.

---

1   [1974] 1 All ER 146, [1973] 1 WLR 1317   *j*
2   [1975] 2 All ER 870, [1976] Fam 210
3   [1966] 2 All ER 403, [1967] P 113
4   [1971] 2 All ER 704, [1971] 1 WLR 357
5   [1974] 1 All ER 146 at 156, [1973] 1 WLR 1317 at 1327
6   [1974] 1 All ER 146 at 152, [1973] 1 WLR 1317 at 1323

I hope that this judgment will serve to clear up some of the misunderstanding which

a appears to have existed at the time of the *Oakdale* case[1].

To conclude, I propose in this case, and whenever it is convenient to do so, to exercise the jurisdiction that was exercised by Chancellor Tristram in the *Chislehurst* case of 1897. It seems altogether easier and shorter than to authorise a sale under the 1943 Measure, since it involves only the parties directly concerned with the transaction and the court itself.

b *Faculty authorising sale granted.*

Solicitors: *Beaumont & Son* (for the petitioners); *Edward Woolf* (for the council); *Official Solicitor to the Church Commissioners for England.*

K Mydeen Esq   Barrister.

c   APPENDIX

IN THE COMMISSARY COURT OF THE CITY AND DIOCESE OF CANTERBURY.

IN THE MATTER of a Petition for a faculty for the sale of a plot of unconsecrated land being part of other land surrounding enclosing and belonging to the consecrated church of Christ Church, Chislehurst in the County of Kent and the Diocese of Canterbury.

d The Reverend William Fleming (Incumbent) and James Battens Esq JP and Robert Whyte Esq JP (the Churchwardens of Christ Church) v The Parishioners of the Parish of Chislehurst.

5th August 1897.

e Order of Chancellor Tristram:

'The Judge having considered the same decreed a faculty to issue sanctioning the sale of a plot of land measuring 17 perches and marked with the letter Z on the plan annexed to the petition and forming part of a larger plot of land conveyed to the Ecclesiastical Commissioners for England on the 29th day of November 1871 by the late Nathaniel William John Strode of Camden Place Chislehurst Esquire as a free gift for the erection

f of a church thereon to Miss Harriet Quincey of the "Arab's Tent" immediately adjoining but henceforth to be called Stowcroft for the sum of £150. The Judge being satisfied upon the evidence that the said plot of land had not been consecrated and that from its position it was of no available use for the extension of the church and that its retention would not be for the benefit of the parishioners directed that the said William Fleming should as incumbent execute a Deed of Conveyance of the said Plot of land to the said

g Harriet Quincey containing a covenant by the purchaser for herself her heirs and assigns that she would not at any time hereafter erect on any part of the said plot of land any erection or building whatsoever or use or permit the same or any part thereof to be used in such a manner as to be a nuisance or annoyance to the owners or occupiers of adjoining property. The Judge also directed that the purchase money should be paid to an account on behalf of the Incumbent and Churchwardens of the said church to be applied in

h payment in the first place of the costs incident to the obtaining of the faculty hereby decreed and in the next place the balance to be applied in diminution of a subsisting debt of about £500, due to Martins Bank Limited of Lombard Street in the City of London for money advanced by them for the purchase of the Parsonage House belonging to the said church. The Judge further decreed that on the Deed of Conveyance being produced to the Registrar of the Court the faculty should issue to the said Harriet Quincey granting

j to her her heirs and assigns the free and undisturbed use of the said plot of land in consideration of the payment of the said sum of £150 for all time to come. Subject nevertheless to the covenant hereinbefore mentioned and to the further covenant by the

---

1   [1975] 2 All ER 870, [1976] Fam 210

said Harriet Quincey that she would forever after maintain along the present boundary
on the church side of the said plot of land a suitable fence or wall of not less than a height
of 5′6″.′

Henry Fielding (Registrar).

Re a Company

COURT OF APPEAL, CIVIL DIVISION
LORD DENNING MR, SHAW AND TEMPLEMAN LJJ
31st JULY 1979

*Appeal – Right of appeal – Exclusion of right of appeal – Error of law – Statute misconstrued
– Judge mistakenly declining jurisdiction – Statute providing judge's decision 'not appealable' –
Whether misconstruction of statute an error of law going to jurisdiction – Whether right of appeal
against judge's decision – Companies Act 1948, s 441(3).*

*Company – Officer – Offence in connection with management of company's affairs – Subordinate
manager defrauding customers for company's benefit – Whether manager an 'officer' of company
– Whether fraud 'an offence in connection with the management of the company's affairs' –
Companies Act 1948, s 441(1).*

A subordinate manager of a company sent false statements to customers of the company
demanding payment of more than was due. A number of customers paid the inflated
statements without query and as the company benefited by the overpayments the
company itself was suspected of fraud. In order to obtain proof of the company's
involvement the Director of Public Prosecutions applied to a judge under s 441(1)[a] of the
Companies Act 1948 for authority to inspect the books or papers of the company. The
Director claimed that he had reasonable cause to believe that 'an officer' of the company
had committed 'an offence in connection with the management of the company's affairs',
that evidence of the offence would be found in the company's books or papers, and that
an order should be made under s 441. The judge held that he had no jurisdiction to
grant the application because the subordinate manager was not 'an officer' of the
company and the suspected fraud was not 'an offence in connection with the management
of the company's affairs' because it was not a breach of the laws regulating the
management of the company's affairs. The Director appealed. On the hearing of the
appeal the question arose whether the Director had a right to appeal, since s 441(3)[b] stated
that the decision of a judge on an application under s 441 'shall not be appealable'.

Held – There was a right of appeal against the judge's decision, and the appeal would be
allowed, for the following reasons—
　(i) The judge had mistakenly refused jurisdiction as a result of misconstruing the 1948
Act and accordingly had made an error of law going to jurisdiction, which gave rise to
a right of appeal notwithstanding the exclusionary words of s 441(3) of that Act (see
p 286 e to g, p 287 d e j and p 288 d e, post); dicta of Lord Reid, of Lord Pearce and of Lord
Wilberforce in *Anisminic Ltd v Foreign Compensation Commission* [1969] 1 All ER at 213–
214, 233, 246, and of Lord Denning MR in *Pearlman v Keepers and Governors of Harrow
School* [1979] 1 All ER at 372 applied.
　(ii) Since s 455 of the 1948 Act provided that 'an officer' of a company 'included a
director, manager or secretary' and since in the context of the Act 'a manager' was not
restricted to the directors or general manager but included anyone who exercised
supervisory or managerial control reflecting the general policy of the company or relating
to its general administration, it followed that the subordinate manager who had carried

---

a　Section 441(1), so far as material, is set out at p 286 b c, post
b　Section 441(3), so far as material, is set out at p 286 e, post

out the suspected fraud was 'an officer' of the company for the purposes of s 441 (see
a p 286 *j* to p 287 *a d e j* and p 288 *c d*, post).

(iii) Since s 441 dealt with criminal acts and was intended to ensure that they were not
concealed behind the corporate facade of a company, 'an offence in connection with the
management of the company's affairs' in that section was not restricted either to internal
misconduct in which the company itself was the victim or to offences under the 1948
Act, but extended to the suspected fraud by the subordinate manager in the instant case
b (see p 286 *a*, p 287 *a* to *e h j* and p 288 *b* to *e*, post).

Notes

For the production of a company's books where an offence is suspected, see 7 Halsbury's
Laws (4th Edn) para 762.

For the Companies Act 1948, ss 441, 455, see 5 Halsbury's Statutes (3rd Edn) 423, 429.
c

Cases referred to in judgments

Anisminic Ltd v Foreign Compensation Commission [1969] 1 All ER 208, [1969] 2 AC 147,
  [1969] 2 WLR 163, HL, Digest (Cont Vol C) 281, 2557b.
Pearlman v Keepers and Governors of Harrow School [1979] 1 All ER 365, [1979] QB 56,
  [1978] 3 WLR 736, CA.
d

Cases also cited

R v Board of Trade, ex parte St Martin Preserving Co Ltd [1964] 2 All ER 561, [1965] 1 QB
  603, DC.
Registrar of Restrictive Trading Agreements v W H Smith & Son Ltd [1969] 3 All ER 1065,
  [1969] 1 WLR 1460, CA.
e *SBA Properties Ltd v Cradock* [1967] 2 All ER 610, [1967] 1 WLR 716.

Appeal

The Director of Public Prosecutions appealed against an order of Vinelott J made on 6th
April 1979 dismissing an application made by the Director pursuant to s 441 of the
Companies Act 1948 for an order authorising a detective inspector and a government
f officer to inspect all books, records, correspondence and other papers belonging to, or
under the control of, a named company and requiring a named director of the company
to produce the company's books, records, correspondence and other papers for the
purpose of the inspection. The facts are set out in the judgment of Lord Denning MR.

Robin Auld QC and *Clive Nichols* for the Director of Public Prosecutions.
g *Donald Rattee QC* for the Official Solicitor as amicus curiae.
The company was not represented.

LORD DENNING MR. Suspicion has fallen on a company. So much so that there is
reasonable cause to believe that an offence has been committed. It would appear that
h fraudulent statements were sent out to customers in which the company demanded
more money than it was entitled to: and the customers paid on those demands. In order
to prove the fraud, it will be necessary to have access to the invoices and accounts which
the company itself received from its suppliers. The matter was referred to the Director
of Public Prosecutions. He wanted to see the company's papers. He made an application
under s 441 of the Companies Act 1948. That enables the Director of Public Prosecutions
j or the Board of Trade or a chief officer of police to go to a judge of the High Court and
tell him that he has reasonable cause for believing that an offence is being committed in
connection with the management of a company's affairs. If the High Court judge is
satisfied that the provisions of the section have been complied with, then he is able to
make an order authorising somebody to inspect the books or papers of the company and
require the secretary or other officers of the company to produce the books and papers for

inspection. It is certainly an important power. It is analogous to a search warrant. It is
justifiable on public policy grounds: because companies are so impersonal that all sorts *a*
of frauds can be concealed beneath their cloaks. It has substantial safeguards in that the
application has to be made by a very responsible officer and is only to be granted by a
High Court judge.

When the Director of Public Prosecutions applied under s 441, the judge refused to
make an order. He limited the range of offences to which it applied. The section says:

> '(1) If . . . there is shown to be reasonable cause to believe that any person has, *b*
> while an officer of a company, committed an offence in connection with the
> management of the company's affairs and that evidence of the commission of the
> offence is to be found in any books or papers of or under the control of the company,
> an order may be made . . .'

The judge said that the only offences 'in connection with the management of the *c*
company's affairs' were offences (and I will read his words)—

> 'which are breaches, whether active or involving a failure to comply with some
> positive requirement, against the laws regulating the management of a company's
> affairs. It may be that such offences extend beyond offences against the express
> provisions of the Companies Act 1948 and extend, for instance, to a fraud
> perpetrated by directors against their company.' *d*

Having come to that limited construction of the words 'an offence in connection with the
management of the company's affairs', he refused any jurisdiction in the matter and
declined to make the order which the Director of Public Prosecutions sought.

The first question which arises is: can the Director of Public Prosecutions appeal to this
court? Section 441(3) provides: 'The decision of a judge of the High Court . . . on an *e*
application under this section shall not be appealable.' In my opinion, that subsection is
not a bar to the appeal to this court. There are many cases now which show that if a
judge misconstrues a statute by giving himself jurisdiction when he has none or by
refusing jurisdiction when he has it, then he makes an error which goes to the
jurisdiction: and there is an appeal to this court, no matter how wide the words which
seem to exclude it. For authority in this regard I need only refer to *Anisminic Ltd v Foreign* *f*
Compensation Commission[1], and especially to what was said by Lord Reid, by Lord Pearce
and by Lord Wilberforce, to which I would add a few words of my own in the later case
of *Pearlman v Keepers and Governors of Harrow School*[2]: '. . . no court . . . has any jurisdiction
to make an error of law on which the decision of the case depends.' It seems to me that
in this case, if the judge made an error of law in construing the words of the section, if
he construed the words 'an offence' etc too narrowly, then he made an error of law which *g*
made him refuse jurisdiction when he ought to have entertained it. So the appeal can be
entertained here in this court.

Then the question arises as to the meaning of the words of s 441. We need not pause
on the words 'reasonable cause to believe'. They do not give rise to any controversy
here. But it is necessary to consider the meaning of the words 'an officer of a
company'. The word 'officer' in relation to a body corporate is defined in s 455 of the *h*
Act. Not really 'defined': for it is only 'included'. It includes a director, manager or
secretary. Its meaning may depend on the context in which it is used and in this case on
the whole phrase, 'while an officer of the company, committed an offence in connection
with the management of the company's affairs'. The officer here referred to is a person
in a managerial situation in regard to the company's affairs. I would not restrict these
words too closely. The general object of the Act is to enable the important officers of the *j*
State to get at the books of the company when there has been a fraud or wrongdoing. It

---

1   [1969] 1 All ER 208 at 213–214, 233, 246, [1969] 2 AC 147 at 171, 195, 210
2   [1979] 1 All ER 365 at 372, [1979] QB 56 at 70

seems to me that whenever anyone in a superior position in a company encourages,
a directs or acquiesces in defrauding creditors, customers, shareholders or the like, then
there is an offence being committed by an officer of the company in connection with the
company's affairs.

Take this particular case. It would appear that in one of the departments there was a
subordinate manager who was conducting false accounts for the company's benefit,
getting in more money for the company than the company ought to have had. In such
b a case, when there is a fraud for the benefit of the company, it may be inferred that the
officers of the company knew of it or acquiesced in it. When a fraud is committed for
the benefit of a company, nine times out of ten the proper inference is that an officer of
the company would be a party to it. But when the fraud is not for the benefit of the
company itself but for the individual himself alone, then you may have to look into it
more closely. It may still be an offence in connection with the company's affairs, but you
c have to be more certain that an officer of the company did it or acquiesced in it. Each
case which comes before the court has to be considered by the judge in the light of all the
circumstances put before him to see whether it is a proper case which comes within the
section.

In this particular case it does seem to me that the judge misdirected himself on the
material which was put before the court. I think properly directed the judge should
d have come to the conclusion that it was a case where the section did apply and an order
should have been made.

I would allow the appeal accordingly.

SHAW LJ. I agree. This appeal comes before this court as an appeal against the
dismissal by the judge of an application under s 441 of the Companies Act 1948. It is in
e truth an appeal against his refusal to make any order under that section because he
renounced jurisdiction, holding that the terms of the section did not bring the matter
properly before him. As Lord Denning MR has said, that was a wrong view.

The judge also considered that the party said to be an officer of the company of whom
it was alleged that he had committed some offence in connection with the management
of the company's affairs was not to be regarded as an officer or a manager within the
f definition in s 455 of the 1948 Act. The expression 'manager' should not be too narrowly
construed. It is not to be equated with a managing or other director or a general
manager. As I see it, any person who in the affairs of the company exercises a supervisory
control which reflects a general policy of the company for the time being or which is
related to the general administration of the company is in the sphere of management.
He need not be a member of the board of directors. He need not be subject to specific
g instructions from the board. If he fulfils a function which touches the central
administration of the company, that in my view is sufficient to constitute him an officer
or manager of the company for the purposes of s 441 of the 1948 Act.

Counsel for the Official Solicitor has maintained that the reference in the section to an
offence in connection with the management of a company's affairs relates to and only to
some internal misconduct by an officer in regard to the company itself, that is to say
h some misconduct of which the company is the victim. That is, in my view, too narrow
a construction. It would hardly warrant conferring the power which the section does on
a judge of the High Court, especially as it can be invoked only on the application of the
Director of Public Prosecutions, the Board of Trade or a Chief Officer of Police. The
judge's view that the offences with which the section is concerned are only those created
under the provisions of the 1948 Act was also in my judgment too limited.
j I would allow the appeal and make the order sought.

TEMPLEMAN LJ. I agree. For the reasons given by Lord Denning MR and Shaw LJ
I am quite satisfied that we have jurisdiction to consider this appeal.

On the question of construction, I take the view that where Parliament conferred
express power on a judge of the High Court to make an order on the application of the

Director of Public Prosecutions, the Board of Trade or a chief officer of police, it is unlikely that Parliament was intending to take a very large sledge-hammer to crack a *a* very small nut. It is far more likely that Parliament was intending to confer an extensive and weighty power which required adequate safeguards, which are to be found in s 441.

In his very helpful argument counsel for the Official Solicitor referred us to other sections of the Companies Act 1948 in which some similar expressions are to be found; and he put forward all the reasons which could be put forward to justify the conclusion of the judge that s 441 must be limited by what counsel happily called the contextual *b* framework of the 1948 Act. For myself I do not accept that. Section 441 is dealing with crime. It is dealing with power to prevent crime being hidden behind a facade and the corporate capacity of a company; and, for the reasons which Shaw LJ has already pointed out, unless the normal meaning of the words of s 441 are to be applied in their wider connotation the section can have very little effect.

So far as the definition of 'manager' is concerned, I agree that the functions performed *c* by the gentleman named in the present application are quite sufficient to constitute him a manager; and in any event on the evidence which we have seen it seems to me that there is reasonable cause at least to fear and believe that some of his activities must have been known to the directors.

Section 441 does not convict anybody. It merely enables a judge of the High Court on the application of the experienced and responsible officials who are mentioned in the *d* section to make quite sure that when there is a slightly unpleasant aroma hanging around somebody should be sent in to trace the source and find out what is going on.

For these reasons I agree with Lord Denning MR and Shaw LJ that the appeal should be allowed.

Appeal allowed.   *e*

Solicitors: *Director of Public Prosecutions*; *Official Solicitor*.

Frances Rustin   Barrister.

Practice Direction   *f*

FAMILY DIVISION

Child – Practice – Order for return of child – Arrival of child in England by air – Direction that *g* *airline and immigration officer supply information relating to arrival.*

Where a person seeks an order for the return to him of children about to arrive in England by air and desires to have information to enable him to meet the aeroplane, the judge should be asked to include in his order a direction that the airline operating the flight, and, if he has the information, the immigration officer at the appropriate airport, *h* should supply such information to that person.

To obtain such information in such circumstances in a case where a person already has an order for the return to him of children, that person should apply to a judge ex parte for such a direction.

Issued with the concurrence of the Lord Chancellor.   *j*

18th January 1980   Sir John Arnold P.

Westminster City Council v Haymarket Publishing Ltd

CHANCERY DIVISION
DILLON J
17th, 18th OCTOBER 1979

Rates – Surcharge on unused commercial building – Unpaid surcharge constituting charge on land comprised in hereditament – Scope of charge – When charge imposed land subject to legal mortgage and owner's interest consisting merely of equity of redemption – Mortgagee exercising power of sale under mortgage and selling land to defendant – Whether defendant liable for surcharge – Whether charge for unpaid surcharge having priority over defendant's interest in land – Whether 'charge on the land' imposing charge on all existing interests at time charge created whether charge including mortgagee's interest – Whether charge imposed only on owner's interest at that date consisting of equity of redemption – General Rate Act 1967, ss 17A(1), 17B(3).

On 3rd January 1974 a company acquired the fee simple in commercial premises. The next day the company charged the premises by a legal mortgage to a bank to secure payment of moneys owing to the bank. The premises remained empty and unused until 24th October 1975. Under s 17A(1)[a] of the General Rate Act 1967 the owner of the premises was liable to a rating surcharge amounting to £16,940 in respect of the period the premises remained unused. On 19th March 1976 the bank demanded payment of the moneys owing to it and on 21st April 1976 the rating authority demanded payment of the rating surcharge. By s 17B(3)[b] of the 1967 Act a rating surcharge was a 'charge on the land' comprised in the hereditament in question. On 22nd April the rating authority registered a charge in the local land registry in respect of the rating surcharge. The company failed to pay both the bank and the rating authority. On 15th July 1977 the bank, exercising its power of sale, contracted to sell the premises to the defendant. After the contract had been completed and the defendant had become the registered proprietor of the premises, the rating authority took out a summons seeking, inter alia, a declaration that the charge under s 17B(3) was imposed on all existing interests in the premises and was therefore imposed on the bank's interest as legal mortgagee and accordingly, took priority over, and bound, the defendant's interest in the premises. The defendant contended that a charge under s 17B(3) was imposed only on the interest of the owner of the premises, that under the scheme of the 1967 Act only one interest at any one time could be the interest of the owner, that when the charge was imposed the owner was the company whose interest then was merely the equity of redemption subject to the bank's mortgage, and that accordingly the charge was imposed only on the equity of redemption and the defendant's interest was not bound by the charge.

Held – On the true construction of s 17B(3) of the 1967 Act a 'charge on the land' imported a charge on all interests in the land when the charge arose. The charge under s 17B(3) therefore bound the bank's interest in the premises as mortgagee and, as the defendant's interest was claimed from the bank, the charge also had priority over and bound the defendant's interest in the premises. The court would therefore make a declaration to that effect (see p 293 c and e, post).

Dicta of Jessel MR in *Birmingham Corpn v Baker* (1881) 17 Ch D at 786 and of Fry LJ in *Guardians of Tendring Union v Dowton* [1891] 3 Ch at 269 applied.

---

a   Section 17A(1), so far as material is set out at p 290 g, post
b   Section 17B(3), so far as material, is set out at p 290 j, post

Notes

For the rating surcharge on unused commercial buildings, see Supplement to 32 **a** Halsbury's Laws (3rd Edn) para 51A3.

For the General Rate Act 1967, ss 17A, 17B (as inserted by the Local Government Act 1974, s 16), see 44 Halsbury's Statutes (3rd Edn) 1309, 1310.

Cases referred to in judgment

Birmingham Corpn v Baker (1881) 17 Ch D 782, 46 JP 52, 26 Digest (Repl) 606, 2616. **b**
Guardians of Tendring Union v Dowton [1891] 3 Ch 265, 61 LJ Ch 82, 65 LT 434, CA, 26
Digest (Repl) 607, 2623.

Cases also cited

Banister v Islington London Borough Council (1973) 71 LGR 239, DC.
Brent London Borough Council v Alfa Romeo (Great Britain) Ltd (1977) 75 LGR 685, DC.   **c**
Bristol Corpn v Virgin [1928] 2 KB 622, DC.
Paddington Borough Council v Finucane [1928] Ch 567, [1928] All ER Rep 428.

Adjourned summons

By an originating summons dated 14th May 1979 the plaintiffs, Westminster City Council ('the rating authority'), claimed against the defendant, Haymarket Publishing Ltd, (1) payment of the sum of £16,940·93, being the amount of a surcharge payable to **d** the rating authority by virtue of ss 17A and 17B of the General Rate Act 1967, (2) a declaration that under those statutory provisions and under s 7 of the Local Land Charges Act 1975 that sum was charged on the premises in question, 22 Lancaster Gate and 12–13 Lancaster Mews, London w2, (3) a declaration that the charge, being registered in the local land charges registry on 22nd April 1976, had priority over (a) the defendant's interest in the premises and (b) the entirety of the interests therein, (4) possession of the **e** premises, (5) an order that the charge be enforced by sale of the premises, and (6) such interest as the court might declare. The facts are set out in the judgment.

W J Mowbray QC and Colin Braham for the rating authority.
Peter Millett QC and Gregory Hill for the defendant.
f

DILLON J. I am concerned in this case with the scope and priority of the charge in respect of the rating surcharge on unused commercial property which is imposed by ss 17A and 17B of the General Rate Act 1967. These sections were introduced into the 1967 Act by the Local Government Act 1974 and have effect from 8th February 1974. Their relevant provisions are as follows. Section 17A says:
g

> '(1) If for a continuous period exceeding six months a commercial building is not used for the purpose for which it was constructed or has been adapted, its owner shall pay in respect of that period (the "period of non-use") a surcharge additional to the rates (if any) payable apart from this section.
> '(2) Subsection (1) of this section will not apply where—(a) the owner has tried his best to let the building, or [another condition which is not relevant in the present **h** case].'

In sub-ss (3) and (4) there are alternative conditions. Subsection (3) applies where the owner is in occupation of the building throughout the period of non-use, and sub-s (4) applies where the owner is not in occupation of the building throughout the period of non-use. Section 17B(3) says:
j

> 'A surcharge imposed under section 17A of this Act in respect of a hereditament shall until recovered be a charge on the land comprised in the hereditament; and for the purposes of the application to such a charge of section 15 . . . of the Land Charges Act 1925 this Act shall be deemed to be a similar statute to the Acts mentioned in subsection (1) of that section.'

Section 17B(6) makes Sch 1 of the General Rate Act 1967 apply for the purposes of
a s 17A with minor modifications, and then s 17B(7) provides that in ss 17A and 17B 'owner'
means the person entitled to possession, and where different persons are entitled to
possession of a hereditament during different parts of a period of non-use a surcharge in
respect of that period shall be apportioned between them according to the length of each
part and levied accordingly.

In Sch 1 of the General Rate Act 1967, para 13 provides: 'Any amount due . . . shall,
b without prejudice to the operation of any other enactment under which it is recoverable,
be recoverable as a simple contract debt in any court of competent jurisdiction.'

The premises with which I am concerned in these proceedings are 22 Lancaster Gate
and 12–13 Lancaster Mews, London w2. These premises were acquired in fee simple by
Shop Investments Ltd ('the company') on 3rd January 1974 and on the next day they
were charged by the company by way of legal mortgage with the payment to National
c Westminster Bank Ltd ('the bank') of all moneys and indebtedness due from the company
to the bank. The legal charge to the bank contains nothing to cut down the ordinary
immediate right of a legal mortgagee to possession of the mortgaged property.

On 8th February 1974 when ss 17A and 17B came into effect the premises, which were
commercial premises, were empty and unused and it is common ground that they
remained empty and unused until 24th October 1975 and that the rating surcharge is
d payable by the owner in respect of the premises for that period. The total amount is
£16,940·93. The premises remained empty after 24th October 1975 but it is common
ground that no surcharge is payable in respect of time after that date because of the
efforts then being made to let the premises. On 19th March 1976 the bank served a
demand on the company for payment of the amount due under the legal charge. This
amount was at all material times in excess of £6 million because the company had
e guaranteed its parent company's obligations to the bank. On 21st April 1976 the rating
authority served a demand on the company for the payment of the £16,940·93 rating
surcharge, and on the following day the rating authority's charge in respect of the
surcharge was duly registered in the land charges register as a local land charge. The
amount has not yet been paid.

On 15th July 1977 the bank in exercise of its powers as legal mortgagee contracted to
f sell the premises to the present defendant, Haymarket Publishing Ltd, for a sum of
£220,000. A few weeks later this contract was duly completed and the defendant is now
the registered proprietor of the premises at HM Land Registry. In the July 1977 contract
the bank agreed to indemnify the defendant against the rating authority's charge for the
rating surcharge if that charge is binding on the defendant.

By virtue of s 17B(3) of the General Rate Act 1967 the surcharge while unpaid is
g declared to be a charge on the land. It is common ground between counsel for the rating
authority and counsel for the defendant that this wording can only mean either (1) a
charge on all interests, legal or equitable, in the premises including the bank's interest as
mortgagee, or (2) merely a charge on the interest, such as it was at the relevant time, of
the owner in the premises. Counsel's first contention for the rating authority is that the
charge is a charge on all interests in the premises including the bank's. It is common
h ground that if this is correct the charge binds the defendant because the charge on this
contention had priority to the bank's interest and the defendant's claim under the
bank. Counsel's second contention for the rating authority is that, even if the charge is
only a charge on the interest of the owner in the premises, the bank was at all relevant
times an owner or the owner of the premises whether or not the company was also an
owner. It is common ground that, if this is right, again the charge binds the defendant.
j Counsel for the defendant by contrast contends that the charge is only a charge on the
interest of the owner of the premises, that under the scheme of the Act only one interest
at any one time can be the interest of the owner and that the owner at the relevant times
was the company whose interest was merely the equity of redemption subject to the
bank's charge. Counsel for the rating authority concedes that, if that is right, the
defendant is freed from the rating authority's charge.

In support of his second contention counsel for the rating authority relies on the well established rule that by virtue of his legal estate a legal mortgagee is entitled to possession *a* of the mortgaged property even before the ink is dry on the mortgage; certainly before demand and before any default on the part of the mortgagor. I prefer the view of counsel for the defendant that it is inconsistent with the scheme of the Act for there to be several owners of a property at a time, not being mere joint owners of the same legal estate like partners or trustees.

Subsections (3) and (4) of s 17A are concerned in the alternative with the situation *b* where the owner is or is not in occupation of the premises, and I do not find these readily workable if there is one owner who is in occupation and another owner in respect of a different interest who is not in occupation. Section 17A(2) refers to the situation where the owner had tried his best to let the building and this hardly fits the situation where there is one owner, the mortgagor, who is trying his best to let and another owner, the mortgagee, who has not been concerned to do anything because the interest under his *c* mortgage had been duly paid. Moreover, I cannot conceive that Parliament intended to impose a personal liability to pay the surcharge recoverable as a simple contract debt on a mortgagee, let alone a second or subsequent mortgagee, who was not at the relevant time a mortgagee in possession in the accepted sense of that term. However, it is unnecessary for me to express any final view on this since I have reached a clear conclusion that counsel for the rating authority is right on his first contention. *d*

In support of this contention counsel for the rating authority has referred me to a line of established authorities on earlier Acts, such as Public Health Acts and the Highways Acts, where charges on land created by statute in favour of local authorities had been held to be charges on all the interests in the land, including the interests of chargees under subsisting mortgages, and not merely charges on the equity of redemption subject to all prior mortgages: see particularly *Birmingham Corpn v Baker*[1]. The material terms of the *e* relevant statute, s 257 of the Public Health Act 1875, are set out as follows:

> 'Where any local authority have incurred expenses for the repayment whereof the owner of the premises for or in respect of which the same are incurred is made liable under this Act or by any agreement with the local authority, such expenses may be recovered, together with interest at a rate not exceeding £5 per centum per annum, from the date of service of a demand for the same till payment thereof, *f* from any person who is the owner of such premises when the works are completed for which such expenses have been incurred, and until recovery of such expenses and interest the same shall be a charge on the premises in respect of which they were incurred . . .'

Jessel MR said[2]:
g
> 'Now, the houses, *per se* being inanimate, they cannot bear the burden. If there be a charge on the houses it is a charge on the total ownership—if I may call it so, on the proprietorship; not on any particular section or portion of the proprietorship, but on the whole.'

See also the judgment of Fry LJ in *Guardians of Tendring Union v Dowton*[3] where he said: *h* 'All the Act does is to create a charge on the premises—that is, on the land—that is, on all the interests of the owners of the land.' He went on to explain that the charge did not override a restrictive covenant in favour of the owners of other property for reasons which are not relevant to this present case.

Counsel for the defendant has sought to distinguish these authorities. He has said, correctly, that they were decisions under other Acts, and under those other Acts the *j* definition of the term 'the owner' was somewhat different. He has pointed out that

1   (1881) 17 Ch D 782
2   17 Ch D 782 at 786
3   [1891] 3 Ch 265 at 269

under recent Public Health Acts and Highways Acts the charge is expressly stated in the
a Act to be on the land and each and every interest in the land: see s 291(1) of the Public
Health Act 1936 and s 264(1) of the Highways Act 1959. But this does not, in my
judgment, invalidate the reasoning of the earlier decisions under the earlier Acts.
Counsel for the defendant has contended in particular, as a ground for distinguishing the
earlier decisions, that in all those cases moneys had been laid out by the local authorities
in carrying out works which were calculated to benefit the owners of all interests in the
b relevant premises including mortgagees. It is quite true that in the reported cases the
judges have pointed out that the works concerned would benefit the owners of all
interests in the premises. But I think they have done so not as the ratio of their decisions
but as an indication why the decisions they have reached are intelligible or in accordance
with commercial sense: see per Lord Halsbury LC in *Guardians of Tendring Union v
Dowton*[1]. The real ratio is that the words in the relevant statute, 'charge on the land',
c naturally import a charge on all interests in the land, that is to say, a charge on the
proprietorship or total ownership. The emphasis of the judgments is on the interests
rather than on the benefits. It would be impossible for the court, in applying such
sections which create statutory charges, to enter on an enquiry whether the matters
which have brought about the creation of the statutory charge were or were not beneficial
to the owners of all or any of the interests in the land concerned. The true beneficiaries
d may well be other sections of the community, users of the public highway or occupiers
of neighbouring premises, and any benefit to any owner of an interest in the subject
premises may on any view be incidental. It would be equally impossible as a matter of
construction for the meaning of such words as 'a charge on the land' in a public statute
to vary from case to case, depending on whether or not the matters which had given rise
to the imposition of the charge were or were not in some sense beneficial to the owners
e of particular interests in the land.

I conclude, therefore, that the rating authority's charge for £16,940·93 under s 17B has
priority over and binds the defendant's interest in the land and all other interests in the
land and I will so declare.

Declaration accordingly.
f

Solicitors: *Edward Woolf* (for the rating authority); *Wilde, Sapte & Co* (for the defendant).

Evelyn M C Budd   Barrister.

---

1   [1891] 3 Ch 265 at 268

Pritchard v Briggs and others   *a*

COURT OF APPEAL, CIVIL DIVISION

STEPHENSON, GOFF AND TEMPLEMAN LJJ

15th, 16th, 19th, 20th, 21st, 22nd FEBRUARY, 11th APRIL 1979

Option – Option to purchase – Implied term – Implied term that grantor would retain subject- *b*
matter of option during option period – Option not exercisable until after grantor's death –
Grantee accepting lease from grantor of part of option land at high rent because lease granted him
option to purchase whole of land at favourable price after grantor's death – Right of pre-emption
of option land granted prior to grant of option – Right of pre-emption exercised before grantor's
death – Whether term to be implied in option that grantor would not sell land during option
period.   *c*

Option – Pre-emption – Creation of interest in land – Option to purchase land granted
subsequently to grant of right of pre-emption – Right of pre-emption registered as land charge
prior to grant and registration of option – Right of pre-emption exercised before option exercised
– Grantor of right of pre-emption and option patient under Mental Health Act – Sale of land
purportedly pursuant to exercise of right of pre-emption – Authorisation of sale by Court of *d*
Protection – Payment of two cheques together amounting to purchase at market value – Right of
pre-emption providing for purchase at low price – Whether right of pre-emption taking priority
over option – Whether right of pre-emption creating interest in land – Whether sale pursuant to
exercise of right of pre-emption genuine sale pursuant to right – Whether order of Court of
Protection constituting lawful justification for sale – Law of Property Act 1925, s 204 – Mental
Health Act 1959, s 116.   *e*

L and his wife owned certain land on which there was an hotel, a house and garage
premises. In 1944 they sold the hotel to R but retained the rest of the land ('the retained
land'). The conveyance of the hotel to R contained a covenant giving a right of pre-
emption to R and his successors by L and his wife, on behalf of themselves and their
successors in title, that so long as the survivor of them was alive and R was alive they   *f*
would not sell the retained land without giving R or his successors in title the option of
purchasing the retained land for £3,000 together with the fixtures and petrol pumps on
the garage premises at valuation. On 17th December 1944 the right of pre-emption was
registered under the Land Charges Act 1925 as an estate contract. L and his wife retired
to live in the house on the retained land. R subsequently sold the hotel and the benefit
of the right of pre-emption to M. In 1954 M sold the hotel and the benefit of the right   *g*
of pre-emption to the first and second defendants. In 1959 L and his wife granted the
plaintiff a lease of the garage premises for five years at a rent of £156 per annum. The
lease contained a covenant by L and his wife, on behalf of themselves and their successors
in title, that on the death of the survivor of them the plaintiff was to have an option to
purchase the whole of the retained land for £3,000 within three months of the survivor's
death. In February 1964 L and his wife granted the plaintiff a further lease of the garage   *h*
premises for a term of 21 years from 1st October 1963 at an escalating rent, commencing
at £520 per annum and rising to £780 per annum in the sixth year. That lease
incorporated the option over the retained land granted by the previous lease. The
plaintiff, who knew about the right of pre-emption granted by the 1944 conveyance, was
prepared to pay the high rents reserved by the 1964 lease because he would obtain a
favourable option to purchase the retained land. The option was registered as an estate   *j*
contract on 10th February 1964. In 1969 L's wife died and the legal and beneficial
interest in the retained land became vested in L. In 1971 L became ill and unable to
manage his affairs. His nephew, the third defendant, was appointed receiver of his estate
under the Mental Health Act 1959. The nephew wished to realise L's only asset, the
retained land, to provide for L. The nephew knew about the right of pre-emption under

the 1944 conveyance and about the plaintiff's option. He negotiated with the first
a defendant for the sale of the retained land to him and the second defendant. The first
defendant was prepared to purchase it for a price exceeding the £3,000 payable under the
right of pre-emption. The nephew and the first and second defendants each received
legal advice (i) that the right of pre-emption had priority over the plaintiff's option, (ii)
that due exercise of the right would override the option, (iii) that there was a risk that
correspondence between L and M in 1953 had exhausted the right of pre-emption, and
b (iv) that if the right of pre-emption were exercised the plaintiff would be entitled to
claim damages for breach of his option from L's estate and claim damages from the
nephew. In 1972, in consequence of the negotiations and with the consent of the Court
of Protection, it was agreed between the nephew and the first and second defendants that
if the first and second defendants paid the sum of £11,150 in consideration of the
nephew waiving any claim that the right of pre-emption had been exhausted, and
c undertook to indemnify the nephew and L and his executors against any claim by the
plaintiff in respect of his option, the first and second defendants would be given an
opportunity to exercise the right of pre-emption and purchase the retained land at
£3,000 and the fixtures and petrol pumps on the garage premises at £1. In accordance
with that agreement, the first and second defendants on 7th August handed the nephew
two cheques, one for £11,150 and one for £3,000. The Court of Protection, which had
d been advised that the sale of the retained land to the first and second defendants would
override the plaintiff's option, made an order authorising the nephew to sell the land to
them. On 15th January 1973 L died before completion of the contract of sale of the
retained land but the contract was completed by a conveyance dated 16th February
executed by L's executors, who were the nephew and the fourth defendant. On 12th
March, within three months of L's death, the plaintiff served notice on the executors
e purporting to exercise his option to purchase the retained land. The first and second
defendants disputed his right to exercise the option and claimed vacant possession of the
garage premises. The plaintiff brought an action against all the defendants, claiming,
inter alia, specific performance of the contract of sale of the retained land which, he
alleged, had been created by the exercise of the option, or, alternatively, damages for
breach of that contract. The defendants contended, inter alia, (i) that it had been
f recognised throughout by L and the plaintiff that the option was subject to the right of
pre-emption and that it was an implied term of the option that it would only be
exercisable if the survivor had not disposed of the retained land in his or her lifetime, (ii)
that the right of pre-emption was an interest in land and took priority over the plaintiff's
option by reason of prior registration, and (iii) that the sale to the first and second
defendants of the retained land was a due exercise of their right of pre-emption and not
g a sale at market value because the documents by which the sale had been effected showed
that there were two transactions, namely the payment of the £11,150 in consideration
of the waiver of the claim that the right of pre-emption had been exhausted and the
payment of the £3,000 for the land in pursuance of the right of pre-emption. The
judge[a] upheld the defendants' contentions and dismissed the action. The plaintiff
appealed.

h

Held – The plaintiff was entitled to specific performance of the contract resulting from
the exercise of his option to purchase, and the appeal would accordingly be allowed and
the judge's order set aside, for the following reasons—

    (i) On the true construction of the option clause the plaintiff had an unqualified right
to call for the conveyance of the retained land to him if within three months of the death
j of the survivor of L and his wife he gave notice and paid £3,000; in the circumstances
there were no grounds for implying into the option clause a term that the option would
only be exercisable if the survivor had not disposed of the land in his or her lifetime (see
p 302 *f g*, p 303 *h*, p 304 *e f*, p 330 *c d* and p 331 *j* to p 332 *b*, post).

---

a   [1978] 1 All ER 886

(ii) A right of pre-emption, unlike an option to purchase, did not create an interest in land because it did not give the grantee a present right, or even a contingent right, to call *a* for the conveyance of the legal estate. It created a mere spes and could not become an interest in land until the condition on which it depended was satisfied (ie by the grantor offering the land to the grantee) and the right was converted into an option. It followed that once the plaintiff's option had been granted and registered it took priority over the right of pre-emption (see p 304 *h* to p 305 *a*, p 305 *d*, p 311 *d e*, p 313 *g*, p 329 *b* and p 333 *a*, post); *London and South Western Railway Co v Gomm* [1881–5] All ER Rep 1190 *b* and *Mackay v Wilson* (1947) 47 SR(NSW) 315 applied; *Manchester Ship Canal Co v Manchester Racecourse Co* [1901] 2 Ch 37 explained.

(iii) In any event, even if the right of pre-emption had created an interest in land, it would not, by reason of prior registration, have taken priority over the plaintiff's option because, on the evidence, the first and second defendants had not acquired the retained land in the exercise of the right of pre-emption. The land had been sold to them at *c* market value and the sale was unprotected and in breach of the terms of the plaintiff's option to purchase (see p 313 *g h*, p 318 *a*, p 331 *b c* and p 333 *b c*, post); *Inland Revenue Comrs v Duke of Westminster* [1935] All ER Rep 259 explained.

(iv) The order of the Court of Protection could not constitute lawful justification for the sale of the retained land to the first and second defendants and therefore could not, by virtue of s 116(1)*b* of the Mental Health Act 1959 and s 204*c* of the Law of Property *d* Act 1925, operate to give them a good title to the retained land free from any interest that the plaintiff might have. After the grant and registration of the plaintiff's option to purchase, L and his wife could only sell, and the first and second defendants could only purchase, the retained land subject to the plaintiff's option, and the Court of Protection could not, and did not purport to, do any more than L or his wife would have done (see p 321 *a* to *c*, p 331 *b* and p 333 *c*, post); *Re Hall Dare's Contract* (1882) 21 Ch D 41, *Mostyn* *e* *v Mostyn* [1893] 3 Ch 376 and *Jones v Barnett* [1899] 1 Ch 611, [1900] 1 Ch 370 considered.

Per Stephenson and Templeman LJJ, Goff LJ dissenting. A registered right of pre-emption is binding on a successor in title of the grantor (see p 331 *c* and p 332 *e f*, post).

Decision of Walton J [1978] 1 All ER 886 reversed.

Notes   *f*

For options to purchase and rights of pre-emption, see 29 Halsbury's Laws (3rd Edn) 298–299, paras 593–594, and for cases on the subject, see 37 Digest (Repl) 83–84, 214–220.

For the Law of Property Act 1925, s 204, see 27 Halsbury's Statutes (3rd Edn) 625.

For the Mental Health Act 1959, s 116, see 25 ibid 143.

Cases referred to in judgments   *g*

Alderdale Estate Co v McGrory [1917] 1 Ch 414, CA; *rvsd* [1918] AC 503, [1918–19] All ER Rep 1184, 87 LJ Ch 435, 119 LT 1, HL, 44 Digest (Repl) 142, *1215*.

Bank of New Zealand v Simpson [1900] AC 182, 69 LJPC 22, 82 LT 102, PC, 17 Digest (Reissue) 376, *1396*.

Birmingham Canal Co v Cartwright (1879) 11 Ch D 421, 48 LJ Ch 552, 40 LT 784, 37 Digest (Repl) 91, *266*.   *h*

Brimelow v Casson [1924] 1 Ch 302, [1923] All ER Rep 40, 93 LJ Ch 256, 130 LT 725, 45 Digest (Repl) 564, *1390*.

Camden Nominees Ltd v Slack [1940] 2 All ER 1, [1940] Ch 352, 109 LJ Ch 231, 163 LT 88, 45 Digest (Repl) 307, *214*.

Canadian Long Island Petroleums Ltd v Irving Industries (Irving Wire Products Division) Ltd (1974) 50 DLR (3d) 265, [1974] 6 WWR 385, Digest (Cont Vol D) 720, *32a*.   *j*

---

b   Section 116(1), so far as material, provides: 'Section two hundred and four of the Law of Property Act, 1925 (by which orders of the High Court are made conclusive in favour of purchasers) shall apply in relation to orders made ... by the judge as it applies in relation to orders of the High Court.'

c   Section 204 is set out at p 318 *f g*, post

Carington (Lord) v Wycombe Railway Co (1868) LR 3 Ch App 377, 37 LJ Ch 213, 18 LT 96,
a   LJJ, 11 Digest (Reissue) 318, *2027*.

Churchill v Walton [1967] 1 All ER 497, [1967] 2 AC 224, [1967] 2 WLR 682, 14(1) Digest
(Reissue) 126, *842*.

Cooper v Phibbs (1867) LR 2 HL 149, 16 LT 678, HL, 22 Digest (Reissue) 173, *1446*.

Essex County Roman Catholic Separate School Board and Antaya, Re (1978) 80 DLR (3d) 405.

First National Securities Ltd v Chiltern District Council [1975] 2 All ER 766, [1975] 1 WLR
b   1075, 40 P & CR 38, Digest (Cont Vol D) 756, *925ed*.

Gardner v Coutts & Co [1967] 3 All ER 1064, [1968] 1 WLR 173, 19 P & CR 79, Digest
(Cont Vol C) 863, *347a*.

Halifax (City) v Vaughan Construction Co Ltd [1961] SCR 715.

Hall Dare's Contract, Re (1882) 21 Ch D 41, 51 LJ Ch 671, 46 LT 755, CA, 40 Digest (Repl)
63, *440*.

c *Imperial Chemical Industries Ltd v Sussmann* (28th May 1976) unreported.

Inland Revenue Comrs v Dowdell O'Mahoney & Co Ltd [1952] 1 All ER 531, [1952] AC 401,
33 Tax Cas 259, 31 ATC 126, [1952] TR 85, 45 R & IT 204, HL; *rvsg* [1950] 1 All ER
969, 33 Tax Cas 259, 28(1) Digest (Reissue) 612, *2262*.

Inland Revenue Comrs v Duke of Westminster [1936] AC 1, [1935] All ER Rep 259, 19 Tax
Cas 490, 104 LJKB 383, 153 LT 223, HL, 28(1) Digest (Reissue) 507, *1845*.

d *Jones v Barnett* [1900] 1 Ch 370, 69 LJ Ch 242, 82 LT 37, CA; *affg* [1899] 1 Ch 611, 68 LJ
Ch 244, 80 LT 408, 40 Digest (Repl) 64, *451*.

Kirkness v John Hudson & Co Ltd [1955] 2 All ER 345, [1955] AC 696, [1955] 2 WLR 1135,
36 Tax Cas 28, 34 ATC 142, [1955] TR 145, 48 R & IT 352, HL, 28(1) Digest (Reissue)
463, *1668*.

London and County Banking Co v Lewis (1882) 21 Ch D 490, 47 LT 501, CA, 28(2) Digest
e   (Reissue) 973, *101*.

London and South Western Railway Co v Blackmore (1870) LR 4 HL 610, 39 LJ Ch 713, 23
LT 504, 35 JP 324, HL, 12 Digest (Reissue) 626, *4438*.

London and South Western Railway Co v Gomm (1882) 20 Ch D 562, [1881–5] All ER Rep
1190, 51 LJ Ch 530, 46 LT 449, CA; *rvsg* 20 Ch D 562, 51 LJ Ch 193, 45 LT 505, 37,
Digest (Repl) 81, *203*.

f *Lumley v Gye* (1853) 2 E & B 216, [1843–60] All ER Rep 208, 22 LJQB 463, 118 ER 749,
34 Digest (Repl) 210, *1474*.

Lumley v Wagner (1852) 1 De GM & G 604, [1843–60] All ER Rep 368, 21 LJ Ch 898, 19
LTOS 264, 42 ER 687, LC, 28(2) Digest (Reissue) 1056, *749*.

Mackay v Wilson (1947) 47 SR(NSW) 315, 64 WN 103, 31(1) Digest (Reissue) 162, ******430*.

MacManaway, Re [1951] AC 161, PC, 36(1) Digest (Reissue) 562, *248*.

g *Manchester Ship Canal Co v Manchester Racecourse Co* [1900] 2 Ch 352, 69 LJ Ch 850, 83 LT
274; *affd* [1901] 2 Ch 37, 70 LJ Ch 468, 84 LT 436, CA, 37 Digest (Repl) 83, *218*.

Mogul Steamship Co v McGregor, Gow & Co (1889) 23 QBD 598, [1891–4] All ER Rep 263,
58 LJQB 465, 61 LT 820, 53 JP 709, 6 Asp MLC 455, CA, 45 Digest (Repl) 275, *6*.

Mostyn v Mostyn [1893] 3 Ch 376, 62 LJ Ch 959, 69 LT 741, 2 R 587, CA, 40 Digest (Repl)
63, *441*.

h *Murray v Two Strokes Ltd* [1973] 3 All ER 357, [1973] 1 WLR 823, 26 P & CR 1, Digest
(Cont Vol D) 757, *962 d e*.

Prenn v Simmonds [1971] 3 All ER 237, [1971] 1 WLR 1381, HL, 17 Digest (Reissue) 259,
1264.

Quinn v Leathem [1901] AC 495, [1900–3] All ER Rep 1, 70 LJPC 76, 85 LT 289, 65 JP 708,
HL, 45 Digest (Repl) 560, *1373*.

j *Sharp v Union Trustee Co of Australia Ltd* (1944) 69 CLR 539.

Smith v Morrison, Smith v Chief Land Registrar [1974] 1 All ER 957, [1974] 1 WLR 659, 27
P & CR 321, Digest (Cont Vol D) 759, *941c*.

Smithies v National Association of Operative Plasterers [1909] 1 KB 310, [1908–10] All ER
Rep 455, 78 LJKB 259, 100 LT 172, CA, 45 Digest (Repl) 564, *1393*.

South Wales Miners' Federation v Glamorgan Coal Co Ltd [1905] AC 239, [1904–7] All ER

Rep 211, 74 LJKB 525, 92 LT 710, HL; *affg* [1903] 2 KB 545, CA, 45 Digest (Repl) 562, 1381.

Tulk v Moxhay (1848) 2 Ph 774, [1843–60] All ER Rep 9, 1 H & Tw 105, 18 LJ Ch 83, 13 LTOS 21, 41 ER 1143, LC, 40 Digest (Repl) 342, 2774.

Woodall v Clifton [1905] 2 Ch 257, [1904–7] All ER Rep 268, 74 LJ Ch 555, 92 LT 292; *affd* [1905] 2 Ch 266, CA, 37 Digest (Repl) 83, 219.

Woodroffe v Box (1954) 92 CLR 245.

Appeal

The plaintiff, Robert Ellis Pritchard, brought an action against the defendants, (1) Christopher Baskin Briggs, (2) Joyce Briggs, his wife, (3) Arthur Harry Inman and (4) George Ledger Hawksworth, the executors of Arthur Lockwood deceased, claiming against all the defendants (a) specific performance of an alleged contract to sell to the plaintiff property at Pen-y-Gwryd, Beddgelert in the county of Caernarvon constituted by an option to purchase the property granted to the plaintiff by a lease of premises on the property, dated 3rd February 1964, and notices dated 12th March 1973 whereby the plaintiff purported to exercise the option; (b) if and so far as was necessary an order setting aside a conveyance dated 16th February 1973 made between the third and fourth defendants of the one part and the first and second defendants of the other part. Alternatively the plaintiff claimed against the third and fourth defendants damages for breach of the alleged contract, and against the first, second and third defendants damages for conspiracy. By their defence the first and second defendants denied that the option was binding on them, and alleged that the plaintiff had taken the option with notice of their prior right of pre-emption, that he was bound by the right of pre-emption, that at all times since 16th February 1973 he had been bound to give vacant possession of the premises leased to him in accordance with the terms of the right of pre-emption and that he had wrongfully retained possession of the premises. The first and second defendants counterclaimed for possession of the premises, mesne profits and costs. The plaintiff served a third party notice on the third and fourth defendants claiming the following relief in the event of the first and second defendants' counterclaim succeeding: (i) damages for breach of the covenant of quiet enjoyment contained in the lease, and (ii) an indemnity against any sum which the first and second defendants might recover in the counterclaim against the plaintiff for mesne profits. On 24th June 1977 Walton J[1] dismissed the action, the counterclaim and the third party proceedings. The plaintiff appealed against the dismissal of the action. The facts are set out in the judgment of Goff LJ.

Richard Scott QC and *Malcolm Waters* for the plaintiff.
H E Francis QC and *John Boggis* for the defendants.

Cur adv vult

11th April. The following judgments were read.

GOFF LJ (prepared as the first judgment and read by Stephenson LJ). This is an appeal from a judgment given on 24th June 1977 by Walton J[1], whereby he dismissed the plaintiff's action for specific performance of a contract for the sale of certain land and premises at Pen-y-Gwryd in Snowdonia, which contract had resulted from the exercise by him of a certain option, dismissed a counterclaim by the first and second defendants for possession of that same property, and also third party proceedings by the plaintiff as defendant to counterclaim against the third and fourth defendants. The plaintiff appeals

---

1   [1978] 1 All ER 886, [1978] 2 WLR 317

a against the dismissal of the action, but there is no appeal against the dismissal of the counterclaim or of the third party proceedings.

The history of the matter is as follows. In 1933 a certain Major and Mrs Lockwood acquired lands in the Snowdonia National Park in the parish of Beddgelert and situate on both sides of a road there. On one side the property includes the Pen-y-Gwryd Hotel, which is very well known, and adjoining it a dwelling-house and gardens called Hafod-y-Gwynt. On the other side of the road the property includes a small petrol filling station

b having two or three pumps and ancillary buildings. There is also a car park, which, save that it is used by coaches, is not a facility going with the hotel. There is also on that side a large lake which was made by the major and intended to provide an amenity for the hotel.

The third defendant is a nephew of Major and Mrs Lockwood, and at one time he managed the hotel for them for a period of about three years whilst the major was in

c Burma.

In 1944 Major Lockwood decided to retire. He and his wife, therefore, sold the hotel which was bought by a Mr Riddett. The conveyance to him is dated 14th August 1944 and it contained a provision which is a central feature of this action, and it is in these terms:

d '(4) The Vendors to the intent and so that the covenant hereinafter contained shall at all times hereafter be binding on such of the lands and premises conveyed by the Principal Deed and a Conveyance dated the fourth day of February One thousand nine hundred and twenty five made between Sir Richard William Bulkelly Baronet of the one part and the said Arthur Lockwood of the other part as are not hereby assured (which lands are hereinafter referred to as the retained lands) and enure for

e the benefit and protection of the lands hereby conveyed and of every part of such lands DO hereby for themselves and their successors in title jointly and each of them DOTH for himself or herself and his or her successors in title separately COVENANT with the Purchaser and his successors in title the owner or owners for the time being of the land hereby conveyed that: (A) NO building or part of a building now or hereafter on the retained lands or any part thereof shall at any time hereafter be used

f as a hotel or road house or for the reception of paying guests (B) THAT so long as the Purchaser shall live and the Vendors or the survivor of them shall also be alive the Vendors will not nor will either of them sell or concur in selling all or any part of the retained lands without giving to the Purchaser the option of purchasing the retained lands and the fixtures and petrol pumps thereon at the price in the case of the retained lands of Three thousand pounds and in the case of the fixtures and

g petrol pumps of a valuation thereof to be made in accordance with Clause 3 of the Conditions of Sale known as the Law Society's Conditions of Sale (1934). The option shall be given in writing and shall not be revoked or altered within Twenty one days from the giving thereof and all rights of the Purchaser under this provision (B) shall cease unless the offer is accepted within Twenty one days from the receipt by the Purchaser of the offer. If the offer is accepted the title shall commence as to part

h with the Principal Deed and as to the remainder with the said Conveyance dated the fourth day of February One thousand nine hundred and twenty five and the sale shall be completed and vacant possession given to the Purchaser at the expiration of one month after the acceptance of the offer and the said Conditions of Sale shall apply to the contract.'

j It will be observed that the preamble is in the form usually adopted when imposing restrictive covenants, para (A) is an ordinary covenant of that nature and para (B) which gives a right of pre-emption is entirely negative in form. I will refer to the land and premises to which that right relates as the retained lands.

On completion of this sale Major and Mrs Lockwood went to live at Hafod-y-Gwynt. The right of a pre-emption contained in cl 4(B) of the conveyance of 1944, whatever its true construction and effect may be, was duly registered as a class C(iv) land charge on 17th December 1944. On that same day, Mr Riddett sold the hotel to a Mr Mather and the conveyance to him contained an express assignment of the right of pre-emption. About the same time the first two defendants, Mr and Mrs Briggs, became the managers of the hotel for Mr Mather and later they bought it from him. The conveyance to them is dated 28th August 1954 and again there was an express assignment of the right of pre-emption, which, therefore, undoubtedly became vested in the first and second defendants.

In the previous year, 1953, Major and Mrs Lockwood had made an oral agreement with the plaintiff to sell to him the petrol filling station for £300 and he paid a deposit of £7. Mr Mather objected that this would be a breach of his right of pre-emption, and the sale was abandoned. Whether or not the plaintiff at this time obtained full information about the right of pre-emption, it is common ground that he was at all material times fully aware of its existence, quite apart from any knowledge imputed to him by its registration as a land charge.

Instead of the proposed sale, Major and Mrs Lockwood gave the plaintiff a weekly tenancy at 12s 6d a week, which was followed by a five-year term on 1st October 1953. When this expired he was granted a new lease on 22nd January 1959 for a further five years from 1st October 1958 at a rent of £156 per annum. This is a very important document because it saw the birth and contained the terms of an option to buy the freehold reversion, which was repeated in a subsequent lease dated 3rd February 1964 which is the option exercised by the plaintiff. That lease contained in cl 3(a) the usual landlord's covenant for quiet enjoyment, in cl 3(c) an option to renew the term for a further five years, and in cl 3(d) an option to purchase the reversion, which was in these terms:

'... if the tenant shall or his successors in title after the death of the survivor of the Landlords desire to purchase [the retained lands] and shall before the expiration of three months of the death of the said survivor give notice in writing to the Personal Representatives of the said survivor ... then the Landlords hereby covenant so as to bind their respective estates that the Personal Representatives of the survivor will upon the expiration of such notice and upon payment of the sum of Three Thousand Pounds together with all arrears of rent up to the expiration of the notice and interest on the said sum of Three Thousand Pounds from the expiration of the notice until actual payment at the rate of £5 per centum per annum convey [the retained lands] to the Tenant in fee simple. The National Conditions of Sale for the time being in force shall govern the terms of the sale as between the said Personal Representatives and the Tenant or his successors in title.'

In 1953 there was an exchange of correspondence between Major Lockwood and Mr Mather with a view to seeing if a sale to him could be arranged, but nothing came of this, and it has no materiality for present purposes save that it was later set up by or on behalf of Mr Inman, acting for Major Lockwood, that it had caused the right of pre-emption to become spent. Indeed, the plaintiff actually pleaded that it had produced that result, but abandoned this contention at the trial on inspection of the relevant correspondence.

The 1959 lease having expired there were negotiations between Major and Mrs Lockwood on the one hand and the plaintiff on the other for a new lease. The plaintiff complained that the rent he was being asked to agree to pay was too high. Major Lockwood sought to make the option one at market value ruling at the time of its exercise instead of a fixed £3,000. In the end a compromise was reached. The plaintiff gave way and accepted the proposed new rent, and Major Lockwood agreed that the option should remain unchanged.

Accordingly, the lease of 1964 was granted for a term of 21 years from 1st October 1963 at an escalating rent, commencing at £520 per annum and rising to £780 in the sixth year. This new lease was endorsed on the lease of 1959 and contained by reference the same option to purchase the reversion. This option was registered as a class C(iv) land charge on 10th February 1964.

Having regard to their ages, Major and Mrs Lockwood and the plaintiff must all have
a contemplated that the lease of 1964 would be still subsisting at the death of the survivor
of the two lessors. Mrs Lockwood in fact died in 1969 aged 93 years.

The loss of his wife shattered Major Lockwood, who became very ill from that time
onwards. For a time the plaintiff looked after him and he moved into Hafod-y-Gwynt
for that purpose. The learned judge expressed somewhat stringent criticisms of the
plaintiff's behaviour in this regard, but as he pointed out it has no relevance to this case,
b and I mention it only to say in fairness to the plaintiff that he maintains that this criticism
was not well founded. The plaintiff left Hafod-y-Gwynt in July 1971 at the request of Mr
Inman.

Major Lockwood grew worse, and on 8th January 1971 he was taken to hospital. Later
he was discharged to a convalescent home and then went on to a nursing home. He was
never able to return to his home at Hafod-y-Gwynt, and ultimately he died on 15th
c January 1973. His will was duly proved on 9th February 1973 by Mr Inman and the
fourth defendant. The events which gave rise to these proceedings occurred during the
major's illness.

In June 1971, Mr Inman applied under the Mental Health Act 1959 to be appointed
receiver for Major Lockwood, and he was so appointed on 26th October 1971.

Mr and Mrs Briggs had for many years been anxious to buy the retained lands and on
d 13th October 1971 Mr Briggs wrote to Mr Inman suggesting a meeting which took place
at the end of that month. At that time Mr and Mrs Briggs did not know of the plaintiff's
option, but they became aware of it about this time.

Protracted negotiations followed which resulted in a sale by Mr Inman to the Briggses
in 1972, which they claim was an exercise by them of their rights under cl 4 (B) of the
conveyance of 14th August 1944.

e I must return to review what happened at this time. Suffice it to say now that the
Briggses, relying on their right of pre-emption, claim that the sale to them, albeit later
in time than the creation of the plaintiff's option, has priority over it. I should, however,
observe in passing that on 19th September 1972 an articled clerk employed by Mr
Inman's solicitors swore an affidavit in support of an application to the Court of
Protection for authority to carry out that transaction in which he said:

f   'I Hilary Langley articled clerk [and then he names the solicitors] make oath and
          say as follows: 1. I have the conduct of this matter. 2. The copy letters exhibited
          herewith . . . relate to the sale of the property known as Hafod-y-Gwynt which has
          been agreed between Arthur Harry Inman, acting as Receiver for his Uncle, Arthur
          Lockwood, and Christopher Baskin Briggs and Joyce Briggs of Pen-y-Gwryd Hotel,
          Nant Gwynant in the County of Caernarvon at a price of £14,150. 3. To my
g   knowledge the terms of the agreed sale are acceptable to all parties.'

The affidavit was sworn on 19th September 1972.

Major Lockwood having died on 15th January 1973, the plaintiff served notice
exercising his option and it is common ground that it was in all respects a valid exercise,
if and so far as the option was good against Mr and Mrs Briggs.

h On 8th March 1973 their solicitors wrote to the plaintiff's solicitors informing them
of the sale to the Briggses and contending that the option was bad against them, but
offering to recognise him as tenant provided he performed his obligations under the lease
of 1964 and on 13th March 1973 Major Lockwood's executors' solicitors replied to the
plaintiff's notice exercising his option by a letter in which they contended that the option
was void. The plaintiff, who was still unaware of the details of the transaction with Mr
j and Mrs Briggs, insisted that his exercise of his option was valid against all the defendants,
and accordingly on 27th April 1973 the writ in this action was issued, whereby the
plaintiff claimed (1) specific performance of the contract to purchase the retained lands
for £3,000 arising on the exercise of his option, (2) alternatively, damages against Major
Lockwood's executors for breach of contract, (3) alternatively, damages against the first
three defendants for conspiracy to interfere with his contractual rights.

The defendants asserted that the sale to Mr and Mrs Briggs was a due exercise of their right of pre-emption and, therefore, took priority over the plaintiff's option by reason of prior registration, and they counterclaimed for possession. The plaintiff served a third *a* party notice on the executors claiming damages for breach of the covenant for quiet enjoyment, which would arise, of course, only if the plaintiff's claim for specific performance should fail. The learned judge upheld the defendant's claim to priority and that is the main question in issue on this appeal.

The learned judge said obiter that if he had held the exercise of the option was good against Mr and Mrs Briggs then he would have thought it right to grant specific *b* performance. The defendants say that, even if they are otherwise wrong, that relief should be refused on discretionary grounds, and by a respondent's notice they have maintained this claim before us. By an additional respondent's notice they seek to defeat the plaintiff's claim altogether on the following grounds:

'(1) The Order dated 6th October, 1972 of the Court of Protection constituted lawful justification for the sale to [Mr and Mrs Briggs], even if such sale was a breach *c* of the option to purchase contained in the Plaintiff's lease.

'(2) By virtue of Section 204 of the Law of Property Act 1925 and Section 116, Sub-section(1) of the Mental Health Act 1959 the said Order operated to give to [Mr and Mrs Briggs] a good title to the Retained lands free from any equitable interest which the Plaintiff may have had therein.

'(3) By virtue of Section 2, Sub-section(1)(iv) of the Law of Property Act 1925 the *d* Plaintiff's equitable interest in the retained lands was overreached by the conveyance thereof to [Mr and Mrs Briggs] and was transferred to the proceeds of sale viz the sum of £3,000 paid by [Mr and Mrs Briggs].

'(4) It follows that [the defendants] had not committed the alleged breach of contract or the alleged tort of conspiracy, and that the Plaintiff is not entitled to relief by way of specific performance or damages against any of them.' *e*

The learned judge dismissed the counterclaim on the ground that, in any event, Mr and Mrs Briggs had accepted rent from the plaintiff and so acknowledged his lease, although not of course, the option to purchase. There is no appeal against this part of the judgment. So we are not concerned with that question or with the third party claim, which is thereby rendered irrelevant. *f*

In my judgment the first question to be determined in this case is: what is the proper construction of the option clause? On its face it is a clear, unambiguous and unequivocal agreement by Major and Mrs Lockwood that if the plaintiff should give notice within three months after the death of the survivor and pay the purchase price of £3,000 together with all arrears of rent and interest then the personal representatives of the survivor would convey the retained lands to him. There is no condition that it should be *g* so only if the survivor should not have disposed of them in his or her lifetime.

However, counsel for the defendants sought, first as a pure matter of construction and alternatively by necessary implication, to say that it must be so qualified, and in support of this argument he relied (a) on evidence given by the plaintiff in cross-examination as to his understanding of the effect of the option clause, and the undoubted fact that before entering into the lease of 1964 the plaintiff knew not only that the right of pre-emption *h* was registered, but also the full terms thereof, or at least his solicitors did, and (b) on the correspondence between the solicitors leading up to the option clause.

In my judgment as a matter of construction apart from implication this is wholly untenable. Counsel for the defendants stressed the following questions and answers in the cross-examination of the plaintiff:

j

'Q. Do you agree that the idea of both Major Lockwood and yourself was this, that if he still had this land in hand at his death you were to have the option to buy it? A. I understood that I was to have it, yes.
'Q. If it was still in hand? A. After death.
'Q. After death, yes. If he still had the land in his hands after his death so that it

went into the hands of his personal representative, you were to have the option to buy the land from the personal representative. That was the idea, was it not? A. Yes.

'Q. But you knew, of course, at this time, did you not, that the owner of the hotel had a prior claim on the land if Major Lockwood decided to sell it in his lifetime? A. I was told that, yes.

'Q. Yes, you understood that? A. Yes.'

On the other hand, these further questions and answers followed immediately:

'Q. And, of course, if Major Lockwood had decided to sell it in his lifetime, he would have had to offer it first to the owner of the hotel, would he not? A. But I understood that once he had made it after death that it would automatically cancel the first one.

'Q. You thought it would automatically cancel the first? A. Yes. That was my own opinion.'

It is true that the learned judge said in his judgment[1]:

'It is perfectly true that in re-examination, when he saw what the effect of his answers might be, he told me that Major Lockwood said that he would not let him (the plaintiff) down, and that the property would be his, but in order to justify this statement by Major Lockwood, the plaintiff invented (as I am completely satisfied) the story that Major Lockwood was annoyed with the Briggs and did not want them to have the land.'

But with all respect, I am not really satisfied that the plaintiff was saying that when the option clause was entered into it was the common intention, or his intention, that the option should only be exercisable if Major Lockwood (and I will refer to him alone as he was the survivor) did not sell the land in his lifetime to anybody he chose. Be that as it may, there is no claim to rectification, and direct evidence of intention is not admissible, nor are negotiations save as factual background: see per Lord Wilberforce in *Prenn v Simmonds*[2]:

'In my opinion, then, evidence of negotiations, or of the parties' intentions . . . ought not to be received, and evidence should be restricted to evidence of the factual background known to the parties at or before the date of the contract, including evidence of the "genesis" and objectively the "aim" of the transaction.'

Even if direct evidence of intention were admissible, which it is not, still one could not read the option clause as if the subject-matter were the land if, but only if, remaining unsold at the death of Major Lockwood, or as being subject to a condition cancelling the option in the event of a sale, apart from the right of pre-emption, because that was operative 'so long as Mr Riddett should live and the Lockwoods or the survivor should also be alive' so that the plaintiff's knowledge of the right of pre-emption can be no reason for leaving Major Lockwood free despite the option clause to sell in his lifetime after the death of Mr Riddett.

Further in my judgment there are no grounds for implying any such limitation or condition. Counsel for the defendants relied on the decision of the Privy Council in *Bank of New Zealand v Simpson*[3] where Lord Davey said: 'Extrinsic evidence is always admissible, not to contradict or vary the contract, but to apply it to the facts which the parties had in their minds and were negotiating about.' However, any limitation to unsold land apart from a sale under the right of pre-emption would in my judgment

---

1   [1978] 1 All ER 886 at 898–899, [1978] 2 WLR 317 at 332
2   [1971] 3 All ER 237 at 241, [1971] 1 WLR 1381 at 1385
3   [1900] AC 182 at 187

contradict the written terms. Then he relied on *Alderdale Estate Co v McGrory*[1] where
Lord Cozens-Hardy MR said this: *a*

> 'Now what is the law as to the nature of the right to a good title in a case where
> there is no express provision for a good title? It is, I think, taken to be settled in
> accordance with the opinion of Sir Edward Fry and other authorities that it is an
> implied term of such a contract that a good title shall be furnished. But it being
> an implied term, and not an express term, evidence may be admitted to show that   *b*
> the implied term ought not to be relied upon if it can be shown that to the
> knowledge of both parties there were certain incumbrances—such as restrictive
> covenants, or a right of way, or that sort of thing—known to both parties to exist,
> and it was also known that these incumbrances were from their nature and other
> circumstances irremovable, or practically irremovable.'

Counsel for the defendants submitted that if the plaintiff wanted to exercise his option *c*
he could not object if the land had been sold in Major Lockwood's lifetime, but here
again that would be true, if at all, if, but only if, purchased by the Briggses in exercise of
the right of pre-emption, otherwise the lack of title in the personal representatives would
not be due to the known blot on the title but to something done by Major Lockwood
quite outside it.

Counsel for the defendants then placed his argument both on construction and *d*
implication on a lower plane and contended that because of the plaintiff's knowledge of
the right of pre-emption the option was exercisable only if the right of pre-emption had
not been exercised (as the argument assumes it was) during the lifetime of Major
Lockwood.

It seems to me, however, that that is not a matter of implication but of priorities. The
right of pre-emption was prior in point of time and duly registered and, therefore, would *e*
override the option if it was a right creating an interest in land, and if the sale and
conveyance to the Briggses was an exercise of that right, but not otherwise. Moreover,
even if, contrary to my view, one should imply into the unqualified option a term that
it should be subject to the right of pre-emption so as to give that right overriding effect,
even though it be not an interest in the land, still the option would not be overridden
unless that sale and conveyance was an exercise of that right.   *f*

So as it seems to me we have next to determine (a) whether the right of pre-emption
did create an interest in land, and (b) if it did then whether the purchase by the Briggses
was indeed made in exercise of that right.

On question (a) I start with the famous analysis made by Jessel MR in *London and South
Western Railway Co v Gomm*[2] which is in these terms:

> 'The right to call for a conveyance of the land is an equitable interest or equitable *g*
> estate. In the ordinary case of a contract for purchase there is no doubt about this,
> and an option for repurchase is not different in its nature. A person exercising the
> option has to do two things, he has to give notice of his intention to purchase, and
> to pay the purchase-money; but as far as the man who is liable to convey is
> concerned, his estate or interest is taken away from him without his consent, and
> the right to take it away being vested in another, the covenant giving the option   *h*
> must give that other an interest in the land.'

In my judgment a right of pre-emption, and particularly that in the present case which
is in purely negative form, does not satisfy this test. Counsel for the defendants argued
that it does because it fetters one of the important rights inherent in ownership, that of
freedom of alienation. I cannot accept that, however, because a right of pre-emption *j*
gives no present right, even contingent, to call for a conveyance of the legal estate. So far
as the parties are concerned, whatever economic or other pressures may come to affect

---

1 [1917] 1 Ch 414 at 417
2 (1882) 20 Ch D 562 at 581, [1881–5] All ER Rep 1190 at 1193

the grantor, he is still absolutely free to sell or not. The grantee cannot require him to *a* do so, or demand that an offer be made to him. Moreover, even if the grantor decides to sell and makes an offer it seems to me that so long as he does not sell to anyone else he can withdraw that offer at any time before acceptance.

The learned judge said[1]:

> *b* '... there would appear to be no essential difference from the point of view of creating an interest in land, between an option on the one hand and a right of preemption on the other. In the well-known option case, *London and South Western Railway Co v Gomm*[2], Kay J in the court of first instance put it happily thus[3]: "... a present right to an interest in property which may arise at a period beyond the legal limit is void..." and thus the option in that case was in any event void as infringing the rule against perpetuities. But the point of his remark is that it is, so far as I can *c* see, equally applicable to a right of pre-emption; it is a present right to an interest in property which may arise in the future... It is, however, difficult to see why in theory the fact that the condition is one which may be controllable by the owner of the land should make any difference.'

With respect I find myself unable to accept this reasoning. The condition, being one which leaves the grantee's interest subject to the volition of the grantor, is different in *d* kind from other conditions, does prevent a present interest from arising, and takes the case out of the principle enunciated by Jessel MR.

The distinction is well stated by Street J in his judgment in the Australian case of *Mackay v Wilson*[4] in a passage which I respectfully adopt and which reads as follows:

> *e* 'Speaking generally, the giving of an option to purchase land *prima facie* implies that the giver of the option is to be taken as making a continuing offer to sell the land, which may at any moment be converted into a contract by the optionee notifying his acceptance of that offer. The agreement to give the option imposes a positive obligation on the prospective vendor to keep the offer open during the agreed period so that it remains available for acceptance by the optionee at any moment within that period. It has more than a mere contractual operation and *f* confers upon the optionee an equitable interest in the land, the subject of the agreement: see, for example *per Williams J.* in *Sharp* v. *The Union Trustee Co. of Australia Ltd.*[5] But an agreement to give "the first refusal" or "a right of preemption" confers no immediate right upon the prospective purchaser. It imposes a negative obligation on the possible vendor requiring him to refrain from selling the land to any other person without giving to the holder of the right of first refusal the opportunity of purchasing in preference to any other buyer. It is not an offer *g* and in itself imposes no obligation on the owner of the land to sell the same. He may do so or not as he wishes. But if he does decide to sell, then the holder of the right of first refusal has the right to receive the first offer which he also may accept or not as he wishes. The right is merely contractual and no equitable interest in the land is created by the agreement.'

h Turning to English authority there is the extremely important and controversial case of *Manchester Ship Canal Co v Manchester Racecourse Co*[6] in the Court of Appeal and three, or perhaps I should say four, decisions at first instance. The three are *Birmingham Canal Co v Cartwright*[7], *Murray v Two Strokes Ltd*[8] (a decision of Goulding J) and *Imperial*

---

1   [1978] 1 All ER 886 at 899, [1978] 2 WLR 317 at 333
j 2   (1882) 20 Ch D 562, [1881–5] All ER Rep 1190
3   20 Ch D 562 at 573
4   (1947) 47 SR(NSW) 315 at 325
5   (1944) 69 CLR 539 at 558
6   [1900] 2 Ch 352, [1901] 2 Ch 37
7   (1879) 11 Ch D 421
8   [1973] 3 All ER 357, [1973] 1 WLR 823

Chemical Industries Ltd v Sussman[1] (a decision of Oliver J). The fourth is *First National Securities Ltd v Chiltern District Council*[2].

The first of these is not an entirely satisfactory authority because Fry J gave no reasons why he held that the right of pre-emption could be enforced against a stranger to whom the relevant mines and minerals had actually been conveyed; but unless he was making the same mistake as Kay J made in *London and South Western Railway Co v Gomm*[3], that is to say not appreciating that the alienee, being a stranger to the contract, could not be bound unless the contract created an interest in land, he must have held that such it was. Walton J said[4]:

> 'But the mere fact that he was overruled on the question of perpetuity shows that the Court of Appeal in *Gomm's* case[5] approved his decision that the right of pre-emption created an interest in land. Otherwise his decision on the perpetuity point would not have been wrong, but right for the wrong reason.'

I do not go as far as that, for in my judgment the case was wrongly decided on any view, since if the right of pre-emption did create an interest in land it was void for perpetuity, and if it did not then it sounded in contract only and so could not be enforced against the stranger. Nevertheless, this is authority, not binding on this court, in favour of the view that a right of pre-emption does create an interest in land.

Murray v Two Strokes Ltd[6] is, of course, a direct decision to the contrary, but it is based on Goulding J's view that the judgment in the *Manchester Ship Canal* case[7] contains a considered statement by the Court of Appeal that a right of pre-emption does not create an interest in land, which is a vexed question which we now have to resolve. Moreover, when he came to decide the *First National Securities* case[2] that same learned judge doubted whether the *Manchester Ship Canal* case[7] might not be of limited application depending on the statutory validation of an otherwise invalid agreement.

In the *Imperial Chemical Industries* case[1], on an interlocutory application for an interim injunction, Oliver J refused relief on the ground, amongst others, that as the law stood the plaintiffs had no reasonable chance of establishing that a right of pre-emption affecting shares created an interest therein enforceable against third parties.

That was again largely based on the *Manchester Ship Canal* case[7], but that learned judge, in a thorough and, if I may say so with respect, carefully analysed review of the law, gave what Walton J himself described[4] as 'very persuasive reasons why this should be the case' and he reviewed the effect of various relevant provisions of the 1925 property legislation which had not previously been considered in this connection in any case. First, Oliver J said:

> 'The critical distinction between a purchaser's option and a mere right of first refusal lies, as it seems to me, not in the number of conditions which have to be fulfilled before there comes into being a fully effective contract for the sale of the land but in the fact that an option vests in the offeree the right to call for a conveyance of the land without any further intervention of the offeror. It is not inappropriate to describe this right as "an interest in land" for the offeror has parted with his dominion over the land and can no longer control its disposition. The equitable right to call for a conveyance springs up independently of his volition.

1 (28th May 1976) unreported
2 [1975] 2 All ER 766, [1975] 1 WLR 1075
3 (1882) 20 Ch D 562 at 582, [1881–5] All ER Rep 1190 at 1194
4 [1978] 1 All ER 886 at 900, [1978] 2 WLR 317 at 334
5 (1882) 20 Ch D 562, [1881–5] All ER Rep 1190
6 [1973] 3 All ER 357, [1973] 1 WLR 823
7 [1901] 2 Ch 37

a   This appears clearly from the judgment of Jessel MR in *London and South Western Railway Co v Gomm*[1], where, he says this [and then Oliver J read the passage which I have already cited, and continued:] The grantor of a right of pre-emption is not in that position, and the disposition of the land remains a decision which is his and his alone. No doubt if he evinces a desire to sell and thus creates the conditions in which he has undertaken to make an offer, that undertaking can be enforced inter partes, but the decision whether to create such conditions remains his and cannot be
b   demanded or influenced by the offeree.'

Secondly, he pointed out that in the case of an option what is enforced is the contract resulting from the acceptance of the irrevocable offer, whereas in the case of a right of pre-emption there is, ex hypothesi, no contract for sale unless the offer is made and accepted, and what is enforced (and I add indirectly by injunction) is the obligation to make the offer. Thirdly, he instanced the case of a 'put' option which could hardly be
c   thought to give an interest in land. With all this reasoning with respect I entirely agree.

Oliver J also derived assistance from the decision of Cross J in *Gardner v Coutts & Co*[2]. There the grantor had given the property away and was sued for breach of contract. No claim was made against the assignee. Cross J implied a term that the grantor would not make a gift 'so as to defeat the first refusal'[3]. Oliver J said, in his judgment in *Imperial Chemical Industries Ltd v Sussman*[4]:

d   'There does not appear to be any report of the amount of damages assessed, but I think that it follows from the learned judge's ground of decision that they must have been assessed on the footing that the right of first refusal had indeed been defeated. But this was, of course, so only on the footing that no interest in land was created.'

e   However, since no claim was made against the successor, and it was not argued that the plaintiff was not entitled to damages because she could have, but had not, pursued her claim against the land, and as there would be no remedy at all even in contract without the implication, I do not think that this case really helps very much one way or the other.

So I now turn to the *Manchester Ship Canal* case[5]. It must be observed that as the offending contract had not been completed relief could be, and was, given by injunction
f   on the principle of *Lumley v Wagner*[6], so that the view expressed by Vaughan-Williams LJ giving the judgment of the court (himself, Rigby and Stirling LJJ) whether intended to be a statement of general principle or limited to the particular facts was obiter. Nevertheless, it was, I think, a considered view of the whole court, and in general must have great weight in solving the present problem.

The learned judge, however, disagreed with both Goulding J's view in *Murray v Two*
g   *Strokes Ltd*[7] and with Oliver J[4] and said that the Court of Appeal were not laying down any general principle but were merely accepting the argument of Upjohn KC that the agreement could not bind the land, because apart from the statute it was void, both for uncertainty and perpetuity, and the statute only made it 'valid and binding on the parties thereto'[8], and his further argument that the contract could not bind the land because it did not fix a price or provide any machinery for its ascertainment. Walton J said[9] in his
h   judgment:

---

i   1 (1882) 20 Ch D 562 at 581, [1881–5] All ER 1190 at 1193
   2 [1967] 3 All ER 1064, [1968] 1 WLR 173
   3 [1967] 3 All ER 1064 at 1069, [1968] 1 WLR 173 at 179
j   4 (28th May 1976) unreported
   5 [1901] 2 Ch 37
   6 (1852) 1 De GM & G, [1843–60] All ER Rep 368
   7 [1973] 3 All ER 357, [1973] 1 WLR 823
   8 [1901] 2 Ch 37 at 43
   9 [1978] 1 All ER 886 at 902, [1978] 2 WLR 317 at 336

'What the Court of Appeal was doing was no more than deciding that, although they were bound by the section to hold the clause valid (although it would not *a* otherwise have been) as a matter of contract, they were not prepared to hold that it created an interest in land, since that interest would have been of a completely novel type. Non constat that if, in their view, cl 3 had provided proper machinery for ascertaining a price and time for completion the result would have been the same.'

For my part with all respect I do not agree. First, as it seems to me, if validated *b* between the parties, it ought to be as enforceable against strangers as if it had been initially valid. The statute did not say 'but not further or otherwise', and I do not think the contract could be held validated for one purpose and not for another.

Secondly, apart from the statute the right would not be novel, but void. When validated, surely it could not be any different in principle from an ordinary properly constituted right of pre-emption by contract. The objection about the price and terms *c* disappears, and the contract as validated gives a valid right to an offer capable of acceptance. Moreover, if the Court of Appeal had intended no more than the learned judge sees in what they said I think they would have expressed it very differently from the unqualified statement in *Manchester Ship Canal Co v Manchester Racecourse Co*[1]:

'Then it was objected that clause 3 could not be enforced against the Trafford Park *d* Company, who are only alienees of the land. Farewell J., thought that clause 3 created an interest in land, and that this objection could be thus answered. We do not think that clause 3 does create an interest in land, nor do we think that there is anything in the decisions in *Tulk* v. *Moxhay*[2] or in *London and County Banking Co.* v. *Lewis*[3] which gets over the objection.'

e

So, in my judgment, the *Manchester Ship Canal* case[4], though not an absolutely binding authority, does strongly support the view that in general a right of pre-emption does not create an interest in land.

We were, however, referred to two Canadian cases and one Australian decision. The first of these was *City of Halifax v Vaughan Construction Co Ltd*[5]. This is a clear decision that a right of pre-emption does create an interest in land. I cite from the judgment of *f* Judson J[6]:

'What is the juridical nature of this right to reconveyance? I do not think that it is distinguishable from what has been called a right of pre-emption or a right of first refusal. An owner of land contracts that if he decides to sell he will give X the first right to buy at a stated price or at a price to be determined according to a *bona fide* offer made by another. The owner may decide never to sell and X cannot compel *g* him to sell. Nevertheless, X has an equitable interest in the land. The rights of the city in this case are superior to those held by one who has merely a right of pre-emption because Vaughan had no uncontrolled right to determine whether or not it would reconvey. Unless it complied with the building covenants within a reasonable time, the city could have enforced a reconveyance. The rule is that a *h* right of pre-emption will be specifically enforced and its violation restrained by injunction. (Fry, Specific Performance[7]; *Birmingham Canal Co.* v. *Cartwright*[8]).'

---

1   [1901] 2 Ch 37 at 50
2   (1848) 2 Ph 774, [1843–60] All ER Rep 9
3   (1882) 21 Ch D 490   *j*
4   [1901] 2 Ch 37
5   [1961] SCR 715
6   [1961] SCR 715 at 720
7   6th Edn (1920) p 24
8   (1879) 11 Ch D 421

However, in the later case of *Canadian Long Island Petroleums Ltd v Irving Industries Ltd*[1],
a also in the Supreme Court of Canada, in which the *Halifax* case[2] was not cited, the court
came to the opposite conclusion. I cite from the judgment of Martland J[3]:

'An option gives to the optionee, at the time it is granted, a right, which he may
exercise in the future, to compel the optionor to convey to him the optioned
property. As Jessel, M.R., puts it in [*London and South Western Railway Co v Gomm*[4]]:
b ". . . but as far as the man who is liable to convey is concerned, his estate or interest
is taken away from him without his consent, and the right to take it away being
vested in another, the covenant giving the option must give that other an interest
in the land." In other words, the essence of an option to purchase is that, forthwith
upon the granting of the option, the optionee upon the occurrence of certain events
solely within his control can compel a conveyance of the property to him. Clause
c 13 did not give to the respondents any present right to require in the future a
conveyance of Sadim's undivided one-half in the land. It was not specifically
enforceable at the time when the agreement was executed. The respondents were
not given any right to take away Sadim's interest without its consent. Their right
under that clause was a contractual right, *i.e.*, the covenant of Sadim that if it was
prepared to accept any offer to sell its interest, the respondents would then, and only
d then, have a 30-day option to purchase on the same terms. The contingency in this
clause is resolved solely upon the decision of Sadim to sell.'

This later decision was afterwards followed in the Ontario High Court of Justice in the
case of *Re Essex County Roman Catholic Separate School Board and Antaya*[5].

In the Australian case of *Woodroffe v Box*[6] no question of binding successors was
e involved. The problem was simply whether as a matter of construction the executors of
the deceased covenantor were bound to make an offer to the covenantee or whether it
still remained an obligation which would not arise unless and until they decided to sell.
This case turned on a question of construction and does not, I think, really assist in
resolving the present problem.

Such being the state of the authorities, apart from the 1925 property legislation, the
f effect of which I must next consider, I would come to the conclusion that a right of pre-
emption does not create an interest in land for two main reasons: (1) *Gomm's* case[7] appears
to me to establish a logical distinction excluding rights of pre-emption; and (2) in the
Manchester Ship Canal case[8] the Court of Appeal, as I think, went out of their way to
overrule Farwell J in principle and not only on construction.

We were, however, referred to a number of provisions in the 1925 property statutes
g which are clearly framed on the assumption that a right of pre-emption does create an
interest in land. First, s 2(3) of the Law of Property Act 1925 reads as follows:

'The following equitable interests and powers are excepted from the operation of
subsection (2) of this section, namely . . . (iv) the benefit of any contract (in this Act
referred to as an "estate contract") to convey or create a legal estate, including a
h contract conferring either expressly or by statutory implication a valid option to
purchase, a right of pre-emption or any other like right . . .'

1   (1974) 50 DLR (3d) 265
j 2   [1961] SCR 715
3   (1974) 50 DLR (3d) 265 at 277
4   (1882) 20 Ch D 562 at 581, [1881–5] All ER Rep 1190 at 1193
5   (1978) 80 DLR (3d) 405
6   (1954) 92 CLR 245
7   20 Ch D 562, [1881–5] All ER Rep 1190
8   [1901] 2 Ch 37

I turn next to the Land Charges Act 1925, s 10(1), which begins:

> 'The following classes of charges on, or obligations affecting, land may be *a*
> registered as land charges in the register of land charges, namely ... Class C ... (iv)
> Any contract by an estate owner or by a person entitled at the date of the contract
> to have a legal estate conveyed to him to convey or create a legal estate, including a
> contract conferring either expressly or by statutory implication a valid option of
> purchase, a right of pre-emption or any other like right (in this Act referred to as *b*
> "an estate contract") ...'

Then s 13(2) invalidates unregistered land charges against a purchaser of the land with
this proviso:

> 'Provided that, as respects a land charge of Class D and an estate contract created
> or entered into after the commencement of this Act, this subsection only applies in *c*
> favour of a purchaser of a legal estate for money or money's worth.'

We were also referred to ss 58(2) and 61(2) of the Settled Land Act 1925, which so far
as material are as follows. Section 58(2) provides:

> 'A tenant for life may, with the consent in writing of the trustees of the
> settlement, at any time, by deed or writing, either with or without consideration in *d*
> money or otherwise ... release, or agree to release, any other land from any
> easement, right or privilege, including a right of pre-emption, affecting the same for
> the benefit of the settled land, or any part thereof.'

Then s 61(2) provides:

> 'For the purpose of the three last preceding sections "consideration in money or *e*
> otherwise" means ... (e) the release of the settled land, or any part thereof, or any
> other land, from any easement, right or privilege, including a right of pre-emption,
> or from the burden of any restrictive covenant or condition affecting the same.'

But most important of all, in my view, is s 186 of the Law of Property Act 1925 which
reads as follows: *f*

> 'All statutory and other rights of pre-emption affecting a legal estate shall be and
> be deemed always to have been capable of release, and unless released shall remain
> in force as equitable interests only.'

We were also referred to s 9(2) of the Perpetuities and Accumulations Act 1964 which
is in these terms: *g*

> 'In the case of a disposition consisting of the conferring of an option to acquire for
> valuable consideration an interest in land, the perpetuity period under the rule
> against perpetuities shall be twenty-one years, and section 1 of this Act shall not
> apply: Provided that this subsection shall not apply to a right of pre-emption
> conferred on a public or local authority in respect of land used or to be used for *h*
> religious purposes where the right becomes exercisable only if the land ceases to be
> used for such purposes.'

This also indicates that the legislature regarded certain statutory rights of pre-emption
as creating interests in land, but it does not really add to the significance of the 1925
statutes. *j*

I think also that I can at this juncture dispose of ss 58 and 61 of the Settled Land Act
1925 which are, I think, neutral and do not throw any light on the matter one way or the
other, but the other provisions which I have cited certainly do proceed on the basis that
a right of pre-emption is an interest in land and are not really explicable on any other
basis.

To explain away the *Birmingham Canal* case[1], and these statutes, counsel for the plaintiff
argued (1) that a right of pre-emption is not ab initio an interest in land, but it becomes
so the moment the condition on which it depends is satisfied, (2) that if the condition is
that of the grantor selling or desiring to sell so that a sale to a third party is a breach of the
right of pre-emption that right becomes an interest in land at latest eo instanti the
property is conveyed, if not earlier on the decision, offer or agreement to sell, and so, as
an interest in land, it binds the purchaser provided it has been duly registered, and (3)
that if the condition is not that of selling or offering for sale or deciding to sell so that the
conveyance to a third party does not make the right of pre-emption exercisable one has
to look to see whether the condition is not within the volition of the new owner, and if
it be not, then it automatically crystallises into an interest in land, because it then satisfies
the test in *Gomm's* case[2].

As an example, if A agrees with B that if he, A, ceases to carry on his business at
Blackacre then he will offer or sell Blackacre to B, and then he sells and conveys to C, but
does not cease to carry on his business there, having taken a lease or irrevocable licence
from C to enable him to continue it, the right of pre-emption at once becomes an interest
in land binding and enforceable against C because C has no control over the condition.

I find myself unable to accept this line of argument, for, the question being whether
the right is of such a nature as to bind a successor in title, and starting from the premise
that it is not an interest in land, and so does not, I do not for myself see how the fact that
a successor in title comes on the scene can change its nature so as to make it binding on
him. In my judgment principle and logic alike require that the right of pre-emption
must be from the start and throughout either an interest in land capable of binding a
successor in title, or a mere personal contract which is not so capable. Of course, if an
offer be made to the grantee of the right which he accepts then an interest in land is in
any event created, but that is another matter.

There are two cases which at first sight might be thought to support counsel's
argument for the plaintiff. They are *Lord Carington v Wycombe Railway Co*[3] and *London
and South Western Railway Co v Blackmore*[4], both dealing with the statutory right of pre-
emption under s 128 of the Lands Clauses Consolidation Act 1845. In the first of these,
Selwyn LJ, when dealing with the defence of waiver or release, said[5]:

> '[That] contention . . . is, I think, at once disposed of by a consideration of the
> nature of the right itself. For this right of pre-emption is one which continues after,
> and notwithstanding a sale and conveyance, and may indeed be said to arise upon
> and in consequence of such sale and conveyance.'

The point there, however, was not whether the right was binding on a successor after
a conveyance by the railway company to a third party in breach of the right of pre-
emption, but whether it existed at all, that is to say whether it was created by the
purchase by the railway company, notwithstanding that after serving notice to treat they
had reached agreement with the vendor and had taken a conveyance which combined a
form suitable for a conveyance under the Lands Clauses Consolidation Act 1845 and a
form suitable for a conveyance made independently of the Act. It was argued that the
purchase was not a compulsory one, but a purchase by agreement, and the vendor in such
a case, if he desires to have a right of pre-emption, ought to reserve it[6]. So this case
throws no light on our problem one way or another.

---

1   (1879) 11 Ch D 421
2   (1882) 20 Ch D 562, [1881–5] All ER Rep 1190
3   (1868) LR 3 Ch App 377
4   (1870) LR 4 HL 610
5   LR 3 Ch App 377 at 386
6   LR 3 Ch App 377 at 379–380

In the second case, *London and South Western Railway Co v Blackmore*[1], Lord Hatherley
LC said:

> 'Now, in the case referred to of *Lord Carington v. The Wycombe Railway Company*[2],
> it was decided, and I think very justly decided, that when directors, upon the best
> consideration they could give to the case, had not only said: "This land is
> superfluous," but had put the land, as such, up for sale and sold it, the Court will say
> to them: "The time has arrived at which you are to make the offer to the adjoining
> owners." Because, how absurd it would be to say the land shall not be sold to anyone
> else without a previous offer being made, and yet, when the land is actually sold and
> conveyed to someone else, then the persons who ought first to have had the offer are
> not to be entitled to come to the Court; that after your right has been attempted to
> be pretermitted by this actual conveyance and sale, your only right is to come and
> interpose between the actual conveyance and sale if you have time so to do, or to
> have the conveyance set aside; but that you are not entitled to say that your right of
> pre-emption has arisen, that you must wait for that some time longer, because the
> company having attempted to deprive you of your right, and having been foiled in
> that attempt, have now the opportunity of holding back and saying: "If we are not
> allowed to deprive you of this right we shall not offer the land for sale at all until the
> end of the ten years." I apprehend that the Legislature meant that right of pre-
> emption to arise at the very moment when the company chose to sell.'

The question there, however, was whether, the company having within the ten years
allowed by s 127 of the Lands Clauses Consolidation Act 1845, sold in breach of the right
of pre-emption, the adjoining owners could then enforce their right to buy, or could only
have the conveyance set aside leaving the railway company free to retain the land for the
remainder of the ten years. The court was not considering whether the right of pre-
emption created an interest in land ab initio or only as from the moment of the land
becoming superfluous. So in the end this case also does not seem to me to help.

Thus, as I see it, one is forced to choose between three alternatives: either (1) the
conclusion I have so far reached is wrong, or (2) the legislation proceeded on a mistaken
basis as to what the law was, or (3) it has amended the law.

The first view would commend itself to the learned judge, who said[3]:

> 'Apart from the foregoing, the first observation which strikes one immediately is
> that in general there can be no question but that the framers of the 1925 legislation
> knew their land law to perfection; and the assumption contained in the Land
> Charges Act 1925, s 10, class C(iv), that for this purpose there is no relevant
> distinction between an option properly so-called a right of pre-emption, is one
> which one feels instinctively to be correct. The framers of that legislation, in other
> words, are not likely to have got it wrong.'

However, the law was at best uncertain, so that they may have got it wrong, and for my
part I do not feel that any of these statutory provisions are sufficient to dissuade me from
the view I have formed as to what the law was before 1st January 1926.

Further, apart from s 186, which I confess has caused me great difficulty, it seems to
me that these sections cannot have changed the law, because, as has been pointed out
more than once, there is a difference between an Act which is passed under a
misapprehension as to the law, and an amending Act. As Lord Simonds said in *Kirkness
v John Hudson & Co Ltd*[4]:

---

1   (1870) LR 4 HL 610 at 620
2   (1868) LR 3 Ch App 377
3   [1978] 1 All ER 886 at 900, [1978] 2 WLR 317 at 334
4   [1955] 2 All ER 345 at 352, [1955] AC 696 at 714

a
'. . . . it is an excellent example of the proposition to which reference was made in the report of the Committee of the Privy Council in *Re MacManaway*[1], and again by my noble and learned friend, LORD RADCLIFFE, in *Inland Revenue Comrs. v. Dowdall, O'Mahoney & Co., Ltd.*[2], that the beliefs or assumptions of those who frame Acts of Parliament cannot make the law.'

b
Apart from s 186 none of the provisions to which we have been referred seems to me to contain anything to alter the law. They merely assume it to be what I would hold it was not. Section 186, however, contains a provision which might have an amending effect because it contains these words, 'unless released shall remain in force as equitable interests only'. This does seem to be an express enactment that all statutory and other rights of pre-emption shall have effect as equitable interests, and, therefore, as interests in land.

c
Oliver J's explanation that one has first to see apart from the section whether the right is one which creates an interest in land, and if not then it does not affect a legal estate and so is not within the section, is, I venture to say, subject to two serious criticisms. First, with all respect, he made a slip in forgetting for the moment that whereas an option to renew the term does run with the land, an option to purchase the reversion does not: see *Woodall v Clifton*[3]. Secondly, as Walton J pointed out[4], if the statutory right of pre-
d
emption under the Lands Clauses Consolidation Act 1845, s 128 is not within s 186, the section would appear to be, as he expressed it, a piece of 'spectacular non-legislation'.

With regard to the second, it may be that that statutory right of pre-emption does create an interest in land because of the statutory duty to sell all superfluous land at the latest at the end of ten years contained in s 127. I would wish to reserve that for consideration if and when the occasion arises. The statutory right is also different from
e
a private right in an important particular as Oliver J pointed out in *Imperial Chemical Industries Ltd v Sussman*[5] that conveyances in defiance of the statutory pre-emption rights were, at any rate before 1st January 1926, liable to be set aside as beyond the power of the statutory undertaking: see *London and South Western Railway Co v Blackmore*[6].

Even so, it seems to me that Oliver J was right in saying that s 186 deals only with rights affecting a legal estate, and, therefore, does not make a right of pre-emption an
f
interest in land because, not being an interest in land, it does not affect the legal estate. It may be that this makes s 186 nugatory except as confirming that statutory rights of pre-emption may be released, but that is the consequence of the legislation having been framed on a wrong view of the law. In the end, I think, like the other statutory provisions I have had to consider, s 186 itself falls within the principle stated by Lord Simonds in *Kirkness v John Hudson & Co Ltd*[7].

g
I reach the conclusion, therefore, that a right of pre-emption does not create an interest in land and so Mr and Mrs Briggs cannot on any showing claim priority over the plaintiff's option. Lest, however, I be wrong about that I will go on to consider the second half of the problem. Assuming that the right of pre-emption did create an interest in land capable of taking priority over the option, still, in order to establish priority, Mr and Mrs Briggs must show that they acquired the retained lands in exercise
h
of their right of pre-emption, but in my judgment that they cannot do. In my view Mr Inman did not offer the land to them at £3,000 at all, but at the market value of £14,000, plus £150 for certain fixtures and fittings, or if he did offer it at £3,000 it was not under the right of pre-emption but pursuant to a new negotiated bargain.

---

j
1 [1951] AC 161
2 [1952] 1 All ER 531, [1952] AC 401
3 [1905] 2 Ch 257, [1904–7] All ER Rep 268
4 [1978] 1 All ER 886 at 904, [1978] 2 WLR 317 at 338
5 (28th May 1976) unreported
6 (1870) LR 4 HL 610 at 620
7 [1955] 2 All ER 345, [1955] AC 696

The detailed facts are as follows. Mr and Mrs Briggs were for a long time anxious to buy the retained land and at the end of October at the suggestion of Mr Briggs there was *a* a meeting between Mr Inman and Mr Briggs, acting for himself and his wife, at which Mr Briggs made it clear that he was prepared to pay more than £3,000. However, both parties were concerned about the option clause, and both sides took counsel's opinion on several occasions, and ultimately counsel conferred together.

Mr Inman's solicitors put forward an argument that the right of pre-emption had expired in 1953 when there had been a proposal to sell to Mr Mather, but this was *b* disputed. This was, of course, a two-edged sword, because, whilst it would mean that the Briggses could not claim any right to purchase at £3,000, Mr Inman would be unable to sell, because the plaintiff's option must then have priority.

Ultimately, a scheme was devised by counsel, which they thought would enable Mr Inman to obtain market value for the property, and yet the sale would be an exercise by Mr and Mrs Briggs of their right of pre-emption, and an agreement in principle was then *c* made between Mr Inman and Mr Briggs for a sale at a total consideration of £14,150, £14,000 being the figure given by the valuers as the market price. Of this £14,150, £11,150 was to be paid as consideration for Mr Inman acknowledging that the right of pre-emption had not been extinguished in 1953, and to induce him to sell, so that, as it was argued, the right of pre-emption would become exercisable, and the price for the land was to be the remaining £3,000, but subject to contract, subject to the matter being *d* carried out in accordance with counsel's scheme and subject to the approval of the Court of Protection which was duly given.

The next step was an offer made to Mr and Mrs Briggs by letter dated 30th May 1972 in a form settled by counsel and approved by the Court of Protection. That letter is vitally important and I must read it in extenso:

e

'I refer to the fact that I, as the receiver of Mr Arthur Lockwood, and you as the owners of property by reason of being the successors in title of Mr Owen Elliott Riddett, have been in discussion regarding the possibility of Mr Arthur Lockwood acting by me with the authority of the Court of Protection selling the following assets. (1) The property (referred to below as "the relevant property") referred to as "the retained lands" in a conveyance dated the fourteenth day of August 1944 and *f* made between Mr Lockwood and his wife Florence Gertrude Lockwood (since deceased) of the one part and Mr Owen Elliott Riddett of the other part less land with a frontage of 32 feet 8 inches to Capel Curig–Beddgelert Road conveyed to you on the 31st July, 1967 and (ii) Mr Lockwood's interest if any in the fixtures and petrol pumps on the relevant property. In the said 1944 conveyance "the retained lands" are defined or described as the lands and premises comprised in a Deed dated *g* the 18th August, 1906 and a conveyance dated the 4th February 1925 other than the lands and premises conveyed by the said 1944 conveyance. More broadly, the retained lands comprise (a) what I refer to below as "the garage property" namely the site of a car park and petrol filling station shown coloured red on the plan on a lease dated the twenty second day of January 1959, and made between Mr and Mrs Lockwood of the one part and [the plaintiff] . . . of the other part (b) the dwelling *h* house and garage and the land being the site thereof held therewith and known as Hafod-y-Gwynt Penygwryd and (c) the lake and camping ground at Penygwryd. You are aware that there were provisions in the said 1944 conveyance (and I know that you claim to be entitled to the benefit of them), which conferred by means of convenants by Mr and Mrs Lockwood, in respect of the "retained lands" a right of acquisition under circumstances and in accordance with the provisions set out *j* therein. I refer to the contents of the said 1944 conveyance material in this connection as "the 1944 option provisions'. You are aware of the contents of the said lease and also that by a lease of the 3rd February, 1964 made between Mr and Mrs Lockwood on the one part and [the plaintiff] of the other part, the garage property was demised to [the plaintiff] for twenty-one years from the 1st October,

1963 at a yearly rent (now £780) on the terms (with some modifications) contained
in the said 1959 lease including (without modification) the terms of an option in
respect of the whole of the retained lands expressed in Clause 3(c) of the said 1959
lease. I refer below to the option right conferred by the said Clause 3(c) as read with
the provisions of the said 1964 lease as "the 1959/1964 option rights". You and I are
aware of the following items of registration of estate contracts against the names of
Mr and Mrs Lockwood on the Land Charges Registry in London, namely registration
dated the 27th September, 1944, in respect of the 1944 option provision and
registration dated the 10th February, 1964 in respect of the 1959/1964 option
rights. I know that you have claimed and maintained the claim that the benefit of
the 1944 option provisions is vested in you and I have agreed and accept that if the
benefit of the 1944 option provisions still exists, it is vested in you. But I have
claimed against you, and I refer below to this claim as "Mr Lockwood's claim", that
because of correspondence between Mr Lockwood and Mr Mather which took place
in 1953 and was begun by a letter dated the 17th January, 1953, and sent by Mr
Lockwood to Mr Mather, the rights under the 1944 option provisions ceased in
1953 and, therefore, that there is no benefit of the 1944 option provisions and
accordingly no benefit of the 1944 option provisions is vested in you. I am aware
that Mr Lockwood's claim can be and has been resisted by you. I write this letter on
behalf of Mr Lockwood with the authority of the Court of Protection, to offer that
if you, Mr and Mrs Briggs will: (1) Pay (on acceptance of this offer) to Mr Lockwood
the sum of £11,150 (2) Jointly and severally agree with me to keep me and my
personal representatives and my estate and jointly and severally agree with Mr
Lockwood to keep him and his personal representatives and his estate fully
indemnified at all times against all loss damages expenses or costs incurred by me or
my personal representatives or my estate in the one case or by Mr Lockwood or his
personal representatives or his estate in the other by reason (in either case) of any
claims or demands actions or proceedings of [the plaintiff] or any persons claiming
or professing to claim under [the plaintiff] and whether as his assigns or personal
representatives or otherwise howsoever under or in respect of the 1959/1964 option
rights. Mr Lockwood will withdraw Mr Lockwood's claim to the intent that as
between him and you you shall be entitled or agreed to be entitled to all the benefit
of and to exercise the rights conferred by the 1944 option provisions in respect of
the relevant property. The offer above contained will be open for acceptance in
writing by you by actual delivery of such written acceptance to me at any time up
to and including the 30th June, 1972. The offer is made and if accepted by you
must be accepted by you, subject to the following terms: (a) On acceptance you will
pay to me, acting on behalf of Mr Lockwood, the said sum of £11,150. (b) Mr
Lockwood's obligations as regards conveyance and delivery of possession of the
relevant property and fixtures and petrol pumps consequent on an exercise by you
of your rights under the 1944 option provisions, shall be deemed to be fully
performed by (1) His (subject to the payment of the price for the relevant property
and for Mr Lockwood's interest (if any) in the fixtures and petrol pumps) delivering
a conveyance to you in fee simple made by him acting by me under an order of the
Court of Protection of the relevant property subject to and with the benefit of the
said lease of 1964 (as read with the said lease of 1959) and subject to the exceptions
and reservations and covenants contained in the said Deed of 1925 and to the rights
of drainage granted by the said 1944 conveyance and the restrictive covenants (but
excluding (b) set out in Clause 4 of the said 1944 conveyance) and (2) his giving
vacant possession at the completion of the purchase of the whole of the relevant
property other than the property comprised in the said 1964 lease (or now treated
as so comprised by [the plaintiff] provided further that you will accept the title from
Mr Lockwood alone on his conveying as beneficial owner and be satisfied of his
beneficial ownership on being shown his own original ownership of one half and
that he has become entitled as the sole beneficiary in respect of Mrs Lockwood's

fully administered estate to the other half of the beneficial ownership. (c) You will
enter into a Deed of Covenant to be settled and approved by the Court to be   *a*
prepared at Mr Lockwood's expense with me in my personal capacity and with Mr
Lockwood to contain the terms of indemnity set out at (2) of paragraph 7 above. I,
on behalf of Mr Lockwood and with the authority of the Court of Protection,
undertake with you that if you accept the offer made above, I on behalf of Mr
Lockwood will within three days of your said acceptance send or procure to be sent
to you a notice, intended to be consistent with the 1944 option provisions, that Mr   *b*
Lockwood gives to you the option pursuant to the 1944 option provisions and not
to be revoked or altered within 21 days, to purchase the relevant property at the
price of £3000 and all (if any) the interest of Mr Lockwood in fixtures and petrol
pumps at the price of £1 (or such other less price for such interest if any as you and
I on behalf of Mr Lockwood agree on). The giving of that notice by me will be
subject to your confirming that you have continued to be and are the estate owners   *c*
in fee simple of the property comprised in the said conveyance of 1944.'

This was not immediately acceptable, and on 21st June 1972 Messrs Foysters, the
Briggses' solicitors, sent what was in effect a counter-offer in the following terms:

'C. If our clients duly exercise the said option, on completion of the conveyance
to be made to them pursuant to the said option (which conveyance as mentioned   *d*
above will contain no reference to [the plaintiff's] lease or his option) our clients are
to execute a separate Deed, to which they, Mr Lockwood and your client will be
parties, and by which our client will (a) release Mr Lockwood and his personal
representatives from all claims and demands under the covenants for title implied
on his part in the said conveyance so far as the same relate to [the plaintiff's] lease or
the option therein contained but not further or otherwise (b) covenant with Mr   *e*
Lockwood to keep Mr Lockwood and his personal representatives and his estate
fully indemnified at all times against all loss damages expenses or costs incurred by
Mr Lockwood or his personal representatives or his estate by reason of any claims
demands actions or proceedings by [the plaintiff] or any persons claiming or
professing to claim under [the plaintiff] and whether as his assigns or personal
representatives or otherwise howsoever in respect of his lease or the option therein   *f*
contained and (c) covenant with your client to keep your client and his personal
representatives and his estate fully indemnified at all times against one half of all loss
damages expenses or costs incurred by your client or his personal representatives or
his estate by reason of any such claims demands actions or procedings as aforesaid.'

On 11th July 1972 Mr Inman wrote to Mr Briggs formally saying that he could not
agree to the 50% sharing of damages and costs should he be proceeded against by the   *g*
plaintiff, and he informed his solicitors to the same effect.Then Mr Inman's solicitors
wrote officially to Mr Briggs's solicitors:

'The proposition put forward in your letter is not acceptable; our client might be
prepared to consider it were it not for the suggestion that he should bear one half of
any liability which might arise against him personally. Apart from the point we   *h*
have mentioned above the terms suggested in your letter do not appear to be
radically different from those suggested by Mr Turner [of counsel] and if your
clients are to proceed at all we would suggest that it should be in the manner
outlined by him.'

The demand for a full indemnity was accepted on 20th July 1972. Then there was a   *j*
burst of activity on 7th August 1972. Mr Inman's solicitors replied on that day saying:

'Before we make any decision on the amendment to the letter of 21st June, we
should be pleased if you would confirm the following points: 1. That the sum of
£11,150 is paid to our client in consideration of our client not pursuing his
contention that the option granted to your clients predecessors in title by the 1944

a conveyance is no longer exercisable and that when paid to our client it becomes irrecoverable. The further sum of £3000 will be payable on the exercise of the option being the consideration stated in the 1944 conveyance. 2. Our clients, their personal representatives and their respective estates will be fully indemnified by your clients against any loss, damages, costs or expenses arising from any claim made by any successors in title immediate or not of Mr and Mrs Briggs under the covenants for title in the conveyance to them consequent on or by reason of any
b claims or demands of [the plaintiff] or any persons claiming or professing to claim and whether as his assigns or personal representatives or otherwise in respect of his lease or the option therein contained. Since such an indemnity will not appear in the actual conveyance to your clients we would prefer that the indemnity be included in the Deed of Covenant with our client. We should be pleased to hear from you on these points.'

c   Mr Inman wrote to Mr and Mrs Briggs extending 'the time for the acceptance of my offer until the 10th August 1972'. Mr and Mrs Briggs gave two cheques, one for £11,150 and the other for £3,000; and Mr Inman wrote out and signed a formal offer of the retained lands at £3,000. That was in these terms:

d   'Thank you for your letter of the 7th August, 1972 enclosing a cheque for £11,150 which is paid in accordance with the terms agreed between us through our respective solicitors in letters dated 30th May, 21st June, 13th July, 20th July and 7th August, 1972. In accordance with Clause 4(b) in the conveyance dated the 14th August 1944 made between Arthur Lockwood and Florence Gertrude Lockwood (1) and Owen Elliott Riddett (2) I, as Receiver of Mr Arthur Lockwood, now offer to you the offer to purchase the property referred to as the "retained lands" . . . at the
e   price of £3,000 and the fixtures and petrol pumps thereon at a price of £1. This option shall remain open to you for 21 days, that is until the twenty eighth day of August 1972. . . . The Law Society's Conditions of Sale (1934) shall apply to the contract and completion shall take place one month after your acceptance hereof.'

     Also on that same 7th August 1972 the Briggses' solicitors endorsed on one copy of that letter the following acceptance: 'On behalf of C. B. Briggs and J. Briggs we hereby
f accept the offer contained in the letter of which this is a copy', signed Foysters and dated 7th August 1972, and they also wrote on the same day to Mr Inman's solicitors: 'We write to confirm that the terms set out in your letter of today's date are agreed.'

     Major Lockwood died on 15th January 1973 and the retained lands were conveyed by his personal representatives to Mr and Mrs Briggs on 16th February 1973. In the circumstances no question of modifying the covenants for title arose. This conveyance
g contained the usual certificate for stamp duty purposes in the following terms:

     'It is hereby certified that the transaction hereby effected does not form part of a larger transaction or of a series of transactions in respect of which the amount or value or the aggregate amount or value of the consideration exceeds £10,000.'

     This must clearly be wrong on any showing.
h   Counsel for the defendants argues that there was a two stage contract made between 30th May and 7th August 1972, the first being a payment to Mr Inman in consideration for his releasing his claim that the right of pre-emption had been lost in 1953, and to induce him to decide to sell so as to give Mr and Mrs Briggs the right to call for an offer at £3,000 under the right of pre-emption, and the second the making and acceptance of such an offer. The truth is, however, in my view that it is impossible to separate them,
j because the first part contained a term by which Mr Inman obliged himself to make the offer.

     Moreover, the right of pre-emption was not worded so as to arise in the event of the Lockwoods deciding to sell, whatever that might mean precisely, but that they would not sell, which must mean elsewhere, without first offering the property to the Briggses. Mr Inman never decided to sell or contemplated selling to anyone other than the Briggses, or that he would sell to anyone, the Briggses included, for £3,000, and he sold to them only because he was able to negotiate a sale at market value.   *a*

In my judgment there was but one agreement, not two, and the legal effect of that agreement was a sale at market value. Even if, however, it be right to divide the transaction into two parts, still the £3,000 offer was made, not because the right of pre-emption bound Mr Inman to make it, but because Mr Inman by the first part of the May to August transaction bound himself to make it on payment of £11,150. That was a new contract made in August and I do not see how it can be related back to the priority of the   *b* right of pre-emption. With respect, I do not agree with the learned judge that this conclusion flies in the teeth of the decision of the House of Lords in *Inland Revenue Comrs v Duke of Westminster*[1]. Care must be taken to see that the principle laid down there is not taken out of its context. As Lord Halsbury LC said in *Quinn v Leathem*[2]:

'. . . there are two observations of a general character which I wish to make, and one is to repeat what I have very often said before, that every judgment must be read   *c* as applicable to the particular facts proved, or assumed to be proved, since the generality of the expressions which may be found there are not intended to be expositions of the whole law, but governed and qualified by the particular facts of the case in which such expressions are found.'

Now, in *Inland Revenue Comrs v Duke of Westminster*[1] the parties sought to say that a   *d* covenanted annuity should be treated as wages, that being, it was said, the substance of the matter, but it was not the legal effect of what was done. Although the duke expected that his gardener would be satisfied with the annuity and would not also ask for wages and that expectation was communicated to and assented to by him, it was made clear that it was not wages and that he could claim his wages if he wished.

In the present case, however, the conclusion I have reached appears to me to be in   *e* every respect the legal consequence of what was done, and not merely the economic result, although the parties sought to make it appear otherwise.

Then counsel for the defendants set up as a defence that this was a sale by the authority of the court and, therefore, by virtue of s 116 of the Mental Health Act 1959, s 204 of the Law of Property Act 1925 applies, which so far is correct. The last mentioned section reads as follows: *f*

'(1) An order of the court under any statutory or other jurisdiction shall not, as against a purchaser, be invalidated on the ground of want of jurisdiction, or of want of any concurrence, consent, notice, or service, whether the purchaser has notice of any such want, or not.

'(2) This section has effect with respect to any lease, sale, or other act under the authority of the court, and purporting to be in pursuance of any statutory power   *g* notwithstanding any exception in such statute.

'(3) This section applies to all orders made before or after the commencement of this Act.'

That being so, he submits that Mr and Mrs Briggs got a good title and the plaintiff's interest under his option was transferred to the proceeds of sale by virtue of the Law of   *h* Property Act 1925, s 2(1)(iv), which reads as follows:

'A conveyance to a purchaser of a legal estate in land shall overreach any equitable interest or power affecting that estate, whether or not he has notice thereof, if . . . (iv) the conveyance is made under an order of the court and the equitable interest or power is bound by such order, and any capital money arising from the transaction   *j* is paid into, or in accordance with the order of, the court.'

---

1   [1936] AC 1, [1935] All ER Rep 259
2   [1901] AC 495 at 506, [1900–3] All ER Rep 1 at 7

I pause there to observe that the purchase money was paid in accordance with the order
a of the court, and that s 204 replaces without material alteration s 70(1) of the
Conveyancing Act 1881. Thus, so the argument runs, the plaintiff's claim against the
land and the proceeds of sale is in effect totally defeated, because the proceeds, it is said,
were £3,000 only, and so he would have to pay £3,000 under his option to acquire
£3,000. Even if the defendants were right in saying that s 2(1)(iv) applies to give them
a good title still in my view the proceeds of sale were not £3,000 but £14,150.

b   However, in my judgment, this argument is unsound in principle. Counsel for the
defendants based it on the decision of this court in *Mostyn v Mostyn*[1], and in particular
this passage in the judgment of Lopes LJ:

'This section was considered in the Appeal Court in *In re Hall Dare's Contract*[2]. In
that case Sir *George Jessel* after reading the 70th section, said[3]: "The only reason
suggested why the sale here should not be protected by that section is that the
c section is not to apply where it can be seen upon the face of the order that the order
is wrong. But who is to see it? The purchaser cannot see it. It is true a learned
lawyer acquainted with all the provisions of the Act may find it out, but in no other
sense does it appear on the face of the order. No person not familiar with the
provisions of the *Settled Estates Act* would find anything on the face of this order to
lead him to suspect that it was wrong. Now to ask us to hold that whenever there
d appears on the face of an order something which would lead a person of sufficient
learning and acquainted with the practice to the conclusion that the order is
irregular, the 70th section does not apply, would be asking us to repeal a very plain
enactment which was made for the protection of purchasers. The purchaser sees an
order for sale made by the Court which has jurisdiction in the matter, and he is not
to trouble himself any further. If any mistake has been made still he is to get a good
e title, all claims of the persons interested in the estate being transferred to the
purchase-money." The purchasers in this case are, in my opinion, protected by the
order of sale of the 23rd July, 1892, from puisne incumbrances.'

In *Re Hall Dare's Contract*[2] it was in truth a matter of validating an order which the
court intended to make and had full power to make, dispensing with the concurrence or
f consent of certain interested parties, but the order was irregular because they should have
been specifically named whereas they were in fact designated by a generic description,
and it is to be observed that in *Jones v Barnett*[4] Lord Lindley MR said:

'In that case there was a mere irregularity. It is a very different thing to say that
s 70 enables the Court to sell the property of the wrong man. An order of the Court
g does not bind persons who are not parties to it.'

Mostyn v Mostyn[5] was distinguished in *Jones v Barnett*[6], both by Romer J[7] at first
instance and in the Court of Appeal. In that case the court had made an order for the sale
of certain leasehold property in the mistaken belief that it belonged to a certain judgment
debtor whereas in truth he had some years previously assigned the lease to his sister
h whose title was unimpeachable. The court held that the purchaser could not claim title
under s 70(1) of the Conveyancing Act 1881. Romer J said[8]: 'And when the argument

1   [1893] 3 Ch 376 at 381
2   (1882) 21 Ch D 41
j 3   21 Ch D 41 at 46
4   [1900] 1 Ch 370 at 373
5   [1893] 3 Ch 376
6   [1900] 1 Ch 370
7   [1899] 1 Ch 611, [1900] 1 Ch 370
8   [1899] 1 Ch 611 at 617

of the defendant's counsel upon s. 70 is fully developed, it is found of necessity to lead, if sound, to very astonishing conclusions.' Again he said[1]:

    'An owner of an estate might suddenly find himself wholly deprived of it by an order of Court in some proceeding he had never heard of, and without any intention on the part of the Court to affect him, and then be told that he had no remedy except possibly to follow (if he could) any moneys that might have been paid by a purchaser.'

Romer J obviously found difficulty in *Mostyn v Mostyn*[2] about which he said[3]:

    'So far as the actual decision in that case is concerned it was only one determining a question of form of conveyance which had arisen in an administration action as between vendors and purchasers. But one reason given for their decision by the Lords Justices undoubtedly was that certain puisne mortgagees who were strangers to the action were bound under the section by the order for sale. Speaking with all respect, I do not clearly see how they arrived at that conclusion, especially as they also held that the first mortgagees, who had agreed to join in the sale, were not bound by the order, and that as those mortgagees were not before the Court or parties to the contract for sale the Court had no power to compel them to submit to the purchasers' requirements. I gather, however, that the Court, having regard to the conditions of sale and other circumstances of the case, came to the conclusion that the Court by its orders did intend to bind, and had bound, the puisne mortgagees and their interests in the property ordered to be sold, though those puisne mortgagees were strangers to the action. This being so, the case is quite distinguishable from the case now before me, where, having regard to the fact that the sale was ordered under the provisions of the Judgments Act, 1864, and was clearly intended to be a sale of the debtor's interest of which the creditor had obtained equitable execution, I am satisfied that the plaintiff's interest in the property was not intended to be, and was not in fact, bound.'

In *Jones v Barnett*[4] in the Court of Appeal, Lindley MR dealt with *Mostyn v Mostyn*[2] as follows:

    'In neither of the cases which have been referred to had the Court made an order for the sale of the wrong man's property. In *In Re Hall Dare's Contract*[5], the Court was not selling property of a person other than it supposed. There was merely an objection to the regularity of the form of the order. There is no doubt some little difficulty by reason of what the Court said in *Mostyn v. Mostyn*[2]. But the decision was only that the purchaser would get a good title without the concurrence of some puisne incumbrancers, and, if the Court had jurisdiction to sell, it became a mere question of regularity in the machinery. We are asked to go much further than that. I do not propose to redraft s. 70. But it should be observed that it begins by assuming that the Court has made an order under its jurisdiction, statutory or otherwise, and the words "shall not be invalidated on the ground of want of jurisdiction" are introduced to cover any irregularity of procedure which might possibly affect the jurisdiction and invalidate the order. I am not disposed to cut down the operation of the section, but the effect which it is now sought to give to it is so obviously wrong that it is impossible to consider that to have been the

1   [1899] 1 Ch 611 at 618
2   [1893] 3 Ch 376
3   [1899] 1 Ch 611 at 619–620
4   [1900] 1 Ch 370 at 374–375
5   (1882) 21 Ch D 41

intention of the Legislature. They could not have intended to enable the Court to
sell the property of B. when it supposed it was selling the property of A., B. not
being a party to the proceedings.'

Now in the present case, the retained lands were the property of the patient, but
subject to the plaintiff's option of which the Court of Protection was fully aware. It did
not, however, in my judgment make, purport to make, or intend to make an order for
the sale of the property free from that option. All it intended, and did, by its order was
to authorise a sale by the receiver, which it was advised and supposed would overreach
that option, not by virtue of any power in the court so to order, but because it was
thought, erroneously, that the transaction when carried out would so operate. The court
had no power to order a sale, free from incumbrances vested in persons not parties to the
proceedings. All that it had power to do, and purported to do, was to authorise Mr
Inman to act in the name and on behalf of Major Lockwood to do what he could himself
have done had he not become a patient. The position is in my view parallel with the case
envisaged in a note to s 204 in Wolstenholme and Cherry's Conveyancing Statutes[1]. It
is there stated:

> ' "Under the authority of the Court": *semble*, if the court merely gives leave to
> exercise a statutory power out of court, for instance, if the court authorises the sale
> of a mansion house by a tenant for life (Settled Land Act, 1925, s. 65), the order
> merely brings the power into force; if the tenant for life has a bad title, a purchaser
> from him would get no better title by reason of the order, for it is only intended to
> bind the persons interested under the settlement, not persons claiming by title
> paramount.'

I agree with that note which in my judgment also covers the present case.

And so, in my judgment, there is no answer to the plaintiff's claim unless it be that on
some discretionary ground specific performance ought not to be granted. But the
learned judge said that had he taken a different view of the priorities he would not have
seen any sufficient reason for refusing specific performance, and I agree with that view.
Once it is established that Mr and Mrs Briggs are not in a position to claim for their
contract and conveyance the priority of the right of pre-emption, then it is, at least, a case
of a purchase of property subject to a registered land charge and with actual knowledge
in fact of the precise nature of that charge. Moreover they schemed, and I do not use that
word in any pejorative sense, but they did in fact scheme, to defeat that option if they
could. They failed in that attempt; but surely then they cannot say the plaintiff should
not have the equitable remedy which would ordinarily be appropriate.

I feel considerable sympathy with Mr and Mrs Briggs in that, although they must have
known there was a risk (otherwise they would not have been required to give
indemnities), still they did have the advice of counsel and they knew that Mr Inman was
acting under the authority of the Court of Protection. Nevertheless, with all respect to
the learned judge, I am unable to see any defence to this action and in my judgment the
appeal should be allowed and an order made for specific performance of the contract
resulting from the exercise by the plaintiff of his option.

In the circumstances the question of conspiracy is of minor importance, since the
plaintiff will have suffered little (if any) damage from it. Counsel for the plaintiff did say,
however, that he wished to maintain this as an additional claim to enable him to recover
any damage over and above that afforded by the decree for specific performance, which
damages he thought could only be for delay. I must, therefore, consider this aspect of the
case also.

Counsel for the defendants argued that it must fail in limine because Mr Inman was
acting under the directions of the court and, therefore, he could not be liable, and so,
whatever the position of Mr Briggs might be, there could not be the minimum of two

---

1   13th Edn (1972) vol 1, p 335

persons necessary to support a charge of conspiracy. I cannot accept that. The orders of
the Court of Protection would, of course, have protected Mr Inman from any claim by *a*
a person interested in the estate of Major Lockwood if that estate had suffered loss
through the transaction with Mr and Mrs Briggs, and also, of course, would entitle him
to indemnity out of that estate in respect of any personal liability incurred by him as the
result of carrying out what he was authorised to do. Such orders could not, however, in
my view override the rights of the plaintiff or protect Mr Inman from any liability at his
suit on the ground that the transaction authorised by the court and carried into effect was *b*
unlawful as against him.

The questions then are what are the ingredients of the tort, and has it been established
on the facts? The tort is that of interference with contractual rights and its nature and
ambit are stated by Lord Macnaghten in *Quinn v Leathem*[1], where he said:

'. . . that a violation of legal right committed knowingly is a cause of action, and that *c*
it is a violation of legal right to interfere with contractual relations recognised by
law if there be no sufficient justification for the interference.'

Moreover, it is well established that it does not have to be malicious in the sense of being
done from spite or ill will (see per Lord Macnaghten in *South Wales Miners' Federation v
Glamorgan Coal Co Ltd*[2]: 'It is settled now that malice in the sense of spite or ill-will is not
the gist of such an action'). The cause of action and the fact that malice is not an *d*
ingredient of it was stated in the same case by Lord James in these terms[3]:

'As to the word "wrongfully" I think no difficulty arises. If the breach of the
contract of service by the workmen was an unlawful act, any one who induces and
procures the workmen, without just cause or excuse, to break such a contract also
acts unlawfully, and thus the allegation that the act done was wrongfully done is *e*
established. But the word "maliciously" has also to be dealt with. The judgment of
Bingham J. proceeds on the ground that "to support an action for procuring a breach
of contract it is essential to prove actual malice". I cannot concur in this view of the
law.'

See also *Lumley v Gye*[4].

Now it is clear that both Mr Inman and Mr Briggs knew all the relevant facts, they *f*
agreed together, and they intended to defeat the plaintiff's contractual rights under his
option. 'So', says counsel for the plaintiff, 'my case is proved', and prima facie that must
be so, but counsel for the defendants raises a number of defences. First, he says that this
tort cannot be committed, whether by a single individual or by conspirators, unless they
know that what they are doing is unlawful. They cannot be liable if they honestly
believe either that what they are doing does not interfere with the plaintiff's contractual *g*
rights or that they have a prior right which entitles them to do so.

He submitted that the plaintiff must prove that Mr Inman and Mr Briggs knew that
the transaction would inevitably constitute a breach of contract by Major Lockwood, but,
at most, all they knew was that there was some risk or possibility that the plaintiff might
sue for breach of contract, and he relied on the learned judge's finding that '. . . neither
of them did know that the arrangement into which they entered was or might be a *h*
breach of any such contractual rights'[5].

He also drew attention to passages in the evidence showing the state of mind of Mr
Briggs and Mr Inman respectively. As to Mr Briggs the following question was asked:
'Q. It was in relation to the option that the danger arose, was it not? A. Yes, I understood

j

1   [1901] AC 495 at 510, [1900–3] All ER Rep 1 at 9
2   [1905] AC 239 at 246, [1904–7] All ER Rep 211 at 214
3   [1905] AC 239 at 250, [1904–7] All ER Rep 211 at 216–217
4   (1853) 2 E & B 216, [1843–60] All ER Rep 208
5   [1978] 1 All ER 886 at 907, [1978] 2 WLR 317 at 341

that our option if exercised during Major Lockwood's lifetime would extinguish the
a other one which was exercisable after his death.' Again, he was asked:

'Q. Do you remember the passage in it under which Major Lockwood undertook
that if [the plaintiff] exercised his option, his, Major Lockwood's, personal
representatives would convey the property to [the plaintiff]? A. Yes.
'Q. If you purchased the property they could not do that? A. No.
b 'Q. Would it not be clear to you that that would represent a breach of Major
Lockwood's contractual obligation to [the plaintiff]? A. No, I thought that was
purely a matter of law as to which option was the important one.
'*Walton J.* I think you have been trying to say this for a long time, Mr Briggs.
You thought as I gather from a lot of half-answers, if I may put it this way, you have
given, you thought your option was superior in every way to [the plaintiff's], and if
c you exercised your option, if you were in a position to exercise it because there was
some doubt about it, but if that was cleared up and you were in a position to exercise
your option, then [the plaintiff's] option had gone for good? A. Yes, your Lordship.
'Q. That is what you thought? A. That is exactly what I believed.'

Counsel for the defendants says Mr Briggs's state of mind was clear. He thought that
d the exercise of the right of pre-emption by him in Major Lockwood's lifetime would
extinguish the plaintiff's option. But he was asked: 'But Major Lockwood would be
liable to an action in damages from [the plaintiff]. Do you understand that?' and he
answered: 'Yes.' The next question was: 'That is one of the things the indemnity was
wanted in respect of?', and again he answered: 'Yes.'
Concerning Mr Inman, counsel for the defendants said, at most, he thought it possible
e that the plaintiff might sue the executors or Mr Inman himself for damages for breach
of contract after Major Lockwood's death, but he did not know that the 1972 transaction
then constituted or would inevitably be a breach. He thought it lawful. In support of
this counsel for the defendants drew our attention to the following passages in the cross-
examination:

f 'Q. Listen carefully to this question and do not assent to it unless you are satisfied
that it does reflect your views. I think it does and I am therefore putting it to you.
You had Mr Turner's opinion. You had had the letters, or letter, I do not know how
many, from Foysters in which they had been referring to actions which might
follow if the scheme worked as you had hoped it was going to do, and liabilities and
damages that might follow. You had had the opinion from Mr Turner some time
g previously in which he had drawn your attention to your personal risk in the
matter. And you appreciated that what was being done was something that was
going to give [the plaintiff] a right of action in damages when your uncle died?
A. That was a possibility.
'Q. Was it not more than a possibility, was it not a virtual certainty? A. Nobody
had told me that at the time.
h 'Q. It was not certain that [the plaintiff] would do anything, but had you not
understood from what Mr Turner had said, clearly said in his opinion, that what was
being done would be a breach of Major Lockwood's contractual obligations to [the
plaintiff]? A. This is back to the kernel in the nut. I suppose I must say I was alive
to the dangers. What else could I do?
'*Walton J.* Yes, but the point is did you consider them dangers or certainties? A.
j I did not consider them certainties. If I had considered them certainties it would
have been a foolish act to have gone ahead with it.
'*Counsel for the plaintiff.* Except that you were being covered by indemnities. A.
As I mentioned a little earlier on, the fact that my position was going to be made
secure, or an attempt was going to be made to make it secure, did not influence it
at all. The fact that I was going to expose myself did influence it that it was all off.

But I would not have proceeded had I not thought this was a rightful thing to do.

'Q. I follow that, but your solicitors had advised you that it was? A. Yes.   *a*

'Q. So that point was certain. Right or wrong, and you are not a lawyer and you are not expected to know, but right or wrong the learned judge will find in due course, your solicitors had advised you it was all right to go on? A. Yes.

'Q. Nobody would blame you for accepting that advice? A. Absolutely. Yes, I accepted that advice and because I had the Court of Protection's approval it seemed to me as a layman that it had been sifted through all these hands and I was doing the *b* right thing. Everybody has a different point of view. The Court of Protection was concerned only with my uncle's welfare, and indeed I only considered my uncle's welfare. So we were at one on that, and it was on that basis that I agreed.

'Q. Again I would like to suggest you did realise that it was going to be a breach of [the plaintiff's] contract, but you thought because the solicitors had said it was all right and the Court of Protection accepted it that it was a proper thing for you to *c* do? A. Absolutely, I agree to that.'

Read literally, Mr Inman appears in that last answer to be agreeing that he realised 'it was going to be a breach of [the plaintiff's] contract', but I think all he was assenting to was that he thought it was all right.

Then this was put to him: *d*

'Q. Mr Inman I wonder if I could just summarise because I have been rather a long time cross-examining and I want to be quite clear that you know what I am putting to you and equally what I am not putting. I want to tell you first of all what I am not putting to you, what I am accepting out of your evidence. I am accepting, Mr Inman, that your dominant and primary motive in selling (and by that I am speaking of getting the £14,150 so do not take me up on that) was to get money for *e* your uncle's welfare? A. Yes.

'Q. You follow that. I am accepting that you thought what you were doing was lawful? A. Yes.

'Q. I say that you had a subsidiary motive in wanting to help if you could, Mr Briggs, but that you had no motive of personal gain or improper spite or anything *f* of that sort? A. Correct.

'Q. In the reasons behind the transaction? A. Perfectly true.

'Q. And I am also accepting that under advice you genuinely believed there was nothing the matter with the transaction and no reason why you should not do it? A. Perfectly true.

'Q. But I am saying, now I am coming to the positive side of what I am saying, and I say it purely in respect of 30th October 1971 down to 18th April 1972, at some *g* time or another over that period you knew of the plaintiff's option, that it was an option entitling him to buy for £3,000, exercisable at Mr Lockwood's death. You knew that Mr Briggs knew that too? A. Yes, I told Mr Briggs.

'Q. You knew because Mr Turner had said so or your solicitors had said so and you accepted it from one or the other, which it does not matter, but you knew in one of those ways or another that the sale to Mr Briggs in Major Lockwood's lifetime *h* must be a breach of the plaintiff's option? A. I was aware of the facts.

'Q. Will you go that far with me. Will you accept that as I put it to you? A. I did not realise that it would be as strong as a breach.

'Q. Can I just ask you what you did think it would be? A. I always thought that if the sale went through during my uncle's lifetime that this satisfied the Briggs's *j* option. We are back to this difficulty that we cannot get over.'

Finally Mr Inman was asked this question:

'Q. In your conversations with your solicitors was the seriousness of the possibility of an action—I am sorry I am putting that a bit inaccurately. In your conversations

with your solicitors was the seriousness of the possibility of an action being brought
by [the plaintiff] in respect of the sale to Mr Briggs discussed? A. I would say it was,
yes.

'Q. In these discussions so far as you can recollect casting your mind back, was
reference made to Mr Turner's opinions on that subject? A. Oh indeed.

'Q. So far as you can recollect did your solicitors accept Mr Turner's opinions on
that subject? A. Absolutely.

'Q. And did you accept your solicitors and Mr Turner's opinions on that
subject? A. Perfectly.'

So far as authority is concerned, counsel for the defendants relies on *Smith v Morrison*[1]
where Plowman J said:

'In my judgment [the solicitor's] state of mind at the time of, and in relation to,
the transfer to Coyles was not such as to render Coyles liable to a claim for inducing
a breach of contract. I have already stated what [the solicitor's] state of mind was—
one of honest doubt—and that, in my judgment, is not enough to bring him within
the principles of liability enunciated in the cases to which I have referred.'

In my judgment, however, that case is distinguishable, because the learned judge's
finding there was that although the solicitor who acted for Coyles had seen the document
alleged to be a prior contract he did not know that there was a contract at all. That
learned judge's finding as to the solicitor's state of mind is as follows[2]:

'At this point I must say something about the state of mind of [the solicitor] at
completion, because his was the decision to complete. He knew of the
correspondence between his firm and Dale & Newbery, to which I have already
referred. Miss Foinette kept him constantly informed of the position. She reported
to him her telephone conversation with Dale & Newbery on 8th December, after
they had seen Mr Morrison. They had told her first, that there was a doubt whether
the memoranda signed by Mr Morrison were complete when he signed them;
secondly that he was emphatic that he never entered into any binding contract with
Mr Smith; and thirdly that Mr Smith had told Mr Morrison that there would be
some tax advantage if the deposit were split between the farm and the bungalow.
[The solicitor], whose evidence I accept, said in chief that he believed, and still
believes, that those statements of Mr Morrison, reported by Dale & Newbery, were
true. He said that the decision whether to complete or not was not an easy decision,
but that if Dale & Newbery, who knew more about the position as between Mr
Smith and Mr Morrison than he did, felt free to complete, Coyles should do so
within the priority period. He believed that there were serious doubts whether Mr
Smith had a binding contract. He said that he was not, and would not have been,
a party to any collusion with Mr Morrison so as to defeat Mr Smith, and that he did
not refrain from making any enquiry lest the answer should prove embarrassing.'

In the present case, however, both Mr Inman and Mr Briggs did know that there was
a contract with the plaintiff and its terms. I refer again to Mr Inman's evidence:

'Q. But I am saying, now I am coming to the positive side of what I am saying,
and I say it purely in respect of 30th October 1971, down to 18th April 1972, at
some time or another over that period you knew of the plaintiff's option, that it was
an option entitling him to buy for £3,000 exercisable at Mr Lockwood's death. You
knew that Mr Briggs knew that too? A. I told Mr Briggs.

'Q. You knew because Mr Turner had said so or your solicitors had said so and
you accepted it from one or the other, which it does not matter, but you knew in

---

1   [1974] 1 All ER 957 at 974, [1974] 1 WLR 659 at 677–678
2   [1974] 1 All ER 957 at 967–968, [1974] 1 WLR 659 at 670

one of those ways or another that the sale to Mr Briggs in Major Lockwood's lifetime must be a breach of the plaintiff's option? A. I was aware of the facts.' *a*

Counsel for the plaintiff relies, and in my judgment rightly relies, on *Churchill v Walton*[1] where Viscount Dilhorne said:

'The question is "What did they agree to do?" If what they agreed to do was, on the facts known to them, an unlawful act, they are guilty of conspiracy and cannot excuse themselves by saying that, owing to their ignorance of the law, they did not realise that such an act was a crime. If, on the facts known to them, what they agreed to do was lawful, they are not rendered artificially guilty by the existence of other facts, not known to them, giving a different and criminal quality to the act agreed on.'

(The reference in the headnote in the Law Reports[2] to Viscount Dilhorne's speech badly *c* needs correction.) There the accused was held not guilty because he did not know the facts. He did not know that the oil was being used without repayment of the rebate, but it clearly establishes liability in a criminal case if one does know the facts, even though one does not know one is acting unlawfully.

Counsel for the defendants submits that that principle should be limited to criminal cases, but I see no reason why that should be so. Accordingly in my judgment this *d* defence fails.

Secondly, and rather akin to the first point, counsel for the defendants submitted that Mr Inman and Mr Briggs cannot be held liable because they acted under a mistake, not as to the law generally but on a question of private right, and he relied on *Cooper v Phibbs*[3]. That, however, was a case of setting aside an agreement on the ground of mutual mistake, and the House of Lords held that, being a matter of private right, it was a *e* mistake of fact. I cannot see that that has any application to the present case.

Thirdly, he claims justification and submits that, if A enters into a contract to sell to B for £10,000, and then next day to sell to C for £15,000, B is entitled to persuade and procure A to fulfil the contract with him though he knows that it will procure a breach of the second contract. In support of this submission he relies on the following passage *f* in the judgment of Buckley LJ in *Smithies v National Association of Operative Plasterers*[4]:

'But, lastly, it is said that the act was justified. No doubt there are circumstances in which A. is entitled to induce B. to break a contract entered into by B. with C. Thus, for instance, if the contract between B. and C. is one which B. could not make consistently with his preceding contractual obligations towards A., A. may not only induce him to break it, but may invoke the assistance of a Court of Justice to make *g* him break it.'

The difficulty in his way, however, is that on the view that I hold that the right of pre-emption did not create an interest in land, and even if it did, still on my interpretation of the facts, that Mr and Mrs Briggs do not claim under it but under a new contract made in 1972, this case is the converse of that in *Smithies's* case[5], which therefore cannot help *h* counsel for the defendants.

So the only justifications which can be pleaded are the duty which Mr Inman had to act with a single eye to the benefit and protection of Major Lockwood's estate, and the legitimate interest Mr and Mrs Briggs had in trying to get priority under the right of pre-emption if they could; but in my judgment these cannot be sufficient. That there is a

j

1 [1967] 1 All ER 497 at 503, [1967] 2 AC 224 at 237
2 [1967] 2 AC 224 at 225, [1967] 2 WLR 682 at 683
3 (1867) LR 2 HL 149
4 [1909] 1 KB 310 at 337, [1908–10] All ER Rep 455 at 467
5 [1909] 1 KB 310, [1908–10] All ER Rep 455

defence of sufficient justification is clear from the authorites I have cited, but there is not
a a great deal of authority on the question of what is sufficient.

One starts with a dictum of Lord James in the *South Wales Miners'* case[1]:

> 'The action of the defendants in going, as I have said, to the extent of inducing
> and procuring the commission of an unlawful act places them in a very different
> position to that occupied by a person whose duty it is to offer advice to one who
b > needs to be guided or protected.'

There the learned judge speaks of a duty.

There is only one case in which the defence has succeeded, *Brimelow v Casson*[2], and
there again it was based on a duty, albeit a moral one, and the facts were very strong
indeed. The conduct of the party whose contracts were interfered with was utterly
disgraceful and the circumstances produced were in the nature of a public scandal.
c Russell J quoted from the judgment of Romer LJ in the *South Wales Miners'* case[3] and
added a general enumeration of the factors which ought to be taken into account in
considering this question of justification. Russell J[4] quoted Romer LJ as saying:

> 'I respectfully agree with what Bowen L.J. said in the *Mogul Case*[5], when
> considering the difficulty that might arise whether there was sufficient justification
d > or not: "The good sense of the tribunal which had to decide would have to analyze
> the circumstances and to discover on which side of the line each case fell." I will
> only say that, in analyzing or considering the circumstances, I think that regard
> might be had to the nature of the contract broken; the position of the parties to the
> contract; the grounds for the breach; the means employed to procure the breach;
> the relation of the person procuring the breach to the person who breaks the
e > contract; and I think also to the object of the person in procuring that breach.'

Then Russell J reached his conclusion saying[6]:

> 'They adopt this course as regards the plaintiff as the only means open to them of
> bringing to an end his practice of underpayment, which, according to their
> experience, is fruitful of danger to the theatrical calling and its members. In these
f > circumstances, have the defendants justification for their acts? That they would
> have the sympathy and support of decent men and women I can have no doubt.
> But have they in law justification for those acts? As has been pointed out, no
> general rule can be laid down as a general guide in such cases, but I confess that if
> justification does not exist here I can hardly conceive the case in which it would be
> present. These defendants, as it seems to me, owed a duty to their calling and to its
g > members, and, I am tempted to add, to the public, to take all necessary peaceful
> steps to terminate the payment of this insufficient wage, which in the plaintiff's
> company had apparently been in fact productive of those results which their past
> experiences had led them to anticipate. "The good sense" of this tribunal leads me
> to decide that in the circumstances of the present case justification did exist.'

h
On the other hand in *Camden Nominees Ltd v Slack*[7], whilst there was considerable
reason for the defendants' conduct in inducing the tenants to withhold their rents to
force or induce the landlords to perform their obligations, the defence of justification

---

j 1 [1905] AC 239 at 249, [1904–7] All ER Rep 211 at 216
  2 [1924] 1 Ch 302, [1923] All ER Rep 40
  3 [1903] 2 KB 545 at 574
  4 [1924] 1 Ch 302 at 311, [1923] All ER Rep 40 at 46–47
  5 (1889) 23 QBD 598 at 618–619, [1891–4] All ER Rep 263 at 281
  6 [1924] 1 Ch 302 at 312–313, [1923] All ER Rep 40 at 47
  7 [1940] 2 All ER 1, [1940] Ch 352

failed. There Simonds J after carefully reviewing the cases came to that conclusion, saying[1]:

> 'In the present case, if I rightly understand his argument, counsel for the defendants has pleaded that the defendants are justified in their otherwise actionable wrong on two grounds—namely, (i) that they and those whom they would persuade to break their contracts have a common interest in making the landlord perform his obligations, and (ii) that there is such a state of affairs here existing—that is, on the one side tenants who are weak and on the other landlords who are strong, and take advantage of their strength—that it is justifiable for the defendants to use a weapon which would otherwise be wrongful. In my judgment, there is no validity in either of these contentions. The defendants owed no duty to their fellow-tenants; they sought their co-operation for their own ends, though no doubt a successful campaign would have been for the benefit of all alike. The end which they sought—namely, the performance by the landlord of his obligations—was one which could be reached by process of law.'

He distinguished *Brimelow v Casson*[2] and said[3]:

> 'I would only add, in deference to the argument addressed to me, which I think was intended to be founded on *Brimelow* v *Casson*[2], that neither that case nor any other case supports the view that those who assume the duty of advising the withholding of rent or any other breach of contract can justify their action by protesting that they are performing a public service. Advice which is intended to have persuasive effects is not distinguishable from inducement, and there is no reason to suppose that the giving of such advice is justifiable except by those persons in whom the law recognises a moral duty to give it.'

And so I come back to what Russell J said in *Brimelow v Casson*[2], and good sense in this case seems to show it to be on the wrong side of the line. After all, albeit perfectly honestly, and being advised that they could effectively defeat the plaintiff's option and were entitled to do so, I cannot see that even Mr Inman, who had of course to do the best he could for the patient's estate, still less Mr Briggs, who was simply pursuing his own interest, had any moral duty to interfere with the plaintiff's option, and to put it at its lowest they did appreciate that what they were doing might not merely defeat the plaintiff's contract by the exercise of a right having priority, but not having priority, cause a breach of it.

In my judgment, therefore, the plaintiff is also entitled to an enquiry as to damages for this conspiracy, but the costs should be reserved and if this be pursued it may not prove a fruitful venture for the plaintiff.

TEMPLEMAN LJ. The question is whether a right of pre-emption exercisable during the lifetime of the grantor is subject to an option subsequently granted but only exercisable after the death of the grantor. In my judgment the answer to the question depends on whether the grant of the option made the right of pre-emption exercisable.

Rights of option and rights of pre-emption share one feature in common: each prescribes circumstances in which the relationship between the owner of the property which is the subject of the right and the holder of the right will become the relationship of vendor and purchaser. In the case of an option, the evolution of the relationship of vendor and purchaser may depend on the fulfilment of certain specified conditions and will depend on the volition of the option holder. If the option applies to land, the grant of the option creates a contingent equitable interest which, if registered as an estate

1　[1940] 2 All ER 1 at 10–11, [1940] Ch 352 at 365
2　[1924] 1 Ch 302, [1923] All ER Rep 40
3　[1940] 2 All ER 1 at 11, [1940] Ch 352 at 366

contract, is binding on successors in title of the grantor and takes priority from the date
a of its registration. In the case of a right of pre-emption, the evolution of the relationship
of vendor and purchaser depends on the grantor, of his own volition, choosing to fulfil
certain specified conditions and thus converting the pre-emption into an option. The
grant of the right of pre-emption creates a mere spes which the grantor of the right may
either frustrate by choosing not to fulfil the necessary conditions or may convert into an
option and thus into an equitable interest by fulfilling the conditions. An equitable
b interest thus created is protected by prior registration of the right of pre-emption as an
estate contract but takes its priority from the date when the right of pre-emption
becomes exercisable and the right is converted into an option and the equitable interest
is then created. The holder of a right of pre-emption is in much the same position as a
beneficiary under a will of a testator who is still alive, save that the holder of the right of
pre-emption must hope for some future positive action by the grantor which will elevate
c his hope into an interest. It does not seem to me that the property legislation of 1925 was
intended to create or operated to create an equitable interest in land where none existed.
By a conveyance dated 14th August 1944 Major and Mrs Lockwood created a right of
pre-emption over certain retained land. They covenanted that until the death of the
survivor of them they—

d 'will not nor will either of them sell or concur in selling all or any part of the
retained lands without giving . . . the option of purchasing the retained lands . . .
[for] Three thousand pounds . . . The option shall be given in writing and shall not
be revoked or altered within Twenty one days . . . and . . . shall cease unless the offer
is accepted within Twenty one days from the receipt . . . If the offer is accepted
. . . the sale shall be completed and vacant possession given . . . at the expiration of
one month.'

e
Thus the relationship of vendor and purchaser could not be established unless the
Lockwoods chose to offer the retained lands to the holder of the right of pre-emption or,
in breach of covenant, contracted to sell the retained lands to a third party without first
offering the lands to the option holder for £3,000. If and when these conditions were
fulfilled, the holder of the right of pre-emption would be entitled to buy and therefore
f entitled to an equitable interest. The right of pre-emption was duly registered as an
estate contract and became vested in the first and second defendants, Mr and Mrs Briggs.
By a lease dated 3rd February 1964 the Lockwoods created an option over the retained
lands. They covenanted with the plaintiff that if he, after the death of the survivor of the
Lockwoods, desired to purchase the retained lands and gave notice within three months
to the personal representatives of the survivor then the personal representatives would
g convey the retained lands to the plaintiff in fee simple for £3,000. Thus the relationship
of vendor and purchaser could be established by the plaintiff deciding to purchase. The
plaintiff was entitled to buy, albeit in the future, and therefore the plaintiff was entitled
to an equitable interest. The option was duly registered as an estate contract.
Mrs Lockwood was survived by Major Lockwood. In August 1972, Major Lockwood,
by his receiver acting under the authority of the Court of Protection and as part of
h contractual arrangements made at that time, and in accordance with the provisions of the
1944 conveyance, gave the Briggses a 21-day option to purchase the retained lands for
£3,000. The Briggses exercised the option and paid the purchase price. Major Lockwood
died on 15th January 1973. The third and fourth defendants proved his will and
conveyed the retained lands to the Briggses on 16th February 1973. On 12th March
1973 the plaintiff served notice on the personal representatives of Major Lockwood
j exercising his option to purchase the retained lands conferred by his 1964 lease. The
plaintiff now claims the retained lands from the Briggses for £3,000.
If the 1944 conveyance had provided that the Lockwoods would not sell in their
lifetime or grant an option to purchase after their death without first offering the
retained lands to the Briggses for £3,000, then the grant of the plaintiff's option in
breach of the terms of the right of pre-emption would have converted the Briggses' right

of pre-emption into an option and conferred on them an equitable interest in priority to the equitable interest conferred on the plaintiff by his option. But the 1944 conveyance **a** only provided that the Lockwoods would not sell in their lifetime without first offering the retained land to the Briggses. The grant of the plaintiff's option exercisable after the death of the survivor of the Lockwoods was not a sale by the Lockwoods in their lifetime. The right of pre-emption during the life of Major Lockwood did not become exercisable by the grant of an option exercisable after his death. The right of pre-emption therefore did not become an option and did not create an equitable interest **b** until after and subject to the grant of the plaintiff's option and the creation of an equitable interest in his favour ranking in priority to any subsequent equitable interest obtained by the Briggses and enforceable against the legal estate ultimately acquired by them.

On behalf of the Briggses it was submitted that on its true construction the plaintiff's option was only exercisable if the Lockwoods did not sell. If the personal representatives **c** of the survivor of the Lockwoods did not succeed to the retained lands or if they only succeeded to the retained lands subject to a contract of sale entered into by the Lockwoods or the survivor of them, then the plaintiff's option could not and was not intended to take effect. There is no support for this submission to be found in the words of the grant of the plaintiff's option. Support is claimed from the surrounding circumstances but the only relevant and admissible surrounding circumstance was the existence of the right of **d** pre-emption. In my judgment the mere existence of a prior right of pre-emption during the life of the Lockwoods cannot affect the construction of the grant of an option exercisable after the death of the Lockwoods.

It was further submitted that if the Briggses had bought the land in exercise of their right of pre-emption they were entitled to vacant possession and to a title free from encumbrances. The option in favour of the plaintiff was an encumbrance and therefore **e** if the Briggses exercised their right of pre-emption they were entitled to a conveyance free from the plaintiff's option.

The submissions on behalf of the Briggses ignore the fact that they were not entitled to buy or bound to purchase. The Lockwoods were never bound to offer to sell to the Briggses and the Briggses never were in a position to insist that an option be granted to them to purchase free from encumbrances or at all. If an offer or option of any kind, **f** whether subject to or free from encumbrances, were forthcoming, the Briggses were free to accept or decline an offer or to exercise or allow to lapse an option.

Before the grant of the Briggses' right of pre-emption, the Lockwoods were free to enter into any transaction disposing or fettering their powers of disposition of the retained lands. By the Briggses' right of pre-emption, the Lockwoods entered into a transaction in favour of the Briggses whereby the Lockwoods fettered their powers of **g** disposition so that the Lockwoods in their lifetime could only sell to the first or to a third party with the consent of the Briggses. But, by the Briggses' right of pre-emption, the Lockwoods were not bound to sell to the Briggses at all. Notwithstanding the grant of the Briggses' right of pre-emption the Lockwoods remained free to enter into any transaction in favour of the plaintiff whereby the Lockwoods fettered their powers of disposition so that the Lockwoods could not sell in their lifetime to the Briggses or to **h** anyone else. Notwithstanding the grant of the Briggses' right of pre-emption the Lockwoods remained free to enter into any transaction in favour of the plaintiff whereby the Lockwoods fettered their powers of disposition so that the Lockwoods could only sell to the Briggses or to a third party subject to the right of the plaintiff to buy the land after the death of the survivor of the Lockwoods for £3,000. The Lockwoods entered into such a transaction without thereby making the Briggses' right of pre-emption exercisable **j** according to its terms. That transaction took the form of a grant of an option exercisable after the death of the survivor of the Lockwoods. That option created a contingent future equitable interest which when registered as a land charge achieved priority as from the date of registration and bound the Lockwoods, the Briggses, and every other owner of the land.

After the grant of the plaintiff's option Major Lockwood was not in a position to make
a an offer to the Briggses or to grant an option to the Briggses pursuant to their right of pre-
emption or at all save subject to the plaintiff's option. After the registration of the
plaintiff's option, the Briggses could not accept an offer or exercise an option granted by
Major Lockwood pursuant to the right of pre-emption or at all save subject to the
plaintiff's option. In short Major Lockwood could only sell and the Briggses could only
purchase subject to the plaintiff's option; the Court of Protection could not and did not
b purport to do more than Major Lockwood could himself have done.

It follows that the Briggses must convey the retained land to the plaintiff for £3,000
and otherwise on the terms specified in the plaintiff's option. I have had the advantage
of reading the judgment of Goff LJ in draft. That judgment contains a comprehensive
comment on and analysis of the relevant authorities. The weight of authority, as I
understand, is in favour of the conclusions which I have reached as a matter of principle
c and convenience and there is no authority to the contrary which is binding on this court.
I agree with the result arrived at by Goff LJ on this part of the case but I am unable to
accept what appears to be his further conclusion that a registered right of pre-emption is
not binding on a successor in title of the grantor even though the acquisition of the
successor's interest made the right of pre-emption exercisable.

In my judgment no question of damages for conspiracy arises. If, as I hold, the
d plaintiff's option was not capable of being defeated, the plaintiff was entitled as soon as
he exercised his option to specific performance and must rest content with that and with
any ancillary relief obtainable for delay or otherwise.

STEPHENSON LJ. Major and Mrs Lockwood made two promises. (1) By cl 4(B) of
the 1944 conveyance they promised Mr Riddett and his successors in title that they
e would not sell the retained lands so long as he should live or they or the survivor of them
should also be alive without giving Mr Riddett the option of purchasing the retained
lands at £3,000. The promise contained in that covenant gives the defendants, Mr and
Mrs Briggs, any right to the retained lands which they may have. (2) By cl 3(d) of the
1959 lease they promised the plaintiff that after the death of the survivor of them his or
her personal representatives would convey the retained lands to the plaintiff for £3,000
f if he desired to purchase them. The promise contained in that covenant and repeated in
the 1964 lease gives the plaintiff any right to the retained lands which he may have.

Both promises were kept until 1972. I can see no inconsistency in the two promises,
only that the second promise confined the first to a promise not to sell the retained lands
during the lifetime of Mr Riddett and the Lockwoods or the survivor of them. To
render the two promises inconsistent and produce a breach of promise it is necessary to
g imply a term in one or the other of them.

The 1944 promise did not promise to offer the retained lands to Mr Riddett either
before or after the death of the last of the Lockwoods. The promise of what is called an
option of purchasing was only a promise to offer it if the retained lands were for sale
during those lives. By the 1944 covenant the defendants got no promise of an offer after
that death. Indeed, they got no promise of an offer at any time should the Lockwoods
h keep the retained lands until they were both dead. I find it not necessary but impossible
to imply into the cl 4(B) covenant any extension of the limited right expressly conferred
on the defendants or any positive obligation to offer the option to purchase the land
except in the circumstances, which might never happen, of a sale or a decision to sell by
a living Lockwood.

Quite different was the 1959 promise. That promised to sell the retained lands to the
j plaintiff if he wanted them after the Lockwoods were dead. It expressly imposed a
positive obligation to offer the option to purchase the land in circumstances which were
bound to happen sooner or later. If Major Lockwood had kept his mind, I would assume
that he would have kept both promises and lived on owning the retained lands until his
death, when his personal representatives would have sold them to the plaintiff. However
that may be, I find it unnecessary to imply into the cl 3(d) covenant, any limitation of the

right expressly conferred on the plaintiff such as that pleaded by amendment in para 7
of the statement of claim, that is that the Lockwoods and their survivor could not sell the   *a*
retained lands during their, his or her lives. That is not an implication except in the
sense that it must be implicit in any promise to sell something to A that you will not sell
it to B. More important for the decision of this appeal, I find it not necessary but
impossible to imply any such term as counsel for the defendants suggests, eg that the
plaintiff's option was subject to the retained lands being still retained in Lockwood
ownership at the death of the survivor of the Lockwoods. Whether or not the 1944   *b*
covenant increased the purchase price of the land conveyed, the 1959 covenant certainly
increased the rent payable under the leases of 1959 and 1964. And the second was a more
valuable promise than the first. The second made the plaintiff an irrevocable offer and
gave him a right eventually to call for a conveyance of the land whether the Lockwoods
or their personal representatives wished to convey or not. So the plaintiff got what is in
law or legal terminology (though not so described in the leases) an option to purchase   *c*
satisfying the test imposed by Jessel MR in *London and South Western Railway Co v Gomm*[1].
The first gave the defendants no right to call for a conveyance unless the Lockwoods or
the survivor of them decided to sell, and that they need never do. So all the defendants
got was a promise of an offer in circumstances which the Lockwoods or their survivor
could prevent from happening: what textbook writers and judges and some but perhaps
not all statutes have distinguished from an option to purchase as a right of pre-emption   *d*
(though not so described in the conveyance).

Now unless that right of pre-emption, which may never become exercisable because
the grantor has it in his power to permit or prevent its exercise, is as good as that more
valuable right to buy first, which will become exercisable independently of the volition
of the grantor, that weaker right cannot, in my opinion, prevail over or defeat the
stronger right.   *e*

The 1944 conveyance refers to giving the option of purchasing but as a future act, not
as a present right; and counsel for the plaintiff has satisfied me that what is granted as a
right of pre-emption on the true construction of the grant is only properly called an
option when the will of the grantor turns it into an option by deciding to sell and thereby
binding the grantor to offer it for sale to the grantee. That it thereby becomes an interest
in land is a change in the nature of the right to which, unlike Goff LJ, I see no insuperable   *f*
objection in logic or in principle. And, as I understand his opinion on this point, its
consequences would be that a right of pre-emption could never be enforceable against a
successor in title whether it is registered or not.

I accordingly prefer the opinion of Templeman LJ on this point.

The weaker right must therefore create an equitable interest in the retained lands if it
is to claim priority over the stronger. If it does create such an interest it clearly has   *g*
priority, because it had prior registration as an obligation affecting land and an estate
contract, class C(iv), under s 10 of the Land Charges Act 1925. But again counsel for the
plaintiff has satisfied me on the authority of *Gomm's* case[1] and the somewhat unsatisfactory
decision of this court in *Manchester Ship Canal Co v Manchester Racecourse Co*[2] that the
1944 covenant did not create an interest in land, whereas the 1959 covenant did.

The best way to understand the latter case is, in my opinion, to be found in the   *h*
judgment of the Supreme Court of Canada delivered by Martland J in *Canadian Long
Island Petroleums Ltd v Irving Industries Ltd*[3]. I cannot accept counsel's submission for the
defendants that the only reason for this court holding that the agreement by the
Manchester Racecourse Co to give the Manchester Ship Canal Co the first refusal of

   j

---

1   (1882) 20 Ch D 562, [1881–5] All ER Rep 1190
2   [1900] 2 Ch 352
3   (1974) 50 DLR (3d) 265

certain lands did not create an interest in land was that no price was named in the
a agreement and no means of ascertaining it pointed out.

The distinction between these two types of agreement and their legal consequences is
in my opinion nowhere better stated than by Street J in *Mackay v Wilson*[1], previously
cited by Goff LJ. If this view of their legal consequences is correct, as Goulding and
Oliver JJ have considered it to be and as I agree that it is, that is, in my judgment, an end
of the defence to the plaintiff's case. But if I am wrong on this point, I agree that what
b Mr Inman did on legal advice and with the authority of the Court of Protection in 1972
was a conveyance to the defendants of the retained lands at the market price, not an
exercise of the 1944 right of pre-emption, and was therefore a breach of the 1959
promise to the plaintiff.

I agree with all that Goff LJ has said about what the Court of Protection could do, did
and purported to do. For the reasons he gives the court's approval did not alter the nature
c of what the Briggses and Mr Inman did or its legal effect, or validate an invalid transaction
or protect them from any tort they may have committed.

But I agree with Templeman LJ for the reasons he gives that no question of conspiracy
or tort arises. If, however, I thought the plaintiff entitled to an enquiry as to damages for
conspiracy if proved and it were therefore necessary to consider the nature of the tort and
the validity of the defences to the claim for those damages in the light of the evidence
d and the authorities, I would respectfully agree with Goff LJ's view of the law and the
facts.

I feel sympathy for the defendants. Their counsel came before Walton J to meet a case
resting largely on an allegation by amendment of an implied term, to which I have
already referred, and an allegation that the defendants' right of pre-emption derived
from the 1944 covenant had been extinguished by the correspondence of 1953. But the
e second allegation was abandoned at the outset of the trial and the first allegation took
second place in this court, if not at the trial, to an argument on the true construction of
the 1944 covenant which has been accepted by this court. So the defendants acting on
legal advice and in perfect good faith and with the approval of the Court of Protection
have paid £14,150 for land which I feel bound to hold, differing after many days'
argument from the judge, they are not entitled to have but must sell for £3,000, and
f they will have to pay considerably more in costs.

Much as I regret having to differ from Walton J, and to hold that the defendants are
in the wrong, the plaintiff is, in my judgment, clearly in the right and so entitled to have
the land at much less than the market price.

I agree that the appeal must be allowed, the order of Walton J set aside, and an order
made for specific performance of the contract resulting from the exercise by the plaintiff
g of his option, as proposed by Goff LJ, but, as proposed by Templeman LJ, there should be
no order for an enquiry as to damages, although the plaintiff will be entitled to any
ancillary relief obtainable for delay.

Appeal allowed. Order of Walton J set aside. Order for specific performance. No order for an
h *enquiry as to damages.*

Solicitors: *Tuck & Mann & Geffen*, agents for *Gwyndaf-Williams & Roberts*, Portmadoc (for
the plaintiff), *Foysters*, Manchester (for the defendants).

Frances Rustin   Barrister.

j _____

1 (1947) 47 SR(NSW) 315 at 325

Property Discount Corporation Ltd v Lyon Group Ltd and others

CHANCERY DIVISION
GOULDING J
23rd, 24th, 31st JULY 1979

Contract – Agreement for lease – Building agreement providing for grant of lease by owner to developer on completion of buildings – Plans required to be approved by owner's surveyor – Whether agreement creating interest in land – Whether agreement conferring power to require grant of lease – Whether mortgage of interest under agreement creating equitable charge affecting land.

Company – Charge – Registration – Equitable charge affecting land – Charge registered in name of company creating it and not in name of legal owner of estate – Whether registration effective as registration under land charges legislation – Whether purchaser for value of land affected by actual notice of charge although no registration under land charges legislation – Companies Act 1948, s 95(1) – Land Charges Act 1972, s 3(1)(7).

A building agreement made between W Ltd and L Ltd in February 1968 provided for L Ltd to enter on W Ltd's land and develop it by erecting certain buildings in accordance with plans to be approved by W Ltd's surveyors, such approval not to be unreasonably withheld. Any variation in the building work was to be made only by mutual agreement. The agreement further provided that on completion of each building without default by L Ltd, W Ltd was to grant a lease of the appropriate part of the land to L Ltd for a term of 99 years at such rent and with such provisions in the lease as appeared from the building agreement, and that until any lease was granted to L Ltd its interest in the land was to be that of a tenant at will. Under the agreement L Ltd could not assign or deal with its interest under the agreement without W Ltd's consent, which was not to be unreasonably withheld in respect of an assignment by mortgage or charge for the purpose of financing the development. By a mortgage dated 31st July 1968 L Ltd *f* assigned to the plaintiff as mortgagee all its interest under the building agreement as security for sums to be advanced by the plaintiff to finance the development. The mortgage contained a covenant to execute a legal mortgage if any lease was granted under the agreement whilst moneys remained due under the mortgage. L Ltd registered particulars of the mortgage under s 95[a] of the Companies Act 1948 but the mortgage was not registered under the Land Charges Act 1925. Pursuant to the building agreement W *g* Ltd granted two leases to L Ltd who in turn assigned them for value to the defendants who thereafter remained in possession of the land comprised in the leases. Moneys secured by the mortgage remained due from L Ltd to the plaintiff. In proceedings for the enforcement of the mortgage the question arose whether the defendants' interests under the leases were subject to the equitable charge created by the mortgage. The plaintiff contended that their interests were subject to the charge because they had *h*

---

a Section 95, so far as material, provides:

'(1) Subject to the provisions of this Part of this Act, every charge created after the fixed date by a company registered in England and being a charge to which this section applies shall, so far as any security on the company's property or undertaking is conferred thereby, be void ... unless the prescribed particulars of the charge together with the instrument, if any, by which the charge is *j* created or evidenced, are delivered to or received by the registrar of companies for registration in manner required by this Act within twenty-one days after the date of its creation ...

'(2) This section applies to ... (d) a charge on land, wherever situate, or any interest therein ...

'(10) In this Part of this Act—(a) the expression "charge" includes mortgage ...'

acquired the leases with actual notice of the charge since the building agreement
a conferred an equitable interest in the land on L Ltd and the charge created by the
mortgage was therefore an equitable charge affecting land, that as such it was registrable,
and had been registered, under s 95 of the 1948 Act, further, that registration constituted
registration of the charge under the consolidating Land Charges Act 1972 (by virtue of
s 3(7)*[b]* of that Act), and that the deemed registration under the 1972 Act constituted, by
virtue of s 198(1)*[c]* of the Law of Property Act 1925, actual notice of the charge to the
b defendants. The defendants contended that the building agreement did not confer any
interest in land on L Ltd and that the mortgage was not an equitable charge affecting
land registrable under s 95 of the 1948 Act, alternatively, that the mortgage contained
two separate equitable charges, a charge on L Ltd's chose in action entitling it to require
the grant of leases by W Ltd (which had become spent on the grant of the leases by W
Ltd) and a charge on the leases when granted conferred by the covenant to execute a legal
c mortgage (which had not been lawfully registered), and, in the further alternative, that
registration under s 95 of the 1948 Act did not effect registration under the 1925 Act
because the charge was not registered in the name of the estate owner, ie W Ltd, as
required by s 3(1)*[d]* of the 1972 Act.

Held – The defendants' interests were subject to the equitable charge created by the
d mortgage for the following reasons—
(i) A contract gave an interest in land if it gave the power to require a grant of the land
without further permission of the owner. On the true construction of the building
agreement, L Ltd had acquired a present right to the future grant of leases on completion
of the buildings and W Ltd had parted with dominion over the land and could no longer
dispose of it at will. It followed that the agreement had conferred on L Ltd an interest
e in land notwithstanding (a) that the works required under the agreement were subject
to the approval of W Ltd's surveyors, (b) that completion of the agreement might have
been prevented by a supervening impossibility outside either party's control, such as the
refusal of planning permission, and (c) that at the date of the mortgage the development
was at such an early stage that it was unlikely that specific performance of the agreement
would have been granted (see p 339 *a* to *g*, post); dicta of Jessel MR and of Sir James
f Hannen in *London and South Western Railway Co v Gomm* [1881–5] All ER Rep at 1193,
1196 and *Pritchard v Briggs* p 294, ante, applied.
(ii) The charge constituted by the mortgage was a single continuing charge on both L
Ltd's chose in action against W Ltd and on the leases when granted by W Ltd, and it
could not be split into two charges. It followed that, as L Ltd had an equitable interest
in the land at the date of the mortgage, the mortgage was an equitable charge affecting
g land which was registrable under s 95 of the 1948 Act (see p 339 *g* to *j*, post).
(iii) Registration of an equitable charge under s 95 of the 1948 Act, although it had to
be effected in the name of the company creating the charge and could not be effected in
the name of the owner of the underlying legal estate, nevertheless operated as effective
registration of the charge for the purpose of the 1972 Act even though the 1972 Act

h ───────────────────────────────────

b Section 3(7), so far as material, provides: 'In the case of a land charge for securing money created
by a company before 1st January 1970 . . . registration under [inter alia, s 95 of the Companies Act
1948] shall be sufficient in place of registration under this Act, and shall have effect as if the land
charge had been registered under this Act.'

c Section 198(1) provides: 'The registration of any instrument or matter in any register kept under
j the Land Charges Act 1972 or any local land charges register shall be deemed to constitute actual
notice of such instrument or matter, and of the fact of such registration, to all persons and for all
purposes connected with the land affected, as from the date of registration or other prescribed date
and so long as the registration continues in force.'

d Section 3(1) provides: 'A land charge shall be registered in the name of the estate owner whose
estate is intended to be affected.'

required registration of an equitable mortgage to be made in the name of the legal owner
of the estate. It followed that if, contrary to the facts, L Ltd had not become at the date *a*
of the assignments to the defendants the legal owner (under the leases granted to it) the
defendants would still have had to be treated as having had actual notice of the mortgage
at that date (see p 340 *e* to *j*, post).

Notes

For registration of a charge by a company and for the effect of registration under the *b*
Land Charges Act 1972, see 7 Halsbury's Laws (4th Edn) para 862. For cases on the
subject, see 10 Digest (Reissue) 857–868, 4946–4994.

For the Law of Property Act 1925, s 198, see 27 Halsbury's Statutes (3rd Edn) 618. As
from 1st August 1977 s 198 has been amended by the Local Land Charges Act 1975,
s 17(2), Sch 1.

For the Companies Act 1948, s 95, see 5 ibid 189. *c*
For the Land Charges Act 1972, s 3, see 42 ibid 1600.

Cases referred to in judgment

Barrett v Hilton Developments Ltd [1974] 3 All ER 944, [1975] Ch 237, [1974] 3 WLR 545,
29 P & CR 300, CA, Digest (Cont Vol D) 756, 926*cb*.
London and South Western Railway Co v Gomm (1882) 20 Ch D 562, [1881–5] All ER Rep *d*
1190, 51 LJ Ch 530, 46 LT 449, 40 Digest (Repl) 331, 2716.
Pritchard v Briggs p 294, ante, [1979] 3 WLR 868, CA.

Case also cited

Eastham v Leigh London Provincial Properties Ltd [1971] 2 All ER 887, [1971] Ch 871, CA.

Adjourned summons *e*

By an originating summons dated 19th March 1979 the third defendant, ITT Distributors
Ltd, applied for a direction that the preliminary point of law be tried whether on the
basis of agreed facts and the documents referred to in the agreed statement of facts the
interests of the third defendant and of the second defendant, J H Fenner & Co (Holdings)
Ltd, in property comprised in two leases assigned to them respectively were subject to a
charge created by a mortgage dated 31st July 1968 made between the plaintiff, Property *f*
Discount Corpn Ltd, as mortgagee, and the first defendant, Lyon Group Ltd, as
mortgagor. The facts are set out in the judgment.

Martin Nourse QC and *Jonathan Simpkiss* for the third defendant.
Benjamin Levy for the second defendant.
Donald Rattee QC and *Vivian Chapman* for the plaintiff. *g*
The first defendant was not represented.

Cur adv vult

31st July. **GOULDING J** read the following judgment: The present application arises
in proceedings commenced by originating summons dated 25th September 1975 for the *h*
enforcement of an equitable mortgage ('the mortgage') dated 31st July 1968. It was
made between the first named defendant company, Lyon Group Ltd (by an earlier name)
as borrower and the plaintiff, Property Discount Corpn Ltd, as lender, and it related to
property fronting Penarth Road in Cardiff. Lyon Group Ltd ('Lyon') has not been
represented before me and is, I think, in liquidation. I am required to try, as a
preliminary point of law, a particular question raised on a statement of facts agreed *j*
between the plaintiff and the remaining two defendant companies.

The statement of facts begins by reciting an agreement in writing ('the building
agreement') dated 27th February 1968 and made between Western Ground Rents Ltd
and Lyon. It provided that Lyon should during a specified period enter on land
belonging to Western Ground Rents Ltd and build and complete on the site certain

factories, warehouses, offices and roads according to plans, elevations etc, to be first
a approved of in writing by the surveyor of Western Ground Rents Ltd, whose approval
should not be unreasonably withheld. The work was to be carried out in conformity
with all statutory requirements and to be varied only as should be mutually agreed by the
parties in writing and to be completed to the reasonable satisfaction of Western Ground
Rents Ltd or its surveyor. The building agreement contained the usual powers of re-
entry on default, and other provisions usual in such documents. It provided that until
b the grant of leases the interest of Lyon in the site should only be that of a tenant at will,
and that Lyon should not assign or deal with its interest under the building agreement
except with the consent of Western Ground Rents Ltd which consent was not to be
unreasonably withheld to an assignment by way of mortgage or charge for the purpose
of financing the development. Another clause declared that no interest in the premises
could be acquired by the deposit of the building agreement, with an exception in favour
c of any mortgage or charge in respect of which consent should have been given as
aforesaid. The building agreement further provided that on completion of each of the
intended buildings, without default on the part of Lyon, Western Ground Rents Ltd
would forthwith grant to Lyon a lease of the appropriate part of the site with the
building thereon for a term of 99 years from the date of the building agreement at such
a rent and with such provisions as appeared from the building agreement and from a
d form of lease identified by contemporaneous signature. Finally, Western Ground Rents
Ltd agreed with Lyon to make certain advances of money in connection with the
construction of roads and sewers on the site and the infilling thereof.

The statement of facts then refers to the mortgage. The mortgage began by reciting
the building agreement and an agreement on the part of the plaintiff to make advances
to Lyon not exceeding a total of £80,768. By cl 1 of the mortgage, Lyon, as beneficial
e owner, assigned by way of equitable charge to the plaintiff all the interest of Lyon under
the building agreement and the benefit thereof, together with all buildings to be built on
the site etc, as security for, and charged with the payment to the plaintiff of, all sums to
be advanced to Lyon by the plaintiff pursuant to the following covenant, with interest
thereon. By cl 2 the plaintiff covenanted with Lyon to make advances not exceeding
£80,768 by instalments regulated by architect's certificates. Clause 3 of the mortgage
f contained a series of covenants by Lyon with the plaintiff (a) to repay the advances with
interest, (b) to comply with the terms of the building agreement, (c) to insure the
buildings, (d) not to procure the grant of any lease without the plaintiff's consent, such
consent not to be unreasonably withheld, and to make payments in reduction of principal
on the grant or sale of each lease, and (e) if any lease should be granted to Lyon while
money remained owing on the security of the mortgage, to execute forthwith a proper
g legal mortgage of the land comprised in such lease. I need not rehearse the various
stipulations contained in cl 4 of the mortgage, but I ought to mention that cl 5
empowered the plaintiff, in the name of Lyon or otherwise, to demand from Western
Ground Rents Ltd the execution of any lease which Lyon might neglect or refuse to take
up.

The statement of facts next shows that on 12th August 1968, particulars of the
h mortgage were duly registered pursuant to s 95 of the Companies Act 1948, and adds
that no registration was effected under the Land Charges Act 1925.

The statement of facts then records the grant to Lyon, pursuant to the building
agreement, of a lease dated 7th November 1969 of part of the development known as
Unit 7, the assignment of that lease for value on 9th July 1973 by Lyon to the third
defendant, ITT (Distributors) Ltd, the similar grant to Lyon of a lease dated 15th
j December 1969 of another part known as Unit 8 and the assignment of that second lease
for value on 22nd January 1973 by Lyon to the second defendant, J H Fenner & Co
(Holdings) Ltd. I shall call the second and third defendants together 'the leaseholders'.

The statement of facts concludes by stating that certain moneys secured by the
mortgage are still due to the plaintiff from Lyon, and that the leaseholders are in
possession of the land subject respectively to the two before-mentioned leases.

The question posed for the preliminary decision of the court is, whether on the basis of the facts stated and documents referred to in the statement of facts, the interest of the *a* leaseholders under their respective leases in the property comprised therein are subject to the charge created by the mortgage.

The plaintiff's case is quite simply stated. Counsel says that the building agreement conferred on Lyon an equitable interest in the land. The mortgage thus was or contained an equitable charge affecting land, capable of registration as a land charge of class C under the Land Charges Act 1925 which was in force at the time the mortgage was executed. *b* That charge was, however, by law required to be registered under s 95 of the Companies Act 1948, being a charge created by a company registered in England on land or an interest in land. It was in fact so registered in due time, as appears from the statement of facts. Now s 10(5) of the Land Charges Act 1925 provided that in the case of a land charge for securing money created by a company, such registration in the Companies Registry should be sufficient in place of registration under the 1925 Act, and should have *c* effect as if the land charge had been registered under that Act. Section 3(7) of the Land Charges Act 1972, which replaced the 1925 Act, preserves the foregoing provision so far as regards land charges created, as the mortgage was, before 1st January 1970. Therefore, the mortgage has effect as if registered under the Land Charges Act 1925. By s 198 of the Law of Property Act 1925 the registration of any instrument or matter under the provisions of the Land Charges Act 1925 is deemed to constitute actual notice of such *d* instrument or matter to all persons and for all purposes connected with the land affected. Thus, it is submitted, the leaseholders acquired their respective leases with actual notice of the mortgage and cannot claim to be purchasers for value without notice thereof. Accordingly, their interests are now subject to the charge contained in the mortgage.

The leaseholders attack the plaintiff's contentions on a number of alternative grounds. *e* I can state them shortly, as follows. 1. The building agreement did not confer on Lyon any interest in land, and so the mortgage did not contain any land charge or other obligation capable of affecting Lyon's successors in title. 2. Alternatively, the mortgage contained two separate equitable charges, one on Lyon's right to require the grant of leases, the other (given by way of covenant to execute a legal mortgage) on the leases when granted. The first was spent when leases were granted and so cannot affect the *f* interests of the leaseholders. The second was for more than one reason never lawfully registered, and, therefore, the leaseholders took free from it by virtue of s 13 of the Land Charges Act 1925 in the case of the second defendant, and of s 4 of the Land Charges Act 1972 in the case of the third defendant (the latter Act having come into force on 29th January 1973) fortified in each case by s 199 of the Law of Property Act 1925. 3. In the further alternative, registration under s 95 of the Companies Act 1948 was not in this *g* instance equivalent to registration under the Land Charges Act 1925 because Lyon was not at the date of the mortgage the owner of any legal estate in the land. I will examine those three arguments one by one.

The first point, that the building agreement conferred no interest in land, was chiefly expounded by counsel for the third defendant. As appears from the classic judgment of Jessel MR in *London and South Western Railway Co v Gomm*[1] a contract for the sale or lease *h* of a parcel of land gives the purchaser an interest in the land, because the right to call for a grant of land is itself an equitable interest in the land. The purchaser, on performing his side of the bargain, can demand the promised estate in the land, and if necessary enforce his claim by an action for the specific performance of the contract. Now counsel for the third defendant says, in the first place, that at the date of the mortgage, as appears from its date and from its terms, the work of development under the building agreement *j* was still at an early stage, that in those circumstances the court would not have decreed specific performance against Lyon at the suit of Western Ground Rents Ltd, nor by mutuality would it have decreed specific performance against Western Ground Rents Ltd at the suit of Lyon.

1　(1882) 20 Ch D 562 at 581, [1881–5] All ER Rep 1190 at 1193

a Counsel for the plaintiff says, and in my judgment rightly, that that consideration is not enough to prevent the immediate acquisition by Lyon of an interest in the land at the date of the building agreement. A contract gives an interest in land if it puts it in the purchaser's power to require a grant of land without the further permission of the owner: see what Jessel MR said, in the passage that I have cited, about the holder of an option. He said this[1]:

b 'A person exercising the option has to do two things, he has to give notice of his intention to purchase, and to pay the purchase-money; but as far as the man who is liable to convey is concerned, his estate or interest is taken away from him without his consent, and the right to take it away being vested in another, the covenant giving the option must give that other an interest in the land.'

Again, Sir James Hannen[2] said in the same case: '. . . I must say that it appears to me to

c be a startling proposition that the power to require a conveyance of land at a future time does not create any interest in that land.' The point is developed at greater length in the judgment of Goff LJ in *Pritchard v Briggs*[3]. Counsel for the plaintiff says that, for present purposes, Lyon may be regarded in the same light as a person who contracts to take a long lease at a fine or premium. The latter has to find the money. Lyon had to do the building. In each case, having simply done what he promises, the contracting party can

d exact execution of the lease.

Counsel for the third defendant endeavoured to show that the last analogy is a false one. But for the limited purpose for which it was used, I do not think it is. The various requirements of the building agreement for approval by, or for the satisfaction of, Western Ground Rents Ltd or its surveyor are carefully hedged by such expressions as 'not to be unreasonably withheld' or 'reasonable satisfaction'. Variations in the works

e required by the building agreement are to be such only as shall be mutually agreed by the parties. Changes in the agreed form of lease are limited to those necessary to meet any special circumstances, and so on. It is true that the completion of the building agreement might have been prevented by supervening impossibility outside the control of either party. The subsoil might have proved incapable of bearing the intended buildings, or the planning authority might have refused to permit development of the

f site. Such chances are not, in my view, relevant. As between the parties, Western Ground Rents Ltd had parted with dominion over the land and could no longer dispose of it at will. Lyon, on the other hand, had a present right to the future grant of leases on completion of the respective buildings, and so had, in my judgment, acquired an interest in the land, an interest which it later assigned by way of charge to the plaintiff.

The leaseholders' second argument was fully deployed by counsel for the second

g defendant. However, he failed to persuade me that the contents of the mortgage can be split in the way he wants. When Lyon expressly assigned by way of equitable charge to the plaintiff all Lyon's interest under the building agreement, and the benefit thereof, it gave the plaintiff, in my judgment, a single continuing equitable charge that operated (as between Lyon and the plaintiff) both on Lyon's chose in action enforceable against Western Ground Rents Ltd and on each term of years as granted to Lyon, the leases being

h in truth the only real benefit of the building agreement to Lyon. The covenant to execute legal mortgages I regard as an ancillary or supplemental provision, though no doubt sufficient of itself to constitute an equitable charge if it stood alone. I think that, if the leaseholders are to be treated as having had actual notice of the mortgage when the leasehold interests were assigned to them, their consciences are affected by the charge contained in cl 1 of the mortgage, with or without the addition of cl 3(e).

j That conclusion makes it unnecessary for me to examine the grounds on which counsel for the second defendant claimed that any land charge constituted by cl 3(e) was

---

1   (1882) 20 Ch D 562 at 581, [1881–5] All ER Rep 1190 at 1193
2   20 Ch D 562 at 586, [1881–5] All ER Rep 1190 at 1196
3   See pp 304–313, ante

never validly registered. Such a charge, he said, must have been an estate contract, that is a land charge of class C(iv) as defined by s 10(1) of the Land Charges Act 1925 and not *a* a general equitable charge within class C(iii). He suggested that this would be so even without the statutory requirement that a class C(iii) land charge must be an equitable charge not included in any other class of land charge. However, he also relied on that requirement if necessary, thus raising the question whether class C(iv) is to be considered a separate class of land charges for this purpose or only a subdivision of class C.   If the charge constituted by cl 3(e) was only an estate contract, counsel said, it could not be *b* eligible as a charge on land or an interest therein for registration under s 95 of the Companies Act 1948. Alternatively, the charge could only take effect on each leasehold term at the moment the respective lease was granted to Lyon: it took effect by operation of equity, not as a charge created by a company: therefore it could not have been registered under s 95. If the 1948 Act required registration at all, it was registration under s 97, not s 95, and even had that been done, it would not have been equivalent to *c* a land charge registration.

I think that I ought not to express any opinion on these far ranging submissions, since I have as the ground of my judgment rejected that dissecting construction of the mortgage which alone makes them relevant.

The leaseholders' third objection to the plaintiff's contentions was explained to me by counsel for the third defendant. It has been common ground in the debate in this court *d* that an equitable mortgage affecting land, if not secured by deposit of the legal title deeds, is capable of registration as a land charge, even though the mortgagor may himself have had only an equitable interest in the land affected. No one, I observe in passing, has referred in argument to s 137 of the Law of Property Act 1925. However, in such a case, that is where a merely equitable interest is mortgaged, s 3 (1) of the Land Charges Act 1972 requires registration in the name, not of the mortgagor, but of the owner of the *e* underlying legal estate. That appears clearly from the observations of the Court of Appeal regarding registration of a sub-purchaser's contract in *Barrett v Hilton Developments Ltd*[1]. But registration under s 95 of the Companies Act 1948 is necessarily under the name of the company which creates the charge: see s 98 of the 1948 Act. In such circumstances, counsel for the defendant submits that s 10(5) of the Land Charges Act 1925 or s 3(7) of the Land Charges Act 1972 cannot operate to bring about an effective *f* land charge registration by way of registration under s 95 of the 1948 Act. The result would be so anomalous, so inconsistent with the scheme of the 1925 property legislation, so productive of practical difficulties, says counsel, that it cannot have been intended by the legislature. He would have me read the two subsections as though each ended with the words 'shall have effect as if the land charge had been registered *in the name of the company* under this Act' (counsel's emphasis), thus giving no protection unless the *g* company is the owner of the legal estate concerned. I have felt this to be the most difficult part of the case, for the enactment is not very satisfactory on either view. If counsel for the plaintiff is right, it is a potential trap for purchasers. No difficulty could arise on the assumed facts of the present case, for Lyon subsequently acquired the legal terms of years, and the leaseholders, as purchasers thereof from Lyon, must, or ought to, have made a company search against Lyon's name. But one can imagine circumstances *h* wherein a purchaser might be afflicted by statutory notice of a charge given by a company whose name would not appear on the title and whose existence he could not possibly discover. On the other hand, if the view of counsel for the third defendant is preferred, the enactment is a potential trap for lenders, since it says in terms that registration under s 95 of the 1948 Act shall be sufficient in place of registration under the Land Charges Act. *j*

Confronted by such a problem, I think it my duty to choose the more literal construction of the statutes, that is, to decide in favour of the plaintiff.

---

1   [1974] 3 All ER 944 at 948, [1975] Ch 237 at 244

a Accordingly, all the leaseholders' alternative contentions fail, and my answer to the question formulated by a summons in this action dated 11th June 1976, as amended on 19th March 1979, and also set out at the foot of the statement of facts, is Yes, and I so declare.

Order accordingly.

b Solicitors: *Slaughter & May* (for the third defendant); *Barlow, Lyde & Gilbert* (for the second defendant); *Linklaters & Paines* (for the plaintiff).

Evelyn M C Budd   Barrister.

c
Kandalla v British Airways Board (formerly British European Airways Corporation)

QUEEN'S BENCH DIVISION
d GRIFFITHS J
2nd, 3rd, 4th, 5th, 18th OCTOBER 1979

Fatal accident – Damages – Deceased's loss of future earnings – Damages recoverable for benefit of deceased's estate to be calculated 'without reference to any loss or gain to his estate consequent on his death' – Claim on behalf of deceased's estate for damages for deceased's loss of future earnings – Whether claim for loss of future earnings surviving for benefit of his estate – Whether
e *damages for deceased's loss of future earnings a 'gain to his estate consequent on his death' – Law Reform (Miscellaneous Provisions) Act 1934, s 1(2)(c).*

The plaintiff, an Iraqi doctor, and his wife lived in Baghdad. They had two daughters, K and L, who were their only children. The daughters were doctors and worked as such in *f* England, where they shared a flat. The plaintiff was a wealthy man and visited them regularly and gave them sums of money. By the summer of 1972 life in Baghdad was becoming increasingly uncomfortable for him and his wife on account of the political situation there. In June 1972 the daughters were killed in England in an air crash when travelling on one of the defendants' aeroplanes. The daughters were then aged 31 and 27. Neither was married. The plaintiff and his wife came to England for the funeral and *g* thereafter did not return to Iraq but went to live instead in Beirut. The plaintiff tried to set up in practice there but did not succeed in doing so and being unable to get the bulk of his fortune out of Iraq, he and his wife lived in straitened circumstances in Beirut. They inherited their daughters' estates which together amounted to £16,000. The plaintiff brought an action against the defendants claiming damages (i) under the Carriage by Air Act 1961 on behalf of himself and his wife as dependants of the deceased, *h* (ii) under the Fatal Accidents Acts 1846 to 1959 on behalf of himself and his wife as dependants of the deceased, and (iii) under the Law Reform (Miscellaneous Provisions) Act 1934 on behalf of the estates of the deceased. At the date of the trial the plaintiff was aged 74 and his wife 68. The defendants admitted liability but contended that by virtue of art 22 of the Warsaw Convention, as set in Sch 1 to the 1961 Act, their liability was limited to £22,372·23 in respect of each of the deceased. In order to recover more than *j* the admitted liability the plaintiff would, by virtue of the Carriage by Air Act 1961, have had to prove that the air crash had been caused by recklessness combined with knowledge that damage would probably result. The parties agreed that in the circumstances the court should assess the damages likely to be awarded so that the parties could see whether any purpose would be served by embarking on a trial of the issue of recklessness. The parties agreed that £750 in respect of each daughter could be recovered under the Law

Reform (Miscellaneous Provisions) Act 1934 on behalf of the estates of the deceased for
loss of expectation of life. The plaintiff submitted, inter alia, that each estate was also *a*
entitled to recover a substantial sum in respect of the earnings which the daughters
might have been expected to earn during their working lives if they had not been
prematurely killed. The defendants contended (i) that such a claim did not survive for
the benefit of a deceased's estate and that it was only where a victim brought an action in
his own lifetime that he could be awarded damages in respect of the 'lost years'; (ii) that
even if, as a matter of principle, a claim for the lost years under the Law Reform *b*
(Miscellaneous Provisions) Act 1934 was not to be treated differently from a claim by a
living plaintiff, such damages were in fact expressly excluded by s 1(2)(c)[a] of the 1934 Act
because they were a 'gain to [the daughters'] estate[s] consequent on [their] death'. The
judge was satisfied (i) that the plaintiff and his wife had been intending to leave Baghdad
and live in their old age with their daughters in England, (ii) that the daughters were
competent doctors and would have been capable of making sufficient money to support *c*
their parents, and (iii) that they would have provided for them if the plaintiff and his
wife were not permitted to bring their money out of Iraq.

Held – (i) On the assumption that the daughters would have been prepared to use up to
one-quarter of their net available income on supporting their parents, then for the
purpose of the Fatal Accidents Acts the total value of the parents' dependency (prior to
any deduction on account of the fact that they had inherited their daughters' estates) was *d*
£54,000, which, in the circumstances, was to be apportioned on the basis of £21,000 to
the plaintiff and £33,000 to his wife (see p 347 h j and p 348 a to d, post).

(ii) In principle a claim under the Law Reform (Miscellaneous Provisions) Act 1934 for
the lost years could survive for the benefit of a deceased's estate. Furthermore, a
deceased's estate was not prevented by s 1(2)(c) of the 1934 Act from recovering damages
for the lost years, because on the true construction of s 1(2)(c) it applied only to a gain (or *e*
loss) to the estate that arose as a result of the death itself and independently of the fact that
the death was caused by the defendants' wrongful act; it therefore applied to a gain (or
loss) such as an annuity, insurance money etc that would have accrued on death regardless
of the fact that the death was caused by personal injuries attributable to the fault of the
defendants, (see p 349 h j, p 350 d, p 351 g h and p 352 a b, post); *Slater v Spreag* [1935] All
ER Rep 900, *Rose v Ford* [1937] 3 All ER 359, *Oliver v Ashman* [1961] 3 All ER 323 and *f*
Pickett v British Railway Engineering Ltd [1979] 1 All ER 774 considered.

(iii) However, on the evidence, the court could not make any award for the lost years
over and above that which had been assessed for the parents' support, and in the
circumstances £54,000 would be awarded under the Law Reform (Miscellaneous
Provisions) Act 1934 in respect of the lost years and would be apportioned equally
between the estates. To that sum would be added the £750 in respect of each daughter *g*
for loss of expectation of life. The total sum that could be recovered under the 1934 Act
on behalf of each estate was therefore £27,750, subject to the question of limitation of
liability under the Carriage by Air Act 1961 (see p 352 c to e, post).

(iv) If the daughters' estates passed in equal shares to their parents the plaintiff's claim
on behalf of himself and his wife under the Fatal Accidents Acts would be extinguished
because they would each receive more from the estate than the value of their Fatal *h*
Accidents Acts claims (see p 352 e f, post).

Notes

For damages for 'lost years', see 12 Halsburys Laws (4th Edn) para 1154.

For the Law Reform (Miscellaneous Provisions) Act 1934, s 1(1), see 13 Halsbury's
Statutes (3rd Edn) 115. *j*

For the Fatal Accidents Act 1959, s 2, see 23 ibid 802. Section 2 of the Fatal Accidents
Act 1959 has been consolidated in s 4 of the Fatal Accidents Act 1976.

For the Carriage by Air Act 1961, Sch 1, art 22, see 2 ibid 617.

---

[a] Section 1, so far as material, is set out at p 350 e, post

Cases referred to in judgment

a *Oliver v Ashman* [1961] 3 All ER 323, [1962] 2 QB 210, [1961] 3 WLR 669, CA; *affg*
    [1960] 3 All ER 677, [1961] 1 QB 337, [1960] 3 WLR 924, 36(1) Digest (Reissue) 313,
    1267.

Pickett v British Rail Engineering Ltd [1979] 1 All ER 774, [1978] 3 WLR 955, [1979] 1
    Lloyds Rep 519, HL.

Rose v Ford [1937] 3 All ER 359, [1937] AC 826, 106 LJKB 576, 157 LT 174, HL, 36(1)
b   Digest (Reissue) 382, 1530.

Slater v Spreag [1936] 1 KB 83, [1935] All ER Rep 900, 105 LJKB 17, 153 LT 297, 36(1)
    Digest (Reissue) 382, 1529.

Preliminary issue

The plaintiff, Fuad Abdulkarim Kandalla, the administrator of the estates of Ludi
c Marylone Abdulkarim Kandalla and Kay Teresa Kandalla deceased, brought an action
against the defendants, British European Airways Corporation (now the British Airways
Board), claiming (i) under the Carriage by Air Act 1961 damages on behalf of himself and
his wife, Mary Kandalla, the mother of the deceased, as dependants of the deceased, (ii)
under the Fatal Accidents Acts 1846 to 1959 damages on behalf of himself and his wife
as dependants of the deceased, and (iii) under the Law Reform (Miscellaneous Provisions)
d Act 1934 damages on behalf of the estate of each of the deceased. By an order of Master
Creightmore made on 6th October 1975 it was ordered that the issue of damages be tried
as a preliminary issue. The facts are set out in the judgment.

Martin Graham QC and *Mark West* for the plaintiff.
Thomas Morison QC and *Timothy Walker* for the defendants.

e
Cur adv vult

18th October. **GRIFFITHS J** read the following judgment. The plaintiff, Dr Fuad
Abdulkarim Kandalla, brings this action to recover damages in respect of the death of his
daughters, Dr Kay Kandalla and Dr Ludi Kandalla, both of whom died in the Trident air
f disaster at Heathrow on 18th June 1972.

The claims are brought under both the Fatal Accidents Acts and the Law Reform
(Miscellaneous Provisions) Act 1934. The defendants, the British Airways Board, admit
liability to pay damages but contend that their liability is limited to the sum of
£22,372·23 in respect of each of the deceased. In order to recover more than these sums
the plaintiff would have to prove that the accident had been caused by recklessness
combined with the knowledge that damage would probably result: see the Carriage by
g Air Act 1961. The parties have therefore agreed that the court should, as a preliminary
issue, assess the damages so that it can be seen whether or not any purpose will be served
by embarking on the trial of the issue of recklessness.

The plaintiff and his wife claim as dependants of their daughters, claiming that their
daughters would have supported them in their old age. The plaintiff also claims that he
h is entitled to recover a very substantial sum of damages pursuant to the Law Reform
(Miscellaneous Provisions) Act 1934 in respect of the future earnings that his daughters
might have been expected to make had they not been prematurely killed in the
accident. In order to assess these claims it is first necessary to review the family history
up to the time of death.

The plaintiff and his wife are of Iraqi nationality and are now aged 74 and 68
j respectively. The plaintiff commenced his career in Iraq as a school master but changed
to medicine and qualified as a doctor in Beirut in 1937. He then came to England for
approximately a year during which time he worked at St Thomas's Hospital and the
London School of Tropical Medicine and Hygiene. He returned to Baghdad in 1939 and
commenced in private practice. After the war, in 1947 he went for one year to America
working at Harvard under the cardiologist, Dr Paul White, and at Michigan under Dr

Wilson making a particular study of ECG techniques. In 1948 he returned to Baghdad where he continued to practise until he left with his wife to fly to England in order to *a* attend his daughters' funeral in 1972; since that date he has never returned to Baghdad. He stayed in England for approximately six months and then went to Beirut where he has been living ever since. He is a Christian and claims that he was subjected to persecution by the authorities in Baghdad which made life intolerable and forced him to leave his native country.

His daughters (his only children) were both educated in Baghdad at a French convent *b* school and then went to the university in Baghdad where they studied medicine. As soon as they had qualified in Baghdad each of them came to England, where they had studied and practised medicine ever since, both of them obtaining English qualifications. Neither of them ever returned to Baghdad.

Kay, the elder daughter, was born on 8th May 1940 and was 31 at the date of her death. She qualified as a doctor in Baghdad in 1963. She then came to England, studied *c* at Bristol University and qualified in England in 1966. Until the end of 1970 she appears to have worked in the National Health Service holding appointments at a number of hospitals as a house physician and house surgeon, making obstetrics and gynaecology her speciality. She had sat and passed the preliminary examinations for membership of the Royal College of Gynaecologists. It is clear from the numerous medical references which have been put in evidence that she was a very competent doctor. This view of her ability *d* was supported by the evidence of Dr Harling for whom she did a locum in August 1971. It has not been an easy matter to determine precisely what Dr Kay Kandalla was doing since she finished her last hospital appointment in 1970. There is evidence that she took a number of sessions for the student health service at the University of London in 1971. In 1972 she obtained a training certificate from the Family Planning Association and there is evidence that she did some work as a locum. There is also evidence that she *e* carried out a number of abortions in a private clinic. Although it is said that both girls wrote regularly to their parents, I have seen no letters from them; and although the parents visited them regularly (the plaintiff says at least once a year) they were unable to give me any accurate information as to their daughters' work. The picture has, in fact, had to be reconstructed largely from documents found in their flat after their death; therefore it is not easy to form any clear picture of their earnings at the date of their *f* death. House physicians and house surgeons at that time were not generously renumerated and the highest paid of these various appointments appears only to have been in the order of £2,000 per annum. No assistance is to be found from a study of her various bank accounts as they show no regular payments into the account during 1972.

The career of the younger sister, Ludi, who was born on 10th October 1944 and therefore 27 when she died, followed a similar pattern. She qualified in Baghdad in 1966 *g* and then came to this country obtaining her English qualifications in 1970. Like her sister she held various appointments at different hospitals as a house surgeon and house physician and in particular she was a senior house officer at the Royal London Homoeopathic Hospital from 1st November 1970 until 3rd July 1971. Dr Harling, who worked at the London Homoeopathic Hospital, was able to assess Ludi's competence for me and I accept her evidence that she also was a good doctor. *h*

The two sisters shared a flat in Wetherby Gardens. Dr Harling tells me that she knew that they were carrying out medical abortions but they did not discuss it in any detail with her, as they knew she disapproved of it. I have come to the conclusion that these two doctors were probably practising primarily as abortionists at the time of their death, but I have no means of assessing what their earnings were. It is, however, I think, reasonable to assume that they were earning at least as much as, probably substantially *j* more than, they would have earned in an appointment in the National Health Service. I am also satisfied that they were both competent doctors and, if they had chosen to do so, could have earned livings as general practitioners earning at least the average wage of a general practitioner. In addition to their skill as doctors they both enjoyed the advantage of being fluent in English, French and Arabic.

Now in addition to the money that they earned from their profession the plaintiff tells
a me that he was giving substantial sums of money to his daughters. The plaintiff,
according to his evidence and an affidavit that he swore in the course of these proceedings,
was living in affluent circumstances in Baghdad employing a medical staff in his own
private clinic and enjoying a high standard of living. When the daughters first came to
England he was permitted to send to each of them £1,000 per annum to assist in their
further education and this he said continued for approximately six years. He says that he
b also attended at various medical conferences and congresses outside Iraq and on these
occasions he would smuggle money out of Iraq and give it to his daughters, and would
in addition live frugally himself and therefore be able to hand over to them part of the
official allowance he had for the purpose of attending the conferences. At one stage in
the course of his evidence he calculated that in all he had probably provided his daughters
with something in the order of £45,000 since they left Baghdad. If he did, they appear
c to have spent most of it because their combined estates in England came to a total sum
of approximately £9,000 to which has to be added a sum of a little under £7,000 in
respect of a deposit of Swiss francs in the name of Kay Kandalla in a Swiss bank. At this
point I am bound to say that I did not regard the plaintiff as a very reliable witness. He
is now 74, he looked old for his years and frail, and I do not think that his memory is
wholly reliable. Although I do not think that I could place any particular reliance on
d figures, I am satisfied that he was smuggling money out to his daughters but I am not
certain of the precise amounts or the particular purpose. I suspect that it was all part of
a plan to get as much of his assets as he could out of Iraq. I am satisfied that at one stage
he managed to get $30,000 out of Iraq which unfortunately he invested in the ill-fated
IOS fund. He lost the entire sum but it is confirmed by Mr Dickens, his solicitor, that he
did make this disastrous investment and that he consulted Mr Dickens about it in
e England in 1970.

I suspect that the plaintiff was exaggerating the sums that he says he transferred to his
daughters in the belief that by persuading me of his generosity to them I would the more
readily accept that they in their turn would feel it their moral duty to support him and
his wife in their old age. But that he did regularly visit them and give them some sums
of money I do accept, and the fact that he made regular visits is supported by the evidence
f of Dr Harling.

Now the plaintiff's case is that he and his wife had made a firm decision to come to
England and live with his daughters who would support them out of their professional
earnings in this country. The plaintiff says that it had been decided that they would
come to England at the end of the summer of 1972 and he gave various months between
July and September during the course of his evidence. Apart from one matter which I
g shall mention shortly, no single piece of documentary evidence has been produced to
support such a settled intention; no letters from the daughters; no letters from the
parents; no evidence whatever of the sort of preparations that would be necessary for
such a momentous move, for, after all, the parents would be uprooting themselves from
their lifetime home in Baghdad to come to a new country. I do not think that there was
a fixed plan to move at the end of the summer of 1972. However, I do accept that life
h was becoming progressively more uncomfortable for the plaintiff and his wife in
Baghdad and that they did plan at some propitious moment to join their daughters in
England. The elder daughter Kay became a naturalised citizen of the United Kingdom
on 28th May 1970 and if, after retirement, the parents had been unable to remove
sufficient funds from Baghdad on which to have been able to live (which seems to me to
be highly probable) they would then have had every prospect of being admitted to this
j country as dependants of the elder daughter pursuant to the Immigration Rules[1] which
came into effect on 30th January 1973.

The plaintiff's wife told me that it had always been their intention eventually to come

---

1   Statement of Immigration Rules for Control on Entry (H of C Papers (1972–73) nos 79 and 81

to England from the moment that their daughters left Baghdad to qualify and practise in this country. The plaintiff, as I have said, said that they were coming at the end of the summer. Dr Harling in her evidence told me that Kay had spoken of the daughters saving to buy a house for the parents either in this country, or possibly in America, and Mr Dickens the solicitor also said that he understood that the parents were coming to live in this country. There is another piece of evidence which supports the view that preparations were being made to leave Baghdad and it comes from a publication entitled 'Two Thousand Men of Achievement'. In the 1970 edition of this publication the plaintiff's particulars and photograph appear and his address is given as Baghdad, but in the 1972 publication his address is given as Wetherby Gardens which is the flat at which his daughters lived. I have seen the letter that he wrote to the publishers dated 25th March 1972 in which he said, 'Please notice that my home address is changing and unreliable and therefore I have written the change of my address into a reliable address for the time being', and he then gives the address in Wetherby Gardens; and in due course the 1972 volume came out with that address. Be it noted that this letter to the publishers was written three months before his daughters were killed.

The plaintiff told me that he obtained permission from the President of Iraq to fly to this country with his wife for the funeral of his daughters and whilst he was over here he decided that he would never again return to Baghdad. After about six months he and his wife went to Beirut where they have lived ever since. His evidence was given emotionally and it was not always easy to understand precisely what he was trying to say, but the general tenor was that he was politically unacceptable in Baghdad, was harrassed by the authorities and that it would not be safe for him to return there. He has attempted to set up practice in Beirut but with the civil war that has raged there for a number of years it has not been possible for him to earn a living as a doctor. I should also add that as he is now 74 years of age and appears old for his years, in my judgment he is unlikely on that ground to pursue his professional career. He sent his wife to Baghdad to sell his possessions but says that he only got a very poor price for the medical equipment and the lease of the house. He managed to arrange for his medical library, of which he is very proud, to be sent to Beirut but he says that he was cheated out of his other possessions and, in particular, a valuable collection of Persian carpets. The upshot of it is, he says, that he has been compelled to live first on the moneys he received from his daughters' estate and the small sums he was able to get out of Iraq which have long since been exhausted and has ever since been dependant on the charity of relatives without which he and his wife would now be destitute.

Although I feel unable to rely on much of the detail of the plaintiff's evidence, I do accept the evidence that he and his wife have given that they now live in very straitened circumstances in Beirut. I accept that he has no significant part of his wealth out of Iraq, and I further accept that he has been forced out of that country by the political situation. I am unwilling to believe that a man and wife who have spent a married life living in Baghdad in prosperous circumstances would willingly leave it if they could continue to live there in comfort and safety. People do not willingly uproot themselves when they are approaching 70 years of age. I do not overlook the fact that the plaintiff gave a somewhat false picture of his departure from Iraq in an affidavit that he swore in the course of these proceedings from which it appeared that what he was saying was that he had been forced to flee from Iraq with his wife to Beirut and that it was from Beirut that he intended to come to join his daughters in England. In fact the position was, as I have said, that he was able to leave Iraq because of the death of his daughters and then decided not to go back.

My conclusion is that the plaintiff and his wife were intending to leave Iraq and live with their daughters but that they were hoping to be able to make arrangements to get part of their fortune out with them. If however that had not proved possible, I believe they would nevertheless have left Iraq to live in their old age as dependants of their daughters. The departure from Iraq was I think precipitated by the death of the daughters but not caused by it. I believe the probabilities are that the plaintiff would

have been unable to bring out any substantial part of his funds. I see no reason to
a suppose it would be more likely that he would be successful in getting out funds, if his
daughters had not been killed, than has in fact proved to be the case since their death.
I cannot accept the submission of the defendants that but for this accident he would in
all probability have continued living in Baghdad; for if that be so I ask myself, why did
he not return to Baghdad after the funeral? – a question to which neither I nor the
defendants can provide an answer.

b   I turn now to consider the question of valuing the dependency for the purpose of the
Fatal Accidents Acts and this does present formidable difficulties. As I have already
pointed out, there is no firm evidence as to the income that the two daughters were
earning at the date of their death; it is really a matter of conjecture based on the
assumption that it was probably more than they could have been earning in the National
Health Service as junior hospital doctors. They were however both undoubtedly
c competent and well trained doctors with the advantage of speaking several languages and
I have come to the conclusion that their earning capacity must be taken to be at least
equal to that of the average general practitioner. If they had chosen to enter general
practice, no doubt it would have taken a year or so to work up to the national average but
that they were capable of doing so I have no doubt. I have by agreement been provided
with figures showing the national average earnings of general practitioners in this
d country from 1972 to the present date. These figures show that the net earnings, after
deduction of tax, for an unmarried doctor with the advantage of a dependants' allowance
has risen from £4,071·50 for the year 1972–3 to the sum of £9,084·50 for the year 1979–
80. But the question remains, how much of this money would the two daughters have
been able or prepared to make available for the support of their parents? They were both
unmarried at the time of their deaths; there was some evidence from the father about
e conversations that he had at the funeral that suggested they might have been engaged;
on the other hand the evidence of Dr Harling tended to lead to a contrary conclusion.

     The next question is how much of their income would have been needed for the
support of their parents? This would depend on how much of their fortune the parents
could have removed from Iraq and what, if any, earning capacity might have been left
to the plaintiff after his arrival in this country. His evidence suggested that he hoped to
f work with his daughters in some form of clinic. The defendants have argued that
because the daughters appear to have been living up to and beyond the limit of their own
earnings at the date of their deaths it should be assumed that they would have had no
money available to look after their parents. I cannot accept this. They may well have
been spending all their earnings on themselves up to the time of their deaths; they were
young and as yet the parents did not need their support. They may not yet have been
g ready to settle down to the rigours of full time medical practice. Once faced, however,
with the responsibility for their parents, I think it can be anticipated that they would
have applied their undoubted earning capacities to providing for their parents. Between
them they were clearly capable of making sufficient money to support their parents.

     What I suppose would have happened if the parents had come to this country would
have been that they would have lived with either one or both their daughters and would
h thus have been provided with a home, food, clothing and such reasonable comforts as
their daughters' available incomes could provide. I can only approach the matter
broadly. The plaintiff suggests that I should allocate two-fifths of the daughters' income
to the support of their parents, but with the many imponderables I think this is too high
a percentage. I propose to assume that the two daughters would have been prepared to
spend up to a quarter of their available net income for the support of their parents and
j to make the further assumption that this dependency would have commenced in the
year 1973–4. In considering the question of the proportion of the income to be applied
I have not, of course, overlooked the fact that the girls might have married and thus have
had less of their income available for their parents' support because of their own
immediate families' needs. However, as I propose to ignore the possibility of marriage
and dependants for the purpose of assessing the Law Reform (Miscellaneous Provisions)

Act 1934 claims as will appear later, I have not given any great weight to this factor in valuing the Fatal Accidents Acts claim.

Taking this then as my starting point the total net available income from both daughters from the tax year 1973–4 to the end of the tax year 1979–80 was to the nearest round figure £72,000; thus I allow as a loss of dependency a quarter of this figure, namely £18,000, to take one up to the end of the current tax year, ie April 1980, which I apportion equally between the plaintiff and his wife. The plaintiff is now 74 with a life expectation, according to the life expectation tables, of 8·59 years; his wife is 68 with a life expectation of 14·97 years. I shall quantify the plaintiff's continuing dependency at five years purchase and the wife's at nine years purchase. The current net income of the two daughters would be approximately £19,000, a quarter of which is £4,750. Accordingly I shall allow five years purchase at £4,750 which I shall round up to the sum of £24,000, which I again apportion equally between the plaintiff and his wife. Finally I shall allow a further four years purchase on the wife's claim at the rate of £3,000 per annum. I allow rather more than half the joint dependency to the wife because in fact it costs proportionately more to provide support for one person than it does for two people living together. This then is a further £12,000; thus the total dependency before considering any deductions that have to be made because the parents have inherited their daughters' estates comes to the total sum of £54,000 apportioned as to £21,000 to the plaintiff and £33,000 to his wife.

It will now be convenient to consider the claim under the Law Reform (Miscellaneous Provisions) Act 1934. The conventional sums can be recovered on behalf of both estates for loss of expectation of life which the parties have agreed should be assessed in the figure of £750 in respect of each daughter. But in addition to this the plaintiff submits that the estate is also entitled to recover a very substantial sum of money in respect of the earnings that the two daughters might have been expected to earn during their working lives if they had not been prematurely killed. This sum, it is submitted, should be calculated in the case of women of these ages on a basis of 15 years purchase and it should comprise their total net earnings less such proportion as they might reasonably have been expected to spend on themselves. A claim of this nature, conveniently referred to as 'the claim for the lost years' was recently allowed by the House of Lords in the case of a living plaintiff whose life expectation had been materially shortened by reason of industrial disease: see *Pickett v British Rail Engineering Ltd*[1]. In so deciding the House of Lords overruled the earlier decision of *Oliver v Ashman*[2] in which the Court of Appeal had held that no such claim could lie. By deciding as they did the House of Lords mitigated the hardship suffered by the family of the plaintiff from the result of the decision in *Oliver v Ashman*[2]. If an injured plaintiff whose life expectation has been shortened sues and recovers damages, his dependants lose their rights to bring a subsequent action under the Fatal Accidents Acts: thus if a man of 40 has had his life expectation reduced to three years and cannot recover as damages his earnings during the 'lost years' so that they are available to provide for his family after his death, his family will be worse off than if he had brought no action at all for his personal injuries and left them to sue after his death.

The same dilemma does not arise in a case such as the present where the wage earner has been killed in the accident and claims are brought both under the Law Reform (Miscellaneous Provisions) Act 1934 for damages on behalf of the estate and under the Fatal Accidents Acts, for both actions can run concurrently. Justice can be done to the parents by an award under the Fatal Accidents Acts, and any sums for the 'lost years' awarded under the Law Reform (Miscellaneous Provisions) Act 1934 which exceed the value of the Fatal Accidents Acts damages will be a pure windfall for the parents.

If the plaintiff's submission is right it will undoubtedly result in a very considerable increase in the total damages awarded in fatal claims. Its impact will be felt principally in two ways: first in the case where a deceased leaves dependants but by his will leaves his

---

1   [1979] 1 All ER 774, [1978] 3 WLR 955
2   [1961] 3 All ER 323, [1962] 2 QB 210

estate elsewhere. Not only will the estate be able to recover the full value of the sums he

a spent on his dependants, but the dependants will also be able to recover the like sum under the Fatal Accidents Acts. This may be a somewhat unusual state of affairs, for I suspect that most people leave their estates to those who are dependent on them; and it is in this situation that the major effects will be felt. When valuing a Fatal Accidents Acts claim, usually some deduction falls to be made from the award because of the value of the estate. Take the present case. I have assessed the capital sum representing the total

b sums that the parents would have received from the deceased at £54,000; the joint estate of the deceased was £16,000 which the parents inherit. But for the air disaster the overwhelming probability was that this money would never have come to the parents as they would have died before their daughters and so it would be deducted pound for pound reducing the value of the Fatal Accidents Acts claim to £38,000. Furthermore, damages awarded for loss of expectation of life are deducted pound for pound from the

c Fatal Accidents Acts claim if they pass under the estate to the dependant making the claim. So, there is another £1,500 (£750 in respect of each daughter) which would have to be deducted from the Fatal Accidents Acts claim, reducing it to £36,500. As a further illustration, consider the position of a very high earner of 38 years of age who is also possessed of a large fortune. Suppose he is contributing £10,000 per annum to the support of his wife and family during his lifetime and on his death leaves them an estate

d of, say, £500,000. The interest on the estate is more than adequate to replace the dependency of £10,000 per annum and so the accelerated benefit from the estate extinguishes any Fatal Accidents Acts claim. But if the estate can bring a claim for the 'lost years' the family will in fact recover a further large sum, say £150,000, being 15 years purchase of £10,000 per annum. Perhaps in this illustration it will be truer to say that the defendant will have to pay the extra £150,000 rather than the family will

e recover it, for a large slice of it may be destined to the Revenue via capital transfer tax.

I have no enthusiasm for these results that seem to flow inevitably from deciding that a claim for the 'lost years' survives for the benefit of the estate. It does the deceased no good for, unlike the living plaintiff who recovers for the 'lost years', the deceased can derive no comfort from the thought that he can make proper provision for his dependants or any other objects of his bounty. In fact in most cases it will merely

f provide a windfall for the dependants, who will, as I have illustrated, recover not only fair compensation for their pecuniary loss as they have hitherto done under the Fatal Accidents Acts but an additional sum over and above such loss. The damages will, of course, almost always be paid by insurance companies, but the ability to pay such damages will have to be passed on to the general public through increased premiums; so it is the public who will be paying these extra damages which appear to me to breach the

g underlying basis on which damages are assessed, namely that they should be fair compensation for the loss sustained.

In these circumstances I confess that I have striven to find a legitimate judicial basis on which to reject the plaintiff's submissions. The defendants submit that there are two routes open to me.

First, they submit that as *Pickett v British Rail Engineering Ltd*[1] is an authority dealing

h with the claim of a living plaintiff it leaves me free to refuse to make an award for the 'lost years' in a claim brought on behalf of the estate, and that I should adopt a different method of calculating the damage in the case of a Law Reform (Miscellaneous Provisions) Act 1934 claim from that of a claim by a living plaintiff. In *Rose v Ford*[2] the House of Lords held that a claim for loss of expectation of life was not confined to a living plaintiff but survived for the benefit of his estate because the effect of s 1(1) of the 1934 Act was

j to keep the same claim that had vested in the living person alive for the benefit of his estate. In *Oliver v Ashman*[3] Holroyd Pearce LJ considered the same argument as is now

1   [1979] 1 All ER 774, [1978] 3 WLR 955
2   [1937] 3 All ER 359, [1937] AC 826
3   [1961] 3 All ER 323, [1962] 2 QB 210

addressed to the court and rejected it on the grounds that the opinions in *Rose v Ford*[1] leave no room for distinguishing between a claim brought by a living plaintiff and a   *a* claim brought on behalf of a dead plaintiff in respect of the years of which he has been deprived. It is true that *Oliver v Ashman*[2] was overruled, but that was because the House of Lords held that the Court of Appeal had been wrong to hold that a living plaintiff had no claim for the 'lost years'. There is no hint in any of the opinions that their Lordships considered that Holroyd Pearce LJ was wrong in regarding the claim for the 'lost years' as surviving for the benefit of the estate. Lord Scarman expressly assumes it to be so, for   *b* he says[3]: 'A plaintiff (*or his estate*) should not recover more than that which would have remained at his disposal after meeting his own living expenses.' (Emphasis mine).

Furthermore, the possibility of double recovery for the 'lost years' under both the Law Reform (Miscellaneous Provisions) Act 1934 and the Fatal Accidents Acts which arises in cases when the dependants do not inherit the estate only occurs in the case of a claim brought on behalf of the estate, because in the case of a living plaintiff judgment in the   *c* claim extinguishes the right to claim under the Fatal Accidents Acts. The problem of double recovery is discussed in the speeches of Lord Wilberforce, Lord Salmon and Lord Scarman which must be taken as showing that their Lordships considered that the claim for the 'lost years' survived for the benefit of the estate. I therefore feel compelled to reject the defendants' first submission. If the claim for loss of expectation of life survives, I can see no legitimate judicial reason why the claim for the 'lost years' should not also   *d* survive.

The defendants secondly submit that if it is not permissible as a matter of principle to treat the claim for the 'lost years' under the Law Reform (Miscellaneous Provisions) Acts 1934 differently from the claim of a living plaintiff such damages are in fact expressly excluded by virtue of s 1(2)(*c*) of the 1934 Act which provides:

> 'Where a cause of action survives as aforesaid for the benefit of the estate of a   *e* deceased person, the damages recoverable for the benefit of the estate of that person . . . (*c*) where the death of that person has been caused by the act or omission which gives rise to the cause of action, shall be calculated without reference to any loss or gain to his estate consequent on his death, except that a sum in respect of funeral expenses may be included.'

f

The defendants submit that earnings awarded in respect of the 'lost years' would be a gain to the estate consequent on the death of the deceased within the meaning of sub-para (*c*) and are thus not recoverable. This subsection was considered by McKinnon J in *Slater v Spreag*[4]. In that case the claim under the Law Reform (Miscellaneous Provisions) Act 1934 originally had included a claim for the 'lost years'. It was not pursued, but the following passage appears in the judgment[5]:

g

> 'There was a pleaded claim under a third head—namely, the loss of future earnings. I should have been of the opinion that the head was excluded by s. 1, sub-s. 2(*c*) of the Act of 1934, but I do not discuss it in detail as counsel for the plaintiff has stated he now makes no claim for damages under that head.'

The subsection was referred to by Lord Atkin and Lord Wright in *Rose v Ford*[1]. Lord   *h* Atkin said[6]:

> 'I can see the possibility of discussion in the provision of sect. (2)(*c*) that the damages "shall be calculated without reference to any loss or gain to his estate consequent on his death." Plainly this does not mean that his estate is not to gain by

j

1   [1937] 3 All ER 359, [1937] AC 826
2   [1961] 3 All ER 323, [1962] 2 QB 210
3   [1979] 1 All ER 774 at 798, [1978] 3 WLR 955 at 981–982
4   [1936] 1 KB 83, [1935] All ER Rep 900
5   [1936] 1 KB 83 at 87–88, [1935] All ER Rep 900 at 902
6   [1937] 3 All ER 359 at 363, [1937] AC 826 at 835

the award of any damages at all for this would be absurd. Can the damages include a calculation of the loss of income which the deceased would have received during normal expectation of life, but would not have saved so as to increase his estate? I express no opinion.'

Lord Wright said[1]:

'Again, sect. 1(2)(c) is especially significant, because it particularises certain classes of losses and gains. It presupposes that damages may, in general, be calculated where death has been caused by the wrong, but excludes from the calculation losses or gains to the estate consequent on the death. I need not examine the full scope of this proviso which is not directly material to this appeal. Obvious instances of what are referred to are such items as, on the one side, insurance moneys falling due on death, and, on the other, annuities ceasing on death. These are irrelevant to the question of what damages can survive, because the dead man could neither have collected such gains nor experienced such losses. They are subsequent to, and only remotely, for present purposes, connected with his death. Funeral expenses form a clear example of the same category.'

I do not find this section easy to construe. If given its literal meaning it would exclude all damages recovered by the estate, for they are all a gain to the estate consequent on the death of the deceased, but, as Lord Atkin said, such a construction would be absurd. If damages for loss of expectation of life, which are an attempt to put a money value on the years of life that have been lost, are not a gain to the estate consequent on death within the meaning of the subsection (for which we have the authority of *Rose v Ford*[2]), why should the lost earnings during those same years be a gain consequent on the death?

It is interesting to observe that this subsection is not referred to in any of the speeches in *Pickett v British Rail Engineering Ltd*[3] and if the defendants' construction is correct the question of double recovery discussed in those speeches cannot arise, for the claim for the 'lost years' will be excluded from claims made on behalf of the estate. Furthermore the Law Commission[4] recommended that the rule in *Oliver v Ashman*[5] should be reversed so that a living plaintiff could recover for the 'lost years', but recognised that this would result in the claim for the 'lost years' surviving for the benefit of the estate with the result that a defendant would be paying damages twice over to the dependants under the Fatal Accidents Acts and to the beneficiary under the will. Accordingly they recommended that legislation should provide that claims for damages for the lost period should not survive to the estate: see also the passages to the like effect in the speech of Lord Scarman in *Pickett v British Rail Engineering Ltd*[3]. I am unwilling to believe that their Lordships and the Law Commissioners failed to perceive that the simple solution to the dilemma of double recovery lay in the provisions of s 1(2)(c).

I am unable to follow the opinion expressed by McKinnon J in *Slater v Spreag*[6]. In my judgment the subsection must be construed as applying to those gains and losses to the estate that arise as a result of the death itself and independently of the fact that the death was caused by the defendant's wrongful act; that is, to those gains and losses that would have accrued on death regardless of the fact that death was caused by personal injuries attributable to the fault of the defendant. Examples are annuities and insurance moneys referred to by Lord Wright in *Rose v Ford*[2]. I read the subsection as of similar intent to the more clearly expressed provision in the Fatal Accidents Act 1959, s 2(1) of which provides:

1   [1937] 3 All ER 359 at 368, [1937] AC 826 at 842
2   [1937] 3 All ER 359, [1937] AC 826
3   [1979] 1 All ER 774, [1978] 3 WLR 955
4   Report on Personal Injury Litigation—Assessment of Damages (1973) Law Com 56
5   [1961] 3 All ER 323, [1962] 2 QB 210
6   [1936] 1 KB 83, [1935] All ER Rep 900

'In assessing damages in respect of a person's death in any action under the Fatal Accidents Act 1846 . . . there shall not be taken into account any insurance money, *a* benefit, pension or gratuity which has been or will be paid as a result of the death.'

And so I conclude that the terms of s 1(2)(c) do not prevent the estate recovering damages for the 'lost years'.

How then am I to value this claim for the 'lost years' brought on behalf of the estate? The award is not to include sums that the deceased would have spent on themselves (see *Pickett v British Rail Engineering Ltd*[1]) and the burden lies on the plaintiff to satisfy the *b* court of the sum that it would be proper to award. I have already given my reason for concluding that these daughters would have provided a large sum for the support of their parents which I have quantified at £54,000. It is suggested that an even larger award than this is justified on the assumption that in addition to spending money on their parents they would have married and provided for other dependants. It was suggested that I should therefore give 15 years purchase of two-fifths of their incomes. If I did this *c* it would mean that I was speculating whether they would marry, speculating whether they would have children and then awarding a sum of money the only social justification of which is to provide support for husbands and children when in fact no such dependants do or can exist. This seems to me an absurdity. In my view there is no material before the court on which it could properly make an award for the 'lost years' over and above that which it assesses for the parents' support. *d*

Accordingly I award under the 1934 Act the sum of £54,000 in respect of the 'lost years' which I apportion equally between the estates, to which must be added £750 each for loss of expectation of life. Thus the total sum that can be recovered on behalf of each estate is £27,750, subject to the question of limitation of liability under the Carriage by Air Act 1961.

As to the claims under the Fatal Accidents Act, on the assumption that the estates pass *e* in equal shares to the parents it would appear that they will each receive more from the estate than the value of their Fatal Accidents Acts claims which will therefore be extinguished. But if this assumption is shown to be false by reason of the incidence of taxation or the laws of inheritance there will be liberty to apply and address further argument on this question.

f

Judgment accordingly.

Solicitors: *Kennedys*, agents for *Hugh F Dickens*, Potters Bar (for the plaintiff); *Hewitt, Woollacott and Chown* (for the defendants).

K Mydeen Esq   Barrister. *g*

---

1   [1979] 1 All ER 774, [1978] 3 WLR 955

Customs and Excise Commissioners v Oliver

QUEEN'S BENCH DIVISION
GRIFFITHS J
3rd DECEMBER 1979

Value added tax – Supply of goods or services – Supply – Second-hand car dealer selling stolen cars at public auction – Whether sales a 'supply' of goods – Finance Act 1972, ss 1, 2, 5.

The taxpayer was a second-hand car dealer. He sold at auction cars which he had either stolen or which he knew to have been stolen. The Customs and Excise Commissioners assessed the taxpayer to value added tax on the proceeds of those sales. The taxpayer appealed to a value added tax tribunal, which allowed the appeal, holding that the sales, being sales of stolen articles, did not comply with the legal requirements of the law of contract and accordingly did not constitute a 'supply' within ss 1[a], 2[b] and 5[c] of the Finance Act 1972, with the result that no value added tax was assessable on the proceeds of those sales. The Crown appealed.

Held – For the purposes of ss 1, 2 and 5 of the 1972 Act the 'supply' of goods meant the passing of possession in goods under an agreement by which the supplier agreed to part with and the recipient to take 'possession', which in that context meant control of the goods in the sense of having the facility of their immediate use. The sale of stolen cars at auction was therefore a 'supply' within the meaning of that expression in the 1972 Act, and the taxpayer was accordingly liable to value added tax on the proceeds of the sales. The appeal would therefore be allowed (see p 355 *f* to *h*, post).

Notes
For the meaning of 'supply', see 12 Halsbury's Laws (4th Edn) para 871.
For the Finance Act 1972, ss 1, 2, 5, see 42 Halsbury's Statutes (3rd Edn) 163, 164, 165.

Case referred to in judgment
Carlton Lodge Club v Customs and Excise Comrs [1974] 3 All ER 798, [1975] 1 WLR 66, [1974] STC 507.

Appeal
The Crown appealed against the decision of a value added tax tribunal sitting in Manchester (chairman Mr P S Rae-Scott) allowing the appeal by the taxpayer, John Richard Brian Oliver, against a notice of assessment to value added tax dated 16th February 1978. The facts are set out in the judgment.

Simon D Brown for the Crown.
The taxpayer did not appear.

GRIFFITHS J. This is an appeal by the Commissioners of Customs and Excise from the decision of a value added tax tribunal which allowed an appeal by the taxpayer against the commissioners' notice of assessment of value added tax, dated 16th February 1978.
The facts out of which the assessment arose are as follows. The taxpayer is a dishonest second-hand car dealer. One form of dishonesty that he practised was selling at auction motor cars which are known in criminal circles as 'ringers', ie motor cars that had in fact been stolen but which had been clothed with a new and false identity by fitting number plates to them which had been taken from wrecked motor cars and filing off the chassis

---

a   Section 1, so far as material, is set out at p 354 *f*, post
b   Section 2, so far as material, is set out at p 354 *g h*, post
c   Section 5, so far as material, is set out at p 354 *j* to p 355 *a*, post

numbers and engine numbers on the stolen cars and stamping in their place the chassis
and engine numbers of the wrecked motor cars.

It came to light in the course of investigations into the taxpayer's books that a number
of cars which he had either stolen or which he knew to have been stolen and whose
identities had been changed in the manner I have described had been sold by him at
public auction, for which he had received the proceeds of sale, and accordingly he was
assessed in the sum of about £320 value added tax on those transactions.

The taxpayer appealed against this assessment on the impudent assertion that as the
cars were stolen he could not be assessable to value added tax. He added, perhaps more
realistically, that he was unable to pay in any event.

Before the value added tax tribunal he neither appeared nor argued his case, and it is
no surprise that he has not appeared before this court today.

The members of the tribunal concluded rightly that the sales at auction were void
because the subject of the sales was stolen property. They also concluded rightly that
mere illegality as such would be no bar to the imposition of value added tax on the
transaction, and they further concluded that the sales were within the course of the
business of a second-hand car dealer carried on by the taxpayer. However, they came to
the conclusion that value added tax was not assessable because there was no supply of
goods within the meaning of the Finance Act 1972, and as I understand their approach
from their decision, it was this: that in order to determine whether or not there is a
supply of goods within the meaning of that Act, one has first to look at the nature of the
transaction under which the goods passed, decide under what heading the nature of that
transaction might most appropriately be labelled, and then, only if that was a transaction
which complied in all respects with the legal requirements of such a transaction, could
there be said to be a supply. So here they said that this clearly purported to be a supply
by means of sale, and as it was a sale of a stolen article it was a void sale, therefore the
transaction did not comply with the legal requirements of the law of contract, and
accordingly there was no supply.

I am bound to say that I think that this was an entirely mistaken approach to the
problem. There is no definition of 'supply' in the Act itself, but it is quite clear from the
language of the Act that 'supply' is a word of the widest import. The tax is introduced
by s 1(1) of the 1972 Act which reads:

> 'A tax, to be known as value added tax, shall be charged in accordance with the
> provisions of this Part of this Act on the supply of goods and services in the United
> Kingdom (including anything treated as such a supply) and on the importation of
> goods into the United Kingdom.'

The scope of the tax is set out in s 2, which provides:

> '(1) Except as otherwise provided by this Part of this Act the tax shall be charged
> and payable as follows.
> '(2) Tax on the supply of goods or services shall be charged only where—(a) the
> supply is a taxable supply; and (b) the goods or services are supplied by a taxable
> person in the course of a business carried on by him; and shall be payable by the
> person supplying the goods or services.'

Section 5 again deals with supply, and it reads:

> '(1) The following provisions apply for determining for the purposes of this Part
> of this Act what is a supply of goods or services.
> '(2) Supply of goods includes all forms of supply and, in particular, the letting of
> goods on hire and the making of a gift or loan of goods; but supply of services does
> not include anything done otherwise than for a consideration . . .
> '(5) Schedule 2 to this Act shall have effect with respect to matters to be treated
> as a supply of goods . . .
> '(7) Subject to the preceding provisions of this section, the Treasury may by order
> provide with respect to any description of transaction—(a) that it is to be treated as

a supply of goods and not as a supply of services; or (b) that it is to be treated as a
a   supply of services and not as a supply of goods; or (c) that it is to be treated as neither
a supply of goods nor a supply of services.'

In *Carlton Lodge Club v Customs and Excise Comrs*[1], a question arose whether the
provision of drink to members by an unincorporated club was a supply of drink within
the meaning of the 1972 Act, and so assessable for value added tax. The facts I take from
the headnote. The club was an unincorporated members' club. It did not seek to make
b   a profit. It was essentially a drinking club, in the sense that it was a place where members
could, on making payment, obtain a drink of alcoholic liquor. It was licensed under the
Licensing Acts, and it was registered for the purpose of value added tax but applied for
its registration to be cancelled, claiming that the serving of intoxicating liquor to
members on the club premises did not constitute the supply of goods or services within
s 1(1) of the 1972 Act since the liquor was already the property of the club members and
c   the payment made by a member for a drink merely constituted the consideration for the
release by other members of their share in the drink. It was held that the words 'supply
of goods or services' in s 1 of the Act meant 'furnishing or serving goods or services' and
were not limited to the supply of goods and services by way of sale. Accordingly, in
serving drinks to members, the club was engaged in the supply of drinks to them and
was therefore liable to pay value added tax on that supply, and in the course of giving the
d   judgment of the court Milmo J pointed out[2] that it was not a sale but that the issue before
the court was not whether or not it was a sale but whether there was a supply within the
meaning of the 1972 Act. And later he said[3], having cited the provisions of s 5 and Sch 2:

'The relevance for the present purpose, as I see it, of this schedule is that it is
clearly designed to ensure the widest possible interpretation of what constitutes "a
e   supply of goods".'

I ask myself this question: if any layman had asked the purchaser of one of the stolen
motor cars who had supplied him with the car, he would I think have unhesitatingly
answered by giving the name of the taxpayer. The fact that it subsequently turned out
that it had been supplied under a contract of sale that was in fact void would be neither
here nor there, and I am content to adopt the definition of 'supply' for the purposes of
f   this case put forward by counsel for the commissioners. 'Supply' is the passing of
possession in goods pursuant to an agreement whereunder the supplier agrees to part
with and the recipient agrees to take possession. By 'possession' is meant in this context
control over the goods, in the sense of having the immediate facility for their use. This
may or may not involve the physical removal of the goods.

In my judgment this transaction that took place at auction was a 'supply' within the
g   meaning of that expression in the 1972 Act, and it is neither here nor there that in fact
the taxpayer was thoroughly dishonest and the unfortunate purchaser might at some
later date have to part with the car. The taxpayer received the money for the sale and he
must pay the tax on it.

Accordingly, I would allow this appeal.

h   *Appeal allowed.*

Solicitors: *Solicitor for the Customs and Excise.*

Evelyn M C Budd   Barrister.

j   1   [1974] 3 All ER 798, [1974] STC 507, [1975] 1 WLR 66
    2   [1974] 3 All ER 798 at 800, [1974] STC 507 at 509, [1975] 1 WLR 66 at 68
    3   [1974] 3 All ER 798 at 800, [1974] STC 507 at 509, [1975] 1 WLR 66 at 69

Bell v Alfred Franks & Bartlett Co Ltd and another

a

COURT OF APPEAL, CIVIL DIVISION
MEGAW, SHAW AND WALLER LJJ
6th, 7th, 8th NOVEMBER 1979

b

Landlord and tenant – Business premises – Tenancy – Exclusion of statutory protection – Business user in breach of covenant in lease – Consent – Acquiescence – Consent to breach by immediate landlord or predecessor in title – Predecessor in title noticing business user of premises in breach of covenant and not objecting – Whether 'consent' to business user – Whether standing by and not objecting to breach is consent or merely acquiescence – Whether consent requiring positive action accepting breach – Whether tenancy within statute – Landlord and Tenant Act 1954, s 23(4).

c

Landlord and tenant – Business premises – Occupied for business purposes – Flat and garage let to company – Covenant to use garage for standing 'private cars' only – Garage used by company to store cartons of samples and cars in garage used to transport customers and to carry cartons – Whether garage occupied for business purposes – Whether business user in breach of covenant to use garage for private cars only.

d

In 1964 A, the leasehold owner of premises comprising a flat and garage, let the premises to the defendant company under a written agreement. The agreement contained a covenant by the defendants to use the garage 'for standing a private car only' (subsequently amended to 'two private cars') and to use the flat as a 'private' dwelling only. Over a long period F, a director of the company, used the garage to store cartons of samples collected for the company's business and used the two cars kept in the garage, a Rolls-Royce and a Bentley, to transport customers of the business and to carry the cartons. A, who was often in the vicinity of the garage and sometimes conversed with F, observed this user of the garage and cars but did not object to it or request the defendants to stop it. On the expiry of the letting the defendants became yearly tenants under the terms of the agreement. In 1975 there was an assignment of A's lease to the plaintiff, the immediate landlord, who was unaware of the use of the garage and cars in connection with the defendants' business. In April 1977 the plaintiff gave the defendants notice to quit in the form appropriate to terminate a residential tenancy but not a business tenancy. The defendants remained in possession and in December 1978 the plaintiff brought a claim for possession in the county court. By their defence the defendants contended, inter alia, that the garage was occupied for the purposes of their business and if that user was in breach of the covenant in the agreement, A, the plaintiff's predecessor in title, had 'consented' to the breach so that, by virtue of s 23(4)[a] of the Landlord and Tenant Act 1954 (which provided for the Act to apply to a business user, notwithstanding a covenant to the contrary, if 'the immediate landlord or his predecessor in title has consented to the breach or the immediate landlord has acquiesced therein'), Part II of the 1954 Act applied to the tenancy and the notice to quit served by the plaintiff was ineffective. The county court judge upheld that contention and dismissed the claim for possession. The plaintiff appealed, claiming possession of the garage, possession of the flat being no longer in issue. On the appeal the defendants contended that both the storage of the cartons and the use of the cars for the business constituted occupation of the garage for business purposes and that such user was not prohibited by the covenant in the agreement.

e

f

g

h

j

---

a Section 23(4) is set out at p 359 *b*, post

Held – The appeal would be allowed for the following reasons –

a   (i) The word 'private car' in the context of the covenant in the agreement meant a car which was both constructed and used for private purposes. It followed that the keeping of cars used for business purposes in the garage, and as the storage of cartons there, was a breach by the defendants of the covenant to use the garage for standing private cars only (see p 359 *j* to p 360 *b*, p 361 *d* and p 362 *c* and *g h*, post).

(ii) In s 23(4) of the 1954 Act relating to conduct which brought a tenancy within Part
b II of the Act notwithstanding a breach of covenant against business user, the 'consent' of a landlord who was a predecessor in title was used in antithesis to the 'acquiescence' of an immediate landlord. 'Acquiescence' involved no more than a passive standing by without objecting to a breach of covenant, whereas, by contrast, 'consent' required a positive, affirmative act accepting the breach, such as a written or oral acceptance or even an implied acceptance by conduct. On the evidence, A had merely acquiesced in the
c business user of the garage and had not consented to it. It followed that the tenancy of the garage had not been brought within Part II of the Act and that the notice to quit was effective to terminate the tenancy, and the plaintiff was therefore entitled to an order for possession of the garage (see p 359 *c d*, p 360 *b* to *f* and *j* to p 361 *a c d* and *j* to p 362 *c* and *j* to p 363 *a*, post).

d **Notes**

For tenancies protected by Part II of the Landlord and Tenant Act 1954, see 23 Halsbury's Laws (3rd Edn) 885, para 1707.

For the Landlord and Tenant Act 1954, s 23, see 18 Halsbury's Statutes (3rd Edn) 355.

Cases cited

e *Ambler, Doe d v Woodbridge* (1829) 9 B & C 376, 109 ER 140.
Atkin v Rose [1923] 1 Ch 522.
Blackstone (David) Ltd v Burnetts (West End) Ltd [1973] 3 All ER 782, [1973] 1 WLR 1487.
Chapman v Freeman [1978] 3 All ER 878, [1978] 1 WLR 1298, CA.
Cheryl Investments Ltd v Saldanha, Royal Life Saving Society v Page [1979] 1 All ER 5, [1978]
   1 WLR 1329, CA.
f *City and Westminster Properties (1934) Ltd v Mudd* [1958] 2 All ER 733, [1959] Ch 129.
Daimar Investments Ltd v Jones (1962) 112 LJ 424, Cty Ct.
Hillil Property and Investment Co Ltd v Naraine Pharmacy Ltd (1979) 123 Sol Jo 437, CA.
McG (formerly R) v R [1972] 1 All ER 362, sub nom *McGill v Robson* [1972] 1 WLR 237.
Sayers v Collyer (1888) 28 Ch D 103, [1881–5] All ER Rep 385.
Sheppard, Doe d v Allen (1810) 3 Taunt 78, 128 ER 32.
g *Sweet v Parsley* [1969] 1 All ER 347, [1970] AC 132, HL.

Appeal

The plaintiff, John Arnaud Bell, brought a claim in the Bloomsbury and Marylebone County Court against the first defendants, Alfred Franks & Bartlett Co Ltd, the tenants of premises comprising a flat at 9 Devonshire Close, London W1 and a garage, and
h against the second defendant, David Blank, to whom the first defendants had sublet the flat, claiming possession of the flat and garage. On 11th January 1979 his Honour Judge Leslie found that the garage was occupied by the first defendants for business purposes in breach of a covenant in the tenancy but that the plaintiff's predecessor in title, Mr Harold John Allen, had consented to the breach within s 23(4) of the Landlord and Tenant Act 1954; that therefore, by virtue of s 23(4), the tenancy was brought within Part II of the 1954 Act, and since the notice to quit served by the plaintiff was ineffective
j to determine a tenancy of business premises, the plaintiff's claim for possession failed. The plaintiff appealed against the dismissal of his claim for possession of the garage. The facts are set out in the judgment of Shaw LJ.

Andrew Pugh for the plaintiff.
J J Davis for the defendants.

SHAW LJ delivered the first judgment at the invitation of Megaw LJ. This is an appeal from that part of a judgment of his Honour Judge Leslie given on 11th January 1979 at *a* the Bloomsbury and Marylebone County Court which dismissed the plaintiff's claim for possession of a garage at 9 Devonshire Close in the west of London. At the hearing, a flat in proximity to the garage was also the subject-matter of the litigation, but this appeal is concerned only with the garage. The matter in contention was whether that garage had been occupied by the first defendants for business purposes. That issue arises because the plaintiff purported to give a notice to quit which was not in the form required by the *b* Landlord and Tenant Act 1954 in relation to a business tenancy and, therefore, would have been abortive if the garage had in fact been occupied for business purposes.

The history, which was dealt with by the county court judge, is a long one and it is not necessary to recount it in the detail with which it was necessary for counsel for the plaintiff to present it to this court. As long ago as the end of 1949 a gentleman named Ward, who occupied 94 Harley Street (which is adjacent to 9 Devonshire Close), let the *c* garage there to the first defendants (whom I shall call 'the defendant company'). In 1964 Mr Ward assigned, or agreed to assign, the lease to a gentleman named Allen, who was a dental surgeon practising at No 94, and on 23rd September 1964 Mr Allen, by a written agreement, let the garage in question, together with the flat to which I have referred, to the defendant company. The term was for three and a quarter years beginning on 29th September 1964, and therefore it expired by effluxion of time somewhere at the end of *d* December 1967. The agreement, by cl 2(4), setting out the tenant's covenants, provided that the tenant undertook to 'use the said garage for standing a private car only' and then, since the agreement comprised the flat also, it went on to say 'and the flat only as and for a private dwelling-house'. It is important to note that the same word 'private' is used in relation to the car and also in relation to the dwelling-house, because the question arises as to whether '*private* car' was merely a description of the character of the vehicle or was *e* a reference to the nature of the use to which it would normally be put.

In September 1975 there was an assignment of Mr Allen's lease to the plaintiff. By that time the covenant to which I have just referred had been relaxed because it was amended so as to provide that two private motor cars might stand there instead of one. For some long time before the assignment to the plaintiff there is no question but that a Mr Franks, who was a director and moving spirit in the defendant company, had used the garage *f* from time to time to take in and store samples collected for his company's business. Two cars which were put there, one a Bentley and another a Rolls-Royce, were used, so the evidence went, in order to assist the objects of the company by carrying prospective customers to and fro and also for the purpose of conveying samples. That was the business use which was relied on in order to establish the character of the occupation of the garage as being for business purposes within the provisions of s 23 of the Landlord *g* and Tenant Act 1954.

The plaintiff having given the notice to quit, discontinued the action which he had started. It was not until 15th December 1978 that the action under which the present appeal arises was begun. In that action the plaintiff claimed possession of the flat (which is not now in issue) and also of the garage. This was on the ground that the agreement under which the defendant company held, made in 1964, had expired at the end of *h* December 1977. The defence, in general terms, was that the notice was ineffective because it was not such a notice as is required in the case of a business tenancy by the Landlord and Tenant Act 1954. In that way the critical issue from the standpoint of this appeal is whether the judge was right in finding (as he did) that the occupancy of the garage was within the 1954 Act.

Section 23, which is the first section in Part II of the Act, which is headed 'Tenancies *j* to which Part II applies', provides by sub-s (1):

'Subject to the provisions of this Act, this Part of the Act applies to any tenancy where the property comprised in the tenancy is or includes premises which are *a*   occupied by the tenant and are so occupied for the purposes of a business carried on by him or for those and other purposes.'

If a business is carried on in contravention of a covenant excluding such user, sub-s (4) provides as follows:

b   'Where the tenant is carrying on a business, in all or any part of the property comprised in a tenancy, in breach of a prohibition (however expressed) of use for business purposes which subsists under the terms of the tenancy and extends to the whole of that property, this Part of this Act shall not apply to the tenancy unless the immediate landlord or his predecessor in title has consented to the breach or the immediate landlord has acquiesced therein.'

c   Thus if a breach of the prohibition has occurred but it can be said to have been acquiesced in by the immediate landlord the activity constituting the breach will nonetheless give rise to a business tenancy. If the acquiescence of the immediate landlord is not relied on (and it was not in this case, as is conceded) one has to look back to his predecessor in title (who in the present case was Mr Allen) and see whether he consented to that use. Mere acquiescence by a predecessor in title would not be sufficient to confer on the tenant the protection of the 1954 Act to a tenant of business premises.

d   Mr Allen, who is unfortunately now deceased, had a long and friendly association with Mr Franks. Mr Allen carried on his practice as a dentist at 94 Harley Street and he very often was in the vicinity of the garage; he was able to observe what was going on there; he was able to see that from time to time there were parcels containing samples left there; and he also saw from time to time one or other of the vehicles which the company used, namely the Rolls-Royce or the Bentley, but not a van, or a lorry, or anything of the *e*   nature that might be called a commercial vehicle. It is contended that, because over this long history Mr Allen did not require that activities of that kind in the garage should stop as being in contravention of the tenant's covenants in the agreement, that amounted to consent.

That is really the short point which the judge had to decide so far as the occupancy of the garage was concerned. Two matters were relied on before him by counsel on behalf *f*   of the defendants to show that there was a business user of the premises and that there had been consent to them. One was the presence of cartons containing samples for the business, fortified by conversations, which were part of the evidence, between Mr Allen and Mr Franks and which had reference to the contents of the cartons, such as sunglasses and things of that kind. The other was the fact that the cars themselves were used in order to convey customers of the defendant company as well as goods belonging to it.

g   The first question is, did either of those activities constitute a business use? There can be no doubt that the bringing in of samples in cartons, and so forth, might well constitute such a business use even though it was intermittent and not continuous. The evidence suggested that there was nearly always something of that kind there, and the judge held that that was in this respect such a use. He made no finding as to the effect of the presence of these motor cars from time to time. That prompted counsel for the *h*   defendants to submit, on the basis of his cross-notice, that he should have found that the motor cars were there for business purposes, so that on that foundation also the premises were occupied for such purposes and, therefore, there existed a business tenancy which was protected under the Landlord and Tenant Act 1954.

It is convenient to deal with that part of his submission first because it raises the narrow question of interpretation of the meaning of the word 'private' in the context of *j*   the agreement under which the defendant company held the garage. It seems to me that in conjunction with the sentence which follows it, which refers to the use of the flat as a 'private' dwelling-house, 'private' there must mean used for some personal or domestic purpose; not merely a car which is constructed for such purpose, but which is indeed used for such purpose. A dwelling-house, of course, is a house which people normally dwell in. A 'private' dwelling-house is one actually used for domestic purposes. So construing that agreement, one has got to take note of the conjunction of the use of that word in two different aspects, one relating to the garage and the other relating to the flat, No 9. It would follow that use of the word 'private' there means for private purposes. The fact that it used the phrase 'for standing two private cars' did not mean two private cars used for business purposes thus introducing the element of business occupancy into the letting of the garage any more than it did into the letting of the flat at the same time. So I would hold against the defendant's submission on that matter under the cross-notice.

That leaves for decision only the question whether there had been at some stage in the history a consent to the use of the garage against the prohibition contained in the agreement. This is a semantic and philosophical question which requires definition of the distinction between 'acquiescence' and 'consent'. It is quite clear that what s 23(4) intended was to ensure that the immediate landlord should not be bound by mere (and I use that word deliberately) acquiescence on the part of the immediate predecessor in title, because that goes far to giving to the tenant a protection and exposing the immediate landlord to an undue risk to which he ought not to be exposed. What is meant by acquiescence? It may involve no more than a merely passive attitude, doing nothing at all. It requires as an essential factor that there was knowledge of what was acquiesced in. In this case it is not in controversy that there was such knowledge on the part of the plaintiff's predecessor in title that the garage was used in the way in which it was.

If acquiescence is something passive in the face of knowledge, what does 'consent' mean? In the context of the contrast implicit in the subsection, the only practical and sensible distinction that can be drawn is that if acquiescence can arise out of passive failure to do anything, consent must involve a positive demonstrative act, something of an affirmative kind. It is not to be implied, because the resort to implication betokens an absence of express affirmation. The only sense in which there can be implied consent is where a consent is demonstrated, not by language but by some positive act other than words which amounts to an affirmation of what is being done and goes beyond mere acquiescence in it. It may lead, in this context, to a false conclusion to speak of 'implied consent', which is what the learned judge said was the proper inference to be drawn from the long history of acquiescence. I would prefer for myself to say 'consent' involves something which is of a positive affirmative kind and that is what is required by s 23(4) if the immediate landlord is to be deprived of the opportunity of taking advantage of a breach of a prohibition contained in the terms of the tenancy.

The judge, in his very careful judgment, having examined the evidence, expressed himself in this way in regard to the garage: 'The question is whether the plaintiff's notice to quit was effective to terminate the letting to the first defendants, and that depends on the use of the garage'. He then set out what the contentions of the parties were and went on to say this:

'It is true that the plaintiff and his witness saw no cartons, but having heard the evidence I find that the defendants have been using the premises for the purposes of a business, namely for the storage of cartons containing samples and goods, although contrary to the lease and contrary to the head lease. Mr Allen [he was the predecessor in title of the plaintiff] knew of this and must have waived the breach. It is possible that the plaintiff is entitled to bring proceedings for forfeiture but that is not what the court is concerned with in the present case.'

Then having set out s 23(4) in his judgment he said: '. . . in my view that section applies to this case.' That was following what he had previously said, that Mr Allen knew what was going on 'and must have waived the breach'. However, the inference from the history of Mr Allen's relationship with Mr Franks and his knowledge of the activities of the defendant company gives rise, so it seems to me, to no stronger inference than that there was acquiescence on the part of Mr Allen. An examination of the evidence as a whole reveals nowhere that any such positive consent, positive affirmation or permission was actually given at any time. So far as the immediate landlord is concerned, that

a appears to be fortified by the earlier part of the history when Mr Franks, who was himself, incidentally, a solicitor although he was engaged in business as well, had asked that the tenancy should be in the name of his company. That was not necessarily because the company wanted it. There might have been convenience, or financial advantage, in having the company as the tenant of the garage instead of Mr Franks himself.

I have not dealt with all the elaborate submissions that counsel for the plaintiff

b presented before this court. That is not to say that they were without interest, but it seems to me that the only ones that really go to the heart of this case are: first, the issue as to whether or not the judge was right in coming to the conclusion that there had been a business use; secondly, whether he was right in saying that the premises were occupied for the purposes of the business; and, thirdly, whether he was right in finding, as he did, that there had been a consent within the meaning of s 23(4). In my view, what is

c decisive of the appeal is that there was no acquiescence on the part of the plaintiff and no consent by Mr Allen. Accordingly, the requirements of the 1954 Act were not called into play. The notice to quit was effective to terminate the tenancy and the plaintiff is entitled to an order for possession of the garage premises.

I would allow the appeal.

d **WALLER LJ.** I agree, and I agree with the judgment which Shaw LJ has just delivered. I only add a few words on the question of consent because we are differing from a very experienced judge on that one finding which he made.

Shaw LJ has already read s 23 of the Landlord and Tenant Act 1954, and in particular sub-s (4), and I need only repeat the last few lines of that section which say:

e '. . . this Part of this Act shall not apply to the tenancy unless the immediate landlord or his predecessor in title has consented to the breach or the immediate landlord has acquiesced therein.'

The judge, in considering that part of the case, made the finding already quoted by Shaw LJ, namely that, having dealt with the storage of cartons about which evidence was given by Mr Franks, he said: 'Mr Allen knew of this and must have waived the breach. It is

f possible that the plaintiff is entitled to bring proceedings for forfeiture, but that is not what the court is concerned with in the present case'.

So that, in effect, was the view the judge formed in that paragraph, and then he went on to consider whether or not the consent had to be formal and said:

'When a landlord knows about a breach as Allen did, and the breach clearly goes on for a substantial period of time, as this one did, and the landlord can even accept

g a sample which should not be there, then one can only infer that he did consent. The parties were on amicable terms and Mr Allen took no steps to cause this wrongful user to cease and he never even objected. I find, therefore, that the premises were used for business purposes notwithstanding the prohibition and that it was consented to by Mr Allen.'

h When one looks at the evidence on which the judge made that finding, perhaps the high-water mark is shown in a quotation from the evidence of Mr Franks. He said at the end of his evidence-in-chief: 'He never objected.' Although there are other passages which clearly show acquiescence that answer is the only one on which the judge could found the finding that there was consent.

Shaw LJ has already mentioned, and I do not wish to repeat it, but I would emphasise,

j the distinction which is drawn in s 23(4) between the predecessor of the landlord and the immediate landlord. In order to avoid being taken out of the Act the tenant has to show that the immediate predecessor consented to the breach whereas it would be sufficient for him to show acquiescence on the part of the present landlord. The contrast between those words is, in my view, significant. Acquiescence clearly can cover a great many matters, and it seems to me the words of the judge where he says: 'Mr Allen knew of this

and must have waived the breach,' were very clear evidence of acquiescence, but
acquiescence is something which has to be contrasted with consent and, in my judgment, *a*
consent requires some positive action on the part of the landlord or his predecessor,
usually no doubt in words, perhaps in writing, possibly, if gestures were absolutely clear,
it could conceivably be by gesture but, in my view, careful proof of such an intention
would be required. Normally one would look for some express statement, either in
writing or orally, by the landlord. The answer which I have quoted clearly shows
something far short of that, because there is the answer: 'He [that is Allen] never *b*
objected'. In my judgment, having regard to the matters that I have mentioned, it is not
possible to draw an inference from that evidence that the predecessor consented to the
use for business purposes. Accordingly, I also would allow the appeal.

MEGAW LJ. I agree with the conclusions reached by Shaw and Waller LJJ and with the *c*
reasons given by them. We did not consider it necessary to trouble counsel for the
defendants to make submissions on a number of points which had been raised by counsel
for the plaintiff in support of the appeal. That was because it was apparent, and accepted
by counsel, that if counsel for the defendants were wrong on the point which he wished
to raise in the cross-notice and were wrong on the issue as to consent, then none of those
other issues fell to be decided.   *d*
   One of those issues on which we did not hear counsel for the defendants and on which,
therefore, I do not find it necessary to express anything in the nature of a concluded view,
was the conclusion reached by the judge that here it was shown on the evidence that the
premises were occupied for the purposes of the business carried on by the first
defendants. I will assume, therefore, without expressing any view on it, that the judge
was right in deciding that question in favour of the first defendants, the tenants. On that *e*
assumption, counsel for the defendants put forward, by virtue of his cross-notice, as I
understood it, the proposition that the case thus inevitably fell within the purview of
s 23(1) and (2) of the Landlord and Tenant Act 1954, and then he went on to submit that
for one simple reason s 23(4) did not apply to take it out again. Subsection (4) depends
on the carrying on of a business having been in breach of a prohibition on use for
business purposes; and, said counsel for the defendants, here there was no covenant in the *f*
relevant tenancy agreement which in any way precluded the first defendant from using
the garage for business purposes. That was a point which depended on the construction
of cl 2(4) of the agreement of 23rd September 1964, which imposed an obligation on the
tenant 'To use the said garage for standing a private car only and the flat only as and for
a private dwelling house'. Whatever may be the meaning of 'private' or 'private car' in
other contexts, I am satisfied that on the true construction of the words of that clause, *g*
first the keeping of cartons of goods in the garage was in breach of that covenant to use
the garage for standing a private car only; and, secondly, that the using of the garage in
order to keep one or more cars there which were used to a substantial degree for the
business of the defendants (they being a limited liability company) was an infringement
of that covenant. If a car is used to a substantial degree for business purposes it is not a
private car for the purposes of this covenant any more than the use of a house for the *h*
purposes of a business would be the using of the house as a private dwelling-house.
   That point having gone, unless the judge was right in the view which he has taken that
there was here consent on the part of the plaintiff's predecessor in title, Mr Allen, then
the plaintiff was entitled to succeed. I agree with Shaw and Waller LJJ that in the context
of s 23(4) of the Act, whatever consent or acquiescence may mean in different contexts,
in that context 'consent' is put in plain antithesis to 'acquiescence'; and that, therefore, if *j*
something falls within the description 'acquiescence', it is not consent. The difference
which is pointed out between the two in this context is that 'consent' involves some
affirmative acceptance, not merely a standing by and absence of objection. The
affirmative acceptance may be in writing, which is the clearest obviously; it may be oral;
it may conceivably even be by conduct, such as nodding the head in a specific way in

a response to an express request for consent. But it must be something more than merely standing by and not objecting.

I agree that the appeal falls to be allowed.

Appeal allowed; order for possession against first defendants but not second defendant; order stayed for 28 days.

b Solicitors: *Manches & Co* (for the plaintiff); *Frank Charlesly & Co* (for the defendants).

Mary Rose Plummer   Barrister.

c # Newstead (Inspector of Taxes) v Frost

HOUSE OF LORDS

LORD DIPLOCK, VISCOUNT DILHORNE, LORD SALMON, LORD FRASER OF TULLYBELTON AND LORD KEITH OF KINKEL

17th, 18th DECEMBER 1979, 31st JANUARY 1980

d *Income tax – Foreign possessions – Income arising from possessions out of United Kingdom – Partnership between taxpayer and Bahamian company – Partnership activities carried on outside United Kingdom – Taxpayer's motive for entering into partnership to avoid tax on overseas earnings – Object of partnership to exploit taxpayer's talents as television personality – Objects of company including 'all kinds of financial commercial trading or other operations' –*
e *Partnership carrying on genuine commercial trade of exploiting taxpayer's talents – Taxpayer entitled to 95% of partnership profits – No part of profits remitted to United Kingdom – Whether income arising from foreign possessions – Whether motive for entering into partnership overriding genuine commercial nature of partnership – Partnership Act 1890, s 1 – Income and Corporation Taxes Act 1970, ss 109(2), 122(2)(3).*

f The taxpayer who had established himself in the United Kingdom as a television entertainer and author wished to exploit his talents abroad, particularly in the United States, but wished to remain resident in the United Kingdom. A tax saving scheme was devised for the taxpayer whereby in February 1967 he entered into partnership with a 'shell' Bahamian company activated solely for the purpose of the agreement. Under cl 3 of its memorandum of association the company was authorised, inter alia, to carry on and execute 'all kinds of financial commercial trading or other operations'. The objects
g of the partnership agreement between the taxpayer and the company were to enter into the businesses of 'exploiting copyrights and . . . television and film consultants and advisers publicity agents and providers of publicity services . . . producing television programmes, films, stage plays and other entertainment and . . . exploiting the services of producers, actors, directors, writers and artistes'. The agreement provided that the
h partnership business was to be carried on outside the United Kingdom and that the profits were to be divided in the proportions of 95% to the taxpayer and 5% to the company. During the relevant period all the partnership activities, including the control and management of the partnership, took place outside the United Kingdom. The exploitation of the taxpayer's talents in the United States proved to be very successful and the profits of the partnership, which arose mainly from the taxpayer's activities in the
j United States, were divided in accordance with the agreement. No part of the taxpayer's share of the profits was remitted to the United Kingdom. The Crown assessed the taxpayer to income tax for the years 1969–70 to 1971–72 on the basis that the taxpayer's share of the partnership profits was in reality the profits of his trade, business or vocation. The taxpayer appealed to the General Commissioners who held that during the relevant period a genuine partnership had existed between the taxpayer and the

company with the taxpayer providing the profit-earning contribution and the company
providing administrative and secretarial services and financial and fiscal advice, that the   *a*
taxpayer's activities outside the United Kingdom had been performed under the
partnership and all of its activities had taken place outside the United Kingdom, that
therefore the income in question had arisen from 'possessions out of the United
Kingdom', within s 109(2)*ᵈ* of the Income and Corporation Taxes Act 1970, and was
chargeable under Case V of Sch D, but that as the income had been derived from the
carrying on by the taxpayer of his profession in partnership, within s 122(2)(*b*)*ᵇ* of the   *b*
1970 Act, he was chargeable to tax in respect of the income, under s 122(3)(*b*) of the Act,
only to the extent to which it had been received by him in the United Kingdom. On
appeal by the Crown, the judge*ᶜ* and the Court of Appeal*ᵈ* upheld the commissioners'
decision. The Crown appealed to the House of Lords contending, inter alia, (i) that the
commissioners' finding that during the relevant years there was a partnership between
the taxpayer and the company in respect of the taxpayer's activities was erroneous in law   *c*
because the company, being a limited company, could not perform those activities, and
acts done by one partner which another partner could not perform could not be regarded
as acts done for the partnership, and that accordingly that the income in question was not
income derived from the partnership business and was therefore not income arising
from 'possessions out of the United Kingdom' within s 109(2) of the 1970 Act, (ii) that
the arrangement between the taxpayer and the company was not a valid partnership   *d*
since they carried on business in common to avoid tax and not with 'a view of profit' as
required by the definition of a partnership in s 1 of the Partnership Act 1890, and (iii)
that the company had no power under the objects of the agreement in cl 3 of its
memorandum of association to carry on the business of the partnership because the
words 'other operations' in cl 3 was to be construed ejusdem generis with the words
'financial commercial trading' and the carrying on of the partnership business was not   *e*
such an activity and therefore there was no partnership between the taxpayer and the
company.

Held – The appeal would be dismissed for the following reasons—
    (i) Although the object of the partnership was to avoid tax, before it could achieve that
object it had to make profits and it therefore came within the definition of a partnership   *f*
contained in s 1 of the 1890 Act (see p 366 *e*, p 368 *j* to p 369 *a* and p 370 *c* to *e*, post).
    (ii) The partnership agreement between the taxpayer and the company was not invalid
on the ground that the company could not perform the objects of the partnership,
because the purpose of the agreement was not for both parties to be television entertainers
and authors but merely to exploit and procure engagements for such performers. Nor
was the agreement invalid on the ground that the taxpayer was to be one of those   *g*

---

a   Section 109, so far as material, provides:
      '(1) Tax under Schedule D shall be charged under the Cases set out in subsection (2) below . . .
      '(2) The Cases are . . . Case V—tax in respect of income arising from possessions out of the
    United Kingdom . . .'
b   Section 122, so far as material, provides:
      '(1) Subject to the provisions of this section and sections 123 and 124 below, income tax   *h*
chargeable under . . . Case V of Schedule D shall be computed on the full amount of the income
arising in the year preceding the year of assessment, whether the income has been or will be
received in the United Kingdom or not . . .
      '(2) Subsection (1) above shall not apply . . . (*b*) to any income which is immediately derived by
a person from the carrying on by him of any trade, profession or vocation, either solely or in
partnership . . .
      '(3) In the cases mentioned in subsection (2) above, the tax shall . . . be computed . . . (*b*) in the   *j*
case of tax chargeable under Case V, on the full amount of the actual sums received in the United
Kingdom in the year preceding the year of assessment from remittances payable in the United
Kingdom . . .'
c   [1978] 2 All ER 241, [1978] STC 239
d   [1979] 2 All ER 129, [1979] STC 45

performers and therefore could not enter into a valid partnership to exploit his own
a skills, since the taxpayer was no different in that respect from any other artiste or
performer exploited by the partnership (see p 366 *e*, p 368 *f g* and p 370 *c* to *e*, post).

(iii) It was within the power of the company to enter into the partnership agreement
since the business of the partnership was a form of financial operation, or, if not, it came
within 'all kinds of . . . other operations' and was thus intra vires cl 3 of the company's
articles of association (see p 366 *e* and p 370 *a* and *c* to *e*, post).

b (iv) It followed therefore that since the partnership between the taxpayer and the
company was a valid partnership and not a sham the activities of the taxpayer were
partnership activities, with the consequence that the taxpayer's income therefrom, being
income from the partnership, was income arising from overseas possessions for the
purposes of s 109(2) of the 1970 Act, and by virtue of s 122 thereof the taxpayer was not
liable to United Kingdom income tax for the years in question on his earnings in the
c United States not remitted to the United Kingdom (see p 366 *e*, p 368 *h* and p 370 *b* to *e*,
post).

Decision of the Court of Appeal [1979] 2 All ER 129 affirmed.

Notes

For tax in respect of income arising from possessions out of the United Kingdom, see 23
d Halsbury's Laws (4th Edn) paras 611–618, and for cases in the subject, see 28(1) Digest
(Reissue) 301–311, *1031–1082*.

For the existence of a partnership, see 23 Halsbury's Laws (4th Edn) para 1348, and for
cases on the subject, see 28(1) Digest (Reissue) 232, 234, 566, *710, 712, 723, 2084*.

For the tax liability of a partner resident in the United Kingdom of a partnership
controlled abroad, see 23 Halsbury's Laws (4th Edn) para 849, and for a case on the
e subject, see 28(1) Digest (Reissue) 301, *1031*.

For the Income and Corporation Taxes Act 1970, ss 109, 122, see 33 Halsbury's Statutes
(3rd Edn) 154, 173.

For the Partnership Act 1890, s 1, see 24 ibid 501.

Case referred to in opinions

f De Beers Consolidated Mines Ltd v Howe (Surveyor of Taxes) [1906] AC 455, 5 Tax Cas 198,
15 LJKB 858, 95 LT 221, 13 Mans 394, HL, 28(1) Digest (Reissue) 366, *1339*.

Cases also cited

Bishop (Inspector of Taxes) v Finsbury Securities Ltd [1966] 3 All ER 105, 43 Tax Cas 591,
HL.
g Brighton College v Marriott (Inspector of Taxes) [1926] AC 192, [1925] All ER Rep 600,
10 Tax Cas 213, HL.
Bullen v Sharp (1865) LR 1 CP 86.
Carson (Inspector of Taxes) v Peter Cheyney's Executor [1958] 3 All ER 573, [1959] AC 412,
38 Tax Cas 240, HL.
Christophers v White (1847) 10 Beav 523, 50 ER 683.
h Collins v Carey (1839) 2 Beav 128, 48 ER 1128.
Colquhoun v Brooks (1889) 14 App Cas 493, [1886–90] All ER Rep 1063, 2 Tax Cas 490,
HL.
Cox v Hickman (1860) 8 HL Cas 267, 11 ER 431, HL.
Davis (Inspector of Taxes) v Braithwaite [1931] 2 KB 628, 18 Tax Cas 198.
Esplen (William), Son and Swainston Ltd v Inland Revenue Comrs [1919] 2 KB 731.
j FA & AB Ltd v Lupton (Inspector of Taxes) [1971] 3 All ER 948 [1972] AC 634, 47 Tax Cas
580, HL.
Hall (George) & Son v Platt (1954) 35 Tax Cas 440.
Holme v Hammond (1872) LR 7 Exch 218.
Inland Revenue Comrs v Maxse [1919] 1 KB 647, 12 Tax Cas 41, CA.
Poulton v London and South Western Railway Co (1867) LR 2 QB 534.

Rolloswin Investments Ltd v Chromolit Portugal Cutelarias e Produtos Metálicos SARL [1970]
2 All ER 673, [1970] 1 WLR 912.   *a*
San Paulo (Brazilian) Railway Co Ltd v Carter (Surveyor of Taxes) [1896] AC 31, HL.

Appeal

This was an appeal by the Crown against a decision of the Court of Appeal[1] (Buckley,
Roskill and Goff LJJ) dated 30th June 1978 dismissing an appeal by the Crown against a
decision of Browne-Wilkinson J[2] dated 28th November 1977 whereby on a case stated [3] *b*
by the Commissioners for the General Purposes of the Income Tax he dismissed an
appeal by the Crown against a decision of the General Commissioners dated 19th March
1975 allowing an appeal by the taxpayer, David Paradine Frost, against assessments to tax
under Case II of Sch D of the Income Tax and Corporation Taxes Act 1970 on profits
derived from his activities as an entertainer and author in the United States of America
for the years of assessment 1969 to 1972 inclusive. The facts are set out in the opinion *c*
of Viscount Dilhorne.

Conrad Dehn QC, J E Holroyd-Pearce QC and *A G Wilson* for the Crown.
D C Potter QC, Andrew Park QC and *R Mathew* for the taxpayer.

Their Lordships took time for consideration.   *d*

31st January. The following opinions were delivered.

LORD DIPLOCK. My Lords, I have had the advantage of reading in draft the speech
prepared by my noble and learned friend Viscount Dilhorne and I agree with it. For the
reasons given by him I would dismiss this appeal.   *e*

VISCOUNT DILHORNE. My Lords, the taxpayer, who had by 1966 established
himself as a very successful entertainer on television in this country, in that year
considered using his talents overseas and, in particular, in the United States. He wished
to continue to reside in the United Kingdom and to avoid or reduce his liability to United
Kingdom income tax on his earnings abroad. Under Sch D, Case II tax is chargeable on *f*
the annual profits or gains arising or accruing to a person residing in the United
Kingdom from a profession, whether carried on in the United Kingdom or elsewhere.
   With this object in view his solicitors sent to the Trust Corpn of Bahamas Ltd a draft
of a partnership agreement to be entered into between the taxpayer and a Bahamian
company. On 8th February 1967 the Pembina Investment Co Ltd, a 'shell' company
held by the trust corporation, changed its name to Leander Productions Ltd and on 17th *g*
February an 'Indenture of Partnership' was entered into between the taxpayer and
Leander Productions Ltd. The business of the partnership was to be carried on under the
name Leander Enterprises and the agreement provided that 99% of the capital assets of
the partnership should belong to the taxpayer and 1% to the company; and that the
taxpayer should be entitled to 95% of the annual profits of the partnership and the
company to 5%.   *h*
   The source of all the income of the partnership was the taxpayer's activities in the
United States. In March 1969 Leander Enterprises entered into a contract with
Hellespont NV, a company situate in Curacao, under which that company acquired the
sole and exclusive benefit of the exploitation of the assets of Leander Enterprises. The
Hellespont company was owned by Tamarisk Investments Ltd, a Bahamian company.
After this date moneys earned by the taxpayer's activities were channelled through the *j*
Hellespont company and through the Tamarisk company to the partnership which

---

1   [1979] 2 All ER 129, [1978] 1 WLR 1441, [1979] STC 45
2   [1978] 2 All ER 241, [1978] 1 WLR 511, [1978] STC 239
3   The case stated is set out at [1978] 2 All ER 244–248

received substantially the whole benefit of the moneys earned by the taxpayer. These
two companies were created on the advice of the trust corporation and the taxpayer's
earnings were paid to these companies with view to avoiding United States tax.

The taxpayer was assessed to income tax under Case II for the year 1969–70 in the sum
of £30,000, for the year 1970–71 in the sum of £29,256 and for the year 1971–72 in the
sum of £115,398, each assessment being made on the basis that his earnings in the
United States in those years were liable to tax under Case II.

It is convenient to refer to the provisions of the Income and Corporation Taxes Act
1970 rather than to the relevant provisions of the earlier Acts which were replaced by
that Act.

Section 153(1) of the Act reads as follows:

> 'Where any trade or business is carried on by two or more persons in partnership,
> and the control and management of the trade or business is situated abroad, the
> trade or business shall be deemed to be carried on by persons resident outside the
> United Kingdom, and the partnership shall be deemed to reside outside the United
> Kingdom, notwithstanding the fact that some of the members of the partnership
> are resident in the United Kingdom and that some of its trading operations are
> conducted within the United Kingdom.'

The taxpayer claims that as the control and management of the business of the
partnership was situated abroad (that was a term of the partnership agreement) its
business is to be deemed to have been carried on by persons resident outside the United
Kingdom with the consequence that his profits from his activities are not to be regarded
as having accrued to a person residing in the United Kingdom and so are not assessable
under Case II.

Further it is contended on his behalf that Case V of Sch D is the case applicable. Under
that case tax is to be charged 'in respect of income arising from possessions out of the
United Kingdom, not being income consisting of emoluments of any office or
employment'.

Section 122 of the 1970 Act provides by sub-s (1) that the income tax chargeable under
Case V is to be computed on the income arising in the year preceding the year of
assessment 'whether the income has been or will be received in the United Kingdom or
not'. Subsection (2) states that sub-s (1) is not to apply to 'any income which is
immediately derived by a person from the carrying on by him of any trade, profession
or vocation, either solely or in partnership'. In the case of such income sub-s (3) provides
that tax shall be charged only on the full amount of the actual sums received in the
United Kingdom in the year preceding the year of assessment from remittances payable
in the United Kingdom.

The taxpayer contended that as no part of his earnings in the United States were
remitted to the United Kingdom in the years in respect of which he was assessed to tax
on his earnings in the United States he should not have been assessed to tax in any sum
in respect thereof.

The Crown did not contend that the taxpayer's income from the carrying on of his
profession in the United States was not immediately derived by him from carrying on of
his profession, either solely or in partnership, though the payments for his activities were
received first by the Hellespont company and then from that company by the Tamarisk
company and then from that company by the partnership. So for the purposes of this
appeal, one must assume that s 122(2) applies.

The Crown challenged the conclusions of the commissioners, which were upheld by
Browne-Wilkinson J[1] and by the Court of Appeal[2] (Buckley, Roskill and Goff LJJ), on a
number of grounds.

Their main contention was that the commissioners' findings that during the relevant

---

1   [1978] 2 All ER 241, [1978] 1 WLR 511, [1978] STC 239
2   [1979] 2 All ER 129, [1978] 1 WLR 1441, [1979] STC 45

years there was a partnership between the taxpayer and the company was erroneous in law. It was said acts done by one partner which another partner could not perform could not be regarded as acts done for the partnership. Reliance was placed on the following passage in Lindley on Partnership[1]:

'Speaking generally, no person can do by his agent what he cannot do himself; and although each member of a firm is a principal as regards his own conduct, he is the agent of his co-partners; and he cannot therefore do for the firm what they cannot do. In other words, the disability of one of the partners affects the whole firm, so that the legal capacity of the firm is no greater than that of the partner with the least legal capacity.'

As Lord Loreburn LC said in De Beers Consolidated Mines Ltd v Howe (Surveyor of Taxes)[2]: 'A company cannot eat or sleep.' Neither can it be a television entertainer or author and so it was said that there could not be in law a partnership between the taxpayer and the company which covered their appearances as television entertainers or their being authors. But the partnership agreement was not an agreement between them that they should entertain on television or write books. Clause 1 of the agreement as amended provided that they should become and remain partners—

'in the business of exploiting copyrights and interests in copyrights and in the business of television and film consultants and advisers publicity agents and providers of publicity services and facilities and in the business of producing television programmes, films, stageplays and other entertainment and using and exploiting the services of producers, actors, directors, writers and artistes, and material and facilities which may be used for the production of television programmes, films, stageplays and other entertainments, and in the business of television, films and stage advisers and agents throughout the world outside the United Kingdom . . .'

Under this clause the partnership could procure engagements for artistes and enter into contracts undertaking that they would appear and perform, but it was said on behalf of the Crown that a man cannot exploit his own skills and that he consequently cannot enter into a valid partnership agreement to exploit his own skills. There is a difference, it was said, between A exploiting his own skills and A exploiting the skills of others. While recognising that there is a difference between the persons whose skills are to be exploited, I am in agreement with Buckley LJ in being unable to see any reason why the taxpayer and the company could not agree to join in exploiting the taxpayer's skills. Just as they could procure engagements for other artistes and contract that they would appear and perform, so could they procure engagements for the taxpayer and undertake that he would appear to fulfil them. I see nothing to prevent such an agreement being made and I cannot construe this clause as only covering the exploitation of the activities of artistes other then the taxpayer.

I cannot regard the partnership agreement as invalid either on the ground that the taxpayer bound himself to do what the company could not do or on the ground that under it he undertook to do what he could not do, and so I conclude that the receipts from his activities were receipts of the partnership.

The commissioners, after referring to the definition of a partnership in s 1 of the Partnership Act 1890, held that during the relevant years there was a partnership between the taxpayer and the company[3]. This conclusion can only mean that they were satisfied that the taxpayer and the company were carrying on business in common with a view of profit. The Crown challenged this conclusion, contending that the business carried on in common was with a view to avoiding tax. While it is clear that the partnership was formed with that object, it must also have been formed with a view of

1   13th Edn (1971) p 44
2   [1906] AC 455 at 158, 5 Tax Cas 198 at 212
3   [1978] 2 All ER 241 at 248, [1978] STC 239 at 246

profit. It was intended that profits should be made, for if they were not made as a result
a of the taxpayer's activities there would have been no tax to be avoided. I therefore reject
this contention.

Before Browne-Wilkinson J[1] but not before the commissioners, the Crown contended
that it was not within the power of the company to enter into the partnership
agreement. Whether this was so depends on the objects of the company as stated in its
memorandum of association. Clause 3 of that memorandum sets out the objects of the
b company and cl 3(6) reads as follows:

> 'To carry on business as bankers, capitalists, financiers, concessionaires and
> merchants and to undertake and carry on and execute all kinds of financial
> commercial trading or other operations and generally to undertake and carry out all
> such obligations and transactions as an individual capitalist may lawfully undertake
> and carry out.'
c
The paragraph ends with the following statement:

> 'And it is hereby declared that the objects of the company as specified in each of
> the foregoing paragraphs of this clause . . . shall be separate and distinct objects of
> the Company and shall not be in anywise limited by reference to any other
> paragraph or the order in which the same occur or the name of the Company.'
d
That name was, as I have said, when the company was formed the Pembina Investment
Co Ltd, and while no doubt the objects are entirely suitable for an investment company,
it was submitted for the Crown that they were not wide enough to empower the
company to carry on the business of the partnership. This contention, which did not
appear to be the one on which most reliance was placed, perhaps because it had not been
e advanced before the commissioners, is to my mind the most formidable of those put
forward on behalf of the Crown. Whether or not it is well founded depends on the
construction to be placed on cl 3(6) of the memorandum. It was submitted that the
words 'other operations' should be construed ejusdem generis with 'financial commercial
trading'. The difficulty I feel about accepting this argument is that I am unable to find
genus in the clause. Carrying on the partnership business was not carrying on the
f business of bankers or of capitalists, financiers, concessionaires or merchants nor was it an
activity which one would normally associate with the activities of an individual
capitalist. So whether or not the carrying on of the partnership business was ultra vires
the company appears to depend on the meaning to be given to the words 'all kinds of
financial commercial trading or other operations'.

Reading cl 3(6) as a whole, it gives me the impression that it was intended to cover
g every kind of activity that an investment company might want to carry on and that the
words 'other operations' were inserted ex abundanti cautela to cover any kind of such
activity if any, not covered by the words 'financial commercial trading'. Noscitur a
sociis.

In one sense the business of the partnership was financial. The clause covered all kinds
of financial operations. 'Commercial' has a very wide meaning. It is not infrequently
h contrasted with 'industrial'. I doubt if the business of the partnership, which included
the exploitation of the talents of artistes, is properly to be described as a commercial
operation, but if it is not a financial or commercial operation it certainly is covered by the
words 'all kinds of . . . other operations'. It is true that if they are given an unlimited
meaning, it is hard to see the purpose of the other words in cl 3(6) or indeed the object
of including the other paragraphs of cl 3 for a statement that the object of the company
j was to carry on and execute all kinds of operations would cover all the other stated
objects.

This question has now been considered by four learned judges, all very experienced in
construing the memorandum and articles of association of companies, and they have

---

1   See, however, [1978] 2 All ER 241 at 247, [1978] STC 239 at 245

rejected the Crown's contention and have held that it was not ultra vires of the company to enter into the partnership agreement to carry on the business stated in that *a* agreement. Having read and studied their judgments carefully, I am not prepared to dissent from their conclusion, for with some hesitation I think that the business of the partnership can be regarded as a kind of financial operation, and, if not, as covered by the words 'all kinds of . . . other operations'.

It follows that in my opinion the taxpayer by entering into the partnership agreement, which the Crown did not allege was a sham, with a 'shell' Bahamian company of which *b* the directors were repeatedly changed and were nominated by the trust corporation to give them training and experience and which provided only 'financial, administrative, secretarial and fiscal services and an advisory contribution', the taxpayer providing the 'profit earning contribution' with the taxpayer being entitled to 95% of the profits and 99% of the assets of the partnership, is not liable to be taxed under Case II and has successfully avoided liability to the United Kingdom income tax on his earnings in the *c* year in question in the United States.

In my opinion this appeal should be dismissed with costs.

LORD SALMON. My Lords, for the reasons set out in the speech of my noble and learned friend Viscount Dilhorne, with which I agree, I also would dismiss this appeal.

LORD FRASER OF TULLYBELTON. My Lords, I have had the advantage of *d* reading in draft the speech prepared by my noble and learned friend Viscount Dilhorne and I agree with it. For the reasons given by him I would dismiss this appeal.

LORD KEITH OF KINKEL. My Lords, I also would dismiss this appeal for the reasons set out in the speech of my noble and learned friend Viscount Dilhorne, with *e* which I agree entirely.

Appeal dismissed.

Solicitors: *Solicitor of Inland Revenue*; *Harbottle & Lewis* (for the taxpayer).

f

Mary Rose Plummer　Barrister.

Federated Homes Ltd v Mill Lodge Properties Ltd

COURT OF APPEAL, CIVIL DIVISION
MEGAW, BROWNE AND BRIGHTMAN LJJ
23rd, 26th, 27th, 28th, 29th NOVEMBER 1979

Restrictive covenant affecting land – Annexation of benefit – Annexation by statute – Covenant relating to or touching and concerning covenantee's land – Sufficient description of covenantee's land for purpose of annexation – Conveyance containing covenant not expressly or impliedly annexing benefit of covenant – Whether benefit of covenant annexed and running with covenantee's land under statute – Whether covenant annexed to land enuring only for benefit of land as a whole or for benefit of every part of it – Law of Property Act 1925, s 78(1).

In 1970 M Ltd, the owner of a site which included three areas of land, the red, green and blue land, obtained outline planning permission to develop the site by erecting a certain number of dwellings. The permission was valid for three years. In February 1971 M Ltd as vendor conveyed the blue land to the defendants. By a restrictive covenant in cl 5(iv) of the conveyance the defendants covenanted with the vendor that in carrying out the development of the blue land they would not build 'at a greater density than a total of 300 dwellings so as not to reduce the number of units which the vendor might eventually erect on the retained land under the existing planning consent'. The 'retained land' was described as 'any adjoining or adjacent property' retained by M Ltd and therefore meant the red and green land, together with some additional land. By a series of transfers the plaintiffs became the owners of the red and the green land. In the case of the green land the transfers contained an unbroken chain of express assignments of the benefit of the restrictive covenant. However, in the case of the red land, the transfer to the plaintiffs did not contain any express assignment of the benefit of the covenant and the chain of assignments of the benefit of the covenant was broken. In 1977 the plaintiffs obtained planning permission to develop the red and green land. They then discovered that the defendants had obtained permission to develop the blue land at a higher density than permitted by the restrictive covenant, and that that density was likely to prejudice development of the red and green land. The plaintiffs accordingly brought an action to restrain the defendants from building on the blue land at a density which would be in breach of the restrictive covenant. By their defence the defendants contended, inter alia, that, if the restrictive covenant was capable of assignment and was not spent on the lapse of the 1970 planning permission, the benefit of the covenant had not been transmitted to the plaintiffs. The judge held that the covenant was capable of assignment and was not spent, but that the benefit of it had not been annexed to the retained land because the conveyance to the defendants had not expressly or impliedly annexed it and because s 78[a] of the Law of Property Act 1925 did not have the effect of annexing the benefit of the covenant to the retained land. However, he held that in the case of the green land, the unbroken chain of assignments of the benefit of the covenant vested the benefit of it in the plaintiffs as the owner of the green land, and that under s 62 of the 1925 Act, which implies general words into a conveyance of land, the benefit of the covenant was carried to the plaintiffs as the owners of the red land. The judge granted the plaintiffs an injunction restraining breach of the covenant by the defendants. The defendants appealed. On the appeal, the court having concluded that the restrictive covenant was capable of assignment and was not spent, the question arose whether the benefit of it had been transmitted to the plaintiffs as the owner of the red land.

---

a   Section 78 is set out at p 378 *h j*, post

Held – Where there was a restrictive covenant which related to or touched and concerned the covenantee's land, s 78(1) of the 1925 Act had the effect of annexing the *a* benefit of the covenant to the covenantee's land, and did not merely provide a statutory shorthand for shortening a conveyance. The language of s 78(1) implied that such a restrictive covenant was enforceable at the suit of (i) the covenantee and his successors in title, (ii) a person deriving title under him or them and (iii) the owner or occupier of the benefited land, and, therefore, under s 78(1) such a covenant ran with the covenantee's land and was annexed to it. Since cl 5(iv) of the conveyance to the defendants showed *b* that the restrictive covenant was for the benefit of the retained land and that land was sufficiently described in the conveyance for the purposes of annexation, the covenant related to, or touched and concerned, the land of the covenantee (M Ltd) and s 78(1) had the effect of annexing the benefit of the covenant to the retained land for the benefit of M Ltd, its successors in title and the persons deriving title under it or them including the owners for the time being of the retained land. Furthermore, if on the proper *c* construction of a document a restrictive covenant was annexed to land, prima facie it was annexed to every part of the land. It followed that s 78(1) had caused the benefit of the restrictive covenant to run with the red land and be annexed to it, and that the plaintiffs, both as the owners of the red land and as the owners of the green land, were entitled to enforce the covenant against the defendants. The appeal would therefore be dismissed (see p 378 *h*, p 379 *b* to *d* and *g h*, p 381 *b c* and *f* to *j* and p 382 *a b* and *d*, post).   *d*

Shelfer v City of London Electric Lighting Co [1891–4] All ER Rep 838 and *Smith v River Douglas Catchment Board* [1949] 2 All ER 179 applied.

Dictum of Romer LJ in *Drake v Gray* [1936] 1 All ER at 376 considered.

Notes

For annexation of covenants to retained land, see 16 Halsbury's Laws (4th Edn) para 1353, and for cases on the subject of burden and benefit of covenants, see 40 Digest (Repl) *e* 339–343, 2764–2783.

For the Law of Property Act 1925, ss 62, 78, see 27 Halsbury's Statutes (3rd Edn) 438, 462.

Cases referred to in judgments

Drake v Gray [1936] 1 All ER 363, [1936] Ch 451, 105 LJ Ch 233, 155 LT 145, CA, 40 *f* Digest (Repl) 341, 2771.

Rogers v Hosegood [1900] 2 Ch 388 [1900–3] All ER Rep 915, 69 LJ Ch 652, 83 LT 186, CA, 40 Digest (Repl) 340, 2769.

Russell v Archdale [1962] 2 All ER 305, [1964] Ch 38, [1962] 3 WLR 192, 14 P & CR 24, Digest (Cont Vol A) 1315, 2783a.

Shelfer v City of London Electric Lighting Co, Meux's Brewery Co v City of London Electric *g* *Lighting Co* [1895] 1 Ch 287, [1891–4] All ER Rep 838, 64 LJ Ch 216, 72 LT 34, CA, 28(2) Digest (Reissue) 1017, 435.

Smith v River Douglas Catchment Board [1949] 2 All ER 179, 113 JP 388, 47 LGR 627, sub nom *Smith and Snipes Hall Farm Ltd v River Douglas Catchment Board* [1949] 2 KB 500, CA, 41 Digest (Repl) 58, 371.

Tophams Ltd v Earl of Sefton [1966] 1 All ER 1039, [1967] 1 AC 50, [1966] 2 WLR 814, *h* HL, Digest (Cont Vol B) 643, 2885b.

Union of London and Smith's Bank Ltd's Conveyance, Re, Miles v Easter [1933] Ch 611, [1933] All ER Rep 355, 162 LJ Ch 241, 149 LT 82, CA, 40 Digest (Repl) 329, 2702.

Williams v Unit Construction Co Ltd (1951) 19 Conv NS 262, CA.

Cases also cited   *j*

Doherty v Allman (1878) 3 App Cas 709, HL.

Ecclesiastic Comrs for England's Conveyance, Re [1936] Ch 430, [1934] All ER Rep 118.

Johnson v Agnew [1979] 1 All ER 883, [1979] 2 WLR 487, HL.

Kelly v Barrett [1924] 2 Ch 379, [1924] All ER Rep 503, CA.

Marten v Flight Refuelling Ltd [1961] 2 All ER 696, [1962] Ch 115.

Prenn v Simmonds [1971] 3 All ER 237, [1971] 1 WLR 1381, HL.

a   *Reardon Smith Line Ltd v Hansen-Tangen, Hansen-Tangen v Sanko Steamship Co* [1976] 3 All ER 570, [1976] 1 WLR 989, HL.

Shayler v Woolf [1946] 2 All ER 54, [1946] Ch 320, CA.

Suisse Atlantique Société D'Armement Maritime SA v N V Rotterdamsche Kolen Centrale [1966] 2 All ER 61, [1967] 1 AC 361, HL.

b **Appeal**

This was an appeal by the defendants, Mill Lodge Properties Ltd, against so much of the judgment of Mr John Mills QC, sitting as a deputy judge of the High Court in the Chancery Division, given on 29th June 1979, as held that a restrictive covenant in a conveyance dated 26th February 1971, conveying part of a development site ('the blue land') to the defendants, which restricted the density of development of the blue land to

c   300 dwellings so as not to adversely affect the retained land, related to the covenantee's land and enured for the benefit of the covenantee's successors in title; that the plaintiffs, Federated Homes Ltd, who had purchased the retained land, were entitled in equity to the benefit of the covenant and were, therefore, entitled to enforce it against the defendants and that an injunction should be granted to restrain the defendants, whether by themselves, their directors, servants or agents or otherwise, from building on the blue

d   land in breach of the covenant. The facts are set out in the judgment of Brightman LJ.

Leolin Price QC and *Martin Mann* for the defendants.
M A F Lyndon-Standford QC and *R G B McComber* for the plaintiffs.

e   **BRIGHTMAN LJ** delivered the first judgment at the invitation of Megaw LJ. This is an appeal from a judgment of Mr Mills QC, sitting as a deputy judge of the High Court in the Chancery Division. The dispute relates to a large development site near Newport Pagnell in Buckinghamshire. This site consists of four areas of land of roughly equal size which can, for convenience, be called the red, green, pink and blue land. There were also included in the development site certain additional bits of land which I shall ignore.

f   The plaintiff company is now the owner of the red and the green land. The defendant company, Mill Lodge Properties Ltd (which I shall call 'Mill Lodge'), is the owner of the blue land. The plaintiff company claims to be entitled to the benefit of a restrictive covenant which is said to debar Mill Lodge from building more than 300 houses on the blue land. Mill Lodge is in the process of exceeding that density by building an additional 32 houses in conformity with a new planning permission which it has

g   obtained. The judge decided against Mill Lodge and granted an injunction.

In September 1970 a company called Mackenzie Hill Ltd (which I shall refer to as 'Mackenzie Hill') was about to become the owner of the site. On 18th September the Buckinghamshire County Council, as planning authority acting through the Newport Pagnell Urban District Council as its agent, granted outline planning permission to Mackenzie Hill to develop the site by the provision of housing and associated amenities.

h   There were a number of conditions attached to the permission, of which the important ones were these:

> '1. The approval of the County Council shall be obtained to the number, siting, design and external appearance of the buildings (except the schools), and the means of access thereto before the development is commenced . . .

j   > '2. This permission shall be null and void if the approval of the County Council to all the matters referred to in the last preceding condition has not been applied for in writing within three years [i e by September 1973].

> '4. This permission shall enure only for the benefit of the applicants and their subsidiaries.

> '5. This permission shall relate to the erection of a Church/community centre, a

shopping cluster, a petrol filling station, a public house, and approximately 1,250 private residential dwellings . . .'

Condition 8 specified the rate of development, but this topic was covered in a revised form by the agreement to which I shall next refer.

On the same day as the planning permission Mackenzie Hill entered into an agreement with the urban district council, which has been called the phasing agreement. By this agreement the council undertook to construct roads and sewers through the site and Mackenzie Hill agreed to contribute towards the cost. Clause 7, so far as material, reads as follows (in the clause the expression 'Developers' means Mackenzie Hill and 'H.1' means the development site):

'(a) If the Developers shall desire to sell the whole or any part of H.1, they shall forthwith inform the Council and the terms and conditions of such sale or sales shall include the disclosure of this Agreement to the purchasers and provisions to safeguard the Council's position under this Agreement which shall be to the satisfaction of the Council . . . PROVIDED that this sub-clause shall not apply to the sale of any single completed dwelling to an individual purchaser.

'(b) The Developers shall have the right to assign the burden and benefit of this Agreement but shall not be released from their obligations hereunder on any such assignment unless the proposed assignees shall have first furnished the Council with a Bond . . .'

By cl 9(a) Mackenzie Hill agreed that the rate of development should not exceed 50 houses by the end of 1970 and a further 125 houses in each of the years 1971 and 1972. The rate of development was then to be reviewed with the possibility of an increase, but not a decrease, in the rate. On that basis the development would be completed in or before the year 1980 according to whether or not the rate of development ultimately exceeded a minimum of 125 houses a year. That rate of development differed slightly from the rate laid down in the planning permission and that, no doubt, was the reason for cl 9(e) of the phasing agreement, whereunder Mackenzie Hill covenanted with the council that they would enter into an agreement under seal with the council on or before 14th December 1970 incorporating the terms of cl 9(a).

It seems to me, reading cll 7 and 9(e), that the urban district council contemplated that Mackenzie Hill might not itself develop, but might part with the development in favour of someone else. Furthermore, as it was the urban district council which had, on the same day as the phasing agreement, in its capacity as agent for the Buckinghamshire County Council, granted the planning permission to Mackenzie Hill, the planning permission ought fairly to be read in conjunction with the phasing agreement.

On 26th February 1971 Mackenzie Hill and its mortgagee sold and conveyed the blue land to Mill Lodge. By cl 3 the conveyance was expressed to be subject to and with the benefit of the phasing agreement. Clause 5(iv) set out the covenant which is the subject-matter of this action. It reads as follows:

'The Purchaser hereby covenants with the Vendor that . . . (iv) in carrying out the development of the "blue" land the Purchaser shall not build at a greater density than a total of 300 dwellings so as not to reduce the number of units which the Vendor might eventually erect on the retained land under the existing Planning Consent.'

There was a simultaneous conveyance of the pink land to a company called Gough Cooper (Midland) Ltd (which I shall abbreviate to 'Gough Cooper'). Clause 6 of the Mill Lodge conveyance provided that the blue land was sold with the benefit, so far as the same related to the blue land, of the agreements and undertakings on the part of Gough Cooper contained in the Gough Cooper conveyance. Clause 7 of the Mill Lodge conveyance contained a covenant by Mackenzie Hill with Mill Lodge expressed to be for the benefit of the blue land and every part thereof that Mackenzie Hill would not build houses on the red and the green land, with an immaterial exception, before the date on a   which Mill Lodge had erected or had permission from the planning authority under any revised phasing agreement to erect 300 dwellings on the blue land or 1st January 1975, whichever should happen first, but not in any event earlier than 1st January 1974.

The Mill Lodge conveyance contains no express definition of the retained land. There is, however, a reference in cl 2 to 'any adjoining or adjacent property retained by the Vendor'. I read 'the retained land' in cl 5(iv) as meaning just that. I do not accept the submission of the plaintiff's counsel that the retained land included the pink land; cl 6
b   makes it clear that the pink land was not retained, but was being simultaneously conveyed to Gough Cooper. Counsel invited us to look at the contract of sale at Mill Lodge for the purpose of resolving an ambiguity as to the meaning of the retained land, but I see no ambiguity. I, therefore, conclude that the retained land means the red and the green land and the small additional areas comprised in the site, other, of course, than the blue and the pink land. To avoid confusion, I think I ought to explain that the expression 'the green land' is made use of in the Mill Lodge conveyance, but it means
c   both the red and the green land as I use those expressions in this judgment.

The Gough Cooper conveyance is not, in my view, relevant to the construction of the Mill Lodge conveyance, but it is permissible to refer to it as part of the backcloth against which the Mill Lodge conveyance was made, since the Gough Cooper conveyance is referred to in the Mill Lodge conveyance as a document of simultaneous execution.
d   Clause 4 of this conveyance was obviously intended to cover the same subject-matter as cl 5(iv) of the Mill Lodge conveyance and was in the following terms:

> 'The Purchaser for itself and its successors in title hereby covenants with the Vendor and its successors in title that the Purchaser shall not build on the land hereby conveyed at a greater density than a total of Three Hundred dwellings so as not to reduce the number of units which the Vendor might eventually erect on the
e   > land edged green on the said plan under the existing Planning Consent obtained by the Vendor in respect of the whole of the land edged red edged blue and edged green on the said plan.'

Clause 6 of the Gough Cooper conveyance is the counterpart of and has much the same wording as cl 7 of the Mill Lodge conveyance, in effect binding Mackenzie Hill to give
f   precedence to the purchaser's building programme in the operation of the phasing agreement.

A month later Mackenzie Hill sold and conveyed the red and the green land to William Brandt's Sons & Co Ltd (which I shall call 'Brandt's'). Brandt's was in fact Mackenzie Hill's mortgagee of the blue and the pink land at the time of the earlier conveyance, but nothing turns on that. The conveyance to Brandt's was dated 25th March 1971 and it contained an express assignment of the benefit of the covenant
g   contained in the Mill Lodge and the Gough Cooper conveyance.

Just under a year later Brandt's sold and conveyed the green land to the plaintiffs. This conveyance, which was dated 25th February 1972, likewise contained an express assignment of the benefit of those covenants.

Shortly afterwards Brandt's and the plaintiff company conveyed the red land to BTA
h   Trading Co Ltd. In that conveyance the plaintiff was the purchaser and BTA was the sub-purchaser. This conveyance, which is dated 1st March 1972, also contained an express assignment of the benefit of the covenants. Following that conveyance BTA's title became registered at the Land Registry.

On 18th March 1975 BTA, which by then had changed its name to UDT Properties Ltd, sold and conveyed the red land to the plaintiff company. This conveyance was in
j   the form of a transfer applicable to registered land. It did not contain any express assignment of the benefit of the covenants in the Mill Lodge and the Gough Cooper conveyances.

The original outline planning permission granted in 1970 lapsed in 1973 because approval of the county council to all the matters referred to in condition 1 had not been applied for in respect of the total site within three years. In fact, Mill Lodge proceeded

with the separate development of the blue land under new planning permissions granted
in 1971 and 1972 for a total of 300 dwellings.   *a*

Towards the end of 1977 the plaintiff company applied for planning permission in
respect of the red and the green land. The balance of density left available for these areas,
having regard to the Mill Lodge and Gough Cooper conveyances, was approximately 650
dwellings if the principle of the 1970 planning permission still applied. The application
was, in fact, for a much greater density, but after a planning inquiry the 1970 density of
about 1,250 dwellings for the entire site was reaffirmed. It was at about this time that   *b*
the plaintiff company discovered that, on 9th January 1975, Mill Lodge had obtained
planning permission for the erection of an additional 32 dwellings on the blue land. It
is not in dispute that the existence of such additional dwellings would or might prejudice
the plaintiff company in relation to the development that might be permitted on the red
and the green land; and, therefore, if the plaintiff company's rights would be infringed
by the building of the further 32 dwellings, the plaintiff company would suffer damage.   *c*

In September 1978, after much prevarication on the part of Mill Lodge, the plaintiff
company issued a writ to restrain Mill Lodge from building on the blue land at a greater
density than a total of 300 dwellings in breach, it was alleged, of cl 5(iv) of the Mill Lodge
conveyance. The defences raised by Mill Lodge so far as relied on in this appeal were as
follows: (1) the covenant in cl 5(iv) was said to be personal to Mackenzie Hill so that the
benefit thereof was incapable of assignment to the plaintiff company; (2) alternatively,   *d*
it was said that the covenant became spent when the 1970 planning permission became
void at the end of the three year period; (3) it was said that, if the covenant was assignable
and was not spent, then the benefit did not become vested in the plaintiff company by
assignment or otherwise.

That, in broad effect, was how the defence was pleaded so far as relevant for present
purposes. In a reserved judgment the learned deputy High Court judge held that the   *e*
covenant was not personal to Mackenzie Hill and was not spent when the original
planning permission lapsed. As regards the transmission of the benefit of the covenant,
he held that the benefit was not annexed to the red and the green land, so that it did not
automatically pass on conveyances of the red and the green land. However, he found, as
was clearly the fact, that there was an unbroken chain of assignments between transferor
and transferee of the green land, so that the benefit of the covenant was now vested, by   *f*
reason of such assignments, in the plaintiff company as the present owner of the green
land. There was no such unbroken chain of assignments in the case of the red land; but
the judge considered that s 62 of the Law of Property Act 1925, which implies general
words into a conveyance of land, was apt to carry the benefit of the covenant from UDT
Properties Ltd, the previous assignee of such benefit, to the plaintiff company when the
registered transfer in its favour was made. The defence, therefore, failed. The judge   *g*
rejected a submission that damages would be the proper remedy. He granted an
injunction against building in excess of the permitted density and gave liberty to apply
for a mandatory injunction.

I deal first with the question of construction, on which two issues arise: whether the
covenant was personal to Mackenzie Hill and whether it is spent.

Counsel for the defendants pointed out that the planning permission was expressed by   *h*
condition 4 to enure for the benefit of Mackenzie Hill and its subsidiaries. That meant
that a purchaser from Mackenzie Hill, not being a subsidiary company, had no legal
right as between itself and the Buckinghamshire County Council to rely on the planning
permission as authority to carry out development which would otherwise be contrary to
planning legislation. Possibly the condition was inserted to enable the planning
authority to object to development by somebody of whom it did not approve. Counsel   *j*
for the defendant sought to argue from this that the covenant in the Mill Lodge
conveyance was personal to Mackenzie Hill and not assignable. It was designed, he
submitted, to protect a non-assignable planning permission and therefore should itself be
treated as non-assignable.

I do not think that the defendants can gain much comfort from the form of the planning permission. The planning permission was certainly not exclusive to Mackenzie

a Hill because it was available to a subsidiary of Mackenzie Hill; so the benefit was clearly assignable to that extent. Theoretically, and not I think as a matter of reality, there was nothing in the planning permission to prevent the assignment of the benefit. The only restriction was that the proprietor who ultimately relied on the permission would have to be either Mackenzie Hill or a subsidiary. There could, in theory, be any number of intermediate transfers of the land, with the benefit of the permission, through persons

b who would not have been themselves qualified to rely on the permission. I think this is a narrow point and I do not stress it.

Counsel for the defendants also relied on the fact that cl 5 is penned as a covenant with the vendor (no mention of assigns) and that it is linked with the number of dwellings which the vendor (again no mention of assigns) might erect on the retained land.

But, apart from these considerations, I entirely agree with the learned deputy High

c Court judge when he said that it is neither necessary nor natural nor sensible to read the covenant as personal to Mackenzie Hill. Generally speaking, the benefit of a contract between businessmen is assignable without mention of assignability unless the contract is of a personal nature, which the restrictive covenant was not. Furthermore, cl 3 of the Mill Lodge conveyance stated that the property was sold subject to and with the benefit of the phasing agreement and, as I have already mentioned, cll 7 and 9(e) of that

d agreement in terms contemplated that Mackenzie Hill might sell the development site in whole or part. So it is hardly possible to argue that the parties *must* have contracted on the basis that Mackenzie Hill personally would develop the retained land. I conclude that the restrictive covenant was not personal, but was assignable, which seems to me to correspond with business realities.

If there were still any doubt, s 78 of the Law of Property Act 1925, in my view, sets

e that doubt at rest. For it provides that a covenant relating to any land of the covenantee shall be deemed to have been made with the covenantee and his successors in title, which presupposes assignability. I shall have occasion in due course to examine this section at greater length.

I turn to the defence that the covenant is now spent as the 1970 planning permission has lapsed. The concluding words of cl 5(iv) are: 'so as not to reduce the number of units

f which the vendor might ultimately erect on the retained land under the existing planning consent'. As no dwellings can now be erected in reliance on the original planning consent, the covenant has, it was argued, lost its purpose. This resolves itself into the question whether the concluding words form an integral part of the restrictive covenant or are merely explanatory of the covenant without controlling it. I think that the answer is largely a matter of impression and is not susceptible of prolonged

g argument. It does, however, seem to me a little unlikely that the parties intended to tie the restrictive covenant to the original planning permission so that the covenant and the permission should stand and fall together. There would seem no purpose in such rigidity. There must always have been a strong possibility, if not a likelihood, that a developer would have to apply for a new planning permission at some stage (as happened) because the three-years deadline for seeking planning approval for the siting, design and

h external appearance of the buildings and the means of access thereto does not fit easily into the ten-year phasing of the development.

There is the additional consideration that, if the covenant were linked to the 1970 planning permission, it is difficult to see its value. The 1970 planning permission was to become void if detailed approval were not applied for in relation to the entire site within three years. As Mackenzie Hill was selling off and therefore not developing the blue and

j the pink land, the 1970 planning permission seems to me to have had a very doubtful future. It could hardly have been anticipated that Mackenzie Hill would be applying for detailed approval for the development of land which was going to be developed by others. There was no covenant by Mill Lodge or Gough Cooper to apply for detailed approval within the three-year period; so the covenant, if linked to and dependent on the 1970 planning permission, becomes somewhat of a nonsense as counsel for the defendant was, I think, constrained to admit. I think that the more natural and businesslike construction of the sub-clause is to read the reference to the existing planning permission as explanatory and not as controlling.

Having reached the conclusion that the restrictive covenant was capable of assignment and is not spent, I turn to the question whether the benefit has safely reached the hands of the plaintiff company. The green land has no problem, owing to the unbroken chain of assignments. I am disposed to think that that is sufficient to entitle the plaintiff company to relief, and that the plaintiff company's right to relief would be no greater at the present time if it were held that it also had the benefit of the covenant in its capacity as owner of the red land. However, the judge dealt with both areas of land and I propose to do the same.

An express assignment of the benefit of a covenant is not necessary if the benefit of the covenant is annexed to the land. In that event, the benefit will pass automatically on a conveyance of the land, without express mention, because it is annexed to the land and runs with it. So the issue of annexation is logically the next to be considered.

The judge said:

'The next heading with which I must deal is "annexation", to which I will now come. It is a somewhat technical thing in the law of restrictive covenants. A good deal of argument was addressed to me on annexation by both sides. Submissions are made about express annexation, implied annexation, that is to say, annexation implied from surrounding circumstances, and annexation by assignment. In my judgment, there was in this case no "annexation" of the benefit of the covenant to the retained land or any part of it. Section 78, in particular, of the Law of Property Act does not have the effect of annexing the benefit of the covenant to anything. It is simply a statutory shorthand for the shortening of conveyances, which it perhaps has done to some extent in this case. Annexation depends on appropriate drafting, which is not here in this case, in spite of a recent process which can perhaps be called "a widening of the law" in these matters. The attendant circumstances moreover, positively militate against annexation because, as counsel for the defendants rightly pointed out to me (though he did so in the course of his argument on construction) the restriction in this particular case is of limited duration and plainly not applicable to ultimate purchasers of plots of the land intended to be benefited. "Annexation", in my judgment, is for the parties to the covenant itself to achieve if they wish to, and (though those parties may no doubt provide for annexation at a later stage) I am not satisfied or prepared to hold that there is any such thing as "delayed annexation by assignment" to which the covenantor is not party or privy.'

The reference to 'delayed annexation by assignment' is to a proposition that a covenant can, on a later assignment, thereby become annexed to the land by the act of the assignor and the assignee alone.

In my judgment the benefit of this covenant was annexed to the retained land, and I think that this is a consequence of s 78 of the Law of Property Act 1925, which reads:

'(1) A covenant relating to any land of the covenantee shall be deemed to be made with the covenantee and his successors in title and the persons deriving title under him or them, and shall have effect as if such successors and other persons were expressed. For the purposes of this subsection in connexion with covenants restrictive of the user of land "successors in title" shall be deemed to include the owners and occupiers for the time being of the land of the covenantee intended to be benefited.

'(2) This section applies to covenants made after the commencement of this Act, but the repeal of section fifty-eight of the Conveyancing Act, 1881, does not affect the operation of covenants to which that section applied.'

Counsel for the defendants submitted that there were three possible views about s 78. One view, which he described as 'the orthodox view' hitherto held, is that it is merely a statutory shorthand for reducing the length of legal documents. A second

a view, which was the one that counsel for the defendants was inclined to place in the forefront of his argument, is that the section only applies, or at any rate only achieves annexation, when the land intended to be benefited is signified in the document by express words or necessary implication as the intended beneficiary of the covenant. A third view is that the section applies if the covenant in fact touches and concerns the land of the covenantee, whether that be gleaned from the document itself or from evidence

b outside the document.

For myself, I reject the narrowest interpretation of s 78, the supposed orthodox view, which seems to me to fly in the face of the wording of the section. Before I express my reasons I will say that I do not find it necessary to choose between the second and third views because, in my opinion, this covenant relates to land of the covenantee on either interpretation of s 78. Clause 5(iv) shows quite clearly that the covenant is for the

c protection of the retained land and that land is described in cl 2 as 'any adjoining or adjacent property retained by the Vendor'. This formulation is sufficient for annexation purposes: see *Rogers v Hosegood*[1].

There is in my judgment no doubt that this covenant 'related to the land of the covenantee', or, to use the old-fashioned expression, that it touched and concerned the land, even if counsel for the defendants is correct in his submission that the document

d must show an intention to benefit identified land. The result of such application is that one must read cl 5(iv) as if it were written: 'The purchaser hereby covenants with the vendor and its successors in title and the persons deriving title under it or them, including the owners and occupiers for the time being of the retained land, that in carrying out the development of the blue land the purchaser shall not build at a greater density than a total of 300 dwellings so as not to reduce the number of units which the

e vendor might eventually erect on the retained land under the existing planning consent.' I leave out of consideration s 79 as unnecessary to be considered in this context, since Mill Lodge is the original covenantor.

The first point to notice about s 78(1) is that the wording is significantly different from the wording of its predecessor, s 58(1) of the Conveyancing and Law of Property Act 1881. The distinction is underlined by sub-s (2) of s 78, which applies sub-s (1) only to

f covenants made after the commencement of the Act. Section 58(1) of the earlier Act did not include the covenantee's successors in title or persons deriving title under him or them, nor the owners or occupiers for the time being of the land of the covenantee intended to be benefited. The section was confined, in relation to realty, to the covenantee, his heirs and assigns, words which suggest a more limited scope of operation than is found in s 78.

g If, as the language of s 78 implies, a covenant relating to land which is restrictive of the user thereof is enforceable at the suit of (1) a successor in title of the covenantee, (2) a person deriving title under the covenantee or under his successors in title, and (3) the owner or occupier of the land intended to be benefited by the covenant, it must, in my view, follow that the covenant runs with the land, because ex hypothesi every successor in title to the land, every derivative proprietor of the land and every other owner and

h occupier has a right by statute to the covenant. In other words, if the condition precedent of s 78 is satisfied, that is to say, there exists a covenant which touches and concerns the land of the covenantee, that covenant runs with the land for the benefit of his successors in title, persons deriving title under him or them and other owners and occupiers.

This approach to s 78 has been advocated by distinguished textbook writers: see Dr Radcliffe in the Law Quarterly Review[2], Professor Wade in the Cambridge Law Journal[3]

j under the apt cross-heading 'What is wrong with section 78?', and Megarry and Wade on

---

1   [1900] 2 Ch 388, [1900–3] All ER Rep 915
2   (1941) 57 LQR 203
3   [1972] CLJ 157

the Law of Real Property[1]. Counsel pointed out to us that the fourth edition of Megarry
and Wade's textbook indicates a change of mind on this topic since the third edition was   *a*
published in 1966.

Although the section does not seem to have been extensively used in the course of
argument in this type of case, the construction of s 78 which appeals to me appears to be
consistent with at least two cases decided in this court. The first is *Smith v River Douglas
Catchment Board*[2]. In that case an agreement was made in April 1938 between certain
landowners and the catchment board under which the catchment board undertook to   *b*
make good the banks of a certain brook and to maintain the same, and the landowners
undertook to contribute towards the cost. In 1940 the first plaintiff took a conveyance
from one of the landowners of a part of the land together with an express assignment of
the benefit of the agreement. In 1944 the second plaintiff took a tenancy of that land
without any express assignment of the benefit of the agreement. In 1946 the brook
burst its banks and the land owned by the first plaintiff and tenanted by the second   *c*
plaintiff was inundated. The two important points are that the agreement was not
expressed to be for the benefit of the landowner's successors in title; and there was no
assignment of the benefit of the agreement in favour of the second plaintiff, the tenant.
In reliance, as I understand the case, on s 78 of the Law of Property Act 1925, it was held
that the second plaintiff was entitled to sue the catchment board for damages for breach
of the agreement. It seems to me that that conclusion can only have been reached on the   *d*
basis that s 78 had the effect of causing the benefit of the agreement to run with the land
so as to be capable of being sued on by the tenant.

The other case, *Williams v Unit Construction Co Ltd*[3], was decided by this court in
1951. There a company had acquired a building estate and had underleased four plots
to Cubbin for 999 years. The underlessors arranged for the defendant company to build
houses on the four plots. The defendant company covenanted with Cubbin to keep the   *e*
adjacent road in repair until adopted. Cubbin granted a weekly tenancy of one house to
the plaintiff without any express assignment of the benefit of the covenant. The plaintiff
was injured owing to the disrepair of the road. She was held entitled to recover damages
from the defendant for breach of the covenant.

We were referred to observations in the speeches of Lord Upjohn and Lord Wilberforce
in *Tophams Ltd v Earl of Sefton*[4] to the effect that s 79 of the Law of Property Act 1925   *f*
(relating to the burden of covenants) achieved no more than the introduction of statutory
shorthand into the drafting covenants. Section 79, in my view, involves quite different
considerations and I do not think that it provides a helpful analogy.

It was suggested by counsel for the defendants that if this covenant ought to be read
as enuring for the benefit of the retained land, it should be read as enuring only for the
benefit of the retained land as a whole and not for the benefit of every part of it; with the   *g*
apparent result that there is no annexation of the benefit to a part of the retained land
when any severance takes place. He referred us to a passage in *Re Union of London and
Smith's Bank Ltd's Conveyance, Miles v Easter*[5], which I do not think it is necessary for me
to read.

The problem is alluded to in Megarry and Wade on the Law of Real Property[6]:

'In drafting restrictive covenants it is therefore desirable to annex them to the   *h*
covenantee's land "or any part or parts thereof". An additional reason for using this
form of words is that, if there is no indication to the contrary, the benefit may be
held to be annexed only to the whole of the covenantee's land, so that it will not pass
with portions of it disposed of separately. But even without such words the court

1   4th Edn (1975) p 764
2   [1949] 2 All ER 179, [1949] 2 KB 500
3   (1951) 19 Conv NS 262
4   [1966] 1 All ER 1039 at 1048, 1053, [1967] 1 AC 50 at 73, 81
5   [1933] Ch 611, [1933] All ER Rep 355
6   4th Edn (1975) p 763

j

a
may find that the covenant is intended to benefit any part of the retained land; and small indications may suffice, since the rule that presumes annexation to the whole only is arbitrary and inconvenient. In principle it conflicts with the rule for assignments, which allows a benefit annexed to the whole to be assigned with part, and it also conflicts with the corresponding rule for easements.'

I find the idea of the annexation of a covenant to the whole of the land but not to a part

b
of it a difficult conception fully to grasp. I can understand that a covenantee may expressly or by necessary implication retain the benefit of a covenant wholly under his own control, so that the benefit will not pass unless the covenantee chooses to assign; but I would have thought, if the benefit of a covenant is, on a proper construction of a document, annexed to the land, prima facie it is annexed to every part thereof, unless the contrary clearly appears. It is difficult to see how this court can have reached its decision in *Williams v Unit Construction Co Ltd*[1] unless this is right. The covenant was, by inference,

c
annexed to every part of the land and not merely to the whole, because it will be recalled that the plaintiff was a tenant of only one of the four houses which had the benefit of the covenant.

There is also this observation by Romer LJ in *Drake v Gray*[2]. He was dealing with the enuring of the benefit of a restrictive covenant and he said:

d
'... where ... you find, not "the land coloured yellow", or "the estate", or "the field named so and so", or anything of that kind, but "the lands retained by the vendor", it appears to me that there is a sufficient indication that the benefit of the covenant enures to every one of the lands retained by the vendor, and if a plaintiff in a subsequent action to enforce a covenant can say, "I am the owner of a piece of land or a hereditament that belonged to the vendor at the time of the conveyance",

e
he is entitled to enforce the covenant.'

In the instant case the judge in the course of his judgment appears to have dismissed the notion that any individual plotholder would be entitled, even by assignment, to have the benefit of the covenant that I have been considering. I express no view about that. I only say this, that I am not convinced that his conclusion on that point is correct. I say no more about it.

f
In the end, I come to the conclusion that s 78 of the Law of Property Act 1925 caused the benefit of the restrictive covenant in question to run with the red land and therefore to be annexed to it, with the result that the plaintiff company is able to enforce the covenant against Mill Lodge, not only in its capacity as owner of the green land, but also in its capacity as owner of the red land.

For these reasons I think that the judge reached the correct view on the right of the

g
plaintiff company to enforce the covenant, although in part he arrived there by a different route.

There remains only the question whether we ought to interfere with the remedy granted by the judge of an injunction against the building of the 32 extra dwellings. *Shelfer v City of London Electric Lighting Co*[3] is authority for the proposition that a person who has the benefit of a restrictive covenant is, as a general rule, entitled to an injunction

h
on the trial of the action as distinct from an award of damages unless (1) the injury to the plaintiff's legal rights is small, (2) it is capable of being estimated in terms of money, (3) it can adequately be compensated for by a small payment, and (4) it would be oppressive to the defendant to grant an injunction. In my view, the first, third and fourth of these conditions have not been shown to be satisfied. I would, therefore, uphold the injunction and I would dismiss this appeal.

j

1 (1951) 19 Conv NS 262
2 [1936] 1 All ER 363 at 376, [1936] Ch 451 at 465
3 [1895] 1 Ch 287, [1891–4] All ER Rep 838

BROWNE LJ. I agree that this appeal should be dismissed for the reasons given by Brightman LJ. I agree so entirely with the judgment that he has delivered that there is *a* nothing I can usefully add.

MEGAW LJ. I also agree with the conclusion reached by Brightman LJ for the reasons given by him. There is only one matter on which I would desire to add a few words. That is in respect of the passage quoted by Brightman LJ towards the end of his judgment from the judgment of Romer LJ in *Drake v Gray*[1]. It is right to observe that the passage *b* which Brightman LJ read has been the subject of criticism by Buckley J in *Russell v Archdale*[2]. Buckley J suggests that the passage in question in Romer LJ's judgment is obiter dictum and that there is difficulty in accepting the distinction which Romer LJ there drew between, on the one hand, land described as the land marked yellow on the plan or the estate of the vendor known as such and such a name and, on the other hand, reference to the remaining land or retained land. It is, however, right to point out that *c* Buckley J says[2]: 'No doubt every case of this kind, being one of construction, must be determined on the facts and the actual language used', and he goes on to say that, with the utmost respect to Romer LJ, he cannot see that the distinction is a valid one.

For myself, I would regard the observations made in the passage which Brightman LJ read from Megarry and Wade[3] as being powerful reasons, and I find great difficulty in understanding how, either as a matter of principle, or as a matter of practical good sense *d* in relation to a legal relationship of this sort, it can be said that a covenant, which ex hypothesi has been annexed to the land as a whole, is somehow or other not annexed to the individual parts of that land.

I agree that the appeal should be dismissed.

Appeal dismissed. Leave to appeal to the House of Lords refused.   *e*

Solicitors: *Blythe, Dutton, Holloway*, agents for *Coffin, Mew & Clover*, Havant (for the defendants); *Eatons* (for the plaintiffs).

Mary Rose Plummer   Barrister.

f

---

1 [1936] 1 All ER 363 at 376, [1936] Ch 451 at 465
2 [1962] 2 All ER 305 at 312, [1964] Ch 38 at 47
3 Law of Real Property (4th Edn, 1975) p 763

Ellesmere Port and Neston Borough Council v Shell UK Ltd and another

and related appeals

a

b
COURT OF APPEAL, CIVIL DIVISION
MEGAW, SHAW AND WALLER LJJ
10th, 11th, 15th OCTOBER, 9th NOVEMBER 1979

c
Rates – Local valuation court – Appeal – Jurisdiction – Direction giving effect to contention of appellant – Contention of appellant – Valuation officer and ratepayer agreeing figure lower than proposal figure – Rating authority not a party to agreement – Valuation court finding agreed figure correct and directing alteration of valuation list accordingly – Rating authority appealing to Lands Tribunal – Whether tribunal having jurisdiction to make higher assessment than that determined by valuation court – Whether 'the contention of the appellant' is the proposal figure or is limited to the agreed or a lower figure – General Rate Act 1967, s 76(5).

d
Rates – Local valuation court – Appeal – Parties entitled to be heard – Rating authority – Valuation officer and ratepayer reaching agreement on figures – Rating authority not party to agreement – Rating officer and ratepayer putting forward agreed figures before valuation court and calling no other evidence – Rating authority wishing to contest agreed figures – Whether rating authority entitled to be heard on agreed figures – General Rate Act 1967, s 76(4).

e
Proposals for altering the valuation list in respect of certain hereditaments were made by both the valuation officer and the ratepayers, and both made cross-objections to each other's proposals. No proposals or objections were made by the rating authority. After negotiating for three years the ratepayers and the valuation officer reached agreement on assessments which were lower than the figures in the proposals. Since there had been objections to the proposals, the proposals had to be transmitted to the local valuation court and by ss 73 and 74 of the General Rate Act 1967 those transmissions constituted
f
appeals to the valuation court against the objections. Before the valuation court, the valuation officer and the ratepayers put forward the agreed figures but did not call any other evidence. The rating authority exercised its right under s 76(4)*[d]* of the 1967 Act to appear and be heard as a party to the appeal and sought to question the agreed figures and to prove that they were too low. The valuation court decided that as the figures were agreed, the rating authority had no right to be heard, and directed that the valuation list
g
be altered in accordance with the agreed figures. The rating authority appealed to the Lands Tribunal. The ratepayers raised a preliminary point of law, namely that the tribunal had no jurisdiction to increase the agreed figures found by the valuation court. The tribunal held that it had jurisdiction. The ratepayers appealed to the Court of Appeal, contending that where opposing parties had agreed a figure which was lower than the figure in the proposal the valuation court, and therefore the Lands Tribunal, had
h
no jurisdiction to direct a higher figure to be entered in the valuation list because, under s 76(5) of the 1967 Act, the valuation court was required 'to give effect to the contention of the appellant' (ie the person making the proposal), so far as it appeared to be well founded, and once the parties had agreed a lower figure than the figure in the proposal the appellant thereby limited his 'contention' to the agreed, or a lower, figure, and it could no longer be said that his 'contention' was the higher figure in the proposal. The
j
ratepayers further contended that, once figures had been agreed, there was no issue for the valuation court to determine.

---

a Section 76, so far as material, is set out at p 388 *b* to *d*, post

Held – The appeals would be dismissed for the following reasons —

(i) The figures which were in 'contention' within s 76(5) of the 1967 Act were those *a*
contained within the proposal figure on the one hand and the figure put forward in the
objection on the other. The 'contention of the appellant' within s 76(5) was, therefore,
his proposal and not any other figure. It followed that unless there was, before the
valuation court made its determination, an agreement on an alteration of the valuation
list under s 72(1)*b* of the Act, and that agreement was made by all the persons interested
including, by s 72(2)(e), the rating authority, the valuation court's jurisdiction was *b*
limited to giving effect to the proposal in whole or in part, according to whether on
consideration of the validity of the objection the proposal appeared well founded. Since
the rating authority was not a party to the agreement between the valuation officer and
the ratepayers, the agreement did not come within s 72(1) and, though the agreement
might be of persuasive value, it did not alter the jurisdiction of the valuation court or
entitle it to treat the agreed figures as the limit of the 'contentions' of the valuation officer *c*
and the ratepayers. The valuation court's jurisdiction remained to give effect to the
various proposals, in whole or in part, in the light of the validity of the objections to
them. It followed that the Lands Tribunal (whose jurisdiction corresponded to that of
the valuation court when the appeal before it was constituted) had jurisdiction to make
higher assessments than those which had been determined by the valuation court, so
long as its assessments were not higher than those in the proposals (see p 389 *a b g h*, p 390 *d*
d to p 391 *c* and p 392 *f g*, post).

(ii) Moreover, since it was implicit in Part V of the 1967 Act that no conclusion on the
compilation or alteration of the valuation list could be reached without the co-operation
of the rating authority and the Act required that at every stage the rating authority must
be involved unless under s 72(2)(e) it had notified its desire not to be included in the
proceedings, and having regard to the unambiguous terms of s 76(4), the rating authority *e*
was entitled, despite the agreement between the rating officer and the ratepayers, to
appear and call evidence before the valuation court, and the court should have taken such
evidence into account in deciding whether the 'contentions' of the valuation officer and
ratepayers were well founded (see p 389 *c* to *j*, p 390 *h j*, p 391 *c* and p 392 *c d*, post).

Per Megaw and Waller LJJ. Since an appeal to the Court of Appeal from the Lands
Tribunal is only on a question of law, and questions of fact are for the tribunal, it is *f*
undesirable, in the absence of very exceptional circumstances, for the Court of Appeal to
admit evidence not given before the tribunal; although, therefore, the court has
jurisdiction to admit such evidence, it should be sparingly exercised. If evidence
tendered before the Lands Tribunal is rejected and it is desired to contend that the
rejection is wrong, that contention should be dealt with as a question of law, and not as
a ground for re-submitting the evidence in the Court of Appeal (see p 389 *g h* and p 391 *g*
f g, post).

Notes

For powers and decisions of a local valuation court, see 32 Halsbury's Laws (3rd Edn) 125,
para 169, and for parties entitled to appear and be heard before the court, see ibid 123–
124, para 168.   *h*

For the General Rate Act 1967, s 76, see 27 Halsbury's Statutes (3rd Edn) 169.

Cases referred to in judgments

Ellerby v March [1954] 2 All ER 375, [1954] 2 QB 357, 118 JP 382, 52 LGR 397, CA, 38
    Digest (Repl) 716, 1509.
Morecambe and Heysham Corpn v Robinson [1961] 1 All ER 721, [1961] 1 WLR 373, 125 JP *j*
    259, 59 LGR 160, CA, Digest (Cont Vol A) 1294, 887a.

b   Section 72 is set out at p 387 *f* to *h*, post

Cases also cited

a   *Brixham Urban District Council, Re Application by* [1954] 3 All ER 501n, DC; on appeal (1955) 48 R & IT 187, CA.
R v East Norfolk Local Valuation Court, ex parte Martin [1951] 1 All ER 743, DC.
River Wear Comrs v Adamson (1877) 2 App Cas 743, [1874–80] All ER Rep 1, HL.
Sheffield (City of) v Meadow Dairy Co Ltd (1958) 2 RRC 395, CA.

b   **Cases stated**

These were five appeals, by case stated, by ratepayers against decisions of the Lands Tribunal dated 21st February 1978 on a preliminary point of law, namely whether the Lands Tribunal had jurisdiction to increase the assessments which were the subject of the appeals. In each case a rating authority and the valuation officer were the respondents to the appeal. In the first and third appeal, Shell UK Ltd was the ratepayer and the rating
c   authorities were respectively, Ellesmere Port and Neston Borough Council and Chester City Council. In the second appeal, UKF Fertilizers Ltd was the ratepayer and Ellesmere Port and Neston Borough Council the rating authority. In the fourth and fifth appeals, Burmah Oil Trading Ltd was the ratepayer and Ellesmere Port and Neston Borough Council and Chester City Council respectively the rating authorities. The facts are set out in the judgment of Waller LJ.

d
David Widdicombe QC and *Matthew Horton* for Shell UK Ltd.
Charles Fay for Burmah Oil Trading Ltd.
Matthew Horton for UKF Fertilizers Ltd.
Alan Fletcher for the valuation officer.
William Glover QC and *Susan Hamilton* for Ellesmere Port and Neston Borough Council.
e   *Rt Hon Viscount Colville of Culross QC* and *Susan Hamilton* for Chester City Council.

Cur adv vult

9th November. The following judgments were read.
f
WALLER LJ (delivering the first judgment at the invitation of Megaw LJ). These are five appeals against decisions of the Lands Tribunal called on and heard together at the request of all parties. The case stated by the Lands Tribunal is in identical terms in each case and raises the same point for the decision of this court. In each case it is the ratepayer who is appealing and the rating authority and the valuation officer who are supporting
g   the decision of the Lands Tribunal. The ratepayers own pipelines and oil refineries and, in the case of UKF Fertilizers Ltd, manufacturing plant and, although in reality in each case one hereditament, each is divided into a number of items which are divided between two rating authorities. The sums involved are very great; in the case of Shell UK Ltd, for instance, a total amount amounting to some £2,600,000 odd. Some of the proposals were by the ratepayer for reductions and some were by the valuation officer for
h   new items with a stated valuation.

We were told that, over a period of three years, the ratepayers and the valuation officer were in negotiation and that at the end of that time agreement was reached between them at figures which, in the case of Shell, produced a total of some £2,150,000. Since in each case there had been an objection to the proposal by the valuation officer, or the ratepayer as the case might be, it was necessary to go to the local valuation court to effect
j   any alteration to the valuation list. Before the local valuation court neither the valuation officer nor the ratepayers called evidence, but each put forward their agreed figures. The rating authority, however, appeared and claimed the right to ask questions and call evidence. The local valuation court, having heard argument, decided that the figures were agreed and that the rating authority had no further right to be heard. The rating authority appealed to the Lands Tribunal and the ratepayers took the preliminary point

that the Lands Tribunal had no jurisdiction to increase the figures found by the local valuation court.

Counsel on behalf of each of the appellants submit that it is unfair and contrary to the spirit of rating legislation since 1948 that the rating authority should stand by for three years without even objecting to the proposals and then be allowed to go before the local valuation court and seek to argue and prove that the figures should be higher than that which had been agreed.

I do not propose to refer at this stage to the earlier legislation, namely the Local Government Act 1948 and the Rating and Valuation (Miscellaneous Provisions) Act 1955, because they can only be relevant if there is an ambiguity in the current statute, namely the General Rate Act 1967 and, in particular, Part V. Section 67 deals with the publication of a new valuation list and then there follow a number of sections dealing with alterations to the current valuation list. Section 69 deals with proposals for alteration of the current valuation and enables anyone aggrieved to make a proposal for amendment either by adding an hereditament or altering its description or value.

Section 69 reads:

'(1) . . . any person (including a rating authority) who is aggrieved—(a) by the inclusion of any hereditament in the valuation list; or (b) by any value ascribed in the list to a hereditament or by any other statement made or omitted to be made in the list with respect to a hereditament; or (c) in the case of a building or portion of a building occupied in parts, by the valuation in the list of that building or portion of a building as a single hereditament, may at any time make a proposal for the alteration of the list so far as it relates to that hereditament.

'(2) . . . the valuation officer may at any time make a proposal for any alteration of a valuation list and in particular, in addition to the proposals authorised or required by, or by virtue of, the following provisions of this Act, namely, paragraph 6(1) of Schedule 1, paragraph 4(1) of Schedule 4, paragraph 8(4) of Schedule 5, paragraph 13 of Schedule 6 and paragraph 15 of Schedule 7, shall from time to time make such proposals as may be requisite—(a) for deleting from the list any premises exempted from rating by virtue of section 33(1)(b) of this Act; (b) for excluding from the list any premises which form part of a hereditament shown in the list and which, by virtue of section 33(1)(a) or (b) of this Act, are not liable to be rated, and for including in the list, as one or more separate hereditaments, so much of any such hereditament as remains liable to be rated; (c) for altering the list in consequence of any event whereby premises cease to be within the exemption from rating conferred by section 32(3), 33(1) or 34(1) of this Act.

'(3) Without prejudice to any right exercisable by rating authorities by virtue of subsection (1) of this section, where—(a) it appears to a rating authority that a hereditament in their rating area which is not included in the list ought to be included therein; and (b) the valuation officer gives notice in writing to the rating authority that he does not intend to make a proposal for inserting that hereditament in the list, the rating authority, at any time within twenty-eight days after the date on which that notice was given, may make a proposal for the alteration of the list by the insertion of that hereditament therein . . .

'(5) Every proposal under this section must—(a) be made in writing; and (b) specify the grounds on which the proposed alteration is supported; and (c) comply with any requirements of any regulations made by the Minister with respect to the form of such proposals and otherwise with respect to the making thereof, and every such proposal made otherwise than by the valuation officer must be served on the valuation officer.'

Section 70 makes provision for objections to proposals:

'(1) The valuation officer shall, within twenty-eight days after the date on which a proposal under section 69 of this Act is served on him, or within seven days after *a* the date on which such a proposal is made by him, as the case may be, transmit a copy thereof, together with a statement in writing of the right of objection conferred by subsection (2) of this section, to each of the following persons, not being the maker of the proposal, that is to say—(*a*) the occupier of the hereditament to which the proposal relates; and (*b*) the rating authority for the area in which the hereditament in question is situated.'

b And by s 70(2) the owner or occupier or the rating authority may within 28 days of service serve notice of objection on the valuation officer. Where the proposal was made by the ratepayer the valuation officer must give him notice of objection by the rating authority. The valuation officer's duty is under s 74(1) and he has to object within three months. In this case the proposals for alterations were made by both the ratepayer (in all cases) and the valuation officer in the cases of proposed new entries in the valuation list.

c The ratepayer objected to the valuation officer's proposals and the valuation officer in due course objected to the ratepayer's proposals but no objection was made by the rating authority.

Section 71 deals with unopposed proposals:

d '(1) Where in the case of any proposal under section 69 of this Act—(*a*) no notice of objection is served within the time limited by section 70(2) of this Act, or every such notice is unconditionally withdrawn; and (*b*) either—(i) the proposal was made by the valuation officer; or (ii) the valuation officer is satisfied that the proposal is well-founded; or (iii) at the end of the period of four months beginning with the date on which the proposal was served on the valuation officer, that officer has not given a notice under section 74(1) of this Act, the valuation officer shall cause the valuation list to be altered so as to give effect to the proposal.'

e There then comes s 72 which deals with agreed alterations after proposals but before determination by the local valuation court. If the requirements of the section are fulfilled it becomes the duty of the valuation officer to cause the alteration to be made in the valuation list:

f '(1) Where, in the case of any proposal under section 69 of this Act, the requirements of section 71 of this Act are not satisfied, but—(*a*) all the persons referred to in subsection (2) of this section agree on an alteration of the valuation list (whether the alteration is that specified in the proposal or another alteration); and (*b*) the agreement is reached without, or before the determination of, any appeal to a local valuation court, or reference to arbitration, with respect to an objection to the proposal, the valuation officer shall cause that alteration to be made in the valuation list.

g '(2) The persons referred to in subsection (1)(*a*) of this section are—(*a*) the valuation officer; (*b*) the person who made the proposal, where the proposal was not made by the valuation officer; (*c*) any person who has served and who has not unconditionally withdrawn a notice of objection to the proposal; (*d*) the occupier of the hereditament to which the proposal relates, if he is not included by virtue of *h* paragraph (*b*) or (*c*) of this subsection; (*e*) the rating authority (if not included by virtue of paragraph (*b*), (*c*) or (*d*) of this subsection), unless they have notified the valuation officer that they do not desire to be included by virtue of this paragraph either generally or as respects a class of hereditament which includes the hereditament to which the proposal relates.'

j It is not suggested that in this case s 72 had been complied with. Under s 73 the valuation officer is under a duty to transmit proposals to which there has been an objection to the clerk to the local valuation court and s 74 makes provision for proposals to which the valuation officer objects to be so transmitted. Under either section the transmission has effect as an appeal to the local valuation court and by virtue of s 76—

'(1) Where a copy of a proposal is transmitted to the clerk to a local valuation panel and by virtue of section 73(2), 74(3) or 75 of this Act that transmission has effect as an appeal to a local valuation court against an objection to the proposal, it shall be the duty of the chairman or a deputy chairman of that panel to arrange for the convening of such a court.

'(2) The procedure of a local valuation court shall, subject to any regulations made in that behalf by the Minister, and . . . be such as the court may determine; and the court—(a) shall sit in public, unless the court otherwise order on the application of any party to the appeal and upon being satisfied that the interests of one or more parties to the appeal would be prejudicially affected; and (b) may take evidence on oath and shall have power for that purpose to administer oaths . . .

'(4) On the hearing of an appeal to a local valuation court—(a) the appellant; and (b) the valuation officer, when he is not the appellant; and (c) the owner or occupier of the hereditament to which the appeal relates, when he is not the appellant; and (d) the rating authority for the rating area in which the hereditament in question is situated, when that authority are not the appellant; and (e) the objector, where he is not one of the persons aforesaid, shall be entitled to appear and be heard as parties to the appeal and examine any witness before the court and to call witnesses.

'(5) Subject to the provisions of this Act, after hearing the persons mentioned in subsection (4) of this section, or such of them as desire to be heard, the local valuation court shall give such directions with respect to the manner in which the hereditament in question is to be treated in the valuation list as appear to them to be necessary to give effect to the contention of the appellant if and so far as that contention appears to the court to be well founded; and the valuation officer shall cause the valuation list to be altered accordingly.'

As I have already indicated, the rating authority exercised their right to appear and be heard as parties to the appeal but the local valuation court, having heard argument, decided that the figures were agreed. In effect, the question which is posed for the opinion of this court is: were the local valuation court right in deciding that the agreed figures stood?

The case for the appellants is put in two ways: (1) in the case of proposals for new entries and valuations made by the valuation officer the 'contention' of the valuation officer was not the proposal figure but was the agreed figure or some lower figure. This argument is based on the wording of s 76(5) where it says:

'. . . the local valuation court shall give such directions with respect to the manner in which the hereditament in question is to be treated in the valuation list as appear to them to be necessary to give effect to the contention of the appellant if and so far as that contention appears to the court to be well founded . . .'

It was submitted that, once the valuation officer reduced his own figure, his 'contention' was the new figure as a maximum; and it was not open to the local valuation court to go above the new figure because its jurisdiction was limited to 'so far as that contention appears to the court to be well founded'; (2) it was submitted that in the case of proposals by the occupiers for a lower figure than in the valuation list once there was agreement with the valuation officer there was no justiciable issue, ie no dispute. This argument did not depend on the meaning of the word 'contention', but on the simple submission that there was no issue for the local valuation court to try.

On the meaning of 'contention' it was submitted that, once the valuation officer agreed a lower figure than that in the valuation list or in his proposal, as the case might be, this lower figure would be the limit of his contention and it would not be possible to say that the higher figure in the proposal was his contention. *Morecambe and Heysham Corpn v Robinson*[1], when carefully considered, does not support this limited view of 'contention'. Furthermore, the decision is really on the question of whether contention

---

1   [1961] 1 All ER 721, [1961] 1 WLR 373

refers to the figures or refers to the arguments. I do not find any help from other
a   authorities cited to us. In this case the valuation officer published a valuation list with
valuations in it. These valuations were communicated to all concerned including the
rating authority. The occupier made a proposal of a nominal figure. In my judgment,
the limits of contention were contained in the valuation list figure on the one hand and
the figure in the proposal on the other and, unless all parties agreed, no agreement
between the two parties could alter that. In other instances, where the valuation officer
b   made proposals, the limits of contention would be that figure on the one hand and that
made in any objection on the other.

We were referred also to *Ellerby v March*[1], a decision which was concerned with
appearances before the Lands Tribunal. There the argument is on appeal from the local
valuation court which is the court of first instance. In my opinion the decision does not
apply to proceedings before the local valuation court.

c   Subsidiary arguments by the ratepayers that the words of s 76(4) entitling the rating
authority to be present at the local valuation court do not give the rating authority the
right to attack and overrule an agreement between the valuation officer and the ratepayer
were to the effect that there were other possible ways of achieving an alteration without
the rating authority's concurrence. One argument was based on making a number of
proposals for one hereditament and then withdrawing all but one. Another was founded
d   on s 81(1) where there could be a partial withdrawal of the proposal. In my opinion these
arguments do not assist the appellants. The fact that it is possible to point to one anomaly
is no argument for ignoring or restricting the meaning of plain words in the statute. It
is implicit throughout the part of the Act that I have set out above that no conclusion can
be reached without the co-operation of the rating authority. The rating authority could
adopt one of three possible courses of action: first, it could object in accordance with the
e   provisions of s 70 and thereafter it would be an active party to the dispute; secondly, it
could notify the valuation officer that it did not desire to be included (see 72(2)(e));
thirdly, it could do nothing until it could see whether things were going wrong, ie,
whether their rateable values were to be reduced to figures which they regarded as being
too low. If they were, then the rating authority could attack the figure and call evidence
before the local valuation court. The sections I have mentioned above require that at
f   every stage the rating authority must be involved unless it has notified the valuation
officer that it does not desire to be included (see s 72(2)(e)).

I said earlier that I was not looking at the statutes which preceded the 1967 Act unless
there was an ambiguity about the General Rate Act 1967. Although there may be some
anomalies I do not find any ambiguity about the words which say that the rating
authority 'shall be entitled to appear and be heard as parties to the appeal and examine
g   any witness before the court and to call witnesses' and I therefore do not need to examine
these earlier statutes.

I am of opinion that the president of the Lands Tribunal came to a correct decision in
law and that the Lands Tribunal has jurisdiction to increase the assessments which are the
subject of these appeals.

Since preparing this judgment I have had the advantage of reading in draft the
h   judgments which Megaw and Shaw LJJ are about to deliver and I agree with them both.

SHAW LJ. I agree with the judgment which has just been delivered.

The scheme embodied in Part V of the General Rate Act 1967, for the maintenance
and alteration of valuation lists, recognises that, apart from other possible parties, the
j   valuation officer, the ratepayer and the rating authority must always have an interest in
the compilation and alteration of a valuation list which relates to the area of that
authority and is a hereditament for which the ratepayer has a liability.

_____

1   [1954] 2 All ER 375, [1954] 2 QB 357

This concurrence of interest is made clear from a cursory examination of the relevant provisions of the Act beginning with s 69.

Where a proposal has been made and has been met with a notice of objection which is persisted in, the valuation officer is required within the limits of time prescribed by s 73 to transmit a copy of the proposal and of every notice of objection to the local valuation panel, and by s 76(1) this step in the procedure prescribed under the Act shall 'take effect as an appeal to a local valuation court against an objection to the proposal'.

By s 76(5) after due hearing (a matter which gives rise to one aspect of this appeal and to which I shall later refer)—

'the local valuation court shall give such directions . . . as appear to them to be necessary to give effect to the contention of the appellant if and so far as that contention appears to the court to be well founded.'

As I understand these provisions they not only determine and delimit the function and jurisdiction of the valuation court but they also define the role of the party responsible for the proposal. That role is to challenge and refute the objections and as a necessary corollary to support the proposal. The function of the valuation court is to assess the impact of the contentions of the appellant (and in particular where the appellant is the valuation officer) on the force of the objections. The court may reject the objections or accept them in whole or in part with the consequence that the proposal may be left intact or may be reduced or obliterated. Even if the appellant does not seek to support his proposal in its entirety it is still for the court to decide to what extent the objections to it have been refuted by facts proved before them. The appellant cannot modify his proposal (unless he withdraws it altogether) save as provided by s 72; and the court cannot determine on a more onerous proposal than that which was objected to since it is the objections to that proposal which constitute the matter in contention rather than the primary validity of the proposal itself.

Thus the jurisdiction of the court is measured by the area of controversy lying between the proposal and the matters of objection. The court will refuse to give effect to these last to the extent that the appellant's contentions appear to the court to be well founded. Prima facie the contention of the appellant must be that the objections are ill-founded. Otherwise he is virtually putting forward a new proposal and must follow the procedural requirements appertaining to a fresh proposal unless there is an agreement to which all interested bodies or persons are parties in accordance with the requirements of s 72(2) of the Act. It is pertinent to observe that s 72(1)(b) provides that such an agreement may be reached without or before the determination of any appeal to a local valuation court with respect to an objection to the proposal.

No such agreement to which the rating authority was a party was made in the present case. The agreement between the valuation officer and the ratepayer could be no more than persuasive before the valuation court. Their jurisdiction remained what it had been from the outset, namely, to allow the appeal in whole or in part and by rejecting or upholding the objections in whole or in part correspondingly to uphold the proposal in its entirety or partially.

As to the operation of sub-s (4) of s 76 it seems to me plain that any of the persons or bodies enumerated in paras (a), (b), (c), (d) and (e) are entitled to intervene in the appeal and to be heard as parties. Whether they support or oppose the objections will depend on their interest; but the valuation court will take account of the results of their intervention in deciding whether and in what measure the contention of the appellant that the objections are untenable is well founded.

I see no substance in the suggestion made by the appellants that it is unfair on the part of the rating authority to come in as a party to the appeal when they have taken no earlier action. There was neither need nor obligation to do so. When the proposal has been made and met with an objection the issue is defined and all parties whose interests may be affected have a status to intervene at the hearing.

When the matter is taken to the Lands Tribunal its jurisdiction corresponds to that

a which the valuation court had when the appeal before it was constituted; this may be
stated shortly in the formula that it is to decide the outcome by consideration of the
validity of the objections rather than by addressing itself to the propriety of the
proposal. It may therefore, in the result, arrive where the amount is in issue at a higher
figure than that determined by the valuation court. What it cannot do is to find a figure
higher than the proposal itself for it, like the valuation court, has no jurisdiction to
entertain a different proposal from that to which objection has been made.

b It follows that the answer to the question posed by the case in each of the appeals is in
the affirmative and that the Lands Tribunal can make a higher assessment than that
determined by the valuation court so long as their assessment so found is not greater than
that contained in the proposal.

I would accordingly dismiss these appeals.

c
MEGAW LJ. I agree with the conclusions and with the reasons expressed in the
judgment of Waller LJ on each of the points raised by the appellants in these appeals. I
agree that the decision of the president of the Lands Tribunal was correct in law.

There are two procedural matters to which I should refer. The responsibility of
formulating, for consideration by the president of the Lands Tribunal, the question or
d questions of law on which they sought to contend before this court that the decisions
were wrong, rested with the respective appellants. It is unfortunate that the appellants
formulated one general question, instead of formulating two separate questions. This is
particularly to be regretted since the appellants put in the forefront of their criticism of
the president's decision the submission that he failed to recognise that there were two
separate points of law. Before us it emerged that the appellants' submissions involved
e that if we were to decide one of the two points of law against them, but were to uphold
their submission on the other point of law, it would be impossible for the court to answer
the question asked other than by some such formula as 'The Lands Tribunal has
jurisdiction unless . . .', or 'The Lands Tribunal does not have jurisdiction except if and
in so far as . . .'

We were asked on behalf of one of the appellants, Shell UK Ltd, by original motion,
f for leave to adduce additional evidence in the form of a lengthy affidavit and exhibits.
Since an appeal to this court from the Lands Tribunal is only on questions of law, and
since questions of fact are for the tribunal itself, it is obviously in the highest degree
undesirable that, in the absence of very exceptional circumstances, this court should
admit evidence not given before the tribunal. The court has jurisdiction to do so; but it
should be very sparingly exercised. If evidence tendered in the Lands Tribunal has been
g rejected, and it is desired to contend that the rejection was wrong, that should be dealt
with as a question of law: not as a ground for simply re-submitting the evidence in this
court.

We decided that the only course open to us was to look at the proposed evidence
provisionally. Two of the parties to these appeals, the valuation officer and one of the
rating authorities, said that, if the evidence were to be admitted, they would wish to put
h in affidavits in reply on certain matters of fact. In the end, they did not do so, perhaps
because it became evident that the evidence was, at best, of little real significance to the
issues of law which we had to decide.

The proposed evidence turned out to be, to a considerable extent, argument, which, if
relevant, should not have been put forward in an affidavit. The affidavit dealt also with
facts and figures concerned with the particular assessment. Such facts and figures, it was,
j I think, accepted on behalf of the party seeking to adduce the evidence, could not directly
affect a decision of general principle to be reached on the construction of statutory
provisions: which principle, when ascertained, must be equally applicable to all
assessments, large or small, complex or simple. It was contended that some of the facts
set out in the affidavit would be helpful to the court as what was called 'background' in
reaching its decision on the issues of law. In the end, I think it is right to say that the

affidavit was used only for the purpose of drawing illustrations, or examples, from an exhibit thereto.

We were not asked to give a definite ruling, following our decision to look at the evidence provisionally. I think we ought now to give such a ruling. In all the circumstances, it seems to me to be better to treat the evidence as admitted. But if I had thought that anything in it was material to the decision of this court, as putting in evidence facts which were not before the Lands Tribunal, I should have regarded it as necessary to consider further, with the assistance of counsel, whether the proper course would not have been to remit the relevant appeal to the Lands Tribunal for further consideration on the basis of the evidence now adduced.

The point which, logically, I should have thought, was the appellants' first point was dealt with second in the arguments for the appellants and has thus been dealt with as the second point in the judgment of Waller LJ. If it were right, the answer to the question of law posed would be that the Lands Tribunal have no jurisdiction to increase any of the figures found by the local valuation court in any of the appeals. I have been unable to understand how, in the absence of some express provision in s 76(4) of the General Rate Act 1967 affecting the position in cases such as those with which we are concerned, it can be said that the words of that subsection are consistent with the appellants' contention that the rating authority is precluded from being heard as parties to the appeal: that is, from saying, if they see fit, 'we require the appellant ratepayer to prove his case on this appeal'. It was suggested, if I understood the submission correctly, that the rating authority could, indeed, 'be heard as parties to the appeal', to the extent of challenging the validity of the agreement as to figures between the ratepayer and the valuation officer. I do not understand either what sort of 'invalidity' is here contemplated, or why the words of the statute should be treated as being so limited in effect. In substance, also, as I see it, the appellants' argument on this point cannot stand in the light of the provisions of s 72 of the Act. They are intended to provide for agreed alterations of the proposals, and not to leave it open for the rights of a rating authority under s 76(4) to be circumvented by a purported 'agreed alteration of the proposals' which does not comply with the requirements of s 72 as to such agreement.

As regards the appellants' other point, it would, if right, as I have already said, not require or entitle this court to say that the Lands Tribunal had no jurisdiction to increase the values accepted by the local valuation court. The court would have to answer the question with a qualification. If I understood correctly, it was accepted at the end of the argument before us that the question was whether 'the contention' of the appellant in s 76(5) is to be treated as being the proposal for the alteration of the list as set out in what I may call the relevant 'pleading', or is the figure (where it is an appeal as to the proper figure) which the appellant is putting forward before the local valuation court at the final moment before the local valuation court has to consider its decision. I think that both reason and convenience support the view that it is the former.

Appeals dismissed. Application for leave to appeal to the House of Lords refused. Motion to adduce additional evidence by Shell UK Ltd granted.

Solicitors: *F D Duffield* (for Shell UK Ltd and UKF Fertilizers Ltd); *Allen & Overy* (for Burmah Oil Trading Ltd); *Solicitor of Inland Revenue; J B Bickerton,* Ellesmere Port (for Ellesmere Port and Neston Borough Council); *D M Kermode,* Chester (for Chester City Council).

Mary Rose Plummer   Barrister.

Belmont Finance Corporation v Williams Furniture Ltd and others (No 2)

COURT OF APPEAL, CIVIL DIVISION
BUCKLEY, GOFF AND WALLER LJJ
8th, 12th, 13th, 14th, 15th, 16th, 19th, 20th, 21st, 22nd MARCH, 25th MAY,
13th, 31st JULY 1979

Company – Shares – Purchase of shares with financial assistance of company – Arm's length transaction – Bona fide commercial transaction – Parties agreeing sale and purchase of company – Purchase financed by selling inflated asset to company and using money so obtained to buy company – Seller of company obtaining services of property expert in return – Transaction fair and bona fide as regards buyer and seller – Whether company's shares purchased with financial assistance from company – Whether transaction illegal – Whether parties liable to company in conspiracy or as constructive trustees – Companies Act 1948, s 54.

The first defendant (a company known as 'Williams') owned all the shares in the second defendant (a company known as 'City') which in turn owned all the shares in the plaintiff company ('Belmont'). The chairman of all three companies was J. The third defendant, G, was the controlling shareholder of another company ('Maximum') which was engaged in property development. The fourth to sixth defendants were associates of G and owned the balance of the shares in Maximum. In 1963 G and his associates wished to purchase Belmont in order to use its assets to finance the property development projects of other companies owned by them. At the same time J, who was impressed by G, wanted to obtain the benefit of G's expertise and flair in property development for the Williams group of companies. Accordingly, on 3rd October, G and his associates agreed with Williams and City to sell Maximum to Belmont for £500,000 and to buy the share capital of Belmont from City for £489,000. In addition Williams and City agreed to lend Belmont £200,000 for 12 months secured on the capital of Maximum, G guaranteed to Belmont that the aggregate pre-tax profits of Maximum and its subsidiaries for the six years to 31st May 1968 would be not less than £500,000, and City agreed to subscribe for 230,000 £1 preference shares in Belmont out of the £489,000 it received for the sale of Belmont. Although G and J negotiated at arm's length, neither J, City nor Belmont sought or received an independent valuation of the worth of Maximum. It was realised by the parties involved that there was a possibility that the transaction might involve a breach of s 54(1)[a] of the Companies Act 1948 which made it unlawful for a company to give 'any financial assistance for the purpose of . . . a purchase . . . made . . . by any person of or for any shares in the company'. G's solicitors obtained counsel's opinion that the proposed purchase of Maximum by Belmont, being a bona fide purchase at a proper price, would not contravene s 54. A copy of that opinion was given to the directors of City. At board meetings of City and Belmont held on 11th October it was resolved that the agreement of 3rd October should be implemented, and the transaction was completed later that day. Belmont subsequently went into liquidation with debts of £176,269. The receiver of Belmont obtained an independent valuation of Maximum on the basis of advising Belmont of a fair price to pay for Maximum as at 3rd October 1963. That valuation suggested that Maximum was worth only £60,069 at that date and not £500,000. The receiver accordingly commenced an action on behalf of Belmont against, inter alios, Williams, City and G alleging (i) that the price of £500,000 for Maximum had

---

a   Section 54(1), so far as material, provides: 'Subject as provided in this section, it shall not be lawful for a company to give, whether directly or indirectly, and whether by means of a loan, guarantee, the provision of security or otherwise, any financial assistance for the purpose of or in connection with a purchase or subscription made or to be made by any person of or for any shares in the company, or, where the company is a subsidiary company, in its holding company . . .'

been arrived at to enable G and his associates to purchase Belmont with the money provided by Belmont in contravention of s 54, (ii) that the defendants had wrongfully conspired together to carry into effect the sale and purchase of Belmont's share capital in contravention of s 54, and (iii) that the defendants were liable as constructive trustees, both as having received money which was held in trust for Belmont in such circumstances as to render them accountable for it and as having knowingly participated in a dishonest and fraudulent design on the part of those holding money in trust for Belmont. Belmont claimed damages. At the trial, J, on behalf of Williams and City, asserted that he genuinely believed that buying Maximum for £500,000 was a good commercial proposition for Belmont because he and Belmont were buying G's ability to make money. The judge accepted that and, having decided that the agreement of 3rd October was a bona fide commercial transaction, dismissed the claim. Belmont appealed.

Held – The appeal would be allowed for the following reasons—

(i) A breach of s 54 of the 1948 Act occurred if a company, without regard to its own commercial interests, bought something from a third party with the sole purpose of putting the third party in funds to acquire shares in the company, notwithstanding that the price paid was a fair price. Thus, even though the agreement for the purchase of the share capital of Maximum by Belmont was a satisfactory commercial transaction for both Williams and City and for G and his associates, it nevertheless contravened s 54 even if the £500,000 paid by Belmont for Maximum had been a fair price, because it was not a commercial transaction in its own right but merely part of a scheme to enable G and his associates to acquire Belmont at no cash cost to themselves, was not a transaction in the ordinary course of Belmont's business, and did not enable Belmont to acquire anything which it genuinely needed for its own purposes. It followed that the belief of Williams and City (acting through J) that Maximum's shares were worth £500,000 was not in any event a good defence to a breach of s 54. The fact that Maximum was, on the evidence, worth only some £60,000 and not £500,000 at the time merely reinforced the fact that the transaction contravened s 54 (see p 402 *f g*, p 403 *c* to *j*, p 406 *e*, p 407 *j*, p 408 *b* to p 409 *j*, p 410 *c*, p 413 *d* and p 414 *d* to *h*, post); *Re V G M Holdings* [1942] 1 All ER 224 and *Gradwell (Pty) Ltd v Rostra Printers Ltd* 1959 (4)SA 419 considered.

(ii) Having regard to the fact that, as a director of both companies, J's knowledge of the objects of the agreement was to be imputed to Williams and City, the claim of conspiracy had been established against the defendants because (a) they had combined to participate in a common intention to enter into the agreement of 3rd October, to procure that Belmont entered into it, and then to ensure that it was implemented, (b) that combination had been to effect an unlawful purpose, namely the provision of financial assistance to G and his associates to acquire Belmont using money provided by Belmont, in contravention of s 54 of the 1948 Act, and (c) that had resulted in damage to Belmont (see p 404 *c* to *h*, p 406 *e*, p 413 *d*, p 414 *j* to p 415 *a*, p 416 *b c* and p 417 *d* to *f*, post); *Mulcahy v R* (1868) LR 3 HL 306 and dictum of Lord Simon LC in *Crofter Hand Woven Harris Tweed Co Ltd v Veitch* [1942] 1 All ER at 147 applied.

(iii) Having regard to J's genuine belief that Maximum's shares were worth £500,000, it could not be said that City had knowingly participated in a dishonest and fraudulent design on the part of Belmont's directors, and City was not therefore liable as a constructive trustee on that account. However City was liable to Belmont as a constructive trustee of the £489,000 received for the sale of the share capital of Belmont because that money had been misapplied by the directors of Belmont by virtue of the breach of s 54 and City, through its directors, had known of the whole circumstances of the transaction, and had accordingly received trust funds (ie funds belonging to Belmont of which Belmont's directors were trustees) in such a way as to become accountable for them (see p 405 *c* to *h*, p 406 *b* to *f*, p 411 *a b*, p 412 *e* to p 413 *b d* and p 417 *f*, post); dictum of Lord Selbourne LC in *Barnes v Addy* (1874) LR 9 Ch App at 251–252 applied.

Quaere whether there is a breach of s 54 when company A legitimately enters into a transaction in its own commercial interests and not solely as a means of financially

a
assisting B to buy shares in it, but nevertheless partly with the object of putting B in funds to acquire shares in it or with the knowledge that B so intends to use the proceeds of sale (see p 402 h j, p 406 e, p 407 j to p 408 b, p 413 d and p 414 g h, post).

Notes
For the ingredients of the tort of conspiracy, see 37 Halsbury's Laws (3rd Edn) 128, para 222.

b
For the provision of financial assistance by a company for the purchase of its own shares, see 7 Halsbury's Laws (4th Edn) para 208, and for cases on the subject, see 9 Digest (Reissue) 403–405, 2378–2379.

For constructive trusts, see 38 Halsbury's Laws (3rd Edn) 855–856, paras 1440–1441, and for cases on the subject, see 47 Digest (Repl) 101–113, 727–814.

For pleading fraud, see 30 Halsbury's Laws (3rd Edn) 17, para 36.

c
For the Companies Act 1948, s 54, see 5 Halsbury's Statutes (3rd Edn) 163.

Cases referred to in judgments
Barnes v Addy (1874) LR 9 Ch App 244, 43 LJ Ch 513, 30 LT 4, LC and LJJ, 47 Digest (Repl) 191, *1593*.
Belmont Finance Corpn Ltd v Williams Furniture Ltd [1979] 1 All ER 118, [1979] Ch 250,

d
[1978] 3 WLR 712, CA.
Churchill v Walton [1967] 1 All ER 497, [1967] 2 AC 224, [1967] 2 WLR 682, 131 JP 277, 51 Cr App R 212, HL, 14(1) Digest (Reissue) 126, *842*.
Cooper v Simmons (1862) 7 H & N 707, 31 LJMC 138, 5 LT 712, 26 JP 486, 8 Jur NS 81, 158 ER 654, 12 Digest (Reissue) 731, *5283*.
Crofter Hand Woven Harris Tweed Co Ltd v Veitch [1942] 1 All ER 142, [1942] AC 435, 111

e
LJPC 17, 166 LT 172, HL, 45 Digest (Repl) 534, *1175*.
Fenwick, Stobart & Co Ltd, Re, Deep Sea Fishery Co's (Ltd) Claim [1902] 1 Ch 507, 71 LJ Ch 321, 86 LT 193, 9 Mans 205, 9 Digest (Reissue) 585, *3492*.
Gradwell (Pty) Ltd v Rostra Printers Ltd 1959 (4) SA 419.
Kamara v Director of Public Prosecutions [1973] 2 All ER 1242, [1974] AC 104, [1973] 3 WLR 198, 137 JP 714, 57 Cr App R 880, HL; *affg* sub nom *R v Kamara* [1972] 3 All ER

f
999, [1973] QB 660, [1973] 2 WLR 126, 57 Cr App R 144, CA, Digest (Cont Vol D) 151, *863a*.
Lands Allotment Co, Re [1894] 1 Ch 616, [1891–94] All ER Rep 1032, 63 LJ Ch 291, 70 LT 286, 1 Mans 107, 7 R 115, CA, 9 Digest (Reissue) 560, *3351*.
Mulcahy v R (1868) LR 3 HL 306, 14(1) Digest (Reissue) 119, *800*.
Payne (David) & Co Ltd, Re, Young v David Payne & Co Ltd [1904] 2 Ch 608, 73 LJ Ch 849,

g
91 LT 777, 11 Mans 437, CA, 9 Digest (Reissue) 511, *3058*.
R v I C R Haulage Ltd [1944] 1 All ER 691, [1944] KB 551, 113 LJKB 492, 171 LT 180, 108 JP 181, 42 LGR 226, 30 Cr App R 31, CCA, 13 Digest (Reissue) 351, *2981*.
Russell v Wakefield Waterworks Co (1875) LR 20 Eq 474, 44 LJ Ch 496, 32 LT 685, 10 Digest (Reissue) 1363, *8755*.
Shaw v Director of Public Prosecutions [1961] 2 All ER 446, [1962] AC 220, [1961] 2 WLR

h
897, 125 JP 437, 45 Cr App R 113, HL; *affg* sub nom *R v Shaw* [1961] 1 All ER 330, CCA, 14(1) Digest (Reissue) 139, *965*.
V G M Holdings Ltd, Re [1942] 1 All ER 224, [1942] Ch 235, 111 LJ Ch 145, CA, 9 Digest (Reissue) 677, *4043*.
Wallersteiner v Moir (No 2) [1975] 1 All ER 849, [1975] QB 373, 508n, [1975] 2 WLR 389, CA, Digest (Cont Vol D) 570, *518a*.

j
Cases also cited
Carl-Zeiss-Stiftung v Herbert Smith & Co (a firm) (No 2) [1969] 2 All ER 367, [1969] 2 Ch 276, CA.
Competitive Insurance Co Ltd v Davies Investments Ltd [1975] 3 All ER 254, [1975] 1 WLR 1240.

Heron II, The, Koufos v C Czarnikow Ltd [1967] 3 All ER 686, [1969] 1 AC 350, HL.
Jefford v Gee [1970] 1 All ER 1202, [1970] 2 QB 130, CA.
Selangor United Rubber Estates Ltd v Cradock (No 3) [1968] 2 All ER 1073, [1968] 1 WLR 1555.
Wallersteiner v Moir [1974] 3 All ER 217, [1974] 1 WLR 991, CA.
Yuill v Yuill [1945] 1 All ER 183, [1945] P 15, CA.

Appeal

The plaintiff, Belmont Finance Corpn Ltd ('Belmont'), by a receiver appointed out of court under debentures issued by the company, brought an action against the defendants, (1) Williams Furniture Ltd (formerly Easterns Ltd) ('Williams'), (2) City Industrial Finance Ltd ('City'), (3) James Peter Grosscurth, (4) Andreas Demetri, (5) Kenneth Maund, (6) John Sinclair Copeland, (7) Archie Spector and (8) Frank Victor Smith, seeking (i) a declaration that a transaction effected by an agreement dated 3rd October 1963 made between the first three defendants and Belmont was unlawful and void under s 54 of the Companies Act 1948, (ii) damages and (iii) all necessary accounts and enquiries. Further and in the alternative Belmont claimed against the seventh and eighth defendants a declaration that they were guilty of misfeasance and breach of trust in relation to Belmont, as its directors, in procuring Belmont to enter into an unlawful agreement and/or in procuring the purchase by Belmont of certain shares at a price which to the knowledge of those defendants was greatly in excess of the true value of the shares, and compensation for such misfeasance and breach of trust.

The third defendant was a bankrupt and did not enter an appearance to the action. Shortly before the trial Belmont reached a compromise with the fifth defendant. Early in 1970 the action was discontinued against the eighth defendant on compassionate grounds. At the trial of the action Belmont asserted that on the pleadings in the statement of claim it was entitled to claim additional relief against all defendants, on the basis of constructive trust.

On 30th July 1976, at the close of Belmont's case, Foster J dismissed the action on the grounds that there was no case to answer on the claim for conspiracy and that it was not open to Belmont, on the case as pleaded, to claim relief on the basis of constructive trust. Belmont appealed to the Court of Appeal[1] (Buckley, Orr and Goff LJJ) which on 18th February 1977 allowed the appeal holding that Belmont was not barred from pursuing the claim for conspiracy. The Court of Appeal also allowed Belmont to amend its statement of claim to allege breach of a constructive trust by the defendants. The case was remitted to Foster J who on 6th December 1977, after the trial of the action, dismissed Belmont's claim. Belmont appealed. During the course of the hearing of the appeal Belmont reached a compromise with the fourth and sixth defendants. The seventh defendant was not made a respondent to the appeal and therefore as against him the case stood dismissed. The facts are set out in the judgment of Buckley LJ.

Michael Miller QC and *M J Roth* for Belmont.
Martin Nourse QC and *Brian Parker* for Williams and City.
Nicholas Stewart for the fourth and sixth defendants.
The third defendant did not appear.

Cur adv vult

25th May. The following judgments were read.

BUCKLEY LJ. This is the plaintiff's appeal against a judgment of Foster J, who on 6th December 1977 dismissed this action. The action is brought by a receiver and manager appointed out of court by the holders of debentures created by the plaintiff company ('Belmont'). The receiver sues in Belmont's name under the direction of the court, but

---

1   [1979] 1 All ER 118, [1979] Ch 250

the action is being fought in the interests of depositors with Belmont, the business of
a which was that of deposit bankers financing mainly hire-purchase transactions. Belmont
is now in compulsory liquidation. We are told that under the terms of the debentures
the claims of depositors rank in priority to the claims of the debenture holders and that
there are no assets to meet the claims of the depositors apart from the fruits of this action.

The action arises out of a sale of the share capital of Belmont which is claimed to have
been in breach of the Companies Act 1948, s 54, which makes it illegal for a company to
b give financial assistance for or in connection with the purchase of its own shares.

Immediately before the transaction out of which the claim arises Belmont was a
wholly-owned subsidiary of the second defendant, City Industrial Finance Ltd ('City').
City was and is a wholly owned subsidiary of the first defendant, Williams Furniture Ltd
('Williams') formerly called Easterns Ltd. Williams was then owned or controlled by a
Colonel Lipert. He was anxious to sell Belmont because its business was not proving to
c be profitable and also partly because it did not form a particularly useful adjunct of the
business of dealing in furniture in which the rest of his companies were engaged.

The third defendant, James Peter Grosscurth, and associates of his, owned or controlled,
amongst other companies, two companies called Rentahome Ltd ('Rentahome') and
Maximum Finance Ltd ('Maximum') engaged directly or indirectly in property
development. All or substantially all the issued shares of Maximum, which consisted of
d 50,000 £1 ordinary shares, were beneficially owned by Mr Grosscurth, the fifth
defendant Kenneth Maund and the sixth defendant John Sinclair Copeland, although
some of these were registered in the name of the fourth defendant Andreas Demetri. Mr
Grosscurth controlled both companies. Mr Grosscurth, with the concurrence of Mr
Maund and Mr Copeland, was anxious to buy Belmont for use as a means of financing
property development projects of other companies in their group. He and Colonel
e Lipert entered into negotiations. While these negotiations were proceeding there was a
change in the control of Williams. A Mr James and a Mr Norman Williams owned the
share capital of a company called W & S Williams (Kilburn) Ltd which carried on a
furniture business. As a result of what has been termed a reverse takeover, Messrs James
and Norman Williams early in September 1963 acquired a controlling interest in
Williams (the first defendant) in exchange for their shares in W & S Williams (Kilburn)
f Ltd, which thus became a subsidiary of Williams. Thereafter the negotiations with Mr
Grosscurth were conducted by Mr James and his representatives in the place of Colonel
Lipert. They resulted in due course in an agreement dated 3rd October 1963 ('the
agreement') which gives rise to the present action.

Early in those negotiations in answer to an enquiry by Colonel Lipert as to how Mr
Grosscurth proposed to finance the deal, Mr Grosscurth stated in a letter dated 5th June
g 1963 that his present intention was 'to arrange the consideration for the purchase of
Belmont from Belmont's own resources . . . by selling to Belmont the whole of the issued
share capital of Rentahome Limited'. Later, in a letter dated 2nd September 1963 to Mr
James, Mr Grosscurth said that for fiscal reasons he was unable to sell shares in Rentahome
and suggested as an alternative that Belmont should purchase the whole of the share
capital of Maximum for £500,000.

h The parties to the agreement were Mr Grosscurth, Belmont, City (then called Belmont
Industrial Finance Ltd) and Williams (then called Easterns Ltd). By cl 2 Mr Grosscurth
agreed to sell, or procure the sale of, the whole share capital of Maximum to Belmont for
£500,000 in cash and Belmont agreed to buy it at that price. By cl 4, subject to and on
completion of the foregoing sale, City agreed to sell and Mr Grosscurth agreed to buy, or
procure the purchase of, all the issued share capital of Belmont for £230,000 and a
j further sum to be ascertained in accordance with cl 5, which turned out to be £259,000,
making a total purchase price of £489,000. Both transactions were to be completed on
11th October 1963, the latter sale being completed immediately after the former. By
cl 7 on completion of the latter sale City agreed to subscribe for 230,000 £1 5%
cumulative redeemable preference shares of Belmont, and Mr Grosscurth agreed to
subscribe for 20,000 like shares and 50,000 £1 ordinary shares of Belmont, in every case

at par. By cl 9 City and Williams agreed to lend Belmont £200,000 for 12 months from *a*
completion at 9¼% per annum secured on the capital of Maximum. By cl 13(h) Mr
Grosscurth undertook and warranted to Belmont that the aggregate profits of Maximum
and its subsidiaries for the period from 22nd May 1962 to 31st May 1968, net of all
expenses but subject to tax, should be not less than £500,000, and that in default Mr
Grosscurth should pay to Belmont by way of liquidated damages a sum equal to the
deficiency less income tax and profits tax at the rates in force on 31st May 1968. This
undertaking or warranty was to be secured on the whole of the issued share capital of *b*
Rentahome. The preference shares of Belmont were to be redeemed in accordance with
a prescribed programme and Mr Grosscurth covenanted with City that, if they were not
so redeemed, he would purchase them at par within 28 days of the several redemption
dates.

The outcome of the agreement when completed was (1) that, whereas previously (a)
Mr Grosscurth and his associates had owned all the capital of Maximum, of which a *c*
company which I shall call Cityfield was a wholly owned subsidiary, and (b) Mr James
and his associates had owned a controlling interest in Williams, of which City was a
wholly owned subsidiary and Belmont a wholly owned sub-subsidiary, after completion
(i) Mr Grosscurth and his associates owned all the capital of Belmont, of which Maximum
was a wholly-owned subsidiary and Cityfield a wholly-owned sub-subsidiary, and (ii) City
had parted with Belmont, (2) that City received £489,000, out of which it subscribed at *d*
par for 230,000 £1 5% cumulative redeemable preference shares of Belmont retaining
£259,000 in cash, and Mr Grosscurth and his associates received £11,000 in cash, (3) that
the paid-up capital of Belmont was increased by an amount of £300,000 consisting of
230,000 preference shares subscribed by City, 20,000 like shares subscribed by Mr
Grosscurth and 50,000 ordinary shares subscribed by Mr Grosscurth, (4) that Belmont
had £200,000 on loan from Williams and City for 12 months, which altogether with the *e*
proceeds of the new share capital, restored to Belmont for the time being the £500,000
cash employed in buying Maximum, (5) that Belmont had the undertaking of Mr
Grosscurth that the profits of Maximum and its subsidiaries for the period 22nd May
1962 to 31st May 1968, net of all expenses but subject to tax, should be not less than
£500,000 (representing net profits after tax at the rates of tax then in force of £156,250),
such undertaking being secured on the share capital of Rentahome, and (6) that the *f*
programme for the redemption of the preference shares was such that they would
become due for redemption by prescribed instalments in each of the sixth to the
twentieth years following allotment.

The sealing of the agreement by Belmont was resolved on at a board meeting of
Belmont on 3rd October 1963 at which three directors only of that company were
present, namely Mr Norman Williams, the seventh defendant Mr Spector, and a Mr *g*
Foley. Its completion was carried out at two board meetings of Belmont, one of which
was held at noon on 11th October 1963 and the other at 2.30 pm on the same day. The
directors present at each of those meetings were the seventh and eighth defendants,
Messrs Spector and Smith, a Mr Kellman and Mr Foley. At the earlier meeting it was
resolved that Belmont should purchase the issued share capital of Maximum for
£500,000. The necessary transfers were approved and sealed by Belmont and the *h*
secretary was instructed to arrange for the transfers to be stamped and presented for
registration. The minute of the later meeting records:

> 'It was confirmed that Messrs. Gouldens [who were the solicitors advising Mr
> Grosscurth and his associates] had obtained Counsel's Opinion, a copy of which was
> produced at the meeting, stating that the transaction did not in his opinion
> contravene section 54 of the Companies Act 1948.'   *j*

At that meeting, which was also attended by Mr Grosscurth and his associates, all the
rest of the formal steps necessary to implement the agreement were carried out. The
opinion of counsel there referred to is dated 27th September 1963 and was obtained by
Messrs Gouldens on behalf of their clients without any reference to Belmont or anyone

on Belmont's behalf, or any suggestion by anyone on Belmont's behalf that such an
a opinion should be obtained. I must revert to this opinion later.

For the sake of completeness I should say that the execution of the agreement by
Williams was resolved on at a board meeting of Williams on 3rd October 1963 at which
the directors present were Mr Norman Williams and a Mr Burke. The execution of the
agreement by City was resolved on at a board meeting of City on the same date at which
the directors present were Mr Norman Williams, a Mr Harries and Mr Spector. At a
b board meeting of City at 1.30 pm on 11th October 1963, at which the directors present
were Mr Harries, Mr Smith and Mr Spector, it was, according to the minute, confirmed
that Messrs Gouldens had obtained counsel's opinion, a copy of which was produced at
the meeting, stating that the agreement did not in counsel's opinion contravene s 54 of
the 1948 Act. Share transfers of all the shares of Belmont were then approved and sealed
as follows: 116,668 ordinary £1 shares in favour of Mr Grosscurth, 41,666 like shares in
c favour of Mr Maund, 41,666 like shares in favour of Mr Demetri, making a total of
200,000 shares.

It was further resolved that City should subscribe for 230,000 preference shares of
Belmont and the secretary was authorised to draw and present a cheque in favour of
Belmont for £230,000 accordingly. A letter from Messrs Binder Hamlyn & Co,
chartered accountants, was produced to the meeting confirming that that firm held a
d memorandum of deposit of all the issued share capital of Rentahome together with the
relevant certificates and blank transfers executed by the registered holders, and that the
same would not be removed from Messrs Binder Hamlyn & Co until the liability of Mr
Grosscurth to Belmont had been determined. The shares transferred to Mr Demetri
were to be held by him as nominee for Mr Grosscurth and Mr Copeland.

At 3rd and 11th October 1963 the boards of directors of City and Belmont respectively
e consisted of the following persons: City—James, Norman Williams, Harries, Voss,
Spector and Smith; Belmont—James, Norman Williams, Spector, Smith, Kellman and
Foley. Foley was also the secretary of Williams, City and Belmont. Of these gentlemen,
Harries and Foley were members of what I shall refer to hereafter as Mr James's team.
None of the rest, apart from Mr James himself, appears to have taken any effective part
in the affair, save in so far as they appeared at the board meetings of 3rd and 11th
f October, but no explanation of the transactions was given to them at either of those
board meetings or apparently at any other time. They did what they were told to do.
Mr Norman Williams, Mr Harries and Mr Foley all died before the action came to trial.
Harries and Foley, who both died in 1972, had made written statements, but no use was
attempted to be made of these under the Civil Evidence Act 1968 at the trial. Mr Spector
was alive at the time of the trial, but his health was said to be such that he was unfit to
g be cross-examined. He was then legally aided and represented by counsel, who asked
that Mr Spector should be permitted to give evidence by way of answers to interrogatories;
but in the face of opposition by counsel for Williams and City to this proposal the judge
refused to allow that course to be taken. Consequently the judge heard no evidence from
Mr Spector. Mr Spector is not a respondent to this appeal. So far as he is concerned the
judgment stands.

h It is perhaps convenient to mention also at this point (i) that the action was
discontinued against Mr Smith in 1970 on compassionate grounds and (ii) that all claims
by Belmont against Mr Maund were compromised shortly before the first trial on
payment of a certain sum by Mr Maund to Belmont, when the proceedings were
discontinued against him. Neither of these two gentlemen has given evidence. Late in
the course of this appeal the plaintiff came to terms with Mr Copeland and Mr Demetri
j and all proceedings against them have been stayed. Mr Grosscurth himself has gone
bankrupt and was not available at the trial to give evidence, being abroad.

This action was commenced by Belmont's receiver on 30th September 1969 against
Williams, City, Grosscurth, Demetri, Maund, Copeland, Spector and Smith. The fourth,
fifth and sixth defendants were, as I have already indicated, associates of Mr Grosscurth.
The seventh and eighth defendants were directors of Belmont until the board of that

company was reconstituted at the board meeting held at 2.30 pm on 11th October 1963 after the completion of the agreement. In the statement of claim Belmont alleged that the agreement was in contravention of s 54 of the 1948 Act and that the defendants conspired to carry it into effect whereby Belmont had suffered damage. Belmont claimed as against all the defendants a declaration that the agreement was unlawful and void under s 54 and damages with ancillary relief, and as against the defendants Spector and Smith that they were guilty of misfeasance and breach of trust in procuring Belmont to enter into the agreement or alternatively in procuring Belmont to buy the share capital of Maximum at £500,000, which was to their knowledge greatly in excess of its true value, with consequential relief.

The earlier history of the action appears from the report of an earlier appeal to this court[1]. I shall not repeat now what is there recorded. Under the leave to amend which was then obtained, Belmont amended its statement of claim to introduce an allegation that, as all the defendants well knew, the price paid for the capital of Maximum was an inflated price, or alternatively that the defendants shut their eyes to the fact that such price was an inflated one or wilfully refrained from enquiring into the question whether such price was a proper or an inflated one. They further alleged that the price of £500,000 was arrived at by all the defendants dishonestly to facilitate the purchase of Belmont's capital in contravention of s 54. They also alleged that the banker's draft for £489,000 by which the purchase price for the capital of Belmont was satisfied, as City knew or ought to have known, was or represented moneys of Belmont misapplied by the defendants Spector and Smith in breach of trust in giving financial assistance to the purchasers of the capital of Belmont for their purchase thereof from City. They also alleged that £122,500, part of the £489,000, was the purchase price of 41,666 Belmont shares bought by Grosscurth and Copeland and that as Copeland well knew the £122,500 was or represented moneys of Belmont misapplied by the defendants Spector and Smith in breach of trust in giving financial assistance as aforesaid. Based on these new allegations Belmont by amendment to the prayer of its statement of claim raised new claims against City and Copeland as constructive trustees in respect of the sums of £489,000 and £122,500 respectively.

The first question for consideration is whether the agreement did contravene s 54 of the 1948 Act. Only if the answer to that question is affirmative does the question whether the defendants or any of them are guilty of conspiracy arise, for it is the illegality of the agreement, if it be illegal, which constitutes the common intention of the parties to enter into the agreement a conspiracy at law.

There is little judicial authority on the section. In *Re V G M Holdings*[2] this court had to consider whether under the section in the form in which it stood in the Companies Act 1929, which did not contain the word 'subscription', the section covered a case where money which a company had provided had been used to assist a subscription for the company's own shares. Lord Greene MR said[3]:

'There could, I think, be no doubt that, if that question were answered in favour of the liquidator, the 15,980*l* was provided by the company by way of financial assistance, because whether a company provides the money by way of gift or by way of loan or by buying assets from the person who is purchasing the shares at a fraudulent overvalue, all those transactions, it seems to me, would fall within the phrase "financial assistance."'

The transaction there in question was a fraudulent one. V G M Holdings Ltd bought all the share capital of Century, which was worthless, from Vanbergen for £8,301 and Vanbergen used the money to pay a call on shares which he held in V G M. The court,

---

1   [1979] 1 All ER 118, [1979] Ch 250
2   [1942] 1 All ER 224, [1942] Ch 235
3   [1942] Ch 235 at 240; cf [1942] 1 All ER 224 at 226

however, held that the transaction did not involve a purchase of V G M shares and so was
a not within the section. In reliance on the reference by Lord Greene MR to a purchase at
a fraudulent overvalue, it was suggested to us that the section does not apply to any case
in which the company which is alleged to have given financial assistance got fair value
for its money. I think that Lord Greene MR must be understood to have been speaking
in the context of the facts of the case before him and not to have intended to attempt to
put any limit on the scope of the section.

b   Our attention was also drawn to a South African case of *Gradwell (Pty) Ltd v Rostra
Printers Ltd*[1]. The contract in that case was a little complicated, but the facts can be
summarised as follows. Company A sold to company B all the shares in company C and
a debt of £40,258 due from company C to company A. The price was £32,245. The
contract was conditional on company B being able to borrow £30,000 on the security of
company C's assets. That sum was to be applied in discharging an existing mortgage of
c company C's assets and in reducing company C's debt to company A. To the extent that
the debt to company A was reduced, the cash so received by company A was to be treated
as paid on account of the purchase price, that is to say, the price payable by company B
was to be reduced by the amount that the debt to company A, which formed part of the
subject-matter of the sale, was reduced. The statutory provision there under consideration
was for present purposes identical with s 54(1) of the 1948 Act.

d   The case eventually came before the Appellate Division of the Supreme Court of South
Africa. In the following passage Rostra is company A, Crowden is company B and 'the
company' is company C. Schreiner JA, who delivered what was effectively the judgment
of the court, said[2]:

> 'We were pressed by counsel for Crowden with the importance of the purpose of
> the whole transaction. The purpose of Crowden and Rostra was inevitably that of
e > the company, the actions of which were entirely controllable by Rostra. The
> purpose must be taken to have been to help Crowden to buy and Rostra to sell the
> company's shares. But this does not carry Crowden to success. Unless what was to
> be done would amount to giving of financial assistance within the meaning of the
> sub-section the purpose and the connection would not be important. Having
> money available the company could part with it in various ways that would enable
f > the recipient to purchase the company's shares with the money. It could for
> instance buy an asset, not required for the purposes of its business, in order to
> provide the seller of the asset with money with which to buy the shares. It was
> contended on behalf of Crowden that this would be giving financial assistance. If
> the purchase of the asset were effected at a price known to be inflated, this would no
> doubt be the giving of financial assistance. It would indeed be equivalent to a gift
g > and would clearly involve a reduction of the company's capital. It was one of the
> illustrations given by LORD GREENE in *In re V. G. M. Holdings Ltd*.[3] It is, I think,
> significant that the MASTER OF THE ROLLS did not mention the case of the purchase
> of an asset at a fair price with the object of enabling the seller of the asset to buy the
> shares. But whatever may be the position in such a case the paying off of an existing
> debt seems to be decidedly more difficult to bring within the notion of giving
h > financial assistance. The payer's assets and liabilities are put into a different form
> but the balance is unchanged. And the same applies to the financial position of the
> payee. Here the company would have no more and no less after the completion of
> the transaction than before. And the same would apply to Rostra. The company
> would owe more to its mortgagee and correspondingly less to Rostra. The price to
> be paid by Crowden would be less by the difference in the value of the assets to be
j > acquired. Its financial position would be unchanged—only its investment would be

---

1   1959 (4) SA 419
2   1959 (4) SA 419 at 425–426
3   [1942] 1 All ER 224 at 226, [1942] Ch 235 at 240

smaller. Where there is an anticipation of the date when a debt becomes due and payable the position may possibly be different, but where the debt is presently due *a* and payable and the debtor can have no answer to the creditor's demand for payment, it would be straining the language to hold that by paying his debt the debtor gives the creditor financial assistance.'

In that passage the learned judge reserves the question of what the effect would be if company B were to purchase from company A an asset not required for the purposes of *b* its business but at a fair price.

Foster J treated as a proposition of law, accepted by counsel for Belmont, that a company does not give financial assistance in connection with a purchase of its own shares within the meaning of s 54 by reason only of its simultaneous entry into a bona fide commercial transaction as a result of which it parts with money or money's worth, which in turn is used to finance the purchase of its own shares. He went on to find that *c* the negotiations in the present case were at arm's length and that on the one side Mr James genuinely believed that to buy the capital of Maximum for £500,000 was a good commercial proposition for Belmont and on the other side Mr Copeland honestly believed that in October 1963 the value of the capital of Maximum with Mr Grosscurth's guarantee of Maximum's profits under cl 13(h) of the agreement secured on Rentahome's share capital was not less than £500,000. On these findings he reached the conclusion *d* that the agreement was a bona fide commercial transaction, on which ground he dismissed the action.

This reasoning assumes, as I understand it, that if the transaction under consideration is genuinely regarded by the parties as a sound commercial transaction negotiated at arm's length and capable of justification on purely commercial grounds, it cannot offend against s 54. This is, I think, a broader proposition than the proposition which the judge *e* treated as having been accepted by counsel for Belmont. If A Ltd buys from B a chattel or a commodity, like a ship or merchandise, which A Ltd genuinely wants to acquire for its own purposes, and does so having no other purpose in view, the fact that B thereafter employs the proceeds of the sale in buying shares in A Ltd should not, I would suppose, be held to offend against the section; but the position may be different if A Ltd makes the purchase in order to put B in funds to buy shares in A Ltd. If A Ltd buys something from *f* B without regard to its own commercial interests, the sole purpose of the transaction being to put B in funds to acquire shares in A Ltd, this would, in my opinion, clearly contravene the section, even if the price paid was a fair price for what is bought, and a fortiori that would be so if the sale to A Ltd was at an inflated price. The sole purpose would be to enable (ie to assist) B to pay for the shares. If A Ltd buys something from B at a fair price, which A Ltd could readily realise on a resale if it wished to do so, but the *g* purpose, or one of the purposes, of the transaction is to put B in funds to acquire shares of A Ltd, the fact that the price was fair might not, I think, prevent the transaction from contravening the section, if it would otherwise do so, though A Ltd could very probably recover no damages in civil proceedings, for it would have suffered no damage. If the transaction is of a kind which A Ltd could in its own commercial interests legitimately enter into, and the transaction is genuinely entered into by A Ltd in its own commercial *h* interests and not merely as a means of assisting B financially to buy shares of A Ltd, the circumstance that A Ltd enters into the transaction with B, partly with the object of putting B in funds to acquire its own shares or with the knowledge of B's intended use of the proceeds of sale, might, I think, involve no contravention of the section, but I do not wish to express a concluded opinion on that point.

The reasoning of the judge's judgment appears to me, with deference to him, to *j* overlook the word 'only' in the suggested proposition of law.

[His Lordship then considered the judge's favourable assessment of Mr James as a witness and the failure of Mr James or any of his associates to obtain a valuation of Maximum and went on to consider an independent valuation made in July 1974 by Mr Howard Williams, a partner in Messrs Mann Judd & Co, a London firm of chartered

accountants, who were instructed by Belmont's receiver as if to advise Belmont of a fair
a price to pay for the share capital of Maximum as at 3rd October 1963. The valuation
report of Messrs Mann Judd & Co valued the total issued share capital of Maximum as at
3rd October 1963 at not more than the 'value of the underlying consolidated "tangible"
assets of the company, that is, £60,069'. His Lordship then pointed out that Mr James
had genuinely believed that the transaction was a good commercial proposition for
Belmont without having any good grounds for that belief, and then continued:] After
b careful consideration I do not feel that we should be justified in disturbing the judge's
finding that Mr James genuinely believed that the agreement was a good commercial
proposition for Belmont. It was a belief which, on his view of the commercial aspects of
the case, Mr James could have sincerely held.

In truth the purchase of the share capital of Maximum was not a commercial
transaction in its own right so far as Mr James and his group of companies were
c concerned: it was part of the machinery by which City obtained £489,000 for the share
capital of Belmont, £259,000 in cash and £230,000 by redemption of the redeemable
preference shares subscribed in Belmont. It was not a transaction whereby Belmont
acquired anything which Belmont genuinely needed or wanted for its own purposes: it
was one which facilitated Mr Grosscurth's acquiring Belmont for his own purposes
without effectively parting with Maximum. That the purpose of the sale of Maximum
d to Belmont was to enable Mr Grosscurth to pay £489,000 for Belmont was at all relevant
times known to and recognised by Mr James and the members of his team as well as by
Mr Copeland. There is no good reason disclosed by the evidence to suppose either that
Mr Grosscurth and his associates could have sold Maximum to anyone else for £500,000
or that Belmont could have disposed of Maximum for £500,000 to anyone else at any
time. The purchase of the share capital of Maximum may have been intra vires of
e Belmont (a matter which we have not been invited to consider), but it was certainly not
a transaction in the ordinary course of Belmont's business or for the purposes of that
business as it subsisted at the date of the agreement. It was an exceptional and artificial
transaction and not in any sense an ordinary commercial transaction entered into for its
own sake in the commercial interests of Belmont. It was part of a comparatively
complex scheme for enabling Mr Grosscurth and his associates to acquire Belmont at no
f cash cost to themselves, the purchase price being found not from their own funds or by
the realisation of any asset of theirs (for Maximum continued to be part of their group
of companies) but out of Belmont's own resources. In these circumstances, in my
judgment, the agreement would have contravened s 54 of the 1948 Act even if £500,000
was a fair price for Maximum. I think, however, that Mr Howard Williams's report and
evidence clearly establish that £500,000 was in truth an inflated price. To the extent that
g it exceeded £60,000 or thereabouts it was speculative and depended on the continued
availability of Mr Grosscurth to direct Maximum's affairs and his willingness to do so.
The view that Belmont was buying Mr Grosscurth's services for a period of some five
years or until Maximum had earned £500,000 gross profits is, in my view, untenable.
As I remarked in the course of the argument, Belmont was not buying Grosscurth;
Grosscurth was buying Belmont. The business of Cityfield, which was Maximum's main
h source of profit, was admittedly speculative and was financed by borrowing. Moreover,
its profits as stated in its annual accounts were ascertained on a basis which Mr Copeland
agreed was imprudent, though not improper, profits being brought into account before
they were received. A considerable part of such profits had to be written off because the
contracts on which they depended fell through. It is, in my judgment, manifest on the
evidence, particularly that of Mr Howard Williams, that the existence of the warranty
j could not have added an amount anywhere near £440,000 to the saleable value of
Maximum, if indeed it added anything.

It follows that in my judgment the agreement was unlawful, for it was a contract by
Belmont to do an unlawful act, viz to provide financial assistance to Mr Grosscurth and
his associates for the purpose of, or in connection with, the purchase of Belmont's own
share capital.

The next question is whether in these circumstances the alleged conspiracy is established in respect of those defendants against whom the action is still on foot, ie the first three defendants. To obtain in civil proceedings a remedy for conspiracy, the plaintiff must establish (a) a combination of the defendants, (b) to effect an unlawful purpose, (c) resulting in damage to the plaintiff (*Crofter Hand Woven Harris Tweed Co Ltd v Veitch*[1] per Lord Simon LC). The classic definition of conspiracy is that in *Mulcahy v R*[2]:

'A conspiracy consists not merely of the intention of two or more, but in the agreement of two or more to do an unlawful act, or to do a lawful act by unlawful means.'

I have used the word 'combination' rather than the word 'agreement' used in that definition and by Lord Simon LC, because the word 'agreement' in this context does not mean an agreement in any contractual sense but a combination and common intention to do the act which is the object of the alleged conspiracy. That Lord Simon LC was so using the word is, in my opinion, clear from later passages in his speech: see also the other speeches in the *Crofter Hand Woven* case[3].

The unlawful purpose in this case was the provision of financial assistance in contravention of s 54 of the 1948 Act. That the purpose of the sale of Maximum to Belmont was to enable Mr Grosscurth to pay £489,000 to City for the share capital of Belmont was known to all concerned. For reasons which I gave in my judgment on the earlier appeal in this action[4], the alleged conspiracy sued on must, in my view, have preceded the signing of the agreement, but its object is made clear by the agreement, namely that Belmont should give the financial assistance to Mr Grosscurth which the carrying out of the agreement would afford him. Williams and City were parties to the agreement and so, in my opinion, are fixed with the character of parties to the conspiracy. Moreover, Mr James knew perfectly well what the objects of the agreement were. He was a director of both Williams and City. Mr Harries and Mr Foley, who also knew the objects of the agreement, were a director and the secretary respectively of City. Mr Foley was also the secretary of Williams. Their knowledge must, in my opinion, be imputed to the companies of which they were directors and secretary, for an officer of a company must surely be under a duty, if he is aware that a transaction into which his company or a wholly-owned subsidiary is about to enter is illegal or tainted with illegality, to inform the board of that company of the fact. Where an officer is under a duty to make such a disclosure to his company, his knowledge is imputed to the company (*Re David Payne & Co Ltd*[5], *Re Fenwick, Stobart & Co Ltd*[6]). In these circumstances, in my opinion, Williams and City must be regarded as having participated with Mr Grosscurth in a common intention to enter into the agreement and to procure that Belmont should enter into the agreement and that the agreement should be implemented. That Mr Grosscurth was a party to that common intention is, in my opinion, indisputable.

In my judgment, the alleged conspiracy is established in respect of these three defendants, and they are not exempt from liability on account of counsel's opinion or because they may have believed in good faith that the transaction did not transgress s 54. If all the facts which make the transaction unlawful were known to the parties, as I think they were, ignorance of the law will not excuse them: see *Churchill v Walton*.[7] That case was one of criminal conspiracy, but it seems to me that precisely similar principles must apply to a conspiracy for which a civil remedy is sought. Nor, in my

1 [1942] 1 All ER 142 at 147, [1942] AC 435 at 440
2 (1868) LR 3 HL 306 at 317
3 [1942] 1 All ER 142, [1942] AC 435
4 [1979] 1 All ER 118 at 127, [1979] Ch 250 at 263
5 [1904] 2 Ch 608
6 [1902] 1 Ch 507
7 [1967] 1 All ER 497 at 503, [1967] 2 AC 224 at 237

opinion, can the fact that their ignorance of, or failure to appreciate, the unlawful nature
a of the transaction was due to the unfortunate fact that they were, as I think, erroneously
advised excuse them (*Cooper v Simmons*[1], and see *Shaw v Director of Public Prosecutions*[2],
where the appellant had taken professional legal advice).

If they had sincerely believed in a factual state of affairs which, if true, would have
made their actions legal, this would have afforded a defence (*Kamara v Director of Public
Prosecutions*[3]); but on my view of the effect of s 54 in the present case, even if £500,000
b had been a fair price for the share capital of Maximum and all other benefits under the
agreement, this would not have made the agreement legal. So a belief in the fairness of
the price could not excuse them.

I now come to the constructive trust point. If a stranger to a trust (a) receives and
becomes chargeable with some part of the trust fund or (b) assists the trustees of a trust
with knowledge of the facts in a dishonest design on the part of the trustees to misapply
c some part of a trust fund, he is liable as a constructive trustee (*Barnes v Addy*[4] per Lord
Selborne LC).

A limited company is of course not a trustee of its own funds: it is their beneficial
owner; but in consequence of the fiduciary character of their duties the directors of a
limited company are treated as if they were trustees of those funds of the company which
are in their hands or under their control, and if they misapply them they commit a
d breach of trust (*Re Lands Allotment Co*[5], per Lindley and Kay LJJ). So, if the directors of
a company in breach of their fiduciary duties misapply the funds of their company so
that they come into the hands of some stranger to the trust who receives them with
knowledge (actual or constructive) of the breach, he cannot conscientiously retain those
funds against the company unless he has some better equity. He becomes a constructive
trustee for the company of the misapplied funds. This is stated very clearly by Jessel MR
e in *Russell v Wakefield Waterworks Co*[6], where he said:

'In this Court the money of the company is a trust fund, because it is applicable
only to the special purposes of the company in the hands of the agents of the
company, and it is in that sense a trust fund applicable by them to those special
purposes; and a person taking it from them with notice that it is being applied to
f other purposes cannot in this Court say that he is not a constructive trustee.'

In the present case, the payment of the £500,000 by Belmont to Mr Grosscurth, being
an unlawful contravention of s 54, was a misapplication of Belmont's money and was in
breach of the duties of the directors of Belmont. £489,000 of the £500,000 so misapplied
found their way into the hands of City with City's knowledge of the whole circumstances
of the transaction. It must follow, in my opinion, that City is accountable to Belmont as
g a constructive trustee of the £489,000 under the first of Lord Selborne LC's two heads.

There remains the question whether City is chargeable as a constructive trustee under
Lord Selborne LC's second head on the ground that Belmont's directors were guilty of
dishonesty in buying the shares of Maximum and that City with knowledge of the facts
assisted them in that dishonest design. As I understand Lord Selborne LC's second head,
a stranger to a trust notwithstanding that he may not have received any of the trust fund
h which has been misapplied will be treated as accountable as a constructive trustee if he
has knowingly participated in a dishonest design on the part of the trustees to misapply
the fund; he must himself have been in some way a party to the dishonesty of the
trustees. It follows from what I have already held that the directors of Belmont were
guilty of misfeasance but not that they acted dishonestly. No attack appears to have been

j 1   (1862) 7 H & N 707
2   [1961] 2 All ER 446, [1962] AC 220
3   [1973] 2 All ER 1242 at 1252, [1974] AC 104 at 119
4   (1874) LR 9 Ch App 244 at 251–252
5   [1894] 1 Ch 616 at 631, 638, [1891–94] All ER Rep 1032 at 1034, 1038
6   (1875) LR 20 Eq 474 at 479

made at the trial on the honesty of either Mr Norman Williams or Mr Spector, who were two of the three directors of Belmont present at the board meeting of 3rd October 1963, or on the honesty of Mr Smith and Mr Kellman, who with Mr Spector were three of the four directors present at the Belmont board meetings of 11th October 1963. The other director present at those three meetings was Mr Foley. The evidence establishes that the scheme was not explained to Mr Spector, Mr Smith or Mr Kellman. They did what they were told to do. In this respect they clearly failed to discharge their duties as directors, but it has not been shown that they were dishonest. The position of Mr Norman Williams was not investigated. Mr Foley, as one of Mr James's team, was presumably aware of all the relevant facts. There was, so far as I am aware, no evidence directed to establishing dishonesty on his part. Any finding of dishonesty by Mr Foley would have had to be reached by inference. The judge made no finding that any of these gentlemen acted dishonestly. His judgment clearly implies that in his view they did not. Mr James was not present at either of the board meetings. It was not suggested that it was on his personal instructions that Messrs Spector, Smith and Kellman acted as they did at the board meetings. It would seem probable that it was Mr Foley who ran the meetings. Even if the instructions should be regarded as given by Mr James and relayed through Mr Foley, the judge's finding that Mr James honestly believed that the transaction was in Belmont's interests, which as I have said I would not feel justified in disturbing, makes it impossible, in my view, to hold that there was any dishonesty about the proceedings of the Belmont board. So Lord Selborne LC's second head of liability as a constructive trustee cannot, in my judgment, apply in this case.

For these reasons, in my opinion, Belmont is entitled to judgment against the first three defendants for conspiracy and against City as a constructive trustee. I would allow this appeal accordingly. What precise form the relief flowing from this should take may require further argument.

GOFF LJ. I agree with all that Buckley LJ has said. As, however, we are differing from the learned judge I feel that I ought to add my reasons in my own words.

In my view, with every respect to Foster J, he misdirected himself in two fundamental respects. In the first place he took the view at the outset that the matter was remitted to him to try an allegation of dishonesty and nothing else, saying '. . . and the case was remitted to me to finish the trial but now on the basis of an allegation of dishonesty'. This may, I think, have been occasioned by the way in which the defendants put their argument, although Belmont's counsel certainly made it clear that he was submitting that he did not have to prove fraud, unless in the end he was forced to rely on one particular claim, and in that, in my judgment, Belmont's counsel was correct.

Belmont presented its case originally as one of conspiracy and nothing else, and it has never resiled from that claim, or placed less reliance on it, but the first trial came to an abrupt end because the judge accepted a submission on behalf of the defendants that they had no case to answer on the ground that Belmont was itself a party to the agreement of 3rd October 1963, and therefore a party to the alleged conspiracy and thus precluded from maintaining any claim based on it.

We rejected that ruling, and so on the remission the judge had to try that issue, which had so far never been tried. That case, however, does not depend on any allegation of fraud, and so with all respect, taking the view he did that all he had to consider was an allegation of fraud, he could not, and did not, properly consider the issue of conspiracy. Secondly, when the judge gave his ruling at the conclusion of Belmont's case at the first trial, its counsel applied for leave to amend so as to add, not substitute, a claim for relief on the basis of constructive trust. The judge refused to allow any amendment, but we also overruled him on that point. It is true that we held that for this purpose Belmont must allege and prove fraud, which it did in the final version of its statement of claim. However, the constructive trustee claim was formulated, both in the finally amended statement of claim and in argument before us, in the two alternative ways stated by Lord

Selborne LC in *Barnes v Addy*[1], namely, receiving trust funds in such a way as to become
a accountable for them and knowing participation in a dishonest and fraudulent design on
the part of the trustees. The second of those ways does depend on fraud or dishonesty,
but the first does not, and in saying that fraud was essential, we were dealing only with
the second class of case, and with the argument of Belmont's counsel, which we rejected,
that even there fraud is not a necessary part of the cause of action.

In my judgment, therefore, in addition to the conspiracy case the judge had at the
b second trial to decide, quite apart from any question of fraud, whether any, and if so
which, of the defendants had received money, being or representing money held in trust
for Belmont, in such circumstances as to render them accountable as constructive
trustees. Again, however, with all respect he failed to direct his mind to this, because no
doubt of the mistaken view he had on the question that it was fraud or nothing. This is
highlighted, I think, when one sees that in his recital of the significant paragraphs in the
c statement of claim, the judge stopped short at para 20 and did not read or mention para
20A at all, that being the paragraph alleging receipt of trust money and constructive
trusteeship on that footing.

The second fundamental misdirection, in my judgment, was that the judge placed too
wide a construction on the proposition advanced by counsel in his opinion on the effect
of s 54 of the Companies Act 1948, and accepted by counsel for Belmont as an accurate
d statement of the law. With all respect, the judge failed to give due, or any, weight to the
words 'by reason only' in that opinion, which words in my view are highly important.
That being so, the judge directed himself that—

> 'there remains for me to decide a question of fact, namely: was the purchase by
> Belmont of all the shares in Maximum a *bona fide* [the judge's emphasis] commercial
> transaction [and] was the purchase price of £500,000 a commercial one?'

e
That, however, was in my judgment plainly too narrow, for the judge had also to
consider as a matter of the utmost importance what was the purpose of the purchase by
the plaintiff company.

With these preliminary observations I shall proceed to consider the case in
conspiracy. To succeed on this issue Belmont must establish that the agreement of 3rd
f October 1963 was a breach of s 54 of the 1948 Act and, therefore, illegal and that the
value of the Maximum shares was significantly less than £500,000, since otherwise
Belmont suffered no damage which is not too remote.

For reasons which I shall give presently, the shares were not in my view worth
anything like that amount, and if that be so I do not understand it to be seriously
disputed but that there was a breach of the section. In any case in my judgment, for
g reasons which will appear later, on that basis there most plainly was.

Even so, in my view it is necessary to consider further whether there would have been
a breach even if the shares had been of that value because the defendants raise the defence
that, as the judge found, Mr James genuinely believed that they were. If there would be
a breach of trust even if that were true, this cannot help them because there would still
be an offence even if the facts had been as he believed, and they knew all other relevant
h facts, namely the purpose of the transaction and the existence and general effect of s 54.
If, however, there would be no breach unless the value of the Maximum shares did not
amount to £500,000, then unless one can go behind the judge's finding, as we are asked
to do, this belief would in my judgment afford a complete defence to the charge of
conspiracy.

Then was the agreement a breach of s 54, and was it so even if the shares in Maximum
j were worth £500,000? I have already said that I agree with everything in Buckley LJ's
judgment and I repeat this in particular with regard to the construction of s 54. I too
would wish to leave open the question whether, when the transaction is of a kind which

---

1   (1874) LR 9 Ch App 244 at 251–252

A Ltd could in its own commercial interests legitimately enter into and the transaction is genuinely entered into by A Ltd in its own commercial interests and not merely as a *a* means of assisting B financially to buy shares of A Ltd, the circumstance that A Ltd enters into the transaction with B partly with the object of putting B in funds to acquire its own shares, or with the knowledge of B's intended use of the proceeds of sale, would involve a contravention of s 54. It is not necessary to decide that problem for the purposes of this case. In my view the section was breached even if the Maximum shares were worth £500,000 because the only, or main, purpose was to put Grosscurth and his associates in *b* possession of funds to buy Belmont's shares from City.

In my judgment this conclusion is established by the following considerations.

1. There is no evidence that Belmont wished to buy the shares in Maximum for any purpose of its own, or even that it was looking for an opening to expand or diversify its undertaking.

2. Mr Grosscurth stated his intention in categorical terms in his letter of 5th June *c* 1963:

'My present intention is to arrange the consideration for the purchase of Belmont from Belmont's own resources, and this I propose to accomplish by selling to Belmont the whole of the issued share capital of Rentahome Limited.'

3. The sixth defendant, Mr Copeland, was aware of this purpose. In evidence-in-chief *d* he said:

'Q. Were you aware during this transaction that Mr Grosscurth's intention was to sell assets to Belmont and use the proceeds to acquire the share capital of Belmont? A. Yes.'

and in cross-examination: *e*

'Q. Mr Copeland, is it a fair statement that Mr Grosscurth's object in selling Maximum Finance Ltd shares to Belmont in 1963, that his object was by that sale to obtain the money with which he was purchasing the shares of Belmont? A. Yes.
'Q. And that is reflected, is it not, in a letter which I think you have seen . . . ? A. Is that the letter of 2nd September?   *f*
'Q. Yes. A. Yes, I have it now.
'Q. And you remember in para 4 of that it is proposed that Belmont should purchase from Mr Grosscurth the whole of the share capital of Maximum for £500,000: "This will enable me to avoid showing a large loan in Belmont's accounts and deal with the section 54 difficulty"? A. Yes.
'Q. He proposed to buy the shares of Belmont with bridging finance originally, *g* and now he is proposing in para 5 to repay the bridging loan out of the proceeds of sale of Maximum? A. Yes.
'Q. So does that confirm what you have just told my Lord as to Mr Grosscurth's contemporary object? A. Yes.
'Q. You yourself signed this letter on Mr Grosscurth's behalf? A. Yes.
'Q. So I can take it that you knew at the time that that was Mr Grosscurth's *h* intention? A. Yes.'

Moreover, this was Mr Copeland's own intention also:

'Q. In selling your shares of Maximum to Belmont, therefore, I understand that it was your purpose to obtain the money to buy the Belmont shares with? A. Yes.'
                                                                                                        j
4. Mr James also knew of Mr Grosscurth's intention, and of s 54. This he admitted in cross-examination. I quote as follows:

'Q. Third, that you knew at the time that Mr Grosscurth's intention in selling Maximum to Belmont for £500,000 was to obtain finance for his acquisition of the share capital of Belmont. A. This was put to Queen's Counsel and he said that it was all right to do so, and on his advice we did so.

'Q. Please answer my question, Mr James. A. I do not see any other way of answering it.

'Q. My question was did you know that Mr Grosscurth's purposes in selling Maximum for £500,000 to Belmont was to obtain finance for the purchase by him of the shares of Belmont? A. Yes.'

5. The subject-matter of the sale to Belmont was changed, because it was, for fiscal reasons affecting the vendors only, found to be unwise for them to sell Rentahome. The judge relied on this change as a factor showing that the transaction as a whole was a bona fide commercial one. He said: 'Mr James did not adopt these proposals without a great deal of enquiry and certain vital changes were made, in particular the substitution of Maximum for Rentahome', but that was entirely to suit the convenience of the vendors. There is no evidence that anyone ever considered whether the change was beneficial to Belmont, or whether it called for any reduction in price.

6. There was never any attempt by anybody on behalf of Belmont to make or obtain a valuation of the shares in Maximum. True, Mr James said it was not merely a matter of valuing the assets but of assessing the value of the prospective profits and this, he felt, depended not so much on valuation as on his assessment of the supposed extraordinary flair and expertise of Mr Grosscurth, and when it came to the question of value the judge fully accepted this, saying that he did not think that Messrs Mann Judd & Co were properly instructed, that is to say, to value the deal as a whole and not to value Maximum in isolation. I do not think that that criticism was well founded, and I shall return to it when I come to consider the question of value. The fact remains, however, that no independent advice was sought on this aspect of the matter and the price of £500,000 was originally dictated, as it seems to me, by two considerations: (a) the price which City must receive to prevent its showing a loss in its books because of the price that it, or its predecessors, had paid on the acquisition of Belmont; (b) the necessity of providing Grosscurth and his associates with a matching sum so that they could pay that price, as can be seen from a letter of 28th May 1963 from Colonel Lipert and the offer of 27th May 1963 enclosed therewith.

7. The shares in Maximum were not a readily marketable security on which Grosscurth and his associates could readily have raised money elsewhere. They were shares in a private company, newly formed, and the purchase of the shares by Belmont involved it in a speculative venture.

8. There was a particular advantage to the vendors in selling Maximum to Belmont and, at the same time, buying all the shares in that company, as they thereby acquired Belmont, which they wanted, and retained Maximum within their empire.

9. By the agreement of 3rd October 1963, the sale of Maximum to Belmont and the purchase of the shares in Belmont were integrated as parts of one entire transaction, and by cll 4 and 6 the sale of the shares in Belmont was expressly made subject to, and to take effect immediately after, the sale of the Maximum shares to Belmont. This nexus alone would, I think, be sufficient to establish breach of s 54 irrespective of the value of the Maximum shares, but, taken in conjunction with all the other factors I have rehearsed, there can be no doubt, for in my judgment there is a breach of the section whenever the company does not merely know that its vendor intends to use the proceeds of sale for the purpose of purchasing or subscribing for its shares, but it is the company's purpose, or one of the company's purposes, in buying the property to place him in funds to do so, even if it gets full value for its money. In my judgment, therefore, the defence of honest belief must fail; the claim in conspiracy should have succeeded, and the judge was in error in dismissing the action.

I confess, however, that I have felt very grave doubt about the judge's finding in this respect. What Mr James wanted to do was to buy a controlling interest in all Grosscurth's ventures. He stressed in his evidence that it must be all, and that control was essential.

The evidence leaves a strong impression in my mind that when he could not get this, he
simply fell back on the arrangement to sell Belmont's shares, for City wanted to be rid of *a*
them, and adopted the price of £500,000 negotiated for Rentahome, which had valuable
assets, although the substitution of Maximum made it a very different proposition, and
that he did shut his eyes to the value of Maximum. However, the judge said: 'Mr James
was an impressive and truthful witness', and he found as a fact that he (Mr James)
genuinely believed that the agreement was a good commercial proposition for Belmont
to purchase Maximum's shares for £500,000, and seeing that he was charged with fraud, *b*
and all the events took place some 13 or 14 years previously and seeing the very
favourable impression that Mr James made on the learned judge, I have come to the
conclusion that it would not be right for this court to disturb that finding.

Accordingly, in my judgment this defence would have succeeded had I taken the view
that if this belief had been true in fact there would have been no breach of the section;
but, as I have said, I do not. A company, of course has no mind of its own, only the mind *c*
of its directors, and this was its mind through Mr James. It is true that he left the details
to Foley, Harries and Duck (who had been associated with Mr Jones for a number of years
and has been described as his right-hand man), that the statement of the first two were
not put in evidence and that Mr Duck was not called. However, on the basis on which
Mr James proceeded, that the bulk of the value lay not in the assets but in the judgment
and expertise of Mr Grosscurth, and that he was sufficiently bound to Belmont by the *d*
guarantee, there was nothing left for them to investigate or do. Commercial assessment
would obviously be a matter on which Mr James's views would prevail.

The measure of damages on this claim is, in my judgment, the difference between the
true value of the Maximum shares, including therein such allowance (if any) as may be
proper over and above the value of the net tangible assets in respect of future profitability
on the one hand, and £500,000 on the other. *e*

Before I develop that further, I shall consider which of the defendants are liable on this
claim. Grosscurth plainly must be, and Williams and City also, in my judgment, because
they were both parties to the agreement of 3rd October 1963, and Mr James, who was
chairman of both, knew the offending purpose. Having regard to the various settlements
and arrangements which have been made, this is not now a live issue against anyone else.

[His Lordship then considered the evidence relating to the true value of Maximum at *f*
the time of the sale to Belmont. His Lordship continued:]

Having carefully weighed all these matters, I would accept Messrs Mann Judd & Co's
valuation in principle, that is, the net tangible assets only, without any addition for
goodwill, save that I think something should be added for the guarantee. This should,
in my view, be substantially less than the actuarially discounted value of £156,250, since
whilst Rentahome had substantial assets there was no telling what its position and that *g*
of Grosscurth might be at the end of the five or six years before the guarantee could
become enforceable. Moreover, Belmont, Grosscurth and Rentahome would all be
engaged in or about the same kind of business and, as in fact actually happened, could all
fail together. I would hear argument from counsel before deciding on a precise figure.

I turn next to the first limb of Belmont's case on constructive trust, that is to say,
'knowing receipt'. This is now relevant as against City only. As I have said, this does not *h*
depend on proof of fraud, nor in my judgment is Mr James's belief that 'the agreement
was a good commercial proposition for Belmont to purchase Maximum's shares for
£500,000' any answer.

What Belmont has to show is that the payment of the £500,000 was a misfeasance,
which for this purpose is equivalent to breach of trust, that City received all or part of this
money, and that it did so knowing, or in circumstances in which it ought to know, that *j*
it was a breach of trust. In fact City received £489,000 and that is the basic measure of
any liability under this head. It is true that City received this through Grosscurth as a
payment for the shares in Belmont, but this was intended by all parties and made
pursuant to the agreement of 3rd October 1963. In my judgment, therefore, the money
received by City was clearly part of the original £500,000 of Belmont's money.

Then was the payment of the £500,000 a breach of trust? In my judgment it was, on
a two counts. First, and obviously, because, as I have held, the agreement was unlawful
and the payment was made by Belmont for an illegal purpose, namely to facilitate the
purchase by Grosscurth and his associates of Belmont shares.

Secondly, it was a misfeasance in my judgment for the following reasons. Belmont
parted with sound assets in return for which it received shares which, making full
allowance for prospective profits and the benefit of the guarantee, were not worth
b anything like the sum paid for them and it committed itself to a speculative venture.
However much store Mr James set by Mr Grosscurth's ability, everything depended on
that, and Belmont had no sufficient control over him. It is highly significant that Mr
James wanted 51% if he put in his own or City's money, and Belmont did not get that.
This stands out when one sees that both Mr James and Mr Copeland attributed the failure
which ensued to Grosscurth, both saying he got too much money too soon and had no
c proper financial control.

All this was done without an independent board capable of considering the transaction
from Belmont's point of view, since Mr James de facto controlled the board of Belmont,
and he, or his team, simply told the other directors what to do. Mr James himself said
so, and Mr Kellman, who was the only independent director and who was called by
Belmont, made his own position quite clear. He said he regarded himself as an executive
d director in a subordinate position. Further, the board did not even have any independent
advice of any kind, whether from accountants, merchant bankers, lawyers or anyone
else.

The opinion on s 54 of the 1948 Act was obtained by the solicitors acting for the
Grosscurth side; Mr Mesquita (the partner in Messrs Gouldens concerned with the
matter) made this quite clear in his letter to Mr Duck of 14th October 1963, in which he
e said:

'I confirm having handed you at your request copy of the Opinion of counsel
dated 27th September 1963, and I have noted that you have incorporated a reference
to this Opinion in the minutes of Belmont Industrial Finance Limited. To this of
course I make no objection, but I think that it should be put on record that this
f Opinion was obtained by my clients without any reference to your clients, or any
suggestion from your clients that an Opinion on this point should be obtained.'

As was to be expected, Mr Mesquita provided his clients, Mr Grosscurth, Mr Maund
and Mr Copeland, with copies of the opinion, but there is nothing to show or suggest that
he sent it to any of the directors of Belmont, or informed them of its existence before the
g board meeting at 2.30 pm on 11th October, at which it is recorded as having been
produced. It was also produced earlier on that same day at the board meeting of City,
which took place at 1.30 pm, but there is no documentary evidence to suggest that it was
shown, even to that board, any earlier. As Buckley LJ has pointed out, Mr James's
evidence shows clearly that he personally never saw the opinion at any time. His
evidence was that he left all the details to his team, Messrs Harries, Foley and Duck, and
h legal matters in particular to Mr Duck. He was sure Messrs Harries and Foley would not
have proceeded unless they had been satisfied on the particular aspect of s 54. In spite of
this evidence, the defendants did not put in the statements that they had from Messrs
Harries and Foley, nor did they call Mr Duck, who was available to give evidence and was
actually in court part of the time. In these circumstances I see no reason to infer that Mr
Spector, Mr Smith or Mr Kellman saw the opinion at any time before the agreement was
j entered into on 3rd October.

The only valuation obtained was that of Mr Cass, which Mr Copeland directed to be
sent to himself, and he could not recall having sent it to the board of Belmont, and Mr
Demetri, his bookkeeper and right-hand man, was not called. So there is at least no
evidence that this was produced to the board of Belmont, and in my view the evidence
really leads positively to the inference that it was not. Further, it is clear on the evidence

that no enquiries were made about the assets or Maximum's prospects on behalf of the
board of Belmont.   *a*

Yet there was an obvious and inescapable conflict of duty and interest between the
position of Mr James as chairman of the board of Belmont, and his position as chairman
of the board of City. Counsel for Williams and City argued that this was not altogether
so, because City subscribed for 230,000 preference shares in Belmont and also lent it a
large sum of money, £200,000, and thus was concerned for the success of Belmont. This
is true as far as it goes, but it does not go anywhere nearly far enough. As chairman of *b*
City it was his interest and duty to see that the shares in Belmont were disposed of,
because it was not making sufficient profits for the group's liking, and to get as high a
price as possible, and in particular one which would include £230,000 for goodwill. As
chairman of Belmont, it was his duty to consider, with a single eye to the future welfare
of that company and the safety of its assets and the protection of the depositors, whether
to purchase the Maximum shares at all and, if so, to keep the price as low as possible and *c*
in particular to take the opportunity of reopening negotiations with a view to a reduction
of the price when Grosscurth sought to substitute the Maximum shares for those of
Rentahome. This very important aspect of the matter seems to me, with very great
respect, to have been overlooked by the judge, who said:

> 'It must be remembered that there were two factions in this deal. On the one
> hand was Mr John James who had recently taken over Williams and City and on the *d*
> other hand Mr Grosscurth and his two associates. I cannot find any evidence of
> collaboration between the two groups. They were very much at arm's length.'

In my view there were not two, but three, since on the James side was Belmont as well
as City and their interests were clearly not the same as those of City.

Then did City know, or ought it to have known, of the misfeasance or breach of *e*
trust? In my judgment the answer to that question must plainly be Yes, for they are
fixed with all the knowledge that Mr James had. Now, he had actual knowledge of all
the facts which made the agreement illegal and his belief that the agreement was a good
commercial proposition for Belmont can be no more a defence to City's liability as
constructive trustees than in conspiracy.

Apart from this, clearly, in my judgment, Mr James knew or ought to have known all *f*
the facts that I have rehearsed, showing that there was in any event a misfeasance apart
from illegality. He knew of the conflict of interest, and indeed, said in his evidence that
he sought (though he failed) to obtain a further term in the guarantee for the protection
of Belmont's depositors that a sum of £60,000 should actually be set aside each year. Yet
neither he nor his team took any steps whatever to see that Belmont was separately
advised.   *g*

In my judgment, therefore, City are liable in damages as constructive trustees. 'The
long arm of equity' is long enough to catch this sort of transaction.

What then is the measure of damages? Belmont did in fact receive dividends on the
Maximum shares, amounting to approximately £60,000 before the collapse, and its
counsel rightly concedes that it must give credit for that amount. But must it bring into
account, either in addition or substitution, the full value to it of the transaction as a whole *h*
at 3rd October 1973, notwithstanding that in the end all was lost? In my judgment the
answer is No, because the loss was inherent in and, though not expected, could be
foreseen from the start. True, there was a sharp deterioration in the economic situation,
but that was one of the risks inherent in the speculation, and Mr Copeland himself said
in his evidence that he thought that as things turned out Mr Grosscurth would have
failed apart from that because, as I have said, he got too much money too soon and did *j*
not have, or exercise, the necessary financial control.

This leaves only the second head of constructive trusteeship, and in my judgment that
cannot be supported without going behind the judge's finding as to Mr James's genuine
belief, which I have already said I am not prepared to do. He may have been carried away
by his enthusiasm over Mr Grosscurth, but if he genuinely believed that the agreement

a was a good commercial proposition for Belmont, he cannot be held to have been fraudulent. If he had been wilfully shutting his eyes to the truth, his belief would not have been genuine.

The judge also acquitted Mr Copeland of fraud, and it is not suggested that anyone else was guilty of fraud. The junior directors committed breaches of duty, but they were not fraudulent.

b On the judge's findings, therefore, in my judgment this part of Belmont's case has not been made out.

Apart from this, however, it has succeeded and I would therefore allow the appeal, discharge the judge's order and give judgment for Belmont: (i) in conspiracy against Williams, City and Grosscurth, for the sum of £500,000, less the value of the Maximum shares on 3rd October 1963, on the basis set out in this judgment; the actual figure will have to be decided after further argument, if necessary, when the parties have had an *c* opportunity of considering this judgment, (ii) against City as constructive trustees for £489,000, less the precise amount of the dividends to be brought into account. I would hear counsel on the question of interest on these sums.

Belmont is entitled to pursue this judgment as it thinks fit, but cannot, of course, recover in the aggregate more than £500,000 less the value of the Maximum shares as valued in accordance with this judgment, or £489,000 less the dividends, whichever be *d* the greater.

WALLER LJ. I agree with the judgment of Buckley LJ, and were it not that we are differing from the final conclusion of the learned judge I would be content to say no more. However, as we are differing, and as the matter is one of considerable importance, I will on the substance of the case briefly set out my own reasons.

e The judge came to the conclusion and I quote: 'There can be no doubt that Mr Grosscurth used the £500,000 which he received from Belmont to purchase its shares for £489,000.' He also came to the conclusion that Mr James was a truthful witness who genuinely believed that the agreement was a good commercial proposition. Similarly he accepted that Mr Copeland honestly believed that the value of Maximum was not less than £500,000. We have been referred to a number of passages in the evidence of both *f* Mr James and Mr Copeland which are not easy to reconcile with such a conclusion. There were passages in Mr James's evidence on four different topics which, were it not for the judge's findings to the contrary, would appear to show that his evidence was unreliable. But the judge had the advantage of seeing Mr James in the witness box for four days and we have not had that advantage. Furthermore he was giving evidence about events which had taken place 14 years before the hearing. I will return to this *g* subject again but I am of the opinion that the passages to which we have been referred are insufficient to justify disturbing the judge's assessment.

It was however part of counsel's case for Belmont, both before the judge and before this court, that although he suggested there was dishonesty it was not necessary for him to prove dishonesty in order to succeed. In other words there could be a breach of s 54 of the Companies Act 1948 without dishonesty on the part of either members of the *h* James group or of the Grosscurth group, which included of course Mr Copeland.

The details of the transactions between the two groups have already been set out in the judgment of Buckley LJ. I propose however to set out briefly the effect of what happened on 11th October 1963. At the beginning of the day the Grosscurth group owned, among other things, Maximum. At the same time the James group owned City and also Belmont, again among others. They proposed to sell Belmont for £500,000 which *j* would enable them to show a book value for the goodwill as the same as the group had paid for Belmont. The first transaction that took place was that Belmont purchased Maximum for £500,000. The next stage was, with the £500,000 they had received from Belmont, the Grosscurth group paid City £489,000 for Belmont, which included of course Maximum. At the end of the day therefore the Grosscurth group owned everything that they owned at the beginning of the day, that is including Maximum,

plus Belmont which had paid out £500,000 for Maximum. The James group owned
everything that they owned at the beginning of the day except Belmont, but they had ***a***
received £489,000 for the sale of Belmont. They also had an obligation to subscribe to
preference shares in Belmont which by now was in the Grosscurth group. From the
point of view of the two groups it was easy to see that the situation was satisfactory. The
Grosscurth group had acquired Belmont at no cost to themselves and the James group
had sold Belmont for £489,000, which would mean that the goodwill price was that
which they had paid for it years before. But the question with which we are concerned ***b***
is Belmont. Had Belmont benefited from a transaction in which the company had paid
£500,000 for Maximum even if Maximum was worth £500,000?

Another way of looking at the transaction is to isolate the transaction in which
Belmont purchased the shares of Maximum for £500,000. At that time Belmont was in
the James group and had been concerned with the hire-purchase of furniture. Maximum
on the other hand had been in the Grosscurth group (it had been formed just six months ***c***
before) and was concerned with the financing of house building. After Belmont had
purchased Maximum, Belmont remained in the James group. Even assuming Maximum
was worth £500,000 can it possibly be said that this was a genuine commercial
transaction? Can it be said it was in the interests of Belmont to purchase Maximum?
After the purchase Belmont had virtually no assets except Maximum and, as I have
already said, was still in the James group. If it be said that the surrounding circumstances ***d***
have to be taken into account and must include the sale of Belmont then it becomes clear,
in my view, that the whole purpose of the sale was to provide funds for this purchase.
There could be no other object in the transaction except to provide finance. It had no
independent commercial purpose. In my opinion the above facts alone compel this
conclusion. But this conclusion is underlined because it had been Grosscurth's plan, at
least since 5th June 1963, when he wrote saying: '. . . My present intention is to arrange ***e***
the consideration for the purchase of Belmont from Belmont's own resources . . .' In my
judgment, having eliminated any other purpose from this transaction, it is impossible to
avoid the conclusion that Belmont was giving financial assistance for the purpose of the
purchase of its shares and that therefore there was a breach of s 54 of the 1948 Act
whether or not Maximum was worth £500,000.

So far as the evidence shows there was no discussion of this purchase at any board ***f***
meeting of Belmont. If there had been such a meeting and the question had been posed,
'Why are we purchasing Maximum?', the only answer which could have been given
would be: 'In order to enable the Grosscurth group to purchase shares in Belmont', or to
use the words of the section, in order to give financial assistance to Grosscurth and his
associates for the purpose of the purchase of shares in the company, namely Belmont. To
avoid a contravention of s 54 it is not sufficient, in my view, to show that the company ***g***
is purchasing an asset which is worth the price being paid. The company must also show
that the decision to purchase is made in the commercial interests of the company. If this
were so, then the fact that the proceeds are used by the seller for the purchase of shares
in the company would not necessarily infringe s 54. That would only happen if the
decision was made partly with the intention on the part of the board that the proceeds
should be used for the purchase of shares in the company. ***h***

The next question is whether or not the defendants were guilty of conspiracy. A
conspiracy is an agreement between two or more persons to effect an unlawful purpose
which results in damage to somebody (see *Crofter Hand Woven Harris Tweed Co Ltd v
Veitch*[1] per Viscount Simon LC). A person is a party to a conspiracy if he knows the
essential facts to constitute that conspiracy even though he does not know that they
constitute an offence (see *Churchill v Walton*[2]). Since there was a breach of s 54 and the ***j***
defendants through their directors made all the arrangements and knew all the facts

1   [1942] 1 All ER 142 at 147, [1942] AC 435 at 440
2   [1967] 1 All ER 497, [1967] 2 AC 224

constituting the breach, it would follow that they conspired together to contravene s 54,

a the object of their conspiracy being Belmont, and if Belmont suffered damage they are liable.

I next consider whether Belmont in fact suffered damage. This could only arise if Maximum was not worth £500,000 when it was bought by Belmont. Belmont relied on the independent evidence of Mr Williams, who was presented with the same information as had been given to Mr Cass by Mr Copeland. Mr Cass was not called but he valued

b Maximum at £500,000 having seen the accounts and made enquiries about them. The accounts gave an unduly optimistic picture because they showed profits which had not been received and Mr Williams regarded this as an imprudent basis; Mr Copeland agreed. Furthermore they included two contracts which by the time of the valuation had been cancelled. Finally Mr Cass relied on a warranty different from, and better than, that which in fact had been given by Mr Grosscurth. Maximum was a company that had

c only been functioning for some six months and Mr Copeland said: 'I have to agree that the business of Cityfield, indeed of Maximum, were largely speculative ventures.' There was no independent evidence to set against that of Mr Williams. Instead there was the evidence of Mr James and of Mr Copeland about the value of Grosscurth's guarantee. It was common ground between counsel that if a company had a history of profits of £100,000 per year over five years it would be properly valued at £500,000, that is to say,

d it would be appropriate to apply a multiplier of five in these circumstances. Mr James, who said he would have paid £250,000 for a 51% share of Grosscurth's empire, emphasising the importance of having financial control, nevertheless urged the value of the warranty by Grosscurth and valued the business of Maximum at £276,000 applying a multiplier of five to the profits after tax. This figure was based on the actual profits of Maximum and Cityfields. This took into account the profitability due to Grosscurth.

e The warranty, which could not be enforced for five years, could not add very much to this valuation.

In my judgment the failure of the defendants to call Mr Cass, and the failure to call independent witness when they had a representative of Messrs Peat Marwick & Mitchell in court, throws grave doubt on the reliability of the estimates made by Mr James and Mr Copeland, both of whom were interested parties. Mr James was valuing a speculative

f business as if it were a reliable business with a five year history of profits. To back his own judgment with his own money would be one thing, but to use it as support for a purchase by a company of which he was a director was a very different matter. Mr Copeland also was an interested party and apparently in the negotiations had not observed the important error in Mr Cass's description of the warranty and chose to take no notice of the contrast between Mr Cass's view of the warranty and counsel's view that the

g warranty should be ignored. Furthermore, Mr Copeland did not appear to be aware of the part of the profits which had in fact been cancelled. When one adds to this the fact that £500,000 had been agreed as a proper valuation for Rentahome, whose assets were considerable, and the same figure was used when Maximum was substituted with assets which were very much smaller, the absence of an independent valuation which could be tested in the witness box is a fatal weakness in the case for the defendants. In my opinion

h a proper approach would be to accept Mr Williams's figure and to add to it some modest figure to represent the value of the warranty. In Mr Williams's view (and there is no independent evidence to the contrary) the shares of Maximum were not worth more than £60,000. In addition I would add something more for the prospect of future profits backed by the warranty. Both Mr James and Mr Copeland thought that this business, although Copeland regarded it as speculative, had good prospects of profits and thought

j that the guarantees which Grosscurth had given would ensure those profits. The value of a warranty which cannot be called on for five years is itself speculative and must be very severely discounted. I have no doubt that Maximum was not worth £500,000 or anything approaching such a figure. If I am asked to make my own assessment on the evidence I would add something like £75,000, or at the most £100,000, to the £60,000 assessed by Mr Williams.

If I am wrong in the conclusion that a breach of s 54 can be established even though the price paid for the asset is a fair price, and if it is necessary to prove that the price was an inflated one, then I must consider the state of mind of City and Williams about the price being paid: see the words of Lord Hailsham LC in *Kamara v Director of Public Prosecutions*[1]:

'It seems fairly clear that while a mistake of law is not a good defence, a sincere belief in a state of facts which if true would render the illegal conduct legal would be a good answer to any charge of conspiracy.'

A company acts through its officers and can be a party to a conspiracy (see *R v I C R Haulage Ltd*[2]). If there were responsible officers of City who were shutting their eyes to the value of Maximum, it would not avail City that there was another officer who honestly believed that Maximum was worth £500,000. As I have already mentioned, counsel for Belmont has submitted that this court should reverse the assessment of the judge that Mr James was a truthful and honest witness. He has drawn attention to a number of matters in the course of the evidence which are not consistent with the view expressed by the judge. Nevertheless, as I have already said, I am of opinion that the view of the judge is a view that cannot be disturbed. But Mr James in his evidence repeated again and again that he left the decisions and arrangements for this transaction to Mr Foley, Mr Harries and Mr Duck. The history of it is as follows: the original proposal was that Grosscurth was going to sell Rentahome to Belmont for £500,000. This was a transaction which was under discussion for some time, a fact which appears from the correspondence. Mr James came into the City group in late August and took over the negotiations with Mr Grosscurth. Some time before 2nd September the plan to sell Rentahome was dropped and Maximum was put in its place. Maximum was a company which had only been in existence for six months. There is no evidence that any enquiry was made by anybody from the James group about Maximum and Mr Copeland did not remember any enquiry being made of him apart from Mr Cass. There is no document of any kind showing that enquiries were made. Mr James knew of no enquiry; he left it to his subordinates and relied on their judgment.

Both Mr James and Messrs Smith, Harries and Foley had the same interests and indeed had the same conflicting interests. As directors of Williams and of City (in Mr Foley's case as secretary) they were concerned to see that they received a price for Belmont which included a price for goodwill which was no less than that which was paid on its acquisition. As directors of Belmont they should have been concerned to see that the integrity of the company was preserved. The James group lost nothing by this transaction. The Grosscurth group were only concerned to provide enough finance to cover the purchase of Belmont. With such a conflict of interest it was in my opinion essential that those representing Belmont should have had an independent valuation of Maximum. Mr James, when discussing Rentahome, said he would want to check the books and have an independent valuation before offering to purchase. Furthermore one would expect that there would be independent advice as to the legality of the transaction. Mr Copeland in the Grosscurth group did both. We are no longer concerned with the case against Mr Copeland or with the merits of the valuation of Mr Cass or the details of the legal advice which Mr Copeland received. There is, however, no evidence that the valuation was ever seen by any director of Belmont or anybody in the James group and there is no evidence that the opinion of counsel was communicated to anybody within the James group until the transaction was being completed. The state of the evidence was such as to produce a prima facie case that when Maximum was substituted for Rentahome those responsible in the James group were ignoring any question of valuation. When so much reliance was placed by Mr James on Mr Foley and Mr Harries and on Mr Duck being his right-hand man it was unfortunate that both Mr

Foley and Mr Harries had died before the hearing of this case. But each of them had
made a statement and this could have been put in under the provisions of the Civil
Evidence Act 1968. It is difficult to believe that such statements would ignore this
question if in fact there had been a valuation. Mr Duck was alive at the time of the
hearing and did attend on at least one day, but he was not called as a witness. I find the
complete absence of evidence from these three as significant. In my opinion evidence
was required from City, or City's officers, to show a sincere belief that Maximum was
worth £500,000. City only called Mr James. City did not put in the statement of Mr
Harries or Mr Foley whom James said he had told to get on with it. Nor did City call Mr
Duck, who was Mr James's right-hand man. Mr James was obviously a strong personality
and only the judge's finding of truthfulness prevents me from saying he must have
deliberately decided not to have a valuation. But since he left all the negotiations to be
done by others, the court is not concerned with his belief. It is not necessary to decide
who made, or was a party to making, the decision not to obtain independent advice.
Williams and City have, in my opinion, failed to show that those who were entrusted
with the arranging of the purchase by Belmont of the shares in Maximum had a sincere
belief that they were worth £500,000. In the absence of such evidence the inference to
be drawn is that a decision was deliberately taken not to obtain a valuation. Having
regard to the matters I have already mentioned, this would indicate, in my opinion, a
lack of belief that Maximum was worth the price being paid.

It follows that even if it were necessary to prove knowledge of an inflated price to
establish conspiracy on the part of City I would hold that inasmuch as those on whom Mr
James relied deliberately refrained from obtaining a valuation they must be taken as
knowing the price was too high. Indeed, to use the words of Lord Hailsham LC[1], City
completely failed to show that there was a sincere belief, on the part of those negotiating,
in the value of Maximum at £500,000.

I conclude therefore on this aspect of the case that Williams and City were a party to
a conspiracy to commit a breach of s 54 of the Companies Act 1948 and that as a result
of that conspiracy Belmont suffered damage, and that accordingly Williams and City are
liable to Belmont for the damage suffered. I have not sought to identify the other
conspirators. Suffice it to say that Grosscurth was clearly one, and that is sufficient to
establish the conspiracy.

On the question of constructive trust, I do not wish to add anything to that which has
been said by Buckley and Goff LJJ.

Having given judgment on the merits of the appeal, the court heard argument from
counsel with respect to the remedies available to Belmont.

Michael Miller QC and *M J Roth* for Belmont.
Martin Nourse QC and *Brian Parker* for Williams and City.
The third, fourth and sixth defendants did not appear.

Cur adv vult

31st July. **BUCKLEY LJ.** The judgment I am about to read is the judgment of the
court.

Having already decided the merits of this appeal, we now have to determine what
remedies Belmont is entitled to. We have found that Belmont is entitled to judgment
against the first three defendants for conspiracy and against City as a constructive trustee.

We will deal first with the claim in conspiracy. Counsel for Belmont submits that as
in the event Maximum was a total loss, having been wound up in a state of complete
insolvency, the whole of the £500,000 invested in Maximum by Belmont has been lost
as a result of the conspiracy. The wrong suffered by Belmont was, counsel submits, that

1   See *Kamara v Director of Public Prosecutions* [1973] 2 All ER 1242 at 1252, [1974] AC 104 at 119

the conspirators caused Belmont to buy Maximum. The purchase was a speculative
venture and the loss was foreseeable as at least a possible consequence. The measure of a
damages should consequently, acccording to counsel, be £500,000 less any sums proper
to be brought into credit against that amount. Having regard to the ways in which
Belmont's case has been pleaded and presented here and below, Belmont is willing to give
credit for the fair value of Maximum at the time of the transaction, although it does not
concede that it is legally bound to do so. This would result in a net figure (which is now
agreed) of £439,941. b

Counsel for Williams and City, on the other hand, says that the wrong suffered by
Belmont was that it was induced to pay too much for Maximum, and that in assessing the
damages account must be taken not only of the fair value of Maximum at the date of the
purchase but of any other advantage obtained by Belmont under the agreement. In this
connection he submits that the value of Mr Grosscurth's guarantee must be taken into
account as well as any benefits consequent on City's subscription of new capital in c
Belmont. He further submits that an enquiry is necessary to ascertain to what extent the
collapse of Maximum was foreseeable at the date of the agreement because, as he
submits, any damage which was not then reasonably foreseeable cannot be recovered.

In our principal judgments delivered earlier in this appeal certain provisional views
were expressed which touched on the question of the measure of damages in this case
and the elements to be taken into account in measuring them. Having now heard d
argument on the subject we have reached the following conclusions.

The loss of the entire investment by Belmont of £500,000 in Maximum was, in our
view, a reasonably foreseeable possible consequence of that investment. The fact that Mr
Grosscurth's guarantee of the profits of Maximum might prove to be of no value, as was
the case in the event, was also in our view a reasonably foreseeable possible event. It is for
the defendants to establish either that the damage resulting to Belmont from the e
conspiracy was less than £500,000 and by how much, or that there are matters which
were not gone into at the trial but which require further investigation before the
damages can be assessed. Before the learned trial judge this did not arise because he held
in favour of the defendants on liability; but we have not been satisfied that there are any
such matters apart from two dividends declared by Maximum and received by Belmont
before Maximum was liquidated. These dividends were of a substantially less amount f
than the amount for which Belmont is prepared to give credit in respect of the fair value
of Maximum at the date of the purchase. We think that Belmont was under no
obligation to allow this credit and, since it exceeds the amount of the dividends, no
further sum needs to be credited in reduction of the loss in respect of the dividends.

Counsel for Williams and City submits that some allowance should be made in respect
of benefits received by Belmont from the subscription by City of £230,000 new capital g
of Belmont. We feel unable to accept this for three reasons. First, the subscription was
made in pursuance of the agreement of 3rd October 1963 which, as we have held, was
an illegal agreement. Secondly, the £230,000 made a circular journey from Belmont to
Mr Grosscurth and his associates, from Mr Grosscurth and his associates to City and from
City to Belmont. This enabled Belmont to the extent of £230,000 to provide the
£500,000 for the purchase of Maximum without recourse to any of Belmont's other h
assets. The sums invested in the purchase of Maximum have been wholly lost.
Accordingly Belmont obtained no advantage from the subscription apart from the
dividends declared by Maximum. Thirdly, the use by City of £230,000 thus received
indirectly from Belmont in subscribing for shares in Belmont was itself a breach of s 54
of the Companies Act 1948. In these circumstances it is, in our judgment, not open to
City to rely on the subscription in abatement of Belmont's claim against City as a j
constructive trustee.

Counsel for Williams and City also submitted that there should be an enquiry as to
damages, but this could only increase the amount of the loss suffered by Belmont by
reason of the further costs involved, and in any case we see no reason for directing an
enquiry.

Accordingly we quantify the damages in conspiracy at £439,941.

a These being damages at common law for a tort, we think that there is no reason in the circumstances of this case to import the equitable rule under which compound interest is sometimes ordered where a defendant in a fiduciary position has wrongly employed funds in his hands or under his control in his fiduciary capacity for his own personal gain (see *Wallersteiner v Moir (No 2)*[1]). We award Belmont simple interest on the £439,941 from 11th October 1963 to the date of judgment at 1% per annum above bank rate or the

b minimum lending rate for the time being in force from time to time.

Belmont must give credit against the £439,941 and interest for the amounts received from Mr Maund (£5,000) and Mr Copeland (£20,000) on the settlement of the claims against them, with interest thereon at the rate already mentioned from the date of receipt of such sums respectively down to the date of judgment.

We now turn to the remedy in constructive trust. By an order of this court in this

c matter dated 18th February 1977 Belmont was given leave to amend its statement of claim in certain respects on terms that in taking an account of what sums were due to Belmont by (inter alios) City credit should be given for whatever right of contribution City might have against the defendants Maund and Smith or either of them. It is common ground that an enquiry must be directed to ascertain what amounts are proper to be brought into credit in this respect. Counsel for Williams and City has submitted

d that City should also be given credit in this respect for any benefits received by Belmont under the agreement. Belmont is willing to give credit for the dividends declared by Maximum amounting to £23,525 and to account to City for any further sums received hereafter from the liquidator of Maximum or otherwise in respect of Belmont's holding of shares in Maximum. Apart from these matters we do not think that City is entitled to any further credit against its liability as constructive trustee.

e In our view, City is accountable for the whole of the £489,000, subject only to the deduction of such credits as we have mentioned. There is no evidence that any part of the £489,000 was employed by City for its own commercial advantage in earning profits for City, and consequently we do not consider that whatever net sum is due from City to Belmont under the claim in constructive trust should carry compound interest. In this case also we award simple interest at the rate already mentioned from 11th October

f 1963 down to the date of judgment.

Belmont cannot recover more from City than whichever is the greater of the damages recoverable from City in conspiracy and the sum recoverable from City as a constructive trustee.

Appeal allowed. Leave to appeal to House of Lords.

g

Solicitors: *Sidney Pearlman & Greene* (for Belmont); *Freshfields* (for Williams and City); *Gentle Mathias & Co* (for the fourth and sixth defendants).

J H Fazan Esq   Barrister.

h

1 [1975] 1 All ER 849, [1975] QB 373

Bremer Vulkan Schiffbau Und Maschinenfabrik v South India Shipping Corporation

a

Gregg and others v Raytheon Ltd

b

COURT OF APPEAL, CIVIL DIVISION

LORD DENNING MR, ROSKILL AND CUMMING-BRUCE LJJ

15th, 16th, 17th, 19th, 22nd, 23rd, 24th, 25th OCTOBER, 23rd NOVEMBER 1979

Arbitration – Practice – Want of prosecution – Dismissal of claim – Power of arbitrator to *c*
dismiss claim for want of prosecution – Whether arbitrator having same power as courts in
litigation to dismiss claim for want of prosecution.

Arbitration – Practice – Want of prosecution – Injunction restraining claimant from proceeding
with arbitration – Claimant's delay prejudicing fair hearing and just result – Claimant's conduct
justifying dismissal of claim for want of prosecution – Whether implied term in contract to *d*
arbitrate that claimant not to be so dilatory as to frustrate purpose of contract – Whether breach
of that term a repudiation of contract entitling respondent to rescind – Whether respondent's
right to rescind and right to fair hearing can be protected by injunction – Whether court
empowered under inherent jurisdiction to issue injunction restraining claimant.

e

In two separate arbitrations the respondents, being dissatisfied with the lack of progress
on the part of the claimants, brought actions claiming injunctions restraining the
claimants from proceeding with the arbitrations. The respondents in each case contended
that the claimants' dilatoriness had been such that if the claims had been litigated rather
than arbitrated they would have been dismissed for want of prosecution.

The first case concerned a dispute over the design and construction by the respondents *f*
of five bulk carriers for the claimants. The ships were delivered between November
1965 and December 1966. The claimants, the shipowners, commenced arbitration
proceedings in January 1972 but did not deliver their points of claim until April 1976,
over nine years after the delivery of the last vessel. No further proceedings had been
taken in the arbitration and in April 1977 the respondents brought their action for an
injunction. They claimed that 16 of their important witnesses were dead, retired or had *g*
left their employment, and that their position at the hearing would be prejudiced.

The second case concerned a dispute over the sale in 1970 of the total shareholding in
a publishing company by the respondents to the claimants. The contract included
various warranties by the respondents as to the state of the company and provided for any
dispute between the parties to be settled by arbitration in Geneva under the rules of the
International Chamber of Commerce ('the ICC'). Some months after taking over the *h*
company, the claimants claimed a total of £500,000 for alleged breaches of the warranties
by the respondents, who denied liability. In 1972 the dispute was referred to arbitration
under the ICC rules although by agreement the venue was changed to London. In 1973
arbitrators were appointed and they ordered the delivery of pleadings and discovery. On
a number of occasions a date for hearing was set but each time it had to be vacated
because the claimants, who as the purchasers of the company had all the relevant papers, *j*
had not given proper discovery. In 1975 the arbitrators adjourned the proceedings
generally with liberty to either party to restore. Nothing happened until November
1978 when the claimants offered inspection of several thousand documents. In
December 1978 the respondents issued a writ seeking an injunction restraining the
claimants from proceeding with the arbitration.

Both actions were heard together and the judge[a] held (i) that arbitrators had the same

a powers as a court to dismiss a claim for want of prosecution, (ii) that it was an implied term of the contract to arbitrate that both parties would use their reasonable endeavours to bring the matter to a speedy conclusion, (iii) that inordinate delay prejudicing the other party or putting a fair trial at risk struck at the root of the contract to arbitrate and amounted to a repudiation of it entitling the other party to apply for an injunction, and (iv) that in both cases the respondents would be seriously prejudiced if the arbitrations

b proceeded after such lengthy delays and they were therefore entitled to the injunctions sought. The claimants in both cases appealed contending, inter alia, that there was no duty on either party or the tribunal to move the arbitration forward, alternatively that if the term implied by the judge was correct the respondents had been equally at fault in doing nothing, and that in any event the court's power to issue injunctions in respect of arbitrations was restricted to cases where there was misconduct by the arbitrator or

c where there was a dispute whether a person was properly a party to the agreement to arbitrate. In addition the claimants in the second case contended that respondents' appropriate remedy was to apply not to an English court but to the Court of Arbitration of the ICC in Paris since that body would as a matter of practice withdraw the request for arbitration of a party that was dilatory.

d **Held** – The appeals would be dismissed for the following reasons—

(i) An arbitrator had no power to dismiss an arbitration for want of prosecution because (per Lord Denning MR) an order made by an arbitrator was exhortatory only and not mandatory and (per Roskill LJ) arbitrators did not possess the powers of a court (see p 425 *j* to p 426 *a*, p 428 *g*, p 436 *b*, p 437 *d*, p 439 *g* and p 447 *g*, post); *Re an*

e *arbitration between Unione Stearinerie Lanza and Weiner* [1917] 2 KB 558 applied; *Crawford v A E A Prowting Ltd* [1972] 1 All ER 1199 approved.

(ii) Terms could be implied in a contract to arbitrate in the same way as in any other contract. However, the term proposed by the judge that each party should use his reasonable endeavours to bring the arbitration to a speedy conclusion could not be implied in the contracts because it would require a respondent to force a dilatory

f claimant into action when a respondent was under no such obligation. But there was implied as a matter of law a term imposing a duty on a claimant not to be so dilatory in proceeding that there could no longer be a fair hearing or a just result thus causing the whole purpose of the contract to be frustrated. Breach of that implied term by a claimant amounted to a repudiation of the contract entitling the respondent to rescind and also to sue for an injunction and/or damages. Delay which in the High Court would cause an action to be struck out for want of prosecution amounted to such a breach of

g that implied term (see p 430 *g* to p 431 *b*, p 441 *d e*, p 442 *b* to *e* and p 447 *g*, post); *Universal Cargo Carriers Corpn v Citati* [1957] 2 All ER 70 applied; *Liverpool City Council v Irwin* [1976] 2 All ER 39 considered.

(iii) In respect of arbitrations to which the Arbitration Act 1979 did not apply, where the claimants had been guilty of repudiatory conduct which gave the respondents a right

h to rescind the arbitration contract, that right, coupled with the respondents' legal or equitable right to a fair hearing which was denied by the claimants' repudiatory conduct, would be protected by the court by the issue of an injunction restraining the claimants from continuing with the arbitration. Furthermore, the court could award damages to the respondents, without reference to their prospects of success in the arbitration, in respect of wasted expenditure incurred by them, since that was loss or damage which

j flowed naturally and directly from the claimants' repudiatory conduct (see p 430 *d*, p 446 *d* to *j*, p 447 *a g h* and p 448 *a*, post); *Pickering v Cape Town Railway Co* (1865) LR 1 Eq 84 and dictum of Lord Diplock in *The Siskina* [1977] 3 All ER at 824 applied; *North London*

---

a   [1979] 3 All ER 194

Railway Co v Great Northern Railway Co (1883) 11 QBD 30 explained; dictum of Lord Macmillan in *Heyman v Darwins Ltd* [1942] 1 All ER at 347 distinguished.

(iv) Since the claimants in both appeals had been guilty of inordinate delay which would have caused their claims to have been struck out for want of prosecution had they been actions in the High Court, the judge had been right to issue injunctions against the claimants in both cases and to award damages against the claimants in the second case. Furthermore the claimants in the second case could not rely on the rules of the ICC as a defence because whatever the practice of the ICC Court of Arbitration may have been the ICC rules did not confer on the ICC Court of Arbitration power to dismiss a claim for want of prosecution (see p 431 *f g*, p 432 *b*, p 439 *f g* and p 447 *g*, post).

Per Lord Denning MR. The principle that the court will restrain a dilatory claimant from proceeding with the arbitration may also be applicable to dilatory respondents (see p 432 *a*, post).

Decision of Donaldson J [1979] 3 All ER 194 affirmed on other grounds.

Notes
For the court's power to restrain arbitration proceedings by injunction, see 2 Halsbury's Laws (4th Edn) para 518, for an arbitrator's powers generally, see ibid, para 577, and for cases on restraint of arbitration by injunction, see 3 Digest (Reissue) 95–98, 484–500.

For dismissal of actions for want of prosecution, see 30 Halsbury's Laws (3rd Edn) 410, para 771.

Section 5 of the Arbitration Act 1979 which came into force on 1st August 1979 and applies to all arbitrations commenced after that date and to arbitrations commenced before that date if the parties have agreed that it should do so (in which case the Act applies from 1st August 1979 or the date of the agreement, whichever is the later) provides that, if any party to an arbitration fails within the time specified or a reasonable time to comply with an order made by an arbitrator, then on the application of the arbitrator or a party the High Court may authorise the arbitrator to proceed with the arbitration in default of appearance or any other act by the party.

Cases referred to in judgments
Allen v Sir Alfred McAlpine & Sons Ltd, Bostic v Bermondsey and Southwark Group Hospital Management Committee, Sternberg v Hammond [1968] 1 All ER 543, [1968] 2 QB 229, [1968] 2 WLR 366, CA, Digest (Cont Vol C) 1091, 2262b.
André et Compagnie SA v Marine Transocean Ltd, The Splendid Sun (4th May 1979) unreported.
Associated Bulk Carriers Ltd v Koch Shipping Inc, The Fuohsan Maru [1978] 2 All ER 254, [1978] 1 Lloyd's Rep 24, CA, 3 Digest (Reissue) 76, 390.
Beddow v Beddow (1878) 9 Ch D 89, 47 LJ Ch 588, 3 Digest (Reissue) 97, 495.
Birkett v James [1977] 2 All ER 801, [1978] AC 297, [1977] 3 WLR 38, HL.
Bristol Corpn v John Aird & Co [1913] AC 241, [1911–13] All ER Rep 1076, 82 LJKB 684, 108 LT 434, 77 JP 209, HL, 3 Digest (Reissue) 84, 91, 434, 460.
Chandris v Isbrandtsen Moller Co Inc [1950] 2 All ER 618, [1951] 1 KB 240, CA, 3 Digest (Reissue) 202, 1241.
County & District Properties Ltd v Lyell [1977] Court of Appeal Transcript 314.
Crawford v A E A Prowting Ltd [1972] 1 All ER 1199, [1973] 1 QB 1, [1972] 2 WLR 749, 3 Digest (Reissue) 116, 637.
Crighton and the Law Car and General Insurance Corpn Ltd, Re an arbitration between [1910] 2 KB 738, 80 LJKB 49, 103 LT 62, 3 Digest (Reissue) 174, 1049.
Dalmia Dairy Industries Ltd v National Bank of Pakistan [1978] 2 Lloyd's Rep 223, CA.
Danforth Travel Centre Ltd v BOAC (1972) 29 DLR (3d) 141, [1972] 3 OR 633, 3 Digest (Reissue) 99, *389.
Den of Airlie Steamship Co v Mitsui & Co Ltd and British Oil and Coke Mills Ltd (1912) 106 LT 451, 12 Asp MLC 169, 17 Com Cas 116, CA, 3 Digest (Reissue) 96, 491.
Frota Nacional de Petroleiros v Skibsaktielskapet Thorsholm [1957] 1 Lloyd's Rep 1, CA.

Heyman v Darwins Ltd [1942] 1 All ER 337, [1942] AC 356, 111 LJKB 241, 166 LT 306,
a   HL, 3 Digest (Reissue) 88, 453.
Jackson v Barry Railway Co [1893] 1 Ch 238, [1891–4] All ER Rep 661, 68 LT 472, 2 R
      207, CA, 3 Digest (Reissue) 97, 496.
Japan Line Ltd v Aggeliki Charis Compania Maritima SA, The Angelic Grace [1979] Court of
      Appeal Transcript 507.
Kitts v Moore [1895] 1 QB 253, 64 LJ Ch 152, 74 LT 676, 12 R 43, CA, 3 Digest (Reissue)
b   96, 488.
Lister v Romford Ice & Cold Storage Co Ltd [1957] 1 All ER 125, [1957] AC 555, [1957] 2
      WLR 158, 121 JP 98, [1956] 2 Lloyd's Rep 505, HL, 34 Digest (Repl) 145, 996.
Liverpool City Council v Irwin [1975] 3 All ER 658, [1976] QB 319, [1975] 3 WLR 663, CA;
      affd in part [1976] 2 All ER 39, [1977] AC 239, [1976] 2 WLR 562, 74 LGR 392, 32 P
      & CR 43, HL.
c   Maunsell v Midland Great Western (Ireland) Railway Co (1863) 1 Hem & M 130, 2 New Rep
      268, 32 LJ Ch 513, 8 LT 347, 826, 9 Jur NS 660, 71 ER 58, 3 Digest (Reissue) 96, 490.
Miller (James) and Partners Ltd v Whitworth Street Estates (Manchester) Ltd [1970] 1 All ER
      796, [1970] AC 583, [1970] 2 WLR 728, [1970] 1 Lloyd's Rep 269, HL, 3 Digest
      (Reissue) 280, 1867.
Moorcock, The (1889) 14 PD 64, [1886–90] All ER Rep 530, 58 LJP 73, 60 LT 654, CA, 12
d   Digest (Reissue) 751, 5395.
Murrayfield Real Estate Co Ltd v C Bryant & Son Ltd [1978] Court of Appeal Transcript 473.
North London Railway Co v Great Northern Railway Co (1883) 11 QBD 30, 52 LJQB 380, 48
      LT 695, CA, 3 Digest (Reissue) 95, 485.
Pickering v Cape Town Railway Co (1865) LR 1 Eq 84, 13 LT 357, 570, V-C and LC, 3
      Digest (Reissue) 97, 493.
e   Shell UK Ltd v Lostock Garage Ltd [1977] 1 All ER 481, [1976] 1 WLR 1187, CA.
Siskina, The, Owners of cargo lately laden on board the vessel Siskina v Distos Compania Naviera
      SA [1977] 3 All ER 803, [1979] AC 210, [1977] 3 WLR 818, [1978] 1 Lloyd's Rep 1,
      HL.
Smith & Service and Nelson & Sons, Re an intended arbitration between (1890) 25 QBD 545,
      59 LJQB 533, 63 LT 475, 6 Asp MLC 555, CA, 3 Digest (Reissue) 104, 128, 545, 699.
f   Sneddon v Kyle (1902) 2 SR (NSW) Eq 112, 19 WN 182, 3 Digest (Reissue) 98, *376.
Unione Stearinerie Lanza and Weiner, Re an arbitration between [1917] 2 KB 558, 117 LT
      337, sub nom Lanza v Weiner 86 LJKB 1236, 3 Digest (Reissue) 327, 2252.
Unitramp v Garnac Grain Co Inc, The Hermine [1979] 1 Lloyd's Rep 212, CA.
Universal Cargo Carriers Corpn v Citati [1957] 3 All ER 234, [1957] 1 WLR 979, [1957] 2
      Lloyd's Rep 191, CA; affg [1957] 2 All ER 70, [1957] 2 QB 401, [1957] 2 WLR 713,
g   [1957] 1 Lloyd's Rep 174, 3 Digest (Reissue) 282, 1876.
Wilson Sons & Co v Conde d'Eu Railway Co (1887) 51 JP 230, 3 Digest (Reissue) 174, 1047.

Cases also cited
Angelia, The, Trade and Transport Inc v Iino Kaiun Kaisha Ltd [1973] 2 All ER 144, [1973]
      1 WLR 210.
h   Ben & Co Ltd v Pakistan Edible Oil Corpn Ltd [1978] The Times, 13th July.
Carron Iron Co v Maclaren (1855) 5 HL Cas 416, 10 ER 961, HL.
City General Insurance Co Ltd v Robert Bradford & Co Ltd [1970] 1 Lloyd's Rep 520.
Compagnie Française de Télévision v Thorn Consumer Electronics Ltd [1978] RPC 735, CA.
Connolly Brothers Ltd, Re, Wood v Connolly Brothers Ltd [1911] 1 Ch 731, 80 LJ Ch 409, CA.
Curtis v Potts (1814) 3 M & S 145, 105 ER 565.
j   Denmark Productions Ltd v Boscobel Productions Ltd [1968] 3 All ER 513, [1969] 1 QB 699,
      CA.
Doleman & Sons v Ossett Corpn [1912] 3 KB 257, 81 LJKB 1092, CA.
Exormisis Shipping SA v Oonsoo [1975] 1 Lloyd's Rep 432.
Farrar v Cooper (1890) 44 Ch D 323, 59 LJ Ch 506.
Gibraltar, Government of v Kenney [1956] 3 All ER 22, [1956] 2 QB 410.

Giddings v Giddings (1847) 10 Beav 29, 50 ER 492.

Gouriet v Union of Post Office Workers [1977] 3 All ER 70, [1978] AC 435, HL.   *a*

Halfdan Grieg & Co A/S v Sterling Coal & Navigation Corpn, The Lysland [1973] 2 All ER 1073, [1973] QB 843, CA.

Hodgkinson v Fernie (1857) 3 CBNS 189, 140 ER 712.

Imperial Metal Industries (Kynoch) Ltd v Amalgamated Union of Engineering Workers [1979] 1 All ER 847, [1979] ICR 23, CA.

Jugoslavenska Oceanska Plovidba v Castle Investment Co Inc, The Kozara [1973] 3 All ER 498, *b* [1974] QB 292, CA.

Leeds Industrial Co-operative Society Ltd v Slack [1924] AC 851, [1924] All ER Rep 259, HL.

London and Blackwall Railway Co v Cross (1886) 31 Ch D 354, CA.

London Export Corpn Ltd v Jubilee Coffee Roasting Co Ltd [1958] 1 All ER 494, [1958] 1 WLR 271; *affd* [1958] 2 All ER 411, [1958] 1 WLR 661, CA.

Malmesbury Railway Co v Budd (1876) 2 Ch D 113.   *c*

Miliangos v George Frank (Textiles) Ltd [1975] 3 All ER 801, [1976] AC 443, HL.

Mylne v Dickinson (1815) Coop G 195, 35 ER 528, DC.

Myron (Owners) v Tradax Export SA Panama City RP, The Myron [1969] 2 All ER 1263, [1970] 1 QB 527.

R v Leyland Justices, ex parte Hawthorn [1979] 1 All ER 209, [1979] QB 283, DC.

R v National Joint Council for the Craft of Dental Technicians (Disputes Committee), ex parte *d* *Neate* [1953] 1 All ER 327, [1953] 1 QB 704, DC.

R v Wandsworth Justices, ex parte Read [1942] 1 All ER 56, [1942] 1 KB 281, DC.

Rasu Maritima SA v Perusahaan Pertambangan Minyak Dan Gas Bumi Negara (Pertamina) and Government of Indonesia (as interveners) [1977] 3 All ER 324, [1978] QB 644, CA.

Sissons v Oates (1894) 10 TLR 392, DC.

Star International Hong Kong (UK) Ltd v Bergbau-Handel GmbH [1966] 2 Lloyd's Rep 16.   *e*

Third Chandris Shipping Corpn v Unimarine SA, The Pythia, The Angelic Wings, The Genie [1979] 2 All ER 972, [1979] QB 645, CA.

Wood v Leake (1806) 12 Ves 412, 33 ER 156.

Interlocutory appeals

Bremer Vulkan Schiffbau Und Maschinenfabrik v South India Shipping Corpn   *f*

By a writ issued on 25th April 1977 the plaintiffs, Bremer Vulkan Schiffbau Und Maschinenfabrik ('Bremer'), a body corporate of West Germany, sought as against the defendants, South India Shipping Corpn Ltd ('South India Shipping'), a body corporate of India, (i) an injunction restraining South India Shipping by themselves or their agents from proceeding with, pursuing or taking any further step in a reference to arbitration in which South India Shipping were the claimants and Bremer were the respondents, *g* commenced pursuant to an arbitration clause in a contract between the parties dated 6th August 1964 and in which the Rt Hon Sir Gordon Willmer was appointed sole arbitrator by an agreement dated January 1972, or (ii) alternatively, a declaration that the arbitrator had power to make and issue a final award in the reference dismissing South India Shipping's claim on the grounds only that they had failed to prosecute their claims in the reference with diligence and had been guilty of gross and inexcusable delay causing *h* serious prejudice to Bremer and/or that the dispute could not fairly be tried at the likely time of the hearing. On 10th April 1979, Donaldson J[1] granted the injunction. South India Shipping appealed.

Gregg and others v Raytheon Ltd

By a writ issued on 1st December 1978 the plaintiffs, Newton Gregg, Lucile Gregg and *j* Malcolm Kelly ('the Greggs'), sought as against the defendants, Raytheon Ltd ('Raytheon'), a body corporate of Massachusetts, USA, (i) an injunction against the continuance of an arbitration commenced by Raytheon against the Greggs and another party concerning

1   [1979] 3 All ER 194, [1979] 3 WLR 471

a disputes arising out of a contract dated 2nd June 1970 between the Greggs and the other party and Raytheon, by reason of Raytheon's inordinate and inexcusable delay in prosecuting the arbitration, together with the Greggs's costs of the arbitration as damages for breach of contract or under the court's inherent jurisdiction, the costs to be assessed by a taxing master, and (ii) a declaration that the arbitrators in the arbitration had power to strike out Raytheon's claim in the arbitration for want of prosecution. On 10th April 1979 Donaldson J[1] granted the injunction. Raytheon appealed.

b   The facts in each appeal are set out in the judgment of Lord Denning MR.

Gerald Butler QC and *Giles Caldin* for South India Shipping.
Kenneth Rokison QC and *David Grace* for Bremer.
Mark Saville QC and *V V Veeder* for Raytheon.
Mark Waller QC and *Julian Chichester* for the Greggs.

c

Cur adv vult

23rd November. The following judgments were read.

LORD DENNING MR. When I was young, a sandwich-man wearing a top-hat used *d* to parade outside these courts with his boards back and front, proclaiming 'Arbitrate, don't litigate'. It was very good advice so long as arbitrations were conducted speedily: as many still are in the City of London. But it is not so good when arbitrations drag on for ever.

These cases mark a new development in the law of arbitrations: parallel to the development 11 years ago when we started to strike out actions at law for want of *e* prosecution. That development has had some beneficial results. It has taught practitioners that they must observe the time schedules provided by the rules of court. They must enter in their diaries the latest dates by which writs must be issued and served, pleadings delivered, discovery made, and cases set down for trial. They must keep those dates or get them extended by consent; else they may find themselves in serious trouble. The consequences have, I believe, been beneficial. Many actions are *f* started as 'try-ons'. The plaintiff's claim is weak, but it is hoped that the defendants will pay up or settle. Where the try-on is unsuccessful, and the defendants resist it, the plaintiff or his advisers lose heart. Sooner or later they let things slide. At length the defendant applies to dismiss it for want of prosecution. The plaintiff's advisers then take fright, lest they be held responsible. But the court is adamant. The action is struck out. Other actions are much more genuine. The claim is well founded, but the *g* plaintiff's advisers become busy with other things. They put this case on one side until they have more time to deal with it. Before long they forget about it altogether. This may be their own fault; or it may be the fault of the plaintiff himself for not reminding them; or for not doing what the advisers ask of him. But whatever it is, the time may come when the delay is so inordinate and so inexcusable that a fair trial is impossible. In that case too the court is strict. It strikes the action out. Not for want of sympathy with *h* the plaintiff: but out of justice to the defendant. During the lapse of time, witnesses will have died, memories will have faded, documents will have been lost, all of which might have served him to defend himself against the plaintiff. It is not fair to the defendant to make him fight a case with his hands tied behind his back. So here too the plaintiff or his advisers have to take the consequences. The action is struck out for want of prosecution.

j   Now in the year 1979 we are invited to make a like development in regard to arbitrations. Three recent cases now show that, in arbitrations, as well as in courts of law, cases may last 'so long as to turn justice sour'. They show, too, that an arbitrator has far

1   [1979] 3 All ER 194, [1979] 3 WLR 471

less power than a judge. If the parties drag their feet, the arbitrator can do nothing to
quicken them up. He cannot dismiss a claim for want of prosecution. He cannot strike   *a*
out a dilatory plea which is put in just to gain time. He must abide the pleasure of the
parties. He has no sanctions with which to enforce his orders. Seeing that he can do
nothing, the question is: can the courts do anything about it?

Just see what has happened in these three cases. In the first case it is *13 years* since five
big bulk carriers were built and delivered to the owners ('South India Shipping'). They
have sailed the oceans ever since earning money for their owners. The owners now make   *b*
claims for damages against the builders ('Bremer'). Starting modestly, the claims now
come to a large figure. It is so large that you could buy two of the five ships with it.
They say that the five ships were badly designed and badly built those 13 years ago. Most
of the engineers who worked on them have died or retired. The arbitration was not
started for over five years. The parties appointed Sir Gordon Willmer, who had recently
retired from this court. They could not have picked anyone better. But that was nearly   *c*
eight years ago, when he was 72. The parties have not been near him since. He is now
80. The arbitration has only got so far as points of claim. They cover 137 pages of
foolscap with masses of detail. They go into all the alleged defects of 13 years ago and the
damage said to result from them in the succeeding years. If the arbitration is to proceed,
it will need several years more to prepare for the hearing. The arbitrator will have died,
or got past it. A new arbitrator will have to be appointed. A fair trial is quite   *d*
impossible. Much of the delay is due to the claimants, South India Shipping. They went
to sleep off and on for months at a time. Not even a snore was heard. Time and again
they said they were just about to deliver full points of claim. Eventually, after a whole
year without a word, they delivered those portentous points of claim. The judge has held
that their delay was inordinate and inexcusable, and that the builders, Bremer, had
suffered serious prejudice from it. Is the arbitration to be allowed to go on?   *e*

In the second case it is *nine years* since some shareholders called Gregg in a publishing
company sold their holding to purchasers called Raytheon. The Greggs gave several
assurances to Raytheon about the amount of business being done by the publishing
company. The transaction was completed in 1970 those nine years ago when Raytheon
took over the business. A few months later Raytheon complained that the business was
not what it was represented to be. They claimed £500,000 as damages. The matter was   *f*
referred to arbitration in accordance with the rules of the International Chamber of
Commerce: but by agreement the arbitration was to be held in London. Over *six years*
ago, in 1973, three arbitrators were appointed, all very suitable, Mr Desmond Miller QC,
Mr Michael Mustill QC and Mr I A H Davison. Those arbitrators ordered pleadings and
discovery. Over the years pleadings were delivered, but discovery was never complete.
Time and time again the arbitrators fixed dates for hearing, but time and time again   *g*
these were abandoned. The reason every time was because Raytheon had not given
proper discovery. It was a case where full discovery was essential. Raytheon had bought
the shares and were in control of the publishing company. They would have all the
papers showing what business the publishing company did before and after the deal,
showing whether the assurances were broken or not, and if so, what the damages were.
They promised many a time to get the documents from the United States of America.   *h*
Eventually, in July 1975, over four years ago, the three arbitrators adjourned the case
generally with liberty to either party to restore. It never has been restored. The claimants
Raytheon went silent for three whole years. When they bestirred themselves, two of the
arbitrators had gone off and put on new suits. Mr Desmond Miller QC had left the Bar
and become a man of business. Mr Michael Mustill QC had become a judge of the High
Court. So it looks as if one or two new arbitrators will have to be appointed. It was only   *j*
last November 1978, after three years of silence, that Raytheon's solicitor wrote offering
inspection of thousands of documents. It will take a long time before these can be
analysed and the case is ready to be heard. And then much will depend on oral
conversations ten years before when the shares were sold. The judge held that the delay

of Raytheon was inordinate and inexcusable and that the prejudice to Greggs would be
a most serious. Is the arbitration to be allowed to go on?
   The third case[1] is not before us, but it is so pertinent that I would mention it. In 1969,
ten years ago, the Splendid Sun carried 10,400 tons of maize from Mexico to Venezuela.
On arriving at the discharging port, she grounded and suffered damage of over
$US200,000. The owners claimed damages from the charterers for not nominating a
safe port. In that same year, 1969, two experienced commercial arbitrators in the City
b of London were appointed, Mr Cedric Barclay for the owners and Mr Lynn for the
charterers. Nothing happened for eight whole years. Then on 3rd January 1978 the
owners delivered points of claim. By this time Mr Lynn had died, though Mr Barclay is
still going strong. Lloyd J has held that the delay has been such as to frustrate the
arbitration agreement. Is the arbitration to be allowed to go on? The case was decided
by Lloyd J on 4th May 1979.
c   We had a good deal of discussion about the facts in our two cases, especially whether
there had been acquiescence by one party in the delay of the other. All I need say on this
is that, so far as our court cases are concerned, even when there has been acquiescence up
to a point, nevertheless, if the claimant is thereafter guilty of further delay, he does so at
his peril: because on an application to dismiss for want of prosecution, the court can and
should look at the whole of the case from beginning to end. If, owing to the claimant's
d inexcusable and inordinate delay, before and after the acquiescence, a fair trial is
impossible, the case may be struck out for want of prosecution. I agree entirely with the
observation of Donaldson J[2] on this point. I do not think we need pause on the
unreported cases of *County & District Properties Ltd v Lyell*[3] or *Murrayfield Real Estate Co
Ltd v C Bryant & Son Ltd*[4]. They should be left in the oblivion to which the law reporters
quite rightly consigned them.
e   I see no reason to differ from the judge's assessment of the facts in these cases. So I turn
to the law.

The powers of an arbitrator
   One question is of importance: has an arbitrator any power to dismiss a claim for want
of prosecution? If he has such a power, I should have thought that any application
f should be made to him rather than to the courts. At present, however, there are two
conflicting decisions at first instance. In *Crawford v A E A Prowting Ltd*[5], Bridge J held
that an arbitrator had no power to dismiss a claim for want of prosecution. In our
present case of *Bremer Vulkan Schiffbau v South India Shipping Corpn*[6] Donaldson J has held
that an arbitrator has the power.
   To decide between these two, I would say this: the powers of an arbitrator are derived
g from the agreement of the parties. In the ordinary way the parties agree simply to refer
any matters in dispute to arbitration without saying what powers the arbitrator is to
have. In this situation his powers are to be defined by the law itself. Scrutton J once said
that he has 'inherent powers as a judicial officer': see *Re an arbitration between Crighton
and the Law Car and General Insurance Corpn Ltd*[7]. He also has the powers set out in s 8(1)
of and Sch 1 to the Arbitration Act 1934, and repeated in s 12(6) of the Arbitration Act
h 1950. These require the parties to do 'all other things which, during the proceedings on
the reference, the arbitrator or umpire may require'[8].

---

1   *André et Compagnie SA v Marine Transocean Ltd, The Splendid Sun* (4th May 1979) unreported
2   [1979] 3 All ER 194 at 198
j 3   [1977] Court of Appeal Transcript 314
4   [1978] Court of Appeal Transcript 473
5   [1972] 1 All ER 1199, [1973] 1 QB 1
6   [1979] 3 All ER 194 at 201, 204
7   [1910] 2 KB 738 at 745
8   Arbitration Act 1950, s 12(1)

Apart from previous authority, I would have been disposed to think that an arbitrator would have the power to do, and to require the parties to do, all the same things as a *a* judicial officer could do. He could require the delivery of pleadings, and the disclosure of documents. He could allow or disallow the amendment of pleadings. He could fix a day for hearing, and so forth. If his orders were disobeyed, I should have thought that he could have imposed sanctions for non-compliance. But there is a decision going back for over 60 years now which says he has no power to inflict sanctions for disobedience. It is *Re an arbitration between Unione Stearinerie Lanza and Weiner*[1]. An Italian buyer *b* bought goods from an English seller. The contract contained an arbitration clause. The Italian buyer claimed damages in an arbitration here in London. The English seller asked the arbitrator to order the Italian buyer to put up security for costs. That would have been automatic in a court of law, because the claimant was resident abroad. But it was held that the arbitrator had no power to make an order for security for costs. The reason, as I see it, was because, implicit in such an order, there would be an implied *c* sanction: namely, that unless security were given, the proceedings would be stayed. Viscount Reading CJ[2] said that 'the words in clause (*f*) [of Sch 1 to the Arbitration Act 1889] . . . do not give the power to order a stay of proceedings'.

Likewise, suppose that an arbitrator made a peremptory order for delivery of points of claim adding that 'unless' they were delivered in seven days the proceedings would be stayed. Such an 'unless' order would be beyond the powers of the arbitrator, because in *d* the words of Viscount Reading CJ[2], 'the words in clause (*f*) . . . do not give the power to order a stay of the proceedings'.

This view of the law has been accepted by practitioners: and the parties at arbitrations have taken advantage of it. Especially defendants who want to get more time. They will instruct their arbitrator to delay as much as he can. They will say they are not ready. They will manufacture counterclaims or set-offs. They will get up to no end of tricks, *e* such as were described by MacKinnon J in 1927[3] and by me in *Associated Bulk Carriers Ltd v Koch Shipping Inc, The Fuohsan Maru*[4]. In 1978 the Commercial Court Committee in their Report on Arbitration[5] observed:

> 'A favourite ploy by those who seek delay is to ignore the time table fixed by the arbitrator or to fail to comply with directions for the delivery of a defence or for discovery. Parties to an action in the Commercial Court who adopted similar tactics *f* would receive short shrift, since the Court would strike out the claim or counterclaim or debar the defendants from defending.'

In this situation I am afraid we must recognise that arbitrators are impotent. They can make all sorts of orders for pleadings, discovery and the like: but they are exhortatory only. Either party can cock a snook at the arbitrator. Either can disobey with *g* impunity. It is only the court that can bring a party to book.

Parliament has just given some remedy in s 5 of the Arbitration Act 1979; but it only applies to arbitrations started after 1st August 1979[6].

The powers of the court

It is some confirmation of this view that Parliament has intervened to correct the *h* position. It has set out some specific orders which the court can make in aid of an arbitration. In s 8 of the Arbitration Act 1934, as read with Sch 1 to that Act, now replaced by s 12(6) of the 1950 Act, it says that—

j

1   [1917] 2 KB 558
2   [1917] 2 KB 558 at 561–562
3   Report of Committee on the Law of Arbitration (March 1927), Cmd 2817
4   [1978] 2 All ER 254 at 257, [1978] 1 Lloyd's Rep 24 at 26
5   Cmnd 7284 (July 1978), para 57
6   Arbitration Act 1979 (Commencement) Order 1979, SI 1979 No 750

'The . . . Court shall have, for the purpose of and in relation to a reference, the same power of making orders in respect of—(a) security for costs; (b) discovery of documents . . . as it has for the purpose of and in relation to an action or matter in the High Court.'

In case, therefore, a party to an arbitration desires security for costs, or discovery, which the other refuses to give, he can apply to the court. Then the court can make an order and apply sanctions to enforce obedience. It can make a peremptory order saying that 'unless' such and such is done within such and such a time, the proceedings in the arbitration shall be stayed. Just as it could stay proceedings in an action. So, although the arbitrator has no power to inflict sanctions, the court has the power.

Some may say that s 12(6) of the 1950 Act is exhaustive: that the court can only intervene in the cases specified in paras (a) to (h) of that subsection, and in no others. I do not take that view. That section was enacted so as to make it clear that the courts can intervene in those cases at any rate, leaving it open to the courts to intervene in any other cases in which its inherent jurisdiction enables it so to do. We have recently held that the powers of the court are not to be found exclusively in the statute, but also in its inherent jurisdiction: see *Japan Line Ltd v Aggeliki Charis Compania Maritima SA, The Angelic Grace*[1].

The inherent jurisdiction of the court

There is a difference between the powers of the court *after* an award has been made and *before* it. It is quite clear that, *after* it has been made, the court can set it aside if the arbitrator has wholly or partially exceeded his jurisdiction, or if he has been guilty of misconduct, or if there is an error of law on the face of the award. *Before* any award is made, the court can restrain the parties and the arbitrator from proceeding further with it in these cases: first, where one party brings an action impeaching the supposed arbitration agreement, saying that there was no binding agreement (see *Maunsell v Midland Great Western (Ireland) Railway Co*[2] and *Kitts v Moore*[3]); and second, where the arbitrator has done something or other which shows him to be unfit or incompetent to continue with the arbitration (see *Beddow v Beddow*[4] and *Jackson v Barry Railway Co*[5]).

Counsel for Raytheon submitted that those two were the only cases where the courts would restrain an arbitrator from continuing. He said that there was no general jurisdiction in equity to prevent an arbitrator from continuing. He relied on *North London Railway Co v Great Northern Railway Co*[6]. Two trains were in collision. One railway company said it was the fault of the other company's signalman. The other railway company said it was the fault of the first company's driver. One company started arbitration proceedings. The other company said the dispute was not within the arbitration clause, and started an action at law. The Court of Appeal refused to stay the arbitration pending the trial of the action. They realised that the arbitration might be futile, because the dispute might not be within the arbitration clause. Yet they allowed the arbitration to go on. Both the arbitration and the action went on together. Nowadays it is obvious that the two proceedings would not be allowed to continue side by side. Either the arbitration should be stayed, or the action should be stayed. The procedure of these courts has altered so much in the last 100 years that that case cannot, in my view, afford any guidance to us today.

On the other side counsel for the Greggs referred us to a case in 1865 of *Pickering v Cape Town Railway Co*[7]. There was a contract for the construction of a railway. It contained

---

1   [1979] Court of Appeal Transcript 507
2   (1863) 1 Hem & M 130, 71 ER 58
3   [1895] 1 QB 253
4   (1878) 9 Ch D 89
5   [1893] 1 Ch 238 at 249, [1891–4] All ER Rep 661 at 666
6   (1883) 11 QBD 30
7   (1865) LR 1 Eq 84

an arbitration clause, but instead of proceeding under it, the company took possession of
the works. The company afterwards sought to insist on going to arbitration. Page Wood
V-C restrained them. He said[1] that if—

> 'the Court should be of opinion that they have debarred themselves from
> exercising those rights [to take arbitration proceedings] by the course of conduct
> which they have adopted, there arises an equity, which prevents them from
> prosecuting proceedings, however they might otherwise be entitled to do so . . .'

In the next edition of Russell on Arbitration[2] that case was cited as authority for this
proposition: 'Parties, however, sometimes conduct themselves in such a manner as to
induce the Court of Chancery to restrain them from proceeding in a reference.'

That proposition was accepted in New South Wales in *Sneddon v Kyle*[3], and underlies
a case in Ontario, *Danforth Travel Centre Ltd v BOAC*[4]. In the text to a note in Halsbury's
Laws of England[5], it is said:

> 'The court has jurisdiction to interfere in arbitration proceedings on equitable
> grounds where the parties have by their conduct excluded themselves from the
> benefit of their contract to arbitrate.'

Following these persuasive authorities, I am of opinion that this court has an inherent
jurisdiction to restrain arbitration proceedings where it would be right and just to do so:
and it may be right and just when the claimant has been guilty of such inexcusable and
inordinate delay that a fair hearing is impossible. In other words, the court can dismiss
the claim for want of prosecution, just as it can an action.

Frustrating delay

There is, however, another way of reaching the same result. It must be remembered
that the parties, having agreed to submit their differences to arbitration, are bound to
pursue that method of proceeding. Co-operation by both is essential to its success. On
the one hand it is the duty of the claimant to proceed with reasonable despatch so that the
respondents are not prejudiced by delay. On the other hand it is the duty of the
respondent not to baulk the claimant by devious manoeuvres.

Those duties are, in my opinion, imposed by law; and not by any application of the
Moorcock[6] principle. They are imposed by more general considerations, such as Viscount
Simonds remarked in *Lister v Romford Ice & Cold Storage Co Ltd*[7]; and Lord Wilberforce
and Lord Edmund-Davies approved in *Liverpool City Council v Irwin*[8]; and I spelt out in
Shell UK Ltd v Lostock Garage Ltd[9] (the first category of implied terms).

So there is, in my opinion, a duty imposed by law on the claimant to use reasonable
despatch. He may often break that duty with impunity. Delay often does no harm to
the respondent. Even unreasonable delay may do no harm to anyone but the claimant
himself. But sometimes the delay may reach such proportions as to frustrate the very
object of the venture, the very purpose of the arbitration itself, so that there cannot be a
fair hearing and the arbitrator cannot reach a just result. When the delay is as great as
this, when it is so great as to frustrate the arbitration itself, the respondent is entitled to
treat the contract of arbitration as at an end: see the cases collected by Devlin J in

---

1 (1865) LR 1 Eq 84 at 87–88
2 Russell on Arbitration (7th Edn, 1891) p 204
3 (1902) 2 SR (NSW) Eq 112
4 (1972) 29 DLR (3d) 141
5 21 Halsbury's Laws (3rd Edn) p 406, para 852; 24 Halsbury's Laws (4th Edn) para 1038
6 *The Moorcock* (1889) 14 PD 64, [1886–90] All ER Rep 530
7 [1957] 1 All ER 125 at 133, [1957] AC 555 at 576
8 [1976] 2 All ER 39 at 44, 54–55, [1977] AC 239 at 254–255, 266–267
9 [1977] 1 All ER 481 at 487, [1976] 1 WLR 1187 at 1196

Universal Cargo Carriers Corpn v Citati[1]. That was the approach favoured by Lloyd J in
André et Compagnie SA v Marine Transocean Ltd, The Splendid Sun[2], when he said: '. . . the
test should be the same as in other cases of delay, namely, such delay as would frustrate
the arbitration agreement.'

Frustrating delay in this sense is equivalent to a repudiation of the arbitration
agreement, which the respondent can elect to accept, and, on doing so, can apply to
dismiss the claim for want of prosecution. He can also claim as damages the cost to
which he has been put in preparing for the arbitration thus rendered fruitless.

International Chamber of Commerce rules

Before us counsel for Raytheon raised a point which was not taken below. It only
applies to the shares case where the arbitration was to be held 'in Geneva, Switzerland
under the rules then prevailing of the International Chamber of Commerce'. By
agreement London was substituted for Geneva. The proper law of the contract was
governed by the laws of England and of the State of Delaware; but the procedure was
governed by the law of England: see *James Miller and Partners Ltd v Whitworth Street
Estates*[3] by Lord Wilberforce.

Counsel for Raytheon took us through the rules of the ICC. He showed us that, in
addition to the three arbitrators named by the parties, there was a 'Court of Arbitration'
in Paris which exercised some kind of supervision over the arbitration proceedings. He
submitted that, under the rules, the Court of Arbitration in Paris was the superior
authority in matters of procedure: and that, if one of the parties was guilty of
unreasonable delay, the remedy was to apply to the Court of Arbitration in Paris. He
relied on the practice as set out in an affidavit by Dr Eisemann, at one time the head of
the secretariat of the ICC; and also on art 31, which says that—

> 'In any circumstances not specifically provided for above, the Court of Arbitration
> . . . shall act on the basis of these Rules and make their best efforts for the award to
> be enforceable at law.'

I do not propose to go into the rules in detail. Suffice it to say that I do not find in them
any power in the Court of Arbitration in Paris to inflict sanctions on a party, or to dismiss
a claim for want of prosecution. There is a further difficulty in this case. No terms of
reference were drawn up by the arbitrators so as to satisfy art 19. No hearing could be
held until the terms of reference were drawn up.

I regard the arbitration in London under the ICC rules as virtually equivalent to an
ordinary English arbitration. The Court of Arbitration in Paris is a body with
administrative functions only. It has no power to interfere in the judicial process of the
arbitrators. If there is inordinate and inexcusable delay, the courts in England can take
a hand, but no one else.

I would reject, therefore, the point on the ICC.

Conclusion

In the end I think we should make the new development which we are invited to
make. We should develop the law as to arbitration on the same lines as we did 11 years
ago for the law of actions. The judges in the courts below, Donaldson and Lloyd JJ, have
pointed the way. Both are most experienced in the ways of arbitrations. By their
opinions we set great store. They have struck out these three commercial claims for
want of prosecution. I would do the same. In doing so, I do not overlook the further
development which is foreshadowed. It may often happen that it is the respondents who
cause the delays. They may put up one excuse after the other, so as to gain more time,
or so as to avoid payment of a just demand. If the arbitrator has no power to bring them

---

1   [1957] 2 All ER 70 at 80–82, [1957] 2 QB 401 at 430–434
2   (4th May 1979) unreported
3   [1970] 1 All ER 796 at 809–810, [1970] AC 583 at 616

to book, can the courts intervene? If our decision today is correct, the principle underlying it may, I only say 'may', apply to respondents as much as to claimants. If the *a* respondents to an arbitration are guilty of such wilful delay as to frustrate the arbitration agreement itself, they may be said to have broken the agreement and be liable in damages. The damages would be assessed according to the chance which the claimants had of succeeding in the arbitration. I throw that out only by the way because one has to look ahead as far as one can when new developments are made new law. There are exciting times ahead. But for the reasons I have given I would uphold the decision of *b* Donaldson J in these two cases, and dismiss the appeal.

ROSKILL LJ. These two appeals from decisions of Donaldson J dated 10th April 1979 raise, as the judge said at the outset of his judgment, questions of great importance relating to the conduct of arbitrations in this country and especially in relation to the conduct of those arbitrations to which s 5 of the Arbitration Act 1979 will not apply. *c* Before us the appeal in *Gregg v Raytheon Ltd* was argued before the appeal in *Bremer Vulkan Schiffbau Und Maschinenfabrik v South India Shipping Corpn*, though before the judge the cases were apparently heard in the reverse order. I shall call the first appeal 'the Raytheon appeal' and the second 'the Bremer appeal'. In each action the judge has held that the appellants ('Raytheon' and 'South India Shipping'), who were the defendants in the two actions and the respective claimants in the two arbitrations, had been guilty of *d* inordinate and inexcusable delay which had caused such prejudice to the plaintiffs in each of the two actions ('the Greggs' and 'Bremer'), who were the respective respondents in the two arbitrations and of course in these appeals, that had the appellants commenced these proceedings in the High Court by way of action instead of by arbitration in accordance with the arbitration clauses in the respective agreements under which the disputes concerned arose such proceedings would have been dismissed by the High Court *e* for want of prosecution in accordance with the principles laid down in *Birkett v James*[1] and *Allen v Sir Alfred McAlpine & Sons Ltd*[2]. The judge[3] summarised those principles in six succinct paragraphs. Subject to what I say in the next sentences on the question of acquiescence (see para 5 of the judge's summary) I accept as correct and gratefully adopt the judge's summary without repetition. Counsel for South India Shipping argued that acquiescence was an absolute bar and that, once there was acquiescence in delay, the *f* existence of that delay ceased to be relevant. Only further delay is relevant. Since I take the view, as did the judge, that there was no acquiescence in the Bremer case, this point does not arise for decision. But as at present advised, I think the argument of counsel for South India Shipping is inconsistent with what Salmon LJ said in *Allen v Sir Alfred McAlpine & Sons Ltd*[4].

The question for decision before Donaldson J was, and in this court is, whether those *g* principles have any application to the conduct of arbitration in this country. Until the present cases no court has held that they have. But the judge has held first that an arbitrator (I include an umpire in that word) has power to dismiss for want of prosecution and to make an award to that effect. He has further held that in such a case the courts have power to intervene and prevent a dilatory claimant in an arbitration from further proceeding with his claim by granting an injunction restraining him from so doing. *h* The judge based this conclusion on the view that unjustified delay by a claimant struck at the root of an agreement to arbitrate which a respondent might treat as repudiatory conduct and accept as such, thus bringing to an end the agreement to arbitrate, and enabling him to obtain an injunction and also, where appropriate, damages, eg for wasted expenditure.

j

---

1   [1977] 2 All ER 801, [1978] AC 297
2   [1968] 1 All ER 543, [1968] 2 QB 229
3   [1979] 3 All ER 194 at 197–198, [1979] 3 WLR 471 at 474–476
4   [1968] 1 All ER 543 at 563–564, [1968] 2 QB 229 at 272

a The judge's first conclusion that an arbitrator had power to dismiss for want of prosecution was contrary to an earlier decision of Bridge J in *Crawford v A E A Prowting Ltd*[1], where Bridge J had held that there was no such jurisdiction vested in an arbitrator. The argument that the court had power in effect to achieve the same result by an injunction was not and indeed could not have been advanced in that case, since the matter came before Bridge J by way of case stated by an arbitrator who had been invited to dismiss the claimants' claim in that arbitration for want of prosecution.

b Before us, counsel for Raytheon, the appellants in the Raytheon appeal, argued as almost his last submission that Donaldson J had reached the wrong conclusion on the facts of that case. Counsel for South Indian Shipping, the appellants in the Bremer appeal, devoted virtually the whole of his argument to a like submission and was content for the rest to adopt (with one exception) counsel's submissions for Raytheon on the other issues so far as relevant to the Bremer appeal. In neither appeal did this court find c it necessary to call on counsel for the respondents to support the judge's conclusions on the facts of the case, for, notwithstanding the arguments of counsel for each of the appellants, I think the judge's conclusions on the facts in each case are quite unassailable. For my part I would in each case have unhesitatingly reached the same conclusion as did Donaldson J. But even if I had felt any doubt as to the correctness of either or both of his conclusions, which I do not, I would not have been willing to d interfere with his exercise of his discretion on a matter of this kind, assuming, of course, he was right in applying to arbitrations the same principle as is now clearly established to apply to actions in the High Court.

It follows that for the first time this court is asked to decide whether, first, arbitrators have power to dismiss for want of prosecution in such circumstances and make an award to that effect, and, secondly, whether or not they have such power, the court has power e to interfere in such circumstances by injunction. It is convenient to mention at this juncture that since the instant decisions, in *André et Compagnie SA v Marine Transocean Ltd, The Splendid Sun*[2] Lloyd J granted an injunction restraining claimants in an arbitration from proceeding with their claim. The question whether arbitrators had power to strike out did not arise for decision. The delays in that case were even worse than in the instant cases since the arbitration in question had been begun in 1969 and no steps had been f taken thereafter for over eight years. Lloyd J stated that, as is the fact, until the instant cases, no court had granted an injunction such as Donaldson J granted.

But following Donaldson J's decision Lloyd J granted such an injunction, resting his decision on the submission that the delay in question was such as would frustrate the agreement to arbitrate, a submission apparently not advanced before or considered by Donaldson J. As will later emerge, I think Lloyd J was right to rest his decision on this g foundation rather than on that enunciated on this branch of the case by Donaldson J if, which still remains to be considered, the court has any power to interfere by injunction in the circumstances under consideration.

It should be mentioned that neither of the two counsel for the respective respondents, who, as plaintiffs, obtained injunctions from Donaldson J, found it easy to support that part of the judge's judgment which held that arbitrators had power to dismiss for want h of prosecution and to make an award to that effect. Counsel for the Greggs dealt with this question only towards the end of many submissions, while counsel for Bremer, whose help we had invited in order to make sure that no point favourable to the judge's view had inadvertently been overlooked, recognised his difficulty in supporting this part of the judgment.

It is strange that if arbitrators have this power it has never been invoked, at any rate in j such a way as to obtain a decision of the court on its existence. The inadequacy of the powers of arbitrators to deal with delays, often deliberate delays, has long been a matter of complaint. Many of the proposals of the powerful committee over which MacKinnon J

---

1   [1972] 1 All ER 1199, [1973] 1 QB 1
2   (4th May 1979) unreported

presided in 1927[1] were directed towards strengthening the Arbitration Act 1889 so as to
avoid delays which by 1927 were already notorious. Those of the proposals which were *a*
ultimately adopted found their place on the statute book in the Arbitration Act 1934. As
recently as 1978 the Commercial Court Committee, over which Donaldson J himself
presided, in a report[2] bewailed the constant delay and discussed the 'favourite ploy' by
those seeking delay. Paragraph 57, which bears the rubric 'Sanctions in case of delay or
failure to comply with the arbitrator's directions' merits quotation in full:

> 'A favourite ploy by those who seek delay is to ignore the time table fixed by the *b*
> arbitrator or to fail to comply with directions for the delivery of a defence or for
> discovery. Parties to an action in the Commercial Court who adopted similar tactics
> would receive short shrift since the Court would strike out the claim or counterclaim
> or debar the defendant from defending. In cases which fall within section 12(6) of
> the 1950 Act it is possible for parties to obtain an order from the High Court and for
> that Court to apply sanctions in the event of default. However, this is not widely *c*
> known, does not cover all forms of foot-dragging and involves at least two
> attendances on the High Court—first to obtain an order and further attendances to
> invoke sanctions. What is required is power for the High Court to apply sanctions
> for disobedience of orders made by the arbitrator. This too is a suitable subject for
> the attention of an Arbitration Rules Committee.'
>
> *d*

That report was in part responsible for the passing of the Arbitration Act 1979,
including s 5. But in neither the report of MacKinnon J's committee nor in this report
of the Commercial Court Committee does one find any hint or suggestion that arbitrators
have so readily to hand this lethal weapon which the judge in his judicial capacity has
held to exist.

On the other hand, it must be said that before *Allen v Sir Alfred MacAlpine & Sons Ltd*[3] *e*
and the other related cases it had not readily occurred to practitioners that this weapon
of striking out was available to dispose of personal injury and other actions of seemingly
indefinite duration, and perhaps it is not surprising that the possibility of using this
weapon had not occurred to those engaged in arbitrations rather than litigation.
Nonetheless complaints of delays in arbitration have been of as long, or longer, standing
as complaints of the law's delays, and it has at long last in 1979 been thought necessary *f*
to deal with this problem by legislation.

In my view it is necessary to consider the correctness of the judge's view both as a
matter of history and of principle. Until well into the last century the courts looked
askance at arbitrations. The procedure was suspect as tending to oust the jurisdiction of
the courts, and indeed one finds traces of this attitude in decided cases well into this
century notwithstanding the passing, first, of the Common Law Procedure Act 1854 and, *g*
secondly, of the Arbitration Act 1889.

As Lord Moulton pointed out in his speech in *Bristol Corpn v John Aird & Co*[4], it was not
until the Common Law Procedure Act 1854 that Parliament gave to the courts the
limited power of stay which s 11 of that statute accorded in cases where the parties had
agreed that existing or future differences should be referred to arbitration, provided, of
course, the other conditions in that section were also satisfied. Until then if one of the *h*
parties to a submission refused to proceed to arbitration the other was left to a useless
remedy in an action for damages (see also in this connection the judgment of this court
in *Re an intended arbitration between Smith & Service and Nelson & Sons*[5], where it was held
that the only remedy for unilateral revocation of a submission to arbitration, before s 1

j

---

1 Cmd 2817
2 Report on Arbitration (July 1978), Cmnd 7284
3 [1968] 1 All ER 543, [1968] 2 QB 229
4 [1913] AC 241 at 256–257, [1911–13] All ER Rep 1076 at 1080–1081
5 (1890) 25 QBD 545

of the Arbitration Act 1889 was enacted, lay in an action for damages for breach of
a contract). But the Common Law Procedure Act 1854 is singularly silent as to the powers
as distinct from the duties of arbitrators; for example, s 15 provided that an arbitrator
should, save in circumstances for which the section made provision, make his award
within three months of his appointment. Those and other sections of the 1854 Act
dealing with arbitrations were repealed by Sch 2 to the Arbitration Act 1889. That
statute in s 4 re-enacted, in a somewhat different form, s 11 of the 1854 Act. By s 2 of
b and Sch 1 to the 1889 Act, nine provisions respectively lettered (a) to (i) were ordered to
be implied into submissions to arbitration unless the parties had otherwise provided.
The former s 15 found new and extended life in paras (c), (d) and (e) of that schedule,
provisions which were castigated by the MacKinnon committee as of no practical value
(see para 5 of that report[1]). It is to be observed that para (f) created an implied obligation
on parties to give evidence and also discovery, but notwithstanding that provision no
c sanctions were provided for any failure so to do. Curiously enough, Sch 1 to the 1889
Act contained no express power to order pleadings or indeed to allow amendments to
pleadings, nor was any power given to arbitrators to order a claimant to give security for
costs in cases where in an action a court would order such security to be given.

It is difficult to think that, if between 1889 and 1934, when some of the
recommendations of the MacKinnon committee took effect in the Arbitration Act 1934,
d anyone had been bold enough to assert that an arbitrator had power to dismiss an
arbitration for want of prosecution and to make an award to that effect without more
ado, such a submission would have been favourably received in any court of law. That
that is so is supported, I think, by two decisions in this period, especially the second, to
neither of which was Donaldson J referred when this matter was before him. In *Re an
arbitration between Crighton and the Law Car and General Insurance Corpn Ltd*[2], a Divisional
e Court which included Scrutton J held that an arbitrator had both inherent power and also
power under para (f) of Sch 1 to the 1889 Act to order pleadings and to allow or to refuse
amendments to them. No doubt it was this decision which made it unnecessary for the
MacKinnon committee to recommend that this apparent gap in Sch 1 to the 1889 Act be
filled by legislation. More important, in *Re an arbitration between Unione Stearinerie Lanza
and Weiner*[3] the Divisional Court held that an arbitrator had no power to order security
f for costs. That court declined to extend Scrutton J's reasoning in *Re Crighton*[2] to the
length necessary to enable security for costs to be ordered by an arbitrator. Viscount
Reading CJ said[4]:

g
'I do not think Scrutton J. meant by those words to imply that an arbitrator under
a submission by agreement was in the same position as and had all the powers of a
judge. I think he meant that he had power to ascertain the facts and, under clause
(f), power to order points of claim to be delivered, and, that that being so, he must
have the power also, sitting as the person to decide the questions, to allow an
amendment. I do not think he meant anything more than that.'

h This decision led to the recommendation of the MacKinnon committee that the court,
not, be it noted, arbitrators, should be given power (inter alia) to order security for costs,
a provision subsequently enacted in the 1934 Act and now finding its place in s 12(6)(a)
of the Arbitration Act 1950.

It was faintly suggested that we should overrule the *Unione Stearinerie* case[3]. It would

j

1   Cmd 2817
2   [1910] 2 KB 738
3   [1917] 2 KB 558
4   [1917] 2 KB 558 at 561

be completely wrong for us to do so even if I had any doubts (which I have not) as to its correctness. When a decision has been accepted for over 60 years and its consequences *a* remedied by statute, though not so as to give arbitrators power to order security for costs, it would indeed be strange for the Court of Appeal to hold at this late stage that this latter power had always existed.

I cannot but think that if the judge had been referred to this decision, and in particular to the passage I have just quoted from the judgment of Viscount Reading CJ, he would not have reached the conclusion that he did, namely that parties by their agreement to *b* arbitrate impliedly clothed the arbitration tribunal with jurisdiction to give effect to their rights and remedies to the same extent and in the same manner as a court, subject only to certain well-recognised exceptions.

The judge relied on the decision of this court in *Chandris v Isbrandtsen-Moller Co Inc*[1] as supporting his view. With great respect, I do not think that that decision goes so far as the judge thought. An arbitrator may award interest on damages in a proper case for the *c* reasons given by this court in the *Chandris* case[1]. But that is not to say, as the judge sought to say, that an arbitrator has in all the circumstances all the powers of the court, subject only to the exceptions which he mentioned. I venture to think that the members of this court who decided the *Chandris* case[1] would have been surprised to learn that they had impliedly held that an arbitrator had power to dismiss for want of prosecution and had also impliedly reversed the decision in the *Unione Stearinerie* case[2]. *d*

So far I have dealt with the question only by considering the history of the relationship between the courts and arbitrators and what I conceive to be the principle which has to be applied in these cases. But we were referred to an ill-reported case, *Wilson Sons & Co v Condé d'Eu Railway Co*[3]. This was a decision of the Divisional Court (Day and Wills JJ) in which it appears to have been held that an arbitrator, seemingly vested with all the powers of a judge at nisi prius, nonetheless had no power to strike out the claims that *e* were before him, but that he must adjudicate on them (see the brief report of the successful argument of the then Attorney-General and also of the judgment of the court). This decision was before the 1889 Act, but for what it is worth supports the conclusion at which I have independently arrived.

One reason which Bridge J[4] gave for holding that there was no power in an arbitrator to dismiss for want of prosecution was what he suggested was the different position of a *f* respondent in an arbitration from that of a defendant in an action. He described the position of a defendant in an action as 'relatively privileged', because such a defendant could sit back, do nothing, and then apply to dismiss the action against him for want of prosecution. In the case of an arbitration Bridge J thought there was an obligation on both parties to enable the matter to be prepared for trial. Donaldson J[5] disagreed with this view, suggesting that save in what he called 'look-sniff' arbitrations, arbitrations and *g* actions were indistinguishable in principle in their adversarial characteristics.

Counsel for Raytheon submitted that on this issue Donaldson J was wrong and Bridge J was right and that arbitrations were inquisitorial rather than adversarial in their character. He relied on what he claimed to be the duty of an arbitrator to make his award promptly and referred to the penalties for which provision is made in s 13 of the Arbitration Act 1950 for the removal of an arbitrator from office and deprivation of *h* remuneration. I think, with respect, this submission is without foundation. The subsection is dealing with an arbitrator who will not go forward when everyone wishes him to do so. But an arbitrator who insisted on proceeding against the wishes of the parties and attempted to make an award when they were not ready to proceed might at least in some cases find himself accused of misconduct.

j

1   [1950] 2 All ER 618, [1951] 1 KB 240
2   [1917] 2 KB 558
3   (1887) 51 JP 230
4   In *Crawford v A E A Prowting Ltd* [1972] 1 All ER 1199 at 1203, [1973] 1 QB 1 at 7
5   [1979] 3 All ER 194 at 199, [1979] 3 WLR 471 at 477–478

With great respect to any view of Bridge J, I find it difficult to distinguish between
a litigation and arbitrations on the grounds which he suggested. Both to my mind are
essentially adversarial. Even in a case where each party has appointed an arbitrator and
the arbitrators meet and agree on their award before appointing an umpire I think the
proceedings can properly be characterised as adversarial. If the commercial judge tries
an action in the Commercial Court, it is by concession an adversarial process. If he is
invited and agrees to hear precisely the same dispute as an arbitrator or umpire under s 4
b of the Administration of Justice Act 1970, I find it difficult to see how or why the whole
character and quality of the proceedings suddenly changes. Indeed an arbitrator or
umpire who, in the absence of express agreement that he should do so, attempted to
conduct an arbitration along inquisitorial lines might expose himself to criticism and
possible removal.

On this point, therefore, I respectfully prefer the reasoning of Donaldson J to that of
c Bridge J. I take the view that almost all arbitration proceedings and certainly the instant
arbitration proceedings were essentially adversarial in their character. As will appear
later in this judgment, I do not think that a respondent in an arbitration is in an in any
way different position from a defendant in an action. Neither is under any obligation to
stir his adversary into action. The dictum which Donaldson J[1] quoted in his judgment
about sleeping dogs seems to me to apply equally to sleeping claimants in an arbitration
d as to sleeping plaintiffs in an action.

If Donaldson J's view that arbitrators do, with certain exceptions, possess all the powers
of a court, were right, one wonders why the express powers listed in s 12(6) of the 1950
Act were necessary, since an arbitrator would already have possessed the greater number
of these powers pursuant to some inherent powers vested in him.

In support of Raytheon's appeal counsel advanced two further arguments, neither of
e which, he frankly admitted, had been advanced by counsel appearing for Raytheon
before Donaldson J.

The first was that even if the criticism of the first part of the judge's judgment were
well-founded his conclusion could be supported on the ground that the position was
different in the case of what counsel for Raytheon called an 'institutional' arbitration, by
which phrase I understood him to mean an arbitration conducted in accordance with the
f rules of and under the supervision of some organisation of arbitration such as, in the
Raytheon appeal, the International Chamber of Commerce ('ICC'), or perhaps the
Institute of Arbitrators in this country. The second was that even if the three arbitrators
appointed by the parties under the ICC rules had no jurisdiction to dismiss for want of
prosecution nonetheless under those rules the respondents' remedy was to apply to the
ICC 'Court of Arbitration', a body for which their rules make provision, for an
g appropriate order which he claimed that court could make under the rules. He relied in
this connection on an affidavit by Dr Eisemann, a former Secretary-General of the Court
of Arbitration of the ICC. To this affidavit the respondents replied with an affidavit from
Dr Mann whose experience in the field of international arbitration requires no
endorsement from this court. We admitted these affidavits notwithstanding formal
objection from counsel for the Greggs.

h   The arbitration clause in the contract concerned in the Raytheon appeal, which was
dated 2nd June 1970, will be found in cl 11 of that contract. It reads thus:

> 'In the event that any dispute or controversy shall arise between the parties
> hereto, the same shall be resolved by arbitration in Geneva, Switzerland under the
> rules then prevailing of the International Chamber of Commerce. The laws of
> England and the laws of the State of Delaware shall be deemed equally applicable to
j > this agreement and in the event of conflict between the two bodies of law the
> Arbitrator shall be free to apply whichever of the said laws will in his opinion most
> equitably secure the results contemplated herein. The decision of the Arbitrator(s)

1   [1979] 3 All ER 194 at 198, [1979] 3 WLR 471 at 476

shall be final and binding upon both parties and judgment thereon may be entered in any court of competent jurisdiction.'

Thus the originally intended place of arbitration was Geneva. But this was later changed to London by agreement between the parties and with the consent of the ICC. It was argued that this change cannot have been intended to import into the agreement to arbitrate all the striking-out procedure applicable to English High Court actions. Since I take the view that by English law an arbitrator has no such power, the interesting discussion we had on the extent of the applicability of the lex fori to arbitrations which is elaborated in Dr Mann's affidavit and also in an article he wrote, 'Lex Facit Arbitrium' in a presentation Book of Essays, 'Liber Amicorum', requires no further consideration.

But I find it difficult to accept the distinction suggested by counsel for Raytheon between institutional and non-institutional arbitration, for which he claimed some support in a textbook entitled 'Handbook of Institutional Arbitration in International Trade'[1]. No doubt institutions concerned with furthering arbitration as a means of disposal of disputes seek emancipation from control of the courts of the countries where such arbitrations take place, perhaps in the belief that such freedom facilitates expedition of decision. Dr Mann's affidavit shows the limited success of such attempts and this court recently had to consider similar problems in relation to ICC arbitrations in *Dalmia Dairy Industries Ltd v National Bank of Pakistan*[2], to which frequent reference was made during the arguments. For my part, I am unable to accept that there can be any logical distinction between arbitrations of one kind and the other according to whether some label such as 'institutional' can be attached. In each case the relevant question is: on what terms and conditions have the parties agreed to go to arbitration? That question must be answered without regard to any attachment of suggested labels.

Ultimately counsel for Raytheon did not argue that the three named arbitrators had power to dismiss for want of prosecution. But he contended that the respondents had pursued the wrong remedy and that to achieve their objective they should have applied, not to the arbitrators, nor to the courts of this country, but to the ICC Court of Arbitration. To some extent this submission overlaps with the question whether or not the court has power to grant and, if it has power, should grant an injunction, for clearly if an alternative remedy existed an English court would be less willing to grant a discretionary remedy such as an injunction.

I therefore turn to the ICC rules. We are concerned with the 1955 edition, which were those in force at the date of the relevant contract. I think it is clear that for the purpose of the present proceedings we must interpret those rules in accordance with English principles of construction. There is no evidence that the law of Delaware is any different from our own. Section B(1) of those rules deals with the Court of Arbitration and arbitrators and arts 6 and 7 set out the method of appointment of and the functions of the Court of Arbitration. Article 13 gives further powers to the Court of Arbitration. Article 26 reads:

> 'Before completing the awards the arbitrator will submit the same to the Court of Arbitration. The Court may lay down modifications as to its form and, if need be, draw the arbitrator's attention even to the points connected with the merits of the case, but with due regard to the arbitrator's liberty of decision. No award shall under any circumstances be issued until approved as to its form by the Court of Arbitration.'

Article 31, much relied on by counsel for Raytheon, reads:

> 'General rule. In any circumstances not specifically provided for above the Court of Arbitration and the arbitrator shall act on the basis of these rules and make their best efforts for the award to be enforceable at law.'

---

1   Cohn, Domke and Eisemann (eds) (1977)
2   [1978] 2 Lloyd's Rep 223

In addition I should refer to arts 1, 2, 3 and 4 of the Statutes of the Court of Arbitration set out in an appendix.

In para 40 of his affidavit Dr Eisemann claims that ICC arbitrations are more expeditious than others. I do not stop to consider whether this assertion would be universally accepted. Paragraph 37 of his affidavit states:

> 'If the claimant were merely stalling for time, no extension would be granted and the claimant would be warned by the ICC Secretariat or the arbitrators on behalf of the Court of Arbitration that unless he remedied his dilatory conduct within a specified time the Court of Arbitration would treat his Request for Arbitration as withdrawn, settle the fees of the arbitrators and reimburse the deposit paid by the Respondents.'

It is true that Dr Mann does not contradict this statement. Accepting therefore for present purposes that this is what does or may happen in practice, but construing the rules as a matter of English law, I feel bound to say that I see nothing in those rules which justifies such a course of action as a matter of contract. I derive some comfort for this conclusion from an article in the Handbook on Institutional Arbitration, to which I have already referred. In a passage dealing with ICC arbitration under the most recent rules (we were told that art 13 of the most recent rules is virtually identical with art 19 of the rules with which we are concerned), the writer says[1]:

> 'The first of the "anti-frustrating" measures provided by the Rules are those which enable the preliminaries to the proceedings to go ahead, once certain time limits have been reached. The second is that provided in Article 13, where a party fails to cooperate in the definition of the precise limits of the dispute, and of the points on which the arbitrators are to rule. This obviously does not mean that there is any default procedure, since no party can ever be deprived of its right to defend its interest.'

This passage hardly supports the submissions of counsel for Raytheon or suggests that Dr Eisemann's para 37 is justified by the rules, whatever may happen in practice. Moreover to my mind para 37 suggests something more akin to action of an administrative nature than to action with any contractual force or effect behind it. I am of the clear view therefore that the respondents could not have found any satisfactory remedy by application to the Court of Arbitration.

Thus far I have reached these conclusions:

1. There is no power in an arbitrator to dismiss an arbitration for want of prosecution. In this I respectfully disagree with Donaldson J and agree with Bridge J, though for reasons which I fear differ from his.

2. The submissions of counsel for Raytheon regarding the possible distinction between 'institutional' and other arbitrations and especially his submission on the ICC rules regarding an application to the Court of Arbitration fail.

3. It must follow that unless the court can interfere by injunction, as the judge has held, an aggrieved respondent in an arbitration is without remedy save himself to press the proceedings forward, which as a defendant in an action he would be under no obligation to do and which in an arbitration might well not be in his interest.

Underlying the view of the judge that the court had power to interfere by injunction was the undoubted fact that the relationship between the parties to an arbitration agreement was a contractual one. An agreement to arbitrate might, like any other contract, be broken or become incapable of performance. If the particular breach in question took the form of repudiatory conduct, then there was no difference in principle between conduct evincing an intention not to perform an agreement to arbitrate and such conduct evincing an intention not to perform any other type of contract. Such

---

1 Cohn, Domke and Eisemann (eds), Handbook of Institutional Arbitration in International Trade (1977) p 24

conduct could be accepted by the innocent party as a repudiation and a claim to rescind
would follow coupled with a claim for damages and an injunction where either or both *a*
of these were the appropriate remedies. Such an injunction could then be granted in
support of the innocent party's contractual right to cancel.

The judge further took the view that terms could be implied into an agreement to
arbitrate as into any other contract. In addition to the implication, which I have for the
reasons already given felt unable to accept, that parties to an arbitration impliedly clothe
the arbitrators with jurisdiction to give effect to their rights and remedies to the same *b*
extent and in the same manner as a court, the judge also held that it was 'implicit' in, by
which he meant an implied term of, an agreement to arbitrate that each party would use
his reasonable endeavours to bring the matter to a speedy conclusion. In the light of the
judge's findings of fact, he held that each of the appellants had been guilty of repudiatory
conduct by failing to proceed with reasonable despatch, repudiatory conduct which each
of the respondents was entitled to accept as bringing the agreement to arbitrate to an end. *c*

Counsel for Raytheon was quick to attack the implied term theory both in principle
and in its application to the facts of these cases. In principle, he said, there was no need
to imply any such term as being both reasonable and necessary in order to make the
agreement to arbitrate work. The Arbitration Act 1950, like its predecessors, in the
absence of any contrary agreement imported by statute certain implied terms into a
submission to arbitration, for example s 12(1). There was therefore no need in order to *d*
make the agreement to arbitrate work to imply any other terms and no justification for
so doing. Moreover, whereas in the Raytheon appeal the complaint was of delay in
giving discovery, the respondents had ready to hand a statutory remedy by application
to the High Court under s 12(6)(*b*), a submission much relied on by counsel for Raytheon
in his argument on the facts that the respondents were responsible for much, if not all,
of the delay by failing to pursue their statutory rights under that provision, as indeed *e*
they had indicated in correspondence at one time that they intended to do.

Counsel for Raytheon also contended that the judge's implied term imposed an equal
obligation on both parties to proceed with due diligence. Whatever might be said
against the appellants in this connection, the respondents had equally done nothing and
therefore were equally in breach of their obligation vis-à-vis the appellants, as the
appellants were to the respondents, if the judge's implied term were correctly imported *f*
into the agreement to arbitrate. Counsel for Raytheon further argued that if a respondent
in an arbitration did nothing, it was for the arbitration tribunal itself to get the arbitration
moving, and that if a respondent did nothing to galvanise that tribunal into action, the
respondent was without more ado acquiescing in the delay.

Counsel for South India Shipping, however, did not adopt this part of the argument
of Raytheon's counsel, contenting himself with the submission that there was no duty on *g*
either party or on the arbitration tribunal to move an arbitration forward. In addition,
counsel for Raytheon argued that the respondents' submission and the judge's view that
an agreement to arbitrate could be repudiated for breach of the implied term which the
judge held to exist involved that the innocent party was purporting to revoke his
submission to arbitration, which, counsel for Raytheon argued, he was not entitled to do
without the leave of the court, in view of the provisions of s 1 of the Arbitration Act *h*
1950. This further argument had not been advanced before the judge and we therefore
do not know whether, had he thought this submission well-founded, he would have
granted the necessary leave under that section. Both respondents before us sought and
obtained leave to amend their writs to seek such leave if it should prove necessary. For
my part, in the light of the judge's reasoning in his judgment, I feel little doubt that he
would, if he had thought it necessary so to do, have granted leave to revoke. *j*

The submission that a term such as that which the judge held must be implied into
this agreement to arbitrate was in the court below based on what in lawyers' shorthand
is known as the *Moorcock*[1] principles. Those principles were recently restated by the

---

1   (1889) 14 PD 64, [1886–90] All ER Rep 530

majority of this court in *Liverpool City Council v Irwin*[1], in terms later unanimously
a approved by the House of Lords[2]. Counsel for Raytheon devoted the greater part of his
attack on the implication made by the judge to showing that it was neither reasonable
nor necessary to imply such a term so as to make this agreement to arbitrate work. This
is, however, not the only basis on which a court will imply a term into a contract. As the
House of Lords held in *Liverpool City Council v Irwin*[2], there are certain classes of contracts
to which a court will, in the absence of agreement to the contrary, attach an implied term
b as a matter of law. Thus in that case the House of Lords held that the particular implied
term there in question attached to the contract concerned, which was a contract for the
letting of a flat, as a legal incident of that contract (see per Lord Wilberforce and per Lord
Edmund-Davies[3]). There are plenty of other examples of the operation of this principle
in the law of contract. For example, ss 13 and 14 of the Sale of Goods Act 1893, and s 39
of the Marine Insurance Act 1906 attach certain implied conditions to contracts of the
c particular class with which those two statutes are respectively concerned, and each of
those statutory provisions merely reproduces the relevant antecedent common law.

Sale of goods law, landlord and tenant law and marine insurance law are all part of our
general law of contract. To each as to other types of contract the law will or may attach
certain particular implied terms as legal incidents of the relevant contract. I see no
reason in principle why contracts to refer disputes to arbitration should not also be
d treated as part of our general law of contract, be governed by the same legal principles
and have attached to them where appropriate one or more implied terms as incidents of
those particular contracts, those implied terms if necessary being in addition to those
other implied terms for which the relevant legislation makes statutory provision.

Counsel for Raytheon's attack on the implication into the agreement to arbitrate
which the judge held to be correct has to my mind considerable force. Counsel for the
e Greggs found difficulty in supporting the judge's implied term. Adroitly he rested this
part of his submission on a different basis. Founding himself on the decision in *Universal
Cargo Carriers Corpn v Citati*[4], he argued that following the reasoning of the House of
Lords in *Liverpool City Council v Irwin*[2] there attached to this agreement to arbitrate and
to other similar agreements as a legal incident of such agreements a duty not to be guilty
of such delay as would frustrate the whole purpose of the arbitration in question. In the
f *Citati* case[4] the delay which was ultimately held to be frustrating delay of a repudiatory
character was the charterer's failure to load the ship within such time as did not wholly
destroy the commercial purpose of the adventure so that the shipowner thereupon
became entitled to throw up the charterparty by reason of the charterer's repudiatory
conduct.

By parity of reasoning counsel for the Greggs argued that a claimant in an arbitration
g who, like a plaintiff in an action, has the conduct of the case and who is guilty of
prejudicial delay of such a kind as would, in an action, lead to that action being struck out
by the court was equally guilty of frustrating delay of a repudiatory character, thus
enabling the innocent party, the respondents in the Raytheon appeal, to rescind the
agreement to arbitrate.

This is indeed a formidable submission. As I have already said, agreements to arbitrate
h are but part of the general law of contract. The *Citati*[4] doctrine is of general application.
It is not limited to contracts of particular types. This court recently applied that same
principle in *Unitramp v Garnac Grain Co Inc, The Hermine*[5], a decision against which I
understand the House of Lords has recently refused leave to appeal.

j

---

1   [1975] 3 All ER 658, [1976] QB 319
2   [1976] 2 All ER 39, [1977] AC 239
3   [1976] 2 All ER 39 at 44, 54–55, [1977] AC 239 at 254–255, 266–267
4   [1957] 2 All ER 70, [1957] 2 QB 401
5   [1979] 1 Lloyd's Rep 212

Counsel for Raytheon sought to meet this argument by submitting that the Arbitration Act 1950 was a complete code and that therefore there was no justification for attaching *a* by implication to any agreement to arbitrate any further legal obligations beyond those for which the statute provided, that such an agreement to arbitrate was not inefficacious or futile without making the implication, especially as the aggreived party could always invoke his statutory remedies and, in particular, in the Raytheon appeal, a remedy under s 12(6) from the court.

The short answer to this submission seems to me to lie in the fact that it presupposes, *b* contrary to my view, that a respondent in an arbitration is under some obligation to galvanise a dilatory claimant into action, for example by an appropriate application to the High Court under s 12(6) of the 1950 Act. In my view, for the reasons already given, a respondent is under no such obligation. He can sit back and wait. If this conclusion be right, I see little or no difficulty in attaching to an agreement to arbitrate as a legal incident of such a contract an implied obligation in point of law on the claimant who, *c* like a plaintiff in the action, has the conduct of the case not to be guilty of such dilatory conduct in the prosecution of his claim as will defeat the whole purpose of the agreement to arbitrate by making a fair hearing before the arbitration tribunal impossible because of the lapse of time involved. This is merely another way of saying that a claimant must in such circumstances not be guilty of frustrating delay of a repudiatory character and it is difficult to think of a better example of frustrating delay of a repudiatory character *d* than delay of such a kind as would in an action cause the High Court to strike out the action in its entirety for want of prosecution.

Thus far I accept the judge's view that a term can properly be implied into the agreement to arbitrate which reflects what I regard as the obligation of a claimant not to delay the prosecution of his claim. But I venture to think that the correct basis for implying such a term is that which I have just stated rather than that which the judge *e* adopted and that the correct implication is also that just stated rather than that suggested by the judge.

In this connection it should be mentioned, as counsel for Bremer told us, that the suggestion of implying a term originally emanated from the judge during the hearing of the Bremer action and not from counsel arguing that case. Counsel for Bremer frankly admitted to us that he displayed little enthusiasm for the judge's suggestion *f* when the judge first made it and the judge thereupon appeared to drop the suggestion (we have been shown the relevant extract from the transcript which contains the interchange between the judge and counsel for Bremer on this topic). But, during the subsequent hearing of the Raytheon case, the judge seemingly revived the idea and ultimately it has formed the basis of this part of his judgment.

Counsel for Raytheon also argued that before the innocent party can treat delay of a *g* repudiatory character as giving him the right to rescind the contract he must give the guilty party notice making time of the essence. No doubt in certain classes of contract, for example where an innocent party has allowed a guilty party to think that a specific obligation as to timeous performance will not be insisted on, such a notice making time of the essence would be required and a failure to comply with that notice established before rescission could successfully be sought for non-compliance. But in my judgment *h* the present is not such a case. The whole basis of the reasoning in the *Citati* case[1] is inconsistent with this submission. The guilty party remains under a continuing obligation to prosecute his claim and there will come a time, not always very easy to determine in point of fact, when the innocent party can say to the guilty party, 'enough and no more', and rescind without giving the guilty party any further locus penitentiae. In my view, therefore, this further submission fails. *j*

As to the submission on s 1 of the Arbitration Act 1950, the short answer is that the rescission with which we are concerned is of the agreement to arbitrate, and not of the

1   [1957] 2 All ER 70, [1957] 2 QB 401

appointment of the arbitrators. It is, however, clear that logically the latter appointments

a must disappear as an inevitable consequence of the rescission of the agreement to arbitrate. Section 1 is only concerned with revocation of the appointment of an arbitrator and not with an agreement to arbitrate. I do not think the dictum of Denning LJ in *Frota Nacional de Petroleiros v Skibsaktielskapet Thorsholm*[1] is any authority for the contrary view. That was a case where the arbitration in question was continuing. There was no suggestion in that case of a repudiation of the agreement to arbitrate. But even if I be

b wrong in the views I have just expressed and leave is required under s 1, I would unhesitatingly give such leave, as I feel reasonably certain that the judge would have done had this issue been raised before him. Finally, on this branch of the case, counsel for Raytheon argued that there was no clear acceptance of the repudiation by the respondents for he contended that the writ treated the arbitrators as still having power to strike out and that therefore the declaration sought in the writ affirmed the agreement

c to arbitrate. I do not think this submission is sound; at best it is certainly highly technical. The writ claims an injunction on the footing that the agreement to arbitrate was not subsisting. The claim for a declaration was really no more than a claim for an alternative remedy, namely striking out by the arbitrators consequently on the rescission of the agreement to arbitrate.

I now turn to the question whether the court has power to grant an injunction

d restraining the appellants from proceeding with the arbitrations. I approach this question on the basis that the respondents have established a right to rescind owing to frustrating delay which the respondents have exercised. Counsel for Raytheon argued that before s 5 of the Arbitration Act 1979 was enacted the court had no such power.

It is true that such a power, if it exists, has never, at least in recent times, been exercised to restrain the prosecution of an arbitration in support of a claim that the arbitration

e agreement has been rescinded by repudiatory conduct of one of the parties to that agreement. But if the main submission of Raytheon's counsel be right and I am right in disagreeing with the judge's views that the arbitration tribunal itself has no power to strike out, it follows that there is no power anywhere to prevent a dilatory claimant guilty of frustrating delay from ultimately proceeding with his claim notwithstanding the impossibility of the issues between him and the respondent being fairly tried. This

f of course gives the claimant a grossly unfair advantage.

Counsel for Raytheon argued that the cases where injunctions had been granted in connection with the prosecution of arbitrations fell into two classes: first, misconduct of the arbitrators, and, secondly, where there was a dispute whether a particular party was or was not a party to the agreement to arbitrate. He claimed that the respondents by their submissions were trying to add a third class to these two.

g In support of the first part of his suggested dichotomy he relied on a recent decision of this court, *Japan Lines Ltd v Aggeliki Charis Compania Maritima SA, The Angelic Grace*[2], where it was stated by Lord Denning MR that the High Court had jurisdiction to supervise the conduct of arbitrators in order to make sure that they were not guilty of 'real misconduct'. In support of the second part of his suggested dichotomy counsel for Raytheon relied on the decision of this court in *Kitts v Moore*[3], where this court granted

h an injunction to a plaintiff who sought to impeach an alleged agreement to arbitrate by alleging that he was not bound by it: see the judgments of Lindley and A L Smith LJJ[4].

In the present case it was urged there was no 'impeaching' of the agreement to arbitrate since it was admitted that initially each of the respondents had been bound by it. There was no suggestion that either agreement to arbitrate was void or voidable on the ground of fraud or mistake. Counsel for Raytheon relied on *Den of Airlie Steamship*

j

---

1 [1957] 1 Lloyd's Rep 1 at 5
2 [1979] Court of Appeal Transcript 507
3 [1895] 1 QB 253
4 [1895] 1 QB 253 at 259–260, 262

Co v Mitsui & Co Ltd and British Oil and Coke Mills Ltd[1], as illustrating a case where a court would not grant an injunction to restrain a defendant from proceeding with an *a* arbitration, saying that there was in such a case no initial impeaching of the agreement to arbitrate.

In answer to these submissions counsel for the Greggs demonstrated, as he submitted, the development of the relevant equitable jurisdiction before the passing of the Supreme Court of Judicature Act 1873 by taking us through many 19th century authorities, not all of which were referred to before the judge. I do not propose to examine all these *b* cases, in some of which injunctions were granted and in others injunctions were refused. I think reference to three of the cases only will suffice. First and foremost is *Pickering v Cape Town Railway Co*[2], a decision of Page Wood V-C later varied by Lord Cranworth LC. The *Pickering* case[2] has had a curious history and we are indebted to counsel for the Greggs and his learned junior for having traced this history through. It was treated in the seventh edition of Russell on Arbitration[3] as authority for the proposition that *c* 'Parties, however, sometimes conduct themselves in such a manner as to induce the Court of Chancery to restrain them from proceeding in a reference'. That passage and the relevant reference to the *Pickering* case[2] was, however, later dropped in subsequent editions of Russell on Arbitration and the case is not mentioned in the current[4] or indeed any recent edition of that work. It is however cited in Halsbury's Laws of England[5] as authority for the proposition that— *d*

> 'The Court has jurisdiction to interfere in arbitration proceedings on equitable grounds where the parties have by their conduct excluded themselves from the benefit of their contract to arbitrate.'

In *Pickering's* case[2] there was a contract between the plaintiffs and the defendants for the building of a railway in the former Cape Colony. That contract contained an *e* arbitration clause and a certain Mr Hawkshaw was appointed what was called 'standing referee'. Disputes arose and the defendants then resorted to the Supreme Court of the Cape Colony to eject the plaintiff from the site. Later the defendants sought to insist on their right to go to arbitration in respect of matters arising from the plaintiff's ejection from the site. The plaintiff sought and obtained from Page Wood V-C an injunction restraining the arbitrator from proceeding to make an award. Page Wood V-C stated the *f* position thus[6]:

> 'We have nothing in this Court in the nature of a writ of prohibition authorizing the Court to proceed against an arbitrator, and the only jurisdiction that exists to stop the proceedings before arbitration is founded upon the conduct of the parties. If, for example, Defendants are seeking to enforce certain rights which they conceive they are entitled to exercise under a deed for submission to a reference, and the *g* Court should be of opinion that they have debarred themselves from exercising those rights by the course of conduct which they have adopted, there arises an equity, which prevents them from prosecuting proceedings, however they might otherwise be entitled to do so under the particular jurisdiction which is beyond the control of this Court.'

 h

Lord Cranworth LC subsequently discharged this injunction[7]. As I read the very brief report[7] of Lord Cranworth LC's judgment, he discharged the injunction because it had

---

1   (1912) 106 LT 451
2   (1865) LR 1 Eq 84   *j*
3   (1891) p 204
4   19th Edn (1977)
5   24 Halsbury's Laws (4th Edn) para 1038
6   LR 1 Eq 84 at 87–88
7   LR 1 Eq 84 at 89–90

in his opinion been premature to grant it before the relevant facts had been fully
a ascertained. It is important to note that Lord Cranworth LC is reported as having said[1]:

> 'The Vice-Chancellor might have come to a correct conclusion as to the parties
> having by their conduct excluded themselves from the benefit of their contract to
> arbitrate, but his Lordship could not see his way to that conclusion until the cause
> was heard.'

b I do not read this passage as disagreeing with Page Wood V-C's statement of basic
principle on which the Court of Chancery would proceed in granting relief to a plaintiff
seeking to restrain a defendant from proceeding with an arbitration under an arbitration
clause.

Counsel for Raytheon strongly argued that the *Pickering* case[2] was no authority for the
proposition that the court could or would interfere with an arbitration because owing to
c delay a fair trial was no longer possible. *Pickering*[2] was, he said, a case where the
agreement to arbitrate had been impeached. He reinforced this submission that
Pickering[2] was no authority for the wider proposition by urging that nothing could be
more unfair than an arbitrator whose award could be shown to have proceeded on a
wrong view of either of the facts or the law or both. Yet there was ample authority in
such cases that the court would not interfere. If, therefore, before 1979 the case did not
d come within s 12(6) of the 1950 Act, no one had power to interfere.

I shall return to this submission later, but it will be convenient next to consider the
two other principal cases. In *Beddow v Beddow*[3] Jessel MR enjoined an arbitrator from
acting because of his own unfitness. This case on its facts, of course, falls comfortably
within counsel for Raytheon's first category. But Jessel MR said[4]:

> *e* '. . . it appears to me that the only limit to my power of granting an injunction is
> whether I can properly do so. For that is what it amounts to. In my opinion, having
> regard to these two Acts of Parliament, I have unlimited power to grant an
> injunction in any case where it would be right or just to do so: and what is right or
> just must be decided, not by the caprice of the Judge, but according to sufficient
> legal reasons or on settled legal principles.'

f In the third and last of these cases, *North London Railway Co v Great Northern Railway
Co*[5], this court refused to grant an injunction where the plaintiff asserted that the
arbitrator had no jurisdiction to hear the dispute. The court, after considering the
judgment of Jessel MR in *Beddow v Beddow*[3], held that it had no jurisdiction to grant the
injunction sought because if there were no jurisdiction in the arbitrator to hear and
determine the arbitration there would be no legal injury and no legal right in the
g plaintiff which he was entitled to protect by injunction (see the judgments of Brett and
Cotton LJJ[6]). Cotton LJ pointed out that *Beddow v Beddow*[3] proceeded on the basis that
the plaintiff had a legal and equitable right to protect by injunction.

At the present day the problem to which *North London Railway Co v Great Northern
Railway Co*[5] gave rise could, and no doubt would, be swiftly solved by an action for a
declaration that the arbitrator had no jurisdiction. The *North London Railway* case[5]
h clearly troubled the judge. I do not think the *North London Railway* case[5] decides more
than, as is indeed clear law, that the court will not grant an injunction save in support of
some legal or equitable right: see the recent restatement of this principle by Lord
Diplock in *The Siskina*[7]. Lord Diplock in that passage appears to treat this as the ratio
decidendi of the *North London Railway* case[5]. Curiously enough it does not seem to have

j
1   (1865) LR 1 Eq 84 at 89–90
2   LR 1 Eq 84
3   (1878) 9 Ch D 89
4   9 Ch D 89 at 93
5   (1883) 11 QBD 30
6   11 QBD 30 at 35–36, 40–41
7   [1977] 3 All ER 803 at 824, [1979] AC 210 at 256

been argued in that case that the plaintiffs had a legal or equitable right to be protected by injunction against wasted costs in an arbitration in which such costs would be *a* irrecoverable if the arbitrator had no power to determine the dispute. He would indeed be a brave lawyer who, where a problem of this kind arises, advises his clients that they can safely stay away from such an arbitration and risk the arbitrator deciding the issue of jurisdiction against them merely in order to save costs which might prove to be irrecoverable.

There is always a tendency where courts, whether of equity or of common law, possess *b* some power whether equitable, at common law or by statute and over a long period of time can be shown to have exercised or refused to exercise that power in widely differing cases to seek to group those cases and to categorise them and then, having drawn up those categories, to limit the exercise of those powers to such cases and to contend that there is no wider power which may be exercised in other cases which do not fall within those categories. With respect, I think this is the basic fallacy which underlies counsel for *c* Raytheon's suggested dichotomy. No doubt many of the cases I have referred to and others to which we were referred in argument and which were also referred to by Donaldson J in his judgment can be grouped or categorised as counsel for Raytheon suggests. But to accept that grouping or categorisation is not to say that every future case must fall within such a group or category before such an injunction can be granted. Equity has never proceeded along tramlines. In the instant case, as already stated, the *d* respondents have in my view a legal right to rescind the arbitration agreement. They also have a right, whether it be called an equitable right does not matter, to a fair hearing before the arbitration tribunal. The appellants' conduct has led to their having acquired this legal right to rescind. Their right to a fair hearing cannot now be fulfilled because of the appellants' conduct.

Why then, when there is no other remedy available, should the court not interfere and *e* protect both those rights by injunction? Without an injunction the appellants can go on with the hearing which ex hypothesi cannot be fair to the respondents.

I think, therefore, that the judge was entirely right to grant the injunctions in both these cases. It would in my judgment be a lamentable gap in our jurisprudence were claimants in arbitration to be preferred to plaintiffs in litigation, as would be the case if the judge were wrong in that they can drag out arbitrations indefinitely, being *f* arbitrations to which the 1979 Act does not apply, without any penalty being imposed on them.

That leaves the question of damages. This only arises in the Raytheon appeal. The respondents claim as damages their wasted expenditure and the judge ordered the quantum of such damage to be assessed by a taxing master. Counsel for Raytheon argued that the respondents were not entitled to damages unless they could show that *g* they would have, or at least had stood, a good chance of winning the arbitration. I do not think this submission is well founded. In some cases, for example, an action for negligence against solicitors may require proof of the prospects of success as an essential prerequisite of a successful claim for damages for what would have been gained in the action which the solicitors have negligently failed to bring is the measure of the plaintiff's loss in his action for negligence. But the question in the Raytheon appeal is: what loss or *h* damage flows naturally and directly from the appellants' repudiatory conduct? My answer is that the damage which flows naturally and directly from their breach is the wasted expenditure which has been incurred by the appellants to no useful purpose because of the determination of the arbitration by rescission of the agreement to arbitrate and by the injunction. In reaching this conclusion I have not lost sight of the dictum of Lord Macmillan in *Heyman v Darwins Ltd*[1] that the remedy for breach of an agreement *j* to arbitrate is enforcement and not damages. That statement, however, must be read in

1   [1942] 1 All ER 337 at 347, [1942] AC 356 at 374

its context and not divorced from it. Lord Macmillan was not intending to override the

a earlier decisions to which I have already referred which emphasise the contractual character of an agreement to arbitrate, a breach of which can in certain circumstances give rise to a claim for damages. In my judgment, therefore, the respondents in the Raytheon appeal are entitled to damages on the basis determined by the judge.

It remains to mention two other matters for the sake of completeness. The first is a submission which counsel for Raytheon sought to raise for the first time in this court.

b There were, he correctly pointed out, only three respondents in the Raytheon appeal who were the three plaintiffs in the original action. But when one looks at cl 9 of the agreement between the appellants and the respondents one finds that the indemnity on which the appellants sought to rely in the arbitration was jointly and severally given by four persons, the fourth being a Mr Teasdale. Mr Teasdale was not a plaintiff in the proceedings presently before the court and is not a respondent to this appeal. Therefore,

c argued counsel for Raytheon, the respondents' cause of action was incomplete without Mr Teasdale being joined either as a plaintiff or as a defendant. This became known as the 'Teasdale point'. Mr Teasdale unfortunately is an undischarged bankrupt. Naturally his trustee in bankruptcy is interested as to any terms on which leave to join Mr Teasdale might be granted. Since this was a new point taken for the first time in this court, counsel for Raytheon could only take it with leave and we were only prepared to grant

d such leave on terms which counsel for Raytheon declined to accept. The Teasdale point, therefore, disappears.

The second matter was raised by counsel for South India Shipping. He sought to introduce for the first time in this court controversial evidence as to German law on the implication of terms into contracts of which German law is the proper law. Since it seemed to us that it would be impossible to resolve this issue even if it be relevant, as to

e which I express no opinion, without hearing the expert witnesses cross-examined, we declined to allow the matter to be raised for the first time before us. Clearly, if this were intended to be raised as an issue in these proceedings, the matter ought to have been investigated before Donaldson J so that he might make his findings of fact on the disputed questions of German law which would be available for us. We therefore declined to allow this matter to be raised.

f In the result, for the reasons which I have given, I would dismiss both appeals. I would venture to add this. In the addendum to this judgment Lord Denning MR has referred to the position of a respondent who was guilty of inordinate and frustrating delay as were the plaintiffs in the present two cases. I prefer to express no view as to the position which might arise in that event, which does not now arise for decision and was not presented in argument before us.

g
CUMMING-BRUCE LJ. I agree that both appeals should be dismissed on the grounds stated by Lord Denning MR and Roskill LJ. I take the same view as Roskill LJ of *North London Railway Co v Great Northern Railway Co*[1]. The power to intervene by injunction only falls to be exercised in support of a legal or equitable right as stated by Lord Diplock in *The Siskina*[2], and the respondents in each case have established a legal right to accept the

h repudiation of the arbitration agreements arising from the repudiatory conduct of the appellants. The decision of Page Wood V-C in *Pickering v Cape Town Railway Co*[3] is correctly stated in Halsbury's Laws of England[4] as authority for the proposition quoted in the judgments which have just been delivered. The fact that the courts have not been asked before to intervene by injunction in a case of repudiatory delay is explained by the history of the procedural remedy of striking out an action at law for want of prosecution.

j
1   (1883) 11 QBD 30
2   [1977] 3 All ER 803 at 824, [1979] AC 210 at 256
3   (1865) LR 1 Eq 84
4   24 Halsbury's Laws (4th Edn) para 1038

A new chapter began with *Allen v Sir Alfred McAlpine & Sons Ltd*[1]. The principles which were therein explained and applied are as relevant to proceedings taken pursuant to an *a* agreement to arbitrate as to proceedings at law.

Appeals dismissed. Leave to appeal to the House of Lords.

Solicitors: *Richards, Butler & Co* (for South India Shipping); *Norton, Rose, Botterell & Roche* (for Bremer); *Lovell, White & King* (instructed only on the appeal) (for Raytheon); *Herbert* *b* *Smith & Co* (for the Greggs).

Sumra Green   Barrister.

---

1   [1968] 1 All ER 543, [1968] 2 QB 229

^a Co-operative Retail Services Ltd v Secretary of State for the Environment and others

COURT OF APPEAL, CIVIL DIVISION
STEPHENSON AND BRANDON LJJ
b 22nd OCTOBER 1979

Town and country planning – Appeal to Minister against refusal of permission for development – Local inquiry – Adjournment – Application for adjournment to allow applicant to prepare case and instruct counsel – Secretary of State refusing adjournment – Whether jurisdiction to quash Secretary of State's decision – Whether Secretary of State's refusal a 'decision . . . on an appeal'
c – Town and Country Planning Act 1971, ss 36, 242(3)(b).

Natural justice – Public inquiry – Duty to hear parties – Opportunity to be heard – Adjournment of inquiry – Local inquiry into refusal of planning permission – Application for adjournment to allow applicant to prepare case and instruct counsel – Secretary of State refusing adjournment – Inspector having power to adjourn inquiry in interests of natural justice – Town and Country
d Planning (Inquiries Procedure) Rules 1974 (SI 1974 No 419), r 10(8).

In April 1978 a firm of developers applied for planning permission to build a large supermarket. The planning authority not having granted permission within the prescribed period the application was deemed, under s 37 of the Town and Country Planning Act 1971, to have been refused. The developers appealed to the Secretary of
e State under s 36^a of the 1971 Act against the deemed refusal. On 27th July 1979 the Secretary of State appointed an inspector to hold a local inquiry into the appeal, and, after consultation with the planning authority and the developers, fixed 23rd October 1979 as the date on which the inquiry was to be held. On 20th August 1979 the applicants, who were apprehensive of the effect of the proposed supermarket on their own business, requested the Secretary of State to adjourn the inquiry in order to give them more time
f to prepare their case and to instruct counsel to appear on their behalf at the inquiry. The Secretary of State refused that request and two further such requests made by the applicants. On 10th October the applicants applied to the High Court by notice of motion for the Secretary of State's refusals to be quashed, contending, inter alia, that the refusal to adjourn the inquiry constituted a breach of natural justice. The judge held that the refusal was not a 'decision' of the Secretary of State on an appeal under s 36 of the
g 1971 Act and therefore, by virtue of s 242(1)(e) and (3)(b)^b, he had no jurisdiction to hear the notice of motion. The applicants appealed.

Held – The appeal would be dismissed for the following reasons—
    (i) The decision of the Secretary of State to refuse an adjournment of the inquiry was not a 'decision of the Secretary of State on an appeal under section 36 of [the 1971 Act]'
h within s 242(3)(b) of that Act because it was merely a decision in the cause of an appeal and did not finally dispose of it, and accordingly the judge lacked jurisdiction to deal with the application (see p 452 *e f* and p 453 *f*, post); *Chalgray Ltd v Secretary of State for the Environment* (1976) 33 P & CR 10 doubted.
    (ii) In any event, even if there were jurisdiction, there was no evidence that the Secretary of State's refusal to adjourn the inquiry had resulted in a breach of the rules of
j natural justice, having regard to the fact that, under r 10(8) of the Town and Country Planning (Inquiries Procedure) Rules 1974, the inspector had a wide and unfettered

---

a   Section 36, so far as material, is set out at p 451 *g*, post
b   Section 242, so far as material, is set out at p 451 *h*, post

discretion to adjourn the inquiry if he thought it necessary in the interests of justice to any objector or any party to do so (see p 452 *g h* and p 453 *b* to *d f g*, post); dictum of Lord *a* Denning MR in *Ostreicher v Secretary of State for the Environment* [1978] 3 All ER at 86 applied.

Notes

For the powers of the Secretary of State and challenging his decision, see 37 Halsbury's Laws (3rd Edn) 331–332, paras 436–437. *b*

For the requirement of natural justice that a party should be given sufficient notice to enable him to prepare his case, see 1 Halsbury's Laws (4th Edn) para 75.

For the Town and Country Planning Act 1971, ss 36, 37, 242, see 41 Halsbury's Statutes (3rd Edn) 1628, 1630, 1854.

For the Town and Country Planning (Inquiries Procedure) Rules 1974, r 10, see 21 Halsbury's Statutory Instruments (Third Reissue) 204. *c*

Cases referred to in judgments

Button v Jenkins [1975] 3 All ER 585, 139 JP 828, 74 LGR 48, DC.
Chalgray Ltd v Secretary of State for the Environment (1976) 33 P & CR 10.
Ostreicher v Secretary of State for the Environment [1978] 3 All ER 82, [1978] 1 WLR 810, 142 JP 532, 76 LGR 445, CA. *d*

Cases also cited

Ellinas v Department of the Environment [1977] JPL 249.
Gill & Co (London) Ltd v Secretary of State for the Environment [1978] JPL 373.
R v Secretary of State for the Environment, ex parte Ostler [1976] 3 All ER 90, [1977] QB 122, CA. *e*

Appeal

Co-operative Retail Services Ltd ('the Co-operative') appealed against the decision of Phillips J on 19th October 1979 whereby he held that he had no jurisdiction to quash the decisions of the first respondent, the Secretary of State for the Environment, on 31st August, 7th September and 4th October 1979 not to adjourn the hearing of a local inquiry into the appeal under s 36 of the Town and Country Planning Act 1971 by the *f* third respondents, William Morrison Supermarkets Ltd ('Morrison'), against the failure of the second respondents, the City of Wakefield Metropolitan District Council, to decide within the prescribed period an application to demolish certain existing brickwork and construct a supermarket with associated car parking facilities at Westgate Brickworks, Dewsbury Road, Wakefield. The second respondents put in an affidavit supporting the appeal. The facts are set out in the judgment of Stephenson LJ. *g*

Patrick Ground for the Co-operative.
David Latham for the Secretary of State.
Duncan B W Ouseley for Morrison.
The second respondents were not represented.

h

STEPHENSON LJ. This is an important appeal and I regret that in view of the lateness of the hour and the urgency of the matter I must deal with it shortly and, therefore, run the risk of doing a considerable injustice to the careful submissions made by both counsel, particularly those made by counsel for the appellants.

What we have before us are orders of Phillips J, made on 19th October 1979, in effect refusing to interfere with a decision of the Secretary of State for the Environment *j* refusing to grant an adjournment of a public inquiry fixed for tomorrow, 23rd October, at the suit of the appellants, Co-operative Retail Services Ltd ('the Co-operative'), and the City of Wakefield Metropolitan District Council, the planning authority for the area. The public inquiry is concerned with an appeal by the third respondents, William Morrison (Supermarkets) Ltd ('Morrison'), against a decision refusing them planning *a* permission to carry out some demolition work and erect a large supermarket, which is obviously going to have a considerable effect, if it is permitted, on the nearby premises of the Co-operative and it could have a considerable effect, one would have thought, on the planning of the whole area.

In the correspondence which we have seen, namely in the months of August and September 1979, the Co-operative have been repeatedly attempting to get the Secretary of State to adjourn the hearing and holding of this public inquiry on the ground that they *b* cannot be ready in time. I would not like to be thought insensitive to the difficulties of getting specialist counsel and specialist experts to support opposition to an appeal which, of course, may be unsuccessful even if unopposed, because the Co-operative and the planning authority are not appellants; they are resisting this appeal of Morrison.

The Secretary of State has, in letters which I shall not read, taken, if I may say so, a hard line, not always choosing his words particularly well and being perhaps rash enough to *c* indicate an unbending policy which might be thought not to take adequate account of the objections that were being put; but I bear in mind the authority which counsel for the Secretary of State has cited to us, *Ostreicher v Secretary of State for the Environment*[1], and in particular what Lord Denning MR said:

d '... there is a distinction between an administrative inquiry and judicial proceedings before a court. An administrative inquiry has to be arranged long beforehand. There are many objectors to consider as well as the proponents of the plan. It is a serious matter to put all the arrangements aside on the application of one objector out of many. The proper way to deal with it, if called on to do so, is to continue with the inquiry and hear all the representatives present; and then, if one objector is unavoidably absent, to hear his objections on a later day when he can be *e* there. There is ample power in the rules for the inspector to allow adjournments as and when reasonably required.'

That, of course, was said in reference to a very different case to this, but nevertheless it states matters which have to be borne in mind in considering the second ground on which we are asked to allow this appeal.

Phillips J dismissed the motions before him on the ground that he had no jurisdiction *f* to hear them. He was sitting as a single judge of the High Court, to hear an appeal under s 245 of the Town and Country Planning Act 1971, and by RSC Ord 94, r 1 a single judge is the person to hear a matter of that kind.

What was said by counsel for the Co-operative to the judge, and has been said to us, is that what is being questioned is a decision of the Secretary of State on an appeal under s 36 of the 1971 Act, as provided by s 242(3)(*b*). Section 36 of the 1971 Act deals with *g* appeals against planning decisions. It sets out a number of matters and by sub-s (6) states: 'The decision of the Secretary of State on any appeal under this section shall be final'. That, like all the other subsections of the Act has to be read with s 242, which provides by sub-s (1):

h 'Except as provided by the following provisions of this Part of this Act the validity of ... (*e*) any such action on the part of the Secretary of State as is mentioned in subsection (3) of this section, shall not be questioned in any legal proceedings whatsoever.'

By s 242(3) the action referred to in sub-s (1)(*e*) includes: '(*b*) any decision of the Secretary of State on an appeal under section 36 of this Act'. The opening words of s 242(1) let in the provision of s 245 for questioning the validity of, inter alia, such a decision on an *j* appeal: see s 245(3).

The judge was referred to ss 36, 242 and 245, and the first question he had to decide was: are these decisions decisions of the Secretary of State on an appeal under s 36? 'It is a short but not necessarily easy question,' he said, in a note of his judgment which has

---

1   [1978] 3 All ER 82 at 86, [1978] 1 WLR 810 at 816

been agreed but has not been submitted to the judge for approval because it had not been
typed, 'namely whether in s 242(3)(b) they constitute a decision of the Secretary of State *a*
on an appeal. In my judgment they do not.'

He was referred to *Chalgray Ltd v Secretary of State for the Environment*[1], which is a
decision of Slynn J, and *Button v Jenkins*[2], which was applied in that case, but he took the
view that what was in contemplation when Parliament referred to a decision on an
appeal, both in s 36(6) and in s 242(3)(b), was a decision which disposes of an appeal, not
a decision in the course of an appeal but one dealing with its final outcome. Then Phillips *b*
J considered that this decision, and this cannot be doubted, was not a decision disposing
of the appeal: it was a decision letting the appeal go on but refusing to alter the date on
which it was to be started; and so he came to the conclusion that it was not for him,
under the section which empowered him to deal with the matter, to grant the relief
sought, but it was possible to apply for judicial review to a Divisional Court.

It is now conceded that he was right about that possibility and if this were a decision *c*
on an appeal under s 36 there would also be that possibility because by s 242(4) it is
provided that:

> 'Nothing in this section shall affect the exercise of any jurisdiction of any court in
> respect of any refusal or failure on the part of the Secretary of State to take any such
> action as is mentioned in subsection (3) of this section.'
>   *d*

It seems to me that if the Secretary of State refuses to do his statutory duty, or fails to do
his statutory duty by not making a decision which he ought to make, he is then subject
to the supervisory jurisdiction, the judicial reviewing jurisdiction, of the Divisional
Court.

For my part, after hearing the interesting arguments addressed to us, I am in complete
agreement with the view of Phillips J on this point. It may be in a sense a procedural *e*
wrangle. It is a matter, as the judge said, of some importance, but it seems to me that
looking at ss 242 and 245 this decision of the Secretary of State is not a decision on an
appeal under s 36 of the 1971 Act. I think some support for the view which the judge
took is to be derived from s 246 of the Act which starts off in sub-s (1) with these words:
'Where the Secretary of State gives a decision in proceedings on an appeal . . .' *Button v
Jenkins*[2], on which counsel for the Co-operative relied, both here and before Phillips J, was *f*
a decision on that section and on those words, and it may well be that the decision in this
case was a decision in proceedings on an appeal, but it was not in my view a decision on
the appeal.

If there is anything in Slynn's J decision which indicates a different view from that
taken by Phillips J, or can be taken to define the words used in a different way to that in
which they are defined by Phillips J, I would not be disposed to follow it. I see no reason *g*
to suppose the decision by Slynn J was wrong and have every reason to suppose that
Phillips J was right in saying that he was not departing from that decision in reaching the
decision which he did on the main point. I would, however, like to add, that if I were
wrong on this point, and Phillips J was wrong on this point, we have listened to full
argument on the question whether the Secretary of State's decision does result in a breach
of the rules of natural justice, or in other words, does deny justice to the Co-operative or *h*
to the planning authority. In my view, it does not. It is, of course, true that the
inspector will know that the Secretary of State has repeatedly refused to adjourn the date
of this inquiry, and he will not be able to put that out of his mind. Nevertheless, he has,
as indicated in the passage quoted from Lord Denning MR's decision in the *Ostreicher*
case[3], a complete discretion of his own under the rules to adjourn if he thinks it is
necessary in the interests of justice to any objector or any party to do so. We were *i*

1   (1976) 33 P & CR 10
2   [1975] 3 All ER 585
3   [1978] 3 All ER 82 at 86, [1978] 1 WLR 810 at 816

referred to the terms of r 10(8) of the Town and Country Planning (Inquiries Procedure)
a Rules 1974[1], which gives him a wide and unfettered discretion from time to time to
adjourn. One knows that adjournments are ordered by inspectors handling public
inquiries in order to enable further objections to be taken or pursued.

I am not indicating in any way whether the inspector should yield to arguments
addressed to us in the course of this appeal, if and when he is asked to do what the
Secretary of State refuses; but it is very apparent that the Secretary of State by refusing to
b delay the start of this inquiry has in no way decided that the inquiry is to be continued
and to proceed to a determination by the inspector without adjournments if an
adjournment is asked for.

The notice given was adequate. There are, no doubt, great administrative pressures in
these cases and I have carefully considered the possible injustice to the parties who
complain that they have not been given more time. If I thought that they would have
c no opportunity of pressing those objections but would be bound to do the best they can
without any possibility of a further adjournment being granted, I might feel able to take
the view that natural justice was being breached by the hard line taken by the Secretary
of State. But I am not satisfied on the material we have that it would not be possible for
all the parties to put adequately before the inspector, at any rate before the end of the
inquiry, the objections which they wish to put before him, and I am by no means
d satisfied that if they were to try to persuade the inspector to grant an adjournment, their
attempts would necessarily be defeated. There seems to be a real possibility that they
may be successful in obtaining an adjournment, but that is a matter for the inspector and
he has that duty to consider any applications that may be made to him, and to decide
them independently of what the Secretary of State has already decided. There is a
difference between a decision to postpone the start of a widely advertised inquiry which
e may cause great inconvenience, and a decision de die in diem to adjourn in order to
enable particular points or material to be put before the inspector as the inquiry goes
on. For those reasons I would dismiss the appeal.

BRANDON LJ. I agree that the appeal should be dismissed on the two grounds stated
by Stephenson LJ. The first ground is that the decision of the Secretary of State to refuse
f a postponement of the inquiry was not a decision on an appeal under s 36 of the Town
and Country Planning Act 1971, within the meaning of s 242(3)(*b*) of that Act. There
was accordingly no jurisdiction in the judge to deal with the application. The second
ground which is alternative is that, if that is wrong, then the decision to refuse
postponement of the inquiry has not been shown on the evidence before us to have been
contrary to justice. Therefore the court has no power to interfere with that decision.

g I should like to make some observations about *Chalgray Ltd v Secretary of State for the
Environment*[2], which was relied on by counsel for the Co-operative. In the headnote of
that case, the second part of the decision is stated in this way:

> '. . . That the words in section 242(3)(*b*) "any decision of the Secretary of State on
> an appeal under section 36 of the Act" were not necessarily limited to the decision
> or orders or final result specified in section 36(3); and that the Secretary of State's
h > declining to consider the appeal was a decision on an appeal under section 36.'

Even if that decision made by Slynn J is correct, it does not assist the Co-operative on the
facts of this case because there has not been any refusal to consider the appeal. I am
bound to say, however, that I have doubts about the correctness of that decision on the
law by Slynn J. It seems to me very arguable that the expression 'any decision of the
j Secretary of State on an appeal under section 36', as used in s 242(3)(*b*), is limited to
decisions or orders or final results arrived at under s 36(3). I further think that, where
there is a refusal to consider an appeal, the case might well come within s 242(4) of the

---

1   SI 1974 No 419
2   (1976) 33 P & CR 10 at 11

Act. It is not, however, necessary to decide that question in this case. I only wish to express my doubts about this because the case has been relied on and I would not like it *a* thought that I regard it as necessarily correct.

Appeal dismissed. Leave to appeal to the House of Lords refused.

Solicitors: *Bower, Cotton & Bower*, agents for *Bury & Walkers*, Barnsley (for the Co-operative); *Treasury Solicitor*; *Warren, Murton & Co*, agents for *Last, Suddards & Co*, *b* Bradford (for Morrison).

Patricia Hargrove   Barrister.

Meadows v Clerical, Medical and General Life Assurance Society

CHANCERY DIVISION
SIR ROBERT MEGARRY V-C
25th, 30th OCTOBER 1979

Landlord and tenant – Business premises – Application for new tenancy – Judgment for forfeiture before issue of application for new tenancy – Subsisting claim by tenant for relief from forfeiture – Landlord seeking to dismiss application for new tenancy on ground that tenancy had already come to an end by forfeiture – Whether tenant entitled to apply for new tenancy – Whether judgment for forfeiture resulting in 'coming to an end of . . . tenancy by . . . forfeiture' – Whether tenancy not coming to an end by forfeiture until claim for relief determined – Whether undue delay in applying for relief indicating application not genuine and forfeiture fully effective – Landlord and Tenant Act 1954, s 24(2).

S Ltd, who held premises under a lease from the defendants, granted an underlease of part of the premises to the plaintiff for a term of 14 years less three days from 24th June *f* 1965. The plaintiff occupied the premises for business purposes, and for the purposes of Part II of the Landlord and Tenant Act 1954 the defendants were the plaintiff's landlords. On 23rd December 1978 the defendants served on the plaintiff a notice under Part II of the 1954 Act terminating his tenancy on 24th June 1979, on the grounds of breach of covenant and the defendants' intention to reconstruct the premises. On 25th January 1979 the plaintiff served a counter-notice under the 1954 Act, claiming a new tenancy. On 30th January S Ltd issued a writ against the plaintiff claiming forfeiture of the *g* underlease on the ground of breaches of his repairing covenant. On 9th April the plaintiff swore an affidavit in the forfeiture proceedings claiming relief against forfeiture. On 10th April a Queen's Bench master made a consent order in the forfeiture proceedings, that judgment for possession, and for damages to be assessed, be entered for S Ltd, that the plaintiff's claim for relief against forfeiture, and the assessment of *h* damages, be adjourned generally on the plaintiff undertaking to make quarterly payments to S Ltd equivalent to the amount of the current rent, and that execution of the judgment for possession be stayed meanwhile. On 20th April the plaintiff, within the period prescribed by Part II of the 1954 Act, issued an originating summons against the defendants applying for the grant of a new tenancy under the 1954 Act. The defendants took out a summons asking the court under its inherent jurisdiction to dismiss the *j* originating summons on the ground that when it was issued the plaintiff had no tenancy to which Part II of the 1954 Act could apply, since by then his underlease had 'come to an end . . . by . . . forfeiture' within s 24(2)[a] of the 1954 Act by the order of 10th April.

---

a   Section 24, so far as material, is set out on p 458 *h*, post

The plaintiff contended that, on the true construction of s 24(1) and (2), the underlease
a was continued for the purpose of the 1954 Act until the forfeiture was perfected by the
determination of the application for relief against forfeiture, and therefore the originating
summons was valid and ought not to be dismissed.

Held – A tenancy of business premises in respect of which there was a judgment for
forfeiture coupled with a subsisting application for relief against forfeiture was not a
b tenancy which had 'come to an end . . . by . . . forfeiture', within s 24(2) of the 1954 Act,
since the right to apply for relief was part of the process of forfeiture, and, until that
process was completed by the application for relief being determined, the tenancy could
be restored by the grant of relief and could not be said to have come to an end. Because
there was a subsisting application by the plaintiff for relief against forfeiture, and there
had not been undue delay in seeking the relief, the underlease had not come to an end
c under s 24(2) and remained a tenancy to which Part II of the 1954 Act applied, within
s 24(1). It followed that under s 24(1) the plaintiff was entitled to apply to the court for
a new tenancy, notwithstanding the judgment for forfeiture. Accordingly his originating
summons was valid and would not be dismissed. The defendants' summons therefore
failed and would be dismissed (see p 458 *h* to p 459 *c* and p 460 *d* post).
> *Dendy v Evans* [1910] 1 KB 263 applied.
d > *City of Westminster Assurance Co Ltd v Ainis* (1975) 29 P & CR 469 considered.
> Per Curiam. Undue delay in seeking relief against forfeiture may indicate that the
claim to relief is not genuine and ought to be disregarded (see p 460 *c d* post).

Notes
For termination of tenancies to which Part II of the Landlord and Tenant Act 1954
e applies, see 23 Halsbury's Laws (3rd Edn) 887, para 1709.
> For the Landlord and Tenant Act 1954, s 24, see 18 Halsbury's Statutes (3rd Edn) 557.

Cases referred to in judgment
Canas Property Co Ltd v KL Television Services Ltd [1970] 2 All ER 795, [1970] 2 QB 433,
> [1970] 2 WLR 1133, 21 P & CR 601, CA, 31(2) Digest (Reissue) 810, 6717.
f *City of Westminster Assurance Co Ltd v Ainis* (1975) 29 P & CR 469, CA, Digest (Cont Vol
> D) 589, 6891a.
Dendy v Evans [1910] 1 KB 263, [1908–10] All ER Rep 589, 79 LJKB 121, 102 LT 4, CA,
> 31(2) Digest (Reissue) 810, 6715.
Driscoll v Church Comrs for England [1956] 3 All ER 802, [1957] 1 QB 330, [1957] 3 WLR
> 996, 7 P & CR 371, CA, 31(1) Digest (Reissue) 415, 3309.
g *Serjeant v Nash, Field & Co* [1903] 2 KB 304, [1900–3] All ER Rep 525, 72 LJKB 630, 89
> LT 112, CA, 31(2) Digest (Reissue) 842, 6956.

Summons
By an originating summons dated 20th April 1979 the plaintiff, Harry Meadows, the
tenant under an underlease dated 30th December 1965 of premises at 160 New Bond
h Street, London w1, applied for the grant of a new tenancy of the premises pursuant to
Part II of the Landlord and Tenant Act 1954. By a summons dated 23rd May 1979 the
defendants, the Clerical, Medical and General Life Assurance Society, the landlords of the
premises, applied for an order that the plaintiff's originating summons be dismissed on
the ground that his underlease was forfeited by an order dated 10th April 1979 and a
judgment signed on that date pursuant to the order made in an action entitled *A Sulka*
j *& Co v Meadows*, and there was not, therefore, at the date of the issue of the originating
summons any tenancy held by the plaintiff to which Part II of the 1954 Act could
apply. The facts are set out in the judgment.

Edwin Prince for the plaintiff.
Benjamin Levy for the defendants.

Cur adv vult

30th October. **SIR ROBERT MEGARRY V-C** read the following judgment: This *a* is another example of simple facts posing a new and not very easy problem of law. Put shortly, the question is whether a business tenant whose lease has been forfeited for breach of covenant but whose application for relief against forfeiture has yet to be determined is a 'tenant', within Part II of the Landlord and Tenant Act 1954 who can claim a new tenancy under the Act.

The matter arises thus. By an underlease dated 30th December 1965, a company *b* called A Sulka & Co Ltd (which I shall call 'Sulka') granted an underlease of part of business premises in New Bond Street, London, to Mr Meadows, the plaintiff, for 14 years less three days from 24th June 1965. The business carried on by the plaintiff on his premises is that of a club or licensed restaurant. Sulka held the premises under a lease from the defendants, the Clerical, Medical and General Life Assurance Society, and Sulka *c* occupy another part of the premises themselves for business purposes. Sulka are thus the head tenants of the whole and the plaintiff is a sub-tenant of part; and Sulka, I understand, had only a nominal reversion on the term granted to the plaintiff. For the purposes of s 44 of the 1954 Act the defendants, and not Sulka, are 'the landlord' in relation to the plaintiff's tenancy. On 23rd December 1978 the defendants served on the plaintiff a notice under the Act dated 22nd December 1978 to determine his tenancy on 24th June *d* 1979 on the grounds of breaches of covenant, and their intention to demolish or reconstruct the holding, and so on. The plaintiff duly served a counter-notice dated 25th January 1979, and then on 20th April 1979, within the requisite period, issued an originating summons against the defendants claiming the grant of a new tenancy under the Act.

Thus far, there is nothing remarkable. However, at some stage the defendants *e* discovered that other proceedings had been taken in relation to the plaintiff's tenancy. On 30th January 1979, Sulka, having served a notice on the plaintiff under s 146 of the Law of Property Act 1925, issued a writ against him, claiming forfeiture of his underlease on the ground of breaches of his repairing covenant. On 9th April 1979 the plaintiff swore an affidavit in those proceedings claiming relief against forfeiture; and on 10th April 1979 (that is, ten days before the plaintiff issued his originating summons claiming *f* a new tenancy under the Landlord and Tenant Act 1954) an order was made by a Queen's Bench master in chambers. This was a consent order that judgment should be entered for Sulka against the plaintiff for recovery of the premises held by the plaintiff under his underlease and for damages to be assessed, that the plaintiff's application for relief against forfeiture and the assessment of damages should be adjourned generally on the plaintiff undertaking to make quarterly payments to Sulka (without prejudice to their rights in *g* the action) equivalent to the amount of the current rent, and that execution of the judgment for possession be stayed meanwhile. The formal judgment is, of course, to the same effect, save that, for no reason that anyone could give, it failed to comply with the elementary requirement that an order made by consent should state this on the face of it. But nobody disputes that the judgment was in fact by consent.

In those circumstances, the defendants have taken out a summons in the proceedings *h* by originating summons under the Landlord and Tenant Act 1954, seeking under the inherent jurisdiction to have the originating summons dismissed. The ground on which the summons is based is that when the originating summons was issued the plaintiff had no tenancy to which Part II of that Act applied, since his underlease had been forfeited by virtue of the Queen's Bench order made ten days earlier, if not before. In its essentials, the case made by counsel for the defendants could hardly be more simple. When the *j* plaintiff issued his originating summons his underlease had ceased to exist at least ten days earlier; he was therefore not a 'tenant' who held a 'tenancy' to which s 24(1) of the 1954 Act applied; there was thus no 'tenancy' for that subsection to prolong and no 'tenant' who could apply for a new tenancy; and s 24(2) makes it explicit that sub-s (1) did not prevent 'the coming to an end of a tenancy by . . . forfeiture'. The plaintiff's claim

to a new tenancy was accordingly hopeless and should be dismissed without more ado.
a The plaintiff's claim for relief against forfeiture, which stood adjourned sine die, could make no difference to this.

Counsel for the plaintiff accepted much of these contentions. However, he contended that in s 24(1) 'tenant' and 'tenancy' ought to be construed in a way which carried out the purpose of Part II of the Act in protecting tenants. Accordingly, the subsection should be treated as including a forfeited tenancy if there was a subsisting claim to relief against
b forfeiture which, if successful, would result in the existence of a tenancy which on any footing was within the subsection. Furthermore, he contended that in s 24(2) 'forfeiture' must mean a perfected forfeiture, and not a forfeiture which is still liable to be set aside as a result of a subsisting application for relief against it. In a forfeiture case, the two subsections, when read together, mean that a tenancy which otherwise would be within the Act is continued under it until the forfeiture is perfected and is no longer liable to be
c set aside under a subsisting application for relief.

A number of authorities were discussed in argument, but none of them had any direct bearing on this problem. It seems clear that the mere issue of a writ claiming forfeiture of a lease does not bring about a forfeiture. On the other hand, there is authority for saying that as soon as such a writ is served, there is a forfeiture, though not until judgment will it be determined whether the forfeiture was justified. There is also
d authority for saying that it is clear that 'the lease is not terminated until judgment is given for possession', though, when given, the judgment relates back to the issue of the writ: see *City of Westminster Assurance Co Ltd v Ainis*[1], per Cairns LJ. That was a case in which authorities for the proposition that the lease is terminated by service of the writ without awaiting judgment do not seem to have been cited: see, for instance, *Serjeant v Nash, Field & Co*[2] and *Canas Property Co Ltd v KL Television Services Ltd*[3], both decisions of
e the Court of Appeal. Fortunately I do not have to discuss this apparent conflict, since on any footing there had been both service of the writ and a judgment for forfeiture well before the plaintiff issued his originating summons under the 1954 Act.

I think the starting point is that before Sulka issued and served their writ, the plaintiff was plainly and admittedly a tenant who could claim the protection of the 1954 Act. The plaintiff is still in occupation of his premises and carrying on his business there. If
f he obtains relief against forfeiture, the effect will be as if the underlease had never been forfeited. Thus in *Dendy v Evans*[4] it was held that an assignee of a forfeited lease could, after obtaining relief against forfeiture, sue an underlessee for rent falling due after the date of the forfeiture. When the plaintiff in the present case issued his originating summons under the 1954 Act, his underlease, though forfeited, was the subject of a subsisting application for relief which, if it succeeded, would restore his underlease to its
g full effect as if it had never been forfeited; and in that case, the originating summons must be valid. That being so, ought the originating summons to be dismissed as claimed by the defendants?

There are, of course, curiosities in the status of a forfeited lease which is the subject of an application for relief against forfeiture. Until the application has been decided, it will not be known whether the lease will remain forfeited or whether it will be restored as if
h it had never been forfeited. But there are many other instances of such uncertainties. When the validity of a notice to quit is in dispute, until that issue is resolved it will not be known whether the tenancy has ended or whether it still exists. The tenancy has a trance-like existence pendente lite; none can assert with assurance whether it is alive or dead. The status of a forfeited underlease which is the subject of an application for relief seems to me to be not dissimilar; at least it cannot be said to be dead beyond hope of
j resurrection.

---

1   (1975) 29 P & CR 469 at 471
2   [1903] 2 KB 304, [1900–3] All ER Rep 525
3   [1970] 2 All ER 795, [1970] 2 QB 433
4   [1910] 1 KB 263, [1908–10] All ER Rep 589

Counsel for the plaintiff relied on *Driscoll v Church Comrs for England*[1]; and, although the issue was different in a number of respects, I think that the case is helpful. Under s 84 *a* of the Law of Property Act 1925, a tenant, Mr Driscoll, applied to the Lands Tribunal for the discharge or modification of certain restrictions as to user in his leases. Before his application was heard, the landlord had issued and served writs claiming forfeiture of the leases for breach of covenant and the tenant had applied for relief for forfeiture. On the tenant's appeal from the Lands Tribunal's refusal to discharge or modify the covenants, the landlords contended (inter alia) that the tenant had no locus standi to apply to the *b* Lands Tribunal as a 'person interested' under s 84(1) of the 1925 Act, since the leases had gone, and so there were no covenants left which could be discharged or modified. On this contention, Denning LJ, who delivered the leading judgment, said[2]:

> 'I do not agree with that argument, for this reason, that, although a writ is an unequivocal election, nevertheless, until the action is finally determined in favour of the landlord, the covenant does not cease to be potentially good. For instance, the *c* forfeiture may not be established; or relief may be granted; in which case the lease is re-established as from the beginning. That appears from *Dendy v. Evans*[3] following what Sir Richard Henn Collins, M.R., said in *Serjeant v. Nash, Field & Co.*[4] It seems to me that so long as the covenant is potentially good, [Mr Driscoll], or anyone in like position, has a locus standi to apply to the tribunal for a modification of the covenant.'   *d*

Hodson and Morris LJJ[5] concurred in rejecting this contention of the landlord, and although they were less explicit than Denning LJ on the point, I do not think that they were in any way disagreeing with Denning LJ. I may say that in that case the application to the Lands Tribunal had been made before the writ had been issued, and so at a time when on any footing there had been no forfeiture; but nothing seems to have turned on *e* this.

Obviously a person may be a 'person interested' without being a tenant; and I am concerned with what is a 'tenant' and a 'tenancy' within the Landlord and Tenant Act 1954, Part II, and not with a 'person interested' under the Law of Property Act 1925, s 84(1). Nevertheless, the concept of a covenant being 'potentially good' necessarily involves the lease being 'potentially good', awaiting the determination whether or not *f* relief against forfeiture will be granted. Does a tenancy which formerly was plainly within the Act get driven out of the Act when it becomes a tenancy which is only 'potentially good'? Does it thereupon cease to be a 'tenancy' within the meaning of s 24(1) of the 1954 Act? The definition of 'tenancy' in s 69(1) of the Act does not help in answering this question.

I turn to the language of the subsections mainly in point. By s 24(1), 'A tenancy to *g* which this Part of this Act applies shall not come to an end unless terminated in accordance with the provisions of this Part of this Act . . .'; and the subsection then authorises 'the tenant under such a tenancy [to] apply to the court for a new tenancy . . .' Pausing there, but for the forfeiture, the tenancy in issue in this case would have expired at common law on 21st June 1979, but would then have been continued under s 24(1). There is then s 24(2); and it is on this, rather than on s 24(1), that I think the case *h* in the main turns. Section 24(2) provides:

> 'The last foregoing subsection shall not prevent the coming to an end of a tenancy by notice to quit given by the tenant, by surrender or forfeiture, or by the forfeiture of a superior tenancy . . .';

j

1   [1956] 3 All ER 802, [1957] 1 QB 330
2   [1956] 3 All ER 802 at 806, [1957] 1 QB 330 at 340
3   [1910] 1 KB 263, [1908–10] All ER Rep 589
4   [1903] 2 KB 304, [1900–3] All ER Rep 525
5   [1956] 3 All ER 802 at 809, 812 [1957] 1 QB 330 at 344, 348

and then there are some exceptions which I need not read. It will be observed that mere

a forfeiture is not enough: there must be 'the coming to an end' of the tenancy 'by forfeiture'. Furthermore, the phrase 'the coming to an end' of the tenancy is shared by a 'notice to quit given by the tenant' and by 'surrender'. Has a forfeited tenancy which is the subject of a subsisting application for relief which may restore the tenancy as if it had never been forfeited a tenancy which has come to an end for these purposes, at any rate in the sense in which a tenancy which has been surrendered has come to an end?

b   The point is not easy, but in my judgment the answer is No. I think that such a tenancy is a tenancy which may or may not have truly come to an end, and that the subsection is contemplating a tenancy which has in fact come to an end. The right of a tenant to apply for relief is part of the process of forfeiture, and until that process is complete, I do not think that the tenancy has come to an end within the meaning of s 24(2) of the 1954 Act. The plaintiff's tenancy in this case had accordingly not been

c taken out of the operation of s 24(1), and it continued under it, thus enabling the plaintiff to apply for a new tenancy. I do not think that it matters much whether the form that any relief would take would be the restoration of the old lease or the grant of a new lease on the terms of the old: in either case the relief would relate back to the date of the forfeiture and so produce a tenancy which was within the Act when the originating summons was issued.

d   This conclusion does not seem to me to be affected by the majority decision in *City of Westminster Assurance Co Ltd v Ainis*[1], a case to which I have already referred. In that case, the landlords obtained judgment in default of appearance for possession against the tenants under a lease on the ground of non-payment of rent and breach of covenant. The tenants then applied for relief against the forfeiture, and were granted it conditionally on complying with certain conditions, some of which could be performed in the future.

e While certain conditions had yet to be complied with, the landlords took proceedings for possession against some squatters who had occupied the premises, and the squatters contended that the right to sue for possession was in the tenants and not in the landlords. Over the dissent of MacKenna J, Cairns and Lawton LJJ rejected this contention and reversed the decision of Cusack J, holding that the landlords were entitled to sue the squatters for possession. The order giving relief was construed as being an

f order which did not restore to the tenants the rights of lessees under the forfeited lease until the conditions had been complied with. In the meantime, the tenants, if they remained in possession, would, in the words of Cairns LJ[2], be there 'not as tenants under the lease but as tenants at will or on sufferance'. Lawton LJ[3] treated the order for relief as imposing a fetter on the landlords' right to possession against the tenants. This fetter operated in favour of the tenants alone, and not in favour of the whole world, so that as

g against others the landlords were entitled to possession. On compliance with all the conditions the tenants were to be restored to their rights as lessees, but until then they were not to have the rights of lessees. This approach seems to assume the continued existence of the lease in some form, despite the forfeiture, with the order operating to qualify the tenants' rights under the lease. I do not think that there is anything in the case which shows that in such a case the lease has come to an end by forfeiture within the

h meaning of s 24(2).

Counsel for the defendants contended that to hold that the plaintiff in this case was entitled to claim a new tenancy would mean that a tenant who deliberately dragged out his proceedings for relief from forfeiture could thereby obtain an unmerited extension of his tenancy in a case in which in the end he would obtain no relief. He pointed out that in the present case the order was made with the plaintiff's consent, and under it the

j claim for relief against Sulka stood adjourned generally. The defendants. who were not

---

1   (1975) 29 P & CR 469
2   (1975) 29 P & CR 469 at 472
3   (1975) 29 P & CR 469 at 473

parties to those proceedings, could not say when it would be determined. Furthermore, in those proceedings the plaintiff had admitted the extent of the work required to be *a* done under his repairing covenant, but contended that under s 18 of the Landlord and Tenant Act 1927 (relating to diminution in the value of the reversion) he had a good defence to the claim for damages if the defendants intended, as they asserted, to demolish or reconstruct the premises, and so on, within the meaning of the Landlord and Tenant Act 1954, s 30(1)(*f*). The plaintiff was thus waiting to see what events would bring, and had little incentive to have his application for relief determined promptly.   *b*

I can, of course, see the force of this. I can also see some force in counsel for the plaintiff's contention that, if the Act is held not to apply, landlords may find in timely proceedings for forfeiture a means of depriving some tenants of the protection which they ought to have. I agree that the Act should, if possible, be construed in such a way as to prevent it being manipulated by either landlords or tenants so as to produce results contrary to its purpose. I think that at least something of the sting would be taken out *c* of counsel for the defendants' contention if it is held, as I think it should be, that undue delay in seeking relief may indicate that the claim to relief is unreal and so ought to be disregarded. I do not consider that at present there is any question of that in this case. Furthermore, I do not think that a decision now that the originating summons should not be dismissed could preclude the defendants from seeking the dismissal of the originating summons at a later date on the ground that there is no longer any genuine *d* application for relief, and so the forfeiture has by then become fully effective. Doubtless such an application would have its problems, but at least it could be made. All that I decide is that the originating summons was not a nullity when it was issued, and that as matters stand today the plaintiff has not ceased to have a tenancy to which the Act applies.

Perhaps I may add that I am conscious that this judgment has not attempted to analyse *e* the attributes of a lease during the twilight period between its forfeiture and the determination of an application for relief against the forfeiture. There are plainly conceptual difficulties in almost any approach, and these, understandably, have not been fully explored during argument. My duty is not one of carrying out a jurisprudential analysis but merely one of finding what I hope is a safe resting place for my decision. For the reasons that I have given, I hold that this summons fails and should be dismissed.   *f*

Summons dismissed.

Solicitors: *Kingsley, Napley & Co* (for the plaintiff); *Frere, Cholmeley & Co* (for the defendants).

Azza M Abdallah   Barrister. *g*

a # McEniff v General Dental Council

PRIVY COUNCIL
LORD EDMUND-DAVIES, LORD SCARMAN AND LORD LANE
27th NOVEMBER 1979

b *Dentist – Professional misconduct – Infamous or disgraceful conduct in a professional respect – Striking off register – Dentist charged with knowingly enabling persons employed by him who were not registered medical or dental practitioners to carry out work amounting to practice of dentistry – What constitutes such conduct – Whether infamous or disgraceful conduct in a professional respect – Dentists Act 1957, s 25(1)(b).*

c A patient of a registered dentist complained that he allowed unqualified members of his staff to insert fillings in her teeth after he had done the necessary drilling. As a result of the complaint he was charged before the Disciplinary Committee of the General Dental Council with knowingly enabling persons employed by him who were not registered medical or dental practitioners or enrolled ancillary dental workers to carry out work amounting to the practice of dentistry as defined in s 33 of the Dentists Act 1957, and d with being guilty of infamous or disgraceful conduct in a professional respect. He admitted that on four occasions he had allowed an unqualified person to insert fillings in the patient's teeth after he had completed the drilling, but claimed that he had been forced to do so because he had not been able to recruit qualified staff, and that he always inspected the work done by his unqualified staff before the patient left the surgery. He contended that his conduct did not in the circumstances amount to infamous or e disgraceful conduct in a professional respect. At the hearing counsel for the dental council referred to the leading cases on infamous or disgraceful conduct, and the legal assessor advised the committee that infamous or disgraceful conduct meant serious misconduct in a professional respect and that it was for the committee, applying their own knowledge and experience, to decide the appropriate standard each practitioner should adhere to, not being a special standard greater than was ordinarily to be expected f but the ordinary standard of the profession. The dentist was found guilty and, pursuant to s 25(1)(b)[a] of the 1957 Act, his name was ordered to be struck off the register. He appealed (1) against conviction on the ground that the legal assessor had misdirected the committee by failing to draw a distinction between merely negligent conduct and infamous or disgraceful conduct, and on the ground that his maltreatment of the patient could not be stigmatised as infamous or disgraceful conduct in a professional respect; (2) g against sentence, on the ground that the penalty of striking off was excessive in the circumstances.

Held – The appeal would be dismissed for the following reasons—
(1) There were no grounds for setting aside the finding of guilty since, although the legal assessor had not drawn a distinction between mere negligent conduct and infamous h or disgraceful conduct, the disciplinary committee had been duly reminded of the decisions which had long been recognised as accurately stating the relevant law, and the advice tendered by the assessor had not contained a defect which could fairly be thought to have been of sufficient significance to the result to invalidate the committee's decision, and in any event the dentist's admitted misconduct could support a finding of infamous or disgraceful conduct in a professional respect (see p 464 h to p 465 b, post); *Sivarajah v* j *General Medical Council* [1964] 1 All ER 504 applied; *Allinson v General Council of Medical Education and Registration* [1891–4] All ER Rep 768, *R v General Medical Council* [1930] 1 KB 562 and *Felix v General Dental Council* [1960] 2 All ER 391 considered.
(2) The sentence of striking off was not wrong or unjustified in the particular

---

a   Section 25(1), so far as material, is set out at p 462 j to p 463 a, post

circumstances and there were therefore no grounds for setting it aside (see p 465 *c d* and p 466 *e*, post); *Fox v General Medical Council* [1960] 3 All ER 225 and *McCoan v General Medical Council* [1964] 3 All ER 143 applied.

     Observations on the penalty provisions of the Dentists Act 1957 regarding the necessity for other, lesser penalties apart from striking off the register (see p 465 *d* to *j* and p 466 *e*, post).

Notes

For disciplinary proceedings against registered dentists and for appeals against striking off the register, see 26 Halsbury's Laws (3rd Edn) 94, 104, paras 213, 236, and for cases on professional misconduct, see 33 Digest (Repl) 568, *303–305*.

     For the Dentists Act 1957, ss 25, 33, see 21 Halsbury's Statutes (3rd Edn) 727, 734.

Cases referred to in judgment

Allinson v General Council of Medical Education and Registration [1894] 1 QB 750, [1891–4]   All ER Rep 768, 63 LJQB 534, 70 LT 471, 58 JP 542, 9 R 217, CA, 33 Digest (Repl) 519,   25.

Dubois v General Dental Council [1978] Privy Council Appeal No 18 (unreported).

Felix v General Dental Council [1960] 2 All ER 391, [1960] AC 704, [1960] 2 WLR 934, PC,   33 Digest (Repl) 567, 299.

Fox v General Medical Council [1960] 3 All ER 225, [1960] 1 WLR 1017, 124 JP 467, PC,   33 Digest (Repl) 522, 47.

McCoan v General Medical Council [1964] 3 All ER 143, [1964] 1 WLR 1107, PC, Digest   (Cont Vol B) 518, 26a.

R v General Medical Council [1930] 1 KB 562, 99 LJKB 217, 142 LT 390, 94 JP 94, 28 LGR   159, CA, 33 Digest (Repl) 519, 22.

Sivarajah v General Medical Council [1964] 1 All ER 504, [1964] 1 WLR 112, PC, Digest   (Cont Vol B) 519, 47Aa.

Solicitor, Re a [1956] 3 All ER 516, [1956] 1 WLR 1312, DC, 43 Digest (Repl) 434, 4614.

Solicitor, Re a [1960] 2 All ER 621, [1960] 2 QB 212, [1960] 3 WLR 138, DC, 43 Digest   (Repl) 434, 4615.

Appeal

This was an appeal by Patrick Joseph McEniff from a determination of the Disciplinary Committee of the General Dental Council, made on 16th May 1979, that the appellant had been guilty of infamous or disgraceful conduct in a professional respect and that his name should be erased from the dentists register. The facts are set out in the judgment of the Board.

Roy Beldam QC and *Bernard Hargrove* for the appellant.
Anthony Hidden QC and *Timothy Straker* for the General Dental Council.

LORD EDMUND-DAVIES. This is an appeal from a determination of the Disciplinary Committee of the General Dental Council, made on 16th May 1979, by which the appellant, a registered dentist, was found to have been guilty of infamous or disgraceful conduct in a professional respect and his name was ordered to be erased from the register.

     The appeal (which is against both finding and sentence) is said to involve the construction of s 25 of the Dentists Act 1957, the relevant parts of which read as follows:

     '(1) A registered dentist who either before or after registration . . . (b) has been   guilty of any infamous or disgraceful conduct in a professional respect, shall be   liable to have his name erased from the register.

'(2) A person's name shall not be erased under this section . . . (c) on account of his adopting or refraining from adopting any particular theory of dentistry.'

The appellant was charged in the following terms:

'That being a registered dentist: Between about 1 October, 1975, and 31 January, 1976, you knowingly enabled persons employed by you who were not registered medical or dental practitioners or enrolled ancillary dental workers to carry out work amounting to the practice of dentistry as defined in section 33 of the Dentists Act 1957. And that in relation to the facts alleged you have been guilty of infamous or disgraceful conduct in a professional respect.'

The facts can be shortly stated. The appellant qualified in 1964 and has practised for many years in Northern Ireland. The charge arose from a complaint made by Miss Teresa Elizabeth McGrath by a letter which she sent to the Central Services Agency in Northern Ireland. The nature of her complaint was that, in treating Miss McGrath as a patient, on approximately nine or ten occasions the appellant had drilled her teeth but the fillings were inserted by unqualified staff. It was said on the appellant's behalf that he had tried unsuccessfully for two years to recruit qualified staff and had in consequence to manage with a Mrs Blake, who was a qualified dental surgery assistant, and a Miss Ellis, a receptionist. It was not suggested on his behalf that either of them was an 'ancillary dental worker' within the meaning of s 41 of the Act.

A hearing of Miss McGrath's complaint took place before the Services Committee of the Central Services Agency on 3rd October 1978, and this led to a report being presented to the Disciplinary Committee by the Department of Health and Social Services.

It was admitted on behalf of the appellant that on four occasions—namely 24th October, 11th December, 19th December 1975 and 23rd January 1976—Miss McGrath attended the appellant's surgery as a patient and was treated by him, and that on each of these occasions either Miss Ellis or Mrs Blake treated her by inserting the filling after drilling had been completed by the appellant. He claimed that he always inspected the work done before Miss McGrath left the surgery, but accepted that in treating her in this way he was not offering the full services of professional dentistry, and that by allowing unqualified persons to do the packing he was increasing the risk of a filling becoming loose, with resultant pain, discomfort, or waste of the patient's time.

The conviction has been attacked on two grounds: (1) that the legal assessor misdirected the disciplinary committee as to what constituted infamous or disgraceful conduct in a professional respect; and (2) that the appellant's maltreatment of Miss McGrath could not be so stigmatised.

As to (1), reference must first be had to the opening of the case before the Disciplinary Committee by counsel for the General Dental Council. Having outlined the facts, he continued:

'May I pause now only to say one or two words on the law, of which you will be fully familiar, and no doubt you will be advised by your learned legal assessor in any event. You will remember that the test of what is infamous conduct in a professional respect was laid down clearly in *Allinson v General Council of Medical Education and Registration*[1]. Lopes LJ in fact devised the test, with the assistance of the other judges, and the immortal words are these: "'If it is shewn that a medical man, in the pursuit of his profession, has done something with regard to it which would be reasonably regarded as disgraceful or dishonourable by his professional brethren of good repute and competency', then it is open to the General Medical Council to say that he has been guilty of 'infamous conduct in a professional

---

1   [1894] 1 QB 750 at 763, [1891–4] All ER Rep 768 at 772

respect'." There is some assistance equally in *R v General Medical Council*[1]. Scrutton LJ said: "It is a great pity that the word 'infamous' is used to describe the conduct of a medical practitioner who advertises. As in the case of the Bar so in the medical profession advertising is *serious* misconduct in a professional respect and that is all that is meant by the phrase 'infamous conduct'; it means no more than serious misconduct judged according to the rules written or unwritten governing the profession." [Counsel's emphasis.] Your committee will be aware of *Felix v General Dental Council*[2].'

At the conclusion of the evidence and speeches of counsel, the legal assessor, exercising his indubitable right under r 4 of the General Dental Council Disciplinary Committee (Legal Assessor) Rules 1957[3] to advise the disciplinary committee of his own motion where it appears desirable to do so, concluded his short observations by saying:

'As far as what constitutes infamous or disgraceful conduct is concerned, to which both advocates have referred, for me the words of Scrutton LJ[1] of *serious* misconduct in a professional respect mean quite plainly that it is for the committee, applying their own knowledge and experience, to decide what is the appropriate standard each practitioner should adhere to, not a special standard greater than is ordinarily to be expected, but the ordinary standard of the profession. I think I have said very little that is in any way new to any member of the committee, but having regard to the submissions made to you I thought I ought at least to say what I have said.' (My emphasis.)

These observations have been criticised as wrong in law in that they failed to draw a distinction between mere negligent conduct and infamous or disgraceful conduct. The submission is that there was a misdirection, in that, although in his opening remarks counsel for the General Dental Council had made passing reference to *Felix v General Dental Council*[2], the legal assessor failed to remind the disciplinary committee of an important passage in the speech of Lord Jenkins, who, in delivering the judgment of this Board in that case, said[4]:

'Granted that ... the full derogatory force of the adjectives "infamous" and "disgraceful" in s. 25 of the Act of 1957 must be qualified by the consideration that what is being judged is the conduct of a dentist in a professional respect, which falls to be judged in relation to the accepted ethical standards of his profession, it appears to their Lordships that these two adjectives nevertheless remain as terms denoting *conduct deserving of the strongest reprobation*, and, indeed, so heinous as to merit, when proved, the extreme professional penalty of striking-off.' (Emphasis mine.)

Although the facts in *Felix v General Dental Council*[2] were quite unlike those of the present case, these observations are of compelling significance. For it has respectfully to be said that although prolonged veneration of the oft-quoted words of Lopes LJ[5] has clothed them with an authority approaching that of a statute, they are not particularly illuminating. It is for this reason that their Lordships regard Lord Jenkins's exposition as so valuable that, without going so far as to say that his words should invariably be cited in every disciplinary case, they think that to do so would be a commendable course. But having said that, it has to be added that the committee in the instant case were duly reminded of decisions which have long been approved of by this Board as accurately

1 [1930] 1 KB 562 at 569
2 [1960] 2 All ER 391, [1960] AC 704
3 SI 1957 No 1470
4 [1960] 2 All ER 391 at 399–400, [1960] AC 704 at 720
5 [1894] 1 QB 750 at 763, [1891–4] All ER Rep 768 at 772

stating the relevant law.   And their Lordships have in mind in this context the following
a observations of Lord Guest in *Sivarajah v General Medical Council*[1]:

> 'The committee are masters both of the law and of the facts.   Thus what might
> amount to a misdirection in law by a judge to a jury at a criminal trial does not
> necessarily invalidate the committee's decision.   The question is whether it can
> "fairly be thought to have been of sufficient significance to the result to invalidate
> the Committee's decision"[2].'

b

In their Lordships' judgment, it cannot be said that the advice tendered by the legal
assessor in this case contained such a defect, and the first ground of criticism must
therefore be rejected.

Little needs to be added regarding the second ground of appeal against finding.
Whether the misconduct of the appellant, freely admitted by him with complete
c candour, was such as to justify his being convicted as charged was essentially for the
committee.   Their Lordships desire to say no more than that had a finding of not guilty
been pronounced it could well have been greeted by surprise.   Indeed, by allowing his
unqualified staff to insert fillings, the appellant implicated both himself and them in
contravention of s 34 of the 1957 Act and all three of them could have been subjected to
summary proceedings in a magistrates' court.

d   Their Lordships turn accordingly to the appeal against sentence, it being urged that,
in all the circumstances of the case, the penalty of erasure was excessive.   It has to be said,
and not for the first time, that the penalty provisions of the Dentists Act 1957 need to be
reconsidered.   As recently as this year the matter was raised by Lord Diplock in *Dubois v
General Dental Council*[3] in the following words which their Lordships respectfully regard
as well worthy to be recorded:

e

> '. . . under s 25 of the Dentists Act 1957 the *only* punishment for professional
> misconduct which the Disciplinary Committee has jurisdiction to impose is to erase
> the dentist's name from the Register.   Unlike the corresponding statutory provisions
> applicable to doctors the Act has not been amended to permit the imposition of the
> milder penalty of suspension for a period not longer than twelve months in cases
f > involving what may properly be regarded as the less serious breaches of the
> professional code.   In the case of dentists the only way in which the gravity of the
> offence can be reflected in the punishment he is compelled to undergo by reason of
> the erasure of his name from the Register, is the length of time that he is made to
> wait before an application for restoration of his name to the Register under s 30 of
> the Act, is granted; but the minimum period that must elapse before he can make
> such application is ten months.'   (Emphasis Lord Diplock's.)

g
Section 25 provides merely that a registered dentist found guilty under sub-s (1)(*b*) 'shall
be *liable* to have his name erased from the Register' (emphasis mine).

The committee is therefore free to do no more than deliver a homily in suitable cases,
and it appears that this is by no means uncommon.   Or it may resort to the device of
postponing sentence to a date sufficiently far distant to enable the committee in due
h course to judge whether the wrong-doer has learnt his lesson, and then at the adjourned
hearing to do no more than deliver what is again in the nature of an unofficial
admonition.   But if the committee does not regard either of these courses as appropriate,
it has no alternative but to order erasure from the register.

In all the mitigating circumstances of the present case, their Lordships would have
been in no degree surprised had the disciplinary committee elected to postpone sentence,
j but that course evidently did not commend itself.   The only remaining alternative to

---

1   [1964] 1 All ER 504 at 507, [1964] 1 WLR 112 at 117
2   See *Fox v General Medical Council* [1960] 3 All ER 225 at 229, [1960] 1 WLR 1017 at 1023 per Lord
     Radcliffe
3   [1978] Privy Council Appeal No 18

erasure would therefore be to take no action at all in respect of the s 25 finding, save, in
effect, to grant an absolute discharge and accompany it possibly by a homily if such were *a*
deemed desirable. Section 29 of the 1957 Act provides that appeals in disciplinary cases
lie to this Board, and, in relation to a similar provision contained in s 36 of the Medical
Act 1956, it was held in *Fox v General Medical Council*[1] that the Board's position in such
appeals is analogous to that of the Court of Appeal hearing an appeal from the judge
sitting alone. Their Lordships can see no reason for holding that similar appeals, brought
under the Dentists Act 1957, should be regarded any differently. The attitude to be *b*
adopted by this Board in these circumstances is well-established by such decisions as
McCoan v General Medical Council[2], where Lord Upjohn said:

> 'The powers of the Board to correct the determination of the committee on the
> hearing of such an appeal are in terms unlimited, but in principle, where a
> professional body is entrusted with a discretion as to the imposition of the sentence
> of erasure their lordships should be very slow to interfere with the exercise of that *c*
> discretion . . . Their lordships are of the opinion that LORD PARKER, C.J., may have
> gone too far in *Re a Solicitor*[3], when he said that the appellate court would never
> differ from sentence in cases of professional misconduct, but their lordships agree
> with LORD GODDARD, C.J., in *Re a Solicitor*[4] when he said that it would require a very
> strong case to interfere with sentence in such a case, because the Disciplinary
> Committee are the best possible people for weighing the seriousness of the *d*
> professional misconduct. No general test can be laid down, for each case must
> depend entirely on its own particular circumstances. All that can be said is that, if
> it is to be set aside, the sentence of erasure must appear to their lordships to be
> wrong and unjustified.'

Adopting that test and applying it to the proved circumstances of the present case, *e*
their Lordships, while adhering to the view earlier expressed regarding the severe
sentence of erasure, are unable to say that it was wrong or unjustified.

It follows that, in relation to both finding and sentence, their Lordships must humbly
advise Her Majesty that the appeal should be dismissed. There will be no order as to
costs.

f

Appeal dismissed.

Solicitors: *Hempsons* (for the appellant); *Waterhouse & Co* (for the General Dental Council).

Christine Ivamy   Barrister.

1   [1960] 3 All ER 225, [1960] 1 WLR 1017
2   [1964] 3 All ER 143 at 147, [1964] 1 WLR 1107 at 1112–1113
3   [1960] 2 All ER 621, [1960] 2 QB 212
4   [1956] 3 All ER 516, [1956] 1 WLR 1312

a

R v Chatwood and others

COURT OF APPEAL, CRIMINAL DIVISION
BRIDGE LJ, FORBES AND SHELDON JJ
19th OCTOBER 1979

b *Criminal evidence – Admissions and confessions – Personal knowledge – Admission by party of something of which he has actual knowledge – Accused identifying controlled drug and admitting possession to police – Accused an experienced drug user – Police having no other evidence of identity of drug or possession – Whether accused's identification and admission prima facie evidence of unlawful possession of controlled drug – Misuse of Drugs Act 1971, s 5(1).*

c Where an experienced drug user admits possession of a substance which he himself identifies as a controlled drug that admission and identification are sufficient to provide prima facie evidence of the nature of the substance and of unlawful possession of a controlled drug contrary to s 5(1)[a] of the Misuse of Drugs Act 1971. An admission in such circumstances is quite different from an admission made by an accused that he has committed a crime, since it is a question of law whether the accused's acts amount to the crime charged (see p 470 c to g, p 471 g and p 472 a to c, post).

d *Bird v Adams* [1972] Crim LR approved.
Mieras v Rees [1975] Crim LR 224 and *R v Wells* [1976] Crim LR 518 explained.

Notes

For admissibility of evidence in criminal proceedings, see 11 Halsbury's Laws (4th Edn) para 364, and for cases on the subject, see 14(2) Digest (Reissue) 549–552, 4494–4517.

e For the Misuse of Drugs Act 1971, s 5, see 41 Halsbury's Statutes (3rd Edn) 884.

Cases referred to in judgment

Bird v Adams [1972] Crim LR 174, DC.
Haughton v Smith [1973] 3 All ER 1109, [1975] AC 476, [1974] 2 WLR 1, 38 JP 31, 58 Cr App R 198, HL, 14(1) Digest (Reissue) 113, 756.

f *Mieras v Rees* [1975] Crim LR 224, DC.
R v Wells [1976] Crim LR 518, CA.

Appeals

The appellants, Roy Chatwood, Christopher Michael Patrick Egan, Paul Thomas Flaherty and Harry Proctor, appealed against their convictions at the Crown Court at Preston on 28th March 1979 before his Honour Judge Openshaw and a jury of possessing controlled

g drugs contrary to s 5(1) of the Misuse of Drugs Act 1971. The appellant Anthony William Kenneth Walker applied for leave to appeal against a sentence of three years' imprisonment imposed by Judge Openshaw at the Crown Court at Preston on 26th March 1979 for supplying a Class A controlled drug. The facts are set out in the judgment of the court.

h *R C W Bennett* for the appellants Chatwood, Egan and Flaherty.
Edmund Perez for the appellant Proctor.
A R D Stuttard for the Crown.
The appellant Walker did not appear.

FORBES J delivered the following judgment of the court: On 26th March 1979, at the

j Crown Court at Preston, these four appellants pleaded not guilty to a number of related offences concerned with the possession of controlled drugs. In addition, Egan was charged with theft.

---

a Section 5(1) provides: 'Subject to any regulations under section 7 of this Act for the time being in force, it shall not be lawful for a person to have a controlled drug in his possession.'

The case arose out of the finding of the body of a drug addict named Fisher by the side of a motorway in Lancashire in the middle of June 1978. Subsequently the police made *a* extensive enquiries among those involved in the abuse of drugs in the area, including these four appellants, Chatwood, Egan, Flaherty and Proctor. Each of them denied having anything to do with Fisher's death, but each admitted, orally and in writing, to police officers, that they had been in possession of the various drugs specified in the indictment. Egan too admitted that he had stolen £3 from the wallet of the dead youth, apparently to pay for the transport of the body to the motorway.   *b*

The case was complicated by the fact that both the forensic scientist called for the Crown and one of the experienced police officers from the drug squad were asked questions about the nature of the drug heroin itself. The forensic scientist (cautious as scientists usually are) said that he could not tell whether a substance was heroin without analysing it. The police officer (with nine years' experience with the drug squad) said effectively that, while he might have a pretty good suspicion about a substance being *c* heroin, he could not be certain.

On the basis of that evidence, submissions were made to the trial judge that there was insufficient evidence to go to the jury in the case of these men, because the only evidence against them was their own belief that the drug that they had administered to themselves was heroin or pethidine (whichever it may have been in the individual cases) and that that belief was not good enough.   *d*

Those submissions were supported by reference to a number of cases, to one or two of which I shall have to turn in a moment.

The three appellants Chatwood, Egan and Flaherty did not give evidence but Proctor did. Proctor, in his evidence, maintained that the substance with which he had injected himself was flour. The cogency of that evidence was somewhat eroded, because evidence had been given by the detective sergeant in the prosecution case that during the course *e* of questioning Proctor, having admitted possessing heroin, had gone on to say: 'How can you prove it was heroin? I could say it was flour; in fact I probably will say it was flour when it comes to court. It was poor stuff, it made me sick after cranking it.' 'Cranking it' is the cant term for injecting it, as I understand it. The evidence of the interview goes on:

'Q. How long have you been abusing drugs? A. Since I was about thirteen years *f* old. I'm not as fit now as when I first started, I'll tell you that. They do say it's habit forming. I was a registered addict at one time.

'Q. If you have been taking drugs for this length of time, you of all people should know the difference between heroin and flour. A. I know the difference all right; that was heroin I got off that lad. Poor stuff, I know, but you [ie the police] have got to be one step ahead. You have to prove it was heroin.'   *g*

In the face of that statement, that he knew perfectly well that it was heroin, the jury convicted him, quite clearly disbelieving his evidence that he thought it was flour and accepting the evidence of that statement that it was heroin.

There is that distinction between the case of Proctor and the others, that he did give evidence, unlike the others, and that the jury were able to test that evidence against what *h* he had said in his statement.

The case got off, if one may put it this way, on the wrong foot by the fact that in their submissions counsel for the defendants relied on the case in the House of Lords of *Haughton v Smith*[1]. *Haughton v Smith*[1] was a case concerned with the question whether a person could be guilty of an attempt to commit a crime (in that case handling stolen goods) when his belief that he was committing it turned out to be erroneous. I need not *j* go into the details of their Lordships' opinions in the House. It is sufficient to say that really the proposition which that case established was that merely to have an intention to commit a crime, without more, could not be a crime. If I may turn round the usual

---

1   [1973] 3 All ER 1109, [1975] AC 476

a aphorism, mens non facit reum nisi actus sit reus. The case was not concerned in any way with any question of proof that the goods were stolen, or of whether an admission by a defendant that the goods were stolen goods amounted to evidence of that fact, or anything of that kind at all. It was a case concerned solely with this issue about attempt. In fact of course in that case, and I need not go into the facts, the prosecution had established by their evidence that the goods were not in fact stolen at the time they were handled.

b *Mieras v Rees*[1], on which much reliance was placed in the Crown Court, was a case to the like effect. The account of that case in the report is inaccurate. The defendant was not charged, as is said there, with unlawfully supplying a substance, believing it to be a controlled drug: he was, in fact, charged with attempting (under s 19 of the Misuse of Drugs Act 1971) to commit an offence under s 4(3) by unlawfully supplying a substance believing it to be a controlled drug, in this case one called STP. The only evidence against c him was his own statement that he supplied the substance believing it to be STP, but had subsequently been told that it was not in fact STP, but something similar. Once again this case was clearly concerned with attempt and not with whether there was prima facie evidence that the substance supplied was a controlled drug. Had there been such evidence, the proper charge would have been one of supplying it under s 4(3), as was pointed out by Michael Davies J in the judgment of that case. Having dealt with the d defendant's statement to which I have just referred, he goes on:

'It is perfectly plain that the difficulty which the prosecution were in was apparent to them before the informations were laid, the difficulty being that the prosecution was quite unable to prove that the substance which had been supplied by the appellant was STP. If they had been able so to prove, the appropriate charge which no doubt would have been brought would have been one of actually supplying that e substance. So it was thought with ingenuity, but in my judgment without any justification as a matter of law and fact, that the prosecution's difficulty could be overcome by preferring informations alleging an attempt to commit an offence even though, as I have said, the court would be bound to conclude that the appellant had not indeed supplied STP.'

f Then Michael Davies J goes on to refer to the opinion of Lord Reid in *Haughton v Smith*[2] and of Lord Morris of Borth-y-Gest, and to point out that the decision in *Haughton v Smith*[3] effectively disposed of the argument, in the circumstances set out in *Mieras v Rees*[1], that this could properly be an attempt to commit a crime at all. *Mieras v Rees*[1] has nothing whatever to do with any question of evidence. It was not a question of whether there g was prima facie evidence led by the prosecution. In *Mieras v Rees*[1], in fact, the only evidence of the nature of the substance was the statement by the defendant that he had been told that it was not in fact STP. The decision is based on acceptance of that statement as evidence of the nature of the substance. The Divisional Court was apparently content to do this without hesitation and untroubled by any nice question about whether or not the statement was admissible as being based on hearsay.

h The case which is in fact concerned with the question of whether an admission of possession of a controlled drug is prima facie evidence that the substance was in fact such a drug is *Bird v Adams*[4]. In that case the appellant had been charged with unlawful possession of a controlled drug. The only evidence as to the substance in possession of which he was found was his own admission that it was LSD. I take up the tale from the j transcript of the judgment of Lord Widgery CJ in that case:

---

1   [1975] Crim LR 224
2   [1973] 3 All ER 1109 at 1119, 1122, [1975] AC 476 at 497, 500
3   [1973] 3 All ER 1109, [1975] AC 476
4   [1972] Crim LR 174

'Now when the case was heard before the magistrates, at the conclusion of the
prosecution case, which really consisted of nothing more than the evidence of the   *a*
police officer to which I have referred, there was a submission of no case to answer,
and the basis of the submission was this, that although the appellant had admitted
possession of what he thought to be LSD, there was no independent proof that the
drug was in fact LSD, and that it might have been some innocuous substance sold
to the appellant under a fraudulent description, and so it was submitted that there
was no case to answer because the vital element of the prosecution case, namely that   *b*
the drug was a prohibited drug, had not been established by an admission of the
appellant who himself could not know whether that which he carried was or was
not the genuine drug. Now the justices rejected that suggestion; at least they were
not influenced by it. They held there was a case to answer and on the case
proceeding the appellant gave no evidence and he was duly convicted. Counsel
before us today returns to the original submission in the case and says that the   *c*
justices should have upheld the submission of no case because the admission of the
appellant in the circumstances of this case was of no evidential value at all. Now it
is clear from the authorities which have been put before us that there are many
instances where an admission made by an accused person on a matter of law in
respect of which he is not an expert is really no admission at all. There are bigamy
cases where a man has admitted a ceremony of marriage in circumstances in which   *d*
he could not possibly have known whether in truth he had been married or not
because he was no expert on the marriage ceremonial appropriate in the particular
place. It is quite clear that there are cases of that kind where the person making the
admission lacks the necessary background knowledge to be able to make the
admission at all. Again we have been referred to *Comptroller of Customs* v. *Western
Lectric Co Ltd*[1], where a man made an admission in regard to the country of origin   *e*
of certain goods when he had no idea at all where the goods had come from. Again
it was held that this admission was worthless because it was an admission of a fact
as to which he had no knowledge at all, and in respect of which no valid admission
can be made. Counsel submitted that the present case is a like case with that, but in
my judgment this is not so. If a man admits possession of a substance which he says
is a dangerous drug, if he admits it in circumstances like the present where he also   *f*
admits that he has been peddling the drug, it is of course possible that the item in
question was not a specific drug at all but the admission in those circumstances is
not an admission of some fact about which the admitter knows nothing. This is the
kind of case in which the appellant had certainly sufficient knowledge of the
circumstances of his conduct to make his admission at least prima facie evidence of
its truth and that was all that was required at the stage of the proceedings at which   *g*
the submission to the justices was made.'

In view of some remarks about subsequent cases involving handling stolen goods,
which counsel submitted on behalf of the first three appellants, I think perhaps I should
read a short passage from the judgment of Lawson J which followed. He said:

'I would just add this, that the situation in my judgment seems very similar to the   *h*
situation which can and frequently does arise when people are charged with
handling stolen goods under s 22 of the Theft Act 1968. In many cases it is not
possible for those responsible for prosecutions to prove that goods are in fact stolen
goods. It may not be known from what source they emanate, but if the person
charged has made some statement relating to the circumstances in which he
acquired possession of these goods, it is quite legitimate and proper for inferences to   *j*
be drawn from evidence of that statement that the goods are in fact stolen. This is
in fact a common situation and a situation which seems to me to be very close to the
present case.'

1   [1965] 3 All ER 599, [1966] AC 367

It should be said that in the current edition of Archbold[1], there is a note of the decision

a in *Bird v Adams*[2] followed by this statement: 'In *Mieras* v. *Rees*[3], on very similar facts, the defendant's appeal was allowed.' From what has been said above, it will be apparent that neither the facts nor the principles of law in *Mieras v Rees*[3] were at all similar to those in *Bird v Adams*[2].

The last case to which I shall refer is *R v Wells*[4]. When examined, that case proceeds entirely on the same reasoning as *Bird v Adams*[2]. Ormrod LJ, giving the judgment of the

b court, said:

'The point in this case is, in our view, this. At no time has it been suggested by Miss Wells that her belief that she had smoked cannabis with Mr Cooke and that she had taken "speed" with him was erroneous. There is even now no suggestion by her

c that she might have been mistaken about that admission. All that is said is it is on the prosecution to prove positively that she had been, at the relevant time or times, in possession of either cannabis or amphetamine as the case may be. But the best evidence that she has been in possession of these articles at some time might well be her admission, particularly when her admission is still not retracted.'

d It is true that at one point he said that, unlike the case he was dealing with, *Mieras v Rees*[3] was a plea of not guilty. But in its context this remark was necessary only to draw the distinction between that situation and the situation where there was a plea of guilty, because Ormrod LJ had just been outlining the principles on which the courts allow a plea of guilty to be withdrawn, principles which the court in *Mieras v Rees*[3] had not had to consider. He went on to point out that *Mieras v Rees*[3] was a case concerned with

e attempt, which was the true distinction between that case and the one before him. He continued by saying this:

'What is said is that the prosecution in a drug case must identify the drugs in question positively by scientific evidence before a court can accept a plea of guilty

f to possession. One has only got to state the proposition in those terms to see how absurd it must be. If one needs to take it to its logical conclusion, it is necessary to point out it is no answer to say this young woman was convicted on her own expression of opinion. In the last analysis all the evidence as to the nature of the substance is an expression of opinion. Scientists perhaps express more reliable opinions than people who have not got the advantages of scientific techniques of

g identifying substances. But in the last analysis, everybody is expressing an opinion.'

So here these drug abusers were expressing an opinion, and an informed opinion, that, having used the substance which they did use, it was indeed heroin, because they were experienced in the effects of heroin.

h The difficulty is that the commentary in the Criminal Law Review on *R v Wells*[4] misunderstands both the ratio of that case and, indeed, the facts of *Mieras v Rees*[3]. This commentary appears to have misled also the editor of the latest edition of Phipson on Evidence[5], for the second supplement reiterates the inaccurate summary given in the Criminal Law Review.

j

1   Pleading, Evidence and Practice in Criminal Cases (40th Edn, 1979) para 1398
2   [1972] Crim LR 174
3   [1975] Crim LR 224
4   [1976] Crim LR 518
5   12th Edn (1976) 2nd Supplement

This court considers that the law is stated, if we may say so respectfully, with complete accuracy by Lord Widgery CJ in *Bird v Adams*[1] in the passage to which I have referred. *a* Applying that law to this case, it is apparent that the statements of the accused in this case, either orally to the police officer, or when reduced to writing, were sufficient to provide prima facie evidence of the nature of the substance which had been in their possession. One of them, Proctor, as I have indicated, gave evidence, but what I have said about his statement to the police and the fact that he was found guilty by the jury indicates quite clearly that the jury disbelieved his explanation that it was flour and *b* believed his earlier statement to the police that he knew it was heroin.

This court is of the view that the statements of the accused provide, having regard to the circumstances of this case, prima facie evidence of the identity of the substance. As that is the only point on the appeals against conviction, the appeals against conviction are accordingly dismissed.

The court also has before it an application by one other accused who was concerned in *c* this matter, a man called Walker. He in fact pleaded guilty to possessing controlled drugs and also to supplying a Class A controlled drug. He was sentenced to three years' imprisonment on the supply charge and six months' imprisonment concurrent on each of the possession counts, but consecutive to the three years. There is an application for leave to appeal against that sentence on the ground that it was excessive. A sentence of three years for supplying heroin cannot, in the view of this court, be regarded as excessive *d* or as wrong in principle. The application is accordingly refused.

Appeals dismissed.

Solicitors: *Registrar of Criminal Appeals*; *L & R Wilkinson*, Blackburn (for the Crown).

e

Dilys Tausz   Barrister.

---

1   [1972] Crim LR 174

R v Adams

COURT OF APPEAL, CRIMINAL DIVISION
CUMMING-BRUCE LJ, PHILLIPS AND MICHAEL DAVIES JJ
29th OCTOBER, 2nd NOVEMBER 1979

Criminal law – Obscene publications – Power of search and seizure – Validity of warrant – Use of same warrant for more than one entry, search and seizure – Whether warrant permitting only one entry, search and seizure while in force – Whether warrant able to be used from time to time while in force – Whether seizure of articles under invalid warrant precluding conviction for possessing obscene articles – Obscene Publications Act 1959, ss 2(1), 3(1).

Criminal evidence – Exclusion of evidence – Discretion – Evidence seized under invalid search warrant – Seizure of obscene articles – Defendant admitting articles obscene and in his possession for publication for gain – Whether articles admissible in evidence – Whether seizure of evidence under invalid warrant oppressive.

On 6th April 1977 the police, acting under a search warrant issued on that day under s 3(1)[a] of the Obscene Publications Act 1959 and valid for 14 days, entered and searched the defendant's bookshop and seized certain articles. A summons against the defendant alleging an offence against s 2(1)[b] of that Act was issued but later withdrawn, but proceedings for forfeiture of the seized articles were taken and a forfeiture order was made. On 12th April 1977 three police officers purporting to act under the same warrant entered and searched the shop and seized further articles. The defendant was charged in respect of those articles with possessing them for publication for gain, contrary to s 2(1) of the 1959 Act. He pleaded not guilty. At the trial the articles were exhibited as evidence. The defendant admitted that the articles were obscene and in his possession for publication for gain but, in the absence of the jury, submitted (i) that a warrant issued under s 3(1) authorised only one entry, search and seizure of premises while it was in force and therefore the entry, search and seizure on 12th April were unauthorised and unlawful, and (ii) that the judge ought to exercise his discretion to exclude the articles seized on 12th April as evidence, and direct the jury that there was no evidence to support a conviction. The judge ruled against the defence on the first submission and therefore held that it was unnecessary to rule on the second submission. The defendant changed his plea to guilty and was convicted. He appealed on the ground that the judge's ruling on the final submission was erroneous in law. At the hearing of the appeal the Crown contended that s 3(1) of the 1959 Act was wide enough to authorise entry, search and seizure on more than one occasion within the period the warrant was in force.

Held – (i) Although a search warrant under s 3(1) of the 1959 Act could be issued if a magistrate was satisfied that obscene articles were kept 'from time to time' for publication for gain, there was nothing in s 3(1) to show that a warrant could be used from time to time during the period it remained in force, and it followed that on the true construction of s 3(1) a warrant issued under that section authorised only one entry, search and seizure of premises, and when that had been carried out the warrant was spent. The judge's ruling had therefore been wrong because the entry, search and seizure on 12th April had not been authorised by the warrant issued on 6th April and were unlawful, since the warrant had been spent by the entry, search and seizure on 6th April (see p 478 g to p 479 b and d, post); *Dickinson v Brown* (1794) 1 Esp 218 considered.

---

a   Section 3(1) is set out at p 476 *e f*, post
b   Section 2(1), so far as material, provides: 'Subject as hereinafter provided, any person who, whether for gain or not, publishes an obscene article or who has an obscene article for publication for gain (whether gain to himself or gain to another) shall be liable . . . (b) on conviction on indictment to a fine or to imprisonment for a term not exceeding three years or both.'

(ii) However, the judge had no discretion to exclude the articles as evidence, because (a) s 2(1) of the 1959 Act did not require strict compliance with s 3(1) as a condition for conviction under s 2(1), and (b) the manner in which the evidence had been obtained, i e under the warrant issued on 6th April, could not be said to have been oppressive merely because the police had made an error regarding the validity of the warrant for the purpose of the entry, search and seizure on 12th April. It followed that the appeal would be dismissed (see p 480 *a b*, post); *R v Sang* [1979] 2 All ER 1222 applied; *Spicer v Holt* [1976] 3 All ER 71 distinguished.

Per Curiam. If objection is to be taken to the admissibility of evidence in a criminal trial, that evidence should not be opened by the Crown, much less admitted in evidence and taken into the cognisance of the jury before the objection is taken (see p 476 *c*, post).

Notes

For powers of search and seizure in respect of obscene articles, see 11 Halsbury's Laws (4th Edn) para 1020.

For the court's discretion to admit evidence wrongfully obtained, see 17 ibid para 12, and for a case on the subject, see 14(2) Digest (Reissue) 469, *3913*.

For the Obscene Publications Act 1959, ss 2, 3, see 8 Halsbury's Statutes (3rd Edn) 480, 482.

Cases referred to in judgment

Dickinson v Brown (1794) 1 Esp 218, Peake 307, 170 ER 334 NP, 14(1) Digest (Reissue) 210, *1527*.

R v Curl (1727) 2 Stra 788, 1 Barn KB 29, 17 State Tr 153, 93 ER 849, 15 Digest (Reissue) 1035, *8970*.

R v Sang [1979] 2 All ER 1222, [1979] 3 WLR 263, HL; *affg* [1979] 2 All ER 46, [1979] 2 WLR 439, 68 Cr App R 240, CA.

Scott v Baker [1968] 2 All ER 993, [1969] 1 QB 659, [1968] 3 WLR 796, 132 JP 422, 52 Cr App R 566, DC, Digest (Cont Vol C) 928, *322c*.

Spicer v Holt [1976] 3 All ER 71, [1977] AC 987, [1976] 3 WLR 398, 140 JP 545, 63 Cr App R 270, [1976] RTR 389, HL.

Case also cited

Jeffrey v Black [1978] 1 All ER 555, [1978] QB 490, DC.

Appeal

This was an appeal by the defendant, John Adams, against his conviction on 21st September 1978 in the Crown Court at Manchester before the recorder, Mr George Carman QC, and a jury on one count of publishing an obscene article, contrary to s 2(1) of the Obscene Publications Act 1959, and on two counts of possessing obscene articles for publication for gain, contrary to s 2(1) of the 1959 Act. The facts are set out in the judgment of the court.

James H Gregory for the defendant.
Michael Shorrock for the Crown.

Cur adv vult

2nd November. **CUMMING-BRUCE LJ** read the following judgment of the court: On 6th April 1977, on the application of a police constable, a justice of the peace issued a search warrant, pursuant to s 3(1) of the Obscene Publications Act 1959, in the following terms:

'SEARCH WARRANT.

'OBSCENE PUBLICATIONS ACT 1959.

'BEFORE THE MAGISTRATES' COURT SITTING AT CROWN SQUARE, IN THE CITY OF MANCHESTER.

a 'To Brian Webb. P.C. 1517 A Police Constable of the Greater Manchester Police Force, and to all other Police Constables of the said force.

'Whereas it appears to me the undersigned Stipendiary Magistrate (Justice of the Peace for the County of Greater Manchester) by the information on oath of P.C. 1517 Brian Webb that there is reasonable ground for suspecting that in the premises (shops, store etc.) situate at 290 Cheetham Hill Road, Cheetham, Manchester 8 in the said City, obscene articles, to wit, books (or as the case may be) are kept for

b publication for gain, and that the said premises are occupied by The Forum Bookshop.

'You are therefore hereby commanded within fourteen days from the date hereof to enter, if need be by force, and search the said premises and to seize and remove any articles found therein which you or any of you have reason to believe to be obscene articles kept for publication for gain, and to bring such articles so seized

c before a Justice of the Peace for the said City.

'And if any articles are so seized, to seize and remove any documents found therein which relate to a trade or business carried on at the said premises.

'Dated this 6th day of April 1977.'

It was signed by a 'Justice of the Peace for the County of Greater Manchester, or The
d Stipendiary Magistrate'.

On the same day the police entered the defendant's bookshop, searched and seized a quantity of stock pursuant to the authority given in the warrant. A summons was issued to the defendant on 6th April alleging an offence under s 2 of the Obscene Publications Act 1959, but was later withdrawn, but proceedings were taken for forfeiture of goods seized on 6th April. The defendant did not contest those proceedings, and the
e magistrates' court made an order of forfeiture.

On 12th April a police officer visited the shop in the guise of a member of the public and made a purchase of an obscene magazine. An hour or so later a number of police officers, armed with the search warrant that had been issued on 6th April, made a second raid on the shop. They entered, searched and seized a number of publications and three films, all of which were admittedly obscene.

f The defendant was charged with offences under s 2 of the 1959 Act, committed to the Crown Court for trial, and came up for trial at the Crown Court in Manchester on 21st September 1978.

The indictment contained three counts. In the first he was charged with publishing an obscene article contrary to s 2(1) of the 1959 Act. The particulars were that he on 12th April 1977 sold an obscene article. He pleaded guilty.

g In the second and third counts he was charged with possessing obscene articles for publication for gain contrary to the same subsection. The particulars were that on 12th April 1977 he had obscene articles (namely magazines and films seized on 12th April) for publication for gain. He pleaded not guilty to both counts, and was put in charge of the jury. The trial took a curious course. Counsel for the Crown opened the case to the jury and described or showed to the jury the magazines and films which were the subject of
h the second and third counts. The defence made formal admissions that (i) the articles were obscene and (ii) the defendant had been in possession of the same for publication for gain. Three police officers gave evidence of the entry, search and seizure of the articles on 12th April, and the articles were made exhibits. The witnesses stated that the entry, search and seizure on 12th April were carried out by the authority of the warrant issued on 6th April. The Crown admitted that there had been a previous entry, search and
j seizure on 6th April on the authority of the same warrant and that the summonses under s 2 issued in respect of events on 6th April had been later withdrawn.

Against that background counsel for the defence in the absence of the jury made two submissions to the recorder. First, he submitted that the entry, search and seizure on 12th April were unlawful because there could only be one entry, search and seizure made on the authority of the warrant issued on 6th April. That entry, search and seizure had been made on 6th April. The warrant, having been executed, was spent. The entry, search and seizure on 12th April were not therefore authorised by any warrant, and were unlawful.

The second submission was that if the recorder upheld the first submission he had a discretion to exclude the evidence of the obscene articles seen and seized on 12th April, that he should exercise that discretion by excluding the evidence, and direct the jury that there was no evidence to support a conviction in spite of the admissions earlier made by the defence. The recorder ruled against the first submission of the defence, and therefore did not not have to rule on the second submission. After that ruling, the defendant changed his plea, and pleaded guilty to counts 2 and 3, without prejudice to an appeal on the correctness of the recorder's ruling on the submission. On the direction of the recorder the jury returned verdicts of guilty on counts 2 and 3, and the defendant was duly sentenced.

We have not heard argument on the point, but, as presently advised, it seems clear that the procedure was irregular. If objection is to be taken to the admissibility of evidence, that evidence should not be opened by the Crown, much less admitted and taken into cognisance of the jury before the objection is taken. In this case the evidence of the police as to the entry on 12th April under the purported authority of the warrant issued on 6th April should have been proved, followed by the statement of the Crown that an earlier entry, search and seizure had occurred on 6th April under the authority of the same warrant. The submission as to admissibility of evidence of articles seized should have been made at that stage, so that the admission or exclusion of that evidence to the jury might follow the recorder's ruling. As it happens nothing turns on this irregularity, and having disposed of it, we turn to the substance of this appeal.

The first point is a question of construction of s 3(1) of the Obscene Publications Act 1959. The subsection reads:

> 'If a justice of the peace is satisfied by information on oath that there is reasonable ground for suspecting that, in any premises in the petty sessions area for which he acts, or on any stall or vehicle in that area, being premises or a stall or vehicle specified in the information, obscene articles are, or are from time to time, kept for publication for gain, the justice may issue a warrant under his hand empowering any constable to enter (if need be by force) and search the premises, or to search the stall or vehicle, within fourteen days from the date of the warrant, and to seize and remove any articles found therein or thereon which the constable has reason to believe to be obscene articles and to be kept for publication for gain.'

Counsel for the defendant submits that a warrant thereunder issued authorises a single entry, search and seizure, to be carried out within 14 days from the date of the warrant. This, he submits, is the natural meaning of the words in s 3(1). If Parliament intended to authorise a number of quite separate entries, searches and seizures, extending throughout the period of 14 days, express words authorising such an invasion of privacy and property rights would be found in the subsection.

He invites us to compare with s 3(1) the draftsman's language in s 152(1) of the Licensing Act 1953, re-enacted in s 187(1) of the Licensing Act 1964, which reads:

> 'If a justice of the peace is satisfied by information on oath that there is reasonable ground for believing that any intoxicating liquor is sold by retail or exposed or kept for sale by retail at any place in the county or borough for which he is justice, being a place where that liquor may not lawfully be sold by retail, he may issue a search warrant under his hand to a constable authorising him at any time or times within one month from the date of the warrant to enter that place, which shall be named in the warrant, by force if need be, and search the place for intoxicating liquor and seize and remove any intoxicating liquor that the constable has reasonable grounds for supposing to be in the place for the purpose of unlawful sale there or elsewhere, and the vessels containing the liquor.'

He points to similar language in s 23(3) of the Misuse of Drugs Act 1971:

> 'If a justice of the peace (or in Scotland a justice of the peace, a magistrate or a sheriff) is satisfied by information on oath that there is reasonable ground for suspecting—(a) that any controlled drugs are, in contravention of this Act or of any regulations made thereunder, in the possession of a person on any premises; or (b) that a document directly or indirectly relating to, or connected with, a transaction or dealing which was, or an intended transaction or dealing which would if carried out be, an offence under this Act, or in the case of a transaction or dealing carried out or intended to be carried out in a place outside the United Kingdom, an offence against the provisions of a corresponding law in force in that place, is in the possession of a person on any premises, he may grant a warrant authorising any constable acting for the police area in which the premises are situated at any time or times within one month from the date of the warrant, to enter, if need be by force, the premises named in the warrant, and to search the premises and any persons found therein and, if there is reasonable ground for suspecting that an offence under this Act has been committed in relation to any controlled drugs found on the premises or in the possession of any such persons, or that a document so found is such a document as is mentioned in paragraph (b) above, to seize and detain those drugs or that document, as the case may be.'

Counsel for the Crown submits that the language of s 3(1) of the Obscene Publications Act 1959 is on its face wide enough to authorise any number of entries, searches and seizures within that period stated by the warrant.

He submits that this construction is consistent with the control of the mischief aimed at by the statute, as the justice of the peace may issue his warrant if he 'is satisfied . . . there is reasonable ground for suspecting that, in any premises . . . obscene articles are, or are from time to time, kept . . .' So, if the justice is satisfied that obscene articles are from time to time kept on the premises, it is likely that Parliament enabled him to issue a warrant which authorised entries and searches, if need be from time to time within the statutory period of 14 days. And this, the wider construction, for which he contended, would achieve. He relied also on the practical inconveniences which would, or might, flow from the more restrictive construction. What if the search and seizure could not be finished properly on a single day? Why should not the police depart at nightfall and return to continue what in effect would be a single but continuing transaction of search and seizure proceeding intermittently over a period of days. Counsel for the defendant indeed at first conceded that such a transaction, namely a search which was not completed on the first occasion, might continue after an interval of time under the authority of one warrant, though he later sought to withdraw that concession after appreciating that though the search might sensibly be regarded as a continuing search, the transaction must involve more than one entry as an entry cannot readily be regarded as a continuing event.

Counsel for the Crown also relied on the existence on the statute book for a long period of years of many statutes giving powers of search for different purposes in much the same terms as s 3(1), and relied on the fact that there is no trace of any authority to the effect that such words should be given a restrictive construction. Examples of such statutes are s 42 of the Larceny Act 1916, later re-enacted, and s 42 of the Children Act 1975. It would be curious, he submitted, if a police officer who had searched premises for stolen goods without success and then remembered that he had not searched the place where the goods were most likely to be concealed was then unable to return without a second warrant; or if on a search for a child the search was unsuccessful because the child temporarily had been taken out for a walk, but the police could not enter and search again without another warrant if they discovered that the child had been taken into the premises shortly after the first search had been completed.

We were not referred to any authority on the point either in relation to the statute under consideration or to any other statute authorising entry and search in language similar to s 3(1) of the 1959 Act. We have observed that in the 21st edition of Moriarty's Police Law[1] the editor expresses his opinion as follows:

'SEARCH WARRANT—A warrant to search usually authorises the person to whom it is addressed and his assistants, to enter, by force if necessary, the place or premises named, to search every place and thing inside, to seize and take away any articles mentioned in the warrant, and to arrest the persons named in the warrant or the persons in whose possession the articles named are found. A search warrant remains in force until executed or when any limitation of time ends. It is usually "executed" when a search has been made, whether the articles named are found or not, but some search warrants authorise entry at any time or times.'

And we understand that the chief constable of Manchester would welcome guidance on the question whether a warrant issued under s 3(1) is executed and spent when there has once been an entry and search made under its authority.

We derive assistance from consideration of the history of legislation in respect of search for obscene articles. Publication of obscene matter was a misdemeanor at common law within the jurisdiction of a temporal court, and the first successful prosecution for this offence recorded in Halsbury's Laws of England[2] is *R v Curl*[3]. The first statute giving a power of search was the Obscene Publications Act 1857, the preamble to which states: 'WHEREAS it is expedient to give additional Powers for the Suppression of the Trade in Obscene Books, Prints, Drawings, and other Obscene Articles ...' The power of search is enacted in s 1. The relevant words are:

'It shall be lawful for any ... Magistrate ... upon Complaint made before him ... that any Obscene Books ... are kept in any House ... to give Authority by Special Warrant to any Constable ... into such House ... to enter in the Daytime, and, if necessary, to use Force, by breaking open Doors or otherwise, and to search for and seize any such Books ... found in such House ... and to carry all the Articles so seized before the Magistrate ... issuing the said Warrant ... and such Magistrate ... shall thereupon issue a Summons calling upon the Occupier of the House ... which may have been so entered by virtue of the said Warrant to appear within Seven Days ... to show Cause why the Articles so seized should not be destroyed ...'

In that Act there is no express limitation of time for which the warrant remains in force, and the only restriction on the power of search is that it must be made in the daytime. It is manifest in the view of this court that Parliament did not intend such a warrant to subject the owner to an unlimited number of searches throughout an unlimited period of time. We construe the section as authorising a single entry, search and seizure. Section 1 of the 1857 Act remained in force until its repeal by the Obscene Publications Act 1959, and its replacement in altered form by s 3(1) of that Act. The changes material to the question of construction are the following: (i) the magistrate may issue a warrant not only if he is satisfied that obscene articles 'are kept' but also if he is satisfied that they 'are from time to time, kept'; (ii) entry may be by night as well as by day; (iii) the warrant remains in force for a limited time: 'empowering any constable to enter (if need be by force) and search the premises, within fourteen days from the date of the warrant ...'

It is to be observed that by the 1959 Act the jurisdiction is extended to include the case where the magistrate is satisfied that obscene articles are kept from time to time. There is nothing in the subsection to express an intention that the power of entry and search should be exercised more than once, or that it may be exercised from time to time throughout the 14 days that the warrant remains in force. In our view Parliament did

---

1 (1972) p 55
2 10 Halsbury's Laws (3rd Edn) 666, para 1274
3 (1727) 2 Stra 788, 93 ER 849

not by the language of the subsection show an intention to impose a more onerous
a interference with the owner's right of privacy or right of property than had been enacted
by the 1857 Act, other than to lift the prohibition on searches during the night. It
follows that as before a warrant authorises one and only one entry, search and seizure of
articles. After that entry search and seizure the warrant is executed and spent, and a
second warrant must be obtained to authorise a second entry.

We have not founded our decision on consideration of statutes concerned with other
b mischiefs, and express no view on the powers of entry or search enacted in different
contexts. If any issue arose in connection with a warrant issued under another statute, it
would fall to be resolved in consideration of the relevant Act of Parliament.

We have however observed that as long ago as 1794 in *Dickinson v Brown*[1] the court of
King's Bench doubted the legality of a second arrest on a warrant which had already been
used to effect an arrest of the plaintiff on an earlier occasion; and a passage in Hawkins'
c Pleas of the Crown[2] implies the same view of the illegality of a second arrest on a single
warrant. It is however relevant in relation to the draftsman's technique to observe that
in s 3(1) of the 1959 Act the power to issue the warrant was extended to the case where
the articles are kept 'from time to time'. The draftsman has not inserted any such words
in that part of the subsection which deals with the powers authorised by warrant,
although such a drafting technique was adopted in s 152(1) of the Licensing Act 1953 and
d the Misuse of Drugs Act 1971 to confer an express power of searches from time to
time. These considerations fortify, rather than found, our conclusion.

It follows that the recorder was in error on the only submission that he considered.
Before us, counsel for the defendant's second submission falls for consideration. As the
entry, search and seizure on 12th April were not authorised by the warrant, should the
case be sent back to the court of trial to consider, as a matter of discretion, whether the
e evidence of the articles seized on 12th April should be excluded from the evidence before
the jury? Counsel recognised that the decision and speeches in the House of Lords in *R
v Sang*[3] placed great difficulties in his way. He sought to distinguish it on the analogy of
the reasoning in *Scott v Baker*[4] approved in *Spicer v Holt*[5]. He submitted that s 3 of the
1959 Act prescribes a statutory procedure, and compliance with that procedure is a
necessary step towards procuring a conviction for the offence in s 2. We do not agree.
f The ground of decision in *Spicer v Holt*[5] is to be collected from the passage in the speech
of Lord Dilhorne where he stated[6]:

'Section 1(1) of the [Road Safety Act 1967] created and defined the new offence
and s 6(1) of the [Road Traffic Act 1972] now defines it in the same terms, but these
sections not only define it but lay down the only way in which the offence can be
proved. It is a driving offence but guilt can only be proved by the result of an
g analysis of blood or urine provided by the accused later . . .'

This section of the Road Traffic Act 1972 may be contrasted with and distinguished
from the provisions of the Obscene Publications Acts of 1857 and 1959. Before the 1857
Act obscene publication was a misdemeanour at common law. The 1857 Act was an Act
to give additional powers for the suppression of the trade in obscene articles. The
h common law misdemeanour was untouched, but the Act provided a new power of
search and a summary procedure for forfeiture. The 1959 Act provided, by s 1, a new
test of obscenity for the purposes of the Act.

By s 2 a new statutory offence was created, and by s 2(4) the common law offence was
abolished in any case where it is the essence of the offence that the matter is obscene.

j
1   (1794) 1 Esp 218, 170 ER 334
2   8th Edn (1824) vol 2, ch 13, s 9
3   [1979] 2 All ER 1222, [1979] 3 WLR 263
4   [1968] 2 All ER 993, [1969] 1 QB 659
5   [1976] 3 All ER 71, [1977] AC 987
6   [1976] 3 All ER 71 at 75, [1977] AC 987 at 996

There is no restriction in s 2 on the evidence which may be adduced to prove the offence
or on the procedure for obtaining such evidence. Section 3 enacts new powers replacing *a*
the powers of search in the 1857 Act, and there is nothing to suggest that strict
compliance with the procedure in s 3 is a necessary condition of a conviction under s 2.
The comparison with the Road Traffic Act 1972 does not therefore assist the defendant.
The relevant principles are those explained in *R v Sang*[1]. There is no material suggesting
that the error of the police as to the continuing validity of the warrant after the search on
6th April was oppressive in the sense that the adjective is used in *R v Sang*[1]. If the case *b*
went back, and the court, in the exercise of discretion, excluded the evidence, such
exclusion would be contrary to law.

For those reasons the appeal is dismissed and the conviction upheld.

Appeal dismissed.

c

Solicitors: *Registrar of Criminal Appeals* (for the defendant); *D S Gandy*, Manchester (for
the Crown).

Dilys Tausz   Barrister.

d

Iraqi Ministry of Defence and others v
Arcepey Shipping Co SA (Gillespie Brothers
& Co Ltd intervening)
The Angel Bell

e

QUEEN'S BENCH DIVISION
ROBERT GOFF J
5th, 7th, 13th NOVEMBER 1979

Injunction – Interlocutory – Danger that defendant may transfer assets out of jurisdiction – *f*
Injunction restraining removal of assets out of the jurisdiction – Variation of injunction –
Intervener seeking variation to enable defendant to use proceeds of insurance to repay loan made
by intervener – Proceeds of insurance sole asset of defendant – Defendant denuded of assets if
proceeds of insurance used to repay loan – Plaintiff having large claim against defendant –
Whether court should order variation of injunction to enable defendant to repay loan out of
proceeds of insurance.

g

Contract – Illegality – Enforceability of contract – Loan – Plaintiff alleging loan by intervener to
defendant illegal – Defendant denying loan illegal and wishing to repay it – Intervener seeking
variation of injunction restraining removal of defendant's assets from jurisdiciton to allow
repayment of loan – Whether variation of injunction would have effect of enforcing loan.

h

In 1974 the interveners, who carried on business as a confirming house in sale transactions
between sellers in England and foreign buyers, lent £270,000 to the defendants, a
Panamanian company, for the purpose of buying ships, the intention being that the
defendants would provide security to the interveners by giving them mortgages over the
ships and by assigning an insurance policy on one of the ships to them. Documents were
executed with the intention of achieving that result. In the event the defendants *j*
purchased only one ship, and insurance of it was effected in London. In 1976 the ship
sank with cargo owned by the plaintiffs on board. The plaintiffs brought an action

1   [1979] 2 All ER 1222, [1979] 3 WLR 263

a against the defendants claiming damages of about $US 3 million in respect of the loss of their cargo. The defendants had no assets within the jurisdiction but they had the prospect of recovering the proceeds of the insurance on the ship. On 9th June 1977 the plaintiffs obtained a Mareva[a] injunction restraining them from dealing with their assets within the jurisdiction and from removing any of their assets from the jurisdiction save in so far as the court might order to the contrary on the application of other parties. At that time only part of the interveners' advance had been repaid, the amount of principal

b and interest outstanding being £200,000. The proceeds of the insurance, including interest earned on deposit, was about £240,000. The interveners applied to the court for an order varying the injunction so that the loan could be repaid out of the proceeds of the insurance. The plaintiffs contended any payment of the insurance proceeds to the interveners would be in breach of the Mareva injunction, and further that the interveners had been carrying on the business of unregistered moneylenders and that therefore the

c loan by them to the defendants was illegal and void. The interveners denied that they were carrying on such business and asserted that the loan was a one-off transaction forming no part of their usual business.

Held – The injunction would be varied in the manner sought by the interveners for the following reasons—

(i) Although the whole point of the Mareva jurisdiction was to enable the plaintiff to

d proceed by stealth so as to pre-empt any action by the defendant to remove his assets from the jurisdiction (whether by his own act or by a transfer to a collaborator within the jurisdiction), and to achieve that result a Mareva injunction was necessarily in a wide form, it did not follow that, having granted such an injunction, the court should not thereafter permit a qualification to it to allow a transfer of assets by the defendant if the money was required for a purpose which did not conflict with the policy underlying the

e Mareva jurisdiction (see p 485 h to p 486 b and p 487 a g, post); dictum of Mustill J in *Third Chandris Shipping Corpn v Unimarine SA* [1979] 2 All ER at 978 applied.

(ii) The effect of the plaintiffs' contention that payment would be a breach of the injunction was to seek for themselves a priority, in the event of the defendants' insolvency, to which they were not entitled in English law. The purpose of the Mareva jurisdiction was not in any way to improve the position of claimants in an insolvency but

f to prevent the injustice of a foreign defendant removing his assets from the jurisdiction when they might otherwise have been available to satisfy a judgment; a Mareva injunction was not a form of pretrial attachment but a relief in personam which prohibited certain acts in relation to the assets in question (see p 486 b to f and p 487 a g, post); *Cretanor Maritime Co Ltd v Irish Marine Management Ltd* [1978] 3 All ER 164 applied.

g (iii) Although the court would not enforce an illegal contract directly or indirectly, it would not be enforcing the loan transaction, even indirectly, by varying the injunction to enable the defendants to repay to the interveners the loan they had received. The interveners were not asking that the transaction should be enforced but merely that the defendants should be free to repay the loan if they thought fit so to do. It was not inconsistent with the policy underlying the Mareva jurisdiction for a defendant to be free

h to repay a loan in such circumstances since he was not seeking to avoid his responsibilities to the plaintiff if the latter should ultimately obtain a judgment but was merely seeking in good faith to make payments which he considered he should make in the ordinary course of business (see p 487 b to e and g, post).

Notes

j For injunctions restraining the disposition of property, see 24 Halsbury's Laws (4th Edn) para 1018.

Cases referred to in judgment

Chartered Bank v Daklouche p 205, ante, CA.

---

a   See *Mareva Compania Naviera SA v International Bulkcarriers SA* p 213, ante

Cretanor Maritime Co Ltd v Irish Marine Management Ltd, The Cretan Harmony [1978] 3 All
    ER 164, [1978] 1 WLR 966, [1978] 1 Lloyd's Rep 425, CA.   *a*
Etablissement Esefka International Anstalt v Central Bank of Nigeria [1979] 1 Lloyd's Rep 445,
    CA.
Mareva Compania Naviera SA v International Bulkcarriers SA p 213, ante, [1975] 2 Lloyd's
    Rep 509, CA.
Nippon Yusen Kaisha v Karageorgis [1975] 3 All ER 282, [1975] 1 WLR 1093, [1975] 2
    Lloyd's Rep 137, CA, Digest (Cont Vol D) 534, 79a.   *b*
Rasu Maritima SA v Perusahaan Pertambangan Minyak Dan Gas Bumi Negara (Pertamina)
    and Government of Indonesia (as interveners) [1977] 3 All ER 324, [1978] QB 644, [1977]
    3 WLR 518, [1977] 2 Lloyd's Rep 397, CA.
Siskina (Cargo owners) v Distos Compania Naviera SA, The Siskina [1977] 3 All ER 803,
    [1977] 3 WLR 818, [1978] 1 Lloyd's Rep 1, HL.
Third Chandris Shipping Corpn v Unimarine SA, The Pythia, The Angelic Wings, The Genie *c*
    [1979] 2 All ER 972, [1979] QB 645, [1979] 3 WLR 122, [1979] 2 Lloyd's Rep 184, CA.

Application

On 9th June 1977 Jupp J granted the plaintiffs, Iraqi Ministry of Defence, Iraqi Stores Co,
Middle East Traders, Renco, Abu Dhabi Furnitures and Ministry of Water and Electricity,
an injunction restraining the defendants, Arcepey Shipping Co SA, the owners of the *d*
vessel Angel Bell, by their agents of servants or otherwise, from dealing with their assets
within the jurisdiction and from removing any of those assets out of the jurisdiction. On
21st June 1977 Kerr J ordered the injunction to continue. On 22nd October 1979 the
interveners, Gillespie Brothers & Co Ltd, applied to intervene in the action between
the plaintiffs and the defendants seeking an order varying the injunction to enable the
defendants to repay a loan made by the interveners to the defendants and secured by *e*
certain mortgages and assignments of insurance policies on the Angel Bell. The plaintiffs
contested the validity of the mortgages and the assignments. On 16th March 1979
Donaldson J held that the interveners were equitable mortgagees and assignees. The facts
are set out in the judgment.

J S Hobhouse QC and *Alan Pardoe* for the plaintiffs.   *f*
Anthony D Colman QC and *Nigel Teare* for the interveners.

The defendants were not represented.

                                                         Cur adv vult

13th November. **ROBERT GOFF J** read the following judgment: There is before the *g*
court an application by Gillespie Brothers & Co Ltd, who are interveners in this action.
Their application is for an order varying a Mareva[1] injunction which was ordered at the
instance of the plaintiffs in the action restraining the defendants in the action from
dealing with their assets within the jurisdiction of the court and from removing any of
such assets from the jurisdiction.

    The matter arises as follows. The plaintiffs in the action were the owners of cargo *h*
shipped on a vessel called the Angel Bell. The defendants, who are a Panamanian
company, were the owners of the vessel. On 18th February 1976 the Angel Bell sank
with the plaintiffs' cargo on board. The plaintiffs then commenced proceedings against
the defendants claiming damages in a sum of about $US 3 million in respect of the loss
of their cargo. On 9th June 1977 they obtained the Mareva injunction by the order of
Jupp J, and on 21st June 1977 the injunction was continued by Kerr J. At that time the *i*
defendants had no assets within the jurisdiction but they had the prospect of recovering
the proceeds of insurance policies on the Angel Bell, which were policies written in

---

1   See *Mareva Compania Naviera SA v International Bulkcarriers SA* p 213, ante

London by Lloyd's underwriters and by various companies. The brokers for these
a policies were a company called Brandts Marine Ltd. Subsequently their name was
changed to Grindley Brandts Marine Ltd.

Now this is where the interveners come on the scene. It appears that in 1974 they had
lent a sum of £270,000 to the defendants for the purpose of buying ships, including the
Angel Bell. The intention was that the defendants should provide security to the
interveners by giving the interveners mortgages over the Angel Bell and other ships and
b by assigning an insurance policy on the Angel Bell to the interveners. Documents were
executed with the intention of achieving this result. Obviously, if this had been
effectively done, the interveners would be entitled by virtue of such security to receive
the insurance proceeds on the Angel Bell. But when the plaintiffs realised that the
interveners claimed the insurance proceeds, they saw the only assets which they might
recover towards the satisfaction of their claim disappearing out of the window. Only
c part of the interveners' advance had been repaid, leaving outstanding principal and
interest in a sum which had been agreed at £200,000. The proceeds of the insurance,
including interest earned on deposit, are only about £240,000. So if the interveners are
entitled to £200,000 there will be little left to satisfy the plaintiffs' claim, bearing in
mind that the defendants are a Panamanian one-ship company whose only ship has sunk.

The plaintiffs have therefore argued that the interveners have no right to the insurance
d proceeds. They discovered that the mortgages were never registered in Panama, so they
claimed that they were ineffective, to which the interveners responded that they had an
equitable mortgage on the Angel Bell. The plaintiffs also argued that the insurance
moneys were not in fact assigned to the interveners so as to give the interveners any legal
or beneficial interest in the policies or their proceeds.

Now, the interveners having intervened in the action between the plaintiffs and the
e defendants, an issue was ordered to be tried as between the interveners and the plaintiffs
concerning the interveners' rights as mortgagees and the effectiveness of the assignment
of the insurance moneys. It is right however that I should record that the defendants
have at all material times conceded that they have no interest in the insurance moneys,
and have maintained that such moneys should be paid to the interveners, with the
consequence that, when the brokers collected the insurance moneys they acted on the
f interveners' instructions and, subject only to the possible effect of the Mareva injunction
in this case, the brokers would pay the moneys over to the interveners as assignees.
However, the plaintiffs' solicitors have warned them that they would be acting contrary
to the Mareva injunction if they did so, and in consequence they have not done so.

The issue between the interveners and the plaintiffs was tried by Donaldson J in
February 1979, and on 16th March 1979 he gave judgment in favour of the interveners
g on both aspects, holding that the interveners were equitable mortgagees of the Angel Bell
and assignees of the policies with title to sue on the policies. It might be thought that
that would have been an end of the matter; but not so. First of all, the plaintiffs have
served notice of appeal against Donaldson J's decision. Secondly, they have taken another
point. The interveners, I have been told, carry on business as a confirming house in
which, in sale transactions between sellers in this country and foreign buyers, they
h provide a service to buyers for a fee, viz they intervene in the sale transaction, making
themselves liable to the sellers for the price but having themselves recourse over against
the buyers. In this way they provide the sellers with security, in the sense that the sellers
thereby have recourse against a party in this country. Frequently they give credit to the
foreign buyers in the form of bills for 120 or 180 days. The plaintiffs are now saying that
the interveners have been carrying on the business of unregistered moneylenders and
j that therefore the loan by the interveners to the defendants was illegal and void under
legislation which though now repealed was in force at the material time. This the
interveners deny. They say that they were not carrying on business as moneylenders at
all, and furthermore that the loan to the defendants was a one-off transaction forming no
part of their usual business.

This point was taken by the plaintiffs just before the hearing of the issue before

Donaldson J, and he gave the plaintiffs leave to amend their pleadings to raise it; but, involving as it did very substantial discovery, it was not dealt with on the hearing before him. However, on 31st July 1979 he ordered that this matter should be the subject of another issue to be tried in February 1980. Four days have been set aside for the hearing. The substantial discovery involved has since been taking place. Meanwhile the pending appeal from Donaldson J's first decision has been allowed to stand over.

So that is the state of the proceedings as between the plaintiffs and the interveners. However, now the interveners have advanced a different contention which they believe should, if right, decide the whole matter in their favour without any need to proceed any further with the various issues raised by the plaintiffs and with consequent saving of costs. This contention has its origin in certain observations made by Donaldson J on the occasion of the hearing of the issue in February 1979 and in his judgment in March 1979. I quote from the judgment:

'[The interveners] sought and were granted leave to intervene in the action, on the grounds that they too had claims against the defendants, having lent them money and further that their claims were secured on the proceeds of these insurance policies. I ordered that an issue be tried as to [the intervener's] claims and whether they were indeed secured creditors. This is the issue with which I am now concerned. Lest this procedure be regarded as a precedent, let me confess at once that I may have been mistaken in making this order. The Mareva jurisdiction is still in a formative stage. Its original purpose is clear. It was to prevent foreign defendants making themselves judgment-proof by removing their assets from the jurisdiction or by disposing of those assets within the jurisdiction to shareholders or others who might be amicably disposed, and doing so before judgment and execution. But in ordering this issue, I have inadvertently gone much further and, by implication, have suggested that the interveners' right to obtain a judgment against the defendants and to levy execution on the insurance proceeds depends on their being secured creditors. This would not be the position if the defendants were an English company against whom no winding-up petition had been presented. In other words, I seem to be in danger of creating a new legal concept: the quasi-winding up of foreign companies at the suit of those who are not yet judgment creditors of that company. As the parties do not wish to explore this aspect at the present time, suffice it to say that in any other case I shall require to be persuaded that the approach adopted in this case is correct.'

Prompted by these observations the interveners now seek to have the Mareva injunction varied by the addition of the words: 'Save that [the brokers] shall be permitted to pay to [the interveners] the sum of £200,000 being part of the proceeds of certain policies of insurance on the vessel Angel Bell.'

The basis of the interveners' contention is as follows. They say that, whatever be the result of the issues tried and pending between them and the plaintiffs, the injunction should be lifted to enable the defendants and the brokers to pay back the money which the interveners advanced to the defendants. They say that for the defendants or the brokers to pay the money to the interveners would be to pay money in good faith in the ordinary course of business, and that Mareva injunctions were not designed to prevent transactions of this kind. The plaintiffs however oppose the interveners' application. They say that the whole purpose of the Mareva jurisdiction is to freeze the assets of a defendant within the jurisdiction until after the litigation between the plaintiffs and the defendants has been resolved by judgment or agreement between the parties.

Counsel for the interveners and counsel for the plaintiffs have taken me right through the authorities on the Mareva jurisdiction from the first case, *Nippon Yusen Kaisha v Karageorgis*[1] up to *Third Chandris Shipping Corpn v Unimarine SA*[2]. I am satisfied from the

---

1   [1975] 3 All ER 282, [1975] 1 WLR 1093
2   [1979] 2 All ER 972, [1979] QB 645

authorities that the fundamental purpose of the Mareva jurisdiction is to prevent foreign
a parties from causing assets to be removed from the jurisdiction in order to avoid the risk
of having to satisfy any judgment which may be entered against them in pending
proceedings in this country. There are numerous statements in the authorities to this
effect, beginning with the *Mareva* case[1] itself. In that case Lord Denning MR said:

> 'If it appears that the debt is due and owing, and there is a danger that the debtor
> may dispose of his assets so as to defeat it before judgment, the court has jurisdiction
b > in a proper case to grant an interlocutory judgment . . . so as to prevent him
> disposing of those assets.'

There are many other statements to the same effect. Thus in *Rasu Maritima SA v
Perusahaan Pertambangan Minyak Dan Gas Bumi Negara (Pertamina) and Government of
Indonesia (as interveners)*[2] Lord Denning MR quoted with approval a passage from the
c judgment of Kerr J (who sat in first instance in that case) which included the following
words:

> '. . . on being apprised of the proceedings, the defendant is liable to remove his
> assets, thereby precluding the plaintiff in advance from enjoying the fruits of a
> judgment which appears irresistible on the evidence before the court. The
d > defendant can then largely ignore the plaintiff's claim in the courts of this country
> and snap his fingers at any judgment which may be given against him. It has
> always been my understanding that the purpose and scope of the exercise of this
> jurisdiction is to deal with cases of this nature.'

Similar statements are to be found in the judgments of Lord Denning MR and
Brandon LJ in *Etablissement Esefka International Anstalt v Central Bank of Nigeria*[3]. Lord
e Denning MR said[4]: 'The Mareva injunction is only to be granted where there is danger
of the money being taken out of the jurisdiction so that if the plaintiffs succeed they are
not likely to get their money.' Brandon LJ[5] said, basing his judgment on a ground
mentioned by Lawton LJ: '. . . there is no material from which the Court could conclude
that the assets of the defendants were likely to be removed from the jurisdiction so as to
avoid payment of any judgment which the plaintiffs might obtain.'
f   Other statements to the same effect are to be found in *Chartered Bank v Daklouche*[6] per
Lord Denning MR and in *Third Chandris Shipping Corpn v Unimarine SA*[7] per Mustill J,
where he said that: 'The whole point of the Mareva jurisdiction is that the plaintiff
proceeds by stealth, so as to pre-empt any action by the defendant to remove his assets
from the jurisdiction', and in the Court of Appeal per Lord Denning MR[8].
     Counsel for the plaintiffs submitted that the purpose of the Mareva jurisdiction was to
g freeze a foreign defendant's assets in this country to ensure that there is a fund available
in this country from which the plaintiff will be able to satisfy a judgment. In support of
this he relied in particular on the form of the order usually made in these cases which
restrains the defendant from dealing with his assets within the jurisdiction and from
removing his assets from the jurisdiction. I do not however see that the usual form of
the order as such assists his argument. As was made plain by Mustill J in the *Third
h Chandris* case[9], the point of the Mareva jurisdiction is to proceed by stealth, to pre-empt
any action by the defendant to remove his assets from the jurisdiction. To achieve that

1   See p 215, ante
2   [1977] 3 All ER 324 at 334, [1978] QB 644 at 660–661
j 3   [1979] 1 Lloyd's Rep 445
4   [1979] 1 Lloyd's Rep 445 at 448
5   [1979] 1 Lloyd's Rep 445 at 449
6   See p 210, ante
7   [1979] 2 All ER 972 at 978, [1979] QB 645 at 653
8   [1979] 2 All ER 972 at 985, [1979] QB 645 at 669
9   [1979] 2 All ER 972, [1979] QB 645

result the injunction must be in a wide form because, for example, a transfer by the defendant to a collaborator in the jurisdiction could lead to the transfer of the assets *a* abroad by that collaborator. But it does not follow that, having established the injunction, the court should not thereafter permit a qualification to it to allow a transfer of assets by the defendant if the defendant satisfies the court that he requires the money for a purpose which does not conflict with the policy underlying the Mareva jurisdiction.

Counsel for the plaintiffs also relied on certain passages in the speeches of Lord Diplock and Lord Hailsham of St Marylebone in *The Siskina*[1]. But it is to be observed that in that *b* case their Lordships expressly disclaimed the task of pronouncing on the validity or scope of the jurisdiction: see especially per Lord Diplock[2], with whose speech all their Lordships agreed. In truth, counsel for the plaintiffs, although he disavowed this purpose, was really seeking for his clients a priority to which they are not entitled in English law. It was not in dispute before me that in English law a party who claims unliquidated damages against a company is not entitled to present a petition for the winding up of the *c* defendant company before he has a judgment. But if counsel for the plaintiffs is right, his clients will be enabled, at least where the defendant company is a foreign company, to achieve the status of a judgment creditor before they have a judgment. Hence the concern expressed by Donaldson J.

For my part I do not believe that the Mareva jurisdiction was intended to rewrite the English law of insolvency in this way. Indeed it is clear from the authorities that the *d* purpose of the Mareva jurisdiction was not in any way to improve the position of claimants in an insolvency but simply to prevent the injustice of a foreign defendant removing his assets from the jurisdiction which otherwise might have been available to satisfy a judgment. This appears not only from the statements of principle, to which I have already referred, but is consistent also with the proposition established by the Court of Appeal in *Cretanor Maritime Co Ltd v Irish Marine Management Ltd*[3], which clearly laid *e* down that a Mareva injunction is not a form of pretrial attachment but a relief in personam which prohibits certain acts in relation to the assets in question.

In the light of the *Cretanor* case[3] counsel for the plaintiffs was at pains to disclaim a proprietary interest in the assets or the position of a secured creditor by virtue of the Mareva injunction; but from the very nature of his submission he was claiming for his clients a ranking among the creditors of the defendants in the event of their insolvency *f* which otherwise they would not be entitled to. I find it difficult to see why, if a plaintiff has not yet proceeded to judgment against a defendant but is simply a claimant for an unliquidated sum, the defendant should not be free to use his assets to pay his debts. Of course, if the plaintiff should obtain a judgment against a defendant company, and the defendant company should be wound up, its previous payments may thereafter be attacked on the ground of fraudulent preference, but this is an entirely different matter *g* which should be dealt with at the stage of the winding up. It is not to be forgotten that the plaintiff's claim may fail, or the damages which he claims may prove to be inflated. Is he in the meanwhile, merely by establishing a prima facie case, to preclude the bona fide payment of the defendant's debts? When taxed with this point counsel for the plaintiffs suggested that in such circumstances the appropriate course of a defendant's creditors was to proceed to judgment because the enforcement of judgments by *h* execution would not constitute breaches of the Mareva injunction against the defendant. This I consider to be an unsatisfactory answer. It does not make commercial sense that a party claiming unliquidated damages should, without himself proceeding to judgment, prevent the defendant from using his assets to satisfy his debts as they fall due and be put in the position of having to allow his creditors to proceed to judgment with consequent loss of credit and of commercial standing. On the approach of counsel for *j*

---

1   [1977] 3 All ER 803 at 822, 828, [1979] AC 210 at 253, 260–261
2   [1977] 3 All ER 803 at 822–823, [1979] AC 210 at 254
3   [1978] 3 All ER 164, [1978] 1 WLR 966

a the plaintiffs a jurisdiction which found its origin in the prevention of an abuse would be transmuted into a rewriting of our established law of insolvency.

For these reasons I am unable to accept the submissions of the plaintiffs in the present case. There remains however the point that the interveners are seeking to recover a debt which the plaintiffs say is illegal and void as a moneylending transaction. Whatever may be the merits of the plaintiffs' submission, it is an issue which has yet to be resolved; and I have to consider whether it would right to amend the present Mareva injunction to

b permit payment by the defendants of the interveners' claim in these circumstances. The plaintiffs submit that I should not do so, for to do so might be to enforce an illegal transaction. I do not think that this is right. No doubt the court will not enforce, directly or indirectly, an illegal contract; but by lifting the Mareva injunction in the present case to enable the defendants to repay to the interveners the loan they have received would not be to enforce the transaction, even indirectly. A reputable

c businessman who has received a loan from another person is likely to regard it as dishonourable, if not dishonest, not to repay that loan even if the enforcement of the loan is technically illegal by virtue of the Moneylenders Acts. All the interveners are asking is that the defendants should be free to repay such a loan if they think fit to do so, not that the loan transaction should be enforced. For a defendant to be free to repay a loan in such circumstances is not inconsistent with the policy underlying the Mareva jurisdiction.

d He is not in such circumstances seeking to avoid his responsibilities to the plaintiff if the latter should ultimately obtain a judgment; on the contrary, he is seeking in good faith to make payments which he considers he should make in the ordinary course of business. I cannot see that the Mareva jurisdiction should be allowed to prevent such a payment. To allow it to do so would be to stretch it beyond its original purpose so that instead of preventing abuse it would rather prevent businessmen conducting their businesses as

e they are entitled to do.

It is true that, as counsel for the plaintiffs pointed out, no such limit on the Mareva jurisdiction has been recognised in the previous cases; but, as I see it, no case has yet come before the courts in which this point arose for consideration. It has only arisen in the present case because here there is, so far as I am aware, only one asset available and that asset is not large enough to satisfy both the claim of the interveners and the claim of the

f plaintiffs. It is for that reason that the plaintiffs are seeking to restrain not a removal of the assets from the jurisdiction but a payment to another party who claims to be a creditor within the jurisdiction. Having studied the previous authorities, I am satisfied that they are not concerned with the question in this case, and that, not only is there nothing in them inconsistent with the submissions of the interveners in the present case but, on the contrary, the policy underlining the Mareva jurisdiction as revealed in these

g authorities is entirely consistent with these submissions.

For these reasons I accept the submission of the interveners. It follows that the Mareva injunction granted in this case must be qualified, and I shall be grateful for the assistance of counsel on the precise terms of the order.

Judgment for the interveners.

h

Solicitors: *Clyde & Co* (for the plaintiffs); *McHale & Co* (for the interveners).

K Mydeen Esq   Barrister.

Frobisher (Second Investments) Ltd v Kiloran Trust Co Ltd and another

CHANCERY DIVISION
WALTON J
22nd NOVEMBER 1979

Landlord and tenant – Service charge – Flat – Restriction on recovery of service charge – Recovery in advance – Lease providing for payment in advance of interim sums on account of service charge – Interim sums paid into separate bank account maintained by landlord's managing agents to meet service costs during year – Whether landlord entitled to require interim sums to be paid in advance – Whether interim sums held by managing agents as stakeholders – Whether interim sums received by managing agents trust moneys – Housing Finance Act 1972, s 91A (1)(b).

Landlord and tenant – Service charge – Flat – Restriction on recovery of service charge – Supervening legislation rendering recovery of service charge in advance unlawful – Landlord obliged to borrow in financial market in order to carry out obligations under lease if unable to recover service charge in advance – Whether landlord entitled to include interest charges in fees payable to him for carrying out obligations under lease – Whether term implied in lease that tenant should pay interest charges – Housing Finance Act 1972, s 91A.

Under a long lease of a flat the landlords covenanted with the tenant to observe and perform during the term of the lease certain obligations with respect to, inter alia, keeping the demised premises in repair, keeping them insured, paying water rates, etc. The tenant covenanted to pay to the landlords twice a year a 'contribution' which was defined as being a proportion of 'the amount which the [landlords] shall from time to time have expended during the [preceding] year . . . in . . . meeting the outgoings costs expenses and liabilities incurred by them in carrying out their obligations under [the lease]'. The lease further provided that the tenant was to pay 'on account of the Contribution' interim sums, certified by the landlords' managing agents as being reasonable, half yearly in advance. The managing agents paid the interim sums into a separate service charge bank account which they maintained to meet the day-to-day costs during the year. The questions arose (i) whether the interim sums were a service charge to which s 91A[a] of the Housing Finance Act 1972 applied, (ii) if so, whether the landlords were entitled to require the interim sums to be paid in advance, and (iii) if they were not entitled to payment in advance, whether they were entitled to recover from the tenant the cost of borrowing in the financial market the moneys required by them to meet their obligations under the lease. The landlords contended that the interim sums were trust moneys held by the managing agents as stakeholders, that therefore they were no part of the service charge and that it was only when the contribution had been ascertained and had become payable that the agents were entitled to put the moneys towards the discharge of the contribution.

Held – (i) The contribution provided for in the lease was in fact a service charge and since the lease provided that the interim sums were to be paid on account of the contribution, i e that they were to be paid on account of the service charge, it followed that they were part of the service charge, and since on the true construction of s 91A(1)(b) of the 1972 Act a service charge was only recoverable from the tenant of a flat once the landlord had defrayed the cost or, at least, incurred liability to pay the cost of chargeable

---

a   Section 91A, so far as material, is set out at p 492 c d, post

a items, it followed that the landlords were not entitled to require the interim payments to be made in advance on account of estimated or proposed expenditure to be incurred for services, repairs, maintenance or insurance (see p 491 *h j*, p 492 *b c* and *e* to *g*, p 493 *d e* and p 495 *e f*, post).

(ii) The interim sums were not held by the landlords' managing agents as stakeholders, since stakeholders held money of third parties which was to be applied in a particular way on the occurrence of a particular event, whereas the managing agents maintained a
b separate service charge bank account to meet the day-to-day costs during the year. Nor were the interim sums trust moneys because (a) in the absence of necessity a trust would not be imported into a purely commercial matter and (b) for the interim sums to be trust moneys, to be applied at the end of each year in meeting the contribution, it would be the duty of the managing agents to keep all those moneys together throughout the year, and it was apparent from the lease that that was not the intention of the parties (see p 492
c *j* to p 493 *d*, post).

(iii) The fees payable to the landlords' managing agents were paid for carrying out the general management and administration of the property, which, on the true construction of the lease, could not include interest paid on money borrowed by the agents in order to carry out their obligations thereunder. Nor could a term be implied in the lease as a matter of necessary implication that, in the event of supervening legislation rendering
d the payment of the service charge in advance unlawful, the tenant was to pay interest on the money which the landlords might then be obliged to borrow in order to meet their obligations under the lease. The doctrine of implying a term to give efficacy to an agreement did not apply where there had been a disturbance to contractual arrangements as the result of the intervention of a statute. In such a case it was to be left to the statute to make consequential provision (see p 494 *a* to *c g h* and p 495 *f g*, post); *The Moorcock*
e [1886–90] All ER Rep 530 and *Finchbourne Ltd v Rodrigues* [1976] 3 All ER 581 distinguished.

Notes

For service charges in respect of a flat, see Supplement to 23 Halsbury's Laws (3rd Edn) paras 1120–1122.
f For implied contractual terms, see 9 Halsbury's Laws (4th Edn) paras 351–358, and for cases on the subject, see 12 Digest (Reissue) 746–754, 5371–5411.

For the Housing Finance Act 1972, s 91A (as inserted by the Housing Act 1974, s 124), see 44 Halsbury's Statutes (3rd Edn) 599.

Cases referred to in judgment

Finchbourne Ltd v Rodrigues [1976] 3 All ER 581, CA.
g *Moorcock, The* (1889) 14 PD 64, [1886–90] All ER Rep 530, 58 LJP 73, 60 LT 654, 6 Asp MLC 373, CA, 12 Digest (Reissue) 751, 5395.

Case also cited

Barclays Bank Ltd v Quistclose Investments Ltd [1968] 3 All ER 651, [1970] AC 567, HL.

Adjourned summons

h By originating summons dated 16th August 1979 Frobisher (Second Investments) Ltd ('the landlords'), the lessors in whom was vested the reversion of a lease dated 25th November 1965 of flat 34, Campden House, 29 Sheffield Terrace, Kensington, London W8, and made between Campden House Chambers Ltd and George Maylam and Deborah Smith, sought the following relief: (1) a declaration that the interim payments for which provision was made in the proviso to the eighth schedule to the lease were
j charges to which s 91A of the Housing Finance Act 1972 applied; (2) a declaration that the landlords were entitled to require the interim payments to be made in advance on account of estimated or proposed expenditure to be incurred for the purposes referred to in the seventh schedule to the lease before such expenditure had been incurred; (3) a declaration that the landlords were entitled to recover from the tenants as lessees the appropriate proportion of the costs of borrowing in the financial market the moneys

required to make the expenditure referred to in the seventh and eighth schedules until such time as the payments referred to in the eighth schedule were made to the landlords; and (4) a declaration that the landlords were entitled to recover from the tenants as lessees fees or reimbursement of interest charges paid to the agents employed by the landlords to manage the block of flats in which flat 34 was situate in respect of the agents' expenditure on the matters specified in the seventh schedule in respect of borrowing in order to effect that expenditure. The defendants, Kiloran Trust Co Ltd and Vernon Aidan Ravenscroft, were assignees of the lease and entitled to the unexpired residue of its term as tenants. The facts are set out in the judgment.

Benjamin Levy for the landlords.
Paul de la Piquerie for the tenants.

WALTON J. The matter before me arises out of the impact of s 91A of the Housing Finance Act 1972, which was added by the Housing Act 1974, on a lease in a fairly standard form. The lease was made on 25th November 1965 between Campden House Chambers Ltd, as lessors, and George Maylam and Deborah Smith, as lessees. The reversion is now vested in the plaintiffs, Frobisher (Second Investments) Ltd ('the landlords'), and the lease is now vested in the defendants, Kiloran Trust Co Ltd and Vernon Aidan Ravenscroft ('the tenants').

The lease was a demise, in consideration of the payment of a premium, of a flat in a block of property described in the first schedule to the lease as Campden House, 29 Sheffield Terrace in the Royal Borough of Kensington. The lease is a long lease at a low rent, so that the provisions of the Rent Acts do not apply to it. By the fourth clause of the lease the lessors covenanted with the lessee 'from time to time and at all times during the said term to observe and perform each and every of the obligations on the lessors' part set out in the Seventh Schedule'. That is in substance the services to be provided by the lessors, which I will have to look at a little more closely in a moment. The lessees undertook to pay in respect of that 'the contribution', and we will see in a moment how 'the contribution' is in fact defined.

The schedule of matters which the landlords undertook to do were the kind of things that one frequently finds in a block of flats, e g to keep the reserved property in good order, repair and condition, to keep the property insured, to pay all premiums necessary for effecting and maintaining insurance, to apply all moneys received under insurance in respect of loss or damage in rebuilding and reinstating the property, to pay the charges incurred in the water rates on the whole of the property, electricity charges in connection with part of the property, the cost of maintaining and renting a public GPO telephone, and a clause to which I shall have to refer in more detail later but which for present purposes may be taken as requiring the landlords to pay the reasonable and proper fees payable by them to their managing agents for the time being for carrying out the general management and administration of the property. Then there was another clause concerning the cleaning and maintaining of part of the reserved property, the dustbins, paying the rent and performing the covenants in the head lease. Then there are two matters with which we are not concerned, employing and maintaining a porter, providing a supply of hot water, and repairing and keeping the lifts in running order.

One of the covenants on the part of the tenant contained in the sixth schedule is that the tenant will pay the rent and 'the contribution' and interim sums on the days and in the manner stipulated in the lease. That takes us on to the eighth schedule, which deals with 'the contribution', and 'the contribution' is a yearly sum equal to a percentage, which would vary from flat to flat, but which in the case of the flat with which we are concerned is 0·3%—

> 'of the amount which the [landlords] shall from time to time have expended
> during the year immediately preceding the date next hereunder mentioned in (a)
> meeting the outgoings costs expenses and liabilities incurred by them in carrying

out their obligations under the provisions of the Seventh Schedule hereto (except
paragraphs 6 and 7 thereof) and (b) in paying from time to time the costs and
expenses of and incidental to making repairing maintaining amending and
cleansing all or any ways roads pavements gutters sewers channels drains pipes
watercourses walls party walls party structures fences and other conveniences which
shall belong to or be used for the Premises in common with any other part or parts
of the Property or which shall form part of the Reserved Property such contribution
to be paid on the 25th day of March in every year The amount of such Contribution
shall be ascertained and certified by the [landlords'] Managing Agents acting as
experts and not as arbitrators once each year throughout the term on the 25th day
of March in each year (or if such ascertainment shall not take place on the said 25th
day of March then the said amount shall be ascertained as soon thereafter as may be
possible as though such amount had been ascertained on the aforesaid 25th day of
March) commencing on the 25th day of March 1964 and such certificate shall
contain full details and figures relating to all the component elements comprised
therein and a copy thereof shall be supplied to the [tenant] at the request of the
[tenant] and without charge to him (but not more frequently than once in every
yearly period. . .)'

Then it is provided:

'(1) That the [tenant] shall (if required by the [landlords]) Pay such a sum on
account of the Contribution payable by the [tenant] under this Schedule as the
[landlords'] Managing Agents shall certify as being a reasonable interim sum (in this
Lease referred to as "interim sum" or in the plural as "interim sums") to be paid on
account of the Contribution Such interim sums shall be paid (if required as
aforesaid) half yearly in advance on the 25th day of March and the 29th day of
September in every year commencing on the quarter day next following the date of
this Lease in respect of the period from the date hereof to the next following half
yearly day
'(2) That the Contribution payable by the [tenant] hereunder (or such balance as
shall remain after giving credit for any interim sum) shall be paid by the [tenant] or
any proper balance found to be repayable to the [tenant] shall be so repaid to him on
the 24th day of June next following the year ending on the 25th day of March to
which such contributions shall relate or as soon thereafter as may be possible [then
there is a proviso limiting the contribution for a comparatively short period from
the commencement of the lease]
'(3) That (without prejudice to any other remedy or right) the [landlords] shall
not be entitled to re-enter under the provisions in that behalf herein contained in
respect of non-payment only of any interim sum.'

So the general scheme is quite clear. Twice a year, on 25th March and 29th September,
the tenant is required to pay interim sums certified by the managing agents as being
reasonable. At the end of the year at the next 25th March or shortly thereafter there is
worked out what the contribution properly comes to. The sums which have been paid
on account are set against that, and then either the tenant has to pay the balance, if it is
a balance against him, or, if it is a balance in his favour, he receives the balance back.

There can, I think, be no doubt whatsoever, and it is not challenged in any way, that
the contribution proper is in fact a service charge. For present purposes, that is to say, for
the purposes of s 91A of the Housing Finance Act 1972, the expression 'service charge'
means—

'any charge for services, repairs, maintenance or insurance, being a charge which
is payable as part of, or in addition to, the rent, and which varies or may vary
according to any costs (including charges for overheads) incurred from time to time
by or on behalf of the landlord or any superior landlord.'

That is a definition to be found in s 90(12) of the Housing Finance Act 1972, and it applies to s 91A, because in sub-s (7) of s 91A there is to be found this definition: *a*

> 'In this section "chargeable items" means any items for which a service charge may be payable, and other expressions used in this section have the meanings assigned to them by section 90(12) above.'

The difficulty which is created by s 91A lies in this, that if one reads the opening words of s 91A it is I think abundantly clear that a service charge strictu sensu can only be   *b* recovered in respect of expenditure which has already been incurred or defrayed by the landlord and cannot be recovered in respect of prospective matters, however clear it is that those matters, when actually carried out, will be properly chargeable items and costs proper to be brought into account as part of the service charge.

That is because s 91A in its opening words, and I only intend to read the opening words because there are very grave difficulties thereafter, with which, fortunately, I am in no   *c* wise concerned in this case, begins as follows:

> '(1) A service charge shall only be recoverable from the tenant of a flat—(a) in respect of the provision of chargeable items to a reasonable standard; and (b) to the extent that the liability incurred or amount defrayed by the landlord in respect of the provision of such items is reasonable . . .'
>   *d*

Counsel for the tenants has argued that that result is brought about not only by the wording of s 91A(1)(b) but also by the wording of s 91A(1)(a):

> 'A service charge shall only be recoverable from the tenant of a flat—(a) in respect of the provision of chargeable items to a reasonable standard . . .'

But, in my judgment, he is putting too great a burden on that wording, and if that   *e* wording stood alone, there would be no reason to restrict the service charge that may be recovered to past items. But, however, when one gets to para (b), 'to the extent that the liability incurred or amount defrayed by the landlord in respect of the provision of such items is reasonable . . .' it appears to me perfectly clear that the landlord must have defrayed the cost, or at any rate incurred liability to pay the cost, before it can be recovered from the tenant.   *f*

Therefore, I am faced in this case with the simple point, simple, that is, to state, but difficult to solve, whether the interim sums are or are not properly to be designated as a service charge. In my judgment, they are to be so designated. It seems to me that the wording of the lease is too strong to enable me to do anything else, because the first proviso to the eighth schedule, which I have already read, provides that the interim sums are to be paid on account of the contribution or, spelling that out, the interim sums are   *g* sums paid on account of the service charge, and it appears to me that sums paid on account of the service charge are part of the service charge.

Counsel for the landlords has sought to argue that the interim sums are a kind of trust fund or moneys held by the landlords' managing agents as stakeholders, and that therefore they really have nothing to do with the service charge, save that when the contribution is ascertained and becomes payable, then the landlords' managing agents,   *h* on behalf of the tenants, are entitled to put those moneys towards the discharge of the contribution, and that is the first time that those moneys become part of or are used to discharge the service charge.

But that seems to me to ignore the realities of the matter. Clearly the interim sums are paid so as to enable the managing agents to have money in hand to discharge the costs of the landlords, which are properly recoverable by means of the contribution, as and   *j* when they arise without waiting for the contribution to be ascertained; and because that is so, it appears to me that the suggested analogies of the landlords' managing agents being stakeholders or alternatively trustees of the money just will not fit the circumstances of the case in any way at all. They are not stakeholders of the money, because stakeholders hold the money of third parties, to be applied in a particular way

when a particular event happens. But I cannot see that there is anything in the lease to
a prevent the landlords' managing agents from applying the moneys as they receive them
to whatever appropriate purpose they think fit. Indeed, we know that that is precisely
what happens, because in fact the managing agents maintain a separate service charge
bank account, and they maintain that to meet the day-to-day costs during the year.
Similarly it seems to me that there is no possibility here of treating the moneys as trust
moneys in any way. First of all, one does not import the question of trust into a matter
b of this nature, which is a purely commercial matter, unless one has to do so, but, even
more importantly, if those moneys were trust moneys to be applied in the way that has
been suggested, ie only at the end of the year in meeting the contribution, it seems to me
that it would be the duty of the managing agents to keep all those moneys together all
during the year until the specified event happened, and that that is not what is intended
is perfectly apparent.

c   So it seems to me that the provision for repayment if by any chance the interim sums
do exceed the contribution payable by the tenant is a matter which very sensibly rests
purely in contract as between the landlord and the tenant, and does not in any way rest
in trust or on some concept of the managing agents being stakeholders.

   I realise, of course, that that is a most unfortunate conclusion so far as the landlords are
concerned, but I have reached that conclusion on the argument which has been placed
d before me. Having reached that conclusion, I did not require counsel to address me on
it, but I am by no means certain that that is the only way of putting the matter against
the landlords. At the very lowest, the interim sums are some form of security for the fact
that the contribution will ultimately be paid; and the opening words of s 91A are that a
service charge shall only be recoverable from the tenant of a flat to the extent that the
liability incurred etc; and it seems to me that, even if one could, by some attribution of
e a label, call the interim sums something other than a 'service charge', the exemption of
the interim sums would still be a matter of recovering the service charge and thus
invalidated by the opening words of s 91A(1).

   This now leads me to the second point, which is this. Counsel for the landlords says:
'Well, if now it is impossible to recover the costs in advance in this way, this is going to
create very difficult problems for the landlords', and I should not like the landlords to
f think that I do not fully sympathise with the fact that that is precisely and exactly what
my decision will do. I can see their very great difficulties which will result. What
counsel for the landlords says is that it will mean that the landlords, or the landlords'
managing agents, will have to borrow moneys in order to carry out their obligations
under the lease, and he naturally wishes on behalf of the landlords to include the costs of
the borrowed money, that is to say, the interest which will be payable on it, in the
g matters which can be recovered from the tenants.

   The only clause in the lease, I think it is fair to say, to which he can really point as
providing any ground for such a submission is to be found in cl 3(iv) of the seventh
schedule. Of course, if it is in cl 3(iv) of the seventh schedule, then it will be one of the
matters which the tenant will have to reimburse pursuant to the provisions of the eighth
schedule. But I must now read cl 3(iv) in detail:

h

   'The reasonable and proper fees payable by the [landlords] to its Managing Agents
   for the time being for carrying out the general management and administration of
   the Property including (but without prejudice to the generality of the foregoing) all
   fees payable to such Agents in connection with the collection of the rents the
   Contribution and the interim sums payable by the respective owners of the Flats
j the payment of the rent under the Head Lease and other outgoings payable by the
   [landlords] in respect of the Property or any part thereof and the preparation of all
   accounts in connection with the calculation and assessment of the Contribution and
   interim sums and arrangements for the supervision of any works which may be
   carried out pursuant to paragraph 1 of this Schedule and (if undertaken by such
   Agents) preparation of Specifications in connection therewith.'

I am afraid that at the end of the day I cannot find in there any real reference of any description to 'interest'. It seems to me that what that clause is dealing with are the fees *a* payable to the managing agents. They are fees payable for carrying out the general management and administration of the property. Then the clause goes on to specify, without prejudice to the generality of that phrase, various matters: fees payable to the agents in connection with the collection of the rents, fees payable to the agents in connection with the collection of the contribution, fees payable to the agents in connection with the collection of the interim sums, fees payable to the agents in *b* connection with the payment of the rent under the head lease, fees payable to the agents in connection with the payment of other bills payable by the landlords in respect of the property or any part thereof, fees payable to the agents in respect of the preparation of accounts and in connection with the calculation and assessment of the contribution and interim sums and fees payable to the agents in respect of the arrangements for the supervision of any works and preparation of specifications. It does not seem to me that *c* one can fairly say that in that wording there is any general phrase which one could fairly read as including interest payments of the general nature with which we are dealing.

Moreover, it would be very surprising indeed if one could, and for this reason: it may very well be that the present landlords are impecunious landlords, I know not, but the landlords might, far from being impecunious, have very large sums of money under their control, in which case they would not need to borrow any other money at all; and *d* if that were the situation and interest was going to be charged, one would have expected to find a clause specifically dealing with it and mentioning the interest on sums expended, or words to that effect, somewhere in the lease, and one does not, unfortunately, find any such words.

Counsel for the landlords then says: 'Well, be that so, it must be implied as a matter of necessary implication in this lease following the doctrine of *The Moorcock*[1] that if the *e* statute were to render the payment of the service charge in advance unlawful, the tenant would immediately start paying interest on moneys expended in the manner in which it will now become necessary for the landlords to incur that interest.'

While the doctrine of *The Moorcock*[1] is a very useful doctrine indeed, and I would be the last person to refuse to apply it if I thought it could be properly applied, counsel for the tenants says that, so far from a tenant saying 'Of course that must be the case', if he *f* was asked at the commencement of the lease 'Supposing a statute intervened to make your payments in advance unlawful, I assume that you will be quite willing to pay interest on the moneys that the landlords have to borrow?', so far from saying 'Of course', the tenant might very well reply 'Well, I don't know about that. I shall want to know a very great deal more about the whole matter. I am not sure I am going to agree to that'.

Whether that be so or not, I do not think that in fact one can apply the doctrine of *The* *g* *Moorcock*[1], because I know of no case, and counsel for the landlords has been unable to cite any case to me, in which the doctrine of *The Moorcock*[1] has been applied when there has been a disturbance to contractual arrangements as the result of a statute. It seems to me that, if there is a disturbance of contractual relationships because a statute intervenes, then it must be left to the statute to say what is to happen consequentially on its intervention, and that one cannot foist on the parties what some outside body thinks *h* would have been what they would have agreed to in circumstances which neither of them can possibly have contemplated under any circumstances. Indeed, if I am right on the construction that I have given to s 91A (and I say 'if I am right', because, unfortunately, this appears to be the first case on that section, and it is likely, I imagine, to go to a higher court), the legislature has set its face against the tenant paying in advance for anything except liabilities actually incurred by the landlord; and in order to imply a clause taking *j* the fullest possible advantage of that fact, which could undoubtedly be done in future leases, one would have to reconstruct the whole system of liability completely; and it

---

1   (1889) 14 PD 64, [1886–90] All ER Rep 530

seems to me that it is not a proper use of *The Moorcock*[1] to imply a term reconstructing
a the position as between the landlord and tenant only partially.

Therefore, for those reasons, I feel unable to accept counsel's submissions for the
landlord on *The Moorcock*[1] on that point of principle. Moreover, although I do not,
having done that, need to decide it, I feel at any rate a lurking suspicion that if the tenant
had been asked 'What are the parties going to do if statute intervenes to frustrate any part
of your bargain?', he would have said 'Well, that must be left to statute. I am not going
b to agree to any particular term in advance', because it must be recalled that implied terms
do not, as it were, get written into the contract as one goes along. One goes back to the
inception of the contract and asks the question then and says 'Is that the term to which
both of you would agree if asked by the officious bystander?' It seems to me that it must
at the very least be dubious whether the tenant would not have said 'Well, if statute
intervenes, I shall have to read the statute and see what it says. I am not going to agree
c in advance what is going to happen'.

Counsel for the landlords pressed me on this aspect of the case very much with the
decision in *Finchbourne Ltd v Rodrigues*[2], where the Court of Appeal had no hesitation in
implying a term that various matters should be carried out fairly and reasonably in a
lease and that maintenance of the property should not be left to the landlords' discretion
to adopt the highest conceivable standard of maintenance for the block of flats and to
d charge the tenant with that cost. It seems to me that that case, as it were, speaks for
itself. Obviously, in order to give business efficacy to a block of flats leased in the Mile
End Road, one assumes a Mile End Road standard of maintenance, just as if the flats were
in Park Lane one would assume a Park Lane standard of maintenance. It seems to me
that the readiness of the Court of Appeal to adopt, as it were, the current standard for the
block of flats in that particular case does not in any way assist me in this matter at all.

e Therefore, at the end of the day, for those reasons, I have come to the conclusion that
the interim payments for which provision is made in the proviso to the eighth schedule
to the lease are charges to which s 91A of the Housing Finance Act 1972 applies, and I
have come to the conclusion that the landlords are not entitled to require the said, or any,
interim payments to be made in advance on account of estimated or proposed
expenditure to be incurred for the purposes referred to in the seventh schedule to the
f lease, or for any of such purposes, before such expediture has been incurred; and also I
have come to the conclusion that the landlords are not entitled to recover from the
tenants the appropriate proportion of the cost of borrowing in the financial market the
moneys required to make the expenditure referred to in the seventh and eighth schedules
until such time as the payments referred to in the eighth schedule are made to the
landlords, nor would that in the slightest be changed if, instead of the landlords incurring
g the interest charges, those charges were incurred by the managing agents themselves.

Declarations accordingly.

Solicitors: *Lieberman Leigh & Co* (for the landlords); *Thwaytes* (for the tenants).

h   Jacqueline Metcalfe Barrister.

---

1   (1889) 14 PD 64, [1886–90] All ER Rep 530
2   [1976] 3 All ER 581

Practice Direction

FAMILY DIVISION

Practice – Family Division – Counsel's fees – Interlocutory fees – Scale of fees to be allowed on taxation.

The Senior Registrar of the Family Division, in consultation with the Senate of the Inns of Court and the Bar, has decided that the scale of fees set out hereafter would be proper to be allowed on taxation in respect of instructions and briefs delivered on or after 1st February 1980.

It is emphasised that the list is intended only to be a guide as to the broad range of fees applicable to the average 'weight' of each item of work, and higher or lower fees may be allowed in appropriate cases.

The items in the list are those most frequently found in the most common kind of case, but the list itself is not exhaustive. For example, it will be observed that brief fees relating to contested suits or to ancillary relief have not been dealt with, since it is considered that conditions vary too much for them to be included in a scale.

The Senior Registrar confirms his predecessor's view that, when, in circumstances which merit it, counsel gives an oral opinion in the course of a conference, his fee therefor may be substituted for the routine conference fee. The taxing officer will require to be satisfied that it was appropriate to have dealt with the matter orally. It should not be assumed that, as a matter of course, the fee given for such an oral opinion will be the same fee as for one in writing.

Answer (plain denial)	£8
Answer (with no cross-charge)	£15
Answer (with cross-charge)	£25–£35
Request for particulars	£10
Particulars	£10–£40
Reply (plain denial)	£8
Reply (other than a plain denial)	£15–£25
Advice on evidence	£15–£50
Opinion (comprehensive)	£25–£50
Opinion (limited)	£15–£25
Notice of appeal or counter-notice	£20–£30
*Affidavit (main)	£20–£50
*Affidavit (minor supporting)	£8–£15
Brief – registrar (procedural)	£25–£35
Brief – judge (ex parte injunction)	£25–£35
Brief – judge (injunction)	£30–£100
Brief – judge (uncontested application in chambers)	£30
Consultation (Queen's Counsel)	£20 first half hour
	£15 thereafter
Conference (junior counsel)	£10 first half hour
	£8 thereafter

*If drafted with other affidavits an omnibus fee may be allowed.

1st February 1980

R L BAYNE-POWELL
Senior Registrar.

Khan v Khan

FAMILY DIVISION
SIR JOHN ARNOLD P AND WATERHOUSE J
16th OCTOBER 1979

*Husband and wife – Summary proceedings – Maintenance order – Order for limited period –
Whether court having power to make order limited in time – Matrimonial Proceedings
(Magistrates' Courts) Act 1960, s 2(1)(b).*

The power of a magistrates' court under s 2(1)(b)[a] of the Matrimonial Proceedings
(Magistrates' Courts) Act 1960 to make an order containing a provision that the husband
pay to the wife 'such weekly sum as the court considers reasonable in all the circumstances
of the case' entitles the court to qualify the duration of the order, as well as the amount
payable. Accordingly, an order under s 2(1)(b) may be limited in time (see p 500 *a b* and
g h, post).

Dictum of Sir George Baker P in *Chesworth v Chesworth* (1973) 118 Sol Jo 183 approved.
Per Sir John Arnold P. It is not inconsistent with s 2(1)(b) of the 1960 Act to make the
weekly payments variable in relation to successive periods (see p 500 *h j*, post).

Notes

For matrimonial orders made by a magistrates' court, see 13 Halsbury's Laws (4th Edn)
para 1288.

For the Matrimonial Proceedings (Magistrates' Courts) Act 1960, s 2, see 17 Halsbury's
Statutes (3rd Edn) 246.

Cases referred to in judgments

Chesworth v Chesworth (1973) 118 Sol Jo 183, DC, Digest (Cont Vol D) 438, 8051a.
Graves v Graves (1973) 117 Sol Jo 679, DC.

Appeal

This was an appeal by the husband, Mohammed Sajid Khan, against an order made on
27th March 1979 by the stipendiary magistrate at Birmingham Magistrates' Court,
whereby it was found that the husband deserted the wife, Fazeelath Sajid Khan, on 15th
February 1978 and it was directed that the husband should pay the wife £18 per week.
The appeal proceeded against the quantum of the order only. The facts are set out in the
judgment of Waterhouse J.

Eleanor Platt for the husband.
John Freeman for the wife.

WATERHOUSE J delivered the first judgment at the invitation of Sir John Arnold P.
This is an appeal from a decision made by the stipendiary magistrate at Birmingham
Magistrates' Court on 27th March 1979. He had before him complaints by a wife of
desertion by her husband from 15th February 1978, and of wilful neglect to maintain
her from 2nd May 1978. The learned magistrate found both the complaints proved.
There is no child of the marriage and, accordingly, his order was limited to maintenance
of the wife, which he assessed at £18 per week. I should interpolate that, since the order,
the husband has paid an average of about £6 per week, pending the outcome of the
present appeal.

---

a   Section 2(1), so far as material, is set out at p 500 *b*, post

The notice of appeal includes grounds of appeal directed to the magistrate's findings on both complaints, and an appeal on quantum in relation to the maintenance order itself. Counsel for the husband has now said that he wishes to proceed only with the appeal on quantum, and it is on that footing that I will deal with the matter.

The marriage was short lived. Both parties are Moslems and were natives of India, although the wife came to England at a young age. She was only about 17 years old when she married and her husband was in his late twenties. The marriage took place on 14th May 1977 and the final separation occurred only nine months later, on 15th February 1978. After the parting, the wife went to live with her own parents and the husband went to live with his sister. It is perhaps material to mention that the magistrate, in setting out the reasons for his decision, gave some account of the married life in which he said that the wife not only had no home of her own during the marriage, because they were living with the husband's sister, but had no allowance from him and no money of her own. She told the court that no attempt was made to provide her with a home of her own. The wife's father said that he had agreed to provide £1,000 towards a house, of which he had paid £500. The husband said that they looked at flats and houses but the magistrate was satisfied that no serious attempt had been made to find independent accommodation.

The finding of the magistrate in relation to the charge of desertion was that the husband constructively deserted his wife in February 1978. The basic facts were that the wife's father, who was a building contractor in Birmingham, went to Croydon and had a long interview with the husband. The latter said that he would not have his wife back if she attended a marriage ceremony that she wished to attend. The husband said to the father that, if the wife went to the wedding, she was not to come back, and in front of the wife herself said: 'I am telling you in front of your father, you are not to come back again.' It was in those circumstances that the father took his daughter back to Birmingham, where she has lived ever since; and the magistrate went on to find that there was no genuine offer by the husband to return.

At the stage when the matter came before the magistrate, the wife had received no maintenance in the intervening period, and the magistrate said that the wife had suffered humiliation in her married life: no house or income had been supplied, and she had been told to go.

In the course of the hearing, the evidence was mainly directed to the circumstances in which the parting had occurred, and the events that followed. The evidence about the means of the parties and the potential income of the wife was brief. The magistrate took the view that it was a straightforward case where there should be an order for maintenance. The evidence before him indicated that the husband's income was £2,580 net per annum, and, grossed up, that would produce a figure between £3,300 and £3,500. With the consent of the wife, there has been produced to us in court today the P 60 certificate of income tax deducted for the year to April 1979, which indicates that the husband's gross income was £3,844, subject to a deduction of £250 in respect of national insurance and no doubt some further small deductions appropriate to cover the travelling expenses incurred by the husband in earning his income. He is employed, and has at all material times been employed, by the Commonwealth Secretariat.

The wife's position was that she had never worked; in cross-examination she said that she learned housework at school and that she took CSE's but had no time to take 'O' levels. She had been to a college after school until her marriage. She said also that it was her idea to go to college during the marriage, and she did start in September 1977, but she only went to two classes because a quarrel with her husband caused her to discontinue the course. She said that she would have liked to go on and pass 'O' levels, but she told the magistrate that she was taking a correspondence course because she could not get into college; and this court has been told that she has continued with that correspondence course since the magistrates' court hearing. There was very little evidence, therefore, before the magistrate as to the real potential of the wife and her earning capacity. The husband himself concentrated in his evidence on the details of the

history of the marriage, and did not supply any additional information about his wife's
a capacity, or indeed about Moslem practice in relation to employment. It has been urged
on behalf of the wife throughout that it is not Moslem practice for a married woman to
go out to earn an income, and the court has been invited to take judicial notice of this
practice, on the assumption that it continues to apply to parties who are separated.

For my part, I am quite unable to accept the argument that one should take judicial
notice of the Moslem practice in this regard. It is plainly a matter about which there
b should be evidence, if it is to be relied on as a relevant factor.

Thus, the position in this case was that the wife had been deserted in February 1978
and by the time the matter came before the magistrate she had been deserted for a period
of 15 months. She had had the advantage of living with her parents during that period,
and it is clearly a case in which consideration had to be given to her earning capacity in
the future. The general principle applicable to a case of this kind was stated in *Graves v*
c *Graves*[1]. In that case, the parting had occurred only about 12 months after the marriage;
there was no child; and both parties were in their early twenties. Ormrod J said[1] that the
appeal emphasised the difference between the approach of justices and that of the judges
of the Family Division when considering financial matters in similar circumstances:

d 'Where a marriage was of short duration and the parties were young a nominal
order was the appropriate order unless there were children or the wife was
handicapped in some way which prevented her from working. At the time of the
hearing before the justices the wife was not working, but she was a state enrolled
nurse and the justices should have taken into account her potential earning
capacity. The wife was now employed fulltime in a hospital.'

e

The present case is, of course, plainly distinguishable from *Graves v Graves*[1] because
there the young wife had a profession, and indeed, by the time of the hearing of the
appeal to the Divisional Court, she had been able to resume that profession. The present
wife is in receipt of social security benefits totalling £13·90 per week, but she has no
additional income, and there was no evidence before the magistrate that she was, as yet,
f in a position to earn her living outside her parents' home. One would infer, however,
from the fact that she was living with her parents that she must have been providing
some services in the home in return for the board and lodging afforded to her by them.

On behalf of the husband, it has been urged by counsel that the approach of the
magistrate should have been that the wife was capable of earning an income in the near
future, and that the order should have catered for that finding of fact. Counsel for the
g husband suggests that either the order should have been for a limited period in order to
encourage the wife to train herself for employment at an early date or that it should have
been assessed at such a modest level that there would be active encouragement to the
wife to find employment at the earliest opportunity.

The jurisdiction of the court to make an order for a limited term has been stated in
Chesworth v Chesworth[2]. The dicta in that case were obiter because the court, comprising
h Sir George Baker P and Dunn J, was dealing with an offer of maintenance for a limited
period; but Sir George Baker P said that[2]—

'it was accepted by the wife's counsel that only a nominal order was appropriate.
The husband was willing to pay £3·50 a week to the wife for a limited period of
j

---

1   (1973) 117 Sol Jo 679
2   (1973) 118 Sol Jo 183

nine months while she reorganised her life. Doubts had been expressed whether justices had power to make such an order limited in time. Justices had power to *a* make orders unlimited in time, and it was commonsense to make limited orders as well.'

I respectfully agree with what was said by Sir George Baker P in that case. Section 2(1) of the Matrimonial Proceedings (Magistrates' Courts) Act 1960 provides that the court *b* may make a matrimonial order containing any one or more of the following provisions, namely, '(b) a provision that the husband shall pay to the wife such weekly sum as the court considers reasonable in all the circumstances of the case'. In the absence of any express fetter, it seems abundantly clear that the order may be either unlimited in time or limited in time; and there is no such fetter in the statute.

Looking at the whole of the facts of this case, and the rather limited evidence about the parties' finances that was before the learned stipendiary magistrate, I consider that it is a *c* case in which it is right for a time limit to be placed on the order for maintenance. The amount of £18 per week was assessed at a level rather less than one-third of the joint incomes, and provides adequately for the wife in her particular circumstances whilst she is seeking to train herself and obtain satisfactory employment. However, a substantial period has now elapsed since the desertion occurred in February 1978. For my part, I think that, if the order of the magistrate had been limited to a period of 12 months from *d* the date thereof, that would have provided satisfactory maintenance for the wife for an adequate period, that is, just over two years from the date of the desertion, and that any maintenance thereafter should be at a reduced rate.

I consider, therefore, that this is a case in which the appeal should be allowed to the extent of inserting in the magistrates' court order a time limit of 12 months, so that the maintenance at the rate of £18 a week will terminate at the end of March 1980. The *e* position thereafter requires separate consideration; it is right that there should continue to be some small maintenance for the wife but it should be assessed on an entirely different basis. Having regard to the whole of the history and the obligations and means of the parties, I would propose that from 27th March 1980 the rate of maintenance should be £5 per week.

f

SIR JOHN ARNOLD P. I agree. I would like just to add a word in relation to the matter which was considered in *Chesworth v Chesworth*[1] to which Waterhouse J has referred. The provision in the Matrimonial Proceedings (Magistrates' Courts) Act 1960 *g* is a provision that the husband shall pay to the wife 'such weekly sum as the court considers reasonable in all the circumstances of the case'. In my view, the word 'such' is not limited to defining the amount of the weekly sum but carries with it an ability to qualify that sum in every relevant respect, in terms of duration in particular so far as this case is concerned, as well as amount. Nor does there seem to me to be anything inconsistent with that provision in making the weekly payments of a variable nature, in *h* relation to successive periods. The order which we make in the terms suggested by Waterhouse J is, of course, in line with what we regard as reasonable and expectable in the present circumstances. If we are wrong, and there is a really valid reason why, at the end of the 12-month period, the wife is not able to earn an adequate living, then she can deploy those matters on an application to vary before the magistrate; and equally, if the basis on which the continuing payment of £5 a week is ordered, namely that expectably *j* the wife will at any rate for some little time to come be earning less than she might otherwise have earned if she had been more experienced and therefore some small

___

1　(1973) 118 Sol Jo 183

subsidy would be appropriate, turns out to be a pessimistic point of view, then equally
a the husband can apply for an appropriate variation.

Accordingly, the appeal will be allowed to the extent indicated.

Appeal allowed.

Solicitors: *Stocken & Co* (for the husband); *Evershed & Tomkinson*, Birmingham (for the
b wife).

Georgina Chambers   Barrister.

c

M Golodetz & Co Inc v Czarnikow-Rionda Co Inc

The Galatia
d
COURT OF APPEAL, CIVIL DIVISION
MEGAW, SHAW AND WALLER LJJ
31st OCTOBER, 1st NOVEMBER 1979

Sale of goods – C and f contract – Bill of lading – Payment to be made against clean bill of lading
e *– Bill of lading stating that goods shipped in apparent good order and condition – Bill also stating*
that goods subsequently discharged on account of fire damage – Bill tendered to buyers – Bill
rejected by buyers on ground that it was not a clean bill of lading – Whether bill 'clean' – Whether
buyers entitled to reject bill.

The sellers contracted to sell to the buyers 12,000 to 13,200 tonnes of sugar c and f
f Bandarshapur, Iran. The contract provided, inter alia, that payment was to be made
against a complete set of signed clean 'on board' bills of lading evidencing that freight
had been paid. After part of the consignment of sugar had been loaded, a fire broke out
on the ship, as a result of which 200 tonnes of sugar were damaged and had to be
discharged. The remainder of the consignment was loaded and carried to its
destination. The sellers tendered two bills of lading to the buyers. The first was in
g respect of the 200 tonnes of sugar which had been lost and the second was in respect of
the balance of the consignment. The first bill in its printed clauses acknowledged
shipment of the goods in apparent good order and condition. In addition it bore a
typewritten note stating that the cargo covered by the bill had been discharged because
it had been damaged by fire and/or water. The second bill was taken up and paid for by
the buyers but the first bill was rejected by them on the ground that it was not a 'clean'
h bill of lading. The sellers claimed that the typewritten note did not prevent it being a
clean bill of lading and that they were entitled to be paid the price of the 200 tonnes of
sugar which had been lost.

Held – The bill of lading was 'clean' and the buyers should have accepted it, because (i)
there was nothing in it to qualify the admission that at the time of shipment the goods
j were in apparent good order and condition, and (ii) there was no evidence that it was not
a document which would ordinarily and properly have been accepted in the trade as
being an appropriate document. Accordingly the sellers were entitled to be paid the
price of the 200 tonnes of sugar which had been lost (see p 506 *b* and *e* to p 507 *a* and *g h*,
post). *Hansson v Hamel & Horley Ltd* [1922] All ER Rep 237 applied.

Decision of Donaldson J [1979] 2 All ER 726 affirmed.

Notes

For the tender of documents and the requirements that the bill of lading must be clean,   *a*
see 3 Halsbury's Laws (4th Edn) paras 141–142, and for cases on the subject, see 39 Digest
(Repl) 704–711, 1949–1985.

Case referred to in judgments

Hansson v Hamel & Horley Ltd [1922] AC 36, [1922] All ER Rep 237, 91 LJKB 433, 127 LT
74, 15 Asp MLC 546, 27 Com Cas 321, 10 Ll L Rep 199, 507, HL, 39 Digest (Repl) 706,   *b*
1956.

Cases also cited

Biddell Brothers v E Clemens Horst Co [1911] 1 KB 214.
British Imex Industries Ltd v Midland Bank Ltd [1958] 1 All ER 264, [1958] 1 QB 542.
Horn v Minister of Food [1948] 2 All ER 1036.   *c*
Munro Brice & Co v War Risks Association Ltd [1918] 2 KB 78, [1916–17] All ER Rep 981.
Rugg v Minett (1809) 11 East 210, 103 ER 985.
Spillers Ltd v J W Mitchell Ltd (1929) 33 Ll L Rep 89.

Appeal

By a written contract, dated 26th February 1975, M Golodetz & Co Inc ('the sellers') sold   *d*
a quantity of sugar to Czarnikow-Rionda Co Inc ('the buyers'). The contract incorporated
the rules of the Refined Sugar Association, including the rules relating to arbitration and
the rules relating to contracts. Disputes arose between the parties and in accordance with
the contract they were referred to a panel of arbitrators appointed by the Council of the
Refined Sugar Association. The matters referred to arbitration were (i) a claim by the
sellers for $US180,720 representing the price of 2,008 bags of sugar or alternatively   *e*
damages of the same amount in respect of the buyers' alleged failure to accept such goods
or to take up and pay for the shipping documents in respect thereof, (ii) a counterclaim
by the buyers for $US3,012 as damages in respect of the sellers' alleged failure to present
documents to the buyers in respect of the 2,008 bags of sugar in conformity with the
provisions of the contract, (iii) a claim by the sellers (in the event that the claim in matter
(i) did not succeed) for damages in respect of the buyers' alleged failure to comply with   *f*
the provisions of the contract as to insurance. The parties asked the arbitrators to make
an interim award ('the first award') in the form of a special case. The first award, dated
14th February 1977, set out in para A the facts found by the arbitrators, and in para B the
questions of law for the decision of the court, which were:

'On the facts found and on the true construction of the contract (1) Whether the   *g*
Sellers are entitled to the price of the 2,008 bags of sugar alternatively to damages for
the [buyers'] failure to accept the same or to take up and pay for the shipping
documents in respect thereof. If the answer to (1) be "No", (2) Whether the Buyers
are entitled to any, and if so what, damages against the Sellers for the [the sellers']
failure to make a contractual presentation of documents in respect of the 2,008 bags
of sugar?'   *h*

Paragraph C was in the following terms:

'1. Subject to the decision of the Court on the question of law set out above WE
FIND AND HOLD:—(a) Under the said contract between [the sellers] and [the buyers]
Bills of Lading presented for payment were required to be clean "On board" Bills of
Lading evidencing freight having been paid. (b) The Bills of Lading presented by   *j*
[the sellers] in respect of the said 2,008 bags of sugar were Bills of Lading evidencing
freight having been paid. (c) The said Bills of Lading were not clean "On Board"
Bills of Lading within the meaning of the said contract by reason of the notation
referred to in paragraph A.8 hereof. (d) [The buyers] were entitled to reject the
documents in respect of the said 2,008 bags on the ground that the Bills of Lading

were not clean "On Board" Bills of Lading. (e) [The buyers] are now estopped or

a precluded from contending that the said documents were capable of rejection on
any other ground except that mentioned in (d) above. (f) [The sellers] are not
entitled to the price of the said 2,008 bags of sugar or to damages for [the buyers']
failure to accept the same or to take up and pay for the shipping documents in
respect thereof. (g) [The sellers] were not under any obligation to tender documents
in respect of any quantity in excess of the said 12,999·20 metric tons and [the

b buyers] are not entitled to damages in respect of [the sellers] failure to deliver more
than that quantity or in respect of their failure to tender a clean "On Board" Bill of
Lading in respect of the said 2,008 bags.

'2. Accordingly WE AWARD AND ADJUDGE that the claim by [the sellers] and the
counterclaim by [the buyers] hereof both fail.

c [Paragraph 3 made provision for the costs of the reference up to the date of the award.]

'4. If, however, the Court should answer the question of law in paragraph B(1)
hereof in the affirmative WE AWARD AND ADJUDGE that [the buyers] shall forthwith
pay to [the sellers] the sum of U.S.$ 180,720 together with interest at the rate of 6
per cent from 21st April 1975 to the date hereof . . .

'5. If the Court should answer the question of law in paragraph B(2) hereof in a

d manner different from that mentioned in paragraph C.1(g) above we respectfully
request that the Court remit the award to us under Section 22 of the Arbitration Act
1950, with the appropriate directions.

'6. AND FINALLY WE AWARD AND DIRECT that if this case shall not have been set
down for hearing within six weeks of the date of publication (or within such further
time as the Court may order) then our Award in paragraphs C.2 and C.3 hereof shall

e be and become our final Award in relation to the said claim and counterclaim.'

On 30th March 1977 the arbitrators dealt with the sellers' claim in respect of the
buyers' alleged failure to insure the goods. At the request of the buyers the arbitrators,
on 9th September 1977, stated their second award in the form of a special case.

f Paragraphs 1 to 3 thereof set out the nature of the dispute, the contentions of the parties,
the findings of fact and the arbitrators' holdings (subject to the opinion of the court on
the questions of law stated in para 4). Paragraphs 4 to 8 were in the following terms:

'4. The questions of law for the decision of the Court are: Whether on the facts
found and on the true construction of the contract between the parties:—(1) The

g buyers have fulfilled their obligations to effect insurance cover and if not (2)
Whether the sellers are entitled to any, and if so what, damages for the buyers'
breach of contract.

'5. Subject to the decision of the Court on the questions of law set out above WE
FIND AND HOLD:—(1) That [the buyers] failed to comply with their obligations in

h relation to the insurance of the said 2,008 bags. (2) That [the sellers] have not
suffered any loss by reason of such failure because any claim against the insurers
would, on balance of probabilities, have failed for the reason given in paragraph
3(28) hereof.

6. Accordingly WE AWARD AND ADJUDGE that the claim by [the sellers] which is the
subject of this Award fails.

j [Paragraph 7 made provision for the costs of the reference from the date of the
first award up to the date of the second award.]

'8. AND FINALLY WE AWARD AND DIRECT that, if this case shall not have been set
down for hearing within 6 weeks of the date of publication or within such further
time as the Court may order, then our Award in paragraph 6 shall be and become
our Final Award in relation to the said claim by [the sellers].'

On 16th March and 7th October 1977 the special cases were set down for hearing by the High Court for the determination of the question raised in para B of the first award *a* and para 4 of the second award. In relation to the first award Donaldson J[1] held on 20th November 1978 (i) that the first question of law in para B should be answered in the affirmative, (ii) that the award contained in para C2 should be set aside and (iii) that the alternative award contained in para C4 should be upheld. In relation to the second award Donaldson J[1] held on 20th November that his decision in relation to the first award rendered it unnecessary for him to decide the questions of law stated in para 4 but that *b* he would have answered question (i) in the negative and held that the sellers were entitled to recover an amount equal to the price as damages for the buyers' failure to insure the goods. The buyers appealed against his decision. The facts are set out in the judgment of Megaw LJ.

Gordon Pollock QC and *Christopher C Russell* for the buyers.   *c*
Kenneth Rokison QC and *Martin Moore-Bick* for the sellers.

MEGAW LJ. This is an appeal from the judgment of Donaldson J[1] delivered on 20th November 1978, wherein he gave his decisions on two awards, each in the form of a special case stated by the Council of the Refined Sugar Association to whose arbitration disputes had been referred by the parties to a contract. That contract was dated 26th *d* February 1975 and by its express terms that contract was made subject to the rules of that association. The parties were, respectively, the sellers under the contract in question, M Golodetz & Co Inc of New York, and the buyers under the contract, Czarnikow-Rionda Co Inc of New York. The two awards were dated respectively 14th February 1977 and 9th September 1977. The arbitral tribunal, members of the Council of the Refined Sugar Association (I shall call them 'the arbitrators'), decided in favour of the *e* buyers in both awards. The learned judge, on the cases stated, decided both in favour of the sellers. As requested by the parties, he heard the arguments on the two special cases together and gave one single judgment, although separate formal orders were made. That was a proper and sensible procedure. The first of the two awards was expressed to be an interim award and the second of them a supplementary award.

It is not necessary for me to go in any detail into the facts. The full text of the two *f* awards, as well as the judgment of Donaldson J, will be found reported in the All England Law Reports[1]. Reference may be made to that report by anyone who should be interested in further details of the facts or the terms of the awards or of the judgment. On the view that I take of this appeal, no important question of principle falls to be decided. The decision is one which depends on special and unusual facts.

A number of the contentions which were raised before the learned judge have not *g* been renewed in argument in this court, I have no doubt for good and sufficient reason.

The contract was for the sale of 12,000–13,000 tonnes of sugar on c and f terms to Bandarshapur in Iran. Although the contract did not so specify, shipment took place from an Indian port, Kandla. Payment under the contract was to be made cash against documents on first presentation in New York. The shipment period was March/April 1975. The contract provided that its terms and conditions were to be in accordance with *h* the rules of the Refined Sugar Association. The relevant parts of the relevant rules, rr 22 and 23, headed respectively 'Insurance' and 'Payment', are set out in the judgment appealed from[2]. Rule 23 included provision that, in respect of a c and f contract, payment was to be 'against a complete set . . . of signed clean "On Board" Bills of Lading evidencing freight having been paid . . .'

j

---

1   [1979] 2 All ER 726
2   [1979] 2 All ER 726 at 735–736

It was arranged by or on behalf of the sellers that the sugar would be carried in a vessel,
a the Galatia. She arrived at Kandla on 20th March 1975. On 24th March, by which time
part of the sugar had been loaded, a fire broke out on board and 2,008 bags, that is, 200·8
tonnes of sugar, were damaged by fire and water. The sugar was discharged. It could not
be made suitable for reloading. The rest of the cargo, which totalled 12,999·2 tonnes,
was safely loaded and was carried to Bandarshapur in the Galatia.

The intention had been, apparently, that there should be one single set of three bills of
b lading, but, following the fire, two separate sets of bills of lading were prepared and
signed on behalf of the shipowners and made available to the sellers. (For simplicity, I
shall refer to the set of three bills of lading as a bill of lading.) One of the bills of lading
was for 12,999·2 tonnes. No question arises about it or about that part of the contract
goods. The other bill of lading was for 200·8 tonnes.

There were in the course of the arbitration various other complaints about that bill of
c lading. One by one they have dropped away. But the complaint which was the original
complaint, when the bills of lading were first tendered by the sellers to the buyers and
when the 200 tonnes bill of lading was rejected, still remains. That complaint relates to
the fact that, on the face of the bill of lading, presumably before the signature was put on
the bill, there was put on it a typewritten notation, which was in these terms: 'Cargo
covered by this Bill of Lading has been discharged Kandla view damaged by fire and/or
d water used to extinguish fire for which general average declared.' That notation
accurately stated the facts. It was contended on behalf of the buyers, in rejecting that bill
of lading, that it was not a 'clean' bill of lading. I do not find it necessary to refer to the
precise terms of the various ways in which it was expressed in the correspondence which
passed between the parties at the time of the rejection.

The issue in the first arbitration was, and the first issue before us is, whether the buyers
e were entitled to reject that bill of lading. The award made by the arbitrators reads:
'(c) The said Bills of Lading were not clean "On Board" Bills of Lading within the
meaning of the said contract by reason of the notation referred to in paragraph A.8
hereof'. (That is, the notation above set out.)

The relevant question of law which was stated for the decision of the court in that
award is:

f
> 'On the facts found and on the true construction of the contract (1) Whether the
> Sellers are entitled to the price of the 2,008 bags of sugar alternatively to damages for
> the [buyers'] failure to accept the same or to take up and pay for the shipping
> documents in respect thereof.'

A further question was stated, which does not now call for an answer.
g The learned judge held that the correct answer to the question was in the affirmative.
This is because, in the learned judge's view, the bill of lading was a clean bill of lading and
the buyers should have accepted it and paid the price.

I think that, without disrespect to the very interesting and careful arguments which
have been put before us by counsel on that issue, I can deal with them quite shortly.

The learned judge was asked, on behalf of the buyers, to uphold the arbitrators' view
h of the matter on a large number of grounds. The first ground was that the bill of lading
was not 'clean' and that, therefore, it did not comply with the provisions of the contract
for a clean 'On Board' bill of lading; and that, indeed, was what the arbitrators appear to
have held in their award. The learned judge, having gone into the authorities, arrived
at the conclusion that a clean bill of lading is one in which there is nothing to qualify the
admission that the goods were in apparent good order and condition at the time of
j shipment.

Counsel for the buyers accepted in this court that the meaning of 'clean', in respect of
'clean bill of lading', was, indeed, as he put it, the correct meaning of the word 'clean'.
There is also authority to that effect. But, said counsel, although that is the correct
meaning of 'clean', it has another, wider, meaning in which it can be used: namely, that
a bill of lading is not 'clean' if it contains a clause the effect of which is to make the bill

of lading unacceptable or unmerchantable, so that it would not be accepted in the ordinary way in the trade as being a proper document. He says that, on the true *a* construction of the award with which we are concerned, the arbitrators ought to be taken to have been using the words 'not clean' in that wider sense. They ought not to be taken to have been using the words in the narrower sense.

I have no doubt but that the learned judge was right in saying that, on the correct approach in law, this bill of lading, with the typewritten notation on it, is a 'clean' bill of lading in the proper sense of that word; and therefore, if indeed the arbitrators' finding *b* that it was not a 'clean' bill of lading is a finding which has got to be treated as using the word 'clean' in its proper legal sense, the arbitrators had erred in law. That is the view the learned judge took.

However, counsel for the buyers, as I have said, submits that, on the construction of the award as a whole and by reference to various documents which passed between the parties, and, I think he also submits, as a matter of ordinary good sense, the arbitrators *c* ought, by way of necessary inference, to be taken as saying that the bill of lading was not 'clean' in the sense that it was not a document which would ordinarily and properly have been accepted in the trade as being an appropriate document. That there is such a requirement in relation to bills of lading is, I think, sufficiently clear. The authority in that regard which is usually quoted, and which was quoted by the learned judge in this case, is a passage from the speech of Lord Sumner in *Hansson v Hamel & Horley Ltd*[1]. The *d* passage cited by the learned judge contains these words:

> 'These documents have to be handled by banks, they have to be taken up or rejected promptly and without any opportunity for prolonged inquiry, they have to be such as can be re-tendered to sub-purchasers, and it is essential that they should so conform to the accustomed shipping documents as to be reasonably and readily *e* fit to pass current in commerce.'

Donaldson J unreservedly accepted that proposition. He said that if the arbitrators had found that a bill of lading in this form was not acceptable in the trade his decision 'would, of course, have been different'. In that event he would have upheld their decision on this issue. But the learned judge found himself unable to take the view that that was what the arbitrators were to be treated as having said, either by the words that they used or by *f* any inference that could properly be drawn in respect of them from the award as a whole or any relevant matters referred to therein. For myself, I find that view supported by the fact that, in the second award[2] dealing with what has been called the 'insurance' issue, the self-same arbitrators, in dealing with the question whether a policy of insurance taken out by the buyers was in accordance with the contract, made an express finding, first, that the policy was defective in certain stated respects, and then went on to say: 'We further *g* find and/or hold that the policy was not one which was usual or merchantable in the trade.'

The arbitrators, therefore, when they were minded to find that a document was not one which was usual or merchantable in the trade, were prepared to express the view specifically. That lends strength, in my view, to the conclusion reached by the learned judge. I would agree with him, in any event, that here it cannot be assumed or accepted, *h* even on a balance of probability (if that were the appropriate test), that the arbitrators were intending to say, 'We, having considered this matter, find here that this document is one which was unusual and which was not merchantable in the trade'. In my judgment, accepting the conclusion of the learned judge, the arbitrators here must be taken, incorrectly as a matter of law, to have held that the bill of lading in question was not 'clean' by reason of the notation referred to. If the arbitrators have not found that *j* this bill of lading, with its notation, is not reasonably and readily fit to pass current in commerce, there is no reason for the court so to hold.

1   [1922] 2 AC 36 at 46, [1922] All ER Rep 237 at 241
2   See [1979] 2 All ER 726 at 730–734

No other grounds are now put forward in favour of the buyers on this issue. I am
a satisfied that the decision of the learned judge was correct on this issue.

However, I should say, as we have had interesting submissions on each side whether
or not this bill of lading could properly be regarded as one which should have been, in
some way, unacceptable, that I think there is great force in the submissions which
counsel put forward on behalf of the sellers. But in saying that, I am not departing in any
way from the view which the judge expressed, that if this had been what the arbitrators
b had said, he would have accepted it. So would I, on that hypothesis.

That being so, it is agreed between the parties that, so far as this court is concerned, the
answer on this first issue makes it unnecessary to decide the other two issues. As to one
of them, the judge would have decided it in favour of the sellers if it had arisen. But it
did not arise if his decision on the first issue was right. As to the third issue, it may be
that the judge was disposed to the view that it would not, in any event, have been open
c to the sellers to argue, in view of the form of the question of law. But the third issue also
does not arise, if the first issue is decided in favour of the sellers.

I merely mention that the second question was the question as to the right of the
sellers to obtain damages from the buyers, having regard to the fact, which was strongly
contested before the arbitrators but which is now not challenged on behalf of the buyers,
that the insurance policy which they purported to take out, in compliance with their
d duty under the contract (for the contract by incorporating r 22 of the rules of the
association put the duty of insuring the goods on the buyers), was not a policy which
fulfilled their own contractual obligation under the contract. Although that is accepted,
it is said in this court that the only damages to which the sellers would be entitled by
reason of that breach of contract by the buyers would be the loss of the chance, whatever
the chance might have been, that if a proper insurance policy had been taken out the
e sellers would, if they were wrong on the first issue, have been entitled to recover their
loss from the insurers under the proper policy of insurance. It was said that, in the
circumstances and having regard to what was said to be facts as found by the arbitrators,
the arbitrators must be taken to have arrived at a conclusion of fact that, if the proper
policy had been issued, the sellers would not have been able to recover one penny of the
insurance money from the insurers in respect of the 200 tonnes which had been destroyed
f by fire.

Since this hypothetical question does not arise if the sellers are right on the first issue,
I find it unnecessary to consider it. We have had interesting argument on it from
counsel for the buyers. We have not heard counsel for the sellers on it. I therefore
express no view about it. But by reason of what I regard as being the correct decision of
the learned judge on the first issue, I would dismiss the appeal.
g

SHAW LJ. For the reasons given by Megaw LJ, I agree that this appeal should be
dismissed.

WALLER LJ. I also agree.

h *Appeal dismissed.*

Solicitors: *Ince & Co* (for the buyers); *Thomas Cooper & Stibbard* (for the sellers).

Christine Ivamy   Barrister.

Ashby and another v Secretary of State for the Environment and another

COURT OF APPEAL, CIVIL DIVISION
STEPHENSON, GOFF AND EVELEIGH LJJ
31st OCTOBER, 1st NOVEMBER, 11th DECEMBER 1979

Town and country planning – Permission for development – Stopping up or diversion of highway – Power to authorise diversion – Development obstructing footpath completed or partly completed before diversion authorised – Whether power to authorise diversion where development already completed or partly completed – Whether retrospective authority to divert highway is authority which 'is necessary . . . to enable development to be carried out' – Town and Country Planning Act 1971, s 209(1).

In 1962 outline planning permission was granted for housing development on land through which there was a public footpath. Approval of detailed plans for the development was given in September 1975. The development involved the obstruction of the footpath. The builder began development on the line of the footpath in January 1976 before a diversion order diverting the route of the footpath was made by the local authority. Later in 1976 the local authority made a diversion order under s 210 of the Town and Country Planning Act 1971. The order was confirmed by the Secretary of State on 3rd November 1977. At the date of his decision much of the development under the planning permission on the line of the footpath had been completed but some work remained to be done. The applicants applied to a judge to quash the Secretary of State's decision as being ultra vires on the grounds, inter alia, that development obstructing the footpath having already been carried out at the date of the decision, the Secretary of State could not be satisfied, within s 209(1)[a] of the 1971 Act, that it 'is necessary' to divert the footpath 'to enable development to be carried out in accordance with planning permission', and that was so even if some of the development on the line of the footpath remained to be completed at the date of the decision. The judge refused to quash the Secretary of State's decision. The applicants appealed, contending that under s 209(1) the Secretary of State had no power to ratify past unlawful development on a highway because the words 'to be carried out' in s 209(1) only empowered authorisation of a diversion for the purpose of future development which had not yet begun. The Secretary of State contended that s 209(1) empowered authorisation of a diversion even though the development obstructing the highway had been completed, or, alternatively, that at the date of his decision some development on the line of the footpath remained to be done and there was, therefore, a situation where authorisation of the diversion could enable development 'to be carried out' within s 209(1).

Held (per Goff and Stephenson LJJ) – Since the words 'to be carried out' in s 209(1) of the 1971 Act were words of futurity, s 209(1) did not empower authorisation of a diversion where all the permitted development on the line of the highway had already been completed. For a local authority or the Secretary of State to be satisfied that a diversion order 'is' necessary to enable development under a planning permission 'to be carried out', within s 209(1), there had at least to be, at the date of the authorisation, some development remaining to be carried out on the line of the highway because then that which remained to be carried out could not be carried out until the development already carried out was rendered lawful by a diversion order, with the consequence that it was necessary to make a diversion order to enable the remaining development to be carried

---

a   Section 209(1) is set out at p 510 *h*, post

out within s 209(1). In ascertaining if any development on the line of the highway
a remained to be carried out, it had to be borne in mind that development began to be
carried out as soon as any work was done, even if that work was unlawful, and it could
not be said that no development was carried out until all the work was completed. Since,
at the date of the Secretary of State's decision, development on the line of the highway
was still being carried out and had not been completed, the Secretary of State had power
to authorise diversion of the footpath, even though the diversion order would validate
b the unlawful development which had already been carried out. It followed (Eveleigh LJ
concurring because in his view s 209 gave the Secretary of State power to make an order
with retrospective effect) that the appeal would be dismissed (see p 512 *a*, p 513 *d h j*,
p 514 *b f* to *h* and p 515 *f* and *j* to p 516 *b*, post).

Per Goff LJ. In exercising the discretion under s 210(1) of the 1971 Act to authorise
diversion of a highway, the local authority or the Secretary of State should disregard the
c fact that the highway has already been obstructed, for they ought not, on the one hand,
to make an order which otherwise would not be made because the loss to the developer
if no order is made will be out of proportion to the public's loss occasioned by making the
order, nor, on the other hand, should they refuse to make an order which otherwise
would be made in order to punish the developer (see p 515 *b* to *d*, post).

d
Notes
For the stopping up and diversion of highways to enable development to be carried out,
see 37 Halsbury's Laws (3rd Edn) 178, para 289.

For the Town and Country Planning Act 1971, s 209, see 41 Halsbury's Statutes (3rd
Edn) 1822.
e

Case referred to in judgments
Wood v Secretary of State for the Environment (27th June 1975) unreported.

f
Cases also cited
David (Thomas) (Porthcawl) Ltd v Penybont Rural District Council [1972] 3 All ER 1092,
[1972] 1 WLR 1526, CA; *affg* [1972] 1 All ER 733, [1972] 1 WLR 354, DC.
Lucas (F) & Sons Ltd v Dorking and Horley Rural District Council (1964) 63 LGR 491.
R v Secretary of State for the Environment, ex parte Hood [1975] 3 All ER 243, [1975] QB
g   891, CA; *rvsg* [1975] 1 All ER 102, [1974] 1 WLR 1479.

Appeal
By notice of motion dated 9th March 1978 the appellants, Kenneth Ashby and Andrew
Ashby (suing on their own behalf and on behalf of all other members of the Ramblers
h Association), moved for an order that the decision of the first respondent, the Secretary
of State for the Environment, made on 2nd November 1977 confirming an order, the
Kirklees (Broad Lane Estate, Upperthong) Public Path Diversion Order 1976, made
under s 210 of the Town and Country Planning Act 1971 by the second respondent, the
Kirklees Metropolitan Council, and the 1976 order, be quashed and set aside. On 13th
July 1978 Sir Douglas Frank QC, sitting as a deputy judge of the High Court, dismissed
j the application. The appellants appealed. The facts are set out in the judgment of
Eveleigh LJ.

Barry Payton for the appellants.
Jeremy Sullivan for the Secretary of State.
The second respondents were not represented.

Cur adv vult

a

11th December. The following judgments were read.

EVELEIGH LJ (read by Stephenson LJ). This is an appeal against the refusal of the deputy judge to quash a decision by the Secretary of State concerning a footpath diversion order made by the second respondent ('the local authority') under s 210 of the Town and Country Planning Act 1971.

b

In 1962 outline planning permission was granted for housing development on an area of land through which ran a public footpath. Approval of the details of residential development for 40 houses was given on 5th September 1975 to a Mr Woodhead, a builder. The proposed development involved obstruction of the footpath at a number of points and so the question of diversion arose. On 4th September the advisory panel on footpaths of the Kirklees Metropolitan Council accepted a proposed route for the diversion. In January 1976 the builder laid out an alternative footpath and started work on a house, no 25, which obstructed the footpath before the local authority had published a diversion order and of course before any application was made to the Secretary of State. For that he was fined £80 and ordered to pay £100 costs.

c

On 15th March 1976 the local authority made a diversion order in respect of a new route. After objections had been received and a public meeting had rejected this diversion, the local authority devised another new route for the footpath which became the subject of the Kirklees (Broad Lane Estate, Upperthong) Public Path Diversion Order 1976. After a local inquiry, the Secretary of State confirmed the order. It is this decision which is the subject of the present appeal.

d

Section 210(1) of the Town and Country Planning Act 1971 reads:

e

'Subject to section 217 of this Act, a competent authority may by order authorise the stopping up or diversion of any footpath or bridleway if they are satisfied as mentioned in section 209(1) of this Act.'

Section 217(1) reads:

'An order made under section 210 ... of this Act shall not take effect unless *f* confirmed by the Secretary of State, or unless confirmed, as an unopposed order, by the authority who made it.'

As the order made under s 210 was opposed, confirmation by the Secretary of State was required. Section 217(2) reads:

'The Secretary of State shall not confirm any such order unless satisfied as to every *g* matter of which the authority making the order are required under section 210 ... to be satisfied.'

Thus, the local authority and the Secretary of State have to be satisfied of the matters referred to in s 209. Section 209(1) reads:

'The Secretary of State may by order authorise the stopping up or diversion of any *h* highway if he is satisfied that it is necessary to do so in order to enable development to be carried out in accordance with planning permission granted under Part III of this Act, or to be carried out by a government department.'

And it is on the interpretation of this subsection that this appeal depends. For the appellants, emphasis is placed on the words 'to be carried out'. It is said that these words *j* relate to the future and cannot apply where development has begun or alternatively and a fortiori where development has been completed. It is argued that there is no power to ratify past activities which would only encourage developers to 'jump the gun'. The whole of Part X of the 1971 Act in which the relevant sections are contained and provisions in Sch 20 and s 215 of the Act for objectors to be heard and inquiries to be held

indicate that the purpose of those provisions is to prevent premature unlawful
a development where a highway will be obstructed. In the present case, therefore, the
order and the Secretary of State's decision were invalid and the developer's only course is
to apply under s 111 of the Highways Act 1959 for an order for diversion of the highway.

The Secretary of State (the local authority do not appear) claims that s 209 on its proper
construction does give power to the Secretary of State to act although development has
been completed and although the highway has already been obstructed. Alternatively it
b is claimed that all of the permitted development had not been completed, that
development in accordance with planning permission remained to be done and
consequently there was a situation where the Secretary of State's decision could enable
development to be carried out in the future.

The Secretary of State's alternative submission makes it necessary to see what work had
actually been done. Work on house no 25 was begun in January 1976 and part of the
c house went over the footpath. Two houses, nos 20 and 21, were about 18 feet apart and
one was on the east of the footpath and the other on the west. The tarmac drives to the
garages of these houses were linked or merged and between them covered the line of the
footpath over the distance from the pavement to the garages. The footpath crossed the
gardens of the houses and also the plots of two further houses, nos 34 and 36, which were
to the north of nos 20 and 21. Although the public could still walk along the footpath
d line, except that no 25 encroached over it, the path would be totally isolated from public
use when the various plots were fenced.

House no 25 appeared to have been completed externally but inside it had not been
decorated. A floorboard 14 feet long was missing and some cupboards had not been
completely installed in the kitchen. Houses numbered 20 and 21 also appear to have
been completed from the outside but inside neither had been decorated. Radiators and
e sanitary fittings had not been installed in house no 21 and floorboards had not been
nailed down in the larder of house no 20.

In his report to the Secretary of State the inspector remarked that a footpath had not
yet been legally diverted and—

f   'For this reason Mr Woodhead is unable to sell the 3 plots and houses and to
complete the development so far as he is concerned and so to enable the buildings
to be occupied as dwellinghouses. So long as the public has a right to walk through
these plots, people are not likely to buy the houses. The development permitted on
plan C, away from the line of the path is also incomplete, and cannot be completed
until the alternative route is known, along which the path will be diverted.'

He went on to say that he considered that it would be unfair to the developer to
g require him to pull down house no 25 (and possibly another house).

An application to stop up or divert a highway may be made with the Secretary of
State's consent to a magistrates' court under ss 110 and 111 of the Highways Act 1959.

Part X of the Town and Country Planning Act 1971 contains provisions for
safeguarding the public interest before a final order is made. The considerations
governing the making of an order are not precisely the same as those under the Highways
h Act 1959, although in some situations the order might well be obtainable under the
procedure of either Act. The effect of Part X of the 1971 Act is to provide a
comprehensive scheme in that Act for the development of land and the consequential
interference with highways under the supervision of the Secretary of State. It is tidy and
logical and ensures a consistent approach in deciding the merits of conflicting interests.

I turn now to consider the construction of s 209. The Secretary of State is empowered
j to 'authorise the stopping up or diversion of any highway'. Stopping up or diversion
may refer to the past or the future. The words are as applicable to a highway which has
already been diverted as to one which it is intended to divert. I cannot accept the
argument that the word 'authorise' is inappropriate to something already done. The first
meaning in the Shorter Oxford Dictionary for the verb 'to authorise' is given as 'To set up
or acknowledge as authoritative. To give legal force to; to sanction, countenance'.

Where 'authorise' embodies the idea of future conduct, it is defined in the second
meaning in that dictionary. I read s 209 as saying that the Secretary of State may **a**
acknowledge as authoritative or give legal force to or sanction the stopping up and
consequently he may deal with a highway that has been stopped up or one that will be
stopped up. Indeed, the above meaning of the word is borne out by s 209(4), which
provides: 'An order may be made under this section authorising the stopping up or
diversion of any highway which is temporarily stopped up or diverted under any other
enactment.'   **b**

The Secretary of State has to be 'satisfied that it is necessary to do so'. This means that
it is necessary to authorise the stopping up or the diversion. We then come to the words
so strongly relied on by the appellants, 'in order to enable development to be carried out
in accordance with planning permission granted under Part III of this Act . . .' Counsel
for the appellants would have us read this as though 'carried out' were equivalent to
'begun'. I cannot so read it. For something to be carried out it must of course be begun, **c**
but bearing in mind the use of the past participle it must also contemplate completion.
The section is not concerned with the possibility of the works being carried out from a
physical or practical point of view. It is an enabling section and is concerned to remove
what would otherwise be a legal obstacle (not a physical obstacle) to development. In
other words, the authorisation has to be necessary in order to enable development to be
carried out lawfully. If it has not yet been carried out lawfully, the purpose for which the **d**
Secretary of State is given power to 'authorise' is still there as the basis for the exercise of
that power. Thus far, then, I see nothing in the words of the section themselves to
prevent the Secretary of State from authorising an already existing obstruction of the
highway caused by development already carried out to completion. Counsel for the
appellants, however, says that the legislature must be taken to have intended to
discourage unlawful development and furthermore to deny assistance in any way to a **e**
developer who, as he puts it, 'has jumped the gun'.

The development covered by the section is 'development in accordance with planning
permission granted under Part III of the Act'. It is relevant therefore to see what
development may be permitted under Part III. Section 32(1) reads:

> 'An application for planning permission may relate to buildings or works
> constructed or carried out, or a use of land instituted, before the date of the **f**
> application, whether—(a) the buildings or works were constructed or carried out
> . . . or (b) the application is for permission to retain the buildings or works, or
> continue the use of the land, without complying with some condition subject to
> which a previous planning permission was granted.'

Clearly the legislature did envisage the possibility of legalising that which had already **g**
been done without permission. There is, however, no reference in s 32 to the obstruction
of a highway. As the Act envisages authorisation by the Secretary of State for
development purposes and provides a comprehensive scheme (as I have already stated),
it seems to me illogical that in a particular case where planning permission may be
granted, namely under s 32, the Secretary of State should have no power to authorise the
stopping up. This would presumably be the case if 'to be carried out' made authorisation **h**
impossible when the work had already obstructed the highway.

If the construction of s 209 is in any way ambiguous, I would resolve the ambiguity
in favour of consistency in the operation of the scheme for every kind of permitted
development envisaged by the Act. Developers who act unlawfully would have to be
dealt with by the penal provisions applicable to their conduct.

The matter does not stop there, however. Section 32(2) reads: **j**

> 'Any power to grant planning permission to develop land under this Act shall
> include power to grant planning permission for the retention on land of buildings
> or works constructed or carried out, or for the continuance of a use instituted, as
> mentioned in subsection (1) of this section; and reference in this Act to planning

a   permission to develop land or to carry out any development of land, and to
applications for such permission, shall be construed accordingly.'

The words 'and references in this Act to planning permission to develop land or to
carry out any development of land . . .' are of importance. The references are not limited
to the sections contained in Part III of the Act. It is true that 'applications for such
permission' will be made under Part III, but there are references to 'planning permission
to develop land' and to 'the carrying out of any development of land' elsewhere than in
b   Part III. Section 209 refers to 'development to be carried out in accordance with planning
permission granted under Part III', that is to say, 'planning permission to develop land',
the expression used in s 32. Putting it another way, 'planning permission granted under
Part III of this Act' (the words of section 209) is 'planning permission to develop land'.
Consequently, by virtue of s 32(2), the words in s 209 must be construed to include
planning permission for the retention on land of buildings or works constructed or
c   carried out etc, as mentioned in s 32(1). This makes it quite clear to my mind that
Parliament cannot be said to have intended that there should be no authorisation when
a highway had already been obstructed or when the development had already been
carried out. In other words, it emphasises that what is being applied for is an order to
enable development to be carried out lawfully. This must be so because ex hypothesi in
a case to which s 32 refers, the development has already been carried out on the ground.
d   It is perfectly permissible, consequently, to read s 209 as saying that the Secretary of State
may authorise the stopping up of any highway if he is satisfied that it is necessary to do
so in order to enable development which has been carried out on the ground to be
legalised.

I appreciate that it can be argued that the power of the Secretary of State to authorise
development ex post facto should be limited to a case where planning permission has
e   been applied for by virtue of s 32 itself. However, once one recognises that s 209 can
apply to an application under s 32, the future tense as contended for by counsel for the
appellants cannot be upheld. An argument seeking to limit retrospective authorisation
to the s 32 case can only be based on the argument that the developer who 'jumps the
gun' must be denied the procedure under s 209 if it is conceivably possible to do so. Such
an argument really rests on an inferred intention to penalise such a person by forcing on
f   him the procedure provided by the Highways Act 1959. While the conditions for the
exercise of the power to make an order under that Act are not the same as those contained
in the 1971 Act, there are many cases where an order could be made under either Act.

Counsel for the appellants has contended that in this present case the application falls
to be dealt with under s 111 of the Highways Act 1959. I do not see that any worthwhile
advantage is to be obtained in this way. It is surely better for the Secretary of State, who
g   may have to consider the merits of the development permission, to consider at the same
time the highway question. Moreover, it does not always follow that the developer is
blameworthy. Genuine mistakes can occur. A builder might be prepared to say that he
will pull the house down and start again. Why should not the Secretary of State give his
authority in such a case? I regard s 209 as saying that if development is of a kind which
involves obstruction of a highway, then the Secretary of State can give his authority so
h   that the development can be carried out legally. Until his authority is given development,
although carried out on the ground, has not been carried out legally. The Secretary of
State is concerned to give legal status to a development of which he approves. He is not
concerned to enquire how far, if at all, the work has been done.

I would dismiss this appeal.

j   **GOFF LJ.** I much regret that I am unable to accept Eveleigh's LJ conclusion that s 209
includes power for the Secretary of State to make a completely retrospective order,
although on a more restricted construction of the section which I am prepared to adopt
I agree that this appeal should be dismissed.

I feel the force of his argument and I would like to adopt it, or any other process of

reasoning which would enable me to arrive at the conclusion that the Secretary of State's
powers under s 209 are fully retrospective, since that would avoid the possible anomaly *a*
which will arise if (ignoring de minimis) an order may be made where the work is nearly
finished, although not if it has been completed. It would also protect an innocent
wrongdoer, as in *Wood v Secretary of State for the Environment*[1], where an order had
actually been obtained before work started, but it was void for a technical irregularity
and it was assumed that a further order could not be made under s 209 or s 210.

However, I am driven to the conclusion that this is not possible in view of the words *b*
of futurity 'to be carried out' which occur in s 209, and I think this is emphasised by the
sharp contrast with the expression in s 32 'constructed or carried out, or a use of land
instituted, before the date of the application'.

Moreover, with all respect, I do not think that any anomaly is involved, in that if the
work be started without planning permission the developer will have to have recourse to
s 32, and that contains no provision for authorising work on the highway. The answer, *c*
to my mind, is that if the work has been finished ss 209 and 210 do not apply, whether
or not planning permission was obtained before the work was done or started, and if it
has not been finished the permission granted would have to be not only under s 32 to
retain the work so far done, but also to authorise the rest, and that would bring in ss 209
and 210. I do not see how the local authority or the Secretary of State can be satisfied that
an order is necessary 'in order to enable development to be carried out' without *d*
ascertaining the factual situation in order to see whether there is in fact any part of the
relevant permitted development left to be carried out or whether it has all been
completed.

Moreover, one cannot escape this difficulty by holding that in law there has been no
development until the work is completed, because development occurs as soon as any
work is done, and to say otherwise for the purposes of ss 209 and 210 would be *e*
inconsistent with the definition of development in s 22(1) and with s 23(1). Any work
is a development, even if contrary to planning control: see s 87(2). It cannot be any the
less a development because it is unlawful for an entirely extraneous reason, namely that
it is built on the highway. Nor, I think, can it be said that the local authority or the
Secretary of State have to perform a paper exercise, looking only at the plan and ignoring
the facts. This is possibly what the legislature ought to have said, but it has not said it. *f*
It would be necessary to do unwarranted violence to the language. One would have to
read the section as if it said 'to be carried out or remain' or 'it is or was necessary'.

So I turn to the more limited alternative. Can it be said that, if development on the
highway has not been completed, then what remains to be done does show that it is
necessary to make an order to enable development to be carried out none the less so
because the order will as from its date validate the unlawful exercise? *g*

In my judgment, the answer to that question should be in the affirmative, on the
simple ground that what remains to be done cannot be carried out so long as what has
already been done remains unlawful and liable to be removed, at all events where the
new cannot physically stand alone, and it would be a very narrow distinction to draw
between that kind of case, for example building an upper storey or putting on a roof, and
a case where what remains to be done can stand alone but is only an adjunct, for example *h*
a garage, of what has to be removed, the house.

If necessary, I would say that any further building on the site of the highway, even
though it is physically stopped up by what has been done already, is itself a further
obstruction which cannot be carried out without an order.

Much reliance was placed by the appellants on para 3 of Sch 20, but I do not think that
presents any unsurmountable difficulty. The words 'is to be stopped up, diverted or *j*
extinguished' clearly refer only to the effect of an order, because the paragraph reads on
'by virtue of the order'. So it is in no way inconsistent with an order being made to give
validity to what remains to be done and indirectly to what has been done in fact but

---

1   (27th June 1975) unreported.

unlawfully. The positioning of the notice is a little more difficult, because the ends or an
a end of the relevant part of the highway may already have disappeared, but the notice can
still be given on the face of whatever obstruction has been constructed. The general
sense of the paragraph is perhaps against my construction, but it is only an administrative
provision and certainly does not, in my view, exclude it.

Section 90(1), which draws a distinction between carrying out and continuing, has
caused me some difficulty, but this distinction is not repeated in the final provision in
b sub-s (5) and I do not feel driven by this section from the alternative construction which
I have proposed, which is beneficial and which I would adopt.

When it comes to the exercise of discretion, in my view the local authority or the
Secretary of State should disregard the fact that the highway has already been obstructed,
for he ought not on the one hand to make an order he otherwise would not have made
because the loss to the developer if no order be made would be out of all proportion to
c the loss to the public occasioned by the making of the order, for that loss the developer
has brought on himself, nor on the other hand should the local authority or the Secretary
of State, in order to punish the developer, refuse to make an order which he otherwise
would have made. Punishment for the encroachment, which must in any event be
invalid for the period down to the making of the order, is for the criminal law.

I should add finally that counsel for the appellants made much of the public policy of
d preserving amenities for ramblers; but in many cases this is not the point, because even
if no order be made the developer may well, either before or after development starts, be
able to obtain planning consent for revised plans and develop the site, so making the
highway no longer a place for a ramble. The relevant considerations will be the
desirability (if any) of keeping any substituted way off the estate roads, and the
convenience of the way as a short cut, whether or not to a place where one can ramble,
e and if a diversion is proposed the relative convenience of the old and new way, whether
any different diversion would be better and whether in suitable cases diversion is
necessary or whether the way may simply be stopped up.

For these reasons, I agree that this appeal should be dismissed.

f

STEPHENSON LJ. I am attracted by the construction put by Eveleigh LJ on s 209 of
the Town and Country Planning Act 1971, but I agree with Goff LJ that it does violence
to the language of the section and, for the reasons he gives, I cannot accept it.

Sections 209 and 210 require the Secretary of State or the local authority to be satisfied
that to authorise a diversion order *is* necessary in order to enable development *to be*
g *carried out* in accordance with planning permission granted under Part III of the Act.
They do not require, or permit, either to be satisfied that it *was* necessary to authorise a
diversion order, or that it is necessary to authorise one ex post facto, in order to enable
development *to have been carried out.* I cannot give what seem to me reasonably plain
words that strained meaning unless it can be confidently inferred from their context or
other provisions in the 1971 Act that that meaning would express Parliament's
h intention. And I do not find in any of the provisions of this Act to which we have been
referred, including s 32, or in the provisions of the Highways Act 1959, any clear
indication that what appears to be a requirement that a Secretary of State or a local
authority should be satisfied on the facts that something cannot be done in the future
without a diversion order is intended to be a requirement that a Secretary of State or local
authority should be satisfied on paper that something done in the past unlawfully needs
j to be legalised by a diversion order.

I am, however, in agreement with the view that, on the facts of the case, development
was still being carried out which necessitated the authorisation of a diversion order at the
time when the diversion order was authorised and confirmed. I agree with the deputy
judge that on the inspector's findings of fact it was then still necessary to enable a by no
means minimal part of the permitted development to be carried out.

In my judgment, development which consists of building operations, and it may be development which consists of change of use, as to which I express no concluded opinion, is a process with a beginning and an end; once it is begun, it continues to be carried out until it is completed or substantially completed. That fact of life may produce the deplorable result that the earlier the developer 'jumps the gun' the better his chance of completing the development before the Secretary of State or the local authority comes to consider whether it is necessary to authorise a diversion order. But it may not save the developer from unpleasant consequences and it does not enable me to attribute to the legislature an intention which it has not expressed.

I agree that the appeal fails.

Appeal dismissed.

Solicitors: *Franks Charlesley & Co*, agents for *Pearlman Grazin & Co*, Leeds (for the appellants); *Treasury Solicitor.*

Patricia Hargrove   Barrister.

Hall v Avon Area Health Authority (Teaching)

COURT OF APPEAL, CIVIL DIVISION
STEPHENSON, WALLER AND CUMMING-BRUCE LJJ
3rd, 4th DECEMBER 1979

Practice – Stay of proceedings – Medical examination of plaintiff at defendant's request – Refusal to submit to examination – Refusal to submit unless plaintiff's doctor present – Uneducated and unskilled plaintiff – Whether general rule that plaintiff need not submit to examination by defendant's doctor unless plaintiff's doctor present – Whether necessary to have reasonable grounds for having plaintiff's doctor present – Whether fact that plaintiff a woman in her fifties a reasonable ground.

In 1977 the plaintiff, a woman aged 52, fell and was injured in the course of her employment as a domestic at the defendants' hospital. She brought an action against the defendants claiming damages for personal injury. In accordance with RSC Ord 38, r 37 a master ordered that the plaintiff and the defendants exchange medical reports. The defendants' solicitors wrote to the plaintiff's solicitors requesting that the plaintiff submit to an examination by the defendants' nominated surgeon. The plaintiff's solicitors agreed 'on the usual terms', which, they stated, included a condition that the plaintiff's doctor should be present. On the defendants' application, the district registrar made an order which had the effect of staying the action until the plaintiff submitted unconditionally to examination by the defendants' surgeon. The plaintiff appealed to a judge who found that the defendants' request for the plaintiff's examination was reasonable but, without requiring evidence in support, he also found that it was reasonable that a woman aged 52 should be accompanied by her doctor at a medical examination in order to protect her interests and, if necessary, to confirm whether the defendant's doctor had accurately recorded the examination. Accordingly, the judge exercised his discretion to set aside the registrar's order. The defendants appealed to the Court of Appeal against the judge's order, contending, inter alia, that it should be the exception rather than the general rule of practice for a plaintiff's doctor to attend an examination by the defendant's doctor, since it would cause delay and extra expense.

a They further contended that a plaintiff had to disclose good reasons for imposing such a condition and the mere fact that the plaintiff was a female aged 52 was not a sufficient reason. For the plaintiff it was contended that it was necessary in the case of unskilled and uneducated plaintiffs to impose such a condition as a general rule of practice because otherwise such plaintiffs could feel aggrieved by a medical examination at which no one was present to represent them, and, further, that the judge was entitled to hold that the plaintiff's age and sex justified imposing the condition.

b **Held** – Where there was a reasonable request for medical examination of a plaintiff by the defendant's nominated doctor, the court had to have good and substantial reasons put before it, either by counsel on instructions or, where appropriate, on affidavit, before it was entitled to impose a condition that the plaintiff's doctor should be present at the examination. It followed that the imposition of such a condition should not be the c general practice and that, unless good reasons were advanced which outweighed the disadvantages in increased expense, delay and (per Cumming-Bruce LJ) waste of doctors' time, the court should not impose the condition. It was not a good ground for imposing such a condition that the plaintiff was a woman aged 52, or that her surgeon might be able to testify that the report of the defendants' surgeon was inaccurate, or that in other cases plaintiffs from a similar background had felt aggrieved by their examination by a d defendant's doctor. It followed that the judge had no evidence before him to show it was reasonable to impose the condition and that he had exercised his discretion on improper grounds. The appeal would accordingly be allowed (see p 525 g to j, p 526 b and f to j, p 527 c to e and p 528 c to e, post).

Starr v National Coal Board [1977] 1 All ER 243 applied.

Per Stephenson and Waller LJJ. If a plaintiff is in a nervous state, or if the defendant's e nominated doctor has a reputation for being hostile to plaintiffs, it might be reasonable for the plaintiff's solicitor to insist on a third party being present at a medical examination by the defendant's doctor, though (per Stephenson LJ) the need for such a condition may often be met by a joint medical examination (see p 526 e f and p 527 b, post).

Notes
f For the circumstances in which an action may be stayed, see 30 Halsbury's Laws (3rd Edn) 407, para 768, and for cases on the subject, see 51 Digest (Repl) 1003–1008, 5374–5404.

For disclosure of medical evidence, see 13 Halsbury's Laws (4th Edn) para 53.

Cases referred to in judgments
g *Edmeades v Thames Board Mills Ltd* [1969] 2 All ER 127, [1969] 2 QB 67, [1969] 2 WLR 668, [1969] 1 Lloyd's Rep 221, CA, Digest (Cont Vol C) 1102, 5371a.
Lane v Willis, Lane v Beach (Executor of estate of George William Willis) (deceased) [1972] 1 All ER 430, [1972] 1 WLR 326, CA, Digest (Cont Vol D) 1068, 5371c.
Pickett v Bristol Aeroplane Co Ltd [1961] The Times, 17th March, CA.
Starr v National Coal Board [1977] 1 All ER 243, [1977] 1 WLR 63, CA.

h **Cases also cited**
Clarke v Martlew [1972] 3 All ER 764, [1973] QB 58, CA.
McGinley v Burke [1973] 2 All ER 1010, [1973] 1 WLR 990.
Murphy v Ford Motor Co Ltd (1970) 114 Sol Jo 886, CA.
Worrall v Reich [1955] 1 All ER 363, [1955] 1 QB 296, CA.

j **Interlocutory appeal**
In an action by the plaintiff, Mrs Betty Hall, claiming damages for personal injury against the defendants, Avon Area Health Authority (Teaching), Master Lubbock (for Master Creightmore), by an order dated 4th January 1979, ordered that the plaintiff and the defendants mutually disclose medical reports within 28 days after setting down, such

reports to be agreed if possible, and that unless such reports were agreed the parties were
to be at liberty to call medical witnesses limited to one witness for each party whose *a*
report had been so disclosed. By a letter dated 19th January 1979 the defendants'
solicitors requested that their nominated surgeon should examine the plaintiff for the
purpose of preparing a report on her. On 25th January the plaintiff's solicitors replied
that the plaintiff would be available for examination by the defendants' surgeon on the
usual terms, which included a term that a doctor nominated by the plaintiff's solicitor
was present. By a summons dated 9th March the defendants applied to have the *b*
plaintiff's action stayed until such time as she was prepared to be medically examined by
the defendants' surgeon without, inter alia, the attendance of the plaintiff's medical
adviser. By an order dated 21st March the deputy district registrar, Mr Sansbury,
ordered, in effect, that all proceedings in the action be stayed until the plaintiff submitted
unconditionally to examination by the defendants' surgeon. The plaintiff appealed to a
judge and on 27th July Kenneth Jones J ordered that the appeal be allowed and the *c*
deputy district registrar's order be set aside, and that all further proceedings in the action
be stayed until the plaintiff had been examined by the defendants' surgeon, provided
that, inter alia, such examination took place in the presence of the surgeon named by the
plaintiff. By a notice of motion and notice of appeal dated 17th August the defendants
moved the Court of Appeal for leave to appeal from the order of Kenneth Jones J and
gave notice, in the event of leave being granted, of appeal from the order. The facts are *d*
set out in the judgment of Stephenson LJ.

C S Rawlins for the defendants.
Edward Bailey for the plaintiff.

STEPHENSON LJ. The plaintiff in this action has refused to undergo a medical *e*
examination by an orthopaedic surgeon nominated by the defendants, the Avon Area
Health Authority, unless the examination is conducted in the presence of a doctor
nominated by her or her solicitors.
   Kenneth Jones J held on 27th July 1979 that she was entitled to refuse on that
condition. He allowed her appeal from an order of the deputy district registrar staying
her action, or intending to stay her action, until she submitted to that examination *f*
without her doctor being present, and he subjected the stay to the proviso that (among
other things) the examination should take place in the presence of a surgeon nominated
by her. Was the judge plainly wrong?
   Counsel for the defendants has submitted that he was and that we should remove the
condition. Counsel for the plaintiff has submitted that the judge was right and we
should not interfere with his exercise of his discretion.   *g*
   I am bound to say that my first reaction to this application for leave to appeal was
hostile. Why should not the plaintiff have her doctor or surgeon there? Why should she
be prevented from pursuing her claim unless she agreed to be examined without him?
What injustice could possibly result from her insisting on his presence? And even if I
might have reached a different decision, how could it be said that Kenneth Jones J was
not entitled to exercise his discretion as he did? But counsel for the defendants has *h*
persuaded me, in spite of my reluctance to reverse an exercise of discretion by this
learned judge and of all that counsel for the plaintiff has forcibly urged in support of his
order, that we ought to give leave to appeal and to allow the appeal.
   The plaintiff's case is an uncomplicated one, as appears from paras 1 and 2 of her
statement of claim, which was served on 15th September 1978:
                                                                                              j
      '1. At all material times the Plaintiff was employed by the Defendants as a
      domestic at their premises Hortham Hospital, Almondsbury, Bristol of which
      premises the Defendants were at all relevant times the occupiers and on which the
      Plaintiff, during the course of her said employment, was a visitor.
      '2. On 8th November 1977 at about 8.05 a.m. the Plaintiff was walking along the

driveway leading towards Avon Ward when she was caused to slip and fall to the ground by a patch of mud and wet leaves which were lying on the said driveway.'

Then it was alleged that her fall was caused by the negligence and/or breach of statutory duty of the defendants and it was alleged in para 4 that, by reason of the defendants' negligence and/or breach of duty as employer or occupier, the plaintiff sustained personal injury and suffered loss and damage, the only particulars given being '(a) Shock and severe pain. (b) Major rupture of the rotator cuff of the right shoulder'. The paragraph goes on:

> 'The Plaintiff was aged 52 at the time of the accident. Details of her injuries and treatment therefor appear in a medical report dated 26th June 1978 by Mr. W. G. J. Hampson. The Plaintiff will have a permanent marked limitation of movement in her right shoulder and this may well prevent her from continuing her employment as a domestic and will restrict her ability to obtain other employment.'

The report referred to in that paragraph was, by a mistake, not in fact delivered with the statement of claim to the defendants' solicitors and, of course, it was a report of an examination made not in the presence of any representative, medical or otherwise, of the defendants. Mr Hampson, who was the author of that report, unfortunately died before these proceedings came on for trial. His death was not immediately known to the plaintiff's solicitors.

The defence delivered on 8th November 1978 is in ordinary form denying liability and damage and alleging contributory negligence on the part of the plaintiff.

On 4th January 1979 Master Lubbock made an order for directions and by the first paragraph of that order he ordered that—

> 'The Plaintiff and the Defendant do mutually disclose medical reports within 28 days after setting down. Such reports be agreed if possible. Unless such reports are agreed, the parties be at liberty to call medical witnesses limited to one witness for each party whose report has been so disclosed.'

That order for mutual disclosure was in accordance with the practice laid down in RSC Ord 38, r 37. That provides:

> '(1) Where in an action for personal injuries an application is made under rule 36(1) [which I need not read] in respect of oral expert evidence relating to medical matters, then, unless the Court considers that there is sufficient reason for not doing so, it shall direct that the substance of the evidence be disclosed in the form of a written report or reports to such other parties and within such period as the Court may specify . . .'

Orders made under that rule provide now for the mutual exchange of medical reports contemporaneously on the principle of reciprocity, which is recognised also, for instance, in RSC Ord 38, r 36 and r 38, and in Ord 25, r 6(1). In the Supreme Court Practice[1] will be found valuable notes referring to the authorities which establish this principle and explaining the machinery of simultaneous exchange and its reason.

On 19th January 1979 (well before the end of the period laid down in the order for directions, to which I have referred) the defendants' solicitors wrote to the plaintiff's solicitors:

> 'As you know, we do not yet have a Medical Report on your client. We would like to instruct Mr. M. P. McCormack, Orthopaedic Surgeon of 18, Richmond Hill, Bristol 8 to examine your client and prepare a report on her for the purpose of defending the action. Would you please ascertain whether your client has any personal objections to Mr. McCormack and, if she has not, please confirm this and we will instruct him.'

---

1   (1979) vol 1, pp 441, 622, paras 25/6/2, 38/35/5

To that the plaintiff's solicitors replied on 25th January:

'We confirm that facilities will be available to you to have our client examined by *a* Mr. McCormack on the usual terms, namely: 1. A doctor nominated by us is present. 2. You agree to meet the fees of the doctor nominated by us. 3. You agree to reimburse our client her reasonable expenses including any loss of wages for attending the Medical Examination. 4. You agree to let us have a sight of your doctor's report. We note that you are waiting to hear from Counsel and we await hearing from you as soon as possible.'   *b*

So there the plaintiff's solicitors are putting forward four, what they call 'usual,' terms, which are conditions precedent to their client's being examined by Mr McCormack, the orthopaedic surgeon nominated by the defendants, to whom they, by their silence, have no personal objections. It is admitted, and the judge so found, that the request contained in the defendants' solicitors' letter of 19th January was a reasonable request.   *c*

Thereafter, the defendants' solicitors took out a summons and the deputy district registrar made an order, neither of which I need read.

On 26th June the plaintiff appealed against the registrar's order as it was intended to be made, to stay the plaintiff's action unless she submitted to an examination by Mr McCormack without the presence of a doctor nominated by her. On 26th June, apparently, the judge had his first hearing of the plaintiff's appeal. The hearing dealt *d* mainly with the question of reciprocity in making any report by Mr McCormack available to the plaintiff and any report by a doctor nominated by the plaintiff available to the defendants. But on 27th July, when the hearing was resumed, that matter had been resolved and the sole issue was the first condition which the plaintiff's solicitors were seeking to impose on the examination as a 'usual term'.

We have the advantage of a full note of the judge's judgment, approved by him, and *e* that note begins with these two sentences:

'This matter can be taken shortly. The defendants wish to have the plaintiff examined by their own doctor. The plaintiff started by agreeing or consenting to such examination only on certain conditions, these conditions being . . .'

and then he sets out the four conditions. In a note appended to the agreed note of his *f* judgment, dated 5th September 1979, the judge added:

'According to my recollection the only issue here was whether condition 1 [the first "usual term"] was reasonable. I decided that it was. On that basis the defendants agreed that conditions 3 and 4 were reasonable. The plaintiff at the outset abandoned condition 2.'
          g

The plaintiff's solicitors had given an undertaking in accordance with all the cases which were cited to us, ending with *Starr v National Coal Board*[1]. The reasonableness of condition 1 was the only outstanding issue between the parties.

The judge referred to *Starr's* case[1] and quoted from it what Scarman LJ had said[2]:

'So what is the principle of the matter to be gleaned from those cases? In my judgment the court can order a stay if, in the words of Lord Denning MR in *h* *Edmeades'* case[3], "the conduct of the plaintiff in refusing a reasonable request [for medical examination] is such as to prevent the just determination of the cause". I think that those words contain the principle of the matter. We are, or course, in the realm of discretion. It is a matter for the discretion of the judge, exercised judicially on the facts of the case, whether or not a stay should be ordered.'
          j

1   [1977] 1 All ER 243, [1977] 1 WLR 63
2   [1977] 1 All ER 243 at 249, [1977] 1 WLR 63 at 70
3   *Edmeades v Thames Board Mills Ltd* [1969] 2 All ER 127 at 129, [1969] 2 QB 67 at 71

Kenneth Jones J went on to say: 'In this case it is not disputed that the defendants'
a request for a medical examination is a reasonable request.' Later he said:

'Really the question is whether the conduct of the plaintiff in insisting on these
two conditions (1 and 4) prevents a just determination of the cause. I have no doubt
that the court has to see whether these conditions are reasonable in all the
circumstances of the case.'

b Further he added:

'It seems to me abundantly obvious that it is reasonable. She is not insisting on
a joint examination. She is not insisting that her doctor should in any way impede
or interfere with the examination. She is only asking that he be present to protect
her interests in the widest sense. It seems to me that that is a very modest request
indeed and I am surprised that any defendant looking at it dispassionately can really
c contend otherwise. It seems entirely reasonable that a lady aged 52 should be
accompanied at a medical examination. It is better that the person to accompany
her should possess some professional skill. She might have asked for her solicitors
to be present but it is obviously right that the person should be another doctor. He
can safeguard her interests. He can witness the examination as it takes place,
d witness what is said by the plaintiff to the defendants' doctor and he can in due
course confirm whether the defendants' doctor's account is an accurate one. It may
be that the defendants' doctor has recorded her answers not quite accurately. He
may have to report that the defendants' doctor's account is not quite accurate but
that is not necessarily impropriety. That is all part of the examination. The matter
is so completely obvious that it does not require further elaboration. It is urged on
e me that I should require evidence of why a doctor nominated by her should be
present and that affidavits should be sworn. I see no need for evidence where a
female plaintiff of 52 is required to undergo a medical examination. If she was
requiring her doctor to take some part in the examination that would be different.'

So, with the undertaking given to get rid of condition 4, the order of 27th July was
made by the judge. By that order he ordered:
f
'1. The Plaintiff's appeal be allowed and the order made by Mr. Deputy District
Registrar Sansbury on the 21st day of March, 1979 be set aside.
'2. All further proceedings in this action be stayed until such time as the Plaintiff
shall have been medically examined by Mr. M. P. McCormack F.R.C.S. provided
that (a) Such examination shall take place in the presence of Mr. P. J. Witherow
F.R.C.S., a surgeon nominated by the Plaintiff. [He was nominated to take the place
g of the deceased Mr Hampson.] (b) The Defendants do pay the Plaintiff's own
reasonable expenses of attending such examination. (c) The Defendants shall
disclose to the Plaintiff's Solicitors a copy of any report which they obtain from Mr.
M. P. McCormack in exchange for any report which the Plaintiff's Solicitors may
obtain from Mr. P. J. Witherow and any other reports on which the Plaintiff intends
to rely.
h '3. The costs of the Plaintiff's appeal and of the Defendant's application to the
Deputy District Registrar be the Plaintiff's in any event.
'4. Leave to appeal be refused.'

I need not, I think, refer to any of the cases to which counsel for the defendants has
directed our attention: most of them are cited in the notes in the Supreme Court
j Practice[1] to which I have already referred. None of those cases, including *Starr's* case[2],
deals with a conditional refusal of this kind. The observations which were made by the

1 (1979) vol 1, pp 441, 622, paras 25/6/2, 38/35/5
2 [1977] 1 All ER 243, [1977] 1 WLR 63

members of this court in *Starr's* case[1] relate to an unconditional refusal. That is made
plain by what Scarman LJ said[2]:

'The question which the learned judge had to decide, and which is now before
this court, is whether the plaintiff was entitled to refuse to be examined by a
particular doctor.'

Later Scarman LJ said this[3]:

'There are a number of propositions of law which are not in dispute, and I
mention them straight away so that one may approach and consider that which *is*
in issue between the parties. It is accepted that, where a plaintiff refuses to undergo
a medical examination requested by a defendant, the court does have an inherent
jurisdiction to grant a stay until such time as he submits to such examination when
it is just and reasonable so to do. It is also recognised that a stay, if granted, does
either shut out the plaintiff from the seat of justice or compel him against his will
to submit to a medical examination; and, of course, that is an invasion of his
personal liberty.'

Then he said[4]:

'So what is the principle of the matter to be gleaned from those cases? In my
judgment the court can order a stay if, in the words of Lord Denning MR in
Edmeades' case[5] . . .'

and then he went on to cite the rest of the passage which has already been read in a
quotation from the judgment of the judge in this case. After that passage Scarman LJ
said[6]:

'For myself, I find talk about "onus of proof" in such a case inappropriate. There
is, I think, clearly a general rule that he who seeks a stay of an action must satisfy the
court that justice requires the imposition of a stay. In the exercise of the discretion
in this class of case, where a plaintiff has refused a medical examination, I think the
court does have to recognise (and here I think *Pickett's* case[7] is helpful) that in the
balance there are, amongst many other factors, two fundamental rights which are
cherished by the common law and to which attention has to be directed by the
court. First, as mentioned in *Pickett's* case[7] by Willmer and Donovan LJJ, and by
Sachs LJ in *Lane's* case[8], there is the plaintiff's right to personal liberty. But on the
other side there is an equally fundamental right—the defendant's right to defend
himself in the litigation as he and his advisers think fit; and this is a right which
includes the freedom to choose the witnesses that he will call. It is particularly
important that a defendant should be able to choose his own expert witnesses, if the
case be one in which expert testimony is significant . . . And so in every case, as I see
it, the particular facts of the case on which the discretion has to be exercised are all-
important. The discretion cannot be exercised unless each party does expose the
reasons for his action. I have already indicated that I do not regard this as a question
of onus of proof. There is, in my judgment, a duty on each party in such a situation
to provide the court with the necessary material known to him, so that the court,
fully informed, can exercise its discretion properly. However, I would add this

1   [1977] 1 All ER 243, [1977] 1 WLR 63
2   [1977] 1 All ER 243 at 245, [1977] 1 WLR 63 at 65
3   [1977] 1 All ER 243 at 247, [1977] 1 WLR 63 at 67–68
4   [1977] 1 All ER 243 at 249, [1977] 1 WLR 63 at 70
5   [1969] 2 All ER 127 at 129, [1969] 2 QB 67 at 71
6   [1977] 1 All ER 243 at 249–250, [1977] 1 WLR 63 at 70–71
7   *Pickett v Bristol Aeroplane Co Ltd* [1961] The Times, 17th March
8   *Lane v Willis, Lane v Beach* [1972] 1 All ER 430 at 435–436, [1972] 1 WLR 326 at 333

a comment: that at the end of the day it must be for him who seeks the stay to show that, in the discretion of the court, it should be imposed.'

Scarman LJ then applied those principles and stated the first question to be: 'Was the defendants' request for the examination of the plaintiff by Dr X a reasonable request?' He found that it was. He asked himself the second question: 'Granted the reasonableness of the defendants' request, was the plaintiff's refusal of it unreasonable?' He answered that question: 'Yes, it was.'

b The judgments of Geoffrey Lane and Cairns LJJ both contain passages to which I will refer. Geoffrey Lane LJ said[1]:

'One has to do one's best to extract from the decisions such principles as seem best to accord with reason and with practice and with fairness. The court clearly has inherent jurisdiction to order a stay when the justice of the case demands such a stay. There are not infrequent occasions when justice demands that the plaintiff should undergo medical examination by a doctor appointed on behalf of the defendants. There are circumstances in which refusal by the plaintiff to undergo such examination should in justice be met by the imposition of a stay.'

Cairns LJ said[2]:

d 'If the defendant has put forward the name of a particular doctor and can show that an examination by *a* doctor is necessary in his interests and that this particular doctor is apparently well qualified to examine the plaintiff, the plaintiff then has to give reasons for objecting to him. He must at least be able to show that there is some substantial ground on which he or his advisers have formed the opinion that the doctor in question lacks the proper qualifications or is likely to conduct his examination and to make his reports unkindly or unfairly.'

In their notice of appeal the defendants complained that the judge held that the plaintiff had a legal right to insist on her nominated doctor being present at her examination by the defendants' nominated surgeon. I can find nothing of the kind in the judgment of the judge. He quoted Scarman LJ's observations that the matter is a matter of discretion and it seems to me that the judge treated it throughout as a matter
f of discretion. I therefore would not read ground (1) of the notice of appeal, but I read ground (2):

'That there were no grounds or material upon which the Learned Judge could properly have exercised any discretion vested in him in favour of the Plaintiff by making it a condition of any examination by the said Mr. M. P. McCormack F.R.C.S. on behalf of the Defendants that it should only take place in the presence
g of the said Mr. P. J. Witherow F.R.C.S.'

I also read from ground (3):

'The Learned Judge should have held that, the Defendants having made a reasonable request for a medical examination by an orthopaedic surgeon to whom the Plaintiff raised no objection . . . (b) As no reason for imposing such a condition
h was given by the Plaintiff herself, or by her Solicitors or by her Counsel and no evidence was tendered to suggest that there were any or reasonable grounds for imposing it, the Plaintiff was not entitled to have it inserted as a term of the order. (c) The mere fact that the Plaintiff was a female aged 52 was not a sufficient reason for the Court to exercise its discretion in her favour by inserting the condition in the order.'

j Counsel for the defendants relies on those grounds and submits that, by claiming condition 1 to be a 'usual term' required by solicitors, wider considerations are raised and,

---

1   [1977] 1 All ER 243 at 254, [1977] 1 WLR 63 at 75
2   [1977] 1 All ER 243 at 256, [1977] 1 WLR 63 at 78

if the judge's judgment is upheld, this court will be deciding that the court is absolved
from finding reasons for a particular plaintiff insisting on this term or condition, that it a
is a usually reasonable requirement which the courts should not remove but enforce. So
here we are not concerned with this case in isolation but with the effect which our
decision may have on other cases and other plaintiffs, and in particular members of the
trade union which has acted for this plaintiff and instructed these solicitors of hers will
be taking the same point if the judge's order stands.

Counsel for the defendants, accordingly, submits first that the interests of justice and b
the just determination of personal injuries litigation involve four things. First, that the
imposition of this condition should be the exception rather than the rule. Second, that
if a plaintiff refuses to undergo an examination unless this condition is performed, he or
she must disclose his or her reasons for seeking to do so. I think he relies on *Starr's* case[1]
and, in particular, some of the passages I have quoted from the judgments of Cairns,
Scarman and Geoffrey Lane LJJ. Those principles, he submits, apply to any condition c
which involves the court's exercise of its discretion.

The third thing is that the principle of reciprocity must not be infringed. It is a
consistent theme running through the disclosure and exchange of medical reports and to
depart from it can cause an injustice or an imbalance of justice in the determination of
personal injuries litigation. He points out that, in this case as in others, it would be quite
impracticable for the defendants to have their medical man present at the first d
examination or the early examinations of a plaintiff by his or her nominated medical
man. Yet this condition requires the presence of the plaintiff's medical man at the
defendant's medical man's first examination.

Fourth, if allowed to become a general rule of practice, and not the exception, the
imposition of this condition would have the inevitable consequence that there will be a
widespread adoption of this practice and that will cause delay in getting medical reports e
and will cause injustice and extra expense. He added that it will cause the alienation of
medical men from assisting the court in litigation of this kind. They may not always
easily be persuaded to examine the parties to litigation, knowing that if they do they may
or will have to take time off from their practices to give evidence in support of their
reports. Their reluctance will be increased if they are called on to be present with, as it
were, a watching brief at medical examinations in which they can take no part. They f
may find that a burdensome and frustrating duty and be further deterred from giving
their assistance in this type of litigation.

Those submissions are, of course, in addition to those which he elaborated in his
grounds of appeal, namely, that in this case no good reason has been put forward for this
lady requiring this medical man to be present at her examination by this other medical
man. He submits, on the authority particularly of *Starr's* case[1], that such reasons must g
be put forward and they must be reasons sufficient to outweigh, when it comes to the
exercise of the court's discretion, those increases in delay and costs, which may ultimately
fall on the defendants, caused by insisting on this condition, and those other consequences:
the one-sided presence of the other side's doctor after an earlier examination where only
the plaintiff's side has been present, and the possible deterrent effect on doctors generally.

Counsel for the plaintiff does not shrink from our treating this as a test case. He h
submits that the experience of his instructing solicitors is that members of this union
with a background like the plaintiff's, a union for whom they have acted in claims
against other defendants, have, during the last nine months to a year, complained of the
medical examinations to which they have submitted by doctors nominated by
defendants, in the absence of anybody on their own side. It is in consequence of this
general experience of those solicitors that they have evolved this practice of requiring this j
condition, without consulting each plaintiff for whom they are acting, although each
plaintiff is, of course, informed by them of what they are doing or have done to protect

_____

1   [1977] 1 All ER 243, [1977] 1 WLR 63

the plaintiff's interests in this way. By this condition counsel's instructing solicitors hope
to protect unskilled and uneducated plaintiffs from being badgered or upset, as he put it,
a by medical examinations in the absence of anybody representing their own side, and
from being led to feel that they are being unjustly treated, even if their feelings are
irrational. They also hope, by this condition, to increase the chances of agreement
between the medical men on each side and of the consequent settlement of their claims.

He frankly conceded that this condition would be required where a plaintiff was not
a woman of 52 but a man of 25, provided that he came from the same unskilled,
b uneducated sort of background as this lady; but he submitted that it was even more
reasonable to require such a condition for a 52-year-old woman.

He did not argue that the court should enforce unreasonable conditions if justice
would, nonetheless, not be thereby prevented from being done; but he did claim that it
was reasonable for parties like the plaintiff to stand on their right to personal liberty by
having their own nominated doctor present when it could not prejudice the defendants
c or their nominated doctor's examination or cause the defendants any injustice.

He conceded that the costs of the attendance of a medical man like Mr Witherow
might be relevant to the exercise of the judge's discretion, but he submitted that any
delay resulting from the adoption of this practice was minimal and that the question of
possibly deterring the medical profession if this practice were to be adopted was not put
to the judge or supported by anything but speculation. He pointed out that the taxing
d master could disallow the costs of the attendance of such a medical man if he thought
proper, but on any view these considerations on which counsel for the defendants relies
could not outweigh the importance of protecting unskilled working men or women, and
this plaintiff in particular, not only from injustice but from any sense of injustice,
however unreasonable, which medical examination by the other side's medical man
alone might implant in their minds.

e Counsel for the plaintiff argued that the judge was entitled to hold, as he undoubtedly
did, that the plaintiff's age and sex justified the solicitors requiring this condition
without any reason, substantial or otherwise, being put before him on affidavit or in
argument. And he did not throw over what seems to have been the other ground on
which the judge decided in the plaintiff's favour, namely, that her own surgeon would
be able to check any inaccuracy in the defendants' surgeon's report of his examination of
f her. But, as I understood him, he rested his case mainly on the experience of his solicitors
in other cases that other clients felt aggrieved by such medical examinations, a submission
he was prevented from making to the learned judge, because the judge stopped him and
called on counsel for the defendants before he could make it. From the note of the
judge's judgment the judge clearly regarded this as a plain case and that is confirmed by
his having asked counsel for the defendants (so he told us) whether the plaintiff was not
g entitled to have someone to protect her interests when she went into the 'den of lions'.

In my judgment, the court ought to have good or substantial reasons put before it on
instructions or, in an appropriate case, on affidavit, if it is to impose conditions of this
kind on a reasonable request for a medical examination of a plaintiff by a doctor
nominated by a defendant. This is just as necessary in a case like the present as in cases,
like Starr[1], of out-and-out refusal. The judge rightly treated this conditional acceptance
h as a refusal of a reasonable request, but I cannot agree with his opinion that it was a
reasonable refusal because the plaintiff was a woman of 52 or because the surgeon
nominated by her solicitors might have testified to the inaccuracy of the other surgeon's
report. Nor would it have been reasonable because in other cases other previously
injured parties had been injured in their feelings by the way in which they were
examined by other doctors for other defendants. All professions have their black sheep
j and good men have 'off days'. Courts of law, as well as the parties to litigation and their
solicitors, must give a Fellow of the Royal College of Surgeons, of high standing in his
profession of orthopaedic surgeon, credit for being fair and considerate in his treatment

---

1   [1977] 1 All ER 243, [1977] 1 WLR 63

of those whom he examines on behalf of the other side and fair and accurate in his
recording of such examination, and for needing no third party, whether medically *a*
qualified or not, to prevent him from misleading the court by inaccuracies or, I would
add, to restrain him, as was suggested (though not by the judge) from confusing the
party examined by unfair interrogation.

None of the reasons advanced to support the practice, which alone can justify the
judge's order, makes this plaintiff's conditional refusal to be examined reasonable or
outweighs the disadvantages in increased expense and delay which it may cause, even in *b*
such a simple case as this. I do not put into the scale the lack of reciprocity necessarily
resulting, or the possible deterrent effect on the medical profession's willingness to take
part in examinations of parties if they are required to hold a watching brief at an
examination in which they take no part, because I think there is nothing in the first
factor and not much in the second, though I may be underestimating that consideration.

I accept that the plaintiff's solicitors require this (I think) unreasonable condition in *c*
what they conceive to be the best interests of this plaintiff and other parties for whom
they act. And I am not to be taken as saying that it would be unreasonable in every case
or that it could never be imposed by a judge. I do, however, find it difficult to see what
advantage a medical man has over a solicitor or a friend in the protection of a plaintiff
from being harassed or disturbed or inaccurately reported. I cannot understand why a
partner or legal executive in the firm of solicitors handling this plaintiff's case as local *d*
agents would not have secured the purpose of her union's solicitors better than Mr
Witherow, a specialist, who by the accident of Mr Hampson's death, was as unfamiliar to
her as was Mr McCormack.

What I have said about this condition is not intended to deprive the plaintiff of the
help and comfort of any third party's presence at any medical examination by any doctor
on behalf of any defendant. If, for example, the particular plaintiff were in a nervous *e*
state or confused by a serious head injury, or if the defendant's nominated doctor had a
reputation for a fierce examining manner, or if the plaintiff asked for her nominated
doctor to be present, it might be reasonable for her solicitors to insist, for her, on such a
condition, though the need for it might often be met, I would have thought, by a joint
medical examination, which was never suggested by the plaintiff's advisers and which
her counsel submitted was something which the defendants' advisers ought to have *f*
suggested. But there is nothing of that kind here. On the bare facts of this case, and they
are perhaps so bare as to make it a good test case, I can find no reason for not staying the
plaintiff's action unless she submits to this examination by Mr McCormack
unconditionally.

I would, accordingly, grant the defendants leave to appeal, allow the appeal and set
aside para 2(a) of the judge's order. That would leave the stay subject to sub-paras (b) and *g*
(c) only.

WALLER LJ. I agree with the judgment of Stephenson LJ. I would only add this. In
my experience, the order which was sought here is an unusual order and, although the
plaintiff's solicitors in their letter describe the terms as 'usual terms', counsel for the
plaintiff frankly said it was only for the last nine months that those instructing him had *h*
sought to enforce this condition. It has become clear in the course of the argument that
this is not a special case: it is an attempt to change the practice. In my judgment, the case
for change has not been made out. If this change were to be made it would cost money
and the extent of the cost over the country as a whole would be or might be great.

Counsel for the plaintiff has based his case on the members of the union for whom *j*
those instructing him appear, but that case would apply very widely indeed to members
of other unions throughout the country. If this became a common order it might well
make doctors less ready to involve themselves in personal injury litigation, because it
would involve highly skilled professional men sitting quietly while one of their fellow
consultants was making an examination. It would also cause delays, because, although

counsel rather minimised this, there would be the difficulty of two busy professional

a men having to make an appointment which fitted them both rather than just one, and
that would cause delay.

There may be cases where such an order would be justifiable: for example, a very
nervous plaintiff. In such a case it might well be, indeed it probably would be, preferable
to have some other person present rather than a consultant whom he or she has probably
only seen once. Another case might be the sort of case which arose in *Starr v National*

b *Coal Board*[1], where it was thought that the consultant who the defendants wished to
examine the plaintiff was one who tended to be hostile to plaintiffs. In such circumstances
it might (I do not say it would) be a good ground for saying that the consultant on the
other side should be present.

Starr v National Coal Board[1] is authority for the view that it is not a ground for refusing
but it might be a good ground for having somebody present. In this case there were no

c such grounds and, although the judge has based his decision on the age and sex of the
plaintiff, when one asks where the line has to be drawn her counsel promptly concedes
that he would be making a similar application even if the age and sex were both
different. The real grounds put before us are that plaintiffs sometimes come back from
medical examination by the defendant's consultant unhappy and worried, a worry which
may be irrational.

d Having heard the argument, because, like Stephenson LJ, initially I was disposed to
uphold the judge's decision, in my view there were in fact no grounds on which the
judge could properly exercise his discretion as he did. Furthermore, if he had been told
the real grounds on which the application was made, it would not have strengthened the
case in any way. Indeed, those real grounds would have demonstrated the flimsy nature
of the case for this change of practice. I would allow the appeal.

e

CUMMING-BRUCE LJ. I agree. It is clear now that in this court we have obtained
a much more comprehensive picture of the history of the conditions that the plaintiff's
solicitors sought in their letter of 25th January 1979 than was available to the judge.
Counsel for the plaintiff told this court that most of the time at the hearing before the

f judge was taken up with discussion of the notice of appeal and when counsel was himself
addressing the judge it was very quickly apparent that the judge, partly as a matter of
first impression, had formed a strong view in his favour, which emerges from the
judgment. So counsel for the plaintiff did not have the opportunity of developing his
argument in the way in which it has been developed in this court. But it emerged from
counsel's candid submission to this court that the conditions sought to be imposed on

g 25th January were not in any sense the result of any initiative or sense of need on the part
of the personal plaintiff, but were founded entirely on the experience of the plaintiff's
solicitors in the conduct of litigation.

I agree with Stephenson and Waller LJJ that such initiative on the part of the solicitors
is entirely within their professional competence and I would not for a moment criticise
them for the initiative that they took in this case. But, as appears from counsel for the

h plaintiff's submission in this court, the strongest consideration which moved the
solicitors to ask for the conditions on which they tried to insist was a subjective feeling
of which they had become aware on the part of previous clients who had complained
about the way in which they had been received, examined and treated in the course of
the examination, although an analysis of the reaction of those clients showed that
frequently their reaction had been irrational. It was in order to give a reasonable

j reassurance to clients who had to be subjected to a medical examination on the part of the
defendants' doctors that the conditions put forward in the letter were prompted.

It may be too dramatic a metaphor, but it seems to me that the remedy proposed by
the solicitors was a sledge-hammer to crack a nut. It seems to me entirely reasonable that

---

1   [1977] 1 All ER 243, [1977] 1 WLR 63

solicitors, as a result of their professional experience in litigation, should advise plaintiffs that it would be sensible to have someone with them to reassure them when they go to *a* a medical examination, whether the examination be by a doctor nominated on their behalf by their own solicitors or examination by a doctor nominated by the defendants. The person who could usually give reassurance, perfectly adequately, would be a relative or a friend, who in the ordinary way would not expect any remuneration, or in some (perhaps rare) cases a member of the staff of the plaintiff's solicitors' firm, preferably someone to whom the plaintiff had previously been introduced in order to gain *b* confidence.

Such a solution would avoid the objections which counsel for the defendants has so forcibly brought to our notice about the conditions required by the plaintiff's solicitors in this case. To require a medical consultant to be present to act as a chaperone, although he has no personal function to perform in the course of the examination by the defendant's surgeon, seems to me to be a serious addition to the costs of the litigation and *c* also an inexcusable requirement, on the part of the processes of litigation and justice, of the precious time of highly qualified consultants, whose professional business includes the examination of litigants for the purposes of litigation, but whose primary concern is with diagnosis and treatment of patients in order to alleviate their sufferings.

In my view, the court should hesitate long before encouraging or permitting any such addition to the time and expense in the conduct of personal injury cases as is proposed by *d* the solicitors in this case.

For those reasons, in addition to the reasons stated by Stephenson and Waller LJJ, with which I fully agree, I agree that this appeal should be allowed.

Leave to appeal granted. Appeal allowed. Leave to appeal to the House of Lords refused.

e

Solicitors: *Gillhams* (for the plaintiff); *Gouldens*, agents for *Bevan Hancock & Co*, Bristol (for the defendants).

Patricia Hargrove   Barrister.

Duport Steels Ltd and others v Sirs and others

QUEEN'S BENCH DIVISION
KENNETH JONES J
25th JANUARY 1980

COURT OF APPEAL, CIVIL DIVISION
LORD DENNING MR, LAWTON AND ACKNER LJJ
26th JANUARY 1980

HOUSE OF LORDS
LORD DIPLOCK, LORD EDMUND-DAVIES, LORD FRASER OF TULLYBELTON, LORD KEITH OF KINKEL, AND LORD SCARMAN
1st, 7th FEBRUARY 1980

Trade dispute – Acts done in contemplation or furtherance of trade dispute – In contemplation or furtherance of – Claim by party that he has acted in furtherance of trade dispute – Union in dispute with nationalised steel corporation deciding to extend strike action to private steel sector – Extension of strike not having immediate adverse trade or industrial effect on corporation – Union honestly and sincerely believing that extension of strike would advance their cause in their dispute with corporation – Whether union acting 'in . . . furtherance of' trade dispute – Trade Union and Labour Relations Act 1974, s 13(1) (as substituted by the Trade Union and Labour Relations (Amendment) Act 1976, s 3(2)).

Injunction – Interlocutory – Trade dispute – Claim by party against whom injunction sought that he had acted in contemplation or furtherance of trade dispute – Likelihood of that party's succeeding at trial of action in establishing matters which would afford defence to action – Discretion to grant injunction – Judge at first instance refusing injunction – Whether Court of Appeal entitled to substitute own exercise of discretion and grant injunction – Trade Union and Labour Relations Act 1974, s 17(2) (as inserted by the Employment Protection Act 1975, Sch 16, Part III, para 6).

The appellants were members of the executive council of a trade union which was in dispute with the British Steel Corporation ('BSC') over pay and which in the course of that dispute had called those of its members employed by BSC out on strike. BSC ran the public sector of the steel industry and produced 50% of the steel produced in the United Kingdom. BSC maintained that they could not increase their pay offer to the union's members unless that increase was directly funded by the government. In order to bring pressure to bear on the government the union decided to extend the strike to the private sector even though there was no dispute with the private steel companies. They hoped that a total shutdown of steel production would cause manufacturers, workers and members of the public to persuade the government to subsidise the payment of higher wages by BSC. Faced with the extension of the strike, 16 private steel companies issued a writ seeking injunctions against the appellants restraining them from (i) inducing the companies' employees to break their contracts of employment by coming out on strike, or (ii) inducing any members of the union to interfere with the supply of steel to or from the companies' premises or to picket those premises. At the hearing in chambers of an application by the companies for interlocutory injunctions, the appellants claimed that their action in extending the strike to the private sector was done 'in . . . furtherance of a trade dispute' and they were therefore accorded immunity by s 13(1)[a] of the Trade

---

a   Section 13(1) provides: 'An act done by a person in contemplation or furtherance of a trade dispute shall not be actionable in tort on the ground only—(a) that it induces another person to break a

Union and Labour Relations Act 1974 from any action in tort against them. It was not
disputed that the appellants honestly and sincerely believed that by extending the strike
into the private sector they were advancing or furthering the union's cause in the dispute
with BSC. The companies contended however that an act was not 'done . . . in
furtherance of a trade dispute' unless it was intended to have an immediate adverse trade
or industrial effect on the other party to the dispute, and extending the strike to the
private sector was not going to have that effect on BSC. The judge rejected that argument
and held that as it was highly probable that the appellants' defence would succeed at the
trial of the action he ought therefore, having regard to s 17(2)[b] of the 1974 Act, to exercise
his discretion by refusing the injunctions. The companies appealed to the Court of
Appeal which granted the injunctions on the grounds that the union's extension of the
strike to the private sector had generated a second dispute between the union and the
government which was separate from the union's dispute with BSC, that the second
dispute was not a 'trade dispute' because the government were not the employers, that
therefore the union's action had not been 'in . . . furtherance of a trade dispute', and
further (per Lord Denning MR) that the acts done were too remote to be regarded as 'in
. . . furtherance of' the trade dispute. The appellants appealed to the House of Lords
against the grant of the injunctions.

Held – The appeal would be allowed and the injunctions discharged for the following
reasons—

(i) Applying the principle that an act was done 'in . . . furtherance of a trade dispute'
within s 13(1) of the 1974 Act if the person doing the act honestly believed that it might
further the cause of those taking part in the dispute, the appellants came within the
ambit of s 13(1) and were accordingly protected against an action in tort since it was not
disputed that they honestly and sincerely believed that by extending their strike to the
private sector they were advancing or furthering their cause in their dispute with BSC.
The fact that they might at the same time be bringing into existence a second and
separate dispute with the government or that the extension of the strike to the private
sector would not have an immediate adverse trade or industrial effect on BSC was
irrelevant (see p 545 c to g, p 546 g h, p 547 g, p 548 g to p 549 a g, p 550 j and p 552 g to
p 553 d, post); *Express Newspapers Ltd v MacShane* p 65, ante, followed.

(ii) In any event the discretion conferred by s 17(2) of the 1974 Act to grant or refuse
an injunction, if the person against whom the injunction was sought claimed that he was
acting in furtherance of a trade dispute, was a discretion conferred on the judge at first
instance and not on the Court of Appeal, and since there was no indication that the judge
had wrongly exercised his discretion the Court of Appeal had been wrong to substitute
their own exercise of the discretion. The judge had correctly decided that it was highly
probable that the appellants' claim to immunity would succeed at trial and that the
nature and gravity of a lengthy strike which extended to the private sector was not so
serious as to bring the case within that exceptional category in which an injunction
would be granted unless there was a high degree of probability that the defence of
statutory immunity would succeed at trial (see p 544 j to p 545 b, p 546 j to p 547d, p 548
g h, p 549 c to g and p 553 g to p 554 a, post); *NWL Ltd v Woods* [1979] 3 All ER 614
followed.

---

contract or interferes or induces any other person to interfere with its performance; or (b) that it
consists in his threatening that a contract (whether one to which he is a party or not) will be broken
or its performance interfered with, or that he will induce another person to break a contract or to
interfere with its performance.'

b Section 17(2) provides: 'It is hereby declared for the avoidance of doubt that where an application
is made to a court, pending the trial of an action, for an interlocutory injunction and the party
against whom the injunction is sought claims that he acted in contemplation or furtherance of a
trade dispute, the court shall, in exercising its discretion whether or not to grant the injunction,
have regard to the likelihood of that party's succeeding at the trial of the action in establishing the
matter or matters which would, under any provision of section 13, 14 (2) or 15 above, afford a
defence to the action.'

a   **Per Curiam.** It endangers public confidence in the political impartiality of the judiciary, which is essential to the continuance of the rule of law, if judges, under the guise of interpretation, provide their own preferred amendments to statutes which experience of their operation has shown to have had consequences that members of the court before whom the matter comes consider to be injurious to the public interest. So, in relation to s 13(1) of the 1974 Act, for a judge (who is always dealing with an individual case) to ask whether Parliament really intended that the acts done in the

b   particular case should have the benefit of immunity is to risk straying beyond his constitutional role as interpreter of the enacted law and assume a power to decide at his own discretion whether to apply the general law to a particular case. The legitimate questions for a judge to ask in his role as interpreter of the enacted law are whether Parliament, by the words that it has used in the statute to express its intentions, has defined the category of acts that are entitled to the immunity, and whether the acts done

c   in the particular case fall within that description (see p 542 *c* to *f*, p 548 *g h*, p 549 *g*, p 550 *e* to *j* and p 551 *d* to *g*, post).

     Per Lord Scarman. If Parliament is minded to amend the 1974 Act, instead of seeking to close 'open-ended expressions' such as those which have given rise to bitter and damaging litigation, the draftsman should be bold and tackle his problems head-on. If he is to put a limitation on the immunities in s 13, he should do so by limiting the heads

d   of tortious liability where immunity is conferred; if he is to strengthen the availability of interlocutory relief in industrial relations, he should include clear guidelines in the statute; and, if he is to limit secondary or tertiary blacking or picketing, the statute must declare whose premises may be picketed and how far the blacking or picketing may extend. Open-ended expressions will bring the judges inevitably into the industrial arena exercising a discretion which may well be misunderstood by many and damage

e   confidence in the administration of justice (see p 544 *a* to *d*, post).

Notes

For the legal liability of trade unions, see Supplement to 38 Halsbury's Laws (3rd Edn) para 677B.3.

     For the Trade Union and Labour Relations Act 1974, s 13(1) (as substituted by the Trade Union and Labour Relations (Amendment) Act 1976, s 3(2)), see 46 Halsbury's

f   Statutes (3rd Edn) 1941, and for s 17(2) of the 1974 Act (as inserted by the Employment Protection Act 1975, s 125, Sch 16, Part III, para 6), see 45 ibid 2438.

Cases referred to in judgments and opinions

Associated Newspapers Group Ltd v Wade [1979] 1 WLR 697, [1979] ICR 664, CA.

Beaverbrook Newspapers Ltd v Keys [1978] ICR 582, CA.

British Broadcasting Corpn v Hearn [1978] 1 All ER 111, [1977] 1 WLR 1004, [1977] ICR

g   685, CA.

Express Newspapers Ltd v MacShane p 65, ante, [1980] 2 WLR 89, HL; *rvsg* [1979] 2 All ER 360, [1979] 1 WLR 390, [1979] ICR 210, CA.

Inland Revenue Comrs v Hinchy [1960] 1 All ER 505, [1960] AC 748, [1960] 2 WLR 448, 38 Tax Cas 625, [1960] TR 33, 39 ATC 13, 53 R & IT 188, HL, 28(1) Digest (Reissue)

h   579, 2159.

London (City of) v Wood (1701) 12 Mod Rep 669, 88 ER 1592, 13 Digest (Reissue) 258, 2293.

NWL Ltd v Woods, NWL Ltd v Nelson [1979] 3 All ER 614, [1979] 1 WLR 1294, [1979] ICR 867, HL.

Scruttons Ltd v Midland Silicones Ltd [1962] 1 All ER 1, [1962] AC 446, [1962] 2 WLR 186,

j   [1961] 2 Lloyd's Rep 365, HL, 12 Digest (Reissue) 53, 275.

United Biscuits (UK) Ltd v Fall [1979] IRLR 110.

Interlocutory application

By a writ dated 24th January 1980 the plaintiffs, Duport Steels Ltd, Ductile Steels Ltd, British Rolling Mills Ltd, Brymbo Steel Works Ltd, Glynwed Steels Ltd, Sheerness Steel Co Ltd, GKN (South Wales) Ltd, GKN Wire Products Ltd, GKN Reinforcements Ltd,

Firth Brown Ltd, Lee Steel Strip Ltd, Hadfields Ltd, Osborn Steels Ltd, Osborn Steel
Extrusion Ltd, Edgar Allen Balfour Steels Ltd and William Oxley & Co Ltd, sought   *a*
against the defendants, William Sirs, Leslie Bramley and E Makepiece (sued on their own
behalf and on behalf of all members of the executive council of the Iron and Steel Trades
Confederation ('the ISTC')), injunctions (i) restraining the defendants from instructing,
or interfering with the plaintiffs' businesses by instructing members of the ISTC to break
their contracts of employment with the plaintiffs or from inducing or procuring those
members to break their contracts of employment by striking or interfering with the   *b*
supply or delivery of steel or steel products to, from or on behalf of the plaintiffs or by
taking any other industrial action, (ii) restraining the defendants from instructing
members of the ISTC to interfere with the plaintiffs' businesses by picketing at or
adjacent to the plaintiffs' premises, (iii) ordering the defendants to withdraw and revoke
any instructions or advice to members of the ISTC to engage in any strike or picketing
or to interfere with the supply or delivery of steel or steel products to, from or on behalf   *c*
of the plaintiffs or to take any other industrial action in breach of their contracts of
employment or in any way that would interfere with the plaintiffs' businesses, and
damages.

Alexander Irvine QC and *Christopher Carr* for the plaintiffs.
J Melville Williams QC and *John Hendy* for the defendants.
                                                                                      d

KENNETH JONES J[1]. In this case the defendants are sued as officers of the Iron and
Steel Trades Confederation ('the ISTC') on behalf of all members of that union. They are
in dispute with the British Steel Corporation ('BSC') and since 2nd January 1980 have
been on strike. Steps have now been taken by the defendants to bring about a strike in
the private sector. The plaintiffs are a number of steel producing companies in that
private sector. They seek from me interim injunctions, having as their purpose the   *e*
prevention of the strike which is called to start at 6.00 am on Sunday, 27th January.
    I have come to the conclusion that I am unable in the proper administration of the law
to grant those injunctions. I come to that conclusion solely because I am constrained
from doing so, in my judgment, by the decision of their Lordships in *Express Newspapers
Ltd v MacShane*[2]. I am told by counsel for the plaintiffs that the immediate sequel of a
refusal to grant the injunctions will be an appeal to the Court of Appeal. Bearing that in   *f*
mind, it seems unnecessary for me to give a lengthy judgment here, or to do more than
express in outline my reasons for arriving at the decision at which I have arrived.
    These proceedings are subject to s 17 of the Trade Union and Labour Relations Act
1974, as amended. It is not necessary for me to read the subsection applicable, sub-s (2),
but what I have to concern myself with is the likelihood of the defendants succeeding at
the trial of the action in establishing that the acts in calling this strike are done in   *g*
contemplation or furtherance of a trade dispute. It is clear from the speeches of the
majority of the House of Lords in *Express Newspapers Ltd v MacShane*[2] that the test is a
subjective one. If the defendants say that they are acting in contemplation or in
furtherance of a trade dispute, I can only examine that statement in two respects. First
to decide whether or not there is a trade dispute. Secondly to decide whether or not that
belief is honestly held.   *h*
    There is no dispute here but that there is a trade dispute between the defendants and
BSC. Counsel for the plaintiffs would have me say that there is no honest belief that the
defendants are acting in contemplation or in furtherance of that trade dispute because no
person in their situation could reasonably think that calling a strike in the private sector
is in furtherance of the dispute with BSC. This is a somewhat fine argument, as I am sure
counsel will concede, although not conceding that it is lacking in legal merit for that   *i*

---

1   This version of his Lordship's judgment was agreed by counsel and has been approved by Kenneth
     Jones J
2   Page 65, ante

reason. As I understand it, what he contends is that an act can only be in furtherance of
a a trade dispute in so far as it is directed to a party who is a stranger to the dispute if it is
designed to cause that party to bring pressure to bear on the other party to the dispute
within the industrial or commercial relationship which exists between that stranger and
the party to the dispute. Counsel, while making that contention, for the moment
confines himself to submitting that his contention or argument is sufficient to make it
less than highly probable that the defendants would succeed in due course in showing
b that their act was in furtherance of this trade dispute. He advances that argument
because in *Express Newspapers Ltd v MacShane*[1] Lord Scarman particularly contemplated
that in granting an interlocutory injunction the court may well be entitled to have
regard to the consequences of allowing the strike to proceed, ie not granting an
injunction, and he quoted the words of Lord Diplock in *NWL Ltd v Woods*[2], where Lord
Diplock said:

c
> '. . . but this does not mean that there may not be cases where the consequences
> to the employer or to third parties or the public and perhaps the nation itself, may
> be so disastrous that the injunction ought to be refused, unless there is a high degree
> of probability that the defence will succeed.'

I am persuaded this should read 'that the injunction ought not to be refused . . .'[3]
d   Counsel for the plaintiffs says this strike would be disastrous; and although there may
be a probability that the defendants will succeed, because of the argument to which I
have just referred, there is no high degree of probability. Dealing with that argument,
it appears to me that it involves putting a gloss on the words in ss 13 and 17 of the 1974
Act. The only question is whether the act contemplated is to be done in contemplation
or furtherance of a trade dispute. I see no warrant within the Act for the importing of
e any further words indicating that the act should be effective only within the commercial
relationship existing here between the private sector and BSC. In my view counsel's
argument fails. There is a probability that this defence will succeed. Indeed I would go
so far as to say that there is a high degree of probability that the defence will succeed here.
   The other limb of counsel's argument for the plaintiffs is that the disaster which would
be consequent on a strike, and which is to be put in the scale in favour of granting an
f injunction, is so tremendous that that should certainly outweigh any degree of
probability of success in the defence. There is ample evidence that this strike will bring
in its train disaster or, without using any emotive word, considerable and heavy loss. It
may well be that it is designed to do precisely that. It is not surprising that such would
be the consequence. In any event, if and in so far as counsel is availing himself only of
this escape route, suggested by Lord Scarman in *Express Newspapers Ltd v MacShane*[1], for
g my part I would, with great respect, agree with the views expressed by Lord Wilberforce[4]
whether, if a subjective test is right, any such escape route does exist. Lord Salmon also
had well in mind the consequences the decision of the House might inadvertently result
in danger to human life. His view was that, to remove that possibility, the time had
come for the law, if that was its effect, to be altered[5].
   Be that as it may, I feel myself constrained to hold that Mr Bramley, the president of
h the ISTC, having stated clearly that this act complained of, although tortious, he honestly
believes to be done in furtherance of the dispute with BSC, the law makes Mr Bramley
really the judge of that, not I, and that, he having so stated and there really being no

---

j   1   See p 79, ante
     2   [1979] 3 All ER 614 at 626, [1979] 1 WLR 1294 at 1307
     3   Lord Diplock has since agreed that the word 'not' was omitted from the transcript of his Lordship's
         opinion in *NWL Ltd v Woods*
     4   See pp 71–72, ante
     5   See p 75, ante

sufficient evidence to the contrary, nor any sufficient weight that I can attach to counsel's
argument for the plaintiffs to which I have already referred, it is highly probable that the *a*
defendants will establish their defence.

In these circumstances, despite the forbidding consequences, I find myself unable to
grant the injunctions.

Injunctions refused.

K Mydeen Esq   Barrister. *b*

Interlocutory appeal
The plaintiffs ('the private sector companies') appealed to the Court of Appeal.

Alexander Irvine QC and *Christopher Carr* for the private sector companies.
J Melville Williams QC and *John Hendy* for the defendants.   *c*

LORD DENNING MR. It is important to distinguish between the public sector and
the private sector of the steel industry. The public sector is under the control of the
British Steel Corporation ('BSC'). It accounts for 40% to 50% of the production of crude
steel and the processing of it. But there is an important private sector which covers about *d*
20% of the rest of the industry. It is run by many private companies. The turnover is
something in the region of £1,500 million a year in the private sector.

At the beginning of this year there was a dispute between the workers in BSC and their
employers, BSC itself, in regard to wages. Through their union, the Iron and Steel Trades
Confederation ('the ISTC'), the workers in the public sector demanded higher wages. As
they did not achieve what they desired, they called a strike (I think the first for many,
many years in the industry) on 2nd January 1980. They called out all the workers in the *e*
public sector, and brought the whole of that great sector to a standstill.

The strike does not seem to have achieved the objective which the union desired. So,
on Wednesday, 16th January, an important decision was made by the union or its
representatives. They made the decision that they would call out the members of the
union who were employed in the private sector.   *f*

Let it be said at once that those workers in the private sector had no dispute whatever
with their employers. All was peaceful and contented. They were ready to go on, and
wanted to go on, with their work, processing the steel, making it, supplying it, and so
forth. When the union suggested, indeed, ordered, that those in the private sector
should come out, ballots were taken in some cases. These showed that the workers in the
private sector did not want to come out. We know that the majority in a secret ballot did *g*
not. There is other evidence to show that many others of them did not want to come
out. Nevertheless, if ordered to do so by their union, they would have no option;
because, if they did not obey the union call, they would lose their union card and in due
course their employment.

On 16th January of this year there was a meeting of the executive council of the
union. They came to a decision to extend the dispute into the private sector. They *h*
decided to call out all those men; and the date they chose for this action was 27th January
at 6.00 am.

Meanwhile the movement of all steel throughout the United Kingdom was to cease
from 6.00 am on Thursday, 17th January.

So there was a most important decision. The ISTC decided to call out the men, who
had no quarrel whatever with their own employers, or between the employers and the *j*
men. They decided to call them out in regard to a dispute with which they were not in
any way concerned. So the question must be asked, and is asked: why did the trade
union extend the strike to the private sector?

It is amply shown by a letter which was written by Mr William Sirs on 17th January
and by instructions which were given to all the branches. I will read a sentence or two

from the letter, because it is quite plain to my mind that by this time the trade union had
a determined that the one way in which they could achieve their ends, or might hope to
achieve their ends, was by bringing pressure to bear on the government. They knew, as
is indeed so by an Act of Parliament, that BSC is in many respects under the general
direction and control of the Secretary of State. That appears in s 4 of the Iron and Steel
Act 1975, which provides:

b   'The Secretary of State may, after consultation with the Corporation, give to the
         Corporation directions of a general character as to the exercise and performance by
         the Corporation of their functions (including the exercise of rights conferred by the
         holding of interests in companies) in relation to matters which appear to him to
         affect the national interest; and the Corporation shall give effect to any directions so
         given.'

c They knew that the government had declined to print any more money for the purpose
of increasing the wages of the workers. In these circumstances, the trade union seems to
have directed its attack on the government.
    On 17th January Mr Sirs wrote to the Independent Steel Employers Association. He
said:

d   '. . . whilst agreeing that there is no dispute with any independent steel employer,
         [the executive council of the ISTC] were firmly of the opinion that this dispute is
         becoming politically stage-managed by the Conservative Government. We feel that
         with not being made an offer of any new money, that we are being singled out for
         a direct Government and British Steel Corporation attack. It is because of the
         political intervention that my Executive Council feel that we should now take the
e   action of involving the private sector in the public battle against the Government
         attitude.'

They knew that they were going against all the industrial agreements which had been
made, because the letter goes on to say:

f   'I recognise the fact that our procedure agreements do exist and we do not have
         a dispute with you, nevertheless these points have been made to our Executive, who
         have ultimately taken this decision.'

    That letter was sent by Mr Sirs to the independent employers. Then on 21st January
Mr Sirs sent out a general direction to the union branches:

g   '. . . It was apparent [he said] that the strike was developing into a confrontation
         between the Government and the trade unions. It was also apparent that the
         continued operation of the private sector was not only having the effect of
         prolonging the [trade] dispute but was creating a feeling of injustice within other
         trade unions.'

    There was further evidence, such as a statement broadcast on the BBC on 16th
h January. The trade unions 'decided to step up their pressure this afternoon: and they left
no doubt that their aim was to force Government intervention'. Passage after passage in
the newspapers, and on the evidence, show that the action taken against the private sector
was in order to bring pressure to bear on the government: so as to make the government
alter its policy and increase the payments to BSC—out of the taxpayers' money, I
suppose.
j   That action taken was ratified, we are told, unanimously by all the 21 members of the
executive council on 24th January, which was last Wednesday. This action is timed to
take place at six o'clock tomorrow morning.
    There is evidence of the disastrous effect which this action will have, not only on all the
companies in the private sector, but on much of British industry itself. The private
sector, as I have said, has a turnover (if it continues to work) of £1,500 million a year.

The turnover in the private sector is about £30 million a week. If the men are called out in the private sector, all these companies would have to shut down at enormous loss. Not only will they have to shut down, but all the firms which they supply will not be able to carry on with their work. They will not be able to make their steel. British Leyland, who depend on 80% of their supplies from the private sector, will have to shut down much of their works too. Not only that, we will lose trade here in this country, and our competitors abroad will clap their hands in anticipation of being able to send their products into England because our industry is at a standstill.

In these circumstances, it is not surprising that 16 of the big private steel companies in this country have come to the courts, hoping they can get here in time, to restrain the three principal members of this union (Mr Sirs, Mr Bramley and Mr Makepiece) calling this disastrous strike, which is going to injure British industry so much.

The judge below heard the application yesterday afternoon. He felt that he had to refuse it because of the recent case in the House of Lords of *Express Newspapers Ltd v MacShane*[1]. He inferred from that case that the majority of the House held that the test was purely subjective; and that if the trade union leaders honestly believed that what they were doing was in furtherance of a trade dispute they would have complete immunity; and the courts can do nothing, because they would be exempt from judicial review.

We have gone through that case, and have read the judgments. They are not nearly so clear on the point as some would believe, but I will deal with them as we come to consider the case. But, first, there is a preliminary point to be considered: what was the dispute here? Was it a trade dispute? Section 29 of the Trade Union and Labour Relations Act 1974 defines a 'trade dispute'. It is quite plain that the dispute between the workers and the employers of BSC was certainly a trade dispute. It was 'a dispute between employers and workers ... connected with ... terms and conditions of employment': see s 29(1)(a). Beyond all doubt, it was a trade dispute. In regard to any acts done in contemplation or furtherance of that dispute, they were entitled to immunity under s 13 of the 1974 Act.

But was that the only dispute in this case? On the evidence which I have read, it seems to me that there is good ground at least for thinking that, besides that initial dispute, there was a second dispute—not between the unions and the private steel companies, because they were all in agreement and were happy working together—but a dispute between the union and the government of this country. I have read enough already to show that the union leaders were complaining of 'political stage management' by the Conservative government. They were engaged 'in a public battle against the Government's attitude'. There was 'a confrontation between the union and the Government'. All this goes to show that there is evidence that there was a second dispute here: a dispute between the union and the government, in which the union were seeking to bring pressure to bear on the government to make them change their attitude and provide more money, or take other steps in relation to BSC, so as to bring them to heel.

It seems to me that that second dispute cannot be regarded as a trade dispute within s 29 at all. In so far as the acts done, or the calling out of these workers, was in furtherance of that second dispute, they are entitled to no immunity whatsoever. It is not a trade dispute. It is not a dispute between employers and workers. It is a dispute between the union and the government.

Then it was suggested by counsel for the defendants that in any event it was in furtherance of that earlier dispute with BSC. That may be a question on the facts. It does not depend on a state of mind, or anything of that kind. I must say that it seems to me arguable that this step taken of calling out all the employees in the private sector, stopping all the movement of steel into and out of the country, was taken in furtherance of a dispute with the government: to try and bring the government to heel, and not in furtherance of the original dispute. If that be so, then they are not protected; because

---

1   Page 65, ante

they are only protected for acts done in contemplation or furtherance of the original
a trade dispute.

That is the first part of the case. But I would say at this point that there is a question
on remoteness. Some acts may be too remote to be in furtherance of a trade dispute.
There was only one member of the House of Lords who dealt with the question of
remoteness. That was Lord Wilberforce; and he certainly expressed the law as I have
always understood it to be. In *Express Newspapers Ltd v MacShane*[1] he said:

b
> '... it is always open to the courts, indeed their duty, with open-ended expressions
> such as those involving cause, or effect, or remoteness, or in the context of this very
> Act, connection with [or, I would add, 'furtherance of'] ... to draw a line beyond
> which the expression ceases to operate. This is simply the common law in action.
> It does not involve the judges in cutting down what Parliament has given; it does
> involve them in interpretation in order to ascertain how far Parliament intended to
c > go.'

In the cases which we have had very recently in this court, particularly in *Associated
Newspapers Group Ltd v Wade*[2], we granted an injunction especially because the act was
too remote to be considered in furtherance of the dispute. It is significant that that case
was not overruled by the House of Lords, nor was it said to be erroneous. I need only
d repeat what I said in that case[3]:

> 'Some acts are so remote from the trade dispute that they cannot properly be said
> to be "in furtherance" of it. When conduct causes direct loss or damage to the
> employer himself (as by withdrawing labour from him or stopping his supplies) it
> is plainly "in furtherance" of the dispute with him. But when trade unions choose
> not to cause damage or loss to the employer himself, but only to innocent third
e > persons—who are not parties to the dispute—it is very different. The act done may
> then be so remote from the dispute itself that it cannot reasonably be regarded as
> being done "in furtherance" of it ... [I cited two cases which have not been
> overruled, *Beaverbrook Newspapers Ltd v Keys*[4], and *United Biscuits (UK) Ltd v Fall*[5]].
> Thus when strikers choose to picket, not their employers' premises, but the premises
> of innocent third persons not parties to the dispute—it is unlawful. "Secondary
f > picketing" it is called. It is unlawful at common law and is so remote from the
> dispute that there is no immunity in regard to it.'

The House did not say that that case was wrongly decided.

Apart from that point, it seems to me, as I have said, that it is arguable in this case that
there is no immunity for these acts done in calling out the private sector, because those
g acts were done in furtherance of the dispute with the government. It was not a trade
dispute at all. It is arguable that they were not done in furtherance of the original trade
dispute with BSC.

Seeing that it is arguable, I come to the other point in this case. It arises out of the
amended s 17 of the statute, which is in para 6 of Part III of Sch 16 to the Employment
Protection Act 1975. Section 17(2) says, in respect to an interlocutory injunction, that
h 'the court shall, in exercising its discretion whether or not to grant the injunction, have
regard to the likelihood of that party's succeeding at the trial of the action'. That section
was much considered by the House of Lords in two recent cases: *NWL Ltd v Woods*[6] and
the recent case of *Express Newspapers Ltd v MacShane*[7]. It is very interesting to see how
the House of Lords have been dealing with s 17. They point out that it does not mean

j 1   See p 70, ante
2   [1979] 1 WLR 697
3   [1979] 1 WLR 697 at 713
4   [1978] ICR 582
5   [1979] IRLR 110
6   [1979] 3 All ER 614, [1979] 1 WLR 1294
7   Page 65, ante

that the likelihood of success is to be the paramount or sole consideration in granting or refusing an injunction; there are other matters to be considered. In particular, damage to the employers, or to the public, or even to the nation can be considered in considering whether to grant or refuse an injunction. Although he put it in the form of a double negative, I would quote what Lord Diplock said (removing the double negative and putting it into the affirmative) in *NWL Ltd v Woods*[1]:

'. . . there may be cases where the consequences to the employer or to third parties or the public and perhaps the nation itself, may be so disastrous that the injunction ought to be granted, unless there is a high degree of probability that the defence will succeed.'

Then Lord Fraser of Tullybelton[2] speaks to the same effect. He said that the likelihood is not to be regarded as of overriding or paramount importance. And Lord Scarman, on that point, said[3]:

'. . . I do not rule out the possibility that the consequences to the plaintiff (or others) may be so serious that the court feels it necessary to grant the injunction, for the subsection does leave a residual discretion with the court.'

That seems to me to be the view of the majority of the House of Lords in *NWL Ltd v Woods*[4]. It was taken up by Lord Scarman in particular in *Express Newspapers Ltd v MacShane*[5]. It had not been raised by counsel in the court, but he thought it so important that he brought it up himself. He referred to that passage, which I have quoted from Lord Diplock, and went on to say[6]:

'. . . in a case where action alleged to be in contemplation or furtherance of a trade dispute endangers the nation [that is the point here, 'endangers the nation'] or puts at risk such fundamental rights as the right of the public to be informed and the freedom of the Press, it could well be a proper exercise of the court's discretion to restrain the industrial action pending trial of the action. It would, of course, depend on the circumstances of the case; but the law does not preclude the possibility of the court exercising its discretion in that way.'

Those passages which I have read from the judgments of the House of Lords do show that there is a residual discretion in the courts to grant an injunction restraining such action as in this case, where it is such as to cause grave danger to the economy and the life of the country, and puts the whole nation and its welfare at risk. In those circumstances, the courts have a residual discretion to grant an injunction unless it is clear, or in the highest degree probable, that there is a defence which is likely to succeed.

I have said enough in this case to show that there is a very good ground for argument that the so-called defence, the immunity, is not likely to succeed. To call out these private steel workers, who have no dispute at all with their employers, would have such a disastrous effect on the economy and well-being of the country that it seems to me only right that the court should grant an injunction to stop these people being called out tomorrow morning, to stop all this picketing and to stop all these people who are preventing the movement of steel up and down the country.

It seems to me that this is a case where, in our residual discretion, we should grant the injunctions in the terms asked. I would allow the appeal.

LAWTON LJ. On 2nd January 1980 the Iron and Steel Trades Confederation ('the ISTC') called out on strike its members employed by the British Steel Corporation

1 [1979] 3 All ER 614 at 626, [1979] 1 WLR 1294 at 1307
2 [1979] 3 All ER 614 at 627, [1979] 1 WLR 1294 at 1309
3 [1979] 3 All ER 614 at 633, [1979] 1 WLR 1294 at 1315
4 [1979] 3 All ER 614, [1979] 1 WLR 1294
5 Page 65, ante
6 See p 79, ante

a ('BSC'). No doubt when they did so they hoped that the strike would be a short one and that victory would come to them. The history of the last two decades tends to show that, when there have been disputes between unions and nationalised industries, there has usually been government intervention, followed fairly quickly by a settlement to the advantage of the strikers.

b Unfortunately for the ISTC on this occasion there was no government intervention of this kind; and by 16th January it became clear that there was not going, in the foreseeable future, to be any. There was going to be no quick victory. The dispute was likely to go on for a long time. What was to be done? The members of the ISTC were likely to suffer hardship if the strike went on for too long. It is clear from a letter which was sent out by Mr Sirs, the general secretary of the ISTC, to all branch secretaries, what the decision was and why a decision was made in the terms it was. I will read from the opening paragraph of the letter:

c   'Dear Colleagues ... I wish to inform you that at the joint ISTC and NUB Executive Council meeting held on Wednesday 16th January 1980, a progress report was submitted on the strike of our members employed by the British Steel Corporation. Arising from that report and subsequent discussion it was apparent that the strike was developing into a confrontation between the Government and the trade unions.'

d That was what the situation was; and, as a result of finding that that was the situation, it was decided (to use Mr Sirs's words) 'to involve the private sector'. The union had no dispute with the private sector at all. Why did they want to involve the private sector? The answer from the evidence which has been filed is clear, namely, by involving the private sector, pressure could be brought to bear on the government. There would be a *e* stoppage of steel going from the private sector to industry; and industry would in consequence grind to a halt. There would be mass unemployment, and then both workers and employers would start beseeching the government to intervene. The whole purpose of the decision of 16th January was by starting a strike in the private sector to bring pressure to bear on the government.

f Trade unions are entitled to bring pressure to bear on the government provided they do it in lawful ways. But one of the privileges they are not entitled to have when doing so is the immunity given by s 13 of the Trade Union and Labour Relations Act 1974, as amended, if what they are doing is done otherwise than in contemplation or furtherance of a trade dispute. So the question arises at once whether what happened after 16th January in relation to the private sector was in contemplation or furtherance of a trade dispute. It is arguable, indeed, strongly arguable, that a strike, the object of which is to *g* coerce the government to change its policies, is not a trade dispute at all within the meaning of s 29 of the Act.

In those circumstances, the question at once arises: was there one dispute here, namely a trade dispute with BSC which would attract the immunity given by s 13, or were there two disputes, the one with the private sector not attracting the immunity given by the Act? This is a matter of some complexity, as counsel for the defendants ('the ISTC') *h* pointed out. The information before the court at the moment is scanty; and, before any firm decision could be reached as to what led the union to behave as it did, it would have to be the subject of much more evidence than the court has at the present time. Suffice for this purpose to say that prima facie it looks as if the decision to involve the private sector was made not for any purpose connected with terms and conditions of employment in that sector but for the purpose of coercing the government.

j If that is so, the courts have jurisdiction to decide whether what was done was a trade dispute within the meaning of the 1974 Act: see *Express Newspapers Ltd v MacShane*[1] per Lord Diplock. It follows, therefore, that the courts are entitled to look at the evidence to see whether what was done in relation to the private sector was a trade dispute. It is only

---

1   See p 72, ante

if they decide that there was a trade dispute that the tests in *Express Newspapers Ltd v MacShane*[1] come into operation. If there was a trade dispute with the private sector, then on the evidence what the defendants did was in furtherance of that dispute. But they have first to satisfy the court that there was a trade dispute with the private sector.

In my judgment, on the evidence, it is strongly arguable that what was happening after 16th January was not in furtherance of a trade dispute with the private sector. It follows, so it seems to me, that s 17(2) of the 1974 Act has little significance because, once there is a strong case for thinking that the union has behaved in a way which does not confer the immunity given by the 1974 Act, then an injunction should be granted.

I too would grant the relief which is requested.

ACKNER LJ. We are, of course, not deciding this action. We have only to consider whether in the exercise of our discretion we should give the pretrial relief of an injunction. I agree with Lord Denning MR and Lawton LJ that there is a seriously arguable question which involves deciding whether or not there were two disputes, one with BSC and the other with the government. If there was a second dispute, then it appears to be common ground that that in itself could not be a trade dispute because the government are not the employers of the defendants. Accordingly, if the acts sought to be restrained are to be done in furtherance of *that second dispute*, they could not be 'in furtherance of a trade dispute'.

Counsel for the private sector companies has raised yet another point, which I think is arguable as well, and that is this: can action aimed at the government, who are not the employers, to coerce the government to change its policy by visiting disastrous consequences on the community at large, be action in furtherance of a trade dispute within the meaning of the section? That Parliament should have intended immunity in such circumstances is, to say the least, surprising. 'Stark' as the effect of the subjective interpretation may be, this still remains in my judgment an arguable question. Having considered, as required by s 17(2) of the 1974 Act, the likelihood of the defendants' establishing a defence under s 13 of the Act and generally the balance of convenience, I too agree that the relief should be granted and the appeal allowed.

Appeal allowed. Injunctions granted in terms of writ. Leave to appeal to the House of Lords refused.

Sumra Green   Barrister.

Interlocutory appeal
The defendants appealed to the House of Lords.

J Melville Williams QC and *John Hendy* for the appellants.
Alexander Irvine QC and *Christopher Carr* for the private sector companies.

LORD DIPLOCK. My Lords, for the reasons that I will give in writing later I do not think that there are any relevant differences between this case and the case of *Express Newspapers Ltd v MacShane*[1] that was recently decided by this House. In my opinion the present appeal is governed by that decision and the Court of Appeal were wrong in holding that it was not. I would accordingly allow the appeal and discharge the injunctions.

LORD EDMUND-DAVIES. My Lords, being of a like mind, I concur with the noble and learned Lord on the Woolsack in holding that this appeal should be allowed and the injunctions discharged.

---

1   Page 65, ante

LORD FRASER OF TULLYBELTON. My Lords, I also agree with the opinion
a expressed by my noble and learned friend on the Woolsack and I too would allow this
appeal.

LORD KEITH OF KINKEL. My Lords, I too for reasons which I will prepare and
make available in writing would allow this appeal.

b **LORD SCARMAN.** My Lords, for reasons which I intend to embody in a speech
which I shall be preparing, I also would allow this appeal.

7th February. The following written opinions were given.

LORD DIPLOCK. My Lords, as recently as 13th December 1979, this House decided
c in *Express Newspapers Ltd v MacShane*[1] that on the true interpretation of s 13(1) of the
Trade Union and Labour Relations Act 1974, as substituted by s 3(2) of the Trade Union
and Labour Relations (Amendment) Act 1976, the test whether an act was 'done by a
person in contemplation or furtherance of a trade dispute' and so entitled him to
immunity from a part of the common law of tort, is purely subjective; ie provided that
the doer of the act honestly thinks at the time he does it that it may help one of the parties
d to a trade dispute to achieve their objectives and does it for that reason, he is protected by
the section.
   That conclusion as to the meaning of words that have been used by successive
Parliaments since the Trade Disputes Act 1906, to describe acts for which the doer is
entitled to immunity from the law of tort over an area that has been much extended by
the 1974 and 1976 Acts, is (as I pointed out in the *MacShane* case[2]) one which is
e intrinsically repugnant to anyone who has spent his life in the practice of the law or the
administration of justice. Sharing those instincts it was a conclusion that I myself
reached with considerable reluctance, for given the existence of a trade dispute, it
involves granting to trade unions a power, which has no other limits than their own self-
restraint, to inflict by means which are contrary to the general law, untold harm to
industrial enterprises unconcerned with the particular dispute, to the employees of such
f enterprises, to members of the public and to the nation itself, so long as those in whom
the control of the trade union is vested honestly believe that to do so may assist it, albeit
in a minor way, in achieving its objectives in the dispute.
   My Lords, at a time when more and more cases involving the application of legislation
which gives effect to policies that are the subject of bitter public and parliamentary
controversy, it cannot be too strongly emphasised that the British Constitution, though
g largely unwritten, is firmly based on the separation of powers: Parliament makes the
laws, the judiciary interpret them. When Parliament legislates to remedy what the
majority of its members at the time perceive to be a defect or a lacuna in the existing law
(whether it be the written law enacted by existing statutes or the unwritten common law
as it has been expounded by the judges in decided cases), the role of the judiciary is
confined to ascertaining from the words that Parliament has approved as expressing its
h intention what that intention was, and to giving effect to it. Where the meaning of the
statutory words is plain and unambiguous it is not for the judges to invent fancied
ambiguities as an excuse for failing to give effect to its plain meaning because they
themselves consider that the consequences of doing so would be inexpedient, or even
unjust or immoral. In controversial matters such as are involved in industrial relations
there is room for differences of opinion as to what is expedient, what is just and what is
j morally justifiable. Under our Constitution it is Parliament's opinion on these matters
that is paramount.
   A statute passed to remedy what is perceived by Parliament to be a defect in the

---

1   Page 65, ante
2   See p 72, ante

existing law may in actual operation turn out to have injurious consequences that
Parliament did not anticipate at the time the statute was passed; if it had, it would have *a*
made some provision in the Act in order to prevent them. It is at least possible that
Parliament, when the 1974 and 1976 Acts were passed, did not anticipate that so
widespread and crippling use as has in fact occurred would be made of sympathetic
withdrawals of labour and of secondary blacking and picketing in support of sectional
interests able to exercise 'industrial muscle'. But if this be the case it is for Parliament,
not for the judiciary, to decide whether any changes should be made to the law as stated *b*
in the Acts, and if so, what are the precise limits that ought to be imposed on the
immunity from liability for torts committed in the course of taking industrial action.
These are matters on which there is a wide legislative choice, the exercise of which is
likely to be influenced by the political complexion of the government and the state of
public opinion at the time amending legislation is under consideration.

It endangers continued public confidence in the political impartiality of the judiciary, *c*
which is essential to the continuance of the rule of law, if judges, under the guise of
interpretation, provide their own preferred amendments to statutes which experience of
their operation has shown to have had consequences that members of the court before
whom the matter comes consider to be injurious to the public interest. The frequency
with which controversial legislation is amended by Parliament itself (as witness the 1974
Act, which was amended in 1975 as well as in 1976) indicates that legislation, after it has *d*
come into operation, may fail to have the beneficial effects which Parliament expected or
may produce injurious results that Parliament did not anticipate. But, except by private
or hybrid Bills, Parliament does not legislate for individual cases. Public Acts of
Parliament are general in their application; they govern all cases falling within categories
of which the definitions are to be found in the wording of the statute. So in relation to
s 13(1) of the 1974 Act, for a judge (who is always dealing with an individual case) to pose *e*
himself the question, 'Can Parliament really have intended that the acts that were done
in this particular case should have the benefit of the immunity?' is to risk straying
beyond his constitutional role as interpreter of the enacted law and assume a power to
decide at his own discretion whether or not to apply the general law to a particular
case. The legitimate questions for a judge in his role as interpreter of the enacted law are,
'How has Parliament, by the words that it has used in the statute to express its intentions, *f*
defined the category of acts that are entitled to the immunity? Do the acts done in this
particular case fall within that description?'

The first of these questions was answered by this House in the *MacShane* case[1] in the
way I have already mentioned. The principal question in this appeal is whether the
Court of Appeal were right in overruling Kenneth Jones J's finding that it was highly
probable that the acts complained of in the instant case did fall within the category of acts *g*
entitled to the immunity.

The relevant facts that were in evidence before the judge and the Court of Appeal are
to be found set out with customary clarity and simplicity in the judgment of Lord
Denning MR. Except that I think it necessary to transcribe in full one letter on which
the argument has mainly turned, I need do no more than restate them here in summary
form. *h*

The British Steel Corporation ('BSC') is a public authority established under the Iron
and Steel Act 1975 to run the nationalised sector of the steel industry. It produces some
50% of home produced steel in the United Kingdom and for that purpose employs a
workforce numbering some 150,000, of whom about 95,000 are members of the trade
union known as the Iron and Steel Trades Confederation ('the ISTC'). Under the 1975
Act the Secretary of State is empowered by s 4 to give to BSC general directions as to the *j*
exercise and performance of its functions, and under Part II of the Act (ss 14–24) he is
entitled to exercise a relatively close control over the finances of BSC and in particular
over its borrowings. In effect, if BSC is operating at a loss, as it notoriously has been

---

1   Page 65, ante

doing for some time past, the Secretary of State holds the purse strings. It is also in
a evidence, what is in any event a matter of public knowledge, that, before the
commencement of the strike by ISTC members which has given rise to the events with
which this appeal is concerned, the government had announced its decision not to
provide any public funds to enable BSC to meet its operating losses after 31st March
1980. Thereafter it must pay its own way and meet its operating costs, including its
current wages bill out of its current earnings.

b In the latter part of 1979 negotiations began between the ISTC and BSC on wage rates
for 1980. Owing to the financial stringency which BSC would experience in 1980, little
progress was made; and on 2nd January the executive council of the ISTC called a strike
of its members employed by BSC. This is the trade dispute in furtherance of which the
union claims the subsequent steps that are the subject of the instant appeal were taken.

Alongside the nationalised sector of the iron and steel industry there is a private
c sector. It consists of about a hundred companies producing some 17½% of the steel
produced in the United Kingdom and employing as part of their total workforce some
15,000 people who are members of the ISTC. It is common ground that there was no
existing trade dispute between these workers and any of their employers in the private
sector.

By 17th January the executive council of the ISTC were growing dissatisfied at the
d progress that the strike was making even with the aid of some sporadic secondary
picketing and sympathetic blacking of movements of steel by members of other trade
unions. Accordingly they resolved to call out on strike their members employed in the
private sector on 26th January unless a wage settlement with BSC had been reached by
then.

On the same date notice of this resolution was sent to the Independent Steel Employers
e Association which represents employers in the private sector. It is convenient to set out
this letter in full because it contains a contemporary explanation by the general secretary
of the ISTC of the purpose of the executive council in resolving on this extension of the
strike:

f
'Dear Mr Hale,
'I refer to your telegram and that of Mr. Alec Mortimer received yesterday. These
telegrams were read to the members of my Executive Council who, after a full and
detailed discussion on the position of the Steel Strike with the Corporation, and
whilst agreeing that there is no dispute with any independent steel employer, were
firmly of the opinion that this dispute is becoming politically stage-managed by the
g Conservative Government. We feel that with not being made an offer of any new
money, that we are being singled out for a direct Government and British Steel
Corporation attack. It is because of the political intervention that my Executive
Council feel that we should now take the action of involving the private sector in
the public battle against the Government attitude. Therefore a recommendation
will be confirmed next which states as follows:— "That in the event of the dispute
h with the British Steel Corporation not being settled by Saturday, 26th January, 1980
instructions are being given to all of our members in the private steel industry to
withdraw their labour." I recognise the fact that our procedure agreements do exist
and we do not have a dispute with you, nevertheless these points have been made
to our Executive, who have ultimately taken this decision. I did manage to extend
the period of time before the action will be taken. This will give us the opportunity
j to try and resolve the dispute. I would suggest that it could be very helpful if you
and all of your affiliated organisations could write to the Government complaining
about their role in this matter which leaves a lot to be desired. Perhaps also
pressures upon the Corporation to settle the issue would be helpful now not only to
the B.S.C. but to the private sector.'

An affidavit of Mr Bramley, the President of the ISTC, that was filed in these proceedings, stated that there were other purposes too, concerned with maintaining the morale of the BSC strikers, retaining the sympathy of members of other trade unions at home and abroad who were adversely affected by the strike, and avoiding confusion between steel that was to be 'blacked' and steel that was not. I regard these, however, as subsidiary to the main purpose as disclosed in the letter. That was to speed up the time when the shortage of steel for manufacturing industry would really begin to bite so that those manufacturers whose businesses would sustain serious losses, those workers who would lose their jobs and members of the public who would suffer hardship, would be induced to put the maximum pressure on the government to revoke its previous decision and to loosen the purse-strings to BSC to an extent that would provide it with a subsidy from public moneys sufficient to enable it to pay to its workforce wages higher than it would be commercially possible for it to pay out of operating earnings.

Faced with this threat the 16 companies operating in the private sector who are the respondents to this appeal ('the private sector companies') issued a writ on 23rd January claiming injunctions against the three appellants who are sued in a representative capacity on behalf of themselves and all other members of the executive council of the ISTC. The injunctions sought were against inducing the private sector companies' employees to break their contracts of employment by coming out on strike, and against inducing any members of the ISTC to interfere with the supply of steel to or from the companies' works or to picket the companies' premises.

Having given the requisite notice to the ISTC under s 17(1) of the Trade Union and Labour Relations Act 1974 the private sector companies applied to the judge in chambers for interlocutory injunctions in terms of the writ. The application was heard in chambers on the afternoon of Friday 25th January by Kenneth Jones J. In a brief oral judgment the judge held that the case was indistinguishable from the *MacShane* case[1] the report of which had just been published. He rejected the only argument addressed to him on behalf of the companies on which it was sought to draw a distinction between that case and the instant case. He held that it was highly probable that the defence that the executive council of the ISTC had acted in furtherance of a trade dispute would succeed. In the exercise of his discretion, he accordingly refused to grant any of the injunctions.

An appeal against this decision was heard by the Court of Appeal (Lord Denning MR, Lawton and Ackner LJJ) at a special sitting held on Saturday 26th January 1980. They reversed the judge's decision, granted the private sector companies the injunctions that they sought and, somewhat surprisingly, refused the executive council of the ISTC leave to appeal to your Lordships' House.

The decision of the Court of Appeal was unanimous. The reasons given by the individual members of the court were not identical but in oral judgments delivered ex tempore with little time for mutual consultation this is neither surprising nor illegitimate, since the task before the court was to consider the degree of likelihood that the executive council of the ISTC would establish that the act of calling on their members in the private sector to join the strike was done in furtherance of the trade dispute between the union and BSC. One possible argument that could be advanced against the executive council's immunity might carry weight with one member of the court, an alternative argument might be preferred by another. The court acting collectively might legitimately take into account the cumulative merits of the various arguments which commended themselves to one or other of its members.

A feature of the judgments which appears to me to be less legitimate is the absence of any recognition that the task on which the Court of Appeal was engaged was not one of exercising an original discretion of its own to grant or to withhold an interlocutory injunction but of reviewing the exercise by a High Court judge of an original discretion which was his alone and which he had exercised in favour of withholding an injunction. Apart from a passing observation in the judgment of Lord Denning MR that

1   Page 65, ante

the speeches of the majority of this House in the *MacShane* case[1] as to the purely

a subjective nature of the relevant test of entitlement to immunity under s 13(1) of the 1974 Act was not nearly as clear as the judge had thought, no deference was paid to his exercise of a discretion which the law had entrusted to him; there was no examination of his reasons for exercising it in the way he did. Indeed, both Lord Denning MR and Ackner LJ in their judgments refer to the exercise of 'our' discretion by the Court of Appeal.

b All three members of the Court of Appeal took the view that the original trade dispute between the ISTC and BSC about wages had by 17th January generated a second dispute in which the parties were the ISTC and the government; that this second dispute did not fall within the definition of 'trade dispute' because the government were not the employers, and that the calling out of workers in the private sector was an act done in furtherance of that second dispute. It will be convenient to refer to this as the 'two

c disputes argument'.

My Lords, if all this be accepted as an accurate description of the situation on 17th January, how does this prevent the act of calling out the workers in the private sector from being an act done in furtherance of the trade dispute between the ISTC and BSC which was still subsisting? If the executive council honestly believed that a principal reason why BSC would not agree to raise wages to the level that the ISTC was demanding

d was because the government was adhering to a policy of refusing to provide BSC with the money to do so out of public funds, what could be better calculated to promote the success of the ISTC's demands in its trade dispute with BSC than to take steps to create a nation-wide shortage of steel which would induce the victims of the shortage to put pressure on the government to change its policy? There may be some who would deplore this conduct; harsh words descriptive of it may come readily to the tongue; but

e it seems to me that, whatever else may be fairly said about it, it cannot be said with any plausibility that it was not done in furtherance of the existing trade dispute with BSC.

The two disputes argument had not been advanced before Kenneth Jones J. Counsel for the private sector companies had relied on a different argument to which I shall be adverting later. The two disputes argument originated from a suggestion proffered from the Bench during the hearing in the Court of Appeal; not unnaturally, in the haste

f of a Saturday morning hearing, counsel for the private sector companies was reluctant at that stage to reject it. Further reflection, however, prior to the hearing in this House, led him to the conclusion that the two disputes argument cannot rationally be supported; he has not sought to uphold the judgments of the Court of Appeal on this ground. In the circumstances I do not find it necessary to analyse those judgments in order to pinpoint what I believe to be the fallacies in the trains of reasoning which led individual members

g of the court to accept the two disputes argument as plausible. Suffice it to say that, for the reason I have already indicated briefly, I do not think it is.

Lord Denning MR advanced an alternative reason for allowing the appeal which is not echoed in either of the other judgments. He was unwilling to accept that the majority speeches in this House in the *MacShane* case[1] had expressed a clear opinion that the test of whether an act was done in furtherance of a trade dispute was purely subjective. This

h led him to conclude that this House had not rejected a test based on remoteness that he himself had adumbrated and adopted in three earlier cases[2]. These cases, he said, had not been specifically singled out by name in the *MacShane* case[1] as being overruled. He inferred from this that it was arguable that they still remained good authority. In the *MacShane* case[1] this House was not concerned to decide whether the actual decisions in any of a series of previous cases in the Court of Appeal were wrong. What was considered

j was whether any of three different tests which had been adumbrated in those cases as

---

1   Page 65, ante
2   *Beaverbrook Newspapers Ltd v Keys* [1978] ICR 582; *United Biscuits (UK) Ltd v Fall* [1979] IRLR 110; *Associated Newspapers Group Ltd v Wade* [1979] 1 WLR 697

applicable to determine whether an act was done by a person in contemplation or furtherance of a trade dispute was right in law or not. Among the three tests rejected as wrong in law was the test of remoteness the authorship of which was specifically ascribed in my own speech to Lord Denning MR. Recognising this, counsel for the private sector companies has not felt able to support the judgment of the Court of Appeal on this ground either.

There remains the argument for distinguishing the instant case from the *MacShane* case[1] that counsel for the companies had addressed to Kenneth Jones J at first instance. He had been diverted by the two disputes argument from developing it in the Court of Appeal. It formed the only ground on which he felt able to rely in inviting this House to overrule the exercise of his discretion by the judge. It receives no mention in the judgments of Lord Denning MR and Lawton LJ, but it attracts what may have been intended as a brief reference in the judgment of Ackner LJ who treats it as arguable.

I do not however find the argument easy to formulate with precision. It starts with a question in a form which I have suggested presents the court with an insidious temptation to cross the boundary between interpretation and legislation: can Parliament in passing the 1974 and 1976 Acts have intended the immunity conferred by it to extend to acts the object of which was to coerce governments by the infliction of great damage on an innocent public?

Parliament may not have expected when it passed the 1974 and 1976 Acts that trade union leadership would use the immunity granted to them by s 13(1) in such a way as to produce consequences so injurious to the nation; but if there is some legal limit on the immunities under the existing legislation it must be found as a matter of construction of the simple words, 'An act done by a person in contemplation or furtherance of a trade dispute' to be found in s 13(1). That Parliament contemplated that such an act might be directed at putting pressure on (or, if you prefer the word, coercing) a Minister to alter government policy where that policy relates to terms and conditions of employment is evident from s 29(2)(b) of the 1974 Act which brings within the definition of a trade dispute a dispute between workers and a Minister of the Crown if the dispute relates 'to matters which cannot be settled without that Minister exercising a power conferred upon him by or under an enactment'. It is not necessary for present purposes to consider whether the dispute between the ISTC and the Secretary of State comes within this description by reason of his statutory powers of control over the finances of BSC; but the existence of the provision disposes of the suggestion that Parliament intended that the mere fact that an act is done with the purpose of coercing government is sufficient in itself to take the act outside the immunity.

Faced by this difficulty counsel for the private sector companies submitted that as a matter of construction the expression 'An act done ... in ... furtherance of a trade dispute' is confined to acts which are intended to have an immediate adverse trade or industrial effect on the opposite party to the trade dispute or to set up a train of trade or industrial causes and effects which will have an adverse consequence of that kind on the opposite party. Like Kenneth Jones J I find elusive the concept of a train of causes and effects which is confined to causes and effects that can be described as 'trade or industrial', and is presumably supposed to be broken by the interposition of a cause and its effect which cannot be so described. There is clearly no principle of construction which would justify reading into the plain and simple words of s 13(1) additional words (and counsel was quite unable to suggest what they would be) to give effect to so elusive a context.

I turn last to the question of discretion. The effect of s 17(2) of the 1974 Act, as inserted by the Employment Act 1975, Sch 16, Part III, para 6, and on the judge's discretion whether or not to grant an interlocutory injunction was discussed by this House in *NWL Ltd v Woods*[2]. The judge, before whom the only argument against the executive council's claim to immunity was that to which I have just referred, took the

1 Page 65, ante
2 [1979] 3 All ER 614, [1979] 1 WLR 1294

view that there was a high degree of probability that the claim to immunity would
a succeed. He took account of the evidence that if the threatened strike in the private
sector were to continue for any considerable length of time, it would bring in its train
consequences of crippling gravity to the manufacturing industries of this country, to
workers employed in them and to the nation as a whole. In refusing to grant the
injunctions he followed the guidance given in my own speech in *NWL Ltd v Woods*[1].

My Lords, it is the exercise by the judge of a discretion vested in him, not in the Court
b of Appeal itself, that your Lordships are required to review. It has not been asserted
before your Lordships that there is any real possibility that the executive council's claim
to immunity will fail on either of the grounds referred to in the judgments of the Court
of Appeal. As to the only remaining ground on which it was argued in this House, as it
was before the judge, that the executive council's claim to immunity for their action in
extending the strike to the private sector might fail, I agree with his assessment of the
c likelihood of this argument ever succeeding. In my view, there is so high a degree of
probability that it falls little short of certainty that it would not. I can see no ground on
which this House would be entitled to interfere with the judge's exercise of his discretion.

The nature and gravity of the damage which would be caused if the strike as extended
to the private sector continues for any length of time is not in itself exceptional.
Comparatively recent experience has shown that almost any major strike in one of the
d larger manufacturing or service industries, if it is sufficiently prolonged, may have the
effect (figuratively) of bringing the nation to its knees. It is the ability in the last resort
to carry out a threat to do this without involving any breach of the civil or criminal law
as it now stands that gives to trade unions, individually and collectively, their 'industrial
muscle'. In practice, one side or the other to the dispute gives way and a settlement is
arrived at, either with or without government intervention, before this point is reached.
e If the national interest requires that some limits should be put on the use of industrial
muscle, the law as it now stands must be changed and this, effectively as well as
constitutionally, can only be done by Parliament, not by the judges.

As a means of controlling abuse of industrial muscle, injunctions granted in civil
actions depend for their efficacy on the respect which the majority of those taking part
in industrial action pay to the law as laid down by the judges. Civil actions cannot be
f brought against trade unions, but against individual defendants only; and only those
individuals are bound to observe the injunction. Everyone else involved in the industrial
action can carry on with impunity doing that from which the individual defendants
have been restrained.

If judges were to grant injunctions notwithstanding that they know that it is highly
probable that the acts that they are enjoining are perfectly lawful, it is unlikely that
g voluntary respect for the law as laid down and applied by courts of justice will continue
to have any influence in controlling industrial action.

It was for these reasons that I expressed myself in favour of allowing this appeal.

LORD EDMUND-DAVIES. My Lords, a judge's sworn duty to 'do right by all
manner of people after the laws and usages of this realm' sometimes puts him in
h difficulty, for certain of those laws and usages may be repugnant to him. When that
situation arises, he may meet it in one of two ways. First, where the law appears clear,
he can shrug his shoulders, bow to what he regards as the inevitable, and apply it. If he
has moral, intellectual, social or other twinges in doing so, he can always invoke Viscount
Simonds LC, who once said (in *Scruttons v Midland Silicones Ltd*[2]):

j   'For to me heterodoxy or, as some might say, heresy, is not the more attractive
         because it is dignified by the name of reform. Nor will I easily be led by an
         undiscerning zeal for some abstract kind of justice to ignore our first duty, which is

---

1   [1979] 3 All ER 614 at 626, [1979] 1 WLR 1294 at 1307
2   [1962] 1 All ER 1 at 7, [1962] AC 446 at 467

to administer justice according to law, the law which is established for us by Act of Parliament or the binding authority of precedent.'

Alternatively, a judge may be bold and deliberately set out to make new law if he thinks the existing legal situation unsatisfactory. But he risks trouble if he goes about it too blatantly, and if the law has been declared in statutory form it may prove too much for him, dislike it though he may. For, as Holt CJ said in 1701, '. . . an Act of Parliament can do no wrong, though it may do several things that look pretty odd . . .' (see *City of London v Wood*[1]). From time to time some judges have been chafed by this supremacy of Parliament, whose enactments, however questionable, must be applied. In *Inland Revenue Comrs v Hinchy*[2] Lord Reid said:

'What we must look for is the intention of Parliament, and I also find it difficult to believe that Parliament ever really intended the consequences which flow from the Crown's contention. But we can only take the intentions of Parliament from the words which they have used in the Act and, therefore, the question is whether these words are capable of a more limited construction. If not, then we must apply them as they stand, however unreasonable or unjust the consequences and however strongly we may suspect that this was not the real intention of Parliament . . . One is entitled and, indeed, bound to assume that Parliament intends to act reasonably and, therefore, to prefer a reasonable interpretation of a statutory provision if there is any choice. But I regret that I am unable to agree that this case leaves me with any choice.'

My Lords, the principal task in this case at all its stages has been that of considering the meaning and ambit of the words, 'An act done by a person in contemplation or furtherance of a trade dispute' in s 13(1) of the Trade Union and Labour Relations Act 1974. Similar words have appeared in United Kingdom statutes for over a hundred years (see eg s 3 of the Conspiracy and Protection of Property Act 1875) and they have many times been judicially considered.

Doubtless, they have sometimes been more favourably regarded from the Bench than at other times. They were considered by this House as recently as December 1979 in *Express Newspapers Ltd v MacShane*[3]. That decision was naturally binding on Kenneth Jones J and on the members of the Court of Appeal who have had to deal with this case. In reality, though not in strict law, it is also presently binding on this House. At first instance it was applied without qualification. But in the Court of Appeal it was restrictively applied and held to have no operation on certain grave and recent developments from what indubitably was in origin a trade dispute.

The proper impact of the decision in *MacShane*[3] on the instant appeal, and particularly in relation to the restrictive approach of the Court of Appeal, has been considered with, if I may say so, admirable clarity in the speech of my noble and learned friend Lord Diplock. This I have had the advantage of reading in draft. I respectfully agree with what he has written, and I feel that, particularly at this interlocutory stage, I cannot usefully add to it. Suffice it to say that, for the reasons he gives, I too would allow this appeal and discharge the injunctions granted below. This I regard as the inevitable outcome of the statutory provision. That this outcome is unpalatable to many has already been made clear. What should be equally clear is that the provision is not the work of the judges but of Parliament, and it is to Parliament alone that those who find this state of the law insupportable may now appeal.

LORD FRASER OF TULLYBELTON. My Lords, I respectfully agree with my noble and learned friends Lord Diplock and Lord Scarman that the acts of the appellants

1   (1701) 12 Mod Rep 669 at 687–688, 88 ER 1592 at 1602
2   [1960] 1 All ER 505 at 512, [1960] AC 748 at 767–768
3   Page 65, ante

in calling out members of the ISTC who are employed by firms in the private sector of
the steel industry were acts done in furtherance of a trade dispute that was already in
existence between the ISTC and BSC. That conclusion is inevitable in the light of the
decision of this House in *Express Newspapers Ltd v MacShane*[1]. In that case, Lord
Wilberforce did not agree with the majority, who held that the test whether an act was
'in . . . furtherance of a trade dispute' was subjective. He considered that the test was
whether the act was reasonably capable of furthering a trade dispute but he nevertheless
agreed with the majority decision that the act of extending the strike in that case to the
Press Association was in furtherance of the existing trade dispute. In my opinion, it is
abundantly clear that if the 'reasonably capable' test had been applicable in this case, its
application would have led to the same result as the application of the subjective test; the
act of calling out the members of the ISTC in the private sector would still have been held
to be in furtherance of the trade dispute with BSC.

I come now to consider the discretion under s 17(2) of the 1974 Act. I wish to explain
in my own words the kind of matters which in my opinion a judge ought to have in
mind when exercising his discretion. For the reason that I stated in *NWL Ltd v Woods*[2],
I consider that the duty of the court, both in England and in Scotland, is to 'have regard
to' the likelihood that the party against whom an interlocutory injunction is sought will
succeed in establishing the defence that his threatened action would be in contemplation
or furtherance of a trade dispute, but without giving overriding effect to that matter. It
follows that in a case where the court considers that the defence is highly likely to be
established it will be slow to grant an interlocutory injunction against acts which would
be protected by the defence. But even in such a case the court has the duty to have regard
also to the probable effects of the threatened act. If the court considers, on the available
evidence, that the threatened act would probably have an immediate and devastating
effect on the applicant's person or property, eg by ruining plant which could not be
replaced without large expenditure and long delay, the court ought to take that into
account. Similarly, if the probable result of the threatened act would be to cause
immediate serious danger to public safety or health, and if no other means seemed to be
available for averting the danger in time, the court would in my opinion not be
exercising its discretion wrongly if it were to grant an interim injunction. But the kinds
of instance which I have suggested do not embrace the facts of the present case where the
probable injury to the respondents, the private sector companies, although undoubtedly
very serious, is not so immediate as to tip the scale in favour of granting an injunction.

I would allow this appeal.

LORD KEITH OF KINKEL. My Lords, I agree with the reasons for allowing this
appeal which have been stated by my noble and learned friend Lord Diplock, and which
I have had the opportunity of reading in draft.

In *Express Newspapers Ltd v MacShane*[1] this House authoritatively decided that, in
considering whether an act was done 'in . . . furtherance of' a trade dispute within the
meaning of s 13(1) of the Trade Union and Labour Relations Act 1974, it was necessary
for the court to examine the state of mind of the person doing the act in order to ascertain
whether his honest purpose was to promote the success of his side in the dispute. It
rejected the view that on a proper construction of the enactment it was permissible to
have regard to the remoteness of the act done from the immediate source of the dispute,
or the extent to which it had reasonable prospects of furthering the dispute, otherwise
than in connection with testing the genuineness, on the evidence as a whole, of the
purpose professed by the defendant.

In the present case there are no reasonable grounds, on the evidence available at this
interlocutory stage, for doubting that the action taken by the defendants was taken with

---

1   Page 65, ante
2   [1979] 3 All ER 614 at 629, [1979] 1 WLR 1294 at 1310–1311

the genuine purpose of promoting their union's side of its trade dispute with the BSC.
That dispute is over wages. It is apparent that there is little or no prospect of BSC being *a*
able to pay higher wages to its workers, on conditions acceptable to them, unless the
government, which has power to do so, makes available to BSC, in sufficient quantity to
allow of increased wages, money levied from the general body of taxpayers. So action on
the part of the union designed to result in pressure being applied to the government to
make such money available is plainly directed to improving the prospects of the union's
wages claim being met. Even if the quality of the action properly fell to be tested *b*
objectively, which is not the position, the test would in my opinion be satisfied.

The Court of Appeal took the view that the action designed to bring pressure to bear
on the government was taken in pursuance of a political dispute which was something
separate and distinct from the trade dispute with BSC. Having regard to the
considerations which I have mentioned, that was not, in my opinion, a tenable view.
Further, it was not a view which was urged on the Court of Appeal by counsel for the *c*
private sector companies. His argument, as he made plain in his most attractively
presented address to this House, was to quite a different effect. It was that in order to
qualify as an act in furtherance of a trade dispute the act relied on must be designed to
operate through a sequence of cause and effect of an industrial character. An act designed
to operate otherwise than by interfering in some way with the processes of manufacturing
and marketing of the employer's product, so it was maintained, did not qualify. This *d*
argument was considered and rejected by Kenneth Jones J at first instance. It was barely
noticed in the judgments of the Court of Appeal. In my opinion it is unsound. However
desirable its outcome might be thought to be, I can find no warrant in the terms of s 13(1)
for implying into the width of the language there used a limitation such as is contended
for.

Perusal of the judgments in the Court of Appeal makes it clear that their conclusion *e*
was strongly influenced by consideration of the injustice involved, in their view, in
subjecting to serious economic loss, inconvenience and distress, employers and workers
in the private sector of the steel industry, who had no concern at all with the dispute
between the union and the BSC, and also of the disastrous economic consequences to the
country as a whole of the action taken by the defendants. Such considerations cannot
properly distract the court from its duty of faithfully interpreting a statutory provision *f*
according to its true intent, notwithstanding that events have shown the provision to be
capable of being relied on to enable privileged persons to bring about disastrous
consequences with legal impunity. There is nothing in the apparent policy of the Act,
or the 1976 amending Act, which might warrant a restrictive interpretation of s 13(1) of
the 1974 Act. Indeed, that policy seems to have been to enlarge, not to abridge, the
privileges by way of immunity conferred on trade unions, their officials and members. *g*
If these privileges should prove to have been exercised with insufficient sense of
responsibility, to the serious detriment of the national interest, then it is for the force of
public opinion to seek their curtailment through the democratic processes available to
it. The considerations for and against such curtailment can be properly and definitely
debated only in Parliament. It is no part of the function of a court of law to form
conclusions about the merits of the issue. The one public interest which courts of law are *h*
properly entitled to treat as their concern is the standing of and the degree of respect
commanded by the judicial system. Involvement in political controversy, particularly in
the legislatively governed field of industrial relations, is calculated to damage that
interest. In the interpretation of statutes the courts must faithfully endeavour to give
effect to the expressed intention of Parliament as gathered from the language used and
the apparent policy of the enactment under consideration. *j*

I have therefore concluded that the appeal must be allowed.

LORD SCARMAN. My Lords, this appeal raises two specific questions as to the
interpretation of a statute, the Trade Union and Labour Relations Act 1974, as
amended. But below the surface of the legal argument lurk some profound questions as

to the proper relationship in our society between the courts, the government and Parliament. The technical questions of law pose (or should pose) no problems. The more fundamental questions are, however, very disturbing; nevertheless it is on my answer to them that I would allow the appeal. My basic criticism of all three judgments in the Court of Appeal is that in their desire to do justice the court failed to do justice according to law. When one is considering law in the hands of the judges, law means the body of rules and guidelines within which society requires its judges to administer justice. Legal systems differ in the width of the discretionary power granted to judges: but in developed societies limits are invariably set, beyond which the judges may not go. Justice in such societies is not left to the unguided, even if experienced, sage sitting under the spreading oak tree.

In our society the judges have in some aspects of their work a discretionary power to do justice so wide that they may be regarded as lawmakers. The common law and equity, both of them in essence systems of private law, are fields where, subject to the increasing intrusion of statute law, society has been content to allow the judges to formulate and develop the law. The judges, even in this, their very own field of creative endeavour, have accepted, in the interests of certainty, the self-denying ordinance of stare decisis, the doctrine of binding precedent; and no doubt this judicially imposed limitation on judicial lawmaking has helped to maintain confidence in the certainty and even-handedness of the law.

But in the field of statute law the judge must be obedient to the will of Parliament as expressed in its enactments. In this field Parliament makes and unmakes the law the judge's duty is to interpret and to apply the law, not to change it to meet the judge's idea of what justice requires. Interpretation does, of course, imply in the interpreter a power of choice where differing constructions are possible. But our law requires the judge to choose the construction which in his judgment best meets the legislative purpose of the enactment. If the result be unjust but inevitable, the judge may say so and invite Parliament to reconsider its provision. But he must not deny the statute. Unpalatable statute law may not be disregarded or rejected, merely because it is unpalatable. Only if a just result can be achieved without violating the legislative purpose of the statute may the judge select the construction which best suits his idea of what justice requires.

Further, in our system the stare decisis rule applies as firmly to statute law as it does to the formulation of common law and equitable principles. And the keystone of stare decisis is loyalty throughout the system to the decisions of the Court of Appeal and this House. The Court of Appeal may not overrule a House of Lords decision; and only in the exceptional circumstances set out in the practice statement[1] of 26th July 1966 will this House refuse to follow its own previous decisions.

Within these limits, which cannot be said in a free society possessing elective legislative institutions to be narrow or constrained, judges, as the remarkable judicial career of Lord Denning MR himself shows, have a genuine creative role. Great judges are in their different ways judicial activists. But the Constitution's separation of powers, or more accurately functions, must be observed if judicial independence is not to be put at risk. For, if people and Parliament come to think that the judicial power is to be confined by nothing other than the judge's sense of what is right (or, as Selden[2] put it, by the length of the Chancellor's foot), confidence in the judicial system will be replaced by fear of it becoming uncertain and arbitrary in its application. Society will then be ready for Parliament to cut the power of the judges. Their power to do justice will become more restricted by law than it need be, or is today.

In the present case the Court of Appeal failed to construe or apply the statute in the way in which this House had plainly said it was to be construed and applied. This failure was recognised, significantly and courageously, by counsel for the respondents, the private sector companies, who at the outset of his argument in this House said he would

---

1   Note [1966] 3 All ER 77, [1966] 1 WLR 1234
2   Table Talk of John Selden (Pollock, ed) (1927) p 43

not be relying on the reasoning of the Court of Appeal. It was, he recognised, contrary to the ruling of the majority of this House in the recent case of *Express Newspapers Ltd v MacShane*[1]. Instead of relying on the grounds selected by the Court of Appeal for reversing the judge's decision to refuse the private sector companies the injunctions they were seeking, counsel advanced a skilful and serious argument on the construction of the statute, which could plausibly be said to be open to him notwithstanding the decision in *MacShane's* case[1]. He had advanced it before the judge in chambers, who considered and rejected it. He advanced it before the Court of Appeal, who so far as one can gather from the terms of their judgments, did not think it even merited consideration, for not one of the three judges dealt with it, though Ackner LJ did refer to it. My Lords, I regret to have to say it, but in my opinion the Court of Appeal in this case, for the most laudable of motives, their desire to achieve a just result, strayed beyond the limits set by judicial precedent and by our (largely unwritten) Constitution. Their decision was contrary to the statute as authoritatively interpreted by your Lordships' House.

The two questions which arise on the statute are: first, the true construction of the words 'an act done by a person in contemplation or furtherance of a trade dispute' in s 13 of the 1974 Act, the section which confers on persons contemplating or already engaged in a trade dispute certain immunities from tortious liability; secondly, the extent of the discretion possessed by the court where s 17(2) of the 1974 Act, as amended, applies.

Section 13

There are two sectors in the British steel industry: the public sector, in which the British Steel Corporation ('BSC') is the employer, and a much smaller private sector, which includes a number of private employers, among them the 16 plaintiffs in this action. It is common ground that there exists in the present case a trade dispute between the union and BSC. It is a dispute about wages. The union wants 'more money on the table'. BSC say that they cannot provide it; nor is the government, who under the Iron and Steel Act 1975 retain ultimate financial control of BSC, willing to provide it. In these circumstances, as Lord Denning MR said in his judgment[2], the union 'came to a decision to extend the dispute into the private sector'. It was apparent to the union, as Mr Sirs said in a letter written to union branches and quoted in his judgment by Lord Denning MR[2], 'that the continued operation of the private sector was not only having the effect of prolonging the [trade] dispute but was creating a feeling of injustice within other trade unions'. The extension of the dispute was intended to put pressure on the government to find the money which would enable BSC to make an offer acceptable to the union and so to put an end to the trade dispute. Whether or not this extension brought into existence a second and separate dispute with the government (as the Court of Appeal thought), it was certainly an act done in furtherance of the wages dispute with BSC in the sense in which this House interpreted the section in *MacShane's* case[1]. The executive council of the union honestly and sincerely believed that by extending the strike into the private sector they were advancing, or furthering, their cause in the wages dispute.

This analysis of the situation, which the private sector companies in this House have not suggested is false, disposes of the reasons given by the Court of Appeal for considering it 'arguable' that what was done was not in furtherance of the trade dispute. And counsel did not contend to the contrary.

His argument assumed that the acts of the appellants were done in furtherance of the trade dispute. But he argued that on a true construction of the section the acts which attract immunity must be acts having industrial or commercial consequences and designed to bring pressure on a person or persons who could themselves bring industrial

---

1   Page 65, ante
2   See p 535, ante

or commercial pressure on the employer who was in dispute with the union. Applying
a this criterion to the facts of this case, he submitted that the private sector had no power
to coerce, or exert industrial or commercial pressure on, BSC. It was neither a customer
nor a supplier of BSC, but a competitor. The purpose of extending the strike to the
private sector was, therefore, political in character, i e to induce the private sector to bring
pressure on the government to provide the money needed to satisfy the union.

The plausibility of the submission derives from the fact that it is directed to the quality
b of the act required for immunity and not to the question whether or not it is in
contemplation or furtherance of a trade dispute. Nevertheless, it must be rejected. First,
the Act imposes no express limitation on the character of the act which attracts immunity
other than that it must be done in contemplation or furtherance of a trade dispute.
Secondly, an analysis of the submission reveals that it is an attempt to define acts
qualifying for immunity by reference to their purpose. But the only purpose mentioned
c by the statute is the advancement of a trade dispute.

In brief, the statute is not expressly limited in the way counsel suggests; and, in the
light of Parliament's legislative purpose as analysed in *NWL Ltd v Woods*[2] and *MacShane's*
case[2], it cannot be said that Parliament intended that it should be. To the question 'Could
Parliament have conceivably intended that any act which a trade disputant honestly
believed would further his side of the dispute should attract the immunity provided by
d the section?' the answer is simply 'Yes, and this House in its judicial examination of the
legislative purpose of the statutory provisions has already so answered the question'.

Section 17(2)

This subsection requires that, where an application is made for an interlocutory
injunction against a party claiming that he acted in contemplation or furtherance of a
e trade dispute, the court shall have regard to the likelihood of his succeeding at the trial
in establishing that he so acted. The subsection does not deprive the court of its
discretion; and in both *NWL Ltd v Woods*[1] and *MacShane's* case[2] are to be found dicta
recognising that the court has a residual discretion to grant an injunction notwithstanding
the likelihood of such a defence succeeding at trial, e g where the consequences to the
employer or to third parties or the public and perhaps the nation itself might be
f disastrous if it were refused (per Lord Diplock[3] and myself in *NWL Ltd v Woods*[3]) or
where the action sought to be enjoined endangered a fundamental right of the public
such as the freedom of the press (per myself in *MacShane's* case[4]). But it would require
an altogether exceptional case, some examples of which my noble and learned friend
Lord Fraser of Tullybelton has given in his speech.

In the instant case the high probability is that the defence would succeed at the trial.
g Indeed, my Lords, I think it 'a virtual certainty' (to borrow Lord Diplock's words in *NWL
Ltd v Woods*[5]). The economic damage threatened by the extension of the strike to the
private sector, though very serious, is not so immediate as to justify intervention by the
court granting relief to which it is probable that the plaintiffs are not entitled. There is
time for the parties to come to terms or for the government to act either by intervention
or by taking emergency powers or by some other executive or legislative action. When
h disaster threatens, it is ordinarily for the government, not the courts, to act to avert it.

But, my Lords, there is a further ground for holding the Court of Appeal to have been
in error in granting the injunctions. Injunctive relief is discretionary, and the discretion
is the judge's. An appellate court may intervene if the judge misdirected himself in law,
took into account irrelevant matters or failed to take into account relevant matters. The

j

1   [1979] 3 All ER 614, [1979] 1 WLR 1294
2   Page 65, ante
3   [1979] 3 All ER 614 at 626, 633, [1979] 1 WLR 1294 at 1307, 1315
4   See p 79, ante
5   [1979] 3 All ER 614 at 626, [1979] 1 WLR 1294 at 1307

judge exercised his discretion in this case by refusing the injunctions, and there is no indication in his short and admirable judgment that he fell into any of these errors of *a* law.

My Lords, for these reasons, as well as for those set forth in the speech of my noble and learned friend Lord Diplock I would allow the appeal and discharge the injunctions.

If the law is unacceptable, the remedy lies with Parliament, not the judges. And if Parliament is minded to amend the statute, I would suggest that, instead of seeking to close what Lord Wilberforce has aptly called 'open-ended expressions' (in *MacShane's* *b* case[1]) such as those which have now given rise to bitter and damaging litigation (e g *British Broadcasting Corpn v Hearn*[2], *NWL Ltd v Woods*[3] and *Express Newspapers Ltd v MacShane*[4]), the draftsman should be bold and tackle his problems head on. If he is to put a limitation on the immunities in s 13, let him do so by limiting the heads of tortious liability where immunity is conferred; if he is to strengthen the availability of interlocutory relief in industrial relations, let him include clear guidelines in the *c* statute. And, if he is to limit secondary or tertiary blacking or picketing, the statute must declare whose premises may, or may not, be picketed and how far the blacking or picketing may extend. 'Open-ended expressions' will bring the judges inevitably into the industrial arena exercising a discretion which may well be misunderstood by many and which can damage confidence in the administration of justice.

d

Appeal allowed. Injunctions discharged.

Solicitors: *Russell Jones & Walker* (for the appellants); *Allen & Overy* (for the private sector companies).

                                          Mary Rose Plummer   Barrister. *e*

1   See p 70, ante
2   [1978] 1 All ER 111, [1977] 1 WLR 1004
3   [1979] 3 All ER 614, [1979] 1 WLR 1294
4   Page 65, ante

a

Practice Note

COURT OF APPEAL, CRIMINAL DIVISION
LORD WIDGERY CJ, ROSKILL LJ AND CAULFIELD J
14th FEBRUARY 1980

b *Criminal law – Appeal – Leave to appeal – Application – Unmeritorious appeals – Direction that time spent in custody after lodging application not to count towards sentence – Counsel not to settle grounds of appeal unless proposed appeal properly arguable.*

At the sitting of the court **LORD WIDGERY CJ** made the following statement. In 1970 the then Lord Chief Justice, Lord Parker CJ, found it necessary to issue a reminder of the power, both of the full court and of the single judge, when refusing an application c for leave to appeal, to direct that part of the time, during which a person was in custody after lodging his application, should not count towards sentence: see the Practice Note of 17th March 1970[1].

The power was then being exercised only rarely at the single judge stage and the reminder was necessary due to the serious delays caused to meritorious appeals by the huge number of hopeless appeals which had also to be considered. It led immediately to d an improvement in the situation.

A similar reminder is necessary now. Again, meritorious appeals are suffering serious and increasing delays, due to the lodging of huge numbers of hopeless appeals. Again, the power at the single judge stage is being rarely used.

In order to accelerate the hearing of those appeals in which there is some merit, single judges will, from 15th April 1980, give special consideration to the giving of a direction e for loss of time, whenever an application for leave to appeal is refused. It may be expected that such a direction will normally be made unless the grounds are not only settled and signed by counsel, but also supported by the written opinion of counsel. Advice on appeal is, of course, often available to prisoners under the legal aid scheme. Counsel should not settle grounds, or support them with written advice, unless he f considers that the proposed appeal is properly arguable. It would, therefore, clearly not be appropriate to penalise the prisoner in such a case, even if the single judge considered that the appeal was quite hopeless.

It is also necessary to stress that, if an application is refused by the single judge as being wholly devoid of merit, the full court has power, in the event of renewal, both to order loss of time, if the single judge has not done so, and to increase the amount of time ordered to be lost if the single judge has already made a direction, whether or not g grounds have been settled and signed by counsel. It may be expected that this power too will, as from 15th April 1980, normally be exercised.

Steps will be taken to see that the terms of this Practice Note, which is made after consultation both with those Lords Justices who habitually preside in this court and with the judges, are brought to the attention of prisoners who contemplate lodging a notice h of appeal.

N P Metcalfe Esq   Barrister.

---

1   [1970] 1 All ER 1119, [1970] 1 WLR 663

j

Photo Production Ltd v Securicor Transport Ltd

HOUSE OF LORDS

LORD WILBERFORCE, LORD DIPLOCK, LORD SALMON, LORD KEITH OF KINKEL AND LORD SCARMAN

12th, 13th, 14th NOVEMBER 1979, 14th FEBRUARY 1980

Contract – Fundamental breach – Effect on exception clause – Exclusion of applicability of exception clause – Destruction of subject-matter of contract – Defendants contracting to guard factory against fire but instead causing fire which destroyed factory – Whether breach of contract eliminating exception clause – Whether defendants able to rely on exception clause to limit their liability.

The plaintiffs, a company which owned a factory, entered into a contract with the defendants, a security company, by which the defendants were to provide security services at the factory, including night patrols. While carrying out a night patrol at the factory an employee of the defendants deliberately lit a small fire which got out of control. The factory and stock inside, together valued at £615,000, were completely destroyed. The plaintiffs sued the defendants for damages on the ground that they were liable for the act of their employee. The defendants pleaded, inter alia, an exception clause in the contract, to the effect that 'under no circumstances' were the defendants to be 'responsible for any injurious act or default by any employee ... unless such act or default could have been foreseen and avoided by the exercise of due diligence on the part of the [defendants] as his employer; nor, in any event, [were the defendants to] be held responsible for ... any loss suffered by the [plaintiffs] through ... fire or any other cause, except in so far as such loss [was] solely attributable to the negligence of the [defendants'] employees acting within the course of their employment ...' No negligence was alleged against the defendants for employing the employee. The trial judge held that the defendants were entitled to rely on the exception clause. The Court of Appeal[a] reversed his decision, holding that there had been a fundamental breach of the contract by the defendants which precluded them from relying on the exception clause. The defendants appealed to the House of Lords.

Held – The appeal would be allowed for the following reasons—

(i) There was no rule of law by which an exception clause in a contract could be eliminated from a consideration of the parties' position when there was a breach of contract (whether fundamental or not) or by which an exception clause could be deprived of effect regardless of the terms of the contract, because the parties were free to agree to whatever exclusion or modification of their obligations they chose and therefore the question whether an exception clause applied when there was a fundamental breach, breach of a fundamental term or any other breach, turned on the construction of the whole of the contract, including any exception clauses, and because (per Lord Diplock) the parties were free to reject or modify by express words both their primary obligations to do that which they had promised and also any secondary obligations to pay damages arising on breach of a primary obligation (see p 560 *b* to *d*, p 561 *c* to *f*, p 565 *b*, p 566 *c* to *e*, p 567 *f g*, p 568 *a h* and p 570 *a* to *d*, post); *Suisse Atlantique Société d'Armement Maritime SA v NV Rotterdamsche Kolen Centrale* [1966] 2 All ER 61 explained and applied; *Charterhouse Credit Co Ltd v Tolly* [1963] 2 All ER 432, *Harbutt's Plasticine Ltd v Wayne Tank and Pump Co Ltd* [1970] 1 All ER 225 and *Wathes (Western) Ltd v Austins (Menswear) Ltd* [1976] 1 Lloyd's Rep 14 overruled.

---

a   [1978] 3 All ER 146

(ii) Although the defendants were in breach of their implied obligation to operate
a their service with due and proper regard to the safety and security of the plaintiffs'
premises, the exception clause was clear and unambiguous and protected the defendants
from liability (see p 564 *c* to *f*, p 568 *d e*, p 569 *e f* and p 570 *b c*, post).

Per Curiam. (i) In commercial matters generally, when the parties are not of unequal
bargaining power and when the risks are normally borne by insurance, the parties should
be left free to apportion the risks as they think fit, having regard to difficulties of
b deciding at what point the breach in fact becomes fundamental and the date at which the
termination is to be fixed (see p 561 *j* to p 562 *b*, p 568 *b c*, p 569 *f g* and p 570 *b c*, post).

(ii) Much of the difficulty regarding the 'termination' of a contract and its effect on
the plaintiff's claim for damages arises from uncertain or inconsistent terminology; in
particular (per Lord Wilberforce) the use of 'rescission' as an equivalent for discharge,
though justifiable in some contexts, may lead to confusion in others, and (per Lord
c Diplock) the expression 'fundamental breach' should be confined to an event resulting
from the failure by one party to perform a primary obligation which has the effect of
depriving the other party of substantially the whole benefit which it was the intention
of the parties that he should obtain from the contract, so that the party not in default may
elect to put an end to all primary obligations of both parties remaining unperformed,
while 'breach of condition' should be confined to the situation where the contracting
d parties have agreed, whether by express words or by implication of law, that any failure
by one party to perform a particular primary obligation irrespective of the gravity of the
event that has in fact resulted from the breach shall entitle the other party to elect to put
an end to all primary obligations of both parties remaining unperformed (see p 562 *e* to
h, p 565 *e f* and p 566 *h* to p 567 *a*, post).

Observations on, and analysis of, the primary and secondary obligations arising under
e a contract (see p 565 *g* to p 567 *e*, post).

Decision of the Court of Appeal [1978] 3 All ER 146 reversed.

Notes

For the doctrine of fundamental breach of contract, see 9 Halsbury's Laws (4th Edn) paras
372, 545.
f   For rules of construction in relation to exclusion clauses and the effect of breach of such
clauses, see ibid paras 370–380.

Cases referred to in opinions

Alderslade v Hendon Laundry Ltd [1945] 1 All ER 244, [1945] KB 189, 114 LJKB 196, 172,
g   LT 153, CA, 3 Digest (Reissue) 469, *3116*.
Angelia, The, Trade and Transport Inc v Iino Kaiun Kaisha Ltd [1973] 2 All ER 144, [1973]
1 WLR 210, [1972] 2 Lloyd's Rep 154, Digest (Cont Vol D) 823, *1355a*.
Boston Deep Sea Fishing and Ice Co Ltd v Ansell (1888) 39 Ch D 339, [1886–90] All ER Rep
65, CA, 1(2) Digest (Reissue) 662, *4525*.
Charterhouse Credit Co Ltd v Tolly [1963] 2 All ER 432, [1963] 2 QB 683, [1963] 2 WLR
h   1168, CA, Digest (Cont Vol A) 649, *43c*.
Hain Steamship Co Ltd v Tate & Lyle Ltd [1936] 2 All ER 597, 155 LT 177, 19 Asp MLC 62,
41 Com Cas 350, 55 Ll L Rep 159, HL, 41 Digest (Repl) 385, *1737*.
Harbutt's Plasticine Ltd v Wayne Tank and Pump Co Ltd [1970] 1 All ER 225, [1970] 1 QB
447, [1970] 2 WLR 198, [1970] 1 Lloyd's Rep 15, CA, 12 Digest (Reissue) 475, *3407*.
Hardwick Game Farm v Suffolk Agricultural and Poultry Producers Association Ltd [1966] 1
j   All ER 309, [1966] 1 WLR 287, [1966] 1 Lloyd's Rep 197, CA; on appeal sub nom
Henry Kendall & Sons (a firm) v William Lillico & Sons Ltd [1968] 2 All ER 444, [1969] 2
AC 31, [1968] 3 WLR 110, [1968] 1 Lloyd's Rep 547, HL, Digest (Cont Vol C) 853,
781b.
Heyman v Darwins Ltd [1942] 1 All ER 337, [1942] AC 356, 111 LJKB 241, 166 LT 306,
HL, 2 Digest (Repl) 492, *435*.

Hong Kong Fir Shipping Co Ltd v Kawasaki Kisen Kaisha Ltd [1962] 1 All ER 474, [1962] 2
    QB 26, [1962] 2 WLR 474, [1961] 2 Lloyd's Rep 478, CA, 41 Digest (Repl) 363, *1553*.   *a*
Johnson v Agnew [1979] 1 All ER 883, [1979] 2 WLR 487, HL.
Karsales (Harrow) Ltd v Wallis [1956] 2 All ER 866, [1956] 1 WLR 936, CA, 26 Digest
    (Repl) 666, *35*.
Kenyon, Son & Craven Ltd v Baxter Hoare & Co Ltd [1971] 2 All ER 708, [1971] 1 WLR
    519, [1971] 1 Lloyd's Rep 232, 3 Digest (Reissue) 451, *3019*.
Levison v Patent Steam Carpet Cleaning Co Ltd [1977] 3 All ER 498, [1978] QB 69, [1977]   *b*
    3 WLR 90, CA.
Morris v C W Martin & Sons Ltd [1965] 2 All ER 725, [1966] 1 QB 716, [1965] 3 WLR
    276, [1965] 2 Lloyd's Rep 63, CA, 3 Digest (Reissue) 436, *2958*.
Moschi v Lep Air Services Ltd [1972] 2 All ER 393, [1973] AC 331, [1972] 2 WLR 1175,
    HL, Digest (Cont Vol D) 368, *625a*.
Suisse Atlantique Société d'Armement Maritime SA v NV Rotterdamsche Kolen Centrale [1966]   *c*
    2 All ER 61, [1967] 1 AC 361, [1966] 2 WLR 944, [1966] 1 Lloyd's Rep 529, HL,
    Digest (Cont Vol B) 652, *2413a*.
UGS Finance Ltd v National Mortgage Bank of Greece [1964] 1 Lloyd's Rep 446, CA.
Ward (R V) Ltd v Bignall [1967] 2 All ER 449, [1967] 1 QB 534, [1967] 2 WLR 1050, CA,
    Digest (Cont Vol C) 858, *2522a*.
Wathes (Western) Ltd v Austins (Menswear) Ltd [1976] 1 Lloyd's Rep 14, CA.   *d*

Appeal

This was an appeal by the defendants, Securicor Transport Ltd ('Securicor'), against a
decision of the Court of Appeal[1] (Lord Denning MR, Shaw and Waller LJJ) dated 15th
March 1978 allowing an appeal by the plaintiffs, Photo Production Ltd, from a judgment
of MacKenna J given on 7th April 1976 whereby he dismissed the plaintiffs' action   *e*
against Securicor claiming damages for breach of contract between the parties dated 2nd
January 1968 and/or the negligence of Securicor in the employment of or for the acts
done by their servant, George Andrew Musgrove, or for the negligence of other servants
or agents of Securicor which caused the destruction by fire of the plaintiffs' factory at
Gillingham, Kent, on the night of 18th/19th October 1970. The quantum of damages
was agreed at £615,000 but liability was disputed. The facts are set out in the opinion   *f*
of Lord Wilberforce.

Richard Yorke QC, Anthony Machin QC and *Roger Toulson* for Securicor.
Michael Wright QC and *John Crowley* for Photo Production Ltd.

Their Lordships took time for consideration.
                                                                                  g
14th February. The following opinions were delivered.

LORD WILBERFORCE. My Lords, this appeal arises from the destruction by fire of
a factory owned by the respondents ('Photo Productions') involving loss and damage
agreed to amount to £615,000. The question is whether the appellants ('Securicor') are   *h*
liable to the respondents for this sum.
    Securicor are a company which provides security services. In 1968 they entered into
a contract with Photo Productions by which for a charge of £8 15s 0d (old currency) per
week it agreed to 'provide their Night Patrol Service whereby four visits per night shall
be made seven nights per week and two visits shall be made during the afternoon of
Saturday and four visits shall be made during the day of Sunday'. The contract   *j*
incorporated printed standard conditions which, in some circumstances, might exclude
or limit Securicor's liability. The questions in this appeal are (i) whether these conditions

---

1   [1978] 3 All ER 146, [1978] 1 WLR 856

can be invoked at all in the events which happened and (ii) if so, whether either the exclusion provision, or a provision limiting liability, can be applied on the facts. The trial judge (MacKenna J) decided these issues in favour of Securicor. The Court of Appeal[1] decided issue (i) in Photo Productions' favour invoking the doctrine of fundamental breach. Waller LJ in addition would have decided for Photo Productions on issue (ii).

What happened was that on a Sunday night the duty employee of Securicor was one Musgrove. It was not suggested that he was unsuitable for the job or that Securicor were negligent in employing him. He visited the factory at the correct time, but when inside he deliberately started a fire by throwing a match onto some cartons. The fire got out of control and a large part of the premises was burnt down. Though what he did was deliberate, it was not established that he intended to destroy the factory. The judge's finding was in these words:

'Whether Musgrove intended to light only a small fire (which was the very least he meant to do) or whether he intended to cause much more serious damage, and, in either case, what was the reason for his act, are mysteries I am unable to solve.'

This, and it is important to bear it in mind when considering the judgments in the Court of Appeal, falls short of a finding that Musgrove deliberately burnt or intended to burn Photo Productions' factory.

The condition on which Securicor relies reads, relevantly, as follows:

'Under no circumstances shall the Company [Securicor] be responsible for any injurious act or default by any employee of the Company unless such act or default could have been foreseen and avoided by the exercise of due diligence on the part of the Company as his employer; nor, in any event, shall the Company be held responsible for; (a) Any loss suffered by the customer through burglary, theft, fire or any other cause, except insofar as such loss is solely attributable to the negligence of the Company's employees acting within the course of their employment . . .'

There are further provisions limiting to stated amounts the liability of Securicor on which it relies in the alternative if held not to be totally exempt.

It is first necessary to decide on the correct approach to a case such as this where it is sought to invoke an exception or limitation clause in the contract. The approach of Lord Denning MR in the Court of Appeal was to consider first whether the breach was 'fundamental'. If so, he said, the court itself deprives the party of the benefit of an exemption or limitation clause. Shaw and Waller LJJ substantially followed him in this argument.

Lord Denning MR in this was following the earlier decision of the Court of Appeal, and in particular his own judgment in *Harbutt's Plasticine Ltd v Wayne Tank and Pump Co Ltd*[2]. In that case Lord Denning MR distinguished two cases: (a) the case where as the result of a breach of contract the innocent party has, and exercises, the right to bring the contract to an end; and (b) the case where the breach automatically brings the contract to an end, without the innocent party having to make an election whether to terminate the contract or to continue it. In the first case Lord Denning MR, purportedly applying this House's decision in *Suisse Atlantique Société d'Armement Maritime SA v NV Rotterdamsche Kolen Centrale*[3], but in effect two citations from two of their Lordships' speeches, extracted a rule of law that the 'termination' of the contract brings it, and with it the exclusion clause, to an end. The *Suisse Atlantique* case[3] in his view—

'affirms the long line of cases in this court that when one party has been guilty of a fundamental breach of the contract . . . and the other side accepts it, so that the

1   [1978] 3 All ER 146, [1978] 1 WLR 856
2   [1970] 1 All ER 225, [1970] 1 QB 447
3   [1966] 2 All ER 61, [1967] 1 AC 361

contract comes to an end . . . then the guilty party cannot rely on an exception or
limitation clause to escape from his liability for the breach.'

a

See (*Harbutt's* case[1]). He then applied the same principle to the second case.

My Lords, whatever the intrinsic merit of this doctrine, as to which I shall have
something to say later, it is clear to me that so far from following this House's decision
in the *Suisse Atlantique* case[2] it is directly opposed to it and that the whole purpose and
tenor of the *Suisse Atlantique* case[2] was to repudiate it. The lengthy, and perhaps I may say
sometimes indigestible speeches of their Lordships, are correctly summarised in the
headnote[3]—

b

'(3) That the question whether an exceptions clause was applicable where there
was a fundamental breach of contract was one of the true construction of the
contract.'

That there was any rule of law by which exception clauses are eliminated, or deprived of
effect, regardless of their terms, was clearly not the view of Viscount Dilhorne, Lord
Hodson or myself. The passages invoked for the contrary view of a rule of law consist
only of short extracts from two of the speeches, on any view a minority. But the case for
the doctrine does not even go so far as that. Lord Reid, in my respectful opinion, and I
recognise that I may not be the best judge of this matter, in his speech read as a whole,
cannot be claimed as a supporter of a rule of law. Indeed he expressly disagreed with
Lord Denning MR's observations in two previous cases (*Karsales (Harrow) Ltd v Wallis*[4]
and *UGS Finance Ltd v National Mortgage Bank of Greece*)[5] in which he had put forward the
'rule of law' doctrine. In order to show how close the disapproved doctrine is to that
sought to be revived in *Harbutt's* case[6] I shall quote one passage from the *Karsales* case[7]:

c

d

'Notwithstanding earlier cases which might suggest the contrary, it is now settled
that exempting clauses of this kind, no matter how widely they are expressed, only
avail the party when he is carrying out his contract in its essential respects. He is not
allowed to use them as a cover for misconduct or indifference or to enable him to
turn a blind eye to his obligations. They do not avail him when he is guilty of a
breach which goes to the root of the contract.'

e

Lord Reid[8] comments as to this that he could not deduce from the authorities cited in
the *Karsales* case[4] that the proposition stated in the judgments could be regarded as in any
way 'settled law'. His conclusion is stated thus[9]: 'In my view no such rule of law ought
to be adopted', adding that there is room for legislative reform.

f

My Lords, in the light of this, the passage from the *Suisse Atlantique* case[10] cited by Lord
Denning MR has to be considered. For convenience I restate it:

'If fundamental breach is established, the next question is what effect, if any, that
has on the applicability of other terms of the contract. This question has often
arisen with regard to clauses excluding liability, in whole or in part, of the party in
breach. I do not think that there is generally much difficulty where the innocent

g

h

---

1 [1970] 1 All ER 225 at 235, [1970] 1 QB 447 at 467
2 [1966] 2 All ER 61, [1967] 1 AC 361
3 [1967] 1 AC 361 at 362
4 [1956] 2 All ER 866, [1956] 1 WLR 936
5 [1964] 1 Lloyd's Rep 446
6 [1970] 1 All ER 225, [1970] 1 QB 447
7 [1956] 2 All ER 866 at 868–869, [1956] 1 WLR 936 at 940
8 [1966] 2 All ER 61 at 73, [1967] 1 AC 361 at 401
9 [1966] 2 All ER 61 at 76, [1967] 1 AC 361 at 405
10 [1966] 2 All ER 61 at 71, [1967] 1 AC 361 at 398

j

a party has elected to treat the breach as a repudiation, bring the contract to an end and sue for damages. Then the whole contract has ceased to exist including the exclusion clause, and I do not see how that clause can then be used to exclude an action for loss which will be suffered by the innocent party after it has ceased to exist, such as loss of the profit which would have accrued if the contract had run its full term.'

b It is with the utmost reluctance that, not forgetting the 'beams' that may exist elsewhere, I have to detect here a mote of ambiguity or perhaps even of inconsistency. What is referred to is 'loss which will be suffered by the innocent party after [the contract] has ceased to exist' and I venture to think that all that is being said, rather elliptically, relates only to what is to happen in the future, and is not a proposition as to the immediate consequences caused by the breach; if it were, that would be inconsistent with the full and reasoned discussion which follows.

c It is only because of Lord Reid's great authority in the law that I have found it necessary to embark on what in the end may be superfluous analysis. For I am convinced that, with the possible exception of Lord Upjohn whose critical passage, when read in full, is somewhat ambiguous, their Lordships, fairly read, can only be taken to have rejected those suggestions for a rule of law which had appeared in the Court of Appeal and to have firmly stated that the question is one of construction, not merely of course
d of the exclusion clause alone, but of the whole contract.

Much has been written about the *Suisse Atlantique* case[1]. Each speech has been subjected to various degrees of analysis and criticism, much of it constructive. Speaking for myself I am conscious of imperfections of terminology, though sometimes in good company. But I do not think that I should be conducing to the clarity of the law by adding to what was already too ample a discussion a further analysis which in turn would
e have to be interpreted. I have no second thoughts as to the main proposition that the question whether, and to what extent, an exclusion clause is to be applied to a fundamental breach, or a breach of a fundamental term, or indeed to any breach of contract, is a matter of construction of the contract. Many difficult questions arise and will continue to arise in the infinitely varied situations in which contracts come to be breached: by repudiatory breaches, accepted or not, anticipatory breaches, by breaches of
f conditions or of various terms and whether by negligent, or deliberate, action, or otherwise. But there are ample resources in the normal rules of contract law for dealing with these without the superimposition of a judicially invented rule of law. I am content to leave the matter there with some supplementary observations.

1. The doctrine of 'fundamental breach' in spite of its imperfections and doubtful parentage has served a useful purpose. There were a large number of problems,
g productive of injustice, in which it was worse than unsatisfactory to leave exception clauses to operate. Lord Reid referred to these in the *Suisse Atlantique* case[2], pointing out at the same time that the doctrine of fundamental breach was a dubious specific. But since then Parliament has taken a hand: it has passed the Unfair Contract Terms Act 1977. This Act applies to consumer contracts and those based on standard terms and enables exception clauses to be applied with regard to what is just and reasonable. It is
h significant that Parliament refrained from legislating over the whole field of contract. After this Act, in commercial matters generally, when the parties are not of unequal bargaining power, and when risks are normally borne by insurance, not only is the case for judicial intervention undemonstrated, but there is everything to be said, and this seems to have been Parliament's intention, for leaving the parties free to apportion the risks as they think fit and for respecting their decisions.

j At the stage of negotiation as to the consequences of a breach, there is everything to be said for allowing the parties to estimate their respective claims according to the contractual provisions they have themselves made, rather than for facing them with a

---

1 [1966] 2 All ER 61, [1967] 1 AC 361
2 [1966] 2 All ER 61 at 76, [1967] 1 AC 361 at 406

legal complex so uncertain as the doctrine of fundamental breach must be. What, for example, would have been the position of Photo Productions' factory if instead of being *a* destroyed it had been damaged, slightly or moderately or severely? At what point does the doctrine (with what logical justification I have not understood) decide, ex post facto, that the breach was (factually) fundamental before going on to ask whether legally it is to be regarded as fundamental? How is the date of 'termination' to be fixed? Is it the date of the incident causing the damage, or the date of the innocent party's election, or some other date? All these difficulties arise from the doctrine and are left unsolved by *b* it.

At the judicial stage there is still more to be said for leaving cases to be decided straightforwardly on what the parties have bargained for rather than on analysis, which becomes progressively more refined, of decisions in other cases leading to inevitable appeals. The learned judge was able to decide this case on normal principles of contractual law with minimal citation of authority. I am sure that most commercial *c* judges have wished to be able to do the same (cf *The Angelia, Trade and Transport Inc v Iino Kaiun Kaisha Ltd*[1], per Kerr J). In my opinion they can and should.

2. *Harbutt's Plasticine Ltd v Wayne Tank and Pump Co Ltd*[2] must clearly be overruled. It would be enough to put that on its radical inconsistency with the *Suisse Atlantique* case[3]. But even if the matter were res integra I would find the decision to be based on unsatisfactory reasoning as to the 'termination' of the contract and the effect of *d* 'termination' on the plaintiffs' claim for damage. I have, indeed, been unable to understand how the doctrine can be reconciled with the well accepted principle of law, stated by the highest modern authority, that when in the context of a breach of contract one speaks of 'termination' what is meant is no more than that the innocent party or, in some cases, both parties are excused from further performance. Damages, in such cases, are then claimed under the contract, so what reason in principle can there be for *e* disregarding what the contract itself says about damages, whether it 'liquidates' them, or limits them, or excludes them? These difficulties arise in part from uncertain or inconsistent terminology. A vast number of expressions are used to describe situations where a breach has been committed by one party of such a character as to entitle the other party to refuse further performance: discharge, rescission, termination, the contract is at an end, or dead, or displaced; clauses cannot survive, or simply go. I have come to *f* think that some of these difficulties can be avoided; in particular the use of 'rescission', even if distinguished from rescission ab initio, as an equivalent for discharge, though justifiable in some contexts (see *Johnson v Agnew*[4]) may lead to confusion in others. To plead for complete uniformity may be to cry for the moon. But what can and ought to be avoided is to make use of these confusions in order to produce a concealed and unreasoned legal innovation: to pass, for example, from saying that a party, victim of a *g* breach of contract, is entitled to refuse further performance, to saying that he may treat the contract as at an end, or as rescinded, and to draw from this the proposition, which is not analytical but one of policy, that all or (arbitrarily) some of the clauses of the contract lose, automatically, their force, regardless of intention.

If this process is discontinued the way is free to use such words as 'discharge' or 'termination' consistently with principles as stated by modern authority which *Harbutt's* *h* case[2] disregards. I venture with apology to relate the classic passages. In *Heyman v Darwins Ltd*[5] Lord Porter said:

> 'To say that the contract is rescinded or has come to an end or has ceased to exist may in individual cases convey the truth with sufficient accuracy, but the fuller

j

1 [1973] 2 All ER 144 at 164, [1973] 1 WLR 210 at 232
2 [1970] 1 All ER 225, [1970] 1 QB 447
3 [1966] 2 All ER 61, [1967] 1 AC 361
4 [1979] 1 All ER 883, [1979] 2 WLR 487
5 [1942] 1 All ER 337 at 360–361, [1942] AC 356 at 399

expression that the injured party is thereby absolved from future performance of his obligations under the contract is a more exact description of the position. Strictly speaking, to say that, upon acceptance of the renunciation of a contract, the contract is rescinded is incorrect. In such a case the injured party may accept the renunciation as a breach going to the root of the whole of the consideration. By that acceptance he is discharged from further performance and may bring an action for damages, but the contract itself is not rescinded.'

Similarly Lord Macmillan[1]; see also *Boston Deep Sea Fishing and Ice Co Ltd v Ansell*[2] per Bowen LJ. In *Moschi v Lep Air Services Ltd*[3] my noble and learned friend Lord Diplock drew a distinction (relevant for that case) between primary obligations under a contract, which on 'rescission' generally come to an end, and secondary obligations which may then arise. Among the latter he included an obligation to pay compensation, ie damages. And he stated in terms that this latter obligation 'is just as much an obligation arising from the contract as are the primary obligations that it replaces'. My noble and learned friend has developed this line of thought in an enlightening manner in his opinion which I have now had the benefit of reading.

These passages I believe to state correctly the modern law of contract in the relevant respects; they demonstrate that the whole foundation of *Harbutt's* case[4] is unsound. A fortiori, in addition to *Harbutt's* case[4] there must be overruled *Wathes (Western) Ltd v Austins (Menswear) Ltd*[5] which sought to apply the doctrine of fundamental breach to a case where, by election of the innocent party, the contract had not been terminated, an impossible acrobatic, yet necessarily engendered by the doctrine. Similarly, *Charterhouse Credit Co Ltd v Tolly*[6] must be overruled, though the result might have been reached on construction of the contract.

3. I must add to this, by way of exception to the decision not to 'gloss' the *Suisse Atlantique*[7], a brief observation on the deviation cases, since some reliance has been placed on them, particularly on the decision of this House in *Hain Steamship Co Ltd v Tate & Lyle Ltd*[8] (so earlier than the *Suisse Atlantique*[7]) in the support of the *Harbutt*[4] doctrine. I suggested in the *Suisse Atlantique*[7] that these cases can be regarded as proceeding on normal principles applicable to the law of contract generally, viz that it is a matter of the parties' intentions whether and to what extent clauses in shipping contracts can be applied after a deviation, ie a departure from the contractually agreed voyage or adventure. It may be preferable that they should be considered as a body of authority sui generis with special rules derived from historical and commercial reasons. What on either view they cannot do is to lay down different rules as to contracts generally from those later stated by this House in *Heyman v Darwins Ltd*[9]. The ingenious use by Donaldson J in *Kenyon, Son & Craven Ltd v Baxter Hoare & Co Ltd*[10] of the doctrine of deviation in order to reconcile the *Suisse Atlantique* case[7] with *Harbutt's* case[4], itself based in part on the use of the doctrine of deviation, illustrates the contortions which that case has made necessary and would be unnecessary if it vanished as an authority.

1   [1942] 1 All ER 337 at 346–347, [1942] AC 356 at 373
2   (1888) 39 Ch D 339 at 361
3   [1972] 2 All ER 393 at 403, [1973] AC 331 at 350
4   [1970] 1 All ER 225, [1970] 1 QB 447
5   [1976] 1 Lloyd's Rep 14
6   [1963] 2 All ER 432, [1963] 2 QB 683
7   [1966] 2 All ER 61, [1967] 1 AC 361
8   [1936] 2 All ER 597
9   [1942] 1 All ER 337, [1942] AC 356
10   [1971] 2 All ER 708, [1971] 1 WLR 519

4. It is not necessary to review fully the numerous cases in which the doctrine of fundamental breach has been applied or discussed. Many of these have now been superseded by the Unfair Contract Terms Act 1977. Others, as decisions, may be justified as depending on the construction of the contract (cf *Levison v Patent Steam Carpet Cleaning Co Ltd*[1] in the light of well-known principles such as that stated in *Alderslade v Hendon Laundry Ltd*[2].

In this situation the present case has to be decided. As a preliminary, the nature of the contract has to be understood. Securicor undertook to provide a service of periodical visits for a very modest charge which works out at 26p per visit. It did not agree to provide equipment. It would have no knowledge of the value of Photo Productions' factory; that, and the efficacy of their fire precautions, would be known to Photo Productions. In these circumstances nobody could consider it unreasonable that as between these two equal parties the risk assumed by Securicor should be a modest one, and that Photo Productions should carry the substantial risk of damage or destruction.

The duty of Securicor was, as stated, to provide a service. There must be implied an obligation to use care in selecting their patrolmen, to take care of the keys and, I would think, to operate the service with due and proper regard to the safety and security of the premises. The breach of duty committed by Securicor lay in a failure to discharge this latter obligation. Alternatively it could be put on a vicarious responsibility for the wrongful act of Musgrove, viz starting a fire on the premises; Securicor would be responsible for this on the principle stated in *Morris v C W Martin & Sons Ltd*[3]. This being the breach, does condition 1 apply? It is drafted in strong terms, 'Under no circumstances, any injurious act or default by any employee'. These words have to be approached with the aid of the cardinal rules of construction that they must be read contra proferentem and that in order to escape from the consequences of one's own wrongdoing, or that of one's servant, clear words are necessary. I think that these words are clear. Photo Productions in fact relied on them for an argument that since they exempted from negligence they must be taken as not exempting from the consequence of deliberate acts. But this is a perversion of the rule that if a clause can cover something other than negligence it will not be applied to negligence. Whether, in addition to negligence, it covers other, e g deliberate, acts, remains a matter of construction requiring, of course, clear words. I am of opinion that it does and, being free to construe and apply the clause, I must hold that liability is excluded. On this part of the case I agree with the judge and adopt his reasons for judgment. I would allow the appeal.

LORD DIPLOCK. My Lords, my noble and learned friend Lord Wilberforce has summarised the facts which have given rise to this appeal. The contract which falls to be considered was a contract for the rendering of services by the defendants ('Securicor') to the plaintiffs ('Photo Productions'). It was a contract of indefinite duration terminable by one month's notice on either side. It had been in existence for some 2½ years when the breach that is the subject-matter of these proceedings occurred. It is not disputed that the act of Securicor's servant, Musgrove, in starting a fire in the factory which they had undertaken to protect was a breach of contract by Securicor; and, since it was the cause of an event, the destruction of the factory, that rendered further performance of the contract impossible, it is not an unnatural use of ordinary language to describe it as a 'fundamental breach'.

It was by attaching that label to it that all three members of the Court of Appeal found themselves able to dispose of Securicor's defence based on the exclusion clause restricting its liability for its servants' torts in terms which Lord Wilberforce has already set out, by holding that where there had been a fundamental breach by a party to a contract there

1 [1977] 3 All ER 498, [1978] QB 69
2 [1945] 1 All ER 244, [1945] KB 189
3 [1965] 2 All ER 725 at 739, [1966] 1 QB 716 at 739

a was a rule of law which prevented him from relying on any exclusion clause appearing in the contract, whatever its wording might be.

The Court of Appeal was, I think, bound so to hold by previous decisions of its own, of which the first was *Harbutt's Plasticine Ltd v Wayne Tank and Pump Co*[1]. It purported in that case to find support for the rule of law it there laid down in the reasoning of this House in *Suisse Atlantique Société d'Armement Maritime SA v Rotterdamsche Kolen Centrale*[2].

b I agree with Lord Wilberforce's analysis of the speeches in the *Suisse Atlantique* case[2], and with his conclusion that this House rejected the argument that there was any such rule of law. I also agree that the *Harbutt's Plasticine* case[1] and the subsequent cases in which the so-called 'rule of law' was applied to defeat exclusion clauses should be overruled, though the actual decisions in some of the later cases might have been justified on the proper construction of the particular exclusion clause on which the defendant relied.

My Lords, the contract in the instant case was entered into before the passing of the

c Unfair Contract Terms Act 1977. So what we are concerned with is the common law of contract, of which the subject-matter is the legally enforceable obligations as between the parties to it of which the contract is the source. The 'rule of law' theory which the Court of Appeal has adopted in the last decade to defeat exclusion clauses is at first sight attractive in the simplicity of its logic. A fundamental breach is one which entitles the party not in default to elect to terminate the contract. On his doing so the contract

d comes to an end. The exclusion clause is part of the contract, so it comes to an end too; the party in default can no longer rely on it. This reasoning can be extended without undue strain to cases where the party entitled to elect to terminate the contract does not become aware of the breach until some time after it occurred; his election to terminate the contract could not implausibly be treated as exercisable nunc pro tunc. But even the superficial logic of the reasoning is shattered when it is applied, as it was in *Wathes*

e *(Western) Ltd v Austins (Menswear) Ltd*[3], to cases where, despite the 'fundamental breach', the party not in default elects to maintain the contract in being.

The fallacy in the reasoning, and what I venture to think is the disarray into which the common law about breaches of contract has fallen, is due to the use in many of the leading judgments on this subject of ambiguous or imprecise expressions without defining the sense in which they are used. I am conscious that I have myself sometimes

f been guilty of this when I look back on judgments I have given in such cases as *Hong Kong Fir Shipping Co Ltd v Kawakasi Kisen Kaisha Ltd*[4], *R V Ward Ltd v Bignall*[5], *Moschi v Lep Air Services Ltd*[6], and in particular *Hardwick Game Farm v Suffolk Agricultural and Poultry Producers Association Ltd*[7], when commenting unfavourably on the then budding doctrine of fundamental breach in a portion of my judgment in the Court of Appeal that did not subsequently incur the disapproval of this House[8].

g My Lords, it is characteristic of commercial contracts, nearly all of which today are entered into not by natural legal persons, but by fictitious ones, ie companies, that the parties promise to one another that something will be done, for instance, that property and possession of goods will be transferred, that goods will be carried by ship from one port to another, that a building will be constructed in accordance with agreed plans, that services of a particular kind will be provided. Such a contract is the source of primary

h

---

i 1 [1970] 1 All ER 225, [1970] 1 QB 447
2 [1966] 2 All ER 61, [1967] 1 AC 361
j 3 [1976] 1 Lloyd's Rep 14
4 [1962] 1 All ER 474, [1962] 2 QB 26
5 [1967] 2 All ER 449, [1967] 1 QB 534
6 [1972] 2 All ER 393, [1973] AC 331
7 [1966] 1 All ER 309, [1966] 1 WLR 287
8 Sub nom *Henry Kendall & Sons (a firm) v William Lillico & Sons Ltd* [1968] 2 All ER 444, [1969] 2 AC 31

legal obligations on each party to it to procure that whatever he has promised will be
done is done. (I leave aside arbitration clauses which do not come into operation until a
party to the contract claims that a primary obligation has not been observed.)

Where what is promised will be done involves the doing to a physical act, performance
of the promise necessitates procuring a natural person to do it; but the legal relationship
between the promisor and the natural person by whom the act is done, whether it is that
of master and servant, or principal and agent, or of parties to an independent sub-
contract, is generally irrelevant. If that person fails to do it in the manner in which the
promisor has promised to procure it to be done, as, for instance, with reasonable skill and
care, the promisor has failed to fulfil his own primary obligation. This is to be
distinguished from 'vicarious liability', a legal concept which does depend on the
existence of a particular legal relationship between the natural person by whom a
tortious act was done and the person sought to be made vicariously liable for it. In the
interests of clarity the expression should, in my view, be confined to liability for tort.

A basic principle of the common law of contract, to which there are no exceptions that
are relevant in the instant case, is that parties to a contract are free to determine for
themselves what primary obligations they will accept. They may state these in express
words in the contract itself and, where they do, the statement is determinative; but in
practice a commercial contract never states all the primary obligations of the parties in
full; many are left to be incorporated by implication of law from the legal nature of the
contract into which the parties are entering. But if the parties wish to reject or modify
primary obligations which would otherwise be so incorporated, they are fully at liberty
to do so by express words.

Leaving aside those comparatively rare cases in which the court is able to enforce a
primary obligation by decreeing specific performance of it, breaches of primary
obligations give rise to substituted secondary obligations on the part of the party in
default, and, in some cases, may entitle the other party to be relieved from further
performance of his own primary obligations. These secondary obligations of the contract
breaker and any concomitant relief of the other party from his own primary obligations
also arise by implication of law, generally common law, but sometimes statute, as in the
case of codifying statutes passed at the turn of the century, notably the Sale of Goods Act
1893. The contract, however, is just as much the source of secondary obligations as it is
of primary obligations; and like primary obligations that are implied by law secondary
obligations too can be modified by agreement between the parties, although, for reasons
to be mentioned later, they cannot, in my view, be totally excluded. In the instant case,
the only secondary obligations and concomitant reliefs that are applicable arise by
implication of the common law as modified by the express words of the contract.

Every failure to perform a primary obligation is a breach of contract. The secondary
obligation on the part of the contract breaker to which it gives rise by implication of the
common law is to pay monetary compensation to the other party for the loss sustained
by him in consequence of the breach; but, with two exceptions, the primary obligations
of both parties so far as they have not yet been fully performed remain unchanged. This
secondary obligation to pay compensation (damages) for non-performance of primary
obligations I will call the 'general secondary obligation'. It applies in the cases of the two
exceptions as well.

The exceptions are: (1) where the event resulting from the failure by one party to
perform a primary obligation has the effect of depriving the other party of substantially
the whole benefit which it was the intention of the parties that he should obtain from the
contract, the party not in default may elect to put an end to all primary obligations of
both parties remaining unperformed (if the expression 'fundamental breach' is to be
retained, it should, in the interests of clarity, be confined to this exception); (2) where the
contracting parties have agreed, whether by express words or by implication of law, that
any failure by one party to perform a particular primary obligation ('condition' in the
nomenclature of the Sale of Goods Act 1893), irrespective of the gravity of the event that
has in fact resulted from the breach, shall entitle the other party to elect to put an end to

a all primary obligation of both parties remaining unperformed (in the interests of clarity, the nomenclature of the sale of Goods Act 1893, 'breach of condition', should be reserved for this exception).

Where such an election is made (a) there is substituted by implication of law for the primary obligations of the party in default which remain unperformed a secondary obligation to pay monetary compensation to the other party for the loss sustained by him in consequence of their non-performance in the future and (b) the unperformed primary *b* obligations of that other party are discharged. This secondary obligation is additional to the general secondary obligation; I will call it 'the anticipatory secondary obligation'.

In cases falling within the first exception, fundamental breach, the anticipatory secondary obligation arises under contracts of all kinds by implication of the common law, except to the extent that it is excluded or modified by the express words of the contract. In cases falling within the second exception, breach of condition, the *c* anticipatory secondary obligation generally arises under particular kinds of contracts by implication of statute law; though in the case of 'deviation' from the contract voyage under a contract of carriage of goods by sea it arises by implication of the common law. The anticipatory secondary obligation in these cases too can be excluded or modified by express words.

When there has been a fundamental breach or breach of condition, the coming to an *d* end of the primary obligations of both parties to the contract at the election of the party not in default is often referred to as the 'determination' or 'rescission' of the contract or, as in the Sale of Goods Act 1893, 'treating the contract as repudiated'. The first two of these expressions, however, are misleading unless it is borne in mind that for the unperformed primary obligations of the party in default there are substituted by operation of law what I have called the secondary obligations.

e The bringing to an end of all primary obligations under the contract may also leave the parties in a relationship, typically that of bailor and bailee, in which they owe to one another by operation of law fresh primary obligations of which the contract is not the source; but no such relationship is involved in the instant case.

I have left out of account in this analysis as irrelevant to the instant case an arbitration or choice of forum clause. This does not come into operation until a party to the contract *f* claims that a primary obligation of the other party has not been performed; and its relationship to other obligations of which the contract is the source was dealt with by this House in *Heyman v Darwins Ltd*[1].

My Lords, an exclusion clause is one which excludes or modifies an obligation, whether primary, general secondary or anticipatory secondary, that would otherwise arise under the contract by implication of law. Parties are free to agree to whatever *g* exclusion or modification of all three types of obligations they please within the limits that the agreement must retain the legal characteristics of a contract and must not offend against the equitable rule against penalties, that is to say, it must not impose on the breaker of a primary obligation a general secondary obligation to pay to the other party a sum of money that is manifestly intended to be in excess of the amount which would fully compensate the other party for the loss sustained by him in consequence of the *h* breach of the primary obligation. Since the presumption is that the parties by entering into the contract intended to accept the implied obligations, exclusion clauses are to be construed strictly and the degree of strictness appropriate to be applied to their construction may properly depend on the extent to which they involve departure from the implied obligations. Since the obligations implied by law in a commercial contract are those which, by judicial consensus over the years or by Parliament in passing a *j* statute, have been regarded as obligations which a reasonable businessman would realise that he was accepting when he entered into a contract of a particular kind, the court's view of the reasonableness of any departure from the implied obligations which would

1 [1942] 1 All ER 337, [1942] AC 356

be involved in construing the express words of an exclusion clause in one sense that they are capable of bearing rather than another is a relevant consideration in deciding what *a* meaning the words were intended by the parties to bear. But this does not entitle the court to reject the exclusion clause, however unreasonable the court itself may think it is, if the words are clear and fairly susceptible of one meaning only.

My Lords, the reports are full of cases in which what would appear to be very strained constructions have been placed on exclusion clauses, mainly in what today would be called consumer contracts and contracts of adhesion. As Lord Wilberforce has pointed *b* out, any need for this kind of judicial distortion of the English language has been banished by Parliament's having made these kinds of contracts subject to the Unfair Contract Terms Act 1977. In commercial contracts negotiated between businessmen capable of looking after their own interests and of deciding how risks inherent in the performance of various kinds of contract can be most economically borne (generally by insurance), it is, in my view, wrong to place a strained construction on words in an *c* exclusion clause which are clear and fairly susceptible of one meaning only even after due allowance has been made for the presumption in favour of the implied primary and secondary obligations.

Applying these principles to the instant case, in the absence of the exclusion clause which Lord Wilberforce has cited, a primary obligation of Securicor under the contract, which would be implied by law, would be an absolute obligation to procure that the *d* visits by the night patrol to the factory were conducted by natural persons who would exercise reasonable skill and care for the safety of the factory. That primary obligation is modified by the exclusion clause. Securicor's obligation to do this is not to be absolute, but is limited to exercising due diligence in their capacity as employers of the natural persons by whom the visits are conducted, to procure that those persons shall exercise reasonable skill and care for the safety of the factory.

For the reasons given by Lord Wilberforce it seems to me that this apportionment of *e* the risk of the factory being damaged or destroyed by the injurious act of an employee of Securicor while carrying out a visit to the factory is one which reasonable businessmen in the position of Securicor and Photo Productions might well think was the most economical. An analogous apportionment of risk is provided for by the Hague Rules[1] in the case of goods carried by sea under bills of lading. The risk that a servant of Securicor *f* would damage or destroy the factory or steal goods from it, despite the exercise of all reasonable diligence by Securicor to prevent it, is what in the context of maritime law would be called a 'misfortune risk', something which reasonable diligence of neither party to the contract can prevent. Either party can insure against it. It is generally more economical for the person by whom the loss will be directly sustained to do so rather than that it should be covered by the other party by liability insurance. This makes it *g* unnecessary to consider whether a later exclusion clause in the contract which modifies the general secondary obligation implied by law by placing limits on the amount of damages recoverable for breaches of primary obligations would have applied in the instant case.

For the reasons given by Lord Wilberforce and in application of the principles that I have here stated, I would allow this appeal. *h*

LORD SALMON. My Lords, the contract with which this appeal is concerned is a very simple commercial contract entered into by two highly experienced business enterprises, the appellants, whom I shall call 'Securicor' and the respondents, whom I shall call 'Photo Productions'.

This appeal turns in my view entirely on certain words in the contract which read as *j* follows:

---

1 See the Carriage of Goods by Sea Act 1971, Sch

a
'Under no circumstances shall [Securicor] be responsible for any injurious act or default by any employee of [Securicor] unless such act or default could have been foreseen and avoided by the exercise of due diligence on the part of [Securicor] as his employer.'

We are not concerned with the Unfair Contract Terms Act 1977 since the present contract was entered into before that Act was passed. Accordingly, I prefer to express no view about the effect of that Act as the result of this appeal depends solely on the

b common law.

The facts relevant to this case are very short. Indubitably, one of Securicor's servants called Musgrove committed an injurious act or default which caused Photo Productions' factory to be burned down, and as a result, Photo Productions suffered a loss of £615,000. This disaster occurred when Musgrove was visiting the factory on patrol one Sunday night and deliberately threw a lighted match on some cartons lying on the floor

c of one of the rooms he was inspecting. Whether Musgrove intended to light only a small fire or to burn down the factory and what his motives were for what he did were found by the learned trial judge to be mysteries which it was impossible to solve.

No one has suggested that Securicor could have foreseen or avoided by due diligence the act or default which caused the damage or that Securicor had been negligent in employing or supervising Musgrove.

d
The contract between the two parties provided that Securicor should supply a patrol service at Photo Productions' factory by four visits a night for seven nights a week and two visits every Saturday afternoon and four day visits every Sunday. The contract provided that for this service Securicor should be paid £8 15s 0d a week. There can be no doubt that, but for the clause in the contract which I have recited, Securicor would have been liable for the damage which was caused by their servant Musgrove whilst

e indubitably acting in the course of his employment: see *Morris v C W Martin & Sons Ltd*[1]. To my mind, however, the words of the clause are so crystal clear that they obviously relieve Securicor from what would otherwise have been their liability for the damage caused by Musgrove. Indeed the words of the clause are incapable of any other meaning. I think that any businessman entering into this contract could have had no doubt as to the real meaning of this clause and would have made his insurance

f arrangements accordingly. The cost to Photo Productions for the benefit of the patrol service provided by Securicor was very modest and probably substantially less than the reduction of the insurance premiums which Photo Productions may have enjoyed as a result of obtaining that service.

Clauses which absolve a party to a contract from liability for breaking it are no doubt unpopular, particularly when they are unfair, which incidentally, in my view, this clause

g is not. It is, I think, because of the unpopularity of such clauses that a so called 'rule of law' has been developed in the Court of Appeal to the effect that what was characterised as 'a fundamental breach of contract', automatically or with the consent of the innocent party, brings the contract to an end; and that therefore the contract breaker will then immediately be barred from relying on any clause in the contract, however clearly worded, which would otherwise have safeguarded him against being liable, inter alia, in

h respect of the damages caused by the default: see for example *Karsales (Harrow) Ltd v Wallis*[2], per Denning LJ and *Harbutt's Plasticine Ltd v Wayne Tank and Pump Co Ltd*[3].

I entirely agree with my noble and learned friend Lord Wilberforce's analysis of the *Suisse Atlantique* case[4] which explains why the breach does not bring the contract to an end and why the so-called 'rule of law' on which Photo Productions rely is therefore non-

j
───────────────────────────────

1 [1965] 2 All ER 725, [1966] 1 QB 716
2 [1956] 2 All ER 866 at 868–869, [1956] 1 WLR 936 at 940
3 [1970] 1 All ER 225, [1970] 1 QB 447
4 [1966] 2 All ER 61, [1967] 1 AC 361

existent. This proposition is strongly supported by the passage recited by Lord Wilberforce in Lord Porter's speech in *Heyman v Darwins Ltd*[1].

Any persons capable of making a contract are free to enter into any contract they may choose; and providing the contract is not illegal or voidable, it is binding on them. It is not denied that the present contract was binding on each of the parties to it. In the end, everything depends on the true construction of the clause in dispute about which I have already expressed my opinion.

My Lords, I would accordingly allow the appeal.

LORD KEITH OF KINKEL. My Lords, I agree with the speech of my noble and learned friend Lord Wilberforce, which I have had the advantage of reading in draft and to which I cannot usefully add anything.

Accordingly I too would allow the appeal.

LORD SCARMAN. My Lords, I have had the advantage of reading in draft the speech delivered by my noble and learned friend Lord Wilberforce. I agree with it. I would, therefore, allow the appeal.

I applaud the refusal of the trial judge, MacKenna J, to allow the sophisticated refinements into which, before the enactment of the Unfair Contract Terms Act 1977, the courts were driven in order to do justice to the consumer to govern his judgment in a commercial dispute between parties well able to look after themselves. In such a situation what the parties agreed (expressly or impliedly) is what matters; and the duty of the courts is to construe their contract according to its tenor.

Appeal allowed.

Solicitors: *Berrymans* (for Securicor); *Stanleys & Simpson, North* (for Photo Productions Ltd).

Mary Rose Plummer   Barrister.

---

1 [1942] 1 All ER 337 at 360–361, [1942] AC 356 at 399

a
Woodar Investment Development Ltd v Wimpey Construction UK Ltd

HOUSE OF LORDS

LORD WILBERFORCE, LORD SALMON, LORD RUSSELL OF KILLOWEN, LORD KEITH OF KINKEL AND LORD SCARMAN

b 19th, 20th, 21st, 22nd NOVEMBER 1979, 14th FEBRUARY 1980

Contract – Repudiation – Rescission – Attempted rescission amounting to repudiation – Purchaser wishing to withdraw from contract with vendor for sale of land – Purchaser purporting to rely on term of contract to rescind – Judge holding that purchaser not entitled to rescind – Whether purchaser's erroneous attempt to rescind amounting to repudiation and entitling vendor to
c *damages.*

The vendors agreed to sell and the purchasers to buy 14 acres of land for development for a price of £850,000 with provision for payment on completion of a further £150,000 to a third party who had no legal connection with the vendors. The contract further provided for the purchasers to be entitled to rescind the contract if prior to completion
d a statutory authority 'shall have commenced' to acquire the property by compulsory acquisition. In fact at the date the contract was signed the Minister had already commenced compulsory purchase proceedings for part of the property. It later became clear that there was a prospect of planning permission being granted for most of the land, but in the meantime land prices had fallen drastically and the purchasers wished to withdraw from the contract. After taking legal advice they purported to rescind the
e contract because of the Minister's actions, stating in a letter accompanying the notice of rescission that '. . . the contract is now discharged'. The rescission was not accepted by the vendors, although their representative stated that he would let the court decide the issue and that he assumed both parties would abide by the result. The vendors accordingly brought an action against the purchasers seeking a declaration that the purchasers were not entitled to rescind the contract. By their defence and counterclaim
f the purchasers sought a declaration that they had validly rescinded the contract. Thereafter the vendors brought a second action against the purchasers claiming that the notice of rescission and the defence and counterclaim together amounted to a repudiation, which they accepted and which consequently entitled them to sue for damages. Included in their claim was a claim for damages on behalf of the third party. The two actions were consolidated, and at the trial the judge held (i) that the purchasers were not entitled to
g rescind, because they only had power to do so in respect of compulsory purchase proceedings commenced after the date of the contract and the Minister's actions on which they had purported to rely had commenced before the contract, (ii) that by wrongly insisting on the right to rescind the purchasers had repudiated the contract, and (iii) that the vendors were entitled to recover £312,000 damages on their own account and £150,000 on behalf of the third party. On appeal the purchasers conceded that they
h were not entitled to rescind. The Court of Appeal, by a majority, affirmed the judge's decision on liability but reduced the damages to £137,943 payable to the vendors and £135,000 to be held on behalf of the third party. On appeal to the House of Lords on the issues of whether the purchasers' attempted rescission amounted to a repudiation of the contract and whether the vendors were entitled to recover more than nominal damages on behalf of the third party.

j
Held (Lord Salmon and Lord Russell of Killowen dissenting) – Unjustified rescission of a contract did not always amount to repudiation, and, although a party who had withdrawn from a contract might have had every motive for so doing, it was necessary, when deciding whether he had in fact repudiated it, to consider the circumstances and the party's conduct as a whole. On that basis, because the purchasers in attempting to

rescind were in fact relying (albeit erroneously) on the contract itself rather than refusing
to be bound by it and because there was no evidence that they intended to abandon it or   *a*
refuse future performance if the court decided against them, their erroneous and
unsuccessful attempt at rescission did not amount to a repudiation. Furthermore (Lord
Salmon and Lord Russell concurring) because the purchasers' defence and counterclaim
had not carried their notice of rescission any further, their pleadings also did not amount
to a repudiation. Accordingly, the appeal would be allowed (see p 574 *c* to *h*, p 575 *e* and
j, p 576 *c d*, p 577 *c*, p 582 *h j*, p 584 *g*, p 586 *c d*, p 587 *c d* and *g h*, p 588 *c* to *e*, p 589 *a*   *b*
b and p 590 *a* to *f*, post).

Dicta of Lord Coleridge CJ in *Freeth v Burr* (1874) LR 9 CP at 213, *Spettabile Consorzio
Veneziano di Armamento e Navigazione v Northumberland Shipping Co Ltd* [1918–19] All ER
Rep 963, *James Shaffer Ltd v Findlay Durham & Brodie* [1953] 1 WLR 106 and *Sweet &
Maxwell Ltd v Universal News Services Ltd* [1964] 3 All ER 30 applied.

Federal Commerce and Navigation Ltd v Molena Alpha Inc [1979] 1 All ER 307   *c*
distinguished.

Observations on the unsatisfactory state of the law regarding the recovery of damages
for the benefit of third parties and (per Lord Salmon, Lord Keith of Kinkel and Lord
Scarman) the need for the House of Lords to review the law in an appropriate future case
(see p 576 *e* to p 577 *b*, p 583 *c*, p 584 *h* to p 585 *h*, p 588 *f* to p 589 *a* and p 590 *h* to p 591
f, post).   *d*

Jackson v Horizon Holidays Ltd [1975] 3 All ER 92 explained.

Dictum of Lord Denning MR in *Jackson v Horizon Holidays Ltd* [1975] 3 All ER at 95–
96 disapproved.

Tweddle v Atkinson [1861–73] All ER Rep 369, *Beswick v Beswick* [1967] 2 All ER 1197
and dictum of Lush LJ in *Lloyd's v Harper* (1880) 16 Ch D at 321 referred to.
                                                                                        e

Notes
For repudiation of contract by rescission, see 9 Halsbury's Laws (4th Edn) para 548, and
for cases on the subject, see 12 Digest (Reissue) 413–415, 3042–3048.

Cases referred to in opinions
Beswick v Beswick [1967] 2 All ER 1197, [1968] AC 58, [1967] 3 WLR 932, HL, 12 Digest   *f*
(Reissue) 49, 256.
Bradley v H Newsom Sons & Co [1919] AC 16, 88 LJKB 35, 119 LT 239, 14 Asp MLC 340,
24 Com Cas 1, HL, 12 Digest (Reissue) 423, 3078.
Federal Commerce and Navigation Co Ltd v Molena Alpha Inc [1978] 3 All ER 1066, [1978]
QB 927, [1978] 3 WLR 309, [1978] 1 Lloyd's Rep 581, CA; affd [1979] 1 All ER 307,
[1979] AC 757, [1978] 3 WLR 991, [1979] 1 Lloyd's Rep 201, HL.   *g*
Freeth v Burr (1874) LR 9 CP 208, [1874–80] All ER Rep 750, 43 LJCP 91, 29 LT 773, 12
Digest (Reissue) 413, 3042.
Frost v Knight (1872) LR 7 Exch 111, [1861–73] All ER Rep 221, 41 LJ Ex 78, 26 LT 77,
Ex Ch, 12 Digest (Reissue) 418, 3050.
Heyman v Darwins Ltd [1942] 1 All ER 337, [1942] AC 356, HL.
Jackson v Horizon Holidays Ltd [1975] 3 All ER 92, [1975] 1 WLR 1468, CA, Digest (Cont   *h*
Vol D) 113, 259a.
Johnstone v Milling (1886) 16 QBD 460, 55 LJQB 162, 54 LT 629, 50 JP 694, CA, 12 Digest
(Reissue) 412, 3033.
Lloyd's v Harper (1880) 16 Ch D 290, 50 LJ Ch 140, 43 LT 481, CA, 47 Digest (Repl) 277,
2393.
Mersey Steel and Iron Co v Naylor, Benzon & Co (1884) 9 App Cas 434, [1881–5] All ER Rep   *j*
365, 53 LJQB 497, 51 LT 637, HL, 12 Digest (Reissue) 413, 3038.
New Zealand Shipping Co Ltd v A M Satterthwaite & Co Ltd [1974] 1 All ER 1015, [1975]
AC 154, [1974] 2 WLR 865, [1974] 1 Lloyd's Rep 534, [1974] 1 NZLR 505, PC, Digest
(Cont Vol D) 114, 99a.
Radford v De Froberville [1978] 1 All ER 33, [1977] 1 WLR 1262, 35 P & CR 316.

Shaffer (James) Ltd v Findlay Durham & Brodie [1953] 1 WLR 106, CA, 12 Digest (Reissue)
414, 3046.

Smyth (Ross T) & Co Ltd v T D Bailey, Son & Co [1940] 3 All ER 60, 164 LT 102, 45 Com
Cas 292, HL, 39 Digest (Repl) 611, 1239.

*Spettabile Consorzio Veneziano di Armamento e Navigazione v Northumberland Shipbuilding Co
Ltd* (1919) 121 LT 628, [1918–19] All ER Rep 963 88 LJKB 1194, CA, 12 Digest
(Reissue) 425, 3087.

Sweet & Maxwell Ltd v Universal News Services Ltd [1964] 3 All ER 30, [1964] 2 QB 699,
[1964] 3 WLR 356, CA, 12 Digest (Reissue) 415, 3048.

Tweddle v Atkinson (1861) 1 B & S 393, [1861–73] All ER Rep 369, 30 LJQB 265, 4 LT 468,
25 JP 517, 121 ER 762, 12 Digest (Reissue) 48, 237.

Appeal

The defendants, Wimpey Construction UK Ltd ('Wimpey'), appealed against the
judgment of the Court of Appeal (Lawton and Goff LJJ, Buckley LJ dissenting in part)
given on 26th October 1978 varying an order made by Fox J on 21st December 1976
awarding the plaintiffs, Woodar Investment Development Ltd ('Woodar'), £462,000
damages, for breach of a contact dated 21st February 1973 for the sale by Woodar and
purchase by Wimpey of 14·41 acres situated at Cobham, Surrey, such damages to include
the sum of £150,000 for the use and benefit of a third party nominated by Woodar,
Transworld Trade Ltd. By its order of 26th October 1978 the Court of Appeal reduced
the damages to £272,943 including £135,000 for the use of Transworld Trade Ltd. The
facts are set out in the opinion of Lord Wilberforce.

Jonathan Parker QC and *S Acton* for Wimpey.
Leolin Price QC and *Nicholas Stewart* for Woodar.

Their Lordships took time for consideration.

14th February. The following opinions were delivered.

LORD WILBERFORCE. My Lords, the appellants ('Wimpey') are defendants in this
action brought by the respondents ('Woodar') on a contract of sale dated 21st February
1973. This contract, in which Woodar were the vendors and Wimpey the purchasers,
related to 14 acres of land at Cobham, Surrey, near to the site later occupied by the Esher
by-pass road. There was the prospect of planning permission being granted for
development. The purchase price was £850,000 and there was a special condition
(condition I) that on completion Wimpey should pay £150,000 to a company called
Transworld Trade Ltd. Completion was fixed for the earliest of three dates, namely (i)
two months from the granting of outline planning permission for the development of
the property, (ii) 21st February 1980, (iii) such date as Wimpey should specify by not less
than 14 days' notice in writing.

The contract contained a special condition, condition E, under which there was
reserved to Wimpey power to rescind the contract in either of three events. The first
related to failure to obtain outline planning permission, the second to failure to obtain
an easement giving access to the property, and the third condition (E(a)(iii)), was in the
following terms:

> '[If prior to the date of completion] any Authority having a statutory power of
> compulsory acquisition shall have commenced to negotiate for the acquisition by
> agreement or shall have commenced the procedure required by law for the
> compulsory acquisition of the property or any part thereof.'

On 20th March 1974 Wimpey sent to Woodar a notice in writing purporting to
rescind the contract under this provision. The notice stated that the ground relied on
was that the Secretary of State for the Environment had commenced the procedure
required by law for the compulsory acquisition of 2·3 acres of the property.

It was in fact known to both parties at the date of the contract that certain steps had

already been taken in relation to these 2·3 acres. In 1970 the Minister had given notice
of a draft compulsory purchase order to the then owner, and this fact had been published
in the local press. Notice had been given of the appointment of an inspector to hold a
public inquiry, and this was held. A compulsory purchase order was made on 8th
November 1973. On these facts, Woodar contended that special condition E(a)(iii) could
not be invoked by Wimpey because the relevant procedure for compulsory purchase had
started before the date of the contract, and so did not come within the words 'shall have
commenced'. This contention was upheld by Fox J at the trial and was not the subject of
appeal, so that Wimpey's claim to invoke the condition has failed.

This gives rise to the first issue in this appeal: whether, by invoking special condition
E(a)(iii), and in the circumstances, Wimpey are to be taken as having repudiated the
contract. Woodar so claim, and assert that they have accepted the repudiation and are
entitled to sue Wimpey for damages.

My Lords, I have used the words 'in the circumstances' to indicate, as I think both sides
accept, that in considering whether there has been a repudiation by one party, it is
necessary to look at his conduct as a whole. Does this indicate an intention to abandon
and to refuse performance of the contract? In the present case, without taking Wimpey's
conduct generally into account, Woodar's contention, that Wimpey had repudiated,
would be a difficult one. So far from repudiating the contract, Wimpey were relying on
it and invoking one of its provisions, to which both parties had given their consent. And
unless the invocation of that provision were totally abusive, or lacking in good faith,
(neither of which is contended for), the fact that it has proved to be wrong in law cannot
turn it into a repudiation. At the lowest, the notice of rescission was a neutral document
consistent either with an intention to preserve, or with an intention to abandon, the
contract, and I will deal with it on this basis, more favourable to Woodar. In order to
decide which is correct Wimpey's conduct has to be examined.

One point can, in my opinion, be disposed of at once. Woodar, in March 1974, started
proceedings against Wimpey: this is one of the actions consolidated in the litigation
before us. They claimed a declaration that Wimpey's notice of rescission was not valid,
and Wimpey, by their defence asserted the contrary and they counterclaimed for a
declaration to that effect. Woodar now contend that if the original notice did not amount
to a repudiation, the defence and counterclaim did. I regard this contention as
hopeless. Wimpey's pleading carried the matter no further: it simply rested the matter
on the contract. It showed no intention to abandon the contract whatever the result of
the action might be. If the action were to succeed (ie if Wimpey lost) there was no
indication that Wimpey would not abide by the result and implement the contract.

The facts indicative of Wimpey's intention must now be summarised. It is clear in the
first place that, subjectively, Wimpey in 1974 wanted to get out of the contract. Land
prices had fallen, and they thought that if the contract was dissolved, they could probably
acquire it at a much lower price. But subjective intention is not decisive: it supplied the
motive for serving the notice of rescission; there remains the question whether,
objectively regarded, their conduct showed an intention to abandon the contract.

In early 1974 there was a possibility that some planning permission might be
granted. If it were, and unless Wimpey could take valid objection to it, completion
would (under the conditions) have to follow in two months. Therefore, if a notice of
rescission were to be given, it had to be served without delay, ie before the planning
permission arrived. In this situation, Wimpey's advisers arranged a meeting with a Mr
Cornwell, who was acting for Woodar, or as an intermediary with power to commit
Woodar, to discuss the matter. This took place on 7th March 1974 and is recorded as a
disclosed aide memoire dated the next day. This document was prepared by Wimpey,
and we have not had the benefit of Mr Cornwell's evidence on it: he died before the
trial. But the rest of the correspondence is fully in line with it and I see no reason to
doubt its general accuracy. After recording each side's statement of position, the
document contained, inter alia, these passages: 'He [Mr Cornwell] stated that if we
attempted to rescind the contract, then he would take us to court and let the judge decide

a
whether the contract could be rescinded on the point we were making.' This 'point' was undoubtedly that relating to the compulsory purchase of the 2·5 acres. The aide memoire continues:

> 'I told him that our Legal Department would be serving the Notice to Rescind the Contract within a short while—this would ensure that the company was fully protected and was prudent. He assured me that he would accept it on that basis and not regard it as a hostile act.'

b
The notice was then served on 20th March 1974. On 22nd March Woodar's solicitors wrote that they did not accept its validity. On 30th May 1974 Mr Cornwell wrote a long letter to Sir Godfrey Mitchell, president of Wimpey. I refer to one passage:

c
> ' . . . within a few days of the original meeting, a notice of rescission was served upon the vendor company by your organisation that the contract was to be rescinded. Simultaneously with that notice of rescission, proceedings were instituted and there the matter remains so far as the legal situation is concerned and both parties, from the legal point of view, must now await the decision of the court as to the validity of the claim made by Messrs. George Wimpey & Co. Limited that they are entitled to rescind this contract upon the grounds which they have so stated.'

d
On 4th June 1974 Mr Cornwell wrote again: 'All I need say now is that we will retire to our battle stations and it goes without saying I am sure that you will abide by the result as I will.'

My Lords, I cannot find anything which carries the matter one inch beyond, on Wimpey's part an expressed reliance on the contract (in condition E(a)(iii)), on Woodar's
e
side an intention to take the issue of the validity of the notice (nothing else) to the courts, and an assumption, not disputed by Wimpey, that both sides would abide by the decision of the court. This is quite insufficient to support the case for repudiation. There is only one other matter relied on. At the date of the contract (21st February 1973) there were arrangements made for a loan of £165,000 to be made to Woodar by the National Westminster Bank. Wimpey guaranteed, subject to three months' notice of termination,
f
Woodar's indebtedness to the bank up to £165,000 and agreed with the bank to meet interest and other charges. As between Wimpey and Woodar it was agreed that Wimpey should indemnify Woodar against all interest on the loan for seven years or until the contract should be 'fulfilled or discharged'. These arrangements did not form part of the contract of sale but were collateral to it.

When the notice of rescission was served on 20th March 1974, it was accompanied by
g
a covering letter, of the same date, referring to the loan arrangements stated which:

> 'The undertaking was limited to seven years from the date of exchange, or until the Contract was fulfilled or discharged. As the Contract is now discharged by the enclosed Notice, [Woodar] will now be liable for the charges incurred in respect of this loan.'

h
Wimpey also gave three months' notice to the bank terminating the guarantee. Again, in my opinion, this carried the matter no further. It simply drew the attention of Woodar to the consequences which would follow from rescission of the contract, nothing more. Woodar, in fact understood it as such, for they wrote to the bank on 8th April 1974 stating that proceedings had been instituted against Wimpey for a declaration 'which, if successful, will reinstate the arrangements which you now give notice you
j
intend to bring to an end.'

My Lords, in my opinion, it follows, as a clear conclusion of fact, that Wimpey manifested no intention to abandon, or to refuse future performance of, or to repudiate the contract. And the issue being one of fact, citation of other decided cases on other facts is hardly necessary. I shall simply state that the proposition that a party who takes action relying simply on the terms of the contract and not manifesting by his conduct an ulterior intention to abandon it is not to be treated as repudiating it, is supported by *James Shaffer Ltd v Findlay Durham & Brodie*[1] and *Sweet & Maxwell Ltd v Universal News Services Ltd*[2].

In contrast to these is the case in this House of *Federal Commerce and Navigation Co Ltd v Molena Alpha Inc*[3] which fell on the other side of the line. Of that I said:

> 'The two cases relied on by the owners (*James Shaffer Ltd v Findley Durham & Brodie*[1] and *Sweet & Maxwell v Universal News Services Ltd*[2]) ... would only be relevant here if the owners' action had been confined to asserting their own view, possibly erroneous, as to the effect of the contract. They went, in fact, far beyond this when they threatened a breach of contract with serious consequences.'

Spettabile Consorzio Veneziano di Armamento e Navigazione v Northumberland Shipbuilding Co Ltd[4], though in some factual respects distinguishable from the present, is nevertheless, in my opinion, clear support for Wimpey.

In my opinion, therefore, Wimpey are entitled to succeed on the repudiation issue, and I would only add that it would be a regrettable development of the law of contract to hold that a party who bona fide relies on an express stipulation in a contract in order to rescind or terminate a contract should, by that fact alone, be treated as having repudiated his contractual obligations if he turns out to be mistaken as to his rights. Repudiation is a drastic conclusion which should only be held to arise in clear cases of a refusal, in a matter going to the root of the contract, to perform contractual obligations. To uphold Woodar's contentions in this case would represent an undesirable contention of the doctrine.

The second issue in this appeal is one of damages. Both courts below have allowed Woodar to recover substantial damages in respect of condition I under which £150,000 was payable by Wimpey to Transworld Trade Ltd on completion. On the view which I take of the repudiation issue, this question does not require decision, but in view of the unsatisfactory state in which the law would be if the Court of Appeal's decision were to stand I must add three observations.

1. The majority of the Court of Appeal followed, in the case of Goff LJ with expressed reluctance, its previous decision in *Jackson v Horizon Holidays Ltd*[5]. I am not prepared to dissent from the actual decision in that case. It may be supported either as a broad decision on the measure of damages (per James LJ) or possibly as an example of a type of contract, examples of which are persons contracting for family holidays, ordering meals in restaurants for a party, hiring a taxi for a group, calling for special treatment. As I suggested in *New Zealand Shipping Co Ltd v A M Satterthwaite & Co Ltd*[6], there are many situations of daily life which do not fit neatly into conceptual analysis, but which require some flexibility in the law of contract. *Jackson's* case[5] may well be one.

I cannot agree with the basis on which Lord Denning MR put his decision in that case. The extract on which he relied from the judgment of Lush LJ in *Lloyd's v Harper*[7] was part of a passage in which Lush LJ was stating as an 'established rule of law' that an agent (sc an insurance broker) may sue on a contract made by him on behalf of the principal (sc the assured) if the contract gives him such a right, and is no authority for the proposition required in *Jackson's* case[5], still less for the proposition, required here, that,

1   [1953] 1 WLR 106
2   [1964] 3 All ER 30, [1964] 2 QB 699
3   [1979] 1 All ER 307 at 315, [1979] AC 757 at 780
4   (1919) 121 LT 628, [1918–19] All ER Rep 963
5   [1975] 3 All ER 92, [1975] 1 WLR 1468
6   [1974] 1 All ER 1015 at 1020, [1975] AC 154 at 167
7   (1880) 16 Ch D 290 at 321

a if Woodar made a contract for a sum of money to be paid to Transworld, Woodar can, without showing that it has itself suffered loss or that Woodar was agent or trustee for Transworld, sue for damages for non-payment of that sum. That would certainly not be an established rule of law, nor was it quoted as such authority by Lord Pearce in *Beswick v Beswick*[1].

   2. Assuming that *Jackson's* case[2] was correctly decided (as above), it does not carry the present case, where the factual situation is quite different. I respectfully think therefore
b that the Court of Appeal need not, and should not have followed it.

   3. Whether in a situation such as the present, viz where it is not shown that Woodar was agent or trustee for Transworld, or that Woodar itself sustained any loss, Woodar can recover any damages at all, or any but nominal damages, against Wimpey, and on what principle, is, in my opinion, a question of great doubt and difficulty, no doubt open in this House, but one on which I prefer to reserve my opinion.
c I would allow the appeal.

LORD SALMON. My Lords, this case raises a point of law of considerable importance in relation to the repudiation of contracts.

   Between July 1969 and February 1973 prolonged negotiations took place between Mr Ronald Cornwell and Wimpey for the purchase by Wimpey of 14·41 acres of freehold
d land known as Mizen's Nurseries at Cobham. In January 1973 Wimpey learnt from Mr Cornwell that the vendors were to be Woodar. By February 1973 the purchase price had been agreed at £1 million. In that month Mr Cornwell proposed that part of the purchase price should be paid to him as European agent for Transworld Trade Ltd, and a few days later it was agreed that that part of the purchase price should amount to £150,000 and be paid to Transworld direct.

e It was also arranged that the contract should provide for a loan of £165,000, secured by a charge on the land (the subject-matter of the contract) to be made to Woodar by Wimpey through their bank and that Wimpey should be responsible for servicing the loan. Wimpey were, however, advised that the loan should be treated separately from the contract, otherwise the contract might be void as constituting a clog on the equity of redemption under the charge. Accordingly, on 21st February 1973 Wimpey's bank lent
f Woodar £165,000 and Woodar executed a legal charge on the land in respect of the loan. Wimpey gave a written undertaking to the bank to meet all interest and other charges in respect of the loan until 21st February 1980 '*or until the contract should be fulfilled or discharged*' (emphasis mine). The facts which I have related are all taken out of Wimpey's printed case.

   The written contract for the purchase of the land by Wimpey from Woodar was also
g executed on 21st February 1973. It specified the purchase price as £850,000 and laid down at the end of the contract in condition I that on the completion of the purchase of the whole or any part of this land, Wimpey should pay Transworld £150,000.

   I will now turn to the material clauses in the contract. Condition E(a) so far as relevant reads:

h 'This Contract shall be absolutely binding on both parties . . . for a period of seven years from the date hereof but there shall be reserved to [Wimpey] only the power to rescind this contract if prior to the date of completion . . . (iii) any Authority having a statutory power of compulsory acquisition shall have commenced to negotiate for the acquisition by agreement or shall have commenced the procedure required by law for the compulsory acquisition of the property or any part thereof.'

j This condition, quite obviously, refers only to any such negotiation or procedure commenced after the execution of the contract and prior to completion but not to any

---

1 [1967] 2 All ER 1197, [1968] AC 58
2 [1975] 3 All ER 92, [1975] 1 WLR 1468

negotiation or procedure which had commenced and of which both parties were well aware before they executed the contract.

Condition E(c), so far as relevant, reads:

'The power to rescind reserved to [Wimpey] by sub-clause (a) ... shall be exercisable by the service of a notice in writing to that effect upon [Woodar] ... and [Wimpey] liability under ... this Contract shall from the date of service of such notice cease.'

Condition E(g) provides that completion shall take place on the earliest of the three dates it mentions, namely (i) two months after the date on which outline planning permission for the development of the property was granted, (ii) 21st February 1980, (iii) such date as Wimpey should specify but not by less than 14 days' written notice.

Returning to condition E(a)(iii) of the contract, it is common ground that Wimpey and Woodar both knew, well before the contract between them was executed, (1) that in 1970 the Minister of the Environment had given notice of a draft compulsory purchase order in respect of 2·3 acres of the 14·41 acres covered by the contract, (2) that this fact had been published in the local press, and (3) that notice had also been given of the appointment of an inspector to hold a public inquiry which he had duly held. Indeed, there is a provision in the contract under condition G which, so far as relevant, reads:

'It is hereby agreed that [Woodar] shall not require [Wimpey] to include in the Transfer to [Wimpey] any part ... of the land hereby agreed to be sold which shall be required by the Surrey County Council ... or any Statutory Authority ... and the purchase price shall be abated at the rate of £70,000 per acre ... for any part ... of the land hereby agreed to be sold which shall not be included in the Transfer to [Wimpey].'

It is to be observed that if the land is priced in the contract at £70,000 an acre, the 14·41 acres sold under the contract would, in fact, be priced at about £1 million.

By March 1974 there had been a very alarming slump in the value of land. It is quite clear from one of Wimpey's internal memoranda, written at the beginning of that month, that Wimpey had no intention of honouring their contract by paying the agreed price of £70,000 an acre for the land; and that they intended to repudiate the contract but would gladly enter into a new contract with Woodar to buy the land at £48,000 an acre, on otherwise the same terms as those of the existing contract. The relevant part of the memorandum reads as follows:

'Revised broadsheets have been prepared taking account of the reduced selling price of houses and increased building costs and these indicate that currently to show 20% profit we can offer £48,000 per acre, to show 15% profit £53,000 per acre. The indications are that this piece of land could obtain outline planning permission within the next 4 months, in which case we as a company would be obliged to perform in accordance with the obligations of our contract to purchase subject to the various conditions. We propose arranging a meeting with Mr. Cornwell to discuss formally with him: (a) Our intention to rescind the contract so that he is obliged to pay the interest on the loan thereafter from that date. (b) To make him a proposal that we are prepared to proceed with the purchase of the land at the reduced figure of £48,000 per developable acre subject, of course, to the same terms and conditions.'

On 20th March 1974 a notice was sent to Woodar by Wimpey in the following terms:

'Pursuant to Clause E(c) of a Contract dated the Twenty-first day of February 1973 and made between Woodar Investment Development Limited of the one part and George Wimpey & Co., Limited of the other part the said George Wimpey & Co., Limited hereby rescinds the said Contract on the ground that within the meaning of Clause E(a)(iii) of the said Contract the Secretary of State for the Environment has

a
commenced the procedure required by law for the compulsory acquisition of part
of the property (a Compulsory Purchase Order relating to the land edged red on the
plan annexed hereto having been made).'

I am afraid that I am entirely unable to agree with the proposition that this notice of
rescission was a neutral averment consistent either with the intention to preserve or with
an intention to abandon the contract. To my mind it was served with the clearly
expressed intention of bringing the contract to an end. This notice was accompanied by
b a letter of the same date, the last paragraph of which reads as follows:

> 'When Contracts for the sale and purchase of the above land were exchanged, an
> undertaking was given by [Wimpey] indemnifying Woodar Investment Develop-
> ment Limited against all interest charges payable to the National Westminster Bank
> Limited as a result of a loan by them to you of a sum of £165,000·00. The
> undertaking was limited to seven years from the date of exchange *or until the*
c *Contract was fulfilled or discharged. As the Contract is now discharged* by the enclosed
> Notice, Woodar Investment Development Limited will now be liable for the charges
> incurred in respect of this loan.' (Emphasis mine.)

My lords, it was conceded in this House on behalf of Wimpey that they had no right
to rescind, discharge or repudiate the contract. In my respectful opinion, Wimpey had
d made it crystal clear by their notice and letter of 20th March that they purported to bring
their liability under the contract to an end by rescinding and discharging it; and that
they had no intention of paying the contract price for the land in question. If this does
not go to the root of the contract and evince an unequivocal intention no longer to be
bound by it, and therefore amounts to a repudiation of the contract, I confess that I
cannot imagine what would.

In the court of first instance, Wimpey sought to justify their notice and letter of 20th
e March 1974 on the ground that prior to the execution of the contract of 21st February
1973, steps had been taken for the compulsory acquisition of 2·3 acres out of the 14·41
acres the subject matter of the contract. I have already described these steps and I shall not
repeat them. It is common ground that all these steps were well known both to Wimpey
and to Woodar at the time they were taken. The point was nevertheless argued on behalf
f of Wimpey before the trial judge that because of these steps having been taken when
they were, Wimpey were entitled under condition E(a)(iii) of the contract to rescind the
contract and refuse to perform it. The learned trial judge made short work of that point
and decided that it was untenable. The point was so obviously bad that it was wisely
decided by counsel on behalf of Wimpey not to be worth taking in the Court of Appeal.
It was however accepted by Woodar that on 20th March 1974, Wimpey honestly believed
in the point which they later abandoned. I do not understand how Wimpey's honest
g belief in a bad point of law can in any way avail them. In *Federal Commerce Navigation Co
Ltd v Molena Alpha Inc*[1] Lord Denning MR said:

> 'I have yet to learn that a party who breaks a contract can excuse himself by saying
> that he did it on the advice of his lawyers; or that he was under an honest
> misapprehension. Nor can he excuse himself on those grounds from the
h consequences of a repudiation.'

I gratefully adopt that passage which seems to me to be particularly apt in the present
case. It certainly was never questioned in your Lordships' House when the appeal from
the decision of the Court of Appeal in the *Federal Commerce* case[2] was dismissed.

In *Freeth v Burr*[3] Lord Coleridge CJ said:

j
> '... where the question is whether the one party is set free by the action of the
> other, the real matter for consideration is whether the acts or conduct of the one do

1   [1978] 3 All ER 1066 at 1082, [1978] QB 927 at 979
2   [1979] 1 All ER 307, [1979] AC 757
3   (1874) LR 9 CP 208 at 213, [1874–80] All ER Rep 750 at 753

or do not amount to an intimation of an intention to abandon and altogether to refuse performance of the contract.'   *a*

In *Mersey Steel and Iron Co Ltd v Naylor, Benzon and Co*[1] Lord Selborne LC, after approving what Lord Coleridge CJ said in *Freeth v Burr*[2], went on to say:

> '. . . you must examine what the conduct is, so as to see whether it amounts to a renunciation, to an absolute refusal to perform the contract, such as would amount to a rescission if he had the power to rescind, and whether the other party may *b* accept it as a reason for not performing his part . . .'

In *Spettabile Consorzio Veneziano di Armamento e Navigazione v Northumberland Shipbuilding Co Ltd*[3] Atkin LJ said:

> 'A repudiation has been defined in different terms—by Lord Selborne as an absolute refusal to perform a contract; by Lord Esher as a total refusal to perform it; *c* by Bowen, L.J. in *Johnstone v Milling*[4] as a declaration of an intention not to carry out a contract when the time arrives, and by Lord Haldane in *Bradley v H. Newsom, Sons, & Co. Limited*[5] as an intention to treat the obligation as altogether at an end. They all come to the same thing, and they all amount, at any rate to this, that it must be shown that the party to the contract made quite plain his own intention not to perform the contract.'   *d*

In *Heyman v Darwins Ltd*[6] Lord Wright said:

> 'There is a form of repudiation, however, where the party who repudiates does not deny that a contract was intended between the parties, but claims that it is not binding because of the failure of some condition or the infringement of some duty fundamental to the enforceability of the contract, it being expressly provided by the *e* contract that the failure of condition or the breach of duty should invalidate the contract . . . But perhaps the commonest application of the word "repudiation" is to what is often called the anticipatory breach of a contract where the party by words or conduct evinces an intention no longer to be bound, and the other party accepts the repudiation and rescinds the contract. In such a case, if the repudiation is *f* wrongful and the rescission is rightful, the contract is ended by the rescission, but only as far as concerns future performance. It remains alive for the awarding of damages . . . for the breach which constitutes the repudiation.'

In my opinion, the repudiation in the present case exactly fits the repudiation which Lord Wright explains in the passage which I have just cited.

I do not recall that any of these definitions of a repudiation of a contract have ever, *g* until now, been questioned. The fact that a party to a contract mistakenly believes that he has the right to refuse to perform it cannot avail him. Nor is there any authority for the proposition that if a party to a contract totally refuses to perform it, this refusal is any the less a repudiation of the contract because he honestly but mistakenly believes that he is entitled by a condition of the contract to refuse to perform it.

It would indeed be unfortunate if the law were otherwise. A mistake in the *h* construction of a contractual condition, even such a glaringly obvious mistake as the present, can apparently easily be made especially perhaps when the market price has fallen far below the contract price. It is acknowledged in this case that the mistake was

---

1   (1884) 9 App Cas 434 at 439, [1881–5] All ER Rep 365 at 368   *j*
2   (1874) LR 9 CP 208 at 213, [1874–80] All Rep 750 at 753
3   (1919) 121 LT 628 at 634–635, [1918–19] All ER Rep 963 at 968
4   (1886) 16 QBD 460
5   [1919] AC 16, [1918–19] All ER Rep 625
6   [1942] 1 All ER 337 at 350, [1942] AC 356 at 378–379

an honest one. If, however, a case arose in which a mistake of this kind was alleged to be
a an honest mistake, but not acknowledged to be so, it would be extremely difficult, if not
impossible to prove the contrary.

James Shaffer Ltd v Findlay Durham & Brodie[1] and Sweet & Maxwell Ltd v Universal News
Services Ltd[2] were strongly relied on on behalf of Wimpey. Those two cases were very
different from each other and even more different from the present case; in my opinion
they certainly lend no more support to Wimpey than they did to the appellants in the
b Federal Commerce case[3]. Indeed, if anything they are of some help to Woodar. In the
former case, Singleton LJ said[4] '. . . is it possible to say that the defendants . . . showed an
intention to abandon and altogether to refuse the performance of the contract? . . . I
think not.' Morris LJ said[5]: 'I have no doubt that [the defendants] wanted to go on with
the contract.' In the latter case, Harman LJ said[6]

c
'. . . repudiation really is not in the picture here at all, because if the defendant
company was not wholly justified in the attitude it took up [on the construction of
the agreement], the plaintiff company was not wholly justified in its attitude either
and could only treat the defendant company's refusal to comply with its demands
as repudiation if its demands were wholly right. Therefore . . . repudiation does not
really arise: but as it was the ground of the judgment of the learned judge below I
d think that I ought to say something about it . . . there was not that absolute refusal
to go on which is necessary to arrive at a conclusion that an agreement . . . has been
entirely repudiated.'

Pearson LJ said much the same.

The present case is, however, quite different from the James Shaffer case[1] and the Sweet
& Maxwell case[2] because Wimpey made it very plain by their notice and letter of 20th
e March 1974 that they had no intention to go on with the contract and buy the land at the
contract price.

Spettabile Consorzio Veneziano di Armamento e Navigazione v Northumberland Shipbuilding
Co Ltd[7] was also strongly relied upon on behalf of Wimpey. The facts of that case were
very strange and clearly distinguishable from the present. Goff LJ in the Court of Appeal
made a long and masterly analysis of that case with which I agree and gratefully adopt.
f I do not consider that that case is, in reality, of any help to Wimpey.

I cannot accept that the majority of the Court of Appeal concentrated too much
attention on Wimpey's rescission notice of 20th March 1974 and not enough on its
surrounding circumstances. In any event, it seems to me that those surrounding
circumstances supported Woodar's case rather than Wimpey's. I think that it is obvious
from the surrounding circumstances that Wimpey had made up their mind at the
g beginning of March 1974 (and never changed it) that, in no circumstances would they
comply with their contractual obligation to buy the land in question at the price of
£70,000 per acre. This is made clear by the language of their memorandum which I
have already cited and which appears to have been written a day or two before Wimpey's
aide memoire of 8th March 1974 on which Wimpey rely. I do not understand how that
document can be evidence against Woodar, even if Mr Cornwell were still alive. Nor do
h I think that even if the document were admissible in evidence it could be accepted as
being accurate in every detail. Looking at the document as a whole, however, it seems

---

j
1   [1953] 1 WLR 106
2   [1964] 3 All ER 30, [1964] 2 QB 699
3   [1979] 1 All ER 307, [1979] AC 757
4   [1953] 1 WLR 106 at 121
5   [1953] 1 WLR 106 at 124
6   [1964] 3 All ER 30 at 39, [1964] 2 QB 699 at 729
7   (1919) 121 LT 628, [1918–19] All ER Rep 963

to support Woodar's case rather than Wimpey's. It indicates (1) that Wimpey made plain
to Mr Cornwell what was recorded in the memorandum which I have cited, (2) that Mr *a*
Cornwell was anxious to effect a compromise and suggested that 'the money could be
paid to him over a period of up to say five years, or that the price could be lowered or a
combination of both', (3) that Wimpey replied that 'the mere extension of five years
would not be attractive to us, *but that if the land value was vastly reduced we would still like
to remain with the deal*' (emphasis mine), and (4) that Mr Cornwell then said 'that he would
go away and consider the lowest price that he could afford to sell it to us and that below *b*
that price he would fight us through the Courts'.

On 22nd March 1974, two days after the notice of rescission was served by Wimpey,
Woodar's solicitors wrote that they did not accept its validity. By a writ of summons
endorsed with a statement of claim served on 29th March 1974 Woodar, amongst other
things, claimed against Wimpey a declaration that their notice of 20th March 1974 did
not rescind the contract. It may well be that Woodar considered that once they *c*
commenced legal proceedings, Wimpey would throw in their hand. If so, they were
mistaken, for Wimpey served a defence and counterclaim on 18th May 1974 alleging
that the notice of rescission of 20th March 1974 was valid and counterclaimed a
declaration that the contract had been rescinded by that notice.

Mr Cornwell, who seems to have done all the negotiations on behalf of Woodar, was
obviously anxious if possible to settle rather than embark on lengthy and expensive *d*
litigation. He was no doubt disappointed when Wimpey made it clear by their defence
and counterclaim that they intended to fight. He probably, I think, wrote his lengthy
letter of 30th May 1974 in one last effort to effect a settlement. Wimpey have sought to
make much of this letter which in my view helps Woodar rather than Wimpey. It seems
to make it very plain that Mr Cornwell had consulted counsel on the notice of rescission
and had been advised that it constituted a wrongful repudiation of the contract. I cite *e*
one brief passage from it: '. . . unless some compromise is reached and quickly, then I
shall feel obliged to sell immediately in the best possible circumstances with a certain
knowledge, so far as counsel's advice is concerned, that we have a complete redress
against [Wimpey].' Of course there was nothing to stop the parties waiting and doing
nothing until the litigation constituted by the first action was over as Mr Cornwell said
earlier in his letter. But there was nothing to prevent Woodar from selling immediately *f*
and bringing another action claiming damages, *once they had accepted* the repudiation to
which I have already referred.

At the time when Mr Cornwell's letter of 4th June 1974 was written, on which my
noble and learned friend Lord Scarman places considerable reliance, Woodar had not
accepted the repudiation: and a repudiation, however wrongful is nugatory until
accepted by the other contracting party. *g*

The result of the first action must have been in Woodar's favour. They could have
waited until completion was due under the contract, which could not have been later
than 21st February 1980. Wimpey might then perhaps have completed the contract or
they might have failed to complete it, in which event they would have had no defence
to an action for specific performance or damages. There was, however, nothing to
compel Woodar to confine themselves to the first action. They had a free choice to do so *h*
or to accept the wrongful repudiation which would enable Woodar to bring the second
action claiming damages for an anticipatory breach of the contract.

I entirely agree with my noble and learned friend Lord Wilberforce that Wimpey's
counterclaim in the first action did not amount to a repudiation of the contract. For the
reasons I have given, however, their repudiation of the contract had, in my view, been
effected by the notice of rescission dated 20th March 1974 and supported by the letter of *j*
the same date.

Although I cannot agree with Buckley LJ that the contract was not wrongfully
repudiated, I do agree with his view that, if Wimpey's notice of 20th March 1974 did not
constitute a wrongful repudiation of the contract of 21st February 1973, the proceedings
launched by Woodar against Wimpey on 29th March 1974 could not preclude them

a from accepting that repudiation and bringing another action against Wimpey claiming damages for an anticipatory breach of contract. And this is what Woodar did. On 10th July 1974, through their solicitors, they accepted the wrongful repudiation of 20th March 1974 and then launched their action for damages for an anticipatory breach of contract. The two actions were consolidated and duly tried by Fox J who found that Wimpey had wrongfully repudiated the contract of 21st February 1973 and gave judgment in favour of Woodar for, in all, £462,000 damages.

b The Court of Appeal by a majority affirmed Fox J's decision on liability but reduced the damages to £272,943.

My Lords, for the reasons I have stated, I would dismiss the appeal on the issue of liability. Since, as I understand, the majority of your Lordships are for allowing the appeal on liability, the interesting question in relation to damages in respect of the claim for £150,000 does not now arise. I do, however, agree with what my noble and learned
c friend Lord Wilberforce has said about the finding of the majority of the Court of Appeal (Goff LJ with reluctance) on this topic. I would add that, in my opinion, the law as it stands at present in relation to damages of this kind is most unsatisfactory; and I can only hope that your Lordships' House will soon have an opportunity of reconsidering it unless in the meantime it is altered by statute.

d
LORD RUSSELL OF KILLOWEN. My Lords, the contention advanced by the purchaser ('Wimpey') was that it was entitled to rescind the contract by notice of rescission under special condition E(a)(iii) of the contract, because the relevant authority had 'commenced the procedure' required by law for compulsory acquisition not earlier than the making of the compulsory purchase order on 8th November 1973, subsequent
e to the contract. Fox J held that this was incorrect; and that even if it were a correct construction of the contract there should be rectification to make it clear that steps taken by the authority in that connection prior to the contract constituted commencement of the relevant procedure and were not intended to afford a ground for rescission under the special condition. From that holding there was and is no appeal.

Consequently there was no justification in law for the notice of rescission, and the first
f question in this appeal is whether the notice of rescission was capable of being accepted by the vendor ('Woodar') as a renunciation or repudiation of the contract by Wimpey. An affirmative answer to that question was assumed, or not disputed, before Fox J, and was given by the majority in the Court of Appeal (Buckley LJ dissenting).

The difference of opinion on this point in the Court of Appeal and in your Lordships' House turns on a question which can be shortly stated. If a party to a contract has a
g power thereunder totally to rescind and renounce all liability to perform any part of its obligations under a contract, and in terms purports absolutely so to rescind and renounce on grounds that in law are not justified, can there ever be circumstances which enable the rescinder to dispute the renunciatory and repudiatory quality of his action?

My Lords, in my opinion the answer to that question is in the negative.

I do not of course dispute that a mistaken concept of the rights of a party under the
h contract, and action (or inaction) on the basis of that mistaken concept, need not constitute such a renunciation of the contract as to be capable of being accepted as repudiation of the contract. Nor do I dispute that repudiation is a serious matter not lightly to be found. Nor do I dispute that in most cases repudiation or non-repudiation falls to be decided having regard to all the circumstances of a case. But I deny that a clear case of the purported exercise of a power of rescission, a total renunciation of all future
j obligation to perform any part of the contract, such as now concerns your Lordships, can by any circumstances be watered down or deprived of its repudiatory quality. I further assert that it is fallacious to deny that totally renunciatory and repudiatory quality on the ground that because the action is purportedly taken under a clause in the contract it is somehow affirming rather than repudiating the contract. The notice of rescission given in this case by Wimpey was wholly unequivocal, in effect saying that Wimpey would not

in any circumstances fulfil the contract: and that flat statement is not to be regarded as otherwise than renunciatory of the contract because Wimpey genuinely thought that it was entitled in law to take that attitude.

It is of course true that in previous discussion with Mr Cornwell (for Woodar) it was indicated that Wimpey's right to rescind on the ground suggested would be challenged by Woodar in proceedings. But I see no ground in that for watering down the absolute nature (or colour) of the notice of rescission as being somehow conditional on the rectitude in law of Wimpey's stance. Indeed I do not accept a view that the notice of rescission could have been (i) expressed to be conditional on its justification in law but (ii) *then* operative to terminate all liability of Wimpey under the contract, as it was manifestly intended to be because it was feared that shortly a planning permission would be forthcoming (though it was not) which would trap Wimpey irrevocably into an unprofitable bargain.

I can, my Lords, envisage a situation in which a party in the position of Woodar might state unequivocally in advance that if Wimpey were to serve the notice which it did serve, Woodar would not, when it was shown in proceedings that the notice was unjustified, treat it as repudiatory. But that would achieve a position in which Woodar would be debarred from asserting repudiation, rather than constitute a circumstance qualifying the fundamental renunciatory character of the purported exercise by Wimpey of the power. But it cannot be said that such a position was achieved by anything said by Mr Cornwell in this case.

I am, my Lords, not led to a contrary view by the circumstances of the *Spettabile* case[1] at first instance. There the view was taken that if originally a communication would have indicated a repudiatory attitude, subsequent approach to the court by the 'repudiator' for a decision on the rights of the case should be taken as withdrawal of the original repudiation. That is not this case. The resort to the court was not by Wimpey, and Wimpey never withdrew its notice of rescission to abide the outcome of the litigation.

It was suggested that the proceedings by Woodar for declaration and/or rectification somehow constituted an election not to accept the rescission as a repudiation, so that Woodar's later purported acceptance of it as such was ineffective. In common with, I believe, all your Lordships I cannot accept that. Woodar was obliged to take the steps that it did in order to establish that the notice was unjustified in law and *therefore* an unjustified repudiation.

Accordingly in my opinion Wimpey wrongfully repudiated the contract by its notice of rescission, and Woodar accepted that repudiation so as to entitle it to damages for total breach.

In arriving at my conclusion I do not rely on the reference to interest payments in the covering letter enclosing the rescission notice, or on the defence or counterclaim of Wimpey. These seem to me to add nothing to the repudiatory nature of the notice itself.

In conclusion on this point I cannot agree that, if my opinon were correct, it would be an unfortunate step in the law. If a party takes such a bold step he risks disaster. If he plunges in without first testing the temperature by a construction summons asking whether the rescission remedy is available to him he runs the risk of catching a severe cold.

There is no question on this appeal as to quantum of damage save under the heading of damages for breach of special condition I, under which Wimpey agreed on completion of the sale to pay £150,000 to Transworld, a Hong Kong company. Transworld was in some way connected with Mr Cornwell, who died before action. No evidence connects Transworld with Woodar, the party to the contract. No evidence suggests that Woodar could suffer any damage from a failure by Wimpey to pay £150,000 to Transworld. It is clear on the authority of *Beswick v Beswick*[2] that Woodar on completion could have

---

1 (1919) 121 LT 628, [1918–19] All ER Rep 963
2 [1967] 2 All ER 1197, [1968] AC 58

secured an order for specific performance of the agreement to pay £150,000 to
a Transworld, which the latter could have enforced. That would not have been an order
for payment to Woodar, nor (contrary to the form of order below) to Woodar for the use
and benefit of Transworld. There was no suggestion of trust or agency of Woodar for
Transworld. If it were necessary to decide the point, which in the light of the views of
the majority of your Lordships on the first point it is not, I would have concluded that
no more than nominal damages had been established by Woodar as a consequence of the
b refusal by Wimpey to pay Transworld in the light of the law of England as it now stands.
I would not have thought that the reasoning of Oliver J in *Radford v De Froberville*[1]
supported Woodar's case for substantial damages. Nor do I think that on this point the
Court of Appeal was correct in thinking it was constrained by *Jackson v Horizon Holidays
Ltd*[2] to award substantial damages. I do not criticize the outcome of that case: the
plaintiff had bought and paid for a high class family holiday; he did not get it, and
c therefore he was entitled to substantial damages for the failure to supply *him* with one.
It is to be observed that the order of the Court of Appeal as drawn up did not suggest that
any part of the damages awarded to him were 'for the use and benefit of' any member
of his family. It was a special case quite different from the instant case on the Transworld
point.

I would not, my Lords, wish to leave the *Jackson* case[2] without adverting with respectful
d disapproval to the reliance there placed by Lord Denning MR, not for the first time, on
an extract taken from the judgment of Lush LJ in *Lloyd's v Harper*[3]. That case was
plainly a case in which a trustee or agent was enforcing the rights of a beneficiary or
principal, there being therefore a fiduciary relationship. Lord Denning MR in *Jackson's*
case[4] said this:

> 'The case comes within the principle stated by Lush LJ in *Lloyd's v Harper*[5]: "...
e > I consider it to be an established rule of law that where a contract is made with A. for
> the benefit of B., A. can sue on the contract for the benefit of B. and recover all that
> B. could have recovered if the contract had been made with B. himself". [Lord
> Denning continued:] It has been suggested that Lush LJ was thinking of a contract
> in which A was trustee for B. But I do not think so. He was a common lawyer
> speaking of the common law.'
f
I have already indicated that in all the other judgments the matter proceeded on a
fiduciary relationship between A and B; and Lush LJ in the same passage made it plain
that he did also, for he said[5]:

> 'It is true that the person [B] who employed him [the broker A] has a right, if he
> pleases, to take action himself and sue upon the contract made by the broker for
g > him, for he [B] *is a principal party to the contract*.' (Emphasis mine.)

To ignore that passage is to divorce the passage quoted by Lord Denning MR from the
fiduciary context in which it was uttered, the context of principal and agent, a field with
which it may be assumed Lush LJ was familiar. I venture to suggest that the brief
quotation should not be used again as support for a proposition which Lush LJ cannot
h have intended to advance.

In summary therefore, in disagreement with the majority of your Lordships, I would
have dismissed this appeal on repudiation. Had I been correct I would, as at present
advised, have allowed the appeal on the Transworld point, and awarded only nominal

j

1   [1978] 1 All ER 33, [1977] 1 WLR 1262
2   [1975] 3 All ER 92, [1975] 1 WLR 1468
3   (1880) 16 Ch D 290
4   [1975] 3 All ER 92 at 95–96, [1975] 1 WLR 1468 at 1473
5   16 Ch D 290 at 321

damages on that point to Woodar, and not substantial damages to be paid to Woodar 'for the use and benefit of' Transworld, a form of order which I cannot see was justified.

LORD KEITH OF KINKEL. My Lords, in deciding the issue of repudiation which arises in this appeal, the guiding principle is that enunciated by Lord Coleridge CJ in *Freeth v Burr*[1]:

> 'In cases of this sort, where the question is whether the one party is set free by the action of the other, the real matter for consideration is whether the acts or conduct of the one do or do not amount to an intimation of an intention to abandon and altogether to refuse performance of the contract.'

The matter is to be considered objectively—per Bowen LJ in *Johnstone v Milling*[2]:

> 'The claim being for wrongful repudiation of the contract it was necessary that the plaintiff's language should amount to a declaration of intention not to carry out the contract, or that it should be such that the defendant was justified in inferring from it such intention. We must construe the language used by the light of the contract and the circumstances of the case in order to see whether there was in this case any such renunciation of the contract.'

The importance of looking at the whole circumstances of the case was emphasised by Lord Selborne LC in *Mersey Steel & Iron Co Ltd v Naylor, Benzon & Co*[3] and by Singleton LJ in *James Shaffer Ltd v Findlay Durham & Brodie*[4].

There is a tract of authority which vouches the proposition that the assertion by one party to the other of a genuinely held but erroneous view as to the validity or effect of a contract does not constitute repudiation. In the *Spettabile*[5] case the plaintiffs sent to the defendants a letter claiming that certain contracts were no longer binding on them and followed it up with service of a writ seeking declarations to that effect. The Court of Appeal held that the plaintiffs' conduct did not amount to repudiation of the contracts. Warrington LJ said[6] with reference to the letter:

> 'It seems to me that that is not telling the defendants that whatever happens, whatever is the true state of the case, whether the contracts are binding on the plaintiffs or not, they will not perform them: but that they have instructed their solicitors to take proceedings with the object of having it determined that the contracts are not binding upon the plaintiffs and are at an end ... [and with reference to the writ] ... I think that it is desirable to say this, that in my opinion where one party to a contract conceives that he is no longer bound by the contract or has a right to have it rescinded or declared null and void, and issues a writ for the purpose of obtaining that which he believes to be his right, he does not by that mean to repudiate the performance of the contract in any event. It seems to me that he submits to perform it if the court, as the result of the action, comes to the conclusion that he is bound to perform it, and it cannot be taken to be an absolute repudiation.'

Atkin LJ, after observing that it must be shown that the party to the contract made quite plain his own intention not to be bound by it, said[7]:

> '... the substance [of the writ] appears to me to be this: that the plaintiffs in the action are asking the court to declare whether or not they are any longer bound by

1 (1874) LR 9 CP 208 at 213, [1874–80] All ER Rep 750 at 753
2 (1886) 16 QBD 460 at 474
3 (1884) 9 App Cas 434 at 438–439, [1881–5] All ER Rep 365 at 367–368
4 [1953] 1 WLR 106 at 116
5 (1919) 121 LT 628, [1918–19] All ER Rep 963
6 121 LT 628 at 633, [1918–19] All ER Rep 963 at 965–966
7 121 LT 628 at 635, [1918–19] All ER Rep 963 at 968

the contracts. It appears to me that that is an entirely different state of facts altogether from an intimation by the plaintiffs, apart from the courts of law, that they in any event are not going to perform the contracts. It is something quite different from a repudiation. So far from expressing the intention of the parties not to perform the contracts, it appears to me to leave it to the court to say whether or not the contract is to be performed, and if the court says it is, then it impliedly states that it will be performed. I think, therefore, there was no repudiation of the contract.'

In two other cases it was held by the Court of Appeal that the expression by one party to a contract of a genuine but erroneous view as to the obligations which on a proper construction of it were thereby imposed did not infer an intention to repudiate the contract. These cases are *James Shaffer Ltd v Findlay Durham & Brodie*[1] and *Sweet & Maxwell Ltd v Universal News Services Ltd*[2]. Finally, it is worth observing that in *Ross T Smyth & Co Ltd v T D Bailey, Son & Co*[3] Lord Wright said: '... a mere honest misapprehension, especially if open to correction, will not justify a charge of repudiation.'

So in the present case the question comes to be whether, having regard to all the circumstances, the conduct of Wimpey in relation to their invocation of condition E(a)(iii) of the contract was such that a reasonable person in the position of Woodar would properly infer an intention 'in any event' (to use the expression employed by Warrington and Atkin LJJ in the *Spettabile* case[4]) to refuse to perform the contract when the time came for performance.

The terms of condition E(a)(iii) have been quoted by my noble and learned friend Lord Wilberforce. It conferred on Wimpey the right lawfully to rescind the contract in the event there described. Wimpey had come to find the contract burdensome in view of the dramatic collapse of the property market. They accordingly desired to be relieved of it and took legal advice as to whether there existed grounds on which they might lawfully do so. The advice received was to the effect that condition E(a)(iii) provided such a ground. Wimpey did not, however, at once give notice of rescission under the clause. They sought an interview with Mr Cornwell, as representing Woodar, which took place on 7th March 1974 and proceeded on the lines described in the aide memoire which is in evidence. Wimpey informed Mr Cornwell of their position as regards the application of condition E(a)(iii) and proposed a renegotiation of the contract, failing which they stated their intention to serve notice of rescission in terms of the clause. Mr Cornwell contested the correctness of their position, and expressed the intention, that if Wimpey served notice of rescission, of taking the matter to court and obtaining a decision on their right to do so. Wimpey served their notice of rescission about two weeks later, clearly in the expectation, which was duly and promptly realised, that Woodar would initiate legal proceedings in order to test its validity. In my opinion there was nothing in Wimpey's conduct up to this point, there being no dispute about the genuineness of their belief that they were entitled to terminate the contract on the stated ground, which might reasonably be treated as inferring that it was their intention to refuse performance in the event of a judicial determination that belief was erroneous. The letters written by Mr Cornwell to Sir Godfrey Mitchell on 30th May and 6th June 1974, the material parts of which have been quoted by my noble and learned friend Lord Wilberforce, clearly indicate that he himself did not draw any such inference. I am unable to regard Wimpey's conduct as evincing an intention 'altogether to refuse performance of the contract' as Lord Coleridge CJ put it in *Freeth v Burr*[5], or as constituting 'an absolute repudiation' in the sense in which Atkin LJ used that expression in the *Spettabile* case[4].

1   [1953] 1 WLR 106
2   [1964] 3 All ER 30, [1964] 2 QB 699
3   [1940] 3 All ER 60 at 72
4   (1919) 121 LT 628, [1918–19] All ER Rep 963
5   (1874) LR 9 CP 208 at 213, [1874–80] All ER Rep 750 at 753

I would accept without hesitation the statement of Lord Denning MR in *Federal Commerce and Navigation Co Ltd v Molena Alpha Inc*[1] that a party who breaks a contract *a* cannot excuse himself by saying that he did it on the advice of his lawyers, or that he was under an honest misapprehension. If in the present case the time for performance had passed while Wimpey were still maintaining their position based on the erroneous interpretation of condition E(a)(iii), they would have been in breach of contract and liable in damages accordingly. Lord Denning MR goes on to say: 'Nor can he excuse himself on those grounds from the consequences of a repudiation.' That may be so, but *b* it is first necessary to determine whether or not there has been a repudiation.

The doctrine of repudiatory breach is largely founded on considerations of convenience and the opportunities which it affords for mitigating loss, as observed by Cockburn CJ in *Frost v Knight*[2]. It enables one party to a contract, when faced with a clear indication by the other that he does not intend to perform his obligations under it when the time for performance arrives, to treat the contract, if he so chooses, as there and then at an end and *c* to claim damages as for actual breach. Where one party, honestly but erroneously, intimates to the other reliance on a term of the contract which, if properly applicable, would entitle him lawfully to rescind the contract, in circumstances which do not and are not reasonably understood to infer that he will refuse to perform his obligations even if it should be established that he is not so entitled, legal proceedings to decide that issue being in contemplation, I do not consider it in accordance with ordinary concepts of *d* justice that the other party should be allowed to treat such conduct as a repudiation. Nor, in my opinion, are there any considerations of convenience which favour that course.

I would add that in my view the lodging by Wimpey of their defence and counterclaim in answer to Woodar's first writ did not constitute further conduct on their part which can itself be regarded as having a repudiatory character. They thereby demonstrated nothing more than an adherence to their position as they had earlier expressed it. *e* Further, the action taken by Wimpey in relation to the guarantee arrangements with the National Westminster Bank appear to me to have been no more than a natural consequence of the view taken by Wimpey as to their right to terminate the contract.

In the circumstances the issue regarding Woodar's right to damages in respect of alleged breach of Wimpey's obligation under the contract to pay £150,000 to Transworld does not arise for decision. It is desirable, however, that I should express my agreement *f* with my noble and learned friend Lord Wilberforce that the decision in favour of Woodar on this issue, arrived at by the majority of the Court of Appeal, was not capable of being supported by *Jackson v Horizon Holidays Ltd*[3]. That case is capable of being regarded as rightly decided on a reasonable view of the measure of damages due to the plaintiff as the original contracting party, and not as laying down any rule of law regarding the recovery of damages for the benefit of third parties. There may be a *g* certain class of cases where third parties stand to gain indirectly by virtue of a contract, and where their deprivation of that gain can properly be regarded as no more than a consequence of the loss suffered by one of the contracting parties. In that situation there may be no question of the third parties having any claim to damages in their own right, but yet it may be proper to take into account in assessing the damages recoverable by the contracting party an element in respect of expense incurred by him in replacing by other *h* means benefits of which the third parties have been deprived or in mitigating the consequences of that deprivation. The decision in *Jackson v Horizon Holidays Ltd*[3] is not, however, in my opinion, capable of being supported on the basis of the true ratio decidendi in *Lloyd's v Harper*[4], which rested entirely on the principles of agency.

I would also associate myself with the observations of my noble and learned friend Lord Scarman as to the desirability of this House having an opportunity of reviewing, in *j*

1   [1978] 3 All ER 1066 at 1082, [1978] QB 927 at 979
2   (1872) LR 7 Exch 111 at 114, [1861–73] All ER Rep 221 at 225
3   [1975] 3 All ER 92, [1975] 1 WLR 1468
4   (1880) 16 Ch D 290

some appropriate future case, the general attitude of English law towards the topic of jus
a quaesitum tertio.

My Lords, I would allow the appeal.

LORD SCARMAN. My Lords, for the reasons given by my noble and learned friend
Lord Wilberforce I would allow Wimpey's appeal. In my judgment Wimpey did not
commit, or threaten to commit, a repudiatory breach of contract. The principle of the
b modern law is now 'perspicuous', as Lord Wilberforce observed in *Federal Commerce and
Navigation Co Ltd v Molena Alpha Inc*[1]. To be repudiatory, the breach, or threatened
breach, must go to the root of the contract. If an anticipatory breach is relied on, the
renunciation must be 'an intimation of an intention to abandon and altogether to refuse
performance of the contract'; or, put in other but equally clear words, 'the true question
is whether the acts or conduct of the party evince an intention no longer to be bound by
c the contract': per Lord Coleridge CJ in *Freeth v Burr*[2]. The emphasis on communication
of the party's intention by his acts and conduct is a recurring theme in the abundant case
law. Two well-known cases illustrative of the emphasis are *Mersey Steel and Iron Co
v Naylor, Benzon & Co*[3] and *Bradley v H Newsom, Sons & Co*[4] (see in particular the speech
of Lord Wrenbury).

Difficulty, however, does arise in the application of the principle to particular facts, as
d the difference in judicial opinion in the present case shows. The dividing line between
what is repudiatory and what is not emerges from three very persuasive dicta to be found
in the case law. When the *Federal Commerce* case[5] was in the Court of Appeal, Lord
Denning MR said:

> 'I have yet to learn that a party who breaks a contract can excuse himself by saying
> that he did it on the advice of his lawyers: or that he was under an honest
e > misapprehension ... I would go by the principle ... that, if the party's contract,
> objectively considered in its impact on the other party, is such as to evince an
> intention no longer to be bound by his contractual obligations, then it is open to the
> other party to accept his repudiation and treat the contract as discharged from that
> time onwards.'

f In the *Spettabile* case[6] Atkin LJ said of the various definitions of repudiation: 'They all
come to the same thing, and they all amount at any rate to this, that it must be shown
that the party to the contract *made quite plain* his own intention not to perform the
contract' (emphasis mine). In *James Shaffer Ltd v Findlay Durham & Brodie*[7] the Court of
Appeal had under consideration a breach of a long term supply contract where the
defendant, who had undertaken to pass on orders of not less than a specified value each
g year, failed to do so. He honestly believed his failure was not a breach of contract; but
the Court of Appeal held that it was, his construction of the contract being erroneous in
law. The court held, however, that the breach did not evince an intention not to be
bound by the contract. Singleton LJ, who referred to *Freeth v Burr*[8] and the *Spettabile*
case[9], made this comment[10]:

> 'Streatfield J. said that this was a very difficult case and near the line. I think that
h > that is a true description. Sometimes when a case is put in one particular way it has

---

1   [1979] 1 All ER 307 at 314, [1979] AC 757 at 778
2   (1874) LR 9 CP 208 at 213, [1874–80] All ER Rep 750 at 753
3   (1884) 9 App Cas 434, [1881–5] All ER Rep 365
j 4   [1919] AC 16, [1881–5] All ER Rep 365
5   [1978] 3 All ER 1066 at 1082, [1978] QB 927 at 979
6   (1919) 121 LT 628 at 634–635, [1918–19] All ER Rep 963 at 698
7   [1953] 1 WLR 106
8   LR 9 CP 208, [1874–80] All ER Rep 750
9   121 LT 628, [1918–19] All ER Rep 963
10   [1953] 1 WLR 106 at 120

great appeal, and, when it is put in the other way, it has an almost equal appeal. I
do not think that it is right to look at the interview of May 18 alone; as I understand *a*
the law, it is our duty to have regard to the circumstances.'

Morris LJ and Upjohn J[1] said the same thing.

My Lords, as I see it, the error of the majority of the Court of Appeal in the instant case
was, notwithstanding some dicta to the contrary, to concentrate attention on one act, ie
the notice of rescission with its accompanying letter. They failed to give the consideration
which the law requires of all the acts and conduct of the defendants in their dealings with *b*
Mr Cornwall, the 'alter ego' of Woodar. The law requires that there be assessed not only
the party's conduct but also, 'objectively considered', its impact on the other party. The
error is neatly exposed in Goff LJ's terse conclusion: 'In my judgment rescission is
repudiation, and if it cannot be justified by the terms of the contract it is wrongful and
a breach.' Goff LJ was, with respect, concentrating too much attention on one act isolated
from its surrounding circumstances and failing to pay proper regard to the impact of the *c*
party's conduct on the other party.

In this case the contract provided for the possibility of rescission by Wimpey. But the
notice of rescission, which Wimpey gave, was not, in the circumstances which existed
when it was given, one which Wimpey had any contractual right to give. But they
honestly believed the contract did give them the right. When one examines the totality
of their conduct and its impact on Mr Cornwell it is plain, as shown by my noble and *d*
learned friend Lord Wilberforce's analysis of the facts, that Wimpey, though claiming
mistakenly to exercise a power given them by the contract to bring it to an end, were not
evincing an intention not to be bound by the contract. On the contrary, they believed
they were acting pursuant to the contract. And Mr Cornwell well understood the
situation. As he put it in his final letter to Sir Godfrey Mitchell, the president of
Wimpey: '. . . all I need say now is that we will retire to our battle stations and it goes *e*
without saying I am sure that you will abide by the result as I will.' It never occurred to
Mr Cornwell that Wimpey, if held not to have been entitled to give notice of rescission,
would refuse to perform the contract. In fact, it would seem that he believed exactly the
contrary. Such was the impact on him of Wimpey's conduct.

It being the view of the majority of the House that there was no repudiation, the
appeal must be allowed, with the result that there is no need to consider the other issues *f*
raised. But, because of its importance, I propose to say a few words on the question of
damages.

Woodar agreed to sell the land to Wimpey for £850,000. They also required Wimpey
to pay £150,000 to a third party. The covenant for this payment was in the following
terms: 'I. Upon completion of the purchase of the whole or any part of the land the
purchaser shall pay to Transworld Trade Limited of 25 Jermyn Street, London, S.W.1. a *g*
sum of £150,000.' No relationship of trust or agency was proved to exist between
Woodar and Transworld. No doubt, it suited Mr Cornwell to split up the moneys
payable under the contract between the two companies; but it is not known, let alone
established by evidence (though an intelligent guess is possible) why he did so, or why
Woodar desired this money to be paid to Transworld. It is simply a case of B agreeing *h*
with A to pay a sum of money to C.

B, in breach of his contract with A, has failed to pay C. C, it is said, has no remedy,
because the English law of contract recognises no 'jus quaesitum tertio': see *Tweddle
v Atkinson*[2]. No doubt, it was for this reason that Transworld is not a party to the suit.
A, it is acknowledged, could in certain circumstances obtain specific performance of the
promise to pay C: see *Beswick v Beswick*[3]. But, since the contract in the present case is
admitted (for reasons which do not fall to be considered by the House) to be no longer in *j*

---

1   [1953] 1 WLR 106 at 124, 127
2   (1861) 1 B & S 393, [1861–73] All ER Rep 369
3   [1967] 2 All ER 1197, [1968] AC 58

existence, specific performance is not available. A's remedy lies only in an award of damages to himself. It is submitted that, in the absence of any evidence that A has suffered loss by reason of B's failure to pay C, A is only entitled to nominal damages.

I wish to add nothing to what your Lordships have already said about the authorities which the Court of Appeal cited as leading to the conclusion that Woodar is entitled to substantial damages for Wimpey's failure to pay Transworld. I agree that they do not support the conclusion. But I regret that this House has not yet found the opportunity to reconsider the two rules which effectually prevent A or C recovering that which B, for value, has agreed to provide.

First, the jus quaesitum tertio. I respectfully agree with Lord Reid that the denial by English law of a jus quaesitum tertio calls for reconsideration. In *Beswick v Beswick*[1], Lord Reid, after referring to the Law Revision Committee's recommendation[2] that the third party should be able to enforce a contractual promise taken by another for his benefit, observed: 'If one had to contemplate a further long period of Parliamentary procrastination, this House might find it necessary to deal with this matter.' The committee reported in 1937; *Beswick v Beswick*[3] was decided in 1967. It is now 1979; but nothing has been done. If the opportunity arises, I hope the House will reconsider *Tweddle v Atkinson*[4] and the other cases which stand guard over this unjust rule.

Likewise, I believe it open to the House to declare that, in the absence of evidence to show that he has suffered no loss, A, who has contracted for a payment to be made to C, may rely on the fact that he required the payment to be made as prima facie evidence that the promise for which he contracted was a benefit to him and that the measure of his loss in the event of non-payment is the benefit which he intended for C but which has not been received. Whatever the reason, he must have desired the payment to be made to C and he must have been relying on B to make it. If B fails to make the payment, A must find the money from other funds if he is to confer the benefit which he sought by his contract to confer on C. Without expressing a final opinion on a question which is clearly difficult, I think the point is one which does require consideration by your Lordships' House.

Certainly the crude proposition for which Wimpey contends, namely that the state of English law is such that neither C for whom the benefit was intended nor A who contracted for it can recover it if the contract is terminated by B's refusal to perform, calls for review, and now, not 40 years on.

Appeal allowed.

Solicitors: *P J Ward* (for Wimpey); *Sharpe Pritchard & Co* (for Woodar).

Mary Rose Plummer   Barrister.

---

1   [1967] 2 All ER 1197 at 1201, [1968] AC 58 at 72
2   Sixth Interim Report (1937) Cmd 5449, p 31
3   [1967] 2 All ER 1197, [1968] AC 58
4   (1861) 1 B & S 393, [1861–73] All ER Rep 369

Practice Direction

FAMILY DIVISION

Practice – Matrimonial causes – Trial – Directions for trial – Applications for property adjustment and lump sums – Pre-trial review – Registrar to consider possibility of settlement of case or to clarify issues – Directions as to discovery.

From 1st April 1980 by way of experiment in the Divorce Registry the substantive appointment for directions in all applications for property adjustment and lump sums will include a pre-trial review at which the registrar will consider the possibility of settlement of the case, or clarification of the issues. Where the case continues to be contested the registrar will give directions, particularly as to discovery, designed to elicit all necessary information but to save costs by excluding over-detailed requests for it.

With a view to achieving these objectives the following procedure should be followed in these cases:

1. The applicant's affidavit in support of the application should have annexed to it a list setting out the capital of the deponent, and any loans debts and other charges against capital. The list should also set out all the deponent's sources of income and the income from each source. A copy of this list with a similar list in respect of the respondent's means, set out on the same page, should be annexed to his affidavit. Where the deponent is employed he should exhibit his last three pay slips or, if he is the director of any company, the last three accounts of that company. Where the deponent is self-employed he should exhibit his accounts for the past three years or other appropriate information as to his means.

2. After affidavits have been filed, general mutual discovery should take place without order 14 days from the last affidavit, unless some other period is agreed, with inspection seven days thereafter.

3. Where a dispute arises as to the value of any property a valuation should be made by an agreed valuer or, in default of agreement, by an independent valuer chosen by the President of the Royal Institution of Chartered Surveyors. The valuation should be produced at the appointment for directions and pre-trial review.

4. Any questionnaire should be delivered to the other side at least 21 days before the said appointment. At the pre-trial review directions will be given by the registrar as to what disputed items on discovery or in the questionnaire are to be dealt with. Where the registrar considers that to answer any question would entail considerable expense and that there is doubt whether the answer would provide any information of value, he may make the order for the question to be answered at the questioner's risk as to costs. The registrar may refuse to order an answer to a question if he considers that its value would be small in comparison with the property or income of the party to whom the question is addressed.

5. If after the pre-trial review there are relevant changes in the income or capital position of either party, these should be set out in an affidavit annexing a list of the changes as compared with the earlier list.

6. Where the issue of conduct is raised on the affidavits, the registrar will enquire whether it is being pursued and, if so, will order particulars to be given of the precise allegations relied on.

7. To ensure the success of this procedure it is essential that pre-trial reviews should be attended either by counsel or by a representative of solicitors who is fully conversant with the facts of the case.

12th February 1980

R L BAYNE-POWELL
Senior Registrar.

Tomlinson v Tomlinson

FAMILY DIVISION
SIR JOHN ARNOLD P AND WOOD J
22nd OCTOBER 1979

Husband and wife – Maintenance – Procedure – Magistrates' court – Presence of witness during hearing – Court's power to order witness to withdraw – Discretion to admit his evidence – How discretion to be exercised – Magistrates' Courts Act 1952, s 57.

A husband who was ordered to pay his wife maintenance applied to the justices for an order reducing the amount on the ground that his wife was cohabiting with, and being maintained by, another man, H. The wife and H attended the hearing of the application. She did not have a solicitor present and decided that she would go through the trial unrepresented. At the outset the husband drew the justices' attention to H's presence in court. They made no order excluding him. H was therefore present when the husband gave his evidence and was cross-examined by the wife, and also when the wife gave her evidence. She denied that she was cohabiting with H and being maintained by him. She wanted to call H as a witness in support of her case but, when the husband pointed out that H had been present throughout the hearing, the justices refused to allow her to do so. They made an order reducing the amount of the maintenance to a nominal sum. The wife appealed against the order on the ground, inter alia, that they were wrong in law, or alternatively had exercised their discretion wrongly, in refusing to allow her to call H as a witness.

Held – (i) A witness in matrimonial proceedings in the magistrates' courts was not under any obligation to leave the court unless the justices made an order excluding him. Where they received an application for such an order, they should, unless they were satisfied that it would not be an appropriate step to take in the circumstances, order the witness to withdraw. If a party was not represented and they thought that the case was one in which a witness should be excluded, they should suggest to the party who was not represented that he should make an application to that effect. Such an order could never apply, however, to one of the parties themselves or their solicitors or to expert witnesses (see p 596 *g h* and p 597 *d*, post).

(ii) If a witness remained in court after an order had been made excluding him, and his evidence was then offered to the court, the justices had a discretion to admit that evidence notwithstanding that the witness had remained in court in apparent defiance of their ruling. Such a discretion was in no way inconsistent with s 57*[a]* of the Magistrates' Courts Act 1952 which gave justices power to exclude witnesses from the hearing (see p 597 *a* to *d*, post).

(iii) It followed that the justices had exceeded their powers by refusing to allow the wife to call H to give evidence because no order had been made requiring him to withdraw. The appeal would accordingly be allowed, and since H's evidence might have affected the justices' decision in respect of the maintenance order a rehearing would be ordered (see p 595 *d e*, p 596 *e f* and p 597 *d*, post).

Notes

For the exclusion of witnesses from domestic courts until they are called for examination, see 29 Halsbury's Laws (4th Edn) para 376.

For the Magistrates' Courts Act 1952, s 57, see 21 Halsbury's Statutes (3rd Edn) 233.

---

a   Section 57, so far as material, is set out at p 597 *c*, post

Case referred to in judgments

R v Briggs (1930) 22 Cr App R 68, CCA, 14(2) Digest (Reissue) 625, 5080.   *a*

Appeal

This was an appeal by Carol Ann Tomlinson ('the wife') against an order made by the Wigan justices on 9th March 1979, whereby they had, on an application by David Barry Tomlinson ('the husband'), directed that the amount of maintenance which he was required to pay under an order dated 4th April 1978 should be reduced from £12 per *b* week to 5p per annum. The facts are set out in the judgment of Sir John Arnold P.

Martyn Bennett for the wife.
J S Thrower for the husband.

SIR JOHN ARNOLD P. This is an appeal from the Wigan justices who on 9th March *c* 1979 heard an application by Mr David Barry Tomlinson ('the husband') for a reduction of the maintenance which he had been ordered to pay to his wife, that application being based on the proposition that his wife was cohabiting with and being maintained by another man. The other man in question was one Derek Holmes. There has been no argument on the hearing of the appeal that in order for such a ground to be a valid *d* ground for the reduction of the amount of a maintenance order it is necessary to satisfy both of the requirements in proof before the justices, namely that the person being maintained is cohabiting with another man and that she is being maintained by that other man.

The justices made the order sought and indeed reduced the amount of maintenance to a purely nominal sum. From that order the wife appeals. She brings forward three grounds for her appeal. She says that there was no or no sufficient evidence to enable the *e* justices to find that she was cohabiting with and being maintained by Mr Holmes. On refinement of that proposition in argument it is found to be simply that the second part of the combined proposition was not supported by the evidence. There was no doubt that there was sufficient evidence for the justices to find, if they were so disposed, that the, wife was cohabiting with Mr Holmes.

The second ground is that there was no evidence before the justices of the income of *f* Mr Holmes. The way that point arises is this: in the absence of any direct evidence of payments by Mr Holmes to the wife for any purpose which could justly be regarded as maintenance, there might have been, it is thought by the wife, some possibility that the court might have inferred the fact of such maintenance from a consideration of the availability of the wherewithal to maintain.

Thirdly, that the justices were wrong in law or alternatively in the exercise of their *g* discretion to refuse to permit the wife to call as a witness of fact Mr Holmes, in support of her contention that she was neither cohabiting with nor being maintained by him.

It is that last matter which seems to me not only to be the most important of the matters which were raised in the notice of appeal but also to give rise to wider considerations than those which intimately affect this particular case.

The facts which were adduced in evidence as regards the proposition that the wife was *h* being maintained by Mr Holmes were two, and two only. One was that Mr Holmes from time to time bought toys for the wife's children, and the other was that on occasions he left his van at the wife's premises to enable her to run her mother about, there being some evidence that she was looking after her mother to some extent.

It is for consideration whether, without more, those two matters could really be *j* enough to enable justices to hold that they were facts from which the inference of some degree of maintenance could be drawn.

But they are very much bound up with the rest of the matter because if Mr Holmes had been called those two matters could, and could with propriety, have been more deeply investigated. For my part, I have preferred to place my judgment in this appeal

on the basis not of the first ground, that is, there being no evidence from which the
justices could legitimately infer the fact of maintenance, but on the matter of the
evidence of Mr Holmes. Similarly, in relation to the second ground of appeal, the fact
that there was no evidence of the income of Mr Holmes must be intimately bound up
with the fact that he gave no evidence at all.

I come then to the third ground. What happened was this: the wife, after some
hesitation, it seems, not having a solicitor present in the court, decided that she would go
through the trial unrepresented. Of course, the justices knew that perfectly well.

At the beginning of the evidence, when the husband was in the witness box, within
a matter of minutes of starting his evidence he said, according to the notes of evidence
taken down by the clerk: 'I want the order reduced because another man has been living
with my wife. His name is Derek Holmes. He is in court today.' Then the husband
gave his evidence. He was cross-examined by his wife, and then a Mr Worthington, an
enquiry agent, gave his evidence about the comings and goings of Mr Holmes from the
wife's premises. Then the wife gave her evidence. Then, in the words of the justices in
their reasons, the wife proposed to call a witness, that was Mr Holmes, but it was pointed
out by the husband's solicitors that the witness had been in court throughout the hearing
and the wife did not pursue her intention of calling him as a witness, but in fact, as we
heard from both sides today, the reason why the wife did not pursue her intention of
calling him as a witness was because she was told by the justices that she would not be
allowed to do so.

That in my judgment was an absolutely wrong thing for the justices to do. Since it
seems to me to be tolerably clear that the evidence of Mr Holmes, if it had been given,
might have altered the view which the justices took, the refusal to permit him to be
called appears to me to be a fatal defect and one which must necessarily involve a further
hearing of this complaint.

In the course of the argument on the appeal it has been brought to our attention that
there is something of a confusion in the various authoritative pronouncements which
have been made concerning the general matter of the presence or otherwise of witnesses
in court during the hearing of a matter of controversy in the magistrates' court. As long
ago as 1908 the then President of the Probate, Divorce and Admiralty Division, Sir John
Gorrell Barnes P, said that with regard to contested probate and matrimonial cases his
view was that the old Admiralty rule should be adopted, namely that all witnesses should
remain out of court until they had given their evidence[1]. He then noticed that it might
be unpleasant for counsel to have to apply for a direction that the witnesses should
remain out of court and concluded that in future in all contested cases the witnesses
should remain out of court, subject of course to a relaxation of that rule where there was
no need for it to be enforced.

That was plainly intended to be a ruling as to the practice in the High Court in the
division over which the President presided. But it would be very bad practice that there
should be different rules pertaining in different courts. Therefore, it is plainly desirable
that there should be a degree of consistency in the matter.

In 1967, in the Supreme Court Practice[2] there is a note to be found on this subject in
relation to the Matrimonial Causes Rules 1957[3], which were the rules then in
operation. The note is appended to the rule which provided that evidence should in
ordinary circumstances be given orally and in open court. The direction[1] given by Sir
John Gorrell Barnes P in 1908 is noted and then the comment in the Supreme Court
Practice is this:

> 'This practice has fallen into desuetude and the present practice in probate and
> divorce suits is to allow the exclusion of witnesses to depend on the discretion of the
> Judge, either on the application of counsel or at the Judge's own instance.'

---

1 *Practice Note* (1908) 24 TLR 263
2 Vol 2, p 444, para 1666
3 SI 1957 No 619

In Stone's Justices' Manual[1] the matter is discussed in relation to proceedings in magistrates' courts generally. The note is to this effect:

a

'It is a common practice when a case is called on for hearing to order the witnesses on both sides to leave the court; but if a person who has disobeyed such order by remaining in the court should be offered in evidence by either party, his testimony cannot, it seems, be excluded.'

But there is no authority given for that statement at all.   b

The note then observes that in accordance with a ruling given in 1858 the plaintiff himself could not be included in the order to withdraw. There is a further note that in accordance with a case decided in 1930, *R v Briggs*[2], in the absence of an order, a witness may stay in court until he is called.

Finally in the current Supreme Court Practice[3] the note is to this effect:

c

'On the application of either party the Court may at any time order all witnesses on both sides, other than the one under examination, to withdraw but not to leave the Court again after evidence so as to communicate with other witnesses before they give evidence.'

The only other matter which I think it is necessary to mention is that in 1974 a direction was given by Goulding J during the hearing of a probate action in the Chancery   d
Division[4]. He merely says that the practice note[5] by Sir John Gorrell Barnes P appears never to have been overruled and it was not thenceforth to apply to the trial of probate actions in the Chancery Division, where the ordinary practice stated in the Supreme Court Practice for 1973[6] (which we are told is the same as that which I have quoted from 1979) should be followed.

In those circumstances, it is apparent that, by excluding the evidence of a witness who   e
had been in court during the hearing of a case in relation to which there had never been any order whatever that the witnesses should withdraw, the justices were going beyond what on any of the various practices which I have indicated could possibly be justified. In my judgment, that is by itself enough to make it imperative that this case should be reheard. However, it is desirable to take this opportunity of indicating what I think should be the practice in matrimonial proceedings in magistrates' courts on this subject.   f

I do not think that it is enough in relation to proceedings in which parties are frequently unrepresented merely to say that the court should be permitted to exclude witnesses on an application being made, because necessarily, if the matter is to be limited to that, unrepresented parties would be very likely to omit to make an application out of sheer ignorance where an application ought to be made in accordance with the best principles of the administration of justice.   g

It seems to me that the right course is this: witnesses should not be under any obligation to leave the court, except where an order is made excluding them; that the proper course for justices to pursue, if an application is made to them, would be to exclude the witnesses, unless they were satisfied that that would not be an appropriate step to take; but that, if they think it is a case in which perhaps the witnesses should be excluded, then where a party is not represented they should suggest that perhaps he   h
might like to make an application to that effect. This of course does not apply and never has applied to the parties themselves or their solicitors or their expert witnesses. Those are never excluded from the court.

Then it seems to me that there is one more matter to be considered: what should happen if a witness remains in court or a person remains in court after an order has been

j

1   1979 Edn, vol 1, p 535
2   (1930) 22 Cr App R 68
3   1979, vol 1, p 589, para 38/1/4
4   *Re Nightingale (deceased), Green v Nightingale* [1975] 1 WLR 80n
5   (1908) 24 TLR 263
6   Vol 1, p 553, para 38/1/4

made excluding witnesses and his testimony is then offered to the court? In that case
a there should it seems to me be, and there is some indication that there already is, a
discretion to admit that witness's evidence, notwithstanding that he has remained in
court in apparent defiance of a ruling. Of course the magistrates, if they were satisfied
that contumacy or deception was involved, would be likely to exercise their discretion by
excluding the testimony. But, on the other hand, if the case were one in which the
possibility of that person being called as a witness was not apparent at the time when the
b exclusion order was made and the person remained, then they might well exercise their
discretion the other way. But it being a discretion it would have to be exercised in every
case in accordance with the merits of the occasion.
    In s 57 of the Magistrates' Courts Act 1952 the provision in sub-s (2) is that—

c
> '. . . no person shall be present during the hearing and determination by a
> magistrates' court of any domestic proceedings, except . . . (b) parties to the
> case . . . witnesses and other persons directly concerned in the case . . .'

Then in sub-s (6) it is provided: 'Nothing in this section shall affect the exercise by a
magistrates' court of the power to direct that witnesses shall be excluded until they are
called for examination.' If the discretion which I have suggested should be exercised in
fact exists, as I think it does exist, then there is nothing in the section to render it
d inoperable.

WOOD J. I agree.

Appeal allowed. Case remitted to the justices for rehearing.

e Solicitors: *G Isherwood & Co*, Wigan (for the wife); *White & Leonard*, agents for *Taylors,
Bridge, Baron & Sykes*, Wigan (for the husband).

                                                    Georgina Chambers   Barrister.

R v Wilkinson

f
QUEEN'S BENCH DIVISION
ROBERT GOFF J SITTING WITH CHIEF MASTER MATTHEWS AND MR M J A THUM AS ASSESSORS
3rd, 4th, 5th, 8th, 9th, 10th OCTOBER, 21st NOVEMBER 1979

*Legal aid – Taxation of costs – Criminal proceedings – Solicitor's fees – Method of charging for
preparation of case for trial – Solicitors adopting method based on hourly expense rate recorded
g on time record sheet by partner etc occupied directly on work for client – Whether that method
providing reliable basis for taxation of costs.*

*Legal aid – Taxation of costs – Criminal proceedings – Solicitor's fees – Attendance at trial –
Whether fee should be daily attendance fee or be calculated on same basis as that for preparation
of case for trial – Legal Aid in Criminal Proceedings (Fees and Expenses) Regulations 1968 (SI
h 1968 No 1230), regs 2, 7(6) (as substituted by the Legal Aid in Criminal Proceedings (Fees and
Expenses) (Amendment) Regulations 1977 (SI 1977 No 875), reg 10(4)).*

In 1977 a firm of solicitors acted for a legally aided defendant in connection with his trial
at the Crown Court. The trial lasted several days, the defendant was represented by
junior counsel, and K, a partner in the firm of solicitors, was present throughout.
j Afterwards the solicitors submitted their bill of costs to the Crown Court for taxation.
They calculated their remuneration according to the method outlined in a Law Society
booklet on costs[a], that method being based on an hourly expense rate for each time
recorder (ie a partner, assistant solicitor, legal executive, clerk or articled clerk whose

---

a The Expense of Time (2nd Edn, 1976)

time was occupied directly on work for clients and who recorded on a time record sheet details of all time spent). For the preparation for trial the solicitors claimed an amount *a* based on the expense rate for a partner of £22·66 per hour with a mark up of 50% for care and conduct, and for attendance at the trial they claimed an amount calculated in the same way, ie based on the attendance of K at the hourly rate of £22·66 and a percentage mark-up for care and conduct. The taxing officer rejected the solicitors' method of calculating their remuneration. He allowed the 50% mark-up in respect of preparation for trial but reduced the hourly rate to £15, and in accordance with the current practice *b* based on reg 2[*b*] of the Legal Aid in Criminal Proceedings (Fees and Expenses) Regulations 1968 of allowing a solicitor only a daily fee for court attendance without any mark-up for care and conduct, he merely allowed the solicitors the scale fee of £50 per day. The solicitors applied for a review of taxation, and sought to justify the amount claimed by adducing evidence of expense rates of other firms of solicitors in the area calculated in a similar way on the basis of the Law Society's booklet. They contended, inter alia, that, *c* in accordance with a recommendation of the Law Society, a solicitor's court attendance should be remunerated on the same basis as his preparation for trial. The taxing officer refused to change his assessment, and the solicitors appealed to the chief taxing master. The master also rejected the solicitors' method of calculating their remuneration, and at their request certified that there were two points of principle of general importance for the decision of the High Court, namely (i) whether a taxing officer ought to accept, as *d* sufficient evidence of the broad average direct cost of work done in the particular area by a principal solicitor in 1977, the expense rates shown in tables prepared by a group of solicitors practising in that area's Crown Court, on the basis of the method suggested in the Law Society's booklet, and (ii) whether, in computing the allowance to be made for attendance at court on the trial, the proper amount should be ascertained by multiplying the time actually and reasonably engaged in any one day by the relevant expense rate of *e* the appropriate fee earner and adding thereto a further sum for care and conduct calculated as a percentage of the time charge. Following the issue of the certificate the solicitors applied by summons to the High Court for a review of taxation of their costs.

Held – (i) Although the Law Society's booklet was laudable in many ways, it did not, in its present form, provide a reliable basis for the taxation of costs. Nevertheless taxing *f* officers should not entirely disregard calculations of expenses submitted to them on the basis of the booklet but should merely regard such calculations with reserve and treat them as no more than one matter to be taken into account (see p 608 *f* and *j* to p 609 *a*, post).

(ii) It would be a fundamental change to depart from the provisions of regs 2 and 7(6)[*c*] of the 1968 regulations and allow a solicitor's court attendance to be remunerated on the same basis as his preparation for the trial and it was not open to the court to make such *g* a change. In the circumstances, therefore, it would not be appropriate to interfere with the costs as assessed by the master (see p 610 *j* to p 611 *d*, post).

Per Curiam. It may be that the Law Society should re-examine its booklet in the light of this judgment and then invite the Lord Chancellor's Department to consider with them, possibly with the aid of accountants and the Chief Taxing Master, (i) whether it is *h* possible to arrive at more acceptable figures, or ranges of figures, for solicitors' hourly expense rates for various types of work in various areas, for the general guidance of taxing officers, and (ii) whether solicitors' remuneration for court attendance should be on the basis of an hourly expense rate plus a mark-up for care and conduct instead of on the basis of a fixed fee (see p 608 *g h* and p 611 *d* to *f*, post).

Notes   *j*
For taxation of costs generally, see 36 Halsbury's Laws (3rd Edn) 158–167, paras 209–222.

---

b   Regulation 2, so far as material, is set out at p 609 *d*, post
c   Regulation 7(6), so far as material, is set out at p 610 *a* to *c*, post

For the Legal Aid in Criminal Proceedings (Fees and Expenses) Regulations 1977, regs
a   7, 10, see 6 Halsbury's Statutory Instruments (3rd Reissue) 37, 39.

Cases referred to in judgment
Eastwood (deceased), Re [1974] 3 All ER 603, [1975] Ch 112, [1974] 3 WLR 454, CA.
Lazarus (Leopold) Ltd v Secretary of State for Trade and Industry [1976] The Times, 8th
   April.

b **Summons for review of taxation**
On 26th January 1979 Master Clews allowed an appeal by a firm of solicitors, Messrs
Stunt & Son ('the solicitors'), against an assessment by a taxing officer at the Crown Court
at Chelmsford of the fees incurred by them in the criminal trial in that court intituled
R v Wilkinson to the extent of increasing from £15 to £16 the expense rate allowed by the
taxing officer for the work done by a principal solicitor in their firm but refused (i) to
c   accept a claim by the solicitors for an expense rate of £22·66 or (ii) to compute the
allowance for attendance at court on the basis of a time charge or to add anything further
for profit costs. Following that decision, the solicitors requested a certificate from Master
Clews under reg 10(1) of the Legal Aid in Criminal Proceedings (Fees and Expenses)
Regulations 1968[1] and in response to that request he issued a certificate on 1st May 1979
stating that two questions which the solicitors wished to have decided by the High Court
d   involved points of principle of general importance, namely (i) whether, in allowing
pursuant to reg 1(1) of the 1968 regulations, such fees and expenses as appeared to him
to be fair remuneration for work actually and reasonably done a taxing officer ought to
accept, as sufficient evidence of the broad average direct cost of work done in the
Chelmsford area by a principal solicitor in 1977, the expense rates shown in the tables
prepared by a group of solicitors practising in the Crown Court at Chelmsford, on the
e   basis of the method suggested in the Law Society's publication The Expense of Time (2nd
Edn, 1976), and (ii) whether in computing the allowance to be made for attendance at
court on the trial, the proper amount should be ascertained by multiplying the time
actually and reasonably engaged in any one day by the relevant expense rate of the
appropriate fee-earner and adding thereto a further sum for care and conduct calculated
as a percentage of the time charge. By a summons dated 11th May 1979 the solicitors
f   applied for a review of the taxation of their fees. As both questions certified by the
master were of fundamental importance to the calculation of solicitors' charges the
Attorney-General intervened. The facts are set out in the judgment.

Robert Gatehouse QC and *Anthony Sumption* for the solicitors.
Mark Potter for the Attorney-General.

g
                                                                              Cur adv vult

21st November. **ROBERT GOFF J** read the following judgment: This is an appeal by
a firm of solicitors, Messrs Stunt & Son of Chelmsford ('the solicitors'), against a review
by a taxing master, Master Clews, of an assessment by a taxing officer of their fees
h   incurred in a criminal case, *R v Wilkinson*.
The matter arises as follows. The defendant in the criminal proceedings was charged
with attempting to murder his wife on 18th July 1977 by dropping a live hair-dryer into
her bath while she was bathing. Legal aid was granted to the defendant, and the
solicitors were instructed to act on his behalf, Mr Kemp being the partner concerned.
The trial took place at Chelmsford Crown Court on 24th, 25th, 28th and 29th November
j   1977; the defendant was represented by junior counsel and at the conclusion of the trial
was acquitted. On 13th January 1978 the solicitors submitted their bill of costs to the
clerk of the Crown Court at Chelmsford for taxation. In their bill of costs, they claimed
a sum of £4,949·73 in respect of preparation for trial, plus a 50% mark-up for care and

---
1   SI 1968 No 1230

conduct, and a further £717·75 for typing and copying, making a total of £8,142·34 in respect of preparation for trial. For attendance at the trial, they claimed a total of £945·98 based on attendance by the partner concerned (Mr Kemp) for the whole trial at a rate of £22·66 per hour, attendance by an assistant solicitor and secretary for part of the trial at rates of £12·43 and £10 per hour respectively, and a small claim of £11·33 in respect of attendance by Mr Kemp on the occasion of a bail application before a judge; on these sums, a mark-up of one-third was claimed for profit, bringing the total claim for attendance at court to £945·98. The taxing officer at the Crown Court however allowed only £2,733 for preparation for trial, and £207 for attendance at court. The principal differences between the sums claimed and the sums allowed were as follows:

(1) *Preparation for trial.* The claim was based on an expense rate for partners of £22·66 per hour; the taxing officer allowed only £15 per hour. A charge of £1·50 a page was claimed for letters written, but they were allowed at a rate of 75p for short letters and £1·50 for long letters. A charge of 35p a page was claimed for letters received, but these were allowed at 35p for short letters and 70p for long letters. Routine untimed telephone calls were claimed and allowed at £1 each. Only part of the time claimed in respect of attendance by a partner on the defendant and his witnesses, and of his preparation and consideration of the documents for trial, was allowed. The effect of these and certain other minor reductions was to reduce the basic expenses claimed from £4,949·73 to £1,630. The 50% mark-up was allowed; but the reduction in the expenses from £4,949·73 to £1,630 meant that the mark-up was only £815 instead of the £2,474·86 claimed. The taxing officer allowed £100 (instead of £248) for typing; and £187 (instead of £469·75) for copying. Hence the total of £2,733 allowed.

(2) *Attendance at court.* The taxing officer allowed a daily attendance fee of £50 per day for the partner, and £7 for the bail application; nothing was allowed for the assistant solicitor or secretary, and no mark-up was given. Hence the total of £207 allowed.

The solicitors were dissatisfied with this assessment, and on 28th April 1978 Mr Kemp wrote to the chief clerk of the Crown Court at Chelmsford asking for a review of the taxation. On 1st June 1978 the taxing officer replied: apart from a trivial item, he made no changes in his assessment. He gave his reasons for his decision in a document dated 21st June 1978. The solicitors then exercised their right of appeal to the Chief Taxing Master under para 9 of the Legal Aid in Criminal Proceedings (Fees and Expenses) Order 1968[1]. The appeal was heard by Master Clews, and on 26th January 1979 he published his decision in which to some extent he allowed the appeal. He revised the figure allowed for partner's time in preparation for trial from £15 to £16 per hour; and he restored periods of time (9½ hours and 50 hours) in respect of partner's time spent in attendance on the defendant and his witnesses and in preparation and consideration of documents. The effect of these revisions was to increase the total sum allowed for preparation for trial by £1,550, so that a total of £4,283 (instead of £2,733) was allowed, as against £8,142·34 claimed. The amount allowed for attendance at court remained unchanged at £207, as against £945·98 claimed.

Following the decision of Master Clews, the solicitors, by letter dated 9th February 1979, requested a certificate from the master under reg 10(1) of the 1968 order, and in response to that request Master Clews issued a certificate on 1st May 1979 in respect of two specific points of principle of general importance (to which I shall refer later) and at the same time expanded his reasons for his earlier decision. Pursuant to that certificate the solicitors now appeal to the High Court.

Such in bald outline is the background to this appeal. Behind it however lie a circumstance which explains the importance which Master Clews attached to the appeal. In 1972 the Law Society published a booklet entitled The Expense of Time[2]; a second edition of the booklet was published in 1976. In the preface to the booklet the author, Mr Thomas Woodcock, stated that it dealt with 'the first but essential stage in deciding what is fair and reasonable remuneration, namely establishing the *expense* to

---

1   SI 1968 No 1230
2   2nd Edn (1976)

the solicitor of doing his work'. Mr Kemp based his calculation of the expense rate of his
a own time (£22·66 per hour), which was used in drawing up his firm's bill of costs
submitted to the taxing officer, on the formula proposed in The Expense of Time; and
he subsequently sought to provide justification for that approach by adducing in evidence
expense rates for partners in other firms of solicitors in Chelmsford calculated on the
same basis. This approach was however rejected both by the taxing officer and by Master
Clews. The taxing officer, in his letter of 1st June, stated that he felt the booklet had little
b relevance to taxation of costs in the Crown Court; and Master Clews gave detailed reasons
why he considered that The Expense of Time did not provide a satisfactory basis for
taxation of solicitors' costs. The appeal before me, which enjoyed the support of the Law
Society, was really directed towards persuading the court to reject the reasoning of
Master Clews, and to give its seal of approval to the approach in The Expense of Time.
Indeed, one of the two questions which Master Clews certified as involving a point of
c principle of general importance was the question whether—

> 'a taxing officer ought to accept, as sufficient evidence of the broad average direct
> cost of work done in the Chelmsford area by a principal solicitor in the year 1977,
> the expense rates shown in the tables prepared by a group of solicitors practising in
> the Chelmsford Crown Court, on the basis of the method suggested in the
> publication of the Law Society entitled "The Expense of Time" (2nd Edition 1976).'

d

There is, however, a second question of principle raised in the case. Hitherto, the
practice has been for taxing officers and taxing masters to approach the taxation of costs
for court attendance on a different basis from that adopted in taxation of other costs. The
general principle of taxation, following *Re Eastwood*[1] and *Leopold Lazarus Ltd v Secretary
of State for Trade and Industry*[2], has been that a solicitor's remuneration should consist of
e two elements: first, a sum computed on the basis of an hourly rate which represents the
'broad average direct cost' of undertaking the work; and second, a sum, usually expressed
as a percentage mark-up of the broad average direct cost, for care and conduct. The first
element is generally known as the 'A' factor: the second as the 'B' factor. The total of the
A factor and the B factor (if any) constitutes the solicitor's total remuneration. However,
for court attendances in all criminal and civil cases the practice has been to allow a daily
f fee; furthermore no addition has been made to the daily fee for care and conduct,
although the taxing officer may take this omission into account, in an appropriate case,
in assessing the B factor to be awarded in respect of the work done in preparing the case
for trial. In the present case the solicitors, again with the support of the Law Society,
sought to challenge this practice; they submitted that solicitors' costs for attendance at
court should be assessed in the same way as other costs, viz on the basis of the broad
g average direct cost expressed as an hourly rate plus a percentage mark-up for care and
conduct. Accordingly, the second question certified by Master Clews was whether the
solicitors should be allowed—

> 'for attendance at Court on the trial, [an] amount . . . ascertained by multiplying
> the time actually and reasonably engaged in any one day by the relevant expense
> rate of the appropriate fee-earner and adding thereto a further sum for care and
> conduct calculated as a percentage of the time charge.'

h

Since both questions are of fundamental importance to the calculation of solicitors'
charges, the Attorney-General intervened in the action, and the court has had the
assistance of counsel who appeared on behalf of the Attorney-General and who was
instructed by the Treasury Solicitor. The court wishes to express its indebtedness to
j counsel for the Attorney-General, and also to counsel who appeared on behalf of the
solicitors, supported by the Law Society, for their assistance in elucidating the problems
in the case, which are of considerable complexity. I also wish to express my gratitude to

1   [1974] 3 All ER 603, [1975] Ch 112
2   [1976] The Times, 8th April

the two assessors who sat with me, the Chief Taxing Master (Master Matthews) and Mr Thum, for the extremely helpful advice which they have provided to the court.

I propose to deal with the matter as follows. First, I shall consider the Law Society's submission based on The Expense of Time. Second, I shall consider the Law Society's submission concerning the daily fee for court attendance. Third, I shall consider whether, in the light of my conclusion on the first two points, I should interfere in the taxation of the solicitors' costs in the present case.

1. *The Expense of Time*

I must first summarise the system proposed in The Expense of Time for establishing the expense to the solicitor of doing his work. The aim of the system is expressed to be 'to produce an *hourly expense rate* for each *time recorder*'[1]. Both these expressions are defined. A time recorder is defined as 'A partner, assistant solicitor, legal executive, clerk or articled clerk whose time is occupied directly on work for clients and who records on a *time record sheet* details of all time spent'. The hourly expense rate is defined as 'The actual expense of one hour of a *Time Recorder's chargeable time*', chargeable time being itself defined as 'Time occupied directly on work for clients'[2].

The booklet proposes that the hourly expense rate for any particular firm should be established as follows:

(1) First, the relevant figure for chargeable time has to be established. The booklet points out that where an office works a 35 hour week (ie five working days per week of seven hours each) then 1,820 hours are worked in a year. It continues[1]:

'The number of working hours representing *chargeable time* varies from firm to firm. The correct figure for any particular firm will appear in due course from its own records. In the meantime the number of chargeable hours might reasonably be estimated at 1,000 per annum . . .'

For the purposes of computing the actual chargeable time used in any one firm, it is recommended that *all* chargeable time should be recorded in the time record sheet, except for short letters and short telephone calls, which should be allowed for at the rate of six minutes for each such letter or call. It is not clear from the booklet whether 'overtime' (ie time spent directly on work for clients outside usual office hours) should be included in chargeable time: the definition of 'chargeable time' suggests that it should, but the estimate of 1,000 hours appears to be based on a proportion of the office working hours (apparently making allowance for such matters as hours not so spent by reason of other work, holidays, sickness, etc) which would not include overtime, and this appears to be the view taken by the Law Society.

(2) Next, the expenses of the firm have to be established. This is done by adjusting the expense figure in the latest profit and loss account of the firm in five respects (I quote from the booklet[3]):

'(i) The addition of a *notional salary* for each partner to reflect the fact that partners make a working contribution which justifies a basic reward. (ii) A provision for partners' pensions to reflect the fact that the recommendation for determining *notional salaries* is based on a salary scale which includes a non-contributory pension funded entirely by the employer. (iii) Updating salaries and other items of normal expenditure either by the substitution of known current figures or by a percentage increase to the figures for the previous year based on the current rate of inflation. (iv) The substitution of the *market rent* of the office premises for the figure (if any) which appears in the latest profit and loss account.

1   The Expense of Time (2nd Edn, 1976) p 7
2   Ibid pp 5–6
3   Ibid p 8

a This adjustment is appropriate only where no rent is paid, or where the office premises are rented but the landlord/tenant relationship is such (for example where the landlord is a partner or a relative of a partner or former partner in the firm) that the rent actually payable was not fixed by reference to normal market factors. (v) Interest on the *working capital* provided by the partners.'

In the glossary to the booklet, a notional salary is defined as 'the amount used in the various calculations to represent the salary which a partner would receive as an employee *b* for the working contribution he makes'. However, in the text it is stressed that, since the object is to calculate an expense rate and not the amount actually to be charged to the client, it is better to have one uniform hourly expense rate for all the more experienced partners in a firm, and another for the less experienced partners: where partners do exceptional work, this can be reflected in the amount actually to be charged over and above the expense rate. The booklet makes the following proposal for fixing notional *c* salaries[1]:

'The best criterion for fixing *notional salaries* would be the market value of assistant solicitors in private practice with equivalent age and experience. As this market is a limited one these *notional salaries* can perhaps best be estimated by reference to scales of salaries paid to solicitors employed outside private practice. *d* The Council suggest the *notional salaries* for profit sharing partners are based on the scale of salary of the Career Grade of lawyers in the Civil Service current from time to time with the addition where appropriate of the London weighting allowance. The present Career Grade is that of Senior Legal Assistant.'

However, the booklet adds the caveat that, although the council's suggestions are likely to be suitable for most firms, it is for each firm to select the figures it calculates to be *e* appropriate bearing in mind that in the end the firm may be called on to justify the figures by reference to market factors.

(3) Next, the hourly expense rate for each time recorder is calculated as follows[2]:

'Step 1. Calculate the total of all *Time Recorders' salaries, actual* or *notional*. Step 2. Calculate the total of *adjusted expenses*. Step 3. Calculate the total of the *other* *f* *overheads* by deducting the total of all *Time Recorders' salaries, actual* or *notional*, from the total of *adjusted expenses*. Step 4. *Hourly expense rates* are calculated for each *Time Recorder* by allocating to each *Time Recorder* his own *salary, actual* or *notional*, a per capita share of one half of the *other overheads* and a proportionate to salary share of the other half of the *other overheads* and dividing the resultant sum by the *Time Recorder's* number of hours worked on client's matters (his *chargeable time*).'

g The booklet then goes on to consider how, taking into account the expense to the firm of dealing with it, calculated on the basis of the time spent and the hourly expense rate, any particular matter should be charged out to the client. For this, the booklet recommends that all the relevant circumstances should be taken into account, including for example complexity, skill, the amount involved, the importance of the matter to the client, etc.

h Such is the system proposed in The Expense of Time. Its origin and purpose were explained to the court in a helpful affidavit sworn by Mr Woodcock himself. There is no doubt that the booklet constitutes a most praiseworthy effort to promote the calculation of the expense of time to solicitors on a scientific and uniform basis, primarily for managerial purposes, but also as a means to assist solicitors in calculating their charges and justifying them on taxation. Inevitably, during the course of the argument, it was *j* subjected to critical examination, both by counsel for the Attorney-General and by the court; and certain criticisms will be made of it in this judgment. This does not alter the

1   The Expense of Time (2nd Edn, 1976) p 9
2   Ibid p 10

fact that the booklet, which must be the fruit of very considerable work, contains many useful features and constitutes a most valuable step towards the more scientific assessment of solicitors' costs.

In the course of his argument, however, counsel for the solicitors made certain claims for the booklet which were not justified. He claimed that it had received the seal of approval from the Royal Commission[1]: I do not consider that, on a fair reading of the report of that body, such a claim can be justified. He also claimed that the booklet had, after study, been approved by Messrs Peat, Marwick, Mitchell & Co, the accountants, as a method of calculating solicitors' expense rates. I consider that that also was putting the case for the document too high. There was placed before the court a helpful report on the document by Messrs Peat's, in which it is stated that 'the basis set out in The Expense of Time is a practical method of calculating expense rates although it is acknowledged that in theory at least it would be possible to adopt a more sophisticated approach'; the report goes on to approve certain features of the system, but also proposes certain qualifications regarding overtime, interest on clients' accounts and articled clerks. I do not consider that this report can reasonably be said to constitute approval of the system. It is true, however, that The Expense of Time formed in part the basis of a remuneration survey carried out by the Law Society in 1976 for the purpose of their evidence to the Royal Commission[1]. The survey states that, of the total of 6,485 firms which received the Law Society's questionnaire, answers were received from 4,230 firms (about two-thirds) which formed the basis of the survey. Of these firms, 2,185 kept time sheets; but only 1,592 kept time sheets for all fee earners, and only 527 kept time sheets for all work, and it was stated that only 446 firms maintained a full time recording system. The survey also states that, of the 4,230 firms which provided answers, 1,174 used The Expense of Time basis for calculating hourly expense rates. It is, however, plain from the figures I have already given that among these 1,174 firms the methods of time keeping must have varied. Furthermore, the survey records that those who use The Expense of Time basis interpreted the expression 'chargeable hours' in a number of different ways, including (a) the number of hours worked in normal office time directly chargeable to clients; (b) the number of hours whether worked in or out of normal office time directly chargeable to clients; or (c) the number of hours actually spent on the business of the firm whether in or out of normal office time and whether directly chargeable to clients or not. Of these, comments the survey, The Expense of Time requires the calculation to be done on the first basis: a conclusion which, of course, excludes all 'overtime'. It is however apparent that figures for average hourly expense rates set out in this survey based on these samples cannot provide any very precise guide to the expense rates which would derive from a widespread uniform application of The Expense of Time, first because of the statistically small size of the relevant sample, and secondly because of the variations in the methods of time keeping and calculation used by the firms concerned. Nor does the survey provide information about the profitability of different categories of work.

I now turn to consider whether The Expense of Time can provide a useful basis for the taxation of solicitors' costs. It is clear from the question certified by Master Clews, and indeed from the correspondence on which that question was based, that the submission made to him was that calculations founded on The Expense of Time were capable of providing 'sufficient evidence' of the broad average direct cost of work done by a principal solicitor in the relevant area at the relevant time. However, in the course of argument, counsel for the solicitors did not put his argument in such an extreme form, recognising that to do so would place an undue fetter on the taxing officer's discretion; his submission was rather that The Expense of Time should be taken into account by the taxing officer in exercising his discretion, though it was plain from his argument that the purpose of that submission was to persuade the court to hold that The Expense of Time

---

1   Royal Commission on Legal Services (1979) Cmnd 7648

did provide a reliable guide for the calculation of the expense rate, to which taxing
a officers should attach great importance in the taxation of costs. However, after careful
consideration of the document and of the submissions of counsel, I have come to the
conclusion that there are very serious difficulties in the way of the submission of counsel
for the solicitors.

The first criticism derives from the system itself. The system proposed by The
Expense of Time is dependent on assumptions relating to the number of chargeable
b hours and notional salaries for profit sharing partners. It proposes that (pending the
calculation of accurate figures for each firm in the light of experience) it would be
reasonable for firms to work on the basis of 1,000 chargeable hours per annum; and it
proposes that notional salaries for profit sharing partners should be based on the scale of
salary of career grade lawyers (senior legal assistants) in the Civil Service. The
incorporation in the system of each of these assumptions makes it, in my judgment,
c unreliable as a scientific guide to the assessment of solicitors' hourly expense rates.

I take first the assumption relating to the number of chargeable hours. Counsel for
the solicitors sought to defend the recommended estimate of 1,000 chargeable hours per
annum. He relied on three matters: certain paragraphs in the Law Society's remuneration
survey, certain evidence from Centre-File Ltd which provides computer services for
(inter alia) solicitors, and the evidence of Mr Kemp himself. The survey recorded that
d the average chargeable hours per annum of very large firms, which kept time records by
computer, were (for principals) 985 hours for firms with 15 to 19 principals, and 1,080
hours for firms with more than 20 principals. Somewhat higher figures were given for
salaried partners, assistant solicitors and legal executives; and lower figures for articled
clerks. The Law Society sought justification for these figures by pointing out that, with
deductions for weekends, bank holidays etc leave and sick leave, there were 223 working
e days in the year making 1,561 normal working hours per annum, and by stating that it
was clear from records maintained by Centre-File Ltd that one-third of normal working
time cannot be charged directly to clients. From all this they inferred that 1,040
chargeable hours 'cannot be far wrong'. It is however fair to point out that this conclusion
was based on a statistically small sample of one type of firm and that it ignored overtime
altogether. If the Law Society's figures are right, and overtime is taken into account, the
f figures should be considerably higher than 1,040; but I must confess that I doubt if there
is a sufficiently firm statistical basis for the Law Society's figure. The evidence of Mr
Gladstone of Centre-File Ltd was that, on the basis of records kept for 125 firms, the
average annual chargeable hours recorded by full time fee-earners (including partners)
was 1,005, and for partners alone 970. The figures included overtime. From the
recorded figures for partners in 11 firms, with 10, 11 or 12 partners, the average figure
g was 912 hours. It was pointed out that firms using this service had every incentive to
record their hours, since otherwise they could not bill their clients; even so there must
be doubt whether all had done so, and the statistical basis of this evidence is a very small
sample of firms. Indeed it is not easy to reconcile Mr Gladstone's evidence with the Law
Society's remuneration survey. Finally, there were Mr Kemp's own figures of 967
chargeable hours per annum.

h Counsel's submission for the solicitors was that these matters contributed the only
really hard evidence available, and that they provided strong support for the estimated
average figure of 1,000 hours. I am bound to say that I am unable to accept this
submission. I cannot say that the figure of 1,000 hours is necessarily wrong; I can only
say that the evidence available is insufficient to establish it as a reliable figure. It is plain
that the taxing masters do not accept it. I was informed by the assessors that a very wide
j range of figures is used by various firms of solicitors, ranging from 800 to 1,400 hours
per annum at the extremes. Mr Thum, the solicitor assessor who sat with me, told the
court that he personally worked on a figure (including overtime) of 1,200 hours, although
this was calculated on a somewhat optimistic basis. Master Clews works on 1,100 hours;
and the Chief Taxing Master told the court that, although until recently they worked on
1,200 hours, the figure of 1,100 hours was now widely used by taxing masters, the figure

being founded on their general experience of what they learn from solicitors in the innumerable taxations which take place. It is right to observe that overtime can make *a* a considerable difference; an average of one hour's overtime a day on each working day could lead to an extra 200 chargeable hours a year, quite apart from overtime worked at weekends. In all the circumstances, it is impossible for me to hold that there is a satisfactory basis for the Law Society's figure of 1,000 hours; likewise, it is impossible for me to hold that Master Clews erred in proceeding on the basis of 1,100 hours.

I turn next to the recommendation made in The Expense of Time that the notional *b* salary for each partner should be based on the scale of salary of the career grade of lawyers in the Civil Service, ie senior legal assistant; for partners outside London the appropriate notional salary so derived would in 1976 have been £8,750 for senior partners, and £7,914 for junior partners. Now counsel for the solicitors found this adoption of Civil Service salaries as the appropriate criterion very difficult to defend. The Expense of Time itself states that the best criterion for fixing notional salaries would be 'the market value *c* of assistant solicitors in private practice with equivalent age and experience'; and I am satisfied that the Civil Service salaries provide no useful guide to such market value, because they simply are not comparable. Putting on one side such matters as non-contributory pensions, the civil servant's salary represents his full remuneration for work of a different kind, in a profession to which entry is gained on a competitive basis, which will involve promotion in graduated steps, and which provides no opportunity to make *d* extra profits but does provide a certain security.

I cannot see how in these circumstances the salary paid to a lawyer in the Civil Service, of any grade, can provide any useful guide to what might be the market value of an assistant solicitor in private practice, or to the notional salary for a partner in a firm of solicitors, particularly as there has to be added to the solicitor's notional salary the 'B' factor for care and conduct. Even if it were useful to have regard to the Civil Service rates *e* of salary, I suspect that the grade chosen is too high. But the choice appears to me to be an arbitrary one; and calculations founded on it cannot, in my judgment, provide a reliable guide to solicitors' expense rates for the purpose of taxation of costs.

When he found himself driven into a corner on this point, counsel for the solicitors had recourse to certain figures published in the Royal Commission's report[1] which, I was told, were not available at the time of the preparation of the second edition of The *f* Expense of Time. These figures are to be found in table 16.76 of the report, and relate to November 1976 salaries of full-time salaried partners and assistant solicitors by year of admission. Counsel for the solicitors concentrated on the column concerned with solicitors admitted in the ten years 1961–1970, which showed the following figures for November 1976 salaries:

average	£6,379
highest decile	£9,871
3rd decile	£7,590
median	£6,050
7th decile	£5,010
lowest decile	£3,832

g

Counsel for the solicitors submitted that these figures provided the best evidence available *h* for assessing notional salaries for partners of Mr Kemp's standing by reference to the market value for assistant solicitors in private practice, as recommended by The Expense of Time, subject to an increment to allow for inflation between November 1976 and the date when the work was done. He further submitted that the appropriate rate to take was the figure for the highest decile (£9,871). I do not however feel able to accept this submission. In the first place the table relates to full-time salaried partners as well as *j* assistant solicitors; the formula in The Expense of Time relates only to the latter. Next, the table draws no distinction between the various types of assistant solicitor, or the types of work they do. It is notorious that highly intelligent and well qualified young men in

---

1 Royal Commission on Legal Services (1979) Cmnd 7648, vol 2, p 526, table 16.76

large firms, who have not yet achieved a partnership, may be highly paid; so also may

a assistant solicitors engaged on difficult or highly profitable work, such as commercial work or conveyancing. It does not follow, with all respect to Mr Kemp, that an assistant solicitor in private practice with equivalent age and experience to his would command a salary in the highest decile. Support for this view is to be found in the report in table 16.75, which relates the salary figures to the size of the firm; it is significant that for firms of three or four partners, the salary figure given for the highest decile is £5,999, whereas

b for firms with ten or more partners it is £8,748. The salary figure of £5,999 in table 16.75 in the report is very close to the median figure of £6,050 in table 16.76. Accordingly, if it is right to use these tables as a guide, they point to a figure in the region of £6,000 in November 1976, which is significantly lower than the Civil Service salaries for senior legal assistants current at that time. But I feel that, without further information, it would be unwise to place too much reliance on these figures as providing,

c in any particular case, an appropriate guide for the assessment of notional salaries under the system advocated in The Expense of Time. Indeed, such evidence as was available to the court of salaries paid to assistant solicitors in firms in Chelmsford indicated a level of salary considerably lower than that for which counsel for the solicitors contended.

For these two reasons alone, I am unable to say that The Expense of Time in its present form provides a sufficiently reliable guide to be used as a basis for taxation of solicitors'

d costs. It is right that I should record that figures were placed before the court by counsel for the Attorney-General which showed that, if calculations were made on the basis of 1,100 hours chargeable time and partners' notional salary of £6,000 (as opposed to 1,000 hours and the recommended Civil Service rates in 1976), this would effect a very significant reduction (in some cases of almost one-third) in the hourly expense rate, primarily due to the difference in notional salary; I need not go into the details of this

e calculation in my judgment, since the figures as such were unchallenged, but I comment that comparatively small variations in chargeable hours and notional salary can affect substantially the resultant expense rate, which points to the need for maximum precision in this exercise. The Chief Taxing Master also produced calculations of partners' profits based on the charging rates adopted by Mr Kemp in the present case, on the basis of The Expense of Time. These calculations were necessarily hypothetical to some degree; but

f they tended to the conclusion that the resulting profits of partners would, if based on fees so calculated, be surprisingly high compared with the median profits recorded in the Law Society's survey as having been actually received by solicitors in 1976. My conclusion is however simply based on the demonstrated facts that the figure of 1,000 hours lacks sufficient evidence to support it, and that the adoption of Civil Service rates for assessing partners' notional salaries is likely to be positively misleading; but I wish to

g point out that any error arising from the adoption of an inaccurate basis for the calculation of expense rates will be compounded when the 'B' factor is applied to the figure so calculated.

I should add that there are certain other criticisms of The Expense of Time which are, in my judgment, well founded. In particular, no provision is made for the necessarily speculative element of interest on clients' account, and clarification is needed of the

h method of treating articled clerks, who are in any event unlikely to work for 1,000 chargeable hours (as apparently envisaged in the booklet[1]). I have already referred to the omission of overtime in dealing with the question of chargeable hours; and it has not been established how 'non-chargeable time' has been calculated, or whether it has been calculated consistently. It is also doubtful whether any allowance should be made for the provision for partners' pensions or, if any such allowance should be made, whether it

j should be based on the net amounts actually paid in previous years. However, on the positive side I wish to add that, on the evidence before me, I consider it right that an allowance should be made for interest on working capital, and that rent for offices should be allowed at the 'market rent' in those cases in which no rent is paid or the rent paid is not fixed by reference to normal market factors.

---

1   The Expense of Time (2nd Edn, 1976) p 16

There are however other more fundamental objections to the submission advanced by counsel for the solicitors. If a taxing officer is presented by a firm of solicitors with a particular expense rate calculated on the basis of The Expense of Time, it is in practice impossible for him to check whether it is accurate or not. He may well possess neither the time nor the training to enable him to check the relevant accounts on which the calculations are based, or indeed the calculations themselves. This problem is compounded by two further factors. First, as is apparent from the Law Society's remuneration survey, there is at present no consistency in the method of operating the system, in particular in the method of assessing the number of chargeable hours; there is also, on the evidence before the court, some variation in the practice of attributing overheads to fee earners. Secondly, the taxing officer's task will be made all the more difficult if he is required to consider not only the calculation of the hourly expense rate of a partner in one firm, but also (as in the present case) the calculation of the rates of partners of other firms in the neighbourhood. In this connection, it is to be borne in mind that an ordinary Crown Court taxation does not take place on an opposed hearing, so that there is no adversary to assist the officer in the detection of shortcomings or errors in the figures presented to him.

Another point is that The Expense of Time system produces no separate figures for different types of work. All the overheads of each firm are attributed to all the fee earners, without regard to the type of work done, whether the work be of a type which in fact attracts small overheads (eg legal aid criminal work) or larger overheads (eg commercial work, including commercial conveyancing work). Finally, there is a point of a more general nature. If taxation of costs were to be based on a system such as The Expense of Time, taxed costs would tend to float on the actual expenses of the relevant firm, rather in the manner of an index-linked pension. Now it can be said with force that there are market forces which militate against solicitors allowing their expenses to rise uncontrolled; the taxation of costs by an independent body, unfettered by any rigid system of computing expense rates, does however impose an element of discipline which, together with market forces, provides some resistance to uncontrolled increases in expense rates.

For all these reasons, I have come to the conclusion that The Expense of Time, laudable though it is in many ways, does not in its present form provide a reliable basis for the taxation of costs; and I also conclude that it will be difficult in practice for any such system to form such a basis without some prior monitoring by an appropriate body. I reach this conclusion with some regret, because I regard with considerable sympathy the aim of the Law Society to place the calculation of solicitors' charges on a more scientific basis, and I have great respect for the work which has been done under their auspices. I very much hope that this judgment, negative though it is, will assist rather than impede the continuation of that work. One solution of the problem which may prove attractive to all concerned would be for the Law Society to re-examine The Expense of Time in the light of this judgment and then invite the Lord Chancellor's Department to consider with them, no doubt with the aid of accountants, and possibly also with the aid of the Chief Taxing Master, whether it is possible to arrive at more acceptable figures, or ranges of figures, for solicitors' hourly expense rates for various types of work in various areas, for the general guidance of taxing officers. Whether such figures are capable of being produced, I do not know, although the implementation of the recommendations of the Royal Commission[1] in their report might assist in their production, and might also assist in such figures being kept up to date. I do not envisage that such figures, even if produced, would deprive the taxing officer of his overall discretion; but they might introduce an element of greater certainty into the present system, and might also serve to reduce the feeling among many solicitors, which I have no doubt is sincerely felt, that they are being under-remunerated under the present system for criminal legal aid work.

---

1   Royal Commission on Legal Services (1979) Cmnd 7648, vol 1, ch 37

a In the result I answer the first question certified by Master Clews in the negative. I only wish to add this. I am not saying that taxing officers should necessarily disregard altogether calculations of hourly expense rates submitted to them based on The Expense of Time; but I do consider that they should regard such calculations with some reserve, having regard to the comments made in this judgment, and that they should at present treat them as no more than one matter to be taken into account when they come to tax costs.

b I do not wish to leave this part of the case without paying a tribute to the very carefully drafted reasons prepared by Master Clews, which formed the basis of much of the discussion before the court. It is unnecessary for me to refer to these reasons in any detail; but in fact much of the criticism advanced by Master Clews in his reasons has survived the argument and is now reflected in this judgment.

c
2. The daily fee for court attendance
The present practice of taxing masters and taxing officers is to allow a solicitor a daily fee for court attendance, without any mark-up for care and conduct. This practice is challenged in the present case, the proposal of the Law Society being that court attendance should be remunerated on the same basis as preparation for trial.

d The practice derives from reg 2 of the Legal Aid in Criminal Proceedings (Fees and Expenses) Regulations 1968. Regulation 2(1) and (3) provides as follows:

'(1) Where a person is granted legal aid under the provisions of section 73 of the Criminal Justice Act 1967 . . . his solicitor and counsel shall (subject to the following provisions of these Regulations) be allowed basic fees in accordance with the provisions of the Schedule to these Regulations . . .

e '(3) Where a hearing has not been concluded on the day on which it started, there shall be allowed to the solicitor, in respect of the second or every subsequent day or part thereof, a daily fee in accordance with the provisions of the Schedule to these Regulations.'

f So I turn to the schedule. Under the heading 'Solicitor', fees are specified in two columns, referring respectively to (1) a basic fee for hearing and preparation therefor, and (2) a daily fee, and related to (a) the Court of Appeal, (b) the Crown Court and (c) magistrates' courts. I was astonished to learn that the figures specified in this schedule have remained unaltered since 1960, and so have remained unaltered throughout one of the worst periods of inflation in the history of this country. In the result, by today's standards the figures can only be regarded as derisory. Thus the solicitor's daily fee in the Court of
g Appeal is specified as not exceeding £15·75; in the Crown Court, not exceeding £21 where no counsel is instructed and in other cases not exceeding £15·75; in the magistrates' courts, not exceeding £9·45 where no counsel is instructed.

The only concession which has been made by those responsible for this legislation is an amendment made in 1977 to para 7 of the regulations. Regulation 7(6) of the regulations originally provided as follows:
h

'(6) If it appears to the taxing authority having taken into account all the relevant circumstances referred to in paragraph (1) of this regulation that nevertheless owing to exceptional circumstances the sums payable by virtue of these Regulations or any of them would not provide fair remuneration for the work actually and reasonably done by the solicitor or counsel, as the case may be (whether in respect of the whole
j work or a particular item of work, including work done in respect of advice on appeal or giving notice of appeal or application for leave to appeal), he shall certify accordingly; and, where he so certifies, any limitation contained in these Regulations on the amount of any fee payable shall not apply.'

In 1977, by the Legal Aid in Criminal Proceedings (Fees and Expenses) (Amendment)

Regulations 1977[1], this was replaced by the following paragraph:

'(6) If it appears to the taxing authority having taken into account all the relevant *a*
circumstances referred to in paragraph (1) of this Regulation that the nature,
importance, complexity or difficulty of the work or the time involved, including
time spent at the court on any day waiting for the case to be heard if the case was in
that day's list, was such that the sums payable by virtue of these Regulations or any
of them would not provide fair remuneration for the work actually and reasonably
done by the solicitor or counsel, as the case may be (whether in respect of the whole *b*
work or a particular item of work, including work done in respect of advice on
appeal or giving notice of appeal or application for leave to appeal), he shall certify
accordingly; and, where he so certifies, any limitation contained in these Regulations
on the amount of any fee payable shall not apply.'

This amendment was no doubt intended to ameliorate the position created by the *c*
retention of the long-outdated figures in the schedule. I was not surprised to learn,
however, that this method of amending legislation has placed taxing officers in a position
of great difficulty. On its face, the new para 7(6) appears to contemplate that the taxing
authority should give a certificate where the case exhibits features which require him to
do so; in practice, taxing officers treat it as a means of escape from the straitjacket of the
schedule, all interpreting the new para 7(6) very liberally, and some in consequence now *d*
disregarding the schedule altogether. This attitude is most understandable in the
circumstances; but the present situation cannot be described as satisfactory. The court
has every sympathy for those government departments whose duty it is to do all they can
to keep inflation under control, and counsel for the Attorney-General did his valiant best
to defend the schedule; but the result of preserving fixed scales unchanged over the past
19 years has not only been to provoke justified resentment on the part of the legal *e*
profession and measured criticism by the Royal Commission, but to drive those
responsible for the taxation of costs to shut their eyes to what has become oppressive
legislation. The time for change must be long overdue; indeed, it is difficult to see how
fixed scales of fees can be justified at all in an inflationary age, unless machinery is
provided for their regular scrutiny and frequent revision.

At all events, the preservation of the scales in the schedule added an edge to the Law *f*
Society's argument that a solicitor's court attendance should be remunerated on the same
basis as his preparation for the trial. The argument so advanced by them appears to me,
in practical terms, most persuasive. First, solicitors generally bill their clients on the basis
of an hourly expense rate; it is difficult to see why this should not apply to court work as
much as to other work. Second, the principles applicable to the assessment of costs for
preparatory work, with the built-in 'B' factor for care and conduct, are as well fitted to the *g*
assessment of costs for court appearance. Third, by assessing costs on an hourly expense
rate, the taxing officer can make a more scientific assessment based on the length of the
solicitor's court attendance, including waiting time and travelling time. Fourth, under
the present system, under which the taxing officer allows no mark-up for care and
conduct on court attendances, he is driven to reflect the lack of such mark-up in the 'B'
factor allowed on preparation for trial; such a system is somewhat crude and unscientific, *h*
and it would be far better to provide for a separate mark-up on court attendances,
especially as there must be many cases where counsel is instructed for the court hearing
and the mark-up on a solicitor's preparatory work would be justifiably higher than his
mark-up on his attendance in court.

Having regard to the force of these arguments, I feel greatly tempted to accede to the
Law Society's submissions on this point. But on reflection, I do not think it would be *j*
right for a court to introduce this fundamental change, particularly as any such change
as I made in this case would be confined to legally aided criminal proceedings. The

---

1   SI 1977 No 875

assessment of a solicitor's costs in such proceedings is regulated by the 1968 regulations;
a and those regulations contemplate that his attendance in court should be remunerated on
the basis of a daily fee. This is so not only in cases where the schedule applies (as to which
see reg 2(1) and (3), quoted above), but also in cases where, by virtue of a certificate
granted under reg 7(6), the scales in the schedule do not apply, for the sub-rule provides
that in such event 'any limitation contained in these Regulations *on the amount of any fee
payable* shall not apply'. For years, it has been the practice for the taxing masters and
b taxing officers so to assess costs; this practice is reflected in the taxing officers' Notes for
Guidance in Crown Court Cases[1]. It would be a fundamental change for taxing officers
to adjust their practice to the assessment of all solicitors' costs in legally aided criminal
cases in the manner now proposed by the Law Society. How fundamental this change
would be is illustrated by the fact that, at present, a daily fee is allowed whether or not
the person from the solicitor's office in court is a qualified solicitor, articled clerk or legal
c executive, or is some other employee from the office; if costs were to be assessed on the
basis of an hourly expense rate, it is at least possible that no costs would be allowed where
the person attending court was not a fee-earner, because the costs of such a person
attending court would form part of the firm's overheads and would therefore be reflected
in the hourly expense rate of the solicitors and articled clerks in the firm. I do not
consider that it is open to me to make so fundamental a change. I must therefore answer
d the second question certified by Master Clews in the negative.

But once again I wish to express the hope that this judgment, though negative, may
not be unproductive. I wish to draw to the attention of those concerned the comments
I have made on the continuance in force of the schedule to the 1968 regulations, and
invite them to consider whether, in the light of this judgment, it is desirable that the
schedule should in any event be allowed to stand in its present form. It is possible that,
e if consultations take place between the Lord Chancellor's Department and the Law
Society on the lines I have already envisaged in the first part of this judgment, their scope
might be widened to embrace the whole question of solicitors' remuneration for court
attendances, and in particular the question whether such remuneration should no longer
be on the basis of a fee but rather on the basis of an hourly expense rate plus a mark-up
for care and conduct.

f
3. *Review of the taxation of the solicitors' costs in the present case*
The argument before me was directed towards the two questions certified by Master
Clews. Having answered both those questions in the negative, I do not consider that it
would be right for me to interfere with the costs assessed by Master Clews on his review
of the taxing officer's taxation.

g
Application dismissed.

Solicitors: *Stunt & Son*; *Treasury Solicitor*.

K Mydeen Esq   Barrister.

h _____

1   (1978) paras 95–97

United Kingdom Association of Professional Engineers and another v Advisory, Conciliation and Arbitration Service

HOUSE OF LORDS

LORD WILBERFORCE, LORD DIPLOCK, LORD EDMUND-DAVIES, LORD KEITH OF KINKEL AND LORD
SCARMAN

29th NOVEMBER, 3rd, 4th DECEMBER 1979, 14th FEBRUARY 1980

*Trade union – Recognition – Reference of recognition issue to Advisory, Conciliation and
Arbitration Service – Duty of Service to improve industrial relations and encourage extension of
collective bargaining – Duty of Service to prepare report setting out findings and recommendations – Scope of duties – Recognition sought by small union – Opposition by larger unions and by
employers' federation – Report by Service recommending non-recognition – Whether Service
performing statutory duties properly in making report – Employment Protection Act 1975,
ss 1(2), 12(4).*

UKAPE, a small trade union wishing to represent professionally qualified engineers
employed by an engineering company, applied to the company for recognition for
collective bargaining purposes. The company, which was a member of the Engineering
Employers' Federation ('the EEF') and which had already recognised for negotiating
purposes certain large unions representing a number of employees in the company's
employment, refused to recognise UKAPE which thereupon referred the recognition
issue to the Advisory, Conciliation and Arbitration Service ('ACAS'), a special body set up
under the Employment Protection Act 1975 to hear such issues and make recommendations for their settlement. Under s 1(2)*ᵃ* of the 1975 Act ACAS was charged with the
general duty of promoting the improvement of industrial relations, and in particular
with encouraging the extension of collective bargaining and the development and,
where necessary, reform of collective bargaining machinery. ACAS proceeded to hold
an enquiry into the recognition issue which revealed, inter alia, (i) that 84% of the
professionally qualified engineers in the company's employment wanted UKAPE to
represent them for negotiating purposes, (ii) that the large unions which had established
collective bargaining arrangements in the engineering industry opposed recognition of
UKAPE, (iii) that two of those unions threatened to take industrial action if recognition
was accorded to UKAPE, and (iv) that the EEF opposed recognition of UKAPE. ACAS
was required, by s 12(4)*ᵇ* of the 1975 Act, to make a written report setting out its
findings, any advice in connection with those findings and any recommendation for
recognition and the reasons for it, or its reasons for not making any recommendation.
In its report on the UKAPE reference, ACAS purported to set out its 'findings', then stated
that it would only recommend recognition if it were consistent with established
collective bargaining arrangements in the company and the industry, and concluded that
it would not recommend recognition of UKAPE because (i) it would be inconsistent with
existing collective bargaining arrangements in the company and the engineering
industry, (ii) it would lead to fragmentation of those arrangements, and (iii) it would
arouse strong opposition from the EEF and the large unions, representing respectively
the majority of employers and workpeople in the industry, with a risk of industrial
action by the unions which would be damaging to the industry. UKAPE brought an
action against ACAS seeking a declaration that its report was a nullity and of no effect on

---

a   Section 1(2) is set out at p 617 *j*, post
b   Section 12(4), so far as material, is set out at p 619 *c d*, post

the ground that ACAS had failed properly to discharge its duties under ss 1(2) and 12(4)
a of the 1975 Act. The judge granted the declaration and the Court of Appeal[c] upheld his
decision. ACAS appealed to the House of Lords.

Held – The appeal would be allowed for the following reasons—

(i) The duty of ACAS under s 1(2) of the 1975 Act in considering whether to
recommend recognition was to consider all the factors involved and to decide whether
b the particular extension of collective bargaining sought by the proposed recognition was
to be encouraged, having regard to the likely effect of such an extension of collective
bargaining on industrial relations and whether it would be consistent or inconsistent
with the development and, where necessary, reform of machinery for collective
bargaining. ACAS was not required to encourage the extension of collective bargaining
if it would lead to a worsening of industrial relations. ACAS had correctly appreciated
c its duty under s 1(2) and had correctly directed itself in law, since the threat of industrial
strife if UKAPE were to be recognised was a relevant factor for ACAS to consider, and it
was not to be inferred that because it attached importance to that factor and followed a
course which would avert industrial strife it had ceased to exercise its own independent
and impartial judgment (see p 614 *f g*, p 615 *e f* and p 620 *g* to p 621 *e*, post).

(ii) Moreover, there was nothing in their report to suggest that ACAS had unlawfully
d fettered its discretion. The statement in the report that any recommendation for the
recognition of a trade union in the company should be consistent with established
collective bargaining arrangements within both the company and the industry was to be
read in the context of the report, and on that basis was a conclusion arising reasonably
from the consideration of matters which ACAS was bound to consider under the 1975
Act rather than a refusal to consider the evidence or a misdirection as to its statutory duty
e (see p 614 *f g*, p 615 *e f* and p 621 *e* to *g*, post).

(iii) Section 12(4) of the 1975 Act did not prescribe the matters on which ACAS was
required to make findings but merely that it should set out in its report such findings as
it did make. Accordingly, provided the report showed that there had been a full
examination of the issue referred and that its conclusion was reasonable in the context of
the findings set out, it was for ACAS to decide what findings it would make. Since the
f conclusion that recognition of UKAPE would constitute a risk to good industrial relations
and lead to a fragmentation of existing arrangements for collective bargaining in the
industry followed logically and reasonably from the findings in the report, it was
unnecessary for ACAS to make specific findings whether UKAPE had enough members
working for the company and in the engineering industry to form an effective group for
collective bargaining purposes and whether UKAPE members in the company's
g employment needed union recognition for collective bargaining purposes. Accordingly
the omission of ACAS to make specific findings on those matters did not nullify the
report. It followed that ACAS had performed its duties under s 12(4) of setting out the
findings on the principal matters of fact and opinion relevant to the recognition issue and
its duty under s 1(2) to examine 'fully and fairly' the case for the extension of collective
bargaining (see p 614 *f g*, p 615 *e f* and p 622 *c* to *f*, post).

h   Decision of the Court of Appeal [1979] 2 All ER 478 reversed.

Notes

For the duties of the Advisory, Conciliation and Arbitration Service under the
Employment Protection Act 1975, ss 1(2), 12(4), see Supplement to 38 Halsbury's Laws
(3rd Edn) para 677A.2.

j   For the Employment Protection Act 1975, ss 1, 12, see 45 Halsbury's Statutes (3rd
Edn) 2374, 2384.

---

c [1979] 2 All ER 478

Cases referred to in opinions

Anisminic Ltd v Foreign Compensation Commission [1969] 1 All ER 208, [1969] 2 AC 147, [1969] 2 WLR 163, HL, 30 Digest (Reissue) 209, *313*.

Associated Provincial Picture Houses Ltd v Wednesbury Corpn [1947] 2 All ER 680, [1948] 1 KB 223, [1948] LJR 190, 177 LT 641, 112 JP 55, 45 LGR 635, CA, 45 Digest (Repl) 215, *189*.

Grunwick Processing Laboratories Ltd v Advisory, Conciliation and Arbitration Service [1978] 1 All ER 338, [1978] AC 655, [1978] 2 WLR 277, [1978] ICR 231, CA & HL.

Padfield v Minister of Agriculture, Fisheries and Food [1968] 1 All ER 694, [1968] AC 997, [1968] 2 WLR 924, HL, Digest (Cont Vol C) 280, *1237a*.

Appeal

The plaintiffs, the United Kingdom Association of Professional Engineers ('UKAPE') and Andrew Thow Butchart, a member of UKAPE and an employee of W H Allen Sons & Co Ltd, brought an action against the defendants, the Advisory, Conciliation and Arbitration Service ('ACAS'), claiming a declaration that a report of ACAS dated 3rd October 1977, recommending that UKAPE should not be recognised by W H Allen Sons & Co Ltd for collective bargaining purposes, was a nullity and of no effect and that ACAS had failed to discharge its duty pursuant to s 12(1) and (4) of the Employment Protection Act 1975, namely to report on the recognition issue in accordance therewith. On 30th June 1978 May J granted the declaration and on 17th January 1979 the Court of Appeal[1] (Lord Denning MR, Lawton and Brandon LJJ) affirmed his decision. ACAS appealed to the House of Lords with leave of the Court of Appeal. The facts are set out in the opinion of Lord Scarman.

P D J Scott QC and *Henry Brooke* for ACAS.
Bernard Marder QC and *Caroline Alton* for the plaintiffs.

Their Lordships took time for consideration.

14th February. The following opinions were delivered.

LORD WILBERFORCE. My Lords, the issues arising in this case have been so fully analysed, and the conclusions on them so clearly stated, by my noble and learned friend Lord Scarman that I can see no need to add any observations of my own. For the reasons given by his Lordship I would allow this appeal.

LORD DIPLOCK. My Lords, I agree with my noble and learned friends that this appeal must be allowed; and there is little that I can usefully add to their reasons for doing so.

In making their report on a recognition issue the Advisory, Conciliation and Arbitration Service ('ACAS') are under a statutory duty to set out their findings and their reasons why they decided to make the recommendation that they made, or, as in the instant case, not to make a recommendation at all. The principal addressees of a report are the unions and employees concerned in the issue and reports are written in a style which although it is readily understood by those who are accustomed to the conduct of industrial relations is less familiar to judges who are confronted with applications for judicial review. It seems to me that much of the difficulty in the instant case has arisen from the fact that ACAS, as a body highly experienced in these matters, consider that candour is out of place in stating reasons for their decisions in recognition disputes since plain speaking might be harmful to industrial relations and to ACAS's own role as adviser and conciliator in future disputes. Meanings that are conveyed by indirection and by inference only but can be 'read between the lines' quite clearly by those accustomed to

---

1   [1979] 2 All ER 478, [1979] 1 WLR 570

the jargon in which industrial relations are conducted, would appear to be a common
a feature of communications in this field.

Reading between the lines of the report on the reference by the United Kingdom
Association of Professional Engineers ('UKAPE') I find quite plain the reasons for ACAS's
refusal to recommend that UKAPE should be recognised as representing in collective
bargaining with their employer the grades of employees whom they seek to represent,
despite the wishes of a very large majority of those employees that UKAPE should do
b so. The overriding consideration in ACAS's view is that no new union should be
permitted to intrude in the existing bargaining arrangements at W H Allen's factory
(which are governed by the industry-wide agreement between the Engineering
Employers' Federation ('EEF') and the Confederation of Shipbuilding and Engineering
Unions ('CSEU')) if this would arouse the opposition of the CSEU, backed as it was by
threat of industrial action. If this was ACAS's view as to what was best for industrial
c relations at W H Allen's factory it does not seem to me to be possible for a court charged
with the function of judicial review of ACAS's decision to say that no reasonable body of
persons experienced in industrial relations could have come to that conclusion. Nor can
it be said that ACAS has paid no regard to its duty to promote the extension of collective
bargaining. The reference in the 'Conclusions' to the understandings between the EEF
and the CSEU as to the criteria for non-procedural categories, conveys by indirection to
d those employees who want to be represented in collective bargaining with their
employer, the advice of ACAS that if they want to achieve their object the way to do it
is to join the Technical, Administrative and Supervisory Section of the Amalgamated
Union of Engineering Workers ('TASS') or the Association of Scientific, Technical and
Managerial Staffs of the CSEU ('ASTMS'), instead of UKAPE.

e **LORD EDMUND-DAVIES.** My Lords, for the reasons developed in the speech of
my noble and learned friend Lord Scarman, which I have had the advantage of reading
in draft, I would allow the appeal.

LORD KEITH OF KINKEL. My Lords, I have had the opportunity of considering
in draft the speech prepared by my noble and learned friend Lord Scarman. I agree with
f it, and for the reasons there expressed I would allow the appeal.

LORD SCARMAN. My Lords, the issue which brings these parties to the courts, and
now to your Lordships' House, is whether an employer, W H Allen Sons & Co Ltd,
should recognise a union, the United Kingdom Association of Professional Engineers
('UKAPE') for the purpose of collective bargaining on behalf of a group of its employees
g at their factory premises in Bedford. It raises questions as to the interpretation of the
Employment Protection Act 1975 ('the Act'). UKAPE is an independent trade union
with some 5,000 members. Membership is limited to professional engineers and others
of compararable status in the engineering industry. The union is not affiliated to the
Trades Union Congress ('the TUC'): nor is it a member of the Confederation of
h Shipbuilding and Engineering Unions ('CSEU') with whom the Engineering Employers'
Federation ('EEF'), to which W H Allen Sons & Co Ltd belong, have procedure and
recognition arrangements covering manual and staff employees in the industry.

In June 1976, UKAPE, having secured a certificate of independence pursuant to s 8 of
the Act, submitted a request for recognition for the purpose of collective bargaining on
behalf of senior engineering staff. This grade of staff is not covered by the procedural
j arrangements between the company and the CSEU. The company rejected the request
on the ground that it would create disharmony to industrial relations in the company
and the industry 'rather than advance and develop' collective bargaining. UKAPE's
response was to refer a 'recognition issue' to ACAS pursuant to s 11 of the Act. On 3rd
October 1977 ACAS announced that they had completed their examination of the issue
referred to them by the union and had sent copies of their report to the parties concerned.

The report ended thus:

'For these reasons [ie those stated in the report] we make no recommendation in *a* respect of UKAPE's application under s 11 of the Employment Protection Act 1975, for recognition at W H Allen Sons and Co Ltd.'

Dissatisfied, UKAPE issued a writ in the Queen's Bench Division on 28th November 1977 in which they challenged the validity of the report and sought declarations that the report was a nullity and that ACAS had failed to discharge its statutory duties. On 29th *b* June 1978, May J delivered a reserved judgment granting the declarations sought. ACAS appealed. On 17th January 1979 the Court of Appeal[1] upheld the judge. Now ACAS appeals with the leave of the Court of Appeal.

The appeal turns on an examination of the report against the background of the duties imposed on ACAS by the Act. The report covers 14 pages and consists of 34 paragraphs and one appendix. It is drafted in language unfamiliar to lawyers, but, no doubt, well *c* understood by management, trade union officials and others concerned in the conduct or study of industrial relations. The history of the dispute, the complex union pattern in the engineering industry which is reflected in the recognition arrangements at W H Allen's factory, and the enquiries and consultations of ACAS are set out in the first 13 paragraphs. The views of the EEF and of the unions affected, including, of course, the views of UKAPE, are outlined in paras 14 to 25. In para 26 ACAS explains that it *d* extended its enquiry to include all technical staff as a result of the view of the company that there were difficulties in defining a viable negotiating group along the lines proposed by UKAPE. In para 27 ACAS makes a finding that 'in the area claimed by UKAPE there was an overwhelming wish to have terms and conditions determined by collective bargaining: ie 84% of [those who answered its questionnaire]'. ACAS further finds that 106 employees in the area of the UKAPE claim (79% of those who answered) wanted *e* UKAPE to represent them, and concludes that UKAPE has very strong support not only within the area of its claim but within the wider technical group. Paragraph 28 summarises the views of the company and the CSEU staff unions: they believed recognition of UKAPE would lead to 'fragmentation' of collective bargaining in the industry. The report notes that this was also the view of the EEF. The conclusions of ACAS are set out in paras 31 to 34. Paragraph 31 emphasises that the wishes of the *f* workers concerned are always an important factor; but other factors have also to be taken into account:

'... for example the shape of any negotiating group, the organisational structures and employment policies designed by management, the views of all the parties concerned and any existing bargaining procedures including industry wide arrangements to which the employer is a party.'   *g*

Paragraph 32 contains a specific reminder of the overall duty with which ACAS is charged by s 1(2) of the Act. The last sentence of para 33 expresses the conclusion which leads logically to the refusal to recommend recognition of UKAPE: 'Any recommendation for the recognition of a trade union in W H Allen must be consistent with established collective bargaining arrangements in the company and industry.' Finally in para 34 *h* ACAS sums up its conclusions as follows:

'In our view recognition of UKAPE by the company for collective bargaining for the staff covered by their claim, would be inconsistent with the existing procedural arrangements established in the company and within the industry. A recommendation in favour of UKAPE would lead to further fragmentation of these arrangements and would not in our view promote the improvement of industrial *j* relations. We also cannot disregard the implications for industrial relations within the engineering industry of any recommendation which would be strongly opposed

---

1   [1979] 2 All ER 478, [1979] 1 WLR 570

a   by the EEF and the CSEU representing respectively the great majority of the
employers and workpeople in the industry. Engineering is of critical importance
to Britain and its system of industrial relations has been developed voluntarily for
more than one hundred years. Both employers and unions have sought, despite
many difficulties and setbacks, to reduce fragmentation of representation and it is
in the interests of good industrial relations that this trend should be encouraged.
For these reasons we make no recommendation in respect of UKAPE's application

b   under s. 11 of the Employment Protection Act 1975, for recognition at W H Allen
Sons and Co Ltd.'

The jargon of the report may be unattractive and unfamiliar to the ear of the lawyer:
but the reasoning is plain and is based on matters which it was certainly the duty of
ACAS to consider. Nevertheless all the judges below concluded that the report offended
the Act. It has not been shown, nor is it now submitted, that there was any lack of due

c process or natural justice in the way ACAS went about its statutory task of examining and
enquiring into the issue. The report, and only the report, is challenged. The reasons for
the challenge which succeeded in the courts below may be summarised as follows: (1)
that the report reveals a misconception by ACAS of the purpose and policy of Part I of the
Act so profound as to vitiate its reasoning and conclusion: in other words, that the report
is based on an erroneous assumption as to the nature of the duty with which ACAS is

d charged by the statute (the 'section 1(2) point'); (2) that, by concluding in para 33 of the
report that 'Any recommendation for the recognition of a trade union in W H Allen
must be consistent with established collective bargaining arrangements in the company
and industry', ACAS unlawfully fettered the discretion conferred on it by the Act (the
'industrial strife point' which led Lord Denning MR to the view that, influenced by the
pressure of 'the big battalions', ACAS failed to do its statutory duty); (3) that, required by

e s 12(4) to prepare a written report setting out its findings, ACAS failed to include in the
report the findings necessary to enable it to render a decision whether or not to
recommend recognition (the 'findings point'); (4) that the refusal to recommend
recognition of a union which enjoyed such strong support was a breach of art 11 of the
European Convention for the Protection of Human Rights and Fundamental Freedoms[1]
(the 'European Convention' point).

f   May J at first instance and Lord Denning MR in the Court of Appeal decided the case
on the first two grounds, which are themselves interrelated since both raise the question
as to the proper construction of s 1(2) of the Act. Lord Denning MR alone of the judges
also expressed the view that there was an infringement of the European Convention.
Lawton and Brandon LJJ decided the case on the third ground, though they differed
from each other as to the findings which in their view ACAS ought to have set out in the

g report. Lawton LJ also expressed his agreement with the judge and Lord Denning MR
on the second ground, but expressed no opinion as to the construction of s 1(2) of the
Act. Brandon LJ, however, took a different view from that of the judge and Lord
Denning MR on the s 1(2) point.

It will be necessary to analyse in detail the judgments below, all of which were
reserved. But before I do so it will be convenient to comment on Part I of the Act and the

h principles of judicial review so far as relevant to this appeal.

First, the Act. Part I consists of 21 sections and establishes machinery for promoting
the improvement of industrial relations. Section 1(1) establishes ACAS. Section 1(2)
formulates its overall duty in the following terms:

j   'The Service [ACAS] shall be charged with the general duty of promoting the
improvement of industrial relations, and in particular of encouraging the extension
of collective bargaining and the development and, where necessary, reform of
collective bargaining machinery.'

---

1   Rome, 4th November 1950; TS 71 (1953); Cmd 8969

As its name implies, ACAS exists to make available to those concerned with industrial relations a service of advice, conciliation and arbitration. None of these services is *a* judicial in character. A glance at ss 2, 3 and 4 of the Act reveals that these services are to assist others to resolve by negotiation or, if the parties consent, by arbitration, their industrial problems. Advice, including guidance and conciliation, not decision-making is the keynote of these provisions.

The advisory role of ACAS is fundamental to a proper understanding of its statutory functions. ACAS, who, as Lord Diplock said in *Grunwick Processing Laboratories Ltd v* *b* *Advisory, Conciliation and Arbitration Service*[1], may properly be described as a statutory body independent as well as expert in industrial relations, is empowered not only to advise parties to a trade dispute but also, whether requested or not, to 'provide, without charge, to employers, employers' associations, workers and trade unions such advice as it thinks appropriate on any matter concerned with industrial relations or employment policies': see s 4(1). It may also provide 'general advice': see s 4(2). And it may issue *c* codes of practice offering 'such practical guidance as the Service [ACAS] thinks fit for the purpose of promoting the improvement of industrial relations': see s 6(1). Parliament's intention is clear. ACAS is to be trusted to advise and guide all who are concerned with industrial relations. No one is to tell ACAS what standards and criteria to adopt. ACAS is the chosen instrument for promoting good industrial relations.

There is a notable exception to the purely advisory role of ACAS: its duties in *d* connection with trade union recognition, which are imposed by ss 11 to 16 of the Act. Before summarising the effect of these sections, I propose to refer briefly to the industrial and Parliamentary history which preceded their enactment, since it throws some light not only on the powers and duties of ACAS under the Act but on the role which the courts are required to play in this field.

Recognition problems have troubled industrial relations for very many years. They *e* have given rise to disputes not only between unions and employers but also between union and union. The complexities of these disputes are endless. They can constitute a major obstacle to the maintenance of industrial peace and to the improvement of industrial relations. In an inter-union quarrel they can make a mockery of the epithet 'collective' when applied to bargaining. They can impede effective collective bargaining. The TUC has, therefore, its own procedures for handling inter-union *f* disputes: but its jurisdiction extends only to unions affiliated to it. And in some industries (as in the engineering industry) management and unions have negotiated agreements at national or company or workshop level (or at all three levels) designed to resolve recognition problems. But until 1971 there was no legal sanction which could be imposed on an employer who refused unreasonably to recognise a union. The Industrial Relations Act of that year made it possible to compel an employer in certain circumstances *g* to recognise a trade union. It introduced an elaborate process which included a judicial element, whereby in certain circumstances an employer could ultimately be required by law to recognise a union as a bargaining agent for his employees, or some of them. That Act was repealed in 1974, but Parliament soon showed that it was not prepared to allow the law to revert to its pre-1971 state. No doubt, as Lord Denning MR observed in the Court of Appeal, Parliament, when enacting Part I of the 1975 Act, had in mind the *h* report of the Royal Commission on Trade Unions (the Donovan Commission). The Royal Commission, which reported in 1968[2], had exposed the need for an independent body to resolve recognition disputes if collective bargaining was to be developed successfully and proposed an independent tribunal to which recognition disputes could be referred. It does not follow that in 1975, Parliament accepted the machinery recommended in 1968 to meet the need. Much turbulent water had swirled under the *j* bridge of the law between 1968 and 1975: and it is not to be assumed that Parliament, though it accepted the need, also accepted the remedy proposed seven years earlier. In

---

1 [1978] 1 All ER 338 at 357, [1978] AC 655 at 686
2 Royal Commission on Trade Unions and Employers' Associations 1965–1968 (Lord Donovan, Chairman) (June 1968) Cmnd 3623

a the result, all that can be properly said is that the uncontrolled freedom of an employer to choose either recognition or refusal has gone. The 1971 machinery with its judicial element for determining whether an employer should recognise a union has also gone. In its place Parliament has chosen to establish machinery for determining the issue, which relies on the recommendation of an independent and expert advisory body, ACAS.

b I come now to the sections which create this machinery. Section 11 provides that a recognition issue may be referred by an independent trade union to ACAS. The issue has to be one which arises from a request by a union, but it may involve others besides the requesting union and the employer. Indeed, the real battle may not be against the employer, but between competing unions. There are many possible permutations. For instance, in the present case the struggle is between a union not affiliated to the TUC, a consortium of unions affiliated to the TUC, an employer and an employers' association.

c ACAS, accordingly, in examining the issue is to consult 'all parties who it considers will be affected' and to make 'such inquiries as it thinks fit': see s 12(1). It is also obliged to ascertain the views of the workers concerned: see s 14. ACAS, true to its role as the statutory conciliator, is always to encourage 'settlement of the issue by agreement': see s 12(3). But, if the issue be neither settled nor withdrawn, ACAS 'shall prepare a written report setting out its findings, any advice in connection with those findings and any *d* recommendation for recognition and the reasons for it, or, where no such recommendation is made, the reasons for not making any recommendation': see s 12(4). Thus the subsection leaves to the judgment or discretion of ACAS what goes into the report, what findings it thinks fit to make, what advice it chooses to offer in connection with its findings, whether it will make a recommendation or not, and its reasons for making or not making a recommendation.

e Section 12(5) provides that a recommendation for recognition shall specify certain matters which the subsection sets out. Section 12(6) empowers ACAS, if it recommends recognition, to impose such conditions as it thinks fit on the union: but, if it does impose conditions, it must set them out in the report.

The sanction of the law is to be found in ss 15 and 16. A trade union, in whose favour a recommendation for recognition has been made, may by observing the requirements *f* of s 15 refer to ACAS a complaint that the employer is failing to comply with the recommendation. ACAS must attempt to settle the matter by conciliation. If conciliation fails, the trade union may apply, in accordance with the provisions of the section, for an award by the Central Arbitration Committee. The committee cannot compel recognition: but it can impose on the employer the terms and conditions the union recommends for incorporation into his employees' contracts of service.

g The purpose of Part I of the Act being to promote the improvement of industrial relations, Parliament has selected machinery which consists of an independent, expert, advisory service, ACAS and an arbitral body, the Central Arbitration Committee. The courts have no part to play other than to exercise their function of judicial review in the event of a challenge to the legality of any act or omission on the part of the bodies entrusted by statute with the duty of promoting the improvement of industrial *h* relations. Since the Act makes no provision for appeal to the courts in the event of a party's dissatisfaction with an ACAS report, it is plain that it is Parliament's intention that recognition issues are for ACAS and the Central Arbitration Committee. It is their discretion, their judgment, which is to determine such issues.

Of course, it does not follow that the courts have no role to play. Judicial review of the lawfulness of the actions of the two statutory bodies is available to an aggrieved party or *j* person. Judicial review is the modern term to describe the very ancient supervisory jurisdiction vested in the superior courts to declare the law and to require compliance with it. It is this jurisdiction which the union has invoked. However, redress by way of injunction is not available against ACAS, its functions being performed 'on behalf of the Crown' notwithstanding its independence: see Sch 1 to the Act, para 11(1).

In the case of a statutory body the scope of judicial review depends on the statute but it can never be wholly eliminated. The courts will examine the action, or lack of action,

of a statutory body in order to determine whether it has complied with the statute: see
Padfield v Minister of Agriculture, Fisheries and Food[1].

The courts will determine any challenge that may be made to the jurisdiction or
extent of authority conferred on the body: see *Anisminic Ltd v Foreign Compensation
Commission*[2]. But the courts will not substitute their judgment for that of the statutory
body on matters which the statute has provided are for its decision. The extent to which
the courts are able to interfere with the judgment or discretion of such a body was laid
down in the classic judgment delivered by Lord Greene MR in *Associated Provincial
Picture Houses Ltd v Wednesbury Corpn*[3]. In the course of it Lord Greene MR observed[4]:

> '. . . a person entrusted with a discretion must direct himself properly in law. He
> must call his own attention to the matters which he is bound to consider. He must
> exclude from his consideration matters which are irrelevant . . . Similarly, you may
> have something so absurd that no sensible person could ever dream that it lay
> within the powers of the authority.'

The language of the judgment is very different from the language of industrial
relations: but the principle is clear and applicable. The courts will not tell a statutory
body how it is to conduct its business or what decision, report or recommendation it is
to make. They will invalidate the exercise of a statutory body's judgment or discretion
only if satisfied that no reasonable person charged with the body's responsibilities under
the statute could have exercised its power in the way that it did. Applying the principle
to this case, the courts will not invalidate the ACAS report unless satisfied that no
reasonable advisory, conciliation and arbitration service with a due appreciation of its
statutory duties and responsibilities, could have reported is it did.

Each member of the Court of Appeal, for the reasons which he gives, reached the
conclusion that ACAS misdirected itself in law, failed to consider matters which it was
bound to consider, and reported in a way which no reasonable body in its position and
with its statutory duties could have done. With all respect, I do not find that their
reasons support their conclusion.

I turn now to consider the four grounds of challenge to the report which attracted
support from one or more of the judges below. First, the s 1(2) point. Is the subsection
to be interpreted as requiring ACAS to give priority to the duty to encourage the extension of collective bargaining, if faced with a conflict between that duty and the
general duty of promoting the improvement of industrial relations? I cannot read the
subsection as laying down any such priority. It is inconceivable that Parliament intended
that ACAS must recommend recognition, even if to do so would be to worsen industrial
relations; and the language of the subsection does not compel any such conclusion. The
subsection formulates the various objectives of a statutory policy which it is for ACAS to
implement as, in the exercise of its independent and expert judgment, it thinks best in
individual cases. The specified objectives are the strands of a complex fabric of duty and
are meaningful only so long as they remain knitted together in a pattern of industrial
policy. As I interpret the subsection, ACAS has to consider all the factors and, in reaching
its own decision whether or not the particular extension of collective bargaining which
would result from a recognition recommendation is to be encouraged, must have regard
to its likely effect on industrial relations and its consistency, or inconsistency, with the
development and, where necessary, the reform of collective bargaining machinery. I
agree with the interpretation put on the subsection by Brandon LJ[5]:

> '. . . s 1(2) should not be interpreted as requiring ACAS to encourage the extension
> of collective bargaining, or to develop or reform collective bargaining machinery,
> in a case where to do so would lead, not to the improvement, but to the worsening
> of industrial relations.'

---

1   [1968] 1 All ER 694, [1968] AC 997
2   [1969] 1 All ER 208, [1969] 2 AC 147
3   [1947] 2 All ER 680, [1948] 1 KB 223
4   [1947] 2 All ER 680 at 682–683, [1948] 1 KB 223 at 229
5   [1979] 2 All ER 478 at 492, [1979] 1 WLR 570 at 590

In my judgment, ACAS correctly appreciated its duty under s 1(2) of the Act, and correctly directed itself in law.

Secondly, the industrial strife point. May J offered this analysis, with which I respectfully agree, of the attitude of ACAS as revealed in the report:

> 'To recommend recognition of UKAPE might well lead to industrial strife initiated by the larger CSEU affiliated trade unions . . . this clearly would not improve industrial relations within the industry . . . their [ACAS's] principal and indeed overriding duty to promote good industrial relations required them to desist from making any recommendation for recognition [of UKAPE].'

The judge, on his interpretation of s 1(2), which for the reasons already given I think was erroneous, held that ACAS had misconceived its priorities. But Lord Denning MR in the Court of Appeal went further. He asked himself, 'Ought ACAS to be influenced by implications of this kind?' and answered with an emphatic No. He said[1] that 'It would make ACAS the tool of the powerful trade unions. It would cease to be an independent and impartial tribunal . . .'

For the reasons already given I have no doubt that the threat of industrial strife if UKAPE were to be recognised was a relevant matter for ACAS to consider, and that it was for ACAS, not the courts, to determine what weight should be given it. If, of course, as Lord Denning MR appears to suggest, ACAS surrendered in the face of threats by the big unions so that it failed to exercise its own independent judgment, it would assuredly be in breach of the Act, and its report a nullity. But the mere fact that it attached importance to the risk of industrial strife and favoured a course which it believed would avert it is no sufficient ground for concluding that it had ceased to exercise its own independent and impartial judgment.

Is there, then, anything in the report which would suggest that ACAS had abjectly retreated from its duty? One passage, ie the last sentence of para 33, has been suggested as an indication that ACAS had unlawfully fettered its discretion. That sentence, read in isolation, could be construed as meaning that ACAS had closed its mind against the possibility of any recommendation for recognition in W H Allen Sons & Co Ltd which was inconsistent with the established arrangements between the industry, the company and the CSEU. But, if the sentence be read, as it must be, in the context of the report, it is a conclusion reached after a careful examination of the relevant factors: it is not a refusal to consider the evidence, or, as Lawton LJ thought, a misdirection as to its statutory duties. Further, for the reasons already given, it cannot be said to be a perverse conclusion, ie one which no reasonable advisory, conciliation and arbitration body charged with the statutory duties of ACAS could have reached in the circumstances of this case. Indeed, it was a conclusion arising reasonably from the consideration of matters which under the Act ACAS was bound to consider.

The third ground of challenge is that on which, in their different ways, Lawton and Brandon LJJ founded their judgments. Lawton LJ held that any reasons given for not making a recommendation must be based on findings of fact set out in the report and that ACAS failed to make findings on two crucial questions. The first was whether UKAPE had enough members working for the company and in the engineering industry to form an effective group for collective bargaining purposes. It was not enough, according to Lawton LJ, to find that UKAPE had 'very strong support within the area of its claim'. The second question was whether the UKAPE members in the company's employment really did need for the purpose of collective bargaining that the union be recognised.

Brandon LJ interpreted s 12(4) of the Act as requiring ACAS to make and set out in its report such findings as the nature of the case required. He criticised the report for failing to include findings on 'four vital matters'[2]:

---

1   [1979] 2 All ER 478 at 484, [1979] 1 WLR 570 at 580
2   [1979] 2 All ER 478 at 490–491, [1979] 1 WLR 570 at 589

'(1) Whether the workers to whom UKAPE's claim related constituted an identifiable and viable group for the purposes of collective bargaining. (2) Whether the existing arrangements under which the pay and conditions of the group were determined were adequate. (3) If not, whether separate arrangements for collective bargaining for the group were needed. (4) If so, whether such need could be adequately met (a) by UKAPE or (b) by some other union or unions.'

Lawton LJ held that by failing to set out findings on these matters ACAS was in breach of its statutory duty in two respects. First, it failed to set out necessary findings as required by s 12(4). Secondly, it failed to examine 'fully and fairly' the case for the extension of collective bargaining and so failed to do its duty under s 1(2) of the Act.

This approach to the report and its findings appears to me to be essentially appellate in character: but Parliament has not provided for any appeal to the courts. A court exercising the supervisory function, which is all that a court may do in a case such as this, must, of course, look closely at the terms of s 12(4). That subsection does not prescribe on what questions ACAS is to make findings, but only that it shall set out in the report the findings it does make. Unless, therefore, no reasonable body charged with ACAS's statutory duties could, on the findings which ACAS in fact set out in the report, have reached the conclusion not to recommend recognition, the courts cannot interfere: their interference would be a substitution of the court's judgment for the opinion of ACAS.

The conclusion that recognition of UKAPE would constitute a risk to good industrial relations and lead to a fragmentation of existing arrangements for collective bargaining in the industry does follow logically and reasonably from the findings in the report. This conclusion being the reason why ACAS refused to recommend recognition, it was unnecessary to make the specific findings the omission of which led Lawton and Brandon LJJ to declare the report a nullity. And it might well have appeared to ACAS unwise to set out findings which were not required to support its conclusion. It does not need the facts of this case to remind us how highly sensitive and complex is the world of industrial relations, a world in which it is as dangerous to say too much as in some cases it is to say too little. Provided, therefore, a report shows that there has been a full examination of the issue referred, and that its conclusion is reasonable in the context of the findings set out, it is left to the judgment of ACAS to decide what findings it will make. In my judgment, for the reasons given, the report satisfies this test. This ground of challenge, therefore, also fails.

Finally, the point on the European Convention. I agree with Lord Denning MR that art 11 of the convention and the common law recognise and protect the right of association, which in the present context includes the right to join a trade union. But it does not follow from the existence of the right that every trade union which can show it has members employed by a particular company or in a particular industry has a right to recognition for the purposes of collective bargaining. I would be surprised if either the convention or the common law could be interpreted as compelling so chaotic a conclusion. If the common law is to be so understood (and I do not accept that it is), Parliament has averted the mischief by the Act. And, if it be a possible interpretation of the European Convention, I shall not adopt it unless and until the European Court of Human Rights declares that it is correct. Suffice it to say that I understand why counsel for UKAPE did not seek to support this ground of challenge in your Lordships' House. Until such time as the Act is amended or the convention both becomes part of our law and is authoritatively interpreted in the way proposed by Lord Denning MR, the point is a bad one.

I would allow the appeal.

Appeal allowed.

Solicitors: *Treasury Solicitor* (for ACAS); *Gregory, Rowcliffe & Co* (for the plaintiffs).

Mary Rose Plummer   Barrister.

Liff v Peasley and another

COURT OF APPEAL, CIVIL DIVISION

STEPHENSON AND BRANDON LJJ

19th, 23rd, 24th OCTOBER, 14th NOVEMBER 1979

b *Practice – Parties – Adding defendant – Amendment of writ – Date from which added defendant becomes party to proceedings – Action against added defendant time-barred at date writ amended – Whether joinder taking effect from date of original writ or from date writ amended – Whether added defendant entitled to plead defence of limitation on basis that joinder takes effect from date writ amended.*

c *Practice – Parties – Adding defendant – Amendment of writ – Defendant entering unconditional appearance to amended writ – Defendant serving defence that action time-barred – Defendant applying for order to strike out joinder – Whether entry of unconditional appearance precluding defendant from objecting to joinder – Whether defendant ceasing to be a party because he had improperly been made a party or because he had ceased to be a proper party on service of defence pleading statute of limitation – RSC Ord 15, r 6(2)(a).*

d *Limitation of action – Court's discretion to override time limit in personal injury or fatal accident claim – Matters to which court may have regard – Action claiming damages for personal injury sustained in road accident – First defendant's insurers disclaiming liability – Motor Insurers' Bureau liable to meet judgment against first defendant – Plea of limitation of action raised by second defendant when added – Whether discretion to override time limit should be exercised – Whether fact that Motor Insurers' Bureau would meet judgment a matter to be taken into* *e* *consideration – Limitation Act 1939, s 2D(1)(a)(3) (as inserted by the Limitation Act 1975, s 1).*

On 25th October 1973 the plaintiff was injured while travelling as a passenger in a car driven by S, when the car collided with another car driven by P. There was evidence that P was solely to blame for the accident. On 1st August 1975, within the primary limitation period prescribed for the action under s 2A of the Limitation Act 1939, the *f* plaintiff issued a writ against P claiming damages. P's insurers repudiated liability and notified the Motor Insurers' Bureau ('the MIB') who nominated other insurers for P. The primary limitation period expired on 2nd October 1976. The plaintiff delivered his statement of claim against P in June 1977 and P delivered a defence in September in which he alleged that the collision was wholly or partly caused by the negligence of S. At the instance of the MIB the plaintiff and P applied ex parte to join S as a defendant to *g* the action, and on 5th October 1978 a master ordered that S be joined as second defendant and that the plaintiff be given leave to amend the statement of claim. On 22nd January 1979 another master gave leave to amend the writ to join S. The solicitors for S entered an unconditional appearance to the amended writ and, after accepting service of the amended statement of claim, served a defence pleading that the action against S was time-barred. Subsequently S challenged his joinder and applied (i) for an *h* order that the claim against him be struck out as being time-barred, notwithstanding s 2D[a] of the 1939 Act, or (ii) alternatively, for an order under RSC Ord 15, r 6[b] that he should cease to be a party to the action because he had been improperly joined. The

***

a Section 2D, so far as material, provides:

j '(1) If it appears to the court that it would be equitable to allow an action to proceed having regard to the degree to which—(a) the provisions of section 2A ... of this Act prejudice the plaintiff or any person whom he represents ... the court may direct that those provisions shall not apply to the action, or shall not apply to any specified cause of action to which the action relates ...

'(3) In acting under this section the court shall have regard to all the circumstances of the case ...'

b Rule 6, so far as material, is set out at p 631 *e* to *g*, post

judge made no order on the first application and dismissed the second application. S
appeared. On the appeal the plaintiff and P contended (i) that, because S had entered an   *a*
unconditional appearance instead of following the usual procedure whereby a person
objecting to joinder entered a conditional appearance and applied to set aside the
amended writ, he (a) had lost his right to have the joinder set aside since he could not
contend that he had been improperly joined and (b) was not entitled to rely on the statute
of limitation as a defence because the true basis of the court's practice not to allow joinder
of a person as defendant to an existing action if the claim against him was already time-   *b*
barred ('the rule of practice') was that the joinder was deemed to relate back to the date
of the original writ ('the relation back' theory), (ii) that, accordingly, the action against S
was deemed to have begun on the date of the original writ and was therefore deemed to
have begun in time, and (iii) that his plea that the action was time-barred was not
available to him.

                                                                   c

Held – The appeal would be allowed, and an order made that S cease to be a party to the
action, for the following reasons—
    (i) The joinder, contrary to the rule of practice, of a person as a defendant when the
claim against him was time-barred was not a mere irregularity of process which could be
waived by entry of an unconditional appearance to the amended writ, because the
joinder took away an accrued right of defence under the 1939 Act. Accordingly, even   *d*
though S had been properly joined (which he had been, because at the date of the
master's order it had not been known whether he would plead the limitation defence)
and had entered an unconditional appearance to the amended writ, he was not precluded
from objecting to his joinder. Since the claim against him was already time-barred when
he was joined, he was entitled to an order under RSC Ord 15, r 6(2)(*a*), that he cease to be
a party to the action, because either he was a person 'who has been improperly . . . made   *e*
a party', within r 6(2)(*a*), or, as soon as it was known that he would plead the limitation
defence, he had 'ceased to be a proper party', within r 6(2)(*a*) (see p 630 *g h*, p 638 *a* to *g*,
p 640 *c* to *g* and p 643 *h j*, post).
    (ii) Assuming, however, that the entry of an unconditional appearance did preclude
S from objecting under Ord 15, r 6 to his joinder, he would be entitled to plead the 1939
Act because the true basis of the rule of practice was not the 'relation back' theory but that   *f*
the action against a person joined as defendant was deemed to have been commenced
against him from the date on which the writ was amended, so that if the action was then
time-barred there was no useful purpose in allowing the joinder. Accordingly, the
joinder of S took effect only from the date on which the writ had been amended, and not
from the date of the original writ. On that basis, the court would summarily dismiss the
action against him on the ground that it was time-barred (see p 636 *c d*, p 637 *h*, p 638 *g*,   *g*
p 642 *f g* and p 643 *e f* and *j* to p 644 *a*, post); *Byron v Cooper* (1844) 11 Cl & Fin 556,
Mitchell v Harris Engineering Co Ltd [1967] 2 All ER 682 and *Seabridge v H Cox & Sons
(Plant Hire) Ltd* [1968] 1 All ER 570 applied; *Weldon v Neal* (1887) 19 QBD 394, *Mabro v
Eagle Star and British Dominions Insurance Co Ltd* [1932] All ER Rep 411 and *Lucy v W T
Henley's Telegraph Works Co Ltd* [1969] 3 All ER 456 considered.
    (iii) Furthermore, the court would not exercise its discretionary power under s 2D of   *h*
the 1939 Act to extend the primary limitation period because (a) the plaintiff was not
prejudiced by s 2A, within s 2D(1)(*a*), since he had a cast-iron case against P, and the MIB
were required to satisfy any judgment against P, and (b) the presence of the MIB in the
case was one of the circumstances of the case to which, under s 2D(3), the court was
required to have regard (see p 629 *h* to p 630 *b e* and *f* and p 638 *j* to p 639 *a*, post); *Firman
v Ellis* [1978] 2 All ER 851 and *Walkley v Precision Forgings Ltd* [1979] 2 All ER 548   *j*
applied.
    Per Brandon LJ. Although the Court of Appeal is bound by the authorities to hold
that the rule of practice exists and to continue to apply it, the court is not bound to hold
that the 'relation back' theory is the true basis of the rule, for two reasons: first, it was
never necessary for the decision in any of the reported cases from 1877 onwards to decide
whether that theory or the theory that no useful purpose would be served by the joinder

was the true one, and it was sufficient simply to formulate and apply the rule, and,
a second, the authorities do not speak with one voice but provide support for and against
both theories. Moreover, the 'relation back' theory is inconsistent with RSC Ord 15,
r 8(4)^c and CCR Ord 15, r 2^d, whereas the 'no useful purpose' theory is consistent with
both of those rules (see p 641 *f* to *h* and p 643 *d e*, post).

Notes
b For the effect of misjoinder, see 30 Halsbury's Laws (3rd Edn) 394, para 735, and for cases
on the subject, see 50 Digest (Repl) 450–463, *1469–1575*.
   For the Limitation Act 1939, s 2D (as inserted by the Limitation Act 1975, s 1), see 45
Halsbury's Statutes (3rd Edn) 850.

Cases referred to in judgments
c *Ashley v Taylor* (1878) 10 Ch D 786, 48 LJ Ch 406, 39 LT 573, CA, 50 Digest (Repl) 461,
   1559.
   Braniff v Holland & Hannen and Cubitts (Southern) Ltd [1969] 3 All ER 959, [1969] 1 WLR
   1533, CA, 32 Digest (Reissue) 727, *5275*.
   Byron v Cooper (1844) 11 Cl & Fin 556, 8 Jur 991, 8 ER 1212, HL, 32 Digest (Reissue) 727,
   5273.
d *Challinor v Roder* (1885) 1 TLR 527, DC, 50 Digest (Repl) 113, *939*.
   Davies v Elsby Brothers Ltd [1960] 3 All ER 672, [1961] 1 WLR 170, CA, 32 Digest
   (Reissue) 725, *5257*.
   Firman v Ellis [1978] 2 All ER 851, [1978] QB 886, [1978] 3 WLR 1, CA, 32 Digest
   (Reissue) 742, *5341*.
   Gawthrop v Boulton [1978] 3 All ER 615, [1979] 1 WLR 268.
e *Hattam v National Coal Board* [1978] The Times, 27th October.
   Lucy v W T Henley's Telegraph Works Co Ltd [1969] 3 All ER 456, [1970] 1 QB 393, [1969]
   3 WLR 588, CA, Digest 32 (Reissue) 727, *5274*.
   Mabro v Eagle Star and British Dominions Insurance Co Ltd [1932] 1 KB 485, [1932] All ER
   Rep 411, 101 LJKB 205, 146 LT 433, CA, 32 Digest (Reissue) 726, *5263*.
   Mitchell v Harris Engineering Co Ltd [1967] 2 All ER 682, [1967] 2 QB 703, [1967] 3 WLR
f 447, CA, Digest (Cont Vol C) 1076, *830a*.
   Plowden v Thorpe (1840) 7 Cl & Fin 137, West 42, 4 Jur 211, 7 ER 1019, HL.
   Puerto Acevedo, The [1978] 1 Lloyd's Rep 38.
   Riches v Director of Public Prosecutions [1973] 2 All ER 935, [1973] 1 WLR 1019, CA,
   Digest (Cont Vol D) 1038, *563a*.
   Seabridge v H Cox & Sons (Plant Hire) Ltd [1968] 1 All ER 570, [1968] 2 QB 46, [1968] 2
g WLR 629, CA, Digest (Cont Vol C) 1085, *1602a*.
   Sneade v Wotherton Barytes and Lead Mining Co [1904] 1 KB 295, 13 Digest (Reissue) 436,
   3614.
   Sterman v E W & J W Moore Ltd (a firm) [1970] 1 All ER 581, [1970] 1 QB 596, [1970] 2
   WLR 386, CA, 32 Digest (Reissue) 723, *5244*.
   Walkley v Precision Forgings Ltd [1979] 2 All ER 548, [1979] 1 WLR 606, HL.
h *Weldon v Neal* (1887) 19 QBD 394, 56 LJQB 621, CA, 32 Digest (Reissue) 728, *5278*.

Cases also cited
   Browes v Jones & Middleton (a firm) (1979) 123 Sol Jo 489, CA.
   Steward v North Metropolitan Tramways Co (1886) 16 QBD 556, CA.
j *Vallance v Birmingham and Midland Land and Investment Corpn* (1876) 2 Ch D 369, CA.

   Interlocutory appeal
   By a writ issued on 14th August 1975 the plaintiff, Raymond Jack Liff, brought an action
   against the first defendant, Ian Stanley Peasley, claiming damages for personal injuries

---
c Rule 8(4), so far as material, is set out at p 634 *f* to *h*, post
d Rule 2, so far as material, is set out at p 635 *c*, post

sustained in a road accident on 25th October 1973. By an order dated 5th October 1978
Master Warren ordered that Timothy John Spinks be joined as second defendant in the *a*
action and gave leave for the statement of claim to be amended. On 22nd January 1979
Master Creightmore gave leave to amend the writ to join the second defendant. The
second defendant entered an unconditional appearance to the amended writ and
subsequently on 5th March 1979, served a defence pleading, inter alia, that the plaintiff's
cause of action against him was statute-barred under s 2 of the Limitation Act 1939. By
a summons dated 12th March 1979, as amended, the second defendant applied for an *b*
order that (1) notwithstanding s 2 of the 1939 Act as amended, the plaintiff's claim
against him be struck out as being statute-barred, (2) further or in the alternative the
second defendant be struck out of the action having been improperly joined, and (3)
further or in the alternative the action against the second defendant be dismissed for
want of prosecution. On 26th July Mr T P Russell QC sitting as a deputy judge of the
High Court made no order on the first application and dismissed the second and third *c*
applications. The second defendant appealed seeking (1) an order that s 2A of the 1939
Act should apply to the plaintiff's cause of action against him and that the plaintiff's
claim against him was statute-barred, (2) further or in the alternative an order under RSC
Ord 15, r 6 that the second defendant was improperly made a party to the proceedings
in that he was joined after the expiry of the limitation period and that the second
defendant cease to be a party to the proceedings, and (3) further or in the alternative an *d*
order that the action against the second defendant be dismissed for want of prosecution.
The facts are set out in the judgment of Stephenson LJ.

John M Cherry for the second defendant.
Mark Tennant for the plaintiff.
Jonathan Woods for the first defendant.

e

Cur adv vult

14th November. The following judgments were read.

STEPHENSON LJ. This is an appeal by leave of Mr T P Russell QC sitting as a deputy
judge of the High Court in the Queen's Bench Division from his refusal on 26th July *f*
1979 to grant three applications by Mr Timothy John Spinks, the appellant.
   Mr Spinks has been joined as a defendant to an action brought against Mr Ian Stanley
Peasley by Mr Raymond Jack Liff by writ issued on 14th August 1975. Mr Liff was
injured in a cross-roads collision between a Ford Cortina motor car driven by Mr Spinks,
in which he was a passenger, and a Triumph motor car driven by Mr Peasley on 25th
October 1973. By summons dated 12th March 1979, Mr Spinks asked the judge in
chambers to order: '1. That notwithstanding Section 2 of the Limitation Act, 1939 as *g*
amended, the Plaintiff's claim against the Second Defendant be struck out as being
statute barred.'
   By amendment at the hearing of the summons on 26th July 1979 he asked the deputy
judge to order two other things:

   '2. That further or in the alternative that the Second Defendant be struck out of *h*
   the action having been improperly joined.
   '3. Further or in the alternative the action against the Second Defendant be
   dismissed for want of prosecution.'

The deputy judge made no order on the application under item 1, and dismissed the
applications under items 2 and 3.
   By his notice of appeal Mr Spinks asks this court for the same three things, two in *j*
slightly different form:

   '1. For an order that the provisions of Section 2A of the Limitation Act, 1939 as
   amended shall apply to the Plaintiff's cause of action against the Second Defendant
   and that the Plaintiff's claim against the Second Defendant is statute barred.

'2. Further or in the alternative for an order under Order 15 Rule 6 that the Second Defendant was improperly made a party to the proceedings in that he was joined after the expiry of the limitation period and that the second defendant cease to be a party to the proceedings.

'3. Further or in the alternative for an order that the action against the Second Defendant be dismissed for want of prosecution.'

In this court counsel has submitted that Mr Spinks was improperly joined as a party, because he was joined too late according to the Rules of the Supreme Court and to the practice established by binding authority. His submissions and those of counsel for Mr Liff and Mr Peasley require consideration of the peculiar history of Mr Liff's action, of the Rules of Court and of a number of decided cases.

First the history. The accident which injured Mr Liff took place on 25th October 1973. The Cortina Mr Spinks was driving was apparently owned by his brother and insured with the Norwich Union ('the Norwich'). They acted promptly and on 18th November 1973 obtained a statement from an independent eye-witness named Kennard blaming Mr Peasley only. Traffic lights were not working at the time of the accident, but Mr Spinks stopped and tried to cross carefully while Mr Peasley tried to cross much too fast without stopping. On 8th December 1973 the police obtained a statement from another independent eye-witness named Stevens which was equally favourable to Mr Spinks.

On 28th May 1974 Mr Peasley was convicted of careless driving. On 3rd September 1974 Mr Peasley's insurers, Zurich Insurance ('the Zurich') notified the Norwich of Mr Liff's claim against their insured. On 1st August 1975 Mr Liff issued his writ against Mr Peasley alone, and on 1st September 1975 the Norwich heard again from the Zurich. After a further year's silence the Norwich wrote again to the Zurich on 2nd October 1976 and heard from the Zurich on 9th December 1976 that the Zurich was not involved. By that time the three years primary period of limitation had expired on 2nd October 1976.

The Zurich has in fact repudiated liability and brought the matter to the attention of the Motor Insurers' Bureau ('the MIB') who nominated the Sun Alliance ('the Sun') as insurer concerned for Mr Peasley.

This action appears to have been taken at the end of 1975 and the beginning of 1976, but the Zurich did not advise Mr Peasley's solicitors until June 1977 and the Sun did not approach the Norwich until January 1978. Meanwhile on 27th June 1977 Mr Liff delivered his statement of claim against Mr Peasley, and on 22nd September 1977 Mr Peasley delivered his defence claiming that the collision was caused wholly or partly by the negligence of Mr Spinks.

On 23rd January 1978, 4½ years after the accident, the Sun wrote to the Norwich as follows:

'Your Insured T J Spinks. R J Liff v I S Peasley. *Motor Accident 25th October 1973.* It would appear from our papers that this is the first time we have approached you in the above connection. You will be familiar with the circumstances of the accident and will therefore have knowledge of how the various parties are involved. Our interest arises on behalf of the Motor Insurers Bureau who are undertaking Mr Peasley's defence following the decision of his insurers not to indemnify. An Action has been started by Mr R J Liff who was a passenger in your Insured's Ford Cortina MVK 201E against Mr Peasley for the injuries he received and we have had a defence entered. You will be aware, we trust, that the MIB Agreement relieves them of any responsibility to satisfy any judgment if there is any other known party upon whom a minimum of 1% contributory negligence can be proven. It will be the duty of that person's insurers to satisfy any judgment. Your Insured is not yet named in the proceedings but our Solicitors consider this step should be taken and notwithstanding the possibility that the Limitation Defence will be raised on his behalf it is felt that the Court would, in its discretion, allow the action to proceed against him. In this event we are satisfied the required degree of negligence could be held to attach. We are therefore providing you with the opportunity to consider your position and to ask whether or not you wish to take over the handling of the claim that has been brought by Mr Liff. May we have your decision as quickly as possible as our solicitors have asked for our further instructions.'

It is clear from this letter that it was at the instance of the MIB that Mr Liff brought Mr Spinks into his action. At the same time the Sun suggested to Mr Liff's solicitors that they should join Mr Spinks as a defendant.

On 5th October 1978 Master Warren made the following order. It is headed: 'RAYMOND JACK LIFF Plaintiff and IAN STANLEY PEASLEY first Defendant and TIMOTHY JOHN SPINKS Second Defendant.'

It then continues:

'UPON HEARING the Solicitors for the parties IT IS ORDERED THAT Timothy John Spinks be joined as Second Defendant in this Action and that the Plaintiff has leave to amend the Statement of Claim as shown in the document initialed by the Master and to re-serve the Amended Statement within fourteen days with leave to the Defendant to serve an amended Defence (if so advised) in fourteen days thereafter and the costs incurred and thrown away by the amendments be costs in the cause.'

That order calls for the following comments. (1) The 'Solicitors for the parties' were the solicitors for Mr Liff and Mr Peasley, although Mr Spinks was wrongly entitled a party as second defendant. For as far as he was concerned, the application was ex parte and he was not represented at its hearing. (2) The order gives Mr Liff leave to amend the statement of claim, but not the writ, and gives the defendant (presumably the first defendant, Mr Peasley) leave to serve an amended defence, but gives no directions as to service on the newly joined second defendant.

On 13th October 1978 Mr Liff's solicitors informed Mr Spink's brother that Mr Spinks had been joined as a second defendant and asked him to pass their letter to his insurers. So the Norwich were informed and instructed solicitors, who wrote to Mr Liff's solicitors on 11th December 1978 as follows:

'With reference to our telephone call of the 8th instant, we confirm that on the instructions of his motor insurers, the Norwich Union, we act for the second defendant. Before we enter an Appearance we should be grateful if you would let us have a copy of the Amended Writ which presumably you served but which must have gone astray. We have a copy of the Amended Statement of Claim and of the First Defendant's Defence: should there be any other Pleadings, we should welcome copies of them as well. No doubt you will extend our time for appearing pending receipt of the above documents.'

A reminder on 19th December apparently stirred Mr Liff's solicitors into appreciating that, perhaps in consequence of the form of Master Warren's order, the writ had not been amended as required by RSC Ord 15, r 8(1). So on 22nd January 1979 they got Master Creightmore to give leave to amend the writ and sent Mr Spinks's solicitors a copy on 25th January. On 30th January Mr Spinks's solicitors wrote to Mr Liff's solicitors as follows:

'We acknowledge receipt of your letter of the 25th instant. We enclose our Memorandum of Appearance on behalf of the Second Defendant on your assurance that the Writ has been served. Unfortunately we have been unable so far to trace the whereabouts of Mr Spinks and any information which your client or you can give us in that respect would be appreciated. [Then there is a P.S. which says:] The endorsement as to service on your Writ specifies that service was on the 30th of last November but the amendment is said to have been made on the 22nd January. Which is wrong please? We do not have a copy of the amending Order. May we have one.'

The appearance they entered was unhappily unconditional. The reply of 1st February
a from Mr Liff's solicitors explained how the writ had not been amended but not how the
endorsement of service antedated the leave to amend, and asked Mr Spinks's solicitors to
accept service of the statement of claim.

On 2nd February Mr Spinks's solicitors wrote to Mr Liff's solicitors as follows:

> 'Thank you for your letter of the 1st February. A copy of the Amending Order
> was not, however enclosed. In the particular circumstances of this case, whilst we
b > will continue our preparations, we shall need an Order amending the Writ, before
> we can accept service of the Statement of Claim. Thereafter, we would like a fixed
> date. We suggest that you should have the date vacated, and at the same time apply
> to the Clerk of the Lists for a new fixture. The sooner this is done the earlier the
> fixture is likely to be. Please keep us closely informed about this.'

c It was not until 6th February 1979 that they wrote:

> 'We have now seen Counsel on this matter. Counsel advises that as and when our
> client is properly joined in the action, we should make an early application to strike
> out your client's claim against our client, by reason of delay. This will be a
> Summons for the Judge in Chambers, supported by Affidavit. We shall therefore
> be proceeding accordingly.'
d
On 2nd March in response to a further letter they wrote:

> 'We accept service of the amended Statement of Claim, and enclose Defence,
> service of which please accept by post and acknowledge. We have served the
> Defence, as Counsel settled the same a little while ago, whilst we were waiting to
> hear from you, so that the Pleadings can be in proper order. We are however
e > forthwith applying to the Judge in Chambers to strike out the Plaintiff's claim, as
> we told you we would in our letter of the 6th February. The Summons and
> supporting affidavit will be served in the course of the next few posts.'

On 5th March they served Mr Spinks's defence, which ended with a plea that the
plaintiff's cause of action was statute-barred by s 2 of the Limitation Act 1939.
f   I take first the last point which we have been asked to consider, not because it comes
first in logic or in argument but because I find it the easiest to decide. This is the point
under s 2D of the Limitation Act 1939, introduced into that Act by s 1 of the Limitation
Act 1975: would it be equitable to allow Mr Liff's action to proceed against Mr Spinks
having regard to the provisions of s 2D and to prevent Mr Spinks from relying on the
expiry of the primary limitation period of three years provided by s 2A if it is otherwise
g available to him as a defence to this action? See the speech of Lord Diplock in *Walkley v
Precision Forgings Ltd*[1]. We have heard argument on a subsidiary point whether this
question should be decided on a summons to strike out the claim against the added
defendant, or at the trial, or after a separate action has been directed to be brought, and
we have been referred to the views expressed in *Firman v Ellis*[2], in *Walkley's case*[3],
especially per Lord Wilberforce, and in *Hattam v National Coal Board*[4].
h   In the course of what turned out to be a long hearing we were supplied with fresh
evidence to enable us to decide whether it was equitable to override the three years' time
limit and 'disapply' the provisions of s 2A. I have come to the conclusion that if Mr
Spinks can rely on the primary limitation period Mr Liff ought not to be allowed to
override it. If in refusing to make any order on para 1 of the summons the judge
exercised his discretion to grant to Mr Liff a discretionary limitation period on the
j material and submissions before him, on the material before us I would refuse to grant
Mr Liff that relief.

---

1   [1979] 2 All ER 548, [1979] 1 WLR 606
2   [1978] 2 All ER 851 at 863, 866, 869, [1978] QB 886 at 909, 913, 916
3   [1979] 2 All ER 548 at 556, [1979] 1 WLR 606 at 610
4   [1978] The Times, 27th October

I can state my reasons shortly. I am first not satisfied that the provisions of s 2A have prejudiced Mr Liff to any degree, so the condition required by s 2D(1)(a) for exercising　*a* the discretion is not fulfilled: compare *Walkley's* case[1]. Mr Liff has a cast-iron case against Mr Peasley. His claim may turn out to be beyond Mr Peasley's means to satisfy. We have affidavit evidence that Mr Peasley has only limited resources in capital and income, but we have no evidence to suggest that the MIB will not satisfy any judgment against Mr Peasley. We have evidence in a statement made to the police by Mr Spinks himself and in statements from other witnesses of matters which might prove some contributory　*b* negligence on Mr Spinks's part. Hence the MIB's request to Mr Liff to join him in his action. But we have seen the MIB agreement of 22nd November 1972 which does not 'relieve them of any responsibility to satisfy any judgment if there is any other known party upon whom a minimum of 1% contributory negligence can be proved', as stated in the Sun's letter dated 23rd January 1978, which I have read. This appears to be a misleading reference to cl 5 of the agreement, 'Conditions Precedent to Liability', and the　*c* following provision:

> '(1) M.I.B. shall not incur any liability under clause 2 of this Agreement unless . . . (c) *if so required by M.I.B.* and subject to full indemnity from M.I.B. as to costs the person bringing the proceedings has taken all reasonable steps to obtain judgment against all the persons liable in respect of the injury or death of the third party, and, in the event of such a person being a servant or agent, against his principal.'
>
> *d*

What Mr Liff or his legal advisers did or did not do *before* they were first required by the MIB to do anything is not a ground for relying on this condition; and counsel for Mr Peasley, and instructed on behalf of the Sun and the MIB, did not suggest any failure to take all reasonable steps to obtain judgment against Mr Spinks *after* being so required.

Counsel for Mr Peasley submitted that in 'having regard to all the cirumstances of the　*e* case', as required by s 2D(3), we should disregard the insurance position, or if we had regard to it we should disregard the presence of the MIB. I would consider it unrealistic and inequitable to disregard the insurance position or the important part of it occupied by the MIB. Ormrod and Geoffrey Lane LJJ both considered the insurance position in *Firman v Ellis*[2]. I would do the same, not least in an appeal which would never have come before the court but for the MIB. I make no criticism of their action in initiating the　*f* joinder of Mr Spinks, but I regard it as an important circumstance which tells against granting Mr Liff a discretionary limitation period.

On the view I take of the outcome of Mr Liff's claim against Mr Peasley and the MIB's liability to satisfy it, I need not consider any prejudice to Mr Spinks under s 2D(1)(b) or any other matters under s 2D(3).

I can go back to consider the question whether Mr Spinks was properly or improperly　*g* joined. I have no doubt that he was properly joined by Master Warren's order of 2nd March 1978. Whatever the defects in the form of that order, it was properly made, because when made it was not known whether Mr Spinks would plead s 2 of the 1939 Act, and it was properly made ex parte: see, e g, *The Puerto Acevedo*[3] and *Ashley v Taylor*[4].

But when Mr Spinks's solicitors were notified through his brother and his insurers of the joinder they did not enter a conditional appearance, or no appearance, and apply　*h* under RSC Order 12, r 8 to set aside or discharge Master Warren's order. That rule provides:

> '(1) A defendant to an action may at any time before entering an appearance therein, or, if he has entered a conditional appearance, within fourteen days after entering the appearance, apply to the Court for an order setting aside the writ or　*j*

1　[1979] 2 All ER 548, [1979] 1 WLR 606
2　[1978] 2 All ER 851 at 865, 868, [1978] QB 886 at 912, 916
3　[1978] 1 Lloyd's Rep 38
4　(1878) 10 Ch D 786

service of the writ, or notice of the writ, on him, or declaring that the writ or notice has not been duly served on him or discharging any order giving leave to serve the writ or notice on him out of the jurisdiction.

'(2) An application under this Rule must be made—(a) in an Admiralty action *in rem*, by motion; (b) in any other action in the Queen's Bench Division, by summons; (c) in any other action, by summons or motion.'

Instead, they entered an unconditional appearance and proceeded to serve a defence before intimating their intention to take out a summons to strike out the claim against them. The effect of entering an unconditional appearance is stated in the notes to RSC Ord 12, r 1 in the Supreme Court Practice[1], as follows:

'Where a defendant enters an ordinary appearance, without any condition or protest reserving his right to object to the irregularity of the writ or service, or the jurisdiction of the Court, he is debarred from raising an objection afterwards. The effect, therefore, of an ordinary or unconditional appearance is a waiver of irregularity, if any, as well as submission to the jurisdiction of the Court . . .

'On the other hand, the effect of an unconditional appearance is not a waiver of the defendant's right to dispute the plaintiff's claim, though it is sometimes a waiver of the right to raise a defence against the validity of the action.'

It is submitted by counsel for Mr Peasley and counsel for Mr Liff that by their action Mr Spinks's solicitors have waived his objection to his joinder, have lost his right to challenge it, and cannot now apply under RSC Ord 15, r 6 to have Mr Liff's claim against him struck out. The judge was therefore right to dismiss the second application. RSC Ord 15, r 6 provides:

'(1) No cause or matter shall be defeated by reason of the misjoinder or nonjoinder of any party, and the Court may in any cause or matter determine the issues or questions in dispute so far as they affect the rights and interests of the persons who are parties to the cause or matter.

'(2) At any stage of the proceedings in any cause or matter the Court may on such terms as it thinks just and either of its own motion or on application—(a) order any person who has been improperly or unnecessarily made a party or who has for any reason ceased to be a proper or necessary party, to cease to be a party . . .

'(3) An application by any person for an order under paragraph (2) adding him as a party must, except with the leave of the Court, be supported by an affidavit showing his interest in the matters in dispute in the cause or matter or, as the case may be, the question or issue to be determined as between him and any party to the cause or matter.'

On the wording of this rule we are asked on the one hand to say by a restrictive interpretation and application of it that Mr Spinks is not improperly or unnecessarily made a party to Mr Liff's action. On the other hand counsel for Mr Spinks asks us to hold that Mr Spinks is improperly or unnecessarily made a party or, on the suggestion of Brandon LJ, has ceased to be a party properly or necessarily joined. Counsel for Mr Spinks concedes that there is no other rule under which he can now get Mr Spinks out of Mr Liff's action but asks us to give the rule a sensible or even generous construction. So we have to decide whether Mr Spinks can now be said to be improperly before the court as a defendant, and to decide that question we have to examine the practice relating to defendants in Mr Spinks's situation and the reasons for the practice.

There is no doubt about the practice long established before the 1975 Act. It is not to permit a person to be made a defendant in an existing action at a time when he could have relied on a statute of limitation as barring the plaintiff from bringing a fresh action against him. The reason for this practice, or rather the way in which this practice is

---

1   Supreme Court Practice 1979, vol 1, pp 99–100, paras 12/1/3–12/1/4

justified or the legal basis on which it is rested, is, curiously more doubtful. There appear
to be two alternative bases: (1) the action against the added defendant relates back to the *a*
date of the original writ, the plaintiff is deemed to have begun his action against the
defendant when he began it against the original defendant, and so the defendant is
deprived of his right to rely on the statute of limitations; (2) the action against the added
defendant is begun at the date of the amendment joining him in the action, and so he can
rely on the statute as barring the plaintiff from suing him. In most cases it will not
matter which of the two possible dates is regarded as the date of the commencement of *b*
the action brought against the added defendant. If he applies to set aside the order
joining him as co-defendant, he will succeed, either because he would be deprived of his
right to rely on the statute if the earlier date were preferred or because he would be able
to rely on the statute and defeat the plaintiff's claim if the later date were preferred. But
in this case the added defendant has elected to plead the statute in answer to the
plaintiff's claim before challenging the plaintiff's right to make him a defendant. Can *c*
he at that later stage allege that his joinder, though properly made in the first instance,
is improper, only if he can successfully rely on the statute, because he was not sued until
the later date, so that it would be pointless and unnecessary that he should be, or remain,
a defendant? But if he cannot rely on the statute because he is deemed to have been sued
from the earlier date, how can he then deny that he is, and remains, a proper and
necessary party to the action?   *d*
   There is a formidable line of authority which appears to rest the practice on relating
the introduction of a new defendant, or a new plaintiff, or a new cause of action, into an
existing action back to the date when that action first began. And that amendments
relate back to the date of the claim they amend is a principle not confined to statutes of
limitation: see *Sneade v Wotherton Barytes and Lead Mining Co*[1] per Lord Collins MR.
   There are, however, at least three decisions, one at first instance, one in this court and *e*
one in the House of Lords, which decide or seem to decide that an action is not brought
against a new defendant (whatever may be the date for a new plaintiff or a new cause of
action) until he is brought into the action by amendment; and the later date derives
support from the wording of some rules and from some judgments in this court.
   It was by 1887 the settled rule of practice that amendments were not admissible when
they prejudiced the rights of the opposite party as existing on the date of such *f*
amendments. So said Lord Esher MR in *Weldon v Neal*[2], where this court, consisting of
Lord Esher MR and Lindley and Lopes LJJ, affirmed a decision of the Divisional Court
striking out paragraphs adding to a statement of claim fresh causes of action because the
amendments would deprive the defendant of the benefit of the statute of limitations.
   In *Mabro v Eagle Star and British Dominions Insurance Co Ltd*[3] this court upheld a refusal
to join a plaintiff on the same ground. Scrutton LJ[4] restated that practice and that basis *g*
of it:

   'In my experience the Court has always refused to allow a party or a cause of
   action to be added where, if it were allowed, the defence of the Statute of Limitations
   would be defeated. The Court has never treated it as just to deprive a defendant of
   a legal defence.'
                                                                                        h
And Greer LJ[5] made it clear that—

   'The objection to joining [the new plaintiff] was that if he were joined and
   treated as a plaintiff from the time the writ was issued the defendants would be
   deprived of the benefit of the Statute of Limitations.'
                                                                                        j

1   [1904] 1 KB 295 at 297
2   (1887) 19 QBD 394 at 398
3   [1932] 1 KB 485, [1932] All ER Rep 411
4   [1932] 1 KB 485 at 487, [1932] All ER Rep 411 at 412
5   [1932] 1 KB 485 at 489, [1932] All ER Rep 411 at 413

The decision concerned a new plaintiff, but not only did Scrutton LJ state the rule as
a covering any new party or cause of action but he expressly disapproved the decision in
Challinor v Roder[1] that a new defendant could be joined after the statute had run, and
approved the opinion of Grove J that he could not be so joined and deprived of the
benefit of the statute.

In *Davies v Elsby Brothers Ltd*[2] this court followed the principle of *Mabro's* case[3] and
applied it to the substitution of a defendant, Pearce LJ[4] in a rather obscure passage
b considering the purpose of the addition or substitution of a new defendant to be to
deprive him of the benefit of the statute.

This 'long line of authority' was referred to by Lord Denning MR and by Russell LJ in
Mitchell v Harris Engineering Co Ltd[5] with comments which suggest it must be considered
in the light of the rules of court, to which I shall return.

Finally, *Mabro's* case[3], 'the reasoning which appears to underline [quaere 'underlie']' it
c and the principle enunciated in it, were approved and applied to dismiss applications to
join new defendants by Mackenna J and a majority of this court, after a consideration of
all the relevant rules, in *Lucy v Henley's Telegraph Works Co Ltd*[6]. Megaw LJ, with whose
judgment Edmund Davies LJ agreed, said[7]:

d 'I am unaware of any case in which leave to amend a writ has been given in such
circumstances; namely, where the joinder of a new defendant would be calculated
to defeat a right as to limitation which he would have had if an action were to be
brought by the plaintiff against him alone. As I understand it, *Mabro's case*[3] . . . is
authority for the proposition that it cannot be done. That case was concerned with
an application to amend the writ so as to join a plaintiff. It was held that leave
would not be granted where the effect would be to prevent the defendant from
e relying on the Statute of Limitations. The same principle applies in relation to the
joinder of a defendant. Where, as here, a direct action against a proposed defendant
can be defeated by a plea of limitation, the plaintiff cannot escape that consequence
by seeking to join the proposed defendant as a party in pre-existing proceedings
. . . [An] amendment to add a completely new and different defendant is not
permissible where a relevant period of limitation affecting the proposed defendant
f has expired.'

In *The Puerto Acevedo*[8] Lord Denning MR reiterated his dissenting view in *Lucy's* case[9]
and other cases[10] that the practice had changed since *Mabro's* case[3] was decided, and all
three members of this court gave leave to a plaintiff to join a defendant ex parte, Bridge
g LJ expressly preserving the new defendant's right to apply to set the joinder aside.

In *Gawthrop v Boulton*[11] Walton J felt able to hold, and I read from the headnote—

'That when leave to join an additional defendant to an existing action was given,
the joinder took effect as from the date when the order for joinder was stamped in

h

---

1   (1885) 1 TLR 527
2   [1960] 3 All ER 672, [1961] 1 WLR 170
3   [1932] 1 KB 485, [1932] All ER Rep 411
4   [1960] 3 All ER 672 at 674, [1961] 1 WLR 170 at 173
5   [1967] 2 All ER 682 at 685, 687–688, [1967] 2 QB 703 at 717, 721
6   [1969] 3 All ER 456 at 459, 463, 468–469, [1970] 1 QB 393 at 399, 405, 411–412
7   [1969] 3 All ER 456 at 468–469, [1970] 1 QB 393 at 411–412
8   [1978] 1 Lloyd's Rep 38
9   [1969] 3 All ER 456, [1970] 1 QB 393
10 See for example *Sterman v E W & J W Moore* [1970] 1 All ER 581 at 584–585, [1970] 1 QB 596
    at 604
11 [1979] 1 WLR 268 at 269

the Central Office and had no retrospective effect back to the date of issue of the writ; and that the joinder of K as a defendant would not therefore prejudice any defence which K might have under the Limitation Act 1939 . . .'

He accordingly added K as a defendant. In an interesting judgment he based his decision on principle and a decision of this court in *Seabridge v H Cox & Sons (Plant Hire) Ltd*[1]. He considered that a later decision of this court in *Braniff v Holland & Hannen and Cubitts (Southern) Ltd*[2] left open the question whether the Statute of Limitation ceased to run against an additional defendant from the date of the issue of the writ or from the date when he is added as a party, and he distinguished the *Mabro*[3] and *Lucy*[4] cases.

In *Seabridge's* case[5] this court held—

'allowing the appeal, that, on the construction of the new rule 8(4) of Ord. 15, a writ amended in the prescribed manner by being taken to the central office, filed and stamped, took effect against the added defendant at the moment when it was stamped at the central office; that under Ord. 15, r. 8(2) once the writ was amended the rules as to service applied as against the added defendant as they did to an original defendant on the issue of a writ, so that a plaintiff had 12 months from the date when the amendment was made within which to serve the added defendant; and that, accordingly, since the amendment had been made within 3 years of the accident, the service was regular and the writs were not statute-barred.'

By RSC Ord 15, r 8:

'(1) Where an order is made under rule 6 the writ by which the action in question was begun must be amended accordingly and must be endorsed with—(a) a reference to the order in pursuance of which the amendment is made, and (b) the date on which the amendment is made; and the amendment must be made within such period as may be specified in the order or, if no period is so specified, within 14 days after the making of the order.

'(2) Where by an order under rule 6 a person is to be made a defendant, the rules as to service of a writ of summons shall apply accordingly to service of the amended writ on him, but before serving the writ on him the person on whose application the order was made must procure the order to be noted in the cause book . . .

'(4) Where by an order under rule 6 or 7 a person is to be added as a party or is to be made a party in substitution for some other party, that party shall not become a party until—(a) where the order is made under rule 6 the writ has been amended in relation to him under this rule and (if he is a defendant) has been served on him . . . and where by virtue of the foregoing provision a person becomes a party in substitution for some other party, all things done in the course of the proceedings before the making of the order shall have effect in relation to the new party as they had in relation to the old, except that entry of appearance by the old party shall not dispense with entry of appearance by the new.'

In that case the amended writ was stamped in the central office on the very day when the three year limitation period expired, but it was not served on the added defendant until a few days later. The court was referred to the old rule, RSC Ord 16, r 11, which had provided that the proceedings against a party added should 'be deemed to have begun only on the service of such writ', and CCR Ord 15, r 2 which was in the same

1   [1968] 1 All ER 570, [1968] 2 QB 46
2   [1969] 3 All ER 959, [1969] 1 WLR 1533
3   [1932] 1 KB 485, [1932] All ER Rep 411
4   [1969] 3 All ER 456, [1970] 1 QB 393
5   [1968] 2 QB 46 at 46–47

terms. (Compare *Mitchell's* case[1] per Russell LJ.) *Mabro's*[2], *Mitchell's*[3] and *Davies's*[4] cases

a were all cited. But this court held that the action against the added defendant was begun in time because the writ had been amended in time, though not served in time. The whole argument was addressed to the question whether the writ dated from when the defendant was added or from when he was served. It was not argued that it dated from the issue of the original writ and that possibility was not referred to in the judgment of Lord Denning MR with which Diplock and Salmon LJJ agreed. The decision rested

b simply on the wording of the rule and the fact that the limitation period had not expired at the date of the amendment. As a result of the decision, CCR Ord 15, r 2, was amended to read as follows:

> *c* 'Where any person is added or substituted as defendant, except under Rule 11 of this Order, the amended originating process shall be served on the added or substituted defendant according to the Rules applicable to the service of the originating process, and the proceedings as against him shall be deemed to have begun on the date of the amendment.'

Rule 11 is not without interest, for it reads:

> *d* 'Where a person other than the defendant appears on the return day and admits that he is the person whom the plaintiff intended to sue, or ought to have sued, he may, if the plaintiff consents, be substituted for the defendant, and the proceedings shall continue as if he had originally been made defendant.'

In *Braniff's* case[5] this court affirmed a judge's order setting aside a writ and service, where the master had granted an extension of time for amending the writ to add a defendant so as to keep alive or create a cause of action otherwise barred by the Limitation

e Act.

In the leading judgment, with which Davies LJ agreed, Widgery LJ stated that the provisions of RSC Ord 20, r 5, including specific exemptions enabling the court to allow amendments ' after any relevant period of limitation current at the date of issue of the writ has expired', did not mean that in general there was any relaxation of the principle in *Weldon v Neal*[6]. But he went on to follow *Seabridge's* case[7] in holding that the amended

f writ takes effect against the added defendant only when the amendment is completed in accordance with RSC Ord 15, r 8. From that he concluded that there was no writ available against the added defendant, but he left open what he appears to have regarded as a separate question, whether there was no action brought against the added defendant until the final amendment of the writ.

Cross LJ, with whom also Davies LJ agreed, reserved the question whether the

g amendment of the writ by adding the second defendant could relate back to the date of the issue of the writ against the first defendant, but on the assumption that it did relate back thought the master wrong and the judge right.

In *Lucy's* case[8] this court held, by a majority, that writs in actions requiring leave within s 1(1) of the Limitation Act 1963, which had not been 'brought before the end of the period of twelve months from the date on which the deceased died' as required by

h s 3(4) of the Act, could not be amended by adding another defendant as the joinder would deprive the added defendant of the defence afforded by s 3(4). *Mabro's*[2], *Davies's*[4]

---

j
1   [1967] 2 All ER 682 at 687, [1967] 2 QB 703 at 711, 720
2   [1932] 1 KB 485, [1932] All ER 411
3   [1967] 2 All ER 682, [1967] 2 QB 703
4   [1960] 3 All ER 672, [1961] 1 WLR 170
5   [1969] 3 All ER 959, [1969] 1 WLR 1533
6   (1887) 19 QBD 394
7   [1968] 1 All ER 570, [1968] 2 QB 46
8   [1969] 3 All ER 456, [1970] 1 QB 393

and *Seabridge's*[1] cases were cited, and, as I have said earlier, *Mabro's* case[2] was approved and followed, unaffected by the provisions of RSC Ord 15, r 6, and Ord 20, r 5, and *a* (though the judgments do not refer to it) by the decision in *Seabridge's* case[1].

I regret that I am unable to reconcile *Seabridge's*[1] and *Lucy's*[3] cases in the way suggested by Walton J. The decision in *Seabridge's* case[1] is not inconsistent with the decision in *Lucy's* case[3], but their ratios are.

Again I find it difficult to see any distinction in principle between adding a plaintiff or a defendant, or a cause of action, when deciding the question when an action is brought *b* or begun. But were it not for the authorities to which I have referred I would have no difficulty in holding that the wording of RSC Ord 15, r 8 determines that question as it was decided in *Seabridge's*[1] and *Gawthrop's*[4] cases and regulates the practice concerning the joinder of defendants in a manner which may distinguish the practice concerning the joinder of plaintiffs or causes of action.

The settled practice is, in my judgment, the important matter, not the legal basis of it, *c* which in most cases is of no relevance. But if that basis is of importance there is, I think, high, if not overriding, authority for the opinion that for the purpose of considering whether an action is statute-barred it is brought or begun against an additional defendant at the date of his being brought into it. In the middle of the last century, the House of Lords (per Lord Cottenham LC and Lord Brougham) had twice to consider whether persons who had been added by an order of the court as defendants to a bill for tithes filed *d* within one year after the date fixed by s 3 of the Tithes Act 1832 were defendants in a suit or action commenced within that time.

On the first occasion Lord Cottenham LC expressed strong doubts about the question whether they could not claim the benefit of s 3, without deciding it: see *Plowden v Thorpe*[5]. On the second they decided that the suit, as against such defendants, must be taken to have commenced at the date at which they were actually introduced into the *e* bill; that they could not, by relation backwards be treated as defendants to the original bill, and that they were consequently entitled to the protection of the provisions of the statute. In *Byron v Cooper*[6] Lord Brougham said:

'The first miscarriage in the Court below, however, was to consider the whole defendants to the suit, the whole nine Appellants, as excluded from the operation of the Act. The ground of this opinion was that the bill being originally filed before *f* the 16th August 1833, and the four last-named Appellants being, under an order of the Court of Exchequer, made defendants to that same bill, were as much excluded by the 3d section of the Act as if they had been made originally defendants to the bill filed on the 5th of August, 1833. This is as great and as manifest an error as could well be committed. It is contrary to the whole nature and constitution of a tithe suit, and to the very species of rights which come in question in such a suit. There *g* is no privity whatever between the different defendants. There could be no objection taken for the omission of one or more by the others being made parties to the bill. The defences may be quite separate, and are necessarily quite independent one of the other. One defence may be of a totally different kind from the others. One defendant or class of defendants may set up a former modus; one defendant or class of defendants may set up a composition real, which covers his land and none *h* other in the parish. One may set up a defence *de non decimando*, and no modus at all, as showing that his lands were abbey lands. In short, it is quite clear that each party

---

1 [1968] 1 All ER 570, [1968] 2 QB 46
2 [1932] 1 KB 485, [1932] All ER Rep 411
3 [1969] 3 All ER 456, [1970] 1 QB 393
4 [1978] 3 All ER 615, [1979] 1 WLR 268
5 (1840) 7 Cl & Fin 137 at 164, 7 ER 1019 at 1030
6 (1844) 11 Cl & Fin 556 at 579–580, 8 ER 1212 at 1221

j

a may stand in a different relation towards the plaintiff and towards the suit, from all his co-defendants. No more need be said to prove how erroneous is the view taken of the case below, whereby this is considered as one suit and one defence. The parson is permitted to add new defendants to his amended bill, in order to save delay and expense; but each defendant so added is to be considered as sued by the proceeding which makes him a defendant, and the date of his being added is the date of the suit's commencement *quoad* him; consequently the four last-named and

b last-added defendants in this case were only sued in November 1834, and *quoad* them the bill and the suit bear the date of November 1834. They do not fall, therefore, within the description of the 3d section of the statute. They are not defendants, to use the words of that statute, "in a suit or action commenced within one year" after the 16th of August 1832, being the last day of the Session in which the Act passed . . . As against them, therefore, the bill should have been at once

c dismissed, and with costs.'

I approach and apply that case with caution, but counsel for Mr Peasley has not succeeded in persuading me that there was anything in the peculiarities of a tithe suit or in the rules of procedure and practice of the 1840's which weakens the authority of that decision for the proposition ·which it appears to support that when a defendant has a

d separate defence he should not be added after the relevant period of limitation has expired because the date of his being added to a suit commenced in time is the date of the suit's commencement quoad him. That proposition seems to me to accord with what is restated in RSC Ord 15, r 8(4).

How then can effect be given in this case to the practice that a person in Mr Spinks's position should not be added by the court to defend himself against a claim brought against another in good time but not against him until the time for suing him has long

e run out?

In none of the cases in which the practice of protecting a defendant has operated has it been necessary for the court to decide when the action is brought or commenced or when or how the defendant must claim the protection of the practice. Plaintiffs have been allowed to correct their mistakes, defendants have been allowed to set aside service

f of writs under RSC Ord 12, rr 7 and 8, but never has a defendant been deprived of the protection. That he may be deprived by exceptional circumstances other than those provided for by RSC Ord 20, r 5, is, I think, still a minority view, a minority view which has distinguished support (see the references given in the Supreme Court Practice[1]) and which is itself based on the need to relax the doctrine of relation back. I would apply to the present case the two sentences from Rees J's judgment in *Pheasant v Smith*[2] cited by Lord Denning MR in *Firman v Ellis*[3]:

g

'. . . on the present state of the authorities, I am not satisfied that power exists to add a defendant after a limitation period has expired . . . [and] even if the power did exist, I am not satisfied that it should be exercised otherwise than in exceptional circumstances, and I can find no such circumstances in the present case.'

h If free to do so I would hold that Mr Spinks can plead the Limitation Act 1939 successfully because Mr Liff's action had not been brought against him until he was joined.

It would then be a waste of time to let the action against him go to trial provided he made clear his intention to plead the statute. Unless there were some special reason, I would not think it right to do what Walton J did in *Gawthrop v Boulton*[4] and join him as

j a defendant but would dismiss the action against him at the earliest opportunity:

1 1979, vol 1, p 346, para 20/5–8/7
2 (11th February 1974) unreported
3 [1978] 2 All ER 851 at 861, [1978] QB 886 at 907
4 [1978] 3 All ER 615, [1979] 1 WLR 268

compare *Riches v Director of Public Prosecutions*[1], where one of the grounds on which an action was struck out as vexatious and an abuse of the process of the court was that it was bound to be defeated by a plea of the Limitation Act.

If, however, it was rightly conceded that Mr Spinks must bring himself within RSC Ord 15, r 6, I would hold that Mr Spinks has been improperly and/or unnecessarily made a party, or has by reason of his pleaded defence of s 2 of the Limitation Act 1939 ceased to be a proper or necessary party, and order him to cease to be a party under Ord 15, r 6(2)(*a*).

But that is the order which I would make if I am compelled by the weight of authority to hold that the action was brought against Mr Spinks when brought against Mr Peasley.

I am not satisfied that the joinder of Mr Spinks was an irregularity within RSC Ord 2, r 1, to which objection can only be taken under Ord 2, r 2, or a failure to comply with the rules, or made without jurisdiction; I am satisfied that by submitting to the jurisdiction there has been no waiver of the benefit accrued to him by lapse of the primary limitation period, notwithstanding the steps which his legal advisers took and their failure to apply to set the joinder aside. It is true that that was the procedure adopted in most if not all of the cases where a defendant has succeeded in defeating such a joinder. But if he was sued by a separate writ he could choose whether to apply to set it aside or to enter an appearance and serve a defence pleading the statute. An unconditional appearance would not then waive his right to plead the statute and be dismissed from the action. There would be nothing like the assent provided for by CCR Ord 15, r 11. It would be unjust, in my judgment, if he should be in a worse position when he has lost his right to defend the claim if allowed to go on against him simply because his legal advisers may have made a procedural slip or have chosen to pursue his right to the benefit of the statute by a less summary or inexpensive method than is open to them under the rules. In this case of all cases, where the plaintiff has made no mistake in not suing a second defendant initially, and has only sought to add him at the instance of a stranger to the action, it would be ridiculous to depart from the established practice of protecting a person in Mr Spinks's position by permitting the plaintiff to take advantage of a procedural error which was made many years later and has prejudiced no one.

I am satisfied that it is open to Mr Spinks's advisers to apply now under RSC Ord 15, r 6, on a properly liberal construction of its wording to make an order under r 6(2)(*a*) whatever the orthodox legal basis for protecting a person joined as Mr Spinks was.

Having had the privilege of reading the draft of the judgment which Brandon LJ is about to deliver, I am convinced, more especially by his comments on the assumption underlying RSC Ord 20, r 5, that we should allow the appeal on this ground alone without expressing any final opinion on the true foundation for the practice of protecting persons in Mr Spinks's position.

I would allow the appeal and order that Mr Spinks ceases to be a party.

I should add that I would not dismiss the action against him for want of prosecution. That ground of application, as counsel for Mr Spinks submitted, highlights the absurdity of relating the action against Mr Spinks back to the beginning of the action against Mr Peasley. For if deemed to have started his action against Mr Spinks in 1975, Mr Liff has indeed been dilatory in prosecuting it by taking no step at all until 1978, yet he would be in a stronger position to resist its dismissal than a plaintiff who had in fact sued both in 1975.

BRANDON LJ. I agree with Stephenson LJ that this is not a case in which the court should exercise its discretionary power under s 2D of the Limitation Act 1939, as amended, to extend the primary period of limitation of three years prescribed by s 2A(4)(*a*). It follows that the case must be approached on the footing that the time allowed to the plaintiff for beginning an action against Mr Spinks in respect of the

---

1   [1973] 2 All ER 935, [1973] 1 WLR 1019

collision expired in October 1976 long before the writ was amended so as to add Mr
a Spinks as defendant.

It is an established rule of practice that the court will not allow a person to be added as
defendant to an existing action if the claim sought to be made against him is already
statute-barred and he desires to rely on that circumstance as a defence to the claim.
Alternatively, if the court has allowed such addition to be made ex parte in the first place,
it will not, on objection then being taken by the person added, allow the addition to
b stand. I shall refer to that established rule of practice as 'the rule of practice'.

There are two alternative bases on which the rule of practice can be justified. The first
basis is that, if the addition were allowed, it would relate back so that the action would
be deemed to have been begun as against the person added, not on the date of
amendment, but on the date of the original writ; that the effect of such relation back
would be to deprive the person added of an accrued defence to the claim on the ground
c that it was statute-barred; and that this would be unjust to that person. I shall refer to
this first basis of the rule of practice as the 'relation back' theory.

The second and alternative basis for the rule is that, where a person is added as
defendant in an existing action, the action is only deemed to have been begun as against
him on the date of amendment of the writ; that the defence that the claim is statute-
barred therefore remains available to him; and that, since such defence affords a complete
d answer to the claim, it would serve no useful purpose to allow the addition to be made.
I shall refer to this second and alternative basis of the rule of practice as the 'no useful
purpose' theory.

An application by a plaintiff for leave to add a person as defendant in an existing action
is, or should ordinarily, be made ex parte under RSC Ord 15, r 6(2)(*b*). If the application
is allowed, the writ must then be amended under r 8(1), and served on the person added
e under r 8(2) of the same order. If the person added as defendant, having had the
amended writ served on him, objects to being added on the ground that the claim against
him was already statute-barred before the writ was amended, the ordinary practice is for
him to enter a conditional appearance under RSC Ord 12, r 7, and then to apply to set
aside the amended writ and the service of it on him under Ord 12, r 8. Then, if he
establishes that the claim against him was statute-barred before the writ was amended,
f he is entitled as of right, in accordance with the rule of practice, to the relief for which
he has asked, unless the case is of the special kind covered by RSC Ord 20, r 5(3).

Provided that the person added as defendant follows the ordinary practice described
above, he gets the benefit of the rule of practice, and it is not material to consider which
of the two alternative bases for that rule, that is to say the 'relation back' theory on the one
hand or the 'no useful purpose' theory on the other, is the true one. In the present case,
g however, the solicitors acting for Mr Spinks did not follow the ordinary practice. Instead,
after they had accepted service on him of the amended writ, they entered an
unconditional appearance in the action on his behalf, and later, after accepting service of
the amended statement of claim, they served a defence containing a plea that the claim
against him was statute-barred.

It was contended for the plaintiff and the original defendant, Mr Peasley, that, because
h the solicitors for Mr Spinks dealt with the matter in this way, he had now lost his right
either (a) to have the addition of him as defendant set aside or otherwise got rid of, or (b)
to rely on the defence that the claim against him was statute-barred.

This contention was based on two propositions. The first proposition was that, because
the solicitors for Mr Spinks had entered an unconditional appearance on his behalf,
instead of entering a conditional appearance and then applying to set aside the amended
j writ and service of it, it was now too late for him to contend that he should not have been
added as defendant in the first place. The second proposition was that, since the true
basis of the rule of practice was the 'relation back' theory, the action must now be deemed
to have been begun as against Mr Spinks on the date of the original writ; it must be
deemed therefore to have been begun in time, so that the plea that the action was statute-
barred was no longer available to him.

I should regard it as very unjust if these consequences should flow from what, if the argument is correct, was no more than a procedural error on the part of the solicitors for Mr Spinks. The solution in that case might be to allow Mr Spinks to amend his appearance so as to make it conditional instead of unconditional and to apply belatedly to set aside. Leaving aside that possible solution, however, the question to be considered is whether the argument relied on for the plaintiff and the original defendant is correct or not.

I consider, first, whether, because the solicitors for Mr Spinks entered an unconditional appearance on his behalf, he is now precluded from contending that he should not have been added as defendant in the first place. The argument that he was so precluded was put in two ways. It was said, first, that the entry of an unconditional appearance operated as a waiver of any right to have the addition set aside. It was said, secondly, that, apart from RSC Ord 12, rr 7 and 8, there was no rule of court under which an application to set aside, or otherwise get rid of, the addition could now be made by Mr Spinks or allowed by the court.

I do not accept either of these arguments. With regard to the first argument, the entry of an unconditional appearance operates, no doubt, as a waiver of any irregularity in the process of which the person entering it was, or should have been, aware. In my view, however, the addition of a person as defendant contrary to the rule of practice is not, and should not be treated as being, a mere irregularity. Such addition involves rather, if the 'relation back' theory is correct, the taking away of an accrued right of defence, and the right to complain of it cannot therefore be waived in such a manner. With regard to the second argument, I think that there is another rule of court, besides RSC Ord 12, rr 7 and 8, under which an application to get rid of the addition can be made by Mr Spinks and allowed by the court. That rule is RSC Ord 15, r 6(2)(a), which provides:

'At any stage of the proceedings in any cause or matter the court may on such terms as it thinks just either of its own motion or on application—(a) order any person who has been improperly or unnecessarily made a party or who has for any reason ceased to be a proper or necessary party, to cease to be a party . . .'

In my view, since the claim against Mr Spinks was already statute-barred before he was added as defendant, and he desired to rely on that circumstance as a defence to the claim, he is a person who has been improperly made a party within the meaning of RSC Ord 15, r 6(2)(a) above; alternatively, if he was properly made a party on the ex parte application, because it was not then known for certain whether he wished to rely on the claim being statute-barred, then, as soon as it became apparent that he did wish to rely on that defence, he ceased to be a proper party within the meaning of that rule. Either way an order that he cease to be a party should be made.

If the view about RSC Ord 15, r 6(2)(a), which I have just expressed is correct, it is sufficient to dispose of this case, and it becomes unnecessary to go on to consider the correctness of the second limb of the argument for the plaintiff and the original defendant based on the 'relation back' theory. Since the matter was argued at some length before us, however, I think that I should express some provisional views on it.

The crucial question here is this: when the original writ in an action is amended by adding a person as defendant, on what date is the action deemed to have been begun, for the purposes of any relevant statute of limitation, as against the person added? Is it the date of the original writ or is it the date of the amendment?

This problem arises not only in relation to amendments involving the addition of a person as defendant. It also arises in relation to amendments involving the addition of a person as plaintiff or the addition of a new cause of action. It does not, however, follow necessarily from this that the problem falls to be resolved in the same way in all three cases, although one might well expect this to be so.

Disregarding for the moment the case law on the subject, I should have thought that, if a relevant rule of court prescribed at what time an action is to be deemed to have been *a* begun as against a person added as defendant, that is the time which should be taken for the purpose of answering the question posed above.

In fact the relevant rules of court, both in the High Court and the county court do, as I understand them, prescribe in terms the time at which an action is to be deemed to have been begun as against a person added as defendant.

In the High Court RSC Ord 15, r 8(4), provides:

b 'Where by an order under rule 6 or 7 a person is to be added as a party or is to be made a party in substitution for some other party, that person shall not become a party until—(*a*) where the order is made under rule 6, the writ has been amended in relation to him under this rule and (if he is a defendant) has been served on him . . .'

In the county court, CCR Ord 15, r 2, provides:

c 'Where any person is added or substituted as defendant, except under Rule 11 of this Order, the amended originating process shall be served on the added or substituted defendant . . . and the proceedings as against him shall be deemed to have been begun on the date of amendment.'

The exception under CCR Ord 15, r 11, referred to in this rule, is not directly relevant for *d* present purposes, although it is, as Stephenson LJ has said, not without interest.

Both these rules, in their present form, are of comparatively recent origin. The earlier High Court rule, then RSC Ord 16, r 11, provided that proceedings should be deemed to have been begun as against a person added as defendant on the date of service of the amended writ. The earlier county court rule contained a similar provision.

It was held by this court in *Seabridge v H Cox & Sons (Plant Hire) Ltd*[1] that the effect of *e* the present High Court Rule, RSC Ord 15, r 8(4)(*a*), set out above, is that, where a person is added as defendant, the action is deemed to have been begun as against him on the date of amendment of the writ, and not, as under the earlier High Court rule, then RSC Ord 16, r 11, on the date of service of the amended writ on him. The present county court rule, CCR Ord 15, r 2, is a revised version of the earlier rule, designed to bring the position in the county court into line with the position in the High Court as it was *f* declared to be in *Seabridge v H Cox & Sons (Plant Hire) Ltd*[1]. There are, perhaps, difficulties about the interpretation put on the present High Court rule in that case. Since we are bound by it, however, no purpose would be served by referring to them.

It seems to me that the 'relation back' theory, which involves that the date on which an action is deemed to have been begun as against a person added as a defendant is the date of the original writ, is inconsistent with the rules of court, both in the High Court *g* and the county court, to which I have just referred. By contrast it seems to me that the 'no useful purpose' theory, which involves that the date on which an action is deemed to have been begun as against a person added as a defendant is the date of amendment of the writ, is consistent with those rules. If it were permissible, therefore, to choose between the two theories by reference to the relevant rules of court alone, without regard to the case law on the subject, I should have no hesitation in concluding that the 'no useful *h* purpose' theory was the correct one.

Much of the case law, however, though by no means all, supports the opposite conclusion. The 'relation back' theory was treated as the true basis of the rule of practice by this court in *Mabro v Eagle Star and British Dominions Insurance Co Ltd*[2] (a case of adding a plaintiff) and again in *Lucy v W T Henley's Telegraph Works Co Ltd*[3] (a case, like the

j

---

1   [1968] 1 All ER 570, [1968] 2 QB 46
2   [1932] 1 KB 485, [1932] All ER Rep 411
3   [1969] 3 All ER 456, [1970] 1 QB 393

present one, of adding a defendant). The 'relation back' theory is also supported, in relation to adding a new cause of action, by *Weldon v Neal*[1], another decision of this court. *a*

There are other cases in this court, however, the judgments in which support, or tend to support, the 'no useful purpose' theory rather than the 'relation back' theory. These are *Mitchell v Harris Engineering Co Ltd*[2] (see the judgment of Russell LJ) and *Seabridge v H Cox & Sons (Plant Hire) Ltd*[3]. The latter case was applied at first instance in *Gawthrop v Boulton*[4].

Other relevant cases in this court are *Davies v Elsby Brothers Ltd*[5], in which the judgment *b* of Pearce LJ seems to lend some support to either theory in turn, and *Braniff v Holland & Hannen and Cubitts (Southern) Ltd*[6], in which the question whether the 'relation back' theory was correct was expressly left open.

Finally I would refer to *Byron v Cooper*[7], a decision of the House of Lords which, though it relates to a special statute and an earlier mode of procedure, appears to me to be inconsistent, in principle, with the 'relation back' theory. *c*

There is one other matter to be mentioned. The Rule Committee, in framing the new provisions of the present RSC Ord 20, r 5, appears to have assumed that the 'relation back' theory was the true basis of the rule of practice. I say that because paras (2), (3), (4) and (5) of r 5 are designed to allow amendments in certain circumstances which would or might otherwise infringe the rule of practice, and these paragraphs would not serve their intended purpose of defeating a defence of time-bar if the amendments allowed under *d* them did not relate back to the date of the original writ but only took effect from the date of amendment. The fact that the Rule Committee made that assumption is clearly a matter of some weight to be taken into account. It cannot, however, of itself be decisive of the question under discussion.

There is, in my view, a high degree of artificiality and unreality about the 'relation back' theory. There is no reason to quarrel with the general proposition that an *e* amendment of a writ or a pleading relates back to the original date of the document amended, as stated by Lord Collins MR in *Sneade v Wotherton Barytes and Lead Mining Co*[8]. This seems to me to be an entirely sensible proposition so long as the amendment concerned does not involve the addition of a new party, either as plaintiff or defendant, or the raising of a new cause of action, but involves only the modification, by addition, deletion or substitution, of pleas or averments made between existing parties in respect *f* of a cause or causes of action already raised. Where, however, the amendment concerned involves the addition of a new party or the raising of a new cause of action, it appears to me to be unrealistic and contrary to the common sense of the matter to treat it as relating back in the same way.

The artificiality and unreality of the 'relation back' theory to which I have just referred cannot be more forcibly illustrated than by the nature of the relief asked for in the *g* alternative by Mr Spinks in his amended summons in this case. In para 3 he asks for an order that the action against him be dismissed for want of prosecution. He asks for that order on the footing that, if the action against him is to be treated as having been begun on the date of the original writ, that is to say, 1st August 1975, then the plaintiff has been guilty of inexcusable delay over about 3½ years in prosecuting such action. To such absurdities do artificiality and unreality inevitably lead. *h*

1   (1887) 19 QBD 394
2   [1967] 2 All ER 682 at 687, [1967] 2 QB 703 at 720
3   [1968] 1 All ER 570, [1968] 2 QB 46
4   [1978] 3 All ER 615, [1979] 1 WLR 268
5   [1960] 3 All ER 672 at 674, [1961] 1 WLR 170 at 173
6   [1969] 3 All ER 959, [1969] 1 WLR 1533
7   (1844) 11 Cl & Fin 556, 8 ER 1212
8   [1904] 1 KB 295 at 297

j

The 'relation back' theory also creates problems in cases where there is an arguable
a question whether the claim against the person added or sought to be added as defendant
is statute-barred or not. Such a question may arise where there is doubt about the date on
which the relevant cause of action arose, or an issue whether the plaintiff can rely on
suspension or interruption of the relevant period of limitation on one ground or another.
In such cases it will not usually be possible to resolve the question whether the claim is
statute-barred or not on the hearing of the ex parte application by the plaintiff to add the
b new defendant, or, if leave is then given, on the hearing of the subsequent inter partes
application by the new defendant to set aside the order by which he was added. It will
instead be necessary to have pleadings and discovery on the question and a proper trial of
it. If the 'relation back' theory applies, and no special order is made, the addition of the
new defendant will of itself take away his right to rely on the time bar, and so make the
question whether he would, before such addition, have been entitled to rely on it or not
c a purely academic question. In order to get over this difficulty the order giving leave to
add the new defendant will have to be made on special terms, namely that the addition
shall not relate back but shall take effect from the date of amendment of the writ only.
These considerations again point to the inappropriateness of treating amendments which
involve the addition of a new party or the raising of a new cause of action as relating back.

This court is undoubtedly bound, by the authorities to which I have referred, to hold
d that the rule of practice exists and to continue to apply it. I do not consider, however,
that this court is also bound to hold that the 'relation back' theory is the true basis of that
rule, and that for two reasons. The first reason is that it was never necessary for the
decision in any of the reported cases from 1877 onwards to decide whether the one
theory or the other was the true one. It was sufficient simply to formulate and apply the
rule. The second reason is that the authorities do not, as I have indicated, speak with one
e voice on the subject, but on the contrary provide support both for and against both
theories.

Feeling free therefore to form my own opinion on the matter, I have reached the
provisional conclusion, it is not necessary to reach a final conclusion, that the 'no useful
purpose' theory, rather than the 'relation back' theory, should be regarded as the true
basis of the rule of practice.

f I appreciate that this view, if correct, creates problems with regard to the effectiveness
of para (3), and possibly but not necessarily also paras (4) and (5), of RSC Ord 20, r 5, as
at present framed. These difficulties could, however, be overcome by adding an express
provision that, where amendments of the kinds covered by those three paragraphs are
made, they shall relate back to the date of the original writ. This is, after all, the result
which those new provisions of the rule are, in substance, intended to achieve.

g The argument against Mr Spinks was, as I indicated earlier, based on two
propositions. The first proposition was that, because his solicitors had entered an
unconditional appearance on his behalf, he was now precluded from complaining about
his being added as defendant. The second proposition was that, since the addition of Mr
Spinks as defendant related back to the date of the original writ, the defence that the
claim was statute-barred was no longer available to him.

h For the reasons given earlier I have reached the conclusion that the first proposition is
erroneous. I hold that Mr Spinks is not precluded from complaining of his being added
as defendant, but is on the contrary entitled to an order under RSC Ord 15, r 6(2)(*a*), that
he cease to be a party. I am further content to decide the appeal on that ground alone,
without expressing any final view with regard to the second proposition.

If I had reached the conclusion, however, that the first proposition was correct, I should
j have been prepared to decide the appeal on the alternative ground that the second
proposition was erroneous. I should in that event not merely have expressed the
provisional view, but held as a matter of decision, that the addition of Mr Spinks as
defendant did not relate back to the date of the original writ but took effect only from the
date of amendment, so that the defence that the claim was statute-barred remained
available to him. On that basis I should again have allowed the appeal and made an order

summarily dismissing the action as against Mr Spinks on the ground that the claim
raised against him in it was statute-barred and was therefore bound to fail: see *Riches v*   ***a***
Director of Public Prosecutions[1].

Appeal allowed. Leave to appeal to the House of Lords granted.

Solicitors: *Greenwood & Co* (for the second defendant); *Outred & Co*, Weybridge (for the
plaintiff); *Stevens* (for the first defendant).   ***b***

Patricia Hargrove   Barrister.

Attorney-General v New Statesman and Nation Publishing Co Ltd

c

QUEEN'S BENCH DIVISION
LORD WIDGERY CJ AND PARK J
13th, 14th DECEMBER 1979, 15th JANUARY 1980

d

*Contempt of court – Publication concerning legal proceedings – Disclosure of jury room secrets
– Whether mere disclosure punishable as contempt – Whether necessary to show tendency to
imperil finality of verdict or to have other adverse effect on jury system.*

The jury at a trial which attracted much publicity acquitted the accused. Afterwards two
journalists, who had been commissioned by the editor of a magazine to write an article
about the trial, interviewed a juror who was willing, without reward, to divulge what   ***e***
had happened in the jury room because he felt that some aspects of the case should be
made public. The journalists then wrote an article incorporating his account of a
significant part of the jury's deliberations. The editor of the magazine believed that
nothing but good could come from publication of the article and decided to publish it.
Following publication of the article, the Attorney-General applied under RSC Ord 52,   ***f***
r 9, for an order that the publishers of the magazine were in contempt of court on the
ground that the article interfered with the due administration of justice because it tended
to imperil the finality of jury verdicts and thereby diminish public confidence in the
general correctness and propriety of such verdicts and to affect adversely the attitude of
future jurors and the quality of their deliberations. The Attorney-General conceded that
publication of the article could not have interfered in any way with the administration
of justice in the particular case to which it referred and that the article itself was   ***g***
unexceptionable since it showed that the jury had approached their task in a sensible and
responsible manner.

Held – (i) Although the mere disclosure of the secrets of the jury room was not
necessarily a contempt of court, if such disclosure or any other similar activity tended to
imperil the finality of jury verdicts or to affect adversely the attitude of future jurors and   ***h***
the quality of their deliberations it was capable of being a contempt. Whether a
disclosure was in fact a contempt had to be judged in the light of the circumstances in
which the publication took place (see p 649 *c d* and *f* and p 650 *c*, post); *Attorney-General
v Leveller Magazine Ltd* [1979] 1 All ER 745 applied; dicta of Lord Hewart CJ in *R v
Armstrong* [1922] All ER Rep at 156–157 and of Bankes LJ and of Atkin LJ in *Ellis v*   ***j***
Deheer [1922] All ER Rep at 452, 454–455 considered.
    (ii) Since the sole ground on which the allegation of contempt was based was the
disclosure of some of the secrets of the jury room in the particular trial, but there were,

---

1   [1973] 2 All ER 935, [1973] 1 WLR 1019

a   apart from that, no special circumstances which called for condemnation, the publication of the article did not amount to a contempt. Accordingly the application would be dismissed (see p 649 *g* and p 650 *c d*, post).

Notes

b   For contempts outside the court, see 9 Halsbury's Laws (4th Edn) paras 7–14, and for cases on criminal contempt, see 16 Digest (Repl) 17–45, *102–396*.

Cases referred to in judgment

Attorney-General v Leveller Magazine Ltd [1979] 1 All ER 745, [1979] AC 440, [1979] 2 WLR 247, 68 Cr App R 342, HL.

Ellis v Deheer [1922] 2 KB 113, [1922] All ER Rep 451, 91 LJKB 937, 127 LT 431, 86 JP 169, 20 LGR 625, CA, 14 (1) Digest (Reissue) 429, *3643*.

c   *R v Armstrong* [1922] 2 KB 555, [1922] All ER Rep 153, 91 LJKB 904, 127 LT 221, 86 JP 209, 27 Cox CC 232, 16 Cr App R 149, CCA, 14(2) Digest (Reissue) 522, *4258*.

R v Holmes (22nd June 1979) unreported.

R v Martin (1848) 5 Cox CC 356, 16 Digest (Repl) 45, **181*.

d   **Cases also cited**

Attorney-General v Times Newspapers Ltd [1973] 3 All ER 54, [1974] AC 273, HL.

Langdell v Sutton (1737) Barnes 32, 94 ER 791.

R v Dyson (1972) 1 OR 744, 5 CCC (2d) 401.

R v Thompson [1962] 1 All ER 65, CCA.

R v Twiss [1918] 2 KB 853, CCA.

e   **Application**

By notice of motion the Attorney-General applied for an order under RSC Ord 52, r 9, against the publishers of the New Statesman magazine, New Statesman and Nation Publishing Co Ltd ('the publishers'), for contempt of court in publishing in the issue of the magazine dated 27th July 1979 an article entitled 'Thorpe's Trial: How the Jury Saw

f   It'. The facts are set out in the judgment of the court.

Simon D Brown and *Andrew Collins* for the Attorney-General.
Geoffrey Robertson and *Andrew Nicol* for the publishers.

Cur adv vult

g   15th January.   **LORD WIDGERY CJ.** The judgment I am about to read, composed by Park J, is the judgment of the court.

In these proceedings counsel for the Attorney-General moves for an order under RSC Ord 52, r 9, against New Statesman and Nation Publishing Co Ltd, the publishers of the New Statesman, requiring them to be punished in respect of a publication said to be a

h   contempt of court.

The publication complained of is an article in the New Statesman magazine dated 27th July 1979 entitled 'Thorpe's Trial: How the Jury Saw It'. The article contains a juror's account of significant parts of the jury's deliberations in the course of arriving at their verdicts in *R v Holmes*[1] tried at the Central Criminal Court between 8th May and 22nd June 1979. Both the trial itself and the long committal proceedings which preceded it

j   were sensational and received saturation coverage in the daily press. The jury, having considered their verdicts for 52 hours, acquitted all the accused.

The editor of the New Statesman, Mr Bruce Page, was of the opinion that the jury's verdict did not dispose of a number of important issues ventilated in the course of the

---

1   (22nd June 1979) unreported

trial, namely the future of Mr Thorpe and the Liberal Party, the behaviour of senior
politicians of all parties when allegations were made to them about Mr Thorpe's conduct *a*
in 1971, the propriety of the behaviour of certain newspapers in offering lucrative
contracts to witnesses prior to their testimony in court, and the workings of a legal
system which had operated in a way which had enabled men who had admitted, through
their counsel, to discreditable conduct (albeit behaviour not the subject of any charge in
the indictment) to emerge without a conviction for any criminal offence.

Mr Bruce Page therefore commissioned two reputable and experienced journalists to *b*
write a three part series of articles: the first, published in the magazine on 6th July 1979,
was about Mr Thorpe's financial career; the second, published on 13th July 1979, was
about the manner in which leading politicians had dealt with Mr Thorpe and the
allegations against him made some years before he was charged with any criminal
offence; and the third was to deal with legal issues in the trial, and in particular with the
question whether the prosecution should have proceeded against the accused on lesser *c*
charges and whether large payments, escalating in the event of a conviction, by
newspapers to witnesses ought to be prohibited.

It came to the notice of the two journalists that a juror was willing, without reward,
to divulge what had happened in the jury room. He did this because he felt that some
aspects of the case ought to be made public. They interviewed him. Mr Bruce Page was
told; he formed the opinion that the juror's comments provided important evidence *d*
which should be incorporated in the third article in the series. This was done and the
article was published on 27th July 1979. It records the juror as saying, inter alia, that all
the jury were agreed that the accused were guilty of a conspiracy of some kind, that 11
of them, after little more than an hour's deliberation on the first day, agreed that it was
not proved that there had been a conspiracy to murder and that, on a charge of incitement
to murder, the jury could not accept the uncorroborated word of a prosecution witness *e*
who had agreed to accept money from a newspaper, the amount to be increased in the
event of a conviction.

It is accepted by the Attorney-General that Mr Bruce Page's decision to publish the
article was taken with the best intentions, that he honestly believed that nothing but
good would result from its publication and that the article would never involve him in
proceedings for contempt. *f*

It is conceded that the publication could not in any respect interfere with the administration of justice in the Thorpe case and that, where the article refers to the juror's
comments, it is unexceptionable since the words published demonstrate that the jury
approached its task in a sensible and responsible manner, but it is contended that, despite
this, mischief is done by the article by reason of its impact on the administration of
justice. It is argued that the article involves an interference with the due administration *g*
of justice as a continuing process, in that the disclosure of what happened in the jury
room tends or will tend (a) to imperil the finality of jury verdicts and thereby diminish
public confidence in the general correctness and propriety of such verdicts and (b) to
affect adversely the attitude of future jurors and the quality of their deliberations. It is
said that nothing must be permitted to be published which might tend to deter a person
likely to be called for jury service from playing his full part as a juror in any trial. *h*

We were reminded that, until a few years ago, it was accepted that the secrets of the
jury room had to be treated as secret. The solemn obligation by jurors to observe secrecy
was well maintained and breaches of the obligation were kept at an acceptable level. It
had never been necessary to invoke the law of contempt in respect of such breaches, but
that law had always been available for use in any case in which the administration of
justice would have been imperilled. Recently, however, the solemn obligation of secrecy *j*
has been shown to be breaking down; a considerable number of publications involving
jury room revelations, some more objectionable than others, have occurred. Accordingly,
in view of the apparently diminishing respect for the convention of observance of jury
secrecy and the risk of escalation in the frequency and degree of the disclosures, it has
become right for the Attorney-General to invoke the law of contempt in relation to this

article in the New Statesman since it represents a departure from the norm and is a
a serious and dangerous encroachment into the convention of jury secrecy.

On the other hand, it is also conceded that there are strong arguments in support of the
view that certain categories of disclosure fall outside the law of contempt, eg where
serious research is being carried out, but, even then, any disclosures would have to be
such as to ensure that the trial could not be identified, or where the disclosure occurred
in social discussion, but even that could in some circumstances be so undesirable as to
b constitute contempt.

Accordingly we have been invited to draw a distinction between these categories of
disclosure which probably fall outside the law of contempt and the general principle of
that law and to hold, by applying the general principle, that this article constitutes
contempt. The general principle has recently been stated in *Attorney-General v Leveller
Magazine Ltd*[1] by Lord Diplock:

c
'... although criminal contempts of court may take a variety of forms they all
share a common characteristic: they involve an interference with the due
administration of justice either in a particular case or more generally as a continuing
process. It is justice itself that is flouted by contempt of court, not the individual
court or judge who is attempting to administer it.'

d Counsel's submissions for the publishers can be briefly summarised. Once a trial is
concluded, he says, there is no interference with the administration of justice and no
contempt is therefore committed by the disclosures of what happened in the jury
room. Although the publication of such disclosures has in the past been deplored by
judges, no proceedings for contempt have ever been taken in this country against those
responsible for them. Accordingly, if this court were to condemn the article in the New
e Statesman as contempt, the effect would be to extend the law of contempt and thereby
to create a new offence, which is something Parliament alone ought to do.

There can be no doubt that amongst the actions which can have the effect of interfering
with the due administration of justice is interference with a juror. This may take place
in a number of different circumstances and with a number of different consequences. For
example, a person interested in the result of a trial may meet a juror before the trial
f occurs and seek to induce him to give a false verdict or otherwise distort the ends of
justice, or such a person, seeking to influence a juror's decision, may occupy a position in
court from which he can glower at the juror and generally put him in a frame of mind
in which he may be induced to find a particular verdict. But we are concerned with an
alleged contempt occurring after the conclusion of the trial. An example of this kind of
contempt would be when a juror was attacked or threatened after the trial pursuant to
g a desire for vengeance from a disappointed litigant or a member of the convicted person's
family. See, for example, *R v Martin*[2].

To attack or threaten a juror after the trial in order to obtain revenge or for some other
purpose connected with the discharge of his duty as a juror would almost certainly be a
contempt of court.

On the other question whether, after a trial has been concluded, it is contempt to
h approach and interview a juror and thereafter to publish in a newspaper the secrets of the
jury room as revealed by the juror, it is helpful to have some regard to observations made
by learned judges in the past.

In the notorious case of the poisoner Armstrong[3], the writer of an article published in
some newspapers claimed to report a statement to him by the foreman of the jury as to
what had occurred in the jury room after the jury had retired. The matter was brought
j to the attention of the Court of Criminal Appeal. After giving the court's reasons for
dismissing Armstrong's appeal against conviction, Lord Hewart CJ said[4]:

1   [1979] 1 All ER 745 at 749, [1979] AC 440 at 449
2   (1848) 5 Cox CC 356
3   *R v Armstrong* [1922] 2 KB 555, [1922] All ER Rep 153
4   [1922] 2 KB 555 at 568–569, [1922] All ER Rep 153 at 156–157

'It remains to mention a separate matter. Reference has been made in the course of the argument to the fact that, after verdict, there appeared in some newspapers an account of what the writer said was said to him about the evidence, with a complete lack of reserve, by a member of the jury. Whether what was published was, in fact, said, is not certain. But it is at least certain that it was published. In the opinion of this Court nothing could be more improper, deplorable and dangerous. It may be that some jurymen are not aware that the inestimable value of their verdict is created only by its unanimity, and does not depend upon the process by which they believe that they arrived at it. It follows that every juryman ought to observe the obligation of secrecy which is comprised in and imposed by the oath of the grand juror. If one juryman might communicate with the public upon the evidence and the verdict so might his colleagues also, and if they all took this dangerous course differences of individual opinion might be made manifest which, at the least, could not fail to diminish the confidence that the public rightly has in the general propriety of criminal verdicts. Whatever the composition of a British jury may be, experience shows that its unanimous verdict is entitled to respect. That respect, with all that it involves, is not lightly to be thrown away, and it is a matter of supreme importance that no newspaper and no juryman should again commit the blunder, to use no harsher word, which has disfigured some of the reports relating to matters connected with the trial of this case.'

At much the same time (which was 1922) the Court of Appeal in *Ellis v Deheer*[1] heard an application for a new trial of an action tried before a jury on the ground that the verdict as delivered by the foreman was not the verdict of the whole jury. In the course of his judgment Bankes LJ made reference to the report of the jurors' disclosures in *R v Armstrong*[2]. He said[3]:

'It has for many years been a well accepted rule that when once a verdict has been given it ought not to be open to an individual juryman to challenge it, or to attempt to support it if challenged. I have spoken of this as a rule of law, but it has also been generally accepted by the public as a rule of conduct, that what passes in the jury room during the discussion by the jury of what their verdict should be ought to be treated as private and confidential. I may say that I saw the other day with astonishment and disgust the publication in a newspaper of a statement by the foreman of the jury in an important criminal trial as to what took place in the jury room after the jury had retired. I do not think it necessary to express any opinion as to whether such a publication amounts to a contempt of Court, but I feel confident that anyone who read that statement will realize the importance of maintaining the rule.'

Warrington LJ agreed. Atkin LJ[4] said:

'I wish to express my complete agreement with what has fallen from my Lord with regard to the general rule that the Court does not admit evidence of a juryman as to what took place in the jury room, either by way of explanation of the grounds upon which the verdict was given, or by way of statement as to what he believed its effect to be. The reason why that evidence is not admitted is twofold, on the one hand it is in order to secure the finality of decisions arrived at by the jury, and on the other to protect the jurymen themselves and prevent their being exposed to pressure to explain the reasons which actuated them in arriving at their verdict. To my mind it is a principle which it is of the highest importance in the interests of justice to maintain, and an infringement of the rule appears to me a very serious

---

1 [1922] 2 KB 113, [1922] All ER Rep 451
2 [1922] 2 KB 555, [1922] All ER Rep 153
3 [1922] 2 KB 113 at 118, [1922] All ER Rep 451 at 452
4 [1922] 2 KB 113 at 121–122, [1922] All ER Rep 451 at 454–455

interference with the administration of justice. I do not propose to decide (for it is not before us) whether such a publication on the part of the press as my Lord has referred to of the reasons of a particular juryman for arriving at his decision is or is not a contempt of Court, and content myself with expressing my complete adherence to the views on the subject expressed by the other members of the Court.'

As the observations of these learned judges demonstrate, there are powerful arguments against breaching the secrets of the jury room. Serious consequences may flow from an approach to a juror, particularly after a trial which has attracted great publicity, followed by the publication of an account of what the juror had said about the discussion in the jury room. If not checked, this type of activity might become the general custom. If so, it would soon be made to appear that the secrecy of the jury room had been abandoned, and if that happened, it is not beyond the bounds of possibility that trial by jury would go the same way.

The virtue of our system of trial by jury lies in the fact that, once the case is over and the jury has returned its verdict, the matter is at an end. In our judgment, therefore, any activity of the kind under consideration in this case which, to use the language of the Attorney-General's statement, tends or will tend to imperil the finality of jury verdicts, or to affect adversely the attitude of future jurors and the quality of their deliberations, is capable of being a contempt. But that is not to say that there would be of necessity a contempt because someone had disclosed the secrets of the jury room.

What then is the test to apply in deciding whether or not such activity is or is not a contempt of court? In *Attorney-General v Leveller Magazine Ltd*[1] the House of Lords considered the question whether the publication in a magazine of the name of a witness in criminal proceedings who had been allowed to conceal his identity was in all the circumstances of the case a contempt of court. Lord Edmund-Davies said[2]:

'So the liability to be committed for contempt in relation to publication of the kind with which this House is presently concerned must depend on all the circumstances in which the publication complained of took place. It may be objected that, in an area where the boundaries of the law should be defined with precision, such a situation confronts those engaged in the public dissemination of information with perils which cannot always be foreseen or reasonably safeguarded against.'

This passage of Lord Edmund-Davies's supports our view that each case of disclosure has to be judged in the light of the circumstances in which the publication took place. In the instant case, the sole ground on which the allegation of contempt is based is the publication of some of the secrets of the jury room in this particular trial. Apart from that, there are no special circumstances which, it is suggested, call for condemnation.

One of the most interesting documents shown to us in the course of counsel's submissions was the Tenth Report of the Criminal Law Revision Committee[3]. On 27th July 1967 the then Home Secretary had asked the committee to consider—

'whether statutory provision should be made to protect the secrecy of the jury room; and in particular whether and, if so, subject to what exemptions and qualifications, it should be an offence to seek information from a juror about a jury's deliberations or for a juror to disclose such information.'

In the report, the committee, consisting of distinguished judges and lawyers, set out the reasons for their opinion that they did 'not deem it immediately necessary or desirable to make any statutory provisions to protect the secrecy of the jury room'[4]. Evidently

1 [1979] 1 All ER 745, [1979] AC 440
2 [1979] 1 All ER 745 at 761–762, [1979] AC 440 at 465
3 Secrecy of Jury Room (1968) Cmnd 3750
4 Ibid p 4, para 4

they did not take the view that there was already a sufficient obligation imposed by the common law to protect that secrecy. On the contrary, the report says[1]:

'Should any newspaper be tempted to take advantage of the freedom which at present exists to approach jurors for information in order to prolong the sensationalism of a criminal trial, we should hope that intervention by the Press Council, which exercises so valuable an influence in maintaining standards of journalism, would be effectual to check any such abuse.'

The evidence before us shows that for a number of years the publication of jury room secrets has occurred on numerous occasions. To many of those disclosures no exception could be taken because, from a study of them, it would not be possible to identify the persons concerned in the trials. In these cases, jury room secrets were revealed in the main for the laudable purpose of informing would-be jurors what to expect when summoned for jury service. Thus, it is not possible to contend that every case of post-trial activity of the kind with which we are concerned must necessarily amount to a contempt.

Looking at this case as a whole, we have come to the conclusion that the article in the New Statesman does not justify the title of contempt of court. That does not mean that we would not wish to see restrictions on the publication of such an article, because we would. But our duty is to say what the law is today and to see whether today the activity in question is a contempt of court.

We are unable to say that it is and we would therefore refuse the application.

Application refused.

Solicitors: *Director of Public Prosecutions*; *Stanleys & Simpson North* (for the publishers).

N P Metcalfe Esq Barrister.

Whitehouse v Jordan and another

COURT OF APPEAL, CIVIL DIVISION
LORD DENNING MR, LAWTON AND DONALDSON LJJ
30th, 31st OCTOBER 1st, 5th, 6th, 7th, 8th, NOVEMBER, 5th DECEMBER 1979

Medical practitioner – Negligence – Test of liability – Error of judgment – Hospital registrar testing forceps delivery – Registrar pulling foetus several times with obstetric forceps – Baby born with brain damage – Whether error of clinical judgment negligence – Whether negligence to be inferred from fact baby born with brain damage – Whether doctor negligent.

Appeal – Evidence – Finding of fact of trial judge – Interference with finding of fact – Finding depending on credibility of witness heard by trial judge – Baby born with brain damage – Claim in negligence against doctor on ground he pulled too hard and too long on forceps – Evidence of doctors present at delivery that forceps not used improperly – Evidence accepted by judge – Judge nevertheless finding doctor pulled too hard and long on basis of mother's evidence – Whether court entitled to reverse finding.

The defendant, a senior hospital registrar, was in charge of the delivery of the plaintiff as a baby following a high risk pregnancy. After the mother had been in labour for 22 hours the defendant decided to carry out a test to see whether forceps could be used to assist the delivery. In doing so the defendant followed a suggestion by his head of department, a consultant professor of obstetrics, in his case notes on the mother. The

---

1   Secrecy of Jury Room (1968) Cmnd 3750, p 4, para 5

defendant pulled on the baby with forceps five or six times and then fearing for the safety
a of the mother and child he carried out a Caesarean section quickly and competently. The
plaintiff was born with severe brain damage and, acting by his father, brought an action
in negligence against the defendant alleging want of professional skill and care by pulling
too hard and too long on the forceps and so causing the brain damage. At the trial there
was evidence by a junior registrar who was present at the delivery that the defendant's
use of the forceps was not violent or untoward. There was also eminent medical opinion
b that it was a matter of clinical judgment based on experience as to how hard and how
many times a doctor should pull on obstetric forceps. The mother gave evidence and
although her description of what had happened was not physically possible, the judge
interpreted it as meaning that the forceps were applied with such force that she was
pulled to the bottom of the delivery bed. There was also in evidence a report prepared
by the consultant professor shortly after the birth and after discussion with the defendant,
c in which the professor stated that the defendant had 'disimpacted' the baby's head prior
to the Caesarean section. Although the professor gave evidence that he had used the
term 'disimpacted' to denote that only slight force was needed to free the head before
delivery, the trial judge interpreted the term in its medical sense, namely that the baby's
head had become wedged or stuck in the birth canal because of the use of the forceps and
force was required to move it. Because of his interpretation of the professor's report and
d the mother's evidence the judge found that the defendant had pulled too hard and too
long on the forceps causing the foetus to become wedged in the birth canal, that in
unwedging the foetus he had caused asphyxia which in turn had caused cerebral palsy
and that in so using the forceps he fell below the high standard of professional
competence required by law, and was therefore negligent. The defendant appealed.

e **Held** – The appeal would be allowed for the following reasons—
   (i) An error of clinical judgment by a medical practitioner did not of itself amount to
negligence in the legal sense. Accordingly (Donaldson LJ dissenting), even if the finding
that the defendant had pulled too hard and too long with the forceps was accepted, that
did not constitute a finding of negligence, for the defendant's decision to continue
pulling on the forceps was merely an error of clinical judgment or (per Lord Denning
f MR) was not, on the evidence, improper at all (see p p 658 a to h and p 661 h j, post);
dictum of Denning LJ in *Roe v Ministry of Health* [1954] 2 All ER at 139 applied.
   (ii) (Donaldson LJ dissenting) In any event the court was entitled to, and would,
reverse the judge's finding that the defendant had pulled too hard and too long with the
forceps because that finding was based on an unjustified interpretation of the professor's
report and the mother's evidence, especially as the latter contradicted the evidence of the
doctors who were present at the delivery and the rest of the mother's evidence had been
g rejected by the judge, and (per Lawton LJ) because, in this particular instance, the
appellate court was entitled to disregard the trial judge's assessment of the reliability of
a witness (see p 657 e to h, p 658 h, p 660 d e and p 661 e, post); *The Hontestroom* [1927] AC
37 applied.
   Per Curiam. An inference of negligence should not necessarily be drawn from the fact
h that a baby is born with brain damage sustained in the course of delivery (see p 658 a,
p 661 h and p 663 c, post).
   Per Lawton LJ. (i) Allegations of negligence against medical practitioners should be
considered as serious, and the standard of proof is, therefore, a high degree of probability
(see p 659 b, post); dictum of Denning LJ in *Hornal v Neuberger Products Ltd* [1956] 3 All
ER at 973 applied.
j (ii) As long as liability in this type of case rests on proof of fault judges will have to go
on making decisions they would prefer not to make. The victims of medical mishaps of
this kind should be cared for by the community, not by the hazards of litigation (see
p 661 j, post).

Notes
For the duty to exercise the special skill required in the practice of a profession, see 28

Halsbury's Laws (3rd Edn) 19, para 17, and for cases on the subject, see 33 Digest (Repl) 526, 65–74.

Cases referred to in judgment

Hatcher v Black [1954] The Times, 2nd July.

Hontestroom (Owners) v Owners of Steamship Sagaporack, Owners of Steamship Hontestroom v Owners of Steamship Durham Castle [1927] AC 37, 95 LJP 153, 136 LT 33, 17 Asp MLC 123, HL, 51 Digest (Repl) 815, 3712.

Hornal v Neuberger Products Ltd [1956] 3 All ER 970, [1957] 1 QB 247, [1956] 3 WLR 1034, CA, 22 Digest (Reissue) 47, 268.

Hucks v Cole (8th May 1968) unreported.

Roe v Ministry of Health, Woolley v Ministry of Health [1954] 2 All ER 131, [1954] 2 QB 66, [1954] 2 WLR 915, CA, 33 Digest (Repl) 533, 107.

Cases also cited

Barnett v Chelsea and Kensington Hospital Management Committee [1968] 1 All ER 1068, [1969] 1 QB 428.

Bolam v Friern Hospital Management Committee [1957] 2 All ER 118, [1957] 1 WLR 582.

Chin Keow v Government of Malaysia [1967] 1 WLR 813, PC.

Meek v Fleming [1961] 3 All ER 148, [1961] 2 QB 366, CA.

Portland Managements Ltd v Harte [1976] 1 All ER 225, [1977] QB 306, CA.

Powell v Streatham Manor Nursing Home [1935] AC 243, HL.

Praed v Graham (1889) 24 QBD 53, CA.

Wheat v E Lacon & Co Ltd [1966] 1 All ER 582, [1966] AC 552, AC.

Appeal

By a writ dated 14th December 1972 the plaintiff, Stuart Charles Whitehouse, an infant suing by his father and next friend Victor Edward Whitehouse, claimed damages against Mr J A Jordan, Professor H C McLaren, a consultant professor of obstetrics at Queen Elizabeth Hospital, Edgbaston, and the United Birmingham Hospital Board for personal injuries sustained on or about 7th January 1970 in the course of his birth at the Queen Elizabeth Hospital, Edgbaston, Birmingham. By notice of discontinuance dated 31st March 1976 the plaintiff discontinued his action against the second defendant, Professor McLaren. On 26th September 1976 Eileen Whitehouse, the plaintiff's mother, was substituted as his next friend. At the trial of the action Bush J gave judgment on 1st December 1978 for damages against the first and third defendants in the sum of £100,000. They appealed. The grounds of the appeal were (1) that the judge misdirected himself in holding that there was any sufficient evidence that the first defendant pulled too hard and too long when using forceps, (2) that the judge failed to consider and find whether, if the first defendant made any error, it was an error of clinical judgment as opposed to negligence, and (3) that the judgment was against the weight of evidence. The facts are set out in the judgment of Lord Denning MR.

Ian Kennedy QC and *Bernard Hargrove* for the first defendant.
Ian Morris for the third defendants.
Michael Wright QC and *Desmond Perrett* for the plaintiff.

Cur adv vult

5th December. The following judgments were read.

LORD DENNING MR. Being born is dangerous for the baby. So much so that an eminent professor in this case tells us that: 'Throughout history, birth has been the most dangerous event in the life of an individual and medical science has not yet succeeded in eliminating that danger.' He parodies the psalmist by referring to 'the valley of the shadow of birth'.

This has its legal consequences. It follows that, when a baby is still-born or dies soon

a after birth or is born damaged or deformed, that fact is no evidence of negligence on the part of the doctors or nurses attending the birth. It does not speak for itself. The maxim res ipsa loquitur does not apply. That was conceded here.

During the pregnancy this was regarded as a high-risk case. So much so that the mother was treated at the specialist maternity unit of the Birmingham Maternity Hospital. That unit is held in the highest regard by the medical profession. The doctor

b in charge of the unit was Professor H C McLaren of international reputation.

The delivery was expected to be troublesome. A very good team was gathered for it. The child was delivered by a very able and promising senior registrar, Mr Jordan. Soon afterwards he attained the status of a consultant. He was assisted by a good younger man, Dr Skinner, and two midwives. Also there was the anaesthetist. At hand were the paediatricians to take over the baby. With that assembly of skill, you would not think

c that anything would go wrong on the medical side. Nor did it by their accounts. None of them noticed anything untoward at all. Their evidence was that Mr Jordan skilfully carried out a 'trial of labour' to see if the baby could be safely delivered by forceps. As a result of the trial, it appeared that it would not be safe for the baby. So Mr Jordan decided to switch over to a Caesarean section: and that was performed most skilfully.

Yet despite all that skill and care, the baby was born with severe brain damage. The

d doctors diagnose him as suffering from 'cerebral palsy and mental deficiency'. He is now nearly ten years of age but he is no better than a baby of nine months. He cannot speak. He cannot think. He cannot sit up, or stand or walk. He cannot feed himself. He cannot control his bowels or his bladder. He can only swallow soft foods. He is a helpless cripple. He will need constant care and attention all his life.

Naturally enough his mother is greatly distressed. She toils day and night for him.

e The saddest part of it is that she blames it all on the hospital and particularly on Mr Jordan, the surgeon who delivered the child. Ever since the child was born, she and her husband have sought an inquiry. They invoked the aid of the press, the media and their member of Parliament. When an inquiry was refused, she obtained legal aid to press the case against the hospital and the surgeon. It is sometimes said that you cannot get one medical man to give evidence against another: just as it is said that you cannot get one

f lawyer to give evidence against another. This case shows how wrong that is. In this case two of the most eminent obstetricians in the country have given evidence against the surgeon: and two equally eminent have given evidence for him. Eminent counsel have been engaged to press the case against him: and counsel equally eminent to defend him. The expense must have been colossal. All borne on both sides by the taxpayers of this country.

g Now I must go into detail. The mother, Mrs Whitehouse, was a little woman. She was only 4 feet 10½ inches tall. She was aged 30 years and this was her first baby. During her pregnancy she visited the hospital at intervals on 13 occasions. She was a very nervous, tense woman. She had an instinctive revulsion against her vagina being examined. So much so that the doctors found it impossible to discover by clinical examination the position of the baby. They wanted to take a lateral X-ray to show it, but

h this she declined. On 31st December 1969, just a week before she was confined, she was examined by the head of the unit, Professor H C McLaren. He made this note: 'High head. Relaxed well. This is a tight outlet, I think. Declines lateral X-ray. So awaiting head fixing. Trial of labour is my guess.'

That note meant that the baby's head was still too 'high'. It had not yet 'engaged'. That is, it had not got down to that point where the widest part of the head was level with

j the brim of the outlet. The professor thought it might be best to have 'trial of labour'. That means that the surgeon would have to go cautiously and try forceps and gradually see whether the baby could be delivered safely or not.

A week later, soon after midnight on 6th January 1970, the mother began to have her labour pains. She was taken into the hospital at two o'clock in the morning. She was seen by the doctors and nurses on several occasions during the rest of the night and the

next day. Their notes recorded on three occasions quite clearly, 'Vertex engaged'. That
meant that the baby's head had come down so far that the widest part of the head was **a**
level with the brim of the outlet: and that the time for delivery was approaching.

The labour was prolonged. Hour after hour passed. Twenty-two hours until it was
eleven o'clock at night. She was in a labour ward. The doctor on duty at the time was
a young Dr Skinner. He had been qualified for five years and was working on a research
fellowship in obstetrics. Mr Jordan, a senior registrar, was off duty. He was working on
a research project upstairs. Soon after 11 o'clock he went down to have a word with Dr **b**
Skinner. Whilst they were having a cup of coffee, Dr Skinner's 'bleep' went. It was a
message from the midwife that a patient was fully dilated. It was Mrs Whitehouse. Dr
Skinner told Mr Jordan: 'This may be difficult. I doubt if I can do it myself. I shall need
help.' Mr Jordan said: 'I think I had better come myself.' They changed their clothes
into operating clothes and went to the delivery room to which Mrs Whitehouse had been
moved. From that moment Mr Jordan took charge. He read the notes and discussed the **c**
case with Dr Skinner. He examined the patient. He found that the head of the baby was
'engaged' but that the mother was so small that normal delivery was out of the
question. This was his note: 'Abdomen: Sinciput still palpable. Head engaged. Pelvis:
Small gynaecoid. Normal delivery out of the question.'

So he decided to do 'trial of labour' such as Professor McLaren had suggested in his
notes. All those concerned were there. Dr Skinner was close beside him. The **d**
anaesthetist was there. Two midwives were there. The baby's head was 'engaged' but it
was a little out of straight. So he turned it with forceps called Kielland's forceps till it was
straight. This was easily done. Then he tried to see if he could urge the baby towards the
outlet. For this he used other forceps called Simpson's forceps. He managed to get the
baby down some way. He could have pulled it right down and out, but it was so tight
a fit that he feared that the baby might be damaged on the way. So he stopped pulling **e**
and switched over to a Caesarean section. These were his notes on this most crucial stage:

'Forceps began at 23.45 6/1/70. Head rotated to O.A. [occiput anterior] with
Kiellands—no problem. Kiellands removed and Simpsons forceps applied. A very
tight fit. No episiotomy. After pulling with 5 or 6 contractions, it was obvious that
vaginal delivery would be too traumatic—for Caesarean section.'

f

The charge against Mr Jordan arises out of that very note which he made. It is said that
he pulled too long and too hard: and that in so doing he was guilty of such want of skill
and care that it was he who was the cause of this baby's cerebral haemorrhage. I will
return to this later: and meanwhile get on with the story.

As soon as Mr Jordan decided on a Caesarean section, Mrs Whitehouse was moved
from the delivery room into the next room. She was made ready for the operation. The **g**
team got ready too with fresh sterile gowns and so forth. She was given a general
anaesthetic. Mr Jordan made an incision in her abdomen. He removed the baby and
handed it at once to the paediatricians. It took two minutes. Everyone in the case agrees
that this stage was all superbly done. Mr Jordan's note says:

'Caesarean section—patient given G.A. [general anaesthetic] Op. started at 00.23
7/1/70   **h**
'Child delivered 00.25 7/1/70
'Subumbilical mid-line incision. Standard lower segment Caesarean section.'

Mr Jordan stayed to look after the mother. The paediatricians took over the baby.
It was in a very poor shape. It was not breathing and the pulse was almost nil. The
paediatricians applied all their resuscitative techniques. It took them 35 minutes before **j**
the baby breathed spontaneously on its own. One of the greatest paediatricians of our
time, Professor Ronald Illingworth, said: 'It is a matter of opinion whether the ventilation
and other resuscitative measure should have been continued so long, when there was no
spontaneous respiration for 35 minutes.' Seeing this boy's present condition, most
would say: 'What a pity they did not let him die.'

The evidence of the medical men

a   This case has been considered by some of the most eminent men in the country. They have studied the hospital notes and seen both child and mother. The great preponderance of opinion is that neither Mr Jordan nor the hospital were guilty of any negligence. Professor L B Strang (London), Professor J P M Tizard (Oxford), Dame Josephine Barnes (Charing Cross Hospital) and Professor Sir John Dewhurst (London) all say so. I would summarise their view by quoting the concluding three paragraphs of Sir John Dewhurst's

b report:

> 'How hard one should pull on the forceps and how many times one should pull in this kind of case is again a matter of clinical judgment based on experience. Force of pull on a pair of obstetric forceps is not measured but is judged by the operator in the light of his previous experience. Mr. Jordan says that he exerted traction 5 or 6 times co-incidental with the uterine contractions and that he relaxed the lock of
>
> c the forceps between these pulls. He then concluded *not* that delivery was not possible but that *safe* delivery was not possible and proceeded to Caesarean section. I see nothing improper in this course of action nor in the manner of implementing it. One cannot argue that because the child *probably* suffered some intracranial damage (although even this is uncertain) he pulled too hard. Children have
>
> d sustained intracranial damage from a normal delivery; the hardness of all babies heads is not the same and they are not all similarly resistant to pressure. I find no evidence to support an allegation of negligence on Mr. Jordan's part and I recommend that he be strongly defended.' (Emphasis mine.)

In addition I may say that Professor Sir John Stallworthy (Oxford, now retired) at first made a report saying that Mr Jordan was not negligent. He said that he had dealt with

e the case 'with courage and skill'. But afterwards Sir John Stallworthy joined with Sir John Peel (also Oxford, retired) in holding that Mr Jordan was negligent. Their joint report was the justification for the continuance of this action to trial. But their joint report has been subjected to severe criticism and has been shown to be mistaken on some very important points.

In the first place, their joint report suffers to my mind from the way it was prepared.

f It was the result of long conferences between the two professors and counsel in London and it was actually 'settled' by counsel. In short, it wears the colour of special pleading rather than an impartial report. Whenever counsel 'settle' a document, we know how it goes. 'We had better put this in', 'We had better leave this out', and so forth. A striking instance is the way in which Professor Tizard's report was 'doctored'. The lawyers blacked out a couple of lines in which he agreed with Professor Strang that there was no

g negligence.

There is also evidence of serious mistakes in the joint report itself. The two professors said that the baby's head was 'not engaged', whereas the hospital notes made it clear that those on the spot had found that it was 'engaged'. And the judge so found.

The two professors also said that the pulling was so hard that Mrs Whitehouse was 'lifted from the bed' which they explained as meaning that she was pulled down off the

h bed and lifted back on to it again. That was contrary to all the evidence in the case, including that of Mrs Whitehouse herself. The two professors did not have the benefit of the evidence of Dr Skinner. He said that nothing of the kind took place.

The two professors also criticised the hospital for not having made a pelvic assessment: without paying sufficient regard to the fact that Mrs Whitehouse was so tense that it could not be done: and she refused an X-ray.

j   The defects in the joint report of the two professors are so great that, to my mind, it cannot stand up against the reports of the other distinguished men in the case.

Professor McLaren's report

The judge, however, decided against Mr Jordan. He did so largely on a report made by Professor McLaren, the head of the unit. Professor McLaren was not in the hospital when the baby was born. He was back home recovering from flu. But he was responsible for the unit. So he made enquiries and made a report. It was sent to Mrs Whitehouse's *a* own general practitioner. This was about two months after the child was born. Mr Jordan saw it before it was sent off. He made no corrections in it. So the judge took it as evidence against him. The report denies that there was any negligence. Professor McLaren says: 'My own view is that both Mr and Mrs Whitehouse are naturally very distressed although there is no evidence that she had anything but first-class obstetric care.' *b*

But the judge has used the report as most telling evidence against Mr Jordan, because of this sentence in it:

> 'A trial of forceps was carried out under epidural anaesthesia the head rotating with ease with Kiellands forceps. Descent, however, did not follow traction and *in the interest of the child* the head was disimpacted prior to speedy delivery by Caesarean Section.' (Emphasis mine.) *c*

Again:

> 'The baby, alas, was seriously affected by this well conducted trial of labour and forceps. Possibly at Caesarean Section the disimpaction of the head was critical and cerebral haemorrhage followed.'

There was much discussion as to the strict meaning of that word 'disimpacted'. None *d* of the doctors save Professor McLaren were familiar with it in this context. But 'impacted', in the context of obstetrics, appears in Steadman's Medical Dictionary[1]. It runs: 'Denoting a fetus that, because of its large size or narrowing of the pelvic canal, has become wedged and incapable of spontaneous advance or recession.'

Now here is the crucial point of the case. Professor McLaren says that he meant it to denote that no more than some slight force was needed to free the baby's head. Whereas *e* the judge said: 'It is with regret that I find it difficult to accept Professor McLaren's explanation of his use of the word "impacted".' Counsel for the plaintiff elaborated the report for us. He said that 'Descent did not follow traction' meant that, on none of the pulls, was there any progress: and yet Mr Jordan went on pulling for five or six pulls: 'impacted' meant it was jammed tight and required much force to move it. In short, Professor McLaren's report was interpreted as a condemnation of Mr Jordan, whereas *f* that was the last thing that Professor McLaren thought.

Mrs Whitehouse's evidence

Mrs Whitehouse in her evidence blamed Mr Jordan for everything. She said that it was he who examined her on three occasions beforehand when it was really Dr Hall. The judge disbelieved her. He said: 'That Mrs Whitehouse believes what she says I have no doubt, but that she is wrong I am sure.' *g*

The crucial part of her evidence was about the pulling. She said: 'It was like a deadened electric shock that lifted me up off the table, up off the bed.' She told the two retired professors, it is in their joint report, that she suffered shocks and was lifted from the bed. They interpreted this as meaning that she was pulled down off the bed and had to be lifted back. That was quite wrong. All those present said that nothing of the kind *h* occurred. The judge acknowledged that Mrs Whitehouse's description could not be accurate: but nevertheless he made this finding:

> 'Though Mrs Whitehouse's description of what occurred to her when the forceps were applied may not be exact in detail, I believe her, in so far as her description can be taken to be understood, as a pulling of her towards the bottom of the delivery bed in a manner and with such force as to be inconsistent with a trial of forceps properly *j* carried out.'

If this were the case, surely Dr Skinner and the others there would have seen it. Yet they gave evidence that there was no such pulling at all.

1   23rd Edn (1976)

a The point is so important that I will read the evidence of Dr Skinner about it. He was there only a yard away from Mr Jordan, watching all very closely, as he was thinking of writing this case up. This is his examination-in-chief:

'Q. Was there anything in the way you saw Mr Jordan deal with this case which excited any degree of disapprobation on your part? A. Definitely not.

b 'Q. Was there any question that you could see of violent pulling of the forceps by Mr Jordan? A. Definitely not. I have never ever seen Mr Jordan violently pull forceps in my life.

'Q. It was suggested somewhere that the forceps were used in such a way that the patient was lifted from the bed. Did you see anything like that? A. No. Physically lifted off the bed?

'Q. Yes. A. Definitely not.

c 'Q. If you had seen something of that nature do you think you would have remembered it? A. I am sure that I would have remembered it from the fantasticness of it.'

Then in cross-examination:

'Q. You have no recollection of her having to be moved back into a better
d position on the table? A. Continually moved back following forceps?

'Q. Following tractions. A. No, oh no.'

In view of that evidence, I do not think the judge should have accepted Mrs Whitehouse's evidence at all about the pulling. She was not in a state to know what was going on.

e *The judge's findings of fact*

We were reminded once again of the caution to be observed before interfering with the findings of fact by a trial judge. The cases on it are well known. But this case is different. The medical notes, made at the time, were accepted as accurate. The evidence of all those present was accepted as truthful and accurate, except for Mrs Whitehouse. The judge did not disbelieve any of them. None of this evidence disclosed any negligence
f by Mr Jordan at all. The judge found against him for two reasons: (i) the judge's interpretation of the report of Professor McLaren, especially of the word 'disimpacted'; (ii) the judge's interpretation of the evidence of Mrs Whitehouse.

The judge concluded that Mr Jordan 'pulled too hard and too long so that the foetus became wedged or stuck'.

g *My assessment*

I must say that I think those two points are quite insufficient to convict Mr Jordan of negligence. Professor McLaren's report itself refutes any suggestion of negligence. It is not right, therefore, to read it as if it contained an admission of negligence. The judge read too much into the word 'disimpacted'. As to Mrs Whitehouse's evidence, she was shown to be wrong in so many respects that it is not right to accept her evidence in
h contradiction of all those present at the time.

I would therefore myself reverse the judge's finding that Mr Jordan 'pulled too hard and too long'. He acted with every care and skill. The damage to the baby was one of those unfortunate things which happen in the best of hospitals, despite all care.

j *Standard of proof*

The key sentence of the judge was this:

'In getting it wedged or stuck, or unwedged or unstuck, Mr Jordan caused asphyxia which in turn caused the cerebral palsy. In this respect Mr Jordan fell below the very high standard of professional competence that the law requires of him.'

The first sentence suggests that, *because* the baby suffered damage, *therefore* Mr Jordan was at fault. In other words res ipsa loquitur. That would be an error. In a high-risk case, damage during birth is quite possible, even though all care is used. No inference of negligence should be drawn from it.

In the second sentence the judge required Mr Jordan to come up to 'the very high standard of professional competence that the law requires'. That suggests that the law makes no allowance for errors of judgment. This would be a mistake. Else there would be a danger, in all cases of professional men, of their being made liable whenever something happens to go wrong. Whenever I give a judgment, and it is afterwards reversed by the House of Lords, is it to be said that I was negligent? That I did not pay enough attention to a previous binding authority or the like? Every one of us every day gives a judgment which is afterwards found to be wrong. It may be an error of judgment but it is not negligent. So also with a barrister who advises that there is a good cause of action and it afterwards fails. Is it to be said on that account that he was negligent? Likewise with medical men. If they are to be found liable whenever they do not effect a cure, or whenever anything untoward happens, it would do a great disservice to the profession itself. Not only to the profession but to society at large. Take heed of what has happened in the United States. 'Medical malpractice' cases there are very worrying, especially as they are tried by juries who have sympathy for the patient and none for the doctor, who is insured. The damages are colossal. The doctors insure but the premiums become very high: and these have to be passed on in fees to the patients. Experienced practitioners are known to have refused to treat patients for fear of being accused of negligence. Young men are even deterred from entering the profession because of the risks involved. In the interests of all, we must avoid such consequences in England. Not only must we avoid excessive damages. We must say, and say firmly, that, in a professional man, an error of judgment is not negligent. To test it, I would suggest that you ask the average competent and careful practitioner: 'Is this the sort of mistake that you yourself might have made?' If he says: 'Yes, even doing the best I could, it might have happened to me', then it is not negligent. In saying this, I am only reaffirming what I said in *Hatcher v Black*[1] (a case I tried myself), *Roe v Ministry of Health*[2] and *Hucks v Cole*[3]. Perhaps I may remind you of the saying of John Bradford over 450 years ago. On seeing some criminal taken to execution he exclaimed: 'But for the Grace of God, there goes John Bradford.' So now if this judgment against Mr Jordan stands, all the doctors in England will say: 'But for the Grace of God, there go I.'

Applying this test I am clearly of opinion that, even accepting the judge's view that Mr Jordan pulled too hard and too long, it was not negligent. It was at worst an error of judgment. For myself I would not go as far as that. I think that Sir John Dewhurst's assessment was correct. There was nothing improper at all. Let it not be thought that I am wanting in sympathy for the mother. It is a most grievous thing for her. But it is not a thing which will be cured by money damages. Everyone will rally round to help her as they have already done during these last ten years. She should be grateful for all that has been done for her without laying blame on the doctors. I would allow the appeal accordingly.

LAWTON LJ. At about 25 minutes past midnight on 7th January 1970 the infant plaintiff was born. He was seriously handicapped. His distraught mother has blamed the obstetrician, Mr Jordan, who delivered him, for his grave disabilities. She has alleged that he was negligent.

In what way was he said to have been negligent? The statement of claim alleged that he had failed in his duty to the infant plaintiff in nine respects. By the end of the evidence there was only one allegation worthy of consideration, namely that Mr Jordan,

1 [1954] The Times, 2nd July
2 [1954] 2 All ER 131, [1954] 2 QB 66
3 (8th May 1968) unreported

a when attempting by the use of Simpson's forceps to find out whether he could ease the baby through his mother's pelvic ring, pulled too hard and too long, with the result that the baby suffered brain damage. The judge decided that this allegation had been proved. The defendants have challenged that finding.

The standard of proof which the law imposed on the infant plaintiff was that required in civil cases, namely proof on the balance of probabilities, but as Denning LJ said in *Hornal v Neuberger Products Ltd*[1]: 'The more serious the allegation the higher the degree

b of probability that is required.' In my opinion allegations of negligence against medical practitioners should be considered as serious. First, the defendant's professional reputation is under attack. A finding of negligence against him may jeopardise his career and cause him substantial financial loss over many years. Secondly, the public interest is put at risk, as Denning LJ pointed out in *Roe v Ministry of Health*[2]. If courts make findings of negligence on flimsy evidence or regard failure to produce an expected

c result as strong evidence of negligence, doctors are likely to protect themselves by what has become known as defensive medicine, that is to say, adopting procedures which are not for the benefit of the patient but safeguards against the possibility of the patient making a claim for negligence. Medical practice these days consists of the harmonious union of science with skill. Medicine has not yet got to the stage, and maybe it never will, when the adoption of a particular procedure will produce a certain result. As

d Denning LJ said in *Roe v Ministry of Health*[3]:

> 'It is so easy to be wise after the event and to condemn as negligence that which was only a misadventure. We ought always to be on our guard against it, especially in cases against hospitals and doctors. Medical science has conferred great benefits on mankind, but these benefits are attended by considerable risks . . . We cannot take the benefits without taking the risks.'

e
Obstetrical forceps must have saved the lives of many mothers and babies since they were first used a very long time ago; but it is common knowledge that babies on whom they are used sometimes suffer injury, fortunately in most cases it is only slight. The doctor in each case has to decide for himself whether to apply forceps and continue to do so or to stop and deliver the baby by Caesarean section. There are risks in either procedure;

f and the evidence in this case was that delivery through the pelvic ring, if it could be effected, was less risky than by Caesarean section.

It follows, so it seems to me, that the evidence in this case requires careful examination. I have reminded myself, however, that I am not taking part in the retrial of the infant plaintiff's claim. I have kept in mind Lord Sumner's admonition to appellate judges about reversing the conclusions of fact made by a trial judge. They should not do so, so

g he said, unless he has failed to use, or has palpably misused, the advantages he has had of seeing and hearing the witnesses: see *The Hontestroom*[4].

There were two questions which had to be answered in the infant plaintiff's favour if he was to succeed. First, had the brain damage he sustained been caused by anything Mr Jordan had done or had omitted to do? In acting as he did, had Mr Jordan been negligent?

h As to the first question the trial judge found that the injury sustained by the infant plaintiff had been caused by what Mr Jordan did whilst using forceps. On the evidence, as the trial judge himself accepted, there were powerful arguments in favour of a different view; but the trial judge was entitled to make this finding and he cannot be criticised for doing so.

The second question is the one which matters. Whatever Mr Jordan did was in the

j presence of witnesses. Present were the mother, a junior registrar (Dr Skinner), an

---

1   [1956] 3 All ER 970 at 973, [1957] 1 QB 247 at 258
2   [1954] 2 All ER 131 at 139, [1954] 2 QB 66 at 86–87
3   [1954] 2 All ER 131 at 137, [1954] 2 QB 66 at 83
4   [1927] AC 37 at 47

anaesthetist and two midwives. Both Mr Jordan and Dr Skinner said that nothing
untoward had happened. The midwives and the anaesthetist were not called, which is *a*
not surprising as the medical and nursing staff in large hospitals move around a lot and
these events had occurred nearly nine years before the trial. The mother gave an account
of what had happened. The trial judge accepted the substance of it. What he said about
this part of her evidence was this:

> 'Though Mrs Whitehouse's description of what occurred to her when the forceps *b*
> were applied may not be exact in its clinical detail, I believe her, in so far as her
> description can be understood as a pulling of her toward the bottom of the delivery
> bed and in a manner and with such force as to be inconsistent with a trial of forceps
> properly carried out.'

This was the only relevant part of the mother's evidence which he did accept. What she
said had happened could not have happened. All the medical witnesses who were asked *c*
about the details of her account agreed that even if Mr Jordan had pulled too hard he
could not have caused the physical movements which she described. Professor Sir John
Stallworthy suggested that she might have been pulled off the delivery bed. She might;
but this is not what she said had happened and if it had happened those present would
have had to act to get her back on the delivery bed. Dr Skinner would surely have
remembered an event of this kind as it was his task to make the mother as comfortable *d*
as possible whilst Mr Jordan was using the forceps. In my judgment the trial judge
should not have accepted that the mother could give any worthwhile evidence on the
question whether Mr Jordan pulled too hard and too long. This is, in my opinion, one
of the rare cases in which an appellate judge is entitled to disregard a trial judge's
assessment of the reliability of a witness. In Lord Sumner's words in *The Hontestroom*[1] the
trial judge in this case 'palpably misused his advantage' in having seen and heard the *e*
mother. These advantages could not be used, as the trial judge used them, to turn an
account of what had happened which physically could not have taken place, into one
which could. That is what he did, as the following passage in his judgment shows:

> 'According to Mrs Whitehouse when the forceps were applied "It felt like a
> deadened electric shock that lifted my hips off the table" and she described her *f*
> buttocks and hips being lifted off the table. This cannot be an accurate description
> since the pull is downwards, but it *could be* that she was pulled towards the bottom
> of the delivery bed depending on the amount of force used.' (Emphasis mine.)

It cannot be right that a finding of negligence against an experienced obstetrician should
rest on a speculation as to what might have happened to the mother.

The trial judge went on to say: 'Perhaps the strongest piece of evidence that something *g*
untoward was done is the report by Professor McLaren' (who was Mr Jordan's superior
and head of the department). This report could only be evidence against Mr Jordan if he
knew what was in it and agreed with its contents. The trial judge seems to have decided
that Mr Jordan should be deemed to have accepted that it set out the substance of his then
recollection as to what had happened. On the evidence he was so entitled to decide; but
for my part, had I been trying the case, I would have been most hesitant about inferring that *h*
Mr Jordan had described what had happened in the very words which Professor McLaren
had used and in the same sense as he had used them. This is what the trial judge seems
to have done.

In his evidence Mr Jordan described what he had done. It did not amount to an
admission that the baby's head had become wedged or stuck in the mother's pelvic
ring. What he was saying was that when he first used the Simpson's forceps there was *j*
'a small degree of progress' and that he exerted about six pulls in all. There was
satisfactory progress until the fifth when there was no movement. He was asked in cross-
examination how he could justify pulling once more. He answered as follows:

---

1   [1927] AC 37 at 47

a
'The reason is that at this stage when one gets this, one realises that is the point at which one has to make a decision: "Can one, or should one, continue?" What one wants to know is, is there at this particular moment, and this is the crucial part as far as a trial of forceps is concerned, would this little extra pressure, or traction, deliver this head past that bony structure [ie the ischial spines] or not? In these circumstances realising this was the point at which the decision had to be made finally, as to continue or go back, it is justified to see whether or not a little more,

b
a little extra traction with other contractions would be enough to overcome the resistance one is feeling.'

There is nothing in the judgment to indicate that the trial judge rejected any part of Mr Jordan's evidence. He merely associated him with Professor McLaren's use of the word 'disimpacted' in the latter's report. In my judgment there was nothing in Mr Jordan's evidence to justify the inference that he had got the baby's head wedged or

c
stuck. There was evidence pointing to the opposite inference. The delivery by Caesarean section was rapid, which it was unlikely to have been had the head become wedged or stuck between or in the region of the ischial spines. Further, no signs of trauma on the baby's body were noted after delivery. What Mr Jordan described in his evidence was consistent with one meaning of the word 'impacted' as defined in Steadman's Medical Dictionary[1], viz 'incapable of spontaneous advance or recession'. 'Disimpacted' would

d
mean getting rid of this condition. Mr Jordan said that this is what he did, pushing the head up a little way within the forceps. This is normal practice when the foetal head is incapable of spontaneous advance or recession.

In my judgment there was no justification for the judge's finding, based on Professor McLaren's report, that Mr Jordan got the baby's head 'wedged, stuck or jammed'. The only other evidence relevant to this crucial issue of pulling too long and too hard came

e
in the opinions of Professor Sir John Stallworthy and Sir John Peel which were shown to be mistaken in some respects. Lord Denning MR has commented on their evidence. I agree with what he has said. As expert witnesses they had to advise on the facts given to them by the mother. No doubt they used their long experience to decide what was credible in the mother's account of what had happened and what was not. They did, however, somewhat surprisingly accept her version of what had occurred on the delivery

f
bed and based their opinions on it. For the reasons already given that version could not have been accurate. Its inaccuracy must weaken the opinions based on it.

As Lord Denning MR has said in his judgment, there was weighty expert evidence in favour of Mr Jordan. The trial judge was entitled to decide which evidence he preferred and I have reminded myself that this court should not, without good cause, differ from him in the assessment of witnesses. Save, however, for a critical comment on Professor

g
McLaren's explanation for his use of the word 'disimpacted', the trial judge did not say that he did not accept the evidence of the experts called on behalf of the defendants. He may have held the same opinion as I do, to wit that the expert evidence made the case understandable but the decision in the end depended on whether it had been proved that Mr Jordan pulled too hard and too long. This was not a case in which any inference to that effect could be drawn from the fact that the infant plaintiff had been born with brain

h
damage which he had sustained in the course of delivery. In my judgment the most which was proved against Mr Jordan was that when he asked himself the question whether he should go on using forceps or proceed at once to Caesarean section he gave himself an answer which subsequent events showed was wrong. It was based on his clinical judgment. Neither he nor any other doctor can always be right. Being wrong is not the same as being negligent. In my judgment negligence was not proved against

j
Mr Jordan. I have come to this conclusion with sorrow, knowing as I do what anguish the parents have suffered and the grave disabilities which the infant plaintiff will have to bear until death. As long as liability in this type of case rests on proof of fault judges will

---

1   23rd Edn (1976)

have to go on making decisions which they would prefer not to make. The victims of medical mishaps of this kind should, in my opinion, be cared for by the community, not *a* by the hazards of litigation.

I would allow Mr Jordan's appeal and that of the hospital authority whose case stands or falls with that of Mr Jordan.

DONALDSON LJ (read by Lawton LJ). No one could fail to feel the greatest sympathy for all concerned in this case. For Stuart Whitehouse, born gravely brain damaged. For *b* his mother who has fought so hard on his behalf. For Mr Jordan, a young obstetrician of the highest skill and repute, who is said on this one occasion to have failed to exercise the degree of skill required of him. And last, but by no means least, for the trial judge, Bush J, who had to put aside all conflicting sympathies, weigh the evidence dispassionately and reach a decision in circumstances in which any decision would be distasteful.

Counsel for Mr Jordan, criticised the judge for having failed to distinguish in the *c* reasons for his decision between negligence and an error of clinical judgment.

It is not now, and never has been, the law that a doctor is liable to his patients simply because the treatment prescribed or carried out by him was unsuccessful. The law recognises that doctors have to practise their profession on and beyond the frontiers of the unknown, that they have sometimes to take calculated risks, that they have sometimes to make inspired guesses. It is nothing to the point to look at the situation *d* with hindsight and to conclude that if a different decision had been made the result would or might have been more successful. And were it otherwise we should all suffer. As Denning LJ said in *Roe v Ministry of Health*[1]:

'Doctors would be led to think more of their own safety than of the good of their patients. Initiative would be stifled and confidence shaken. A proper sense of *e* proportion requires us to have regard to the conditions in which hospitals and doctors have to work. We must insist on due care for the patient at every point, but we must not condemn as negligence that which is only misadventure.'

It is said that the judge lost sight of the fact that the plaintiff had to establish negligence. The basis of this submission was in part that he nowhere referred to 'errors of clinical judgment' and contrasted such errors with negligence. I can understand the *f* omission, because it is a false antithesis. If a doctor fails to exercise the skill which he has or claims to have, he is in breach of his duty of care. He is negligent. But if he exercised that skill to the full, but nevertheless takes what, with hindsight, can be shown to be the wrong course, he is not negligent and is liable to no one, much though he may regret having done so. Both are errors of clinical judgment. The judge was solely concerned with whether or not the defendant's actions were negligent. If they were not, it was *g* irrelevant whether or not they constituted an error of clinical judgment. The question which Bush J asked himself was whether there had been any failure by the defendant 'to exercise the standard of skill expected from the ordinary competent specialist having regard to the experience and expertise which that specialist holds himself out as possessing', and added the proviso that 'the skill and expertise which we are considering is that applying in 1969–70'. In my judgment, that was not only the correct question, *h* it was the only relevant question.

I have now to consider whether he gave the right answer on the evidence. At and immediately after the birth, little was known except that the baby was very ill. Both the nature and the cause of the illness had yet to be determined. This was difficult and took a great deal of time. There were differences of opinion between experts and some of them changed their opinions as further facts emerged. Sir John Stallworthy and Sir John *j* Peel, who were called to give evidence in support of the plaintiff's case, were criticised for changing their minds. But their problem was that they were being asked by the plaintiff's advisers not only to express an opinion on what the defendant should or should

1   [1954] 2 All ER 131 at 139, [1954] 2 QB 66 at 86–87

not have done, but also to decide what he had in fact done and in what circumstances he
a had done it. In other words, they were being asked to constitute themselves not only
expert advisers, for which they were fully qualified, but also judges of fact without
having the benefit of hearing all the evidence and having it probed as it was at the
hearing. As their view of the facts changed, so necessarily did their expert opinions.

Initially the judge was confronted with a number of allegations and issues. However,
having heard and considered a very large amount of factual and expert evidence (there
b were 11 working days of evidence) he reached the conclusion on the balance of
probabilities that the brain damage suffered by the plaintiff was not the result of inherent
maldevelopment, that it was caused by asphyxia or anoxia and that this asphyxia or
anoxia was caused by some event occurring during the 40 minutes between the
beginning of the trial of forceps and the delivery of the baby by Caesarean section. These
findings are now accepted.

c On those findings it is common ground that if this asphyxia or anoxia was caused by
the fault of anyone, it was that of the defendant. However, Bush J expressly and rightly
reminded himself that 'it is important always to bear in mind that it is absolutely
impossible and wrong to say that because a child is born anoxic or with cerebral palsy,
then the man on the end of the forceps must be at fault.'

No one now criticises Mr Jordan for deciding that it was in the best interests of both
d mother and child that delivery should, if possible, be per vaginam. No one contends that
he should have waited longer to see whether such a delivery could take place without the
use of forceps. Indeed if Mr Jordan had been consulted earlier, it is unlikely that he
would have waited so long. That being so, all are now agreed that before proceeding to
a Caesarean delivery, it was right to consider whether a safe forceps delivery was
possible. In the light of a number of considerations which I need not enumerate, there
e was very real doubt whether this could be achieved. It followed that this doubt had to
be resolved and the accepted way of doing so was to undertake a 'trial of forceps'.
Accordingly, no one now criticises Mr Jordan for deciding to undertake and for
undertaking such a trial.

It is of the essence of a trial or test of forceps that it is a tentative procedure designed
to find out whether there is some unacceptable obstruction in the birth canal. It is
f therefore essential that the operator proceed with gentleness and care. Above all, he has
to be conscious of the risk of injury to the baby if he meets such an obstruction and uses
undue force to try to overcome it. The most likely area for meeting such an obstruction
is when the broadest part of the baby's head is in the region of the ischial spines. The
judge found, and this is now accepted, that when the trial of forceps began, the baby's
head was in a position which was of the order of five centimetres above that which it
g would occupy when its broadest part was in the region of those spines. It must, of course,
be remembered that a trial of forceps which leads to the conclusion that an actual forceps
delivery is possible is not divorced in time from that delivery. One follows the other
without a break and the need to be tentative in applying traction to some extent
disappears once the operator is satisfied that there is no unacceptable obstruction.
However, that stage, which would have been reached once the baby had travelled a
h distance of the order of only five centimetres, was never reached. At all relevant times,
it behoved Mr Jordan to be both gentle and tentative in all that he did.

Mr Jordan before abandoning the trial of forceps exerted traction during five or six
successive contractions. He said that failure to achieve movement with the first pull was
fairly common, but that one would expect to feel some descent of the head with the
second and succeeding pulls. Not unnaturally, he had no recollection of what progress
j was achieved with each individual pull, but he assumed that this is what occurred in the
present case and that he must have encountered some difficulty with the penultimate
pull. This would have been confirmed with the last pull. He had then concluded that
whilst a forceps delivery, as opposed to the trial on which he was engaged, was not
impossible, it would or might involve trauma for the baby.

Sir John Peel gave evidence that, whilst it was difficult to be dogmatic, one or two pulls should be sufficient to tell the operator whether the baby was coming down satisfactorily. He also said that if progress was being made with five or six pulls, he *a* would have expected the baby's head to be down on the perineum, which it was not. On the other hand, Mr Jordan said that whilst it was not uncommon to achieve delivery in two or three pulls, he had delivered babies which required more than six pulls. Whether he was there referring to a trial of forceps as contrasted with an actual delivery is open to doubt, but I will assume that he was referring to a trial.

Sir John Dewhurst explained that the operator had to feel whether there was some *b* minor disproportion between the size of the baby's head and the size of the narrowest part of the birth canal. This was not easy and the necessary skill was acquired by experience. He had to avoid pulling past a point where there was such a disproportion, because doing so might involve damage to the baby and such damage could take the form of asphyxia. Indeed, if pulling caused the asphyxia which occurred in this case, it was, in Sir John Dewhurst's view, axiomatic that Mr Jordan had used too much force. It *c* was equally axiomatic that Mr Jordan had used too much force if he had used sufficient force to jam the baby's head in the sense that it required force to get it out again. Mr Jordan denied that he had used such force, but he said that he had pushed the baby's head back upwards using the forceps before he proceeded to the Caesarean section.

Clearly against this evidential background, the judge had to consider what other evidence there was which might indicate whether Mr Jordan exceeded reasonable limits *d* either in the number of pulls or in the force applied. He had the contemporary notes and he also had a report by Professor H C McLaren, the head of the maternity unit. Professor McLaren had not been present at the birth and had no first-hand knowledge of the circumstances. He had, therefore, consulted with Mr Jordan before he wrote it. He had also handed it to Mr Jordan, who had read it before passing it on to the hospital administrator for whom it had been prepared. *e*

Now I fully accept that Professor McLaren could have got the facts wrong or he could have expressed himself badly. I also accept that Mr Jordan could have failed to read the professor's report carefully, could have misunderstood it or could have felt inhibited from expressing disagreement. But that report contained the following three passages which clearly had to be considered and probed.

(i) 'A trial of forceps was carried out under epidural anaesthesia the head rotating with *f* ease with Kiellands forceps. Descent, however, did not follow traction and *in the interest of the child* the head was disimpacted prior to speedy delivery by Caesarean section.' (Emphasis mine.)

'Impacted' according to Steadman's Medical Dictionary[1], in the context of obstetrics denotes 'a fetus that, because of its large size or narrowing of the pelvic canal, has become wedged and incapable of spontaneous advance or recession'. *g*

(ii) 'It could be that a congenital weakness of a blood vessel existed so that the fixing of the head in the pelvis and its disimpaction for Caesarean section led to a leaking of blood in the skull.'

(iii) 'The baby, alas, was seriously affected by this well conducted trial of labour and forceps. Possibly at Caesarean section the disimpaction of the head was critical and cerebral haemorrhage followed.' *h*

Both Professor McLaren and Mr Jordan were questioned at length about this report. The professor said that he should not have used the word 'disimpacted' because he did not intend to convey that he understood (necessarily from Mr Jordan) that the baby's head had become stuck or wedged. Mr Jordan said that 'Descent did not follow traction' was a loose and inaccurate description of what occurred and I think that in the end he was making the same comment with regard to the use of the word 'disimpacted'. Asked why *j* he did not demur at the wording of the report, he said that he was a little naive in those days, more naive than at the time of the hearing.

The judge had also to consider the evidence of Mrs Whitehouse, the mother. She had

---

1   23rd Edn (1976)

said that when Mr Jordan pulled it felt like an electric shock which lifted her up off the
a table. This evidence was rightly criticised on the basis that any pull would have been
downward rather than upward and the judge concluded that 'it could be that she was
pulled towards the bottom of the delivery bed depending on the amount of force used.
She was a little woman and it would be a question of degree whether this indicated in
itself the excessive use of force'. Later in his judgment he said: 'I believe her in so far as
her description can be understood as a pulling of her towards the bottom of the delivery
b bed in a manner and with such force as to be inconsistent with a trial of forceps properly
carried out.'

However, before expressing that view Bush J had said that 'perhaps the strongest piece
of evidence that something untoward was done is the report of Professor McLaren'. He
regretfully rejected the professor's explanation of his use of the word 'impacted' and by
implication found that Mr Jordan had accepted the report as substantially accurate,
c giving the word its dictionary meaning. The judge's conclusion was expressed in these
words:

> 'In all these circumstances I am doubtful whether Mr Jordan was in fact
> undertaking a trial of forceps as opposed to an attempt at vaginal delivery which
> failed, and in the course of which the baby was wedged, stuck or jammed, and
> which on anyone's view of the matter would be unjustified. However, in any event,
d > if it were a trial of forceps then he pulled too hard and too long so that the foetus
> became wedged or stuck. In getting it wedged or stuck, or unwedged or unstuck,
> Mr Jordan caused asphyxia which in its turn caused the cerebral palsy. In this
> respect Mr Jordan fell below the very high standard of professional competence that
> the law requires of him.'

e I have been able to detect no error of law in the judge's approach to this problem and
in the end I think that it was virtually conceded that the appeal turned on a single issue
of fact. This was whether Mr Jordan pulled too hard and too long so that the foetus
became wedged or stuck. In such circumstances it is not a matter of discretion, but of
justice and judicial obligation, for an appellate court to consider to what extent the fact
that the trial judge was able to see and hear the witnesses puts him in a better position
f than it is in seeking to reach a correct conclusion. If the trial judge's estimate of the
reliability of the witnesses must have formed any substantial part of the reasons for his
judgment, whether or not he says so, his conclusions of fact should not be disturbed,
unless it can be shown that he has in some way failed to use the unique advantages which
he had or that he has in some way misused them: see the speech of Lord Sumner in *The
Hontestroom*[1].

g It is within the experience of all judges that from time to time counsel produce a
phrase in argument which, like a flash of lightning, suddenly illuminates the whole
landscape revealing the problem in all its stark reality. So far as I am concerned, this
happened in this appeal when counsel for Mr Jordan said 'The trouble about this case is
that it got lost in the small print'. We had reached the end of the reading of an endless
succession of exerpts from the transcript, and I thought that he must be referring to the
h appeal. In fact, he was referring to the trial before Bush J, but he should not have been.
Time after time as the argument went on I found myself speculating on how the
questions were posed and how the answers were given. Did the witness display any
hesitation in his answers? Did he appear to be embarrassed by the question? Did the
answer have the ring of reliability? Did he or she carry conviction? Speaking for myself,
I was wholly lost in the small print.

j There is only one finding by the judge with which I feel able to quarrel. He seems to
have found that Mrs Whitehouse was pulled towards the bottom of the bed in the sense
that her body was moved. This cannot be right. He had already declined to accept her
evidence in almost every other respect. In this he was no doubt correct. It is no criticism

---

1 [1927] AC 37 at 47

of Mrs Whitehouse to say that she was so emotionally involved, so bitter, so convinced that Mr Jordan was to be blamed, and had had so long to mull over the traumatic events *a* of the birth, that it would have been remarkable if she had been an objective and reliable witness on any crucial matter. She had in fact said that it felt as if her hips were lifted upwards. This cannot in fact have happened. What it felt like to her is quite another matter. But that can hardly assist, since the lower part of her body was under the influence of an epidural anaesthetic and in such circumstances sensations can clearly be entirely misleading. Nor can she have been moved on the bed to any unusual extent *b* without the knowledge of Dr Skinner, whose hand she was gripping tightly. But he claimed to have no recollection of any such unusual movement and there is no indication that the judge rejected his evidence.

But having said that, I still have to decide whether the judge's conclusion was wrong and I am not satisfied that it was. Reading the judgment as a whole, it seems to me that Mrs Whitehouse's evidence was treated as no more than consistent with or, at most, *c* confirmatory of Professor McLaren's report and that even if Bush J had put her evidence to one side, he would still have reached the same conclusion.

Mr Jordan is entitled to think and to say that the judge's judgment was wrong. I cannot. But I can and do say this, if it is of any comfort to him. There are ve ƒ few professional men who will assert that they have never fallen below the high standards rightly expected of them. That they have never been negligent. If they do, it is unlikely *d* that they should be believed. And this is as true of lawyers as of medical men. If the judge's conclusion is right, what distinguishes Mr Jordan from his professional colleagues is not that on one isolated occasion his acknowledged skill partially deserted him, but that damage resulted. Whether or not damage results from a negligent act is almost always a matter of chance and it ill becomes anyone to adopt an attitude of superiority.

I would dismiss the appeal.

e

Appeal allowed. Leave to appeal to the House of Lords refused.

21st February 1980. *The Appeal Committee of the House of Lords (Lord Diplock, Lord Salmon and Lord Scarman) granted leave to appeal.*

f

Solicitors: *Hempsons* (for the defendants); *Roper Morris & Co*, Birmingham (for the plaintiff).

Frances Rustin Barrister.

Nabi v British Leyland (UK) Ltd

COURT OF APPEAL, CIVIL DIVISION
MEGAW, BROWNE AND BRIGHTMAN LJJ
12th, 13th, 30th NOVEMBER 1979

Damages – Personal injury – Loss of earnings – Deduction of unemployment benefit – Benefit payable out of fund financed by contributions from state, employers and employees – Employee injured as a result of employer's negligence – Employee receiving unemployment benefit – Whether unemployment benefit deductible from damages awarded for employee's loss of earnings.

An employee brought an action against his employers claiming damages in respect of personal injuries which he sustained in an accident in the course of his employment. The trial judge found that the employers had been negligent and that the employee had become unemployed as a result of their negligence. In calculating the special damages in respect of the employee's loss of earnings to the date of the trial, the judge took into account the amount which the employee had received by way of unemployment benefit under s 12(1)(a) of the Social Security Act 1975 and reduced the sum he would have awarded accordingly. The employee appealed, contending that the judge should not have taken the benefit into account because it was not an alternative to, or continuation of, the wages which he had received during his employment but was paid from a fund to which he, and the employers and the state, had contributed on the basis that they were insuring the employee against the risk of unemployment; it therefore had a combination of the characteristics of insurance and state benevolence and in consequence fell within the category of post-accident receipts which were not deductible in assessing damages.

Held – Although in assessing, as against a negligent employer, the special damages to be awarded to an injured employee for his loss of earnings, a disablement pension or a contributory pension was not deductible despite the fact that both employer and employee were contributories, the court was bound by previous authority to hold that unemployment benefit was deductible even though both employer and employee contributed to the fund from which it was paid. It followed that the appeal would be dismissed (see p 676 *a* to *e*, post).

Parsons v B N M Laboratories Ltd [1963] 2 All ER 658 applied.

Parry v Cleaver [1969] 1 All ER 555 considered.

Notes

For deduction for benefits received or receivable assessing damages in tort, see 12 Halsbury's Laws (4th Edn) para 1152, and for cases on the subject, see 17 Digest (Reissue) 87–90, 32–46.

Cases referred to in judgment

Bourgeois v Tzrop (1957) 9 DLR (2d) 214, 36(1) Digest (Reissue) 332, *2690.

Bowker v Rose [1978] The Times, 3rd February, [1978] Court of Appeal Transcript 164.

Bradburn v Great Western Railway Co (1874) LR 10 Exch 1, [1874–80] All ER Rep 195, 44 LJ Ex 9, 31 LT 464, 36(1) Digest (Reissue) 337, *1344*.

British Transport Commission v Gourley [1955] 3 All ER 796, [1956] AC 185, [1956] 2 WLR 41, [1955] 2 Lloyd's Rep 475, 34 ATC 305, 49 R & IT 11, HL, 17 Digest (Reissue) 88, *35*.

Browning v War Office [1962] 3 All ER 1089, [1963] 1 QB 750, [1963] 2 WLR 52, CA, 36(1) Digest (Reissue) 319, *1292*.

Cackett v Earl [1976] The Times, 15th October.

Daish v Wauton [1972] 1 All ER 25, [1972] 2 QB 262, [1972] 2 WLR 29, CA, 36(1) Digest (Reissue) 322, *1314*.

Eldridge v Videtta (1964) 108 Sol Jo 137, 36(1) Digest (Reissue) 325, *1325*.

Fitzpatrick v Moore [1962] NILR 152, 36(1) Digest (Reissue) 332, *2691*.

Foxley v Olton [1964] 3 All ER 248, [1965] 2 QB 306, [1964] 3 WLR 1155, 36(1) Digest (Reissue) 325, *1323*.

Hewson v Downs [1969] 3 All ER 193, [1970] 1 QB 73, [1969] 2 WLR 1169, 36(1) Digest (Reissue) 320, *1297*.

Lindstedt v Wimborne Steamship Co (1949) 83 Ll L Rep 19.

Parry v Cleaver [1969] 1 All ER 555, [1970] AC 1, [1969] 2 WLR 821, [1969] 1 Lloyd's Rep 183, HL, 36(1) Digest (Reissue) 320, *1295*.

Parsons v B N M Laboratories Ltd [1963] 2 All ER 658, [1964] 1 QB 95, [1963] 2 WLR 1273, [1963] TR 183, 42 ATC 200, CA, 17 Digest (Reissue) 90, *45*.

Payne v Railway Executive [1951] 2 All ER 910, [1952] 1 KB 26, CA, 36(1) Digest (Reissue) 319, *1291*.

Redpath v Belfast and County Down Railway [1947] NILR 167, 18 Digest (Reissue) 197, *997*.

Shaw v Cape Insulation Co Ltd (18th July 1977) unreported, QBD at Manchester.

Washington v Norwest Holst Ltd (30th July 1976) unreported, QBD at Liverpool.

Cases also cited

Brooks v Gloucester Aircraft Co Ltd (1964) unreported; cited [1964] 3 All ER at 249, [1965] 2 QB at 308, 310.

Cheeseman v Bowaters United Kingdom Paper Mills Ltd [1971] 3 All ER 513, [1971] 1 WLR 1773, CA.

Cunningham v Harrison [1973] 3 All ER 463, [1973] QB 942, CA.

Eley v Bedford [1971] 3 All ER 285, [1972] 1 QB 155.

Gohery v Durham County Council [1978] Court of Appeal Transcript 236 (noted in Kemp & Kemp, The Quantum of Damages, vol 12, paras 5–011/1 and 5–323).

Turner v Ministry of Defence (1969) 113 Sol Jo 585, [1969] Court of Appeal Transcript 278A.

Appeal

By a writ issued on 29th April 1976 the plaintiff, Guhulam Nabi, brought an action against the defendants, British Leyland (UK) Ltd, his employers, claiming damages for personal injuries suffered and losses and expenses incurred as the result of an accident which occurred in the course of his employment with the defendants on 10th June 1975 arising out of the negligence and/or breach of statutory duty of the defendants or their agents. On 13th July 1978 Smith J, sitting without a jury at Leeds, held that the accident was caused entirely by the defendants' negligence in leaving dangerous machinery unfenced in breach of their statutory duty under s 14 of the Factories Act 1961, and awarded the plaintiff damages of £11,211·30 made up as follows: £2,000 general damages for pain and suffering and loss of amenity; £3,662 special damages for loss of earnings to the date of trial and £549·30 interest thereon at the rate of 5% from 10th June 1975; £5,000 special damages for loss of future earnings. In calculating the loss of earnings the judge took into account the sum of £1,062 which the plaintiff had received by way of unemployment benefit. The plaintiff appealed contending that unemployment benefit should not have been taken into account in calculating those damages. The facts are set out in the judgment of the court.

T P Russell QC and *Janet Smith* for the plaintiff.
Christopher Rose QC and *K Goddard* for the defendants.

Cur adv vult

30th November. **BRIGHTMAN LJ** read the following judgment of the court: This
a appeal raises the question whether sums received by an injured workman by way of
unemployment benefit under s 12(1)(a) of the Social Security Act 1975 ought to be taken
into account in assessing as against his negligent employers the damages to be awarded
for his consequent loss of earnings. Smith J held that such sums should be taken into
account and the damages reduced accordingly.

   The plaintiff was injured by an accident which occurred during the course of his
b employment on 10th June 1975. The accident was held by the trial judge to be due to
the fault of the employers who had left dangerous machinery unfenced in breach of their
statutory duty[1]. Damages were awarded under three heads (leaving aside interest):
general damages for pain and suffering and loss of amenity; special damages in respect of
loss of earnings to date; and special damages in respect of loss of future earnings. The
first head of special damages was calculated as follows. The judge assessed the loss of
c earnings at £4,724 without regard to social security. He then took into account the fact
that the plaintiff had received the sum of £1,062 by way of unemployment benefit, and
reduced the sum of £4,724 by that amount, thereby arriving at a figure of £3,662. The
question at issue, as already indicated, is whether the judge correctly had regard to that
sum of £1,062.

   The Social Security Act 1975 came into force in April of that year. The scheme of the
d Act, so far as relevant for present purposes, is as follows. The funds required for paying
benefits are provided by means of contributions payable by employees, employers, self-
employed persons and others, together with supplements paid by the Treasury.
Employers and employees make what are called Class 1 contributions (s 1). A Class 1
contribution is a percentage of the employee's earnings subject to upper and lower
limits; the employer's contribution is somewhat larger than the employee's contribution
e (s 4). Section 12 specifies the eight contributory benefits payable. One of these is
unemployment benefit. To qualify for unemployment benefit, a claimant must have
made a certain minimum number of contributions (s 14). The duration of the benefit
is confined to a year (s 18, the 312 days therein mentioned being the equivalent of a
year). The claimant is thereafter disqualified from unemployment benefit until he has
resumed employment for a certain period and thus made further Class 1 contributions.
f It is evident from this brief outline of the scheme that, in relation to unemployment
benefit, it bears some similarity to an insurance scheme, in that payments are made by
a person which have the effect of entitling him to a benefit on the happening of an event
which may or may not occur.

   As regards some of the contributory benefits described in s 12, the sort of issue which
arises in the instant case has been resolved by statute. Section 2 of the Law Reform
g (Personal Injuries) Act 1948 (as amended by the National Insurance Act 1971) provides
that in assessing damages for personal injuries, one half of sickness benefit and invalidity
benefit shall be taken into account against loss of earnings. Widow's benefit and death
grant are to be left wholly out of account under s 2[2] of the Fatal Accidents Act 1959 (as
amended by the Social Security Act 1973). Unemployment benefit and retirement
pensions are however untouched by statute in this context.
h   In order to reach a reasoned conclusion whether unemployment benefit should or
should not be taken into account in assessing the damages payable to a person who is
unemployed in consequence of the wrongful act of another, one needs to search for the
principle to be applied. Prima facie damages are compensation for net loss. If the victim
of a personal injury or any other wrong is in receipt of a benefit which he would not have
received had the wrongful act not been done, that benefit, in a broad sense, reduces his
j loss and is usually intended to do so.

---

1   Section 14 of the Factories Act 1961
2   See now s 4 of the Fatal Accidents Act 1976

As pointed out by Lord Reid in *Parry v Cleaver*[1] there are three questions to be
answered in this type of case. First, what did the plaintiff lose as a result of the accident, *a*
ie what are the sums which he would have received but for the accident and which by
reason of the accident he can no longer get? The answer in the present case, down to date
of judgment, is £4,724. Secondly, what are the sums which he did in fact receive as a
result of the accident, ie sums which he would not have received but for the accident?
It may be convenient to refer to such sums as post-accident receipts. In the instant case,
the answer is £1,062 so far as relevant for present purposes. Thirdly, should the latter *b*
sum be deducted from the former in assessing the damages? So analysed the problem we
have to consider is not resolved by *British Transport Commission v Gourley*[2], which only
governs the answer to the first question.

There are two large and clearly defined areas in which post-accident receipts are
disregarded at common law, that is to say, the proceeds of insurance and the proceeds of
benevolence. The first exception is usually considered to have been established by *c*
Bradburn v Great Western Railway Co[3], although, as Lord Reid pointed out in *Parry's case*[4],
it was recognised in Scotland as long ago as 1818[5]. The ratio of Bramwell B's decision in
the *Bradburn* case[3] was that 'The plaintiff is entitled to retain the benefit which he has
paid for'. The approach of Pigott B was[6]:

> 'He does not receive that sum of money because of the accident, but because he
> has made a contract providing for the contingency; an accident must occur to entitle *d*
> him to it, but it is not the accident, but his contract, which is the cause of his
> receiving it.'

There is probably no substantial distinction between the two reasons. The victim of an
injury can keep for himself a benefit for which he has paid; the wrongdoer cannot
appropriate it to himself by way of a reduction in his liability. For the exclusion of the *e*
proceeds of benevolence it is convenient to turn to *Redpath v Belfast and County Down
Railway*[7], a decision of Andrews LCJ. A railway company in an action by a passenger for
personal injuries, sought unsuccessfully to administer interrogatories to elicit whether
the plaintiff had been the recipient of benefit out of a distress fund raised locally for the
victims of the accident. The decision in favour of the plaintiff was based on a number of
grounds; it was not the accident but an extraneous factor, namely, the existence of the *f*
charity fund, which gave the plaintiff his advantage, echoing the approach of Pigott B;
the circumstance relied on in mitigation of damages arose independently of the cause of
action and was not actually attributable to it; admittedly a sequence but not a
consequence, it arose as a result of a novus actus interveniens.

In *Parry v Cleaver*[8] Lord Reid expressed the view that unemployment benefit could be
regarded as a combination of insurance and national benevolence. There is no sensible *g*
reason for distinguishing between public and private benevolence; so said this court in
Daish v Wauton[9], which established the non-deductibility from lost future earnings of the
benefit of state maintenance under the national health service legislation. If both
insurance payments and the fruits of public and private benevolence are to be disregarded,
one may ask oneself why it is logical to take into account payments which can properly
be regarded as a combination of insurance and benevolence. *h*

---

1   [1969] 1 All ER 555 at 557, [1970] AC 1 at 13
2   [1955] 3 All ER 796, [1956] AC 185
3   (1874) LR 10 Exch 1, [1874–80] All ER Rep 195
4   [1969] 1 All ER 555 at 558, [1970] AC 1 at 14 *j*
5   *Forgie v Henderson* (1818) 1 Murr 413
6   LR 10 Exch 1 at 3, [1874–80] All ER Rep 195 at 197
7   [1947] NILR 167
8   [1969] 1 All ER 555 at 562, [1970] AC 1 at 19
9   [1972] 1 All ER 25 at 33–34, [1972] 2 QB 262 at 272

So far as reported decisions are concerned, the question of deductibility of
a unemployment benefit against lost earnings arose in Northern Ireland about a year
before the same point arose in this country. In *Fitzpatrick v Moore*[1] the plaintiff had
suffered personal injuries as the result of the admitted negligence of his employers. The
defendants sought to deduct from damages for loss of earnings the unemployment
benefits received by the plaintiff before he resumed employment. We were told by
counsel that the Northern Ireland legislation under which this case was decided did not
b materially differ from the English legislation applicable to the plaintiff's case. In
Fitzpatrick's case[2] Lord MacDermott LCJ said:

> 'While the plaintiff, during the second period of his unemployment [nothing
> turns on the word 'second'], was suffering a loss of earnings because of the accident,
> he was not receiving his unemployment benefits because of the accident. He was
> receiving them, while he remained in benefit by virtue of his contributions, because
c > he was unemployed, and neither the defendant's negligence nor the accident which
> resulted therefrom had anything directly to do with his entitlement to those
> benefits. The fact that his contributions and his benefits were exacted and granted
> under statute does not, in my opinion, affect the matter. To distinguish on that
> score between the present case and *Bradburn's case*[3] would be to ignore the principle
> of remoteness and to raise fine distinctions which the law relating to damages could
d > very well do without.'

There is also a Canadian case, *Bourgeois v Tzrop*[4], in which the Appeal Division of the
New Brunswick Supreme Court reached the same conclusion in 1957. The plaintiff's
claim was for damages for personal injuries suffered while being carried as a passenger in
a car owned and driven by the defendant. The question arose whether the unemployment
e insurance benefits received by the plaintiff should be applied to reduce the damages for
which the defendant was liable in respect of the plaintiff's loss of earnings. It was said
that this point had not previously been decided by any Canadian court. It was held that
the benefits were not deductible. After a review of the authorities, including the English
cases, the reasons were expressed as follows in the judgment of the court[5]:

f > 'The amount of $159 paid to the plaintiff under the provisions of the *Unemployment
> Insurance Act* was derived partly from monies provided by Parliament, partly from
> contributions by employed persons, including the plaintiff, and partly from
> contributions by the employers of those persons. Both Tzrop and his employer, in
> respect of him, made weekly contributions in equal amounts to the Unemployed
> Insurance Fund ... The benefits, which the plaintiff did receive would have been
> paid if his injuries had been sustained without any negligence on the part of the
g > defendant. The payments received by the plaintiff were received not because he
> was injured but because he was entitled to unemployment insurance benefits by
> reason of having been employed in an occupation coming within the scope of the
> *Unemployment Insurance Act*. The accident in which the plaintiff was injured was not
> the *causa causans* of the receipt by the plaintiff of the unemployment insurance
h > benefits but the *causa sine qua non*. The *causa causans* was his employment having
> been within the scope of the *Unemployment Insurance Act*. There is no statutory
> provision requiring the deduction of unemployment insurance benefits from
> damages allowed to an injured employee in respect to the injuries which caused the
> unemployment in respect to which the benefits were paid ... I am unable to
> distinguish between unemployment insurance benefits and a pension for naval

j

1   [1962] NILR 152
2   [1962] NILR 152 at 159
3   (1874) LR 10 Exch 1, [1874–80] All ER Rep 195
4   (1957) 9 DLR (2d) 214
5   9 DLR (2d) 214 at 224

service . . . The wrongdoer should not get the benefit of the fortuitous circumstance
that the plaintiff's employment entitled him to unemployment insurance benefits.'   *a*

'Naval service' was a reference to the decision of this court in *Payne v Railway Executive*[1].

The problem came before this court in *Parsons v B N M Laboratories Ltd*[2] on appeal
from a decision of a Queen's Bench master who had decided that unemployment benefit
should be disregarded. In that case the plaintiff claimed damages for wrongful
dismissal. The master assessed damages at £1,200 representing the plaintiff's loss of
salary and commission. Unemployment benefit of £59-odd had been received by the   *b*
plaintiff under the National Insurance Act 1946, which was broadly similar to the present
legislation. During the course of the argument the Court of Appeal was referred to
Bourgeois v Tzrop[3] but oddly not to *Fitzpatrick v Moore*[4]. The court unanimously reversed
the master's decision. Sellers LJ said[5]:

> 'With the employer as a contributing party I do not regard the payment as   *c*
> comparable to benefits received under a purely personal insurance policy or by way
> of pension or benefit arising out of a man's employment. In the one case the
> employee has paid a premium and in the other he has a contract of employment and
> his services given under it form the reward (equivalent to a premium) which
> entitles him to the benefit. I can see no reason why a defaulting party should obtain
> the benefit of a payment for which he has not paid any part of the premium or   *d*
> given the services which command the benefit. In such matters I would apply the
> decision of this court in *Payne* v. *Railway Executive*[1]. That case was applied in
> Canada in support of a similar question to that which we have to consider here, but
> although I was a party to the decision in *Payne* v. *Railway Executive*[1], at first instance,
> with respect I would not so apply it, but would distinguish it. I would adhere to
> what was said in *Payne* v. *Railway Executive*[1] and by DONOVAN, L.J., in *Browning* v.   *e*
> *War Office*[6], but I think that where, as here, the employer has made a contribution
> to the unemployment insurance he should get the benefit of it, if he finds it
> necessary to put one of his employees into unemployment, even in circumstances
> where he is liable to compensate him in damages.'

Harman LJ said[7]:
                                                                                      f
> 'Unemployment insurance is a sum receivable by contract made by the employed
> man and his employer each of whom contributes to the state on the footing that if
> and when the servant is unemployed the state will make good part of his earnings
> to him. I do not think such a payment is truly analagous to insurance moneys, as
> in the leading case of *Bradburn* v. *Great Western Ry. Co.*[8], where there was a purely
> voluntary contract made by the plaintiff. This is a contribution which he is bound   *g*
> to make with the very object of mitigating the damage which inability to work will
> do him. It is just as if his employer continued to pay part of his wages. The loss he
> suffers is pro tanto diminished and therefore cannot be charged against the
> wrongdoer.'

Pearson LJ[9] expressed himself in a similar manner:
                                                                                      h
> 'The dismissal caused the plaintiff to become unemployed, and therefore entitled,
> as a matter of general right under the system of state insurance and not by virtue of

---

1   [1951] 2 All ER 910, [1952] 1 KB 26
2   [1963] 2 All ER 658, [1964] 1 QB 95
3   (1957) 9 DLR (2d) 214
4   [1962] NILR 152   *j*
5   [1963] 2 All ER 658 at 669, [1964] 1 QB 95 at 120
6   [1962] 3 All ER 1089, [1963] 1 QB 750
7   [1963] 2 All ER 658 at 675–676, [1964] 1 QB 95 at 120
8   (1874) LR 10 Exch 1, [1874–80] All ER Rep 195
9   [1963] 2 All ER 658 at 684, [1964] 1 QB 95 at 143

a   any private insurance policy of his own, to receive unemployment benefit. The effect of the dismissal was not to deprive him of all income but to reduce his income by substituting unemployment benefit for his salary. It would be unrealistic to disregard the unemployment benefit, because to do so would confer on the plaintiff, to the extent of £59, a fortuitous windfall in addition to compensation.'

This decision was applied by John Stephenson J two years later in a personal injuries case, *Foxley v Olton*[1].

b   We were invited by the plaintiff to review these two decisions in the light of the House of Lords' conclusion in *Parry v Cleaver*[2]. In that case a police constable had been injured in a traffic accident in January 1963 as a result of the defendant's admitted negligence. On 30th June 1964 he was discharged from the police force as the result of his injuries. In October 1964 he obtained other but less well-paid employment. In the action he claimed damages in respect (inter alia) of his net annual loss of earnings pending normal

c   retirement at 48 in 1975. However, as from 1st July 1974, he received a police disablement pension (called 'an ill-health award') payable to him during his life. There was no dispute that he was entitled to damages representing the difference between the wages he would have earned in the force and his civilian wages until he would have retired at the age of 48. The problem was whether, during the period when he was under 48 and was still claiming loss of wages, he must give credit for the disablement

d   pension which he received from his employers during what should have been, but for the accident, his working time on full pay in the force.

    Although there was no actual disablement pension fund in existence, it was agreed between the parties, and the case proceeded on the basis, that he should be treated as if there had been a fund in existence to which he contributed, the remainder necessary for paying the benefit being provided by the police authority, so that in effect employer and

e   employee were the contributories, and the sole contributories, to the notional fund.

    The House decided by a majority against deductibility; the majority consisted of Lord Reid, Lord Pearce and Lord Wilberforce. Lord Reid, in reviewing the authorities which he described as not consistent with each other, dealt first with the case of 'benevolence'. He said[3] that *Redpath's* case[4] was readily supported on the ground that—

f   'It would be revolting to the ordinary man's sense of justice, and therefore contrary to public policy, that the sufferer should have his damages reduced so that he would gain nothing from the benevolence of his friends or relations or of the public at large, and that the only gainer would be the wrongdoer. We do not have to decide in this case whether these considerations also apply to public benevolence in the shape of various uncovenanted benefits from the welfare state, but it may be

g   thought that Parliament did not intend them to be for the benefit of the wrongdoer.'

As regards insurance Lord Reid said[3]:

        'I think that the real and substantial reason for disregarding them is that the plaintiff has bought them and that it would be unjust and unreasonable to hold that the money which he prudently spent on premiums and the benefit from it should

h   inure to the benefit of the tortfeasor. Here again, I think that the explanation that this is too remote is artificial and unreal. Why should the plaintiff be left worse off than if he had never insured? In that case he would have got the benefit of the premium money; if he had not spent it he would have had it in his possession at the time of the accident grossed up at compound interest.'

j   A contributory pension is in no different position. The benefits received, so far as attributable to the employer's contribution, are delayed remuneration for current

1   [1964] 3 All ER 248, [1965] 2 QB 306
2   [1969] 1 All ER 555, [1970] AC 1
3   [1969] 1 All ER 555 at 558, [1970] AC 1 at 14
4   [1947] NILR 167

work. The pension itself is a form of insurance: the employee does not get back exactly what he paid in, but an amount which is dependent on how things turn out; it may be less or more than the contributions from himself and his employer. Lord Reid referred to *Parsons's* case[1] and *Foxley's* case[2], but said they were not directly relevant, and added[3]:

> 'In *Foxley* v. *Olton*[2] JOHN STEPHENSON, J., followed *Parson's* case[1] in taking unemployment benefit into consideration, but refused to take national assistance grants into consideration following a decision of VEALE, J., in *Eldridge* v. *Videtta*[4]. I find it difficult to draw a distinction between unemployment benefit and national assistance. The former could be regarded as a combination of insurance and national benevolence while the insurance element is absent from the latter. But there are here other considerations besides those with which I have dealt. There has been no full argument about them and I do not propose to express any concluded opinion on the matter.'

Lord Pearce made no mention of *Parsons's* case[1] and *Foxley's* case[2]. Lord Wilberforce referred to *Parsons's* case[1] but left the matter open. He said[5]:

> 'As regards some of the social protections which injured plaintiffs may enjoy, Parliament has intervened with a compromise solution, providing that half of certain payments over a period are to be deducted in assessing the loss—see Law Reform (Personal Injuries) Act 1948, s. 2, but this type of solution is not open to the courts. They have to grapple with each type of benefit as it arises, and they have done so sometimes by setting themselves to ascertain what is "fair", sometimes by attempting to squeeze the appropriate answer from, or to explain the answer arrived at by reference to, such words (and I do not wish to deprecate their utility) as "compensatory", "loss", "collateral" or "caused". On the whole, reasonably consistent results have been achieved. As regards private insurance policies taken out by the injured man, the courts have adhered to *Bradburn's* case[6]—it has been approved in this House and in other common law jurisdictions; as regards receipts from voluntary funds it has been decided in Northern Ireland that no deduction should be made (*Redpath* v. *Belfast and County Down Ry.*[7]). The decision was put either on public policy or on the intention of the subscribers, see per SIR JAMES ANDREWS, L.C.J. Decisions have been given regarding some forms of social benefit (e.g., *Parsons* v. *B. N. M. Laboratories, Ltd.*[1]): I do not think that we ought to consider these at this time'.

Lord Morris, in his dissenting judgment, did not refer to *Parsons's* case[1]. Lord Pearson said that he adhered to his decision in *Parsons's* case[1].

In the instant case Smith J treated deduction of unemployment benefit as settled practice. He said:

> 'All I propose to say on this issue, which is whether or not a sum paid by way of unemployment benefit to the plaintiff should or should not be deducted, is that I am going to follow the reasoning in the case which Hollings J decided last year. There is also the authority of the decision of the late Finer J[8]. Both Hollings and

---

1 [1963] 2 All ER 658, [1964] 1 QB 95
2 [1964] 3 All ER 248, [1965] 2 QB 306
3 [1969] 1 All ER 555 at 562–563, [1970] AC 1 at 19
4 (1964) 108 Sol Jo 137
5 [1969] 1 All ER 555 at 579, [1970] AC 1 at 39
6 (1874) LR 10 Exch 1, [1874–80] All ER Rep 195
7 [1947] NILR 167
8 *Orme v Walmsley* (unreported)

a   Finer JJ were in favour of deductibility. Therefore I am going to say the sum of
£1,062 paid by way of unemployment benefit should be deducted from the
plaintiff's damages.'

Hollings J's case was *Shaw v Cape Insulation Co Ltd*[1] decided on 18th July 1977. It contains
some indication of the current practice. Hollings J said:

b   'Now I did have occasion to consider the deductibility of unemployment benefit
in an earlier case last year, *Washington v Norwest Holst Ltd*[2], and gave judgment at
Liverpool on 30th July 1976. I have retained my notes of that judgment, and I have
reconsidered it in the light of the submissions of Mr Playford and, in particular, of
Mr Russell. I should state that in my judgment the proper way to deal with these
benefits is to deduct unemployment benefit but not to deduct supplementary
benefit, and I will try to make as brief as possible my reasons for this. This question
c   involves consideration of previous decisions both of the Court of Appeal and of first
instance and also depends on whether the decision of the House of Lords in *Parry
v Cleaver*[3] has had any effect, and if so what effect, on this question. In two decisions
at first instance in this jurisdiction, it has been held that unemployment benefit is
deductible: Cassels J in *Lindstedt v Wimborne Steamship Co*[4] and John Stephenson J in
Foxley v Olton[5]; and I add there a recent decision of Milmo J reported in The Times,
d   though no reason was set out there, when he deducted unemployment benefit and
industrial rehabilitation allowance and supplementary benefit, in *Cackett v Earl*[6].'

He then referred to the cases of *Fitzpatrick*[7], *Parsons*[8], *Foxley*[5] and *Parry*[3]. He came to the
conclusion that he was bound by the *Parsons's* case[8] but even apart from such authority
he would have so held. He said:

e   'I agree with the submission that for the period that the plaintiff received
unemployment benefit, the plaintiff did not suffer a complete loss of earnings;
unemployment benefit is paid in lieu of wages or when wages cannot be earned for
any reason. Taking the views that I do, that unemployment benefit is a recognised
substitute for wages, provided by statute, and that the insurance element is
essentially notional or even illusory, I consider any sum received should be
f   deducted.'

No transcript or other note was available of Finer J's judgment[9].
We were pressed by the plaintiff's counsel to allow this appeal on the basis that
Parsons's case[8] was wrongly decided, and that we were at liberty and indeed obliged to
depart from it on the ground that the ratio decidendi could not be supported in the light
g   of the majority conclusions in *Parry's* case[3]. Unemployment benefit, it was submitted,
was the product in part of contributions made by the employee over perhaps many
years. It was a form of state insurance, not an alternative to or continuation of the wages
which had been received by the plaintiff during his employment. The effect of the social
security scheme was that both employee, employer and the state were contributing to
the insurance of the employee against the risk of unemployment. The benefits therefore
h   partake partly of the character of insurance and partly of the character of benevolence.

---

1   (18th July 1977) unreported
2   (30th July 1976) unreported
j   3   [1969] 1 All ER 555, [1970] AC 1
4   (1949) 83 Ll L Rep 19
5   [1964] 3 All ER 248, [1965] 2 QB 306
6   [1976] The Times, 15th October
7   [1962] NILR 152
8   [1963] 2 All ER 658, [1964] 1 QB 95
9   *Orme v Walmsley* (unreported)

Furthermore, social benefits have come through a series of decisions of the courts not to be deductible from the damages payable by the wrongdoer, save so far as they are subject to the statutory compromise imposed by the 1948 Act: see, for example, *Hewson v Downs*[1] (state retirement pension), *Daish v Wauton*[2] (maintenance under the national health service), *Bowker v Rose*[3], decided by this court on 2nd February 1978 (mobility allowance and attendance allowance). So ran the argument of the plaintiff.

It was also urged on us that *Parsons's* case[4] was not decisive of the instant case, because the damages were in respect of breach of contract and not, as here, in respect of personal injuries. That appears to us to be a distinction without a difference.

We appreciate the force of the plaintiff's main argument. In the end it comes down to the question whether *Parsons's* case[4] was overruled by *Parry's* case[5]. We have no doubt that the time has come for *Parsons's* case[4] to be reviewed, as indeed was indicated in *Parry's* case[5], but we do not think that such review can properly be conducted by this court. There is no such inconsistency between the two decisions as would entitle us to depart from our previous decision. The law in relation to unemployment benefit is at present that laid down in *Parsons's* case[4], and so it must remain until the House of Lords or the legislature decides otherwise.

For these reasons the appeal will be dismissed.

Appeal dismissed. Leave to appeal to the House of Lords.

Solicitors: *Brian Thompson*, Manchester (for the plaintiff); *A W Mawer & Co*, Manchester (for the defendants).

Mary Rose Plummer   Barrister.

---

1   [1969] 3 All ER 193, [1970] 1 QB 73
2   [1972] 1 All ER 25, [1972] 2 QB 262
3   [1978] The Times, 3rd February
4   [1963] 2 All ER 658, [1964] 1 QB 95
5   [1969] 1 All ER 555, [1970] AC 1

a   Von Ernst & Cie SA and others v Inland
        Revenue Commissioners

COURT OF APPEAL
BUCKLEY, BRIDGE AND TEMPLEMAN LJJ
b   22nd, 23rd, 26th, 27th, 30th NOVEMBER 1979

*Capital transfer tax – Exemptions and reliefs – Excluded property – Government securities in
foreign ownership – Trust fund consisting of exempt government securities held on discretionary
trusts in favour of settlor's children and United Kingdom charities – Settlor's children neither
domiciled nor resident in the United Kingdom – Trustees appointing trust fund to settlor's*
c *children – Whether exempt Government securities liable to tax – Whether charities beneficially
entitled to trust fund before appointment by trustees – Whether charities 'known person for whose
benefit the settled property . . . might be applied' – Whether distribution payment to charity capital
distribution – Whether legislation passed before capital transfer tax introduced capable of
exempting transfer from liability to tax – Finance (No 2) Act 1931, s 22(1) – Finance Act 1975,
Sch 5, paras 6(2), 11(11), Sch 6, para 10(2), Sch 7, para 3(1)(2).*
d

Under a settlement dated 29th August 1967 ('the 1967 settlement') a trust fund was held
on discretionary trusts for the benefit of the children of the settlor and two named
charities in the United Kingdom, one a company with exclusively charitable objects, the
other an unincorporated association. The trustees had power, with the consent of the
e settlor, to advance the whole of the fund to the trustees of another settlement for the
benefit of the settlor's children. In 1976, the trustees of the 1967 settlement were all
resident outside the United Kingdom, and the only living objects of the discretionary
trusts (apart from the charities) were the settlor's two infant children, both of whom
were resident and domiciled outside the United Kingdom. On 22nd March 1976, the
trustees of the 1967 settlement purchased £4,205,875 nominal 10½% Treasury Stock
f 1976 ('the exempt securities'). On 24th March, the settlor established another settlement
('the 1976 settlement'), having the same trustees as the 1967 settlement, under which the
trust fund was held in trust for the two infant children of the settlor as the trustees of the
1976 settlement might appoint and, subject thereto, on discretionary trusts for the
benefit of those two children during a trust period. On the same day, the trustees of the
1967 settlement, in exercise of their power to advance, appointed that the exempt
g securities should be held on the trusts of the 1976 settlement. On 25th March the
trustees of the 1976 settlement appointed funds subject to that settlement on trust to
divide the same into two equal parts and pay the income of one such part to each of the
settlor's two children with remainders over. It was common ground that immediately
before the appointment of 25th March there was no interest in possession in the exempt
securities and that, in consequence of the appointment, the settlor's two children
h immediately became entitled to interests in possession in the whole of the exempt
securities. The Crown took the view that, in consequence of the appointment on 25th
March, a capital distribution was to be treated as having been made out of property
comprised in the settlement by virtue of Sch 5, para 6(2)[a], to the Finance Act 1975, and
served on the trustees a notice of determination specifying the amount of capital transfer
tax chargeable on the distribution. The trustees sought a declaration that in ascertaining
j their liability to capital transfer tax in consequence of the deed of appointment the part
of the trust fund which consisted of the exempt securities did not fall to be taken into
account, contending that the securities were 'excluded property' within Sch 7, para

_____

a   Paragraph 6(2) is set out at p 682 *e f*, post

3(1)(*b*)[*b*], to the 1975 Act. The judge[*c*] refused to make the declaration, holding that, under **a**
the scheme of the 1975 Act, characterisation of exempt securities as 'excluded property'
within Sch 7, para 3(1)(*b*), depended on the beneficial ownership of those securities before
the event giving rise to the charge to tax, that in the circumstances the exempt securities
were not such excluded property immediately before the appointment to the children
and that, accordingly, on the appointment there was a capital distribution out of property
comprised in the settlement for the purposes of charge to tax under Sch 5, para 6(2), to
the Act. The trustees appealed to the Court of Appeal contending further that the **b**
exempt securities were 'excluded property' under Sch 7, para 3(2)[*d*], and that, in any
event, the securities were exempt from capital transfer tax by virtue of s 22(1)[*e*] of the
Finance (No 2) Act 1931.

Held – (i) Whether a particular transaction affecting exempt securities was exempt from
capital transfer tax depended on the true construction of the specific provisions applicable
to such a transaction contained in the 1975 Act, and if those provisions did not provide **c**
exemption the taxing provisions of the Act came into operation and the provisions of the
1931 Act could not provide any exemption therefrom (see p 681 *a b*, p 685 *b c* and p 688
f, post).

(ii) Although on a literal reading Sch 5, para 6(2), to the 1975 Act contemplated a
logical impossibility, viz a person becoming entitled to an interest in possession at a time **d**
when no such interest subsisted, on its true construction the sequence of events
contemplated was first the existence of settled property in which no interest in possession
subsisted and second the creation of an interest in possession in that property. Such a
construction brought para 6(2) into line with the rest of the 1975 Act by looking at the
state of affairs before rather than after the event giving rise to a potential charge to tax in
order to determine whether any relevant exclusion from liability was applicable, and
whether a particular property escaped liability to capital transfer tax on a transfer inter **e**
vivos or on the death of the owner as 'excluded property' within Sch 7, para 3(1), to the
1975 Act depended on whether it correctly answered that description in the hands of the
transferor or the deceased and not whether it would answer that description in the hands
of the transferee or the beneficiary who inherited on death. Before the appointment on
25th March 1976, no one was entitled to an interest in possession in the exempt securities **f**
and accordingly those securities were not 'excluded property' under Sch 7, para 3(1)(*b*), to
the Act for the purposes of charge to tax on the appointment taking effect (see p 681 *j*,
p 683 *b* to *f* and *j*, p 685 *b c* and p 686 *f* to *j*, post).

(iii) An unincorporated charity or a company with exclusively charitable objects could
not be an object for whose benefit settled property or income from it could be applied or
which might become beneficially entitled to an interest in possession in settled property
within the meaning of Sch 7, para 3(2), and accordingly was not within the scope of the **g**
phrase 'known person for whose benefit the settled property . . . might be applied' under
that paragraph. Thus the inclusion of the two charities as the possible objects of the
discretionary trust was not fatal to the exemption given by para 3(2) if it was otherwise
applicable. Furthermore, by virtue of Sch 6, para 10(2)[*f*], property given to a charity was
not a capital distribution within Sch 5, para 6, and consequently the inclusion of a charity **h**
in a discretionary class could not render exempt securities held on discretionary trusts for
that class non-excluded if those securities would be otherwise excluded. It followed that,
since, apart from the charities, the only beneficiaries under the trust were neither
domiciled nor resident in the United Kingdom, the exempt securities were 'excluded
property' within Sch 7, para 3(2), and, therefore, by virtue of Sch 5, para 11(11)[*g*], were not **j**

---

b Paragraph 3(1) is set out at p 681 *h*, post
c [1979] STC 478
d Paragraph 3(2) is set out at p 683 *h*, post
e Section 22(1), so far as material, is set out at p 680 *f g*, post
f Paragraph 10(2), is set out at p 684 *j*, post
g Paragraph 11(11) is set out at p 682 *g h*, post

a property comprised in a settlement within Sch 5, para 6(2). Accordingly the appointment of 25th March 1976 did not result in the making of a capital distribution out of the exempt securities within Sch 5, para 6(2). The appeal would therefore be allowed (see p 684 *f* to p 685 *c* and p 688 *c* to *f*, post).

Notes

For exempt government securities which are excluded property, see 19 Halsbury's Laws
b (4th Edn) para 758.

For the Finance Act 1975, Sch 5, paras 6, 11, Sch 6, para 10, and Sch 7, para 3, see 45 Halsbury's Statutes (3rd Edn) 1889, 1894, 1909, 1918.

For the Finance (No 2) Act 1931, s 22, see 34 ibid 813.

Cases referred to in judgment

Construction Industry Training Board v Attorney-General [1972] 2 All ER 1339, [1973] Ch
c 173, [1972] 3 WLR 187, CA, 8(1) Digest (Reissue) 291, 359.

Finger's Will Trusts, Re, Turner v Ministry of Health [1971] 3 All ER 1050, [1972] Ch 286, [1971] 3 WLR 775, 8(1) Digest (Reissue) 353, 847.

French Protestant Hospital, Re [1951] 1 All ER 938, [1951] Ch 567, 13 Digest (Reissue) 261, 2332.

Inland Revenue Comrs v Graham's Trustees 1971 SLT 46.
d *Larter (Inspector of Taxes) v Skone James* [1976] 2 All ER 615, [1976] 1 WLR 607, [1976] STC 220.

Smith's Settlement Trusts, Re, Executor, Trustee and Agency Co of South Australia Ltd v Inland Revenue Comrs [1951] 1 All ER 146, [1951] Ch 360, [1950] TR 355, 21 Digest (Repl) 50, 200.

Soldiers', Sailors' and Airmen's Families Association v Attorney-General [1968] 1 All ER 448,
e [1968] 1 WLR 313, 8(1) Digest (Reissue) 430, 1693.

Cases also cited

Ayerst (Inspector of Taxes) v C & K (Construction) Ltd [1975] 2 All ER 537, [1976] AC 167, [1975] STC 345, HL.

Camille and Henry Dreyfus Foundation Inc v Inland Revenue Comrs [1955] 3 All ER 97,
f [1956] AC 39, 36 Tax Cas 126, HL; *affg* [1954] 2 All ER 466, [1955] Ch 672, 36 Tax Cas 126, CA.

Gasque v Inland Revenue Comrs [1946] KB 80, 23 Tax Cas 210.

Hastings-Bass (deceased), Re, Hastings v Inland Revenue Comrs [1974] 2 All ER 193, [1975] Ch 25, [1974] STC 211, CA.

Appeal
g Under a settlement made on 29th August 1967 ('the 1967 settlement') and varied pursuant to an order of 14th December 1972, the plaintiffs, Von Ernst & Cie SA, Jean-Paul Aeschimann and Kenneth Porter, held a trust fund on discretionary trusts for the benefit of the children of the settlor, Mrs Vivien Louise Duffield, and two charities, Annacastle Ltd, a company limited by guarantee with exclusively charitable objects, and the Charles Clore Foundation, an unincorporated charity. On 24th March 1976, the
h settlor executed another settlement ('the 1976 settlement') having the same trustees as the 1967 settlement under which the trust fund was held in trust for the two infant children of the settlor as the trustees of the 1976 settlement might appoint and subject thereto on discretionary trusts for the benefit of those two children during a trust period. On the same day the trustees of the 1967 settlement, in exercise of their power to advance, appointed that £4,205,875 nominal 10½% Treasury Stock 1976, which
j formed part of the trust fund of the 1967 settlement, should be held on the trusts of the 1976 settlement. On the following day, the trustees of the 1976 settlement executed a deed of appointment appointing the Treasury Stock equally to the settlor's two children. At all material times the settlor's children were domiciled and resident outside the United Kingdom. On 2nd February 1978, the Inland Revenue Commissioners sent to each of the trustees a notice of determination under Sch 5, para 6(2), to the Finance Act

1975 to the effect that, in consequence of the deed of appointment, the trustees were
liable to capital transfer tax in the sum of £2,900,993. By an originating summons dated a
3rd March 1978 the trustees appealed to the High Court pursuant to para 7(3) of Sch 4 to
the 1975 Act, seeking, inter alia, by para 1, a declaration that in ascertaining the liability
(if any) of the trustees to capital transfer tax under Sch 5, para 6(2), in consequence of the
deed of appointment made on 25th March 1976 the part of the trust fund which
consisted of the Treasury Stock did not fall to be taken into account, on the ground that
the Treasury Stock constituted 'excluded property' within Sch 7, para 3(1)(b) to the 1975 b
Act, and, by para 2, a declaration that no capital transfer tax was chargeable in
consequence of the deed of appointment. On 26th March 1979 Browne-Wilkinson J[1]
declined to make the declarations and confirmed the determination made on the trustees
subject to an agreed reduction in the amount of tax chargeable on the capital distribution
to £2,804,936·75. The trustees appealed to the Court of Appeal contending further (a)
that the Treasury Stock held by them constituted excluded property within Sch 7, para c
3(2), to the 1975 Act, and accordingly was not comprised in the settled property
chargeable with capital transfer tax in consequence of the deed of appointment, and (b)
that, in any event, by reason of s 22(1)(b) of the Finance (No 2) Act 1931, the holding of
the Treasury Stock was not liable to capital transfer tax.

C N Beattie QC and Robert Walker for the trustees.
D J Nicholls QC and Peter Gibson for the Crown.   d

- Cur adv vult

30th November. The following judgments were read.

BRIDGE LJ (delivering the first judgment at the invitation of Buckley LJ). This is an
appeal from a judgment of Browne-Wilkinson J[1] given on 26th March 1979, refusing the e
declarations sought by the appellant plaintiffs ('the trustees') in their originating
summons and confirming the determination by the Board of Inland Revenue (subject to
an agreed variation of the figures) that a capital distribution had been made by the
trustees attracting capital transfer tax under para 6 of Sch 5 to the Finance Act 1975.

The facts are concisely and accurately summarised in the judgment of the learned
judge and I need not repeat them. The point at issue relates to a transaction affecting a f
holding of 10½% Treasury Stock 1976. These are securities issued subject to a condition,
authorised by the Finance (No 2) Act 1931, s 22(1), that they shall be exempt from
taxation 'so long as the securities are in the beneficial ownership of persons who are
neither domiciled nor ordinarily resident in the United Kingdom'. It will be convenient
to refer to them as exempt securities. For the purposes of capital transfer tax, imposed
by Part III of the Finance Act 1975, the effect of s 29 and Sch 7, para 3(1)(b), is to provide g
that exempt securities are excluded property 'if they are settled property and [a person
neither domiciled nor ordinarily resident in the United Kingdom] is beneficially entitled
to an interest in possession in them'.

Immediately before 25th March 1976 the exempt securities with which we are
concerned were held on discretionary trusts and were thus comprised in a settlement in
which no interest in possession subsisted. By a deed of appointment made on 25th h
March 1976, two named individuals, neither of them domiciled or ordinarily resident in
the United Kingdom, became entitled to interests in possession in the exempt
securities. The question at issue is whether in consequence of this appointment capital
transfer tax became chargeable under Sch 5, para 6(4), to the Finance Act 1975 'as on the
value transferred by a chargeable transfer'. Three distinct points have been canvassed
before us. First, is the transaction exempt from tax by virtue of the Finance Act 1975, j
Sch 7, para 3(1)(b)? Secondly, is the transaction exempt from tax independently of the
provisions of the Finance Act 1975 by the operation of s 22(1) of the Finance (No 2) Act
1931? Thirdly, is the transaction exempt from tax by virtue of the Finance Act 1975, Sch

1 [1979] 1 WLR 1325, [1979] STC 478

7, para 3(2)? The second and third points were raised for the first time in this court. I have set out the points in the order in which they were argued before us for the trustees but I find it convenient to dispose of the second point first since this can be done in a few sentences. It is to my mind clear beyond argument that whether or not any particular transaction affecting exempt securities is exempt from capital transfer tax must depend on the true construction of the specific provisions applicable to such a transaction contained in the Finance Act 1975. If those provisions provide exemption, well and good; if those provisions do not provide exemption, the taxing provisions of the Finance Act 1975 come into operation and the provisions of the Finance (No 2) Act 1931 cannot provide any exemption from them.

I turn now to the first point which the judge decided in favour of the Crown. This point depends on the true construction of the provisions of Sch 5, para 6, but to see the overall scheme of the Act of which the crucial provisions form part it is convenient to set out the main taxing provisions and in particular to see how they operate in relation to exempt securities. I shall read them omitting immaterial words.

Section 19(1): 'A tax, to be known as capital transfer tax, shall be charged on the value transferred by a chargeable transfer.'

Section 20(2) and (3):

'(2) Subject to subsections (3) and (4) below, a transfer of value is any disposition made by a person ("the transferor") as a result of which the value of his estate immediately after the disposition is less than it would be but for the disposition; and the amount by which it is less is the value transferred by the transfer.

'(3) For the purposes of subsection (2) above no account shall be taken of the value of excluded property which ceases to form part of a person's estate as a result of a disposition.'

Section 22(1):

'On the death of any person after the passing of this Act tax shall be charged as if, immediately before his death, he had made a transfer of value and the value transferred by it had been equal to the value of his estate immediately before his death, but subject to the following provisions of this section.'

Section 23(1):

'For the purposes of this Part of this Act, a person's estate is the aggregate of all the property to which he is beneficially entitled, except that the estate of a person immediately before his death does not include excluded property.'

Section 24 contains general provisions relating to 'excluded property' but the relevant definition of 'excluded property' for present purposes is in Sch 7, para 3(1), to which I have already referred. It reads:

'Where securities have been issued by the Treasury subject to a condition authorised by section 22 of the Finance (No. 2) Act 1931 (or section 47 of the Finance (No. 2) Act 1915) for exemption from taxation so long as the securities are in the beneficial ownership of persons neither domiciled nor ordinarily resident in the United Kingdom the securities are excluded property—(a) if they are not settled property and are in the beneficial ownership of such a person; or (b) if they are settled property and such a person is beneficially entitled to an interest in possession in them.'

Pausing there, it is in my judgment abundantly clear from the language of the provisions I have read that the question whether a particular property escapes taxation on a transfer inter vivos or on the death of the owner as 'excluded property' depends on whether it correctly answers to that description in the hands of the transferor or the deceased, not on whether it will answer to that description in the hands of the transferee or the beneficiary who inherits on death. I found the contention of counsel for the trustees to the contrary, with respect, to be quite unarguable.

Against that background I turn to Sch 5, which is brought into effect by s 20(1). Paragraph 1(1) provides: *a*

'The following provisions of this paragraph apply for determining what is to be taken for the purposes of capital transfer tax to be a settlement, and what property is, accordingly, referred to as property comprised in a settlement or as settled property; and who is the settlor and a trustee in relation to a settlement.'

It is common ground that the phrases 'property comprised in a settlement' and 'settled   *b* property' are synonymous.

Paragraph 3(1) provides: 'A person beneficially entitled to an interest in possession in settled property shall be treated as beneficially entitled to the property in which the interest subsists.' This provision, it will be observed, has the effect, together with s 22, of charging capital transfer tax on settled property on the death of the life tenant unless he is entitled to exemption as a non-resident holder of exempt securities under Sch 7, para   *c* 3(1)(b), or unless the property is otherwise excluded property.

Paragraph 4 contains provisions for imposing tax on the disposal or other termination inter vivos of interests held under a settlement, but again gives exemption in favour of the non-resident beneficiary on the disposal or termination of his interest in exempt securities or other excluded property.

Paragraph 6 provides as follows: *d*

'(1) Where a distribution payment is made out of property comprised in a settlement and at the time the payment is made no interest in possession subsists in the property or in the part of it out of which the payment is made, the payment is in this Schedule referred to as a capital distribution.

'(2) Where a person becomes entitled to an interest in possession in the whole or any part of the property comprised in a settlement at a time when no such interest   *e* subsists in the property or that part, a capital distribution shall be treated as being made out of the property or that part of the property; and the amount of the distribution shall be taken to be equal to the value at that time of the property or, if the interest is in part only of that property, of that part . . .

'(4) Tax shall be charged on any capital distribution as on the value transferred by   *f* a chargeable transfer . . .'

These provisions must be read in conjunction with para 11(7), which provides:

'"Distribution payment" means, subject to sub-paragraph (8) below, any payment which—(a) is not income of any person for any of the purposes of income tax and would not for any of those purposes be income of a person not resident in the United Kingdom if he were so resident; and (b) is not a payment in respect of costs   *g* or expenses; and "payment" includes the transfer of assets other than money.'

and para 11(11) which provides: 'References to settled property shall be construed as referring only to property which is not excluded property.'

The argument of counsel for the trustees is essentially a simple one. He submits that when the appointment of 25th March 1976 took effect the beneficiaries thereunder did   *h* not 'become entitled to an interest in possession in . . . property comprised in a settlement' under para 6(2) because at the very moment of their entitlement arising the property in question ceased to be 'settled property' under Sch 6 by virtue of para 11(11).

Counsel for the trustees sought to support his argument by extracting from certain earlier authorities relating to estate duty and capital gains tax the general principle that in applying what has been called a mutation tax one must always determine the incidence   *j* and amount of the tax by reference to the state of affairs existing after, not before, the occurrence of the event relied on as giving rise to the charge to tax. He relied on *Re Smith's Settlement Trusts*[1], *Inland Revenue Comrs v Graham's Trustees*[2] and *Larter (Inspector*

1   [1951] 1 All ER 146, [1951] Ch 360
2   1971 SLT 46

of Taxes) v *Skone James*[1]. In reference to a taxing statute which left the matter at large, or
a threw up an ambiguity on the point which could not otherwise be resolved, I can
appreciate that it would be proper to pray in aid the principle derived from these
decisions. But if the provisions of the particular statute on their true construction point
to an opposite conclusion these decisions are, in my judgment, of no relevance.

As the judge pointed out, Sch 5, para 6(2), read quite literally, contemplates a logical
impossibility, viz a person becoming entitled to an interest in possession at a time when
b no such interest subsists. The sequence contemplated must clearly be first the existence
of settled property in which no interest in possession subsists, secondly the creation of an
interest in possession in that property. When that sequence of events occurs the sub-
paragraph provides that 'a capital distribution shall be treated as being made out of the
property'. The property out of which the capital distribution is treated as being made is
property in which no interest in possession subsists. This brings para 6(2) into line with
c sub-para (1), which provides in effect a definition of what amounts to a capital
distribution. The two elements essential to a capital distribution are (1) a payment out
of property comprised in a settlement and (2) the making of the payment at a time when
no interest in possession subsists in the property. Counsel for the trustees concedes, I
think, that a distribution payment out of property held on discretionary trusts to a
beneficiary for an absolute interest would be an actual capital distribution under para 6(1)
d which (subject to the new point raised under Sch 7, para 3(2)) would inevitably attract tax
under para 6(4). This concession being rightly and, as I think inescapably, made, it
follows in my judgment equally inescapably that the capital distribution which is to
be treated as being made in the event contemplated by para 6(2) attracts tax in exactly the
same way. This construction would, in my judgment, be the right one to apply to
the language of para 6 considered in isolation. But it is powerfully reinforced by the
e consideration that it brings the paragraph wholly into line with the rest of the Act as
looking at the state of affairs before rather than after the event giving rise to a potential
charge to tax in order to determine whether any relevant exclusion from liability is
applicable.

Accordingly, on the only point which was argued before the learned judge, I reach a
conclusion entirely in accord with his. I have attempted to set out my reasons for doing
f so in my own language but I would also wish gratefully to adopt the learned judge's
admirably lucid and to my mind wholly convincing reasoning.

All that has been said so far in this judgment has been based on the assumption, which
was accepted as correct in the court below, that the trustees cannot claim exemption
from capital transfer tax in respect of the appointment made on 25th March 1976 in
reliance on Sch 7, para 3(2). But now in this court that assumption is challenged and it
g is submitted that, even if one must, in applying paras 6(2) and 11(11) of Sch 5, consider
whether the exempt securities were excluded property when still subject to a discretionary
trust, one can reach a conclusion in favour of the exemption claimed by applying Sch 7,
para 3(2) to the facts of the case. That sub-paragraph provides as follows:

'If the securities are settled property and no interest in possession subsists in them
h   the condition of sub-paragraph (1)(b) above shall be treated as satisfied if it is shown
that all known persons for whose benefit the settled property or income from it has
been or might be applied or who might become beneficially entitled to an interest
in possession in it are persons neither domiciled nor ordinarily resident in the
United Kingdom.'

For the purpose of considering the application of this provision, we have to look at the
j facts as they were immediately before the appointment of 25th March 1976. The
exempt securities were then subject to discretionary trusts of which the only individual
beneficiaries were neither domiciled nor ordinarily resident in the United Kingdom.
But it is common ground that on failure of the trusts in favour of those beneficiaries the
property would have been held on constructive discretionary trusts for two named

1   [1976] 2 All ER 615, [1976] 1 WLR 607, [1976] STC 220

charities in the United Kingdom, one a company limited by guarantee with exclusively
charitable objects, the other an unincorporated charitable foundation. I should add that
the limited company was qualified to take under the discretionary trusts only so long as
its objects remained exclusively charitable.

A number of questions have been canvassed on the construction of Sch 7, para 3(2), but
the only question I find it necessary to decide is whether either or both of the charities
who might have received payments of the income or capital out of the exempt securities
fall within the words 'known persons for whose benefit the settled property or income
from it . . . might be applied or who might become beneficially entitled to an interest in
possession in it'.

Junior counsel for the trustees submitted in summary that the trustees of an
unincorporated charity have no 'benefit' from, nor 'beneficial entitlement' to, trust
moneys within the meaning of this provision and that likewise a company with
exclusively charitable objects has no 'benefit' from, nor 'beneficial entitlement' to, the
company's assets. The true beneficiaries in each case, counsel submitted, are the objects
of the charity. This submission was developed by reference to a number of authorities
concerned with various aspects of the status, functions and duties of charitable
corporations. I do not refer to these in detail since, in my view, they certainly do not
resolve nor in the end throw much significant light on the question we have to decide
which depends on the true construction of the particular statutory provision to be
applied.

Counsel for the Crown understandably concentrated his argument on the charitable
company, though he did not concede that the trustees of the unincorporated charity
were not 'known persons for whose benefit the settled property or income from it . . .
might be applied or who might become beneficially entitled to an interest in possession
in it'. With respect to the company, he submitted that a company formed under the
Companies Acts, though its objects may be exclusively charitable, is nevertheless not a
trustee of its assets. I assume for the purpose of this judgment that that submission is
well founded. It must inevitably follow from that, according to counsel's submission for
the Crown, that all receipts by the company are for its benefit and that the company is
beneficially entitled to all its assets.

In the end this question falls to be decided according to the proper meaning to be
given to the concepts of 'benefit' and 'beneficial entitlement' in Sch 7, para 3(2). I find it
difficult to see how it could properly be said that the trustees of an unincorporated
charity 'might become beneficially entitled' to property within the meaning of the
provision and consequently I should be inclined equally to exclude them from the scope
of the phrase 'known persons for whose benefit the settled property . . . might be
applied'. If this view is right and the inclusion of an unincorporated charity as the
possible object of a discretionary trust is not fatal to the exemption given by Sch 7, para
3(2), if it is otherwise applicable, I should be reluctant to find myself driven to the
opposite conclusion if the charity which may take under the discretionary trust is a
limited company qualified to take only so long as its objects remain exclusively
charitable. I can imagine no possible ground of fiscal policy which could make such a
distinction sensible or reasonable.

But the decisive factor which has confirmed me in the conclusion that this point
should be decided in favour of the trustees is derived from a consideration of another
provision in the Act. Schedule 6, para 10(2) and (3), provide, as follows:

'(2) Notwithstanding anything in paragraph 6 of Schedule 5 to this Act, where
property is given to a charity by the making of a distribution payment within the
meaning of that paragraph, the distribution payment is not a capital distribution for
the purposes of that Schedule.

'(3) For the purposes of this paragraph property is given to charities if it becomes
the property of charities or is held on trust for charitable purposes only.'

It follows from this that no payment out of a discretionary trust in favour of a charity a   attracts capital transfer tax at all. That being so, it would seem to me utterly paradoxical that the mere possibility of such a payment being made out of a particular discretionary trust should deprive that trust of the immunity from taxation which it would otherwise enjoy under Sch 7, para 3(2) on a capital distribution of exempt securities.

On that short ground I would accordingly allow the appeal and substitute for the learned judge's order a declaration in the terms claimed in para 1 of the trustees' originating summons.

b

TEMPLEMAN LJ. I agree with the judgment that has just been delivered and, having had an opportunity of reading in draft the judgment which Buckley LJ is about to deliver, I agree with that also.

c
BUCKLEY LJ. I agree with the judgment which Bridge LJ has delivered, but as the case may be one of some general interest I propose to state my reasons in my own language.

The question in this case is whether in the circumstances of the case the $10\frac{1}{2}$% Treasury Stock comprised in the settled fund was 'excluded property' for the purposes of the Finance Act 1975, Part III, on 25th March 1976 when the settlor's two children (whom d   I shall call Arabella and George) became entitled to interests in possession in the settled fund under the appointment of that date. It is common ground that the fund in question was 'property comprised in a settlement' and 'settled property' for the purposes of the Act. By virtue of s 21, Sch 5 to the Act applies to such property.

Immediately before 25th March 1976 the fund was held on discretionary trusts, and it is common ground that in that state of affairs no interest in possession subsisted in the e   fund within the meaning of the Act. Accordingly under para 6(2) of Sch 5 a 'capital distribution' must be treated as having been made out of the property comprised in the settlement on Arabella and George becoming entitled to interests in possession. The label 'a capital distribution' is given by para 6(1) of Sch 5 to a 'distribution payment' made out of settled property at a time when no interest in possession subsists in it; and by f   virtue of para 11(7) of the schedule 'distribution payment' means, putting it shortly, any payment (which may include a transfer of assets other than money) which is not the income of any person for income tax purposes and would not be so if he was resident in the United Kingdom. The combined effect of these provisions is that on 25th March 1976 payments of a capital nature are to be treated as having been made out of the trust fund to Arabella and George together equal to the value at that time of the settled g   property except to the extent that the settled property consisted of 'excluded property' (see para 11(11)). Tax became payable under para 6(4) on the value so ascertained.

Section 29 of the Act gives statutory effect to certain exemptions and reliefs contained in Sch 7 to the Act. The relevant paragraph of that schedule for present purposes is para 3, which specifies in what circumstances securities issued on such conditions as in fact apply to the $10\frac{1}{2}$% Treasury Stock in the present case constitute excluded property. Sub-h   paragraph (1)(b) of that paragraph provides that such securities are excluded property if they are settled property and a person who is neither domiciled nor ordinarily resident in the United Kingdom (a qualification which both Arabella and George had at all material times) is beneficially entitled to an interest in possession in them. Paragraph 3(2) contains an alternative ground on which such securities may qualify as excluded property, to which I must return later.

j   Counsel for the trustees, relying on *Re Smith's Settlement Trusts*[1], *Inland Revenue Comrs v Graham's Trustees*[2] and *Larter (Inspector of Taxes) v Skone James*[3], contended that for the

---

1   [1951] 1 All ER 146, [1951] Ch 360
2   1971 SLT 46
3   [1976] 2 All ER 615, [1976] 1 WLR 607, [1976] STC 220

purposes of para 3(1)(*b*) of Sch 7 one must consider the beneficial interests which arise on the event which occasions the charge to tax, that is to say that in the present case it is the *a* interests in possession which arose in Arabella and George on the execution of the appointment that are relevant, and not the discretionary trusts which were in operation immediately before that appointment. His argument can, I hope, be fairly summarised thus. A capital distribution is only to be treated under para 6(2) of Sch 5 as being made if and when a person becomes entitled to an interest in possession in settled property. At that moment the settlement is transmuted from being one under which no interest in *b* possession subsists to being one under which a person is entitled to an interest in possession. Since this transmutation is the cause of the charge to tax arising, the charge to tax must be regarded as arising after (no doubt immediately after, but nevertheless after) the transmutation. Therefore the taxing provisions must be applied in the light of the interests subsisting as the result of the transmutation, not of those which subsisted immediately before the transmutation.   *c*

Counsel for the trustees suggested that precisely the same principles must also apply to other cases in which a transfer of value occurs, or is to be treated as having occurred, for the purposes of the tax. Thus in a case of an out and out transfer of property by a transferor inter vivos (to which s 20 is applicable) counsel for the trustees says that whether exempt securities are excluded property must depend not on the domicile and ordinary residence of the transferor but on those of the transferee. In the same way on *d* a transfer on death (to which s 22 is applicable) he says that the answer to the question must depend on the state of affairs following the death and not on that immediately preceding the death. In the case of a change in beneficial ownership occurring on a cesser of a life interest (to which Sch 5, para 3(1), s 23 and s 22(1) are applicable) counsel for the trustees says that the answer must depend on the state of affairs following the death of the life tenant and not on that immediately preceding his death. In my judgment none of *e* these contentions can stand up against the express language of the relevant provisions. Section 20(3) provides that no account shall be taken of the value of excluded property 'which ceases to form part of [the transferor's] estate' as a result of a disposition. Section 23, which falls to be read with s 22, provides that the estate of the deceased immediately before his death does not for the purposes of the Act include excluded property. The same provision is applicable on the termination of a life interest. This language, in my *f* opinion, clearly points to the identification of excluded property by reference to the state of affairs while the property in question forms part of the estate of the transferor or of the deceased owner or life tenant. In my judgment, analysis of para 6(1) and (2) of Sch 5 leads to the same conclusion. When a person becomes entitled to an interest in possession in settled property in which no such interest has hitherto subsisted, what is to be treated as being made out of that property is a 'capital distribution', which by definition (see para *g* 6(1)) is a payment out of settled property at a time when no interest in possession in it subsists. This, in my opinion, focuses attention on the state of affairs which existed immediately before the transmutation. At that stage in the present case no one who was neither domiciled nor ordinarily resident in the United Kingdom had any interest in possession in the Treasury Stock. Indeed at that stage no one at all had any interest in possession in the stock. If anyone had had such an interest, para 6 would not have *h* applied.

I consequently reach the conclusion that the Treasury Stock was not excluded property by virtue of para 3(1)(*b*) of Sch 7 for the purposes of the charge to tax which arose in this case on the appointment taking effect.

The cases referred to earlier, on which counsel for the trustees relies, are decisions on other statutes. I reach my conclusion on this part of the present case on the construction *j* of the language used in the relevant provisions of the Finance Act 1975. I do not think the cases are of assistance on that question of construction.

I turn, therefore, to para 3(2) of Sch 7, which has already been read by Bridge LJ. No point was taken on this before Browne-Wilkinson J. The question here is whether in the present case it can be said that immediately before the appointment took effect 'all

known persons for whose benefit the settled property or income from it has been or
a might be applied or who might become beneficially entitled to an interest in possession
in it' were persons who were neither domiciled nor ordinarily resident in the United
Kingdom.

At that stage the settled fund was held on a discretionary trust for a class of
discretionary objects consisting of Arabella and George and their respective issue (of
whom there were and never have been any in existence) subject to a power of
b appointment in favour or for the benefit of Arabella and George or either of them. If no
appointment had been made under that power, and if Arabella and George had both died
before the end of the last mentioned trust period without issue, or their issue failing
during that trust period, the trusts of the 1976 settlement would have become exhausted
and one would be thrown back on the trusts of the 1967 settlement then capable of
subsisting, under which an incorporated charity called Annacastle Ltd (which was
c introduced to the 1967 settlement by the variation of trusts order of 14th December
1972), and an unincorporated charity called the Charles Clore Foundation, would have
become objects of the trusts.

The appointment of 25th March 1976 was made under the power of appointment
contained in the 1976 settlement. As in accordance with my judgment already expressed
the question whether the Treasury Stock was excluded property for the purposes of the
d notional capital distribution which must be treated as having been made on that
appointment taking effect has to be answered in reference to the state of affairs which
existed immediately before the appointment took effect, I need not consider in detail the
terms of that appointment. The only known persons or bodies who might have to be
taken into account for the purposes of para 3(2) of Sch 7 in relation to that notional capital
distribution are Arabella, George, Annacastle Ltd and the Charles Clore Foundation.

e Annacastle Ltd is a company incorporated under the Companies Act 1948 having
objects of a wide character but exclusively charitable. Its memorandum of association
forbids in a familiar form any payment or transfer of assets directly or indirectly to any
member of the company and provides that on liquidation surplus assets shall not be paid
to or distributed among the members but shall be applied for charitable purposes. The
company has power in law to alter its objects and so could introduce non-charitable
f objects, but this is, I think, irrelevant because the variation of trusts order makes
Annacastle Ltd an object of the trusts of the 1967 settlement for so long only as its objects
remain exclusively charitable.

In these circumstances the question arises whether Annacastle Ltd was, at 25th March
1976, a 'known person for whose benefit the settled property or income from it had been
or might be applied or who might become beneficially entitled to an interest in possession
g in it'.

Junior counsel, who argued this part of the case on behalf of the trustees and did so, if
I may say so, very well, accepted that Annacastle Ltd was a known person, but contended
that it was not a person capable of being benefited or of becoming beneficially entitled
for the purpose of para 3(2). He says that the only persons or purposes capable of
benefiting from money or property received by Annacastle Ltd are the objects of the
h charitable purposes of the company, and these are unascertained purposes and unknown
persons. Counsel for the Crown submits that Annacastle Ltd is not a trustee of its assets:
it owns its assets absolutely and can do what it likes with them within its statutory
powers like any other company incorporated under the Companies Acts. It can, he says,
own property beneficially.

We were referred to certain authorities which give support to the view that a company
j incorporated for exclusively charitable purposes is in the position of a trustee of its funds
or at least in an analogous position. The authorities were *Re French Protestant Hospital*[1],
Soldiers', Sailors' and Airmen's Families Association v Attorney-General[2], *Construction Industry*

1   [1951] 1 All ER 938, [1951] Ch 567
2   [1968] 1 All ER 448, [1968] 1 WLR 313

Training Board v Attorney-General[1] and *Re Finger's Will Trusts, Turner v Ministry of Health*[2].

In the first two of these cases it seems to me that it was assumed, rather than decided, *a* that a corporate charity was in the position of a trustee of its funds. In the third, the question was what was meant by the words 'in the exercise of the court's jurisdiction with respect to charities' in the Charities Act 1960, s 45(1). In the course of my judgment in that case I certainly did express the view that the court would exercise its jurisdiction over corporate charities on the basis that their assets were held on charitable trusts and it appears to me that Plowman J, as I understand his very short judgment, agreed with me *b* in that respect. *Re Finger's Will Trusts*[2] turned on a question of whether or not a bequest to a charitable corporation, which ceased to exist in the testatrix's lifetime, demonstrated a general charitable intention capable of permitting a cy-près application. I do not think that it is a decision which is of assistance for present purposes.

On this part of the case, as on the earlier part, I do not think that authority helps us much. We have to construe para 3(2). In my judgment a corporation which is by its *c* constitution debarred from using or acquiring assets for the purpose of making or obtaining any profit for itself or its corporators, and which serves the purpose only of machinery for carrying on exclusively charitable activities, is not an object for whose *benefit* settled property or income from it can be applied or which might become *beneficially* entitled to an interest in possession in settled property within the meaning of para 3(2). For the purposes of applying para 3(2) I think one must look at the character *d* of such a body to see whether it, rather than the purposes which it exists to serve, is capable of benefiting within the meaning of the paragraph and, in my judgment, it is not capable of doing so. It is a mere conduit pipe, just as in my view the trustees of an unincorporated charity are.

It is, in my view, significant that by para 10 of Sch 6 property given to charity is not a capital distribution for the purposes of Sch 5. If settled property given to charity is *e* exempt, it would be strange if the inclusion of a charity in a discretionary class could render exempt securities held on discretionary trusts for that class non-excluded if those securities would otherwise be excluded property.

I would consequently allow this appeal on this latter ground.

On the point which has been argued under the Finance (No 2) Act 1931, I am in entire agreement with Bridge LJ.   *f*

Appeal allowed. Leave to appeal to the House of Lords.

Solicitors: *Titmuss, Sainer & Webb* (for the trustees); *Solicitor of Inland Revenue.*

J H Fazan Esq   Barrister. *g*

1   [1972] 2 All ER 1339, [1973] Ch 173
2   [1971] 3 All ER 1050, [1972] Ch 286

Castanho v Brown & Root (UK) Ltd and another

QUEEN'S BENCH DIVISION
PARKER J
29th, 30th OCTOBER, 19th NOVEMBER 1979

Practice – Discontinuance of action – Discontinuance by plaintiff – Action brought in England claiming damages for personal injuries – Defendant ordered to make interim payments on admitting liability – Plaintiff commencing action in America in hope of getting higher damages – Plaintiff purporting to discontinue English action – Defendant applying for order to strike out notice of discontinuance and for injunction to restrain plaintiff continuing proceedings in America and commencing other proceedings there or elsewhere – Whether notice of discontinuance should be struck out – Whether injunction should be granted.

The plaintiff, a Portuguese national residing in Portugal, was employed by the defendants, a Panamanian company, as an oiler on one of their ships. In February 1977 he sustained very severe personal injuries in an accident which occurred on board the ship when she was at an English port. As a result he brought an action in England against the defendants claiming damages in respect of his injuries. On 22nd March 1978 a consent order was made requiring the defendants to make an interim payment of £7,250 to the plaintiff, which they did. In June the defendants admitted liability by letter. About that time the plaintiff was approached by a firm of American lawyers, who sought to persuade him to hand over the case to them and to give them authority to enforce his claim in America on a contingency fee basis. The plaintiff was reluctant to do so. In December 1978 there was an order, not by consent, that the defendants should make a further interim payment of £20,000, which they did. About that time the plaintiff's English solicitors were approached by the American lawyers, and, following discussions between the American lawyers, the English solicitors and the plaintiff, the latter were persuaded that the plaintiff was likely to obtain much higher damages in America. On 7th February 1979, while the English action was still pending, process was issued in the plaintiff's name in a state court in Texas claiming, against the defendants and certain other companies, damages in respect of the plaintiff's accident. The following day the plaintiff signed a power of attorney in favour of the American lawyers giving them exclusive power to represent him in the prosecution of his claim in America and providing, inter alia, for them to be paid out of the amounts received or recovered by the plaintiff and for the action in England not to be concluded prior to the decision in the American action and that in the event of the English action being reactivated by the defendants the course to be followed would be decided by agreement between the American lawyers and the English solicitors or in default of agreement by the English solicitors. The plaintiff also signed an agreement with his English solicitors that he would pay their fees if they were not paid by the American lawyers. On 6th April the defendants entered a special appearance in the American action objecting to the jurisdiction of the Texas court. On 30th April they delivered their defence in the English action in which they formally admitted liability. The following day they issued a summons for directions and applied for an injunction restraining the plaintiff from continuing the American action and from commencing further proceedings in America or elsewhere in respect of his accident. Within 14 days of the service of the defence, the English solicitors, with the plaintiff's authority, gave notice of discontinuance. Their purpose in so doing was to improve the plaintiff's position in respect of the defendants' efforts to stay the American proceedings. On 6th June, when the defendants' summons for directions came on for hearing, it was directed that it should be treated as an application to strike out the plaintiff's notice of discontinuance, and was adjourned to a date to be fixed. On 26th June the defendants filed a notice in Texas calling on the plaintiff's attorney to show his authority for bringing an action there. On 18th July, while the action in the Texas state court was still pending, the American lawyers launched an action in the plaintiff's name in a federal court in Texas claiming, in respect of the same accident, $US5 million compensatory damages and $US10 million punitive damages. The following day the action in the Texas state court was terminated by the filing of a nonsuit. In September the defendants filed a motion to dismiss and to show authority for bringing the action in the federal court. In October their applications in the English action for an order striking out the notice of discontinuance and for an injunction to restrain the plaintiff from continuing the action in the federal court and commencing further proceedings in America or elsewhere were referred to a judge in chambers. At the hearing before him it was stated (i) that the plaintiff was prepared to submit to orders (a) setting aside the notice of discontinuance if the £27,250 paid to him was not repaid and (b) restraining the action in the federal court until the money was repaid, (ii) that the American lawyers were prepared to make the repayment, and (iii) that if the federal court declined jurisdiction the plaintiff would consider himself free to, and would seek to, start a fresh action against the defendants in England.

Held – (i) The notice of discontinuance would be struck out and the English action would remain in being because (a) if the plaintiff had required leave to discontinue, the court would have granted leave only on condition that he would bring no fresh action in England, and, since the plaintiff would not in the circumstances have accepted such a term, leave would have been refused, and (b) although in fact he did not require such leave, the court could, in its inherent jurisdiction, make an order striking out a notice of discontinuance if it was necessary to prevent an abuse of process. On the evidence it was necessary because it would be an abuse of process for the plaintiff to use the machinery of discontinuance without leave in order to improve his position in the American proceedings while remaining free to commence a fresh action in England if those proceedings failed (see p 697 a to h, post).

(ii) In the circumstances the court had jurisdiction to grant the injunction and would do so because (a) the defendants had satisfied the court that they were subject to its jurisdiction and that justice could be done between the parties in England at substantially less inconvenience and expense than in America, (b) having regard to the fact that the plaintiff was merely forum shopping in bringing an action in Texas and any award he received in England would not be lower than a comparable award in Portugal where he resided, the grant of the injunction would not deprive the plaintiff of any real legitimate personal or juridical advantage, and (c) in the circumstances the refusal of the injunction would be unjust to the defendants (see p 699 b to e and p 700 b to f, post); *MacShannon v Rockware Glass Ltd* [1978] 1 All ER 625 applied.

Notes

For the discontinuance of an action, see 30 Halsbury's Laws (3rd Edn) 409, para 770, and for cases on the subject, see 51 Digest (Repl) 570–574, 2036–2080.

Cases referred to in judgment

Atlantic Star, The, The Atlantic Star (Owners) v The Bona Spes (Owners) [1973] 2 All ER 175, [1974] AC 436, [1973] 2 WLR 795, [1973] 2 Lloyd's Rep 197, HL, 11 Digest (Reissue) 645, 1777.

Christiansborg, The (1885) 10 PD 141, 54 LJP 84, 53 LT 612, 5 Asp MLC 491, CA, 11 Digest (Reissue) 645, 1774.

Conybeare v Lewis (1880) 13 Ch D 469, 51 Digest (Repl) 575, 2086.

MacShannon v Rockware Glass Ltd [1978] 1 All ER 625, [1978] AC 795, [1978] 2 WLR 362, HL.

Newcomen v Coulson (1878) 7 Ch D 764, 47 LJ Ch 429, 38 LT 275, 51 Digest (Repl) 575, 2087.

Tropaioforos, The, (No 2) [1962] 1 Lloyd's Rep 410.

Adjourned summonses

a Brown & Root (UK) Ltd and Jackson Marine SA, the defendants in an action by the plaintiff, Inocencio Fernando Castanho, claiming damages for personal injuries sustained in an accident on 11th February 1977, applied by summons dated 1st May 1979, and amended pursuant to leave of the court, for an injunction restraining the plaintiff (1) from continuing an action in Texas and (2) from commencing, causing to be commenced, continuing or prosecuting further proceedings in the United States of America or

b elsewhere in respect of his accident. On 14th May the plaintiff filed a notice of discontinuance of the action pursuant to RSC Ord 21, r 2. On 6th June when the defendants' summons for directions dated 1st May 1979 came on for hearing it was directed that it be treated as an application to strike out the notice of discontinuance, and was adjourned to a date to be fixed. The applications were heard in chambers but judgment was delivered in open court. The facts are set out in the judgment.

c

Timothy Walker for the defendants.
J Melville Williams QC and *John Hendy* for the plaintiff.

Cur adv vult

19th November. **PARKER J** read the following judgment: These are two chambers
d applications in an action commenced by writ dated 29th September 1977. In the action the plaintiff claims damages for very severe personal injuries suffered in an accident which occurred on 11th February 1977. He is now a paraplegic. Both applications raise points of considerable general importance. For that reason, and with the agreement of the parties, this judgment is given in open court.

The plaintiff is of Portuguese nationality and resides in Portugal. The first defendants
e are a United Kingdom company and the second defendants are a Panamanian company. The accident took place aboard the m v American Moon at Great Yarmouth. It is admitted in the action that this vessel was owned by the second defendants and that they employed the plaintiff thereon as an oiler. After the accident the plaintiff was in hospital in England until, in about October 1977, he returned to Portugal on the advice of his doctors. He has remained there ever since.

f Until February 1979 the action proceeded without unusual incident, the principal events being as follows: (i) on 22nd March 1978 there was an order by consent that the second defendants should pay £7,250 by way of interim payment under RSC Ord 29, rr 10–12 and this sum was duly paid, (ii) on 28th March 1978 the statement of claim was delivered, (iii) on 9th June 1978 the second defendants admitted liability by letter, and (iv) on 8th December 1978 there was an order, not by consent, that the second defendants
g should make a further interim payment of £20,000; this, like the earlier sum, was paid, the date of payment being 18th December 1978.

Two months later, on 7th February 1979, process, allegedly on the authority of the plaintiff, was issued in the District Court of Harris County, Texas, claiming damages in respect of the same accident. Such process was issued by an American firm of attorneys, Benton Musselwhite Inc. The defendants named were the defendants in the action here
h and also three other Jackson Marine companies and Brown & Root Inc.

The evidence does not reveal how this firm came to get in touch with the plaintiff in the first instance, but it is plain, and not disputed by counsel for the plaintiff, that they approached him on their own initiative, that is to say they were 'touting' for work on an international scale. However they may have learnt that contact with the plaintiff might be profitable, by June 1978 contact had been made and the evidence reveals that in June
j and July 1978 the plaintiff was being pressed to hand over his case to them and to sign a power of attorney giving them full authority to enforce his claim in America on a contingency fee basis. Such fee was to be one-third of all recovery if the claim were settled before filing suit and 40% if suit were filed before any settlement were achieved. Nothing was to be paid in the event of failure of the claim.

Quite apart from the question of the desirability or otherwise of contingency fees as such, this arrangement would appear to be a direct incentive to lawyers *not* to settle before filing suit, however favourable might be the terms obtainable, and thus one *a* which a properly advised plaintiff would be unwilling to accept.

Despite the efforts of the American lawyers, the plaintiff did not, at that time, yield to their persuasion and expressed himself to the second defendants' loss adjuster's Portuguese agents as wishing his claims to remain with those then handling them, that is to say Messrs Birnberg & Co, his solicitors in the action here.

When Messrs Birnberg first heard of the activities of the American lawyers is not clear, *b* but it was before 27th November 1978 when they issued a summons for the second interim payment, and was in fact not later than about 5th September 1978, when the defendants' solicitors wrote to them drawing attention to the fact that the plaintiff was being approached.

In December 1978 Messrs Birnberg were visited by the American firm and had inconclusive discussions with them. In January 1979 there were further discussions *c* between the two sets of lawyers, this time in the presence, or partly in the presence, of the plaintiff and his wife, in Portugal. As a result of those discussions and subsequent events which I shall mention shortly, the plaintiff, on 8th February 1979, the day *after* process had been issued in the Texan State Court, signed a power of attorney in favour of Benton Musselwhite and also an agreement with Messrs Birnberg. Before committing themselves to any association with the American lawyers or any special agreement with *d* the plaintiff, Messrs Birnberg took advice both from counsel and the Law Society. The exchange of letters with the Law Society dated 12th and 14th December 1978 was exhibited. The advice which they received was, in effect, that they would be acting properly so long as they charged properly for all work done and so long as it was provided that their charges would be paid either by the American lawyers or by the plaintiff, whatever the result of the claims. I have not quoted from their letter to the Law Society *e* but it is right that I should state that it makes it clear that the object of the exercise so far as they were concerned was simply to try to obtain the highest possible damages for the plaintiff.

As the conduct of Messrs Birnberg has been the subject of very serious criticism on behalf of the defendants and as they were concerned not merely in the making of their own agreement with the plaintiff but also with the content of the power of attorney in *f* favour of the American lawyers, it would in any event be necessary to consider those documents closely. Quite apart from the conduct of Messrs Birnberg, however, the documents have an important bearing on other matters. I shall consider the two documents in turn.

The power of attorney followed, but was more extensive than, the document previously submitted to the plaintiff for signature. It gave to the American lawyers *g* exclusive powers to represent him in the prosecution of his claim in America in respect of his accident and, like its predecessor, provided for them to be paid one-third of all amounts received or recovered by out of court settlement or other means if the claims were settled prior to the filing of judicial petition, and 40% if a petition were filed; for them to advance all moneys necessary for preparation for trial or settlement and for nothing to be payable by the plaintiff in respect thereof in the event of failure of his *h* claim.

It went, however, further than its predecessor in a number of respects. It provided: (1) for Messrs Birnberg to be used by the American lawyers in connection with the American action and for their fees in this connection to be liquidated by the American lawyers out of their contingency fees, (2) for the American lawyers to communicate with the plaintiff exclusively through Messrs Birnberg, (3) for Messrs Birnberg to have *j* exclusive authority to engage any specialist necessary for the construction for the plaintiff of any special accommodation or facilities in Portugal, (4) for the American lawyers to pay the plaintiff's wages pending final settlement in the event that his employers ceased to do so, (5) for sums expended in the case, other than general legal costs, to be limited to $US10,000 (except with the express consent of Messrs Birnberg), and to be deducted from any recovery, and (6) for the action here not to be concluded prior to a decision in

a the United States and that, in the event that the action here should be reactivated by the defendants, the course to be followed should be decided by agreement between the American lawyers and Messrs Birnberg or, in default of agreement, by Messrs Birnberg.

This power of attorney, as ultimately granted on 8th February, contained certain amendments which had not been agreed by the American lawyers when they were in Portugal, but they were agreed by telephone between Mrs Bowden of Messrs Birnbergs

b and the American lawyers on 5th February, and Mrs Bowden then instructed the American lawyers to proceed with the action in Texas and asked a Mr Valente, the architect employed in connection with the plaintiff's accommodation, to have it sworn by the plaintiff as soon as possible.

It was, as I have said, on 7th February that the American action was launched and not until 8th February that the power of attorney was granted. Hence the American action

c was commenced on Mrs Bowden's instructions by telephone. Whether this was sufficient authority in Texas it is unnecessary to investigate or decide, because the action then in being has since come to an end by a nonsuit being filed. It is, however, to be noted (1) that Mrs Bowden's instructions were given without any attempt at settlement having been made and that as a result she was committing her client to a 40% fee notwithstanding that a satisfactory settlement attracting the lesser one-third fee was

d never attempted, (2) that the power of attorney provides not only for the American lawyers to finance the action but also, if necessary, to finance the plaintiff personally, (3) that it expressly provides for the action here to be kept alive, and (4) that it appears to contemplate that Messrs Birnberg's remuneration will come wholly out of the American lawyers' contingency fees.

Item (2) above, the provision for personal finance, is provided for in a clause which was

e covered over when the power of attorney was produced in connection with the Texas proceedings and also as originally produced in the proceedings before me. However, the full text was finally put in evidence and there was also produced Messrs Birnberg's agreement with the plaintiff which provided that in the event of their fees not being paid by the American lawyers they would be paid by the plaintiff. This disposes of the defendants' charge that Messrs Birnbergs were themselves acting on a contingency fee

f basis, a charge which, in view of the terms of the power of attorney and Messrs Birnberg's failure to disclose their own arrangements, was entirely understandable.

Why the clause providing for personal finance was covered up I do not know. It may well have been because it was felt that, if disclosed, it would encourage the second defendants to cease paying the plaintiff's wages, or it may be because, although contingency fees are permissible in America, the same is not or was feared not, to be true

g of agreements to provide personal financial support. There was some suggestion that the latter was the true reason but on the evidence I can draw no such conclusion. For the purpose of these applications I regard both the existence of the clause itself and its non-disclosure as neutral matters.

One further clause only of Messrs Birnberg's agreement with the plaintiff calls for mention, namely cl 1, which specifically provided that the action here should be

h continued but not determined pending the determination of the American action.

With this account of how the action in the Texas courts came to be launched I can now continue the chronological history of events.

On 6th April 1979 the defendants in the American action (other than the two who were American corporations), that is to say, including the defendants in the action here, entered a special appearance objecting to the jurisdiction of the Texas courts.

j On 30th April (effectively 1st May) the defendants delivered their defence in the action here in which the second defendants formally admitted liability, and on 1st May they (1) issued a summons for directions in the action here and (2) issued a summons in the action here seeking an injunction to restrain the plaintiff from continuing the American action and from commencing further proceedings in the United States or elsewhere in respect of his accident.

At that time it is not disputed that this court had jurisdiction to grant such an injunction and that it continued to do so until, on 14th May, Messrs Birnbergs gave notice of discontinuance which, it is now accepted, was within the time limited by RSC Ord 21, r 2. Prima facie the effect of this notice was to terminate the action here, but under the terms of RSC Ord 21, r 4, the plaintiff would subsequently be able, if he wished, to commence a fresh action. The plaintiff's prime contention is that the effect of the discontinuance is to deprive this court of jurisdiction to grant the injunction sought.

In face of the terms of both the power of attorney and the plaintiff's agreement with Messrs Birnberg it would appear that Messrs Birnberg had no authority to discontinue the action here. Towards the end of the hearing, however, a further affidavit on behalf of the plaintiff was put in and also, on an undertaking to have it sworn, a draft affidavit to be sworn by the plaintiff. It was in due course duly sworn and filed. In para 3 of that affidavit the plaintiff states that he wishes to proceed in America rather than in England and that the action of Messrs Birnbergs in discontinuing the English action so as to proceed in America as quickly as possible was done with his full consent and authority. This appeared somewhat doubtful in the light of the contents of an affidavit of Mr P J Farthing sworn on behalf of the defendants, but was sought to be supported by a last minute affidavit of Mrs Monjardino of the Portuguese Consulate who, due to language difficulties, acted as the channel of communication between Mrs Bowden of Messrs Birnbergs and the plaintiff, an earlier affidavit by the deponent not being satisfactory on the point.

In her second affidavit Mrs Monjardino states that some days before attending a meeting with Mrs Bowden and the American lawyers on 16th May she had spoken to the plaintiff by telephone about the possibility of the action in England having to be stopped in order that the American action might proceed, and that he had expressed himself as agreeable if Mrs Bowden so advised.

Mrs Monjardino does not mention having passed this information to Mrs Bowden before the meeting on 16th May, and unless she did so it is plain that in discontinuing on 14th May Mrs Bowden was acting contrary to the specific terms of cl 1 of the agreement between the plaintiff and Messrs Birnberg without any justification.

To have taken such action without authority would, however, be a serious matter and it may be that Mrs Monjardino, in the flurry of filing additional evidence in the closing stages of the hearing, merely omitted some communication which she had with Mrs Bowden. Had the matter of such authority in the event turned out to be of crucial importance I should have felt it necessary to investigate the matter further. In view, however, of the fact that I have not found it of crucial importance it was unnecessary to pursue it or to make any finding on the question of authority. For the purposes of these applications I treat the notice as having been given with authority.

The defendants' summons for directions came on for hearing on 6th June when it was directed to be treated as an application to strike out the plaintiff's notice of discontinuance and adjourned for a date to be fixed.

On 18th June both the second defendants' solicitor and counsel for the plaintiff gave evidence in Texas on the effect of a notice of discontinuance of the action here. This was in connection with the defendants' attempt to stay the Texas proceedings, but there was no attempt then to obtain any decision. The plaintiff's memorandum of authorities to the Texas court, however, shows that, in order to persuade the Texas court not to stay the action there, it was important for the plaintiff to establish that the action here had been terminated and it was not disputed that the notice of discontinuance here was expressly for the purpose of improving the plaintiff's position in resisting the defendants' efforts to stay the Texas proceedings.

On 26th June the defendants in Texas filed a notice under r 12 of the Rules of Civil Procedure in Texas calling on the plaintiff's attorney to show his authority to bring the American action and there then occurred a most remarkable manoeuvre. On 18th July, while the original action was still pending, the American lawyers launched an action in

the Beaumont Division of the Federal District Court for the Eastern District of Texas in
a respect of the same accident. There were fewer defendants, the first defendants in the
action here being amongst those not included, but the second defendants here were still
included. In these proceedings the plaintiff claimed $US5 million compensatory damages
and $US10 million punitive damages and requested trial by jury.

On the following day the original American action was brought to an end by the filing
of a nonsuit. Service of the second American action was effected on 22nd August, and on
b 11th September the defendants filed motion to dismiss and to show authority for
bringing the action.

The last procedural events are that on 2nd October Master Elton referred the
application to strike out the notice of discontinuance to be heard by the judge in
chambers at the same time as the summons for an injunction, and that I gave leave to
amend para 2 of that summons so as to cover the second American action.

c Before coming to the issues between the parties I must mention certain further
matters. The reasons for proceedings in America were said to be the prospect of greater
damages there than are likely to be obtained here and increased ease and certainty of
enforcing any judgment obtained.

The reasons for stopping in the Texas state court and starting afresh in the federal
courts was stated to be that such courts were more liberal in accepting jurisdiction over
d foreigners and that an earlier hearing date was likely, it being stated that the motion to
stay was likely to be heard in November and tried before the end of January.

That awards of damages in America are higher than in this country I accept, but the
evidence before me, which on this point I do not rehearse, does not convince me that
there will be any difficulty in obtaining satisfaction of a judgment obtained in the courts
of this country. As to hearing date, the evidence shows that the estimates of hearing
e dates are unlikely to be fulfilled. So far as liberality in relation to extended jurisdiction
is concerned I had no satisfactory evidence as to the likelihood of the federal court
accepting jurisdiction on the facts of this case. What appears to me to matter is the
attitude which would be adopted by the court when acquainted fully with the facts,
including in particular: (a) that the plaintiff apparently required considerable persuasion
before allowing the American lawyers to embark on an action at all; (b) that by the time
f he was so persuaded he had already obtained orders for and been paid £27,250 in an
English action; (c) that the original action had been commenced whilst the English
action was pending; (d) that having given notice of discontinuance in the English action
the federal action was commenced while the original American action was still pending;
(e) that in addition to financing the original action, which is apparently perfectly proper
in America, the American lawyers had undertaken to finance the plaintiff personally
g during its pendency; (f) that in proceedings before me it was stated (1) that the plaintiff
was prepared to submit to orders (a) setting aside the notice of discontinuance unless the
£27,250 were repaid within 28 days, and (b) restraining the federal action until it was
repaid, and (2) that the American lawyers proposed to make this repayment, the
plaintiff's authority both for submitting to such orders and making such payments being
considered to derive solely from the power of attorney of 8th February 1978, and finally
h (3) that if the federal court declined jurisdiction the plaintiff would consider himself free
to and would seek to start over again in England.

As to the likely attitude of the federal court in such circumstances, I had no evidence
but it appears to me that they are matters which, however liberal the federal court might
be in general, might cause them to have some doubt in the present instance. Furthermore,
the federal court will, on the motion, have to consider the authority to bring the action
j and also possibly to discontinue the original action.

I have set out the history at considerable length for I am being asked to strike out a
notice of discontinuance which, under the rules, the plaintiff was entitled to serve
without leave, and to restrain proceedings in a foreign court when, if the notice of
discontinuance is not struck out, the applicant will, it is said, not be engaged in an action
pending here.

I shall consider first the question of striking out the notice of discontinuance, the giving of which without leave was only possible due to the fact that, as the events and *a* correspondence reveal, the defendants were hoping to settle and had not delivered their defence either within the time limited, or within extensions granted.

That a notice of discontinuance terminates an action in the ordinary way is beyond doubt, but it does not determine altogether the jurisdiction of the courts in the action, for in every case the defendant is, under RSC Ord 62, r 10 entitled to tax his costs and, if the taxed costs are not paid within four days, the defendant may sign judgment for *b* them. Also, if such costs are not paid, the court may stay any fresh action for the same or substantially the same cause of action until such costs are paid. Furthermore, the court may, after discontinuance, make such order as may be necessary to give effect to rights acquired by the defendant during the course of the proceedings, such as rights under an undertaking in damages: see *Newcomen v Coulson*[1]. In general, however, a notice of discontinuance terminates the action and thus will, for example, automatically terminate *c* an appeal: see *Conybeare v Lewis*[2].

Where interim payments have been made under RSC Ord 29 the rules contain no provision to cover the case of discontinuance. RSC Ord 29, r 16, only provides for the court to make orders with respect to interim payments on giving or making a final judgment or order determining the defendant's liability to the plaintiff and for giving effect to that determination. This rule cannot apply to a discontinuance, for the essence *d* of such procedure is that the claim is not determined at all and that the plaintiff is free to bring a fresh action unless leave is required and it is made a term of leave that no such action shall be brought. There can be no doubt that if, in any case where interim payments had been made, leave to discontinue were required, the court could, under RSC Ord 21, r 3(1) make it a term of giving leave that the payments should be repaid. There can also be no doubt that a court has power under the same rule to make it a term *e* of the grant of leave that the plaintiff shall bring no fresh action for the same or substantially the same cause of action.

If, therefore, the notice of discontinuance had been one day later or delivery of the defence one day earlier, so that the plaintiff required leave to discontinue, there would have been power to adopt either or both of these courses. Furthermore, where leave is required the court would also, in my judgment, as an alternative to making it a term that *f* no fresh action should be brought, make it a term that no foreign proceedings should be instituted or continued. This must follow from the existence of the power in the courts to put a plaintiff to his election whether to proceed in this country or in a foreign court: see *The Christianborg*[3].

Although, however, the above powers would exist in such circumstances, it does not follow that all or any of them would be exercised. A plaintiff is in the ordinary way *g* entitled to discontinue on payment of taxed costs and still be free to commence a fresh action later. If he has received interim payments he would in the absence of special circumstances no doubt also be ordered to repay them as a term of the grant of leave unless the defendant were content, provided that the plaintiff were prohibited from bringing a fresh action, to let him retain them. Assuming, however, that the plaintiff were prepared to repay, possibly with interest, the question arises as to the circumstances *h* in which, under the general power in RSC Ord 21, r 3, to impose such terms as it thinks just, a court would make it a term either that no fresh proceedings be brought here or that no foreign proceedings should be instituted or continued.

That a plaintiff may in certain circumstances conduct proceedings both in this country and in a foreign court is clear on the authorities. Where he seeks to do so the question whether one and if so which set of proceedings should be stayed depends on what, in the *j*

particular circumstances of each case, justice demands: see *MacShannon v Rockware Glass*
a *Ltd*[1].

In the circumstances of this particular case justice would in my judgment have
demanded at least that discontinuance be allowed only on terms that no fresh action
should be brought in England. It would in such circumstances be an injustice to the
defendant, even on repayment of the interim payments with interest, to allow a
discontinuance desired for the purpose of strengthening the plaintiff's case for persuading
b the foreign court to accept jurisdiction, yet leave him open to be pursued again in these
courts if the American courts, despite the fact that there was no pending action in
England, declined jurisdiction. To impose such a term would not work injustice to the
plaintiff. He could accept the term and discontinue or he could continue the action here
and seek to continue or institute American proceedings. Unless he were certain of being
able to continue the proceedings in America he would clearly not accept the term and
c discontinue for by so doing he would be committing himself to a possible chance of
recovering a greater sum at the price of repaying money received and, with liability
admitted, the certainty of a large award here in a comparatively short time.

Hence, had an application for leave been necessary, I conclude that it would only have
been granted on terms that the plaintiff would not have accepted and consequently that
leave would have been refused.

d I have considered the powers available on an application for leave and the probable
result of such an application, for they have an important bearing on the application to
strike out. On such an application the power to order repayment of the interim
payments must, if it exists, depend on the inherent jurisdiction of the courts to prevent
an abuse of their own process. Such jurisdiction has been used in many connections but
never in circumstances such as are here present. I have, however, no doubt that it covers
e such a case for nothing could be more clearly an abuse of process than for a plaintiff,
having received interim payments, to discontinue without repaying them. Indeed this
is not disputed, for counsel for the plaintiff, by offering to submit to an order to strike out
unless the repayments are made, accepts the jurisdiction to make such an order. If the
jurisdiction is there at all it must also be wide enough to allow the making of an
unconditional order to strike out if that is necessary to prevent an abuse of process. In
f my judgment it is an abuse of process to use the machinery of discontinuance without
leave to improve the plaintiff's position in American proceedings if he is then left free,
on failure of those proceedings, to commence afresh here. This would be the case on
discontinuance without leave. I have already held that it would be unjust on an
application for leave to allow such a result, and for the same reasons I consider it to be an
abuse of process. I accordingly order that the notice of discontinuance be struck out with
g the result that the action here remains in being.

The next question is whether an injunction restraining the continuance of the
American proceedings or the institution of other proceedings should be granted. If my
conclusion on the application to strike out is correct it is not disputed that jurisdiction
exists, but, since this case may go further, I express my views shortly on the question
whether there is jurisdiction here, even assuming that the action here has terminated
h save for taxation of costs and any order for the repayment of the interim payments. In
such event the situation would be that of a foreign national resident outside the
jurisdiction, with no assets here and with no action proceeding here, seeking an
injunction to restrain proceedings in a foreign court. This situation arose in *The*
Tropaioforos (No 2)[2]. In that case Megaw J held that there was jurisdiction on two
grounds, one of which does not arise here, but the other of which was that the connection
j of the applicant with this country was sufficient to ground jurisdiction notwithstanding
that an action which he had brought in England had finally terminated in a decision

1   [1978] 1 All ER 625, [1978] AC 795
2   [1962] 1 Lloyd's Rep 410

adverse to him. Adopting this test I hold that the plaintiff has, even if the action has
terminated, sufficient connection with this country to ground jurisdiction. His claim is *a*
in respect of a tort committed within the jurisdiction, the natural forum for trying
which is in England. He has and retains payments made in the English proceedings. He
has solicitors here and is subject to the jurisdiction of the courts here in respect of costs
and orders for repayment. His arrangements with the American lawyers and Messrs
Birnberg are such that the American proceedings can only be advanced with the assistance
of Messrs Birnberg, and in any event much of the evidence, documentary and oral, must *b*
be obtained from England. This, in my judgment, is sufficient connection to ground
jurisdiction even if the action has been terminated.

Should an injunction then be granted? Counsel for the plaintiff submits that it should
not, on the basis (1) that a plaintiff is prima facie entitled to proceed both here and
elsewhere concurrently, (2) that proceeding in America gives him the legitimate
advantage of the prospect of very much higher compensatory damages (even after *c*
deduction of the American lawyers' 40%) and the separate additional remedy of very
large punitive damages, and (3) that it will work no injustice to the defendants if the
action there is allowed to proceed.

Counsel for the defendants, on the other hand, submits (1) that it would be an injustice
to the defendants if the action is allowed to proceed, because they have admitted liability
here which they might not have done in America, (2) that they have paid moneys here *d*
that would not have been obtainable in America, (3) that the American proceedings
would be more expensive and are being pursued for the benefit of the American lawyers
and not the plaintiff, and (4) that the American proceedings are brought without
authority.

I find it unnecessary to decide whether the federal action was brought without
authority for an injunction on this ground would be valueless. With regard to the *e*
allegation that the proceedings are being pursued for the benefit of the American lawyers
and not the plaintiff, it is plain that they will, if they continue, probably be of great
benefit to the American lawyers. The total claims in the federal action are for
$US15 million ($5 million compensatory damages and $10 million punitive damages)
and the evidence is that recent awards for paraplegics have been between $2 million and
$4 million, with the exception of one award of $638,000. It is therefore plain that the *f*
American lawyers stand to make a very large sum out of American proceedings. If, for
example, the jury were to award $4 million compensatory damages to the plaintiff the
American lawyers would retain $1·6 million, and even if the award were as low as the
exceptional $638,000, they would retain $255,200, leaving the plaintiff in this event
with $382,000, or approximately £190,000. Bearing in mind recent very large awards
in the courts here it is therefore at least possible that an award in America will leave the *g*
plaintiff with less than he might obtain here. Furthermore, it must be borne in mind
that, had there been no American proceedings, the action here might well have already
been determined with a large award already paid and the plaintiff might by now have the
action with all its worries behind him. When there is added to this the fact that the
American lawyers are prepared, without reference to the plaintiff and for the purpose of
assisting them in persuading the American court to accept jurisdiction, to pay £27,250 *h*
in order to achieve discontinuance of an action which could result in a large award in
favour of the plaintiff in a very short time, there is clearly much force in counsel's
argument for the defendants. I am, however, not prepared on the evidence to hold that
the American action is being pursued in disregard of the plaintiff's interests. Although
it is plainly of great benefit to the American lawyers that it should be pursued and their
advice to the plaintiff may, as a result, be less than objective, I am prepared to accept that *j*
they do consider it to be in his interests as well as their own that the action should
proceed. I am satisfied that Messrs Birnberg so consider.

This leaves for consideration the questions whether, assuming authority and that the
American action is being pursued for the plaintiff's benefit, that action and any other
proceedings should be restricted by injunction.

The authorities for the most part concern the question of staying an action in these
a courts, but they nevertheless afford valuable guidance. In *The Atlantic Star*[1] the question
was whether, where an action had been commenced in the Belgian courts, an action here
in respect of the same matters should be stayed. The House of Lords decided that it
should be, on the basis that taking into account advantages to the plaintiff on the one
hand and disadvantages to the defendant on the other the defendants ought not to be
required to face proceedings here as well.

b In *MacShannon v Rockware Glass Ltd*[2], Scotsmen living and working in Scotland and
having suffered personal injuries in Scotland sought to proceed in England but were not
permitted to do so and were left to pursue their claims in Scotland. Lord Diplock[3] stated
the rule thus:

> 'In order to justify a stay two conditions must be satisfied, one positive and the
c > other negative: (a) the defendant must satisfy the court that there is another forum
> to whose jurisdiction he is amenable in which justice can be done between the
> parties at substantially less inconvenience and expense, and (b) that the stay must
> not deprive the plaintiff of a legitimate personal or juridical advantage which would
> be available to him if he invoked the jurisdiction of the English court.'

So stated the rule does not take into account prejudice or injustice to the defendant,
d but it is plain from the speeches in the case that this factor comes equally into
consideration.

If, with necessary amendments, this is applied to the present case it appears to me that
the defendants clearly satisfy head (a) of the rule. The questions therefore to be
determined are in my judgment as follows. (1) Will an injunction deprive the plaintiff
of a legitimate personal or juridical advantage he would have in the American
e proceedings? (2) Will the refusal of an injunction cause prejudice or injustice to the
defendant? (3) Weighing up the above two matters, does justice between the parties
require an injunction?

The legitimate advantages which the plaintiff claims and of which he will be deprived
if an injunction is granted are the increased damages which he is likely to get in an
American court. That increased damages can be a legitimate advantage I have already
f said I accept. It was indeed recognised in *MacShannon v Rockware Glass Ltd*[2]. The
importance of such a matter will, however, inevitably vary not only with the amount or
size of the expected increase and the certainty or otherwise of obtaining it, but with other
matters as well, such as whether, in a particular case, early termination of the case is more
important medically than higher damages which may be obtained if termination is
delayed. Even, however, in cases where the expected increase is very considerable and
g relatively certain it may be of little weight. The object of the court is to see that justice
is done between the parties. If, for example, two English plaintiffs residing in England
suffer identical industrial injuries in respect of which both can and do sue in England,
but one, by the accident that the defendant in his case has an office and assets in Texas,
can sue in Texas also, the fact that he could recover more compensation in Texas and
perhaps punitive damages also cannot in my judgment, even if it is a legitimate
h advantage, be regarded as of much weight. The object of damages is to provide just
compensation and what is required for this purpose must vary between country and
country according to their respective costs and standards of living. In the case supposed
both plaintiffs will obtain here an award considered just by the courts of this country in
the circumstances prevailing here. I can see no injustice in preventing one of the two
plaintiffs from seeking to obtain an award, which although it might be just, reasonable
j and necessary in the light of costs and standards prevailing in Texas, would be grossly
excessive here. If this is not right there is a direct encouragement to 'forum shopping'

---

1   [1973] 2 All ER 175, [1974] AC 436
2   [1978] 1 All ER 625, [1978] AC 795
3   [1978] 1 All ER 625 at 630, [1978] AC 795 at 812

which has been frequently criticised by the courts and which Lord Reid in *The Atlantic Star*[1] regarded as undesirable. The question of real importance appears to me to be, not *a* whether the plaintiff will obtain a higher award in another jurisdiction but whether the award he is likely to obtain here is likely to be lower than awards in the country where he lives, in this case Portugal. If this were so, and it is not suggested here, the fact that, by going to Texas, he could obtain an award more in line with awards in his own country would no doubt be a legitimate and considerable advantage. As there was nothing here by way of suggestion or evidence to lead me to the conclusion that an English award *b* would be regarded as unjustly low in Portugal, where the plaintiff resides and intends to reside, and as an award here is likely to be obtained more quickly and less expensively than a probably higher award in Texas, I regard any advantage to the plaintiff in this respect as being, even if legitimate, of little weight.

What then of the defendants? They have admitted liability here and accorded the plaintiff here the advantage of interim payments which he could not have obtained in *c* America. The plaintiff deliberately sued them here and if the proceedings continue in America they will undoubtedly be put to extra expense. It would, I consider, be unjust to expose them to an action in America and I so consider whether or not I am right in deciding that the action here is still in being. If it is not the plaintiff can start again here, pursue his claim in its natural forum and obtain economically an award which is not shown to be any less than justice requires. *d*

I should mention also two further matters. Where a foreign plaintiff seeks to sue in his own country as well as here the case is different from that in which a foreign plaintiff seeks to sue in another country, not his own. The latter is a pure case of forum shopping as is the present case. Furthermore, the case is different again where the plaintiff has already put the defendants to expense in resisting one attempted action in the other country, has then abandoned that action and is seeking to proceed with another, and *e* thereby put the defendants to yet further expense. That is also the situation here. These matters added to those already mentioned satisfy me that justice demands in the present case that an injunction should be granted and I accordingly grant an injunction in the terms of para (2) of the summons as amended.

Notice of discontinuance struck out. Injunction granted. *f*

Solicitors: *B M Birnberg & Co* (for the plaintiff); *Clyde & Co* (for the defendants).

K Mydeen Esq   Barrister.

g

1   [1973] 2 All ER 175 at 181, [1974] AC 436 at 454

a # R v Governor of Pentonville Prison, ex parte Budlong and another

QUEEN'S BENCH DIVISION
LORD WIDGERY CJ AND GRIFFITHS J
b 12th, 13th, 14th, 15th, 16th, 19th, 30th NOVEMBER 1979

Extradition – Committal – Evidence – Formal documents – Whether formal document setting out particulars of offence required to be put before magistrate – Whether Minister's order or foreign warrant of arrest required to give particulars of offence – Extradition Act 1870, s 20, Sch 2.

c *Extradition – Committal – Extradition crime – Double criminality – Definition of crime in foreign country not identical with definition of English crime – Burglary – Trespass essential ingredient of English crime of burglary but not of foreign crime of burglary – Whether if foreign crime substantially similar to English crime principle of double criminality satisfied — Extradition Act 1870, s 26.*

d *Extradition – Restrictions on surrender – Political offence – What constitutes political offence – Unlawful entry into US government offices by members of Church of Scientology – Allegation that entry effected to obtain information for purpose of changing US government policy towards church – Whether the unlawful entry a political offence or simply extraditable offence of burglary.*

e *Extradition – Restrictions on surrender – Right of national of member country of EEC to move freely between EEC countries – Whether extradition unlawfully restricting that right – EEC Treaty, arts 48, 234.*

The two applicants, an English national and a United States national, were senior members of the Church of Scientology resident in England. The United States government requested their extradition to stand trial in the United States on charges of *f* burglary. The evidence placed before the metropolitan magistrate dealing with the issue of committal warrants for the two applicants showed that members of the church, acting on the applicants' written instructions, had unlawfully entered certain government offices in the United States as trespassers, and taken photocopies of the contents of confidential government files relating to the church's affairs. The magistrate was satisfied that burglary was an extraditable offence and that a prima facie case of burglary had been *g* made out against the applicants under both American and English law (ie s 9[a] of the Theft Act 1968). Accordingly he issued committal warrants pending the applicants' extradition to America. Although trespass was an essential ingredient of burglary under s 9 of the 1968 Act it was not an essential ingredient under American law[b]. The applicants applied for writs of habeas corpus on the grounds, inter alia, that (i) the

h
---

a Section 9, so far as material, provides:
   '(1) A person is guilty of burglary if—(a) he enters any building or part of a building as a trespasser and with intent to commit any such offence as is mentioned in subsection (2) below; or (b) having entered any building or part of a building as a trespasser he steals . . . anything in the building or that part of it . . .
j   '(2) The offences referred to in subsection (1)(a) above are offences of stealing anything in the building or part of a building in question.'
b Ie § 1801(b) of Title 22, District of Columbia Code which, so far as material, provides: '. . . whosoever shall, either in the night or in the daytime, break and enter, or enter without breaking any dwelling . . . or other building or any apartment or room, whether at the time occupied or not . . . with intent to break and carry away any part thereof . . . or to commit any criminal offense, shall be guilty of burglary in the second degree . . .; and § 105 of Title 22 which,

(Continued on p 702)

magistrate did not have before him a formal document giving particulars of the crime alleged, since both the Secretary of State's order made under s 7[c] of, and in the form set out in Sch 2 to, the Extradition Act 1870, and the American warrants of arrest merely referred to the crime of burglary without giving particulars, (ii) it would be against the principle of double criminality to extradite the applicants because the crime of burglary was not identical under English and American law, (iii) the offences were political in character, and therefore by virtue of s 7 not extraditable, since the Church of Scientology was engaged in protracted litigation with various United States Government departments and the applicants had organised entry into United States Government offices as part of an attempt to change government policy towards the church, (iv) the extradition was merely a means of indirectly enforcing a foreign public law, namely the United States Freedom of Information Act which the applicants had breached in organising the burglary, and (v) in respect of the applicant who was a United Kingdom national, the extradition would be a restriction on her right to move freely between countries within the EEC, as guaranteed by art 48[d] of the Treaty of Rome.

Held – The applications for habeas corpus would be refused for the following reasons—

(i) In extradition proceedings the only formal documents required to be put before the magistrate were the Minister's order under s 7 of the 1870 Act and the foreign warrant of arrest, neither of which were required to set out particulars of the offence. By virtue of s 20 and Sch 2 to the 1870 Act, all that was required to be specified in the Minister's order under s 7 was a general description of the crime. Furthermore, in assessing whether there were sufficient facts established to constitute an offence against English law the magistrate was required to look at the evidence, rather than the documents, put before him (see p 706 b to f, p 708 b to g and p 717 f, post); dicta of Stephen J in *R v Jacobi and Hillier* (1881) 46 LT at 597 and of Cave J in *Re Bellencontre* [1891] 2 QB at 136 applied; *R v Governor of Brixton Prison, ex parte Gardner* [1968] 1 All ER 636 distinguished and doubted.

(ii) An 'extradition crime' within the definition in s 26[e] of the 1870 Act referred merely to an act or omission which would have amounted to the commission of an extraditable crime if it had been done in England, and the definition of the crime in the foreign country was not required to be identical with the definition of the English crime, although the crime had to be substantially similar in concept in both countries. Since the crime for which extradition of the applicants was requested was substantially similar to the extraditable English crime of burglary, and since there was prima facie evidence that the conduct in question amounted to commission of the English crime of burglary, it followed that the principle of double criminality had not been breached and that the committal orders were properly made, notwithstanding that the definitions of burglary in English and American law were not identical (see p 712 d to h and p 717 f, post); dicta of Cockburn CJ and of Blackburn J in *Re Windsor* (1865) 6 B & S at 528 and 530, of Wills J in *Re Bellencontre* [1891] 2 QB at 140–141, of Lord Russell CJ in *Re Arton (No 2)* [1896] 1 QB at 517 and of Darling J in *R v Dix* (1902) 18 TLR at 232 applied.

(iii) The offences were not political in character for the purposes of s 7 of the 1870 Act because the burglaries were not carried out to challenge the political control or government of the United States but merely to further the interests of the church. Nor

---

(Continued from p 701)

    so far as material, provides: 'In prosecutions for any criminal offense all persons advising, inciting or conniving at the offense, or aiding or abetting the principal offender, shall be charged as principals . . .'

c   Section 7 is set out at p 705 *fg*, post

d   Article 48, so far as material, provides: '1. Freedom of movement for workers shall be secured within the Community . . . 3. It shall entail the right, subject to limitations justified on grounds of public policy . . . (b) to move freely within the territory of Member States . . .'

e   Section 26, so far as material, is set out at p 712 *bc*, post

a could it be contended that the real purpose of the extradition was to punish the applicants for breach of a foreign public law, because under the extradition treaty the United States had undertaken not to try the applicants for any offence other than that for which they were extradited and to entertain their allegation would be to impute bad faith to the United States Government (see p 714 *d* to *f* and *h* to p 715 *c* and p 717 *f*, post); *Re Arton* [1896] 1 QB 108, *Re Kolczynski* [1955] 1 All ER 31 and dictum of Viscount Radcliffe in *Schtraks v Government of Israel* [1962] 3 All ER at 540 applied.

b   (iv) For reasons of common sense, art 48 of the Treaty of Rome was to be interpreted as not applying to the exercise by a member state of its power to extradite an accused person under an extradition treaty (see p 717 *e f*, post).

Notes
For extradition crimes, see 18 Halsbury's Laws (4th Edn) paras 213–214 and for cases on
c the subject, see 24 Digest (Repl) 991–994, *21–39*, and for cases on proceedings before the magistrate, see ibid, 998–1004, *60–109*.
    For political crimes, see 18 Halsbury's Laws (4th Edn) para 217.
    For the Extradition Act 1870, ss 7, 20, 26, Sch 2, see 13 Halsbury's Statutes (3rd Edn) 254, 264, 265, 267.
    For the EEC Treaty, arts 48, 234, see 42A ibid 751, 328.

d
Cases referred to in judgments
Arton, Re [1896] 1 QB 108, 65 LJMC 23, 73 LT 687, DC, 24 Digest (Repl) 995, *43*.
Arton, Re, (No 2) [1896] 1 QB 509, 65 LJMC 50, 74 LT 249, 60 JP 132, 18 Cox CC 177, DC, 24 Digest (Repl) 991, *21*.
Bellencontre, Re [1891] 2 QB 122, 60 LJMC 83, 64 LT 461, 55 JP 694, 17 Cox CC 253, DC,
e 24 Digest (Repl) 997, *52*.
Bulmer (HP) Ltd v J Bollinger SA [1974] 2 All ER 1226, [1974] Ch 401, [1974] 3 WLR 202, [1974] CMLR 91, Digest (Cont Vol D) 316, *1*.
Castione, Re [1891] 1 QB 419, [1886–90] All ER Rep 640, 60 LJMC 22, 64 LT 344, 55 JP 328, 17 Cox CC 225, DC, 24 Digest (Repl) 993, *36*.
Factor v Laubenheimer (1933) 290 US 276.
f *Knoors v Secretary of State for Economic Affairs* [1979] 2 CMLR 357, ECJ.
Kolczynski, Re [1955] 1 All ER 31, sub nom *R v Brixton Prison (Governor), ex parte Kolczynski* [1955] 1 QB 540, [1955] 2 WLR 116, 119 JP 68, DC, 24 Digest (Repl) 993, *37*.
R v Bouchereau [1978] QB 732, [1978] 2 WLR 250, [1978] ECR 1999, 66 Cr App R 202, ECJ.
g *R v Dix* (1902) 18 TLR 231, DC, 24 Digest (Repl) 991, *27*.
R v Governor of Brixton Prison, ex parte Gardner [1968] 1 All ER 636, [1968] 2 QB 399, [1968] 2 WLR 512, 132 JP 187, DC, Digest (Cont Vol C) 370, *158b*.
R v Jacobi and Hillier (1881) 46 LT 595, DC, 24 Digest (Repl) 997, *50*.
R v Pentonville Prison (Governor), ex parte Ecke [1974] Crim LR 102, DC.
R v Pentonville Prison (Governor), ex parte Myers (6th December 1972) unreported, DC.
h *R v Saunders* [1979] 2 All ER 267, [1979] 3 WLR 359, [1979] 2 CMLR 216, ECJ.
Schtraks v Government of Israel [1962] 3 All ER 529, [1964] AC 556, [1962] 3 WLR 1013, HL; affg sub nom *Re Shalom Schtraks* [1962] 2 All ER 176, sub nom *R v Brixton Prison Governor, ex parte Schtraks* [1963] 1 QB 55, [1962] 2 WLR 976, DC, Digest (Cont Vol A) 575, *4a*.
Shapiro v Ferrandina (1973) 478 F 2d 894.
j *Tzu-Tsai Cheng v Governor of Pentonville Prison* [1973] 2 All ER 204, [1973] AC 931, [1973] 2 WLR 746, sub nom *R v Pentonville Prison Governor, ex parte Cheng* 137 JP 422, HL, Digest (Cont Vol D) 338, *39b*.
Windsor, Re (1865) 6 B & S 522, 5 New Rep 96, 34 LJMC 163, 12 LT 307, 29 JP 327, 11 Jur NS 807, 10 Cox CC 118, 122 ER 1288, 24 Digest (Repl) 991, *24*.
Wright v Henkel (1902) 190 US 40.

Cases also cited

Government of India, Ministry of Finance (Revenue Division) v Taylor [1955] 1 All ER 292, *a*
   [1955] AC 49, HL.
Huntingdon v Attrill [1893] AC 150, PC.
Kakis v Government of the Republic of Cyprus [1978] 2 All ER 634, [1978] 1 WLR 779, HL.
Malone v Metropolitan Police Comr [1979] 2 All ER 620, [1979] Ch 344.
R v Brixton Prison (Governor), ex parte Soblen [1962] 3 All ER 641, [1963] 2 QB 243, CA.
R v Chief Immigration Officer, Heathrow Airport, ex parte Salamat Bibi [1976] 3 All ER 843, *b*
   [1976] 1 WLR 979, CA.
R v Governor of Winson Green Prison, Birmingham, ex parte Littlejohn [1975] 3 All ER 208,
   [1975] 1 WLR 893, DC.
R v Thompson (1979) 69 Cr App R 22, [1979] 1 CMLR 390; *on appeal* [1979] 1 CMLR 47,
   ECJ.
Schemmer v Property Resources Ltd [1974] 3 All ER 451, [1975] Ch 273.   *c*
Van Duyn v Home Office (No 2) [1975] 3 All ER 190, [1975] Ch 358, ECJ.
Wyatt v McLoughlan [1974] IR 378.

Motions for habeas corpus

The applicants, Mr Morrison Budlong and Mrs Jane Kember, members of the Church of
Scientology, moved for writs of habeas corpus ad subjiciendum, under s 11 of the *d*
Extradition Act 1870, directed, in the case of Mr Budlong, to the governor of Pentonville
Prison and, in the case of Mrs Kember, to the governor of Holloway Prison, to which the
applicants had respectively been committed under committal warrants issued on 25th
May 1979 under s 10 of the 1870 Act by Mr W E C Robins, the metropolitan magistrate
of Bow Street Magistrates' Court, sitting at Wells Street Magistrates' Court, pending their
extradition to the United States of America for trial on ten charges of burglary alleged to *e*
have been committed there. The applicants contended that the warrants were
unlawful. The facts are set out in the judgment of Griffiths J.

William Denny QC and *Anthony Hooper* for the applicant Mr Budlong.
Louis Blom-Cooper QC, Alan Newman and *Hannah Burton* for the applicant Mrs Kember.
D W Tudor Price and *Colin Nicholls* for the United States Government.   *f*
Nicolas Bratza as amicus curiae.

Cur adv vult

30th November. The following judgments were read.

GRIFFITHS J (delivering the first judgment at the invitation of Lord Widgery CJ). In *g*
these proceedings the applicants move for writs of habeas corpus on the ground that the
extradition warrants issued by the metropolitan magistrate dated 25th May 1979 and on
which they are held pending extradition to the United States of America are unlawful.
   The Government of the United States seeks the extradition of the applicants to face ten
charges of burglary committed between January and May 1976 and for which they were
indicted by a grand jury on 15th August 1978. The evidence placed before the magistrate *h*
revealed the following facts. Between January and May of 1976 members of the Church
of Scientology unlawfully as trespassers entered various offices of the United States
Internal Revenue Service and the United States Department of Justice in the District of
Columbia and therein, making use of government property, took photocopies of the
contents of confidential government files relating to the affairs of the Church of
Scientology and its adherents. They replaced the original documents in the files but stole *j*
the photocopies. Eventually the actual burglars were caught red-handed and they then
revealed that they were acting on the written instructions of the applicants who are
senior members in the hierarchy of the Church of Scientology residing in this country.
   The magistrate, being satisfied that the facts revealed a prima facie case of burglary
against the applicants, both according to the relevant law of the United States, namely

§§ 1801(b) and 105 of Title 22, District of Columbia Code, and according to English law
and that burglary was an extraditable crime within the extradition treaty made between
the Government of the United Kingdom and the Government of the United States of
America, he issued warrants committing the applicants to prison to await extradition.
They have in fact both since been allowed bail pending the outcome of these proceedings.

In this court the magistrate's warrants have been attacked on a variety of grounds, but
there has been no suggestion that the evidence before the magistrate did not establish a
prima facie case of burglary against the applicants both according to American and
English law.

The pleading point

The first ground of attack was conveniently described by counsel for the applicants as
the pleading point. His complaint is that there was no formal document before the
magistrate that contained sufficient particulars of the applicants' offence to show that it
constituted the crime of burglary according to English law. It is submitted that before
the magistrate can begin to consider the evidence in support of the application for an
extradition warrant he must have all the necessary ingredients to establish the English
offence formally set out in some document; and as there was no formal document in this
case that alleged the burglars entered 'as trespassers' the magistrate should have refused
to consider the matter further because trespass is an essential element of the English
crime of burglary (see s 9 of the Theft Act 1968).

In order to examine this submission it is necessary to consider the steps by which
extradition is obtained to see what formal documents are required to be placed before the
magistrate. The first step is the request for extradition. This is made through diplomatic
channels and the material that must accompany the request is set out in Article VII of the
extradition treaty between the two governments, given statutory force by Order in
Council[1].

This is the material on which the legal advisers in the Home Office will consider
whether they should advise the Secretary of State to take the next step in the extradition
procedure, which is to refer the request to a metropolitan magistrate pursuant to s 7 of
the Extradition Act 1870, which provides:

> 'A requisition for the surrender of a fugitive criminal of any foreign state, who is
> in or suspected of being in the United Kingdom, shall be made to a Secretary of State
> by some person recognised by the Secretary of State as a diplomatic representative
> of that foreign state. A Secretary of State may, by order under his hand and seal,
> signify to a police magistrate that such a requisition has been made, and require him
> to issue his warrant for the apprehension of the fugitive criminal. If the Secretary
> of State is of opinion that the offence is one of a political character, he may, if he
> think fit, refuse to send any such order, and may also at any time order a fugitive
> criminal accused or convicted of such offence to be discharged from custody.'

When the magistrate receives the order from the Secretary of State, it is his duty to
enquire into the evidence and, if sufficient, to issue his warrant, as plainly appears from
the terms of ss 8 and 10. Section 8 provides:

> 'A warrant for the apprehension of a fugitive criminal, whether accused or
> convicted of crime, who is in or suspected of being in the United Kingdom, may be
> issued—1. By a police magistrate on the receipt of the said order of the Secretary of
> State, and on such evidence as would in his opinion justify the issue of the warrant
> if the crime had been committed or the criminal convicted in England.'

Section 10 provides:

> 'In the case of a fugitive criminal accused of an extradition crime, if the foreign
> warrant authorising the arrest of such criminal is duly authenticated, and such

---

1   SI 1976 No 2144, Sch 1

evidence is produced as (subject to the provisions of this Act) would, according to the law of England, justify the committal for trial of the prisoner if the crime of *a* which he is accused had been committed in England, the police magistrate shall commit him to prison, but otherwise shall order him to be discharged.'

The form of the Secretary of State's order is prescribed by s 20 which provides:

'The forms set forth in the second schedule to this Act, or forms as near thereto as circumstances admit, may be used in all matters to which such forms refer, and *b* in the case of a British possession may be so used, mutatis mutandis, and when used shall be deemed to be valid and sufficient in law.'

The 'Form of Order of Secretary of State to the Police Magistrate' contained in Sch 2 requires the Secretary of State to do no more than insert the name of the crime for which extradition is asked. The order in the present case is in the form prescribed by Sch 2 and names the crime as burglary. As such it is deemed to be valid and sufficient in law by *c* s 20.

The only other document of a formal nature that is required to be before the magistrate is the foreign warrant authorising the arrest of the criminal. It cannot have been intended that this foreign warrant should set out all the ingredients of the English offence for, as Stephen J said in *R v Jacobi and Hiller*[1] 'if it were necessary for the warrant to set forth precisely the crime ... every magistrate [in a foreign country] who issued a *d* warrant ... would have to be acquainted with the law of England'. Such an oppressive requirement would, of course, make extradition unworkable. There is nothing in the treaty that requires any other formal document to be before the magistrate and no authority has been cited to show that extradition has ever been refused on this ground. I am quite satisfied that in extradition proceedings there is no requirement for any formal documents to be before the magistrate other than the order of the Secretary of *e* State and the warrant of arrest, neither of which, for the reasons I have given, are required to set out all the particulars of the English offence. It is to the evidence that the magistrate is directed to look to see whether there are sufficient facts established to constitute an offence contrary to English law and not to any formal document. I am glad to find that this is so, for it would be deplorable if the technicalities of English procedure *f* were introduced to thwart an otherwise proper request for extradition.

In support of his submission, counsel for Mr Budlong relied on the decision of this court in *R v Governor of Brixton Prison, ex parte Gardner*[2], followed in this court in *R v Governor of Pentonville Prison, ex parte Myers*[3]. *Gardner's* case[2] is a decision under the Fugitive Offenders Act 1967, as was *Myers's* case[3], which Act provides for the return from the United Kingdom of persons who have committed crimes in the Commonwealth.

The facts of *Gardner's* case[2] were that warrants had been issued in New Zealand *g* alleging against Gardner the offence of obtaining by false pretences. Because the warrants only disclosed a pretence as to future conduct they did not at that date disclose any offence according to English law. The 1967 Act makes provision for the arrest and return of persons accused in a Commonwealth country of a 'relevant offence'. A relevant offence is defined in the terms in s 3(1) of the Act:

h

'For the purposes of this Act an offence of which a person is accused or has been convicted in a designated Commonwealth country or United Kingdom dependency is a relevant offence if—(a) in the case of an offence against the law of a designated Commonwealth country, it is an offence which, however described in that law, falls within any of the descriptions set out in Schedule 1 to this Act, and is punishable under that law with imprisonment for a term of twelve months or any greater *i* punishment; (b) in the case of an offence against the law of a United Kingdom

1   (1881) 46 LT 595 at 597
2   [1968] 1 All ER 636, [1968] 2 QB 399
3   (6th December 1972) unreported

dependency, it is punishable under that law, on conviction by or before a superior court, with imprisonment for a term of twelve months or any greater punishment; and (c) in any case, the act or omission constituting the offence, or the equivalent act or omission, would constitute an offence against the law of the United Kingdom if it took place within the United Kingdom or, in the case of an extra-territorial offence, in corresponding circumstances outside the United Kingdom.'

Section 5(2) requires the requesting country to furnish the Secretary of State with the following information:

'(a) in the case of a person accused of an offence, a warrant for his arrest issued in that country . . . together . . . with particulars of the person whose return is requested and of the facts upon which and the law under which he is accused or was convicted, and evidence sufficient to justify the issue of a warrant for his arrest under section 6 of this Act.'

Section 5(3) provides:

'On receipt of such a request the Secretary of State may issue an authority to proceed unless it appears to him that an order for the return of the person concerned could not lawfully be made, or would not in fact be made, in accordance with the provisions of this Act.'

Section 6 then provides that a magistrate on receipt of the authority to proceed may issue a warrant of arrest and s 7 provides for the committal if, after hearing evidence, the court is satisfied that the offence in respect of which the authority to proceed has been issued is a relevant offence and that the evidence discloses a prima facie case. Nowhere in the Act is there any requirement as to the form in which the authority to proceed should be drawn. This is, as I have already illustrated, in contrast to the Extradition Act 1870 which does prescribe the form in which the order of the Secretary of State should be drawn.

Lord Parker CJ, having considered the general framework of the 1967 Act, concluded that the authority to proceed had to be drawn with sufficient particularity to disclose all the ingredients of a relevant offence. He said[1]:

'It seems to me that what is clearly contemplated here is that a request coming forward to the Secretary of State must set out in some form, and no doubt the most usual form is the warrant or warrants of arrest, the offence or offences of which the fugitive is accused, in this case in New Zealand. Not only must it supply a general description which will fulfil the provisions of s. 3(1)(a), but it must condescend to sufficient detail to enable the matter to be considered under s. 3(1)(c). Similarly, as it seems to me, it is contemplated that the Secretary of State, in giving his authority to proceed under s. 5(1) should again set out the offences to which his authority is to relate in sufficient detail for the matter to be considered again not only under para. (a) but also under para. (c) of s. 3(1).'

The authority to proceed in *Gardner's* case[2] stated:

'A request having been made to the Secretary of State by or on behalf of the Government of New Zealand for the return to that country of [the applicant] who is accused of the offences of obtaining money by false pretences; attempting to obtain money by false pretences . . . the Secretary of State hereby orders that a metropolitan stipendiary magistrate proceed with the case in accordance with the provisions of the Fugitive Offenders Act, 1967.'

Lord Parker CJ continued[1]:

'So far as this case is concerned, as I have said, the authority to proceed was in perfectly general terms, and this court naturally has not seen and could not look at

---

1   [1968] 1 All ER 636 at 641, [1968] 2 QB 399 at 415
2   [1968] 1 All ER 636 at 640, [1968] 2 QB 399 at 413

the request from the Commonwealth power. But it seems to me, however, perfectly plain that this authority to proceed, albeit in general terms, must be taken as *a* relating to the offences of which the applicant was accused in New Zealand, and on which the request was made for his return.'

As those offences did not disclose an offence known to English law which is an essential element of a 'relevant offence', it was held that the authority to proceed was not in respect of a relevant offence and the application succeeded.   *b*

I can see no reason why these decisions should be applied to proceedings under the 1870 Act. They turn on the construction of the Fugitive Offenders Act 1967, the shape and provisions of which are not in any way on all fours with the 1870 Act. However, the applicants submit that because art III of the treaty requires similar information to be submitted to the Secretary of State by the country requesting extradition to that required to be submitted by a Commonwealth country under s 3 of the 1967 Act, it follows that *c* the Secretary of State's order under the 1870 Act shall contain the same particulars as, pursuant to *Gardner's* case[1], are required to be set out in the authority to proceed under the 1967 Act. I cannot see why that result should necessarily follow, but the conclusive answer to the submission is to be found in the terms of s 20 of the 1870 Act which expressly provides that the order shall be valid if it follows the form prescribed in Sch 2, which form does not require the order to do other than state the general description of *d* the crime for which extradition is asked.

The point is also covered by authority. In *Re Bellencontre*[2], Cave J said:

'The duty of the Secretary of State is to call the attention of the police magistrate to what he is required to do under the Extradition Treaty, and it is enough if he draws attention to the particular crime under the 3rd article of the Extradition *e* Treaty, and that is fraud by a bailee, which expresses in general terms what is expressed rather more specifically in the French warrant.'

Because, in my view, the *Gardner*[1] and *Myers*[3] cases do not support the applicants' argument, it is not necessary to consider if they were correctly decided. But I would not wish anything I have said to be taken as expressing my own endorsement of the *f* decisions. It seems to me that they lead to the surprising conclusion that the success or failure of a Commonwealth country to extradite a criminal who has offended against their laws may depend on the drafting of particulars in a document, namely the authority to proceed, for which they are not responsible.

For the reasons I have given the pleading point fails.

g

Double criminality

The second submission is founded on the fact that under the relevant American law, § 1801(*b*) of Title 22 District of Columbia Code, entry as a trespasser is not an essential element of the crime of burglary whereas under English law trespass is an essential element of the crime (see the Theft Act 1968, s 9).

It is admitted that the facts of this case show that the burglars obtained entry to the *h* various government offices as trespassers, but it is argued that because the applicants, when they are tried in America could be convicted without proof that the entry involved a trespass, they are thereby placed in peril of being convicted of a crime in America for which they could not be convicted in this country. The applicants submit that this offends against the principle of double criminality under which a criminal is only to be extradited for the commission of a crime punishable by the laws of both countries. *j*

1 [1968] 1 All ER 636, [1968] 2 QB 399
2 [1891] 2 QB 122 at 136
3 (6th December 1972) unreported

a The prosecution submit that the true rule is that a criminal is to be extradited if his crime falls within the general description of a crime specified in the extradition treaty and the facts of the offence, that is the conduct complained of, show it to be a criminal offence punishable by the laws of both countries. As the facts of these offences show a prima facie case of burglary against both the laws of the District of Columbia and this country, the prosecution submit that extradition should be ordered.

b The law of extradition depends not on any common law principles, but on statute. Ultimately the question before this court has to be solved by deciding whether on their true construction the extradition treaty and the 1870 Act, which by art 3 of the United States of America (Extradition) Order 1976[1] is applied to the treaty, permit extradition in this case. None of the authorities that have been cited bear directly on the question we have to decide, but I believe they provide valuable guidance to the correct approach to the construction of the statutory provisions.

c In *Re Windsor*[2] extradition to the United States was demanded under a treaty making forgery an extraditable offence. The facts alleged against a bankteller revealed that he had made a false entry in a bank book for fraudulent purposes which would amount to forgery under the definition in the New York statute; they did not, however, constitute the offence of forgery in English law. The principal ground given for refusing extradition was that the local statute of New York did not make the offence forgery by

d the general law of the United States and, hence, the crime of forgery had not been committed in either country. This ground has been disapproved by the Supreme Court of the United States (see *Wright v Henkel*[3]), and is not relied on in this case. There are, however, two short passages in Re Windsor[4] dealing with the concept of double criminality. Cockburn CJ said: 'the true construction of [the Extradition Act 1843] is, that its terms, specifying the offences for which persons may be given up, must be

e understood to apply to offences which have some common element in the legislation of both countries.' Blackburn J said[5]: 'Forgery is one of the crimes specified, and that must be understood to mean any crimes recognised throughout the United States and England as being in the nature of forgery.' From the two expressions 'some common element' and 'in the nature of' it is apparent that the court was not looking for the crime to be defined in identical terms in both countries.

f In *Re Bellencontre*[6] the French authorities demanded extradition of a French subject accused in France of 19 separate charges of embezzling or misappropriating money delivered to him as a notary. The court found that as to 15 of the charges the evidence disclosed no crime punishable by English law, but that in the case of the four remaining charges the evidence did show an offence contrary to the French Penal Code and English law within the extradition treaty and that extradition ought to be granted in respect of

g those four charges.

In the course of his judgment Wills J said[7]:

h 'The substance of the Extradition Act, 33 & 34 Vict. c. 52, seems to me to require that the person whose extradition is sought should have been accused in a foreign country of something which is a crime by English law, and that there should be a primâ facie case made out that he is guilty of a crime under the foreign law, and also of a crime under English law. If those conditions are satisfied, the extradition ought to be granted. We cannot expect that the definitions of description of the crime when translated into the language of the two countries respectively, should exactly correspond. The definitions may have grown up under widely different

j 1 SI 1976 No 2144, Sch 1
    2 (1865) 6 B & S 522, 122 ER 1288
    3 (1902) 190 US 90
    4 (1865) 6 B & S 522 at 528, 122 ER 1288 at 1291
    5 6 B & S 522 at 530, 122 ER 1288 at 1291
    6 [1891] 2 QB 122
    7 [1891] 2 QB 122 at 140–141

circumstances in the two countries; and if an exact correspondence were required in mere matter of definition, probably there would be great difficulty in laying down what crimes could be made the subjects of extradition. Now this difficulty has been met, as it seems to me, by the first schedule to the Extradition Act, 1870 (33 & 34 Vict. c. 52), which describes what are the various extradition crimes. In this case, the man has been accused of a number of things which clearly fall within article 408 of the French Code, and therefore are crimes in France, and crimes which clearly fall under number 18 in the French part of the Treaty of Extradition. One looks, then, to see whether in the corresponding English section, No. 18 of article 3, there is a crime described by English law which crime has been made out by the evidence. It seems to me that there is no difficulty in saying which of the definitions it falls under.'

This passage clearly indicates that in considering extradition it is the actual facts of the offence which are all important rather than the definition of the crime in the foreign law.

In *Re Arton (No 2)*[1], extradition was demanded for 'faux' which is the French equivalent of forgery. The facts did not disclose the offence of forgery according to English law, but did disclose the offence of falsification of accounts, which is an extradition crime and within the French and English treaties. Lord Russell CJ said[2]:

'Is extradition to be refused in respect of acts covered by the treaty, and gravely criminal according to the law of both countries, because in the particular case the falsification of accounts is not forgery according to English law, but falls under that head according to French law? I think not. To decide so would be to hinder the working and narrow the operation of most salutary international arrangements.'

Here again the emphasis is placed not on the definition of the crime but on the acts that constitute the criminal conduct. In a later passage he continued[2]:

'We are here dealing with a crime alleged to have been committed against the law of France; and if we find, as I hold that we do, that such a crime is a crime against the law of both countries, and is, in substance, to be found in each version of the treaty, although under different heads, we are bound to give effect to the claim for extradition.'

Here, too, it is the substance of the two offences that must correspond, not their precise definitions.

R v Dix[3] is another case in which the description of the crime was different in the two countries, but the facts revealed criminal acts punishable under the laws of both countries and within the extradition treaty. The accused was charged with larceny by embezzlement according to American law. It was held that as the evidence showed fraud by a bailee banker under the Larceny Act, an offence within the treaty, the accused could be extradited. Darling J said[4]: '... the essential thing was to see whether what the evidence showed *prima facie* that the prisoner had done was a crime in both countries and within the treaty.' Once more the court is looking to the actual criminal conduct to decide if extradition should be granted.

The case most comparable to the present facts is the unreported decision of this court in *R v Governor of Pentonville Prison, ex parte Ecke*[5] decided on 3rd December 1973. The German Government asked that the accused should be extradited on a number of charges of fraudulent trading, the dishonesty alleged being a false representation as to a future intention and not as to an existing fact. The date of the treaty[6] was 1960 at which date

1   [1896] 1 QB 509
2   [1896] 1 QB 509 at 517
3   (1902) 18 TLR 231
4   (1902) 18 TLR 231 at 232
5   [1974] Crim LR 102
6   See Federal Republic of Germany (Extradition) Order 1960, SI 1960 No 1375, Sch 1

a false representation as to a future intention was not a criminal offence in England.

a Article 2 of the treaty provided: 'Extradition shall be reciprocally granted for the following crimes, provided that the crime charged constitutes an extradition crime according to the laws of the territory from which and to which extradition is desired.' The list of crimes included in the English version under para 17 are: 'Fraud by a bailee, banker, agent, factor or trustee, or by a director, member or public officer of any company; fraudulent conversion; or obtaining money, valuables, security, or goods by

b false pretences.' In the German version para 17 consisted of two words meaning, in English, 'fraud'. It was submitted that an offence could not be an extraditable offence within the meaning of the treaty unless it was an offence with all its English constituents, and that as a false pretence as to a future event was not an English offence in 1960, when the treaty was made, it was not an extradition crime under the treaty. The fact that since the Theft Act 1968, a misrepresentation as to a future event will found a criminal charge

c was said to be beside the point for to accept it as now coming within the treaty would be to amend the treaty unilaterally. This argument was rejected: the court held that the words descriptive of the offence in the treaty were to be given their general meaning, general to the lawyer and layman alike, their ordinary international meaning, and not a particular meaning they may have attracted in England. Giving the words a liberal meaning, treating them not as words of art but as words of general description, the

d accused's activities came within both the English and German versions of art 17. The court pointed out that the requirement that the facts alleged must amount to an offence in English law would have protected him from extradition if his offences had been committed before 1968.

It was helpful to have citation of three American authorities, two decisions of the Supreme Court (*Wright v Henkel*[1] and *Factor v Laubenheimer*[2]), and one decision of the

e Court of Appeal of the second circuit (*Shapiro v Ferrandina*[3]). None of them bear directly on the problem in this case, but they show no difference in their general approach to extradition to that adopted by the courts in this country. I will do no more than cite briefly from the opinion of the court in *Wright v Henkel*[4]:

'Treaties must receive a fair interpretation, according to the intention of the contracting parties, and so as to carry out their manifest purpose. The ordinary

f technicalities of criminal proceedings are applicable to proceedings in extradition only to a limited extent . . . The general principle of international law is that in all cases of extradition the act done on account of which extradition is demanded must be considered a crime by both parties . . .'

Finally, in reference to the definition of the crime under the American and British

g statutes[5]: 'Absolute identity is not required. The essential character of the transaction is the same, and made criminal by both statutes.'

With the guidance of these authorities I turn back to the statutory provisions. Article III of the treaty provides:

'(1) Extradition shall be granted for an act or omission the facts of which disclose an offence within any of the descriptions listed in the Schedule annexed to this

h Treaty, which is an integral part of the Treaty, or any other offence, if: (*a*) the offence is punishable under the laws of both Parties by imprisonment or other form of detention for more than one year or by the death penalty; (*b*) the offence is extraditable under the relevant law, being the law of the United Kingdom or other territory to which this Treaty applies by virtue of sub-paragraph (1)(*a*) of Article II;

j

1 (1902) 190 US 40
2 (1933) 290 US 276
3 (1973) 478 F 2d 894
4 (1902) 190 US 40 at 57–58 per Fuller CJ
5 (1902) 190 US 40 at 58

and (c) the offence constitutes a felony under the law of the United States of America.'

_a

The first requirement is satisfied: burglary is in the schedule. The facts do disclose acts that would be recognised by layman and lawyer alike as falling within the concept of burglary, and it matters not that the two crimes are not identically defined. Sub-paras (a) and (c) also are satisfied. Burglary in both countries is punishable by imprisonment for more than one year and it is a felony under American law.

I turn to sub-para (b). For the offence to be extraditable under the law of the United *b* Kingdom it must be an extradition crime as defined by s 26 of the Extradition Act 1870, for it is only in respect of an extradition crime that the magistrate has power to commit an accused person under s 8. The definition in s 26 reads: 'The term "extradition crime" means a crime which, if committed in England or within English jurisdiction, would be one of the crimes described in the first schedule to this Act.'

Now I come to what I consider to be the nub of the case. Is this definition to be *c* construed as meaning that the crime as defined in the foreign law must contain all the essential ingredients of one of the English crimes described in the schedule, in which case the applicants' submission succeeds because the American definition of burglary does not require trespass as an essential element? Alternatively, does the definition mean that an 'extradition crime' has been committed if that which the accused has done would have amounted to the commission of one of the crimes in the schedule if it had been done in *d* England? If this is the true meaning of the definition, the applicants fail for the evidence shows that they committed the crime of burglary according to English law.

In my judgment, the second construction is to be preferred. The first construction would give rise to all the difficulties inherent in attempting to apply extradition on the unlikely foundation that foreign definitions of crimes, often in different languages and operating in very different legal systems, will accord with English definitions. The *e* authorities show that the courts do not expect or look for such identity of definition.

On the other hand, an English court should have no difficulty in deciding whether a given set of facts does or does not constitute a crime according to English law. The authorities that have been cited stress the importance that the facts of the case should disclose an offence against the law of both countries and appear to me to lean heavily towards this interpretation of the definition. I appreciate that this construction may in *f* theory result in the possibility of conviction in a foreign country which would not occur here. Although a theoretical possibility, it is I think a very unlikely result and, certainly so far as I can see, there is not a remote chance of it in the present case. This construction still leaves the accused with the protection that he is only to be extradited for a crime that is substantially similar in concept in both countries and I do not believe that this will result in any injustice. *g*

I therefore summarise by saying that double criminality in our law of extradition is satisfied if it is shown: (1) that the crime for which extradition is demanded would be recognised as substantially similar in both countries, and (2) that there is a prima facie case that the conduct of the accused amounted to the commission of the crime according to English law.

I therefore conclude that double criminality does not have the meaning contended for *h* by the applicants and their objection fails.

Are the offences of a political character?

Extradition will not be granted if the offence with which the accused is charged is of a political character. An offence of a political character is an elusive concept and probably defies any completely satisfactory definition. It is probably not desirable to attempt one *j* because, as Lord Radcliffe said in *Schtraks v Government of Israel*[1], it is virtually impossible to find one that does not cover too wide a range. It is submitted that the offences were of a political character because the applicants were engaged in an attempt to change the

---

1   [1962] 3 All ER 529 at 539, [1964] AC 556 at 589

policy of the United States Government towards the Church of Scientology and that the
a burglaries were committed to further this end. The applicants rely on passages in the
opinions in *Schtraks v Government of Israel*[1] per Lord Reid, and *Tzu Tsai Cheng v Governor
of Pentonville Prison*[2] per Lord Diplock, which refer to an offence of a political character
being one aimed at changing the policy of the foreign government. But these words of
their Lordships must be read in the full context of their speeches which make it clear that
they were considering offences committed in the course of a struggle against a foreign
b government from which the accused had sought asylum in this country. As society
becomes more sophisticated, and populations increase, so the scope of government
increases with the inevitable result that the policies of government affect the everyday
life of the individual over an ever widening range of his daily activities.

In respect of any government policy there will probably be a substantial number of
people who disagree with it and would wish to change it, but it should not be thought
c that if they commit a crime to achieve their ends it necessarily becomes an offence of a
political character. In only two of the reported cases have our courts held that the offence
was of a political character: in *Re Castioni*[3] in which the accused had killed a member of
the government in the course of an armed uprising that overthrew the government, and
in *Re Kolczynski*[4] in which a number of Polish seamen mutinied and sailed their vessel to
England where they sought asylum for they feared prosecution for their political
d opinions if they should be returned to Poland. The idea underlying an offence of a
political character is expressed by Lord Radcliffe in *Schtraks v Government of Israel*[5] in the
following language:

> 'In my opinion the idea that lies behind the phrase "offence of a political character"
> is that the fugitive is at odds with the state that applies for his extradition on some
> issue connected with the political control or government of the country. The
e > analogy of "political" in this context is with "political" in such phrases as "political
> refugee," "political asylum" or "political prisoner."'

Counsel for Mrs Kember has taken the court through a great deal of evidence in the
course of his submission on this aspect of the case. The evidence reveals that the Church
of Scientology has been engaged in a protracted struggle with the Internal Revenue
f Services Department of the United States to secure exemption from taxes on the grounds
that it is a religious foundation, and that it has also fought another long battle through
the courts against the Food and Drugs Administration to establish that they were entitled
to use a device known as an E-Meter as a part of their religious practice. It is also apparent
from the documents that the Internal Revenue Services Department and the Food and
Drugs Administration entertained grave doubts about the bona fides of the Scientologists
g and that they had received a number of reports suggesting various forms of criminal
activity and chicanery on the part of the church and its members. The material before
us also shows that these departments of the United States Government were not alone in
their distrust of Scientology and its practices. The State of Victoria passed legislation
against it and this country has refused to permit entry to those wishing to enter the
employment of the Church of Scientology. It should, however, be stated that the
h Church of Scientology has achieved a substantial degree of success in the American
litigation; the Internal Revenue Service in June and July 1975 finally conceded exempt
status for tax purposes to all but one of its churches in the United States, and subject to
certain safeguards the courts have permitted the use of the E-Meter.

Counsel for Mrs Kember submitted that the burglaries were planned in order to gain
access to the information that had been collected by the Internal Revenue Service and

j

---

1   [1962] 3 All ER 529 at 535, [1964] AC 556 at 583
2   [1973] 2 All ER 204 at 209, [1973] AC 931 at 945
3   [1891] 1 QB 419
4   [1955] 1 All ER 31, [1955] 1 QB 540
5   [1962] 3 All ER 529 at 540, [1964] AC 556 at 591

Department of Justice so that the Church of Scientology could inform themselves as to the false reports circulating about it between government departments, and identify and *a* deal with the particular persons within the departments who were hostile to the church.

I am prepared to accept that this was one motive for the burglaries. Guardian order 1361 dated 21st October 1974, which seems to be the seminal document that initiated the break-ins, does refer to employees of the government departments concerned as, I quote, 'suppressive psychotics utilising the IRS as a substitute for standard justice procedures on scientology' and later it refers to the 'suppressive psychotics being *b* identified and handled'. We were not told just how it was proposed to handle them. But this was only one of the guardian orders put in evidence, and it is manifest from the terms of other orders that a very important purpose of the burglaries was to obtain information that would help in the litigation. By way of examples only, I quote from the guardian order dated 5th December 1975: 'Place an agent in the US Attorneys Office DC as a first action as this office should cover all Federal agencies that we are in litigation *c* with or may be in the litigation with', and the guardian order dated 27th March 1976: 'An excellent B1 success over the last year was the obtaining of non-FOI [non-Freedom of Information Act] data that resulted in aiding our overall strategy to get the CofS tax exemptions.'

I am unable to accept that organising burglaries either for the purpose of identifying persons in government offices hostile to the Scientologists, or for the purpose of gaining *d* an advantage in litigation, or even for the wider purpose of refuting false allegations thus enabling a better image of the Church of Scientology to be projected to the public, comes anywhere near being an offence of a political character within the meaning of the Extradition Act 1870.

The applicants did not order these burglaries to take place in order to challenge the political control or government of the United States; they did so to further the interests *e* of the Church of Scientology and its members, and in particular the interest of Ron L Hubbard, the founder of Scientology. In my view, it would be ridiculous to regard the applicants as political refugees seeking asylum in this country, and I reject the submission that these were offences of a political character.

The public law argument   *f*

It is a well established rule that our courts will not enforce a foreign revenue, penal or public law. This means that our courts will not try and either punish or give a remedy for the breach of such a law committed in a foreign country. Counsel for Mrs Kember submits that the United States Government is attempting by indirect means to enforce a public law of the United States, namely the Freedom of Information Act. He says the real purpose behind the request for extradition is to punish the applicants not for *g* burglary but for stealing confidential government information protected by the Freedom of Information Act. This could not be achieved by extradition proceedings because a breach of that Act is not an extradition crime, and so, it is said, resort is had to the offence of burglary. Although in the course of his argument counsel for Mrs Kember said he was not suggesting any bad faith on the part of the Government of the United States, it seems to me that bad faith is necessarily implicit in this submission. Under the treaty the *h* United States give their undertaking that the accused will not be tried for any offence other than that for which they are extradited; if in the face of this undertaking they were ostensibly tried for burglary but in fact punished for the commission of a different offence, I should regard that as flagrant bad faith. When the offence has not been shown to be of a political character our courts will not entertain allegations of bad faith on the part of the requesting country: see *Re Arton*[1] and *R v Governor of Brixton Prison, ex parte* *j* *Kolczynski*[2].

---

1   [1896] 1 QB 108
2   [1955] 1 All ER 31, [1955] 1 QB 540

This is sufficient to dispose of the submission, but there is in fact a further ground for
a rejecting it. In the course of the proceedings in the United States, Judge Richey has given
the following ruling:

'The government will not be permitted to rely on any alleged conversion of
government information for a violation of section 641 in this case. However the
government may proceed on the theory that copies made from government
resources are owned by the government.'
b
This makes it doubly unthinkable that their punishment will not be for burglary but
for stealing confidential information. This objection therefore fails.

The construction of s 3(1) of the Extradition Act 1870
Section 3(1) provides:
c
'A fugitive criminal shall not be surrendered if the offence in respect of which his
surrender is demanded is one of a political character, or if he proves to the satisfaction
of the police magistrate or the court before whom he is brought on habeas corpus,
or to the Secretary of State, that the requisition for his surrender has in fact been
made with a view to try or punish him for an offence of a political character.'

d   Counsel for Mrs Kember addressed an argument to the court on the construction of
s 3(1). He submitted that stealing confidential information was a political act and that
the requisition for surrender was made with a view to punishing the applicants for this
offence, and that they were thus protected by the second limb of s 3(1). For the reasons
I have already given this submission would fail on the facts, but it is also bound to fail on
the construction of the section. It is submitted that, even if the crime for which
e extradition is asked is not an offence of a political character within the first limb of the
section, the second limb allows the fugitive criminal to show that the requesting country
intends to try or punish him for some other political offence. This was the construction
of the section adopted by Lord Russell CJ in *Re Arton*[1]. But since that date the section has
been construed in two modern authorities: by Lord Goddard CJ in *Re Kolczynski*[2], and by
Lord Parker CJ[3] in the Divisional Court and by Lord Radcliffe[4], Lord Reid[5] and Lord
f Evershed[6] in the House of Lords in the *Schtraks* case[7]. They have all rejected Lord Russell
CJ's construction and held that the second limb of the section does no more than permit
the accused to show by evidence that the offence for which extradition is asked is in truth
of a political character, although it might not appear to be so from the evidence produced
by the country requesting extradition. In my judgment, this court is bound by that
weight of authority to apply this construction.

g
The law of the European Economic Community
The final submission is made on behalf of Mrs Kember only and by virtue of her status
as a national of the United Kingdom. It is submitted that the order of committal to await
extradition is a restriction on her right to move freely between countries within the
community guaranteed by art 48 of the Treaty of Rome and can only be justified on
h grounds of public policy under art 48(3), and in accordance with the provisions of
Council Directive 64/221/EEC of 25th February 1964.
The basis of this submission is that extradition is closely analogous to deportation. In
R v Bouchereau[8] the European Court of Justice on a reference from the Marlborough

1   [1896] 1 QB 108
. 2   [1955] 1 All ER 31 at 35–38, [1955] 1 QB 540 at 549–553
j 3   [1962] 2 All ER 176 at 187–192, [1963] 1 QB 55 at 81–89
4   [1962] 3 All ER 529 at 538–541, [1964] AC 556 at 587–592
5   [1962] 3 All ER 529 at 533–536, [1964] AC 556 at 580–585
6   [1962] 3 All ER 529 at 545, [1964] AC 556 at 599
7   [1962] 3 All ER 529, [1964] AC 556
8   [1978] QB 732

Street Magistrates' court held that a recommendation for deportation made by a criminal court in this country was a measure within the meaning of art 3(1) and (2) of EEC Directive 64/221 and could only be made on grounds of public policy. The case concerned a French national convicted of the unlawful possession of drugs and it was accepted that a deportation order would constitute a restriction on his freedom of movement within art 48. Directive 64/221 applies only to foreign nationals and therefore has no direct application to the facts of the present case; it is concerned with the behaviour of member states towards foreign nationals in relation to entry to or expulsion from their territory. However, it has been argued that a member state is under a duty to treat its own nationals no less favourably than foreign nationals, for which the authority of *Knoors v Secretary of State for Economic Affairs*[1] was cited, and that as extradition is equivalent to deportation a member state can only extradite one of its own nationals if it applies the same criteria as it is required to apply by Directive 64/221 in the case of foreign nationals.

If this submission is right, it will impose a formidable fetter on extradition. It will mean that extradition can only be ordered on grounds of public policy based exclusively on the personal conduct of the individual concerned (see art 3 of the Directive). In *R v Bouchereau*[2] the European Court said in the course of their judgment:

'27. The existence of a previous conviction can . . . only be taken into account in so far as the circumstances which gave rise to that conviction are evidence of personal conduct constituting a present threat to the requirements of public policy.
'28. Although, in general, a finding that such a threat exists implies the existence in the individual concerned of a propensity to act in the same way in the future, it is possible that past conduct alone may constitute such a threat for the requirements of public policy.'

This concept is easily understood in the law of deportation. A man should not be banished for a crime for which he has been punished unless he remains a present threat to society. But how do you apply it to extradition? The whole basis of extradition is that the accused has offended against society in another country; in all probability he is no threat to our society. Does that then mean he is not to be extradited to face justice where he has committed the crime? I cannot believe that it can have been the intention of those who drew the Treaty of Rome that it should have the effect of so emasculating the process of extradition.

It is submitted by counsel who appeared as amicus curiae that the restrictions on the freedom of an individual imposed by extradition are unaffected by art 48. In *R v Saunders*[3] the European Court of Justice held that art 48 did not aim to restrict the power of member states to lay down restrictions within their own territory on the freedom of movement of all persons subject to their jurisdiction in implementation of domestic criminal law. I regard extradition as far more closely analogous to the implementation of domestic criminal law than to deportation. It is in no true sense a banishment from our shores as is deportation; indeed s 3(2) of the Extradition Act 1870 specifically provides that there will be no extradition unless the foreign state undertakes to allow the accused to return to this country after he has been dealt with for the extradition crime. Extradition is no more than a step that assists in the implementation of the domestic criminal law of the foreign state. This country has extradition treaties with other member states entered into before the Treaty of Rome.

Article 234 of the treaty provides:

'The rights and obligations arising from agreements concluded before the entry into force of this Treaty between one or more Member states on the one hand, and

---

1   [1979] 2 CMLR 357
2   [1978] QB 732 at 759
3   [1979] 2 All ER 267, [1979] 3 WLR 359

a one or more third countries on the other, shall not be affected by the provisions of this Treaty.'

It would be a curious result if extradition could be granted on generally accepted principles between member states who had entered into extradition treaties before the Treaty of Rome but on very different principles, introducing the concept of public policy already discussed, between member states who made or, I suppose, amended, extradition treaties after the Treaty of Rome. Again I cannot think that this result can have been b intended.

Counsel for Mrs Kember wishes us to refer to the European Court of Justice the following question:

> 'Whether a Member-State, in considering an application for the extradition (whether to another Member-State or to a Third party) of a worker who is a national c of that first Member-State, must have regard to the provisions of Article 48(3) of the Treaty establishing the E.E.C.'

Article 48(3) requires the justification to be on grounds of public policy.

If we did refer this question we should undoubtedly have to refer a number of supplementary questions to elucidate how the concept of public policy was to be applied to extradition.

d Lord Denning MR, in *H P Bulmer Ltd v Bollinger SA*[1] laid down guidelines to assist the courts in deciding whether to refer a question to the European Courts of Justice. The court should refer the point unless it considers it to be reasonably clear and free from doubt.

I have come to the clear conclusion that, borrowing the words of Advocate-General Warner in his opinion in *R v Saunders*[2], it is common sense that dictates that art 48 e should be interpreted as manifestly not intended to apply to the exercise of the power of this country to extradite an accused person to the United States of America. Accordingly I would not make any reference to the European Court of Justice.

For the reasons I have given I would refuse the writ of habeas corpus to these applicants.

f **LORD WIDGERY CJ.** I agree with the judgment which has just been delivered.

Applications refused. Leave to appeal to the House of Lords refused.

Solicitors: *Stephen M Bird*, East Grinstead (for the applicants); *Director of Public Prosecutions* (for the United States Government); *Treasury Solicitor*.
g

N P Metcalfe Esq   Barrister.

---

1 [1974] 2 All ER 1226, [1974] Ch 401
2 [1979] 2 All ER 267 at 276, [1979] 3 WLR 359 at 366

Stewart Chartering Ltd v C & O Managements SA and others
The Venus Destiny

QUEEN'S BENCH DIVISION
ROBERT GOFF J
21st DECEMBER 1979

Judgment – Default of appearance – Application for leave to enter judgment – Jurisdiction – Writ containing or including claim other than for liquidated demand etc – Writ containing claims for liquidated demand and injunction to restrain defendant from removing assets from jurisdiction – Plaintiff granted injunction – Whether claim for injunction in writ precluding plaintiff from entering judgment in claim for liquidated demand in default of appearance by defendant – RSC Ord 13, r 6.

Where a writ is indorsed with a claim for a Mareva injunction[a], the court may in an appropriate case, by virtue of its inherent jurisdiction to prevent an abuse of its process, grant leave to the plaintiff to enter judgment in default of appearance by the defendant notwithstanding RSC Ord 13, r 6[b], which precludes a plaintiff from entering judgment in default of appearance in every case in which the indorsement on the writ contains or includes a claim for other than a liquidated demand, unliquidated damages, detention of goods or possession of land, since otherwise, if the plaintiff was unable to proceed to judgment without abandoning the injunction, it would be open to the defendant to defeat the purpose of the Mareva proceedings by declining to enter an appearance. If the court so acts, it can also order that the Mareva injunction continue in force after the judgment, in aid of execution (see p 719 f to h, post).

Notes

For judgment in default of appearance, see 26 Halsbury's Laws (4th Edn) paras 509–511, and for cases on the effect of default of appearance where the writ contains or includes a claim other than for liquidated demand etc, see 50 Digest (Repl) 397–398, 1075–1093.

Application for leave to enter judgment

By a writ dated 2nd August 1979 the plaintiffs, Stewart Chartering Ltd, brought an action against the defendants, C & O Managements SA of Athens, Greece, and Palirima

---

a　See *Mareva Compania Naviera SA v International Bulkcarriers SA* p 213, ante
b　Rule 6 provides:
　　'(1) Where a writ is indorsed with a claim of a description not mentioned in Rules 1 to 4 [which mention a claim for a liquidated demand (r 1), a claim for unliquidated damages (r 2), a claim for detention of goods (r 3) and a claim for possession of land (r 4)], then, if any defendant fails to enter an appearance, the plaintiff may, after the time limited for appearing and upon filing an affidavit proving due service of the writ on that defendant and, where the statement of claim was not indorsed on or served with the writ, upon serving a statement of claim on him, proceed with the action as if that defendant had entered an appearance.
　　'(2) Where a writ issued against a defendant is indorsed as aforesaid, but by reason of the defendant's satisfying the claim or complying with the demands thereof or any other like reason it has become unnecessary for the plaintiff to proceed with the action, then, if the defendant fails to enter an appearance, the plaintiff may, after the time limited for appearing, enter judgment with the leave of the Court against that defendant for costs.
　　'(3) An application for leave to enter judgment under paragraph (2) shall be by summons which must, unless the Court otherwise orders, and notwithstanding anything in Order 65, rule 9, be served on the defendant against whom it is sought to enter judgment.'

a Shipping Co Ltd of Nicosia, Cyprus, (i) claiming £23,101·33 for ship management services rendered by them for the defendants in connection with the second defendants' vessel mv Venus Destiny and (ii) seeking an injunction restraining the defendants from removing from the jurisdiction or otherwise disposing of any assets of the defendants' including in particular the proceeds of a hull insurance policy on the mv Venus Destiny save in so far as the assets exceeded the sum of £32,500. On 17th August, on an ex parte application, his Honour Judge Hawser QC sitting as a judge of the High Court granted
b the plaintiffs leave to serve the writ out of the jurisdiction and an injunction in the terms of the writ. Notice of the writ was served on the defendants. On 21st December the plaintiffs applied ex parte in the Commercial Court for leave to enter judgment.

Jonathan Hirst for the plaintiffs.

c **ROBERT GOFF J.** There is before the court an ex parte application for leave to sign judgment in default of appearance in an action for a liquidated sum brought against the defendants outside the jurisdiction who have been properly served with proceedings pursuant to leave granted under RSC Ord 11. In the ordinary course, no appearance having been entered, judgment could be entered for the sum claimed without leave of the court; but the matter is complicated by the fact that, in order to obtain a Mareva injunction[1], the writ is indorsed in addition with a claim for an injunction. In such
d circumstances, having regard to the provisions of RSC Ord 13, r 6, it is not possible for the plaintiffs simply to enter judgment in default of appearance; and in the present case, the Chief Clerk in the Judgment Room has quite rightly declined to permit the plaintiffs so to proceed.

I am therefore presented with the paradoxical situation that, because the plaintiffs have obtained an injunction designed to prevent the defendants from removing assets
e from the jurisdiction in order to prevent the plaintiffs from satisfying any judgment, they are inhibited from signing judgment in default of appearance which is, in the present situation, the next step which would ordinarily be taken by them with a view to enforcing their claim.

The solution to this problem lies, in my judgment, in the inherent jurisdiction of the court to control its own process, and in particular to prevent any possible abuse of that
f process. If the plaintiffs were unable to obtain a judgment in the present case without abandoning their Mareva injunction, it would be open to a defendant to defeat the very purpose of the proceedings simply by declining to enter an appearance. Such conduct would be an abuse of the process of the court; and in my judgment the court has power to take the necessary steps, by virtue of its inherent jurisdiction, to prevent any such abuse of its process. The appropriate action to be taken by the court in such circumstances
g is, in my judgment, to grant leave to the plaintiffs, in an appropriate case, to enter judgment in default of appearance, notwithstanding that the writ is indorsed with a claim for an injunction. If the court so acts, it can also order that the Mareva injunction continue in force after the judgment, in aid of execution. The purpose of a Mareva injunction is to prevent a defendant from removing his assets from the jurisdiction so as to prevent the plaintiff from obtaining the fruits of his judgment; from this it follows
h that the policy underlying the Mareva injunction can only be given effect to if the court has power to continue the Mareva injunction after judgment, in aid of execution.

In my judgment, the present case is an appropriate case for the court so to proceed. I therefore give leave to the plaintiffs to enter judgment; and I shall also order that the Mareva injunction continue in force in aid of execution.

j *Leave to the plaintiffs to enter judgment. Injunction to continue in force in aid of execution.*

Solicitors: *Constant & Constant* (for the plaintiffs).

K Mydeen Esq   Barrister.

---

1   See *Mareva Compania Naviera SA v International Bulkcarriers SA* p 213, ante

Grant and others v Allen and another

Mobile home – Agreement offered by site owner to occupier of mobile home – Dispute – Occupier dissatisfied with terms of agreement – Date of commencement of agreement omitted – Term that owner could move mobile home for purpose of better management of park – Term imposing on occupier obligation to pay commission to owner where mobile home not sold to assignee of agreement – Term giving owner right of access to pitch for purpose of inspecting and maintaining property other than his own – Application to court to determine matter in dispute – Criteria to be applied in determining matter in dispute – Whether terms offered valid – Mobile Homes Act 1975, ss 3 (f)(h)(i)(j), 4(1)(a)(2)(a)

The owners of a caravan park offered to enter into written agreements with occupiers of mobile homes pitched there on the terms of a printed form of draft agreement in purported compliance with their duty under ss 1, 2 and 3 of the Mobile Homes Act 1975. The draft contained blank spaces for the insertion of such matters as the dates of commencement and termination of the agreement, and the date from which the pitch fee was payable. The occupiers declined to accept the offer and applied to the court for relief on the grounds that they were dissatisfied with certain clauses of the draft agreement, including, inter alia, (i) cl 2(D) which provided that the owners should have the right to move the mobile home to another part of the park for the purpose of carrying out essential works to the pitch or park or for the better management of the park, (ii) cl 3(1) which obliged the occupier to pay a pitch fee to the owners but without stating the amount of the fee or the date from which it was payable, (iii) cl 3(12) which required the occupier to permit the owners to enter the pitch for the purpose of inspecting, maintaining and repairing fences, sheds and outbuildings whether the property of the owners or otherwise, and (iv) cl 6(c) which provided that the owners were entitled to receive a commission from the occupier if the occupier assigned the agreement without selling to the assignee or disposing of the mobile home otherwise than by sale. The county court judge, acting under s 4(7), determined the amount of the pitch fee for the purposes of cl 3(1), and ordered that it should be payable from 1st January 1976, which was the date he determined for the commencement of the agreement, and approved the disputed clauses in the terms proposed by the owners. Three of the occupiers appealed, contending that under the Act the judge had no power, in the absence of agreement between the parties, to determine that the commencement of the agreement should be backdated to a date earlier than his decision or that the pitch fee should be payable from the date thus fixed, and that the clauses as proposed were in conflict with the provisions of the Act and therefore should not have been approved.

Held – (i) A judge had power under the 1975 Act to order a retrospective date for the commencement of an agreement if he thought it was reasonable to do so, and on the evidence the backdating of the commencement of the agreement and the date from which the weekly pitch fee was payable was reasonable. Accordingly, to that extent the appeal would be dismissed (see p 726 j to p 727 a, post).

(ii) The effect of ss 3 and 4 of the 1975 Act was that, in order to comply with the provisions of the Act, an agreement was, in any event, required to contain terms and conditions as prescribed by paras (a) to (j) of s 3, and could in addition, if the parties so agreed or if the court thought it reasonable, contain other terms and conditions. In determining a dispute about a particular term or condition in an agreement the court was required to ensure that the term or condition, if and to the extent that it was approved by the court, complied with s 3 and was reasonable (see p 724 h to p 725 b and p 727 e to g, post).

(iii) Since s 3(*h*) set out the maximum and not the minimum right of an owner to
a move a mobile home (ie for the purpose of carrying out essential works on the site), to
the extent to which cl 2(D) extended that right to give the owners the right to move the
occupier's mobile home for the purposes of the better management of the park, that
clause was inconsistent with s 3(*h*) and would, to that extent, be deleted (see p 727 *j* to
p 728 *d*, post).

(iv) Since the purpose of s 3 was to ensure that an agreement included certain basic
b terms which were just to both the owner and the occupier and which preserved a fair
balance between their respective rights and obligations, paras (*i*) and (*j*)[a] of that section
should be construed as impliedly prohibiting the imposition on an occupier of an
obligation to pay a commission to an owner except in the case expressly provided for in
para (*j*), ie on the sale of the mobile home to a third party, and to the extent to which cl
6(c) provided otherwise it would be deleted (see p 729 *j* to p 730 *b*, post).
c   (v) Since s 3(*f*)[b] provided for undertakings on the part of the occupier as to the repair
and maintenance of the mobile home and such other provisions as might be necessary to
maintain the standards reasonably required by the owner in relation to the occupation of
the site, and since, so far as it related to the owner's right of access for the purpose of
inspecting, maintaining and repairing property other than their own, cl 3(12) would be
interpreted as conferring a right only exercisable by the owner pursuant to the provisons
d of s 3(*f*), cl 3(12) would, in order to avoid doubt, be modified to such an extent as to
achieve that object (see p 728 *f* to p 729 *a*, post).
Taylor v Calvert [1978] 2 All ER 630 considered.
Per Curiam. Where the owner of a protected site supplies the occupier of a mobile
home stationed or to be stationed on that site with a draft agreement containing blank
spaces relating to crucial matters which have not been filled in, it is not a draft agreement
e which complies with s 1(4) of the 1975 Act, and the offer of an agreement on the terms
contained in it is not therefore an offer which complies with s 1(2) of the Act.
Accordingly the occupier's appropriate course is to apply to the court for the grant of an
agreement complying with s 3 of the Act on the ground that the site owner has, within
s 4(1)(*a*) of the Act, failed without reasonable excuse to comply with s 1, and the court's
duty on such an application is to make an order under s 4(2)(*a*) for the grant of an
f agreement complying with s 3 and containing such terms and conditions as the court
thinks reasonable (see p 723 *hj*, post).

Notes
For disputes between occupiers of mobile homes and site owners, see Supplement to 23
Halsbury's Laws (3rd Edn) para 1850.
g   For the Mobile Homes Act 1975, ss 1, 2, 3, 4, see 45 Halsbury's Statutes (3rd Edn) 1586,
1587, 1588, 1589.

Case referred to in judgment
Taylor v Calvert [1978] 2 All ER 630, [1978] 1 WLR 899, 37 P & CR 36, CA.

h
Appeal
Mr T A Fisher and 28 other occupiers of mobile homes stationed on a site owned by the
respondents, John S Allen and Neil A Allen ('the owners'), at Redlands Caravan Site,
Lighthorne, Warwickshire, appealed against an order of his Honour Judge Colin Sleeman
made in the Warwick County Court on 19th July 1978, whereby, on an application
j under s 4(5) of the Mobile Homes Act 1975, he directed that certain clauses contained in
a draft of an agreement offered by the owners to the occupiers should be in the terms
proposed by the owners and that the weekly pitch fee of £40 should be payable from 1st

a   Paragraphs (*i*) and (*j*), so far as material, are set out at p 729 *bc*, post
b   Paragraph (*f*), so far as material, is set out at p 728 *h*, post.

January 1976. Before the hearing of the appeal Mr Fisher and 25 of the occupiers
withdrew from the proceedings. At the hearing of the appeal the only remaining *a*
appellants were Wilfred Grant, Lawrence Francis Flint and Robert Malcolm ('the
occupiers'). The facts are set out in the judgment.

Joseph Harper for the occupiers.
Brian Ash for the owners.

b

Cur adv vult

14th December. **BRANDON LJ** read the following judgment of the court: This is an
appeal against an order of his Honour Judge Sleeman made in the Warwick County
Court and dated 19th July 1978. The order was made in proceedings brought by *c*
occupiers against owners under the Mobile Homes Act 1975 ('the Act'). The purpose of
the proceedings was to obtain the decision of the court on disputes between the parties
about the terms of certain clauses contained in a draft agreement into which the owners
had offered to enter with the occupiers pursuant to the Act.

The appeal is brought by some only of the occupiers who were applicants in the court
below and concerns some only of the clauses in dispute there. Those clauses relate to four *d*
matters: first, the date from which the weekly pitch fee should first be payable (cl 3(1));
secondly, the right of the owners to move an occupier's mobile home for certain purposes
(cl 2(D)); thirdly, the obligation of an occupier to permit the owners to enter on his pitch
for certain purposes (cl 3(12)); fourthly, the right of the owners to be paid a commission
by an occupier on an assignment by him of an agreement unaccompanied by a sale of the
mobile home to which the agreement relates (cl 6(c)(ii)). *e*

The learned judge approved these four clauses in the terms proposed by the owners.
The occupiers appeal on the ground that the clauses as proposed are in conflict with the
provisions of the Act and should not therefore have been approved.

The Act came into force on 1st October 1975. The purpose of the Act, as stated in the
long title, was to amend the law relating to mobile homes and residential caravan sites.
The scheme of the Act, as appears from its main provisions, was to bring into being, as *f*
between the owners of protected sites as defined in the Act of the one part and persons
occupying mobile homes stationed on such sites as their only or main residences of the
other part, written agreements containing all the terms and conditions of the occupation,
including certain particular terms and conditions prescribed by the Act. Such agreements
were to be brought into being either voluntarily by the consent of the two parties
concerned or, in the absence of such consent, compulsorily through orders made by a *g*
county court on the application of one party or the other.

Among the sites to which the Act applied when it came into force was one known as
Redlands Caravan Site, Lighthorne, Warwickshire. The owners of that site were Mr
John S Allen and Mr Neil A Allen, and on it there were stationed, with their permission,
a substantial number of mobile homes occupied by persons as their only or main
residences. *h*

Under s 1(2) and (4) of the Act it became the duty of the owners, by 1st January 1976,
to offer to enter into written agreements with the occupiers, and in this connection to
supply them with drafts of the agreements proposed. Under s 2 the agreements had to
be for a term of at least five years. Under s 3 the agreements had to contain all the terms
and conditions of the occupation, including terms and conditions of the kinds specified
in paras (*a*) to (*j*) of that section.

On or about 15th December 1975 the owners, with the intention of complying with *j*
their duty under ss 1, 2 and 3 of the Act referred to above, offered to enter into written
agreements with the occupiers on the terms of a printed form of draft agreement which
they supplied to them. The draft agreements so supplied were, however, incomplete in
that they contained a number of clauses with blank spaces in them which had not been

filled in. Among the spaces not filled in were spaces in which there should have been
a inserted three crucial matters: the date of the commencement of the agreement (cl 1(g)),
the date of the termination of the agreement (cl 2), and the amount of the pitch fee and
the date from which it was to be paid (cl 3(1)).

By notice in writing dated 11th February 1976 the occupiers declined to accept the
offer made by the owners, and on 9th March they, or most of them, issued an originating
application in the Warwick County Court seeking relief in the matter. The application
b was stated to be made by Mr T A Fisher on behalf of himself and 28 other occupiers
named in a schedule. The owners were named as respondents.

It is a matter for consideration under which provisions of the Act the application
should be regarded as having been made. There are under the Act four kinds of case in
which an owner or an occupier is entitled to apply to a county court for relief in
connection with the bringing into being of an agreement and the court is required to
c grant it to him. The first kind of case is where an owner has failed without reasonable
excuse to make an offer as required by s 1. In such a case an occupier may apply to the
court under s 4(1)(a), and the court is then required under s 4(2)(a) to make an order for
the grant of an agreement which complies with s 3 and contains such terms and
conditions as the court thinks reasonable.

The second kind of case is where an owner has made an offer to an occupier of an
d agreement on terms and conditions which have been accepted by the occupier, but fails
to implement the offer within one month of such acceptance. In such a case the occupier
may apply to the court under s 4(1)(b), and the court is then required to do one of two
things: if it is satisfied that terms and conditions have been agreed, it is required under
s 4(2)(b)(i) to make an order for the grant of an agreement containing those terms and
conditions; alternatively, if it is not so satisfied, it is required under s 4(2)(b)(ii) to make
e an order, as under s 4(2)(a), for the grant of an agreement which complies with s 3 and
contains such terms and conditions as the court thinks reasonable.

The third kind of case is where an owner has made an offer to an occupier of an
agreement as required by s 1, but the occupier has failed without reasonable excuse to
inform the owner within three months of the offer being made whether he accepts the
terms and conditions contained in the agreement. In such a case the owner may apply
f to the court under s 4(3), and the court is then required under s 4(4) to make an order, as
under s 4(2)(a) and s 4(2)(b)(ii), for the grant of an agreement which complies with s 3 and
contains such terms and conditions as the court thinks reasonable.

The fourth kind of case is where an owner has offered to enter into an agreement as
required by s 1, but the occupier to whom the offer has been made is dissatisfied with one
or more of the terms or conditions of the agreement offered. In such a case the occupier
g may apply to the court under s 4(5), within three months of the date of the offer, for the
determination of the matter in dispute, and the court is then required under s 4(7) to
determine the matter in dispute and to make such order as is necessary to give effect to
its determination.

We said earlier that the offer made by the owners in the present case was made with
the intention of complying with ss 1, 2 and 3. It appears to us, however, that, since the
h draft agreement supplied contained blank spaces relating to crucial matters which had
not been filled in, it was not a draft agreement which complied with s 1(4), and the offer
of an agreement on the terms of it was not therefore an offer which complied with
s 1(2). If this is the correct view of the matter, the present case was, strictly speaking, the
first kind of case referred to above, that is to say one in which the owners had failed
without reasonable excuse to make an offer as required by s 1. It would follow that the
j occupiers' right to apply to the court for relief was that given to them by s 4(1)(a), namely
a right to apply for the grant of an agreement complying with s 3, and the court's duty
on such an application was that prescribed by s 4(2)(a), namely to make an order for the
grant of an agreement complying with s 3 and containing such terms and conditions as
the court thought reasonable.

It appears, however, that the occupiers disregarded the circumstance that the draft agreement supplied contained blank spaces relating to crucial matters which had not been filled in, and did not therefore present or prosecute their application to the county court under s 4(1)(a) on the basis referred to above. On the contrary, despite some ambivalence in the wording of the particulars of claim annexed to the originating application, we think it is clear that the occupiers presented and prosecuted their application under s 4(5) on the basis that the owners had offered an agreement pursuant to the requirements of s 1 and that they were dissatisfied with some only of the terms and conditions contained in it. We think it is also clear that the learned judge, in dealing with the application, regarded himself, on the same basis, as discharging the duty placed on him by s 4(7).

While it may not have been strictly correct, for the reasons which we have given, for the occupiers' application to have been made under s 4(5) rather than s 4(1)(a), and dealt with by the learned judge therefore under s 4(7) rather than s 4(2)(a), that is the way in which the proceedings were in fact conducted, for understandable reasons, in the court below. In these circumstances it seems to us that it is now too late to say that the proceedings ought to have been conducted differently. Accordingly, whatever the technicalities of the matter, we consider that this court must deal with the appeal as an appeal from an order duly made under s 4(7) on an application duly made under s 4(5). As will appear later, however, the adoption of this approach does not alter the fact that the draft agreement was incomplete in certain crucial respects, nor can it eliminate certain problems in relation to one of the disputed clauses which arise from that fact.

We have said that the application was stated to be made by Mr T A Fisher on behalf of himself and 28 other occupiers named in a schedule. The appellants were further named in the title of the notice of appeal, as the applicants were named in the title of the proceedings below, as T A Fisher and others. It appears now, however, that only three of the original 29 occupiers remain in the field as appellants, those being Mr Wilfred Grant, Mr Lawrence Francis Flint and Mr Robert Malcolm. That being so, the record should be amended by substituting the names of those three persons as appellants in the title of the proceedings on the appeal.

The occupiers' application was heard by the learned judge on 2nd and 3rd March and 27th April 1977. The occupiers presented their case to him, as we indicated earlier, on the basis that they accepted parts of the draft agreement offered by the owners, but were dissatisfied with certain clauses in it, on which they asked for his ruling. There had in fact been prolonged negotiations between the representatives of the parties prior to the hearing in the course of which various clauses previously in dispute had been agreed, and this process of reducing the number of clauses in dispute by agreement continued during the hearing itself. On 27th April 1977 the judge gave judgment on the clauses remaining in dispute. Unfortunately, however, there then ensued a prolonged disagreement between the parties with regard, first, to what clauses had been agreed and, secondly, to what the judge had decided in relation to the clauses not agreed. As a result of this disagreement there was a further hearing before the judge on 10th April 1978, and finally, on 19th July 1978, the order now appealed from was drawn up.

The occupiers accept the decision of the learned judge on some of the disputed clauses, their appeal being confined to his decision on the four clauses, cll 3(1), 2(D), 3(12) and 6(C)(ii), to which we referred earlier.

In order to decide the points which the appeal raises in relation to those clauses, it is necessary to consider first on what principles, that is to say according to what criteria, the county court should discharge its duty of determining disputes under s 4(7). The Act is not as clear about this as it might be. So far as the task of the court in dealing under s 4(2)(a), s 4(2)(b)(ii) and s 4(4) with applications made by an occupier under s 4(1)(a), s 4(1)(b) and s 4(3) respectively is concerned, the duty of the court is stated to be to order the grant of an agreement which complies with s 3 and contains such terms and conditions as the court thinks reasonable. The court is thereby given specific criteria according to which it is to act. By contrast, so far as the task of the court in dealing under s 4(7) with an application by an occupier under s 4(5) is concerned, the duty of the court

is stated only to be to determine the matter in dispute and to make such order as is
a necessary to give effect to its determination. The court is thereby given no specific
criteria according to which it is to act.

It seems to us that the legislature must have intended that the court should apply the
same criteria in determining a matter in dispute under s 4(7) as it is required to apply
when ordering the grant of an agreement under s 4(2)(*a*), s 4(2)(*b*)(ii) and s 4(4), that is to
say, the court should determine a dispute about a particular term or condition in an
b agreement by ensuring that such term or condition, if and to the extent that it is
approved by the court, complies with s 3 and is reasonable. We turn to examine the four
clauses remaining in dispute on that basis.

Clause 3(1) of the draft agreement deals with the obligation of the occupier to pay a
pitch fee to the owner. The clause is in skeleton form, containing blank spaces in which
particulars relating to three matters are intended to be inserted. These three matters are
c (a) the amount of the pitch fee, (b) the intervals at which it is to be paid and (c) the date
from which it is to be paid. Unfortunately, in the draft agreement as supplied by the
owners to the occupiers, and as also put before the court below, no particulars with
regard to any of these three matters had been inserted. The failure of the owners to fill
in item (c), the date from which the pitch fee is to be paid, is linked with their similar
failure to insert in cl 1(g) the date of the commencement of the agreement.
d Since the spaces in cl 3(1) were left blank in this way, there were no proposals by the
owners in relation to items (a), (b) and (c) above to which the occupiers could object, and
accordingly no dispute in relation to those items which the judge could properly
determine in the manner contemplated by s 4(5) and (7) of the Act. As regards item (b),
it appears to have been agreed that the pitch fee should be paid weekly. As regards item
(a), the judge was invited to decide the proper amount of the weekly pitch fee on the basis
e of expert evidence about it called on either side. As regards item (c), there is a dispute
between the parties about what happened. According to counsel for the owners it was
agreed that whatever weekly pitch fee was fixed by the judge should be payable from 1st
January 1976. According to counsel for the occupiers, on the other hand, there was no
agreement on the matter.

The learned judge decided by his order what the amount of the weekly pitch fee
f payable under cl 3(1) should be, and there is no appeal from his decision on that. He
further ordered that the date from which the pitch fee should be payable should be 1st
January 1976. It seems likely that he did so in the belief that, since the expert evidence
on both sides about the amount of the pitch fee was related to that date, there was no
dispute on the matter. This is supported by the fact that there is no reference in his note
of the proceedings to any evidence or argument directed to the question what the date
g should be.

The case sought to be put forward for the occupiers on the appeal is that, whatever
may have been the basis of the judge's order in this respect, he had no jurisdiction under
the Act to determine that the pitch fee should be payable retrospectively from a date
earlier than the date of his decision.

If it were clear beyond doubt that it was agreed between the parties in the court below
h that the pitch fee should be payable from 1st January 1976 we should not think it right
to allow the occupiers to take this point on appeal. In our view, however, it is not clear
beyond doubt that there was such an agreement, and, in these circumstances, the
occupiers should not be precluded from taking the point.

By s 3(c) of the Act an agreement entered into under it has to include the date of
commencement of the agreement, and by s 3(d) it has to include the annual charge to be
j made and the intervals at which payment is to be made. It would be usual, we think, for
the pitch fee provided for in an agreement to be payable from the date of the
commencement of the agreement. The question for decision therefore really is whether
the judge had power under the Act to determine on 27th April 1977 that the date of the
commencement of the agreement should be 1st January 1976. The case for the occupiers
is, as we have said, that the judge had no such power. The case for the owners is that he

had power to decide the matter in that way if it was reasonable to do so, and that it was reasonable in this case.

The main argument put forward for the occupiers was that, if the date of commencement of an agreement could be fixed retrospectively in this way, the effect would be to deprive an occupier of the benefits which it was the purpose of the Act should be conferred on him by the agreement. In particular the occupier would, it was said, be deprived, first, of the right of security of occupation for a period of at least five years, as provided for by ss 2(1) and 3(c), and, secondly, of the right at any time during such period to assign the benefit of the agreement and to sell his mobile home on site, as provided for by s 3(i) and (j). Since the fixing of a retrospective date of commencement would in these respects be inconsistent with the Act, it should be regarded as impliedly prohibited by it.

In considering this question it is necessary, we think, to bear in mind the sort of timetable for the bringing into being of an agreement between an owner and an existing occupier provided for in the Act. Under s 1(2) an agreement had to be offered by an owner by 1st January 1976. Under s 4(1)(b), if the occupier accepted the offer and the owner did not then enter into an agreement within one month, the occupier could apply to the court for the grant of an agreement. Under s 4(3), if the occupier did not signify his acceptance or non-acceptance of the offer within three months of its being made, the owner could apply to the court for the grant of an agreement. The legislature must further have contemplated that, if it became necessary for the court to deal with the matter, it would be able to do so without any long delay of the kind which occurred in this case.

This timetable indicates that it was the intention of the legislature that agreements should be brought into being, either voluntarily or compulsorily, as soon as reasonably practicable after 1st January 1976. That being so, we do not see anything inconsistent with the Act in an agreement, though not brought into being on that date but only for practical reasons some months later, having that date as its date of commencement. It seems to us that there is no reason why the parties themselves should not agree that the agreement, when entered into, should take effect retrospectively from that date; nor any reason why the court, when ordering the grant of an agreement on the application of either party, or determining a dispute about the date of commencement alone or along with other matters, should not make an order which produces the same result.

So far as the argument that a retrospective date of commencement would deprive an occupier of his right to security of occupation for a period of at least five years is concerned, we do not consider that this would in practice be the result, for the court would clearly protect an occupier's right of occupation by interim injunction pending an agreement being brought into being. Indeed the reality of the matter is rather the other way, in that, if an occupier was protected by injunction until the date on which an agreement was brought into being, and the agreement, instead of being retrospective, commenced only from that date, the occupier would in effect be getting security of occupation for longer than the minimum period of five years.

So far as the argument that a retrospective date of commencement would deprive an occupier of his rights to assign the agreement and to sell his mobile home on site throughout a minimum period of five years is concerned, we accept that there is some force in the argument. We do not, however, regard it as sufficiently strong to lead to the conclusion that a retrospective date of commencement is so inconsistent with the Act as to be impliedly prohibited by it.

While the matter is not altogether easy, the conclusion which we have reached is that the judge had power under the Act to order a retrospective date of commencement, including a date as early as 1st January 1976, if he thought it reasonable to do so.

This conclusion does not entirely dispose of the matter, for it is not clear whether the judge considered whether it was reasonable to backdate the commencement of the agreement to 1st January 1976 or not. If, as seems likely, he believed that there was no dispute between the parties on the matter, he may well not have considered the question

of reasonableness at all. That being so, we think that it is necessary for this court to form
a its own view on the matter. Our view is that the backdating was reasonable in the
circumstances of this case and we would therefore uphold the judge's order relating to it.

Clause 2(D), as contained in the owners' draft, reads:

b
'The Owner shall be permitted to have reasonable access to the Pitch and shall
have the right (if necessary) to move the mobile home to another part of the Park
(i) for the purpose of carrying out essential works to the Pitch or the Park subject
(a) to reinstatement of the Mobile Home at the cost of the Owner either in the
original position or in a position reasonably equivalent to its original position and
(b) to reconnection of all services and (ii) (subject to Clause 4(5) hereof) for the better
management of the Park.'

Clause 4(5) referred to in para (ii) above contains various safeguards for the benefit of the
c occupier which it is not necessary to detail.

Clause 2(D), as so framed, follows substantially for the most part the wording of para
(*h*) of s 3 of the Act. That paragraph, however, provides only for the right of the owner
to move the mobile home for the purpose specified in para (i) of cl 2(D), ie the purpose
of carrying out essential work to the site, and does not provide for such right for the
purpose specified in para (ii) of cl 2(D), ie the better management of the park.

d The case for the owners is that, in so far as cl 2(D) gives them the right to move the
mobile home not only for the purpose specified in para (*h*) of s 3, but also for a further
purpose not so specified, it is a reasonable term to have in the agreement. The case for
the occupiers is that cl 2(D), in so far as it extends the owners' right to move the mobile
home in this way, is inconsistent with s 3(*h*), and so is not in compliance with that
section.

e The effect of ss 3 and 4 of the Act is that an agreement under it must, in any event,
contain terms and conditions as prescribed by s 3(*a*) to (*j*) which we shall call the
mandatory terms; and may, if the parties so agree, or, although they do not agree, the
court thinks it reasonable, contain other terms and conditions as well, which we shall call
the optional terms. No difficulty should normally arise in deciding whether an
agreement contains the mandatory terms. Further, so long as the optional terms
f contained in an agreement relate only to subject-matters different from those to which
the mandatory terms relate, no difficulty should normally arise in deciding whether they
are reasonable or not. Difficulty does arise, however, where an agreement contains
optional terms which relate to the same subject-matters as those to which the mandatory
terms relate. Such terms may confer rights or impose obligations in relation to matters
covered by the mandatory terms, which vary the rights conferred or obligations imposed
g by the mandatory terms themselves. Where optional terms have this effect, can they be
approved by the court if it thinks that they are reasonable, or must they be disapproved
by the court on the ground that they involve a departure from, and do not therefore
comply with, s 3?

Clause 2(D) contains an example of the kind of optional term which gives rise to the
problem referred to above. Apart from para (ii) at the end of it, cl 2(D) represents no
h more than a mandatory term according with s 3(*h*). Paragraph (ii), however, is an
optional term which relates to the same subject-matter as para (*h*) and varies the rights
and obligations of the parties under that paragraph. It does this by conferring on the
owner the right to move an occupier's mobile home, and imposing on the occupier a
corresponding obligation to allow his mobile home to be moved, in circumstances
outside those specified by para (*h*) itself. The question then is whether, having regard to
j this effect of cl 2(D)(ii), the clause complies with para (*h*).

The answer to this question depends on whether para (*h*) is construed as defining the
minimum or the maximum right to move the occupier's mobile home which the owner
is to have. Is the owner to have at least the right given, or the right given and no
more? The paragraph itself provides no answer to the question, but the answer is, in our
view, to be found in a consideration of the purposes of the Act taken as a whole. One of

the main purposes of the Act, if not the main purpose, was to give occupiers security of occupation. Such security involves not only the right of an occupier to occupy his pitch *a* for a substantial period of years, but also the right to occupy it without disturbance by having his mobile home moved from time to time. In the light of this main purpose of the Act, we think that para (*h*), in so far as it gives an owner the right to move an occupier's mobile home for the purpose of carrying out essential work to the site, should be construed as defining the maximum rather than the minimum right of an owner in this respect.   *b*

It was contended for the owners that cl 2(D)(ii) was a proper term to include in the agreement on the ground that without it the owners might be prevented from complying with the requirements of their site licence. We do not consider that there is any real force in this argument for, if and to the extent that the owners were obliged to carry out work to the site for the purpose of complying with the requirements of their site licence, such work would be essential work and therefore already covered by cl 2(D)(i) *c* which follows s 3(*h*).

We would accordingly uphold the occupiers' case on cl 2(D) and vary the clause by deleting para (ii).

Clause 3(12), as contained in the owners' draft, requires the occupier:

> 'To permit the Owner his servants and agents with or without workman [sic] at *d* all reasonable hours to enter upon the Pitch for the purpose of:—(i) inspecting and maintaining the services provided at the Park (ii) inspecting maintaining and repairing fences sheds and outbuildings whether the property of the Owner or otherwise (iii) ascertaining whether there is or has been any breach of this Agreement (iv) removing the mobile home in accordance with the rights in that regard contained in Clause 2(D) hereof.'   *e*

The object of cl 3(12) appears to be to amplify the general right of reasonable access to the pitch given by cl 2(D) (in accordance with s 3(*h*)) by specifying particular cases in which access is to be permitted. The occupiers raise only one objection to the clause, which is that para (ii) ought not to extend to access for the purpose of inspecting, maintaining and repairing property other than that of the owners.

In considering this objection to cl 3(12) regard has to be had to the earlier provisions *f* of cl 3(5) and (6). By cl 3(5) the occupier undertakes to keep the mobile home in a sound state of repair and condition and to keep the exterior thereof clean and tidy, and by cl 3(6) he undertakes to keep the pitch and all fences, outbuildings and gardens thereon in a neat and tidy condition. Each of these two clauses further provides that, if the occupier fails to comply with his undertaking, the owner may give 28 days' notice in writing requiring the occupier to do so, and, if the occupier then fails to take all reasonable steps to comply *g* with his undertaking during that period, the owner may enter on the pitch and carry out such work as may be necessary and the cost of such work shall be payable by the occupier forthwith.

These two clauses appear to accord with s 3(*f*), under which an agreement is to include—   *h*

> 'undertakings on the part of the occupier . . . as to repair and maintenance of the mobile home . . . and such other provisions as may be necessary to maintain the standards reasonably required by the owner in relation to the occupation . . . of the site . . .'

It seems to us that the right of access given by cl 3(12)(ii) should be interpreted as being *j* a right only exercisable by the owner pursuant to the provisions of cl 3(5) and cl 3(6), and further that, if the right is interpreted in that limited way only, there is nothing in it which conflicts with cl 3 or is unreasonable. It would be better, however, for the avoidance of doubt, if some further words were added to para (ii) of cl 3(12) in order to make this limitation clear. The addition at the end of para (ii) of the words 'pursuant to

the provisions of clause 3(5) and (6) above', or such other similar wording as may be
a agreed between the parties, would achieve the object which we have indicated.

We would accordingly uphold the occupiers' objection to cl 3(12) to the limited extent
of adding such further words and no more.

It remains to consider cl 6(c)(ii). In order to explain the dispute between the parties in
relation to this clause it will be convenient to set out first the terms of s 3 (*i*) and (*j*).
Under those paragraphs an agreement has to include—

b
   '(*i*) provision for the right of the occupier to assign the agreement, subject to
   reasonable conditions including the obtaining of the owner's consent which shall
   not be unreasonably withheld and the entry by the assignee into direct undertakings
   with the owner; (*j*) provision for the right of the occupier to sell a mobile home on
   site to a purchaser approved by the owner, whose approval shall not be unreasonably
   withheld: Provided that . . . (iv) the owner shall be entitled to receive such
c   commission on the sale to a third party as may be provided for in the agreement.'

In the draft agreement as offered by the owners cl 6(A) provides for the right of the
occupier to assign the benefit of the agreement subject to the owner's consent which is
not to be unreasonably withheld and to certain other conditions to which it is not
necessary to refer. Clause 6(B) further provides for the right of the occupier to sell the
d mobile home on site to a purchaser approved by the owner whose approval shall not be
unreasonably withheld, subject again to certain conditions to which it is not necessary to
refer. These two clauses appear to accord, so far as they go, with paras (*i*) and (*j*) of s 3 set
out above.

Then comes cl 6(c) relating to owner's commission. This provides:

e
   '(i) On the sale of the Mobile Home the Owner shall be entitled to receive from
   the Occupier a commission of   per cent of the actual consideration paid by
   the Purchaser . . . (ii) On the assignment of this Agreement in a case where the
   Mobile Home is not sold to the assignee or on disposal of the Mobile Home
   otherwise than by sale the Owner shall be entitled to receive from the Occupier a
   commission of   per cent of the fair market value of the Mobile Home . . .'

f In the court below two matters relating to this clause were in dispute: first, whether
para (ii) should be included at all; and, second, what the amount of the commission
should be. With regard to the first matter, the learned judge decided that para (ii) was
reasonable and should be included. With regard to the second matter, he fixed the
amount of the commission payable under both paragraphs at 12%. In this court the
occupiers, while accepting 12% as the proper amount of commission for the purposes of
g para (i), renewed their objection to para (ii) being included at all. Their ground of
objection was that, since para (ii) provided for the payment of commission in
circumstances other than those covered by paras (*i*) and (*j*) of s 3, cl 6(c) did not in this
respect comply with that section.

The point so raised is similar to, though not entirely the same as, the point discussed
earlier in relation to cl 2(D). It can be put in this way. Paragraph (*j*) of s 3 expressly
h provides for the payment of commission on the sale of a mobile home by an occupier to
a purchaser. It does not provide for the payment of a commission on a disposal of the
mobile home to another person otherwise than by sale. Further para (*i*) of s 3 does not
provide for the payment of commission on an assignment of the agreement alone
without any accompanying sale. In these circumstances should paras (*i*) and (*j*) of s 3 be
construed not merely as entitling an owner to receive a commission on the sale of the
j mobile home, but also as impliedly prohibiting the imposition on an occupier of an
obligation to pay a commission otherwise than on such a sale?

Paragraphs (*i*) and (*j*) of s 3 do not expressly exclude the right of an owner to receive,
and the corresponding obligation of an occupier to pay, a commission otherwise than on
a sale of the mobile home to a purchaser. The purpose of s 3, however, is to ensure that
an agreement includes certain basic terms which are just to both the owner and the

occupier, and which preserve a fair balance between their respective rights and
obligations. Having regard to that purpose we think that paras (i) and (j) of s 3 should be   *a*
construed as impliedly prohibiting the imposition on an occupier of an obligation to pay
a commission to an owner except in the one case expressly provided for in para (j).

We would accordingly uphold the occupiers' case that cl 6(c)(ii) is in conflict with s 3
and should not therefore be included in the agreement.

We have reached the conclusions on the four disputed clauses which we have expressed
without reference to any previous decision on the interpretation of the Act. It is right to   *b*
observe, however, that the effect of the Act has been considered by this court in one
previous case, *Taylor v Calvert*[1], which was cited to us. In that case the owners of a
protected site had offered the occupiers of mobile homes stationed on it written
agreements for a minimum period of five years. The occupiers, being dissatisfied with
the terms offered, applied to the county court under s 4(5) of the Act for a determination
of the disputed matters. The judge, acting under s 4(7), amended the agreements, inter   *c*
alia, by extending the five-year periods. On appeal it was contended for the site owners
that the judge had no jurisdiction to require agreements to be for periods of over five
years, and that contention was upheld by this court.

The ground of the decision was that the discretion of a county court judge under s 4(7)
of the Act did not extend to his fixing a period of occupation longer than the minimum
of five years prescribed by ss 2(1) and 3(c): see the judgment of Lord Denning MR[2].   *d*

There are passages in the judgment of Lord Denning MR which suggest that a county
court judge has an unlimited discretion to insert any other terms and conditions which
he thinks reasonable in relation to all other matters besides the length of the period of
occupation, and these passages were very naturally relied on by counsel for the owners in
the present case. The court in *Taylor v Calvert*[1], however, was solely concerned with the
power of the judge to fix a longer period of occupation than five years, and the extent of   *e*
his powers in relation to other terms and conditions was not in issue. In these
circumstances we do not, with respect, regard the observations relied on as affording any
authoritative guidance in relation to the different problems raised by the present appeal.

There is one other point to be noticed about *Taylor v Calvert*[1]. That is that the
agreements there concerned ran from 1st January 1976, and, for what it is worth, which
is not much, no objection to their doing so was taken by the occupiers in that case.   *f*

Counsel for both sides invited this court, if it should allow the occupiers' appeal in
whole or in part, not to make a specific order itself for variation of the agreement, but to
remit the case to the county court judge to order such variations as would give effect to
our decision. The result of our judgment is that we would allow the appeal in part, that
is to say so far as cll 2(D), 3(12) to a limited extent, and cl 6(c)(ii) are concerned, and we
would accordingly remit the case to the county court to give effect to our judgment in   *g*
relation to those clauses.

Appeal allowed in part in regard to cll 2(D), 3(12) and 6(c)(ii). Case remitted to county court.

Solicitors: *Penmans*, Coventry (for the occupiers); *Price Atkins*, Stratford-upon-Avon (for
the owners).   *h*

Patricia Hargrove   Barrister.

---

1   [1978] 2 All ER 630, [1978] 1 WLR 899
2   [1978] 2 All ER 630 at 633, [1978] 1 WLR 899 at 903

_a_ # Newbury District Council v Secretary of State for the Environment

Newbury District Council v International Synthetic Rubber Co Ltd

_b_

HOUSE OF LORDS

VISCOUNT DILHORNE, LORD EDMUND-DAVIES, LORD FRASER OF TULLYBELTON, LORD SCARMAN AND LORD LANE

14th, 15th, 16th, 17th, 21st, 22nd JANUARY, 28th FEBRUARY 1980

_c_ *Town and country planning – Development – Use classes – Repository – Use of building to store civil defence vehicles and synthetic rubber – Whether used as 'repository' – Town and Country Planning (Use Classes) Order 1950 (SI 1950 No 1131), Sch, class X.*

Town and country planning – Change of use – Conditions attached to permission for change of use _d_ – Permission for temporary change of use of existing building – Condition attached that building be removed at the end of period of permission – Whether condition valid – Town and Country Planning Act 1971, s 29(1).

In 1941 the Crown requisitioned, and became the owner of, land in a rural area which was then converted into an airfield. From 1955 until 1959 two hangars built on the _e_ airfield during wartime were used to store civil defence vehicles while the rest of the airfield was returned to agricultural use. In 1959 the former owner of the land received planning permission to use the hangars to store agricultural products subject to their removal by 31st December 1970, and subsequently in 1961 he and his family trustees purchased the freehold of the hangar site from the Crown. They then leased it back to the Crown for a term of 40 years at a nominal rent. In 1962 a rubber company received _f_ planning permission to use the hangars as warehouses subject to their removal by 31st December 1972, and subsequently purchased the 40-year lease from the Crown at auction. The particulars of sale referred to the county council's policy, stated in the county development plan, of securing the removal of wartime buildings built in open countryside. The company used the hangars to store synthetic rubber and in 1970 applied for a 30-year extension of their planning permission. The local district council _g_ refused the application on the grounds that the hangars were an undesirable intrusion into a rural landscape. The company continued to use the hangars after 1972 and in 1973 the council served enforcement notices on them. The company appealed to the Secretary of State who, after a local inquiry, decided that the condition requiring the removal of the hangars was invalid and that as the company had started using them before 1963 they had an indefeasible right under s 87 of the Town and Country Planning Act 1971 to _h_ continue using them. In so deciding the Secretary of State applied a policy that it was in all cases unreasonable to impose a condition requiring the removal of a building on the expiry of permission for a temporary change of use of an existing building. The local planning authority appealed to the Divisional Court which dismissed their appeal. The authority appealed to the Court of Appeal, contending that under s 29(1)[a] of the 1971 Act they were required when granting planning permission to 'have regard to the _j_ provisions of the development plan' and could grant permission 'subject to such conditions as they [thought] fit'. On the hearing of the appeal the rubber company contended that as the hangars had previously been used as a 'repository' by the Crown and as they themselves were continuing to use them for that purpose or purposes of the

---

_a_   Section 29(1) is set out at p 745 _f_, post

same class the use came within class X^b of the schedule to the Town and Country Planning (Use Classes) Order 1950 and therefore planning permission was not necessary *a* to continue that use. The Court of Appeal^c allowed the authority's appeal, holding (i) that the condition imposed was not unreasonable in the circumstances since the rubber company had bought at auction knowing that they would be required to remove the hangars at the end of the temporary use, and (ii) that the hangars had not been used as a 'repository', ie a place where goods were stored as part of a storage business, when used to store civil defence vehicles or synthetic rubber, and accordingly permission had been *b* required to change the use. The Secretary of State and the company appealed to the House of Lords. On the appeal the local planning authority further contended that in taking up the planning permission in 1962 the rubber company had waived any previous use rights or protection from enforcement proceedings attached to the hangars.

Held – The appeal would be allowed for the following reasons—   *c*
  (i) On the true construction of class X of the 1950 order a 'repository' was not restricted to a building where goods were kept or stored in the course of a trade or business but extended to any place the principal use of which was storage. The hangars had therefore been used as a repository when used by the Crown to store civil defence vehicles and the rubber company had not been required to obtain permission for a change of use since they already had an existing use right (see p 737 *d* to *g*, p 741 *c g*, *d* p 743 *c g*, p 744 *c*, p 750 *d* to *h*, p 751 *b d* and p 759 *a b*, post); dicta of Havers J in *Horwitz v Rowson* [1960] 2 All ER at 886 and of Lord Denning MR in *G Percy Trentham Ltd v Gloucestershire County Council* [1966] 1 All ER at 703 disapproved.
  (ii) The rubber company were not precluded from relying on their existing use right merely because they had subsequently applied for planning permission, since the grant of planning permission in 1962 had not created a new planning unit (see p 738 *h* to p 739 *e* *c*, p 741 *c*, p 742 *b c*, p 744 *h*, p 745 *c*, p 754 *a* to *c*, p 760 *f* and p 761 *a*, post); *Mounsdon v Weymouth and Melcombe Regis Corpn* [1960] 1 All ER 538 applied; *Prossor v Minister of Housing and Local Government* (1968) 67 LGR 109 explained.
  (iii) The Secretary of State had been correct in deciding that the local planning authority's condition that the hangars be removed was invalid, since, regardless of the Secretary of State's reasons for so deciding, the condition was ultra vires and void because *f* it was extraneous to the proposed use and did not fairly or reasonably relate to the permitted development (see p 741 *a* to *c* and *j* to p 742 *a*, p 747 *a* to *d*, p 756 *b* to *g*, p 757 *a b* and p 762 *d e* and *j* to p 763 *a*, post).
  Decision of the Court of Appeal [1979] 1 All ER 243 reversed.

Notes   *g*
For conditions attaching planning permission, see 37 Halsbury's Laws (3rd Edn) 304, para 414, and for cases on the subject, see 45 Digest (Repl) 340–343, 56–64.
  For the Town and Country Planning Act 1971, s 29, see 41 Halsbury's Statutes (3rd Edn) 1619.
  The Town and Country Planning (Use Classes) Order 1950. Sch, class X has been replaced by the Town and Country Planning (Use Classes) Order 1972, Sch, class X. For *h* the 1972 order see 21 Halsbury's Statutory Instruments (3rd Reissue) 141.

Cases referred to in opinions
Associated Provincial Picture Houses v Wednesbury Corpn [1947] 2 All ER 680, [1948] 1 KB 223, [1948] LJR 190, 177 LT 641, 112 JP 55, 45 LGR 635, CA, 45 Digest (Repl) 215, 189.   *j*
Brayhead (Ascot) Ltd v Berkshire County Council [1964] 1 All ER 149, [1964] 2 QB 303, [1964] 2 WLR 507, 128 JP 167, 62 LGR 162, 15 P & CR 423, DC, 45 Digest (Repl) 348, 81.

---

b   Class X is set out at p 736 *f*, post
c   [1979] 1 All ER 243

a *Chertsey Urban District Council v Mixnam's Properties Ltd* [1964] 2 All ER 627, [1965] AC 735, [1964] 2 WLR 1210, 128 JP 405, 62 LGR 528, 15 P & CR 331, [1964] RVR 632, HL, 45 Digest (Repl) 359, *126.*

City of London Corpn v Secretary of State for the Environment (1971) 71 LGR 28, 23 P & CR 169, Digest (Cont Vol D) 924, *64b.*

Crabb v Arun District Council [1975] 3 All ER 865, [1976] Ch 179, [1975] 3 WLR 847, CA, Digest (Cont Vol D) 312, *1205a.*

b *East Barnet Urban District Council v British Transport Commission* [1961] 3 All ER 878, [1962] 2 QB 484, [1962] 2 WLR 134, 126 JP 1, 60 LGR 41, 13 P & CR 127, DC, 45 Digest (Repl) 329, *17.*

Fawcett Properties Ltd v Buckingham County Council [1960] 3 All ER 503, [1961] AC 636, [1960] 3 WLR 831, 125 JP 8, 50 LGR 69, 12 P & CR 1, HL, 45 Digest (Repl) 342, *60.*

Gray v Minister of Housing and Local Government (1969) 68 LGR 15, CA, Digest (Cont Vol
c C) 963, *30r.*

Hall & Co Ltd v Shoreham-by-Sea Urban District Council [1964] 1 All ER 1, [1964] 1 WLR 240, 128 JP 120, 62 LGR 206, 15 P & CR 119, CA, 45 Digest (Repl) 342, *61.*

Halsall v Brizell [1957] 1 All ER 371, [1957] Ch 169, [1957] 2 WLR 123, Digest (Cont Vol B) 641, *2719a.*

Horwitz v Rowson [1960] 2 All ER 881, [1960] 1 WLR 803, 124 JP 424, 58 LGR 252, 11
d P & CR 411, 45 Digest (Repl) 328, *15.*

Ives (ER) Investments Ltd v High [1967] 1 All ER 504, [1967] 2 QB 379, [1967] 2 WLR 789, CA, Digest (Cont Vol C) 828, *925c.*

Kent County Council v Kingsway Investments (Kent) Ltd, Kent County Council v Kenworthy [1970] 1 All ER 70, [1971] AC 72, [1970] 2 WLR 397, 134 JP 127, 21 P & CR 58, HL, Digest (Cont Vol C) 970, *61a.*

e *Kingston-upon-Thames Royal London Borough Council v Secretary of State for the Environment* [1974] 1 All ER 193, [1973] 1 WLR 1549, 138 JP 131, 72 LGR 206, 26 P & CR 480, DC, Digest (Cont Vol D) 923, *61c.*

Leighton and Newman Car Sales Ltd v Secretary of State for the Environment (1976) 32 P & CR 1.

Mounsdon v Weymouth and Melcombe Regis Corpn [1960] 1 All ER 538, [1960] 1 QB 645,
f [1960] 2 WLR 484, 124 JP 231, 58 LGR 144, 11 P & CR 103, 45 Digest (Repl) 326, *8.*

Petticoat Lane Rentals Ltd v Secretary of State for the Environment [1971] 2 All ER 793, [1971] 1 WLR 1112, 135 JP 410, 69 LGR 504, 22 P & CR 703, DC, Digest (Cont Vol D) 932, *119a.*

Prossor v Minister of Housing and Local Government (1968) 67 LGR 109, DC, Digest (Cont Vol C) 971, *61b.*

g *Pyx Granite Co Ltd v Ministry of Housing and Local Government* [1959] 3 All ER 1, [1960] AC 260, [1959] 3 WLR 346, 123 JP 429, 58 LGR 1, 10 P & CR 319, HL; *rvsg* [1958] 1 All ER 625, [1958] 1 QB 554, [1958] 2 WLR 371, 56 LGR 171, 9 P & CR 204, CA, 45 Digest (Repl) 336, *37.*

R v London Borough of Hillingdon, ex parte Royco Homes Ltd [1974] 2 All ER 643, [1974] 1 QB 720, [1974] 2 WLR 805, 138 JP 505, 72 LGR 516, 28 P & CR 251, DC, Digest (Cont
h Vol D) 925, *64c.*

Swallow and Pearson (a firm) v Middlesex County Council [1953] 1 All ER 580, [1953] 1 WLR 422, 117 JP 179, 51 LGR 253, 3 P & CR 314, 45 Digest (Repl) 346, *75.*

Trentham (G Percy) Ltd v Gloucestershire County Council [1966] 1 All ER 701, [1966] 1 WLR 506, 130 JP 179, 64 LGR 134, CA, Digest (Cont Vol B) 689, *30d.*

j **Appeal**

On 31st May 1962 the Hungerford Rural District Council acting as agent for the Berkshire County Council, the predecessor of Newbury District Council ('the local planning authority'), granted to International Synthetic Rubber Co Ltd ('ISR') planning permission to use two hangars at Membury Airfield, Lambourn Woodlands, Berkshire, as warehouses on condition that the buildings were removed at the expiration of the period ending 31st December 1972 and that the use should be confined to storage and no materials should be stored which gave rise to offence by reason of smell. On 30th December 1969 planning permission was granted for an extension to offices near the hangars subject to a condition requiring removal at the expiration of the period ending 31st December 1972. On 5th November 1970 ISR applied for planning permission to use the hangars for a further 30 years from 31st December 1972. On 4th January 1971 the local planning authority refused their application. ISR appealed to the Secretary of State for the Environment against that refusal. On 12th November 1973, while the appeal to the Secretary of State was pending, the local planning authority served two enforcement notices on ISR requiring compliance with the conditions of removal. ISR appealed to the Secretary of State against the enforcement notices. On 5th February 1975 an inspector appointed by the Secretary of State to hold an inquiry into the appeals reported to the Secretary of State who issued his decision letter on 24th July 1975 in which he held that the condition requiring removal was invalid and that the planning permission itself was void. The local planning authority appealed. On 18th February 1977 the Divisional Court of the Queen's Bench Division (Lord Widgery CJ, Michael Davies and Robert Goff JJ) dismissed the appeal. The local planning authority appealed to the Court of Appeal. On 13th July 1978 that court[1] (Lord Denning MR, Lawton and Browne LJJ) allowed their appeal and refused the Secretary of State and ISR leave to appeal. The Secretary of State and ISR appealed to the House of Lords pursuant to leave granted by the House on 16th November 1978. The facts are set out in the opinion of Viscount Dilhorne.

John Newey QC and *Christopher Symons* for the Secretary of State.
David Widdicombe QC and *Anthony J Anderson* for ISR.
Peter Boydell QC, R M K Gray and *James May* for the local planning authority.

Their Lordships took time for consideration.

28th February. The following opinions were delivered.

VISCOUNT DILHORNE. My Lords, on 7th May 1962 the appellants, the International Synthetic Rubber Co Ltd (hereafter referred to as 'ISR'), sent to the Hungerford Rural District Council who were then acting for the Berkshire County Council, then the local planning authority, an application dated 3rd May 1962 for permission to use two hangars on what had been Membury Airfield as warehouses for the storage of synthetic rubber. They said that they were prospective buyers of the hangars from the Air Ministry and that as a considerable capital outlay would be involved, 'it would be appreciated if the planning authorities could see their way to giving their permission to cover as long a period forward as is possible'.

ISR were then occupying one of the hangars under a lease granted to them by the Secretary of State for Air for nine years commencing on 8th May 1961.

On 31st May 1962 the Hungerford Rural District Council gave that company permission to use the two hangars as warehouses subject to two conditions, one being that 'The buildings shall be removed at the expiration of the period ending December 1972'.

The written statement of the Berkshire County Council which accompanied the county map in February 1960, said:

'Problems have arisen from time to time regarding the use of buildings on sites relinquished by government departments. These are often suitable in design for industrial or storage use, although frequently their location in open countryside renders them unsuitable in location as permanent centres of employment and detrimental to landscape amenities. The local planning authority will normally only permit permanent changes of use in localities appropriate in the light of their

a
general policy objectives for the distribution of employment; otherwise they will seek to secure the removal of the buildings. Temporary periods of changed use may be permitted in particular circumstances.'

On 26th July 1962 ISR bought the two hangars and the Secretary of State's leasehold interest in the land under a lease for 40 years which commenced on 30th November 1961.

b
ISR did not, as they could have done, appeal against the imposition of the condition that the hangars should be removed. On 4th November 1969 they applied for planning permission to make an extension to an existing office on the airfield. They were given permission to do so subject to the condition that at the expiration of the period ending 31st December 1972 the building should be removed.

On 5th November 1970 ISR applied for an extension of the permission to use the hangars as warehouses for 30 years. On 4th January 1971 this application was refused
c and on 25th June 1971 ISR appealed against this refusal.

The two hangars and the extension to the office were not removed at the expiration of the period ending 31st December 1972, and on 12th November 1973, the hangars and extension still not having been removed, the Hungerford Rural District Council served two enforcement notices on ISR requiring their removal within three months.

ISR appealed against these notices to the Secretary of State for the Environment.
d Although the case in respect of the enforcement notice relating to the office extension differed in some respects from that relating to the notice applying to the hangars, it was agreed that the result of the appeal as to the notice in respect of the office extension should depend on and follow the result of the appeal as to the notice about the hangars. No separate argument was therefore advanced in connection with the office extension.

These appeals were brought under s 88 of the Town and Country Planning Act 1971
e which provides for an appeal against an enforcement notice on any of seven grounds. In this case only the first two are relevant. They are as follows:

'(a) that planning permission ought to be granted for the development to which the notice relates or, as the case may be, that a condition or limitation alleged in the enforcement notice not to have been complied with ought to be discharged; (b) that the matters alleged in the notice do not constitute a breach of planning control.'

f
In the notice of appeal relating to the hangars it was asserted, firstly, that the condition as to the removal of the hangars was void with the result that the permission granted in 1962 was unconditional, and, secondly, that the authorised use of the hangars on 1st July 1948, the date when the Town and Country Planning Act 1947 came into force, was 'warehouse/storage' and that the hangars were used for 'warehouse/storage purposes
g throughout the period 1948/62'.

If the authorised use of the hangars on 1st July 1948 was 'warehouse/storage' and that use had not been abandoned or if the 'existing use' of the hangars was for 'warehouse/storage purposes', it was not necessary to apply for planning permission to use the hangars for those purposes.

The first question to be considered in this appeal appears to me to be: was planning
h permission necessary for the use by ISR of the hangars as warehouses?

Before making his decision on these appeals the Secretary of State directed a local inquiry. The inspector who held the inquiry reported on 5th February 1975. His findings of fact were accepted by the Secretary of State and the relevant findings were as follows: that Membury Airfield ceased to be operational in 1947; that from 1947 to 1953 the hangars were used as a storage depot on behalf of the Ministry of Agriculture,
j Fisheries and Food; that in 1953 the airfield was transferred to the United States Air Force and the use then made of the hangars is not known; that in 1954 it became a sub-depot of No 3 Maintenance Unit at Milton; that from 1955 to 1959 the hangars were used by the Home Office for the storage of Civil Defence vehicles; and that in 1959 an eleven year permission was granted for the use of the hangars for the storage of fertilisers subject to the condition that at the end of that period the hangars would be removed.

The inspector concluded on these facts that there was a clearly established use of the hangars when in Crown occupation prior to 1959 for storage and that the only gap in *a* their use for storage was when they were used by the United States Air Force and that after that, use for storage was resumed. In his view the application for permission to use them for the storage of fertilisers in 1959 was unnecessary and ISR did not require planning permission to use them for storage as that was their previous use.

The Secretary of State in his decision letter of 24th July 1975 held that when the hangars were used for storage purposes from 1947 to 1953 and again from 1955 to 1959 *b* the hangars formed an independent planning unit. He held that the Home Office use of them was not use as wholesale warehouses nor was it use as repositories coming within class X of the Town and Country Planning (Use Classes) Order 1950[1].

It was not contended by the appellants that the use by the Home Office was use as wholesale warehouses but it was submitted that the hangars were then used as repositories. *c*

By the Town and Country Planning (Use Classes) Order 1948[2] (which came into force on the same day as the Town and Country Planning Act 1947) it was provided by para 3(1):

> 'Where a building or other land is used for a purpose of any class specified in the Schedule to this Order, the use of such building or other land . . . shall not be deemed for the purposes of the Act to involve development of the land.' *d*

Class X in the schedule read as follows: 'Use as a wholesale warehouse for any purpose, except storage of offensive or dangerous goods'; and class XI as follows: 'Use as a repository for any purpose except storage of offensive or dangerous goods.' 'Repository' was defined in this order as meaning 'a building (excluding any land occupied therewith) where storage is the principal use and where no business is transacted other than incidentally to *e* such storage'.

The meaning of 'wholesale warehouse' was also defined.

In 1950 this order was replaced by the Town and Country Planning (Use Classes) Order 1950. The purpose of this order was to amalgamate certain of the use classes so that a wider range of changes of use might take place without involving development requiring planning permission. *f*

Classes X and XI of the 1948 order were amalgamated and class X in the 1950 order read as follows: 'Use as a wholesale warehouse or repository for any purpose.' In subsequent use classes orders, this has not been altered.

The definitions of 'repository' and 'wholesale warehouse' were omitted from the 1950 and subsequent use classes orders but, if it had been the intention that these words should bear a different meaning from that they bore from 1948 to 1950, I would have expected *g* that to have been made clear.

In my opinion the definition of 'repository' in the 1948 order is an excellent definition of the meaning that would ordinarily be given to that word.

The Secretary of State based his decision on a sentence of Lord Denning MR's in his judgment in *G Percy Trentham Ltd v Gloucestershire County Council*[3]. Lord Denning MR had pointed out that under class X a building used as a repository for storing furniture *h* could be used as a repository for storing archives without getting planning permission and then went on to say[4]: 'A repository means a place where goods are stored away, to be kept for the sake of keeping them safe, *as part of a storage business*' (my emphasis).

In an earlier case, *Horwitz v Rowson,*[5] Havers J had said: '"Repository", I think, means a building wherein goods are kept or stored, and I think that the keeping or storing must be in the course of a trade or business.' *j*

---

1   SI 1950 No 1131
2   SI 1948 No 954
3   [1966] 1 All ER 701, [1966] 1 WLR 506
4   [1966] 1 All ER 701 at 703, [1966] 1 WLR 506 at 512
5   [1960] 2 All ER 881 at 886, [1960] 1 WLR 803 at 810

He did not say why he thought that nor did Lord Denning MR say why he thought
a that the storage must be part of a storage business. It may be that the conjunction of
'wholesale warehouse' and 'repository' in class X of the 1950 order led to the view that as
use as a wholesale warehouse would be use for a business purpose, use as a repository
must also, to come within class X, be for a business purpose but if this was so, the history
of the order shows, in my opinion, that it was not well founded. A place may be used as
a repository for archives without being used as part of a business, eg a muniment
b room. The merger of classes X and XI of the 1948 order into class X of the 1950 order was
not done with the object of altering the meaning to be given to the word 'repository' but
to extend the changes of use that might be made without planning permission.

All the members of the Divisional Court (Lord Widgery CJ, Michael Davies and
Robert Goff JJ) and all the members of the Court of Appeal[1] (Lord Denning MR, Lawton
and Browne LJJ) agreed that the use of the hangars by the Home Office was not use as a
c repository.

Despite the unanimity of judicial opinion and despite the strong view expressed by
Lord Denning MR[2] that 'no one conversant with the English language would dream of
calling these hangars a "repository" when filled with fire-pumps or synthetic rubber' and
that of Lawton LJ[3] that—

d   'As a matter of the ordinary modern usage of the English language . . . no literate
        person would say that the use to which the Home Office had put the hangars in the
        1950s was or that the company are now, using them as a repository.'

I feel compelled to say that to describe the use of the hangars when so filled as use for a
repository is, in my opinion, a perfectly accurate and correct use of the English
language. They were when used by the Home Office used as repositories for fire-pumps
e and so to describe them is just as correct as it is to describe a burial place as a repository
for the dead.

The Secretary of State cannot be blamed for holding that they were not used as
repositories coming within class X in the light of what was said in *G Percy Trentham Ltd
v Gloucestershire County Council*[4] but in my view it is wrong to say that to come within that
class use as a repository must be use as part of a storage business.

f   My conclusion on this part of the case is that the use by the Home Office was use as a
repository coming within class X and that, consequently, unless that use was abandoned
(and that was not established) or unless ISR cannot now rely on that use in consequence
of 'blowing hot and cold', ISR can now, by virtue of class X, use the hangars as wholesale
warehouses without planning permission.

g *Blowing hot and cold*

The respondents contended that the appellants were precluded from relying on
existing use rights and class X as they had taken up and implemented the permission
granted to them on 31st May 1962. This contention found favour with Lord Denning
MR. He said[5] that in 1962 ISR had two inconsistent courses open to them—

h   'One was to apply for a grant of planning permission; the other was to rely on any
        existing use rights that might be attached to the site. Once they opted for planning
        permission, and accepted it without objection, they had made their bed and must
        lie on it. No doubt they did not know of the past history, but that was only because
        they did not choose to rely on it. They should not be allowed to bring it up again
        now.'

j _____

1   [1979] 1 All ER 243, [1978] 1 WLR 1241
2   [1979] 1 All ER 243 at 250, [1978] 1 WLR 1241 at 1250
3   [1979] 1 All ER 243 at 252, [1978] 1 WLR 1241 at 1253
4   [1966] 1 All ER 701, [1966] 1 WLR 506
5   [1979] 1 All ER 243 at 250, [1978] 1 WLR 1241 at 1250–1251

I do not know whether ISR before they applied for planning permission in May 1962 and before they had acquired the hangars could have found out the past history but, *a* however that may be, I find this passage from Lord Denning MR's judgment difficult to reconcile with his acceptance of the argument advanced in *Gray v Minister of Housing and Local Government*[1] that the fact that a man applies for planning permission does not debar him from afterwards alleging that he was entitled to rely on 'existing use' rights.

Lawton LJ did not find it necessary to decide this question and Browne LJ did not agree with Lord Denning MR on this. *b*

It was not until the decision in *Prossor v Minister of Housing and Local Government*[2] that any support can be found for the proposition that application for, followed by the grant and use of, planning permission prevented reliance on existing use rights. In that case permission was given for the rebuilding of a petrol station subject to the condition that no retail sales other than of motor accessories should take place thereon. After the rebuilding secondhand cars were displayed for sale on the site. An enforcement notice *c* was served. In the course of his judgment, with which the other members of the court agreed, Lord Parker CJ said[3]:

'. . . assuming that there was . . . an existing use right running on this land for the display and sale of motor cars, yet by adopting the permission granted in April, 1964, the appellant's predecessor, as it seems to me, gave up any possible existing use *d* rights in that regard which he may have had. The planning history of this site, as it were, seems to me to begin afresh on April 4, 1964, with the grant of this permission, a permission which was taken up and used . . .'

The correctness of this decision was doubted by Winn LJ but not by Lord Denning MR in *Gray v Minister of Housing and Local Government*[1]. There the planning permission was *e* to build premises twice the size of premises which had been destroyed by fire. Lord Denning MR doubted whether, having obtained that permission and having taken advantage of it by building the new premises, the appellants could afterwards rely on existing rights. Winn LJ did not think it necessary to decide the case on that ground. He thought that there was no sufficient proof of existing use rights.

These two cases were reviewed in *Petticoat Lane Rentals Ltd v Secretary of State for the* *f* *Environment*[4]. In that case Widgery LJ, with whose judgment Lord Parker CJ agreed, while thinking that the *Prossor* case[2] was rightly decided, though it was a case which should be applied with some little care. In the *Petticoat Lane* case[4] planning permission was given for the erection of a building on a clear site and the building was put up. Widgery LJ said[5]:

'Where that happens . . . one gets in my judgment an entirely new planning unit *g* created by the new building. The land as such is merged in that new building and a new planning unit with no planning history is achieved. That new planning unit, the new building, starts with a nil use, that is to say immediately after it was completed it was used for nothing, and thereafter any use to which it is put is a change of use, and if that use is not authorised by the planning permission, that use *h* is a use which can be restrained by planning control.'

My Lords, there are a number of cases, of which *Mounsdon v Weymouth and Melcombe Regis Corpn*[6] is one, in which it has been held that a grant of planning permission does not

j

1   (1969) 68 LGR 15
2   (1968) 67 LGR 109
3   67 LGR 109 at 113
4   [1971] 2 All ER 793, [1971] 1 WLR 1112
5   [1971] 2 All ER 793 at 796, [1971] 1 WLR 1112 at 1117
6   [1960] 1 All ER 538, [1960] 1 QB 645

not prevent it being subsequently contended that no such permission was necessary on
a account of existing use rights and I do not myself think that the decision in the *Prossor*
case[1] is sustainable on the basis that the obtaining and taking up of planning permission
in itself prevents reliance on such rights.

If, however, the grant of planning permission, whether it be permission to build or for
a change of use, is of such a character that the implementation of the permission leads to
the creation of a new planning unit, then I think that it is right to say that existing use
b rights attaching to the former planning unit are extinguished. It may be that in the
Prossor case[1] the erection of the new building created a new planning unit. If it did, and
it is not very clear from the report, then in my view that case was rightly decided.

It is clear that in this case the grant of the planning permission in May 1962 did not
create a new planning unit and so, in my opinion, ISR were not precluded from relying
on the existing use rights attaching to the site.

c If, contrary to my view, planning permission was necessary for the use of the hangars
by ISR, the validity of the condition attached to that permission has to be determined.

The validity of the condition.
Section 29(1) of the Town and Country Planning Act 1971 requires a local planning
authority when dealing with an application for planning permission to have regard to
d the provisions of the development plan so far as material 'and to any other material
considerations', and gives the planning authority power, subject to the provisions of a
number of sections (which have no relevance to this case) to grant planning permission,
either unconditionally or subject to such conditions as it thinks fit or to refuse permission.

The power to impose conditions is not unlimited. In *Pyx Granite Co Ltd v Ministry of
Housing and Local Government*[2] Lord Denning said:

e   'Although the planning authorities are given very wide powers to impose "such
        conditions as they think fit", nevertheless the law says that those conditions, to be
        valid, must fairly and reasonably relate to the permitted development. The
        planning authority are not at liberty to use their powers for an ulterior object,
        however desirable that object may seem to them to be in the public interest.'

f As Lord Reid said in *Chertsey Urban District Council v Mixnam's Properties Ltd*[3], this
statement of law was approved by this House in *Fawcett Properties Ltd v Buckingham
County Council*[4].

It follows that the conditions imposed must be for a planning purpose and not for any
ulterior one, and that they must fairly and reasonably relate to the development
permitted. Also they must not be so unreasonable that no reasonable planning authority
g could have imposed them (*Associated Provincial Picture Houses Ltd v Wednesbury Corpn*[5];
Hall & Co Ltd v Shoreham-by-Sea Urban District Council[6], per Willmer, Harman and Pearson
LJJ; *City of London Corpn v Secretary of State for the Environment*[7]; *London Borough of
Hillingdon, ex parte Royco Homes Ltd*[8]).

The conditions in this case were clearly imposed for planning purposes. Did they
fairly and reasonably relate to the proposed development? If they did not, it is
h unnecessary to consider whether they were so unreasonable that no planning authority
could reasonably have imposed them. The Secretary of State came to the conclusion that
the condition that the hangars should be removed at the end of the period during which

---

j
1   (1968) 67 LGR 109
2   [1958] 1 All ER 625 at 633, [1958] 1 QB 554 at 572
3   [1964] 2 All ER 627 at 632, [1965] AC 735 at 751
4   [1960] 3 All ER 503, [1961] AC 636
5   [1947] 2 All ER 680, [1948] 1 KB 223
6   [1964] 1 All ER 1 at 8, 13, 17–18, [1964] 1 WLR 240 at 248, 255, 261
7   (1971) 71 LGR 28
8   [1974] 2 All ER 643, [1974] 1 QB 720

their use as warehouses was permitted did not fairly and reasonably relate to their use as warehouses. The Court of Appeal held that he was wrong.

In 1968 the Ministry of Housing and Local Government published a circular[1] entitled 'The Use of Conditions in Planning Permissions' as guidance to the use of the power. In the paragraph headed 'Is the condition relevant to the development to be permitted?' the following appears:

'A condition requiring the removal of an existing building, whether on the application site or not, will only be reasonable if the need for that removal springs directly from the fact that a new building is to be erected. It may so spring, for example, if with both buildings on it, the site would be overdeveloped. But the grant of permission for a new building or for a change of use cannot properly be used as a pretext for general tidying-up by means of a condition on the permission.'

The attention of the inspector was drawn to this paragraph and it was contended that he and the Secretary of State had reached the conclusion that the condition did not fairly and reasonably relate to the permission granted on the ground that, in view of this statement in the circular, a condition requiring the removal of a building could not be attached to a permission relating to its use. If they had decided this question on this ground, they were in my opinion, wrong. Although it may be that only in exceptional cases could it be held that a condition requiring the removal of buildings fairly and reasonably related to the grant of permission for their use, such cases may occur.

I do not, however, think that the inspector or the Secretary of State decided this question on this ground. The inspector held:

'. . . the condition that such substantial and existing buildings as the two hangars should be removed would appear to flow from a general wish to restore the area as a whole rather than from any planning need arising from the actual purpose for which the permission was sought. It was not necessary to that purpose, or to the protection of the environment in the fulfilment of that purpose: it was a condition extraneous to the proposed use.'

So he held that the condition was void.

The Secretary of State in his decision letter said:

'The Inspector's conclusions have been considered. It is evident that the Local Planning Authority imposed the condition to remove the hangars to safeguard their long term policy for industrial development in rural areas and to secure the future improvement of the amenity of the area of the appeal site. It is considered however in the circumstances of this case where planning permission was sought merely for a change of use of existing substantial buildings, that a condition requiring the removal of those buildings after the expiration of a specified number of years was not sufficiently related to the change of use in respect of which the planning permission was granted and was unreasonable.'

This appears to me in substance to be a repetition in different language of the inspector's conclusion. The Secretary of State agreed with him as to the object the local planning authority had sought to achieve. They both emphasised the substantial nature of the existing buildings. The contention that the Secretary of State misdirected himself by holding that a condition requiring demolition of a building could not be attached to a use permission does not appear to me established.

If in the circumstances of this case the condition imposed was not, in the Secretary of State's opinion, fairly and reasonably related to the permission granted, the courts cannot interfere with his conclusion unless it is established that he misdirected himself or reached a conclusion to which he could not reasonably have come. That has not been done.

---

1   Circular 5/68 dated 6th February 1968

The Secretary of State held that the condition which in his view was invalid was not
a severable from the permission granted and that consequently this permission was void.
In my opinion he was entitled so to do and I consequently conclude that the enforcement
notices were invalid and also that, as the use of the hangars by ISR started before 1st
January 1964, no enforcement notice can now be served.

I would allow the appeals and restore the order of the Divisional Court. In my opinion
the proper order as to costs should be that no order should be made in respect of the
b Secretary of State's costs and that the Newbury District Council should pay ISR's costs in
this House and in the Court of Appeal.

LORD EDMUND-DAVIES. My Lords, I seek to do no more than add some short
comments on the three main issues involved in these appeals, as I share in the common
agreement of your Lordships that the appeals must be allowed and the order of the
c Divisional Court restored, and this for the reasons advanced in the speech of my noble
and learned friend Viscount Dilhorne.

Of the three issues, the first logically calling for consideration is whether, on the true
construction of class X of the Town and Country Planning (Use Classes) Order 1950[1], the
use by the Home Office of the former aircraft hangars between 1955 and 1959 for the
long-term storage of civil defence vehicles constituted use as a 'repository'. A negative
d answer to that question has hitherto been given throughout by the Secretary of State, the
Divisional Court and the Court of Appeal. But the true answer, as I think, is that there
was a class X user of the hangars right back to 1950, when the use classes order of that
year put 'wholesale warehouse' and 'repository' uses for the first time in the same user
class. It is common ground that the ISR user was as a wholesale warehouse, and the sole
dispute on this aspect of the case relates to the nature of the Home Office four-years'
e user. If, as ISR assert, it was as a 'repository', it follows that the later user by them
involved no material change of user and therefore no 'development', and, accordingly, no
planning permission was necessary. The issue accordingly resolved itself into the proper
meaning of the term 'repository'. Havers J said in *Horwitz v Rowson*[2]: '"Repository", I
think, means a building wherein goods are kept or stored, and I think that the keeping
or storing must be in the course of a trade or business.' This was followed by the obiter
f dictum of Lord Denning MR in *G Percy Trentham Ltd v Gloucestershire County Council*[3],
that 'A repository means a place where goods are stored away, to be kept for the sake of
keeping them safe, *as part of a storage business*' (my emphasis). But, my Lords, the
relevant words of the use classes order itself are 'repository for any purpose', and the
qualification judicially imposed was, with respect, contrary both to the order itself and
to the generally accepted meaning of 'repository'. There is, I hold, no material difference
g (as far as the uses order is concerned) between a furniture repository or a repository for
archives (cited by Lord Denning MR as typical uses of the word) and the use of the
hangars by ISR as a wholesale warehouse. It follows, accordingly, that no planning
permission was required by them in turning the hangars to such use.

My Lords, as to the earlier issue raised, that relating to the interpretation of ss 29 and
30 of the Town and Country Planning Act 1971, I desire to say no more than that, in my
h judgment, counsel for ISR went farther than he need in submitting that a condition for
removal of buildings could *never* be attached to a planning permission restricted to
change of use. It is true that such was the view expressed in the Ministry circular 5/68,
issued in 1968 ('The Use of Conditions in Planning Permissions') and followed by the
Secretary of State in the present case. But whether a removal condition may properly be
imposed in *some* circumstances, wholly different from those of the present case, may on
j another occasion call for careful consideration. For present purposes it is sufficient to

---

1   SI 1950 No 1121
2   [1960] 2 All ER 881 at 886, [1960] 1 WLR 803 at 810
3   [1966] 1 All ER 701 at 703, [1966] 1 WLR 506 at 512

hold, as I do, that, in the circumstances of the instant case, the condition for removal of the hangars did not fairly or reasonably relate to the permitted development.   *a*

The third issue ('blowing hot and cold') was not advanced at the inquiry and was therefore never considered by the Secretary of State. Nor was it raised in the notice of motion to the Divisional Court, though it was adverted to at the hearing, Michael Davies J restricting himself to saying, 'I do not think there is any comfort for the appellant [Newbury District Council] in it', and Robert Goff J expressing himself similarly. In the Court of Appeal it was sympathetically received by Lord Denning MR alone. Counsel *b* for the Secretary of State expressed alarm in this House at the prospect of the view expressed by Lord Denning MR receiving acceptance by your Lordships, envisaging as one of the possible results the destruction even of what had long been regarded as established rights of user. I restrict myself to saying that I am in respectful agreement with all your Lordships in holding that, on the facts of this case, the 'hot and cold' doctrine should be regarded as having no application.   *c*

LORD FRASER OF TULLYBELTON. My Lords, these appeals, which were heard together, raise questions of planning law as it affects two hangars built by the Royal Air Force on Membury Airfield during the war. The hangars now belong to the International *d* Synthetic Rubber Co Ltd ('ISR'), who are the appellants in one appeal. The appellant in the other appeal is the Secretary of State for the Environment. The respondents in both appeals are Newbury District Council. After the war the hangars were used for storing various things but it is unnecessary to go further back than 1955. From 1955 to 1959 they were used by the Home Office for the long-term storage of civil defence vehicles, including 'Green Goddess' fire engines. In 1959 planning permission was given for the *e* hangars to be used for the storage of agricultural products, subject to a condition that the buildings were to be removed at the expiration of a period ending 31st December 1970. Thereafter one of them was used for a time for storing fertilisers and agricultural goods. On 31st May 1962 planning permission was granted to ISR by the predecessors of the respondents as planning authority, for use of the hangars as 'warehouses'. The permission was not expressed to be for a limited period, but it was subject to two *f* conditions, one of which was that 'the buildings be removed at the expiration of the period ending 31st December, 1972'. In July 1962 ISR, having been granted planning permission, bought the hangars and proceeded to use them as warehouses.

In 1970, when the time for demolition was drawing near, they applied for an extension of the planning permission for 30 years, but their application was refused by the respondents. ISR appealed to the Secretary of State against the refusal, and on 12th *g* November 1973, while the appeal was pending, an enforcement notice was served on them requiring them to comply with the condition that the hangars be removed. (A separate enforcement notice was served on ISR at the same time relating to the removal of another small building. This notice was also the subject of an appeal which forms part of the present proceedings, but we heard no separate argument about it and I need not refer to it again.) ISR appealed to the Secretary of State against the enforcement notice, *h* and against the refusal to extend the planning permission for 30 years. After a public inquiry, the Secretary of State upheld ISR's appeal against the enforcement notice on the ground that the condition attached to the planning permission of 1962 was invalid and was not severable from the rest of the notice. But he rejected an argument for ISR to the effect that no planning permission had been required in 1962 because the hangars had been in use since 1947 for a purpose in the same use class as wholesale warehouse. He *j* dismissed the appeal against the refusal to extend planning permission for 30 years. The Divisional Court refused an appeal against the Secretary of State's decision. The Court of Appeal allowed an appeal by the respondents and held that the enforcement notice was valid but they again rejected the argument that planning permission had been unnecessary. It will be convenient to consider that argument first.

Was planning permission necessary in 1962 for use of the hangars as warehouses?

a   The Town and Country Planning (Use Classes) Order 1950[1] provides in para 3 that where a building or other land is used for a purpose specified in the schedule to the order, the use of the building or land for any other purpose of the same class shall not be deemed to involve development of the land in the sense of the Town and Country Planning Acts. The result is that planning permission for a change of use within the class is not required. Class X in the schedule is as follows: 'Use as a wholesale warehouse or

b   repository for any purpose.' It was common ground that the hangars had been used since 1959 as wholesale warehouses. It was also common ground that if the use of the hangars by the Home Office from 1955 to 1959 had been as 'repositories' such use would be within class X of the order and that therefore no planning permission would be required to use them as wholesale warehouses. The question in dispute is whether the use by the Home Office for the long-term storage of civil defence vehicles was use as a 'repository'.

c   The Secretary of State and all the learned judges who have so far considered this question have held that the Home Office did not use the buildings as repositories. It is therefore only with diffidence that I reach the opposite conclusion, as I feel bound to do. In the Court of Appeal, Lord Denning MR said[2] that it was a matter of impression depending on the meaning that one gives to the word 'repository' in one's own vocabulary. He went on[3]: 'My opinion is that no one conversant with the English language would dream of

d   calling these hangars a "repository" when filled with fire-pumps or synthetic rubber.' Lawton and Browne LJJ agreed with Lord Denning MR's view and they also expressed agreement with the statement by Lord Denning MR in *G Percy Trentham Ltd v Gloucestershire County Council*[4] as follows: 'A repository means a place where goods are stored away, to be kept for the sake of keeping them safe, *as part of a storage business*' (my emphasis). That statement was quoted by the Secretary of State in his decision letter in

e   the present appeal and he naturally and properly relied on it in making his decision. But the words emphasised were not strictly necessary to the decision in the *Trentham* case[5]. They seem to have been taken from an earlier statement, which was also obiter, by Havers J in *Horwitz v Rowson*[6]. I am about to explain why the words in italics are not correct.

The question is not simply what the word 'repository' means in ordinary speech, but

f   what it means as used in class X of the schedule to the 1950 order. The two meanings are not necessarily identical. In ordinary speech the word is seldom used, but when used it is applied mainly to two things, a furniture repository and a repository for documents. In the latter sense it may be applied either to a building such as the Public Record Office or to places such as a safe or a desk in which a person's will or codicils are likely to be found after his death; in neither case is the storage 'as part of a storage business'. But the

g   Shorter Oxford English Dictionary gives the word a much more general meaning. It gives the first meaning of 'repository' as 'a vessel, receptacle, chamber, etc. in which things are, or may be, placed, deposited or stored'. In this order the meaning is not restricted, because class X includes repository 'for any purpose'. It seems to me that buildings used for the long-term storage of vehicles fall clearly within that description. The reason why the draftsman preferred the word repository to the commoner word

h   'store' may be that 'store' is sometimes used to include a retail shop such as a 'department store'.

If it were permissible to refer to the 1948 use classes order, which was repealed and replaced by the 1950 order, the matter would, I think, be even clearer because in the 1948 order 'repository' is defined as meaning 'a building . . . where storage is the principal

---

j   1   SI 1950 No 1131
      2   [1979] 1 All ER 243 at 249, [1978] 1 WLR 1241 at 1249–1250
      3   [1979] 1 All ER 243 at 249–250, [1978] 1 WLR 1241 at 1250
      4   [1966] 1 All ER 701 at 703, [1966] 1 WLR 506 at 512
      5   [1966] 1 All ER 701, [1966] 1 WLR 506
      6   [1960] 2 All ER 881 at 886, [1960] 1 WLR 803 at 810

use and where no business is transacted other than incidentally to such storage'. In the
schedule to the 1948 order, use as a wholesale warehouse and use as a repository were in   *a*
separate use classes, numbered X and XI respectively. But in the schedule to the 1950
order those classes were amalgamated and the definition of repository was omitted.
Comparison of the two orders is of course permissible, but there is no way in which the
courts can know for certain what was the purpose of these changes. In any event, what
matters is their effect which has to be ascertained by construing the 1950 order and not
by relying on the explanatory note attached to it which is not part of the order but is   *b*
intended merely to indicate its general purport. In these circumstances I do not think it
would be legitimate to assume that the meaning of repository was the same in both
orders, or to use the 1948 definition as an aid to construing the 1950 order. I shall
therefore disregard the 1948 order.

It follows from what I have said that in my opinion the change of use from repositories
to wholesale warehouses was a change between two uses, both of which were within class   *c*
X. It was therefore not development and did not require planning permission. So,
unless ISR are precluded from relying on the Home Office use of the buildings as
repositories, it is immaterial whether the enforcement notice was valid or not.

Blowing hot and cold
In the Court of Appeal Lord Denning MR held that, even if the hangars had been used
as 'repositories' by the Home Office, ISR would not now be entitled to rely on existing use   *d*
rights derived from that use, because they had accepted and acted on the grant of
planning permission in 1962, which was subject to the condition of removal, and they
could not turn round now and say they did not need planning permission after all. That
would be blowing hot and cold and should not be allowed. He applied the maxim of law
and equity, qui sentit commodum sentire debet et onus. Counsel for the local planning
authority said that the planning authority had been prejudiced by ISR's apparent   *e*
acceptance of the planning permission with its attached condition for nearly ten years,
and I was at first attracted by the argument. The principle for which he contended was
stated by him thus: 'The planning history of a site starts afresh when the acceptance and
implementation of planning permission is inconsistent with reliance on earlier existing
use rights.' I doubt whether that formulation really applies to the circumstances of the
present case, because the implementation of the 1962 planning permission can hardly be   *f*
said to have been inconsistent with reliance on earlier existing use rights during the
period before 31st December 1972. During that period there was nothing to show
whether ISR's use of the hangars was in reliance on the planning permission of 1962 or
on earlier existing use rights. But apart from that point which arises on the facts of this
appeal, I am of opinion that the principle contended for is unsound. It would introduce
an estoppel or bar, personal to the particular party, which is quite inappropriate in this   *g*
field of law, which is concerned with rights that run with land. To do so would lead to
uncertainty and confusion. It would also interfere with the convenient practice whereby
prospective vendors or purchasers of land apply for planning permission as a precaution
if there is doubt about whether their proposals are already permissible or not. It would,
moreover, be inconsistent with a number of decided cases, including *Mounsdon v
Weymouth and Melcombe Regis Corpn*[1].   *h*

The only circumstances in which existing use rights are lost by accepting and
implementing a later planning permission are, in my opinion, when a new planning
unit comes into existence as in *Prossor v Minister of Housing and Local Government*[2]. That
was a case where planning permission had been given for the rebuilding of a petrol
service station and the rebuilding had been carried out. Lord Parker CJ said[3]:

'... by adopting the permission granted in April, 1964, the appellant's predecessor,   *j*
as it seems to me, gave up any possible existing use rights in that regard which he

1   [1960] 1 All ER 538, [1960] 1 QB 645
2   (1968) 67 LGR 109
3   67 LGR 109 at 113

may have had. The planning history of this site, as it were, seems to me to begin
afresh on April 4, 1964, with the grant of this permission, a permission which was
taken up and used . . .'

Prossor's case[1] was approved in *Leighton and Newman Car Sales Ltd v Secretary of State for
the Environment*[2], where the facts were very similar, and in *Petticoat Lane Rentals Ltd v
Secretary of State for the Environment*[3], where a new building was erected covering the
whole of an area of open land. Such physical alteration will normally be made only in
implementation of planning permission for erection of new buildings, but it might be
made in implementation of planning permission for a change of use in some
circumstances. For example, as was suggested in argument, there is the case of a single
dwelling house being divided into separate flats by purely internal alterations, for which
the only planning permission required would be for a change of use. Accordingly I do
not think that the principle should be limited to cases of planning permission for
rebuilding, although it will only seldom apply to planning permission for change of use.

For these reasons I do not consider that ISR are precluded from relying on their
existing use rights derived from the Home Office use of the site. It follows that there is
nothing to prevent their continuing to use the hangars as warehouses or, if they choose,
reverting to using them as repositories.

Validity of the enforcement notice

Having regard to the opinion which I have already expressed, it is not strictly necessary
to consider this matter, but as we were urged by counsel for all the parties to give what
guidance we could I shall express my opinion on the questions that arise.

The power on which the respondents relied to justify the condition attached to the
planning permission granted in 1969 was derived from s 17(1) of the Town and Country
Planning Act 1962, but it is more convenient to refer to s 29(1) of the Town and Country
Planning Act 1971, which does not differ from the earlier enactment in any material
respect. Section 29(1) provides as follows:

'Subject to the provisions of sections 26 to 28 of this Act, and to the following
provisions of this Act, where an application is made to a local planning authority for
planning permission, that authority, in dealing with the application, shall have
regard to the provisions of the development plan, so far as material to the
application, and to any other material considerations, and—(a) subject to sections
41, 42, 70 and 77 to 80 of this Act, may grant planning permission, either
unconditionally or *subject to such conditions as they think fit . . .*'

The words that I have emphasised would appear on their face to confer an unlimited
power, but it is plain that the power is subject to certain limitations. If authority for that
proposition is needed it is to be found in the speech of Lord Reid in *Kent County Council
v Kingsway Investments (Kent) Ltd*[4]. In order to be valid, a condition must satisfy three
tests. First, it must have a planning purpose. It may have other purposes as well as its
planning purpose. But if it is imposed solely for some other purpose or purposes, such
as furtherance of the housing policy of the local authority, it will not be valid as a
planning condition: see *R v London Borough of Hillingdon, ex parte Royco Homes Ltd*[5].
Second, it must relate to the permitted development to which it is annexed. The best
known statement of these two tests is that by Lord Denning in *Pyx Granite Co Ltd v
Ministry of Housing and Local Government*[6] which has been followed and applied in many
later cases. Lord Denning said there[7]:

1   (1968) 67 LGR 109
2   (1976) 32 P & CR 1
3   [1971] 2 All ER 793, [1971] 1 WLR 1112
4   [1970] 1 All ER 70 at 73, [1971] AC 72 at 86
5   [1974] 2 All ER 643, [1974] 1 QB 720
6   [1958] 1 All ER 625, [1958] 1 QB 554
7   [1958] 1 All ER 625 at 633, [1958] 1 QB 554 at 572

'Although the planning authorities are given very wide powers to impose "such conditions as they think fit", nevertheless the law says that those conditions, to be valid, must fairly and reasonably relate to the permitted development. The planning authority are not at liberty to use their powers for an ulterior object, however desirable that object may seem to them to be in the public interest.'

One reason, relevant to the instant case, why it would be wrong to secure removal of buildings by the use of a condition unrelated to the permitted development is that it would enable the planning authority to evade its liability to pay compensation for removal under s 51 of the 1971 Act. Thirdly, the condition must be 'reasonable' in the rather special sense of *Associated Provincial Picture Houses Ltd v Wednesbury Corpn*[1]. Thus it will be invalid if it is 'so clearly unreasonable that no reasonable planning authority could have imposed it' as Lord Widgery CJ said in *Kingston-upon-Thames Royal London Borough Council v Secretary of State for the Environment*[2].

There was no dispute between the parties that tests substantially in the terms I have set out were those relevant for the present purpose. It may not be strictly necessary to specify the second of these tests separately, as it may be included within the third, but I think it is desirable to set it out as a separate test lest it be overlooked.

It remains to ascertain whether the Secretary of State applied these tests in the present case. Clearly the condition for the removal of the buildings was imposed in furtherance of the authority's planning policy, and it therefore satisfied the first test. I think it also satisfies the third test. The second test raises more difficulty. The reasons for the Secretary of State's decision on this part of the appeal are given in para 8 of his decision letter, which included the following passage:

'It is evident that the local planning authority imposed the condition to remove the hangars to safeguard their long-term policy for industrial development in rural areas and to secure the future improvement of the amenity of the area of the appeal site. It is considered, however, in the circumstances of this case, where planning permission was sought merely for a change of use of existing substantial buildings, that a condition requiring the removal of those buildings after the expiration of a specified number of years was not sufficiently related to the change of use in respect of which the planning permission was granted and was unreasonable. It is therefore concluded that the condition was invalid. The allegation that [ISR] failed to comply with the condition is therefore inappropriate. The appeal succeeds on ground (b) and the enforcement notice is being quashed.'

Ground (b) is a reference to s 88(1)(b) of the 1971 Act which provides that an appeal may be taken to the Secretary of State against an enforcement notice on the ground '(b) that the matters alleged in the notice do not constitute a breach of planning control'. I am not sure whether para 8 is intended to mean that a condition for removal of buildings could never, as a matter of law, be sufficiently related to planning permission which was merely for a change of use (as distinct from permission for the erection of buildings), or that, on the facts in this case, it was not related to the permission. On the whole I am inclined to think that the former view is correct, because the only circumstance of the case which is mentioned is that planning permission has been sought 'merely for a change of use of existing substantial buildings'. I am also influenced by the fact that that appears to be the opinion of the Secretary of State's department as set out in the circular 5/68, dated 6th February 1968, issued by the former Ministry of Housing and Local Government with its accompanying memorandum on 'The Use of Conditions in Planning Permissions', para 9 of which includes the following sentence:

'A condition requiring the removal of an existing building, whether on the application site or not, will only be reasonable if the need for that removal springs directly from the fact that *a new building is to be erected*.' (My emphasis.)

---

1   [1947] 2 All ER 680 at 682, [1948] 1 KB 223 at 229
2   [1974] 1 All ER 193 at 196, [1973] 1 WLR 1549 at 1553

That statement is, in my opinion, too absolute and the words emphasised are not
a supported by authority. If (as I am inclined to think) it explains the reason on which the
Secretary of State's decision was based, then the reason was, in my opinion, erroneous in
law. But even if that is so, I am satisfied that, if the Secretary of State had correctly
appreciated that a condition for removal of buildings attached to permission for change
of use might be valid, he would nevertheless have certainly decided that in the
circumstances of this case it was not sufficiently related to the permission and was
b therefore invalid. There was nothing that I can see about the change of use to a wholesale
warehouse which required or justified a condition for removal of the buildings. The
reason why the planning authority ordered their removal was to improve or restore the
amenity of the neighbourhood by getting rid of ugly buildings. No doubt that was a
very proper object, but it had nothing particularly to do with the use of the buildings as
warehouses. The fact that the permission was in substance a temporary permission, as
c the Court of Appeal held, does not seem to me to be relevant to this matter.

Accordingly I am of opinion that, even giving this condition the benevolent treatment
to which, like a byelaw, it is entitled, it was invalid. If planning permission had been
required for the change of use in 1962, the Secretary of State would have been right in
so deciding and also in deciding that, as the condition could not be severed from the
permission, the permission itself was invalid, although his reason for doing so was (on
d my reading of his letter) wrong.

I would allow the appeal by ISR with costs here and below against Newbury District
Council. The Secretary of State must bear his own costs throughout.

LORD SCARMAN. My Lords, the House has under consideration two appeals. Both
the Secretary of State for the Environment and the International Synthetic Rubber Co
e Ltd ('ISR') appeal against the reversal by the Court of Appeal of the decision of the
Divisional Court dismissing the appeal of the Newbury District Council ('the local
planning authority') from a decision of the Secretary of State allowing ISR's appeal against
an enforcement notice served on them by the Hungerford Rural District Council as
agent for the local planning authority to whose statutory functions and duties the
Newbury District Council has succeeded. Newbury District Council, as local planning
f authority, seek to uphold a condition imposed by Hungerford Rural District Council on
a planning permission granted to ISR on 31st May 1962 to use two ex-Royal Air Force
hangars as warehouses for the storage of synthetic rubber. The condition was that 'the
buildings shall be removed at the expiration of the period ending December 31st
1972'. The Secretary of State, holding that the condition was invalid, quashed the
enforcement notice. The Divisional Court agreed. But the Court of Appeal, ruling that
g the condition was valid, upheld the enforcement notice. This House gave leave to
appeal.

The Secretary of State announced his decision by letter dated 24th July 1975. He
accepted the facts as found by his inspector after a public inquiry held by him in January
1975. The appeal site comprises two large aerodrome hangars on either side of an
unclassified road and enclosed in a perimeter fence at the former Membury airfield some
h five miles north-west of Hungerford and just south of the M4 motorway. The freehold
was vested in the Crown until 1961, when it was returned to the Gilbey family who had
owned the land before the war.

The airfield is an area allocated on the county map for service requirements but is
surrounded for the most part by land in agricultural use ('white' on the map, indicating
that it is not planned to disturb the existing use). The airfield was operational until
j 1947. From 1947 until 1953 the two hangars were used by the Ministry of Agriculture,
Fisheries and Food 'as a buffer storage depot'. In 1953 the depot was cleared and the
airfield transferred to the United States Air Force for their use. The nature of the USAF
use is not known. In 1954 the Royal Air Force took over the airfield (including the
hangars) for use as a sub-depot of No 3 Maintenance Unit. From 1955 to 1959 the
hangars were used by the Home Office for the storage of civil defence vehicles. In 1959

planning permission was granted to Mr J S Gilbey (a member of the family whose land it had been before the war) for use of the hangars for the storage of agricultural products *a* (including fertiliser). Permission was conditional on the buildings being removed at the expiration of the period ending 31st December 1964, which was later extended to 31st December 1970. A certain Mr James was allowed to use, and did use, one of the hangars for the storage of agricultural products and fertiliser. In 1961 ISR began to use one hangar for the storage of synthetic rubber.

In 1962 there occurred the planning application and permission with which these *b* appeals are directly concerned. On 3rd May 1962 ISR applied for permission to use the two hangars 'as warehouses for the storage of synthetic rubber', declaring (with strict accuracy only so far as one hangar was concerned) that they were already in use for that purpose. On 31st May 1962 planning permission was granted subject to conditions. The relevant terms of the permission were that the local planning authority permitted 'use of two hangars on Membury airfield as warehouses . . . subject to compliance with *c* the conditions specified hereunder:—1. the buildings shall be removed at the expiration of the period ending December 31st 1972 . . .' The reasons for the conditions were stated to be: '1. To accord with the local planning authority's policy regarding industrial development in rural areas. 2. To safeguard the amenities of the area.' ISR did not appeal against the conditions. But two months later, in July 1962, they took a long lease of the site, and put both hangars to use as warehouses. *d*

On 5th November 1970 ISR applied for planning permission to use the hangars as warehouses for a further 30 years (ie until the expiry of their lease) from 31st December 1972. Clearly ISR saw their right of use as based on a temporary permission expiring at the end of 1972. Permission was refused, and on 25th June 1971 ISR appealed to the Secretary of State.

ISR did not remove the hangars by 31st December 1972, but continued their use of *e* them. On 12th November 1973 the local planning authority served an enforcement notice requiring ISR to remove them. ISR appealed to the Secretary of State against the notice.

After stating the facts, the inspector, who took the public inquiry, concluded—

'that there was a clearly established use of the appeal hangars when in Crown *f* occupation, prior to 1959, for storage. Food-stuffs were stored from 1947 to 1953, then the hangars were part of a sub-depot for No. 3 Maintenance Unit at Milton, then from 1955 to 1959 they were used for storing civil defence vehicles.'

He noted that, after a gap in 1953, when the USAF had the use of the airfield, the storage use was resumed and commented that 'The application for permission for storage in 1959 [the Gilbey application] appears to have been unnecessary'. Though his report *g* contains a very helpful discussion of what he calls 'the legal implications' of the facts, he was careful to leave them to the Secretary of State. He contented himself with two recommendations confined to the planning aspects of the case: the first that, if the Secretary of State decided that there had been a breach of planning control, the condition for removal of the hangars should not be discharged, and the second that the planning appeal should be dismissed. *h*

Three questions arise on these facts. First, was planning permission required when it was granted in 1962? I shall call this the existing use point. Secondly, if it was not, can ISR now rely on an existing use right and so avoid the condition imposed, that the hangars should be removed by the end of 1972? I shall call this the estoppel point. Thirdly, if planning permission was required, was the condition one which the local planning authority could lawfully impose? The first question turns on the true *j* construction of the 1950 use classes order[1], the effective order in 1962. The second and third questions raise points of great importance in the law of planning control and its enforcement.

1   SI 1950 No 1131

Existing use

a   The Town and Country Planning Act 1971 consolidated the statute law relating to town and country planning in England and Wales. Part III (ss 22–53) provides for general planning control, and Part V (ss 87–111) for the enforcement of planning control. Section 22(1) (which reproduces the earlier law) defines development as meaning 'the carrying out of building, engineering, mining or other operations in, on, over or under land, or the making of any material change in the use of any buildings or

b   other land.' Subsection (2) provides that certain operations or uses of land shall not be taken to involve development of the land including—

> '(*f*) in the case of buildings or other land which are used for a purpose of any class specified in an order made by the Secretary of State under this section, the use thereof for any other purpose of the same class.'

c   This provision has been a feature of the legislation ever since the Town and Country Planning Act 1947. A use classes order had been made under that Act in 1948[1]. It was revoked and replaced by the 1950 use classes order, which is the effective order for the purposes of these appeals. (In its turn it has been replaced by subsequent orders.) Where a building or other land is used for a purpose of any class specified in the schedule to the order, its use for any other purpose of the same class shall not be deemed to involve

d   development of the land (art 3(1)). The schedule specifies, amongst other classes, 'Class X—Use as a wholesale warehouse or repository for any purpose'.

The purpose of the use classes order becomes evident when one reaches s 23(1) of the Act, which provides that subject to the provisions of the section 'planning permission is required for the carrying out of any development of land'. Since a change of use within a class is not deemed to involve development, planning permission for the change of use

e   is not required. The effect, therefore, of class X is that premises previously used as a repository for any purpose may be used as a wholesale warehouse, and vice versa. In neither case does the law deem any development to be involved or require the grant of planning permission. A comparison of the 1950 order with that of 1948, which it revoked, is, in my judgment, permissible and instructive. The 1950 order amalgamated certain use classes to be found in the earlier order, thus permitting a wider range of

f   changes of use to take place without the requirement of planning permission. The 1948 order placed use as a wholesale warehouse in class X and use as a repository in class XI; it also included definitions of 'wholesale warehouse' and 'repository'. The 1950 order has no definition of either term; but, since the purpose of the order is the amalgamation of certain use classes to be found in the 1948 order, it is legitimate, for the purpose of construing the order, to note the meaning of these terms in the two use classes which the

g   1950 order has amalgamated into one (the new class X). The 1948 order provided that 'wholesale warehouse' means a building where business, principally of a wholesale nature, is transacted, and that 'repository' means a building where storage is the principal use and where no business is transacted other than incidentally to such storage.

It is common ground that ISR use the hangars as wholesale warehouses. If, therefore, the lawful prior use was that of a 'repository for any purpose', planning permission was

h   unnecessary, for there would be an existing use right entitling ISR to use them as wholesale warehouses.

It is also common ground (though at one time the local planning authority was disposed to deny it) that the Crown use, which began in 1947 and with two 'service' breaks continued until 1959, was lawful. The inspector has found and the Secretary of State has accepted that this use was 'for storage purposes'. In other words, the hangars

j   were buildings in respect of which there had been lawfully established an existing storage use prior to the arrival of the ISR on site.

The sole issue, therefore, is as to the meaning to be given to the words 'repository for any purpose' where they appear in the order. ISR's submission is that repository is (as

---

1   SI 1948 No 954

defined in the 1948 order) a building used for storage, and that class X includes such use 'for any purpose'. The Secretary of State and the local planning authority submit that the *a* context requires that a limitation be placed on the words 'for any purpose', namely a limitation to the purposes of a storage business. This construction found favour with the Divisional Court and the Court of Appeal. Reliance was placed on *G Percy Trentham Ltd v Gloucestershire County Council*[1], a decision of the Court of Appeal. In that case the Court of Appeal reached the unsurprising conclusion that use as a farm shed was not use as a repository, Diplock LJ commenting that nowhere, except in a court of law, did he think *b* it would be argued 'with gravity' that ordinary farm buildings are properly described as 'repositories'. In his judgment, however, Lord Denning MR essayed a definition of repository. He said[2]: 'A repository means a place where goods are stored away, to be kept for the sake of keeping them safe, as part of a storage business.' The Court of Appeal applied this definition in this case. After hearing counsel's submissions for ISR (no doubt very persuasive, if his argument in this House be any guide), Lord Denning MR felt that *c* his 'one answer' must be 'a matter of impression'. So far, I agree. But then he added[3]: 'My opinion is that no one conversant with the English language would dream of calling these hangars a "repository" when filled with fire-pumps or synthetic rubber.' I cannot, with respect, agree. I find that neither the standard English dictionaries nor my experience of the English language as writer and student suggest that the qualification 'as part of a storage business' is to be embodied in the ordinary meaning of the word *d* 'repository'. The primary and literal meaning of 'repository' is what anyone acquainted with its Latin origin would expect, a place or receptacle where things are stored. But there is also an old established secondary meaning, 'a place where things are kept or offered for sale: a warehouse, store, shop or mart'[4]. But this meaning is not limited to use 'as part of a storage business'. It embraces any business use, as distinct, for example, from a repository used for domestic, museum or academic purposes. Two questions, therefore, *e* arise. First, is 'repository' used in the order in its primary, or literal, sense? Secondly, if not, is the term 'use as a repository' a reference to a general business use or to a use limited to that of a storage business?

The language of the class is wide enough to permit the primary, or literal, meaning. But the context, I think, makes the secondary, but well established, meaning the more likely. In this respect, I note that Havers J, in *Horwitz v Rowson*[5], defined 'repository' as *f* a building wherein goods were kept in the course of trade or business. Although the various classes scheduled to the order make strange reading and include some oddly assorted bedfellows, they are classes. The order being part of the apparatus of planning control, I look for a planning link between the several members of each class, and this is not difficult to ascertain, though the linkage is looser in some classes than in others. So far as class X is concerned, if each of the two specified uses is a business use, the planning *g* link between them is established without doing any violence to the English language. But I cannot go the step further which was taken by Lord Denning MR in the *Trentham* case[1] and construe the business use as limited to that of a storage business. The words 'for any purpose', though consistent with a general limitation of the class to business use, negative the possibility of limiting use as a repository to a specific type of business. The express limitation of 'wholesale' on the warehouse use is to be contrasted with the express *h* extension of the repository use to such use 'for any purpose'.

The question for decision is, therefore, whether the Crown use of the hangars for storage purposes between 1947 and 1959 was a business use. The word 'business' is apt to include official or governmental business as well as commercial business. The relevance of business to planning is that it is associated with a certain character of

j

1   [1966] 1 All ER 701, [1966] 1 WLR 506
2   [1966] 1 All ER 701 at 703, [1966] 1 WLR 506 at 512
3   [1979] 1 All ER 243 at 250, [1978] 1 WLR 1241 at 1250
4   Shorter Oxford English Dictionary, 1944 edition and repeated in subsequent revisions
5   [1960] 2 All ER 881, [1960] 1 WLR 803

development and a certain level of activity on and adjacent to the land, e g the type of
a buildings and the level of traffic movement. As such, it matters not whether the Crown
is storing goods in the hangars for the purposes of public business or a wholesaler for his
private business purposes or any other commercial enterprise for its business purposes.
To quote the 1948 order, 'where storage is the principal use and where no business is
transacted other than incidentally to such storage', the nature or purpose of the business
for which the repository is used is immaterial for planning purposes. The one essential
b limitation, which is to be compared with the 'wholesale' limitation on warehouse use, is
implicit in the word 'repository', namely, that the principal use is storage. So understood,
class X does embrace the Home Office and Ministry of Agriculture, Fisheries and Food
use. Counsel for the local planning authority sought to avoid this conclusion by
submitting, correctly, that not all uses of land are included in the use classes order. He
urged on the House the proposition that the Crown use was 'sui generis' (in English, a
c distinct, unique use), and not covered by class X. I do not accept his proposition.
Properly considered, the Crown use was as much a storage use for its business as would
be that of any commercial enterprise for its business.

Accordingly, I think the *Trentham*[1] limitation, 'as part of a storage business', was
erroneous and that class X is wide enough to include the Crown use in this case. The
Crown did, and ISR do, use the hangars for storage, each for the purposes of their
d business: and no business is transacted on the site save that which is incidental to
storage. My conclusion is, therefore, that the planning permission obtained by ISR in
1962 was unnecessary. There was an existing use right by virtue of class X of the use
classes order.

The estoppel point ('blowing hot and cold').
e The Court of Appeal did not have to decide whether ISR by taking up and then
exercising the 1962 planning permission had estopped themselves from relying on their
existing use right, for the court was unanimous that no such right existed. But, as your
Lordships are agreed that planning permission was unnecessary, the point does now arise
for decision.

In the Court of Appeal, Lawton LJ found the point attractive, but, since it did not arise,
f expressed no final opinion. Browne LJ did not find the point attractive. He said[2]:

'I will only say that as at present advised I am afraid that I do not agree with Lord
Denning MR on this point, except where the circumstances are as in *Prossor v
Minister of Housing and Local Government*[3], and the cases which have followed and
applied that decision, viz where a new planning unit, and indeed in those cases a
new physical unit, has been created.'

g Lord Denning MR, however, was prepared to lay down a broad general principal. He
said[4]:

'Blowing hot and cold
'In case I am wrong about "repository", I must turn to the final point, which is
this. Seeing that [ISR] accepted the grant of planning permission in 1962 (subject
h to the condition of removal), can they now turn round and say that they did not
need planning permission at all, being entitled, as they say, to use the hangars for
storing rubber without any permission at all? Counsel for [ISR] submitted that
they could. He referred to *Mounsdon v Weymouth and Melcombe Regis Corpn*[5] and
East Barnet Urban District Council v British Transport Commission[6]. But counsel for the

---

j 1   [1966] 1 All ER 701 at 703, [1966] 1 WLR 506 at 512
2   [1979] 1 All ER 243 at 255, [1978] 1 WLR 1241 at 1256
3   (1968) 67 LGR 109
4   [1979] 1 All ER 243 at 250, [1978] 1 WLR 1241 at 1250
5   [1960] 1 All ER 538, [1960] QB 645
6   [1961] 3 All ER 878, [1962] 2 QB 484

planning authority on the other side referred to *Brayhead (Ascot) Ltd v Berkshire County Council*[1], *Prossor v Ministry of Housing*[2], *Gray v Minister of Housing and Local Government*[3], *Petticoat Lane Rentals Ltd v Secretary of State for the Environment*[4] and *Kingston-upon-Thames Royal London Borough Council v Secretary of State for the Environment*[5]. To my mind the maxim of law and equity applies here: qui sentit commodum sentire debet et onus. He who takes the benefit must accept it with the burdens that go with it. It has been applied recently in *Halsall v Brizell*[6] and *E R Ives Investment Ltd v High*[7]. It is an instance of the general principle of equity considered in *Crabb v Arun District Council*[8] and it is, in my view, particularly applicable in planning cases. At any rate in those cases where the grant of planning permission opens a new chapter in the planning history of the site.'

His last sentence is an echo of *Prossor's* case[2] which, I think, was correctly decided. But, as I shall endeavour to show, it does not follow from the correctness of *Prossor's* case[2] that 'the general principle' of equitable estoppel is applicable to planning cases.

As every law student who has read the opening chapters of Snell on The Principles of Equity (now in its 27th edition (1973)) knows, equity, as a body of law ancillary to the common law, developed so as to provide a protection for interests in property which was more effective than the remedies available at law. The Court of Chancery acted on the conscience of the legal owner of property. Equitable interests were strictly not proprietary in character, but rights in personam. Although they have developed a proprietary character, they are not enforceable against all the world. The purchaser for value without notice is not bound. In the field of property law, equity is a potent protection of private rights, operating on the conscience of those who have notice of their existence. But this is no reason for extending it into the public law of planning control, which binds everyone.

The case law does not support Lord Denning MR's view. In *Swallow and Pearson v Middlesex County Council*[9] Parker J refused to hold that the plaintiffs, having treated an enforcement notice as a good notice, were estopped from denying its validity. He said[10]: '. . . no person can waive a provision or a requirement of the law which is not solely for his benefit but is for the public benefit.'

In *Mounsdon v Weymouth and Melcombe Regis Corpn*[11] a Divisional Court, which included Lord Parker CJ, referred to 'the principle' applied in *Swallow's* case[9] with approval and held that appellants who had obtained a conditional planning permission were not precluded from arguing that it was unnecessary.

Although the point was not argued, this House in *Pyx Granite Co Ltd v Ministry of Housing and Local Government*[12] implicitly accepted Lord Parker CJ's view, for in that case the appellant company, though it had obtained a conditional planning permission, was granted a declaration that their development was authorised by the Malvern Hills Act 1924[13] and so did not require permission.

1   [1964] 1 All ER 149, [1964] 2 QB 303
2   (1968) 67 LGR 109
3   (1969) 68 LGR 15
4   [1971] 2 All ER 793, [1971] 1 WLR 1112
5   [1974] 1 All ER 193, [1973] 1 WLR 1549
6   [1957] 1 All ER 371, [1957] Ch 169
7   [1967] 1 All ER 504 at 507, [1967] 2 QB 379 at 394
8   [1975] 3 All ER 865 at 871–872, [1976] Ch 179 at 187–188
9   [1953] 1 All ER 580, [1953] 1 WLR 422
10 [1953] 1 All ER 580 at 582, [1953] 1 WLR 422 at 426
11 [1960] 1 All ER 538, [1960] 1 QB 645
12 [1959] 3 All ER 1, [1960] AC 260
13 14 & 15 Geo 5 c xxxvi

Counsel for ISR referred us to other cases to the same effect, notably *East Barnet Urban*
a *District Council v British Transport Commission*[1], in which Lord Parker CJ was a member of
the court.

My Lords, I agree with the view so consistently expressed by Lord Parker CJ that it is
wrong to introduce into public administrative law concepts such as equitable estoppel
which are essentially aids to the doing of justice in private law. I forebear to discuss the
cases on which Lord Denning MR founded his view to the contrary because counsel for
b the local planning authority did not seek to rely on them. Indeed he based his argument
on *Prossor's case*[2], the principle of which is independent of any equitable doctrine.
Suffice it to say of the authorities mentioned by Lord Denning MR in the passage which
I have quoted that, if and in so far as they suggest (and I do not think that they do) that
equitable estoppel has a place in the law of planning control, they are incorrect in law and
should not be followed.

c In *Prossor's case*[2] Lord Parker CJ enunciated a genuine planning principle. The
appellant's predecessor in title had obtained planning permission for the rebuilding of a
petrol service station on a by-pass. It was subject to a condition that no retail sales other
than the sale of motor accessories should be carried out on the site. The appellant
displayed on the site secondhand cars for sale. Being served with an enforcement notice,
he claimed an existing use right. Though it was held that he had not established an
d existing use right, the Divisional Court also held that, by reason of the exercise of the
planning permission to rebuild, the appellant was bound by the condition attached to the
permission.

The case has nothing whatever to do with equitable estoppel. The permission was for
a new operational development of the site, ie the rebuilding. Lord Parker CJ put it
thus[3]: 'The planning history of this site, as it were, seems to me to begin afresh on
e April 4, 1964, with the grant of this permission, a permission which was taken up and
used . . .'

Prossor's case[2] has been followed in a number of cases. Their effect is accurately
summarised by Browne LJ in the passage from his judgment which I have already
quoted. *Prossor's case*[2] was approved by the Court of Appeal in *Gray v Minister of Housing*
and Local Government[4] and by the Divisional Court (Lord Widgery CJ presiding) in
f *Petticoat Lane Rentals Ltd v Secretary of State for the Environment*[5]. It has never, however,
been applied, so far as the research of counsel have been able to ascertain, to a change of
use case. In every case the permitted development which has been held to begin a new
planning history has been operational in character ie it altered the physical nature of the
land by building, mining or other engineering works.

Counsel for ISR submitted at the outset of his argument (and at that stage he was
g supported by counsel for the Secretary of State) that the principle in *Prossor's case*[2] is not
applicable to a 'change of use' case, where there is no building or other physical operation
covered by the planning permission. Clearly it will be much more difficult to establish
the creation of a new planning unit or the beginning of a new chapter of planning
history where the unnecessary permission which has been granted subject to conditions
purports to authorise only a change of use. But such cases can exist, as at a later stage in
h the argument counsel for the Secretary of State was able to show, eg where permission
is granted to change the use of residential premises in single occupation to a multi-
occupation use. There is in such a case a wholly new departure, a new chapter of planning
history. It would be a negation of sound planning if the conditions attached to the multi-
occupation use could be avoided merely because prior to such use the premises had the

j
1   [1961] 3 All ER 878, [1962] 2 QB 484
2   (1968) 67 LGR 109
3   67 LGR 109 at 113
4   (1969) 68 LGR 15
5   [1971] 2 All ER 793, [1971] 1 WLR 1112

benefit of an existing residential use in single occupation. I conclude, therefore, that *Prossor's*[1] principle is of general application where it can be shown that a new planning *a* unit has been brought into existence by the grant and exercise of a new planning permission. But, where *Prossor's* case[1] does not apply, the grant of an unnecessary planning permission does not preclude a landowner from relying on an existing use right.

On the facts of this case, it is, however, not possible to apply the *Prossor*[1] principle. Planningwise, on the facts as found by the inspector and accepted by the Secretary of *b* State, there was no departure from the previous use substantial enough to justify the inference that a new unit had been created or a new planning history begun. I, therefore, reject the submission to the contrary made on behalf of the council.

The validity of the condition   *c*

My Lords, it is strictly unnecessary for me to express a view on the validity of the condition. But the House has heard full argument on the point, and I have reached the clear conclusion that the Secretary of State's decision that the condition was invalid cannot be said to be incorrect in law. I think it right, therefore, to state briefly the reasons for my conclusion.

The Divisional Court agreed with the Secretary of State. But the Court of Appeal *d* upheld the enforcement notice, ruling that the condition for the removal of the hangars was valid. In their view, it fairly and unreasonably related to the permitted development, i e the temporary use of the hangars as warehouses for the storage of synthetic rubber.

The Court of Appeal was entitled to reverse the Secretary of State only if he could be shown to have made an error in law, see s 246 of the 1971 Act. The law is, I think, well settled save for one small area of doubt. Counsel for ISR opening the appeal, suggested *e* that the law requires three tests of validity, all of which, he submitted, must be satisfied. Counsel for the Secretary of State agreed with him. Counsel for the local planning authority suggested that there were really only two. The difference between them is semantic, not substantial. The three tests suggested are (1) the condition must fairly and reasonably relate to the provisions of the development plan and to planning considerations affecting the land, (2) it must fairly and reasonably relate to the permitted *f* development, and (3) it must be such as a reasonable planning authority, duly appreciating its statutory duties, could have properly imposed. As counsel for the local planning authority said, test (3) is almost invariably wrapped up in the first two; but it is possible, though unusual, that a condition could in an exceptional case satisfy the first two tests but fail the third.

My Lords, I accept the submission of the Secretary of State and ISR that there are these *g* three tests. The legal authority for the tests is to be found in the 1971 Act and its judicial interpretation. Section 29(1) of the Act, substantially re-enacting s 14(1) of the 1947 Act, provides as follows:

'Subject to the provisions of sections 26 to 28 of this Act, and to the following provisions of this Act, where an application is made to a local planning authority for *h* planning permission, that authority, in dealing with the application, shall have regard to the provisions of the development plan, so far as material to the application, and to any other material considerations, and—(a) subject to sections 41, 42, 70 and 77 to 80 of this Act, may grant planning permission, either unconditionally or subject to such conditions as they think fit; or (b) may refuse planning permission.'   *j*

Though the subsection speaks of 'such conditions as they think fit', its opening words impose a limitation on the powers of the local planning authority including the

1   (1968) 67 LGR 109

discretionary power to impose conditions. In dealing with the application for permission,
a they shall have regard to the development plan 'so far as material to the application, and
to any other material considerations,' I construe 'material considerations' in the context
of the subsection as a reference to planning considerations.

The subsection therefore expressly mentions the first two tests. The third test arises
from the application to the planning law of the reasonableness test as enunciated by Lord
Greene MR in *Associated Provincial Picture Houses Ltd v Wednesbury Corpn*[1].
b This view of the subsection and its predecessor has been accepted by a line of
authoritative judicial decisions, the most notable of which are *Pyx Granite Co Ltd v
Ministry of Housing and Local Government*[2] when in the Court of Appeal, and *Fawcett
Properties Ltd v Buckingham County Council*[3]. In the *Pyx Granite* case[4] Lord Denning said
that 'conditions . . . must fairly and reasonably relate to the permitted development'. In
Fawcett's case[3] this House, in effect, adopted the three tests. Lord Cohen[5] considered that
c the relevant questions which the court must answer were, as Megarry QC had submitted,
whether the scope of the condition was 'unrelated to the policy declared in the outline
plan or to any other sensible planning policy'. Lord Denning repeated his formula in the
Pyx Granite case[4], adding, with a reference to the *Wednesbury* case[1], that 'they [ie the local
planning authority] must produce a result which does not offend against common
sense'. Lord Jenkins[6] quoted Lord Denning's formulation in the *Pyx Granite* case[4] with
d approval.

Fawcett's case[3] renders it unnecessary to cite further authority, though there is plenty
in the books, to establish the three tests. They have been recognised and adopted by the
courts and this House.

The small area of doubt which remains is whether a condition for the removal of
existing buildings can ever satisfy the tests if the permitted development is limited to a
e change of use. The doubt is whether in such a case the condition could *ever* be said fairly
and reasonably to relate to the permitted development. Indeed, the Court of Appeal has
interpreted the Secretary of State's decision as based on the view that in law no such
condition can be imposed on a 'change of use permission'. Browne LJ[7] put their view of
the Secretary of State's decision succinctly: '. . . it is a holding of law that such a condition
can *never* be valid' (my emphasis).

f My Lords, if the Secretary of State really did base his decision on this view of the law,
I would agree with the Court of Appeal that he erred in law. The point is not covered by
any clear authority. But I would reject such a view of the law as being wrong in
principle. First, the acceptance of an inflexible rule would, so far as it extends, preclude
the application in change of use cases of the three recognised tests of validity. There
would be substituted a rule of thumb for the exercise of the Secretary of State's judgment
g on the facts of the appeal.

Secondly, so various are the circumstances and interests affected by a planning
permission that I would think it wrong, in the absence of an express statutory
prohibition, to assert that, as a matter of law, a condition requiring the removal of
buildings already in existence can never fairly or reasonably relate to a permission
limited to a change of use. And the 1971 Act contains no express prohibition, for s 29(1)
h leaves the imposition of conditions to the discretion of the local planning authority (and
to the Secretary of State on appeal). The validity of a condition must, therefore, depend
in all cases on the application of the three tests to the particular facts. If the permitted

---

j 1   [1947] 2 All ER 680, [1948] 1 KB 223
2   [1958] 1 All ER 625, [1958] 1 QB 554
3   [1960] 3 All ER 503, [1961] AC 636
4   [1958] 1 All ER 625 at 633, [1958] 1 QB 554 at 572
5   [1960] 3 All ER 503 at 506, 507, [1961] AC 636 at 660, 662
6   [1960] 3 All ER 503 at 522, [1961] AC 636 at 685
7   [1979] 1 All ER 243 at 253, [1978] 1 WLR 1241 at 1253

change of use is unlimited in time, it may well be fair and reasonable to require the
removal of some existing buildings as a condition of the permission. But, if the   *a*
permitted change of use should be for a limited period, the reasonableness of the
condition may be more difficult to establish. In either case, the planning history, the
situation of the land, the circumstances of all those interested in the land and the
existence of other statutory powers to achieve the same planning purpose would be
relevant considerations.

In his decision letter the Secretary of State gave the following reasons for holding the   *b*
condition invalid. He said, in para 8:

> 'It is considered however in the circumstances of this case where planning
> permission was sought merely for a change of use of existing substantial buildings,
> that a condition requiring the removal of those buildings after the expiration of a
> specified number of years was not sufficiently related to the change of use in respect   *c*
> of which the planning permission was granted and was unreasonable. It is therefore
> concluded that the condition was invalid.'

These words do not suggest to me that the Secretary of State committed himself to the
view of the law which the Court of Appeal has attributed to him. He noted that
permission was sought 'merely for a change of use of existing substantial buildings'; he   *d*
considered that the removal condition was 'not sufficiently related to the change of use
and was unreasonable. With the greatest respect, the Court of Appeal has misinterpreted
the Secretary of State's reasons. He did not hold that a condition for removal of buildings
attached to a 'change of use permission' could never be valid. He held that in the
circumstances of this case the condition was not sufficiently related to the permitted
change of use. The condition certainly related to the development plan and to planning   *e*
considerations and so satisfied the first test. But did it satisfy the second test? Was it
fairly and reasonably related to the permitted development, ie a temporary change of
use? This was for the Secretary of State in the light of all the circumstances to decide; and
he decided it. I would comment only that the Secretary of State, being the ultimate
authority on planning questions arising in the enforcement of planning control, is the   *f*
appropriate authority to determine whether a condition 'sufficiently', ie fairly and
reasonably, relates to the permitted development.

The Court of Appeal was led into error by their belief that the Secretary of State based
his conclusion on a statement to be found in the Ministry of Housing and Local
Government Circular 5/68[1]. Lord Denning MR put it thus[2]:

> 'The present view of the ministry is contained in a circular which was issued in   *g*
> 1968 and is numbered 5/68. It is to the effect that, when an applicant applies for
> permission to *change the use of an existing building*, the local planning authority, when
> granting permission, can impose a condition limiting the period of time during
> which the building may be so used: but cannot impose a condition requiring the
> building to be *removed* at the end of that time. The crucial sentence in the circular
> is this: "A condition requiring the removal of an existing building, whether on the   *h*
> application site or not, will only be reasonable if the need for that removal springs
> directly from the fact that a new building is to be erected."' (Lord Denning's
> emphasis.)

I agree that the circular has no legal effect and that, if in the sentence quoted it purports
to lay down a rule of law, it is wrong. But how can it be said, as Lord Denning MR said[2],   *j*
that this sentence in the circular represents 'the present view of the ministry' on the

---

1 The Use of Conditions in Planning Permissions (circular 5/68 dated 6th February 1968)
2 [1979] 1 All ER 243 at 248, [1978] 1 WLR 1241 at 1247

law? The answer has to be, only if the Secretary of State's letter of decision is to be read
a as saying so. But, my Lords, it says nothing of the sort.

I conclude, therefore, that the Secretary of State made no error of law. That being so,
his view, that a condition requiring the removal of existing substantial buildings was not
sufficiently related to the temporary change of use for which permission was granted in
this case, is unappealable: see s 246 of the 1971 Act.

My Lords, for all these reasons I would allow the appeals. I agree with the order for
b costs proposed by my noble and learned friend Viscount Dilhorne.

LORD LANE. My Lords, Royal Air Force Station Membury was a wartime airfield
built on requisitioned farming land. There were, apart from the usual concrete runways,
perimeter tracks, hardstandings and so on, and two hangars in which repair and
maintenance of aircraft could be carried out. The last aeroplane left Membury in about
c 1947. The hangars have since then had a chequered history. They are now (albeit
functionally useful) an eyesore in otherwise pleasant countryside and, if aesthetic
considerations were the only criterion, ought to be removed. The local planning
authority (now Newbury District Council) contend that that is also the position in law,
and the Court of Appeal have upheld that contention. They have decided that the
present owners, the International Synthetic Rubber Co Ltd ('ISR'), are in law obliged to
d remove the hangars.

The history of the site, so far as it is known and material, is as follows. From 1947 to
1953 the hangars were used as a food storage depot by the Ministry of Agriculture,
Fisheries and Food. For brief periods in 1953 the United States Air Force and in 1954 the
Royal Air Force used the airfield for purposes which are not known. From 1955 to 1959
the Home Office stored civil defence vehicles, fire-pumps and suchlike, in the hangars.
e In 1959 planning permission was given for the use of the hangars for storage of
agricultural products, subject to the condition that the hangars should be removed by a
date later extended to 31st December 1970. In May 1962 permission was granted to ISR
as follows: 'Use of two hangars at Membury Airfield as warehouses'. That was qualified
by two conditions—

f   '(1) The buildings shall be removed at the expiration of the period ending
December 31st, 1972. (2) The use shall be confined to storage and no materials
shall be stored which give rise to offence by reason of smell.'

For this reason: '(1) To accord with the local planning authority's policy regarding
industrial development in rural areas. (2) To safeguard the amenities of the area.'

The freehold title of the site was vested in the Crown until 1961. On 30th November
g 1961 the site was sold to the former owner and then leased back to the Crown for a period
of 40 years. In July 1962 (ie after receipt of the permission) the lease was assigned and
the hangars were sold to ISR. The terms of the particulars of sale imply, surprisingly,
that the hangars were being treated as chattels, distinct from the realty. Nothing now
turns on that point because the parties are all agreed that the hangars were and are, as one
would expect, part of the realty.

h   Since then ISR has used the hangars continuously for the storage of synthetic rubber.
In November 1970 they applied for a postponement of the removal date to 2002. That
was refused. By 31st December 1972 ISR had taken no steps to comply with the
condition by removing the hangars. In November 1973, therefore, the local authority
served an enforcement notice. ISR appealed under s 88 of the Town and Country
Planning Act 1971. An inquiry was held in January 1975. The Secretary of State's
j decision letter was published in July of that year. He allowed the appeal on the grounds
that the condition imposed by the local authority was ultra vires and void. He further
decided that the condition could not properly be severed from the permission and that
the planning permission as a whole was void. If this conclusion is right, there is nothing
at present to stop ISR continuing to use the hangars as warehouses. This is because they
started to use them as warehouses before 1963, and s 87(1) of the 1971 Act provides them

in these circumstances with immunity. The Secretary of State's view of the matter was
upheld by the Divisional Court. The Court of Appeal, however, held that the condition *a*
was not ultra vires, that the enforcement notice was lawful and should be obeyed.

The issues are these. First, was any planning permission necessary in 1962, that is, was
there an existing use which absolved ISR from the need for permission to use the hangars
as warehouses? Secondly, if such was the case, are ISR debarred from asserting that that
is so? This has been referred to as the 'blowing hot and cold point'. Thirdly, was the
condition requiring the removal of the hangars outside the proper powers of the local *b*
planning authority and therefore void? If the first two questions are decided in favour
of the Secretary of State and ISR, the third, although remaining important, would not
affect the outcome whichever way it was decided.

Existing use

The use which ISR assert was sufficient to render planning permission unnecessary in *c*
1962 was the Home Office's storage of civil defence vehicles from 1955 to 1959. That is
the basis on which the case has been fought throughout.

The Town and Country Planning (Use Classes) Order 1950[1] provides by reg 3(1) as
follows:

> 'Where a building . . . is used for a purpose of any class specified in the Schedule
> to this Order, the use of such building . . . for any other purpose of the same class *d*
> shall not be deemed for the purposes of the Act to involve development of the land.'

Class X of the schedule is 'Use as a wholesale warehouse or repository for any purpose.'

The present use is undoubtedly as a wholesale warehouse. If the previous use was as
a 'repository for any purpose', it follows that no permission was necessary because
permission is only required for development, and if the change was only from one class *e*
X use to another there was no development.

All those who have hitherto considered the matter have come to the conclusion that
the use by the Home Office as a store for civil defence vehicles was not use as a
'repository'. That being so, one naturally hesitates to differ, but I fear I must. The first
meaning of the word given in the Oxford English Dictionary is 'A vessel, receptacle,
chamber, etc. in which things are, or may be placed, deposited or stored'. The hangars *f*
fell plainly within this definition. The Court of Appeal held that a repository means 'a
place where goods are stored away to be kept for the sake of keeping them safe, as part
of a storage business'. If those last six words properly form part of the definition then the
Home Office use did not constitute the building a repository. But are those words
justified? Their origin is probably to be found in a judgment of Havers J in *Horwitz v
Rowson*[2]: '"Repository", I think, means a building wherein goods are kept or stored, and *g*
I think that the keeping or storing must be in the course of a trade or business.' No
reasons are given for this conclusion. The same view was expressed (obiter) by Lord
Denning MR in *G Percy Trentham Ltd v Gloucestershire County Council*[3] and reiterated by
him in the present case. As to the other point of view, exemplified by the Oxford
English Dictionary, Lord Denning MR said[4]:

> 'The one answer I can give to this argument is that it is a matter of impression, *h*
> depending on the meaning one gives to the word "repository" in one's own
> vocabulary. My opinion is that no one conversant with the English language would
> dream of calling these hangars a "repository" when filled with fire-pumps or
> synthetic rubber.'

No doubt there are few people, however, conversant with the English language, who *j*
would use the word 'repository' at all. The question is: what does it mean in the 1950

1   SI 1960 No 1131
2   [1960] 2 All ER 881 at 886, [1960] 1 WLR 803 at 810
3   [1966] 1 All ER 701 at 703, [1966] 1 WLR 506 at 512
4   [1979] 1 All ER 243 at 249–250, [1978] 1 WLR 1241 at 1249–1250

order? The word 'store' might perhaps have been employed, but that would have led to
a confusion because the word is now commonly used to mean retail shop (eg 'village
store'). To my mind 'repository' simply means a storage place. If there were any real
doubt about the matter it would, I think, be resolved by the words which follow, namely
'for any purpose'. It is difficult to see how those words can possibly mean 'for any
purpose provided it is a business purpose'. That is what the contention of the local
planning authority entails. In my opinion ISR had an existing use right under class X
b and no planning permission was necessary.

Blowing hot and cold

The local authority contends further that even if the use made of the hangars by the
Home Office fell within class X of the 1960 order, nevertheless it is not open to ISR to rely
on that existing use by reason of their applying for, receiving and using the planning
c permission of May 1962. In short they cannot now assert that no planning permission
was necessary in the face of their 1962 actions.

This contention has been put in a number of different ways. Lord Denning MR put
it thus[1]:

> *d* 'The truth is that, back in 1962, they had two inconsistent courses open to them.
> One was to apply for a grant of planning permission; the other was to rely on any
> existing use rights that might be attached to the site. Once they opted for planning
> permission, and accepted it without objection, they had made their bed and must
> lie on it. No doubt they did not know of the past history, but that was only because
> they did not choose to rely on it. They should not be allowed to bring it up again
> now.'

e Lawton LJ found it unnecessary to decide the point. Browne LJ felt unable to agree
with the dictum of Lord Denning MR on this aspect of the case, except in so far as it
applies to circumstances where a new planning unit has been created. Nor does counsel
for the local planning authority seek to argue that the doctrine is of any more than
narrow application. He contends, on the strength primarily of the decisions in *Prossor
f v Minister of Housing and Local Government*[2] and *Leighton and Newman Car Sales Ltd v
Secretary of State for the Environment*[3], that where planning permission is 'sought, granted
and implemented' (as he puts it) the planning history starts afresh and any previous
existing use must be ignored. Alternatively the planning history starts afresh where 'the
acceptance and implementation' of the planning permission is inconsistent with reliance
on earlier existing right. It is inconsistent here, because the permission together with the
g condition as to removal of the hangars cannot live with the existing use right. In
Prossor's case[2] the local planning authority granted permission for the rebuilding of a
petrol station with a condition prohibiting any retail sales other than of motor
accessories. The appellant nevertheless displayed secondhand motor cars on the site. An
enforcement notice was served but the appellant claimed that the site had existing use
rights for the sale of secondhand cars. The Minister upheld the enforcement notice. On
h appeal to the Divisional Court Lord Parker CJ[4] had this to say:

> '... assuming that there was at all material times prior to April, 1964, an existing
> use right running on this land for the display and sale of motor cars, yet by adopting
> the permission granted in April, 1964, the appellant's predecessor, as it seems to me,
> gave up any possible existing use rights in that regard which he may have had. The
> *j* planning history of this site ... seems to me to begin afresh on April 4, 1964, with

1   [1979] 1 All ER 243 at 250, [1978] 1 WLR 1241 at 1250–1251
2   (1968) 67 LGR 109
3   (1976) 32 P & CR 1
4   67 LGR 109 at 113

the grant of this permission, a permission which was taken up and used, and the sole
question here is: has there been a breach of that condition?'   *a*

The facts in *Leighton and Newman Car Sales Ltd v Secretary of State for the Environment*[1]
were very similar to those in *Prossor's case*[2]. Browne LJ in delivering the judgment of
the court said[3]:

> '[Counsel for the appellants] made some criticism of *Prossor v. Minister of Housing* *b*
> *and Local Government*[2] . . . but . . . there is nothing to throw any doubt on the actual
> decision in that case, which was that where (as in the present case) there has been an
> application for a new planning permission and a grant of permission subject to an
> express condition prohibiting a previous established use, and the new permission
> has been acted on, the previous use is extinguished.'
>
> *c*

Taken out of context, those words seem to widen the scope of *Prossor's case*[2]. They
must, however, be read against the facts of the case which show that this was an extensive
development involving not only the original site but the addition of two adjoining sites
and the creation of access to the highway from the two new sites. It was, in short, the
classic *Prossor*[2] situation of a new planning unit being born.

The other cases relied on by counsel for the local planning authority all tell the same *d*
story. *Gray v Minister of Housing and Local Government*[4] was another rebuilding case.
Petticoat Lane Rentals Ltd v Secretary of State for the Environment[5] concerned planning
permission to erect a building on an area of open land, a cleared bomb-site. Widgery LJ
in the course of his judgment in the Divisional Court said[6]:

> 'For my part I also think that it [sc *Prossor's case*[2]] was entirely correctly decided, *e*
> but I think that in extending and applying it we should tread warily and allow our
> experience to guide us as that experience is obtained . . . but I am quite confident
> that the principle of *Prosser's case*[2] can be applied where, as here, one has a clear
> area of land subsequently developed by the erection of a building over the whole of
> that land. Where that happens . . . one gets in my judgment an entirely new
> planning unit created by the building. The land as such is merged in that new *f*
> building and a new planning unit with no planning history is achieved.'

Those words seem to me to express precisely and accurately the concept underlying
Prossor's case[2]. The holder of planning permission will not be allowed to rely on any
existing use rights if the effect of the permission when acted on has been to bring one
phase of the planning history of the site to an end and to start a new one. It may not *g*
always be as easy as it was in the *Petticoat Lane Rentals case*[5] to say whether that has
happened. There will no doubt be borderline cases difficult to decide, but that does not
affect the principle. We were asked by counsel for the Secretary of State to say that the
principle can only apply where the permission granted is to build or rebuild or the like
and can never apply to cases where the permission is simply to change the use. I do not
consider that any such limitation would be proper. It is not the reason for the break in *h*
planning history which is important. It is the existence of the break itself, whatever the
reasons for it may have been. No doubt it will usually be a case of permission to build
which will attract the doctrine, but I myself would not altogether rule out the possibility

j

1   (1976) 32 P & CR 1
2   (1968) 67 LGR 109
3   (1976) 32 P & CR 1 at 10
4   (1969) 68 LGR 15
5   [1971] 2 All ER 793, [1971] 1 WLR 1112
6   [1971] 2 All ER 793 at 796, [1971] 1 WLR 1112 at 1117

that in some circumstances the permitted change of use might be so radical as to fulfil the

a criteria of *Prossor's* case[1].

In the present case there is no such break in the history. The change of use from repository to wholesale warehouse could not by any stretch of the imagination be said to have started a new planning history or created a new planning unit. Indeed no one has so contended. ISR succeed on this point.

b *Was the condition void?*

The Town and Country Planning Act 1971 provides:

> '29.—(1) . . . where an application is made to a local planning authority for planning permission, that authority, in dealing with the application, shall have regard to the provisions of the development plan . . . and to any other material considerations and—(*a*) . . . may grant planning permission, either unconditionally
>
> *c* or subject to such conditions as they think fit . . .
>
> '30.—(1) Without prejudice to the generality of section 29(1) . . . conditions may be imposed on the grant of planning permission thereunder . . . (*b*) for requiring the removal of any buildings or works authorised by the permission, or the discontinuance of any use of land so authorised, at the end of a specified period
>
> . . .'

d

Despite the breadth of the words 'subject to such conditions as they think fit', subsequent decisions have shown that to come within the ambit of the 1971 Act and therefore to be intra vires and valid a condition must fulfil the following three conditions: (1) it must be imposed for a planning purpose; (2) it must fairly and reasonably relate to the development for which permission is being given; (3) it must be reasonable, that is

e to say, it must be a condition which a reasonable local authority properly advised might impose.

The first test arises directly from the wording of the material sections of the 1971 Act. The second test comes from the same sections as interpreted by Lord Denning in *Pyx Granite Co Ltd v Ministry of Housing and Local Government*[2] and approved in this House by Lord Keith of Avonholm and Lord Jenkins in *Fawcett Properties Ltd v Buckingham*

f *County Council*[3] and by Lord Reid and Lord Guest in *Chertsey Urban District Council v Mixnam's Properties Ltd*[4]. The third test is probably derived from *Associated Provincial Picture Houses Ltd v Wednesbury Corpn*[5], and ensures that the Secretary of State, if he is asked to review the actions of a local planning authority, may, even if tests (1) and (2) are quite satisfied, nevertheless allow an appeal on much broader grounds, if the effect of the condition would be to impose an obviously unreasonable burden on the appellant.

g Decisions of the local planning authority should not, however, lightly be set aside on this ground. As Lord Guest said in *Chertsey Urban District Council v Mixnam's Properties Ltd*[6]:

> 'There should, however, in my view be a benevolent interpretation given to the discretion exercised by a public representative body such as the appellants in carrying out the functions entrusted to them by Parliament. Courts should not be
>
> *h* astute to find that they have acted outside the scope of their powers.'

In the present case there is no doubt that the removal of these hangars by 1972 together with their use meantime as a wholesale warehouse was the fulfilment of a planning purpose. The idea was in accordance with the development plan and amply fulfilled the first test.

j 1 (1968) 67 LGR 109
2 [1958] 1 All ER 625, [1958] 1 QB 554
3 [1960] 3 All ER 503, [1961] AC 636
4 [1964] 2 All ER 627, [1965] AC 735
5 [1947] 2 All ER 680, [1948] 1 KB 223
6 [1964] 2 All ER 627 at 637, [1965] AC 735 at 760–761

It is on the second test, whether one treats it as part of test (3) (as counsel for the local planning authority suggests one should) or as a matter to be considered separately, that difficulty arises. The Court of Appeal has, unlike the Divisional Court, found that the obligation to demolish the hangars after ten years did truly relate to the permitted development. Since the permitted development consisted not in permission to build but in a change of use of the hangar to the purpose of a warehouse, it is at first sight hard to see how the conclusions of the Divisional Court can be faulted. As Robert Goff J said in his judgment:

'I cannot see how a condition that the buildings be removed related to the permitted development in the present case, which was the use of the building as a warehouse for synthetic rubber.'

The Court of Appeal took the view that the application by ISR should be interpreted as an application for temporary use of the two hangars as warehouses, and that the permission should be read as permission for temporary use. So interpreted, it is said, a condition which specified a period of temporary use and a condition which required removal of the hangars at the end of that period both related to the permitted development. Assuming that those glosses on both the application and the permission are legitimate, it still seems to me, with respect to the reasoning of the Court of Appeal, that a condition requiring the hangars to be demolished cannot fairly be said to relate to the use of the hangars as warehouses. The fact that the use is to be temporary does not bring the requirement to demolish into any closer relationship with the permitted development. In my opinion the Secretary of State arrived at the correct conclusion, namely that the condition did not relate to the permitted development, was void and therefore failed, taking with it the permission to which it was annexed.

It is not altogether clear on what precise basis the Secretary of State reached this decision. We have been shown a circular emanating from the Ministry in 1968[1] containing certain guidelines which it suggests should be observed by local planning authorities when considering applications for planning permission. Paragraph 9 of that document states as follows:

'*Is the condition relevant to the development to be permitted?* Unless it can be shown that the requirements of the condition are directly related to the development to be permitted, the condition is probably *ultra vires* . . . The condition must be expedient having regard to the development which is being permitted; and where the condition requires the carrying out of works, or regulates the use of land, its requirements must be connected with the development permitted on the land which forms the subject of the planning application.'

So far there can be no criticism. These suggestions are simply an amplification of the second test. At the end of para 9, however, come the following words:

'A condition requiring the removal of an existing building, whether on the application site or not, will only be reasonable if the need for that removal springs directly from the fact that a new building is to be erected.'

That is too sweeping a proposition. No doubt a condition requiring the removal of a building will usually relate to the permission only if the permission has been to erect a new building. There may however be exceptional cases, and some possibilities were suggested in argument, where a requirement to remove could properly be said to relate to a mere permission to change the use. In short the test is: does the condition fairly relate to the permission? and not: does the condition spring directly from the fact that a new building is to be erected? It is not clear which test the Secretary of State applied here. The decision at which he arrived was correct whichever test he applied.

---

1 The Use of Conditions in Planning Permissions (Ministry of Housing and Local Government circular 5/68 dated 6th February 1968)

a   Since the decision was correct, the provisions of RSC Ord 94, r 12(5) do not require this House to remit the matter to the Secretary of State for rehearing.

I would allow the appeal and restore the order of the Secretary of State. I agree with the order for costs proposed by my noble and learned friend Viscount Dilhorne.

Appeal allowed.

b   Solicitors: *Treasury Solicitor*; *Herbert Smith & Co* (for ISR); *Sharpe Pritchard & Co* (for the local planning authority).

                                               Mary Rose Plummer   Barrister.

c

Hanlon v Law Society

COURT OF APPEAL, CIVIL DIVISION

LORD DENNING MR, SIR JOHN ARNOLD P AND DONALDSON LJ

2nd, 5th NOVEMBER, 4th DECEMBER 1979

d

Legal aid – Certificate – Scope of certificate – Matrimonial cause – Certificate to prosecute suit for divorce, to continue property proceedings and to apply for an injunction – Single contribution assessed 'in respect of proceedings' – Proceedings – Whether certificate covering ancillary proceedings regardless of prolongation or extent – Legal Aid Act 1974, s 9(6).

e   *Legal aid – Charge on property recovered for deficiency of costs – Property recovered or preserved in proceedings – Recovered or preserved – Property adjustment order in matrimonial proceedings – Matrimonial home ordered to be transferred to wife absolutely – Wife already having equitable interest in home because of her contribution to marriage – Whether matrimonial home 'recovered or preserved' by wife – Legal Aid Act 1974, s 9(6) – Legal Aid (General) Regulations 1971 (SI 1971 No 62, as amended by SI 1976 No 628), reg 18(10)(c).*

f

Legal aid – Charge on property recovered for deficiency of costs – Enforcement of charge – Discretion of Law Society – Matrimonial home occupied by wife and children of family – Court likely to postpone order for possession if charge sought to be enforced – Wife wishing to sell matrimonial home and buy smaller house – Whether Law Society bound to enforce charge – Whether Law Society having discretion to postpone enforcement – Whether charge able to be

g   *transferred to substitute home – Legal Aid Act 1974, s 9(6) – Legal Aid (General) Regulations 1971 (SI 1971 No 62, as amended by SI 1976 No 628), regs 18(10)(c), 19(2).*

The husband and wife were married in 1957. In 1963 a matrimonial home was purchased in the husband's name with a mortgage. The parties contributed equally in money and work to the family and the marriage. In 1971 the wife was granted an

h   emergency legal aid certificate to prosecute a suit for divorce and to apply for an injunction restraining the husband from entering the matrimonial home or otherwise molesting her. The certificate was extended from time to time until 1972 when a full certificate was granted 'to prosecute a suit for divorce and to continue proceedings under [s 17 of the Married Women's Property Act 1882] and to apply for an injunction'. The wife was required to make a contribution of £115 towards the costs of the proceedings.

j   She was granted a decree of divorce, was given custody of the two daughters of the marriage, and a property adjustment order was made under s 24 of the Matrimonial Causes Act 1973 requiring the husband to transfer the matrimonial home, the equity in which was worth about £10,000, to the wife absolutely. The wife incurred costs totalling £8,025, made up of £925 for the main suit and applications for an injunction, £1,150 for applications for custody and access, and £5,950 in respect of the property adjustment order. The costs, which were not recoverable from the husband because he also was legally aided, fell to be recovered from the legal aid fund administered by the Law *a* Society. When the certificates were originally granted no charge on a matrimonial home could arise in favour of the legal aid fund, but by the time the property adjustment order had been made, and by virtue of s 9(6)*ᵃ* of the Legal Aid Act 1974 and reg 18(10)*ᵇ* of the Legal Aid (General) Regulations 1971, as amended in 1976, if a legally aided person's contribution was less than the net liability of the legal aid fund on his account, a sum equal to the deficiency became a first charge for the benefit of the fund on any property *b* 'recovered or preserved for him in the proceedings' other than the first £2,500 of the value of property recovered or preserved by virtue of an order made under s 24 of the 1973 Act. The wife wished to sell the matrimonial home and buy a smaller house in which she and the daughters could live. She applied to the court to ascertain whether the legal aid fund was entitled to a charge on the matrimonial home and, if it was, to what extent and whether there was a discretion as to its enforcement. The judge held that the *c* fund was entitled to a charge for £8,025 attaching to the matrimonial home subject to both the existing mortgage and the first £2,500 of the home's value, which was exempt. The wife appealed, contending that the legal aid certificate related to three separate proceedings, viz the main suit, the custody and access proceedings, and the proceedings for the property adjustment order, and that, if the charge did exist, it existed only in relation to the costs involved in the property adjustment proceedings. The *d* question also arose whether property was 'recovered or preserved' for a party when a property adjustment order was made.

Held – (i) The wife's legal aid certificate covered not only the suit for divorce itself but also the ancillary proceedings that arose out of it, no matter how prolonged or extensive they were, and so covered the cost of the proceedings for custody and access and for the transfer of the matrimonial home, because (per Lord Denning MR) that was the well- *e* established practice and was the plain meaning of the wide form of the certificate, and (per Sir John Arnold P and Donaldson LJ) the words 'the proceedings' in s 9(6) of the 1974 Act meant any proceedings in respect of which a single contribution to the legal aid fund had been assessed, and a single contribution had been levied in relation to the totality of the wife's proceedings. It followed that the deficiency referred to in s 9(6) was that by which the wife's contribution was less than the net liability of the legal aid fund incurred *f* on her account in those proceedings, that a sum equal to that deficiency was charged on any property recovered or preserved for her in those proceedings, and that the whole of the cost, less the wife's contribution of £115, was the subject of the charge (see p 770 *c d*, p 774 *b* to *f* and p 780 *c d*, post).

(ii) (Donaldson LJ dissenting) For the purposes of reg 18(10) of the 1971 regulations the wife had 'recovered or preserved' the matrimonial home by virtue of the property *g* adjustment order made under s 24 of the 1973 Act, because (per Lord Denning MR, Sir John Arnold P dissenting) either she had 'recovered' the whole of the house since she had obtained the full legal and beneficial title in it whereas before she had only had an uncertain equitable share in it, or, alternatively, she had not only 'recovered' the husband's share but had also 'preserved' her own share because she had secured it with the protection of the full legal title, or because (per Sir John Arnold P) in transferring *h* property from one party to another pursuant to a property adjustment order under s 24(1)(*a*) of the 1973 Act the other party could accurately be said to have 'recovered' the property thus ordered to be transferred. It followed that (Donaldson LJ concurring if, contrary to his view, the matrimonial home had been 'recovered or preserved') the whole

a   Section 9(6) is set out at p 769 *h*, post   *j*
b   Regulation 18(10), so far as material, provides: 'The provisions of this regulation shall not apply to
     . . . (*c*) the first £2,500 of any money, or the value of any property, recovered or preserved by virtue
     of—(i) an order made, or deemed to be made, under the provisions of section . . . 24 . . . of the
     Matrimonial Causes Act 1973 . . . and such payments, money or property shall not be the subject
     of a charge within the terms of section 9(6) of the Legal Aid Act 1974.'

a of the matrimonial home other than the first £2,500 of its value was subject to the charge (see p 770 *j* to p 771 *a d e* and *h*, p 772 *a*, p 774 *a* and *f* to *j* and p 781 *h* to p 782 *a*, post); *Till v Till* [1974] 1 All ER 1096 considered.

b (iii) Although the Law Society had an element of choice in the enforcement of the charge it was restricted to adopting that course which was most beneficial to the legal aid fund rather than that which was most beneficial to the chargee, unless that coincided with the best interests of the fund. Since, on an application for the enforcement of a charge by an order for possession of a matrimonial home occupied by a wife who was looking after children, the court usually sought to secure a roof over her head and could well postpone any order for possession, and since it was contrary to the interest of the fund to make an application to the court which was likely to fail, it followed that the Law Society, in carrying out its duty to act reasonably in the interests not of the community as a whole nor of the assisted person as an individual but of the legal aid fund itself, had *c* a discretion to postpone the enforcement of its charge in appropriate cases. However (Lord Denning MR dissenting), it could not be said that the substitution of a security was the enforcement of the charge within reg 19(2)*c* of the 1971 regulations and the Law Society had no discretion under that regulation to make such a substitution. It followed (Donaldson LJ dissenting) that the appeal would be dismissed (see p 773 *e f*, p 774 *a*, p 779 *c* to *j* and p 782, post).

d **Notes**

For charges for the benefit of the legal aid fund on property recovered or preserved, see 30 Halsbury's Laws (3rd Edn) 506–507, paras 940–941.

For financial provision and property adjustment orders on divorce and the matters to which the court must have regard, see 13 Halsbury's Laws (4th Edn) paras 1052–1053, 1060.

e For the Legal Aid Act 1974, s 9, see 44 Halsbury's Statutes (3rd Edn) 1048.

For the Legal Aid (General) Regulations 1971, reg 18, see 5 Halsbury's Statutory Instruments (Third Reissue) 331 and Supplement thereto.

Cases referred to in judgments

Catlow v Catlow (1877) 2 CPD 362, 43 Digest (Repl) 323, *3374.*

f Cooke v Head (No 2) [1974] 2 All ER 1124, [1974] 1 WLR 972, CA, Digest (Cont Vol D) 1008, *927a.*

Foxon v Gascoigne (1874) 9 Ch App 654, 43 LJ Ch 729, 31 LT 289, 43 Digest (Repl) 323, *3373.*

Gissing v Gissing [1970] 2 All ER 780, [1971] AC 886, [1970] 3 WLR 255, 21 P & CR 702, HL, 27(1) Digest (Reissue) 311, *2303.*

g Greer v Young (1883) 24 Ch D 545, 52 LJ Ch 915, 49 LT 224, CA, 43 Digest (Repl) 320, *3350.*

Hyde v White, White v Hyde [1933] P 105, [1933] All ER Rep 226, 149 LT 96, 102 LJP 71, 43 Digest (Repl) 325, *3393.*

Pelsall Coal and Iron Co v London and North Western Railway Co (No 3) (1892) 8 Ry & Can Tr Cas 146, 8 TLR 629, 43 Digest (Repl) 322, *3365.*

h Philippine, The (1867) LR 1 A & E 309, 16 LT 34, 2 Mar LC 476, 43 Digest (Repl) 322, *3366.*

Till v Till [1974] 1 All ER 1096, [1974] QB 558, [1974] 2 WLR 447, CA, Digest (Cont Vol D) 416, *6149a.*

Wachtel v Wachtel [1973] 1 All ER 829, [1973] Fam 72, [1973] 2 WLR 366, CA, Digest (Cont Vol D) 425, *6962Aa.*

j Wagg v Law Society [1957] 2 All ER 274, [1957] Ch 405, [1957] 3 WLR 20, 50 Digest (Repl) 488, *1709.*

Westacott v Bevan [1891] 1 QB 774, 60 LJQB 536, 65 LT 263, DC, 43 Digest (Repl) 324, *3380.*

---

c   Regulation 19(2) is set out at p 773 *b*, post

Western Bank Ltd v Schindler [1976] 2 All ER 393, [1977] Ch 1, [1976] 3 WLR 341, 32
    P & CR 352, CA.   *a*
Wimbourne v Fine [1952] 2 All ER 681, [1952] Ch 869, 43 Digest (Repl) 330, *3444*.

Cases also cited
Blatcher v Heaysman [1960] 2 All ER 721, [1960] 1 WLR 663, CA.
Cedar Holdings Ltd v Green [1979] 3 All ER 117, [1979] 3 WLR 31, CA.
Currie & Co v The Law Society [1976] 3 All ER 832, [1977] QB 990.   *b*
Fuld (deceased), Re [1967] 2 All ER 649, [1968] P 727.
Jessel v Jessel [1979] 3 All ER 645, [1979] 1 WLR 1148, CA.
Law Society v Rushman [1955] 2 All ER 544, [1955] 1 WLR 681, CA.
Loescher v Dean [1950] 2 All ER 124, [1950] Ch 491.
Pudephatt v Leith (No 2) [1916] 2 Ch 168, [1916–17] All ER Rep 624.
Williams & Glyn's Bank v Boland [1979] 2 All ER 697, [1979] 2 WLR 550, CA.   *c*

Interlocutory appeal
By an order dated 6th February 1976 Mr Registrar Kenworthy ordered that the wife,
Mary Isabella Hanlon, should make a lump sum payment of £5,000 to the husband,
Peter James Hanlon, within three months of the date of the order and that on such
payment the husband should transfer the matrimonial home, 106 Trinity Lane, *d*
Waltham Cross, Hertfordshire, to the wife subject to the existing mortgage charge, and
further ordered that the husband should make to the two daughters of the family, as
from 6th February, periodical payments at the rate of £6 a week for each child until they
respectively attained the age of 17 years or further order. The wife appealed and on 26th
April 1977 Rees J set aside the registrar's order and ordered that the matrimonial home
should be transferred forthwith into the joint names of the parties on trust for sale as *e*
tenants in common in equal shares and that the sale of the property should be postponed
until the youngest surviving child of the family attained the age of 17 years or until the
earlier remarriage of the wife or further order. He also increased the order for periodical
payments to the two daughters to £7 per week for each child. The Court of Appeal[1a]
(Stamp, Orr and Ormrod LJJ) on 17th October 1977 allowed an appeal by the wife and
varied the order of Rees J to provide that the husband should transfer the legal estate in *f*
the matrimonial home with all his equitable interest therein to the wife absolutely,
subject to the existing mortgage charge, and that the periodical payments to the
daughters should be reduced to the nominal sum of 5p per annum. Throughout the
proceedings both parties had been legally aided. The wife was granted an emergency
civil aid certificate on 28th July 1971 and a full certificate on 19th January 1972, and her
contribution was assessed at £115. The costs incurred by the legal aid fund on the wife's *g*
behalf amounted to £8,025, made up of £925 for the divorce suit and applications for
an injunction to restrain the husband from entering the matrimonial home or otherwise
molesting the wife, £1,150 for applications for custody and access, and £5,950 in respect
of the property adjustment order. On 26th October 1977 the Court of Appeal adjourned
the question of the imposition of the statutory charge to allow the Law Society to be
represented. On 3rd February 1978 the court refused a request by the wife to ante-date *h*
its order to the date of Mr Registrar Kenworthy's order. The wife wished to sell the
matrimonial home and obtain alternative accommodation for herself and the two
daughters of the marriage. The Law Society informed her that if the former matrimonial
home were sold the charge would have to be satisfied from the proceeds of sale since it
had no power to register the charge against a replacement home. On 8th May 1979 the
wife took out an originating summons against the legal aid fund in the name of the Law *j*
Society, challenging the existence or, alternatively, the amount of the charge. On 21st
June Reeve J declared that the Law Society were entitled to a charge of £8,025 in respect
of the costs incurred by the legal aid fund on account of the wife and that the charge

---

1a [1978] 2 All ER 889, [1978] 1 WLR 592

attached to the house, subject to the existing mortgage and the first £2,500 of the value
a of the wife's interest in the property. The wife appealed. The facts are set out in the
judgment of Lord Denning MR.

Joseph Jackson QC and *Nicholas Wall* for the wife.
Duncan Matheson for the Law Society.

b   *Cur adv vult*

4th December. The following judgments were read:

LORD DENNING MR. Costs loom large. They are often more important than the
issues in the litigation itself. Especially in cases between husband and wife, where both
c are legally aided, and the legal aid fund has a charge on the matrimonial home. Let me
recite the facts in this case.

Here is a couple whose marriage has unfortunately broken down. He is a police
officer. She is a community nursing sister. They were married in 1957, separated in
1971 and divorced in 1974. They have four children. Two sons who are out in the
d world. Two girls who are 15 and 13.

In 1963 they bought the matrimonial home in Waltham Cross, Hertfordshire. It was
taken in the husband's name. It is now worth about £14,000, with a mortgage of about
£3,600. So the equity is about £10,000. Both went out to work and contributed to the
outgoings. It is probable that, if the title were worked out, the wife would be entitled
beneficially to a considerable share in the equity in the house; but it was never
e investigated, and we cannot be sure about it.

If you forget about the costs for the moment, the courts have made an order which
looks fair enough. The husband has given up his title to the house and his share in it,
whatever it is. The house has been transferred to the wife, so that she is now the full
beneficial owner of it. But, in return for that undoubted benefit, she has to undertake
the responsibility for all the outgoings on the house, such as the mortgage instalments
f and the rates and repairs; and she has to maintain the children. The husband has lost his
share in the house, but he is not badly off. He is living rent-free in a flat provided by the
police authorities; and he is not contributing anything for the maintenance of the wife
and children.

Thus far the order of the courts seems fair enough. But now the legal aid fund have
come down on the wife. They say that they have a charge on the whole of the
matrimonial home (so as to recoup themselves for all the costs they have incurred on her
g behalf throughout) made up as follows:

(i)	divorce proceedings, including application for injunction	£925·00
(ii)	custody and access proceedings	£1,150·00
(iii)	transfer of property proceedings under ss 23 and 24 of the Matrimonial Causes Act 1973	£5,950·00
h

	£8,025·00

Under the regulations, the first £2,500 is not caught by the charge. So the priorities
j are: first, a sum of £3,600 outstanding on the mortgage; second, the wife's £2,500;
third, the charge of £8,025 to the legal aid fund. The house is only worth about
£10,000. So the charges will more than exhaust it. None of the charges can be realised
unless the house is sold.

The wife cannot afford to do the repairs on this house. So she would like to sell it and
get something smaller. But the legal aid fund say that, if it is sold, they will feel bound

to enforce their charge. They will require her to pay over the proceeds of sale to them
to meet their charge, less the £2,500. If that happened, it would mean that she would   *a*
have sold her house and have only the £2,500. She would not be able to buy another, or
to get alternative accommodation of any sort. She would be in a desperate plight. She
has applied to the court so as to ascertain whether the legal aid fund were entitled to a
charge at all, and, if so, to what extent, and whether they have a discretion as to its
enforcement.

b

Summary of the statutory provisions
   Ever since legal aid was introduced in 1949, the legal aid fund has been given a charge
on any property 'recovered or preserved' for the legally assisted person: see s 3(4) of the
Legal Aid and Advice Act 1949, now replaced by s 9(6) of the Legal Aid Act 1974.
   Before 1976. I will first consider the position before 1976. If the husband or wife got
an order in his or her favour under s 17 of the Married Women's Property Act 1882, it   *c*
was subject to the charge in favour of the legal aid fund: see reg 17(10) of the Legal Aid
(General) Regulations 1962.[1] But, if he or she got an order for a lump sum or for the
transfer to him or her of the matrimonial home under ss 2 and 4 of the Matrimonial
Proceedings and Property Act 1970 (now replaced by ss 23 and 24 of the Matrimonial
Causes Act 1973), it was *not* subject to the charge: see reg 18(10) of the Legal Aid
(General) Regulations 1971, as originally enacted[2]. The result was that after 1970 a   *d*
legally aided husband or wife always applied for a lump sum or a transfer of the
matrimonial home under those provisions. None applied for a beneficial share under
s 17 of the 1882 Act.
   After 1976. I will next consider the position after 1976. In 1976 there was an
amendment[3] made to the 1971 regulations which substituted a new reg 18(10). The
first £2,500 was exempt but the rest was made subject to the charge. This applied both   *e*
to lump sums and to matrimonial homes, but not to periodical payments. If the wife
was awarded a lump sum, the first £2,500 was exempt from the charge, but the rest
not. If she was awarded the matrimonial home, the first £2,500 of the value of any
property recovered or preserved was exempt, but the rest was not. It was subject to a
charge in favour of the legal aid fund.
   Transitional cases. There was a special provision to deal with transitional cases. They   *f*
were cases where the legal aid certificate was issued before the regulations were
amended. In such a case the regulations[4] expressly provided that the charge should not
apply to an order made before 1st August 1976, but that it did apply to orders made after
1st August 1976.

Application to the present case   *g*
   Both wife and husband have been legally aided. They were granted full certificates to
bring and defend divorce proceedings respectively. The wife's contribution was £115.
The husband's was £149·50. The certificates were granted in 1971 and 1972. At that
time there was no charge on the matrimonial home whatever in favour of the legal aid
fund. So they could go on with the divorce and the ancillaries that followed it, with no
expense over and above their contributions and with no risk of any charge on the   *h*
matrimonial home. Then in 1976 there was a complete change. The regulations were
amended so as to give the legal aid fund a charge for the costs on the matrimonial home.
I do not know whether the husband or wife knew what this meant; or whether it was
explained to them. But it was destined to have a most important impact on the
litigation.

j

----

1   SI 1962 No 148
2   SI 1971 No 62
3   Legal Aid (General) (Amendment No 2) Regulations 1976, SI 1976 No 628
4   SI 1971 No 62, reg 18(10)(*d*), as substituted by SI 1976 No 628, reg 2, and by SI 1977 No 1293,
    reg 7.

These are the principal facts. The matrimonial home was bought in 1963, and
a conveyed into the name of the husband alone. Both husband and wife went out to
work. I should imagine that the wife contributed to the outgoings and got a share in the
equity in the house, possibly one-half, perhaps more, but we cannot be sure.

In 1976 Mr Registrar Kenworthy ordered the wife to make to the husband a lump
sum payment of £5,000, and ordered that the house should be transferred into the sole
name of the wife on her paying that £5,000 to the husband. He ordered the husband to
b pay £6 a week for each of the two younger children. The wife accepted that decision for
ten months. She then found that she could not raise the £5,000, because there was
already a mortgage debt of £3,600 charged on the house; and it was only worth
£14,000. So she applied for leave to appeal out of time and was granted it. On 26th
April 1977 Rees J allowed the appeal. He ordered that the matrimonial home should be
transferred into the joint names of the husband and wife in equal shares on trust for sale,
c but the sale to be postponed until the younger child reached the age of 17. He also
increased the payments for the children to £7 a week each. The wife appealed to the
Court of Appeal. On 17th October 1977 the Court of Appeal[1] allowed the appeal. They
ordered the husband to transfer the matrimonial home to the wife absolutely, and
relieved the husband of any payment for the children, save for a nominal amount of 5p
per annum. Later on the wife applied to the Court of Appeal, asking that the order be
d backdated to 6th February 1976 (the date when Mr Registrar Kenworthy made his
order), because at that date there was no charge on lump sums or matrimonial homes.
But the Court of Appeal held that it could not properly ante-date its order so as to escape
the charge. The order stood as on 17th October 1977 (ie after 1st August 1976). So the
house was subject to the charge. The costs were £8,025. They would eat up the value
of the matrimonial home, save for £2,500 for the wife.
e   Now it must be noted that all those steps were taken by the wife on legal aid. The area
committee granted it to her without any further contribution. This grant was justified
by the results. She won all her appeals. And yet, if the legal aid fund are right, her
success will prove worthless to her. They will have a charge by which she can be
deprived of the very house for which she fought so long. She will have to pay all the costs
just as if she had not been legally aided at all.
f   In May 1979 the wife took out a summons against the legal aid fund (in the name of
the Law Society) challenging the existence of any charge on the home, or, alternatively,
the amount of it. On 21st June 1979 Reeve J declared that the Law Society was entitled
to a charge for the costs of £8,025 incurred by the wife, and that it attached to the whole
of the house, subject to (i) the existing mortgage to the building society and (ii) £2,500
for the wife.
g   She now appeals to this court.

Section 9(6) of the Legal Aid Act 1974
Ever since 1949 the relevant section has remained unaltered. It is now s 9(6) of the
1974 Act. It says:

h   'Except so far as regulations otherwise provide, any sums remaining unpaid on
account of a person's contribution to the legal aid fund in respect of any proceedings
and, if the total contribution is less than the net liability of that fund on his account,
a sum equal to the deficiency shall be a first charge for the benefit of the legal aid
fund on any property (wherever situate) which is recovered or preserved for him in
the proceedings.'

j *The proceedings*
Counsel for the wife submitted that there were here three separate proceedings,
namely (i) the divorce suit itself, (ii) the custody and access proceedings and (iii) the

---

1   *Hanlon v Hanlon* [1978] 2 All ER 889, [1978] 1 WLR 592

property proceedings: so that the charge on the home, he contended, would only be for
the costs incurred under head (iii), and not the costs under heads (i) and (ii).   *a*

I would have liked to have adopted this view, but I think it is not possible. The
opening words of s 9(6) show that we must look at the contribution made by the wife to
the legal aid fund. What was her contribution? And in respect of what proceedings?
For this we must turn to the legal aid certificate. It was granted on 11th February 1971—

> 'To Prosecute a Suit for Divorce and to continue proceedings under the Married
> Women's Property Act Section 17 and to apply for an injunction . . .   *b*
> 'Contribution to be paid. The Supplementary Benefits Commission have made
> the following determination Disposable Income £645 Disposable Capital
> £Nil   Maximum Contribution £115·00.'

That certificate does not say exactly what is covered by the words 'To Prosecute a Suit
for Divorce'. But we have been shown the notes for guidance issued by the Law Society,   *c*
and have been told the practice. It is quite plain that a certificate in that wide form
covers not only the suit for divorce itself, but also many of the ancillary proceedings that
may arise in or out of it, no matter how prolonged and how expensive they may be. It
covers all the costs of the proceedings for custody and access and of the proceedings for
transfer of the matrimonial home.

In view of that well-established practice, I feel that the wife's contribution of £115 was   *d*
made in respect of *all* the proceedings which were taken in the divorce suit, and that it
includes the three items of divorce, custody and access, and property. It follows that the
whole of these costs (less £115) are the subject of the charge.

'Recovered or preserved for him'   *e*

In this case everything depends on the true interpretation of those few words in the
statute, 'recovered or preserved for him'. They go back to the Solicitors Act 1860, s 28,
and have been interpreted in many cases since that time. All in different contexts. Now
we have to consider them in relation to a context about the matrimonial home. Before
I go further, I would like to mention a point which occurred to this court itself, but was   *f*
not taken by counsel. It was whether the words 'recovered or preserved' had any
application to a property adjustment order. In the Solicitors Acts those words were used
in relation to 'any suit, matter or proceeding'. They referred to a suit, matter or
proceeding in which one party claimed property or damages and the other party disputed
it. In that context the words were appropriate enough. If the plaintiff succeeded in
getting property or money, by a judgment or a settlement, it was 'recovered' through the   *g*
instrumentality of his solicitor. If the defendant successfully resisted the claim and
vindicated his title to property or money, it was 'preserved' by the instrumentality of his
solicitor.

But in the property adjustment order (under ss 23 and 24 of the Matrimonial Causes
Act 1973) we have a new concept altogether. The court takes the rights and obligations
of the parties all together, and puts the pieces into a mixed bag. Such pieces are the right   *h*
to occupy the matrimonial home or have a share in it, the obligation to maintain the wife
and children, and so forth. The court then takes out the pieces and hands them to the
two parties, some to one party and some to the other, so that each can provide for the
future with the pieces allotted to him or to her. The court hands them out without
paying any too nice a regard to their legal or equitable rights but simply according to
what is the fairest provision for the future, for mother and father and the children. We   *j*
have to consider whether, in such a distribution, the words 'property . . . recovered or
preserved' can properly be applied. Those words are intelligible enough when used in
connection with ordinary legal proceedings which determine legal rights and
obligations. They are difficult to apply to modern family transfers made to fit the future.

But, however difficult the application, I think it must be done. I say this because of the

wording of the amended reg 18(10) of the 1971 regulations[1]. It clearly assumes that,
a when a transfer is made in a property adjustment order, property is 'recovered or
preserved' just as in other proceedings in the courts of law. We also know that many
charges have been levied and enforced on matrimonial homes which have been
transferred under property adjustment orders. They come, I believe, now to well over
£1,000,000. It is too late now to suggest that it cannot be done.

So I turn to the task of applying the words to a property adjustment order. To simplify
b the argument, I propose to take a typical case in which the matrimonial home is legally
vested in the husband, but in which the wife has, by her contribution, acquired a
beneficial interest. It may often be a half-share; but sometimes it is more, and sometimes
less. Now let me assume that there is a dispute whether she is entitled to any share at all,
or, if she is, what her share is. Or, at any rate, let me assume that they have not agreed
on what her share is. In such a case, when the court comes to make a property
c adjustment order under s 24 of the 1973 Act, let me assume that it does what is often
done: it orders the husband to transfer the whole interest in the house, legal and
equitable, to the wife, and in return he is relieved of making periodic payments to her,
or, they are much reduced: see the instances given in *Wachtel v Wachtel*[2].

In such a case I think it can properly be said that the wife has 'recovered' the whole of
the house: because she has got the full legal and beneficial title in it, whereas previously
d she had only an uncertain equitable share in it. Alternatively, if it be said that she has
'recovered' her husband's share, then I would say that she has also 'preserved' her own
share: because she has secured her share by shielding it with the protection of the full
legal title. It has been secured to her just as much as the plaintiff's share was secured in
Hyde v White[3]. So together she has 'recovered or preserved' the whole house for herself;
and it is subject to the legal charge: see *Till v Till*[4].
e It was contended, however, that in such a case she has only 'recovered' her husband's
share; and that she has not 'preserved' her own share because it was hers all the time. So
the legal aid fund have only a charge on the husband's share. I was much attracted by
this argument at one time. But I do not think it can stand. For this reason: her
husband's share is and always was uncertain. It has never been ascertained by the court
or by agreement. So there can never be a legal charge on it. You cannot have a legal
f charge on any equitable share in a house when that share is unascertained and
unascertainable. I see no practical method of ascertaining the husband's previous share
after the house has been transferred to the wife.

In order to avoid this difficulty, counsel for the wife said that it did not apply in this
particular case. He submitted that, before this adjustment order was made, it was
accepted by all concerned that the husband and wife had each a half-share in the house.
g I do not think that is correct. It was negatived by Ormrod LJ in the Court of Appeal
when he said[5]:

'Up to now everybody has been approaching the case on the footing that the
interests of these two parties in their property were equal. That seems to me a
doubtfully accurate assumption or premise.'

h So this case is like the typical case where the shares are unascertained. Even if we assume,
however, that the parties were entitled each to a half-share in equity, I still think that, by
the adjustment order, the wife not only 'recovered' the husband's half-share, but also
'preserved' her own by shielding it with the protection of a full legal title.

---

j 1 SI 1971 No 162, reg 18(10), as substituted by SI 1976 No 628, and amended by SI 1977 Nos 1293,
1715
2 [1973] 1 All ER 829 at 840–841, [1973] Fam 72 at 96
3 [1933] P 105, [1933] All ER Rep 226
4 [1974] 1 All ER 1096 at 1101, [1974] QB 558 at 569
5 [1978] 2 All ER 889 at 893, [1978] 1 WLR 592 at 597

I find myself therefore in agreement with Reeve J. The wife 'recovered or preserved' the whole house. It is subject to the charge in respect of the costs incurred on her behalf. *a* I would add that I am grateful to him for pointing out a slip or two I made in *Till v Till*[1] and *Cooke v Head (No 2)*[2]. I do make mistakes sometimes.

The policy of the legislature

Thus far I have considered the legislation in our traditional English way, by looking at the actual words used and interpreting them as best I can. But I would venture to *b* consider it in the wider purposive way fashionable in Europe, by considering the underlying policy behind the Act and regulations.

On the one hand there is this broad social policy: no one should be hindered by lack of means from bringing his case before the courts, or contesting that of his opponent. He should make a contribution, as much as he can reasonably afford, towards the costs, but having paid that contribution, he should not be called on to pay more. In this case it was *c* only £115. He should be entitled to carry on all the proceedings covered by his certificate, no matter how long and expensive they might be, without further expense to him. In this case the costs come to £8,025. According to this policy, the whole of that £8,025 should be borne by the taxpayers at large, less only the £115 contributed by the legally aided person.

On the other hand, there is a limit to the money to be gotten out of the taxpayers. *d* There is a broad economic policy to be considered as well. The moneys provided by the state should not be used so as to finance ill-advised litigation, or to prolong disputes at the state's expense, when they ought to be settled reasonably between the parties themselves. All of us in this court know what happens in a wide certificate such as this. The parties are very concerned about the custody or access to their children. So concerned that they will contest cases up to this court, quite hopeless cases, all at the *e* expense of the state, when they would not dream of appealing if they had to pay the costs themselves. That still happens. But there is no reason why it should happen any longer (since 1976) when a legally aided person does exceedingly well out of it by recovering a large lump sum or a valuable house, which he can sell at a large profit. If parties choose to contest about it, then it may be fair that some part of the cost should be borne by that asset itself. The whole expense should not be borne by the taxpayers of this country. *f*

In 1976 the legislature considered those opposing policies. In consequence regulations were made which were of a compromise nature[3]. Whenever, as a result of legal aid, a husband or wife 'recovered or preserved' a lump sum or the matrimonial home, he was allowed to retain the sum of £2,500 free. It was exempt from any charge in respect of the costs paid by the taxpayers on his behalf. Only £2,500 was free. Above that sum the legal aid fund had a charge on the property. *g*

By insisting on the charge, the legislature imposes a restraint on litigation between husband and wife, when both are legally aided. It acts as a sanction against an assisted person who requests legal advisers to conduct him or his case unreasonably.

So far as cases are concerned, I would note that long ago in *Wagg v Law Society*[4] Harman J thought the first policy was of overriding importance. A legally aided person should not be asked to pay any more than his assessed contribution. But in *Till v Till*[5] this court *h* thought that the second policy was to operate. It gave the legal aid fund a charge for costs over and above the contribution.

In our present case the economic policy prevails. The amending regulations ensure

---

1   [1974] 1 All ER 1096, [1974] QB 558   *j*
2   [1974] 2 All ER 1124, [1974] 1 WLR 972
3   Legal Aid (General) (Amendment No 2) Regulations 1976, SI 1976 No 628, substituting reg 18(10)
     in the Legal Aid (General) Regulations 1971, SI 1971 No 62
4   [1957] 2 All ER 274, [1957] Ch 405
5   [1974] 1 All ER 1096 at 1103, [1974] QB 558 at 570

a that the legal aid fund should have a charge on the matrimonial home for all the costs incurred on behalf of the wife, over and above her £2,500 which is exempt.

Discretion

Thus far I am in agreement with the judgment of Reeve J. But he did not go on to consider a most important point which was much discussed before us. It is the question
b of discretion. Regulation 19(2) of the 1971 regulations says that 'The Law Society may enforce any such charge in any manner which would be available if the charge had been given inter partes'. The word 'may' gives a wide discretion. We discussed it in *Till v Till*[1]. At that time I thought it gave a limited discretion. I said that the legal aid fund were *bound* to enforce the charge, if they could, but they had a discretion as to the *way* in which to do it. In the light of the facts in this case, I have altered my mind about it. I
c start with this. The wife is not indebted to the legal aid fund at all. They cannot sue her for these costs of £8,025. They cannot get a judgment against her. No interest runs on the sum. They only have a charge on the house for it. Then how are they to enforce it? It is said that, like any mortgagee, they can sue her for possession and turn her out; and then, having got vacant possession, they can sell it and recoup themselves out of the proceeds, leaving nothing for her. Are they bound to go to that length? Are they to be
d like the hard-hearted mortgagees of the 19th century, foreclosing and obtaining possession, turning out the innocent and grinding the faces of the poor? Are they to do it so as to recover the costs of litigation, which they themselves sanctioned and approved? I cannot believe that either Parliament, when it gave the charge, or the Lord Chancellor, when he made the regulations, thought the legal aid fund were bound to do this. In my opinion they are not so bound. They have a discretion under which they can and should
e enforce the charge when it is just and reasonable to do so, and to the extent that it is just and reasonable, but not when it is unjust and unreasonable. You must remember that, in order to enforce the charge by getting possession, the legal aid fund must get an order of the court; and the court would, I am sure, not make an order except when it was just and reasonable to do so.

It is for these reasons that I think the practice of the legal aid fund has been correct in
f the past. They have not sought to evict the wife or family from the matrimonial home so long as they are living there. They have only sought to enforce the charge when the house is sold; and then only against the proceeds. That is fair enough; and it is only to be justified by recognising that they have a discretion to do what is just and reasonable.

Likewise in the present case I think that if the wife is advised to sell the house so as to get something smaller, the legal aid fund are perfectly at liberty to accept a substitute
g charge on the smaller house. If the wife should make a handsome profit on the deal, it may be fair enough that some part of it should go in part payment of the charge. But I cannot think it right that the legal aid fund should baulk the transaction altogether. That would mean her staying in a dilapidated house, unable to afford the repairs, simply so that the legal aid fund could in some years' time, when she dies, enforce the charge against it.
h   I realise, of course, that in entrusting the legal aid fund with this wide discretion, a grave responsibility is placed on them, which they would perhaps rather avoid. But it is better thus than that injustice should be done to a wife placed as this wife is. I observe that the Royal Commission on Legal Services thinks that there should be no charge on the matrimonial home at all[2]. Pending this change the legal aid fund should have a discretion whether to enforce it and to what extent. Applied to this case it means that
j they have a discretion to agree to a substitute charge on a new house.

---

1   [1974] 1 All ER 1096 at 1101, [1974] QB 558 at 568
2   Royal Commission on Legal Services, Final Report (1979) Cmnd 7648, vol 1, p 149, para 13.64

Conclusion

Whilst holding that the legal aid fund have a charge, I would hold that any injustice *a* to the wife can be relieved by the exercise of a wise discretion as to its enforcement.

SIR JOHN ARNOLD P. It is provided by s 9(6) of the Legal Aid Act 1974 that the deficiency in the legal aid fund between what the fund pays out and what the fund receives back by way of contribution from the assisted person is to be a first charge on any property which is recovered or preserved for that person in the proceedings. It is in my *b* judgment plain that the words 'the proceedings' have the same meaning as the words 'any proceedings' used earlier in the subsection, that is to say that they mean any proceedings in respect of which a contribution to the legal aid fund has been assessed. It may be that the proceedings so defined are, or are usually, all the proceedings mentioned in a single legal aid certificate; but this is not because they are mentioned in the certificate, but because a single contribution has been assessed in relation to the whole of *c* the proceedings so included.

The wife's contribution is shown in the offer of legal aid, made to her by the Law Society and accepted by her, as being a contribution 'towards ... the case', and, in the context in which it appears in that document, it is in my judgment clear that the case is the totality of the proceedings mentioned earlier in the offer, namely the prosecution of a suit for divorce, an application under s 17 of the Married Women's Property Act 1882 *d* and an application for an injunction. No further proceedings were ever embraced in any new offer and acceptance, nor was any amendment ever made in the description of proceedings included in the offer which I have mentioned. It follows that all the legally aided proceedings in this case, whether relating to dissolution of marriage, or children, or financial relief in the form of periodical payments or adjustment of property, were undertaken as part of the prosecution of a suit for divorce, and all these proceedings are *e* in my judgment comprised within the ambit of the proceedings referred to in s 9(6) of the 1974 Act. It follows that the deficiency referred to in that subsection is that by which the wife's contribution is less than the net liability of the legal aid fund incurred on her account in those proceedings and that a sum equal to that deficiency is charged on any property recovered or preserved for the wife in those proceedings.

By the order finally made in those proceedings by this court on 17th October 1977 the *f* husband was ordered to transfer to the wife the legal estate in the property at Waltham Cross, together with all his equitable interest therein, and in my view the property recovered or preserved for the wife in the proceedings in question is the property recovered or preserved by means of that order. A bare legal estate is not property, in the sense of that which is in my view in contemplation in the subsection, nor in my view does the transfer of the legal estate in any way affect the question of what was 'recovered *g* or preserved'. The answer to that question would in my judgment have been exactly the same if the legal estate had been left outstanding in the husband or had been transferred to some third party. In no way did the transfer of the legal estate to the wife in my judgment protect or preserve any equitable interest that she herself may have had or that the husband transferred to her. In my view what the wife relevantly recovered by means of the order was the equitable interest referred to therein, namely that of the husband. *h* The language of the order closely follows that of s 24(1)(a) of the Matrimonial Causes Act 1973. Such an order is generically referred to as a property adjustment order in s 21(2)(a) of that Act but it is there made clear that the method of property adjustment to be employed is that of a transfer of property from one party to another party. It seems to me that where such an order is made that other party can accurately be said to recover the property thus ordered to be transferred. The use of the word 'recovered' in s 9(6) cannot *j* have any connotation of the regaining of something by the party recovering, since it is under this provision alone that there exists a charge on damages obtained in an action for contract or tort, a context from which regaining is wholly absent. Nothing is said in the order in relation to any equitable interest in the property of the wife. It does not seem possible therefore to say that this was thereby recovered. Nor does it seem to me to be

accurate to say that it was preserved, since my understanding is that at no point in the
a litigation was any application on the part of the husband for a transfer to him of any
equitable interest of the wife put forward or considered, and no court could in this
litigation legitimately have transferred any such interest away from the wife.

Whether this is the right view depends on two matters: first, whether it can properly
be said that the equitable interest of one tenant in common in whose favour an order is
made for a transfer of the remaining equitable interest has thereby recovered or preserved
b his own equitable interest; and, secondly, whether, in the instant case, the wife had an
equitable interest. If the first question be answered in the negative and the second to
some extent in the affirmative, it would in my judgment follow that to that extent the
wife is exempt in her ownership of the property from any charge in favour of the fund.

There is no authority bearing in any relevant way on the construction of the words
'recovered or preserved' in s 9(6) of the 1974 Act or any predecessor section, but it has
c been held in *Till v Till*[1] in this court that the words have the same meaning as in s 72 of
the Solicitors Act 1957[2] which conferred on solicitors the right to apply for a charging
order on property recovered or preserved through their instrumentality in any suit,
matter or proceeding. We have been referred to numerous cases under the corresponding
sections in successive Solicitors Acts and it is necessary to examine those of them in which
the order was made. In *Foxon v Gascoigne*[3] Jessel MR, in a decision which was upheld by
d the Lords Justices on appeal, said:

> 'Now what does that expression "actual recovery or preservation" mean?
> Generally I apprehend it means that where the Plaintiff claims property, and
> establishes a right to the ownership of the property in some shape or other, there the
> property has been recovered; *that where a Defendant's right to the ownership of property*
> *e* *is disputed and that right has been vindicated by the proceedings there the property has been*
> *preserved.*' (My emphasis.)

He then proceeds to include in 'preservation' a case where there has been physical
protection of some property, a conception not relevant in the present case. It seems
therefore that Jessel MR considered that the charge could extend under the then operative
f section only to property of which the ownership was affected in the proceedings, either
by an effective alteration in its ownership or by an effective protection of its antecedent
title or its integrity.

In *The Philippine*[4] it was held that property recovered or preserved included some shares
in a ship to the extent that the plaintiff had by means of the proceedings established a
right to their transfer for a sum less than he would have had to pay if the suit had never
g been instituted. In *Catlow v Catlow*[5] a solicitor was held entitled to a charging order on
a trust fund representing the proceeds of certain chattels which had been the subject of
a successful action in detinue undertaken by the solicitor against the fiduciary holders of
the goods, the judgment in detinue not having been able at first to be enforced and the
fiduciaries having later lodged the proceeds in court.

Greer v Young[6] was a case in which two proceedings had been brought, respectively
h against the estates of a delinquent trustee and of his co-trustee who although not
personally delinquent was said to be liable for the defaults of the other. Both suits were
successful to the extent of dividends payable out of the two estates. The solicitors acting
in the second action were held entitled to a charge on the dividends recovered in that
action but not on those recovered in the other action in which they had not acted.

j 1   [1974] 1 All ER 1096, [1974] QB 558
2   Now the Solicitors Act 1974, s 73
3   (1874) 9 Ch App 654 at 657
4   (1867) LR 1 A & E 309
5   (1877) 2 CPD 362
6   (1883) 24 Ch D 545

In *Westacott v Bevan*[1] there was an action for work done under a contract for repairs and a counterclaim for damages for delay in completing the work. A sum of money was paid into court by the defendants with a denial of liability and not taken out. In the event the action and counterclaim both succeeded and the balance of that recovered in the action after a set-off of that recovered on the counterclaim was smaller than the sum which had been paid into court. The plaintiff's solicitors had obtained a charging order over the sum paid into court and that was discharged on appeal, there being substituted a charging order limited to the balance of the successful claim over the successful counterclaim.

In *Pelsall Coal and Iron Co v London and North Western Railway Co (No 3)*[2] before the Railway and Canal Commission, the solicitors obtained a charging order against certain railway wagons limited to the amount of a lien to which the railway company claimed to be entitled over the wagons and which had been eliminated in a compromise of the application, the property in the wagons having been preserved to the extent of the alleged lien thus eliminated.

Hyde v White[3] concerned a probate action in which the plaintiff had unsuccessfully propounded three wills and which had ended with a grant of representation as on an intestacy. The plaintiff's solicitors claimed a charging order on the interest of the plaintiff under that intestacy and succeeded. Lord Merrivale P said[4]:

'She claimed so much of the estate as was disposed of in her favour under a will of 1926 and in the alternative under two wills of 1929 and those claims failed, but there still remained the question of what her interest was in the estate . . . and that was an inchoate interest until there was some effective order of the Court. That was the position until that right had been ascertained. In these circumstances I do not think that a merely narrow construction must be put on the words of the section but that they must be read with regard to the intention of the Legislature. I think that this is a property which has been preserved, that is to say, that has been secured to the plaintiff in these proceedings.'

Whilst the reasoning is not spelled out in detail it seems to me that Lord Merrivale P was relying on the circumstance that the plaintiff's share on an intestacy was not something which could be established until the propounded wills had been eliminated and that this was what was achieved in the proceedings.

This case was followed in *Wimbourne v Fine*[5], where the plaintiff claimed in the alternative the ownership of a business and an interest in it as a partner. Her claim succeeded on the second alternative basis and a partnership account was ordered. This was compromised and the plaintiff's solicitor applied for a charging order on a sum of money coming to the plaintiff as a result of the compromise. The solicitor's claim succeeded. Harman J said[6]:

'The object of the suit, it is true, was to obtain the whole of this money for the plaintiff, but in the upshot she became entitled to only part of it. Nevertheless, the fund in question was put into safe custody in this way to abide the result of the suit and, it seems to me . . . to have been "recovered or preserved". The fact that the plaintiff got an answer which was not welcome to her does not seem to me to be relevant, because it is clear, for instance, from *Hyde v. White, White v. Hyde*[3], that money can be recovered or preserved, notwithstanding such a result.'

1   [1891] 1 QB 774
2   (1892) 8 Ry & Can Tr Cas 146
3   [1933] P 105, [1933] All ER Rep 226
4   [1933] P 105 at 107–108, [1933] All ER Rep 226 at 228
5   [1952] 2 All ER 681, [1952] Ch 869
6   [1952] 2 All ER 681 at 685, [1952] Ch 869 at 874

Later on, Harman J in exercising his discretion to grant a charging order said[1]:

'I think I must have regard to the fact, so far as the plaintiff is concerned, that what she eventually got was something she might possibly have had before the action started: she was offered in the defence to be treated as a partner.'

What was recovered or preserved in that action was therefore a sum of money first quantified at the stage of the compromise representing on that compromise what was then for the first time accepted as between plaintiff and defendants as the value of a partnership share, the right of the plaintiff to which share was not disputed.

None of these cases seems to me to decide that the proprietor of an equitable interest in property who claims in an action a further equitable interest in that property and whose equitable interest is not in that action disputed can be said to have recovered or preserved his own equitable interest or anything in respect of it, and indeed Jessel MR's dictum in *Foxon v Gascoigne*[2] contradicts such a proposition. Nor in my view does any of those cases embody or express a principle whereby anything more can be seen to have been recovered or preserved than the additional equitable interest successfully claimed by the plaintiff.

I turn then to examine the question whether the wife did in this case have an equitable interest of her own so that that of the husband which she obtained by the order of the Court of Appeal represented something less than the totality of the equitable interest in the property. In the affidavit which he swore on 16th March 1979 the wife's solicitor referred to an affidavit sworn by the husband on 1st May 1974, in answer to the wife's application for a property adjustment order in which he said, 'The position would be eased a great deal if the matrimonial home could be sold and the net proceeds divided equally between my wife and myself', a matter which is referred to in the judgment of Rees J of 26th April 1977. When the matter came before the registrar there does not appear to have been any contest in relation to the existing financial interests which were not referred to at all in the parties' evidence-in-chief. A passage in the cross-examination of the husband, as reported in the notes of evidence which are before us, refers to the wife having a half share in the property and raises the question whether she would be able to buy another property if given a one-third interest. Without some idea of the method of question and answer which produced the evidence thus noted, it is not possible in my judgment to say that this passage involved any departure on either side from a position in which each was equally entitled. The registrar's order was that the husband should transfer the house to the wife and that the wife should pay the husband a lump sum of £5,000. The net value of the equity in the house was by agreement taken to be £10,000, so that there is here no departure from the position of equality. In his judgment given on appeal from the registrar, Rees J observes that it was argued that whatever order the court made the wife should obtain more than 50% of the equity in the house and continues: 'It was suggested she should receive either the whole house, that is to say to have the husband's 50% interest transferred to herself, or at least two-thirds instead of one-half.' It is evident therefore that Rees J regarded the case as being argued on the basis that the starting position was that each was equally entitled. Finally, when the case was tried in the Court of Appeal, Ormrod LJ, giving what was in effect the unanimous judgment of the court, said[3]:

'Up to now everybody has been approaching the case on the footing that the interests of these two parties in this property were equal. That seems to me to be a doubtfully accurate assumption, or premise. Putting them as shortly as I can, the facts are these. Over 14 years of cohabitation these two parties no doubt contributed broadly equally to this family in terms of money, in terms of work and so on. From

1 [1952] 2 All ER 681 at 688, [1952] Ch 869 at 880
2 (1874) 9 Ch App 654 at 657
3 [1978] 2 All ER 889 at 893–894, [1978] 1 WLR 592 at 597–598

1971 onwards, that is now for over five years, the wife has had the upbringing of *a*
these four children and has been working full time as a community nurse. She has
maintained the house as well as she could during those years, and on any view she
has taken a considerable load off the shoulders of the husband over a period of five
years, and she will continue to take a large load off his shoulders from now on until
the youngest child leaves home, which of course will not necessarily by any manner
of means be in five years' time. A family like this will not simply dissolve
completely on the 17th birthday of the youngest child. In fact, of course, she will *b*
be, as the mother of this family, maintaining the nucleus of the home effectively for
a considerable number of years until the girls are married and settled on their own,
and the boys are similarly married and settled on their own; that is what it really
means in real life. So in my view she has made a very large contribution to this
family.'

It is clear in my judgment that Ormrod LJ was there referring to the sort of financial *c*
contribution which is regarded in *Gissing v Gissing*[1] as justifying the inference of a
common intention of spouses that the wife should share in the beneficial interest and was
recognising that the parties in the present case had both acknowledged the existence of
such an interest and that it was an equal interest; the only criticism that Ormrod LJ was
making was that this recognition did not perhaps reflect the largest size of such interest
which the wife might have claimed if there had been no agreement on the proportion. *d*
I accordingly do not agree with the assessment of the situation made by Reeve J, whose
order is appealed from, that all that the husband was doing was 'recognising that in the
light of s 25 and the decided cases, that was the order which would probably be made in
her favour under s 24'. In my judgment therefore this wife had, from a time earlier than
that at which she proceeded with her application for financial relief, an equal interest in
the property, and consequently the property recovered or preserved in the proceedings *e*
did not exceed the other moiety.

It is however argued on behalf of the wife that it was less than this. The reason put
forward was that the order of the Court of Appeal not only gave to the wife her husband's
beneficial interest in the property, but, at the same time, and in compensation therefor,
defined the periodical payments to be made by the husband to the children while they
were respectively under 17 years of age at a nominal amount, while by the order of *f*
Rees J they had been fixed at £7 per week each. So it is said that the true measure of the
property recovered by the wife was the value of the husband's 50% beneficial interest less
the capitalised value of the periodical payments ordered by Rees J, or at least some capital
value representing the true worth of the claim in that regard. To a possible objection to
this argument, that the claim for periodical payments was that of the children, whilst the
property was recovered by the wife, it is answered that the wife has a duty to maintain *g*
her children which would have been relieved pro tanto by periodical payments made by
their father. If it be right that the proceedings in question are all the proceedings from
their initiation before the registrar until their end in the Court of Appeal, the comparison
which must be made in relation to this argument must be that between the position at
the commencement of the proceedings and that after the Court of Appeal's order. At the
commencement, the wife had a claim for a capital financial adjustment, a claim for *h*
periodical payments for herself, although not a strong one since she was working, and,
indirectly as above mentioned, a claim for periodical payments in respect of the
children. None of these claims was quantified and they could be quantified only in the
proceedings. At the end of the proceedings, she received, as I think, the value of one-half
of the equity in the house, and nothing more, except such value as might be attached to
the nominal order for periodical payments to the children. In these circumstances it *j*
seems to me that what she recovered in the proceedings was everything which the Court
of Appeal's order gave her, and that it is not possible to cut that down by reference to

1   [1970] 2 All ER 780, [1971] AC 886

some other order which might have been obtained in the proceedings if they had had a
a different result. If the matter rested with me, therefore, I would allow the appeal, and
declare that the charge extends to one undivided half share in the net proceeds of sale of
the house, less the first £2,500 in value of that share.

The other issues raised in this appeal concern the realisation of the charge given to the
Law Society by s 9(6) of the Legal Aid Act 1974. The property in question is one which
it is very expensive to maintain and which, if she could, the wife would very much like
b to leave in favour of some other less expensive property, but she could not acquire the
latter if, on a sale of the existing property, the Law Society's charge had to be satisfied out
of the proceeds of sale. It is argued for the wife that this result can be avoided by the
exercise by the Law Society of a discretion that it is said to have to substitute the new
house as the security for the charge. This discretion is said to arise under reg 19(2) of the
Legal Aid (General) Regulations 1971, where it is provided that 'The Law Society may
c enforce any such charge in any manner which would be available if the charge had been
given inter partes'. I can only say that in my view it is quite impossible to describe the
substitution of a security as the enforcement of a charge, and I can find no ground for
saying that the Law Society has any discretion under this regulation to make such a
substitution. The powers of the Law Society in administering the legal aid fund,
including any charges accruing under s 9(6), are in my judgment altogether circumscribed
d by the relevant statutory provisions, and, although there is an element of choice imported
into reg 19(2) by the use of the permissive 'may', it does not, in my judgment, extend
beyond the selection by the Law Society, as between the courses open to it, of that which
is most beneficial to the legal aid fund. In particular, it does not in my view permit the
Law Society to deal with charges in such a way as is most beneficial to a chargee, unless
that way coincides with the best interests of the fund. This is relevant to the other
e argument which is put forward in this part of the appeal, to the effect that the Law
Society has a discretion to postpone the realisation of the charge, for the duration of the
wife's life, or at least for so long as she wishes to occupy the property. In my judgment
the Law Society has such a discretion only if it believes that, by dealing with the matter
in this way, the best interests of the fund will be served. The matter is one for the Law
Society, but there is in my judgment solid ground on which they could take such a
f view. The main purpose which the courts of the Family Division, and, indeed, county
courts when exercising this jurisdiction, strive to serve when they make orders dealing
with matrimonial homes, particularly in cases where these are to continue to be occupied
by a wife who is looking after children, is most frequently to secure a roof over her head,
and that purpose is no doubt one which would be taken into most careful consideration
by any other court which had to exercise a discretion the exercise of which involved the
g question whether that purpose could continue to be served. The Law Society has the
power of sale conferred by s 101 of the Law of Property Act 1925 on mortgagees, the Law
Society being the proprietor of such a charge as is mentioned under the definition of a
mortgage in s 205 of that Act. The Law Society has a right to apply to the court for
possession of the property with a view to the exercise of its power of sale and in so doing
would in my view have to demonstrate that the court ought to make the order at once
h and not postpone it to enable the wife to continue to occupy the property. This is
because of the provisions of s 36 of the Administration of Justice Act 1970, as interpreted
by this court in *Western Bank Ltd v Schindler*[1]. An application for an order for possession
which failed would or might cause a detriment to the legal aid fund in respect of costs
thrown away, and it may very well be that the Law Society would, for this reason, think
that an attempt to oust a former wife from the former matrimonial home by the making
j of such an application would be one that it should for this reason not undertake.

The danger to the continued occupation of such a wife in such a home which is
thrown up by the considerations which I have mentioned is such as to make the task of

1   [1976] 2 All ER 393, [1977] Ch 1

the judges of the Family Division and all other judges exercising similar functions under
s 24 of the Matrimonial Causes Act 1973 extremely difficult effectively to perform, and *a*
it is in my view most desirable that the regulations should be amended so as to permit
the purpose of the exercise of that jurisdiction of providing a home for a spouse and
children, or a spouse alone, to be carried into effect, by the conferment on the Law
Society of an appropriate discretion in that regard.

DONALDSON LJ (read by Lord Denning MR). Section 9(6) of the Legal Aid Act 1974 *b*
creates a charge in favour of the legal aid fund 'if the total contribution is less than the net
liability of that fund on [the legally assisted person's] account'. 'Net liability' is defined
by s 9(9) as being, in effect, what the fund pays out on the legally assisted person's behalf
less what it recoups under orders for costs made in his favour with respect to those
proceedings. If, therefore, 'proceedings' were to be construed restrictively, it would be
possible to calculate the net liability of the fund with respect to each phase of the *c*
proceedings, and indeed this has been done in this case. The figures are £925 for the
main suit and interlocutory injunction, £1,150 for custody and access and £5,950 for
periodical payments and property proceedings. However, there are no settled principles
which would enable anyone to allocate the wife's contribution between these phases, and
accordingly it is impossible to ascertain the deficiency which forms the basis of the
charge under the section. For this reason, in addition to the matters of construction to *d*
which Sir John Arnold P has referred, I am satisfied that the 'proceedings' referred to in
s 9(6) are the totality of the proceedings in respect of which the wife received legal aid.

The charge
   Let me turn to the charge itself. It is imposed on 'any property (wherever situated)
which is recovered or preserved for [the legally assisted person] in the proceedings'. I *e*
agree with Sir John Arnold P that we are bound by the decision of this court in *Till v Till*[1]
to hold that the words have the same meaning as they bear in s 72 of the Solicitors Act
1957[2]. Any difference between the effect of the two sections must therefore depend on
the presence of the words 'through his instrumentality' in s 72. This is not a material
difference in the present appeal.
   For present purposes the issue is whether the wife 'recovered or preserved' any, and if *f*
so what, property in the proceedings. In all the cases under the Solicitors Acts which
were cited to us, one party or the other was asserting an existing right in law or equity
and was calling on the court to give effect to that right or alternatively was calling on the
court to vindicate a denial that an alleged right existed. The case which comes nearest to
being an exception to this general description is *Hyde v White*[3], where the plaintiff needed
a grant of representation as on an intestacy before she could become entitled to her share *g*
in the estate. But this is mere machinery. Ignoring her claims under the wills which
were held to be unfounded, before the action began she had a statutory right to her share
on the basis of an intestacy, subject only to obtaining this formal grant. She was
therefore recovering property in exactly the same sense as anyone who claims a debt,
damages in contract or tort, or any order designed to give effect to a determination that
the plaintiff has an existing legal or equitable right in respect of property. *h*
   In the present case this court ordered the husband to 'transfer the legal estate in the
property at 106 Waltham Cross, together with all his equitable interest therein to [the
wife] absolutely, subject to the existing charge . . .' In doing so, it was not ascertaining
that the wife had any legal or equitable right to this property and giving effect to that
right. It was exercising its discretionary powers under s 24 of the Matrimonial Causes
Act 1973. It is of the essence of those provisions that the court, far from giving effect to *j*
existing rights, is entitled and, in appropriate cases, bound to override those rights with

a view to creating a situation in which, so far as it is practicable and, having regard to the
a parties' conduct, just to do so, the parties are placed in the same financial position in
which they would have been if the marriage had not broken down and each had properly
discharged his or her financial obligations and responsibilities towards the other: see
s 25. Indeed it only made this order as part of a package which limited the husband's
liability to maintain the children to a nominal amount and thereby placed an additional
burden on the wife. This seems to me to be a wholly different exercise to that on which
b the courts were engaged in any of the reported cases on the effect of the Solicitors Acts.
Accordingly, I find those cases of no assistance.

   The crucial question is whether I would express myself aptly if I said that the wife had
'recovered' property in the proceedings and, although it is not directly in issue, that the
husband had 'preserved' any property which was not transferred to the wife. I am bound
to say that it seems to me to be an all or nothing situation. Every piece of property
c involved in the joint matrimonial adventure was either recovered by one party or, as the
case may be, preserved by the other or none of it was either recovered or preserved. In
exercising its powers under s 24 of the 1973 Act the court looks at the whole financial
position of the parties jointly and severally during the marriage and at the whole
financial position of the parties severally after the breakdown of that marriage. It
notionally pools all the assets and redistributes them in such a way as to produce as little
d change in real terms as possible. Every individual asset of each of the parties is at risk
even if, in the nature of things, calamity in the form of a transfer to the other party to the
marriage is unlikely to strike at all such assets. Can the result of this process really be
described as a recovery or a preservation of property? I think not. The fact that
reg 18(10) of the Legal Aid (General) Regulations 1971[1] assumes that s 9(6) of the 1974
Act is applicable to property the subject-matter of a s 24 order is a reason for my re-
e examining my own view of the applicability of the section. But it is not a permissible aid
to construction. I have re-examined the arguments but remain of the same opinion. It
follows that, in my judgment the legal aid fund has no charge on this property under
s 9(6) of the 1974 Act. I would, therefore, allow the appeal.

   I have also considered what would be the position if, contrary to my view, the wife
'recovered' property within the meaning of s 9(6) of the 1974 Act. Before the proceedings
f began, the husband was the legal owner of the matrimonial home. He had recognised
the interest of the building society as mortgagees, but he had never recognised any
interest of the wife. After the proceedings had concluded and effect had been given to
this court's order, the wife was the legal owner of the property, whilst the husband's
unquantified equitable interest had been transferred to her and extinguished.

   Whilst it is true that the husband conducted the proceedings on the basis that the best
g for which he could hope was that the wife would end up with a 50% equitable interest
in the house, he never acknowledged that she had such an interest. There was, for
example, no declaration of trust in her favour. As I see it, it does not matter whether the
husband or his advisers reached this conclusion on the basis that the wife already had a
50% equitable interest in the house on a *Gissing v Gissing*[2] basis or on the basis that the
court would exercise its powers under the Matrimonial Causes Act 1973 to transfer assets
h in such a way as to produce a result which was no less favourable to the wife. Even if the
wife had an existing 50% interest before the proceedings began, in the absence of an
unequivocal concession of this fact by the husband, she needed a court order in order to
make her interest effective. Accordingly, if I am wrong in thinking that a property
adjustment order under s 24 of the Matrimonial Causes Act 1973 does not result in the
recovery or preservation of any property, I should be of opinion that Reeve J was right
j and that in the proceedings the wife recovered the whole value of the former matrimonial

---

1   SI 1971 No 62, reg 18(10), as substituted by SI 1976 No 628 and amended by SI 1977 Nos 1293,
    1715
2   [1970] 2 All ER 780, [1971] AC 886

home, less only the interest of the building society, i e she recovered her own pre-existing equitable interest and that of the husband.   *a*

Deferred enforcement and transfer of the charge

This leaves the question of the enforcement of the charge. If I am right in the views which I have expressed, there is no charge in this case. However, there are other cases in which there may be a charge on the matrimonial home, e g where rights of title to, or possession of, property are determined under s 17 of the Married Women's Property Act *b* 1882.

If the legal aid fund's right to payment of 'a sum equal to the deficiency' mentioned in s 9(6) of the Legal Aid Act 1974 was a liability independent of, but secured by, the charge on any property recovered or preserved, I think that the Law Society could accept a substitute security if it was in the interest of the fund so to do. This would involve neither enforcement nor waiver of the primary liability. The Law Society would simply *c* be accepting an alternative security for that liability.

This is the case with charges under the Solicitors Acts. There the client has a contractual obligation to pay his solicitor's bill of costs and the charge is merely security for that liability. But the position is different in the case of legal aid. There is no contractual liability on the assisted person to pay the legal aid fund anything beyond the initial periodical contributions. The fund's right to any further payment is purely *d* statutory and takes the form of the s 9(6) charge. That operates only on property recovered or preserved. I have considered whether the Law Society could agree, on behalf of the fund, to release the statutory charge in consideration of the assisted person contracting to pay the fund an amount equal to the charge and to secure this obligation by a charge on other property. In many situations this might well be sensible. But I do not see how such action could possibly be described as enforcing the statutory charge *e* within the authority given by reg 19(2) of the Legal Aid (General) Regulations 1971. It is a waiver of that charge for consideration. I have, therefore, regretfully concluded that the Law Society has no power to transfer the charge to other property.

When it comes to postponing enforcement, the position is different. The Law Society is under an obligation to act reasonably in the interests not of the community as a whole nor of the assisted person as an individual, but of the legal aid fund itself. It must be *f* contrary to the interest of that fund to make applications to the court for possession of the dwelling-house if such applications will or are likely to fail. There is, therefore, ample power to postpone enforcement in appropriate cases.

The future   *g*

If at any time Parliament were to reconsider the terms of the Legal Aid Act 1974, some thought might be given to possible ways of making the limited amount of money available for legal aid go a little further and be more equitably distributed. My own suggestions would be these. First, the scheme for assessing contributions is based on the philosophy that, however great the cost of the litigation, the legally assisted person cannot be expected to contribute more than (a) a proportion of his disposable income in *h* a single year, (b) a proportion of his readily disposable capital at the time when he applies for legal aid and (c) whatever results eventually from the operation of the charge on property recovered or preserved. Much larger contributions could be made if they were spread over a longer period than one year and took account of disposable income over that longer period. If the average citizen decides to incur expenditure of the same magnitude as the cost of litigation on, for example, the purchase of a car or other *j* 'consumer durable', he will spread the cost over more than one year by means of a personal loan from a bank, or hire-purchase or credit sale contract. Why cannot he treat legal aid in the same way, spreading his contributions over a period of up to three or even five years, the amount of the periodic payments taking account of his disposable income throughout that period?

Second, could not provision be made for the charge to be transferable to other
a substitute property provided that this was considered to be in the public interest and the
interest of the fund? If the owner cannot afford to maintain the house, the security
afforded by the charge will diminish progressively. Furthermore, the time will arrive
when the house ceases to be habitable and is sold only at site value, leaving the assisted
person to be rehoused in scarce public sector housing.

Third, could not machinery be provided for assessing how much, if anything, the
b assisted person could reasonably be expected to pay by way of periodic instalments in
reduction of the amount of the charge, beginning after the litigation has been
concluded? If there was default in making these payments, the legal aid fund would be
in a much stronger position in seeking to enforce the charge and could, of course, be
given a specific statutory right to do so notwithstanding s 36 of the Administration of
Justice Act 1970.

c   Fourth, consideration might be given to the special situation in relation to costs, where
both or all parties are legally aided. Section 13 of the Legal Aid Act 1974 already deals
with the costs of successful unassisted parties. But what about the costs of successful
assisted parties? The hardship of a successful unassisted party is that he is left to pay his
own costs despite his success. Bearing in mind the existence of the charge, the hardship
of a successful assisted party against another assisted party is even greater. By definition
d he is less well off than an unassisted party, but in so far as he recovers property or his
property is preserved, he may well be as much liable for his own costs as is an unassisted
party.

These are, however, matters for Parliament and not for me. I merely put them
forward for consideration.

e *Appeal dismissed. Leave to appeal to the House of Lords.*

Solicitors: *Smith & Harrison*, Waltham Cross (for Mrs Hanlon); *Law Society.*

Sumra Green   Barrister.

Practice Direction   *a*

FAMILY DIVISION

Divorce – Practice – Children – Custody – Joint custody order – Petitioner and respondent to be given opportunity to be heard – Matrimonial Causes Act 1973, s 41.

b

It sometimes happens that the judge who is considering the arrangements for the children under s 41 of the Matrimonial Causes Act 1973 is invited by one or both parties to make a joint custody order. Such orders are being sought more often now than formerly and variations of practice have been noticed in different parts of the country. With a view to securing uniformity of approach it is hereby directed as follows:

1. Where a petitioner and a respondent have reached an agreement as to which of *c* them should have the care and control of the child, or children, and are further agreed that legal custody should be vested in the two of them jointly and only one of them appears on the appointment, the court ought not on that appointment to make an order which is inconsistent with the agreement. If the court is unwilling to make the agreed order, it should adjourn the matter to give each party the opportunity to be heard.

2. Where a petition contains a prayer for custody and the respondent has indicated in *d* writing (in the acknowledgment of service or otherwise) that he (or she) wishes to apply for custody to be vested in the two of them jointly, the court should proceed on the basis that the question of custody is in issue, and should not make an order for custody, or joint custody, except with the agreement of both parties or after giving each of them the opportunity to be heard.

This direction is issued with the concurrence of the Lord Chancellor.

e

18th February 1980   SIR JOHN ARNOLD P.

Inland Revenue Commissioners v Helen Slater Charitable Trust Ltd

CHANCERY DIVISION
SLADE J
26th, 30th NOVEMBER 1979

Income tax – Exemption – Charity – Donations from one charity to another – Donations accumulated by recipient charity – Whether donations 'applied to charitable purposes' – Income and Corporation Taxes Act 1970, s 360(1)(c).

Capital gains tax – Exemptions and reliefs – Charity – Donations from one charity to another – Donations accumulated by recipient charity – Whether donations 'applied for charitable purposes' – Finance Act 1965, s 35(1).

In February 1970 a trust and a foundation were each incorporated as a company limited by guarantee. Both companies were registered charities and had been set up to work in tandem, the trust's main function being to raise funds for the foundation. In the years 1973 to 1975, out of its income and gains, the trust made large donations to the foundation, which, except for a small sum, were added by the foundation to its own capital. A claim by the trust for exemption from tax under s 360(1)[a] of the Income and Corporation Taxes Act 1970 and s 35(1)[b] of the Finance Act 1965 in respect of income and gains which it had donated to the foundation, but which had been added to the foundation's funds, was refused. The trust appealed contending that the donations to the foundation were an application of its income and gains for charitable purposes within s 360(1)(c) of the 1970 Act and s 35(1) of the 1965 Act and that no further enquiry how the foundation had made use of them was necessaary. The Special Commissioners upheld the trust's contention and allowed the appeal. The Crown appealed contending that the disputed payments by the trust to the foundation amounted to the mere addition of income to capital through the use of a parallel body and, therefore, did not amount to 'applications' of income by the trust, and could not qualify for relief under s 360(1)(c) of the 1970 Act or s 35(1) of the 1965 Act.

Held – A charitable corporation which, acting intra vires, made an outright transfer of money applicable for charitable purposes to any other charity in such manner as to pass to the transferee full title to the money was to be taken, by the transfer itself, to have applied such money for charitable purposes, within the meaning of s 360(1) of the 1970 Act and s 35(1) of the 1965 Act, unless the transferor knew or ought to have known that the money would be misapplied by the transferee. It followed that the trust had applied the money for charitable purposes and was entitled to exemption under s 360(1)(c) of the 1970 Act and s 35(1) of the 1965 Act, without having to show how the money had been dealt with by the foundation. The appeal would accordingly be dismissed (see p 795 *j* to p 796 *b* and *f g*, post).

Notes
For exemption of charities from income tax and capital gains tax, see 23 Halsbury's Laws (4th Edn) paras 1066–1071 and 5 ibid para 137.
For the Finance Act 1965, s 35, see 34 Halsbury's Statutes (3rd Edn) 906.
For the Income and Corporation Taxes Act 1970, s 360, see 33 ibid 477.
Section 35 of the Finance Act 1965 was replaced by s 145 of the Capital Gains Tax Act 1979 with effect from 6th April 1979.

---

a Section 360(1), so far as material, is set out at p 790 *e f*, post
b Section 35(1) is set out at p 790 *g*, post

Cases referred to in judgment

General Nursing Council for Scotland v Inland Revenue Comrs 1929 SC 664, 14 Tax Cas 645, *a*
28(1) Digest (Reissue) 486, *1238.

Hastings-Bass, Re, Hastings v Inland Revenue Comrs [1974] 2 All ER 193, [1975] Ch 25,
[1974] 2 WLR 904, [1974] STC 211, 53 ATC 87, [1974] TR 87, CA, Digest (Cont Vol
D) 518, 1139a.

Henriksen (Inspector of Taxes) v Grafton Hotel Ltd [1942] 1 All ER 678, [1942] 2 KB 184, 24
Tax Cas 453, 111 LJKB 497, 167 LT 39, 28(1) Digest (Reissue) 182, 550. *b*

Inland Revenue Comrs v Educational Grants Association Ltd [1967] 2 All ER 893, [1967] Ch
993, [1967] 3 WLR 41, 44 Tax Cas 93, 46 ATC 71, [1967] TR 79, CA, 28(1) Digest
(Reissue) 478, 17227.

Morris (B) Ltd v Lunzer [1942] 1 All ER 77, [1942] 1 KB 356, 111 LJKB 625, 166 LT 143,
CA, 39 Digest (Repl) 348, 822.

Mostyn (Lord) v London (Surveyor of Taxes) [1895] 1 QB 170, 3 Tax Cas 294, 64 LJQB 106, *c*
71 LT 760, 59 JP 390, 15 R 49, DC, 28(1) Digest (Reissue) 249, 782.

Ofrex Foundation (Trustees of George Drexler) v Inland Revenue Comrs [1965] 3 All ER 529,
[1966] Ch 675, [1965] 3 WLR 1168, 42 Tax Cas 524, 44 ATC 295, [1965] TR 307, 28(1)
Digest (Reissue) 480, 1733.

Williams v Papworth [1900] AC 563, 69 LJPC 129, 83 LT 184, PC, 47 Digest (Repl) 282,
2454. *d*

Case stated

1. At a hearing before the Commissioners for the Special Purposes of the Income Tax
Acts held on 11th October 1978, the Helen Slater Charitable Trust Ltd ('the trust')
appealed against the decision of the Board of Inland Revenue on its claim to exemption
from tax under s 360(1) of the Income and Corporation Taxes Act 1970 and s 35(1) of the *e*
Finance Act 1965 in respect of income and gains for the accounting periods ended 31st
March 1973 to 1975 inclusive.

2. The question for decision was whether the trust was entitled to exemption under
those sections in respect of income or gains which it paid to another charitable body, the
Slater Foundation Ltd ('the foundation'), and which the foundation had not itself
distributed by the end of the year in which the payments were received. *f*

3. The commissioners heard no oral evidence.

[Paragraph 4 listed the agreed documents put before the commissioners.]

5. The salient facts, taken from the agreed statement of facts and the other documents
which were put before the commissioners, are set out in paras 8.1 to 8.9 below.

6. The contentions advanced on behalf of the trust are summarised in para 8.10
below. *g*

7. The contentions advanced on behalf of the Crown are summarised in para 8.11
below.

8. The commissioners who heard the appeal took time to consider their decision and
gave it in writing on 9th November 1978 as follows:

'1. The [trust], being a registered charity, is entitled to exemption from income *h*
tax under section 360 of the Income and Corporation Taxes Act 1970 and from
Capital Gains Tax under section 35 of the Finance Act 1965 in so far as its income
and gains are "applied to charitable purposes only."

'2. The trustees maintain that the whole of the Trust's income and capital gains
for the three years under appeal was so applied. The Board of the Inland Revenue
have rejected that claim in respect of certain sums which the Trust paid over to *j*
another registered charity, the Slater Foundation Ltd ("the Foundation"), and which,
by the end of the year in question, the Foundation had not disbursed in furtherance
of charitable objects but had added to its own funds.

'3. The sums in dispute are £578,479 for the Trust's accounting year to 31 March
1973, £5,050 for the year to 31 March 1974 and £12,225 for the year to 31 March

1975. The question for our determination is whether those sums, being part of the Trust's income or gains, were applied to charitable purposes only.

'4. The Trust and the Foundation were both incorporated in February 1970 as companies limited by guarantee with no share capital. Each had then a different name (the Trust having been incorporated as Univale Ltd and the Foundation as Basilicon Ltd) which was changed to its present name on 6 July 1970. The three general objects of each company are similar (although not identical in all respects):— (i) (in both cases) to relieve suffering amongst the aged, impotent or poor; (ii) (in both cases) to advance education; (iii) (in the case of the Foundation) to further such other charitable objects as the company may think fit; (iii) (in the case of the Trust) to further such other charitable objects as the company may think fit and in particular but without prejudice to the generality of the foregoing to make grants to such associations, trusts, societies or corporations as are established for charitable purposes only.

'5. In the Memorandum of each company those three general objects are followed by a number of specific objects and powers of a detailed kind, subject in each case to a proviso that the company is established for charitable purposes only and that all its objects and powers are to be construed in the light of that limitation.

'6. It is an agreed fact that the Trust and the Foundation were established as a joint operation whereby money would from time to time, pass from the Trust to the Foundation. They were intended to operate in tandem and the trustee/directors have, in practice, at all material times been common to both companies. Mr and Mrs Slater have been directors throughout the companies' existence: there have been some changes among the other directors.

'7. The Trust's accounts show that its net income for the three year period (ie the balance of its income from dividends, interest, rents, covenanted payments and capital gains over its expenses) was disposed of as follows:—

(i) Year to 31 March 1973—net income	£739,219	
Donation to European charity		£ 75,000
Donation to the Foundation		£639,318
Undistributed		£ 24,901
		£739,219
(ii) year to 31 March 1974—net income	£ 5,050	
Donation to the Foundation		£ 5,050
(iii) year to 31 March 1975—net income	£ 12,225	
Donation to the Foundation		£ 12,225

'8. For the same three years the Foundation's net income (excluding donations from the Trust) was £10,963, £83,867 and £77,325 respectively. At the beginning of the period it had funds in hand (described in the accounts as the Accumulated Fund) of £263,265 which, after some fluctuation during the period, stood at £515,554 at 31 March 1975. Its donations to other charitable bodies totalled £115,815 in the first year, £89,511 in the second year and £295,473 in the third year.

'9. On those figures there seemed to us to be room for debate as to how far the Foundation should be treated as having distributed in each year the money received from the Trust; but no argument was addressed to us on that point. For the purpose of this appeal the Trust accepts the Revenue's calculation that £578,479 out of the first year's donation and the whole of the donation in each of the other years was added to the Foundation's funds and was not distributed in the year of receipt. We have accordingly considered the rival contentions on that agreed basis.

'10. The Trust contends that, by giving money to another registered charity whose *bona fides* has not been challenged, it has applied its income for charitable purposes and no further enquiry is necessary as to the use which the recipient charity has made of it. Not every charity can engage in relief work "in the field" and *a* the making of grants to further the work of other charities is a well-recognised method of furthering charitable objects. The donor charity is entitled to assume that the money will be used for charitable purposes unless it has knowledge that the recipient intends to misapply it (which is not suggested in this case). Moreover, even if it were appropriate to consider the Foundation's application of the money, the Trust's claim would be established. The addition of money to a charity's general *b* endowment fund, provided that it is appropriated to charitable purposes only, is itself the application of money to charitable purposes.

'11. The Inland Revenue contends that these two charities set up to work together under a common directorship, should be considered as one. The Trust's part in the operations is, in effect, to raise funds for the Foundation. The Trust itself did not "apply" its income at all in any realistic sense, but left its application to the *c* Foundation. The accumulation of money generally for future use in a charity's work (as opposed to the building up of a fund for a specific purpose), does not amount to an "application" of that money within the meaning of the relevant statutory provisions.

'12. Neither party could point to authority as to the effect of accumulation of income in relation to the statutory provisions which we had to consider. For the *d* Trust we were referred to dicta of Lord Sands in *The General Nursing Council for Scotland v Commissioners of Inland Revenue*[1] which suggested that income carried to the credit of a charity's reserve fund would be applied for a charitable purpose; but it was not necessary to decide that point for the purposes of the case and Lord Blackburn (the only other member of the Court of Session who mentioned it) appeared to take a somewhat different view. For the Crown it was pointed out that *e* in *Ofrex Foundation Trustees v Commissioners of Inland Revenue*[2] Cross J (as he then was) regarded it as arguable that if charitable income has been accumulated it has not yet been applied to a charitable purpose.

Conclusion

'13. We accept that the Trust and the Foundation are separate entities and that it *f* is the application of the Trust's income which is for question. We also accept, as a general proposition, that it is a proper application of a charity's income to make donations for the furtherance of another charity's work. It would be highly inconvenient if, in order to satisfy the requirements of section 360, the donor charity had to follow its donation into the accounts of the recipient charity and produce evidence as to its application by that body. In our view the section imposes, *g* in principle, no such requirement. The mere fact of donation to another charity will normally satisfy the requirements of the section.

'14. A general proposition of that kind may, no doubt, need to be modified in relation to particular facts. Circumstances could, we think, arise in which it would be proper to look beyond the immediate disposition of a charity's income, as for example where income was knowingly channelled through an associated charitable *h* company under common control to a non-charitable object. We doubt whether, in such a case, the donor could rely on the separation of identity between the two bodies to establish a claim to exemption under section 360. However there is no evidence to suggest that those considerations apply to the present case. We have to decide this case on the basis that the Trust's donations to the Foundation were to be used for the general furtherance of the Foundation's authorised charitable objects. *j* On that basis we hold that the sums in dispute were applied by the Trust to charitable purposes only.

1   1929 SC 664 at 671, 14 Tax Cas 645 at 653
2   [1965] 3 All ER 529 at 539, [1966] Ch 675 at 701, 42 Tax Cas 524 at 537

a '15. We should have reached the same conclusion even if we had accepted the Crown's argument that it was necessary to look through the transfer of money from the Trust to the Foundation and treat the Trust's income as being, in effect, applied by the Foundation in augmenting its own funds in the years under appeal. We share Lord Sands' view, expressed in the *General Nursing Council for Scotland* case[1], that the addition of income to the reserve fund of a charity can in itself be the application of that income for a charitable purpose, at any rate in the absence of any *b* special indication to the contrary.

'16. For these reasons we allow the appeals and admit the Trust's claim in respect of each of the disputed amounts of income.'

9. The Crown immediately after the determination of the appeal declared its dissatisfaction therewith as being erroneous in point of law and on 5th December 1978 required the commissioners to state a case for the opinion of the High Court pursuant to *c* s 56 of the Taxes Management Act 1970.

10. The question of law for the opinion of the court was whether, on the facts stated in this case, the commissioners' decision was erroneous in point of law.

C H McCall for the Crown.
Andrew Park QC for the trust.

d

Cur adv vult

30th November. **SLADE J** read the following judgment: This is an appeal by the Crown from a decision of the Commissioners for the Special Purposes of the Income Tax Acts by way of case stated. It relates to the nature and extent of the special exemptions from tax given to charities by s 360(1) of the Income and Corporation Taxes Act 1970 and *e* s 35(1) of the Finance Act 1965.

The facts are to be found set out in the case stated together with an agreed statement of facts, which is annexed to and forms part of it. The salient facts may be summarised as follows. In February 1970 a company now known as the Helen Slater Charitable Trust Ltd was incorporated at the instance of Mrs Helen Slater under the then name of Univale Ltd. I will for brevity call it 'the trust', though it must throughout be borne in mind that *f* it is a corporate body. Also in February 1970 a company now known as the Slater Foundation Ltd was incorporated at the instance of Mrs Slater's husband, Mr J D Slater, under the name of Basilicon Ltd. I will call it 'the foundation'. Both companies were incorporated as companies limited by guarantee with no share capital; each of them is a registered charity.

The three general objects of each company are similar, although not identical in all *g* respects; that is to say, (1) in both cases, to relieve suffering amongst the aged, impotent or poor; (2) in both cases, to advance education; (3) in the case of the foundation, to further such other charitable objects as the company may think fit; (4) in the case of the trust, to further such other charitable objects as the trust may think fit and, in particular, but without prejudice to the generality of the foregoing, to make grants to such associations, trusts, societies or corporations as are established for charitable purposes *h* only. In the memorandum of each company those three general objects are followed by a number of specific objects and powers of a detailed kind, subject in each case to a proviso that the company is established for charitable purposes only and that all its objects and powers are to be construed in the light of that limitation.

Paragraph 6 of the commissioners' decision records further findings of fact as follows:

j 'It is an agreed fact that the Trust and the Foundation were established as a joint operation whereby money would, from time to time, pass from the Trust to the Foundation. They were intended to operate in tandem and the trustee/directors have, in practice, at all material times been common to both companies. Mr and

---

1   1929 SC 664, 14 Tax Cas 645

Mrs Slater have been directors throughout the companies' existence: there have been some changes among the other directors.'

For the accounting year ended 31st March 1973, the trust's net income (that is to say, the balance of its income from dividends, interest, rents, covenanted payments and capital gains after its expenses) amounted to £739,219, of which £75,000 was donated by it to a European charity, £639,318 was donated by it to the Foundation and £24,901 was undistributed. For present purposes it is common ground that £578,479 out of this donation to the foundation was added to the foundation's funds and was not distributed in the year of receipt. For the accounting year ended 31st March 1974 the trust's net income amounted to only £5,050, of which the whole was donated by it to the foundation. For present purposes, it is common ground that the whole of this sum was added to the foundation's funds and was not distributed in the year of receipt. For the accounting year ended 31st March 1975 the trust's net income amounted to £12,225, of which the whole was donated by it to the foundation. Again, for present purposes, it is common ground that the whole of this sum was added to the foundation's funds and was not distributed in the year of receipt.

The Crown refused a claim by the trust to exemption from tax under s 360(1) of the 1970 Act and s 35(1) of the Finance Act 1965, in respect of income and gains for the three relevant accounting periods. The trust appealed against this refusal to the Special Commissioners, who allowed the appeal and admitted the trust's claim in respect of each of the disputed amounts of income; that is to say, £578,479 for the year to 31st March 1973; £5,050 for the year to 31st March 1974; and £12,225 for the year to 31st March 1975. The Crown now appeals from the Special Commissioners' decision.

Section 360(1)(c) of the 1970 Act, so far as material, provides:

'The following exemptions shall be granted on a claim in that behalf to the Board ... (c) exemption—(i) from tax under Schedule C in respect of any interest, annuities, dividends or shares of annuities, (ii) from tax under Schedule D in respect of any yearly interest or other annual payment, and (iii) from tax under Schedule F in respect of any distribution, where the income in question forms part of the income of a charity, or is, according to rules or regulations established by Act of Parliament, charter, decree, deed of trust or will, applicable to charitable purposes only, and so far as it is applied to charitable purposes only . . .'

Then, s 360(2), as amended, provides: 'A charity shall in respect of tax on chargeable gains be allowed exemption in accordance with section 35 of the Finance Act 1965.' Subsection (3) defines 'charity' as meaning 'any body of persons or trust established for charitable purposes only'.

Section 35(1) of the Finance Act 1965, provides: 'Subject to subsection (2) of this section a gain shall not be a chargeable gain if it accrues to a charity and is applicable and applied for charitable purposes.'

Subsection (2) then contains certain provisions which are expressed to take effect if property held on charitable trusts ceases to be subject to charitable trusts, but I do not think I need read it.

It follows from s 360(1) of the 1970 Act and s 35(1) of the 1965 Act (which I shall henceforth call 'the two subsections') that the trust, being a registered charity of which the income is applicable to charitable purposes only, must be entitled to exemption from income tax, and from tax that would otherwise be payable on chargeable gains, in so far as its income and gains are 'applied to charitable purposes only' within the meaning of the two subsections, but no further. Section 35(1) in fact uses the phrase 'applied for charitable purposes', but this slight difference in the language of the two subsections seems to me immaterial and I shall use the two phrases interchangeably.

The trust claims that the whole of the disputed sums have been 'applied for charitable purposes' within the relevant meaning. The grounds on which it so claimed before the commissioners are to be found summarised in para 10 of the commissioners' decision as follows:

a
'The Trust contends that, by giving money to another registered charity whose *bona fides* has not been challenged, it has applied its income for charitable purposes and no further enquiry is necessary as to the use which the recipient charity has made of it. Not every charity can engage in relief work "in the field" and the making of grants to further the work of other charities is a well-recognised method of furthering charitable objects. The donor charity is entitled to assume that the money will be used for charitable purposes unless it has knowledge that the recipient

b
intends to misapply it (which is not suggested in this case). Moreover, even if it were appropriate to consider the Foundation's application of the money, the Trust's claim would be established. The addition of money to a charity's general endowment fund, provided that it is appropriated to charitable purposes only, is itself the application of money to charitable purposes.'

c
The grounds on which the Crown opposed this claim before the commissioners are to be found summarised in para 11 of the commissioners' decision as follows:

'The Inland Revenue contends that these two charities set up to work together under a common directorship, should be considered as one. The Trust's part in the operations is, in effect, to raise funds for the Foundation. The Trust itself did not "apply" its income at all in any realistic sense, but left its application to the

d
Foundation. The accumulation of money generally for future use in a charity's work (as opposed to the building up of a fund for a specific purpose), does not amount to an "application" of that money within the meaning of the relevant statutory provisions.'

The commissioners in the event preferred the arguments of the trust as they are summarised in the commissioners' decision.

e
Before me, the grounds on which the trust has claimed that it is entitled to the relevant reliefs have been substantially the same as they were before the commissioners. The Crown's case has been put slightly differently from the arguments summarised in para 11 of the commissioners' decision. Counsel for the Crown has not contended before me that the trust and the foundation should be treated as one body. This seems to me plainly correct; in law, they must be regarded as separate, distinct entities. He has, however,

f
submitted that the facts as found by the commissioners show that the foundation was what he called 'a parallel body' to the trust, in the sense that both bodies were set up to act together by husband and wife respectively, they have at all material times had the same control and the same generality of purpose, and they have at all material times operated in tandem, to use the commissioners' phrase.

In my judgment, the submission that the foundation has at all material times been a

g
parallel body to the trust in this sense is justified on the facts as found, and I do not think it has really been disputed on behalf of the trust.

From this starting point of fact, counsel for the Crown goes on to submit three propositions of law. (1) If income of a charity is to qualify for relief under the two subsections, it is not enough that it should simply belong to the charity in question; there has to be a positive 'application' of the income within the meaning of the two

h
subsections. (2) The simple addition of income to capital does not amount to an 'application' within such meaning, unless the accumulation is made for a specific charitable purpose. (3) If such simple accumulation does not amount to an application, then no more does the addition of income to capital through the use of a parallel body.

In the present case, counsel for the Crown went on to submit, in effect, the disputed payments by the trust to the foundation amounted to the mere addition of income to

j
capital through the use of a parallel body. Accordingly, he submitted, they did not amount to 'applications' of income by the trust, and cannot qualify for relief under the two subsections.

I find no difficulty in accepting the first of counsel's three propositions for the Crown. The wording of the two subsections makes it clear that for income of a charity or gains accruing to a charity to qualify for relief thereunder, it does not suffice for the

income in question merely to be the income of a charity: it has to be both 'applicable' and *a*
'applied' for charitable purposes within the meaning of the subsections. The present
dispute and the accuracy or otherwise of counsel's second and third propositions for the
Crown turn on the meaning of the phrases 'applied to charitable purposes' or 'applied for
charitable purposes' in the context of the present facts.

In support of the second of his three principal propositions counsel for the Crown
referred me to a number of authorities, some in the context of the Income Tax Acts and
others not, where the meaning of the word 'applied' has been considered by the court. *b*
In *General Nursing Council for Scotland v Inland Revenue Comrs*[1], that council claimed
exemption from income tax with respect to the income on its investments under
s 37(1)(b) of the Income Tax Act 1918, of which I think the wording was in all material
respects similar to that of s 360 of the 1970 Act. The Court of Session rejected the claim
on the grounds that the council was not established for charitable purposes only. Lord
Sands and Lord Blackburn, however, went on to make certain obiter observations on the *c*
meaning of the phrase 'and so far as the same are applied to charitable purposes only',
which appeared at the end of s 37(1)(b). Lord Sands said in this context[2]:

> 'It does not import that the exemption is to be allowed only when the income has
> been spent, or falls immediately to be spent, for some charitable purpose. If the
> directors of a charitable trust deem it desirable that a capital sum should be
> accumulated for the service of the trust or that a reserve fund should be formed for *d*
> the greater security of the trust, the income carried to the credit of any such account
> is, in my view, applied to a charitable purpose. If testamentary trustees were
> directed to apply part of an estate to charitable purposes, it would, as it appears to
> me, be quite unreasonable to suggest that they had failed so to apply it if they made
> it over to the capital fund of a charitable institution. Surplus income of the charity
> which the managing body find it possible to use in the same way seems to me to be *e*
> on the same footing and to be applied to a charitable purpose.'

Lord Blackburn, however, took what is at least at first sight a rather different view, less
favourable to the taxpayer. He said[3]:

> 'Some income then which otherwise would be entitled to exemption is not to be
> exempt unless it is actually applied to charitable purposes, and I agree with Lord *f*
> Sands that these words are apt to apply to the income in question, assuming that the
> Council was itself a charitable institution. I should hesitate to give them so strict a
> construction as to attach to small sums necessarily carried forward in the accounts
> of a charitable trust from one year to another to enable the trust to be conducted in
> a businesslike manner. But it seems to me that they do require that the income, if
> not actually expended on a charitable purpose during the year of assessment, must *g*
> at least be appropriated to expenditure on charity in the immediate future . . . But
> so long as the Council merely apply the income accruing from year to year to
> increasing the capital sum, then even had they been a body established for charitable
> purposes I would have hesitated to agree that it was being applied to charitable
> purposes only and therefore entitled to exemption.'

In the light of these and other judgments to which I shall be referring, counsel for the *h*
Crown accepted and submitted that the setting aside of income for a specific charitable
project could well amount to an 'application for charitable purposes' within the meaning
of the two subsections; for it could amount to an 'appropriation to expenditure on
charity', within the meaning of Lord Blackburn's words. He submitted, however, that
mere retention for the general purposes of a charity, without a positive determination *j*
that it shall be set aside for a particular purpose, does not amount to an 'application'

---

1   1929 SC 664, 14 Tax Cas 645
2   1929 SC 664 at 671, 14 Tax Cas 655 at 653–654
3   1929 SC 664 at 674, 14 Tax Cas 655 at 656–657

within such meaning. Even Lord Sands, he pointed out, used the phrase 'If the directors
a of a charitable trust deem it desirable', which seems to imply that there must be some
conscious, positive exercise of a discretion.

The Crown thus accepts, counsel explained, that money can be 'applied for charitable
purposes', within the meaning of the two subsections, even though it is not immediately
spent. If, for example, the directors of a charity decide to set aside income to fund an art
gallery or to finance research, the setting aside is capable of constituting an application,
b in the Crown's view, since there has been a positive exercise of the discretion of the
directors, who have decided how to deal with the money. There is, however, in the
Crown's submission, a crucial distinction to be drawn between the positive exercise of a
discretion in this manner and a mere retention for the general purposes of a charity,
which in reality involves the postponement of the decision how the money is to be
finally dealt with. So long as such postponement continues, he submitted, it cannot be
c said that the money has been 'applied'.

If, as I understand, this summary broadly represents the practice of the Inland Revenue
in regard to income which is set aside for charitable purposes, it seems that Cross J may
have stated the practice a little too broadly in *Ofrex Foundation (Trustees of George Drexler)
v Inland Revenue Comrs*[1] where he said:

d
> '. . . it might be argued that if charitable income has been accumulated it has not
> yet been applied to a charitable purpose and that accordingly no refund is due. I
> understand, however, that in practice accumulations are treated as having been
> applied for charitable purposes.'

Counsel for the Crown sought to support his submission that there can be no
application of money in the absence of a definite, specific decision as to what should be
e done with it, by reference to a number of further cases. In *Williams v Papworth*[2] the Privy
Council considered a direction in a settlement that an annuity should be 'applied by the
said trustees or trustee for the maintenance and education of such children or child as
aforesaid'. The appellant argued that the trustees had a discretionary power to apportion
the annuity among the children according to their several necessities. The appellant
relied, inter alia, on the use of the word 'applied'. Lord Macnaghten rejected this
f argument saying[3]: 'But the word "applied" does not import a power of selection: it
simply means "devoted to" or "employed for the special purpose of".'

Counsel for the Crown also referred to *Lord Mostyn v London (Surveyor of Taxes)*[4], where
it was held that moneys, which had been received for fines on the renewal of certain
leases and had been placed on temporary deposit at a bank, had not been 'applied as
productive capital' within the meaning of a provision of the Income Tax Act 1842.
g Wright J said[5]:

> 'The word "applied" must mean something more than what has been done in the
> present case, for the fines here cannot be said to have been applied, but are rather
> held in suspense until it is decided how they are to be applied. I think that a
> temporary deposit such as this is not an application of productive capital, for that
h > must mean something more than a deposit by way of loan.'

Collins J said[6]:

> 'There must be some element of permanence, and, as Wright J., has said, it is not
> enough that the money should be held in suspense until the owner has determined
> how he will ultimately apply it.'

j
1   [1965] 3 All ER 529 at 539, [1966] Ch 675 at 701, 42 Tax Cas 524 at 537
2   [1900] AC 563
3   [1900] AC 563 at 567
4   [1895] 1 QB 170, 3 Tax Cas 294
5   [1895] 1 QB 170 at 173, 3 Tax Cas 294 at 296
6   [1895] 1 QB 170 at 173, 3 Tax Cas 294 at 297

Counsel for the Crown also referred to *B Morris Ltd v Lunzer*[1], where the Court of
Appeal considered the meaning of the phrase 'appropriates or applies' in the context of *a*
s 25(2) of the Finance (No 2) Act 1940. The facts of that case are far away from the
present, if only because the subsection was directed to the appropriation or application of
goods and not money. Lord Greene MR however, reading the judgment of the court,
made the following general comment[2]: '. . . whatever the words "appropriates or applies"
may mean in relation to the facts of any individual case, they point to some final and
unconditional act.' Likewise, the Crown submits, if directors of a company holding its *b*
assets for general charitable purposes receive money as income and simply add such
income to capital, without making a final annexation of it to a particular end, they
cannot be said to have 'applied' it within the meaning of the two subsections: they have
merely held their decision in suspense.

In the light of authorities such as these, it becomes obvious that, in particular cases,
difficult borderline questions may arise whether money has been 'applied for charitable *c*
purposes' within the meaning of the two subsections. Three points were, I think, more
or less common ground in argument, though not perhaps covered by formal concessions
on both sides. First, moneys which a charity has expended either on its proper running
expenses or on exclusively charitable relief work 'in the field', to use the commissioners'
phrase, must be ordinarily regarded as having been applied for charitable purposes.
Secondly, one of the purposes of the phrase, 'so far as the same are applied for charitable *d*
purposes', as appearing in the two subsections, must be to exclude from the relief thereby
given any income which, though being that of a charity and applicable for charitable
purposes, has in fact been applied for non-charitable purposes. The Court of Appeal
decision in *Inland Revenue Comrs v Educational Grants Association Ltd*[3] is one example
where certain income did not qualify for the exemption because it had been applied for
demonstrably non-charitable purposes. Thirdly, however, it is unlikely that the *sole* *e*
purpose of the legislature in including the relevant phrase in the two subsections was that
to which I have last referred. Counsel submitted on behalf of the Crown, and counsel for
the trust I think accepted, that the legislature, in using the affirmative phrase 'so far as
applied' etc, must have intended to impose an affirmative requirement that the income
should have been dealt with in some way or other. It was, I think, common ground that
merely to receive income and do nothing with it would not amount to an 'application' *f*
thereof.

The area of doubt concerns the nature and extent of the dealing with the income that
is necessary to constitute an 'application'. Counsel for the Crown, relying particularly on
the dictum of Lord Blackburn in *General Nursing Council for Scotland v Inland Revenue
Comrs*[4] and the other authorities which I have mentioned, submitted, as I have said, that
a simple addition of income receipts to capital does not qualify for relief unless it is made *g*
for a specific charitable purpose. Counsel for the trust while accepting that the mere
holding of moneys in suspense would not constitute an application, submitted, so far as
was necessary for his argument, that counsel's proposition for the Crown was too
narrowly stated. He submitted that income of a charity can properly be said to have been
'applied for charitable purposes', if it is used to augment its endowments by way of
accumulation. *h*

I confess that the propositions of both sides on this point leave me with a number of
doubts, and do not strike me as wholly satisfactory. I am not sure, for example, that I can
see any satisfactory logical distinction between (a) the case where the directors or trustees
of a charity make a conscious decision to accumulate, because they think that this is the
best way to further a specific charitable object which they have decided to support (for
example, to fund a particular form of research), and (b) the case where the directors or *j*

1   [1942] 1 All ER 77, [1942] 1 KB 356
2   [1942] 1 All ER 77 at 80, [1942] 1 KB 356 at 362
3   [1967] 2 All ER 893, [1967] Ch 993, 44 Tax Cas 93
4   1929 SC 664, 14 Tax Cas 645

a   trustees make a conscious decision to accumulate, because they think that this is, in all the circumstances, the best way to further the general objects of the charity. One example of case (b) might arise where the charity was likely to be faced with heavy building expenditure in a few years' time and its managers thought it only prudent to create a reserve fund of investments to meet it. In either case (a) or case (b) the decision to accumulate would ordinarily be revocable, so that in this sense, even in case (a), it could be said that the decision was no more than a temporary one. It seems to me at least

b   a possible view that the reliefs must be available in both case (a) and case (b) or in neither of them.

However, in the event, I find it unnecessary to express any final view on the second of counsel's three main propositions for the Crown, or as to the extent if any to which income which is accumulated, whether for the general purposes of the charity or for a specific purpose, can be said to be 'applied for charitable purposes' within the meaning

c   of the two subsections. My reasons are these. Whatever other doubts may arise in other contexts as to the meaning of the phrase 'applied for charitable purposes', it seems to me that, ordinarily, income must be said to have been thus 'applied' by charitable corporation A, if it is transferred outright to charitable corporation B, being itself a corporation with exclusively charitable objects. A disposition of assets by one corporation in favour of another corporation, in such manner as to pass the whole title in such assets to the

d   transferee, must, in my judgment, ordinarily amount to an 'application' of such assets within the normal use of legal terminology. In *Re Hastings-Bass*[1], it was held, inter alia, that trustees of one settlement had 'applied' trust funds within the meaning of s 32 of the Trustee Act 1925 in advancing the funds to the trustees of another settlement, even though, on the particular facts, the advance had created only a limited beneficial interest in income and no effective beneficial trust of capital of the funds advanced (see per

e   Buckley LJ[2]). The present example seems to me a fortiori.

On behalf of the Crown, counsel, in answer to a question which I put to him, expressly accepted that if one charitable corporation, acting intra vires, transfers money applicable for charitable purposes to another corporation established for exclusively charitable purposes, *whose management is as a matter of fact entirely separate and distinct from that of the transferor corporation*, the transfer will by itself amount to an 'application' of such money

f   within the meaning of the two subsections, except in the case where the transferor has knowledge that the recipient intends to misapply it. In these hypothetical circumstances, and subject to this exception, he accepted that the transfer will entitle the transferor to claim relief under the two subsections, without having to show what use the recipient charity has made of the money.

Does it, then, make any difference that the recipient corporation in the present case,

g   namely the foundation, is a 'parallel body' to the trust, as I have found it to be within the terminology of counsel for the Crown? He submits that it makes the whole difference. Everything in the end, he submits, must depend on the purpose or motive of the transferor corporation. If its purpose or motive has been to enable accumulation to take place within the parallel transferee corporation, there cannot be said to have been an 'application' by the transferor.

h   I do not feel able to accept this submission. The 1965 Act and the 1970 Act could well have contained provisions ancillary to the two subsections providing, in effect, that a transfer of income or gains to a connected body should not be treated as an 'application' for the purposes of the two subsections. In many other contexts the Income Tax Acts contain special provisions designed to cover dealings between connected persons or bodies. There are, however, no such special provisions applicable in the present case. In

j   their absence, the following general proposition is in my judgment correct in law. Any charitable corporation which, acting intra vires, makes an outright transfer of money applicable for charitable purposes to any other corporation established exclusively for

---

1   [1974] 2 All ER 193, [1975] Ch 25, [1974] STC 211
2   [1974] 2 All ER 193 at 293–204, [1975] Ch 25 at 42, [1974] STC 211 at 221–222

charitable purposes, in such manner as to pass to the transferee full title to the money, must be taken, by the transfer itself, to have 'applied' such money for 'charitable *a* purposes', within the meaning of the two subsections, unless the transferor knows or ought to know that the money will be misapplied by the transferee. In such circumstances, and subject to the last-mentioned exception, the transferor corporation is in my judgment entitled to claim exemption under the two subsections, without having to show how the money has been dealt with by the transferee.

There is no suggestion on the facts of the present case that there was any question of *b* the moneys being misapplied by the foundation. The good faith of the Trust and of the foundation has not been questioned.

It follows from all this that I must effectively reject counsel's principal proposition for the Crown and that I find it unnecessary to make a decision on his second proposition. I answer his third principal proposition as follows. If an 'application' of moneys takes place through an outright transfer of such moneys by charitable corporation A to *c* charitable corporation B, for present purposes it matters not whether the purpose or motive of the transfer may have been to enable corporation B to add such income to its general funds of capital. Once the court were to begin to introduce the concept of 'parallel bodies' into the construction of the two subsections, then, in the absence of statutory definition, intolerably difficult questions of degree would arise; and I do not think that such introduction can be justified by the wording of the subsections. *d*

In conclusion, I would make this observation. Counsel for the Crown submitted that, if the trust's contentions be correct, this opens up an easy avenue to tax avoidance by the setting up of parallel charitable companies or trusts. In this context, however, counsel for the trust fairly reminded me of what was said by Lord Greene MR in *Henriksen* (*Inspector of Taxes*) v *Grafton Hotel Ltd*[1]:

> 'It frequently happens in income tax cases that the same result in a business sense *e* can be secured by two different legal transactions, one of which may attract tax and the other not. This is no justification for saying that a taxpayer who has adopted the method which attracts tax is to be treated as though he had chosen the method which does not or *vice versa*.'

The subsections may give rise to very difficult questions of construction in other cases, *f* particularly where only one charitable corporation or trust is involved and its income has not been fully distributed. On the present facts, however, the trust has distributed and applied all the disputed sums of income by paying them to the foundation, so that these difficult questions do not arise. I think that the trust has plainly brought itself within the wording of the relevant exemptions on the facts of the present case. In my judgment, therefore, the commissioners were right to admit the trust's claim in respect of each of *g* the disputed amounts of income, and I must dismiss this appeal.

In conclusion, I should like to express my appreciation to counsel on both sides for their interesting and helpful arguments.

Appeal dismissed.

h

Solicitors: *Solicitor of Inland Revenue*; *Clifford-Turner* (for the trust).

Rozanna Malcolm   Barrister.

---

1   [1942] 1 All ER 678 at 683, [1942] 2 KB 184 at 193, 24 Tax Cas 453 at 460

j

Hawkins v Bepey and others

QUEEN'S BENCH DIVISION
BROWNE LJ AND WATKINS J
23rd, 24th OCTOBER, 2nd NOVEMBER 1979

Criminal law – Appeal – Death of prosecutor before appeal heard – Effect – Information laid by chief inspector of police in accordance with chief constable's instruction that informations were to be laid by chief inspectors – Justices dismissing information on ground no case to answer – Chief inspector appealing and requesting case stated – Chief inspector entering into recognisance to prosecute appeal without delay – Chief inspector dying before appeal heard – Whether appeal lapsing on his death – Whether chief constable real prosecutor – Whether chief inspector prosecuting as representative of chief constable – Whether recognisance given in representative capacity.

The chief constable of a police force issued instructions, similar to instructions issued by other chief constables, that informations laid by the police in magistrates' courts should, as a general rule, be laid by a chief inspector or inspector of the force. A chief inspector laid informations against the respondents alleging certain offences, but he was not himself involved in the investigation of the offences. At the end of the prosecution's case the justices accepted a submission by the respondents that there was no case to answer and dismissed the informations. The chief inspector appealed against the decision and asked the justices to state a case. He entered into a recognisance to prosecute the appeal without delay. After the case was stated but before the appeal came on for hearing the chief inspector died. The respondents contended that there was no jurisdiction to hear the appeal since as a matter of public policy the appeal lapsed on the death of the chief inspector for he alone was the prosecutor and the recognisance to prosecute the appeal was a personal recognisance enforceable only against him or against his estate, which had no pecuniary or other interest in the appeal entitling it to prosecute the appeal.

Held – In laying the informations in accordance with the chief constable's instruction the chief inspector had been acting in a representative capacity for the chief constable or the police force, and not in a personal capacity, since he was merely obeying, as was his duty, the instruction validly given by the chief constable. It followed that the real prosecutor was the chief constable or the police force, and not the chief inspector, and that the recognisance entered into to prosecute the appeal had been tendered on behalf of the chief constable or the police force. Accordingly, as the chief constable was before the court as the prosecutor, the court had jurisdiction to hear the appeal (see p 800 *e f h*, p 801 *f* and p 802 *g*, post).

Dicta of Lush J in *R v Truelove* (1880) 5 QBD at 340, of Lord Parker CJ in *R v Burt, ex parte Presburg* [1960] 1 All ER at 428 and of Lord Denning MR in *R v Metropolitan Police Comr, ex parte Blackburn* [1968] 1 All ER at 769 applied.

Notes
For the effect of the death of parties to a criminal matter, see 11 Halsbury's Laws (4th Edn) para 689.

Cases referred to in judgments

R v Burt, ex parte Presburg [1960] 1 All ER 424, [1960] 1 QB 625, [1960] 2 WLR 398, 124 JP 201, DC, 14(2) Digest (Reissue) 860, 7444.

R v Jefferies [1968] 3 All ER 238, [1969] 1 QB 120, [1968] 3 WLR 830, 14(2) Digest (Reissue) 747, 6267.

R v Metropolitan Police Comr, ex parte Blackburn [1968] 1 All ER 763, [1968] 2 QB 118, [1968] 2 WLR 893, CA, 14(2) Digest (Reissue) 761, 6346.

R v Truelove (1880) 5 QBD 336, 49 LJMC 57, 42 LT 250, 44 JP 346, 14 Cox CC 408, DC, 14(1) Digest (Reissue) 220, 1580.

Cases also cited

Finchley Urban District Council v Blyton (1913) 77 JP Jo 556, DC.   *a*

Garnsworthy v Pyne (1871) 35 JP 21.

Hodgson v Lakeman [1943] KB 15, DC.

Lawford v Leigh Union (1905) 1 Konst Rat App 113.

R v Newport (Salop) Justices, ex parte Wright [1929] 2 KB 416, DC.

R v Rowe [1955] 2 All ER 234, [1955] 1 QB 573, CCA.

R v Spokes, ex parte Buckley (1912) 107 LT 290, DC.   *b*

Richards v Bloxham (Binks) (1968) 112 Sol Jo 543, DC.

Case stated

This was an appeal by a case stated by justices sitting at Tunbridge Wells in respect of their adjudication on 4th April 1977 whereby they dismissed informations laid by Chief Inspector Ernest Walter Hawkins of the Kent Constabulary against the respondents, *c* Derek Jeffrey Bepey, Bepey Transport Services and Wendy Carr, alleging against the first two respondents that on 26th March 1976 they used on a road a motor vehicle of excessive weight for a purpose for which it was unsuitable and likely to cause danger to persons on the road, contrary to reg 90(3) of the Motor Vehicles (Construction and Use) Regulations 1973 and ss 40(5) and 177 of the Road Traffic Act 1972, and alleging against the third respondent that she aided, abetted, counselled and procured the commission of *d* the offence. The justices dismissed the informations because they accepted the respondents' submission at the end of the prosecution's case that there was no case to answer. The chief inspector appealed and asked the justice to state a case. After the case was stated but before the appeal came on for hearing the chief inspector died. The question arose whether on his death the appeal lapsed and there was no jurisdiction to hear it. The facts are set out in the judgment of Watkins J.   *e*

Stephen Hockman for the Chief Constable of the Kent Constabulary.

Camden Pratt for the respondents.

Cur adv vult

2nd November. The following judgments were read.   *f*

WATKINS J (delivering the first judgment at the invitation of Browne LJ). This is an appeal by case stated from a decision of justices sitting at Tunbridge Wells Magistrates' Court on 4th April 1977. On that day they heard informations laid against the respondents, Derek Jeffrey Bepey, Bepey Transport Services and Wendy Carr, alleging that the first two respondents did on 26th March 1976, at Frant Road, Tunbridge Wells, *g* use on a road a motor vehicle of an excessive weight, being a purpose for which it was so unsuitable as to cause or be likely to cause danger to persons on a road, contrary to reg 90(3) of the Motor Vehicles (Construction and Use) Regulations 1973[1] and ss 40(5) and 177 of the Road Traffic Act 1972. The third respondent was alleged to have aided, abetted, counselled and procured the commission of this offence by the first respondent.

At the conclusion of the prosecution's evidence the justices, in response to a submission *h* to that effect made to them on behalf of all the respondents, found there was no case to answer and dismissed the informations. The prosecutor appealed against this decision. He asked the justices to state a case. This they have done and invite this court to decide, inter alia, whether they were correct in law in finding there was no case to answer and whether an order for costs made in favour of the appellant was legally proper.

Before expressing an opinion on these matters it is necessary to examine a very *j* different question, namely whether this court has jurisdiction to hear the appeal since the police officer who laid the informations died on 15th October 1978, which was over a

1 SI 1973 No 24

year after the case had been stated. He was Chief Inspector Ernest Walter Hawkins of the
a Kent police force. That this appeal was not heard before his death is due to no lack of
diligence on his part in prosecuting it. Nor is it attributable to any fault of the
respondents.

It is submitted by counsel on their behalf that, however regrettable the effect of this
may be, the appeal lapsed on the death of Chief Inspector Hawkins. Accordingly, if that
be right, we have no power to hear it and presumably no power to make any order
b whatsoever concerning it save in respect of costs. He asserts that the chief inspector and
none other was the prosecutor. On laying the informations he did so of his own volition
and determination. He acted neither at the behest nor on behalf of anyone. He entered
into a personal recognisance to prosecute this appeal without delay as he was by law called
on to do when requesting the justices to state a case. This was enforceable against him
and is now enforceable against his estate. No other person can be made responsible for
c it. When a party to an appeal who is a prosecutor in a criminal matter dies, public policy
demands that thereupon the appeal should be terminated. It would be unconscionable
or otherwise wrong to allow some other person to take the place of the deceased chief
inspector on the basis that he is an aggrieved person for the purpose of s 87(1) of the
Magistrates' Courts Act 1952 or on any other basis. The deceased chief inspector's estate
has no interest, pecuniary or other, in the appeal since no one will make demands on that,
d no matter what be the outcome of these proceedings.

Counsel for the respondents and counsel instructed by the prosecuting solicitor for the
chief constable and of the Kent police force have referred us to a large number of
authorities, most of which raised the question of the effect of the death of a respondent
to an appeal on its continued existence. In some cases personal representatives of the
deceased respondents have been allowed by this court to continue appeals on establishing
e a pecuniary interest in the subject-matter on appeal. This court does not derive its
jurisdiction and powers entirely from statute.

Widgery LJ in *R v Jefferies*[1] said of the courts which do derive jurisdiction from statute:

f
'Whatever may be the powers of courts exercising a jurisdiction that does not
derive from statute, the powers of this court are derived from, and confined to,
those given by the Criminal Appeal Act, 1907. We take it to be a general principle
that whenever a party to proceedings dies, the proceedings must abate, unless his
personal representatives both have an interest in the subject-matter and can by
virtue of the express terms of a statute (or from rules of court made by virtue of
jurisdiction given by a statute) take the appropriate steps to have themselves
substituted for the deceased as a party to the proceedings.'
g

Jefferies died following his conviction of conspiracy to cheat and defraud and before
his application for leave to appeal could be heard. The court held that it had no
jurisdiction to allow his widow and executrix to continue the application since neither
the Criminal Appeal Act 1907 nor rules made thereunder made provision for the
continuance of an appeal after the death of the 'person convicted'. The right of appeal
h under the Act was strictly personal to the person convicted and there was no inherent
power in the court to permit an appeal to continue after his death.

Regardless of the matter of inherent power, it is further submitted on the respondents'
behalf that it would be grossly unjust to permit an appeal to continue following the death
of a prosecutor and to deny the like consent to the personal representatives of a convicted
person.
j How this court would have viewed an application on behalf of a personal representative
with an interest to continue an appeal following, let me suppose, the death of either the
first or third respondent had that person been convicted does not arise for

---

1   [1968] 3 All ER 238 at 240, [1969] 1 QB 120 at 124

determination. However, as I understand the status and power of this court, it would have by its inherent jurisdiction the right in its discretion to grant such an application. *a* The fate of the application would, I think, depend on the nature and extent of the interest, probably pecuniary only, in the subject-matter of the appeal proved by the personal representative.

Since this is not the issue before us I do not see the necessity to recite the authorities which appear to support this proposition. Nor do I deem it necessary to embark on a review of all those authorities and matters of argument and submission which counsel *b* for the Kent police force provided. He maintains that the chief constable and the personal representative of the chief inspector are 'aggrieved persons'. Thus either one is entitled to continue the appeal. Whether this be so or not, this court as a matter of practice will allow an appeal to proceed wherever it is just and convenient to do so. Whilst those propositions might prove to be meritorious if closely examined, since I believe the jurisdiction to hear this appeal can be securely founded on a wholly different *c* basis I do no more than make mention of them.

There is no doubt that the Kent police force is under the direction and control of its chief constable: see s 5(1) of the Police Act 1964. Using those powers the chief constable has by no 45 of his instructions to the force ruled:

> 'Officers in charge of divisions will as a general rule arrange that all information *d* relative to proceedings in magistrates' courts shall be laid by the chief inspector or inspectors.'

No one suggests that that instruction is in any way improper. A similar instruction exists in other police forces. There is a sound administrative, if no other, reason for it. By obeying this instruction does a chief inspector who lays an information, having had no connection with investigating the offence involved, become *the* prosecutor, that is to *e* say the one and only person thereafter to be so regarded for all purposes? I think not. I believe in carrying out force instruction no 45 Chief Inspector Hawkins was acting in a representative capacity. He was representing his chief constable whose orders he had to obey not as a result of the relationship of master and servant but as a duty arising out of the chief constable's power and obligation to direct and control the force.

In *R v Metropolitan Police Comr, ex parte Blackburn*[1] Lord Denning MR said: *f*

> 'Although the chief officers of police are answerable to the law, there are many fields in which they have a discretion with which the law will not interfere. For instance, it is for the Commissioner of Police, or the chief constable, as the case may be, to decide in any particular case whether enquiries should be pursued, or whether an arrest should be made, or a prosecution brought. It must be for him to decide on *g* the disposition of his force and the concentration of his resources on any particular crime or area. No court can or should give him direction on such a matter.'

The real prosecutor of these respondents was, in my opinion, the chief constable of Kent or the Kent police force. So, as counsel for the chief constable has submitted, in a real sense no party to this appeal has died. The recognisance entered into by the chief *h* inspector was tendered by him on the chief constable's behalf, who is answerable for all the consequences of it.

In coming to this conclusion I have gathered support for it from the following cases which were heard in this court, the facts of which are, as one would expect, different from those in the instant case. So are the legal implications which arise from the very different offences and issues involved in them. But whilst the quotations I use must be *j* viewed in the context of the whole of the judgments from which they are taken, I regard the principle which emerges from them as being of general application in circumstances

---

1   [1968] 1 All ER 763 at 769, [1968] 2 QB 118 at 136

where a police officer dies after laying an information and before the relevant proceedings
a come before the court.

In *R v Truelove*[1] Lush J said:

'The counsel for the defendant mainly relied upon these last words, as shewing
that it is essential that there should be a complainant to appeal against. But I cannot
see why, if upon the death of the complainant some other person takes up the
prosecution, he should not be liable to pay costs if the appeal should be successful.
b It could readily be ascertained as a matter of fact who was the party virtually
prosecuting the appeal. There is nothing to shew that the same person who
originally made the complaint must always be party to the appeal.'

In *Truelove's* case[2] the complainant died before a summons concerning the sale of
obscene books was heard in the magistrates' court.
c In *R v Burt, ex parte Presburg*[3] Lord Parker CJ said:

'That is really an end of this case, but I would like also to say this, and I should
have said it earlier. It has been conceded that although the information was laid by
a particular police constable, he must be taken to have been acting on behalf of the
Metropolitan Police in laying that information. It would be quite artificial to treat
him as a private individual and to say that as a private individual he had been put
d to no expense or loss or trouble because he himself was being paid all the time. Not
only would that be an artificial approach, but if one looks at s. 17(1)[4] of the Costs in
Criminal Cases Act, 1952, it is expressly provided: "'Prosecutor' includes any person
who appears to the court to be a person at whose instance the prosecution has been
instituted, or under whose conduct the prosecution is at any time carried on."
Accordingly, counsel for the applicant conceded, quite rightly, that the prosecutor
e here and the person entitled to costs, if costs be payable, is the Commissioner of
Metropolitan Police or the Metropolitan Police Force. Accordingly, in my
judgment, this application fails.'

The subsequent repeal of the 1952 Act to which Lord Parker CJ referred does not, in
my opinion, affect in any way the principle which clearly emerges as a general
f proposition from what Lord Parker CJ said. I hold, therefore, that the actual prosecutor
in this case now before this court is either the chief constable or the Kent police force.
I will assume him to be the chief constable for the purpose of dealing, as I now do, with
the substantive issues in the appeal in the belief that this court is competent to do so.

In summary form the evidence given to the justices revealed that on 26th March 1976
a police constable who was on motor patrol duty saw a horse-box which contained a horse
g being towed along Frank Road, Tunbridge Wells, by a Land-Rover. The first respondent
was driving the Land-Rover, which belonged to the company of which he is the
managing director, namely, the second respondents, who are haulage contractors. The
horse-box was the property of the third respondent. She was at the wheel of and steering
it. The two vehicles were joined by a rigid metal tow bar.

Apparently the horse-box, which was of Bedford manufacture, had broken down.
h Consequently the third respondent asked the first respondent to tow it to a farm in
Wadhurst.

The constable, an experienced and well-tutored member of the traffic patrol, discovered
on stopping these vehicles that the Land-Rover had servo-assisted hydraulic brakes and
that the Bedford had air-assisted hydraulic brakes. The unladen weight of the Land-

j

1   (1880) 5 QBD 336 at 340
2   5 QBD 336
3   [1960] 1 All ER 424 at 428, [1960] 1 QB 625 at 635
4   The definition of 'prosecutor' in s 17(1) of the 1952 Act was omitted when that Act was consolidated
    in the Costs in Criminal Cases Act 1973

Rover was 1 ton 9 cwt 2 qtr. The laden weight of the Bedford subsequently ascertained
was 4 tons 15 cwt 2 qtr.

Whilst being towed the engine of the Bedford was not running and was not therefore
replenishing the supply of air in the brakes reservoir as it diminished on application of
the brakes by the third respondent. Both respondents seemed to have said that they were
aware of this and had devised a system of signalling which would alert them both to the
need to stop when necessary in order that the Land-Rover's compressor could be used to
replenish the Bedford's reservoir with air. When the level of air was dangerously low a
buzzer sounded automatically in the cab of the Bedford. There would then be very little
air indeed in the reservoir, just enough to apply the brake pedal effectively a couple of
times.

The constable thought that, having regard to the disparity in weight of the vehicles,
the absence of any real control of the Bedford's braking system by the first respondent
and the late warning system of the level of air in the brake reservoir, a potentially
dangerous situation could in an emergency arise. To support his opinion he quoted from
the manufacturer's recommendations about weight and other matters relating to the safe
use of a Land-Rover with a trailer. This evidence the justices, wrongly I think, rejected
as hearsay and inadmissible.

Although he had formed the opinion that the first and third respondents were
engaging in a movement of vehicles which could have been potentially dangerous, he
allowed the towing to proceed to the farm because the horse was becoming agitated.

His evidence was, so it could be said, in a reasonably cogent and persuasive manner
confirmed by that provided by a forensic science officer who, amongst other matters,
dealt with acceptable and comparative braking efficiencies.

It is unnecessary to traverse the totality of the evidence in any further detail. Suffice
it to say that, in my view, the effect of it was such as to render safe a conviction of the
respondents if, as was the fact, the prosecution's evidence remained uncontradicted. In
answer to the direct question they ask I would inform the justices that in my opinion
their finding of no case to answer was wrong.

In the usual way this would lead me to say that the case should be remitted to a fresh
bench of magistrates for rehearing and determination. But we deal with an event which,
as things transpired, did not actually become dangerous, although the likelihood of
danger was present. What is more important, it occurred over three years ago.

As has been said before, this court has an overriding discretion when deciding whether
to remit cases for rehearing. I would exercise it here by declining to remit. Nothing
useful would come from incurring any further expenditure of time and money on this
matter.

BROWNE LJ. I agree. The order of the court will be as Watkins J has proposed, that
is to answer the justices' first question[1] No, but we do not remit the case to the justices.

Order accordingly.

Solicitors: *Sharpe, Pritchard & Co*, agents for *R A Crabb*, Maidstone (for the chief
constable); *Buss, Stone & Co*, Tunbridge Wells (for the respondents).

Jacqueline Charles   Barrister.

---

1 The first question was whether the justices were correct in law accepting the submission of no case
   to answer

Samuels v Linzi Dresses Ltd

COURT OF APPEAL, CIVIL DIVISION

ROSKILL, LAWTON LJJ AND SIR STANLEY REES

28th NOVEMBER 1979

Practice – Time – Extension of time – Non-compliance with order striking out claim or defence unless act done within specified time – Whether jurisdiction to extend time where 'unless' order not complied with – RSC Ord 3, r 5(1).

The defendants to an action failed to comply with an order dated 4th October 1978 for delivery of particulars of their defence and counterclaim within 21 days. On 15th December the judge in chambers made a further order that 'unless' the particulars were served by 2nd January 1979 the defence and counterclaim would be struck out leaving the plaintiff at liberty to sign judgment for damages to be assessed. The defendants failed to serve the particulars by 2nd January and on that date issued a summons asking for an extension of time. By an order dated 5th March the judge granted an extension of time until 9th March 1979. The plaintiff appealed contending that, by virtue of RSC Ord 3, r 5(1)[a], where an 'unless' order was made, i e one striking out the claim or defence unless some act was done within a specified time, there was no jurisdiction to grant an extension of time.

Held – A court had jurisdiction to extend the time where an 'unless' order had been made and not complied with, but the power was to be exercised cautiously and with due regard to maintaining the principle that orders were made to be complied with. Whether an extension of time should be granted was in the discretion of the master or judge in chambers. It followed that the judge had jurisdiction to extend the time, and in all the circumstances had properly exercised his discretion in granting the extension. The appeal would therefore be dismissed (see p 812 *a* to *e* and p 813 *c*, post).

Dictum of Lord Denning MR in *R v Bloomsbury and Marylebone County Court, ex parte Villerwest Ltd* [1976] 1 All ER at 900 applied.

Whistler v Hancock (1878) 3 QBD 83 not followed.

Notes

For the power of a court to enlarge the time fixed by an order for doing an act, see 30 Halsbury's Laws (3rd Edn) 402, para 755, and for cases on the subject, see 50 Digest (Repl) 256–259, 87–115.

Cases referred to in judgments

Allen v Sir Alfred McAlpine & Sons Ltd, Bostic v Bermondsey and Southwark Group Hospital Management Committee, Sternberg v Hammond [1968] 1 All ER 543, [1968] 2 QB 229, [1968] 2 WLR 366, Digest (Cont Vol C) 1091, 2262b.

Birkett v James [1977] 2 All ER 801, [1978] AC 297, [1977] 3 WLR 38, HL.

Brown (J M) Ltd v Dennis Price Ltd [1978] Court of Appeal Transcript 304.

Burke v Rooney (1879) 4 CPD 226, 48 LJQB 601, 43 JP 750, 51 Digest (Repl) 622, 2350.

Carter v Stubbs (1880) 6 QBD 116, 50 LJQB 161, 43 LT 746, CA, 50 Digest (Repl) 256, 91.

Collinson v Jeffery [1896] 1 Ch 644, 65 LJ Ch 375, 74 LT 78, 50 Digest (Repl) 257, 97.

King v Davenport (1879) 4 QBD 402, 48 LJQB 606, 50 Digest (Repl) 275, 95.

Laws (R) Planbuild Ltd v Globe Picture Theatres (Bristol) Ltd (10th February 1978) unreported.

Manley Estates Ltd v Benedek [1941] 1 All ER 248, CA, 50 Digest (Repl) 275, 96.

Pryer v Smith [1977] 1 All ER 218, [1977] 1 WLR 425, CA.

R v Bloomsbury and Marylebone County Court, ex parte Villerwest Ltd [1976] 1 All ER 897, [1976] 1 WLR 362, CA, 13 Digest (Reissue) 533, 4472.

---

a   Rule 5(1) provides: 'The Court may, on such terms as it thinks just, by order extend or abridge the period within which a person is required or authorised by these rules, or by any judgment, order or direction, to do any act in any proceedings.'

Script Phonography Co Ltd v Gregg (1890) 59 LJ Ch 406, 50 Digest (Repl) 256, 90.

Wallis v Hepburn (1878) 3 QBD 84n, 50 Digest (Repl) 140, *1231*.

Whistler v Hancock (1878) 3 QBD 83, 47 LJQB 152, 37 LT 639, 50 Digest (Repl) 141, *1233*.

Interlocutory appeal

In an action between the plaintiff, Algy Samuels, and the defendants, Linzi Dresses Ltd, the defendants were ordered on 4th October 1978 to serve further and better particulars of their defence and counterclaim within 21 days. They failed to comply with the order and by a further order dated 15th December 1978 his Honour Judge Hawser QC, sitting as an official referee, ordered that 'Unless the Further and Better Particulars of the Defence and Counterclaim ordered on the 4th day of October 1978 be served by the 2nd day of January 1979 the Defence and Counterclaim be struck out and that the Plaintiff be at liberty to sign judgment for damages to be assessed'. The defendants failed to serve the particulars by 2nd January. On that date they issued a summons applying for an extension of time until 8th January 1979. After adjournments of the summons it was heard on 19th February by Judge Hawser who gave judgment on 5th March granting the defendants an extension of time until 9th March. The plaintiff appealed from that order on the grounds that the judge erred in law in holding that he had jurisdiction to make an order extending time for service of the particulars, and that he ought to have ordered the defence and counterclaim to be struck out. The facts are set out in the judgment of Roskill LJ.

Alistair McGregor for the plaintiff.

M J Segal for the defendants.

ROSKILL LJ. This is an interlocutory appeal from his Honour Judge Hawser QC, sitting as an official referee. The judge, on 5th March 1979, gave an extension of time to the defendants in this action (the respondents in this appeal) for delivery of further and better particulars of their defence and counterclaim. They had failed to comply with an 'unless' order, which had been made some weeks previously.

The history of this matter is set out, with admirable clarity, in the judge's judgment, and I cannot do better than quote from that judgment. In the opening paragraph, he explains how the plaintiff, a Mr Samuels, was employed by the defendants, and how—

'On the 3rd May 1977 Mr Samuels issued a writ claiming certain rather complicated accounts and enquiries, payment of the sums thereby found to be due and damages for breaches of his contract of employment. By the defence and counterclaim dated 21st July 1977 the defendants denied that the plaintiff was entitled to any further sums than those already paid to him and denied the allegations of alleged breaches of contract. They also pleaded a set-off. The counterclaim contained serious allegations of misconduct by the plaintiff and claimed payment of secret profits he was alleged to have made and damages for breaches of the implied terms of contract. On 12th July 1978 the plaintiff issued a summons for directions which was heard on 4th October 1978. One of the orders then made was that the defendants should comply with a request for further and better particulars of the defence and counterclaim, which request runs to nearly five pages. The order was that the defendants should serve such particulars within 21 days. On 16th November 1978 the plaintiff issued a summons for an order that the defendants' defence, set-off and counterclaim herein be struck out and that the plaintiff have leave to enter judgment against the defendants in accordance with the statement of claim, the defendants having failed to comply with para 1 of the order of the court, dated 4th October 1978. That, of course, was the order for further and better particulars. This summons was heard on the 15th December 1978 when an order was made in this form: [and I quote the judge's quotation] that unless the further and better particulars of the defence and counterclaim ordered on 4th October 1978 be served by 2nd January 1979, the defence and counterclaim be *a*   struck out and that the plaintiff be at liberty to sign judgment for damages to be assessed.'

The judge went on:

'The particulars were not served on 2nd January 1979 but the document containing the particulars, which runs to some 19 pages, was handed to the plaintiff's solicitors on 5th January 1979.'

b   I interpose that we are therefore concerned with a case where the defendants were three days out of time, and of course time was running over the Christmas holiday and during the Christmas vacation. The judge went on:

'On 2nd January 1979 the defendants issued a summons, asking for an order extending the time for serving the further and better particulars until 8th January *c*   1979. After various adjournments this summons was heard by me on 19th February 1979, when the matter was fully argued. At that hearing counsel for the defendants gave the following explanation for the failure to comply with the "unless" order the details of which explanation were not challenged by the plaintiff. Counsel received instructions to settle the further and better particulars on 21st December 1978. He prepared a draft running to some 19 pages, which contained certain gaps requiring *d*   further instructions from the clients. This draft was collected from his chambers by the defendants' solicitors on the very day he completed it, namely 28th December. The defendants' solicitors tried to contact their clients on 28th or 29th December, but failed to do so. On 29th December they spoke to someone in the plaintiff's solicitors' office, who was not himself dealing with the matter. They also wrote to the plaintiff's solicitors on that date explaining the difficulties which had arisen and asking for an extension to 5th January 1979. On 2nd January they again telephoned *e*   the plaintiff's solicitors, and this time were able to speak to the person dealing with the matter. He said he had strict instructions not to consent to an extension but agreed not to sign judgment if a summons was taken out. This, as I have stated, was done that day. The plaintiff had not signed judgment against the defendants. No date for the trial had yet been fixed nor was this asked for or dealt with on the *f*   hearing of the summons for direction.'

The judge then made it plain that if he had jurisdiction to grant the extension which the defendants sought, he would in the exercise of his discretion grant that extension. He held that he had such jurisdiction, and he exercised his discretion accordingly.

I have dealt with the facts at some length because, in his admirable argument, counsel for the plaintiff submitted to us that even if contrary to his main submission the judge *g*   had jurisdiction, the judge was wrong in exercising his discretion as he did. With respect, this is a matter entirely for the discretion of the judge in chambers or, as in this case, sitting as an official referee. There was ample material, on the facts which I have just read from the judgment, on which, assuming jurisdiction, the judge could properly exercise his discretion as he did, and it seems to me quite impossible for this court to interfere with the exercise of his discretion *if* there is jurisdiction. The all important *h*   question is whether or not there was jurisdiction. The judge, in a long and careful judgment, held that there was.

The question whether where an 'unless' order has been made and the time is allowed to run out without that order being properly complied with, further extensions of time can be granted has been a vexed one in recent times. The matter has been directly before this court on no less than three recent occasions (and I will refer to each in due course) on *j*   two of which, as it happens, I was a member of the court. The matter has also been more than once before one or other of the judges who sit as official referees. There was before Judge Hawser an earlier decision of his Honour Judge Edgar Fay QC, also sitting as an official referee, in *R Laws Planbuild Ltd v Globe Picture Theatres (Bristol) Ltd*[1], a decision

---

1   (10th February 1978) unreported

which we had the benefit of reading in one of the three cases which I have just mentioned, *J M Brown Ltd v Dennis Price Ltd*[1] which came before Stephenson LJ and *a* myself on 18th May 1978. In that judgment, Judge Fay held that he had the jurisdiction which Judge Hawser in the present case has also held that he had. In the case before Stephenson LJ and myself, we found it unnecessary to decide that question, but Stephenson LJ made it clear that he was not in any way suggesting that Judge Fay's decision was wrong.

The strength of the argument in favour of this appeal, and against the views expressed *b* by Judge Fay and Judge Hawser, lies in a decision of the Divisional Court of the Queen's Bench Division, oft quoted and oft criticised, *Whistler v Hancock*[2], a case decided over 100 years ago on 11th January 1878. The Divisional Court consisted of Cockburn CJ and Manisty J, and the appeal was brought from an order of Fry J at chambers. An order had been made under the then RSC Ord 29, r 1 dismissing an action for want of prosecution unless a statement of claim should be delivered within a week. The week expired; no *c* statement of claim had been delivered. A summons was then taken out to extend the time, and Fry J, reversing the decision of the master, held that the master had no jurisdiction to make such an order. The plaintiff appealed to the Divisional Court: in those days appeals from the judge in chambers went not, as at the present time, to this court, but to the Divisional Court.

Cockburn CJ, in giving judgment, said[3]: *d*

'This is a very plain case. The defendant obtained an order that unless the statement of claim were delivered within a week the action should be at an end. The plaintiff took out a summons to set aside the appearance, and if he could have obtained an order to that effect before the week was out, he would have been the victor; but before his summons could be heard he fell under the operation of the *e* order dismissing the action, and the action was at an end. It cannot be contended that the taking out of a summons to set aside the appearance in the meantime could keep the action alive after the period when by the operation of the master's order it was defunct. For these reasons, I think the master had no jurisdiction, and the order of Fry, J., was right.'

Manisty J agreed. *f*

The very next day there was an almost identical case, *Wallis v Hepburn*[4], before the Divisional Court of the Exchequer Division. *Wallis v Hepburn*[4] is reported as a note immediately following the report of *Whistler v Hancock*[2]. By a strange coincidence, counsel who had been counsel for the plaintiff, and thus had been on the losing side in *Whistler v Hancock*[2], appeared for the defendant in *Wallis v Hepburn*[4], and was able triumphantly to refer the Divisional Court of the Exchequer Division to the judgment *g* of the Divisional Court of the Queen's Bench Division on the previous day. As a result, that Divisional Court followed *Whistler v Hancock*[2] and held that there had been no jurisdiction to make the order in question, 'the action being then dead . . .'

Thus in 1878 there were two decisions, one of the Divisional Court of the Queen's Bench Division and one of the Divisional Court of the Exchequer Division, that where an 'unless' order was made and not complied with there was no jurisdiction to extend the *h* time.

At that time, the Rules of the Supreme Court were scheduled to the Supreme Court of Judicature Acts 1873 and 1875, and the relevant order to which the Divisional Court had been referred was Ord 57. The relevant rule, Ord 57, r 6, reads:

j

1 [1978] Court of Appeal transcript 304
2 (1878) 3 QBD 83
3 3 QBD 83 at 83–84
4 (1878) 3 QBD 84

'A Court or a Judge shall have power to enlarge or abridge the time appointed by
a   these Rules, or fixed by any order enlarging time, for doing any act or taking any
proceeding, upon such terms (if any) as the justice of the case may require, and any
such enlargement may be ordered although the application for the same is not made
until after the expiration of the time appointed or allowed.'

As Lawton LJ said during the argument, if one reads the then Ord 57, r 6 and then
b   applies its language to the facts of the two cases to which I have referred, it is not readily
apparent why each of those two cases did not fall within the express language of the
rule. However, the two Divisional Courts, after being referred to that order and that
rule, held otherwise.

The next case is *King v Davenport*[1]. I can take the facts sufficiently from the headnote:

'An order having been made on the 6th of May dismissing the action for want of
c   prosecution if the statement of claim were not delivered within fourteen days on
the 19th of May the plaintiff took out a summons returnable the next day, the last
of the fourteen days, for further time to deliver the statement of claim. The
summons was, on the 20th, adjourned by the consent of the parties in writing
indorsed thereon, till the 21st, and on the 21st a master made an order giving seven
days more for delivery of statement of claim. Pollock, B., rescinded the order of the
d   master on the ground that he had no jurisdiction, the action being at an end on the
20th May.'

The order of Pollock B was appealed to the Divisional Court (Cockburn CJ and
Mellor J). They affirmed the order of Pollock B on the ground there was no jurisdiction
further to extend the time. That case therefore is in line with *Whistler v Hancock*[2].

The next case, in order of date, is *Script Phonography Co Ltd v Gregg*[3]. This was a
e   decision of North J. The note in the Supreme Court Practice[4] to RSC Ord 3, r 5, which
says that this was a decision of the Court of Appeal, is, with respect, wrong.

The headnote in *Script Phonography Co Ltd v Gregg*[3] is as follows:

'When an order has been made in chambers dismissing an action unless the next
step is taken by the plaintiff within a specified time, and the plaintiff does not take
f   that step within the specified time nor appeal against the order, the order takes
effect, and the time for taking the step cannot subsequently be extended, the action
having become dead, notwithstanding that the order has not been drawn up or
served upon the plaintiff before it became operative.'

North J, giving judgment, began with these words[5]: 'It appears to me that the cases of
Whistler v. *Hancock*[2] and *King* v. *Davenport*[1], and cases like them, have settled the law on
g   the point which is now before me.' He then concluded his judgment by saying: 'I do not
see how I can set up a dead action, and I must dismiss this application, with costs.'

Next, chronologically, is *Collinson v Jeffery*[6], a judgment of Kekewich J. Kekewich J
distinguished the cases to which I have referred on the ground really that the case before
him was a redemption action. In that action the order was made—

h   'giving the plaintiff leave to lodge the mortgage money in court, and that "in
default of such lodgment within two months from the date of this order, the action
be dismissed with costs." Under a bonâ fide mistake the plaintiff failed to lodge the
money in court until after the two months fixed by the Order . . .'

---

j   1   (1879) 4 QBD 402
2   (1878) 3 QBD 83
3   (1890) 59 LJ Ch 406
4   1979, vol 1, p 18, para 3/5/5
5   59 LJ Ch 406 at 407
6   [1896] 1 Ch 644

Kekewich J held that—

> 'notwithstanding the expiration of the two months, the action was not dead, but *a*
> that the Court had jurisdiction, at the instance of the plaintiff, to extend the time
> limited by the order so as to include the actual date of lodgment.'

Kekewich J's reasons for distinguishing the earlier cases to which he was referred will
be found in the judgment[1]. I feel bound to say that I find the suggested grounds of
distinction difficult to follow, because he appears to have founded his distinction on the *b*
words of the order before him that 'this action do stand dismissed until further order'.
But Kekewich J did not appear to have had drawn to his attention the fact that, as
North J's judgment[2] to which I have referred shows, the order there had provided that
this action 'do stand dismissed for want of prosecution', yet North J did not feel able to
distinguish *Whistler v Hancock*[3] and the other cases on that ground.

Meanwhile there had been the decision of this court in *Carter v Stubbs*[4]. I emphasise, *c*
before returning to *Carter v Stubbs*[4], there had been no earlier decisions of this court
approving the *Whistler v Hancock*[3] line of cases. In *Carter v Stubbs*[4] the question arose in
a somewhat different way. There was not an attempt to extend the time because of non-
compliance with a so-called 'unless' order; there was an application for leave to appeal
against the original order. The decision in *Carter v Stubbs*[4] (and it was a strong Court of
Appeal: Lord Selborne LC and Baggallay and Brett LJJ) was that a judge had jurisdiction *d*
under RSC Ord 57, r 6 (which I read a few moments ago) to enlarge the time for
appealing against an order dismissing the action for want of prosecution even after the
order had taken effect and the action had, therefore, stood dismissed; and that he also had
jurisdiction, when he so enlarged the time for appealing, to vary or amend the order
dismissing the action, and in the exercise of such jurisdiction his discretion was not
limited by any fixed or arbitrary rule. *e*

Lord Selborne LC described *Whistler v Hancock*[3] and *Wallis v Hepburn*[5] as very different
from the instant case. He said[6]:

> 'In those cases the order dismissing the action was in force and not appealed
> against, and also there was no application to enlarge the time for appealing, but
> some other orders were asked to be made for extending the time for doing
> something in the action, and it was there held rebus existentibus that there was no *f*
> power to make such orders, as the action was no longer in existence. Those cases
> have no application here, where the form of the order is for enlargement of the time
> for appealing against the order dismissing the action, and an Order of this kind is
> within the meaning of Order LVII., rule 6, which expressly says that such
> enlargement may be ordered after the expiration of the time allowed for doing the
> act.' *g*

Accordingly, it was not necessary for this court to consider whether or not *Whistler v
Hancock*[3] and the other cases were correct; they were distinguished on the ground that
the relief which was sought in *Carter v Stubbs*[4] was a relief to which the then Ord 57, r 6
applied.

Baggallay LJ agreed with Lord Selborne LC, but it is right to point out that Brett LJ, *h*
while holding that the judge in chambers had jurisdiction to make the order, added[7]:

---

1   [1896] 1 Ch 644 at 646   *j*
2   In *Script Phonography Co Ltd v Gregg* (1890) 59 LJ Ch 406 at 407
3   (1878) 3 QBD 83
4   (1880) 6 QBD 116
5   (1878) 3 QBD 84
6   6 QBD 116 at 118
7   6 QBD 116 at 120–121

a
'The cases of *Whistler* v. *Hancock*[1] and *Wallis* v. *Hepburn*[2] were cited to shew there was no jurisdiction to make these orders; but in those cases it was held that the Court had no jurisdiction to do what they were asked to do, because there had been no order in either of those cases to enlarge the time for appealing against the order dismissing the action, and that order existing and having taken effect, the cause was dead. In *Burke* v. *Rooney*[3], however, a different cause was pursued, and there application was made by the plaintiff, similar to that which has been made here, to

b
extend the time for appealing against the order, so that he might afterwards get it varied or set aside, and it was held that there was jurisdiction to extend the time. I am clearly of opinion that the decision in that case [that is *Burke v Rooney*[3]] was right although *Whistler* v. *Hancock*[1] and *Wallis* v. *Hepburn*[4] were also rightly decided.'

Brett LJ alone of the members of this court in *Carter v Stubbs*[4] expressed that view, and counsel for the plaintiff has rightly accepted that there is no binding decision of this court

c
which compels us to accept, at the present date, that *Whistler v Hancock*[1] and that line of cases were rightly decided.

As Lawton LJ pointed out during the argument, this court is always slow not to follow cases which have stood for a long time without challenge. But *Whistler v Hancock*[1] has not passed unassailed in recent times. In *Manley Estates Ltd v Benedek*[5], a decision of this court, MacKinnon and du Parcq LJJ, this court, reversing Stable J, distinguished *Whistler*

d
v Hancock[1] on the basis that in the case then before the court the action in question was not dead. Stable J had followed *Whistler v Hancock*[1]. But MacKinnon LJ after referring to that case, said[6]:

'Counsel for the respondents relies, and there was reliance below, on cases of a totally different nature, where, after an action was dismissed—and, therefore, judgment entered for the defendant—it was held that the plaintiff could not make

e
an application to enlarge the time in that action, as the action had disappeared. Here, the action has not disappeared. It is in existence, and there is actually a judgment which has not been prosecuted to execution. I think that, within the words of that rule, there was jurisdiction in the master to enlarge the time.'

Thus we have yet another way suggested of distinguishing *Whistler v Hancock*[1]. More

f
recently this question came before this court in *R v Bloomsbury and Marylebone County Court, ex parte Villerwest Ltd*[7]. There, the Divisional Court had allowed an order of certiorari to issue to quash the order of the judge in the Bloomsbury and Marylebone County Court under which it had been directed that if a sum of money were paid into court by a certain date, the judgment in favour of the landlord should be set aside. This court, Lord Denning MR, Geoffrey Lane LJ and myself, reversed the Divisional Court.

g
Lord Denning MR, after referring to *Manley Estates Ltd v Benedek*[5], said[8]:

'I have one further observation to make. It is about *Whistler v Hancock*[1]. It seems there to be suggested that if a condition is not fulfilled the action ceases to exist, as

h

1   (1878) 3 QBD 83
2   (1878) 3 QBD 84
3   (1879) 4 CPD 226
4   (1880) 6 QBD 116
5   [1941] 1 All ER 248
6   [1941] 1 All ER 248 at 251
7   [1976] 1 All ER 897, [1976] 1 WLR 362
8   [1976] 1 All ER 897 at 900, [1976] 1 WLR 362 at 366

though no extension of time can be granted. I do not agree with that line of reasoning. Even though the action may be said to cease to exist, the court always *a* has power to bring it to life again, by extending the time. In my opinion, the county court judge had ample jurisdiction to make the order he did.'

Geoffrey Lane LJ and I did not think it necessary to express any view about *Whistler v Hancock*[1]; we decided the appeal on the basis that the county court judge, like a judge of the High Court, had inherent jurisdiction to extend the time. Lord Denning MR asked *b* whether if a man, on his way to court in time, with money in his pocket, was run down in an accident, or were robbed, there was no power to remedy the injustice if in such circumstances the money was not paid into court in time? This court took the view that a court had inherent power to remedy such injustice. In addition, the correctness of *Whistler v Hancock*[1] was expressly doubted by Lord Denning MR.

Then came the unreported decision[2] of Stephenson LJ and myself, to which I have referred. Once again the court did not find it necessary to rule on the correctness or *c* otherwise of *Whistler v Hancock*[1], although as I have already said, Stephenson LJ was at pains to say that he was not suggesting that Judge Fay's view was in any way incorrect.

The last of the three cases I have mentioned where this problem arose before the court (Megaw, Scarman and Browne LJJ) is *Pryer v Smith*[3]. Megaw LJ said[4]:

'Various authorities were cited to the learned judge which have again been cited, *d* together with additional authorities, in this court. In particular, the defendant relied on *Whistler v Hancock*[1], a decision of the Queen's Bench Divisional Court on 11th January 1878. That authority was followed in *King v Davenport*[5], in 1879. I do do not propose to go into the question of law, involving difficult, and in some respects obscure, questions of procedure, because, in the view that I have formed on another aspect of this case, it is unnecessary for the decision of this appeal so to do; *e* and, indeed, in those circumstances, any view which I were to express about that matter of law would, I think, be obiter and unlikely perhaps to be helpful.'

Judge Hawser has given a judgment which involves this court expressing a definite view on this controversial issue. These various authorities are set out in the note to RSC Ord 3, r 5[6]. The note opens with these words:
f
'Where an order is made dismissing an action for want of prosecution unless some act is done within a specified time, and the act is not in fact done within that time, the action ceases to exist and thereafter no order can be made extending the time for doing the act.'

That succinctly summarises the cases starting with *Whistler v Hancock*[1]. The note goes on: *g*

'Accordingly if an application for extension of time is not made and heard before the time limited by the order has expired, the only remedy is to appeal from the order dismissing the action, and (if necessary) to apply at the same time for an extension of time for appealing. On the other hand, if an order is made setting aside a default judgment on condition that a payment is made, or step taken, within a *h* specified time, even after the lapse of that time it can be extended on application. The action is not dead: there is an unexecuted judgment (*Manley Estates v. Benedek*[7]).'

---

1 (1878) 3 QBD 83
2 *J M Brown Ltd v Dennis Price Ltd* [1978] Court of Appeal transcript 304   *j*
3 [1977] 1 All ER 218, [1977] 1 WLR 425
4 [1977] 1 All ER 218 at 222, [1977] 1 WLR 425 at 429–430
5 (1879) 4 QBD 402
6 Supreme Court Practice 1979, vol 1, p 18, para 3/5/5
7 [1941] 1 All ER 248

a
Then this paragraph had been added:

> 'If a condition is not fulfilled within a specified time, even though the action may be said to cease to exist, the court always has power to bring it to life again by extending the time (*per* Lord Denning M.R. in *R. v. Bloomsbury and Marylebone County Court, ex parte Villerwest Ltd*[1]). See, however [and I am not quite sure why 'however'], *Pryer v. Smith*[2] [per Megaw LJ].'

b
It has been suggested that we should, by our decision in the present case, preserve these very artificial distinctions which these cases have suggested. It is suggested that this court can legitimately draw a distinction between striking out a claim, such as was done in *Whistler v Hancock*[3], and striking out a defence. That seems, with respect, to be illogical and the illogicality is, to my mind, made worse where there is not only a defence *c* but also a counterclaim and as so often happens, the counterclaim overlaps with the defence. Counsel for the plaintiff rightly pointed out that strictly a counterclaim is a separate cause of action and logically would, if this argument be right, have to be dealt with by reference to the same principles as would apply to striking out a claim.

It seems to me that at this date we are entitled in this court to review the whole position de novo. As Lawton LJ pointed out, those early cases are all contemporary *d* illustrations of the court exercising the power to strike for want of prosecution. In recent times, since *Allen v Sir Alfred McAlpine & Sons Ltd*[4] and of course *Birkett v James*[5], this court has adopted a much more realistic approach to questions of striking out for want of prosecution, and it is difficult to think that, if the *Allen v Sir Alfred McAlpine & Sons Ltd*[4] and *Birkett v James*[5] principles were applied, the claims would have been struck out in any of those cases.

e
As Megaw LJ pointed out in *Pryer v Smith*[2], early decisions on procedural matters are often obscure and have to be regarded with some caution. It was pointed out during the argument that new Rules of the Supreme Court resulted from changes effected by the Supreme Court of Judicature Acts 1873 and 1875. Those are all early decisions under those rules when the new practice had not been fully worked out and of course the courts were still greatly influenced by the practice which had prevailed before the Judicature *f* Acts.

Today the position is very different. There are many decisions of this court and of course there is the decision of the House of Lords in *Birkett v James*[5], as to the principles which should be applied in striking out claims for want of prosecution. One principle now clearly established is that the court will not, generally speaking, strike out a claim for want of prosecution where a plaintiff is free to issue a fresh writ. In the instant case *g* the defendants would be free, if their counterclaim were struck out, to issue a fresh writ covering the matters raised by the counterclaim. There would be no issue of estoppel or res judicata.

Accordingly, it seems to me quite wrong that today a claim should be struck out simply because of these decisions now a century old. I think the judge in the present case, and Judge Fay in the earlier case[6] to which I have referred and, if I may say so, Lord *h* Denning MR in the *Villerwest* case[7], were all correct in taking the view that *Whistler v Hancock*[3] should no longer be followed.

---

j
1   [1976] 1 All ER 897 at 900, [1976] 1 WLR 362 at 366
2   [1977] 1 All ER 218 at 222, [1977] 1 WLR 425 at 429–430
3   (1878) 3 QBD 83
4   [1968] 1 All ER 543, [1968] 2 QB 229
5   [1977] 2 All ER 801, [1978] AC 297
6   *R Laws Planbuild Ltd v Globe Picture Theatres (Bristol) Ltd* (10th February 1978) unreported
7   [1976] 1 All ER 987, [1976] 1 WLR 362

To say that there is jurisdiction to extend the time where an 'unless' order has been made and not complied with is not to suggest, let this be absolutely plain, that relief *a* should be automatically granted to parties who have failed to comply with the orders of the court otherwise than on stringent terms either as to payment of costs or as to bringing money into court or the like. Orders as to time, and in particular as to the time for delivery of pleadings and particulars, are made not to be ignored but to be complied with. In the present case, long before the problem caused by the 1978 Christmas holidays arose, there had been serious delay in complying with various orders, and the *b* defendants were at mercy when they came before Judge Hawser. They had not done that which they ought to have done. They were not, save perhaps at the very last moment, deserving of any sympathy. But at the last moment they had made a real effort to comply with the order and they were perhaps unlucky that their efforts did not meet with success.

In my judgment, therefore, the law today is that a court has power to extend the time *c* where an 'unless' order has been made but not been complied with; but that it is a power which should be exercised cautiously and with due regard to the necessity for maintaining the principle that orders are made to be complied with and not to be ignored. Primarily it is a question for the discretion of the master or the judge in chambers whether the necessary relief should be granted or not.

I think that Judge Hawser was in law entitled to grant the relief sought and to exercise *d* his discretion in the way he did. The appeal should be dismissed.

LAWTON LJ. I agree with the judgment delivered by Roskill LJ, and have only a few words to add. The concept of the action coming to an end through non-compliance with an 'unless' order derived from the language used by Cockburn CJ in *Whistler v Hancock*[1]. He said this: *e*

> 'The plaintiff took out a summons to set aside the appearance, and if he could have obtained an order to that effect before the week was out, he would have been the victor; but before his summons could be heard he fell under the operation of the order dismissing the action, and the action was at an end. It cannot be contended that the taking out of a summons to set aside the appearance in the meantime could keep the action alive after the period when by the operation of the master's order it *f* was defunct.'

The concept of death to the action was underlined in the note, printed in the same report, of *Wallis v Hepburn*[2], when the reporter said: '. . . the action being then dead . . .'

The concept of the action being dead is one which does not fit in, as Roskill LJ has pointed out, with the modern approach to striking out for want of prosecution.   *g*

Further, the illogicality of its purported application to this case is shown by the order which is under consideration in this appeal because on the face of that order it is clear that the litigation is not dead; it is very much alive. The relevant part of the order reads as follows:

> 'Unless the further and better particulars of the defence and counterclaim ordered *h* on the 4th day of October 1978 be served by the 2nd day of January 1979 the defence and counterclaim be struck out and that the plaintiff be at liberty to sign judgment for damages to be assessed.'

The litigation was to go on. A distinction between striking out a defence and striking out a counterclaim lacks reality.

As Roskill LJ has pointed out, the consequences of this decision has been that time and *j* time again, in recent years, attempts have been made to distinguish it. It was wrong in

---

1   (1878) 3 QBD 83 at 83–84
2   (1878) 3 QBD 84

the first place. In my judgment it was contrary to the wording of RSC Ord 57 as set out
a in the schedules to the Supreme Court of Judicature Acts 1873 and 1875. Roskill LJ has
sounded a note of warning about these earlier decisions on procedure made before this
court as a division of the Supreme Court of Judicature had had an opportunity of seeing
how the new rules were working. The decisions in 1878 and 1879 were probably
coloured by the old practice. Schedule 1 to the Supreme Court of Judicature Act 1875,
which set out the Rules of Court, has this note: 'Where no other provision is made by the
b Act or these Rules the present procedure and practice remain in force.'
The approach of the courts to coercive orders has been greatly changed by the decision
of the House of Lords in *Birkett v James*[1].

SIR STANLEY REES. I agree with the judgments delivered by Roskill and Lawton
LJJ, and have nothing further to add.
c
Appeal dismissed.

Solicitors: *Benjamin & Benjamin* (for the plaintiff); *Paisner & Co* (for the defendants).

Avtar S Virdi Esq   Barrister.
d

Practice Direction

e FAMILY DIVISION

*Minor – Custody – Application – Applications which may be made to registrar – Wardship and
guardianship proceedings – Application for access where other party consents to access and only
issue is extent of the access – Such applications to be made in first instance to registrar unless
f exceptional circumstances make it desirable to apply to a judge.*

By a Practice Direction of 3rd November 1977[2] it was provided that on an application in
a matrimonial cause for an agreed custody order or for an order for access to a child where
the only question at issue is the extent of such access, the application should in the first
instance be made to a registrar, unless there are exceptional circumstances making it
desirable for the matter to be brought before a judge for decision.
g The judges of the Family Division are of the opinion, and it is accordingly hereby
directed, that applications of like nature made in wardship and guardianship cases
proceeding in the Principal Registry including applications for an agreed care and control
order should be dealt with in the same manner.

h Issued with the approval of the President.

R L BAYNE-POWELL
4th March 1980   Senior Registrar.

---

j 1 [1977] 2 All ER 801, [1978] AC 297
2 [1977] 3 All ER 944, [1977] 1 WLR 1226

Re Gray's Inn Construction Co Ltd   *a*

COURT OF APPEAL, CIVIL DIVISION
BUCKLEY, GOFF LJ AND SIR DAVID CAIRNS
16th, 17th, 18th, 19th, 22nd OCTOBER, 5th DECEMBER 1979

Company – Compulsory winding-up – Disposition of property after commencement of winding- *b*
up – Validation by court – Principles on which discretion to validate exercisable – Continuation
by bank of company's account after commencement of winding-up – Account overdrawn at date
of commencement of winding-up – Payments made into account after that date – Continuation of
account resulting in trading loss – Pre-liquidation debts paid out of account – Whether
transactions on account should be validated – Whether bank liable to pay liquidator credits
covering overdraft, payments to creditors for pre-liquidation debts and amount of trading loss   *c*
– Companies Act 1948, s 227.

On 3rd August 1972 a creditor of a company carrying on a building business presented
a petition to wind up the company. Immediately prior to 3rd August the company was
trading at a loss and had an unsecured overdraft of £5,322 on its bank account. Between
3rd and 9th August the company credited sums of £2,570 to the account. A further sum
of £100 was credited on 11th August. The winding-up petition was advertised on 10th   *d*
August and the bank became aware of the petition before 15th August, although the
manager of the branch where the company banked was not aware of it until 17th
August. The court made a compulsory winding-up order in respect of the company on
9th October. The bank, in accordance with its practice but without obtaining a
validating order from the court, decided to allow the company to continue operating the
account, which the company did from 3rd August to 9th October ('the relevant   *e*
period'). In allowing the company to operate the account during the relevant period the
bank neither considered whether that was in the interests of the unsecured creditors nor
ensured that pre-liquidation debts were not paid out of the account after commencement
of the winding up. Throughout the relevant period sums totalling £25,313 were paid
into the account, mainly in the form of third parties' cheques, and sums totalling   *f*
£24,129 were paid out to third parties including sums totalling £4,824 paid to creditors
for goods and services supplied before the commencement of the winding up.
Throughout the period the account was overdrawn. In October 1976 the liquidator
applied by summons for: (i) a declaration that the bank's receipt of the sums credited to
the account throughout the relevant period constituted dispositions of the company's
property which were void under s 227[a] of the Companies Act 1948 and (ii) an order for
payment to the liquidator of the amount of the credits; or alternatively (iii) a declaration   *g*
that the amounts debited to the account during the relevant period were dispositions of
the company's property which were void under s 227 and (iv) an order for payment of
those amounts by the bank to the liquidator. At the hearing of the summons the
liquidator limited his claim to payment by the bank of the trading loss sustained by the
company by remaining in business during the relevant period, which was found to be   *h*
£5,000. The judge held that payments into the account by the company during the
relevant period were not dispositions of the company's property within s 227. He also
decided to exercise his discretion under s 227 by validating the payments out during the
period, even though the decision to continue the account had involved the creditors in
a trading loss of £5,000, on the ground that the court should absolve the bank from
liability where, as the judge found, the decision to continue the account was based on   *j*
adequate information about the company and was reasonable at the time. The liquidator
appealed.

---

a   Section 227 is set out at p 818 *d*, post

Held – The appeal would be allowed for the following reasons—

a   (i) The payments into the account during the relevant period constituted dispositions of the company's property within s 227 of the 1948 Act, and all payments out of the account, and not merely the excess over payments in, during the relevant period likewise constituted dispositions of the company's property (see p 818 *e f* and *j* to p 819 *a* and p 826 *c d*, post).

(ii) The court's discretion under s 227 should be exercised in the context of the
b liquidation provisions of the 1948 Act and the court should not, in exercising that discretion, validate any transaction which would result in a pre-liquidation creditor being paid in full at the expense of other creditors who would only receive dividends, unless to do so would benefit the unsecured creditors as a whole (see p 819 *g*, p 820 *a* to *e*, p 821 *d e* and p 826 *c d*, post).

(iii) Where a bank allowed a company in liquidation to have facilities on an existing
c account without obtaining a validating order then, even though the decision was based on adequate information and was reasonable at the time, if in the event the creditors incurred a loss, the court would not necessarily absolve the bank from liability, particularly where it had not taken steps to inform itself that the company was trading at a loss (see p 825 *a b* and p 826 *c d*, post); dictum of Oliver J in *Re J Leslie Engineers Co Ltd* [1976] 2 All ER at 95 applied; dictum of Lord Cairns LJ in *Re Wiltshire Iron Co* (1868) LR
d 3 Ch App at 447 considered.

(iv) The bank ought not, however, to be penalised further than was necessary to restore to the fund of assets available for distribution in the liquidation the amount of any loss. Amounts which had been paid out of the account to pre-liquidation creditors during the relevant period ought primarily to be recovered from those creditors, the bank being treated as liable to make good those amounts only to the extent by which any
e such amounts which were not recovered might exceed any dividends which would have been payable in respect thereof if they had been recovered. Sums amounting to £2,570 which had been credited to the account after presentation of the petition but before advertisement ought to be validated, as well as the £100 credited on the day following advertisement, but subsequent credits to the extent of the balance of the pre-liquidation overdraft ought not to be validated, without prejudice to any right of the bank to prove
f in respect of that balance. Since the bank had not applied for a validating order and had taken the risk of going on without an order, it followed that it was vulnerable to an order to restore to the company the post-liquidation trading loss of £5,000 (see p. 822 *b e f* and *j* to p 823 *f*, p 825 *f* and p 826 *c d*, post).

Per Curiam. Where the court is satisfied that it is in the interests of the general body of creditors of a company which is in the course of being wound up that the company be
g permitted to continue trading, the court's proper course is to freeze the company's bank account as at the date of presentation of the winding-up petition by discontinuing all further dealings on the existing account as from that date and requiring all subsequent dealings to be on a new and separate account (see p 821 *f* to *h* and p 826 *c d*, post).

Notes
h For the retrospective effect of a winding-up order on the disposition of property, see 7 Halsbury's Laws (4th Edn) para 1209, and for cases on the subject, see 10 Digest (Reissue) 979–981, 5899–5913.

For the Companies Act 1948, s 227, see 5 Halsbury's Statutes (3rd Edn) 297.

Cases referred to in judgments
j *Civil Service and General Store Ltd, Re* (1887) 57 LJ Ch 119, 58 LT 220, 10 Digest (Reissue) 979, 5904.

Clayton's Case, Devaynes v Noble, Baring v Noble (1816) 1 Mer 572, [1814–23] All ER Rep 1, 35 ER 781, 3 Digest (Reissue) 570, 3669.

Clifton Place Garage Ltd, Re [1970] 1 All ER 353, [1970] Ch 477, [1970] 2 WLR 243, CA, 10 Digest (Reissue) 980, 5910.

Leslie (J) Engineers Co Ltd (in liquidation) [1976] 2 All ER 85, [1976] 1 WLR 292.
Levy (AI) (Holdings) Ltd [1963] 2 All ER 556, [1964] Ch 19, [1963] 2 WLR 1464, 10 Digest *a*
(Reissue) 980, 5912.
Liverpool Civil Service Association, Re, ex parte Greenwood (1874) LR 9 Ch App 511, 43 LJ
Ch 609, 30 LT 451, 10 Digest (Reissue) 929, 5413.
Neath Harbour Smelting and Rolling Works, Re (1887) 56 LT 727, 10 Digest (Reissue) 1026,
6274.
Park Ward & Co Ltd, Re [1926] Ch 828, 95 LJ Ch 584, 135 LT 575, [1926] B & CR 94, 10 *b*
Digest (Reissue) 903, 5277.
Steane's (Bournemouth) Ltd, Re [1950] 1 All ER 21, 10 Digest (Reissue) 980, 5909.
Wiltshire Iron Co, Re, ex parte Pearson (1868) LR 3 Ch App 443, 37 LJ Ch 554, 18 LT 38,
10 Digest (Reissue) 979, 5899.

c

Cases also cited

Mal Bower's Macquarie Electrical Centre Pty Ltd (in liquidation), Re [1974] 1 NSWLR 254.
Millar v National Bank of Scotland Ltd (1891) 28 SLR 884.
Operator Control Cabs Ltd, Re [1970] 3 All ER 657.
Yeovil Glove Co Ltd, Re [1964] 2 All ER 849, [1965] Ch 148, CA.   *d*

Appeal

By a summons dated 27th October 1976 Richard Eaglesfield Floyd, the liquidator of
Gray's Inn Construction Co Ltd ('the company'), applied for (i) a declaration that the *e*
receipt of amounts totalling £22,183·55 by the National Westminster Bank Ltd ('the
bank') from the company between 3rd August and 9th October 1972 constituted
dispositions of the company's property which were void pursuant to s 227 of the
Companies Act 1948, (ii) an order that the bank pay the liquidator that sum with interest
thereon at such rate as the court might think fit, (iii) alternatively a declaration that
debits caused or permitted by the bank to be made to the company's account with the *f*
bank at their branch office at Tavistock Square, London WC1 between 3rd and 9th·
October 1972 in amounts totalling £21,693·22 and/or the payments to which the same
related constituted dispositions of the company's property which were void under s 227,
and (iv) further to (iii), an order that the bank pay the liquidator the sum of £21,693·22
with interest. By a judgment given on 18th July 1978 Templeman J ordered that all
dispositions of the company's property made or allowed by the bank after 3rd August *g*
1972 be deemed valid. The liquidator appealed seeking (i) a declaration that the receipt
by the bank from the company between 3rd August and 9th October 1972 of sums
totalling £25,313·31, or alternatively £22,183·55, constituted dispositions of the
company's property which were void under s 227, (ii) an order that the bank pay to the
liquidator part of the said sums amounting to £13,259·92, or alternatively £5,000, or
alternatively £1,184·91 together with interest thereon, (iii) alternatively to (i) and (ii), a *h*
declaration that debits caused or permitted by the bank to be made to the company's
account with the bank at their Tavistock Square branch between 3rd August and 9th
October 1972 in sums totalling £24,455·55, or alternatively £21,693·22 and/or the
payments to which the same related constituted dispositions of the company's property
which were void under s 227, (iv) further to (iii), an order that the bank pay the
liquidator part of the said sums amounting to £13,259·92, or alternatively £5,000, or *j*
alternatively £1,184·91, with interest thereon. The facts are set out in the judgment of
Buckley LJ.

David Oliver for the liquidator.
Philip Heslop for the bank.

Cur adv vult

a 5th December. The following judgments were read.

BUCKLEY LJ. This is an appeal from an order of Templeman J under the Companies Act 1948, s 227, validating all transactions on the current banking account of the company, Gray's Inn Construction Co Ltd, between 3rd August 1972, when a petition *b* for the compulsory winding up of the company was presented by a creditor, and 9th October 1972, when an order was made on that petition for the winding up of the company.

The company, which was incorporated in 1969, carried on a building business. It maintained a current account with the National Westminster Bank at its Tavistock Square branch in London. It seems that the company did not engage in large building *c* projects or in speculative building on its own account, but mainly undertook relatively small contracts of which it seems to have secured a considerable number. The company's current account appears to have been normally overdrawn. At any rate it was in debit throughout the period covered by the evidence, and it is apparent that the company found difficulty in keeping within the overdraft limit of £5,000 imposed by the bank. The overdraft was unsecured by the company, but was guaranteed by Mr Chapman, the *d* managing director, whose guarantee was secured.

The company was indebted to another company, named Field-Davis Ltd, of which it had at one time been a subsidiary, in a sum of over £4,000. The origin of this debt does not appear from the evidence, but it seems possible that it may have been a loan made by Field-Davis Ltd to the company to provide working capital in the company's early days. On 3rd August 1972 Field-Davis Ltd presented a petition for the winding up of the *e* company founded on that debt. The petition was advertised on 10th August 1972 and came to the notice of the manager of the Tavistock Square branch of the bank on 17th August. It is, however, evident that it must have come to the notice of the head office of the bank before 17th August, though on what date is not clear. On 9th October the court made a compulsory winding-up order. The bank continued throughout the period 3rd August to 9th October to accept payments into the account, mainly if not *f* entirely in the form of third parties' cheques paid in by the company and collected by the bank; it also continued to honour cheques drawn on the account, making sure, so far as it was able to do so, that all such cheques were drawn in the ordinary course of the company's business but without attempting to distinguish between pre-liquidation debts and post-liquidation debts. In so doing the branch manager was acting in accordance with an internal directive issued by the bank's head office to all branches. This dealt as *g* follows with the action to be taken on notice of presentation of a petition:

> 'Normally the account whether overdrawn or in credit may be continued for all bona fide transactions which are in the normal course of business, i.e. wages and current purchases until a winding-up order is made. The Bank is accepting some risk in adopting this course as the winding-up will, if pursued, commence from the date of the petition and the Bank is relying on the Court to confirm those *h* transactions which are allowed on the account after notice of the petition and before the winding-up order is made. Managers must therefore advise the Area Manager as soon as notice is received. All entries on the account during this period must be scrutinised very carefully and where there are unusual transactions, further reference should be made to the Area Manager.'

j Immediately before 3rd August the account was overdrawn to the extent of £5,322 (I ignore pence). At 9th October it was overdrawn to the extent of £4,464. Sums amounting to £25,313 had been paid in during this period, sums amounting to £24,129 had been paid out and the bank had debited the account with sums amounting to £326 for interest and bank charges. The amount of the overdraft during this period fluctuated, the highest figure being in excess of £7,000 and the lowest less than £3,600.

On 27th October 1976 the liquidator issued a summons for a declaration that the
receipt by the bank from the company between 3rd August and 9th October (inclusive) *a*
of the amounts credited to the account during that period constituted dispositions of the
property of the company which were void pursuant to the Companies Act 1948, s 227,
and an order that the bank should pay the amount of those sums to the liquidator with
interest, or, alternatively, a declaration that the amounts debited to the account during
the period constituted dispositions of property of the company which were likewise void,
and an order that the bank should pay the amount of those sums to the liquidator with *b*
interest. At the hearing, however, the liquidator did not press for this relief in full; he
limited his claim to the amount which the company lost by remaining in business after
the presentation of the petition, which the liquidator calculated to amount to £13,260.
The judge said that reconstruction (and I think he was referring to reconstruction of the
trading figures during the relevant period) was difficult on the information before the
court, that it was not possible to be certain that harm was caused by the company *c*
continuing in business after 3rd August 1972, that the probability was that creditors
were worse off by not less than £4,000 nor more than £8,000, and that for the purposes
of the summons he assumed and found that the creditors were worse off to the extent of
£5,000. That finding is not now sought to be disturbed. It was, I think, a finding that
there had been a trading loss of £5,000.

The Companies Act 1948, s 227, is in the following terms: *d*

'In a winding up by the court, any disposition of the property of the company,
including things in action, and any transfer of shares, or alteration in the status of
the members of the company, made after the commencement of the winding up,
shall, unless the court otherwise orders, be void.'

The judge proceeded on the basis, which he held to be the position in law, that *e*
payment of moneys to the credit of a company's account, whether it is in credit or not,
do not constitute a disposition of the company's property. That is a view with which,
with deference to the judge, I feel unable to agree. When a customer's account with his
banker is overdrawn he is a debtor to his banker for the amount of the overdraft. When
he pays a sum of money into the account, whether in cash or by payment in of a third
party's cheque, he discharges his indebtedness to the bank pro tanto. There is clearly in *f*
these circumstances, in my judgment, a disposition by the company to the bank of the
amount of the cash or of the cheque. It may well be the case, as counsel for the bank has
submitted, that in clearing a third party's cheque and collecting the amount due on it,
the bank acts as the customer's agent, but as soon as it credits the amount collected in
reduction of the customer's overdraft, as in the ordinary course of banking business it has
authority to do in the absence of any contrary instruction from the customer, it makes *g*
a disposition on the customer's behalf in its own favour discharging pro tanto the
customer's liability on the overdraft. Counsel for the bank was constrained in the course
of the argument to accept that this is so. In the present case the company's account with
the bank was overdrawn, so I need not consider what the position would have been if any
cheque had been paid in when the account was in credit, but I doubt whether even in
those circumstances it could be properly said that the payment in did not constitute a *h*
disposition of the amount of the cheque in favour of the bank.

Counsel for the bank does not dispute that all payments out of the company's account
to third parties, not being payments to agents of the company as such, are dispositions of
the company's property; but he contends (as I understand his argument) that they are
only relevant for the purposes of s 227 to the extent that payments out during the
relevant period exceed payments in. That all such payments out must be dispositions of *j*
the company's property is, I think, indisputable, but I cannot accept counsel's
contention. The section must, in my judgment, invalidate every transaction to which it
applies at the instant at which that transaction purports to have taken place. I cannot see
any ground for saying that the invalidation can be negatived by any subsequent
transaction.

It follows, in my judgment, that unless validated under the section all the payments
a into and all the payments out of the company's account during the period 3rd August to
9th October 1972 were invalid. No one, however, suggests that the bank should repay
to the liquidator £25,313 and that all the recipients of the £24,129 should repay to the
liquidator the sums so received by them. The problem is how in these circumstances the
discretionary power of the court under the section to validate dispositions which would
otherwise be invalid should be exercised.

b Templeman J said in the course of his judgment:

'This present case, however, inevitably involves consideration of the dilemma
which confronts a bank when a company requests the continuation of banking
facilities after the presentation of a winding-up petition, but there are no plain
indications on the one hand that the petition is misconceived or on the other hand
c that the company ought to be immobilised immediately.'

He went on to say that a bank faced with such a request should weigh the likely benefits
and dangers of the company continuing in business against the benefits and losses which
may be the consequences of an immediate cessation of business, and that, if the bank
d comes to the conclusion that the risks of allowing the company to continue in business
are worth taking in the interests of the company and its creditors, the bank must
thereafter remain satisfied that the company does not make payments which are not
normal and reasonable expenditure in the ordinary course of business, and that there are
no indications that the financial position of the company is deteriorating and no signs
that the confidence of the bank in the directors is misplaced. He reviewed the facts of the
e present case and concluded that the decision to allow banking facilities for normal trade
was made after proper consideration by a prudent and conscientious bank manager who
knew sufficient about the company's affairs to reach a reasonable conclusion, and who
prescribed and enforced proper safeguards for the operation of the company's banking
account. If in the event the creditors were worse off by £5,000 or more, that loss could
not, he said, fairly be recovered from the bank. On these grounds he validated all the
f dealings on the account during the period 3rd August to 9th October 1972.

In *Re Steane's (Bournemouth) Ltd*[1], Vaisey J said that the legislature, by omitting to
indicate any particular principles which should govern the exercise of the discretion
vested in the court by the section, must be deemed to have left it entirely at large and
controlled only by the general principles which apply to every kind of judicial discretion.
I do not at all dissent from that statement beyond saying that the discretion must, in my
g opinion, be exercised in the context of the liquidation provisions of the Companies Act
1948.

It is a basic concept of our law governing the liquidation of insolvent estates, whether
in bankruptcy or under the Companies Acts, that the free assets of the insolvent at the
commencement of the liquidation shall be distributed rateably amongst the insolvent's
unsecured creditors as at that date. In bankruptcy this is achieved by the relation of the
h trustee's title to the bankrupt's assets back to the commencement of the bankruptcy. In
a company's compulsory winding up it is achieved by s 227. There may be occasions,
however, when it would be beneficial, not only for the company but also for its unsecured
creditors, that the company should be enabled to dispose of some of its property during
the period after the petition has been presented but before a winding-up order has been
made. An obvious example is if the company has an opportunity by acting speedily to
j dispose of some piece of property at an exceptionally good price. Many applications for
validation under the section relate to specific transactions of this kind or analogous
kinds. It may sometimes be beneficial to the company and its creditors that the company

---

1   [1950] 1 All ER 21 at 25

should be enabled to complete a particular contract or project, or to continue to carry on *a*
its business generally in its ordinary course with a view to a sale of the business as a going
concern. In any such case the court has power under s 227 to validate the particular
transaction, or the completion of the particular contract or project, or the continuance of
the company's business in its ordinary course, as the case may be.

In considering whether to make a validating order the court must always, in my
opinion, do its best to ensure that the interests of the unsecured creditors will not be
prejudiced. Where the application relates to a specific transaction this may be susceptible *b*
of positive proof. In a case of completion of a contract or project the proof may perhaps
be less positive but nevertheless be cogent enough to satisfy the court that in the interests
of the creditors the company should be enabled to proceed, or at any rate that proceeding
in the manner proposed would not prejudice them in any respect. The desirability of the
company being enabled to carry on its business generally is likely to be more speculative
and will be likely to depend on whether a sale of the business as a going concern will *c*
probably be more beneficial than a break-up realisation of the company's assets. In each
case, I think, the court must necessarily carry out a balancing exercise of the kind
envisaged by Templeman J in his judgment. Each case must depend on its own
particular facts.

Since the policy of the law is to procure so far as practicable rateable payments of the
unsecured creditors' claims, it is, in my opinion, clear that the court should not validate *d*
any transaction or series of transactions which might result in one or more pre-liquidation
creditors being paid in full at the expense of other creditors, who will only receive a
dividend, in the absence of special circumstances making such a course desirable in the
interests of the unsecured creditors as a body. If for example it were in the interests of
the creditors generally that the company's business should be carried on and this could
only be achieved by paying for goods already supplied to the company when the petition *e*
is presented but not yet paid for, the court might think fit in the exercise of its discretion
to validate payment for those goods.

Where a third party proposes to enter into a transaction with a company which is liable
to be invalidated under s 227, the third party can decline to do so until the company has
obtained a validating order, or it might itself seek a validating order, or it can enter into
the transaction in anticipation of the court making a retroactive validating order at a later *f*
date. In the present case the bank adopted the last course. A third party who does that
takes the risk of the court refusing to make the order.

It may not always be feasible, or desirable, that a validating order should be sought
before the transaction in question is carried out. The parties may be unaware at the time
when the transaction is entered into that a petition has been presented; or the need for
speedy action may be such as to preclude an anticipatory application; or the beneficial *g*
character of the transaction may be so obvious that there is no real prospect of a liquidator
seeking to set it aside, so that an application to the court would waste time, money and
effort. But in any case in which the transaction is carried out without an anticipatory
validating order the disponee is at risk of the court declining to validate the transaction.
It follows, in my view, that the parties when entering into the transaction, if they are
aware that it is liable to be invalidated by the section, should have in mind the sort of *h*
considerations which would influence the court's decision.

A disposition carried out in good faith in the ordinary course of business at a time
when the parties are unaware that a petition has been presented may, it seems, normally
be validated by the court (see *Re Wiltshire Iron Co*[1], *Re Neath Harbour Smelting and Rolling
Works*[2] and *Re Liverpool Civil Service Association*[3]), unless there is any ground for thinking
that the transaction may involve an attempt to prefer the disponee, in which case the *j*
transaction would probably not be validated. In a number of cases reference has been
made to the relevance of the policy of ensuring rateable distribution of the assets: see *Re*

1   (1868) LR 3 Ch App 443
2   (1887) 56 LT 727 at 729
3   (1874) LR 9 Ch App 511 at 512

Civil Service and General Store Ltd[1], *Re Liverpool Civil Service Association*[2] and *Re Leslie*
a Engineers Co Ltd[3]. In the last mentioned case Oliver J said[4]:

> 'I think that in exercising discretion the court must keep in view the evident
> purpose of the section which, as Chitty J said in *Re Civil Service and General Store Ltd*[1],
> is to ensure that the creditors are paid pari passu.'

But, although that policy might disincline the court to ratify any transaction which
b involved preferring a pre-liquidation creditor, it has no relevance to a transaction which
is entirely post-liquidation, as for instance a sale of an asset at its full market value after
presentation of a petition. Such a transaction involves no dissipation of the company's
assets, for it does not reduce the value of those assets. It cannot harm the creditors and
there would seem to be no reason why the court should not in the exercise of its
discretion validate it. A fortiori the court would be inclined to validate a transaction
c which would increase, or has increased, the value of the company's assets, or which
would preserve, or has preserved, the value of the company's assets from harm which
would result from the company's business being paralysed (*Re Wiltshire Iron Co*[5], *Re Park*
Ward & Co Ltd[6], where the business of the company was eventually sold as a going
concern presumably to the advantage of the creditors, and *Re Clifton Place Garage Ltd*[7]).
In *Re A I Levy (Holdings) Ltd*[8] the court validated a sale of a lease which was liable to
d forfeiture in the event of the tenant company being wound up, and also validated, as part
of the transaction, payment out of the proceeds of sale of arrears of rent which had
accrued before the presentation of the petition for the compulsory liquidation of the
company. If that case was rightly decided, as I trust that it was, the court can in
appropriate circumstances validate payment in full of an unsecured pre-liquidation debt
which constitutes a necessary part of a transaction which as a whole is beneficial to the
e general body of unsecured creditors. But we have been referred to no case in which the
court has validated payment in full of an unsecured pre-liquidation debt where there was
no such special circumstance, and in my opinion it would not normally be right to do so,
because such a payment would prefer the creditor whose debt is paid over the other
creditors of equal degree.

So I ask myself what the court would have done if an application had been made at or
f about 10th August 1972 for an order that all dealings in the ordinary course of business
on the company's current account pending an order for the winding up of the company
should be valid. For this purpose I will assume that the court would have been satisfied
that it would be in the interests of the general body of creditors that the company should
be permitted to continue trading and to use the services of the bank for that purpose. In
such circumstances the court should not, and would not in my judgment, have made an
g order which would result in the preferential discharge of the existing overdraft on the
company's account. The proper course in such circumstances, in my opinion, would be
to freeze the existing overdraft as at 3rd August 1972. The practical method of achieving
this in accordance with normal banking practice would, I imagine, be to discontinue all
further dealings on that account as from 3rd August 1972, and to require all subsequent
dealings to be on a new and separate account. The effect of such an order would have
h been that at and after 3rd August 1972 the old account would have remained overdrawn
to the extent of £5,322, which would be provable in the winding up. The new account
would initially have been neither in debit nor in credit. On this footing the court might

j 1 (1887) 57 LJ Ch 119
   2 (1874) LR 9 Ch App 511
   3 [1976] 2 All ER 85, [1976] 1 WLR 292
   4 [1976] 2 All ER 85 at 95, [1976] 1 WLR 292 at 304
   5 (1868) LR 3 Ch App 443
   6 [1926] Ch 828
   7 [1970] 1 All ER 353, [1976] Ch 477
   8 [1963] 2 All ER 556, [1964] Ch 19

well have been disposed to allow the bank to operate the new account subject to safeguards directed to ensuring that it would only do for so long as the company was *a* trading at a profit or that continued trading would be likely to benefit the general body of creditors. A bank cannot, of course, spend all or even a great deal of its time in conducting a day-to-day surveillance of a customer's business, and the court, if asked to make a prospective order, must do its best to make a realistic assessment of the risk involved of any system of safeguards falling short of failing safe, but we are not in this case concerned with a prospective order. It seems to me that, when the matter came *b* before Templeman J, he was bound to deal with it in the light of all the facts then known to him, including the fact, according to his finding, that the company had traded at a loss. The bank, having taken the risk of going on without the protection of a validating order, must, it seems to me, take the consequences.

If the old account had been frozen in the way I have supposed between 3rd August and 9th October 1972, the credits to the new account would have been £25,313; the debits, *c* including interest and charges, would have amounted to £24,455; so that, if the post-liquidation operations were segregated from the pre-liquidation current account, the new account would have been in credit at 9th October 1972 to the extent of £858, to which amount the liquidator would have been entitled as an asset of the company.

Templeman J took the view that, as the bank had acted in good faith in the belief that the petition would be dismissed and that the company would continue in business, it *d* would be unfair to the bank to make the bank answerable for any of the £5,000 loss. He said that the bank could not be required to insure the creditors against loss. Having come to the conclusion that harm would have resulted if the company had ceased to trade and that it did not appear to the bank manager that harm would be occasioned if the company were allowed banking facilities after 17th August 1972 for the purpose of continuing normal trade, he made the order appealed from. I ask myself, however, why *e* the creditors should suffer for the loss, the bank not having protected itself by the precaution of obtaining an order of the court. In my judgment, the learned judge should in principle have ensured that the creditors did not suffer. On the other hand I see no reason why the bank should be penalised further than may be necessary to restore to the fund of assets available for distribution among the creditors the amount of the loss.

It may be suggested that this approach is one which must increase the dilemma *f* referred to by the judge in a passage which I have cited from his judgment. I do not think that this is really so. If a bank decides to continue to afford facilities to a corporate customer against whom a winding-up petition has been presented, having an account in debit at the date of the presentation of the petition, the bank can itself freeze that account and insist on all subsequent dealings being dealt with on a separate account. It can require personal assurances from the directors of the company that no payments out of *g* the new account will be made in discharge of pre-liquidation debts and that all payments out of the new account shall be in respect of liabilities incurred in the ordinary course of business subsequent to the presentation of the petition. It can institute such checks on the profitability of the company's trading as it thinks fit.

Having regard to the way in which the current account was operated in the present case, under the rule in *Clayton's Case*[1], the earliest credits on and after 3rd August 1972 *h* up to an aggregate amount of £5,322, if valid, would be treated as appropriated to discharge pro tanto the overdraft existing immediately before 3rd August 1972. Sums amounting to £2,570 were credited to the account between 3rd August 1972 and 9th August 1972 (both included); further sums amounting to £4,666 were credited to the account before 17th August 1972. Sums amounting to £2,928 were debited to the account between 3rd August and 9th August (both included) and further sums *j* amounting to £3,483 were debited before 17th August 1972.

On the facts of this case it seems to me that it was proper for the learned judge in the exercise of his discretion to validate the credits amounting to £2,570 which were

1   (1816) 1 Mer 572, [1814–23] All ER Rep 1

credited to the account before advertisement of the petition. Of the credits to the

a account between 10th August and 17th August 1972, £100 was credited on 11th August and £4,566 on 15th August. Although the branch manager was not aware of the presentation of the petition until 17th August, I think that the bank must be treated as having been aware of the presentation of the petition before 15th August. In these circumstances I would not disturb the validation of the £100. The aggregate amount of £2,670 so validated would have the effect of reducing the pre-liquidation overdraft of

b £5,322 to £2,652. In my judgment, the bank was not justified in appropriating any subsequent credits to the discharge of this outstanding pre-liquidation debt. I would accordingly refuse to validate the next credits to the account after 11th August 1972 up to a sum of £2,652, and would order repayment of that sum by the bank to the liquidator but without prejudice to the right of the bank (if any) to prove in the liquidation in respect of that sum as part of the £5,322 due to the bank on the overdraft

c at the commencement of the winding up.

It appears from the affidavit of Mr Cookey-Gam, the accountant who conducted an investigation into payments made by and to the company, that during the period 3rd August to 9th October 1972 the company paid out of its current account with the bank for goods and services supplied before the commencement of the winding up an aggregate sum of £4,824. These payments were a consequence of the failure of the bank

d to take any steps to ensure so far as it could, as in my judgment it should have done, that no payments were made out of the current account after the commencement of the winding up in payment of pre-liquidation debts. In these circumstances, in my judgment, subject to the qualification I shall mention in a moment, the bank is vulnerable to a refusal to validate the next £4,824 of credits to the account and to an order for repayment of that sum by the bank to the liquidator.

e It seems to me, however, that primarily these sums, amounting in the aggregate to £4,824, should be recovered from the creditors to whom they were paid, and that the bank should in any event only be required to repay them to the extent that the amounts, if any, which prove to be irrecoverable from those creditors exceed the dividends which would be payable in respect of them.

These repayments of £2,670 and £4,824 would restore to the fund of assets available

f for distribution amongst the unsecured creditors all the sums mistakenly applied in payment of pre-liquidation debts, but those from whom they have been recovered will be entitled to prove in the winding up in respect of the amounts recovered.

This, however, would not restore the fund of assets distributable amongst the unsecured creditors to its state as at 3rd August 1972. There is still the trading loss of £5,000 to be considered. Before expressing my own view about this, it is right that I

g should indicate how the judge approached this problem. He said:

> 'It follows that before a bank allows a company to continue to operate its bank account, the bank must know enough about the company's finances to be able to determine whether there is a reasonable chance that the company will avoid or mitigate the effects of compulsory liquidation. The bank must know enough about the company's activities to be able to determine the probable effect of an immediate
> *h*   cessation of business and the probable effect of remaining in business until the winding-up petition is heard. The bank must have grounds for trusting the integrity and competence of the directors . . . If in the event the decision taken by the bank involves the creditors in loss, the court will nevertheless absolve the bank from liability provided the decision was based on adequate information and was reasonable at the time.'

j

The judge found that the branch manager lectured the directors from time to time on the danger of over-trading and the need to press for prompt payment from debtors in order to keep within the overdraft limit, but he also found that there were no indications of serious over-trading, and that there was no evidence of unprofitable trading. The directors assured the branch manager that proposals for clearing the petitioner's debt

over a period had been submitted to and agreed by the petitioner. No creditors gave
notice of an intention to support the petition.   *a*

The judge made the following findings:

> 'The directors informed the bank manager that they were optimistic for the
> future of the company: current turnover was £15,000 to £16,000 per month, with
> monthly outgoings in the region of £10,000. Order books were full. Work in
> progress amounted to £168,000. Debtors stood at £24,000 and new contracts   *b*
> totalling £102,500 had been signed. The current account was expected to move
> into permanent credit in the foreseeable future. The liquidator agrees that the
> factual information given by the directors to the bank manager was broadly
> accurate.'

He found that the branch manager warned the directors that until the petition was
withdrawn the company's account would be under close scrutiny and that only bona fide   *c*
trading transactions would be permitted and that he also stressed that borrowing must
in no circumstance exceed the overdraft limit of £5,000. In fact, from 3rd to 15th
August the overdraft was substantially in excess of £5,000 by a margin of around
£2,000; on 17th and 22nd August it was more than £500 in excess of £5,000, and on
30th and 31st August it was again in excess of £5,000, the excess of the latter date being
more than £1,100, notwithstanding that the account was scrutinised by the bank every   *d*
day.

Templeman J said:

> '... the bank manager did ask himself whether it would be beneficial to the
> company to be allowed to continue to operate its bank account and to continue in
> business and he had sufficient information with which to answer that question. If   *e*
> it was beneficial to the company to continue, it was beneficial to the creditors. The
> bank manager was informed that an agreement had been reached which would
> result in the petition being dismissed. The bank manager was provided with
> figures from which it appeared that the company was trading at a profit. The bank
> manager was not told how much the company owed but he was told that the bank
> account would be in credit in the foreseeable future. The bank manager had no   *f*
> reason to suppose from this information that the company was trading at a loss or
> was over-trading or was for any reason insolvent. The liquidator admits that the
> information given to the bank manager was in general accurate. If the bank
> manager had asked for more detailed information the result would have been the
> same. At the least there appeared a reasonable chance that the company would
> avoid liquidation and that the creditors would be paid in full. The information that   *g*
> work in progress amounted to £168,000 and new contracts for £102,000 had been
> signed signified that if the company immediately ceased to trade the results could
> be disastrous to the company and thus to the creditors. At the least it appeared that
> the effects of remaining in business, even if the winding-up petition succeeded,
> were likely to be less harmful than the effects of an immediate cessation of
> business. The bank manager had no reason to distrust the integrity or competence   *h*
> of the directors. The danger of over-trading which had manifested itself in the past
> appeared to have been averted judging by the history of the past months. Provided
> that the company kept within its existing overdraft of £5,000 and made no unusual
> payments there was no reason to think that the financial position of the company
> would deteriorate ... In my judgment the circumstances of this company were
> such that harm would have resulted if the company had ceased to trade on 3rd or   *j*
> 10th or 17th August. It did not appear that harm would be occasioned if the
> company were allowed banking facilities after 17th August for the purpose of
> continuing its normal trade. It is not certain that any greater harm resulted from
> the decision to continue in business than the harm which would have been suffered
> if the company had ceased to carry on business.'

The correctness of the judge's conclusion in respect of the trading loss depends, I think,
a on whether he was right in saying that, if in the event the decision taken by the bank
involved the creditors in loss, the court would nevertheless absolve the bank from
liability provided that the decision was based on adequate information and was reasonable
at the time. In my judgment, and with deference to the judge, that is too benevolent a
view, particularly in a case in which the bank was unsuccessful in putting into operation
precautions which would effectively alert the bank to the fact that the company was
b trading at a loss.

It is evident that the judge had prominently in mind what was said by Lord Cairns LJ
in *Re Wiltshire Iron Co*[1] where he said:

> 'But where a company actually trading, which it is in the interest of every one to
> preserve, and ultimately to sell, as a going concern, is made an object of a winding-
> up Petition, which may fail or may succeed, if it were to be supposed that
c > transactions in the ordinary course of its current trade, *bonâ fide* entered into and
> completed, would be avoided, and would not, in the discretion given to the Court,
> be maintained, the result would be that the presentation of a Petition, groundless or
> well-founded, would, *ipso facto*, paralyze the trade of the company, and great injury,
> without any counterbalance of advantage, would be done to those interested in the
> assets of the company.'
d

It will be observed that Lord Cairns LJ there supposes a case of a company actually
trading which it is in the interests of everyone to preserve and ultimately to sell as a going
concern. It has not been suggested in the present case that anyone ever addressed his
mind to the question whether it would be in the interests of the unsecured creditors that
the company's business should be continued with a view to a sale as a going concern
e notwithstanding the possibility of trading losses meanwhile.

If the bank had applied for a prospective validating order at or about 10th or 17th
August 1972, it is possible that the court would have been prepared to authorise
continued banking facilities subject to certain precautions. Precisely what those
precautions would have been I cannot say, but they would or should have been devised
to ensure, as far as was practicable, that the company would not be supported in
f unprofitable trading unless this would be likely to benefit the general body of
creditors. The bank made no such application; as I have already said, it took the risk of
going on without an order. It is accordingly in my judgment also vulnerable to an order
to restore to the company the amount lost by post-liquidation unprofitable trading, viz
£5,000.

The liquidator has been moderate in his demands on this appeal. In saying so, I do not
g intend in any way to criticise him for the course he has taken in what has been, I think,
a difficult case. By his notice of appeal he has claimed repayment by the bank of three
alternative sums, which he asserts to have been the amounts to the extent of which the
creditors have been prejudiced. They are £13,259·92, which was the liquidator's
estimate of the trading loss during the relevant period; alternatively £5,000, which was
the amount of the loss as found by the judge, and in the further alternative £1,184·91,
h which was the amount by which credits exceeded debits on the current account during
the period 3rd August to 10th October 1972, plus the £326 debited in respect of bank
charges and interest. The liquidator now accepts the judge's finding that the loss
amounted to £5,000. Accordingly he does not claim repayment of more than that sum.

In these circumstances I would allow this appeal, discharging the order of Templeman
J and substituting an order to the following effect: (1) validating payments into the
j company's current account with the bank on and after 3rd August 1972 in order of
priority of date up to a sum of £2,670; (2) declaring invalid the payment into that
account of the next £5,000 paid in after 3rd August 1972, and ordering repayment of
that sum by the bank to the liquidator for the account of the company without prejudice

1   (1868) LR 3 Ch App 443 at 447

to the right (if any) of the bank to prove in the liquidation in respect of a sum of £2,652 as part of the £5,322 due by the company to the bank immediately before 3rd August *a* 1972; (3) validating as between the company and the bank all other transactions on the account on and after 3rd August 1972, but on the footing that no credits to the account which are so validated shall be treated as discharging any part of the £2,652.

I have made no reference to any interest on the sum repayable to the liquidator. I would like to hear submissions by counsel on that point.

Counsel for the liquidator has submitted that certain of the findings of the judge were *b* unjustified by the evidence. I do not think that I need deal with those submissions in any detail. I need only say that I have not been satisfied on any of the findings in question that there was not sufficient evidence before the judge on which he could make such finding. I differ from the judge not on the basis of fact but on the principles on which the discretion under the section should be exercised.

c

GOFF LJ. Having had the advantage of reading Buckley LJ's judgment whilst it was still in draft, and of discussing the case with him on several occasions, I am happy to say, with respect, that I agree in its entirety with the judgment which Buckley LJ has just delivered.

SIR DAVID CAIRNS. I also am in the position of being able to agree.   *d*

Appeal allowed.   Leave to appeal to the House of Lords.

Solicitors: *W F Prior & Co* (for the liquidator); *Wilde, Sapte & Co* (for the bank).

J H Fazan Esq   Barrister.

Carter v Carter

a

COURT OF APPEAL, CIVIL DIVISION
ORR, ORMROD AND GOFF LJJ
14th DECEMBER 1979

b
c

Divorce – Financial provision – Right to apply – Periodical payments – Right not to be taken away without party's consent – Wife consenting to dismissal of claim for periodical payments if husband's half share in home transferred to her – Judge making order transferring half share to her subject to a charge in husband's favour for half the value of his share – Judge making 'no order' for periodical payments – Subsequently judge purporting to vary order under slip rule by substituting 'application ... dismissed' instead of 'no order' – Whether jurisdiction to dismiss wife's claim – Whether consent to dismissal – Whether variation of order permitted under slip rule – Matrimonial Causes Act 1973, s 23(1) – CCR Ord 15, r 12.

d
e

Following the parties' divorce the wife applied in ancillary proceedings for a property adjustment order in respect of the matrimonial home, which was owned by the parties jointly, and for periodical payments for herself. There were previous orders for periodical payments. In the ancillary proceedings the wife offered to forgo her claim for periodical payments in return for the transfer to her of the husband's half share in the house. The judge's order dated 8th June 1979 required the husband to transfer his share in the house to the wife subject to a charge in his favour for half the value of his share, and stated that there should be 'no order for periodical payments'. After the order was drawn up the judge had the matter restored to his list, because he had overlooked the outstanding arrears of periodical payments under the previous orders, and, on 30th October, purported to vary the order of 8th June under the slip rule (CCR Ord 15, r 12[a]) by substituting for the words 'no order for periodical payments' an order that the wife's application for periodical payments 'be dismissed'. The wife appealed.

f
g
h

Held – The judge had no jurisdiction to make the order of 30th October dismissing the wife's application for periodical payments and the appeal would therefore be allowed, for the following reasons—

(i) A party's statutory right under s 23(1)[b] of the Matrimonial Causes Act 1973 to apply for one of the orders set out in s 23(1) could not be taken away by an order of the court unless the party consented to the order. Since the wife had consented to forgo her claim for periodical payments only if the whole of the husband's share in the house was transferred to her, and not if the transfer of the husband's share was to be subject to a charge in his favour for half the amount of his share, it followed that she had not consented to the court dismissing her claim for periodical payments (see p 829 *h* to p 830 *b*, p 831 *a* and 832 *c*, post); *Minton v Minton* [1979] 1 All ER 79 distinguished.

(ii) Since the order of 30th October introduced a major change into the order as drawn on 8th June, it could not come within the slip rule (see p 830 *d* and p 832 *c*, post).

Per Curiam. Where there is an agreement between husband and wife disposing of their financial claims it should be made clear by their legal advisers and the court whether it is the parties' intention to bar the wife from making any further claim for relief, or whether that matter is left open. The order of the court should therefore state clearly either that a claim for periodical payments or other relief is dismissed, or that it is left open (see p 831 *g* to *j* and p 832 *c*, post).

j

---

a   Rule 12 is set out at p 830 *c*, post

b   Section 23(1), so far as material, provides: '(1) On granting a decree of divorce ... (whether ... before or after the decree is made absolute), the court may make any one or more of the following orders, that is to say—(*a*) an order that either party to the marriage shall make to the other such periodical payments, for such term, as may be specified in the order ...'

Notes

For waiver and dismissal of claims for financial provision, see 13 Halsbury's Laws (4th
Edn) para 1158.

For the Matrimonial Causes Act 1973, s 23, see 43 Halsbury's Statutes (3rd Edn) 564.

Cases referred to in judgments

Jessel v Jessel [1979] 3 All ER 645, [1979] 1 WLR 1148, CA.

Minton v Minton [1979] 1 All ER 79, [1979] AC 593, [1979] 2 WLR 31, HL.

Appeal

This was an appeal by Sylvia Joan Carter ('the wife') from an order made on 30th October
1979 by his Honour Judge Smithies at Bournemouth County Court in ancillary
proceedings following the wife's divorce from the husband, John Maurice Carter,
whereby the judge varied an earlier order made by him on 8th June 1979 in the
proceedings, purporting to act under CCR Ord 15, r 12 (the 'slip rule'). The facts are set
out in the judgment of Ormrod LJ.

Peter Mauleverer for the wife.
T G Field-Fisher QC and *Sheila McKinney* for the husband.

ORMROD LJ delivered the first judgment at the invitation of Orr LJ. This is in form
an appeal from an order made on 30th October 1979 by his Honour Judge Smithies at
Bournemouth County Court in ancillary proceedings following a divorce between the
husband and wife.

It is not necessary to go into the history either of this marriage or of the preceding
litigation between the parties beyond saying that both the marriage and the litigation
seem to have been quite unusually stormy. Matters came almost to a head on 8th June
1979 when the learned judge had before him a claim by the wife for a property
adjustment order, a periodical payments order and other ancillary relief. There had
previously been an order for periodical payments for the wife and children, the last of
those orders being on 14th December 1977 when an order was made for £37 per week
to be paid to the wife, the wife assuming responsibility for the mortgage repayments on
the matrimonial home, and a total of £20 per week in all for the children, of whom there
are effectively two. The proceedings in June were mainly about the former matrimonial
home. It is a house in Dorset owned by the parties jointly and it is subject to a mortgage.

The judge, having heard the evidence, which was voluminous so far as affidavits went,
and also having heard oral evidence, did not give a reasoned judgment. I do not for a
moment criticise him for that. What he did do at the end of the argument was to say
what his conclusions were. We are very much assisted by a helpful note which was taken
by junior consel for the husband before us and who was then counsel for the husband.
Her note of what the judge said reads thus:

'I value the equity at £21,000. I order that the [wife] and [husband] hold the
former matrimonial home on trust for the [wife] and children subject to a charge
in favour of the [husband] in the sum of £5,250. I make no order for periodical
payments for the [wife] or children. Liberty to the [husband] to apply to enforce
the charge when a home is no longer required for the [wife] and children unless the
parties otherwise agree, or on death or re-marriage or co-habitation with another
man, without leave of the court.'

Then there is an order as to costs which does not matter. The judge then invited the
parties' counsel and solicitors between them to draw up minutes of the order. In the
events which have now come to light the parties have come, at the fifty-ninth minute of
the eleventh hour, to an arrangement between themselves which makes it unnecessary
to go in great detail through the matter.

There are, however, at least one or two important points which have arisen in the
a course of argument in this case and it would be, I think, right for this court to express a
view about them. It is clear that the judge intended that the legal representatives of the
parties should draft the order. Unfortunately a muddle occurred in the court office.
Counsel went away and proceeded to draw up minutes of the order. Whether they were
finally settled or not we have not been told, nor have we seen a draft (no doubt rightly),
because unknown to counsel and solicitors acting for the wife the court office was in fact
b drawing up the order itself. Some officer in the court office drew up the order, no doubt
thinking that it was an ordinary case, and this order appears in our papers. The parts of
it which matter are these: the order says:

> 'Upon hearing counsel for both parties
> 'It is declared that the [wife] and [husband] hold the matrimonial home, 73,
> Horseponds Lane, East Morden, Wareham, Dorset, on trust for the [wife] absolutely
c > subject to a charge in favour of the [husband] in the sum of £5,250.
> 'It is ordered that the said charge be not enforced otherwise on[1] death, marriage
> or co-habitation of the [wife] without leave of the court.
> 'Liberty to the [husband] to apply if the property for the time being subject to the
> charge is not reasonably required for both the [wife] and the children of the
> family. [Then, and this is the important part:] AND IT IS ORDERED that there be no
d > order for periodical payments.'

That order as drawn did not satisfy either party when it appeared. It does not seem to
have met with the judge's approval either, because he himself, we are told, restored the
matter to his list to deal with an item which had been overlooked, namely the
outstanding arrears of periodical payments which amounted, we are told, to something
e like £2,000. So that led to the case being restored, but meanwhile it seems clear that
neither side was satisfied with the order in the form in which it appears.

So the matter came back before the judge on 30th October 1979 as I have already
mentioned. There was a long discussion between counsel and the judge and he gave a
long judgment. The upshot was that he varied the order of 8th June in some considerable
detail purporting to act under the slip rule. The first part of the order of 30th October
f is not now of particular significance. It rewrote the provisions relating to the former
matrimonial home without very materially altering them. The important change made
in the order related to the periodical payments. The June order, as I have already said,
specifically provided that there be no order for periodical payments for the wife or the
children. The order as varied on 30th October by the judge deleted the words 'There be
no order for periodical payments' and substituted for them: 'The [wife's] application for
g periodical payments for herself and the dependent children of the family be dismissed.'

In my judgment, for two quite separate reasons, the judge had no jurisdiction to make
the order in that latter form. Firstly, it is conceded by counsel for the husband, very
properly, that the one thing the judge clearly had no jurisdiction to do was to dismiss the
children's claim for periodical payments. In my judgment neither had he jurisdiction to
dismiss the wife's claim for periodical payments unless she consented to it, which she did
h not. My reason for saying that is simply this: s 23 of the Matrimonial Causes Act 1973
provides in sub-s (1): 'On granting a decree of divorce, a decree of nullity of marriage or
a decree of judicial separation or at any time thereafter . . . the court may make any one
or more of the following orders'. Then the various periodical payments orders are set
out. Reference is made to a lump sum order and various other matters are dealt with.
In my judgment the effect of s 23(1) is to give the parties concerned a statutory right to
j apply for one or other of the orders set out in that section. That statutory right, as I see
it, cannot be taken away by the court unless the party concerned consents to such an
order. There is no one who could possibly consent in such circumstances on behalf of the
children, and the wife did not consent in respect of her own rights. So in my view the

---

1 'otherwise on': sic

judge never had any power to dismiss the wife's claim for periodical payments in the circumstances of this particular case. She had offered to agree to forgo her claim to periodical payments in return for the transfer to her of the husband's half share in the house. She never agreed, and was never asked to agree, to forgo her claim for periodical payments in return for a transfer of the husband's share of the house to her subject to a charge, which means in effect that the husband would transfer half his interest (that is one-quarter of the whole) to the wife, leaving a quarter of the value of the house in his hands. It is true, of course, that if inflation proceeds at the present rate the wife would have got progressively a greater and greater proportion of the house in the end, because of course the real value of the charge, expressed as it is in a sum of money, would progressively decrease.

The second reason is that in my judgment it was miles outside the provisions of the slip rule. The slip rule is CCR Ord 15, r 12. It reads: 'Clerical mistakes in judgments or orders or errors arising therein from any accidental slip or omission may at any time be corrected by the court.' Having regard to what the judge said at the conclusion of the submissions to him, as recorded by counsel for the husband, it could not conceivably be referred to as a 'clerical mistake' or an 'accidental slip'. It may be accidental in the sense that the judge did not express what he had in his mind with sufficient clarity, but however that may be the order of 30th October introduces a major change in the order as drawn on 8th June, so it was, in my judgment, way outside the slip rule.

Reference was made in the course of argument, quite rightly, to a judgment in the House of Lords in *Minton v Minton*[1]. That case, in my judgment, decides two propositions only. The first proposition, and the important one, is that a party with a claim to financial relief under either s 23 or s 24 of the Matrimonial Causes Act 1973 may validly agree to forgo any such claim for ever in the future. The issue that was before the House in *Minton v Minton*[1] was whether, there being no order in terms dismissing the wife's claim for periodical payments, the court retained nonetheless, in spite of the agreement between the parties, jurisdiction to entertain a new application for periodical payments. The House of Lords, and it is all set out in Lord Scarman's speech, decided that an adult party could bar his or her claim under those two sections by making an appropriate agreement. There is nothing in *Minton v Minton*[1] to suggest that such a claim can be barred in any other way.

The other proposition which *Minton v Minton*[1] decides is that it is not necessary for the court specifically to dismiss the claim. Whether or not the claim is barred depends on the construction of the agreement between the parties. In *Minton v Minton*[1] what had happened was that an agreement had been reached between the parties which provided, inter alia, for payment by the husband to the wife of maintenance at the rate of 5p per annum until the matrimonial home was conveyed to her. Obviously the purpose was to preserve her right to claim periodical payments in the event of anything going wrong with the conveyance. The agreement went on to provide that when the matrimonial home had been conveyed to her such nominal payment should cease. The construction placed on that agreement, and for my part I would say the only possible construction, was that the wife was agreeing that on the conveyance to her of the former matrimonial home, her application for periodical payments would in effect be dismissed. The House held that that was good enough. In my judgment there is nothing else established by *Minton v Minton*[1], often quoted as it now is in this and many other courts for all sorts of other propositions. For my part I respectfully agree with the observations on *Minton v Minton*[1] to be found in the judgments of Lord Denning MR and Geoffrey Lane LJ in *Jessel v Jessel*[2].

1   [1979] 1 All ER 79, [1979] AC 593
2   [1979] 3 All ER 645 at 648, 650, [1979] 1 WLR 1148 at 1153, 1156

That deals with the relevant parts of the appeal in relation to the order of 30th
a October. The judge had no power, in my view, to make an order dismissing either the
wife's claim for periodical payments or the children's claim. So that necessitates the
allowing of this appeal from that order. .

Fortunately, with the great assistance of counsel on both sides, these parties who have
been warring for years have now realised that it is essential to tidy up their affairs and
they have reached an agreement. What has been agreed between the parties now is this,
b that the husband will now agree to the order which the wife originally suggested in her
affidavit in May 1978, namely that he should transfer to her his interest in the former
matrimonial home, subject to the mortgage, in respect of which she will undertake to
indemnify him in respect of all sums falling due under the mortgage. She has not
consented to an order dismissing her claim for periodical payments in full because there
is one outstanding matter which neither counsel can deal with by consent, nor we in this
c court, and that is this: these two parties have been carrying on a business of a butcher and
fish and chip shop in partnership together. That business has collapsed for one reason or
another. There were substantial debts and we are told by counsel for the husband that
there are still some debts, the amount of which is not entirely clear, still outstanding. In
respect of those debts, of course, under the law the husband and wife are both responsible.

Counsel for the wife would be prepared to consent to her claim for periodical payments
d being dismissed if she could get an indemnity from the husband against any claim made
against her in respect of the partnership debts. Counsel for the husband has not the
necessary instructions to consent to that, so we are not able at the moment to go as far as
dismissing her claim for periodical payments, but it has been agreed by counsel that the
best we can do in the circumstances is to make the order I have indicated transferring the
husband's interest to the wife and an order for nominal maintenance for the wife of 5p
e a year, such order to be discharged and her claim dismissed if and when she receives the
necessary undertaking from her former husband to indemnify her against any
partnership liability which may fall on her. In order to do that, it will be necessary to
give leave to the wife to appeal against the order of 8th June. For some reason the judge
did not seem to think that he had power to give her leave to appeal. He clearly had. He
did not have the power to give her leave to appeal out of time, but we can do that, so I
f would give her leave to appeal and to extend her time for appealing until today (no doubt
the notice of appeal can be amended) and vary the order of 8th June in the way I have
indicated.

There may be other details of this order to be settled by counsel. There are a number
of other minor matters outstanding which we ought to deal with if we can.

There is only one other point I would like to mention and that is that the phrase in the
g order of 8th June 'no order for periodical payments' is ambiguous. Whether the judge
intended to discharge the order of December 1977 or not one does not know. One can
only presume that he did, but if he did, the order does not say so; it simply says 'no
order'. It is arguable that, having said 'no order' the original order stands. It should be
emphasised that where agreements are made between husband and wife for disposal of
their financial claims, one on the other, it is extremely important that the legal advisers
h to both sides and the court, whether it be registrar or judge, should make it perfectly
clear whether the intention is that the wife should be barred from making any further
claim for periodical payments or any other relief, or whether the matter is being left
open. That means that for the sake of clarity these orders should state clearly either that
the claim for periodical payments or other relief is to be dismissed, or that it is left
open. We will have to go back to the old 'nominal order' in order to make it perfectly
j clear that the claim remains in existence. Parties must make up their minds which of the
two alternatives they want, otherwise the court will have great difficulty in construing
some of these agreements to decide whether or not there is, or was, the necessary consent
to forgo the statutory right of the parties concerned.

In those circumstances I would allow the appeal. I would discharge the order of 30th
October 1979 in whole or in part, depending on how much of it counsel for the husband

wishes to retain in respect of the other matters. I would give leave to appeal from the order of 8th June 1979 and set that order aside and substitute for it an order that the husband within 14 days (or whatever is the convenient time) transfers his interest in the former matrimonial home to the wife absolutely, she undertaking to indemnify him in respect of all debts arising under the existing mortgage. I would make a nominal order for periodical payments for the wife and for the children on the basis that she is now free to apply for maintenance for the children whenever she is so advised. There will be a further order that, in the event of the husband giving an undertaking in writing to indemnify the wife against liablity for any outstanding partnership debts, the nominal order for periodical payments for the wife shall be dismissed. That I feel is all that we need do.

ORR LJ. I agree.

GOFF LJ. I agree. One of the minor matters to be provided for in the order is what is to be done about the application for periodical payments for the children. Ormrod LJ has pointed out that that could not be dismissed and therefore the paragraph in the order of 30th October 1979, which was a new paragraph purporting to dismiss the wife's application of 8th June 1979, will have to be discharged or varied to enable her to make application for periodical payments for the children or to vary the order for herself in the event of her failing to get the undertaking. Counsel for the wife has suggested that the proper way would be to give her liberty to apply to the registrar for directions as to the claim in respect of the children. That, speaking for myself, would appear to be the right thing to do so far as she is concerned. Of course there will be no application if she gets the undertaking unless circumstances change.

Appeal allowed.

Solicitors: *Gregory Rowcliffe & Co*, agents for *Humphries, Kirk & Miller*, Wareham (for the wife); *Jacobs & Reeves*, Poole (for the husband).

Avtar S Virdi Esq   Barrister.

a Gandolfo v Gandolfo (Standard Chartered Bank Ltd, garnishee)

COURT OF APPEAL, CIVIL DIVISION
MEGAW, BROWNE LJJ AND SIR STANLEY REES
b 7th DECEMBER 1979

Execution – Garnishee order – Debt due to creditor pursuant to undertaking given by debtor to court – Husband undertaking to pay school fees of child of marriage – Wife in consequence receiving lower amount under order for periodical payments for benefit of child – Husband falling into arrears with fees – Wife applying for order against husband's bank for payment of arrears to her out of husband's account – Whether jurisdiction to make garnishee order against bank –
c Whether husband's undertaking amounting to 'order' for payment of school fees – Whether order 'obtained' by wife – CCR Ord 27, r 1.

The husband was ordered by a county court in September 1972 to pay the wife periodical payments of £1,000 per annum for herself and, on the basis of the husband's undertaking to the court to pay the school fees of the child of the marriage, periodical payments of
d £250 per annum for the benefit of the child. The husband fell into arrears with both the periodical payments and the school fees. His salary was paid into a bank account, and on 8th June 1978 the wife issued a garnishee summons against this bank for an order that the bank as garnishee pay the amount of the arrears to her out of the account. By an order dated 13th July 1979 a county court judge ordered the bank to pay the wife, inter alia, £3,211 in respect of the arrears of school fees. The husband appealed, contending
e that (i) under CCR Ord 27, r 1[a], a garnishee order could be made only if the wife had 'obtained a judgment or order' for the payment of the school fees whereas they were in fact payable by virtue of his undertaking rather than a judgment or order, and (ii) the undertaking was to pay the school fees to the school and could not therefore be regarded as having been 'obtained' by the wife.

f **Held** – Applying the principle that in an appropriate case an undertaking given to the court and embodied in a written order had the same effect as a judgment or order in terms of the undertaking, it was appropriate to treat the husband's undertaking to pay the school fees as equivalent to an order for their payment within CCR Ord 27, r 1, because it was an integral part of the order of September 1972 and if it had not been given the periodical payments for the child would probably have been increased.
g Furthermore, the undertaking was equivalent to an order 'obtained' by the wife because it was not in terms an undertaking to pay the fees to the school and the wife was the person who was going to have to pay the school fees and was the only person who could have obtained such an order. Accordingly the judge had had jurisdiction under Ord 27, r 1, to make the garnishee order, and the appeal would be dismissed (see p 838 *c* to *j*, post).
h   *Milburn v Newton Colliery Ltd* (1908) 52 Sol Jo 317 and *Biba Ltd v Stratford Investments Ltd* [1972] 3 All ER 1041 applied.

Notes
For when garnishee proceedings may be instituted and what debts are attachable, see 17 Halsbury's Laws (4th Edn) paras 526–527.

j **Cases referred to in judgments**
Biba Ltd v Stratford Investments Ltd [1972] 3 All ER 1041, [1973] Ch 281, [1972] 3 WLR 902, [1973] RPC 799, Digest (Cont Vol D) 257, 535aa.
Milburn v Newton Colliery Ltd (1908) 52 Sol Jo 317, 16 Digest (Repl) 57, 535.

---

a   Rule 1 is set out at p 835 *j* to p 836 *a*, post

Appeal

By an order made in the Stoke-on-Trent County Court on 25th September 1972 Frederick *a*
Lewis Gandolfo ('the husband') was ordered to pay Muriel Gandolfo ('the wife') periodical
payments for herself of £1,000 a year, and, on the basis of the husband's undertaking to
the court to pay the school fees of the child of the marriage, was ordered to make further
periodical payments of £250 a year to the wife for the benefit of the child. The husband
fell into arrears with the periodical payments and the payment of the school fees. On 8th
June 1978 the wife issued a garnishee summons against the Standard Chartered Bank Ltd *b*
('the bank') alleging that the bank was indebted to the husband and applying for an order
that the bank pay to the wife a sum in respect of the arrears of school fees and a further
sum in respect of the arrears of maintenance. By an order dated 13th July 1979 his
Honour Judge Taylor in the Stoke-on-Trent County Court ordered that the garnishee
summons should be adjourned generally on the terms that (i) the bank pay forthwith to
the wife the sum of £427·42 in respect of the arrears of maintenance and (ii) the bank *c*
pay to the wife on 3rd August 1979 the sum of £3,311·20 in respect of the arrears of
school fees. The judge refused leave to appeal. By leave of the Court of Appeal given on
30th July 1979 the husband appealed from the order of 13th July. The grounds of the
appeal were that the judge had no jurisdiction under CCR Ord 27, rr 1, 10 to order the
bank to pay to the wife the sum of £3,211·20 because the school fees were payable by
virtue of the husband's undertaking to the court on 25th September 1972 and not under *d*
a judgment or order obtained by the wife, within Ord 27, r 1. The facts are set out in the
judgment of Browne LJ.

J E Mitting for the husband.
M S E Grime for the wife.
The garnishee did not appear and was not represented.   *e*

BROWNE LJ delivered the first judgment at the invitation of Megaw LJ. This is an
appeal by a husband, as I shall call him, from a decision of his Honour Judge Taylor in the
Stoke-on-Trent County Court on 13th July 1979. That decision was given on a garnishee
summons taken out by the wife against the husband. The substance of the judge's order
was that he ordered the garnishee summons to be adjourned generally on terms that the *f*
garnishee, who is the Standard Chartered Bank Ltd, should pay to the wife a sum of £427
odd forthwith and should pay to her on 3rd August 1979 a sum of £3,211 odd. He
refused leave to appeal, but leave to appeal was given by this court on 30th July 1979.

To make the appeal intelligible, it is necessary to say something about the background,
though not, I think, very much. The parties were formerly husband and wife, and there
is one child, a boy. It is not quite clear how old he is now, but apparently he is still at *g*
school. The story, so far as we are concerned, begins with an order of the Stoke-on-Trent
County Court of 25th September 1972. That order provided that the wife withdrew her
claim under the Married Women's Property Act 1882 and that the husband acknowledged
that the entire equitable estate in the matrimonial home was to be vested solely in his
wife. By para 4 it was ordered that the husband should make periodical payments at the
rate of £1,000 a year payable monthly in advance to the wife, it being recited that the *h*
husband was then resident abroad and not liable to British income tax. So that sum was
to be paid gross. The order goes on:

'And it is further ordered that as from the like date [ie 1st October 1972] and
upon the basis of the Respondent [ie the husband] undertaking to the Court to
continue to pay the school fees at the present preparatory school and such other *j*
schools as may be agreed, the Respondent make further periodical payments of
£250 per annum (payable monthly in advance as aforesaid) to and for [the son] the
younger child of the family, until he shall attain the age of 17 years, or until further
order (the receipt of the Petitioner/Applicant [ie the wife] given from time to time
to be a good and sufficient discharge on behalf of such child of the family).'

There was then an order, also of the Stoke-on-Trent County Court, dated 27th February
a 1976 which varied the periodical payments to the wife to £2,500 a year. As appears
from the order, the husband did not appear on that occasion, and, without going into any
details, it is plain from the subsequent documents before us that he has challenged that
order. In particular, discussions took place in Zambia, in Lusaka, where the husband was
working, in 1978, as a result of which the husband said that an agreement had been
reached that the wife would waive any rights she might have, if she had any, under the
b 1976 order. In return the husband agreed to pay arrears, as I understand it, under the
1972 order and school fees, neither of which he has done.

I do not think it is necessary to say any more about that agreement in 1978, although
we have a considerable body of evidence about it in our papers. It is necessary to mention
it though because, as we are told by counsel, the main issue before the county court judge
on 13th July was the effect of that agreement in Lusaka in 1978. The judge held that its
c effect was indeed to release the husband, putting it generally, from any obligations under
the 1976 order, and that, therefore, the only arrears of periodical payments with which
he had to deal were arrears under the 1972 order.

We have the judge's note and we also have a note taken by counsel for the husband,
who appeared as counsel in the court below. The judge's own note, reads as follows:

> *d* 'Applying Ord 27, r 10 [that is, of the County Court Rules] Garnishee should pay
> to J. Creditor those sums due to today under Order of 1972 from which should be
> deducted only those payments actually made by the J. Debtor or deducted from his
> salary. Arrears on '72 basis. £3,211·20'

That was arrears of school fees. We were told that some school fees had been paid by the
husband, but that nothing had been paid since, I think, March 1976. Then the next
e figure is £427·42. That was the arrears of the periodical payments under the 1972 order
in favour of both the wife and the child. That made a total of £3,638·62. The judge
deducted from the arrears under the 1972 order sums which had been paid by the
Ministry of Overseas Development, who were the employers of the husband, direct to
the Department of Health and Social Security, which had been paying supplementary
benefit to the wife. Having deducted those payments which had been made by the
f Ministry of Overseas Development to the Department of Health and Social Security,
there was left that figure of £427·42 to which I have referred. The judge, I think
recording counsel for the husband's argument, goes on to say:

> 'Says I cannot garnishee school fees—which are on top of the figures given—
> because they are paid as a result of an undertaking and not a "judgment or order"
> under r 1.'

g
He then made the order to which I have referred.

Counsel for the husband's note of the judgment is rather fuller. It says:

> 'I may not be absolutely right, but I include school fees in the order. Order 27,
> r 1 says that a judgment creditor may take proceedings by way of garnishee to
> enforce a judgment or order for the payment of money. Order 27, r 10 seems to
> *h* throw my discretion wider. It permits me to make such an order as to payment "as
> may be just". In the circumstances of this case, the judgment debtor's undertaking
> to pay school fees being an integral part of an order for the payment of money,
> justice requires me to order payment of those fees. Accordingly, the money payable
> under the undertaking should be paid by the garnishee to the judgment creditor.'

j
I should refer first, I think, to CCR Ord 27, rr 1 and 10. CCR Ord 27, r 1 provides:

> 'Any person who has obtained a judgment or order (in this Order called "the
> judgment creditor") for the payment of money may take proceedings to obtain
> payment to him of the amount of any debt owing or accruing to the judgment
> debtor from any other person (in this Order called "the garnishee") or so much

thereof as may be sufficient to satisfy that judgment order and the costs of the garnishee proceedings.'

The Standard Chartered Bank Ltd, the garnishee here, has money belonging to the husband because, as I understand it, the Ministry of Overseas Development, as it then was, had paid the whole or part of his salary into the bank in London.

CCR 27, r 10 provides:

'If no amount is paid into court or the amount paid into court under Rule 7 of this Order is not accepted, the judge may, after hearing the judgment creditor, the garnishee and the judgment debtor or such of them as appear, determine the question of the liability of the garnishee, and may make such order as to the payment to the judgment creditor of any sum found to be due from the garnishee to the judgment debtor and as to costs as may be just . . .'

I do not think I need read the rest of that rule.

With all respect to the judge, I do not myself feel that r 10 has any bearing on the problem which we have to consider. It is dealing with the situation where the garnishee disputes his liability to the judgment debtor. Accordingly, I return to r 1.

Counsel for the husband submits that the county court had no jurisdiction to make a garnishee order in respect of the school fees, for two reasons. He says that the undertaking embodied in the order of 1972 was not a 'judgment or order' within the meaning of CCR Ord 27, r 1 and he says that it was not 'obtained' by the wife in this sense, as I understand it, that the money was not necessarily going to be paid to the wife. It could have been paid direct to the school. Counsel for the husband says that if the order should be read as meaning that payment should be made to the child, he does not rely on the second point. However, he does say that in so far as the order should be read as meaning payment to the school, then he does rely on his second point.

So far as the first point is concerned, I think I should refer to the definitions of 'judgment' and 'order' in CCR Ord 49, r 2. By that rule '"judgment" means the final decision of the court in an action' and '"Order" means the final decision of the court in a matter and also any decision of the court other than a final decision in any proceedings.'

We were referred by counsel for the wife to two authorities. The first was *Milburn v Newton Colliery Ltd*[1]. That was an action brought by a landowner against a colliery company which had been discharging poisonous water into a burn and thence into the River Coquet. The plaintiffs moved for an injunction (I suppose for an interlocutory injunction, but it is not absolutely clear) against the defendants, and on the hearing the defendants—

'undertook "to pump all standage water (being water in the dip of the colliery preventing the working of the coal therein) out of the colliery by the 1st March, 1908, and to so treat such water that when same enters the plaintiffs' water such water shall be free from pollution so as not to be injurious to fish life."'

Thereafter, after the undertaking, the defendants did allow more water, which was still poisonous, to get into the burn, and I suppose thence into the plaintiffs' river:

'The plaintiffs moved for leave "to sue out a writ of sequestration directed to commissioners to be therein named to sequester the goods, chattels, and personal estate and the rents, issues, and profits of the real estate of the defendants for the contempt of this court committed by the said defendants in that they have broken the undertaking on their part contained in an order made in this action on the 15th day of November, 1907." [The report goes on:] The defendants for their defence relied on their evidence, and also took the objection that R.S.C., Ord. 42 r. 31, does not apply to a breach of an undertaking.'

---

1 (1908) 52 Sol Jo 317

Warrington J in giving judgment said:

> 'Now several objections have been taken by the defendants to the application. The first which I must mention, although it was not pressed strongly, was to the jurisdiction of the court to give leave to issue a writ of sequestration for a breach of an undertaking. Now, Ord. 42, r. 31, of the Rules of the Supreme Court provides, "Any judgment or order against a corporation wilfully disobeyed may, by leave of the court or a judge, be enforced by sequestration against the corporate property, or by attachment against the directors or other officers thereof, or by writ of sequestration against their property."'

So it will be observed that that rule, like the county court rule with which we are concerned, refers to 'any judgment or order', and there it was an undertaking, and in that case an undertaking to do positive acts. The judgment continues as follows:

> 'Now, I do not think that this rule was intended to alter the practice of the court as it existed before these rules were promulgated. The practice of the Court of Chancery was not to treat an undertaking as distinct from an injunction with regard to a breach, and for the purpose of enforcing an undertaking that undertaking is equivalent to an order – that is to say, an undertaking, if broken, would involve the same consequences on the persons breaking that undertaking as would their disobedience to an order for an injunction.'

The judge then referred to an earlier authority[1], and went on:

> 'Now, it seems to me on that, that an undertaking ought to be treated as equivalent to an order, and RSC, Ord. 42, r. 31 must be read with that in view.'

Then he dealt with the evidence, and granted the plaintiffs' application.

That case was followed by Brightman J in *Biba Ltd v Stratford Investments Ltd*[2]. That was a case of a negative undertaking. The headnote[3] reads:

> 'A company gave an undertaking that it would not infringe, whether by its directors, officers or by their servants or agents, the registered trade mark "Biba" which was the property of the plaintiff, nor advertise for sale or sell shirts under or by reference to the word "Biba". The plaintiff subsequently alleged that the undertaking had been breached by the company and moved for the committal of a director of the company for contempt.'

Then the headnote continues:

> 'On a preliminary point as to whether the director, who had neither aided nor abetted the contempt, could be liable to committal proceedings under R.S.C., Ord. 45, r. 5, for breach by the company of its undertaking, the question arose whether Ord. 45, r. 5, applied only to a case where an order had been disobeyed and not to the breach of an undertaking. *Held*, that for the purposes of R.S.C., Ord. 45, r. 5, an undertaking, given to the court and embodied in a written order of the court, to abstain from an act, had the same effect as an order or judgment enjoining that act, and was thus equivalent to an injunction; it followed that the director was liable to proceedings for contempt . . .'

RSC Ord 45, r 5, which I need not read in full, again uses the words 'judgment or order'. It provides that 'Where . . . (b) a person disobeys a judgment or order requiring him to abstain from doing an act', then it may be enforced by various means.

In the *Biba* case[4] Brightman J said:

---

1   *London and Birmingham Railway Co v Grand Junction Canal Co* (1835) 1 Ry & Can Cas 224
2   [1972] 3 All ER 1041, [1973] Ch 281
3   [1973] Ch 281
4   [1972] 3 All ER 1041 at 1045, [1973] Ch 281 at 287

'I approach the case before me on the basis that Mr Lawson [that is, the director] adopted a purely passive role and did not aid and abet a contempt in any way. The question to be decided is whether, despite this purely passive role, he can be made liable under RSC Ord 45, r 5, in consequence of the breach by the company (which I assume to have taken place) of an undertaking, as distinct from disobedience to an order. In my view, I ought to follow and apply the decision of Warrington J in *Milburn v Newton Colliery Co Ltd*[1]. That is a clear authority, to my mind, that an undertaking given to the court and embodied in the written order of the court, whereby a party undertakes to abstain from doing an act, has the same effect for the purposes of RSC Ord 45, r 5, as a judgment or order enjoining that act. It is a common practice for a plaintiff in these sort of proceedings to accept an undertaking offered by a defendant as a substitute for the imposition of an injunction. I think it would be a pity to disturb that practice by giving a lesser quality to an undertaking than to an injunction. I therefore gladly follow the decision of Warrington J and I adopt his view that an undertaking to the court is equivalent to an injunction for the purposes of RSC Ord 45, r 5.'

Having regard to those authorities, it is in my view appropriate in a particular case to treat an undertaking as being equivalent to an order for the purposes of CCR Ord 27, r 1 or the corresponding Rules of the Supreme Court. I am not saying it would be appropriate in all cases, but in my judgment this is a case in which it would be appropriate. It is quite plain from the 1972 order, which I have read, that the undertaking was an integral part of the order.

So far as the child is concerned, the part of the order which I have already read provides that 'upon the basis of the [husband] undertaking to the Court to continue to pay the school fees' the husband is to make periodical payments of £250 a year to and for the boy, the receipt of the wife to be a good and sufficient discharge on behalf of the child.

It is quite plain, for example, that if the undertaking had not been given, periodical payments for the boy would almost certainly have been increased, in order to cover the school fees.

As to the other point, that this was really an undertaking to pay the school fees to the school, and therefore it cannot be regarded as being an order obtained by the wife, I think there are certainly two answers to that. In the first place, it does not say so. It does not purport to be an order in favour of the school. The school was not, of course, a party to the proceedings. The only person who could have obtained this order, in my judgment, was the wife, who was obtaining it in her own right, because she was going to pay the school fees for herself or on behalf of the child. It does not matter which.

It seems to me that all the merits in this case are in favour of our applying and following the two authorities to which we were referred.

As counsel for the wife pointed out, if this particular undertaking in this case cannot be enforced by garnishee proceedings, highly complicated alternative proceedings would have to be taken, probably by way of transfer of this part of the case to the High Court, and a motion for a sequestration order, leaving the wife to enforce her periodical payments and the boy's periodical payments in the county court.

It seems to me that every argument of good sense and convenience, and on the merits, is in favour of the order which the judge made, and in my judgment he had jurisdiction to do so and was justified in doing so, having regard to the authorities to which I have referred.

Accordingly, I would follow and apply those authorities and dismiss the appeal.

SIR STANLEY REES. I agree, and have nothing to add.

MEGAW LJ. I also agree with the conclusion arrived at by Browne LJ, for the reasons given by him.

---

1   (1908) 52 Sol Jo 317

There is one thing only which I desire to add, and in saying this I am confident that my
a brethren will both agree with it. I would like to express the appreciation of the court to
counsel for the wholly admirable way in which they have addressed their arguments to
this court. It was a matter of some complexity, some intricacy; it was a matter which
required to be explained to the court, and both counsel have confined their submissions
to within a period of half an hour each. They have put their arguments with complete
lucidity, complete clarity, and have said everything that is to be said on behalf of their
b respective parties. If all submissions to the court were of that quality, the task of the
court would be infinitely easier.

BROWNE LJ. I should like to associate myself very warmly with what Megaw LJ has
said.

c **SIR STANLEY REES.** I would too.

Appeal dismissed.

Solicitors: *Pritchard Englefield & Tobin* (for the husband); *William H Lill & Co*, Altrincham,
(for the wife).
d
Mary Rose Plummer   Barrister.

e # Verrall v Great Yarmouth Borough Council

COURT OF APPEAL, CIVIL DIVISION
LORD DENNING MR, ROSKILL AND CUMMING-BRUCE LJJ
18th OCTOBER 1979

f *Specific performance – Defence to action – Licence – Contract to let hall to political party –
Wrongful repudiation of contract – Political party claiming specific performance of contract –
Defence that licence to use hall was of short duration – Defence that repudiation occurred before
licensee entered into possession – Defence that public disorder might result if contract performed
– Whether specific performance could and should be ordered.*

g At the end of 1978 the National Front, a political party whose views were vigorously
opposed by other political parties, applied to the Conservative controlled council at Great
Yarmouth for permission to hold their annual conference at one of the council's halls on
26th and 27th October 1979. The conference was to be a private meeting, open only to
members of the National Front and such members of the press as were invited. The
council were aware of all the difficulties which might ensue if they let the National Front
h hire the hall, such as persons and bodies opposed to the National Front's views forcibly
attempting to prevent the conference being held, but nevertheless they resolved to allow
the National Front to hold the conference in their hall. Accordingly, on 4th April 1979
the council entered into a contract with the National Front to let out the hall for £6,000,
which the National Front paid forthwith. In the local government elections held shortly
afterwards, the council's decision became a major issue. A Labour controlled council
j were returned and in fulfilment of an election pledge almost immediately resolved that
the approval for the use of the conference hall by the National Front should be rescinded
and that their money should be refunded. The National Front made numerous attempts
to find another place to hold their conference but were unable to do so. They therefore
brought an action against the council seeking specific performance of the contract of 4th
April or alternatively damages for breach of contract, and in due course applied for

summary judgment under RSC Ord 14. Before the hearing of the application, the
council served a defence in which they admitted repudiation of the contract without   *a*
lawful excuse but contended that specific performance was not appropriate because, inter
alia, it was likely that the National Front's use of the hall would provoke breaches of the
peace, and that damages were an adequate remedy. The judge dealt with the case under
RSC Ord 14 and made an order for specific performance. The council appealed,
contending (i) that they had shown that they had an arguable defence and that therefore
the judge should not have dealt with the case under RSC Ord 14, (ii) that specific   *b*
performance could not be granted in respect of a transient interest such as a mere
contractual licence to use premises for two days only, (iii) that specific performance of an
executory licence could not be granted before the licensee had entered into possession
thereunder, and (iv) that, in any event, in view of the risk of public disorder and its
attendant consequences, the judge should not have exercised his discretion in favour of
granting the order of specific performance.   *c*

Held – The appeal would be dismissed for the following reasons—

(i) The judge was entitled to deal with the case under RSC Ord 14 because all the issues
were clear and the points of substance could be decided in the RSC Ord 14 proceedings
without a trial having to be ordered (see p 843 *e*, p 846 *a* to *d* and p 848 *g*, post).

(ii) There was no reason why the court could not order specific performance of a   *d*
contractual licence of short duration, such as that granted to the National Front, having
regard (per Roskill LJ) to the fact that it was the duty of the court to protect any interest
in land, whether an estate or a licence, by injunction or specific performance if it were
appropriate to do so (see p 843 *f*, p 846 *e* to *h*, p 847 *c* to *e* and p 848 *g*, post); dictum of
Darling J in *Gilbey v Cossey* [1911–13] All ER Rep at 645 and *Winter Garden Theatre
(London) Ltd v Millenium Productions Ltd* [1947] 2 All ER 331 applied; *Glasse v Woolgar and*   *e*
Roberts (No 2) (1891) 41 Sol Jo 573 and dictum of Lord Greene MR in *Booker v Palmer*
[1942] 2 All ER at 677 disapproved.

(iii) Furthermore the court could, in an appropriate case, order specific performance
where a licensee's licence had wrongfully been repudiated before he entered into
possession (see p 844 *b* and *d* to *g*, p 847 *e* to *g* and p 848 *b* and *g* to p 849 *a*, post); *Winter
Garden Theatre (London) Ltd v Millenium Productions Ltd* [1947] 2 All ER 331 applied;   *f*
Thompson v Park [1944] 2 All ER 477 not followed.

(iv) There were no grounds for interfering with the judge's exercise of his discretion
since he had taken into account all relevant matters, including freedom of speech and of
assembly and the sanctity of contracts, before deciding to make the order for specific
performance (see p 844 *h*, p 845 *h* and p 848 *c d*, post).

Notes   *g*

For contractual licences, see 9 Halsbury's Laws (4th Edn) para 530, for the nature of
licences generally, see 23 Halsbury's Laws (3rd Edn) 430, para 1026, and for cases on
licences, see 31(1) Digest (Reissue) 201–232, 1678–1891.

Cases referred to in judgments   *h*

Booker v Palmer [1942] 2 All ER 674, 87 Sol Jo 30, CA, 31(1) Digest (Reissue) 219, 1793.
Gilbey v Cossey (1912) 106 LT 607, [1911–13] All ER Rep 644, DC, 31(1) Digest (Reissue)
   67, 493.
Glasse v Woolgar and Roberts (No 2) (1897) 41 Sol Jo 573, CA, 31(1) Digest (Reissue) 84,
   652.
Hart v Hart (1881) 18 Ch D 670, 50 LJ Ch 697, 45 LT 13, 27(1) Digest (Reissue) 278,   *j*
   2065, 27(2) Digest (Reissue) 719, 5573.
London Borough of Hounslow v Twickenham Garden Developments Ltd [1970] 3 All ER 326,
   [1971] Ch 233, [1970] 3 WLR 538, 69 LGR 109, 31(1) Digest (Reissue) 217, 1775.
Luganda v Service Hotels Ltd [1969] 2 All ER 692, [1969] 2 Ch 209, [1969] 2 WLR 1056,
   20 P & CR 337, CA, 31(2) Digest (Reissue) 1129, 8742.

Thompson v Park [1944] 2 All ER 477, [1944] KB 408, 113 LJKB 561, 170 LT 207, CA,
a   31(1) Digest (Reissue) 219, *1792*.
Warder v Cooper [1970] 1 All ER 1112, [1970] Ch 495, [1970] 2 WLR 975, 21 P & CR
      336, 31(2) Digest (Reissue) 1080, *8449*.
Wilson v West Hartlepool Railway Co (1865) 2 De GJ & Sm 475, 5 New Rep 289, 34 LJ Ch
      241, 11 LT 692, 11 Jur NS 124, 46 ER 459, 44 Digest (Repl) 45, *315*.
Winter Garden Theatre (London) Ltd v Millenium Productions Ltd [1947] 2 All ER 331, [1948]
b   AC 173, [1947] LJR 1422, 177 LT 349, HL; *rvsg* [1946] 1 All ER 678, 115 LJ Ch 297,
      175 LT 434, CA, 45 Digest (Repl) 201, *83*.

Cases also cited
American Cyanamid Co v Ethicon Ltd [1975] 1 All ER 504, [1975] AC 396, HL.
c *Chandler v Kerly* [1978] 2 All ER 942, [1978] 1 WLR 693, CA.
    DHN Food Distributors Ltd v London Borough of Tower Hamlets [1976] 3 All ER 462, [1976]
      1 WLR 852, CA.
    De Brassac v Martyn (1863) 2 New Rep 512, 9 LT 287.
    Director of Public Prosecutions v Luft, Director of Public Prosecutions v Duffield [1976] 2 All ER
      569, [1977] AC 962, HL; *rvsg* [1976] 1 All ER 519, [1977] AC 962, DC.
d *Errington v Errington and Woods* [1952] 1 All ER 149, [1959] 1 KB 290, CA.
    Foster v Robinson [1950] 2 All ER 342, [1951] 1 KB 149, CA.
    Hurst v Picture Theatres Ltd [1915] 1 KB 1, [1914–15] All ER Rep 836, CA.
    Lavery v Pursell (1888) 39 Ch D 508, 57 LJ Ch 570.
    Lever v Koffler [1901] 1 Ch 543, 70 LJ Ch 395.
    Miller v Jackson [1977] 3 All ER 338, [1977] QB 966, CA.
e *Tanner v Tanner* [1975] 3 All ER 776, [1975] 1 WLR 1346, CA.
    White & Carter (Councils) Ltd v McGregor [1961] 3 All ER 1178, [1962] AC 413, HL.
    Wood v Leadbitter (1845) 13 M & W 838, [1843–60] All ER Rep 190.

Appeal
f By a writ indorsed with a statement of claim, dated 6th August 1979, the plaintiff,
Richard Verrall (suing on behalf of himself and as representing all members of the
National Front), brought an action against the defendants, the Great Yarmouth Borough
Council, seeking (i) an order for the specific performance of an agreement, partly oral and
partly in writing, made in April 1979 whereby the council agreed to hire to the National
Front the use of their hall on the Wellington Pier in Great Yarmouth on 26th and 27th
g October 1979 for purposes of the National Front's annual conference; alternatively (ii)
damages, (iii) further or other relief. On 31st August the plaintiff issued a summons for
summary judgment under RSC Ord 14. On 24th September the council served their
defence on the plaintiff. In it they contended, inter alia, that specific performance should
not be granted because (i) the proposed user of the hall by the National Front would be
likely 'by reason of the provocative racial and political policies and violence practised and
h preached by the [National Front]' (a) to invite and/or cause breaches of the peace and/or
violence, (b) to involve substantial expense to the taxpayers and ratepayers in the
provision of police and other safeguards against breaches of the peace and/or violence, (c)
to involve industrial action effectively preventing the proposed user and conference
taking place, and materially to interfere with the amenities of the inhabitants and visitors
to Great Yarmouth in respect of the pier and otherwise, (ii) the proposed user would
j require the constant supervision of the court, and (iii) damages would be an adequate
remedy. On 28th September Master Lubbock in chambers ordered (i) that the plaintiff
be at liberty to enter judgment for damages to be assessed against the council and (ii) that
the plaintiff's application for specific performance be refused. The plaintiff appealed
against the latter part of the order. On 11th October Tasker Watkins J allowed the appeal
and gave judgment for the plaintiff for specific performance of the agreement. The

council appealed against his decision. The facts are set out in the judgment of Lord
Denning MR.   *a*

Gavin Lightman and *Alan Boyle* for the council.
John Beveridge QC and *Christopher Moger* for the plaintiff.

LORD DENNING MR. The National Front is a political party. This is one of its
principles: 'The National Front stands for the preservation of the national and ethnic
character of the British people and is wholly opposed to any form of racial integration *b*
between British and non-European peoples.' It therefore is opposed to all non-European
immigration into Britain and is committed to a programme for the resettlement overseas
of those non-European people already here. Later it says: 'The National Front is
implacably opposed to Communism and all other forms of Marxian Socialism.' Those
principles are abhorrent to many. Nevertheless it is a political party. It is entitled to
make its views known, so long as it does so peaceably and without inflaming others to *c*
violence.
   The National Front has been in existence for some years. At the end of last year, 1978,
it made arrangements for its annual conference to be held this year, 1979, in Great
Yarmouth at the Wellington Pier pavilion on 26th and 27th October 1979. To that end
it entered, by its officers, into negotiations with the officers of the Great Yarmouth
Borough Council. The council was at that time controlled by a Conservative majority. *d*
They were fully aware of all the difficulties which might ensue, even the tumults and
disturbances which might ensue, if the conference were held there. In the course of the
negotiations, there was much discussion in the council. The public in the gallery made
their voices heard against any such conference being held. Nevertheless, after two or
three meetings, the council deliberately decided to allow the National Front to hold its
conference there.   *e*
   To show that it was a deliberate decision, I will read one or two letters which passed.
The first is a letter of 15th March 1979 from the chairman of the executive council of the
National Front to the chief executive officer of the council:

   'I believe that some elements in the opposition to our Conference are claiming
   that our application has no merit because it is merely a stunt for publicity *f*
   purposes. Let me assure you that claim is quite untrue. This is a sincere application
   for a facility to hold our Annual Conference, which is to be held in October each
   year. We are prepared to meet any reasonable conditions which the Council deems
   fit to impose in the way of hire charge and insurance. The sincerity of our
   application arises from the fact that Great Yarmouth Borough Council is one of the
   few Councils in Britain to have taken a principled stand on freedom of speech and *g*
   freedom of assembly, by deciding that it will hire out its facility to any lawful
   political party, including ours, irrespective of its political colours. This is why we
   have made our application, because so many other Councils have allowed themselves
   to be pressured by communist elements, left-wing Trades Councils and church
   groups into denying us such facilities on political grounds. This is why we are
   putting our faith in the decision of your Council.'   *h*

That letter was written before any contract was concluded. In the light of it, and after
hearing arguments on both sides, on 27th March 1979 the council of Great Yarmouth
approved the letting of the hall for the conference. They referred the details to a
committee. There was a substantial fee for the hire of the hall. There were also to be
safeguards by way of insurance. Arrangements were made with the police so as to ensure
security during the conference.   *j*
   The contract was concluded on 4th April 1979 by a letter from the chief executive
officer's department, saying: '. . . the Council have now agreed to let you have the
accommodation on the following terms . . .' They set out the terms. Over £6,000 was
to be paid down by the National Front for the facility of holding their conference in the
Wellington Pier pavilion, and this sum was paid down at once.

But there was an election pending for a new council on 3rd May. This coming
a conference was a big issue in the election at Great Yarmouth. The Labour Party were
against it. On 12th April 1979 the local paper, the Yarmouth Mercury, came out with
the headline, 'Labour "will reverse decision" if elected'. It was plain that if the Labour
Party got into power at the election it would do its best to reverse the decision about
allowing the National Front to hire the hall. That is what happened. On 3rd May 1979
the Labour Party came into control at Great Yarmouth. One of the first things the new
b council did was to hold a special meeting on 15th May. It passed a resolution that the
approval for the use of the conference hall by the National Front be rescinded, the offer
of facilities be withdrawn, and any payment sent back. So there it was. The new Labour
controlled council put everything into reverse.

Faced with this difficulty, the National Front tried to find a place elsewhere in which
to hold their conference. They tried both in England and Wales. They are trying even
c now. No other town or city will receive them. So they have brought proceedings in the
courts by a writ issued on 6th August 1979. They claim that a contract was made for the
use of this conference hall for those two days, that it has been repudiated, and they claim
specific performance of that contract.

The matter has come speedily before the courts. It came before Tasker Watkins J.
After hearing the case argued for a day and a half, Tasker Watkins J (and I would like to
d pay tribute to his judgment, which was prepared very quickly) came to the conclusion
that the National Front should be entitled to go ahead with their conference and hold it
in the Wellington Pier pavilion. He granted a decree of specific performance accordingly
ordering the borough council to hold to their contract and allow the National Front to
come in.

Counsel took some technical points on behalf of the Labour controlled council. First,
e he said that this was an arguable case and ought not to be dealt with under RSC Ord 14.
I reject that point. In many cases now, when all the issues are clear and the point of
substance can be decided as well now as hereafter, we have repeatedly decided matters
under the RSC Ord 14 procedure.

Second, he referred us to a passage in Halsbury's Laws of England[1] on landlord and
f tenant law: 'A letting for a single day to view a procession cannot be specifically enforced',
citing *Glasse v Woolgar and Roberts (No 2)*[2]. That case is quite out of date. He cited other
cases too saying that a lease for a year could not be specifically enforced. But I do not
think we need go through them now. Suffice it to quote *Gilbey v Cossey*[3] where Darling J
said:

g
> 'At one time it was said in the Courts of Chancery that there could not be a decree
> for the specific performance of an agreement from year to year, upon the ground
> that it was inconceivable that a case could be heard within a twelvemonth. That
> idea, however, has now been given up, and the court would make such an order
> before a tenancy of this kind would have expired.'

So that point fails. Third, counsel on behalf of the council submitted that the council
h could determine the licence effectively despite the contract. He relied on *Thompson v
Park*[4]. In that case two schoolmasters amalgamated their schools. The one who was in
the school gave a licence to the other to come onto the premises. Later on he revoked the
licence. The other then forced his way in. The court granted an injunction to stop the
other from entering the premises. Goddard LJ said as to a licence[5]:

j

1   23 Halsbury's Laws (3rd Edn) 464, para 1077, note (*s*)
2   (1897) 41 Sol Jo 573
3   (1912) 106 LT 607 at 608, [1911–13] All ER Rep 644 at 645
4   [1944] 2 All ER 477, [1944] KB 408
5   [1944] 2 All ER 477 at 479, [1944] KB 408 at 410

'Whether it has been rightly withdrawn or wrongly withdrawn matters nothing for this purpose. The licensee, once his licence is withdrawn, has no right to re-enter on the land . . . If he does, he is a common trespasser.' *a*

Basing himself on that dictum and on a passage in Salmond on Torts[1], counsel for the council said that a licensor has a *power effectively* to determine the licence. He may not have a *right* to do so *lawfully*, but he has a *power* to do so *effectively*. So that the licensee could not get specific performance of the licence, but only damages.

That is not good law. The decision of the House of Lords in *Winter Garden Theatre* *b* *(London) Ltd v Millenium Productions Ltd*[2] has made all the difference. Viscount Simon said[3]:

'. . . a third variant of a licence for value . . . occurs, as in the sale of a ticket to enter premises and witness a particular event, such as a ticket for a seat at a particular performance at a theatre or for entering private ground to witness a day's sport. In *c* this last class of case, the implication of the arrangement, however it may be classified in law, plainly is that the ticket entitles the purchaser to enter and, if he behaves himself, to remain on the premises until the end of the event which he has paid his money to witness.'

Since the *Winter Garden* case[2], it is clear that once a man has entered under his contract of licence, he cannot be turned out. An injunction can be obtained against the licensor *d* to prevent his being turned out. On principle it is the same if it happens before he enters. If he has a contractual right to enter, and the licensor refuses to let him come in, then he can come to the court and in a proper case get an order for specific performance to allow him to come in. An illustration was taken in the course of the argument. Supposing one of the great political parties, say the Conservative Party, had booked its hall at Brighton for its conference in September of this year; it had made all its *e* arrangements accordingly; it had all its delegates coming; it had booked its hotels, and so on. Would it be open to the Brighton corporation to repudiate that agreement, and say that the Conservative Party could not go there? Would the only remedy be damages? Clearly not. The court would order the corporation in such a case to perform its contract. It would be the same in the case of the Labour Party, or whoever it may *f* be. When arrangements are made for a licence of this kind of such importance and magnitude affecting many people, the licensors cannot be allowed to repudiate it and simply pay damages. It must be open to the court to grant specific performance in such cases.

So I hold that the observations in *Thompson v Park*[4] are no longer law. I agree with what Megarry J said about them in *London Borough of Hounslow v Twickenham Garden Developments Ltd*[5]. *g*

All technical objections being on one side, we come to the real point in the case: whether or not, as a matter of discretion, we should order specific performance of this contract.

Tasker Watkins J ordered the new council to perform the contract. He did so because of the importance of freedom of speech and freedom of assembly. These are among our *h* most precious freedoms. Freedom of speech means freedom not only for the views of which you approve, but also freedom for the views of which you most heartily disapprove. This is a land, in the words of the poet[6], where—

j

---

1 17th Edn (1977) p 75
2 [1947] 2 All ER 331, [1948] AC 173
3 [1947] 2 All ER 331 at 335, [1948] AC 173 at 189
4 [1944] 2 All ER 477, [1944] KB 408
5 [1970] 3 All ER 326 at 338–339, [1971] Ch 233 at 248–250
6 Tennyson, 'You ask me why', ll 8–12

'A man may speak the thing he will.
A land of settled government.
A land of just and old renown,
Where Freedom slowly broadens down
From precedent to precedent.'

But, mark you, freedom of speech can be abused. It can be used so as to promote violence; to propagate racial hatred and class warfare; and to undermine the structure of society itself. History provides examples. Such as when Hitler led the Germans to believe that they were the master race, and inflamed them so that they expelled and massacred the Jews. Or when the communists have used their freedom to destroy the freedom of others. If there were any evidence that the National Front were abusing this freedom, it might turn the scale. But there is no evidence of it here.

Freedom of assembly is another of our precious freedoms. Everyone is entitled to meet and assemble with his fellows to discuss their affairs and to promote their views; so long as it is not done to propagate violence or do anything unlawful. On this point I would stress, and it is very important that it should be stressed, that this is a private meeting of this political party. I will read what Mr Verrall said in his affidavit:

'The conference which is to be held in Great Yarmouth is a private meeting. It is open to members and to invited members of the press only. Each person attending the meeting will be required to produce a current membership card validated by a regional officer of the National Front. A panel of senior members of the National Front will scrutinise the credentials of every person seeking entry to the meeting. There have been twelve such conferences in the past. There has never been any trouble inside such a meeting.'

That is the meeting which is contemplated. It is essential under the constitution of this party that it should hold the meeting; that it should elect its officers and members for the ensuing year and the like; and that it should do all such things as are done at an annual conference of this kind.

The evidence is that if there is any trouble it will not be at the meeting at all. If it does occur, it will be outside caused by opponents of the National Front. There are societies such as the Anti-Nazi League who object to all the goings-on of the National Front. Their members may threaten or assault the members of the National Front; or try to stop their meeting. It would then be those interrupters who would be the destroyers of freedom of speech. They cannot be allowed to disrupt the meeting by mass pickets, or by violent demonstrations, and the like. The police will, I hope, be present in force to prevent such disruptions.

In this case, in April the Great Yarmouth Borough Council made a deliberate decision. They took everything into account. They had all information before them. They must have decided that the dangers were not such as to lead them to withhold the use of their hall for the conference. The dangers are just the same now. The newly constituted council is bound by what the old constituted council did. The newly constituted council must honour the contract. I see no sufficient reason for not holding the council to their contract. In the interests of our fundamental freedoms, freedom of speech, freedom of assembly, and the importance of holding people to their contracts, we ought to grant specific performance in this case, as the judge did.

I would therefore dismiss the appeal.

ROSKILL LJ. I begin my judgment by echoing what Lord Denning MR said about the admirable quality as well as the brevity of counsel's arguments and also the judgment given by the judge, Tasker Watkins J.

Four points have been put by counsel on behalf of the defendants ('the council') as the basis of challenging the judge's judgment. First, it was said that these were RSC Ord 14 proceedings, and that the council had shown there was an arguable defence. Secondly, it was said that, as a matter of law, the courts would not grant specific performance of what has been described in some of the 19th century cases as a transient interest. *a* Thirdly, it was said that, as a matter of law, the courts would not grant specific performance of an executory licence before the licensee had taken possession thereunder. Fourth and last, it was said that reasons of public policy disentitled the plaintiff to equitable relief such as the judge had granted.

Lord Denning MR has covered the ground fully, but I would like to add a few words on each of those points. As to the first, that these are RSC Ord 14 proceedings, I think *b* there is nothing in that submission. I ventured to ask counsel for the council this morning what advantage would be gained, if, instead of dealing with this matter now, we ordered it to be tried at an expedited trial tomorrow, possibly before Tasker Watkins J. I confess I found some difficulty in following his answer; but in his reply this afternoon, after further reflection, he suggested an answer might be found in the fact that he would wish, at the trial, to call evidence to investigate what had been the cause *c* of notorious disturbances at a number of meetings and confrontations at which the National Front and other political parties had been involved. I cannot think that that is a relevant consideration in the present case, and I can imagine few matters less suitable for such enquiry in an action for damages for breach of contract or specific performance. We have often said in this court in recent years that where there is a clear-cut issue raised in RSC Ord 14 proceedings, there is no reason why the judge in *d* chambers, or, for that matter, this court, should not deal with the whole matter at once. Merely to order a trial so that the matters can be re-argued in open court is to encourage the law's delays which in this court we are always trying to prevent. The first point fails.

As to the second, the submission that as a matter of law the courts should not grant specific performance in cases of a transient interest, the high-water mark of the doctrine *e* is perhaps to be found (I do not propose to trace it through the 19th century) in an observation of Lord Greene MR in *Booker v Palmer*[1], where he is reported as saying: 'If a licence is revoked in breach of a contract, the remedy is damages and nothing else, the reason being that the licensee has no estate in the land at all.' There is much earlier authority in support of that view; and at that time I do not doubt that that view correctly represented the law. *f*

Following that was the decision of this court consisting of Goddard and du Parcq LJJ in *Thompson v Park*[2]. With all respect to the observation[3] of Lord Denning MR that that was a decision of two Lords Justices which, for that reason, we need not necessarily follow, I should feel compelled to follow that decision if I thought it were still consistent with other and later cases; but to my mind, with very great respect to the memory of Lord Greene MR and of both Goddard and du Parcq LJJ, I do not think that the reasoning *g* underlying those decisions can stand alongside the later decision of the House of Lords in the well-known case of *Winter Garden Theatre (London) Ltd v Millenium Productions Ltd*[4], though the decision in *Thompson v Park*[2] can readily be supported for the reasons given by Megarry J in *London Borough of Hounslow v Twickenham Garden Developments Ltd*[5]. At one point in his argument, no doubt because of a momentary lapse of memory, counsel for the council did say that *Thompson v Park*[2] was not referred to in the House of Lords. *h* With respect, reference to Sir Valentine Holmes KC's argument in the Law Reports[6] shows that it was there referred to.

Lord Denning MR has read part of the speech of Viscount Simon[7]. I stress, as Lord Denning MR did, Viscount Simon's emphasis on the word 'entry' in the relevant passage.

1 [1942] 2 All ER 674 at 677
2 [1944] 2 All ER 477, [1944] KB 408
3 During the course of argument
4 [1947] 2 All ER 331, [1948] AC 173
5 [1970] 3 All ER 326 at 339, [1971] Ch 233 at 250
6 [1948] AC 173 at 181
7 [1947] 2 All ER 331 at 335, [1948] AC 173 at 189

j

a I will not repeat what he read, but I would add a reference to Lord Uthwatt's speech. He said[1]:

> 'I merely confess my present inability to see any answer to the propositions of law stated by LORD GREENE, M. R., in his judgment in the case under appeal. The settled practice of the courts of equity is to do what they can by an injunction to preserve the sanctity of a bargain. To my mind, as at present advised, a licensee who has refused to accept the wrongful repudiation of the bargain which is involved in an *b* unauthorised revocation of the licence is as much entitled to the protection of an injunction as a licensee who has not received any notice of revocation, and, if the remedy of injunction is properly available in the latter case against unauthorised interference by the licensor, it is also available in the former case. In a court of equity, wrongful acts are no passport to favour.'

c No doubt anticipating reliance on that passage, counsel for the council admitted at the outset that his clients are hopelessly in breach of contract and that their conduct was unlikely to find favour in a court of law. He accepted that they have, without lawful excuse, repudiated the contract and must, regrettably from their point of view, pay damages. In my judgment the old view, such as it was, that courts of equity would not protect a so-called transient interest can no longer be supported, at any rate to its full extent. There has been a number of cases, of which *Luganda v Service Hotels Ltd*[2] is one, *d* and *Warder v Cooper*[3], a decision of Stamp J at first instance, is another, where the courts have protected by injunction an interest in land created by statute, in the one case by the Rent Act and in the other case by another statute[4]. It seems to me that, since the fusion of law and equity, it is the duty of the court to protect, where it is appropriate to do so, any interest, whether it be an estate in land or a licence, by injunction or specific performance as the case may be.

e I come to the third point. It appears to be the fact so far as citation of authority goes, that there is no reported case where a licensee, whose licence has been wrongly repudiated before he has entered into possession, has been granted equitable relief, and I do not understand counsel for the plaintiff to dispute that that is so. That has been strenuously relied on by counsel for the council as showing that, as a matter of law, the courts cannot grant relief to a licensee whose licence has not been entered on. With respect, I am not *f* in the least persuaded that that is so. Lord Denning MR has given two examples: one of a great political party, whatever its political colour or views, on the eve of its conference when the local authority with which it has made arrangements for accommodation repudiates the bargain at the last moment. Another perhaps equally good is of the Earl's Court Motor Show, supposing the licensee at Earl's Court found his licence repudiated at the last moment. I find it difficult to believe that a court in those circumstances could *g* not, let alone would not, grant equitable relief by way of specific performance or a mandatory injunction to require the licensor to fulfil his obligations. How much more is that so, in my judgment, where, as here, there has been a long standing contract entered into by the licensee for which that licensee has given full consideration. We were referred to a 19th century decision of Kay J in *Hart v Hart*[5], where he referred to the judgment of Turner LJ in *Wilson v West Hartlepool Railway Co*[6]:

h
> '. . . that when an agreement for valuable consideration between two parties has been partially performed, the Court ought to do its utmost to carry out that agreement by a decree for specific performance. I think, if I do not misquote the

j 1 [1947] 2 All ER 331 at 343, [1948] AC 173 at 202–203
2 [1969] 2 All ER 692, [1969] 2 Ch 209
3 [1970] 1 All ER 1112, [1970] Ch 495
4 *Luganda v Service Hotels Ltd* [1969] 2 All ER 692, [1969] 2 Ch 209 (the Rent Act 1965 and the Rent Act 1968); *Warder v Cooper* [1970] 1 All ER 1112, [1970] Ch 495 (the Rent Act 1965)
5 (1881) 18 Ch D 670 at 685
6 (1865) 2 De G J & Sm 475 at 494–497, 46 ER 459 at 466–467

words, Lord Justice *Turner* went as far as this: It is the duty of the Court, as far as it is possible to do so, to ascertain the terms of the agreement, and to give effect to it. That is, as I understand, the rule of equity, that although there may be considerable vagueness in the terms, and although it may be such an agreement as the Court would hesitate to decree specific performance of, if there had not been part performance, yet when there has been part performance the Court is bound to struggle against the difficulty arising from the vagueness.'

I do not in the present case think there is any vagueness whatever. Large sums were extracted from the plaintiff, no doubt with propriety, by the local authority for the protection of their property, and those sums were paid before the repudiation took place. Accordingly, I think it is open to this court, as Tasker Watkins J thought, to grant equitable relief.

That leaves the last point, whether or not in his discretion the judge should have granted this relief. I agree with him. For my part, but for the argument of counsel for the council, I would have gratefully adopted Tasker Watkins J's judgment on this issue as my own. When one has before this court so careful a judgment on the exercise of discretion, it would be flying in the face of authority to presume to interfere.

It is said that if we insist on this contract being fulfilled there is a risk of public disorder, and evidence has been sought to be given that there have been other disorders on other occasions. I venture to echo what Lord Denning MR and Tasker Watkins J have said about the right of free speech. It would be a sorry day if this court, fearful because an attempt might be made to prevent those who wish to air their views, however unpopular, prevented the performance of due contractual rights for which they have paid, merely because others might seek to disrupt a private meeting by the use of unlawful force. If, as has happened in the past in times of national emergency such as the last war to which Lord Denning MR has referred, the government of the day has found it necessary to stop free expressions of opinion because they are thought contrary to the national good, there are and have been in the past ways and means of stopping them. But, unless and until some political organisations are proscribed as unlawful or legislation such as the Public Order Act 1936 is extended to make their activities unlawful, it is the duty of the court to treat all political parties as equal before the law and (irrespective of whether particular views may be distasteful to the courts or to some members of the public) allow those views to find expression particularly at a meeting which it is said is going to be private.

I have ventured to deal with this matter at some little length in deference to the arguments of counsel for the council, but for my part I feel no doubt that this appeal should be dismissed.

CUMMING-BRUCE LJ. I agree. I only add a word by reason of the manifest interest of the case to the parties, and I suspect more widely.

Counsel for the council made a powerful submission that the relief of specific performance is not available in the circumstances that have arisen; and if I thought that *Thompson v Park*[1] was not inconsistent with subsequent authority I would think it my duty to follow it. But I am clearly of the view that it is inconsistent with subsequent authority, and, in particular, with the ratio of this court in *Winter Garden Theatre (London) Ltd v Millenium Productions Ltd*[2] as affirmed in the speeches of the House of Lords in the appeal in the same case[3] and, in particular, the speeches of Viscount Simon and Lord Uthwatt. I take the view that it is open to this court to review critically the ratio in *Thompson v Park*[1], and that, having regard to what was said by Lord Greene MR in the *Winter Garden* case[2] and affirmed in the House of Lords[4], it is now quite clear law that the

1 [1944] 2 All ER 477, [1944] KB 408
2 [1946] 1 All ER 678 at 680
3 [1947] 2 All ER 331 at 335–337, 343, [1948] AC 173 at 189–191, 202–203
4 [1947] 2 All ER 331, [1948] AC 173

proposition on which counsel for the council depended, drawn from *Thompson v Park*[1],

a is no longer to be regarded as the law. I do not think it is necessary, interesting though I found his submissions, to add anything to what was said on the other legal arguments which have been propounded in this case.

On the matter of discretion, I would only say this. Anyone who has been at the scene of mob violence is likely to regard with deep horror and distaste the risks of personal injury and to personal property which the antics of infuriated political enthusiasts are

b likely to cause. Having been in some such situations in other countries myself, I am very much alive to the apprehensions that the threats of mobs must arouse in the minds of responsible people in Yarmouth. But, when that is said, one has to consider, as did the judge whose discretion it was in the first instance to exercise, that it was his duty to consider, as he did, the implications of the course that the Great Yarmouth Borough Council invite this court to take. A solemn contractual obligation for valuable

c consideration has been entered into. The Great Yarmouth Borough Council are under a legal duty, which they no longer dispute, to comply with that obligation. They deliberately repudiate it. The reason that they deliberately repudiate it is because, after a change of political party in the local government elections, they take a different view of the pros and cons of the bargain from the view taken by their predecessors on the council who made the contract. In that situation, although there is a solemn legal

d obligation whereby the National Front are entitled to hold their annual general meeting in the hall that has been licensed to them, because of the threats of mobs and the fear of unlawful violence on the part of groups who, I suppose, if they are not already in Yarmouth are intending to go to Yarmouth in order to prevent this political party from exercising its constitutional right, they invite the court to step in and say, 'Free speech should be silenced. The constitutional rights enjoyed in this country, at any rate since

e the Bill of Rights[2], should come to an end'. If that proposition is right, then, if you look at the other side of the penny, those political enthusiasts described as 'left-wing bodies' who wish to hold meetings, who wish to organise politically, would find themselves faced with the same difficulty because the ferocious mobs who take the opposite view will claim the assistance of the court to prevent them speaking or holding meetings.

Such implications appear to me to be profoundly dangerous. If there is a case for

f silencing a group which wishes to organise as a political party, it is for the Crown in Parliament by statute to restrict the right of free speech or free association. It is not appropriate to come to this court and invite the court to begin a slide down such a slippery slope.

For those reasons I too would dismiss the appeal.

g *Appeal dismissed.*

Solicitors: *Sharpe, Pritchard & Co*, agents for *R D Ogden*, Great Yarmouth (for the council); *Ward Bowrie*, agents for *Reed-Herbert, Gegan & Co*, Leicester (for the plaintiff).

Sumra Green　Barrister.

h ───

1　[1944] 2 All ER 477, [1944] KB 408
2　1 Will & Mar sess 2 c 2 (1688)

Roome and another v Edwards (Inspector of Taxes) *a*

COURT OF APPEAL, CIVIL DIVISION
BUCKLEY, BRIDGE AND TEMPLEMAN LJJ
15th, 16th, 19th, 20th, 30th NOVEMBER 1979

b

Capital gains tax – Settlement – Settled property – Trustees of a settlement appointing part of trust fund of settlement to different beneficiaries under different trusts – Transfer of beneficial interests in residue of fund to two Cayman Island companies – Replacement of trustees of original fund by Cayman Island trustees – Beneficial interests assigned to Cayman Island companies becoming vested in one company and that company becoming absolutely entitled as against Cayman Island trustees – Whether separate settlement created in respect of appointed fund – Finance Act 1965, s 25(3)(11), Sch 10, para 12(1).

c

Under a settlement made in 1944, a trust fund ('the 1944 fund') was settled on trustees to hold the fund for the wife for life, then for the husband for life and thereafter for such of their issue as the husband and wife or survivor thereof should appoint. In October 1955 the husband and wife executed a deed of appointment and release (i) irrevocably *d* appointing a fund ('the 1955 fund') consisting of part of the 1944 settlement in trust for one of their daughters absolutely when she reached the age of 25 and (ii) surrendering the wife's life interest in the investments making up the 1955 fund. Thereafter the fund representing the balance of the 1944 settlement ('the main fund') and the 1955 fund were administered separately, although until 1972 they had common trustees. That segregation was necessary because in each case the persons for the time being entitled to *e* the income (ie the wife and the daughter respectively) and the eventual beneficiaries of the capital of the respective funds were different. In 1972 the original trustees of the 1944 fund were replaced by trustees in the Cayman Island and the husband and wife and their two daughters each assigned for substantial consideration their beneficial interests in the main fund to two Cayman Island companies, one of which on 13th April assigned its reversionary interest to the other, so that for the purposes of a deemed disposal under *f* s 25(3)[a] of the Finance Act 1965 the assignee company became absolutely entitled to the main fund. In consequence the trustees of the 1955 fund, who were resident in the United Kingdom, were assessed to capital gains tax for the year 1972–73 on gains accruing to the Cayman Island trustees on the basis that on 13th April the appointed fund and the main fund were subject to the same settlement and therefore, under s 25(11)[b] of, and Sch 10, para 12(1)[c] to, the 1965 Act, they and the Cayman Island trustees together *g* constituted a single body of trustees for the purpose of liability to capital gains tax. The Special Commissioners upheld the assessment in principle. On appeal by the trustees of the 1955 fund the judge[d] held that, although the main fund and the 1955 fund constituted a single settlement and the trustees of both funds were to be regarded as a single body of trustees, tax could not be recovered from the trustees of the 1955 fund because para 12 could not make persons liable for any tax arising on the disposal of assets *h* if they had no control over the assets. The Crown appealed.

Held – The appeal would be dismissed for the following reasons—
(i) For the purposes of capital gains tax a settlement was the state of affairs brought about or deemed to have been brought about in respect of particular assets by a document or documents, and where a settlement originally or as the result of an appointment *j*

---

a   Section 25(3), so far as material, is set out at p 855 *c*, post
b   Section 25(11) is set out at p 856 *f*, post
c   Paragraph 12(1), so far as material, is set out at p 853 *a*, post
d   [1979] STC 546

created different trusts of different properties then different states of affairs brought
a about by one or more documents, and thus two different settlements, were created.
Because the burden of capital gains tax should fall equitably only on those beneficiaries
interested in the capital assets which produced the gain, it followed that where different
beneficiaries were interested in different capital assets capital gains tax was to be assessed
as if those assets were comprised in different settlements (see p 854 *c d* and *f* to *h*, p 855
j to p 856 *a*, p 857 *f* and p 860 *g*, post); dictum of Romer J in *Re Ogle's Settled Estates*
b [1927] 1 Ch at 233 adopted.

(ii) The effect of the appointment in 1955 was not to vary a single settlement
comprising both funds, but merely to alter the 1944 fund in certain respects so that for
the purposes of capital gains tax two separate settlements were created, one consisting of
two documents (the 1944 settlement and the 1955 appointment) and affecting the 1955
fund, and the other consisting only of the 1944 settlement and affecting the main
c fund. The trustees of the 1955 fund were therefore not liable for the capital gains tax
accruing and payable in respect of the fund (see p 855 *d*, p 856 *a* to *c*, p 857 *f* and p 860
b to *g*, post).

Notes

d For capital gains tax in relation to settled property, see 5 Halsbury's Laws (4th Edn), paras
45–48.

For the Finance Act 1965, s 25, Sch 10, para 12(1), see 34 Halsbury's Statutes (3rd Edn)
884, 970.

As from 6th April 1979 s 25 of, and para 12 of Sch 10 to, the 1965 Act have been
replaced by the Capital Gains Tax Act 1979, ss 52–54, 55(1)(4)(6) and s 48 respectively.

e
Cases referred to in judgments

Hoare Trustees v Gardner (Inspector of Taxes), Hart (Inspector of Taxes) v Briscoe [1978] 1 All
ER 791, [1978] 2 WLR 839, [1978] STC 89.
Ogle's Settled Estates, Re [1927] 1 Ch 229, 96 LJ Ch 113, 136 LT 300, 40 Digest (Repl) 790,
2720.

f
Cases also cited

Brotherton v Inland Revenue Comrs [1978] 2 All ER 267, [1978] 1 WLR 610, [1978] STC
201, CA.
Canadian Eagle Oil Ltd v R [1945] 2 All ER 499, [1946] AC 119, 27 Tax Cas 205, HL.
g *Cape Brandy Syndicate v Inland Revenue Comrs* [1921] 2 KB 403, 12 Tax Cas 358, CA.
Jamieson v Inland Revenue Comrs [1963] 2 All ER 1030, [1964] AC 1445, 41 Tax Cas 43,
CA.
Joynson's Will Trusts, Re, Gaddum v Inland Revenue Comrs [1954] 2 All ER 294, [1954] Ch
567.
Mangin v Inland Revenue Comrs [1971] 1 All ER 179, [1971] AC 739, PC.
h *Muir (or Williams) v Muir* [1943] AC 468, HL.
Penton's Settlements, Re, Humphreys v Birch-Reynardson [1968] 1 All ER 36, [1968] 1 WLR
248.
Phipps v Ackers (1842) 9 Cl & Fin 583, [1558–1774] All ER Rep 381, HL.
Potts' Executors v Inland Revenue Comrs [1951] 1 All ER 76, [1951] AC 443, 32 Tax Cas
211, HL.
j *Rank Xerox Ltd v Lane (Inspector of Taxes)* [1979] 3 All ER 657, [1979] 1 WLR 594, [1979]
STC 740, HL.
Symons, Re, Symons-Jeune v Bunbury, [1927] 1 Ch 344.
Wankie Colliery Co v Inland Revenue Comrs [1921] 3 KB 344, CA; *on appeal* [1922] AC 51,
HL.
Wood, Re, Wodehouse v Wood [1913] 2 Ch 574, CA.

Appeal

The Crown appealed from the order of Brightman J[1] made on 23rd February 1979 *a* whereby, on a case stated[2] by the Commissioners for the Special Purposes of the Income Tax Acts, he allowed an appeal by the respondents, John Watford Roome and Thomas Graham Denne ('the taxpayers'), against the determination of the commissioners dismissing the taxpayers' appeal against the assessment to capital gains tax made on them. The facts are set out in the judgment of Templeman LJ.

b

D J Nicholls QC and *Peter Gibson* for the Crown.
D C Potter QC and *Robert Walker* for the taxpayers.

Cur adv vult

30th November. The following judgments were read.

c

TEMPLEMAN LJ (delivering the first judgment at the invitation of Buckley LJ). This is an appeal by the Crown from a decision of Brightman J[1]. The facts are clearly set out in his judgment. The first question which arises is whether the exercise of a special power of appointment created a separate settlement for the purposes of capital gains tax. The answer depends on the provisions and intendment of the capital gains tax legislation and the nature and effect of the appointment. *d*

The Finance Act 1965, which introduced capital gains tax, provided in s 20(4), so far as material, that:

'Capital gains tax shall be charged . . . on the total amount of chargeable gains accruing to the person chargeable in the year of assessment, after deducting any allowable losses accruing to that person in that year of assessment and, so far as they have not been allowed as a deduction from chargeable gains accruing in any previous *e* year of assessment, any allowable loss accruing to that person in any previous year of assessment . . .'

By ss 19, 22(10) and 23 of the 1965 Act every gain accruing on the disposal of assets shall be a chargeable gain and every loss on disposal shall be an allowable loss.

In relation to settlements, where trust assets are vested in trustees in trust for *f* beneficiaries entitled to limited interests in those assets, the persons chargeable to capital gains tax resulting from gains and losses made on the disposition of trust assets must be identified and made liable for the tax. In addition the annual computation of capital gains tax on the difference between capital gains and allowable losses in respect of trust assets must be separated from the computation of capital gains tax on the difference between chargeable gains and allowable losses made by a beneficiary in the disposition *g* of his own absolute property and from the computation of capital gains tax on the difference between chargeable gains and allowable losses made by a trustee in the disposal of his own personal estate. If under a settlement, trust assets held by two trustees in trust for a life tenant and remainderman are sold or otherwise disposed of, then any chargeable gain thus made, or allowable loss thus suffered, must be brought into account for the purpose of assessing capital gains tax in respect of the settlement, but it would be illogical *h* to allow or compel the life tenant or remainderman or either of the trustees to bring into account gains and losses which are not attributable to trust assets. Finally the burden of the capital gains tax attributable to trust assets must ultimately fall on the capital of the trust assets in such manner that the beneficiaries interested in that capital and no one else bear the burden in proportion to, and in accordance with, their respective interests.

For the purpose of identifying the persons chargeable to capital gains tax resulting *j* from chargeable gains and allowable losses made on the disposal of trust assets, s 25(1) provides that:

---

1   [1979] 1 WLR 860, [1979] STC 546
2   The case stated is set out at [1979] STC 548–555

'In relation to settled property, the trustees of the settlement shall . . . be treated as being a single and continuing body of persons (distinct from the persons who may from time to time be the trustees) . . .'

Paragraph 12(1) of Sch 10 to the 1965 Act provides: 'Capital gains tax chargeable in respect of chargeable gains accruing to the trustees of a settlement . . . may be assessed and charged on and in the name of any one or more of those trustees . . .'

For the purpose of collecting capital gains tax, ss 7, 8 and 12 of the Taxes Management Act 1970 impose a duty of giving notice and making returns of capital gains and allowable losses on every person who is chargeable to capital gains tax.

For the purpose of separating chargeable gains accruing to trustees and capital gains tax payable in respect of dispositions of trust assets from capital gains and tax of a beneficiary in respect of his absolute property or of a trustee in respect of his personal assets, para 12(2) of Sch 10 to the 1965 Act provides that chargeable gains accruing to trustees and capital gains tax chargeable on or in the name of the trustees of a settlement shall not be regarded as accruing to or chargeable on any other person, nor shall any trustee be regarded as an individual.

Thus, so far as settled property is concerned, the trustees make separate annual returns based on chargeable gains and allowable losses arising from the disposition of trust assets and pay any resultant capital gains tax out of the capital of those assets. The burden of tax, being borne by capital, affects and falls equitably on the beneficiaries interested under the settlement according to their respective interests. A life tenant will suffer the loss of income on the money paid out in tax and the remainderman will suffer the loss of capital.

No difficulty arises when one trust fund is held by one set of trustees under trusts declared by one trust instrument in favour of one set of beneficiaries.

In the present case two different trust funds are held by two different sets of trustees on trusts declared by one principal instrument and several subsidiary trust instruments in favour of two different sets of beneficiaries.

By a marriage settlement dated 24th March 1944 a trust fund was settled on the wife for life, with remainder to the husband during his life on protective trusts, with remainder to the issue of the marriage as the husband and wife should by deed appoint, with remainders over.

By an appointment dated 20th October 1955 certain specified assets comprised in the marriage settlement were appointed and released by the husband and the wife and became held on trust for Jane, a daughter of the marriage, during the life of the wife; then for the husband on protective trusts during his life (preserving the interest accorded to him by the marriage settlement) and then for Jane, who was seven years old, contingently on her attaining the age of 25 years with remainder to Jane's children. The appointed fund comprised in the 1955 appointment was necessarily segregated from the unappointed main fund which remained held on the original trusts of the 1944 marriage settlement. This segregation was necessary, firstly because the person for the time being entitled to the income of the appointed fund, namely Jane, was different from the person entitled to the income of the main fund, namely the wife, and secondly because the beneficiaries who became eventually entitled to the capital of the appointed fund were, or might be, different from those who eventually became entitled to the capital of the main fund.

That was the position when the Finance Act 1965 came into operation. The marriage settlement trustees held the appointed fund and the main fund. The marriage settlement trustees were the persons accountable for the capital gains tax in respect of the appointed fund and the main fund. But the beneficiaries interested in the appointed fund were different from those interested in the main fund to a substantial degree. In these circumstances, in order to ensure that the burden of capital gains tax fell equitably on the beneficiaries interested, it became necessary to treat the appointed fund and the main fund for capital gains tax purposes as though they were comprised in two separate settlements. If the trustees sold an asset comprised in the appointed fund at a profit and sold an asset comprised in the main fund at a loss, the Revenue would suffer if the loss on one fund was set off against the gain on the other fund. Moreover, the beneficiaries *a* interested in the appointed fund would pay less tax and ultimately, if the main fund made a profit in a subsequent year, the beneficiaries interested in the main fund would pay more tax than the tax attributable to the disposition of assets comprised in the appointed fund on the one hand and the disposition of the assets comprised in the main fund on the other hand.

In my judgment, therefore, the 1955 appointment resulted for the purposes of capital *b* gains tax in two settlements, one settlement which affected the appointed fund and consisted of two documents, namely the 1944 marriage settlement and the 1955 appointment, and the original settlement which affected the main fund and consisted only of the 1944 marriage settlement. Capital gains tax must be calculated and charged separately on the two separate funds comprised in the two different settlements.

In *Re Ogle's Settled Estates*[1] Romer J considered the meaning of a settlement for the *c* purposes of the Settled Land Act 1925. Of course that decision, being based on the 1925 Act, does not determine the construction of the 1965 Act dealing with capital gains tax. Nevertheless a settlement for the purposes of capital gains tax is in my judgment, and adopting the words of Romer J[2], 'a state of affairs in relation to certain "assets" brought about, or deemed to have been brought about by one or more documents . . .'

The trustees of the 1944 settlement in every year from 1965 onwards correctly made *d* two tax returns. The returns relating to the appointed fund dealt with income arising from the assets comprised in the appointed fund and held in trust for Jane. That return also disclosed chargeable gains and allowable losses made in the relevant year of assessment by dispositions of the assets comprised in the appointed fund and the trustees paid capital gains tax out of the appointed fund if the gains exceeded the losses, or carried forward a net loss if the losses exceeded gains. The return relating to the main fund dealt *e* with income arising from assets comprised in the main fund and held in trust for the wife. That return also disclosed chargeable gains and allowable losses and resulted in payment out of the main fund of any capital gains tax attributable to dispositions of the assets of the main fund or the carrying forward of any net losses incurred by the main fund. The just claims of the Revenue and the correct attachment of the burden of liability for capital gains tax could only be maintained if the different trusts affecting the *f* appointed fund and the main fund respectively created different settlements.

A deed of settlement which creates different trusts of different properties is one settlement in the eyes of an equity lawyer. The settlement remains one settlement in common parlance if by the exercise of a power of appointment or otherwise the trusts affecting part of a trust fund are altered. If a trust fund is settled on, or appointed to, different beneficiaries in aliquot shares, the trustees of the trust fund may treat the whole *g* trust fund for capital gains tax purposes as one settlement; but that is because capital gains tax payable in respect of any dispositions of any of the assets comprised in the trust fund paid out of any capital of the trust fund will fall proportionally and equitably on the beneficiaries interested in the whole of the trust fund in different shares. But where a settlement originally, or as a result of an appointment, creates different trusts of different properties, then for capital gains tax purposes there are created different states of affairs *h* brought about by one or more documents and thus creating two different settlements.

The learned judge held that in the present case there was one single settlement which comprised the appointed fund held on the trusts of the 1944 settlement and the 1955 appointment and the main fund held on the trusts of the 1944 settlement alone. The learned judge considered that if there were two settlements for capital gains tax purposes, it must follow that the 1944 settlement was partially brought to an end by the 1955 *j* appointment. He considered that the 1944 settlement in relation to the appointed fund and the main fund would continue until such time as both funds were wholly discharged

1   [1927] 1 Ch 229
2   [1927] 1 Ch 229 at 233

from all the trusts, powers and provisions of the 1944 settlement. In my judgment the
a 1944 settlement was not brought to an end by the 1955 appointment in relation to the
appointed fund, but was altered in certain respects, alterations which were of a kind
which made it necessary for the appointed fund to be treated as comprised in a separate
settlement consisting of the 1944 settlement and the 1955 appointment for the purposes
of capital gains tax.

Counsel for the Crown, submitted that if the 1955 appointment created a separate
b settlement of the appointed fund consisting of the 1944 settlement and the 1955
appointment, then the trustees of that separate settlement became 'absolutely entitled' to
the appointed fund as against the trustees of the 1944 settlement within the meaning of
s 25(3) of the Finance Act 1965. That subsection provides:

> *c* 'On the occasion when a person becomes absolutely entitled to any settled
> property as against the trustee all the assets forming part of the settled property to
> which he becomes so entitled shall be deemed to have been disposed of by the
> trustee, and immediately reacquired by him in his capacity as a trustee within
> section 22(5) of this Act, for a consideration equal to their market value.'

It follows, counsel for the Crown submitted, that if the 1955 appointment had been
made after 1965 or if any alteration to any settlement takes place by way of an
d appointment or assignment, or in any other manner so as to create a separate settlement,
then capital gains tax immediately becomes payable as a result of s 25(3). In my
judgment the trustees of the 1944 settlement, and the separate trustees subsequently
appointed of the appointed fund, did not become absolutely entitled to the appointed
fund as against the trustees of the 1944 settlement within s 25(3). Some of the trusts,
powers and provisions of the 1944 settlement remained effective. The separate
e settlement consisted of a state of affairs to which both the 1944 settlement and the 1955
appointment were relevant.

Whether a separate settlement is created by the exercise of a power of appointment for
the purposes of capital gains tax depends on the property comprised in the appointment
and the beneficial interests thereby created. If a separate settlement is created by an
appointment after 1965 it does not follow that anyone becomes absolutely entitled to the
f appointed fund, thus to make capital gains tax payable pursuant to s 25(3) of the Finance
Act 1965. That again depends on the circumstances. For example, if a power of
appointment merely conferred on a husband a life interest in specified assets if he
survived his life tenant wife, the appointment would create a separate settlement for
capital gains tax purposes in order that the burden of capital gains tax attributable to the
assets in which the husband did not have an expectant interest should not fall on the
g assets appointed in his favour, or vice versa; but in my judgment no person by that
appointment would become absolutely entitled to the appointed fund as against the
trustees of the settlement for the purposes of s 25(3) of the Finance Act 1965.

On the other hand, in *Hoare Trustees v Gardner (Inspector of Taxes)*[1], trustees in exercise
of a power declared trusts which were wholly exhaustive of the property thereby taken
out of an existing settlement and settled on entirely new trusts. Brightman J held that
h the trustees holding on entirely new trusts became absolutely entitled as against the
trustees of the old trusts. In the present case the separate settlement was not exhaustive
of the 1944 settlement powers and trusts but consisted of the 1944 settlement as altered
by the 1955 appointment.

In the present case it suffices that capital gains tax is a tax on capital and that the
burden of the tax must fall equitably on the beneficiaries and only on the beneficiaries
j interested in the capital assets which produce the gain. It follows that where different
beneficiaries are interested in different capital assets, capital gains tax must be assessed,
charged and paid as if those capital assets were comprised in different settlements,

---

1   [1978] 1 All ER 791, [1978] 2 WLR 839, [1978] STC 89

irrespective of the number or kind of documents involved. In my judgment the
appointed fund by virtue of the 1955 appointment became for the purposes of the *a*
assessment charge and payment of capital gains tax comprised in a different settlement
from the settlement of the main fund when the Finance Act 1965 came into operation,
and at all times thereafter.

In 1972 the trustees of the appointed fund ceased to be the same persons as the trustees
of the main fund as a result of the appointment of separate trustees of the appointed
fund. Later in 1972 capital gains tax became payable in respect of assets comprised in the *b*
main fund. Since the appointed fund and the main fund were, for the reasons I have
advanced, comprised in different settlements for the purposes of capital gains tax, it
follows that the trustees of the appointed fund are not liable for the capital gains tax
payable in respect of the main fund.

The learned judge reached the same conclusion, but for different reasons. He rejected
the argument, which I have accepted, that the appointed fund and the main fund were *c*
held on the trusts of separate settlements, but accepted the argument that a trustee of a
settlement was only liable for capital gains tax payable as a result of dispositions of
property vested in him. The trustees of the appointed fund were therefore not liable for
the capital gains tax payable in respect of the main fund, which was vested in different
trustees. I find this argument impossible to sustain in view of the provisions of s 25(1),
25(11) and para 12(1) of Sch 10 to the 1965 Act. If, contrary to the views I have already *d*
expressed, the appointed fund and the main fund remained comprised in one settlement
only, then in my judgment the trustees of the appointed fund are trustees in whom part
of the property comprised in the settlement is vested and are treated, together with the
trustees of the main fund, as the trustees of the settlement, each of whom is liable for
capital gains tax on the whole.

Section 25(1) of the 1965 Act, to which I have already referred, provides that the *e*
trustees of the settlement shall be treated as being a single and continuing body of
persons. Section 25(11) provides:

> 'For the purposes of this section, where part of the property comprised in a
> settlement is vested in one trustee or set of trustees and part in another (and in
> particular where settled land within the meaning of the Settled Land Act, 1925 is
> vested in the tenant for life and investments representing capital money are vested *f*
> in the trustees of the settlement), they shall be treated as together constituting and
> in so far as they act separately as acting on behalf of a single body of trustees.'

This subsection is plainly not confined to the particular instance given of a strict
settlement under the Settled Land Act 1925. Junior counsel for the taxpayers gave
several instances in which it would be necessary or desirable for part of the property *g*
comprised in one settlement to be vested in one set of trustees and part in another. In my
judgment all the instances he gave would fall within s 25(11) and all the trustees would
be treated as constituting a single body of trustees. Paragraph 12(1) of Sch 10 to the Act
provides that capital gains tax chargeable in respect of chargeable gains accruing to the
trustees of a settlement may be assessed and charged on any one or more of those
trustees. The learned judge was naturally impressed with the unfairness which might *h*
result if for example in the present case, on the hypothesis that the main fund and the
appointed fund were comprised in the same settlement, any one trustee of the appointed
fund might be made liable for all the capital gains tax attributable to the main fund
despite the fact that the assets of the appointed fund under his control might not be equal
in value to the tax assessed. The facts of this case as set out in the judgment of the learned
judge emphasise the fact that possible unfairness by the Revenue to an individual *j*
taxpayer can be more than matched by the unfairness of an individual taxpayer towards
the general body of taxpayers. It is very rarely that parts of trust funds become vested in
different sets of trustees without the consent or acquiescence of all the trustees. The
Revenue are not bound to assess every trustee and I apprehend that they will be slow to
do so if through no fault of his own a trustee never obtains control of part of a fund

which becomes liable to capital gains tax. But if a trustee were responsible for part of the
a fund being moved beyond his control and beyond the grasp of the Revenue for the
lawful recovery of tax, the trustee might well find himself assessed to capital gains tax on
the whole of the fund. In the present instance the trustees could not complain about
unfairness if the Revenue were able to levy capital gains tax against them on capital gains
attributable to the main fund. The trustees participated in the scheme, a perfectly lawful
scheme, which was operated in the present case, and it was open to them to protect
b themselves by indemnities before doing so. I do not find the harshness of the results, or
possible results, so intimidating as to overcome what I believe to be the plain meaning
and effect of s 25(1), s 25(11) and para 12(1) of Sch 10 to the Finance Act 1965.

Counsel for the trustee taxpayers, mounted a complicated and ingenious argument
partly based on the fact that sometimes s 25 refers to 'the trustees of the settlement',
sometimes to 'the trustees' and sometimes to 'the trustee'. The fact remains that the
c trustees of a settlement constitute a single and continuing body of persons and any one
of them is liable for capital gains tax. Counsel for the taxpayers also mounted an
alternative argument which depended, as I understand it, on the fact that by s 22(5) of the
Act in relation to assets held by a trustee for another person absolutely entitled as against
the trustee, capital gains tax legislation applies as if the acts of the trustee were the acts of
the beneficiary. He said that this had happened in the present case and that s 25(3),
d which imposes tax when a person becomes absolutely entitled to settled property against
the trustee, in some way avoided the implications of s 25(1). If I have misunderstood the
argument it is not for want of trying and, so far as I understand it, the argument seems
to me to be based on a fallacy. Section 25(3) applies when a person becomes absolutely
entitled to any settled property. Capital gains tax thereupon becomes payable by the
trustee. Subsequent actions which take place before the trustee actually hands the trust
e property over to a beneficiary fall within s 22(5).

In the result, whilst disagreeing with the reasons given by the learned judge, I concur
in his conclusions and would dismiss the appeal.

BRIDGE LJ. I agree.
f

BUCKLEY LJ. I agree that this appeal should be dismissed for the reasons given by
Templeman LJ, but, as we are differing from the learned judge about the reasons which
led him to his conclusion, I propose to put my judgment in my own language.

Capital gains tax was created and is regulated by Part III of the Finance Act 1965,
g which has been subsequently amended in some respects. The tax is charged on
chargeable gains, less allowable losses, accruing on actual or notional disposals of
property. The person liable is the person to whom the chargeable gain accrues. When
that person is the absolute beneficial owner both at law and in equity of the property
disposed of, he is the person liable to the tax. If however, although he is the legal owner,
he is a mere nominee of, or a bare trustee for, another person who is the absolute
beneficial owner, the beneficial owner is the person liable for the tax (s 22(5)). If the
h property is held by the legal owner on any trust other than a bare trust in favour of a
beneficial owner absolutely entitled to the property, it is 'settled property' as defined in
s 45(1). In that case s 25 applies.

Section 25(1) provides as follows:

j   'In relation to settled property, the trustees of the settlement shall for the purposes
of this Part of this Act be treated as being a single and continuing body of persons
(distinct from the persons who may from time to time be the trustees), and that
body shall be treated as being resident and ordinarily resident in the United
Kingdom unless the general administration of the trusts is ordinarily carried on·
outside the United Kingdom and the trustees or a majority of them for the time
being are not resident or not ordinarily resident in the United Kingdom.'

Then there is a proviso, which I do not think I need read.

The Act provides no definition of the word 'settlement' but in this context it seems to   *a*
me clearly to mean the trusts which make the property settled property for the purposes
of the Act. So one has to investigate what were the trusts of the particular property
which has been actually or notionally disposed of and who were the trustees holding that
property on those trusts.

Section 25(1) confers on those trustees a quasi-corporate capacity as a single and
continuing body distinct from the individuals who are the trustees, and fixes the   *b*
residence of that quasi-corporate body for the purposes of the tax. The subsection also
has the effect (1) of segregating chargeable gains and allowable losses on trust assets from
chargeable gains and allowable losses in respect of disposals of the individual trustees'
own property and (2) of avoiding complications which might arise out of changes in the
trusteeship between a date when an allowable loss was incurred on the disposal of a trust
asset and a later date when a chargeable gain has been realised on another asset of the   *c*
same trust against which the allowable loss should be taken into account.

This machinery works straightforwardly if the chargeable gain accrues on a disposal of
a piece of settled property which forms part of a corpus of settled property all held by one
set of trustees on one set of trusts. The trustees are liable for the tax and when it is paid
they, or those of them who pay the tax, are entitled under the general law to be
indemnified out of the capital of the trust fund with the consequence that the incidence   *d*
of the tax falls on the beneficiaries under the trusts in accordance with their several
interests in the trust fund in the way Templeman LJ has described.

Complications are liable to arise, however, if the corpus of the settled fund is not all
held on one and the same set of trusts. No such complications arise, I think, where ab
initio two settlements are comprised in one trust instrument, as would be the case where
a settlor by one instrument, whether inter vivos or by will, settled fund A on trust for X   *e*
for life with remainders, and fund B on trust for Y for life with different remainders.
These can be clearly recognised as two distinct settlements, although the trustees may be
the same in each case and although administrative provisions may be contained in the
trust instrument which are common to both settlements. But where, as in the present
case, one fund is initially settled on trusts which apply to the whole fund but include
powers of appointment by the exercise of which at a later date one part of the fund comes   *f*
to be held on different trusts from other parts, complications may arise.

This would not, I think, be the case so long as the different trusts affect undivided
shares of the settled corpus. Suppose for instance that a fund were held in trust for A for
life and subject thereto as to one-fifth of the fund for B for life with remainder to B's
issue, and as to four-fifths thereof for C for life with remainder to his issue. Unless and
until appropriations were made to the one-fifth share and the four-fifths share, the whole   *g*
fund must, in my view, be held on one trust, for every beneficiary is interested in an
undivided share of every asset of the fund. One could not identify any asset as belonging
to the one-fifth share or to the four-fifths share exclusively. But once specified assets are
appropriated to a particular share or part of a settled fund, whether by appointment or
appropriation, a different state of affairs exists. If one were to ask on what trusts a
particular trust asset which has been appropriated to the one-fifth share is held, these   *h*
would manifestly be different trusts from those affecting an asset appropriated to the
four-fifths share. As soon as such a state of affairs comes into existence it would, in my
view, be a quite accurate use of language to say that the one-fifth share and the four-fifths
share were distinct settled properties held on distinct trusts and so were the subjects of
distinct settlements notwithstanding that their distinctness may have arisen from acts or
events which have occurred later than the original declaration of trust from which they   *j*
have a common origin.

In such circumstances, as Templeman LJ has made clear, common sense and fairness
appear to demand that the several parts of the original fund should be treated as distinct
for the purposes of the tax. The question is, I think, whether on the true interpretation
of the Act they are to be regarded as the subject matters of separate, distinct settlements,

or as parts of property comprised in a single settlement. In this connection it is necessary
a to consider s 25(1) in conjunction with s 25(11) and (12). Section 25(11), which deals
with the position were 'part of the property comprised in the settlement is vested in one
trustee or set of trustees and part in another', read by itself, could equally well apply to
circumstances where the two parts of the settled property were held by different trustees
but on the same beneficial trusts (as would be the case in the particular instance given in
the subsection where settled land is vested in the tenant for life and investments of capital
b moneys of the settlement are held by the trustees of the settlement) and to circumstances
where one part of settled property is vested in one set of trustees on certain beneficial
trusts and another part is vested in another set of trustees on different beneficial trusts.
The subsection does not, in my opinion, provide a key to the solution of the problem of
construction.

Section 25(12) provides as follows:

c   'If there is a life interest in a part of the settled property and, where that is a life
          interest in income, there is no right of recourse to, or to the income of, the
          remainder of the settled property, the part of the settled property in which the life
          interest subsists shall while it subsists be treated for the purposes of subsections (4),
          (5), (6) and (7) of this section as being settled property under a separate settlement.'

d Subsections (5), (6) and (7) of s 25 were repealed in 1971, as also were the references in
sub-s (12) to those three subsections. At the same time sub-s (4) was amended so as to
read:

          'On the termination at any time after 6th April 1965 of a life interest in possession
          in all or any part of settled property, the whole or a corresponding part of each of the
          assets forming part of the settled property and not ceasing at that time to be settled
e   property, shall be deemed for the purposes of this part of this Act at that time to be
          disposed of and immediately reacquired by the trustee for a consideration equal to
          the whole or a corresponding part of the market value of the asset.'

For the purposes of the construction of the rest of the section, however, I must consider
the section as originally enacted.
f Subsection (4) in its original form provided, inter alia, for reasons which I do not fully
understand, that if a life interest in possession in part of settled property terminated,
there should be a deemed disposal and re-acquisition of 'all the assets forming part of the
settled property' (which I take to mean all the assets constituting the settled property)
except any which then ceased to be settled property. The consequence of this without
modification would appear to be that if a life interest in an undivided share of a settled
g fund or in a part of a settled fund consisting of specific assets terminated, there would be
a deemed disposal and re-acquisition of the whole settled fund except any part which
then ceased to be settled. Subsection (12) appears to me to have been designed, in part at
any rate, to avoid this consequence. Subsection (12) is, I think, designed to deal with
special cases within sub-ss (4), (5), (6) and (7) and does not, in my opinion, throw light on
any other part of s 25. In particular I do not think that it gives rise to an inference that
h a diversity of contemporaneous income interests under the trusts declared by a trust
instrument can only give rise to separate settlements of various parts of the settled
property for the limited purposes specified in sub-s (12).

It is, perhaps, worth drawing attention in passing to the fact that sub-s (4) as amended,
with its reference to 'a corresponding part of each of the assets forming part of the settled
property', seems to have in view a case where the relevant part of the settled property
j consists of an undivided share. I should not, however, be taken to express any decided
opinion about this.

Subsections (5), (6) and (7) as originally enacted do not seem to me to help to solve the
problem under consideration. So one is left with sub-ss (1) and (11). For reasons which
I have already given, I get no help from sub-s (11). In my judgment, the proper approach
to the construction of sub-s (1) is to look at the item of settled property in question, that

is to say, the property the disposal of which has given rise to a chargeable gain, and to enquire what the trusts are which make that property settled property within the meaning of the Act. Those trusts are, in my opinion, the settlement referred to in the subsection. One must then discover who are the trustees of that settlement. They are the persons who are chargeable with any capital gains tax payable in respect of any actual or notional disposal of that asset.

On the facts of the present case, when on 13th April 1972 Royal Oak Investments Ltd became absolutely entitled to the main fund as against the Cayman Island trustees by whom alone that fund was then held, the main fund was the subject matter of a settlement subsisting under the 1944 marriage settlement, the Variation of Trusts Act Order of 28th February 1972 and the appointment of 15th March 1972. That settlement was, in my judgment, a separate and distinct settlement for the purposes of s 25 from the settlement which then existed in respect of the fund then representing the specific assets appointed in favour of Jane by the appointment of 20th October 1955. In my view there were two separate settlements of two distinct funds for the purposes of the section from the commencement of the Finance Act 1965. They were separate settlements because by virtue of the appointment of 20th October 1955 specific assets then became subject to trusts under which the beneficial interests were different from the beneficial interests which then and thereafter subsisted under the 1944 marriage settlement in respect of the main fund. No part of the property comprised in either of those two settlements was held by one set of trustees while another part of the property comprised in that same settlement was held by another set of trustees. Consequently s 25(11) is not, in my opinion, applicable.

I agree with Templeman LJ that the 1944 marriage settlement was not brought to an end by the 1955 appointment, either in respect of the assets comprised in that appointment or at all. As regards the specific assets comprised in the appointment, its effect was that thereafter those assets were held on the trusts of the 1944 settlement as modified by the appointment. This would not in ordinary parlance bring the 1944 settlement to an end or involve any notional transfer of the appointed assets from the trustees of the 1944 settlement to themselves as the trustees of another settlement, but it did, in my view, bring about a new state of affairs in which thenceforth it was not true to say that the appointed fund and the main fund were still the subject-matters of one and the same settlement for the purposes of the tax.

I also agree with Templeman LJ in thinking that, if contrary to the view which I have formed, the 1955 appointed fund and the main fund ought to be treated as parts of property comprised in one settlement, s 25(11) and para 12(1) of Sch 10 to the Act make it impossible to hold that the Cayman Island trustees alone are assessable in respect of the notional disposal of the main fund.

For these reasons, although differing from the learned judge, I would dismiss this appeal.

Appeal dismissed. Leave to appeal to House of Lords.

Solicitors: *Solicitor of Inland Revenue*; *Withers* (for the taxpayers).

Rengan Krishnan Esq   Barrister.

a

R v Saville

COURT OF APPEAL, CRIMINAL DIVISION
LORD WIDGERY CJ, BRIDGE LJ AND WOOLF J
24th JANUARY 1980

b *Crown Court – Order – Amendment – Jurisdiction – Criminal bankruptcy order in respect of several offences – Order made in single sum and not apportioned between offences – Judge purporting to cure that defect more than 28 days later by apportioning sum between offences – Whether order 'varied' – Whether alteration merely proper exercise of court's inherent power to remedy mistake in order – Whether alteration valid though made more than 28 days after original order – Courts Act 1971, s 11(2) – Powers of Criminal Courts Act 1973, s 39(3)(a).*

c

The appellant was convicted of a number of offences involving dishonesty against his employers resulting in loss or damage being caused to them. The trial judge sentenced the appellant to imprisonment and in addition made a criminal bankruptcy order against him under s 39[a] of the Powers of Criminal Courts Act 1973. The order was made in the sum of £35,000 which was specified as being a lump sum in respect of all the *d* offences and, contrary to s 39(3)(a), was not apportioned between the offences. More than two months later the failure to comply with s 39(3)(a) was pointed out to the judge and he then purported to rectify the order by dividing the sum of £35,000 into amounts attributable to each offence. The appellant appealed against the order contending that as originally drawn up it was void, because of the failure to comply with s 39(3)(a), and that the purported amendment contravened s 11(2)[b] of the Courts Act 1971 since it amounted *e* to a variation of the order made more than 28 days after the original order was made.

Held – Since all the judge had done in altering the bankruptcy order was to exercise his inherent jurisdiction to remedy a mistake in an inchoate order, he had not, for the purposes of s 11(2) of the 1971 Act, 'varied' the order, and was not therefore required to make the alteration within 28 days after the original order. Accordingly the alteration *f* had been properly made, and the appeal would be dismissed (see p 865 *d e*, post).

R v Michael [1976] 1 All ER 629 applied.
R v Menocal [1979] 2 All ER 510 distinguished.

Notes
For variation of an order made by the Crown Court, see 11 Halsbury's Laws (4th Edn)
g paras 333–350.
For criminal bankruptcy orders, see ibid para 803.
For the Courts Act 1971, s 11, see 41 Halsbury's Statutes (3rd Edn) 299.
For the Powers of Criminal Courts Act 1973, s 39, see 43 Halsbury's Laws (3rd Edn) 334.

h **Cases referred to in judgment**
R v Menocal [1979] 2 All ER 510, [1979] 2 WLR 876, 143 JP 511, sub nom *Customs and Excise Comrs v Menocal* 69 Cr App R 148, HL.
R v Michael [1976] 1 All ER 629, [1976] QB 414, [1975] 3 WLR 731, 140 JP 265, 14(2) Digest (Reissue) 859, 7437.

j **Case also cited**
Director of Public Prosecutions v Anderson [1978] 2 All ER 512, [1978] AC 964, HL.

---

a   Section 39, so far as material, is set out at p 862 *f* to *h*, post
b   Section 11(2) is set out at p 863 *f*, post

Appeal

On 2nd December 1977 in the Crown Court at Winchester before Lawson J the appellant, *a* Peter Davies Saville, pleaded guilty to six counts in an indictment of obtaining property by deception from his employers. On 19th April 1978 in the same court, before Ackner J, he pleaded guilty to a charge in another indictment of conspiracy to defraud his employers. Ackner J remanded him in custody for sentence and on 26th April sentenced him to a total of five years' imprisonment in respect of the offences under both indictments. On the same day the judge also made a criminal bankruptcy order against *b* the appellant, under s 39 of the Powers of Criminal Courts Act 1973, in a lump sum of £35,000 specified to be in respect of all the offences. On 19th July, Ackner J amended the order by specifying what proportion of the £35,000 resulted from each offence. The appellant appealed against the bankruptcy order on the ground that as originally made it was void since it had failed to comply with s 39(3) and that the purported amendment of it on 19th July amounted to a variation of the order made more than 28 days from the *c* date of the order, in contravention of s 11(2) of the Courts Act 1971. The facts are set out in the judgment of the court.

Robin Barrett for the appellant.
Michael Brodrick for the Crown.

LORD WIDGERY CJ delivered the following judgment of the court: On 26th April *d* 1978 three indictments had been preferred against the appellant, Peter Davies Saville. They were in respect of acts of dishonesty done when he was in a position of trust. But he pleaded guilty to the charges which arose so far as our case today is concerned, and he was sentenced to prison for a substantial period and a criminal bankruptcy order was made in respect of him in the sum of £35,000. Thanks to counsel's economy of language, we are not bound to look into those background matters today, because the *e* sole argument is concerned with the £35,000.

Before I deal with the facts of the matter, it will be convenient to look briefly at the statutory provisions under which that power to make criminal bankruptcy orders was conferred. The particular authority is in ss 39 and 40 of the Powers of Criminal Courts Act 1973. Section 39(1) reads: *f*

'Where a person is convicted of an offence before the Crown Court and it appears to the court that—(a) as a result of the offence, or of that offence taken together with any other relevant offence or offences, loss or damage (not attributable to personal injury) has been suffered by one or more persons whose identity is known to the court; and (b) the amount, or aggregate amount, of the loss or damage exceeds £15,000; the court may, in addition to dealing with the offender in any other way *g* (but not if it makes a compensation order against him), make a criminal bankruptcy order against him in respect of the offence or, as the case may be, that offence and the other relevant offence or offences.'

Subsection (3) imposes certain obligations on a court when making a criminal bankruptcy order. By s 39(3)— *h*

'A criminal bankruptcy order shall specify—(a) the amount of the loss or damage appearing to the court to have resulted from the offence or, if more than one, each of the offences. . . .'

Other similar provisions are made in regard to specifying persons. Those are not of materiality in this case.

The whole argument on behalf of the appellant is derived from the fact that under *j* s 39(3)(a) there was an obligation to specify the amount of loss or damage, and if it was more than one offence, each of the offences.

If one goes to Sch 2 to the 1973 Act, it is possible to see the general pattern in which criminal bankruptcy orders fit into the general law of bankruptcy. The importance of specifying the amount in regard to each offence is due to the fact that the figure specified

under s 39 becomes for most practical purposes throughout the bankruptcy a statement
a of petitioning creditors' debts, there being not the usual machinery available for the
petitioning creditor to call his debt as he would in an ordinary bankruptcy. So it is
obviously quite important that the provisions of s 39(3) should be meticulously
obeyed. But at the same time the consequence in this instance is, in practice, very little
indeed.

I make that statement good by going to the circumstances and seeing what
b happened. The case was before the learned trial judge, Ackner J, on 26th April 1978. It
is evident that he was told that the amount for which the criminal bankruptcy order was
appropriate was £35,000. In the criminal bankruptcy order which was in due course
made on that day the figure of £35,000 was specified as a lump sum in respect of all the
offences. In point of fact, since there were more than one offence, the figure of £35,000
should have been allocated in accordance with the statute.

c The point is totally unimportant in the present instance, because there was only one
creditor concerned, that is to say the appellant's employers, who were the only persons
who remained as creditors in the order. Therefore that division amongst them is a
matter of no consequence. But at the same time it ought to have been done, and when
the matter was brought to the judge's attention, as it was on 19th July, he readily agreed
that the amount should be divided into the various damage in the offences, and this was
d in due course done.

Now the matter comes before us on appeal by counsel that the order was defective
when first made, and that it was not possible for the judge to do, as he attempted to do
on 19th July, to make good this defective order.

The main reason why it is contended that the first order should not be made good by
the judge is because reference is made to s 11 of the Courts Act 1971, and it is contended
e that within the terms of s 11 is to be found the only situation in which the kind of
alteration which appears to be contemplated can be made.

This is what s 11(2) says:

'Subject to the following provisions of this section, a sentence imposed, or other
order made, by the Crown Court when dealing with an offender may be varied or
f   rescinded by the Crown Court within the period of 28 days beginning with the day
on which the sentence or other order was imposed or made, or where subsection (3)
below applies, within the time allowed by that subsection.'

There is undoubtedly within that paragraph a general and important power whereby the
Crown Court can make orders varying or rescinding certain decisions within the period
of 28 days. But the period of 28 days had elapsed in the instant case, and therefore it was
g not possible for the prosecution to rely on that.

We were referred to one authority in the House of Lords dealing with these criminal
bankruptcy orders and indeed dealing with the very section with which we are
concerned. The case we were referred to, to which considerable importance is attached,
is *R v Menocal*[1]. The headnote reads[2]:

h   'The appellant, who had money in her possession, was arrested on a charge of
contravening section 304 of the Customs and Excise Act 1952 by being knowingly
concerned in the fraudulent evasion of the prohibition in section 3(1) of the Misuse
of Drugs Act 1971 against the importation of a controlled drug. She pleaded guilty
to the charge and was sentenced to a term of imprisonment. More than three
months after the imposition of the sentence of imprisonment, on an application for
j   an order forfeiting the money found in her possession on arrest, the court inferred
that the whole of the money had been provided to her to assist in the importation,

---

1   [1979] 2 All ER 510, [1979] 2 WLR 876
2   [1979] 2 WLR 876

and a forfeiture order was made, expressed to be under section 27 of the Act of 1971
or, alternatively, under section 43 of the Powers of Criminal Courts Act 1973. She a
appealed against the order of forfeiture on the grounds that it was made without
jurisdiction since, inter alia, the time within which the sentence might be varied
under section 11(2) of the Courts Act 1971 had expired. The Court of Appeal
dismissed the appeal. On appeal by the appellant:—*Held* that by virtue of the
definition of "sentence" in section 57 of the Courts Act 1971 the word "sentence" in
section 11(2) of that Act included a forfeiture order made against the offender; that b
section 11(2) laid down very clearly that any sentence or other order might be varied
or rescinded by the Crown Court within 28 days, but that there was no power in the
Crown Court to vary or rescind a sentence or any other order after the expiry of that
period, and that accordingly, in the circumstances, the appeal must be allowed.'

When one looks at s 57 of the Courts Act 1971 and the definition of 'sentence', one sees c
why the House of Lords came to that view: '"sentence" in relation to an offence, includes
any order made by a court when dealing with an offender ...' including a
recommendation for deportation. So it has a wide meaning. It includes any order made
by the court when dealing with an offender, and the question is whether, in the
circumstances of the instant case, it can be said, as it was said in *R v Menocal*[1], that there
was a variation or attempted variation. d

The learned trial judge, Ackner J, took the view that he was not varying his sentence
when he made the fresh disposition on 19th July. He regarded the order as being
inchoate at that time and considered that if he made the appropriate alterations and gave
them the authority of the court, they would then be valid for all purposes.

However the House of Lords unquestionably, on the facts which I have read from the
headnote, took the view that the word 'sentence' had a wide meaning and held in that e
case that there had been an attempt to vary the sentence out of time.

We do not think that *R v Menocal*[1] is really a case which should sway us today, because
the factual differences are so numerous. In *R v Menocal*[1] the court did attempt to vary
what was undoubtedly a sentence on a matter which had not passed through the minds
of the parties or their advisers during the trial. Some substantial time after the trial
someone had the idea of making a forfeiture order and that was done. It was a case in f
which the penalty against the accused had been increased after the date of the hearing in
respect of a matter on which no one had exercised their minds at the time.

Comparing the situation in the instant case, here, as I have pointed out more than
once, there was only one creditor. It was purely an exercise of futility that the amount
should be split up as the Act provides. Never mind. These things do happen. Maybe it
is necessary sometimes for acts of futility to be acted out. But in this instance we cannot g
believe, considering all the circumstances, and comparing them with *R v Menocal*[1], that
we should regard ourselves to be bound by *R v Menocal*[1] because of the extreme difference
between the two cases.

We are reinforced in that view by the assistance given to us by counsel for the Crown,
who cited the ruling of his Honour Judge Rubin in *R v Michael*[2]. There the defendant
had been tried and acquitted on an indictment containing a large number of counts. h
Application was made at the end of the proceedings for the defence costs to be paid out
of central funds. Although no specific reference was made to the costs of the committal
proceedings, it was the court's intention to include those costs in the order. The record
showed that the order was for the defence costs to be paid out of central funds under

j

---

1   [1979] 2 All ER 510, [1979] 2 WLR 876
2   [1976] 1 All ER 629, [1976] QB 414

s 3. The taxing officer excluded the costs of the committal proceedings on the ground
a that they had not been included in the order. The matter was brought back to the judge
and it was held[1]—

> 'that "may" in section 3(9) of the Costs in Criminal Cases Act 1973 made it clear
> that the court had a discretion whether to include the costs of the committal
> proceedings in an order for the defence costs to be paid out of central funds; that it
> *b* followed that an order for costs under s 3(1)(*b*) of the Act, without specific reference
> to committal proceedings, referred only to the costs of the trial on indictment and,
> accordingly, the order was defective in that it did not reflect the intention of the
> court to include the costs of the committal proceedings.'

There is a passage in the judgment of Judge Rubin, in which he says[2]:

> *c*   'In my judgment these cases [he is referring to the authorities already cited]
> establish that this court, as a court of record, has an inherent jurisdiction to remedy
> mistakes in its record. There are two other cases to which I must refer which show,
> in my judgment, that an omission from an order should be rectified if it is of such
> a character that if it had been mentioned before the order had been entered the
> omission would have been supplied as a matter of course without further argument.'

d We cannot have a better illustration of that principle being applied than the principle
which is sought to be adopted today.
   Having regard to the existence of the power, having regard to the total unimportance
of the alteration performed, we think that distinguishes this case from the earlier
authorities to the contrary to which I have referred. We consider the judge properly
made the adjustment which he made and it can properly be regarded as an adjustment
e of an inchoate order which at that moment existed.
   In those circumstances the appeal is dismissed.

Appeal dismissed.

The court refused leave to appeal to the House of Lords but certified under s 33(2) of the Criminal
f *Appeal Act 1968 that the following point of law of general public importance was involved in the*
decision: if, in purported performance of its duty under s 39(3)(a) of the Powers of Criminal
Courts Act 1973, and there being two or more relevant offences, the Crown Court computes the
loss or damage as a single sum, can the court subsequently apportion that sum between the relevant
offences otherwise than under s 11 of the Courts Act 1971?

g Solicitors: *Registrar of Criminal Appeals; Director of Public Prosecutions.*

N P Metcalfe Esq   Barrister.

---

1   [1976] QB 414 at 415
2   [1976] 1 All ER 629 at 632, [1976] QB 414 at 419

Imperial Tobacco Ltd and another v Attorney-General

a

HOUSE OF LORDS

VISCOUNT DILHORNE, LORD EDMUND-DAVIES, LORD FRASER OF TULLYBELTON, LORD SCARMAN AND LORD LANE

23rd, 24th, 28th, 29th, 30th JANUARY, 6th MARCH 1980

b

Gaming – Lottery – Competition – Scheme involving distribution of prizes by chance – No payment or contribution by participants to obtain chance of winning prize – No skill involved – Purchasers of packets of cigarettes receiving ticket with packet – Ticket listing six possible prizes – If three prizes corresponding purchaser entitled to that prize – Packets of cigarettes sold at normal price – Whether scheme a lottery or competition – Lotteries and Amusements Act 1976, ss 2(1)(b), 14(1)(b).

c

Administrative law – Declaratory judgment – Declaration sought whether scheme an unlawful lottery or competition – Concurrent criminal proceedings against plaintiffs in respect of scheme – Jurisdiction of civil court to grant declaration as to validity of scheme.

The respondents, a tobacco company, launched a sales promotion campaign, known as 'Spot Cash', for a particular brand of cigarettes whereby in every packet of cigarettes there *d* was a ticket with six spaces covered with silver foil. When the spaces were rubbed with a coin possible prizes were disclosed and if three of the prizes corresponded the ticket holder was entitled to collect that prize. The prizes ranged from a free packet of cigarettes to £5,000. The scheme was advertised as being free, and packets of cigarettes containing the cards were sold at the normal retail price. The Director of Public Prosecutions laid informations against the respondents and their senior officers charging *e* them with (i) distributing tickets in an unlawful lottery contrary to s 2(1)(b)[a] of the Lotteries and Amusements Act 1976, and (ii) conducting an unlawful competition contrary to s 14(1)(b)[b] of that Act. The Director indicated to the respondents his intention of proceeding with the charges on indictment in the Crown Court rather than summarily before magistrates. Before the charges were tried the respondents issued an originating summons in the Commercial Court seeking a declaration that their scheme was lawful. *f* The Crown took the preliminary point that the Commercial Court had no jurisdiction to grant the declaration sought, or, if it had, that it ought to exercise its discretion by declining to grant the declaration, on the ground that the case was already before a criminal court of co-ordinate jurisdiction, ie the Crown Court. The judge held that he had jurisdiction to hear the originating summons and would have granted the declaration if the respondents' scheme had been lawful, but he went on to hold that the scheme was *g* an unlawful lottery, because the purchaser was buying both the cigarettes and the ticket, and also an unlawful competition, because the purchaser competed with others for the limited number of prizes available. The respondents appealed. At the hearing of the appeal the Crown conceded that the court had jurisdiction to grant the declaration but again took the point that the court ought to exercise its discretion not to do so because a court of co-ordinate jurisdiction was already seised of the matter. The Court of Appeal[c] *h*

---

a Section 2(1), so far as material, provides: 'Subject to the provisions of this section, every person who in connection with any lottery promoted or proposed to be promoted either in Great Britain or elsewhere . . . (b) sells or distributes, or offers or advertises for sale or distribution, or has in his possession for the purpose of sale or distribution, any tickets or chances in the lottery . . . shall be guilty of an offence.'

b Section 14, so far as material, provides:

j

'(1) . . . it shall be unlawful to conduct in or through any newspaper, or in connection with any trade or business or the sale of any article to the public . . . (b) any other competition in which success does not depend to a substantial degree on the exercise of skill . . .

'(3) Any person who contravenes this section shall, without prejudice to any liability to be proceeded against under section 2 above, be guilty of an offence . . .'

c [1979] 2 All ER 592

upheld the judge on the issue of jurisdiction but held that the scheme was lawful, since
a participants in the scheme neither paid for their opportunity to participate nor competed
against one another for the prizes, and accordingly granted the declaration. The Crown
appealed.

Held – The appeal would be allowed for the following reasons—

(i) In order to establish an unlawful lottery it was not necessary to prove that money
paid by the participants in return for obtaining a chance of winning was used to provide
b prizes or was paid into a fund out of which the prizes were provided. What was essential
was that there was a distribution of prizes by lot or chance and that the chance of
winning was secured by a payment, contribution or consideration by those taking part;
and where, in order to get the chance of a prize, a customer had to pay for an article,
albeit at the normal price, that amounted to a payment, contribution or consideration for
the chance of a prize. On that basis the purchase of a packet of cigarettes in the
c respondents' scheme was the consideration in return for which the card containing the
chance of a prize changed hands, and that made the scheme a lottery contrary to s 2(1)(*b*)
of the 1976 Act, regardless of the fact that it was impossible to ascribe any part of the
purchase price to the value of the chance so obtained (see p 872, *b c*, p 874 *f g*, p 876 *f g*,
p 877 *j*, p 879 *b* to *d* and p 880 *c h*, post); *Taylor v Smetten* (1883) 11 QBD 207 and dictum
of Lord Widgery CJ in *Reader's Digest Association v Williams* [1976] 3 All ER at 739
d applied; *Willis v Young and Stembridge* [1907] 1 KB 448 and dictum of Sheriff Mowat in
Douglas v Valente 1968 SLT at 87 disapproved.

(ii) However, the respondents' scheme was not a competition since for the purposes of
s 14(1)(*b*) of the 1976 Act a competition involved the exercise of some degree of skill and
under the respondents' scheme no effort or striving or dexterity was required of the
participants. The respondents had not therefore contravened s 14(1)(*b*) (see p 875 *a*,
e p 876 *f g*, p 879 *d e h* and p 882 *b* to *d*, post); *Whitbread & Co Ltd v Bell* [1970] 2 All ER 64
overruled.

(iii) Where criminal proceedings were properly instituted and were not vexatious or
an abuse of the process of the court, it was not a proper exercise of judicial discretion for
a judge in a civil court to grant the defendant in the criminal proceedings a declaration
that the facts alleged by the prosecution did not in law prove the offence charged, because
f to make such a declaration would be to usurp the function of the criminal court without
binding it, and would thus inevitably prejudice the criminal trial one way or the other.
Accordingly the declaration ought not to have been granted (see p 875 *f j*, p 876 *d* to *g*,
p 879 *f* to *h* and p 884 *c* to *e*, post).

Decision of the Court of Appeal [1979] 2 All ER 592 reversed.

Notes
g For lotteries and competitions, see 4 Halsbury's Laws (4th Edn) paras 4–6, 142, 151, and
for cases on the subject, see 25 Digest (Repl) 489, 493–495, 509–513, 504, 511–527, 604–
622.

For power and discretion to make declaratory judgments, see 1 Halsbury's Laws (4th
Edn) paras 185–187, and for cases on the subject, see 30 Digest (Reissue) 189–222, 202–
h 359.

For the Lotteries and Amusements Act 1976, ss 2, 14, see 46 Halsbury's Statutes (3rd
Edn) 645, 659.

Cases referred to in opinions
Atkinson v Murrell [1972] 2 All ER 1131, [1973] AC 289, [1972] 3 WLR 465, 136 JP 611,
    HL; *affg* [1972] 2 All ER 31, [1972] 2 QB 274, [1972] 2 WLR 509, DC, Digest (Cont
j Vol D) 363, 518*a*.
Bartlett v Parker [1912] 2 KB 497, 81 LJKB 857, 106 LT 869, 76 JP 280, 23 Cox CC 16,
    DC, 25 Digest (Repl) 494, 525.
Caminada v Hulton (1891) 60 LJMC 116, 64 LT 572, 55 JP 727, 17 Cox CC 307, sub nom
    R v Hulton 7 TLR 491, DC, 25 Digest (Repl) 509, 604.
Connolly Brothers Ltd, Re, Wood v Connolly Brothers Ltd [1911] 1 Ch 731, 80 LJ Ch 409, 104
    LT 693, CA, 16 Digest (Repl) 222, 1109.

Director of Public Prosecutions v Bradfute and Associates Ltd [1967] 1 All ER 112, [1967] 2
QB 291, [1967] 2 WLR 459, 131 JP 117, DC, Digest (Cont Vol C) 403, *618a*.   *a*
Douglas v Valente 1968 SLT (Sh Ct) 85.
Hall v McWilliam (1901) 85 LT 239, 65 JP 742, 20 Cox CC 33, 17 TLR 561, DC, 25 Digest
(Repl) 494, *523.*
Hobbs v Ward (1929) 93 JP 163, 45 TLR 378, 27 LGR 610, DC, 25 Digest (Repl) 512, *617.*
Howgate v Ralph (1929) 141 LT 512, 93 JP 127, 27 LGR 432, 28 Cox CC 633, DC, 25
Digest (Repl) 498, *553.*   *b*
Hunt v Williams (1888) 52 JP 821, DC, 25 Digest (Repl) 494, *522.*
Kerslake v Knight (1925) 94 LJKB 919, [1925] All ER Rep 679, 133 LT 606, 89 JP 142, 23
LGR 574, 28 Cox CC 27, 17 TLR 561, DC, 25 Digest (Repl) 495, *527.*
London Borough of Ealing v Race Relations Board [1972] 1 All ER 105, [1972] AC 342, [1972]
2 WLR 71, 136 JP 112, 70 LGR 219, HL, Digest (Cont Vol D) 260, *156a.*
McCollom v Wrightson [1968] 1 All ER 514, [1968] AC 522, [1968] 2 WLR 578, 132 JP   *c*
261, 66 LGR 343, HL, Digest (Cont Vol C) 397, *340a.*
Minty v Sylvester (1915) 84 LJKB 1982, 114 LT 164, 79 JP 543, 13 LGR 1085, 25 Cox CC
247, 31 TLR 589, DC, 25 Digest (Repl) 494, *526.*
Morris v Blackman (1864) 2 H & C 912, 28 JP 199, 10 Jur NS 520, 159 ER 378, 25 Digest
(Repl) 494, *519.*
Munnich v Godstone Rural District Council [1966] 1 All ER 930, [1966] 1 WLR 427, 130 JP   *d*
202, 64 LGR 141, 18 P & CR 1, CA, 30 Digest (Reissue) 221, *355.*
Pyx Granite Co Ltd v Ministry of Housing and Local Government [1959] 3 All ER 1, [1960] AC
260, [1959] 3 WLR 346, 123 JP 429, 58 LGR 1, 10 P & CR 319, HL, 45 Digest (Reissue)
336, *37.*
R v Harris (1866) 10 Cox CC 352, 25 Digest (Repl) 494, *520.*
Reader's Digest Association Ltd v Williams [1976] 3 All ER 737, [1976] 1 WLR 1109, 141   *e*
JP 52, DC.
Taylor v Smetten (1883) 11 QBD 207, 52 LJMC 101, 48 JP 36, DC, 25 Digest (Repl) 494,
521.
Thames Launches Ltd v Corpn of Trinity House of Deptford Strond [1961] 1 All ER 26, [1961]
Ch 197, [1961] 2 WLR 16, [1960] 2 Lloyd's Rep 407, 28(2) Digest (Reissue) 1106, *1042.*
Whitbread & Co Ltd v Bell, Bell v Whitbread & Co Ltd [1970] 2 All ER 64, [1970] 2 QB 547,   *f*
[1970] 2 WLR 1025, 134 JP 445, DC, Digest (Cont Vol C) 400, *509a.*
Willis v Young and Stembridge [1907] 1 KB 448, 76 LJKB 390, 96 LT 155, 71 JP 6, 21 Cox
CC 362, DC, 25 Digest (Repl) 493, *511.*

Appeal

The Attorney-General appealed against the decision of the Court of Appeal[1] (Lord
Denning MR, Ormrod and Browne LJJ) given on 9th March 1979 allowing the appeal of   *g*
the respondents, Imperial Tobacco Ltd and Imperial Group Ltd, against the decision of
Donaldson J on 23rd January 1979 that certain schemes operated by the respondents
were both an unlawful lottery and an unlawful competition. By leave of the Court of
Appeal given on 9th March 1979 the Director of Public Prosecutions was struck out as a
defendant to the respondents' action. The facts are set out in the opinion of Viscount
Dilhorne.   *h*

Peter Taylor QC, Simon Brown and *Andrew Collins* for the Attorney-General.
Stanley Brodie QC and *Stephen Nathan* for the respondents.

Their Lordships took time for consideration.

6th March. The following opinions were delivered.

VISCOUNT DILHORNE. My Lords, the start of this litigation was the taking out by   *j*
the respondents on 13th December 1978 of an originating summons in the Commercial
Court to secure a declaration that schemes they had operated on and after 9th October
1978 were lawful and did not contravene the Lotteries and Amusements Act 1976, in
other words, a declaration that they were not guilty of criminal offences. Those schemes

1   [1979] 2 All ER 592, [1979] QB 555

were called 'Spot Cash', 'Trade Spot Cash', 'Special Trade Spot Cash' and 'Wholesalers Spot
a Cash'.

For the year 1978–79 the respondents had allocated £19,800,000 for advertising and
promoting the sale of Players cigarettes. For their Spot Cash promotion 262,250,000
cards were printed, 260 million of those cards were to be inserted in packets of Players
King Size cigarettes. The packets which contained a card had on their outsides a strip
bearing the words 'SPOT CASH closes 31.3.79.' and so could be distinguished from the
b packets of King Size cigarettes which did not contain a card. The purchaser of a packet
so marked, would, if the card contained had the same amount of money, it might be
£5,000, £1,000, £100 or £10 or £1, or the words 'Free Packet' printed on it three times,
win a prize of the amount so printed or a free packet of King Size cigarettes as the case
might be. The purchaser of such a packet paid no more for it than he would have had
to pay for a packet which did not contain a card. The Spot Cash scheme was widely
c advertised as free and as a game not involving skill. The remaining 2,250,000 cards were
distributed without anything having to be purchased to obtain a card. Members of the
public could obtain them from retailers or on application to the respondents. Cards were
also allocated to wholesalers and sales representatives to encourage the promotion of the
Spot Cash scheme.

The scheme proved very successful. In the short time it was operated, from 9th
d October to 27th November 1978 sales of King Size cigarettes increased by 39·9%. Mr
Douglas, a director of the Imperial Group Ltd and a solicitor, in an affidavit sworn in
these proceedings, said that the value of sales effected by the success of the Spot Cash
promotion ran into 'tens of millions of pounds'.

In a statement prepared by the respondents it was said: 'The idea of "Spot Cash" as (for
want of any better expression) a "free lottery" evolved during the summer months of
e 1978.' That the 2,250,000 cards were cards giving chances in a 'free lottery' is not
disputed. The respondents in the light of the legal advice they had received, believed
that the 260 million cards in the packets of cigarettes were also free and that consequently
they were not conducting an unlawful lottery. Although their receipts from the sale of
their King Size cigarettes increased so substantially, they did not charge for any card. It
was essential in their view that a money payment should be made for the chance if the
f distribution of prizes by lot or chance was to constitute an unlawful lottery.

The British American Tobacco Co, one of the respondents' principal competitors, were
advised that the Spot Cash scheme was an unlawful lottery. They did not, as they might
have done, launch a private prosecution to test the matter. They applied to the Attorney-
General for his consent to the institution of a relator action by them against the
respondents. The Attorney-General did not consent and after his refusal, a prosecution
g was started on the instructions of the Director of Public Prosecutions by the laying of
informations in Nottingham Magistrates' Court. Lord Denning MR in the course of his
judgment in this case, wondered why consent to the institution of such an action had
been refused. The fact that it was refused does not surprise me. If I had been Attorney-
General at the time, I would have refused any consent without any hesitation. If the Spot
Cash scheme was an unlawful lottery, criminal offences had already been committed
h when the application was made and the proper place for the determination of the
respondents' guilt or innocence was a criminal and not a civil court.

Summonses in the Nottingham Magistrates' Court were taken out not only against
Imperial Tobacco Ltd but also against three directors and a senior manager. I do not
know why these four individuals were selected from the board of directors and
managers. I would have thought that it would have sufficed to prosecute the company.
j On 24th November 1978 a letter was sent by a principal assistant director in the office
of the Director of Public Prosecutions to the respondents. That letter stated that counsel
had advised the Director that three of the schemes were unlawful lotteries and four of
them unlawful competitions. It said:

'The Director would like to receive your assurance that you will discontinue these
promotions immediately, pending the outcome of the trial . . . It is the Director's
intention to proceed on indictment . . . In the event of your giving the assurance

which is now sought, it will become unnecessary for the Director to consider what further steps can be taken to prevent further breaches of the law.'

Mr Douglas replied to this on 30th November. Among other things, he said that it was believed that the scheme was lawful but that all advertising of it had been terminated, that the manufacture of packets of cigarettes containing the cards had been stopped and that the promotion would be run down as soon as possible. He asked that the summonses against the individual defendants who were honourable men and who had done no more than carry out their proper functions, should be withdrawn. On 7th December 1978 the same principal assistant director replied. In his letter he appears to have expressed his personal views. It was not expressed to be written on behalf of the Director. He was not satisfied about what had been done to stop the promotion and in the course of his letter he said:

> 'I do not regard the proceedings which I have instituted as being in any way a "test case" but rather as a prosecution for contravention of the statute, and I take the view that any continuation of the promotion constitutes further illegality. In these circumstances, I am quite unable to give any assurance as to the courses I might take, and in particular as to the presentation of the prosecution's case at the Crown Court. You also ask me to withdraw the proceedings instituted against the individual defendants. I am not willing to do so.' (Emphasis mine.)

It appears from this letter that it was this gentleman's view, despite having been informed that legal advice had been obtained that the scheme was lawful, that there was no defence to the prosecution. All prosecutions for criminal offences created by statute are, of course, prosecutions for contravention of a statute. This letter appeared to the respondents to contain a threat to prosecute wholesalers and retailers as well and led to Mr Douglas writing, saying that the company had been content to let the issue be determined in the magistrates' court or the Crown Court but that as it appeared from the letter of 7th December that there was appreciable risk of further criminal proceedings against the company and others in the trade they had decided to try to get the legality of the scheme determined at the earliest possible date and for that purpose had taken out the originating summons. I do not propose to make any further observations on the letters which emanated from the Director's office. I have not heard what explanation there may be for correspondence which at first sight appears difficult, if not impossible, to justify.

I have set these matters out at this length as they explain why the unusual course of seeking a ruling as to innocence of criminal offences from the Commercial Court was followed.

The case was heard by Donaldson J. He had to decide whether the Spot Cash scheme was (1) an unlawful lottery, (2) an unlawful competition and (3) whether, if he came to the conclusion that it was neither, it was a proper exercise of his discretion to grant a declaration to that effect. He held that it was an unlawful lottery and an unlawful competition but that if he had come to the other conclusion, it would have been a proper exercise of his discretion to have granted the declaration sought. The Court of Appeal[1] (Lord Denning MR, Ormrod and Browne LJJ) held that the scheme was lawful and granted the declaration.

In both courts it had been argued for the Attorney-General that the issue of the originating summons was an abuse of process and that the issue should be decided in a criminal and not a civil court. That argument was not pursued in this House but as the question is of great and far-reaching importance and as it would not be right for their Lordships to uphold the decision of the Court of Appeal unless they were satisfied that the granting of the declaration after a criminal prosecution had been started could be regarded as a proper exercise of judicial discretion, their Lordships heard argument on this question.

So the same three issues as were decided below have to be considered by this House.

_____
1   [1979] 2 All ER 592, [1979] QB 555

Was the Spot Cash scheme an unlawful lottery?

a   In this connection one can ignore the cards which were, or were to be, distributed but were not to be inserted in the packets of cigarettes. They formed a very small proportion of the total. We are concerned only with the distribution of the 260 million cards in the packets of Players King Size cigarettes.

Section 1 of the Lotteries and Amusements Act 1976 declares that all lotteries which do not constitute gaming, are, except as provided by that Act, unlawful lotteries. The

b   Spot Cash scheme does not come within any of the exceptions. The Act does not define a lottery nor does any other Act.

In *Whitbread & Co Ltd v Bell*[1] Lord Parker CJ, with whose judgment the other members of the court agreed, said:

> 'Nowhere in the history of lotteries or in this Act is there a statutory definition of a lottery. At least it consists of the distribution of prizes by chance, that is to say,
c   cases where there is no element of skill whatever on the part of the participant . . . It is clear, however, and indeed admitted, that that is not a complete definition . . . There is, as far as I know, no case of a successful prosecution for running a lottery which has not involved some payment or contribution by the participants, and indeed the trend of authority has all been the other way. There must be some payment or contribution, if not towards the prizes themselves, at any rate towards
d   funds, ie profits, out of which prizes are provided.'

He cited the following passage from the judgment of the sheriff-substitute (J S Mowat) in *Douglas v Valente*[2]:

> 'I am satisfied that the whole trend of judicial decision and the majority of judicial observations, as well as the more recent dictionary definitions, favour the view that
e   in its ordinary sense a lottery involves contribution to the prize fund by the participants.'

Lord Parker CJ agreed with this subject to the reference to the prize fund being interpreted as including profits out of which the prizes are provided.

In my speech in *Atkinson v Murrell*[3] I cited both these passages. In that case it was not necessary to consider whether contribution to the prize fund or to funds out of which the
f   prizes were paid was an essential ingredient of an unlawful lottery and if that is the case, whether *Bartlett v Parker*[4] was wrongly decided. In that case those who bought 6d tickets for a dance had a chance of winning a bicycle given as a prize by the Rudge-Whitworth Co. The point was taken that the money paid for the ticket did not contribute to the prize, but it was held by the court (Ridley, A T Lawrence and Pickford JJ) that that was immaterial and that there was an unlawful lottery. In *Atkinson v Murrell*[5] the only
g   question to be decided was whether what would clearly have been an illegal lottery if the money paid for a chance had been paid to the promoters and had provided the prizes or had been contributed to funds out of which the prizes were paid, was not an unlawful lottery by reason of the fact that the participants paid money direct to the winners. I said that it was and that all the *Whitbread* case[6] had decided was that for there to be an unlawful lottery, the participants must pay for their chances. I agreed with what
h   Griffiths J[7] had said in the Divisional Court, namely:

> 'Whereas it is true that most lotteries involve a scheme which creates an identifiable prize fund, I can find no reason to conclude that this is an essential feature of a lottery, provided the scheme achieves the overall object of the distribution of money by chance.'

j   1   [1970] 2 All ER 64 at 66, 67 [1970] 2 QB 547 at 555
2   1968 SLT (Sh Ct) 85 at 87
3   [1972] 2 All ER 1131 at 1133, [1973] AC 289 at 294
4   [1912] 2 KB 497
5   [1972] 2 All ER 1131, [1973] AC 289
6   [1970] 2 All ER 64, [1970] 2 QB 547
7   [1972] 2 All ER 31 at 38, [1972] 2 QB 274 at 282–283

There are no doubt many cases in which the money paid by participants contributes to the prizes and in such cases if the distribution of the prizes is by chance, it is easy to conclude that it is a lottery. Proof that the money so contributed goes into a fund out of which the prizes are paid may not be so easy and if such proof is necessary, then it would be easy to avoid the conclusion that there was a lottery by arranging that the prizes came from an independent source.

My Lords, despite the final words in the passage I have cited from Lord Parker CJ's judgment and what was said in *Douglas v Valente*[1] I am satisfied that it is not necessary to prove that the money paid by participants was used to provide the prizes or towards funds out of which the prizes are provided to establish the existence of an unlawful lottery. What is essential is that there is a distribution of prizes by lot or chance and that the chances should be secured by some payment or contribution by those who take part.

In *Reader's Digest Association Ltd v Williams*[2] Lord Widgery CJ said:

'A lottery is the distribution of prizes by chance where the persons taking part in the operation, or a substantial number of them, make a payment or consideration in return for obtaining their chance of a prize. There are really three points one must look for in deciding whether a lottery has been established: first of all, the distribution of prizes; secondly, the fact that this was to be done by means of a chance; and thirdly, that there must be some actual contribution made by the participants in return for their obtaining a chance to take part in the lottery.'

In that case he said there was 'no such contribution' and 'there was no actual payment or consideration in my judgment tendered by the participant in order to take part in the prize draw'.

Lord Parker CJ spoke of 'some payment or contribution'; Lord Widgery CJ of 'a payment or consideration' and an 'actual contribution'. Usually, I think, money is parted with to secure a chance. I suspect that Lord Parker CJ and Lord Widgery CJ did not refer only to payment because in their view it would suffice to constitute an unlawful lottery if there was any consideration given to secure the chance. However this may be, the question to be decided in this case is, was there a payment of money for the chance of winning a prize when someone paid for a packet of Players King Size cigarettes bearing the identifying strip. If there was, it was an unlawful lottery. If there was not, it was indeed a free lottery. The respondents say that as no more was paid for a packet with a card in it than was paid for a packet of the same cigarettes, no part of the price paid was attributable to the card and so there was no payment for the chance. Counsel for the Attorney-General contended that where payment for an article, albeit at the normal price, is necessary to obtain the chance, that in law amounts to payment for a chance.

Lord Denning MR in the course of his judgment referred to a large number of cases which he thought had been wrongly decided. For the seventy years preceding 1968 he thought the courts had erred and that it was then that their mistake was discovered. I regret that I am unable to agree. I have looked at all the cases to which he referred and with one possible exception, they were in my opinion all rightly decided. In my view none of them lend support to the view that for a lottery to be unlawful, where the chance is obtained with something else, it must be shown that the price is 'loaded' and that part of it is attributable to the chance.

In *Morris v Blackman*[3] the promoter of an entertainment announced that at the end of it, he would distribute among the audience 'a shower of gold and silver treasures on a scale utterly without parallel'. It was a matter of chance whether the buyer of a ticket got anything and if he did, what he got. Here the payment for a ticket entitled the purchaser to see the entertainment and to secure a chance in a lottery.

In *R v Harris*[4] Montague Smith J said the case came within the Lotteries Act: 'as the subscribers were induced to part with their money in the hope of obtaining, not only

1   1968 SLT (Sh Ct) 85 at 87
2   [1976] 3 All ER 737 at 739, [1976] 1 WLR 1109 at 1113
3   (1864) 2 H & C 912
4   (1866) 10 Cox CC 352 at 352–353

their alleged shilling's worth [of goods] but something of much greater value, the right
to which was to be ascertained by chance.'

The facts of *Taylor v Smetten*[1] bear some resemblance to those of this case. There
packets of tea were sold at 2s 6d a packet. Each packet had in it a coupon entitling the
purchaser to a prize, the prizes varying in character and value. Delivering the judgment
of the court, Hawkins J said[2]:

> 'There can be no doubt that the appellant in enclosing and announcing the
> enclosure of the coupon in the packet of tea, did so with a view to induce persons to
> become purchasers and realise a profit to himself; and, although it was admitted by
> the respondent that the tea was good and worth all the money, it is impossible to
> suppose that the aggregate prices charged and obtained for the packages did not
> include the aggregate prices of the tea and the prizes.'

The court held that there was a lottery. This decision was not based on any presumption
that the price of the tea was 'loaded' so as to include the price of the chance. It was clear
in that case, and indeed accepted, that a purchaser bought for 2s 6d a packet of tea and a
chance of winning a prize.

In *R v Hulton*[3] (more fully reported under the name of *Caminada v Hulton*[4]) copies of a
handicap book were sold for a penny. Attached to them were coupons. If the purchaser
of a book filled in the coupon and predicted a number of winners of races, he won a
prize. For the defendant it was contended that the filling up of the coupon involved the
exercise of skill and Day J held that there was no lottery 'for there was no contrivance or
device to obtain money by chance'. The decision did not turn, as I read the reports, on
whether anything was paid for the coupon and I cannot regard it as in any way
inconsistent with the cases to which I have referred or as an authority for the proposition
that to constitute a lottery, there must be a payment atributable to the chance. Lord
Denning MR is, I fear, mistaken in thinking that this decision was overlooked ten years
later in *Hall v McWilliam*[5]. The report of that case in Cox's Criminal Law Cases[6] shows
that it was referred to both in argument and in the judgment of Ridley J. There it was
contended for the publisher of a newspaper that the halfpenny paid for the paper was
exhausted in its purchase and that no part of it could be allocated to the chance. This
argument was rejected not only by Ridley J but also by Bigham J, Ridley J[7] saying: 'The
purchaser gives the halfpenny not only for the paper but for the chance of becoming the
owner of the lucky spots', and Bigham J[8] saying: 'What he [the publisher] did was to sell
a newspaper to purchasers and with the newspaper to sell a chance of getting a prize in
a lottery.'

In *Kerslake v Knight*[9] where goods were sold with a ticket giving the chance of a prize,
Lord Hewart CJ is reported as follows: 'It was also contended that there was no sale of
tickets, because the price of the goods was not increased, and they were fair value for the
money.' He thought that the purchaser bought for one undivided price an article and a
chance: 'The ticket was just as much bought as if it had been priced separately.'

Lord Denning MR thought that the mistaken view of the courts for 70 years was
noticed in *McCollom v Wrightson*[10]. I must confess my inability to find anything in the
speech of Lord Hodson, with which the other members of the House agreed, to that
effect. Lord Hodson said it was unnecessary to consider whether *Willis v Young and
Stembridge*[11] was rightly decided. In that case numbered medals were distributed free

1   (1883) 11 QBD 207
2   11 QBD 207 at 211
3   (1891) 7 TLR 491
4   60 LJMC 116, 17 Cox CC 307
5   (1901) 17 TLR 561, 85 LT 239
6   20 Cox CC 33
7   17 TLR 561 at 562
8   20 Cox CC 33 at 38
9   (1925) 41 TLR 555 at 557
10   [1968] 1 All ER 514, [1968] AC 522
11   [1907] 1 KB 448

among members of the public. The holders of winning numbers won a prize. The
winning numbers were published in a newspaper. It was not necessary to buy a paper to *a*
win a prize. This operation was designed to increase and did increase the circulation of
the paper. Although no payment was made for the medal, it was held that those who
received the medals contributed collectively sums of money which constituted the fund
from which the profits of the paper were drawn 'and also the money for the prize
winners came'. In this case too, I do not find it necessary to consider whether that case
was rightly decided. I doubt if it was. It may have led to Lord Parker's reference in the *b*
Whitbread case[1] to contributions towards funds out of which prizes are provided.
However this may be, that case is of no assistance in the present case.

I do not find in any of the other cases to which Lord Denning MR referred any
criticism or rejection of what I take to be the ratio decidendi of the cases he thought
wrongly decided. That ratio I take to be that where a person buys two things for one
price, it is impossible to say that he paid only for one of them and not for the other. The *c*
fact that he could have bought one of the things at the same price as he paid for both, is
in my view immaterial.

I regret too that I cannot agree with the conclusion reached on this by Ormrod LJ. In
his judgment he said that the conclusion that there was a payment for a chance assumed
that a customer in a tobacconist's shop stipulated for the cigarettes and a coupon and that
the tobacconist supplied both. I see no reason for any such assumption. If a customer *d*
asked for a packet identified by the strip on its outside and the tobacconist supplied it, I
see no reason for any other conclusion than that the customer paid for both. If one
packet in ten contained a coupon, all the packets being outwardly identical, and the
purchaser knew that if he bought a packet he had a chance of winning a prize, in my
view the purchaser was clearly participating in a lottery (see Hunt v Williams[2]).

In the course of the judgments in the Court of Appeal reference was made to the *e*
mischief at which the 1976 Act was directed. While I do not think that that affects the
question that has now to be decided, I think it by no means certain that the Act was
directed at the same mischief as the ancient Acts. For a very long period lotteries have
been unlawful but in recent years we have seen some relaxation. Under the 1976 Act
some lotteries are now lawful. It may have been thought that a more general relaxation
would not meet with the approval of a considerable section of the population. However *f*
this may be and whatever the mischief at which the 1976 Act was directed, it cannot
affect the determination of the question: was there a payment for a chance when in
return for the money paid, the customer secured a chance as well as a packet of
cigarettes? In my opinion there was.

Was the Spot Cash scheme an unlawful competition?   *g*
It has long been the law that for there to be a lottery, the distribution of the prizes
must solely depend on chance. If the winning of a prize involved the exercise of any
skill, then it was not a lottery. Ingenious schemes were devised which closely resembled
lotteries but which were not unlawful on account of some degree of skill being
required. In the Betting and Lotteries Act 1934 this loophole was stopped and now s 14
of the 1976 Act, a consolidation Act, makes it an offence for any person to conduct 'in *h*
connection with any trade or business or the sale of any article to the public' a competition
in which success does not depend to a substantial degree on the exercise of skill.

The section does not define 'competition'. It was submitted for the Attorney-General
that all lotteries are competitions and that a lottery conducted in connection with a trade
or business or the sale of any article to the public consequently contravenes the section.
I do not think that this can be right. Apart from the improbability of Parliament ever *j*
intending to enact that all unlawful lotteries should be competitions coming within this
section and so making a person who committed a criminal offence in conducting a
lottery also guilty of an offence under this section, the legislative history appears to me

1   [1970] 2 All ER 64, [1970] 2 QB 547
2   (1888) 52 JP 821

to show that the net was being spread to catch schemes which due to the exercise of skill
a were not caught by the provisions as to lotteries. That leads me to the conclusion that a
competition, to come within the section, must be one which involves the exercise of
some degree of skill. If it is a substantial degree, then no offence is committed. I can find
nothing in the section to suggest that only competitions which the competitor must pay
to enter are within the section and I disagree with Lord Denning MR as to this but I agree
with him in holding that it was wrong in the *Whitbread* case[1] to hold that there was an
b unlawful competition.

Subsection (3) of s 14 provides that contravention of it is, 'without prejudice to any
liability to be proceeded against' in respect of a lottery, an offence. I do not think that this
subsection throws any light on the meaning to be given to the word 'competition.' I
think that this subsection was probably inserted ex abundanti cautela to guard against
the possibility that a scheme may be so devised that it is in part a lottery and in part a
c competition and to make it clear that a conviction for conducting an unlawful
competition is no bar to a conviction in respect of a lottery.

In my opinion the Spot Cash scheme was not a competition coming within the section.
I now turn to what I think is the most important question in this appeal.

Could the court in the proper exercise of its discretion grant the declaration sought?

Donaldson J thought it could but did not grant it as he thought that the Spot Cash
d scheme was a lottery and an unlawful competition. The Court of Appeal, holding that
it was neither, granted it. That decision, if it stands, will form a precedent for the
Commercial Court and other civil courts usurping the functions of the criminal courts.
Publishers may be tempted to seek declarations that what they propose to publish is not
a criminal libel or blasphemous or obscene. If in this case where the declaration sought
was not in respect of future conduct but in respect of what had already taken place, it
e could properly be granted, I see no reason why in such cases a declaration as to future
conduct could not be granted. If this were to happen, then the position would be much
the same as it was before the passing of Fox's Libel Act 1843 when judges, not juries,
decided whether a libel was criminal, blasphemous or obscene.

Such a declaration is no bar to a criminal prosecution, no matter the authority of
the court which grants it. Such a declaration in a case such as the present one, made after
f the commencement of the prosecution, and in effect a finding of guilt or innocence
of the offence charged, cannot found a plea of autrefois acquit or autrefois convict,
though it may well prejudice the criminal proceedings, the result of which will depend
on the facts proved and may not depend solely on admissions made by the accused. If a
civil court of great authority declares on admissions made by the accused that no crime
has been committed, one can foresee the use that might be made of that at the criminal
g trial.

The justification for the Court of Appeal taking this unusual and unprecedented
course (no case was cited to us where a civil court had after the commencement of a
prosecution, granted a declaration that no offence had been committed) was said to be the
length of time it would have taken for the matter to be determined in the criminal
courts. I can well see the advantages of persons being able to obtain rulings on whether
h or not certain conduct on which they propose to embark will be criminal and it may be
a defect in our present system that it does not provide for that. Here, I wish to
emphasise, it was not a question whether future conduct would be permissible but
whether acts done were criminal. It was said that the administration of justice would
belie its name if civil courts refused to answer reasonable questions on whether certain
conduct was or was not lawful. I do not agree. I think that the administration of justice
j would become chaotic if after the start of a prosecution, declarations of innocence could
be obtained from a civil court.

What was the urgency in the present case? The operation of the scheme began in
October 1978. It was to end on 31st March 1979. It may be that far too much time
elapses nowadays before accused persons are tried on indictment but why should these

1 [1970] 2 All ER 64, [1970] 2 QB 547

respondents be singled out for special treatment? I do not see that there was any particular urgency or that there was any special reason for the respondents to be treated differently from other accused. If the case had been tried summarily in the magistrates' court at Nottingham, I doubt if it would have taken longer, or an appreciable time longer to reach this House. All the cases on lotteries to which I have referred were, with one exception, tried in the magistrates' courts. The exception is R v Harris[1] where the trial was on indictment. In my opinion a magistrates' court is the best court for the determination of the question, where there is a genuine dispute, whether or not a scheme is an unlawful lottery or unlawful competition, for whatever the result, there can be an appeal by way of case stated on facts found by the magistrates. There can, of course, be no appeal should a trial on indictment result in a verdict of not guilty. In this case the Director said that he would seek trial on indictment, presumably because it was felt that the magistrates would not have power to impose a heavy enough penalty. Whether in a case such as this, when the respondents honestly believed in the light of the legal advice they had received that the scheme was lawful, a Crown Court would have imposed a heavier penalty than the magistrates may be open to doubt.

My Lords, it is not necessary in this case to decide whether a declaration as to the criminality or otherwise of future conduct can ever properly be made by a civil court. In my opinion it would be a very exceptional case in which it would be right to do so. In my opinion it cannot be right to grant a declaration that an accused is innocent after a prosecution has started.

While I would allow the appeal on this ground alone, I have felt it to be desirable to state my opinion on the questions on which the Court of Appeal and Donaldson J pronounced.

As it is clear that the originating summons was taken out in order, if possible, to avoid threatened prosecutions of wholesalers and retailers I think that the proper order as to costs in this case is that there should be no order, as to costs in this House, the Court of Appeal and in the Commercial Court.

LORD EDMUND-DAVIES. My Lords, the speech of my noble and learned friend Viscount Dilhorne contains a close and careful consideration of the many cases cited to this House on the subject of the modern law relating to lotteries. The reasons he gives and those developed by my noble and learned friend Lord Lane in a speech which I venture to describe as one of outstanding clarity and cogency, have convinced me that no advantage would accrue were I to carry out my original intention of contributing one of my own. I have therefore destroyed the draft on which I had been engaged. In its place, let me say simply that, being in respectful agreement with my noble and learned friends, I concur in holding that this appeal should be allowed and in the proposed order as to costs.

LORD FRASER OF TULLYBELTON. My Lords, the respondents (plaintiffs in the action) seek a declaration that a scheme which they introduced in 1978 for promoting the sales of certain brands of their cigarettes was lawful and did not contravene the Lotteries and Amusements Act 1976 as being either a lottery or an unlawful competition. The correct answer to the apparently simple questions thus raised are surprisingly difficult to ascertain. Donaldson J held that the scheme was both a lottery and an unlawful competition. His decision on both points was reversed by the Court of Appeal, where Lord Denning MR and Ormrod and Browne LJJ were unanimously of opinion that the scheme was lawful. During the argument before this House, I must confess that my opinion on the lottery question veered from side to side as the argument proceeded. But I have eventually reached the view that the appellants' argument must prevail and that the scheme was a lottery. The competition point seems to me much less difficult, and I am clearly of opinion that the scheme was not a competition at all, and therefore not an unlawful competition.

---

1 (1866) 10 Cox CC 352

The scheme has already been described by my noble and learned friend Viscount
a Dilhorne and I need not repeat what he has said.

The word 'lottery' is not defined in the 1976 Act and has apparently never been
defined in any statute. But there is a considerable number of reported decisions, many
of which have been referred to by Viscount Dilhorne in his speech, on the question of
whether particular schemes were lotteries. Without going through the cases again, I
respectfully accept the statement of the essentials of a lottery by Lord Widgery CJ in
b *Reader's Digest Association Ltd v Williams*[1] as follows:

> 'A lottery is the distribution of prizes by chance where the persons taking part in
> the operation, or a substantial number of them, make a payment or consideration
> in return for obtaining their chance of a prize. There are really three points one
> must look for in deciding whether a lottery has been established: first of all, the
> distribution of prizes; secondly, the fact that this was to be done by means of a
> *c* chance; and thirdly, that there must be some actual contribution made by the
> participants in return for their obtaining a chance to take part in the lottery.'

No question arises in the instant appeal with regard to the first two of those points. The
question that arises is on the third point and it is this: what is meant by an 'actual
contribution made by the participants *in return for* their obtaining a chance to take part
d in the lottery'?

Counsel for the respondents says it means that a participant must pay in cash for the
chance, that is he must buy the chance. If he buys another article, in this case a packet
of cigarettes, for its normal price and receives in addition a free chance to win a prize, that
free chance is a gift and he pays nothing for it. He is therefore not entering a lottery.
Reliance was placed by the respondents on their advertisements, one of which contained
e this statement: 'A Spot Cash game ticket comes FREE with every packet of John Player
King Size ... marked with ... the Spot Cash tear tape.' I am unable to accept that
argument because I do not think that the ticket, or really the chance which it represented,
was free in the relevant sense. In this context the word 'free' is ambiguous. It might
mean 'free of any charge *at all*'. If the word had been used in that sense, the respondents'
advertisement would not have been true because unless a participant buys the cigarettes
f he will not get the chance; a man with no money cannot get the chance. I disregard as
de minimis the relatively small number of cards that were available to the public from
dispensers without payment. They were too few in proportion to the number enclosed
in packets to affect the answer, and I did not understand it to be suggested that they had
any bearing on the point.

The other possible meaning of 'free' is 'free of any *extra* charge'. That is the sense in
g which the respondents used the word, but, although it was true in that sense, it is in my
opinion not enough for their argument. Of course, if the price of packets containing a
card had been 'loaded' that would have been fatal to the respondents' case, but absence of
'loading' is by no means conclusive in their favour. Lord Denning MR was mistaken in
saying that *R v Hulton*[2] held that there was no lottery because the presumption that the
price had been 'loaded' had in that case been rebutted. The case is also reported under the
h name *Caminada v Hulton*[3], where the judgment of Day J is reported in full, and evidently
proceeded on the ground that the scheme was not a lottery because 'there was no
contrivance or device to obtain money by chance'. The case was not, as Lord Denning
MR thought, overlooked in *Hall v McWilliam*[4] but it was cited as *Caminada v Hulton*[3] and
distinguished.

In my opinion, a scheme will be a lottery if the prizes are distributed by chance and if
j persons are induced to make a money payment, or to give other valuable consideration
in order to obtain a chance of winning a prize. It is immaterial that no part of the price
can be allocated to the chance. That is the conclusion to which the long line of cases

1   [1976] 3 All ER 737 at 739, [1976] 1 WLR 1109 at 1113
2   (1891) 7 TLR 491
3   (1891) 17 Cox CC 307
4   (1901) 17 TLR 561, 20 Cox CC 33

referred to by Viscount Dilhorne leads. In particular *Taylor v Smetten*[1] seems to me to be indistinguishable in principle from the present case. In that case the promoter had sold *a* packets of tea for 2s 6d each. In each packet was a coupon entitling the purchaser to a prize, but the purchasers did not know until after buying the packets what prizes they were entitled to, and the prizes varied in value. The promoter was convicted of keeping a lottery, notwithstanding that the tea was good and worth all the money. Hawkins J[2] said that a participant—

'bought the tea coupled with the chance of getting something of value by way of *b* a prize, but without the least idea what the prize might be . . . To us it seems utterly immaterial whether a specific article was or was not conjoined with the chance, and as the subject-matter of the sale.'

In that case as in the instant appeal, the chance was the subject-matter of a contract of sale. But the result would have been the same if the contract had been of some other *c* kind, for example a contract to give the chance in return for the participant entering into a separate collateral contract. I do not think it is necessary to go into the question of contract at all; the material question is whether some consideration has to be given, in order to acquire a chance. The participant must, of course, give the consideration knowing that it will give him a chance to win a prize; if he pays his money without knowing that, the scheme will not be a lottery: see *Minty v Sylvester*[3], per Lord Reading *d* CJ.

Of the cases brought to our notice, where prizes were distributed by chance, without the exercise of skill or dexterity, the only ones that escaped classification as lotteries were those in which the chance was truly free in the sense of being available to a participant whether he bought anything else or not. Those cases were the *Reader's Digest* case[4], *Whitbread & Co Ltd v Bell*[5] and *Douglas v Valente*[6]. In *Douglas v Valente*[6] the sheriff *e* evidently thought that the payment of 1s 0d for life membership of the National Sporting Klub, although it was a condition precedent to participating in the scheme, was not closely enough related to obtaining a chance to be regarded as paid in exchange for a chance. On that view of the facts I think the decision was right. The decision in *Willis v Young and Stembridge*[7] has been treated with some reserve in later cases. In *McCollom v Wrightson*[8] Lord Hodson said it was 'unnecessary to consider whether the case [of *Willis*[7]] *f* was rightly decided', and in *Whitbread & Co Ltd v Bell*[9] Lord Parker CJ said that it was a case 'which depends entirely, as I see it, on its very special facts'. I would go further; in my opinion *Willis's* case[7] was wrongly decided because the medals which gave the chance of a prize were distributed free and not only to persons who bought the newspaper. That case may be contrasted with *Kerslake v Knight*[10] where each copy of the newspaper was sold together with a numbered ticket for what the judge described as 'one undivided *g* price', and where the card gave a chance of a prize to anyone who exhibited it in his window. I am with respect unable to agree with Browne LJ in the Court of Appeal that *Kerslake v Knight*[10] was wrongly decided. It seems to me to fit exactly into line with *Taylor v Smetten*[1] and other cases.

In *Douglas v Valente*[11] Sheriff-substitute Mowat said:

'I am satisfied that the whole trend of judicial decision and the majority of judicial *h*

---

1   (1883) 11 QBD 207
2   11 QBD 207 at 212
3   (1915) 31 TLR at 590
4   [1976] 3 All ER 737, [1976] 1 WLR 1109
5   [1970] 2 All ER 64, [1970] 2 QB 547   *j*
6   1968 SLT (Sh Ct) 85
7   [1907] 1 KB 448
8   [1968] 1 All ER 514 at 517, [1968] AC 522 at 528
9   [1970] 2 All ER 64 at 67, [1970] 2 QB 547 at 556
10 (1925) 94 LJKB 919, [1925] All ER Rep 679
11 1968 SLT (Sh Ct) 85 at 87

observations, as well as the more recent dictionary definitions, favour the view that in its ordinary sense a lottery involves contribution to the prize fund by the participants.'

In *Whitbread & Co Ltd v Bell*[1] Lord Parker CJ, after quoting that passage from *Douglas v Valente*[2], said: 'I entirely agree, subject, possibly, to the deletion of the words "to the prize fund", unless by that is meant to include a fund out of which the prizes are provided.' But even with Lord Parker CJ's gloss, I consider that the sheriff's-substitute statement in *Douglas v Valente*[2] was erroneous. I do not think it is necessary for the participants' payments to contribute in any way to the prize fund or to profits from which prizes are provided. In *Atkinson v Murrell*[3], Viscount Dilhorne, with whom the other Law Lords agreed, said that the *Whitbread* case[4] 'decided no more than that for there to be a lottery, the participants must pay for their chances'. The actual decision in *Atkinson v Murrell*[5] was that a scheme that would otherwise have been a lottery does not cease to be a lottery if it provides that each participant shall send a contribution direct to the winner as a contribution to his prize. That decision is consistent with the view which I think is correct that the destination of the participants' payments is immaterial. Thus in *Bartlett v Parker*[6], where the prize was a bicycle presented by an outside firm as an advertisement, and the participants' payments made no contribution to the cost of the bicycle or to the profits of the firm that had presented it, the scheme was held to be a lottery. *Bartlett*[6] was referred to in argument in *Atkinson v Murrell*[5], and it was not disapproved, or mentioned at all, in the speeches in this House.

For these reasons I am of opinion that this scheme was a lottery. On the other hand I do not think it was a competition because no effort or striving or dexterity was required from the participants. No doubt persons who are competing for a limited number of prizes may be said to be in competition with one another for the prizes, but I do not think that, merely because the number of prizes is limited, they are engaged in 'a competition' if the distribution of prizes is dependent wholly on chance. I agree with Viscount Dilhorne that the history of the legislation supports the view that the distinction between a lottery and a competition is that the award of prizes in the former depends purely on chance and in the latter it depends at least partly on skill. In the present case obviously there was no element of skill. Accordingly I agree with the Court of Appeal on this matter, and I think that the decision in *Whitbread & Co Ltd v Bell*[4], on the competition point was wrong.

I am in entire agreement with my noble and learned friends that this is not a case in which the discretion of the court should have been exercised to make the declaration. By doing so the civil court, in my opinion, improperly intruded into the domain of the criminal court, notwithstanding that criminal proceedings had already been begun. We were not referred to any reported case where such intrusion had occurred and in my opinion it ought not to be permitted except possibly in some very special circumstances which are not found here.

Having regard to my opinion on the lottery point, I would allow the appeal. I agree with Viscount Dilhorne that there should be no order as to costs in this House or below.

LORD SCARMAN. My Lords, I have had the advantage of reading in draft the speeches of my noble and learned friends Viscount Dilhorne and Lord Lane. I agree with them. I would allow the appeal. But, for the reasons given by my noble and learned friend Viscount Dilhorne, I would not allow the Attorney-General any costs here or below.

1 [1970] 2 All ER 64 at 68, [1970] 2 QB 547 at 557
2 1968 SLT (Sh Ct) 85 at 87
3 [1972] 2 All ER 1131 at 1133–1134, [1973] AC 289 at 294–295
4 [1970] 2 All ER 64, [1970] 2 QB 547
5 [1972] 2 All ER 1131, [1973] AC 289
6 [1912] 2 KB 497

LORD LANE. My Lords,

1 *Lottery*

By s 1 of the Lotteries and Amusements Act 1976: 'All lotteries which do not constitute gaming are unlawful, except as provided by this Act'. If the Spot Cash scheme devised by Imperial Tobacco was in law a lottery it does not fall within any of those exceptions and its promotion was an offence.

The Act provides no definition of lotteries. The draftsman would, however, choose his words against the background of decided cases, of which there is no shortage. There is no dispute between the parties as to the elements broadly speaking which have to be proved. First, there must be a distribution of prizes; secondly, that distribution must depend on chance; thirdly, the customer or participant must give some form of payment or consideration for the chance. The word 'contribution' is sometimes used. That is equally correct if it is used simply as a synonym for payment. What is not required is that there should be any contribution by the participant to the prize-fund: see *Atkinson v Murrell*[1]. The only point at issue is what may constitute the necessary payment, consideration or contribution. I am conscious that one is treading on the frontiers between fact and law in such an enquiry, but one has in the end to decide whether on the undisputed facts of this case any verdict other than one of guilty would have been open.

The object of the respondents' scheme, details of which have already been described by my noble and learned friend Viscount Dilhorne, was to encourage sales of their King Size cigarettes. Smokers were tempted to buy these cigarettes by the inclusion in the Spot Cash packets of a card which, if the customer was lucky, might entitle him to a prize. There were other ways of obtaining these cards legitimately without buying a packet of cigarettes, but one suspects that they were introduced in an attempt to avoid the effect of the 1976 Act. They formed only a miniscule part of the scheme as a whole and can be disregarded for the purpose of this appeal. Packets containing cards cost the same as those which did not. The question is this: where, in order to get the chance of a prize, the customer has to pay for an article (albeit at the normal price), does that amount to the necessary payment, contribution or consideration made or given in return for the chance of a prize? Donaldson J considered that it did, the members of the Court of Appeal were unanimously of the view that it did not.

Counsel for the respondents emphasised the fact that the promoters of the scheme honestly believed it to be free and said as much in all their advertisements, for example, 'FREE game ticket in every special pack'. What the promoters said or believed, however, is irrelevant. The word 'free' has more than one meaning. From the promoters' point of view no doubt it might be said, 'We are giving this card away free with every packet'. It would only be free in the sense of 'without extra charge'. From the customer's point of view the card would not properly be described as free. He would, one imagines, consider himself to be buying the packet and the card. He would have a legitimate complaint if he asked and paid for a Spot Cash packet only to discover there was no card inside. The whole object of the scheme was to induce him to ask for a special packet of the respondents' King Size cigarettes and hand over 57p to the tobacconist. The fact that it may not be possible to ascribe any part of that price to the value of the chance so obtained does not affect the matter. Whether one calls it payment or contribution or consideration it seems to me as a matter of first impression at least that the purchase of the cigarettes is indeed the consideration in return for which the card changes hands. That makes the scheme a lottery.

That conclusion accords with the preponderance of authorities starting with *Taylor v Smetten*[2] (packets of tea). A series of decisions followed: *Minty v Sylvester*[3] (theatre seat); *Kerslake v Knight*[4] (newspaper); *Howgate v Ralph*[5] (tea); *Hobbs v Ward*[6] (dog food); *Director*

1   [1972] 2 All ER 1131, [1973] AC 289
2   (1883) 11 QBD 207
3   (1915) 84 LJKB 1982
4   (1925) 94 LJKB 919, [1925] All ER Rep 679
5   (1929) 141 LT 512, 93 JP 127
6   (1929) 93 JP 163

of Public Prosecutions v Bradfute and Associates Ltd[1] (cat food). All are consistent with the
a conclusion I have expressed. The 'mistake' in these cases which Lord Denning MR said
was perceived in various later cases culminating in *Reader's Digest Association Ltd v
Williams*[2], was not, I venture to suggest, a mistake at all. Nor was it perceived as such.
The *Reader's Digest* case[2] was a case where no payment, contribution or consideration
could on any view of the facts be said to have been required. The decision of the
Divisional Court that there was no lottery was wholly consistent with authority and
b constituted no departure from the earlier cases. *McCollom v Wrightson*[3] was, according to
Lord Denning MR, the case in which the 'mistake' was first noticed. That case was
concerned with gaming, not lotteries. It emphasised that 'gaming' only takes place
where there is a chance of losing as well as of winning; where 'some stake has been
hazarded'. It is true that the appellants there, in support of subsidiary argument, cited
two lottery cases, namely, *Willis v Young and Stembridge*[4] and *Minty v Sylvester*[5], but their
c Lordships found it unnecessary to make any pronouncement at all on the correctness of
those decisions. Lord Denning MR[6] then went on to consider *Douglas v Valente*[7] which
he said was 'followed by Lord Parker CJ in *Whitbread & Co Ltd v Bell*[8], with the approval
of the House of Lords in *Atkinson v Murrell*[9]'.

Douglas v Valente[7] was decided on the basis that to prove a lottery there must be a
contribution by the customer to the prize fund. The sheriff-substitute went on to find
d on the facts (no doubt correctly) that no such contribution had been made. Of that
decision Lord Parker CJ in *Whitbread & Co Ltd v Bell*[10] had this to say: 'I entirely agree,
subject, possibly, to the deletion of the words "to the prize-fund", unless by that is meant
to include profits out of which the prizes are provided.'

Lord Parker CJ's reservations about *Douglas v Valente*[7] were proved well founded by
the decision of this House in *Atkinson v Murrell*[9] already referred to. This was a chain-
e letter case, very different on its facts from the present. It did however make it abundantly
clear that although in a lottery the participant must pay for his chance to participate, yet
it is not an essential ingredient that there should be any prize fund, let alone contribution
to it, provided the scheme had the overall object of the distribution of money by chance.

Thus the basis on which the Court of Appeal felt themselves entitled to say that all the
Divisional Court cases from 1901 to 1967 were wrongly decided is itself unsound. There
f is no necessity to prove that the participant stands to lose what he has paid if he is unlucky
(as Lord Denning MR held). That is to import notions of gaming into the definition of
lottery which is not justified.

The law is correctly stated by Lord Widgery CJ in *Reader's Digest Association Ltd v
Williams*[11]:

g   'A lottery is the distribution of prizes by chance where the persons taking part in
          the operation, or a substantial number of them, make a payment or consideration
          in return for obtaining their chance of a prize. There are really three points one
          must look for in deciding whether a lottery has been established: first of all, the
          distribution of prizes; secondly, the fact that this was to be done by means of a
          chance; and thirdly, that there must be some actual contribution made by the
h   participants in return for their obtaining a chance to take part in the lottery.'

The difficulties which have arisen in some of the cases, in particular *Willis v Young and*

---

1   [1967] 1 All ER 112, [1967] 2 QB 291
2   [1976] 3 All ER 737, [1976] 1 WLR 1109
3   [1968] 1 All ER 514, [1968] AC 522
j 4   [1907] 1 KB 448
   5   (1915) 84 LJKB 1982
6   [1979] 2 All ER 592 at 601, [1979] QB 555 at 577
7   1968 SLT (Sh Ct) 85
8   [1970] 2 All ER 64, [1970] 2 QB 547
9   [1972] 2 All ER 1131, [1973] AC 289
10   [1970] 2 All ER 64 at 68, [1970] 2 QB 547 at 557
11   [1976] 3 All ER 737 at 739, [1976] 1 WLR 1109 at 1113

Stembridge[1], have been caused not so much by any confusion about the law as by somewhat bizarre conclusions about the facts. In that case there was plainly evidence on *a* which the magistrate could reach the conclusion he did. The Divisional Court nevertheless saw fit to allow the prosecutor's appeal, I think wrongly.

2 Competition

As in the case of lotteries, so with competitions Parliament has not seen fit to provide any definition. There are two meanings. The first is the passive 'competition' between, *b* for example, 50 people who enter a raffle when there is only one prize. In one sense of the word each of the 50 is competing with the other 49 for the prize. The second is the active exercise of skill, or strength or prowess of some sort, a striving to do better than other contestants in the hope of excelling them. That is the sense in which I believe the word 'competition' is used in the 1976 Act. The mischief which s 14 (re-enacting the relevant provisions of the 1934 Act) sought to meet was the evasion of the law relating *c* to lotteries by the requirement that some small degree of skill should be exercised by the participants. If the first meaning is the true one then almost all lotteries would be competitions, a result which Parliament would be unlikely to intend. The second meaning is to my mind the natural one and must have been intended. I respectfully agree with the judgment of Browne LJ on this aspect of the matter, and consider, as he does, that *Whitbread's* case[2] was wrongly decided so far as it purported to give to *d* 'competition' the other meaning. The respondents' scheme was not a competition.

3 Jurisdiction and discretion

The history of this prosecution is unhappy. Disregarding, as one must, the possibly deleterious effects of smoking, this lottery, as Lord Denning MR rightly observed, was light entertainment and also good advertising. No one was likely to complain about the light entertainment, but the good advertising was another matter. A 39% increase in the *e* sales of the respondents' King Size cigarettes meant that rival concerns would be suffering a corresponding drop.

Hence the first complaint from a trade rival; hence the initiation of proceedings. Given that the Director of Public Prosecutions was convinced (rightly as it transpires) that the promotion of this lottery was an offence, nevertheless the following matters *f* should have been clear to him. First, that so far as the public was concerned (as opposed to rival tobacco companies) this lottery could hardly be said to be causing harm to anyone. Secondly, whatever views he might have had about its illegality, that there was ample room for the opposite view to be honestly held by others. Thirdly, that the respondents had taken skilled advice and did honestly hold the opposite view. Fourthly, that if the scheme was brought to a premature end the financial loss to the respondents was likely to be considerable. *g*

We did not have the advantage of any explanation from the Director of Public Prosecutions, and so one must not be too censorious, but I confess I find it difficult to understand how in those circumstances it was decided to have the matter tried in the Crown Court rather than before the justices, with all the delay which that would entail; why it was necessary to charge individuals rather than the company alone; and particularly, why it was thought proper to threaten to charge the small fry, wholesale and *h* retail tobacconists and so on. It seems as though everything was being done which might inject venom into a situation where plainly no venom was necessary or justified. Putting it as charitably as possible, it was a maladroit performance. It is not surprising that the respondents took the action they did and sought a declaration.

Understandable though that action was, was it right, even assuming there was no *i* illegal lottery, that a declaration in these circumstances should be granted? Although the *j* appellant contested this aspect of the matter before Donaldson J and the Court of Appeal he did not do so before this House. It would not however be right in a matter of such great importance for your Lordships to let it pass without expressing a view.

---

1 [1907] 1 KB 448
2 [1970] 2 All ER 64, [1970] 2 QB 547

a There is no doubt that there is jurisdiction to grant a declaration in these circumstances. Anyone is on principle entitled to apply to the court for a declaration as to their rights unless statutorily prohibited expressly or by necessary implication: see *Pyx Granite Co Ltd v Ministry of Housing and Local Government*[1] and *London Borough of Ealing v Race Relations Board*[2]. There was no such prohibition here; but was the learned judge right to exercise his discretion as he did, as the Court of Appeal thought he was?

The high-water mark of the respondents' case is the decision in *Thames Launches Ltd v*
b *Trinity House Corpn*[3]. In April 1960 the plaintiff took civil proceedings by way of an originating summons in the Chancery Division against the defendant. Six months later, two summonses against the plaintiff's servant were issued out of the magistrates' court on an information laid by a servant of the defendant. These summonses raised substantially the same questions of law as did the originating summons. The plaintiff moved to restrain the prosecution of the criminal proceedings until the determination of the civil
c action. Buckley J held that he had jurisdiction to stay the criminal proceedings and further, that it would in the circumstances be proper for him so to do because the criminal proceedings were vexatious. They sought to obtain relief in respect of a particular matter against a defendant who as plaintiff in another court had already instituted proceedings designed to decide the same matter between the same parties. The prosecution of the criminal proceedings was therefore restrained by injunction.
d Buckley J said[4]:

> 'Jurisdiction of that kind, in my judgment, is very clearly a jurisdiction which must be exercised with the greatest care; and this court, I think, would be very slow to interfere with the course of criminal proceedings unless it was clear that the issues in the civil proceedings and the criminal proceedings really raised in substance the
e same issue and that if the civil proceedings succeeded the criminal proceedings must necessarily fail ... In other words, the court must be satisfied that to allow the criminal proceedings to be proceeded with pending the decision of the civil proceedings would really be vexatious.'

Re Connolly Brothers Ltd[5], a decision of the Court of Appeal, concerned two civil actions. Lord Cozens-Hardy MR said[6]:
f
> 'It is enough to say that the jurisdiction ... ought to be exercised if the court comes to the conclusion that the defendant in the High Court action, the plaintiff in the foreign action—in this case, the Palatine action—acted vexatiously in instituting the proceedings in the foreign action; and ... I have no hesitation in saying that the proceedings taken ... in the Palatine action were vexatious and unreasonable to such an extent that the court ought to exercise the jurisdiction
g which it plainly possesses to grant an injunction.'

Munnich v Godstone Rural District Council[7] was a case where the applicant for declaratory relief had already been convicted in criminal proceedings for having failed to comply with the provisions of a planning enforcement notice under the Town and Country Planning Act 1947. He pleaded guilty and was fined. Two months later he issued a writ
h seeking a declaration that no valid enforcement notice had been served and that he was entitled to 'deemed' unconditional planning permission. Thereafter a further summons was issued by the planning authority for continued contravention of the enforcement notice. The magistrates refused his request for an adjournment, held the notice to be valid and convicted and fined him. He abandoned his intention to appeal by way of case stated. The Court of Appeal rejected the application for a declaration on the basis that the

j _____
1 [1959] 3 All ER 1, [1960] AC 260
2 [1972] 1 All ER 105, [1972] AC 342
3 [1961] 1 All ER 26, [1961] Ch 197
4 [1961] 1 All ER 26 at 29–30, [1961] Ch 197 at 204
5 [1911] 1 Ch 731
6 [1911] 1 Ch 731 at 744
7 [1966] 1 All ER 930, [1966] 1 WLR 427

enforcement notice was in fact valid. They expressed the view however that had the enforcement notice been invalid they would have granted the relief sought, because *a* the issue was one of law and was the only method whereby the litigant could have his valuable property rights determined. In that case therefore the criminal proceedings had ended.

Counsel appearing before your Lordships' House were unable to find any case in which a defendant in criminal proceedings already properly and not vexatiously instituted had applied for a declaration that the criminal proceedings were unfounded or *b* based on a misapprehension as to the true meaning of the criminal statute. I do not find that dearth of authority surprising. It would be strange if a defendant to proper criminal proceedings were able to pre-empt those proceedings by application to a judge of the High Court whether sitting in the Commercial Court or elsewhere. What effect in law on the criminal proceedings would any pronouncement from the High Court in these circumstances have? The criminal court would not be bound by the decision. In *c* practical terms it would simply have the inevitable effect of prejudicing the criminal trial one way or the other.

Where there are concurrent proceedings in different courts between parties who for practical purposes are the same in each, and the same issue will have to be determined in each, the court has jurisdiction to stay one set of proceedings if it is just and convenient to do so or if the circumstances are such that one set of proceedings is vexatious and an *d* abuse of the process of the court. Where, however, criminal proceedings have been properly instituted and are not vexatious or an abuse of the process of the court it is not a proper exercise of the court's discretion to grant to the defendant in those proceedings a declaration that the facts to be alleged by the prosecution do not in law prove the offence charged.

I would allow the appeal. I agree that in the circumstances there should be no order *e* as to costs.

Appeal allowed.

Solicitors: *Treasury Solicitor*; *Trower, Still & Keeling* (for the respondents).

Mary Rose Plummer   Barrister. *f*

Inland Revenue Commissioners v McMullen and others

HOUSE OF LORDS

g

LORD HAILSHAM OF ST MARYLEBONE LC, LORD DIPLOCK, LORD SALMON, LORD RUSSELL OF KILLOWEN AND LORD KEITH OF KINKEL

28th, 29th, 30th JANUARY, 6th MARCH 1980

Charity – Education – Educational purposes – Sport – Promotion and encouragement of sport *h* *– Trust to promote, encourage and provide facilities for pupils of schools and universities to play association football and other games – Whether educational charity – Whether encouragement of sport subservient to general charitable purpose.*

The Football Association Youth Trust was established by a deed dated 30th October 1972, made between the Football Association and the trustees of the deed. The objects of the *j* trust, as set out in cl 3(a) of the deed, were 'to organise or provide or assist in the organisation and provision of facilities' which would enable and encourage students at schools and universities 'to play Association Football or other games or sports and thereby to assist in ensuring that due attention is given to the physical education and development of such pupils as well as to the development and occupation of their minds and with a view to furthering this object' to provide such things as facilities, playing fields,

equipment, lectures, demonstrations and coaching of association football or other games
a and sports at schools and universities. The Charity Commissioners decided to register
the trust as a charity, pursuant to s 4 of the Charities Act 1960. The Crown objected to
the registration and on appeal to the High Court, the judge*ᵃ* held, inter alia, that the trust
could not be classified as an educational charity because its object was merely the
encouragement of games and sports and that object had not been made subservient to the
advancement of education. On appeal, the Court of Appeal*ᵇ* upheld that view and added
b that it was a trust for the encouragement of games and sports which were not required
to be enjoyed as part of a school or university curriculum. On appeal to the House of
Lords,

Held – The appeal would be allowed for the following reasons—
    (i) On the true construction of cl 3(a) of the trust deed, the word 'thereby' and the
c phrase which followed it denoted an additional purpose of the trust rather than merely
the result which it was hoped would follow from encouraging students to play association
football or other games or sports. The purpose of the deed was therefore not merely to
organise the playing of association football in schools or universities but also to promote
the physical education and development of students as an addition to their formal
education (see p 889 *g h*, p 890 *a b*, p 894 *a* to *f* and p 895 *a* to *e* and *h*, post).
d   (ii) On that construction the trust established by the deed was a valid charitable trust,
because, having regard to the educational theory that the provision of sporting facilities
contributed to providing a balanced education, it was for the advancement of education,
and furthermore was limited to students at universities and schools (see p 891 *j* to p 892
a and *h* to p 893 *d f j*, p 894 *b* and p 895 *a* to *c* and *h*, post).
    Per Lord Hailsham LC, Lord Diplock, Lord Salmon and Lord Keith. In construing a
e trust deed where the intention is to set up a charitable trust and where there is an
ambiguity, a benign construction should be given if possible (see p 890 *c*, p 894 *b* and
p 895 *b c*, post).
    Decision of the Court of Appeal [1979] 1 All ER 588 reversed.

Notes
f For the meaning of charitable purposes, see 5 Halsbury's Laws (4th Edn) paras 502, 504–
507, for charities for educational purposes, see ibid paras 522–527, for cases on charitable
purposes, see 8(1) Digest (Reissue) 23–302, *1–431*, and for cases on educational purposes
in particular, see ibid 256–266, *112–157*.
    For recreational charities, see 5 Halsbury's Laws (4th Edn) paras 544–547.
    For the Charities Act 1960, s 4, see 3 Halsbury's Statutes (3rd Edn) 594.

g **Cases referred to in opinions**
    Bain, Re, Public Trustee v Ross [1930] 1 Ch 224, [1929] All ER Rep 387, 99 LJ Ch 171, 142
        LT 344, CA, 8(1) Digest (Reissue) 317, *566*.
    Brisbane City Council v Attorney-General for Queensland [1978] 3 All ER 30, [1979] AC 411,
        [1978] 3 WLR 299, PC.
    Bruce v Deer Presbytery (1867) LR 1 Sc & Div 96, HL, 8(1) Digest (Reissue) 334, *700*.
h *Chesters, Re* (25th July 1934) unreported.
    Dupree's Deed Trusts, Re, Daley v Lloyds Bank Ltd [1944] 2 All ER 443, [1945] Ch 16, 114
        LJ Ch 1, 171 LT 384, 8(1) Digest (Reissue) 261, *141*.
    Hopkins' Will Trusts, Re, Naish v Francis Bacon Society Inc [1964] 3 All ER 46, [1965] Ch
        669, [1964] 3 WLR 840, 8(1) Digest (Reissue) 257, *120*.
    Houston v Burns [1918] AC 337, 87 LJPC 99, 118 LT 462, HL, 8(1) Digest (Reissue) 324,
j   *609*.
    Income Tax Special Purposes Comrs v Pemsel [1891] AC 531, [1891–4] All ER Rep 28, 61
        LJQB 265, 65 LT 621, 55 JP 805, 3 Tax Cas 53, HL, 8(1) Digest (Reissue) 236, *1*.
    Incorporated Council of Law Reporting for England and Wales v Attorney-General [1971] 3 All

────────────────────────

a   [1978] 1 All ER 230
b   [1979] 1 All ER 588

ER 1029, [1972] Ch 73, [1971] 3 WLR 853, 47 Tax Cas 321, CA, 8(1) Digest (Reissue) 260, *137*.

Inland Revenue Comrs v Baddeley [1955] 1 All ER 525, [1955] AC 572, [1955] 2 WLR 552, 48 R & IT 157, 35 Tax Cas 661, 34 ATC 22, HL, 8(1) Digest (Reissue) 238, *6*.

Inland Revenue Comrs v Yorkshire Agricultural Society [1928] 1 KB 611, [1927] All ER Rep 536, 97 LJKB 100, 138 LT 192, 13 Tax Cas 58, CA, 28(1) Digest (Reissue) 475, *1704*.

Mariette, Re, Mariette v Governing Body of Aldenham School [1915] 2 Ch 284, [1914–15] All ER Rep 794, 84 LJ Ch 825, 113 LT 920, 8(1) Digest (Reissue) 257, *119*.

Mellody, Re, Brandwood v Haden [1918] 1 Ch 228, [1916–17] All ER Rep 324, 87 LJ Ch 185, 118 LT 155, 82 JP 128, 8(1) Digest (Reissue) 261, *138*.

Nottage, Re, Jones v Palmer [1895] 2 Ch 649, [1895–9] All ER Rep 1203, 64 LJ Ch 695, 73 LT 269, 12 R 571, CA, 8(1) Digest (Reissue) 300, *418*.

Scottish Burial Reform and Cremation Society Ltd v Glasgow City Corpn [1967] 3 All ER 215, [1968] AC 138, [1967] 3 WLR 1132, 132 JP 30, [1967] RA 272, 1967 SC (HL) 116, HL, 8(1) Digest (Reissue) 301, *424*.

Ward's Estate, Re, Ward v Ward (1937) 81 Sol Jo 397, 8(1) Digest (Reissue) 261, *140*.

Webber, Re, Barclays Bank Ltd v Webber [1954] 3 All ER 712, [1954] 1 WLR 1500, 8(1) Digest (Reissue) 265, *156*.

Weir v Crum-Brown [1908] AC 162, 77 LJPC 41, 98 LT 325, HL, 8(1) Digest (Reissue) 315, *549*.

Appeal

The first three defendants, Anthony Derek McMullen, Professor Sir Harold Thompson and Leonard Thomas Shipman, the trustees of the Football Association Youth Trust, appealed against the decision of the Court of Appeal[1] (Stamp and Orr LJJ, Bridge LJ dissenting) on 18th October 1978 dismissing the trustees' appeal from a judgment of Walton J[2] given on 13th July 1977 whereby he (i) allowed an appeal by the Crown from a decision of the Charity Commissioners for England and Wales, (ii) reversed the commissioners' determination that the trust was a charity, and should be entered in the register of charities under s 4 of the Charities Act 1960, and (iii) declared that the trust was not entitled to be registered as a charity because its objects were not charitable or exclusively charitable. The fourth defendant was, pursuant to RSC Ord 108, r 5(2), the Attorney-General. The facts are set out in the opinion of Lord Hailsham LC.

Andrew Morritt QC and *Spencer G Maurice* for the trustees.
David Rattee QC and *Christopher McCall* for the Crown.
John Mummery for the Attorney-General.

Their Lordships took time for consideration.

6th March. The following opinions were delivered.

LORD HAILSHAM OF ST MARYLEBONE LC. My Lords, by a deed dated 30th October 1972 between the Football Association Ltd, described as 'the donor', and three persons named as the original trustees the donor purported to set up a trust to be known as the Football Association Youth Trust. The sole question for decision in the appeal before the House is whether the deed was effective in setting up a valid charitable trust. The Charity Commissioners decided that it was so effective, overriding the objections of the Crown. Walton J[2] decided that it was not, and in his conclusion was supported by a majority (Stamp and Orr LJJ) of the Court of Appeal[1], who, however, in reaching this conclusion, did so for reasons not merely different from but, in some respects, diametrically opposed to the reasons which found favour with Walton J. Bridge

---

1   [1979] 1 All ER 588, [1979] 1 WLR 130
2   [1978] 1 All ER 230, [1978] 1 WLR 664

a LJ, dissenting from the majority, supported the view of the Charity Commissioners. There is thus ample room for a legitimate difference of opinion. Happily, in your Lordships' House, opinion appears to be substantially unanimous that the appeal should be allowed.

Four questions arose for decision below. In the first place neither the parties nor the judgments below were in agreement as to the proper construction of the trust deed itself. Clearly this is a preliminary debate which must be settled before the remaining *b* questions are even capable of decision. In the second place the trustees contend and the Crown disputes that, on the correct construction of the deed, the trust is charitable as being for the advancement of education. Thirdly, the trustees contend and the Crown disputes that if they are wrong on the second question the trust is charitable at least because it falls within the fourth class of Lord Macnaghten's categories as enumerated in *Income Tax Special Purposes Comrs v Pemsel*[1] as a trust beneficial to the community within *c* the spirit and intendment of the preamble to the statute 43 Eliz 1 c 4[2]. Fourthly, the trustees contend and the Crown disputes that, even if not otherwise charitable, the trust is a valid charitable trust as falling within s 1 of the Recreational Charities Act 1958, that is as a trust to provide or to assist in the provision of facilities for recreation or other leisure time occupation provided in the interests of social welfare.

In the events which happened, their Lordships have been greatly assisted by helpful *d* arguments from counsel for the trustees and the Crown and by a valuable contribution from counsel instructed on behalf of the Attorney-General as guardian of charities. Since we have reached the view that the trust is a valid educational charity their Lordships have not sought to hear argument nor, therefore, to reach a conclusion on any but the first two disputed questions in the dispute. Speaking for myself, however, I do not wish my absence of decision on the third or fourth points to be interpreted as an indorsement of *e* the majority judgments in the Court of Appeal nor as necessarily dissenting from the contrary views contained in the minority judgment of Bridge LJ. For me at least the answers to the third and fourth questions are still left entirely undecided.

I now turn to the question of construction, for which it is necessary that I reproduce the material portions of the deed. The first recital in the deed reads as follows:

f 'WHEREAS:—(1) The First Donor is desirous of establishing a charitable trust which would have as the main objects the furtherance of education of Schools and Universities in any part of the United Kingdom encouraging and facilitating the playing of Association Football or other games and sports at such Schools and Universities and thus assisting to ensure that due attention is given to the physical education and character development of pupils at such Schools and Universities as aforesaid as well as the development and occupation of their minds and the *g* organisation or provision or assistance in the organisation or provision of facilities for physical recreation for young people in the interests of social welfare in any part of the United Kingdom.'

Some reliance was placed on this recital in argument, but, since I do not find the remainder of the deed ambiguous I need only say that for the purposes of what follows I have drawn no assistance from it.

h The interpretation clause of the deed (cl 1), so far as material, reads as follows:

'(a) [Defines 'the Trust'] (b) [Defines 'the Trustees'] (c) "Schools" has the same meaning as in the Education Act 1944 (d) "Universities" means Universities, Training Colleges for Teachers, or other institutions of Further Education (including Professional and Technical Education approved by the Trustees) (e) [Defines 'the *j* Trust Fund'].'

The clause of the deed which is effectively for construction is cl 3, which I now reproduce in extenso. It reads:

1   [1891] AC 531 at 583, [1891–4] All ER Rep 28 at 55
2   Charitable Uses Act 1601

'THE objects of the Trust are:—

'(a) to organise or provide or assist in the organisation and provision of facilities
which will enable and encourage pupils of Schools and Universities in any part of
the United Kingdom to play Association Football or other games or sports and
thereby to assist in ensuring that due attention is given to the physical education and
development of such pupils as well as to the development and occupation of their
minds and with a view to furthering this object (i) to provide or assist in the
provision of Association Football or games or sports equipment of every kind for the
use of such pupils as aforesaid (ii) to provide or assist in the provision of courses
lectures demonstrations and coaching for pupils of Schools and Universities in any
part of the United Kingdom and for teachers who organise or supervise playing and
coaching of Association Football or other games or sports at such Schools and
Universities as aforesaid (iii) to promote provide or assist in the promotion and
provision of training colleges for the purpose of training teachers in the coaching of
Association Football or other games or sports at such Schools and Universities as
aforesaid (iv) to lay out manage equip and maintain or assist in the laying out
management equipment and maintenance of playing fields or appropriate indoor
facilities or accommodation (whether vested in the Trustees or not) to be used for
the teaching and playing of Association Football or other sports or games by such
pupils as aforesaid

'(b) to organise or provide or assist in the organisation or provision of facilities for
physical recreation in the interests of social welfare in any part of the United
Kingdom (with the object of improving the conditions of life for the boys and girls
for whom the same are provided) for boys and girls who are under the age of
twenty-one years and who by reason of their youth or social and economic
circumstances have need of such facilities.'

I pause here only to say that no question arises as to cl 3(b) above which clearly
corresponds to the language of the Recreational Charities Act 1958. Controversy
therefore revolves solely around cl 3(a), since it is obvious that, if this cannot be shown
to be solely for charitable purposes, the whole trust ceases to be a charitable trust. Walton
J[1], adopting for this purpose the construction propounded for the Crown, construed the
words between 'thereby' and 'object' where they occur in cl 3(a) of the deed as if they
'only express the draftsman's erroneous view of the effect of the earlier part of cl 3(a), and
cannot control the operation of that part'. Stamp LJ appears, though not quite
unequivocally, to differ. After reciting Walton J's view, he said[2]:

'In my view, however, the proper approach to the construction of para (a) is to
construe "physical education and development", which I find an elusive phrase, as
connoting something which the playing of association football will assist in
ensuring.'

And later[3]:

'But in relation to association football the settlor has made it clear that, for the
purposes of the trust, facilities which do enable and encourage pupils to play that
game are to be regarded as "thereby" assisting in ensuring that due attention is given
to their physical education and development.'

Orr LJ claimed[4] to prefer the view of Stamp LJ by saying that the proper approach to
the words in question is to construe 'physical education and development' as—

'denoting something which the playing of association football will assist in
ensuring, with the result that the trust has the single object of physical education
and development of the pupils.'

1   [1978] 1 All ER 230 at 239, [1978] 1 WLR 664 at 673
2   [1979] 1 All ER 588 at 591, [1979] 1 WLR 130 at 134
3   [1979] 1 All ER 588 at 591, [1979] 1 WLR 130 at 135
4   [1979] 1 All ER 588 at 594, [1979] 1 WLR 130 at 138

a

In his dissenting judgment Bridge LJ took a view fundamentally differing from any of the above. Since I agree with it entirely, I quote the entire passage[1]:

'For convenience of reference I set out the words of the clause which define the object divided into two parts: the first part is ". . . to organise or provide or assist in the organisation and provision of facilities which will enable and encourage pupils of Schools and Universities in any part of the United Kingdom to play Association

b

Football or other games or sports". The second part is: ". . . and thereby to assist in ensuring that due attention is given to the physical education and development of such pupils as well as to the development and occupation of their minds . . ." The ensuing words "and with a view to furthering this object" must refer back to both the first and second parts envisaged as defining a composite object to which all that follows in sub-clauses (i) to (iv) is subordinate. The judge, apparently confining his attention to the first part, declared[2] that this was "on its face simply a trust to

c

promote the playing of games". He explained[3] his disregard of the second part as based on acceptance of the submission that it only expresses "the draftsman's erroneous view of the effect of the [first part], and cannot control the operation of that part". With all respect to the judge, I am quite unable to accept this approach. I know of no canon of construction whereby one part of a document, being in no way repugnant, can be thus dismissed as expressing a mistaken interpretation by the

d

draftsman himself of what he intended by some other part. All parts of a document must be read as conveying the totality of the draftsman's intention and so far as possible harmonised on the premise that each part was included as having some positive role to play in expressing that intention. Applying these principles I can see no difficulty in harmonising the two parts of cl 3(a) or in assigning to both a significant effect in denoting the object which this clause empowers the trustees to

e

promote. The first part of the clause places no limitation on the kind of games or sports which are to be facilitated and encouraged and if it stood alone, would include purely sedentary games. But the second part makes clear that it is only such games or sports as are capable of promoting physical education or development as are intended. This is an obvious and simple demonstration of the necessity for giving some effect to the second part of the clause in controlling the operation of the first

f

part. I see no reason, however, why it should not be construed as indicating to the trustees not only the nature of the games or sports which they are to encourage but also the wider considerations they must keep in mind in deciding whether or not in any particular circumstances it is appropriate that particular sporting facilities should be provided at the expense of the trust.'

g

I agree with this opinion, and, as I understand them, also with the summaries of it propounded by my noble and learned friends Lords Keith and Russell to the effect that what the deed means is that the purpose of the settlor is to promote the physical education and development of pupils at schools and universities as an addition to such part of their education as relates to their mental education by providing the facilities and assistance to games and sports in the manner set out at greater length and in greater detail

h

in the enumerated sub-clauses of cl 3(a) of the deed.

By one passage in the reasoning of Bridge LJ which I have set out above, I have been particularly assisted to my conclusion on the point of construction. This was pointed out in the course of an argument advanced by counsel for the trustees in his reply. One thing which was conceded on both sides about the construction of the deed was that it could not apply to sedentary games like chess or games of cards. That this is so is apparent from

j

the whole clause of the deed, but the restrictive sense admitted to be its meaning could not be applied to what has been called the first part of the clause unless to the words between 'thereby' and 'object' are given a sense controlling and limiting the first part as

1   [1979] 1 All ER 588 at 595–596, [1979] 1 WLR 130 at 140
2   [1978] 1 All ER 230 at 236, [1978] 1 WLR 664 at 670
3   [1978] 1 All ER 230 at 239, [1978] 1 WLR 664 at 673

well as the second part of the clause in the manner contended for by the trustees. The
word 'thereby' cannot therefore bear the purely consequential meaning assigned to it by   *a*
the three judgments appealed from and must bear the controlling and purposive
meaning contended for by the trustees and supported by Bridge LJ. In short, in the
context, the words 'and thereby' bear, and can only bear, a meaning something like 'in
such a way as to' and not the meaning attributed to it on behalf of the Crown as
reflecting, whether erroneously on the part of the draftsman (as per Walton J[1]) or
correctly or incorrectly in the mind of the settlor (as per Stamp and Orr LJJ[2]) the results   *b*
automatically effected by the first part of the deed. Moreover, if this were not enough,
I find the word 'object' in the singular at the end of the phrase far more consistent with
this view than with the other.

On a proper analysis, therefore, I do not find cl 3(a) ambiguous. But, before I part with
the question of construction, I would wish to express agreement with a contention made
on behalf of the trustees and of the Attorney-General, but not agreed to on behalf of the   *c*
Crown, that in construing trust deeds the intention of which is to set up a charitable
trust, and in others too, where it can be claimed that there is an ambiguity, a benignant
construction should be given if possible. This was the maxim of the civil law: semper in
dubiis benigniora praeferenda sunt. There is a similar maxim in English law: ut res
magis valeat quam pereat. It certainly applies to charities when the question is one of
uncertainty (*Weir v Crum-Brown*[3]) and, I think, also where a gift is capable of two   *d*
constructions one of which would make it void and the other effectual (cf *Bruce v Deer
Presbytery*[4], *Houston v Burns*[5] per Lord Findlay LC and *Re Bain, Public Trustee v Ross*[6]). In
the present case I do not find it necessary to resort to benignancy in order to construe the
clause, but, had I been in doubt, I would certainly have been prepared to do so.

The views of the trial judge and of the Court of Appeal on the remaining questions
were obviously coloured largely by their construction of the deed from which I have   *e*
found it necessary to differ. So is my own, and I must now turn to the deed, construed
in the manner in which I have found it necessary to construe it, to consider whether it
sets up a valid charitable trust for the advancement of education.

It is admitted, of course, that the words 'charity' and 'charitable' bear, for the purposes
of English law and equity, meanings totally different from the senses in which they are
used in ordinary educated speech or, for instance, in the Authorised Version of the Bible   *f*
(contrast, for instance, the expression 'cold as charity' with the Authorised Version of
1 Corinthians 13 and both of these with the decisions in *Incorporated Council of Law
Reporting for England and Wales v Attorney-General*[7], *Inland Revenue Comrs v Yorkshire
Agricultural Society*[8], *Brisbane City Council v Attorney-General for Queensland*[9]). But I do not
share the view, implied by Stamp and Orr LJJ in the instant case[10], that the words
'education' and 'educational' bear, or can bear, for the purposes of the law of charity,   *g*
meanings different from those current in present day educated English speech. I do not
believe that there is such a difference. What has to be remembered, however, is that, as
Lord Wilberforce pointed out in *Re Hopkins' Will Trusts*[11] and in *Scottish Burial Reform and
Cremation Society Ltd v Glasgow City Corpn*[12], both the legal conception of charity, and
within it the educated man's ideas about education are not static, but moving and
changing. Both change with changes in ideas about social values. Both have evolved   *h*

1   [1978] 1 All ER 230 at 239, [1978] 1 WLR 664 at 673
2   [1979] 1 All ER 588 at 591, 594, [1979] 1 WLR 130 at 134, 138
3   [1908] AC 162 at 167
4   (1867) LR 1 Sc & Div 96 at 97
5   [1918] AC 337 at 341–342
6   [1930] 1 Ch 224 at 230, [1929] All ER Rep 387 at 390
7   [1971] 3 All ER 1029, [1972] Ch 73
8   [1928] 1 KB 611, [1927] All ER Rep 536
9   [1978] 3 All ER 30, [1979] AC 411
10 [1979] 1 All ER 588 at 591, 594–595, [1979] 1 WLR 130 at 135, 139
11 [1964] 3 All ER 46 at 51, [1965] Ch 669 at 678
12 [1967] 3 All ER 215 at 223, [1968] AC 138 at 154

with the years. In particular in applying the law to contemporary circumstances it is
a extremely dangerous to forget that thoughts concerning the scope and width of education
differed in the past greatly from those which are now generally accepted.

In saying this I do not in the least wish to cast doubt on *Re Nottage*[1], which was referred
to in both courts below and largely relied on by the Crown here. Strictly speaking *Re
Nottage*[1] was not a case about education at all. The issue there was whether the bequest
came into the fourth class of charity categorised in Lord Macnaghten's classification of
b 1891[2]. The mere playing of games or enjoyment of amusement or competition is not
per se charitable, nor necessarily educational, though they may (or may not) have an
educational or beneficial effect if diligently practised. Neither am I deciding in the
present case even that a gift for physical education per se and not associated with persons
of school age or just above would necessarily be a good charitable gift. That is a question
which the courts may have to face at some time in the future. But in deciding what is
c or is not an educational purpose for the young in 1980 it is not irrelevant to point out
what Parliament considered to be educational for the young in 1944 when, by the
Education Act of that year in ss 7 and 53 (which are still on the statute book), Parliament
attempted to lay down what was then intended to be the statutory system of education
organised by the state, and the duties of the local education authorities and the Minister
in establishing and maintaining the system. Those sections are so germane to the present
d issue that I cannot forbear to quote them both. Section 7 provides (in each of the sections
the emphasis being mine):

'The statutory system of public education shall be organised in three progressive
stages to be known as primary education, secondary education, and further
education; and it shall be the duty of the local education authority for every area, so
far as their powers extend, to contribute towards *the spiritual, moral, mental, and*
e   *physical development of the community by securing that efficient education throughout those*
stages shall be available to meet the needs of the population of their area'

and in s 53 of the same Act it is said:

'(1) It shall be the duty of every local education authority to secure that the
facilities for primary secondary and further education provided for their area include
f   adequate facilities for recreation *and social and physical training*, and for that purpose
a local education authority, with the approval of the Secretary of State, may establish
maintain and manage, or assist the establishment, maintenance, and management
of *camps, holiday classes, playing fields, play centres, and other places (including*
playgrounds, gymnasiums, and swimming baths not appropriated to any school or college),
at which facilities for recreation and for such training as aforesaid are available for persons
g   *receiving primary secondary or further education, and may organise games, expeditions*
and other activities for such persons, and may defray or contribute towards the expenses
thereof.
'(2) A local education authority, in making arrangements for the provision of
facilities or the organisation of activities under the powers conferred on them by the
last foregoing subsection shall, *in particular, have regard to the expediency of co-*
h   *operating with any voluntary societies or bodies whose objects include the provision of*
facilities or the organisation of activities of a similar character.'

There is no trace in these sections of an idea of education limited to the development
of mental vocational or practical skills, to grounds or facilities the special perquisite of
particular schools, or of any schools or colleges, or term time, or particular localities, and
j there is express recognition of the contribution which extra-curricular activities and
voluntary societies or bodies can play even in the promotion of the purely statutory
system envisaged by the Act. In the light of s 7 in particular I would be very reluctant
to confine the meaning of education to formal instruction in the classroom or even the

1   [1895] 2 Ch 649, [1895–9] All ER Rep 1203
2   See *Income Tax Special Purposes Comrs v Pemsel* [1891] AC 531 at 583, [1891–4] All ER Rep 28 at 55

playground, and I consider them sufficiently wide to cover all the activities envisaged by
the settlor in the present case. One of the affidavits filed on the part of the Crown *a*
referred to the practices of ancient Sparta. I am not sure that this particular precedent is
an entirely happy one, but from a careful perusal of Plato's Republic I doubt whether its
author would have agreed with Stamp LJ in regarding 'physical education and
development' as an elusive phrase, or as other than an educational charity, at least when
used in association with the formal education of the young during the period when they
are pupils of schools or in statu pupillari at universities.   *b*

It is, of course, true that no authority exactly in point could be found which is binding
on your Lordships in the instant appeal. Nevertheless, I find the first instance case of *Re
Mariette*[1], a decision of Eve J, both stimulating and instructive. Counsel for the Crown
properly reminded us that this concerned a bequest effectively tied to a particular
institution. Nevertheless, I cannot forbear to quote a phrase from the judgment, always
bearing in mind the danger of quoting out of context. Eve J said[2]:   *c*

> 'No one of sense could be found to suggest that between those ages [10 to 19] any
> boy can be properly educated unless at least as much attention is given to the
> development of his body as is given to the development of his mind.'

Apart from the limitation to the particular institution I would think that these words
apply as well to the settlor's intention in the instant appeal as to the testator's in *Re* *d*
Mariette[1], and I regard the limitation to the pupils of schools and universities in the
instant case as a sufficient association with the provision of formal education to prevent
any danger of vagueness in the object of the trust or irresponsibility or capriciousness in
application by the trustees. I am far from suggesting either that the concept of education
or of physical education even for the young is capable of indefinite extension. On the
contrary, I do not think that the courts have as yet explored the extent to which elements *e*
of organisation, instruction or the disciplined inculcation of information, instruction or
skill may limit the whole concept of education. I believe that in some ways it will prove
more extensive, in others more restrictive than has been thought hitherto. But it is clear
at least to me that the decision in *Re Mariette*[1] is not to be read in a sense which confines
its application for ever to gifts to a particular institution. It has been extended already in
Re Mellody[3] to gifts for annual treats for schoolchildren in a particular locality (another *f*
decision of Eve J), to playgrounds for children (*Re Chesters*[4], possibly *not* educational, but
referred to in *Inland Revenue Comrs v Baddeley*[5]); to a children's outing (*Re Ward's Estate*[6]),
to a prize for chess to boys and young men resident in the City of Portsmouth (*Re
Dupree's Deed Trusts*[7], a decision of Vaisey J), and for the furthering of the Boy Scouts'
movement by helping to purchase sites for camping, outfits etc (*Re Webber*[8], another
decision of Vaisey J). In that case Vaisey J is reported as saying[9]:   *g*

> 'I am very surprised to hear that anyone suggests that the Boy Scouts Movement,
> as distinguished from the Boy Scouts Association or the Boy Scouts Organisation, is
> other than an educational charity. I should have thought that it was well settled and
> well understood that the objects of the organisation of boy scouts were educational,
> and none the less educational by reason of the fact that the education is, no doubt,
> of a very special kind.'   *h*

It is important to remember that in the instant appeal we are dealing with the concept
of physical education and development of the young deliberately associated by the settlor

---

1 [1915] 2 Ch 284, [1914–15] All ER Rep 794
2 [1915] 2 Ch 284 at 288, [1914–15] All ER Rep 794 at 797
3 [1918] 1 Ch 228, [1916–17] All ER Rep 324
4 (25th July 1934) unreported   *j*
5 [1955] 1 All ER 525 at 536, [1955] AC 572 at 596
6 (1937) 81 Sol Jo 397
7 [1944] 2 All ER 443, [1945] Ch 16
8 [1954] 3 All ER 712, [1954] 1 WLR 1500
9 [1954] 3 All ER 712 at 713, [1954] 1 WLR 1500 at 1501

with the status of pupillage in schools or universities (of which, according to the evidence,
a about 95% are within the age group 17 to 22). We are not dealing with adult education,
physical or otherwise, as to which some considerations may be different. Whether one
looks at the statute or the cases, the picture of education when applied to the young
which emerges is complex and varied, but not, to borrow Stamp LJ's epithet, 'elusive'.
It is the picture of a balanced and systematic process of instruction, training and practice
containing, to borrow from s 7 of the 1944 Act, both spiritual, moral, mental and
b physical elements, the totality of which, in any given case, may vary with, for instance,
the availability of teachers and facilities, and the potentialities, limitations and individual
preferences of the pupils. But the totality of the process consists as much in the balance
between each of the elements as of the enumeration of the thing learned or the places in
which the activities are carried on. I reject any idea which would cramp the education
of the young within the school or university syllabus, confine it within the school or
c university campus, limit it to formal instruction, or render it devoid of pleasure in the
exercise of skill. It is expressly acknowledged to be a subject in which the voluntary
donor can exercise his generosity, and I can find nothing contrary to the law of charity
which prevents a donor providing a trust which is designed to improve the balance
between the various elements which go into the education of the young. That is what
in my view the object of the instant settlement seeks to do.
d   I am at pains to disclaim the view that the conception of this evolving, and therefore
not static, view of education is capable of infinite abuse or, even worse, proving void for
uncertainty. Quite apart from the doctrine of the benignant approach to which I have
already referred, and which undoubtedly comes to the assistance of settlors in danger of
attack for uncertainty, I am content to adopt the approach of my predecessor Lord
Loreburn LC in *Weir v Crum-Brown*[1], to which attention was drawn by counsel for the
e Attorney-General, that if the bequest to a class of persons, as here capable of application
by the trustees, or, failing them, the court, the gift is not void for uncertainty. Lord
Macnaghten also said[2]:

> 'The testator has taken pains to provide competent judges. It is for the trustees to
> consider and determine the value of the service on which a candidate may rest his
> claim to participate in the testator's bounty.'

f
   Mutatis mutandis, I think this kind of reasoning should apply here. Granted that the
question of application may present difficulties for the trustees, or, failing them, for the
court, nevertheless it is capable of being applied, for the concept in the mind of the settlor
is an object sufficiently clear, is exclusively for the advancement of education, and, in the
hands of competent judges, is capable of application.
   I also wish to be on my guard against the 'slippery slope' argument of which I see a
g reflection in Stamp LJ's reference to 'hunting, shooting and fishing'. It seems to me that
that is an argument with which Vaisey J dealt effectively in *Re Dupree's Deed Trusts*[3] 126
in which he validated the chess prize. He said:

> 'I think this case may be a little near the line, and I decide it without attempting
> to lay down any general propositions. One feels, perhaps, that one is on rather a
h > slippery slope. If chess, why not draughts: if draughts, why not bezique, and so on,
> through to bridge, whist, and, by another route, stamp collecting and the acquisition
> of birds' eggs? When those particular pursuits come up for consideration in
> connection with the problem whether or no there is in existence a charitable trust,
> the problem will have to be faced and dealt with.'

   My Lords, for these reasons I reach the conclusion that the trust is a valid charitable gift
j for the advancement of education, which, after all, is what it claims to be. The conclusion
follows that the appeal should be allowed, the judgments appealed from be reversed, the

---

1   [1908] AC 162 at 167
2   [1908] AC 162 at 169
3   [1944] 2 All ER 443 at 445, [1945] Ch 16 at 20

order for registration made by the commissioners restored, and that costs here and in the Court of Appeal should follow the event. Costs before Walton J were the subject of an agreement between the parties. The Attorney-General asked for his costs against the Crown in the event of its failure and in my opinion is also entitled to an order for these.

LORD DIPLOCK. My Lords, I have had the advantage of reading in draft the speech prepared by my noble and learned friend on the Woolsack, and I agree with it. For the reasons given by him I would allow the appeal.

LORD SALMON. My Lords, I, too, agree with the speech of my noble and learned friend on the Woolsack and, for the reasons which he states, I would allow the appeal.

LORD RUSSELL OF KILLOWEN. My Lords, the ground in this appeal has been so amply covered in the speech of my noble and learned friend Lord Hailsham LC that I can be brief.

The question is whether the trusts of the deed, in particular of cl 3(a), are exclusively for charitable purposes as being for the promotion of education. (I expressly say nothing one way or the other on the questions which, if the answer is in the affirmative, do not arise: namely under the fourth of Lord Macnaghten's categories[1], and under s 1 of the Recreational Charities Act 1958.)

I cannot accept the approach to construction of cl 3(a) which jettisons the second part of the first sentence ('and thereby') as being no more than the draftsman's idea of the outcome or possible outcome of the provision of facilities under the first part. As has been pointed out the second part has at least the operative function of demonstrating that 'games' does not include sedentary pastimes. In my opinion in deciding whether the clause demonstrates that the purpose of the deed is the promotion of education the clause must be considered so to speak 'in the round', with all parts contributing to the decision. Those persons who are intended to be benefited are all pupils undergoing a formal course of education in the narrower sense of that word. I would construe the stated object of the trust as being to promote the physical education and development of pupils as supplementary to the provision made for them by those formal courses for their mental development and occupation by providing facilities to enable and encourage them to play football and other games and sports. The four sub-paragraphs of cl 3(a) do not depart from this concept: they are all provisions expressed to be with a view to furthering it; sub-para (i) provides for the provision of relevant equipment for the use of such pupils; sub-para (ii) deals with the provision of courses, lectures, demonstrations and coaching (clearly in the relevant field) for such pupils, and also for teachers who organise or supervise playing of the relevant games as sports *at* such schools and universities, the benefit in such latter cases to the pupils being at one remove; sub-para (iii) relates to the provision of training colleges to train such last-mentioned teachers; sub-para (iv) relates to the provision etc of outdoor or indoor facilities to be used for such teaching of and playing by such pupils. I have summarised those sub-paragraphs, but not, I consider, so as to depart from their fair construction.

I appreciate that the present trust is different from instances (in the cases) in which provision is made by the provision of facilities etc for the encouragement of sports at a particular school or other educational establishment, where their supervision is under the direct control of the body there responsible for the formal education in the narrower sense of the pupils, and where the facilities are for use during educational terms. But suppose an area containing three schools, short of space for (for example) the physical exercise involved in playing football; suppose the provision by the trust of a field equipped for that purpose, for the use only of pupils of such schools, under the management and control of an appointee of the trustees; that would not in my opinion deny to the trust a sufficient nexus with the education (in the narrower sense) of those pupils to qualify the trust as one of which the purpose is the promotion of education. Nor so if the facility was available to those pupils out of term time.

The crux of the decision of the majority in the Court of Appeal appears to be (a) the

---

1   See *Income Tax Special Purposes Comrs v Pemsel* [1891] AC 531 at 583, [1891–4] All ER Rep 28 at 55

assertion that the promotion of physical education and development by the encourage-
a ment of the playing of games and sports is not a charitable purpose and (b) it is not
converted to a charitable purpose by limiting the objects of the trust to those who happen
to be pupils of schools and universities. I reserve my view on the first assertion; but in
my opinion the second does a good deal less than justice to current views on the value of
what is proposed as a contribution to the concept of education of the young. I find
myself in sympathy with the views expressed by Bridge LJ[1], fully quoted by my noble
b and learned friend on the Woolsack.

In my opinion this appeal should be allowed on the ground that this trust is established
for charitable purposes only, the promotion of education.

LORD KEITH OF KINKEL. My Lords, I have had the advantage of reading in
draft the speech of my noble and learned friend Lord Hailsham LC, and I agree with it.

In my opinion there are only two points in this appeal which require to be considered
c and resolved in order to arrive at the correct disposal of it.

The first point is concerned with the true construction and effect of the second branch
of cl 3(a) of the trust deed, which opens with the words 'and thereby'. It was argued for
the Crown that this did no more than express an erroneous view on the part of the
draftsman as to the consequences of organising or providing sporting facilities such as are
described in the earlier part of the clause. This argument I cannot accept. In the first
d place the words must surely be read, if such reading is reasonably open, as intended to
have some operative effect, rather than as being mere surplusage. It was conceded that
the words must have at least some effect, by excluding sedentary games from the
category of those for which facilities might lawfully be provided under the first part of
the clause. I consider it to be a correct conclusion, taking the words in their context, that
they are intended to express the main abstract purpose of the deed, namely that of
e securing that the due attention is given to the physical education and development of
pupils at schools and universities in the United Kingdom.

The second point is whether a trust having this object is properly to be regarded as
constituted for exclusively charitable purposes as being one for the advancement of
education. A trust for the mere promotion of a particular sport or sports does not qualify
as charitable under this head: see *Re Nottage*[2]. On the other hand a gift to a particular
f educational establishment for the purpose of improving the sporting facilities available
to the pupils there does so qualify: see *Re Mariette*[3]. In the present case the purpose of the
trust is plainly to improve the sporting facilities, particularly as regards the playing of
association football, available to pupils undergoing formal courses of education at schools
and universities in the United Kingdom. It has long been recognised that the provision
of such facilities tends to promote the success of formal education processes with which
g it is associated. In my opinion the link which by this trust deed is required to be
established between the facilities to be provided and persons undergoing courses of
formal education at schools and universities must necessarily lead to the conclusion that
the trust is for the promotion of education, and that its purposes are therefore exclusively
charitable.

In the circumstances it is unnecessary to consider whether the trust is apt to qualify as
h charitable under the fourth category in *Pemsel's* case[4], or under the Recreational Charities
Act 1958, and I reserve my opinion on these matters.

My Lords, I would allow the appeal.

Appeal allowed.

j Solicitors: *Cheethams* (for the trustees); *Solicitor of Inland Revenue*; *Treasury Solicitor.*

Mary Rose Plummer   Barrister.

---

1   [1979] 1 All ER 588 at 595–596, [1979] 1 WLR 130 at 140
2   [1895] 2 Ch 649, [1895–9] All ER Rep 1203
3   [1915] 2 Ch 284, [1914–15] All ER Rep 794
4   [1891] AC 531 at 583, [1891–4] All ER Rep 28 at 55

Engineers' and Managers' Association v Advisory, Conciliation and Arbitration Service and another (No 2)

HOUSE OF LORDS

LORD WILBERFORCE, LORD DIPLOCK, LORD EDMUND-DAVIES, LORD KEITH OF KINKEL AND LORD SCARMAN

5th, 6th, 10th DECEMBER 1979, 6th MARCH 1980

Trade union – Recognition – Reference of recognition issue to Advisory, Conciliation and Arbitration Service – Duty of Service to ascertain opinion of workers to whom issue relates – Whether Service has a discretion to defer making inquiries – Employment Protection Act 1975, ss 12, 14.

In the course of a recognition dispute at an engineering factory where about 300 professional engineers were employed, a professional association ('UKAPE') which was not affiliated to the Trades Union Congress ('the TUC') applied on 9th July 1976 to the Advisory, Conciliation and Arbitration Service ('ACAS') for recognition for the purposes of collective bargaining at the factory. Two unions ('EMA' and 'TASS') which were affiliated to the TUC also wished to represent the professional engineers in collective bargaining at the factory. At the end of 1976 a complaint by TASS to the TUC about EMA's recruiting of new members at the factory was referred to a disputes committee of the TUC in accordance with the TUC's rules. On 16th March 1977 the committee decided that EMA should cease recruiting at the factory, existing EMA members there should transfer to TASS, and EMA should not proceed with any claim for recognition. In defiance of the committee's decision, EMA referred the recognition issue to ACAS on 27th April. ACAS had not at that stage reached a decision on UKAPE's application and was thus faced with two applications for recognition and also the decision of the TUC's disputes committee. It delayed taking any action until June when, under pressure to carry out its duty under ss 12[a] and 14(1)[b] of the Employment Protection Act 1975 to 'ascertain the opinions of workers to whom the [recognition] issue relates', it drafted a questionnaire asking the professional engineers which trade union they wished to represent them. EMA agreed to the form of the questionnaire but UKAPE did not and while that was being discussed EMA issued a writ against the TUC on 13th October claiming, inter alia, that the decision of the disputes committee was ultra vires and invalid. Because of the issue of the writ, ACAS postponed sending out the questionnaire and on 14th December informed EMA and UKAPE that 'for the time being' it could not proceed with its inquiries in relation to the recognition issue. On 25th January 1978 EMA brought an action against ACAS seeking a declaration that ACAS was in breach of its duties under the Act and that it was bound to investigate and report on the recognition issue. On 7th April 1978 the judge held that ACAS had a discretion to postpone the

---

a   Section 12, so far as material, provides:

'(1) . . . when a recognition issue is referred to the Service under section 11 above the Service shall examine the issue, shall consult all parties who it considers will be affected by the outcome of the reference and shall make such inquiries as it thinks fit . . .

'(4) If the issue has not been settled and the reference not withdrawn the Service shall prepare a written report setting out its findings, any advice in connection with those findings and any recommendation for recognition and the reasons for it, or, where no such recommendation is made, the reasons for not making any recommendation . . .'

b   Section 14(1), so far as material, provides: 'In the course of its inquiries into a recognition issue under section 12 . . . above the Service shall ascertain the opinions of workers to whom the issue relates by any means it thinks fit . . .'

investigations and, because of the uncertainty existing at the time when ACAS made that
a decision, it had not wrongly exercised its discretion. EMA appealed. By the time the
appeal came on for hearing in May 1979 the date for the trial of EMA's action against the
TUC had been fixed for March 1980. The Court of Appeal understood ACAS to submit
that it did not intend to proceed with its inquiries until the litigation between EMA and
the TUC had been finally concluded, and on that basis the Court of Appeal[c] held that,
taking the position as at the date of the hearing of the appeal, ACAS had erred in law in
b deferring its inquiries until the outcome of the litigation between EMA and the TUC.
The Court of Appeal accordingly granted the declaration sought by EMA. ACAS
appealed to the House of Lords and there contended that its submissions had been
misunderstood by the Court of Appeal and that it had merely postponed its inquiries 'for
the time being' when EMA had issued its writ against the TUC and had thereafter
periodically reviewed that decision.

c
    Held (Lord Diplock and Lord Keith dissenting) – The appeal would be allowed for the
following reasons—
    (i) Although ACAS was under a statutory duty under s 12(1) and (4) of the 1975 Act to
proceed with reasonable expedition in the preparation of its report, it had power to defer
its inquiries, consultations or report if that would promote the improvement of industrial
d relations (including the extension of collective bargaining) or if a failure to defer its
inquiries, consultations or report would worsen industrial relations or put the extension
of collective bargaining at risk. Since ascertaining the views of the employees to whom
the recognition issue related was part of the inquiries ACAS was required to make, it
followed that it had a discretion to defer ascertaining those views if it was in the interests
of industrial relations and collective bargaining so to do (see p 898 g, p 903 j, p 910 b c and
e e and p 912 b, post).
    (ii) Whether ACAS had deferred ascertaining the views of the employees for an
unreasonable length of time depended on whether ACAS's decision so to do was one
which no reasonable body charged with the statutory duties imposed on ACAS could
have arrived at. Having regard to (a) the fact that ACAS had only suspended its inquiries
'for the time being' and not until the litigation between EMA and the TUC was finally
f resolved, and (b) the fact that ACAS thereafter reviewed its decision periodically, ACAS's
decision could not be said to have been unreasonable (see p 898 g, p 904 g to p 905 c, p 910
e to g, p 911 g h and p 912 a b and g, post).
    Decision of Court of Appeal [1979] 3 All ER 227 reversed.

Notes
    For the reference of a recognition issue to the Advisory, Conciliation and Arbitration
g Service, see Supplement to 38 Halsbury's Laws (3rd Edn) para 677A.2.
    For the Employment Protection Act 1975, ss 12, 14, see 45 Halsbury's Statutes (3rd
Edn) 2384, 2386.

Cases referred to in opinions
h *Grunwick Processing Laboratories Ltd v Advisory, Conciliation and Arbitration Service* [1978]
    1 All ER 338, [1978] AC 655, [1978] 2 WLR 277, [1978] ICR 231, CA and HL.
Lim Poh Choo v Camden and Islington Area Health Authority [1979] 2 All ER 910, [1980] AC
    174, [1979] 3 WLR 44, HL.
United Kingdom Association of Professional Engineers v Advisory, Conciliation and Arbitration
    Service p 612, ante.

j   **Appeal**
    By a writ dated 25th January 1978, the plaintiffs, the Engineers' and Managers'
Association ('EMA'), brought an action against the first defendants, the Advisory,
Conciliation and Arbitration Service ('ACAS'), claiming the following relief: (i) a

declaration that ACAS, in refusing and/or failing to investigate and/or report on a
recognition issue dated 27th April 1977 concerning all category 3 and 4 engineers not   *a*
covered by the Technical, Administrative and Supervisory Section ('TASS') procedural
classes at GEC Reactor Equipment Ltd, Whetstone, Leicestershire, referred to it under
s 11 of the Employment Protection Act 1975, on the sole ground that the issue was
alleged to be the subject-matter of a complaint to the Trades Union Congress ('the TUC')
of alleged breaches of the TUC Disputes Principles and Procedures[1] ('the Bridlington
agreement'), was acting in breach of its statutory duties and unlawfully, (ii) a declaration   *b*
that ACAS in refusing and/or failing to investigate and/or report on the recognition issue
on the sole ground that the issue was the subject-matter of a complaint to the TUC was
acting in breach of its statutory duties and unlawfully, (iii) a declaration that ACAS in
refusing or failing to investigate and/or report on the recognition issue on the ground
that the issue was the subject of a High Court action between the TUC and EMA
concerning the application of the Bridlington agreement was acting in breach of its   *c*
statutory duties and unlawfully, (iv) a declaration that ACAS in refusing and/or failing to
investigate and/or report on the recognition issue on the sole ground that the issue had
. been the subject-matter of a complaint to the TUC and that a disputes committee of the
TUC had issued an award thereon was acting in breach of its statutory duties and
unlawfully, and (v) a declaration that ACAS was bound in pursuance of its statutory
duties under s 12 of the 1975 Act to investigate or report on the issue which had been   *d*
referred to it. By notice of motion dated 10th February 1978 EMA applied for
declarations in the same terms as those in the writ. On 3rd March 1978 the United
Kingdom Association of Professional Engineers ('UKAPE') was joined as second defendant
to the proceedings by leave of Templeman J. The parties agreed that the motion should
be treated as the trial of the action. On 7th April 1978 Oliver J[2] dismissed the motion.
On 14th May 1979 the Court of Appeal[3] (Lord Denning MR, Lawton and Cumming-   *e*
Bruce LJJ) allowed an appeal by EMA and granted a declaration that ACAS was bound in
pursuance of its statutory duties under s 12 of the 1975 Act to investigate and/or report
on the issue which had been referred to it. ACAS appealed to the House of Lords
pursuant to leave granted by the House on 27th June 1979. The facts are set out in the
opinion of Lord Scarman.

f

Peter Scott QC and *Henry Brooke* for ACAS.
Simon Goldblatt QC and *Peter C L Clark* for EMA.
Mr C K Hickling, deputy general secretary, for UKAPE.

Their Lordships took time for consideration.

g

6th March. The following opinions were delivered.

LORD WILBERFORCE. I agree that this appeal must be allowed for the reasons
given by my noble and learned friend Lord Scarman.

h

LORD DIPLOCK. My Lords, this appeal raises the question whether the Advisory,
Conciliation and Arbitration Service ('ACAS') was in breach of its statutory duties under
ss 12 and 14 of the Employment Protection Act 1975, when over a period of two years
from December 1977 to December 1979 it refused to proceed with its inquiries into a
recognition dispute that had been referred to it by a trade union, the Engineers' and
Managers' Association ('EMA') in April 1977.   *j*

---

1   (1976)
2   [1978] ICR 875
3   [1979] 3 All ER 227, [1979] 1 WLR 1113

a Largely owing to uncertainty as to what happened at the hearing in the Court of Appeal, I have found this a difficult case to decide. My mind has wavered often both during the hearing in this House and thereafter. Moreover, since the hearing an event has occurred which makes the outcome of this appeal to your Lordships' House of no practical importance to either party to it. The reason on which ACAS relied as justifying the lengthy suspension of its inquiries into the recognition dispute was the contemporaneous existence throughout that period of a pending action between EMA *b* and the Trades Union Congress ('TUC'). That action has now been settled and what ACAS regarded as a continuing obstacle to its proceeding expeditiously with its inquiries has been removed.

In these circumstances it might be thought that a body of whose title 'conciliation' forms a conspicuous part might have withdrawn its appeal, even after the conclusion of the hearing, when an event occurred which deprived success or failure in it of any *c* practical consequences other than in the incidence of costs. ACAS, however, has expressed a wish that this House should proceed to delivery of judgment. The reason why ACAS wants this to be done is for its own guidance as to the limits of its discretion to suspend its inquiries into particular recognition disputes if circumstances should again arise that are analogous to those which were present in the instant case.

My Lords, the appeal is one on which, as will appear, your Lordships are narrowly *d* divided and that division of opinion is, in the main, due to incertitude as to what happened in the course of the hearing in the Court of Appeal. I fear that this may diminish any guidance which this House is able to give.

The relevant facts are to be found set out in the speech of my noble and learned friend Lord Scarman to which reference may be made. I will not take time in repeating them here.

e No one disputes that ACAS has a very wide discretion how it will conduct a recognition issue that has been referred to it under s 11 of the 1975 Act; but conduct it, in some way or another, it must. It cannot decline to proceed on a reference, untimely though it may think the reference to be, except in the limited circumstances described in s 12(2), which have no application to the instant case. Having started on a reference, ACAS cannot abdicate its functions under ss 12 and 14 to examine the issue and to consult all parties *f* who it considers will be affected by the outcome, to ascertain the opinions of workers to whom the issue relates, to make such other inquiries as it thinks fit and to make a written report conformably with s 12(4). The crucial question for the Court of Appeal and for this House is whether ACAS's refusals since November and December 1977 to proceed further with the conjoined references of UKAPE and EMA (which I will refer to as 'the reference') does amount to an abdication of its statutory functions, or, as the majority of *g* your Lordships think, was a mere adjournment of the proceedings on the reference in the lawful exercise of a statutory discretion to decide how references can best be conducted.

My Lords, the Court of Appeal was greatly influenced by the consideration that the persons most vitally affected by ACAS's decision to postpone proceeding with the reference were the group of more than 300 professional engineers in the two highest *h* grades employed at Whetstone ('the unrepresented engineers') who were excluded from a place at the collective bargaining table with their employers but wanted to be represented there by a trade union of their own choice. They were not parties to the reference; they had no means of hastening its progress; yet, so long as the recognition issue remained pending before ACAS and ACAS were unwilling to issue a report, their right to be represented at a collective bargaining would remain in limbo. This is because *j* with two rival unions, EMA and UKAPE, as claimants for recognition by the employers against the opposition of yet a third union, the Technical, Administrative and Supervisory Section of the Amalgamated Union of Engineering Workers ('TASS'), the employers could not safely settle the issue by agreement with either of the claimant unions, lest ACAS in its report should ultimately recommend recognition of the other, with all the consequences which that would entail under ss 15 and 16 of the 1975 Act.

A recognition issue relating to the unrepresented engineers had been referred to ACAS by UKAPE as long ago as July 1976. The rival claim of EMA to represent the same group a was referred to ACAS as a recognition issue in April 1977. By the time the question of the lawfulness of ACAS's inaction since November 1977 came before the Court of Appeal in May 1979, the unrepresented engineers' right of representation at collective bargaining had already been in limbo for close on three years covering successive rounds of pay bargaining during a period of inflation and erosion of differentials. Unless ACAS were to change its mind their representation would remain in limbo until March 1980 at the b earliest. By then ACAS's failure to proceed with the reference would have lasted for some two and a half years and the reference itself for nearly four years without any report being forthcoming.

My Lords, the long title of the 1975 Act makes it clear that the purpose of Part I is to establish machinery for the improvement of industrial relations. ACAS provides the most important part of that machinery, and s 1(2), which defines the functions of ACAS, c makes clear the intention of Parliament in 1975 that, so far as practicable, collective bargaining as to terms and conditions of employment should be extended. To the great majority of the people of this country their contracts of employment are the most important contracts in their lives. The wages for which these contracts provide determine the material standard of living which they and their dependent families can enjoy. In providing, by means of the reference of recognition issues to ACAS, machinery d for coercing employers to recognise trade unions as representing groups of workers in collective bargaining the dominant intention of Parliament must have been to benefit the groups represented rather than to subordinate this to increasing the power of the trade unions; though such increased power might be an inevitable and not unwelcome by-product.

If this be so, ACAS, in exercising its functions in relation to recognition issues referred e to it under s 12 where there are rival trade unions seeking to represent the workers to whom the issue relates, cannot, consistently with the policy of the Act, sit back and passively await the outcome of a power struggle between rival unions fought out in some other forum of their choice and in their own good time. Once the issue has been referred to it ACAS is, in my view, required to play a more active role than this in protecting the interests of those workers whom Parliament intended to be the primary beneficiaries of f the machinery which the Act provides for dealing with recognition. In particular ACAS should bear in mind that where there are rival unions claiming to be recognised the practical effect of prolonging the reference by its own inaction will be to prolong the period during which those workers will, for the reasons I have indicated, continue to be deprived of the possibility of acquiring the right to be represented at all in collective bargaining about the terms of their contracts of employment. ACAS is in my view g under a duty to play an active part in ending the impasse.

The continuing deprivation suffered by the unrepresented engineers of any practical possibility of obtaining representation in collective bargaining with the employers so long as ACAS refrained from issuing a report seems to me to be relevant also to the question whether the Court of Appeal was right in taking into consideration events that had occurred and in particular the time that had elapsed since the final judgment of h Oliver J[1] against which the appeal was brought. Additionally to the reasons given by your Lordships for holding that the Court of Appeal was entitled to do so, provided that it could be done without unfairness to ACAS, I would add the fact that the unrepresented engineers, two-thirds of whom had in December 1977 petitioned ACAS to proceed with the reference and report before March 1978, had no means themselves of hurrying up the progress either of the reference itself or of the action by EMA against the TUC on j which ACAS had decided that any further progress in the reference should depend.

My Lords, I do not underestimate the difficulty of the task that confronted ACAS

---

1   [1978] ICR 875

when called on to examine and report on the recognition issues that had been referred to
a it by UKAPE and EMA. The problem of what trade union, if any, should represent the
unrepresented engineers in collective bargaining with their employers was bedevilled by
the rivalry of the three trade unions who had been engaging in competitive recruiting
campaigns among them. Longest on the scene had been TASS, a union affiliated to the
TUC, a member of the Confederation of Shipbuilding and Engineering Unions ('CSEU')
and, as such, a party to the industry-wide procedural agreement with the Engineering
b Employers' Federation ('EEF') and to the existing collective bargaining agreements at
Whetstone as representing, inter alios, some lower grades of engineers. Its recruiting
campaign among the unrepresented engineers however had had but minimal success
despite the fact that it had extended over several years. EMA was affiliated to the TUC
but it was not a member of the CSEU, as its membership had until recently been
confined to comparable grades of employees in the electricity supply industry. It had
c succeeded in recruiting rather more than one-third of the unrepresented engineers at
Whetstone. The third claimant union was UKAPE; it is not affiliated to the TUC and is
not a member of the CSEU. It had been less successful in recruiting the unrepresented
engineers than EMA but, in the short time that it had been on the scene, it had already
done better than TASS. The consequences of this inter-union rivalry was complicated by
the intervention of the TUC in application of the Bridlington principles[1]. By the time
d EMA had become a party to the reference in April 1977 conciliation between EMA and
TASS by use of TUC machinery had failed and EMA had already been directed by an
award of a disputes committee of the TUC to cease recruiting at Whetstone and not to
proceed with any claim for recognition. These directions were confirmed on 28th
September 1977 by the General Council of the TUC under threat of disaffiliation. So
there was the possibility that if EMA persisted in continuing as a party to the reference
e it would do so as an unaffiliated union. The initiation by EMA of its action against the
TUC claiming that these directions were invalid and the TUC's undertaking given on the
application for an interlocutory injunction meant that the question whether EMA would
continue to be a union affiliated to the TUC would not be answered for an indefinite
period dependent on when EMA's action against the TUC was settled or came on for trial
and judgment was delivered in it. At the time of ACAS's decision in December 1977 to
f put a halt for the time being to the proceedings on the reference, it was justifiably
thought by ACAS that the period of uncertainty would be short; but by the time the
matter came before the Court of Appeal it was plain that it would continue until at least
March 1980, and from what it had been told in the course of the hearing the court was
under the impression, whether mistakenly or not, that ACAS's continuing intention,
from which it had never deviated, was to await the decision of that action before
g proceeding any further with the reference.

My Lords, the difficulties arising out of doubts as to the future status of EMA as a trade
union affiliated to the TUC or whether, if its then current action against the TUC should
fail, EMA would continue to be a party to the reference may well have needed to be
resolved before ACAS felt justified in deciding whether to make a recommendation for
the recognition of either of the claimants in the reference, EMA or UKAPE. But the Act
h requires ACAS to come to a decision *whether or not* to make a recommendation for
recognition in the circumstances as they exist when the reference is proceeding, not to
wait indefinitely for those circumstances to change. Even if the circumstances are such
that it finds itself unable to make any recommendation it must none the less prepare a
written report which must set out its reasons for not making any recommendation for
recognition, the findings on which these reasons are based and any advice it thinks
j appropriate to give in connection with those findings. Its advice need not be directed
only to the trade unions and employers who are the parties to the reference, but may be
proffered also to the persons most vitally affected by the report, the workers to whom the
recognition issue related. The advice may indicate what change of circumstances would

---

1   See TUC Disputes Principles and Procedures (1976)

be likely to lead ACAS to recommend the recognition of some particular trade union for the purpose of collective bargaining on behalf of the unrepresented engineers, whether *a* that union was claimant in the reference or not. This, as I pointed out, was what in effect ACAS did in *United Kingdom Association of Professional Engineers v Advisory, Conciliation and Arbitration Service*[1] which this House heard immediately before the instant case.

This is not to say that ACAS has no discretion to postpone further progress with a reference for a reasonable time if it thinks that the postponement is likely to enable it to make a recommendation or to ascertain with greater certainty the circumstances which *b* are likely to exist when its decision either to make or not to make a recommendation will take effect. But the existence of uncertainty as to the status of one of the claimant unions as an affiliate of the TUC is in itself a relevant circumstance which may justify making no recommendation for recognition; and, once it is plain that the uncertainty is likely to continue for so long a period that it will cover successive rounds of negotiations of pay claims, ACAS in my view would be abdicating its functions under s 12 if it did not then *c* proceed with the reference.

In the instant case it was not plain that EMA's status as an affiliated union would remain undecided for more than a very few months when ACAS made its decision in December 1977 not to proceed with the next step in the reference until the action by EMA against the TUC had been disposed of; nor do I think that it was plain in April 1978 when the trial took place before Oliver J. By May 1979, however, when the matter came *d* before the Court of Appeal it had become abundantly clear that EMA's future status as an affiliated union of the TUC would not be decided until March 1980 at the earliest and not even then if the action, as well it might be, were taken to appeal. It may be that the Court of Appeal was mistaken in its belief that ACAS had by that date already reached a final decision that, unless required by the court to do so, it would take no further step in the reference until EMA's affiliated status had been resolved; but another eight months *e* elapsed before the matter came before this House. It was then plain that ACAS from first to last had never once deviated from that policy and had no present intention of departing from it. So, in view of the light that its conduct since May 1978 has thrown on its intentions then, I would uphold the judgment of the Court of Appeal[2] declaring that ACAS was under a statutory duty to get on with the next step in the reference, and this involved ascertaining the opinions of the unrepresented engineers. *f*

It remains to deal with the two grounds on which ACAS has relied to justify its policy of waiting until the action between EMA and the TUC had been disposed of. Both of them as it seems to me confirm ACAS's failure to appreciate what the 1975 Act requires of it. The first is ACAS's contention that the blame for the long delay in ascertaining EMA's future status as an affiliated union rests with EMA itself for 'dragging its feet' in its action against the TUC. This may be so; it was a matter of disputed fact before the *g* Court of Appeal; but like Cumming-Bruce LJ I do not think it matters whether it is so or not. A reference of a recognition issue to ACAS bears no resemblance to a lis between the employers and the trade unions whose claim to recognition by those employers has been refused. It may affect the interests of other unions and of many other persons; it is bound to affect vitally the interests of the workers to whom the issue relates. In granting a wide discretion to ACAS as to the way a reference is to be conducted Parliament should *h* not be taken to have intended that the workers' interests in the outcome of the reference should be subordinated to those of the trade unions who were seeking to be recognised as representing them or should be allowed to suffer because of tactics adopted in the reference by any of those unions. Part of ACAS's functions must surely be to do its best to prevent this happening.

The second matter is ACAS's claim that to proceed to the next stage in the reference, *j* the ascertainment of the opinions of workers to whom the issue relates, would have

---

1 Page 612, ante
2 [1979] 3 All ER 227, [1979] 1 WLR 1113

necessitated the putting of hypothetical questions so long as the action between EMA and
a the TUC was undecided, and that hypothetical questions would not produce answers that
ACAS could treat as reliable.   The unrepresented engineers are men with professional
qualifications and presumably not of the lowest level of intelligence.   I do not find it
credible that they are incapable of understanding and answering the simple questions
posed in the questionnaire that ACAS had prepared in September 1977 or, if ACAS
thinks fit, additional questions involving the hypotheses (a) that EMA would be
b disaffiliated from the TUC or (b) that it would withdraw its claim to recognition.   The
answers to those questions would represent the current opinions of the workers on them,
however ill-informed their opinions might appear to be to ACAS with its great experience
of industrial relations.   From the various ways in which it has been put by ACAS in
argument, it is clear to me that ACAS's real objection to proceeding to ascertain the
opinions of the unrepresented engineers, whether by means of a questionnaire or in
c some other way, is that it did not think that those opinions, if obtained at a time when
EMA's affiliated status was undecided, would provide material on which they would feel
able to base any recommendation for recognition.   Assuming that this were so, and
ACAS must be the judge of this, it may be a reason for its reporting that it does not make
any recommendation for recognition.   It is not in my view a valid reason for refusing to
comply with its statutory duty under s 14 to ascertain the opinions of workers to whom
d the issue relates in the circumstances as they now exist, which included uncertainty as to
EMA's status.

So, on the ground that ACAS had, by May 1979, demonstrated that it had not simply
exercised a discretion how the reference should be conducted but had abdicated its
statutory functions under s 12 to go on with the reference, I would have dismissed this
appeal.

e
LORD EDMUND-DAVIES.   My Lords, this appeal is concerned with the duties and
responsibilities imposed on ACAS by the Employment Protection Act 1975 and to the
extent to which its manner of discharging (or neglecting) those duties and responsibilities
is open to be controlled by the courts.   The outcome of the appeal turns, in particular, on
whether ACAS is fettered in deferring the disposal of a recognition issue referred to it
f under s 11(1) of the Act.

The relevant dates are startling, for it was as long ago as 9th July 1976 that UKAPE
referred its recognition issue to ACAS, and it was on 27th April 1977 that the rival claim
of EMA was similarly referred.   On 14th December 1977 ACAS resolved not to proceed
'for the time being' with its inquiries into those recognition issues.   By a writ dated 25th
January 1978 EMA claimed declarations that ACAS was in breach of its statutory duties
g in not prosecuting them.   On 10th February 1978 EMA gave notice of motion for
interim relief, and, when the matter came before Oliver J on 5th April, this was treated
by consent as the trial of the action.   In the result, the learned judge decided in favour of
ACAS, and I am in respectful agreement with your Lordships that, on the facts as they
then stood, that judgment was unimpeachable.   Nevertheless, it may well be that (as my
noble and learned friend Lord Keith observed in the course of counsel's submissions) at
h least some of the later complications would have been avoided had the motion not been
so treated and the action had proceeded to trial in the ordinary and more formal
manner.   Be that as it may, there is little room for doubt that, later on, lassitude largely
took control over ACAS.   So much so that, when the case reached the Court of Appeal in
May 1979, ACAS had not taken a single step towards resolving EMA's reference, and by
the time this appeal came before this House last December absolutely no progress had
j been made.

This is a lamentable tale, and, had what exactly happened in the Court of Appeal been
beyond all doubt, I should have been driven to the conclusion that the unanimous view
of that court that ACAS had unwarrantably failed in its statutory duties was right and,
indeed, inevitable.   For, although ACAS indubitably has an inherent right of deferment
and postponement in proper cases, such extraordinary delay as occurred here called for

a clear and convincing explanation. But the conclusion of the Court of Appeal was that the case presented for ACAS itself demonstrated that, so far from reasonably postponing *a* the disposal of EMA's recognition issue, that body had, in effect, abandoned the task. The Court of Appeal rightly held that, although an appellate court; it was in all the circumstances entitled to have regard to what had happened not only after the issue of the writ but also to events (and non-events) since the hearing before Oliver J. It concluded therefrom that ACAS had manifestly decided to postpone dealing with the recognition issue until such time as EMA's case against the TUC had been finally disposed *b* of.

Now, had that been so, virtual abandonment of its statutory duty would have been clear and EMA's entitlement to the relief sought established. The funereal course of events (both in the past and in the foreseeable future) leading to that inexorable conclusion was thus described by Cumming-Bruce LJ[1]:

> 'But on any view, if the first instance trial [of *EMA v TUC*] takes place in March *c* 1980, even assuming (which is a very big assumption) that there is no appeal to this court, there then remains before finality on the question of the affiliation of [EMA] with the TUC the many steps to be taken ... So that now it does not look as if there is any prospect of the uncertainty arising from the decision of [EMA] to claim a declaration against the TUC being resolved certainly for another 18 months, and I would have thought probably for a good deal longer. So the effect of the decision *d* taken by ACAS in December 1977 is now seen in this court to involve necessarily ... a decision to keep the application for recognition both by EMA and UKAPE on ice for a period not less than about *three* years from the date of the applications before even proceeding to enquire of the opinion of workers. [Emphasis mine. These depressing factors led Cumming-Bruce LJ to say:] I cannot accept that such a long postponement can be regarded as a proper exercise of the undoubted discretion *e* vested in ACAS to determine its manner of proceeding and how to set about finding out the opinion of workers and its undoubted discretion to give itself reasonable time before attempting to proceed to enquiry.'

Now that conclusion, which was arrived at also by Lord Denning MR and by Lawton LJ seems to have been based substantially on the belief that counsel for ACAS had informed *f* the Court of Appeal that, as Cumming-Bruce LJ put it[2]: ... it is *not* the intention of ACAS to proceed to enquiry stage until the uncertainties flowing from the litigation and the dispute between EMA and the TUC have been *finally* resolved' (emphasis mine). But learned counsel himself has in strenuous terms informed your Lordships that this belief entertained by the members of the Court of Appeal was quite mistaken. He asserted that, so far from indicating or accepting that ACAS had ever adopted a *final* stand, he had *g* intimated to that court that, having decided on 14th December 1977 simply '... not to proceed with its inquiries on the references for the *time being* until EMA's claims against the TUC had been determined in the courts or withdrawn', ACAS had thereafter reviewed the position periodically and had throughout kept an open mind on how and when it should next proceed.

My Lords, the difference between the clear understanding of the Court of Appeal and *h* the distinction drawn before your Lordships by counsel may be thought by some to be narrow. But counsel insisted that it is substantial and important, and that justice would be denied ACAS were what he asserts was the mistaken view taken by the Court of Appeal to prevail. As he, in effect, put it, to say 'Come what may, we, ACAS, will *not* proceed with the recognition references until the *EMA v TUC* litigation is finally disposed of' is materially different from keeping the matter open, periodically reviewing it and *j* reaching a fresh conclusion each time in the light of the developing situation; the former

---

1　[1979] 3 All ER 227 at 239, [1979] 1 WLR 1113 at 1130
2　[1979] 3 All ER 227 at 240, [1979] 1 WLR 1113 at 1130

involves abandonment by ACAS of its statutory duty, the latter merely a reasonable and
a permissible postponement.

I have naturally found this conflict between court and counsel considerably
embarrassing. But, having reflected long on the matter, I feel I cannot exclude from my
mind the possibility that the latter attitude may indeed have been the one adopted by
ACAS. If it was, can it be condemned out of hand as one which no reasonable body,
charged with the statutory duties imposed on ACAS, could properly have arrived at?
b After considerable hesitation, I do not think it can. But, even so, with the passing of
time, much, *much* time, can it be said that what may well have been reasonable at one
stage had later become clearly unreasonable? This has proved a far more difficult
question. But, having heard from counsel the sort of considerations which ACAS
believed relevant to its assessment of the situation, I am unable to say that, singly or
cumulatively, they ought not to have carried some weight.
c On the whole, I have therefore come to the conclusion that this appeal should be
allowed. But for me it has been a knife-edge decision and one which ACAS should not
regard as recognising any sort of right in it to make a habit of dilatoriness. If it does, it
will surely come to grief. For it is fettered by the requirements of reason, and, if those
are not met, condemnation must follow.

d **LORD KEITH OF KINKEL.** My Lords, I agree with the speech of my noble and
learned friend Lord Diplock, and would accordingly dismiss the appeal.

LORD SCARMAN. My Lords, the question for the House in this appeal is whether
ACAS was entitled in the circumstances in which it found itself first to take, and then to
continue, its decision to defer its inquiries into a recognition issue referred to it pursuant
e to s 11(1) of the Employment Protection Act 1975 by the respondent trade union, the
Engineers' and Managers' Association. A subsidiary question arises as to the extent of the
power of the Court of Appeal and this House to have regard to events occurring between
trial and the hearing of the appeal.

The history which lies behind the appeal is complex. The motives and intentions of
the actors are not always clear. But the facts necessary for a decision are few.
f First, some words as to the parties and persons directly affected by the appeal.

The House has under consideration a further chapter in the chequered and complicated
story of the struggle between a number of unions to secure recognition as the collective
bargaining agent of the professional engineers (and others of comparable status)
employed in the engineering industry. The unions in contention are the United
Kingdom Association of Professional Engineers ('UKAPE'), the Engineers' and Managers'
g Association ('EMA'), and the Technical, Administrative and Supervisory Section ('TASS')
of the Amalgamated Union of Engineering Workers ('AUEW'). The employees, for
whose favour the unions compete, are vitally affected by, but not participants in, the
struggle. They are 'in consimili casu' with my fair lady at a mediaeval tourney, for whose
favour the jousting champions compete. Apart from voicing their opinions, hopes and
expectations, they stand, like her, on the sidelines, watching and waiting for the master
h of the tournament, for them ACAS, to decide on which competitor to confer the accolade
of recognition, ie the right to be treated as their champion.

In the present case, there are some 300 workers to whom the recognition issue
relates. They are professional, or equivalently high grade, engineers employed by the
General Electric Co Ltd at Whetstone, near Leicester. Over 100 of them are members of
EMA; some 90 of them belong to no union; the remaining 100 are, it appears, more or
j less equally divided between UKAPE and TASS. In other words, at least 200 of them
wish to be represented by a union, and EMA has a membership which is double that of
any other union.

The engineering industry has had for many years a number of 'procedural' agreements
with staff unions who are members of the Confederation of Shipbuilding and
Engineering Unions ('CSEU'). TASS, as a section of the AUEW, is a party to these

agreements. They establish negotiating arrangements for the purpose of collective
bargaining as to the terms and conditions of employment of a great number of workers;   *a*
but they do not cover senior professional engineers. TASS, though it includes some
qualified engineers amongst its members, has not made headway in its effort to extend
its membership amongst the more highly qualified workers at Whetstone. UKAPE, a
union which is not affiliated to the Trades Union Congress ('TUC') and whose rules limit
membership of the union to professional engineers and other employees of comparable
status, has had some success in attracting members amongst the workers with whom this   *b*
case is concerned and would do much better if it could secure recognition by the
employers. EMA, a union which prior to 22nd April 1977 was known as the Electrical
Power Engineers' Association and is the plaintiff in the present case, is, like TASS,
affiliated to the TUC. In recent years it has sought to extend to the engineering
industry. In its campaign to recruit senior engineers and managers as members, it has
caused offence to TASS.   *c*

The struggle between the unions burst into flame in the late seventies. It may be told,
so far as this appeal is concerned, by setting out the critical dates and noting against them
the relevant facts.

9th July 1976. UKAPE refers to ACAS a recognition issue arising from its rejected
request to be recognised by the company for the purpose of collective bargaining on
behalf of graduate engineering staff employed at Whetstone.   *d*

16th March 1977. Award by TUC disputes committee in favour of TASS on a
complaint that EMA by recruiting for members at Whetstone was in breach of the
Bridlington agreement which since 1939 has regulated inter-union disputes between
unions affiliated to the TUC. The award imposed a ban on EMA recruiting.

22nd April 1977. EMA changes its name from the Electrical Power Engineers'
Association to EMA.   *e*

27th April 1977. In defiance of a requirement of the Bridlington agreement not to
invoke the 1975 Act without consultation and agreement with other affiliated union(s)
affected, EMA refers its recognition issue to ACAS, which, with the consent of UKAPE
and EMA, decides to conduct the two references together.

July to early October 1977. ACAS proceeds with its examination and inquiries. In
particular, ACAS with the help of those interested in the reference prepares a draft   *f*
questionnaire designed to ascertain the opinions of the workers concerned.

28th September 1977. TUC informs EMA that the union must either comply with the
award or face disciplinary proceedings. In other words, the TUC serves notice on EMA
that, if it continues to recruit and to proceed with its reference, it faces the possibility of
expulsion from the TUC. EMA requests ACAS to suspend its inquiries while it considers
its position. ACAS agrees.   *g*

13th October 1977. EMA issues a writ against the TUC 'the TUC action' claiming a
declaration that the disputes committee award was invalid.

14th October 1977. EMA requests ACAS to proceed with the reference and to report
as soon as possible. EMA's strategy is clear: to immobilise the TUC while it seeks a
recognition recommendation from ACAS.

8th November 1977. On EMA's application for an injunction in the TUC action, the   *h*
Chancery Division (Browne-Wilkinson J), on the TUC undertaking until judgment or
further order not to impose any penalty on EMA for non-compliance with the disputes
committee award, and by consent, gives directions intended to make possible an early
trial of the action; the statement of claim is to be delivered within seven days and, after
close of pleadings and exchange of lists of documents, the parties are to attend the master
on 6th February 1978 to enable the action to be set down and the parties to apply for an   *j*
early trial. EMA in the event took 98 days to deliver a statement of claim; there were
delays associated with discovery; the action has not yet reached trial, which is now
expected in February 1980. The inference is inescapable: that EMA has, to put it kindly,
made haste slowly in the hope that ACAS would report with a recommendation in its
favour before the court ruled on the validity of the TUC committee's award.

9th November 1977. ACAS decides 'to defer its enquiries' for the present. The anxieties
a of ACAS and the reasons for its decision are best explained by the words of its press notice
of this date:

'The Council of ACAS today considered further whether to proceed with its
enquiries into the references for trade union recognition concerning the United
Kingdom Association of Professional Engineers (UKAPE), The Engineers' and
b Managers' Association (EMA) and GEC Reactor Equipment Limited, Whetstone.
Two references have been made under Section 11 of the Employment Protection
Act 1975. The first by UKAPE made on July 9, 1976 and the second by EMA on
April 27, 1977, both concern the same group of engineers employed by GEC REL
at Whetstone. It has been agreed with the parties that the two references can be
conducted together. Apart from the recognition references to ACAS, the matter
c was already the subject of a dispute between EMA and TASS which had been
referred to the TUC Disputes Committee. The award of the Committee has been
challenged and is now the subject of a writ by the EMA, which is still sub judice.
However today it is being further discussed between the TUC and the EMA with a
view to seeking a solution. The outcome is not known. In considering whether to
proceed with its own enquiries under S12 of the Employment Protection Act the
d Council took account of the above position and also of the probability that if it
decided to go ahead with its enquiries its decision might be the subject of legal
challenge by UKAPE, whilst if it decided to defer enquiries it might be challenged
by EMA. The Council is most anxious to act lawfully and has taken full account of
the advice of its legal advisers. It is very conscious of its duty under S(12)3 of the
Employment Protection Act to have regard to the desirability of encouraging a
e settlement by agreement and where appropriate by conciliation. It has also taken
account of the Code of Practice on Industrial Relations[1] which provides in para 85
that the "Responsibility for avoiding disputes between trades unions about
recognition is principally with the unions themselves and, in the case of affiliated
unions, with the Trades Union Congress. Unions concerned should make full use
of available procedures". The Council believes that it would be helpful if the issue
f between the TUC and the EMA were resolved since the outcome would be one of
the factors which the council would need to take into account in its own
examination. The Council is also anxious not to exacerbate the problem by
untimely action of its own and has decided to defer its enquiries for the present.
The Council intends in the meantime to seek further legal guidance and will
consider the matter at its next meeting.'

g
18th November 1977. Solicitors for EMA protest against ACAS's decision, call for ACAS
to proceed with the EMA reference and, in particular, for the questionnaire to be sent to
the workers concerned. EMA's consent to its reference being conducted together with
that of UKAPE is withdrawn.
14th December 1977. ACAS reaffirms its decision 'not to proceed, for the time being',
h with the two references. A press notice is issued by ACAS as follows:

'At its meeting today the Council of ACAS reconsidered its position with regard
to proceeding on the references for trade union recognition concerning the United
Kingdom Association of Professional Engineers (UKAPE), the Engineers' and
Managers' Association (EMA) and GEC Reactor Equipment Limited (Whetstone).
j The Council decided that it would not proceed, for the time being, with its inquiries
on those references. In reaching its decision, it took particular account of the
implications of the writ which has been served on the TUC by EMA, one of the
applicant unions. This writ which is still outstanding seeks to challenge an award

1 (HMSO, 1972)

by a TUC Disputes Committee in respect of a recognition and recruitment issue
concerning the group of employees who are the subject of the EMA reference.'   *a*

Almost immediately some 200 of the engineers at Whetstone present a petition of
protest to ACAS.

25th January 1978. EMA issue the writ in this action, claiming against ACAS
declarations that ACAS in refusing or failing to proceed on its reference is in breach of its
statutory duties, and that it is bound by s 12 of the 1975 Act to examine and report on
EMA's recognition issue.   *b*

10th February 1978. EMA's notice of motion for interim relief.

8th March 1978. The writ is, by leave, amended so as to allow UKAPE, at its request,
to become a defendant. UKAPE's attitude to the case, put lucidly in this House as in the
Court of Appeal by one of its officers, is that it is content, indeed it would wish, that
ACAS proceed with both references, provided it adds to its workers' questionnaire a
question designed to discover their second choice of a union for recognition if their first   *c*
choice fails to secure ACAS's recommendation. This represented a change of attitude by
UKAPE, for in a letter dated 30th September 1977 the union had requested ACAS to
defer the questionnaire until the issue between EMA and the TUC had been resolved.

7th April 1978. EMA's motion being treated by consent as the trial of the action,
Oliver J[1] gives judgment for ACAS. The speed in this action is to be contrasted with the
delays in the TUC action.   *d*

14th May 1979. The Court of Appeal[2] allows EMA's appeal, and declares that ACAS is
bound to proceed with the reference and report on the recognition issue.

December 1979. Hearing of ACAS's appeal in this House.

The chronological table reveals the very serious delay imposed on the conduct of the
reference by the decision of ACAS taken on 14th December 1977 and maintained ever
since. For some 3½ to 4 years the workers affected who wish to be represented by a union   *e*
have waited, but are still without any decision on either reference. The reasons for
ACAS's suspension of its inquiries into the two references have been explained in the
press notices and in the evidence of one of its senior officers, Mr Norcross. In an affidavit
of 16th February 1978 he said:

'8. In these circumstances it appeared to the Defendants that it was inappropriate   *f*
and untimely to proceed with the next stage of their inquiries, which will involve
seeking the opinions of workers to whom the recognition issues relate, for so long
as the Plaintiffs' challenge to the legal validity of the recruitment bar has not been
determined by the Court or withdrawn by the Plaintiffs. The Defendants considered
that it would not have been meaningful to put hypothetical questions to workers at
a time when it was not known whether the recruitment ban was lawfully made and   *g*
could be lawfully enforced, and when it was within the Plaintiffs' power to break
this deadlock by proceeding expeditiously with its action against the T.U.C. or by
withdrawing their challenge to the legal validity of the recruitment bar. Moreover,
the UKAPE had specifically requested the Defendants to defer issuing a questionnaire
to workers until this issue was resolved one way or the other on the grounds that the
employees could not complete the questionnaire meaningfully in such   *h*
circumstances.

'9. The Defendants were also of the opinion that they could not have reached a
proper conclusion on the basis of the results of such survey. In any case the
Defendants were of the opinion that they were not only entitled but had a duty, on
industrial relations grounds, to take into account any relevant Award of the T.U.C.
Disputes Committee before they could reach a conclusion on the Plaintiffs'   *j*
reference.'

1   [1978] ICR 875
2   [1979] 3 All ER 227, [1979] 1 WLR 1113

Put shortly, the TUC action was, as Oliver J observed, the determining factor. In his
a second affidavit, sworn on 17th March 1978, Mr Norcross described the attitude of ACAS
in these words:

> 'ACAS would like to proceed with the conduct of the references but considers that
> it would be untimely to do so in the light of the legal action between the EMA and
> the TUC, which is still pending.'

b   I turn now to consider whether ACAS has power to defer or suspend proceedings on
a reference, and, if it has, the extent of the power. The answer depends on the
interpretation to be put on ss 11 to 16 of the 1975 Act.

Section 11(1) entitles an independent trade union to refer a recognition issue to
ACAS. A recognition issue arises from a request by a trade union for recognition by an
employer for the purpose of collective bargaining: see ss 11(2) and (3). A reference
c having been made, ACAS becomes bound to examine the issue, to consult affected
parties, and to make such inquiries as it thinks fit. If the issue is not settled and the
reference is not withdrawn, ACAS 'shall prepare a written report': see ss 12(1) and (4).
Thus the union may settle with the employer at any time, or unilaterally withdraw the
reference, in either of which events ACAS has nothing further to do; and the workers to
whom the issue relates have no right to compel either the union or ACAS to proceed.
d Indeed it is the duty of ACAS to seek a settlement of the issue by agreement, using in
appropriate cases its statutory powers of conciliation: see s 12(3). If ACAS has to prepare
a report, it must set out in the report its findings, any advice it chooses to offer in
connection with its findings, and any recommendation for recognition it decides to
make. Whether it makes, or decides not to make, a recommendation, it must give the
reasons for its decision in the report: see s 12(4).
e   The processing by ACAS of a recognition issue is, therefore, not forensic in character
though it embodies a judicial element substantial enough to impose on ACAS in the
conduct of the reference the obligations of natural justice. ACAS can make no order nor,
if it recommends recognition, is there available under the law any process which can
compel an employer to recognise a trade union. The law provides in ss 15 and 16 of the
1975 Act for pressure, which many employers would, no doubt, wish to avert by
f choosing recognition; but neither ACAS nor the Central Arbitration Committee, to
whom a trade union may apply if an employer fails to comply with an ACAS
recommendation, nor the courts of the land can order recognition.

Accordingly, ACAS's power, whatever its extent, to defer its inquiries or the
preparation of its report is not to be compared, except in terms of the broadest generality,
with a court's discretion to adjourn the hearing of a case. It is a power the nature of
g which depends on ACAS's statutory functions, duties and responsibilities.

ACAS, it can be said with confidence, has the following duties. It must do what the
statute says it shall do. It must exercise its powers in a way in which the circumstances
of each particular case it considers best suited to advance the purpose and policy of the
statute. These are the improvement of industrial relations, and the extension of collective
bargaining. It must ensure that those whom it consults, and it is under a statutory duty
h to 'consult all parties who it considers will be affected' (s 12(1)), eg other trade unions, the
TUC, employers' associations, and to 'ascertain the opinions of workers to whom the issue
relates' (s 14(1)), have a proper opportunity of making their views known. But subject
to the mandatory duties imposed on it by the statute it may conduct its examination of
the issue and its inquiries in whatever way it thinks best.

The 1975 Act, as Lord Diplock observed in *Grunwick Processing Laboratories Ltd v*
j *Advisory, Conciliation and Arbitration Service*[1], imposes no time limit on the conduct of the
reference. ACAS is clearly under a duty, arising from the mandatory words of s 12(1)
and (4), to proceed with reasonable expedition; but equally clearly it has a power to defer

---

1   [1978] 1 All ER 338 at 359, [1978] AC 655 at 688

its inquiries and consultations. If, for example, ACAS thinks there is a chance of the settlement of the issue by agreement, it may defer its inquiries and must defer the *a* preparation of a report until it knows whether it will be necessary to report on the issue. Equally clearly, ACAS has a power to defer the preparation of a report until it has made the inquiries which it thinks appropriate to the reference.

To sum up the effect of the statute, I interpret it as conferring on ACAS a discretion to suspend inquiry or to defer the preparation of its report if it is of the opinion that a period of suspension or deferment would promote the improvement of industrial relations *b* (including the extension of *collective* bargaining). Conversely if ACAS should be of the opinion that industrial relations would be worsened (or *collective* bargaining put at risk) if it did not for a period suspend inquiries or defer preparation of its report, it has the power, at its discretion, to defer action. Since ascertainment of the views of the workers to whom the recognition issue relates is a part, albeit a mandatory part, of its inquiries, this discretionary power extends also to this phase of the inquiry. *c*

Both the chance of settlement of the issue and (as with EMA in early October 1977) the possibility of withdrawal of the reference are instances in which the power may be exercised. But the power is not limited. It is a general power to be exercised reasonably, and consistently with the general duty imposed on ACAS by s 1(2) of the 1975 Act as construed by this House in *United Kingdom Association of Professional Engineers v Advisory, Conciliation and Arbitration Service*[1]. *d*

The statute imposes no cut-off point, no time limit. If, however, under the guise of deferment ACAS in effect terminates its conduct of the reference, refusing to complete its examination or to proceed to a report, it will be acting ultra vires the statute, for it can terminate proceedings only if the issue has been settled or the reference has been withdrawn.

In my judgment, therefore, ACAS has a discretion to defer inquiries for a period. For *e* the reasons given in the *UKAPE* case[1], the exercise of its discretion is not reviewable by the courts unless ACAS can be shown either to have misdirected itself in law, or to have failed to observe the requirements of natural justice, or to have failed to consider relevant matters, or to have conducted the reference in a way in which no reasonable advisory conciliation or arbitration service, paying due regard to the statute, could have conducted it. I therefore, agree with the formulation by my noble and learned friend Lord Diplock *f* of the crucial question presented by the appeal: has ACAS by the deferment in this case abdicated its statutory function to proceed with the reference? The courts cannot intervene, unless satisfied that it has.

The test of reasonableness being not what the court, or this House, thinks would have been the reasonable course to have pursued but whether it has been shown that no reasonable advisory, conciliation and arbitration service could properly have made and *g* then continued its deferment decision in the circumstances in which ACAS found itself, it is not possible, in the light of Mr Norcross's evidence, and applying this test, to hold that the decision of 14th December 1977 was unreasonable. I agree on this point with the trial judge. Indeed, I find only one error in his judgment. He said that he had to look at the time when the decision was taken, and not as it was at trial. For reasons, which I shall mention briefly when dealing with the subsidiary question, I think that he should *h* have considered the reasonableness not only of the initial decision to defer but also of the decision to maintain the deferment in the circumstances which existed at trial. Nevertheless the case for deferment was much the same in April 1978 when he gave judgment as it had been in December 1977. In particular, there was still, notwithstanding 'E.M.A.'s own dilatoriness' (the judge's comment[2], with which I agree), a reasonable prospect of an early, or at least a not too distant, trial in the TUC action. The matters to *j* which ACAS had attached importance in the previous November and December remained relevant and real. Their weight was in April 1978, as at the earlier time, not for the court but for ACAS to decide.

---

1   Page 612, ante
2   [1978] ICR 875 at 893

It is submitted, however, that 13 months later, when the case reached the Court of
a Appeal, the lapse of time was such that it was now unreasonable on the part of ACAS to
persist any longer in deferring proceedings on the reference. This was the view of all
three members of the Court of Appeal. It is unfortunate that this question was dealt
with not on the basis of evidence directed to the situation then obtaining but on
statements by counsel. Nevertheless enough is known to enable a conclusion to be
reached. The Court of Appeal understood counsel for ACAS to have said that 'his
b instructions were that ACAS were not going to proceed with their enquiries until the
validity of the award [ie the award of the disputes committee which was the subject of
the TUC action] was determined': see per Lord Denning MR[1] and Cumming-Bruce
LJ[2]. Exactly what counsel said is a matter of doubt. But he did not intend to convey,
nor, as we have been told and I accept, was it ACAS's view, that, come what may, it would
in no circumstances resume its inquiries until the validity or invalidity of the award was
c finally determined. Misunderstanding of ACAS's view arose because evidence was not
taken, as it should have been if matters subsequent to trial were to be relied on, as to what
its view was in May 1979. But, my Lords, it cannot be doubted that ACAS's view in May
1979, and indeed today, remains the same as it had been on 14th December 1977,
namely that 'it would not proceed, for the time being, with its inquiries' and that it was
taking 'particular account of the implications of' the TUC action.
d The question, therefore, is whether in May 1979 the various factors referred to by Mr
Norcross in the evidence to which I have referred and, in particular, the difficulties
created by the TUC action were such that, notwithstanding the lapse of another 18
months without a decision in that action, ACAS could reasonably refuse to resume the
conduct of the reference. All the factors mentioned by Mr Norcross remained relevant;
but there now had to be weighed in the balance the serious frustrations of the workers
e concerned arising from the delay. And there was one further relevant consideration:
trial in the TUC action was now expected in February or March 1980.
The passage of time had not lessened the difficulties of eliciting the opinions of the
workers fairly and accurately. Because of the failure of EMA to bring the TUC action to
trial, ACAS was in no better position in 1979 than it had been in 1977 either to reach a
proper conclusion on the survey of workers' opinion or to report. The difficulty in the
f way of making a recommendation for recognition remained as formidable as it had been
in 1977. If ACAS proceeded to a report, it might well find it impossible to make any
recommendation, a result which would do little to relieve the frustrations of the
workers. And it still remained ACAS's duty, on industrial relations grounds, to take
account of the TUC award, if lawful, before determining EMA's reference: see para 85 of
the Code of Practice to which reference was made in the press notice of 9th November
g 1977.
Can it, therefore, be said that ACAS in May 1979 was acting as no reasonable body
with its statutory duties could properly act? Was its decision to continue with the
deferment an abdication of its statutory function? In my judgment No. Workers do not
have a right to have the trade union of which they are members recognised for the
purpose of collective bargaining, even if a substantial number of them belong to
h the union; for no employer can be compelled to recognise a trade union. The opinions
of the workers are a relevant matter of great importance, which ACAS is bound to
ascertain before it recommends, or refuses to recommend, recognition. But ACAS is not
bound to recommend in accordance with their opinion. ACAS has to form its view as to
what is best for the promotion of improved industrial relations and the extension of
collective bargaining. The Court of Appeal erred in substituting its judgment for that of
j ACAS. In the confused situation which EMA had allowed to persist by not pursuing the
TUC action with sufficient expedition it was not unreasonable of ACAS to continue the
suspension of its inquiries; and it may well remain in the true interests of the workers to

---

1   [1979] 3 All ER 227 at 235, [1979] 1 WLR 1113 at 1124–1125
2   [1979] 3 All ER 227 at 240, [1979] 1 WLR 1113 at 1130

defer a report until the facts exist in which a recognition recommendation can be made.

The appeal reached this House in December 1979. Trial in the TUC action was then *a* only a few months away. It must now be reasonable to await the outcome of the trial, if there be any validity in the reasons adduced by Mr Norcross for the decision to defer inquiries.

For these reasons, my Lords, I would allow the appeal.

My Lords, I have reached my conclusion on the merits of the appeal as I see them. In so doing I have assumed that the answer to the subsidiary question is that the Court of *b* Appeal and this House may, if justice requires it, have regard to events subsequent to trial in determining an appeal. In my view, the assumption is sound in law. I agree with Lord Denning MR[1] that the Court of Appeal was in duty bound, if it thought it necessary in order to do justice, 'to rehear the case *as at the time of rehearing*; and ought to give such judgment as ought to be given if the case came *at that time* before the court of first instance' (Lord Denning MR's emphasis). By parity of reasoning, it is the duty of a trial *c* judge to take account of the situation of the parties as it exists at time of trial. I think, however, the proposition is not as general as might appear from the judgment of Lord Denning MR. I know of no case of authority in the books in which an appellate court has reversed a judgment for the defendant where there was no cause of action, actual, imminent or threatened when the writ was issued; and, if there be any such case, I think it would be wrong in principle. The power to reverse or modify a judgment at first *d* instance in the light of subsequent events arises most frequently in connection with the remedy or relief to be granted. If it be damages, the appeal court can and, if justice so requires, ought to take account of developments since trial: see *Lim Poh Choo v Camden and Islington Area Health Authority*[2]. If the relief is equitable, eg injunction or specific performance, the duty is well established. If the relief sought, as here, is declaratory, it is a matter of discretion. But, if an appellate court is disposed to allow an appeal on the *e* basis of events subsequent to trial, it must be astute to ensure that it does so on evidence. Evidence, of course, embraces admissions, including admissions by counsel. However, in the present case, a statement by counsel was an insecure foundation for forming a view whether ACAS, a statutory body whose duties lay in a complex and specialised field, had since trial abdicated its statutory functions. The Court of Appeal did less than justice to ACAS in relying on what it understood counsel to be saying. *f* Justice required that the court made plain the view it was likely to form in the absence of further evidence as to events subsequent to trial and invite ACAS to file evidence. We now know that, had this been done, Mr Norcross would have sworn a further affidavit explaining the attitude of ACAS in 1979. I have no doubt that he would have had plenty to say. Fortunately, for the reasons already given, enough is known of ACAS's position to enable a judgment to be formed whether in May 1979 it was abdicating its statutory *g* function. In my opinion, it was not.

Appeal allowed.

Solicitors: *Treasury Solicitor ; Lawford & Co* (for EMA).

h

Mary Rose Plummer   Barrister.

1 [1979] 3 All ER 227 at 236, [1979] 1 WLR 1113 at 1126
2 [1979] 2 All ER 910, [1980] AC 174

a
De Falco v Crawley Borough Council
Silvestri v Crawley Borough Council

COURT OF APPEAL, CIVIL DIVISION
LORD DENNING MR, BRIDGE LJ AND SIR DAVID CAIRNS
3rd, 4th, 5th, 6th, 12th DECEMBER 1979

b

Housing – Homeless person – Duty of housing authority to provide accommodation – Remedy for breach of duty – Whether applicant entitled to declaration that local authority in breach of duty or that adverse decision invalid – Whether applicant entitled to injunction – Whether applicant restricted to applying for judicial review – RSC Ord 53.

c *Housing – Homeless person – Preliminary duty to house pending enquiries – Enforcement of duty by interim mandatory injunction – Principles applicable to grant of interim injunction – Decision by authority that applicant became homeless intentionally – Applicant alleging decision invalid – Applicant bringing action claiming mandatory injunction – Application for interim injunction – Whether applicant required to show strong prima facie case that decision invalid – Housing (Homeless Persons) Act 1977, s 3(4).*

d

Housing – Homeless person – Person becoming homeless intentionally – National of EEC country coming to England with family to seek work because unemployed in own country – No indication that secure accommodation not available for him in own country – Whether housing authority satisfied he was intentionally homeless – Whether authority entitled to conclude applicant deliberately left available accommodation in own country – Whether housing authority bound to
e *follow advice contained in Code of Guidance – Housing (Homeless Persons) Act 1977, ss 12(1), 17(1)(4).*

Housing – Homeless person – Person becoming homeless intentionally – Duty to house intentionally homeless person for such period as will give him reasonable opportunity to secure accommodation – What amounts to reasonable period – Whether regard may be had to period prior to notification
f *of authority's decision – Housing (Homeless Person) Act 1977, s 4(3).*

The plaintiffs, two Italians, were unemployed in Italy and came to England with their wives and young children to seek work. There was nothing to indicate that they did not have secure accommodation in Italy. At first they stayed with relatives in Crawley but after a time the relatives could no longer accommodate them. The plaintiffs applied to
g the Crawley Borough Council ('the local authority') for accommodation under the Housing (Homeless Persons) Act 1977. Under EEC law[a] the plaintiffs were to be treated in the United Kingdom, in regard to housing, in the same way as indigenous nationals. There was a housing shortage in Crawley but since the plaintiffs were homeless and had a priority need (having dependent children) the local authority were under a duty, by virtue of s 3(4)[b] of the 1977 Act, to house them pending the authority's enquiries under
h s 3(1) and a final decision. The local authority accommodated them in guest houses for five or six weeks. Following their enquiries the local authority decided that the plaintiffs had become homeless intentionally since they had come to England without ensuring that they had permanent accommodation here. Having reached that decision the

---

j *a*   See EEC Treaty, arts 48 to 51; and EEC Council Regulation 1612/68, which, so far as material, is
         set out at p 924 *h*, post
     b   Section 3, so far as material, provides:
         '(1) If—(a) a person applies to a housing authority for accommodation or for assistance in
         obtaining accommodation, and (b) the authority have reason to believe that he may be homeless
         or threatened with homelessness, the authority shall make the appropriate inquiries.
                            (Continued on p 914)

authority had a duty under s 4(2)(b) and (3)(b)c of the Act merely to house the plaintiffs
and their families for no longer than was reasonable to enable them to find other **a**
accommodation for themselves. By a letter dated Friday 2nd November 1979 the
authority notified each of the plaintiffs that the authority had decided that they had
become homeless intentionally and gave their reasons for so deciding, and required them
to leave the guest houses on Tuesday 6th November. The plaintiffs and their families left
on that date. By writs dated 12th November each plaintiff brought an action against the
local authority claiming (i) declarations that the determination that they became **b**
homeless intentionally was invalid, that the local authority were under a duty to house
them under s 4(5) of the Act, and that the authority were in breach of their duty under
s 4(3) to afford them reasonable opportunity to secure other accommodation, and (ii)
mandatory injunctions requiring the authority to provide accommodation for them.
The plaintiffs applied for interim mandatory injunctions in those terms pending the
hearing of the actions. Because of the proceedings the local authority, on 12th **c**
November, rehoused the plaintiffs and their families in the guest houses pending the
outcome of the proceedings. On 22nd November Chapman J refused to grant the
interim injunctions. The plaintiffs appealed. On the appeal the local authority
contended, inter alia, that the plaintiffs' proper remedy was an application for judicial
review of the authority's decision under RSC Ord 53, and not an action claiming
declarations and an injunction. **d**

Held – The appeals would be dismissed for the following reasons—
  (i) Where a housing authority failed to perform its duty under the 1977 Act an
applicant could either bring an action claiming a declaration that the authority were in
breach of duty or that the decision under the Act adverse to the applicant was invalid, and
could also claim an injunction in the action, or the applicant could apply under RSC Ord **e**
53 for judicial review of the authority's decision (see p 920 g, p 923 f to h and p 926 j,
post); *Thornton v Kirklees Metropolitan Borough Council* [1979] 2 All ER 349 applied.
  (ii) However, where an injunction was claimed and it was held that the housing
authority had not validly decided under s 4(5) of the 1971 Act that the applicant had
become homeless intentionally, interim relief in the form of a mandatory injunction
requiring the housing authority to secure accommodation for the applicant pending a **f**
valid decision, would be granted, but only where the applicant made out a strong prima
facie case that the decision was invalid. The principles governing the grant of prohibitory
injunctions on interlocutory applications had no relevance to the grant of a mandatory
injunction requiring the housing authority to perform their duty because the plaintiffs

---

(Continued from p 913)   **g**
  '(2) In subsection (1) above "appropriate inquiries" means—(a) such inquiries as are necessary to
satisfy the authority whether the person who applied to them is homeless . . . and (b) if the
authority are satisfied that he is homeless . . . any further inquiries necessary to satisfy them—(i)
whether he has a priority need, and (ii) whether he became homeless . . . intentionally.
  '(4) If the authority have reason to believe that the person who applied to them may be
homeless and have a priority need, they shall secure that accommodation is made available for his **h**
occupation pending any decision which they may make as a result of their inquiries (irrespective
of any local connection he may have with the area of another housing authority).'
c Section 4, so far as material, provides:
  '. . . (2) Where . . . (b) [the housing authority] are satisfied that . . . [a person] became homeless
. . . intentionally, their duty is to furnish him with advice and appropriate assistance.
  '(3) Where . . . (b) they are subject to a duty towards him by virtue of subsection (2)(b) above,
they shall secure that accommodation is made available for his occupation for such period as they **j**
consider will give him a reasonable opportunity of himself securing accommodation for his
occupation . . .
  '(5) Where—(a) they are satisfied—(i) that he is homeless, and (ii) that he has a priority need, but
(b) they are not satisfied that he became homeless intentionally, their duty . . . is to secure that
accommodation becomes available for his occupation. . .'

could not give a worthwhile undertaking as to damages, and further (per Lord Denning
a MR) such an interlocutory mandatory injunction should not be granted unless certiorari
and mandamus would have been granted had the application been for judicial review of
the authority's decision (see p 922 *a b*, p 923 *j* to p 924 *d f g* and p 926 *j*, post); *American
Cyanamid Co v Ethicon Ltd* [1975] 1 All ER 504 distinguished.

(iii) The local authority's decision that the plaintiffs became homeless intentionally
was a valid decision because (a) although the authority were required under s 12(1)[d] of
b the 1977 Act to have regard to the Code of Guidance[e] issued by the Secretary of State to
housing authorities, they were not bound to follow the code or the instruction in it that
a person giving up accommodation to move in with relatives or friends who then
decided they could no longer accommodate him was not to be regarded as being
intentionally homeless, and (per Lord Denning MR) that instruction did not apply to
persons coming from another Common Market country; and (b) in all the circumstances,
c the authority's reason for finding that the plaintiffs became homeless intentionally (ie
because they came to England without ensuring that they had permanent accommodation) satisfied the requirements of s 17(1) and (4)[f] of the Act since the authority were
entitled to conclude that the plaintiffs had deliberately left accommodation which was
available to them in Italy and that, having regard to the housing situation in Crawley, it
would have been reasonable for them to have continued to occupy their accommodation
d in Italy; moreover in reaching their decision the authority had neither disregarded any
relevant factors nor taken into account any irrelevant factors. It followed that, as the
decision was valid, interim injunctions would not be granted (see p 921 *b* to *d* and *g h*,
p 925 *c* to *f* and p 926 *f g*, post).

(iv) (Bridge LJ dissenting) In allowing the plaintiffs only four days to find other
accommodation the local authority were not in breach of their duty under s 4(3) of the
e 1977 Act because (per Lord Denning MR) the five or six weeks they were in the guest
houses prior to the notice was to be taken into account in assessing whether they had had
a reasonable time in which to find other accommodation. But in any event (Bridge LJ
concurring), as they had been allowed to stay in the guest houses from 12th November
until the determination of the appeal, they could not now complain that they had not
been afforded reasonable opportunity to secure other accommodation (see p 922 *c d* and
f p 925 *j* to p 926 *a* and *h* to p 927 *a*, post).

Per Bridge LJ. The period contemplated by s 4(3) commences when the local
authority's decision adverse to the applicant on the issue of intentional homelessness is
communicated to him, and the local authority cannot rely on any prior opportunity the
applicant has had of himself securing accommodation, which ex hypothesi has not been
successful, to curtail the period which will afford reasonable opportunity to secure
g accommodation after the decision is communicated (see p 925 *h*, post).

---

d Section 12(1), so far as material, provides: 'In relation to homeless persons . . . a relevant authority
    shall have regard in the exercise of their functions to such guidance as may from time to time be
    given by the Secretary of State.'
h e Housing (Homeless Persons) Act 1977 Code of Guidance (England and Wales) (HMSO, 1977) para
    2.18.
f   Section 17, so far as material, provides:
        '(1) Subject to subsection (3) below, for the purposes of this Act a person becomes homeless
    intentionally if he deliberately does or fails to do anything in consequence of which he ceases to
    occupy accommodation which is available for his occupation and which it would have been
    reasonable for him to continue to occupy . . .
j   '(3) An act or omission in good faith on the part of a person who was unaware of any relevant
    fact is not to be treated as deliberate for the purposes of subsection (1) or (2) above.
        '(4) Regard may be had, in determining for the purposes of subsections (1) . . . above whether
    it would have been reasonable for a person to continue to occupy accommodation, to the general
    circumstances prevailing in relation to housing in the area of the housing authority to whom he
    applied for accommodation or for assistance in obtaining accommodation.'

Notes

For a housing authority's duties to a homeless person, see 22 Halsbury's Laws (4th Edn) *a* para 513.

For remedies available on a breach of statutory duty, see 36 Halsbury's Laws (3rd Edn) 440–443, paras 664–669, and for cases on the subject, see 44 Digest (Repl) 346–350, 1810–1850.

For the EEC Treaty, arts 48–51, see 42A Halsbury's Statutes (3rd Edn) 751–753, 860.

For EEC Council Regulation 1612/68, see ibid 755–768 *b*

For the Housing (Homeless Persons) Act 1977, ss 3, 4, 12, 17, see 47 ibid 317, 318, 326, 330.

Cases referred to in judgments

American Cyanamid Co v Ethicon Ltd [1975] 1 All ER 504, [1975] AC 396, [1975] 2 WLR 316, [1975] RPC 513, HL, Digest (Cont Vol D) 536, 152a.

Associated Provincial Picture Houses Ltd v Wednesbury Corpn [1947] 2 All ER 680, [1948] 1 *c* KB 223, [1948] LJR 190, 177 LT 641, 112 JP 55, 45 LGR 635, CA, 45 Digest (Repl) 215, 189.

Meade v London Borough of Haringey [1979] 2 All ER 1016, [1979] 1 WLR 637, [1979] ICR 494, 77 LGR 577, CA.

R v Bristol City Council, ex parte Browne [1979] 3 All ER 344, [1979] 1 WLR 1437, DC. *d*

Secretary of State for Education and Science v Metropolitan Borough of Tameside [1976] 3 All ER 665, [1977] AC 1014, [1976] 3 WLR 641, 75 LGR 190, HL.

Secretary of State for Employment v Associated Society of Locomotive Engineers and Firemen (No 2) [1972] 2 All ER 949, [1972] 2 QB 455, [1972] 2 WLR 1370, [1972] ICR 19, CA, Digest (Cont Vol D) 974, 1514.

Thornton v Kirklees Metropolitan Borough Council [1979] 2 All ER 349, [1979] QB 626, *e* [1979] 3 WLR 1, 77 LGR 417, CA.

Tickner v Mole Valley District Council (29th October 1979) unreported.

Cases also cited

Anisminic v Foreign Compensation Commission [1969] 1 All ER 208, [1969] 2 AC 147, HL.

Hubbard v Vosper [1972] 1 All ER 1023, [1972] 2 QB 84, CA. *f*

K (H) (an infant), Re [1967] 1 All ER 226, [1967] 2 QB 617, DC.

Leary v National Union of Vehicle Builders [1970] 2 All ER 713, [1971] Ch 34.

Minister of Health v Bellotti [1944] 1 All ER 238, [1944] 1 KB 298, CA.

NWL Ltd v Woods [1979] 3 All ER 614, [1979] 1 WLR 1294, HL.

Redland Bricks Ltd v Morris [1969] 2 All ER 576, [1970] AC 652, HL.

Roebuck v National Union of Mineworkers (Yorkshire Area) [1977] ICR 573. *g*

Smith v Inner London Education Authority [1978] 1 All ER 411, CA.

Stevenson v United Road Transport Union [1977] ICR 893, CA.

Appeals

By writs dated 12th November 1979 the plaintiffs, Vicenzo De Falco and Antonio Silvestri, respectively brought actions against the Crawley Borough Council ('the local *h* authority') each seeking (1) a declaration that the local authority had not validly determined that the plaintiffs were intentionally homeless pursuant to s 3(2)(b) of the Housing (Homeless Persons) Act 1977, (2) a declaration that the local authority were under a duty to secure that accommodation became available for the plaintiffs and their families pursuant to s 4(5) of the 1977 Act; (3) a declaration that the local authority had not validly determined that accommodation was available for the plaintiffs' occupation *j* for such period as would give them a reasonable opportunity of themselves securing accommodation for their occupation, pursuant to s 4(3) of the 1977 Act, (4) an injunction ordering the local authority to provide accommodation for the plaintiffs and their families, and (5) damages. The plaintiffs applied in the action for interim mandatory injunctions requiring the local authority to provide the plaintiffs and their families with *a* accommodation pending the hearing of the actions. By a judgment given in open court on 22nd November 1979 (the applications having been heard in chambers) Chapman J refused to grant interim mandatory injunctions. The plaintiffs appealed seeking orders that mandatory injunctions in the terms applied for be granted. The facts are set out in the judgment of Lord Denning MR.

John R Macdonald QC and *Andrew Bano* for the plaintiffs.
b *Anthony Scrivener QC* and *Graham Stoker* for the local authority.

Cur adv vult

12th December. The following judgments were read.

LORD DENNING MR. Every day we see signs of the advancing tide. This time it is
c two young families from Italy. They had heard tell of the Common Market. Naturally enough, because it all stemmed from a treaty made at Rome. They had heard that there was freedom of movement for workers within the Community. They could come to England without let or hindrance. They may have heard, too, that England is a good place for workers. In Italy the word may have got round that in England there are all sorts of benefits to be had whenever you are unemployed. And, best of all, they will look
d after you if you have nowhere to live. There is a special new statute there which imposes on the local authority a duty to house you. They must either find you a house or put you up in a guest house. 'So let's go to England', they say, 'That's the place for us'. In that telling I have used a touch of irony, but there is a good deal of truth behind it. You will see it as I recount the story.

e *Community law*
        But, before doing this, I would draw attention to the Community law. It is set out in arts 48 to 51 of the EEC Treaty and arts [2] to [18] of the regulations of 15th October 1968[1]. It is well summarised in an explanatory document[2] issued by the Department of the Environment to local authorities. It reads thus:

f   'Nationals of European Community (EEC) countries do not require permission to
        work in the United Kingdom, and once employed are subject to all legislation and
        regulations governing the employment of UK nationals . . . They are entitled to the
        same treatment as indigenous nationals with regard to pay, working conditions,
        access to housing and property, training, social security and trade union rights.
        They also have the right to be joined by their family and immediate dependants,
        and these family members in turn have the same rights as the workers themselves.'
g

The De Falcos
        The De Falcos have lived all their lives in Italy. Their home was in Naples, at 86 Corso Vitto Rio Emanuele, Marano, Napoli. He is aged 27. She is 24. They have a baby son of 11 months old. The husband, Vincenzo De Falco, had been out of work in Italy for
h over a year. So he decided to bring his wife and baby over to England. They did not speak a word of English, but they had got to know of the Common Market, and that under it there is freedom of movement for workers. They had heard that they were entitled to come to England and seek a job here, so that they could live here indefinitely. Now the wife had a brother, Mr Morrone, living in Horsham. So they arranged to come and stay with her brother. He lived at 84 Drake Close, Horsham,
j Sussex. They gave up their home in Italy and came with the baby and their belongings,

---

1   EEC Council Regulation 1612/68
2   ELP 21 (1978) revised, prepared by the Employment Service Division of the Manpower Services
    Commission and the Central Office of Information

lock, stock and barrel, to England. They left Italy on 22nd February 1979 and came to
stay with her brother. It was a two-bedroomed house. Her brother let them have one *a*
room rent free. The husband tried to get work, but did not succeed for about three
months. Then he got a job at Gatwick Airport, in the canteen. He earned £64 a week
net. His wife got a job as a hospital cleaner at £17 a week net. About this time the
brother's wife became pregnant. The brother told the De Falcos that they would have to
leave. So they did leave in June 1979, and went to stay with another relation, a brother-
in-law, at 26 The Birches, Three Bridges, Crawley. A month or two later, in August *b*
1979, the brother-in-law gave them a month's notice to quit. He said he had relatives
coming from Italy to stay with them. So the De Falcos would have to leave by 21st
September 1979. At once they determined to take advantage of our new legislation for
housing the homeless. As soon as they got notice to quit, on 21st August 1979, the wife
went along to the office of the Crawley Borough Council. She could not speak English.
So her sister-in-law, Mrs Morrone, went with her and acted as interpreter. The wife *c*
asked for accommodation for her husband and herself and their baby from 21st
September 1979.

Now the Crawley Borough Council were concerned about this request. They were
uncertain about people coming from the Common Market. They asked the Department
of the Environment, and were told that they had just the self-same rights as true born
Englishmen with regard to pay, working conditions, access to housing and property, *d*
training, social security and trade union rights.

So the Crawley Borough Council felt that they must treat the De Falco family just the
same as if they had come from Yorkshire or any other part of England. On that footing,
as soon as the De Falcos were turned out on 21st September 1979, the council were bound
to provide accommodation for them. That is clear from the Housing (Homeless Persons)
Act 1977. That Act, in s 3(4), placed a duty on the council to provide accommodation for *e*
a family with young children, if they were homeless. So it was the duty of the Crawley
council to house the De Falcos. There were no council houses available. So the council
did the only thing they could. They put them up at a guest house called Furzedown
Guest House, 11 Brighton Road, Horley. It was near the airport where Mr De Falco was
working. It cost the council £100 a week. The De Falcos made a contribution of £19·20
a week. *f*

The Silvestris

The Silvestris are also Italian. He is 25. She is 20. They have two small daughters,
aged three years and one year. They first came to England three years ago and stayed
here for nearly two years. He then worked at a factory in the Crawley area. They shared
a flat with his brother-in-law. But the brother-in-law was given a council house; and Mr *g*
Silvestri could not afford the flat on his own. So he went back to Italy with his wife and
family. That was in September 1978. They lived in Naples and he got work there. He
hoped that it would be permanent. But after nine months the work turned out not to
be permanent. He has not told the reason. Maybe he got the sack. We do not know.
All we do know is that he could not find any other work in Naples. So he decided to
come back to England. They were living in Naples in very crowded conditions there, *h*
but that was not the reason he left. He left because he could find no other work there.
He got in touch with a brother-in-law living in Redhill. He told him that two flats were
coming available at 14 Gloucester Road, Redhill, and that he might have one of them.
So Mr Silvestri bought the tickets and made arrangements to come over, with his wife
and two babies and all their belongings. But three days before he was due to leave Italy
his brother-in-law sent a message that the flats were no longer available. Nevertheless, as *j*
they had made all their arrangements, the Silvestris came over. They arrived on 29th
June 1979. They went to stay with various relatives and friends for a few weeks at a
time. He obtained work as a solderer. We do not know his wages. I expect they were
very good. But they could not stay indefinitely with relatives and friends. So they went
to the Crawley council on 30th August and asked the council to house them. They could

not speak English much. The council explained to them that, if they became homeless,
a the council might be prepared to find them temporary accommodation, but they ought
to try to find other accommodation.

On 29th September they were staying with his brother-in-law. He told them to
leave. So they went to the council. The council by this time knew they were bound to
provide accommodation for them. The council put them up in a guest house at Hope
Cottage, 3 Meath Green Lane, Horley, Surrey. It cost the council £60 a week. He
b contributed £16·70 a week.

The statutory duty

So I have reached the point where the local authority put up these two families in guest
houses. That was a very proper thing to do. These two families with small children
c came into the category of persons who had a 'priority need' within s 2(1)(*a*) of the 1977
Act. They were homeless and had applied for accommodation. So the local authority
were under a duty to make appropriate enquiries (see s 3(1) and (2)), and to house them
pending a decision (see s 3(4)). But then the council had to make appropriate
enquiries. The object of these was to decide whether these families were 'intentionally
homeless' or not (see s 3(2)). For a great deal depended on it. The statute is not at all easy
d to follow, but I will try and explain it in simple language.

If the council are satisfied that the family became homeless intentionally, they are
bound to house them for a *short* time, but they are not bound to house them forever.
They are bound to house them for such time as they consider reasonable, so as to enable
them to look for accommodation for themselves, but not indefinitely. After a short time
the family must make their own arrangements themselves. That is how I interpret
e s 4(2)(*b*) and (3)(*b*).

But if the family became homeless *unintentionally*, the local authority *are* bound to
house them indefinitely. They must either let them have a council house, or put them
into a guest house, or find other accommodation for them somewhere (see s 4(5)). The
family are not bound to look for anything for themselves. This means that families who
are 'unintentionally homeless' go to the top of the people in need, getting priority over
f the young marrieds or the key workers, and everybody else.

This puts the local authorities in a very vulnerable position. They can be beseiged by
the 'unintentional homeless' and forced to house them indefinitely. There is only one
ray of hope for the authorities. It is contained in s 17(4). They can have regard to the
housing situation in their own area. If they are already overcrowded, they can say to the
applicant, if the facts warrant it: 'You ought to have stayed where you were before. You
g ought not to have landed yourself on us when it would have been reasonable for you to
stay where you were.'

Our two cases

The local authority made appropriate enquiries. It took them about six weeks. As a
result by the beginning of November 1979 they were 'satisfied' that each of these two
h families became *homeless intentionally*. It then became their duty under s 8(1) and (4)(*b*) to
notify the families of their reasons. They did this by a letter to each of the husbands on
Friday, 2nd November 1979 in these words:

'(a) The Council is satisfied that you were rendered homeless on [21st September
1979 for the De Falcos and on 29th September 1979 for the Silvestris], (b) the
j Council is satisfied that you have a "priority need for accommodation" ... (c) the
Council is of the view that you became homeless intentionally because you came to
this Country without having ensured that you had permanent accommodation to
come to. In these circumstances, the Council is under no obligation to rehouse you
on a permanent basis, and I must therefore inform you that the Council is not
prepared to pay for your present accommodation after the night of Monday 5th

November, 1979, and the owner of the accommodation has been advised accordingly. The Council is not prepared to assist you after that date.'   *a*

Both those families received that letter on Saturday morning, 3rd November. They stayed in their guest houses until the time given, that is until Tuesday, 6th November. They then left and went to stay with relatives or friends. And at the same time they immediately got in touch with a charitable organisation for the homeless called Shelter. That organisation got in touch with its own solicitors. Those solicitors at once got legal aid and issued a writ against the council. They said that the council's decision was invalid; and they claimed an injunction in these wide terms: 'An injunction ordering the defendants to provide accommodation for the occupation of the plaintiff and his family.'   *b*

Faced with this challenge the council gave way temporarily. They put the two families back into the guest houses, and paid for them, pending the conclusion of the proceedings. The families were only out for four or five days. On 22nd November   *c* Chapman J held that the council's decision was perfectly valid; but as the two families have brought an appeal to us, the council have allowed them to stay in the guest houses, and have paid for them, pending our decision.

The procedure   *d*

During the hearing, a point was raised about the procedure adopted by the plaintiffs. They issued writs in the High Court claiming declarations and an injunction. It was suggested that they should have applied for judicial review, because that was the more appropriate machinery.

Now the interesting thing is that this new Act, the Housing (Homeless Persons) Act 1977, contained nothing about remedies. It does not say what is to be done if the local   *e* authority fails to perform any of the duties imposed by the statute. It has been held by this court that, if the council fails to provide accommodation as required by s 3(4), the applicant can claim damages in the county court: see *Thornton v Kirklees Metropolitan Borough Council*[1]. I am very ready to follow that decision and indeed to carry it further, because this is a statute which is passed for the protection of private persons, in their capacity as private persons. It is not passed for the benefit of the public at large. In such   *f* a case it is well settled that, if a public authority fails to perform its statutory duty, the person or persons concerned can bring a civil action for damages or an injunction: see *Meade v London Borough of Haringey*[2], Wade on Administrative Law[3] and the Law Commission's Report on Remedies in Administrative Law[4]. No doubt such a person could, at his option, bring proceedings for judicial review under the new RSC Ord 53. In those proceedings he could get a declaration and an injunction equally well. He could   *g* get interim relief also. So the applicant has an option. He can either go by action in the High Court or county court, or by an application for judicial review.

The challenge

The plaintiffs' challenge the decision of the council in this respect. They say that their finding that they were 'intentionally homeless' was bad. I must, therefore, repeat the   *h* reason given by the council in their letter of the 2nd November 1979:

> '. . . the Council is of the view that you became homeless intentionally because you came to this Country without having ensured that you had permanent accommodation to come to.'

j

1   [1979] 2 All ER 349, [1979] QB 626
2   [1979] 2 All ER 1016 at 1023–1024, [1979] 1 WLR 637 at 646
3   4th Edn (1977) pp 633–634
4   Law Com.73 (1976) Cmnd 6407, para 22

That finding is very concise; but I think it can be expanded in the light of all the
a surrounding circumstances. It tells the families: 'You left Italy and came to Crawley
where we are absolutely crowded out. You ought not to have come here unless you had
arranged for permanent accommodation here. As it is, you came with only the most
precarious accommodation with relatives and friends. You really cannot expect us to
house you at the expense of all our other people. You ought to have stayed in Italy
where, so far as we know, you had accommodation which you could continue to occupy
b quite well.'

So stated the reason complies entirely with the provisions of the statute. Every word
in it satisfies the detailed provisions of s 17 of the 1977 Act. I do not think the plaintiffs
have any grounds for upsetting the finding of 'intentional homelessness'. Throughout
this statute there are words which require the local authority to be 'satisfied' or 'not
satisfied' on this, that or the other. In using that word, I have no doubt that the framers
c of the statute had before them the law as stated by me in *Secretary of State for Employment
v Associated Society of Locomotive Engineers and Firemen (No 2)*[1], and in *Secretary of State for
Education and Science v Metropolitan Borough of Tameside*[2], and by Lord Wilberforce[3], and
endorsed in the context of this Act by Lord Widgery CJ in *R v Bristol City Council, ex parte
Brown*[4]. I do not see that the council took anything into account which they ought not
to have taken into account or vice versa: nor do I see that their finding was in any way
d unreasonable: nor do I see anything unfair in their conduct of their enquiries.

The Code of Guidance

The most forceful way in which the case was put for the plaintiffs was that they did not
observe the Code of Guidance[5]. That states:

e   'In assessing whether a person has become homeless intentionally it will be
relevant to consider the most immediate cause of that homelessness rather than
events that may have taken place previously. It would be inappropriate to treat as
intentionally homeless a person who gave up accommodation to move in with
relatives or friends who then decided after a few months that they could no longer
continue to accommodate him.'

f   Now, if that paragraph were to be treated as a binding statute, the council ought not
to have looked at the position of these families when they left Italy. They ought to have
looked at the position when their relatives or friends in England threw them out. That
the council did not do.

But I am quite clear that the code should not be regarded as a binding statute. The
council, of course, had to have regard to the code (see s 12 of the 1977 Act) but, having
g done so, they could depart from it if they thought fit. This is a case in which they were
perfectly entitled to depart from it. That paragraph may be all very well for people
coming from Yorkshire or any other part of England. But it should not, or, at any rate,
need not, be applied to people coming from Italy, or any other country of the Common
Market. There is a great difference between the two positions. This is shown by s 5 of
the Act which shows that people coming from another area in England may not have a
h claim to accommodation.

---

j 1   [1972] 2 All ER 949 at 967–968, [1972] 2 QB 455 at 493
    2   [1976] 3 All ER 665 at 670–671, [1977] AC 1014 at 1024–1025
    3   [1976] 3 All ER 665 at 681–682, [1977] AC 1014 at 1047
    4   [1979] 3 All ER 344, [1979] 1 WLR 1437
    5   Housing (Homeless Persons) Act 1977 Code of Guidance (England and Wales) (HMSO, 1977) para
        2.18

The granting of an interlocutory injunction

This is not the same sort of case as *American Cyanamid Co v Ethicon Ltd*[1] because the *a* plaintiffs here cannot give any worthwhile undertaking in damages. No injunction should be granted against the council unless the plaintiffs make out a strong prima facie case that the council's finding of 'intentional homelessness' was invalid. I would go further. It should not be granted unless it is a case in which, on an application for judicial review, certiorari would be granted to quash their decision: and mandamus issued to command them to consider the case afresh. We were shown the unreported decision of *b* Stephen Brown J in *Tickner v Mole Valley District Council*[2]. He granted an interlocutory injunction, ordering the council to provide accommodation for some caravan dwellers. I think that decision was erroneous.

The time allowed

A subsidiary point was taken because it was said that the council in their letter of 2nd *c* November 1979 allowed too short a time. It was only until after the night of 5th November. That is four days. That was insufficient, it was said, to satisfy s 4(3). In this regard, I think that regard can be had to the five or six weeks which they had already been in the guest houses. They had had all that time in which to find other accommodation. In any event, they have had four or five extra weeks now in which to find it. So there is no substance in their complaint. *d*

Conclusion

The local authority at Crawley are very concerned about these two cases. They have Gatwick Airport within their area. If any family from the Common Market can fly into Gatwick, stay a month or two with relatives, and then claim to be unintentionally homeless, it would be a most serious matter for their overcrowded borough. They *e* should be able to do better than King Canute. He bade the rising tide at Southampton to come no further. It took no notice. He got his feet wet. I trust the councillors of Crawley will keep theirs dry against this new advancing tide.

I would dismiss this appeal.

BRIDGE LJ. The Housing (Homeless Persons) Act 1977 confers valuable rights on a *f* select category of homeless persons and imposes burdensome duties on local authorities with limited housing resources. A person has an absolute right to look to the authority to secure that accommodation becomes or remains available for his occupation if (a) he is homeless or threatened with homelessness, (b) he has a priority need for accommodation as defined in s 2 of the Act, and (c) he did not become homeless intentionally. It is for the local authority in each case to determine whether an applicant for accommodation fulfils *g* these qualifications. Pending their determination, if they have reason to believe that the applicant for accommodation may be homeless and have a priority need, they have an interim duty to secure that accommodation is made available for his occupation under s 3(4). Normally, I apprehend, no difficulty will arise with respect to the issues of homelessness, actual or threatened, or priority need. In the present appeals it is common *h* ground that each applicant qualifies under both these heads. The contentious issue in both these appeals is, as it is likely to be in most such cases, whether the local authority have rightly determined that the applicant, in each case, became homeless intentionally. Such a determination can only be properly made if the local authority are satisfied pursuant to s 17 (1) that the applicant deliberately did or failed to do something in consequence of which he ceased to occupy accommodation which was available for his *j* occupation and which it would have been reasonable for him to continue to occupy.

---

1   [1975] 1 All ER 504, [1975] AC 396
2   (29th October 1979) unreported

This enquiry clearly involves two distinct questions: (i) Was accommodation available for
a his occupation? (ii) Would it have been reasonable for him to continue to occupy that
accommodation? In relation to the second question, the local authority can have regard
to the general circumstances prevailing in relation to housing in their area under s 17(4).

It is common ground and clearly right that the court's power to review any decision
of a local authority under this Act is not appellate but supervisory. The court can only
interfere in accordance with the well-known principles which find their classic expression
b in the judgment of Lord Greene MR in *Associated Provincial Picture Houses Ltd v
Wednesbury Corpn*[1].

Two important questions of principle arise which have not previously been considered
in this court. First, when an applicant for accommodation under the Act wishes to
challenge in the courts a decision adverse to him on the issue of intentional homelessness,
what is the appropriate procedure for him to adopt. Secondly, in any proceedings where
c such a decision is challenged, can the court grant interim relief in the form of a
mandatory injunction requiring the local authority to secure accommodation for the
applicant's occupation and if so on what principles should the court act in deciding
whether such relief ought to be granted?

On the procedural issue, counsel for the local authority submits that the only
appropriate course is to apply for judicial review under RSC Ord 53. He points out that
d the local authority making a decision adverse to an applicant are required by s 8(4) of the
Act to notify him of their reasons, so that there will always be a speaking order open to
attack. If the decision is defective, it can be quashed by certiorari, if necessary at an
expedited hearing, whereupon the local authority's interim duty to secure accommodation for the applicant's occupation under s 3(4) will revive and continue until a fresh valid
decision has been made. So long as the decision stands, it represents, counsel submits, an
e insuperable obstacle to the grant of any interim relief in an ordinary action. Moreover,
the essentially public character of the duties performed by a local authority under the act
makes it more fitting that when their action is challenged its validity should be
determined in proceedings under RSC Ord 53 in the Divisional Court of the Queen's
Bench Division rather than in an action in either the Queen's Bench Division or the
county court.

f   I see the force of these contentions but I am unable to accept them. It has already been
decided in this court in *Thornton v Kirklees Metropolitan Borough Council*[2] that an action for
damages lies against a local authority for breach of duty under the Act and can be
brought in the county court. There the question of jurisdiction alone was in issue and
it was conceded for the purpose of deciding that question that the pleaded breach of duty
must be assumed. Whether or not technically binding on us (being a decision of a court
g of two judges) the correctness of that decision has not been challenged before us. If an
ordinary action lies in respect of an alleged breach of duty, it must follow, it seems to me,
that in such an action the plaintiff as well as claiming damages or an injunction as his
remedy for the breach of duty can claim any declaration necessary to establish that there
was a relevant breach of duty, and, in particular, a declaration that a local authority's
decision adverse to him under the Act was not validly made.

h   The question whether and in what circumstances interim relief can appropriately be
granted in the form of a mandatory injunction is more difficult. Counsel for the local
authority is, of course, right in saying that a declaration to the effect that a local
authority's decision adverse to an applicant was not validly made cannot be granted on
an interim application. But I do not think he is right in his submission that either this
consideration or the availability of the alternative remedy of an application for judicial
j review would in all cases present decisive reasons why the court's discretion to grant an
interlocutory mandatory injunction should not be exercised. If, on the material before

---

1   [1947] 2 All ER 680 at 682–683, [1948] 1 KB 223 at 228–229
2   [1979] 2 All ER 349, [1979] QB 626

it on an interim application, the court can see clearly that the local authority have erred in a way which invalidates their decision adverse to the applicant, I can see no reason in principle why it should not give effect to that view by requiring the local authority to secure accommodation for the applicant's occupation on the footing that the interim housing duty under s 3(4) pending a valid decision ought to be performed. To take this course would not be to usurp the local authority's decision-making function. In a case where an interim mandatory injunction was made, it would be open to the local authority to proceed at once to make a fresh decision on the question of intentional homelessness and if they could show that the fresh decision while avoiding the errors which invalidated the original decision was nevertheless still adverse to the applicant, they could apply at once to have the interim injunction discharged.

I have no doubt therefore that the court may properly exercise its discretion to grant a mandatory injunction on an interlocutory application in an appropriate case. In considering what principles should govern the exercise of this discretion, I do not think much assistance is to be derived from authority. In particular I am satisfied that the principles expounded by Lord Diplock in *American Cyanamid Co v Ethicon Ltd*[1] governing the grant of prohibitory injunctions on interlocutory applications have no relevance to the case we are considering. A dispute between an applicant who claims entitlement to be provided with accommodation, and a local authority who dispute that entitlement, exhibits sufficiently unusual features to make a comparison even with other types of litigation where a mandatory injunction may be granted on an interim application difficult and possibly misleading. I think the appropriate principles can only be derived from a consideration of the likely consequences to the parties to such a dispute of granting or withholding relief. In a case where the applicant is entitled to relief but it is withheld, he will be rendered homeless when he should have been housed. This is an injury which is sufficiently traumatic and hardly compensable in damages. On the other hand, if the local authority are required to provide accommodation to which the applicant is not entitled, this may, as the figures we have been given in the present case show, impose a heavy financial burden on the ratepayers with no prospect of recompense by way of a cross-undertaking in damages. What is perhaps more important, a mandatory injunction to provide accommodation for a particular applicant who ought not to enjoy priority may operate to the detriment of others on the local authority's housing list by interfering with the local authority's own system of priorities for the fair distribution of limited housing resources. In the light of these considerations, I think the court inevitably must make the best assessment it can, on an interim application for a mandatory injunction, of the strength of the applicant's claim to impugn the local authority's decision adverse to him and should only grant the relief sought if a strong prima facie case is made out.

The facts relevant to the present appeals have been fully set out in the judgment of Lord Denning MR. It is accepted that, the plaintiffs now being employed in this country, the fact that they came here from Italy is no bar to their claim to be accommodated under the Act if it is otherwise well founded. This follows from EEC Regulation 1612/68, art 9(1) which provides:

'A worker who is a national of a Member State and who is employed in the territory of another Member State shall enjoy all the rights and benefits accorded to national workers in matters of housing . . .'

The local authority gave as their reason for deciding that each plaintiff became homeless intentionally 'because you came to this Country without having ensured that you had permanent accommodation to come to'. This is attacked essentially on three grounds. (i) That it disregards the advice given by the Secretary of State in the Code of Guidance[2] (issued pursuant to s 12 of the 1977 Act) at para 2.18 that:

1 [1975] 1 All ER 504, [1975] AC 396
2 Housing (Homeless Persons) Act 1977 Code of Guidance (England and Wales) (HMSO, 1977)

'In assessing whether a person has become homeless intentionally it will be
a   relevant to consider the most immediate cause of that homelessness rather than
events that may have taken place previously. It would be inappropriate to treat as
intentionally homeless a person who gave up accommodation to move in with
relatives or friends who then decided after a few months that they could no longer
continue to accommodate him.'

b   (ii) That it has regard to an irrelevant consideration, viz, that the applicant came to the
United Kingdom from Italy. (iii) That there is no affirmative finding by the local
authority, nor was there material to justify a finding, that the plaintiffs on leaving Italy
deliberately did or failed to do anything in consequence of which they ceased to occupy
accommodation which was available for their occupation and which it would have been
reasonable for them to continue to occupy.

The first ground of attack is not well founded since, although the authority must 'have
c   regard' to the guidance given under s 12, that guidance is of no direct statutory force or
effect and the local authority are not bound to follow it in any particular case.

I think there is some considerable force in each of the second and third of the plaintiffs'
contentions, but is it sufficient to carry the day at this stage?

Counsel submits that the local authority's formally stated reason should be construed
benevolently and in the light of the evidence of the authority's officers. He points out
d   that according to that evidence, which is not challenged, both plaintiffs gave as their
reason for leaving Italy and coming to this country, not their lack of suitable
accommodation, but their lack of employment. He submits that this afforded a sufficient
basis for the local authority to conclude, and we should infer that they did conclude,
under s 17(1) and (4), (a) that both plaintiffs deliberately left accommodation which was
available to them in Italy, and (b) that, having regard to the general circumstances
e   prevailing in relation to housing in Crawley, it would have been reasonable, in each case,
for the plaintiff to have continued to occupy that accommodation.

On this main issue I have felt throughout the argument and still feel a considerable
difficulty in reaching a clear-cut decision whether or not the case mounted for either of
the plaintiffs is of sufficient strength to warrant granting him the interim relief he
f   seeks. The rival contentions are, in my view, very finely balanced. But finding that the
judge of first instance and the other two members of this court are all of one mind that
an interlocutory injunction should not be granted, I am certainly not prepared to dissent
from their view.

A subsidiary point taken on behalf of the plaintiffs was that the local authority, when
they notified their decision as to intentional homelessness by letter posted on Friday, 2nd
November, and required each plaintiff to vacate the accommodation provided by the
g   local authority, which he was then occupying, by Tuesday, 6th November, they failed in
their duty under s 4(3) of the Act to secure that accommodation was made available for
each plaintiff's occupation for such period as they considered would give him a reasonable
opportunity of himself securing accommodation for his occupation.

In my judgment the period contemplated by s 4(3) is one which commences when the
local authority's decision adverse to the applicant on the issue of intentional homelessness
h   is communicated to him, and the local authority cannot rely on any prior opportunity
the applicant has had of himself securing accommodation for his occupation, which ex
hypothesi has not been successful, to curtail the period which will afford a further
reasonable opportunity after the local authority's decision is made and communicated.
On this basis the period allowed by the notices of 2nd November was so short that no
reasonable authority could have thought it sufficient to satisfy the requirements of the
j   section. But since the issue of the writs in these actions on 12th November the plaintiffs
have again been provided with accommodation by the local authority until now and it
cannot now be said that the time which has elapsed since the receipt of the notices of 2nd
November, or indeed since 12th November, has not amounted to such a period as the
local authority might properly consider as affording the reasonable opportunity

contemplated by s 4(3). It will now be up to the local authority to decide whether to allow any further time. In this matter, as in any other committed to their decision by the Act, so long as they exercise their discretion on proper grounds, we have no power to substitute our decision for theirs. Accordingly in relation to this subsidiary ground of claim it would not be appropriate that any injunction should issue.

For these reasons I would dismiss these appeals.

SIR DAVID CAIRNS. Once a housing authority have reason to believe that an applicant for housing accommodation may be homeless and may have a priority need they are obliged, if they consider that he may be intentionally homeless, to secure accommodation for him while they make enquiries about the matter (s 3(4) of the Housing (Homeless Persons) Act 1977). Then they must not thereafter deprive him of accommodation on the ground of intentional homelessness unless (a) they are satisfied that he is intentionally homeless (s 4(2)), and (b) he has had such time as they consider will give him a reasonable opportunity of finding accommodation for himself (s 4(3)).

In dealing with homeless immigrants from a Common Market country a housing authority may be faced with difficult problems. They are bound to treat such a person as favourably as if he had come from another part of England. In one respect they may have to treat him more favourably because they cannot rely on s 5 of the Act to throw responsibility on to the housing authority of some other area. And when the applicant may have come from a secure home abroad it may well be impracticable to make as full enquiries as would be available with an applicant from another part of England to discover, for the purpose of s 17 of the Act, whether he had deliberately done or failed to do anything in consequence of which he had ceased to occupy accommodation which was available for him and which it would have been reasonable for him to continue to occupy.

In the present cases it appears that each plaintiff was asked where he last lived before leaving Italy, when he went to live there, when he left there, the nature of the accommodation and why he left. There was nothing in the answers received to indicate in either case that the accommodation was insecure or that there was any reason for leaving it except the wish to come and work in England. In my view the local authority were not bound to press their enquiries further. They were entitled to assume that each plaintiff, if he had left his home in Italy because he was expelled from it or because it did not constitute reasonable accommodation for him and his family, would have mentioned this as the reason, or an additional reason, for leaving.

I would therefore hold that the local authority were in no breach of duty up to the time when they declared themselves satisfied that each plaintiff was intentionally homeless.

I find more difficult the question whether the local authority ever directed their minds to the question of what period would give each plaintiff a reasonable opportunity of securing accommodation for himself. If they did consider that matter, one would not have expected them to think that a period of two or three days was sufficient. But it is for the authority and not for the court to decide the question and it is not so clear that the matter was not considered, nor that there were no circumstances to justify so short a notice, as would in my view make it right for the court to hold that the local authority were in breach of duty in refusing to accommodate the plaintiffs after the night of 5th November.

If there was at that stage any breach of duty, I should be prepared to hold that the plaintiffs were entitled to bring actions for any damages suffered and to apply for an injunction to restrain the local authority from withdrawing accommodation until they had had a reasonable opportunity to find accommodation for themselves. But they have been fortunate in that they were only excluded from the guest houses for a short time, and have been housed there ever since notwithstanding the refusal of Chapman J to grant injunctions. I should certainly not be prepared to find that they had not had a sufficient

opportunity to find other accommodation by 22nd November, when the case was before
a the judge, even less that they still today have not had such an opportunity.

Accordingly I would dismiss the appeals.

I would only add, in justice to King Canute, that he was not at all surprised when he
did not hold back the waves; his obsequious courtiers had flattered him by saying that he
could hold back the tide, and he carried out the exercise to show them how wrong they
were.

b
LORD DENNING MR. The books differ on that story.

Appeals dismissed.

Solicitors: *Rates, Wells & Braithwaite* (for the plaintiffs); *Sharpe, Pritchard & Co* (for the
c local authority).

Frances Rustin   Barrister.

Dodd Properties (Kent) Ltd and another v Canterbury City Council and others

COURT OF APPEAL, CIVIL DIVISION
MEGAW, BROWNE AND DONALDSON LJJ
10th, 11th, 12th, 21st DECEMBER 1979

Damages – Measure of damages – Repairs to building – Cost of repairs – Pile driving operations causing damage to next door building – Owners deferring carrying out repairs until after trial of action 10 years later – Owners deferring repairs partly for lack of finance and partly for commercial reasons – Whether damages to be assessed at date physically reasonable to commence repairs – Whether owners entitled to damages to be assessed at date of hearing.

The plaintiffs were respectively the owners and lessees of a building in which the second plaintiffs operated a garage and car sales business. In 1968 a multi-storey car park was erected next door to the plaintiffs' building. The defendants were respectively the contractors for the construction of the car park and the sub-contractors for its foundations. As a result of pile-driving operations for the foundations serious structural damage was caused to the plaintiffs' building. The plaintiffs brought an action against the defendants in negligence and/or nuisance. The first plaintiffs claimed damages for the cost of repairs to the building and the second plaintiffs claimed damages for losses arising out of the prospective interruption to their business if and when the repairs were carried out. Liability was at first denied by the defendants but was admitted shortly before the hearing of the action in 1978, but the issue of quantum remained contested. The first plaintiffs had not carried out any repairs at the date of hearing, claiming that to have done so in 1970 (which was the earliest date when it was physically possible to have carried out repairs) would have caused them a degree of financial stringency and that in any event it would not have made commercial sense for them to have repaired the building before they were sure of recovering the expenditure from the defendants, because that expenditure was not going to produce a corresponding increase in income. The plaintiffs accordingly contended that the damages should be assessed as at the date of hearing, being £30,327 for the cost of repairs and £11,951 for the disruption to the business. The defendants contended that the damages should be assessed as at 1970, being £11,375 for the repairs and £4,108 for the disruption. The judge[a] held that the damages were to be assessed as at 1970 because that was the date when it was reasonable for the plaintiffs to have commenced carrying out the repairs. In so holding the judge decided that any financial stringency caused to the first plaintiffs by carrying out the repairs in 1970 was an extrinsic factor and irrelevant. The plaintiffs appealed.

Held – The appeal would be allowed for the following reasons—
(i) Where a building was damaged by a tortious act and put in need of repair, the cost of repairs was to be assessed according to the broad and fundamental principle regarding damages, namely that they were compensatory and should as far as possible put the injured party in the same position as if the wrong had not been committed. Applying that principle, the cost of repairs was to be assessed at the earliest date when, having regard to all the circumstances, they could reasonably be undertaken, rather than the date when the damage occurred (see p 933 f to p 934 b, p 936 g to p 937 c, p 938 f g, p 939 c and p 941 d e, post); dictum of Lord Blackburn in *Livingstone v Rawyards Coal Co* (1880) 5 App Cas at 39 and *Birmingham Corpn v West Midland Baptist (Trust) Association (Inc)* [1969] 3 All ER 172 applied; dictum of Lord Wilberforce in *Miliangos v George Frank (Textiles) Ltd* [1975] 3 All ER at 813 distinguished; dictum of Denning LJ in *Philips v Ward* [1956] 1 All ER at 876 disapproved.

a [1979] 2 All ER 118

a (ii) The financial stringency (which did not amount to impecuniosity or financial embarrassment) in which the plaintiffs would have been placed had they carried out the repairs in 1970, the fact that it made commercial sense to postpone the repairs until the outcome of the action, the fact that the plaintiffs were not in breach of any duty owed by them to the defendants for their failure to carry out the repairs earlier, and were thus for practical purposes not under a duty to mitigate the damages if they could not afford to do so, and the fact that the defendants had wrongly denied liability, leaving the plaintiffs

b to establish their rights by litigation, were all circumstances to be considered in deciding the date at which the cost of repairs was to be assessed. Taking those circumstances into account and applying the compensatory principle of damages to the facts, the cost of the repairs was to be assessed as at the date of the action, ie 1978 (see p 933 *c d*, p 934 *d* to *f* and *h j*, p 935 *c* to *h*, p 936 *a b g h*, p 937 *h* to p 938 *b e* and p 941 *a* to *e*, post); dictum of Lord Collins in *Clippens Oil Co Ltd v Edinburgh and District Water Trustees* [1907] AC at

c 303 applied; *The Edison* [1933] All ER Rep 144 distinguished; dictum of Oliver J in *Radford v De Froberville* [1978] 1 All ER at 44 approved.

Decision of Cantley J [1979] 2 All ER 118 reversed.

Notes

For the plaintiff's duty to mitigate loss, see 12 Halsbury's Laws (4th Edn) paras 1193–1195, and for cases on the subject, see 17 Digest (Reissue) 124–133, 242–302.

d   For the measure of damages in an action for nuisance, see 28 Halsbury's Laws (3rd Edn) 164, para 234, and for cases on the measure of damages in tort, see 17 Digest (Reissue) 112–119, 168–208.

Cases referred to in judgments

Archer v Moss, Applegate v Moss [1971] 1 All ER 747, [1971] 1 QB 406, [1971] 2 WLR 541,
e   CA, 7 Digest (Reissue) 393, 2426.
Birmingham City Corpn v West Midland Baptist (Trust) Association (Inc) [1969] 3 All ER 172, [1970] AC 874, [1969] 3 WLR 389, 133 JP 524, 67 LGR 571, 20 P & CR 1052, [1969] RVR 484, HL, 11 Digest (Reissue) 149, 209.
Clark v Woor [1965] 2 All ER 353, [1965] 1 WLR 650, 7 Digest (Reissue) 393, 2424.
Clippens Oil Co Ltd v Edinburgh and District Water Trustees [1907] AC 291, 76 LJPC 79, HL,
f   17 Digest (Reissue) 210, 814.
East Ham Borough Council v Bernard Sunley & Sons Ltd [1965] 3 All ER 619, [1966] AC 406, [1965] 3 WLR 1096, 64 LGR 42, [1965] 2 Lloyd's Rep 425, HL, 7 Digest (Reissue) 358, 2312.
Hickman v Haynes (1875) LR 10 CP 598, 44 LJCP 358, 32 LT 873, 12 Digest (Reissue) 442, 3194.
g *Johnson v Agnew* [1979] 1 All ER 883, [1979] 2 WLR 487, HL.
Liesbosch, Dredger (Owners) v Owners of Steamship Edison [1933] AC 449, 102 LJP 73, sub nom *The Edison* [1933] All ER Rep 144, 149 LT 49, 18 Asp MLC 380, 38 Com Cas 267, 45 Ll L Rep 123, HL; *varying* [1932] P 52, CA, 17 Digest (Reissue) 103, 113.
Livingstone v Rawyards Coal Co (1880) 5 App Cas 25, 42 LT 334, 44 JP 392, HL, 17 Digest (Reissue) 89, 38.
h *Miliangos v George Frank (Textiles) Ltd* [1975] 3 All ER 801, [1976] AC 443, [1975] 3 WLR 758, [1976] 1 Lloyd's Rep 201, HL, Digest (Cont Vol D) 691, 64c.
Ogle v Earl Vane (1868) LR 3 QB 272, 9 B & S 182, 37 LJQB 77, Ex Ch; *affg* (1867) LR 2 QB 275, 36 LJQB 175, 39 Digest (Repl) 819, 2815.
Philips v Ward [1956] 1 All ER 874, [1956] 1 WLR 471, CA, 47 Digest (Repl) 564, 35.
Radford v De Froberville [1978] 1 All ER 33, [1977] 1 WLR 1262, 35 P & CR 316.
j

Cases also cited

Alberta Caterers Ltd v R Vollan (Alta) Ltd (1977) 81 DLR (3d) 672, Alta SC.
Batty v Metropolitan Property Realizations Ltd [1978] 2 All ER 445, [1978] QB 554, CA.
British Westinghouse Electric and Manufacturing Co Ltd v Underground Electric Railways of London Ltd [1912] AC 673, [1911–13] All ER Rep 63, HL.

Bunclark v Hertfordshire County Council (1977) 243 Estates Gazette 381, 455.
Celia (Steamship) (Owner) v Owners of Steamship Volturno [1921] AC 544, [1921] All ER Rep **a**
  110, HL.
Davies v Taylor [1972] 3 All ER 836, [1974] AC 207, HL.
Di Ferdinando v Simon, Smits & Co [1920] 3 KB 409, [1920] All ER Rep 347, CA.
Jens and Jens v Mannix Co Ltd [1978] 5 WWR 486, BC SC.
Jones v Griffith [1969] 2 All ER 1015, [1969] 1 WLR 795, CA.
Kitchen v Royal Air Forces Association [1958] 2 All ER 241, [1958] 1 WLR 563, CA.   **b**
Kingsway, The [1918] P 344, [1918–19] All ER Rep 360, CA.
London, Chatham and Dover Railway Co v South Eastern Railway Co [1893] AC 429, HL.
Monarch Steamship Co Ltd v A/B Karlshamns Oljefabriker [1949] 1 All ER 1, [1949] AC 196,
  HL.
Pickett v British Rail Engineering Ltd [1979] 1 All ER 774, [1980] AC 136, HL.
Taylor (C R) (Wholesale) Ltd v Hepworths Ltd [1977] 2 All ER 784, [1977] 1 WLR 659.   **c**

Appeal
By a writ issued on 20th February 1973 the first plaintiffs, Dodd Properties (Kent) Ltd,
as owners of, and the second plaintiffs, Marlowe Garage (Canterbury) Ltd, as lessees and
occupiers of, the premises known as Marlowe Garage, Rose Lane, Canterbury, where the
second plaintiffs carried on a garage and car sales business, claimed damages against the **d**
defendants, Canterbury City Council, Truscon Ltd and Frankipile Ltd, for negligence
and/or nuisance by the defendants and each of them in the course of the construction of
a multi-storey car park on land adjacent to the plaintiffs' premises in and about April
1968 whereby the defendants caused damage to the plaintiffs' premises. The second and
third defendants admitted liability for the damage except for one minor matter but
contested quantum. On 28th July 1978 Cantley J[1] held that the first defendants were **e**
also liable and ordered the defendants to pay to the first plaintiffs damages of £11,375
and the second plaintiffs damages of £4,108. The plaintiffs appealed as to quantum.
The first defendants were not parties to the appeal, having received an undertaking of
indemnity from the other defendants. The facts are set out in the judgment of Megaw
LJ.

                                                                                        f
Roger Titheridge QC and *Michael McMullan* for the plaintiffs.
Oliver Popplewell QC, Stephen Desch and *Antony Edwards-Stuart* for the second and third
  defendants.

                                                                                        g

                               Cur adv vult

21st December. The following judgments were read.

MEGAW LJ. This is an appeal from a judgment of Cantley J[1]. The first plaintiffs, **h**
Dodd Properties (Kent) Ltd, are the owners of a building in Rose Lane, Canterbury,
known as Marlowe Garage. The second plaintiffs, Marlowe Garage (Canterbury) Ltd,
have been the occupiers of Marlowe Garage as lessees of the first plaintiffs. They carry on
their business there as motor car dealers and they sell petrol, oil and car accessories.
    In 1968 the first defendants, the Canterbury City Council, erected a large multi-storey
car park close to Marlowe Garage. The second defendants, Truscon Ltd, were the main **j**
contractors; the third defendants, Frankipile Ltd, were their sub-contractors for the
foundations of the car park. As a result of their operations, damage was caused to the

---

1   [1979] 2 All ER 118

plaintiffs' building. Liability was for long denied, but shortly before the action came on
a for hearing before Cantley J in 1978, liability was admitted in nuisance by the second and
third defendants, though the extent of the damage was in issue, and also the basis of
assessment of the amount of the damages to which the plaintiffs were entitled. The first
defendants did not formally admit liability. But they took no part in the proceedings,
having received an undertaking of indemnity from the other defendants.

The judge held that the first defendants also were liable. They are not parties to the
b appeal. There is no dispute as to liability. The issues are as to damages. No question of
fact is now in dispute, the judge's findings of fact are accepted as to the extent of the
physical damage and as to other matters.

On the question of the extent of the damage, the judge to a large degree accepted the
evidence of the defendants' experts. On their evidence, the necessary repairs would, at
the prices prevailing at the time of the hearing in 1978, cost about £30,000. On the
c evidence of the plaintiffs' expert, the repairs required were much greater and the cost
much higher.

The question which remained, and which is the primary issue before us, is this: by
reference to which of two dates is the cost of the repairs to be ascertained, for the purposes
of arriving at the amount of the defendants' liability for their tort? The plaintiffs say that
the relevant date for this purpose is the date of the hearing, or of the judgment; that is,
d that the 1978 prices are relevant and decisive. The defendants say that the relevant date
is 1970 and the relevant prices are the 1970 prices. As a result of inflation, the difference
between the computations at those respective dates is very large. The 1978 figure, for
the repairs which the judge held to be required, is £30,327. The 1970 figure, for the
same work, is approximately £11,375.

The second plaintiffs also have a claim. It gives rise to the same issue as to the proper
e date of assessment. The second plaintiffs' claim arises out of prospective interruption of
their business during the time that would be required for the carrying out of the
appropriate repairs, if and when that work is done. The figure, if the repairs were to be
carried out in 1978 would be £11,951. In 1970 the corresponding amount would have
been £4,108.

Taking the first and second plaintiffs' potential entitlements together, the sums payable
f by the defendants as damages (apart from any question of interest) would be: on the 1970
assessment, £15,483; on the 1978 assessment, £42,278.

Cantley J held that in law, in the circumstances, judgment had to be given on the 1970
basis. He also awarded interest, making the total payable by the defendants to the first
and second plaintiffs £22,974·20.

Against that judgment, the plaintiffs appeal and the defendants cross-appeal. The
g plaintiffs say that the judge was wrong in law to make his assessment of damages on the
basis of the cost of the repairs in 1970. They say that he should have taken the 1978
computation. They say, in the alternative, that, if they should be wrong on this, which
is their first and main contention, then the judge ought to have awarded interest from
an earlier date and at a higher rate. They accept that, if they are right on their first
contention, that is, the acceptance of 1978 as the date by reference to which the cost of
h the repairs is to be assessed, then they could not claim interest.

The defendants' cross-appeal raises an issue affecting the damages of the second
plaintiffs only. The defendants say that, since the judge held that it was only 'just about
established' that it was probable that the repairs would in fact be carried out after his
judgment, he ought not to have awarded to the second plaintiffs the full amount of the
prospective loss to them arising from the interruption of their business which would be
j caused by those potential repairs. The judge, say the defendants, should have awarded
the second plaintiffs only, say, 60% of the total prospective loss by interruption, because
the chance that the loss would in fact occur was no greater than a chance of that order.

On the first, and main, issue raised by the plaintiffs, it is necessary to see what the
judge found were the reasons why the repairs for this damage to the Marlowe Garage,
caused in 1968, had still not been carried out when the action was heard in 1978.

Because I think it is important to see precisely what the the judge held in this respect, I
shall quote the judge's own words[1]:   *a*

> 'I find that the first plaintiffs could probably have raised the money for repairs but
> this would have increased their annual losses and their financial stringency. As a
> commercial decision, judged exclusively from the point of view of the immediate
> and short-term welfare of the companies, it was reasonable to postpone incurring
> the very considerable expense of these repairs while no harm was being done to the
> building by the delay in repairing it and while these three rich defendants with   *b*
> apparent if not genuine belief in the validity of their defences were firmly denying
> liability to make even a contribution.'

The judge then referred to the well-known and much-discussed case of *Owners of Dredger
Liesbosch v Owners of Steamship Edison*[2]. He said[3]: 'In the case of destruction of a chattel,
the normal measure of the damage is its market value at the time of the loss. That was *c*
the measure of damage applied in the *Liesbosch* case[2].' The judge then cited from the
judgment of Denning LJ in *Philips v Ward*[4]:

> 'The general principle of English law is that damages must be assessed as at the
> date when the damage occurs, which is ususally the same day as the cause of action
> arises . . . A fall thereafter in the value of money does not in law affect the figure, for
> the simple reason that sterling is taken to be constant in value.'   *d*

Although this may not affect the statement of 'the general principle', I think that the
reasoning as to sterling having to be taken to be constant in value is unfortunately no
longer good law, having regard to the facts of life and the recent authoritative decisions,
including *Miliangos v George Frank (Textiles) Ltd*[5].

Cantley J then said[6]:   *e*

> 'No authority has been cited to me and in my very limited opportunity lately I
> have discovered none for myself where a court has considered the time at which
> damages are to be assessed in the cases of buildings damaged and put in need of
> repair by a tortious act. If there is no authority on that precise point, it may be
> because no one has ever before thought to contend that the general principle did not *f*
> apply to it. The general principle is that damages must be assessed as at the date
> when the damage occurs. In my view, that general principle applies here. It is not,
> of course, to be rigidly applied as a rule of thumb, fixing the time rigidly by the
> calendar and the clock. The damage may be concealed by some fault of the wrong-
> doer or not reasonably discoverable by the victim until some time after it has first
> appeared: see, e g, *East Ham Corpn v Bernard Sunley & Sons Ltd*[7] and *Archer v Moss,
> Applegate v Moss*[8]. Moreover, repairs cannot usually be put in hand at once and at *g*
> prices ruling at the very date of damage. There may have to be inspections and
> specifications and tenders and an available contractor may have to be found before
> the work can be started. Furthermore, the nature and circumstances of the damage
> may be such that it would be imprudent and possibly wasteful to begin the work
> before waiting longer to ensure that no further damage is going to develop from the *h*
> same cause. This is particularly true when the foundations of a building have been

---

1   [1979] 2 All ER 118 at 124
2   [1933] AC 449, [1933] All ER Rep 144
3   [1979] 2 All ER 118 at 125   *j*
4   [1956] 1 All ER 874 at 876, [1956] 1 WLR 471 at 474
5   [1975] 3 All ER 801, [1976] AC 443
6   [1979] 2 All ER 118 at 126
7   [1965] 3 All ER 619, [1966] AC 406
8   [1971] 1 All ER 747, [1971] 1 QB 406

a
disturbed by vibrations. I would put it in this way. The appropriate damages are the cost of repairs at the time when it was reasonable to begin repairs. Whether the time is reasonable must be judged objectively and not taking into account such matters as impecuniosity or financial stringency which, in the words of Lord Wright in the *Liesbosch* case[1], are extrinsic'.

b
The judge then held that it was reasonable for the plaintiffs not to begin repairs until 1970 even though the damage had all occurred, and was known, in 1968. On that basis he adopted 'as the measure of damage . . . the cost of repairs on the prices ruling in 1970', ie £11,375.

There is no dispute in this case but that the appropriate measure of damages on this claim of the first plaintiffs is by reference to the cost of the repairs required. The defendants do not challenge the judge's acceptance of the 1970 figures. That means that
c
they do not now contend that the judge should have taken the lower prices for the repair work prevailing in 1968 when the tort was committed.

It is important to bear in mind that we are not concerned with any suggestion that the plaintiffs were under a duty towards the defendants to repair the premises damaged by the defendants' wrongdoing. The plaintiffs did not lose their right to recover damages from the defendants because they did not effect the repairs. True, in certain
d
circumstances with which we are not concerned here, such as the building being destroyed by fire before the repairs were carried out, the amount of the plaintiffs' entitlement to damage might have become nil. But what we are concerned with here is: by reference to what date is the amount of the recoverable loss to be calculated, during a period when the cost of the necessary work is rising as time goes on? Since the defendants do not suggest that the judge was wrong in taking the 1970 prices instead of
e
the 1968 prices, it is accepted, and I think necessarily and rightly accepted, by the defendants that there are circumstances in which the proper amount of damages, where, as here, the damages are to be computed by reference to the cost of repairs, have to be computed by reference to that cost at a date later than the date of the wrongdoing which caused the damage.

The general principle, referred to in many authorities, has recently been recognised by
f
Lord Wilberforce in *Miliangos v George Frank (Textiles) Ltd*[2], namely that 'as a general rule in English law damages for tort or for breach of contract are assessed as at the date of the breach'. But in the very passage in which this 'general rule' is there stated, it is stressed that it is not a universal rule. That it is subject to many exceptions and qualifications is clear. Cantley J in the present case rightly recognised that that was so, in the passage from his judgment which I have recently read.

g
Indeed, where, as in the present case, there is serious structural damage to a building, it would be patently absurd, and contrary to the general principle on which damages fall to be assessed, that a plaintiff, in a time of rising prices, should be limited to recovery on the basis of the prices of repair at the time of the wrongdoing, on the facts here, being two years, at least, before the time when, acting with all reasonable speed, he could first have been able to put the repairs in hand. Once that is accepted, as it must be, little of
h
practical reality remains in postulating that, in a tort such as this, the 'general rule' is applicable. The damages are not required by English law to be assessed as at the date of breach.

The true rule is that, where there is a material difference between the cost of repair at the date of the wrongful act and the cost of repair when the repairs can, having regard to all the relevant circumstances, first reasonably be undertaken, it is the latter time by
j
reference to which the cost of repairs is to be taken in assessing the damages. That rule conforms with the broad and fundamental principle as to damages, as stated in Lord

---

1   [1933] AC 449, [1933] All ER Rep 144
2   [1975] 3 All ER 801 at 813, [1976] AC 443 at 468

Blackburn's speech in *Livingstone v Rawyards Coal Co*[1] where he said that the measure of damages is—

> 'that sum of money which will put the party who has been injured, or who has suffered, in the same position as he would have been in if he had not sustained the wrong for which he is now getting his compensation or reparation.'

In any case of doubt, it is desirable that the judge, having decided provisionally as to the amount of damages, should, before finally deciding, consider whether the amount conforms with the requirement of Lord Blackburn's fundamental principle. If it appears not to conform, the judge should examine the question again to see whether the particular case falls within one of the exceptions of which Lord Blackburn gave examples, or whether he is obliged by some binding authority to arrive at a result which is inconsistent with the fundamental principle. I propose to carry out that exercise later in this judgment.

The judge has held, in a passage which I have already read, that as a commercial decision, judged exclusively from the plaintiffs' point of view, it was reasonable to postpone incurring the expense of the repairs up to, for so I understand what the judge says, the time when the action had been heard and liability decided, resulting in a judgment which, when complied with, would have put the plaintiffs in funds. The reasons why that deferment of repairs was reasonable from the plaintiffs' point of view included the fact, not that they were 'impecunious' (meaning poverty-stricken or unable to raise the necessary money) but that the provision of the money for repairs would have involved for them a measure of 'financial stringency'. Other reasons, consistent with commercial good sense, why the repairs should be deferred include those mentioned in evidence by a director of the plaintiff companies, whose evidence was accepted by the judge as truthful and reliable. If there had been no money problem, he said, he would still not have spent money on the building before he was sure of recovering the cost from the defendants. It would not have made commercial sense to spend this money on a property which would not produce corresponding additional income. So long as there was a dispute, either as to liability or amount of compensation, he would have done no more than to keep the building weatherproof and 'in working order'.

If that was, as the judge held, reasonable from the point of view of the plaintiffs as being grounds for deferring the carrying out of repairs, and if the time at which the cost of the repairs falls to be completed in order to ascertain the amount of damages is the time when it has become reasonable to do the repairs, why did the judge reject 1978, for which the plaintiffs contended, and accept 1970 for which the defendants contended?

There are, as I see it, two possible answers to that question. The first answer is that what is reasonable has to be looked at from the point of view of both parties and a balance struck. The judge's findings of reasonableness of the deferment from the point of view of the plaintiffs does not, therefore, conclude the matter. But I do not think that that was the answer intended to be given by Cantley J. He nowhere refers to the question in any such form and there is no indication of any attempt by him to strike a balance. If a balance had to be struck, surely it would be right, even in a climate of indulgence to contract-breakers or tortfeasors, that the scales should move heavily in the favour of the innocent party as against the wrongdoer, in any comparison of respective disadvantages or unfairnesses? It has to be borne in mind that these were defendants who were wrongly maintaining a denial of any liability and thereby leaving the plaintiffs faced with all the potentially heavy expenditure of money required for the mere purpose of establishing by litigation what we now know to have been their rights. Moreover, as the plaintiffs concede, they could not claim interest on the amount of their compensation starting to run before the date when the money was expended on repairs. So the defendants, being liable, as we now know, to recompense the plaintiffs for the tort which the defendants committed in 1968, will have enjoyed the free use for their own account

---

1   (1880) 5 App Cas 25 at 39

of the money which would have been the appropriate compensation at that date, with
a the opportunity of earning compound interest thereon, from 1968 until the date of
judgment. If that were the ground on which the judge held in favour of the defendants
on this issue, I would respectfully hold that it was a wrong ground. But I do not think
that the judge did so hold.

The second possible answer is that which I believe to have influenced the judge. He
thought that the decision in the *Liesbosch* case[1] precluded him from taking into account,
b in considering the reasonableness of the deferment of repairs, any part of the deferment
which was caused by 'financial stringency'.

The *Liesbosch* case[1] has been the subject of much debate and much speculation, and a
considerable measure of disagreement, as to its ratio decidendi and the scope of its
application, particularly in the light of later House of Lords decisions: see, eg, the
discussion of the case by the learned author of the title Damages in Halsbury's Laws of
c England[2]. I agree with the analysis of the *Liesbosch* case[1] and the comments thereon in
the judgment which Donaldson LJ will deliver hereafter. I do not think that, on any fair
view of the ratio decidendi of the *Liesbosch* case[1], it applies to the issue with which we are
concerned. Amongst other reasons, there are these two. First, it was not 'financial
stringency', let alone 'impecuniousness' as in the *Liesbosch* case[1], which on any fair view,
on the judge's findings, was *the* cause, or even, I think, an effective cause, of the decision
d to postpone repairs. The 'financial stringency' which would have been created by
carrying out the repairs was merely one factor among a number of factors which
together produced the result that commercial good sense pointed towards deferment of
the repairs. The second reason which I would mention is that, once it is accepted that the
plaintiffs were not in any breach of any duty owed by them to the defendants in failing
to carry out repairs earlier than the time when it was reasonable for the repairs to be put
e in hand, this becomes, for all practical purposes, if not in theory, equated with a
plaintiff's ordinary duty to mitigate his damages. Lord Wright in his speech in the
Liesbosch case[3] accepted Lord Collins's dictum in *Clippens Oil Co Ltd v Edinburgh and
District Water Trustees*[4]: '. . . in my opinion the wrong-doer must take his victim talem
qualem, and if the position of the latter is aggravated because he is without the means of
mitigating it, so much the worse for the wrong-doer . . .' I agree with the observations of
f Oliver J in *Radford v De Froberville*[5] as to the relationship between the duty to mitigate
and the measure, or amount, of damages in relation to a question such as the question
with which we are here concerned. A plaintiff who is under a duty to mitigate is not
obliged, in order to reduce the damages, to do that which he cannot afford to do,
particularly where, as here, the plaintiff's 'financial stringency', so far as it was relevant
at all, arose, as a matter of common sense, if not as a matter of law, solely as a consequence
g of the defendant's wrongdoing.

My provisional answer to the question raised in the first issue would thus be that the
damages in this case are to be assessed by reference to the 1978 cost of repairs. I now
carry out that exercise which I mentioned earlier. Once it is accepted, as it is accepted by
the parties, that the damages fall to be computed by the cost of repairs to the building,
and once the *Liesbosch* case[1] and *Philips v Ward*[6] are out of the reckoning, there is no
h exception of which I am aware which is relevant here to exclude the application of Lord
Blackburn's fundamental principle. On the relevant facts as found by the judge, the
1978 cost of the repairs gives the answer which accords with that principle. The
calculation of damages by reference to the 1970 cost of repairs would not so accord.

---

j   1   [1933] AC 449, [1933] All ER Rep 144
     2   12 Halsbury's Laws (4th Edn) para 1144, n 4
     3   [1933] AC 449 at 461, [1933] All ER Rep 144 at 158–159
     4   [1907] AC 291 at 303
     5   [1978] 1 All ER 33 at 44, [1977] 1 WLR 1262 at 1272
     6   [1956] 1 All ER 874, [1956] 1 WLR 471

On that issue, I would allow the appeal.

The result is that the plaintiffs' alternative ground of appeal, as to the appropriate *a* calculation of interest, does not arise, for it is a necessary part of their submission on the first issue that, damages being referable to the deferment of repairs, interest is not payable up to the date of the hearing. In the circumstances, I think it better to say nothing on that point, on which the argument on either side was commendably brief.

If I am right in my conclusion on the main issue in the appeal, I think that the cross-appeal, whatever its merit in law might otherwise have been, ceases to have validity. *b* Early in this judgment, I summarised the issue raised by the cross-appeal. I need not repeat it. I find difficulty in reconciling two passages in the judgment as to the probability of repairs being carried out. The judge, referring to the evidence of Mr Smith, a director of the plaintiff companies, said[1]: 'However, Mr Smith, who I think was being careful to say no more than the truth and no more than he knew, said that in all probability the repairs will be done.' The acceptance of the truthfulness and the *c* reliability of that evidence by the man who was in the best position to give the best evidence on that question would appear to be conclusive. How can the judge's acceptance of it be reconciled with what he says a few lines later: 'Having regard to what Mr Smith said, I think the probability . . . is just about established'? If Mr Smith was truthful and reliable in saying 'in all probability', that results in much more than probability being 'just about established'. *d*

However, fortunately, it is not necessary to resolve that difficulty, since the judge went on to say 'although I would be more confident of the extent of the second plaintiffs' loss if the first plaintiffs were recovering the present day costs of the repairs so that they could, with a light heart, carry out the full repairs . . .' As in my judgment the plaintiffs are entitled to recover the 1978 cost of the repairs, this court should not remit this Methuselah of an action for a further hearing by the judge on that issue. We should *e* make our own assessment what the discount, if any, should be. In my opinion, the discount, if the law requires any discount (I do not find it necessary to decide this) would be de minimis. As the law requires us to disregard the trivial, I propose to disregard it, as I think Cantley J would have disregarded it, if he had reached the same conclusion as I have reached on the main issue.

So I would allow the appeal, and direct that judgment be entered for the first plaintiffs *f* for £30,327, without interest up to the date of Cantley J's judgment, and for the second plaintiffs for £11,951, also without interest up to that date. I would dismiss the cross-appeal.

BROWNE LJ. I agree that this appeal should be allowed and the cross-appeal dismissed, for the reasons given by Megaw LJ and the reasons which will be given by Donaldson LJ *g* in the judgment he will deliver very soon. I can summarise my own reasons fairly shortly, because they are in substance the same as theirs.

The first principle for the assessment of damages is that the injured person should, so far as money can do it, be put in the same position as if the wrong (in this case the tort) had not been committed against him: see Halsbury's Laws of England[2], and, e g, the authority cited by Megaw LJ, *Livingstone v Rawyards Coal Co*[3] per Lord Blackburn. This *h* the damages of £11,375 awarded to the first plaintiffs, for the cost of repairs in 1970, glaringly fail to do. By the time of the hearing in 1978 the cost had risen to £30,327. In fact, the repairs had not been done by that time, and the cost will probably have risen still further by the time they are done, but the plaintiffs do not make any further claim beyond the cost at the date of the hearing.

j

---

1 [1979] 2 All ER 118 at 127
2 12 Halsbury's Laws (4th Edn) para 1129
3 (1880) 5 App Cas 25 at 39

It is not disputed that in this case the measure of the first plaintiffs' damages is the cost
a of repair, as opposed to the other possible measure in a case of this sort, ie the diminution
in the value of the building. The only question is the time as at which that cost shall be
taken.

The general rule, both in contract and in tort, is that damages should be assessed as at
the date when the cause of action arises, but they may be assessed as at some later date.
In my view, Cantley J was plainly right in saying[1] 'The appropriate damages are the cost
b of repairs at the time when it was reasonable to begin repairs'. In *Johnson v Agnew*[2] Lord
Wilberforce said:

'The general principle for the assessment of damages is compensatory, ie that the
innocent party is to be placed, so far as money can do so, in the same position as if
the contract had been performed. Where the contract is one of sale, this principle
normally leads to assessment of damages as at the date of the breach, a principle
c recognised and embodied in s 51 of the Sale of Goods Act 1893. But this is not an
absolute rule; if to follow it would give rise to injustice, the court has power to fix
such other date as may be appropriate in the circumstances. In cases where a breach
of a contract for sale has occurred, and the innocent party reasonably continues to
try to have the contract completed, it would to me appear more logical and just
rather than tie him to the date of the original breach, to assess damages as at the date
d when (otherwise than by his default) the contract is lost. Support for this approach
is to be found in the cases. In *Ogle v Earl Vane*[3] the date was fixed by reference to
the time when the innocent party, acting reasonably, went into the market; in
Hickman v Haynes[4] at a reasonable time after the last request of the defendants (the
buyers) to withhold delivery. In *Radford v De Froberville*[5], where the defendant had
covenanted to build a wall, damages were held measurable as at the date of the
e hearing rather than at the date of the defendant's breach, unless the plaintiff ought
reasonably to have mitigated the breach at an earlier date.'

Lord Wilberforce, of course, was there speaking of damages for breach of contract, but
I have no doubt that the same principle applies to this case, where it is common ground
that the measure of damages is the cost of repairs. I think this view is supported by
f analogy by the decision of the House of Lords in *Birmingham City Corpn v West Midland
Baptist (Trust) Association*[6].

In this case, it was common ground, and the judge accepted, that it was reasonable to
postpone the doing of the repairs from 1968, when damage was first discovered, until
1970, and that 1970 was the earliest date as at which the cost of repairs should be
assessed. The defendants contended that the assessment should not be any further
g postponed; Cantley J accepted this contention, and assessed the damages on the cost of
repairs in 1970.

In the course of the passage of the judgment which Megaw LJ has already read, the
judge[7] held that 'As a commercial decision, judged exclusively from the point of view
of the immediate and short term welfare of the companies, it was reasonable to postpone
incurring the very considerable expense of these repairs ...' Like Megaw LJ, I
h understand this to mean that it was in this sense reasonable to postpone doing the repairs
until after the hearing. This finding was based on the evidence of Mr Smith, a director
of both the plaintiff companies and a chartered accountant, which is set out in the

---

j
1 [1979] 2 All ER 118 at 126
2 [1979] 1 All ER 883 at 896, [1979] 2 WLR 487 at 499
3 (1867) LR 2 QB 275; *affd* LR 3 QB 272
4 (1875) LR 10 CP 598
5 [1978] 1 All ER 33, [1977] 1 WLR 1262
6 [1969] 3 All ER 172, [1970] AC 874
7 [1979] 2 All ER 118 at 124

judgment and has been summarised already by Megaw LJ. He gave a number of reasons for the decision. Only one of what he said were the relevant factors was financial, and I **a** think that the judge's finding on this point falls far short of the 'impecuniosity' or 'financial embarrassment' in the *Liesbosch*[1] sense.

The judge said[2]: 'Whether the time is reasonable must be judged objectively and not taking into account such matters as impecuniosity or financial stringency which, in the words of Lord Wright in the *Liesbosch* case[1], are extrinsic.' I am afraid I do not clearly understand what the judge meant by 'objectively' in that sentence. If he meant that the **b** decision to postpone, although reasonable from the point of view of the plaintiff companies, was not reasonable from the point of view of a hypothetical reasonable commercial man, I cannot agree; it seems to me that any commercial man in the circumstances with which Mr Smith was faced could reasonably, and probably would, have come to the same decision.

The judge relied on *Philips v Ward*[3] and *Clark v Woor*[4], in which Lawton J simply **c** followed and applied *Philips v Ward*[3]. I agree with Megaw LJ that the reasoning of Denning LJ in *Philips v Ward*[3] can no longer be regarded as good law.

That leaves only the *Liesbosch* case[1]. I do not propose to analyse that difficult case, because I entirely agree with Megaw and Donaldson LJJ, that, for the reasons they give, it did not compel Cantley J to take the 1970 cost of repairs. I will only say that, like Megaw LJ, I agree with the observations of Oliver J in *Radford v De Froberville*[5] as to the **d** relationship between the duty to mitigate and the measure of damages in a case such as this.

I would, therefore, allow the first plaintiffs' appeal and vary the judgment by substituting £30,327 for £11,375. I think it necessarily follows that the appeal of the second plaintiffs should also be allowed, and their damages increased from £4,108 to £11,951. The plaintiffs' alternative ground of appeal as to interest therefore does not **e** arise, and, like Megaw LJ, I think it better to say nothing on that point. I agree that the cross-appeal should be dismissed, for the reasons given by Megaw LJ.

DONALDSON LJ. The general object underlying the rules for the assessment of damages is, so far as is possible by means of a monetary award, to place the plaintiff in the position which he would have occupied if he had not suffered the wrong complained of, **f** be that wrong a tort or a breach of contract. In the case of a tort causing damage to real property, this object is achieved by the application of one or other of two quite different measures of damage, or, occasionally, a combination of the two. The first is to take the capital value of the property in an undamaged state and to compare it with its value in a damaged state. The second is to take the cost of repair or reinstatement. Which is appropriate will depend on a number of factors, such as the plaintiff's future intentions **g** as to the use of the property and the reasonableness of those intentions. If he reasonably intends to sell the property in its damaged state, clearly the diminution in capital value is the true measure of damage. If he reasonably intends to continue to occupy it and to repair the damage, clearly the cost of repairs is the true measure. And there may be in-between situations.

Happily there is no issue in the present case as to which measure of damage falls to be **h** applied. It is the cost of reinstatement. The primary issue is as to how and, more particularly, on what date those costs are to be assessed. This is a very significant issue in the light of the increase in costs over the period between the occurrence of the damage in 1968 and the trial in 1978.

j

1   [1933] AC 449, [1933] All ER Rep 144
2   [1979] 2 All ER 118 at 126
3   [1956] 1 All ER 874, [1956] 1 WLR 471
4   [1965] 2 All ER 353, [1965] 1 WLR 650
5   [1978] 1 All ER 33 at 44, [1977] 1 WLR 1262 at 1272

a Counsel for the defendants submits, and I for my part would readily accept, that the general rule is that damages fall to be assessed as at the date when the cause of action arose. The rule is so stated by Lord Wilberforce in *Miliangos v George Frank (Textiles) Ltd*[1]. And I am inclined to think that in normal circumstances this would be applicable where the relevant measure of damage was diminution in the capital value of the property. But it is only a general or basic rule and is subject to many exceptions. Thus damages for personal injury, excluding consequential loss to which other principles

b apply, are assessed in the light of the value of money at the date of the hearing. The issue here is whether the assessment of damages based on the cost of repair or reinstatement is another exception, as counsel for the plaintiffs contends. I think that it is.

In *Birmingham City Corpn v West Midland Baptist (Trust) Association (Inc)*[2] the House of Lords was faced with the problem of whether the reasonable cost of equivalent reinstatement, which was the basis of compensation under the Land Compensation Act

c 1961, involved taking costs which prevailed at the date of the notice to treat or those which prevailed at the earliest date when the claimants might reasonably have begun rebuilding. The decision was in favour of the latter. Lord Reid[3] cited with approval various statements on the measure of compensation which assume that the assessed cost of reinstatement would be sufficient to enable the owner to undertake the work if he acted reasonably. In an era of rising costs, this could only happen if compensation was

d assessed on the basis of costs applicable at the time at which reinstatement would in fact occur, on the assumption that the owner acted reasonably. Again Lord Morris of Borth-y-Gest said[4]:

e 'The reasonable cost, depending on the facts of particular cases, will be the actual reasonable cost which a claimant has incurred or can be expected to incur; it will be such cost at the time when equivalent re-instatement reasonably does or should take place.'

Whilst this is not a decision on the measure of damages in tort, I think that the reasoning is directly applicable to the present problem. It is also only common sense, for, as counsel for the plaintiffs pointed out, it would be wholly unfair to the defendant to charge him with the costs applicable to reinstatement in 1968 when the damage occurred

f if the actual reinstatement took place at a later date when improved technology had reduced the cost. That this happy situation has not in fact arisen does not affect the point of principle.

In the absence of special and extraneous factors, there is no divergence between the interest of a plaintiff and a defendant on the choice of the most propitious moment at which to effect reinstatement. Both wish to achieve the maximum economy, at least so

g long as the plaintiff is in doubt whether he will be entitled to a full indemnity from the defendant. It follows that, in a case in which a plaintiff has reinstated his property before the hearing, the costs prevailing at the date of that operation which were reasonably incurred by him are prima facie those which are relevant. Equally in a case in which a plaintiff has *not* effected reinstatement by the time of the hearing, there is a prima facie presumption that the costs then prevailing are those which should be adopted in

h ascertaining the cost of reinstatement. There may indeed be cases in which the court has to estimate costs at some future time as being the reasonable time at which to reinstate, but that is not this case.

This is, however, only a prima facie approach. It may appear on the evidence that the plaintiff, acting reasonably, should have undertaken the reinstatement at some date earlier than that in fact adopted or, as the case may be, earlier than the hearing. If so, the

j

---

1   [1975] 3 All ER 801 at 813, [1976] AC 443 at 468
2   [1969] 3 All ER 172, [1970] AC 874
3   [1969] 3 All ER 172 at 176, [1970] AC 874 at 894
4   [1969] 3 All ER 172 at 183, [1970] AC 874 at 903

relevant costs are those ruling at that earlier date. Whether this is regarded as arising out of the primary measure of damage, ie that the relevant time is when the property should *a* have been reinstated or whether it is regarded as being a reflection of a plaintiff's duty to mitigate his loss, may not matter.

In the present case Cantley J accepted that the relevant date was when it was reasonable to begin repairs. However, in deciding what was reasonable, he considered himself bound by the decision of the House of Lords in the *Liesbosch* case[1] to disregard such factors as impecuniosity or financial stringency experienced by the plaintiffs. Accordingly, *b* although he considered that the plaintiffs had acted reasonably in deferring reinstatement until after the hearing, he felt constrained to adopt September 1970 costs, the delay until then being justified exclusively on other grounds, namely, the need to make sure that no further damage would occur before repairs were started. Dealing with the latter delay he said[2]:

> 'I find that the first plaintiffs could probably have raised the money for repairs but *c* this would have increased their annual losses and their financial stringency. As a commercial decision, judged exclusively from the point of view of the immediate and short term welfare of the companies, it was reasonable to postpone incurring the very considerable expense of these repairs while no harm was being done to the building by the delay in repairing it and while these three rich defendants with apparent if not genuine belief in the validity of their defences were firmly denying *d* liability to make even a contribution.'

Whatever the difficulties inherent in the *Liesbosch*[1] decision, and it is not at once apparent why a tortfeasor must take his victim as he finds him in terms of exceptionally high or low profit earning capacity, but not in terms of pecuniosity or impecuniosity which may be their manifestations, it binds this court as much as it bound Cantley J *e* unless and until it is reviewed by the House of Lords. However, it is important to see precisely what it did decide.

The Edison fouled the Liesbosch's moorings, carried her out to sea and sank her. The ordinary measure of damage was the cost of buying another similar vessel, the cost of getting her to the Liesbosch's old moorings and any loss of profit consequent on the disruption of commercial operations whilst the substitute vessel was being obtained and *f* delivered. However, the plaintiffs contended for a different and special measure of damage. Substitute dredgers were available for purchase but the plaintiffs could not afford to buy them. Instead they hired another dredger, the Adria, which was larger than the Liesbosch, more expensive to operate and for which they had to pay a very high rate of hire. Eventually the port authority, for whom the plaintiffs were working, bought the Adria and resold her to the plaintiffs under a credit sale contract. The *g* plaintiffs claimed the cost of hiring the Adria until the port authority bought and resold her to them, the cost of purchasing the Adria and the excess cost of working her as compared with the Liesbosch together with unrecovered overhead charges and lost profit whilst they were without any dredger. The ordinary measure of damage is based on market rates. The measure of damage claimed by the plaintiffs was quite different, namely, one based on their actual loss and expenditure. *h*

As I understand Lord Wright's speech, he took the view that in so far as the plaintiffs in fact suffered more than the loss assessed on a market basis, the excess loss flowed directly from their lack of means and not from the tortious act, or alternatively it was too remote in law. In·modern terms, I think that he would have said that it was not foreseeable.

j

---

1   [1933] AC 449, [1933] All ER Rep 144
2   [1979] 2 All ER 118 at 124

The position of the plaintiffs in the present case seems to me to be quite different.
a They were not impecunious in the *Liesbosch*[1] sense of one who could not go out into the market. On the contrary, they were financially able to carry out the work of reinstatement in 1970. However, on the judge's findings, they were commercially prudent in not incurring the cash flow deficiency which would have resulted from their undertaking the work in the autumn of 1970 and waiting for reimbursement until after the hearing, particularly when the defendants were denying liability and there was a
b dispute as to what works could and should be done by way of reinstatement. In my judgment, the decison in the *Liesbosch* case[1] has no application to such a situation, which is distinguishable.

If the decision whether to adopt 1970 or 1978 costs turns on whether, bearing in mind the likelihood that prices would rise, the plaintiffs should have undertaken the work in 1970 in pursuance of their duty to mitigate their damage, there is another ground for
c distinguishing the *Liesbosch* case[1] and for taking full account of the plaintiffs' financial position. This is that Lord Wright's explanation of the decision in *Clippens Oil Co Ltd v Edinburgh and District Water Trustees*[2], where Lord Collins said that the tortfeasor must take his victim as he found him, including any lack of means, was that that decision represented the rule in relation to the duty to minimise damage.

I would therefore allow the appeal by the plaintiffs and, for the reasons stated by
d Megaw LJ, would dismiss the defendants' cross-appeal.

Appeal allowed. Judgment below varied by substituting as the amount of damages, for the first plaintiffs, £30,327, and, for the second plaintiffs, £11,951. Cross-appeal dismissed. Leave to appeal to the House of Lords refused.

e Solicitors: *Lewis & Dick* (for the plaintiffs); *Hewitt, Woollacott & Chown* (for the second and third defendants).

Mary Rose Plummer   Barrister.

_____

f 1   [1933] AC 449, [1933] All ER Rep 144
2   [1907] AC 291 at 303

Domb and another v Isoz   *a*

COURT OF APPEAL, CIVIL DIVISION
BUCKLEY, BRIDGE AND TEMPLEMAN LJJ
27th, 28th, 29th NOVEMBER 1979

Sale of land – Exchange of contracts – Authority of solicitor – Exchange by telephone – Vendor's
solicitor holding vendor's and purchaser's parts of contract duly signed – Vendor's and ***b***
purchaser's solicitors agreeing to exchange contracts by telephone – Whether such exchange
resulting in binding contract.

Sale of land – Exchange of contracts – Agreement subject to contract – Parts exchanged required
to be in identical terms – Purchase price of house to include fittings and fixtures – Purchase price
apportioned in vendor's part of contract – Purchase price not apportioned in purchaser's part of ***c***
contract – Whether contract able to be rectified – Whether exchange of parts resulting in
concluded contract.

Sale of land – Damages for breach of contract – Damages in substitution for specific performance
– Date of assessment – Purchaser claiming specific performance of contract for sale of house –
Purchaser then buying another house – Purchaser subsequently electing to claim damages in lieu ***d***
of specific performance – Date at which damages should be assessed – Whether damages should
be assessed at date of purchase of other house or date of election to claim damages.

The plaintiffs were proposing to buy the defendant's house and its fittings and fixtures
for £32,500. On 22nd December 1977 their solicitors sent the plaintiffs' part of the ***e***
contract, duly signed, to the defendant's solicitor and asked him (i) to confirm that the
price might be apportioned on the basis of £30,000 for the house and £2,500 for the
fittings and fixtures, and (ii) to hold the enclosed contract to their order until they were
able to agree by telephone that contracts might be exchanged. By 9th February 1978 the
defendant's solicitor also had in his possession the defendant's part of the contract. Before
it had been signed the defendant's solicitor had added a clause apportioning the purchase ***f***
price in the way mentioned in the letter from the plaintiffs' solicitors. That clause was
not in the part of the contract signed by the plaintiffs. On 9th February the defendant's
solicitor rang the plaintiffs' solicitors and they agreed that the contracts should be treated
as immediately exchanged by telephone at that moment. The defendant's solicitor never
forwarded the defendant's part of the contract to the plaintiffs' solicitors. The defendant
refused to proceed with the sale of the house whereupon the plaintiffs brought an action ***g***
against her claiming an order for specific performance or, alternatively, damages. The
defendant contended that a binding contract had not been concluded (i) because, in the
absence of express agreement to the contrary, her solicitor had authority only to exchange
contracts in the customary manner, e g by physical or postal delivery of her part of the
contract to the plaintiffs' solicitors, and he could not agree to act as the plaintiffs' agent to
receive delivery of it, and (ii) because the two parts of the contract were not in identical ***h***
terms. The judge dismissed the action. The plaintiffs appealed. Between the date of the
trial and the hearing of the appeal they bought another house and at the hearing of the
appeal elected to claim damages in lieu of specific performance.

Held – The appeal would be allowed, and an enquiry ordered as to damages, for the
following reasons—   ***j***
    (i) A client impliedly and ostensibly authorised his solicitor to effect exchange in any
manner which the law recognised as amounting to exchange. In law, exchange of
contracts was effected as soon as each part of the contract, signed by the vendor or
purchaser as the case might be, was in actual or constructive possession of the other party
or his solicitor; possession by an agent of the party or by an agent of his solicitor was

sufficient provided that person had control over the document and could at any time
a procure its actual physical possession. On the evidence, from the time of the telephone
conversation on 9th February 1978 the defendant's part of the contract was in the
effective control and constructive possession of the plaintiffs' solicitors and the plaintiffs'
part of the contract was held to the defendant's order. Accordingly there was an effective
exchange of contracts (see p 948 *e* to *j*, p 949 *c*, p 950 *e* to *j* and p 952 *f* to p 953 *c*, post).

(ii) The fact that the defendant's solicitor had written an additional clause into the part
b of the contract signed by the defendant did not affect the plaintiffs' right to relief because
both parties intended that the sale should include the fixtures and fittings, and if the
clause gave rise to any substantial difference between the two parts of the contract as
signed, the remedy of rectification would be available (see p 949 *g h*, p 951 *a* and p 954
b c, post); *Harrison v Battye* [1974] 3 All ER 830 distinguished.

(iii) The damages should be assessed as at the date at which the plaintiffs elected to
c pursue the remedy of damages in lieu of specific performance (see p 950 *b* to *d*, p 951 *a*
and p 954 *b c*, post); dictum of Lord Wilberforce in *Johnson v Agnew* [1979] 1 All ER at
896 applied.

Per Templeman LJ. In order to avoid uncertainty in such cases about the terms and
effect of a telephone conversation, it is desirable that a short formula which effects an
exchange of contracts by telephone should be devised and adopted by the legal profession
d (see p 953 *j*, post).

Cases referred to in judgments
Eccles v Bryant [1947] 2 All ER 865, [1948] Ch 93, [1948] LJR 418, CA, 12 Digest
(Reissue) 78, 416.
Harrison v Battye [1974] 3 All ER 830, [1975] 1 WLR 58, CA, Digest (Cont Vol D) 114,
417a.
e *Johnson v Agnew* [1979] 1 All ER 883, [1979] 2 WLR 487, HL.

Cases also cited
Caldwell v Sumpters (a firm) [1972] 1 All ER 567, [1972] Ch 478, CA.
Compass v Thomas (1973) 117 Sol Jo 306.
Damodaran s/o Raman v Choe Kuan Him [1979] 3 WLR 383, PC.
f *King v O'Shee* (1951) 158 EG 83.

Appeal
This was an appeal by the plaintiffs, Alfred Hyman Domb and Irene Stella Domb, against
a judgment of Mr Brian Dillon QC sitting as a Deputy High Court judge given on 31st
July 1978, whereby he dismissed their action against the defendant, Cecile Clair Isoz, for,
g inter alia, specific performance of an alleged agreement in writing for the sale of a house
known as 34 Erskine Hill, London NW11. Between the date of the trial of the action and
the hearing of the appeal the plaintiffs bought another house and at the hearing of the
appeal they elected to claim damages for breach of contract in lieu of specific
performance. The facts are set out in the judgment of Buckley LJ.

h Peter Millett QC and Roger Toulson for the plaintiffs.
Gerald Godfrey QC and Nicholas Stewart for the defendant.

BUCKLEY LJ. In this action the plaintiffs sue as purchasers for specific performance
of a contract of sale by the defendant to them of property known as 34 Erskine Hill,
London NW11. Alternatively they claim damages for breach of contract. The action
j was tried before Mr Brian Dillon QC sitting as a deputy judge of the Chancery Division,
on 31st July 1978. At that stage the plaintiffs were seeking specific performance of the
contract. The learned deputy judge dismissed the action on the ground that there was
no concluded contract. The plaintiffs appeal from that dismissal. Since judgment they
have bought another house and consequently at the opening of this appeal the plaintiffs
elected to seek damages rather than specific performance.

The contract in question formed one of a chain of transactions, as so frequently occurs nowadays when domestic accommodation is being disposed of on the market; there *a* were three transactions involved. The plaintiffs were proposing to sell their house, 38 Chelmsford Square, Willesden, to a Mr Petsas. The plaintiffs' solicitors acting in that matter were the firm of Yudolph & Brooke and the partner in that firm who was acting for the plaintiffs in the matter was a Mr Redstone. Mr Petsas' solicitors were Messrs Lickfolds. The plaintiffs were proposing to acquire 34 Erskine Hill from the defendant, and in that matter again Mr Redstone was acting for the plaintiffs. The defendant was *b* represented by the firm of William Heath & Co in the person of a Mr Bond, who was a salaried solicitor employed by that firm.

The defendant was proposing to acquire a flat or maisonette in Westbourne Terrace, London, from a Mr Holding. In respect of that transaction Mr Bond was the solicitor acting for the defendant and, by coincidence, Messrs Yudolph & Brooke were the solicitors acting for Mr Holding. But it was not Mr Redstone who was acting for Mr *c* Holding; it was Mr Brooke, another partner in that firm. I shall refer to those three transactions as the first, the second and the third transaction. This action relates to the second transaction.

On 22nd December 1977 Mr Redstone wrote a letter to Mr Bond (for the sake of simplicity I shall refer to them by their individual names rather than by the names of their firms) in relation to the second transaction. In that letter he said: 'We enclose *d* herewith our clients' part of the contract together with their cheque in your favour for £2,950 the balance of the deposit the sum of £300 being held by Messrs Benham & Reeves your clients' Agents.'

Then there comes a passage which relates to a separate matter, but I shall read it now while I am on the letter:

> 'We are instructed that there are included in the sale for the avoidance of doubt *e* the following:—(1) Garden shed. (2) All bathroom fittings. (3) All kitchen fitted units including wall and floor units, electric hob and the wall oven. Our clients are of the opinion that the reasonable value that may be ascribed to the above fixtures and fittings is £2,500 and would you, therefore, please confirm that the price of £32,500 may be apportioned as to £30,000 for the property and £2,500 for the above mentioned items. The transfer from your client to our clients will then be at *f* £30,000. [Then I omit two irrelevant short paragraphs and read on:] Would you please hold the enclosed contract and deposit cheque to our order until we are able to agree with you on the telephone that contracts may be exchanged and agree a completion date which we are fairly fluid on as we should be receiving in the course of the next day or so our clients' contract for the sale of their present property and we wish to effect simultaneous exchange of contracts on both transactions.' *g*

Immediately before 9th February 1978, which was a crucial date in the history of this matter, the position with regard to the three transactions was as follows; I read from the judgment of the trial judge:

> '*The first transaction*
> 'On 20th December 1977 Messrs Lickfolds had sent to Mr Redstone the part of *h* the contract for the purchase of 38 Chelmsford Square signed by Mr Petsas and a cheque for the deposit. They had expressed eagerness on Mr Petsas' part for early completion and had authorised Mr Redstone to exchange at any time by inserting a completion date 14 to 28 days from exchange and sending the vendors' part. Subsequently, by further letters, Messrs Lickfolds had sought to put a degree of pressure for an early exchange on the plaintiffs. By 9th February Mr Redstone had *i* in his hands the part of this contract signed by the plaintiffs and was in a position to exchange if he could tie up the second transaction.
>
> '*The second transaction*
> 'On 22nd December 1977 Mr Redstone sent to Messrs William Heath and Co the

part of the contract for the purchase of 34 Erskine Hill signed by the plaintiffs and a cheque for the deposit. The relevant paragraph of his letter reads as follows [and then the judge read a passage from the letter I have just referred to, and the judgment goes on:] By 9th February, Mr Bond of William Heath and Co had in his hands the part of this contract signed by the defendant and was in a position to exchange if he could tie up the third transaction. There was, in fact, a difference between the part of the contracts signed by the plaintiffs and the part signed by the defendant; this raises an entirely separate point to which I shall refer later.

'*The third transaction*

'The title to 40 Westbourne Terrace was sub-under leasehold and a bit complicated although registered. Mr Bond had had some difficulty in getting hold of documents which he needed to see before he would agree to an exchange of contracts. Mr Brooke did not hold these documents since he had not acted on Mr Holding's purchase. Accordingly, Mr Bond had got in touch with the solicitors who had then acted and on the morning of 9th February he received from them the documents he wanted. He had in his hands the part of this contract signed by the defendant and he had been told by the defendant that Mr Holding had told her that 2nd March 1978 would be acceptable to Mr Holding as a completion date. Mr Bond did not, however, know that Mr Brooke had not yet received Mr Holding's signed part of the contract. Moreover, though Mr Bond believed from what the defendant had told him that Mr Holding would have told Mr Brooke that 2nd March was an acceptable completion date, I am not satisfied that Mr Holding had in fact mentioned this date to Mr Brooke.'

On 9th February 1978 Mr Bond telephoned Messrs Yudolph & Brooke and spoke in the first instance to Mr Brooke. He told Mr Brooke that he had received the outstanding documents, and there was some discussion about inspection of the register and the obtaining of evidence that there was no encumbrance affecting the title. At that stage Mr Bond asked to be transferred to Mr Redstone, and the switchboard at Yudolph & Brooke's transferred Mr Bond to Mr Redstone and another conversation took place between them. According to the judge's findings, Mr Bond and Mr Redstone agreed on 2nd March 1978 as the completion date for the second transaction. Mr Redstone then proposed that the contracts should be treated as immediately exchanged by telephone as of the moment they were speaking, and that this should be irrevocable and without benefit of second thoughts; and Mr Bond, fully understanding that proposal, agreed to it.

Mr Bond was then transferred back again by the switchboard to Mr Brooke, and some reference was made between them to 2nd March as a proposed completion date for the third transaction; Mr Brooke said that he would have to obtain instructions about that from Mr Holding. I should observe here that after that conversation Mr Redstone despatched to Messrs Lickfolds the plaintiffs' part of the contract for the sale comprised in the first transaction, and Mr Bond, on that same day, dictated a letter in the following terms addressed to Messrs Yudolph & Brooke:

'Dear Sirs, *Re: 34 Erskine Hill, N.W.11.* As arranged, we enclose our client's signed part of the Contract having dated both as of 9th February and having inserted in each as the completion date 2nd March next as arranged.'

Mr Brooke made contact with Mr Holding and was instructed by Mr Holding to insist on a six-week completion period, with the consequence that he was unable to comply with Mr Bond's request that the completion date for the third transaction should be 2nd March, and with the ultimate result that the contract between Mr Holding and the defendant went off, and the defendant never succeeded in acquiring the premises in Westbourne Terrace.

The learned judge took the view that the effect of the conversation on the telephone of 9th February between Mr Bond and Mr Redstone was that they thereby purported to

dispense with exchange of the contracts relating to the second transaction, and to bind
their clients immediately to a contract in the terms of the documents which they had *a*
already signed but which, on the judge's view, had not been exchanged.

With deference to the learned judge, I take a different view. Mr Redstone and Mr
Bond did not purport to dispense with exchange of the contracts; they purported to
effect an exchange of the two parts of the contract. The question is, I think, whether they
succeeded in achieving their object.

By that conversation Mr Redstone released Mr Bond from the obligation under which *b*
he had hitherto been in consequence of the letter of 22nd December, to hold the
plaintiffs' part of the contract relating to the second transaction to Mr Redstone's order.
Mr Bond, by the same transaction, by implication if not expressly, undertook to transmit
the defendant's part of the same contract to Mr Redstone.

In the course of the oral evidence at the trial Mr Redstone, in cross-examination, was
asked the following question:
                                                                                          c
'Q. But what I understand the conversation to mean is this: first of all, that the
pieces of paper which we had from you were released from being held to your
order. That is the first consequence. A. Yes.'

The pieces of paper there referred to are, of course, the plaintiffs' part of the contract.
Then:
                                                                                          d
'Q. So that the [plaintiffs'] piece which he had been holding for you came over to
us. A. Yes; that is a consequence.
'Q. That is one thing we accept as agreed, and there is no dispute that Mr Bond
said words which involved him in the obligation, as he thought, to send the other
piece signed by [the defendant] back to your firm . . .'

Mr Bond, also in cross-examination, was asked the following questions and gave the *e*
following answers, relating to the same event:

'Q. You now held the [plaintiffs'] part of the contract? A. Oh yes, yes.
'Q. To your client's order in fact, in practice. A. Yes.
'Q. And you felt yourself, as a result of the conversation, to be under an obligation
to send [the defendant's] part to Mr Redstone? A. Yes.   *f*
'Q. Without trying to define what sort of an obligation it was, did you regard that
as a legal obligation? A. I would think it was a professional rather than a legal
obligation.
'Q. A professional rather than a legal? A. Yes.
'Q. It was an obligation you owed on behalf of your client though? A. In so far
as one is acting as a solicitor, one is generally acting for a client at the same time.
'Q. Yes. A. The two do obviously tend to become a little confused at times.   *g*
'Q. The obligation, using the word you yourself used, the obligation related to a
document that was your client's document originally, [the defendant's] document.
A. Yes.
'Q. And that is what your obligation was directed to. Is that right? To sending
it to Mr Redstone. A. Yes.   *h*
'Q. Your client's document. A. Yes, yes.
'Q. Your obligation must necessarily have involved your client. A. Oh yes,
quite.
'Q. In that case, are you saying that this was simply a matter of professional
courtesy between solicitors, or do you go further than that? A. I think something
more than courtesy, most certainly.
'Q. Another expression you used in another part of your evidence was that from *i*
then onwards you were under a duty to send it. A. Yes.
'Q. I ask you again. Was that a legal duty, did you feel? A. As far as I am
concerned, the two terms are . . .
'Q. Synonymous. A. Completely synonymous.'

Counsel for the plaintiff, says that thereafter Mr Bond held the defendant's part of the contract to the order of Mr Redstone, and that Mr Bond could have no right to retain it from Messrs Yudolph & Brooke. I think the question which arises is whether Mr Bond had ostensible authority to do that; if so, did it amount to an exchange of contracts?

Counsel for the defendant has submitted that Mr Bond did have ostensible authority to effect exchange of contracts in relation to 34 Erskine Hill, but he says 'in the customary manner', that is to say, by an exchange carried out in accordance with the settled practice

of conveyancing, for example by physical or postal delivery to the purchaser's solicitors of her part of the contract, and he submits that Mr Bond did not have ostensible authority to effect exchange of contracts in relation to 34 Erskine Hill otherwise than in what he describes as 'the customary manner'. In that respect counsel for the defendant relies on the decision of this court in *Eccles v Bryant*[1]. The headnote of that case in the Law Reports reads[2]:

'Where parties enter into an agreement for the sale of real property "subject to contract," the contract, in the absence of express agreement to the contrary, is not complete until the parties have exchanged their copies in accordance with ordinary conveyancing practice, and until such exchange is effected either party can withdraw.'

In so far as that headnote suggests that the court said anything about what the 'ordinary conveyancing practice' was, I think the headnote goes further than anything that can be found in the judgments.

Lord Greene MR said[3]:

'One thing is quite clear on the facts of this case to my mind, that both firms of solicitors, one of whom—that is the vendors' solicitors—practised in East Grinstead and the other of whom, the purchaser's solicitors, practised in London, when they were instructed to carry this matter through by their respective clients, contemplated and intended from beginning to end to do so in the customary way which is familiar to every firm of solicitors in the country, namely, by preparing the engrossment of the draft contract when agreed in duplicate, the intention being to

do what I have no doubt at this very moment is happening in dozens of solicitors' offices all over the country, namely, to exchange the two parts when signed by their respective clients.'

Further on Lord Greene MR said[4]:

'When parties are proposing to enter into a contract, the manner in which the contract is to be created so as to bind them must be gathered from the intentions of the parties express or implied. In such a contract as this, there is a well-known, common and customary method of dealing; namely, by exchange, and anyone who contemplates that method of dealing cannot contemplate the coming into existence of a binding contract before the exchange takes place. It was argued that exchange is a mere matter of machinery, having in itself no particular importance and no

particular significance. So far as significance is concerned, it appears to me that not only is it not right to say of exchange that it has no significance, but it is the crucial and vital fact which brings the contract into existence. As for importance, it is of the greatest importance, and that is why in past ages this procedure came to be recognised by everybody to be the proper procedure and was adopted. When you are dealing with contracts for the sale of land, it is of the greatest importance to the vendor that he should have a document signed by the purchaser, and to the

purchaser that he should have a document signed by the vendor. It is of the greatest

---

1 [1947] 2 All ER 865, [1948] Ch 93
2 [1948] Ch 93
3 [1948] Ch 93 at 97, cf [1947] 2 All ER 865 at 865–866
4 [1948] Ch 93 at 99–100, cf [1947] 2 All ER 865 at 866–867

importance that there should be no dispute whether a contract had or had not been made and that there should be no dispute as to the terms of it. This particular *a* procedure of exchange ensures that none of those difficulties will arise. Each party has got what is a document of title, because directly a contract in writing relating to land is entered into, it is a document of title. That can be illustrated, of course, by remembering the simple case where a purchaser makes a sub-sale. The contract is a vital document for the purpose of the sub-sale. If he had not got the vendor's part, signed by the vendor, to show to the sub-purchaser, he would not be able to make *b* a good title. If the argument for the purchaser is right and the contract comes into existence before exchange takes place, it would mean that neither party could call upon the other to hand over his part. The non-exchanged part would remain the property of the party who signed it, because exchange would be no element in the contract at all and therefore you could get this position, that the purchaser might wish to resell and would have no right to obtain from the vendor the vendor's *c* signed part.'

I draw attention in particular to the sentence in which Lord Greene MR said that if the argument for the purchaser was right and the contract came into existence before exchange took place, it would mean that neither party could call on the other to hand over his part of the contract. *d*

That judgment, in my opinion, throws no light on what methods of exchange can properly be employed or can be described as 'exchange in accordance with ordinary conveyancing practice'. Nor, I think, do either of the other judgments do so.

In my judgment, the essential characteristic of exchange of contracts is that each party shall have such a document signed by the other party in his possession or control so that, at his own need, he can have the document available for his own use. Exchange of a *e* written contract for sale is in my judgment effected so soon as each part of the contract, signed by the vendor or the purchaser as the case may be, is in the actual or constructive possession of the other party or of his solicitor. Such possession need not be actual or physical possession; possession by an agent of the party or of his solicitor, in such circumstances that the party or solicitor in question has control over the document and can at any time procure its actual physical possession will, in my opinion, suffice. In such *f* a case the possession of the agent is the possession of the principal. A party's solicitor employed to act in respect of such a contract has, subject to express instructions, implied authority to effect exchange of contracts and so to make the bargain binding on his client. This he can, in my judgment, do by any method which is effectual to constitute exchange.

In the present case, in my judgment, Mr Bond on 9th February constituted himself Mr *g* Redstone's agent to hold the defendant's part of the contract to Mr Redstone's order from the moment of the telephonic agreement, and to despatch it to Mr Redstone forthwith, or on Mr Redstone's demand. At the same time Mr Bond became the holder of the plaintiffs' part of the contract to the order of his own client, the defendant, and was discharged from any continuing obligation to hold it to Mr Redstone's order as he had theretofore been bound to do in pursuance of the letter of 22nd December. *h*

It is, I think, erroneous to suggest that any special authority from the defendant would have been necessary to enable Mr Bond to take this course. He had authority to effect exchange, and he had ostensible authority to effect exchange at any time, and he did effect exchange of the defendant's part of the contract for the plaintiffs' part of the contract. From the moment of the telephonic agreement the defendant's part of the contract was in the effective control of Mr Redstone and in his constructive possession. *j* It was no longer the defendant's document.

The judge thought that such a practice was a bad practice. Again with deference, I do not agree. In the present state of the property market, particularly where domestic houses are concerned, chain bargains are of very frequent occurrence. These necessarily require simultaneous contracts for sale and purchase all the way along the chain.

Synchronisation of this kind cannot as a practical matter be secured by physical exchange
a across the table, or by messenger, or by post; the only method which counsel have been
able to suggest involves telephonic agreements which are synchronised, or as nearly
completely synchronised as is humanly possible. The mechanics for carrying out such an
exchange may, I think, vary. There are probably a number of variants that could be
adopted; but the essence is that, as the consequence of the telephonic communication,
the part of the contract signed by each party must be either physically or constructively
b in the hands of the other party or his solicitor, free from any claim of the first party
which would enable him to control the second party in his right to hold and retain the
document and deal with it as he chooses. As the matter must be handled, if not by a
party in person, by solicitors, that is to say by professional men of high integrity who are
officers of the court, amenable to the control of the court in the conduct of their
professional affairs, such a procedure does not, in my view, involve any undesirable
c degree of risk of its leading to errors or confusion.

On these grounds in my judgment the events which occurred in the present case on
9th February constituted an effective exchange of contracts, and the sale by the defendant
to the plaintiffs of 34 Erskine Hill thereby became binding.

When Mr Bond came to deal with the defendant's part of the contract for sale, he
wrote in an additional clause dealing with the position in regard to the fixtures and
d fittings. He added in manuscript a clause to the following effect under the special
conditions of sale:

> 'At completion the Vendor shall sell and the Purchasers shall purchase the garden
> shed, all bathroom fittings and all kitchen fitted units including wall and floor units,
> electric hob and the wall oven, and of the price of £32,500 the sum of £2,500.00
> shall be attributable to the above-mentioned fixtures, fittings and effects.'

e
The point was taken below, and it has been taken in this court, that consequently the part
of the contract signed by the defendant did not accord in all respects with the part of the
contract signed by the plaintiffs, for which reason it is said that there was no concluded
contract between them. Reference has been made to *Harrison v Battye*[1], where it was
held that a sale of land subject to contract was not concluded until the two parts of the
f contract were exchanged in the same terms, and since in that case the vendor's part had
not been amended to show the changed amount of the deposit, the two parts would have
been in different terms if they had in fact been exchanged, and there was no concluded
contract. In that case Sir Eric Sachs pointed out that the position would have been very
different if it had been possible to raise a case for rectification of the defective part of the
contract. In the present case, if the clause which was written in by Mr Bond on the
g defendant's part of the contract gives rise to any substantial difference between the two
parts of the contract as signed by the parties, there could in my judgment be no doubt
whatever that the remedy of rectification would be available, for it is common ground
that both parties intended that the sale should include the fixtures and fittings referred
to, and the apportionment of the price was purely a matter of conveyancing and not of
contract and would be of no significance. In my judgment, the fact that Mr Bond wrote
h that additional clause into the part of the contract signed by the defendant in no way
affects the right of the plaintiffs to relief in the present action.

For these reasons I have reached a different conclusion from that of the learned judge
who, as I said at the outset, took the view that there was no concluded contract because
there had been no exchange of contracts. In my judgment the contract was concluded
and, had the plaintiffs wished to pursue their remedy in specific performance, they
j would have been entitled to specific performance of it. However, they have made the
choice of asking for damages and not for specific performance, so there will have to be an
inquiry as to damages.

---

1   [1974] 3 All ER 830, [1975] 1 WLR 58

The question has been raised as to the date at which damages should be assessed, and in that connection we were referred to *Johnson v Agnew*[1], a decision of the House of *a* Lords. In that case Lord Wilberforce said this[2]:

> 'In cases where a breach of contract for sale has occurred, and the innocent party reasonably continues to try to have the contract completed, it would to me appear more logical and just rather than tie him to the date of the original breach, to assess damages as at the date when (otherwise than by his default) the contract is lost.'
  b

Applying that observation to the present case, it seems to me that the date at which damages should be assessed was yesterday's date, that being the day on which the plaintiffs elected to pursue the remedy of damages in lieu of the remedy of specific performance, which down to that date they had pursued. The fact that between trial and the hearing of the appeal they have bought another house, which is no doubt the reason which now prompts them to be content with damages rather than specific performance, *c* does not in my judgment mean that at the date of that purchase they elected to abandon their right to specific performance; that purchase in no way affected their right to insist on the performance by the defendant of her obligations under the contract for sale which is now under consideration, and had they wished to do so, there would have been no reason why they should not have continued to pursue their remedy in specific performance. *d*

Accordingly, I would direct an enquiry as to damages, indicating that the correct date at which to assess the damages is yesterday.

BRIDGE LJ. A solicitor acting for a vendor or a purchaser who holds his client's signed part of the contract has his client's ostensible authority to effect exchange of contracts; so much is common ground. *e*

With respect to counsel's argument for the defendant, I can see no reason why the transaction which is to constitute the exchange should not be carried into effect in any manner which the law can recognise as amounting to an exchange. If both parts of the contract have been physically exchanged in advance and are held by each solicitor to the order of the other, it is again common ground that each solicitor can then agree by telephone to release his client's part of the contract to be held by the other solicitor on his *f* own client's behalf.

Similarly where, as here, the vendor's solicitor holds the purchaser's part of the contract to the order of the purchaser's solicitor but also holds his own client's part on behalf of his own client, I can see no sensible reason why an agreement that the purchaser's solicitor will release the purchaser's part of the contract to the vendor, and the vendor's solicitor will hold the vendor's part to the order of the purchaser, should not *g* take effect according to its terms. Thereupon the vendor's solicitor has the actual possession of the purchaser's part of the contract, which he holds on behalf of his client, and the purchaser's solicitor on behalf of his client has possession of the vendor's part through the agency of the vendor's solicitor, who has agreed to hold it to his order.

In conveyancing transactions, for a solicitor to hold documents to the order of a party other than his own client is the merest commonplace, and the conduct of conveyancing *h* business, particularly when mortgagees are concerned, could hardly be efficiently conducted if that were not so. If it is within a solicitor's authority, actual or ostensible, to hand over his own client's document to the other party, it is equally within his authority to agree to hold the document to the other party's order.

Accordingly I am satisfied that on the judge's findings of fact an exchange of contracts was here effected by the telephone conversation between Mr Redstone and Mr Bond on *j* 9th February 1978 and that thereupon a binding contract was concluded.

---

1   [1979] 1 All ER 883, [1979] 2 WLR 487
2   [1979] 1 All ER 883 at 896, [1979] 2 WLR 487 at 499

a For these reasons and for those given in the judgment of Buckley LJ, including his reasons relating to the point raised as to the difference between the two parts of the contract, I too would allow the appeal and direct an enquiry as to damages; on the point as to when damages are to be assessed, I also agree with Buckley LJ.

TEMPLEMAN LJ. Conveyancing is a complicated business. A chain of transactions is frequently involved where no vendor will sell until he can purchase and no purchaser
b will buy until he can sell. Each client as vendor and purchaser needs time to make up his mind and change his mind after studying surveys and legal reports and other relevant matters and each client expects everyone else to be ready when he is ready. Skilful conveyancers are required to forge the chain, to see that no bargain is lost and that no one is left without a home. Binding and enforceable undertakings between professional men play an essential part at different stages. Mistakes are bound to occur occasionally and
c each client must be protected by the insurance of his solicitor against financial loss, even though damages will never fully compensate a client for the loss of a bargain or the loss of a home. This appeal illustrates some of the difficulties which can arise and some of the reasons why the Royal Commission on Legal Services[1] came to the conclusion that conveyancing should be confined to members of a trained and responsible profession, which should be improved rather than diluted or invaded.
d Mr Petsas was ready and willing to contract to buy 38 Chelmsford Square from the plaintiffs. The plaintiffs for their part were willing to sell 38 Chelmsford Square to Mr Petsas; by February 1978 all that remained to be done was for the part of the contract signed by the plaintiffs to be delivered by their solicitor, Mr Redstone, to the solicitor acting for Mr Petsas. But although the plaintiffs were willing to sell 38 Chelmsford Square, they were not ready to do so. They were willing to contract to buy 34 Erskine
e Hill from the defendant, and as early as 22nd December 1977 their part of the contract had been sent by Mr Redstone to Mr Bond, the solicitor acting for the defendant. The letter which accompanied the plaintiffs' part of the contract when it was sent by Mr Redstone to Mr Bond contained the following request and direction by Mr Redstone to Mr Bond:

f   'Would you please hold the enclosed contract and deposit cheque to our order until we are able to agree with you on the telephone that contracts may be exchanged and agree a completion date which we are fairly fluid on as we should be receiving in the course of the next day or so our clients' contract for the sale of their present property and we wish to effect simultaneous exchange of contracts on both transactions.'

g What remained to be done to complete a contract in respect of 34 Erskine Hill was for the part of the contract which had already been signed by the defendant and was in the possession of Mr Bond to be delivered to Mr Redstone, and for Mr Redstone to authorise Mr Bond to hold the plaintiffs' part of the contract to the order of the defendant.

But although the defendant was willing to sell 34 Erskine Hill to the plaintiffs, she was not ready to do so. She was willing to contract to buy 40 Westbourne Terrace from Mr
h Holding, but he was not ready to sell and in the event proved unwilling to sell.

Mr Redstone was therefore in fact, as his letter dated 22nd December 1977 disclosed to Mr Bond, acting for clients, the plaintiffs, who were only willing to purchase if they could sell, and Mr Bond was acting for a client, the defendant, who was only willing to sell if she could purchase.

On 9th February 1978 Mr Bond mistakenly believed that Mr Holding was ready and
j willing to sell 40 Westbourne Terrace to the defendant and that therefore a contract for the sale of 34 Erskine Hill by the defendant to the plaintiffs could safely be concluded. Mr Bond telephoned Mr Redstone. At that time Mr Redstone was anxious to complete

---

1   Final Report (Cmnd 7648), ch 21

the exchange of contracts for the purchase by his clients, the plaintiffs, of 34 Erskine Hill
in circumstances which would enable him immediately to complete the exchange of *a*
contracts for the sale by the plaintiffs of 38 Chelmsford Square to Mr Petsas before Mr
Petsas changed his mind or some other incident happened which prevented Mr Redstone
from safeguarding the plaintiffs from loss of bargain or loss of home. Mr Redstone
appreciated that simultaneous, or practically simultaneous, exchange of contracts for the
purchase of 34 Erskine Hill and for the sale of 38 Chelmsford Square was the best way,
and perhaps the only way, of fulfilling his instructions from the plaintiffs. Mr Bond was *b*
willing to exchange contracts for the sale by his client, the defendant, of 34 Erskine Hill
to the plaintiffs, because Mr Bond mistakenly believed that Mr Holding was ready and
willing to sell 40 Westbourne Terrace to the defendant and that if he exchanged contracts
for the sale of 34 Erskine Hill he would be carrying out the instructions of the defendant
and acting in her best interests to see that she did not lose a bargain or lose a home.

Mr Redstone had ostensible authority to exchange contracts on behalf of the plaintiffs *c*
for the purchase of 34 Erskine Hill and Mr Bond had ostensible authority to exchange
contracts on behalf of the defendant for the sale of 34 Erskine Hill.

The telephone conversation which took place between Mr Redstone on behalf of the
plaintiffs, and Mr Bond on behalf of the defendant, was recorded in an attendance note
by Mr Redstone in these terms 'Agreed irrevocable exchange of contracts as at now,
absolutely irrevocable. Completion 2nd March 1978.' The word 'now' was recorded in *d*
capital letters and underlined. Mr Bond, as he said in evidence, appreciated that the
effect of the telephone conversation was that Mr Bond ceased to hold the plaintiffs' part
of the contract to the order of Mr Redstone pursuant to the directions contained in the
letter dated 22nd December 1977 from Mr Redstone but instead held the plaintiffs' part
of the contract on behalf of the defendant. Mr Bond also appreciated that the telephone
conversation involved Mr Bond in the obligation to send to Mr Redstone the part of the *e*
contract signed by the defendant. Mr Bond in his evidence agreed that after the
telephone conversation he held the plaintiffs' part of the contract to the order of his own
client, the defendant, and recognised an obligation to send the part signed by the
defendant to Mr Redstone. In my judgment, as soon as Mr Bond ceased to hold the
plaintiffs' part of the contract to the order of Mr Redstone but was authorised to hold, and
agreed to hold, the plaintiffs' part of the contract to the order of the defendant, the *f*
delivery of the plaintiffs' part of the contract from purchasers to vendor, which was one
of two essential elements in the exchange of contracts, was forthwith completed.
Similarly as soon as Mr Bond knew, appreciated and accepted that he was under a duty
to send the defendant's part of the contract to Mr Redstone, he thereupon held the
defendant's part of the contract to the order of Mr Redstone and that constituted
constructive delivery by Mr Bond to Mr Redstone of the defendant's part of the contract, *g*
which was the second and final essential element in the exchange of contracts. The
exchange of contracts was completed when Mr Bond held the plaintiffs' part of the
contract as agent for the defendant and held the defendant's part of the contract as agent
for Mr Redstone and thus for Mr Redstone's clients, the plaintiffs.

Counsel for the defendant submitted that contracts could only be exchanged by
physical delivery, effected personally or by post, of the vendor's part to the purchaser and *h*
the purchaser's part to the vendor. Delivery to the solicitor as agent for his client
obviously suffices. Counsel submitted that delivery to an agent appointed by the solicitor
would only suffice if the lay client expressly authorised the solicitor to effect exchange by
means of an agent appointed by the solicitor. Moreover, he submitted that a solicitor
acting for one party could not agree to act as agent for the solicitor of the other party to
receive delivery of the relevant part of the contract.   *j*

In my judgment a client impliedly authorises, and ostensibly authorises, his solicitor
to effect exchange of contracts in such manner and by such agents as the solicitor may
think fit. The client confers power to exchange, but is not interested in the machinery
or method of exchange, which are matters for the solicitor and the general law. I see no
reason why one solicitor should not undertake to hold a document to the order of

another solicitor. Such an undertaking is binding on the solicitor who holds the

a document and constitutes constructive delivery of the document to the other solicitor provided that the solicitor who holds the document has ostensible authority to deliver the document to that other solicitor. In the present case Mr Bond had ostensible authority to deliver the defendant's part of the contract to Mr Redstone, and was entitled to effect constructive delivery by undertaking to hold that part on behalf of Mr Redstone and his clients.

b Indeed, immediately after the telephone conversation between Mr Redstone and Mr Bond and in the belief, induced by that conversation, that a contract for the purchase of 34 Erskine Hill had been exchanged, Mr Redstone forthwith concluded the contract for the sale of 38 Chelmsford Square by delivering the part of the contract signed by his clients to the solicitors acting for Mr Petsas.

In my judgment exchange took place on 9th February 1978 for the sale and purchase

c of 34 Erskine Hill. Indeed, Mr Bond dictated a letter on that very day saying: 'As arranged we enclose our client's signed part of the Contract having dated both as of 9th February and having inserted in each as the completion date 2nd March next as arranged.' The term 'as arranged' means 'as promised' and the draft of that letter makes it quite clear that Mr Bond appreciated that a binding contract had come into existence on 9th February. By accident and not design that letter and the defendant's part of the

d contract which should have accompanied it were not despatched on 9th or 10th February, or indeed at all before hostilities broke out.

It was submitted that there are uncertainties and dangers in exchange by telephone. But there are also severe disadvantages in the other two methods of exchange, namely personal exchange and postal exchange. Where three or more solicitors are involved with two or more houses it is impracticable to arrange a time and place for simultaneous

e personal exchange between all the solicitors or their agents. Even if personal exchange were possible in these circumstances, the arrangement would involve delay in negotiation and in implementation and the danger that one vendor or purchaser might change his mind before, or that one solicitor or his agent might be unable to attend the meeting. Each vendor and purchaser would be in danger of losing the bargain. Postal exchange, as the facts in this appeal demonstrate, is uncertain and dangerous because a client who

f is a vendor of one property and the purchaser of another property will not know for certain, when his solicitor posts off his part of a contract to sell, and thus completes exchange of a contract to sell, that his opposite number with regard to the house he is purchasing will in fact post off his part of the contract until the postmen have disgorged all the parts of the contracts which have in fact been posted. A client who is a vendor of one property and the purchaser of another property will not know for certain whether

g he has lost or gained a bargain or a home or both. Exchange by telephone, it seems to me, eliminates, or at any rate substantially reduces, the danger that any client will lose a bargain or be left without a home. Exchange by telephone can only take place after both vendor and purchaser sign contracts in identical form (subject to the question of rectification, which can apply to any contract) so that there is no doubt about the terms of the contract. Exchange by telephone can only take place when a contract signed by a

h client is in the physical possession of his own solicitor or in the possession of the solicitor on the other side who has agreed to hold that part to the order of the despatching solicitor. It is said that there may be uncertainty about the terms and effect of a telephone conversation which creates an exchange of contracts by telephone. This is perhaps a reason why as a matter of professional practice, exchange by telephone should only be carried out by a partner or proprietor of a firm of solicitors. It is a reason why,

j if two solicitors exchange by telephone, they should then and there agree and record identical attendance notes. It is a reason why a short formula which effects exchange by telephone might be devised and adopted by the profession. No doubt the Law Society, which is at present considering the whole procedure of conveyancing, will consider and give guidance to the profession in the light of this appeal. But many important transactions must perforce be carried out or completed by telephone and conveyancing is no exception. At the end of the day professional solicitors must be trusted, and can be trusted, to fulfil their instructions and to fulfil their obligations. In any one year there *a* may be one million instances of a solicitor acting for a client in a conveyancing transaction. A mere handful of transactions lead to uncertainties and only the isolated case is so uncertain that it results in litigation. The facts of the present isolated case reflect only on Mr Bond, who was mistaken in believing that Mr Holding was ready and willing to sell 40 Westbourne Terrace to the defendant. The facts in the present case, and the forceful observations of counsel for the defendant do not persuade me to condemn a *b* practice without which contracts could not be exchanged with the maximum of safety and the minimum of delay.

For these reasons, and for the reasons given by Buckley and Bridge LJJ, with whom I entirely agree, I too would allow the appeal accordingly.

Appeal allowed. Leave to appeal to House of Lords refused.   *c*

Solicitors: *Reynolds Porter Chamberlain & Co* (for the plaintiffs); *Royds Barfield* (for the defendant).

J H Fazan Esq   Barrister.

a   # NV Slavenburg's Bank v Intercontinental Natural Resources Ltd and others

QUEEN'S BENCH DIVISION

LLOYD J

b   5th, 6th, 7th, 8th, 9th, 12th, 13th, 22nd FEBRUARY 1979

Company – Charge – Registration – Charge by overseas company with place of business in England – Company not registered in England – Validity of charge – Particulars of charge not delivered to registrar – Assignment of business including present and future trading stock by way of security – Property of company stored in England subsequent to creation of charge – Whether charge void against foreign liquidators – Whether statutory provisions regarding charges applying to all overseas companies or only those registered in England – Whether foreign liquidators entitled to plead invalidity of charge – Whether floating charge created by overseas company within provisions of Companies Act – Companies Act 1948, ss 95(1), 106

d   *Bills of sale – Security bills of sale – Application of Bills of Sale Acts to corporations – Whether all corporations outside Acts – Whether document creating general charge on future goods exempt from Acts – Bills of Sale Act (1878) Amendment Act 1882, s 17 – Bills of Sale Act 1890, s 1 (as amended).*

In 1974 a company incorporated in Bermuda which had an established place of business in England entered into agreements with a Dutch bank whereby the bank provided the e   company with credit facilities and the company created charges over its assets in favour of the bank. The charges included an assignment to the bank of the company's entire business including its present and future trading stock. The company was not registered in England under s 407[a] of the Companies Act 1948; nor were particulars of the charges registered in accordance with s 95(1)[b]. Subsequently, property of the company was deposited with a storage company in England. In December 1975 the bank decided to f   withdraw further credit facilities from the company and on 29th December the company ceased trading. Under an agreement between the bank and the company dated 20th January 1976 the property stored in England was sold and the proceeds paid into a joint account in England in the names of the parties' solicitors, on the terms that the rights of each in the proceeds were to be the same as their rights in the property before the sale. Subsequently, a petition for the compulsory winding up of the company was presented g   in Bermuda by a creditor, and on 19th April 1976 the Bermudian court made a winding-

---

a   Section 407, so far as material, provides: '(1) Oversea companies which, after the commencement of this Act, establish a place of business within Great Britain shall, within one month of the establishment of the place of business, deliver to the registrar of companies for registration: (a) a certified copy of the charter, statutes or memorandum and articles of the company or other
h   instrument constituting or defining the constitution of the company, and, if the instrument is not written in the English language, a certified translation thereof; (b) a list of the directors and secretary of the company containing the particulars mentioned in the next following subsection; (c) the names and addresses of some one or more persons resident in Great Britain authorised to accept on behalf of the company service of process and any notices required to be served on the company.'

j   b   Section 95, so far as material, provides: '(1) Subject to the provisions of this Part of this Act, every charge created after the fixed date by a company registered in England and being a charge to which this section applies shall, so far as any security on the company's property or undertaking is conferred thereby, be void against the liquidator and any creditor of the company, unless the prescribed particulars of the charge together with the instrument, if any, by which the charge is created or evidenced, are delivered to or received by the registrar of companies for registration in manner required by this Act within twenty-one days after the date of its creation . . .'

up order and appointed liquidators. The Bermudian winding up was similar in character to an English winding up. In an interpleader issue between the bank and the company a the Bermudian liquidators contended by way of preliminary points of law (i) that the charges in respect of the property stored in England were void as against the liquidators under s 95(1) of the 1948 Act because, by virtue of s 106^c of the Act, s 95 extended to the charges; and (ii) alternatively, if the charges were not void under s 95, they were void under the Bills of Sale Acts 1878 and 1882 because the documents creating them were unregistered bills of sale. On the question whether the charges were void under s 95 the b bank contended that (i) s 95 was applied by s 106 only to companies incorporated in Scotland and Northern Ireland and not to all overseas companies; (ii) alternatively having regard to the registrar of companies' practice not to register charges created by an overseas company unless the company was registered under s 407, s 95 was applied by s 106 only to overseas companies which were registered under s 407; (iii) assuming s 95 applied to the charges, the liquidators could not claim that the charges were void against c them since they were liquidators in a foreign winding up and therefore were not 'liquidators' for the purpose of s 95(1), and if they could not plead s 95, they should not be allowed to join as parties to the proceedings an English firm, as representative creditors, to plead their case under s 95; (iv) in any event s 95 did not apply because it did not apply to the creation of a floating charge by an overseas company and therefore did not apply to the charge on the English property; and (v) as the property was sold and the d proceeds paid into the joint account before the liquidators were appointed, the charges were spent before that date, s 95 did not apply and the liquidators, who were not parties to the agreement of 20th January 1976, had no claim to the proceeds.

Held – (1) By virtue of s 106 of the 1948 Act, s 95 applied to the charges on the English property, and the charges were therefore void against the Bermudian liquidators under e s 95(1), for the following reasons—

(a) Since s 95 was applied by s 106 to a company 'incorporated outside England' it applied to all overseas companies, and not merely to those incorporated in Scotland and Northern Ireland. Moreover, despite the practice of the registrar of companies the operation of s 106 was not dependent on registration of the overseas company under s 407, for s 95 did not require registration of a charge to render it valid but merely that f particulars of the charge be delivered to the registrar; it followed that it was sufficient for the operation of s 106 that the overseas company had an established place of business in England, and that the bank could have preserved the validity of the charges by delivering particulars of them to the registrar even though the company was not registered under s 407 (see p 962 d e and h to p 963 a and h to p 964 b, post); *National Provincial and Union Bank of England v Charnley* [1924] 1 KB 431 applied. g

(b) The liquidators, although appointed in a foreign liquidation, were entitled to plead s 95 because notwithstanding that 'liquidator' in s 95(1) primarily meant a liquidator in an English winding up, when that section was applied by s 106 to an overseas company and the foreign winding up was similar in character to an English winding up, the meaning was extended to include a liquidator in a foreign winding up. In any event if the liquidators were not entitled to plead s 95, the court would allow h joinder of an English firm as representative creditors, under RSC Ord 15, r 6(1), to plead the liquidators' case under s 95 (see p 964 e to g and p 965 j to p 966 a, post).

(c) Section 95, in its application to overseas companies, applied to floating charges as well as fixed charges and thus applied to a charge on future property in England and was not confined to a charge on property existing in England when the charge was created. Moreover if the charge initially came within s 95 by virtue of s 106, it remained within j s 95 even if the company ceased to have a place of business in England before the commencement of the liquidation (see p 966 c d and f to h post);

---

c Section 106 is set out at p 962 a b, post

(d) On the true construction of the agreement of 20th January 1976, the charges were
a not spent when the property was sold and the proceeds paid into the joint account, and
the rights of the parties to the litigation, including the Bermudian liquidators, to the
fund, was to be considered as if the property had not been sold and was still in existence.
It followed that the fund remained subject to the charges and that s 95 applied to the
fund (see p 968 *d* and p 969 *h j*, post); *Mercantile Bank of India Ltd v Chartered Bank of India,
Australia and China and Strauss & Co Ltd* [1937] 1 All ER 231 distinguished.

b 　　(2) The documents creating the charges did not come within the Bills of Sale Acts and
accordingly, if the charges had not been void under s 95, they would have been
enforceable against the liquidators, because, on the true construction of s 17*d*, of the Bills
of Sale Act (1878) Amendment Act 1882, the Bills of Sale Acts applied only to individuals
and not to a corporation (see p 974 *d e g* and p 975 *b*, post); *Clark v Balm, Hill & Co* [1908]
1 KB 667 followed.

c 　　Per Curiam. Section 1*e* of the Bills of Sale Act 1890, as amended, which exempts from
the Bills of Sale Acts an instrument 'creating any security on . . . imported goods given
or executed at any time prior to their deposit in a warehouse, factory, or store . . .' does
not cover a document which creates a general charge on all future goods (see p 977 *b*,
post).

d **Notes**
For charges created by an overseas company and for the charges required to be registered,
see 7 Halsbury's Laws (4th Edn) paras 859, 862, and for cases on the subject, see 10 Digest
(Reissue) 861–867, 4966–4989.

　　For the application of the Bills of Sale Acts to charges by companies, see 4 Halsbury's
Laws (4th Edn) paras 654, 655, and for cases on the subject, see 7 Digest (Reissue) 32–34,
157–172.

e 　　For the Companies Act 1948, ss 95, 106, see 5 Halsbury's Statutes (3rd Edn) 189, 197.

　　For the Bills of Sale Act (1878) Amendment Act 1882, s 17, see 3 Halsbury's Statutes
(3rd Edn) 269.

　　For the Bills of Sale Act 1890, s 1, as amended, see ibid, 270.

Cases referred to in judgment
f *Asphaltic Wood Pavement Co Ltd, Re* (1883) 49 LT 159, 7 Digest (Reissue) 32, 157.
Brocklehurst v Railway Printing and Publishing Co [1884] WN 70, Bitt Rep in Ch 117, 7
　　Digest (Reissue) 33, 166.
Clark v Balm, Hill & Co [1908] 1 KB 667, 77 LJKB 369, 15 Mans 42, 7 Digest (Reissue) 33,
　　165.
Cunningham & Co Ltd, Re, Attenborough's Case (1885) 28 Ch D 682, 24 LJ Ch 448, 52 LT
g 　　214, 7 Digest (Reissue) 22, 97.
Deffell v White (1866) LR 2 CP 144, 36 LJCP 25, 15 LT 211, 12 Jur NS 902, 7 Digest
　　(Reissue) 83, 474.
Edmonds v Blaina Furnaces Co, Beesley v Blaina Furnaces Co (1887) 36 Ch D 215, [1886–90]
　　All ER Rep 581, 56 LJ Ch 815, 7 Digest (Reissue) 34, 169.
*Eichholz, Re, ex parte trustee of the property of the deceased debtor v Eichholz, Eichholz's trustee
h 　　v Eichholz* [1959] 1 All ER 166, [1959] Ch 708, [1959] 2 WLR 200, 25 Digest (Repl)
　　175, 38.
Farrell v Alexander [1976] 2 All ER 721, [1977] AC 59, [1976] 3 WLR 145, 32 P & CR
　　292, HL.
Great Northern Railway Co v Coal Co-operative Society [1896] 1 Ch 187, 65 LJ Ch 214, 73 LT
　　443, 2 Mans 621, 7 Digest (Reissue) 34, 172.
j *Jenkinson v Brandley Mining Co* (1887) 19 QBD 568, DC, 7 Digest (Reissue) 33, 168.
Levy v Abercorris Slate and Slab Co (1887) 37 Ch D 260, [1886–90] All ER Rep 509, 57 LJ
　　Ch 202, 58 LT 218, 7 Digest (Reissue) 34, 170.

---

d 　Section 17 is set out at p 970 *f*, post
e 　Section 1 is set out at p 976 *f*, post

Lloyd's Bank Ltd v Bank of America National Trust and Savings Association [1938] 2 All ER 63,
    [1938] 2 KB 147, 107 LJKB 538, 158 LT 301, 43 Com Cas 209, CA, 1(1) Digest   *a*
    (Reissue) 487, *3374*.
Mareva Compania Naviera SA v International Bulkcarriers SA p 213, ante, [1975] 2 Lloyd's
    Rep 509, CA.
Mercantile Bank of India Ltd v Chartered Bank of India, Australia and China and Strauss & Co
    Ltd, Chartered Bank of India, Australia and China v Mercantile Bank of India Ltd and Strauss
    & Co Ltd [1937] 1 All ER 231, 9 Digest (Reissue) 694, *4128*.   *b*
National Provincial and Union Bank of England v Charnley [1924] 1 KB 431, 93 LJKB 241,
    130 LT 465, [1924] B & CR 37, 10 Digest (Reissue) 861, *4963*.
Nye (CL) Ltd, Re [1970] 3 All ER 1061, [1971] Ch 442, [1970] 3 WLR 158, CA, 10 Digest
    (Reissue) 860, *4962*.
Read v Joannon (1890) 25 QBD 300, 59 LJQB 544, 63 LT 387, 2 Meg 275, DC, 7 Digest
    (Reissue) 32, *159*.   *c*
Royal Marine Hotel Co, Kingstown (Ltd), Re [1895] 1 IR 368, 7 Digest (Reissue) 34, *⁕127*.
Row Dal Constructions Pty Ltd (in liq) [1966] VR 249.
Shears v Jacob (1866) LR 1 CP 513, Har & Ruth 492, 35 LJCP 241, 14 LT 286.
Standard Manufacturing Co, Re [1891] 1 Ch 627, [1891–4] All ER Rep 1242, 60 LJ Ch 292,
    64 LT 487, 2 Meg 418, CA, 7 Digest (Reissue) 33, *163*.
Welsted & Co Ltd v Swansea Bank Ltd (1889) 5 TLR 332, 7 Digest (Reissue) 32, *158*.   *d*

Preliminary issues

In an action by the plaintiffs, NV Slavenburg's Bank ('the bank'), a company incorporated
in the Netherlands, against the defendants, Intercontinental Natural Resources Ltd ('the
company'), a company incorporated in Bermuda, Paktank Storage Ltd and the liquidators
of the company, Richard William Kemp and Andrew Mark Homan, the defendants   *e*
applied by a summons dated 19th June 1978 for the trial of preliminary questions of law
raised by the pleadings. On 11th July 1978 Donaldson J granted the application and
ordered the trial of the preliminary questions (i) whether certain charges created by the
company in favour of the bank were void against the liquidators by virtue of s 95 of the
Companies Act 1948 and (ii) if not, whether the documents creating the charges were
void against the liquidators as unregistered bills of sale. The facts are set out in the   *f*
judgment.

W F Stubbs QC and *David Grace* for the bank.
Edward Evans Lombe QC and *L J Libbert* for the defendants.

Cur adv vult
g

22nd February.   **LLOYD J** delivered the following judgment: In this case I am
concerned with preliminary points of law in an interpleader issue between the plaintiffs,
NV Slavenburg's Bank ('the bank'), a company incorporated in the Netherlands, and the
defendants, Intercontinental Natural Resources ('the defendant company'), a company
incorporated in Bermuda. The order directing the interpleader issue was made by
Mocatta J on 23rd March 1976. Subsequently on 19th April 1976 the Supreme Court of   *h*
Bermuda made an order for the compulsory winding up of the company. Joint
liquidators were appointed on 27th May 1976. In May 1977 the joint liquidators applied
to be made parties to the English proceedings. The bank resisted the application but on
26th July 1977 Kerr J directed that the liquidators be joined as second and third
defendants in the issues. There then followed pleadings in which various defences were
raised by the joint liquidators. On 19th June 1978 the defendants applied to the court for   *j*
the trial of certain preliminary questions of law raised by the pleadings. Again, the
application was resisted by the bank but on 11th July 1978 Donaldson J granted the
application. I need not set out verbatim the preliminary questions of law which he
ordered to be tried, more particularly as they have been varied by subsequent agreement
between the parties. But in essence the questions with which I have been concerned are,

first, whether certain charges created in favour of the bank are void against the liquidators
a by virtue of s 95 of the Companies Act 1948, and, second, whether, if not, the document,
or documents, in question are void as unregistered bills of sale. Before coming to the
questions of law I must first give a short account of the facts.

The defendant company was incorporated in Bermuda on 6th February 1974. Until
it went into liquidation it carried on business in the purchase and sale of crude oil and
refined petroleum products. On 1st June 1974 it entered into a so-called service
b agreement with Dycon Petroleum Trading Ltd, a company incorporated in the United
Kingdom. According to an affidavit filed on behalf of the bank it is the sort of agreement
which is not uncommon between an English company and a company incorporated in
a tax haven such as Bermuda.

On 13th June 1974 the defendant company entered into three agreements with the
bank, all in the Dutch language and all governed by Dutch law. The first is called
c 'General credit agreement'. By that agreement the bank was to provide the defendant
company with credit facilities by way of current account. By cl 9 the company agreed
to provide certain collateral securities, as there set out. The second agreement is called
'General agreement of assignment'. By cl 1 the company agreed to assign all present and
future debts to the bank and to execute such assignments in a form prescribed by the
bank. The prescribed form is called 'List of assignment of accounts receivable'. The
d third agreement is called 'Assignment of stocks as security'. By cll 1 to 3 the company
assigned the entire business by way of security to the bank, including present and future
trading stocks. By cl 4(b) the company assigned, or agreed to assign, all claims arising on
the sale of its trading stocks. There was also a provision that all cash payments were to
be collected by the company as agents for the bank. Those are the three principal
agreements on which the bank relies in these proceedings.

e   It was the practice of the defendant company to store petroleum products with a
company called Paktank Storage Co Ltd, which had bulk storage facilities at Grays, Essex,
and at East Ham. Paktank are the second defendants in the action and it was as a result
of their interpleader summons that Mocatta J made the order to which I have referred.
In the course of 1975 Paktank sent a number of telexes to the bank showing the quantity
of the company's products in store at the end of the preceding month. On 3rd December
f 1975 Paktank sent a telex in the following terms:

> 'We hold the following oil products to the account of Intercontinental Natural
> Resources Ltd, Hamilton, Bermuda, and at your disposal, it being understood that
> Intercontinental Natural Resources Ltd has free and complete authority to dispose
> of all or any part of these products and that we are entirely free to accept their
> disposal instructions, subject only to contra instructions from you.'

g
The language of that telex had originally been suggested by the bank, and the bank's
request had been passed on by the defendant company to Paktank. Paktank sent a
similar telex on 18th December 1975 giving the figures at close of business on the
preceding day, showing a total quantity of 12,974 long tons in store. These telexes were
referred to as 'storage reports'.

h   Meanwhile, on 4th December 1975 the bank had decided to withdraw all further
facilities from the company. On 19th December the bank sent a telex to Paktank,
referring to Paktank's storage report of 18th December and asking Paktank to issue them
with a warehouse receipt. The bank went on to direct Paktank not to deliver any
products without the bank's consent. On 19th December Paktank declined to accept the
bank's directions. On 29th December the company ceased trading. On 9th January
j Messrs Linklaters & Paines, on behalf of the bank, demanded immediate delivery of all
the company's products stored by Paktank at Grays and East Ham, and on 12th January
they obtained an ex parte order from Mocatta J for the detention and preservation of the
goods under RSC Ord 29, r 3. They also obtained a Mareva injunction[1] restraining the

---

1   See *Mareva Compania Naviera SA v International Bulkcarriers SA* p 213, ante

defendants from parting with the proceeds of any goods sold prior to 12th January
1976. The parties then entered into negotiations which resulted in the opening of a joint *a*
account at Lloyds Bank in the names of the parties' solicitors. On 20th January 1976
Messrs Linklaters & Paines wrote to the solicitors then acting for the company as follows:

> 'We refer to our various discussions during the past few days, and confirm that
> our clients, NV Slavenburg's Bank, are agreeable to the uplifting on an interim basis
> by Dycon Petroleum Trading Co. Limited of the oil presently stored by Paktank *b*
> Storage Co. Ltd. in the name of Intercontinental notwithstanding the existence of
> the Order of Court of 12th January 1976, pending the signing, it is hoped, of an
> appropriate written agreement setting out more permanent arrangements for the
> uplifting of and payment for the oil and the destination of its proceeds pending the
> conclusion of the present litigation between Slavenburg's, Intercontinental and
> Paktank. [I can omit the next paragraph. The letter continues:] We have opened *c*
> an account styled "Linklaters & Paines/Freshfields" at the City Branch of Lloyds
> Bank Limited [and it then gives the address, and then further down it continues:]
> Withdrawals from the account can only be made on 7 days' notice and they must be
> supported by the signatures of one designated partner in Linklaters & Paines and
> one designated partner in Freshfields or else by an Order of Court. [and then the
> letter concludes:] The purpose of these arrangements, it is hardly necessary to add, *d*
> is to preserve the proceeds of the oil just as the oil itself is, by means of the present
> Court Order, preserved.'

The first payment into the joint account was made on 21st January and payments
continued to be made through the rest of January, and in February and March. By 15th
April the joint account stood at £905,098·21. In October 1976 it was converted into a *e*
dollar account and now stands, with interest, at $1,747,327·02. The joint account
contains three main elements: first, there is a relatively small sum of £63,068, which was
the company's share of the profit arising out of a joint venture for the sale of fuel oil to
the Central Electricity Generating Board. The other party to the joint venture was a
company called Shaw's Fuels Ltd. The defendant company's share of the profit was
specifically assigned to the bank by a 'List of assignment' dated 16th December 1975, and *f*
was paid into the joint account on 29th January 1976. The second element in the joint
account is £256,607·98, being the proceeds of sale of products sold between 1st January
1976 and the date of Mocatta J's order of 12th January 1976. This sum was paid into the
joint account on 15th April 1976. The third element in the joint account represents
proceeds of products sold since 12th January 1976.

The remaining events can be mentioned very briefly. On 15th March 1976 a creditor *g*
in Bermuda presented a petition for the compulsory winding up of the company on the
basis of a judgment debt of $5,195,832. On 19th April, as already mentioned, a winding-
up order was made and the joint liquidators were appointed on 27th May 1976.
Meanwhile on 13th April 1976 the company and the bank reached agreement by telex,
subsequently confirmed by letter, as to the terms on which the joint account had been set
up. The joint liquidators were not, of course, parties in their own names to that *h*
agreement, since they had not yet been appointed. Since the agreement is important for
an understanding of the bank's submissions, I will set out the letter in full.

> 'Dear Sirs, This letter confirms our telex of today as follows: Following legal
> action taken by you in the High Court in London on 12th of January, 1976 on
> behalf of N.V. Slavenburgs Bank arresting all mineral oils owned by us and stored *j*
> with Paktank in the U.K. a joint bank account was set up at Lloyds Bank in the
> names of Linklaters and Paines and Freshfields into which it was agreed the proceeds
> of the sale of such mineral oils should be paid on terms that the right, interest and
> equities of each ourselves and N.V. Slavenburgs Bank in such proceeds of sale should
> be identical to those in the mineral oils from which the proceeds derived.

a   'Since January 21st, 1976 sales of mineral oils have taken place with the consent of Slavenburgs and the proceeds of the sale duly paid to the joint bank account on the terms set out above. In addition on or about 29th January, 1976 Shaws Fuels Ltd. paid into the joint account £63,068·48. This sum did not represent proceeds of sale of mineral oils subject to your arrest but was our share of profit on approx. 40,000 tons of fuel oil delivered to CEGB in December, 1975 the account receivable in respect of which was purported to be assigned by us to Slavenburgs. A further

b   40,000 tons were delivered to CEGB in March under the same contract and the proceeds which will be considerably less than £63,000 are expected to be paid shortly.

'During the first two weeks of January prior to your court proceedings we sold mineral oils from U.K. storage for a total net sale price of £256,607·98 the accounts receivable in respect of these sales were purported to be assigned by us to

c   Slavenburgs. The sales were made to Dycon Petroleum Trading Ltd. and that Company has deposited the said sum of £256,607·98 on Client Account with Messrs. Freshfields to be released only as follows: 1. In accordance with instructions from an authorised signatory of Dycon to pay either us or Slavenburgs. 2. In accordance with joint instructions from us and Slavenburgs to pay either of us. 3. In accordance with an order of the High Court arising from any proceedings

d   between us and Slavenburgs relating to the monies in question.

'Against your Clients agreement 1. That the Joint Account is to be divided into three parts, the first representing proceeds of sale of mineral oils subject to their arrest, the second representing payments made under the CEGB contract and the third representing the proceeds of sale of mineral oils to Dycon Petroleum Trading Limited prior to the arrest and 2. That the rights, titles, interest and equities of

e   Intercontinental Natural Resources Limited and N.V. Slavenburgs Bank in each part of the account shall be identical to the rights, titles, interest and equities that each of them held in the mineral oils and accounts receivable from which each part derived and against your Clients agreeing to amend their pleadings before the High Court to reflect this agreement and to enable the Court to decide the issues pertaining to each of the three parts we will join with your clients in instructing

f   Freshfields to pay the £256,607·98 into the joint account and will instruct Shaws Fuels to pay the balance of the CEGB monies into the joint account.'

A number of facts have been agreed between the parties, and I have been asked to make a number of assumptions for the purpose of dealing with the questions of law which are now before the court. It may well be that the short cut which the court had

g   in mind when ordering the preliminary questions of law will in the end, in this case as in others, prove to have been the longest way round. But, be that as it may, I am satisfied that the points which are now before the court are in no way academic, and in those circumstances my proper course is to attempt to deal with all the points that have been argued.

I now turn to the questions of law. As already mentioned, they fall into two main

h   groups, the first relating to s 95 of the Companies Act 1948, and the second to the Bills of Sale Acts. For the purposes of dealing with the first group of questions I am asked to assume (i) that they are to be determined in accordance with English law and not Dutch law; (ii) that the company had at all material times an established place of business in England within the meaning of s 106 of the Companies Act 1948; (iii) that the documents relied on by the bank, that is to say the general credit agreement, the general

j   agreement of assignment, the assignment of stocks as securities, the list of assignments and storage reports, all create charges within the meaning of s 95(2) of the 1948 Act; (iv) that no particulars of these charges were ever delivered to the registrar for registration pursuant to s 95(1). On those assumptions counsel for the company and the joint liquidators argues that the charges are all void as against the liquidators by virtue of the combined effect of ss 95 and 106. I need not set out the provisions of s 95, but s 106 provides as follows:

> '*Application of Part III to charges created, and property subject to charge acquired, by* *a*
> *company incorporated outside England.* The provisions of this Part of this Act shall
> extend to charges on property in England which are created, and to charges on
> property in England which is acquired, by a company (whether a company within
> the meaning of this Act or not) incorporated outside England which has an
> established place of business in England.'

b

Counsel for the bank takes five points: the first, logically (though not in the order in
which he took them) is that s 106 does not apply because on its true construction it only
applies to companies incorporated in Scotland and Northern Ireland. Counsel supports
that argument in a number of ways. First he says that all other provisions relating to
overseas companies generally are to be found in Part X of the Act; therefore if s 106
relates to overseas companies generally you would expect to find it in Part X and not at *c*
the end of Part III. Secondly, he says that ss 103 and 104 presuppose the existence of a
registered office; and other provisions in Part III create offences. It would be absurd, he
says, that Parliament should have intended such provisions to apply to all overseas
companies. Thirdly, he appeals to the legislative history. He says that the words in
brackets, 'whether a company within the meaning of this Act or not', which, on their
face, are fatal to his argument, were first enacted when the legislature was preoccupied *d*
with the problem of applying the Companies Acts to Northern Ireland, and that they
were introduced for that limited purpose only.

I cannot accept counsel's argument. The language of s 106 is crystal clear. If by
'companies incorporated outside England' the legislature had meant companies
incorporated in Scotland and Northern Ireland, and nowhere else, it would have been
simple enough to say so. Moreover, it is impossible to reconcile counsel's contention *e*
with s 461 of the 1948 Act which provides:

> '*Application to Northern Ireland.* (1) Nothing in this Act, except the provisions
> thereof which relate expressly to companies registered or incorporated in Northern
> Ireland or outside Great Britain, shall apply to or in relation to companies registered
> or incorporated in Northern Ireland.
> '(2) Nothing in this Act, except where it is expressly provided to the contrary, *f*
> shall affect the law in force in Northern Ireland at the commencement of this Act.'

Nor is it correct to say that all provisions relating to overseas companies are contained
in Part X: see Part IX which relates to the winding up of unregistered companies, and, in
particular, s 400. None of the standard textbooks on company law suggest that s 106 is
confined to Scotland and Northern Ireland, and Buckley[1], Palmer[2], Gower[3] and
Pennington[4] all clearly assume the contrary. The editors of Buckley[5] in particular draw *g*
attention to the potential difficulty of applying ss 103 and 104, according to their literal
terms, to all overseas companies. But they do not draw the conclusion that s 106 is on
that account to be treated as inapplicable to all companies incorporated outside England
except those incorporated in Scotland and Northern Ireland.

As for the legislative history, I am guided, and indeed bound, by what was said by the *h*
House of Lords on the construction of consolidation Acts in *Farrell v Alexander*[6]. There
is no difficulty or ambiguity in the meaning of s 106. The words in brackets make it
clear that the section applies to any company whether or not a company as defined in

---

1   Companies Acts (13th Edn, 1957)   *j*
2   Company Law (22nd Edn, 1976)
3   Modern Company Law (4th Edn, 1979)
4   Company Law (4th Edn, 1979)
5   13th Edn (1957) p 247
6   [1976] 2 All ER 721 at 725, 733, 746, [1977] AC 59 at 73, 82, 97

s 455. In those circumstances I do not regard it as desirable to speculate (and it could be
no more than speculation) why the words were introduced into the Companies Act
1929[1]. For those reasons I reject counsel's first argument.

Counsel's second argument is that assuming, contrary to his first argument, s 106
applies to overseas companies generally, it only applies where they have been registered
under Part X. As appears from the affidavit of Mr Hathaway of Linklaters & Paines,
sworn on 21st July 1977, this seems to have been the principal argument relied on by the
bank in resisting the liquidators' application to be joined as parties to the proceedings.
The point is taken in para 3 of the points of reply as follows:

> '. . . if, which is denied, Incon had an established place of business in England no
> registration of the said company or place of business pursuant to the provisions of
> Part X of the Companies Act, 1948, was ever effected by or on behalf of the said
> company. In the premises it was not possible, it was not practicable and it was not
> necessary to register the Plaintiffs' securities pursuant to Section 106 of the
> Companies Act, 1948.'

Counsel for the bank, however, did not put the point in the forefront of his
argument. He described it as *a* point, not *the* point. He supported it by reference to the
practice of the Registrar of Companies as described in a letter dated 24th October 1977.
From that letter it appears that, since overseas companies with a place of business in
England are obliged to register under Part X, the registrar requires the company to
comply with Part X before he will accept particulars of charges for registration under Part
III. The letter continues:

> 'There is no method by which an overseas company can register charges unless it
> has an established place of business in England and therefore should first register
> under section 407, unless it informs the Registrar that it is in the process of
> submitting the necessary documents required under that section, in which case the
> charges would be held for a short period pending registration. If registration was
> not completed within a short period the charges would be returned.'

In contrast, a Scottish company is not, of course, required to register under Part X. In
the case of Scottish companies, therefore, wishing to register a charge under s 95, the
registrar opens a special file.

Against the background of that practice (which I am to assume has continued
uniformly since 1928) counsel for the bank submits, first, that the object of delivering
particulars of charges under s 95(1) is so that they may be registered. He stresses the
words 'for registration', and if the fact is that charges will not be registered unless the
company has first registered under Part X, then s 95 cannot have been intended to apply
to such charges. Secondly, he submits that a chargee is entitled to know where he is, and
it is unsatisfactory that the validity of his charge in the absence of registration should
depend on something which may be so uncertain as whether the company has an
established place of business in England or not.

The fallacy in the argument lies in regarding registration of the charge under Part III
as a condition precedent to its validity. It is clear both from the language of s 95 and
from what was said in *National Provincial and Union Bank of England v Charnley*[2] that it is
delivery of particulars of the charge, together with the instrument (if any) by which it is
created or evidenced that saves the charge, and not its registration. In the *National
Provincial Bank* case[3] Scrutton LJ said, after referring to the language of the section: 'That
makes the avoidance depend on the neglect to send in the particulars. The neglect to
register the charge will not make it void.' Counsel reserved the right to challenge the

---

1   See s 90
2   [1924] 1 KB 431
3   [1924] 1 KB 431 at 447

correctness of that dictum in a higher court. So far as I am concerned, it seems to follow that the bank could have preserved the validity of its charges by delivering particulars **a** within 21 days, despite the unwillingness of the registrar to register the charge without prior registration by the company under Part X. In those circumstances there is really nothing left in counsel's argument under this head. There is certainly nothing in s 106 to suggest that the operation of that section is dependent in any way on the company having registered under Part X, and I am unwilling to imply any such limitation.

Before leaving the point, I should say that counsel for the defendants expressly **b** disclaimed any criticism of the registrar's current practice. Nor would I, myself, wish to criticise it in any way. His reasons for insisting on the company first registering under Part X are clear enough. But they cannot affect the outcome of this case. I reject counsel for the bank's second argument.

Counsel for the bank's third argument is that, assuming ss 95 and 106 apply to the charges in the present case, nevertheless the joint liquidators cannot take advantage of **c** s 95 because 'the liquidator' in s 95 means 'the liquidator in an English liquidation', whereas the joint liquidators were, as I have already mentioned, appointed by the Supreme Court of Bermuda. Counsel's argument is that wherever the word 'liquidator' appears in the Act it means liquidator in an English winding up, whether voluntary or compulsory; that s 95 of the 1948 Act is no exception, and that it cannot be extended to include the person appointed in a foreign liquidation, even though he may happen to be **d** called a 'liquidator'.

I would accept the premise of counsel's argument, but I would not accept the conclusion. The primary meaning of 'liquidator' in s 95 is, no doubt, the liquidator in an English winding up, just as the primary meaning of 'company' in s 95 is an English company. But when applied to a foreign company by s 106 the word 'company' in s 95 must necessarily be given an extended meaning. That being so, I can see no difficulty in **e** doing the same for the word 'liquidator'. For the purpose of s 106 (but only of course for the purpose of s 106) it means either an English liquidator or the foreign equivalent (whether in place of incorporation or elsewhere) as the case may be. Otherwise s 106 would lose much of its impact. It cannot have been intended that wherever there is a foreign winding up there should always have to be a winding up in England under Part IX before s 95 can be operated for the benefit of unsecured creditors. Certainly there is **f** nothing express to that effect and, again, I cannot see why any such limitation should be implied.

There could perhaps be a difficulty where it is uncertain whether a foreign proceeding is in the nature of a winding up. But no such difficulty arises here. I was referred to the Companies Act of Bermuda 1923. From s 38 it appears that so far as practicable companies in Bermuda are wound up in the manner in which English companies are **g** wound up 'under the law and practice in England regulating the winding-up of companies'. I note that the winding-up order in Bermuda was made under the United Kingdom Companies Act 1948 as well as under the 1923 Act, and that one of the two joint liquidators is in fact resident in England. Counsel submits that, though I am entitled to read the Bermudian Companies Act 1923, I am not entitled to draw any conclusion as to its meaning. I need not deal with that submission, although it is hardly **h** a submission which commends itself to me. For I only refer to the 1923 Companies Act in the present connection for the limited purpose of satisfying myself (which I should in any event have thought obvious) that a winding up in Bermuda is a proceeding which the English court will recognise or characterise as a winding up for the purposes of s 95 of the 1948 Act. I hold that the joint liquidators come within the meaning of 'liquidator' in s 95 as applied to the present case by s 106.

In case I should be against him on that point counsel for the defendants applied to join **j** Messrs Sedgwick Forbes & Co, the well known insurance brokers, as fourth defendants in the interpleader issue. Even if the joint liquidators cannot, themselves, take the points under s 95 because they are not liquidators appointed in an English liquidation, there can, he said, be no objection to Messrs Sedgwick Forbes taking the same points as

representative creditors. Counsel for the bank strenuously resisted the application on the
ground that it would be unfair to the bank. The application comes, he says, too late. But
the underlying principle is as stated in RSC Ord 15, r 6 (1):

> 'No cause or matter shall be defeated by reason of the misjoinder or nonjoinder
> of any party; and the Court may in any cause or matter determine the issues or
> questions in dispute so far as they affect the rights and interests of the persons who
> are parties to the cause or matter.'

In the present case the proceedings are still only at the stage of preliminary questions
of law. It would require a very strong case indeed before I would refuse leave to join a
new party at this stage. In fact so far from the defendants being in mercy it is rather the
other way round. Paragraph 22 of Mr Hathaway's affidavit, to which I have already
referred, shows that one of the points taken by the bank in resisting the application to
join the liquidators was that the liquidators would not in any event, as foreign liquidators,
be entitled to take 'an independent point in the litigation'. In the context this must mean
a point under section 95. I will read the relevant paragraph:

> 'Further Incon is a foreign corporation and the Liquidators are acting under a
> foreign winding-up order. No winding-up order has been made in England relating
> to Incon's assets here, nor have Liquidators been appointed in England. In these
> circumstances in my respectful submission the Liquidators while they can act on
> behalf of Incon and in its name cannot act separately from it, take an independent
> point in litigation, or raise matters which the company itself could not raise.'

Subsequently Messrs Cameron, Kemm, Nordon, the solicitors acting for the defendants,
wrote as follows on 22nd August 1977:

> 'As you will be aware, one of the points taken by your Clients at the hearing was
> the question of whether or not the liquidators, being liquidators appointed by the
> Supreme Court of Bermuda, had any locus standi in their own right in the English
> Court. The Judge was not disposed to determine this question on an interlocutory
> application. It was agreed that it would be open to your Clients to take it by way of
> defence in the action if they so wished. However, having regard to the fact that it
> is open to our Clients at any time to apply for Incon to be wound up in England (for
> which purpose the existence of assets in England would be sufficient) and that on
> the making of such a winding-up order there would be liquidators in England who
> would undoubtedly have locus standi it seems to us to be pointless to take this step
> for that purpose alone. Whatever the result of the litigation between our respective
> Clients, your Clients will in any event at the end of the day still be unsecured
> creditors for quite a considerable sum of money and it is not therefore in their
> interest that the assets which will in any event be available for unsecured creditors
> should be further dissipated by the costs of an English winding-up proceeding. We
> should be glad therefore if you would kindly confirm within the next 14 days that
> your Clients will not seek to take the locus standi point by way of defence or by way
> of appeal from the order of Mr. Justice Kerr.'

There was no reply to that letter, nor was the point ever pleaded. Counsel for the bank
says that the point which he is taking on the construction of the word 'liquidator' in s 95
of the 1948 Act is entirely separate and distinct from the so-called locus standi point. For
myself, I cannot see the difference. Certainly there is no difference in substance.
Whichever way the point is put it could have been met by a successful application to the
court for the company to be wound up in England and it was to avoid the pointless
expense of doing that that Messrs Cameron, Kemm, Nordon wrote their letter of 22nd
August 1977. So that even if the points are entirely separate, as counsel maintains, the
defendants were justified in thinking that no technical point of the kind covered by that
letter was going to be taken, which is why the defendants were so surprised (as clearly
they were) when the present point was taken. In those circumstances, I can see no

unfairness whatever in allowing the amendment to meet the point by joining Messrs
Sedgwick Forbes as representative creditors. Accordingly that application is allowed. If
authority is needed for the course which I have taken it is to be found in the decision of
Harman J in *Re Eichholz*[1].

Counsel's last point under this head is that there is in any event no point in joining the
creditors because they cannot be in a better position than the English liquidators. I find
it difficult to follow that argument. I could understand (though I would not accept) an
argument that the creditors have no locus standi in the absence of an English winding
up. But counsel expressly disclaims that argument. His argument is that, on the true
construction of s 95, they are not creditors at all within the meaning of the section. It
seems to me that a creditor is either a creditor or he is not. It cannot depend on whether
the company is being wound up, and, if so, where.

I now turn to the fourth argument. Counsel for the bank submits that s 106 only
applies to charges on property which is in England at the time the charge is created or the
property acquired. I cannot accept that argument either. It would mean that all floating
charges so far as they relate to future property would be outside the scope of the
section. Yet s 95(2)(*f*) expressly covers floating charges. In applying s 95 to overseas
companies Parliament must have intended it to apply to floating charges as well as fixed
charges and must therefore have intended it to apply in the case of future property in
England as well as existing property in England. I reject counsel's main argument under
his fourth head.

There is, however, a subsidiary argument, that, even if a charge were initially brought
within s 95 by s 106, it would cease to be within s 95 if at any time the company ceased
to have an established place of business in England under s 106. For this purpose I have
to qualify the assumption made above, that the company had an established place of
business in England at all material times, and assume instead that, having had such a
place of business, it ceased to have a place of business before the commencement of the
winding up in Bermuda on 15th March 1976. The point can be illustrated in the
following way: suppose on day 1 a foreign company with an established place of business
in England creates a charge on its assets in England. If it fails to deliver particulars of the
charge within 21 days, the charge is potentially void against the liquidator and general
creditors. Suppose on day 30 a liquidator is appointed. What is the position if on, say,
day 25 the company had ceased to have an established place of business in England?
Counsel for the defendants submits that the liquidator's rights are unaffected. He would,
I think, submit the same even if the company had ceased to have a place of business in
England on day 15. Counsel for the bank, on the other hand, submits that the conditions
of s 106 have to be satisfied not only at the date of the creation of the charge but also at
the commencement of the winding up. For until then there is nobody who is in a
position to take advantage of the provisions of s 95. The point is not altogether easy. But
on the whole I prefer counsel for the defendants' submission. Section 106 is, as he says,
a triggering section. If its conditions are satisfied it triggers s 95 in relation to charges at
the moment of their creation. Thereafter the charge is to be treated as if it were for all
purposes a charge created by an English company. If that is right, it does not matter that
the conditions of s 106 ceased to be satisfied the day after the creation of the charge.
Counsel for the defendants referred me to *Re C L Nye Ltd*[2]. But I do not find the case
particularly helpful in this connection. I prefer to rest my decision on what seems to me
the most natural meaning of s 106.

I now turn to the last of the points under s 95. Counsel for the bank submits that there
is nothing here for s 95 to bite on, because the property charged had all been sold and the
proceeds paid into the joint account in the names of the parties' solicitors before the
liquidators were ever appointed. It is settled law, says counsel, that a liquidator cannot

---

1   [1959] 1 All ER 166, [1959] Ch 708
2   [1970] 3 All ER 1061, [1971] Ch 442

a avoid a charge that has ceased to exist or become spent, and the charges here were all spent prior to the appointment of the liquidators, when the products were sold pursuant to the agreement of 20th January 1976. He further submits that the liquidators cannot, themselves, take advantage of that agreement since they were not parties to it, and, in those circumstances, the joint liquidators can lay no claim to the fund for the benefit of the creditors.

b The point was first foreshadowed in the letter from Messrs Linklaters & Paines dated 16th January 1979. As the argument progressed it became an increasingly important part in the bank's case. It was accepted by both sides that, for the sake of simplicity, the relevant date should be regarded as the date of the appointment of the liquidators rather than the commencement of the winding up or the date of the winding-up order.

Now, I agree with counsel for the bank that once a charge is spent there is nothing for s 95 to bite on. That appears sufficiently from the language of the section itself and also c from at least two authorities that were cited. In *Mercantile Bank of India Ltd v Chartered Bank of India, Australia and China, and Strauss & Co Ltd*[1] two banks had lent money to a company on the security of certain documents variously called letters of hypothecation and letters of lien. The company subsequently went into liquidation. The banks each alleged against the other that the other's securities were void for non-registration. Prior to the liquidation the defendant bank had seized the company's assets under the terms d of its security. One of the questions was whether the defendant's security should be regarded as a floating charge or not. Porter J said[2]:

'I do not propose finally to decide that question, because I think it is admitted . . . that, the goods having been seized, the Chartered Bank [that is the defendant bank] has put itself in a different position; and has brought down, as it were, on the e floating charge a perfecting of the charge upon those goods, whatever they may be . . .'

Later on in the same judgment, after referring to a number of authorities, he said[3]:

'On the authority of those cases, it appears that once seizure had taken place, at a f time before liquidation, at any rate, of the company, the security, even if it were originally a floating security, has ceased to be so describable. It has become a definite charge which has been perfected by the seizure of the goods. Therefore, in so far as the Chartered Bank has seized the goods rightfully, it is entitled, in my view, to the benefit of its security.'

g Porter J's decision is authority for the view that once a charge has been perfected by seizure of the goods charged it is too late for the liquidator to intervene.

Counsel for the bank had some doubt whether the decision of Porter J goes all the way for him. But the point was not really contested by counsel for the defendants, so that I need not consider whether his doubts are justified. Certainly it is too late for the liquidators to intervene if the chargee has already been paid prior to the liquidation. That appears from the other decision to which I was referred, namely *Re Row Dal* h *Construction Pty Ltd*[4], a decision of the Supreme Court of Victoria. In that case a bank had lent money to a company on the security of certain book debts which were assigned to the bank. The company subsequently went into liquidation. But before it went into liquidation the bank had been paid the amount of its loan under the assignment. The liquidator sought to recover from the bank the amount paid under the assignment on the ground that the assignment was void as against him for non-registration. It was held

j

---

1   [1937] 1 All ER 231
2   [1937] 1 All ER 231 at 235
3   [1937] 1 All ER 231 at 241
4   [1966] VR 249

that he could not succeed as the bank had already been paid before he came on the
scene. The non-registration was therefore irrelevant. Heron CJ said[1]:   *a*

> 'Had liquidation in this case intervened before the payment of the £6,000 actually
> paid . . . on 31 May, no doubt in that event there would have been a contest as to the
> destination of this sum, the liquidator claiming it as property of the company and
> relying upon non-registration of the assignment to defeat the bank's claim, and the
> bank for its part claiming it as its property by reason of the absolute assignment.
> But as things are the liquidator can derive no assistance from the failure to register   *b*
> under s. 72 [of the Victorian Companies Act 1958]. When he was appointed on
> 6 July 1962, there was no property of the company upon which the bank claimed
> any security, and there was consequently no basis upon which he could call in aid
> s. 72 to defeat the bank's assignment. These considerations are, in my opinion,
> sufficient to dispose of this point.'

c

Counsel for the bank laid particular stress on the penultimate sentence of that passage
which I have just read. He says that the position is precisely the same here because the
only property of the company on which the bank claimed security had been sold and the
proceeds paid into the joint account before the liquidators were appointed.

The real dispute, as it seems to me, on this part of the case is not as to what is the effect
in law of the charge being spent, because it is largely common ground that if a charge is   *d*
spent before liquidation s 95 has nothing to bite on. The real dispute is whether the
charges were indeed spent, or whether the bank can be heard to say that they were spent,
on the facts of this case; for, if counsel is wrong about that, then the rest of his argument
falls to the ground.

There are, I think, considerable difficulties in the way of his submission. In the first
place it is to be noted that the facts of the present case are very different from those in the   *e*
two cases to which I have just referred. The bank has not seized or taken possession of
the property in any way, as in the former case, nor has it been paid, as in the latter. The
money is still in the joint account. It is no more within the control of the bank than it
is within the control of the company. In the absence of agreement between the parties
to this action, the destination of the fund in the joint account is subject to the decision of
this court. Secondly, when one looks at the bank's pleading, it is clear, as counsel for the   *f*
defendants points out, that the basis of the bank's claim to be entitled to the amount in
the joint account are the very charges which the liquidators seek to impugn. It hardly
lies in the bank's mouth to say that the charges are spent, when, at the same time, it
asserts their existence and validity as the basis of its claim against the company.

But I am prepared to assume that the bank could get over both those difficulties. The
real objection to the argument of counsel for the bank, as it seems to me, lies in the   *g*
agreement of 20th January 1976 by virtue of which these products came to be sold. It
is accepted by both parties that one must construe that agreement as amplified by the
letter of 15th April 1976, to which I have already referred. What does that agreement
provide? It provides quite simply that the rights of each party to the proceeds of sale
shall be the same as its rights in the oil. One therefore asks oneself the question: what
rights would the bank have had to the oil if it had still existed? The answer must be that   *h*
the bank's rights would have been liable to have been defeated by the very arguments
which the liquidators are now advancing.

Counsel for the bank puts forward a number of counter-arguments against that simple
view. First, he submits that you must look at the rights of the bank immediately *prior*
to the sale of the products, at which time the liquidators had not been appointed. He
draws attention to the language of the relevant passage in the letter[2] as follows: *j*

---

1   [1966] VR 249 at 258
2   See p 961 *e*, ante

a
'That the rights, titles, interest and equities of Intercontinental Natural Resources Limited and N.V. Slavenburg's Bank, in each part of the account, shall be identical to the rights, titles, interests and equities that each of them held in the mineral oils and accounts receivable from which each part derived.'

b
He says that the word 'held' shows that you are not to look at future events. It seems to me that that is reading far too much into a single word; and it is to be noted that that word does not appear when the effect of the agreement is set out in the first paragraph of the letter. I can see no justification for treating the parties' rights as having been frozen when the agreement was made, still less for treating them as having been frozen in relation to any particular quantity of petroleum products immediately prior to the sale of that quantity.

c
Counsel for the bank's second argument was that 'the bank's rights' means its rights as against the only other party to the agreement at the time it was made, namely the company. The bank's rights cannot, he said, be affected by any 'rights' which the liquidators may acquire under s 95, since the liquidators were not, themselves, parties to the agreement. But that is to draw an entirely artificial distinction between the rights which the liquidators assert in the name of the company for the general benefit of its creditors, which rights are indisputably preserved by the agreement, and the additional

d
rights which they, and they alone, can assert for the benefit of creditors under s 95.
Thirdly, counsel for the bank argues that I cannot assume that a liquidation was inevitable on 20th January 1976, or even likely. But, as counsel for the defendants pointed out, the company can have had no motive for entering into the agreement of 20th January 1976 other than to benefit the general creditors. There was never any doubt about the existence of the company's debt to the bank or its amount. From the start the only dispute has been whether, and if so to what extent, the bank's debt is

e
secured. This must have been as obvious to the bank as it was to the company. It may well be, as counsel for the bank asserts, that a liquidation was not inevitable. But it does not follow, in my judgment, that the liquidators are to be regarded as strangers to the agreement.
Counsel for the bank's fourth, and final, argument was that, whatever the parties may

f
have agreed, the petroleum products did in fact cease to be the property of the company when they were sold, and that thereafter there was nothing to which the charge could apply. The money in the joint account is not 'the company's property' within the meaning of s 95. The parties cannot by their private agreement make s 95 apply to something to which, on its true construction, it does not apply. It seems to me that there is a short answer to that argument. Of course the parties cannot by their private

g
agreement contract themselves out of a public statute. But that is not what these parties have sought to do. They are, in effect, agreeing to be bound by a statute as if it applied, which is a very different thing. I can see no reason why they should not make such an agreement. Indeed such agreements are matters of everyday experience in the commercial world as, for instance, where parties agree to apply the Carriage of Goods by Sea Act 1971 to a bill of lading to which it would not otherwise apply; or to a charterparty,

h
which the Act specifically excludes from its operation. For the above reasons, I cannot accept any of counsel for the bank's submissions as to the construction and effect of the agreement of 20th June 1976. To my mind the meaning is, as I have already said, clear enough, namely that you look at the rights of the parties (and that means all the parties to this litigation, including the liquidators) as if the petroleum products were still in existence. If that is right, then it follows that counsel for the bank's argument that s 95

j
of the 1948 Act has nothing to bite on must be rejected.
There was some further discussion in the course of the hearing as to the nature of the bank's claim to the sums standing in the joint account. I have already mentioned that in their pleading they claim as assignees or chargees. The alternative is to regard them as beneficiaries under a trust. I do not find it necessary to consider that question further, because I take it to have been conceded that if the bank should fail on all the points that

have been argued, then, on the assumptions I have been asked to make, the sum in the
joint account would fall to be paid out to the defendants. If that is not conceded, I would　*a*
so decide.

That concludes the various points which have been argued in relation to s 95, all of
which I have decided against the bank. On the assumptions which I have been asked to
make, I hold that the charges created by the documents on which the bank relies are all
void, so far as any security was conferred thereby, against the third and fourth defendants,
as joint liquidators, and against the fifth defendants, as representative creditors of the　*b*
company. It follows on the same assumptions that the defendants are entitled to have
paid out to them the sum standing in the joint account.

I now come to the second group of questions, namely whether the documents on
which the bank relies are void as unregistered bills of sale. If I am right so far, that is to
say, if its charges are all void against the liquidators or representative creditors under s 95,
then the point does not arise. But as I am dealing with preliminary questions of law on　*c*
a number of assumed facts, some or all of which may not be established at the trial,
counsel for the defendants naturally wishes to be able to support his attack on alternative
grounds. In any event, having heard full argument (more than 50 authorities were cited)
it is obviously right to express my conclusion, if only quite shortly.

The first main issue in relation to the Bills of Sale Acts is whether they apply to
companies at all. Counsel for the bank says they do not. Counsel for the defendants says　*d*
they do but not if the charge falls to be registered under s 95. If for any of the reasons
which counsel for the bank has advanced the present charges are not void under s 95,
then, says counsel for the defendants, the defendants can fall back on the Bills of Sale
Acts.

The general pattern of the Bills of Sale legislation is very well set out in Halsbury's
Laws of England[1]. Very briefly, the 1878 Act is the sole Act in force in relation to　*e*
absolute bills. It is also in force in relation to bills given by way of security, to the rather
limited extent that it has not been amended by the Bills of Sale (1878) Amendment Act
1882. It is agreed by all parties that the documents on which the bank rely, if they are
bills of sale at all, are bills of sale given by way of security and not absolute bills.
Accordingly, I am concerned primarily with the 1882 Act. I need only refer to one
section of it, s 17, which provides:　　　　　　　　　　　　　　　　　　　　　　*f*

　　'*Debentures to which Act not to apply.* 'Nothing in this Act shall apply to any
　debentures issued by any mortgage, loan or other incorporated company, and
　secured upon the capital stock or goods, chattels, and effects of such company.'

While I am primarily concerned with the 1882 Act, I am also concerned indirectly
with the 1878 Act to the extent that it throws light on the question whether the Bills of
Sale Acts as a whole (since they are to be read as one) apply to companies as well as　*g*
individuals, and also to the limited extent to which, as I have already said, it still applied
in relation to security bills.

Before dealing with the submissions on either side, I must refer, in order to make the
submissions intelligible, to the five principal cases in this field. I can start with *Read v
Joannon*[2]. Prior to *Read v Joannon*[2] there were cases in which it had been said, or more　*h*
often assumed, that the Bills of Sale Acts applied to companies as well as individuals: see
Shears v Jacob[3], *Deffell v White*[4], *Re Cunningham & Co Ltd, Attenborough's Case*[5], *Edmonds v
Blaina Furnaces Co Ltd*[6], *Levy v Abercorris Slate and Slab Co*[7], *Jenkinson v Brandley Mining*

1　4 Halsbury's Laws (4th Edn) paras 605–606
2　(1890) 25 QBD 300　　　　　　　　　　　　　　　　　　　　　　　　　　　*j*
3　(1866) LR 1 CP 513
4　(1866) LR 2 CP 144
5　(1885) 28 Ch D 682
6　(1887) 36 Ch D 215
7　(1887) 37 Ch D 260, [1886–90] All ER Rep 509

Co[1], and *Brocklehurst v Railway Printing and Publishing Co*[2]. There were also cases the other

a way: see *Re Asphaltic Wood Pavement Co Ltd*[3] and *Welsted & Co Ltd v Swansea Bank Ltd*[4].

In *Read v Joannon*[5] the question arose in relation to an ordinary company debenture. It had been held in the City of London Court that the debenture was void as against an execution creditor, under the 1878 Act, notwithstanding s 17 of the 1882 Act. The matter then came on appeal before the Divisional Court in July of 1890. In an unreserved judgment Lord Coleridge CJ said[6]:

b

> 'The question is, whether a debenture of an incorporated company requires registration as a bill of sale. I am of opinion—and I think it right to say that my opinion does not stand alone, but is supported by a judge of much greater authority than myself, whom I have had the opportunity of consulting—that such debentures are not bills of sale and are not struck at by either of these Acts of Parliament—that **c** they were never within the Act of 1878, and are expressly exempted from the operation of the Act of 1882.'

Wills J said[7]:

> 'I am of the same opinion; and I agree with my Lord, upon consideration, that **d** debentures of an incorporated company are not, and were never intended to be, within the operation of the Act of 1878.'

Both judgments went on to hold that even if the debenture had fallen within the 1878 Act, considered on its own it was taken out of the 1878 Act by s 17 of the 1882 Act.

In the course of the next term precisely the same question came before the Court of **e** Appeal, consisting of Lord Halsbury LC, Bowen and Fry LJJ, in *Re Standard Manufacturing Co*[8]. There was a very full argument lasting four days. In the course of the argument it was submitted for the execution creditors that debentures were registrable as bills of sale and that that had been the general understanding prior to *Read v Joannon*[5]. It was submitted for the debenture holders that limited liability companies never were within the operation or policy of the Bills of Sale Acts, quite apart from s 17 of the 1882 Act. **f** The point was thus directly before the Court of Appeal. The judgment of the court was given the following February by Bowen LJ. The court held that the debentures were expressly excepted by s 17 from the 1882 Act. But they went on to consider the position under the 1878 Act. The court held that company debentures are not within the 1878 Act. There are three strands to be found in the reasoning. In the first place company debentures are not within the mischief of the Act. The Act was designed to prevent frauds on creditors by secret bills of sale. Company debentures could hardly be described **g** as 'secret documents' since there already existed provision for their registration under the Companies Clauses Consolidation Act 1845 and the Companies Act 1862. Secondly, the language of the Act seemed much more appropriate to individuals than companies; thus in s 12 there is provision that the index of bills of sale to be kept by the registrar is to be arranged according to the 'surnames' of their grantors; thirdly, the court referred to **h** previous authority. The judgment concludes with the following paragraph[9]:

---

1   (1887) 19 QBD 568
2   [1884] WN 70
j 3   (1883) 49 LT 159
4   (1889) 5 TLR 332
5   (1890) 25 QBD 300
6   25 QBD 300 at 303
7   25 QBD 300 at 304–305
8   [1891] 1 Ch 627, [1891–4] All ER Rep 1242
9   [1891] 1 Ch 627 at 647–648, [1891–4] All ER Rep 1242 at 1247–1248

'The view that debentures like the present are not within the *Bills of Sale Act* of 1878 was that adopted by Baron *Pollock*, in the case of *John Welsted & Co.* v. *Swansea* *a* *Bank*[1], and by Lord *Coleridge* and Mr. Justice *Wills* in the case of *Read* v. *Joannon*[2]: see also *Edmonds* v. *Blaina Furnaces Company*[3] and *Levy* v. *Abercorris Slate and Slab Company*[4]. We agree with this view, and we think that this appeal should, therefore, be allowed with costs both here and below, on the ground that the mortgages or charges of any incorporated company for the registration of which other provisions have been made by the *Companies Clauses Act*, 1845, or the *Companies Act*, 1862, are *b* not within the *Bills of Sale Act* of 1878.'

The *Standard Manufacturing* case[5] was followed a year later in an Irish case, *Re Royal Marine Hotel Co, Kingstown (Ltd)*[6]. Porter MR[7] stated the ground of the decision in the *Standard Manufacturing* case[5] as follows:

'It was there decided by the Court of Appeal that a debenture charging the *c* chattels of a limited Company was not void as against execution creditors because it was not registered under the Bills of Sale Acts, on the ground that under the Companies Act of 1862 the Company is bound to keep a register of its mortgages and charges, and that the debenture should have been placed upon such register, and that the Legislature having enacted this particular provision for registering charges given by a Company on its property, impliedly relieved a Company from *d* registering such charges under the Bills of Sale Acts. I agree with [counsel for the unsecured creditors] that this may be a far-reaching decision but I am bound by it.'

Then in 1896 the *Standard Manufacturing Co* case[5] was distinguished by Vaughan Williams J in *Great Northern Railway Co v Coal Co-operative Society*[8]. The case concerned debentures issued by a society registered under the Industrial and Provident Societies Act 1876. By virtue of its registration the society became a body corporate with perpetual *e* succession, a common seal and limited liability. But it was not a limited company within the Companies Act 1862, so that it was not obliged to keep a register of mortgages or charges under s 43 of that Act or under any other Act. Vaughan Williams J held that the debentures were void against the liquidator for non-registration. The primary ground of his decision was that the society, although a corporation, was not an *f* incorporated company within the meaning of s 17 of the 1882 Act. He said[9]:

'The word "company" has come to have a very well recognised meaning. There are various legal companies, but this industrial society does not come within the connotation of that word in any of its accepted legal meanings. And I think that that alone would be sufficient ground for saying that the section was designed by the Legislature in favour of companies, and that if the Legislature had intended to *g* exclude from the operation of the Bills of Sale Act all sorts of corporations, nothing would have been easier for the Legislature to do than to say so in plain terms.'

But Vaughan Williams J went on to consider the broader question whether corporations, be they limited companies within the Companies Act 1862 or not, are within the Bills of Sale Acts at all. He treated the decision in the *Standard Manufacturing* *h*

---

1   (1889) 5 TLR 332
2   (1890) 25 QBD 300
3   (1887) 36 Ch D 215
4   (1887) 37 Ch D 260   *j*
5   [1891] 1 Ch 627, [1891–4] All ER Rep 1242
6   [1895] 1 IR 368
7   [1895] 1 IR 368 at 375
8   [1896] 1 Ch 187
9   [1896] 1 Ch 187 at 194

Co case[1] as being confined to companies for which other provisions for registration had

a been made in the 1845 Act or the 1862 Act. The question whether the Bills of Sale Acts could ever apply to corporations had been 'deliberately and studiously left open'. He said[2]:

b
> 'I think I have now been through the authorities on the point. There is the judgment of the Court of Appeal delivered by Bowen L.J. in *re Standard Manufacturing Co.*[1], which decides that companies for the registration of the mortgages of which provision is made are not within the Act of 1878, and I am asked to go a step further and say that no corporations are within the Bills of Sale Acts. I do not feel disposed to go that step.'

He then concluded[3]:

c
> 'Under those circumstances I am disposed to hold that there is nothing in the Bills of Sale Acts generally or in s. 17 of the Act of 1882 which excludes from the operation of the Bills of Sale Acts debentures issued by an industrial society like the present, and I therefore decide in favour of the liquidator.'

d
The last case to which I must refer is *Clark v Balm, Hill & Co*[4], a decision of Phillimore J. The case concerned a series of debentures issued by a company incorporated in Guernsey but charged on property in England. The question was whether the debentures were void for want of registration. The company was not obliged by the law of Guernsey to keep a register of charges. Phillimore J held, nevertheless, in favour of the debenture

e holders. His conclusion as to the 1878 Act is expressed at the very start of his judgment, namely that all debentures of all incorporated bodies are outside the 1878 Act and that there is 'a little error'[5] in the judgment of Vaughan Williams J in the *Great Northern Railway* case[6]. As for s 17 of the 1882 Act, he accepted that the Court of Appeal in the *Standard Manufacturing* case[1] had not gone the full length and had rightly guarded itself against deciding more than it needed to by limiting its decision to companies which keep

f a register of mortgages or charges. Nevertheless he regarded that distinction as being unsatisfactory. He therefore decided the point left open by the Court of Appeal in accordance with the earlier decision of the Divisional Court in *Read v Joannon*[7]. He said[8]:

g
> 'I myself think that, though the Court of Appeal rightly guarded itself against deciding more than it need do in *In re Standard Manufacturing Co.*[1], I ought to follow and am bound by *Read v. Joannon*[7] which is wider in its terms; and I must say that the reasoning of Wills J. in that case commends itself to my mind.'

He also considered, and rejected, the argument that 'incorporated company' in s 17 of the 1882 Act means 'company incorporated in the United Kingdom'.

h In the light of those cases, all decided within a relatively short space of time, counsel for the defendants submits, first, that the overriding authority is that of the Court of

---

1 [1891] 1 Ch 627, [1891–4] All ER Rep 1242
2 [1896] 1 Ch 187 at 197
j 3 [1896] 1 Ch 187 at 198
4 [1908] 1 KB 667
5 [1908] 1 KB 667 at 670
6 [1896] 1 Ch 187
7 (1890) 25 QBD 300
8 [1908] 1 KB 667 at 671

Appeal in the *Standard Manufacturing Co* case[1]. *Read v Joannon*[2] was approved but only
on the limited ground that the company in that case was one for which the 1862 Act had
provided an alternative system of registration. In the absence of an alternative system of
registration the Bills of Sale Acts apply to individuals and corporations alike. They are all
within the mischief of the Acts. It follows that if for any reason the charges in the
present case are not registrable under s 95 of the 1948 Act they are caught by the Bills of
Sale Acts just as charges given by companies registered under the Industrial and Provident
Societies Act 1876 were held to be within the Acts by Vaughan Williams J[3]. In particular
it would, he said, be absurd that an overseas company with an established place of
business in England which failed to register under Part X should, as a result of its own
failure, escape registration of its charges altogether, i e under the Bills of Sale Acts as well
as under the Companies Act. As for s 17 of the 1882 Act, he says that it shows
conclusively, or is at least a very strong indication, that, but for s 17, companies are
within the Bills of Sale Acts. Otherwise it serves no useful purpose.

These are forceful arguments but I do not think they ought to prevail. The real
difficulty in counsel for the defendants' path is the decision of Phillimore J in *Clarke v
Balm, Hill & Co*[4]. That decision is for all practical purposes the latest decision in the
field. It has stood now for 70 years. Even if I thought it wrong (which I do not) I would
be most reluctant not to follow it. So far as I know, it has never been criticised in any of
the standard textbooks. It is treated as good law in the most recent textbook on the topic,
Gough on Company Charges[5], a book to which I am much indebted. The only support
which counsel for the defendants could find for the opposite view was a single reference
in Halsbury's Laws of England[6]. If *Clark v Balm, Hill & Co*[4] is rightly decided, as I believe
it to be, then it is clear that the present case cannot be distinguished. Both concerned
foreign companies. Both concerned companies for which, on the assumption that I am
making, there was no alternative system of registration. Counsel for the defendants tried
to persuade me that *Clark v Balm, Hill & Co*[4] was wrongly decided. If he could have
shown that the decision was inconsistent with what had been held by the Court of
Appeal in the *Standard Manufacturing Co* case[1], he would, so far as I am concerned, have
succeeded. But there is no such inconsistency. The Court of Appeal decided that certain
corporations were outside the Bills of Sale Acts. It did not decide that all other
corporations are within the Acts. It left the point open; and it was the point which was
left open by the Court of Appeal which Phillimore J decided in the negative.

It is true, of course, that the reasoning in *Clark v Balm, Hill & Co*[4] is difficult, even
impossible, to reconcile with the decision of Vaughan Williams J in the *Great Northern
Railway Co* case[7]. It is also true that Vaughan Williams J was an acknowledged expert in
this field. But as between the two, and with the humility which any judge must feel in
the circumstances, I would prefer the decision of Phillimore J. In the first place, as I have
already mentioned, it is the latest in point of time. Secondly, like Phillimore J, I find it
difficult to see that the publicity afforded by the 1862 Act registration system was ever
a very sound basis for distinguishing between debentures of corporations which fall
within the 1862 Act and those that do not. Thirdly, I would attach rather more
importance than did Vaughan Williams J to the infelicity of the language of the Bills of

1   [1891] 1 Ch 627, [1891–4] All ER Rep 1242
2   (1890) 25 QBD 300
3   In *Great Northern Railway Co v Coal Co-operative Society* [1896] 1 Ch 187
4   [1908] 1 KB 667
5   (1978) pp 381–382, notes 4–6
6   4 Halsbury's Laws (4th Edn) para 800
7   [1896] 1 Ch 187

Sale Acts when applied to corporations. It seems to me clear that, as Bowen LJ says[1], the

a draftsman cannot have had corporations in mind. As for cl 17 of the 1882 Act, the obvious explanation is that given by Phillimore J, namely that it was inserted per majorem cautelam.

It may perhaps be possible to reconcile the two cases on the narrow ground that, while a foreign company is an incorporated company within the meaning of s 17, a society registered under the Industrial and Provident Societies Act 1876, though incorporated,

b is not an incorporated company. But I would prefer to put my decision on the broad ground indicated by Phillimore J, namely that the Bills of Sale Acts apply to individuals only and not to corporations at all.

There is a further point which weighs with me, and which I must mention, even though it did not find much favour with counsel for the bank. Even if the *Great Northern Railway Co* case[2] was correctly decided, and even if the Court of Appeal in *Re Standard Manufacturing Co*[3] is to be taken as having held that the only corporations

c outside the Act are those for which Parliament had provided an alternative system of registration, then it seems to me that Parliament *has* provided just such a system in the present case by virtue of Part III of the Companies Act 1948. Counsel for the defendants' argument in effect came to this, that the Bills of Sale Acts are a catch-all, which apply to all bills of sale as defined unless a charge created by a particular bill of sale happens to be

d registrable under the Companies Act 1948; so that if, for instance, Parliament had provided for a system of registration of charges, but a particular charge, while coming broadly within the system, fell through an unforeseen gap, for example, by non-registration of an overseas company under Part X of the Companies Act 1948, then it would be caught by the Bills of Sale Acts.

I think this is to attribute far too meticulous an intention to the legislature. Assuming Parliament did not intend to exclude all corporations when they enacted the Bills of Sale

e Acts, as I have held that they did, the intention must have been to exclude certain broad categories of corporation, namely those for whom a separate system of registration was provided by the Companies Acts in force from time to time. You then look at the current Companies Act and ask yourself: is the company in question within the registration provisions? If it is, then the Bills of Sale Acts on their true construction do

f not apply, and it is irrelevant that the particular charge may not be registrable. In other words, you look at the company and not at the charge.

If that is right, then it seems to me that on all except one of counsel for the bank's arguments the present company falls outside the Bills of Sale Acts even if the charges were not registrable under the Companies Act. The one exception is counsel's argument that s 106 only applies to companies incorporated in Scotland and Ireland. On all the

g other arguments the company is within the registrable provisions of the 1948 Act even if the particular charge is not registrable, and, accordingly, the Bills of Sale Acts do not apply.

I now turn to the second main issue under the Bills of Sale Acts. Assuming the Bills of Sale Acts are capable of applying to companies, are the documents in the present case debentures issued by an incorporated company within the meaning of s 17 of the 1882

h Act? The point does not arise as a separate point if I am right on the first issue, so I can deal with it quite briefly. Counsel for the defendants argues, first, that 'incorporated company' does not include a company incorporated abroad. In *Clark v Balm, Hill & Co*[4] Phillimore J held that 'incorporated company' at least included a company which, if not a company incorporated according to the law of the United Kingdom, was nevertheless

j
1   See *Re Standard Manufacturing Co* [1891] 1 Ch 627 at 646, [1891–4] All ER Rep 1242 at 1246–1247
2   [1896] 1 Ch 187
3   [1891] 1 Ch 627, [1891–4] All ER Rep 1242
4   [1908] 1 KB 667

incorporated according to the laws in force in one portion of the British Empire under
the sanction of the common Sovereign. Although the British Empire no longer exists, *a*
I see no reason for not applying what Phillimore J said to a company incorporated in
Bermuda.

Secondly, counsel argued that the documents are not debentures within the meaning
of s 17. A debenture, he said, is a document which creates or acknowledges an
indebtedness. It is of the essence of a debenture that it identifies the particular sum
which is due. Accordingly, a document which relates to future indebtedness, that is to *b*
say to a debt which is unquantified at the date of the creation of the document and may
never arise, cannot be a debenture. Thus it was said that the ordinary form of bank
debenture which is taken by a bank as security for sums to be advanced on current
account (sometimes called an 'all-moneys' debenture, as opposed to a 'fixed sum'
debenture) is not a debenture at all.

I was referred to a number of cases. I note that in many of them judges of great *c*
eminence have declined to attempt a definition of what is meant by a debenture. I
certainly do not propose to rush in where they have feared to tread. No doubt it is true
that in general a debenture is a document of which it can usually be said that it creates
or acknowledges an indebtedness. But there is no hard and fast definition. Certainly
none of the cases to which I was referred decide that a document cannot be a debenture
unless the debt to which it relates is quantified at the date of its creation. I am unwilling *d*
to be the first so to decide. Had it been necessary for my decision I would have held that
all the documents on which the bank relies in the present case, with the exception of the
storage report, are debentures of an incorporated company within the meaning of s 17
of the 1882 Act.

I now come to the last question of all. Assuming the documents on which the bank
relies are otherwise within the Bills of Sale Acts, are they exempt by virtue of the Bills of *e*
Sale Act 1890? Section 1 of that Act, as amended by s 1 of the Bills of Sale Act 1891,
provides as follows:

> '*Exemption of letters of hypothecation of imported goods* . . . An instrument charging or
> creating any security on or declaring trusts of imported goods given or executed at
> any time prior to their deposit in a warehouse, factory, or store, or to their being
> reshipped for export, or delivered to a purchaser not being the person giving or *f*
> executing such instrument, shall not be deemed a bill of sale within the meaning of
> the Bills of Sale Acts 1878 and 1882.'

For the purpose of dealing with questions under the 1890 Act, I am to assume (i) that
the relevant petroleum products are imported goods, and (ii) that the assignment of
stocks as security was executed prior to their deposit with Paktank. In those *g*
circumstances, counsel for the bank argues that the assignment of stocks as security is to
be deemed not to be a bill of sale. Counsel for the defendants, on the other hand, submits
that the 1890 Act is not dealing with future goods at all, that is to say with instruments
which charge or create any security of goods generally, but only with particular goods
which can be identified at the time of the creation of the charge, for example a
consignment of goods arriving by a particular ship. In Halsbury's Laws of England[1] *h*
there is a footnote which reads:

> 'It would seem that the statutory provisions contemplated an instrument referring
> to a specific consignment of goods, rather than a general letter of pledge covering all
> goods which may from time to time be imported by the pledgor.'

Counsel were unable to refer to any other authority. The point is a very short one. On *j*
the whole I agree with counsel for the defendants' contention on this point. It seems to
me that what the section contemplates is the sort of document sometimes called a letter

---

1   4 Halsbury's Laws (4th Edn) para 636, note 1

a of hypothecation, but more usually called a trust receipt, which a bank takes when releasing bills of lading held under a documentary credit in order to enable the merchant to take delivery of the goods from the ship's side. In *Lloyds Bank v Bank of America National Trust and Savings Association*[1] the practice in relation to such documents was described as well established and of very long standing. I do not say that the section is necessarily confined to such documents. But I do decide that it was not meant to cover a document which creates, or purports to create, a general charge on all future goods,

b whether imported or not. I would therefore agree with what is said in the note in Halsbury's Laws[2] to which I have already referred, with a proviso that the word 'specific' might prove misleading. For the goods do not have to be specific goods in the strict Sale of Goods Act sense, provided the consignment is sufficiently identified. With regard to the storage reports, counsel for the bank agreed that they could not come within the section because they were only issued after the petroleum products had been deposited

c with Paktank.

On this last issue, therefore, I decide in favour of the defendants. But on the other issues in relation to the Bills of Sale Acts, I decide in favour of the bank.

The overall result is that, on the assumption I have been asked to make, the defendants win outright on the first group of issues, that is to say in relation to s 95 of the Companies Act 1948. But on their alternative case under the Bills of Sale Acts they fail.

d
Order accordingly.

Solicitors: *Linklaters & Paines* (for the bank); *Cameron, Kemm, Nordon* (for the defendants).

K Mydeen Esq   Barrister.

e _____

1   [1938] 2 All ER 63, [1938] 2 KB 147
2   4 Halsbury's Laws (4th Edn) para 636, note 1

Lambert and another v Lewis and others   *a*

COURT OF APPEAL, CIVIL DIVISION
STEPHENSON, ROSKILL AND LAWTON LJJ
24th, 25th, 26th, 30th APRIL, 1st MAY 1979
3rd, 4th, 24th MAY 1979

b

Sale of goods – Implied condition as to fitness – Defective trailer coupling supplied by garage to vehicle owner for use with trailer – Coupling unsafe for purpose for which it was designed by manufacturer – Continued use of coupling by owner after he ought to have known of defective condition – Defective coupling causing trailer to break loose from vehicle and cause damage to another vehicle resulting in death and injury to occupants – Whether continued user of defective coupling by owner in contemplation of parties at time of sale – Whether conduct of owner *c* *breaking chain of causation between suppliers' breach of warranty in supplying defective coupling and the accident – Liability of owner, supplier and manufacturer inter se.*

The plaintiffs, a mother and daughter, were passengers, together with the son, in a car being driven by the father. As the car approached an on-coming Land-Rover towing a *d* trailer the trailer became unhitched, slewed across the road into the path of the car, and caused an accident in which the father and son were killed and the plaintiffs injured. The Land-Rover was being driven by an employee of the owner of the Land-Rover and trailer. The unhitching of the trailer had resulted from the failure of the coupling connecting the trailer to the Land-Rover, the design of the coupling being defective. The plaintiffs brought an action in negligence against the owner of the Land-Rover, the *e* driver, the suppliers who had supplied and fitted the coupling to the Land-Rover, and the manufacturers of the coupling. All four defendants denied negligence, and by a third party notice the owner and the driver claimed against the suppliers an indemnity or contribution in the event of judgment being entered against them, on the grounds that the suppliers had been guilty of a breach of the warranty of fitness for purpose implied by s 14 of the Sale of Goods Act 1893. In fourth party proceedings the suppliers claimed *f* an indemnity in contract and tort from the manufacturers in the event of being held liable to the plaintiffs, the owner or the driver. At the trial the judge found that the coupling was unsafe for the purpose for which it had been designed and for which it was likely to be used. The judge also found that the owner ought to have noticed that a handle on the coupling was missing and ought to have appreciated the significance of it being missing. However, the judge further found that the owner's negligence did not *g* amount to recklessness. On those findings the judge awarded the plaintiffs £45,000 agreed damages, and apportioned liability on the basis of 75% to the manufacturers and 25% to the owner. The plaintiffs' claim against the suppliers was dismissed. In the third party proceedings the judge dismissed the owner's claim against the suppliers for an indemnity, holding that although the suppliers were in breach of the implied warranty of fitness and although the owner's negligence, despite being a superimposed cause, had *h* not broken the chain of causation from the manufacturers through the suppliers and the owner to the accident, nevertheless the owner's negligence was too remote to have been within the contemplation of the parties (i e the owner and the suppliers) at the time the contract of supply was made as being a probable consequence of the breach of warranty. Although not required to decide the fourth party proceedings, the judge stated that he would have dismissed the suppliers' claim against the manufacturers for an *j* indemnity, on the ground that the suppliers had not relied on any express warranty from the manufacturers when purchasing the coupling and therefore could not recover for any negligent misrepresentations made by the manufacturers in their promotional literature or advertising material. On appeal, the court having held that the judge's assessment of the owner's liability at 25% was correct, the issues remained as to the rights and liabilities of the defendants inter se in the third and fourth party proceedings.

Held – (1) In the third party proceedings the suppliers were liable to the owner for the

a following reasons—

(a) On the principle that a seller of goods was responsible for all damage which flowed naturally and directly from a breach of a warranty or condition in the contract of sale or which was presumed to have been within the parties' contemplation as the probable result of a breach, a seller or supplier who sold, in breach of a warranty of fitness, defective goods to a buyer who in turn became liable to pay damages to a third party as

b a result of the defect, was liable to indemnify the buyer for those damages if the buyer's liability to the third party was damage flowing naturally and directly from the breach of warranty. Further, the seller remained liable notwithstanding any negligence by the buyer or some other person which may have been the immediate cause of, and which contributed to, the damage to the third party, if that negligence was reasonably deemed to have been in the contemplation of the buyer and seller as a probable result of the

c breach of warranty and had not broken the chain of causation between the breach and the accident or been so unreasonable as to have been beyond the contemplation imputed to the parties, that being a question of degree in each case. Having regard to the judge's findings that there had been no break in the chain of causation between the manufacturers (and thus the suppliers) and the accident and that the owner had not been reckless, the suppliers were liable to indemnify the owner in respect of the latter's liability to the

d plaintiffs because that liability was, for the purposes of s 53(2) of the 1893 Act, a direct and natural consequence of the suppliers' breach of their implied warranty under s 14 of the 1893 Act to provide a towing hitch that was fit for the purpose for which they knew it was going to be used (see p 993 *f* to *j* and p 997 *h j*, post); *Hadley v Baxendale* [1843–60] All ER Rep 461, and *Mowbray v Merryweather* [1895–9] All ER Rep 941 applied; dictum of Winn LJ in *Hadley v Droitwich Construction Co Ltd* [1967] 3 All ER at 914 disapproved.

e (b) (per Lawton LJ) The suppliers were liable to indemnify the owner because they were prima facie liable for their breach of warranty of fitness of the coupling under s 14 of the 1893 Act and that liability was not affected by the owner's negligence, having regard to the judge's findings that the chain of causation had not been broken and that the owner's negligence was not a sufficiently substantial cause of the accident to make the suppliers' breach of warranty no longer a cause (see p 997 *a b* and *e* to *j* and p 999 *e f*, post)

f (2) In the fourth party proceedings the manufacturers were not liable to the suppliers for the following reasons—

(a) The suppliers could not succeed on a breach of warranty because in the absence of an express warranty the literature supplied by the manufacturers and the claims made in it were not intended to be such a warranty and were not acted on as such by the suppliers (see p 1002 *e f*, post); *Carlill v Carbolic Smoke Ball Co* [1891–4] All ER Rep 127, *Shanklin Pier*

g *Ltd v Detel Products Ltd* [1951] 2 All ER 471, *Wells (Merstham) Ltd v Buckland Sand and Silica Co Ltd* [1964] 1 All ER 41 and *Howard Marine & Dredging Co Ltd v Ogden & Sons (Excavations) Ltd* [1978] 2 All ER 1134 distinguished.

(b) The manufacturers were not liable to the suppliers for any negligent misrepresentation because merely making a statement with the serious intention that others will or may rely on them did not of itself establish the special relationship between the parties

h which was a prerequisite to liability for negligent misrepresentation (see p 1003 *f* to *h*, post); *Hedley Byrne & Co Ltd v Heller & Partners Ltd* [1963] 2 All ER 575 distinguished.

(c) Nor were the manufacturers liable in negligence to the suppliers for their dangerous and defective design by virtue of being the distributors of a dangerous article, because the loss or damage caused to the suppliers by that negligent act was purely financial loss and on the grounds of common sense and authority it was not recoverable

j (see p 1005 *g* to p 1006 *a*, post); *SCM (United Kingdom) Ltd v W J Whittall & Son Ltd* [1970] 3 All ER 245 and *Spartan Steel and Alloys Ltd v Martin and Co (Contractors) Ltd* [1972] 3 All ER 557 followed.

Notes

For contribution and indemnity between joint and several tortfeasors, see 37 Halsbury's Laws (3rd Edn) 137–141, paras 247–250.

Cases referred to in judgments

Anns v London Borough of Merton [1977] 2 All ER 492, [1978] AC 728, [1977] 2 WLR 1024, *a*
75 LGR 555, 141 JP 526, HL.

Ashington Piggeries Ltd v Christopher Hill Ltd, Christopher Hill Ltd v Norsildmel [1971] 1 All
ER 847, [1972] AC 441, [1971] 2 WLR 1051, [1971] 1 Lloyd's Rep 245, HL, Digest
(Cont Vol D) 785, 726a.

*British Oil and Cake Co Ltd v Burstall & Co, Burstall & Co v Rayner & Co, Rayner & Co v
Bowring & Co Ltd* (1923) 39 TLR 406, 39 Digest (Repl) 828, 2896. *b*

Burrows v March Gas and Coke Co (1870) LR 5 Exch 67, 39 LJ Ex 33, 22 LT 24; *affd* (1872)
LR 7 Exch 96, [1861–73] All ER Rep 343, 41 LJ Ex 46, 26 LT 318, 36 JP 517, Ex Ch,
36(1) Digest (Reissue) 58, *196*.

Carlill v Carbolic Smoke Ball Co [1893] 1 QB 256, [1891–4] All ER Rep 127, 62 LJQB 257,
67 LT 837, 57 JP 325, CA; *affg* [1892] 2 QB 484, 12 Digest (Reissue) 66, *342*.

Compania Naviera Maropan SA v Bowaters Lloyd Pulp and Paper Mills Ltd [1954] 3 All ER *c*
563, [1955] 2 QB 68, [1954] 3 WLR 894; *affd* [1955] 2 All ER 241, [1955] 2 QB 68,
[1955] 2 WLR 998, [1955] 1 Lloyd's Rep 349, CA, 41 Digest (Repl) 189, *259*.

Dobell (G C) & Co Ltd v Barber and Garratt [1931] 1 KB 219, 100 LJKB 65, 144 LT 266, 36
Com Cas 87, CA, 2 Digest (Reissue) 163, *991*.

Donoghue v Stevenson [1932] AC 562, [1932] All ER Rep 1, 101 LJPC 119, 37 Com Cas 350,
1932 SC (HL) 31, 1932 SLT 317, HL, 36(1) Digest (Reissue) 144, *562*. *d*

Driver v William Willett (Contractors) Ltd [1969] 1 All ER 665, 36(1) Digest (Reissue) 27,
90.

Hadley v Baxendale (1854) 9 Exch 341, [1843–60] All ER Rep 461, 23 LJ Ex 179, 23 LTOS
69, 18 Jur 358, 2 CLR 517, 156 ER 145, 17 Digest (Reissue) 101, *109*.

Hadley v Droitwich Construction Co Ltd [1967] 3 All ER 911, [1968] 1 WLR 37, CA, 3
Digest (Reissue) 498, *3282*. *e*

Hedley Byrne & Co Ltd v Heller & Partners Ltd [1963] 2 All ER 575, [1964] AC 465, [1963]
3 WLR 101, [1963] 1 Lloyd's Rep 485, HL, 36(1) Digest (Reissue) 24, *84*.

Home Office v Dorset Yacht Co Ltd [1970] 2 All ER 294, [1970] AC 1004, [1970] 2 WLR
1140, [1970] 1 Lloyd's Rep 453, HL, 36(1) Digest (Reissue) 27, *93*.

Howard Marine & Dredging Co Ltd v A Ogden & Sons (Excavations) Ltd [1978] 2 All ER
1134, [1978] QB 574, [1978] 2 WLR 515, CA. *f*

Independent Broadcasting Authority v EMI Electronics Ltd (10th November 1978) unreported,
[1978] Court of Appeal Transcript 670.

Jackson v Watson & Sons [1909] 2 KB 193, 78 LJKB 587, 100 LT 799, CA, 17 Digest
(Reissue) 140, *341*.

Kate, The [1935] P 100, [1935] All ER Rep 912, 104 LJP 36, 154 LT 432, 18 Asp MLC 562,
51 Ll L Rep 321, 42 Digest (Repl) 1143, *9513*. *g*

Kendall (Henry) & Sons (a firm) v William Lillico & Sons Ltd [1968] 2 All ER 444, [1969] 2
AC 31, [1968] 3 WLR 110, sub nom *Hardwick Game Farm v Suffolk Agricultural and
Poultry Producers' Association Ltd* [1968] 1 Lloyd's Rep 547, HL, Digest (Cont Vol C)
853, *781b*.

Krüger & Co Ltd v Moel Tryvan Ship Co Ltd [1907] AC 272, 76 LJKB 985, 97 LT 143, 10
Asp MLC 465, 13 Com Cas 1, HL, 26 Digest (Repl) 232, *1792*. *h*

Monarch Steamship Co Ltd v A/B Karlshamns Oljefabriker [1949] 1 All ER 1, [1949] AC 196,
[1949] LJR 772, 82 Ll L Rep 137, 1949 SC (HL) 1, 1949 SLT 51, HL, 41 Digest (Repl)
362, *1549*.

Morrison Steamship Co Ltd v Owners of cargo lately laden on SS Greystoke Castle [1946] 2 All
ER 696, [1947] AC 265, [1947] LJR 297, 176 LT 66, HL, 41 Digest (Repl) 514, *2887*.

Mowbray v Merryweather [1895] 1 QB 857; *affd* [1895] 2 QB 640, [1895–9] All ER Rep *j*
941, 65 LJQB 50, 73 LT 459, 59 JP 804, 14 R 767, CA, 36(1) Digest (Reissue) 95, *365*.

SCM (United Kingdom) Ltd v W J Whittall & Son Ltd [1970] 3 All ER 245, [1971] 1 QB 337,
[1970] 3 WLR 694, CA, 36(1) Digest (Reissue) 28, *94*.

Shanklin Pier Ltd v Detel Products Ltd [1951] 2 All ER 471, [1951] 2 KB 854, [1951] 2
Lloyd's Rep 187, 39 Digest (Repl) 579, *1030*.

a   *Sims v Foster Wheeler Ltd* [1966] 2 All ER 313, [1966] 1 WLR 769, CA, 7 Digest (Reissue) 437, 2575.

Spartan Steel & Alloys Ltd v Martin & Co (Contractors) Ltd [1972] 3 All ER 557, [1973] QB 27, [1972] 3 WLR 502, CA, 17 Digest (Reissue) 149, 403.

Victoria Laundry (Windsor) Ltd v Newman Industries Ltd [1949] 1 All ER 997, [1949] 2 KB 528, CA, 17 Digest (Reissue) 103, 110.

Vogan & Co v Oulton (1899) 81 LT 435, 16 TLR 37, CA, 17 Digest (Reissue) 165, 478.

b   *Weller & Co v Foot and Mouth Disease Research Institute* [1965] 3 All ER 560, [1966] 1 QB 569, [1965] 3 WLR 1082, [1965] 2 Lloyd's Rep 414, 36(1) Digest (Reissue) 45, 143.

Wells (Merstham) Ltd v Buckland Sand and Silica Co Ltd [1964] 1 All ER 41, [1965] 2 QB 170, [1964] 2 WLR 453, Digest (Cont Vol B) 632, 1078a.

c **Appeal**

By a writ dated 29th August 1973 and subsequently amended and re-amended, the plaintiffs, Iris Frances Lambert (on her own behalf and as administratrix of the estates of her husband George Charles Lambert and her son Kirby George Lambert both deceased, under the Fatal Accidents Acts 1846 to 1959 and on behalf of each of the said estates under the Law Reform (Miscellaneous Provisions) Act 1934) and Tracy Frances Lambert

d (an infant suing by her mother and next friend Iris Frances Lambert) brought an action against the defendants, Donald Richard Lewis (the owner of a Land-Rover and trailer) ('the owner'), Hugh Francis Larkin (the driver of the Land-Rover at the material time) ('the driver'), B Dixon-Bate Ltd (the manufacturers of the towing hitch or coupling by which the trailer was attached to the Land-Rover) ('the manufacturers') and Lexmead (Basingstoke) Ltd (the garage which supplied and fitted the coupling to the Land-Rover)

e ('the suppliers'), claiming damages for personal injuries, loss and damage suffered by each of them by the negligence of the four defendants or any one or more than one of such defendants which gave rise to a road accident on 10th September 1972 in which the plaintiffs were injured and the deceased killed.

The accident occurred when the driver, as servant or agent of the owner, was driving the Land-Rover towing a trailer loaded with builder's rubble and the trailer became

f detached from the Land-Rover and collided with a Reliant motor car owned and driven in the opposite direction by the first plaintiff's husband now deceased. The plaintiffs and Kirby George Lambert now deceased were passengers in the Reliant motor car. All four defendants denied negligence. The owner and driver issued a third party notice against the suppliers claiming an indemnity, damages or contribution in the event of one or other or both of them being held liable to the plaintiffs. The suppliers issued a fourth

g party notice against the manufacturers claiming an indemnity or contribution from the manufacturers in the event that the third party was held liable to the owner and/or the driver.

On 11th November 1977 Stocker J gave judgment for the plaintiffs against the owner, the driver and the manufacturers for a total of £45,000 agreed damages in the proportions of 75% against the manufacturers and 25% against the owner and driver. He

h dismissed the plaintiffs' claim against the suppliers and the third party proceedings brought by the owner and driver against the suppliers. He stated that he would have dismissed the fourth party proceedings brought by the suppliers against the manufacturers if on his judgment the question had arisen for decision.

The owner and driver appealed from so much of the judgment in the main action as adjudged that they were 25% to blame for the accident and asked that that judgment

j should be set aside and judgment entered for the plaintiffs against the manufacturers and for the owner and driver against the plaintiffs. By a respondent's notice the manufacturers admitted liability but contended that the owner and driver were more to blame for the accident than they were and they asked that judgment against them in the main action should be varied to reflect that. The owner also appealed against the dismissal of the third party proceedings. It was conceded on the appeal that judgment should not have been entered against the driver because the negligence alleged against him was quite distinct from the negligence found and proved against his employer, the owner.

The suppliers appealed against the dismissal of their claim for an indemnity against the manufacturers in the fourth party proceedings and asked for an order that the judgment should be set aside and judgment entered for them against the manufacturers for an indemnity in respect of all sums which the suppliers might be held liable to pay to the owner in the event of the owner's appeal in the third party proceedings succeeding.

The facts are set out in the judgments of Stephenson LJ below and at p 999, post.

Roy Beldam QC and *R F Nelson* for the owner and the driver.
Michael Maguire QC and *R Livesey* for the manufacturers.
Michael Turner QC and *Patrick Phillips* for the suppliers.

30th April. **STEPHENSON LJ.** We will give judgment in the action and in the third party proceedings, but we have not yet heard the arguments in the fourth party proceedings[1], and they will depend on the judgments which we now give.

This appeal arises out of a fatal road accident which took place on 10th September 1972; in that accident the first plaintiff and her daughter were injured and her husband, who was driving his motor car perfectly properly, was killed, and their son was also killed.

On 11th November 1977 Stocker J gave judgment for the plaintiffs for £45,000 agreed damages against three out of the four defendants. He gave judgment for the fourth defendants. He dismissed third party proceedings brought by the first defendant against the fourth defendants and although on his findings the question did not arise he stated that he would have dismissed fourth party proceedings brought by the fourth defendants against the third defendants.

The accident, injuries and deaths were caused by a trailer becoming detached from a Land-Rover and slewing across to the offside of the road and into the oncoming car driven by the first plaintiff's husband, containing him and her and their two children.

The defendants were: first Mr Lewis ('the owner'), a farmer who owned the Land-Rover and the trailer; second, Mr Larkin ('the driver'), who was employed by him driving the Land-Rover at the time; third, a company called B Dixon-Bate Ltd ('the manufacturers'), who were the manufacturers of the towing hitch which was found to have failed; fourth, another company, called Lexmead (Basingstoke) Ltd ('the suppliers'), who were the company running the garage which had supplied the owner in January or February 1971 with the Land-Rover and with the towing hitch manufactured by the manufacturers.

There were formulated by the learned judge, in an admirably careful and comprehensive judgment, three issues for him to decide. The first was: why did the trailer become detached from the Land-Rover? His judgment contains a detailed description of the hitch or coupling, and the way in which the trailer was attached to the Land-Rover. I cannot emulate or improve his exposition of the mechanics of it, so I will not repeat it. Suffice it to say that there was supplied by the supplier and fixed to the Land Rover a dual-purpose towing hitch. It consisted in outline of a towing pin which ended at the top in a ball; that ball could be and was locked to the cup attachment on the only trailer which the owner had at the time when he bought this towing hitch, and that was the trailer which became detached and caused the injuries to the Lambert family.

That towing pin was not only locked at the top by the ball and the cup, but it was locked at the bottom by a brass spindle and spiral pin with a handle. The towing hitch was a dual-purpose towing hitch and recommended to the owner as such. He wanted it for two purposes, namely to carry stuff about his own farm land, and also for carrying building materials and rubble in connection with a building business in which he was

---

1   For judgment in those proceedings, see p 999, post

engaged; but that was not the dual purpose for which this Dixon-Bate towing hitch was
a specifically designed.

The advantage of this particular towing hitch was that it could be coupled to a cup-
type attachment on a trailer, as this one was, but it could also be coupled to a ring-type
trailer attachment; and if it had ever come about that the owner had invested in a ring-
type trailer, then he would have been able to attach it to this towing hitch manufactured
by Dixon-Bate if, making use of the handle, he removed the pin and then re-inserted it
b through the ring. But he never had occasion to use it in that way, and he did not intend
at the time he bought it to use it in that way.

What happened, apparently, on 10th September 1972 was that the towing pin, securely
locked at the top, rose out of the jaws of the towing assembly to which it should have
been securely locked at the bottom, and that caused the trailer to become detached from
the Land-Rover and to slew across the road with the fatal consequences I have described.
c On examination after the accident, it was found that the brass spindle and the handle
were missing, and the hitch was very dirty. When the dirt was cleared away, it was
found that only the dirt was keeping the towing pin in position, and expert evidence
showed that submission to a steady upward thrust of 1·05 tons would be enough to bring
the pin out of the jaws once the locking of them had become imperfect, and indeed a
pressure of 0·87 tons would have brought this pin out because the tongue of the locking
d part was substantially worn, and also the protuberance at the bottom of the pin had been
deliberately chamfered to reduce chattering.

That was how the accident had happened according to the judge, and it really was not
disputed. It may be that in passing over a pot-hole or a manhole cover, or something of
that kind on the road the towing pin was forced up and as there was nothing to retain it
but the dirt, it came out and so the trailer became detached from the Land-Rover.
e The second issue formulated by the judge was: which, if any, of the defendant parties
was liable for the detachment of the trailer and the consequent accident? The judge
found that the manufacturers were responsible. He had to ask himself: was their design
or manufacture of this coupling defective or dangerous? If it was, ought they to have
appreciated the defect and foreseen the dangers in view of the history put before him of
failure of this type of coupling, and in view of the expert evidence put before him by I
f think at least three of the parties?

The history of the failure included ten incidents, only disclosed at the start or near the
start of the trial, in none of which had there ever been a complete loss of the handle or
spindle but in at least one of which there had been damage to this handle which was so
near the ground as almost inevitably, one would have thought, to come into contact with
the ground when the Land-Rover and the trailer were driven over rutted farm land.
g The judge answered this question in this way: he held that the coupling was unsafe for
the use for which it was designed and which it was likely to receive, and he concluded
that the designers ought to have realised that the adaptation of a coupling of this sort for
this dual purpose, so that it could be used with the cup-type attachment, did result in a
fundamental change in its function and in the stresses to which it was subjected: it
became subject to vertical stresses to which it would not have been subject when coupled
h to a ring attachment, and that made the handle, and through it the spindle on which the
integrity of the lock depended, vulnerable. He therefore found the manufacturers
responsible in negligence for the plaintiffs' loss and damage, and that finding was not
challenged by the manufacturers.

He assessed and apportioned their responsibility at 75% because he went on to find that
the owner was also responsible in negligence and responsible to the extent of the
j remaining 25%. That finding is challenged by counsel on behalf of the owner in the first
part of his appeal.

The third issue which the judge had to decide was the rights of the defendants inter se,
both in contract and as tortfeasors, and before I come to the first of those, I shall deal with
the judge's findings against the owner.

The judge found that the owner could not have known that the integrity of the lock

depended on the undamaged spindle. That was a concealed mechanism inside the
towing hitch which was supplied, but he should have known, and did know, first, that *a*
the safety of the trailer on the highway depended on the effectiveness of the coupling,
second, how the towing pin could be removed by the handle being depressed and
releasing the lock, and, third, that the security of the towing pin depended on the lock
being operated by the handle.

It is said by counsel for the owner that in this part of his judgment the judge put the
evidence of Mr Hunt[1] in giving his opinion too high. I do not refer to the details of that *b*
because it is undoubtedly true that the opinion of Mr Hunt, the owners's expert, was not
as unqualified a statement as was attributed to him in the judge's summary.

It is also said that the judge misunderstood the test which the owner said he applied,
and which his employees were instructed to apply, every time they coupled the trailer to
the Land-Rover. The evidence was that he and his men stood on the tow-bar facing the
Land-Rover coupled to the trailer, locked the cup onto the ball at the head of the towing *c*
pin, and then moved the coupling up and down rapidly in order to make sure that it was
secure. But the owner's evidence was that he never removed the towing pin; he never
had the curiosity to discover how it was removed and would require to be removed if he
should ever want to fit it to a ring type trailer; and he carried out that test in order to
make sure that the locking of the ball to the cup was secure, and that was all that
concerned him.   *d*

It is also pointed out by counsel for the owner that the Land-Rover with the towing
hitch (but without the trailer) had recently been into the supplier's garage for servicing,
and had been serviced on a ramp by a competent mechanic named Walker, and that
competent mechanic had not noticed, when he was doing the servicing, that this handle,
on which the security of the locking device depended, was missing, although he was a
skilled man and although he had a better opportunity of looking at it from below to *e*
notice the missing handle than the owner, who was only looking down on it from above
as he stood on the tow-bar, rather low down between his legs. But the judge acquitted
Mr Walker and his employers of any negligence in that respect and gave judgment for
the suppliers, holding that their job was only to service in certain respects which did not
include the handle or the locking device.

The judge went on to hold that the owner ought to have noticed that the handle was *f*
missing on one of the many occasions when he stood on the tow-bar and rapidly moved
it up and down, and he ought to have appreciated the significance of the handle being
missing because the evidence was that it had been missing for anything from three to six
months at the time when the accident happened; and if he had noticed the handle being
off, as the judge thought he must have done, he ought to have examined the coupling or
had it examined by an expert, to see if it was safe to use. The judge acquitted the owner *g*
of recklessness; he did not think he was reckless but he thought he was insensitive to the
public safety and to the condition of the vehicle. No doubt he reached that conclusion
relying to some extent on the very poor maintenance of the trailer itself, which had
nothing directly to do with the accident.

Counsel for the owner has forcibly asked: ought this owner of a Land-Rover and
trailer, a farmer, to have noticed that the handle was missing and to have been put on *h*
enquiry? Ought a reasonably prudent farmer in his position, coupling and uncoupling
this trailer to this Land-Rover once or twice a week, to have noticed that the handle was
missing in the three to six months when it was, on the evidence, proved to have been
missing and to have done something about it?

The judge answered those questions Yes. Perhaps the owner was somewhat
unfortunate, but despite counsel's persuasive and able argument, and despite some *j*
sympathy which I feel for the owner, who had been, as I will indicate, supplied with this
towing hitch from reputable manufacturers by his garage who, under the Sale of Goods

---

1   A consulting engineer

Act 1893, warranted it to be safe and suitable for the purpose for which it was known to
a be used, I do not see my way to holding that the judge was not justified in finding the
owner negligent in the respects in which he did find him negligent and responsible to
the extent to which he did find him responsible. I would therefore dismiss the owner's
appeal in the action and leave the liability of the owner where the judge put it.

I come next to the appeal in the third party proceedings. The judge found that the
suppliers, Lexmead (Basingstoke) Ltd, supplied a coupling which was not fit for the
b purpose for which it was to be used within s 14 of the Sale of Goods Act 1893, and also
not merchantable within that section; and he also found that it was likely to cause a
serious accident because it was unfit in the respects which I have tried, shortly, to
indicate. But he found that the owner's negligence was a concurrent, superimposed and
added cause. He found that that negligence, that continued user of the coupling when
he knew or ought to have known that the handle was missing and the towing pin might
c be insecure (the judge thought he did know and was not impressed by his denial that he
ever removed the pin or had been interested enough when working on it to know that
the handle had some connection with the integrity of the lock) did not break the chain
of causation between the plaintiffs' accident and the negligence of the manufacturer,
Dixon-Bate, in designing and marketing a coupling unfit for the purpose and that their
negligence still continued. Nevertheless, he found that this superimposed and added
d cause in the continued use of the coupling on the road by the owner, when he realised or
ought to have realised it was damaged or broken, was an action which would not have
been in the contemplation of the parties at the time the contract was made; and he went
on to apply a statement of Winn LJ in *Hadley v Droitwich Construction Co Ltd*[1], which I
have had some difficulty in understanding, and held that the facts of this case fell within
the principle stated by Winn LJ and therefore that the suppliers were not liable to the
e claim made against them by the owner in the third party proceedings.

The statement of principle on which Stocker J admittedly relied was in these terms[2]

> 'The principle [of *Mowbray v Merryweather*[3]), as HARMAN, L.J., has already stated,
> is this: that in a case where A has been held liable to X, a stranger, for negligent
> failure to take a certain precaution, he may recover over from someone with whom
> he has a contract only if by that contract the other contracting party has warranted
f > that he *need not*—there is no necessity to—take the very precautions for the failure
> to take which he has been held liable in law to the plaintiff.' (Emphasis Winn LJ's.)

That led the judge to take the view that, as he put it, the duty owed by the owner to
the Lamberts was co-extensive with the contractual duty relied on by the owner against
the suppliers; that, as expounded, and I think rightly expounded, by counsel appearing
g for the suppliers, means that the facts constituting the two breaches of duty, one the duty
owed by the owner to the members of the public on the road like Mr and Mrs Lambert,
and the other the contractual duty owed by the suppliers to the owner, were the same in
each case and nothing more could be said against the owner than his continuing to use
the coupling for the purpose for which it was supplied by the suppliers.

That in its turn has led to detailed submissions on *Mowbray v Merryweather*[4] and the
h cases in which it has been applied and distinguished, including *Hadley v Droitwich
Construction Co Ltd*[1]. The other cases in which it has been applied by this court and to
which we have been referred are *Vogan & Co v Oulton*[5] and *Sims v Foster Wheeler Ltd*[6]

j   1   [1967] 3 All ER 911, [1968] 1 WLR 37
      2   [1967] 3 All ER 911 at 914, [1968] 1 WLR 37 at 43
      3   [1895] 1 QB 857; *affd* [1895] 2 QB 640, [1895–9] All ER Rep 941
      4   [1895] 2 QB 640, [1895–9] All ER Rep 941
      5   (1899) 81 LT 435
      6   [1966] 2 All ER 313, [1966] 1 WLR 769

where, as Stocker J rightly said, this court dismissed the suggestion that the introduction
of an apportionment of responsibility between joint tortfeasors by the Law Reform
(Married Women and Tortfeasors) Act 1935 affected in any way the principle laid down
in *Mowbray v Merryweather*[1].

Counsel for the owner submits that that decision applies to decide these third party
proceedings in favour of the owner against the suppliers. He submits that a purchaser
owes no duty to a seller who gives him a warranty, even if the purchaser breaks his duty
of care to a third party, whether one of his own servants, as in many of the cases, or a
stranger; he can still rely on the breach of warranty and recover from the seller or
supplier who gives the warranty the damages he has had to pay for his negligence or
breach of duty to that third party as part of the damage, part of his loss, resulting
naturally in the ordinary course of events from the breach of warranty. Counsel for the
owner further submits that if the negligence of a purchaser (or hirer) amounts to
recklessness, it may break the chain of causation and constitute a novus actus or make
him volens, a person who willingly undertakes the risk of that damage, and such
recklessness may be conduct beyond the reasonable contemplation of the parties and
make the damages which result from it too remote.

That last submission rests on the obiter observations of Devlin J in *Compania Naviera
Maropan SA v Bowaters Lloyd Pulp and Paper Mills Ltd, The Stork*[2], where the judge, having
referred to novus actus interveniens and volenti non fit injuria, said[3]:

> 'If I may return to the case of the sale of goods, from which I have already drawn
> an analogy, in a proper case in which sub-sales are contemplated, a plaintiff may
> recover as part of his damages his liablity to a third party: but if he passed on to a
> third party goods which he knew to be dangerous or defective, or if he incurred
> damages himself by recklessly using such goods, he could not claim to be
> reimbursed,'

and then he referred to what Lord Halsbury said in *Kruger & Co Ltd v Moel Tryvan Ship
Co Ltd*[4].

Counsel for the owner went on to submit that Stocker J was here rejecting recklessness
in favour of insensitivity and he found that the negligence of the owner was only one
third as great as that of the manufacturers, and he has positively stated that there was no
break in the chain of causation between their negligence in designing an unsuitable
coupling and the damages which he has been ordered (and I would hold rightly ordered)
by the judge to pay to the plaintiff in the action.

There being no break in the chain of causation, says counsel for the owner, these
damages are not too remote; they must be deemed to be within the contemplation of the
parties who bought and sold the coupling; put another way, the defective design remains
remote in one sense as a cause, but not too remote because without the breach of
warranty these damages would not have been incurred; and although the owner, by the
negligence found against him by the judge, has added an immediate cause which has
contributed to his liability to pay these damages, they none the less remain attributable
as between him and the seller to the breach of warranty on which he is entitled to rely.

I would make it plain that no counsel has suggested that this court should apportion
the damages as betwen the owner and the suppliers. Either the suppliers are liable to
indemnify the owner, or, as the judge has held, they are not liable to him at all; so that,
if *Mowbray v Merryweather*[1] does apply to achieve the former result and to make the
suppliers liable to the owner, it is a harsh doctrine because if, as one hopes is not the case,
the manufacturers were for any reason unable to satisfy the judgment obtained against

---

1   [1895] 2 QB 640, [1895–9] All ER Rep 941
2   [1954] 3 All ER 563, [1955] 2 QB 68
3   [1954] 3 All ER 563 at 569, [1955] 2 QB 68 at 78
4   [1907] AC 272 at 278

a them by the plaintiffs, the owner might have to satisfy the whole of the plaintiffs' judgment against him and the suppliers might find themselves liable for £45,000 and presumably costs, whereas if the owner had escaped any liability to the plaintiff altogether, they would of course escape also, as the judge has found, but for a different reason.

b 1st May. **STEPHENSON LJ** continued delivering his judgment:
Counsel's submissions on behalf of the suppliers, the third parties, appear to have been accepted by the judge. I begin with what I understand counsel to accept. He first concedes, in this court at any rate, that the suppliers were in breach of contract and that the owner is entitled, therefore, to nominal damages. He also concedes that the suppliers' breach of warranty was a causa sine qua non, and that no duty was owed by the owner c to the suppliers.

I also understand him to concede that there is no difference between the position of the manufacturers and the suppliers, except that the suppliers were not negligent; they were the innocent distributors of the towing hitch negligently designed by the manufacturers. But as far as causation and damage is concerned, there is no difference between the operation of the manufacturers' negligence and the suppliers' breach of warranty. He d also concedes that a serious accident was the likely result of the towing pin coming out with or without manifest damage, such as the missing handle, having already occurred; and one of the other incidents concerning the towing hitch of Mrs Dewey[1] shows that damage to the handle not resulting in its disappearance altogether could produce the same sort of result as the detachment of the trailer as was produced in this case.

But he submits that the normal measure of damages is the difference in value between e the article contracted to be sold and that which was in fact supplied. He submits that there is no finding by the judge that the suppliers' breach caused the damage incurred by the owner in paying the plaintiffs; that there is no finding by the judge of no break in the chain of causation from the suppliers' breach to that damage, but only from the manufacturers' negligence to that damage. He also submits that the judge has found that the owner was independently negligent: he not merely used the towing hitch f negligently in the defective condition in which he obtained it, but with knowledge actual or imputed of its defective and potentially dangerous condition used it and permitted it to be used with the disastrous results which ensued.

He submits further, that the cases show that if the buyer of defective goods had actual or imputed knowledge of the defective goods, the damages suffered by the buyer by reason of his decision to use them do not flow from the breach of warranty that they were g suitable; or if knowing of the defect, a buyer elects to use the goods, whether for purposes of resale or for his own personal use, either (a) he does not rely on the warranty or, (b) he has not acted reasonably, that is to say within the reasonable contemplation of the parties.

So he says that he comes within the principle of *Mowbray v Merryweather*[2] as correctly stated in the judge's judgment and in *Hadley v Droitwich Construction Co Ltd*[3] as correctly understood and applied by the judge in this case. He goes on to submit that to hold h otherwise would be to make the seller, who is in breach of contract, an insurer of the buyer's tort where the tort consists of acts other than those relied on to establish the breach of contract.

Finally he submits that, if he is wrong in that, if the judge wrongly distinguished *Mowbray v Merryweather*[2], and was misled by Winn LJ's[4] interpretation of it, the facts

j ────────────────────────────────

1 In June 1976 Mrs Dewey, a witness who gave oral evidence at the trial, had a coupling manufactured by the third defendants fitted to her Land-Rover
2 [1895] 2 QB 640, [1895–9] All ER Rep 941
3 [1967] 3 All ER 911, [1968] 1 WLR 37
4 [1967] 3 All ER 911 at 914, [1968] 1 WLR 37 at 43

which the judge found nevertheless brought this case within the true principle of
Mowbray v Merryweather[1], and the owner was guilty of independent unreasonable   *a*
conduct outside the contemplation of the parties, and the judge was justified in so
finding and dismissing the third party proceedings.

I start with the statutory provision as to the measure of damages for breach of warranty
by a seller which is to be found in s 53(2) of the Sale of Goods Acts 1893. That well-
known subsection provides: 'The measure of damages for breach of warranty is the
estimated loss directly and naturally resulting in the ordinary course of events from the   *b*
breach of warranty.' Then the section goes on, by sub-s (3), to provide:

> 'In the case of breach of warranty of quality such loss is prima facie the difference
> between the value of the goods at the time of delivery to the buyer and the value
> they would have if they had answered to the warranty.'

It would appear from counsel's argument for the suppliers in this court that that   *c*
difference must be presumed to be nominal, although I know that, according to the
judge's judgment, he argued in the court below that the owner was entitled to the cost
of repair to the spindle and the handle and the replacement of the towing hitch in good
and working order under this prima facie rule. Nevertheless, the judge has not given the
owner anything.

From s 53 of the Sale of Goods Act 1893 I go to *Hadley v Baxendale*[2], and I quote the   *d*
relevant passages in that case quoted in the judgment of this court in *Victoria Laundry
(Windsor) Ltd v Newman Industries Ltd*[3]:

> 'Where two parties have made a contract which one of them has broken, the
> damages which the other party ought to receive in respect of such breach of contract
> should be such as may fairly and reasonably be considered either arising naturally,   *e*
> *i.e.*, according to the usual course of things, from such breach of contract itself, or
> such as may reasonably be supposed to have been in the contemplation of both
> parties, at the time they made the contract, as the probable result of the breach of it.'

Asquith LJ, giving the judgment of the court in the *Victoria Laundry* case[3], went on: 'The
limb of this sentence prefaced by "either" embodies the so-called "first" rule; that prefaced   *f*
by "or" the "second".' I am not sure that both rules are not now embodied concisely in
the phrase more familiar in past times in a criminal connection, 'the natural and probable
consequences' of the breach.

I next adopt what Lord Wright said in *Monarch Steamship Co Ltd v A/B Karlshamns
Oljefabriker*[4]:

> '... the question in a case like the present must always be what reasonable   *g*
> business men must be taken to have contemplated as the natural or probable result
> if the contract was broken.'

The judge rightly held that the owner must prove not only the breach of warranty,
which there is no doubt he did, but damage, the £45,000 or that proportion of it which
he was ordered to pay, resulting from the breach. Did he prove that his liability to pay   *h*
that was caused by the breach of warranty? Well, he found that there was no break in the
chain of causation from the negligence of the manufacturers, and I think it follows from
that finding that the suppliers' breach of warranty was *a* cause, at any rate, of his liability
to pay damages to the plaintiffs.

j

1 [1895] 2 QB 640, [1895–9] All ER Rep 941
2 (1854) 9 Exch 341, [1843–60] All ER Rep 461
3 [1949] 1 All ER 997 at 1001, [1949] 2 KB 528 at 537
4 [1949] 1 All ER 1 at 14, [1949] AC 196 at 224

The judge, correctly in my judgment, set out the effect of the decision of Charles J
a (affirmed by this court) in *Mowbray v Merryweather*[1]. He said:

> '. . . a chain supplied by the defendants was defective and caused an accident to
> the plaintiff's servant, who recovered damages from the plaintiff. It was held that
> the plaintiff's liability to pay damages to the servant was a natural consequence of
> the defendants' breach of contract and was such as might reasonably have been
> supposed to have been in the contemplation of the parties when the contract was
> *b*   entered into and that accordingly the damages were not too remote.'

That seems to me to be an accurate rendering of what was decided in that case.
In his judgment Charles J said[2]:

> '. . . the only question I have to determine is whether the damage done to the
> workman, and which he could only recover from the plaintiffs by shewing want of
> *c*   care in them, may nevertheless be regarded as the natural consequence of the
> defendant's breach of contract; or, in other words, a consequence which might
> reasonably be supposed to have been within the contemplation of the parties.'

That statement was approved by Lord Esher MR[3] in the report of the case in the Court
of Appeal:
d
> 'What is the rule of law on the subject? The test is rightly laid down by Charles
> J. when he says that the question is whether the damages "can be regarded as the
> natural consequence of the defendant's breach of contract, or, in other words, the
> consequences which might reasonably be supposed to have been within the
> contemplation of the parties".'

e Kay LJ[4] put his conclusion in this way:

> 'I think the damages claimed by the plaintiffs must be regarded as the natural
> result of the breach of warranty and one which must be deemed to have been within
> the contemplation of the parties as likely to spring from that breach.'

Rigby LJ said[5]: 'The only question here appears to be whether the damages claimed can
f reasonably be supposed to have been within the contemplation of the parties when the
contract was made.'
The judge, in this case, went on rightly to hold that the decision of this court in *Simms
v Foster Wheeler Ltd* [6] and a later decision of Rees J in *Driver v William Willett (Contractors)
Ltd*[7] showed that the principle in *Mowbray v Merryweather*[8] applied despite the
introduction of the right of contribution between tortfeasors and despite the fact that an
g apportionment in tort may have been made under the Law Reform (Married Women
and Tortfeasors) Act 1935.
So the question for the judge, as for this court, is in my judgment this: were the
owner's liability to the plaintiffs and his loss incurred by discharging that liability the
direct and natural consequences in the ordinary course of events, or within the reasonable
contemplation of the parties as consequences of the breach of warranty, notwithstanding
h the negligent conduct of the owner which was found by the judge to have contributed
to causing that liability and loss? That is the question which was rightly asked by Sir

---

1   [1895] 1 QB 857; *affd* [1895] 2 QB 640, [1895–9] All ER Rep 941
j   2   [1895] 1 QB 857 at 859
3   [1895] 2 QB 640 at 643
4   [1895] 2 QB 640 at 645
5   [1895] 2 QB 640 at 647
6   [1966] 2 All ER 313, [1966] 1 WLR 769
7   [1969] 1 All ER 665
8   [1895] 2 QB 640, [1895–9] All ER Rep 941

Boyd Merriman P, applying *Mowbray v Merryweather*[1], in *The Kate*[2], where he said: 'The question in either case is whether the damage sustained is the natural consequence of the *a* breach of contract, notwithstanding some independent negligence on the part of the plaintiff.' That was a case where a company, which had leased a defective berth from a corporation, were held not to be disentitled by their negligence in accepting assurances that the defect had been repaired and in not warning the master that the berth might still be defective from recovering from the corporation damages paid to the owner of a ship damaged by the defect. *b*

A purchaser, who resells goods which are not as warranted by the seller with notice that they are not as warranted, has been held by this court in *G C Dobell & Co Ltd v Barber and Garratt*[3], following Rowlatt J's decision in *British Oil and Cake Co Ltd v Burstall & Co*[4], to be disentitled from recovering damages paid to a sub-purchaser from the seller who is in breach of his warranty. A purchaser cannot resell defective goods sold with a warranty of fitness with knowledge on his part of the defect which makes them unfit for *c* the purpose, and then claim damages that he has to pay a sub-purchaser from the seller who is in breach. Those damages, as Scrutton LJ said[5], would result from his unreasonable conduct and be too remote a consequence of the original breach of warranty, or, as Greer LJ[6] put it, 'Those damages would neither be the natural nor the probable result of the breach, or such as would in the events that happened have been within the contemplation of the parties', and Lawrence LJ[7] pointed out that the purchaser *d* cannot increase his damages in this way.

So in the context not of the sale of goods but of a berth warranted safe the question was: did the shipowners act unreasonably in making use of the unsafe berth, or fail to mitigate their damage, or deliberately assume the risk of damage? See *Compania Naviera Maropan SA v Bowaters Lloyd Pulp and Paper Mills Ltd*[8], per Singleton, Hodson and Morris LJJ. There Devlin J[9] had referred to the analogy of the sale of goods in the passage I have *e* already cited, and he had also suggested that the shipowners' conduct must amount to a novus actus interveniens or a voluntary assumption of risk to disentitle them from relying on the warranty of safety. But the Court of Appeal contented themselves with finding no unreasonable conduct on the part of the shipowners without holding positively that unreasonable conduct would have been enough, and without having to decide how unreasonable the conduct of one party would have to be, to exonerate the *f* other from liability.

I would agree with counsel for the suppliers that the use a purchaser may himself make of goods after notice that they are defective and not in accordance with a warranty of fitness may be just as unreasonable as reselling them after notice and without warning. That was Rowlatt J's[10] view of the law, though it was inapplicable to the case he had to decide. The use by a purchaser either for his own purpose or for resale *g* illustrates the general rule that a party to a contract should act reasonably even when the other party is in breach and may not increase the liability of the other party by acting unreasonably: see Chalmers on the Sale of Goods[11], a passage on which counsel for the suppliers relies.

h

---

1 [1895] 2 QB 640, [1895–9] All ER Rep 941
2 [1935] P 100 at 113, [1935] All ER Rep 912 at 915
3 [1931] 1 KB 219
4 (1923) 39 TLR 406
5 [1931] 1 KB 219 at 231
6 [1931] 1 KB 219 at 246–247
7 [1931] 1 KB 219 at 238   *j*
8 [1955] 2 All ER 241 at 249, 252, 258, [1955] 2 QB 68 at 94, 99, 107
9 [1954] 3 All ER 563 at 569, [1955] 2 QB 68 at 78
10 See *British Oil and Cake Co v Burstall & Co* (1923) 39 TLR 406
11 17th Edn (1975) p 250

a   But it is remarkable that in all the cases on which counsel for the suppliers relies, except *Hadley's* case[1], the promisee to whom the warranty was given did recover from the promisor who gave the warranty damages which the promisee had become liable to pay to a third party; and in the passage in McGregor on Damages[2] on which he also relies the learned editor states: 'There appear to be no cases in which the buyer's action failed on the ground that he ought to have examined the goods before using them or reselling them.' Where I part company with counsel for the suppliers is at the point where he

b   submits that *any* unreasonable conduct on the part of the promisee disentitles him from recovering from the promisor damages resulting from his own conduct, as not resulting also from the promisor's breach of warranty. That submission seems to me to ignore human nature and common sense, which the law applies to require, for instance, road users to expect a certain amount of negligence on the part of other road users and which would treat unreasonableness in relation to other persons who are in law neighbours in

c   the same way as unreasonableness in relation to the other party to a contract.

Of course, the promisor does not give the promisee a licence to be as careless as he likes with the goods sold or to act as unreasonably in relation to them as he chooses, secure in the knowledge that the promisor will pay for the consequences of the promisee's carelessness however great; but *any* failure by the promisee to take reasonable care in relation to the goods and his use of them is unreasonable, yet it, and its consequences,

d   may be within the contemplation of both promisee and promisor and its consequences may flow from the original breach of warranty.

Mowbray v Merryweather[3] demonstrates that some unreasonable action on the part of the promisee causing liability to pay damages is no bar to recovering those damages as a consequence of the breach of warranty deemed to be contemplated by the promisor, who is not exonerated by that tortious action. Mowbray was held to have relied on

e   Merryweather's warranty and to be entitled to do so, notwithstanding his own negligent failure to inspect the chain.

Counsel for the suppliers says that the owner was rather more careless than Mowbray because he let the goods warranted suitable suffer damage and either did not notice the damage or noticed it and ignored it and went on using it after the latent defects and dangers of the design had become patent.

f   I do not think the defects and the dangers had become patent to the owner's comparatively inexpert eye. On the judge's finding, he was put on enquiry, but that seems to raise a question of degree. Did that extra carelessness take the owner's conduct, as the judge has held, outside the reasonable contemplation of the parties and the principle of *Mowbray v Merryweather*[3]? The judge seems only to have felt himself able to regard it as outside both by limiting the principle of *Mowbray v Merryweather*[3] in

g   accordance with Winn LJ's interpretation of it in *Hadley v Droitwich Construction Co Ltd*[1]. I cannot agree that *Hadley's* case[1] touches this case or decides the question which we have to decide.

In *Hadley's* case[1], Pugsley Ltd hired a mobile crane to Droitwich Construction Co Ltd and in a letter confirming the hiring they thanked Droitwich for their promise to put a competent man in charge of the crane who would carry out the servicing properly.

h   Droitwich in fact put a 16-year-old youth in charge of the crane who operated it for three months. During that time he never inspected it and no servicing was carried out. Three months after the hiring, the plaintiff, an employee of Droitwich, working on the site,

j

1   [1967] 3 All ER 911, [1968] 1 WLR 37
2   13th Edn (1972) para 603, p 428
3   [1895] 2 QB 640, [1895–9] All ER Rep 941

was injured when the superstructure of the crane broke away from its base and fell on
him. He sued both Pugsley and Droitwich for personal injuries. In third party *a*
proceedings against Pugsley, Droitwich claimed that they were entitled to be indemnified
by Pugsley in the event of their being held liable to the plaintiff, on the ground of their
being negligent and in breach of contract in providing them with a defective crane. The
judge found that the accident was caused because there was an excessive clearance
between the rollers which hooked the slewing wheel on the superstructure onto the base
of the crane, and found Droitwich and Pugsley equally liable to the plaintiff for *b*
negligence and he gave judgment for Droitwich in third party proceedings and held that
Pugsley were in breach of the implied term of the contract that the crane would be fit for
the purpose for which it was required and free from defect.

It is plain from the report[1] that the judge was satisfied that the crane driver was
negligent in failing to observe that there was excessive clearance and in failing to adjust
the rollers and failing to make weekly inspections of the crane. He found, further, that *c*
Droitwich never serviced the crane or inspected it, in spite of Pugsley's letter. He stated
that the damage flowing from such a breach was that which could be regarded as a
natural consequence of Pugsley's breach of contract, or, in other words, a consequence
which might reasonably be supposed to have been within the contemplation of the
parties. Applying *Mowbray v Merryweather*[2], he held that Droitwich were entitled to be
indemnified by Pugsley in the manner sought in third party proceedings. He therefore *d*
applied the correct interpretation, in my judgment, of *Mowbray v Merryweather*[2], but he
was held by the Court of Appeal not to be entitled to apply it, as I read, at any rate, two
of the judgments, to the facts of the case. Both Sellers and Harman LJJ decided that the
contractual warranty of suitability of this crane for the purpose for which it was used by
the Droitwich company was qualified by the letter, and that letter, as is plain from what
Sellers and what Harman LJJ said[3], was read by those two Lords Justices as imposing two *e*
conditions (1) that Droitwich should put an experienced man in charge of the crane and
(2) that they should service it properly. Harman LJ said[4]:

> 'Any warrant that the owners may have impliedly given as to fitness of the
> machine for its task was undoubtedly, as I see it, qualified by those two conditions.
> Neither condition was performed: the warranty disappears, as the conditions were *f*
> broken.'

Then he went on to say[4]: '*Mowbray* v. *Merryweather*[2] was quite a different case . . . Here,
owing to the presence of the letter [imposing these two qualifications], the boot is on the
other leg, so it seems to me.'

Where did Winn LJ get from that judgment of Harman LJ the statement of the *g*
principle in *Mowbray v Merryweather*[2] which he attributes to him in his judgment,
which I have already read and which the judge sought here to apply and follow? I have
no doubt that the decision in *Hadley v Droitwich Construction Co Ltd*[5] was right, but I
cannot derive from it any justification for qualifying a warranty of fitness where it is not
expressly qualified, as it was in *Hadley's* case[5] or for reducing it to a warranty that goods
are suitable for use for the contemplated purpose provided that there is no negligence in *h*
employing incompetent servants or in failure to maintain. We are not, I think, entitled

j

1   [1968] 1 WLR 37 at 39–40
2   [1895] 2 QB 640, [1895–9] All ER Rep 941
3   [1967] 3 All ER 911 at 913, 914, [1968] 1 WLR 37 at 41, 42
4   [1967] 3 All ER 911 at 914, [1968] 1 WLR 37 at 42
5   [1967] 3 All ER 911, [1968] 1 WLR 37

by what this court decided in *Hadley's* case[1] or for any other reason to whittle down what
a it decided in *Mowbray v Merryweather*[2] or to devalue the statutory condition or warranty
or a purchaser's right to rely on it, as it seems to me Winn LJ's interpretation of *Mowbray
v Merryweather*[2] would whittle down the decision and devalue the warranty and the
right. It is one thing for A to promise that a crane is safe if B promises to employ a
competent driver to maintain it, and quite another thing for A to promise either
expressly or impliedly that the crane is safe and to *imply* some such promise by B as a
b condition precedent to liability for breach of A's apparently unconditional promise.

On the evidence in this case, the owner had not seen the leaflet in which the
manufacturers called their dual-purpose towing hitch foolproof and such as required no
maintenance; but it would be indeed ironic if in such a case the warranty or condition
implied by s 14, or any of the warranties or conditions implied by s 14, were qualified by
an implied condition that the purchaser should maintain the towing hitch properly,
c keep it clean and make sure that it was undamaged.

If the judge was wrong in his interpretation of *Mowbray v Merryweather*[2], can his
dismissal of the third party proceedings be supported, without a respondent's notice, on
other grounds? I do not regard the absence of a respondent's notice as fatal, but I have
come to the conclusion that the dismissal cannot be supported. The question in my
judgment is not whether the defect in this towing hitch was patent or latent either at the
d time of sale or at the time of the accident. Nor is it whether the purchaser actually knew
or ought to have known of the defect; nor is it whether his negligence was independent,
in the sense that it added something to the user of the defective goods in the way
contemplated; nor whether his conduct was not merely careless but reckless or amounted
to a voluntary assumption of risk. The answers to these questions are all helpful but
none of them is conclusive in answering the real question, which is whether, in all the
e circumstances, the owner's carelessness was so unreasonable as to be beyond the
contemplation of the suppliers, or such as to break the chain of causation between their
breach of warranty and the accident which resulted in the owner's liability to pay the
plaintiffs damages.

Put another way, was his conduct such as to disentitle him from relying on the
warranty given by the suppliers as still playing an effective part in causing the particular
f damage which would not have occurred without his own negligence contributing? Was
it still a causa causans, if you like to use the Latin term?

On the evidence, and on the judge's findings, on his assessment of the owner's conduct
and on his apportionment of the responsibility between him and the manufacturers, the
owner's negligence in my judgment falls on the right side of the line for the owner and
the wrong side of the line for the suppliers. The suppliers, warranty does not disappear,
g the breach of it is not spent, as a result of the owner's intervening and contributing
negligence. The question is simply one of causation. If the effect of the manufacturer's
negligent design was still continuing on 10th September 1972, as the judge found, why
was not the effect of the retailers' breach of warranty still continuing at that date? If the
owner's conduct did not break the chain, his liability and consequent loss by discharging
it were natural and probable results or consequences of the breach still operating
h alongside it, and must be deemed to have been within the contemplation of the
suppliers. The judge was, in my opinion, right to say that the chain of causation was not
broken but wrong to say that the owner's conduct would not have been within the
contemplation of the parties at the time the contract was made between them.

He was, therefore, in my judgment wrong to dismiss the third party proceedings and
I would hold the suppliers liable to indemnify the owner against the damages which he
j has to pay to the plaintiffs.

---

1   [1967] 3 All ER 911, [1968] 1 WLR 37
2   [1895] 2 QB 640, [1895–9] All ER Rep 941

ROSKILL LJ. As regards the appeal by the owner against the learned judge's judgment holding that he was 25% to blame for the tragedy which resulted in two deaths in this *a* young family, I agree with everything that has fallen from Stephenson LJ and beyond expressing my appreciation of the argument of counsel for the owner, I do not find it necessary to add anything. One cannot help, as Stephenson LJ has said, a certain feeling of sympathy with the owner, but on the material before the judge he was entitled to reach the conclusion which he did and, for my part, on that evidence I think that I would have reached the same conclusion. *b*

So far as the appeal on the third party proceedings is concerned, I also agree with what has fallen from Stephenson LJ, but as here we are differing from Stocker J, and not only differing from him but also from the dictum of Winn LJ in *Hadley v Droitwich Construction Co Ltd*[1], and also out of deference to the argument of counsel for the suppliers, I add to what has fallen from Stephenson LJ.

At the opening of his address two days ago, counsel for the suppliers said that it was *c* because of the owner's independent negligence that the owner incurred liability to the plaintiffs, in respect of which the owner now sought indemnity from the suppliers, and he contended vigorously (and supported that contention with a mass of authority) that the fact that there was what he called independent negligence freed his client, the suppliers, from liability to pay to the owner that 25% of the global figure of damages which the owner has to pay to the plaintiffs. He went on to submit that a seller is not the *d* insurer of the independent negligence of his buyer. I entirely agree; he is not. But a seller of goods remains responsible for all damages which flow naturally and directly from any breach of condition or warranty contained in his contract with his buyer.

Stephenson LJ, at the outset of his judgment this morning, referred to s 53 of the Sale of Goods Act 1893. That section, as is well known, merely reproduces the old common law and, as I pointed out to counsel for the suppliers yesterday afternoon when he urged *e* that the relevant measure of damages here was governed by s 53(3), sub-s (2) comes before sub-s (3) and the basic rule is that the measure of damages for breach of warranty is the loss directly and naturally resulting in the ordinary course of events from that breach of warranty. Subsection (3) goes on to declare that in the case of a breach of warranty, with which we are concerned, such a loss is prima facie the difference between the value of the goods when delivered and the value they would have had if they had *f* then answered to the warranty.

It was by reference to sub-s (3) that counsel for the suppliers argued that the sole damage for which his clients were liable, was the difference between the sound and damaged values of this coupling. He contended that that was the sole measure of their liability and that nothing beyond that was recoverable. But with respect, that is simply not the law. One has only to look at some of the illustrations in Chalmers on the Sale of *g* Goods[2], to see that there are many cases (the illustration of *Jackson v Watson & Sons*[3] is perhaps the best example) where a buyer who has suffered damage beyond the getting of poor goods rather than sound contract goods is able to recover his further additional loss. The decision in *Jackson v Watson & Sons*[3] is summarised thus: 'A, a grocer, sells tinned salmon to B which is unfit for food. B's wife is poisoned and dies. B may recover the reasonable expenses of medical attendance and the funeral, and also a reasonable sum *h* for the loss of his wife's services.' But if counsel's basic submission be right, he ought only to have recovered the difference between the value of the poisoned and an unpoisoned tin of salmon.

Now in the real world, when parties make a contract whether for the sale of goods or for anything else, they do not usually contemplate a breach of that contract; they contemplate its performance and their efforts are more directed towards ensuring its *j*

1   [1967] 3 All ER 911 at 914, [1968] 1 WLR 37 at 43
2   17th Edn (1975) p 246
3   [1909] 2 KB 193

fulfulment than towards providing for compensation for its breach. When a breach

a occurs, the law therefore has to impute to them an agreement as to what is to happen in the event of a breach, so that they are, in such circumstances, deemed to have contemplated certain consequences, to use Asquith LJ's phrase as being 'on the cards' as damage flowing naturally and directly from the breach. That is what I venture to think that Kay LJ had in mind in the passage of his judgment in *Mowbray v Merryweather*[1], to which Stephenson LJ drew attention that the damage claimed by the plaintiffs must be considered as being the natural result of the breach of warranty, and one which must be

b deemed to have been within the contemplation of both parties as likely to spring from that breach.

If further authority be required for that proposition it is to be found in *Burrows v March Gas and Coke Co*[2]; it is to be observed that it was the judgment of Martin B[3] which had the approval of this court in *Mowbray v Merryweather*[1].

c The basic rule is as Stephenson LJ has indicated and is, I venture to think, now plain: it is clearly expressed in *Mowbray v Merryweather*[1], a decision binding on this court. Of course to all rules there are qualifications. There are the qualifications to which attention was drawn during the argument mentioned in Chalmers on the Sale of Goods[4], on the liability of a seller to pay damages where he is admittedly in breach. After setting out certain propositions it is said:

d

'These propositions are probably illustrations of the general rule that a party to a contract should act reasonably even when the other party is in breach, and may not increase the liability of the other party by acting unreasonably. There may well be circumstances in which a buyer could reasonably use defective goods even with the knowledge of the defect. Thus, if no alternative goods were available and there was a reasonable prospect that the defective goods would fulfil the purpose for which

e

they were bought, it may sometimes be reasonable to use them for that purpose, and if in such a case the buyer in fact suffered additional loss, such loss might be recoverable from the seller.'

That passage, curiously enough, does not refer to *Mowbray v Merryweather*[1]; indeed,

f *Mowbray v Merryweather*[1] is not referred to anywhere in the present edition of Chalmers on the Sale of Goods[5]. True strictly it is not really a sale of goods case, but it was a claim for damages for breach of a condition indistinguishable from the condition implied in contracts for the sale of goods by s 14(1) of the Sale of Goods Act 1893.

The same problem was considered by Devlin J and by this court in *Compania Naviera Maropan SA v Bowaters Lloyd Pulp and Paper Mills Ltd*[6]. The most relevant passage is in

g Devlin J's judgment[7]. The case concerned an unsafe berth; the argument was that the master had disentitled the owners from recovering damages because of the action which he took going there with the knowledge of its condition at the time he entered and re-entered. Devlin J said:

'To deny the defendants' proposition does not mean that a master can enter ports

h that are obviously unsafe and then charge the charterers with damage done. The

j 1   [1895] 2 QB 640, [1895–9] All ER Rep 941
   2   (1870) LR 5 Exch 67; *affd* (1872) LR 7 Exch 96, [1861–73] All ER Rep 343
   3   LR 5 Exch 67 at 72
   4   17th Edn (1975) p 250
   5   17th Edn (1975)
   6   [1954] 3 All ER 563, [1955] 2 All ER 241, [1955] 2 QB 68
   7   [1954] 3 All ER 563 at 569, [1955] 2 QB 68 at 78

damages for any breach of warranty are always limited to the natural and probable consequences. The point then becomes one of remoteness of damages; or, if it is *a* thought better to put it in Latin, the expressions novus actus interveniens and volenti non fit injuria are ready to hand. There is also the rule that an aggrieved party must act reasonably and try to minimise his damage. A master who entered a berth which he knew to be unsafe (and which perhaps the charterer had nominated in ignorance of its condition) rather than ask for another nomination and seek compensation for any time lost by damages for detention, might find himself in *b* trouble . . . If I may return to the case of the sale of goods, from which I have already drawn an analogy, in a proper case in which sub-sales are contemplated, the plaintiff may recover as part of his damages his liability to a third party: but if he passed on to a third party goods which he knew to be dangerous or defective, or if he incurred damage himself by recklessly using such goods, he could not claim to be reimbursed.'

c

Devlin J referred to a number of cases with which it is not necessary to deal. In passing I would only make this observation. The learned judge there uses the adverb 'recklessly': that adverb does not occur in any of the judgments in the cases which he cites; probably he was only using that word to illustrate one of the extreme cases which he mentioned in the immediately following passage. In my judgment there does not have to be recklessness and nothing less than recklessness on the part of the buyer before a seller can *d* disclaim liability for damage in respect of which the buyer claims an indemnity. It is, as Lawton LJ said yesterday during the course of argument, always a question of degree at what point the damage claimed for ceases to flow naturally and directly from the breach.

The only statement of the law which, to my mind, is out of line with this impressive list of authorities is the dictum of Winn LJ in *Hadley v Droitwich Construction Co Ltd*[1]. As Stephenson LJ has already said, the decision is plainly right if it is treated as a decision on *e* the construction of the rather curiously worded letter there in question. Both Sellers and Harman LJJ said that a condition of this kind implied by s 14(1) could not possibly stand alongside the terms of that letter. In my judgment both Sellers and Harman LJJ were looking at the matter simply in the light of the particular contract there in question and pointing out that the contract in *Hadley's* case[2] was totally different from the contract in *Mowbray v Merryweather*[3]. *f*

But Winn LJ[1] went much further. He seemingly sought to invoke something which Harman LJ had said as supporting his (that is, Winn LJ's) view. With all respect I cannot find in the report of Harman LJ's judgment anything which gives any such support. Winn LJ went on to discuss the *Mowbray v Merryweather*[3] principle. He said[1] it was—

'that in a case where A has been held liable to X, a stranger, for a negligent failure *g* to take a certain precaution, he may recover over from someone with whom he has a contract only if by that contract the other contracting party has warranted that he *need not*—there is no necessity to—take the very precautions for the failure to take which he has been held liable. It does not go farther than that . . .' (Winn LJ's emphasis.)

With very great respect to Winn LJ, I cannot agree with that proposition or that that *h* proposition correctly states what was decided first in *Burrows v March Gas and Coke Co*[4], and secondly, in this court in *Mowbray v Merryweather*[3].

j

1   [1967] 3 All ER 911 at 914, [1968] 1 WLR 37 at 43
2   [1967] 3 All ER 911, [1968] 1 WLR 37
3   [1895] 2 QB 640, [1895–9] All ER Rep 941
4   (1870) LR 5 Exch 67; affd (1872) LR 7 Exch 96, [1861–73] All ER Rep 343

a The law is, as Stephenson LJ has said, that the damage which is recoverable by a buyer from a seller for the seller's breach of warranty in a case such as this is the damage which follows naturally and directly from that breach and such damage does not cease to be recoverable merely because the act which 'triggers off' the casualty giving rise to the liability may be some act, albeit a negligent act, of some other party, or indeed of the buyer himself. That seems to me to be plain. The relevant law was discussed in the House of Lords in *Monarch Steamship Co Ltd v A/B Karlshamns Olejefabriker*[1]. In the

b present case we are concerned with damages for bad design; in that case the court was concerned with the unseaworthiness of a ship. There are, to my mind, certain analogies between physical unseaworthiness of the ship and bad design of a towing coupling; unseaworthiness of a ship will rarely of itself cause a loss. As Lord Wright pointed out, something else usually has to happen before that unseaworthiness has any causative effect. So, in cases of bad design, the breach is usually committed at the moment delivery

c takes place. But the breach remains inoperative in most cases until it manifests itself because something else happens (as in this case namely the owner's negligence) which 'triggers off' an accident which but for the initial breach would not have occurred.

Here the learned judge apportioned liability as to 25% for the owners negligence and as to 75% to bad design by the manufacturers. The learned judge rightly said that there were two concurrent causes: unsuitability of the coupling, and the fact that the owner

d continued to use the coupling for a period of months when it was manifestly defective. I do not consider this failure by the owner broke the chain of causation between the breach of conditions by the suppliers in supplying a coupling which by reason of bad design was unfit for the purpose required.

In my judgment the judge ought to have given judgment for the owner against the suppliers for damages for breach of contract for the full 25%. But the learned judge did

e not do so because of that dictum of Winn LJ[2]. With profound respect to the judge whose judgment in the first two parts of this complicated case appears to me faultless, on the last point he allowed himself to be misled by that dictum which, for the reasons given, I do not think can be supported. It seems to me that these damages did flow naturally and directly, and for my part I cannot see how it can be said the 25% negligence by the owner can free the suppliers from all responsibility. Of course, counsel for the suppliers was not

f slow to make the point that if the owner had been acquitted of all negligence, then there would have been no liability on the suppliers for damages for breach of contract, except perhaps nominal damages for the difference between the value of the coupling in the condition in which it was and in the condition in which it ought to have been.

But if that were enough to enable the suppliers to escape liability, the decision in *Burrows v March Gas and Coke Co*[3] and, indeed, in the *Monarch Steamship* case[4] should have

g been different.

I think that the liability for the owner's negligence to the extent of 25% must fall on those who were in breach of the implied condition under s 14(1), as damages naturally and directly flowing from their breach. For those reasons, as well as those which Stephenson LJ has given, I agree with Stephenson LJ that the appeal in the third party proceedings should be allowed.

h

LAWTON LJ. I agree with the judgments which have been delivered by Stephenson and Roskill LJJ. I add a few comments because I have been disturbed by the length of the arguments which have been put before the court in this case. In saying that, I do not

j

---

1   [1949] 1 All ER 1 at 16, 17, [1949] AC 196 at 227–230
2   *Hadley v Droitwich Construction Co Ltd* [1967] 3 All ER 911 at 914, [1968] 1 WLR 37 at 43
3   (1872) LR 7 Exch 96, [1861–73] All ER Rep 343
4   [1949] 1 All ER 1, [1949] AC 196

criticise counsel; they felt it necessary, because of the way the law has developed, to spend the time they did inviting the court's attention to a long line of cases.   *a*

Their submissions lasted four days. Stephenson and Roskill LJJ have had to deliver long judgments analysing in detail the various cases to which we have been referred. This has led me to consider whether it might not be possible to find a short cut through this morass of case law.

I find it advisable to look for a short cut because cases of this kind are, unfortunately, not all that uncommon. When the damage is slight, or comparatively slight, cases of this   *b* kind are dealt with in the county court. When the damage is more serious, they are dealt with in the High Court, and occasionally, the issues which have been considered in this court, have to be considered by magistrates and, in the Crown Court, by juries. It would be a pity if, in this kind of case, subtleties entered into the law which might make it difficult to apply.

It seems to me that it is possible to find a short cut. I start with the proposition that   *c* when a garage sells a towing hitch to a customer, the probabilities are that there will be a warranty of fitness under the provisions of s 14 of the Sale of Goods Act 1893, as amended. Both the garage proprietor and the customer must surely envisage that, if the towing hitch is not reasonably suitable for towing, then an accident is likely to happen on the highway when the towing hitch is used. What the consequences of the accident will be are unpredictable. There may be nothing more than scratched paintwork on   *d* another vehicle, or, as in this case, people may be killed. It follows, therefore, that both the garage selling the towing hitch and the customer buying it should take care to ensure that accidents do not happen.

In the circumstances of this case, no moral blame of any kind attaches to the suppliers as the garage owners. They bought from reputable wholesalers who, no doubt in turn, bought from reputable manufacturers; but the fact remains that what the garage sold   *e* was liable to cause, and did cause, an accident.

It follows, therefore that prima facie the garage are liable for their breach of warranty. They excuse themselves by alleging that their breach of warranty did not cause the accident because their customer, the owner, was also negligent. That was an argument which was put before Charles J in 1895[1], and rejected by him, and was repeated in this court later that year, and rejected by this court[2]. So the law undoubtedly   *f* is that negligence on the part of a customer which was a cause of the accident and which triggered it off, to use Roskill LJ's phrase, is not always an answer to an allegation of breach of warranty. What the court has to consider is: what was the substantial cause or causes of the accident? There may be two or more causes of an accident. That is what the trial judge found there were in this case. There were two concurrent causes, one was the bad design for which the manufacturers were responsible, and the second was the   *g* negligence of the customer, the owner, in not behaving in relation to the towing hitch as the judge found he should have done.

The trial judge then had to ask himself whether the negligence of the customer was of such degree that the breach of warranty by the suppliers could no longer be said to be a cause of the accident. This is the sort of problem which, at the turn of the century, would have been left to a jury had the judge decided to take a general verdict from   *h* them. The jury would have used their common sense and their knowledge of the world in deciding whether the owner's negligence was such a substantial cause of the accident so as to excuse not only the garage proprietors but the designers of the towing hitch as well.

Stocker J decided that the chain of causation had not been broken. He said, in relation to the negligence of the owner: *j*

1   *Mowbray v Merryweather* [1895] 1 QB 857
2   [1895] 2 QB 640, [1895–9] All ER Rep 941

a

'He would not have known nor could he have been expected to have known that the integrity of the locking mechanism depended on the continued undamaged existence of the spindle, nor that a blow on the handle, sufficient to cause deformation of the spindle might affect the proper working of the spring-loaded lock. What I find the [owner] should have known and by his evidence he did in fact know was that the safety of the trailer on the highway depended on the effectiveness of the coupling.'

b

A little later he said:

'I find that he [that is the owner] ought to have ascertained the physical nature of the lock on which the security of the tow depended. I am not making a finding that he should have known or enquired as to the unseen nature of the lock mechanism within the casting or the materials of which it was composed. He was entitled to assume that both were suitable but he ought, however, to have seen and ascertained that the security of the towing pin depended on the spring-loaded lock operated by a handle.'

c

Later still he said:

'I do not think the [owner] was in any way reckless of the public safety. I think he was insensitive to it and never really turned his mind to the risks involved in the use of a trailer on the highway.'

d

The judge, acting as a jury, came to the conclusion that negligence of that kind did not break the chain of causation. In his judgment the design of the towing hitch was a substantial cause of the accident, and as Stephenson and Roskill LJJ have pointed out, he went further and said it was the major cause because he attributed 75% of the blame to the bad design.

e

Most unfortunately for the suppliers, they must be held responsible for the bad design having regard to the implied warranty of fitness.

As to the judge's finding about causation, no appellate court in my judgment could say that it was unreasonable or perverse or that the consequences of the bad design were so remote as to have played no part in the accident. Essentially, this was a matter of fact for the judge to decide and there was evidence on which he could decide as he did.

f

Accordingly I would hold, like Stephenson and Roskill LJJ, that the appeal against the fourth party should be allowed.

Appeal by the owner in the main action dismissed. Appeal by the owner against the suppliers in the third party proceedings allowed, and judgment entered for the owner against the suppliers for repayment of damages, interest and costs, and interest on such sum since payment. Suppliers' application for leave to appeal to the House of Lords refused.

g

The court then heard argument in the appeal in the fourth party proceedings.

Michael Maguire QC and *R Livesey* for the manufacturers.
Michael Turner QC and *Patrick Phillips* for the suppliers.

h

Cur adv vult

j

24th May. **STEPHENSON LJ** read the following judgment of the court: From the judgment we have already given in the third party proceedings allowing the owner's appeal and holding the suppliers liable to indemnify the owner arises the necessity to decide the fourth party proceedings brought by the suppliers against the manufacturers. The necessity for taking those proceedings arose simply from the fact that the suppliers were unable to identify the stockist or distributor who sold to them the particular Dixon-Bate towing hitch (or trailer coupling) which they sold to the owner.

If they could have identified that party they could, in the absence of special contractual terms, have obtained an indemnity from that party for his breach of contractual condition or warranty, or perhaps for negligent misrepresentation under the Misrepresentation Act 1967, and that party could in turn have been indemnified by the seller of the hitch to him, probably the manufacturers themselves, but without that identification the suppliers must have recourse direct to the manufacturers, with whom they had no contract of sale, but who may be considered in part responsible because they do not identify each coupling by a serial number.

Counsel for the suppliers have addressed to us an ingenious argument that they are none the worse off for that lack of identification. The argument was put before us, as it was put before Stocker J, in three different ways. Having dismissed the third party proceedings it was not necessary for him to consider the argument or pronounce on it; but he did so for the sake of completeness should it be held on appeal, as it has been, that he was wrong to dismiss the third party proceedings, and after considering the argument he rejected it and stated that he would have dismissed the fourth party proceedings.

We agree with him that they should be dismissed and in deference to the interesting arguments of counsel for the suppliers, and also because the judge did not expressly deal with the third way in which they put their case, we shall state our reasons more fully perhaps than we need.

We take their pleaded claim from the judge's judgment with a few additions:

> 'By their fourth party notice the [suppliers] claim by sub-para (4) of para 3 that the [manufacturers] owed a duty to distributors, garages, sellers and/or users, of whom they were one, to exercise reasonable care in the design of the towing hitches to ensure that they were safe to be fitted to vehicles such as Land-Rovers, and were suitable for use when so fitted. The duty is alleged to arise from the matters pleaded in sub-paras (1), (2) and (3) of para 3 of the fourth party notice, namely: (1) The [manufacturers] represent themselves by selling such and other towing hitches on a world-wide scale by promotion and otherwise, being experienced and competent manufacturers of towing hitches which are safely fitted to vehicles such as Land-Rovers and were suitable to be used when so fitted for the purpose of safely towing a trailer. (2) Further the [manufacturers] supply such towing hitches to distributors with the expectation that such distributors will sell them to others, including garages, or are likely to sell them to customers for their use. (3) Yet further the [manufacturers] so pack and sell their said towing hitches to be ready for immediate easy attachment to another vehicle and accordingly knew or ought to have known no intermediate distributor seller garage or user would test, examine or otherwise appraise the qualities of any such towing hitches, or any of them. Alternatively it is claimed that the [manufacturers] by the fact of their manufacture, packing and selling of the hitches, warranted to each distributor who might handle, sell or fit one of their towing hitches, that the same was safe to be fitted to vehicles such as a Land-Rover and was suitable to be used when so fitted for the purpose of towing trailers.'

Then para 4(1) and (2) reads:

> '(1) The towing hitch which the [suppliers] fitted to the [owner's] Land-Rover they acquired from such a distributor who had acquired the same directly or through another from the [manufacturers]. (2) At the same time, when the [suppliers] came to fit the said towing hitch to the said Land-Rover the said towing hitch was in the same condition and packing as was manufactured and sold by the [manufacturers].'

The suppliers relied on the manufacturers' representations, reputation and warranties and carried out no test or examination and fitted the towing hitch to the owner's Land-Rover in such reliance. The suppliers therefore claim under the heads above specified: (1) damages for negligent misrepresentation, and/or (2) damages for the breach of the warranty alleged to have been given to them as distributors. They also alleged (in para 6) a breach of the duty alleged in para 2(4) and claimed damages for that.

The judge dealt first, and so will we, with the argument that the suppliers could
a succeed on a breach of warranty. The allegation of implied collateral warranty, he said—

> '. . . is based on a submission that the following facts are established: 1. The
> [manufacturers] were well known in the trade as manufacturers of a variety of
> towing hitches. 2. [They] had justly acquired not only a good trade reputation but
> also a reputation for quality and safety. 3. [They] sought to improve their reputation
> *b* by obtaining approval of certain of their products from Messrs Rovers, the Ministry
> of Defence, and so on. 4. To the trade and to the public [they] expressly claimed in
> relation to the safe towing trailer coupling that it requires "no maintenance", is
> "foolproof" and "once the pin is pushed home it is locked—absolutely". They also
> claimed that the pin "locked positively and automatically" and "no metallic springs
> to break or rust". 5. [They] were thus making these claims seriously and intending
> *c* that any purchaser should rely on them. It is said that Mr Dixon-Bate said in his
> evidence "Such claims were intended to be serious and to be acted on by users". 6.
> The [manufacturers] did not consider or publicly claim that any instruction or
> warning in relation to a hitch was necessary, nor did they give any indication with
> regard to restrictions of user in relation to the suitability for that purpose of their
> coupling. 7. [They] expressly or by implication claimed no instruction or warning
> *d* was necessary.'

The evidence of the suppliers' witnesses, Mr Baldwin, their parts manager, Mr Curtis,
their salesman, and Mr Wallace, their storeman, was mainly related to documents put
out by the manufacturers in 1960, 1963 and 1966, which were not concerned with
the dual-purpose towing hitch, or put out in 1973 after the purchase of this hitch by the
e suppliers. But it was rightly assumed that there was a document put out by the
manufacturers after the manufacture of the dual-purpose hitch in 1968 and before this
purchase by the suppliers and in the same terms as the 1973 literature. The judge rightly
acted on that assumption and found that Mr Wallace read the claims then made and
relying on the manufacturers' reputation rather than on them believed them to be true.
Counsel for the suppliers relied before the judge, and also before us, on the evidence
f of Mr Dixon-Bate himself that the manufacturers intended these claims to be taken
seriously, and on the decisions of this court in *Carlill v Carbolic Smoke Ball Co*[1] and of
McNair J in *Shanklin Pier Ltd v Detel Products Ltd*[2].
We accept counsel for the suppliers' submission that not much is needed to conclude
that when a warranty of suitability for a particular purpose is expressed or implied in a
contract of sale that warranty has been relied on by the purchaser: see *Henry Kendall &*
g *Sons Ltd (a firm) v William Lillico & Sons Ltd*[3] per Lord Reid and Lord Pearce; *Ashington
Piggeries Ltd v Christopher Hill Ltd*[4] per Lord Wilberforce. But the difficulty is to show
that what the manufacturers stated in the literature advertising and accompanying their
products as to their safety and suitability was intended to be a contractual warranty or
binding promise. It is one thing to express or imply it in a contract of sale, another to
treat it as expressed or implied as a contract, or a term of a contract, collateral to a contract
h of sale. There may be cases where the purchase from an intermediate seller may be
regarded as fortuitous and the original supplier or seller can properly be held liable for
breaches of warranty given by the intermediate seller as well as for those given by him:
see *Wells (Merstham) Ltd v Buckland Sand and Silica Co Ltd*[5]. But that is not, in our
judgment, this case.

j

---

1   [1893] 1 QB 256, [1891–4] All ER Rep 127
2   [1951] 2 All ER 471, [1951] 2 KB 854
3   [1968] 2 All ER 444 at 457, 483, [1969] 2 AC 31 at 84, 115
4   [1971] 1 All ER 847 at 876–877, [1972] AC 441 at 495
5   [1964] 1 All ER 41, [1965] 2 QB 170

In the *Carbolic Smoke Ball* case[1] this court had no difficulty in holding that the suppliers of the ball made a binding promise to pay £100 to any users of the ball on the stated *a* conditions if it failed to prevent them from getting influenza. Their statement that they had deposited £1,000 with a bank showed that their statements were not a mere 'puff' but a sincere promise, and we cannot agree with counsel for the suppliers that the promise to pay £100 merely showed that they were serious and quantified the damages which they would have been liable to pay to an unsuccessful user of their ball as the loss naturally and directly resulting from their breach of contract. It appears from the report *b* of the argument before Hawkins J[2] that the plaintiff there put her case as a claim for liquidated damages for breach of a contract of warranty of prevention of disease; but it could have been put as a claim for a debt. That case is no authority for holding that the manufacturers were saying to the suppliers: 'If you acquire our product we promise it is safe and merchantable and if it is not we will pay you such damages as the law requires.'

A statement relating to the marketed product may be more than a puff and less than *c* a warranty: it may be so important that it may induce a contract, may now amount to a negligent misrepresentation,and may nearly amount to a warranty: see *Howard Marine and Dredging Co Ltd v Ogden & Sons (Excavations) Ltd*[3], where Lord Denning MR and Bridge LJ (Shaw LJ dubitante) held that oral statements made in pre-contract negotiations as to deadweight capacity were not warranties (though, as Roskill LJ pointed out in the course of the argument, any terms as to deadweight capacity in the charterparty, which *d* was the resulting contract, are not given in the reports of the case). But whether the statement is oral or written, made contemporaneously with the contract or earlier, the question is whether it is intended to be binding. When it is written, as here, we doubt if parol evidence of the intention of the person who made it is admissible, though here admitted without objection, but the intention must, we think, be inferred from the construction of the writings against the background of all the circumstances. The *e* construction of these documents in the circumstances of this case leads us to the same conclusion as the judge, that the claims in them 'were not intended to be, nor were they acted on as being express warranties and (though this further finding, if it adds anything, is not strictly necessary) the [suppliers] did not purchase the coupling in reliance on such warranties'.

Nor do we think that the development of the law in the *Shanklin Pier Co* case[4] (and, it *f* may be, in the unreported case of *Independent Broadcasting Authority v EMI Electronics Ltd*[5]) helps the suppliers to a different result. The effect and ratio of the former decision are correctly stated by the judge in his judgment in these terms:

'In that case the defendant paint company made certain express representations as to the quality of its paint and its suitability for use on the plaintiffs' pier which *g* was then to be repaired by contractors. On the strength of that representation the plaintiffs caused the specification for their works to be carried out by contractors to be amended by substituting the defendants' paint for that previously specified. The contractors bought and used the paint, which was unsatisfactory and unsuitable for use on the pier. It was held that the plaintiff company could recover damages on the warranty from the defendant paint company despite the fact that there was no *h* contract other than a collateral one between the plaintiff pier company and the defendant paint company. In my judgment the basis of this decision was that consideration for the representation was the procurement by the plaintiffs of a contract of sale by their contractors with the defendants.'

j

1   [1893] 1 QB 256, [1891–4] All ER Rep 127
2   [1892] 2 QB 484 at 486
3   [1978] 2 All ER 1134, [1978] QB 74
4   [1951] 2 All ER 471, [1951] 2 KB 854
5   [1978] Court of Appeal Transcript 670

There the express representation was clearly an express warranty, for which the
a consideration was the procurement of a particular contract, as the judge pointed out; but
here was no warranty and we find it unnecessary to consider whether that decision could
be extended to the contract of purchase made by the suppliers, or the contract of resale
made by them, and to hold that in consideration of either of those contracts, both in fact
unknown to the manufacturers, they are promising or warranting, either expressly or by
implication, that their claims for their hitch are true, and they are prepared to stand by
b their warranties and pay the suppliers and any other distributors in their position
damages for breach of them, as long (counsel for the suppliers was constrained to add) as
the user of the hitch is reasonable.

The judge went on to hold that this finding that the manufacturers' claims were not
warranted precluded the suppliers from recovering damages from the manufacturers in
tort for negligent misrepresentation. The basis of his finding against counsel's second
c submission was that the House of Lords in *Hedley Byrne & Co Ltd v Heller & Partners Ltd*[1],
had 'limited the ambit of those entitled to sue in respect of negligent misstatement to the
person to whom [we add the words 'the answer to'] 'the enquiry was directed and for the
purposes for which the enquiry was made'. And he appears to have held that even if the
ambit could have been extended to the suppliers they would be defeated by the fact that
they did not rely on the manufacturers' misstatements.

d Counsel for the suppliers does not dispute that a special relationship is necessary
between the maker of the misstatement and the person who suffers damage by acting on
it before the former can be liable for the damage to the latter on the *Hedley Byrne*[1]
principle. He concedes also that it is easier to prove that relationship and the consequent
duty of care if the information or advice contained in the statement is asked for. But he
submits that if the statement is made seriously, not casually, and is intended to be acted
e on and is in fact acted on and it is negligent, it is actionable at the suit of him who acts
on it notwithstanding the maker has forestalled an enquiry for the information or advice
it contains by volunteering the one or the other.

This may sometimes be so. A doctor who goes to the help of an unconscious patient
will be liable to him if he injures him by negligent treatment. But we cannot regard the
manufacturer and supplier of an article as putting himself into a special relationship with
f every distributor who obtains his product and reads what he says or prints about it and
so owing him a duty to take reasonable care to give him true information or good
advice. Bearing in mind what, for instance, Lord Reid and what Lord Pearce said in the
Hedley Byrne case[2], we consider that cases of liability for statements volunteered
negligently must be rare and that statements made in such circumstances as these are not
actionable at the suit of those who have not asked for them. To make such statements
g with the serious intention that others will or may rely on them (and here parol evidence
of intent may be admissible) is not, in our opinion, enough to establish a special
relationship with those others or a duty to them.

So we are again in agreement with the judge's rejection of leading counsel for the
suppliers' argument and we turn to his last submission on which the judge is silent,
probably because at the trial it was no more than a makeweight thrown into the scales
h after his two main arguments. That submission is that the suppliers can recover what
they have to pay the owner from the manufacturers as damages for their negligence not
in words but in deeds, not in what they stated untruly and carelessly but in what they
designed defectively and dangerously. What is sought is an application of the principle
in *Donaghue v Stevenson*[3] to the distributor of a dangerous article in the condition in which
it was originally supplied and to the financial loss which the distributor has suffered

j

1   [1963] 2 All ER 575, [1964] AC 465
2   [1963] 2 All ER 575 at 580, 616–617, [1964] AC 465 at 482, 539
3   [1932] AC 562, [1932] All ER Rep 1

under his contractual liability to reimburse the ultimate user of the article for the financial loss which he has incurred from the injury and damage its use has done to third *a* parties. On the judge's finding that this hitch or coupling was a trap, all that counsel for the suppliers says he has to prove is that the manufacturers contemplated its passing through the suppliers' hands on its way to causing injury and damage of the kind that ultimately resulted to the first plaintiff and her family. The damage which the suppliers have suffered in meeting their liability to the owner for his liability to the plaintiffs is not too remote because that commercial consequence of the defective design manifesting *b* itself was reasonably foreseeable by the manufacturers as a direct and immediate result of marketing the coupling as they did.

The way to this argument is opened by what has been said by Lord Reid and Lord Pearson in *Home Office v Dorset Yacht Co Ltd*[1], and by Lord Wilberforce, with the assent of Lord Diplock, Lord Simon of Glaisdale and Lord Russell of Killowen, in *Anns v London Borough of Merton*[2].   *c*

In the *Dorset Yacht Co* case[3] Lord Reid said:

> 'In later years there has been a steady trend towards regarding the law of negligence as depending on principle so that, when a new point emerges, one should ask not whether it is covered by authority but whether recognised principles apply to it. *Donoghue v Stevenson*[4] may be regarded as a milestone, and the well-known passage in Lord Atkin's speech[5] should I think be regarded as a statement of *d* principle. It is not to be treated as if it were a statutory definition. It will require qualification in new circumstances. But I think that the time has come when we can and should say that it ought to apply unless there is some justification or valid explanation for its exclusion. For example, causing economic loss is a different matter; for one thing, it is often caused by deliberate action. Competition involves traders being entitled to damage their rivals' interests by promoting their own, and *e* there is a long chapter of the law determining in what circumstances owners of land can, and in what circumstances they may not, use their proprietary rights so as to injure their neighbours. But where negligence is involved the tendency has been to apply principles analogous to those stated by Lord Atkin[5] (cf *Hedley Byrne & Co Ltd v Heller & Partners Ltd*[6]).'

Then in the same case Lord Pearson said[7]:   *f*

> 'It may be artificial and unhelpful to consider the question as to the existence of a duty of care in isolation from the elements of breach of duty and damage. The actual damage alleged to have been suffered by the respondents may be an example of a kind or range of potential damage which was foreseeable, and if the act or omission by which the damage was caused is identifiable, it may put one on the trail *g* of a possible duty of care of which the act or omission would be a breach. In short, it may be illuminating to start with the damage and work back through the cause of it to the possible duty which may have been broken.'

Then in *Anns v London Borough of Merton*[2], Lord Wilberforce said:

> 'Through the trilogy of cases in this House, *Donoghue v Stevenson*[4], *Hedley Byrne & Co Ltd v Heller & Partners Ltd*[6] and *Home Office v Dorset Yacht Co Ltd*[8], the position *h*

---

1   [1970] 2 All ER 294 at 297, 319, [1970] AC 1004 at 1026, 1052
2   [1977] 2 All ER 492 at 498–499, [1978] AC 728 at 751
3   [1970] 2 All ER 294 at 297, [1970] AC 1004 at 1026   *j*
4   [1932] AC 562, [1932] All ER Rep 1
5   [1932] AC 562 at 580, [1932] All ER Rep 1 at 11
6   [1963] 2 All ER 575, [1964] AC 465
7   [1970] 2 All ER 294 at 319, [1970] AC 1004 at 1052
8   [1970] 2 All ER 294, [1970] AC 1004

a has now been reached that in order to establish that a duty of care arises in a particular situation, it is not necessary to bring the facts of that situation within those of previous situations in which a duty of care has been held to exist. Rather the question has to be approached in two stages. First one has to ask whether, as between the alleged wrongdoer and the person who has suffered damage there is a sufficient relationship of proximity or neighbourhood such that, in the reasonable contemplation of the former, carelessness on his part may be likely to cause damage

b to the latter, in which case a prima facie duty of care arises. Secondly, if the first question is answered affirmatively, it is necessary to consider whether there are any considerations which ought to negative, or to reduce or limit the scope of the duty or the class of person to whom it is owed or the damages to which a breach of it may give rise (see the *Dorset Yacht* case[1], per Lord Reid). Examples of this are *Hedley Byrne & Co Ltd v Heller & Partners Ltd*[2] where the class of potential plaintiffs was

c reduced to those shown to have relied on the correctness of statements made, and *Weller & Co v Foot and Mouth Disease Research Institute*[3] and (I cite these merely as illustrations, without discussion) cases about "economic loss" where, a duty having been held to exist, the nature of the recoverable damages was limited (see *SCM (United Kingdom) Ltd v W J Whittall & Son Ltd*[4], *Spartan Steel and Alloys Ltd v Martin & Co (Contractors) Ltd*[5]).'

d It is right to note that the passing references of Lord Reid and Lord Wilberforce to economic loss are not expressions of considered judicial approval or disapproval, but nevertheless there are two decisions of this court which, in our opinion, bind us to reject the argument that economic loss is, generally speaking, recoverable, though there are exceptions, as damages for negligence of this kind. One is *SCM (United Kingdom) Ltd v W J Whittall & Son Ltd*[4]; the other *Spartan Steel & Alloys Ltd v Martin & Co (Contractors)*

e *Ltd*[5], the cases mentioned by Lord Wilberforce. It is submitted that those cases decide only that 'pure' financial loss not consequent on physical damage is irrecoverable, and so decide because to hold otherwise would be to broaden the class of persons entitled to the benefit of the neighbourly relationship which founds the duty of care; here there are a limited number of contractors buying and selling, stocking and distributing this article of the manufacturers, and the manufacturers could expect any and all of these couplings

f which they manufactured (according to the evidence at least 35,000) to go through the chain of such contractors to the ultimate user with some such result of its use as happened in this case of physical damage and consequent legal liability. If *Mowbray v Merryweather*[6] declares that legal liability to be a direct and foreseeable consequence of the suppliers' breach of contract, why is it not a direct and foreseeable result of the manufacturers' breach of duty?

g The answer seems to us to be found in principle and on authority, in particular the authority of those two recent decisions of this court, not in a detailed examination of the cases nor in a logical analysis of the distinction between physical damage to the owner's trailer and physical injury to the first plaintiff and her family, or between loss of profits and financial loss incurred by legal liability to pay damages, but in applying common sense to draw a line between circumstances where the financial loss can and cannot be

h held to be recoverable for a breach of duty owed to the party who incurs the loss. Whether we follow the first thoughts of Lord Denning MR in *SCM (United Kingdom) Ltd v W J Whittall & Son Ltd*[4], with which Winn LJ agreed, and consider remoteness, or his

---

j   1   [1970] 2 All ER 294 at 297–298, [1970] AC 1004 at 1027
    2   [1963] 2 All ER 575, [1964] AC 465
    3   [1965] 3 All ER 560, [1966] 1 QB 569
    4   [1970] 3 All ER 245, [1971] 1 QB 337
    5   [1972] 3 All ER 557, [1973] QB 27
    6   [1895] 2 QB 640

second thoughts in *Spartan Steel & Alloys Ltd v Martin & Co (Contractors) Ltd*[1], with which Lawton LJ agreed, and discard everything but policy in setting bounds to duty and damage, we reach the conclusion that the loss which the suppliers incurred by their liability to indemnify the owner against his legal liability to compensate the plaintiffs cannot be recovered from the manufacturers.

We should perhaps add (1) that the introduction by the Trade Descriptions Act 1968 of fresh provisions prohibiting false trade descriptions does not, in our judgment, advance the suppliers' case under any of its three heads, nor do other statutory provisions for consumer protection and safety, and (2) that we read the decision of the House of Lords in *Morrison Steamship Co Ltd v Owners of the cargo lately laden on SS Greystoke Castle*[2] as providing no support for the suppliers' claim, perhaps rather ammunition against it, because the decision rests on the existence of a common adventure between the party who negligently caused the collision and the party who had to pay as a result of it and there is no joint venture of the manufacturers and the suppliers here.

There comes a point where the logical extension of the boundaries of duty and damage is halted by the barrier of commercial sense and practical convenience. In our judgment, the facts of this case do not enable the suppliers to push that barrier back as far as to include themselves and their damage within the range of the manufacturers and the towing hitch which they put into the market, or to surmount the barrier where we think common sense would place it.

Putting aside any sympathy we may feel for the suppliers, or their insurers, we would therefore reject all three grounds on which their appeal is put and dismiss it.

Appeal by driver against plaintiffs allowed by consent. Appeal by owner in third party proceedings allowed. Appeal by owner against manufacturers in main action be dismissed. Appeal of suppliers in fourth party proceedings be dismissed. Suppliers application for leave to appeal to House of Lords refused.

Solicitors: *Stevensons* (for the owner and driver); *Hextall Erskine & Co*, agents for *Laces & Co*, Liverpool (for the manufacturers); *Young, Jones, Hair & Co* (for the suppliers).

Mary Rose Plummer　Barrister.

1　[1972] 3 All ER 557, [1973] QB 27
2　[1946] 2 All ER 696, [1947] AC 265

Practice Direction

FAMILY DIVISION

Minor – Maintenance – Payment to minor – Payment directly to child or to person with whom child has his home – Registration of order in magistrates' court – Right of person with whom child has his home to proceed in his own name for variation, revival or revocation or for enforcement – Orders for payment direct to minor not to be made where of no benefit to parties or no tax advantage – Magistrates' Courts Act 1952, s 53A.

Divorce – Financial provision – Registration of orders – Orders for nominal amounts in favour of spouses or for maintenance pending suit and interim orders not to be registered.

(a) Children's orders

Section 77 of the Domestic Proceedings and Magistrates' Court Act 1978, which came into operation on 1st November 1979, added a new s 53A to the Magistrates' Court Act 1952. This makes provision, inter alia, for a magistrates' clerk to transmit payments under a maintenance order registered in his court, which provides for payment directly to a child, either directly to that child or to the person with whom the child has his home. It also provides that that person may proceed in his own name for variation, revival or revocation of the order and may enforce non-payment either in his own name or by requesting the magistrates to do so.

It is therefore no longer necessary for the High Court or the divorce county court when granting an application for registration to place on the order the wording required by the Practice Direction of 2nd November 1977[1] and that direction is hereby cancelled.

The registration in a magistrates' court of an order made direct to a child entails a considerable amount of work. Accordingly, when the court is considering the form of an order where there are children, care should be taken not to make orders for payment direct where such orders would be of no benefit to the parties or where the parties would derive no immediate tax advantage.

(b) Nominal orders for spouses

Applications for leave to register orders for nominal amounts in favour of spouses only should not be allowed and, except in special circumstances, leave to register should not be granted in respect of orders for maintenance pending suit and interim orders.

Issued with the concurrence of the Lord Chancellor.

R L BAYNE-POWELL
Senior Registrar.

10th March 1980

---

1   [1977] 3 All ER 942, [1977] 1 WLR 1222

Practice Direction

a

FAMILY DIVISION

Practice – Family Division – Applications to the court – Liberty to apply – 'Liberty to apply' not giving right to apply to the court without complying with rules – Non-Contentious Probate Rules 1954 (SI 1954 No 796) – Matrimonial Causes Rules 1977 (SI 1977 No 344), r 122.

b

Judges and registrars of the Family Division have found that there is misunderstanding among practitioners as to the meaning of the words 'liberty to apply'. In one sense there is always liberty to apply since the court can always be applied to by using the proper procedure, but it is emphasised that, except in a few special cases, the words 'liberty to apply' do not give the right to apply to the court without using the procedures comprised *c* in the Matrimonial Causes Rules 1977[1], r 122 and in the Non-Contentious Probate Rules 1954[2], passim.

Under a summons for directions there is always liberty to apply for further directions without taking out a further summons. The court may give liberty to apply as to terms of compromise or as to the minor terms where property is settled. These examples are not exhaustive, but in general applications should not be made under liberty to apply *d* without using the procedures laid down by the rules referred to.

R L BAYNE-POWELL
4th March 1980   Senior Registrar.

e

1   SI 1977 No 344
2   SI 1954 No 796

Shelley v Paddock and another

COURT OF APPEAL, CIVIL DIVISION

LORD DENNING MR, BRANDON AND BRIGHTMAN LJJ

4th, 5th, 8th OCTOBER 1979

Tort – Fraud – Defence of illegality – Unwitting contravention of statute by plaintiff – Exchange control legislation – Payment made by plaintiff to defendant in consequence of defendant's fraud – Contract for sale to plaintiff of house outside United Kingdom in contravention of exchange control legislation – Defendant having no title or authority to sell house – Plaintiff ignorant of exchange control legislation and unaware that payment illegal – Action by plaintiff for damages for fraud – Whether defendant entitled to raise defence of illegality.

The plaintiff agreed to purchase a house in Spain for £9,500 from the defendants who were English nationals resident in Spain. The defendants did not own the house but told the plaintiff that they were selling as agents for the owner, and asked the plaintiff to pay the purchase moneys to them. In fact the defendants had no authority to sell the house. While in Spain the plaintiff paid the defendants £80 in cash as a deposit. The balance of the purchase price she paid into the defendants' bank account in England. Both payments were made in contravention of s 5 of the Exchange Control Act 1947. The plaintiff, who had acted without advice, did not know of the 1947 Act and was not aware that the payments were illegal. The defendants were unable to transfer any legal interest in the house to the plaintiff who thereupon brought an action against the defendants, claiming damages for fraud. At the trial of the action the defendants contended that the sums paid by the plaintiff were irrecoverable since the transaction was contrary to the 1947 Act. The judge[a] rejected that contention and found for the plaintiff. On appeal by the defendants,

Held – The judge had correctly decided that the plaintiff was entitled to recover damages for fraud, since (i) the parties were not equally in the wrong, (ii) the principle that the court would not assist a party who founded his cause of action on an immoral or illegal act did not apply, and (iii) it was fair and just that the defendants should not be allowed to keep the benefit of their fraud. The appeal would accordingly be dismissed (see p 1012 b to p 1013 a, post).

Dictum of Lord Denning in *Kiriri Cotton Co Ltd v Dewani* [1960] 1 All ER at 181 applied.

Dictum of Lord Mansfield CJ in *Holman v Johnson* [1775–1802] All ER Rep at 99, *Boissevain v Weil* [1950] 1 All ER 728 and *Shaw v Shaw* [1965] 1 All ER 638 distinguished.

Decision of Bristow J [1978] 3 All ER 129 affirmed.

Notes

For contracts illegal at common law, see 9 Halsbury's Laws (4th Edn) para 427, and for cases on the subject, see 12 Digest (Reissue) 337–343, 2425–2464.

For the Exchange Control Act 1947, s 5, see 22 Halsbury's Statutes (3rd Edn) 906.

Exchange control regulations were abolished (except as applicable to Southern Rhodesia) as from midnight on 23rd October 1979.

Cases referred to in judgments

Boissevain v Weil [1950] 1 All ER 728, [1950] AC 327, HL, 17 Digest (Reissue) 509, *201*.

Dott v Brickwell (1906) 23 TLR 61, 35 Digest (Repl) 236, *352*.

Holman v Johnson (1775) 1 Cowp 341, [1775–1802] All ER Rep 98, 98 ER 1120, 12 Digest (Reissue) 343, *2464*.

---

a   [1978] 3 All ER 129

Kiriri Cotton Co Ltd v Dewani [1960] 1 All ER 177, [1960] AC 192, [1960] 2 WLR 127, PC, 31(2) Digest (Reissue) 1068,* 2082.

Shaw v Shaw [1965] 1 All ER 638, [1965] 1 WLR 537, CA, 12 Digest (Reissue) 341, 2457.

Cases also cited

Allan (J M) (Merchandising) Ltd v Cloke [1963] 2 All ER 258, [1963] 2 QB 340, CA.

Berg v Sadler and Moore [1937] 1 All ER 637, [1937] 2 KB 158, CA.

Bigos v Boustead [1951] 1 All ER 92.

Harse v Pearl Life Assurance Co [1904] 1 KB 558, [1904–7] All ER Rep 630, CA.

Hughes v Liverpool Victoria Legal Friendly Society [1916] 2 KB 482, [1916–17] All ER Rep 918, CA.

Oom v Bruce (1810) 12 East 225, 104 ER 87.

Parkinson v College of Ambulance Ltd and Harrison [1925] 2 KB 1, [1924] All ER Rep 325.

Selangor United Rubber Estates Ltd v Cradock (No 3) [1968] 2 All ER 1073, [1968] 1 WLR 1555.

Appeal

By a writ dated 14th October 1974 the plaintiff, Dorothy Shelley, brought an action against the defendants, George Frederick Paddock and Carol Ann Paddock, claiming, inter alia, (1) damages as compensation for money fraudulently obtained from her, (2) expenses incurred as a consequence of the fraud, and (3) damages for mental and physical suffering. On 22nd November 1977 Bristow J[1] awarded the plaintiff £10,350 damages and expenses. The defendants appealed. The facts are set out in the judgment of Lord Denning MR.

E Somerset Jones QC and *Daniel Serota* for the defendants.
The plaintiff appeared in person

LORD DENNING MR. Miss Dorothy Shelley was living in Lowestoft in England. She was interested in buying a house in Spain. She saw an advertisement in the Exchange and Mart on 28th March 1974. An agency, Agencia Nero, were advertising the sale of a house, 7 Calle la Salud, Altea near Alicante, for £12,000 freehold. Miss Shelley answered that advertisement. In her letter she said: 'Would you be prepared to accept payment in cash sterling in Spain?' She received a reply from a Mr Paddock, in which he said that the suggestion of payment in that way 'would be most acceptable to us'.

On receiving that acknowledgment, Miss Shelley took advantage of an agent's (Vernon Smith) inspection flight cheap ticket, and went to Spain. When she arrived, she went to the local agent of Vernon Smith. She discovered that he had no houses on offer, and asked him to drop her at the Agencia Nero.

Miss Shelley arrived on 25th April. Between 26th and 29th April she negotiated with Mr and Mrs Paddock. They said that they were estate agents selling the house which belonged to a Mr Hallett, an Englishman who was living in Spain. As a result of those negotiations, she agreed to buy the house for £9,500. The Paddocks said they wanted a deposit. Miss Shelley asked, 'How much?' Mrs Paddock said, 'How much have you got?' Miss Shelley said, '£80'. She had brought that much money with her in cash. Mrs Paddock said, 'That will do'. When Miss Shelley asked about the balance, the Paddocks said that she should pay it into their joint bank account at the Midland Bank in Wembley.

An agreement was drawn up in writing. Miss Shelley has shown it to us:

'In Altea, near Alicante, on the 27th April, 1974, Carol Paddock representing Mr. Hallett, made an agreement between herself and Miss Shelley that Mr. Hallett sold

---

1   [1978] 3 All ER 129, [1979] QB 120

a
to Miss Shelley the house No. 7 Calle la Salud, Altea, Alicante. The price for the sale was £9,500, paid in the following manner: £80 on the signing of the contract and £9,420 on or before the 6th June, 1974.'

There it was. The contract was signed then and there on 27th April.

b
Miss Shelley did not know anything about the need to get exchange control permission. It is quite plain on our statutes ever since 1947 that if a person is going to pay money out of England or take it out, or pay money out of England for the benefit of a person here, it is contrary to ss 5 and 7 of the Exchange Control Act 1947. Miss Shelley did not know anything about that at all. She had not got permission. She did not know it was necessary.

c
Miss Shelley returned to England. She did not hear anything for a time. She became anxious. She was making arrangements to get her furniture sent to Spain. She wrote to the Paddocks about it. Eventually, not having received any satisfactory answer from the Paddocks (as to the exact time when she could take possession), she took the bull by the horns. She arranged to go out by a flight to Spain in order to take over the house. To ensure that she could do so, she paid the balance of the purchase price (£9,420) into the Paddocks' bank account at the Midland Bank in Wembley. On the selfsame night, thinking she had paid for the house, she took the night flight to Alicante.

d
When she arrived at the house, the Paddocks' furniture was still there. She could not get her own furniture in. The long and short of it was that the Paddocks never passed the deeds over to her. The house was never conveyed to her at all. The truth was that they had no authority whatsoever from Mr Hallett to make any contract of sale on his behalf. In fact, the Paddocks were buying the house themselves on instalments from Mr Hallett. They were not paying those instalments, and Mr Hallett, as he was entitled, was ready to take possession of the house from them. Miss Shelley never obtained possession

e
of the house at all.

The Paddocks came to England. The £9,420 was in the bank at Wembley. They took advantage of it and used it to help them get into a house in Gloucestershire.

f
Miss Shelley also came back to England. She was thoroughly disappointed. She had lost her money. She had also lost her furniture. She went to the Bank of England and explained that she knew nothing about the exchange control regulations. She also went to Scotland Yard and told them. The Paddocks were prosecuted. The case was brought to trial; but, for reasons which we have not been told, they were not convicted. Miss Shelley then brought an action against the Paddocks for damages for fraud.

g
The judge[1] decided in her favour. The Paddocks appeal to this court. They are not here themselves. But they obtained legal aid. Counsel is appearing for them. The point raised on their behalf is that this was an illegal transaction. It was in breach of the Exchange Control Act. Miss Shelley did not know that she was breaking the Exchange Control Act when she paid the money into the bank account at Wembley: but, even though she did not know that, it was an illegal transaction. It is said that under English law no person can recover on a transaction which is illegal. For that proposition the cases go back to a statement by Lord Mansfield CJ in *Holman v Johnson*[2]. He said:

h
'The principle of public policy is this; ex dolo malo non oritur actio. No Court will lend its aid to a man who founds his cause of action upon an immoral or an illegal act.'

j
It is said that Miss Shelley founds her cause of action on an illegal act, namely that she paid the money to the bank in Wembley without exchange control permission, contrary to the Exchange Control Act, as the Paddocks were in Spain. Therefore she cannot recover on an illegal act.

1   [1978] 3 All ER 129, [1979] QB 120
2   (1775) 1 Cowp 341 at 343, [1775–1802] All ER Rep 98 at 99

The judge rejected that argument on the ground that the Paddocks were guilty of a fraud all the way through. He put it in no uncertain terms. He said that this was a 'pretty swindle' which operated from the very beginning. The Paddocks pretended that they were acting as agents for Mr Hallett when they were not acting for him at all. They were acting for themselves all the way through, intending to get as much money from Miss Shelley as they could for their own benefit, and meanwhile keeping Mr Hallett quiet, as they did, with an instalment or two. Then, when the money was paid into the bank at Wembley, they used it for themselves knowing that they had no title whatever to convey this property. Even at that stage they could have asked Mr Hallett to transfer the deeds, but they did not. It is plain from the judge's findings that the Paddocks were swindlers right from the beginning who dishonestly obtained £9,500 from Miss Shelley.

In those circumstances, it seems to me that the principle stated by Lord Mansfield CJ does not apply. I know that there are some cases where a person has not been able to recover when he has been guilty of evading the exchange control regulations or similar regulations: see *Boissevain v Weil*[1] and *Shaw v Shaw*[2]. In those cases both parties were participating in the illegal act and there was nothing to choose between them. But it seems to me altogether different when the parties are not in pari delicto. I ventured to summarise such cases in *Kiriri Cotton Co Ltd v Dewani*[3]. In the instant case the property was never conveyed to Miss Shelley. As I said in the *Kiriri* case[4], in circumstances like that—

'. . . it was better to allow the plaintiff to resile from it before it was completed, and to award restitution to him rather than to allow the defendant to remain in possession of his illegal gains.'

It is better to allow Miss Shelley to recover here rather than to allow the Paddocks to remain in possession of their unlawful gains. I went on to say[5]:

'If there is something more in addition to a mistake of law—if there is something in the defendant's conduct which shows that, of the two of them he is the one primarily responsible for the mistake—then it may be recovered back.'

It seems to me plain on each of those principles that these parties are not in pari delicto.

The same principle was applied by Swinfen Eady J in *Dott v Brickwell*[6]. In that case a purported loan of £50 was obtained by fraud. Swinfen Eady J held that, although the transaction was contrary to the Money-lenders Act 1900 and was illegal, the loan had been obtained by fraud and the moneylender could recover in an action for fraud. The parties were not in pari delicto. The Paddocks were guilty of a swindle. It is only fair and just that they should not be allowed to keep the benefit of their fraud. The judge was quite right in holding that the Paddocks are liable despite their plea of illegality.

I would therefore dismiss the appeal.

BRANDON LJ. I have found this case more difficult than the other two members of the court. I still feel some doubt whether the defendants are not entitled to succeed in law even though such a result would appear to any ordinary person to be extremely unfair; but the other members of the court have formed a clear view that the appeal should be dismissed. In these circumstances, although I still have doubts, I do not think that I should be justified in carrying them so far as to dissent from that view.

---

1 [1950] 1 All ER 728, [1950] AC 327
2 [1965] 1 All ER 638, [1965] 1 WLR 537
3 [1960] 1 All ER 177, [1960] AC 192
4 [1960] 1 All ER 177 at 180, [1960] AC 192 at 203
5 [1960] 1 All ER 177 at 181, [1960] AC 192 at 204
6 (1906) 23 TLR 61

BRIGHTMAN LJ. I agree with the judgment of Lord Denning MR.

Appeal dismissed. Application for leave to appeal to the House of Lords refused.

Solicitors: *Philip Conway, Thomas & Co* (for the defendants).

Frances Rustin   Barrister.

Re Clifford's Settlement Trusts
Heaton and another v Westwater and others

CHANCERY DIVISION
SIR ROBERT MEGARRY V-C
22nd, 23rd, 24th OCTOBER 1979

Settlement – Class gift – Distribution date – Compound gift – Trust for children of settlor's son attaining age of 25 before expiration of 21 years from death of settlor or son and for son's other children then living – Whether class closing on eldest child attaining age of 25 – Whether gift to compound class – Whether fact that class closing rule could not apply to one part of compound class precluding rule from applying to other part – Whether fact that application of rule would reduce scope of one limb of gift to improbable but not impossible circumstances sufficient to exclude application of rule.

By a settlement dated 25th August 1954 the settlor directed trustees to hold the trust fund 'in Trust for the children of the Settlor's son . . . born in the Settlor's lifetime or after his death who before the expiration of the period of Twenty one years from the death of the survivor of the Settlor and [the son] shall attain the age of Twenty five years and the other children or child of [the son] living at the expiration of such period'. If more than one child qualified for a share in the trust fund, they were to take equal shares. At the date of the settlement, the son had two children, and subsequently he had two more, one born in 1956 and the other in 1960. On 26th March 1977 the eldest child attained the age of 25 years. In 1979, when the settlor's son was still living, the trustees instituted proceedings to determine whether the class of persons entitled to a share under the settlement had closed when the son's eldest child attained 25 years of age. The trustees contended that the settlement provided for a compound class of the son's children with two different qualifications, namely (a) children born in the settlor's lifetime who attained the age of 25 within 21 years of the son's death and (b) other children, of any age, who were alive 21 years after the son's death and who did not qualify under limb (a), and since the rule[a] that the class of persons entitled to a share of a fund closed when one member of the class became absolutely entitled in advance of the others could not apply to limb (b), there being but a single point of time at which it was to be determined which children were entitled to take and consequently no question of premature closing, it could not apply to the gift as a whole. The trustees further contended that the rule was excluded if its application would prevent one limb of the gift from having any operation save in improbable circumstances, and since the only circumstances in which limb (b) could have any effect were the improbable circumstances of the settlor and the son dying promptly after the making of the settlement that sufficed to show an intention to exclude the rule.

Held – The rule that the class of persons to benefit under a gift closed on one of the members becoming absolutely entitled in advance of the others was a rule which yielded

---
a   *Andrews v Partington* (1791) 3 Bro CC 401, [1775–1802] All ER Rep 209

to a contrary intention, but in determining whether an expression sufficed to exclude the application of the rule the standard was high. It was not enough that there were provisions which merely pointed to the exclusion of the rule if they were nevertheless capable of operating in conformity with it: there had to be an inescapable incompatibility with the operation of the rule. The mere fact that the rule could not apply to part of a compound class was not sufficient to demonstrate any incompatibility of the rule with the other part or with the gift as a whole. Nor was the fact that the application of the rule would reduce the scope of limb (b) to circumstances which, though be no means impossible, were less probable than other circumstances sufficient to exclude the rule, since the question was one of impossibility and not improbability; and, although it might be that 'impossible' could be treated as extending to something which was so improbable as to be unreal, that was not the case with the settlement. In any event the exclusion of the rule could not depend on a mere estimate of a degree of improbability. Accordingly the rule applied and the class of persons entitled to a share under the settlement closed when the son's eldest child attained 25 years of age (see p 1015 *j*, p 1016 *e* to *g* and p 1017 *h* to p 1018 *a* and *d* to *g*, post).

Andrews v Partington [1775–1802] All ER Rep 209, dicta of Russell LJ in *Re Edmondson's Will Trusts* [1972] 1 All ER at 449 and of Buckley J in *Re Wernher's Settlement Trusts* [1961] 1 All ER at 188 applied.

Notes
For the rule in *Andrews v Partington*, see 34 Halsbury's Laws (3rd Edn) 610, para 1067, and 39 ibid 1037–1040, paras 1558–1559, and for cases on the subject, see 49 Digest (Repl) 669–677, 6321–6379.

Cases referred to in judgment
Andrews v Partington (1791) 3 Bro CC 401, [1775–1802] All ER Rep 209, 29 ER 610, LC, 49 Digest (Repl) 669, 6321.
Chapman's Settlement Trusts, Re, Jones v Chapman [1978] 1 All ER 1122, [1977] 1 WLR 1163, CA.
Edmondson's Will Trusts, Re, Baron Sandford of Banbury v Edmondson [1972] 1 All ER 444, [1972] 1 WLR 183, CA, Digest (Cont Vol D) 1034, 6342a.
Henderson's Trusts, Re, Schreiber v Baring [1969] 3 All ER 769, [1969] 1 WLR 651, Digest (Cont Vol C) 873, 1169a.
Wernher's Settlement Trusts, Re, Lloyds Bank Ltd v Mountbatten (Earl) [1961] 1 All ER 184, [1961] 1 WLR 136, Digest (Cont Vol A) 1321, 1166a.

Summons
By an originating summons dated 14th February 1979, the plaintiffs, James Stanley Heaton and John Lewis Clifford, the trustees of a settlement dated 25th August 1954 and made between Lewis Clifford of the one part and the trustees of the other part, sought, by para 1, the determination by the court of the question whether on the true construction of the settlement and in the events which had happened, the first defendant, Jane Anne Westwater, became absolutely and indefeasibly entitled to a one-quarter of the capital under the trusts of the settlement on attaining the age of 25 years, and, by para 2, if the question in para 1 was answered in the negative that an arrangement might be approved under the Variation of Trusts Act 1958. The facts are set out in the judgment.

John Knox QC for the trustees.
T L Dewhurst for the defendants.

SIR ROBERT MEGARRY V-C. This originating summons raises a short but not easy point on the application of the rule in *Andrews v Partington*[1] to a settlement. The

---

1   (1791) 3 Bro CC 401, [1775–1802] All ER Rep 209

main question is as to what amounts to a sufficient intention to exclude the operation of

a the rule. The settlement was made by deed on 25th August 1954 in favour of the settlor's grandchildren, being children of his son, John Lewis Clifford; and the property settled consisted of certain shares. The deed contained only nine clauses, and it became common ground between counsel for the trustees and counsel for the defendants that in the solution of the problem set by cl 2, the other clauses provided little or no assistance. Clause 1 established a trust for sale, cl 2 (to which I shall come back) established the

b principal trust, cl 3 provided for the failure or determination of the trusts in cl 2, cl 4 modified the power of applying income contained in s 31(1) of the Trustee Act 1925, and cl 5 conferred further powers of applying income. There are then provisions for investment and appointing new trustees, and a professional charging clause; and that is all.

With that I can come back to cl 2. This reads as follows:

c   'The Trustees shall hold the Trust Fund In Trust for [(a)] the children of the Settlor's son the said John Lewis Clifford born in the Settlor's lifetime or after his death who before the expiration of the period of Twenty one years from the death of the survivor of the Settlor and the said John Lewis Clifford shall attain the age of Twenty five years and [(b)] the other children or child of the said John Lewis Clifford living at the expiration of such period and if more than one in equal shares.'

d I have read the clause with the insertion of an '(a)' and a '(b)' which do not in fact appear in it, but which were used during argument for convenience of reference; and it was common ground that the concluding words 'and if more than one in equal shares' applied to both (a) and (b).

The state of affairs on 25th August 1954, when the settlement was made and in

e relation to which it must be construed, was as follows. The settlor's son, Mr J L Clifford (whom I shall call 'the son') was then between 31 and 32 years old. He had two children, one aged a little under 2½ years and the other between 2 and 3 months old. Both these children have now attained the age of 25 years. After the settlement was made the son had two more children, one born in 1956 and the other in 1960. Both are now of full age, though neither is yet 25 years old. The son is still living, but the settlor died in 1955,

f just under a year after making the settlement. The period under cl 2 is thus 21 years from the death of the son. Counsel for the trustees assisted the court by arguing the cause of any children of the son yet to be born who may be excluded from cl 2 if the rule in *Andrews v Partington*[1] is applied, and so he contended against any such application. On the other hand, counsel appeared on behalf of the four existing children of the son, and so his contention was that the rule in *Andrews v Partington*[1] applied, with the result that

g no children yet to be born could take any beneficial interest under cl 2. The class, he said, closed when the eldest child attained the age of 25 years on 26th March 1977.

I do not propose to embark on a detailed examination of the rule. I may state it as it appears in Hawkins on the Construction of Wills[2]:

h   'Where there is a bequest of an aggregate fund to children as a class, and the *share of each* child is made payable on attaining a given age, or marriage, the period of distribution is the time when the *first* child becomes entitled to receive his share, and children coming into existence after that period are excluded.'

I shall not attempt to say whether this is a rule of construction, a rule of convenience or even a rule of law. Whichever it is, and even if it is a rule both of construction and convenience, it is clear that it yields to a contrary intention. The real question in this case

j is whether or not a contrary intention has been shown which suffices to exclude the rule. It is well established that the rule arises from the attempt by the court to reconcile

---

1 (1791) 3 Bro CC 401, [1775–1802] All ER Rep 209
2 3rd Edn (1925) p 96

two seemingly inconsistent directions of a settlor or testator. One is that the whole class of the children should be able to take, whenever born. The other is that a child who has *a* reached the requisite age or satisfied the requisite condition should be able to take his share forthwith, without being forced to wait to see whether other children will be born whose claims may diminish the size of the shares to be taken.

From time to time the courts have had to consider whether a sufficient intention to exclude the rule has appeared in the will or settlement. Mere words of comprehensiveness, such as 'all or any' or 'all and every' the children of X, will normally not suffice, nor will *b* words of futurity, such as 'all children whether now living or hereafter to be born': see generally *Re Wernher's Settlement Trusts*[1], approved (and not 'affirmed', as the headnote in the Weekly Law Reports[2] states) in *Re Chapman's Settlement Trusts*[3]. On the other hand, if the gift is to children 'whenever born', the phrase will exclude the rule (*Re Edmondson's Will Trusts*[4]); for the phrase is sufficiently specific and emphatic to be inconsistent with the closing of a class as long as it is still possible for any more children to be born. One *c* way of putting the distinction is to say that phrases such as 'all and every' or 'hereafter to be born' are in no way necessarily inconsistent with the class closing as soon as one member of the class has become absolutely entitled: 'all and every' the children born before then can take, and so can children 'hereafter to be born' before then. In each case, meaning and content are given to the phrases, even though the point of time by which 'all and every' the children, or the children 'hereafter to be born', are to be ascertained is *d* not the indefinite future but a future made finite by reference to the date when the first member of the class becomes absolutely entitled. 'Whenever born', on the other hand, is an expression which cannot easily be qualified by a phrase such as 'before then'. It is an expression which is essentially inconsistent with the application of the rule.

In determining what expressions suffice to exclude the application of the rule, I think that the standard is high. In *Re Edmondson's Will Trusts*[5] Russell LJ, in delivering the *e* judgment of the Court of Appeal, stated the question by reference to clarity. He asked: 'Is it clear from the language of the instrument in the circumstances in which that language is used that the rule is not applicable?' In *Re Wernher's Settlement Trusts*[6] Buckley J said that it is not enough that emphatic words had been used 'unless one finds that the emphasis is expressed in such a way that it is impossible to make it march in step with the application of the rule'. In *Re Chapman's Settlement Trusts*[7] Bridge LJ adopted *f* and applied that test; and Sir John Pennycuick[8] agreed with his judgment. Stamp LJ, I may say, joined with the other two members of the court in approving *Re Wernher's Settlement Trusts*[1]. In other words, it is not enough to find provisions which merely point to the exclusion of the rule if they nevertheless are capable of operating in conformity with it. There must be an inescapable incompatibility with the operation of the rule.

With that, I return to cl 2 of the settlement. Counsel for the trustees emphasised *g* strongly that this clause provided for a compound class of the son's children with two completely different requirements. Under limb (a), the qualification is that of a child attaining the specified age of 25 years within 21 years of the son's death. Under limb (b), there is no requirement of age at all. Nothing is required save that the child should be alive 21 years after the son's death. Under limb (a), children will successively become entitled, whereas under limb (b) they will all become entitled simultaneously. Further, *h*

---

1   [1961] 1 All ER 184, [1961] 1 WLR 136
2   [1977] 1 WLR 1163
3   [1978] 1 All ER 1122, [1977] 1 WLR 1163
4   [1972] 1 All ER 444, [1972] 1 WLR 183
5   [1972] 1 All ER 444 at 449, [1972] 1 WLR 183 at 187
6   [1961] 1 All ER 184 at 188, [1961] 1 WLR 136 at 140–141
7   [1978] 1 All ER 1122 at 1128, [1977] 1 WLR 1163 at 1170
8   [1978] 1 All ER 1122 at 1129, [1977] 1 WLR 1163 at 1171

j

the word 'other' in limb (b) makes it plain that nobody can take under limb (b) if he or

a she becomes entitled under limb (a).

Now it is common ground that the rule would plainly be applicable to limb (a) if it stood alone. Equally plainly, the rule could not apply to limb (b) if that stood alone; for if there is a single point of time at which it is to be determined which children are to take, no question of the premature closing of the class by reason of one member becoming absolutely entitled in advance of the others can possibly arise. The question is thus

b whether the rule applies where there is a compound class made up of these two disparate limbs. Counsel for the trustees contended that this conjunction sufficed to exclude the rule.

In its final form, counsel's argument for the trustees was based on two main submissions. First, he said that the presence of limb (b), to which the rule cannot apply, sufficed to show that the rule was not to apply to the gift at all. In other words, if a

c compound class is defined in terms which include one limb to which the rule is incapable of applying, that necessarily excludes the application of the rule. Second, he said that if the application of the rule would prevent one limb of the words of gift from having any operation save in improbable circumstances, then that sufficed to exclude the rule. In this case, if the rule were to be held to apply to the gift, and it took effect in respect of limb (a), then limb (b) could not operate. The only circumstances in which limb (b)

d could have had any effect were the improbable circumstances of the settlor and the son dying promptly after the making of the settlement. In that case, neither of the two children then living (then aged $2\frac{1}{2}$ years and a few months respectively) could attain the age of 25 years within 21 years of the death of the settlor and the son. Each would then be able to take only by satisfying limb (b) by living until 21 years had elapsed after the death of the settlor and the son. This, said counsel for the trustees, was improbable, for

e the natural expectation when the settlement was executed was that the son would live for many years and that he would or might have further children, as in fact he did. The bare existence of improbable circumstances in which limb (b) could have operated even if the gift was held to be subject to the rule was not enough to leave it within the scope of the rule: instead, it showed that the rule was intended to be excluded.

During the argument, counsel for the defendants drew attention to the possibility that

f in determining whether the rule was excluded, different tests might apply to the words of gift themselves and to other provisions of the instrument, such as the presence of a power of advancement, as in *Re Henderson's Trusts*[1]. Counsel for the trustees accepted that there might indeed be some distinction; but nothing very clear emerged from the discussion, and I do not think that I need say any more about it. There was also some discussion whether *Re Henderson's Trusts*[1] established any test different from that laid

g down in *Re Wernher's Settlement Trusts*[2] and approved in *Re Chapman's Settlement Trusts*[3]: see in particular the reference to 'improbable' events or circumstances in *Re Henderson's Trusts*[1]. However, as I understand it, what was there being considered was whether to construe a clause in the settlement providing (inter alia) for the making of advancements so as to confine it to improbable events and thus to avoid any inconsistency with the rule. In other words, what was in point was the anterior question of the meaning of a

h provision of the settlement and not the degree of collision between that provision and the rule which is requisite to exclude the rule. That degree of collision remains, I think, one of impossibility of marching in step, or necessary incompatibility, and not merely one of an improbability of marching in step.

I return to counsel's first proposition for the trustees, to the effect that if the rule is incapable of applying to one limb of a compound class, it cannot apply to the class at all.

j I do not see why that should be so. It is in the nature of the rule that it should be brought

---

1   [1969] 3 All ER 769, [1969] 1 WLR 651
2   [1961] 1 All ER 184, [1961] 1 WLR 136
3   [1978] 1 All ER 1122, [1977] 1 WLR 1163

into operation by one member of the class attaining the requisite age, even though the attainment of that age by other members of the class can then do nothing to bring the *a* rule into operation. I know of no requirement that every member of the class must be capable of being the one who pulls the trigger, as it were. I can see no impossibility of making the gift to the compound class march in step with the application of the rule, nor anything to make it clear that the rule is not to apply to something to which it is capable of applying. The mere fact that the rule cannot apply to part of a compound class does not appear to me to demonstrate any incompatibility of the rule with the other part, or *b* with the gift as a whole. Inapplicability is one thing, contradiction another. Furthermore, the inconvenience which the rule is intended to obviate is just as much present for those defined by the words of gift in respect of which the rule can operate as it would be if those were the only words of gift. In the present case, exclude the rule and the eldest child, who became 25 years old over 2½ years ago, must wait until the son dies before discovering the minimum size of her share, and, perhaps another 21 years before *c* knowing its exact size. I would be slow to treat the settlement as imposing this inconvenience, in the interests of possible further children to be born to the son later in life, especially as two children of the son were alive when the settlement was made, and the right of a child to take a share absolutely at 25 appears in the foreground of the gift. I accept, of course, that this is difficult terrain in uncharted territory; but, doing the best that I can, I would reject this first proposition. *d*

As for the second proposition, I do not think that it accords with the test laid down in *Re Wernher's Settlement Trusts*[1]. The question is one of impossibility, not improbability. If the application of the rule would deprive limb (b) of all possible effect, I would expect the rule to be excluded. But where, as here, it does not do that but merely reduces the scope of limb (b) to circumstances which, though by no means impossible, are less probable than other circumstances, than I can see nothing to exclude the rule. It may be *e* that 'impossible' would be treated as extending to something which is so improbable as to be unreal: but that is not the case here. The settlor died within a year of the settlement being made, and none can say that the possibility of the son, a man in his early thirties, dying within a year or two of the settlement being made was so remote as to be unreal. In any case, I do not think that the exclusion of the rule can depend on a mere estimate of a degree of improbability. *f*

In the result, my conclusion is that it is not sufficiently clear from the language of this settlement that the rule in *Andrews v Partington*[2] is to be excluded, and so that rule applies to the settlement. Accordingly, the answer to question 1 in the originating summons, asking whether the eldest child became absolutely and indefeasibly entitled to a quarter share of capital under the trusts of the settlement on attaining the age of 25 years, is Yes.

g

Declaration accordingly.

Solicitors: *Ward Bowie*, agents for *Wright & Wright*, Keighley (for all parties).

Azza M Abdallah   Barrister.

---

1   [1961] 1 All ER 184, [1961] 1 WLR 136
2   (1791) 3 Bro CC 401, [1775–1802] All ER Rep 209

Re R-R Realisations Ltd (formerly Rolls-Royce Ltd)

CHANCERY DIVISION
SIR ROBERT MEGARRY V-C
21st, 22nd, 26th NOVEMBER 1979

Company – Voluntary winding-up – Power to apply to court to have question determined – Application by liquidator for liberty to distribute final dividend to members – Late claim by creditor – Likelihood of company's liability to creditor being covered by insurance – Whether liquidator should be allowed to distribute without regard to creditor's claim – Whether creditor should pay costs of distribution being delayed – Companies Act 1948, s 307.

In 1971 a company which manufactured aircraft engines went into voluntary liquidation. The liquidators were subsequently able to realise some of its assets and to pay all the known debts of the company and, in addition, to pay substantial sums to its stockholders. In October 1976, 95 persons were killed when an aircraft powered by engines manufactured by the company crashed in India. According to the findings of an Indian judicial enquiry into the crash, published on 22nd September 1978, a crack in an engine component had caused one of the engines to fail shortly after take-off. On 26th September 1979, after the liquidators of the company had started preparing the final distribution to the stockholders, a solicitor's letter was sent to one of the liquidators informing him that proceedings might be brought against the company by the families of the victims of the accident. No reply to that letter had been despatched by 8th October 1979 when there was a press announcement that the final distribution of £5·5m would be made to ordinary stockholders on 6th December 1979. On 15th October the solicitor again wrote to the liquidator warning him that proceedings might be brought against the company in respect of the aircraft accident. Between 8th and 16th October 55 writs were issued against various defendants, including the company, claiming damages in respect of the accident. No reply was sent to the solicitor's letters until 6th November 1979. The company was insured for £53m in respect of any liability arising out of an accident caused by any defect in its products supplied and the liquidators considered that that was sufficient to cover any liability in respect of the aircraft accident. By November 1979 the company had already incurred expenses totalling £14,700 in preparing for the final distribution to its stockholders and the liquidators estimated that the cost of delaying the distribution by six months would be £86,500. In November 1979 they applied to the court, under s 307[a] of the Companies Act 1948, for (i) an order giving them liberty to distribute the remaining assets of the company without regard to any claims arising out of the aircraft accident, on the ground that they were under an implied statutory duty to complete the liquidation and effect final distribution of the assets within a reasonable time, that there was a correlative duty on creditors to make their claims with all reasonable diligence, and that, if a claim was made at a late stage in the liquidation, the burden lay on the creditor to show that he had acted with such diligence and the plaintiffs had not done so, or, alternatively, (ii) an order giving the liquidators liberty to distribute unless the plaintiffs made proper provision for the payment of the additional costs incurred by a postponement of the proposed distribution.

Held – (1) In deciding whether to make an order under s 307 of the 1948 Act authorising liquidators of a company in a voluntary liquidation to distribute the assets of a company among the company's members, notwithstanding a last-minute claim by persons who contended that they were creditors, the test to be applied was whether in all the

---

[a] Section 307, so far as material, is set out at p 1024 *g h*, post

circumstances of the case it was just to make such an order. There was no rule that the claimants had to establish that they had not been guilty of wilful default or want of due a
diligence, although the presence or absence of any such default or lack of diligence was a factor, and normally an important factor, in determining what was just (see p 1024 e f and p 1026 h, post); *David v Frowd* (1833) 1 My & K 200 and *Re House Property and Investment Co Ltd* [1953] 2 All ER 1525 considered.

(2) On making an order under s 307 of the 1948 Act the court could impose such terms and conditions as in all the circumstances of the case it considered fitting, or could b
make such other order as it thought just. Where an application was made that an order should only be refused or suspended on terms that the claimants bore the expenses thrown away as the result of their tardiness in asserting their claims, that application should itself be subject to the test of what was fitting and just (see p 1026 j, post); *Angell v Haddon* (1816) 1 Madd 529 and *Cattell v Simons* (1845) 8 Beav 243 considered.

(3) Where the order was sought in order to facilitate a distribution among members, c
the court would be more reluctant to grant it than if the distribution was to be made to creditors (see p 1026 j to p 1027 a, post).

(4) The liquidators' application would be refused because (a) it would not be just in all the circumstances to make an order absolute giving the liquidators liberty to distribute the remaining assets of the company, and so prevent the plaintiffs making any effective claim against the company, particularly as the proposed distribution was to members and d
not to creditors, and (b) it would not be just or fitting to make an order nisi on the terms proposed (see p 1027 a to c and e, post).

Notes
For powers and duties of a liquidator in a voluntary winding up, see 7 Halsbury's Laws (4th Edn) paras 1467–1472, and for the power to apply to the court under s 307 of the Companies Act 1948 to have questions determined or powers exercised, see ibid para e
1500.

For the Companies Act 1948, s 307, see 5 Halsbury's Statutes (3rd Edn) 340.

Cases referred to in judgment
Angell v Haddon (1816) 1 Madd 529, 56 ER 194, 24 Digest (Repl) 884, 8831.
Butler v Broadhead [1974] 2 All ER 401, [1975] Ch 97, [1974] 3 WLR 27, 10 Digest f
    (Reissue) 1142, 7107.
Cattell v Simons (1845) 8 Beav 243, 14 LJ Ch 138, 9 Jur 418, 50 ER 90.
David v Frowd (1833) 1 My & K 200, 2 LJ Ch 68, 39 ER 657, 24 Digest (Repl) 856, 8513.
House Property and Investment Co Ltd, Re [1953] 2 All ER 1525, [1954] Ch 576, 10 Digest
    (Reissue) 1151, 7166.
Hull v Falkoner (1865) 5 New Rep 266, 11 LT 761, 11 Jur NS 151, 24 Digest (Repl) 885, g
    8840.
McMurdo, Re, Penfield v McMurdo [1902] 2 Ch 684, 71 LJ Ch 691, 86 LT 814, CA, 9
    Digest (Reissue) 437, 2597.
Ministry of Health v Simpson [1950] 2 All ER 1137, [1951] AC 251, HL; *affg* sub nom *Re
    Diplock's Estate, Diplock v Wintle* [1948] 2 All ER 318, 429, [1948] Ch 465, CA, 24
    Digest (Repl) 814, 8058.   h
Sale Continuation Ltd, Re (24th November 1977) unreported.

Appeal
By a summons dated 2nd November 1979 the joint liquidators of R-R Realisations Ltd (formerly called Rolls-Royce Ltd) ('the company') applied (1) for an order that the liquidators should from thenceforth be at liberty to distribute the assets from time to j
time remaining in their hands amongst the creditors and stockholders of the company without regard to, and without paying or making provision for the payment from such assets (or any part thereof) of, any debt, claim or liability which might be or might be alleged to be owing by the company to any person or persons and which might have arisen out of, or might be alleged to have arisen out of, the crash of a Caravelle aircraft at

Bombay, India, on 12th October 1976, including in particular (but without prejudice to
a the generality of the foregoing) any such claim for, or liability to, damages as had been
made and/or alleged in any of the actions which had been commenced by (amongst
others) the respondents, Nicholas Brian Baker and David Christopher Willis, the
administrators of the estate of Louis Salvadore Cuthinho deceased, against (amongst
others) the company in the Queen's Bench Division; (2) if and in so far as requisite an
order that the respondents be appointed to represent, for the purposes of the application,
b all of the plaintiffs in the above mentioned actions. By an order dated 16th November
1979, Mr Registrar Hunt (i) dismissed the liquidators' application under para (1) of the
summons, but (ii) made a representation order in the terms of para (2) of the
summons. The liquidators appealed against the first part of his order. The facts are set
out in the judgment.

c W F Stubbs QC and D Richards for the liquidators.
Allan Heyman QC and Michael Kennedy for the respondents.

Cur adv vult

26th November. **SIR ROBERT MEGARRY V-C** read the following judgment: This
is an appeal from a decision of Mr Registrar Hunt, dated 16th November 1979, whereby
d he dismissed the summons issued on 2nd November 1979 by the three joint liquidators
of R-R Realisations Ltd, a company formerly entitled Rolls-Royce Ltd. I shall call it 'the
company'. The company ran into financial difficulties towards the end of 1970, and after
it had been in receivership early in 1971, it went into a creditors' voluntary liquidation
on 4th October 1971. The receivers sold the company's aero-engine division to a
company originally called Rolls-Royce (1971) Ltd and subsequently called Rolls-Royce
e Ltd. I shall call this 'the new company'. The receivers also sold the motor division to
Rolls-Royce Motor Holdings Ltd, a company to which I need not refer again. Largely as
a result of these sales, the liquidators were able to pay all the company's debts of which
they knew, and pay substantial sums to the stockholders. The holders of workers' stock
were satisfied in full, and the holders of the ordinary stock have received 55p in the
pound. On 20th January 1975 an order was made giving the liquidators leave to
f distribute the assets without regard to any claims made after 15th February 1975; but
there were still some difficulties in what was plainly a very substantial and complex
liquidation, and further orders dealing with specific problems were made in 1978 and
1979. Finally the liquidators began to make detailed provisions for the final distribution
to the ordinary stockholders, said to be some 80,000 in number. On 8th October 1979
there was a press announcement that a final distribution of 8·41p in the pound would be
g made to ordinary stockholders; and it is proposed to pay this on 6th December 1979.
Some £5·5m is to be distributed in this way.

It is against this background that the summons has to be considered. It arises out of
an aircraft accident at Bombay airport in India on 12th October 1976 in which a
Caravelle aircraft powered by Rolls-Royce engines was destroyed, with the loss of the
lives of the 95 persons on board. The starboard engine, which the company had
h manufactured some 10 or 12 years earlier, failed shortly after take-off, due to a crack in
the engine's 10th-stage compressor disc; and the consequent fire was aggravated by the
failure of the aircrew to cut off the fuel supply to the engine. I make no findings on these
facts, but state the essentials of the findings of Bhasme J of the High Court of Bombay.
He conducted an inquiry into the causes of the accident, and his report was published on
22nd September 1978. Nothing that could be regarded as a claim against the company
j or its liquidators was made on behalf of any of the victims of the accident or their
families until a short solicitors' letter dated 26th September 1979 was delivered by hand,
addressed to a firm of accountants and marked for the attention of 'R. Nicholson Esq.',
who was one of the joint liquidators. This letter enclosed a copy of a letter to the new
company, asking various questions about the provenance of the starboard engine of the
Caravelle, and concluding with a statement that if the information was not provided, it

might be necessary 'to bring proceedings against all existing Rolls Royce companies as might remotely be thought to be involved'. No reply to this letter was sent on behalf of the liquidators, and so on 15th October 1979 the solicitors sent a long letter to Mr Nicholson, with copies to the other liquidators and to a partner in the firm of accountants. There was no reply to this letter either, and so on 31st October 1979 the solicitors sent to the partner in the firm of accountants what might be called a telex before action. Finally, on 6th November 1979, solicitors for the liquidators and the company replied to the solicitors' communications. This delay in dealing with what was plainly a possible claim is most regrettable, and although it was not explained in evidence, I was told on instructions that Mr Nicholson had been on holiday until the end of October; and although the first letter was opened, it was apparently put on one side and not given to anyone to reply to or otherwise deal with. However, I do not think that this makes much difference, save that if the letter had been treated more responsibly, the liquidators might well have postponed taking some of the steps that they took, and in particular the making of the press announcement on 8th October 1979.

The present state of the claims arising out of the accident is as follows. Fifty-five writs have been issued, although four of these appear not to have been issued until the limitation period expired on 12th October 1979. However, in these four cases (and in others) the plaintiffs may be able to obtain leave to sue out of time. The writs have not been served, but a copy of one writ is in evidence. In this, Mr N B Baker and Mr D C Willis (the respondents), who are both partners in a well known firm of London solicitors, sue as administrators of one of the victims of the accident. There are five other plaintiffs, consisting of the deceased's widow, and four infants, each suing by Mr Baker as his or her next friend. These plaintiffs are, I understand, children of the deceased. There are eight defendants, the company and the new company being the first two, and the others being airlines or aviation authorities. The writ is generally indorsed with claims under the Fatal Accidents Act 1976 for damages for the death of the deceased and under the Law Reform (Miscellaneous Provisions) Act 1934 for damages for the loss of expectation of life, earning capacity and consequential loss. All save the administrators claim damages for personal injuries, shock, distress and consequential loss and damage. The claims are based on negligence and breach of statutory duty in, inter alia, the design, manufacture, assembly and maintenance of the aircraft and its starboard engine, and in failing to advise as to the correct maintenance and servicing procedures to be carried out in respect of it. I state the claim as it particularly relates to the company, and with the omission of the ten 'and/ors' with which the two sentences of the indorsement are bespattered. During the hearing it was generally accepted that the other writs were in a closely similar form; and there was no contention that the actions could not properly be brought in England. I should add that all writs were issued under emergency legal aid certificates.

One other matter that I should mention is that of insurance. The combined effect of various transactions, and in particular a deed of indemnity dated 22nd December 1975 and a policy of insurance numbered TP(S) 14211602, is that the company is entitled, through the new company, to the benefit of an insurance policy for $US115m in respect of any liability arising out of any accident caused by any defect in products sold, supplied, repaired or worked on, or any neglect, error or omission in connection with any advice given or any report supplied. I state it shortly.

In those circumstances counsel for the liquidators contends that the liquidators ought to be granted the relief that they seek by their summons, and that Mr Registrar Hunt was wrong in dismissing the summons. The relief sought is that the liquidators should be given liberty to distribute the remaining assets of the company without regard to any claims arising out of the aircraft disaster on 12th October 1976: I summarise it. In essence, the substance of counsel's case is that the claims of the plaintiffs against the company were at present very general and unparticularised, but so far as they could be judged, they were unlikely to succeed; that in any event the insurance cover of $US115m (which comes to nearly £53m) was virtually certain to cover any successful claims, since it was inconceivable that more than an average of £1m would be recovered in each a action; that much time and money had been expended in preparing for the final distribution next month, and that this would be wasted if the distribution was postponed. The direct costs already incurred for printing and data processing are said to be about £14,700, and all of this would be wasted if there had to be a postponement. There is also the cost of maintaining a registrar's department, estimated at a little over £250 a day. A document not in evidence gives £86,500 as the estimated cost of a six month delay, though there is an obvious difficulty is substantiating all of this as being

b wholly wasted expenditure which would be caused by the postponement of the distribution.

During his opening, counsel for the liquidators helpfully provided a typewritten summary of his submissions on the law. I will not set them out in full, but I shall summarise their main thrust. They fall under two heads. The primary submission was that the liquidators should in any event be granted the liberty to distribute that they

c sought. The reason was that they were under an implied statutory duty to complete the liquidation and to effect a final distribution of the assets within a reasonable time. This imposed a correlative duty on creditors to make their claims with all reasonable diligence, and if a claim was made at a late stage in the liquidation, the burden lay on the creditor to show that he had acted with such diligence. The plaintiffs in the actions had not done this, and so the liquidators should be granted the leave to distribute that they sought.

d The secondary submission, made in the alternative, was that the order giving the liquidators the liberty to distribute that they sought should, in effect, instead of being an order absolute, be an order nisi. If a late claim is made, the court may impose terms on the claimant in order to prevent injustice to others being caused by postponing the distribution. Here, substantial sums of money would be wasted if the distribution was halted, both in barren expenditure already incurred and in the additional costs of a

e prolonged liquidation; and even if the plaintiffs' claims all failed, no order for costs in the actions could include these sums. Accordingly, the liquidators should be given the leave to distribute that they sought unless the plaintiffs made proper provision for the payment of the additional expenses that would be entailed by a postponement of the proposed distribution. I may add that counsel for the liquidators properly accepted that the order dated 20th January 1975 giving the liquidators leave to distribute the assets without

f regard to subsequent claims could not properly be relied on in respect of claims such as those made by the plaintiffs, which had not come into existence until after the date of the order.

It was common ground between counsel for the liquidators and counsel for the respondents that there was no authority at all closely in point. But counsel for the liquidators cited a number of cases on the administration of estates as providing helpful

g analogies. Thus he relied on *David v Frowd*[1] as supporting the view that a creditor with a late claim must establish that he has been guilty of no wilful default and has shown no want of reasonable diligence. He also relied on *Angell v Haddon*[2] and *Cattell v Simons*[3] as supporting his alternative contention that if a creditor is permitted to come in late, he will have to bear the costs of revising the distribution.

I think that one has to exercise considerable caution in applying cases on the

h administration of the estate of a deceased person to a voluntary liquidation. One reason is that the effect of a distribution in a voluntary liquidation is quite different from that of a distribution in the administration of estates. The *Diplock* principle of tracing assets into the hands of the beneficiaries under a will (see *Ministry of Health v Simpson*[4]) has no application to the recipients, whether creditors or members, under a distribution of the assets of a company in voluntary liquidation: see *Butler v Broadhead*[5]. Once the liquidators

j 1 (1833) 1 My & K 200 at 209–210, 39 ER 657 at 661
   2 (1816) 1 Madd 529, 56 ER 194
   3 (1845) 8 Beav 243, 50 ER 90
   4 [1950] 2 All ER 1137, [1951] AC 251; *affg* sub nom Re Diplock's Estates [1948] 2 All ER 318, 429, [1948] Ch 465
   5 [1974] 2 All ER 401, [1975] Ch 97

have duly advertised for creditors, any creditor who could have proved his debt in the liquidation has no claim against any of the assets in the hands of the creditors or the members of the company to whom that distribution has been made. What has gone has gone. There is no question of reopening the distribution so as to let in the late claimant, in the way that was done, for example, in *David v Frowd*[1]. If the order that counsel for the liquidators seeks is made, and the distribution is duly made under it, that will be the end of any claim made by the plaintiffs against the company. Counsel for the liquidators also cited *Hull v Falkoner*[2], an ill-reported case; but even when the better report, sub nom *Hull v Falconer*[3], is examined, I do not think that it helps counsel for the liquidators. The case was a plain case of laches by a creditor who had herself instituted a second suit for administration and yet refrained from proving her debt in the first suit even after she had failed to proceed on her own suit. *Re McMurdo*[4], if anything, assists counsel for the respondents, in that a creditor in the administration of an insolvent estate was held to be entitled to come in and prove at any time if there were assets still undistributed and no injustice would be caused. I do not think that counsel for the liquidators could get much more out of that case than that in such cases the court can impose terms on a creditor who seeks to come in and prove late.

There is another point which I think must be carefully borne in mind in considering the cases on administration of estates, and that is the standing of the claimant in relation to those to whom the distribution is to be made. If the claimant is a creditor, it may well be right to be slower to shut him out if the distribution is to be made to beneficiaries than it is if the distribution is to be made to other creditors. Correspondingly, in the voluntary liquidation of a company, it may well be right to give the claimant greater latitude if the distribution is to be to members rather than to other creditors. Just as a man should seek to be just before he affects to be generous, so I think that an especial care is needed to ensure that all creditors are paid before distributions are made to the members. It is only subject to the satisfaction of the company's liabilities that the company's property is distributable among the members: see the Companies Act 1948, s 302. I do not, of course, say that a creditor has an absolute right to come in at any time, however gross his delay, whatever his conduct, and however unjust this would be to others. But I do say that the court should be slower to shut out a creditor as against members than as against other creditors.

In considering what is the appropriate approach in a voluntary winding up, some assistance can, I think, be obtained from the section of the Companies Act 1948 which confers jurisdiction, s 307. The first two subsections run as follows:

'(1) The liquidator or any contributory or creditor may apply to the court to determine any question arising in the winding up of a company, or to exercise, as respects the enforcing of calls or any other matter, all or any of the powers which the court might exercise if the company were being wound up by the court.

'(2) The court, if satisfied that the determination of the question or the required exercise of power will be just and beneficial, may accede wholly or partially to the application on such terms and conditions as it thinks fit or may make such other order on the application as it thinks just.'

It will be observed that sub-s (2) is phrased in terms of what is 'just and beneficial', with a power to impose such terms and conditions as the court 'thinks fit', and to make such other order as the court 'thinks just'. The section is, indeed, in very wide terms, and is capable of application to a great variety of cases; but nevertheless the language chosen is expressed in terms of what is just. That, I think, is plainly something different from mere convenience.

1   (1833) 1 My & K 200, 39 ER 657
2   (1865) 5 New Rep 266
3   11 LT 761
4   [1902] 2 Ch 684

With that in mind, I turn to the only two cases cited to me which deal with voluntary
liquidations. *Re House Property and Investment Co Ltd*[1] was very different. In it, Roxburgh
J rejected a claim by a lessor to have enough of the assets of the company (which was an
original lessee) set aside to meet all future liabilities for the payment of rent and the due
performance of the covenants in the lease. Instead, it was held that the lessor should
prove in the liquidation for the difference in value of the lease with the benefit of the
original lessee's covenants and its value without that benefit. That, of course, is very far
away from the present case; but in his judgment Roxburgh J[2] referred to the implied
obligation imposed by the Companies Act 1948 on liquidators to complete the liquidation
and effect a final distribution of the assets within a reasonable time. I fully accept this;
but I do not think that there flows from this duty any corresponding duty on creditors
to make their claims with all reasonable diligence. Obviously both prudence and
convenience require them to do so; but that is not the same as saying that there is a legal
obligation to do so. I think that the courts must be cautious in laying down any rules
which would in effect shorten the periods available to a claimant under the Statutes of
Limitation. In the case of a company in voluntary liquidation where a final distribution
is in contemplation, the practical effect would be to substitute an undefined period of
diligence for whatever was the appropriate statutory period of years. A doctrine of laches
may be appropriate enough in claims made in equity in the administration of estates, but
I do not think that it should be admitted without compelling reasons in claims at law
made in the statutory process of voluntary liquidation; and I can see no compelling
reasons.

The other case on voluntary liquidation is *Re Sale Continuation Ltd*[3]. This is much more
in point. I am indebted to counsel for the liquidators for a transcript of the judgment.
There, the assets of the company had sufficed to pay 33·5p in the £ in a creditors'
voluntary liquidation. The liquidator wished to pay a final dividend, to convene final
meetings, and to make his final returns; but there was a claimant whose 'excessively stale
claims' had 'long ago been rejected by the liquidator', who sought to have the distribution
postponed until he had litigated his claims. The claimant had neither lodged a formal
proof nor commenced proceedings in support of his claims; and the periods of delay,
which varied with different claims, were of the order of five or seven or nine years or
more, with intermittent activity in some cases, and some periods of complete dormancy
for five or seven years. In those circumstances, Brightman J, who described the delay as
'grotesque', granted an application by the liquidator under s 307 of the 1948 Act for an
order authorising him to distribute the assets without providing for any claims of the
claimant which had not been established. The judge rejected any idea that a claimant
could keep a voluntary liquidator on tenterhooks for an indefinite period by deciding
neither to sue nor to prove nor to proceed under s 307 nor to abandon his claim.

That case differs from the present case in at least two important respects. First, the
delay there was 'grotesque', and that cannot be said of any delay in the present case.
Second, the case was one of an alleged creditor against other creditors, and not as against
members. The judge mentioned as being 'instructive' the words in *David v Frowd*[4]
which require from a tardy creditor in the administration of the estate of a deceased
person proof of no wilful default and no want of reasonable diligence; but I am not at all
sure that in making his decision the judge relied on these words as providing anything
of a test for voluntary liquidation. To say that this burden rests on a person who seeks
to recover assets which have already been distributed in the administration of the estate
of a deceased person by no means leads to the conclusion that the same burden lies on a

1   [1953] 2 All ER 1525, [1954] Ch 576
2   [1953] 2 All ER 1525 at 1545, [1954] Ch 576 at 612
3   (24th November 1977) unreported
4   (1833) 1 My & K 200, 39 ER 657

person who seeks to be included in a distribution of a company's assets which has yet to be made.

   I return to the case before me. The accident occurred on 12th October 1976. Mr Registrar Hunt regarded it as being not merely excusable but eminently reasonable that the plaintiffs should have awaited the publication of the report of the inquiry held by Bhasme J in India, and this did not occur until 22nd September 1978. In this, I entirely agree with the registrar. Even if the plaintiffs knew that the company was in liquidation, I can seen no reason why, in such a technical matter as the cause of an aircraft accident, the plaintiffs should not take advantage of the pending inquiry as a means of discovering the persons and companies against which the claims should be made. True, every conceivable defendant (including the company) could have been notified on a provisional basis; but I do not think that it would have been reasonable to expect this to be done. The first letter to one of the liquidators, delivered on 26th September 1979, contained an enclosure which in its last sentence might well be thought to give warning of a possible claim; and in any case the letter of 15th October 1979 is explicit enough. It was no fault of the plaintiffs that neither of these letters provoked any activity on the part of the liquidators until the following month, or that the liquidators should in the meantime have been proceeding with their arrangements for the final distribution. Of course it would have been better if an earlier notification of possible claims had been sent to the liquidators; but with the complications that arise from the subject-matter being an aircraft accident in India and the multiplicity of plaintiffs I find it impossible to regard the 12 or 13 months in question as being a period of time that ought to bar the plaintiffs' claim. If the claim had been made before the process of arranging the final distribution had begun in June 1979, it would be unthinkable to shut out the plaintiffs. It seems highly probable that the real complaint of the liquidators is founded on the time and money expended during the next three or four months, and in particular on the press announcement having been made on 8th October 1979.

   I turn to the subject of insurance. On the facts as I know them at present, it seems highly improbable that an insurance cover of over £50m would not suffice to meet any claims that succeed. But I know very little of the facts, and I most certainly cannot say that I am sure that the cover will be enough. More important, I do not know whether the insurance company will accept responsibility under the policy if the liability of the company is established. It indeed looks probable that the combined effect of the deed of indemnity and the policy itself will make the insurance company responsible. But questions may arise as to the precise effect of the language of the deed and the language of the policy in relation to the as yet unascertained facts in each individual case. In those circumstances, ought the court to make an order which will in effect destroy any chances of success for the plaintiffs if their claims against the company are well founded but the insurance company escapes liability? To me, the question almost answers itself.

   In the result, I would summarise my conclusions as follows:

   1. In deciding whether to make an order under s 307 authorising liquidators of a company in a voluntary liquidation to distribute the assets of a company among the company's members, notwithstanding a last-minute claim by persons who contend that they are creditors, the test to be applied is whether in all the circumstances of the case it is just to make such an order. There is no rule that the claimants must establish that they have been guilty of no wilful default and no want of due diligence, although the presence or absence of any such default or lack of diligence will of course be a factor, and normally an important factor, in determining what is just.

   2. On making such an order the court may impose such terms and conditions as in all the circumstances of the case it considers fitting, or may make such other order as it thinks just. Where the court is asked to refuse or suspend such an order, any contention that this should be done only on terms that the claimants should bear the expenses thrown away by their tardiness in asserting their claims should itself be subject to the test of what is fitting and just.

   3. Where the order is sought in order to facilitate a distribution among members, the

court will be more reluctant to grant it than if the distribution is to be made to creditors.

a   If I apply those conclusions to the present case, it becomes plain that the application must be refused. I do not think that it would be just to make the order and so shut out the plaintiffs from making any effective claim against the company, particularly as the proposed distribution is to members and not creditors. I can well appreciate that it is highly inconvenient to have the proposed distribution halted in mid-course, and postponed for an indefinite period, with the attendant wasted and additional cost. I do

b   not say that inconvenience and expense may not be of such a degree as to amount to an injustice, but when this is weighed against the proposed virtual extinction of the plaintiffs' claims against the company's assets, I have no doubt where the balance of justice lies. As between injustice and inconvenience of anything like equal degree, it is injustice that must be rejected. As matters stand, I cannot regard the rights of insurance as providing any sufficient substitute. When the claims of the plaintiffs have been

c   sufficiently particularised (and I do not forget that it is not the fault of the liquidators that they lack anything more than the broad indications given by the writ that I have mentioned), it may be possible to get the insurance company to accept the claims subject to liability being established; and the failure of the present application would be no bar to the making of a renewed application when the facts are better known. I would add that if, contrary to my views, the plaintiffs are required to establish that they were guilty

d   of no wilful default and no want of due diligence, I would hold that I can see nothing to establish wilful default, and, with a little hesitation, I would hold that due diligence had been established. 'Due diligence' is a concept which has to be considered in relation to all the facts of the case: and the complications of the air accident, differences of countries and the multiplicity of claims seem to me to regulate the 'diligence' that is 'due'.

As for requiring the plaintiffs to reimburse the wasted expenditure as the price of

e   having the order refused, or some other order made, I need only say that I think that it would be neither just nor fitting to impose any such terms. I know nothing of the financial status of the plaintiffs, and I would not draw any extensive inferences from the fact that the writs were issued under emergency legal aid certificates. Those with no assets in England may be wealthy in India. But any such term might exclude the poor in favour of the wealthy, or require the wealthy to bear more than their fair share. In any

f   case, I do not think that such delay as there has been suffices for any requirement to bear any costs. Furthermore, the expenses thrown away are relatively modest in relation to the £5·5m to be distributed. The liquidators' estimate of the direct costs already incurred which would have to be incurred again if distribution is postponed is £14,700, but counsel for the respondents may be right when he says that not all of this has been thrown away by the delay. At all events, I do not think that it would be right to accede

g   to the application of counsel for the liquidators that unless the plaintiffs within so many days pay a specified sum to the liquidators the order that he sought should be made. At one stage counsel for the liquidators put this sum at £32,300, and at another stage £80,100, though in the end I think he had to accept that he could not sustain the larger sums.

In the result, I think that Mr Registrar Hunt was right in the conclusion that he

h   reached, and I dismiss the appeal. I understand that he made a representation order as prayed in para 2 of the summons, and that order stands. Subject to that, I dismiss the summons.

Appeal dismissed.

Solicitors: *Linklaters & Paines* (for the liquidators); *Frere, Cholmeley & Co* (for the respondents).

Azza M Abdallah   Barrister.

Worsfold v Howe   *a*

COURT OF APPEAL, CIVIL DIVISION
MEGAW, BROWNE AND DONALDSON LJJ
13th DECEMBER 1979

Negligence – Contributory negligence – Collision between vehicles on road – Car emerging from *b*
minor to major road – Driver's vision blocked by stationary vehicle – Driver inching out slowly
in front of stationary vehicle even though vision blocked – Motorcyclist overtaking stationary
vehicle and colliding with emerging car – Whether motorcyclist solely responsible for accident –
Whether driver of emerging car also responsible for accident.

The defendant wished to drive his car out of a minor road and turn right into the
southbound carriageway of a major road. Because of traffic conditions in the northbound *c*
lanes of the major road, a petrol tanker had stopped, leaving a gap in front of it, in the
left-hand northbound lane, obscuring the defendant's view of northbound traffic. The
defendant began to inch his way out past the tanker. The front of his car had reached one
or two feet beyond the tanker when the plaintiff, who was riding his motor cycle in the
right-hand lane and had just passed the tanker collided with the defendant's car. The
plaintiff was injured and claimed damages. The trial judge found that the plaintiff had *d*
been travelling too fast to stop or avoid a collision and was therefore at fault. The judge
stated that he considered the parties to be equally at fault since the defendant had
proceeded beyond his line of vision, but held that he was constrained by authority[a] to
absolve the defendant from any liability on the ground that a driver of a vehicle who
wished to drive across a line of stationary traffic facing in the opposite direction to that
in which he wanted to travel discharged his duty to other drivers if he did so by inching *e*
out into the traffic. The plaintiff appealed.

Held – There was no principle of law that a driver was entitled to emerge blind from a
minor road onto a major road by inching forward beyond his line of vision and that if he
did so very slowly he was under no liability to other traffic on the main road. Since the
judge would have held the parties equally to blame but for the fact that he felt bound by *f*
precedent to hold that the defendant was under no liability, the appeal would be allowed
and judgment entered for the plaintiff for half the agreed damages (see p 1033 *c* and *f* to
p 1034 *b*, post).
    Clarke v Winchurch [1969] 1 All ER 275 explained.

Notes   *g*
For contributory negligence and apportionment of liability, see 28 Halsbury's Laws (3rd
Edn) 87–93, paras 92–97, and for cases on the subject, see 36(1) Digest (Reissue) 270–305,
1084–1227.

Cases referred to in judgments
Clarke v Winchurch [1969] 1 All ER 275, [1969] 1 WLR 69, CA, 36(1) Digest (Reissue) *h*
    274, 1111.
Garston Warehousing Co Ltd v O F Smart (Liverpool) Ltd [1973] RTR 377, CA, 36(1) Digest
    (Reissue) 286, 1168.

Appeal
The plaintiff, Mark Worsfold, appealed against a judgment of his Honour Judge Jones *j*
given at Lincoln County Court on 9th November 1978 dismissing his claim against the
defendant, Henry Cecil Howe, for damages for personal injuries arising out of a collision

_____

a   1e *Clarke v Winchurch* [1969] 1 All ER 275

_a_ between the plaintiff's motor cycle and the defendant's motor car on 1st September 1975. The facts are set out in the judgment of Browne LJ.

Richard Burns for the plaintiff.
Bernard Livesey for the defendant.

_b_ **BROWNE LJ** delivered the first judgment at the request of Megaw LJ. This is an appeal from the decision of his Honour Judge Jones in the Lincoln County Court, given on 9th November 1978. He gave judgment for the defendant on a claim arising from a collision between the plaintiff's motor bicycle and the defendant's car, and the plaintiff appeals.

We are concerned only with liability, the damages having been agreed at £1,200, subject of course to the question of liability. The plaintiff, in his notice of appeal, asks _c_ that judgment should be entered for him for £1,200, or alternatively that there should be a new trial.

The accident took place on 1st September 1975 at about 8 o'clock in the evening. It was daylight, though getting dusk, and the road was dry and visibility was good. The accident took place in the High Street of Lincoln. We have two photographs showing the scene of the accident, looking in opposite directions. At that point High Street, _d_ Lincoln, runs roughly north and south. The plaintiff on his motor bicycle was travelling from south to north on the road.

Looking at the position as the plaintiff was going, the position was that, first of all, there was a pedestrian crossing controlled by a traffic light. Having passed that traffic light going towards the city centre one comes to a level crossing. Then on the left as the plaintiff was going north, there is the entrance to a station yard. Then taking up a _e_ position in which the entrance to the station yard is on the left, there is a junction further up between High Street and a street going off to the right, also controlled by traffic lights. There are two lanes of traffic as one approaches that traffic light and there are arrows on the road showing, in the right-hand lane, an arrow indicating a right turn and, in the left-hand lane, an arrow indicating straight on or turn left.

What happened at the time of the accident was that the plaintiff, as I have said, was _f_ going north. He was then aged 17½. He stopped at the first lot of traffic lights. When the lights changed he moved over towards the offside of his half of the road because he was going to turn right when he got to the second lot of traffic lights.

There was traffic in his nearside lane and, in particular, there were two petrol tankers, each I think about 40 feet long, stopped on their nearside of the road pointing north because traffic had backed up from the second lot of traffic lights. The first of those two _g_ tankers had stopped on the south side of the entrance to the station yard, no doubt to let traffic get into or out of the station yard.

The defendant, in his car, was intending to come out from the station entrance and turn to his right in order to go south. There was a good deal of traffic about at the time, though it was not the rush hour.

What happened was that the driver of the leading tanker, that was the one that was _h_ stopped just south of the station yard entrance, made some sort of sign to the defendant, but the defendant said that he did not regard that as being a signal that it was safe for him to go across the road and turn right. It was merely a signal that so far as the tanker driver was concerned he was going to wait for the defendant. The defendant did move out and when the nose of his car was a foot or two feet beyond the tanker, the plaintiff on his motor cycle ran into the nearside front of the car.

_j_ The judge eventually, as I have said, found for the defendant. Having described the circumstances of the accident (as I hope that I have summarised them), he went on in this way. I should have said that the defendant's evidence was that he had stopped his car at the time of the accident. The plaintiff in his evidence said that the car was moving when he ran into it. The judge found: 'I am quite satisfied that the speed of the motor cycle was neither 10 mph nor 30 mph, but that it was something in between.' I should pause

there and say that there was some conflicting evidence about the speed of the motor
bicycle. The judge went on:

> 'I cannot say precisely how fast it was travelling. It is not necessary for me to
> come to any conclusion as to the precise speed. It is sufficient to say that the plaintiff
> was in my judgment travelling too fast to enable him to stop when he saw
> something emerging from the gap. I do not think that the defendant's car was
> stationary. I think that it was moving forward all the time. The defendant is not
> a liar but I think he is mistaken. I think his recollection is clouded, perhaps by the
> shock of the collision, perhaps by the passage of time. He did what he said he did.
> I think he decided to move out through the gap. He could not see and so he inched
> forward. I find that he was at an angle of greater than five degrees.'

Pausing there, the defendant had said that his car was only at an angle of five degrees.
Going on:

> 'He allowed his car to move forward very, very slowly indeed. I think "inching"
> forward is the best way to describe what he did. At the time of impact I find the
> vehicle was projecting more than one foot and probably beyond two feet from the
> tanker. I cannot think that the plaintiff would be riding within one foot of the
> tanker or indeed within two feet of the tanker.'

Then having described the state of the traffic and saying that the plaintiff had stopped
at the far pedestrian crossing and he then moved over towards the middle of his side of
the road, he went on: 'As he [that is the plaintiff] moved alongside the leading tanker he
could see the gap ahead', that being the gap into the station yard. The judge went on:

> 'He assumed that this gap was for vehicles turning right from the station yard.
> I accept that he contemplated the possibility that vehicles might turn out of the yard
> and that he did not see any vehicle turning out of the yard and thought the way
> ahead was clear. At this stage I am quite sure that he was travelling at a speed which
> was too fast to enable him to stop or otherwise avoid a collision if any vehicle did
> emerge from the gap and he did not reduce his speed to such a speed. At the same
> time as the plaintiff is thus travelling along the length of the two tankers the
> defendant's car is moving through the gap in the traffic and the plaintiff does not see
> it. Suddenly the plaintiff sees it and then it is too late. He tries to avoid it but he is
> too close and travelling too fast. All he can do is to raise his leg in an attempt to
> mitigate injury to it. Maybe he lost control. I make no finding about this. The
> important finding is that he was travelling too fast and this was the cause of this
> accident. In my judgment, and I am quite clear what was the cause of the accident,
> the plaintiff suddenly saw the defendant inching out and was going too fast to do
> anything about it. He drove at this speed even though he contemplated that cars
> might emerge from the gap.'

He continued:

> 'What is the effect in law? I have been referred to *Clarke v Winchurch*[1]. I need not
> repeat the facts of that case. This case is distinguishable from *Clarke's* case[1] because
> this plaintiff was not queue-jumping. But any vehicle travelling along a line of
> stationary traffic has a very heavy duty of care. He must contemplate the possibility
> of vehicles giving warning of their presence by inching out and must so organise his
> driving as to guard against this possibility. This plaintiff did not do that, so he fell
> short of the heavy duty on him and he was to blame for the accident. But the real
> issue is whether the defendant carries any blame. Now I must say that when I first
> heard counsel for the plaintiff opening this case I took the view that a person who
> emerges from a minor into a major road ought not to proceed beyond the line of his

---

1   [1969] 1 All ER 275, [1969] 1 WLR 69

vision and that if he does so, he does so at his own risk and could not rely on other vehicles seeing him. That would have continued to be my view of the matter had I not been referred to *Clarke v Winchurch*[1]. Had it not been for *Clarke v Winchurch*[1], I would have found the parties fifty-fifty to blame, on the basis that the plaintiff had been going too fast and the defendant had gone beyond the line of his vision. I confess to having my confidence shattered by the Court of Appeal's decision in *Clarke*[1]. It is clear that their Lordships' extensive experience extended numerically more largely in areas other than running down actions, although the basis of the decision was common sense rather than anything else. The facts in *Clarke*[1] were almost on all fours with this particular case. The only material distinction was that the facts in *Clarke's* case[1] occurred at the rush hour but that is not the case here although the road was busy. All their Lordships discussed, in *Clarke's* case[1], the duty of a driver who wanted to drive across a line of stationary traffic facing in the direction in which he did not want to go. Their Lordships even described what a counsel of perfection was.'

Then the judge quoted a passage from the judgment of Phillimore LJ in that case, and went on:

'I cannot feel that I can make any distinction between *Clarke's* case[1] and this case. In my judgment the defendant moved out very, very slowly so that what he did was almost perfect. The only question which exercised me was whether the defendant should have waited for the tanker to pass. But in my judgment the defendant was only doing what the defendant in *Clarke's* case[1] did and there is no obligation on him to wait for the tanker to clear before moving out. I do not think there was any obligation on him to wait. I therefore think that I am forced to come to the conclusion that he was exercising all the care he should have done and there was nothing more the defendant could have done to avoid this collision. In fact he acted almost to perfection. Therefore I am driven to the conclusion that he was not in any way to blame for the accident, because when the plaintiff saw the defendant inching out he was going too fast to be able to stop. I therefore am obliged to find against the plaintiff. It may be no comfort to the plaintiff that I am not at all sure that he was travelling at as great a speed as 30 mph. I find against him with regret because he is a young man and an honest young man.'

Counsel, who appeared for the plaintiff in this court and below, submitted that the judge felt that he had been forced by the doctrine of precedent to do an injustice, and submitted that *Clarke's* case[1] was not intended to lay down any principle of law that a driver who inches forward very slowly is entitled to emerge blind from a minor road onto a major road.

It is quite true that in *Clarke's* case[1] the facts were very like the facts in the present case. There were certain differences which I do not think I need go into. That was a case where the first defendant's car was parked in a parking space on the offside of the road facing oncoming traffic. A bus coming towards him had stopped and flashed its lights. The first defendant, the driver of the car, started to pull out and a motor bicycle ridden by the plaintiff came along and ran into him. The plaintiff in that case had sued the car driver and the bus driver who flashed his headlights and the bus driver's employer. The trial judge had held that the bus driver, and through him his employers, were to some extent to blame for the accident, and that they were one-third to blame, and he held that the defendant, the car driver, was not to blame at all. But when the matter got to this court there was an appeal and a cross-appeal, and this court held that the bus driver and his employer were not to blame at all and allowed their appeal, and they dismissed the plaintiff's cross-appeal holding that the driver of the car was to no extent to blame.

---

1   [1969] 1 All ER 275, [1969] 1 WLR 69

It seems to me that the actual decision in that case was simply that this court saw no sufficient reason for disagreeing with the finding of the trial judge that the car driver was *a* not to any extent to blame.

It is quite true that in a passage which is quoted by the judge in the present case Phillimore LJ did say[1]:

'That finding seems to me to be a finding that the car driver came out extremely slowly and extremely carefully. In effect he inched his way out beyond the line of the bus. If it be said (and it is the most formidable point that has been made) that *b* he ought to have just poked his nose out and then stopped, I venture to think that the answer is that that is a counsel of perfection; and the difference between doing that, going out for only a foot or a little more, and travelling very, very slowly for a yard is so small that it is wrong to say that in the one case it would amount to negligence, and in the other it would not. I regard the suggestion of just going out and then stopping as a counsel of perfection.' *c*

Then he went on[1]:

'It appears to me that for this court to interfere with the learned judge's finding that the car driver did all that he could be expected to do involves revising other findings of fact which this court is in no position to do.'
d

Then, having referred to other possibilities, he said[2]:

'But he [that is the trial judge] saw and heard the witnesses, and we have not; and in my opinion we are in no position to substitute our findings of fact for those reached by the learned judge.'

Willmer LJ said[3]: *e*

'On the whole, therefore, accepting (as I think we should) the findings of fact arrived at by the learned judge, who saw the witnesses, I do not think that it would be right for us in this court to impute blame to the car driver.'

Russell LJ dissented and thought that the car driver should, in fact, have stopped as soon as the tip of his bonnet was showing. *f*

It seems to me clear that the judge would have come to a different conclusion but for that decision, and that he did regard that decision as laying down some principle of law which bound him to find, contrary to his own inclination, that the defendant was under no liability at all.

There is, of course, ample high authority about the danger of elevating decisions on the facts in particular cases into principles of law. For the purpose of the present case I *g* think it is enough to refer to what was said in this court in *Garston Warehousing Co Ltd v O F Smart (Liverpool) Ltd*[4]. That again was a case of a car emerging from a side road into a main road, and in that case both the plaintiff and the defendant were held to blame in certain proportions, the emerging car one-third and the other car two-thirds.

Cairns LJ said[5]:

'It does not appear to me that in this case any question of law arises at all. *h* Reference has been made to *Clarke v Winchurch*[6], the circumstances of which bear some resemblance to those in the present case in that the driver had come out from a side road and, it was said, was negligent in not stopping in very much the same

1   [1969] 1 All ER 275 at 279, [1969] 1 WLR 69 at 74
2   [1969] 1 All ER 275 at 280, [1969] 1 WLR 69 at 74
3   [1969] 1 All ER 275 at 281, [1969] 1 WLR 69 at 76
4   [1973] RTR 377
5   [1973] RTR 377 at 382
6   [1969] 1 All ER 275, [1969] 1 WLR 69

a
way as the judge found that the plaintiffs in this case should have stopped. There it was said that the requirement on the driver to stop in those circumstances was a counsel of perfection, and the majority of the Court of Appeal found there was no negligence on his part at all. Russell LJ, who dissented, would have assessed his blame for the accident at no more than 20 per cent, and while it is of some assistance to see the way in which this court dealt with the case which had, as I have said, that feature in common with this case, I certainly do not think that it was laying down

b
any principle of law as to whether or not that constitutes negligence.'

MacKenna J did not say anything specifically about this point, but Buckley LJ said that he agreed with the judgments that had been delivered and, therefore, was agreeing with what Cairns LJ had said in the passage which I have read.

In my judgment, therefore, the judge was not bound by *Clarke's* case[1], which in my opinion laid down no principle of law, to reach the conclusion he did.

c
Counsel for the defendant takes another point. I have already read some passages from the judge's judgment, but I think I should read part of one of them again:

d
'Now I must say that when I first heard counsel for the plaintiff opening this case I took the view that a person who emerges from a minor into a major road ought not to proceed beyond the line of his vision and that if he does so, he does so at his own risk and could not rely on other vehicles seeing him. That would have continued to be my view of the matter had I not been referred to *Clarke v Winchurch*[1]. Had it not been for *Clarke v Winchurch*[1] I would have found the parties fifty-fifty to blame, on the basis that the plaintiff had been going too fast and the defendant had gone beyond the line of his vision.'

e
Counsel for the defendant submits that in that passage the judge is really saying that the defendant was under an absolute or a strict liability in the circumstances of this case when he was coming out from a side turning in front of a stationary vehicle. It seems to me that if one reads that sentence as a whole, and in its context, it is not right to say that the judge was taking the view that there was a strict or absolute liability. It seems to me that he was saying no more than that in those circumstances there is a very high duty on

f
a defendant of taking care.

The position therefore, it seems to me, is this: the judge would have held the parties fifty-fifty to blame but for the fact that he thought that *Clarke's* case[1] either laid down a principle of law or was so close to the present case on the facts that he had no choice but to come to the same conclusion as in *Clarke*[1], ie that the defendant was under no liability at all. In my judgment, the judge misled himself in that respect.

It seems to me to follow that the right thing for this court to do is to allow the appeal

g
and make the finding which the judge would have made if he had not, wrongly in my view, thought he was bound by *Clarke's* case[1] to come to a different conclusion. I am not saying for a moment that if I myself had been trying this case I should have apportioned the responsibility fifty-fifty, but it is not possible for this court to go into the question of apportionment or alter the judge's view about that. Accordingly, I would allow this appeal and order judgment to be entered for the plaintiff for half the agreed figure of

h
£1,200 damages, that is £600.

DONALDSON LJ. I agree.

MEGAW LJ. I also agree. This appeal, if it does nothing else, will I hope confirm what the court has already said in the passage in the judgment of Cairns LJ, which Browne LJ

j
has read from *Garston Warehousing Co Ltd v O F Smart (Liverpool) Ltd*[2], to the effect that the

---

1   [1969] 1 All ER 275, [1969] 1 WLR 69
2   [1973] RTR 377 at 382

decision of this court in *Clarke v Winchurch*[1] was not laying down any principle of law. I also take the view that it would be quite wrong to treat the words used by the learned county court judge in such a literal sense as to suggest that what the judge had had in mind before he saw *Clarke v Winchurch*[1] was that somebody who was carrying out a manoeuvre in a car, as the defendant was doing in this case, was necessarily and absolutely liable if any accident happened. That is not what the learned county court judge was saying.

I agree with the order proposed and with the reasons for it given by Browne LJ.

Appeal allowed. Order below to be set aside. Judgment to be entered for the plaintiff for £600 (being half the agreed total damages), interest agreed at £83.

Solicitors: *Anthony T Clark & Co*, Lincoln (for the plaintiff); *Burton & Co*, Lincoln (for the defendant).

Mary Rose Plummer   Barrister.

---

1   [1969] 1 All ER 275, [1969] 1 WLR 69

a   # R v Corwen Justices, ex parte Edwards

QUEEN'S BENCH DIVISION
LORD WIDGERY CJ, SHAW LJ, PARK, KILNER BROWN AND WOOLF JJ
14th DECEMBER 1979, 21st JANUARY 1980

b

Licensing – Permitted hours – Special order of exemption for special occasion – Special occasion –
Principles to be applied by justices in deciding whether occasion a 'special occasion' – Licensing Act
1964, s 74(4).

In considering an application under s 74(4)[d] of the Licensing Act 1964 for a special order
c   of exemption, justices should consider three questions in the following order. First, is
the occasion which is the subject-matter of the application capable in law of being a
'special occasion'. Second, if it is, whether on the material before the justices the occasion
is in fact a special occasion in the locality. Third, if so, whether as a matter of discretion
the application should be granted. Only if all three questions are answered in the
affirmative can the application be granted, and if the justices answer any one of the
d   questions in the negative the application must fail. It is primarily in relation to the first
question, which is one of law, that previous decisions of the courts can be of assistance to
justices, but they should approach such decisions with caution and not apply them
rigidly, for many of the cases are merely examples of the appropriate conclusion on the
particular facts before the court. Moreover, no previous decision exhaustively defines
what is capable of being a 'special occasion', those being ordinary English words which
e   should be given their ordinary meaning, in which case it will be unnecessary in the
majority of cases to consider the previous decisions in relation to the first question. The
court will normally only intervene in a decision on the second question, which is one of
fact, in the unlikely event of it being shown that there was no material on which the
justices could have reached their decision on that question. In relation to the third
question, which is one of discretion, it will rarely be possible to show that the justices
f   exercised their discretion in a manner capable of challenge in the courts (see p 1037 a to
d and f to j, p 1038 a and p 1039 e, post).
     Observations on the guidance to be obtained from previous decisions (see p 1038 a to
d and p 1039 e, post).
     Martin v Spalding [1979] 2 All ER 1193 approved.

g   **Notes**
     For special orders of exemption, see 26 Halsbury's Laws (4th Edn) para 339, and for cases
on the subject, see 30 Digest (Reissue) 83–85, 625–639.
     For the Licensing Act 1964, s 74, see 17 Halsbury's Statutes (3rd Edn) 1134.

     Cases referred to in judgment
h   *Devine v Keeling* (1886) 50 JP 551, 30 Digest (Reissue) 83, 625.
Knole Park Golf Club v Chief Superintendent, Kent County Constabulary [1979] 3 All ER 829,
     DC.
Lemon v Sargant (1967) [1971] 3 All ER 936, [1972] 1 WLR 72, DC, 30 Digest (Reissue)
     84, 634.
Martin v Spalding [1979] 2 All ER 1193, [1979] 1 WLR 1164, DC.
j   *R v Dewsland and Haverfordwest Justices, ex parte Terry* [1961] The Times, 28th January.
R v Wenlock Justices, ex parte Furber [1978] The Times, 26th July, DC.
R v Woodstock Justices, ex parte Holdsworth (30th May 1977) unreported, DC.

---

a   Section 74(4) is set out at p 1036 f, post

Motion for certiorari

This was an application by Chief Superintendent Percy Manning Edwards of the North a
Wales Police for an order of certiorari to quash a special order of exemption made on 9th
February 1979 under s 74 of the Licensing Act 1964 by the licensing justices of the petty
sessional division of Berwyn sitting at Corwen Magistrates' Court in the county of Clwyd
whereby they granted in respect of the licences for 48 named public houses extensions
of the permitted hours for Saturday 26th May 1979 and Saturday 25th August 1979 (the
Saturdays before the spring and summer bank holiday respectively) from 11 pm to 11.45 b
pm. The grounds of the application were (1) that the order was wrong in law and (2) that
the Saturday before a bank holiday Monday had no particular character which gave it the
quality of a special occasion for the purpose of s 74 of the 1964 Act and in the premises,
the justices erred in law in granting the extensions and their order exceeded their
jurisdiction. The facts are set out in the judgment of Woolf J.

c

Martin Thomas QC and *Michael Farmer* for the applicant.
R J Harvey QC and *Richard Beckett* for the National Association of Licensed Victuallers.

Cur adv vult

d

21st January. The following judgments were read.

WOOLF J (delivering the first judgment at the invitation of Lord Widgery CJ). In this
matter counsel moves on behalf of Percy Manning Edwards, a chief superintendent of
the North Wales police, for an order of certiorari to quash the order made by the e
licensing justices sitting in and for the Petty Sessional Division of Berwyn on 9th
February 1979, granting extensions of permitted hours for Saturday 26th May 1979, and
Saturday 25th August 1979 from 11 pm to 11.45 pm in respect of 48 public houses
situated within the division.

The justices in granting the applications purported to act pursuant to s 74(4) of the
Licensing Act 1964, which provides: f

> '(4) Justices of the peace may—(a) on an application by the holder of a justices' on-
> licence for any premises, or (b) on an application by the secretary of a club registered
> in respect of any premises, make an order (in this Act referred to as a special order
> of exemption) adding such hours as may be specified in the order to the permitted
> hours in those premises on such special occasion or occasions as may be so specified.'

g

This case raises again the question of what is the proper approach which justices should
adopt in the case of such applications and the extent to which this court can interfere
with the decisions which they reach. This is the same question as was considered as
recently as 21st May 1979 by this court in *Martin v Spalding*[1]. Having heard numerous
authorities cited to the court in that case, Lord Widgery CJ and Geoffrey Lane LJ sought
to give general guidance as to the principles to be applied, in the hope that their h
judgments would assist 'materially to dispose of this recurring problem'. Lord Widgery
CJ had a reservation as to whether this object would be achieved, and the present case is
not the only justification for that reservation. There has already been at least one other
case before this court on this very provision since *Martin v Spalding*[1].

In the present case counsel have again taken this court through the relevant authorities
starting with *Devine v Keeling*[2]. Having considered those authorities, this court considers j

---

1 [1979] 2 All ER 1193, [1979] 1 WLR 1164
2 (1886) 50 JP 551

that the principles set out in the judgments in *Martin v Spalding*[1] were correct. In order
a to try to achieve the same object as was sought to be achieved in *Martin v Spalding*[1] and
with the same reservations as to the likelihood of success, I would point out that when
justices are considering applications for a special order of exemption, there are three
questions which they should consider in deciding whether to grant an application which
is made to them in the proper form.

The First Question. Is the occasion which is the subject matter of the application capable
b of being a 'special occasion'? As Lord Widgery CJ said in *Martin v Spalding*[2]: 'In other
words, the justices must look at this matter like a judge looking at a matter of law and ask
themselves whether it is open to anybody to contend that this is a special occasion.'

The Second Question. If the occasion is capable of being a special occasion, whether, on
the material available to the justices, it is in fact a special occasion in the locality in which
the licensed premises in respect of which the application is made are situated?

c *The Third Question.* If it is a special occasion in their locality, whether as a matter of
discretion the application should be granted.

As will be apparent from the questions, if the justices answer any question in the
negative, it is not necessary for them to go on to consider the remaining questions. An
application can only be granted if all three questions are answered in the affirmative.

The first question is a question of law and if any relief is to be obtained from a higher
d court in respect of a decision of the justices, it will normally be because they have
answered the first question in a manner which is wrong in law. The second question is
purely a question of fact and the court will normally only be able to intervene in the
unlikely event of it being shown that there was no material on which the justices could
have come to the decision which they did.

It is to this question that the passage from the judgment of Lord Coleridge CJ in *Devine*
e *v Keeling*[3], which is often cited, applies. Lord Coleridge CJ stated:

> 'I think in this case we cannot interfere with the decision of the justices, for the
> question what is a special occasion must necessarily be a question of fact in each
> locality. Each locality may very well have its own meaning to those words, and it
> is for the justices in each district to say whether a certain time and place come
f within the description.'

Those words should not be taken as applying to the first question.

So far as the justices' answer to the third question is concerned, it will be rare indeed
that it will be possible to show that the justices have exercised their discretion in a
manner which is capable of being challenged in the courts.

g It is primarily in relation to the first question, because it involves a question of law,
that the previous decisions of the courts can be of assistance. However, even in relation
to the first question, the earlier authorities must be approached with some caution.
Many of the decisions do not lay down any principle but merely provide examples of
what is the appropriate conclusion on their particular facts. They should not be applied
rigidly to later situations because the facts are unlikely to be precisely the same.

h Furthermore, none of the earlier decisions purport to lay down an exhaustive
definition as to what is capable of being a special occasion. The words 'special occasion'
are ordinary words in the English language which may be given their ordinary meaning,
and if this is done, in the majority of cases it will not be necessary to look at previous
authorities in order to answer the first question. In borderline cases however the earlier

j

---

1 [1979] 2 All ER 1193, [1979] 1 WLR 1164
2 [1979] 2 All ER 1193 at 1196, [1979] 1 WLR 1164 at 1167
3 (1886) 50 JP 551 at 552

authorities may be of assistance in giving guidance as to the proper approach to the problem or by laying down markers as to what is or is not capable of being a special a occasion.

The main guidance which is to be obtained from these authorities can be summarised as follows:

(1) The occasion can be special from the national or local point of view. A local occasion can include what might be more aptly described as a personal occasion such as a wedding, but the more local or the more personal the occasion, the more carefully it b must be scrutinised (see per Geoffrey Lane LJ in *Martin v Spalding*[1]).

(2) The more frequent the occasion occurs the less likely it is that it will be a special occasion (see *Lemon v Sargant*[2]).

(3) If the occasion is one created by the licensee solely for the purposes of his licensed business, it is unlikely to be capable of being a special occasion. Such a situation must be distinguished from the position of a registered club which creates, for example, sporting c occasions which are celebrated at the club and are capable of being special occasions because they are not created solely for the purpose of the *licensed* business of the club (see *Knole Park Golf Club v Chief Superintendent, Kent County Constabulary*[3]).

Turning to the facts of the present case, the complaint is in respect of the grant of extensions for permitted hours for Saturday 26th May, being the Saturday before the spring bank holiday Monday, and Saturday 25th August 1979, being the Saturday before d the summer bank holiday Monday. It is accepted that extensions were properly granted in respect of the bank holiday Mondays themselves, which are agreed to be special occasions. The justices have filed an affidavit in support of their decision. In that affidavit they say in effect that they consider that in their division the whole bank holiday weekend is a continuing special occasion. They point out that the area attracts a large number of visitors during the summer months, and during bank holiday weekends a e large number of visitors arrive on Friday evenings and stay over the weekend departing for their homes on bank holiday Monday. Because of the tourist attractions of the area the Saturdays prior to the spring and summer bank holidays have a particular character giving them the quality of special occasions. They point out that they came to this conclusion after the case of *R v Wenlock Justices, ex parte Furber*[4], to which I will refer later, had been brought to their attention and carefully considered. f

There is nothing in the evidence which is before the court to suggest that the justices misdirected themselves in any way and if their decision was objectionable it could only be on the basis that the Saturdays in question were not capable of being a special occasion. As to this, I am clearly of the view that it is impossible to say that these particular Saturdays were incapable of being special occasions as they form part of the bank holiday weekend.

g

However a different view was taken in the *Wenlock Justices* case[4] and this court did quash the decision in that case. The respondent did not appear and was not represented in that case and in *Martin v Spalding*[5] Geoffrey Lane LJ preferred the decision of *R v Woodstock Justices, ex parte Holdsworth*[6], which was a decision of this court involving a Saturday before a bank holiday weekend in which this court took a different view. Both those cases should be regarded as being decisions on their own facts. What they illustrate h is that a Saturday before a bank holiday is close to the borderline of a situation which is

1   [1979] 2 All ER 1193 at 1197, [1979] 1 WLR 1164 at 1168

2   [1971] 3 All ER 936, [1972] 1 WLR 72 j

3   [1979] 3 All ER 829

4   [1978] The Times, 26th July

5   [1979] 2 All ER 1193, [1979] 1 WLR 1164

6   (30th May 1977) unreported

not capable of being regarded as a special occasion. An illustration of a case which is
a beyond the borderline is provided by *R v Dewsland and Haverfordwest Licensing Justices*[1].
In that case this court said: 'It was impossible to say that because people attended a seaside
resort on Thursday and Saturday in the summer months that in law amounted to special
occasions.'

In support of the application to this court reliance was placed on an affidavit by
Superintendent Pritchard containing in particular more detailed evidence as to the
b extent to which the area in question is properly to be regarded as a holiday area. Quite
apart from the fact that the justices had no opportunity of dealing with this affidavit, this
court will not go into evidential disputes of this sort in order to review the justices'
conclusion on the second question.

Some complaint was made by the applicant that the justices should not have come to
the conclusion which they did without hearing evidence on the issue. That complaint
c is not justified. The letter in support of the application which was placed before the
justices had attached to it a list which made it clear that the applications for extension
were made because the Saturdays formed part of the holiday weekend and in deciding
whether or not such a holiday weekend is a special occasion, the licensing justices are
perfectly entitled to act on their local knowledge without having evidence called before
them.

d The conclusion of this court as to the decision of the justices in this case is that it was
one which they were entitled to come to and which they appear to have reached after
giving proper consideration to the issues and the material available to them. It follows
that the application for an order of certiorari is dismissed.

SHAW LJ. I agree.

e
LORD WIDGERY CJ. I have the authority of Park and Kilner Brown JJ to say they
agree and I also agree.

Application dismissed.

f Solicitors: *Sharpe Pritchard & Co*, agents for *William Jones & Talog Davies and Aneurin O
Evans*, Ruthin (for the applicant); *Lickfolds, Wiley & Powles* (for the National Association
of Licensed Victuallers).

N P Metcalfe Esq   Barrister.

---

1   [1961] The Times, 28th January

Practice Direction

FAMILY DIVISION

Minor – Custody – Access – Supervised access – Application to court for supervised access – Consent of person to supervise access – Welfare officers should not normally be asked to supervise access.

Where application is made to the court for access to be supervised, every effort should be made, before the matter comes before the court, to obtain the consent of a person likely to be agreeable to both parties to supervise the access. Mutual friends, unprejudiced relatives and godparents are examples of the classes of persons who should be approached.

Only when every effort has been made to enlist the help of such persons and has been unsuccessful should welfare officers and similar persons be involved. Application for such persons to supervise access should never be made without obtaining the consent of the person concerned and every effort should be made to avoid asking them to exercise supervision on Saturdays or Sundays.

In the few instances where it is necessary to ask that supervision should be carried out by welfare officers, the supervision should be confined to a very few occasions, the number of which should be specified in the order. Care must be taken to arrange a place of access which does not cause the welfare officer undue travelling difficulties.

Issued with the concurrence of the Lord Chancellor.

12th March 1980   SIR JOHN ARNOLD P.

a
R v Secretary of State for the Home Department, ex parte Zamir

COURT OF APPEAL, CIVIL DIVISION

STEPHENSON, EVELEIGH AND BRANDON LJJ

29th, 30th NOVEMBER, 21st DECEMBER 1979

b

Immigration – Leave to enter – Non-patrial – Right of entry – Change of circumstances removing basis on which entry certificate granted – Applicant born in Pakistan and applying for entry certificate – Applicant eligible for entry certificate at time of application – Entry certificate granted two years later by which time applicant ineligible – Whether applicant under obligation when entering to disclose change of circumstances affecting his right to enter – Immigration Rules
c for Control on Entry: EEC and Other Non-Commonwealth Nationals (1972–73), paras 10, 39.

The applicant was born in Pakistan in 1957. His parents subsequently came to the United Kingdom and in 1973, when the applicant was 15, application was made on his behalf for an entry certificate, to which at that time he was entitled, under para 39[a] of the Immigration Rules[b], because he was then 'an unmarried and fully dependent son under
d 21 . . . who formed part of the family unit overseas' and whose family had settled in the United Kingdom. There was a delay in the grant of the entry certificate which was not issued until November 1975, when the applicant was 18. In February 1976 the applicant married and in March he arrived in the United Kingdom alone and was given authority to enter for an indefinite period. He was later detained as an illegal entrant, and applied for a writ of habeas corpus, contending that at the date when he applied for an entry
e certificate he had been eligible to obtain one and that it was irrelevant that he may later have become ineligible. It was contended on behalf of the Secretary of State (i) that the applicant was under a duty to disclose a 'change of circumstances' which he knew or ought to have known would materially affect his qualification for entry and (ii) that the applicant's marriage was a 'change of circumstances' since the issue of the certificate which had 'removed the basis of the holder's claim to admission' and therefore the
f applicant could have been refused entry under para 10[c] of the rules on his arrival in the United Kingdom.

Held – In obtaining leave to enter the United Kingdom under para 39 of the Immigration Rules an applicant was under a duty to disclose any information relating to a change of circumstances which he knew or ought to have known would affect his
g application to enter, and if he entered the United Kingdom by deliberately concealing that information either by an untruthful answer or by silence he would have entered pursuant to leave obtained by deceit and in breach of the immigration laws, and would be an illegal immigrant. Since the applicant was not, at the time of his entry, eligible for entry under para 39 of the rules, as he must have known that his marriage constituted a 'change of circumstances' which had removed the basis for his admission, his deliberate
h concealment of his marriage amounted to the practising of a deceit. It followed that the Secretary of State had been entitled to detain the applicant as an illegal entrant with a view to his removal from the United Kingdom (see p 1043 *j*, p 1044 *j* to p 1045 *a* and *d*, p 1046 *e f*, p 1047 *c* to *g* and p 1048 *b* to *g*, post).

With v O'Flanagan [1936] 1 All ER 727 applied.

R v Secretary of State for the Home Department, ex parte Ram [1979] 1 All ER 687
j distinguished.

---

a Paragraph 39 is set out at p 1043 *f*, post

b Statement of Immigration Rules for Control on Entry: EEC and Other Non-Commonwealth Nationals (H of C Paper (1972–73) no 81)

c Paragraph 10, so far as material, is set out at p 1043 *h*, post

Decision of the Divisional Court of the Queen's Bench Division [1979] 2 All ER 849 affirmed.   *a*

Notes
For illegal entry into the United Kingdom, see 4 Halsbury's Laws (4th Edn) paras 976, 1027.

Cases referred to in judgments   *b*
Brownlie v Campbell (1880) 5 App Cas 925, HL, 35 Digest (Repl) 8, 24.
R v Secretary of State for the Home Department, ex parte Hussain [1978] 2 All ER 423, [1978] 1 WLR 700, CA.
R v Secretary of State for the Home Department, ex parte Ram [1979] 1 All ER 687, [1979] 1 WLR 148, DC.
Smith v Kay (1859) 7 HL Cas 750, 30 LJ Ch 45, 11 ER 299, HL, 35 Digest (Repl) 19, *110.* *c*
With v O'Flanagan [1936] 1 All ER 727, [1936] Ch 575, 105 LJ Ch 247, 154 LT 634, CA, 35 Digest (Repl) 32, *233.*

Appeal
Mohammed Zamir appealed against the order of the Divisional Court of the Queen's Bench Division[1] (Lord Widgery CJ, Cumming-Bruce LJ and Neill J) on 14th March 1979 *d* whereby it dismissed the appellant's application for an order of habeas corpus directed to the Secretary of State for the Home Department to instruct the Governor of HM Prison, Winson Green, Birmingham, to release the applicant from detention where he had been detained pursuant to an order of an immigration officer issued under para 16 of Sch 2 to the Immigration Act 1971. The facts are set out in the judgment of Eveleigh LJ.

e
Aydin Turkan for the appellant.
Simon D Brown for the Secretary of State.

                                                                                                   Cur adv vult

21st December. The following judgments were read.

f

EVELEIGH LJ (read by Stephenson LJ). This is an appeal from the decision of the Divisional Court[1] on 14th March 1979 refusing the appellant's application for a writ of habeas corpus.
      The appellant was born on 3rd March 1957. On 11th December 1972 when he was 15 years of age an application was made on his behalf in Pakistan for a United Kingdom *g* entry certificate. His personal particulars were given in part I of the application form, including his date of birth. There was a note to part III of the form saying: 'To be completed if you propose to join relatives already in the United Kingdom.' This part was completed giving the name and address of the appellant's father who was stated to have been in the United Kingdom since 1962. At the top of the application form there *h* appeared an exhortation to read the notes before filling in the form. Note D stated:

> 'The holders of entry certificates will be presumed by the immigration officer in the United Kingdom to be qualified for admission unless he discovers:—(a) that the entry certificate was obtained by fraudulent representations or by concealment of facts which the applicant knew to be material; or (b) that a change of circumstances after issue has removed the basis of the holder's claim to admission; or (c) that the *j* holder should be refused admission on medical grounds, on grounds of criminal record, on security grounds or because he is subject to a deportation order.'

---

1   [1979] 2 All ER 849, [1979] QB 688

On 25th November 1975, when the appellant was 18 years of age, a visa was granted
a which was valid for presentation in the United Kingdom within six months from its
date. There was written on it: 'Settlement to join father.' On 10th February 1976 he
married in Pakistan. On 2nd March 1976 he arrived in this country and on the basis of
the visa was given indefinite leave to enter at Heathrow. He did not disclose his
marriage.

On 31st July 1978 the entry clearance officer in Islamabad informed the Home Office
b Immigration and Nationality Department that he was considering applications for
Mazloom Begum and Mohammed Zamir who wished to enter the United Kingdom for
settlement as the wife and son of the appellant. The entry clearance officer was not
satisfied that the appellant had lawfully entered the United Kingdom on 2nd March
1976. He, therefore, referred the matter to the department for their consideration.

The appellant was interviewed on 30th August 1978 with the help of an Urdu
c speaking interpreter. He was asked if he had mentioned his forthcoming marriage to
the entry clearance officer and said that he had not because the marriage had not been
arranged until about four to five weeks after he had been given his visa. He also said that
he had not informed the entry clearance officer when he actually married because he did
not think it was necessary. He was asked whether on his arrival in the United Kingdom
he had told the immigration officer of his marriage and replied that he had not been
d asked any questions regarding this.

The appellant was also asked how, at the time of his entry into the United Kingdom,
he could regard himself as a dependant of his father when he himself had undertaken
marriage. He was apparently unable to offer any explanation but did admit that he had
come to the United Kingdom purely for work for himself and his wife.

Subsequently, on 2nd October 1978, the appellant was arrested and detained pursuant
e to para 16 of Sch 2 to the Immigration Act 1971.

The respondent contends that the appellant was an illegal immigrant when he came
into this country on 2nd March 1976. It is said that the visa was granted on the basis that
the appellant satisfied the requirements of para 39 of the Rules for Control on Entry[1].
That reads:

f   'Generally, children aged 18 years or over must qualify for admission in their own
      right; but subject to the requirements of *paragraphs 34 and 35* an unmarried and
      fully dependent son under 21 years or an unmarried daughter under 21 who
      formed part of the family unit overseas may be admitted if the whole family are
      settled in the United Kingdom or are being admitted for settlement.'

It is said that the basis of the grant of the visa had ceased to exist because not only was
g the appellant married when he entered, but he was not fully dependent on his father as
his admission that he was coming for work clearly showed. We were then referred to
para 10 of the Rules for Control on Entry, which reads:

      '. . . A passenger who holds an entry clearance which was duly issued to him and
      is still current is not to be refused leave to enter unless the Immigration Officer is
      satisfied that: (*a*) false representations were employed or material facts were
h   concealed, whether or not to the holder's knowledge, for the purpose of obtaining
      the clearance, or (*b*) a change of circumstances since it was issued has removed the
      basis of the holder's claim to admission . . .'

The marriage was clearly a change of circumstances since the visa was issued. While
the appellant had probably ceased to be dependent on his father before the date of issue,
j none the less it is said that the absence of dependency is such a change because it should
not lie in the appellant's mouth to say that the change in dependency occurred before and

---

1   Statement of Immigration Rules for Control on Entry: EEC and Other Non-Commonwealth
      Nationals (H of C Paper (1972–73) no 81)

not after the date of issue. Alternatively, it is said that the lack of dependency was a
material fact which was concealed for the purpose of obtaining the clearance.   *a*

However, the fact remains that entry permission was granted although the
circumstances were such that the immigration officer would have refused permission
had he known the truth. Counsel formulated his submission as follows: 'There is a duty
to disclose a change of circumstances when otherwise the entry document to the entrant's
knowledge or constructive knowledge would speak to an entitlement, namely
qualification for entry which as a result of the change of circumstances he does not or   *b*
might not still have.' He further submits that if the immigrant silently proffers a
passport endorsed with a visa containing information which although accurate when
endorsed he knows or should know may materially mislead the immigration officer
because circumstances have changed, then the immigrant is under a positive duty to
disclose the change of circumstances.

On behalf of the appellant it is submitted that as the application was made when he   *c*
was only 15 years of age he was applying for admission under para 38 of the rules. There
is no mention of marriage in para 38 and consequently that does not constitute the basis
of the claim to admission. Counsel argues that when the visa was issued in November
1975 it was issued on the basis of the application. Consequently it is said that in so far as
the marriage is concerned that was irrelevant and could not operate as a change of
circumstances within para 10 of the rules.   *d*

In so far as dependency is relevant it is submitted that the appellant made no
representations that were untrue and that he was under no duty to disclose the fact, if it
were a fact, that he was not dependent on his father. It is further said that if the visa must
be taken to have been issued on the basis of para 39 there was still no duty to disclose the
marriage. Consequently it is said that there was no deceit on the part of the appellant
which invalidated the permission to enter.   *e*

Counsel has also said that the application was made originally on behalf of a 15-year-
old boy who spoke little English. It was no fault of his that so great a time had elapsed
before the visa was granted. It is wrong to assume that the appellant knew the relevant
provisions of the immigration rules and as he had been asked no pertinent questions he
had done nothing to deceive. Reliance was placed on *R v Secretary of State for the Home
Department, ex parte Ram*[1], to which I will refer later.   *f*

In considering these cases it is always important to keep in mind the provisions of the
Immigration Act 1971 itself. Section 3(1) provides:

> 'Except as otherwise provided by or under this Act, where a person is not
> patrial—(*a*) he shall not enter the United Kingdom unless given leave to do so in
> accordance with this Act; (*b*) he may be given leave to enter the United Kingdom   *g*
> (or, when already there, leave to remain in the United Kingdom) either for a limited
> or for an indefinite period; (*c*) if he is given a limited leave to enter or remain in the
> United Kingdom, it may be given subject to conditions restricting his employment
> or occupation in the United Kingdom, or requiring him to register with the police,
> or both.'

h

An illegal immigrant is defined by s 33(1) as—

> 'a person unlawfully entering or seeking to enter in breach of a deportation order
> or of the immigration laws, and includes also a person who has so entered.'

An immigrant seeking admission, therefore, has no right to enter. He asks for
permission. It must be well known to all such immigrants, particularly to those coming   *j*
from India and Pakistan, that there are certain conditions which have to be fulfilled
before an applicant is eligible for the grant of permission. In such circumstances if a

---

1   [1979] 1 All ER 687, [1979] 1 WLR 148

person knows that he is ineligible, or fears that his circumstances may mean that he is
_a_ ineligible, and deliberately conceals that information either by an untruthful answer or
by silence, he is, to my mind, practising a deceit. It is only right that a person asking for
favourable treatment by another should disclose such information as he feels might be
relevant to the decision to grant his request. It is necessary to examine how far these
matters affect the validity of entry permission in the present case.

In *Ram's* case[1] the court held that the entry permission was not invalid. It is important
_b_ to bear in mind the extent to which the evidence went in that case. The immigration
officer made a mistake. It appears nowhere to have been contended or established that
the immigrant knew of the mistake or that he was deliberately refraining from disclosing
matters which he feared might result in refusal to admit. May J said[2]:

_c_ 'Counsel on the applicant's behalf, I think, accepts that the fact that his client's
passport was then stamped with leave to enter for an indefinite period was a genuine
mistake on the part of the relevant immigration officer, a mistake however in no
way induced by any fraud or dishonesty on the part of the applicant.'

That case, therefore, is not the complete answer from the appellant's point of view, as was
submitted to this court. I must, therefore, examine the present case from the beginning.
_d_ The appellant's age was stated on the application form. Consequently at the time that
the visa was issued, as he was 18, the information which had been disclosed by the
appellant justified a grant under para 39 only. The visa must, therefore, be taken to have
been issued on the basis of that paragraph. The marriage constituted a change of
circumstances within para 10 of the rules. As the change of dependency rests on less
precise information I will deal with the case for the moment on the basis of marriage
_e_ alone being the change in the circumstances. Was there a duty to disclose? In the
Divisional Court Lord Widgery CJ said[3]:

'I think we ought to make a modest increase, a modest step forward, in the law
on this topic in this case, and I would do so by adopting the test of counsel for the
Secretary of State for this intermediate situation. I think, with his submission, that
_f_ there is an obligation on an entrant to disclose changes of circumstances if he knew,
or ought to have known, that those changes were material to the immigration
history.'

It is argued that even if there is a duty of some kind the words 'ought to have known' go
too far. They would cover, it is said, the case where the applicant has no reason even to
_g_ suspect and are inconsistent with the decision in *Ram's* case[1].

Such an argument, in my opinion, ignores the effect of Lord Widgery CJ's introductory
words to that statement of principle. He had referred to the clearly established principle
that[3]—

'if an entrant is guilty of active fraud, if he is guilty of misrepresentation
_h_ deliberately made with a view to obtaining an entry document, that entry document
is vitiated by the fraud.'

He then referred to *Ram's* case[1] and concluded[3]:

'Just as fraud clearly is sufficient, mere error on the part of the immigration
_j_ officer is not enough. But what do we do with the intermediate situation? What

1 [1979] 1 All ER 687, [1979] 1 WLR 148
2 [1979] 1 All ER 687 at 688, [1979] 1 WLR 148 at 150
3 [1979] 2 All ER 849 at 852, [1979] QB 688 at 694

do we do with a case which, in my judgment, is very close to the present case where there has been no disclosure by the applicant in circumstances in which one would *a* expect him, if he were honest, to make disclosure?

I believe that the statement of principle is governed by the words 'in circumstances in which one would expect him, if he were honest, to make disclosure'.

Counsel for the appellant has referred to s 26 of the 1971 Act which creates offences in connection with the administration of the Act, including refusal or failure to furnish information which the immigrant is required to produce when examined by *b* immigration officers for the purpose of deciding whether or not to grant permission to enter. It is also an offence to make a representation which he knows to be false or does not believe to be true. I do not think that it is necessary to show an offence under s 26, as it seems to me counsel was submitting, before permission to enter can be invalidated. Many of the cases where permission to enter has been obtained by deceit will probably disclose evidence of such an offence, because even if the presentation of the *c* entry clearance certificate itself does not contain a representation (which I doubt) very little by way of word or conduct will be needed to amount to an assertion that the immigrant is seeking to enter genuinely as a person within the rule or rules which formed the basis of his entry clearance. A mere statement that the applicant is coming to join his father (which statement may well be made by presenting a visa containing that information) will probably also contain an implied representation that he is a person *d* qualified for admission on that basis. However, whether or not leave to enter can subsequently be invalidated on the grounds of deceit ought not, in my opinion, to be approached by reference to the criminal law. Nor should the question be approached as though the court was dealing with someone who has a vested right. It is not easy to discuss in strictly legal terms the extent to which any right has been conferred on a person who has obtained a concession not as of right but by way of favour. Invited guests *e* are entitled to the utmost respect. Gatecrashers are never welcome and have no rights. In deciding whether or not a person was a gatecrasher the Secretary of State should be entitled to approach the matter on a common-sense basis. It therefore seems to me that when it can be said that a person was neither frank nor honest in the way in which he obtained leave to enter, then his leave can be invalidated when it was given on a misunderstanding as to his qualifications for which misunderstanding some deceit or *f* trickery on his part was responsible.

In my opinion a test by reference to honesty is very appropriate in these cases where we are not concerned with strict interpretation of legal rights. In *With v O'Flanagan*[1] Lord Wright MR said:

> 'The matter, however, may be put in another way though with the same effect, *g* and that is on the ground that a representation made as a matter of inducement to enter into a contract is to be treated as a continuing representation. That view of the position was put in *Smith* v. *Kay*[2] by Lord Cranworth. He says of a representation made in negotiation some time before the date of a contract: "It is a continuing representation . . ."'

Lord Wright MR then went on to say, however[3]: *h*

> 'The underlying principle is also stated again in a slightly different application by LORD BLACKBURN in *Brownlie* v. *Campbell*[4]. I need only quote a very short passage. LORD BLACKBURN says: "when a statement or representation has been made in the

j

---

1   [1936] Ch 575 at 584; cf [1936] 1 All ER 727 at 735
2   (1859) 7 HL Cas 750 at 769, 11 ER 299 at 307
3   [1936] 1 All ER 727 at 735, [1936] Ch 575 at 584
4   (1880) 5 App Cas 925 at 950

a *bona fide* belief that it is true, and the party who has made it afterwards comes to find out that it is untrue, and discovers what he should have said, he can no longer honestly keep up that silence on the subject after that has come to his knowledge, thereby allowing the other party to go on, and still more, inducing him to go on, upon a statement which was honestly made at the time when it was made, but which he has not now retracted when he has become aware that it can be no longer honestly persevered in."'

b Lord Wright MR made it clear that the principle is one of wide application when he said[1]:

'I have discussed the law at some little length because the cases to which I have referred show, I think, that this doctrine is not limited to cases of contracts *uberrimae fidei* or to any cases in which owing to confidential relationship there is a peculiar
c duty of disclosure . . .'

In the present case there was abundant evidence on which the Secretary of State could come to the conclusion that the appellant knew that his marriage would be fatal to his request for admission and deliberately refrained from revealing it. In other words, he entered knowing that his visa did not apply to his circumstances. He informed no one of the marriage. He came without his wife. He waited two years before applying for his
d wife to be allowed to join him. One would have expected him to have made an application before leaving Pakistan. One would have expected his wife to have applied as soon as possible if she and her husband both thought that there was a chance for her to be admitted. Bearing in mind the delay there was before his visa was granted one would have expected them to act at once. The other aspect of the case, namely the dependency question, while providing independent grounds for saying he was an illegal
e immigrant, also lends support to the Secretary of State's conclusion in so far as the concealment of the marriage is concerned.

The notes at the top of the application form referred to the consequences of an entry certificate being obtained by concealment of facts 'which the applicant knew to be material', and to a 'change of circumstances'. I believe that people coming from the appellant's own country must have a fairly good idea of the qualifications and
f disqualifications for entry.

In any event, on the facts of this case, I believe that there is evidence of a positive misrepresentation implicit in the presentation of the passport containing the visa worded as it was. I have had the advantage of reading the judgment of Stephenson LJ and I respectfully agree with what he has said on this matter. I have dealt with the wider point because the case was argued on that basis before this court.
g I would dismiss this appeal.

BRANDON LJ. The Secretary of State for the Home Department has treated the appellant as an illegal entrant, that is to say a person who has entered the United
h Kingdom in breach of the immigration laws. The question for decision on this appeal is whether he had reasonable grounds for doing so.

The principle of law applicable appears to me to be that, where a person enters the United Kingdom pursuant to leave to do so which he obtained by deceit, he enters in breach of the immigration laws and is therefore an illegal entrant: *R v Secretary of State for the Home Department, ex parte Hussain*[2] per Geoffrey Lane LJ. The question therefore
j is whether the Secretary of State had reasonable grounds for concluding that the leave to enter which the appellant was given was obtained by him by deceit.

---

1 [1936] 1 All ER 727 at 735, [1936] Ch 575 at 585
2 [1978] 2 All ER 423 at 429, [1978] 1 WLR 700 at 707

There was considerable discussion during the argument in this case, as there has also been in other cases, of the question whether a person seeking leave to enter is under a duty to disclose material facts even if not asked by an immigration officer about them. I do not consider that it is possible to give a simple answer to that question which will apply in all cases. The categories of deceit, in this field as in others, are never closed, and it must be a question of fact in any particular case whether, even though no false answer to a specific question has been given, deceit has nevertheless been practised.

On the facts of this case I agree with Stephenson LJ, a draft of whose judgment I have had the advantage of reading in advance, that there were reasonable grounds on which the Secretary of State could conclude that the appellant, by allowing earlier representations made by him in obtaining his visa to remain uncorrected in circumstances in which an honest person would have corrected them, obtained leave to enter by deceit.

I agree, therefore, that the appeal should be dismissed.

STEPHENSON LJ. I see no need and indeed no reason to decide whether the evidence which the respondent had to consider could properly have satisfied a jury that the appellant was guilty of an offence against s 26(1)(b) of the Immigration Act 1971, nor whether immigrants are under any general duty to disclose information which they are not positively required by immigration officers to furnish. For I am satisfied that the evidence which the Secretary of State had to consider gave him reasonable grounds for deciding: (1) that the appellant had represented to the entry clearance officer on 11th December 1972 when he applied for a visa that he was a boy 15 years of age, unmarried, dependent on his father, and intending to enter this country in order to join his father; (2) that he continued to represent those things (except his age of 15) to the entry clearance officer on 25th November 1975 when he was granted a visa to enter for that purpose; (3) that when he entered this country on 2nd March 1976 he continued to represent those things (with that exception) to the immigration officer with the intention of obtaining leave to enter, when he knew that those things were (with that exception) no longer true because he had married a wife and intended to enter for the different purpose of obtaining employment for himself and her in this country; (4) that by 2nd March 1976 he must have known that those changes in his circumstances might and almost certainly would disqualify him from entering, and might and almost certainly would, if known to the immigration officer, lead him to refuse leave to enter; (5) that the appellant's misrepresentation, not withdrawn or modified, after he knew it had become false, by his disclosing a change of circumstances which he must have known had removed the basis of his claim to admission, but affirmed and continued by his silence when producing his passport and visa, deceived the immigration officer into granting him leave, which he would have refused if the appellant had acted honestly.

I would accordingly regard the Secretary of State as entitled to decide that the appellant had unlawfully entered this country and should be detained and removed, and I too would dismiss the appeal.

I am not sure whether, in approaching the Secretary of State's decision in this way, I am taking even 'a modest step forward' along the path opened or laid down by previous authority, or whether I am in any real disagreement with Lord Widgery CJ in my reason for upholding the Secretary of State's decision. I would confine the duty to disclose to a duty to disclose changes of circumstances 'material to the immigration history', to which Lord Widgery CJ clearly confined it, but I would derive it from the continuation of a would-be entrant's representation of his qualifying status and intention until withdrawn, as I think Lord Widgery CJ might have done had the Divisional Court's attention been directed (as we were) to With v O'Flanagan[1] or the cases there cited, or to criminal cases of continuing false pretences such as those discussed in Russell on Crime[2].

---

1   [1936] 1 All ER 727, [1936] Ch 575
2   12th Edn (1964), vol 2, pp 1179–1180

Appeal dismissed. Leave to appeal to the House of Lords granted.

a

Solicitors: *Sharpe, Pritchard & Co*, agents for *Taylor, Hall-Wright & Co*, Birmingham (for the appellant); *Treasury Solicitor*.

Frances Rustin   Barrister.

b

Gamlen Chemical Co (UK) Ltd v Rochem Ltd and others

c

COURT OF APPEAL, CIVIL DIVISION
GOFF AND TEMPLEMAN LJJ
3rd, 4th DECEMBER 1979

Solicitor – Lien – Retaining lien – Solicitor discharging himself in course of action – Non-payment
d *of costs – Client instructing new solicitor – Client applying for order that papers in action be*
handed over to new solicitor – Whether solicitor who discharges himself required to hand over
papers to new solicitor against undertaking to preserve his lien on the papers – Whether solicitor
entitled to retain papers until court determines whether he had good cause to withdraw from
action – Whether solicitor remaining client's solicitor until order made declaring that he has
ceased to be client's solicitor – RSC Ord 67, r 6(1).

e

In 1974 a firm of solicitors accepted a retainer to represent the defendants in an action. It was an express term of the retainer that the defendants would make periodical payments on account of costs and they paid large sums for costs and disbursements incurred up to 31st March 1978. In a letter dated 2nd February 1979 the solicitors put in a further bill for £21,000. The defendants protested that the bill was excessive and
f although they paid part of it over £12,000 remained outstanding. The solicitors gave several warnings to the defendants that they would apply to the court to be removed from the record if the outstanding costs were not paid. On 25th June they wrote to the defendants giving notice of intention to apply to be removed from the record and on the same day issued a summons under RSC Ord 67, r 6(1)[a] for an order declaring that they had ceased to be the defendants' solicitors. In a letter dated 3rd July they stated that they
g would withdraw the summons if their outstanding costs were paid but would otherwise proceed with the summons. On 9th July the defendants instructed new solicitors and gave notice of change to the original solicitors who in consequence withdrew their summons. On 24th July the judge, on a motion by the defendants, ordered the original solicitors to deliver all the papers in the action to the new solicitors (on the latter undertaking to hold them subject to the original solicitors' lien for costs) on the ground
h that the original solicitors had discharged themselves from the action, and had not been discharged by the defendants, and consequently the court was entitled to make a mandatory order that they hand over the papers to the new solicitors, and the fact that under r 6(1) they remained on the record was irrelevant. The original solicitors appealed from the judge's order contending, inter alia, (i) that they had been discharged by the defendants when the defendants instructed the new solicitors because they were
j unwilling to meet the original solicitors' bill, (ii) that as a matter of law they would have discharged themselves only if they had proceeded with the summons and obtained an order under Ord 67, r 6, but since they had withdrawn the summons they remained

---

a   Rule 6(1), so far as material, is set out at p 1054 *e* to *g, post*

under r 6(1) the defendants' solicitors for all purposes, (iii) to allow the mandatory order to stand would whittle away their lien for costs and thereby cause them hardship, and *a* (iv) they should be allowed to retain the papers until it was determined whether they had had reasonable cause, because of the non-payment of their costs, to discharge themselves.

Held – The appeal would be dismissed for the following reasons—

(i) The practice whereby a solicitor who discharged himself in the course of an action was required to hand over his client's papers to the client's new solicitor, against *b* undertakings to preserve his lien on the papers for costs and to redeliver the papers to him at the end of the litigation, should still be followed because of the overriding principle that a solicitor discharging himself should not be allowed to exert his lien so as to interfere with the course of justice, and therefore the original solicitor only had a qualified lien on the papers. Accordingly, where a solicitor discharged himself the court would normally make a mandatory order obliging him to hand over the client's papers *c* to the new solicitor against an undertaking to preserve his lien (see p 1057 *c*, p 1058 *b* and *d* to *g* and p 1060 *g h*, post); *Heslop v Metcalfe* (1837) 3 My & Cr 183 and *Robins v Goldingham* (1872) LR 13 Eq 440 followed.

(ii) The proper inference from the facts was that the original solicitors had discharged themselves. Moreover, RSC Ord 67, r 6(1), on its true construction, governed the position between the client and other parties to the litigation and not the position *d* between the client and the solicitor on the record. Accordingly, the r 6 did not prevent the ending of the relationship between the solicitor and client before an order was made under the rule (see p 1055 *e f*, p 1057 *e f*, p 1058 *b*, p 1059 *c d h j* and p 1060 *b* to *d*, post).

(iii) Furthermore, the original solicitors were not entitled to retain the papers pending determination of the issue whether they had had good cause to withdraw from the action and (per Templeman LJ) even if they had had reasonable cause to discharge themselves *e* there were no exceptional circumstances which would justify modifying the usual practice that a solicitor who discharged himself was bound to hand over the papers to the new solicitor, against an undertaking as to his lien (see p 1051 *j* to p 1058 *c* and p 1060 *e* to *h*, post); *Heslop v Metcalfe* (1837) 3 My & Cr 183 followed.

Per Templeman LJ. The court will not automatically make a mandatory order obliging a solicitor who discharges himself to hand over the papers to the new solicitor, *f* for the remedy is equitable in character and an automatic order is inconsistent with the inherent jurisdiction of the court to grant or withhold an equitable remedy. In exceptional cases, therefore, the court may impose terms on the mandatory order where justice so requires (see p 1058 *h*, post).

Notes

g

For a solicitor's retaining lien on documents, see 36 Halsbury's Laws (3rd Edn) 173–176, paras 238–240, for the effect on the lien of a change of solicitors, see ibid 178, para 244, and for cases on the subject, see 43 Digest (Repl) 335–338, 3481–3523.

Cases referred to in judgments

Bluck v Lovering & Co (1886) 35 WR 232, 43 Digest (Repl) 57, 458.   *h*

Heslop v Metcalfe (1837) 3 My & Cr 183, 8 Sim 622, 7 LJ Ch 49, 40 ER 894, LC, 43 Digest (Repl) 337, 3508.

Hughes v Hughes [1958] 3 All ER 179, [1958] P 224, [1958] 3 WLR 500, CA, 43 Digest (Repl) 336, 3501.

Robins v Goldingham (1872) LR 13 Eq 440, 41 LJ Ch 813, 25 LT 900, 43 Digest (Repl) 57, 457.   *j*

Webster v Le Hunt (1861) 25 JP 661, 9 WR 804, 43 Digest (Repl) 58, 466.

Interlocutory appeal

By a notice of motion dated 23rd July 1979 Rochem Ltd, Rochem International Ltd and Rochem (Equipment) Ltd, the defendants in an action brought by Gamlen Chemical Co

(UK) Ltd, applied for an order that Amhurst, Brown, Martin & Nicholson, the defendants'
a original solicitors ('the original solicitors'), deliver (on oath if required) to Douglas
Goldberg & Co, the defendants' new solicitors, all papers in the action and all other
documents in the custody or power of the original solicitors relating to the action and
belonging to the defendants or any of them, on the undertaking of counsel for the
defendants on behalf of the new solicitors to hold all the papers and documents delivered
to the new solicitors under the order subject to the original solicitors' lien for costs. By
b a judgment given on 24th July 1979 Oliver J ordered the original solicitors to hand over
the relevant documents in the action to the new solicitors on certain undertakings being
given by counsel for the defendants on behalf of the new solicitors. The original
solicitors appealed. The facts and the terms of Oliver J's order are set out in the judgment
of Goff LJ.

c *Antonio Bueno* and *Elizabeth Anne Gumbel* for the original solicitors.
James Munby for the defendants.

GOFF LJ. This is an appeal from an order of Oliver J, dated 24th July 1979, which he
made on a motion, whereby he ordered as follows:

> **d** 'UPON the undertaking of Counsel for the Defendants Rochem Limited, Rochem
> International Limited and Rochem (Equipment) Limited, on behalf of the solicitors
> for the said defendants (1) To hold all papers and documents delivered to them by
> Amhurst, Brown, Martin & Nicholson under this Order subject to the lien of the
> said Amhurst Brown, Martin & Nicholson for costs (2) to afford the said Amhurst,
> Brown, Martin & Nicholson and their costs draftsman reasonable access to the said
> papers and documents for the purpose of preparing their bill of costs (3) To defend
> **e** this action in an active manner and (4) To re-deliver the said papers and documents
> to the said Amhurst, Brown, Martin & Nicholson after the conclusion of this action
> LET the said Amhurst, Brown, Martin & Nicholson so soon as may be reasonably
> practicable and in any event forthwith upon the receipt by them of written
> authorities from the Defendants [then a number of defendants are named] deliver
> **f** (on Oath if required) to Douglas Goldberg & Company all papers in this action and
> all other documents in the custody or power of the said Amhurst, Brown, Martin
> & Nicholson relating to this action and belonging to the said defendants or any of
> them.'

Messrs Amhurst, Brown, Martin & Nicholson ('the original solicitors') now appeal
against that order.
g The action is a very complicated one in which the plaintiffs, who are associated with
a large American organisation called Sybron Corpn, are suing the three English
companies whose names I have just read out ('the defendants'), and a number of
individual defendants. I need not go into the details of the action, but, shortly, the
plaintiffs allege a conspiracy against all the defendants, and also various torts and breaches
of contract or abuse of fiduciary duty or confidence against individual defendants.
h The original solicitors acted for all the defendants, and it was an express term of the
retainer that the defendants would make periodical payments on account of costs. I do
not think it would make much difference if that were not so, as in my view a solicitor
cannot be required to go on with long and complicated litigation, without being put in
funds, unless of course, he has expressly agreed so to do. But here, as I say, there was in
fact an express agreement to keep the original solicitors in funds.
j In February 1979 a complication presented itself in that the plaintiffs joined one of the
partners in the original solicitors' firm as a defendant alleging that he was a party to the
conspiracy. I wish to make it clear that at this stage nothing whatever has been proved
against him; but in the circumstances, leading counsel advised that he should be
separately represented, and further that the original solicitors might not be able to go on
acting themselves.

I read from their letter of 2nd February 1979 reporting the position to the defendant, Mr Bove, who appears to control or to be the moving spirit of the three defendant companies. They said: *a*

'As you know, Adrian Churchward was served with the amended Writ in this action on the 16th January and as a firm, we have since taken the advice of Mr. Hamilton, Q.C., whose opinion is that Adrian should be separately represented both by Solicitors and Counsel: Messrs. Reynolds Porter Chamberlain and Co. have accordingly been instructed to act on his behalf. Mr. Adrian Hamilton further *b* advised that Adrian Churchward's Solicitors should serve a searching Request for Further and Better Particulars of the amended Statement of Claim as soon as it has been served and, depending on the answers thereto, seriously consider mounting an application to strike out the Statement of Claim on the ground that it discloses no cause of action. He also advised that in the course of argument at the hearing of a search application we should point out that unless Adrian Churchward is dismissed *c* from the action it will be impossible for Amhurst Brown Martin & Nicholson to continue to act for any of the other Defendants, which means that they will all have to go away and find separate solicitors.'

About the same time a dispute arose between the original solicitors and Mr Bove who asserted that the original solicitors' charges were grossly excessive. Again, we cannot try *d* that issue which can only be resolved by taxation. He also said he had no intention of paying any costs until he should know if the action against Mr Churchward would be dismissed.

I read from his letter of 21st February 1979:

'I have carefully considered your letter dated 2nd February, 1979 and can only *e* come to the conclusion that Amhurst Brown would be happy to desert this Case. Your charge of almost £20,000 for the period from 1st April to 31st December is almost equal to your firm's estimated charges for the entire trial put forward in your letter of 9th June 1973. May I remind you that we have not yet been through a 60 day trial and that you have not prepared briefs for Counsel, just to point out two of the more significant items that I assume were included in the £25,000 estimate. *f* My laymans evaluation of the work involved during the 9 month period would be an amount similar to your charges presented on the 25th April, 1978 for the period from September, 1974 to 31st March, 1978, specifically £5,000 to £6,000. Consequently, I am left exasperated concerning your £20,000 bill and do not know how to proceed. This is especially true when I consider the origins of this entire case and the manner in which it has developed. In addition to the above, you leave me with a situation pregnant with the possibility that we will have to seek new *g* solicitors anyway due to [Mr Churchward's] position. At that time we will have to go out and pay entrance fees to new solicitors to learn what we have already paid you to learn ... To be fair, I must point out that until I know if the action against [Mr Churchward] is dismissed, I have no intention of paying anything more than the £5,000 already paid on account.' *h*

The suggestion that the original solicitors would be happy to desert the case is, of course, refuted and was immediately refuted in the correspondence, and some further payments were made, but, in the upshot, first no steps have been taken to get Mr Churchward out of the action, and secondly there is a balance due to the original solicitors, according to their bills of costs, of £12,961, which does not include any disbursements and which the defendants refuse to pay. *j*

On 23rd February 1979 the original solicitors wrote a long letter to Mr Bove, and in the course of that letter they said:

'If you wish to come and discuss the matter, I am perfectly prepared so to do but I would make it clear at this stage that I am not prepared to entertain any reduction

a

in the amount of my firm's fees so that if your reason for suggesting such a meeting is with a view to try to persuade me to agree such a reduction then we will be wasting each other's time. Having said that, as you obviously consider that our bill is excessive, you are entitled to have the same vetted by a Taxing Master and I would be perfectly happy for this to be done. If my firm's costs are not reduced by more than one-fifth, then you would have to pay the costs of the Taxation in addition to the amount allowed on Taxation. However, this operation would take several

b

months and does not solve the present problem, namely that unless my firm's bill is paid in the very near future, then we shall have no alternative but to apply to the Court to be removed from the record. In these circumstances, I am perfectly willing to agree that you should pay the amount of my firm's costs and disbursements without prejudice to your right to call upon us to have the same Taxed as aforesaid. As I have said, the matter is now rather urgent as we must

c

instruct Counsel to settle an Amended Defence, but I am not prepared to incur any further Counsel's fees until my firm's costs have been paid. I regret therefore that I must ask you to accept this letter as formal notice to the three defendant Companies that if the balance of my firm's costs and disbursements as set out in my firm's bill dated the 2nd February 1979, namely the sum of £16,336 [and I interpose there that that was the figure at that time] is not paid to us by Friday the 2nd March 1979,

d

we will issue a Summons on Monday the 5th March 1979 applying for this firm to be removed from the record as solicitors for the three defendant Companies.'

As Mr Bove was then abroad, the original solicitors extended the deadline until 14th March 1979, and on 8th March 1979 they wrote accordingly:

e

'I am prepared to extend the deadline from Monday 5th March 1979 until Wednesday next the 14th March 1979 but if I have heard nothing by that date then I regret it will be necessary to take the course outlined in my letter of the 23rd February.'

The dispute dragged on after that, and as I have said certain payments were made but the net balance increased to the figure I have mentioned, over £12,000, and on 25th June

f

1979 the original solicitors wrote as follows:

'These circumstances leave me no alternative but to apply to the Court for my firm to be removed from the record as solicitors for the three Defendant companies and a copy of the Summons will be served upon the Companies direct. Furthermore, as my firm's position as regards costs has not been secured, I am writing to all the personal Defendants for whom my firm acts informing them that my firm can no

g

longer act for them unless our position as regards costs is secured satisfactorily,'

and they did, in fact, issue a summons that very day, under RSC Ord 67, r 6, the return day of which was 26th July, and they served it the next day. That summons, as far as material, reads as follows:

h

'... for an Order declaring that the said Amhurst Brown Martin & Nicholson have ceased to be the solicitors acting for the said Defendants in the above action and that the costs of this application be taxed and paid by the said Defendants.'

They also applied for similar relief against the individual defendants.

The matter came before Master Ball on 31st July 1979 and was adjourned by him to give the individual defendants an opportunity of reconsidering their position, but before then letters were written to each defendant on 3rd July in precisely the same form, and

j

I quote from one of them:

'Although Rochem International Limited have paid our costs and disbursements in respect of the period from the commencement of the action down to and including the 31st March 1978, we regret to inform you that a substantial part of our costs for the period from the 1st April 1978 down to the 30th April 1979 remains unpaid. We hope you will readily appreciate that we cannot continue to act either for you or any of the other defendants in regard to this action unless our *a* position in respect of costs is secured. We have accordingly issued a Summons for an Order declaring that we have ceased being the solicitors acting for you in this action and we enclose a copy of such Summons herewith ... If the whole of our outstanding costs have been paid before the said Summons comes on for hearing, then we will be happy to continue to act for you in this action and will withdraw the said Summons. However, if such costs are not paid, then we regret that we shall *b* have no alternative but to seek the order mentioned in such Summons.'

After the matter had come before Master Ball and he had adjourned it, a letter was written to the individual defendants asking four questions:

'(1) Do you wish us to continue to act for you in this action? (2) If so, have you any proposals to make with regard to the satisfaction of the costs dealing with your *c* individual defence? (3) If you have no such proposals to make, do you intend to appoint other solicitors to act for you in this action in our stead? (4) If you do not intend to instruct other solicitors to act for you in this action in our stead, do you intend to file Notice that you will be acting in person in this action in our stead?'

The matter came again before Master Chamberlain on 3rd September, when he made the order as asked against the individual defendants. In the meantime, the original *d* solicitors' summons against the defendant companies was overtaken by events as, on 9th July, the first three defendants instructed new solicitors who duly gave notice of change and applied for and obtained the order now under appeal.

At this stage I must read the relevant order, which is RSC Ord 67, r 6, and so far as material it is in these terms. It is headed 'Withdrawal of Solicitors who have ceased to act for Party': *e*

'(1) Where a solicitor who has acted for a party in a cause or matter has ceased so to act and the party has not given notice of change in accordance with rule 1 ... the solicitor may apply to the Court for an order declaring that the solicitor has ceased to be the solicitor acting for the party in the cause or matter, and the Court or the Court of Appeal, as the case may be, may make an order accordingly, but unless and *f* until the solicitor—(a) serves on every party to the cause or matter (not being a party in default as to entry of appearance) a copy of the order, and (b) procures the order to be entered in the district registry or other appropriate office mentioned in rule 1(2), and (c) leaves at that office a copy of the order and a certificate signed by him that the order has been duly served as aforesaid, he shall, subject to the foregoing provisions of this Order be considered the solicitor of the party till the final *g* conclusion of the cause or matter, whether in the High Court or Court of Appeal...'

Oliver J based his judgment on an old case of *Robins v Goldingham*[1] and he said:

'The principles, I think, are fairly clear; that is to say, that if a client discharges a solicitor the solicitors lien endures and the court has no right (or no title) to call for the documents to be handed over. But, if the solicitor has discharged himself in the *h* course of an action, then the order which is sought on this motion seems to follow as a course, and there is authority for that in *Robins v Goldingham*[1] to which I have been referred. [Then, after reviewing that case, he went on:] I am bound to say, I find the present case really almost wholly indistinguishable from *Robins v Goldingham*[1]. Counsel [for the original solicitors] has forcefully argued that as a result of the rule [ie RSC Ord 67, r 6(1)] to which I have referred, the original *j* solicitors remained on the record, but I do not think that is the point. It seems to me that they have unequivocally intimated, both by taking out the summons on

25th June and then in their further letter of 3rd July, that they were not prepared
a to go on unless some arrangement was made as to their costs. That seems to me to
be a clear case of the solicitor discharging himself.'

Counsel for the original solicitors, who has argued this case very forcefully before this
court also, and has said all that can possibly be said on behalf of his client's case, takes
three points on that judgment. First he says that, in so far as *Robins v Goldingham*[1] was a
decision on the facts, it is distinguishable and he submits that Oliver J should have drawn
b the opposite inference on the facts of this case, secondly he says that *Robins v Goldingham*[1]
was wrongly decided and he asks us to overrule it, and thirdly he repeats the submission
referred to in the extract which I have read from the judgment on the construction of the
rule.

I am wholly unable to accept the first of these contentions. He suggested the following
grounds for distinguishing the two cases. First the correspondence here shows that the
c original solicitors were willing to continue if their costs were paid, whereas the report of
Robins v Goldingham[1] shows that a later letter was written in which the solicitors in that
case positively refused to go on. Secondly he points to the initial agreement in the
present case to pay by instalments as the matter progressed, which he said was not so in
Robins v Goldingham[1]. Thirdly he points out that we have in the present case the
additional element that Mr Bove invoked Mr Churchward's position as a ground for
d refusing to pay the costs.

I agree that each case must depend on its own facts, but in my judgment Oliver J's
view of the inference to be drawn from the facts in the present case was clearly right.

Counsel for the original solicitors said that all his clients were doing was to fire
'warning shots' across the defendants 'bow', but after earlier warnings they took up a
categorical position by their letter of 25th June and by issuing and serving a summons
e forthwith, and that under a rule which applies where a solicitor has ceased to act, and, as
Oliver J pointed out, they emphasised that position in their letters of 3rd July.

For my part, I do not think that they can complain and say 'We did not discharge
ourselves; you discharged us', because the defendants, not being willing to meet the bill,
took the original solicitors at their word and instructed other solicitors and therefore I see
nothing in the first suggested ground of distinction .
f The second is, in my judgment, really insignificant because an agreement to make
interim payment would ordinarily be implied, but in any event there was such an
express bargain in *Bluck v Lovering & Co*[2], in which *Robins v Goldingham*[1] was followed,
and, with all respect to the argument, the third point seems to me to be quite irrelevant
as a ground of distinction.

The attack on *Robins v Goldingham*[1] is mounted on several grounds. First, it is said that
g the court assumed that the solicitor would keep his lien if he was ordered to deliver up
the documents without prejudice to it, and on an undertaking to return them, which
may be technically right, but is not so in fact, and therefore (so the argument runs) the
premise on which the case proceeded was bad. Secondly, he relies on the hardship which
will be inflicted on a solicitor if his lien is whittled away in this way, but that again has
to be balanced against the hardship which will be inflicted on the client if, in the middle
h of the case, he has to change his solicitor and is unable to get hold of the relevant
papers. Thirdly he said that the position is now quite different because when *Robins v
Goldingham*[1] was decided, one was faced with impoverished litigants, whereas now there
is no such problem because of legal aid. Fourthly, he pointed out, perfectly correctly,
that prior to 1932 a solicitor could not get himself removed from the record, but I cannot

j

---

1   (1872) LR 13 Eq 440
2   (1886) 35 WR 232

see how that point affects the matter, save possibly with regard to the third limb of the original solicitors' case, the construction of the rule. Fifthly, counsel for the original *a* solicitors said the client can secure the costs pending taxation, but that does not necessarily save him from hardship or even disaster.

So far as legal aid is concerned, I cannot accept that as any ground for saying the law should now be different or that we should overrule *Robins v Goldingham*[1] because it is well known that there are many litigants whose capital or income is sufficiently large to disqualify them for legal aid, but not sufficient to enable them to proceed with *b* complicated litigation without great difficulty and hardship, and in any case in the present case we are dealing with companies who are not entitled to legal aid.

The problem may have ceased to apply to a number, perhaps a large number of litigants, but the problem is still there and the decision on principle must, as has been observed, fit all cases.

So it really comes down to the first two points: that the order which has been made, *c* if allowed to stand, will whittle away the lien contrary to the assumed basis on which *Robins v Goldingham*[1] proceeded and, secondly, the question of hardship.

In the course of the argument it turned out, although it did not appear from the judgment itself, that *Robins v Goldingham*[1] was one of a number of cases all pointing in the same direction. There is *Bluck v Lovering & Co*[2], which I have already mentioned, and *Webster v Le Hunt*[3], to which we were also referred.   *d*

We did not call on counsel for the defendants but he told us that he would have cited many more such cases. Be that as it may, the distinction on which *Robins v Goldingham*[1] proceeded between a solicitor who is discharged by his client and is, therefore, entitled to retain the papers even in the course of litigation, and the solicitor who discharges himself was clearly recognised in Mr Ormrod QC's argument in *Hughes v Hughes*[4], as late as 1958, where he said[5]: 'An important distinction is drawn between (1) a solicitor who *e* discharges himself, (2) a solicitor who is still acting, and (3) a solicitor who is discharged by his client.'

Mr Ormrod cited three cases in support of that analysis, and we have been referred to one of them, namely *Heslop v Metcalfe*[6], which seems to me to be of the utmost significance in this case, and to afford conclusive reasons why we should not at this late stage reverse the decision in *Robins v Goldingham*[1], because *Heslop v Metcalfe*[6] shows quite *f* clearly that in those days the court had fully adverted to the factual effect on the lien on the making of such an order, and to the hardship which it would impose on a solicitor.

Lord Cottenham LC, giving judgment in that case, said[7]:

'Undoubtedly, that doctrine may expose a solicitor to a very great inconvenience and hardship, if, after embarking in a cause, he finds that he cannot get the necessary funds wherewith to carry it on. But, on the other hand, extreme hardship *g* might arise to the client if—to take the case which is not uncommon in the smaller practice in the country—a solicitor, who finds a poor man having a good claim, and having but a small sum of money at his command, may go until that fund is

h

---

1   (1872) LR 13 Eq 440
2   (1886) 35 WR 232
3   (1861) 9 WR 804   *j*
4   [1958] 3 All ER 179, [1958] P 224
5   [1958] P 224 at 226
6   (1872) LR 13 Eq 440
7   3 My & Cr 183 at 188, 40 ER 894 at 896

a   exhausted, and then, refusing to proceed further, may hang up the cause by
withholding the papers in his hands. That would be great grievance and means of
oppression to a poor client, who, with the clearest right in the world, might still be
without the means of employing another solicitor. The rule of the Court must be
adapted to every case that may occur, and be calculated to protect suitors against
such conduct.'

b   Then later in his judgment Lord Cottenham LC said[1]:

'I then take the law as laid down by Lord Eldon, and, adopting that law, must
hold that Mr. Blunt is not to be permitted to impose upon the Plaintiff the necessity
of carrying on his cause in an expensive, inconvenient, and disadvantageous
manner. I think the principle should be, that the solicitor claiming the lien should
have every security not inconsistent with the progress of the cause.'

c   So all the misgivings that one might have in one's mind, which I confess I have had in
my mind during certain stages of the argument, were there considered and set at rest.
In my judgment, therefore, I would not think it right to overrule *Robins v Goldingham*[2].
That leaves the third head of the argument which is this: that having regard to the
latter part of RSC Ord 67, r 6(1), the original solicitors necessarily continued as the
solicitors for the defendants for all purposes, no order having been obtained on their
d   summons and, therefore, the steps referred to in the earlier part of the order of necessity
not having been taken. He relies on the words '. . . shall, subject to the foregoing
provisions of this Order, be considered the solicitor of the party till the final conclusion
of the cause or matter, whether in the High Court, or the Court of Appeal'.
In my judgment, however, that rule is not dealing with the relationship between the
solicitor on the record and his client, but the position as between other parties to the
e   litigation and the client, they being entitled, until the appropriate steps have been taken
to change the record, to regard the solicitor as being still the solicitor, and to serve him
with pleadings, notices and so forth.
I think that must be the right conclusion for two reasons: first, the opening words of
r 6 refer to a solicitor who has ceased to act, so that the argument would mean that the
latter part of the rule was inconsistent with the former; and secondly, the qualifications
f   in paras (a), (b) and (c) of r 6(1) show quite clearly that the rule is dealing only with
matters of procedure.
These reasons are sufficient to dispose of this appeal, but before I conclude my
judgment, I think I should say a few words about two other points which counsel for the
original solicitors took in his persuasive argument. He said, as is true, that a solicitor can
withdraw for good cause and 'good cause' is 'non payment'. But we cannot decide the
g   questions which the defendants have raised when they say that the original solicitors'
charges are excessive, and also a further charge which they have made, of some kind of
negligence or breach of duty on the part of the original solicitors. They have not yet
formulated that in any definite terms, but one way is suggested in the correspondence in
that they allowed their partner, then an assistant solicitor, to become so involved that the
plaintiffs have seen fit to add him as a defendant. There may be absolutely nothing in
h   this at all, but Mr Churchward still remains a party, and the allegation that he did join
the conspiracy still remains on the record. As it seems to me, we cannot decide the
question of 'good cause' either on the point of the allegation that the charges are excessive
or on the second ground.
The other point is this: counsel for the original solicitors submits that we should
protect the lien until these questions can be decided, but that, as it seems to me, merely
j   brings us back again to the question of hardship, with which I have already dealt, the
overriding principle being that a solicitor who has discharged himself is not allowed so

---

1   (1837) 3 My & Cr 183 at 190, 40 ER 894 at 897
2   (1872) LR 13 Eq 440

to exert his lien as to interfere with the course of justice; he has, as it has been put, only a qualified lien.

Finally, he argued that the conduct of the defendants was repudiatory in refusing to pay the costs, and he says that the original solicitors have accepted that repudiation, but that again can only be right if the defendants are wrong on the points which they have taken, and I do not see how it can affect our judgment at this stage.

For these reasons I agree with the judgment given by the learned judge below, and I would dismiss this appeal.

TEMPLEMAN LJ. I entirely agree. This appeal illustrates the difficulties which arise when a client and his solicitor part company in the midst of litigation. A solicitor who accepts a retainer to act for a client in the prosecution or defence of an action engages that he will continue to act until the action is ended, subject however to his costs being paid. That principle was reaffirmed in *Bluck v Lovering & Co*[1].

If before the action is ended the client determines the retainer, the solicitor may, subject to certain exceptions not here material, exercise a possessory lien over the client's papers until payment of the solicitor's costs and disbursements. Thus in *Hughes v Hughes*[2] Hodson LJ said:

'There is no doubt that a solicitor who is discharged by his client during an action otherwise than for misconduct can retain any papers in the cause in his possession until the costs have been paid. . . This rule applies, as the authorities show, whether the client's papers are of any intrinsic value or not. . .'

The solicitor himself may determine his retainer during an action, for reasonable cause, such as the failure of the client to keep the solicitor in funds to meet his costs and disbursements; but in that case the solicitor's possessory lien, ie his right to retain the client's papers of any intrinsic value or not, is subject to the practice of the court which, in order to save the client's litigation from catastrophe, orders the solicitor to hand over the client's papers to the clients' new solicitors, provided the new solicitors undertake to preserve the original solicitor's lien and to return the papers to the original solicitors, for what they are worth, after the end of the litigation.

This practice was settled many years ago, and as Goff LJ has shown, from the citation which he gave of *Heslop v Metcalfe*[3]; there are convincing reasons why the practice should be followed, and it has been followed in *Webster v Le Hunt*[4] in 1861, *Robins v Goldingham*[5] in 1872 and is to be found also in the argument of counsel in *Hughes v Hughes*[6] in 1958.

Where the solicitor has himself discharged his retainer, the court then will normally make a mandatory order obliging the original solicitor to hand over the client's papers to the new solicitor against an undertaking by the new solicitor to preserve the lien of the original solicitor.

I wish to guard myself against possible exceptions to this general rule. The court in fact is asked to make a mandatory order obliging the original solicitors to hand over the papers to the new solicitors. An automatic order is inconsistent with the inherent, albeit judicial discretion of the court, to grant or withhold a remedy which is equitable in character. It may be, therefore, that in exceptional cases the court might impose terms where justice so required. For example, if the papers are valueless after the litigation is ended and if the client accepts that he is indebted to the original solicitor for an agreed sum and has no counterclaim, or accepts that the solicitor has admittedly paid out

1   (1886) 35 WR 232
2   [1958] 3 All ER 179 at 180, [1958] P 224 at 227–228
3   (1837) 3 My & Cr 183 at 188, 40 ER 894 at 896
4   (1861) 25 JP 661
5   (1872) LR 13 Eq 440
6   [1958] 3 All ER 179, [1958] P 224

reasonable and proper disbursements, which must be repaid, the court might make an
a   order which would only compel the original solicitor to hand over the papers to the new
solicitor, on the usual terms preserving the lien but providing that in the first place the
client pays to the original solicitor a sum, fixed by the court, representing the whole or
part of the moneys admittedly due from the client to the original solicitor. Much would
depend on the nature of the case, the stage which the litigation had reached, the conduct
of the solicitor and the client respectively, and the balance of hardship which might
b   result from the order the court is asked to make.

Applying those principles, the following questions arise in the present case. Firstly,
did the original solicitors discharge the client or did the client discharge the solicitors?
Secondly, if the original solicitors discharged the client, was there reasonable cause for the
solicitors to do so? Thirdly, if there was reasonable cause for the solicitors to discharge
the client, and the solicitors did do so, should the court impose terms on the delivery of
c   the client's papers and documents by the original solicitors to the new solicitor other than
the term which requires the new solicitor to undertake to preserve the lien of the original
solicitors?

As to the first question, in my judgment the evidence clearly shows that it was the
original solicitors who discharged the client. The writ was issued in August 1974; the
relevant clients gave and the original solicitors accepted a retainer to represent the
d   defendants in the action. The clients paid large sums for disbursements and costs
necessarily incurred in complicated interlocutory and other matters to 1st April 1978.
Goff LJ has read the letter dated 2nd February 1979, in which the original solicitors
warned the client that it might be necessary for all the defendants to have separate
representation. At the same time, the solicitors did not at that stage take the step of
advising the clients to go elsewhere, and it was in that letter, as Goff LJ has said, that the
e   original solicitors put in a bill for £21,523. The clients replied, protesting that the
charge ought to be £5,000 or £6,000 and not £20,000, and complaining that 'In
addition to the above, you leave me with the situation pregnant with the possibility that
we will have to seek new solicitors anyway'. On 23rd February 1979, again in a letter
which Goff LJ has read, the original solicitors pointed out that the client was entitled to
taxation and continued: 'However this operation would take several months', and asked
f   the clients to accept the letter as formal notice that if the balance then due exceeding
£16,000 was not paid by Friday, 2nd March, they would issue a summons on 5th March
applying for the solicitors' firm to be removed from the record as solicitors for the three
defendant companies. The deadline was extended until 14th March; there was then a
certain amount of correspondence and payment on account; a further bill was rendered,
and on 11th June, the solicitors gave a seven-day ultimatum saying that if it was not
g   complied with they would have no alternative but to apply to the court to be removed
from the record. Finally the solicitors on 25th June said they were going to apply to the
court, and they did apply to the court by summons of the following day returnable in
July.

In my judgment, not later than the issue and service of this summons, the original
solicitors discharged themselves from their retainer by the clients, subject to the clients
h   accepting the position or paying the original solicitors the amount which they demanded
exceeding £12,000-odd. The clients elected to accept the situation and did so; they
accepted that the original solicitors had withdrawn, and not unnaturally in those
circumstances consulted fresh solicitors who, on 10th and 11th July, gave a written
notice of change and asked the original solicitors to confirm that the summons dated
26th June would be withdrawn.

j   As a result, the original solicitors wrote saying that they did not propose to proceed
with the summons. It follows that the clients, besides disputing the amount of costs
which the original solicitors claimed, also felt a grievance (rightly or wrongly) revolving
round the complication caused by the allegations that a partner in the firm in the original
solicitors had become involved personally in the litigation, and the delay which had
taken place clarifying the position with regard to representation and conflict of interest.

At present, there are no means of knowing whether the original solicitors will be held to be entitled to recover the whole or part of the costs which they claim. They have been *a* paid their disbursements.

Counsel for the original solicitors submitted that all the correspondence which Goff LJ has read, and the issue of the summons, did not amount to the discharge of the client by the solicitors. The solicitors, he said, were discharged by the client when the client instructed fresh solicitors, and that new firm gave notice of change. Goff LJ has already dealt with that argument, and I agree that on a plain reading of the correspondence, it *b* was the original solicitors who, as between themselves and the clients, discharged the clients. The clients then took the step which they were entitled to do, of accepting the repudiation by the original solicitors, and instructed fresh solicitors.

Counsel submitted that, as a matter of law, the original solicitors would only have discharged themselves if they had proceeded with the summons and obtained an order under RSC Ord 67, r 6. That rule has been read and analysed by Goff LJ, and I agree that *c* it governs the position as between the litigants and third parties but has nothing to do with the position as between a client and his own solicitor. The rule plainly implies that a summons will be taken out and an order made after the solicitors have ceased to act, and the provisos to the rule make clear its object, which is to safeguard third parties. It is not a rule which is appropriate to prevent the ending of the relationship of solicitor and client as between them before an order is made under the rule. *d*

I have no doubt that in the present circumstances it was the solicitors who discharged their retainer from the clients.

The second question is whether the original solicitors had reasonable cause to discharge themselves. They were unable to obtain payment of the costs which they claimed to be due, or to reach agreement about the payment of future costs and disbursements. For the purposes of this motion I assume they were not bound to go on. But if the original *e* solicitors had reasonable cause to discharge themselves, and did so, they are, nevertheless, for the reasons given in *Heslop v Metcalfe*[1], to which I have already referred and which Goff LJ has read, bound to hand over the papers of the clients to their new solicitors, against the undertaking of the new solicitors to preserve the lien, for what it is worth, unless there are exceptional circumstances which justify some modification of the usual practice. *f*

That raises the third question, namely are there exceptional reasons why the court should impose terms on the clients modifying the usual practice? In my judgment, there are no grounds for modifying the usual practice. This action was begun in 1974; the original solicitors acted until June 1979 and the action was set down for March 1980, possibly a little optimistically by now. Whether the clients this day can lay their hands on the money to pay the original solicitors' demands, I know not, but the clients dispute *g* the original solicitors' right to be paid in principle and in quantum. It would be disastrous for the clients if their new solicitors could not, at this stage, obtain the papers held by the original solicitors.

For these reasons, and the reasons given by Oliver J and by Goff LJ, I agree that the appeal must be dismissed.

h

Appeal dismissed.

Solicitors: *Amhurst, Brown, Martin & Nicholson*; *Douglas Goldberg & Co* (for the defendants).

Frances Rustin   Barrister.

---

1   (1837) 3 My & Cr 183, 40 ER 894

Re J S (a minor)

COURT OF APPEAL, CIVIL DIVISION

ORR AND ORMROD LJJ

17th, 18th DECEMBER 1979, 22nd JANUARY 1980

Ward of court – Jurisdiction – Declaration of paternity – Whether jurisdiction in wardship proceedings to make bare declaration of paternity – Whether discretion to make declaration should be exercised – Whether court should order blood tests in wardship proceedings – Family Law Reform Act 1969, s 20.

The mother, who lived with R but also had sexual relations with the plaintiff, gave birth to a child in September 1975. The plaintiff claimed that he was the father and took out an originating summons making the child a ward of court. The mother and R were the defendants to the summons. The plaintiff applied for an order for blood tests, under s 20 of the Family Law Reform Act 1969, and although no order was made blood samples were taken from the plaintiff, the mother and the child but not from R who refused to give a sample of his blood. Tests on the samples did not exclude the plaintiff from being the father. The plaintiff issued a summons in the wardship proceedings applying, inter alia, for a declaration that he was the child's father. Because of procedural difficulties the judge assumed jurisdiction and did not hear argument on the court's jurisdiction to grant a bare declaration of paternity. Having considered the serological evidence the judge concluded that on the preponderance of probabilities the plaintiff had not proved he was the father, and dismissed the summons. The plaintiff appealed.

Held – The appeal would be dismissed for the following reasons—

(1) There was no jurisdiction under wardship proceedings to grant a bare declaration of paternity, for such a declaration was not directly relevant to the issues normally dealt with in wardship proceedings. Nor did the court have an inherent jurisdiction to grant such a declaration. Accordingly the judge should have dismissed the summons for want of jurisdiction (see p 1065 c to e, post); *Aldrich v Attorney-General* [1968] 1 All ER 345 applied.

(2) In any event, even assuming that the judge had jurisdiction to make a declaration of paternity, it was a discretionary jurisdiction and ought not, in the particular circumstances, to have been exercised, because—

(a) a declaration of paternity, being merely a finding of fact binding inter parties and made without reference to any specific legal issue between the parties, would prejudge such legal issues and might therefore adversely affect the child's interests by, for example, precluding him from asserting that R was his father (see p 1065 f to h, post);

(b) the court should not exercise the discretion to make a bare declaration of paternity unless the evidence of paternity was conclusive or very nearly so, for the degree of probability in a paternity issue had to be commensurate with the importance of the decision on the issue; and probability in the legal sense differed from mathematical probability of paternity on the serological evidence (see p 1065 h to p 1066 e, post);

(c) the issue of paternity should not be tried in wardship proceedings unless determination of the issue would have a material bearing on some other issue in the proceedings and it was in the child's interest that its paternity should be investigated, in which case there should be an order for the trial of the paternity issue. Since the child had a secure relationship with the mother and R, who fully accepted his role as de facto father with knowledge that there was doubt whether he was the natural father, the issue of paternity should not be allowed to disturb that relationship, and, in any event, paternity could not be conclusively proved without a sample of R's blood, which he had refused to give (see p 1066 g to p 1067 b, post).

Per Curiam. In wardship cases, orders under Part III of the 1969 Act for the use of blood tests should only be made if it appears to be in the child's interests that such tests *a* should be carried out and the results are likely to be conclusive, ie the other adults concerned are willing to provide blood samples (see p 1067 *b*, post).

Notes

For the principles on which the court acts in exercising its jurisdiction over wards of court, see 24 Halsbury's Laws (4th Edn) para 594. *b*

For the power of the court to require use of blood tests, see 1 ibid para 685.

For the Family Law Reform Act 1969, Part III (ss 20–25), see 40 Halsbury's Statutes (3rd Edn) 615.

Cases referred to in judgment

Aldrich v Attorney-General [1968] 1 All ER 345, [1968] P 281, [1968] 2 WLR 413, 32 *c* Digest (Reissue) 24, *168*.

Bater v Bater [1950] 2 All ER 458, [1951] P 35, 114 JP 416, 48 LGR 466, CA, 27(1) Digest (Reissue) 364, *2653*.

Hornal v Neuberger Products Ltd [1956] 3 All ER 970, [1957] 1 QB 247, [1956] 3 WLR 1034, CA, 22 Digest (Reissue) 47, *268*.

L, Re [1968] 1 All ER 20, [1968] P 119, [1967] 3 WLR 1645, CA, 32 Digest (Reissue) 24, *d* *170*.

Interlocutory appeal

By an originating summons dated 14th October 1975 issued by the plaintiff against the first defendant, the mother of a minor, the plaintiff applied to have the minor made a ward of court, and by a notice of wardship the minor became a ward of court on that *e* date. By an order dated 6th November a man, Mr R, with whom the mother was living was made the second defendant to the wardship proceedings. By an order dated 19th June 1978 the Official Solicitor was appointed guardian ad litem of the minor. By a summons dated 15th May 1979 issued in the wardship proceedings the plaintiff applied for an order (i) that he be declared the father of the minor and (ii) that he be granted reasonable access to the minor. By an order made on 30th July Heilbron J ordered (i) *f* that, the issue of paternity having been tried and the court not being satisfied that the plaintiff was the minor's father, the summons dated 15th May 1979 be dismissed, and (ii) that the minor cease forthwith to be a ward of court and the originating summons dated 14th October 1975 be dismissed. The plaintiff appealed from that order. The facts are set out in the judgment of the court.

g

Swinton Thomas QC and *Anthony Hunter* for the plaintiff.
Anthony Hollis QC and *Caroline Willbourne* for the mother.
Mr R appeared in person.
Mathew Thorpe for the minor.

h

Cur adv vult

22nd January. **ORMROD LJ** read the folllowing judgment of the court: This is an appeal from an order of Heilbron J in wardship proceedings relating to a little boy, born on 28th September 1975. The plaintiff is a man whom I will refer to as Mr J, who claims to be the father of this, admittedly, illegitimate child. The learned judge's order was as *j* follows:

'It is ordered that:
'1. The issue of Paternity having been tried and the Court not being satisfied that the Plaintiff is the father of the minor, [JS], the said Plaintiff's summons dated 15th May 1979 be and is hereby dismissed.

'2. The said minor do cease to be a Ward of this Court forthwith and the originating summons herein be and the same is hereby dismissed.'

It is plain from that order that this is a most unusual case. It also raises a number of points of considerable difficulty and importance.

The facts are not in dispute. The mother is a qualified teacher. From 1972 to the present time she has lived in what the judge called a 'continuous relationship' with the second defendant, Mr R, mostly in the London area, except for periods when she was working as a teacher elsewhere. She usually returned 'home' to Mr R at weekends. They have not married because they do not think it is necessary or desirable to do so.

During one of these periods at the end of 1974 she was working away from London and met Mr J. The learned judge found that sexual intercourse took place between the mother and Mr J on two occasions only, namely after a party in November 1974 and during the weekend of 2nd/3rd January 1975. She also had intercourse with Mr R several times at weekends between September and February 1975. In February 1975 she returned to live with Mr R. She said that she had also had sexual relations with a third man, David, in December 1974.

In June 1975 the mother, to her surprise, found that she was five months pregnant. Her periods had apparently always been irregular and, on advice, she had ceased taking the pill in August 1974 and had taken no other precautions, believing herself to be infertile. At the same time she wrote a letter to Mr J, saying, 'I don't know whose baby it is, it could be yours or it could be Chris's [ie Mr R's]'. She added that she would have the child adopted.

After the baby was born she changed her mind and decided to keep the child. Mr R was aware of the circumstances and accepted the position so that, since birth, the child has lived with his mother and Mr R in what, to all intents and purposes, is a normal family except that the adults have not married.

Mr J's response was unexpected. He became obsessed with the thought of the child and insisted on coming to see him. The mother allowed him to visit her from time to time to see the baby, but his visits became increasingly embarrassing and his attitude to the child was more and more obsessive. These visits effectively ceased in 1977. Mr J then became hostile to the mother and Mr R, making threats and even informing the Supplementary Benefits Commission that he thought the mother was defrauding them. He is now obsessed with the desire to obtain a declaration that he is the father of this boy and would, if he could, oust Mr R from the child's life.

The proceedings in this case have been protracted and confused and must have caused great distress and anxiety to the mother and Mr R, whose only wish is to be left in peace to bring the child up as normally as they can. Irregularities in procedure have led to a situation which might have been avoided had the mother and Mr R been legally represented throughout the early stages.

The originating summons was issued as long ago as 14th October 1975. Although intituled in the Guardianship of Minors Acts 1971 and 1973, as well as in the Law Reform (Miscellaneous Provisions) Act 1949, the case has been dealt with throughout under the wardship jurisdiction.

The matter first came before the court on 6th November 1975, when the senior registrar continued the wardship and ordered that Mr R be made a defendant. Neither the mother nor Mr R were present or represented, but counsel for the plaintiff applied for an order for blood tests under s 20 of the Family Law Reform Act 1969. The senior registrar indicated that he would make an order for blood tests on Mr J, the mother, Mr R and the child, but directed that the order should not be drawn up without the consent of the mother's solicitors. The child, of course, was not represented at that stage. The order was never drawn up because no consent was given. However, in November 1976 blood samples were taken from Mr J, the mother and the child. Unfortunately, the mother had discharged her solicitors in August 1976 and was eventually persuaded by Mr J to agree to provide samples from herself and the child. Mr R declined to provide a blood sample.

On 19th November 1976 Professor Barbara Dodd reported on the blood tests on Mr J, the mother and the child. The result was a disappointment to the mother because they *a* did not exclude Mr J as the father. According to the report Mr J was among one per cent of men of Western European origin who could be the father of this child.

On 30th March 1977 an application was made by the plaintiff for a direction that a blood sample be taken from Mr R. The matter came before his Honour Judge Barr, sitting as a deputy High Court Judge. The mother and Mr R appeared in person, Mr J by counsel and the child was still not represented. A direction in terms of the summons was *b* made, but Mr R declined to comply with it. There the matter rested until June 1978 when Mr J issued a summons for access to the child and for the restoration of the originating summons. On 19th June 1978 this summons came on before Heilbron J, who gave directions for statements to be filed by the mother and Mr R and ordered that the Official Solicitor be appointed guardian ad litem to the child. The mother and Mr R were still not legally represented. *c*

It should be noted that the only issue before the court at this stage was that of access to the child by Mr J; no order for the trial of an issue as to paternity had been made or applied for, so that no consideration had been given by the court whether the trial of such an issue would be in the interests of the child or not.

The Official Solicitor submitted his report to the court on 5th October 1978. This report contained a summary of the facts of the case and a clear intimation that the *d* Official Solicitor did not consider that access would be in the best interests of the child. This recommendation can have surprised nobody since it was clear on the affidavit evidence that Mr J had had no contact with the child since soon after birth and had admittedly behaved to the mother in such a way as to make any relationship between them virtually impossible. However, the Official Solicitor did recommend, notwith-standing that no issue as to paternity had been ordered and that the mother was *e* contending that it was not in the child's interest to pursue the question of paternity, that the court should determine it.

The matter came on for hearing before Heilbron J in May 1979 in that state. No doubt, as the evidence emerged, it quickly became apparent that the question of access was a foregone conclusion. All the indications were that access by Mr J could only be harmful to the child, even if he were the natural or biological father. The question of the *f* child's paternity had, therefore, become irrelevant to the decision of the only issue before the court.

In this state of things counsel for the plaintiff at a very late stage, so late according to the learned judge that there was little opportunity for argument, applied for leave to issue a summons out of time asking that 'the plaintiff be declared the father of the minor defendant'. No objection was made and leave was given. *g*

This was the last of several unfortunate errors or irregularities in this case and it was a serious one, for it deprived the learned judge, as she herself observed in her judgment, of the benefit of hearing argument on the most important issue in the case, namely whether the court has jurisdiction to grant a bare declaration of paternity. The learned judge decided to assume in the plaintiff's favour that there was jurisdiction and so proceeded to consider whether she should exercise it. Here she was in a difficulty. *h* Counsel for the mother submitted that it would be wiser on the existing state of the evidence not to determine the paternity issue, since it was obviously unnecessary to do so in the circumstances; counsel for the Official Solicitor, however, urged that it would be better for the court to determine it. So the learned judge considered the evidence and arrived at the conclusion that she was 'not satisfied on the preponderance of probabilities that the plaintiff had proved that he is the father of this child'. It is from that conclusion *j* that the plaintiff now appeals.

The first question in the appeal is whether there is jurisdiction to make an order declaring that A is the father of B. The court, of course, has from time to time to decide the issue of paternity in order to resolve some other issue between the parties, although it is rarely necessary to do so in wardship proceedings: *Re L*[1] was such a case. Biological

a parentage usually has little effect on the problems which the court normally handles in such proceedings.

There is certainly no statutory power to grant such a declaration, for there is no analogue to the powers now contained in the Matrimonial Causes Act 1973, s 45, to grant by decree, declarations of legitimacy, legitimation, or the validity of marriage. The lack of any comparable procedure to determine the paternity of an illegitimate child may

b considerably reduce the practical efficacy of the policy of eliminating so far as possible the differences between the rights of legitimate and illegitimate children enacted by Parliament in Part II of the Family Law Reform Act 1969. The illegitimate child has one irremovable handicap; there is no presumption of paternity and it may be very difficult to prove.

There is, we think, no power to grant such a declaration under the wardship

c proceedings as such for, as we have already pointed out, it is not directly relevant to the issues normally dealt with in wardship proceedings.

If, therefore, there is power to grant such a declaration it will have to be found in the inherent jurisdiction of the court. But no authority for such a proposition was cited by counsel for the plaintiff, nor are we aware of any. On the contrary, for what it is worth, the only case which touches the point, *Aldrich v Attorney-General*[2], a decision of Ormrod J

d at first instance, is against the plaintiff's contention. It is true that that case was concerned with a father who was trying to obtain a declaration that a deceased woman was his legitimate daughter but, in effect, what he was seeking was a declaration of paternity and, in our opinion, the reasoning in that case[3] covers the present appeal.

We would, therefore, hold that the learned judge had no power to make a declaration of paternity and should have dismissed the summons of 19th May 1979. This conclusion

e accords with the view expressed by the Law Commission in their paper of 13th March 1979 entitled 'Family Law, Illegitimacy'[4]. That, of course, disposes of this appeal but, since the matter was dealt with by the judge on the assumption that she had jurisdiction, and we have heard argument on the same assumption, we will deal briefly with some of the submissions which have been made.

The jurisdiction, if it exists, is admittedly discretionary, so the next question is whether

f the learned judge should have decided to exercise it in this case. In our view, she should have refused to do so for a number of reasons. In the first place, the declaration sought by the plaintiff is one of pure fact; it determines no legal rights except the right to apply under s 14 of the Guardianship of Minors Act 1971, which is immaterial in this case because all forms of relief under that Act are available in the wardship proceedings. Such a declaration would be binding only inter partes; it would not affect the rights of persons

g not party to the present proceedings. In fact, the only purpose which it could serve would be to create an estoppel. Such a declaration is no more than a finding of fact formalised in an order of the court and made without reference to any specific legal issue between the parties. Its effect, therefore, is to prejudge such issues, and might adversely affect the interests of the child by, for example, precluding him from asserting in the future that he is the illegitimate son of Mr R.

h In the instant case there is the further objection that to make an order declaring that A is the father of B, largely on serological evidence, is to transmute a mathematical probability into a forensic certainty when there is no necessity to do so. When it is necessary to give effect to statistical evidence of this kind in order to determine the rights of the parties, the court does so on the usual basis of deciding where the onus of proof lies and whether the party on whom it lies has sufficiently discharged it. The weight of the

j

1   [1968] 1 All ER 20, [1968] P 119
2   [1968] 1 All ER 345, [1968] P 281
3   [1968] 1 All ER 345 at 349, [1968] P 281 at 291–292
4   Law Commission Working Paper 74 (1979) p 16

evidence may or may not be sufficient, depending on the issue which the court has to decide. But to make a formal declaration 'in the air' so to speak, is another thing altogether. It poses the question of the standard of proof. Counsel for the plaintiff argued strenuously that the learned judge should have been satisfied on 'the balance of probabilities' that Mr J was the father of the child, but what that much used phrase means in the context of a case like the present is by no means clear.

The concept of 'probability' in the legal sense is certainly different from the mathematical concept; indeed, it is rare to find a situation in which these two usages co-exist although, when they do, the mathematical probability has to be taken into the assessment of probability in the legal sense and given its appropriate weight. Nor is the word 'balance' much clearer. Cases like *Hornal v Neuberger Products Ltd*[1] and *Bater v Bater*[2] which were referred to by Heilbron J, make it clear that, in deciding the balance of probability, the court must take into account the gravity of the decision and determine 'the degree of probability which is proportionate to the subject matter'. Perhaps we should recognise that our time-honoured phrase is not a happy one to express a concept which, though we all understand it, is very elusive when it comes to definition. In the criminal law the burden of proof is usually expressed in the formula 'The prosecution must satisfy you so that you are sure that the accused is guilty'. The civil burden might be formulated on analogous lines, 'the plaintiff (or the party on whom the burden rests) must satisfy the court that it is reasonably safe in all the circumstances of the case to act on the evidence before the court, bearing in mind the consequences which will follow'.

The learned judge, rightly in our opinion, adopted this test. In the course of her judgment she said: 'The degree of probability in an issue of paternity should, in my opinion, be commensurate with the transcending importance of that decision to the child.' We would express the proposition differently. In our judgment, if there is power to make a bare declaration that A is the father of B the court should not exercise its discretion to make such a declaration unless the evidence is conclusive or very nearly so. (We do not think that s 26 of the Family Law Reform Act 1969, which deals with the presumption of legitimacy and provides that it may be rebutted by evidence which shows that it is more probable than not that the person concerned is illegitimate, is in point in the present case where there is no presumption to rebut.)

With respect to counsel and the Official Solicitor, we think that there were other reasons in this case for declining to exercise the power, if it exists, to make a declaration of paternity; indeed, there were strong reasons for not embarking on the enquiry in the first place. In wardship proceedings the interests of the child are paramount and all decisions must be taken in the light of those interests, although it may not be easy to evaluate them correctly. With hindsight it is now clear that it was unnecessary to consider the biological parentage of this child in order to reach a conclusion about access, which was the only live issue. The child is securely based in a two-parent family with the mother and Mr R, who fully accepts his role as de facto father, with the knowledge of the doubt of his being the biological father; the plaintiff is, to all intents and purposes, a stranger to the child. To allow the paternity issue to disturb this settled relationship was, in our view, an undoubted mistake and we find ourselves in full agreement with the mother's attitude. We can only regret that she allowed herself to be persuaded into providing samples of her own and the child's blood. Moreover, when it was known that Mr R was not prepared to provide a blood sample (which could only help Mr J to prove his case once the results of the other blood tests were known), it was clear that paternity could not be conclusively proved and that it could only be a matter of mathematical probabilities. The order in *Re L*[3] was designed to avoid just such a situation.

1   [1956] 3 All ER 970, [1957] 1 QB 247
2   [1950] 2 All ER 458, [1951] P 35
3   [1968] 1 All ER 20, [1968] P 119

a In our judgment in wardship cases the court should proceed very carefully where a question as to paternity is raised. If it is to be raised there should be an order for the trial of the issue, but such an order itself should only be made if the court is satisfied that the determination of this issue will have a material bearing on some other issue that is to be tried, and that it is in the child's interest that this question should be investigated. Similarly, in wardship cases, orders under Part III of the Family Law Reform Act 1969 should only be made if it appears to be in the child's best interests that blood tests should *b* be carried out and that the results are likely to be conclusive, ie that the other adults concerned are willing to provide blood samples. Had this practice been followed in the present case much stress and expense would have been eliminated.

For these reasons, therefore, this appeal must be dismissed, but the order made by the learned judge should be amended by deleting the first paragraph and substituting an order dismissing the plaintiff's summons dated 19th May 1979 for a declaration of *c* paternity.

Appeal dismissed; order amended in accordance with judgment. Leave to appeal to House of Lords refused.

Solicitors: *John H Rosen & Co* (for the plaintiff); *Fisher Meredith* (for the mother); *Official* *d* *Solicitor.*

Avtar S Virdi Esq   Barrister.

Re Aro Co Ltd

e
COURT OF APPEAL, CIVIL DIVISION
STEPHENSON, BRANDON AND BRIGHTMAN LJJ
15th, 16th, 17th, 18th OCTOBER, 22nd NOVEMBER 1979

Company – Winding-up – Stay of pending proceedings – Stay of proceedings where creditor not *f* *a secured creditor at commencement of winding-up – Action in rem against ship – Ship only asset of company in liquidation – Writ in action issued but not served before commencement of winding-up – Plaintiff applying for leave to continue action – Whether plaintiff a secured creditor – Whether mere issue of writ in rem constituting plaintiff a secured creditor – Companies Act 1948, s 231.*

g The applicants had a claim, which arose in 1974, against a company whose only asset was a ship. Another claimant against the company issued a writ in rem against the ship in March 1977 and arrested the ship in May. In order to protect their claim, the applicants filed a praecipe in the Admiralty registry, under RSC Ord 75, r 14, in July. A caveat against release of the ship and distribution of the proceeds of any sale was entered in the caveat book. On 29th July the applicants themselves issued a writ in rem against the *h* ship. Under Admiralty practice it was unnecessary for them to effect a second arrest of the ship as their position was protected by the caveat. Accordingly the applicants neither arrested the ship nor served the writ although it was renewed from time to time along with the caveat. On 29th November a petition for the compulsory winding up of the company was presented and a winding-up order was made in January 1978. The Admiralty marshal sold the ship. The applicants wished to establish their right to resort *j* to the proceeds of sale in priority to the company's unsecured creditors, and accordingly applied in the liquidation, under s 231[a] of the Companies Act 1948, for leave to proceed with the action in rem. The judge[b] refused leave on the ground that the mere issue of

---

a   Section 231 is set out at p 1071 *d*, post
b   [1979] 1 All ER 32

the writ did not invoke the Admiralty jurisdiction and did not, therefore, make the applicants secured creditors. The applicants appealed contending that they were secured *a* creditors, but that, if they were not, the court had a discretion under s 231 to allow the action to continue and should in the circumstances exercise that discretion in the applicants' favour.

Held – The appeal would be allowed, and the applicants given leave to proceed with the action, for the following reasons—   *b*
(i) Whether the mere issue of the writ made the applicants secured creditors, i e persons who had a charge or lien on a ship, did not depend on whether issue of the writ invoked the Admiralty jurisdiction but on whether issue of the writ entitled the applicants to assert as against the world that the ship was security for their claim. Since it was conceded that after the issue of the writ the applicants had been entitled to serve the writ and arrest the ship in the hands of a transferee from the liquidator and all subsequent *c* transferees, the ship had been encumbered with their claim from the date of the issue of the writ. It followed that from that date the applicants had been secured creditors and were to be regarded as such for the purposes of s 231 of the 1948 Act. On that basis it was beyond argument that they should be given leave under s 231 to proceed with the action (see p 1075 *e* to *g*, post); dictum of Brandon J in *The Monica S* [1967] 3 All ER at 749 explained.   *d*
(ii) In any event, even if the applicants had not been secured creditors at the commencement of the winding up, leave to proceed with the action would still be granted under s 231, for the power to give leave to proceed depended on the exercise of the court's discretion rather than on the applicant establishing that he was a secured creditor, and that discretion, like the discretion under s 325(1)^c of the 1948 Act, was a wide discretion to do what was right and fair in all the circumstances. Accordingly, it *e* could be exercised in favour of an applicant who had merely issued a writ in rem even though he had not served it, and was not confined to being exercised in favour of an applicant who had arrested the ship, particularly since to confine it so would be contrary to the Admiralty practice of not requiring second or subsequent arrests of a ship (see p 1075 *g h*, p 1076 *cd* and p 1077 *b* to *d*); *Re Grosvenor Metal Co* [1949] 2 All ER 948, *Re Suidair International Airways Ltd* [1950] 2 All ER 920 and *Re Redman (Builders) Ltd* [1964] *f* 1 All ER 851 applied.
Decision of Oliver J [1979] 1 All ER 32 reversed.

Notes
For the power to stay pending proceedings in a liquidation see 7 Halsbury's Laws (4th Edn) paras 1044, 1359, and for cases on the subject 10 Digest (Reissue) 1098–1100, 6744– *g* 6761.
For actions in rem, see 1 Halsbury's Laws (4th Edn) para 311.
For the Companies Act 1948, s 231, see 5 Halsbury's Statutes (3rd Edn) 299.

Cases referred to in judgment
Banco, The, Monte Ulia (Owners) v Owners of Ships Banco and others [1971] 1 All ER 524, *h*
  [1971] P 137, [1971] 2 WLR 335, [1971] Lloyd's Rep 49, CA, 1(1) Digest (Reissue) 294,
  1763.
Berny, The, Berny (Cargo Owners) v Owners of the ship Berny [1978] 1 All ER 1065, [1979]
  QB 80, [1978] 2 WLR 387, [1977] 2 Lloyd's Rep 533, 1(1) Digest (Reissue) 222, 1281.
Cella, The (1888) 13 PD 82, 57 LJP 55, 59 LT 125, 6 Asp MLC 293, CA, 1(1) Digest
  (Reissue) 295, 1764.   *j*
Europa, The (1849) 13 Jur 856, 1(1) Digest (Reissue) 300, 1799.
Grosvenor Metal Co, Re [1949] 2 All ER 948, [1950] Ch 63, 10 Digest (Reissue) 1103, 6782.

---

c   Section 325, so far as material, is set out at p 1076 *a*, post

Lancashire Cotton Spinning Co, Re, ex parte Carnelley (1887) 35 Ch D 656, 56 LJ Ch 761, 57
LT 511, CA, 10 Digest (Reissue) 1110, 6837.

Lloyd (David) & Co, Re Lloyd v David Lloyd & Co (1877) 6 Ch D 339, 37 LT 83, CA, 10
Digest (Reissue) 902, 5268.

Monica S, The, Monica Smith (Cargo Owners) v Owners of Ship Monica Smith now Monica S
[1967] 3 All ER 740, [1968] P 741, [1968] 2 WLR 431, [1967] 2 Lloyd's Rep 113, 1(1)
Digest (Reissue) 221, 1248.

Redman (Builders) Ltd, Re [1964] 1 All ER 851, [1964] 1 WLR 541, 10 Digest (Reissue)
1170, 7287.

Rio Grande do Sul Steamship Co, Re (1877) 5 Ch D 282, 46 LJ Ch 277, 36 LT 603, 3 Asp
MLC 424, CA, 10 Digest (Reissue) 1111, 6844.

Rio Lima, The (1873) 28 LT 775, 2 Asp MLC 34, 1(1) Digest (Reissue) 298, 1782.

Roundwood Colliery Co, Re, Lee v Roundwood Colliery Co [1897] 1 Ch 373, [1895–9] All ER
Rep 530, 66 LJ Ch 186, 75 LT 641, CA, 10 Digest (Reissue) 1101, 6772.

Suidair International Airways Ltd (in liquidation), Re [1950] 2 All ER 920, [1951] Ch 165, 10
Digest (Reissue) 1106, 6800.

Wanzer, Re [1891] 1 Ch 305, 60 LJ Ch 492, 10 Digest (Reissue) 1101, 6766.

Cases also cited

Anglo-Baltic & Mediterranean Bank v Barber & Co [1924] 2 KB 410, [1924] All ER Rep 226,
CA.

Australian Direct Steam Navigation Co, Re (1875) LR 20 Eq 325.

Berry (Herbert) Associates Ltd v Inland Revenue Comrs [1978] 1 All ER 161, [1977] 1 WLR
1437, HL.

Constellation, The [1965] 3 All ER 873, [1966] 1 WLR 272.

Croshaw v Lyndhurst Ship Co [1897] 2 Ch 154.

Great Ship Co Ltd, Re Parry's Case (1863) 4 De GJ & Sm 63, 46 ER 839, LJJ.

James W Elwell, The [1921] P 351.

Jones v Jones [1970] 3 All ER 47, [1970] 2 QB 576, CA.

London and Devon Biscuit Co, Re (1871) LR 12 Eq 190.

Mons, The [1932] P 109.

Oak Pits Colliery Co, Re (1882) 21 Ch D 332, [1881–5] All ER Rep 1157, CA.

Tervaete, The [1922] P 259, [1922] All ER Rep 387, CA.

Thurso New Gas Co, Re (1889) 42 Ch D 486.

United Africa Co Ltd v Owners of mv Tolten, The Tolten [1946] 2 All ER 372, [1946] P 135,
CA.

Vron Colliery Co, Re (1882) 20 Ch D 442, CA.

Zafiro, The [1959] 2 All ER 537, [1960] P 1.

Appeal

This was an appeal by Texaco Export Inc ('Texaco') against the judgment of Oliver J[1]
given on 14th June 1978 refusing to grant Texaco leave pursuant to s 231 of the
Companies Act 1948, to continue, inter alia, an action in rem against a vessel owned by
Aro Co Ltd ('the company') which was in compulsory liquidation even though Texaco
had issued the writ in the action before the commencement of the winding up. The facts
are set out in the judgment of the court. Owing to shortage of funds the liquidator of the
company did not take part in the hearing of the appeal but was represented when
judgment was given.

Anthony Clarke QC and *N J M Teare* for Texaco.
David A S Richards for the liquidator.

Cur adv vult

---

1   [1979] 1 All ER 32, [1979] Ch 613

22nd November. **BRIGHTMAN LJ** read the following judgment of the court: This
is an appeal from an order of Oliver J[1] dismissing an application by Texaco Export Inc   *a*
('Texaco') for relief under s 231 of the Companies Act 1948. So far as relevant for present
purposes, this section provides:

> 'When a winding-up order has been made . . . no action or proceeding shall be
> proceeded with or commenced against the company except by leave of court . . .'

The relief sought by Texaco was leave to continue an Admiralty action in rem against   *b*
the ship Aro and in personam against her owners Aro Co Ltd ('the company')
notwithstanding the compulsory liquidation of the company. The claim is for a short
delivery of cargo and breach of a contract of carriage, amounting to about $US61,000.
The claim dates back to 1974. In March 1977 Shell Co (Hellas) Ltd ('Shell'), which has a
claim for about $US147,000 for bunkers supplied to the ship, issued a writ in rem against
her. In May 1977 the ship was arrested at the instance of Shell. On 28th July Texaco, in   *c*
order to protect its interests, filed a praecipe in the Admiralty registry under RSC Ord 75,
r 14. Under this procedure a caveat is entered in the caveat book against the release of the
arrested vessel, and against distribution of the proceeds of any sale.

On 29th July 1977 Texaco issued a writ. As this was a writ in rem against the Aro as
well as a writ in personam against her owners, Texaco could have had the ship arrested.
It is however unusual for a second claimant to have an arrested ship further arrested. The   *d*
caveat procedure is considered to make this unnecessary. The costs of a second or
subsequent warrant of arrest are not allowed unless justified by special circumstances.
This is a matter to which it will be necessary to return in more detail later. Subject
perhaps to one point, Texaco at this stage had taken every step which a maritime
claimant might think necessary to protect its interests, having regard to the existence of
the arrest by Shell. There was one step which Texaco did not take. It did not serve the   *e*
writ on the ship.

On 29th November 1977, a petition was presented by a mutual underwriting
association for the winding up of the company. A winding-up order was made in
January 1978. The liquidation accordingly commenced on the former date.

The status of Shell as a secured creditor is not challenged by the liquidator. Various
orders were made by the Companies Court enabling Shell to continue with its action.   *f*
Ultimately, in October 1978, the ship was sold by the Admiralty marshal. She had been
laid up in the Thames estuary since 1975.

With the leave of the Companies Court, Texaco's writ in rem, still unserved, was
renewed from time to time. The writ in personam has been allowed to lapse. Successive
caveats have also been entered at the request of Texaco, a caveat expiring after six
months.   *g*

The net proceeds of sale available for distribution amount to about $240,000. If Shell
is the only maritime claimant against this fund, its debt will absorb all except about
$32,000, which will be available for division among the unsecured creditors. If however
Texaco can establish its right to resort to this fund, Shell will share the fund with Texaco,
and it seems unlikely that there will be anything for the unsecured creditors. The
contest, therefore, is between Texaco on the one hand and Shell and the liquidator (for   *h*
the unsecured creditors) on the other hand.

The liquidator was represented at the hearing in the court below but owing to a
shortage of funds in the liquidation he decided not to take part in the appeal. Shell was
not made a respondent to the summons before the judge, and is not a respondent to the
notice of motion in this court. Texaco's solicitors have been in touch with Shell's
solicitors and invited it to take part in the appeal. Shell did not accept this invitation.   *j*
We have accordingly heard argument only from Texaco's counsel. Although we would
have welcomed argument on both sides we have not felt unduly embarrassed, first
because the judgment under appeal contains a clear exposition of the argument against

---

1   [1979] 1 All ER 32, [1979] Ch 613

Texaco, and secondly because counsel has been at pains to draw our attention to points
a which are against him.

This case is directly concerned only with s 231 of the Companies Act 1948, but it will
be convenient to consider the statutory provisions in greater breadth.

The basic scheme of the companies legislation is that the unsecured creditors of an
insolvent company are to rank pari passu (subject to statutory provisions as to preferential
payments): see *Re Redman (Builders) Ltd*[1]. In order to achieve this result, there are
b provisions which restrict the right of a creditor to make use of procedures outside the
liquidation. Secured creditors are not separately catered for by the 1948 Act or its
predecessors, except that the bankruptcy rules are expressed to apply to the respective
rights of the secured and unsecured creditors: see s 317 of the 1948 Act.

Section 228 (1) of the 1948 Act provides that where a company is being wound up by
the court, any attachment, sequestration, distress or execution 'put in force' against the
c estate or effects of the company after the commencement of the winding up shall be void
to all intents. 'Put in force' means, for example, seizure by the sheriff as distinct from a
sale by him. The date of the commencement of the winding up is the date of the
presentation of the petition or of a preceding resolution for a voluntary winding up.

This section, though absolute in terms, has been held to be subject by implication to
the court's dispensing power which is spelt out by s 231. This is the section with which
d we are primarily concerned. It reads in full:

> 'When a winding-up order has been made or a provisional liquidator has been
> appointed, no action or proceeding shall be proceeded with or commenced against
> the company except by leave of the court and subject to such terms as the court may
> impose.'

e Sections 228 and 231 apply to secured as well as to unsecured creditors. But a secured
creditor is in a position where he can justly claim that he is independent of the
liquidation, since he is enforcing a right, not *against* the company, but *to* his own
property: see *Re David Lloyd & Co*[2], a case under the predecessor of s 231. A striking
illustration of this principle is to be found in *Re Wanzer*[3], under the same section. A
landlord of Scottish property began proceedings after a winding-up order for sequestration
f of the company's goods on the premises in order to answer future rent. North J allowed
the sequestration to continue, being satisfied that under Scottish law the landlord was a
secured creditor at the date of the commencement of the winding up, and therefore in
the same position as a mortgagee.

The foregoing sections date back to the Companies Act 1862. In terms they apply only
to a compulsory liquidation, but the principle is equally applicable to a voluntary
g winding up in the sense that the court will exercise its power to stay under s 307 in
circumstances in which it would not exercise its dispensing power if the liquidation were
compulsory: see *Re Roundwood Colliery Co*[4]. Thus if a winding-up order has been made,
proceedings are automatically stayed but the court may on application by the creditor
allow them to be continued; while in a voluntary winding up, or where a petition has
been presented but not adjudicated on, there is no automatic stay but the court may on
h application by an interested party restrain proceedings. The last-mentioned case usefully
summarises the court's general approach[5]:

> 'The result, as I understand it, is this: that a creditor who has issued execution, or
> a landlord who has levied a distress, before the commencement of the winding-up
> will be allowed to proceed to sale unless there is established the existence of special

j

1 [1964] 1 All ER 85, [1964] 1 WLR 541
2 (1877) 6 Ch D 339
3 [1891] 1 Ch 305
4 [1897] 1 Ch 373, [1895–9] All ER Rep 530
5 [1897] 1 Ch 373 at 381 per Stirling J

reasons rendering it inequitable that he should be permitted to do so. On the other hand the case of *In re Lancashire Cotton Spinning Co.*[1] shews that the creditor who does *a* not issue execution or a landlord who does not levy a distress until after the commencement of the winding-up will not be allowed to proceed unless there are special reasons which render such a course inequitable.'

These provisions are reinforced by s 325 of the 1948 Act, which was introduced by the Companies Act 1929, and applies to both voluntary and compulsory liquidations. This section is specifically directed to the case where the execution or attachment precedes the *b* commencement of the winding up. The effect of the section is that the creditor is expressly precluded from retaining the fruits of the execution or attachment unless (broadly speaking) the process has been completed prior to the commencement of the winding up and (in the case of a voluntary liquidation) prior to his receiving notice of the convening of a shareholders' meeting to consider a winding-up resolution. A dispensing power was introduced by the 1948 Act, in the terms that the rights thereby conferred on *c* the liquidator may be set aside by the court in favour of the creditor to such an extent and subject to such terms as the court may think fit.

Whether or not leave to proceed is given under s 231 and, by implication, under s 228, is a matter for the discretion of the court.

We turn to a consideration of the nature of Texaco's claim. There are two classes of maritime claim which need to be reviewed for present purposes. One gives rise to a *d* maritime lien. This lien attaches to a ship and certain other property (but we need only consider ships) from the moment the claim arises. A familiar example is a salvage claim. The holder of a maritime lien ranks as a secured creditor under the insolvency legislation. Indeed he takes priority over a mortgagee of the ship. Consequently, leave will automatically be given under s 231 to enable the holder of a maritime lien to enforce his charge despite the existence of a winding-up order: see *Re Rio Grande do Sul Steamship* *e* *Co*[2], where the master of a ship entitled to a maritime lien over his ship was allowed to take proceedings in Admiralty in rem despite the existence of the winding-up order.

Another type of maritime claim gives rise to a so-called statutory lien, more accurately described as a statutory right of action in rem. This right of action is regulated at the present day by the Administration of Justice Act 1956. Section 1 of the Act defines the Admiralty jurisdiction of the High Court. It specifies the types of claim which fall *f* within that jurisdiction, including claims which give rise to maritime liens, and those which do not. Paragraphs (g) and (h) of s 1(1) cover claims of the latter class, that is to say, claims for loss of or damage to cargo and claims arising out of contracts for the carriage of goods. The Admiralty jurisdiction may as a rule also be invoked by an action in personam: see s 3(1). It may also be invoked by an action in rem against the ship in any case in which there is a maritime lien for the amount: see s 3(3). Additionally, in the case *g* of para (g) and (h) claims, and in certain other cases with which we are not concerned, the Admiralty jurisdiction may be invoked by an action in rem against the ship if, at the time when the cause of action arises and also at the time when the action is brought, the ship (broadly speaking) is in the same hands; more accurately, where the person who would be liable on the claim in the action in personam was, when the cause of action arose, the owner, charterer of or in possession or in control of the ship and the ship is *h* wholly owned by that person when the action is brought: see s 3(4). That was the position in the case of Texaco's claim (and was also the position in the case of Shell's claim). Texaco accordingly brought an action in rem against the ship, as well as an action in personam against the company. To complete matters, s 3(7) gives the High Court, sitting in Admiralty, jurisdiction to determine questions of title to the proceeds of sale of *j* a ship sold by order of the court.

1   (1887) 35 Ch D 656
2   (1877) 5 Ch D 282

a Following on the issue of the writ, Texaco had an immediate right, without having served the writ, to have the ship arrested by the Admiralty marshal. Nothing would have been required of Texaco, as no caveat against arrest had been entered, except an affidavit verifying the basic facts essential to the existence of its statutory right of action in rem. The justification for this procedure is that ships are owned and trade internationally, and unless a claimant can gain immediate security for a claim he may never have the opportunity effectively to pursue it.

b It is normally not considered necessary, as mentioned above, for the second and subsequent claimants to have an arrested ship further arrested at their several instances. The caveat procedure under RSC Ord 75, r 14 can be traced back for more than a hundred years. Under the Admiralty Court Rules 1859 (see appendix to Williams and Bruce's Jurisdiction and Practice of the High Court of Admiralty[1]) an Admiralty action was begun by filing a praecipe in the registry, as a result of which the cause was entered *c* on behalf of the claimant in the cause book. If the cause was in rem, the claimant was entitled as of right to take out a warrant for the arrest of the ship. Rule 16 provided that:

> 'If, when any property is under arrest of the court, a second or subsequent cause is instituted against the same property, it shall not be necessary to take out a second warrant for the further arrest thereof; but the proctor in such second or subsequent *d* cause may, on filing in the Registry a praecipe and an affidavit, take out a citation in rem, and cause a caveat against the release of the property to be entered in the "Caveat Release Book" hereinafter mentioned.'

The effect of the citation in rem was to prevent the release of the property without notice to the caveator. It operated as an early warning system. The citation in rem procedure *e* was abolished by the Admiralty Court Rules 1871, but the 1883 Rules of the Supreme Court restored the procedure to the extent of allowing a solicitor, who desired to prevent the release of a vessel under arrest, to have a caveat against her release entered in the Caveat Release Book: see the provisions of RSC Ord 29, r 8. The position is now regulated by RSC Ord 75, r 14 to which reference has already been made. There is a note in the Supreme Court Practice[2] which reads as follows:

f > 'Use of the caveat procedure normally makes it unnecessary for a plaintiff in an action *in rem* against property which is under arrest in another action to issue a warrant for the arrest of that property . . . The costs of a second or subsequent arrest are not normally allowed save in special circumstances.'

g The argument proceeded in the lower court on the basis that the only question to be decided was whether Texaco, by commencing an action in rem, though not serving the writ or further arresting the ship, put itself in the position of a secured creditor for the purpose of the principles on which the court exercises its jurisdiction under s 231. We do not think that this is the only question, but we will deal with it first.

The judge refused Texaco leave to proceed under s 231 because he did not consider that *h* Texaco, having merely issued a writ, was in any real sense a secured creditor. It would only become a secured creditor on arresting the vessel or possibly on serving the writ, as between which events it was not necessary for the judge to decide.

In this court Texaco's argument was not expressed to stand or fall by the test whether Texaco was in the position of a secured creditor. Counsel submitted these propositions. (1) The discretion of the court under s 231 is unfettered. The court should do what is fair *j* and just in all the circumstances of the particular case. (2) In general, in exercise of that discretion the court should allow a maritime claimant to commence and to continue an

---

1 (1869) p xxix
2 (1979) vol 1, pp 1185–1186, para 75/14/1

action in rem notwithstanding the fact that a winding up has commenced, in order to ensure the priority of maritime claimants whether the priority is that of the holder of a *a* maritime lien, or a mortgagee, or the holder of a statutory lien, that is to say the holder of a statutory right of action in rem. A claimant who has issued a writ in rem before the commencement of the winding up should in general be allowed to continue his action, notwithstanding the winding up, because he has an accrued right of arrest. When a ship is already in the hands of the court, albeit because of the arrest by other claimants, a claimant who satisfies s 3 of the 1956 Act should be allowed to issue a writ in rem or to *b* continue an action in rem and to share in the proceeds of sale. A claimant who has issued a writ and entered a caveat against release before commencement of the winding up, should be allowed to continue his action, because he is or should be treated as being in the same position as if he had arrested. (3) On the facts of the case the judge should have exercised his discretion in favour of Texaco (a) for one or more of the above reasons or (b) on the particular facts of the case. In particular the solicitors did not have the ship *c* arrested because they relied on what they believed to be the ordinary practice in Admiralty matters.

If Texaco is properly to be regarded as a secured creditor as from the date of the issue of the writ, it is beyond argument that it should be given leave under s 231 to proceed with its action and to establish its claim to share in the proceeds of sale paid into court as the result of the arrest by Shell. A secured creditor for this purpose means a person *d* holding a mortgage, charge or lien on the property of the debtor or any part thereof, as a security for a debt due to him from the debtor. This is the definition of secured creditor in the Bankruptcy Act 1914. It would be eccentric to adopt a different criterion in corporate insolvencies. The first question must therefore be to decide whether Texaco did or did not become a secured creditor when it issued its writ, that is to say whether Texaco acquired a charge or lien by virtue of the issue of a writ in rem. The answer to *e* this question must depend on the nature of an action in rem.

The usual object of suing in rem is to obtain security. The plaintiff becomes entitled on the institution of his suit to the arrest and detention of the subject-matter in the custody of an officer of the court pending adjudication, and on adjudication in his favour to a sale and satisfaction of his judgment out of the net proceeds thereof, subject to other claims ranking in priority to or pari passu with his own. So stated, the rights of a *f* plaintiff suing in rem have points of similarity with the rights of a legal or equitable mortgagee or chargee; such persons are also entitled in appropriate circumstances to have the subject-matter of the charge preserved for their benefit, and if the account is in their favour to have it sold in order to satisfy the debt. The similarity is carried a stage further by the decision in *The Monica S*[1], where it was held that the burden of the statutory right of action in rem in a sub-s (4) case ran with the ship so as to enable the plaintiff to serve *g* the writ on the ship notwithstanding a transfer of ownership since the writ was issued. It must follow from that decision that the plaintiff in rem is entitled to have the ship arrested despite change in ownership, and notwithstanding that the writ has not been served. The case is of critical importance to our decision because, applied to the instant case, it means that, had the liquidator sold the ship, he could only have sold subject to Texaco's claim; this does not seem far removed from saying that the liquidator could *h* only sell a proprietary interest equivalent to a right to redeem. In the court below the liquidator conceded the correctness of *The Monica S*[1] decision, and therefore we have not reviewed it in this court. Suffice it to say that it has not been challenged.

In *The Monica S*[2] it was said: 'It is the arrest that actually gives the claimant security; but a necessary preliminary to an arrest is the acquisition, by the institution of a cause in rem, of a right of arrest.' We do not think that anyone could quarrel with that analysis of the *j* status of the plaintiff in an action in rem. It should not be read as answering in the

---

1 [1967] 3 All ER 740, [1968] P 741
2 [1967] 3 All ER 740 at 749, [1968] P 741 at 754

a negative the question whether a person who has instituted an action in rem, affecting the ship into whosesoever hands she may come, ranks as a person holding a charge or lien.

There are a number of cases which contain language consistent with the proposition that the plaintiff's security arises when an action in rem (in a non-maritime lien case) is begun, and others consistent with the proposition that the critical date is that when the ship is arrested. These cases are competently reviewed in the judgment of Oliver J[1]. None of them is decisive for present purposes, because in none, including *The Cella*[2], was b it necessary for the purpose of the decision to distinguish between the time of the institution of the suit on the one hand and the time of service or arrest on the other. We do not think that a further review of the cases in the course of this judgment would add anything useful to what the judge has already said.

The judge reached the conclusion that Texaco did not become a secured creditor on the issue of the writ in rem because the issue of such a writ did not 'invoke' the c jurisdiction of the Admiralty Court, but was merely the first step towards such invocation: see *The Banco*[3]. The jurisdiction is invoked when the writ is served and the warrant of arrest is executed (per Lord Denning MR[4]) or when the writ is served (per Megaw LJ[5]). Cairns LJ on the other hand expressed the view that the jurisdiction was invoked when the writ was issued[6]. The second of these views was accepted by Brandon J in *The Berny*[7]. Oliver J[8] concluded:

d

'... if it be right that the plaintiff who has issued a writ in rem has not yet invoked the jurisdiction of the Admiralty Court and does not do so until he serves his writ, it is really not possible to describe him in any real sense as a secured creditor.'

The legal nexus, he considered, between the creditor and the res claimed as security was e not established merely by the issue of the writ.

In our judgment there is no particular reason for equating the date of the creation of the status of a secured creditor with the date when the Admiralty jurisdiction can be said to be 'invoked' for the purposes of s 3 of the Administration of Justice Act 1956. It seems more logical to test the position of Texaco by asking whether, immediately before the presentation of the winding-up petition, Texaco could properly assert as against all the f world that the vessel Aro was security for its claim, not whether it could assert that it had invoked the jurisdiction of the Admiralty Court within the meaning of s 3 of the Administration of Justice Act 1956. If it is correct to say, as was not challenged in the court below and is not challenged in this court, that after the issue of the writ in rem Texaco could serve the writ on the Aro, and arrest the Aro, in the hands of a transferee from the liquidator and all subsequent transferees, it seems to us difficult to argue that g the Aro was not effectively encumbered with Texaco's claim. In our judgment Texaco ought to be considered as a secured creditor for the purpose of deciding whether or not the discretion of the court should be execised in its favour under s 231.

There is an alternative approach. The dispensing power in s 231 is not in terms dependent on the claimant's establishing the status of a secured creditor, but on the exercise of the court's discretion. The discretion is conferred by the words 'except by h leave of the court and subject to such terms as the Court may impose'. In s 325(1)(c) the discretion exerciseable by the court in favour of the execution creditor is conferred by the words:

---

j 1 [1979] 1 All ER 32, [1979] Ch 613
2 (1888) 13 P D 82
3 [1971] 1 All ER 524, [1971] P 137
4 [1971] 1 All ER 524 at 533, [1971] P 137 at 153
5 [1971] 1 All ER 524 at 538, [1971] P 137 at 158–159
6 [1971] 1 All ER 524 at 540, [1971] P 137 at 161
7 [1978] 1 All ER 1065, [1979] QB 80
8 [1979] 1 All ER 32 at 47, [1979] Ch 613 at 637

'. . . the rights conferred by this subsection on the liquidator may be set aside by the court in favour of the creditor to such extent and subject to such terms as the court may think fit.'

The nature of this latter discretion has been considered in three recent cases. In *Re Grosvenor Metal Co*[1] Vaisey J said: 'The section seems to give the court a free hand to do what is right and fair according to the circumstances of each case.' In *Re Suidair International Airways Ltd*[2] Wynn-Parry J adopted the same construction of the subsection, as also did Pennycuick J in *Re Redman (Builders) Ltd*[3]. We consider that those cases were correctly decided. The only appreciable difference between the wording of the two sections is that s 325 includes the words 'to such extent' as well as the words 'subject to such terms'. This appears to us a trivial distinction on which to found a decision that the discretion under s 231 is somehow narrower than the discretion under s 325. We adopt the definition of the discretion under s 325 as applied in the three cases mentioned and we consider that the discretion of the court under s 231 gives the court an equal freedom to do what is right and fair in the circumstances.

If the liquidator's contention were correct, it would follow that every plaintiff in rem suing a ship already under arrest would have to cause a further arrest to be made unless he knew for a certainty that there would be no liquidation. Quite apart from causing additional and unproductive expense, this would be contrary to the normal practice well established in Admiralty matters over the years. An object of the citation in rem introduced 120 years ago was to avoid the need for recurrent arrests: see Wiswall's The Development of Admiralty Jurisdiction and Practice since 1800[4]:

'The outlines of the Admiralty procedure . . . were preserved by the 1859 Rules, but some innovations were . . . (3) the introduction of the *citation in rem* for service upon vessels already under arrest, to replace subsequent warrants for subsequent actions *in rem*.'

The statement in the Supreme Court Practice that the costs of a second or subsequent arrest are not normally allowed except in special circumstances does not, so far as we are aware, appear earlier than 1964, but the practice can be traced back to Dr Lushington's day: see the concluding remarks in *The Europa*[5], the implication of which is that a person imposing a second arrest on a arrested ship is at risk as to costs. In *The Rio Lima*[6] a claim for necessaries was the subject-matter of a cause in the Newcastle County Court. The cause was transferred to the High Court, because there were other suits pending in the High Court in which the ship was under arrest. The county court claimant moved for leave to arrest. Sir Robert Phillimore said in the course of argument[7]:

'The registrar tells me that the practice has hitherto been, to issue a warrant for arrest in each suit. It appears to me that the rule 53 is intended to apply rather to the case where the proctor seeking a *caveat* is concerned in a case in which the ship is already under arrest. [The motion was refused; Sir Robert Phillimore added:] I do not see how the plaintiffs can be injured by the issuing of a *caveat* instead of a warrant for the arrest of the ship.'

Again, in Roscoe's Admiralty Jurisdiction and Practice[8], we find this note against Ord 29, r 8: 'If in an action property is under arrest, and in a subsequent action the

---

1   [1950] Ch 63 at 65
2   [1950] 2 All ER 920, [1951] Ch 165
3   [1964] 1 All ER 85, [1964] 1 WLR 541
4   (1970) p 56
5   (1849) 13 Jur 856
6   (1873) 28 LT 775
7   28 LT 775 at 776
8   5th Edn (1931) p 314

a
plaintiff takes out a warrant, he will not be allowed the costs for so doing, since the proper course is to enter a caveat against the release.'

Lastly, if the court's discretion under s 231 is to be exercised only in favour of a plaintiff who arrests, a problem will arise in every case where the second or subsequent claimant is proceeding in the county court. The county court has no jurisdiction to issue a warrant for arrest unless it be shown to the satisfaction of the judge that it is probable that the vessel will be removed out of the jurisdiction before the plaintiff's claim is
b
satisfied (see the County Courts Act 1959, s 83). That could hardly be proved of a vessel which is already in the custody of the Admiralty marshal.

In these circumstances there seems to us a powerful argument for leaving undisturbed a long established practice whereby second and subsequent claimants protect their position by caveat against release rather than by multiple arrests.

c
We see no virtue in confining relief under s 231 in this type of case to a claimant who has served his writ on the ship as distinct from the claimant who has issued his writ but not served. The service of the writ adds nothing to the status of the claimant vis-à-vis the vessel sued. This is established by the issue of the writ. As between plaintiff and defendant, service merely causes time to commence running within which the defendant must enter an appearance in order to avoid being a respondent to a motion for judgment by default.

d
We therefore reach the conclusion that leave ought to be granted to Texaco under s 231 even if it is incorrect to regard Texaco as having been a secured creditor at the commencement of the winding up.

On these two grounds we allow the appeal.

Appeal allowed.

Solicitors: *William A Crump & Son* (for Texaco); *Stokes & Lowless* (for the liquidator).

Patricia Hargrove   Barrister.

The Helene Roth   *a*

QUEEN'S BENCH DIVISION (ADMIRALTY COURT)
SHEEN J
26th, 29th NOVEMBER, 7th DECEMBER 1979

Admiralty – Practice – Action in rem – Writ – Renewal – Change in beneficial ownership of ship *b*
after issue of writ – Whether change in ownership providing good cause for renewal of writ –
Administration of Justice Act 1956, s 3(4) – RSC Ord 6, r 8(2).

Where a writ in rem is issued against a ship in respect of a claim in connection with the
ship under s 1(1)(d) to (r) of the Administration of Justice Act 1956, and subsequently
there is a change in the beneficial ownership of the ship so that the person who would   *c*
have been liable in personam when the cause of action arose is no longer the beneficial
owner, the change in ownership provides, so long as the action has been pursued with
diligence, good cause for renewing the validity of the writ under RSC Ord 6, r 8(2)
because, by reason of the change in ownership, the issue of a second writ in rem would
not invoke the Admiralty jurisdiction under s 3(4)*a* of the 1956 Act since on the issue of
the second writ the ship would not be in the beneficial ownership of the person liable in *d*
personam (see p 1081 *f g* and p 1082 *a b*, post).

Notes

For renewal of writs generally, see 30 Halsbury's Laws (3rd Edn) 303, para 558, and for
cases on the subject, see 50 Digest (Repl) 291–293, 328–346.

For Admiralty jurisdiction in actions in rem, see 1 Halsbury's Laws (4th Edn) para 311, *e*
and for cases on the subject, see 1(1) Digest (Reissue) 219–223, 1240–1251.

For the Administration of Justice Act 1956, ss 1, 3, see 1 Halsbury's Statutes (3rd Edn)
21, 26.

Cases referred to in judgment

Berny, The, Owners of cargo lately laden on the ship Berny v Owners of the ship Berny [1978] 1 *f*
  All ER 1065, [1979] QB 80, [1978] 2 WLR 387, [1977] 2 Lloyd's Rep 533, 1(1) Digest
  (Reissue) 222, 1251.
Monica S, The, Owners of cargo laden on ship Monica Smith v Owners of ship formerly Monica
  Smith now Monica S [1967] 3 All ER 740, [1968] P 741, [1968] 2 WLR 431, [1967] 2
  Lloyd's Rep 113, 1(1) Digest (Reissue) 221, 1248.

                                                                      g

Cases also cited

Aro Co Ltd, Re p 1067, ante, [1980] 2 WLR 453, CA.
Battersby v Anglo-American Oil Co Ltd [1944] 2 All ER 387, [1945] 1 KB 23, CA.
Heaven v Road and Rail Wagons Ltd [1965] 2 All ER 409, [1965] 2 QB 355.
Hewett v Barr [1891] 1 QB 98, CA
Jones v Jones [1970] 3 All ER 47, [1970] 2 QB 576, CA.   *h*
Rena K, The [1979] 1 All ER 397, [1979] QB 377.
Wladyslaw Lokietek, The [1978] 2 Lloyd's Rep 520.

---

a Section 3(4), so far as material, provides: 'In the case of any such claim as is mentioned in
    paragraphs (d) to (r) of subsection (1) of section one of this Act, being a claim arising in connection
    with a ship, where the person who would be liable on the claim in an action in personam was, *j*
    when the cause of action arose, the owner . . . of . . . the ship, the Admiralty jurisdiction of the
    High Court . . . may (whether the claim gives rise to a maritime lien on the ship or not) be invoked
    by an action in rem against—(a) that ship . . . or (b) any other ship which, at the time when the
    action is brought, is beneficially owned [by that person].'

Motion

a By a writ issued on 8th November 1978 the plaintiffs, Clipper Ship Supply Co Ltd, of Montreal, Canada, brought an action in rem against three ships, the Helene Roth, the Viktoria Roth and the Anton Roth, which at the date of the issue of the writ were owned by Joseph Roth (Cyprus) Shipping Co Ltd of Limassol, Cyprus. On 26th November 1979 the Admiralty registrar renewed the writ and thereafter the Helene Roth was arrested in the action. By notice of motion dated 29th November Helene Roth Maritime Co Ltd of

b Limassol, Cyprus ('the applicants'), who on 14th November had become the owners of the Helene Roth, applied for an order that the renewal of the writ and the service thereof be set aside and that the Helene Roth be unconditionally released. As the applicants were not the defendants to the action, Sheen J, on 29th November, gave them leave to intervene in the action pursuant to RSC Ord 75, r 17. The facts are set out in the judgment.

c

Richard Mawrey for the applicants.
Charles Macdonald for the plaintiffs.

Cur adv vult

d

7th December. **SHEEN J** read the following judgment: The plaintiffs in this action are a company incorporated in Canada carrying on business as ship chandlers in Montreal. It is alleged by the plaintiffs that in November 1977 they made disbursements for the ship Royal Clipper as agents at the request of and for the account of Joseph Roth (Cyprus) Shipping Co Ltd (hereinafter referred to as 'Joseph Roth'). As the plaintiffs had not been

e reimbursed by Joseph Roth nearly a year later, they instructed solicitors in London to endeavour to recover the money said to be due to them. On 8th November 1978 their London solicitors issued the writ in this action, which is an action in rem against three ships, all of which are registered at the port of Limassol, Cyprus, and which at the date of the issue of the writ were owned by Joseph Roth. The plaintiffs' solicitors enquired of the intelligence department at Lloyd's whether any of those ships was within the

f jurisdiction. They were told that none of the ships was within the jurisdiction. Thereafter, the plaintiffs' solicitors instructed Lloyd's Intelligence Department to keep a special watch on the ships and to report if any of them came within the jurisdiction. In due course it became apparent that the pattern of trading of all those ships was between ports outside the United Kingdom. By August 1979 the plaintiffs thought that they would be wasting money if they continued to pay Lloyd's Intelligence Department to

g maintain the watch. Accordingly it was discontinued. The writ in this action was allowed to lapse on 8th November 1979. A few weeks later news was received that the ship Helene Roth was in dock in London. The plaintiffs' solicitors received fresh instructions to pursue the claim. Accordingly on Friday, 23rd November, they applied to the Admiralty Registrar under RSC Ord 6, r 8, for an extension of the validity of the writ.

h The claim in this action is a claim made by a Canadian company against a Cypriot company. This court has jurisdiction to hear and determine the questions at issue between the parties because they come within the Admiralty jurisdiction of the High Court as prescribed by s 1(1)(*m*) and (*p*) of the Administration of Justice Act 1956. The claim arises in connection with a ship and the person who would be liable on the claim in an action in personam was, when the cause of action arose, in possession or in control

j of the ship. Accordingly, the Admiralty jurisdiction of the High Court may be invoked by an action in rem against any ship which at the time when the action is brought is beneficially owned as respects all the shares therein by that person: see s 3(4) of the 1956 Act. There is no limit to the time within which such an action may be brought: see the Limitation Act 1939, s 2(6). At the time when application was made for renewal of the writ about two years had elapsed since the cause of action arose. It was not in any sense a stale claim.

When the application came before the registrar on 23rd November it was supported by an affidavit of Mr J L A Foster of the plaintiff's solicitors, which set out the efforts which the plaintiffs' London solicitors had made to keep track of the three ships named in the writ. The registrar refused the application. The reason for this refusal was that the registrar thought he was following to the letter the guidelines set out in the judgment of Brandon J in *The Berny*[1]. I am bound to say that I would have acceded to the application. As was pointed out by Brandon J[2], when the claim is not statute-barred the court's requirements with regard to good and sufficient cause for renewal are considerably less exacting than in cases in which a time bar has arisen. Solicitors who issue a writ have a duty to serve it promptly. Renewal is certainly not to be granted as of course. Solicitors must not be dilatory in the conduct of an action because defendants must be protected against the prejudice which can occur when there is a long delay between the time when the cause of action arises and the service of a writ. If a cause of action is not time-barred and if a writ has been allowed to lapse, then in the vast majority of actions in the Queen's Bench Division a further writ can be issued. But such a course may not be effective in an Admiralty action in rem, for reasons with which I will deal later in this judgment. It is clear to me from the first affidavit of Mr Foster that the plaintiffs' solicitors, far from being dilatory, were taking active steps at some expense to their clients to find an opportunity to serve the writ. They continued to do so until the time when it appeared that their task was hopeless. Their continued vigilance is evidenced by the fact that they discovered that the Helene Roth was in dock in London on her first visit since the writ was issued. I have dealt with this aspect of the matter only because it seems to me that the question which the registrar has to answer is whether the plaintiffs' solicitors have taken all reasonable (not all possible) steps to effect service of the writ. In *The Berny*[1] Brandon J laid down some guidelines which provide a yardstick by which the registrar may test the question whether the plaintiffs' solicitors have been reasonably diligent or whether on the other hand their conduct has been such that their clients must be penalised. On 23rd November the plaintiffs' solicitors were faced with this situation. The registrar had refused to extend the validity of the writ in this action and they did not know how long the Helene Roth would remain within the jurisdiction. They therefore issued another writ in a fresh action. I will refer hereafter to that writ as 'the second writ'.

On Monday, 26th November, Mr Foster swore a further affidavit in which he deposed to the fact that Lloyd's Intelligence Department confirmed on that day that according to their records none of the three ships concerned in this action called within the jurisdiction from 1st August 1979 until the arrival of the Helene Roth in London on 18th November 1979. With this further information available the registrar took the view that it would be proper to renew the writ. This was done, and thereafter the Helene Roth was arrested in this action.

On 29th November solicitors acting on behalf of the owners of the Helene Roth issued a notice of motion which came before me at 2 pm on the same day. On this motion counsel described as 'Counsel for the above-named defendants' moves the court for an order that renewal of the writ and service thereof in this action be set aside and that the Helene Roth now under arrest be unconditionally released.

In support of this motion an affidavit of Mr A C Poynter of the applicants' solicitors was read to me. It emerged from that affidavit that on 14th November 1979 Joseph Roth transferred the ownership of the Helene Roth to Helene Roth Maritime Co Ltd of Limassol. It was on behalf of this latter company that the notice of motion was issued.

1 [1978] 1 All ER 1065 at 1082, [1979] QB 80 at 103
2 [1978] 1 All ER 1065 at 1081–1082, [1979] QB 80 at 102

I pointed out that that company is not the defendant in the action. If no one enters an
a appearance, the action proceeds against the res. Those who are commanded by the writ
to enter an appearance are the owners and persons interested in the ship. 'The owners'
must refer to those who are correctly so described at the date when the writ is issued.
The new owners are, of course, 'persons interested in the ship'. So that only those who
are 'persons (or companies) interested in the ship' can enter an appearance, the Rules of
the Supreme Court make provision for an application by interveners for leave to
b intervene by Ord 75, r 17. I gave leave to Helene Roth Maritime Co Ltd of Limassol to
intervene in the action and to enter an appearance therein. Whoever may be the parties
to the action, the questions or claims which the Admiralty Court must hear and
determine are questions or claims between the plaintiffs and Joseph Roth. Counsel
addressed me on behalf of the applicant interveners. He told me that his clients had
offered security for their liability for the plaintiffs' claim and that this had been refused
c by the plaintiffs' solicitors. It was refused because the applicants could not possibly be
liable to the plaintiffs for the sum claimed.

Counsel submitted that the registrar should not have extended the validity of the writ
in this action. His first ground was that the second writ had been issued in respect of the
same cause of action between the same parties. Certainly the plaintiffs' solicitors intended
that the second writ should be between the same parties, because their clients wanted to
d secure a judgment against Joseph Roth. But the plaintiffs' solicitors were ignorant of the
change of ownership of the Helene Roth. The second writ has not been served. It can
be served on the ship within the jurisdiction, but that would be a sleeveless errand
because the ship cannot be arrested in the second action. The reason for this is that the
person who would be liable on the claim in an action in personam was not at the time of
the issue of the second writ the beneficial owner of all the shares in the ship against which
e the action is brought. I need say no more about the second writ because it can have no
effect on the action commenced by the first writ.

The Admiralty jurisdiction of the High Court cannot be invoked by an action in rem
against a ship in cases to which s 3(4) of the 1956 Act applies if at the time when the
action is brought the ship is not in the beneficial ownership of the person liable in
personam. For this reason it behoves solicitors whose clients wish to take advantage of
f that subsection to issue a writ without delay after the cause of action has arisen. If
solicitors act promptly, it is likely that for the purposes of service the validity of the writ
will expire well before the claim has become stale. If there has been no reasonable
opportunity to serve the writ, its validity ought to be extended. If the ownership of the
ship named in the writ has been changed before an application to renew the writ has
been made, it seems to me that the case for extending its validity is overwhelming. This
g is because, in contrast to the vast majority of Queen's Bench actions, the plaintiff can no
longer successfully invoke the jurisdiction of the High Court by issuing another writ in
rem. It was submitted by counsel for the applicants that the effect of renewing a writ in
such circumstances would be to expose a third party to an action in rem. He further
submitted that if, as in this case, the new owner purchased at a time when the writ could
no longer validly be served, he purchased a ship which had then achieved immunity
h from service. Counsel likened this situation to that of a defendant who has achieved
immunity by a time-bar. I cannot accept this analogy. The existence of a time-bar is
known to the plaintiff's advisers. They are under a duty to pursue an action diligently.
If, due to their inaction, the validity of a writ expires, it is not necessarily unjust that the
plaintiff should lose his right to proceed. But a change of ownership of a ship has a
different quality. The sale may be carried out secretly, and it is voluntary. If it is to have
j the effect for which counsel contends, then the defendants are able to introduce their
own time-bar without bringing it to the notice of the plaintiffs.

Merchant ships move freely all over the world. Sometimes they leave port before
their owners have discharged their debts to those ashore who have supplied the ship with
goods, materials or fuel, or to those who have repaired or equipped the ship, or to agents

who have made disbursements on account of the ship. One of the functions of this court is to assist creditors to obtain satisfaction of their just claims. Accordingly, if a writ in rem is issued before any change in the ownership of a ship has occurred, a subsequent change of ownership would provide good cause for renewing the writ unless those who have conduct of the action have obviously not pursued it with diligence. Counsel for the applicants submitted that this is not the correct approach because the purchaser of the ship may be prejudiced. I do not accept this submission either on the specific facts of this case or as a general proposition. On the facts of this case it is clear that the change of ownership of the Helene Roth was a change within a group of companies. Counsel submitted that the fact that the change of ownership was a change between companies in the same group is irrelevant unless the sale was made with the intention of evading the arrest of the ship. There may be many reasons for the sale of a ship, some good commercial reasons, others provoked by a wish to avoid the possibility of the ship being arrested by a court exercising Admiralty jurisdiction. This court is not concerned with the motive for a change of ownership, but it is concerned with the fact of such a change. I have little doubt that those responsible for making the decisions as to the sale and purchase of the Helene Roth knew full well that a claim was pending against Joseph Roth. The general proposition as to prejudice was dealt with by Brandon J in *The Monica S*[1] when he said:

> '[Counsel] said that a would-be purchaser of a ship would have to reckon with the possibility of numerous claims having already attached to the ship without his having notice of them. I am not much impressed with this argument for this reason. A purchaser always has to reckon with the possibility of maritime liens, and under many foreign laws all or most of the claims which in England only give a right of action in rem give rise to such liens.'

It would be surprising if the interveners had not protected themselves against a claim such as this one by taking an indemnity from the seller against any claims which attached prior to the sale. Even if the applicants did not take this precaution, I should not regard that as a good reason for depriving the plaintiffs of the security of the ship to satisfy any judgment they may obtain. The right to arrest a ship is part of the law of England and is recognised by international convention. It is a valuable weapon in the hands of any court exercising Admiralty jurisdiction. All shipowners are, or should be, aware of it.

For these reasons, the application is dismissed with costs.

Application dismissed. Leave to appeal.

Solicitors: *Bentleys, Stokes & Lowless* (for the applicants); *Coward Chance* (for the plaintiffs).

N P Metcalfe Esq   Barrister.

---

1   [1967] 3 All ER 740 at 758, [1968] P 741 at 769

Millican and another v Tucker and others

COURT OF APPEAL, CIVIL DIVISION
BUCKLEY AND DONALDSON LJJ
15th, 16th, 23rd JANUARY 1980

b *Legal aid – Unassisted person's costs out of legal aid fund – Costs incurred by unassisted party – Costs incurred in proceedings between him and party receiving legal aid – Costs of counterclaim where defendant legally aided – Counterclaim raising issues common to both claim and counterclaim – Judge ordering payment of plaintiff's costs of counterclaim out of legal aid fund and directing that the costs attributable to common issues be apportioned equally to claim and counterclaim – Whether jurisdiction to make direction – Whether costs incurred in claim can be appropriated to counterclaim – Legal Aid Act 1974, s 13(1).*

The plaintiffs were entertainers who entered into management contracts with the individual defendants and the defendant company. Substantial sums by way of royalties were paid to the defendants on behalf of the plaintiffs. The plaintiffs brought an action against the individual defendants and the company claiming declarations that they were induced by the individual defendants' fraud and oppression to enter into the contracts and that the contracts were invalid, and seeking an account of the sums received by the defendants on the plaintiffs' behalf. The plaintiffs were unassisted litigants but the individual defendants obtained legal aid, with nil contributions, which extended to a counterclaim against the plaintiffs. By their defence the defendants denied the allegations made in the claim, and by their counterclaim claimed declarations that the contracts were valid. The issue raised by the claim and the counterclaim were therefore identical. At the trial the defendants raised a new issue in the counterclaim, by an amendment, namely a claim for remuneration on a quantum meruit basis. The action was settled on terms in the plaintiffs' favour and the defendants abandoned their counterclaim. The plaintiffs incurred costs of between £6,000 and £7,000 on the claim and counterclaim. Only a small part of that sum was attributable to the quantum meruit issue. The company was insolvent and since the defendants' legal aid contribution was nil the judge made no order against them for the costs of the counterclaim. The plaintiffs applied under s 13[a] of the Legal Aid Act 1974 for payment of those costs out of the legal aid fund. The judge ordered payment of the costs of the counterclaim out of the fund and directed that the 'costs incurred' in the counterclaim for which payment out of the fund could be ordered were not confined to those costs of the counterclaim which were additional to the costs of the claim (ie the costs on the quantum meruit issue) but extended to half of the costs of issues which were common to the claim and the counterclaim. The Law Society appealed, contending that the judge only had jurisdiction to award out of the fund those costs of the counterclaim which were additional to the costs of the claim.

Held – Costs incurred in connection with a claim could not be appropriated to a counterclaim, either wholly or in part, for the purposes of an order under s 13(1) of the

---

a   Section 13, so far as material, provides:

    '(1) Where a party receives legal aid in connection with any proceedings between him and a party not receiving legal aid (in this and section 14 below referred to as "the unassisted party") and those proceedings are finally decided in favour of the unassisted party, the court by which the proceedings are so decided may, subject to the provisions of this section, make an order for the payment to the unassisted party out of the legal aid fund of the whole or any part of the costs incurred by him in those proceedings . . .

    '(3) Without prejudice to subsection (2) above, no order shall be made under this section in respect of costs incurred in a court of first instance, whether by that court or by any appellate court, unless—(a) the proceedings in the court of first instance were instituted by the party receiving legal aid . . .'

1974 Act for payment of the costs of the counterclaim out of the legal aid fund, because 'costs incurred' in a counterclaim referred solely to the costs occasioned by the *a* counterclaim. On the facts, the costs of the issues common to the claim and the counterclaim were costs incurred in the claim since those issues were raised by the claim and defence and were not costs occasioned by the counterclaim. Neither those costs, nor a portion of them, should therefore have been included in the order for payment of the costs of the counterclaim out of the legal aid fund and accordingly the appeal would be allowed (see p 1088 *a* to *d*, post). *b*

Atlas Metal Co v Miller (1898) 2 QBD 500 and *Medway Oil and Storage Co Ltd v Continental Contractors Ltd* [1928] All ER Rep 330 applied.

Saner v Bilton (1879) 11 Ch D 416 considered.

Notes

For costs awarded against an assisted party, see 30 Halsbury's Laws (3rd Edn) 502, para 933. *c*

For the Legal Aid Act 1974, s 13, see 44 Halsbury's Statutes (3rd Edn) 1053.

Cases referred to in judgments

Atlas Metal Co v Miller [1898] 2 QB 500, 67 LJQB 815, 79 LT 5, CA, 40 Digest (Repl) 473, 577.

Bremen, The [1931] P 166, 100 LJP 122, 145 LT 565, 18 Asp MLC 252, 40 Ll L Rep 177, CA, *d* 42 Digest (Repl) 843, 6240.

Medway Oil and Storage Co Ltd v Continental Contractors Ltd [1929] AC 88, [1928] All ER Rep 330, 98 LJKB 148, 140 LT 98, HL, 40 Digest (Repl) 471, 565.

Saner v Bilton (1879) 11 Ch D 416, 48 LJ Ch 545, 40 LT 314, 40 Digest (Repl) 473, 572.

Stentor, The [1934] P 133, [1934] All ER Rep 545, 103 LJP 105, 152 LT 450, 18 Asp MLC 490, 49 Ll L Rep 9, CA, 1 Digest (Reissue) 389, 2742. *e*

Ward v Morse, Re Brown (1883) 23 Ch D 377, 52 LJ Ch 524, 49 LT 68, CA, 40 Digest (Repl) 471, 556.

Cases also cited

Christie v Platt [1921] 2 KB 17, CA.

Cinema Press Ltd v Pictures and Pleasures Ltd [1945] 1 All ER 440, [1945] KB 356, CA. *f*

Interlocutory appeal

In an action between the plaintiffs, Alan Millican and Thomas Nesbitt, unassisted litigants, and the defendants Leonard William Jesse Tucker, Mardistar Ltd and James Patrick Houlihan, of whom the individual defendants were legally aided, which was settled at the hearing of the action on terms which in effect decided the proceedings in the plaintiffs' *g* favour, the trial judge, Browne-Wilkinson J, by an order made on 26th November 1979, ordered that the plaintiffs' costs incurred in connection with the defendants' counterclaim should be paid out of the legal aid fund and directed that where issues in the proceedings were common to the claim and the counterclaim the costs attributable to those issues should be apportioned as to one half to the claim and as to the other half to the counterclaim. The Law Society appealed from that order on the ground, inter alia, that the *h* judge had no jurisdiction to make such a direction. The facts are set out in the judgment of Donaldson LJ.

Duncan Matheson for the Law Society.

W H Goodhart QC for the plaintiffs.

j

Cur adv vult

23rd January. The following judgments were read.

DONALDSON LJ. In this appeal the legal aid fund challenges an order for costs made against it by Browne-Wilkinson J. The plaintiffs were coal miners and part-time

entertainers. In 1973 they appeared on more than one occasion as singers on the television

a programme Opportunity Knocks. They were a great success. This success did not pass
unnoticed. Mr Tucker and Mr Houlihan, defendants in the action, decided that they
would share in that success. They induced the plaintiffs to appoint them as managers for
a year. Under this contract the defendants' remuneration was no less than 30% of the
plaintiffs' gross receipts.

The plaintiffs greatly impressed the judge as men of the highest integrity, men whom

b the judge said that he admired in every way. Unfortunately (and this is no criticism of
them) they lacked all business acumen. This led them not only to accept the original
management contract, but also a suggestion from the defendants that this should be
superseded by another contract under which the defendants received 35% of the plaintiffs'
gross receipts for a period of three years. But even this did not satisfy the defendants. They
negotiated a contract with Pye, under which a large sum was paid to them on behalf of the

c plaintiffs as advance royalties. They then formed a company, Mardistar Ltd, in which the
plaintiffs had only a 60% interest, later reduced to a minority interest. The remaining
shareholders were, of course, the individual defendants. The plaintiffs were induced to
agree that what remained of their gross earnings after paying the 35% management fee
would be paid to Mardistar Ltd in exchange for a salary of £10 per week, and that this
arrangement should continue for five years.

d The plaintiffs eventually took legal advice. As a result they sued Mr Tucker, Mr
Houlihan and Mardistar Ltd for declarations that the second management contract and the
contract with Mardistar had been induced by oppression and fraud and were not binding
on them. They also claimed an account of all sums received by the defendants on their
behalf. Pending the trial of the action they took such steps as were open to them to ensure
that they and not the defendants received fees payable to them in respect of their activities

e as entertainers.

The individual defendants obtained legal aid. In April 1976 they delivered a defence
denying all the plaintiffs' allegations. A year later Mr Tucker obtained an extension of his
legal aid certificate entitling him to counterclaim against the plaintiffs. The defence was
then amended and a counterclaim delivered. By the counterclaim Mr Tucker sought a
declaration that the second management contract was binding. The company, for its part,

f sought a similar declaration that its contract was binding. Both Mr Tucker and the
company also claimed an account from the plaintiffs. At the trial Mr Tucker added an
alternative counterclaim for remuneration on the basis of a quantum meruit.

The hearing began in March 1979, but after two adjournments the dispute was settled.
The plaintiffs withdrew their allegations of fraud but, subject to that, the settlement
amounted to a total surrender by the defendants. But it was a hollow victory. The three-

g year life of the second management contract had already expired and the Mardistar
contract was due to expire shortly. The large sums of money received by the defendants
had evaporated. Mardistar was insolvent and the plaintiffs had to accept a judgment
against the individual defendants for no more than £2,000. Against this they had incurred
costs amounting to between £6,000 and £7,000, and, the defendants being legally aided
with nil contributions, no part of these costs could be recovered from them. In addition,

h the plaintiffs were faced with a claim by Pye for the repayment of £8,000 of advance
royalties, money which had gone to the defendants. As the judge rightly said, it was a very
hard case.

In these circumstances, the plaintiffs sought an order for costs against the legal aid
fund under s 13 of the Legal Aid Act 1974. They were successful. The judge ordered the
payment by the fund of the plaintiffs' costs of the counterclaim and directed that in

j taxing those costs the costs incurred after the date of the counterclaim on issues common
to both claim and counterclaim should be divided equally between the costs of the claim
and those of the counterclaim. The legal aid fund now challenges the jurisdiction of the
judge to make this order.

Let it be said at once, as the judge himself said, that there is no criticism of the Law
Society for granting legal aid to the defendants. At the stage at which legal aid had to be

granted or refused, those concerned did not know the true facts. They had to rely on what they were told by the defendants.

The making of an order for costs against the legal aid fund at first instance is exceptional, because no less than six conditions have to be satisfied. These are as follows. (1) The proceeding in the court of first instance must have been started by the assisted party. It is now accepted that this condition is met in that the counterclaim, which was instituted by Mr Tucker, is to be regarded as a proceeding separate from the claim. (2) The unassisted party must have succeeded. The counterclaim was settled by abandonment, but it is accepted that this constituted success by the plaintiffs for the purposes of the section. (3) The court must have considered what order for costs should be made against the assisted party. The judge did so and decided that no order for costs should be made, because Mr Tucker was an assisted person with a nil contribution. (4) Apart from the fetter imposed by the Legal Aid Act 1974, an order for costs would have been made against the assisted party for the payment of the unassisted party's costs. This condition is satisfied. (5) In the absence of an order against the legal aid fund, the unassisted party will suffer severe financial hardship. If the judge's order is right, the plaintiffs will recover something of the order of £2,000. Clearly the refusal to make an order having this effect would cause the plaintiffs severe financial hardship, for their means are such that they are now themselves eligible for legal aid. If, however, the order is wrong, any other order would entitle the plaintiffs to some quite insignificant sum and no hardship would be caused by refusing to make it. (6) It must be just and equitable in all the circumstances that provision for the costs incurred by the unassisted party in the proceedings in which the other party was assisted should be made out of public funds. In the most unfortunate circumstances of the present case, it has not been contended that it would be other than just and equitable that the plaintiffs' costs should be met out of public funds.

Where a court orders that claim and counterclaim be dismissed (or allowed) with costs, the rule of taxation is that the claim should be treated as if it stood alone and the counterclaim should bear only the amount by which the costs of the proceedings have been increased by it. This is the rule in *Saner v Bilton*[1], which was approved by the House of Lords in *Medway Oil and Storage Co Ltd v Continental Contractors Ltd*[2]. In the present case almost the whole of the plaintiffs' costs would have been incurred if the claim had stood alone, because the counterclaim did little more than claim declarations which were the mirror image of those claimed by the plaintiffs. This is not to say that the counterclaim was unnecessary, only that it scarcely added to the costs. The counterclaim for an account would, if successful, have added to the costs at the later stage of an enquiry, but that stage was never reached. Whilst it is true that the counterclaim for remuneration on the basis of a quantum meruit did raise a new issue, it is unlikely that it involved the plaintiffs in any significant increase in their costs. A simple order that the legal aid fund pay the plaintiffs' costs of the counterclaim would therefore produce very little benefit.

A trial judge has a wide discretion in deciding what order as to costs should be made inter partes. Browne-Wilkinson J considered that to make such an order in this case would do less than justice to the plaintiffs for two reasons, first, whilst the bringing of the counterclaim may not have appreciably increased the plaintiffs' costs, it made it much more difficult for the plaintiffs to discontinue the action if they thought that the costs were becoming too large; and, second, the counterclaim was a matter of real substance since it made positive claims to recover moneys from the plaintiffs and was not merely defensive. In the circumstances, he thought it right to make a special direction that the costs of common issues be divided equally between the costs of the claim and the counterclaim.

If this order had been made inter partes, it would have been well within the judge's discretion. But it was not. It was made between the plaintiffs and the legal aid fund,

---

1   (1879) 11 Ch D 416
2   [1929] AC 88, [1928] All ER Rep 330

which was not a party to the proceedings, and it was made pursuant to a statutory power
a and not in the exercise of the inherent jurisdiction of the court. The judge recognised
this distinction. Section 13(1) of the Legal Aid Act 1974 authorises the court to 'make an
order for the payment to the unassisted party out of the legal aid fund of the whole or any
part of the costs incurred by him in those proceedings'. In a case in which the assisted
party institutes the counterclaim rather than the claim 'those proceedings' means the
counterclaim. Browne-Wilkinson J therefore directed himself that he could only
b properly order the payment of costs which, on the ordinary meaning of the words, can
properly be called costs of the counterclaim, and that the section made it clear that, in the
context of this action, the legal aid fund was not to bear any part of the costs of the claim
by the plaintiffs.

I agree that *Saner v Bilton*[1], viewed in isolation, might be thought to do no more than
define what is meant by the words 'costs of the counterclaim' where the counterclaim is
c allowed or dismissed with costs. However, I do not think that it is possible to take so
narrow a view of the later cases. For present purposes the most important of these is
Atlas Metal Co v Miller[2]. It is not mentioned in the judgment and may not specifically
have been brought to the attention of the judge. It was, however, referred to and
approved in the *Medway Oil* case[3].

Lindley MR, giving the judgment of the Court of Appeal in the *Atlas* case[4], said:

d   'What are costs of a counter-claim? The answer must be the costs occasioned by
          it. No costs not incurred by reason of the counter-claim can be costs of the counter-
          claim. The fact that if there had been no action the costs of the counter-claim would
          have been larger, because the defendant would then have had to issue a writ and
          take other proceedings, does not make costs not incurred costs incurred, and in
          considering what the costs of a counter-claim really have been in any particular case,
e   the costs saved by not bringing a cross-action cannot be treated as costs incurred.
          The introduction of counter-claims has given litigants advantages in this respect.
          Counter-claims, although cross-actions for all purposes of procedure and evidence,
          cost less than actions, and the party who has to pay the costs of a counter-claim gets
          the benefit of the cheaper procedure. To include in the costs of a counter-claim any
          costs not occasioned by its being a counter-claim, but saved by its being what it is,
f   appears to us wrong in principle and opposed to *Saner v. Bilton*[1] and *Ward v. Morse*[5].'

The order under appeal seeks by the special direction to include in the costs of the
counterclaim costs which were not occasioned by it, but were saved because the issues
had already been raised by the claim and defence. This is permissible inter partes,
because all that the judge is then doing is to make an order that one party should pay part
g of the costs both of the claim and of the counterclaim. Indeed, it may often be right to
do so, because where, as here, both parties are seeking inconsistent declarations as to their
rights, it may be largely a matter of chance, financial ballast or enthusiasm that
determines which party initiates the claim and which the counterclaim. It was to such
an order that Scrutton LJ referred in *The Stentor*[6], when he said:

h   'Each judge, under the present system now set up by Order LXV., r. 1, has
          discretion, and he can make such order as he likes. If he makes an order in common
          form, it is no doubt important that it should be known what the order in common
          form means; but nothing is to bind this Division or any other Division to make any

---

j 1   (1879) 11 Ch D 416
    2   [1898] 2 QB 500
    3   [1929] AC 88 at 97–99, 105, 106, [1928] All ER Rep 330 at 334–335, 338, 339, per Viscount
        Haldane, Lord Carson, Lord Blanesburgh
    4   [1898] 2 QB 500 at 505–506
    5   (1883) 23 Ch D 377
    6   [1934] P 133 at 140, [1934] All ER Rep 545 at 548

particular form of order. If the judge thinks a better result will be obtained, as in *The Bremen*[1], by saying no costs, or by making an express order as to apportionment, he is perfectly at liberty to do it.'

But it is quite clear from the *Atlas* case[2] and the *Medway Oil* case[3] that costs incurred in connection with the claim can never be appropriated to the counterclaim, either wholly or by apportionment, so as to become part of the costs of the counterclaim. However dealt with by the judge's order, they remain part of the costs of the claim. If costs are incurred in connection with the claim and further costs are incurred in connection with the counterclaim, but the parties have aggregated those costs, for example, fees payable to counsel or to the solicitor for instructions to counsel, the judge or the taxing master can divide them on the basis of attributing to the counterclaim the increase in the costs occasioned by the existence of that counterclaim. This is not, however, an exercise of judicial discretion; it is merely doing what the parties ought really to have done themselves.

In my judgment, Browne-Wilkinson J has, inadvertently, done precisely what he set out to avoid, namely to order the legal aid fund to pay part of the plaintiffs' costs of the claim. Accordingly, I would allow the appeal.

BUCKLEY LJ. I entirely agree with the judgment which Donaldson LJ has just delivered and, although we are differing from the judge, I do not think that any useful purpose would be served by my restating in my own words the reasons which Donaldson LJ has given. I would however suggest that consideration should be given, when an appropriate opportunity arises, to amending the Legal Aid Act 1974, s 13, to enable a judge to order payment out of the legal aid fund of any costs incurred by an unassisted person in proceedings against an assisted person which the assisted person would, if he had not been assisted, have been ordered to pay to the unassisted person by reason of the assisted person's having commenced proceedings against the unassisted person, whether such costs are strictly costs of the proceedings so commenced or not.

Appeal allowed ; order of Browne-Wilkinson J in respect of costs in court below discharged. Leave to appeal to the House of Lords refused.

Solicitors: *Area Secretary, Law Society No 13 Legal Aid Area ; Bartlett & Gluckstein, Crawley & de Reya* (for the plaintiffs).

Diana Brahams   Barrister.

---

1   [1931] P 166
2   [1898] 2 QB 500
3   [1929] AC 88, [1928] All ER Rep 330

R v Secretary of State for the Home Department, ex parte Akhtar

QUEEN'S BENCH DIVISION
SHAW LJ AND KILNER BROWN J
21st DECEMBER 1979

Immigration – Detention – Minor – Minor given leave to enter United Kingdom – Minor registered as United Kingdom citizen on application made on his behalf by his alleged father – Evidence subsequently obtained that minor not son of alleged father – Detention of minor pending removal from United Kingdom as illegal immigrant – Whether minor immune from order directing his removal by virtue of registration as United Kingdom citizen – Whether registration as United Kingdom citizen effective – Whether detention lawful – British Nationality Act 1948, ss 7, 20.

On his arrival in the United Kingdom the applicant, a minor, claimed that he was the son of X, an immigrant who had settled in the United Kingdom. The authorities initially had doubts about his alleged relationship to X but he was eventually admitted to the United Kingdom on the basis that he was X's son. X subsequently applied, under s 7^a of the British Nationality Act 1948, for the registration of the applicant as a United Kingdom citizen. The Secretary of State granted the application. Enquiries were later made from which it appeared that the applicant was not X's son. He was detained by order of the Secretary of State pending his removal from the United Kingdom as an illegal immigrant. He applied for a writ of habeas corpus, contending that it was not open to the Secretary of State to treat him as an illegal immigrant and to apply the procedure for removal of an illegal immigrant, because he was a citizen of the United Kingdom by virtue of his registration under the 1948 Act and that registration remained effective until such time as he was deprived, under s 20(2)^b of that Act, of the benefit of that registration following an inquiry conducted in accordance with s 20(6) and (7). At the hearing the applicant conceded that the Secretary of State was, on the evidence, entitled to take the view that he was not X's son.

Held – If the applicant was not X's son, he could not have been validly registered as a citizen of the United Kingdom since under the 1948 Act a minor could be registered as a citizen of the United Kingdom only on an application made under s 7 of that Act in the prescribed manner by his 'parent or guardian'. Since he was not a citizen of the United Kingdom, it followed that it was not necessary for steps to be taken under s 20 of that Act to deprive him of that citizenship, and the Secretary of State could deal with him as an illegal immigrant. Accordingly his detention was not unlawful and the application for a writ of habeas corpus would be dismissed (see p 1092 h to p 1093 b, post).

---

a   Section 7(1), provides: 'The Secretary of State may cause the minor child of any citizen of the United Kingdom and Colonies to be registered as a citizen of the United Kingdom and Colonies upon application made in the prescribed manner by a parent or guardian of the child.'

b   Section 20, so far as material, provides:
    '(1) A citizen of the United Kingdom and Colonies who is such by registration (including a person registered under subsection (6) of section twelve of this Act) or is a naturalised person shall cease to be a citizen of the United Kingdom and Colonies if he is deprived of that citizenship by an order of the Secretary of State made under this or the next following section.
    '(2) Subject to the provisions of this section, the Secretary of State may by order deprive any such citizen of his citizenship if he is satisfied that the registration or certificate of naturalisation was obtained by means of fraud, false representation or the concealment of any material fact . . .'

Notes
For citizenship of minors by registration, see 4 Halsbury's Laws (4th Edn) para 914.   *a*
    For the British Nationality Act 1948, ss 7, 20, see 1 Halsbury's Statutes (3rd Edn) 869,
878.

Case referred to in judgments
R v Secretary of State for the Home Department and the Governor of Horfield Prison, ex parte   *b*
Sultan Mahmood [1978] Court of Appeal Transcript 541.

Motion
By notice of motion dated 6th September 1979 the applicant, Parvaz Akhtar, applied for   *c*
an order directing the issue of a writ of habeas corpus ad subjiciendum to the Secretary
of State for the Home Department for the release of the applicant from detention at the
Latchmere Remand Centre. The facts are set out in the judgment of Shaw LJ.

Ian MacDonald for the applicant.
Simon Brown for the Secretary of State.   *d*

SHAW LJ. This is a motion by leave of Mars-Jones J for a writ of habeas corpus in
respect of the applicant, Parvaz Akhtar, at present detained in the Latchmere Remand   *e*
Centre pending his removal from this country as an illegal immigrant.
    The material history can be shortly stated. The applicant claimed to be Parvaz Akhtar,
the son of Waris Ali, and that he had been born at Mirpur, Pakistan, on 4th September
1958. He first came to this country in 1972 as one of the family of Waris Ali who had
been settled in the United Kingdom for many years. Doubts then arose as to the alleged
relationship between Waris Ali and the applicant. He was at first refused entry but after *f*
an appeal he was admitted in 1975 as a son of Waris Ali. He then went to school and
obtained employment in England. A year or so later Waris Ali applied under s 7 of the
British Nationality Act 1948 for the registration of his son Parvaz Akhtar as a United
Kingdom citizen. The application was granted on the 16th June 1976.
    In March 1979 the applicant went to Denmark together with a daughter of Waris Ali,
the applicant's purported sister. There they parted company and the applicant was sent   *g*
back to England by the Danish authorities. As the result of interrogation and enquiries
on his arrival back in the United Kingdom the original doubts as to his relationship to
Waris Ali were revived. Further enquiry was made. In the result it appeared from the
information then obtained, including the applicant's own admission, that his real identity
was not Parvaz Akhtar, son of Waris Ali, but Abdul Hamid, son of Noor Hussein.
Counsel who has appeared for the applicant in support of this motion conceded, though   *h*
only for present purposes, that the evidence which was assembled after the applicant's
return was adequate to support the conclusion that he was not related to Waris Ali as his
son.
    On behalf of the applicant it was contended (i) that the applicant is immune from any
order directing his removal inasmuch as he is a citizen of the United Kingdom by virtue
of registration under the British Nationality Act 1948 (to which I shall refer as 'the 1948   *j*
Act'); (ii) that before he can be deprived under s 20(2) of the 1948 Act of that citizenship
he is entitled to require that there should be an inquiry constituted and conducted in
accordance with the provisions of s 20 (6) and (7); (iii) that until there has been such an
inquiry his registration as a United Kingdom citizen remains effective and that his
detention as an illegal immigrant is therefore unlawful.

a Counsel for the applicant submitted that it is not open to the Secretary of State to treat the applicant as an illegal immigrant and to apply the procedure of removal or deportation which is appropriate to somebody who can be so classified. What stands inexorably in the way, so it is contended, is the current status of the applicant as a citizen by registration of the United Kingdom. Until by due process under s 20 in the form of the inquiry there prescribed he is deprived of that status, he cannot, so the argument went, be dealt with as an illegal immigrant.

b The assumption underlying that argument, and the essential foundation for it, is that the purported registration of the applicant as a citizen of the United Kingdom was ab initio valid and effective and that it remains so until such time as he may be deprived of the benefit of that registration after due inquiry in accordance with s 20(6) and (7) of the 1948 Act. If the argument be ill-founded and the registration is a nullity from the outset, the applicant can appeal against his deportation or removal only pursuant to the provisions of the Immigration Act 1971 when he is out of this country.

c In the course of the argument reference was made to the unreported case of *R v Secretary of State for the Home Department and the Governor of Horfield Prison, ex parte Sultan Mahmood*[1] in which judgment was given by the Court of Appeal on 26th July 1978. In that case the applicant had sought and been granted registration under s 5A of the 1948 Act as a citizen of the United Kingdom. It appeared that his registration had been procured by a fraud, namely, the assumption by him of the identity of his dead cousin named Javed Iqbal. In the course of his judgment Roskill LJ said:

d

'On those facts it was argued that the appellant's registration evidenced by the certificate [it was common ground that the appellant had taken the oath of allegiance before the application was granted] involved that he had become and now was a citizen of the United Kingdom by registration, and that under s 20 of the 1948 Act he could only be deprived of that status in accordance with that section and not otherwise. It was contended that the Secretary of State was alleging fraud, false representation, the concealment of material facts, and that therefore the case fell fairly and squarely within sub-s (2) of s 20. Accordingly, sub-ss (6) and (7) of that section were applicable and the machinery prescribed by Sch 2 to the 1971 Act was not. This argument has the merit of attractive simplicity and it was forcibly advanced by counsel in this court on behalf of the appellant. But before the provisions of sub-ss (2), (6) and (7) of s 20 can be prayed in aid, in my judgment the appellant must show that he can bring himself within sub-s (1) of that section. He seeks to do so by reliance on the fact of registration as evidenced by the certificate. If it were clear that the appellant was the Javed Iqbal originally named and identified in the Pakistani passport and in the other relevant documents and that the Secretary of State had intended to grant registration to that person, this argument would clearly have great force because it would be to that person so named and identified that the grant would have been directed. But the evidence is that the person was dead. The Secretary of State's intention cannot have been to grant registration to the appellant for he did not know who the appellant was. He wrongly believed the appellant to be Javed Iqbal, which he was not, nor could he have been, for that individual was dead. There are, I think, only three possible effects of the purported registration. First, it was a grant to Javed Iqbal. Secondly, it was a grant to the appellant. Thirdly, it was a grant to nobody but was a nullity. I have given my reasons already for rejecting the first two possibilities. There remains the third, that the purported grant was a nullity. Counsel for the Secretary of State drew an analogy between contracts which are void and contracts which are voidable. This analogy, as I think, is useful though, like most analogies, incomplete. I accept that

e

f

g

h

j

---

1 [1978] Court of Appeal Transcript 541

in some cases it may be difficult to draw a dividing line in these cases between a registration which is a nullity and therefore void, as I think is the case with the present registration, in which case the alleged citizen by registration cannot bring himself within s 20(1) at all, and a registration which is only voidable, in which case the machinery of s 20(2), (6) and (7) has to be invoked to the exclusion of the relevant provisions of the 1971 Act.'

Then Geoffrey Lane LJ in the course of his judgment said:

'It seems to me that the only question to be decided is whether the appellant ever was a citizen of the United Kingdom by registration. I find it difficult to see how he could be. He chose to assume the identity of a dead man, he took the oath of allegiance and filled in the necessary forms in the dead man's name. I find it impossible to say that in those circumstances Sultan Mahmood became a citizen of the United Kingdom any more than did Javed Iqbal.'

That was reiterated by Stephenson LJ in these terms :

'. . . I have come to the conclusion, in spite of the deep impression which the language of s 20, read against that background, and the powerful argument of counsel for the appellant first made on my mind, that the appellant never became a citizen of the United Kingdom and colonies by registration and was not registered as such, any more than Javed Iqbal. On the assumed facts, his fraud was so thorough-going as to take him over the dividing line referred to by Roskill LJ and to keep him outside the section altogether.'

Roskill LJ had referred to the dividing line between a fraud which went to the root of the matter and a fraud which in a sense was merely incidental or collateral.

An examination of the relevant provisions of the 1948 Act shows that the present case is even stronger against the applicant. Section 5A of the Act empowers the Secretary of State to cause a person of full age to be registered as a citizen of the United Kingdom if that person satisfies the Secretary of State as to the matters prescribed in sub-ss (1) and (2) of that section. Once the Secretary of State is so satisfied in regard to such a person he may effectively cause that person to be registered as a citizen. If the Secretary of State has been induced to be so satisfied 'by means of fraud, false representation or the concealment of any material fact' in relation to the prescribed particulars he 'may by order deprive [the person registered] of his citizenship' as is enacted by s 20(2). Those particulars are collateral or incidental to the application for registration. If, however, the applicant for registration is not of full age or is not the person whose identity he claims, the application fails in limine, for the Secretary of State has no power under s 5A to grant registration to a minor or to any person of full age other than the actual named applicant. Any purported grant to a minor or such other person is ultra vires the Secretary of State. It is unnecessary, in my view, to consider the degree or nature of the fraud or to decide whether it is such as to vitiate the registration so as to render it void, or whether it is voidable only, and therefore calls for the inquiry contemplated by s 20(6) and (7) when it is sought to deprive a person of the grant of citizenship by registration.

The power of the Secretary of State to cause a minor to be registered as a citizen of the United Kingdom is derived from s 7 of the 1948 Act. The power arises, however, only within the ambit of the section, that is to say where an application is made on behalf of a 'minor child of a citizen of the United Kingdom' and the application is made 'in the prescribed manner by a parent or guardian of the child'.

If as is conceded, the Secretary of State is entitled, for present purposes, to take the view that Waris Ali is not the father of the applicant who is a minor, it follows that there has never been any due application for registration which would empower the Secretary of State to cause the applicant to be registered as a citizen of the United Kingdom. The applicant has, accordingly, never held that status. There is no occasion to take steps under s 20 to deprive him of citizenship for it has never been effectively conferred on *a* him since the circumstances giving rise to the power of the Secretary of State in this regard have not existed.

In my judgment, therefore, this appeal fails and the application for a writ of habeas corpus is refused.

KILNER BROWN J. I agree.

b *Application dismissed.*

Solicitors: *Yusuf & Miller* (for the applicant); *Treasury Solicitor.*

Sepala Munasinghe Esq   Barrister.

c

R v Wilson

COURT OF APPEAL, CRIMINAL DIVISION
LAWTON LJ, CHAPMAN AND WOOLF JJ
d 18th DECEMBER 1979

Criminal law – Court of Appeal – Jurisdiction – Appeal against sentence – Offender committed to Crown Court for sentence – Crown Court bringing into effect suspended sentence consecutive to sentence imposed for offence for which offender committed to court – Total term less than six months – Whether right of appeal against whole of sentence or only against suspended sentence *e* *brought into effect – Criminal Appeal Act 1968, s 10(3)(a)(c)(iii).*

The appellant was convicted of an offence by a magistrates' court and committed for sentence to the Crown Court. The court imposed a sentence of one month's imprisonment for the offence and also brought into effect a previous suspended sentence of six months' imprisonment by substituting for that term a sentence of two months' imprisonment, *f* to run consecutively to the sentence of one month, making a total of three months' imprisonment imposed on the appellant. The appellant appealed against the whole of the sentence. The Crown contended that where the total sentence passed was less than six months but included a suspended sentence brought into effect, s 10(3)(c)(iii)ᵃ of the Criminal Appeal Act 1968 restricted the right of appeal to an appeal against the suspended sentence and the court had no jurisdiction to consider the sentence for the substantive *g* offence since it was for a term of less than six months and appeal against it was restricted by s 10(3)(a). The appellant contended that although the sentence for the substantive offence in respect of which there was committal to the Crown Court was for less than six months, and was therefore not within para (a) of s 10(3), there was a right of appeal against the whole sentence by virtue of para (c)(iii) of s 10(3) because in dealing with him for the substantive offence the Crown Court had made an order under s 23ᵇ of the Powers *h* of Criminal Courts Act 1973 bringing into effect the suspended sentence.

Held – Since the general policy of the 1968 Act was that the court should look at the whole of the sentence when considering an appeal against sentence, the proper construction of s 10(3)(a) and (c)(iii) of that Act was that when the Crown Court brought into effect a suspended sentence and also imposed a sentence for the substantive offence *j* then, even though the total sentence was less than six months, the appellant was entitled to appeal against the whole of the sentence and not merely against the suspended

---

a   Section 10(3), so far as material, is set out at p 1095 *b* to *d*, post
b   Section 23, so far as material, is set out at p 1095 *j*, post

sentence. It followed that the appellant had a right of appeal against the whole of the
sentence imposed by the Crown Court (see p 1095 g to p 1096 a, post).   a
R v Keelan (1975) 61 Cr App R 212 distinguished.

Notes

For appeal against sentence of the Crown Court after summary conviction, see 11
Halsbury's Laws (4th Edn) para 617.
For the Criminal Appeal Act 1968, s 10, see 8 Halsbury's Statutes (3rd Edn) 696.
          b

Case referred to in judgment

R v Keelan (1975) 61 Cr App R 212, CA.

Appeal

The appellant, James Andrew McNaughton Wilson, was committed to the Crown Court
under s 29 of the Magistrates' Courts Act 1952 for sentence in respect of his conviction   c
on 31st May 1979 at Reading Magistrates' Court of being knowingly concerned in the
fraudulent evasion of the prohibition on importing cannabis. On 13th July at the Crown
Court at Reading (the recorder, Mr Petre Crowder QC, sitting with justices) he was
sentenced to imprisonment for one month in respect of that offence and a suspended
sentence of six months' imprisonment passed on him at the Crown Court at Brighton on
1st April 1977 was brought into effect by substituting for the original term a lesser   d
sentence of two months' imprisonment, to run consecutively to the sentence of one
month. The appellant appealed against the whole of the sentence. The facts are set out
in the judgment of the court.

Philip Cox QC and *Basil Hillman* for the appellant.
David Jeffreys and *Susan Jackson* for the Crown.   e

LAWTON LJ delivered the following judgment of the court: On 31st May 1979 at
Reading Magistrates' Court, the appellant pleaded guilty to being knowingly concerned
in the fraudulent evasion of the prohibition of the importation of cannabis. He was
committed to the Crown Court for sentence pursuant to s 29 of the Magistrates' Courts
Act 1952. The offence for which he was committed, and the only offence, was the one   f
for which he was sentenced by the Crown Court.
    On 13th July 1979 in the Crown Court at Reading he admitted to the breach of six
months' suspended sentence of imprisonment which had been passed in the Crown
Court at Brighton on 1st April 1977. The recorder sentenced him to one months'
imprisonment. The suspended sentence was varied to one of two months' imprisonment
and was ordered to be put into effect consecutively. The result was that the Crown Court   g
at Reading sentenced him to a total of three months' imprisonment.
    He now appeals against that sentence by leave of the single judge. A point has arisen
whether there is jurisdiction in this court to hear his appeal. The problem arises under
s 10 of the Criminal Appeal Act 1968, as amended by the Courts Act 1971, the Criminal
Justice Act 1972 and the Powers of Criminal Courts Act 1973.
    Subsection (1) of s 10 reads as follows: h

> 'This section has effect in providing rights of appeal against sentence when a
> person is dealt with by the Crown Court (otherwise than on appeal from a
> magistrates' court) for an offence of which he was not convicted on indictment.'

    The offence for which the appellant was convicted was not, of course, on indictment.
The relevant part of sub-s (2) is as follows: j

> 'The proceedings from which an appeal against sentence lies under this section are
> those where an offender convicted of an offence by a magistrates' court—(a) is
> committed by the court to be dealt with for his offence before the Crown Court
> . . .'

a
It is relevant to point out the opening words of sub-s (2): 'The proceedings from which an appeal against sentence lies . . .' and the use of the words 'against sentence' contrast with the later words in the subsection, namely '. . . where an offender [is] convicted of an offence . . .'

It follows from sub-s (2) that prima facie, anyone who is sentenced by a Crown Court after committal pursuant to s 29 of the Magistrates' Courts Act 1952, has a right of appeal; but Parliament seems to have intended that that right should be restricted.

b
The restrictions are to be found in sub-s (3) of s 10. The relevant parts read as follows:

c
'An offender dealt with for an offence before the Crown Court in a proceeding to which subsection (2) of this section applies may appeal to the Court of Appeal against sentence in any of the following cases:—(a) where either for that offence alone or for that offence and other offences for which sentence is passed in the same proceeding, he is sentenced to imprisonment for a term of six months or more . . . or (c) where the court in dealing with him for the offence makes in respect of him— (i) a recommendation for deportation; or (ii) an order disqualifying him for holding or obtaining a licence to drive a motor vehicle [under Part III of the Road Traffic Act 1972]; or (iii) [and this is the important part] an order under section 23 of the Powers of Criminal Courts Act 1973 (orders as to existing suspended sentence when person subject to the sentence is again convicted) . . .'

d

e
Counsel, on behalf of the appellant has submitted that the object of para (c) of sub-s (3) is to set out cases where although the sentence is for a term of less than six months, nevertheless, there is a right of appeal. He submits that the right of appeal exists when the person appealing has been made subject to an order under s 23 of the Powers of Criminal Courts Act 1973. That arises from the wording of the section and in particular from the use of the phrase 'may appeal to the Court of Appeal against sentence', the argument being that once the appellant is before the court, because he comes under one of the exceptions in sub-section (3), then the court has power to deal with the whole of his sentence, even though the totality of the sentence may be less than six months.

f
Counsel for the Crown has appeared before us not to oppose the application, but to help the court with the construction of s 10 of the Criminal Appeal Act 1968. He has suggested that there is an alternative construction to be put on sub-s (3), namely that para (c)(iii) only entitles this court to look at and deal with that part of a sentence which is the suspended sentence and if that be so, it follows that the court would not have jurisdiction to deal with the substantive offence in respect of which the appellant was committed under s 29 of the 1952 Act.

g
That would be a very odd situation indeed, because it would mean that this court, when dealing with a suspended part of a sentence, would only be dealing with part of it. The general policy of the Criminal Appeal Act 1968 is that when anyone appeals against sentence, the whole sentencing position must be looked at by the court. Under s 11 of that Act an appellant cannot appeal against one of a number of sentences. The court is empowered to look at all the sentences passed on him.

h
Counsel for the Crown submitted that this construction was in line with the policy of the 1968 Act, viz that appeals are restricted to this court when the sentence is less than six months.

It may well be that what para (a) of sub-s (3) was intending to deal with was not suspended sentences at all. Our attention was drawn to the fact that under the Powers of Criminal Courts Act 1973, which was passed some years after the Criminal Appeal Act 1968, s 23(9) reads as follows:

j

'For the purposes of any enactment conferring rights of appeal in criminal cases any order made by a court with respect to a suspended sentence shall be treated as a sentence passed on the offender by that court for the offence for which the suspended sentence was passed.'

We have to construe sub-s (3)(*a*) of s 10 of the 1968 Act in the light of that general provision in the Powers of Criminal Courts Act 1973, which does make the construction *a* of sub-s (3) difficult, because it seems that with one hand Parliament is restricting appeals against sentences under s 10(3)(*a*), because a suspended sentence does come under that paragraph, but, with the other hand, it is giving a power of appeal against a suspended sentence. In our judgment a sensible construction of the 1968 Act is that when there is a suspended sentence brought into effect, the appellant can appeal not only against the suspended sentence, but against the sentence which has brought the suspended sentence *b* into effect.

It follows, in the circumstances of this case, that there is a right of appeal.

We call attention to the fact that this decision does not in any way, in our judgment, conflict with the decision of this court in *R v Keelan*[1]. Sentences of detention, with which that case was concerned, do not come within the exceptions set out in sub-s (3) of s 10.

We turn now to the facts of this case. On 18th January 1979, the appellant sent from *c* South Africa to his elder brother, who was a student at Reading University, a parcel containing 5·3 grammes of cannabis which was enough to make about 20 reefer cigarettes. The sending was accomplished by hollowing out the inside of a book. The parcel was intercepted at Reading post office and its contents examined. In due course the appellant's brother was arrested and is, we understand, awaiting to be dealt with by the court for this offence. *d*

The appellant himself was questioned on 15th February 1979. He admitted his guilt and made a written statement in the course of which he described how he and his brother were in South Africa for Christmas 1978 and whilst over there they came into possession of some cannabis. The pair of them discussed sending some of it back to England when the brother returned.

The difficulty in this case is this: in 1977 the appellant was charged and convicted on *e* a serious offence relating to drugs. In respect of that offence he received the suspended sentence of six months' imprisonment. We have been told by counsel who appears on his behalf, that in addition he was fined £500. It follows that this offence was committed whilst the period of the suspension was still operating.

Unfortunately, in the Crown Court, the recorder and the magistrates sitting with him, seem to have thought that this offence was committed eight months after the imposition *f* of the suspended sentence. The recorder said this to the appellant when sentencing him: '. . . Within a period of eight months you deliberately cut out that book and sent off that cannabis, and a suspended sentence is something which should not be interfered with . . .' Counsel who appeared for the appellant at once got up and pointed out that it was not a period of eight months, it was a period of 20 months. Even counsel was wrong, it was a period of nearly 22 months; in other words, the period covered by the suspended *g* sentence was almost exhausted.

In those circumstances, it seems to us that there could be a good ground for saying that the rigour of the law ought to have been mitigated substantially in relation to the suspended sentence.

The recorder and his magisterial colleagues did mitigate the sentence, but perhaps in the unusual circumstances of this case, having regard to the passage of time, it might not *h* have been necessary to bring the suspended sentence into effect at all.

The problem still arises, however, as to what should have been done to this young man who is now 22 years of age, for deliberately importing into this country a small quantity of cannabis. We stress that the quantity was small, 5·3 grammes, enough to make 20 reefer cigarettes. Anyone who brings drugs into this country is asking to be dealt with severely and anyone introducing drugs into a university is asking to be dealt with very *j* severely. Drug addiction amongst the young in universities is a problem and our courts have got to do their best to eradicate it; but the fact remains that the cannabis was sent by this young man to his brother and the quantity was such that it seems to us unlikely

---

1   (1975) 61 Cr App R 212

a that there was any element of trafficking in drugs. The probability seems to be that any reefer cigarettes made from the cannabis were intended for his brother. It is possible, we suppose, that they might have been handed round amongst a small circle, but they could not have been handed round very much if there was only enough to make the equivalent of a packet of cigarettes.

What is the right course to take? The appellant, save for these two drug offences, has led a blameless life. He is a hard working young man who has established himself in the *b* catering trade and at the present time is doing well in that trade. He has risked his liberty. He has seen the inside of a prison for a few days. It is to be hoped that the clanging of prison doors behind him has had a salutary effect on him.

With considerable hesitation, we have come to the conclusion, that in all the circumstances of this case, the sentence for the substantive offence and the suspended sentence, can be quashed. There will be substituted for the substantive offence a fine of *c* £500. There will be 14 days to pay with an alternative of one month's imprisonment.

Appeal allowed; sentence quashed; fine substituted.

Solicitors: *Nightingale & Francis & Co*, Reading (for the appellant); *Director of Public Prosecutions.*

d
                                      Sepala Munasinghe Esq   Barrister.

Electrical, Electronic, Telecommunication *e* and Plumbing Union v Times Newspapers Ltd and others

QUEEN'S BENCH DIVISION

O'CONNOR J

f 11th, 12th, 13th, 14th DECEMBER 1979

Trade union – Legal proceedings – Right of union to sue – Defamatory statements relating to reputation of trade union – Trade union not a body corporate because not a special register body – Trade union which was not a special register body seeking to sue in its own name for damages for libel – Whether union able to sue in its own name for damages for defamation in relation to its *g* *reputation as a legal entity – Whether union able to bring representative action for damages for defamation in its own name on behalf of all members of union – Trade Union and Labour Relations Act 1974, s 2(1).*

The plaintiff trade union, which was not a special register body within the meaning of s 30(1)[a] of the Trade Union and Labour Relations Act 1974, brought an action against the *h* defendants claiming damages for libel in respect of an article in the defendants' newspaper which the union alleged injured its reputation. The defendants contended (i) that, notwithstanding that s 2(1)(c)[b] of the Act provided that a trade union which was not a special register body could sue in its own name in proceedings founded on tort, the commission of the tort on which the present action was founded depended on the existence of a legal personality, and therefore the action was not maintainable because, by

j
    a   Section 30(1), so far as material, provides: '. . . "special register body" means an organisation whose name was immediately before [16th September 1974] entered in the special register maintained under section 84 of [the Industrial Relations Act 1971] and which for the time being is a company registered under the Companies Act 1948 or is incorporated by charter or letters patent . . .'
    b   Section 2(1) is set out at p 1102 *g* and p 1103 *e f*, post

virtue of s 2(1), the union was not a body corporate and could not be treated as if it were one and as a mere unincorporated association it had no legal personality of its own to **a** protect, and (ii) that furthermore the union could not maintain an action for damages for defamation on behalf of each and every one of its individual members in the name of the union (without identifying any particular member) in relation to a publication which allegedly impugned their several reputations as members of the union.

Held – The action would be dismissed for the following reasons—(i) A trade union, such **b** as the plaintiff union, which was not a special register body, could not bring an action for damages for defamation, because the provision that such a trade union 'shall not . . . be treated as if it were . . . a body corporate' in s 2(1) of the 1974 Act removed from such unions the quasi-corporate personality which had hitherto been attributed to them and which enabled them to sue for defamation (see p 1104 *d* to *g*, post); *Taff Vale Railway Co v Amalgamated Society of Railway Servants* [1901] AC 426 and *National Union of General and* **c** *Municipal Workers v Gillian* [1945] 2 All ER 593 considered.

(ii) The union could not bring an action for damages for defamation in a representative capacity because a representative action was not available to a number of different individuals where the relief sought was damages (see p 1104 *j*, post).

Notes   **d**
For proceedings by and against trade unions, see 38 Halsbury's Laws (3rd Edn) 378–381, paras 651–655, and for cases on the subject, see 45 Digest (Repl) 593–597, 1480–1509.

For the Trade Union and Labour Relations Act 1974, ss 2, 30, see 44 Halsbury's Statutes 3rd Edn) 1823, 1843.

e

Cases referred to in judgment
Bonsor v Musicians' Union [1954] 1 All ER 822, [1954] Ch 479, [1954] 2 WLR 687, CA; rvsd in part [1955] 3 All ER 518, [1956] AC 104, [1955] 3 WLR 788, HL, 45 Digest (Repl) 539, 1213.
Engineers' and Managers' Association v Advisory, Conciliation and Arbitration Service (No 1) [1979] 3 All ER 223, [1979] 1 WLR 1113, CA.   **f**
National Union of General and Municipal Workers v Gillian [1945] 2 All ER 593, [1946] KB 81, 115 LJKB 43, CA, 45 Digest (Repl) 593, 1484.
R v City of London Court Judge and Payne [1892] 1 QB 273, 61 LJQB 337, 66 LT 135, 7 Asp MLC 140, CA, 1(1) Digest (Reissue) 219, 1240.
Taff Vale Railway Co v Amalgamated Society of Railway Servants [1901] AC 426, 70 LJKB 905, 85 LT 147, 65 JP 596, HL, 45 Digest (Reissue) 595, 1500.   **g**
Vacher & Sons Ltd v London Society of Compositors [1913] AC 107, [1911–13] All ER Rep 241, 82 LJKB 232, 107 LT 722, 45 Digest (Repl) 300, 172.

Preliminary issues
By a writ issued on 21st November 1977 the plaintiff, the Electrical, Electronic, Telecommunication and Plumbing Union, brought an action against the defendants, **h** Times Newspapers Ltd, William Rees-Mogg (the editor of The Times) and Paul Routledge (a journalist employed by Times Newspapers Ltd), claiming, inter alia, damages for libel published in The Times on 18th November 1977. The defendants raised the preliminary point of law that the action was not maintainable at the suit of the plaintiff union, and the following preliminary issues were ordered to be tried: (1) Could a trade union (not being a special register body) maintain an action in its own name for damages for **j** defamation in relation to its reputation as a legal entity whether or not such entity was separate and distinct from its individual members? (2) If the answer to question (1) was in the affirmative, was any such cause of action dependent on proof of damage to the union's property or special damage suffered by the union? (3) Was such a union able to maintain an action for damages for defamation on behalf of each and every one of its

a individual members in the name of the union (without identifying any particular member or members) in relation to a publication which impugned their several reputations as members of the union? The facts are set out in the judgment.

Michael Kempster QC and *Adrienne Page* for the union.
Anthony Lester QC, C Hollander and *C Gray* for the defendants.

b **O'CONNOR J.** In this matter the Electrical, Electronic, Telecommunication and Plumbing Union commenced proceedings against Times Newspapers Ltd and others for libel, in respect of a publication published in The Times in November 1977, which the plaintiff union alleges was defamatory of it.

In those proceedings, and I need not refer to them further (the pleadings have the usual complex and extensive attributes found in actions of defamation), preliminary issues of law have been ordered for trial, and they are:

c
'(1) Can a trade union (not being a special register body) maintain an action in its own name for damages for defamation in relation to its reputation as a legal entity whether or not such entity is separate and distinct from its individual members?
'(2) If the answer to question (1) is in the affirmative, is any such cause of action dependent upon proof of damage to the union's property or special damage suffered
d by the union?
'(3) Is such a union able to maintain an action for damages for defamation on behalf of each and every one of its individual members in the name of the union (without identifying any particular members or member) in relation to a publication which impugns their several reputations as members of the union?'

e Those are the issues which fall for determination at this time.
Now it is important to have clearly in mind that these issues are concerned with the law touching the action of defamation. The issues are in no way concerned with any of the law which may or may not touch on industrial disputes. It is the law of defamation with which I am concerned. As was said by Denning LJ in the Court of Appeal in his dissenting judgment in *Bonsor v Musicians' Union*[1]:

f
'A libel is, of course, in its very nature a wrong to the person, not a wrong to property; and it is apparent that it is only by attributing legal personality to a trade union that it can be permitted to sue for a libel on itself.'

That is only applying to a trade union a much broader principle that the action for defamation is a personal matter because it is the reputation of the person which is defamed, and unless one can attach a personality to a body, it cannot sue for
g defamation. The best examples of this are found in the well-established law that a voluntary unincorporated association cannot maintain an action for libel on itself. Let me give an example. If one says of the Longbeach Anglers' Association that at the competition last Saturday they cheated, there is a defamatory statement; but the Longbeach Anglers' Association cannot maintain an action in respect of it. It may be that
h the individuals of the association who were partaking in the competition could successfully sue by saying that, although they were not named, the defamatory statement pointed at them with sufficient clarity and was so understood by those who knew that they were members of that association to enable them to sue for libel; but the association could not do so, and it could not do so, as I see it, on the principle that it has no personality of its own which is capable of being defamed. It may well be that an unincorporated
j association cannot sue in its own name for anything, but I am restricting what I have to say to defamation. So you have got to have personality which is capable of being defamed before a plaintiff can bring an action for libel.
Of an individual there is no difficulty; so too of a corporate body. That is an extensive

1   [1954] 1 All ER 822 at 837, [1954] Ch 479 at 510

term which it is just as well to have in mind. Corporate bodies are of a very much wider variety than most people think. The obvious example with which we are all familiar is *a* a limited company, but there are a wide variety of corporate bodies which have been set up by charter, by special Act of Parliament, by letters patent and so forth, and they all have corporate existence; and again, the law is clear, that a corporate body has a personality which can be defamed and it can bring an action in its own name for the libel on itself.

Next, it is clear that a partnership can do the same. The individual, as I have said, of *b* course can do so.

How then can an unincorporated body ever sue for libel in its own name? The answer on the cases is, I think, now beyond dispute. It is that the necessary personality must be found in some statute, or alternatively, in some grant which enables one to say of an unincorporated body that it has a sufficient personality which it is entitled to protect by bringing an action in libel. *c*

It is as well, at this stage, to clear out of the way the concept of group libel. Again, it is the law that a statement which is defamatory of a group at large cannot be sued on by the individual members unless the individual member can show that the defamatory statement was understood as referring to him. The examples are easy to think of. A statement that all lawyers are rascals does not allow any lawyer in the land to bring an action for libel. The circumstances of the publication may be such that the defamatory *d* statement identifies an individual or individuals sufficiently to show that the libel was aimed at the individual or individuals. Such an individual can sue.

Now where stands a trade union? It is not necessary for the purposes of this judgment to go into a detailed analysis of the history of trade unions in our law. It is well known that, before they were legalised, they ran foul of the law because they were unlawful combinations in the restraint of trade and suffered disabilities. But that is in the long and *e* distant past. The Trade Union Acts since 1871 have recognised trade unions, but they were without question unincorporated associations, and as such one would have thought that they could neither sue in their own names, nor be sued, and as such could not be defamed in their proper name.

In 1901 in *Taff Vale Railway Co v Amalgamated Society of Railway Servants*[1], the House of Lords got over this difficulty, but in circumstances which were disliked by the trade *f* union movement, by introducing what has come to be called a quasi-corporation, or a near corporation. Quite shortly, what happened was this. Looking at the registration of a trade union under the 1871 Act, and seeing the various matters dealt with in that statute, the House of Lords came to the conclusion that the trade union had a sufficient personality for that reason so that it could be sued in its own name and its funds charged in the action. *g*

The reverse of that coin necessarily followed; if it could be sued so also it could maintain an action in its own name and, as we shall see in a moment, unions soon did so and perfectly properly. The immediate effect of the *Taff Vale* decision[1] was to call for a change in the law to give protection to trade unions (nothing whatever to do with actions of libel, but in their industrial capacity), and in 1906 Parliament passed the Trade Disputes Act in order to reverse the decision of the House of Lords in the *Taff Vale* case[1]: *h* that is, to reverse the decision which had enabled the plaintiffs in that case to sue the union in tort. And in 1906, in the Trade Disputes Act, Parliament passed a blanket section relieving trade unions of liability in tort.

It left quite unaffected the decision of the House of Lords that this unincorporated body, because of the effect of the statute to which it was subject, had a quasi-corporate personality and thus we find that trade unions brought actions in their own name and, *j* I have been told, that they sued for libel as early on as 1913; but it is unnecessary to

1   [1901] AC 426

examine that because the matter was decided, in a decision which is binding on me, in
a 1945, in *National Union of General and Municipal Workers v Gillian*[1].

Now before I look at that case, which was a libel action, let me just look again at an
unincorporated association which has a statute bearing on it. If the statute, when looked
at, seems to give the unincorporated body powers which are only attributable to a person
or a corporate body, because a corporate body is the equivalent of a person, then,
following the decision in the House of Lords in the *Taff Vale* case[2], it is apparent that such
b an unincorporated association has got the necessary personality and that was the basis on
which trade unions could sue for libel. Parliament had given them immunity from
being sued in tort and that was held in the House of Lords to apply to a case where a trade
union was sued for libel. The argument was that the immunity did not extend to a tort
quite unconnected with any of the union's industrial activities or relations; but the
House of Lords applied the section, and stated that the words were clear beyond doubt
c and held that a union could not be sued for libel.

In 1945 the Court of Appeal decided in the case to which I have referred, *National
Union of General and Municipal Workers v Gillian*[1], that the trade union could sue in its
registered name for defamatory statements touching its reputation.

Now the basis of it, quite clearly, is to be found in attributing to the trade union,
because of its position under the Trade Union Acts, the necessary personality. Varying
d words are used in the actual decision. Birkett J, who tried the action at first instance,
came to the conclusion that the effect of the law was to give the union an entity. He put
it this way[3]:

> 'The 1871 Act, in my opinion, designedly created registered trade unions for the
> first time and designedly created a new entity in law, a new *persona*, and I think it
e > must follow that that new entity is in the same position as any other creature of the
> legislature.'

That view was effectively adopted in the Court of Appeal although not with quite the
same vivid certainty.

I do not find it necessary to look at the judgments of the Court of Appeal in *Gillian*[1],
f save to say that the power to sue for libel was shown to stem from the connection which
a trade union has with the Trade Union Acts, and it was given a quasi-corporate capacity.
If one took the words from Birkett J, which I have just read, one might think that the
Acts had created an entirely separate entity, but a reading of the judgment in the Court
of Appeal, and above all, of the speeches in the House of Lords in *Bonsor v Musicians'
Union*[4] shows, in my judgment, that that is not so. The speeches in *Bonsor*[4] were
g divided. Lord Morton and Lord Porter appeared to adopt the legal entity stance. Quite
clearly Lord MacDermott and Lord Somervell did not. They took the view that a trade
union was a quasi-corporation; that it had not got a brand new entity, or a corporate
entity, or personal entity of its own, but that it had, because of the position imposed on
the unincorporated association by the Trade Union Acts, as analysed in the *Taff Vale* case[2],
got a quasi-corporate personality, quite sufficient for it to be separate from its members,
h which was the point in the *Bonsor* case[4] where it was a member who was suing the union
for wrongful expulsion. That left the fifth member of the House, Lord Keith, and his
speech has been much analysed in the argument before me, but I have come to the
conclusion that the best one can do with Lord Keith's thinking is to say that he comes

j

---

1   [1945] 2 All ER 593, [1946] KB 81
2   [1901] AC 426
3   [1945] 2 All ER 593 at 602
4   [1955] 3 All ER 518, [1956] AC 104

down more nearly on the side of Lord MacDermott and Lord Somervell than he does on that of Lord Porter and Lord Morton.

In the end, as will be seen in a little while, it may not much matter, but following those decisions, it seems to me to be clear that the trade union was clothed with a quasi-corporate personality which enabled it to sue in its own name and to be sued in its own name where actions against it were permissible, and that was the basis for a trade union being able to protect its reputation by bringing an action for libel.

So, by the mid 1950s, if not before, the position was quite clear and there was no difficulty in the matter. I have already cited Denning LJ in the Court of Appeal in *Bonsor*[1]. It is interesting to note that in that judgment he took the view that a union was a legal entity. He said: 'I start by observing that as a simple matter of fact, not law, a trade union has a personality of its own distinct from its members.'

Now that, in my judgment, is as true today as it was in 1954 and indeed, one might say from 1901 onwards. In fact, does it have the same legal personality in law? On the law as it stood at the time of the decision in *Bonsor*[2], the answer is quite clearly, Yes, and the problem has arisen as a result of the change in the law which has occurred since that time.

In 1965 a Royal Commission was appointed to inquire into the position of the trade unions, under the chairmanship of Lord Donovan. In its report it considered the position of trade unions and it found that there were certain anomalies and recommended that the position be clarified by passing legislation requiring or saying that trade unions should be bodies corporate. It also made recommendations about the immunity in tort because there were all sorts of matters which were quite outside industrial relations, eg personal injuries that a visitor to union premises might suffer. It has got nothing whatever to do with the industrial capacity of a trade union. There were difficulties, which were set out in the report; and in the Industrial Relations Act 1971 effect was given certainly to the recommendation that unions should be bodies corporate. Now it is well known that that statute met with determined opposition from the trade unions and in due course it was repealed and replaced by the statute which governs their positions today. It is unnecessary, other than the statement which I have made, to look further at the 1971 Act because it has been repealed, and the present position, and the difficulty with which I am confronted, has been created by the Trade Union and Labour Relations Act 1974.

Let me come at once to what the difficulty is. When one looks at the statute, s 1(1) is in terse and quite unequivocal terms: 'The Industrial Relations Act 1971 is hereby repealed'. Thereafter, as transitional provisions, a whole series of matters dealing with different topics in that statute were preserved in Sch 4 to the 1974 Act. That is the end of s 1. Section 2, the side note to which reads, 'Status of trade unions', provides:

'(1) A trade union which is not a special register body shall not be, or be treated as if it were, a body corporate . . .'

In my judgment, those are absolutely clear words. One must remember the position in law at that time. At that time, trade unions if they were registered were not necessarily corporate bodies; they were made corporate bodies. If they were on the provisional register they had the attributes of corporate bodies and could properly be called quasi-corporate associations, and the whole background of the position of trade unions until 1971 was that they were quasi-corporate bodies. It was a matter which was as much in their interest as any possible disability. Nevertheless here we find Parliament telling us what a trade union may not be: it 'shall not be, or be treated as if it were, a body corporate'.

Now it is possible that the words 'or be treated as if it were', got into the statute because

1   [1954] 1 All ER 822 at 836, [1954] Ch 479 at 507
2   [1954] 1 All ER 822, [1954] Ch 479

of the dislike of the decision in the *Taff Vale* case[1]. I do not know and it is not for me to
speculate. It is my task to construe the words and if I find them to be absolutely clear
then, even though the result produced may be one which strikes me as being absurd, I
must give effect to them. That that is a well-known rule of construction is sufficiently
set out by Lord Atkinson in *Vacher & Sons Ltd v London Society of Compositors*[2] (that was
the case in which the House of Lords held that a union could not be sued for libel), where
he said this:

> 'So that if in this case the words in this section are plain and are not controlled by
> other portions of the statute, the contention that to interpret them according to
> their natural and ordinary meaning would result in placing trade unions above the
> law is, for the purposes of the judicial decision of this case, entirely irrelevant. We
> have nothing to do with it.'

He had cited the judgment of Lord Esher MR in *R v City of London Court Judge and Payne*[3]:

> 'If the words of an Act are clear, you must follow them, even though they lead to
> a manifest absurdity. The Court has nothing to do with the question whether the
> Legislature has committed an absurdity.'

It does not follow that the result which I am driven to in the present case is necessarily
an absurdity, but as I have said, it seems to me that those words are absolutely clear and
they are saying that a trade union is not to be a body corporate, and it is not to be treated
as if it were a body corporate. That is, it is removing from the status of a trade union that
which had been accorded to it from 1901 until 1971, when the matter was changed; and
there it is.

Section 2(1) of the 1974 Act goes on, and the words have to be carefully considered:

> '. . . but—(a) it shall be capable of making contracts; (b) all property belonging to
> the trade union shall be vested in trustees in trust for the union; (c) subject to
> section 14 below, it shall be capable of suing and being sued in its own name,
> whether in proceedings relating to property or founded on contract or tort or any
> other cause of action whatsoever; (d) proceedings for any offence alleged to have
> been committed by it or on its behalf may be brought against it in its own name;
> and (e) any judgment, order or award made in proceedings of any description
> brought against the trade union on or after the commencement of this section shall
> be enforceable, by way of execution, diligence, punishment for contempt or
> otherwise, against any property held in trust for the trade union to the like extent
> and in the like manner as if the union were a body corporate.'

If the words 'or be treated as if it were' were not in s 2(1), there would be absolutely no
difficulty because all those powers which are attributed and given to trade unions make
it quite clear that if they are, as the section would say, not a body corporate, they had the
attributes of one and they were to be treated as one, so that they could possess the
necessary personalities which they could protect by the action of defamation; but the
words are there, and the words are saying that that is exactly what is not to be done. I do
not find any ambiguity in them. It was submitted by counsel for the union that the
words should be read as though the words 'as if it were' were not there, namely that a
trade union shall not be, or be treated as, a body corporate, leaving it open to treat them
as a quasi-corporation. I would willingly adopt that construction if I thought it
permissible, because, as I have said, the matters contained in paras (a) to (e) of s 2(1) of the
1974 Act would give a trade union all the attributes of a quasi-corporation, and there
would be no difficulty.

Contrast s 2(1) with s 3(1) which deals with the status of employers' associations.

---

1   [1901] AC 426
2   [1913] AC 107 at 122, [1911–13] All ER Rep 241 at 248–249
3   [1892] 1 QB 273 at 290

Remember that many employers' associations were trade unions technically. Section
3(1) reads: 'An employers' association may be either a body corporate or an unincorporated *a*
association.'

Note the difference. Section 3(2) reads: 'Where an employers' association is
unincorporated . . .' and then there follow paragraphs (*a*) to (*e*) which are identical with
those found in s 2(1). A body corporate has those powers in any event and does not have
to have them given to them by the statute, and so an employers' association which is an
unincorporated association enjoying those powers, in my judgment, there being no *b*
restricting words, is quite plainly a quasi-corporation and has the power and the necessary
personality to protect its reputation by an action for defamation; and it is that which
really creates the difficulty because, as I have said, unless I was absolutely driven to it, I
would not construe the Act as removing from trade unions the personality which enables
them to sue in libel while preserving it for employers' associations, but regretfully I have
to construe the words of the 1974 Act, and s 2(1), to my mind, is not ambiguous and that *c*
is exactly what it does. It gives to the unincorporated body (and trade unions are more
closely defined in s 28 of the Act, which I need not read into this judgment; it shows that
they are unincorporated bodies) certain powers but they are unincorporated bodies
which are not to be treated as if they were corporate bodies and that is the creature which
is to enjoy the powers of making contracts, etc.

The fact that it can sue in tort does not mean that it can complain of the tort of libel. *d*
That is procedural. The tort of libel, as I have already demonstrated, must be founded on
possession of a personality which can be libelled and s 2(1) has removed that personality
from trade unions. I find nothing in the statute to show that those words are
ambiguous. There are many attributes which, but for the presence of the words 'or be
treated as if it were' in s 2(1), would simply confirm that a trade union enjoyed a quasi-
corporate personality and could bring an action in libel in its own name for the protection *e*
of its own reputation, and, as I have said, I am quite clear that apart from the law anybody
would say that a trade union has a separate reputation and should be entitled to protect
it; but there it is. Parliament has deprived trade unions of the necessary personality on
which an action for defamation depends; and to the first question which I have to decide
which is:

> 'Can a trade union (not being a special register body) maintain an action in its *f*
> own name for damages for defamation in relation to its reputation as a legal entity
> whether or not such entity is separate and distinct from its individual members?'

the answer is: 'No. It cannot.'

As I have said, I regret that I have to arrive at that decision but, I repeat, it seems to me
that I am driven to it by the clear words of the statute. *g*

Now as far as the second question is concerned the parties are agreed that it is not one
which I could answer in favour of the defendants because of decisions which are binding
on me; and the matter has not been argued but merely kept open for argument in a
higher court as and when the case reaches it.

The third question does arise, as I have answered the first question in the negative. Let
me repeat it: *h*

> 'Is such a union [that is, a trade union] able to maintain an action for damages for
> defamation on behalf of each and every one of its individual members in the name
> of the union (without identifying any particular members or member) in relation
> to a publication which impugns their several reputations as members of the union?'

I will deal with that matter quite shortly. The answer is No, for the simple reason that *j*
a representative action is not available to a number of different individuals where the
relief sought is damages; and that I think becomes quite obvious if one is thinking of a
libel action because one would be looking at the individual reputation of all the members
of the union and, no matter whether we are talking of 500, 5,000 or half a million, they
would all be different and the damages would be different and for that reason alone it

makes it quite unworkable and impossible to bring a representative action on behalf of
a all the members.

There are other reasons which also make it impossible. Something which is libellous
of the union as a whole in the words complained of, for the reasons I have already given
earlier in this judgment, could only be complained about by those individual members
of the union who could demonstrate that the words identified them in the circumstances
in which they were published; and that rules out all those who could not and so it is quite
b impossible to bring a representative action on behalf of all the members of the union.
To my mind, that is absolutely clear and I need say no more about it.

Now there is one last matter which I have got to deal with under the first question and
that is an alternative argument which was advanced by counsel for the defendants,
namely that, quite apart from the construction of the opening words of s 2(1), the true
construction of para (c) of that subsection also means that a trade union could not sue in
c libel. The submission went considerably wider than that because it would go to all torts;
and the submission was that the words 'Subject to section 14' governed what the union
could sue for, as well as what it could be sued for, or, perhaps more accurately, not sued
for. Section 14 gives the present immunity and it is noticeable that it is not as wide as
that in the 1906 Act. The basis of that submission can be put in the homely phrase of
what is sauce for the goose should also be sauce for the gander, and it was submitted that
d in so far as s 14 gave a trade union immunity from suit in tort, so too, it should be unable
to sue in tort to a like extent. But as I pointed out in argument, I find it quite impossible
to produce a mirror image by looking at s 14 and in any event, I am quite clear that it is
not necessary to give para (c) that construction. The fact that the opening words 'Subject
to s 14' appear at the beginning must, in my judgment, be construed by looking at s 14,
and s 14 gives immunity to the union and does not bar the union from suing in tort; and
e if that be the sole ground for trying to support the answer No to the first question, I
would rule against it and answer the question Yes.

[Following submissions by counsel on costs, his Lordship continued:] In the course of
the argument I was referred to a recent decision in the Court of Appeal subsequent to the
1974 Act, namely *Engineers' and Managers' Association v Advisory, Conciliation and
Arbitration Service (No 1)*[1]. That case arose out of a consideration as to how a trade union
f could appear; and at least one of the issues which had to be decided was whether a trade
union needed to appear by solicitors and counsel, and in the course of giving his
judgment on that topic, Lord Denning MR at the beginning of the judgment, had this
to say[2]:

g 'A question has arisen about the position of the United Kingdom Association of
Professional Engineers (UKAPE). It is a trade union. Mr Hickling, the deputy
general secretary, has come before us. He wants to make representations on its
behalf. The judge's view was that Mr Hickling had no right of audience. The
matter is of such importance that we invited the assistance of the Attorney-General.
[and then comes this passage:] Under s 2 of the Trade Union and Labour Relations
Act 1974 a trade union "shall not be, or be treated as if it were, a body corporate".
Nevertheless, it is a legal entity (see *Bonsor v Musicians' Union*[3]) . . .'

h
Those were words with which Lawton and Cumming-Bruce LJJ agreed. Lawton LJ[4] in
his judgment said of trade unions, 'They are not now unlawful conspiracies: they are
legal entities', but although it was accepted that the words were obiter and not binding
on me, it was submitted that they were of powerful authority and should persuade me
to come to the same conclusions. I regret that I cannot do that for reasons which I hope
j are clear from the judgment which I have given. The matter was never before the court

---

1   [1979] 3 All ER 223, [1979] 1 WLR 1113
2   [1979] 3 All ER 223 at 224, [1979] 1 WLR 1113 at 1115
3   [1954] 1 All ER 822, [1954] Ch 479
4   [1979] 3 All ER 223 at 226, [1979] 1 WLR 1113 at 1117

at all; it was never argued and the whole idea as to the basis of the capacity of the trade union to bring an action in libel was far from the court's thought when considering *a* whether the union could appear by a layman rather than a lawyer.

Judgment for the defendants on preliminary issues (1) and (3); judgment for the plaintiff union on preliminary issue (2); action dismissed.

Solicitors: *Lawford & Co* (for the union); *Alastair J Brett* (for the defendants).   *b*

K Mydeen Esq   Barrister.

c

Kokosinski v Kokosinski

FAMILY DIVISION
WOOD J
24th, 25th, 26th, 29th OCTOBER, 3rd DECEMBER 1979   *d*

Divorce – Financial provision – Conduct of parties – Duty of court to have regard to conduct – Conduct prior to ceremony of marriage – Relevance – Circumstances in which regard should be had to conduct prior to ceremony of marriage – Matrimonial Causes Act 1973, s 25(1).

In 1933 a Pole ('the husband') married a Polish girl and in April 1939 they had a son, *e* W. After the German invasion of Poland in 1939 the husband escaped to England where he met an English girl, X, in 1943. They worked together in a factory until 1946 when the husband left to found an engineering business. In 1947 the husband and X started living together and she contributed her wages towards the maintenance of the household. In July 1950 they had a son, C. In September 1950 a matrimonial home in Kilburn was purchased in the husband's name and in the same month X started working *f* full-time in the husband's business. Her wages continued to go towards the maintenance of the household. In about 1955 X changed her surname to that of the husband by deed poll. In 1957 he bought a bungalow in Wokingham for the use of the family at weekends. The bungalow was bought with money contributed by X and the company but was conveyed into the husband's sole name. In 1959 he gave one share in the company to X, keeping the remaining 4,999 shares himself. Later he transferred 2,499 *g* of them to C. In 1969 the husband was divorced by his wife in Poland. On 1st September 1971 he married X ('the wife'), in accordance with a promise he had made to her that he would do so as soon as his wife in Poland gave him a divorce. Early in 1972 a fresh matrimonial home in Cricklewood was purchased with the husband's or the company's money. The wife and C moved into it but the husband refused to join them. Cohabitation between the husband and wife thereupon ceased and was never *h* resumed. The husband had, over the years, been sending substantial sums of money to his wife in Poland and W, their son. W visited England often and during his visits also worked for the company. In 1975 the husband made a will leaving everything to W. Relations between the wife and C on the one hand and between the husband and W on the other were by then deteriorating fast, and in 1976 C and the wife presented a petition for the winding up of the company. Subsequently the husband agreed to sell his shares *j* in the firm to the wife and C for £40,000. The money was paid by C on 1st July 1977. A week later the wife filed a divorce petition and on 11th November a decree nisi was granted on the basis of the husband's desertion. In 1979 the house in Cricklewood, where the wife had been living, was sold for £42,000 and the loan was repaid. The wife thereupon had to move into a single room in the bungalow at Wokingham which was being occupied by her mother and sister. Shortly afterwards her shares in the company

a were transferred to C under a deed of trust executed by her at the time of their purchase. In 1979 the wife was 56 years old and still working for the company, from which she received £5,700 gross per annum. She had the use of a company car and travelled to the factory from Wokingham five or six days a week. She had in addition assets worth approximately £14,000. The husband continued to occupy the house in Kilburn and, although he offered rent to C, C accepted that he was under a moral

b obligation to house his father. The husband was 69 years old and had capital assets worth approximately £47,545 and an income of between £3,000 and £5,000 per annum. A decree absolute had not yet been granted and the wife applied to the court (i) for an order under s 15(1)*ᵃ* of the Inheritance (Provision for Family and Dependants) Act 1975 and (ii) for an order under s 23(1) of the Matrimonial Causes Act 1973 that the husband should make a lump sum payment to her of £13,500 so that she could buy a flat near her

c work. The husband contended that it would be inappropriate to grant a lump sum order because the court was bound by s 25(1)(*d*)*ᵇ* of the 1973 Act to have regard to 'the duration of the marriage' and the marriage had only lasted a few months, and was also bound by s 25(1)(*f*) to take into account the wife's 'contribution to the welfare of the family' only during the subsistence of the marriage, and could not take into consideration her conduct during the 25 years that the husband and wife were cohabiting prior to their

d marriage.

Held – (i) Although (a) the use of the phrase 'duration of the marriage' in s 25(1)(*d*) of the 1973 Act showed that the period between the ceremony of marriage and the final break-up of cohabitation was likely to be the most material and (b) the word 'family' in s 25(1)(*f*) referred only to the events which had occurred after the ceremony of marriage,

e the court was bound by s 25(1) to have regard to both the conduct of the parties and all the circumstances of the case, under both of which it could take into account behaviour which had occurred outside the span of the marriage, at least in a case where the conduct had affected the finances of the other spouse. It was the function of the court to reach a financial resolution of the problems of the family which was fair, just and reasonable as between the parties, and 'conduct' was a relevant factor not only when the question was

f whether a claim by a wife for financial relief should be cut down but also when the question was whether it should be increased (see p 1115 *f* to *j* and p 1117 *f g*, post); *Harnett v Harnett* [1974] 1 All ER 764, *Jones v Jones* [1975] 2 All ER 12 and *W v W* [1975] 3 All ER 970 applied; *Campbell v Campbell* [1977] 1 All ER 1 distinguished; *Wachtel v Wachtel* [1973] 1 All ER 829 considered.

(ii) The court could not do justice between the parties unless it took into account the

g wife's conduct during the 25 years that she and the husband had been cohabiting prior to the ceremony of marriage. She had been faithful, loving and hard working and had helped to build up the family business, whilst at the same time managing the home and

---

a Section 15, so far as material, provides:

  '(1) On granting a decree of divorce . . . or at any time thereafter, the court may, if the court

h considers it just to do so and the parties to the marriage agree, order that either party to the marriage shall not be entitled on the death of the other party to apply for an order [for family provision] under section 2 of this Act.

  '(2) In the case of a decree of divorce an order may be made under subsection (1) above before . . . the decreee is made absolute . . .'

b Section 25(1), so far as material, provides: 'It shall be the duty of the court in deciding whether to exercise its powers . . . to have regard to all the circumstances of the case including . . . (d) the age

j of each party to the marriage and the duration of the marriage . . . (*f*) the contributions made by each of the parties to the welfare of the family, including any contribution made by looking after the home or caring for the family . . . and so to exercise those powers as to place the parties, so far as it is practicable and, having regard to their conduct, just to do so, in the financial position in which they would have been if the marriage had not broken down and each had properly discharged his or her financial obligations and responsibilities towards the other.'

helping to bring up a son of whom both parents were justly proud. In the circumstances the husband would be ordered to make a lump sum payment to her of £8,000, the order being made under s 15 of the 1975 Act with her consent (see p 1117 g to p 1118 a and p 1119 e f, post).

Notes

For financial provision after a decree of divorce and the matters to which the court must have regard, see 13 Halsbury's Laws (4th Edn) para 1060.

For the Matrimonial Causes Act, ss 23, 25, see 43 Halsbury's Statutes (3rd Edn) 564, 567.

For the Inheritance (Provision for Family and Dependants) Act 1975, s 15, see 45 ibid 517.

Cases referred to in judgment

Armstrong v Armstrong (1974) 118 Sol Jo 579, [1974] Court of Appeal Transcript 137.
Campbell v Campbell [1977] 1 All ER 1, [1976] Fam 347, [1976] 3 WLR 572.
Davis v Johnson [1978] 1 All ER 1132, [1979] AC 264, [1978] 2 WLR 553, HL.
Harnett v Harnett [1974] 1 All ER 764, [1974] 1 WLR 219, CA, Digest (Cont Vol D) 429, 6962Aj.
Jones v Jones [1975] 2 All ER 12, [1976] Fam 8, [1975] 2 WLR 606, CA, Digest (Cont Vol D) 426, 6962Abc.
Trippas v Trippas [1973] 2 All ER 1, [1973] Fam 134, [1973] 2 WLR 585, CA, Digest (Cont Vol D) 421, 6786a.
W v W [1975] 3 All ER 970, [1976] Fam 107, [1975] 3 WLR 752, Digest (Cont Vol D) 428, 6962Ae.
Wachtel v Wachtel [1973] 1 All ER 829, [1973] Fam 72, [1973] 2 WLR 366, CA, Digest (Cont Vol D) 425, 6962Aa.

Case also cited

Chambers v Chambers (1979) 123 Sol Jo 689.

Application and cross-application

On 6th July 1977 the wife filed a divorce petition in which she claimed, inter alia, the following ancillary relief: periodical payments and/or such secured provision and/or lump sum or sums as might be just. On 11th November she was granted a decree nisi on the basis of the husband's desertion. On 13th January 1978 she gave notice of her intention to proceed with her application for ancillary relief. On 24th May the husband gave notice that he intended to apply to the court for periodical payments and/or such secured provision and/or lump sum or sums as might be just. The wife's application and the husband's cross-application were heard in chambers but judgment was delivered in open court. The facts are set out in the judgment.

Nicholas Wilson for the wife.
Nicholas Price for the husband.

Cur adv vult

3rd December. **WOOD J** read the following judgment: In this case I have been asked by the parties to give my judgment in open court. The issues arise on claims by each against the other for financial relief in ancillary matters following a divorce. In his final submissions counsel for the husband did not pursue the husband's claim for ancillary relief and I therefore consider only the wife's claims against the husband. In the main her claim is for a lump sum.

The petitioner ('the wife') was born on 4th December 1922 in the United Kingdom. Her present age is, therefore, nearly 57. She is living at Wokingham, Berkshire, occupying a small single bedroom in a three-bedroom bungalow where also live her

mother, aged 91, and her sister. The husband was born on 16th December 1910 in
a Poland and is now aged nearly 69. He lives at the former matrimonial home in Kilburn,
London.

The marriage took place on 1st September 1971 and cohabitation effectively ceased in
January or February 1972. A petition was filed on 6th July 1977 and a decree nisi was
granted on the basis of the husband's desertion on 11th November 1977. The wife's
application for ancillary relief is dated 13th January 1978 and the husband's cross-
b application 24th May 1979. No decree absolute has been granted.

The facts thus baldly stated indicate a very short marriage and counsel for the husband
relies on this fact more than any other in his submission that this is not a case where any
lump sum should be awarded. However, when the whole picture of the relationship
between this man and this woman is examined, a very different picture presents itself.

The husband was first married in Poland on 26th June 1933. He is Polish by origin,
c coming from a humble home. His first wife was some four years his senior. A son was
born of that marriage on 7th April 1939, named Wojciech, who is now aged 40. The
husband was by occupation an engineer, an expert in hydraulics of landing gear for
aircraft. When the invasion of Poland by Germany occurred he escaped and made his
way to this country. Thereafter he joined the Polish forces and trained in Scotland.
Whilst in Scotland he suffered some injury as the result of which he spent a number of
d months in hospital. After a period of time he came to a hospital in Surrey for a period
of convalescence and left there in 1943.

He was unfit to return to the forces and it was then that he met the wife for the first
time. She was helping to produce aircraft parts and her sister was also working in this
small factory. The husband also started to make small engineering parts and for the
remainder of the war, and until about 1946 or 1947, he and his wife were working
e together and with others in this engineering production. Some time early in 1946 a
small engineering company, E Ltd, was formed by the husband, together with some of
his friends. The factory was in Kilburn, London. During 1947 the husband and the
wife started to live together. From about this time until 1950, when Christopher their
son was born, she worked as a bus conductress. This occupation ceased shortly before his
birth on 22nd July 1950 and she did not return to it after her confinement.

f It was in September 1950 that the matrimonial home in Kilburn, London, was
purchased in the sole name of the husband. In that same month the wife started work
at E Ltd and took Christopher with her to work. She was working to some extent part-
time and during the ensuing summers she took Christopher to the coast for a month or
more by arrangement with the husband. However, when Christopher was able to go to
play-school she was able to work virtually full-time in the company.

g On 7th March 1955 a company, M Ltd, was formed. It was a company with 5,000
authorised and issued £1 shares fully paid and was owned equally by the husband and a
friend, Mr Krzysiak, with whom he had been involved earlier. The company was
formed to acquire as a going concern the business previously run by the husband and Mr
Krzysiak.

It was during 1955 that the wife changed her name to the husband's name by deed
h poll.

In March 1959 the husband bought Krzysiak's 2,500 shares in M Ltd and also his half
of the shares in E Ltd. The consideration was £5,600. After the transaction had been
completed the husband gave one share to his wife and kept the remaining 4,999
himself. Mr Krzysiak retired from the business.

In June 1957 the husband bought a bungalow in Wokingham in his sole name for
j £3,500. The wife contributed some £800 from her savings towards the purchase price,
the remainder of the money coming from the company. This bungalow with some 14
acres of ground was used by the family as a weekend bungalow and the husband was able
to enjoy his recreation of fishing. There came a time when a number of burglaries took
place in the area and for a period the wife's aged parents moved into that bungalow in
order to occupy it and to help maintain it. Her mother helped with the cleaning and her

father, who was a builder by occupation before his retirement, helped by maintaining the grounds.

During 1959 the husband transferred 2,499 shares in M Ltd to Christopher.

On 25th January 1968 the husband conveyed the property at Wokingham to trustees for Christopher and on 9th April 1968 he conveyed the matrimonial home to trustees for Christopher. It has been suggested that the husband may have completed these conveyances in order to deprive himself of assets should a divorce occur at some later stage. I do not think that that is the true situation, nor in fairness to the wife did she in her evidence really so suggest. In my judgment the reason for these conveyances, as indeed the transfer of the 2,499 shares to Christopher, was for the purposes of minimising or escaping estate duty. I am also satisfied that when these transfers were made Christopher had a conversation with his father and it was made clear to Christopher that in the future it was going to be necessary for his parents to make use of those houses.

On 25th November 1969 the husband was divorced by his wife in Poland. This was something which the husband, the wife and indeed Wojciech, had been trying to achieve for many years.

On 18th February 1970 both houses were transferred by trustees to Christopher absolutely. On 1st September 1971, as I have said, the husband and wife were married. In October 1971 Christopher went to Leicester University to read engineering.

In January 1972 it was decided that a fresh matrimonial home would be purchased and occupied. A house in Kingscroft Road, London, was purchased for £22,500 and was placed in Christopher's name. The money all came from the husband or from the company.

Shortly thereafter arrangements were made for a move into that house, but, for reasons of which I am not entirely clear, the husband refused to move. This was the ending of cohabitation between the husband and the wife which had continued since 1947. The husband remained at the matrimonial home and the wife, Christopher and the wife's mother lived at Kingscroft Road in Kilburn.

From January 1972 for a period of about a year the husband visited Kingscroft Road and had some meals there. He was indeed there for Christmas 1972, but continued in his refusal to resume cohabitation.

Pausing at this juncture in the recital of historical facts, I would turn to the relationship over these years between the husband and the wife. It was well-known to them both that it would be impossible for the husband to obtain a divorce in Poland unless his wife there divorced him. The petitioner in these proceedings had spoken to Wojciech about this matter on a number of occasions. The husband had always promised and made it clear that as soon as he could he would be prepared and willing to marry the wife. From 1947 until 1950 the wife had always used her wages towards the maintenance of the home which she and the husband had set up together. He had undoubtedly contributed by buying specific items, but her wages had consistently been used towards the household maintenance. From 1950 onwards, indeed thereafter, the wife has been in full-time employment with the company, save for the limitation when Christopher was young, and her income has been used, virtually in its entirety, towards the maintenance of the household. Until 1972 the husband benefited directly, and thereafter indirectly, in that he has been relieved of his liability to maintain.

The wife looked after the home and gave birth to and brought up Christopher. Christopher was educated at a public school and, as I have said, at Leicester University where he obtained a degree in engineering. He is a son of whom his parents can be proud.

As far as I understand the case for the husband, there is no criticism of this woman in her faithful devotion and support of her husband, in her devotion to her home and her child, and to her hard work in maintaining the home and bringing up this child.

In addition she worked in a most responsible and important position in the business being carried on by M Ltd.

In about 1956 the wife's brother came to work for M Ltd and the number of persons

employed, including the members of the family, varied between 11 and 15. It was a
a small entity, a successful entity and in every sense a family concern. There can be no
doubt that the husband was and is a man who not only likes to work hard, but is also
capable of sustained pressure of work. It is conceded that he was the driving force in the
company, but the back-up of the remaining members of the staff, and in particular of the
wife and her brother on the office side, was of vital importance.

In the early days this wife had given assistance on the production side, but as the
b business grew she spent all her time on administration. Initially she supervised
invoicing, credit control and collection of debts. Gradually she also accepted responsibility
for ordering and collection of materials, delivery of goods and all the wages and internal
accounting.

During the early part of 1974 Christopher started full-time in the employ of M Ltd
and it was at about this time that a serious quarrel broke out between the husband and
c the wife in connection with the company. This was at the time of the 'three day week'
when those employed by the company were paid by the company for the three days and
paid through government sources for the other two. The wife was insistent that the
employees were paid regularly on a Friday even though the reimbursement had not been
recovered from the government and when this occurred she paid them with her own
moneys. The husband had given orders that this was not to take place and when he
d discovered what had occurred he told his wife to stay away from the business. She did
so for a period of some months but was eventually restored to her position and received
her back pay. This attitude by the husband did not surprise those concerned, as he was
an autocratic man who would not suffer anyone to gainsay his word.

The husband used company moneys indiscriminately. Over a substantial period of
time he had been sending money or goods to Poland to Wojciech and his first wife, and
e I am not entirely clear quite what happened to other sums of money removed from the
company. It is clear to me that the husband was a man who worked with cash and as he
explained, 'very rarely in Poland does anyone use cheques'. He was used to carrying large
sums of cash on him and was indignant that anyone should ask for explanation of his
financial activities. It was not proved that he had in fact salted away substantial sums of
money for himself, although the wife was quite clear in her own mind that he had sums
f up to about £100,000 which he had not disclosed to the court. There were grounds for
suspicion but I must caution myself against acting on suspicions.

Wojciech was an engineer like his father and the husband hoped that Christopher
would also be trained as an engineer. His hopes for the future were that his two sons,
Christopher and Wojciech, would come into M Ltd and take over. Eventually it was his
intention to retire and gradually to cease an active participation in the company.

g There is no doubt that this husband has been most generous to Christopher, but I also
have no doubt that very substantial sums of money or goods, as money's worth, have
been transferred to Poland for the benefit of Wojciech and his wife and child, also for
Wojciech's mother. This husband has sought to treat his two sons in broadly the same
way.

Wojciech visited this country on many occasions, both with and without his family.
h Permission was sought for him to work here. This was always refused. Despite the fact
that he was only a visitor, he did work and was paid by the husband through the
company. His failure to obtain permission for Wojciech to work here was a bitter
disappointment to the husband.

Until about 1975 the relationship between Wojciech and Christopher was always
cordial; they used to go on holiday together.
j By his will dated 15th May 1975 the husband left everything to Wojciech.

Between 1974 and 1976 the relationship between the wife and Christopher on the one
hand and the husband and possibly Wojciech on the other had deteriorated fast. The
husband knew that Wojciech was probably not going to be allowed to come into this
country to work and yet with that knowledge had insisted on paying Wojciech from the
company during Wojciech's visits to the United Kingdom. Ultimately there came an

occasion when the wife refused to sign a document which allotted a £4,000 bonus to Wojciech and as a result she and Christopher took advice from a firm of solicitors.

The outcome of this advice was that on 28th June 1976 the wife and Christopher as joint petitioners presented a petition in the Companies Court under s 210 of the Companies Act 1948. The petition made a number of allegations, amongst which were the following: (i) that the husband had persistently and wilfully failed to conduct the affairs of M Ltd in accordance either with the constitution of the company or the provisions of the Companies Acts, (ii) that the husband had misappropriated company funds and (iii) that no dividends had been paid since incorporation with the likely result that an additional burden of taxation would fall on Christopher and his mother.

A receiver was appointed by the court to look into the company's affairs and he discovered that a sum of £24,473 had been wrongfully taken by the husband from the company. This sum was repaid by the husband.

Negotiations took place between solicitors for the petitioners and the husband's present solicitors, who were then also acting for him. The husband was anxious to buy the wife's one share and Christopher's 2,499 shares. He was prepared to pay £60,000. If he had succeeded in this purchase the wife and Christopher would have been deprived of their source of income for the future, as would the wife's brother. They were adamant that they would not sell to the husband and ultimately negotiations were concluded whereby the husband sold his 2,500 shares to the wife and Christopher for £40,000. In order to minimise the incidence of tax, £5,000 was said to be remuneration on retirement and £35,000 as consideration for the shares. The wife, as the husband must have known, had no money with which to purchase these shares and the whole sum was provided by Christopher. The husband had been keen that the wife should have 1,250 shares and indeed they were transferred into her name, but as the purchase price had been provided by Christopher she executed a deed of trust and eventually these shares were transferred to Christopher on 20th March 1979.

The cheque for £40,000 was paid to the husband on 1st July 1977.

It had been clear since 1976 that divorce proceedings would be inevitable and indeed the husband had asked for a divorce during that year. The wife told me that whilst she was involved in the company proceedings, in the course of which she was required to go back through the company accounts and documentation for about 20 years, she was in no position to deal with her immediate matrimonial problems. I accept this. Once, however, this sum of £40,000 had been paid it was clear that her position had to be protected. Her petition was filed on 6th July 1977 and on the following day application was made to freeze the sum of £40,000. The matter came before a deputy circuit judge on 25th July 1977 when by consent a sum of £20,000 was 'frozen'.

On 1st September 1977 Christopher changed his name by deed poll and on 15th September he became engaged to be married. He was married on 24th June 1978 and shortly thereafter purchased a home in Maidenhead for £27,000 subject to a mortgage, where he now lives. A son was born to his wife recently.

Since 1975 or 1976 the situation between Christopher and his father has sadly been such that although Christopher does not bear any particular animosity to his father, he is not prepared to argue with his father or to allow his father to have anything further to do with the business. His father's attitude towards him has clearly been of an antagonistic nature and the father does not now trust Christopher.

I ought to say at this juncture that Christopher impressed me as a witness. I found him to be a perfectly straightforward young man and I accepted him as a truthful witness. At the time he went to university he had contemplated going into the Church, he is a Roman Catholic, but his father clearly wanted him to go into the business and Christopher made his decision at that time.

The £40,000 paid by Christopher for the husband's shares in M Ltd was raised with a bank on the security of the Kingscroft Road property. On 15th January 1979 that property was sold at the instigation of the bank for the sum of £42,000 and the loan from the bank was repaid. It was at this time that the wife had to move to the Wokingham property.

Having given my assessment of Christopher as a witness, it is right that I should
a express my views about husband and wife. The husband is a man of definite ideas, who
is autocratic and with a quick temper. I have no doubt that he was an extremely forceful
character throughout this association and that this wife was wise to fall in with his
wishes. I do not think that he was entirely frank with me over his financial arrangements
of the past or indeed over some of his present activities.

The wife impressed me as a witness and as a woman. I have no doubt that she has been
b entirely loyal throughout. It is clear that there came a time when she and Christopher
took a stand because they saw that a great deal of what had been built up, not only by the
husband but also by the wife, with the help of some members of her family, was at
risk. She is a hard worker and an important cog in the family company.

Before turning to the law I look at the present position.

Christopher owns the former matrimonial home at Kilburn. He also owns the house
c at Wokingham where his grandmother and his aunt live. His mother at present occupies
one bedroom in that house. He also owns his own home in Maidenhead where he lives
with his wife and small son. M Ltd is now owned by him, save for one share which is in
the name of his mother. He is in receipt of a substantial income as chairman of that
company. His uncle (the wife's brother) is the managing director and he also earns a
substantial income.

d The wife travels daily for five or six days a week from Wokingham to the factory in
Kilburn. She has the use of a company car and quite often picks up Christopher from
Maidenhead on her way. She still occupies a position with the company and earns a gross
income of £5,700 a year. The company pays all the outgoings on the company car,
which is mainly for her use. Her capital consists of her jewellery. This was valued nearly
a year ago at a figure of £13,950. She also has a small sum in the bank totalling £360 in
e cash. The value of the jewellery has probably increased slightly and it would, in my
judgment, be fair to assess her to have a capital of approximately £16,000.

Turning now to the husband's present financial position. He has the following capital:
building societies £20,000; short term deposit £11,000; motor caravan £1,500;
krugerrands £5,650; guns, cameras etc £1,540; bank deposit account £620; bank
current account £110; premium bonds £1,050; cash £90; making a total of £41,560,
f less tax liabilities £4,015, which gives a balance of £37,545. It was argued before me
that his tax liabilities could be very much larger, but on the evidence I am inclined to
think that the probabilities are that they will not be materially higher. He occupies the
former matrimonial home in Kilburn. He has sent some cheques to Christopher for rent,
but Christopher refuses to bank them. Christopher appreciates that there is a moral
obligation to house his father and is content to give an undertaking to this court whereby
g his father will continue to occupy the ground and first floor of that house. It is far too
large for him and at present he has a distant relative and another Polish girl living in the
house. The undertaking which Christopher is prepared to give is that he will not seek
possession of the ground floor or first floor of the Kilburn home against his father during
the latter's life nor will he seek to charge him any sum in respect of his occupation.
Christopher is, however, to have liberty to apply to the court on notice to be released
h from this undertaking on the grounds of reasonable financial requirements.

I am satisfied that provided the husband does not seek in the future to undermine the
activities of M Ltd, he will be provided with a roof over his head for the rest of his days.

As to his income, he is in receipt of a state retirement pension, which is £1,319 a year
and he will also have the interest on any capital which remains to him after any order
which I may make. I am satisfied that the husband is anxious to earn an income and
j indeed he has been doing so. The precise details of those earnings were not vouchsafed
to me and the husband's evidence on this aspect was highly unsatisfactory. I am satisfied
that in the future he will receive sums in cash from friends and connections in the Polish
community as well as outside that community. The amount of those earnings is
indeterminate but will undoubtedly contribute towards his overall income.

I do not consider that either party will receive any substantial sums in the future from
other sources.

The wife's case is quite simple. She now lives in a small bedroom of the bungalow at Wokingham. She has to travel daily to London. She needs a flat somewhere near the factory in Kilburn. For this she needs a lump sum. She also says that a lump sum is justified because she has looked after the home, brought up Christopher and over the years helped to build up the prosperity of M Ltd; and although Christopher was and is under some moral obligation to provide a roof for his parents, it is wrong to suggest that he should be obliged to house each parent separately. She is prepared to have her claim for periodical payments dismissed and also asks that the court should make an order under s 15 of the Inheritance (Provision for Family and Dependants) Act 1975.

I find that a reasonable sum required by her for a flat is about £25,000. Having regard to the figures which ultimately became clear, the wife moderated her original claim for a lump sum of £20,000 to one of £13,500.

Counsel for the wife submits that in reaching my decision I should look in particular at s 25(1)(f) of the Matrimonial Causes Act 1973 and bear in mind the general provisions towards the start of that section, namely a duty of the court 'to have regard to all the circumstances of the case.'

For the husband counsel submits that no lump sum at all should be paid for the following reasons. First, he submits that the whole purpose of ss 21 to 25 of the 1973 Act is to ensure justice in the widest sense between a husband and a wife, not between a common law husband and a common law wife. He draws attention to s 25(1)(d) and says that in effect this present marriage only lasted a few months, namely from September 1971 to early 1972. He also submits that s 25(1)(f) (contribution to the family) relates to the same period. Secondly, he points to the fact that Christopher agreed that his father's generosity to him in earlier years was not based solely on fiscal reasons, but also in part as recompense to Christopher's mother as his common law wife, and that therefore she should look to Christopher, not only for a gift, but also for her future maintenance. Thirdly, that had the marriage continued, husband and wife would have been living in a house owned by Christopher, and that by giving her any capital now the court would be putting her in a better position than she would have been had the marriage continued.

Fourthly, he submits that the husband needs every penny of capital which he now has in order to provide some security for the future, whether invested in shares or in some future business. There is, therefore, no capital properly available from which the husband could be expected to make any payment of a lump sum. He further re-emphasised his client's previous generosity to Christopher.

In support of his first main submission counsel for the husband relies strongly on *Campbell v Campbell*[1], and in particular the passage in the judgment of Sir George Baker P which reads[2]:

'Now in this case Mrs Campbell does not take the point, which is so often taken in these short marriage cases by the wife, that the marriage was only short because the husband ended it and she was deprived of her opportunity of being a good wife over the years and of, in the words of Lord Denning MR in *Wachtel v Wachtel*[3] "earning her right to share in the property and to proper and full periodical payments". I think this undoubtedly was a short marriage. There is no doubt about that because from the date of the marriage in the register office to the time the husband left the house was two years and under four months. Each party knew perfectly well what they had taken on when they married. The officious bystander present in the Watford Register Office must have said to himself: "This is a marriage

1 [1977] 1 All ER 1, [1976] Fam 347
2 [1977] 1 All ER 1 at 5–6, [1976] Fam 347 at 352
3 [1973] 1 All ER 829, [1973] Fam 72

that cannot last." There really was no hope for it from the start and it did not last.

a I think this is a good illustration of a marriage which must be treated as a short marriage and to which consideration must be given within s 25 of the Matrimonial Causes Act 1973. Counsel for Mrs Campbell attempts to persuade me that the 3½ years of pre-marital co-habitation should be taken into account in assessing the length of the marriage. The way he puts it is: "She was for 3½ years performing wifely duties before marriage." Now I entirely reject that argument. This was a

b married woman with a large number of children, most of them in care, living with a youngster. There is an increasing tendency, I have found in cases in chambers, to regard and, indeed, to speak of the celebration of marriage as "the paper work". The phrase used is: "We were living together but we never got round to the paper work." Well that is, to my mind, an entirely misconceived outlook. It is the ceremony of marriage and the sanctity of marriage which count; rights, duties and

c obligations begin on the marriage and not before. It is a complete cheapening of the marriage relationship, which I believe, and I am sure many share this belief, is essential to the well-being of our society as we understand it, to suggest that premarital periods, particularly in the circumstances of this case [and I emphasise those words], should, as it were, by a doctrine of relation back of matrimony, be taken as a part of marriage to count in favour of the wife performing, as it is put,

d "wifely duties before marriage". So it comes to this that I take this as a marriage of two years and a month or two, and it ended.'

On the facts of that case it was abundantly clear that neither party was worthy of praise for his or her moral attitudes, nor for his or her contribution to a home, nor the upbringing of a family. Indeed there seemed to have been nothing to show for his or her

e efforts during their relationship. I note that Sir George Baker P stressed in the passage which I have quoted that his decision related to the particular circumstances of that case. I believe it was to s 25(1)(*d*) that Sir George Baker P's mind was being directed in argument.

In approaching problems under ss 21 to 25 of the 1973 Act, a number of propositions are clearly established by authority. The function and duty of the court is to reach a

f physical and financial resolution of the problems of that family which is fair, just and reasonable as between the parties. The court must look to the statutory guidance now provided by s 25 of that Act. Secondly, in exercising this wide discretionary jurisdiction it is important that the court should be careful not to limit its discretion by a narrow construction of the statutory guidelines. It is quite impossible for any judge to foresee the multiplicity of circumstances which may be brought before him.

g Turning to s 25(1)(*d*) itself, the words 'the duration of the marriage' in my judgment clearly mean what they say, but within that phrase it is clear that it is the period between ceremony of marriage and the final break-up of cohabitation which is likely to be the most material.

I turn next to s 25(1)(*f*). In considering the problem before me the word from which I derive some guidance in that subsection is the word 'family'. Reading the 1973 Act as

h a whole, I take the view that 'family' in that context indicates a reference to events post-marriage. In the many contexts in which that word is to be found in the Act, I do not think it can properly be construed to refer to a time prior to the ceremony of marriage.

Section 25 further requires me to have regard to the conduct of the parties, and also to all the circumstances of the case. The latter phrase is very wide, but the word 'conduct' has received judicial attention.

j It is argued, and indeed it is true, that the factor of 'conduct' has for the most part been used in order to cut down the amount of financial relief which the court might otherwise have awarded to a party, and not for the purpose of increasing that amount. In my judgment there is nothing in the language of the section itself which supports this restricted view. My initial approach, therefore, is that any such restriction is unwarranted, and I then turn to authority.

There are four cases in the Court of Appeal from which I derive guidance. These are *Wachtel v Wachtel*[1], *Harnett v Harnett*[2], *Armstrong v Armstrong*[3] and *Jones v Jones*[4].

In *Wachtel v Wachtel*[1] in giving the judgment of the court Lord Denning MR does refer to 'misconduct, guilt or blame', but it is to be noted[5] that he emphasises that 'The crucial finding of fact is that the responsibility for the breakdown of the marriage rested equally on both parties'[6]. Therefore the issue of 'conduct' was not strictly before the court. The judgment was given 'to lay down some guidelines'[7] and at a time when the courts and practitioners had very little experience of the working of the new legislation.

In *Harnett v Harnett*[8], *Wachtel v Wachtel*[1] was considered and in his judgment Cairns LJ said:

'I would add that, speaking for myself, and quite independently of the authority of *Wachtel v Wachtel*[1], I would reach the view that it *is* the intention of the 1970 Act that conduct should be taken into account only in a very broad way—that is to say, only where there is something in the conduct of one party which would make it quite inequitable to leave that out of account having regard to the conduct of the other party as well in the course of the marriage.'

This part of his judgment was expressly referred to in *Armstrong v Armstrong*[3]. In that case conduct was directly in issue and a reduction of the sum to be awarded had been made by Cumming-Bruce J at first instance.

Posing the question which the Court of Appeal in *Armstrong v Armstrong*[3] thought that a judge should put to himself on the issue of conduct, Buckley LJ said this:

'The expression "obvious and gross", as I ventured to say in the course of the argument, obviously is not a definitive expression. The Court of Appeal there, I think, indicated clearly what they had in mind by the use of those words, which they borrowed from the judgment of Ormrod J which was there under appeal. They said in the judgment of the court that it was not right for a court before whom an application came under s 4 of the Matrimonial Proceedings and Property Act 1970 to conduct a post-mortem into the matrimonial affairs of the parties: but that, if the conduct known to the court was such that it would be repugnant to anyone's sense of justice to say that it ought not to be taken into account in considering what financial provision should be made by one party for another, it was proper that it should be taken into account. Language having rather the same effect was used by Cairns LJ in *Harnett v Harnett*[8]: [the passage that I have already cited is then quoted. Then Buckley LJ goes on:] I think that what the learned judge had to apply his mind to in the present case was whether, to a reasonable person, the conduct of the wife as it was known to the court was such that it would really offend that reasonable person's sense of justice if no effect was given to it in arriving at the extent to which relief should be given to Mrs Armstrong under s 4.'

Stephenson LJ posed the question in this way, saying:

1 [1973] 1 All ER 829, [1973] Fam 72
2 [1974] 1 All ER 764, [1974] 1 WLR 219
3 [1974] Court of Appeal Transcript 137
4 [1975] 2 All ER 12, [1976] Fam 8
5 [1973] 1 All ER 829 at 835, [1973] Fam 72 at 90
6 [1973] 1 All ER 829 at 834, [1973] Fam 72 at 87
7 [1973] 1 All ER 829 at 833, [1973] Fam 72 at 87
8 [1974] 1 All ER 764 at 767–768, [1974] 1 WLR 219 at 224

'On the first point as to the wife's conduct, bearing in mind what was said by
_a_   Ormrod J and by Lord Denning MR in giving the judgment of this court in _Wachtel_
v Wachtel[1], and what was said by Cairns and Roskill LJJ in _Harnett v Harnett_[2], the
question we have to ask ourselves seems to me to be: Would it offend a reasonable
man's sense of justice that this wife's conduct should be left out of account in
awarding her maintenance by a lump sum out of the proceeds of this sale and that
it should have no effect on the financial provision which the husband ought to be
_b_   ordered to pay her? Would it be inequitable or unjust to disregard her conduct?'

Armstrong v Armstrong[3] was cited to the Court of Appeal (although on a different
aspect) in _Jones v Jones_[4]. The facts of that case are very different from the present, but I
derive some support for the view which I have formed on the proper meaning of the
word 'conduct' in s 25 from the judgment of Orr LJ[5]:

_c_   'It has not been argued—certainly not pressed—on behalf of the husband that the
word "conduct", where it appears in the closing words of s 25(1) of the Matrimonial
Causes Act 1973, is incapable of applying to something that has happened after the
breakdown of the marriage, or indeed after the decree absolute. The wording in
question is entirely general in its character, and I would not be prepared to limit it
in that way. It was argued that conduct is to be considered as relevant only for the
_d_   purpose of cutting down a claim by a wife to a share of matrimonial property and
cannot be applied so as to increase it. I for myself cannot accept the validity of this
contention. As was pointed out in argument, the question in cases of this kind
involves conflicting claims to matrimonial property, and an increase of one involves
inevitably a decrease of the other. Moreover, in my judgment, this was a case in
which the conduct of the husband had been of such a gross kind that it would be
_e_   offensive to a sense of justice that it should not be taken into account.'

I also note that in his judgment Megaw LJ felt that the particular conduct in issue,
namely a physical attack by the husband on the wife, in that case, could be considered
either under the word 'conduct' or the phrase 'all the circumstances of the case'.
Behaviour which has occurred outside the span of the marriage itself has been taken
into account by a court when exercising its discretion under s 25 of the 1973 Act, at least
_f_   in cases where such conduct has affected the finance of the other spouse: see _W v W_[6] per
Sir George Baker P.
I find nothing therefore in the authorities to suggest that a broad and general approach
to the words 'conduct' and 'in all the circumstances of the case' is undesirable or wrong.
This wife has given the best years of her life to this husband. She has been faithful,
loving and hard-working. She has helped him to build what is in every sense a family
_g_   business. She has managed his home and been a mother to and helped him bring up a
son of whom they are both justly proud. I believe that she has earned for herself some
part of the value of the family business.
Having set out those matters prior to the ceremony of marriage itself, which seem to
me to be relevant, I ask myself whether I can do justice, that which is fair, just and
reasonable between these parties, if I ignore the earlier history and the wife's behaviour
_h_   during those earlier years. To put the question in a different form: would it really offend
a reasonable person's sense of justice to ignore those events and that behaviour? I have

_j_   1   [1973] 1 All ER 829, [1973] Fam 72
     2   [1974] 1 All ER 764, [1974] 1 WLR 219
     3   [1974] Court of Appeal Transcript 137
     4   [1975] 2 All ER 12, [1976] Fam 8
     5   [1975] 2 All ER 12 at 16–17, [1976] Fam 8 at 15
     6   [1975] 3 All ER 970 at 972, [1976] Fam 107 at 110

no doubt that the answer from the reasonable man would be that they must be taken into account and, in my judgment, not only can I take these matters into account, whether under the phrase 'conduct' or 'in all the circumstances of the case' in s 25, but that same section casts a duty on me to do so.

Although in the exercise of my discretion my final decision must be reached on the facts as a whole, balancing one factor against another, it may yet be helpful to consider a number of particular aspects.

I look first at the respective needs of the parties. If I were to award the wife a lump sum of about £8,000, then she would be able to raise about £10,000 from the sale of some of her jewellery and I have no doubt that she could borrow a further sum of about £7,000 from Christopher. It should not be impossible, if necessary, for her to raise a mortgage. She will thus be able to buy a flat near the factory where she will be able to continue working for some years yet. In the normal course of events, her own mother may not survive for more than a few years and on her own retirement she will be able to consider joining her sister at Wokingham. There was no suggestion but that this was a close-knit family. This move would enable her to sell her flat and leave herself with a capital sum to provide some security. At age 60 she will be entitled to a state pension and she will also have the use of a company car for some years ahead. I estimate that the rent and rates of her new flat will involve a payment of approximately £300 per annum. Her present salary is £5,700 per annum.

This husband, provided he does nothing stupid or irresponsible, will have a roof over his head for the remainder of his life. He will therefore be living free of rent but will be responsible for the rates, which are at present about £280 per annum. Thus, his basic outgoings will be very much the same as the wife's. This house is large enough to enable him to arrange for a Polish girl to look after him in exchange for free accommodation.

He is in receipt of a state pension in the net sum of £1,319 per annum. He will have free capital of £29,500, subject to a possible liability for the whole or some part of the costs of these proceedings. He claims that he will once more set up in business. I do not think that this is a real likelihood but if he persists in this wish the sum of £25,000 is, in my judgment, sufficient for his purpose. My reason for saying this is that during the proceedings in the Companies Court the husband, as he told me, was prepared to pay £60,000 to Christopher and his mother for their shares in the company. This sum was not available from his own resources but he told me that it would have been readily available from at least two Polish friends, one of whom had been involved with him originally in the early days of E Ltd. He also informed me that for the future he could borrow from two or three Polish friends and join with them in a partnership or limited company. He would like to have financial control, but this may not be possible. He is full of vitality and I see no reason why any such future business should not be a success if he really is keen to achieve it.

In the recent past the husband has been doing casual work for cash. He is well capable of earning several hundreds of pounds a year from this.

If the husband decides against this business project, then he could possibly buy himself an annuity for £20,000 which would provide him with an annual income of £3,379, of which the interest content would be £1,700. There is no need for him to make capital provision for his dependants, who will all have been adequately provided for. I am conscious of the disadvantages of an annuity in times of inflation; thus if the husband does not wish to purchase an annuity, it seems reasonable to anticipate that he could receive an income of say $10-10\frac{1}{2}\%$ per annum from some building society or gilt edged security. At his age he will be looking for income rather than capital appreciation.

In this case, in my judgment, it is right to compare net incomes rather than gross incomes.

The wife's net income will be: gross earned income of £5,700, less tax etc of £1,708 which gives a balance of £3,992 per annum net. She will also have the use of a car.

The husband's net income will be as follows: state retirement pension £1,319; earnings
a £500 to £750; and either capital of £20,000 invested at 10% yielding £2,000, or an
annuity of £3,379 less tax of £406 yielding £2,973. Thus the bracket would seem to be
£3,819 or £5,042.

Apart from the question of need for the future, if this marriage had continued and this
husband had fulfilled his financial obligations to his wife, in my judgment, he would
have given her some capital before his death. Although the facts of the present case are
b distinguishable, I would refer to the views expressed by Scarman LJ in *Trippas v Trippas*[1],
where he said:

'When it occurred [and he is there referring to the sale of the business for about
£80,000] he made a gift of £5,000 to each of his sons. I think it reasonable to infer
that, had they been living together at that time, the wife could have expected in cash
or in kind some sort of benefit accruing to her from the sale of the business. One
c must bear in mind that this man, with a proper sense of his marital obligations, had,
much earlier in the family life, put the matrimonial home in joint names. I think
it would be reasonable to infer that, had the married life continued, he would have
thought it the decent thing to do to see that some part of this capital sum should be
distributed to his wife as well as between himself and his sons. Of course, even if at
that time nothing in the form of cash had come to the wife had they gone on living
d together, it is clear that she would have benefited generally from the availability of
the capital to her husband. Moreover, since this man was not in pensionable
employment, this sum could properly be regarded as his substitute for a pension;
and I would have thought that, had they lived together until he died, some provision
would have been made for the wife by gift or will or settlement from the capital
sum he received on the sale of the business.'
e

The estimated value of the business today is £120,000. In my judgment, a figure of
£8,000, or one fifteenth of that value, is a reasonable proportion for the wife to have
earned. She has been receiving a regular salary.

Lastly, if this case is to be treated as a short marriage case, then on its facts the sum of
£8,000 is not an unreasonable figure at which to arrive. This marriage was, after all,
f terminated by the desertion of the husband as found in the divorce proceedings.

Thus to summarise my conclusion: I award the wife £8,000 by way of lump sum and
I dismiss her claim for periodical payments and secured provision, and I make an order,
with her consent, under s 15 of the Inheritance (Provision for Family and Dependants)
Act 1975.

Bearing in mind what was said by Sir George Baker P in the passage which I have cited
g from *Campbell v Campbell*[2] it will be said by some that to recognise the relationship which
existed before marriage as relevant to financial redistribution, is to encourage relationships
outside marriage. To them I would answer that the occasions on which a court is likely
to feel that justice requires such recognition are likely to be few, possibly very few. It
would, however, not be helpful to speculate on situations which may never arise. In my
judgment, on the particular facts of the present case my decision will do nothing to
h undermine the institution of marriage.

I would also note that under the provisions of s 1 of the Domestic Violence and
Matrimonial Proceedings Act 1976, a mistress may now be protected in her lover's home
(see *Davis v Johnson*[3]) and by s 1(1)(e) of the Inheritance (Provision for Family and

j

---

1   [1973] 2 All ER 1 at 8, [1973] Fam 134 at 145
2   [1977] 1 All ER 1 at 5–6, [1976] Fam 347 at 352
3   [1978] 1 All ER 1132, [1979] AC 264

Dependants) Act 1975, a mistress can now claim against the estate of a deceased lover who maintained her wholly or in part.   *a*

I would dismiss the cross-application by the husband.

Order that a lump sum of £8,000 to be paid by the husband to the wife. Claim for periodical payments and secured provision dismissed. Order made under the Inheritance (Provision for Family and Dependants) Act 1975, s 15. Cross-application by the husband dismissed.

b

Solicitors: *Speechly, Bircham* (for the wife); *Warmingtons & Hasties* (for the husband).

Georgina Chambers   Barrister.

Winkworth v Christie, Manson & Woods Ltd and another

CHANCERY DIVISION
SLADE J
4th, 5th, 8th OCTOBER, 5th NOVEMBER 1979

Conflict of laws – Personal property – Movables – Title to goods – Lex situs – Title to be determined according to lex situs – Goods stolen from plaintiff in England, taken to Italy and sold to defendant – Defendant sending goods back to England for resale – Plaintiff claiming goods – Whether title to goods to be determined according to lex situs – Whether England lex situs because of connection of goods with England – Whether on grounds of public policy exception should be made to lexi situs rule in the case of stolen goods.

The plaintiff owned certain works of art which were stolen from him in England and subsequently taken to Italy. There they were sold to the second defendant who was unaware that they were stolen. Some time later he sent them back to England to be sold on his behalf by the first defendants, a well-known firm of art auctioneers. The plaintiff brought an action against the defendants in detinue and conversion, and in the course of those proceedings a preliminary issue was directed to be tried, namely whether English or Italian domestic law applied to determine whether the plaintiff or the second defendant had title to the goods. That was on the assumption that under Italian law, but not under English law, the second defendant had acquired a valid title to the goods as against the plaintiff. It was contended by the second defendant that, in accordance with the general rule of private international law that the validity of a transfer of movable property was governed by the law of the country where the goods were situated (the lex situs), Italian law should apply. The plaintiff, while accepting the lex situs rule, contended (i) that it only applied to the disposition or transfer of personal property and therefore, while appropriate to determine the rights of the second defendant and the person from whom he purchased, it had no bearing on the respective proprietary rights of the second defendant and the plaintiff because there had been no disposition or transfer from the plaintiff to the second defendant, (ii) that, because the case had so much connection with England, England should be treated as the lex situs, or (iii) that an exception to the lex situs rule should be made on the grounds of public policy in the case of movables which were stolen or unlawfully taken from one country without the owner's knowledge or consent, dealt with in another country and then returned to the first country.

Held – The rule that if personal property was disposed of in a manner binding according to the lex situs that disposition was binding everywhere applied in appropriate circumstances to a transaction whereby a person acquired title under the lex situs and thereby destroyed the proprietary rights of a former owner who had never himself possessed the property in that country and had never consented to the property going to that country. Nor was there any exception to the rule in the case of goods stolen and removed from one country, dealt with in another country and later returned to the first country. The law to be applied in determining the title to the goods was therefore Italian rather than English law, and that was unaffected by the connection the goods may have had with England, since the introduction of a wholly fictional English situs merely because there happened to be a number of English connecting factors would lead to intolerable uncertainty in the law (see p 1132 c d and f, p 1135 b c and g to p 1136 a and d e, post).

Cammell v Sewell (1860) 5 H & N 728, *Todd v Armour* (1882) 9 R (Ct of Sess) 901 and *Embiricos v Anglo-Austrian Bank* [1905] 1 KB 677 applied.

Notes

For the location of personal property and the assignment of movables, see 8 Halsbury's *a*
Laws (4th Edn) paras 632, 657–658.

Cases referred to in judgment

Aksionairnoye Obschesto A M Luther v James Sagor & Co [1921] 3 KB 532, [1921] All ER Rep
138, 90 LJKB 1202, 125 LT 705, CA, 11 Digest (Reissue) 344, *23*.

Alcock v Smith [1892] 1 Ch 238, 61 LJ Ch 161, 66 LT 126, CA, 11 Digest (Reissue) 413, *b*
480.

Anziani, Re, Herbert v Christopherson [1930] 1 Ch 407, 99 LJ Ch 215, 142 LT 570, 8(2)
Digest (Reissue) 497, *49*.

Bank Voor Handel en Scheepvaart NV v Slatford [1951] 2 All ER 779, [1953] 1 QB 248, 11
Digest (Reissue) 731, *494*.

Cammell v Sewell (1858) 3 H & N 617, 27 LJ Ex 447, 157 ER 615 Ct Ex; *affd* (1860) 5 H *c*
& N 728, 29 LJ Ex 350, 2 LT 799, 6 Jur NS 918, 157 ER 1371, Ex Ch, 11 Digest
(Reissue) 610, *1547*.

Castrique v Imrie (1870) LR 4 HL 414, [1861–73] All ER Rep 508, 39 LJCP 350, 23 LT 48,
3 Mar LC 454, HL, 11 Digest (Reissue) 611, *1550*.

Edgerly v Bush (1880) 81 NY 199.

Embiricos v Anglo-Austrian Bank [1905] 1 KB 677, 74 LJKB 326, 92 LT 305, 10 Com Cas 99, *d*
CA; *affg* [1904] 2 KB 870, 73 LJKB 993, 91 LT 652, 3 Digest (Reissue) 640, *4016*.

Inglis v Robertson and Baxter [1898] AC 616, 67 LJPC 108, 79 LT 224, HL, 11 Digest
(Reissue) 415, *489*.

Simpson v Fogo (1862) 1 Hem & M 195, 1 New Rep 422, 32 LJ Ch 249, 8 LT 61, 9 Jur Ns
403, 1 Mar LC 312, 71 ER 85, 11 Digest (Reissue) 407, *443*.

Todd v Armour (1882) 9 R (Ct of Sess) 901, 33 Digest (Repl) 492,* 72. *e*

Case also cited

Janesich v George Attenborough & Son (1910) 102 LT 605.

f

Preliminary issue

By writ of summons issued on 22nd July 1977, the plaintiff, William Wilberforce
Winkworth, claimed against the defendants, Christie, Manson & Woods Ltd ('Christie's')
and Dr Paolo Dal Pozzo D'Annone ('the second defendant'), sued as Marchese Paolo Da
Pozzo, (1) a declaration that certain Japanese works of art sold by Christie's on behalf of
the second defendant in 59 lots on or about 22nd February 1977 and in a further 43 lots *g*
on or about 1st March 1977 and intended to be sold by Christie's on behalf of the second
defendant in a further 147 lots and a further unspecified number of lots had at all
material times been the property of the plaintiff; (2) an injunction restraining Christie's
(a) paying or accounting to the second defendant or to any person on his behalf any part
of the proceeds of the sales of the works of art, (b) selling, offering for sale, parting with
possession of or otherwise disposing of any of the works of art in their possession, *h*
custody, power or control; (3) an injunction restraining the second defendant from (a)
receiving any part of the proceeds of the sales or directing or authorising any other
person to receive any part of the proceeds on his behalf, (b) selling, offering for sale,
parting with possession of, or otherwise disposing of any of the works of art in his
possession, custody, power or control; (4) an order for the return of the works of art in the
possession, custody, power or control of the defendants, or their value; and (5) damages *j*
for detinue, or conversion. On 16th March 1979, Master Heward ordered that a point of
law raised by the defence and counterclaim of the second defendant be tried as a
preliminary issue, namely 'Whether upon the basis of the agreed facts ... English
domestic law, or Italian domestic law is to be applied to the issue whether the plaintiff or
the defendant Paolo Dal Pozzo D'Annone has title to the goods with which this action

and the . . . counterclaim are concerned and to the proceeds of sale of those goods'. The
a proceedings against Christie's were discontinued by notice of discontinuance served on
4th December 1978. The facts are set out in the judgment.

John Mummery for the plaintiff.
Jonathan Gilman for the second defendant.

b

Cur adv vult

5th November. **SLADE J** read the following judgment: In this action, by an order of
16th March 1979, Master Heward has directed that a point of law, raised by the defence
c and counterclaim of the second defendant, be tried as preliminary issue and that, until
this point shall have been determined, all further proceedings in the action and
counterclaim, except for such determination, be stayed. This judgment relates solely to
the preliminary point of law.

The plaintiff in the action is Mr William Wilberforce Winkworth, a collector of works
of art. The first defendant is Christie, Manson & Woods Ltd ('Christie's'). The second
d defendant is Dr Paolo Dal Pozzo D'Annone, sued as Marchese Paolo Da Pozzo.

In the action the plaintiff seeks a declaration that certain works of art have at all
material times been his property. He seeks an injunction restraining Christie's from,
inter alia, paying to the second defendant any part of the proceeds of sale of these works
of art or disposing of any of them at present in their possession. He seeks an injunction
restraining the second defendant from, inter alia, receiving any part of such proceeds of
e sale or disposing of any of the works of art in his possession. He seeks also an order for
the return of the works, or their value and damages for detinue or alternatively damages
for conversion.

Conveniently, the schedule to the relevant order of the master sets out the agreed facts
on the basis of which the relevant point of law is to be determined. Though I do not
quote from the schedule verbatim, these facts are as follows.

f The goods with which the action and counterclaim are concerned ('the goods'), were
stolen in England from the lawful possession of the plaintiff who was the owner of them
at the time of the theft and was domiciled in England and Wales. They were
subsequently taken to Italy and sold and delivered by a third party to the second
defendant under a contract made in Italy, and as to the contractual rights of the parties
governed by Italian law, the goods also being at the time of such sale and delivery
g physically situated in Italy.

The goods were thereafter delivered by the second defendant to Christie's in England
for the sale there by auction by Christie's on his behalf. Some of the goods were sold in
England by Christie's on his behalf, but before the proceeds of sale were paid over by
them to the second defendant or the balance of the goods were sold, the plaintiff asked
for and received undertakings from Christie's not to part with the proceeds of sale and
h not to part with the possession of the balance of the goods then remaining unsold
pending determination of the issues between the plaintiff and the second defendant.
The plaintiff neither knew of nor consented to the removal of the goods to Italy or any
subsequent dealings with or movements of them up to the time when the said
undertakings were given.

For completeness I should mention two other matters of fact. First, Christie's have not
j been represented at the hearing before me and indeed I understand that proceedings
against them have been discontinued. Secondly, since the undertakings were given by
them not to part with possession of the balance of the goods then remaining unsold, the
remaining goods have, I understand, been sold with the plaintiff's consent, on suitable
arrangements being made for the preservation of the proceeds of sale pending the
resolution of these proceedings.

The point of law which the master has directed should be heard as a preliminary issue is expressed as follows:

> 'Whether upon the basis of the agreed facts set forth in the Schedule to this Order English domestic law or Italian domestic law is to be applied to the issue whether the Plaintiff or the Defendant Paolo Dal Pozzo D'Annone has title to the goods with which this Action and the said Counterclaim are concerned and to the proceeds of sale of those goods . . .'

This is an action in detinue and conversion. The general rule is that the title which must be established by a person bringing an action for detinue or conversion of goods in an English court consists of proof not so much of absolute ownership, as proof that he had at the time of the detention or conversion, either actual possession of the goods or the immediate right to possession of them. On the agreed facts the second defendant has on no footing violated any actual possession of the goods by the plaintiff, who, by reason of the theft, had already lost such possession before the time when the contract of sale was concluded in Italy. As against the second defendant therefore the plaintiff must establish the immediate *right to* possession of the goods. It is accordingly common ground between counsel that the phrase 'title to', as appearing in the question of law formulated for the decision of this court, must be construed as meaning 'the immediate right to possession of'. The distinction may have little or no practical significance on the facts of this case, but must be recorded for the sake of accuracy.

It is common ground that at the time of the theft the plaintiff was the owner of the goods, and that they were in his lawful possession. It is also common ground that he neither knew of nor consented to their removal to Italy or any subsequent dealings with or movements of them up to the time when the undertakings were given by Christie's. There is no suggestion in the agreed facts or on the pleadings that any person not a party to these proceedings ever acquired a title to the goods which would have destroyed the plaintiff's immediate right to possession of them. It is therefore plain that, on any footing, at least until the sale in Italy, nothing had occurred which destroyed such right.

On the other hand, if the effect of the subsequent sale in Italy was to confer on the second defendant a title to ownership of the goods, which is valid even against the plaintiff and is of such a nature that it must now be recognised by the English court, it would necessarily follow that, in the events which have happened, the plaintiff has lost and the second defendant has acquired, the immediate right to possession of them.

In the circumstances, a crucial issue in the present case must be: was the effect of the sale in Italy to confer on the second defendant a title to ownership of the goods which is valid even against the plaintiff? And the question of law now before the court resolves itself to the question whether this issue falls to be determined in accordance with English domestic law or Italian domestic law. The question is one of practical importance for the parties. For, while the point has not been argued before me and I do not purport to decide it, it seems probable that, if English domestic law alone applies, the second defendant, who does not claim to have been a purchaser 'in market overt', within the meaning of s 22(1) of the Sale of Goods Act 1893, would not have acquired a title to these stolen goods which was valid vis-à-vis the plaintiff. On the other hand, the second defendant in para 6 of his defence pleads, inter alia:

> 'Under Italian law a purchaser of movables acquires a good title notwithstanding any defect in the seller's title or in that of prior transferors provided that (1) the purchaser is in good faith at the time of delivery (2) the transaction is carried out in a manner which is appropriate, as regards the documentation effecting or evidencing the sale, to a transaction of the type in question rather than in some manner which is irregular as regards documentation and (3) the purchaser is not aware of any

a
unlawful origin of the goods at the time when he acquires them. The Second Defendant will rely on Articles 1153 and 1154 of the Italian Civil Code in relation to the foregoing.'

In para 7 of his defence, the second defendant goes on to plead, as matters of fact, that he was in good faith at the time of the Italian contract; that he was not aware of any defect of title of the vendor in Italy; that the transaction of purchase was carried out in the suitable and appropriate manner as regards documentation, and that he had b reasonable grounds for believing that his vendor was entitled to dispose of the goods to him. If, therefore, the crucial issue which I have mentioned falls to be determined in accordance with Italian law and the second defendant can establish that its relevant content is as pleaded in para 6 of his defence and that the facts are as pleaded in para 7, I suppose that he may well have acquired a title to the goods, which must be recognised by the English court as being valid, even vis-à-vis the plaintiff.

c
The grounds on which counsel for the second defendant submitted the crucial issue falls to be determined in accordance with Italian law are essentially very simple. There is, he submits, a general rule of private international law that the validity of a transfer of movable property and its effect on the proprietary rights of any persons claiming to be interested therein are governed by the law of the country where the property is situated d at the time of the transfer ('the lex situs'). He specifically recognised that there are five exceptions to this rule. The first is the exception summarised as follows in Dicey and Morris's Conflict of Laws[1]: 'If goods are in transit, and their *situs* is casual or not known, a transfer which is valid and effective by its proper law will (*semble*) be valid and effective in England.'

The second exception to the general rule accepted and asserted by counsel for the second defendant arises where a purchaser claiming title has not acted bona fide. The e third exception is the case where the English court declines to recognise the particular law of the relevant situs, because it considers it contrary to English public policy. The fourth exception arises where a statute in force in the country which is the forum in which the case is heard obliges the court to apply the law of its own country. One example of the application of this exception might have been the former s 24 of the Sale f of Goods Act 1893, recently repealed. Fifthly, counsel for the second defendant recognised that special rules might apply to determine the relevant law governing the effect of general assignments of movables on bankruptcy or succession.

None of these exceptions, however, it was submitted on behalf of the second defendant, has any relevance on the facts of the present case. Save where expressly provided to the contrary, English rules of conflict of laws are preserved or not affected by the Sale of Goods Act 1893. Accordingly, it is submitted, that the general rule of private g international law which it is claimed governs the effect of transfers of movable property must apply in the present case. It is common ground that at the time of the sale and transfer of the goods by the third party to the second defendant, the goods were situated in Italy. Accordingly, counsel for the second defendant submits, in effect the English court is bound to apply Italian law for the purpose of determining whether the second h defendant has acquired ownership of the goods, not only vis-à-vis the transferor, but also vis-à-vis the plaintiff; in other words, for the purpose of determining whether the plaintiff can prove the title necessary to enable him to succeed in these proceedings or whether his title has been divested by the sale in Italy.

At least before the decision in *Cammell v Sewell*[2] there had been some conflict of judicial opinion as to whether the validity of a disposition of movables generally depended on the law of the owner's domicile ('the lex domicilii'), or on the law of the j country where the relevant transaction was concluded ('the lex loci actus'), or on the law

1   9th Edn (1973) p 539
2   (1858) 3 H & N 617, 157 ER 615; *affd* (1860) 5 H & N 728, 157 ER 1371

of the country where the goods were situated at the time of the disposition ('the lex situs'). During the course of argument in the lower court in that case, Pollock CB[1] clearly *a* affirmed the lex situs theory, in one brief sentence which was expressly approved in the majority judgment of the Court of Exchequer Chamber delivered by Crompton J[2] on appeal:

> '"If personal property is disposed of in a manner binding according to the law of the country where it is, that disposition is binding everywhere."'
>
> *b*

The judgment of Page Wood V-C in *Simpson v Fogo*[3] illustrates that the decision in *Cammell v Sewell*[4] did not immediately and finally bury the alternative theories based on lex loci actus or lex domicilii. *Simpson v Fogo*[5], however, was accurately described by Scrutton LJ in *Aksionairnoye Obschestvo A M Luther v Sagor & Co*[6] as having been 'the subject of considerable adverse comment' and counsel on neither side relied on it before me. *c*

The general principle relating to the validity of dispositions of personal property, as formulated by Pollock CB and approved by the Court of Exchequer Chamber, to which I shall refer briefly as 'the principle of *Cammell v Sewell*', has been reaffirmed in many subsequent decisions. I will mention only a few of them. As thus formulated, it was expressly approved by Blackburn J, delivering the joint opinion of himself and Bramwell B, Mellor J, Brett J and Cleasby B in *Castrique v Imrie*[7] when, after quoting the words of *d* Pollock CB, he said:

> 'This, we think, as a general rule, is correct, though no doubt it may be open to exceptions and qualifications.'

The general principle has been subsequently stated in very similar terms, for example, by Maugham J in *Re Anziani*[8]. Devlin J in *Bank Voor Handel En Scheepvaart NV v Slatford*[9] *e* summarised the present position by saying:

> 'There is little doubt that it is the *lex situs* which as a general rule governs the transfer of movables when effected contractually.'

Faced with these and a number of other 20th century authorities on the same lines, *f* counsel for the plaintiff accepted that as a general rule the validity of a transfer of movables is governed by the lex situs and that accordingly the principle of *Cammell v Sewell* would have the effect of rendering Italian law the relevant law for the purpose of determining the rights of the second defendant and the vendor in Italy, from whom he purchased, as between themselves and their respective successors in title. He pointed out, however, that the present case is, in contrast, concerned with the respective proprietary rights of the second defendant and the plaintiff. He pointed out the many *g* circumstances which cumulatively give this case a strong association with England, at least if it be regarded solely from the standpoint of his client. At the time of the theft, the goods were situated in England, in the ownership and lawful possession of a person who was domiciled in England. The plaintiff neither knew of nor consented to the removal of the goods from England or anything which made such removal more probable. The goods have now been voluntarily redelivered to England where they or *h* their proceeds of sale still remain. Finally, it is an English court which is now hearing the matter.

---

1 (1858) 3 H & N 617 at 638, 157 ER 615 at 624
2 (1860) 5 H & N 728 at 744–745, 157 ER 1371 at 1378
3 (1862) 1 Hem & M 195 at 222, 71 ER 85 at 97
4 5 H & N 728, 157 ER 1371 *j*
5 1 Hem & M 195, 71 ER 85
6 [1921] 3 KB 532 at 558, [1921] All ER Rep 138 at 151
7 (1870) LR 4 HL 414 at 429, [1861–73] All ER Rep 508 at 510
8 [1930] 1 Ch 407 at 420
9 [1951] 2 All ER 779 at 786, [1953] 1 QB 248 at 257

Laying emphasis on what may be called these English connecting factors, counsel for
a the plaintiff advanced two main propositions as possible avenues of escape from the
principle of *Cammell v Sewell*. Briefly, the first was that for the purpose of applying this
principle to determine the respective rights of the plaintiff and the second defendant in
the peculiar circumstances of this case, the lex situs should be treated as being English,
rather than Italian law. The second was that if, contrary to this first submission, the
application of the principle of *Cammell v Sewell* would result in the relevant issue being
b determined according to Italian law, then the exceptional facts of the case bring it outside
this principle.

No authority has been cited the facts of which can be said to be precisely on all fours
with the present case, in the sense that all the English connecting factors relied on by
counsel for the plaintiff are present. Since, however, I have found three decisions
especially illuminating in the context of his two principal submissions, I shall refer to
c these decisions in some detail.

The first of them is *Cammell v Sewell*[1] itself. In that case a cargo of timber had been
shipped on board a Prussian vessel in Russia by Russian vendors for delivery to English
purchasers in England. The vessel was then wrecked off the coast of Norway, but the
cargo was safely landed. On learning of the wreck, the English purchasers abandoned
their rights to the cargo. The plaintiffs, English underwriters with whom the timber
d was insured, paid the purchasers as for a total loss, while the purchasers endorsed the
relevant bill of lading to them and delivered it to them. Before the underwriters had
accepted the abandonment, however, a survey had been held, on the instigation of an
agent acting for the ship's master, which had reported that it would be in the interests of
the underwriters and all parties concerned that the whole of the cargo should be sold.
The timber had been accordingly sold in Norway to a Mr Clausen. An agent of the
e plaintiff underwriters then brought proceedings in the Norwegian court to set aside the
sale, but the proceedings failed. The Norwegian purchaser then shipped the timber to
England and sold it to the defendants in the action. The plaintiff underwriters sued these
defendants in trover for its value.

The Court of Exchequer[2] found in favour of the defendants. The plaintiff underwriters
appealed to the Court of Exchequer Chamber[1], which dismissed the appeal. Crompton
f J, delivering the judgment of the majority of the court (Cockburn CJ, Wightman,
Williams, Keating JJ and himself) said[3]:

'If we are to recognise the Norwegian law, and if according to that law the
property passed by the sale in Norway to Clausen as an innocent purchaser, we do
not think that the subsequent bringing the property to England can alter the
g position of the parties.'

Pausing there, *Cammell v Sewell*[1] is thus, in my judgment, clear authority for the
following proposition: the mere circumstances that the goods in the present case have
been brought back to England following the sale to the second defendant and that their
proceeds are now in England do not entitle the English court to decline to apply Italian
h law for the purpose of determining the relevant issue if, but for those circumstances, that
would be the law applicable.

Having pointed out that he was prepared to treat Clausen as an innocent purchaser
Crompton J[4] continued as follows:

j
_____

1 (1860) 5 H & N 728, 157 ER 1371
2 (1858) 3 H & N 617, 157 ER 615
3 5 H & N 728 at 742–743, 157 ER 1371 at 1377
4 5 H & N 728 at 743, 157 ER 1371 at 1377

'Treating him, therefore, as an innocent purchaser, it appears to us that the questions are—did the property by the law of Norway vest in him as an innocent purchaser? and are we to recognise that law? ... The conclusion which we draw from the evidence is, that by the law of Norway the captain, under circumstances such as existed in this case, could not, as between himself and his owners, or the owners of the cargo, justify the sale, but that he remained liable and responsible to them for a sale not justified under the circumstances; whilst, on the other hand, an innocent purchaser would have a good title to the property bought by him from the agent of the owners.'

Crompton J, having thus described the extent under Norwegian law of the captain's authority to sell the goods and pass title thereto, went on to reject any suggestion that the nature of the Norwegian law was so monstrous that it should not be recognised by the English court.

There then follows a paragraph which I think embodies the principal ratio decidendi of the majority judgment. Crompton J[1] said:

'Many cases were mentioned in the course of the argument, and more might be collected, in which it might seem hard that the goods of foreigners should be dealt with according to the laws of our own or of other countries. Amongst others our law as to the seizure of a foreigner's goods for rent due from a tenant, or as to the title gained in them, if stolen, by a sale in market overt, might appear harsh. But we cannot think that the goods of foreigners would be protected against such laws, or that if the property once passed by virtue of them it would again be changed by being taken by the new owner into the foreigner's own country. We think that the law on this subject was correctly stated by the Lord Chief Baron in the course of the argument in the Court below where he says "If personal property is disposed of in a manner binding according to the law of the country where it is, that disposition is binding everywhere." And we do not think that it makes any difference that the goods were wrecked, and not intended to be sent to the country where they were sold. We do not think that the goods which were wrecked here would on that account be the less liable to our laws as to market overt, or as to the landlord's right of distress, because the owner did not foresee that they would come to England.'

Finally, Crompton J rejected arguments that the law of Norway as proved in that case was of such a nature that it should not be regarded (this being the point on which Byles J dissented from the majority) or that on the evidence the purchase was made with knowledge of the lack of the vendor's authority to sell. He concluded that, as the law of Norway gave title to an innocent purchaser, the property vested in Clausen and in the defendants as subpurchasers from him and that, having once so vested, it did not become divested by its being subsequently brought to this country.

I regard the last paragraph which I have quoted from Crompton J's judgment as being of crucial importance in the present case. First, in it the Court of Exchequer Chamber explicitly affirmed the principle of *Cammell v Sewell* as stated by Pollock CB in the court below. Secondly, it makes it plain that the principle is capable of applying so as to bind and destroy the proprietary rights of a third person, even though he was not a party to the relevant disposition and did not consent to it, but asserts his claim by virtue of a title prior in time to that of any such party. It does effectively deprive the plaintiff in the present case of any opportunity to argue that the principle is capable of applying only in determining the rights of the parties to a relevant disposition or their respective successors inter se, and indeed his counsel has not asserted any such broad proposition.

Finally, in my judgment, this paragraph from Crompton J's judgment is clear authority for the proposition that, if a person acquires a title to goods situated in England

---

1 (1860) 5 H & N 728 at 744–745, 157 ER 1371 at 1378

at the date of the purchase, by virtue of a purchase in market overt, and that title is a good
a one under English law, the English court will generally still recognise his title to them
in priority to that of the previous owner, even though such previous owner may be a
foreigner from whom the goods had been stolen and the laws of the previous owner's
country would *not* regard his title as having been divested by the purchase. Furthermore,
I can see no ground for excepting from this conclusion the case where the goods have
been stolen from the foreigner in the foreigner's own country. With reference to the
b hypothetical example given by him, Crompton J expressly stated that it made no
difference that the owner did not foresee that the goods would come to England before
the sale in market overt took place.

The majority of the Court of Exchequer Chamber clearly regarded the protection
afforded to purchasers in market overt under sales taking place in England, even in
respect of goods stolen abroad from foreigners, as being founded not on any inherent
c superiority of English law, nor on any statutory protection afforded to such purchasers;
the case was decided before the passing of the Sale of Goods Act 1893. They regarded it
as founded on the general principle of private international law that, if personal property
is disposed of in a manner binding according to the law of the country where it is, that
disposition is binding everywhere. I think it inevitably follows that they would have
considered the English court as being generally bound to recognise the title to goods of
d a person who has purchased them at a time when they were situated in a *foreign* country,
under a disposition which gave him a valid title to them under the law of *that* country,
even though the previous owner was a person from whom the goods had been stolen in
England, and even though the purchaser would have acquired no title to them on the
exclusive application of English law. Subject to exceptions of the nature summarised by
counsel for the second defendant, the English court will not, I conceive, decline to apply
e a well-established principle of private international law merely because a British subject
will suffer thereby or merely because adherence to the principle must result in the
application of rules of foreign law which it may regard as inferior to its own equivalent
rules. Consistency itself is an important element in the administration of justice.

No case has been cited to me in which the decision in *Cammell v Sewell*[1] has either been
overruled or, I think, even criticised. It is therefore binding on me except in so far as it
f can properly be distinguished on its material facts. If therefore my analysis of it is
correct, it presents at very least a serious obstacle to the plaintiff in the present case and
correspondingly powerful support to the second defendant.

The next case cited to me, which I have found particularly helpful, is a decision of the
Scottish Court of Session in *Todd v Armour*[2]. In that case the plaintiff had been the owner
of a horse which was stolen from his land in Ireland. The next day it was sold in Ireland
g to a Mr Black, who purchased it as a bona fide purchaser for value in market overt. Black
then brought the horse to Scotland where he sold it to the defendant. The plaintiff
brought an action against the defendant in the Scottish court to recover the horse. He
contended that his rights were governed by Scottish law under which an indelible
'vitium reale' attached to stolen goods until they were returned to the original owner.
The Court of Session was, however, satisfied on the evidence that, according to Irish law,
h Black acquired a good title to the horse when he purchased it in market overt in
Ireland. The sheriff-substitute's proof, presented to the court, referred to the principle of
Cammell v Sewell. The Court of Session, while not expressly referring in its judgments to
this principle, proceeded to decide the case in accordance with it. It held, in effect, that
Black had acquired a valid title to the goods under Irish law, vis-à-vis the plaintiff, that
this title should be recognised by the Scottish court and that the defendant had
j accordingly received title to the goods from Black, which should likewise be recognised

---

1 (1860) 5 H & N 728, 157 ER 1371
2 (1882) 9 R (Ct of Sess) 901

by the court. Lord Young[1] put the matter very simply: 'Black had a title to the horse, which was good against the pursuer, and sold it to Armour, thereby giving him an *a* equally good title.' The Court of Session declined to accept the invitation to apply Scottish law, even though at least in the view of the Lord Justice-Clerk[2] the Scottish system of irremovable 'vitium reale' attaching to stolen property was preferable to that obtaining in England and Ireland. Lord Young[3] expressed the opinion that there were 'weighty considerations of reason and good sense' in favour of the view that the court should protect a purchaser in Scotland exactly as the Irish court would have done a *b* purchaser in the same circumstances in Ireland, or even in Scotland, observing that it had not been shown that the Irish court would decline to take notice of a sale in market overt in Scotland.

Todd v Armour[4] is thus a good example of a court faithfully applying the principle of *Cammell v Sewell*, with the result that it recognised the title acquired by a purchaser of stolen goods under the law of a foreign country, by virtue of a purchase in that country, *c* even though such law differed in material respects from the lex fori. Furthermore, the Court of Session applied the law of the foreign country, even though the stolen goods were actually in Scotland at the time of the trial and even though at least one member of the court viewed without favour the content of the law which they felt obliged to apply.

The third decision which I regard as particularly important for present purposes is *Embiricos v Anglo-Austrian Bank*[5]. The facts, as summarised in the headnote to the report, *d* were as follows[6]:

'A cheque on a London Bank was drawn in Roumania in favour of the plaintiffs, who the same day specially indorsed it to a firm in London, and placed it, with a letter, in an envelope addressed to that firm in London. The cheque was stolen from the envelope by one of the plaintiffs' clerks. The cheque was presented at a bank in Vienna by a person who desired that it might be cashed. It then bore an *e* indorsement, which purported to be that of the London firm, but which was in fact forged. The Vienna bank, acting in good faith and without negligence, cashed the cheque, and then indorsed it to the defendants, bankers in London, and then sent it to them by post. The defendants cashed it at the London bank on which it was drawn. The plaintiffs sued the defendants for damages for the wrongful conversion of the cheque. By the Austrian law the defendants had a good title to the cheque as *f* bonâ fide holders for value without gross negligence.'

Walton J[7] in the court below referred to a statement in the then current edition of Dicey's Conflict of Laws[8] that:

'"An assignment of a movable which can be touched (goods) giving a good title thereto according to the law of the country where the movable is situate at the time *g* of the assignment (lex situs) is valid."'

Walton J continued[7]:

'It cannot be disputed that that statement is correct in regard to ordinary chattels; and if this document were not a cheque but a valuable and portable article such as a diamond, which had been stolen from the plaintiffs and sold in Vienna under *h* circumstances which gave the purchasers a good title there to the jewel, the English Courts would recognise that title if it was good according to the Austrian law,

1   (1882) 9 R (Ct of Sess) 901 at 907
2   9 R (Ct of Sess) 901 at 906
3   9 R (Ct of Sess) 901 at 908
4   9 R (Ct of Sess) 901
5   [1904] 2 KB 870, *on appeal* [1905] 1 KB 677
6   [1905] 1 KB 677 at 677–678
7   [1904] 2 KB 870 at 874
8   1st Edn (1896), r 140

a although it might not be good according to English law. The analogy of a sale in market overt seems to me exact. If goods which have been stolen are sold in market overt, the purchaser gets a good title to the goods, although according to the general law of England the thief could give no title to the stolen goods. It is the sale in market overt that gives the title. So if goods are sold in Vienna so as to give a good title to them, then that title will be held to be good in England, although the goods might have been previously stolen, and although the sale in England (not being in *b* market overt) would not have given a title. The question is whether that principle applies not only to ordinary chattels but to a bill, note, or cheque or other negotiable security.'

Walton J concluded that in the light of the decisions of Romer J and the Court of Appeal in *Alcock v Smith*[1] the answer to the question which he had posed was in the affirmative. He accordingly decided in favour of the defendant. His decision was affirmed on the *c* same grounds by the Court of Appeal. Vaughan Williams LJ said[2]:

'I think that the view taken by Walton J. of the effect of the decision in *Alcock* v. *Smith*[1], that the rule that the validity of the transfer of chattels must be governed by the law of the country in which the transfer takes place, applies to a bill or cheque, and applies to the transfer of bills or cheques in cases where the transfer is by *d* indorsement, is right. . .'

Romer LJ[3] said that he saw no reason to depart from the opinion on the relevant question which he himself had expressed in *Alcock v Smith*[1]. In his decision in the latter case, Romer J[4] had expressly referred to *Cammell v Sewell*[5] in the following terms:

'Indeed, the question here being legally only as to the right to hold the bill (the *e* document itself) as between claimants not parties to the bill, the case is not different from that of a sale in *Norway* or *Sweden* of chattels there, which would, in the absence of fraud, be governed by the Norwegian law, notwithstanding the claims of English people, not parties to the sale, who were interested in, or claimed title to the chattels sold.'

f The *Embiricos* decision[6] thus has a number of features significant for present purposes. The Court of Appeal not only reaffirmed the principle of *Cammell v Sewell*, but also applied it in such a manner as to deprive the plaintiffs of the opportunity of relying on English law, even though the cheque had been stolen from them and they had not consented in any way to its going to Austria, where the relevant transfer took place, and even though they were not parties to the transfer.

g These being the most relevant authorities cited to me, I now return to consider counsel's two principle submissions for the plaintiff in slightly greater detail. In support of the first of them, he referred me to a general statement in Halsbury's Laws of England[7] to the effect that the location of property is a matter for English law and that it is possible for property to be regarded as having different locations for different purposes. He accepted that, for the purpose of determining the respective rights in the goods of the *h* Italian vendor and the second defendant as between themselves, the situs of the goods must be regarded as Italy. In his submission, however, it does not follow that the situs of the goods must be regarded as Italian for the purpose of determining the respective

---

j 1 [1892] 1 Ch 238
2 [1905] 1 KB 677 at 683–684
3 [1905] 1 KB 677 at 685–686
4 [1892] 1 Ch 238 at 256
5 (1860) 5 H & N 728, 157 ER 1371
6 [1905] 1 KB 677
7 8 Halsbury's Laws (4th Edn) para 632

proprietary claims of the plaintiff and the second defendant. For the latter purpose, he suggested, on the particular facts of the present case, the court is entitled and obliged to *a* hold that the situs of the goods remained English throughout. They were in England at the date of the theft; they are still here; they never left England with the plaintiff's consent; there was never any voluntary act on his part which connected or was even likely to connect the goods with any foreign system of law. In these circumstances, counsel submitted, the alleged connection of the situs with Italy, for the purpose of determining the plaintiff's rights, is a spurious connection which should be disregarded *b* by the court.

This line of argument was supported by no relevant authority and, though attractively presented by counsel for the plaintiff, in my judgment does not itself avail the plaintiff, for these short reasons. It is in my judgment abundantly clear from the authorities already cited that, in appropriate circumstances, the court is prepared to follow the principle of *Cammell v Sewell* by applying the law of country A, in favour of a person who *c* acquires title to personal property under the law of that country, even though the effect of such application is to destroy the proprietary rights of a former owner, who never himself possessed the property in country A and never consented, expressly or implicitly, to its going to country A. This was the situation in *Cammell v Sewell*[1] itself, where, as Cockburn CJ[2] pointed out in argument, 'the goods were wrecked on the coast of Norway and came there without the owner's consent'. It was the situation also in *Embiricos v* *d* *Anglo-Austrian Bank*[3], where the court applied Austrian law so as to divest the title of the injured original owners, even though they had done nothing to consent to the cheque finding its way to Austria. Furthermore, the plaintiff's English domicile cannot avail him in this context, any more than it availed the English plaintiffs in *Cammell v Sewell*[1]. Nor can the presence of the goods, or their proceeds, in England at the date of the hearing entitle the plaintiff to assert that their situs should be treated as English for the purpose *e* of any application of the principle of that decision. As Crompton J there said[4]: 'we do not think that the subsequent bringing the property to England can alter the position of the parties.'

Accordingly, I think it clear that, if the principle of *Cammell v Sewell* applies at all on the facts of the present case, then the lex situs of the relevant disposition cannot be treated as being English rather than Italian. Intolerable uncertainty in the law would result if *f* the court were to permit the introduction of a wholly fictional English situs, when applying the principle to any particular case, merely because the case happened to have a number of other English connecting factors.

It therefore follows that if the plaintiff is to succeed, he must satisfy the court that the second principal submission made on his behalf is correct, namely that the principle of *Cammell v Sewell* does not apply to this case, because the particular circumstances bring it *g* within an exception to that principle.

I have already mentioned that counsel for the second defendant accepted that there are a number of well-recognised exceptions to this principle. For present purposes the most significant of them is that based on public policy. As is stated in Halsbury's Laws of England[5]—

'Exceptionally, the English court will not enforce or recognise a right conferred *h* or a duty imposed by a foreign law where, on the facts of the particular case, enforcement or, as the case may be, recognition, would be contrary to a fundamental policy of English law. The court has, therefore, refused in certain cases to apply foreign law where to do so would in the particular circumstances be contrary to the interests of the United Kingdom or contrary to justice or morality.'

j

1 (1860) 5 H & N 728, 157 ER 1371
2 5 H & N 728 at 735, 157 ER 1371 at 1374
3 [1905] 1 KB 677
4 5 H & N 728 at 742–743, 157 ER 1371 at 1377
5 8 Halsbury's Laws (4th Edn) para 418

a If therefore a case arose where, by reference to the principle of *Cammell v Sewell*, a person claimed a title to goods in an English court, which he would not be able to establish by reference to English law alone, and the content of the particular foreign law on which he relied was so outrageous that this court regarded it as wholly contrary to justice and morality, then it would, I conceive, probably refuse to recognise the rights conferred on the claimant by the relevant foreign law.

b Counsel for the plaintiff, however, clearly correctly in the absence of evidence, pointed out that for the purpose of the present application, he did not rely on the content of the relevant Italian law as a reason why this court should refuse to recognise any rights of ownership thereby conferred on the second defendant vis-à-vis the plaintiff. He did not assert that such content was contrary to justice or morality. Instead, he asserted a further exception to the principle of *Cammell v Sewell* which, he suggested, must apply on the facts of the present case and was in the following terms: where movables have been

c stolen from country A or otherwise unlawfully taken from the owner in country A and are then removed from country A without the owner's knowledge or consent and are then dealt with in country B without his knowledge or consent and are then returned voluntarily to country A, the law of country A should be applied to determine whether the original owner is or is not still the owner of the movables.

d Counsel for the plaintiff accepted that there is no English authority which directly supports this proposition, but submitted that there is likewise no authority which shows it to be incorrect. Three particular considerations, he suggested, support the conclusion that as a matter of public policy, regardless of the content of the particular law or country B, the court should apply the law of country A, rather than that of country B, in the circumstances which he postulated. First, if at the time of the court hearing, the goods are situated in country A rather than country B, there can be no objection on the grounds

e of ineffectiveness to the court in country A applying its own law. Secondly, he pointed out, in the circumstances postulated, there has been no voluntary act on the part of the original owner, which has led to the connection of the goods with the legal system of country B. Thirdly, in counsel's submission for the plaintiff, the concept of security of titles is an important one and country A is justified in making an exception to the general principle of *Cammell v Sewell*, for the purpose of securing a prior title recognised by its

f own system of law.

As to the first of these three considerations, the presence of the goods in country A at the time of the trial certainly removes one potential practical obstacle which might otherwise deter the court in that country from applying its own law; no court likes to make an order which will probably be unenforceable in practice. In my judgment, however, it affords no further positive support at all to counsel's proposition. There have

g been many cases (for example, *Cammell v Sewell*[1] itself and *Todd v Armour*[2]) in which the court of country A has declined to apply the law of that country, despite the presence of the goods in question in that country at the time of the trial.

As to the second of these considerations urged by counsel for the plaintiff, it appears that in the United States of America the courts of at least a number of States regard the knowledge of an owner that his chattel has been removed into another State as being

h relevant to the question whether the law of that other State should be applied for the purpose of determining whether his title has been divested. I was referred to Beale's Treatise on the Conflict of Laws[3]. There it was submitted that the great weight of authority in the United States of America supported the view that—

'the law of a state into which chattels have been surreptitiously removed without the knowledge of an owner and against his will does not apply its law to oust the

j title of the absent owner. [The author continues:] Such little authority as there is, therefore, is to the effect that a state has no jurisdiction over the title of an absent

---

1 (1860) 5 H & N 728, 157 ER 1371
2 (1882) 9 R (Ct of Sess) 901
3 (1935) pp 298–299

owner in a chattel which has been brought into the state without any act of his sufficient to submit his interest in the chattel to the jurisdiction of the state.'   *a*

I was however also referred to a learned monograph by P A Lalive, The Transfer of Chattels in the Conflict of Laws[1] and an article by Dr J H C Morris, The Transfer of Chattels in the Conflict of Laws[2], in which the theories advanced in this context by Mr Beale have been subjected to searching criticism. Counsel for the plaintiff did not go so far as to adopt any of Mr Beale's wide propositions for the purpose of his argument. He   *b* suggested, however, that the broad considerations of policy which have influenced many American states in protecting the title of an owner who has not consented to his goods being removed to another state are relevant for this court, in determining whether it should formulate the new exception to the rule in *Cammell v Sewell* which he invites me to apply. He also read me a decision of the court of New York in *Edgerly v Bush*[3] in which, on the particular facts, that court held that a plaintiff was entitled to recover for conversion of a horse, which had surreptitiously been removed from one state and sold   *c* in another, under the laws of that other state. Though counsel for the plaintiff suggested that the latter decision of a New York court is persuasive authority in his favour, I find it of no assistance for present purposes, since, with due respect, the judgment of the court is expressed in such confusing language that it is impossible to extract from it any coherent reasons for the ultimate decision.

Despite this second consideration advanced by counsel for the plaintiff in support of   *d* the suggested exception to the principle of *Cammell v Sewell*, there have been a number of English cases (for example *Cammell v Sewell*[4] itself and the *Embiricos* case[5]) in which the court of country A has applied the law of country B to determine the ownership of goods, even though there has been no kind of voluntary act on the part of the original owner which has led to the connection of the goods with the legal system of country B. Furthermore, in the *Embiricos* case[5], the original removal of the property in question   *e* from the plaintiff's possession had been unlawful. I find it impossible to derive from the English cases any principle that the absence of such voluntary act should preclude or even deter the court of country A from applying the law of country B in accordance with the principle of *Cammell v Sewell*. For all these reasons I do not think that the absence of any such voluntary act or the fact of an original unlawful removal constitutes an affirmative   *f* reason why I should adopt the suggested exception to that principle. At best it removes one additional obstacle which might have confronted the plaintiff, if he had expressly or implicitly agreed to the goods going to the foreign country or knew that they were going there (as for example in *Inglis v Robertson and Baxter*[6]).

I turn now to the remaining consideration urged on me by counsel for the plaintiff, namely that, on the facts of his hypothetical case, country A is justified in making an exception to the general principle of *Cammell v Sewell* for the purpose of securing a title   *g* recognised by its own system of law. This, I think, is by far his strongest point. In principle, any court must surely regard, with some initial sympathy, the position of a blameless person, such as the plaintiff in the present case, who, if attention is paid solely to the law of the country of that court, has at all material times had and retained a good title to the goods which are the subject of his claim.

On the other hand, there are other equally powerful, I think more powerful, counter-   *h* balancing considerations. Security of title is as important to an innocent purchaser as it is to an innocent owner whose goods have been stolen from him. Commercial convenience may be said imperatively to demand that proprietary rights to movables shall generally be determined by the lex situs under the rules of private international

---

1 (1955) pp 175–184   *j*
2 British Year Book of International Law 1945, p 232 at 240–241
3 (1880) 81 NY 199
4 (1860) 5 H & N 728, 157 ER 1371
5 [1905] 1 KB 677
6 [1898] AC 616

law. Were the position otherwise, it would not suffice for the protection of a purchaser
a of any valuable movables to ascertain that he was acquiring title to them under the law
of the country where the goods were situate at the time of the purchase; he would have
to try to effect further investigations as to the past title, with a view to ensuring, so far as
possible, that there was no person who might successfully claim a title to the movables
by reference to some other system of law; and in many cases, even with such further
investigations, that could result in no certainty that his title was secure. In these
b circumstances, there are, in my view, very strong grounds of business convenience for
applying the principle of *Cammell v Sewell* even in a case such as the present. Maugham
J said in *Re Anziani*[1] with reference to the principle: 'Business could not be carried on if
that were not so.' This was putting the point very strongly. I think, however, that most
undesirable uncertainty in the commercial world would result if the choice of the system
regulating the validity of a disposition of chattels were to depend not only on the
c situation of the goods at the time of the disposition, but also on the additional factors
suggested on behalf of the plaintiff.

It must be accepted that exclusive reference to the lex situs must cause hardship to a
previous owner in some cases, particularly if his goods have been moved to and sold in
a foreign country without his knowledge or consent. Crompton J, however, in the
passage already quoted in the majority judgment in *Cammell v Sewell*[2], expressly
d recognised that the English law as to stolen goods acquired by a purchaser under a sale in
market overt might seem harsh to a former foreign owner, but expressed the view that
it made no difference that such owner did not intend them to be sent to the country
where they were sold. The English court, I do not doubt, would ordinarily expect a
foreign court to apply the principle of *Cammell v Sewell* and recognise the title of a person
who has acquired a title to goods under English law, by virtue of a purchase in England
e in market overt at a time when they were situated in England. And this will be the case
even though such foreign court, on an exclusive application of its own law, would have
regarded a previous owner, from whom the goods had been stolen, as having a better
title. If this would be the attitude of the English court, it could not, in my judgment,
solely on the pretext of a newly formulated exception to the rule in *Cammell v Sewell*
either logically or reasonably, refuse to recognise the title to goods of a person who has
f acquired a title to them under Italian law by virtue of a purchase in Italy at a time when
they were situated in Italy. And it makes no difference that the English court, on an
exclusive application of its own law, would have regarded the previous owner, from
whom the goods had been stolen in England, as having a better title to them.

I thus summarise my conclusions as follows. (1) The relevant general principle is, in
my judgment, clearly and accurately stated in Cheshire and North's Private International
g Law[3] as follows:

'Therefore, it is now established that the proprietary effect of a particular
assignment of movables is governed exclusively by the law of the country where
they are situated at the time of the assignment. An owner will be divested of his
title to movables if they are taken to a foreign country and there assigned in
circumstances sufficient by the local law to pass a valid title to the assignee. The title
h recognised by the foreign *lex situs* overrides earlier and inconsistent titles no matter
by what law they may have been created.'

(2) The rule, however, is not one of universal application; in particular it is not likely to
be applied in any of the five exceptional cases already mentioned. (3) It is not, however,
contended that any of these five exceptions applies on the facts of the present case. For
j the reasons already given, I cannot accept the plaintiff's submission that the court should
regard such facts as giving rise to a further exception, based on the grounds that the

1 [1930] 1 Ch 407 at 420
2 (1860) 5 H & N 728 at 744–745, 157 ER 1371 at 1378
3 10th Edn (1979) p 527

goods were stolen from the plaintiff in England, then removed to Italy and sold there without the plaintiff's knowledge or consent and have now been returned to England.   *a*

I must therefore accept the second defendant's submission that the relevant question of title falls to be determined in accordance with Italian law. This decision, however, must be subject to one proviso. I have heard no evidence as to the content of Italian law. Though the plaintiff's counsel has not sought to submit that either of these things is likely to occur, it is theoretically possible that the trial judge, on hearing such evidence, could form the view that the particular content of the relevant Italian law was such that   *b* the public policy of this country required him to disregard any rights asserted by the second defendant by reference to such law. Alternatively, it is theoretically possible that the evidence as to Italian law would show that the Italian court would itself apply English law, on the particular facts of the present case, for the purpose of determining the rights of the second defendant vis-à-vis the plaintiff and vice versa. In this event I suppose it would be open to the plaintiff to argue that English law should, in the final result, be   *c* applied by the English court by virtue of the doctrine of renvoi. By this judgment I do not intend to deprive the plaintiff of the right to argue either of these two points at the trial.

In all the circumstances I therefore propose to declare, in answer to the questions put to me, that, on the basis of the agreed facts set forth in the schedule to the order of 16th March 1979, but without prejudice to any submissions which any party may wish to put   *d* forward at the trial, based on evidence as to the particular content of the relevant Italian domestic law, Italian domestic law is to be applied to the issue whether the plaintiff or the second defendant has the immediate right to possession of the goods with which the action and the counterclaim are concerned. I will, however, hear counsel as to the precise form which this declaration should take.

e

Declaration accordingly.

Solicitors: *Dawson Cornwell & Co* (for the plaintiff); *Stallard & Co* (for the second defendant).

Jacqueline Metcalfe   Barrister.

End of Volume 1